MAJOR ♦
20th- ♦
CENTURY ♦
WRITERS ♦

MAJOR 20th-CENTURY WRITERS

A Selection of Sketches from
Contemporary Authors

Contains more than one thousand entries on the most widely studied twentieth-century writers, all originally written or updated for this set.

First Edition

Bryan Ryan, Editor

Volume 3: L-Q

 Gale Research Inc. • *DETROIT* • *LONDON*

∞™ This book is printed on acid-free paper that meets the minimum
requirements of American National Standard for Information Sciences
Permanence Paper for Printed Library Materials, ANSI Z39.48-1984.

♻ This book is printed on recycled paper that meets Environmental
Protection Agency standards.

Library of Congress Catalog Card Number: 90-84380
ISBN 0-8103-7766-7 (Set)
ISBN 0-8103-7914-7 (Volume 3)

Printed in the United States of America.

Published simultaneously in the United Kingdom
by Gale Research International Limited
(An affiliated company of Gale Research Inc.)

CONTENTS

INTRODUCTION

An Important Information Source on 20th-Century Literature and Culture

Major 20th-Century Writers provides students, educators, librarians, researchers, and general readers with an affordable and comprehensive source of biographical and bibliographical information on more than 1,000 of the most influential authors of our time. Of primary focus are novelists, short story writers, poets, and dramatists from the United States and the United Kingdom, but prominent writers from over sixty other nations have also been included. Important figures from beyond the literary realm, nonfiction writers who have influenced twentieth-century thought, are also found here.

The vast majority of the entries in *Major 20th-Century Writers* were selected from Gale's acclaimed *Contemporary Authors* series and completely updated for this publication. About 40 sketches on important authors not already in *CA* were written especially for this four-volume set to furnish readers with the most comprehensive coverage possible. These newly written entries will also appear in future volumes of *Contemporary Authors*.

International Advisory Board

Before preparing *Major 20th-Century Writers*, the editors of *Contemporary Authors* conducted a telephone survey of librarians and mailed a print survey to more than four thousand libraries to help determine the kind of reference tool libraries wanted. Once it was clear that a comprehensive, yet affordable source of information on the best 20th-century writers was needed to serve small and medium-sized libraries, a wide range of resources was consulted: national surveys of books taught in American high schools and universities; British secondary school syllabi; reference works such as the *New York Public Library Desk Reference, Reading Lists for College-Bound Students: The Books Most Recommended by America's Top Colleges, The List of Books*, E. D. Hirsch's *Cultural Literacy*, and volumes in Gale's Literary Criticism series and *Dictionary of Literary Biography*.

A preliminary list of authors drawn from these sources was then sent to an advisory board of librarians and teaching professionals in both the United States and Great Britain. The recommendations made by these advisors helped define the scope of the project and the final list of authors to be included in the four-volume set. Stephen T. Willis, Social Sciences Librarian at the Manchester Central Library in Manchester, England, focused on the literary and nonliterary writers of most interest to British school libraries and public libraries, with special consideration for those authors who are relevant to the GCSE and A-level public examinations. Jacqueline G. Morris of the Indiana Department of Education provided input from an American secondary school perspective; Tim LaBorie of St. Joseph University in Philadelphia and Rev. John P. Schlegel, S.J., the Executive and Academic Vice President of John Carroll University in Cleveland, reviewed the list with college students in mind.

Broad Coverage in a Single Source

Built upon these suggestions, *Major 20th-Century Writers* provides single-source coverage of the most influential writers of our time, including:

- *Novelists and short story writers*: James Baldwin, Saul Bellow, Willa Cather, James Joyce, Franz Kafka, Thomas Mann, Flannery O'Connor, George Orwell, Eudora Welty, and Edith Wharton.

- *Dramatists*: Samuel Beckett, Bertolt Brecht, Eugene O'Neill, and Tennessee Williams.

- *Poets*: W. H. Auden, T. S. Eliot, Robert Frost, Ezra Pound, and William Butler Yeats.

- *Contemporary literary figures*: Chinua Achebe, Don DeLillo, Gabriel Garcia Marquez, Nadine Gordimer, Guenter Grass, John Irving, Toni Morrison, V. S. Naipaul, Joyce Carol Oates, and Thomas Pynchon.

- *Genre writers*: Isaac Asimov, Agatha Christie, Tom Clancy, Stephen King, Louis L'Amour, John le Carre, Ursula K. Le Guin, Danielle Steel, and J. R. R. Tolkien.

- *20th-Century thinkers*: Hannah Arendt, Bruno Bettelheim, Joseph Campbell, Albert Einstein, Sigmund Freud, Mohandas Gandhi, Margaret Mead, Jean Piaget, Bertrand Russell, and Jean-Paul Sartre.

Easy Access to Information

Both the newly written and the completely updated entries in *Major 20th-Century Writers* provide in-depth information in a format designed for ease of use. Individual paragraphs within each entry, labeled with descriptive rubrics, ensure that a reader seeking specific information can quickly focus on the pertinent portion of an entry.

A typical entry in *Major 20th-Century Writers* contains the following, clearly labeled information sections:

- *PERSONAL:* dates and places of birth and death; parents' names and occupations; name(s) of spouse(s), date(s) of marriage(s); names of children; colleges attended and degrees earned; political and religious affiliation when known.

- *ADDRESSES:* complete home, office, and agent's addresses.

- *CAREER:* name of employer, position, and dates for each career post; résumé of other vocational achievements; military service.

- *MEMBER:* memberships and offices held in professional and civic organizations.

- *AWARDS, HONORS:* literary and professional awards received and dates.

- *WRITINGS:* title-by-title chronological bibliography of books written and edited, listed by genre when known; list of other notable publications, such as plays, screenplays, and periodical contributions.

- *WORK IN PROGRESS:* description of projects in progress.

- *SIDELIGHTS:* a biographical portrait of the author's development; information about the critical reception of the author's works; revealing comments, often by the author, on personal interests, aspirations, motivations, and thoughts on writing.

- *BIOGRAPHICAL/CRITICAL SOURCES:* books, feature articles, and reviews in which the writer's work has been treated.

Nationality Index Reveals International Scope

Authors included in *Major 20th-Century Writers* appear alphabetically in an index organized by country of birth and/or citizenship. More than 60 nations are represented, reflecting the international scope of this set.

Genre/Subject Index Indicates Range of Writers' Works

The written works composed by the authors collected in this four-volume set represent not only literary novels, short stories, plays, and poems, but also over 25 other genres and subject areas of fiction and nonfiction.

Acknowledgments

The editor wishes to thank: Barbara Carlisle Bigelow for her editorial assistance; Kenneth R. Shepherd for his technical assistance; and James G. Lesniak and Susan M. Trosky, editors of the *Contemporary Authors* series, for their cooperation and assistance, and for that of their staffs.

Comments Are Appreciated

Major 20th-Century Writers is intended to serve as a useful reference tool for a wide audience, so your comments about this work are encouraged. Suggestions of authors to include in future editions of *Major 20th-Century Writers* are also welcome. Send comments and suggestions to: The Editor, *Major 20th-Century Writers*, Gale Research Inc., 835 Penobscot Bldg., Detroit, MI 48226-4094. Or, call toll-free at 1-800-347-GALE.

MAJOR 20th-CENTURY WRITERS

VOLUME 1: A-D

Abe, Kobo 1924-
Abrahams, Peter 1919-
Achebe, Chinua 1930-
Adamov, Arthur 1908-1970
Adams, Alice 1926-
Adams, Richard 1920-
Adamson, Joy 1910-1980
Adler, Mortimer J. 1902-
Adler, Renata 1938-
Agnon, S. Y. 1888-1970
Aiken, Conrad 1889-1973
Aiken, Joan 1924-
Aitmatov, Chingiz 1928-
Akhmatova, Anna 1888-1966
Albee, Edward 1928-
Alcayaga, Lucila Godoy
  See Godoy Alcayaga, Lucila
Aldiss, Brian W. 1925-
Aleixandre, Vicente 1898-1984
Alexander, Lloyd 1924-
Algren, Nelson 1909-1981
Allen, Woody 1935-
Allende, Isabel 1942-
Allingham, Margery 1904-1966
Alther, Lisa 1944-
Amado, Jorge 1912-
Ambler, Eric 1909-
Amichai, Yehuda 1924-
Amis, Kingsley 1922-
Ammons, A. R. 1926-
Anand, Mulk Raj 1905-
Anaya, Rudolfo A. 1937-
Andersch, Alfred 1914-1980
Anderson, Poul 1926-
Anderson, Sherwood 1876-1941
Andrews, V. C. ?-1986
Andric, Ivo 1892-1975
Angelou, Maya 1928-
Anouilh, Jean 1910-1987
Anthony, Piers 1934-
Antschel, Paul 1920-1970
Aragon, Louis 1897-1982
Arden, John 1930-
Arendt, Hannah 1906-1975
Armah, Ayi Kwei 1939-
Arnow, Harriette Simpson 1908-
  1986
Ashbery, John 1927-
Ashton-Warner, Sylvia 1908-1984
Asimov, Isaac 1920-

Asturias, Miguel Angel 1899-1974
Atwood, Margaret 1939-
Auchincloss, Louis 1917-
Auden, W. H. 1907-1973
Avison, Margaret 1918-
Ayckbourn, Alan 1939-
Azuela, Mariano 1873-1952
Bach, Richard 1936-
Bachman, Richard
  See King, Stephen
Bainbridge, Beryl 1933-
Baker, Russell 1925-
Baldwin, James 1924-1987
Ballard, J. G. 1930-
Bambara, Toni Cade 1939-
Baraka, Amiri 1934-
Barker, Clive 1952-
Barker, George Granville 1913-
Barnes, Djuna 1892-1982
Barnes, Peter 1931-
Barth, John 1930-
Barthelme, Donald 1931-1989
Barthes, Roland 1915-1980
Bashevis, Isaac
  See Singer, Isaac Bashevis
Bassani, Giorgio 1916-
Bates, H. E. 1905-1974
Baum, L. Frank 1856-1919
Baumbach, Jonathan 1933-
Beattie, Ann 1947-
Beauvoir, Simone de 1908-1986
Beckett, Samuel 1906-1989
Behan, Brendan 1923-1964
Bell, Clive 1881-1964
Bell, Marvin 1937-
Bellow, Saul 1915-
Benavente, Jacinto 1866-1954
Benchley, Peter 1940-
Bennett, Alan 1934-
Berger, Thomas 1924-
Berne, Eric 1910-1970
Bernhard, Thomas 1931-1989
Berryman, John 1914-1972
Bester, Alfred 1913-1987
Beti, Mongo
  See Biyidi, Alexandre
Betjeman, John 1906-1984
Bettelheim, Bruno 1903-1990
Bioy Casares, Adolfo 1914-
Birney, Earle 1904-

Bishop, Elizabeth 1911-1979
bissett, bill 1939-
Biyidi, Alexandre 1932-
Blackwood, Caroline 1931-
Blair, Eric 1903-1950
Blais, Marie-Claire 1939-
Blasco Ibanez, Vicente 1867-1928
Blish, James 1921-1975
Blixen, Karen 1885-1962
Blount, Roy, Jr. 1941-
Blume, Judy 1938-
Blunden, Edmund 1896-1974
Bly, Robert 1926-
Bodet, Jaime Torres
  See Torres Bodet, Jaime
Boell, Heinrich 1917-1985
Bogan, Louise 1897-1970
Boll, Heinrich
  See Boell, Heinrich
Bolt, Robert 1924-
Bombeck, Erma 1927-
Bond, Edward 1934-
Bonnefoy, Yves 1923-
Bontemps, Arna 1902-1973
Borges, Jorge Luis 1899-1986
Bova, Ben 1932-
Bowen, Elizabeth 1899-1973
Bowles, Paul 1910-
Boyle, Kay 1902-
Bradbury, Malcolm 1932-
Bradbury, Ray 1920-
Bradford, Barbara Taylor 1933-
Bradley, Marion Zimmer 1930-
Braine, John 1922-1986
Brautigan, Richard 1935-1984
Brecht, Bertolt 1898-1956
Brenton, Howard 1942-
Breslin, James 1930-
Breslin, Jimmy
  See Breslin, James
Breton, Andre 1896-1966
Brink, Andre 1935-
Brittain, Vera 1893(?)-1970
Brodsky, Iosif Alexandrovich 1940-
Brodsky, Joseph
  See Brodsky, Iosif Alexandrovich
Brook, Peter 1925-
Brooke, Rupert 1887-1915
Brookner, Anita 1938-
Brooks, Cleanth 1906-

Brooks, Gwendolyn 1917-
Brophy, Brigid 1929-
Brother Antoninus
   See Everson, William
Brown, Dee 1908-
Brown, George Mackay 1921-
Brown, Rita Mae 1944-
Brown, Sterling Allen 1901-1989
Brownmiller, Susan 1935-
Brunner, John 1934-
Buber, Martin 1878-1965
Buchwald, Art 1925-
Buck, Pearl S. 1892-1973
Buckley, William F., Jr. 1925-
Buechner, Frederick 1926-
Buero Vallejo, Antonio 1916-
Bukowski, Charles 1920-
Bullins, Ed 1935-
Bultmann, Rudolf Karl 1884-1976
Burgess, Anthony
   See Wilson, John Burgess
Burke, Kenneth 1897-
Burroughs, Edgar Rice 1875-1950
Burroughs, William S. 1914-
Bustos Domecq, H.
   See Bioy Casares, Adolfo
   and Borges, Jorge Luis
Butler, Octavia E. 1947-
Butor, Michel 1926-
Byars, Betsy 1928-
Byatt, A. S. 1936-
Cabrera Infante, G. 1929-
Cade, Toni
   See Bambara, Toni Cade
Cain, Guillermo
   See Cabrera Infante, G.
Cain, James M. 1892-1977
Calder, Nigel 1931-
Caldicott, Helen 1938-
Caldwell, Erskine 1903-1987
Calisher, Hortense 1911-
Callaghan, Morley Edward 1903-
   1990
Calvino, Italo 1923-1985
Cameron, Eleanor 1912-
Campbell, John W. 1910-1971
Campbell, Joseph 1904-1987
Camus, Albert 1913-1960
Canetti, Elias 1905-
Capote, Truman 1924-1984
Card, Orson Scott 1951-
Cardenal, Ernesto 1925-
Carey, Peter 1943-
Carr, John Dickson 1906-1977
Carruth, Hayden 1921-
Carson, Rachel Louise 1907-1964
Carter, Angela 1940-
Carter, James Earl, Jr. 1924-
Carter, Jimmy
   See Carter, James Earl, Jr.
Cartland, Barbara 1901-

Carver, Raymond 1938-1988
Casares, Adolfo Bioy
   See Bioy Casares, Adolfo
Castaneda, Carlos 1931(?)-
Cather, Willa
   See Cather, Willa Sibert
Cather, Willa Sibert 1873-1947
Causley, Charles 1917-
Cela, Camilo Jose 1916-
Celan, Paul
   See Antschel, Paul
Celine, Louis-Ferdinand
   See Destouches, Louis-Ferdinand
Cendrars, Blaise
   See Sauser-Hall, Frederic
Cesaire, Aime 1913-
Chandler, Raymond 1888-1959
Char, Rene 1907-1988
Charyn, Jerome 1937-
Cheever, John 1912-1982
Chesnutt, Charles W. 1858-1932
Chesterton, G. K. 1874-1936
Ch'ien Chung-shu 1910-
Childress, Alice 1920-
Chomsky, Noam 1928-
Christie, Agatha 1890-1976
Churchill, Caryl 1938-
Churchill, Winston 1874-1965
Ciardi, John 1916-1986
Cixous, Helene 1937-
Clancy, Thomas L., Jr. 1947-
Clancy, Tom
   See Clancy, Thomas L., Jr.
Clark, Kenneth 1903-1983
Clark, Mary Higgins 1929-
Clarke, Arthur C. 1917-
Clavell, James 1925-
Cleary, Beverly 1916-
Cleese, John 1939-
Clifton, Lucille 1936-
Clutha, Janet Paterson Frame 1924-
Cocteau, Jean 1889-1963
Coetzee, J. M. 1940-
Cohen, Leonard 1934-
Colegate, Isabel 1931-
Colette 1873-1954
Colum, Padraic 1881-1972
Colwin, Laurie 1944-
Commager, Henry Steele 1902-
Commoner, Barry 1917-
Compton-Burnett, I. 1884(?)-1969
Condon, Richard 1915-
Connell, Evan S., Jr. 1924-
Connolly, Cyril 1903-1974
Conrad, Joseph 1857-1924
Conran, Shirley 1932-
Conroy, Pat 1945-
Cookson, Catherine 1906-
Coover, Robert 1932-
Cormier, Robert 1925-
Cornwell, David 1931-

Corso, Gregory 1930-
Cortazar, Julio 1914-1984
Cousins, Norman 1915-
Cousteau, Jacques-Yves 1910-
Coward, Noel 1899-1973
Cowley, Malcolm 1898-1989
Cox, William Trevor 1928-
Cozzens, James Gould 1903-1978
Crane, Hart 1899-1932
Creasey, John 1908-1973
Creeley, Robert 1926-
Crews, Harry 1935-
Crichton, Michael 1942-
Cullen, Countee 1903-1946
Cummings, E. E. 1894-1962
Dahl, Roald 1916-
Dahlberg, Edward 1900-1977
Dailey, Janet 1944-
Daly, Mary 1928-
Dannay, Frederic 1905-1982
Dario, Ruben 1867-1916
Davie, Donald 1922-
Davies, Robertson 1913-
Day Lewis, C. 1904-1972
de Beauvoir, Simone
   See Beauvoir, Simone de
de Bono, Edward 1933-
de Filippo, Eduardo 1900-1984
Deighton, Len
   See Deighton, Leonard Cyril
Deighton, Leonard Cyril 1929-
Delaney, Shelagh 1939-
Delany, Samuel R. 1942-
Delibes, Miguel
   See Delibes Setien, Miguel
Delibes Setien, Miguel 1920-
DeLillo, Don 1936-
Deloria, Vine, Jr. 1933-
del Rey, Lester 1915-
de Man, Paul 1919-1983
de Montherlant, Henry
   See Montherlant, Henry de
Dennis, Nigel 1912-
Desai, Anita 1937-
Destouches, Louis-
   Ferdinand 1894-1961
De Vries, Peter 1910-
Dexter, Pete 1943-
Dick, Philip K. 1928-1982
Dickey, James 1923-
Dickson, Carter
   See Carr, John Dickson
Didion, Joan 1934-
Dillard, Annie 1945-
Dinesen, Isak
   See Blixen, Karen
Diop, Birago 1906-1989
Disch, Thomas M. 1940-
Doctorow, E. L. 1931-
Donleavy, J. P. 1926-
Donoso, Jose 1924-

Doolittle, Hilda 1886-1961
Dos Passos, John 1896-1970
Doyle, Arthur Conan 1859-1930
Drabble, Margaret 1939-
Dreiser, Theodore 1871-1945
Du Bois, W. E. B. 1868-1963
Duerrenmatt, Friedrich 1921-
Duffy, Maureen 1933-
Duhamel, Georges 1884-1966

du Maurier, Daphne 1907-1989
Dunbar, Alice
   See Nelson, Alice Ruth Moore
   Dunbar
Dunbar-Nelson, Alice
   See Nelson, Alice Ruth Moore
   Dunbar
Duncan, Robert 1919-1988

Dunn, Douglas 1942-
Durant, Will 1885-1981
Duras, Marguerite 1914-
Durrell, Gerald 1925-
Durrell, Lawrence 1912-
Durrenmatt, Friedrich
   See Duerrenmatt, Friedrich
Dworkin, Andrea 1946-

VOLUME 2: E-K

Eagleton, Terence 1943-
Eagleton, Terry
   See Eagleton, Terence
Eberhart, Richard 1904-
Echegaray, Jose 1832-1916
Eco, Umberto 1932-
Edgar, David 1948-
Ehrenreich, Barbara 1941-
Einstein, Albert 1879-1955
Ekwensi, Cyprian 1921-
Eliade, Mircea 1907-1986
Eliot, T. S. 1888-1965
Elkin, Stanley L. 1930-
Ellin, Stanley 1916-1986
Ellison, Harlan 1934-
Ellison, Ralph 1914-
Ellmann, Richard 1918-1987
Elytis, Odysseus 1911-
Emecheta, Buchi 1944-
Empson, William 1906-1984
Endo, Shusaku 1923-
Erdrich, Louise 1954-
Erikson, Erik H. 1902-
Esslin, Martin 1918-
Estleman, Loren D. 1952-
Everson, William 1912-
Ewart, Gavin 1916-
Fallaci, Oriana 1930-
Farmer, Philip Jose 1918-
Farrell, J. G. 1935-1979
Farrell, James T. 1904-1979
Faulkner, William 1897-1962
Feiffer, Jules 1929-
Feinstein, Elaine 1930-
Ferber, Edna 1887-1968
Ferlinghetti, Lawrence 1919(?)-
Fermor, Patrick Leigh
   See Leigh Fermor, Patrick
Feynman, Richard Phillips 1918-
   1988
Fiedler, Leslie A. 1917-
Filippo, Eduardo de
   See de Filippo, Eduardo
Fitzgerald, F. Scott 1896-1940
Flanagan, Thomas 1923-
Fleming, Ian 1908-1964
Fo, Dario 1926-
Follett, Ken 1949-
Ford, Ford Madox 1873-1939

Fornes, Maria Irene 1930-
Forster, E. M. 1879-1970
Forsyth, Frederick 1938-
Fossey, Dian 1932-1985
Foucault, Michel 1926-1984
Fowles, John 1926-
Fox, Paula 1923-
Frame, Janet
   See Clutha, Janet Paterson
   Frame
France, Anatole
   See Thibault, Jacques Anatole
   Francois
Francis, Dick 1920-
Frank, Anne 1929-1945
Fraser, Antonia 1932-
Frayn, Michael 1933-
French, Marilyn 1929-
Freud, Anna 1895-1982
Freud, Sigmund 1856-1939
Friday, Nancy 1937-
Friedan, Betty 1921-
Friedman, Milton 1912-
Friel, Brian 1929-
Frisch, Max 1911-
Fromm, Erich 1900-1980
Frost, Robert 1874-1963
Fry, Christopher 1907-
Frye, Northrop 1912-
Fuentes, Carlos 1928-
Fugard, Athol 1932-
Fuller, Buckminster
   See Fuller, R. Buckminster
Fuller, Charles 1939-
Fuller, R. Buckminster 1895-1983
Fussell, Paul 1924-
Gaddis, William 1922-
Gaines, Ernest J. 1933-
Galbraith, John Kenneth 1908-
Gallant, Mavis 1922-
Gallegos, Romulo 1884-1969
Gandhi, Mahatma
   See Gandhi, Mohandas Karam-
   chand
Gandhi, Mohandas Karamchand
   1869-1948
Garcia Lorca, Federico 1898-1936
Garcia Marquez, Gabriel 1928-
Gardam, Jane 1928-

Gardner, Erle Stanley 1889-1970
Gardner, John 1926-
Gardner, John, Jr. 1933-1982
Garner, Alan 1934-
Gascoyne, David 1916-
Gass, William H. 1924-
Gasset, Jose Ortega y
   See Ortega y Gasset, Jose
Geisel, Theodor Seuss 1904-
Genet, Jean 1910-1986
Gide, Andre 1869-1951
Gilbert, Sandra M. 1936-
Gilchrist, Ellen 1935-
Gill, Brendan 1914-
Ginsberg, Allen 1926-
Ginzburg, Natalia 1916-
Giono, Jean 1895-1970
Giovanni, Nikki 1943-
Godoy Alcayaga, Lucila 1889-1957
Godwin, Gail 1937-
Golding, William 1911-
Goodall, Jane 1934-
Goodman, Paul 1911-1972
Gorbachev, Mikhail 1931-
Gordimer, Nadine 1923-
Gordon, Caroline 1895-1981
Gordon, Mary 1949-
Gordone, Charles 1925-
Gould, Lois
Gould, Stephen Jay 1941-
Gouldner, Alvin W. 1920-1980
Goytisolo, Juan 1931-
Grass, Guenter 1927-
Grau, Shirley Ann 1929-
Graves, Robert 1895-1985
Gray, Alasdair 1934-
Gray, Francine du Plessix 1930-
Gray, Simon 1936-
Greeley, Andrew M. 1928-
Green, Julien 1900-
Greene, Graham 1904-
Greer, Germaine 1939-
Grey, Zane 1872-1939
Grieve, C. M. 1892-1978
Grigson, Geoffrey 1905-1985
Grimes, Martha
Grizzard, Lewis 1946-
Grossman, Vasily 1905-1964
Guare, John 1938-

Gubar, Susan 1944-
Guest, Judith 1936-
Guiraldes, Ricardo 1886-1927
Gunn, Thom 1929-
H. D.
    See Doolittle, Hilda
Hailey, Arthur 1920-
Haley, Alex 1921-
Hall, Willis 1929-
Hamilton, Virginia 1936-
Hammett, Dashiell 1894-1961
Hampton, Christopher 1946-
Hamsun, Knut
    See Pedersen, Knut
Handke, Peter 1942-
Hanley, James 1901-1985
Hannah, Barry 1942-
Hansberry, Lorraine 1930-1965
Hardwick, Elizabeth 1916-
Hardy, Thomas 1840-1928
Hare, David 1947-
Harris, Wilson 1921-
Harrison, Tony 1937-
Hartley, L. P. 1895-1972
Hasek, Jaroslav 1883-1923
Havel, Vaclav 1936-
Hawkes, John 1925-
Hayden, Robert E. 1913-1980
Hayek, F. A. 1899-
Hazzard, Shirley 1931-
Head, Bessie 1937-1986
Heaney, Seamus 1939-
Hearne, John 1926-
Heath, Roy A. K. 1926-
Hebert, Anne 1916-
Heidegger, Martin 1889-1976
Heinlein, Robert A. 1907-1988
Heller, Joseph 1923-
Hellman, Lillian 1906-1984
Helprin, Mark 1947-
Hemingway, Ernest 1899-1961
Henley, Beth
    See Henley, Elizabeth Becker
Henley, Elizabeth Becker 1952-
Henri, Adrian 1932-
Henry, O.
    See Porter, William Sydney
Herbert, Frank 1920-1986
Herbert, Zbigniew 1924-
Herr, Michael 1940(?)-
Hersey, John 1914-
Hesse, Hermann 1877-1962
Heyer, Georgette 1902-1974
Heyerdahl, Thor 1914-
Higgins, George V. 1939-
Higgins, Jack
    See Patterson, Harry
Highsmith, Patricia 1921-
Hill, Geoffrey 1932-
Hill, Susan 1942-
Himes, Chester 1909-1984

Hinton, S. E. 1950-
Hiraoka, Kimitake 1925-1970
Hirsch, E. D., Jr. 1928-
Hite, Shere 1942-
Hoban, Russell 1925-
Hochhuth, Rolf 1931-
Hochwaelder, Fritz 1911-1986
Hoffman, Abbie 1936-1989
Hoffman, Alice 1952-
Hofstadter, Douglas R. 1945-
Holroyd, Michael 1935-
Hope, A. D. 1907-
Horgan, Paul 1903-
Housman, A. E. 1859-1936
Howard, Maureen 1930-
Howe, Irving 1920-
Hoyle, Fred 1915-
Hughes, Langston 1902-1967
Hughes, Richard 1900-1976
Hughes, Ted 1930-
Hunter, Evan 1926-
Hurston, Zora Neale 1903-1960
Huxley, Aldous 1894-1963
Huxley, Julian 1887-1975
Ibanez, Vicente Blasco
    See Blasco Ibanez, Vicente
Illich, Ivan 1926-
Infante, G. Cabrera
    See Cabrera Infante, G.
Inge, William Motter 1913-1973
Innes, Michael
    See Stewart, J.I.M.
Ionesco, Eugene 1912-
Irving, John 1942-
Isaacs, Susan 1943-
Isherwood, Christopher 1904-1986
Ishiguro, Kazuo 1954-
Jacobson, Dan 1929-
Jaffe, Rona 1932-
Jakes, John 1932-
James, C. L. R. 1901-1989
James, Clive 1939-
James, Henry 1843-1916
James, P. D.
    See White, Phyllis Dorothy
    James
Jarrell, Randall 1914-1965
Jeffers, Robinson 1887-1962
Jennings, Elizabeth 1926-
Jhabvala, Ruth Prawer 1927-
Jimenez, Juan Ramon 1881-1958
Johnson, Diane 1934-
Johnson, James Weldon 1871-1938
Johnson, Pamela Hansford 1912-
    1981
Johnson, Uwe 1934-1984
Jones, David 1895-1974
Jones, Gayl 1949-
Jones, James 1921-1977
Jones, LeRoi
    See Baraka, Amiri

Jones, Mervyn 1922-
Jong, Erica 1942-
Jordan, June 1936-
Joyce, James 1882-1941
Jung, C. G. 1875-1961
Kafka, Franz 1883-1924
Kammen, Michael G. 1936-
Karnow, Stanley 1925-
Kavan, Anna 1901-1968
Kavanagh, Patrick 1904-1967
Kaye, M. M. 1909-
Kazakov, Yuri Pavlovich 1927-
Kazantzakis, Nikos 1883(?)-1957
Keating, H. R. F. 1926-
Keillor, Garrison
    See Keillor, Gary
Keillor, Gary 1942-
Keller, Helen 1880-1968
Keneally, Thomas 1935-
Kennedy, John Fitzgerald 1917-
    1963
Kennedy, William 1928-
Kenyatta, Jomo 1891(?)-1978
Kerouac, Jack
    See Kerouac, Jean-Louis Lebrid
    de
Kerouac, Jean-Louis Lebrid de
    1922-1969
Kerr, M. E.
    See Meaker, Marijane
Kesey, Ken 1935-
Kidder, Tracy 1945-
Kienzle, William X. 1928-
King, Francis 1923-
King, Larry L. 1929-
King, Martin Luther, Jr. 1929-
    1968
King, Stephen 1947-
Kingston, Maxine Hong 1940-
Kinnell, Galway 1927-
Kinsella, Thomas 1928-
Kinsella, W. P. 1935-
Kipling, Rudyard 1865-1936
Kirk, Russell 1918-
Kis, Danilo 1935-
Kissinger, Henry A. 1923-
Knowles, John 1926-
Koestler, Arthur 1905-1983
Konigsburg, E. L. 1930-
Konwicki, Tadeusz 1926-
Koontz, Dean R. 1945-
Kopit, Arthur 1937-
Kosinski, Jerzy 1933-
Krantz, Judith 1927-
Kroetsch, Robert 1927-
Kueng, Hans 1928-
Kumin, Maxine 1925-
Kundera, Milan 1929-
Kung, Hans
    See Kueng, Hans
Kunitz, Stanley 1905-

VOLUME 3: L-Q

Lagerkvist, Paer 1891-1974
La Guma, Alex 1925-1985
Laing, R. D. 1927-1989
Lamming, George 1927-
L'Amour, Louis 1908-1988
Langer, Susanne K. 1895-1985
Lardner, Ring
    See Lardner, Ring W.
Lardner, Ring W. 1885-1933
Larkin, Philip 1922-1985
Lasch, Christopher 1932-
Laurence, Margaret 1926-1987
Lavin, Mary 1912-
Lawrence, D. H. 1885-1930
Laye, Camara 1928-1980
Layton, Irving 1912-
Leakey, Louis S. B. 1903-1972
Leary, Timothy 1920-
Leavis, F. R. 1895-1978
Lebowitz, Fran 1951(?)-
le Carre, John
    See Cornwell, David
Lee, Harper 1926-
Lee, Laurie 1914-
Leger, Alexis Saint-Leger 1887-
    1975
Le Guin, Ursula K. 1929-
Leiber, Fritz 1910-
Leigh Fermor, Patrick 1915-
Lem, Stanislaw 1921-
L'Engle, Madeleine 1918-
Leonard, Elmore 1925-
Leonov, Leonid 1899-
Lessing, Doris 1919-
Levertov, Denise 1923-
Levi, Primo 1919-1987
Levin, Ira 1929-
Levi-Strauss, Claude 1908-
Lewis, C. S. 1898-1963
Lewis, Norman 1918-
Lewis, Sinclair 1885-1951
Lindbergh, Anne Morrow 1906-
Lippmann, Walter 1889-1974
Little, Malcolm 1925-1965
Lively, Penelope 1933-
Livesay, Dorothy 1909-
Llosa, Mario Vargas
    See Vargas Llosa, Mario
Lodge, David 1935-
London, Jack
    See London, John Griffith
London, John Griffith 1876-1916
Lopez, Barry Holstun 1945-
Lorca, Federico Garcia
    See Garcia Lorca, Federico
Lorde, Audre 1934-
Lorenz, Konrad Zacharias 1903-
Lovecraft, H. P. 1890-1937
Lovelace, Earl 1935-

Lovesey, Peter 1936-
Lowell, Robert 1917-1977
Lowry, Malcolm 1909-1957
Luce, Henry R. 1898-1967
Ludlum, Robert 1927-
Lukacs, George
    See Lukacs, Gyorgy
Lukacs, Gyorgy 1885-1971
Lukas, J. Anthony 1933-
Luria, Alexander R. 1902-1977
Lurie, Alison 1926-
MacBeth, George 1932-
MacDiarmid, Hugh
    See Grieve, C. M.
MacDonald, John D. 1916-1986
Macdonald, Ross
    See Millar, Kenneth
MacInnes, Colin 1914-1976
MacInnes, Helen 1907-1985
MacLean, Alistair 1922(?)-1987
MacLeish, Archibald 1892-1982
MacLennan, Hugh 1907-
MacNeice, Louis 1907-1963
Madden, David 1933-
Mahfouz, Naguib 1911(?)-
Mahfuz, Najib
    See Mahfouz, Naguib
Mailer, Norman 1923-
Mais, Roger 1905-1955
Malamud, Bernard 1914-1986
Malcolm X
    See Little, Malcolm
Malraux, Andre 1901-1976
Mamet, David 1947-
Manchester, William 1922-
Mann, Thomas 1875-1955
Manning, Olivia 1915-1980
Mao Tse-tung 1893-1976
Marcel, Gabriel Honore 1889-1973
Marsh, Ngaio 1899-1982
Marshall, Paule 1929-
Martin, Steve 1945-
Masefield, John 1878-1967
Maslow, Abraham H. 1908-1970
Mason, Bobbie Ann 1940-
Masters, Edgar Lee 1868-1950
Matthews, Patricia 1927-
Matthiessen, Peter 1927-
Matute, Ana Maria 1925-
Maugham, W. Somerset
    See Maugham, William Somerset
Maugham, William Somerset 1874-
    1965
Mauriac, Francois 1885-1970
Maurois, Andre 1885-1967
Maxwell, Gavin 1914-1969
McBain, Ed
    See Hunter, Evan
McCaffrey, Anne 1926-

McCarthy, Mary 1912-1989
McCullers, Carson 1917-1967
McCullough, Colleen 1938(?)-
McEwan, Ian 1948-
McGahern, John 1934-
McGrath, Thomas 1916-
McGuane, Thomas 1939-
McIntyre, Vonda N. 1948-
McKay, Claude
    See McKay, Festus Claudius
McKay, Festus Claudius 1889-1948
McKillip, Patricia A. 1948-
McLuhan, Marshall 1911-1980
McMurtry, Larry 1936-
McPhee, John 1931-
McPherson, James Alan 1943-
McPherson, James M. 1936-
Mead, Margaret 1901-1978
Meaker, Marijane 1927-
Mehta, Ved 1934-
Mencken, H. L. 1880-1956
Menninger, Karl 1893-1990
Mercer, David 1928-1980
Merril, Judith 1923-
Merrill, James 1926-
Merton, Thomas 1915-1968
Merwin, W. S. 1927-
Michaels, Leonard 1933-
Michener, James A. 1907(?)-
Millar, Kenneth 1915-1983
Millay, Edna St. Vincent 1892-
    1950
Miller, Arthur 1915-
Miller, Henry 1891-1980
Millett, Kate 1934-
Milligan, Spike
    See Milligan, Terence Alan
Milligan, Terence Alan 1918-
Milne, A. A. 1882-1956
Milner, Ron 1938-
Milosz, Czeslaw 1911-
Mishima, Yukio
    See Hiraoka, Kimitake
Mistral, Gabriela
    See Godoy Alcayaga, Lucila
Mitchell, Margaret 1900-1949
Mo, Timothy 1950(?)-
Momaday, N. Scott 1934-
Montague, John 1929-
Montale, Eugenio 1896-1981
Montherlant, Henry de 1896-1972
Moorcock, Michael 1939-
Moore, Brian 1921-
Moore, Marianne 1887-1972
Morante, Elsa 1918-1985
Moravia, Alberto
    See Pincherle, Alberto
Morgan, Robin 1941-
Morris, Desmond 1928-

Morris, James
    See Morris, Jan
Morris, Jan 1926-
Morris, Wright 1910-
Morrison, Toni 1931-
Mortimer, John 1923-
Mowat, Farley 1921-
Mrozek, Slawomir 1930-
Muggeridge, Malcolm 1903-
Mukherjee, Bharati 1940-
Munro, Alice 1931-
Munro, H. H. 1870-1916
Murdoch, Iris 1919-
Nabokov, Vladimir 1899-1977
Naipaul, Shiva 1945-1985
Naipaul, V. S. 1932-
Narayan, R. K. 1906-
Nash, Ogden 1902-1971
Naughton, Bill 1910-
Naylor, Gloria 1950-
Nehru, Jawaharlal 1889-1964
Nelson, Alice Ruth Moore Dunbar
    1875-1935
Nemerov, Howard 1920-
Neruda, Pablo 1904-1973
Newby, P. H. 1918-
Ngugi, James T.
    See Ngugi wa Thiong'o
Ngugi wa Thiong'o 1938-
Nichols, Peter 1927-
Nin, Anais 1903-1977
Niven, Larry
    See Niven, Laurence Van Cott
Niven, Laurence Van Cott 1938-
Nixon, Richard M. 1913-
Norton, Andre 1912-
Nye, Robert 1939-
Oates, Joyce Carol 1938-
O'Brien, Edna 1936-
O'Casey, Sean 1880-1964
O'Cathasaigh, Sean
    See O'Casey, Sean
O'Connor, Flannery 1925-1964
Odets, Clifford 1906-1963
Oe, Kenzaburo 1935-
O'Faolain, Julia 1932-
O'Faolain, Sean 1900-
O'Flaherty, Liam 1896-1984
O'Hara, Frank 1926-1966
O'Hara, John 1905-1970

Okigbo, Christopher 1932-1967
Olsen, Tillie 1913-
Olson, Charles 1910-1970
O'Neill, Eugene 1888-1953
Onetti, Juan Carlos 1909-
Oppenheimer, J. Robert 1904-1967
Ortega y Gasset, Jose 1883-1955
Orton, Joe
    See Orton, John Kingsley
Orton, John Kingsley 1933-1967
Orwell, George
    See Blair, Eric
Osborne, John 1929-
Ousmane, Sembene 1923-
Oz, Amos 1939-
Ozick, Cynthia 1928-
Page, P. K. 1916-
Pagnol, Marcel 1895-1974
Paley, Grace 1922-
Panova, Vera 1905-1973
Pargeter, Edith Mary 1913-
Parker, Dorothy 1893-1967
Parker, Robert B. 1932-
Parra, Nicanor 1914-
Parsons, Talcott 1902-1979
Pasolini, Pier Paolo 1922-1975
Pasternak, Boris 1890-1960
Patchen, Kenneth 1911-1972
Paterson, Katherine 1932-
Paton, Alan 1903-1988
Patterson, Harry 1929-
Pauling, Linus 1901-
Paz, Octavio 1914-
p'Bitek, Okot 1931-1982
Peake, Mervyn 1911-1968
Peale, Norman Vincent 1898-
Pearson, Andrew Russell 1897-
    1969
Pearson, Drew
    See Pearson, Andrew Russell
Pedersen, Knut 1859-1952
Percy, Walker 1916-1990
Perelman, S. J. 1904-1979
Perse, Saint-John
    See Leger, Alexis Saint-Leger
Peters, Ellis
    See Pargeter, Edith Mary
Petry, Ann 1908-
Pevsner, Nikolaus 1902-1983

Phillips, Jayne Anne 1952-
Piaget, Jean 1896-1980
Piercy, Marge 1936-
Pilcher, Rosamunde 1924-
Pincherle, Alberto 1907-
Pinter, Harold 1930-
Pirsig, Robert M. 1928-
Plante, David 1940-
Plath, Sylvia 1932-1963
Plimpton, George 1927-
Plomer, William Charles Franklin
    1903-1973
Plowman, Piers
    See Kavanagh, Patrick
Pohl, Frederik 1919-
Pollitt, Katha 1949-
Popper, Karl R. 1902-
Porter, Katherine Anne 1890-1980
Porter, William Sydney 1862-1910
Potok, Chaim 1929-
Potter, Dennis 1935-
Potter, Stephen 1900-1969
Pound, Ezra 1885-1972
Powell, Anthony 1905-
Powers, J. F. 1917-
Powys, John Cowper 1872-1963
Prevert, Jacques 1900-1977
Prichard, Katharine Susannah
    1883-1969
Priestley, J. B. 1894-1984
Pritchett, V. S. 1900-
Proust, Marcel 1871-1922
Puig, Manuel 1932-1990
Purdy, James 1923-
Puzo, Mario 1920-
Pym, Barbara 1913-1980
Pynchon, Thomas 1937-
Python, Monty
    See Cleese, John
Qian Zhongshu
    See Ch'ien Chung-shu
Quasimodo, Salvatore 1901-1968
Queen, Ellery
    See Dannay, Frederic
    and Sturgeon, Theodore
    and Vance, John Holbrook
Queneau, Raymond 1903-1976
Quiroga, Horacio 1878-1937
Quoirez, Francoise 1935-

VOLUME 4: R-Z

Raine, Kathleen 1908-
Rand, Ayn 1905-1982
Ransom, John Crowe 1888-1974
Rao, Raja 1909-
Rattigan, Terence 1911-1977
Ravitch, Diane 1938-
Reed, Ishmael 1938-
Remarque, Erich Maria 1898-1970

Rendell, Ruth 1930-
Rexroth, Kenneth 1905-1982
Rhys, Jean 1894-1979
Rice, Elmer 1892-1967
Rich, Adrienne 1929-
Richler, Mordecai 1931-
Richter, Conrad 1890-1968
Rilke, Rainer Maria 1875-1926

Ritsos, Giannes
    See Ritsos, Yannis
Ritsos, Yannis 1909-
Robbe-Grillet, Alain 1922-
Robbins, Harold 1916-
Robbins, Thomas Eugene 1936-
Robbins, Tom
    See Robbins, Thomas Eugene

Robinson, Edwin Arlington 1869–1935

Robinson, Joan 1903–1983

Rodd, Kylie Tennant 1912–1988

Roethke, Theodore 1908–1963

Rogers, Carl R. 1902–1987

Rogers, Rosemary 1932–

Romains, Jules 1885–1972

Rooney, Andrew A. 1919–

Rooney, Andy
    See Rooney, Andrew A.

Rossner, Judith 1935–

Rostand, Edmond 1868–1918

Roth, Henry 1906–

Roth, Philip 1933–

Roy, Gabrielle 1909–1983

Rozewicz, Tadeusz 1921–

Rubens, Bernice 1923–

Rukeyser, Muriel 1913–1980

Rulfo, Juan 1918–1986

Rushdie, Salman 1947–

Russ, Joanna 1937–

Russell, Bertrand 1872–1970

Sabato, Ernesto 1911–

Saberhagen, Fred 1930–

Sacks, Oliver 1933–

Sackville-West, V. 1892–1962

Sagan, Carl 1934–

Sagan, Francoise
    See Quoirez, Francoise

Saint-Exupery, Antoine de 1900–1944

Saki
    See Munro, H. H.

Salinger, J. D. 1919–

Salisbury, Harrison E. 1908–

Sanchez, Sonia 1934–

Sandburg, Carl 1878–1967

Sanders, Lawrence 1920–

Sandoz, Mari 1896–1966

Sansom, William 1912–1976

Santmyer, Helen Hooven 1895–1986

Saroyan, William 1908–1981

Sarraute, Nathalie 1900–

Sarton, May 1912–

Sartre, Jean-Paul 1905–1980

Sassoon, Siegfried 1886–1967

Sauser-Hall, Frederic 1887–1961

Sayers, Dorothy L. 1893–1957

Schaeffer, Susan Fromberg 1941–

Schlafly, Phyllis 1924–

Schlesinger, Arthur M., Jr. 1917–

Schmitz, Aron Hector 1861–1928

Schwartz, Delmore 1913–1966

Sciascia, Leonardo 1921–1989

Scott, Paul 1920–1978

Seferiades, Giorgos Stylianou 1900–1971

Seferis, George
    See Seferiades, Giorgos Stylianou

Segal, Erich 1937–

Seifert, Jaroslav 1901–1986

Selvon, Samuel 1923–

Sendak, Maurice 1928–

Sender, Ramon 1902–1982

Senghor, Leopold Sedar 1906–

Sepheriades, Georgios
    See Seferiades, Giorgos Stylianou

Setien, Miguel Delibes
    See Delibes Setien, Miguel

Seuss, Dr.
    See Geisel, Theodor Seuss

Sexton, Anne 1928–1974

Shaffer, Peter 1926–

Shange, Ntozake 1948–

Shapiro, Karl 1913–

Shaw, George Bernard 1856–1950

Shaw, Irwin 1913–1984

Sheed, Wilfrid 1930–

Sheehy, Gail 1936(?)–

Sheen, Fulton J. 1895–1979

Sheldon, Alice Hastings Bradley 1915–1987

Sheldon, Sidney 1917–

Shepard, Sam 1943–

Shirer, William L. 1904–

Sholokhov, Mikhail 1905–1984

Siddons, Anne Rivers 1936–

Sillanpaa, Frans Eemil 1888–1964

Sillitoe, Alan 1928–

Silone, Ignazio 1900–1978

Silverberg, Robert 1935–

Simak, Clifford D. 1904–1988

Simenon, Georges 1903–1989

Simon, Claude 1913–

Simon, Kate 1912–1990

Simon, Neil 1927–

Simpson, Dorothy 1933–

Simpson, George Gaylord 1902–1984

Simpson, Harriette
    See Arnow, Harriette Simpson

Simpson, Louis 1923–

Sinclair, Andrew 1935–

Sinclair, Upton 1878–1968

Singer, Isaac Bashevis 1904–

Sitwell, Dame Edith 1887–1964

Skinner, B. F. 1904–1990

Skvorecky, Josef 1924–

Smith, Florence Margaret 1902–1971

Smith, Stevie
    See Smith, Florence Margaret

Smith, Wilbur 1933–

Snodgrass, William D. 1926–

Snow, C. P. 1905–1980

Solzhenitsyn, Aleksandr I. 1918–

Sontag, Susan 1933–

Soyinka, Wole 1934–

Spark, Muriel 1918–

Spencer, Elizabeth 1921–

Spender, Stephen 1909–

Spillane, Frank Morrison 1918–

Spillane, Mickey
    See Spillane, Frank Morrison

Spock, Benjamin 1903–

Stafford, Jean 1915–1979

Stead, Christina 1902–1983

Steel, Danielle 1947–

Stegner, Wallace 1909–

Stein, Gertrude 1874–1946

Steinbeck, John 1902–1968

Steinem, Gloria 1934–

Steiner, George 1929–

Stevens, Wallace 1879–1955

Stevenson, Anne 1933–

Stewart, J. I. M. 1906–

Stone, Irving 1903–1989

Stone, Robert 1937–

Stoppard, Tom 1937–

Storey, David 1933–

Stow, Randolph 1935–

Straub, Peter 1943–

Sturgeon, Theodore 1918–1985

Styron, William 1925–

Susann, Jacqueline 1921–1974

Suzuki, D. T.
    See Suzuki, Daisetz Teitaro

Suzuki, Daisetz Teitaro 1870–1966

Svevo, Italo
    See Schmitz, Aron Hector

Swenson, May 1919–1989

Symons, Julian 1912–

Tagore, Rabindranath 1861–1941

Talese, Gay 1932–

Tate, Allen 1899–1979

Taylor, A. J. P. 1906–

Taylor, Elizabeth 1912–1975

Taylor, Peter 1917–

Taylor, Telford 1908–

Teller, Edward 1908–

Tennant, Kylie
    See Rodd, Kylie Tennant

Terkel, Louis 1912–

Terkel, Studs
    See Terkel, Louis

Theroux, Paul 1941–

Thibault, Jacques Anatole Francois 1844–1924

Thomas, Audrey 1935–

Thomas, D. M. 1935–

Thomas, Dylan 1914–1953

Thomas, Joyce Carol 1938–

Thomas, Lewis 1913–

Thomas, R. S. 1913–

Thompson, Hunter S. 1939–

Thurber, James 1894–1961

Tillich, Paul 1886–1965

Tiptree, James, Jr.
    See Sheldon, Alice Hastings Bradley

Toffler, Alvin 1928-
Toland, John 1912-
Tolkien, J. R. R. 1892-1973
Toomer, Jean 1894-1967
Torres Bodet, Jaime 1902-1974
Torsvan, Ben Traven
  See Traven, B.
Tournier, Michel 1924-
Townsend, Sue 1946-
Traven, B. ?-1969
Tremblay, Michel 1942-
Trevor, William
  See Cox, William Trevor
Trifonov, Yuri 1925-1981
Trillin, Calvin 1935-
Trilling, Diane 1905-
Trilling, Lionel 1905-1975
Troyat, Henri 1911-
Truman, Margaret 1924-
Tryon, Thomas 1926-
Tsvetaeva, Marina 1892-1941
Tuchman, Barbara W. 1912-1989
Tutuola, Amos 1920-
Tyler, Anne 1941-
Tynan, Kenneth 1927-1980
Uchida, Yoshiko 1921-
Unamuno, Miguel de 1864-1936
Undset, Sigrid 1882-1949
Updike, John 1932-
Uris, Leon 1924-
Valery, Paul 1871-1945
Vallejo, Antonio Buero
  See Buero Vallejo, Antonio
Vance, Jack
  See Vance, John Holbrook
Vance, John Holbrook 1916-
Van Doren, Mark 1894-1972
van Lawick-Goodall, Jane
  See Goodall, Jane
Vargas Llosa, Mario 1936-
Vendler, Helen 1933-
Vidal, Gore 1925-
Vine, Barbara
  See Rendell, Ruth
Voinovich, Vladimir 1932-

von Hayek, Friedrich August
  See Hayek, F. A.
Vonnegut, Kurt, Jr. 1922-
Voznesensky, Andrei 1933-
Wain, John 1925-
Walcott, Derek 1930-
Walker, Alice 1944-
Walker, Margaret 1915-
Wallace, Irving 1916-1990
Wallant, Edward Lewis 1926-1962
Wambaugh, Joseph 1937-
Warner, Sylvia Ashton
  See Ashton-Warner, Sylvia
Warner, Sylvia Townsend 1893-1978
Warren, Robert Penn 1905-1989
Waruk, Kona
  See Harris, Wilson
Waterhouse, Keith 1929-
Waugh, Evelyn 1903-1966
Wedgwood, C. V. 1910-
Weinstein, Nathan
  See West, Nathanael
Weldon, Fay 1933(?)-
Wells, H. G. 1866-1946
Welty, Eudora 1909-
Wesker, Arnold 1932-
Wesley, Mary 1912-
West, Jessamyn 1902-1984
West, Morris L. 1916-
West, Nathanael 1903-1940
West, Rebecca 1892-1983
Wharton, Edith 1862-1937
Wheatley, Dennis 1897-1977
White, E. B. 1899-1985
White, Edmund 1940-
White, Patrick 1912-
White, Phyllis Dorothy James 1920-
White, Theodore H. 1915-1986
Wiesel, Elie 1928-
Wilbur, Richard 1921-
Wilder, Thornton 1897-1975
Wilhelm, Kate
  See Wilhelm, Katie Gertrude

Wilhelm, Katie Gertrude 1928-
Will, George F. 1941-
Willard, Nancy 1936-
Williams, Emlyn 1905-1987
Williams, Raymond 1921-1988
Williams, Tennessee 1911-1983
Williams, William Carlos 1883-1963
Williamson, Henry 1895-1977
Willingham, Calder 1922-
Wilson, Angus 1913-
Wilson, August 1945-
Wilson, Colin 1931-
Wilson, Edmund 1895-1972
Wilson, Edward O. 1929-
Wilson, Ethel Davis 1888(?)-1980
Wilson, John Burgess 1917-
Wilson, Robert M. 1944-
Winters, Yvor 1900-1968
Wodehouse, P. G. 1881-1975
Wolf, Christa 1929-
Wolfe, Thomas 1900-1938
Wolfe, Thomas Kennerly, Jr. 1931-
Wolfe, Tom
  See Wolfe, Thomas Kennerly, Jr.
Woodiwiss, Kathleen E. 1939-
Woodward, Bob
  See Woodward, Robert Upshur
Woodward, Robert Upshur 1943-
Woolf, Virginia 1882-1941
Wouk, Herman 1915-
Wright, Charles 1935-
Wright, James 1927-1980
Wright, Judith 1915-
Wright, Richard 1908-1960
Yeats, William Butler 1865-1939
Yerby, Frank G. 1916-
Yevtushenko, Yevgeny 1933-
Yezierska, Anzia 1885(?)-1970
Yglesias, Helen 1915-
Yourcenar, Marguerite 1903-1987
Zelazny, Roger 1937-
Zindel, Paul 1936-
Zukofsky, Louis 1904-1978

MAJOR 20th-CENTURY WRITERS

♦

♦

♦

♦

Volume 3: L-Q

L

La COLERE, Francois
See ARAGON, Louis

*   *   *

LACOLERE, Francois
See ARAGON, Louis

*   *   *

LAGERKVIST, Paer (Fabian) 1891-1974

PERSONAL: Born May 23, 1891, in Vaexjoe, Sweden; died July 11, 1974; son of Anders Johan (a railway linesman) and Johanna (Blad) Lagerquist; married Karen Dagmar Johanne Soerensen, 1918 (marriage dissolved, 1925); married Elaine Luella Hallberg, 1925. *Education:* Attended University of Uppsala, 1911-12.

CAREER: Writer. Theater critic for *Svenska Dagbladet* (newspaper), Stockholm, Sweden, 1919.

AWARDS, HONORS: Literary prize from Samfundet De Nio, 1928; elected to Swedish Academy of Literature, 1940; Ph.D. from University of Gothenburg, 1941; Nobel Prize for Literature, 1951.

WRITINGS:

NOVELS

Det eviga leendet, [Stockholm], 1920, reprinted, Bonnier, 1969, translation by Denys W. Harding and Erik Mesterton published as *The Eternal Smile,* Gordon Fraser, 1934.
Boedeln, [Stockholm], 1933, reprinted, Bonnier, 1966.
Dvaergen, Bonnier, 1944, translation by Alexandra Dick published as *The Dwarf,* L. B. Fisher, 1945.
Barabbas, Bonnier, 1950, translation by Alan Blair with a preface by Lucien Maury and a letter by Andre Gide published as *Barabbas,* Random House, 1951.
Sibyllan, Bonnier, 1956, translation by Naomi Walford published as *The Sibyl,* Random House, 1958.
Ahasverus doed, Bonnier, 1960, translation by Walford published as *The Death of Ahasuerus,* Random House, 1962.
Pilgrim paa havet, Bonnier, 1962, translation by Walford published as *Pilgrim at Sea,* Random House, 1964.
Det Heliga landet, Bonnier, 1964, translation by Walford published as *The Holy Land,* Random House, 1966.
Mariamne, Bonnier, 1967, translation by Walford published as *Herod and Mariamne,* Knopf, 1968.

Also author of *Maenniskor,* 1912, and *Tva sagor om livet,* 1913.

PLAYS

Sista maenskan (three-act), Bonnier, 1917.
Teater: Den svaara stunden [and] *Modern teater: Synpunkter och angrepp* (three one-act plays and essays; first produced together in Duesseldorf at Schauspielhaus, 1918), Bonnier, 1918.
Himlens hemlighet (one-act; produced in Stockholm at Intimate Theatre, 1921).
Den osynlige (three-act; first produced in Stockholm at Royal Dramatic Theatre, 1924), Bonnier, 1923.
Han som fick leva om sitt liv (three-act; first produced at Royal Dramatic Theatre, 1928), Bonnier, 1928.
Konungen (three-act; first produced in Malmoe at City Theatre, 1950), [Stockholm], 1932.
Boedeln (one-act; adapted from Lagerkvist's novel of the same title), first produced in Stockholm at Vasa Theatre, 1934.
Mannen utan sjael (five-act; first produced at Royal Dramatic Theatre, 1938) [Stockholm], 1936, translation by H. Koekeritz published in *Scandinavian Plays of the Twentieth Century,* Volume I, [Princeton, N.J.], 1944.
Seger i moerker (four-act; first produced at Royal Dramatic Theatre, 1940), Bonnier, 1939.
Misommardroem i fattighuset (three-act; first produced in Stockholm at Blanche Theatre, 1941), [Stockholm], 1941, translation by Alan Blair published as *Midsummer Dream in the Workhouse,* Hodge, 1953.
Den Vises sten (four-act; first produced at Royal Dramatic Theatre, 1948), [Stockholm], 1947.
Laat maenniskan leva (one-act; first produced in Goeteborg at City Theatre, 1949), Bonnier, 1949, translation by H. Alexander and L. Jones published in *Scandinavian Plays of the Twentieth Century,* Volume III, [Princeton, N.J.], 1931.
Barabbas (two-act; adapted from Lagerkvist's novel of the same title; first produced at Royal Dramatic Theatre, 1953) Bonnier, 1953.

POETRY

Motiv (with prose pieces), Bonnier, 1914.
Aangest, Bonnier, 1916, reprinted, 1966.
Hjaertats saanger, 1926, reprinted, 1962.
Vid laegereld, [Stockholm], 1932.
Genius, [Stockholm], 1937.

Saang och strid, Bonnier, 1940.
Dikter, Bonnier, 1941.
Hemmet och stjaernan, Bonnier, 1942.
Aftonland, Bonnier, 1953, translation by W. H. Auden and Leif Sjoeberg with an introduction by Sjoeberg published as *Evening Land,* Wayne State University Press, 1975.
Dikter, Bonnier, 1958.
Valda dikter, Bonnier, 1967.
Dikter, Bonnier, 1974.

Also author of *Den lyckliges vaeg,* 1921.

NONFICTION

Gaest hos verkligheten [and] *Det besegrade livet* (autobiography), Bonnier, 1925, *Det besegrade livet* published separately, Bonnier, 1927, *Gaest hos verkligheten* published separately, Bonnier, 1967, translation of *Gaest hos verkligheten* by Erik Mesterton and Denys W. Harding published as *Guest of Reality,* J. Cape, 1936.
Den knutna naeven (essays), [Stockholm], 1934.
Antechnat: Ur efterlaemnade dagboecker och anteckningar (diary), Bonnier, 1977.

OTHER

Onda Sagor (title means "Evil Tales"), [Stockholm], 1924, reprinted, Aldus, 1965.
Den Befriande maenniskan, [Stockholm], 1939.
Verner von Heidenstam: Intraedestal i Svenska akademien den 20 december 1940, Bonnier, 1940.
(With Gunnar De Frumerie) *Frya saanger* (songs), Foereningen svenska tonsaettare (Stockholm), 1945.
(With De Frumerie) *Tre saanger,* Foereningen svenska tonsaettare, 1946.
Sagor, satire och noveller, Bonnier, 1957.
(With Christopher Fry) *Barabbas* (screenplay; adapted from own novel), Columbia Pictures, 1962.
Sjaelarnas maskerad, Aldus, 1962.
Pilgrimen, Bonnier, 1966.

COLLECTIONS

Jaern och maenniskor (short stories), Bonnier, 1915.
Kaos (includes stories, poems, and a play, "Himlens hemlighet"), [Stockholm], 1919.
Kaempande ande (short stories and prose sketches), [Stockholm], 1930.
Skrifter, three volumes, [Stockholm], 1932.
I den tiden (short stories), [Stockholm], 1935.
Prosa, [Stockholm], 1945, published in five volumes, 1949.
Dramatik (includes "Modern teater," "Sista maenskan," "Den svaara stunden," "Himlens hemlighet," "Den osynlige," "Han som fick leva om sitt liv," "Konungen," "Boedeln," "Mannen utan sjael," "Seger i moerker," and "Midsommardroem i fattighuset"), Bonnier, 1946.
The Marriage Feast and Other Stories, translated from the Swedish by Blair and Carl Eric Lindin, Chatto & Windus, 1955, Hill & Wang, 1973.
Boedeln, Den knutna naeven, I den tiden, [and] *Den befriande maenniskan,* Bonnier, 1956.
Prosastycken ur aangest, Den fordringsfulla gaesten, Det eviga leendet, Morgonen, [and] *Onda sagor,* Bonnier, 1962.
Ahasverus doed, Pilgrim paa havet, [and] *Det Heliga landet,* Bonnier, 1966.

SIDELIGHTS: Born into a strongly religious and conservative family, Paer Lagerkvist abandoned his early training and, after a year of studying humanities at the University of Uppsala, left for an extended trip to Paris. There he became acquainted with the modern art movement and was especially influenced by the Fauvist, cubist, and naivist movements that were in vogue at the time. His early writings reflected these artistic principles. Lagerkvist's own artistic principles were delineated in a controversial essay, "Modern Theatre: Points of View and Attack," published in 1918. In the essay Lagerkvist denounced the Scandinavian playwright Ibsen and the naturalism he espoused and turned to the playwright Strindberg as his literary mentor. *Anguish,* Lagerkvist's early book of poetry, has been called the first expressionistic work in Swedish literature, and its publication established his reputation as an important Scandinavian writer.

Lagerkvist's early work was dark, lyrical, and pessimistic. Holger Ahlenius characterized his writings of this era as "one single cry of despair over the bestiality of man." The conflict between the traditional Christian and the modern scientific-determinist views became a departure point for his writing: Lagerkvist's works were largely concerned with man's relationship to God, with the meaning of life, and with the conflict between good and evil. In the thirties, in response to the brutalities of Nazism and fascism, Lagerkvist became, according to Alrik Gustafson, "the most eloquent and rigidly uncompromising Swedish critic of totalitarianism." He became known as a defender of the values of "heroic humanitarian idealism." Lagerkvist described himself as "a believer without faith—a religious atheist." Andre Gide wrote: "It is a measure of Lagerkvist's success that he managed so admirably to maintain his balance on a tightrope which stretches across the dark abyss that lies between the world of reality and the world of faith."

Although Lagerkvist's later works were thematically similar to his earlier works, they became more accessible, less pessimistic and more realistic. They began to express "love, sublimated into a Christian-Platonic mysticism," Ahlenius commented. Eventually Lagerkvist came to believe that good and love could triumph over evil. His play *Han som fick leva om sitt,* published in 1928, is generally regarded as the beginning of his more mature, optimistic period.

Lagerkvist was virtually unknown in the United States until the publication of the English translation of *Barabbas* in 1951, the same year he received the Nobel Prize for Literature. It tells the story of the condemned thief whose place Christ took on the cross. In a review of the novel, Graham Bates remarked: "The work combines the utmost physical realism with an intensity of spiritual conflict not often equaled in the retelling of Biblical tales. Paer Lagerkvist has taken a man barely mentioned in the New Testament and has built him into a character as real, as evil, and as good as he must have been to the men who knew him those centuries ago. This is no outline sketch in black and white but a deeply conceived and richly colored portrait of a man driven beyond the powers of his endurance by a force he could never actually believe in."

Charles Rollo called *Barabbas* a "small masterpiece" and commented: "In a prose style that is swift, sparing, limpid, and hauntingly intense in its effects—a style whose energy and beauty the translator, Alan Blair, has magnificently preserved—Lagerkvist evokes the early Christian era with a selective realism more telling than any ponderously detailed reconstruction of the past. Every image sustains the feeling, 'That is the way things were'; every movement in the story has an unerring rightness." Harvey Breit praised Lagerkvist for taking "a complex moral theme" and constructing the tale "with a craftsman's complete mastery and simplicity," synthesizing "an elaborate, moral vision and austere poetic style."

"All [Lagerkvist's] fiction is freighted with philosophy, but in the best of it narrative structure and scene finely support the burden," critic Richard M. Ohmann wrote. "And in the best of his fiction that burden is overwhelmingly one of doubt and brooding evil, not of reassurance. Uncertainty and suffering are woven into the very fabric of experience as Lagerkvist most powerfully feels it; affirmation in his world is like a candle in the outer darkness." Michele Murray, however, complained that Lagerkvist's writing lacked intensity and specificity, which left his characters without individuality. In a review of *Pilgrim at Sea,* she declared: "Lagerkvist's characters are not even characters, but mere spokesmen, mouthpieces of Good or Evil or Lust or Cupidity, whose sins and virtues are as pallid as they are. Deprived of the density which sustains fiction and summons the power of evocation, Lagerkvist has written, not a Profound Statement of Mankind's Struggle With Good and Evil, . . . but merely a philosophical melodrama, in which phantoms wrestle with vague concepts devoid of both significance and vitality."

Adele Bloch was more appreciative of Lagerkvist's use of archetypal characters and situations. She compared him to Thomas Mann, "whose heroes fashion their natures and destinies according to certain legendary prototypes." She continued: "Fuller recognition of identification with mythical figures is slowly attained by certain individuals, as the generations move towards more civilized levels of conscience. In the case of Lagerkvist's fictional characters, complete self-realization can be gained only after a lifetime of guilt, struggles and re-enactment of some original sins."

Winston Weathers reviewed Lagerkvist's last novel, *Herod and Mariamne,* which he termed "another religious-psychological parable." "At that novel's end," he wrote, "Lagerkvist reminds the reader once more that Herod is representative of a mankind 'that replenishes the earth but whose race shall one day be erased from it, and . . . will leave no memorial.' *Herod and Mariamne* is a bitter novel, a brief, brilliant, haunting work. Yet its bitterness may be a challenge: its chilling 'no' may stimulate the 'yes' of faith."

Lucien Maury summed up Lagerkvist's career in the preface he wrote to the English translation of *Barabbas.* He wrote: "There is scarcely a single aesthetic problem in the realm of literature which Lagerkvist has not striven to define and resolve—not only theoretically, but in the practice of his art—whether in the theatre, the short story, or works of meditation, and verse. . . . It has been a far cry with him from anguish to serenity, to that interior joy which triumphs over all despair; from early revolt to an acceptance which has never been mere resignation, though often it is not far removed from a mood of burning adoration, from a religious sense at one with reason, from faith in the existence of a principle to be found at the source of all our human destiny."

BIOGRAPHICAL/CRITICAL SOURCES:

BOOKS

Contemporary Literary Criticism, Gale, Volume 7, 1977, Volume 10, 1979, Volume 13, 1980, Volume 54, 1989.
Lagerkvist, Paer, *Guest of Reality,* translated from the Swedish by Erik Mesterton and Denys W. Harding, J. Cape, 1936.
Lagerkvist, Paer, *Barabbas,* Random House, 1951.
Mooney, Harry J. and Thomas F. Staley, editors, *The Shapeless God: Essays on Modern Fiction,* University of Pittsburgh Press, 1968.
Sjoeberg, Leif, *Paer Lagerkvist,* Columbia University Press, 1976.
Spector, Robert Donald, *Paer Lagerkvist,* Twayne, 1973.

Weathers, Winston, *Paer Lagerkvist: A Critical Essay,* Eerdmans, 1968.

PERIODICALS

American-Scandinavian Review, December, 1940.
American-Swedish Monthly, November, 1951.
Atlantic, December, 1951, October, 1975.
Commonweal, May 11, 1962, April 3, 1964, January 10, 1969.
International Fiction Review, January, 1974.
New York Times, November 16, 1951.
New York Times Book Review, November 25, 1951.
Saturday Review of Literature, October 27, 1951.

OBITUARIES:

PERIODICALS

Newsweek, July 22, 1974.
New York Times, July 12, 1974.
Time, July 22, 1974.

*   *   *

La GUMA, (Justin) Alex(ander)   1925-1985

PERSONAL: Born February 20, 1925, in Cape Town, South Africa; immigrated to London, England, 1966; died October 11, 1985, in Havana, Cuba; son of Jimmy and Wilhelmina (Alexander) La Guma; married Blanche Valerie Herman (an office manager and former midwife), November 13, 1954; children: Eugene, Bartholomew. *Education:* Cape Technical College, student, 1941-42, correspondence student, 1965; London School of Journalism, correspondence student, 1964.

ADDRESSES: Agent—Hope Leresche & Sale, 11 Jubilee Pl., London SW3 3TE, England.

CAREER: New Age (weekly newspaper), Cape Town, South Africa, staff journalist, 1955-62; free-lance writer and journalist, 1962-85. Member of African National Congress, 1955-85. Member of editorial board, Afro-Asian Writers Bureau, 1965-85.

MEMBER: Afro-Asian Writers Association (deputy secretary-general, 1973-85).

AWARDS, HONORS: Afro-Asian Lotus Award for literature, 1969.

WRITINGS:

NOVELS

And a Threefold Cord, Seven Seas Publishers (East Berlin), 1964.
The Stone Country, Seven Seas Publishers, 1967, Heinemann, 1974.
In the Fog of the Season's End, Heinemann, 1972, Third Press, 1973.
Time of the Butcherbird, Heinemann, 1979.

CONTRIBUTOR

Richard Rive, editor, *Quartet: New Voices from South Africa,* Crown, 1963, new edition, Heinemann, 1968.
Ellis Ayitey Komey and Ezekiel Mphahlele, editors, *Modern African Stories,* Faber, 1964.
Mphahlele, editor, *African Writing Today,* Penguin, 1967.
O. R. Dathorne and Willfried Feuser, editors, *Africa in Prose,* Penguin, 1969.
Charles R. Larson, editor, *Modern African Stories,* Collins, 1971.

OTHER

A Walk in the Night (novelette), Mbari Publications (Ibadan, Nigeria), 1962, published with additional material as *A Walk in the Night and Other Stories,* Northwestern University Press, 1967.

(Editor) *Apartheid: A Collection of Writings on South African Racism by South Africans,* International Publishers, 1971.

A Soviet Journey (travel), Progress Publishers (Moscow), 1978.

Contributor of short stories to magazines, including *Black Orpheus* and *Africa South.*

SIDELIGHTS: Alex La Guma's active opposition to the South African government's racist policies permeates his fiction as it did his life. A member of the Cape Town district Communist party until it was banned in 1950, La Guma worked for a time on the staff of the leftist newspaper *New Age.* He came to the government's notice in 1955, when he helped draw up the Freedom Charter, a declaration of rights; in 1956, he was accused of treason, and in 1961 he was arrested for helping to organize a strike.

Various acts passed by the South African government kept La Guma either in prison or under twenty-four-hour house arrest for some years, including time in solitary confinement. La Guma spent this time writing; he composed the novel *And a Threefold Cord* while he was under house arrest in the early 1960s. He left South Africa in 1966, moving to London, where he remained until 1979, writing and working as a journalist. At the time of his death, he was serving as the African National Congress representative to Cuba.

Much of La Guma's work treats the situations and problems he saw in his native Cape Town. *A Walk in the Night* tells the story of Michael Adonis, a factory worker who has just lost his job because he talked back to his white supervisor. Frustrated, Michael commits a senseless crime; he kills the decrepit old ex-actor Doughty. Intertwined with Michael's fate are the lives of Raalt, a white constable on duty in the district where the murder is committed, and Willieboy, a malingerer and occasional criminal. The novelette, says Shatto Arthur Gakwandi in his *The Novel and Contemporary Experience in Africa,* avoids "being a sermon of despair [while also evading] advocating sentimental solutions to the problems that it portrays. Without pathos, it creates a powerful impression of that rhythm of violence which characterizes South African life." He concludes, "All these characters are victims of a system that denies them the facility of living in harmony with fellow human beings and their frustrations find release in acts of violence against weaker members of their society." The power of La Guma's writing leads John Updike, writing for the *New Yorker,* to say of *In the Fog of the Season's End* that it "delivers, through its portrait of a few hunted blacks attempting to subvert the brutal regime of apartheid, a social protest reminiscent, in its closely detailed texture and level indignation, of Dreiser and Zola."

Several of Alex La Guma's books have been translated into Russian; his work is banned in South Africa.

BIOGRAPHICAL/CRITICAL SOURCES:

BOOKS

Contemporary Literary Criticism, Volume 19, Gale, 1981.

Duerden, Dennis, and Cosmo Pieterse, editors, *African Writers Talking: A Collection of Interviews,* Heinemann, 1972.

Encyclopedia of World Literature in the Twentieth Century, Volume 3, revised edition, Ungar, 1983.

Gakwandi, Shatto Arthur, *The Novel and Contemporary Experience in Africa,* Africana Publishing, 1977.

Mphahlele, Ezekiel, *African Image,* Praeger, 1962, reissued, 1974.

Wanjala, C. L., *Standpoints on African Literature,* East African Literature Bureau (Nairobi, Kenya), 1973.

Zell, Hans M., and others, *A New Reader's Guide to African Literature,* 2nd revised and expanded edition, Holmes & Meier, 1983.

PERIODICALS

Black Scholar, July/August, 1986.
Busara, Volume 8, number 1, 1976.
Journal of Commonwealth Literature, June, 1973.
New Statesman, January 29, 1965, November 3, 1972.
New Yorker, January 21, 1974.
PHYLON, March, 1978.
Sechaba (London), February, 1971.
Times Literary Supplement, January 21, 1965, October 20, 1972.
World Literature Today, winter, 1980.

OBITUARIES:

PERIODICALS

Freedomways, Volume 25, number 3, 1985.
Times (London), November 23, 1985.

*   *   *

LAIDLAW, A. K.
   See GRIEVE, C(hristopher) M(urray)

*   *   *

LAING, R(onald) D(avid)   1927-1989

PERSONAL: Born October 7, 1927, in Glasgow, Scotland; died of a heart attack, August 23, 1989, in St. Tropez, France; son of D. P. M. and Amelia Laing; divorced; married second wife, Jutta; children: (first marriage) five; (second marriage) Adam, Natasha, Max. *Education:* University of Glasgow, M.D., 1951.

ADDRESSES: Home—2 Eton Rd., London NW3 45P, England. *Office*—c/o Katriona Myrlees, 265 Mount Pleasant Rd., London N17, England.

CAREER: Glasgow and West of Scotland Neurosurgical Unit, Glasgow, Scotland, intern, 1951; University of Glasgow, Glasgow, instructor in psychological medicine, 1953-56; Glasgow Royal Mental Hospital, Glasgow, psychiatrist, 1955; Tavistock Clinic, London, England, psychiatrist, 1956-61; Tavistock Institute of Human Relations, London, researcher in family relations, 1961-67; Langham Clinic for Psychotherapy, London, director, 1962-65; Philadelphia Association, London, chairman, beginning in 1964; private practice of psychotherapy, London, beginning in 1967. Speaker at U.S. colleges. *Military service:* British Army, psychiatrist in medical corps, 1951-53.

AWARDS, HONORS: Fellow of Foundations Fund for Research in Psychiatry, 1960-67 and Tavistock Institute of Medical Psychology, 1963-64.

WRITINGS:

The Divided Self: A Study of Sanity and Madness, Quadrangle Books, 1960, also published as *The Divided Self: An Existential Study of Sanity and Madness,* Penguin, 1965.

The Self and Others: Further Studies in Sanity and Madness, Tavistock Publications, 1961, Quadrangle Books, 1962, revised edition published as *Self and Others,* Tavistock Publications, 1969, Pantheon, 1970.

(Translator with David G. Cooper) *Reason and Violence: A Decade of Sartre's Philosophy, 1950-60,* foreword by Jean-Paul Sartre, Humanities, 1964.

(With A. Esterson) *Sanity, Madness, and the Family,* Tavistock Publications, 1964, Basic Books, 1965.

(With A. R. Lee and H. Phillipson) *Interpersonal Perception: A Theory and a Method of Research,* Springer Publishing Co., 1966.

The Politics of Experience, Pantheon, 1967.

The Politics of Experience [and] *The Bird of Paradise,* Penguin, 1967.

Knots (poems), Pantheon, 1970.

The Politics of the Family and Other Essays, Pantheon, 1971.

Do You Love Me? An Entertainment in Conversation and Verse (poems), Pantheon, 1976.

The Facts of Life: An Essay in Feelings, Facts, and Fantasy, Pantheon, 1976.

Conversations With Adam and Natasha, Pantheon, 1977.

Conversations With Children, Lane, 1978.

Sonnets (poems), Pantheon, 1980.

The Voice of Experience, Pantheon, 1982.

Wisdom, Madness, and Folly: The Making of a Psychiatrist (autobiography), McGraw, 1985.

Author of films, including "Birth With R. D. Laing," with Helen Brew; "R. D. Laing's Glasgow"; "Approaches"; and "Existential Psychotherapy," 1985.

Contributor of book reviews to periodicals, including *New Statesman* and *New York Times Book Review.* Contributor of articles to professional journals.

SOUND RECORDINGS

"Politics as Experience," Big Sur Recordings, 1967.

"The Illusion of Achievement," Big Sur Recordings, c. 1967.

"Blowout Center: Supportive Environment," Big Sur Recordings, c. 1967.

"An Interview With R. D. Laing," Harper, 1976.

SIDELIGHTS: R. D. Laing's questioning of some of Western culture's basic assumptions about sanity, madness, and the experience of existence helped fuel a growing disenchantment with the established order during the 1960s and was interpreted by some as having far-reaching political, sociological, and scientific implications. Popular perception, and often misconception, created for the Scottish-born psychiatrist a dual image: to the anti-Establishment political Left he was hailed as a hero, a spokesperson who articulated a growing impatience with society's status quo; to traditionalists in psychiatry he became an apostate, a heretical founding member of the antipsychiatry movement.

A major controversy revolved around Laing's view of schizophrenia. Whereas conventional psychiatry viewed schizophrenia as an illness, Laing felt that schizophrenia represented a form of adaptive behavior, "a strategy for living in an unliveable situation." Based upon his clinical observations, Laing held that the verbal gibberish of schizophrenics was much like multileveled, symbolic poetry and could be studied and analyzed, if viewed from the experiential frame of the patient. He illustrated this point in his first book, *The Divided Self,* by profiling the case histories of two women: one a recovered schizophrenic, the other a schizophrenic whose prognosis was uncertain. Through careful study of the women Laing concluded that the etymology of their disturbances began in childhood as a result of the structure of their families.

"In order to understand schizophrenic patients," explained *Film Quarterly* reviewer Norman Silverstein, "Laing has distinguished between two kinds of families: first, in which family members function in *series,* each going his own way and coming together for occasions, such as to celebrate a wedding or to avoid a scandal; secondly, in which they function in nexus, each member participating in the projects of every other member, so sharing one another's lives as to require close obedience in order to satisfy the demands of the larger unit. Obviously normal families share both serial and nexal features." Laing theorized that family members with low levels of ontological security tend develop feelings of engulfment and depersonalization within a nexal family structure. In such a situation the "weaker" personality can be overwhelmed by and internalize personality features of "stronger" family members, resulting in the beginnings of fragmented or split personalities.

In Laing's model the schizoid personality is further engulfed and depersonalized by a world mechanized and computerized to the point of insanity. The "true" or core personality, powerless in the face of such a world, is forced to submit to reality and act in a mechanical way, hiding behind a false-self. As this false-self develops and grows, the true-self shrinks to the point of psychological death. Laing observed this process clinically and noted its result in *The Divided Self:* "The schizophrenic is desperate, is simply without hope. I have never known a schizophrenic who could say he was loved, as a man, by God the Father or by the Mother of God or by another man. He either *is* God, or the Devil, or in hell, estranged from God. When someone says he is an unreal man or that he is dead, in all seriousness, expressing in radical terms the stark truth of his existence as he experiences it, that is—insanity."

Viewed in this context, what appears to the casual observer to be "crazy" behavior is, when taken from the schizophrenic's perspective, a retreat, an attempt to stave off psychological death and preserve the core personality. In *Psychologists on Psychology,* author David Cohen observed: "In *The Divided Self, . . .* Laing tried to make us, the readers, understand what was going on in the mind of a person diagnosed as schizophrenic. At this point, Laing did not hold the view later attributed to him that no one is mad. He was concerned to show that madness, the actions of the mad, are not so incomprehensible. With enough understanding, you can perceive the method behind the madness."

Laing's clinical experience convinced him that psychotic episodes could serve as a natural healing process if allowed to run their courses under the supervision of a trained and sympathetic therapist. The widespread use of chemotherapy and electroshock treatment, he concluded, disrupts the healing process, brutalizes the patient, and serves only to make schizophrenics more manageable and docile for the benefit of overworked mental hospital staffs.

In 1964 Laing founded the Philadelphia Association, which over the next few years established a series of hostels dedicated to providing more humane treatment for schizophrenics. The most famous of these hostels was Kingsley Hall, located in London, England. Wild rumors about what was taking place inside Kingsley Hall alarmed local residents, who forced the city council to close the hostel in 1970, but other hostels continued the work.

In the mid-1960s Laing seemed to some observers to de-emphasize his role as scientific investigator in favor of that of social critic and political poet. The popular success of *The Politics of Experience* in the late 1960s reinforced this perception and transformed Laing into what Cohen termed "a superstar, some kind of elusive folk hero." Misconceptions about Laing's theories were rampant: He was accused of being anti-family, of saying there was no such thing as insanity, that only the insane were truly sane. Psychiatrist Rollo May, reviewing *The Politics of Experience* for *Saturday Review,* attempted to clear up some of the popular misconceptions: "What is refreshing and exciting in

Laing is not his glorification of the irrational—of which he is sometimes accused by psychiatrists and psychologists who preach adaptation—but his frank challenge: 'Adaptation to what? To society? To a mad world?'. . . . I do not agree with a main criticism of Laing—that he glorifies schizophrenia. Rather, he humanizes it.''

Laing continued to explore and expound upon his early themes in a variety of ways, including poetry and through conversations with children. In 1982 he again examined the nature of experience with the publication of *The Voice of Experience,* and three years later he produced a memoir of the first thirty years of his life, called *Wisdom, Madness, and Folly: The Making of a Psychiatrist.* While Laing asserts in *Wisdom, Madness, and Folly* that "I am not trying to justify myself, or prove that I am right," according to *New York Times Book Review* contributor Carol Tavris, he does describe how he arrived at some of his conclusions about the treatment of socially maladjusted individuals. Learning of such treatments as electroshock and chemotherapy for the mentally ill left him "puzzled, and uneasy," Laing explains, but he adds, "Hardly any of my psychiatric colleagues seemed puzzled or uneasy. This made me even more puzzled and uneasy." He developed his nontraditional theories and treatments in response to his doubts about the traditional ones, but he admits in his memoir that the newer methods seemed little better than the old ones. Tavris called Laing's *Wisdom, Madness, and Folly* an "appealing book" and praised it as an important overview of the influential psychiatrist's early life and theories.

MEDIA ADAPTATIONS: Laing's theories served as the basis of two teleplays scripted by David Mercer, "Morgan!" and "Wednesday's Child," both in 1972. Also in 1972, Kenneth Loach and Peter Robinson filmed "Asylum" (based on Laing's experiences at Kingsley Hall). In 1979, David Edgar staged "Mary Barnes" (also based on Laing's experiences at Kingsley Hall) at the Royal Court Theatre in London, England.

BIOGRAPHICAL/CRITICAL SOURCES:

BOOKS

Boyers, Robert, and Robert Orrill, editors, *Laing and Anti-Psychiatry,* Penguin, 1972.
Cohen, David, *Psychologists on Psychology,* Taplinger, 1977.
Collier, Andrew, *R. D. Laing: The Philosophy and Politics of Psychotherapy,* Pantheon, 1977.
Contemporary Issues Criticism, Volume 1, Gale, 1982.
Evans, Richard I., *R. D. Laing: The Man and His Ideas,* Dutton, 1976.
Friedenberg, Edgar Z., *R. D. Laing,* Viking, 1973.
Howarth-Williams, Martin, *R. D. Laing: His Work and Its Relevance for Sociology,* Routledge & Kegan Paul, 1977.
Laing, R. D., *Wisdom, Madness, and Folly: The Making of a Psychiatrist,* McGraw, 1985.
Roazen, Paul, *Freud and His Followers,* Knopf, 1975.

PERIODICALS

Atlantic Monthly, January, 1971.
Film Quarterly, summer, 1973.
New Statesman, January 19, 1979, July 20, 1979.
New York Times, October 7, 1972, January 15, 1978.
New York Times Book Review, May 30, 1976, February 12, 1978, September 8, 1985.
Psychology Today, February, 1981.
Saturday Review, May 20, 1967.
Times Literary Supplement, September 3, 1982, October 11, 1985.

OBITUARIES:

PERIODICALS

Chicago Tribune, August 25, 1989.
Los Angeles Times, August 25, 1989.
New York Times, August 25, 1989.
Times (London), August 25, 1989.
Washington Post, August 25, 1989.

*   *   *

LAMMING, George (William) 1927-

PERSONAL: Born June 8, 1927, in Barbados; immigrated to England, 1950. *Education:* Attended Combermere High School in Barbados.

ADDRESSES: Home—14-A Highbury Place, London N.5, England.

CAREER: Writer. Worked as schoolmaster in Trinidad, 1946-50; factory worker in England, 1950; broadcaster for British Broadcasting Corp. (BBC) Colonial Service, 1951. Writer in residence and lecturer in Creative Arts Centre and Department of Education, University of West Indies, Mona, Jamaica, 1967-68; visiting professor at University of Texas at Austin, 1977, and University of Pennsylvania. Lecturer in Denmark, Tanzania, and Australia.

AWARDS, HONORS: Kenyon Review fellowship, 1954; Guggenheim fellowship, 1955; Somerset Maugham Award, 1957; Canada Council fellowship, 1962; Commonwealth Foundation grant, 1976; Association of Commonwealth Literature Writers Award; D.Litt., University of West Indies.

WRITINGS:

NOVELS

In the Castle of My Skin, introduction by Richard Wright, McGraw, 1953, with a new introduction by the author, Schocken, 1983.
The Emigrants, M. Joseph, 1954, McGraw, 1955, reprinted, Allison & Busby, 1980.
Of Age and Innocence, M. Joseph, 1958, reprinted, Allison & Busby, 1981.
Season of Adventure, M. Joseph, 1960, reprinted, Allison & Busby, 1979.
Water With Berries, Holt, 1972.
Natives of My Person, Holt, 1972.

CONTRIBUTOR OF POETRY TO ANTHOLOGIES

Peter Brent, editor, *Young Commonwealth Poets '65,* Heinemann, 1965.
John Figueroa, editor, *Caribbean Voices,* two volumes, Evans, 1966.
O. R. Dathorne, editor, *Caribbean Verse,* Heinemann, 1968.

CONTRIBUTOR OF SHORT FICTION TO ANTHOLOGIES

Andrew Salkey, editor, *West Indian Stories,* Faber, 1960.
Salkey, editor, *Stories From the Caribbean,* Dufour, 1965, published as *Island Voices,* Liveright, 1970.
Dathorne, editor, *Caribbean Narrative,* Heinemann, 1966.
Barbara Howes, editor, *From the Green Antilles,* Macmillan, 1966.
Salkey, editor, *Caribbean Prose,* Evans, 1967.
James T. Livingston, editor, *Caribbean Rhythms,* Pocket Books, 1974.

OTHER

The Pleasures of Exile (essays and autobiographical observations), M. Joseph, 1960, reprinted, Allison & Busby, 1984.

(With Henry Bangou and Rene Depestre) *Influencia del Africa en las literaturas antillanas* (title means "The Influence of Africa on the Antillian Literatures"), I.L.A.C. (Montevideo, Uruguay), 1972.

(Editor) *Cannon Shot and Glass Beads: Modern Black Writing,* Pan Books, 1974.

Co-editor of Barbados and Guyana independence issues of *New World Quarterly* (Kingston), 1965 and 1967. Contributor to journals, including *Bim* (Barbados), *Savacou, New World Quarterly, Caribbean Quarterly,* and *Casa de las Americas* (Cuba).

SIDELIGHTS: Barbadian writer George Lamming "is not so much a novelist," asserts *New York Times Book Review* contributor Jan Carew, "as a chronicler of secret journeys to the innermost regions of the West Indian psyche." George Davis, however, believes Carew's assessment does not go far enough. Davis notes in his own *New York Times Book Review* critique, "I can think of very few writers who make better use of the fictional moments of their stories to explore the souls of any of us—West Indian or not."

In Lamming's essay "The Negro Writer in His World," the West Indian explains the universality on which Davis comments. In the essay Lamming maintains that black writers are the same as all other writers who use writing as a method of self-discovery. According to Carolyn T. Brown in *World Literature Today,* in Lamming's opinion, "the contemporary human condition . . . involves a 'universal sense of separation and abandonment, frustration and loss, and above all, of man's direct inner experience of something missing.'"

In Lamming's work the "something missing" is a true cultural identity for the West Indian. This lack of identity is, according to Lamming, a direct result of the long history of colonial rule in the region. Caribbean-born writer V. S. Naipaul explains the importance of this idea in his *New Statesman* review of Lamming's novel *Of Age and Innocence:* "Unless one understands the West Indian's search for identity, [the novel] is almost meaningless. It is not fully realised how completely the West Indian Negro identifies himself with England. . . . For the West Indian intellectual, speaking no language but English, educated in an English way, the experience of England is really traumatic. The foundations of his life are removed." James Ngugi makes a similar observation in his *Pan-Africanist* review of the same novel. "For Lamming," Ngugi writes, "a sense of exile must lead to action and through action to identity. The West Indian's alienation springs . . . from his colonial relationship to England."

Lamming's first four novels explore the West Indian search for identity, a search which often leads to a flight to England followed by, for some, a return to their Caribbean roots. His first novel, *In the Castle of My Skin,* which is nearly universally acclaimed by critics, is a quasi-autobiographical look at childhood and adolescence on Lamming's fictional Caribbean island, San Cristobal. The book "is generally regarded," notes Michael Gilkes in *The West Indian Novel,* "as a 'classic' of West Indian fiction. It is one of the earliest novels of any substance to convey, with real assurance, the life of ordinary village folk within a genuinely realized, native landscape: a 'peasant novel' . . . written with deep insight and considerable technical skill."

Several reviewers compare Lamming's prose style in the book to poetry. In *New Statesman and Nation* Pritchett describes Lamming's prose as "something between garrulous realism and popular poetry, and . . . quite delightful"; while in the *San Francisco Chronicle* J. H. Jackson says Lamming "is a poet and a human being who approaches a question vital to him, humanly and poetically." A *Time* contributor finds the book "a curious mixture of autobiography and a poetic evocation of a native life. . . . It is one of the few authentically rich and constantly readable books produced [thus far] by a West Indian."

Lamming's next novel, *The Emigrants,* follows a group of West Indians who—like Lamming himself—leave their native islands for exile in England, while the two novels that follow, *Of Age and Innocence* and *Season of Adventure,* feature a return to San Cristobal. According to Carew, these last two novels also have a bit of autobiography in them because through their action it seems "as though Lamming [is] attempting to rediscover a history of himself by himself."

In Lamming's novels, as critics note, self-discovery is often achieved through an inquiry into his characters' pasts. For example, while *Yale Review* contributor Michael Cook quotes Lamming's *Of Age and Innocence* description of San Cristobal—"an old land inhabiting new forms of men who can never resurrect their roots and do not know their nature," the reviewer comments that "it is obvious" that in "*Season of Adventure* . . . [Lamming] is committed to his characters' at least trying to discover their roots and their natures." Details of the plot seem to verify Cook's assessment, for the novel traces Fola Piggott's quest to discover whether her father was European or African.

According to Kenneth Ramchand in *The West Indian Novel and Its Background,* "*Season of Adventure* is the most significant of the West Indian novels invoking Africa." In the novel, Ramchand maintains, Lamming invokes "the African heritage not to make statements about Africa but to explore the troubled components of West Indian culture and nationhood." Lamming accomplishes this "without preventing us from seeing that Fola's special circumstances . . . are only a manifestation . . . of every man's need to take the past into account with humility, fearlessness, and receptivity."

After a silence of over a decade Lamming published two new novels almost simultaneously: *Water With Berries* and *Natives of My Person.* Again, his fiction focuses on the effects of history on the present. In both books Lamming uses symbolism to tell his story. In *Water With Berries* Lamming uses a theme previously dealt with in his nonfiction work *The Pleasures of Exile.* A *Times Literary Supplement* reviewer quotes from Lamming's collection of essays: "My subject is the migration of the West Indian writer, as colonial and exile, from his native kingdom, once inhabited by Caliban, to the tempestuous island of Prospero's and his language." Caliban and Prospero are both characters from Shakespeare's *Tempest,* Caliban being the deformed slave of Prospero, ruler of an enchanted island. According to the *Times Literary Supplement* contributor, Lamming also refers to himself in the same book as an "exiled descendent of Caliban."

In *Water With Berries* Lamming uses the plot of *The Tempest* to symbolize the various ills of West Indian society, but critics are divided on the success of the novel. In *World Literature in English* Anthony Boxill notes that Lamming uses *The Tempest* to "help put across his points about disintegration of personality . . ., especially in people who are products of a colonial past. . . . However, the *Tempest* pattern which might have been the strength of this novel proves its undoing. . . . In his unrelenting faithfulness to this . . . pattern Lamming loses touch with the characters he is creating; they cease to be credible." A

Times Literary Supplement contributor similarly states, "Lamming writes very well, but *Water With Berries* does not entirely convince either as a study of the pains of exile, or as an allegory of colonialism. . . . [And,] as for the melodrama of . . . Lamming's *Tempest* myth, it tells us nothing new."

Other critics praise Lamming's novel and disregard its connections to *The Tempest.* Paul Theroux and George Davis, for instance, find the work a very compelling statement on the effects of colonialism. In *Encounter* Theroux claims, "the poetic prose of the narrative has a perfect dazzle. . . . When expatriation is defined and dramatised . . . *Water With Berries* takes on a life of its own, for . . . Lamming is meticulous in diagnosing the condition of estrangement." *New York Times Book Review* contributor Davis writes: "This is an effectively written fictional work. Lamming brings his characters . . . into the same nightmare of arson, perversity, suicide and murder, which, we are forced to feel, is the legacy of the colonial experience."

Natives of My Person, according to Gilkes, "is an exceedingly complex work, full of allegorical and historical meanings and echoes. It is an embodiment of all [Lamming's] themes: a kind of *reviewing* process in which he appears to take stock of things." Boxill notes that the novel "provides richly complex insights into human personality and the history of colonialism." It tells the story of the sixteenth-century voyage of the ship *Reconnaissance* from Europe to America by way of Africa. The chief goal of the ship's commandant is the establishment of a slave-free settlement on the island of San Cristobal, but he is killed by two of the ship's officers before he can accomplish his mission.

Some critics find that Lamming's prose detracts from the novel. In *Book World* Theroux calls Lamming "a marvelously skillful writer" but also refers to the novel's "shadowy action and vaguely poetical momentousness." A *Times Literary Supplement* reviewer complains that Lamming writes "a prose of discovery which is effortful, uncolloquial, and almost always mannered."

While Thomas R. Edwards and Carew also regret the complexity of Lamming's prose they are able to find redeeming qualities in the novel. "Lamming's prose is portentous," Edwards notes in the *New York Review of Books,* "hooked on simile, and anxious to suggest more than it says, inviting questions the story never answers. . . . Yet if reading *Natives of My Person* is a voyage into frustration and annoyance, Lamming's story survives and grows in the mind afterward. . . . This imagined history reveals itself as a version of significances that 'real' history is itself only a version of."

Carew similarly comments on the book's difficult prose but calls the work "undoubtedly . . . Lamming's finest novel." In the book, according to Carew's assessment, Lamming expresses better than in any of his other novels his concerns about the effects of colonization on the West Indies and its people. In *Natives of My Person,* Carew maintains, Lamming "succeeds in illuminating new areas of darkness in the colonial past that the colonizer has so far not dealt with; and in this sense it is a profoundly revolutionary and original work."

BIOGRAPHICAL/CRITICAL SOURCES:

BOOKS

Baugh, Edward, editor, *Homecoming: Essays on African and Caribbean Literature, Culture and Politics,* Laurence Hill, 1972.
Contemporary Literary Criticism, Gale, Volume 2, 1974, Volume 4, 1975.

Cooke, Michael G., editor, *Modern Black Novelists: A Collection of Critical Essays,* Prentice-Hall, 1971.
Gilkes, Michael, *The West Indian Novel,* Twayne, 1981.
Lamming, George, *In the Castle of My Skin,* McGraw, 1954.
Lamming, *Of Age and Innocence,* M. Joseph, 1958.
Lamming, *The Pleasures of Exile,* M. Joseph, 1960.
Massa, Daniel, editor, *Individual and Community in Commonwealth Literature,* University Press (Malta), 1979.
Paquet, Sandra Pouchet, *The Novels of George Lamming,* Heinemann, 1982.
Ramchand, Kenneth, *The West Indian Novel and Its Background,* Faber, 1970.

PERIODICALS

Book World, January 23, 1972.
Canadian Literature, winter, 1982.
Caribbean Quarterly, February, 1958.
Encounter, May, 1972.
New Statesman, December 6, 1958, January 28, 1972, December 19, 1980.
New Statesman and Nation, April 18, 1953.
New Yorker, December 5, 1953, May 28, 1955, April 29, 1972.
New York Herald Tribune Book Review, July 17, 1955.
New York Review of Books, March 9, 1972.
New York Times, November 1, 1953, July 24, 1955, January 15, 1972.
New York Times Book Review, February 27, 1972, June 4, 1972, October 15, 1972, December 3, 1972.
Observer (London), October 8, 1972.
Pan-Africanist, March, 1971.
Punch, August 19, 1981.
San Francisco Chronicle, November 17, 1953, June 24, 1955.
Saturday Review, December 5, 1953, May 28, 1955.
Studies in Black Literature, spring, 1973.
Time, November 9, 1953, April 25, 1955.
Times Literary Supplement, March 27, 1953, February 11, 1972, December 15, 1972, September 4, 1981, October 24, 1986.
World Literature Today, winter, 1983, spring, 1985.
World Literature Written in English, November, 1971, April, 1973, November, 1979.
Yale Review, autumn, 1953, summer, 1973.

*   *   *

L'AMOUR, Louis (Dearborn) 1908-1988
(Jim Mayo; Tex Burns, a house pseudonym)

PERSONAL: Born March 28, 1908 in Jamestown, N.D.; died June 10, 1988, of lung cancer in Los Angeles, Calif.; son of Louis Charles (a veterinarian and farm-machinery salesman), and Emily (Dearborn) LaMoore; married Katherine Elizabeth Adams, February 19, 1956; children: Beau Dearborn, Angelique Gabrielle. *Education:* Self-educated.

ADDRESSES: Home—100 Loring Ave., Los Angeles, CA 90024; and, Durango, Colo. *Agent*—c/o Bantam Books, 666 Fifth Ave., New York, NY 10019.

CAREER: Author and lecturer. Held numerous jobs, including positions as longshoreman, lumberjack, miner, elephant handler, hay shocker, boxer, flume builder, and fruit picker. Lecturer at many universities including University of Oklahoma, Baylor University, University of Southern California, and University of Redlands. *Military service:* U.S. Army, 1942-46; became first lieutenant.

MEMBER: Writers Guild of America (West), Western Writers of America, Academy of Motion Picture Arts and Sciences,

American Siam Society, California Writers Guild, California Academy of Sciences.

AWARDS, HONORS: Western Writers of America Award-Novel, 1969, for *Down the Long Hills;* LL.D., Jamestown College, 1972; Theodore Roosevelt Rough Rider award, North Dakota, 1972; American Book Award, 1980, for *Bendigo Shafter,* Buffalo Bill Award, 1981; Distinguished Newsboy Award, 1981; National Genealogical Society Award, 1981; Congressional Gold Medal, 1983; Presidential Medal of Freedom, 1984; LL.D., Pepperdine University, 1984.

WRITINGS:

NOVELS

Westward the Tide, World's Work, (Surrey, England), 1950, reprinted, Bantam, 1984.
Hondo (expanded version of his story, "The Gift of Cochise"; also see below), Gold Medal, 1953, reprinted with introduction by Michael T. Marsden, Gregg, 1978, original reprinted, Bantam, 1985.
Crossfire Trail (also see below), Ace Books, 1954, reprinted with introduction by Kieth Jarrod, Gregg, 1980, original reprinted, Bantam, 1985.
Heller with a Gun (also see below), Gold Medal, 1954, Bantam, 1985.
Kilkenny (also see below), Ace Books, 1954, reprinted with introduction by Wesley Laing, Gregg, 1980, original reprinted, Bantam, 1984.
To Tame a Land, Fawcett, 1955, reprinted, Bantam, 1985.
Guns of the Timberlands, Jason, 1955, reprinted, Bantam, 1985.
The Burning Hills, Jason, 1956, reprinted, Bantam, 1985.
Silver Canyon (expanded version of his story, "Riders of the Dawn"), Avalon, 1956, reprinted, Bantam, 1981.
Last Stand at Papago Wells (also see below), Gold Medal, 1957, reprinted, Bantam, 1986.
The Tall Stranger (also see below), Fawcett, 1957, reprinted, Bantam, 1986.
Sitka, Appleton, 1957, reprinted, Bantam, 1986.
Radigan, Bantam, 1958, reprinted, 1986.
The First Fast Draw (also see below), Bantam, 1959, reprinted, G. K. Hall, 1989.
Taggart, Bantam, 1959, reprinted, Bantam, 1982.
Flint, Bantam, 1960, reprinted, 1985.
Shalako, Bantam, 1962, reprinted, 1985.
Killoe (also see below), Bantam, 1962, reprinted, 1986.
High Lonesome, Bantam, 1962, reprinted, 1982.
How the West Was Won (based on the screenplay by James R. Webb), Bantam, 1963, reprinted, Thorndike, 1988.
Fallon, Bantam, 1963, reprinted, 1982.
Catlow, Bantam, 1963, reprinted, 1984.
Dark Canyon, Bantam, 1963, reprinted, 1985.
Hanging Woman Creek, Bantam, 1964, reprinted, 1984.
Kiowa Trail (also see below), Bantam, 1965.
The High Graders, Bantam, 1965, reprinted, 1989.
The Key-Lock Man (also see below), Bantam, 1965, reprinted, 1986.
Kid Rodelo, Bantam, 1966, reprinted, 1986.
Kilrone, Bantam, 1966, reprinted, 1981.
The Broken Gun, Bantam, 1966, reprinted, 1984.
Matagorda, Bantam, 1967, reprinted, 1985.
Down the Long Hills, Bantam, 1968, reprinted, 1984.
Chancy, Bantam, 1968, reprinted, 1984.
Conagher, Bantam, 1969, reprinted, 1982.
The Empty Land, Bantam, 1969, reprinted, 1985.
The Man Called Noon, Bantam, 1970, reprinted, 1985.

Reilly's Luck, Bantam, 1970, reprinted, 1985.
Brionne, Bantam, 1971, reprinted, 1989.
Under the Sweetwater Rim, Bantam, 1971.
Tucker, Bantam, 1971.
North to the Rails, Bantam, 1971.
Callaghen, Bantam, 1972.
The Ferguson Rifle, Bantam, 1973.
The Quick and the Dead, Bantam, 1973, revised edition, 1979.
The Man from Skibbereen, G. K. Hall, 1973.
The Californios, Saturday Review Press, 1974.
Rivers West, Saturday Review Press, 1974, reprinted, Dutton, 1989.
Over on the Dry Side, Saturday Review Press, 1975.
The Rider of the Lost Creek (based on on of his short stories), Bantam, 1976.
Where the Long Grass Blows, Bantam, 1976.
Borden Chantry, Bantam 1977.
The Mountain Valley War (based on one of his short stories), Bantam, 1978.
Fair Blows the Wind, Bantam, 1978.
Bendigo Shafter, Dutton, 1978.
The Iron Marshall, Bantam, 1979.
The Proving Trail, Bantam, 1979.
The Warrior's Path, Bantam, 1980.
Comstock Lode, Bantam, 1981.
Milo Talon, Bantam, 1981.
The Cherokee Trail, Bantam, 1982.
The Shadow Riders, Bantam, 1982.
The Lonesome Gods, Bantam, 1983.
Son of a Wanted Man, Bantam, 1984.
The Walking Drum, Bantam, 1984.
Passin' Through, Bantam, 1985.
Last of the Breed, Bantam, 1986.
West of the Pilot Range, Bantam, 1986.
A Trail to the West, Bantam, 1986.
The Haunted Mesa, Bantam, 1987.

Also author of *Man Riding West,* Carroll & Graf.

"SACKETT FAMILY" SERIES; NOVELS

The Daybreakers, Bantam, 1960, reprinted, 1984.
Sackett, Bantam, 1961, reprinted, 1984.
Lando, Bantam, 1962, reprinted, 1985.
Mojave Crossing, Bantam, 1964, reprinted, 1985.
The Sackett Brand, Bantam, 1965, reprinted, 1985.
Mustang Man, Bantam, 1966, reprinted, 1986.
The Skyliners, Bantam, 1967, reprinted, Thorndike, 1986.
The Lonely Men, Bantam, 1969, reprinted, Bantam, 1984.
Galloway, Bantam, 1970.
Ride the Dark Trail, Bantam, 1972, reprinted, 1986.
Treasure Mountain, Bantam, 1972.
Sackett's Land, Saturday Review Press, 1974.
The Man from the Broken Hills, Bantam, 1975.
To the Far Blue Mountains, Dutton, 1976.
Sackett's Gold, Bantam, 1977.
The Warrior's Path, Bantam, 1980.
Lonely on the Mountain, Bantam, 1980.
Ride the River, Bantam, 1983.
Jubal Sackett, Bantam, 1985.

PUBLISHED UNDER HOUSE PSEUDONYM TEX BURNS:
"HOPALONG CASSIDY" SERIES; NOVELS

Hopalong Cassidy and the Riders of High Rock, Doubleday, 1951, Aeonian, 1974.
Hopalong Cassidy and the Rustlers of West Fork, Doubleday, 1951, reprinted, Aeonian, 1976.

Hopalong Cassidy and the Trail to Seven Pines, Doubleday, 1951, reprinted, Aeonian, 1976.

Hopalong Cassidy: Trouble Shooter, Doubleday, 1952, Aeonian, 1976.

ORIGINALLY PUBLISHED UNDER PSEUDONYM JIM MAYO; REPRINTED UNDER AUTHOR'S REAL NAME; NOVELS

Showdown at Yellow Butte (also see below), Ace Books, 1954, reprinted with introduction by Scott R. McMillan, Gregg, 1980, original reprinted, Bantam, 1983.

Utah Blaine (also see below), Ace Books, 1954, reprinted with introduction by Wayne C. Lee, Gregg, 1980, original reprinted, Bantam, 1984.

OMNIBUS VOLUMES

Kiowa Trail [and] *Killoe,* Ulverscroft, 1979.

The First Fast Draw [and] *The Key-Lock Man,* Ulverscroft, 1979.

Four Complete Novels (includes *The Tall Stranger, Kilkenny, Hondo,* and *Showdown at Yellow Butte*), Avenal Books, 1980.

Five Complete Novels (includes *Crossfire Trail, Utah Blaine, Heller with a Gun, Last Stand at Papago Wells,* and *To Tame a Land*), Avenel Books, 1981.

L'Amour Westerns (four volumes), Gregg, 1981.

SHORT STORIES

War Party, Bantam, 1975.

Yondering, Bantam, 1980.

The Strong Shall Live, Bantam, 1980.

Buckskin Run, Bantam, 1981.

Law of the Desert Born, Bantam, 1983.

Bowdrie, Bantam, 1983.

The Hills of Homicide, Bantam, 1984.

Bowdrie's Law, Bantam, 1984.

Riding for the Brand, Bantam, 1986.

Dutchman's Flat, Bantam, 1986.

The Trail to Crazy Man, Bantam, 1986.

The Rider of the Ruby Hills, Bantam, 1986.

Night Over the Solomons, Bantam, 1986.

West from Singapore, Bantam, 1987.

Lonigan, Bantam, 1988.

The Outlaws of Mesquite, Bantam, 1991.

OTHER

Smoke from this Altar (poetry), Lusk (Oklahoma City, Okla.), 1939.

Frontier (essays), Bantam, 1984.

(Author of foreword) Frank C. McCarthy, *Frank C. McCarthy: The Old West,* Greenwich Press, 1981.

The Sackett Companion: A Personal Guide to the Sackett Novels (nonfiction), Bantam, 1988.

A Trail of Memories: The Quotations of Louis L'Amour (excerpts from L'Amour's fiction), compiled by daughter, Angelique L'Amour, Bantam, 1988.

The Education of a Wandering Man (autobiography), Bantam, 1989.

Also author of filmscripts and more than sixty-five television scripts. Contributor of more than four hundred short stories and articles to more than eighty magazines in the United States and abroad, including *Argosy, Collier's,* and *Saturday Evening Post.*

SIDELIGHTS: When describing someone like Western writer Louis L'Amour it was necessary to use terms as wide and grand as the West about which he wrote. He sold more books than nearly every other contemporary novelist. He wrote more mil-lion-copy bestsellers than any other American fiction writer. He was the only novelist in this nation's history to be granted either of the country's highest honors—the Congressional Gold Medal and the Presidential Medal of Freedom—and L'Amour received them both. When he died, nearly two hundred million copies of his books were in print.

L'Amour's achievements were even more remarkable when one considered the obstacles that he overcame to achieve popularity. He had no formal education, spent much of his youth wandering from job to job, and was over forty by the time he published his first novel. Among his first published books were some volumes of poetry and stories about the Far East. "I also wrote some sport stories, some detective stories, and some Western stories. It so happens that the Westerns caught on and there was a big demand for them. I grew up in the West, of course, and loved it, but I never really intended to write Westerns at all," L'Amour told *CA.* After he started publishing his work, his novels were often not even reviewed by critics. As Ned Smith of *American Way* noted, L'Amour suffered the same fate as the majority of Western writers who found themselves "largely greeted with indifference . . . by the critics." James Barron, writing in the *New York Times,* cited L'Amour's comment that explained how he felt about being labeled a writer of "Westerns": "If you write a book about a bygone period that lies east of the Mississippi River, then it's a historical novel. . . . If it's west of the Mississippi, it's a western, a different category. There's no sense to it."

L'Amour ignored criticism or—lack of it—and decided to do what hardly anyone had ever done before, make a living as a Western writer. Surprisingly, L'Amour's determination to persevere led to increased critical interest in his work; the literary establishment eventually could no longer continue to disregard such a popular writer. *Newsweek* contributor Charles Leerhsen noted that as L'Amour entered his fourth decade as a novelist "the critics back East [were] finally reviewing his work—and praising his unpretentious, lean-as-a-grass-fed-steer style."

Some critics maintained that L'Amour's style was the key to his appeal. They applauded his ability to write quick-paced action novels filled with accurate descriptions of the Old West—or whatever other locale in which his protagonists found themselves. "Probably the biggest reason for L'Amour's success . . .," wrote Ben Yagoda in *Esquire,* was "his attention to authenticity and detail. . . . His books are full of geographical and historical information."

Because of what *People* contributor Joseph Pilcher called L'Amour's "painstaking respect for detail," a typical L'Amour novel often seemed to contain as many factual elements as fictional ones. Writing in *Arizona and the West* about L'Amour's novel, *Lando,* Michael T. Marsden noted that in that book alone the writer "instruct[ed] his readers on the historical and cultural importance of Madeira wine, the nature of longhorn cattle, the Great Hurricane of 1844, and the several cultural functions of a Western saloon, all the while providing them with an entertaining romance." In other L'Amour works readers learned such things as how native Americans made mocassins, how to pan for gold, and the finer points of Elizabethan decor.

Some critics felt that all the factual material in L'Amour's novels detracted from their narrative continuity. They also felt that L'Amour's energies might have been better spent developing his characters or varying his plots rather than on research. *New York Times Book Review* contributor Richard Nalley, for example, wrote: "There is wonderful information [in L'Amour's novel, *The Walking Drum,*] . . . but the author's historical research is presented textbook style, in great, undigested chunks.

Although the adventure plot is at times gripping, the uneasy integration of Mathurin [the protagonist] with his surroundings prevents the reader from being entirely swept up in the romance."

In *Western American Literature* John D. Nesbitt observed a similar flaw in L'Amour's *Over on the Dry Side*. According to Nesbitt, in the novel "entertaining narrative effect is lost in favor of flat introduction of historical details and moral speeches." Despite such criticism, L'Amour had an enormous following of readers. In the *Lone Star Review* Steve Berner wrote: "It [was], in fact, pointless to discuss the merits or weaknesses of L'Amour's writings . . . since it [had] little or no effect on either author or his public." According to the *Washington Post*'s Richard Pearson, despite what he called "plots [that] could be predictable" and a technique of narrating that was "wooden," L'Amour was a skilled story teller. L'Amour's agent, C. Stuart Applebaum, observed in a *Detroit News* interview: "For many of his readers, he was the living embodiment of the frontier because of the authenticity of his stories and characters. His readers felt L'Amour walked the land his characters had walked. That was one of the major reasons of his enduring popularity."

L'Amour identified himself as a storyteller in the tradition of Geoffrey Chaucer (fourteenth-century author of *The Canterbury Tales*). Barron cited L'Amour's comment, "I don't travel and tell stories, because that's not the way these days. . . . But I write my books to be read aloud and I think of myself in that oral tradition."

One story that L'Amour seemed not to want to stop telling was the story of the Sackett family, continued in more than a dozen novels. These books explore the lives of the two branches of the Sackett clan and, to a lesser extent, two other frontier families, the Chantrys and the Talons, across three hundred years of history. In a *North Dakota Quarterly* article, Marsden commented that L'Amour's "formal family groupings may well constitute the most ambitious and complex attempt to date to create a Faulknerian series of interrelated characters and events in the popular Western tradition."

The publication of L'Amour's 1984 novel, *The Walking Drum*, caused a stir in literary circles because L'Amour had written a saga of medieval life in Europe instead of a Western. Apparently L'Amour's change of locale did not intimidate his readers, for the book appeared on the *New York Times* hardcover bestseller list five days before its official publication date. In *People* L'Amour explained to Pilcher that he was irritated that most books about the twelfth century dealt only with the Crusades and so, the novelist "decided to tell a swashbuckling adventure story about the period which would also show the history of the times—how people lived and how they worked."

According to *Los Angeles Times* writer Garry Abrams, L'Amour saw the publication of this non-Western novel as "a turning point" in his development as a writer. "From now on, he said, he want[ed] to concentrate less on promotion and more on 'improving my writing. I know how to write and I write fairly well. But you can never learn enough about writing.'" L'Amour concentrated on his writing by branching out in several directions. In 1987, he published *The Haunted Mesa*, which *Washington Post Book World* contributor Tony Hillerman referred to as "part western, part adventure, [and] part fantasy." He wrote *The Sackett Companion: A Personal Guide to the Sackett Novels*, which includes a Sackett family tree as well as background information on the sources behind the novels in the series, and completed his long-planned autobiography, *The Education of a Wandering Man*.

Explaining his approach to fiction writing to Clarence Petersen in the *Chicago Tribune*, L'Amour remarked: "A reader of my books expects to get an entertaining story, and he expects a little bit more. I've got to give him something of the real quality of the West, and I can do that because I'm a storyteller, and I don't have to imagine what happened in the Old West—I know what happened." Descended from pioneers who fought with the Sioux Indians and in the Civil War, L'Amour spent much of his early life traveling the west, working alongside the cattlemen and homesteaders who knew the most about the local history.

L'Amour's informers included one of his employers, a man who had been raised as an Apache Indian, who taught him much about the Indian experience of the American west. The novelist's characters also know much about Indian life, but the claims of their own culture exert a stronger hold. Pearson observed in the *Washington Post*, "Though Mr. L'Amour was often faulted by critics for cardboard, simplistic characters, his western heroes often fought an inner struggle against admiration for the Indian and his way of life on one hand and the need to advance 'civilization' on the other. His were often stories of culture in conflict." The title character of *Bendigo Shafter* describes the conflict felt by many of L'Amour's frontier heroes: "I could have lived the Indian way and loved it. I could feel his spirits move upon the air, hear them in the still forest and the chuckling water of the mountain streams, but other voices were calling me, too, the voices of my own people and their ways. For it was our way to go onward; to go forward and to try to shape our world into something that would make our lives easier, even if more complicated."

L'Amour wrote three novels a year for his publisher for more than thirty years. Even so, by the late 1980s, he had come nowhere near to exhausting the store of research he had gathered as a connoisseur of historical details. At the time of his death in 1988, he had developed outlines for fifty more novels. A year before he died, L'Amour told *CA*, "There's alot of Western material out there that's very fresh. And the Western novel is not dying, it's doing very well. It's selling every place but in the movies. . . . There seem to be some misconceptions about me and my type of writing, which have been perpetuated by several articles that weren't written too well. . . . Too often people start with a cliched idea of a Western writer. That automatically eliminates an awful lot of things that interest me. There's no difference in the Western novel and any other novel, as I said earlier. A Western starts with a beginning and it goes to an end. It's a story about people, and that's the important thing to always remember. Every story is about people—people against the canvas of their times."

MEDIA ADAPTATIONS: More than forty-five of L'Amour's novels and short stories have been adapted into feature films and television movies, including "Hondo," Warner Bros., 1953, "East of Sumatra," Universal, 1953, "Four Guns to the Border," Universal, 1954, "Treasure of the Ruby Hills," Allied Artists, 1955, "Kilkenny," Columbia, 1956, "The Burning Hills," Warner Bros., 1956, "Utah Blaine," Columbia, 1956, "Walk Tall," Allied Artists, 1957, "Last Stand at Papago Wells," Columbia, 1958, "Heller with Pink Tights" (based on his *Heller with a Gun*), Paramount, 1960, "Guns of the Timberlands," Warner Bros., 1960, "Taggart," Universal, 1964, "Kid Rodelo," Paramount, 1966, "Shalako," Cinerama Releasing Corp., 1968, "Catlow," Metro-Goldwyn-Mayer, 1971, "The Broken Gun," Warner Bros., 1972, "The Man Called Noon," Scotia-Barber, 1973, "Down the Long Hills," Disney Channel, 1986, and "The Quick and the Dead," Home Box Office, 1987; the "Sackett Family" series was made into a television miniseries, "The Sacketts."

Many of L'Amour's novels and short stories have been adapted for presentation on audio cassettes, including "Riding for the Brand" (adapted from a short story from *Riding for the Brand*), Bantam, 1987, "Bowdrie Passes Through," (adapted from a short story from *Bowdrie*), Bantam, 1988, "Keep Travelin' Rider" (adapted from a short story from *Dutchman's Flat*), Bantam, 1988, and "One for the Mojave Kid" (adapted from a short story from *Dutchman's Flat*), Bantam, 1988.

BIOGRAPHICAL/CRITICAL SOURCES:

BOOKS

Authors in the News, Volume 2, Gale, 1976.
Contemporary Literary Criticism, Volume 25, Gale, 1983.
Dictionary of Literary Biography Yearbook: 1980, Gale, 1981.
L'Amour, Louis, *Bendigo Shafter,* Dutton, 1978.
Pilkington, William T., editor, *Critical Essays on the Western American Novel,* G. K. Hall, 1980.

PERIODICALS

American Way, April, 1976.
Arizona and the West, autumn, 1978.
Chicago Tribune, June 5, 1984, June 23, 1985, February 25, 1987.
Chicago Tribune Book World, September 9, 1984.
Detroit News, March 31, 1978, June 30, 1985.
Esquire, March 13, 1979.
Globe and Mail (Toronto), May 19, 1984, October 17, 1987.
Lone Star Review, May, 1981.
Los Angeles Times, July 9, 1983, May 30, 1984, August 3, 1986, November 17, 1989.
Los Angeles Times Book Review, March 20, 1983, August 25, 1985, April 3, 1986, August 3, 1986.
New Yorker, May 16, 1983.
New York Times, October 21, 1971, September 23, 1983.
New York Times Book Review, November 24, 1974, April 6, 1975, November 30, 1975, January 2, 1977, March 22, 1981, April 24, 1983, July 1, 1984, June 2, 1985, July 6, 1986.
Newsweek, November 10, 1975, July 14, 1986.
North Dakota Quarterly, summer, 1978.
People, June 9, 1975, July 23, 1984.
Publishers Weekly, October 8, 1973, November 27, 1978, November 4, 1978.
Southwest Review, winter, 1984.
Time, April 29, 1974, December 1, 1980, August 19, 1985, July 21, 1986, August 4, 1986.
Times Literary Supplement, August 26, 1977.
Us, July 25, 1978.
USA Weekend, May 30-June 1, 1986.
Washington Post, March 20, 1981, June 23, 1983, November 30, 1989.
Washington Post Book World, December 12, 1976, March 1, 1981, April 17, 1983, December 2, 1984, June 16, 1985, July 6, 1986, June 14, 1987.
West Coast Review of Books, November, 1978.
Western American Literature, May, 1978, February, 1982.

OBITUARIES:

PERIODICALS

Chicago Tribune, June 19, 1988.
Detroit News, June 13, 1988.
Los Angeles Times, June 13, 1988.
New York Times, June 13, 1988.
Times (London), June 14, 1988.
Washington Post, June 13, 1988.

LANGE, John
See CRICHTON, (John) Michael

* * *

LANGER, Susanne K(nauth) 1895-1985

PERSONAL: Born December 20, 1895, in New York, N.Y.; died after a long illness, July 17, 1985, in New London, Conn.; daughter of Antonio (a lawyer) and Else (Uhlich) Knauth; married William L. Langer, September 3, 1921 (divorced, 1942); children: Leonard C. R., Bertrand W. *Education:* Radcliffe College, A.B., 1920, A.M., 1924, Ph.D., 1926; University of Vienna, graduate study, 1921-22. *Religion:* None.

CAREER: Radcliffe College, Cambridge, Mass., tutor in philosophy, 1927-42; University of Delaware, Newark, assistant professor of philosophy, 1943; Columbia University, New York, N.Y., lecturer in philosophy, 1945-50; Connecticut College, New London, professor, 1954-61, professor emeritus, 1962-85, research scholar in philosophy, 1961-85. Visiting professor of philosophy at New York University, 1945, Northwestern University, 1950, Ohio State University, 1950, University of Washington, 1952-53, and University of Michigan, 1954.

MEMBER: American Philosophical Association.

AWARDS, HONORS: Radcliffe achievement medal, 1950; D.Litt. from Wilson College, 1954, Mt. Holyoke College, 1962, Western College for Women (now Western College), 1962, and Wheaton College, Norton, Mass., 1962; LL. D., Columbia University, 1964; D. Humane Letters, Clark University, 1968.

WRITINGS:

The Cruise of the Little Dipper and Other Fairy Tales, Norcross, 1923.
The Practice of Philosophy, Holt, 1930.
Philosophy in a New Key, Harvard University Press, 1942.
An Introduction to Symbolic Logic, Houghton, 1953.
Feeling and Form, Scribner, 1953.
Problems of Art, Scribner, 1957.
Philosophical Sketches, Johns Hopkins Press, 1962.
Mind: An Essay on Human Feeling, Johns Hopkins Press, Volume 1, 1967, Volume 2, 1972, Volume 3, 1982.

SIDELIGHTS: In a *New York Times Book Review* article, James Lord writes that Susanne Langer has "vitally influenced not only other philosophers but artists and scientists as well in their concepts of function, and her theories are discussed with vivid concern in both studios and studies. Her works as well as her aspirationshave remained serious and life-enhancing, and reflect a lively awareness of the 'state of the art' of the various disciplines from which she draws. This awareness and seriousness of purpose naturally dominate one's impression of her as a person." In an interview with Lord, Langer comments on her work: "I am trying to tie together a number of disciplines into a structure that these disciplines-the arts, biology, neurology, psychology, language, anthropology, and others-won't themselves singly support. I am trying to develop basic concepts which underlie all these sciences or fields of study, and which can rule all such thought.' "

When asked about the satisfaction of her solitary intellectual pursuits, Langer, who has lived alone in an old New England farmhouse for many years, answered: " 'Perhaps the ability to meet difficult problems is my ultimate satisfaction. All of a sudden a light dawns on something which I've been wrestling with for a long time. This happens every few weeks. Then I'm very excited. I know I should stay and work it out completely, but I can't. I get out my canoe or drive to Scarsdale to see my son and his family. I know I have the idea under control, but my excitement has to settle down before I can return to my desk. Whenever you know that you've broken through a difficult problem it gives you a great feeling of security. The greatest security in this tumultuous world is faith in your own mind.' "

BIOGRAPHICAL/CRITICAL SOURCES:

PERIODICALS

New Yorker, August 12, 1967.
Listener, November 30, 1967.
New York Times Book Review, May 26, 1968.

OBITUARIES:

PERIODICALS

Boston Globe, July 19, 1985.
Chicago Tribune, July 21, 1985.
New London Day, July 18, 1985.
New York Times, July 19, 1985.
Time, July 29, 1985.
Washington Post, July 22, 1985.

*   *   *

LARDNER, Ring
    See LARDNER, Ring(gold) W(ilmer)

*   *   *

LARDNER, Ring(gold) W(ilmer) 1885-1933
    (Ring Lardner, Ring W. Lardner, Jr.)

PERSONAL: Born March 6, 1885, in Niles, Mich.; died after a heart attack, September 25, 1933, in East Hampton, N.Y.; son of Henry (in business) and Lena Bogardus (a poet; maiden name, Phillips) Lardner; married Ellis Abbott, June 28, 1911; children: John Abbott, James Phillips, Ringgold Wilmer, Jr., David Ellis. *Education:* Attended Armour Institute of Technology (now Armour College of Engineering at Illinois Institute of Technology), 1901-02. *Politics:* Republican. *Religion:* Episcopalian.

CAREER: South Bend Times, South Bend, Ind., reporter, 1905-07; sports reporter for *Chicago Inter-Ocean, Chicago Examiner,* and *Chicago Tribune,* Chicago, Ill., 1907-10; *Sporting News,* St. Louis, Mo., editor, 1910-11; *Boston American,* Boston, Mass., sportswriter, 1911; *Chicago American,* Chicago, sportswriter, 1911-12; *Chicago Examiner,* Chicago, sportswriter, 1912-13; *Chicago Tribune,* Chicago, columnist, 1913-19; writer for Bell syndicate, beginning in 1919; host of radio column, 1932-33; lyricist, cartoonist, playwright, and writer.

MEMBER: Chicago Press Club, Friars Club, New York Athletic Club, Players Club, Coffee House, Coldstream Golf Club, Lakeville Golf Club, North Hempstead Country Club, Soundview Golf Club, Dutch Treat Club.

WRITINGS:

SHORT STORY COLLECTIONS

Bib Ballads, illustrated by Fontaine Fox, P. F. Volland, 1915, reprinted, University of Michigan Microfilms, 1969.
You Know Me Al: A Busher's Letters (stories originally published in *Saturday Evening Post;* includes "A Busher's Letters Home"), Doran, 1916, reprinted, Macmillan, 1986.
Gullible's Travels, Etc., illustrated by May Wilson Preston, Bobbs-Merrill, 1917, reprinted, University of Chicago Press, 1965.

Treat 'Em Rough: Letters From Jack the Kaiser Killer, illustrated by Frank Crerie, Bobbs-Merrill, 1918.
The Real Dope, illustrated by Preston and M. L. Blumenthal, Bobbs-Merrill, 1919.
Own Your Own Home, illustrated by Fox, Bobbs-Merrill, 1919.
Regular Fellows I Have Met, Wilmont, 1919.
The Big Town: How I and the Mrs. Go to New York to See Life and Get Katie a Husband, illustrated by Preston, Bobbs-Merrill, 1921 (also see below).
How to Write Short Stories (With Samples) (includes "Champion," "A Caddy's Diary," "Alibi Ike," "My Roomy," "Some Like Them Cold," and "Golden Honeymoon"; also see below), Scribner, 1924, Scholarly Press, 1971.
What of It?, Scribner, 1925.
The Love Nest, and Other Stories by Ring W. Lardner (includes "The Love Nest," "A Day With Conrad Green," and "Haircut"; also see below), Scribner, 1926.
Round-Up: The Stories of Ring W. Lardner (includes *How to Write Short Stories (With Samples)* and *The Love Nest, and Other Stories by Ring W. Lardner;* also see below), Scribner, 1929, reprinted as *The Collected Short Stories of Ring Lardner,* Modern Library, 1941, reprinted under original title, Franklin Library, 1981.
Lose With a Smile, Scribner, 1933.
(Under name Ring Lardner) *First and Last,* edited by Gilbert Seldes, Scribner, 1934.

Several of Lardner's works have been recorded on audio cassette.

CORRESPONDENCE

Ring Around Max: The Correspondence Between Ring Lardner and Maxwell Perkins, edited by Clifford M. Caruthers, Northern Illinois University Press, 1973.
Letters From Ring, edited by Caruthers, Walden Press, 1979.

OMNIBUS VOLUMES

Ring Lardner's Best Stories (contains *The Big Town* and *Round-Up*), Garden City Publishing, 1938.
The Portable Ring Lardner, edited and introduced by Gilbert Seldes, Viking, 1946.
The Best Short Stories of Ring Lardner, Scribner, 1957.
Haircut and Other Stories, Scribner, 1961, reprinted, Vintage Books, 1984.
Shut Up, He Explained: A Ring Lardner Selection, edited by Babette Rosmond and Henry Morgan, Scribner, 1962.
The Ring Lardner Reader, edited by Maxwell Geismar, Scribner, 1963.
Ring Lardner's You Know Me Al: The Comic Strip Adventures of Jack Keefe, Harcourt, 1979.
The Best of Ring Lardner, edited by David Lodge, Dent, 1984.

OTHER

(Editor with Edward G. Heeman) *March Sixth, 1914: The Home Coming of Charles A. Comiskey, John J. McGraw, and James J. Callahan,* Blakely, 1914.
My Four Weeks in France, illustrated by Wallace Morgan, Bobbs-Merrill, 1918.
(Under pseudonym Ring W. Lardner, Jr.) *The Young Immigrunts* (essay; originally published in *Saturday Evening Post*), Bobbs-Merrill, 1920.
Symptoms of Being Thirty-Five (essay), Bobbs-Merrill, 1921.
Say It With Oil: A Few Remarks About Wives (essay; originally published in *Saturday Evening Post*), Doran, 1923.
(Under name Ring Lardner) *The Story of a Wonder Man: Being the Autobiography of Ring Lardner,* illustrated by Margaret

Freeman, Scribner, 1927, reprinted, Greenwood Press, 1975.

(Under name Ring Lardner, with George S. Kaufman) *June Moon* (three-act comedy; first produced on Broadway in 1929), Scribner, 1930, reprinted, 1973.

Author of plays, including "Elmer the Great," and of song lyrics.

Work anthologized in *Ellery Queen's Mystery Mix: Twenty Stories From Ellery Queen's Mystery Magazine,* edited by Ellery Queen, Popular Library, 1963, and *Barbed Wires: A Collection of Famous Funny Telegrams,* edited by Joyce Denebrink, Bantam, 1966. Work also collected in *Some Champions: Sketches and Fiction,* edited by Matthew J. Bruccoli and Richard Layman, foreword by Ring Lardner, Jr., Scribner, 1976.

Author of column "In the Wake of the News," *Chicago Tribune,* 1913-19; author of comic strip based on the character Jack Keefe that appears in stories included in *You Know Me Al.*

SIDELIGHTS: Primarily known as a short story writer and newspaper journalist, Ring W. Lardner, like so many of the pioneers of modern American literature, grew up in a comfortable family that was a model of late-Victorian, middle-class values. Son of a successful businessman and the cultured daughter of an Episcopal minister, Lardner was born in 1885 in the small town of Niles, Michigan. In *Ring: A Biography of Ring Lardner,* Jonathan Yardley gives a vivid picture of the world in which Lardner spent his childhood—a world of teas, musicales, and literary societies; energetic local theatrical companies; and riverside picnics. For the affluent Lardners, it also was a world of private tutors and Irish nursemaids. By all accounts, the family environment was unusually loving. Mrs. Lardner was a devotee of serious music and a fairly successful sentimental poet who believed, in contrast with some of her small-town contemporaries, that life was to be enjoyed, not just endured.

This idyllic childhood was hard to leave behind, and in the first years after his graduation from high school at sixteen, Lardner drifted between the worlds of childhood and adulthood. He worked a series of odd jobs, flunked out of the Armour Institute in Chicago, and took several extended "rest" periods at the family home. In 1905 he landed a job almost by accident as a reporter for the *South Bend Times.* He took to the work and became a successful and hardworking journalist for most of the rest of his life. Walton R. Patrick in his Twayne study *Ring Lardner* observes that "probably no other American writer of Lardner's stature remained so long and so closely associated with newspaper work as he." One of his principal assignments was sportswriting, at which he quickly established himself as an original, often approaching his stories from the perspective of the participants rather than just summarizing events.

In 1907 Lardner took a position on the *Chicago Inter-Ocean* newspaper, and for the next twelve years he worked as a reporter and columnist for such papers as the *Chicago Examiner* and the *Chicago Tribune* and, briefly, for the *Boston American.* During these years he covered many sports, especially baseball, and he traveled with the White Sox and the Cubs. Not quite respectable in the early years of the century, the sport was rough and sometimes violent. Many of the players were illiterate or semiliterate farmboys, and other figures who hovered around the game were often unsavory. In 1919, for example, the baseball world was rocked by the disclosure that members of the White Sox had conspired to lose the World Series of that year to the Cincinnati club. They had been bribed by gamblers in what came to be known as the Black Sox Scandal.

Lardner was taken with this strange new world, so different from that of his childhood, and he observed it with an amused detachment. He tuned his ear to the awkward but colorful language of the players; he soaked up their tall tales and boasts; he noted with fascination the effects of the big-city spotlight on these boys from the provinces. From 1913 to 1919 he wrote a column called "In the Wake of the News" that appeared on the sports pages of the *Chicago Tribune* and that allowed him free rein to exploit his years of observations. In 1914 he published ten stories in the *Saturday Evening Post,* six of them about a baseball rookie named Jack Keefe. In 1916 these six stories were published in book form as *You Know Me Al.* Ring Lardner's literary career had begun.

Lardner wrote twenty-six stories about the busher, Jack Keefe. In addition to the six stories appearing in *You Know Me Al,* ten others were collected in *Treat 'Em Rough* (1918) and *The Real Dope* (1919). Because the quality of the stories in the latter two volumes is uneven, it would seem that these works were motivated by his audience's rather than Lardner's own continuing enthusiasm for the character. *You Know Me Al,* however, was not only a great popular success but one of the most original works of fiction to appear in the first two decades of the century. Although Lardner first published the saga of Jack Keefe as a series of discrete stories, the book's chronological development and its cohesiveness of characterization justify considering it in the tradition of the picaresque novel.

You Know Me Al portrays a talented but inconsistent and undisciplined right-handed pitcher's first two years in the major leagues. During that time Jack Keefe joins the Chicago White Sox, is sent to the minors, and then is recalled to the Sox. Along the way he squabbles with his teammates, his manager, and the team's owner. He becomes involved with three different women and within one seven-day period proposes to each in turn. The first two turn him down, and Keefe finally marries Florence, the sister-in-law of a teammate. Their marriage is stormy—Florence is not the shy homebody Keefe expected her to be—but eight months after their marriage a baby boy is born and Keefe is enraptured, although terrified that the baby may turn out to be a left-hander. Keefe apparently never considers the possibility, but readers suspect that he might not be the baby's father. While these domestic affairs run through the book, *You Know Me Al* primarily concerns the day-to-day life of a baseball team, and the book ends with Keefe about to depart on a world tour with the White Sox and the New York Giants.

Lardner drew his portrait of Keefe and the other players from his extensive first-hand knowledge of the actual players of the era. In fact, many of them, such as Ty Cobb and Walter Johnson, as well as White Sox owner Charles A. Comiskey, are portrayed as characters in the book. As Otto Friedrich argues in his study *Ring Lardner,* a major contribution of the busher stories was to undermine forever the all-American image of the professional athlete that had dominated sports fiction. The baseball player as Lardner presented him is often petty, can pull cruel practical jokes, and is undisciplined and self-centered. Keefe, himself, is talented but must always blame his teammates for his failures. In addition, he is too pigheaded to take the usually sound advice of his coaches, and he can be fanatically stingy and supremely egotistical. Ultimately, however, he is not a totally unlikable character because of Lardner's inspired choice of a narrative voice—that of Jack Keefe, himself, as he relays his exploits in a series of letters to his friend Al Blanchard back in their hometown of Bedford, Indiana. Friedrich considers the busher stories "perhaps the most effective dialect narrative since [Mark Twain's] *Huckleberry Finn,*" and readers hear in the opening words of the first story, "A Busher's Letters Home," the voice of another American innocent: "Well, Al old pal I suppose you seen in the paper where I been sold to the White Sox." This sentence establishes the colloquial voice that includes the decidedly nontraditional grammar, usage, and spelling for which Lardner is probably most famous. Maxwell Geismar claims in *Ring Lardner and the Portrait of Folly* that "Lardner's new language . . . made most of the previous attempts at an American style sound rather like the diction of an Oxford don." Equally important, the initial sentence of *You Know Me Al* provides the first hints of the nature of the busher. He braggingly writes to call attention to his success as he will in many of his letters. He also unintentionally points out how little control he has over his own fate; as a professional baseball player, he can be bought and sold. As a man, Jack can sometimes dimly sense what readers come to know: that for all his bravado he hasn't a will strong enough to allow him to take control of his own life.

As in *Huckleberry Finn,* the basis for both humor and social criticism is grounded in the dramatic irony that results from the narrator's insufficient understanding of his world and his relation to it. Like Huck, Jack's sense of self is at odds with reality; but whereas Huck has a sense of himself that underestimates his worth, the busher consistently overestimates his abilities both on and off the playing field. Readers sympathize with Al, the unheard correspondent. He is the true friend who allows Jack to brag, to complain, and occasionally to berate him when some favor he has performed does not meet with Jack's satisfaction. Al can be appreciated for enduring all of his friend's broken promises that he will soon be home for a visit, but Jack also deserves sympathy because he really does wish to come home—his letters are an attempt to maintain contact with what he has been. Lardner makes Jack—the ballplayer always on the road—an archetype of rootless modern humanity, longing for stability and connectedness but never quite striving hard enough to achieve them.

While Lardner worked on the Keefe stories, he also created a new character, Fred Gross, a Chicago detective who bears a resemblance to the busher. He is every bit as vain and self-justifying as Keefe and his letters are just as unintentionally revealing, but he proves to be a much less attractive character. Keefe's failings grow out of his naivete, sadness, and uncertainty. The aptly named Gross is significantly different because of his utter cynicism and total lack of personal restraint. As a hard-boiled version of Keefe, with no endearing qualities, Gross fails to engage readers enough to amuse them. Lardner seems to have realized this since he wrote only seven Fred Gross stories, four of which were collected in *Own Your Own Home* (1919).

In Gullible, another character that he created during this period, Lardner struck a new rich vein of humor. Gullible is a twentieth-century American Gulliver whose travels are mostly attempts to climb the social ladder. Gullible is an urban office worker and apartment dweller who is savvy enough to know that there is a "high polloi" and that it means something to belong to it. He is more intelligent and more glib than the other early characters. Telling his story orally rather than in letters, Gullible, because of his upward strivings, is always perilously in danger of committing malapropisms as well as a seemingly endless range of social gaffes, but he possesses enough insight to see himself ironically as well.

This new character gave Lardner a free hand to explore comically the issue of social class in a supposedly classless society. Keefe and Gross are near the bottom of society, but Gullible and his wife are lower middle class, and thus are aware of social strata both below and above. In *Gullible's Travels, Etc.* (1917), they struggle to disassociate themselves from the lower strata by trying to break off their association with their rummy-playing friends, the Hatches, and by preventing the marriage of "the Wife's" wallflower sister because they are convinced that her suitor is a social climber. They find a number of potential avenues to social advancement: the opera, a Palm Beach vacation, and an invitation to substitute in the fashionable "San Susie" bridge club. All comes to naught and, although "the Wife" remains dissatisfied, Gullible finally seems to be cured of his desire to plunge into "the cesspools o' Society."

Clifton Fadiman suggested in a *Nation* article that *Gullible's Travels, Etc.* punctures the pretensions of both the upper and lower classes "at the same time that it casually rips the cover off the cheap mind of the speaker," but that analysis seems too harsh. In fact, Gullible is one of Lardner's most affectionately drawn characters. He may be a "boob," but that fact is tempered by his own occasional insights, in which he realizes that he is just that. Jack Keefe is redeemed by his naivete; Gullible by his brief, self-deprecating glimpses of himself.

Lardner's best work during these early years is marked by fairly gentle satire—the shared realization of author and reader that all human beings can be petty fools at times but that no great harm will come of it. Lardner continued to write such stories throughout his career, but as the 1920s began, the vision grew darker and the satire more damning in many of his best works. Some of those stories were collected in *How to Write Short Stories (With Samples),* published in 1924.

F. Scott Fitzgerald had urged Lardner to publish a collection of his best stories and even suggested the title and the gag preface. He also persuaded his own publisher, the prestigious Charles Scribner's Sons, to publish it. Patrick calls the book "the turning point" of Lardner's career because it marked the first time that he received thoughtful scrutiny as an important literary artist. Of the ten stories, six dealt with sport, and nine were written in the familiar first-person narrative voice; but the collection displayed enough range to suggest both where Lardner had been and where he was going as a writer.

The most striking story in the collection is "Champion," the chronicle of a boxer's rise to success. "Champion" is one story that seems to bear out Fadiman's assertion that Lardner "just doesn't like people. . . . Certainly he hates his characters," for protagonist Midge Kelly is a monster who is as likely to turn his violent skills against family, business associates, and friends as he is against his opponents in the ring. Patrick calls Kelly "the most vicious character found . . . in Lardner's fiction" and perhaps in all fiction. Ironically, the story ends with a reporter preparing a fatuous bit of puffery about the wonderful traits of the champion as Lardner exposes not just the ugly side of sport but the shameless hypocrisy of sportswriters who deify such figures.

"Champion" is a significant work, not only because it is Lardner's most brutal portrayal of human depravity but also because it is his first important exploration of third-person narration. While some critics, such as Friedrich and Yardley, think the use of the new narrative voice is clumsy and ineffective, it does signal an important discovery for Lardner: that he could use the bone-dry objectivity of the third-person point of view to powerful effect, for this portrait of depravity is made even more chilling by the detachment of its narrator.

The theme of "Champion" is continued more gently and more thoughtfully in "A Caddy's Diary," an account by a young caddy of the ways prominent men and women cheat on the golf course. The caddy is amusedly judgmental of the ways the golfers "sell their souls" for meaningless victories, but he comes to realize that he, too, by assisting them in their deceptions, is selling his soul—for tips and smiles. Again, as Geismar notes in *Ring Lardner and the Portrait of Folly,* the voice of the caddy echoes that of Huckleberry Finn—a young man recounting his own, imperfectly understood complicity with the adult world of deception and compromise. "A Caddy's Diary" is an important transition for Lardner. It is told in an effective first-person voice and demythologizes sport as did the earlier stories; but it also examines the mendacity of the sophisticated and well-to-do, as do many of the later works.

In "Alibi Ike" and "My Roomy," Lardner returned to the familiar world of baseball, and the two stories suggest the range of Lardner's reaction to the sport. "Alibi Ike" is a delightful story in the tall-tale tradition. Ike is a fantastic character who has a ready excuse for every failure or success, on or off the field. The story is narrated by a teammate who tells the story in the spirit of gentle fun. "My Roomy" is a player's account of his roommate, Buster Elliott, truly a buster—of baseballs and everything else that gets in his way. Although not really evil, as is Midge Kelly, he is dangerously unstable. Buster finally is released from the team because of his erratic behavior, and he later writes the narrator that when he returned home and found that his fiance had married the druggist, he attacked both of them with a baseball bat. Lardner always enjoyed the eccentricities of baseball players like Ike, who appeared to be as American as the sport they played; he seemed increasingly aware, however, that the moody random violence of Buster Elliott also was all too typical of his America.

"Some Like Them Cold" is an epistolary story that deals with one of Lardner's principal fictional concerns: the awkward and often deceptive relationships between men and women. The story's central characters, Charles F. Leavis and Mabelle Gillespie, meet briefly at a Chicago train station from which he is departing to make his fortune as a songwriter in New York. Their meeting leads to an exchange of letters in which Mabelle goes to increasingly deceptive lengths to present herself as a cultured homebody. At first Charles seems interested, but it later becomes clear that he has corresponded with Mabelle merely to alleviate his homesickness and gratify his ego. He eventually announces to her his plans to marry a very undomestic, "hot" woman. "Some Like Them Cold" is a good illustration of Lardner's critical but often sympathetic portraits of the ways people bungle into, through, and out of relationships that serve as sounding boards for each person's vanities, fears, or insecurities.

"Golden Honeymoon" is a similar story about a couple, married for fifty years, who decide to go to St. Petersburg for the winter. In Florida they meet one of the wife's former suitors, and the husband spends the rest of his time trying to best the suitor in competition at the checker board and horseshoe pit while his wife slyly roots for her former lover. Critics have split over whether to view the story as a gentle and sympathetic portrait of the narrator's foibles or as a vicious revelation of the barren reality of the conventionally happy marriage. The pathos of the couple's situation, however, seems to blunt intentionally the sharper edges of the story's satire. Like *You Know Me Al,* "Golden Honeymoon" is an adroitly drawn portrait of American rootlessness, a glimpse at the newly emerging culture of the elderly who are cut off from the traditional ties with family and home and who are vainly searching for a new youth and new connections. It is the kind of story in which Lardner's barbed satire is tempered by sympathy for the common human lot.

How to Write Short Stories (With Samples) was a prelude to what Patrick calls the "peak years" between 1924 and 1929, during which Lardner wrote less than he sometimes had in the past but produced consistently better stories. Many of those stories were collected in *The Love Nest, and Other Stories by Ring W. Lardner* (1926), and the volume clearly indicates a second phase in Lardner's career. Only one of the nine stories concerns athletics; most use third person narration; and the stories are less broadly humorous and more darkly satiric than the earlier works. Lardner, now financially secure and socially prominent, aimed his barbs at a higher social class. Most of his stories from the mid- to late-1920s focus on urbanites of the middle to upper-middle classes.

Still, his perhaps most famous story in *The Love Nest* returns to familiar territory. "Haircut" is a first-person narration by a small-town barber who tells a stranger about a local prankster named Jim Kendall while he cuts the stranger's hair. The barber tells his story to praise the local cut-up, but his account quickly reveals the malice that lies behind Kendall's pranks. The barber's story ends with a description of Jim Kendall's being shot and killed by the town "half-wit." The barber assumes that the shooting was accidental, but readers clearly see that it was a case of murder as revenge for the prankster's cruelty. The story is masterfully told, a splendid example of Lardner's finely tuned ear for common speech. It also is a revelation of the dark currents beneath the placid surface of small-town life in the manner of Lardner's contemporaries, Sherwood Anderson and Sinclair Lewis. Finally, it is a shrewd examination of how malice often is masked in humor, a mask which is, after all, the basis of Lardner's own satiric art.

"A Day With Conrad Green," another well-known story from the collection, concerns a day in the life of a theatrical producer who is portrayed as cheap, petty, dishonest, and vain. The fact that the story is a thinly veiled and waspish portrait of the famous Florenz Ziegfeld may account for some of its enduring popularity; but Yardley is correct in his assertion that it is a portrait "etched not in acid but in sour milk," for Green's day simply consists of a series of events designed to show his meanness, without the tension between appearance and reality or intention and actuality that marks Lardner's most successful fiction.

The collection's title story, "The Love Nest," also about an entertainment mogul, establishes and maintains the tension that "A Day With Conrad Green" lacks. "The Love Nest" dissects the marriage of movie producer Lou Gregg and former starlet Celia Sayles. He has married her to have a handsome trinket on his arm and to give him children; she has married him so that he can give her plum movie roles. He has won, however, and has forced Celia to retire. When Bartlett—a newspaper reporter assigned to write a piece of fluff about Gregg's fairy-tale personal life—appears on the scene, the sham of their marriage is revealed. After bringing Bartlett home to meet Celia, Gregg runs off on business and leaves the two alone. Celia begins to drink heavily, and the whole unhappy story of marital manipulation and frustration spills out.

By the mid-1920s, Lardner had abandoned sports as his principal subject, but his stories of unhappy marriages, such as "The Love Nest," portray the relations between husbands and wives as bitter contests fought with as much ferocity and as little mercy as any competition on the ball field or in the boxing ring. This story, like many of the later ones, is bitter satire with little of the humor of Lardner's earlier work. When they succeed, as this story does and as "A Day With Conrad Green" does not, it is because readers can feel some sympathy for a character like Celia who, for all her faults, seems more a victim than a victimizer.

In 1929 Lardner published his last important collection, *Round-Up,* which brought together all the stories from *How to Write Short Stories* and *The Love Nest,* plus sixteen previously uncollected stories. The book rounds up not only Lardner's best writing but also stories that reflect the range of his career. All of his character types are there, from simple baseball players to slick wheeler-dealers, from small-town bumpkins to sophisticated and would-be sophisticated urbanites. In addition, the collection emphasizes the variety of his first- and third-person narrative voices. Finally, the book generously samples the range of Lardner's wit, from stories of rib-poking fun to the dark, acerbic satire of many of the later works. *Round-Up,* in its inclusiveness, is the best monument to Lardner's place among the very finest of American short story writers.

While Lardner's reputation must rest on his stories, the stories actually represent only a portion of his output as a writer. He was a journalist before he was a story writer, and he remained a journalist throughout his career. Even after he left full-time newspaper work, he continued to write columns, profiles, and observations. He also composed song lyrics and wrote plays, including "June Moon"—written in collaboration with George S. Kaufman—which had a successful Broadway run in 1929. And some of his most delightful work was in a series of short, dadaesque plays that Donald Elder in his book-length study *Ring Lardner* has characterized as "a commentary on nothing except the absurdity of everything." Lardner also wrote a mock autobiography, *The Story of A Wonder Man* (1927), which, from the perspective of current critical theory, might be thought of as a deconstruction of the genre of autobiography. Lardner even for a time wrote a comic strip based on the Frank Keefe character.

In all, Lardner published twenty books in a career that spanned only twenty years, cut short by his early death—from a combination of tuberculosis and heart trouble exacerbated by years of heavy drinking and general disregard for his health—in 1933 at the age of forty-eight. The range and volume of his writing reflect Lardner's own estimation of his career: he always insisted that he was a professional writer rather than an artist, that he wrote to make a living rather than to make art. Certainly much of what Lardner wrote was "hack" work, albeit usually of a particularly high quality. Still, in his best short stories Lardner created a body of work that can stand comparison with the work of any artist of his generation.

Many of Lardner's contemporaries expected more of him and felt that he never made full use of his talent. In *The Shores of Light* Edmund Wilson complained of Lardner's apparent lack of "artistic seriousness." For instance, Wilson lamented that, in *How to Write Short Stories,* Lardner compiled "a book of the best things he has written and then, with his title and comic preface, tries to pretend that he has never attempted to write anything good at all." Fitzgerald, who had suggested that title and preface and who was Lardner's friend and neighbor on Long Island during the 1920s, also thought that Lardner never matured as a writer and blamed it on his years as a baseball reporter. As Fitzgerald declared in "Ring," an essay collected in *The Crack-Up:* "During those years when most men of promise achieve an adult education, if only in the school of war, Ring moved in the company of a few dozen illiterates playing a boy's game. . . . [Thus, Lardner] fell short of the achievement he was capable of. . . . However deeply Ring might cut into it, his cake had the diameter of Frank Chance's Diamond. . . . Ring got less of himself on paper than any other American author of the first flight."

Wilson felt that Lardner never took himself seriously enough; Fitzgerald thought his years as a sports journalist stunted his de-

velopment. A generation later, John Berryman offered his opinion in *Commentary* that Lardner was a "squandered talent" because he never recognized his "special gift for . . . nonsense" that could have placed him in the company of "the great fantasists [Edward] Lear and [Lewis] Carroll." Still others, following the lead of Clifton Fadiman's influential *Nation* essay "Ring Lardner and the Triangle of Hate," have argued that Lardner was a misanthrope whose hatred of people, especially himself, blocked his potential to be a fruitful creative artist.

The fact that Lardner's career was a profound disappointment to some commentators should not obscure his very real and considerable accomplishments. They are essentially threefold. First, and most important, Lardner helped to liberate the language of fiction, doing for his generation what Twain had done for his own fifty years earlier. No writer of his time had a better ear for what H. L. Mencken called "common American." No writer more concretely demonstrated the idea that language *is* identity. For this reason, Virginia Woolf felt, as she revealed in *The Moment and Other Essays,* that Lardner wrote "the best prose that has come our way. Hence we feel at last freely admitted to the society of our fellows [through their language]." Readers celebrate Lardner's remarkable linguistic inventiveness for the sheer delight it gives, and also because it paved the way for a generation of otherwise disparate writers, from Ernest Hemingway to Dashiell Hammett, who felt free to eschew the constraints of formal literary English in order to explore the variety of American speech in their writing.

Second, Lardner was instrumental in shaping the way sports and sports heroes are regarded. He began his career as a writer on the eve of a renaissance of interest in sport, the era of Babe Ruth, Red Grange, Jack Dempsey, Bobby Jones, and Bill Tilden. Lardner understood the American love of sport and longing for sports heroes, but he also recognized the dangers in creating idols out of the likes of Jack Keefe and Midge Kelly. In addition, he seemed to understand the ways in which the emergence of big-time sports was an integral part of the newly emerging mass culture of radio, the movies, and national-circulation magazines. In a little over two decades—the span of Lardner's career—baseball had moved from a local amusement played by semiliterate farmboys to a national obsession featuring media-created demigods. Lardner knew that sport was a microcosm of American culture and that the rapid and dislocating change at the ballpark was symptomatic of a new age in American culture.

His third major contribution as a writer was in his insightful chronicling of that new age. In those stories that portrayed the breakdown of cohesion in small-town life, the anchorless drift of urban life, and the failure of individuals to establish honest, meaningful, and nurturant interpersonal relationships, Lardner captured a society struggling with rapid and profound change. In characters like Gullible and stories such as "The Love Nest," "The Golden Honeymoon," and "Some Like Them Cold," Lardner showed human pettiness and even cruelty, but not without sympathy for the difficulty people face in coping with the often painful dislocations of the modern age.

Lardner was not the misanthrope that Fadiman and others have taken him for, because his anger at human failings was always tempered by what Dorothy Parker in her *New Yorker* review called "his strange, bitter pity." In his memoir *The Lardners: My Family Remembered,* Ring Lardner, Jr., recounts the time one of his cousins complained that Charles Dickens was "sentimental and sloppy." Lardner, Sr., responded, "How can you write if you can't cry?" If he had been speaking of the powerful effects of his own work, he might have said, "How can you laugh if you can't cry?"

MEDIA ADAPTATIONS: "Elmer the Great" was adapted into a radio play starring Joe E. Brown and June Travis for the Lux Radio Theatre, October 5, 1966; "Champion" was adapted into a radio play starring Kirk Douglas and Marilyn Maxwell for the American Armed Services Radio Network.

BIOGRAPHICAL/CRITICAL SOURCES:

BOOKS

Bruccoli, Matthew J. and Richard Layman, *Ring Lardner: A Descriptive Bibliography,* University of Pittsburgh Press, 1976.
Caruthers, Clifford M., editor, *Ring Around Max: The Correspondence Between Ring Lardner and Maxwell Perkins,* Northern Illinois University Press, 1973.
Caruthers, Clifford M., editor, *Letters From Ring,* Walden Press, 1979.
Concise Dictionary of American Literary Biography: The Twenties, 1917-1929, Gale, 1989.
DeMuth, James, *Small Town Chicago: The Comic Perspective of Finley Peter Dunne, George Ade, Ring Lardner,* Kennikat Press, 1980.
Dictionary of Literary Biography, Gale, Volume 11: *American Humorists, 1800-1950,* 1982, Volume 25: *American Newspaper Journalists, 1901-1925,* 1984.
Elder, Donald, *Ring Lardner,* Doubleday, 1956.
Evans, Elizabeth, *Ring Lardner,* Ungar, 1979.
French, Warren, editor, *The Twenties: Fiction, Poetry, Drama,* Everett/Edwards, 1975.
Friedrich, Otto, *Ring Lardner,* University of Minnesota Press, 1965.
Geismar, Maxwell, *Writers in Crisis: The American Novel, 1925-1940,* Houghton, 1942.
Geismar, Maxwell, *The Ring Lardner Reader,* Scribner, 1963.
Geismar, Maxwell, *Ring Lardner and the Portrait of Folly,* Crowell, 1972.
Herbst, Josephine, *Gullible's Travels, Etc.,* University of Chicago Press, 1965.
Lardner, Ring, *The Story of a Wonder Man: Being the Autobiography of Ring Lardner,* Scribner, 1927.
Lardner, Ring, Jr., *The Lardners: My Family Remembered,* Harper, 1976.
Mencken, H. L., *The American Language: An Inquiry Into the Development of English in the United States,* 2nd edition, Knopf, 1921.
Mencken, H. L., *Prejudices, Fifth Series,* Knopf, 1926.
Patrick, Walton R., *Ring Lardner,* Twayne, 1963.
Seldes, Gilbert, editor, *The Portable Ring Lardner,* Viking, 1946.
Twentieth-Century Literary Criticism, Gale, Volume 2, 1979, Volume 14, 1984.
Wilson, Edmund, editor, *The Crack-Up,* New Directions, 1956.
Wilson, Edmund, *The Shores of Light: A Literary Chronicle of the Twenties and Thirties,* Farrar, Straus, 1956.
Woolf, Virginia, *The Moment and Other Essays,* Hogarth, 1925.
Yardley, Jonathan, *Ring: A Biography of Ring Lardner,* Random House, 1977.

PERIODICALS

Chicago Tribune, February 28, 1985, March 14, 1985.
Commentary, November, 1956.
Nation, March 22, 1933.
New Yorker, April 27, 1939.
New York Times Book Review, March 31, 1985.

LARDNER, Ring W., Jr.
See LARDNER, Ring(gold) W(ilmer)

*   *   *

LARKIN, Philip (Arthur)   1922-1985

PERSONAL: Born August 9, 1922, in Coventry, Warwickshire, England; died following surgery for throat cancer, December 2, 1985, in Hull, England; son of Sydney (a city treasurer) and Eva Emily (Day) Larkin. *Education:* St. John's College, Oxford, B.A. (with first class honors), 1943, M.A., 1947.

ADDRESSES: Office—Library, University of Hull, Yorkshire, England.

CAREER: Wellington Public Library, Wellington, England, librarian, 1943-46; University College Library, Leicester, England, librarian, 1946-50; Queen's University Library, Belfast, Ireland, sublibrarian, 1950-55; University of Hull, Hull, England, librarian, 1955-85. Visiting fellow at All Souls College, Oxford University, 1970-71; chairman of judges for Booker Prize, 1977; caretaker of National Manuscript Collection of Contemporary Writers for Arts Council of Great Britain; member of standing conference of national and university libraries.

MEMBER: Arts Council of Great Britain (member of literature panel), Poetry Book Society (former chairman), American Academy of Arts and Sciences (honorary member).

AWARDS, HONORS: Queen's Gold medal for Poetry, 1965; Loines Award from National Institute and American Academy of Arts and Letters, 1974; Commander, Order of the British Empire, 1975; Shakespeare prize from FVS Foundation (Hamburg, West Germany), 1976; Commander of Literature, 1978; W. H. Smith & Son Literary Award, 1985, for *Required Writing: Miscellaneous Pieces, 1955-82.*

WRITINGS:

The North Ship (poems), Fortune Press, 1946, new edition, Faber, 1966.
Jill (novel), Fortune Press, 1946, revised edition, St. Martin's, 1964, reprinted, Overlook Press, 1984.
A Girl in Winter (novel), Faber, 1947, St. Martin's, 1957.
XX Poems, [Belfast], 1951.
The Less Deceived (poems), Marvell Press, 1955, 4th edition, St. Martin's, 1958.
Listen Presents Philip Larkin Reading "The Less Deceived" (recording), Marvell Press, 1959.
The Whitsun Weddings (poems), Random House, 1964.
Philip Larkin Reads and Comments on "The Whitsun Weddings" (recording), Marvell Press, c. 1966.
All What Jazz: A Record Diary 1961-1968 (essays), St. Martin's, 1970, updated edition published as *All What Jazz: A Record Diary 1961-1971,* Farrar, Straus, 1985.
(Editor and contributor) *The Oxford Book of Twentieth-Century English Verse,* Oxford University Press, 1973.
High Windows (poems), Farrar, Straus, 1974.
British Poets of Our Time, Philip Larkin: "High Windows," Poems Read by the Author (recording), Arts Council of Great Britain, c. 1975.
Required Writing: Miscellaneous Pieces 1955-1982 (essays), Faber, 1983, Farrar, Straus, 1984.
Collected Poems, edited by Anthony Thwaite, Marvell Press, 1988, Farrar, Straus, 1989.

Also editor, with Louis MacNeice and Bonamy Dobree, of *New Poets 1958.* Contributor to numerous anthologies; contributor of poetry and essays to periodicals. Jazz critic for *Daily Telegraph* (London), 1961-71.

MEDIA ADAPTATIONS: Some of Larkin's poetry and a *Paris Review* interview with him were adapted for stage by Ron Hutchinson and produced as "Larkin" in Los Angeles, CA, 1988.

SIDELIGHTS: Philip Larkin, an eminent writer in postwar Great Britain, was commonly referred to as "England's *other* Poet Laureate" until his death in 1985. Indeed, when the position of laureate became vacant in 1984, many poets and critics favored Larkin's appointment, but the shy, provincial author preferred to avoid the limelight. An "artist of the first rank" in the words of *Southern Review* contributor John Press, Larkin achieved acclaim on the strength of an extremely small body of work—just over one hundred pages of poetry in four slender volumes that appeared at almost decade-long intervals. These collections, especially *The Less Deceived, The Whitsun Weddings,* and *High Windows,* present "a poetry from which even people who distrust poetry, most people, can take comfort and delight," according to X. J. Kennedy in the *New Criterion.* Larkin employed the traditional tools of poetry—rhyme, stanza, and meter—to explore the often uncomfortable or terrifying experiences thrust upon common people in the modern age. As Alan Brownjohn notes in *Philip Larkin,* the poet produced without fanfare "the most technically brilliant and resonantly beautiful, profoundly disturbing yet appealing and approachable, body of verse of any English poet in the last twenty-five years."

Despite his wide popularity, Larkin refused to make poetry his sole means of support by teaching or giving readings. Instead he worked as a professional librarian for more than forty years and wrote in his spare time. In that manner he authored two novels, *Jill* and *A Girl in Winter,* two collections of criticism, *All What Jazz: A Record Diary 1961-1968* and *Required Writing: Miscellaneous Pieces 1955-1982,* and all of his verse. *Phoenix* contributor Alun R. Jones suggests that, as a wage earner at the remote University of Hull, Larkin "avoided the literary, the metropolitan, the group label, and embraced the nonliterary, the provincial, and the purely personal." In *Nine Contemporary Poets: A Critical Introduction,* Peter R. King likewise commends "the scrupulous awareness of a man who refuses to be taken in by inflated notions of either art or life." From his base in Hull, Larkin composed poetry that both reflects the dreariness of postwar provincial England and voices "most articulately and poignantly the spiritual desolation of a world in which men have shed the last rags of religious faith that once lent meaning and hope to human lives," according to Press. Critics feel that this localization of focus and the colloquial language used to describe settings and emotions endear Larkin to his readers. *Agenda* reviewer George Dekker notes that no living poet "can equal Larkin on his own ground of the familiar English lyric, drastically and poignantly limited in its sense of any life beyond, before or after, life today in England."

Throughout his life, England was Larkin's emotional territory to an eccentric degree. The poet distrusted travel abroad and professed ignorance of foreign literature, including most modern American poetry. He also tried to avoid the cliches of his own culture, such as the tendency to read portent into an artist's childhood. In his poetry and essays, Larkin remembered his early years as "unspent" and "boring," as he grew up the son of a city treasurer in Coventry. Poor eyesight and stuttering plagued Larkin as a youth; he retreated into solitude, read widely, and began to write poetry as a nightly routine. In 1940 he enrolled at Oxford, beginning "a vital stage in his personal

and literary development," according to Bruce K. Martin in the *Dictionary of Literary Biography.* At Oxford Larkin studied English literature and cultivated the friendship of those who shared his special interests, including Kingsley Amis and John Wain. He graduated with first class honors in 1943, and, having to account for himself with the wartime Ministry of Labor, he took a position as librarian in the small Shropshire town of Wellington. While there he wrote both of his novels as well as *The North Ship,* his first volume of poetry. After working at several other university libraries, Larkin moved to Hull in 1955 and began a thirty-year association with the library at the University of Hull. He is still admired for his expansion and modernization of that facility.

In a *Paris Review* interview, Larkin dismissed the notion that he studied the techniques of poets that he admired in order to perfect his craft. Most critics feel, however, that the poems of both William Butler Yeats and Thomas Hardy exerted an influence on Larkin as he sought his own voice. Martin suggests that the pieces in *The North Ship* "reflect an infatuation with Yeatsian models, a desire to emulate the Irishman's music without having undergone the experience upon which it had been based." Hardy's work provided the main impetus to Larkin's mature poetry, according to critics. King contends that a close reading of Hardy taught Larkin "that a modern poet could write about the life around him in the language of the society around him. He encouraged [Larkin] to use his poetry to examine the reality of his own life. . . . As a result Larkin abandoned the highly romantic style of *The North Ship,* which had been heavily influenced by the poetry of Yeats, and set out to write from the tensions that underlay his own everyday experiences. Hardy also supported his employment of traditional forms and technique, which Larkin [went] on to use with subtlety and variety." In his work *Philip Larkin,* Martin also claims that Larkin learned from Hardy "that his own life, with its often casual discoveries, could become poems, and that he could legitimately share such experience with his readers. From this lesson [came Larkin's] belief that a poem is better based on something from 'unsorted' experience than on another poem or other art."

Not surprisingly, this viewpoint allied Larkin with the poets of The Movement, a loose association of British writers who "called, implicitly in their poetry and fiction and explicitly in critical essays, for some sort of commonsense return to more traditional techniques," according to Martin in *Philip Larkin.* Martin adds that the rationale for this "antimodernist, antiexperimental stance is their stated concern with clarity: with writing distinguished by precision rather than obscurity. . . . [The Movement urged] not an abandonment of emotion, but a mixture of rationality with feeling, of objective control with subjective abandon. Their notion of what they felt the earlier generation of writers, particularly poets, lacked, centered around the ideas of honesty and realism about self and about the outside world." King observes that Larkin "had sympathy with many of the attitudes to poetry represented by The Movement," but this view of the poet's task antedated the beginnings of that group's influence. Nonetheless, in the opinion of *Washington Post Book World* contributor Chad Walsh, Larkin "seemed to fulfill the credo of the Movement better than anyone else, and he was often singled out, as much for damnation as for praise, by those looking for the ultimate Movement poet." Brownjohn concludes that in the company of The Movement, Larkin's own "distinctive technical skills, the special subtlety in his adaptation of a very personal colloquial mode to the demands of tight forms, were not immediately seen to be outstanding; but his strengths as a craftsman have increasingly come to be regarded as one of the hallmarks of his talent."

Those strengths of craftsmanship and technical skill in Larkin's mature works receive almost universal approval from literary critics. London *Sunday Times* correspondent Ian Hamilton writes: "Supremely among recent poets, [Larkin] was able to accommodate a talking voice to the requirements of strict metres and tight rhymes, and he had a faultless ear for the possibilities of the iambic line." David Timms expresses a similar view in his book entitled *Philip Larkin*. Technically, notes Timms, Larkin was "an extraordinarily various and accomplished poet, a poet who [used] the devices of metre and rhyme for specific effects. . . . His language is never flat, unless he intends it to be so for a particular reason, and his diction is never stereotyped. He [was] always ready . . . to reach across accepted literary boundaries for a word that will precisely express what he intends." As King explains, Larkin's best poems "are rooted in actual experiences and convey a sense of place and situation, people and events, which gives an authenticity to the thoughts that are then usually raised by the poet's observation of the scene. . . . Joined with this strength of careful social observation is a control over tone changes and the expression of developing feelings even within a single poem . . . which is the product of great craftsmanship. To these virtues must be added the fact that in all the poems there is a lucidity of language which invites understanding even when the ideas expressed are paradoxical or complex." *New Leader* contributor Pearl K. Bell concludes that Larkin's poetry "fits with unresisting precision into traditional structures, . . . filling them with the melancholy truth of things in the shrunken, vulgarized and parochial England of the 1970s."

If Larkin's style is traditional, the subject matter of his poetry is derived exclusively from modern life. Press contends that Larkin's artistic work "delineates with considerable force and delicacy the pattern of contemporary sensibility, tracing the way in which we respond to our environment, plotting the ebb and flow of the emotional flux within us, embodying in his poetry attitudes of heart and mind that seem peculiarly characteristic of our time: doubt, insecurity, boredom, aimlessness and malaise." A sense that life is a finite prelude to oblivion underlies many of Larkin's poems. King suggests that the work is "a poetry of disappointment, of the destruction of romantic illusions, of man's defeat by time and his own inadequacies," as well as a study of how dreams, hopes, and ideals "are relentlessly diminished by the realities of life." To Larkin, Brownjohn notes, life was never "a matter of blinding revelations, mystical insights, expectations glitteringly fulfilled. Life, for Larkin, and, implicitly, for all of us, is something lived mundanely, with a gradually accumulating certainty that its golden prizes are sheer illusion." Love is one of the supreme deceptions of humankind in Larkin's world view, as King observes: "Although man clutches at his instinctive belief that only love will comfort, console and sustain him, such a hope is doomed to be denied. A lover's promise is an empty promise and the power to cure suffering through love is a tragic illusion." Stanley Poss in *Western Humanities Review* maintains that Larkin's poems demonstrate "desperate clarity and restraint and besieged common sense. And what they mostly say is, be beginning to despair, despair, despair."

Larkin arrived at his conclusions candidly, concerned to expose evasions so that the reader might stand "naked but honest, 'less deceived' . . . before the realities of life and death," to quote King. Many critics find Larkin withdrawn from his poems, a phenomenon Martin describes in the *Dictionary of Literary Biography* thus: "The unmarried observer, a staple in Larkin's poetic world, . . . enjoys only a curious and highly limited kind of communion with those he observes." Jones likewise declares that Larkin's "ironic detachment is comprehensive. Even the intense beauty that his poetry creates is created by balancing on a keen ironic edge." King writes: "A desire not to be fooled by time leads to a concern to maintain vigilance against a whole range of possible evasions of reality. It is partly this which makes Larkin's typical stance one of being to one side of life, watching himself and others with a detached eye." Although *Harvard Advocate* contributor Andrew Sullivan states that the whole tenor of Larkin's work is that of an "irrelevant and impotent spectator," John Reibetanz offers the counter suggestion in *Contemporary Literature* that the poetry records and reflects "the imperfect, transitory experiences of the mundane reality that the poet shares with his readers." Larkin himself offered a rather wry description of his accomplishments—an assessment that, despite its levity, links him emotionally to his work. In 1979 he told the *Observer:* "I think writing about unhappiness is probably the source of my popularity, if I have any. . . . Deprivation is for me what daffodils were for Wordsworth."

Critics such as *Dalhousie Review* contributor Roger Bowen find moments of affirmation in Larkin's poetry, notwithstanding its pessimistic and cynical bent. According to Bowen, an overview of Larkin's oeuvre makes evident "that the definition of the poet as a modern anti-hero governed by a sense of his own mortality seems . . . justified. But . . . a sense of vision and a quiet voice of celebration seem to be asserting themselves" in at least some of the poems. Brownjohn admits that Larkin's works take a bleak view of human existence; at the same time, however, they contain "the recurrent reflection that others, particularly the young, might still find happiness in expectation." *Contemporary Literature* essayist James Naremore expands on Larkin's tendency to detach himself from the action in his poems: "From the beginning, Larkin's work has manifested a certain coolness and lack of self-esteem, a need to withdraw from experience; but at the same time it has continued to show his desire for a purely secular type of romance. . . . Larkin is trying to assert his humanity, not deny it. . . . The greatest virtue in Larkin's poetry is not so much his suppression of large poetic gestures as his ability to recover an honest sense of joy and beauty." The *New York Times* quotes Larkin as having said that a poem "represents the mastering, even if just for a moment, of the pessimism and the melancholy, and enables you—you the poet, and you, the reader—to go on." King senses this quiet catharsis when he concludes: "Although one's final impression of the poetry is certainly that the chief emphasis is placed on a life 'unspent' in the shadow of 'untruth,' moments of beauty and affirmation are not entirely denied. It is the difficulty of experiencing such moments after one has become so aware of the numerous self-deceptions that man practices on himself to avoid the uncomfortable reality which lies at the heart of Larkin's poetic identity."

Timms claims that Larkin "consistently maintained that a poet should write about those things in life that move him most deeply: if he does not feel deeply about anything, he should not write." Dedicated to reaching out for his readers, the poet was a staunch opponent of modernism in all artistic media. Larkin felt that such cerebral experimentation ultimately creates a barrier between an artist and the audience and provides unnecessary thematic complications. Larkin's "demand for fidelity to experience is supported by his insistence that poetry should both communicate and give pleasure to the reader," King notes, adding: "It would be a mistake to dismiss this attitude as a form of simple literary conservatism. Larkin is not so much expressing an anti-intellectualism as attacking a particular form of artistic snobbery." In *Philip Larkin,* Martin comments that the poet saw the need for poetry to move toward the "paying customer." Therefore, his writings concretize "many of the questions which have perplexed man almost since his beginning but which in modern times have become the province principally of academicians. . . . [Larkin's poetry reflects] his faith in the common reader to recognize and respond to traditional philosophical concerns when stripped of undue abstractions and pretentious labels." Brownjohn finds Larkin eminently successful in his aims: "It is indeed true that many of his readers find pleasure and interest in Larkin's poetry for its apparent accessibility and its cultivation of verse forms that seem reassuringly traditional rather than 'modernist' in respect of rhyme and metre." As Timms succinctly notes, originality for Larkin consisted "not in modifying the medium of communication, but in communicating something different."

Larkin's output of fiction and essays is hardly more extensive than his poetry. His two novels, *Jill* and *A Girl in Winter,* were both published before his twenty-fifth birthday. *New Statesman* correspondent Clive James feels that both novels "seem to point forward to the poetry. Taken in their chronology, they are impressively mature and self-sufficient." James adds that the fiction is so strong that "if Larkin had never written a line of verse, his place as a writer would still have been secure." Although the novels received little critical attention when they first appeared, they have since been judged highly successful. Brownjohn calls *Jill* "one of the better novels written about England during the Second World War, not so much for any conscious documentary effort put into it as for Larkin's characteristic scrupulousness in getting all the background details right." In the *New York Review of Books,* John Bayley notes that *A Girl in Winter* is "a real masterpiece, a quietly gripping novel, dense with the humor that is Larkin's trademark, and also an extended prose poem." Larkin's essay collections, *Required Writing* and *All What Jazz,* are compilations of critical pieces he wrote for periodicals over a thirty-year period, including the jazz record reviews he penned as a music critic for the London *Daily Telegraph.* "Everything Larkin writes is concise, elegant and wholly original," Bayley claims in the *Listener,* "and this is as true of his essays and reviews as it is of his poetry." Elsewhere in the *New York Review of Books,* Bayley comments that *Required Writing* "reveals wide sympathies, deep and trenchant perceptions, a subterranean grasp of the whole of European culture." And in an essay on *All What Jazz* for Anthony Thwaite's *Larkin at Sixty,* James concludes that "no wittier book of criticism has ever been written."

Larkin stopped writing poetry shortly after his collection *High Windows* was published in 1974. In an *Observer* obituary, Kingsley Amis characterized the poet as "a man much driven in upon himself, with increasing deafness from early middle age cruelly emphasizing his seclusion." Small though it is, Larkin's body of work has "altered our awareness of poetry's capacity to reflect the contemporary world," according to *London Magazine* correspondent Roger Garfitt. A. N. Wilson draws a similar conclusion in the *Spectator:* "Perhaps the reason Larkin made such a great name from so small an *oeuvre* was that he so exactly caught the mood of so many of us. . . . Larkin found the perfect voice for expressing our worst fears." That voice was "stubbornly indigenous," according to Robert B. Shaw in *Poetry Nation.* Larkin appealed primarily to the British sensibility; he remained unencumbered by any compunction to universalize his poems by adopting a less regional idiom. Perhaps as a consequence, his poetry sells remarkably well in Great Britain, his readers come from all walks of life, and his untimely cancer-related death in 1985 has not diminished his popularity. Andrew Sullivan feels that Larkin "has spoken to the English in a language they can readily understand of the profound self-doubt that this century has given them. He was, of all English poets, a laureate too obvious to need official recognition."

BIOGRAPHICAL/CRITICAL SOURCES:

BOOKS

Alvarez, A., *All This Fiddle: Essays 1955-1967,* Random House, 1969.
Bayley, John, *The Uses of Division,* Viking, 1976.
Bedient, Calvin, *Eight Contemporary Poets,* Oxford University Press, 1974.
Bloomfield, B. C., *Philip Larkin: A Bibliography,* Faber, 1979.
Brownjohn, Alan, *Philip Larkin,* Longman, 1975.
Contemporary Literary Criticism, Gale, Volume 3, 1975, Volume 5, 1976, Volume 8, 1978, Volume 9, 1978, Volume 13, 1980, Volume 18, 1981, Volume 33, 1985, Volume 39, 1986.
Davie, Donald, *Thomas Hardy and British Poetry,* Oxford University Press, 1972.
Dictionary of Literary Biography, Volume 27: *Poets of Great Britain and Ireland, 1945-1960,* Gale, 1984.
Dodsworth, Martin, editor, *The Survival of Poetry: A Contemporary Survey,* Faber, 1970.
Enright, D. J., *Conspirators and Poets: Reviews and Essays,* Dufour, 1966.
Jones, Peter and Michael Schmidt, editors, *British Poetry since 1970: A Critical Survey,* Carcanet, 1980.
King, Peter R., *Nine Contemporary Poets: A Critical Introduction,* Methuen, 1979.
Kuby, Lolette, *An Uncommon Poet for the Common Man: A Study of Philip Larkin's Poetry,* Mouton, 1974.
Martin, Bruce K., *Philip Larkin,* Twayne, 1978.
Motion, Andrew, *Philip Larkin,* Methuen, 1982.
O'Connor, William Van, *The New University Wits and the End of Modernism,* Southern Illinois University Press, 1963.
Petch, Simon, *The Art of Philip Larkin,* Sydney University Press, 1981.
Rosenthal M. L., *The Modern Poets: A Critical Introduction,* Oxford University Press, 1960.
Rosenthal, M. L., *The New Poets: American and British Poetry since World War II,* Oxford University Press, 1967.
Schmidt, Michael, *A Reader's Guide to Fifty Modern British Poets,* Barnes & Noble, 1979.
Thwaite, Anthony, editor, *Larkin at Sixty,* Faber, 1982.
Timms, David, *Philip Larkin,* Barnes & Noble, 1973.

PERIODICALS

Agenda, autumn, 1974, summer, 1976.
American Scholar, summer, 1965.
Atlantic, January, 1966.
Bucknell Review, December, 1965.
Chicago Review, Volume 18, number 2, 1965.
Contemporary Literature, summer, 1974, autumn, 1976.
Critical Inquiry, Number 3, 1976-77.
Critical Quarterly, summer, 1964, summer, 1981.
Dalhousie Review, spring, 1968, spring, 1978.
Encounter, June, 1974, February, 1984.
Harvard Advocate, May, 1968.
Iowa Review, fall, 1977.
Journal of English Literary History, December, 1971.
Listener, January 26, 1967, March 26, 1970, December 22, 1983.
London Magazine, May, 1964, November, 1964, June, 1970, October-November, 1974, April-May, 1980.
Los Angeles Times, June 13, 1984, October 1, 1988.
Los Angeles Times Book Review, December 1, 1985, July 30, 1989.

Michigan Quarterly Review, fall, 1976.
New Criterion, February, 1986.
New Leader, May 26, 1975.
New Republic, March 6, 1965, November 20, 1976.
New Review, June, 1974.
New Statesman, June 14, 1974, July 26, 1974, March 21, 1975.
Newsweek, June 25, 1984.
New Yorker, December 6, 1976.
New York Review of Books, January 28, 1965, May 15, 1975.
New York Times, June 23, 1984, August 11, 1984.
New York Times Book Review, December 20, 1964, January 12, 1975, May 16, 1976, December 26, 1976, August 12, 1984, November 10, 1985, May 21, 1989.
Observer (London), February 8, 1970, December 16, 1979, November 20, 1983.
Paris Review, summer, 1982.
Phoenix, autumn and winter, 1973-74, spring, 1975.
PN Review, Volume 4, number 2, 1977.
Poetry Nation, Number 6, 1976.
Poetry Review, Volume 72, number 2, 1982.
Prairie Schooner, fall, 1975.
Review, June-July, 1962, December, 1964.
Southern Review, winter, 1977.
Stand, Volume 16, number 2, 1975.
Time, July 23, 1984.
Times (London), December 8, 1983, June 20, 1985, October 22, 1988.
Times Literary Supplement, January 6, 1984.
Tribune Books (Chicago), April 16, 1989.
Virginia Quarterly Review, spring, 1976.
Washington Post, June 3, 1989.
Washington Post Book World, January 12, 1975, May 7, 1989.
Western Humanities Review, spring, 1962, autumn, 1975.

OBITUARIES:

PERIODICALS

Globe and Mail (Toronto), December 14, 1985.
Listener, December 12, 1985.
Los Angeles Times, December 3, 1985.
New Criterion, February, 1986.
New Republic, January 6 and 13, 1986.
New York Review of Books, January 16, 1986.
New York Times, December 3, 1985.
Observer (London), December 8, 1985.
Spectator, December 7, 1985.
Sunday Times (London), December 8, 1985.
Times (London), December 3, 1985, December 14, 1985.
Times Literary Supplement, January 24, 1986.
Washington Post, December 3, 1985.

*   *   *

LASCH, Christopher 1932-

PERSONAL: Born June 1, 1932, in Omaha, Neb.; son of Robert (a journalist) and Zora (a professor; maiden name, Schaupp) Lasch; married Nell Commager, June 30, 1956; children: Robert, Elisabeth, Catherine, Christopher. *Education:* Harvard University, B.A., 1954; Columbia University, M.A., 1955, Ph.D., 1961.

ADDRESSES: Home—47 Parker Dr., Pittsford, N.Y. 14534. *Office*—Department of History, University of Rochester, Rochester, N.Y. 14627.

CAREER: Williams College, Williamstown, Mass., instructor in history, 1957-59; Roosevelt University, Chicago, Ill., assistant professor of history, 1960-61; University of Iowa, Iowa City, assistant professor, 1961-63, associate professor, 1965-66, professor of history, 1965-66; Northwestern University, Evanston, Ill., professor of history, 1966-70; University of Rochester, Rochester, N.Y., professor of history, 1970—, Watson Professor of History, 1979—, chairman of department. Freud Lecturer at University College London.

MEMBER: Organization of American Historians, American Historical Association.

AWARDS, HONORS: Grants from Social Science Research Council, 1960, American Council of Learned Societies, 1968 and 1983, Ford Foundation, 1974, and Guggenheim Foundation, 1975; D.H.L. from Bard College, 1977, and Hobart College, 1981; American Book Award in current interest (paperback), 1980, for *The Culture of Narcissism: American Life in an Age of Diminishing Expectations.*

WRITINGS:

American Liberals and the Russian Revolution, Columbia University Press, 1962.
The New Radicalism in America, 1889-1963: The Intellectual as a Social Type, Knopf, 1965, recent edition, Norton, 1986.
The Agony of the American Left (essays), Knopf, 1969.
The World of Nations, Knopf, 1973, published as *World of Nations: Reflections on American History, Politics, and Culture,* Random House, 1974.
Haven in a Heartless World: The Family Besieged, Basic Books, 1977.
The Culture of Narcissism: American Life in an Age of Diminishing Expectations, Norton, 1977.
(Editor) *Social Thought of Jane Addams,* Irvington, 1982.
The Minimal Self: Psychic Survival in Troubled Times, Norton, 1984.

WORK IN PROGRESS: American Social Thought, 1890-1930.

SIDELIGHTS: Christopher Lasch had already seen a number of his social- and political-minded books published—including *The Agony of the American Left* and *Haven in a Heartless World: The Family Besieged*—before he came out with two new works that drew considerable attention from both critics and the public. With *The Culture of Narcissism: American Life in an Age of Diminishing Expectations* and *The Minimal Self: Psychic Survival in Troubled Times,* Lasch proposes theories that are as disturbing as they are thought-provoking: that American society is eroding from within at an alarming rate; that, fueled by an acquisitive obsession, a fear of old age, and a spiritual void, among other elements, our weakening ways could eventually spell the death of our culture.

More than one critic has compared Lasch to the biblical doomsayer Jeremiah. But most agree that the author's works deserve a hearing. To Jackson Lears of the *Nation,* for instance, *The Culture of Narcissism* "is a powerful indictment of the nonmorality promoted by consumer capitalism, drawing on a wide variety of evidence; it is boldly conceived and gracefully, sometimes eloquently expressed. But in detail, the book is uneven; it suffers from a superficiality in historical explanation and a tendency to substitute assertion for argument." The critic continues that Lasch "clings to some of the honorable values in Victorian culture—moral discipline, parental authority, the work ethic—without making his allegiance explicit. As a result, his critique loses polemical focus; sometimes it degenerates into a repetitive tirade. In short, while *The Culture of Narcissism* is an exciting and suggestive book, it could have been a vastly more persuasive one."

"It seems not to occur to Lasch that the problems he catalogues encyclopedically might affect people in a diversity of ways: that they might affect different classes of people differently, that contemporary life might be more full of surprises—and, who knows, of new beginnings, albeit many of them painful—than he is willing to tolerate," writes a *Harper's* reviewer. "In this he is a bit like a novelist who is so possessed by an idea that he forgets to include in his tale the concealments and surprises of actual experience."

Nicholas von Hoffman, in a *Spectator* article, labels the author "more of a grouch than a polemicist, which is not to say that much of what he seizes on in school, home and government isn't eminently grouchable." Von Hoffman adds that, in Lasch's favor, the author is "intelligent, humane and concerned about durable values without being too impossibly conservative in his views. A good man making a good try." To Robert Boyers, the problem lies not in Lasch but in Lasch's critics. In his *New Republic* review of *The Culture of Narcissism,* Boyers addresses the point that Lasch has become "subject to parody and mislabeling. We hear that his view of the future is 'wholly pessimistic': 'nobody' is taught anything in our schools; if we want to go forward, we have to go back and restore the past, and so on. In fact, Lasch is grim about our prospects, but he counsels not an encompassing pessimism so much as a willingness to see where we are. He advises not that we go back but that we consider the distant and more recent past as a repository of options we can neither evaluate nor dismiss unless we have come to terms with it." Sums up Valerie Lloyd in *Newsweek,* "[Lasch] has brilliantly performed the first job of a social critic by prompting us to look at our reflection—short of vanity."

The Minimal Self is Lasch's follow-up to *The Culture of Narcissism,* and this second volume received as much attention as the first. In *The Minimal Self,* as in his previous work, "Lasch levels his criticism at the false prophets of cultural salvation whose windy predictions often seem the only legacy of the New Left. Here, then, is the source of so much of the confusion among Lasch's critics: his jaundiced look at the New Leftovers of the 1970s and 1980s is often seen as a wholesale indictment of the preceding decade as well," notes *Nation* critic Thomas DePietro.

Atlantic reviewer Mark Crispin Miller also assesses Lasch's critics, finding that "several liberal pundits . . . have charged Lasch with elitism, accusing him of belittling the supposedly progressive aspects of our culture, whose defects, they argue, are merely the price we pay for having a democracy. And a number of feminists have responded by defending narcissism as a salutary female impulse, an alternative to men's cruel, Promethean urge to dominate the world."

One of the author's naysayers is Dennis H. Wrong, who writes in the *New York Times Book Review* that Lasch shows strength in his argument that narcissism "is not synonymous with mere selfishness or indifference to others but implies a weak . . . self prone to festering feelings of vulnerability that are often overcompensated for by outbursts of megalomania." However, Wrong continues, not one of Lasch's theories "does much to bolster [his] sweeping claim that we have evolved a culture of narcissism reflecting a dominant narcissistic personality of our time shaped by the basic character-forming agencies of family, school and work. Mr. Lasch doesn't even attempt to resolve such questions as the representative value of psychiatric patients (his chief source of evidence in the previous book), the psychological variations among class and ethnic subcultures and the precise historical timing of the changes supposed to have brought us to our present fallen psychic state."

Another brand of criticism comes from Bronwyn Drainie, of the Toronto *Globe and Mail.* To Drainie, Lasch's "intellect of staggering vigour and originality" is undermined by the fact that he is "almost incapable of getting his thoughts down on paper in a form mere mortals can read." Moreover, "in the final half of this book, Lasch plunges deep into post-Freudian psychoanalytic theory, leaving most non-specialists far behind. Still, there is enough meat in his first three chapters to make an intellectual feast, even if it is hard chewing at times."

In a *Los Angeles Times* piece, Malcolm Boyd likens *The Minimal Self* to a famous painting of primal power, Edvard Munch's "The Scream": Lasch's "far-reaching, ambitious work is explicitly structured in a scholarly, orderly fashion, accompanied by highly technical prose. Yet a contrapuntal implicit message, imagined in the unforgettable terror of Munch's tortured cry, outshouts it."

BIOGRAPHICAL/CRITICAL SOURCES:

BOOKS

Contemporary Issues Criticism, Volume 1, Gale, 1982.

PERIODICALS

Atlantic, December, 1977, November, 1984.
Globe and Mail (Toronto), December 1, 1984.
Harper's, July, 1979.
Los Angeles Times, October 24, 1984.
Nation, May 24, 1965, June 23, 1969, January 27, 1979, February 2, 1985.
New Republic, April 12, 1969, December 3, 1977, February 17, 1979, December 10, 1984.
Newsweek, January 22, 1979, November 5, 1984.
New Yorker, August 27, 1979.
New York Review of Books, February 23, 1978.
New York Times, December 9, 1978.
New York Times Book Review, March 23, 1969, September 30, 1973, January 15, 1978, January 14, 1979, October 28, 1984.
Saturday Review, June 12, 1965, July 26, 1969.
Time, January 8, 1979.
Times Literary Supplement, July 4, 1980, September 13, 1985.
Washington Post, January 24, 1979.
Washington Post Book World, December 2, 1973, February 4, 1979, December 16, 1984.

*   *   *

LATHROP, Francis
See LEIBER, Fritz (Reuter, Jr.)

*   *   *

LAURENCE, (Jean) Margaret (Wemyss) 1926-1987

PERSONAL: Born July 18, 1926, in Neepawa, Manitoba, Canada; died of cancer, January 5 (some sources say January 6), 1987, in Lakefield, Ontario, Canada; buried in Lakefield, Ontario, Canada; daughter of Robert Harrison (a lawyer) and Verna Jean (Simpson) Wemyss; married John Fergus Laurence (a civil engineer), 1947 (divorced, 1969); children: Jocelyn, David. *Education:* University of Manitoba, B.A., 1947.

ADDRESSES: Home—Lakefield, Ontario, Canada. *Agent*—John Cushman Associates, 24 East 38th St., New York, N.Y. 10016.

CAREER: Writer. Worked as a reporter with the *Winnipeg Citizen;* writer in residence at University of Toronto, 1969-70, and

University of Western Ontario, 1973; Trent University, Peterborough, Ontario, writer in residence, 1974, chancellor, 1981-83.

MEMBER: Royal Society of Canada (fellow).

AWARDS, HONORS: First Novel Award, Beta Sigma Phi, 1961; President's Medal, University of Western Ontario, 1961, 1962, and 1964, for best Canadian short stories; Governor General's Literary Award in fiction ($2,500), 1967, for *A Jest of God,* and 1975; senior fellowships from Canada Council, 1967 and 1971; honorary fellow of United College, University of Winnipeg, 1967; Companion of Order of Canada, 1971; Molson Prize, 1975; B'nai B'rith award, 1976; Periodical Distributors award, 1977; City of Toronto award, 1978; writer of the year award from Canadian Booksellers Association, 1981; Banff Centre award, 1983; numerous honorary degrees from institutions including Trent, Carleton, Brandon, Mount Allison, Simon Fraser, Queen's, McMaster, and Dalhousie universities and universities of Winnipeg, Toronto, and Western Ontario.

WRITINGS:

(Editor) *A Tree for Poverty* (Somali poetry and prose), Eagle Press (Nairobi), 1954.
This Side Jordan (novel), St. Martin's, 1960.
The Prophet's Camel Bell, Macmillan (London), 1963, published as *New Wind in a Dry Land,* Knopf, 1964.
The Tomorrow-Tamer, and Other Stories (short stories), Knopf, 1964.
The Stone Angel (novel), Knopf, 1964.
A Jest of God (novel), Knopf, 1966, published as *Rachel, Rachel,* Popular Library, 1968, published as *Now I Lay Me Down,* Panther, 1968.
Long Drums and Cannons: Nigerian Dramatists and Novelists 1952-1966, Macmillan, 1968.
The Fire-Dwellers (novel), Knopf, 1969.
A Bird in the House (short stories), Knopf, 1970.
Jason's Quest (for children), Knopf, 1970.
The Diviners (novel), Knopf, 1974.
Heart of a Stranger (essays), McClelland & Stewart, 1976, Lippincott, 1977.
Six Darn Cows (for children), Lorimer, 1979.
The Olden Days Coat (for children), McClelland & Stewart, 1979.
The Christmas Birthday Story (for children), Knopf, 1980.
Dance on the Earth: A Memoir, McClelland & Stewart, 1989.

Contributor of short stories to *Story, Prism, Queen's Quarterly, Saturday Evening Post,* and *Post Stories: 1962.*

SIDELIGHTS: Though she was not prolific, Margaret Laurence's fiction made her "more profoundly admired than any other Canadian novelist of her generation," according to Toronto *Globe and Mail* critic William French. Often set in the fictional Canadian small town of Manawaka, her novels and short stories earned praise for their compassion and realism and the skill with which they were told. They also aroused controversy— religious fundamentalists attempted to have one novel, *The Diviners,* banned from schools because it contained explicit descriptions of an abortion and a sexual affair. Laurence frequently explored the predicaments of women in society, and some of her characters are recognized as early feminists. Reviewers judge her work a powerful influence on Canadian writing; in an *Atlantic* review of *The Fire-Dwellers* one writer deemed her "the best fiction writer in the Dominion and one of the best in the hemisphere."

Non-Canadian subjects also appeared in Laurence's works. *The Prophet's Camel Bell* is an account of her experiences while living for two years in the Haud desert of Somaliland (now Somalia), with her husband, sharing the hardships and privations of desert life with their Somali workers. West Africa serves as the setting for the stories in *The Tomorrow-Tamer* and the source of the literature Laurence discussed in *Long Drums and Cannons: Nigerian Novelists and Dramatists 1952-1966.*

MEDIA ADAPTATIONS: The Jest of God was adapted as the film "Rachel, Rachel," starring Joanne Woodward and directed by Paul Newman, Warner Bros., 1968.

BIOGRAPHICAL/CRITICAL SOURCES:

BOOKS

Contemporary Literary Criticism, Gale, Volume 3, 1975, Volume 6, 1976, Volume 13, 1980, Volume 50, 1988.
Dictionary of Literary Biography, Volume 53: *Canadian Writers since 1960, First Series,* Gale, 1986.
Hind-Smith, Joan, *Three Voices: The Lives of Margaret Laurence, Gabrielle Roy, and Frederick Philip Grove,* Clarke Irwin, 1975.
Laurence, Margaret, *Dance on the Earth: A Memoir,* McClelland & Stewart, 1989.
Morley, Patricia, *Margaret Laurence,* Twayne, 1981.
New, W. H., editor, *Margaret Laurence: The Writer and Her Critics,* McGraw Hill Ryerson, 1977.
Thomas, Clara, *Margaret Laurence,* McClelland & Stewart, 1969.
Thomas, *The Manawaka World of Margaret Laurence,* McClelland & Stewart, 1975.
Verduyn, Christi, editor, *Margaret Laurence: An Appreciation,* Broadview Press, 1988.
Woodcock, George, editor, *A Place to Stand On: Essays by and About Margaret Laurence,* NeWest Press, 1983.

PERIODICALS

Atlantic, June, 1969, March, 1970.
Canadian Forum, February, 1969, September, 1970.
Chicago Tribune Book World, December 7, 1980.
Christian Science Monitor, June 12, 1969, March 26, 1970.
Fiddlehead, Number 80, 1969.
Globe and Mail (Toronto), December 14, 1985, January 10, 1987, March 5, 1988, November 4, 1989.
Maclean's, May 14, 1979.
New York Times Book Review, April 19, 1970.
Saturday Night, May, 1969.
World Literature Today, winter, 1982.

OBITUARIES:

PERIODICALS

Globe and Mail (Toronto), January 10, 1987.
Los Angeles Times, January 17, 1987.
Maclean's, January 19, 1987.
New York Times, January 7, 1987.
Publishers Weekly, February 20, 1987.
Times (London), January 7, 1987.
Washington Post, January 7, 1987.

*   *   *

**LAUSCHER, Hermann
See HESSE, Hermann**

LAVERTY, Donald
See BLISH, James (Benjamin)

* * *

LAVIN, Mary 1912-

PERSONAL: Born June 11, 1912, in East Walpole, Mass.; immigrated to Ireland; daughter of Thomas and Nora (Mahon) Lavin; married William Walsh (a lawyer), September 29, 1942 (died, 1954); married Michael MacDonald Scott, 1969; children: (first marriage) Valentine (daughter), Elizabeth, Caroline. *Education:* Early schooling in East Walpole, Mass.; attended Loreto Convent, Dublin, Ireland; University College, Dublin, B.A. (honors), 1934; National University of Ireland, M.A. (first class honors), 1938. *Religion:* Roman Catholic.

ADDRESSES: Home—Abbey Farm, Bective, Navan, County Meath, Eire; Apt. 5, Gilford Pines, Gilford Rd., Sandymount, Dublin 4, Eire.

CAREER: Short story writer, farmer. Taught French at Loreto Convent school.

MEMBER: Irish Academy of Letters (president, 1971-73), Irish P.E.N. (president, 1964-65).

AWARDS, HONORS: James Tait Black Memorial Prize for best book of fiction published in United Kingdom, 1944, for *Tales From Bective Bridge;* Guggenheim fellowships for fiction, 1959, 1961, and 1962; Katherine Mansfield-Menton Prize, 1962, for *The Great Wave, and Other Stories;* D.Litt. from National University of Ireland, 1968; Ella Lyman Cabot fellowship, 1969; Gold Medal from Eire Society (Boston), 1974; Gregory Medal, 1974; award from American Irish Foundation, 1979; Allied Irish Bank award, 1981.

WRITINGS:

Tales From Bective Bridge (short stories), Little, Brown, 1942, revised edition, Poolbeg, 1978.
The Long Ago, and Other Stories, M. Joseph, 1944.
The House in Clewe Street (novel; first published serially in *Atlantic Monthly* as "Gabriel Galloway," 1944-45), Little, Brown, 1945, reprinted, Penguin Books, 1988.
The Becker Wives, and Other Stories, M. Joseph, 1946, published as *At Sallygap, and Other Stories,* Little, Brown, 1947.
Mary O'Grady (novel), Little, Brown, 1950, reprinted, Penguin Books, 1986.
A Single Lady, and Other Stories, M. Joseph, 1951.
The Patriot Son, and Other Stories, M. Joseph, 1956.
A Likely Story (for children), Macmillan, 1957.
Selected Stories, Macmillan, 1959.
The Great Wave, and Other Stories (contains seven stories first published in *New Yorker*), Macmillan, 1961.
The Stories of Mary Lavin, Constable, Volume I, 1964, Volume II, 1973, Volume III, 1985.
In the Middle of the Fields, and Other Stories, Constable, 1967, Macmillan, 1969.
Happiness, and Other Stories, Constable, 1969, Houghton, 1970.
Collected Stories, introduction by V. S. Pritchett, Houghton, 1971.
A Memory, and Other Stories, Constable, 1972, Houghton, 1973.
The Second Best Children in the World (for children), Houghton, 1972.
The Shrine and Other Stories, Houghton, 1977.
Mary Lavin: Selected Stories, Penguin Books, 1981.
A Family Likeness (short stories), Constable, 1985.

Short stories anthologized in numerous collections.

WORK IN PROGRESS: A collection of ten short stories.

SIDELIGHTS: Born in the United States and transplanted to Ireland at an early age, Mary Lavin is "Irish in thought and feeling, and the short story is her most natural form of expression," Edward Weeks writes. He quotes her as saying: "It is in the short story that a writer distills the essence of his thought. I believe this because the short story, shape as well as matter, is determined by the writer's own character. Both are one. Short-story writing—for me—is only looking closer than normal into the human heart." Jean Stubbs of *Books* believes "Miss Lavin possesses the strength of gentleness. A serene radiance illuminates all her writing: the radiance of one who observes, accepts and meditates on the human condition. She has, thank God, eschewed mere cleverness in favour of wisdom, so we hear no strident trumpets, no shattering drums. She invites us to contemplate with her the infinite sadness and beauty of the world, the divine inconsequence of life. . . . She will not allow us to stand by and marvel, she insists that we become participants."

In a review of *In the Middle of the Fields,* Roger Baker of *Books and Bookmen* notes: "There is a curiously dated atmosphere about . . . [these] stories; it is as though the world came to a halt in 1939. Ironically, this may be some kind of tribute to her ability to isolate characters in their own rigidly bounded worlds. She approaches her people and their emotional conflicts with rich, lyrical poeticism that transcends the business of mere topicality. But this failure to pinpoint a specific space in time is somehow detracting to the total effect." Her *Collected Stories* has drawn admiration from reviewers and prompted comparisons with "her most noticeable mentors in the genre, Chekhov and Mansfield, and James and Joyce. From them, presumably, she gets the soul, the brittle beauty, the social intricacy, and the technical virtuosity which are the trademarks of her work," according to R. J. Thompson of Canisius College. "In sum," he concludes, "these stories make apparent her position as one of the most artful and perceptive masters of the story form in our day, a fact well recognized by her Irish countrymen who regard her as the only living equivalent of O'Faolain and O'Flaherty."

MEDIA ADAPTATIONS: One short story was used as the libretto of an opera by South African Eric Chisholm and performed at the South African Festival of Music in London.

BIOGRAPHICAL/CRITICAL SOURCES:

BOOKS

Bowen, Zack, *Mary Lavin,* Bucknell University Press, 1975.
Contemporary Literary Criticism, Gale, Volume 4, 1975, Volume 18, 1981.
Dictionary of Literary Biography, Volume 15: *British Novelists, 1930-1959,* Gale, 1983.
Kelly, Angeline A., *Mary Lavin, Quiet Rebel: A Study of Her Short Stories,* Barnes & Noble, 1980.
Peterson, Richard F., *Mary Lavin,* Twayne, 1978.

PERIODICALS

Best Sellers, July 15, 1971.
Books, January, 1970.
Books and Bookmen, May, 1967.
Library Journal, July, 1970.
Nation, November 8, 1971.
New York Times, July 2, 1971.
New York Times Book Review, March 24, 1970, August 8, 1971, November 25, 1973, October 30, 1977.
Saturday Review, August 7, 1971.

Times Literary Supplement, February 16, 1967, June 3, 1977,
November 29, 1985.
Washington Post Book World, January 8, 1978.

* * *

LAVOND, Paul Dennis
See POHL, Frederik

* * *

LAWRENCE, D(avid) H(erbert Richards) 1885-1930
(Jessie Chambers, Lawrence H. Davison)

PERSONAL: Born September 11, 1885, in Eastwood, Nottinghamshire, England; died of tuberculosis, March 2, 1930, in
Vence, France; originally buried in Vence, France, later cremated and interred at Kiowa Ranch, near Taos, N.M.; son of
John Arthur (a coal miner) and Lydia (a schoolteacher; maiden
name, Beardsall) Lawrence; married Frieda von Richthofen
Weekley, July 13, 1914. *Education:* Nottingham University College, teacher training certificate, 1908.

CAREER: Writer. Worked as a manufacturer's clerk, 1899;
pupil-teacher, 1902-06, first at Eastwood British School, then at
Ilkeston, Derbyshire; Davidson Road School, Croydon, England, junior assistant master, 1908-11.

AWARDS, HONORS: James Tait Black Memorial Prize from
Edinburgh University, 1921, for novel *The Lost Girl.*

WRITINGS:

NOVELS

The White Peacock, Duffield & Co., 1911, new edition, Viking,
1984.
The Trespasser, M. Kennerley, 1912, new edition, Viking, 1983.
Sons and Lovers, M. Kennerley, 1913, new edition, Penguin,
1981.
The Rainbow, Methuen, 1915, expurgated edition, B. W. Hueb-
sch, 1916, new edition, Penguin, 1981.
Women in Love, privately printed for subscribers only (New
York), 1920, M. Secker, 1921, T. Seltzer, 1922, new edition,
Penguin, 1983.
The Lost Girl, M. Secker, 1920, T. Seltzer, 1921, new edition, Vi-
king, 1982.
Aaron's Rod, T. Seltzer, 1922, new edition, Viking, 1972.
The Captain's Doll: Three Novelettes, T. Seltzer, 1923 (published
in England as *The Ladybird. The Fox. The Captain's Doll.,*
M. Secker, 1923, reprinted, Penguin, 1960).
Kangaroo, T. Seltzer, 1923, new edition, Viking, 1974.
(With M. L. Skinner) *The Boy in the Bush,* T. Seltzer, 1924, fac-
simile reprint, Southern Illinois University Press, 1971.
St. Mawr, Knopf, 1925.
St. Mawr, Together With The Princess, M. Secker, 1925.
The Plumed Serpent (Quetzalcoatl), Knopf, 1926, with an intro-
duction by William York Tindall, Knopf, 1951, reprinted,
1963.
Sun, expurgated edition, E. Archer, 1926, unexpurgated edition,
Black Sun Press (Paris), 1928.
Lady Chatterley's Lover, privately printed by Giuseppe Orioli
(Florence), 1928, W. Faro, 1930, expurgated edition,
Knopf, 1932, unexpurgated edition, Heinemann, 1956, with
an introduction by Mark Schorer, Grove, 1959; published
as *The Complete and Unexpurgated Edition of Lady Chatterley's Lover,* including the full text of the famous decision
by Federal Judge Frederick vanPelt Bryan which lifted the

post office ban, Pyramid Books, 1959; published with Law-
rence's preface, "A Propos of *Lady Chatterley's Lover,*"
Heinemann, 1982, reprint of Orioli edition (third manu-
script version), preface by Archibald MacLeish, introduc-
tion by Schorer, Modern Library, 1983.
The Escaped Cock, Black Sun Press, 1929, published as *The Man
Who Died,* Knopf, 1931, New Directions, 1947.
The Virgin and the Gypsy, Knopf, 1930, reprinted, Random,
1984.
The First Lady Chatterley, Dial Press, 1944, published as *The
First Lady Chatterley: The First Version of Lady Chatterley's
Lover,* foreword by Frieda Lawrence, Heinemann, 1972.
The Fox, Sphere, 1971.
John Thomas and Lady Jane, Viking, 1972 (published in En-
gland as *John Thomas and Lady Jane: The Second Version
of Lady Chatterley's Lover,* Heinemann, 1972).
Mr. Noon (unfinished manuscript), edited by Lindeth Vasey,
Cambridge University Press, 1984.

SHORT FICTION

The Prussian Officer and Other Stories, Duckworth, 1914, B. W.
Huebsch, 1916, new edition, Viking, 1984.
England, My England and Other Stories, T. Seltzer, 1922, re-
printed, Books for Libraries Press, 1972.
Glad Ghosts, E. Benn, 1926.
The Woman Who Rode Away and Other Stories, Knopf, 1928,
new edition, Berkley Publishing, 1962.
Rawdon's Roof, Elkin Mathews & Marrot, 1928.
Love Among the Haystacks and Other Pieces, with a reminiscence
by David Garnett, Nonesuch Press, 1930, Viking, 1933, re-
printed, Books for Libraries Press, 1976.
The Lovely Lady, M. Secker, 1932, Viking, 1933, reprinted,
Books for Libraries Press, 1972.
A Modern Lover, Viking, 1934, reprinted, Books for Libraries
Press, 1972.
A Prelude, Merle Press, 1949.
Complete Short Stories, three volumes, Heinemann, 1955 (pub-
lished as *The Collected Short Stories of D. H. Lawrence,*
Heinemann, 1974), Viking, 1961.
The Horse Dealer's Daughter, School of Art Press (Oxford),
1963.
The Rocking-Horse Winner, edited by Dominick P. Consolo, C.
E. Merrill, 1969.
The Princess and Other Stories, Penguin, 1971.
The Mortal Coil and Other Stories, edited by Keith Sagar, Pen-
guin, 1971.
You Touched Me, illustrations by Sandra Higashi, Creative Edu-
cation, Inc., 1982.

POETRY

Love Poems and Others, Duckworth, 1913, M. Kennerley, 1915.
Amores, B. W. Huebsch, 1916.
Look! We Have Come Through!, Chatto & Windus, 1917, B. W.
Huebsch, 1918, published as *Look! We Have Come
Through! A Cycle of Love Poems,* Ark Press, 1958, new edi-
tion, Humanities Research Center, University of Texas,
1971.
New Poems, M. Secker, 1918, B. W. Huebsch, 1920, reprinted,
Haskell House, 1974.
Bay, Beaumont, 1919.
Tortoises, T. Seltzer, 1921, published as *Tortoises: Six Poems,*
Cheloniidae Press (Williamsburg, Mass.), 1983.
Birds, Beasts, and Flowers, T. Seltzer, 1923, M. Secker, c. 1923,
reprinted, Haskell House, 1974.

The Collected Poems of D. H. Lawrence, two volumes, M. Secker, 1928, J. Cape and H. Smith, 1929, single volume edition, M. Secker, 1932.

Pansies, Knopf, 1929, M. Secker, 1929, with fourteen poems not printed in the Secker edition, privately printed for subscribers only, 1929.

Nettles, Faber, 1930.

Last Poems, edited by Richard Aldington and Giuseppe Orioli, G. Orioli, 1932, Viking, 1933, reprinted, Scholarly Press, 1971.

Fire and Other Poems, foreword by Robinson Jeffers, note by Frieda Lawrence, Grabhorn Press, 1940.

The Complete Poems of D. H. Lawrence, Heinemann, 1964, Viking, 1971.

PLAYS

The Widowing of Mrs. Holroyd: A Drama in Three Acts (produced in London at the Kingsway Theatre, December 12, 1926), M. Kennerley, 1914.

Touch and Go: A Play in Three Acts (first produced in Oxford, England, at the Oxford Playhouse, November 5, 1979), T. Seltzer, 1920.

David: A Play (first produced in London at the Regent Theatre, May 22, 1927), Knopf, 1926, M. Secker, 1926, reprinted, Haskell House, 1974.

A Collier's Friday Night (first produced in London at the Royal Court Theatre, November 7, 1973), privately printed, 1940, reprinted, Norwood Editions, 1976.

Complete Plays, Heinemann, 1965, Viking, 1966.

The Daughter-in-Law (first produced in London at the Royal Court Theatre, March 16, 1967), published in the program for performances given March 16 to April 8, 1967, Royal Court Theatre, 1967.

"The Fight for Barbara," first produced in London at the Mermaid Theatre, August 9, 1967.

Plays, introduction by Malcolm Elwin, Heron Books, 1969.

TRAVEL SKETCHES

Twilight in Italy, B. W. Huebsch, 1916, Viking, 1958.

Sea and Sardinia, T. Seltzer, 1921, new edition, Viking, 1963.

Mornings in Mexico, Knopf, 1927, new edition, G. M. Smith, 1982.

Etruscan Places, Viking, 1932, reprinted, 1963.

NONFICTION

(Under pseudonym Lawrence H. Davison) *Movements in European History,* Oxford University Press, 1921, published under name D. H. Lawrence, 1925, reprinted, 1971.

Psychoanalysis and the Unconscious, T. Seltzer, 1921.

Fantasia of the Unconscious, T. Seltzer, 1922.

Studies in Classic American Literature (essays), T. Seltzer, 1923, recent edition, Penguin, 1977.

Reflections on the Death of a Porcupine and Other Essays, Centaur Press, 1925, Indiana University Press, 1963.

Pornography and Obscenity, Faber, 1929, Knopf, 1930, published as *Pornography and Obscenity: An Essay,* Alicat Book Shop, 1948.

Assorted Articles, Knopf, 1930, reprinted, Books for Libraries Press, 1968.

Apocalypse, G. Orioli, 1931, Viking, 1932, reprinted, 1966.

We Need One Another (essays), Equinox, 1933, reprinted, Haskell House, 1974.

Phoenix: The Posthumous Papers of D. H. Lawrence, edited with an introduction by Edward D. McDonald, Viking, 1936, reprinted, 1972.

Sex, Literature, and Censorship: Essays, edited by Harry T. Moore, Twayne, 1953.

The Symbolic Meaning: The Uncollected Versions of Studies in Classic American Literature, edited by Armin Arnold, preface by Harry T. Moore, Centaur Press, 1962.

Phoenix II: Uncollected, Unpublished, and Other Prose Works, Viking, 1968.

Lawrence on Hardy and Painting: Study of Thomas Hardy [and] *Introduction to These Paintings,* Heinemann Educational, 1973.

Study of Thomas Hardy and Other Essays, Cambridge University Press, 1985.

LETTERS

The Letters of D. H. Lawrence, Viking, 1932.

D. H. Lawrence: Reminiscences and Correspondence, M. Secker, 1934.

D. H. Lawrence's Letter to "The Laughing Horse," privately printed, 1936.

Letters to Bertrand Russell, Gotham Book Mart, 1948.

Eight Letters to Rachel Annand Taylor, Castle Press, 1956.

Collected Letters, two volumes, Viking, 1962.

Lawrence in Love: Letters to Louie Burrows, University of Nottingham, 1968.

The Quest for Rananim: D. H. Lawrence's Letters to S. S. Koteliansky, 1914 to 1930, McGill-Queen's University Press, 1970.

Letters From D. H. Lawrence to Martin Secker, 1911-1930, privately printed, 1970.

The Centaur Letters, Humanities Research Center, University of Texas, 1970.

Consciousness, privately printed by the Press of the Pegacycle Lady, 1974.

Letters to Thomas and Adele Seltzer, Black Sparrow Press, 1976.

The Letters of D. H. Lawrence, three volumes, Cambridge University Press, 1979-84.

The Letters of D. H. Lawrence and Amy Lowell, 1914-1925, Black Sparrow Press, 1985.

OTHER

My Skirmish With Jolly Roger, Random House, 1929, revised edition published as *A Propos of Lady Chatterley's Lover, Being an Essay Extended From "My Skirmish With Jolly Roger,"* Mandrake Press, 1930, published as *A Propos of Lady Chatterley's Lover,* M. Secker, 1931, Mandrake Press edition reprinted, Haskell House, 1973.

The Paintings of D. H. Lawrence, introduction by Lawrence, privately printed for subscribers only, Mandrake Press, 1929.

D. H. Lawrence's Unpublished Foreword to "Women in Love," 1919, preface by Nathan van Patten, Gelber, Lilienthal, Inc., 1936.

Ten Paintings, Carcanet, 1982.

Also translator of several books. Work represented in numerous anthologies and collections. Contributor to periodicals, including *Adelphi, Dial, English Review, Equinox,* and *Vanity Fair.*

SIDELIGHTS: During most of his career as a writer D. H. Lawrence sparked controversy, and debate continues to characterize discussion of his life and work. Personally, his elopement with another man's wife, Frieda von Richthofen Weekley, branded him as an interloper. His peripatetic existence, marked by frequent changes of residence, country, and continent, earned him a reputation as a bohemian. Moreover, his personality, capable alternately of charm and malice, provoked extreme reactions from others. Professionally, his work defied not only the conventional artistic norms of his day but also its political, social, and moral values. In his foreword to *D. H. Lawrence and Human Existence* by Father William Tiverton, T. S. Eliot criticized Lawrence for "express[ing] his insights in the form least likely to make them acceptable to most of his contemporaries."

In particular, the sexual explicitness of many of Lawrence's books and paintings outraged public opinion and resulted in several notorious court cases on charges of obscenity and pornography. As late as 1985 Lydia Blanchard, in *D. H. Lawrence's "Lady": A New Look at "Lady Chatterley's Lover,"* defended Lawrence against such accusations by associating him with "the battle against prudery and censorship, with the fight both to destroy the sexual restrictions of the Victorian age and to affirm the phallic reality of the body." Shortly after Lawrence's death, the London *Times* regretted that Lawrence "confused decency with hypocrisy, and honesty with the free and public use of vulgar words." However, in the *Nation and Athenaeum,* E. M. Forster lauded him as "the greatest imaginative genius of our generation."

The scope of Lawrence's "imaginative genius" was large. Best known as a novelist and short story writer, he was also a notable poet and essayist. In *D. H. Lawrence: Novelist,* F. R. Leavis called him "an incomparable literary critic." According to Jeffrey Meyers in *D. H. Lawrence and the Experience of Italy,* his letters are "the greatest in English since [John] Keats and [Lord] Byron"; and his travel books "shift[ed] the center of interest from the external world to the self." In addition, Lawrence completed seven plays, of which two, "The Widowing of Mrs. Holroyd" and "David," were staged during his lifetime. He also painted, especially during the last few years of his life. He admitted in a letter dated May 24, 1928, to Mark Gertler, a professional artist, that his paintings were "rolling with faults." Nevertheless, as he explained in the essay "Making Pictures," collected in *Assorted Articles,* he found in them "a form of delight that words can never give."

In *D. H. Lawrence: Novelist,* Leavis described the strength of Lawrence's prose as "an infallible centrality of judgment" stemming from "an unfailingly sure sense of the difference between that which makes for life and that which makes against it, of the difference between health and that which tends away from health." Along the same lines, Richard Ellmann wrote in an essay for *The Achievement of D. H. Lawrence,* edited by Frederick J. Hoffman and Harry T. Moore, that "Lawrence wrote his poetry, and much of his prose, as a healer." Ironically, he spent most of his life in poor health, fighting tuberculosis of the lungs, which at last proved fatal.

Frail from birth, David Herbert Richards Lawrence, called "Bert" by his family, was the fourth of five children born to Arthur John Lawrence, a coal miner, and Lydia Beardsall Lawrence, a former schoolteacher whom Lawrence described as "superior" in an autobiographical sketch from *Assorted Articles.* Lawrence grew up where he was born, in Eastwood, a Nottinghamshire mining village in the Midlands of England. Late in life he confessed, in an autobiographical fragment published in *Phoenix,* "Nothing depresses me more than to come home to the place where I was born, and where I lived my first twenty years." Physical want and constant bickering between his parents plagued his childhood. In "Discord in Childhood," a lyric poem about those early years, Lawrence described his parents' respective voices as "a slender lash / Whistling she-delirious rage, and the dreadful sound / Of a male thong booming and bruising."

In the standard biography of Lawrence, *The Priest of Love,* Harry T. Moore wrote, "Even more than in the case of other in-

tensely autobiographical authors, [Lawrence's] life helps to illuminate his writings." Lawrence's most widely read novel, *Sons and Lovers* (1913), is an autobiographical account of his youth, "a purgation become the successful work of art," claimed Seymour Betsky in an essay from *The Achievement of D. H. Lawrence.* In a letter dated November 14, 1912, Lawrence referred to the "battle . . . between the mother and the girl, with the son as object," which rages at the center of the novel. It represents Lawrence's divided feelings for his own mother and for Jessie Chambers, the "Miriam" of the novel and many of the early poems, whom Lawrence met when he was sixteen. Like Paul Morel in the novel, the adolescent Lawrence "knitted together with his mother in perfect intimacy." Consequently, when he came into contact with women, theorized Chambers in *D. H. Lawrence: A Personal Record,* there was "a split." In the November 14, 1912, letter Lawrence described the novel, and by implication the personal story it tells, as "a great tragedy."

Not only *Sons and Lovers* but also many of his other novels and tales have some connection with Eastwood and its adjacent countryside and with the people he knew there. Lawrence's first novel, *The White Peacock,* "idealized" his family, friends, and their immediate surroundings, wrote Emile Delavenay in his biography of Lawrence's early years, *D. H. Lawrence: The Man and His Work.* Lawrence's acknowledged masterpieces, *The Rainbow* (1915) and *Women in Love* (1920), drew upon life in Eastwood and on Lawrence's own experience and that of friends and acquaintances, who frequently served as the originals on which he modeled his characters. Even his last major novel, *Lady Chatterley's Lover* (1928), returned to the Midlands, one of Lawrence's enduring symbols, for its setting. "There the natural beauty . . . comes up against industrial ugliness," wrote Moore in *The Priest of Love.* This ironic juxtaposition became one of the most prevalent themes in Lawrence's work.

Retrospectively, in the unpublished foreword to *The Collected Poems of D. H. Lawrence,* Lawrence said that he began writing on a "slightly self-conscious Sunday afternoon, when I was nineteen, and I 'composed' my first two 'poems.' One was 'Guelderroses,' and one was to 'Campions,' and most young ladies would have done better." By this time he had already finished at Nottingham High School, which he attended on scholarship, and had found employment, first briefly as a clerk in a surgical goods firm (the model for Jordan's in *Sons and Lovers*), and then as a primary school pupil-teacher in the British School in Eastwood—the model for Saint Philip's School, in which Lawrence's alter ego Ursula teaches in *The Rainbow.* During this period, recalled his sister Ada Lawrence in *Young Lorenzo: The Early Life of D. H. Lawrence,* he spent more time painting than writing, although he continued to compose lyric poems. After his admission on scholarship to the University of Nottingham when he was twenty-one, he began the first of several notebooks, which he called in the foreword to *Collected Poems* "the foundation of the poetic me," and also began writing fiction, both short stories and the novel to be published as *The White Peacock.* He first appeared in print in the *Nottinghamshire Guardian* with one of his tales, "A Prelude." He had submitted the story under Jessie Chambers's name; she turned over the three-guinea prize to him. Appropriately, the tale's setting is the Haggs, the Chambers family farm, where, Lawrence said in a letter written December 3, 1926, he got his "first incentive to write."

A teaching position brought Lawrence to London for four years, from 1908 to 1912, where his writing career began in earnest and his life took a new turn. Never was literary birth so easy. Chambers sent off several of Lawrence's poems to the *English Review,* a periodical she and Lawrence admired; the editor, Ford Madox

Hueffer (later known as Ford Maddox Ford), not only published them but eventually arranged for the publication of *The White Peacock* as well. This novel was soon followed by *The Trespasser* (1912), which Lawrence based on the experience of Helen Corke, a friend and fellow teacher. In his autobiographical sketch, Lawrence recalled that although Hueffer accused the first novel of having "every fault the English novel can have" and called the second too "erotic," he recognized and praised Lawrence's "genius." Both novels received favorable reviews, the first admired for its "infinite promise," as the March 18, 1911, issue of *Academy* put it; the second for "those temperamental qualities which characterize original work," in the words of *Athenaeum* for June 1, 1912.

Soon after he broke into the literary world, Lawrence met his second mentor, Edward Garnett, a reader for a publishing firm. With Garnett's encouragement, Lawrence had extensively revised *The Trespasser* before its publication. Garnett's sensitive criticism also helped Lawrence to complete *Sons and Lovers* and to put together his first book of verse, *Love Poems and Others* (1913). As a tribute to his friend, whom he regarded as both father and brother, Lawrence dedicated *Sons and Lovers* to him.

Productive as they were artistically, these years were filled with personal crises. As Lawrence wrote in the foreword to *Collected Poems,* first came the "long illness and then the death of my mother; and in the sick year after, . . . I almost dissolved away myself, and was very ill." Because of his near-fatal illness, Lawrence gave up his teaching position and decided to live entirely on the earnings from his writing. He also terminated his relationships with several women, all of whom appear in his early fiction and poetry: Jessie Chambers, Helen Corke, and Louie Burrows—the "Beloved" of the poems and Lawrence's fiancee for almost two years. Then in April, 1912, on the eve of his departure for the continent, Lawrence met Frieda Weekley, the German-born, aristocratic wife of a professor at the University of Nottingham. In a letter to her written soon after their meeting, Lawrence called her "the most wonderful woman in all England." Scarcely one month later, Frieda eloped with Lawrence to Germany, leaving her husband and three small children behind. Thus began the unconventional, wandering life of the next twenty years that took the Lawrences—they married two years later, following Frieda's divorce—first to Italy, back to England during World War I, then to Sicily, Ceylon, Australia, the United States, Mexico, and finally once more to the Mediterranean.

Lawrence completed the final version of *Sons and Lovers* in Italy, where he and Frieda lived from 1912 to 1914. "I tell you I've written a great book," he wrote to Garnett on November 14, 1912. Although Lawrence later denied any intentional use of Freudian theories in writing the novel, early readers like the novelist Ivy Low, niece of a psychoanalyst, were quick to identify Freudian elements in the book. Alfred Booth Kuttner used Freudian theory to discuss the novel in an article for *Psychoanalytic Review,* the first important psychoanalytic study of Lawrence's work. Going one step further, John Middleton Murry, Lawrence's best friend during the war years, justified his theory, through references to *Sons and Lovers,* that Lawrence himself suffered from the Oedipus complex. In *Son of Woman,* his biography of Lawrence, Murry said of Paul Morel and by implication of Lawrence, "All unconsciously his mother had roused in him the stirrings of sexual desire. . . . He felt for his mother what he should have felt for the girl of his choice." However, Dorothy Van Ghent rejected the dominant Freudian interpretation of the novel, proposing in an essay from *D. H. Lawrence: A Collection of Critical Essays,* edited by Mark Spilka, that its central conflict

originates in the clash between "the creative life force witnessed in the independent objectivity of things" and the "human attempt to distort and corrupt selfhood." In her view, the novel alerts readers to "'the drift toward death' which Lawrence thought of as the disease syndrome of his time and of Europe."

Critical reactions to the book ranged from high praise to condemnation. Typical of the diverse reviews, the *Manchester Guardian* of July 2, 1913, judged the book "an achievement of the first quality," but the *Nation* of July 12, 1913, warned of "boredom" and found the plot "commonplace and decadent." In contrast, *Love Poems and Others,* published the same year, won uniformly high praise. Ezra Pound asserted in *Poetry: A Magazine of Verse* that "there is no English poet under forty who can get within shot of him. . . . He has brought contemporary verse up to the level of contemporary prose." In *The Priest of Love,* Moore reported that in a letter to Harriet Monroe, the editor of *Poetry,* Pound wrote, "I think [Lawrence] learned the proper treatment of modern subjects before I did."

Much that Lawrence wrote in Italy was about England. Yet he variously recorded his impressions of Italy in sketches later published as *Twilight in Italy* (1916), *Sea and Sardinia* (1921), and *Etruscan Places* (1932) as well as in fiction—most extensively in *The Lost Girl* (1920) and *Aaron's Rod* (1922)—in poetry—in sections of *Look! We Have Come Through!* (1917) and *Birds, Beasts, and Flowers* (1923)—and in numerous essays and letters. Referring to Italy, Meyers noted that "the sympathetic people, the traditional life, and especially the pagan, primitive element revitalized Lawrence and inspired his astonishing creative achievement. . . . Lawrence's discovery of Italy was also a discovery of himself."

Out of this period came *The Prussian Officer and Other Stories* (1914), Lawrence's first collection of tales. Delavenay stressed that these works placed Lawrence "in the front rank of contemporary English short story writers." R. E. Pritchard commented in *D. H. Lawrence: Body of Darkness* that "in their revised form, [these stories] mark the beginning of the 'true,' unmuffled Lawrence." Looking forward to his later writing, they transcend "conventional understanding of morality, personality, and even life . . . in search of the dark reality buried in the body, where consciousness, individuality, and sexuality are absorbed in the nonhuman source of life." In *D. H. Lawrence at Work: The Emergence of The Prussian Officer Stories,* Keith Cushman stressed the importance of this volume to understanding Lawrence's artistic development. As Janice Hubbard Harris wrote in *The Short Fiction of D. H. Lawrence,* "The individual tales, from 1907 to 1928, constitute a steady program of imaginative acts, each story having the potential to inspire Lawrence toward new projects or warn him of likely dead ends."

Also at this time, Lawrence began "The Sisters"—also called "The Wedding Ring" in manuscript—which after many drafts became *The Rainbow* and *Women in Love.* In *D. H. Lawrence: Novelist,* Leavis claimed that these two novels proved Lawrence "the greatest kind of artist"; they represented "a supreme creative achievement." Because of these works, the critic identified Lawrence as "one of the major novelists of the English tradition." Leavis launched his defense of Lawrence as a novelist in *Scrutiny* in the early 1950s. Until that time, as Hoffman and Moore pointed out, Lawrence's "new, bold, experimental, and anti-traditional writing made it difficult for critics to place him."

In an attempt to explain his unconventional novelistic style to a skeptical Garnett, Lawrence cautioned in a letter of June 5, 1914, "You mustn't look in my novel for the old stable ego of the character. There is another ego, according to whose action the individual is unrecognizable. . . . [D]on't look for the development of the novel to follow the lines of certain characters: the characters fall into the form of some other rhythmic form." In an essay from *The Achievement of D. H. Lawrence,* Mark Schorer defined this "other rhythmic form" as a series of "separate episodes, and these only sporadically developed as 'scenes.' Yet these are meant to form a pattern of psychic relationships, a pattern of psychic movement with a large *general* rhythm, but without the objective or rationalized frame of the old novel." Like many other readers of the time, Garnett preferred the more conventional *Sons and Lovers* to Lawrence's later novels.

Shortly after the publication of *The Rainbow,* Scotland Yard seized over a thousand copies of the book from the publisher and printer. The book was an "orgy of sexiness," according to a 1915 reviewer in *Sphere.* As stated in his introduction to Lawrence's *Apocalypse,* Richard Aldington believed that the underlying motives for the suppression of the book were "that [Lawrence] denounced War. And [Frieda was] German." Whatever the reason, "after the suppression of *The Rainbow* in 1915, Lawrence acquired a bad newspaper reputation as a writer of supposedly salacious books," commented Hoffman and Moore in *The Achievement of D. H. Lawrence.* Consequently, although Lawrence completed *Women in Love* by 1916, publishing it proved impossible for four more years.

Lawrence himself harbored mixed feelings, expressed in a letter of October 3, 1916, about *Women in Love:* "I don't know if I hate it or not. I think everyone else will hate it. . . . I know it is true, the book. And it is another world, in which I can live apart from this foul world which I will not accept or acknowledge or even enter. The world of my novel is big and fearless—yes, I love it, and love it passionately. It only seems to me horrible to have to publish it." Ever afterwards, Lawrence expressed dismay at the thought of publishing any of his best work. As he wrote on March 13, 1928, of the unexpurgated edition of *Lady Chatterley's Lover,* "[T]his tender and phallic novel [is] far too good for the public."

In fact, Lawrence published little during the years spent in England between 1914 and 1918. His increasingly poor health was exacerbated by the English climate and the psychological pressure caused by the suspicions with which others regarded Frieda's German nationality and the couple's outspoken opposition to the war. The military authorities threatened the ailing Lawrence with conscription, calling him periodically for medical examinations. Moreover, Lawrence found himself "very badly off" financially, as he confessed often in letters during these years. His writing brought him little income. Only books of verse, most of which he had written much earlier, appeared during this time: *Amores* (1916); *Look! We Have Come Through!* (1917), "the story, or history, or confession" of his relationship with Frieda; *New Poems* (1918); and *Bay* (1919).

Socially, Lawrence and Frieda formed many close if volatile friendships during the war years. John Middleton Murry and Katherine Mansfield, who shared with them what Lawrence referred to in a letter of March 8, 1916, as a "Blutbruderschaft" (blood-brother relationship), even joined the Lawrences at their cottage in Cornwall until, as Delavenay reported, "the [Murrys] were embarrassed by the violence of [Lawrence's] quarrels with Frieda." Lawrence also socialized with a number of aristocrats interested in him because of his writing, among them Lady Cynthia Asquith and Lady Ottoline Morrell, both of whom appear as characters in Lawrence's fiction. Through Lady Ottoline, Lawrence made the acquaintance of the circle later known as the Bloomsbury Group; he became intimate for a short time with

Bertrand Russell before philosophical differences divided them. He also met the American poet Amy Lowell, who made Lawrence a present of his first typewriter.

With the help of Lady Cynthia, the daughter-in-law of England's prime minister, Lawrence hoped to immigrate to the United States. There he planned to found a colony of like-minded individuals. He referred to his proposed utopia as "Rananim." Lawrence wrote on January 18, 1915, "I want to gather together about twenty souls and sail away from this world of war and squalor and found a little colony where there shall be no money but a sort of communism as far as the necessaries of life go, and some real decency." To prepare for emigration, Lawrence began reading American authors and writing critical essays on them. These were published in 1923 as *Studies in Classic American Literature,* described by Gamini Salgado in *A Preface to Lawrence* as "a milestone in the serious study of early American writers such as [Herman] Melville, [Nathaniel] Hawthorne, [James Fenimore] Cooper and [Edgar Allan] Poe." Lawrence also began articulating in prose some of the psychological and philosophical insights, implicit in his novels and poetry, on which his new community would be based.

In a letter to Russell dated December 8, 1915, Lawrence put forth his idea that there is a seat of consciousness in man other than the brain and the nervous system: "There is a blood-consciousness, which exists in us independently of the ordinary mental consciousness." For Lawrence, the tragedy of modern life was that "the mental and nerve consciousness exerts a tyranny over the blood-consciousness, and that [the] will has gone over completely to the mental consciousness and is engaged in the destruction of [the] blood-being or blood-consciousness." In this letter, as in the novels and poems he wrote at the time, Lawrence stressed the importance of the male-female "sexual connection" in rousing the blood-consciousness of the individual. "Blood knowledge comes either through the mother or through the sex," he declared. Lawrence formulated these ideas systematically in *Psychoanalysis and the Unconscious* (1921) and *Fantasia of the Unconscious* (1922), along with his theories about male-female relationships and the nature of women.

When he was writing *The Rainbow* and *Women in Love,* Lawrence declared in a letter of April 17, 1913, that "I can only write what I feel pretty strongly about: and that, at present, is the relation between men and women. After all, it is *the* problem of today, the establishment of a new relation, or the readjustment of the old one, between men and women." In *Psychoanalysis* Lawrence emphasized the importance of integrity to the individual, the couple, and society: "A soul cannot come into its own through that love alone which is unison. If it stress the one mode, the sympathetic mode, beyond a certain point, it breaks its own integrity, and corruption sets in in the living organism. On both planes of love, upper and lower, the two modes must act complementary to one another, the sympathetic and the separatist. It is the absolute failure to see this that has torn the modern world into two halves, the one half warring for the voluntary, objective, separatist control, the other for the pure sympathetic. The individual psyche divided against itself divides the world against itself and an unthinkable progress of calamity ensues unless there be a reconciliation." Lawrence further cautioned in *Fantasia* that "sex as an end in itself is a disaster: a vice. But the ideal purpose which has no roots in the deep sea of passionate sex is a greater disaster still. And now we have only these two things: sex as a fatal goal, which is the essential theme of modern tragedy: or ideal purpose as a deadly parasite." The only solution, according to Lawrence, is "to keep the sexes pure. And by pure we don't mean an ideal sterile innocence and similarity between boy and girl. We mean pure maleness in a man, pure femaleness in a woman. . . . Women and men are dynamically different in everything."

Such statements, together with Lawrence's presentation of women and of sexuality in his fiction, have provoked conflicting points of view on his basic attitudes to women. Indeed, wrote editor Hilary Simpson in *D. H. Lawrence and Feminism,* "attacks on Lawrence's misogyny and praise for his sensitive portrayals of femininity have co-existed since the inception of the critical debate." Anais Nin thought that Lawrence had a "complete realization of the feelings of women. In fact, very often he wrote *as a woman* would write." In Nin's opinion, expressed in *D. H. Lawrence: An Unprofessional Study,* it was "the first time that a man has so wholly and completely expressed woman accurately." However, in *Son of Woman,* Murry expressed another view of Lawrence's aim in both art and life: "to annihilate the female insatiably demanding physical satisfaction from the man who cannot give it her—the female who has thus annihilated him." Kate Millet less personally attacked Lawrence in *Sexual Politics* as "a counterrevolutionary sexual politician." Even though Lawrence often chose a female as the main protagonist in his fiction, such as Ursula in *The Rainbow* or Kate in *The Plumed Serpent,* Faith Pullin complained in an essay from *Lawrence and Women,* edited by Anne Smith, that "Lawrence is an extremely egotistical writer. In his portraits of women, he is usually defining some aspect of himself, rather than attempting the creation of the other sex. Many critics have argued that Lawrence (whether homosexual or bisexual in fact himself) was the androgynous artist and therefore attuned to the inner experience of both sexes. . . . [But] Lawrence's main object was always to examine the male psyche and to use his women characters to that end." Implicitly disagreeing in another essay from *Lawrence and Women,* Smith saw such female identification as going back deep into Lawrence's childhood and suggested that "his physical weakness as a child caused him to be cast in a feminine role, by himself perhaps as much as by others." Simpson, who noted the "extent to which Lawrence used women as actual or potential collaborators, and women's writing as source material," cited as examples, among others, his borrowing of Helen Corke's diaries to write *The Trespasser* and his collaboration with the Australian writer Mollie Skinner on *The Boy in the Bush* (1924). In a further essay from *Lawrence and Women,* Moore theorized that "Lawrence regarded love—and women—in a way that can only be called religious." Moore added that the woman who knew Lawrence best, Frieda Lawrence, commented, "In his heart of hearts, I think he always dreaded women, felt that they were in the end more powerful than men."

The related idea of male friendship preoccupied Lawrence as well: "Friendship should be a rare, choice, immortal thing, sacred and inviolable as marriage. Marriage and deathless friendship, both should be inviolable and sacred: two great creative passions, separate, apart, but complementary: the one pivotal, the other adventurous: the one, marriage, the centre of human life; and the other, the leap ahead." So Lawrence proposed in an essay of the period, "Education of the People," published only after his death in *Phoenix.* He explored the passion of male friendship most fully in *Women in Love,* in the relationship of Rupert Birkin and Gerald Crich. In *Son of Woman,* Murry equated Lawrence with his character Birkin, labeling both "phallic failures." As Moore reported in *The Priest of Love,* although Murry later denied that "what is generally understood by the word homosexuality" applied to Lawrence, the suspicions he aroused have persisted. In his biography of Lawrence, Moore dismissed, as Frieda had, what he termed "the common charge

of homosexuality" against him and suggested instead that he manifested a "compensatory urge, an identification of a frail body with a strong, through a vicarious athleticism."

These concerns shaped the themes, symbols, and relationships depicted in Lawrence's mature fiction and poetry. Schorer pointed out that the struggle of mental versus blood consciousness manifests itself in Lawrence's mature fiction. In *Women in Love,* for example, it appears as a battle between "Will" and "Being" and between an impulse for death on the one hand and life on the other. "Will"—which may be either sensual or spiritual, a death impulse in either case—said Schorer, "fights 'Being,' that integration of total self which is life. Will is the integration of the drive of the ego toward power, toward domination; it has its inverse in the desire to be overpowered, to be dominated, to yield everything to dissolution. Will is mechanical, and its symbol is therefore the machine; its historical and social embodiment is an industrial society that lives by war. Being is the integration of life forces in total and complete self-responsibility. Its historical embodiment lives in the future."

"In comparison with what came before and after, the works of the period between the war and Lawrence's arrival in America are clearly of a lower order," contended Keith Sagar in *The Art of D. H. Lawrence.* "It is widely accepted that the full-length novels of the period—*The Lost Girl, Aaron's Rod,* and *Kangaroo*—are inferior to *The Rainbow* and *Women in Love.*" Ironically, as Moore pointed out in *The Priest of Love,* one of these weaker books, *The Lost Girl,* brought Lawrence "the only official recognition he ever received during his lifetime: the James Tait Black Prize of Edinburgh University."

Aaron's Rod (1922), *Kangaroo* (1923), and *The Plumed Serpent* (1926), most of which Lawrence wrote in a month while living in Mexico, comprise the "leadership" novels, or "novels of power," as Meyers called them. In them, Lawrence, soured by his experience of war, expressed "scorn for the degenerate mob, hatred of Socialism and revolution, belief in discipline, respect for authority, and admiration for a strong and physically attractive leader." Such attitudes led Bertrand Russell and scholars like William York Tindall to regard Lawrence as sympathetic to fascism. Yet, as Meyers pointed out, Lawrence soon revised his desire for a "natural aristocracy" in which "he who is most alive, intrinsically, is King." Lawrence admitted, "I've hated democracy since the war. But now see I'm wrong calling for an aristocracy. What we want is a flow of life from one to another." Meyers refuted the claim that Lawrence shared any sympathy with the Adolf Hitlers and Benito Mussolinis of the world: "The ideas that grew out of the war were certainly anti-democratic, for Lawrence was an elitist who despised the ignorant masses. But they were not Fascist: that totalitarian, nationalistic and racist movement, founded in Milan in 1919, did not yet exist when Lawrence first formulated his ideas." Moreover, as Meyers argued, Lawrence renounced his belief in leadership and authority and radically changed his political ideas in the last five years of his life.

New Mexico "was the greatest experience from the outside world that I have ever had," wrote Lawrence in an essay entitled "New Mexico" and collected in *Phoenix:* "In the magnificent fierce morning of New Mexico, one sprang awake, a new part of the soul woke up suddenly, and the old world gave way to a new." *Birds, Beasts, and Flowers* (1923), begun in Sicily and completed in New Mexico, bears witness to this "awakening." Many of the poems, such as "The Red Wolf," "Men in New Mexico," and "Autumn at Taos," celebrate the landscape and culture of the American Southwest. In an essay for the *D. H. Lawrence Review* Sandra M. Gilbert concluded that the poems in this volume "not only linked two stages in [Lawrence's] career, they actually played a crucial part in his transformation from the romantic yet realistic novelist of *Women in Love* and *Aaron's Rod* to the mythic romancer of *The Plumed Serpent, The Escaped Cock* [also known as *The Man Who Died*], 'The Woman Who Rode Away,' and *Last Poems.*"

Early in his career, in a letter dated February 9, 1914, Lawrence regretted that "in England, people have got the loathsome superior knack of refusing to consider me a poet at all. 'Your prose is so good,' say the kind fools, 'that we are obliged to forgive you your poetry.' How I hate them." "The claim that Lawrence is a poet of real stature is still contentious," Sagar declared in *The Art of D. H. Lawrence.* In *The Double Agent: Essays in Craft and Elucidation* R. P. Blackmur saw in Lawrence's verse "the ruin of great intentions"; he found it flawed by the "fallacy of the faith in expressive form." Vivian de Sola Pinto admitted in his introduction to Lawrence's *Complete Poems* that "like [William] Wordsworth, [Lawrence] wrote a good deal of bad poetry." Nevertheless, he saw even Lawrence's "bad poems" as important because "they are the experiments of a major poet groping his way towards the discovery of a new kind of poetic art." Salgado commented in *A Preface to Lawrence:* "The fact that Lawrence is without question a great poetic novelist has had the unfortunate effect that his poetry has been either neglected, patronized, or dismissed. With the exception of anthology pieces such as 'Snake' and 'Piano' very few of Lawrence's poems are anything like as well known as they deserve to be."

Lawrence himself, recognizing that his poetry defied the formal conventions of his day, frequently invited his readers to regard it differently from other poetry. In the published preface to *Collected Poems,* he warned that the poems "hang together in a life," thus encouraging the reader to regard them as autobiography. As Aldington said in his introduction to *Last Poems and More Pansies,* "With Lawrence the book is not conceived as something made, something apart from the author, but as a prolongation of his own life." Lawrence defended his experiments in verse with a poetic theory that distinguished "poetry of the present" from "poetry of the beginning and poetry of the end." The latter sort of verse manifests "exquisite finality" and "perfection," as he explained in "Poetry of the Present," his introduction to *New Poems.* Like the poetry of Walt Whitman, he maintained, his own poetry is of the first, or "present," type: it is "never finished. There is no rhythm which returns upon itself, no serpent of eternity with its tail in its own mouth. There is no static perfection." Lawrence wanted to "get rid of stereotyped movements and the old hackneyed associations of sound or sense." He desired to "break the stiff neck of habit" in his verse. As a result, concluded Graham Hough in *The Dark Sun: A Study of D. H. Lawrence,* Lawrence's poems "are so independent of literary tradition that the ordinary categories will hardly serve us." At its best, Hough affirmed, "no one sensitive to the rhythms of English speech can fail to observe the lovely fluidity of movement" of Lawrence's verse.

At Kiowa Ranch, near Taos, New Mexico, a gift to Frieda from Lawrence's flamboyant patroness Mabel Dodge Luhan, Lawrence completed works that reflected his setting: the novelette *St. Mawr* and various short stories, among them "The Princess" and "The Woman Who Rode Away." As Harris reported, Lawrence wrote of *St. Mawr* shortly after finishing it, "It's good—a bit bitter—takes place in England, then moves to this ranch—some beautiful creation of this locale and landscape here." Harris said of the short fiction of this period, "His accomplishments include . . . carving out a new kind of story in the visionary tales by blending realism and exemplum; and pointing the way out of realism toward fabulation."

Like most of Lawrence's work at the time, *St. Mawr* and the full-length novel *The Plumed Serpent* were poorly received by readers in England; the American public and press were more receptive. In reference to the latter book, Sagar wrote in *The Art of D. H. Lawrence,* "*The Plumed Serpent* has been mauled by the critics from Frieda, who called it 'desiccated swelled head', onwards. . . . The wholesale condemnation it has received is indicative, it seems to me, of far deeper failings in the critics than in the book; a failure in imaginative range and flexibility; a failure to meet the basic critical challenge, the challenge to enter wholly, if only temporarily, into the fictional world." Leavis admitted in *D. H. Lawrence: Novelist* that he found the book hard to finish, and Eliseo Vivas condemned it in *The Failure and Triumph of Art* as propaganda instead of the prophecy Lawrence intended. As reported by Moore in *The Priest of Love,* the Mexican philosopher Jose Vasconcelos praised the novel as "one of the best books of fantasy ever written about Mexico." Shortly after finishing the book, Lawrence himself in a letter of June 29, 1925, called it "very different," but asserted, "I think most of it."

Lawrence spent most of his last five years in Italy, near Florence, and in southern France, where he died. His steadily deteriorating health, charted in his letters, altered his habits little: he traveled frequently, changed residences many times, and wrote as prolifically as ever. He also translated several works from Italian into English. During this time he composed some of his most famous short stories, among them "The Rocking Horse Winner," "Sun," and "The Man Who Loved Islands." Venting his spleen against the censors and critics of his work, he delighted in writing the satiric poems collected in *Pansies* and *Nettles.* In addition, he extensively revised the early poetry for inclusion in *Collected Poems,* arranging it to tell the story of his creative urge, which he personified as his "demon." Several important manuscripts survived him, in particular, those published as *Last Poems, Etruscan Places,* and the religious treatise *Apocalypse* (1932). For the most part, however, Lawrence limited himself to shorter forms, often dashing off reviews of books and articles on diverse topics for the income they brought him. He also took up painting again, which he found less taxing than writing. Nevertheless, he found the time and energy to compose two longer fictional works, *Lady Chatterley's Lover* and *The Escaped Cock.*

Indeed, Lawrence not only wrote three versions of *Lady Chatterley's Lover,* he also arranged for the private printing and distribution of the unexpurgated edition. Unlike most of Lawrence's books, it sold briskly and made money for him. Yet, as Squires and Jackson pointed out, "unable to obtain a copyright, Lawrence watched, helpless at first, as pirated editions appeared— and profits disappeared. Not until May 1929 did he combat the pirates with his inexpensive Paris edition of the novel."

Even more than *The Rainbow, Lady Chatterley's Lover* has been the subject of intense controversy. Until 1959 and 1960 respectively the unexpurgated edition of the novel could not be legally published and distributed in the United States and England. Critical debate has been intense since it first appeared. In *D. H. Lawrence: Novelist,* Leavis classed it among Lawrence's "lesser novels" because of its "offenses against taste." According to Squires and Jackson: "Its literary reputation is not yet secure; the scent of pornography clings. Too, a novelist's early work often seems more accessible to readers than does the late work, which is typically darker, more complex, more deeply shaded with ideology."

Recalling his earlier statements on blood-knowledge, Lawrence explained the ideas that shaped the novel in "A Propos of *Lady Chatterley's Lover*": "In fact, thought and action, word and deed are two separate lives which we lead. We need, very sincerely, to keep a connection . . . and this is the real point of the book. I want men and women to be able to think sex, fully, completely, honestly and cleanly. . . . Life is only bearable when the mind and body are in harmony, and there is a natural balance between them, and each has a natural respect for the other." Lawrence maintained here, as he had earlier, that dependence on mental knowledge to the exclusion of blood-knowledge leads to most of the "tragedies" of the modern world, chiefly a "mechanization" of life. Far from being obscene, *Lady Chatterley's Lover* celebrates the creative power of togetherness, "which is religious and poetic," he asserted.

In *The World of the Five Major Novels* Scott Sanders agreed with Lawrence's assessment: "In tracing the sources of human violence to the desire for mastery and the illusion of separateness, Lawrence was echoing a view common to many of the world's religions." Put briefly, Sanders wrote, what the characters of the novel and all modern people confront is "the choice between the way of power and the way of love. . . . What we are shown in the history of Lady Chatterley's loving is the education of one woman's consciousness. . . . In proportion as we are drawn into her loving and altered by it, we are forced to realize along with her that there is no ultimate basis for distinctions between classes, between races, between nations, or between humankind and the rest of nature."

In his introduction to *Selected Letters of D. H. Lawrence,* Aldous Huxley quoted part of a letter written by Lawrence on February 24, 1913, at the start of his writing career: "I often feel one ought to be able to pray before one works—and then leave it to the Lord. Isn't it hard work to come to real grips with one's imagination—throw everything overboard. I always feel as though I stood naked for the fire of Almighty God to go through me—and it's rather an awful feeling. One has to be so terribly religious to be an artist." Huxley, who knew Lawrence well in the last years of his life, commented, "Conversely, he might have added, one has to be terribly an artist, terribly conscious of 'inspiration' and the compelling force of genius, to be religious as Lawrence was religious."

Religious themes, symbols, and allusions occur throughout Lawrence's work, but especially at the end. Impounded during the London exhibition in 1928 for indecency and immorality, Lawrence's paintings often evidence, in fact, religious themes; he regarded these works as sacred, as his frequent references to them in letters make plain. *The Escaped Cock,* a story of resurrection, and *Apocalypse,* which Lawrence worked on during the last months of his life, treat religious topics explicitly. The story of the risen Christ who in his wanderings meets and mates with the goddess Isis exemplifies many of the ideas set forth in *Apocalypse.* In his introduction to that book, Aldington admitted that "from the point of view of scholars Lawrence's book may be quite worthless as an interpretation of the Book of Revelation." He found it interesting "not as the revelation of John of Patmos, but as the revelation of Lawrence." In *Apocalypse* as in *The Escaped Cock,* Lawrence condemned all religion at the time of Christ as having turned from "the old worship and study of vitality, potency, power, to the study of death and death-rewards, death-penalties, and morals. All religion, instead of being a religion of *life,* here and now, became a religion of postponed destiny, death, and reward *afterwards,* 'if you are good.' " In his last works, including his poems and paintings and many of his shorter pieces, the underlying message matches that of *Apoca-*

lypse: "What we want is to destroy our false, inorganic connections, especially those related to money, and reestablish the living organic connection, with the cosmos, the sun and earth, with mankind and nation and family." The Etruscan people, revealed to Lawrence through their art and architecture, summed up his conception of life, according to Aldington in the introduction to *Apocalypse:* "Nations of men and women living an intense, physical life without too much intellect and hatred. And in Etruria at any rate the women enjoyed great liberty and consideration, while the idea of sex and sexual desire as shameful things had never been thought of."

"The hatred which my books have aroused comes back and gets me here," Lawrence, pointing to his chest, told his friend Earl Brewster shortly before the writer's death; Brewster reported the words and gesture in *D. H. Lawrence: Reminiscences and Correspondence.* Because of his rapidly deteriorating physical condition, Lawrence reluctantly agreed to hospital care one month before he died; he entered a sanatorium near Vence, in southern France. In *The Priest of Love,* Moore revealed that Lawrence's doctor, commenting on his famous patient's refusal to rest, even when hospitalized, said that "those very qualities which gave Lawrence such keen perception and such passionate feeling made it quite impossible for him to submit for any length of time to a restricted sanatorium existence." "I'm better in a house," he wrote in a letter dated February 21, 1930. The day before he died, he dragged himself from the nursing home to a rented villa; he died there during the evening of March 2, 1930. Although Lawrence was buried in Vence, five years later Frieda arranged for the cremation of his remains, which she then transported to Kiowa Ranch. They are interred in the small chapel that Frieda built to hold them and that she decorated with Lawrence's personal symbol: the rising phoenix.

MEDIA ADAPTATIONS: A number of Lawrence's works have been adapted for film, including the novels *Sons and Lovers, Women in Love, Kangaroo,* and *Lady Chatterley's Lover,* and the short novel *The Fox.* Works adapted for other media include *The Fox,* which was adapted as a play, and *Lady Chatterley's Lover,* released as a sound recording.

AVOCATIONAL INTERESTS: Painting.

BIOGRAPHICAL/CRITICAL SOURCES:

BOOKS

Aldington, Richard, *Portrait of a Genius, But . . . ,* Heinemann, 1950.

Blackmur, R. P., *The Double Agent: Essays in Craft and Elucidation,* Arrow Editions, 1935.

Brett, Dorothy, *Lawrence and Brett: A Friendship,* Lippincott, 1933.

Brewster, Earl and Achsah Brewster, *D. H. Lawrence: Reminiscences and Correspondence,* M. Secker, 1934.

Bynner, Witter, *Journey With Genius: Recollections and Reflections Concerning the D. H. Lawrences,* J. Day Co., 1951.

Carswell, Catherine, *The Savage Pilgrimage,* Chatto & Windus, 1932.

Cavitch, David, *D. H. Lawrence and the New World,* Oxford University Press, 1969.

Chambers, Jessie (under pseudonym E. T.) *D. H. Lawrence: A Personal Record,* J. Cape, 1935.

Clark, L. D., *Dark Night of the Body,* University of Texas Press, 1964.

Clark, L. D., *The Minoan Distance: The Symbolism of Travel in D. H. Lawrence,* University of Arizona Press, 1980.

Clarke, Colin, *River of Dissolution: D. H. Lawrence and English Romanticism,* Routledge & Kegan Paul, 1969.

Corke, Helen, *Lawrence and Apocalypse,* Heinemann, 1933.

Corke, Helen, *D. H. Lawrence's Princess: A Memory of Jessie Chambers,* Merle Press, 1951.

Corke, Helen, *D. H. Lawrence: The Croydon Years,* University of Texas Press, 1965.

Cowan, James C., editor, *D. H. Lawrence: An Annotated Bibliography,* Northern Illinois University Press, 1981.

Cushman, Keith, *D. H. Lawrence at Work: The Emergence of the Prussian Officer Stories,* University Press of Virginia, 1978.

Daleski, H. M., *The Forked Flame: A Study of D. H. Lawrence,* Faber, 1965.

Delany, Paul, *D. H. Lawrence's Nightmare: The Writer and His Circle During the Years of the Great War,* Basic Books, 1978.

Delavenay, Emile, *D. H. Lawrence: The Man and His Work; The Formative Years, 1885-1919,* Heinemann, 1972.

Dictionary of Literary Biography, Gale, Volume 10: *Modern British Dramatists, 1900-1945,* two volumes, 1982, Volume 19: *British Poets, 1880-1914,* 1983, Volume 36: *British Novelists, 1890-1929: Modernists,* 1985.

Draper, R. P., editor, *D. H. Lawrence: The Critical Heritage,* Routledge & Kegan Paul, 1970.

Farr, Judith, editor, *Twentieth-Century Interpretations of "Sons and Lovers": A Collection of Critical Essays,* Prentice-Hall, 1970.

Ford, George H., *Double Measure: A Study of the Novels and Stories of D. H. Lawrence,* Holt, 1965.

Freeman, Mary, *D. H. Lawrence: A Basic Study of His Ideas,* University of Florida Press, 1955.

Gilbert, Sandra M., *Acts of Attention: The Poems of D. H. Lawrence,* Cornell University Press, 1972.

Goodheart, Eugene, *The Utopian Vision of D. H. Lawrence,* University of Chicago Press, 1983.

Gordon, David J., *D. H. Lawrence as a Literary Critic,* Yale University Press, 1966.

Green, Martin, *The von Richthofen Sisters; the Triumphant and the Tragic Modes of Love: Else and Frieda von Richthofen, Otto Gross, Mar Weber, and D. H. Lawrence, in the Years 1870-1970,* Basic Books, 1974.

Gregory, Horace, *Pilgrim of the Apocalypse,* Viking, 1933.

Harris, Janice Hubbard, *The Short Fiction of D. H. Lawrence,* Rutgers University Press, 1984.

Hochman, Baruch, *Another Ego: The Changing View of the Self and Society in the Work of D. H. Lawrence,* University of South Carolina Press, 1970.

Hoffman, Frederick J. and Harry T. Moore, editors, *The Achievement of D. H. Lawrence,* University of Oklahoma Press, 1953.

Hough, Graham, *The Dark Sun: A Study of D. H. Lawrence,* Duckworth, 1956.

Joost, Nicholas and Alvin Sullivan, *D. H. Lawrence and the Dial,* Southern Illinois University Press, 1970.

Kinkead-Weekes, Mark, editor, *Twentieth-Century Interpretations of "The Rainbow": A Collection of Critical Essays,* Prentice-Hall, 1971.

Lawrence, Ada and G. Stuart Gelder, *Young Lorenzo: The Early Life of D. H. Lawrence,* G. Orioli, 1932.

Lawrence, D. H., *Last Poems and More Pansies,* introduction by Richard Aldington, G. Orioli, 1932.

Lawrence, D. H., *Selected Letters,* introduction by Aldous Huxley, Penguin, 1950.

Lawrence, D. H., *Complete Poems,* introduction by Vivian de Sola Pinto, Heinemann, 1967.

Lawrence, Frieda, *Not I, But the Wind,* Rydal Press, 1934.

Leavis, F. R., *D. H. Lawrence: Novelist,* Chatto & Windus, 1955.

Leavis, F. R., *Thought, Words, and Creativity: Art and Thought in Lawrence,* Chatto & Windus, 1976.

Luhan, Mabel Dodge, *Lorenzo in Taos,* Knopf, 1932.

Mandell, Gail Porter, *The Phoenix Paradox: A Study of Renewal Through Change in the "Collected Poems" and "Last Poems" of D. H. Lawrence,* Southern Illinois University Press, 1984.

Marshall, Tom, *The Psychic Mariner: A Reading of the Poems of D. H. Lawrence,* Viking, 1970.

McDonald, Edward D., *A Bibliography of the Writings of D. H. Lawrence,* Centaur, 1925.

Meyers, Jeffrey, *D. H. Lawrence and the Experience of Italy,* University of Pennsylvania Press, 1982.

Miko, Stephen J., editor, *Twentieth-Century Interpretations of "Women in Love": A Collection of Critical Essays,* Prentice-Hall, 1969.

Miko, Stephen J., *Toward "Women in Love": The Emergence of a Laurentian Aesthetic,* Yale University Press, 1971.

Millet, Kate, *Sexual Politics,* Abacus, 1972.

Moore, Harry T., *The Life and Works of D. H. Lawrence,* Twayne, 1951.

Moore, Harry T., *The Intelligent Heart,* Farrar, Straus & Young, 1954.

Moore, Harry T., *Poste Restant: A Lawrence Travel Calendar,* University of California Press, 1956.

Moore, Harry T., editor, *A D. H. Lawrence Miscellany,* Southern Illinois University Press, 1959.

Moore, Harry T., *The Priest of Love: A Life of D. H. Lawrence,* Farrar, Straus, 1974.

Murfin, Ross C., *The Poetry of D. H. Lawrence: Texts and Contexts,* University of Nebraska Press, 1983.

Murry, John Middleton, *Son of Woman: The Story of D. H. Lawrence,* J.Cape, 1931.

Murry, John Middleton, *Reminiscences of D. H. Lawrence,* J. Cape, 1933.

Nehls, Edward, *D. H. Lawrence: A Composite Biography,* University of Wisconsin Press, Volume I, 1957, Volume II, 1958, Volume III, 1959.

Nin, Anais, *D. H. Lawrence: An Unprofessional Study,* Edward W. Titus, 1932.

Oates, Joyce Carol, *The Hostile Sun: The Poetry of D. H. Lawrence,* Black Sparrow Press, 1973.

Panichas, George, *Adventure in Consciousness: The Meaning of D. H. Lawrence's Religious Quest,* Mouton, 1964.

Partlow, Robert B., Jr., and Harry T. Moore, editors, *D. H. Lawrence: The Man Who Lived,* Southern Illinois University Press, 1980.

Pinion, Frank, *A D. H. Lawrence Companion,* Macmillan, 1978.

Pinto, Vivian de Sola, *D. H. Lawrence: Prophet of the Midlands,* University of Nottingham, 1951.

Powell, Lawrence Clark, *The Manuscripts of D. H. Lawrence,* Los Angeles Public Library, 1937.

Pritchard, R. E., *D. H. Lawrence: Body of Darkness,* Hutchinson University Library (London), 1971.

Roberts, Warren, *A Bibliography of D. H. Lawrence,* Hart-Davis, 1963, revised edition, 1982.

Rolph, C. H., editor, *The Trial of Lady Chatterley,* Penguin, 1961.

Ross, Charles, *The Composition of "The Rainbow" and "Women in Love,"* University Press of Virginia, 1979.

Sagar, Keith, *The Art of D. H. Lawrence,* Cambridge University Press, 1966.

Sagar, Keith, *D. H. Lawrence: A Calendar of His Works,* Manchester University Press, 1979.

Sagar, Keith, *The Life of D. H. Lawrence,* Methuen, 1980.

Sagar, Keith, editor, *A D. H. Lawrence Handbook,* Barnes & Noble, 1982.

Salgado, Gamini, *D. H. Lawrence: "Sons and Lovers,"* Edward Arnold, 1966.

Salgado, Gamini, *A Preface to Lawrence,* Longman, 1982.

Sanders, Scott, *The World of the Five Major Novels,* Viking, 1973.

Simpson, Hilary, editor., *D. H. Lawrence and Feminism,* Northern Illinois Universiry Press, 1982.

Smith, Anne, editor, *Lawrence and Women,* Vision, 1978.

Spender, Stephen, editor, *D. H. Lawrence: Novelist, Poet, Prophet,* Weidenfeld & Nicolson, 1973.

Spilka, Mark, *The Love Ethic of D. H. Lawrence,* Indiana University Press, 1955.

Spilka, Mark, editor, *D. H. Lawrence: A Collection of Critical Essays,* Prentice-Hall, 1963.

Squires, Michael, *The Creation of "Lady Chatterley's Lover,"* Johns Hopkins University Press, 1983.

Squires, Michael and Dennis Jackson, editors, *D. H. Lawrence's "Lady": A New Look at "Lady Chatterley's Lover,"* University of Georgia Press, 1985.

Tedlock, E. W., Jr., *The Frieda Lawrence Collection of D. H. Lawrence Manuscripts,* University of New Mexico Press, 1948.

Tedlock, E. W., Jr., *Frieda Lawrence: The Memoirs and Correspondence,* Heinemann, 1961.

Tedlock, E. W., Jr., *D. H. Lawrence, Artist and Rebel: A Study of Lawrence's Fiction,* University of New Mexico Press, 1963.

Tedlock, E. W., Jr., *D. H. Lawrence and "Sons and Lovers": Sources and Criticism,* New York University Press, 1965.

Tindall, William York, *D. H. Lawrence and Susan His Cow,* Columbia University, 1939.

Tiverton, Father William (pseudonym for Martin Jarrett-Kerr), *D. H. Lawrence and Human Existence,* foreword by T. S. Eliot, Rockliff, 1951.

Twentieth-Century Literary Criticism, Gale, Volume 2, 1979, Volume 9, 1983, Volume 16, 1985, Volume 33, 1989.

Vivas, Eliseo, *The Failure and Triumph of Art,* Northwestern University Press, 1960.

Widmer, Kingsley, *The Art of Perversity: D. H. Lawrence's Shorter Fiction,* University of Washington Press, 1962.

PERIODICALS

Academy, March 18, 1911.

Athenaeum, June 1, 1912.

D. H. Lawrence Review, fall, 1979.

Los Angeles Times Book Review, December 27, 1987.

Manchester Guardian, July 2, 1913.

Nation, July 12, 1913, April 26, 1947.

Nation and Athenaeum, March 29, 1930.

Poetry: A Magazine of Verse II, July, 1913.

Psychoanalytic Review, July, 1916.

Renaissance and Modern Studies, Volume 1, 1957.

Sphere, October, 1915.

Times (London), March 4, 1930.

Times Literary Supplement, May 29, 1987, October 16, 1987.

*   *   *

LAYE, Camara   1928-1980

PERSONAL: Family name, Kamara; personal name, Laye; born January 1, 1928, in Kouroussa, French Guinea (now Guinea), West Africa; died February 4, 1980, in Senegal; son of Kamara Komady (a goldsmith) and Daman Sadan; married; wife's name, Marie; children: four. *Education:* Attended Central School of Automobile Engineering, Ecole Ampere, Conservatoire des Arts et Metiers, and Technical College for Aeronautics and Automobile Construction, all near Paris, France.

CAREER: Worked in a market and at various other jobs in Paris, France, before becoming a motor mechanic for Simca Corp. in a Paris suburb, c. 1953; served as attache at ministry of youth in Paris; returned to Guinea, 1956; worked as engineer for the French colonial regime in Guinea, 1956-58; Government of Guinea, Conakry, diplomat in Liberia, Ghana, and other African countries, beginning 1958; became director of Centre de Recherche et d'Etudes in Conakry; self-exiled from Guinea, 1966; lived for a time in the Ivory Coast; research fellow in Islamic Studies at Dakar University, Senegal, c. 1971; associated with the Institut Francais d'Afrique Noire in Dakar; became a university teacher in Senegal.

AWARDS, HONORS: Prix Charles Veillon, 1954, for *L'Enfant noir.*

WRITINGS:

L'Enfant noir (autobiography), Plon, 1953, translation by James Kirkup, Ernest Jones, and Elaine Gottlieb published as *The Dark Child,* Noonday Press, 1954 (published in England as *The African Child,* Collins, 1959).

Le Regard du roi (novel), Plon, 1954, translation by Kirkup published as *The Radiance of the King,* Collins, 1956, Collier, 1971.

Dramouss (novel), Plon, 1966, translation by Kirkup published as *A Dream of Africa,* Collins, 1968, Collier, 1971.

Le Maitre de la parole: Kuoma Lafolo Kuoma, Plon, 1978, translation by Kirkup published as *The Guardian of the Word,* Random House, 1984.

Contributor of articles and short stories to *African Arts, Black Orpheus, Presence Africaine,* and *Paris-Dakar.*

SIDELIGHTS: Although the author of only four books, Camara Laye was "regarded by many critics of African literature as the continent's major Francophone novelist," according to Charles R. Larson in the *Times Literary Supplement.* Laye's autobiographical book *The Dark Child,* originally published as *L'Enfant noir,* was of historical importance in the development of modern West African literature. It is "the work that can with justice be regarded as having brought French African narrative prose finally into its own," as Abiola Irele explained in *The African Experience in Literature and Ideology.*

Born in Guinea and raised a Moslem in that nation's countryside, Laye first encountered the outside world when he left his family's village to attend high school in Conakry, the capitol of Guinea. In Laye's native village his father, because of his work as a goldsmith, was widely assumed to possess magical powers. Other ancient African superstitions were also commonly held. But in Conakry, society was modern; twentieth century technology was everywhere. The contrast between the two societies startled Laye and made his life in the capital difficult.

But when, after graduating from high school, Laye accepted a scholarship to study engineering in Paris, he found the differences between African and European cultures to be overwhelming. To ease the tension and loneliness of his student life, Laye began to write down remembrances of his childhood in the Guinean countryside. These writings became his first book, *The Dark Child,* published in 1953. Tracing Laye's development from his tribal childhood, through his schooling in Guinea's capital, to his college life in Paris, *The Dark Child* poses questions about the preservation of traditional ways of life in the face of technological progress. As Irele noted in an article for *West Africa,* Laye's autobiography presented "an image of a coherence and dignity which went with social arrangements and human intercourse in the self-contained African universe of his childhood."

Some black critics of the time faulted Laye for not speaking out against colonialism. They saw his concern with traditional African society as an irrelevancy in an age of struggle for African independence. But Gerald Moore pointed out in *Twelve African Writers* that the world of Laye's childhood was largely untouched by colonialism. "Though conquered and administered by France," Moore wrote, "a city like [Laye's native village] was complex and self-sufficient enough to go very much on its own immemorial way. Its people . . . were not constantly obsessed with the alien presence of Europe in their midst." In contrast to this view, Irele believed that because *The Dark Child* celebrated the traditional African ways of life, it was "in fact a form of denial of the assumptions and explicit ideological outgrowth of the French colonial enterprise."

Whatever the final judgement regarding the book's stance on colonialism, *The Dark Child* has been widely praised for the quiet restraint of its prose. Moore explained that *The Dark Child* "is a unique book in many ways, written with a singular and gentle sincerity, yet with very conscious artistic skill. Laye does not proclaim his negritude or announce the coming dawn; he records what his childhood was, what was the quality and the depth of the life from which he sprang." In her study *The Writings of Camara Laye,* Adele King called *The Dark Child* "a carefully controlled story . . . presented with economy and restraint. . . . A particular moment in Laye's life and in the history of Africa has been transformed into a minor classic, in which the autobiographical form has been raised to the level of art." The book, Eric Sellin noted in *World Literature Today,* won Laye "instant acclaim and lasting respect as a limpid stylist."

The book's success lifted Laye from the poverty of his student life and enabled him to devote his full time to writing. A year of intensive effort resulted in his second book, the 1954 novel *The Radiance of the King,* originally published as *Le Regard du roi.* The story takes a white European named Clarence into the African countryside where he is forced to adapt to the traditional culture to survive. He has no means to earn a living unless he can find his way to the king's court and gain a position there. His search for the king forms the basis of the plot. "Clarence's search for the king with whom he hopes to hold an audience," Jeannette Macauley wrote in *Modern Black Novelists: A Collection of Critical Essays,* "becomes an obsession. It's the mirage which lures him on through dark forests with people he doesn't feel anything for, with people who do not understand him."

"Attempts have been made," Neil McEwan reported in his *Africa and the Novel,* "to prove Kafka's 'influence' on the novel: 'an African Kafka' can be praise from some European critics, disparagement from some Africans." But McEwan believed that *The Radiance of the King* ultimately suggests "innumerable European writers" and proposed that "symbolist, allegorical, mythic, archetypal, psychological, and comparative-cultural studies seem called for; indeed there are passages . . . in which one suspects that the author has deliberately provoked and mystified critical attention. . . . It mocks analysis."

Several critics found a religious symbolism in the novel, with David Cook in *Perspectives on African Literature* noting that "the book is, of course, cast in the form of a quest—a spiritual quest; though there is nothing pompous, ponderous or moralistic about it." Likewise, Janheinz Jahn in *Introduction to African Literature: An Anthology of Critical Writings from "Black Orpheus,"* explained that *The Radiance of the King* "is usually considered as an ingenious allegory about man's search for God. But I think that the book cannot be seen in this sense only; it is ambivalent, even multivalent."

Because of the ambiguous nature of Clarence's quest, the novel is not restricted to a single interpretation. As Larson stated in *The Emergence of African Fiction,* "Clarence, who is archetypal of Western man in particular, is symbolic of everyman and his difficulties in adjusting not only to a different culture, but to life itself." King explained that "the novel deals with the theme of any man trying to adjust to a strange society, of every man's homelessness in the world. . . . Making this ordinary European a symbol for Everyman is a way of countering 'black racism,' a way of showing that the essential human experiences go beyond colour."

Critical regard for *The Radiance of the King* has been very favorable, with some commentators placing it among the very best of contemporary African literature. The book's "clever reversals, dreamlike evocations, surreal efforts and implementation in prose of techniques proper to film . . .," Sellin remarked, "have caused some admirers to deem it the finest African novel." Larson, writing in the *Times Literary Supplement,* called the novel Laye's "masterpiece" and explained that it "has long been hailed as the great African novel."

Laye's third book resulted in his forced exile from his native Guinea in 1966. *A Dream of Africa,* originally published as *Dramouss,* commented openly on the dictatorial policies of Guinean leader Sekou Toure, who forced Laye into fleeing the country with his family. He was to live in neighboring Senegal, under the protection of Senegal's president Leopold Senghor, for the remainder of his life.

The novel begins with the narrator, Fatoman, returning to Guinea from Paris, where he has been living in exile for six years. Although he is happy to be back in his homeland again, he soon discovers that his country has serious problems. The independence which it will soon be granted by France is accompanied by political violence and murder. Fatoman warns his people that this will only lead to a new, dictatorial government. "Someone," Fatoman proclaims, "must say that though colonialism . . . was an evil thing for our country, the regime you are now introducing will be a catastrophe whose evil consequences will be felt for decades. Someone must speak out and say that a regime built on spilt blood through the activities of incendiaries of huts and houses is nothing but a regime of anarchy and dictatorship, a regime based on violence."

In 1970, during a visit back to Guinea to see her ailing mother, Laye's wife was arrested and imprisoned as an enemy of the state. Because he feared for her safety, Laye was to publish no more overtly political work. His next book did not appear until 1978 when, after teaching in Senegal for many years, he completed *The Guardian of the Word,* originally published as *Le Maitre de la parole: Kouma Lafolo Kouma.* A marked departure from his earlier works, *The Guardian of the Word* is an epic novel set in thirteenth century West Africa and following the life of the "first Emperor of the ancient Malian empire," as Larson explained in the *Times Literary Supplement.* The novel is based on an oral account of the period popular among Guinean storytellers, or griots; Laye first heard the story from Babu Conde, one of the best known of Guinea's griots. Because the novel focuses in part on the conduct of Mali's first emperor and the standards of behavior which he set, it indirectly comments on the proper conduct of all governments, something Laye could not afford to do openly.

The Guardian of the Word, Alan Cheuse of the *Los Angeles Times Book Review* stated, is "one of those books that transmit from one generation to the next elemental visions on which society is founded—on the laws and customs and manners by which it remains stable." In doing so, the novel recreates a historical period in full detail. "There are fascinating passages," Larson noted in the *Times Literary Supplement,* "devoted to almost all of the important stages of traditional life." Martin Tucker of the *New York Times Book Review* argued that in *The Guardian of the Word,* African history and culture is blended with a European literary sensibility. "Although Laye's last work is filled with surrealistic shades and European psychological insight," he wrote, "it is invigorated by the traditional African vision of the spiritual and historic."

All of Laye's books are written according to predominantly European literary modes, yet they paradoxically affirm traditional African life and culture. He succeeds in combining these discordant elements into a satisfying whole which expresses his individual vision. Speaking of *The Radiance of the King* in particular, McEwan explained that "Laye is an artist in whom sources are entirely absorbed and the question whether this novel is French literature or African seems pointless; it is Camara Laye's." King noted that Laye transcended his cultural background, concluding that his work "belongs within the tradition of classic world literature, describing a personal and cultural dilemma in accents that speak to all mankind."

BIOGRAPHICAL/CRITICAL SOURCES:

BOOKS

Beier, Ulli, editor, *Introduction to African Literature: An Anthology of Critical Writings from "Black Orpheus,"* Northwestern University Press, 1967.
Contemporary Literary Criticism, Gale, Volume 4, 1975, Volume 38, 1986.
Cooke, Michael G., editor, *Modern Black Novelists: A Collection of Critical Essays,* Prentice-Hall, 1971.
Heywood, Christopher, editor, *Perspectives on African Literature,* Africana Publishing, 1971.
Irele, Abiola, *The African Experience in Literature and Ideology,* Heinemann, 1981.
King, Adele, *The Writings of Camara Laye,* Heinemann Educational Books, 1980.
Larson, Charles R., *The Emergence of African Fiction,* Indiana University Press, 1971.
Laye, Camara, *The Dark Child,* Noonday Press, 1954.
Laye, Camara, *A Dream of Africa,* Collier, 1971.
McEwan, Neil, *Africa and the Novel,* Humanities Press, 1983.
Moore, Gerald, *Twelve African Writers,* Indiana University Press, 1980.

PERIODICALS

African Literature Today, January, 1969.
Black Orpheus, November, 1959.
Books Abroad, spring, 1969, spring, 1971.
Los Angeles Times Book Review, September 2, 1984.
New York Times, September 16, 1969.
New York Times Book Review, June 24, 1984.
Observer Review, February 4, 1968.
Times Literary Supplement, May 4, 1967, July 17, 1981.
West Africa, April 7, 1980.
World Literature Today, summer, 1980.

OBITUARIES:

PERIODICALS

AB Bookman's Weekly, May 5, 1980.
Publishers Weekly, March 28, 1980.

*   *   *

LAYTON, Irving (Peter)   1912-

PERSONAL: Original surname, Lazarovitch; name legally changed; born March 12, 1912, in Neamtz, Rumania; immigrated to Canada, 1913; son of Moses and Keine (Moscovitch) Lazarovitch; married Faye Lynch, September 13, 1938; married Frances Sutherland, September 13, 1946; married Aviva Cantor (a writer of children's stories), September 13, 1961; married Harriet Bernstein (a publicist; divorced, March 19, 1984); children: (with Sutherland) Max Rubin, Naomi Parker; (with Cantor) David Herschel; (with Bernstein) Samantha Clara. *Education:* Macdonald College, B.Sc., 1939; McGill University, M.A., 1946.

ADDRESSES: Home—6879 Monkland Ave., Montreal, Quebec, Canada H4B 1J5.

CAREER: Jewish Public Library, Montreal, Quebec, lecturer, 1943-58; high school teacher in Montreal, 1945-60; Sir George Williams University (now Sir George Williams Campus of Concordia University), Montreal, lecturer, 1949-65, poet in residence, 1965-69; University of Guelph, Guelph, Ontario, poet in residence, 1969-70; York University, Toronto, Ontario, professor of English literature, 1970-78; Concordia University, Sir George Williams Campus, Montreal poet in residence 1978—. *Military service:* Canadian Army, Artillery, 1942-43; became lieutenant.

MEMBER: P.E.N.

AWARDS, HONORS: Canada Foundation fellow, 1957; Canada Council award, 1959; Governor-General's Medal for *A Red Carpet for the Sun;* President's Medal, University of Western Ontario, 1961, for poem "Keine Lazarovitch 1870-1959"; Prix Litteraire de Quebec, 1963, for *Balls for a One-Armed Juggler;* Canada Council Special Arts Award, 1967; D.C.L., Bishops University, 1972, and Concordia University, 1975.

WRITINGS:

Here and Now, First Statement, 1945.
Now Is the Place (poems and stories), First Statement, 1948.
The Black Huntsmen, privately printed, 1951.
Love the Conqueror Worm, Contact, 1951.
(With Louis Dudek and Raymond Souster) *Cerberus,* Contact, 1952.
In the Midst of My Fever, Divers, 1954.
The Long Peashooter, Laocoon, 1954.
The Cold Green Element, Contact, 1955.
The Blue Propeller, Contact, 1955.
The Blue Calf, Contact, 1956.
Music on a Kazoo, Contact, 1956.
The Improved Binoculars (selected poems), introduction by William Carlos Williams, Jargon, 1956.
A Laughter in the Mind, Jargon, 1958.
A Red Carpet for the Sun (collected poems), McClelland & Stewart, 1959.

PUBLISHED BY McCLELLAND & STEWART, EXCEPT AS INDICATED

The Swinging Flesh (poems and short stories), 1961.
Balls for a One-Armed Juggler (poems), 1963.
The Laughing Rooster (poems), 1964.

Collected Poems, 1965.
Periods of the Moon, 1967.
The Shattered Plinths, 1968.
Selected Poems, 1969.
The Whole Bloody Bird: Obs, Aphs, and Pomes, 1969.
(Author of introduction) *Poems to Colour: A Selection of Work-shop Poems,* York University, 1970.
Nail Polish, 1971.
The Collected Poems of Irving Layton, 1971.
Engagements: The Prose of Irving Layton, edited by Seymour Mayne, 1972.
Lovers and Lesser Men, 1973.
The Pole-Vaulter, 1974.
Seventy-five Greek Poems, 1974.
The Darkening Fire: Selected Poems, 1945-1968, 1975.
The Unwavering Eye: Selected Poems, 1969-1975, 1975.
For My Brother Jesus, 1976.
The Collected Poems of Irving Layton, 1977.
Taking Sides (prose), 1977.
The Uncollected Poems of Irving Layton, 1936-1959, Mosaic Press, 1977.
The Covenant, 1977.
The Tightrope Dancer, 1978.
The Love Poems of Irving Layton, 1979.
Droppings from Heaven, 1979.
An Unlikely Affair, Mosaic Press, 1980.
For My Neighbors in Hell, Mosaic Press, 1980.
Europe and Other Bad News, 1981.
The Gucci Bag, Mosaic Press, 1983.
Selected Poems, [Seoul], 1985.
A Spider Danced a Cosy Jig, Stoddart, 1984.
Where Burning Sappho Loved, [Athens], 1985.

Works available in translation include *Poemas de amor,* [Madrid], 1980, and *Le Poesie d'amore,* 1983.

EDITOR

(With Louis Dudek) *Canadian Poems, 1850-1952,* Contact, 1952, 2nd edition, 1953.
Pan-ic: A Selection of Contemporary Canadian Poems, [New York], 1958.
(And author of introduction) *Poems for Twenty-seven Cents,* [Montreal], 1961.
Love Where the Nights Are Long: Canadian Love Poems, McClelland & Stewart, 1962.
Anvil: A Selection of Workshop Poems, [Montreal], 1966.
(And author of introduction) *Anvil Blood: A Selection of Workshop Poems,* [Toronto], 1973.

Work represented in numerous anthologies, including, *Book of Canadian Poetry,* edited by A. J. M. Smith, Gage, 1948; *Book of Canadian Stories,* edited by D. Pacey, Ryerson, 1950; *Canadian Short Stories,* edited by R. Weaver and H. James, Oxford University Press, 1952; *Oxford Book of Canadian Verse,* edited by Smith, Oxford University Press, 1960; *How Do I Love Thee: Sixty Poets of Canada (and Quebec) Select and Introduce Their Favourite Poems from Their Own Work,* edited by John Robert Colombo, M. G. Hurtig, 1970.

Contributor of poetry and stories to various periodicals, including *Poetry, Canadian Forum,* and *Sail.* Co-founder and editor, *First Statement* and *Northern Review,* 1941-43; former associate editor, *Contact, Black Mountain Review,* and several other magazines.

SIDELIGHTS: Irving Layton, according to Lauriat Lane, Jr., "is by now *the* living Canadian poet, probably *the* Canadian poet,

a major poet by any standard, in fact—dare one say it?—a great poet." Lane goes on to say that Layton's work can pass two tests of greatness: first, that his best poems can be read and reread without becoming tiresome; and second, that his poetry can stand up to "impersonal, systematic, academic" scrutiny. Desmond Pacey feels that most Canadian poets "have tended—with the conspicuous exception of Bliss Carman—to be exigent or timid, and to confine themselves in the role of minor poets; Layton, on the other hand, sees himself as a major poet and is not afraid to essay the part. He is often criticised for being too prolific, and for publishing everything that he writes, the bad along with the good. I see this not as pride but as a form of humility: Layton knows that he is not always at his best, but he is willing to let us see him in his off-moments as well as in his moments of magical success. More power to him: it enables us to see his development, to measure his best poems by his worst, and to savour the tiny pleasure that can be found even in his mistakes."

Layton told *CA:* "One of my sisters thought I should be a plumber or an electrician; another saw in me the ability to become a peddlar; my third and oldest sister was sure I was devious and slippery enough to make a fine lawyer or politician. My mother, presiding over these three witches, pointed to the fly-spotted ceiling, indicating God by that gesture, and said, 'He will be what the Almighty wants him to be.'

"My devout mother turned out to be right. From earliest childhood I longed to match sounds with sense; and when I was older, to make music out of words. Everywhere I went, mystery dogged my steps. the skinny dead rat in the lane, the fire that broke out in our house on Sabbath eve, the energy that went with cruelty and the power that went with hate. The empty sky had no answers for my queries and the stars at night only winked and said nothing.

"I wrote my first poem for a teacher who was astonishingly beautiful. For weeks I mentally drooled over the white cleavage she had carelessly exposed to a precocious eleven-year-old. So there it was: the two grand mysteries of sexuality and death. I write because I'm driven to say something about them, to celebrate what my limited brain cannot comprehend. To rejoice in my more arrogant moods to think the Creator Himself doesn't comprehend His handiwork. I write because the only solace He has in His immense and eternal solitude are the poems and stories that tell Him—like all creators, He too is hungry for praise—how exciting and beautiful, how majestic and terrible are His works and to give Him an honest, up-to-date report on His most baffling creation, Man. I know whenever I put in a good word for the strange biped He made God's despair is lessened. Ultimately, I write because I am less cruel than He is."

Irving Layton's work has been translated into more than ten languages. His poetry has been read on several recordings.

BIOGRAPHICAL/CRITICAL SOURCES:

BOOKS

Contemporary Literary Criticism, Gale, Volume 2, 1974, Volume 15, 1980.
Dictionary of Literary Biography, Volume 88: *Canadian Writers, 1920-1959, Second Series,* Gale, 1989.

PERIODICALS

Canadian Forum, June, 1969.
Canadian Literature, spring, 1972, autumn, 1972, winter, 1973.
Fiddlehead, spring, 1967, summer, 1967.
New Republic, July 2, 1977.
New York Times Book Review, October 9, 1977.

The Record (Sherbrooke, Quebec), November 2, 1984.
Village Voice, March 31, 1966.

* * *

LEAKEY, Louis S(eymour) B(azett) 1903-1972

PERSONAL: Born August 7, 1903, in Kabete, Kenya; died October 1, 1972, in London, England; Kenyan citizen; son of Harry (a missionary) and Mary (a missionary; maiden name, Bazett) Leakey; married Henrietta Witfrida Avern, 1928 (marriage ended); married Mary Douglas Nicol (an anthropologist and archaeologist), 1935; children: (first marriage) one son, one daughter; (second marriage) Richard, Philip, Jonathan. *Education:* Cambridge University, received M.A. and Ph.D. in anthropology.

CAREER: Anthropologist, palaeontologist, and archaeologist. Member of British Museum East African expedition to Tanganyika Territory (now Tanzania), 1924; leader of East African Archaeological Research expeditions, 1926-27, 1928-29, 1931-32, and 1934-35; Cambridge University, Cambridge, England, fellow of St. John's College, 1929-34, Leverhulme Research Fellow, 1933-35, and Jane Ellen Harrison Memorial Lecturer, 1934; Edinburgh University, Edinburgh, Scotland, Munroe Memorial Lecturer, 1936; researcher into customs of Kikuyu for Rhodes Trust, 1937-39; Coryndon Memorial Museum, Nairobi, Kenya, honorary director, 1941-45, curator, 1945-61, honorary keeper of palaeontology and prehistory department, 1961-62; Oxford University, Oxford, England, Herbert Spencer Lecturer, 1960-61; University of Birmingham, Birmingham, England, Huxley Memorial Lecturer, 1961; Regent's Lecturer at University of California, 1963; Yale University, New Haven, Conn., Siliman Lecturer, 1963-64; University of Illinois at Urbana-Champaign, George R. Miller Professor, 1965; honorary fellow of St. John's College, 1966; Cornell University, Ithaca, N.Y., professor-at-large, 1966-72, Andrew D. White Professor-at-Large, 1968; Nairobi College, Nairobi, honorary professor of human anatomy and histology, 1969. Member of government committee to report on Kikuyu Land Tenure, 1929; Pan-African Congress on Prehistory, general secretary, 1947-51, president, 1955-59; member of board of trustees, Royal Kenya National Parks, 1948-62; trustee of Motor Mart Trust 1957. Interpreter for the defense at the trial of Jomo Kenyatta; lecturer. *Wartime service:* Officer in charge of special branch of Criminal Investigations Division (Scotland Yard), Nairobi, 1939-45, handwriting expert, 1943-51.

MEMBER: British Academy (fellow), Geological Society (fellow), Kenya Wild Life Society (trustee, 1957), New York Academy of Science (life member), Explorers Club (life member), East African Kennel Club (vice-president and committee chairman, 1957; judge of Grand Challenge Class of dog show, 1958; president, 1959-60).

AWARDS, HONORS: Cuthbert Peek Prize, 1933, and Royal Medal, 1964, both from Royal Geographical Society; Andree Medal from Swedish Geographical Society, 1933; Rivers Memorial Medal from Royal Anthropological Institute, 1952; Henry Stopes Memorial Medal from Geological Association of London, 1955; Hubbard Medal from National Geographical Society, 1962; Viking Medal from Wenner-Gren Foundation, 1962; Vega Medal (Sweden), 1963; Richard Hopper Day Memorial Medal from Academy of Natural Sciences of Philadelphia, 1964; Haile Selassie Award, 1968; Welcome Medal from Royal African Society, 1968; Science Medal from Academy for Biological Sciences (Italy), 1968; Commander, National Order of Senegal, 1968;

Prestwich Medal from Geological Society of London, 1969; Andre Dumont Medal from Royal Geographical Society of Belgium, 1969. Honorary degrees include LL.D. from University of California, 1963, and from Guelph University, 1969; D.Sc. from University of East Africa, 1965, and from Oxford University.

WRITINGS:

The Stone Age Cultures of Kenya Colony, Cambridge University Press, 1931, new edition, F. Cass, 1971.

Adam's Ancestors: An Up-to-Date Outline of What Is Known About the Origin of Man, Methuen, 1934, 4th edition published as *Adam's Ancestors: An Up-to-Date Outline of the Old Stone Age (Palaeolithic) and What Is Known About Man's Origin and Evolution,* 1953, Harper, 1960.

The Stone Age Races of Kenya, Oxford University Press, 1935, 2nd edition, Anthropological Publishing, 1970.

Kenya: Contrasts and Problems, Methuen, 1936.

Stone Age Africa: An Outline of Prehistory in Africa, Oxford University Press, 1936, reprinted, Negro Universities Press, 1970.

White African (memoirs), Hodder & Stoughton, 1937, reprinted with new introduction by author, Ballantine Books, 1973.

(With wife, Mary Douglas Nicol Leakey) *Excavations at the Njoro River Cave: Stone Age Cremated Burials in Kenya Colony,* Clarendon Press, 1950.

(With Wilfred Edward Le Gros Clark) *The Miocene Hominoidea of East Africa,* British Museum, 1951.

Olduvai Gorge: A Report on the Evolution of the Hand-Axe Culture in Beds I-IV, Cambridge University Press, 1951.

Mau Mau and the Kikuyu, Methuen, 1952, Day, 1954.

(With Camilla Koffler) *Animals in Africa,* Harper, 1953.

Defeating Mau Mau, Methuen, 1954.

Some East African Pleistocene Suidae, British Museum, 1958.

(With Thomas Whitworth) *Notes on the Genus Simopithecus,* Deighton, Bell, 1959.

First Lessons in Kikuyu, East African Literature Bureau, 1959.

The Progress and Evolution of Man in Africa, Oxford University Press, 1961.

Olduvai Gorge: 1951-61, Cambridge University Press, 1965.

Kenya: Contrasts and Problems, Schenkman Publishing Co., 1966.

The Wild Realm: Animals of East Africa, National Geographic Society, 1969.

(With Vanne Morris) *Unveiling Man's Origins: Ten Decades of Thought About Human Evolution,* Schenkman Publishing Co., 1969.

(Editor) *Fossil Vertebrates of Africa,* Academic Press, Volume 1, 1969, Volume 2, 1971, Volume 3, 1973.

(Editor with Jack Hale Prost and Stephanie Prost) *Adam or Ape: A Sourcebook of Discoveries About Early Man,* Schenkman Publishing Co., 1971.

Aggression and Violence in Man: A Dialogue Between Dr. Louis Leakey and Mr. Robert Ardrey, Munger Africana Library, 1971.

By the Evidence: Memoirs, 1932-1951, Harcourt, 1974.

The Southern Kikuyu Before 1903, three volumes, Academic Press, 1977.

Editor of *Proceedings of Pan-African Congress on Prehistory,* Chatto & Windus, 1952. Contributor to *Encyclopaedia Britannica, Chamber's Encyclopaedia,* and *World Encyclopaedia;* also contributor of articles to scientific journals.

WORK IN PROGRESS: A third volume of memoirs left unfinished at time of death.

SIDELIGHTS: Luck was the term often coined by rival anthropologists and archaeologists to dismiss the work and important discoveries of Louis Leakey. For them, it was merely a case of Leakey being in the right spot at the right time. Overlooked, of course, were the long hours of hard work spent digging with dentist's tools, in 110 degree temperatures, and in the most remote areas of East Africa. Also bypassed was the fact that he was digging in the right spot—Africa, at a time when most other prehistorians believed Asia to be the cradle of the human race. In choosing Africa for his work, Leakey had defied those Cambridge dons who had tried to persuade him to reconsider his theories. But Leakey's instincts, and respect for the country of his birth, served him well.

Born in a thatch and mud hut in a Kikuyu tribe village, Leakey was the son of missionaries who had been the first members of their church to work among African tribes. His parents wrapped him up well in cotton wool in order not only to shield him from the leaking roof but also from the tribesmen, who greeted the new arrival with their customary anticurse spit. Leakey grew up learning Kikuyu first, then English; and he always believed that Kikuyu was his best language. Indeed, he claimed to dream in it. From the tribe's children, he learned Kikuyu customs; from the elders, its laws; and "from a hunter of a neighboring Ndorobo tribe, he learned to track and stalk wild animals." At the age of thirteen, Leakey underwent the Kikuyu rites of manhood, the details of which he always refused to discuss. He accepted the name Wakaruigi, or "Son of the Sparrow." Later, he was made a "first-grade elder" of the tribe, and Kikuyu Chief Koinage often referred to him as the "black man with a white face because he is more of an African than a European."

Tutored by his parents until the age of sixteen, Leakey entered British public school in 1919, and soon learned that he was at a distinct disadvantage because of his untraditional African background. He was unfamiliar with cricket, had never learned to swim (crocodiles had prevented it in Africa), and was "innocent of Greek and of first hand encounter with the theatre." Nevertheless, two years later, Leakey enrolled at Cambridge, from which he subsequently received a Ph.D. In his second year at Cambridge, Leakey incurred a head injury during a rugby game and, as a result, suffered from blinding headaches. At the advice of his physician, he took a leave of absence from his studies and joined an expedition bound for Tanzania. As a young boy, Leakey had been interested in ornithology, but when he came across some stone arrowheads while on the trail of wild birds, he abandoned his study of birds in favor of the search for clues to man's distant past. As a result of his Tanzanian experiences, Leakey pursued this growing interest in anthropology and archaeology, and later led four expeditions to Africa for the British Museum.

In 1929, while on a dig in Kenya, Leakey nearly fell off a cliff. He looked down and noticed a hand ax protruding from the rock. After retrieving the artifact, he estimated its age to be about 200,000 years. Experts confirmed his opinion, and Leakey set out on what was to be his life's work. Equally short of funds (the Rockefeller and Carnegie foundations both supported expeditions in Asia) and time, he soon learned that he would have to divide his energies between earning a living as a lecturer and museum curator and his work in Africa. During World War II, he worked for British military intelligence, and left most of the digging to his wife, Mary, and their young son Jonathan. It was estimated that up until the early 1950s, the Leakeys spent only about a week a year at the Olduvai Gorge in northern Tanzania, even though Leakey had first arrived there in 1931.

It was Leakey's work at Olduvai Gorge that altered the accepted family tree of modern man and restructured evolutionary thought about the origins of humankind. First came the discovery of the protohuman *Zinjanthropus,* the "400 scraps of fossilized bone" which formed the skull of a hominid about 1.75 million years old. Leakey originally believed *Zinjanthropus* to be the missing link between prehumans and *Homo sapiens.* He immediately called a press conference at which, with a characteristically flamboyant style, he proudly displayed the skull of "the oldest well-established toolmaker that had ever been found anywhere." Years later he would be forced to retract his statement, but, for the time being, the discovery of *Zinjanthropus* brought much-needed funding from the National Geographic Society, and enabled the Leakeys to carry on their work. Several years later the Leakeys discovered another skull in the same sedimentary layer from which they had extracted *Zinjanthropus.* It certainly was the skull of a hominid, but it resembled modern man more than *Zinjanthropus* did: gone was the gorillalike bony crest across the top of the skull, and the brain case was shaped like modern man's. All factors pointed to the possibility that both Zinjanthropus and this new creature, whom Leakey called *Homo habilis,* had lived together for some time side-by-side. Then, he estimated, *Zinjanthropus* "traveled down a blind alley of evolution" and became extinct. No longer was a linear theory of human evolution defensible. One result of Leakey's work was the subsequent restructuring of man's genealogy. American anthropologist F. Clark Howell called the discovery of *Zinjanthropus* "the event that opened the present modern era of the truly scientific study of man."

Not all the opinions of other anthropologists were as favorable, however, and Leakey was often accused of giving different names to every fossil that he found. "Yet, as much as Leakey was revered as a discoverer," wrote palaeontologist Stephen Jay Gould, "his theoretical approach found little support among his colleagues. . . . Paleontologists are [either] 'splitters' or 'lumpers.' Splitters are analysts: they emphasize the minutest distinctions among objects and give taxonomic status to every difference they can recognize. Lumpers are synthesists: they search for similarities and group together the organisms that share a basic design despite differences in detail. Leakey was a lavish splitter in an age of lumpers."

In spite of those "characteristics that irritated some parts of the scientific world totally, and all parts some of the time—his 'little weakness of rushing to conclusions without being aware of the facts,' his tendency to invent fresh 'genus' to fit each major discovery and his temperamental readiness to expand his personality to fill the role which fame brought him," Louis Leakey was, as Keith Kyle noted, a "genuine scientist." Unlike many other scientists, however, "the remarkable thing about Leakey," wrote Kyle, "was that he liked people, was extremely fluent in communicating with them, and was possessed of charisma in a very marked degree."

Leakey also had a deep regard for African ways. On one occasion during his digging, some Masai cattlemen had brought their beasts too close to the site, and had actually crushed one skull. "Leakey called a baraza," related Boyce Rensburger, "a meeting to discuss important matters with the elders of local clans. . . . After long discussions in Swahili, all agreed that in exchange for Leakey's building two new dams to water their cattle, the elders would beat any herdsmen caught entering the excavation areas. To Leakey it was a fair bargain, for he felt the Masai had as much right to the areas as he did."

Other Leakey discoveries include the fossil of the *Kenyapithecus,* now called *Ramapithecus,* a pithecoid who inhabited the Kenyan highlands about twenty million years ago, and who, he believed, was the distant link between man and ape. In addition to the fossils of hominids, he also unearthed the remains of the *Afrocherus,* a prehistoric pig almost as large as a rhino, the *Pelorovis,* a Pleistocene sheep that stood six feet tall at the shoulders, and the *Simopithecus jonathani,* a giant baboon.

Leakey's panache is evident both in his books and in his reputation as "a witty teacher and lecturer who packed auditoriums in campuses the world over." He inspired Jane Goodall to continue in her work with chimpanzees, and Dian Fossey's study of the endangered mountain gorilla begun under his tutelage. Among his more than twenty works on Africa and his two volumes of memoirs, *By the Evidence,* according to a *Virginia Quarterly Review* critic, impresses "one with the multiplicity of Leakey's accomplishments and the liberality of his understanding of East African problems." Likewise, a *New Yorker* reviewer noted that it "savors of the satisfied adventurer, of spacious opportunities ingeniously and unapologetically seized." And a critic from the *New York Review of Books* declared: "His autobiographies are a joy to read. . . . They tell us much about life in Kenya and about anthropology, but do not really provide the clues to why, sadly, Louis Leakey was never fully accepted as a first-rate anthropologist."

BIOGRAPHICAL/CRITICAL SOURCES:

BOOKS

Cole, Sonia, *Leakey's Luck: The Life of Louis Seymour Bazett Leakey,* 1903-1972, Collins, 1975.
Leakey, Louis S. B., *White African,* Hodder & Stoughton, 1937, reprinted, Ballantine Books, 1973.
Leakey, Louis S. B., *By the Evidence: Memoirs, 1932-1951,* Harcourt, 1974.

PERIODICALS

American Anthropologist, October, 1935.
Geographical Review, July, 1932.
Listener, August 7, 1975.
Nation, June 5, 1954.
Natural History, November, 1974.
Newsweek, July 15, 1974.
New Yorker, March 24, 1975.
New York Herald Tribune Book Review, August 15, 1954.
New York Review of Books, May 29, 1975.
New York Times Book Review, November 17, 1974.
New York Times Magazine, March 3, 1974.
Science, September 17, 1965.
Spectator, December 12, 1952.
Times Literary Supplement, February 14, 1935, October 24, 1936, December 26, 1952, July 22, 1965, January 29, 1971, November 21, 1975.
Virginia Quarterly Review, spring, 1975.

OBITUARIES:

PERIODICALS

Newsweek, October 16, 1972.
New York Times, October 2, 1972.
Saturday Review, October 28, 1972.

LEAR, Peter
See LOVESEY, Peter (Harmer)

* * *

LEARY, Timothy (Francis) 1920-

PERSONAL: Born October 22, 1920, in Springfield, Mass.; son of Timothy (a U.S. Army captain) and Abigail (a teacher; maiden name, Ferris) Leary; married Marianne Busch (a college instructor), December 12, 1944 (died October 22, 1955); married Nena von Schlebrugge (a model; divorced, 1967); married Rosemary Woodruff (an actress), November 11, 1967 (separated, October, 1971); children: (first marriage) Susan, John Busch. *Education:* Attended Holy Cross College, 1938-39, and U.S. Military Academy, 1940-41; University of Alabama, A.B., 1943; Washington State University, M.S., 1946; University of California, Berkeley, Ph.D., 1950.

ADDRESSES: Box 69886, Los Angeles, Calif. 90069. *Agent*—c/o J. P. Tarcher, 9110 Sunset Blvd., Los Angeles, Calif. 90069.

CAREER: University of California, Berkeley, assistant professor, 1950-55; Kaiser Foundation, Oakland, Calif., director of psychiatric research, 1955-58; Harvard University, Cambridge, Mass., lecturer, 1959-63; founder of League for Spiritual Discovery, 1966—; president of Futique Inc. (electronic books), 1985—. Candidate for governor of California, 1969-70. Appeared in motion pictures, including "John Lennon in Montreal," 1971, "Nice Dreams" (with Cheech and Chong), 1981, and "Return Engagement" (with G. Gordon Liddy). Designer of computer software programs, including "Mind Mirror," 1985, "Life Adventure," 1985, and "Neuromancer," 1986. "Stand-up conversationalist" in Los Angeles nightclubs, 1987; guest speaker at colleges. *Military service:* U.S. Army, 1942-45, psychologist; served in medical corps, became sergeant.

MEMBER: American Psychological Association, Screen Actors Guild.

WRITINGS:

(With Helen Lane and others) *Multilevel Measurement of Interpersonal Behavior: A Manual for the Use of the Interpersonal System of Personality,* Psychological Consultation Service, 1956.
Interpersonal Diagnosis of Personality: A Functional Theory and Methodology for Personality Evaluation, Ronald Press, 1957.
(With Ralph Metzner and Richard Alpert) *The Psychedelic Experience: A Manual Based on the Tibetan Book of the Dead,* University Books, 1964.
(Editor with Gunther M. Weil and Metzner) *The Psychedelic Reader: Selected From the Psychedelic Review,* University Books, 1965.
Psychedelic Prayers After the Tao-te-ching, Poets Press, 1966.
(Author of introduction) David Solomon, *LSD: The Consciousness-Expanding Drug,* Putnam, 1966.
High Priest, illustrations by Allen Atwell and Michael Green, World, 1968.
The Politics of Ecstasy, Putnam, 1968.
Jail Notes, introduction by Allen Ginsberg, World, 1970.
Confessions of a Hope Fiend, Bantam, 1973.
What Does Woman Want? (Adventures Along the Schwartzchild Radius), Peace Press, 1976.
Exo-Psychology: A Manual on the Use of the Human Nervous System According to the Instructions of the Manufacturers, Peace Press, 1977, 2nd edition published as *Info-Psychology.*

A Revision of Exo-Psychology, Falcon Press (Phoenix, Ariz.), 1987.

(With Robert Anton Wilson and George A. Koopman) *Neuropolitics: The Sociobiology of Human Metamorphosis,* edited by Daniel Gilbertson and Koopman, illustrations by Cynthia Marsh, Peace Press, 1977, revised edition published as *Neuropolitique,* Falcon Press, 1988.

The Intelligence Agents, Peace Press, 1979.

The Game of Life, Peace Press, 1980.

Changing My Mind Among Others: Lifetime Writings, Prentice-Hall, 1982.

Flashbacks (autobiography), Houghton, 1983.

How To Use Drugs Intelligently, Tarcher, 1983.

Author, with G. Gordon Liddy, of *Return Engagement;* also author of *The Cybernetic Societies of the Twenty-first Century,* 1987.

SOUND RECORDINGS

"The Psychedelic Experience," Folkways Records, 1966.

"Turn On, Tune In, Drop Out," Mercury, 1967.

"You Can Be Anyone, This Time Around," Douglas, 1970.

"A Retrospective From Behind the Prison Walls" [and] "KPFA Press Conference," Big Sur Recordings, 1974.

"American Culture, 1945-1985," Big Sur Recordings, 1977.

Also recorded on "Give Peace a Chance," by Plastic Ono Band, Apple, 1969, and "Seven Up," 1973.

SIDELIGHTS: Once a psychology professor at Harvard University, in the 1960s Leary became one of America's most controversial and influential figures for his outspoken advocacy of the use of LSD (d-lysergic acid diethylamide) and other mind-expanding, psychedelic drugs. Leary energetically publicized his belief in vast spiritual benefits to be gained in the consciousness expansion experienced through hallucinogen use. Soon he found himself spokesperson for a polymorphic movement that regarded him as a guru of "psychedelic utopians," a visionary "prophet of LSD." Known as "Uncle Tim" to his followers, Leary was viewed as a "corrupter of youth" by those who feared the consequences of drug use. Voicing oft-quoted phrases such as "You have to go out of your mind to use your head" and "Turn on, tune in, drop out," Leary emerged from the turbulent decade in the image, for some, of a charlatan prescribing dangerous practices, and, for others, of a leader of true vision.

Leary's first contact with psychedelics came in 1960, while he was still a lecturer at Harvard, and the incident convinced him that psychedelic drugs provide a potential for psychological growth and development. In what he later described as "the deepest religious experience of my life," Leary was introduced to the hallucinogenic "sacred mushrooms" of Mexican religious ceremonies and at once vowed to devote his career to exploring the psychological benefits of mind-expanding drugs. Excited by this prospect, Leary introduced mescaline, psilocybin (the synthetic equivalent of the sacred mushrooms' active ingredient), and other psychedelics to his associates and students at Harvard. In a series of carefully controlled research projects in which he experimented on himself, on associates Richard Alpert (Ram Dass) and Ralph Metzner, and on graduate students, Leary began to collect data and develop theories about the psychological effects of psychedelic drugs. In 1961 Leary's attention was drawn to LSD, also called "acid," a synthetic psychedelic based on a grain fungus and first produced in 1938. One hundred times stronger than psilocybin, LSD soon became the focus of Leary's research. Experimenting on colleagues, students, and inmate volunteers from a local prison, Leary found LSD useful in the treatment of alcoholism, schizophrenia, and other psycho-physiological disorders. By 1962 LSD "trips" were popular among campus underground and avant-garde youth across the United States, and Leary was regarded as the movement's leader.

Controversy over the use of student volunteers in LSD experimentation led Harvard University to dismiss Leary and Alpert in 1963. Together the scientists founded a privately financed research group, the International Foundation for Internal Freedom (IFIF), to study and promote the use of LSD. The foundation's psychedelic study center in Mexico, however, was soon closed down by the Mexican Government and in August, 1963, Leary moved his operations to an estate in Millbrook, near Poughkeepsie, New York. Called the Castilla Center by its new occupants, the four-thousand-acre estate with its sixty-four-room mansion was donated to Leary's experimentation group by William Mellon Hitchcock, a direct descendant of financier Andrew Mellon. At Millbrook Leary continued his experimentation and attracted an ever-changing group of pilgrims curious about or devoted to the psychedelic experience. Though mainly truth-seeking students, Leary's guests included the era's literary and philosophical luminaries, such as William Burroughs, Thomas Pynchon, Aldous Huxley, Allen Ginsberg, and Alan Watts. The growing sphere of LSD proponents revolved around the Castilla Center and Leary.

Initially Leary focused on the biochemical aspect of LSD use. "What we're doing for the mind," Leary told Paul Krassner in a September, 1966, *Realist* interview, "is what the microbiologists did for the external sciences three hundred years ago when they discovered the microscope." Leary claimed that LSD aided users in tapping primordial knowledge stored in the brain in the form of cellular energy. "The great lesson you learn from LSD, from contacting your cells," Leary explained to Krassner, "is that every generation has to re-enact the whole evolutionary drama, and to live a full life you have to go through the *whole* sequence yourself." Drawing on theories of modern biogenetics, Leary described LSD as "simply a particular evolutionary molecule at exactly the moment when it's needed." Leary viewed LSD as a part of the process of the evolution of the human mind toward higher consciousness and foresaw the drug's regular use in intellectual pursuits. "I predict," Leary told Krassner, "that psychedelic drugs will be used in all schools in the very near future as educational devices—not only drugs like marijuana and LSD, to teach kids how to use their sense organs and their cellular equipment effectively—but new and more powerful psycho-chemicals like RNA [ribonucleic acid] and other proteins which are really going to revolutionize our concepts of ourselves and education."

On a trip to India in 1965 Leary converted to Hinduism and added a spiritual dimension to his psychedelic activities. "I consider my work basically religious, because it has as its goal the systematic expansion of consciousness and the discovery of energies within, which men call 'divine,' " Leary remarked in a September, 1966, *Playboy* interview. After local police, led by G. Gordon Liddy, raided the Millbrook community in April, 1966, and arrested four people for possession of drugs, Leary founded the League for Spiritual Discovery, a religious movement that sought constitutional protection for the right to take LSD as a sacramental substance. The League for Spiritual Discovery, its manifesto read, was a religion "dedicated to the ancient sacred sequence of turning on, tuning in, and dropping out." As its leader, Leary called for "the constitutional right to change your own consciousness," and cited as precedent the Native American Church, which is allowed to use the hallucinogen peyote in its religious ceremonies.

Leary's publications during this period reflect his efforts to provide information and instruction on the use of hallucinogens and, influenced by Eastern philosophies and religious texts, reveal Leary's emphasis on the spiritual possibilities of psychedelics. With Ralph Metzner and Richard Alpert, Leary published, in 1964, *The Psychedelic Experience: A Manual Based on the Tibetan Book of the Dead.* This book relates the death and rebirth cycle experienced through psychedelic drugs to the ancient Buddhist text that prepares followers for the after-death experience. It was followed in 1965 by *The Psychedelic Reader,* a selection of pieces first published in *The Psychedelic Review* and edited by Leary, Metzner, and Gunther M. Weil. Leary's 1966 book, *Psychedelic Prayers After the Tao-te-ching,* is loosely based on a third century B.C. Chinese text that lays down the philosophical system of Taoism, a Chinese philosophy and religion involving mystical contemplation. These three books became part of the canon for LSD converts.

While public outcry against the use of LSD began to crescendo, the League for Spiritual Discovery staged multimedia liturgical celebrations in theatres across the country. The psychedelic extravaganzas, according to Elenore Lester in the *New York Times,* were "an attempt to create electronic age ritual drama by wedding mysticism to technology." With appearances by Alpert, Metzner, and Ginsberg, headliner Leary delivered monologues describing the LSD pathway to divinity, including a psychedelic regimen of marijuana once per day and LSD once per week. Reviewing the celebrations in *Saturday Night,* David McReynolds claimed, "As entertainment the show is excellent. As a religious experience I think it's an almost total failure. As a religious movement, close to fraud. Leary struck me as phony—as playing a game. . . . The 'Leary movement' has something about it that is basically cheap. It is a . . . safe, middleclass religion. . . . The best religious insights gained through LSD will, I believe, find expression outside of Leary's movement."

Contrary to McReynolds's comments, Leary's psychedelic movement was not viewed as a "safe, middleclass religion" by most Americans, who witnessed ever-increasing LSD use. Conservative estimates held that by 1967 at least one million Americans had tried LSD at least once, including ten percent of all college students and fifty thousand persons involved in the LSD movement. Many prominent Americans, including comic Steve Allen, Pentagon civil defense planner Herman Kahn, actor Cary Grant, jazz musician Maynard Ferguson, *Time* magazine founder and editor Henry R. Luce, and playwright Clare Boothe Luce, joined Leary in praising the effects of LSD. And the relatively widespread and continually growing use of psychedelic drugs alarmed the middle-aged, middle-class Americans that Leary overtly decried in his public criticism. As he revealed on a British Broadcasting Corporation (BBC) documentary in 1967, "Our avowed aim is of course to bring down the American Empire. . . . The American way of life [is] completely devoted to the pursuit of automobiles and television." Leary further explained in *Playboy* that the social revolution was already taking place: "Current models of social adjustment—mechanized, computerized, socialized, intellectualized, televised, sanforized—make no sense to the new LSD generation, who see clearly that American society is becoming an air-conditioned anthill."

But Leary did not limit himself to criticism of the existing American lifestyle. He further inflamed middle-class parents by advising students to drop out of school. "All of our schools," Leary commented to the BBC, "are paid for by middle-aged parents who want their children to become robots like them. . . . Drop out of school, because schools' education today is the worst narcotic drug of all." Leary told *Playboy* that he viewed dropping

out as essential to consciousness expansion. "It doesn't concern me at all that young people are taking time out from the educational and occupational assembly lines to experiment with consciousness, to dabble with new forms of experience and artistic expression." Leary further explained that the motivational problems of LSD drop-outs would not remain problems: "In our technological society of the future, the problem will be not to get people to work, but to develop graceful, fulfilling ways of living a more serene, beautiful and creative life. Psychedelics will help to point the way."

Leary increased public outrage by defining the psychedelic experience in sexual terms. At the dawn of the Sexual Revolution, Leary's statements, such as "one of the great purposes of an LSD session is sexual union," had the power to shock and enrage. As Leary himself admitted to *Playboy:* "It's socially dangerous enough to say that LSD helps you find divinity and helps you discover yourself. You're already in trouble when you say that. But then if you announce that the psychedelic experience is basically a sexual experience, you're asking to bring the whole middle-aged, middle-class monolith down on your head."

Reports of deeply disturbing LSD-induced experiences, or "bad trips," as they were called, brought more public censure upon Leary. *Playboy* quoted a study that described LSD-induced psychoses, and in 1967 the parents of a youth who killed himself while under the influence of LSD brought a six-hundred-thousand-dollar lawsuit against Leary. Leary answered by continually stressing his conviction that LSD should be used only under controlled conditions. He told *Playboy* that "it's tremendously important that the LSD session be conducted in a protected place, that the person be prepared and that he have an experienced guide to support and shield him from intrusion and interruption." "The person who has an LSD session in a surrounding which is ugly and disharmonious, whether that be a psychiatric clinic or a pad or a penthouse, is naive and foolish," Leary warned in the *Realist* interview. "Every case of prolonged LSD psychosis," Leary insisted to *Playboy,* "is the fault not of the drug nor of the drug taker, but of the people around him who lose their cool and call the cops or the doctors."

Even as Leary defended his ideas against increasing criticism from some segments of American society, his popularity with American youth soared. Sporting blue and orange buttons that read "Leary Is God," college students attended films based on Leary's psychedelic celebrations and listened to companion recordings. On January 14, 1967, Leary and Ginsberg appeared at a "Human Be-In" in San Francisco that drew fifty thousand participants. A month later the League for Spiritual Discovery opened a psychedelic center near Greenwich Village in Manhattan to dispense information about the psychedelic experience and to provide a place for meditation and spiritual communion. Leary was optimistic about the future of the "LSD generation." He asserted to *Playboy* that "it's the college kids who are turning on—the smartest and most promising of the youngsters. What an exciting prospect: a generation of creative youngsters refusing to march in step, refusing to go to offices, refusing to sign up on the installment plan, refusing to climb aboard the treadmill." In a documentary broadcast by the National Broadcasting Company (NBC) in May, 1967, Leary elaborated: "The kids in the United States who are taking LSD tend to be from our best colleges. . . . It's Berkeley. It's Harvard. It's Yale. It's Chicago where you find the LSD users. These are the kids who are searching. They want more. They don't want Vietnam; they don't want race riots; they don't want IBM computer security checks. They want more."

As more Americans began to question their values and lifestyles, some seeking alternatives within Leary's movement, Leary became convinced that America was on the verge of societal revolution. Leary asserted to *Playboy* that his psychedelic regimen "will enable each person to realize that he is not a game-playing robot put on this planet to be given a Social Security number and to be spun on the assembly line of school, college, career, insurance, funeral, goodbye." "Our side always wins," Leary proclaimed to a Michigan State University audience in December, 1966. "The young generation always wins new rights for itself within 15 or 20 years when it grows up and takes over society . . . you're going to see in your lifetime the LSD orthodoxy, the LSD sacrament." On the 1967 NBC documentary Leary declared: "I predict that within 15 years . . . we'll see an LSD orthodoxy in this country. You will see an LSD President. A pot-smoking Supreme Court." "You'll probably hear my name invoked to put down the next generation of visionaries," he concluded in his Michigan State University speech. "Don't let it happen." When Leary left New York for California in May, 1968, he maintained his optimistic stance. "This summer will be a crucial period in history," Leary was quoted in the *Village Voice*. "I think it will be all right. Can anyone think of something to worry about?"

Although the next few years brought much cause for worry on Leary's part, the self-proclaimed visionary retained his conviction that a new era was beginning. In 1969 Leary announced his campaign for the governorship of California but commented to *Village Voice* reporter Steve Lerner: "It's our hope that by the time the election comes around the state will be so turned on that I won't need to run." Yet Leary's movement seemed already to have lost momentum. Lerner recalled, "I occasionally felt his irrepressible optimism was a hang-over from the flower-power season which wilted so quickly." Indeed, Leary's popularity began to dwindle. *Washington Post* staff writer Philip D. Carter, reporting on the New Worlds Drug Symposium in March, 1969, called Leary a "fading guru," and at an "awakening" on June 25, 1969, in Iowa City, fewer than one thousand participants gathered to hear Leary speak on LSD.

Book critics noted a similar decline in Leary's popularity as author. His two 1968 books, *High Priest* and *The Politics of Ecstasy,* were aimed at a readership that, critics felt, Leary could no longer command. In *High Priest,* a diary of Leary's most important psychedelic experiences, Leary commends the continuation of his movement to his young followers but, as reviewer Rollo May noted in the *New York Times Book Review,* "young people to whom Leary mistakenly entrusts his work, have largely exhausted 'the drug routine,' and moved on to something more complete." *New Republic* critic David Sanford asserted that Leary's "rhetoric has a patina of phoniness. One wonders whether he believes what he says or whether his shows are commercial put-ons designed to seduce and make money." The *Times Literary Supplement* agreed: "One has the impression that one half of Dr. Leary is desperately anxious that what he stands for—the religious dimension of L.S.D.—should be taken seriously, but the other half of him constantly thwarts his purpose, for this second half is obsessively uncritical, sensational and sometimes plain stupid." In *Newsweek* Howard Junker concluded: "The charms of psychedelia have faded, and author Leary suffers accordingly."

Then Leary's life changed dramatically, for in early 1970, after years of litigation, his protracted court battles resulted in convictions and prison sentences. Leary's legal troubles had begun in 1965 when he was arrested in Laredo, Texas. Leary and his daughter had been trying to cross the border to Mexico, but had

been turned back by Mexican officials. On re-entering the U.S., Leary was stopped by American authorities who subsequently found less than half an ounce of marijuana in his vehicle. Leary was tried on the charge of failure to pay tax on the marijuana as he brought it into the country. He was convicted in 1966 and sentenced to thirty years imprisonment, but on appeal the U.S. Supreme Court overturned the decision. The Supreme Court ruling explained that the marijuana tax law of which Leary was in violation was unconstitutional because it required self-incrimination, thus opposing the Fifth Amendment. Leary was then retried in Laredo on smuggling charges and was sentenced, in February, 1970, to ten years imprisonment.

Meanwhile, in December, 1968, Leary was driving a borrowed automobile in Laguna Beach, California, when he was stopped by police. They arrested Leary after discovering two marijuana cigarettes in the car's ashtray. Leary was convicted of possession of marijuana and in March, 1970, was sentenced to ten years imprisonment to be served consecutively, not concurrently, with his Texas sentencing. Bail pending appeal was denied and Leary was sent immediately to a minimum security prison near San Luis Obispo, California. While Leary supporters decried the harsh sentencing as scapegoating, and "Free Timothy Leary" slogans appeared across the country, many felt that after a decade as leader of the psychedelic movement Leary, like his cult, had been justly eclipsed.

Within six months, however, Leary was once again in the news. In mid-September, 1970, Leary's wife Rosemary, in conjunction with the radical Weather Underground, arranged Leary's escape from prison. A month later he and Rosemary appeared in Algeria, where they were granted political asylum. Leary's 1970 book, *Jail Notes,* details scenes from prison and narrates his escape to Algeria. Leary and his wife took up residence in Algiers with fugitive Eldridge Cleaver and Cleaver's exiled Black Panther Party. While with the Panthers, the Learys traveled through the Middle East and attempted to visit commandos in Jordan to express their solidarity with the homeless Palestinians. In February, 1971, however, a rift, reportedly engineered by the FBI, developed between Cleaver and Leary. Leary then spent eighteen months in Switzerland, and eventually arrived in Afghanistan.

As *Crawdaddy* writer Nancy Naglin related, in early 1973 Leary was "kidnapped in Afghanistan by American agents, stuffed into a cab at gunpoint, and under the subterfuge of being taken to Beirut, wound up in California." Leary's 1973 book, *Confessions of a Hope Fiend,* presents adventures from Leary's underground life in Algeria and Switzerland, and recounts his capture in Afghanistan. His lawyer claimed Leary had escaped from prison in a state of involuntary LSD flashback intoxication, but the defense was not effective, and Leary was found guilty of prison escape, receiving a sentence of six months to five years imprisonment. Leary, who in 1966 said "I know that the only real prisons are *internal.* . . . If you're free in mind and heart, you're not in trouble," proclaimed from Folsom prison in December, 1973: "I think I belong in American society. I think that a society that imprisons its philosophers is playing with very bad magic. You can't imprison ideas. . . . It's a scandal, a national scandal, that I'm here."

Leary's eventual release from prison was in part engineered by a mysterious woman named Joanna Harcourt-Smith (or, as *New Yorker* referred to her, Joanna Harcourt-Smith Leary). According to Naglin, Harcourt-Smith met Leary, who was no longer traveling with Rosemary, in Switzerland. Harcourt-Smith was with Leary when he was kidnapped in Afghanistan, accompanied him when he was returned to the United States, and visited him in twenty-nine jails over the course of three years. Naglin credits Harcourt-Smith with the organization of the grand jury before which Leary allegedly testified, in return for parole consideration, against the activists who had orchestrated his prison escape. Leary did testify as a government witness, but, he told *Crawdaddy*'s Naglin, "I didn't get out of prison at all because of any trade or deal." Leary was paroled in March, 1975, but began serving another sentence. He was released April 21, 1976.

Six months later, in September, 1976, Leary lectured to three thousand students at Princeton University. His theme was not drugs, but, in Naglin's words, "a kind of scientific approach to self-development." He advocated *Skylab/*space shuttle activities and efforts to increase human intelligence and life-span in a movement called SMILE (Space Migration, Increased Intelligence, Life Extension). In 1977 Leary published two books. One, *Exo-Psychology*, develops the author's SMILE theories on ways for humans to evolve into pure, intelligent, disembodied energy. *Neuropolitics* presents Leary's essays on figures such as songwriter Bob Dylan and mass murderer Charles Manson, and on institutions such as NASA and the media. Leary's activities in the late seventies included lecture tours and the formation of Starseed, a cooperative to colonize space. In 1982 Leary toured on a debate circuit with convicted Watergate conspirator and former nemesis G. Gordon Liddy, who, as assistant district attorney in Duchess County, New York, was involved in a 1966 raid on Leary's Millbrook community. The debate generated public interest, drawing an audience of two thousand in Berkeley, California. "For if all the world's a stage," commented David N. Rosenthal in the *Detroit Free Press,* "Timothy Leary and George Gordon Liddy are two of its most adept players."

The image of Leary as an insincere performer has followed him throughout his life as a public figure. Yet commentators hesitate to discredit him completely. In 1969 *Village Voice* writer Steve Lerner explained: "Dr. Tim is hard to pin down. His sense of humor about himself, . . . what's going on in America, and everything else allows him to remain elusive, slightly mysterious." Naglin, in 1977, agreed: "Leary runs a thin line between being a pretentious con man and a folksy rainmaker spinning a dozen dreams; then by a single glance or joke, he pokes fun at himself." "Weathered by years of over-exposure," Lerner wrote in 1969, "Dr. Tim seems to have the knack for keeping just ahead of the time without looking like he's just keeping up with the young." "The role Leary relishes is the Pied Piper," Naglin echoed. "He thrives on discovering something—or, in the case of space migration, latching on to it—and then spreading the news. If anybody has managed to manufacture celebrity as well as notoriety out of curiosity, Leary has." In 1967 Leary offered what may be the definitive assessment of his role as bringer of truth: "Chances are that I'm wrong because, as a visionary prophet, you know, it's one out of a hundred that you are right and ninety-nine out of a hundred that you are a nut. That's the chance of the game, but history will tell."

BIOGRAPHICAL/CRITICAL SOURCES:

PERIODICALS

Booklist, October 1, 1977, February 15, 1978.
Books and Bookmen, May, 1970, January, 1974.
Crawdaddy, March, 1977.
Detroit Free Press, January 4, 1973, April 30, 1982.
Esquire, July, 1968.
Fifth Estate, December 15-31, 1966, March 1-15, 1967.
IT, October 18-31, 1968.
L'Express, March 27-April 2, 1967, November 23-29, 1970.
Listener, August 31, 1967.

Los Angeles Times, December 11, 1987, December 22, 1987.
National Review, November 5, 1968.
National Observer, December 18, 1967.
New Republic, October 26, 1968.
Newsweek, November 4, 1968, February 8, 1971, January 29, 1973, March 10, 1975, May 3, 1976, September 13, 1976.
New Yorker, December 3, 1973.
New York Times, December 4, 1966, January 1, 1967, May 7, 1967, March 22, 1970, October 21, 1970, October 28, 1970, September 14, 1971, February 1, 1973.
New York Times Book Review, January 26, 1969.
Playboy, September, 1966, December, 1968.
Psychology Today, July, 1983.
Realist, September, 1966.
Saturday Night, February, 1967.
Spectator, February 21, 1970.
Time, December 8, 1967, May 30, 1969, April 16, 1973.
Times Literary Supplement, March 12, 1970.
Variety, July 2, 1969.
Village Voice, January 12, 1967, January 18, 1967, February 16, 1967, February 23, 1967, August 3, 1967, October 5, 1967, November 30, 1967, May 16, 1968, October 10, 1968, December 12, 1968, May 22, 1969, July 3, 1969.
Washington Post, February 7, 1968, March 3, 1969, March 18, 1970, October 21, 1970, June 10, 1983.
Yale Review, spring, 1969.

*   *   *

LEAVIS, F(rank) R(aymond)   1895-1978

PERSONAL: Born July 14, 1895, in Cambridge, England; died April 14, 1978, in Cambridge; son of Harry Leavis; married Queenie Dorothy Roth (an author and critic), 1929 (died 1981); children: two sons, one daughter. *Education:* Emmanuel College, Cambridge, history tripos and English tripos.

ADDRESSES: Home—12 Bulstrode Gardens, Cambridge, England.

CAREER: Founder and editor with wife, Q. D. Leavis, of *Scrutiny* (a quarterly review), 1932-53; Cambridge University, Downing College, Cambridge, England, fellow, 1936-62, university reader in English, 1959-62, honorary fellow, 1962-64; University of York, Heslington, York, England, honorary visiting professor of English, 1965; University of Wales, Cathays Park, Cardiff, Cheltenham Lecturer, 1968, visiting professor, 1969; University of Bristol, Bristol, England, Churchill Professor of English, 1970.

MEMBER: American Academy of Arts and Sciences (honorary member).

AWARDS, HONORS: Litt.D. from University of Leeds, 1965, and University of York, 1967; LL.D. from University of Aberdeen, 1970.

WRITINGS:

CRITICISM

Mass Civilization and Minority Culture, Gordon Fraser, 1930, reprinted, Folcroft Press, 1969.
D. H. Lawrence, Novelist, Gordon Fraser, 1930, revised edition, Chatto & Windus, 1950, Knopf, 1956, reprinted, Simon & Schuster, 1972.
New Bearings in English Poetry: A Study of the Contemporary Situation, Chatto & Windus, 1932, reprinted, Norwood Edi-

tions, 1976, new edition, George W. Stewart, 1950, reprinted, Penguin Books, 1972.

How to Teach Reading: A Primer for Ezra Pound, Gordon Fraser, 1932, reprinted, Norwood Editions, 1976.

For Continuity (essays), Minority Press, 1933, reprinted, Books for Libraries, 1968.

(With Denys Thompson) *Culture and Environment: The Training of Critical Awareness,* Chatto & Windus, 1933, reprinted, 1960, Greenwood Press, 1977.

(Editor and author of introduction) *Towards Standards of Criticism: Selections from "The Calendar of Modern Letters," 1925-1927,* Lawrence & Wishart, 1933, reprinted, Folcroft Press, 1974.

(Editor and author of introduction) *Determinations: Critical Essays,* Chatto & Windus, 1934, Folcroft, 1969.

Revaluation: Tradition and Development in English Poetry, Chatto & Windus, 1936, reprinted, Greenwood Press, 1975, new edition, 1948, Norton, 1963, reprinted, Chatto & Windus, 1983.

Education and the University: A Sketch for an "English School," Chatto & Windus, 1943, new edition, 1961, reprinted, Books for Libraries Press, 1972, 2nd edition, Cambridge University Press, 1979.

The Great Tradition: George Eliot, Henry James, and Joseph Conrad, George W. Stewart, 1948, new edition, Chatto & Windus, 1962, New York University Press, 1963, reprinted, 1980.

(Editor and author of introduction) John Stuart Mill, *On Bentham and Coleridge,* Chatto & Windus, 1950, George W. Stewart, 1951, published as *Mill on Bentham and Coleridge,* Cambridge University Press, 1980.

The Common Pursuit (essays), Chatto & Windus, 1952, New York University Press, 1964, Hogarth Press, 1984.

Two Cultures? The Significance of C. P. Snow (Richmond Lecture, 1962), Chatto & Windus, 1962, published with new preface, Pantheon, 1963.

(Author of retrospect) *Scrutiny,* Volumes 1-20 reissued in one set, Cambridge University Press, 1963.

"Anna Karenina," and Other Essays, Chatto & Windus, 1967, Pantheon, 1968.

(Editor) *A Selection from Scrutiny,* two volumes, Cambridge University Press, 1968.

(With wife, Q. D. Leavis) *Lectures in America,* Pantheon, 1969.

English Literature in Our Time and the University (Clark Lectures, Trinity College, Cambridge University, 1967), Chatto & Windus, 1969.

(With Q. D. Leavis) *Dickens: The Novelist,* Chatto & Windus, 1970, Pantheon, 1971, 3rd edition, 1973.

Nor Shall My Sword: Discourses on Pluralism, Compassion, and Social Hope, Barnes & Noble, 1972.

Letters in Criticism, edited and introduced by John Tasker, Chatto & Windus, 1974.

The Living Principle: English as a Discipline of Thought, Oxford University Press, 1975.

Thought, Words and Creativity: Art and Thought in Lawrence, Chatto & Windus, 1976.

F. R. Leavis's Recent Uncollected Lectures, edited and introduced by Abdel-Azim Suwailem, Anglo-Egyptian Bookshop, 1976.

Reading Out Poetry, and Eugenio Montale: A Tribute, Queen's University of Belfast, 1979.

The Critic as Anti-Philosopher: Essays and Papers, edited by G. Singh, Chatto & Windus, 1982, University of Georgia Press, 1983.

The Common Pursuit, Hogarth Press, 1984.

Valuation in Criticism and Other Essays, edited by G. Singh, Cambridge University Press, 1986.

Contributor to Marius Bewley's *The Complex Fate,* 1952, and C. Gilliard's *A History of Switzerland,* 1955.

OTHER

D. H. Lawrence (pamphlet), Minority Press, 1930, reprinted, Haskell House, 1972.

Scrutiny: A Retrospect (pamphlet), Cambridge University Press, 1963.

Gerard Manley Hopkins: Reflections after Fifty Years (Hopkins Society Annual Lecture, March 1, 1971), [London], 1971.

F. R. Leavis's Recent Uncollected Lectures, edited with an introduction by Abdel-Azim Suwailem, Anglo-Egyptian Bookshop (Cairo), c. 1976.

Also author of introduction to Samuel L. Clemens's *The Tragedy of Pudd'nhead Wilson,* 1955; author of pamphlets on Gerard Manley Hopkins, D. H. Lawrence, and C. P. Snow.

SIDELIGHTS: F. R. Leavis resigned from his position at Cambridge University after a controversy surrounding the selection of a person of opposing views as a fellow in English. He wrote of his quarterly and its influence on the literary world: "In the strength of the essential Cambridge which it consciously and explicitly represented, *Scrutiny* not only survived the hostility of the institutional academic powers; it became—who now questions it?—the clear triumphant justification to the world of Cambridge as a human centre. In Cambridge it was the vitalizing force that gave the English School its reputation and influence, and its readers in the world at large, small as the subscribing public was, formed an incomparably influential community. . . . It established a new critical idiom and a new conception of the nature of critical thought."

In *New Bearings in English Poetry,* according to D. W. Harding in *Scrutiny,* "Leavis's main concern with separate poems is to relate them to the rest of the poet's work; just as, in turn, the whole of the poet's work is related to the culture in which it was produced. His argument is, in brief, that poetry in the nineteenth century became established in a tradition of remoteness from other human activities, not merely from industrialism, but also from pursuits demanding fine intelligence, such as research and speculation in science." Harding continues that Leavis "looks for an attitude to poetry that will allow it to become not merely the poet's comment on his life but an integral part of his life and growth. He looks too for a way of using language which will make this attitude effective." In a *Spectator* review, Richard Church writes: "Being passionately sincere in his devotion to the cause of keeping literature abreast of the metamorphosis of life, he has planned to fight in desperate earnestness for his principles. For this purpose he wants a clear space, and has accordingly brushed away the whole of the nineteenth century with the exception of one figure, Gerard Manley Hopkins." However, Church believes, "In spite of his bias and his deliberated restrictions, Mr. Leavis is a critic who has added something valuable to the theory of English poetry."

Although a *New Statesman and Nation* contributor suggests that "Leavis's criticism is a train that stops at few stations, and perhaps it is not unfair to add that passengers are expected to travel rather obviously first-class," Geoffrey Grigson states in the *Saturday Review,* "Only those prepared to take trouble, to think, to admit the possibility that they have erred, to be humble, those whose minds are not oyster shells whose age still allows them to grow physically or in understanding, only those should be allowed to read this important book. It is not compromising. It states a view and states it with courage and good pleading, and it is informed with needle insight."

Alan Lelchuk estimated in his review of *"Anna Karenina," and Other Essays:* "Leavis cares for literature and for standards—and in an age when most literary criticism consists of a pedestrian professionalism and when literary standards are too frequently abandoned for this cause or that promotion, Leavis is a welcome reminder that literary criticism can be a serious discipline." Edward Thomas wrote of Leavis: "His lack of style is as bad in its way as the self-conscious style of the belletrists. Leavis does love great literature, and this comes out in his always relevant and sensitive choice of quotation, yet the very contrast between the language of creative literature and his own critical language is to me symptomatic of a wrong-headed if honourable approach."

BIOGRAPHICAL/CRITICAL SOURCES:

BOOKS

Contemporary Literary Criticism, Volume 24, Gale, 1983.
Cornelius, D. K., and Edwin S. Vincent, *Cultures in Conflict: Perspectives on the Snow-Leavis Controversy,* Scott, Foresman, 1964.
Enright, D. J., *Conspirators and Poets,* Dufour, 1966.
Hayman, Ronald, *Leavis,* Rowman & Littlefield, 1977.
McKenzie, D. F., and M. P. Allum, *F. R. Leavis: A Check List, 1924-1964,* Chatto & Windus, 1966.
Narasimhaiah, C. D., and others, editors, *F. R. Leavis: Some Aspects of His Work,* Rao & Raghauan, 1963.
Walsh, William, *F. R. Leavis,* Indiana University Press, 1980.

PERIODICALS

Antioch Review, winter, 1969, spring, 1976.
Books Abroad, summer, 1968, summer, 1969, winter, 1970.
Books and Bookmen, January, 1968.
Book World, August 10, 1969.
Canadian Forum, October, 1968.
Christian Science Monitor, December 3, 1964, January 22, 1968, June 12, 1969.
Commentary, July, 1968.
Commonweal, October 25, 1968.
Listener, November 30, 1967.
London Magazine, March, 1968, April, 1969.
Nation, September 9, 1968, June 9, 1969.
New Leader, August 26, 1968.
New Republic, June 15, 1968, May 22, 1971.
New Statesman, December 8, 1967, January 31, 1969.
New Yorker, June 28, 1969.
New York Herald Tribune Book Review, July 15, 1956.
New York Review of Books, September 26, 1968, June 1, 1978.
New York Times, March 31, 1965.
New York Times Book Review, December 21, 1975.
Observer Review, January 4, 1970.
Saturday Review, May 18, 1963.
South Atlantic Quarterly, winter, 1985.
Spectator, April 12, 1968, September 13, 1975, August 28, 1976.
Times Literary Supplement, November 30, 1967, July 25, 1968, March 20, 1969, December 4, 1969, April 23, 1970, December 25, 1970, July 21, 1972, October 17, 1975, October 1, 1976, December 10, 1982, June 12, 1987.

OBITUARIES:

PERIODICALS

Times (London), February 10, 1983.
Universities Quarterly, winter, 1975.
Washington Post, April 19, 1978.

LEBOWITZ, Fran(ces Ann) 1951(?)-

PERSONAL: Born in Morristown, N.J.; daughter of Harold and Ruth Lebowitz (furniture store proprietors).

ADDRESSES: Home—New York, N.Y.

CAREER: Writer. Previously worked at a number of "colorful and picturesque" jobs in New York City, including bulk mailing, taxi driving, apartment cleaning, poetry reading, and selling advertising for *Changes* magazine.

WRITINGS:

HUMOROUS ESSAYS

Metropolitan Life, Dutton, 1978.
Social Studies, Random House, 1981.

Former author of columns, "I Cover the Waterfront," in *Interview,* and "The Lebowitz Report," in *Mademoiselle,* 1977-79. Contributor of book and film reviews to *Changes* magazine.

WORK IN PROGRESS: A novel.

SIDELIGHTS: "Fran Lebowitz is not only the funniest woman in America," Edmund White writes in the *Washington Post Book World,* "she is also the guardian of the proprieties. Like all satirists she is a moralist, and like most moralists she is conservative. She is for the eternal verities of sleep, civilized conversation and cigarette smoking. The list of what she is against is somewhat longer."

As author of two bestselling books, *Metropolitan Life* and *Social Studies,* and a monthly column published in *Interview* magazine, Lebowitz has become recognized as a talented author of satirical essays on the trendy aspects of urban life. Descriptions of Lebowitz have run the gamut from "daring" by *New York Times* reviewer Anatole Broyard, and "right on the mark" by Jean Strouse in *Newsweek,* to "an unlikely and perhaps alarming combination of Mary Hartman and Mary McCarthy" by John Leonard in the *New York Times.* She has also been compared to various other humorists, notably Erma Bombeck, Dorothy Parker, and Oscar Wilde.

"[Lebowitz] disapproves of virtually everything, particularly fads, trends, and the relaxation of social and personal restraints in general," remarks Vic Sussman in the *Washington Post Book World.* Scot Haller comments in the *Saturday Review:* "Chronicling the baroque customs and bizarre behavior of the American species near the end of the 20th century, Lebowitz sounds like Dorothy Parker in Gomorrah, or Emily Post in hysterics. From cafe society to the coffee-klatsch crowd, no social set or disorder escapes her infectious wrath." And finally, Paul Rudnick observes in *New Times* that "Lebowitz's pose is neither establishment lackey nor avant-garde artiste; she has followed the Noel Coward tradition of an intensely civilized, titillating frivolity. Her work is marvelously entertaining and intentionally superficial; any subversiveness is masked by a declaration of triviality. She can insult anyone she likes, as long as the offense is smothered in charm and wit. It is a remarkably difficult tightrope to navigate."

Lebowitz's first book, *Metropolitan Life,* was generally greeted with overwhelmingly favorable reviews and soon became a bestseller. Richard Locke, for example, describes *Metropolitan Life* as a "remarkable collection of satirical pieces." Continues the critic in his *New York Times Book Review* article: "Though she is young in years, her book *Metropolitan Life* exhibits an exceptional ferocity and tone of camp authority that deserve attention. She may lack the mimetic range and dramatic flair of her distinguished elders—she tends toward the firm didactic statement or a desperate Basic English sneer—but she epitomizes the 70's New York know-it-all fashion-magazine/artistic world, and I confess I'm head over heels at her feet." And A. J. Anderson writes in *Library Journal* of *Metropolitan Life:* "Unpredictable variety is the keynote of [Lebowitz's] musings; she discourses on everything from the pros and cons of children to digital clocks and pocket calculators, always projecting a light-hearted and sometimes nonsensical view of things."

One reviewer who does not agree with those who praise *Metropolitan Life* is Madora McKenzie. In a *Christian Science Monitor* review, McKenzie writes: "Apparently Miss Lebowitz wrote these pieces while sucking on lemon drops, because sour grapes crop up so often. . . . All her imagination and energies are devoted to exposing and ridiculing indignities and indemnities of life; she cannot seem to come up with any palatable alternatives." However, Jill Robinson remarks in the that *Metropolitan Life* "introduces an important humorist in the classic tradition. The satire is principled, the taste impeccable—there is character here as well as personality. . . . Astringent, meticulous with language, Miss Lebowitz is a sort of Edwin Newman for the chic urban-decay set."

In general, Lebowitz's second book, *Social Studies,* was greeted with the same degree of enthusiasm as *Metropolitan Life.* Hall, again writing in *Saturday Review,* declares that "for the most part, *Social Studies* is a textbook example of astute, acerbic social comedy. . . . The quick-witted, quick-tempered Lebowitz may be the funniest chronic complainer on the scene." And Anatole Broyard comments in the *New York Times* that one of Lebowitz's most entertaining qualities is that "she never gets used to anything. She experiences customs and situations as if they were all done on purpose to her. And the funniest thing of all is that she's right."

Reviewing *Social Studies* for the *Los Angeles Times Book Review,* Elaine Kendall maintains that "most of the time [Lebowitz is] both original and brave, taking on subjects everyone would like to laugh at but few people dare—highly charged topics that arouse emotional response, some of it furious." Finally, Peter Grier states in the *Christian Science Monitor* that in *Social Studies* Lebowitz "makes W. C. Fields look like St. Francis of Assisi. . . . Not everyone may think Fran Lebowitz is funny. . . . *Social Studies* might offend you. Then again, as Lebowitz says, 'Being offended is the natural consequence of leaving one's home.' "

In her *Los Angeles Times Book Review* article on *Social Studies,* Kendall speculates on why Lebowitz's form of satire is so successful while that of other writers fails. Kendall writes: "Other satirists bite; Lebowitz nibbles. They're corrosive while she's just tart." Even so, writes Glenn Collins in the *New York Times Book Review,* "Lebowitz's wit will not be appreciated by all of the people all of the time. . . . Fran Lebowitz is not exactly brimming over with human compassion. Hers is not an Up-With-People view." While this may be the case, Kendall states that "the humorist who worries excessively about hurt feelings soon runs out of material and winds up doing trite monographs on smog, the only target with no organization dedicated to its defense. If you want to be funny for more than a week or so, you have to be willing to take chances and risk unpopularity."

Concludes Sussman in the *Washington Post Book World:* "Those unfamiliar with Lebowitz might think her a moralist, an elitist, a snob. She is all those. But she is an equal-opportunity snob, venting her disdain regardless of one's race, disability, sexual persuasion, or for that matter, species. Lebowitz is unashamedly

Lebowitz, thank goodness, a funny, urbane, intelligent one-woman bulwark against cultural ticky-tack, creeping mellowness, and the excesses of what [H. L.] Mencken dubbed 'boobus Americanus.' "

BIOGRAPHICAL/CRITICAL SOURCES:

BOOKS

Contemporary Literary Criticism, Gale, Volume 11, 1979, Volume 36, 1986.

PERIODICALS

Bookviews, September, 1978.
Christian Science Monitor, March 15, 1978.
Crawdaddy, June, 1978.
Esquire, August, 1981.
Harper, May, 1978.
Library Journal, April 1, 1978, August, 1981.
Los Angeles Times Book Review, August 30, 1981.
Ms., May, 1978.
New Statesman, February 19, 1982.
Newsweek, April 10, 1978, September 14, 1981.
New Times, July 10, 1978.
New York, September 14, 1981.
New York Times, March 31, 1978, September 2, 1981.
New York Times Book Review, March 26, 1978, April 23, 1978, July 15, 1979, August 23, 1981, February 28, 1982.
People, September 4, 1978.
Saturday Review, April 15, 1978, August, 1981.
Time, May 29, 1978.
Washington Post Book World, April 30, 1978, June 5, 1978, August 30, 1981.

* * *

le CARRE, John
See CORNWELL, David (John Moore)

* * *

LEE, Andrew
See AUCHINCLOSS, Louis (Stanton)

* * *

LEE, (Nelle) Harper 1926-

PERSONAL: Born April 28, 1926, in Monroeville, Ala.; daughter of Amasa Coleman (a lawyer) and Frances (Finch) Lee. *Education:* Attended Huntington College, 1944-45; studied law at University of Alabama, 1945-49; studied one year at Oxford University. *Politics:* Republican. *Religion:* Methodist.

ADDRESSES: Home—Monroeville, Ala. *Office*—c/o McIntosh & Otis, Inc., 18 East 41st St., New York, N.Y. 10017.

CAREER: Airline reservation clerk with Eastern Air Lines and British Overseas Airways, New York, N.Y., during the 1950s; left to devote full time to writing. Member, National Council on Arts, 1966-72.

AWARDS, HONORS: Pulitzer Prize, 1961, Alabama Library Association award, 1961, Brotherhood Award of National Conference of Christians and Jews, 1961, *Bestsellers'* paperback of the year award, 1962, all for *To Kill a Mockingbird.*

WRITINGS:

To Kill a Mockingbird (novel; Literary Guild selection, Book-of-the-Month Club alternate, *Reader's Digest* condensed book), Lippincott, 1960, Popular Library, 1962, large print edition, National Aid to Visually Handicapped, 1965.

Contributor to *Vogue*.

MEDIA ADAPTATIONS: To Kill a Mockingbird was adapted into a movie by Horton Foote and released in 1962. The book was adapted into a play by Christopher Sergel and produced in England in 1987.

SIDELIGHTS: To Kill a Mockingbird, a first novel, received almost unanimous critical acclaim. It is a story narrated by a six-year-old Southern girl whose father, an attorney, defends a Negro accused of the rape of a white woman. Told with "a rare blend of wit and compassion" (*Booklist*), it moves "unconcernedly and irresistibly back and forth between being sentimental, tough, melodramatic, acute, and funny," according to the *New Yorker*. Keith Waterhouse, a British novelist, believes that "Miss Lee does well what so many American writers do appallingly: she paints a true and lively picture of life in an American small town. And she gives freshness to a stock situation." Richard Sullivan writes: "the unaffected young narrator uses adult language to render the matter she deals with, but the point of view is cunningly restricted to that of a perceptive, independent child. . . . Casually, on the side, as it were, *To Kill a Mockingbird* is a novel of strong contemporary national significance. . . . But first of all it is a story so admirably done that it must be called both honorable and engrossing." Lee considers the novel to be a simple love story.

Lee, whose family is related to Robert E. Lee, writes slowly from noon until evening, completing a page or two a day. She considers the law, with its emphasis on logical thought, an excellent training for a writer.

To Kill a Mockingbird has been translated into ten languages.

AVOCATIONAL INTERESTS: Golf and music.

BIOGRAPHICAL/CRITICAL SOURCES:

BOOKS

Concise Dictionary of American Literary Biography: The New Consciousness, 1941-1968, Gale, 1989.
Contemporary Literary Criticism, Volume 12, Gale, 1980.
Dictionary of Literary Biography, Volume 6: *American Novelists since World War II, Second Series,* Gale, 1980.

PERIODICALS

Atlantic, August, 1960.
Booklist, September 1, 1960.
Chicago Sunday Tribune, July 17, 1960.
Commonweal, December 9, 1960.
New Statesman, October 15, 1960.
Newsweek, January 9, 1961.
New Yorker, September 10, 1960.
New York Herald Tribune Book Review, July 10, 1960.
New York Times Book Review, July 10, 1960, April 8, 1962.
Saturday Review, July 23, 1960.
Times Literary Supplement, October 28, 1960.

*   *   *

LEE, Laurie 1914-

PERSONAL: Born June 26, 1914, in Stroud, Gloucestershire, England; married Catherine Francesca Polge, 1950; children: Jesse Frances. *Education:* Educated in Stroud, England.

ADDRESSES: Home—9/40 Elm Park Gardens, London SW10, England.

CAREER: Poet, writer. Worked as clerk in Stroud, England, and as builder's laborer in London, England; documentary filmmaker for Post Office film unit in Cyprus, India, and Assam during World War II; publications editor for Ministry of Information, 1944-46; worked with Green Park film unit, 1946-47; caption writer in chief for Festival of Britain, 1950-51.

MEMBER: Royal Society of Literature.

AWARDS, HONORS: Atlantic Award, 1944; Society of Authors Travelling Award, 1951; Member of the Order of the British Empire, 1952; Foyle's Poetry Award, 1955; W. H. Smith Award for Literature, 1960, for *Cider With Rosie.*

WRITINGS:

The Sun My Monument (poems), Hogarth, 1944.
Land at War, H.M.S.O., 1945.
(With Ralph Keene) *We Made a Film in Cyprus,* Longmans, Green, 1947.
The Bloom of Candles: Verse From a Poet's Year, Lehmann, 1947.
The Voyage of Magellan: A Dramatic Chronicle for Radio, Lehmann, 1948.
A Rose for Winter: Travels in Andalusia, Hogarth, 1955.
My Many-Coated Man (poems), Deutsch, 1955.
Cider With Rosie (autobiography), Hogarth, 1959, published as *The Edge of Day: A Boyhood in the West of England,* Morrow, 1960.
Laurie Lee: Poems, Vista, 1960.
(With David Lambert) *The Wonderful World of Transportation* (for children), Garden City Books, 1960 (published in England as *Man Must Move: The Story of Transport,* Rathbone Books, 1960).
The First Born, Hogarth, 1964.
As I Walked out One Midsummer Morning (autobiography), Deutsch, 1969.
I Can't Stay Long (collected prose pieces), Deutsch, 1975, Atheneum, 1976.
Selected Poems, Deutsch, 1983.
Two Women, with own photographs, Deutsch, 1983.

SIDELIGHTS: At the age of nineteen, Lee left his home and walked to London, taking little with him except his violin and the determination to never again have an employer. Both have remained with him throughout the years. If writing should fail him, Lee said, he will survive on his violin: "A little time ago I went busking with it just to see what the going rate was. . . . I keep in practice."

Cider With Rosie, one of Lee's best-known works, is a memoir of his boyhood in England which was very warmly received by critics and the reading public. When it was published in the United States under the title *The Edge of Day,* T. S. Matthews stated: "Good books don't always sell; the best seller lists are usually swamped by the second- and third-rate. But now and then, once in a blue moon, a book appears that deserves its success. This time the moon is blue, and *The Edge of Day* is the book."

After publishing *Cider With Rosie,* Lee returned to his home town and bought a cottage there. "It took me a long time to go back," he said. "I had to have some success behind me." According to the London *Times:* "There was some vexation when the villagers recognized themselves in the book, then he was accepted. They even sell his books at the local pub." Lee recalled, "At first they wouldn't touch them with tongs."

In 1975 Lee published a collection of prose pieces written over a thirty-year period, *I Can't Stay Long.* Reviews of the book were somewhat mixed. Robert Nye, for example, found that "little in [the book] is deeply thought or felt through," but he admitted that "there is a niceness in [Lee] both in the old sense of being minutely and delicately precise, and in the modern colloquial sense of being agreeable." Other reviews were more favorable. Sylvia Secker noted: "When Lee drops his purple mantle he can write with a vivid, spare imagery that makes one realize how closely allied are the eyes of the poet and the painter: 'the bright-backed cows standing along the dykes like old china arranged on shelves,' 'motionless canals, full of silver light, lap the houses like baths of mercury.' One is no longer reading but looking at the work of an old Dutch Master." A *New Yorker* writer also praised the book's imagery, citing as example Lee's recollection of adolescence: "I don't think I ever discovered sex, it seemed to be always there—a vague pink streak running back through the landscape as far as I can remember." This type of writing, the *New Yorker* critic said, shows Lee "at his most characteristically expressive." The reviewer further stated, "Lee's writing—almost precious, almost naive—has a tone and intensity that are truly entirely his own, and are inimitably pleasing."

BIOGRAPHICAL/CRITICAL SOURCES:

BOOKS

Dictionary of Literary Biography, Volume 27: *Poets of Great Britain and Ireland, 1946-1960,* Gale, 1984.

PERIODICALS

Christian Science Monitor, April 5, 1976.
New Yorker, February 23, 1976.
New York Times Book Review, March 27, 1960.
Times (London), December 21, 1975.
Times Literary Supplement, January 30, 1976.

*   *   *

LEE, William
  See BURROUGHS, William S(eward)

*   *   *

LEE, Willy
  See BURROUGHS, William S(eward)

*   *   *

LEGER, (Marie-Rene Auguste) Alexis Saint-Leger 1887-1975
(Saintleger Leger, Saint-John Perse)

PERSONAL: Born May 31, 1887, in Saint-Leger-les-Feuilles, French West Indies; brought to France at age of eleven; died September 20, 1975, in Giens, France; son of Amedee (a lawyer) and Mme. Leger (nee Dormoy); married Dorothy Milburn Russell, 1958. *Education:* Attended Universities of Bordeaux and Paris, studied medicine, law, and literature, licencie en Droit; held a diploma from the Ecole des Hautes Etudes Commerciales.

CAREER: French Foreign Office, deputy diplomat in the political and commercial division, 1914-16, served as secretary of the French Embassy in Peking, China, 1916-21; collaborator with French Foreign Minister, Aristide Briand, 1921-32; chef de cabinet, Ministry of Foreign Affairs, 1925-32, counsellor, 1925, minister, 1927; secretary-general of Ministry of Foreign Affairs, and

Ambassador of France, 1932-40, removed from this post as a result of his firm stand against the appeasement of Germany; lost his French citizenship, October 29, 1940; fled to Arachon (France), to England, Canada, and finally arrived in Washington, D.C., in January, 1941; consultant on French poetry at the Library of Congress, 1941-45; his French citizenship was restored in 1945; he returned to France, 1957, and maintained homes in Washington and Giens until his death.

MEMBER: American Academy of Arts and Sciences (honorary), American Academy of Arts and Letters, National Institute of Arts and Letters of America, Modern Language Association of America (honorary fellow), Bayerischen Akademie der Schoenen Kuenste.

AWARDS, HONORS: Knight Commander of Royal Victorian Order; Grand Officer of Legion of Honor; Knight Commander of the Bath; Knight of the Grand Cross of the British Empire; Commander des Arts et des Lettres; honorary degree from Yale University; American Academy and Institute of Arts and Letters Award of Merit, 1950; Grand Prix National des Letters, 1959; Grand Prix International de Poesie (Belgium), 1959; Nobel Prize for Literature, 1960.

WRITINGS:

(Under name Saintleger Leger) *Eloges* (poetry; also see below), Gallimard, 1911, published under pseudonym St.-John Perse, Gallimard, 1925, translation by Louise Varese published as *Eloges and Other Poems,* introduction by Archibald MacLeish, Norton, 1944, revised bilingual edition, without introduction, Pantheon Books, 1956.

UNDER PSEUDONYM ST.-JOHN PERSE

Anabase (poem), Gallimard, 1924, bilingual edition with English translation by T. S. Eliot published as *Anabasis,* Faber, 1930, 2nd edition, revised and corrected, Harcourt, 1949.
Amitie du prince (originally published as part of *Elogues*), R. Davis, 1924, critical edition, Gallimard, 1979.
Pluies (poetry), Editions des Lettres Francaises (Buenos Aires), 1944.
Quatre Poemes (1941-1944), Editions des Lettres Francaises, 1944, published as *Exit* [and] *Poeme a l'etrangere, Pluies, Neiges,* Gallimard, 1945, revised and corrected edition, Gallimard, 1946, bilingual edition with English translation by Denis Devlin published as *Exile and Other Poems,* Pantheon Books, 1949, 2nd bilingual edition, Pantheon Books, 1953.
Vents (epic poem; also see below), Gallimard, 1946, bilingual edition with English translation by Hugh Chisholm published as *Winds,* Pantheon Books, 1952, 2nd bilingual edition, 1961.
Oeuvre poetique de Saint-John Perse, two volumes, Gallimard, 1953, revised edition, 1960.
Amers (poetry; also see below), NRF, 1953, Gallimard, 1957, bilingual edition with English translation by Wallace Fowlie published as *Seamarks,* Pantheon Books, 1958, Harper, 1961.
Etroits sont les vaisseaux (also published as part of *Amers*), NRF, 1956.
Chronique (poem; also see below), Gallimard, 1960, bilingual edition with English translation by Robert Fitzerald published as *Chronique,* Pantheon Books, 1960.
On Poetry (Nobel Prize acceptance speech; also see below), bilingual edition with English translation by W. H. Auden, Pantheon Books, 1961.

L'ordre des oiseaux (poems), Au vent d'Arles, 1962, published as *Oiseaux,* Gallimard, 1963, bilingual edition with translation by Robert Fitzgerald published as *Birds,* Pantheon Books, 1966.

Pour Dante (address; also see below), Gallimard, 1965.

Two Addresses: On Poetry [and] *Dante* (includes Auden's translation of *On Poetry* and Fitzgerald's translation of *Pour Dante*), Pantheon Books, 1966.

Eloges [and] *La gloire des rois, Anabase, Exit,* Gallimard, 1967.

Vents [and] *Chronique,* Gallimard, 1968.

Chante par celle qui fut la . . . (bilingual edition), translation by Richard Howard, Princeton University Press, 1970.

Collected Poems, translations by W. H. Auden and others, Princeton University Press, 1971.

Oeuvres completes, Gallimard, 1972.

Chant pour un equinoxe, Gallimard, 1975, translation by Richard Howard published as *Song for an Equinox,* Princeton University Press, 1977.

Letters, translated and edited by Arthur J. Knodel, Princeton University Press, 1979.

OTHER

(Under name Alexis Leger) *La Publication francaise pendant la guerre, bibliographie restreinte (1940-1945),* four volumes, 1940's.

Exit (poetry), Gallimard, 1942.

(Under name Alexis Leger) *Briand,* Wells College Press, 1943.

(Under name Alexis St. Leger Leger) *A Selection of Works for an Understanding of World Affairs since 1914,* [Washington], 1943.

Contributor to *Nouvelle Revue Francaise, Poetry, Transition, Commerce, Mesa, Partisan Review, Intentions, Sewanee Review, Briarcliff Quarterly, Atlantic, Berkeley Review,* and other publications.

SIDELIGHTS: Diplomatic service and the writing of poetry were dual preoccupations during the greater part of Alexis Saint-Leger's life. It was the poet Paul Claudel, whom Leger met in 1905, who first suggested that Leger enter government service. For twenty-six years he served as a highly distinguished diplomat. At the same time he was writing poetry in secret in his spare time. His early writings were for the most part ignored, though *Anabase* was translated into German by Rainer Maria Rilke (1925), into English by T. S. Eliot (1930), and into Italian by Giuseppe Ungaretti (1931). (Wallace Fowlie recalls the story of Leger's recognition by Marcel Proust, who, in *Cities of the Plain,* published in 1922, includes an episode wherein he mentions a book of poems by a Saintleger Leger.)

From 1924 until 1942 Leger published no poetry, but he continued to write, accumulating five volumes of poems. When he fled Paris in 1940 he left his manuscripts (fifteen years of work) behind. The poems were destroyed by the Nazi police, and today the bulk of his work is by many standards small. He wrote carefully and was reluctant to publish in haste. However, he has, as Wallace Fowlie maintained, "taken his place beside the four or five major poets of modern France: Baudelaire, Mallarme, Rimbaud, Valery, Claudel." Fowlie considers *Anabase* to be "one of the key poems of our age. It represents the poet as conqueror of the word. . . ." Eliot thought it as important as James Joyce's later work.

To conceal his diplomat's identity Leger published under the pseudonym St.-John Perse. Some of the very early poems, however, were published without his consent (especially in *Nouvelle Revue Francaise* and *Commerce,* 1909-10) under the name Saintleger Leger. The name St.-John Perse, perhaps chosen because of Leger's admiration for the Roman poet Persius, was first used for the publication of "Anabase" in *Nouvelle Revue Francaise,* January, 1924.

Solitude and exile were Perse's themes. He was interested in the unity and totality of things. Fowlie wrote: "To man and to every aspiration of man he ascribes some eternal meaning. Everything precarious and ephemeral appears less so in the condition of his poetry." "He is the contemporary poet who comes perhaps closest to considering himself the instrument of superior revelation." His poems praise and celebrate the entire cosmos. His style was dazzling, opulent, set forth in nontraditional stanzas in which, as Fowlie wrote, one finds "language brought back, almost by force, to its essential rhythm, language which uses myths and symbols, language which does not describe but which suggests." Transition between images is often nonexistent. Perse believed that the poet relies on his subconscious, but a subconscious that has been mastered by reason. His literary forebears included Persius, Tacitus, Racine, and Claudel.

Perse was also noted for his brilliant and spellbinding conversations. His knowledge of botany, zoology, geology—anything concerned with nature—was considered encyclopedic, and he avowed passions for horses and boats. His childhood and youth (indeed his entire life) gave his name an almost legendary quality: his nurse on the island of his birth was a secret priestess of Shira; his friends in China were the philosophers of the East; in his spare time he traveled to the Gobi Desert and the South Sea Islands; and he was at one time one of the most powerful officials in France. He recalled his diverse experiences with ease, wrote Pierre Geurre, and spoke "a language of surprising diversity and exactitude, occasionally stopping to find an even more precise word to accurately define his thought. While listening to him, one gets the impression that something in the flow of time or being becomes immobilized and that the magic of word and thought creates a pause around itself."

Perse said he was not a professional writer, and he could hardly be considered bookish. Guerre noted Leger's "instinctive" distrust of books, and recalled an anecdote: "When during the war he worked at the Library of Congress in Washington, American critics, curious about the books he himself read, vainly ransacked the card files trying to find what he had taken out. But for five years Perse had not borrowed one book from the famous national library. As he wrote to a poet friend: 'My hostility to culture springs from homeopathy. I believe that culture should be carried to the utmost limit, at which point it disclaims itself, and ungrateful to itself, cancels itself out.' "

Although Perse spent much of his time since 1941 in America, his allegiance belonged entirely to France. In 1942 he wrote to Archibald MacLeish: "I have nothing to say about France: it is myself and all of myself. . . . For me it is the holy kind, and the only one, in which I can communicate with anything universal, anything essential. Even were I not an essentially French animal, an essentially French clay (and my last breath, as my first, will chemically be French), the French language would still be my only imaginable refuge, the shelter and retreat par excellence, the only locus in this world where I can remain in order to understand, desire, or renounce anything at all."

BIOGRAPHICAL/CRITICAL SOURCES:

BOOKS

Bosquet, Alain, *Saint-John Perse,* Seghers, 1953, revised edition, 1967.

Contemporary Literary Criticism, Gale, Volume 11, 1979, Volume 46, 1988.
Saillet, Maurice, *Saint-John Perse: Poete de Gloire,* Mercure de France, 1952.

PERIODICALS

Christian Science Monitor, October 26, 1960.
Contemporary Review, March, 1961.
Poetry, January, 1961.
Reporter, February 2, 1961.
Washington Post, September 2, 1987.
Yale Review, December 2, 1960.

OBITUARIES:

PERIODICALS

Newsweek, October 6, 1975.
New York Times, September 22, 1975.
Time, October 6, 1975.
Washington Post, September 24, 1975.

* * *

LEGER, Saintleger
See LEGER, (Marie-Rene Auguste) Alexis Saint-Leger

* * *

Le GUIN, Ursula K(roeber) 1929-

PERSONAL: Surname pronounced "Luh-Gwin"; born October 21, 1929, in Berkeley, Calif.; daughter of Alfred L. (an anthropologist) and Theodora Covel Brown (a writer; maiden name, Kracaw) Kroeber; married Charles Alfred Le Guin (a historian), December 22, 1953; children: Elisabeth, Caroline, Theodore. *Education:* Radcliffe College, A.B., 1951; Columbia University, A.M., 1952.

ADDRESSES: Agent—Virginia Kidd, P.O. Box 278, Milford, PA 18337; and Ilse Lahn, Paul Kohner Inc., 9169 Sunset Blvd., Los Angeles, CA 90069.

CAREER: Writer. Department secretary, Emory University, Atlanta, GA. Part-time instructor in French at Mercer University, Macon, GA, 1954-55, and University of Idaho, Moscow, 1956. Visiting lecturer and writer in residence at various locations, including Portland State University, University of California, San Diego, University of Reading, England, Kenyon College, Tulane University, and First Australian Workshop in Speculative Fiction. Creative consultant for Public Broadcasting Service, for television production of *The Lathe of Heaven,* 1979.

MEMBER: Authors League of America, Writers Guild, PEN, Science Fiction Research Association, Science Fiction Writers Association, Science Fiction Poetry Association, Writers Guild West, Planned Parenthood Federation of America, Amnesty International of the USA, Nature Conservancy, National Organization for Women, National Abortion Rights Action League, Women's International League for Peace and Freedom, Phi Beta Kappa.

AWARDS, HONORS: Fulbright fellowship 1953; *Boston Globe-Horn Book* Award, 1968, Lewis Carroll Shelf Award, 1979, *Horn Book* honor list citation, and American Library Association Notable Book citation, all for *A Wizard of Earthsea;* Nebula Award, Science Fiction Writers Association, and Hugo Award, International Science Fiction Association, both for best novel,

both 1970, both for *The Left Hand of Darkness;* Nebula Award nomination, novelette category, 1969, for "Nine Lives"; Newbery Silver Medal Award, and National Book Award for Children's Literature finalist, both 1972, and American Library Association Notable Book citation, all for *The Tombs of Atuan;* Child Study Association of America's Children's Books of the Year citation, 1972, and National Book Award for Children's Books, 1973, both for *The Farthest Shore;* Hugo Award for best novella, 1973, for *The Word for World Is Forest;* Hugo Award nomination, Nebula Award nomination, and *Locus* Award, all 1973, all for *The Lathe of Heaven;* Hugo Award for best short story, 1974, for "The Ones Who Walk Away from Omelas"; American Library Association's Best Young Adult Books citation, 1974, for *The Dispossessed: An Ambiguous Utopia;* Hugo Award, Nebula Award, Jupiter Award, all for best novel, and Jules Verne Award, all 1975, all for *The Dispossessed: An Ambiguous Utopia;* Nebula Award, and Jupiter Award, both for best short story, both 1975, both for "The Day Before the Revolution"; Nebula Award nomination and Jupiter Award, both 1976, both for short story "The Diary of the Rose"; National Book Award finalist, American Library Association's Best Young Adult Books citation, Child Study Association of America's Children's Books of the Year citation, and *Horn Book* honor list citation, all 1976, and Prix Lectures-Jeunesse, 1987, all for *Very Far Away from Anywhere Else;* Gandalf Award nomination, 1978; D.Litt., Bucknell University, 1978; Gandalf Award (Grand Master of Fantasy), 1979; Balrog Award nomination for best poet, 1979; Locus Award, 1984, for *The Compass Rose;* American Book Award nomination, 1985, and Janet Heidinger Kafka Prize for Fiction, University of Rochester English Department and Writer's Workshop, 1986, both for *Always Coming Home.*

WRITINGS:

NOVELS

Rocannon's World (bound with *The Kar-Chee Reign* by Avram Davidson; also see below), Ace Books, 1966.
Planet of Exile (bound with *Mankind Under the Lease* by Thomas M. Disch; also see below), Ace Books, 1966.
City of Illusions (also see below), Ace Books, 1967.
A Wizard of Earthsea (illustrations by Ruth Robbins; also see below), Houghton, 1968.
The Left Hand of Darkness, Ace Books, 1969, reprinted, Chelsea House, 1987.
The Tombs of Atuan (sequel to *A Wizard of Earthsea;* illustrations by Gail Garraty; also see below), Athenaeum, 1970.
The Lathe of Heaven, Scribner, 1971.
The Farthest Shore (sequel to *The Tombs of Atuan;* illustrations by Garraty; Junior Literary Guild selection; also see below), Athenaeum, 1972.
The Dispossessed: An Ambiguous Utopia, Harper, 1974.
Orsinian Tales, Harper, 1976.
Very Far Away from Anywhere Else, Athenaeum, 1976 (published in England as *A Very Long Way from Anywhere Else,* Gollancz, 1976).
The Earthsea Trilogy (includes *The Wizard of Earthsea, The Tombs of Atuan,* and *The Furthest Shore*), Gollancz, 1977.
Three Hainish Novels (contains *Rocannon's World, Planet of Exile,* and *City of Illusions*), Doubleday, 1978.
Malafrena, Putnam, 1979.
The Beginning Place, Harper, 1980 (published in England as *Threshold,* Gollancz, 1980).
The Eye of the Heron and Other Stories (novella; originally published in collection *Millennial Women;* also see below), Panther, 1980, Harper, 1983.

The Visionary (bound with *Wonders Hidden,* by Scott R. Sanders), McGraw, 1984.

Always Coming Home (includes tape cassette of "Music and Poetry of the Kesh," with music by Todd Barton [also see below]; illustrations by Margaret Chodos; diagrams by George Hersh), Harper, 1985, published without cassette, Bantam, 1987.

Tehanu: The Last Book of Earthsea (sequel to *The Farthest Shore*), Atheneum, 1990.

JUVENILES

Solomon Leviathan's Nine Hundred Thirty-First Trip around the World (originally published in collection *Puffin's Pleasures;* also see below), illustrations by Alicia Austin, Puffin, 1976, Cheap Street, 1983.

Leese Webster, illustrations by James Brunsman, Athenaeum, 1979.

The Adventures of Cobbler's Rune, illustrations by Austin, Cheap Street, 1982.

Adventures in Kroy, Cheap Street, 1982.

A Visit from Dr. Katz (picture book), illustrations by Ann Barrow, Atheneum, 1988.

Catwings, illustrations by S. D. Schindler, Orchard, 1988.

Catwings Return, illustrations by Schindler, Orchard, 1989.

POEMS

Wild Angels (collection of early works), Capra, 1974.

(With mother, Theodora K. Quinn) *Tillai and Tylissos,* Red Bull, 1979.

Torrey Pines Reserve (broadsheet), Lord John, 1980.

Hard Words and Other Poems, Harper, 1981.

(With artist Henk Pander) *In the Red Zone,* Lord John, 1983.

Buffalo Gals and Other Animal Presences (short stories and poems), Capra, 1987.

Wild Oats and Fireweed, Harper, 1988.

OTHER

From Elfland to Poughkeepsie (lecture), Pendragon Press, 1973.

The Wind's Twelve Quarters (short stories), Harper, 1975.

Dreams Must Explain Themselves (critical essays), Algol Press, 1975.

Orsinian Tales (short stories), Harper, 1976.

The Water Is Wide (short story), Pendragon Press, 1976.

The Word for World Is Forest (novella; originally published in collection *Again, Dangerous Visions;* also see below), Berkley, 1976.

(Editor) *Nebula Award Stories 11,* Gollancz, 1976, Harper, 1977.

The Language of the Night: Essays on Fantasy and Science Fiction, (critical essays), edited by Susan Wood, Putnam, 1978.

(Editor with Virginia Kidd) *Interfaces: An Anthology of Speculative Fiction,* Ace, 1980.

(Editor with Kidd) *Edges: Thirteen New Tales from the Borderlands of the Imagination,* Pocket Books, 1980.

The Compass Rose (short stories), Harper, 1982.

King Dog: A Screenplay (bound with *Dostoevsky: A Screenplay,* by Raymond Carver and Tess Gallagher), Capra, 1985.

(With Barton) *Music and Poetry of the Kesh* (cassette), Valley Productions, 1985.

(With David Bedford) *Rigel Nine: An Audio Opera,* Charisma, 1985.

(With composer Elinor Armer) *Uses of Music in Uttermost Parts* (music and text), first performed in part in San Francisco, CA, and Seattle, WA, 1986, 1987, and 1988.

Dancing at the Edge of the World: Thoughts on Words, Women, Places (essays), Grove, 1989.

Contributor to anthologies, including *Orbit 5,* 1969, *Orbit 6,* 1970, *Orbit 14,* 1974, *Best SF: 1969,* 1970, *World's Best Science Fiction,* 1970, *Those Who Can,* 1970, *Nebula Award Stories 5,* 1970, *Nebula Award Stories 10,* 1975, *Quark #1,* 1970, *The Dead Astronaut,* 1971, *New Dimensions I,* 1972, *New Dimensions III,* 1973, *Clarion II,* 1972, *Clarion III,* 1973, *Again, Dangerous Visions,* Volume 1, 1972, *The Best from Playboy,* number 7, 1973, *The New Atlantis and Novellas of Science Fiction,* 1975, *Universe 5,* 1974, *The Best from Galaxy,* Volume 2, 1974, *The Best from Galaxy,* Volume 3, 1975, *Dream Trips,* 1974, *Epoch,* 1975, *The New Atlantis and Other Novellas of Science Fiction,* 1975, *The Thorny Paradise,* 1975, *Bitches and Sad Ladies,* 1975, *More Women of Wonder,* 1976, *The Best Science Fiction of the Year #5,* 1976, *Science Fiction at Large,* 1976, 1977, *Future Power,* 1976, *The Altered I: An Encounter with Science Fiction,* 1978, *Puffin's Pleasure,* 1976, *Best Science Fiction Stories of the Year,* Sixth Annual Collection, 1977, *Psy Fi One,* 1977, *The Norton Anthology of Short Fiction,* 1978, *Millennial Women,* 1978, *Cassandra Rising,* 1978, *Dark Imaginings,* 1978. Author of postcard short story, *Post Card Partnership,* 1975, and *Sword & Sorcery Annual,* 1975. Contributor of short stories, novellas, essays, and reviews to numerous science fiction, scholarly, and popular periodicals, including *Science-Fiction Studies, New Yorker, Antaeus, Parabola, New Republic, Redbook, Playgirl, Playboy, New Yorker, Yale Review,* and *Omni.* Author of abridged version of *The Left Hand of Darkness,* for Warner Audio, 1985. Le Guin recorded *Gwilan's Harp* and *Intracom,* for Caedmon, 1977, *The Ones Who Walk Away from Omelas and Other Stories,* and *The Lathe of Heaven,* for Alternate World, 1976, and *The Left Hand of Darkness* for Warner Audio.

MEDIA ADAPTATIONS: The Word for World Is Forest was made into a sound recording by Book of the Road, 1968; *The Tombs of Atuan* became a filmstrip with record or cassette by Newbery Award Records, 1980; an abridged version of *The Earthsea Trilogy* was made into a sound recording by Colophone, 1981; *The Lathe of Heaven* was televised by the Public Broadcasting Service in 1979; "The Ones Who Walk Away from Omelas" was performed as a drama with dance and music at the Portland Civic Theatre in 1981.

SIDELIGHTS: Critics have often found it difficult to classify Ursula Le Guin: while some consider her writing science fiction fantasy, Le Guin herself discounts any narrow genre categorizations. She wrote *CA* that "some of my fiction is 'science fiction,' some of it is 'fantasy,' some of it is 'realist,' [and] some of it is 'magical realism.' " Le Guin has also written several volumes of poetry and essays. "A significant amount of science fiction has been profoundly thoughtful about the situation of contemporary humanity in the light of its possible futures and its imaginable alternatives. In recent years, no [writer] inside the field of science fiction or outside of it [has] done more to create a modern conscience than . . . Ursula K. Le Guin," writes Derek de Solla Price in the *New Republic.* Le Guin, however, "is not competing with Orwell or Hemingway," according to George Edgar Slusser in his book *The Furthest Shores of Ursula Le Guin.* "Her social analysis is acute, but its purpose is not indignation or reform. She has no social program, offers no panaceas." And a *Cambridge Review: Fantasy in Literature* contributor finds Le Guin "an elegant, but not a light writer: not to be trifled with. Superficially, her work charms because it has all the glitter of high intelligence and efficiency."

In his essay on Le Guin in the *Dictionary of Literary Biography,* Brian Attebery writes that the author "has brought to science fiction a new sensitivity to language, a powerful set of symbols and images, and a number of striking and sympathetic characters. She has purposely avoided most technical details in order to concentrate on human problems and relationships. . . . Le Guin's fiction is extraordinarily risky: it is full of hypotheses about morality, love, society, and ways of enriching life expressed in the symbolic language found in myth, dream, or poetry. However, the greater the risk, the greater the reward, and for the reader . . . the reward is a glimpse of something glowing, something very much like truth." Similarly, Joseph D. Olander and Martin Harry Greenberg say in their introduction to *Ursula K. Le Guin* that, while "Le Guin's fiction may be filled with wizards, aliens, and clones, . . . the vision contained in her stories and novels is, above all, concerned with what is most permanent about the human condition." *Modern Fiction Studies* contributor Keith N. Hull notes: "Certainly one of the most important lessons in Le Guin's novels is that humanity is a broader, deeper entity than we ordinarily think and that the definition of humanity requires constant expansion as our experience broadens. Because of this theme, Le Guin's work risks being polemical and sentimental, but her best work exploits it beautifully."

Le Guin first began to receive critical and popular attention with her Earthsea novels, the first being *A Wizard of Earthsea*. The Earthsea trilogy, considered by Le Guin to be among her best work, exemplifies her holistic perspective of the universe, a perspective shaped by Taoist philosophy. As Robert Scholes suggests in a *Hollins Critic* article, "What Earthsea represents, through its world of islands and waterways, is the universe as a dynamic, balanced system . . . which include[s] a role for magic and for powers other than human, but only as aspects of the great Balance or Equilibrium, which is the order of this cosmos. Whereas C. S. Lewis worked out of a specifically Christian set of values, Ursula Le Guin works not with a theology but with an ecology, a cosmology, a reverence for the universe as a self-regulating structure." The theme of equilibrium between opposing forces works on several levels within the trilogy. On the most immediate and recognizable level is the integration of man with himself. In *The Wizard of Earthsea*, the young mage, or wizard, Ged undertakes the journey to maturity and self-knowledge; in *The Tombs of Atuan*, it is the girl-priestess, Tenar; and in *The Furthest Shore*, it is Ged's apprentice Arren. Writing in *Ursula K. Le Guin*, Margaret P. Esmonde suggests that "all of these journeys symbolize the journey every human being must make, one through pain and fear, aided only by trust in the goodness of man, hand holding hand, to the acceptance of mortality." A *Times Literary Supplement* contributor praises the trilogy's depth, and concludes: "After Earthsea-lore, with its weight and substance, most other modern fantasies must ring thin."

"Two Le Guin novels of unquestionably high standing, even among readers who generally do not care for science fiction, are *The Left Hand of Darkness* and *The Dispossessed*," writes Hull. "In these novels Le Guin . . . describes herself as writing science fiction based on 'social science, psychology, anthropology [and] history,'. . . [The result] is an emphasis on culture." *The Left Hand of Darkness* explores the themes of sexual identity, incest, xenophobia, fidelity and betrayal in a tale of an Earth ambassador, Genly Ai, who is sent to the planet of Gethen, which is peopled by an androgynous culture. Through Genly Ai's relationship with a native, Estraven, he learns to question his sexual orientation. As in many of her works, Le Guin successfully combines a social message with an engrossing story. Scholes feels that "the great power of the book comes from the way it interweaves all its levels and combines all its voices and values into an ordered, balanced, whole." In *The Dispossessed*, another character is an alien in a strange culture; the physicist Shevek, however, is also at odds with his home planet's values. He is devoted

to the spread of knowledge, but the development of his theories will inevitably bring his isolated colonial planet and its motherplanet into contact, although the two cultures bitterly oppose one another. Attebery describes the novel's form as "slow, sober, down-to-earth. The writing verges on pure naturalistic reporting, except that the places being written about do not exist on Earth." He adds that *The Dispossessed* "is fuller than any other of [Le Guin's] stories in character and in social and political interplay."

Le Guin has invented many beings to inhabit the alien worlds of her fiction and has endowed them with equally diverse physical and mental characteristics. The Athsheans of *A Word for World Is Forest*, for instance, are an intelligent, hominid species covered with green fur and capable of perceiving reality through daydreams. Several different species live on the planet called Rocannon's World, including a large winged creature much like an angelic robot; the Liuar, a feudal society of very tall, lordly people with yellow hair and dark skin; the Clayfolk, short, pale, intelligent troglodytes; and the Fiia, simple-minded, elfish humanoids. And while Le Guin's societies are sometimes utopian in concept, the inhabitants are capable of very and imperfect human actions. According to the *Cambridge Review* critic, "The satisfaction of [Le Guin's] stories is that her heroes and heroines are constantly on the brink of doing the wrong thing, and sometimes do: a reader holds his breath at every turn."

Le Guin's characters and settings vary widely, and her books take place on many different planets and in varying time spans. Some, like the books of the Earthsea trilogy, take place wholly outside of our defined universe, much as do J.R.R. Tolkien's *Lord of the Rings* and C. S. Lewis's "Chronicles of Narnia." Some of Le Guin's other novels adhere to somewhat more familiar spatial and temporal structures, or are at least set within the parameters of human history. The works which form Le Guin's Hainish Cycle, example (including *Rocannon's World, Planet of Exile, City of Illusions, The Left Hand of Darkness, The Dispossessed: An Ambiguous Utopia*, and many of her short stories), are bound by a common historical context—their characters and cultures originated with a race called the Hain, whose history encompasses Earth.

The unusual work, *Always Coming Home*, concerns a people known as the Kesh, who reside in northern California after a nuclear war. The format moves between poetry and prose, and includes stories, legends, and "autobiography"; along with the book comes a tape of Kesh music. Brian D. Johnson in *Maclean's Magazine* describes *Always Coming Home* as "an 'archaeological dig' into the distant future—a search for 'shards of the broken pot at the end of the rainbow.'" Samuel R. Delaney in the *New York Times Book Review* praises the work: "With high invention and deep intelligence, *Always Coming Home* presents, in alternating narratives, poems and expositions, Ursula K. Le Guin's most consistently lyric and luminous book in a career adorned with some of the most precise and passionate prose in the service of a major imaginative vision." H. J. Kirchhoff in the Toronto *Globe & Mail* expresses the belief that Le Guin "has created an entire culture, not just a cast of characters—an impressive achievement from an impressive writer." And Delaney concludes: "This is her most satisfying text among a set of texts that have provided much imaginative pleasure."

Le Guin's excursions into the world of children's fiction have included *Solomon Leviathan's 931st Trip Around the World, Catwings*, and *Catwings Return*. In *Catwings*, four flying cats, Harriet, James, Thelma and Roger, escape city dangers to live in the country, where they are adopted by two children. *New York*

Times Book Review contributor Crescent Dragonwagon finds Le Guin's "dialogue, humor, skill as a storyteller and emotional veracity combine near-flawlessly in a story that is both contemporary and timeless." She continues: "One of the book's weaknesses is that, other than for their wings, the kittens are not so remarkable, at least as individuals. . . . Still, their collective winged adventures, their looking after one another, and the understated charm of Ms. Le Guin's writing keeps us captivated. . . . [When Susan] whispers to her brother, 'Oh, Hank . . . their wings are furry,' as kitten Harriet whispers to her brother, 'Oh, James . . . their hands are kind'—well, who could fail to recognize the enduring, healing power of love?"

Dancing at the Edge of the World: Thoughts on Words, Women, Places is a collection of essays, addresses and reviews. *Los Angeles Times Book Review* critic Nancy Mairs finds the collection "unpredictable and uneven but, for those very reasons, a trove of delights: insightful, impassioned, sometimes lyrical, often funny. . . . Those who appreciate Le Guin's novels will find the pieces in [*Dancing at the Edge of the World*] no substitute for their intricacies of vision and language. But this volume makes a fine companion, and on occasion a guide, to her fiction, offering insight into the writer at work." And Elizabeth Hand in the *Washington Post Book World* thinks the grouping shows "Ursula Le Guin at her best: insightful, funny, sharp, occasionally tendentious and nearly always provocative."

Eighteen years after the publication of *The Farthest Shore,* Le Guin came out with *Tehanu: The Last Book of Earthsea.* Michael Dirda writes in the *Washington Post Book World* that *Tehanu* "unexpectedly turns the trilogy into a tetralogy." The story concerns both Ged and Tenar, who are now old. Ged abandoned his power at the end of *The Farthest Shore;* Tenar has lived a "normal" life, and is a farmer's widow. Their lives become enmeshed with a little girl's, Therru, who has been raped and burned, but survives. Although Dirda sees the novel as "meditative, somber, even talky," it "builds to a climax of almost pornographic horror, nearly too shocking for its supposedly young adult pages." But, he adds, that while "less sheerly exciting," than the Earthsea Trilogy, *Tehanu* "may be the most moving of them all."

"Can one find a common denominator in the work and thought of Ursula K. Le Guin?" asks author Theodore Sturgeon in a *Los Angeles Times* article. "Probably not; but there are some notes in her orchestrations that come out repeatedly and with power. A cautionary fear of the development of democracy into dictatorship. Celebrations of courage, endurance, risk. Language, not only loved and shaped, but investigated in all its aspects; call that, perhaps, communication. But above all, in almost unearthly terms Ursula Le Guin examines, attacks, unbuttons, takes down and exposes our notions of reality."

BIOGRAPHICAL/CRITICAL SOURCES:

BOOKS

Authors in the News, Volume 1, Gale, 1976.
Children's Literature Review, Volume 3, Gale, 1978.
Contemporary Literary Criticism, Gale, Volume 8, 1978, Volume 13, 1980, Volume 22, 1982, Volume 45, 1987.
Dictionary of Literary Biography, Gale, Volume 8: *Twentieth-Century-American Science Fiction Writers,* Part 1, 1981, Volume 52: *American Writers for Children since 1960: Fiction,* 1986.
Olander, Joseph D., and Greenberg, Martin Harry, editors, *Ursula K. Le Guin,* Taplinger, 1979.
Scholes, Robert, *Structural Fabulation: An Essay on Fiction of the Future,* University of Notre Dame Press, 1975.
Slusser, George Edgar, *The Farthest Shores of Ursula Le Guin,* Borgo, 1976.

PERIODICALS

Book Report, March/April, 1989.
Cambridge Review: Fantasy in Literature, November 23, 1973.
Globe & Mail (Toronto), December 7, 1985.
Hollins Critic, April, 1974.
Los Angeles Times, September 5, 1982.
Los Angeles Times Book Review, September 5, 1982, March 5, 1989.
Maclean's Magazine, November 4, 1985.
Modern Fiction Studies, spring, 1986.
New Republic, February 7, 1976, October 30, 1976.
New York Times Book Review, September 29, 1985, November 13, 1988.
Times Literary Supplement, April 6, 1973, June 3-9, 1988.
Village Voice, February 25, 1986.
Washington Post Book World, October 6, 1985, January 29, 1989, February 25, 1990.

*   *   *

LEIBER, Fritz (Reuter, Jr.) 1910-
(Francis Lathrop)

PERSONAL: Born December 24, 1910, in Chicago, Ill.; son of Fritz (a Shakespearean actor) and Virginia (a Shakespearean actress; maiden name, Bronson) Leiber; married Jonquil Stephens (a writer), January 16, 1936 (died September, 1969); children: Justin. *Education:* University of Chicago, Ph.B., 1932; attended Episcopal General Theological Seminary.

ADDRESSES: Home and office—565 Geary St., Apt. 604, San Francisco, Calif. 94102.

CAREER: Episcopal minister at two missionary churches in New Jersey, 1932-33; Shakespearean actor with father's company, 1934-36; Consolidated Book Publishers, Chicago, Ill., editor, 1937-41; Occidental College, Los Angeles, Calif., instructor in speech and drama, 1941-42; Douglas Aircraft Co., Santa Monica, Calif., precision inspector, 1942-44; *Science Digest,* Chicago, associate editor, 1944-56; free-lance writer, 1956—. Lecturer at science fiction and fantasy writing workshops, Clarion State College, summers, 1968, 1969, 1970, and at San Francisco State University.

MEMBER: Science Fiction Writers of America.

AWARDS, HONORS: Guest of honor at World Science Fiction Convention, 1951, 1979; Hugo Award, World Science Fiction Convention, for best novel, 1958, for *The Big Time,* and 1965, for *The Wanderer,* for best novelette, 1968, for "Gonna Roll the Bones," for best novella, 1970, for "Ship of Shadows," and 1971, for "Ill Met in Lankhmar," and for best short story, 1975, for "Catch that Zeppelin"; Nebula Award, Science Fiction Writers of America, for best novelette, 1968, for "Gonna Roll the Bones," for best novella, 1971, for "Ill Met in Lankhmar," for best short story, 1975, for "Catch that Zeppelin," and Grand Master, 1981, for lifetime contribution to the genre; Mrs. Ann Radcliffe Award, Count Dracula Society, 1970; Gandalf Award, World Science Fiction Convention, 1975; World Fantasy Award, World Fantasy Convention, for best short fiction, 1976, for "Belsen Express," and for best novel, 1978, for *Our Lady of Darkness;* World Fantasy Life Award, World Fantasy Convention, 1976, for life achievement; Locus Award for best collection, 1986, for *The Ghost Light.*

WRITINGS:

SCIENCE FICTION AND FANTASY

Night's Black Agents (short stories), Arkham, 1947, reprinted, Berkley, 1978, abridged edition published as *Tales from Night's Black Agents,* Ballantine, 1961.

The Girl with Hungry Eyes and Other Stories, Avon, 1949.

Gather, Darkness! (novel; originally published in *Astounding Stories,* 1943), Pellegrini & Cudahy, 1950, reprinted, Ballantine, 1979.

(With James Blish and Fletcher Pratt) *Witches Three* (novel), Twayne, 1952.

Conjure Wife (novel; originally published in *Unknown Worlds,* 1943), Twayne, 1953, reprinted, Ace, 1981, published as *Burn, Witch, Burn* (also see below), Berkley, 1962.

The Green Millennium (novel), Abelard, 1953, reprinted, Ultramarine Publications, 1980.

The Sinful Ones (novel; bound with *Bulls, Blood, and Passion* by David Williams), Universal Publishing, 1953, published separately as *You're All Alone,* Ace, 1972.

Destiny Times Three (novel), Galaxy, 1957, bound with *Riding the Torch* by Norman Spinrad, Dell, 1978.

The Big Time [and] *The Mind Spider and Other Stories* (also see below), Ace, 1961.

The Silver Eggheads (novel; originally published in *Magazine of Fantasy and Science Fiction,* 1958), Ballantine, 1961, reprinted, 1979.

Shadows with Eyes (short stories), Ballantine, 1962.

The Wanderer (novel), Ballantine, 1964, reprinted, Tor Books, 1983.

A Pail of Air (short stories), Ballantine, 1964.

Ships to the Stars (short stories; bound with *The Million Year Hunt* by K. Bulmer), Ace, 1964.

Tarzan and the Valley of Gold (novel), Ballantine, 1966.

The Night of the Wolf (short stories), Ballantine, 1966.

The Secret Songs (short stories), Hart-Davis, 1968.

Night Monsters (short stories), Ace, 1969, revised edition, Gollancz, 1974.

A Specter Is Haunting Texas (novel), Walker, 1969.

The Best of Fritz Leiber (short stories), edited by Angus Wells, Doubleday, 1974, revised edition, Sidgwick & Jackson, 1974.

The Book of Fritz Leiber (short stories), DAW Books, 1974.

The Second Book of Fritz Leiber (short stories), DAW Books, 1975.

The Worlds of Fritz Leiber (short stories), Ace, 1976.

The Big Time (novel), Gregg, 1976.

The Mind Spider and Other Stories, Ace, 1976.

Our Lady of Darkness (novel), Berkley, 1978.

Heroes and Horrors (short stories), edited by Stuart D. Schiff, Whispers Press, 1978.

The Change War (short stories), Gregg Press, 1978.

Bazaar of the Bizarre (short stories), Donald M. Grant, 1978.

Ship of Shadows (short stories), Gollancz, 1979, bound with *No Truce with Kings* by Poul Anderson, Tor Books, 1989.

In the Beginning, Cheap Street, 1983.

The Ghost Light: Masterworks of Science Fiction and Fantasy (short stories with an essay), Berkley, 1984.

"FAFHRD AND THE GRAY MOUSER" SERIES; HEROIC FANTASY

Two Sought Adventure: Exploits of Fafhrd and the Gray Mouser (short stories), Gnome Press, 1957.

Swords against Wizardry (short stories), Ace, 1968.

Swords in the Mist (short stories), Ace, 1968.

The Swords of Lankhmar (novel), Ace, 1968.

Swords and Deviltry (novel), Ace, 1970.

Swords against Death (short stories), Ace, 1970.

Swords and Ice Magic (short stories), Gregg, 1977.

Rime Isle (short stories), Whispers Press, 1977.

The Knight and Knave of Swords, Morrow, 1988.

OTHER

(Contributor) Steven Eisner, editor, *The Howard Phillips Lovecraft Memorial Symposium,* privately printed, 1958.

(Contributor) Jack L. Chalker, editor, *In Memoriam: Clark Ashton Smith,* Mirage Press, 1963.

(Contributor) L. Sprague de Camp and George H. Scithers, editors, *The Conan Swordbook,* Mirage Press, 1969.

The Demons of the Upper Air (verse), Roy A. Squires, 1969.

(With wife, Jonquil Leiber) *Sonnets to Jonquil and All* (verse), Roy A. Squires, 1978.

(Contributor) Darrell Schweitzer, editor, *Essays Lovecraftian,* T-K Graphics, 1976.

(Contributor) *Robert Bloch: A Bio-Bibliography,* Graeme Flanagan (Canberra City), 1979.

(Editor with Schiff) *The World Fantasy Awards 2,* Doubleday, 1980.

(Author of introduction) John Stanley, *The Creature Feature Movie Guide; or, An A to Z Encyclopedia of Fantastic Films; or, Is There a Mad Doctor in the House?,* Creatures at Large, 1981.

Work appears in numerous anthologies. Contributor of over two hundred short stories to *Unknown, Fantastic, Weird Tales, Magazine of Fantasy and Science Fiction,* and other magazines.

SIDELIGHTS: Although Fritz Leiber has written a wide variety of science fiction, fantasy, and horror stories, he is best known for his sword and sorcery adventures featuring the two swashbuckling characters Fafhrd and the Gray Mouser. These adventures, written over a period of some forty years, are noted for their witty and colorful language, fast-paced plots, tongue-in-cheek humor, and eroticism. Leiber, writing in the author's note to *The Swords of Lankhmar,* describes the pair of adventurers as "rogues through and through, though each has in him a lot of humanity and at least a diamond chip of the spirit of true adventure. They drink, they feast, they wench, they brawl, they steal, they gamble, and surely they hire out their swords to powers that are only a shade better, if that, than the villains."

Fafhrd, a tall, brawny warrior from the Cold Waste, and the Gray Mouser, a small, quick-moving thief, together seek adventure, romance, and treasure in the world of Nehwon, and invariably encounter crafty wizards, beautiful women, dark horrors, and plenty of sword-wielding adversaries. "In story after story," Lin Carter says of the series in his *Imaginary Worlds,* "[Leiber] has captained us on a voyage of exploration and discovery through the magical lands where his fascinating pair of delicious rogues dwell." "These adventure fantasies," Diana Waggoner writes in *The Hills of Faraway,* "are distinguished by a sophisticated style and an excellent sense of humor."

Fafhrd and the Gray Mouser grew out of a correspondence between Leiber and his friend Harry Fisher during the 1930s. "Harry and I began to create imaginary worlds," Leiber recalls in an interview with Darrell Schweitzer, "solely for the purpose of writing about them in our letters. . . . One of the imaginary worlds originally invented by Harry was the world of Fafhrd and the Gray Mouser." Leiber's son, Justin Leiber, writes in *Starship* that the two characters were loosely based on his father (as Fafhrd) and Fisher (as the Gray Mouser). "When I was a kid," Justin remembers, "both my mother Jonquil and I called Fritz 'Faf' or 'Fafhrd' more than anything else." Leiber and Fisher also invented the pair's home base, the city of Lankhmar, a treacherous, labyrinthian metropolis of evil sorcerers, corrupt priests, and numerous back-alley thieves (organized into a "thieves' guild," of course), widely noted for its easy accommodation of nefarious activity. Their world of Nehwon, vaguely reminiscent of both ancient Rome and medieval Europe, is thought by its inhabitants to be contained within a bubble of air floating in a cosmic sea. Perhaps it is, since Nehwon is a world in which magic works and magical events are commonplace.

The first Fafhrd and the Gray Mouser story, written in 1937, was read and commented upon by the late horror story writer H. P. Lovecraft. Leiber had written to Lovecraft after reading and admiring some of his stories and the two men had begun a regular correspondence. When Leiber mentioned that he also wrote, Lovecraft asked to see one of his stories. After reading it, Lovecraft circulated it among several editors and introduced Leiber to such writers as Robert Bloch and August Derleth. In his interview with Schweitzer, Leiber admits that Lovecraft "had a big effect on my writing and continues to do so." Lovecraft's influence can particularly be seen in Leiber's novel *Our Lady of Darkness.* Raymond L. Hough, writing in *Library Journal,* notes that in *Our Lady* Leiber, like Lovecraft, uses "increasingly fantastic events [to] slowly reveal a brooding, and unnatural horror." In other ways, Leiber has modified the standard elements of a Lovecraftian horror story. He has set the story in urban California, for example, rather than in Lovecraft's inevitable rural New England. A Lovecraft-style ancient curse is blended with the ideas of modern psychology. "Lovecraft fans will recognize the debt," Hough observes, "but they'll enjoy the differences too." Algis Budrys of *The Magazine of Fantasy and Science Fiction* calls *Our Lady* "a major work of fantasy, skillfully created and unimaginably imagined. . . . There are things in this book that no one has ever thought of before."

Before beginning his writing career, Leiber appeared in the films "Camille," produced by Metro-Goldwyn-Mayer in 1937, and "Equinox." His father, Fritz Leiber, Sr., was a professional actor who appeared on the stage and in some forty films. Leiber has noted the theatrical influence in his writing. Speaking to Schweitzer, Leiber remembers that "when I was just a little kid I was exposed to the plays of Shakespeare. . . . I do at times tend to fall into a kind of Shakespearean poetry in my writing. And also I tend to cast stories in a dramatic form. I visualize scenes in my stories as if they were scenes in a play on the stage."

Describing Leiber's place in contemporary science fiction, Budrys writes: "Leiber is one of the best science fiction writers in the world. [He is] one SF writer who has somehow made the Hugo and the Nebula [Awards] seem inadequate." Budrys believes that Leiber's place belongs in mainstream literature. "Leiber is a giant," he maintains, "[a] figure of stature in 20th century literature."

MEDIA ADAPTATIONS: Leiber's novel *Conjure Wife* has been filmed three times: first as "Weird Woman" by Universal in 1944; second as "Conjure Wife" (television film), aired on NBC-TV, 1960; and third as "Burn, Witch, Burn," American International, 1962. Two of Leiber's short stories—"The Girl with the Hungry Eyes," 1970, and "The Dead Man," 1971—were filmed for Rod Serling's "Night Gallery" television series. *The Big Time* has been made into a stage play. TSR Games mar-

kets a board game based on the "Fafhrd and the Gray Mouser" series.

BIOGRAPHICAL/CRITICAL SOURCES:

BOOKS

Carter, Lin, *Imaginary Worlds,* Ballantine, 1973.
Dictionary of Literary Biography, Volume 8: *Twentieth-Century American Science Fiction Writers,* Gale, 1981.
Leiber, Fritz, *The Swords of Lankhmar,* Ace, 1968.
Morgan, Chris, *Fritz Leiber: A Bibliography, 1934-1979,* Morgenstern, 1979.
Moscowitz, Sam, *Seekers of Tomorrow,* World Publishing, 1966.
Schweitzer, Darrell, *Science Fiction Voices #1,* Borgo Press, 1979.
Waggoner, Diana, *The Hills of Faraway: A Guide to Fantasy,* Atheneum, 1978.

PERIODICALS

Amazing Stories, October, 1951.
Analog, May, 1951.
Anduril, Number 6, 1976.
Books and Bookmen, February, 1970.
Fantastic Stories, February, 1970.
Fantasy Crossroads, Number 8, 1976.
Future Science Fiction, November, 1950.
Galaxy, May, 1954.
Luna Monthly, July, 1969.
Magazine of Fantasy and Science Fiction, September, 1968, July, 1969 (special Fritz Leiber issue), September, 1978, February, 1979.
New Statesman, June 6, 1969.
New Worlds, March, 1969.
New York Times Book Review, April 14, 1974.
New York Herald Tribune Book Review, December 21, 1952.
Observer, November 9, 1969.
Punch, November 13, 1968.
Saturday Review, January 10, 1953.
Science Fiction Review, August, 1970, February, 1978, September/October, 1978.
Starship, summer, 1979.
Times Literary Supplement, June 15, 1967, January 8, 1970, May 31, 1974.
Venture Science Fiction, August, 1969.
Washington Post Book World, March 5, 1978.

*   *   *

LEIGH FERMOR, Patrick (Michael) 1915-

PERSONAL: Born February 11, 1915, in London, England; son of Lewis Leigh Fermor and Muriel Eileen Taaffe Ambler; married Joan Elizabeth Eyres-Monsell. *Education:* Attended King's School, Canterbury, England.

ADDRESSES: c/o John Murray, 50 Albemarle St., London W.1, England.

CAREER: Writer; world traveler. Traveled extensively in Europe, Greece, and Balkans, 1935-39; enlisted in Irish Guards, 1939; served as second lieutenant in Intelligence Corps in Middle East and liaison officer in Greek headquarters in Albania; officer of British Military Mission stationed in Greece and Crete, 1940; commander of guerrilla operations in German-occupied Crete, 1942-44, disguised as shepherd, led successful expedition to capture German general; became Major in 1943; team commander of Special Allied Airborne Reconnaissance Force in North Germany, 1945; deputy director of British Institute in Athens, 1945-46; traveled in Caribbean, Central America, Africa, India, and Far East.

MEMBER: Athens Academy (corresponding member), Travellers' Club, White's Club, Pratt's Club, Special Forces, Cercle Huysmans.

AWARDS, HONORS: Officer of the Order of the British Empire, 1943; Distinguished Service Order, 1944; Heineman Foundation Prize for literature, 1950, and Kemsley Prize, 1951, both for *The Traveller's Tree;* Duff Cooper Prize, for *Mani: Travels in the Southern Peloponnese;* W. H. Smith Prize, 1977, for *A Time of Gifts.*

WRITINGS:

The Traveller's Tree, J. Murray, 1950.
(Translator with Roger Senhouse) Colette, *Gigi: Jule De Carnei-han: Chance Acquaintances,* J. Murray, 1952, reprinted, Farrar, Straus, 1976.
A Time to Keep Silence, J. Murray, 1953, reprinted, Penguin, 1989.
The Violins of St. Jacques, J. Murray, 1953, reprinted, Oxford University Press, 1985.
(Translator) George Psychoundakis, *The Cretan Runner,* J. Murray, 1955, reprinted, Transatlantic Arts, 1978.
Mani: Travels in the Southern Peloponnese (Book Society's Choice), J. Murray, 1958.
Roumeli: Travels in Northern Greece, J. Murray, 1966, reprinted, ABC/Clio Press, 1989.
A Time of Gifts, J. Murray, 1977.
(Author of foreword) David Smiley, *Albanian Assignment,* Sphere Books, 1985.
Between the Woods and the Water; On Foot to Constantinople from the Hook of Holland: The Middle Danube to the Iron Gates, Viking, 1985.

Also author, with Stephen Spender, of *The Paintings of Niko Ghika,* and translator of *Forever Ulysses* (Book-of-the-Month-Club selection), 1937. Contributor of articles to various periodicals, including *Atlantic, Spectator, Times Literary Supplement,* and *Holiday.*

WORK IN PROGRESS: A sequel to *A Time of Gifts,* describing a journey on foot from Rotterdam to Constantinople, from 1933-35.

SIDELIGHTS: A Time of Gifts was written from notes made by Patrick Leigh Fermor during his travels in the 1930s. Reviewing the book, Raymond A. Sokolov commented that Leigh Fermor's keen sense of observation came through in his "long breath imagery." The reviewer wrote: "The dialogue captures with wonderful economy the feel of cross-cultural misunderstanding familiar to everyone who travels. Leigh Fermor also records similarly direct and historically irreplaceable impressions of Central European Jews waking up to Hitler's menace, of the last days of the charming, Hapsburgian petty nobility and of the pre-Communist landscape of Hungary and Rumania."

AVOCATIONAL INTERESTS: Ancient and modern history and languages, religion, painting, architecture.

BIOGRAPHICAL/CRITICAL SOURCES:

PERIODICALS

Newsweek, November 5, 1951.
New York Times, December 5, 1986.
New York Times Book Review, November 27, 1977.
Reader's Digest, September, 1953.

Times (London), October 16, 1986.
Times Literary Supplement, October 4, 1985, December 27, 1985.

*   *   *

LEM, Stanislaw 1921-

PERSONAL: Born September 12, 1921, in Lvov, Poland; son of Samuel (a physician); married wife, Barbara (a roentgenologist), August, 1953; children: Tomek (son). *Education:* Studied medicine in Lvov, Poland, 1939-41, 1944-46, and in Krakow, Poland, 1946-48.

ADDRESSES: Home—ul. Narwik 66, 30'436 Krakow, Poland. *Agent*—Franz Rottensteiner, Marchettigasse 9/17, A-1060 Vienna, Austria.

CAREER: Worked as garage mechanic during World War II; Jagellonian University, Krakow, Poland, assistant in "Science Circle," 1947-49; *Zycie Nauki* (monthly magazine; title means "The Life of Science"), editor, 1947-49; writer, 1949—. Teacher at University of Krakow.

MEMBER: PEN.

AWARDS, HONORS: Citations from Polish Ministry of Culture, 1965 and 1973; Polish State Prize for literature, 1976; Austrian State Prize for foreign literature, 1985; Alfred Jurzykowski Foundation award, 1987.

WRITINGS:

IN ENGLISH TRANSLATION

Dzienniki gwiazdowe (also see below; portions translated in *Mortal Engines*), Iskry, 1957, translation by Michael Kandel published as *The Star Diaries,* illustrated by the author, Seabury, 1976, translation by Joel Stern and Maria Swiecicka-Ziemianek published as *Memoirs of a Space Traveler: Further Reminiscences of Ijon Tichy,* Harcourt, 1982.
Czas nieutracony (novel; title means "Time Not Lost"), Volume 1: *Szpital przemienienia,* Wydawnictwo Literackie, 1957, translation by William Brand published as *Hospital of the Transfiguration,* Harcourt, 1988, Volume 2: *Wsrod umarlych* (title means "Among the Dead"), Volume III: *Powrot* (title means "Return"), 1957.
Eden, Iskry, 1959, translation by Marc E. Heine published as *Eden,* Harcourt, 1989.
Sledztwo, Ministerstwa Obrony Narodowej, 1959, translation by Adele Milch published as *The Investigation,* Seabury, 1974.
Solaris, Ministerstwa Obrony Narodowej, 1961, French translation by Jean-Michel Jasienko published as *Solaris,* Denoel, 1966, translation from the French edition by Joanna Kilmartin and Steve Cox published as *Solaris,* Walker & Co., 1970, reprinted, Harcourt, 1987.
Pamietnik znaleziony w wannie, Wydawnictwo Literackie, 1961, translation by Kandel and Christine Rose published as *Memoirs Found in a Bathtub,* Seabury, 1973.
Powrot z gwiazd, Czytelnik, 1961, translation by Barbara Marszal and Frank Simpson published as *Return from the Stars,* Harcourt, 1980.
Niezwyciezony i inne opowiadania, Ministerstwa Obrony Narodowej, 1964, German translation by Roswitha Dietrich published as *Der Unbesiegbare,* Verlag Volk und Welt, 1967, translation from the German edition by Wendayne Ackerman published as *The Invincible,* Seabury, 1973.
Bajki robotow (also see below; translation published in *Mortal Engines;* title means "Fables for Robots"), Wydawnictwo Literackie, 1964.

Cyberiada, Wydawnictwo Literackie, 1965, translation by Kandel published as *The Cyberiad: Fables for the Cybernetic Age,* Seabury, 1974.

Opowiesci o pilocie Pirxie, Wydawnictwo Literackie, 1968, translations by Louis Iribarne published as *Tales of Pirx the Pilot,* Harcourt, 1979, and *More Tales of Pirx the Pilot,* Harcourt, 1981.

Glos pana, Czytelnik, 1968, translation published as *His Master's Voice,* Harcourt, 1984.

Bezsennosc (title means "Insomnia"), Wydawnictwo Literackie, 1971, portions translated by Kandel and published as *The Futurological Congress (From the Memoirs of Ijon Tichy),* Seabury, 1974.

Doskonala proznia, Czytelnik, 1971, translation by Kandel published as *A Perfect Vacuum,* Harcourt, 1979.

Wielkosc urojona, Czytelnik, 1973, translation by Marc E. Heine published as *Imaginary Magnitude* (also see below), Harcourt, 1985.

Katar, Wydawnictwo Literackie, 1976, translation by Iribarne published as *The Chain of Chance,* Harcourt, 1978.

Maska (also see below; portions translated in *Mortal Engines;* title means "The Mask"), Wydawnictwo Literackie, 1976.

Mortal Engines, translated by Kandel, Seabury, 1977.

The Cosmic Carnival of Stanislaw Lem: An Anthology of Entertaining Stories by the Modern Master of Science Fiction, edited by Kandel, Continuum, 1981.

Golem XIV, Wydawnictwo Literackie, 1981, translation published in *Imaginary Magnitude,* Harcourt, 1985.

Microworlds: Writings on Science Fiction and Fantasy, edited by Franz Rottensteiner, Harcourt, 1984.

Biblioteka XXI Wieka, Wydawnictwo Literackie, 1986, translation by Catherine S. Leach published as *One Human Minute,* Harcourt, 1986.

Fiasko, Wydawnictwo Literackie, 1987, translation by Kandel, Harcourt, 1987.

IN POLISH

Astronauci (title means "The Astronauts"), Czytelnik, 1951.

(With Roman Hussarski) *Jacht Paradise* (play), Czytelnik, 1951.

Sezam i inne opowiadania (title means "Sesame and Other Stories"), Iskry, 1954.

Oblok Magellana (title means "The Magellan Nebula"), Iskry, 1955.

Dialogi (nonfiction; title means "Dialogues"), Wydawnictwo Literackie, 1957.

Inwazja z Aldebarana (title means "Invasion from Aldebaran"), Wydawnictwo Literackie, 1959.

Ksiega robotow (title means "Book of Robots"), Iskry, 1961.

Wejscie na orbite (nonfiction; title means "Getting into Orbit"), Wydawnictwo Literackie, 1962.

Noc ksiezycowa (title means "Lunar Night"), Wydawnictwo Literackie, 1963.

Summa technologiae (nonfiction), Wydawnictwo Literackie, 1964.

Wysoki zamek (title means "The High Castle"), Ministerstwa Obrony Narodowej, 1966.

Ratujmy kosmos i inne opowiadania (title means "Let Us Save the Cosmos and Other Stories"), Wydawnictwo Literackie, 1966.

Filozofia prypadku: Literatura w swietle empirii (nonfiction; title means "The Philosophy of Chance: Literature Considered Empirically"), Wydawnictwo Literackie, 1968.

Opowiadania (title means "Stories"), Wydawnictwo Literackie, 1969.

Fantastyka i futurologia (nonfiction; title means "Science Fiction and Futurology"), Wydawnictwo Literackie, 1970.

Opowiadania wybrane (title means "Selected Stories"), Wydawnictwo Literackie, 1973.

Rozprawy i szkice (title means "Essays and Sketches"), Wydawnictwo Literackie, 1975.

Suplement (title means "Supplement"), Wydawnictwo Literackie, 1976.

Powtorka (title means "Repetition"), Iskry, 1979.

Wizja lokalna (title means "The Scene of the Crime"), Wydawnictwo Literackie, 1982.

Prowokacja (title means "Provocation"), Wydawnictwo Literackie, 1984.

Pokoj na Ziemi (title means "Peace on Earth"), Wydawnictwo Literackie, 1987.

(With Stanislaw Beres) *Rozmowy ze Stanislawem Lemem* (title means "Conversations with Stanislaw Lem"), Wydawnictwo Literackie, 1987.

Ciemnosc i plesn (title means "Darkness and Mildew"), Wydawnictwo Literackie, 1988.

Also author of screenplay, "Przekledaniec" (title means "Roly Poly"), Film Polski.

OTHER

(Contributor) *Science Fiction: A Collection of Critical Essays,* Prentice-Hall, 1976.

(Contributor) *The Mind's Eye: Fantasies and Reflections on Self and Soul,* Basic Books, 1981.

Contributor to magazines in Europe and America, including *New Yorker.*

SIDELIGHTS: Polish author Stanislaw Lem is the best known, most widely translated science fiction writer outside the English-speaking world. With more than twenty million books sold in some thirty-six languages, Lem has earned international recognition; he is especially popular in both Germany and the Soviet Union, where he is regarded as a leading contemporary philosopher of science. As George Zebrowski notes in the *Magazine of Fantasy and Science Fiction,* however, Lem's stature as a deep thinker transcends the science fiction genre. "Lem has now reached an all but unattainable position for an SF writer," claims Zebrowski. "He is recognized as one of the world's finest writers." *New York Times* columnist John Leonard calls Lem "a Jorge Luis Borges for the Space Age, who plays in earnest with every concept of philosophy and physics, from free will to probability theory."

The circumstances of Lem's life have predisposed him to a philosophical frame of mind. Before he was born, his father narrowly escaped execution by firing squad—marching to his death, the elder Lem was recognized by a friend passing in the street who persuaded the commander to rescind the order. Later, during the Second World War, Lem himself came within inches of capture by the Nazis when a soldier brushed him as he carried a concealed weapon for the Resistance. These moments of chance salvation affected Lem profoundly; they have found their way into both his fiction and his nonfiction. To quote Paul Delany in the *New York Times Book Review,* Lem's books "are haunted by the whims of chance, the insignificance of individual fate in the perspective of the species, the ease with which a thoughtless move—but, just as well, a thoughtful one—can lead to disaster."

Lem was raised in Lvov, Poland, the son of a prosperous doctor. As he grew he indulged in flights of fancy, creating entire fictitious worlds and then outfitting himself with "papers"—passports, diplomas, and certificates—that gave him the highest honors in his imaginary kingdom. Lem decided to study medicine as his father had, and he was in medical school when World War II began. Jewish by descent, he and his family used forged documents to escape internment in the ghetto, and he continued his studies when he could. When rule by the Soviet Union replaced Nazi occupation after the war, Lem decided not to practice medicine—he would have had to serve as an army doctor. He deliberately flunked his last examination and went to work helping to support his aging parents. The work to which he committed himself was writing, and soon he was selling stories and essays to periodicals in Poland.

"In postwar Poland," writes Delany, "science fiction appealed to Mr. Lem as a genre in which an original mind could still express itself with relative freedom. . . . When he writes allegories of the Cold War, his viewpoint is that of a spectator rather than a partisan; and his books . . . are probably more popular in the Soviet Union than in the United States." Lem's artistic freedom has developed slowly; not surprisingly, his earliest fiction was "fashioned more or less along the obligatory ideological lines of its time," according to Stanislaw Baranczak in the *New Republic.* Having lived through the horrors of a World War, Lem wrote several novels depicting a rosy future of one-world government, free of the nuclear threat. "My first two books—which I now never release for reprinting—there's nothing Communist Party about them, but there is this wonderful world that could evoke in a certain sense the communist utopia," Lem told the *Washington Post.* "Now I won't allow them to be republished because I simply stopped believing in the utopia." Although he became dissatisfied with them in time, Lem's early novels helped to establish his reputation, thereby assuring an audience—and a Polish publisher—for his subsequent work.

Lem first reached a number of Western readers with the novel *Solaris,* a book that explores a favorite Lem theme—man's inadequacies in an alien environment. The account of a scientific expedition sent to study a huge, thinking ocean on the planet Solaris, the novel describes the paranoia and fear of the unknown to which the researchers succumb. Frustrated by their inability to communicate with the inscrutable liquid mass, the researchers bombard it with radiation. In response the being somehow creates physical manifestations based on the humans' most submerged psychological traumas. Hence the novel becomes a study of humanity's inability to comprehend the nature of vastly different intelligences. A similar theme appears in Lem's novels *The Invincible* and *Fiasco,* both of which concern confrontation between humans and phenomena they cannot comprehend.

"Books such as *Solaris* and *Fiasco* do more than present intellectual arguments about the universe in an unmistakably Central European voice," writes John Clute in the *Times Literary Supplement.* "As science fiction of the highest order, and as examples of surreally barbed wit, they are very threatening texts indeed. They demand attentive reading, and they show contempt for those too lazy to pay heed." Zebrowski concludes that Lem "realistically shows us what it would be like to come face to face with genuine 'differentness'—an alien non-human system or being which is beyond our understanding. . . . We go out into the universe only to meet ourselves and fight with ourselves."

Lem's forays into future worlds include not only alien life forms but also advanced technology—cyborgs and computers with vast capabilities that nevertheless reflect the foibles of their creators. *New York Times Book Review* contributor Philip Jose Farmer believes that Lem "has no equal in his literary explorations of machines and their physical and philosophical potentialities. . . . The theme he stresses in most of his work is that machines will

someday be as human as Homo sapiens and perhaps superior to him. Mr. Lem has an almost Dickensian genius for vividly realizing the tragedy and comedy of future machines; the death of one of his androids or computers actually wrings sorrow from the reader." Lem's tales suggest that humanity and technology are locked into a symbiotic relationship that can amplify the consequences of good and evil. According to *Voice Literary Supplement* reviewer David Berreby, the author "doesn't believe technology can change human nature, but he's far too subtle to conclude that technology makes no difference. It extends the reach of human folly and restricts the human imagination to those things that mechanisms make possible." Berreby concludes: "The new tools of relentlessly advancing science change what people can do, but they don't change people."

Very few of Lem's numerous stories, then, depict improvements in the human condition. His characters are almost always victims of clumsiness, psychological vulnerability, crackpot ambition, or incompetence. As Adam Mars-Jones puts it in the *Times Literary Supplement,* however far Lem extrapolates into the future, and however far into the universe he extends his speculations, "he is exploring recognisable human possibilities. The settings may be cosmic, but the morals are terrestrial." Critics find Lem's outlook bleak—in *The Nation,* Kurt Vonnegut called the author "a master of utterly terminal pessimism, appalled by all that an insane humanity may yet survive to do."

Pessimistic or hopeful, darkly comic or ironic, Lem's works abound in subtle philosophy and sociology. *Washington Post* correspondent Jackson Diehl observes that Lem advances a view of man "as a creature unable to find a stable place in the universe or control the consequences of accelerating technological advances." Baranczak concludes: "Lem is one of those writers who is interested more in the essential immutability of human existence than in any superficial evolution that history may provide. Paradoxically, he visualizes the future only to find more proof of his suspicion that human fate has remained, will remain, bound by the same laws of pain, love, and death, no matter what space suits we wear or what utopias we build."

Literary critics have noted that Lem's work resembles that favorite European genre, the fable or fairy tale. Lem is by training a scientist, however, and his books reveal an up-to-date knowledge of medicine, engineering, and cybernetics. The author also enjoys experimenting with form; several of his works offer "book reviews" or "introductions" to books that will be written in the future, and many of his conventional stories offer philosophical speculation and technical data. "In spite of the scientific authority that informs even the lightest of these near-parables, their immediate appeal grows out of the sensibility behind them," writes Peter S. Beagle in the *New York Times Book Review.* "Every Lem story is haunted by a passionate, prophetic understanding of what the human being is going to have to learn and become merely to survive, coupled with an unblinded realism about the nature of the species."

Lem is therefore a philosopher concerned with the moral and ethical consequences of advancing technology, a storyteller who feels that *science* fiction implies an obligation to verisimilitude, and a literary practitioner who is compelled to craft high-quality work. Delany writes: "Starting at the very edge of current theories of artificial intelligence, communications, cosmology and nuclear strategy, [Lem] soars out into dizzy flights of speculation, grafting one field onto another to populate whole new realms of possibility." As the author himself put it in an essay for the *Contemporary Authors Autobiography Series,* "I am trying not to limit the meaning of the name of this category of writing but rather to expand it."

That expansion of science fiction into literary and philosophical terrain has become a Lem trademark. His works have appeared in the *New Yorker,* and his books are widely reviewed for discerning mainstream audiences. "Those who have read any of . . . Lem's numerous books know that even the most timeworn subject can be the occasion for fresh surprises," observes Paul Gray in *Time.* "Lem's international reputation rests on two qualities rarely found together in one mortal: he is both a superb literary fantasist, . . . and a knowledgeable philosopher of the means and meanings of technology. Lem . . . not only builds castles in the air, he also provides meticulous blueprints and rationales for their construction." *Bloomsbury Review* contributor J. Madison Davis declares that with his romantic attitude towards art, Lem "challenges himself constantly in search of the new. . . . If the reader takes the active role Lem demands, reading can take on the quality of conversation with a unique character whose writings should be more appreciated."

Washington Post correspondent Jackson Diehl notes that the author "has avoided confrontation with Polish governments, yet he retains the respect of both dissident writers and western critics, who acknowledge him as a major artist. . . . He seems to be regarded by Polish authorities as a kind of international cultural showpiece, exempted from the normal constraints of East Bloc life in tacit exchange for his retention of citizenship." Lem does not see himself as apolitical; rather, he feels that his work confronts the human condition on a global basis—the human race as a species, not a body politic. "I have always resisted the label of science fiction," he told the *Washington Post.* "I've always believed in science, but I write about the real world. . . . I write about what is happening, only in my own way, in my own terms."

BIOGRAPHICAL/CRITICAL SOURCES:

BOOKS

Contemporary Authors Autobiography Series, Volume 1, Gale, 1984.
Contemporary Literary Criticism, Gale, Volume 8, 1978, Volume 15, 1980, Volume 40, 1986.
Updike, John, *Hugging the Shore: Essays and Criticism,* Vintage Books, 1984.

PERIODICALS

Bloomsbury Review, October, 1985.
Books Abroad, spring, 1975.
Chicago Tribune Books, July 12, 1987, October 23, 1988.
Chicago Tribune Book World, June 8, 1980, February 10, 1985.
Detroit News, April 8, 1979.
Discover, December, 1986.
Los Angeles Times Book Review, March 7, 1982, December 5, 1982, November 11, 1984, September 8, 1985, July 6, 1986, July 13, 1986.
Magazine of Fantasy and Science Fiction, May, 1971, July, 1974, July, 1979, April, 1981.
Nation, May 13, 1978.
New Republic, November 26, 1977, February 7, 1983, November 7, 1988.
New Statesman, June 1, 1979.
Newsweek, February 26, 1979, June 30, 1980.
New Yorker, February 26, 1979, September 8, 1980, January 30, 1984.
New York Review of Books, May 12, 1977.
New York Times, February 9, 1979, January 22, 1982.

New York Times Book Review, August 29, 1976, February 11, 1979, February 17, 1980, May 25, 1982, September 19, 1982, March 20, 1983, September 2, 1984, March 24, 1985, February 9, 1986, June 7, 1987, October 30, 1988.
Partisan Review, summer, 1976.
Science Fiction and Fantasy Book Review, June 5, 1979, June, 1983.
Science-Fiction Studies, July, 1977, November, 1986.
Time, January 29, 1979, September 17, 1984, June 1, 1987.
Times Literary Supplement, November 17, 1978, November 7, 1980, March 19, 1982, March 11, 1983, April 8, 1983, February 8, 1985, December 27, 1985, December 4, 1987, March 3, 1989.
Village Voice, May 16, 1989.
Voice Literary Supplement, June, 1987.
Washington Post, July 11, 1987.
Washington Post Book World, February 28, 1982, February 27, 1983, April 24, 1983, February 24, 1985, October 30, 1988.
World Literature Today, autumn, 1977, summer, 1978, winter, 1980.

—*Sketch by Anne Janette Johnson*

*   *   *

L'ENGLE, Madeleine 1918-

PERSONAL: Name originally Madeleine L'Engle Camp; born November 29, 1918, in New York, N.Y.; daughter of Charles Wadsworth (a foreign correspondent and author) and Madeleine (a pianist; maiden name, Barnett) Camp; married Hugh Franklin (an actor), January 26, 1946; children: Josephine (Mrs. Alan W. Jones), Maria (Mrs. John Rooney), Bion. *Education:* Smith College, A.B. (with honors), 1941; graduate study at New School for Social Research, 1941-42, and Columbia University, 1960-61. *Politics:* "New England." *Religion:* Anglican.

ADDRESSES: Home—924 West End Ave., New York, N.Y.; Crosswicks, Goshen, Conn. 06756.

CAREER: Active career in theater, 1941-47; teacher, Committee for Refugee Education, during World War II; St. Hilda's and St. Hugh's School, Morningside Heights, N.Y., teacher, 1960—. Member of faculty, University of Indiana, 1965-66; writer-in-residence, Ohio State University, 1970, University of Rochester, 1972, Cathedral of St. John the Divine, New York City, 1965—, and Wheaton College, 1976—. Lecturer.

MEMBER: Authors Guild (president, member of council, member of membership committee), Authors League of America (member of council), PEN, Colonial Dames.

AWARDS, HONORS: John Newbery Medal, 1963, Hans Christian Andersen Runner-up Award, 1964, Sequoyah Children's Book Award, 1965, and Lewis Carroll Shelf, 1965, all for *A Wrinkle in Time;* Austrian State Literary Prize, 1969, for *The Moon by Night;* Bishop's Medal, 1970; University of Southern Mississippi Medal, 1978; American Book Award, 1980, for *A Swiftly Tilting Planet;* Smith Medal, 1980; Newbery Honor Award, 1981, for *A Ring of Endless Light;* Sophie Award, 1984; Regina Medal, 1985; Alan Award, National Council of Teachers of English, 1986.

WRITINGS:

18 Washington Square, South: A Comedy in One Act (one-act play), Baker's Plays, 1945.
The Small Rain: A Novel, Vanguard, 1945, published as *Prelude,* 1968.
Ilsa, Vanguard, 1946.

And Both Were Young (juvenile), Lethrop, 1949, reprinted, Delacorte, 1983.

Camilla Dickinson, Simon & Schuster, 1951, published as *Camilla,* Crowell, 1965, reprinted, Delacorte, 1981.

A Winter's Love, Lippincott, 1957, reprinted, Ballantine, 1983.

Meet the Austins (juvenile), Vanguard, 1960.

A Wrinkle in Time (juvenile; also see below), Farrar, Straus, 1962.

The Moon by Night (juvenile), Farrar, Straus, 1963.

The Twenty-Four Days before Christmas: An Austin Family Story (juvenile), illustrations by Inga, Farrar, Straus, 1964, reprinted, Shaw, 1984.

The Arm of the Starfish (juvenile), Farrar, Straus, 1965.

(Contributor) Lee Kingman, editor, *Newbery and Caldecot Medal Books: 1956-65,* Horn Book, 1965.

The Love Letters, Farrar, Straus, 1966.

The Journey with Jonah (play), illustrations by Leonard Everett Fisher, Farrar, Straus, 1967.

The Young Unicorns (juvenile), Farrar, Straus, 1968.

Dance in the Desert (juvenile), illustrations by Symeon Shimin, Farrar, Straus, 1969.

Lines Scribbled on an Envelope, and Other Poems, Farrar, Straus, 1969.

Intergalactic P.S. 3 (juvenile), Children's Book Council, 1970.

The Other Side of the Sun, Farrar, Straus, 1971.

A Circle of Quiet (autobiography), Farrar, Straus, 1972.

"*A Wrinkle in Time*" (phonodisc), Newbery Awards Records, 1972.

A Wind in the Door (juvenile; also see below), Farrar, Straus, 1973.

The Summer of the Great-Grandmother (autobiography), Farrar, Straus, 1974.

Prayers for Sunday (juvenile), illustrations by Lizzie Napoli, Morehouse, 1974.

Everyday Prayers (juvenile), illustrations by Lucille Butel, Morehouse, 1974.

Dragons in the Waters (juvenile), Farrar, Straus, 1976.

(Editor with William B. Green) *Spirit and Light: Essays in Historical Theology,* Seabury, 1976.

The Irrational Season (autobiography), Seabury, 1977.

A Swiftly Tilting Planet (juvenile; also see below), Farrar, Straus, 1978.

The Weather of the Heart (poetry), Shaw, 1978.

Ladder of Angels: Scenes from the Bible Illustrated by the Children of the World, Seabury, 1979.

The Time Trilogy (three volumes; contains *A Wrinkle in Time, Wind in the Door,* and *A Swiftly Tilting Planet*), Farrar, Straus, 1979.

A Ring of Endless Light, Farrar, Straus, 1980.

The Anti-Muffins, illustrations by Gloria Ortis, Pilgrim, 1981.

The Sphinx at Dawn: Two Stories, Harper, 1982.

Walking on Water: Reflections on Faith and Art (poetry), Shaw, 1983.

A Severed Wasp, Farrar, Straus, 1983.

(Author of introduction) Paul F. Ford, *Companion to Narnia: A Complete, Illustrated Guide to the Themes, Characters, and Events of C. S. Lewis's Imaginary World,* Harper, 1983.

A House Like a Lotus, Farrar, Straus, 1984.

And It Was Good: Reflections on Beginnings, Shaw, 1984.

Dare to Be Creative, Library of Congress, 1984.

Trailing Clouds of Glory: Spiritual Values in Children's Books, Westminster, 1985.

Many Waters, Farrar, Straus, 1986.

A Cry Like a Bell, Shaw, 1987.

Awaiting the Child: An Advent Journal, Cowley, 1987.

(Author of introduction) Frances H. Burnett, *A Little Princess,* Bantam, 1987.

The Crosswicks Journal, Harper, 1988.

Two-Part Invention: The Story of a Marriage, Farrar, Straus, 1988.

Sold into Slavery: Joseph's Journey into Human Being, Shaw, 1989.

(Author of foreword) C. S. Lewis, *A Grief Observed,* Harper, 1989.

(Author of preface) Edward N. West, *Outward Signs: The Language of Christian Symbols,* Walker & Co., 1989.

Contributor of stories and poems to magazines.

SIDELIGHTS: Madeleine L'Engle is a writer who resists easy classification. She has successfully published plays, poems, essays, autobiography, and novels for both children and adults. She is probably best known for her trilogy of children's books, *A Wrinkle in Time, A Wind in the Door,* and *A Swiftly Tilting Planet.* These novels combine science fiction and fantasy with L'Engle's constant themes of family love and moral responsibility.

As the daughter of a respected journalist and a gifted pianist, L'Engle was surrounded by creative people from birth. She wrote her first stories at the age of five. She was an only child; in her autobiographies she writes of how much she enjoyed her solitude and of the rich fantasy life she created for herself. Her father's failing health sent him and his wife to Switzerland and young Madeleine to a series of boarding schools, where she found herself very unpopular because of her shy, introspective ways. These unpleasant boarding school memories were the ones L'Engle transformed into her first published novel, written in the first years after her graduation from Smith College.

The novel, entitled *The Small Rain,* features Katherine Forrester, a boarding-school student who finds solace in her music and becomes increasingly dedicated to her art. *The Small Rain* thus featured "one of L'Engle's predominant themes: that an artist must constantly discipline herself; otherwise her talent will become dissipated and she will never achieve her greatest potential," comments *Dictionary of Literary Biography* writer Marygail G. Parker. "It also deals with the theme of the individual making her own choices and the importance those choices will have in her life. L'Engle demonstrates in her first novel the ability to portray strong, believable characters that engage the reader's interest deeply." *Atlantic Monthly* contributor Edward Weeks believes that this first novel was "written with good taste and clear understanding," and that "the undeniable vitality of her writing is good to discover."

Throughout her career L'Engle has won praise for her ability to empathize with and convincingly portray young people. *Camilla Dickinson,* another early novel, has even been favorably compared to J. D. Salinger's classic novel of troubled youth, *The Catcher in the Rye.* "There is a remarkable similarity in these two diverse books," notes Harrison Smith in *Saturday Review.* "Both are told in the first person, and both are concerned with the problems of a sensitive adolescent faced suddenly with the necessity of crossing the dividing line between childhood and maturity." In Smith's view, "Miss L'Engle's 'Camilla Dickinson' has more innate strength and stability than Salinger's Holden Caulfield."

After this promising start, L'Engle's career lagged for several years as she raised her family. As she explains in *A Circle of Quiet:* "During the long drag of years before our youngest child went to school, my love for my family and my need to write were in acute conflict. The problem was really that I put two things first. My husband and children came first. So did my writing." On her fortieth birthday, in 1958, discouraged by several years of rejections, she renounced writing completely, but found that she was unable to stop. She explains, "I had to write. I had no choice in the matter. It was not up to me to say I would stop, because I could not. It didn't matter how small or inadequate [was] my talent. If I never had another book published, and it was very clear to me that this was a real possibility, I still had to go on writing." Soon thereafter, things began to change for the author; her writing began to sell again. Within five years, she had won the prestigious Newbery Medal for *A Wrinkle in Time,* the first book in her science-fantasy trilogy.

L'Engle's trilogy blends science fiction, fantasy, and moral issues in a manner reminiscent of C. S. Lewis, according to some reviewers. In *A Wrinkle in Time,* Meg Murry must use time travel and extrasensory perception to rescue her father, a gifted scientist, from the evil forces that are holding him prisoner on another planet. To release him, Meg must learn the power of love. L'Engle further develops the theme of love as a weapon against darkness in the trilogy's second and third volumes, *A Wind in the Door* and *A Swiftly Tilting Planet.* The trilogy has been criticized as over-complicated and didactic. Some reviewers also call the Murry family impossible to believe, as both parents are brilliant scientsts and all the children are remarkably gifted. Ruth Hill Viguers dismisses such criticism, however. In her *Horn Book* review, she notes that while *A Wrinkle in Time* "makes unusual demands on the imagination," it "consequently gives great rewards." Michele Murray finds L'Engle's story and her characters easy to accept, writing in the *New York Times Book Review,* "Madeleine L'Engle mixes classical theology, contemporary family life, and futuristic science fiction to make a completely convincing tale." And *School Library Journal* contributor Margaret A. Dorsey asserts, "Complex and rich in mystical religious insights, this is breathtaking entertainment."

L'Engle created another memorable family in the four books which feature the Austins—*Meet the Austins, The Moon by Night, The Young Unicorns,* and *A Ring of Endless Light.* Less fantastic than the trilogy, the Austin series treats similarly profound themes: Christian love, death, and the importance of hope in a painful world. The Austins are a close-knit, loving family who solve their problems together. Though L'Engle was again criticized by some reviewers for creating a too perfect set of characters and for over-emphasizing her themes in these books, many other critics praise the Austin series. Geraldine E. LaRocque writes in *English Journal,* "A very unusual novel, both frighteningly realistic and highly imaginative, *The Young Unicorns . . .* maintains Madeleine L'Engle's reputation as one of the finest of the present day authors writing for young people. . . . The book deals with profound questions of philosophy and psychology." *Saturday Review* contributor Alice Dalgliesh believes that the Austins are "as real a family as you find in a book." And though Ruth Hill Viguers admits that the Austin stories contain "passages that some might consider sermonizing," she maintains in a *Horn Book* review that "they are so in character and so spiced with reality and humor that I think young people looking for answers to their many questions will appreciate them."

Though L'Engle claims that she makes no distinction between writing for children and writing for adults, her science-fantasy trilogy and the Austin series are generally classified as juvenile fiction, and feature young people in the central roles. In *A Severed Wasp,* the author again treats the theme of redemption through love, but does so in the context of a story about adults. For her protagonist, L'Engle uses the main character from her first novel, *The Small Rain.* In *The Small Rain,* Katherine was

a young music student struggling to discipline herself; in *A Severed Wasp* she has retired after a long and successful career as a concert pianist. Becoming involved with the community of the Cathedral of St. John the Divine in Manhattan, Katherine is able to impart some of the wisdom she has gained to the community's younger members, as well as come to terms with her own past. " 'A Severed Wasp' continually asserts the importance of connecting one's past with the present, the pieces forming a whole the character must learn to accept," explains Linda Barrett Osborne in the *Washington Post.* Like many of L'Engle's novels, *A Severed Wasp* drew some criticism for over-dramatization. But as John Rowe Townsend summarizes in his *A Sense of Story: Essays on Contemporary Writing for Children,* "Madeleine L'Engle is a curiously-gifted, curiously-learned, curiously-imperfect writer. . . . And yet I find her an extraordinarily interesting writer. She aims high, and will risk a few misses for the sake of the hits."

MEDIA ADAPTATIONS: "A Wrinkle in Time," a filmstrip based on the book of the same title, was produced by Miller-Brody Productions, 1974.

BIOGRAPHICAL/CRITICAL SOURCES:

BOOKS

Arbuthnot, May Hill, *Children and Books,* Scott, Foresman, 1972.
Authors in the News, Volume 2, Gale, 1976.
Children's Literature Review, Gale, Volume 1, 1976, Volume 14, 1988.
Contemporary Literary Criticism, Volume 12, Gale, 1980.
Dictionary of Literary Biography, Volume 52: *American Writers for Children since 1960: Fiction,* Gale, 1986.
Kingman, Lee, editor, *Newbery and Caldecott Medal Books: 1956-1965,* Horn Book, 1965.
L'Engle, Madeleine, *A Circle of Quiet,* Farrar, Straus, 1972.
L'Engle, Madeleine, *The Summer of the Great-Grandmother,* Farrar, Straus, 1974.
L'Engle, Madeleine, *The Irrational Season,* Seabury, 1977.
Newquist, Roy, *Conversations,* Rand McNally, 1976.
Townsend, John Rowe, *A Sense of Story: Essays on Contemporary Writing for Children,* Lippincott, 1971.
Viguers, Ruth Hill, *Margin for Surprise: About Books, Children and Librarians,* Little, Brown, 1964.

PERIODICALS

Atlantic, June, 1945, December, 1969.
Christian Science Monitor, November 2, 1967.
Christianity Today, June 8, 1979.
Dallas News, April 1, 1976.
Detroit News, March 19, 1972.
English Journal, May, 1965, May, 1968, February, 1969, February, 1970, November, 1971, May, 1972.
Horn Book, April, 1961, April, 1965, October, 1965, April, 1968, August, 1969, December, 1969, August, 1973, October, 1978.
Los Angeles Times, May 6, 1980.
New Yorker, December 14, 1968.
New York Herald Tribune Book Review, March 11, 1945, August 26, 1951.
New York Times, November 6, 1979.
New York Times Book Review, March 11, 1945, April 28, 1946, May 22, 1949, August 26, 1951, March 12, 1961, March 18, 1962, April 14, 1963, April l8, 1965, January 21, 1968, May 26, 1968, August l0, 1969, November 30, 1969, February

13, 1972, July 8, 1973, June 20, 1976, September 30, 1979, January 11, 1981.

Saturday Review, September 1, 1951, May 12, 1962, May 11, 1963, April 24, 1965.

School Library Journal, November, 1965, March, 1968, May, 1973.

Spectator, June 3, 1966.

Times Literary Supplement, June 14, 1963, October 16, 1969, April 4, 1975.

Washington Post, January 17, 1983.

Washington Post Book World, November 5, 1967, May 5, 1968, May 11, 1980.

* * *

LEONARD, Elmore (John, Jr.) 1925-

PERSONAL: Born October 11, 1925, in New Orleans, La.; son of Elmore John (a salesman) and Flora Amelia (Rive) Leonard; married Beverly Cline, July 30, 1949 (divorced May 24, 1977); married Joan Shepard, September 15, 1979; children: (first marriage) Jane Jones, Peter, Christopher, William, Katherine. *Education:* University of Detroit, Ph.B., 1950. *Religion:* Roman Catholic.

ADDRESSES: Home—Birmingham, Mich. *Agent*—H. N. Swanson, 8523 Sunset Blvd., Los Angeles, Calif. 90069.

CAREER: Writer. Campbell-Ewald Advertising Agency, Detroit, Mich., copywriter, 1950-61; free-lance copywriter and author of educational and industrial films, 1961-63; head of Elmore Leonard Advertising Company, 1963-66. *Military service:* U.S. Naval Reserve, 1943-46.

MEMBER: Writers Guild of America, West, Mystery Writers of America, Western Writers of America, Authors League of America, Authors Guild.

AWARDS, HONORS: Hombre was named one of the twenty-five best western novels of all time by the Western Writers of America, 1977; Edgar Allan Poe Award, Mystery Writers of America, 1984, for *LaBrava.*

WRITINGS:

WESTERN NOVELS

The Bounty Hunters, Houghton, 1953, reprinted, Bantam, 1985.
The Law at Randado, Houghton, 1955, reprinted, Bantam, 1985.
Escape from 5 Shadows, Houghton, 1956, reprinted, Bantam, 1985.
Last Stand at Saber River, Dell, 1957, reprinted, Bantam, 1985 (published in England as *Lawless River,* R. Hale, 1959, and as *Stand on the Saber,* Corgi, 1960).
Hombre, Ballantine, 1961, reprinted, 1984.
Valdez Is Coming, Gold Medal, 1970.
Forty Lashes Less One, Bantam, 1972.
Gunsights, Bantam, 1979.

CRIME NOVELS

The Big Bounce, Gold Medal, 1969, revised edition, Armchair Detective, 1989.
The Moonshine War (also see below), Doubleday, 1969, reprinted, Dell, 1988.
Mr. Majestyk (also see below), Dell, 1974.
Fifty-Two Pickup (also see below), Delacorte, 1974.
Swag (also see below), Delacorte, 1976, published as *Ryan's Rules,* Dell, 1976.
Unknown Man, No. 89, Delacorte, 1977.
The Hunted (also see below), Dell, 1977.

The Switch, Bantam, 1978.
City Primeval: High Noon in Detroit (also see below), Arbor House, 1980.
Gold Coast (also see below), Bantam, 1980, revised edition, 1985.
Split Images, Arbor House, 1981.
Cat Chaser (also see below), Arbor House, 1982.
Stick (also see below; Book-of-the-Month Club alternate selection), Arbor House, 1983.
LaBrava, Arbor House, 1983.
Glitz (Book-of-the-Month Club selection), Arbor House, 1985.
Bandits, Arbor House, 1987.
Touch, Arbor House, 1987.
Freaky Deaky (Book-of-the-Month Club selection), Morrow, 1988.
Killshot (Literary Guild selection), Morrow, 1989.
Get Shorty, Delacorte, 1990.

OMNIBUS VOLUMES

Elmore Leonard's Dutch Treat (contains *The Hunted, Swag,* and *Mr. Majestyk*), introduction by George F. Will, Arbor House, 1985.
Elmore Leonard's Double Dutch Treat (contains *City Primeval: High Noon in Detroit, The Moonshine War,* and *Gold Coast*), introduction by Bob Greene, Arbor House, 1986.

SCREENPLAYS

"The Moonshine War" (based on Leonard's novel of the same title), Metro-Goldwyn-Mayer, 1970.
"Joe Kidd," Universal, 1972.
"Mr. Majestyk" (based on Leonard's novel of the same title), United Artists, 1974.
"High Noon, Part 2: The Return of Will Kane," Columbia Broadcasting System (CBS), 1980.
(With Joseph C. Stinson) "Stick" (based on Leonard's novel of the same title), Universal, 1985.
(With John Steppling) "52 Pick-Up" (based on Leonard's novel of the same title), Cannon Group, 1986.
(With Fred Walton) "The Rosary Murders" (based on the novel by William X. Kienzle), New Line Cinema, 1987.
"Desperado," National Broadcasting Corp. (NBC), 1988.
(With Joe Borrelli) "Cat Chaser" (based on Leonard's novel of the same title), Viacom, 1989.

Also author of filmscripts for Encyclopaedia Britannica Films, including "Settlement of the Mississippi Valley," "Boy of Spain," "Frontier Boy," and "Julius Caesar," and of a recruiting film for the Franciscans.

OTHER

(Contributor) Dennis Wholey, editor, *The Courage to Change: Personal Conversations about Alcoholism,* Houghton, 1984.

Contributor of about 30 short stories and novelettes to *Dime Western, Argosy, Saturday Evening Post, Zane Grey's Western Magazine,* and other publications during the 1950s.

SIDELIGHTS: "After writing 23 novels, Elmore Leonard has been discovered," Herbert Mitgang remarked in the *New York Times* in 1983. Following three decades of moderate success with his novels and short stories, Leonard began in the early 1980s to receive the kind of attention from reviewers befitting an author whom Richard Herzfelder in the *Chicago Tribune* calls "a writer of thrillers whose vision goes deeper than thrill." While the plots of Leonard's books remain inherently action-packed and suspenseful, he is, says *Washington Post Book World* critic Jonathan Yardley, now being "praised for accomplishments rather more substantial than that of keeping the reader on tenterhooks." These accomplishments, which Yardley describes as raising "the hard-boiled suspense novel beyond the limits of genre and into social commentary," have led critics previously inclined to pigeonhole Leonard as a crime or mystery novelist to dispense with such labels in their assessments of his work. In the process, several critics have chosen to mention Leonard's name alongside those of other writers whose literary works transcend their genre, among them Ross Macdonald and Dashiell Hammett. Such comparisons are "flattering, but hardly accurate," according to Grover Sales in the *Los Angeles Times Book Review.* "Leonard is an original," Sales believes. "His uncanny sense of plot, pace and his inexhaustible flair for the nervous rhythms of contemporary urban speech have caught the spirit of the '80s."

Leonard began his career in the early 1950s as a writer of western stories for magazines. His first sale was a novelette entitled "Apache Agent" to *Argosy* magazine for $90. He eventually turned his hand to novels in the genre, publishing five of them while pursuing a career as an advertising copywriter for a firm in Detroit. Copywriter was not an occupation much to Leonard's liking. "He says matter-of-factly that he hated the work," notes Bill Dunn in a *Publishers Weekly* interview, "but it allowed him precious time and a steady paycheck to experiment with fiction, which he did in the early morning before going off to work." Leonard told Dunn: "Sometimes I would write a little fiction at work, too. I would write in my desk drawer and close the drawer if somebody came in."

Western fiction appealed to Leonard for two reasons: he had always liked western movies, and he was determined that his writing should be a lucrative as well as a creative pursuit. "I decided I wasn't going to be a literary writer, that I wouldn't end up in the quarterlies," he tells Beaufort Cranford in *Michigan Magazine.* "So if I was going to be a commercial writer, I had to learn how to do it." His decidedly professional approach to writing paid off. During the 1950s Leonard sold some thirty short stories and five novels. And two of his stories were also sold to Hollywood: "3:10 to Yuma," a novelette that first appeared in *Dime Western* magazine, starred actor Glenn Ford; "The Tall T" starred Randolph Scott and Richard Boone.

By the early 1960s the western genre had peaked in popularity, and Leonard found that the market for his fiction had dried up. For several years he wrote no fiction at all, devoting his time to free-lance copywriting, primarily for Hurst gear shifters, a popular feature in hot rod cars. He also wrote industrial films for Detroit-area companies and educational films for Encyclopaedia Britannica at a thousand dollars apiece. Finally in 1965, when his agent sold the film rights to his last western novel, *Hombre,* for ten thousand dollars, Leonard had the financial leeway to write fiction again. This time he focused on the mystery-suspense genre. As he tells Gay Rubin of *Detroiter:* "I began writing westerns because there was a market for them. Now of course there is an interest in police stories . . . suspense, mystery, crime."

Despite the shift in genre, Leonard's fiction has remained in many ways the same. In both his western and crime fiction there is an overriding interest in seeing that justice is done. Leonard's prose, lean and hard, has consistently been of the same high quality. And his gunfighters and urban detectives approach their work with the same glib, wisecracking attitude. Writing in *Esquire,* Mike Lupica claims that despite their apparent diversity, all of Leonard's main characters are essentially the same, but "with a different name and a different job. . . . They have all been beat on by life, they all can drop a cool, wise-guy line on you, they are all tough, don't try to push them around."

Leonard's first crime novel, *The Big Bounce,* was rejected by some 84 publishers and film producers before being published as a paperback original by Gold Medal. Unsure about his switch to crime writing because of the trouble he had selling the book, Leonard turned again to westerns, publishing two more novels in the genre. But when the film rights to *The Big Bounce* were sold for $50,000, Leonard abandoned the western genre for good. Since making that decision, all of his subsequent novels have enjoyed both hardcover and paperback editions and have been sold to Hollywood.

The typical Leonard novel, Michael Kernan of the *Washington Post* maintains, is distinguished by "guns, a killing or two or three, fights and chases and sex. Tight, clean prose, ear-perfect, whip-smart dialogue. And, just beneath the surface, an acute sense of the ridiculous." Leonard has said on several occasions that he has been less influenced by other crime writers than by such writers as Ernest Hemingway, John Steinbeck, and John O'Hara. Their lean, unadorned writing style and ability to remain in the background of their stories appealed to Leonard. He tells Charles Champlin of the *Los Angeles Times:* "I became a stylist by intentionally avoiding style. When I go back and edit and something sounds like *writing,* I rewrite it. I rewrite constantly, four pages in the basket for every one that survives." The result impresses Ken Tucker of the *Village Voice,* who calls Leonard "the finest thriller writer alive primarily because he does his best to efface style."

To get his dialogue right, Leonard listens to the way people really talk and copies it down as faithfully as possible. When writing the novel *City Primeval: High Noon in Detroit,* Leonard even sat in at the Detroit police department's homicide squad room for several months, listening to the way that police officers, lawyers, and suspects spoke. His writing is full of slang terms and peculiarities of speech that mark each of his characters as a one-of-a-kind individual. More importantly, he captures the speech rhythms of his characters. Leonard recreates speech so well, Alan Cheuse writes in the *Los Angeles Times Book Review,* that "it's difficult to say . . . who among this novelist's contemporaries has a better ear." Herbert Mitgang of the *New York Times* agrees. The conversations in Leonard's books, Mitgang writes, "sound absolutely authentic." Avoiding narration and description, Leonard moves his novels along with dialogue, letting his characters' conversations tell the story. Speaking of the novel *Freaky Deaky,* Jonathan Kirsch writes in the *Los Angeles Times* that the book "is all dialogue—cool banter, jive talk, interior monologue. Virtually everything we learn about the plot and the characters is imparted through conversation, and so the book reads like a radio script."

When plotting his novels, Leonard allows his characters full rein to create their own story. Before beginning a new book, Leonard creates a handful of vividly imagined characters, the relationships between them, and their basic situation, and then he sets them in action. Leonard has, Michael Kernan remarks in the *Washington Post,* "no idea how it will end." He tells Michael Ruhlman in the *New York Times Book Review:* "I see my characters as being most important, how they bounce off one another, how they talk to each other, and the plot just sort of comes along." This spontaneous plotting technique works well for Leonard but has caused at least one reviewer occasional difficulty. Ben Yagoda of the *Chicago Tribune* describes Leonard's crime novels as being "smoky improvisations grouped around a set of reliable elements. . . . Eventually, the elements congeal into a taut climax, but for the first two-thirds or so of the book, the characters, the reader and, it turns out, the author simmer on the low burner and, in Huckleberry Finn style, 'swap juices,' trying to figure out what's going on.''

Many of Leonard's crime novels feature lower class characters trying to make fast money with a big heist or quick scam. They "fall into crime," according to Tucker, "because it's an easier way to make money than that tedious nine-to-five." George Stade of the *New York Times Book Review* calls Leonard's villains "treacherous and tricky, smart enough to outsmart themselves, driven, audacious and outrageous, capable of anything, paranoid-cunning and casually vicious—and rousing fun." Dick Roraback of the *Los Angeles Times Book Review* claims that "it is the mark of the author's craft that his characters do not seem to be created, 'written.' They simply are there, stalking, posturing, playing, loving, scheming, and we watch and listen and are fascinated. And appalled, yes, or approving, but always absorbed. They never let us off the hook."

Often partially set in Leonard's hometown of Detroit, his stories can range from Florida, where Leonard vacations and where his mother owns a motel, to New Orleans, where he was born. But Leonard shows only the seedy parts of these towns, the places where his characters are likely to be conducting their criminal business or avoiding their pursuers. He has, according to Marcel Berlins of the London *Times,* "a feel for the losers of this world, and for the shabby world they inhabit, with its own rules and its own noble principles." As Yardley explains, "Leonard's viewpoint is not exactly cynical, inasmuch as he admits the possibility of something approximating redemption, but it certainly is worldly and unsentimental. In his world nobody gets a free ticket and the victories that people win, such as they are, are limited and costly; which is to say that his world bears a striking resemblance to the real one."

Although he had been writing critically-acclaimed crime novels for a decade, and his work was being adapted for the screen, Leonard had only a small cadre of fans until the early 1980s when his novels began to attract the attention of a larger audience. With the novel *Stick* in 1982, Leonard suddenly became a bestselling writer. One sign of this sudden success can be seen in the agreeable change in Leonard's finances that year. The paperback rights for *Split Images* earned him $7,000 in 1981; the rights for *Stick* a year later earned $50,000. Then, in 1983, *La-Brava* won an Edgar Award from the Mystery Writers of America as the best novel of the year. And the book sold over 400,000 copies. Leonard's next novel, *Glitz,* hit the bestseller lists in 1985 and was a Book-of-the-Month Club selection. All of his novels since then have also been bestsellers.

Now enjoying popular as well as critical acclaim, Leonard is usually ranked as one of the best crime writers in the country. Donald E. Westlake, writing in the *Washington Post Book World,* calls Leonard "an awfully good writer," while James Kaufmann of the *Christian Science Monitor* reports that "nobody brings the illogic of crime and criminals to life better." Yagoda credits him with having "created a gallery of compelling, off-the-wall villains unequaled in American crime fiction." Tucker praises the absolute realism of Leonard's fictional violence: "The violence in his books is quick, quiet, and brutal; it's the kind that can strike you as being true and realistic even though the actions are utterly beyond your experience. Can an artist receive a higher compliment than that?" Writing in the *New York Times Book Review,* Stephen King goes so far as to find that Leonard's "wit, his range of effective character portrayal and his almost eerily exact ear for the tone and nuances of dialogue suggest [Charles] Dickens to me." Margaret Cannon of the Toronto *Globe and Mail* simply

describes Leonard as "one of the finest American writers of hard-boiled detective fiction."

MEDIA ADAPTATIONS: The novelette "3:10 to Yuma" was filmed by Columbia Pictures, 1957; the story "The Tall T" was filmed by Columbia, 1957; *Hombre* was filmed by Twentieth Century-Fox, 1967; *The Big Bounce* was filmed by Warner Bros., 1969; *Valdez Is Coming* was filmed by United Artists, 1970; *Glitz* is being filmed for television by the National Broadcasting Corp.; and the film rights to most of Leonard's other novels have been sold.

BIOGRAPHICAL/CRITICAL SOURCES:

BOOKS

Authors in the News, Volume 1, Gale, 1976.
Bestsellers 89, Volume 1, Gale, 1989.
Contemporary Literary Criticism, Gale, Volume 28, 1984, Volume 34, 1985.
Wholey, Dennis, editor, *The Courage to Change: Personal Conversations about Alcoholism,* Houghton, 1984.

PERIODICALS

American Film, December, 1984.
Armchair Detective, winter, 1986, spring, 1986, winter, 1989.
Chicago Tribune, February 4, 1981, April 8, 1983, December 8, 1983, February 7, 1985.
Chicago Tribune Book World, April 10, 1983, October 30, 1983.
Christian Science Monitor, November 4, 1983.
Detroiter, June, 1974.
Detroit News, February 23, 1982, October 23, 1983.
Esquire, April, 1987.
Globe and Mail (Toronto), December 14, 1985.
Los Angeles Times, June 28, 1984, May 4, 1988.
Los Angeles Times Book Review, February 27, 1983, December 4, 1983, January 13, 1985.
Maclean's, January 19, 1987.
Michigan Magazine (Sunday magazine of the *Detroit News*), October 9, 1983.
Newsweek, March 22, 1982, July 11, 1983, November 14, 1983, April 22, 1985.
New York Times, June 11, 1982, April 28, 1983, October 7, 1983, October 29, 1983, April 26, 1985, May 2, 1988.
New York Times Book Review, May 22, 1977, September 5, 1982, March 6, 1983, December 27, 1983, February 10, 1985, January 4, 1987.
People, March 4, 1985.
Publishers Weekly, February 25, 1983.
Rolling Stone, February 28, 1985.
Times (London), April 23, 1987.
U.S. News & World Report, March 9, 1987.
Village Voice, February 23, 1982.
Washington Post, October 6, 1980, February 6, 1985.
Washington Post Book World, February 7, 1982, July 4, 1982, February 20, 1983, November 13, 1983, May 1, 1988.

*   *   *

LEONOV, Leonid (Maximovich) 1899-

PERSONAL: Some sources transliterate middle name as Maksimovich; born May 31, 1899, in Moscow, Russia (now U.S.S.R.); son of a poet and journalist; married wife, 1923. *Politics:* No party affiliation.

ADDRESSES: Home—Gerzena 37, Flat 10, Moscow, U.S.S.R.; and c/o Union of Soviet Writers, 52 Ulitsa Vorovskogo, Moscow, U.S.S.R.

CAREER: Writer, 1922—. Deputy to U.S.S.R. Supreme Soviet, 1946-70. Editor of newspaper of 15th Inzenskaia Division,. 1920; secretary of educational division of *Krasnyi voin,* newspaper of Moscow Military District, 1921-22. *Military service:* Red Army, 1918-1920.

MEMBER: U.S.S.R. Academy of Sciences, U.S.S.R. Union of Writers (secretary of board; chairman of board, 1929-32), Serbian Academy of Sciences and Arts.

AWARDS, HONORS: Stalin Prize, 1943, for "The Invasion"; Merited Worker of Arts of Russian Soviet Federative Soviet Republic, 1949; Lenin Prize, 1957, for *The Russian Forest;* Hero of Socialist Labour Award, 1967, for outstanding contribution to Soviet culture and the literature of socialist realism; Hammer and Sickle Gold Medal; Order of Lenin (four times); Order of Red Banner of Labour; Order of Patriotic War.

WRITINGS:

FICTION

Petushikhinskii prolom (novella; title means "The Petushikhino Breakthrough"), [Moscow], 1922.
Konets melkogo cheloveka (novella; title means "The End of Insignificant Man"), [Moscow], 1922.
Barsuki, first published in 1924, translation by Hilda Kazanina published as *The Badgers,* Hutchinson International Authors, 1947.
Vor, [Riga], 1927, translation by Hubert Butler published as *The Thief,* Dial, 1931, revised edition, Khudozhestvennaya Literatura, 1959, Vintage, 1960.
Sot', Khudozhestvennaya Literatura, 1929, translation by Ivor Montagu and Sergei Nolbandov published as *Sot,* foreword by Maxim Gorky, Putnam, 1931, published as *Soviet River,* Dial, 1932, translation by Liv Tudge published as *The River,* Raduga, 1983.
Saranchuki (novella; title means "The Grasshoppers"), Khudozhestvennaya Literatura, 1930, published as *Sarancha,* 1958.
Skutarevski, first published in 1932, translation by Alec Brown published as *Skutarevsky,* Harcourt, 1936.
Doroga na okean, first published in 1935, translation by Norbert Guterman published as *Road to the Ocean,* L. B. Fischer, 1944.
Evgenia Ivanovna (novella), first published in 1938, Sovetskaya Rossiya, 1963.
Vziatie Velikoshumska (title means "The Taking of Velikoshumsk"), Khudozhestvennaya Literatura, 1944, translation by Norbert Guterman published as *Chariot of Wrath,* L. B. Fischer, 1946.
Russkii les, Molodaya Gvardiya, 1953, translation by Bernard Isaacs published as *The Russian Forest,* Progress, 1966, reprinted with new afterword, 1976.

Also author of the novella *Zapiski Andreya Petrovicha Kovyakina* (title means "Kovyakin's Journal"), 1924, and the novel *Provintsialnaya istoriya* (title means "A Provincial Story"), 1927.

PLAYS

Untilovsk (four-act; first produced at the Moscow Art Theater, 1928), [U.S.S.R.], 1928.
Usmirenie Badadoshkina (title means "The Humbling of Badadoshkin"; three-act), [U.S.S.R.], 1929.
Skutarevski (three-act dramatization of Leonov's novel of the same title; first produced in Moscow, 1934), [U.S.S.R.], c. 1933.

Barsuki (title means "The Badgers"; four-act dramatization of Leonov's novel of the same title; first produced in Moscow, 1927), [Moscow], 1935.
Provintsialnaya istoriya (title means "A Provincial Story"; four-act dramatization of Leonov's novel of the same title; written in 1927), [U.S.S.R.], 1935.
Polovchanskie sady (title means "The Orchards of Polovchansk"; four-act; first produced in Moscow, 1939), Khudozhestvennaya Literatura, 1938, translation by J. Robbins published in *Seven Soviet Plays,* introduction by H. W. L. Dana, Macmillan, 1946.
Volk (title means "The Wolf"; also produced under name *Begstvo Sandukova* [title means "Sandukov's Escape"]; four-act; first produced at the Moscow Art Theater, 1939), [U.S.S.R.], 1938.
Metel (title means "The Snowstorm"; four-act), [U.S.S.R.], 1939.
Obyknovenny chelovek (title means "An Ordinary Man"; four-act; first produced in Moscow, 1945), [U.S.S.R.], 1941.
Nashestvie (title means "The Invasion"; four-act; first produced in Leningrad, U.S.S.R., 1942), Iskusstvo, 1942, translation by Gerard Shelley published in *Four Soviet War Plays,* Hutchinson, 1944.
Lyonushka (four-act; first produced at the Moscow Art Theater, 1946), [U.S.S.R.], 1943.
Zolotaya kareta (title means "The Golden Coach"; four-act; first produced at the Moscow Art Theater, 1957), Iskusstvo, 1946.
"Vziatie Velikoshumska" (dramatization of Leonov's novel of the same title), first produced at the Moscow Art Theater, 1958.
"Russkii les" (title means "The Russian Forest"; dramatization of Leonov's novel of the same title), first produced in 1959.
"Begstvo mistera Mak-Kinli" (title means "Mr. McKinley's Escape"; adaptation of Leonov's screenplay of the same title), first produced in 1961.

Also author of play, the title of which means "Gardener in the Shade," produced at the Mayakovsk Theater, 1957.

COLLECTIONS

Dereviannaia koroleva (stories), [Petrograd], 1923.
Rasskazy (stories), [Moscow], 1926.
Gibel' Egorushki, O. D. Strok (Riga), 1927.
Izbrannye proizvedeniia (title means "Selected Works"), [Moscow], 1934.
Izbrannoye (title means "Selections"; includes fiction, plays and miscellaneous writings), Khudozhestvennaya Literatura, 1945.
P'esy (title means "Plays"), Iskusstvo, 1948.
Izbrannoye (title means "Selections"; includes fiction, plays and miscellaneous writings), Khudozhestvennaya Literatura, 1949.
Sobranie sochinenii (title means "Collected Writings"), six volumes, Khudozhestvennaya Literatura, 1953-55.
Teatr (title means "Theater"), two volumes, Iskusstvo, 1960.
Sobranie sochinenii (title means "Collected Writings"), ten volumes, Khudozhestvennaya Literatura, 1960-72, reprinted as *Sobranie sochinenii v desiati tomakh* (title means "Collected Writings in Ten Volumes"), 1981-84, Volume 1: *Povesti i rasskazy,* Volume 2: *Barsuki,* Volume 3: *Vor,* Volume 4: *Sot'* [and] *Sarancha,* Volume 5: *Skutarevsky,* Volume 6: *Doroga na okean,* Volume 7: *P'esy,* Volume 8: *Povesti,* Volume 9: *Russkii les,* Volume 10: *Publitsistika* [and] *Fragmenty iz romana.*

Literatura i vremia: Izbrannaia publitsistika, Molodaya Gvardiya, 1964.

P'esy (title means "Plays"), Sovetskii Pisatel, 1964.

Literaturnye vystupleniia (title means "Literary Speeches"), Sovetskaya Rossiya, 1966.

V gody voiny i posle (includes fiction and plays), Voyenizdat, 1968.

Proza, p'esy, stat'i, rechi, [Moscow], 1971.

P'esy (title means "Plays"), Iskusstvo, 1976.

OTHER

Begstvo mistera Mak-Kinli (screenplay; title means "Mr. McKinley's Escape"), Pravda, 1961.

O prirode nachistotu (essay on nature conservation), Sovetskaya Rossiya, 1974.

Khudozhnika sozdaet trud (essay), Pravda, 1975.

Also author of *V nashi gody,* 1949, *Razdum'ia u starogo kamia* (essay; title means "The Thoughts at the Old Stone"), 1968, and a work published in English translation as "In the War Years and After," 1974. Co-author of a screenplay, the title of which means "This Is the Enemy." Short stories represented in anthologies, including *Short Stories of the Soviet Union,* 1929. Contributor to periodicals.

SIDELIGHTS: Hailed by Russian writer and revolutionary Maxim Gorky as one of the Soviet Union's most important young writers when he emerged on the literary scene in the 1920s, Leonid Leonov is the versatile author of novels, short stories, and plays. International critics lauded his fiction works, which include the novels *The Badgers, The Thief,* and *Road to the Ocean,* but his nonconformism and veiled criticisms of the Communist government often sparked controversy. Yet Leonov's plays—patriotic dramas such as "The Invasion," written to raise Russian morale during World War II—earned him respect from fellow countrymen.

Leonov's prose works of the 1920s followed the traditions of the Russian masters, in particular the realism of Nikolay Gogol and the psychologism of Fyodor Dostoyevsky, yet they were praised for their vitality and original plots. The early novellas, the titles of which mean "The Petushikhino Breakthrough," "Kovyakin's Journal," and "The End of an Insignificant Man," take as subjects bourgeois men who question the social, political, and economic changes introduced by the Bolsheviks, Communist insurgents who overthrew the czarist government in 1917. Betraying their author's affection for Russian traditions and values, Leonov told *CA,* "these works are the original portrait of the difficult times." His first full-length novel, 1924's *The Badgers,* explores the growing hostility between urban and rural societies that the Russian Revolution and the ensuing civil war provoked. Although this theme is common in the literature of that decade, Leonov distinguishes *The Badgers* with his vivid, realistic, and endearing depiction of the peasantry and his atypical conclusion.

Leonov gained great literary and political notice with the publication of his second novel, *The Thief,* in 1927. Called "a fascinating document of the times" by a critic in the *Times Literary Supplement,* the complicated and pessimistic psychological study focuses on Dimitry Vekshin, an ex-soldier who has recently returned from the Civil War. Disgusted by what he perceives as the glorification of the very bourgeois values he had been fighting to overthrow, Dimitry goes underground and becomes a thief. Leonov told *CA* that "Dimitry's tragedy grew from his betraying all moral values and his earnest thirst for them, as he understands the depth of his degradation."

Another *Times Literary Supplement* contributor opined in a critique of *The Thief* that Leonov is "one of the few novelists in Soviet Russia whose chief concern is with problems of individual psychology and whose work has an aesthetic quality related to modern standards in the rest of Europe." Leonov took advantage of *The Thief's* underground setting to depict the many Soviets who became rich by manipulating socialist economic policies. The novel also contains a radical episode in which a petty official proposes a system of thought control by the government. Because of such details as these and its generally unflattering portrayal of Communists, *The Thief* was suppressed after four editions were issued. In 1959, Leonov published another revision, portraying Dimitry as a bandit with no redeeming qualities.

Leonov's novels of the 1930s, *Soviet River, Skutarevsky,* and *Road to the Ocean,* are more society-oriented and marked by well-drawn characters. *Soviet River* is a characteristic Soviet reconstruction novel in that it shows the conflict between the retrograde past and the progressive present, symbolized by peasants sabotaging a huge paper mill on a stream. Gorky deemed the novel especially well written and remarkable for its rich language. *Skutarevsky* is a character study centering on a solitary scientist who finds fulfillment when he is integrated into socialist society. Leonov attempts to conform to Communist ideology in this novel but criticism indicates he is not altogether convincing. He portrays the scientist's family as reactionary; as a *Times Literary Supplement* contributor remarked, "What [Leonov] is still writing would probably please the European public which venerates Dostoyevsky more than a contemporary Russian one which does not."

Leonov followed *Skutarevsky* with *Road to the Ocean.* A complicated novel with intertwining narratives and copious footnotes, *Road to the Ocean* features a high-ranking Communist official who looks back on his life from his deathbed. Despite Leonov's effort to create a work with which all Soviets could identify, the novel was not successful. The novel's rich language, complexity, and subjectivity failed to find an Eastern audience, but a *New York Herald Tribune* critic stated that after reading *Road to the Ocean,* "it is easy to understand why Maxim Gorky spoke of him in the same breath with Russia's greatest novelists, for he has power and scope and depth, clear sight and sympathy and humor, enormous vitality and an ability to people pages in a way impossible to little writers."

During the decade following 1936, when the country was embroiled in World War II, Leonov generally wrote essays, articles, and patriotic dramas to bolster morale. Western and Eastern critics alike judged his dramas of the 1940s the most interesting among the officially approved wartime plays. Reviewers deemed two works, "Lyonushka" and "The Invasion," especially well written. Dealing with the German invasion of the Soviet Union and full of Nazi atrocities and Soviet heroism, "Lyonushka" depicts the activities of a partisan group behind the German lines, while "The Invasion," for which Leonov received a Stalin Prize, features a heroic non-Communist who sacrifices himself to save a partisan leader's life.

After the war Leonov returned to writing novels. *The Russian Forest,* which commences at the beginning of the twentieth century and culminates against the backdrop of the German invasion, is a celebration of nature and chronicles the controversy surrounding the felling of the Russian forests. "What can be said about this complicated philosophical novel with intertwining narratives," Leonov told *CA,* "is that all of Russia, with her problems, lives on its pages; its subjects are embroiled in a war between Man and Nature, Life and Death." *The Russian Forest* won the Lenin Prize in 1957. For the last twenty years Leonov has been working on a new novel, "The Angel."

MEDIA ADAPTATIONS: Nashestvie was adapted for film and made into an opera, composed by Dekhteryov.

AVOCATIONAL INTERESTS: Gardening, especially growing cacti and orchids, wood carving, and photography.

BIOGRAPHICAL/CRITICAL SOURCES:

BOOKS

Brown, Edward J., *Russian Literature since the Revolution,* revised edition, Collier-Macmillan, 1969.
Gibian, George, *Interval of Freedom,* University of Minnesota Press, 1960.
Harjan, George, *Leonid Leonov: A Critical Study,* Arowhena Publishing, 1979.
Mathewson, Rufus W., *The Positive Hero in Russian Literature,* Columbia University Press, 1958.
Muchnic, Helen, *From Gorky to Pasternak,* Random House, 1961.
Simmons, E. J., *Russian Fiction and Soviet Ideology: Introduction to Fedin, Leonov, and Sholokhov,* Columbia University Press, 1958.
Starikova, Ekaterina, *On Craftsmanship: L. Leonov,* translation by Joy Jennings, Raduga, c. 1986.
Struve, Gleb, *Soviet Russian Literature, 1917-1950,* University of Oklahoma Press, 1951.

PERIODICALS

New York Herald Tribune, December 13, 1931, November 26, 1944.
New York Times Book Review, October 25, 1931, May 15, 1932, September 6, 1936, December 16, 1944.
Spectator, May 1, 1936.
Times Literary Supplement, June 25, 1931, December 31, 1931, December 28, 1933, April 25, 1936, January 19, 1967.

*   *   *

LeSIEG, Theo.
    See GEISEL, Theodor Seuss

*   *   *

LESSING, Doris (May)   1919-
(Jane Somers)

PERSONAL: Born October 22, 1919, in Persia; daughter of Alfred Cook (a farmer) and Emily Maude (McVeagh) Tayler; married Frank Charles Wisdom, 1939 (marriage dissolved, 1943); married Gottfried Anton Lessing, 1945 (marriage dissolved, 1949); children: (first marriage) John, Jean; (second marriage) Peter. *Education:* Attended Roman Catholic Convent, then Girls' High School, both in Salisbury, Southern Rhodesia; left school at age 14. *Politics:* Left-wing.

ADDRESSES: Home—24 Gondar Gardens, London NW6 1HG, England. *Agent*—c/o Jonathan Clowes Ltd., 22 Prince Albert Rd., London NW1 7ST, England.

CAREER: Writer. Worked as a nursemaid, a lawyer's secretary, a Hansard typist, and a Parliamentary Commissioner's typist while living in Southern Rhodesia, 1924-49.

AWARDS, HONORS: Prix Medicis Award for work translated into French, 1976, for *The Golden Notebook; The Sirian Experi-*

ments was nominated for the Booker McConnell Prize, 1981; Austrian State Prize for European Literature, 1981; Shakespeare Prize, 1982; W. H. Smith Literary Award, 1986, Palermo Prize, 1987, and Premio Internazionale Mondello, 1987, all for *The Good Terrorist.*

WRITINGS:

FICTION

The Grass Is Singing, Crowell, 1950.
This Was the Old Chief's Country (stories), M. Joseph, 1952.
Five Short Novels, M. Joseph, 1955.
Retreat to Innocence, M. Joseph, 1956.
Habit of Loving (stories), Crowell, 1958.
The Golden Notebook, Simon & Schuster, 1962.
A Man and Two Women (stories), Simon & Schuster, 1963.
African Stories, M. Joseph, 1964, Simon & Schuster, 1965.
Briefing for a Descent Into Hell, Knopf, 1971.
The Temptation of Jack Orkney and Other Stories, Knopf, 1972 (published in England as *The Story of a Non-Marrying Man and Other Stories,* J. Cape, 1972).
The Summer Before the Dark, Knopf, 1973.
The Memoirs of a Survivor, Random House, 1975.
Stories, Knopf, 1978.
(Under pseudonym Jane Somers) *The Diary of a Good Neighbor,* Knopf, 1983 (also see below).
(Under pseudonym Jane Somers) *If the Old Could . . .,* Knopf, 1984 (also see below).
The Diaries of Jane Somers (contains *The Diary of a Good Neighbor* and *If the Old Could . . .*), Random House, 1984.
The Good Terrorist, Knopf, 1985.
The Fifth Child, Knopf, 1988.
The Doris Lessing Reader, Knopf, 1989.

"CHILDREN OF VIOLENCE" SERIES

Martha Quest, M. Joseph, 1952.
A Proper Marriage, M. Joseph, 1954.
A Ripple From the Storm, M. Joseph, 1958.
Landlocked, Simon & Schuster, 1966.
The Four-Gated City, Knopf, 1969.

"CANOPUS IN ARGOS: ARCHIVES" SERIES

Re: Colonized Planet V, Shikasta, Knopf, 1979.
The Marriage Between Zones Three, Four, and Five, Knopf, 1980.
The Sirian Experiments: The Report of Ambien II, of the Five, Knopf, 1981.
The Making of the Representative for Planet 8, Knopf, 1982.
Documents Relating to the Sentimental Agents in the Volyen Empire, Knopf, 1983.

NONFICTION

Going Home, M. Joseph, 1957.
In Pursuit of the English, Simon & Schuster, 1961.
Particularly Cats, Simon & Schuster, 1967.
A Small Personal Voice: Essays, Reviews, Interviews, Random House, 1975.
Prisons We Choose To Live Inside, Harper, 1987.
The Wind Blows Away Our Words, Random House, 1987.

OTHER

"Mr. Dollinger" (play), first produced in Oxford, England, at Oxford Playhouse, 1958.
"Each in His Own Wilderness" (play), first produced in London, England at Royal Court, March 23, 1958.
Fourteen Poems, Scorpion Press, 1959.

"The Truth About Billy Newton" (play), first produced in Salisbury, England, 1961.

Play With A Tiger (play; first produced in London at Comedy Theatre, March 22, 1962; produced in New York City at Renata Theatre, December 30, 1964), M. Joseph, 1962.

MEDIA ADAPTATIONS: The Memoirs of a Survivor was adapted into a film and released in 1983; *The Grass Is Singing* was adapted into a film by Michael Raeburn and released as "Killing Heat" in 1984.

SIDELIGHTS: Jeremy Brooks considers Doris Lessing to be not only the best woman novelist of our time but one of the finest writers of the post-war generation. As Dorothy Brewster notes, "since the conspicuous success in 1950 of her first novel, . . . Doris Lessing . . . has been recognized as one of the most gifted of the younger group of English novelists. . . . Those of Doris Lessing's novels and stories that deal with the people and ways of life of Southern Rhodesia before, during, and after World War II have acquired something of the significance of social and political history. . . . When she came to London, she looked at the English . . . with an alert and fresh vision."

In an introductory note to *Declaration* Tom Maschler says of her: "[She was] educated at the Roman Catholic Convent School in Salisbury for five years, and for one year at the girls' High School. Her mother wanted her to be a pianist, and it was a shock when, in Doris Lessing's own words, 'I discovered suddenly that I had no talent whatsoever.' Left school at fourteen. Started writing at eighteen and composed and destroyed six novels. From 1943, . . . was busy politically taking her first lesson from Communists and Socialists in the R.A.F. For the first time in her life she met people who were prepared to do more about the colour bar than deplore it. 1949: came to England. . . . She says, 'England seems to me the ideal country to live in because it is quiet and unstimulating and leaves you in peace.' "

Many of Lessing's short stories are actually novellas, comprising 25,000 to 45,000 words. Of this form she says: "There is space in them to take one's time, to think aloud, to follow, for a paragraph or two, on a sidetrail—none of which is possible in a real short story." Her success in this genre "is primarily a matter of the swift directness and the generalizing intelligence of the voice itself," writes Robert Garis. "Mrs. Lessing's voice has the Laurentian confidence that one can manage the language of fiction by counting the dollars instead of the pennies. This works because she grasps the story as a whole and because it is usually a big story, not [only] in the number of its words but in the number of its events. . . . Almost every paragraph in the story contains [much action] and all of these actions are rendered with the same sufficiency. Sufficiency doesn't sound like much, but it is what makes the minor stories of Lawrence and Chekhov independently valuable, not just failed major works. It is in fact a sign of major talent, for it derives from good judgment in almost the Johnsonian sense. Like Lawrence and Chekhov, Mrs. Lessing has looked at many different kinds of people with unusual curiosity and intelligence and has arrived at sure judgments about them." Despite the success of her novels, Lessing will continue to write stories. She says: "Some writers I know have stopped writing short stories because, as they say, 'there is no market for them.' Others like myself, the addicts, go on, and I suspect would go on even if there really wasn't any home for them but a private drawer." Her 1972 collection, *The Temptation of Jack Orkney and Other Stories,* contains work done over ten years of literary growth, according to Richard Locke, and for which collection he has the highest praise: "I think it's clear that of all the postwar English novelists Doris Lessing is the foremost creative descendant of that 'great tradition' which includes George Eliot, Conrad, and D. H. Lawrence: a literary tradition of intense social concerns and moral realism, a tradition that scrutinizes marriage and sexual life, individual psychology and the role of ideology in contemporary society. . . . These stories are an excellent place to begin reading or rereading Doris Lessing. It's a voyage very well worth taking, for there are few these days who have the energy and imagination to explore the regions Doris Lessing has now made her own."

J. M. Edelstein believes that, on the basis of *African Stories* alone, "Doris Lessing must be counted as one of the most important fiction writers of our times." As political and social commentaries these stories "confirm in precise and painful detail, like stitches in a wound, the abuse of the native population of Southern Rhodesia by the white settlers of British descent," writes Mary Ellmann. "Doris Lessing's work is an uninterrupted study of loneliness, but here it is particularly the isolation of a few white exiles, claiming vast strange land. . . . For her first thirty years . . . Doris Lessing seems to have listened to Southern Rhodesia as no other writer has been able to do. It remained, even after she had left it, all nature to her. As one associates her English work with flats and offices, one associates the African stories with swollen suns and moons, head-tail grass, and the secret constant stirring of animal life. . . . Africa is for her not only a society in which the white people use their exile like a weapon against the black; but also a place, supporting both white and black, which endlessly enacts the conflict of forms, the effort of every living thing, at the cost of other living things, to achieve what is right for itself, its sustenance and continuation. Africa, not England, impressed the knowledge of necessary cruelty. . . . It is disconcerting, in fact, to come so repeatedly upon instances of anarchic hunger, the form of whose seeming formlessness is painful to trace, within stories of straightforward, even old-fashioned, organization. It is this preoccupation with a necessity, which in moral terms can seem a criminal chaos, that disrupts conventional literary form in *The Golden Notebook.*" Lessing says that she considers Africa to be "the center of a modern battlefield," but, she adds, "there are other things in living besides injustice, even for the victims of it." And, says Edelstein, "It is her knowledge of these larger and 'other things' and her ability to make us see them even while she sustains constantly, like distant drumming, the harsh and bitter realities of life in Africa," which gives these stories their power, accuracy and controlled passion. Africa, concludes Lessing, "is not a place to visit unless one chooses to be an exile ever afterwards from an inexplicable majestic silence lying just over the border of memory or of thought. Africa gives you the knowledge that man is a small creature among other creatures, in a large landscape."

Lessing's major and most controversial novel is *The Golden Notebook,* wherein she brilliantly explores, as a *New Statesman* reviewer noted, what it is like to be "free and responsible, a woman in relation to men and other women, and to struggle to come to terms with one's self about these things and about writing and politics." Lessing considers the book to be "a novel about certain political and sexual attitudes that have force now; it is an attempt to explain them, to objectivize them, to set them in relation with each other. So in a way it is a social novel, written by someone whose training—or at least whose habit of mind—is to see these things socially, not personally." In its structure, the novel is really two novels, divided in four sections, and "the Golden Notebook." Lessing split it into four parts, she says, in order to "express a split person. I felt that if the artist's sensibility is to be equated with the sensibility of the educated person, then it is logical to use different styles to express different kinds of people." She feels that the "personality is very much what is remembered; [the form I used] enabled me to say to the reader: Look, these apparently so different people have got so-and-so in common, or these things have got this in common. If I had used a conventional style, the old-fashioned novel, which I do not think is dead by any means, . . . I would not have been able to do this kind of playing with time, memory and the balancing of people. . . . I like *The Golden Notebook* even though I believe it to be a failure, because it at least hints at complexity." Robert Taubman expresses similar sentiments, although he is a bit confused concerning the book's structure. He calls the book "a very full novel: it not only burst the bounds of the short formal novel, as it set out to do, but overflowed its own bounds as well. It's pretty well inexhaustible on the way women think and behave, notably in the area where their personal feelings and social and political attitudes meet." But, he adds, "its unusual structure is less a matter of subtle organization than of simple, rather haphazard naturalism, . . . [or perhaps] an advance in naturalism." Lessing is still disturbed by some of the comments on this novel. She told Florence Howe: "When [the book] came out, I was astonished that people got so emotional . . . one way or another. They didn't bother to see, even to look at, how it was shaped. I could mention a dozen books by male authors in which the attitudes to women are the obverse, mirror attitudes, of the attitudes to men in *The Golden Notebook*. But no one would say that these men are anti-women. . . . But I articulated the same things from a female point of view, and this is what was interesting. It was taken as a kind of banner." Lessing would not want to be labeled a feminist. She simply states that, "in the last generation women have become what is known as free. . . . The point is they're still fighting battles to get free—and rightly. And men are still—some men, you know—some men resist it. But what is interesting, . . . what interests me in that book, was in fact, the ideas. . . . What I'm trying to say is that it was a detached book. It was a failure, of course, for if it had been a success, then people wouldn't get so damned emotional when I didn't want them to be." This novel, she says, was "extremely carefully constructed. . . . And the way it's constructed says what the book is about. . . . What I was doing is this: I was thinking about the kind of ideas we take for granted, . . . a complex of ideas which could be described as Left—and which were born with the French Revolution. And they're all to do with freedom. They are revolutionary ideas that are no longer revolutionary and have been absorbed into the fabric of how we live. And they're ideas that fit together in a system, broadly speaking, nonreligious in the old sense, and have to do with the individual in relation to his society and the rights of the individual. Which is a new idea and we don't realize how new it is. We take it absolutely for granted." In one of the sections of this book, says Lessing, "I was really trying to express my sense of despair about writing a conventional novel. . . . Actually that [part] is an absolutely whole conventional novel, and the rest of the book is the material that went into making it. One of the things I was saying was: Well, look, this is a conventional novel. God knows, I write them myself. . . . There it is: 120,000 words; it's got a nice shape and the reviewers will say this and that. And the bloody complexity that went into it. And it's always a lie. And the terrible despair. So you've written a good novel or a moderate novel, but what does it actually say about what you've actually experienced? The truth is—absolutely nothing. Because you can't. . . . I know perfectly well that when I've finished ['Children of Violence'] I shall think, Christ, what a lie. Because you can't get life into it . . . no matter how hard you try. . . . At least I think [*The Golden Notebook* is] more truthful because it's more complex. People are like other people. I mean, I don't think we are as extraor-

dinary as we like to think we are. . . . The same people occur again and again in our lives. Situations do. And any moment of time is so complicated."

"Children of Violence," the now completed series of self-contained novels that Lessing calls "a lie," has been widely acclaimed. Marjorie M. Bitker writes: "There seems no doubt that this work will rank with the foremost fictional commentaries on events of our century up to and perhaps beyond the present." "The series' importance," says Florence Howe, "has to do not only with Mrs. Lessing's reputation as author of *The Golden Notebook;* for she is trying to do something even more ambitious here. She is writing *bildungsroman* and at the same time . . . she is producing good political fiction. Her themes are major: the politics of race and war; . . . the West's changing attitude toward the Soviet Union; the shift from the Second World War to the cold war; worldwide revolutionary struggle against the West and capitalism; the problem of violence." To quote Lessing, "Martha did not believe in violence. [Yet] Martha was the essence of violence, she has been conceived, bred, fed, and reared on violence . . . because she had been born at the end of one world war, and had spent all her adolescence in the atmosphere of preparations for another which had lasted five years and had inflicted such wounds on the human race that no one had any idea of what the results would be." In "Children of Violence," according to Walter Allen, "Doris Lessing does for a young woman something very similar to what Arnold Bennett in *Clayhanger* and D. H. Lawrence in *Sons and Lovers* did for a young man, but the closer parallel is probably with George Eliot. . . . Doris Lessing shows her kinship to George Eliot both in her technique here and in her sober, unsentimental scrutiny of behavior, motives and morals." Lessing's intent, writes Howe, is "extremely ambitious" and her success, of course, has been debated. "But the canvas large enough to contain world events and small enough to measure the growth of a human being is one that only the very greatest novelists have tried. Martha's half-conscious identification of her own lot with the Africans', as she struggles against the tyranny of paternalistic personal relations, is a motif that lights the novel. Her personal wars are refractions of that other, greater war. And if she is slow to learn how to manage her wars, who is quick?" Bitker concludes that "the bare bones of the plot are the least of the riches of this work; its nuances, complexities and implications for our own time and country are unforgettable. For we, like Martha, are children of violence."

Briefing for a Descent Into Hell, writes Joan Didion, "is entirely a novel of 'ideas,' not a novel about the play of ideas in the lives of certain characters but a novel in which the characters exist only as markers in the presentation of an idea." Pearl K. Bell, too, claims the book "is not a novel but a tract. . . . [Mrs. Lessing] is making a case for one of the more dubious and treacherous intellectual fads of our time—the apocalyptic view of the British psychiatrist, R. D. Laing, and his follower David Cooper. In this worst of all possible worlds, they contend, schizophrenia is a response to life that is more honest than accepted normality. In all fairness to Mrs. Lessing, it must be said that her commitment to this seductive view of the metaphysics of madness is not the modish tropism it represents in many of Laing's guru-worshipping enthusiasts. . . . Mrs. Lessing arrived at the moral of her quasi-fable ('inner-space fiction,' she calls it) in her own way, through a deep commitment to and then increasing disenchantment with contemporary life. . . . In the *Golden Notebook,* she was tentatively suggesting that what the smug world of normality—with its defensive army of psychiatrists, analysts, tranquilizers, and truth serums—calls insanity is actually a higher and purer intuition about the truth of human existence. With *The Four-Gated City* . . . Mrs. Lessing enlarged these ideas into a substantial thesis that drew her much closer to Laing's position." Exploring further on that theme, Jeffrey Meyers says "Mrs. Lessing 'does not believe that other peoples' crises should be cut short, or blanked out with drugs, or forced sleep, or a pretence that there is no crisis, or that if there is a crisis it should be concealed or masked or made light of.' She feels that certain twilight mental states, what doctors call paranoia, 'have a meaning, are reflections from that other [unconscious] part of ourselves which knows things we don't know.' This complex and compassionate novel, about dead men who awaken with a surge of intuitive insight and are drugged and shocked back to sleep, is a Blakean attack on the limitations of pure Reason." Benjamin De Mott's attitude, in describing *Briefing,* is that "writers who mean to add something to human knowledge in the form of philosophical truth are often more permissive than estheticians about untidy composition, garrulity, repetitiousness, circularity . . . they rarely offer readers the pleasures of a perfect design. But the absence of intellectual novelty and of crispness of design doesn't much diminish this writer's significance. Mrs. Lessing in her fifties remains one of the few writers alive in the West whose instinct to feel forward toward a more habitable world is allowed to breathe without shame, hysteria, or ironical defensiveness. If her course as a thinker leads her toward an arraignment of 'sanity' and normality, it does so not in relish of idle tripping, or of supersubtle epistemological argufying about the nature of reality, but rather as a consequence of her moral sense of what men could become and her conviction that self-reduction is a crime against life."

Lessing is deeply concerned with what she calls "the individual conscience in its relation with the collective." She believes that "the real gap between people of my age and, to choose a point at random, people under thirty [is the rejection of] 'propaganda. . . .' They reject an imaginative understanding of what I am convinced is the basic conflict of our time. The mental climate created by the cold war has produced a generation of young intellectuals who totally reject everything communism stands for; they cut themselves off imaginatively from a third of mankind, and impoverish themselves by doing so." But she also believes that there is a point "where 'committedness' can sell out to expediency. Once you admit that 'art should be willing to stand aside for life,' then the little tracts about progress, the false optimism, the dreadful lifeless products of socialist realism, become inevitable." She feels despair over Vietnam and the possibility of the destruction of the world: "[It is] almost as if there's a permanent boil in the human soul." On the other hand, she is by no means a pessimist: "I believe that the pleasurable luxury of despair, the acceptance of disgust, is as much a betrayal of what a writer should be as the acceptance of the simple economic view of man; both are aspects of cowardice, both fallings-away from a central vision, the two easy escapes of our time into false innocence." Somewhere between isolation and the collective conscience, she believes, is "a resting-point, a place of decision, hard to reach and precariously balanced. . . . The point of rest should be the writer's recognition of man the responsible individual, voluntarily submitting his will to the collective, but never finally; and insisting on making his own personal and private judgments before every act of submission."

Many of Lessing's stories and novels have been called autobiographical. Brewster writes: "The young woman named Martha Quest in the series 'Children of Violence' grows up, like her creator, Doris Lessing, on a farm in Central Africa, has a father and a mother with some traits resembling those ascribed elsewhere by Doris Lessing to her own father and mother, goes at eighteen or so to earn her living in the capital of the colony, as Doris Lessing went to Salisbury, and is there shocked and stimulated by new ideas and new relationships in the rapidly changing conditions of the years before and during World War II. We must assume that Mrs. Lessing, in tracing Martha's development, has not forgotten her own." Martha and Anna Wulf, the protagonist in *The Golden Notebook,* are sometimes discussed as similar characters. Brewster relates, however, that "Mrs. Lessing expressed irritation with a review . . . which equated Martha Quest with Doris Lessing, and then compared Martha Quest with Anna Wulf, presenting the two women as combinations of the author and her characters."

As Brewster notes, Lessing "early in her career chose the straight, broad, direct style of narrative. . . . Her first teachers in fiction were the great nineteenth-century novelists: Tolstoy, Stendhal, Dostoevsky, Balzac, Turgenev, Chekhov—the Realists. . . . She never felt close to the English novel, 'whereas I feel so close to the Russian novel that it's as if they were all my blood brothers.' . . . The artist's sensibility as a mirror for our time has been explored by Proust, Joyce, Lawrence, Mann—the list is Mrs. Lessing's—and she calls this exploration one of the mainstreams of the modern novel. And to her Mann is the greatest. . . . ['His] whole message was that art is rooted in corruption—in illness, above all,' [says Mrs. Lessing who herself believes] that art is rooted in an overwhelming arrogance and egotism: 'There is a kind of cold detachment at the core of any writer or artist.' "

In subsequent novels Lessing has continued to produce work that critiques modern society. In contrast to the realism that marks her earlier novels, though, Lessing's later work—particularly her science fiction series titled "Canopus in Argos: Archives"—has taken startling new forms. In the five volumes of the "Canopus" series, Lessing explores the destruction of life brought about by catastrophe and tyranny. Paul Schlueter in the *Dictionary of Literary Biography* notes that in this series Lessing's "high seriousness in describing earth's own decline and ultimate demise is as profoundly apocalyptic as ever."

Following her foray into science fiction, Lessing again surprised readers and critics by publishing two novels under a pseudonym, Jane Somers. *The Diary of a Good Neighbor* and *If the Old Could* . . . contain typical Lessing themes: relations between women, the question of identity, and psychological conflict. Though Lessing was able to get the books published in both England and the United States, the books were generally ignored by critics and did not sell well. Lessing finally admitted that the works were her creation, saying that she had used the pseudonym to prove a point about the difficulties facing young writers. Without adequate marketing and publicity, noted Lessing, books by unknown writers are generally doomed to oblivion.

Since her pseudonymous period Lessing has written *The Good Terrorist,* a novel about the dreariness facing a group of young rebels in London, and *The Fifth Child,* about a violent, antisocial child who wreaks havoc on his family and society. She has also produced nonfiction tomes, including *The Wind Blows Away Our Words,* about war in Afghanistan during the 1980s. In whatever field she chooses to write, Lessing remains a major literary figure. As Schlueter remarks, "[Her] work has changed radically in format and genre over the years, . . . and she has been more and more willing to take chances fictionally by tackling unusual or taboo subjects. . . . And while it is commonplace to note that Lessing is not a stylist, that she is repetitive, and that her fiction too easily reflects her own enthusiasms at particular moments, . . . the fact remains that she is among the most powerful and compelling novelists of our century."

Lessing has very definite opinions on the responsibilities of a writer. She has said: "As a writer I am concerned first of all with novels and stories, though I believe that the arts continuously influence each other, and that what is true of one art in any given epoch is likely to be true of the others. I am concerned that the novel and the story should not decline as art-forms any further than they have from the high peak of literature; that they should possibly regain their greatness, [i.e., through a return to realism]. . . . I define realism as art which springs so vigorously and naturally from a strongly-held, though not necessarily intellectually-defined, view of life that it absorbs symbolism. I hold the view that the realist novel, the realist story, is the highest form of prose writing. . . . The great men of the nineteenth century had neither religion nor politics nor aesthetic principles in common. But what they did have in common was a climate of ethical judgment; they shared certain values; they were humanists." She believes that contemporary literature, on the contrary, is distinguished by "a confusion of standards and the uncertainty of values." It is now difficult "to make moral judgments, to use words like good and bad," because "we are all of us, directly or indirectly, caught up in a great whirlwind of change; and I believe that if an artist has once felt this in himself, and felt himself as part of it; if he has once made the effort of imagination necessary to comprehend it, it is an end of despair, and the aridity of self-pity. It is the beginning of something else which I think is the minimum act of humility for a writer: to know that one is a writer at all because one represents, makes articulate, is continuously and invisibly fed by, numbers of people . . . to whom one is responsible. . . . Once a writer has a feeling of responsibility, as a human being, for the other human beings he influences, it seems to me he must become a humanist, and must feel himself as an instrument of change for good or for bad. . . . The act of getting a story or a novel published is . . . an attempt to impose one's personality and beliefs on other people. If a writer accepts this responsibility, he must see himself, to use the socialist phrase, as an architect of the soul. . . . [Furthermore,] the novelist has one advantage denied to any of the other artists. The novel is the only popular art-form left where the artist speaks directly, in clear words, to the audience. . . . The novelist talks, as an individual to individuals, in a small personal voice. In an age of committee art, public art, people may begin to feel again a need for the small personal voice; and this will feed confidence into writers and, with confidence because of the knowledge of being needed, the warmth and humanity and love of people which is essential for a great age of literature."

BIOGRAPHICAL/CRITICAL SOURCES:

BOOKS

Brewster, Dorothy, *Doris Lessing,* Twayne, 1965.
Contemporary Literary Criticism, Gale, Volume 1, 1973, Volume 2, 1974, Volume 3, 1975, Volume 6, 1975, Volume 10, 1979, Volume 15, 1980, Volume 22, 1982, Volume 40, 1986.
Dictionary of Literary Biography, Volume 15: *British Novelists, 1930-1959,* Gale, 1983.
Dictionary of Literary Biography Yearbook: 1985, Gale, 1986.
Gindin, James, *Postwar British Fiction,* University of California Press, 1962.
Kostelanetz, Richard, editor, *On Contemporary Literature,* Avon, 1964.
Maschler, Tom, editor, *Declaration,* MacGibbon & Kee, 1959.
Newquist, Roy, editor, *Counterpoint,* Rand McNally, 1964.

Wellwarth, George, *Theatre of Protest and Paradox,* New York University Press, 1964.

PERIODICALS

Chicago Tribune Book World, October 30, 1979, April 27, 1980, January 24, 1982, September 29, 1985.
Commentary, May, 1988.
Commonweal, January 28, 1966, May 7, 1971.
Globe and Mail (Toronto), November 24, 1984, April 6, 1985, December 21, 1985, August 6, 1988.
Kenyon Review, March, 1966.
Los Angeles Times, March 1, 1983, July 6, 1983, May 10, 1984, January 14, 1988.
Los Angeles Times Book Review, March 1, 1981, March 21, 1982, February 10, 1985, October 13, 1985, October 20, 1985, March 27, 1988, April 6, 1988.
Milwaukee Journal, May 29, 1966.
Nation, January 17, 1966, June 13, 1966, March 6, 1967.
New Leader, April 19, 1971.
New Statesman, April 20, 1962, November 8, 1963.
Newsweek, October 14, 1985.
New York Times, October 21, 1972, October 23, 1979, March 27, 1980, January 19, 1981, January 29, 1982, March 14, 1983, April 22, 1984, October 5, 1984, October 23, 1984, July 14, 1985, September 17, 1985, March 30, 1988, June 14, 1988.
New York Times Book Review, March 14, 1971, May 13, 1973, June 4, 1978, November 4, 1979, March 30, 1980, January 11, 1981, February 2, 1982, April 3, 1983, September 22, 1985, January 24, 1988, April 3, 1988.
Partisan Review, spring, 1966.
Saturday Review, April 2, 1966, March 13, 1971.
Time, October 1, 1984, October 7, 1985.
Times (London), March 19, 1981, June 2, 1983, August 12, 1985, October 7, 1985.
Times Literary Supplement, November 23, 1979, May 9, 1980, April 17, 1981, April 2, 1982, June 3, 1983, September 13, 1985, May 8, 1987, October 17, 1987, April 22, 1988.
Tribune Books (Chicago), January 31, 1988, March 20, 1988.
Washington Post, September 24, 1984, October 1, 1984, October 24, 1984.
Washington Post Book World, October 21, 1979, November 4, 1979, April 6, 1980, January 25, 1981, March 21, 1982, April 24, 1983, September 22, 1985, March 20, 1988.
Wilson Library Bulletin, May, 1965.

*　　　*　　　*

LEVERTOV, Denise 1923-

PERSONAL: Born October 24, 1923, in Ilford, Essex, England; came to the United States in 1948, naturalized in 1955; daughter of Paul Philip (an Anglican priest) and Beatrice Adelaide (Spooner-Jones) Levertoff; married Mitchell Goodman (a writer), December 2, 1947 (divorced, 1972); children: Nikolai Gregory. *Education:* Privately educated; also studied ballet.

ADDRESSES: Home—4 Glover Circle, West Somerville, Mass. 02144.

CAREER: Poet, essayist, editor, translator, and educator. Worked in an antique store and a bookstore in London, England, 1946; taught English in Holland, three months; Young Men and Women's Christian Association (YM-YWCA) poetry center, New York City, teacher of poetry craft, 1964; Drew University, Madison, N.J., visiting lecturer, 1965; City College of the City University of New York, New York City, writer in residence, 1965-66; Vassar College, Poughkeepsie, N.Y., visiting lecturer,

1966-67; University of California, Berkeley, visiting professor, 1969; Massachusetts Institute of Technology, Cambridge, visiting professor and poet in residence, 1969-70; Kirkland College, Clinton, N.Y., visiting professor, 1970-71; University of Cincinnati, Cincinnati, Ohio, Elliston Lecturer, 1973; Tufts University, Medford, Mass., professor, 1973-79; Brandeis University, Waltham, Mass., Fannie Hurst Professor, 1981-83; Stanford University, Stanford, Calif., professor of English, 1981—. Co-initiator of Writers and Artists Protest against the War in Vietnam, 1965; active in the anti-nuclear movement. *Wartime service:* Nurse for Britain, 1943-45.

MEMBER: American Academy and Institute of Arts and Letters.

AWARDS, HONORS: Bess Hokin Prize from *Poetry*, 1959, for poem "With Eyes at the Back of Our Heads"; Longview Award, 1961; Guggenheim fellowship, 1962; Harriet Monroe Memorial Prize, 1964; Inez Boulton Prize, 1964; American Academy and Institute of Arts and Letters grant, 1965; Morton Dauwen Zabel Memorial Prize from *Poetry,* 1965; D.Litt., Colby College, 1970, University of Cincinnati, 1973, Bates College, 1984, Saint Lawrence University, 1984; Lenore Marshall Poetry Prize, 1976; Elmer Holmes Bobst Award in poetry, 1983; Shelley Memorial Award from Poetry Society of America, 1984.

WRITINGS:

POETRY

The Double Image, Cresset, 1946.
Here and Now, City Lights, 1957.
Overland to the Islands, Jargon, 1958.
Five Poems, White Rabbit, 1958.
With Eyes at the Back of Our Heads, New Directions Press, 1959.
The Jacob's Ladder, New Directions Press, 1961.
O Taste and See: New Poems, New Directions Press, 1964.
City Psalm, Oyez, 1964.
Psalm Concerning the Castle, Perishable Press, 1966.
The Sorrow Dance, New Directions Press, 1967.
(With Kenneth Rexroth and William Carlos Williams) *Penguin Modern Poets 9,* Penguin (London), 1967.
(Editor) *Out of the War Shadow: An Anthology of Current Poetry,* War Resisters League, 1967.
A Tree Telling of Orpheus, Black Sparrow Press, 1968.
A Marigold from North Vietnam, Albondocani Press-Ampersand, 1968.
Three Poems, Perishable Press, 1968.
The Cold Spring and Other Poems, New Directions Press, 1969.
Embroideries, Black Sparrow Press, 1969.
Relearning the Alphabet, New Directions Press, 1970.
Summer Poems 1969, Oyez, 1970.
A New Year's Garland for My Students, MIT 1969-1970, Perishable Press, 1970.
To Stay Alive, New Directions Press, 1971.
Footprints, New Directions Press, 1972.
The Freeing of the Dust, New Directions Press, 1975.
Chekhov on the West Heath, Woolmer/Brotherston, 1977.
Modulations for Solo Voice, Five Trees Press, 1977.
Life in the Forest, New Directions Press, 1978.
Collected Earlier Poems, 1940-1960, New Directions Press, 1979.
Pig Dreams: Scenes from the Life of Sylvia, Countryman Press, 1981.
Wanderer's Daysong, Copper Canyon Press, 1981.
Candles in Babylon, New Directions Press, 1982.
Poems, 1960-1967, New Directions Press, 1983.

Oblique Prayers: New Poems with Fourteen Translations from Jean Joubert, New Directions Press, 1984.
El Salvador: Requiem and Invocation, William B. Ewert, 1984.
The Menaced World, William B. Ewert, 1984.
Selected Poems, Bloodaxe Books, 1986.
Breathing the Water, New Directions Press, 1987.
Poems, 1968-1972, New Directions Press, 1987.
Door in the Hive, New Directions Press, 1989.

OTHER

(Translator and editor with Edward C. Dimock, Jr.) *In Praise of Krishna: Songs from the Bengali,* Doubleday, 1967.
In the Night: A Story, Albondocani Press, 1968.
(Contributor of translations) Jules Supervielle, *Selected Writings,* New Directions Press, 1968.
(Translator from French) Eugene Guillevic, *Selected Poems,* New Directions Press, 1969.
The Poet in the World (essays), New Directions Press, 1973.
Light Up the Cave (essays), New Directions Press, 1981.
(Translator with others from Bulgarian) William Meredith, editor, *Poets of Bulgaria,* Unicorn Press, 1985.
(Translator from French) Jean Joubert, *Black Iris,* Copper Canyon Press, 1988.

Also contributor to poetry anthologies, such as *The New American Poetry, Poet's Choice, Poets of Today,* and *New Poets of England and America.* Sound recordings of Levertov's poetry include "Today's Poets 3," Folkways, and "The Acolyte," Watershed, 1985. Contributor to numerous journals. Poetry editor, *Nation,* 1961-62, and *Mother Jones,* 1976-78.

Manuscript collections are housed in the following locations: Humanities Research Center, University of Texas at Austin; Washington University, St. Louis, Mo.; Indiana University, Bloomington; Fales Library, New York University, New York City; Beinecke Library, Yale University, New Haven, Conn.; Brown University, Providence, R.I.; University of Connecticut, Storrs, Conn.; Columbia University, New York City; State University of New York at Stony Brook.

SIDELIGHTS: As *World Literature Today* contributor Doris Earnshaw explains, poet and essayist "Denise Levertov was fitted by birth and political destiny to voice the terrors and pleasures of the twentieth century. . . . She has published poetry since the 1940s that speaks of the great contemporary themes: Eros, solitude, community, war." Although born and raised in England, Levertov came to the United States when she was twenty-five years old and all but her first few poetry collections have been described as thoroughly American. Early on, critics and colleagues alike detected an American idiom and style to her work, noting the influences of writers like William Carlos Williams, H. D. (Hilda Doolittle), Kenneth Rexroth, Wallace Stevens, and the projectivist Black Mountain poets. With the onset of the turbulent 1960s, Levertov delved into socio-political poetry and has continued writing in this sphere; in *Modern American Women Poets,* for instance, Jean Gould calls her "a poet of definite political and social consciousness." In the end, however, Levertov refuses to be labeled, and Rexroth in *With Eye and Ear* says she is "in fact classically independent."

Because Levertov never received a formal education, her earliest literary influences can be traced to her home life in Ilford, England, a suburb of London. Levertov and her older sister, Olga, were educated by their Welsh mother Beatrice Adelaide Spooner-Jones until the age of thirteen. The girls further received sporadic religious training from their father Paul Peter Levertoff, a Russian Jew who converted to Christianity and subquently moved to England to become an Anglican minister. In the *Dictionary of Literary Biography,* Carolyn Matalene explains that "the education [Levertov] did receive seems, like Robert Browning's, made to order. Her mother read aloud to the family the great works of nineteenth-century fiction, and she read poetry, especially the lyrics of Tennyson. . . . Her father, a prolific writer in Hebrew, Russian, German, and English, used to buy secondhand books by the lot to obtain particular volumes. Levertov grew up surrounded by books and people talking about them in many languages." Many of Levertov's readers favor her lack of formal education because they see it as an impetus to verse that is consistently clear, precise, and accessible. According to Earnshaw, "Levertov seems never to have had to shake loose from an academic style of extreme ellipses and literary allusion, the self-conscious obscurity that the Provencal poets called 'closed.' " Since Levertov decided at age five to become a poet and wrote poems as a child, it is apparent that her home environment has been integral to the success she has become.

Levertov had confidence in her poetic abilities from the beginning, and several well-respected literary figures believed in her talents, as well. Gould records Levertov's "temerity" at the age of twelve when she sent several of her poems directly to T. S. Eliot: "She received a two-page typewritten letter from him, offering her 'excellent advice'. . . . His letter gave her renewed impetus for making poems and sending them out." Other early supporters included critic Herbert Read, editor Charles Wrey Gardiner, and author Kenneth Rexroth. When Levertov had her first poem published in *Poetry Quarterly* in 1940, Rexroth professed: "In no time at all Herbert Read, Tambi Mutti, Charles Wrey Gardiner, and incidentally myself, were all in excited correspondence about her. She was the baby of the new Romanticism. Her poetry had about it a wistful *Schwarmerei* unlike anything in English except perhaps Matthew Arnold's 'Dover Beach.' It could be compared to the earliest poems of Rilke or some of the more melancholy songs of Brahms."

During World War II, Levertov pursued nurse's training and spent three years as a civilian nurse at St. Luke's Hospital in London helping to rehabilitate returning war veterans. She wrote poetry in the evenings. Her first book of poems, *The Double Image,* was published just after the war in 1946. Although many poems in this collection focused on the war, there was no evidence of the immediacy of the death and desperation of the time. Instead, as noted above by Rexroth, the work was very much in keeping with the British neo-romanticism of the 1940s, for it contained formal verse that some considered artificial and overly sentimental. Some critics detect the same propensity for sentimentality in Levertov's second collection, *Here and Now.* In the *National Review,* N. E. Condini comments in retrospect on both of these volumes: "In *The Double Image,* a recurrent sense of loss prompts [Levertov] to extemporize on death as not a threat but a rite to be accepted gladly and honored. This germ of personal mythology burgeons in *Here and Now* with a fable-like aura added to it. . . . [*Here and Now*] is a hymn to 'idiot' joy, which the poet still considers the best protection against the aridity of war and war's memories. Her weakness lies in a childish romanticism, which will be replaced later by a more substantial concision. Here the language is a bit too ornate, too flowery." Criticism aside, Gould says *The Double Image* revealed one thing for certain: "the young poet possessed a strong social consciousness and . . . showed indications of the militant pacifist she was to become."

Levertov came to the United States in 1948, after marrying American writer Mitchell Goodman, and began developing the style that was to make her an internationally respected American poet. Some critics maintain that her first American poetry collection, *Here and Now,* contains vestiges of the bathos that characterized her first book, but for some, *Here and Now* displays Levertov's newly-found American voice. Rexroth, for one, insists in his 1961 collection of essays entitled *Assays* that "the *Schwarmerei* and lassitude are gone. Their place has been taken by a kind of animal grace of the word, a pulse like the footfalls of a cat or the wingbeats of a gull. It is the intense aliveness of an alert domestic love—the wedding of form and content. . . . What more do you want of poetry? You can't ask much more." By the time her third poetry collection, *With Eyes at the Back of Our Heads,* was published, Gould claims Levertov was "regarded as a bona fide American poet."

Levertov's American poetic voice is, in one sense, indebted to the simple, concrete language and imagery, and also the immediacy, characteristic of Williams Carlos Williams' art. Accordingly, Ralph J. Mills, Jr., remarks in his essay in *Poets in Progress* that Levertov's verse "is frequently a tour through the familiar and the mundane until their unfamiliarity and otherworldliness suddenly strike us. . . . The quotidian reality we ignore or try to escape, . . . Levertov revels in, carves and hammers into lyric poems of precise beauty." In turn, *Midwest Quarterly* reviewer Julian Gitzen explains that Levertov's "attention to physical details permits [her] to develop a considerable range of poetic subject, for, like Williams, she is often inspired by the humble, the commonplace, or the small, and she composes remarkably perceptive poems about a single flower, a man walking two dogs in the rain, and even sunlight glittering on rubbish in a street."

In another sense, Levertov's verse exhibits the influence of the Black Mountain poets, such as Robert Duncan, Charles Olson, and Robert Creeley, whom Levertov met through her husband. Creeley was among the first to publish Levertov's poetry in the United States in *Origin* and *Black Mountain Review* in the 1950s. Unlike her early formalized verse, Levertov now gave homage to the projectivist verse of the Black Mountain era, whereby the poet "projects" himself or herself through content rather than through strict meter or form. Although Levertov was assuredly influenced by several renowned American writers of the time, Matalene believes Levertov's "development as a poet has certainly proceeded more according to her own themes, her own sense of place, and her own sensitivities to the music of poetry than to poetic manifestos." Indeed, when Levertov became a New Directions author in 1959, Matalene explains that this came to be because the editor James Laughlin had detected in Levertov's work her own unique voice.

With the onset of U.S. involvement in the Vietnam War in the 1960s, Levertov's social consciousness began to more completely inform both her poetry and her private life. With poet Muriel Rukeyser and several fellow poets, Levertov founded the Writers and Artists Protest against the War in Vietnam. She took part in several anti-war demonstrations in Berkeley, California, and elsewhere, and was jailed at least once for protesting. More recently she has spoken out against nuclear weaponry and U.S. aid to El Salvador. *The Sorrow Dance, Relearning the Alphabet, To Stay Alive,* and to an extent *Candles in Babylon,* as well as other poetry collections, address many socio-political themes, like the Vietnam War, the Detroit riots, and nuclear disarmament. Her goal has been to motivate others into an awareness on these various issues, particularly the Vietnam War.

In contrast with the generally favorable criticism of her work, commentators tend to view the socio-political poems with a degree of distaste, often noting that they resemble prose more than poetry. In *Contemporary Literature,* Marjorie G. Perloff writes:

"It is distressing to report that . . . Levertov's new book, *To Stay Alive,* contains a quantity of bad confessional verse. Her anti-Vietnam War poems, written in casual diary form, sound rather like a versified *New York Review of Books.*" Gould mentions that some consider these poems "preachy," and Matalene notes that in *Relearning the Alphabet* Levertov's "plight is certainly understandable, but her poetry suffers here from weariness and from a tendency toward sentimentality. . . . *To Stay Alive* is a historical document and does record and preserve the persons, conversations, and events of those years. Perhaps, as the events recede in time, these poems will seem true and just, rather than inchoate, bombastic, and superficial. History, after all, does prefer those who take stands."

In an interview with *Los Angeles Times Book Review* contributor Penelope Moffet just prior to the publication of *Candles in Babylon,* Moffet explains that "the poet probably would not go so far as to describe any of her own political work as 'doggerel,' but she does acknowledge that some pieces are only 'sort-of' poems." Moffet then quotes Levertov: "If any reviewer wants to criticize [*Candles in Babylon*] when it comes out, they've got an obvious place to begin—'well, it's not poetry, this ranting and roaring and speech-making.' It [the 1980 anti-draft speech included in *Candles in Babylon*] *was* a speech." Nevertheless, others are not so quick to find fault with these "sort-of" poems. In the opinion of Hayden Carruth for the *Hudson Review, Staying Alive* "contains, what so annoys the critics, highly lyric passages next to passages of prose—letters and documents. But is it, after *Paterson,* necessary to defend this? The fact is, I think Levertov has used her prose bits better than Williams did, more prudently and economically . . . . I also think that 'Staying Alive' is one of the best products of the recent period of politically oriented vision among American poets." In turn, James F. Mersmann's lengthy analysis of several years of Levertov's poetry in *Out of the Vietnam Vortex: A Study of Poets and Poetry against the War* contains remarkable praise for the social protest poems. For contrast, Mersmann first analyzes Levertov's early poetry: "*Balanced* and *whole* are words that have perhaps best characterized the work and the person of Denise Levertov—at least until the late sixties. . . . There are no excesses of ecstasy or despair, celebration or denigration, naivete or cynicism; there is instead an acute ability to find simple beauties in the heart of squalor and something to relish even in negative experiences. . . . Through poetry she reaches to the heart of things, finds out what their centers are. If the reader can follow, he is welcomed along, but although the poetry is mindful of communication and expression, its primary concern is discovery." However, claims Mersmann, the chaos of the war disrupted the balance, the wholeness, and the fundamental concern for discovery apparent in her work—"the shadow of the Vietnam War comes to alter all this: vision is clouded, form is broken, balance is impossible, and the psyche is unable to throw off its illness and sorrow. . . . A few notes of *The Sorrow Dance* sound something like hysteria, and later poems move beyond desperation, through mild catatonia toward intransigent rebellion. . . . In some sense the early poems are undoubtedly more perfect and enduring works of art, more timeless and less datable, but they are, for all their fineness, only teacups, and of sorely limited capacities. The war-shadowed poems are less clean and symmetrical but are moral and philosophical schooners of some size. . . . The war, by offering much that was distasteful and unsightly, prompted a poetry that asks the poet to add the light and weight of her moral and spiritual powers to the fine sensibility of her palate and eye."

In addition to being a poet, Levertov has taught her craft at several colleges and universities nationwide; she has translated a number of works, particularly those of the French poet Jean Joubert; she was poetry editor of *Nation* from 1961-62 and *Mother Jones* from 1976-78; and she has authored two essay collections, *The Poet in the World* and *Light Up the Cave.* With respect to the essay collections, both were generally very well-received. According to Carruth, *The Poet in the World* is "a miscellaneous volume, springing from many miscellaneous occasions, and its tone ranges from spritely to gracious to, occasionally, pedantic. It contains a number of pieces about the poet's work as a teacher; it contains her beautiful impromptu obituary for William Carlos Williams, as well as reviews and appreciations of other writers. But chiefly the book is about poetry, its mystery and its craft, and about the relationship between poetry and life. . . . It should be read by everyone who takes poetry seriously." Other reviewers also recommend the work to those interested in the craft of poetry since, as *New Republic* commentator Josephine Jacobsen puts it, "Levertov speaks for the reach and dignity of poetry. . . . [The book] makes . . . large claims for an art form so often hamstrung in practice by the trivial, the fake and the chic. It is impossible to read this book, to listen to its immediacy, without a quickening."

The essays in *Light Up the Cave,* in turn, are considered "a diary of our neglected soul," by *American Book Review* critic Daniel Berrigan: "Norman Mailer did something like this in the sixties; but since those heady days and nights, he, like most such marchers and writers, has turned to other matters. . . . Levertov is still marching, still recording the march. . . . The entire book is beyond praise. I think of how, in a sane time, such a book and those who preceded it . . . would form a university course entitled something like: A Renaissance Woman of the Late Twentieth Century. But this is dreaming; it would mean crossing jealous frontiers, violating 'expertise.'" *Library Journal* contributor Rochelle Ratner detects much maturation since the earlier *Poet in the World* and Ingrid Rimland, in the *Los Angeles Times Book Review,* remarks that "the strong impression remains that here speaks a poet intensely loyal to her craft, abiding by an artist's inner rules and deserving attention and respect. . . . This volume is a potpourri: assorted musings, subtle insights, tender memories of youth and strength, political passions, gentle but respectful accolades to other writers. The prose is utterly free of restraints, save those demanded by a fierce, independent spirit insisting at all times on honesty."

Into the 1970s and the 1980s Levertov has continued to produce volume after volume of poetry. She has devoted her writing talents to myriad topics, including the childhood and adolescence of her son, Nikolai Gregory; her female perspective on the world; and her sister, Olga, who died young on the heels of a fanatic activist career. The disruption of balance that infused her poetry during the 1960s and early 1970s war era is also evidenced in the confessional poems she wrote about her 1972 divorce from Mitchell Goodman in *The Freeing of the Dust.* With regard to her 1982 volume *Candles in Babylon, World Literature Today* reviewer John Martone is fond of Levertov's "consciously encyclopedic scope" and believes "she remains in this book one of the most vitally innovative of contemporary poets." Although in his *World Literature Today* review of the 1984 *Oblique Prayers,* George Economou expresses regret that Levertov has not taken any new risks or ventured into a new direction, other critics praise her consistency in providing good art. And all along, Levertov's social and political consciousness rings strong. In summary, according to Berrigan, "our options [in a tremulous world], as they say, are no longer large. . . . [We] may choose to do nothing; which is to say, to go discreetly or wildly mad, letting fear possess us and frivolity rule our days. Or we may, along with admirable spirits like Denise Levertov, be driven sane; by community, by conscience, by treading the human crucible."

BIOGRAPHICAL/CRITICAL SOURCES:

BOOKS

Breslin, James E. B., *From Modern to Contemporary American Poetry, 1945-1965,* University of Chicago Press, 1984.

Dictionary of Literary Biography, Volume 5: *American Poets since World War II,* Gale, 1980.

Gould, Jean, *Modern American Women Poets,* Dodd, 1985.

Hungerford, Edward, editor, *Poets in Progress,* Northwestern University Press, 2nd edition, 1967.

Mersmann, James, *Out of the Vietnam Vortex: A Study of Poets and Poetry against the War,* University Press of Kansas, 1974.

Rexroth, Kenneth, *Assays,* New Directions Press, 1961.

Rexroth, Kenneth, *With Eye and Ear,* Herder & Herder, 1970.

Slaughter, William, *The Imagination's Tongue: Denise Levertov's Poetic,* Aquila, 1981.

Wagner, Linda W., *Denise Levertov,* Twayne, 1967.

Wagner, Linda W., editor, *Denise Levertov: In Her Own Province,* New Directions Press, 1979.

PERIODICALS

American Book Review, January-February, 1983.
Contemporary Literature, winter, 1973.
Library Journal, September 1, 1981.
Los Angeles Times Book Review, June 6, 1982, July 18, 1982.
Michigan Quarterly, fall, 1985.
Midwest Quarterly, spring, 1975.
Nation, August 14, 1976.
National Review, March 21, 1980.
New Republic, January 26, 1974.
New York Times Book Review, January 7, 1973, November 30, 1975.
Village Voice, September 29, 1987.
World Literature Today, winter, 1981, spring, 1983, summer, 1985.

*   *   *

LEVI, Primo   1919-1987
(Damiano Malabaila)

PERSONAL: Born July 31, 1919, in Turin, Italy; died from a fall down a stairwell in an apparent suicide attempt, April 11, 1987, in Turin, Italy; son of Cesare (a civil engineer) and Ester (Luzzati) Levi; married Lucia Morpurgo (a teacher), September 8, 1947; children: Lisa, Renzo. *Education:* University of Turin, B.S. (summa cum laude), 1941. *Religion:* Jewish.

ADDRESSES: Home—Corso Re Umberto 75, Turin, Italy.

CAREER: Chemist and author. Partisan in Italian Resistance, 1943; deported to Auschwitz Concentration Camp in Oswiecim, Poland, and imprisoned there, 1943-45; SIVA (paints, enamels, synthetic resins), Settimo, Turin, Italy, technical executive, 1948-77.

AWARDS, HONORS: Premio Campiello (Venice literary prize), 1963 for *La Tregua,* and 1982, for *Se non ora, quando?;* Premio Bagutta (Milan literary prize), 1967, for *Storie Naturali;* Premio Strega (Rome literary prize), 1979, for *La chiave stella;* Premio Viareggio (Viareggio literary prize), 1982, for *Se non ora, quando?;* co-recipient (with Saul Bellow) of Kenneth B. Smilen

fiction award from Jewish Museum in New York, 1985; Present Tense/Joel H. Cavior literary award, 1986, for *The Periodic Table.*

WRITINGS:

Se Questo e un Uomo, F. de Silva (Turin), 1947, 15th edition, Einaudi (Turin), 1975, translation by Stuart Woolf published as *If This Is a Man,* Orion Press (New York), 1959, published as *Survival in Auschwitz: The Nazi Assault on Humanity,* Collier, 1961 (also see below), new edition, 1966 (published in England as *If This Is a Man,* Bodley Head, 1966), dramatic version in original Italian (with Pieralberto Marche), Einaudi, 1966.

La Tregua, Einaudi, 1958, 8th edition, 1965, translation by Woolf published as *The Reawakening,* Little, Brown, 1965 (also see below; published in England as *The Truce: A Survivor's Journey Home From Auschwitz,* Bodley Head, 1965).

(Under pseudonym Damiano Malabaila) *Storie Naturali* (title means "Natural Histories"; short story collection), Einaudi, 1967.

(With Carlo Quartucci) *Intervista Aziendale* (radio script), Radiotelevisione Italiana, 1968.

Vizio di Forma (title means "Technical Error"; short story collection), Einaudi, 1971.

Il sistema periodico, Einaudi, 1975, translation by Raymond Rosenthal published as *The Periodic Table,* Schocken, 1984.

Abruzzo forte e gentile: Impressioni d'occhio e di cuore, edited by Virgilio Orsini, A. Di Cioccio, 1976.

Shema: Collected Poems, Menard, 1976.

La chiave a stella (novel), Einaudi, 1978, translation by William Weaver published as *The Monkey's Wrench,* Summit Books, c. 1986.

La Ricerca della radici: Antologia personale, Einaudi, c. 1981.

Lilit e altri racconti, Einaudi, 1981, translation by Ruth Feldman published as *Moments of Reprieve,* Summit Books, c. 1986.

Se non ora, quando? (novel), Einaudi, 1982, translation by Weaver published as *If Not Now, When?,* introduction by Irving Howe, Summit Books, c. 1985.

(Translator) Franz Kafka, *Il processo* (title means "The Trial"), c. 1983.

L'altrui mestiere, Einaudi, c. 1985.

Survival in Auschwitz [and] *The Reawakening: Two Memoirs,* Summit Books, 1986.

Autoritratto di Primo Levi, Garzanti (Milan), 1987.

Sommersi e i salvati (originally published in 1986), translation by Rosenthal published as *The Drowned and the Saved,* Summit Books, 1988.

The Collected Poems of Primo Levi, translation by Feldmand and Brian Swann, Faber & Faber, 1988.

The Mirror Maker, translation by Rosenthal, Schocken, 1989.

(With Tullio Regge) *Dialogo,* Princeton University Press, 1989.

The Sixth Day, and Other Stories, Summit Books, 1990.

SIDELIGHTS: Primo Levi told *CA:* "My uncommon experience as a concentration camp inmate and as a survivor has deeply influenced my later life and has turned me into a writer. The two books [*Se Questo un Uomo* and *La Tregua*] are a chronicle of my exile and an attempt to understand its meaning."

If This Is a Man and *The Reawakening,* the English translations of *Se Questo un Uomo* and *La Tregua,* have been widely praised for their portrayal of Levi's imprisonment and subsequent return home. W. J. Cahnman, for example, reviewing *If This Is a Man* in *American Journal of Sociology,* writes: "Here is literally a report from hell: the detached, scientific, unearthly story of a man who descended to the nether world at Auschwitz and returned to the land of the living." Levi's "lack of personal bitterness is almost unnatural, especially when it is realised that he wrote so soon after the German retreat brought him his freedom," notes G. F. Seddon in the *Manchester Guardian.* "Levi's more outstanding virtue is his compassionate understanding of how in these conditions men cease to be men, either give up the struggle or in devious ways win it, usually at the expense of their fellow men." In a 1985 interview published in the *Los Angeles Times,* Levi defended his scientific approach to recounting the horrors of the Holocaust: "It was my duty not to behave as a victim, not to wail and weep, but to be a witness, to give readers material for judgment. This is Divine Law, to be a witness, not to overstate or distort but to deliver and furnish facts. The final judge is the reader."

Sergio Pacifici points out in *Saturday Review* that like *If This Is a Man, The Reawakening,* which chronicles the author's return to Italy, is more than an intimate and accurate diary. "It is a plea for self-restraint and generosity in human relations that may well be heeded in our own critical times," he says. "Levi's lucid and wise reflections on the nature of man deserve more than a mere hearing. *The Reawakening* must take its honored place next to Carlo Levi's *Christ Stopped at Eboli,* Andre Schwartz-Bart's *The Last of the Just,* and *The Diary of Anne Frank.*"

After the successful publication of these first two memoirs, Levi continued to write about the Jewish Holocaust in a variety of works, including two award-winning novels, *La chiave a stella* (published in English as *The Monkey's Wrench*) and *Se non ora, quando?* (published in English as *If Not Now, When?*). Toward the mid-1980s, however, Levi became progressively despondent over what he felt was a general disregard for the immense suffering and loss the Jews experienced during World War II. For reasons not clearly understood, Levi ended his life in 1987 when he jumped down a stairwell in his native town of Turin, Italy. Levi's friend Italian newspaper editor Lorenzo Mundo told Steve Kellerman of the *New York Times* that during the months preceding his death, Levi "would come to visit me and his face looked so discouraged and helpless. He kept saying he was tired, physically and mentally. And he was terribly pessimistic about the destiny of the world and the fate of the spirit of man." Since Levi's death a number of his works have been translated into English, including *The Collected Poems of Primo Levi, The Mirror Maker, The Sixth Day, and Other Stories,* and his final work, *The Drowned and the Saved.*

BIOGRAPHICAL/CRITICAL SOURCES:

PERIODICALS

American Journal of Sociology, May, 1960.
Manchester Guardian, April 22, 1960, February 12, 1965.
New York Times Book Review, November 7, 1965.
Observer, January 26, 1965.
Saturday Review, January 2, 1960, May 15, 1965.
Times Literary Supplement, April 15, 1960, December 3, 1982.

*   *   *

LEVIN, Ira 1929-

PERSONAL: Born August 27, 1929, in New York, N.Y.; son of Charles (a toy importer) and Beatrice (Schlansky) Levin; married Gabrielle Aronsohn, August 20, 1960 (divorced January, 1968); married Phyllis Finkel, 1979 (divorced, 1981); children: (first marriage) Adam, Jared, Nicholas. *Education:* Attended Drake University, 1946-48; New York University, A.B., 1950.

ADDRESSES: Home—New York, N.Y. *Agent*—Harold Ober Associates, 40 East 49th St., New York, N.Y. 10017.

CAREER: Novelist and playwright. *Military service:* U.S. Army, Signal Corps, 1953-55.

MEMBER: Dramatists Guild, Authors Guild, Authors League of America, American Society of Composers, Authors and Publishers (ASCAP).

AWARDS, HONORS: Edgar Allan Poe Award, Mystery Writers of America, 1953, for *A Kiss before Dying,* and 1980, for *Deathtrap.*

WRITINGS:

NOVELS

A Kiss before Dying, Simon & Schuster, 1953.
Rosemary's Baby (also see below), Random House, 1967.
This Perfect Day (also see below; Literary Guild selection), Random House, 1970.
The Stepford Wives (also see below), Random House, 1972.
The Boys from Brazil, Random House, 1976.
Three by Ira Levin (contains *Rosemary's Baby, This Perfect Day,* and *The Stepford Wives*), Random House, 1985.

PLAYS

No Time for Sergeants (adapted from the novel by Mac Hyman; first produced on Broadway at the Alvin Theatre, October 20, 1955; produced on the West End at Her Majesty's Theatre, August 23, 1956), Random House, 1956.
Interlock (first produced on Broadway at the ANTA Theatre, February 6, 1958), Dramatists Play Service, 1958.
Critic's Choice (first produced on Broadway at the Ethel Barrymore Theatre, February 14, 1960; produced in London, England, 1961), Random House, 1961.
General Seeger (first produced on Broadway at the Lyceum Theatre, February 28, 1962), Dramatists Play Service, 1962.
"Drat!, The Cat," with music by Milton Schafer, first produced on Broadway at the Martin Beck Theatre, October 10, 1965.
"Dr. Cook's Garden," first produced on Broadway at the Belasco Theatre, September 26, 1967.
Veronica's Room (first produced on Broadway, 1973), Random House, 1974.
Deathtrap (first produced on Broadway at the Music Box Theatre, February 26, 1978), Random House, 1979.
Break a Leg (first produced on Broadway at the Palace Theatre, April 29, 1979), Samuel French, 1981.

OTHER

Also author of scripts for the television series "Clock," "Lights Out," and "U.S. Steel Hour."

SIDELIGHTS: In his plays and novels, Ira Levin exhibits "a continuing preoccupation with dark matters," states James Lardner in the *Washington Post Book World.* Levin's first novel, *A Kiss before Dying,* is a murder mystery; *Rosemary's Baby* is a horror novel, as are *This Perfect Day* and *The Stepford Wives; The Boys from Brazil* is a thriller about the resurgence of a Nazi underground; and Levin's most successful play, "Deathtrap," is a mystery comedy. Despite his dark themes, Levin's many popular successes have shown him to be "a professional writer with an ear attuned to the elusive tempo of the times," Robert Lima writes in *Studies in American Fiction.*

Levin began his career by writing for television in the early 1950s, scripting for some of the era's top programs. His first novel, a mystery entitled *A Kiss before Dying,* appeared in 1953 to rave reviews. The novel is told in three parts: the first part from the point of view of the supposed killer of a young girl; the other parts from the points of view of the girl's two sisters as they attempt to track down the killer. Writing in the *Chicago Sunday Tribune,* Drexel Drake describes *A Kiss before Dying* as a "remarkably constructed story depicting an inconceivably vicious character in episodes of chilling horror." Anthony Boucher of the *New York Times Book Review* maintains that "Levin combines great talent for pure novel writing—full bodied characterization, subtle psychological exploration, vivid evocation of locale—with strict technical whodunit tricks as dazzling as anything ever brought off." James Sandoe of the *New York Herald Tribune Book Review* was moved to call *A Kiss before Dying* "the most striking debut of the year." The Mystery Writers of America were inclined to agree with Sandoe. They awarded the novel an Edgar Allan Poe Award as the best first novel of 1953.

It was fourteen years before Levin wrote another novel. With the success of his stage adaptation of Mac Hyman's *No Time for Sergeants* in 1955, which ran for more than seven hundred performances on Broadway and launched the career of actor Andy Griffith, Levin devoted many years to writing exclusively for the theater. But in 1967 he returned to the novel with *Rosemary's Baby,* the story of a young couple in the clutches of a modern cult of devil-worshippers. The Satanists want Rosemary, the young wife, to give birth to the son of the Devil, hoping that he may "overcome the influence of God's son, Christ," Lima relates. But Rosemary is a recently lapsed Catholic who may only be hallucinating the devil-worshippers out of religious guilt. She is unsure whether she is truly threatened or merely fantasizing her danger. "One by one, untoward events happen. . . .," a writer for *Time* reports. "Dark signs and other-worldly hints occur; black candles, 'tannis root' or Devil's-fungus, missing articles of clothing." "The delicate line between belief and disbelief is faultlessly drawn. . . .," writes Thomas J. Fleming in the *New York Times Book Review.* "We are with [Levin] entirely, admiring his skill and simultaneously searching out possible, probable and improbable explanations of how he is going to extricate his heroine."

The setting for the novel, a gloomy Manhattan apartment building, is based on a building where Levin once lived. It "had a laundry room kind of like the one in the book," Levin explained to a writer for *Publishers Weekly.* "I would never let my wife go down there alone." Other details in the book are based on items from the daily newspaper. For the time period covered in the novel, some nine months during 1965 and 1966, Levin worked appropriate newspaper stories into *Rosemary's Baby* to make it more realistic. Coincidentally, Pope Paul VI's visit to New York occurred at the same time that Rosemary would have conceived her baby, so Levin worked it into his story. "The contrast between the Papal visit and what was happening to Rosemary produced some highly effective and quite unexpected drama," according to the *Publishers Weekly* article.

Critical appraisal of *Rosemary's Baby* was generally favorable. Barbara Nelson of *Library Journal,* for example, compares Levin's writing in the novel to the work of Shirley Jackson. Both authors, she claims, suggest a "veneer of normality with hideous evil forces busy just beneath the surface." Peter Corodimas of *Best Sellers* also praises the novel, calling it "an exercise in sheer terror and tight craftsmanship" that is "superb." Fleming, however, ultimately judges *Rosemary's Baby* to be "just another Gothic tale" because of its literal resolution. But in her conclusion, Nelson argues that Levin "suspends disbelief so effectively that the unwary reader may well be converted to belief in the supernatural."

Ironically, Levin himself is not a believer in the supernatural. "It's not something I gave much serious attention to," he told

Lardner. But the huge success of *Rosemary's Baby*—with over five million copies sold—and of the subsequent film adaptation by director Roman Polanski inspired other writers to turn to the occult thriller genre. Throughout the 1970s there was "a small tidal wave of other tales of evil and the supernatural," Lardner writes. Levin finds his book so disturbing that he refused to allow his own wife, pregnant at the time he worked on the manuscript, to read it. "I don't think any pregnant woman should read it," he declared in *Publishers Weekly.*

Levin's next two novels, *This Perfect Day* and *The Stepford Wives,* have similarly chilling premises. In *This Perfect Day,* a huge subterranean computer regulates all human behavior. In *The Stepford Wives,* the wives in a suburban community are turned into obedient robots. Alex Keneas of *Newsweek* finds that, in *This Perfect Day,* Levin "knows how to handle plot, twisting here and turning there, so that his story breezes along. . . . For a quick couple of hours it takes you away." Speaking of *The Stepford Wives,* Webster Schott of *Saturday Review* complains that it "is written with a grade school vocabulary, a high school version of syntax, and a best-selling author's understanding of what mass audiences want." But Martin Levin of the *New York Times Book Review* finds a "broad current of humor beneath the horrific surface of this little ambush of Women's Lib, life and the pursuit of happiness."

The Boys from Brazil, Levin's next novel, postulates a Nazi underground in South America led by the infamous Josef Mengele, the doctor who performed hideous experiments at the Auschwitz concentration camp. Mengele's experiments with cloning lead him to attempt a cloning of Adolf Hitler and thereby restore the Nazi movement. He clones 94 babies from Hitler's genes and places the children with parents similar in age and occupation to Hitler's own parents, hoping that at least one of the children will grow up with Hitler's driving ambition for political power. In his review of *The Boys from Brazil,* the critic for the *New Yorker* finds that "the writing is smooth and suspense-inducing, the characters are wafer-thin but plausible, and Mr. Levin once again proves himself to be an author who can tell a fairly far-fetched, silly story with surprising grace."

Many of the characters in the novel are based on actual people. Mengele, for example, is the real doctor from Auschwitz who was long rumored to be hiding in South America. And the novel's hero, Yakov Libermann, who tracks down fugitive Nazis and exposes the cloning plot, is based on the actual Nazi hunter Simon Weisenthal. This use of actual people as fictional characters moves R. Z. Sheppard of *Time* to criticize Levin. Sheppard thinks that "the turning of Josef Mengele into a mad scientist from the pages of a 1940s comic book requires more than a suspension of disbelief. It also requires a suspension of taste. Exploiting such a monster for entertainment and profit is enough to give evil a bad name."

But most reviews of *The Boys from Brazil* judge it to be an entertaining novel. Valentine Cunningham of *New Statesman,* for example, finds that "the plot unfolds utterly enthrallingly to make a superior read in this genre." And Gary Arnold of the *Washington Post* calls it "a snappy pop entertainment synthesis of accumulating suspense, detective work, pseudoscientific speculation and historical wish fulfillment." Writing in *Newsweek,* Peter S. Prescott admits that a Levin novel "is like a bag of popcorn: utterly without nutritive value and probably fattening, yet there's no way to stop once you've started."

The idea for *The Boys from Brazil* came from a newspaper article on cloning in which Hitler and Mozart were given as examples of the wide range of cloning possibilities. "Needless to say,"

Lardner observes, "Levin never gave much thought to a novel about the cloning of Mozart." Levin's ideas for books and plays "are not so much born as incubated," Alfred Gillespie writes in *People*. A story idea is first jotted down in one of Levin's many notebooks and will, over a period of years, be added to and mulled over until it coalesces into a complete plot. The process of writing, too, takes time. Levin admits to being a slow writer. "Drat!, The Cat" took ten years to reach the stage; *Rosemary's Baby* was six years in the making; and *Deathtrap* took six years from initial idea to full production.

Levin's playwriting efforts since his initial success with "No Time for Sergeants" have been only moderately fruitful. Besides "No Time for Sergeants," only "Critic's Choice" enjoyed a substantial run on Broadway. The folding of "Drat!, The Cat" after only a week, Levin told Gillespie, "succeeded only in sending me back to novels." But in 1978, Levin returned to the stage with "Deathtrap," a comedy mystery in involving Sidney Bruhl, a failed playwright who toys with the idea of murdering a young playwright and stealing his play. Filled with twists and turns that keep the audience guessing as to the protagonist's real intentions, "Deathtrap" ran on Broadway for over four years—from February 26, 1978, to June 27, 1982—making it the fourth-longest-running play in Broadway history.

The play's structure—"as convoluted as an artichoke," Richard F. Shepard writes in the *New York Times*—has garnered the most critical attention. Levin succeeds in turning inside-out many cliche mystery situations so that the audience is always surprised by the unexpected. A psychic character, neighbor to the Bruhls, even predicts various plot twists in advance, but her predictions only serve to mislead the audience. According to Walter Kerr of the *New York Times,* "Levin engages us all in an open-handed, evening-long game of hide-and-seek. . . . [He] has brazenly opted for revealing all, showing us the naked machinery, inviting us to compete in putting the pieces into the jigsaw. And surprised us anyway. The sheer cockiness of his method compounds our delight." Sylvie Drake of the *Los Angeles Times* calls the play "two hours of escapist fun, a rollercoaster ride through convolutions of plot and psyches."

"Deathtrap" provides as many laughs as chills, following in the tradition of *Arsenic and Old Lace* and other Broadway thrillers. Sidney Bruhl's witty remarks about the writer's life and the writing of mysteries are a running commentary on the play itself. "All the way through," Shepard remarks, "['Deathtrap'] is laughing at itself and perhaps at the genre on which it is a take-off, although at its moment of murder it wipes the smile off your face." Levin, Lardner writes, "is after laughs as well as screams. . . . 'Deathtrap' is capable of generating both responses, sometimes all but simultaneously." Speaking to Gillespie, Levin defends the thriller tradition in theatre. "Thrillers are satisfying deep down," Levin says, "because they give you the chance to deal safely with violence and murder. . . . They're horror stories with happy endings." "Deathtrap," too, has a happy ending. In addition to its record-breaking run on Broadway, the play was performed by four national touring companies, was made into a film, and won an Edgar Allan Poe Award.

Levin's books have enjoyed sales in the millions of copies, his novels and plays have been made into popular films, and his work has been translated into many languages. His publisher, Random House, prints a minimum of 100,000 copies of every new book he writes. It is no surprise, then, to hear Levin tell Lardner that his primary purpose "will always be to entertain. . . . I really in general tend to resent works of art that make a moral point. In a way, when you write something sheerly to entertain, that's making a moral point, too."

MEDIA ADAPTATIONS: A Kiss before Dying was filmed by United Artists in 1956, *No Time for Sergeants* by Twentieth Century-Fox in 1959, *Critic's Choice* by Warner Bros. in 1962, *Rosemary's Baby* by Paramount in 1968, "Dr. Cook's Garden" by the American Broadcasting Co. in 1970, *The Stepford Wives* by Columbia in 1975, *The Boys from Brazil* by Twentieth Century-Fox in 1978, and *Deathtrap* by Warner Bros. in 1982.

BIOGRAPHICAL/CRITICAL SOURCES:

BOOKS

Contemporary Literary Criticism, Gale, Volume 3, 1975, Volume 6, 1976.

PERIODICALS

Best Sellers, April 15, 1967.
Books and Bookmen, December, 1972.
Chicago Sunday Tribune, October 25, 1953.
Christian Science Monitor, September 27, 1972.
Library Journal, April 15, 1967.
Los Angeles Times, March 29, 1979.
National Observer, June 12, 1967, February 24, 1969.
New Republic, June 20, 1981.
New Statesman, April 16, 1976.
Newsweek, April 17, 1967, March 16, 1970, November 5, 1973, February 23, 1976.
New York, November 12, 1973.
New Yorker, November 21, 1953, November 5, 1973, March 8, 1976.
New York Herald Tribune Book Review, October 18, 1953.
New York Times, October 25, 1953, March 5, 1978, April 30, 1979, August 17, 1981, June 8, 1982, April 23, 1985.
New York Times Book Review, April 30, 1967, October 15, 1972, March 14, 1976.
People, May 15, 1978.
Publishers Weekly, May 22, 1967.
Punch, April 15, 1970.
Saturday Review, April 15, 1967, October 7, 1972.
Studies in American Fiction, autumn, 1974.
Time, June 23, 1967, November 12, 1973, February 23, 1976.
Times Literary Supplement, June 1, 1967.
Village Voice, November 8, 1973.
Washington Post, October 5, 1978, July 22, 1979, July 26, 1979, May 22, 1986.
Washington Post Book World, February 15, 1975.
World, October 10, 1972.

*   *   *

LEVI-STRAUSS, Claude 1908-

PERSONAL: Born November 28, 1908, in Brussels, Belgium; son of Raymond (a painter) and Emma (Levy) Levi-Strauss; married Dina Dreyfus, 1932 (divorced); married Rosemarie Ullmo, 1946 (divorced); married Monique Roman, April 5, 1954; children: (second marriage) Laurent; (third marriage) Matthieu. *Education:* Universite de Paris, licence, 1929, Agregation, 1931, Doctorat es Lettres, 1948.

ADDRESSES: Home—2 rue des Marronniers, Paris 75016, France. *Office*—Laboratoire d'Anthropologie sociale, 52 rue du Cardinal-Lemoine, Paris 75005, France.

CAREER: Universidade de Sao Paulo, Sao Paulo, Brazil, professor of sociology, 1935-39; New School for Social Research, New

York, N.Y., visiting professor, 1942-45; French Embassy, Washington, D.C., cultural counselor, 1946-47; Musee de l'Homme, Paris, France, associate curator, 1948-49; Sorbonne, Ecole Pratique des Hautes Etudes, Paris, director of research, 1950—, College de France, Paris, professor of social anthropology, 1959—.

MEMBER: Academie francaise, National Academy of Sciences, American Academy and Institute of Arts and Letters, British Academy, Royal Academy of the Netherlands (foreign member), Academy of Norway (foreign member), Royal Anthropological Institute of Great Britain (honorary fellow), American Academy of Arts and Sciences, American Philosophical Society, Norwegian Academy of Letters and Sciences, New York Academy of Sciences.

AWARDS, HONORS: Honorary doctorates from University of Brussels, Oxford University, Yale University, University of Chicago, Columbia University, Stirling University, Universite Nationale du Zaire, University of Uppsala, Laval University, Universidad Nacional Autonoma de Mexico, Johns Hopkins University, and Harvard University; Viking Fund Medal, Wenner-Gren Foundation, 1966; Erasmus Prize, 1975; Grand-Officier de la Legion d'Honneur; Commandeur de l'Ordre Nationale du Merite; Commandeur de l'Ordre des Palmes Academiques; Commandeur des Arts et des Lettres; Commandeur de la Coronne de Belgique; Cruzeiro do Sul.

WRITINGS:

La Vie familiale et sociale des Indiens Nambikwara, Societe de Americanistes, 1948.

Les Structures elementaires de la parente, Presses Universitaires de France, 1949, translation by J. H. Bell and J. R. von Strumer published as *The Elementary Structures of Kinship,* Beacon, 1969.

Race et histoire, Gonthier, 1952.

Tristes Tropiques, Plon, 1955, revised edition, Adler, 1968, partial translation by John Russell published as *Tristes Tropiques,* Criterion, 1961 (published in England as *A World on the Wane,* Hutchinson, 1961), complete translation by John Weightman and Doreen Weightman, J. Cape, 1973, Atheneum, 1974.

Anthropologie structurale, Volume 1, Plon, 1958, translation by Claire Jacobson and Brooke Grundfest Schoepf published as *Structural Anthropology,* Basic Books, 1964, Volume 2, Plon, 1973, translation by Monica Layton, Basic Books, 1977.

Entretiens avec Claude Levi-Strauss, edited by Georges Charbonnier, Plon-Julliard, 1961, translation published as *Conversations with Claude Levi-Strauss,* J. Cape, 1969.

La Pensee sauvage, Plon, 1962, translation published as *The Savage Mind,* University of Chicago Press, 1966, revised edition, Adlers Foreign Books, 1985.

Le Totemisme aujourd'hui, Presses Universitaires de France, 1962, translation by Rodney Needham published as *Totemism,* Beacon, 1963, revised edition, Penguin, 1969.

Mythologiques, Plon, Volume 1: *Le Cru et le cuit,* 1964, Volume 2: *Du Miel aux cendres,* 1967, Volume 3: *L'Origine des manieres de table,* 1968, Volume 4: *L'Homme nu,* 1971, translation by J. Weightman and D. Weightman published as *Introduction to a Science of Mythology,* Volume 1: *The Raw and the Cooked,* Harper, 1969, Volume 2: *From Honey to Ashes,* J. Cape, 1973, harper, 1974, Volume 3: *The Origin of Table Manners,* Harper, 1978, Volume 4: *The Naked Man,* Harper, 1981.

The Scope of Anthropology, J. Cape, 1968.

Discours de reception a l'Academie francaise, Institut de France (Paris), 1974.

La Voie des masques, two volumes, Skira, 1975, enlarged edition, Plon, 1979, translation by S. Modelski published as *The Way of the Masks,* University of Washington Press, 1982.

Myth and Meaning: Five Talks for Radio, University of Toronto Press, 1978, Schocken, 1979.

Le Regard eloigne, Plon, 1983, translation by J. Neugroschel and P. Hoss published as *The View from Afar,* Basic Books, 1985.

Paroles donnees, Plon, 1984, translation by Roy Willis published as *Anthropology and Myth: Lectures, 1957-1982,* Blackwell, 1987.

La Potiere jalouse, Plon, 1985, translation by Benedicte Chorier published as *The Jealous Potter,* University of Chicago Press, 1988.

Introduction to the Work of Marcel Mauss, Routledge & Kegan Paul, 1987.

(With Didier Eribon) *De pres et de loin,* Jacobs, 1988.

Comparative Mythology, Johns Hopkins University Press, 1988.

SIDELIGHTS: Often ranked with Jean-Paul Sartre and Andre Malraux as one of France's greatest modern intellectuals, Claude Levi-Strauss is "the last uncontested giant of French letters," as James M. Markham describes him in the *New York Times.* Acclaimed for his studies of primitive mythology and for his autobiographical book *A World on the Wane (Tristes Tropiques),* Levi-Strauss is also credited with founding the movement known as structural anthropology, "the search for underlying patterns of thought in all forms of human activity," as Markham defines it. So pervasive is Levi-Strauss's influence in such diverse fields as language theory, history, and psychology that George Steiner claims in his *Language and Silence: Essays on Language* that "an awareness of Levi-Strauss's thought is a part of current literacy." Marshall D. Sahlins believes the professional attention accorded Levi-Strauss is almost "unparalleled in the history of anthropology."

Tristes Tropiques, Levi-Strauss's study of Brazilian Indians, is "one of the great books of our century," according to Susan Sontag in her *Against Interpretation and Other Essays.* As much a rationale for anthropology as it is a study of a primitive people, the book asks why Western culture is the first to study other cultures and it explores the role of the anthropologist. Sontag finds the book to be "rigorous, subtle, and bold in thought. It is beautifully written. And, like all great books, it bears an absolutely personal stamp; it speaks with a human voice." This personal dimension is noted by Richard A. Shweder in the *New York Times Book Review,* who describes *Tristes Tropiques* as the book in which Levi-Strauss "transformed an expedition to the virgin interiors of the Amazon into a vision quest, and turned anthropology into a spiritual mission to defend mankind against itself."

In his *Introduction to a Science of Mythology,* Levi-Strauss attempts to systematize myths, discover their underlying structures, and expose the process of their creation. James Redfield in *Thinkers of the Twentieth Century* sees the massive four-volume work as "a book about human nature—if we understand that 'nature' here means the mind, which is to say, the sense that things make." "Levi-Strauss was intrigued by the way that languages as well as myths of different cultures resembled each other and appeared to be structured in a similar fashion," Edith Kurzweil explains in *The Age of Structuralism: Levi-Strauss to Foucault.* Steiner credits Levi-Strauss with "seeking a science of mythology, a grammar of symbolic constructs and associations allowing the anthropologist to relate different myths as the structural linguist relates phonemes and language systems. Once the code of myths is deciphered and is seen to have its own logic and translatability, its own grid of values and interchangable significants, the anthropologist will have a tool of great power with which to attack problems of human ecology, of ethnic and linguistic groupings, of cultural diffusion. Above all, he may gain insight into mental processes and strata of consciousness which preserve indices . . . of the supreme event in man's history—the transition from a primarily instinctual, perhaps pre-linguistic condition to the life of consciousness and individualized self-awareness." Although Kurzweil admits that Levi-Strauss's structuralist approach has not been wholly successful in studying mythology, "his theory of the elusive, unconscious structures did lead to the creation of various new subjects of inquiry such as the relationships between the structures of all signs in language, their function within messages, and their rapport with other sign systems, such as music, gestures, [and] body language."

Several observers find that how Levi-Strauss expresses his ideas is as important as what he says. He often presents an intellectual position only to tear it down, uses irony and digression, and ranges over a number of seemingly unrelated subjects—all while displaying a mastery of such diverse fields as linguistics, psychiatry, genetics, and neuroscience. "Levi-Strauss once described his own rather cultivated, but sometimes savage, mind as the intellectual equivalent of slash-and-burn agriculture," Shweder reports. "The prose of Levi-Strauss," Steiner writes, "is a very special instrument, and one which many are trying to imitate. It has an austere, dry detachment. . . . It uses a careful alternance of long sentences, usually organized in ascending rhythm, and of abrupt Latinate phrases. While seeming to observe the conventions of neutral, learned presentation, it allows for brusque personal interventions and asides." "There is more to understanding Levi-Strauss than knowing what he himself has written," adds Godfrey Lienhardt. "Perhaps beyond any other living anthropologist he has established a dialogue with part of the intellectual public, appearing to speak personally to educated general readers and engaging them in his own processes of analysis and reflection." "The outstanding characteristic of his writing . . .," Edmund Leach maintains in his study *Claude Levi-Strauss,* "is that it is difficult to understand; his sociological theories combine baffling complexity with overwhelming erudition." Leach goes so far as to say that "Levi-Strauss is admired not so much for the novelty of his ideas as for the bold originality with which he seeks to apply them. He has suggested new ways of looking at familiar facts; it is the method that is interesting rather than the practical consequences of the use to which it has been put." But Lienhardt identifies Levi-Strauss's writing as "an exhortation to wonder at the complex creativity of mankind, to revere it and finally to see through it."

Levi-Strauss cheerfully admits that his books "are hard to understand" and that he "stands outside of the anthropological mainstream," notes a writer for *Newsweek.* " 'I think,' he says, 'I'm a school by myself.' " With Sartre and Malraux dead, and their leftist politics increasingly discredited, Levi-Strauss now holds a unique and powerful position in the French intelligensia. But though he is widely respected, he refuses to accept the role of "prophet," a role long common among French philosophers. Markham quotes Pierre Bourdieu explaining that "one of [Levi-Strauss's] effects has been to change the nature of the French intellectual, to propose something more modest." David Pace, writing in *Claude Levi-Strauss: The Bearer of Ashes,* reports that Levi-Strauss "has made no real effort to disseminate his ideas of cultural progress to a large popular audience or to translate them into any political movement. On the contrary, he has taken every opportunity to deny the importance of his own speculations on

these topics and to focus attention upon his technical achievements in structural anthropology."

Speaking to Markham, Levi-Strauss identified his deep concern for "a certain number of values which are those of my society and which I consider to be threatened. They are threatened by the Soviet Union, by Islamic fundamentalism, and by the demographic growth of the Third World." Among these values are the importance of a national culture over a world "monoculture" and the ideal of the traditional peasant who lives close to nature. Yet Pace finds "something fundamentally nihilistic about Levi-Strauss's world-view. . . . There is neither a serious effort to protect the things which he sees as threatened nor an attempt to abandon his attachment to them. He himself has described his own position as a 'serene pessimism.' "

"For 25 years," Shweder notes, "[Levi-Strauss] has been the object of adoration and scorn in the English-speaking world." Redfield reports that "it is possible that . . . later ages will speak of our time as the age of Levi-Strauss. . . . He is a maker of the modern mind, and has influenced many who have never read him, and some who have quite mistaken ideas about what he says." As Joan Bamberger writes: "Whatever the future impact of [Levi-Strauss's] work, certainly the anthropological study of myth will never be the same."

BIOGRAPHICAL/CRITICAL SOURCES:

BOOKS

Contemporary Literary Criticism, Volume 38, Gale, 1986.

Girard, Rene, *"To Double Business Bound": Essays on Literature, Mimesis, and Anthropology,* Johns Hopkins University Press, 1978.

Kurzweil, Edith, *The Age of Structuralism: Levi-Strauss to Foucault,* Columbia University Press, 1980.

LaPointe, Francois Y. and Claire C. LaPointe, *Claude Levi-Strauss and His Critics: An International Bibliography of Criticism (1950-1976) Followed by a Bibliography of the Writings of Claude Levi-Strauss,* Garland Publishing, 1977.

Leach, Edmund, *Claude Levi-Strauss,* Viking Press, revised edition, 1974.

Pace, David, *Claude Levi-Strauss: The Bearer of Ashes,* Routledge & Kegan Paul, 1983.

Rossi, Ino, editor, *The Logic of Culture: Advances in Structural Theory and Methods,* J. F. Bergin Publishers, 1982.

Sontag, Susan, *Against Interpretation and Other Essays,* Farrar, Straus, 1966.

Steiner, George, *Language and Silence: Essays on Language, Literature, and the Inhuman,* Atheneum, 1967.

Thinkers of the Twentieth Century, St. James, 2nd edition, 1987.

PERIODICALS

Atlantic, July, 1969.
Book Week, February 9, 1964.
Book World, November 9, 1969.
Commentary, May, 1968.
Globe & Mail (Toronto), May 14, 1988.
Hudson Review, winter, 1967.
Kenyon Review, March, 1967.
Listener, May 23, 1968.
Nation, March 16, 1970.
Natural History, June/July, 1973.
New Republic, July 22, 1969, May 18, 1974.
Newsweek, February 23, 1967.
New York Review of Books, November 28, 1963, October 12, 1967.
New York Times, December 31, 1969, December 21, 1987.

New York Times Book Review, June 3, 1973, April 14, 1985.
Reporter, April 6, 1967.
Saturday Review, December 31, 1966, May 17, 1969.
Spectator, May 12, 1961, March 21, 1969.
Time, June 30, 1967.
Times Literary Supplement, May 12, 1961, June 15, 1967, September 12, 1968.

—*Sketch by Thomas Wiloch*

*   *   *

LEWIS, C(live) S(taples)   1898-1963
(N. W. Clerk, Clive Hamilton)

PERSONAL: Born November 29, 1898, in Belfast, Ireland; died November 22, 1963, of heart failure after an extended illness; son of Albert James (a solicitor) and Flora Augusta (Hamilton) Lewis; married Joy Davidman Gresham, 1956 (died, 1960); children: two stepsons. *Education:* Attended Malvern College, 1913-14; University College, Oxford, A.B. (first class honors), 1923.

ADDRESSES: Magdalene College, Cambridge, England.

CAREER: Philosophy tutor and lecturer, University College, Oxford University, Oxford, England, 1924, fellow and tutor in English literature, Magdalen College, 1925-54; Magdalene College, Cambridge University, Cambridge, England, professor of Medieval and Renaissance English, 1954-63. Ballard Matthews Lecturer, University of Wales, 1941; Riddell Lecturer, University of Durham, 1942; Clark Lecturer, Trinity College, Cambridge, 1944. *Military service:* British army, Somerset Light Infantry, 1918-19; became second lieutenant.

MEMBER: British Academy (fellow, 1955), Royal Society of Literature (fellow, 1948), Athenaeum, Sir Walter Scott Society (president, 1956), Socratic Club (president and speaker), Inklings.

AWARDS, HONORS: Hawthornden Prize, 1936, and Gollancz Memorial Prize for Literature, 1937, both for *The Allegory of Love;* D.D., University of St. Andrews, 1946; fellow, Royal Society of Literature, 1948, British Academy, 1955, University College, Oxford, 1958, and Magdalene College, Cambridge, 1963; Docteur-es-Lettres, Laval University, 1952; honorary fellow, Magdalen College, Oxford, 1955; Library Association Carnegie Medal, 1957, for *The Last Battle;* D.Litt., University of Manchester, 1959; Lewis Carroll Shelf Award, 1962, for *The Lion, the Witch, and the Wardrobe;* honorary doctorate, University of Dijon, 1962, and University of Lyon, 1963.

WRITINGS:

NOVELS

The Pilgrim's Regress: An Allegorical Apology for Christianity, Reason and Romanticism, Dent, 1933, Sheed & Ward, 1935, revised edition, Fount, 1977, reprinted with translations and notes by John C. Traupman, Bantam, 1981.
Out of the Silent Planet (also see below), John Lane, 1938, Macmillan, 1943, reprinted, 1990, abridged with introduction, glossary and notes by Jane Brooks, Macmillan, 1973.
The Screwtape Letters (first published in *Guardian,* 1941), Bles, 1942, Macmillan, 1943, reprinted, New American Library, 1988, revised edition published as *The Screwtape Letters and Screwtape Proposes a Toast* (also see below), Bles, 1961, Macmillan, 1962, reprinted with introduction by Phyllis McGinley (bound with *Mistress to an Age,* by J. Christopher Herold), Time-Life Books, 1981, published as *The*

Screwtape Letters; with, Screwtape Proposes a Toast, drawings by Robert Korn, Macmillan, 1982.
Perelandra (also see below), John Lane, 1943, Macmillan, 1944, reprinted, 1990, new edition published as *Voyage to Venus,* Pan Books, 1960, reprinted, 1983.
That Hideous Strength: A Modern Fairy-Tale for Grownups (also see below), John Lane, 1945, Macmillan, 1946, reprinted, 1990, abridged edition published as *The Tortured Planet,* Avon, 1958.
The Great Divorce: A Dream (first published in weekly installments in *Guardian*), Bles, 1945, reprinted, Collier, 1984.
Till We Have Faces: A Myth Retold, Bles, 1956, Harcourt, 1957, reprinted, 1980.

JUVENILES; ILLUSTRATIONS BY PAULINE BAYNES

The Lion, the Witch, and the Wardrobe (also see below), Macmillan, 1950, reprinted, 1988.
Prince Caspian: The Return to Narnia (also see below), Macmillan, 1951, reprinted, 1988.
The Voyage of the "Dawn Treader" (also see below), Macmillan, 1952, reprinted, Macmillan, 1988.
The Silver Chair (also see below), Macmillan, 1953, reprinted, 1988.
The Horse and His Boy (also see below), Macmillan, 1954, reprinted, 1988.
The Magician's Nephew (also see below), Macmillan, 1955, reprinted, 1988.
The Last Battle (also see below), Macmillan, 1956, reprinted, 1988.

THEOLOGICAL WORKS

The Problem of Pain, Centenary Press, 1940, Macmillan, 1943, reprinted, 1978.
The Weight of Glory (also see below), S.P.C.K., 1942, revised and expanded edition, Macmillan, 1980.
Broadcast Talks: Right and Wrong: A Clue to the Meaning of the Universe and What Christians Believe, Bles, 1942, published as *Broadcast Talks: Reprinted with Some Alterations from Two Series of Broadcast Talks,* Bles, 1942, published as *The Case for Christianity,* Macmillan, 1943, reprinted, 1989.
Christian Behaviour: A Further Series of Broadcast Talks (also see below), Macmillan, 1943.
Beyond Personality: The Christian Idea of God (also see below), Bles, 1944, Macmillan, 1945.
(Editor and author of preface) *George MacDonald: An Anthology,* Centenary Press, 1945, Macmillan, 1947, reprinted, 1986, published as *George MacDonald: 365 Readings,* Collier, 1986.
Miracles: A Preliminary Study, Macmillan, 1947, reprinted, 1978.
The Trouble with X, The Church Union, Church Literature Association, 1948.
Reflections on the Psalms, Harcourt, 1958, Phoenix Press, 1985.
Shall We Lose God in Outer Space? (also see below), S.P.C.K., 1959.
The Four Loves, Harcourt, 1960, Collins, 1987.
The Humanitarian Theory of Punishment, Abingdon, 1972.

LITERARY CRITICISM

The Allegory of Love: A Study in Medieval Tradition, Oxford University Press, 1936, reprinted, 1977.
(With Eustace M. W. Tillyard) *The Personal Heresy: A Controversy,* Oxford University Press, 1939, reprinted, 1965.
Rehabilitations and Other Essays (also see below), Oxford University Press, 1939, reprinted, R. West, 1978.

A Preface to 'Paradise Lost': Being the Ballard Matthews Lectures, Delivered at University College, North Wales, 1941, Oxford University Press, 1942, revised edition, 1960, reprinted Oxford University Press, 1977.

(Editor and author of commentary) Charles Williams, *Arthurian Torso: Containing the Posthumous Fragment of "The Figure of Arthur,"* Oxford University Press, 1948, Eerdmans, 1974.

Hero and Leander (lecture), Oxford University Press, 1952.

English Literature in the Sixteenth Century, Excluding Drama, Clarendon Press, 1954, reprinted, Oxford University Press, 1990, published as *Poetry and Prose in the Sixteenth Century,* 1990.

Studies in Words, Cambridge University Press, 1960, 2nd edition, 1967.

An Experiment in Criticism, Cambridge University Press, 1961.

They Asked for a Paper: Papers and Addresses (also see below), Bles, 1962.

(Author of introduction) *Selections from Layamon's "Brut,"* edited by G. L. Brook, Clarendon Press, 1963.

The Discarded Image: An Introduction to Medieval and Renaissance Literature, Cambridge University Press, 1964.

Studies in Medieval and Renaissance Literature, edited by Walter Hooper, Cambridge University Press, 1967.

Spenser's Images of Life, edited by Alastair Fowler, Cambridge University Press, 1967.

Shelley, Dryden, and Mr. Eliot in Rehabilitations, Richard West, 1973.

(Author of commentary) Charles W. S. Williams, *Taliessin through Logres,* [and] *The Region of the Summer Stars,* [and] *Arthurian Torso* (also see below), Eerdmans, 1974.

Also author of lectures, *Hamlet: The Prince or the Poem?,* H. Milford, 1942, reprinted, Norwood Editions, 1978; *The Literary Impact of the Authorized Version: The Ethel M. Wood Lecture Delivered Before the University of London on 20th March, 1950,* Athlone Press, 1950, Fortress Press, 1963, revised edition, 1967; and *De Descriptione Temporum: An Inaugural Lecture,* Cambridge University Press, 1955.

COLLECTED WORKS

Rehabilitations, 1939, published as *Rehabilitations and Other Essays,* Folcroft, 1980.

The Weight of Glory, and Other Addresses, Macmillan, 1949 (published in England as *Transposition, and Other Addresses,* Bles, 1949), revised edition, 1980.

Mere Christianity (contains enlarged versions of radio talks, *The Case for Christianity, Christian Behaviour,* and *Beyond Personality*), revised and enlarged with new introduction, Macmillan, 1952, reprinted, 1986, anniversary edition, 1981.

The World's Last Night, and Other Essays (contains *Shall We Lose God in Outer Space?*), Harcourt, 1960.

Screwtape Proposes a Toast and Other Pieces, Collins, 1965, published as *Screwtape Proposes a Toast,* Fontana, 1970.

The Complete Chronicles of Narnia, seven volumes (contains *The Lion, the Witch, and the Wardrobe, Prince Caspian: The Return to Narnia, The Voyage of the Dawn Treader, The Silver Chair, The Horse and His Boy, The Magician's Nephew,* and *The Last Battle*), Penguin, 1965, published as *The Chronicles of Narnia,* Macmillan, 1983.

Of Other Worlds: Essays and Stories, edited by Hooper, Bles, 1966, Harcourt, 1967, Collins, 1982.

A Mind Awake: an Anthology of C. S. Lewis, edited by Kilby, Bles, 1968, Harcourt, 1969.

Selected Literary Essays (includes part of *Rehabilitations and Other Essays, De Descriptione Temporum,* part of *They Asked for a Paper: Papers and Addresses*), edited by Hooper, Cambridge University Press, 1969.

C. S. Lewis: Five Best Books in One Volume, Iversen Associates, 1969.

God in the Dock: Essays on Theology and Ethics, edited by Hooper, Eerdmans, 1970 (published in England as *Undeceptions: Essays on Theology and Ethics,* Bles, 1971; new edition published in England as *First and Second Things,* Fount, 1985).

Space Trilogy (boxed set; includes *Out of the Silent Planet, Perelandra,* and *That Hideous Strength*), Macmillan, 1975, reprinted, 1990.

Fern-Seed and Elephants and Other Essays on Christianity, edited by Hooper, Fontana, 1975.

The Dark Tower and Other Stories (includes two unfinished novels), edited by Hooper, Harcourt, 1977.

The Joyful Christian: 127 Readings from C. S. Lewis, Macmillan, 1977.

Six by Lewis (six volumes), Macmillan, 1978.

On Stories and Other Essays on Literature, edited by Hooper, Harcourt, 1982.

The Visionary Christian: One Hundred and Thirty-One Readings from C. S. Lewis, edited by Chad Walsh, Macmillan, 1981.

The Business of Heaven: Daily Readings from C. S. Lewis, edited by Hooper, Harcourt, 1984.

Of This and Other Worlds, edited by Hooper, Fount, 1984.

Boxen Stories, Collins, 1985.

The Seeing Eye and Other Selected Essays from Christian Reflections, Ballantine, 1986.

The Essential C. S. Lewis, Macmillan, 1988.

LETTERS

Beyond the Bright Blur, Harcourt, 1963.

Letters to Malcolm: Chiefly on Prayer, Bles, 1964 (published in England as *Prayer: Letters to Malcolm,* Fontana, 1974).

Letters of C. S. Lewis, edited by brother, W. H. Lewis, Harcourt, 1966.

Letters to an American Lady, edited by Clyde S. Kilby, Eerdmans, 1967, reprinted, Hodder & Stoughton, 1971.

Mark vs. Tristram: Correspondence between C. S. Lewis and Owen Barfield, edited by Hooper, Lowell House Printers, 1967.

They Stand Together: The Letters of C. S. Lewis to Arthur Greeves (1914-1963), edited by Hooper, Macmillan, 1979.

Letters to Children, edited by Lyle W. Dorsett and Marjorie Lamp Mead, foreword by Douglas H. Gresham, Macmillan, 1985.

Letters: C. S. Lewis and Don Giovanni Calabria, Servant (Ann Arbor, MI), 1988.

C. S. Lewis Letters: A Study in Friendship, translation from Latin by Martin Moynihan, Servant, 1988.

POEMS

(Under pseudonym Clive Hamilton) *Spirits in Bondage: A Cycle of Lyrics,* Heinemann, 1919, published under name C. S. Lewis, Harcourt, 1984.

(Under pseudonym Clive Hamilton) *Dymer,* Macmillan, 1926, reprinted, 1950.

Poems, edited by Hooper, Bles, 1964, reprinted, Harcourt, 1977.

Narrative Poems, edited by Hooper, Bles, 1969, Harcourt, 1972.

CONTRIBUTOR

Essays on Malory, edited by J. A. W. Bennett, Clarendon Press, 1963.

Christian Reflections, edited by Walter Hooper, Eerdmans, 1967, Fount, 1981.

(Contributor of letters) Vanauken, Sheldon, *A Severe Mercy: C. S. Lewis and a Pagan Love Invaded by Christ, Told by One of the Lovers,* Harper, 1977.

Eglerio!: In Praise of Tolkien, edited by Anne Etkin, decorations and illustrations by Lucy Matthews, Quest Communications, 1978.

Christian Childhoods: An Anthology of Personal Memories, edited by Celia Van Oss, Crossroad, 1986.

The Collier Christian Library (boxed set; three volumes), Macmillan, 1988.

Contributor to the proceedings of the British Academy and to *Essays and Studies by Members of the English Association.*

OTHER

The Abolition of Man; or, Reflections on Education with Special Reference to the Teaching of English in the Upper Forms of Schools, Oxford University Press, 1943, Macmillan, 1947, reprinted, Fount, 1986.

Vivisection, New England Anti-Vivisection Society, c. 1947.

Surprised by Joy: The Shape of My Early Life (autobiography), Bles, 1955, Harcourt, 1956, reprinted, Fontana, 1974.

(Under pseudonym N. W. Clerk) *A Grief Observed,* Faber, 1961, Seabury, 1963, published under name C. S. Lewis, Walker and Company, 1988, gift edition, 1989.

Essays Presented to Charles Williams, Eerdmans, 1966.

C. S. Lewis at the Breakfast Table, and Other Reminiscences, edited by James T. Como, Macmillan, 1979.

The Grand Miracle, Ballantine, 1983.

Boxen: The Imaginary World of the Young C. S. Lewis (collection of early maps, histories, and sketches), edited by Hooper, Harcourt, 1985.

Present Concerns (essays), edited by Hooper, Harcourt, 1986.

Timeless at Heart, edited by Hooper, Fount, 1988.

Author, with Owen Barfield, of parody, *A Cretaceous Perambulator (the Re-examination Of),* edited by Hooper, Oxford University C. S. Lewis Society, limited edition, 1983. Author of *Love,* a recording of talks by Lewis for American radio broadcast, Creative Resources, 1971.

Lewis's papers are held at the Bodleian Library at Oxford University, Oxford, England, and in the Marion Wade Collection at Wheaton College, Wheaton, Illinois.

MEDIA ADAPTATIONS: The "Chronicles of Narnia" has been made into an animated television film; abridged versions of the "Chronicles" have been recorded by Caedmon, 1978-81; *The Lion, the Witch, and the Wardrobe* became an animated television special presented April 1-2, 1979, on CBS-TV; was produced as a play in Chicago, IL at the Lifeline Theater, December, 1986; was adapted by Jules Tasca, Thomas Tierney, and Ted Drachman as *Narnia the Musical,* which was first presented in London, and subsequently in New York, NY, at St. Stephens Church September 29, 1986; and was presented as a series on PBS-TV in 1989; *Out of the Silent Planet, Perelandra,* and *That Hideous Strength* have been recorded for Books on Tape; *The Four Loves* has been recorded for Catacomb; *Philia, The Four Loves, Agape,* and *Storge* have been recorded for Word Books.

SIDELIGHTS: Whether one approaches C. S. Lewis through the fantasyland of Narnia, the mythic worlds of Malacandra and Perelandra, the playful, satiric letters of senior devil Screwtape to his nephew, underdevil Wormwood, the witty but thoroughly logical theological works, or the critical literary studies which established him as a noted scholar, one finds that each path leads to an encounter with the faith that thoroughly shaped Lewis's life and writing. Phrases such as "apostle to the skeptics" and "defender of the faith" testify to the influence of Lewis's thought upon readers beginning with the mid-twentieth century and continuing through to the present. A *Times Literary Supplement* reviewer commented that "for the last thirty years of his life no other Christian writer in this country had such influence on the general reading public as C. S. Lewis. Each new book from his pen was awaited with an eagerness which showed that thousands of intelligent men and women had acquired a taste for his distinctive idiom and had come to rely on him as a source of moral and intellectual insight."

Critics have pointed out that Lewis's own journey from atheism to a vital Christian faith uniquely qualified him to defend that faith against its severest opponents. Though brought up in a nominally Christian home, while at boarding school Lewis rejected any belief in God. In his autobiography, *Surprised by Joy* the writer described his intellectual and spiritual development from childhood through adolescence and early adulthood. Richard B. Cunningham summarized his journey in *C. S. Lewis: Defender of the Faith.* "Reason and imagination, beginning early in his life and often pulling in opposite directions, were the controlling elements in [Lewis's] intellectual and spiritual pilgrimage. . . . His imagination and reason converged at the point of revelation; and for him revelation pointed to where myth had become fact: the Incarnate God Jesus Christ." Describing the moment of his conversion to theism, which came as a necessary submission to indisputable evidence, Lewis wrote in *Surprised by Joy:* "You must picture me alone in [my] room in Magdalen, night after night, feeling, whenever my mind lifted even for a second from my work, the steady, unrelenting approach of Him whom I so earnestly desired not to meet. . . . In the Trinity term of 1929 I gave in, and admitted that God was God, and knelt and prayed: perhaps, that night, the most dejected and reluctant convert in all England." He further described himself as "a prodigal who is brought in kicking, struggling, resentful, and darting his eyes in every direction for a chance of escape."

Just as the interplay of reason and imagination was instrumental in Lewis's conversion to theism and subsequently to Christianity, so it characterized the body of writings which flowed from his pen in the following years. Propelled by the conviction that reason is related to truth, and imagination connects with meaning, Lewis communicated his ideas in myth, satire, and fantasy, which appealed to the imagination, and in didactic logical treatises, whose arguments addressed the mind. And even though critics distinguished between these genres and assigned his works to one category or another, many acknowledged the interplay within individual works. Cunningham observed: "His literary technique, even in his didactic writing where he relies so heavily on reason and logic, also depends for its impact on the myths, allegories, metaphors, analogies, epigrams, and illustrations provided by his imagination."

Lewis's first scholarly work was *The Allegory of Love.* According to Margaret Patterson Hannay in *C. S. Lewis,* the work "introduces the reader first to the phenomenon of courtly love, then to the literary form of allegory, before presenting detailed studies of medieval allegory. . . . The book thus traces the form of allegorical love poetry from the late eleventh century to the late sixteenth century. Lewis argues that romantic love, something we assume as part of the nature of reality, is a relatively new phenomenon, unknown in classical, biblical, or early medieval times." *The Allegory of Love* includes "the best critical treatment in English of Chaucer's psychological romance, *Troilus and Criseyde,*" Charles A. Brady noted in *America.* And a *Times Lit-*

erary Supplement contributor stated, "This is plainly a great book—one which is destined to outlive its particular conclusions as few works of literary scholarship contrive to do. . . . The book is itself an allegory of love, a scholarly romance, in which a journey among works of poetry, many of them neglected, among erotic and scholastic treatises, most of them little read, is woven together into an imaginative and self-subsistent whole, and made available to the literate common reader as this material had never been before."

Many of his academic colleagues wished that Lewis had remained with strictly scholarly pursuits, but the author felt the need to speak to a wider audience. His science fiction trilogy for adults achieved that goal. The trilogy commenced in *Out of the Silent Planet,* continued in *Perelandra,* and ended in *That Hideous Strength.* While Christian ideas are primary to the works, they also contain mythic and literary themes, such as Greek and Roman fables and the Arthurian legends. Writing on the trilogy, A. K. Nardo in *Extrapolation* found that "as the reader travels with Ransom into Deep Heaven, he too is introduced to worlds where myth comes true and where what are merely artificial constructs to delineate kinds of poetry on earth become living realities in the heroic world of Mars and the pastoral world of Venus. Through identification with Ransom, the reader tastes what, Lewis seems to believe, is almost impossible in the modern world: pure epic and pure lyric experiences." And Brady considered the "Miltonic grandeur of conception [in *Out of the Silent Planet* and *Perelandra*] the greatest exercise of pure imagination in immediately contemporary literature."

Out of the Silent Planet introduces the trilogy's main character, the reticent philologist, Dr. Elwin Ransom, who is kidnapped by an unscrupulous scientist, Dr. Weston, and Devine, his power-hungry accomplice. Weston and Devine transport Ransom to Mars via spaceship, intending him as a human sacrifice to placate the "wild" natives. But the inhabitants of Malacandra, as they themselves call Mars, are far more civilized than the kidnappers, and they adopt Ransom, despite certain suspicions concerning his home planet. The Malacandrans view Earth with intense but careful curiosity, calling it the "silent planet," as it is wrapped in a dark veil that keeps it separated from the rest of the cosmos. Ransom comes to love the Malacandrans despite their peculiarities, and he unites with them in capturing Weston and Devine.

While the book received some negative criticism, it was generally popular with both ordinary readers and reviewers. As a piece of "science fiction," *Out of the Silent Planet* had its drawbacks, however. Brian Murphy noted in *C. S. Lewis:* "A reader of science fiction who delights in technical detail and scientific speculation had better pass on at once. What interests Lewis is what-would-happen-if; he imagines a space ship traveling to Mars and hasn't the slightest interest in how it might get there." Still, Lewis's friend J. R. R. Tolkien, who frequently disagreed with Lewis's literary approach to fantasy, was enthusiastic about the book. In *The Letters of J. R. R. Tolkien,* Humphrey Carpenter reprinted Tolkien's letter to his publisher, Stanley Unwin, concerning a negative review of *Out of the Silent Planet:* "I read [*Out of the Silent Planet*] in the original MS. and was so enthralled that I could do nothing else until I had finished it. My first criticism was simply that it was too short. . . . I at any rate should have bought this story at almost any price if I had found it in print, and loudly recommended it as a 'thriller' by (however and surprisingly) an intelligent man."

Ransom's struggles with Weston continue in *Perelandra.* On this trip, Ransom is transported by supernatural beings to Venus,

which is a watery Eden, covered by floating islands. There Ransom meets a beautiful green woman, who seems completely innocent of all evil. But Weston also appears, and has apparently been sent by evil spirits. Eventually, the philologist realizes that he has been indeed sent to a second Eden, and that Weston is tempting the woman to disobey the few rules that have been established by the world's creator; Ransom finds his job is to keep yet another planet from losing its Paradise. According to R. J. Reilly in *Romantic Religion: A Study of Barfield, Lewis, Williams, and Tolkien,* "The drama of the Incarnation takes on a strange new light in being told by a naked green woman on a floating island on Venus, as the Fall assumes new grandeur by being almost repeated." Leonard Bacon wrote in *Saturday Review* that *Perelandra* "is the result of the poetic imagination in full blast and should never have been written in prose, however excellent." Bacon found the planet's "first couple" "a thoroughly interesting Eve and perhaps the only endurable Adam in literature." He concluded that *Perelandra* is "a truly remarkable book."

In the *Atlantic,* Chad Walsh explained *Perelandra*'s finale, which leads into *That Hideous Strength,* the longest and most complex novel in the series. "As Ransom prepares to return to the Earth, he has a long conversation with the Adam of Venus, and learns that exciting events may be expected on the Earth in a few years. For countless centuries the Earth has been in the grip of the Devil and his assistants, but there are signs that the final struggle is approaching; the Earth may be delivered from evil, and contact re-established between it and the uncorrupted planets." *That Hideous Strength* "represents Lewis's most complex and impressive use of myth in fiction," wrote Charles Moorman in *College English.* The plot focuses on a young married couple who experience the explosion of their quiet university world by the invasion of a revolutionary group known as N.I.C.E. (National Institute of Coordinated Experiments). The wife, Jane Studdock, finds herself on one side of the conflict, headed by Ransom, who is now known as Mr. Fisher-King, while her sociologist husband Mark lands on the other, which is apparently led by Devine in his new identity as Lord Feverstone.

Moorman wrote, "In *That Hideous Strength* Lewis's theme is not a theological dogma, but a moral dilemma. Lewis is here opposing the sanctity and morality of Mr. Fisher-King, who symbolizes the whole weight of an ordered and Christian society, and the chaotic and turbulent secularism of the N.I.C.E. The war between these forces, and thus, in terms of the silent planet myth, between the angels and devils who direct them, is reflected in the inward struggles of a young couple, Mark and Jane Studdock, to choose sides in the great battle, and it is their personal struggles which become the real subject of the last novel." In *Dictionary of Literary Biography,* Eugene McGovern observed, "Lewis packs *That Hideous Strength* with scenes from college politics, bureaucracy, journalism, and married life, and he has much to say about academic ambition, education, equality and obedience, language and abuses of it, scientism and social science, vivisection, magic, the legend of King Arthur, and medieval cosmology. . . . All of this is kept under an impressive control, with the many discursive elements never interfering with the narrative."

The Screwtape Letters contains some of the twentieth-century's best-known descriptions of the bureaucracy of Hell. As the title indicates, the novel's form is a series of letters: all are from Uncle Screwtape, a senior devil, to his nephew, Wormwood, a junior tempter, who is endeavoring to lure a malleable young man to damnation. But the devils find themselves in competition with the Church and with a young Christian woman, whom the demons find "nauseating." Bacon wrote in the *Saturday Review of*

Literature that "whatever you may think of the theses of Mr. Lewis . . . the fact remains that [*The Screwtape Letters*] is a spectacular and satisfactory nova in the bleak sky of satire." A *Commonweal* reviewer felt that while Lewis's "comments on marriage seem inadequate, the author exhibits a remarkable knowledge of human nature." And P. W. Wilson recounted in the *New York Times* Thomas More's observation that the devil " 'cannot endure to be mocked,' and which, if correct, means that somewhere in the inferno there must be considerable annoyance."

Lewis's seven-volume series for children, "The Chronicles of Narnia," is considered his best-loved popular work. While the stories rely heavily on Christian ideas, traces of Greek and Roman mythology also surface in its pages. Some critics have mistaken parts of the fairy tales (in particular the first volume, *The Lion, the Witch, and the Wardrobe*) for a direct allegory of Christ's death and resurrection. But in *Of Other Worlds: Essays and Stories,* Walter Hooper introduced Lewis's comments on his initial creation of the fantastic country of Narnia: "Everything began with images; a faun carrying an umbrella, a queen on a sledge, a magnificent lion. At first there wasn't even anything Christian about them; that element pushed itself in of its own accord." But in the same volume, Hooper presented Lewis's recollection of how he planned the stories to communicate with readers who were uninterested in God. Lewis wrote: "I thought I saw how stories of this kind could steal past a certain inhibition which had paralysed much of my own religion in childhood. Why did one find it so hard to feel as one was told one ought to feel about God or about the sufferings of Christ? I thought the chief reason was that one was told one ought to. . . . But supposing that by casting all these things into an imaginary world, stripping them of their stained-glass and Sunday school associations, one could make them for the first time appear in their real potency? Could one not thus steal past those watchful dragons? I thought one could."

The stories concern varying groups of children who first come into contact with the "other world" of Narnia while living in the country during the bombing of London in World War II. The first and most famous group, Peter, Susan, Edmund, and Lucy Pevensie, have been separated from their parents and are lodging with a kindly, but remote, old professor in his large country estate. During a rainstorm, they engage in a game of hide and seek, and Lucy runs into a large wardrobe that turns out to be a doorway into Narnia. Eventually, Lucy's brothers and sisters also find Narnia, and what follows is an adventure-packed tale that includes themes of betrayal, forgiveness, death, and rebirth. The rest of the Chronicles also concern adventures into Narnia, although, as the children mature, they become "too old" to visit, and a younger cousin and his friend eventually become the new explorers. The Chronicles close with Narnia's end: in the final book, *The Last Battle,* Lewis intertwines the New Testament book of the Revelation into Narnia's history, and concludes an "earthly" world with the opening of an eternal one. Murphy believed that Lewis's style grew throughout the Chronicles. "In *The Lion, the Witch and the Wardrobe,* [Lewis's] tone is a bit self-consciously avuncular, even the slightest bit condescending. But by the second story, *Prince Caspian,* he has an assured and simple narrative tone which becomes, by the end of the Chronicles, a genuinely noble and serious 'high' style—almost a development of and improvement on the style William Morris . . . adopted for his romances."

Despite the books' continual popularity with children, Lewis was not altogether successful with adults. According to *Use of English* contributor Peter Hollindale, "The structure of power in Narnia, with Aslan at its head, is enforced by battle, violence, retributive justice, pain and death. Anything which challenges the power is either evil or stupid, and frequently both." And Penelope Lively in another issue of the same periodical saw an "underlying savagery that . . . makes the books . . . sinister, and the more so because this is what emerges as the most convincing thing about them." Perhaps the problem some critics had with the powerful Aslan, the talking lion who is the series' Christ-figure, was the author's conception of goodness. Hooper in *Imagination and the Spirit: Essays in Literature and the Christian Faith* described this as "none of the mushy, goody-goody sort of thing we sometimes find in people we feel we ought to like, but cannot. Here, in this magnificent Lion, is absolute goodness beyond anything we could imagine. Qualities we sometimes think of as opposites meet in him and blend." Lewis reconciled many apparent opposites in presenting Aslan's character, where ferocity mingled with tenderness, and sternness was followed by humor.

Surprised by Joy was Lewis's chronicle of his own life, explaining how his early childhood led up to his conversion to Christianity. (Lewis's last years were recorded in *A Grief Observed,* written after his wife's death from cancer). The author approached his own story as he would his fiction or his essays. *Nation* contributor May Swenson called the "long drawn out and intricate conversion . . . fascinating because of [Lewis's] intellect and charm, plus the story-telling dexterity of a topnotch mystery writer." T. S. Matthews, however, writing in the *New York Times* found the book left him "cold." Matthews continued, "In his clear, dry, take-it-or-leave-it manner, [Lewis] describes and tries to dissect the most incandescent of human emotions—and takes all the joy out of it." But while a *Times Literary Supplement* contributor agreed that the story "lacks the appalling, double-you-for-damnation sense of crisis which hangs over, say, that of Bunyan," he continued that "the tension of [the] final chapters holds the interest like the close of a thriller."

"*Till We Have Faces* has a special place in [Lewis's] work: the object of either extravagant praise or silent neglect, [and] the novel has an oddly tentative quality," Murphy wrote. "Lewis explored wonderingly in this difficult novel. . . . [and] deeply his own past, his own deepest dreams, and his own deeply hidden images of God." While *Faces* was the author's favorite work, this unusually dark and puzzling novel has confused readers and critics. Although it builds on the themes of sin and redemption, *Faces* operates in a pre-Christian world. The story takes place in the violent, barbaric realm of Glome, where the only civilizing force is expressed through a Greek slave tutor, known as the Fox. "The driving motif of *Till We Have Faces* is the development of the soul, a motif explored allegorically in one of [Lewis's] earliest works, *The Pilgrim's Regress.* Here Lewis has recast the familiar myth of Cupid and Psyche," noted John H. Timmerman in *Religion in Life.* The familiar story is altered by perspective: it is told first-person, from the view of Psyche's ugly and embittered older sister, Orual, who eventually becomes the queen of Glome. *Till We Have Faces* is Orual's story, and relates first-person how she becomes harmful to her beloved sister, whom she loves possessively. McGovern felt that the novel displays Lewis's skill in psychological characterization. "Not before *Till We Have Faces* did Lewis show he could produce a complete and thoroughly convincing portrait, and in this novel he has not one but three impressive creations," and mentions Orual, the Fox, and the faithful soldier, Bardia. Timmerman also saw depth in the work, and stated that "The philosophic cast to the novel is stronger than in any other of [Lewis's] work."

The novel darkens further when Orual desires to observe Psyche's lover and the castle in which the "gods" have placed her. But when Psyche's sisters come to visit, they can see nothing. Nothingness is also the answer given to Orual when she demands of her country's goddess why she has lost Psyche. But Orual eventually comes to an unusual conclusion: "I saw well why the gods do not speak to us openly, nor let us answer. . . . Why should they hear the babble that we think we mean? How can they meet us face to face till we have faces?" Murphy wrote: "This is an answer that is as powerful . . . as it is troubling." He concluded, "Through all his work, but especially [the] last works, Lewis says that life is a preparation—not, as William Butler Yeats said, a preparation for something that never happens—but a readying for seeing God."

Frequently controversial but as popular now as during his lifetime, Lewis excited as much criticism as praise. McGovern quoted Helen Gardner, who said of Lewis: "He aroused warm affection, loyalty, and devotion in his friends, and feelings of almost equal strength among innumerable persons who knew him only through his books. But he also aroused strong antipathy, disapproval, and distaste among some of his colleagues and pupils, and among some readers. It was impossible to be indifferent to him." In his belief that "man does not 'make himself,' " he appeared a reactionary to many twentieth-century minds. Patrick J. Callahan explained in *Science Fiction: The Other Side of Realism—Essays on Modern Fantasy and Science Fiction,* Lewis's conviction that man's "reason is capable of apprehending a rational universe, and thus, that there is a natural moral order. Such a stance places him in opposition to all principles of infinite human progress, to all philosophies of the superman. Lewis would accept Blake's maxim that 'in trying to be more than man, we become less.' "

BIOGRAPHICAL/CRITICAL SOURCES:

BOOKS

Authors & Artists for Young Adults, Volume 3, Gale, 1990.
Callahan, Patrick J., *SF: The Other Side of Realism—Essays on Modern Fantasy and Science Fiction,* edited by Thomas D. Clareson, Bowling Green University Popular Press, 1971.
Carter, Humphrey, with Christopher Tolkien, editors, *The Letters of J. R. R. Tolkien,* Allen and Unwin, 1981.
Children's Literature Review, Volume 3, Gale, 1978.
Contemporary Literary Criticism, Gale, Volume 1, 1973, Volume 3, 1975, Volume 6, 1976, Volume 14, 1980, Volume 27, 1984.
Cunningham, Richard B., *C. S. Lewis: Defender of the Faith,* Westminster Press, 1967.
Dictionary of Literary Biography, Volume 15: *British Novelists, 1930-1959,* Gale, 1983.
Hannay, Margaret Patterson, *C. S. Lewis,* Ungar, 1981.
Hooper, Walter, *Imagination and the Spirit: Essays in Literature and the Christian Faith,* edited by Charles A. Huttar, Eerdmans, 1971.
Lewis, C. S., *Of Other Worlds: Essays and Stories,* edited by Walter Hooper, Harcourt, 1966.
Lewis, C. S., *Surprised by Joy: The Shape of My Early Life,* Harcourt, 1956.
Lewis, C. S., *Till We Have Faces: A Myth Retold,* Eerdmans, 1966.
Murphy, Brian, *C. S. Lewis,* Starmont House, 1983.
Reilly, R. J., *Romantic Religion: A Study of Barfield, Lewis, Williams, and Tolkien,* University of Georgia Press, 1971.
Walsh, Chad, *The Literary Legacy of C. S. Lewis,* Harcourt, 1979.
Wilson, A. N., *C. S. Lewis: A Biography,* Norton, 1990.

PERIODICALS

America, May 27, 1944.
Atlantic, September, 1946.
College English, May, 1957.
Commonweal, March 5, 1943.
Extrapolation, summer, 1979.
Nation, June 2, 1956.
New Republic, February 18, 1967.
New York Times, March 28, 1943; February 5, 1956.
New York Times Book Review, December 26, 1971.
Religion in Life, winter, 1977.
Saturday Review April 8, 1944.
Saturday Review of Literature, April 17, 1943.
Times Literary Supplement, February 28, 1942; October 7, 1955; January 7, 1965; March 23, 1967.
Use of English, winter, 1968; spring, 1977.

—*Sketch by Jani Prescott*

*   *   *

LEWIS, Norman   1918-

PERSONAL: Son of Richard (a chemist) and Louise Lewis; married first wife, Ernestina (marriage ended); married second wife; children: (second marriage) two. *Education:* Educated in Enfield, England.

ADDRESSES: Home—Essex, England. *Agent*—c/o William Collins Sons & Co., Ltd., 14 St. James Place, London S.W.1, England.

CAREER: Writer. *Military service:* British Army, Intelligence Corps, 1939-45.

AWARDS, HONORS: Listing as a notable book of 1979 by *Library Journal,* for *Naples '44.*

WRITINGS:

(And photographer) *Sand and Sea in Arabia,* G. Routledge & Sons, 1938.
Samara (novel), J. Cape, 1949.
Within the Labyrinth (novel), J. Cape, 1950, Carroll & Graf, 1986.
A Dragon Apparent: Travels in Indo-China, Scribner, 1951.
Golden Earth: Travels in Burma, Scribner, 1952.
A Single Pilgrim (novel), J. Cape, 1953, Rinehart, 1954.
The Day of the Fox (novel), Rinehart, 1955.
The Volcanoes Above Us (novel), Pantheon, 1957.
The Changing Sky: Travels of a Novelist, Pantheon, 1959.
Darkness Visible (novel), Pantheon, 1960.
The Tenth Year of the Ship (novel), Harcourt, 1962.
Dragon Tree Island, Collins, 1964.
The Honored Society: A Searching Look at the Mafia, Putnam, 1964 (published in England as *The Honoured Society: The Mafia Conspiracy Observed,* Collins, 1964).
A Small War Made to Order (novel), Harcourt, 1966.
Every Man's Brother (novel), Heinemann, 1967, Morrow, 1968.
Flight From a Dark Equator (novel), Putnam, 1972.
The Sicilian Specialist (novel), Random House, 1974.
Naples '44 (nonfiction), Pantheon, 1978.
The German Company, Collins, 1979.
Cuban Passage (novel), Pantheon, 1982.
Voices of the Old Sea (travel), Hamish Hamilton, 1984, Viking, 1985.
A Suitable Case for Corruption (novel), Hamish Hamilton, 1984.
Jackdaw Cake (autobiography), Hamish Hamilton, 1985.

The March of the Long Shadows, Secker & Warburg, 1987.
The Missionaries, Secker & Warburg, 1988.

Also author of *A Passage to Freedom,* 1982. Contributor to periodicals, including London *Times, New Statesman,* and *New Yorker.*

SIDELIGHTS: Norman Lewis is a distinguished British writer of travel books, novels, and general nonfiction. He spent his childhood in Wales, where he was raised by relatives, whom he described to Caroline Moorehead as "three insane aunts" in a London *Times* profile. He later worked as an assistant to his father, a chemist, and indulged in motorcycle riding. After he began traveling, he showed an ability to learn languages, including Arabic. Early travels took him to Arabia, and in World War II he served in Italy. Since then, he has traveled diverse lands, including South America, Cuba, and China.

Lewis began his writing career in 1938 with the photographic collection *Sand and Sea in Arabia,* and in ensuing years he has further contributed to the travel genre with such volumes as *A Dragon Apparent,* detailing his adventures in Indo-China, *Golden Earth,* about his times in Burma, and *Voices of the Old Sea,* which concerns his experiences in the Mediterranean in the late 1940s. Lewis spent parts of three years in northeastern Spain, where he observed the lives and customs of land workers and fishermen. "At the time, the experiences struck me as nothing," he confided to Moorehead in the *Times.* "But when I look now at what I wrote, then I see it is full of incredible things."

Voices of the Old Sea has been praised as an accomplished work. Tony Lambert described it in the *Times Literary Supplement* as "poetic" and added, "The tone is not merely elegiac; with a novelist's eye for a rounded story as well as an anthropologist's nosiness, Lewis disinters memorable lives and presents a rich array of brave, comic, idiosyncratic and above all dignified characters." Gontran Goulden also lauded *Voices of the Old Sea,* writing in the London *Times* that the volume is "charming, funny, harsh, yet compassionate" and that Lewis exercised "sensitivity and wit."

Lewis's finest nonfiction work is generally considered to be *Naples '44,* which documents his wartime experiences in Naples, Italy. Lewis served there in 1944 as a liaison between other military personnel and the local citizenry. "We had to cope with a city of a million people devastated by warfare," he told Moorehead in her 1983 *Times* article. "It was a concentrated and kaleidoscopic experience." His more provocative tasks included tracking prostitutes and interceding in frequently violent disagreements among villagers. In *Saturday Review,* Ted Morgan called *Naples '44* a "remarkable book" and hailed it as invaluable. "If for some reason I were limited to owning no more than 10 books on World War II," Morgan wrote, "Lewis's would be one of them." Goulden was similarly positive in the *Times,* deeming *Naples '44* "one of the best war books."

While in Italy Lewis also obtained some insights into the Sicilian organized crime network known as the Mafia. In 1964 he published *The Honored Society,* an account of the Mafia's development in the years immediately following World War II. In addition, Lewis provides background into the criminal organization's activities during the 1930s, and he illuminates the often disturbing ties between the Mafia and the American military during the war. *The Honored Society* is considered an essential study on the Mafia, but Lewis, according to Moorehead, refers to the organization "extremely cautiously."

Lewis's various travels and experiences have also informed his novels. *Within the Labyrinth,* for instance, is set in Italy during the Occupation, another period when Lewis was in that country. The novel concerns a British sergeant—Manning—assigned to the war-torn town Malevento. Manning arrives with intentions of merely completing his task, which involves making an inquiry into the whereabouts of a mysterious fellow named Mancuso. He soon finds, however, that fulfilling his duties will not be entirely easy, for a local marshal seems determined to undermine the assignment. Ann Cornelisen, writing in the *New York Times Book Review,* praised *Within the Labyrinth* as a "virtuoso performance" and declared: "Mr. Lewis never allows his plot or characters to wobble off into burlesque. . . . He has a sharp eye for people and their lairs and the wit to describe them both."

Lewis has also produced several suspense novels, including *Cuban Passage.* This work takes place in 1950s Cuba during Fulgencio Batista's dictatorship. *Cuban Passage* concerns Dick, a British teenager in conflict with his mother's illicit lover, a mysterious Cuban government official. Fleeing a trying situation, the youth arrives in Havana and befriends Jerry, a remarkably resourceful American living on the docks. The American, reacting to Dick's account of his lamentable family life, blithely encourages the Brit to develop his more violent aspects. In his *New York Times* review, Anatole Broyard described *Cuban Passage* as "rather good" and added that it is "better than most" suspense novels. Broyard also commended Lewis for possessing "a fine ear" and for being "good at description."

In 1985 Lewis published in still another genre, autobiography. His *Jackdaw Cake* details the first half of his life, recounting life with his three aunts, whom he describes as "dotty," and discussing his early travels, his unconventional marriage to a Sicilian, and his wartime experiences in the Intelligence Corps. Allan Massie, in his review for the London *Times,* deemed *Jackdaw Cake* a "superior chronicle of corners of lunacy" and praised it as "undeniably fascinating."

BIOGRAPHICAL/CRITICAL SOURCES:

PERIODICALS

Christian Science Monitor, July 25, 1979.
Esquire, September, 1979.
Los Angeles Times Book Review, July 4, 1982, October 19, 1986.
New Republic, March 3, 1979.
New Statesman, July 11, 1959, March 17, 1972.
New York Review of Books, February 7, 1980.
New York Times, June 5, 1982.
New York Times Book Review, May 16, 1964, October 8, 1972, February 16, 1975, March 18, 1979, November 25, 1979, July 14, 1985, June 15, 1986, December 25, 1988.
Observer (London), March 12, 1972, October 14, 1979.
Saturday Review, July 7, 1979.
Spectator, September 15, 1979.
Times (London), December 8, 1983, November 24, 1984, November 14, 1985.
Times Literary Supplement, July 10, 1959, June 18, 1964, April 7, 1972, March 3, 1978, May 14, 1982, August 13, 1982, May 4, 1984, December 28, 1984, January 4, 1985, June 5, 1987, July 1, 1988.
Virginia Quarterly Review, autumn, 1979.

*   *   *

LEWIS, (Harry) Sinclair   1885-1951
(Tom Graham)

PERSONAL: Born February 7, 1885, in Sauk Centre, MN; died of paralysis of the heart, January 10, 1951, in Rome, Italy; cremated, and ashes returned to birthplace; son of Edwin J. (a physician) and Emma (Kermott) Lewis; married Grace Livingstone Hegger, April 15, 1914 (divorced, 1928); married Dorothy Thompson, May 14, 1928 (divorced, 1943); children: (first marriage) Wells; (second marriage) Michael. *Education:* Yale University, A.B., 1908.

CAREER: Helicon Home (Upton Sinclair's socialist community), Englewood, NJ, janitor, 1906-07; *Transatlantic Tales,* New York City, assistant editor, 1907; *Daily Courier,* Waterloo, IA, reporter, 1908; worked for a charity organization in New York City, 1908; secretary to Alice MacGowan and Grace MacGowan Cooke in Carmel, CA, 1909; *Evening Bulletin,* San Francisco, CA, staff writer, 1909; Associated Press, San Francisco, staff writer, 1909-1910; *Volta Review,* Washington, D.C., staff member, 1910, Frederick A. Stokes (publisher), New York City, manuscript reader, 1910-12; *Adventure,* New York City, assistant editor, 1912; Publisher's Newspaper Syndicate, New York City, editor, 1913-14; George H. Doran (publisher), New York City, editorial assistant and advertising manager, 1914-15; full-time writer, 1916-51. Writer in residence, University of Wisconsin, Madison, 1942. Acted in several plays, including his own *It Can't Happen Here* and *Angela is Twenty-Two.*

MEMBER: National Institute of Arts and Letters (vice president, 1944), American Academy of Arts and Letters.

AWARDS, HONORS: Pulitzer Prize, 1926, for *Arrowsmith* (declined); Nobel Prize for Literature, 1930; Litt.D., Yale University, 1936; award from *Ebony* magazine for promoting racial understanding in his novel, *Kingsblood Royal.*

WRITINGS:

NOVELS

(Under pseudonym Tom Graham) *Hike and the Airplane* (juvenile), Stokes Publishing, 1912.
Our Mr. Wrenn: The Romantic Adventures of a Gentle Man, Harper, 1914, reprinted, Crowell, 1951.
The Trail of the Hawk: A Comedy of the Seriousness of Life, Harper, 1915.
The Job: An American Novel, Harper, 1917.
The Innocents: A Story for Lovers, Harper, 1917.
Free Air, Harcourt, 1919, reprinted, Scholarly Press, 1970.
Main Street: The Story of Carol Kennicott (also see below), Harcourt, 1920, reprinted, 1989.
Babbitt (also see below), Harcourt, 1922, reprinted, 1989.
Arrowsmith (also see below), Harcourt, 1925, reprinted, Buccaneer, 1982 (published in England as *Martin Arrowsmith,* J. Cape, 1925, reprinted, 1957).
Mantrap, Harcourt, 1926.
Elmer Gantry, Harcourt, 1927, reprinted, New American Library, 1980.
The Man Who Knew Coolidge: Being the Soul of Lowell Schmaltz, Constructive and Nordic Citizen, Harcourt, 1928.
Dodsworth, Harcourt, 1929, reprinted, New American Library, 1972.
Ann Vickers, Doubleday, Doran, 1933, reprinted, Dell, 1962.
Work of Art, Doubleday, Doran, 1934, reprinted, Popular Library, 1962.
It Can't Happen Here (also see below), Doubleday, Doran, 1935, reprinted, New American Library, 1970.
The Prodigal Parents, Doubleday, Doran, 1938.
Bethel Merriday, Doubleday, Doran, 1940, reprinted, Popular Library, c. 1965.
Gideon Planish, Random House, 1943, reprinted, Manor Books, 1974.

Cass Timberlane: A Novel of Husbands and Wives, Random House, 1945, reprinted, Buccaneer, 1982.
Kingsblood Royal, Random House, 1947.
The God-Seeker, Random House, 1949, reprinted, Manor Books, 1975.
World So Wide, Random House, 1951, reprinted, Manor Books, 1974.

PLAYS

Hobohemia, first produced in New York at Greenwich Village Theatre, February 8, 1919.
(With Lloyd Lewis) *Jayhawker: A Play in Three Acts* (first produced in New York at Cort Theatre, November 5, 1934), Doubleday, Doran, 1935.
(With John C. Moffitt) *It Can't Happen Here* (first produced in New York at Adelphi Theatre, October 27, 1936), Dramatists Play Service, 1938.
(With Fay Wray) *Angela Is Twenty-Two,* first produced in Columbus, Ohio, December 20, 1938.

OTHER

John Dos Passos' "Manhattan Transfer," Harper, 1926, reprinted, Norwood, 1977.
Cheap and Contented Labor: The Picture of a Southern Mill Town in 1929, United Feature Syndicate, 1929.
Selected Short Stories, Doubleday, Doran, 1935, reprinted as *Selected Short Stories of Sinclair Lewis,* I. R. Dee, 1990.
From Main Street to Stockholm: Letters of Sinclair Lewis, 1919-1930, edited by Harrison Smith, Harcourt, 1952.
The Man from Main Street; A Sinclair Lewis Reader: Selected Essays and Other Writings, 1904-1950, edited by Harry E. Maule and Melville H. Cane, Random House, 1953.
Moths in the Arc Light [and] *The Cat of the Stars,* edited by Densaku Midorikawa, Taishukan (Tokyo), 1960.
Lewis at Zenith; A Three-Novel Omnibus: Main Street, Babbitt, Arrowsmith, Harcourt, 1961.
I'm a Stranger Here Myself and Other Stories, edited by Mark Schorer, Dell, 1962.
(With Dore Schary) *Storm in the West* (screenplay), Stein & Day, 1963, revised edition, 1981.
To Toby, limited edition, Macalester College, 1967.

Also author of *The American Fear of Literature,* 1931. Author of column, "Book Week," *Newsweek,* 1937-38; columnist, *Esquire,* 1945. The majority of Lewis's manuscripts are kept at Yale University; another large collection is at the University of Texas at Austin.

MEDIA ADAPTATIONS: Samuel Goldwyn filmed *Arrowsmith* in 1931 and *Dodsworth* in 1936; Sidney Howard also wrote a play adaptation of *Dodsworth* that opened in New York at the Shubert Theatre, February 24, 1934; *Elmer Gantry* was adapted as a 1960 United Artists film starring Burt Lancaster; a sound recording of Lewis's short story, "Young Man Axelbrod," was produced by American Forces Radio and Television Services, 1972; a sound recording was made of *Arrowsmith* by American Forces Radio and Television Service, 1973; LP recordings of *It Can't Happen Here* and *Babbitt,* with text read by Michael Lewis, were produced in 1973 and 1974, respectively.

SIDELIGHTS: Sinclair Lewis was the first American to win the Nobel Prize for Literature. Four years before he was awarded this honor in 1930, however, Lewis was also the first author in history to decline the Pulitzer Prize. In a 1926 press statement reprinted in the *Dictionary of Literary Biography Documentary Series,* Lewis justified this refusal by explaining his objection to the provision that the Pulitzer be given to the book "which shall best present the wholesome atmosphere of American life, and the highest standard of American manners and manhood." The conditions could not be applied, Lewis felt, to an author such as himself who had satirized American lifestyles in such works as *Main Street: The Story of Carol Kennicott, Babbitt, Arrowsmith, Elmer Gantry,* and *Dodsworth;* and he objected to the American Academy of Arts and Letters and other institutions that upheld the illusion of a perfect America. Lewis regularly attacked Americans in his books for "their standardized thinking, aggressive provincialism, and self-righteous tyranny over all those who do not rigidly subscribe to their ways," wrote Leo and Miriam Gurko in *College English.* Because these attitudes were contagious, in the author's view, he called such beliefs the "village virus." Using humor through his gift of mimicry, he managed to reveal the problems caused by this uniquely American disease while still appealing to his readers. Thus, commented James Lundquist in his *Sinclair Lewis,* Lewis "was that most unusual phenomenon, an important writer whose appeal to the masses was genuine." Toward the end of his career, however, it is generally felt that Lewis's writing lost much of its satiric edge. As *Sinclair Lewis* author Sheldon Norman Grebstein commented, in the novels that the author published after the 1920s Lewis had "become the historian, not the reformer; . . . the scribe of what has been, rather than the maker of what should be."

Literary historians usually divide Lewis's writing career into three periods: an apprenticeship phase that includes the novels from *Our Mr. Wrenn: The Romantic Adventures of a Gentle Man* to *Free Air,* the 1920s period during which Lewis wrote what are generally considered his most significant books, and the years that are regarded as a time of decline after the publication of *Dodsworth.* His early novels, as Grebstein pointed out, are "novels of and about education . . . [that are] generally characterized by a playful, deliberately facetious approach." Leo and Miriam Gurko also considered this to be a "period of unfocused hesitation" in Lewis's attitude, since some of his novels—*Our Mr. Wrenn, The Innocents: A Story for Lovers,* and *Free Air*—presented a positive viewpoint toward American provincialism, while *The Trail of the Hawk: A Comedy of the Seriousness of Life* and *The Job: An American Novel* were more denigrating. It was a period of experimentation that also hinted at what would come in Lewis's later work. As *Dictionary of Literary Biography* contributor Martin Light observed, for example, in *The Job* the author "tries out his imitation of salesman's talk, later to be developed in the speech of Babbitt"; and in *The Trail of the Hawk* the novelist first addresses the problem of combining "the practical life with the artistic one . . . [which was] a possibility that would puzzle many of Lewis's later protagonists." These ideas, however, would not all come into focus until *Main Street.*

Main Street was Lewis's first popular and critical success. A unique work of fiction, it was praised in a 1920 *New York Times Book Review* article as a "remarkable book. . . . A novel, yes, but so unusual as not to fall easily into a class. There is practically no plot, yet the book is absorbing. It is so much like life itself, so extraordinarily real." Lewis set out to paint a picture of American life in the small town, rather than to tell a story. More specifically, as David Aaron reported in *The American Novel: From James Fenimore Cooper to William Faulkner,* the author wished "to puncture humbug notions about the alleged neighborliness of small towns." To do so, Lewis created the character Carol Kennicott, a young, idealistic woman from the city who moves to the little burg of Gopher Prairie after she marries Will, a simple country doctor. Here, she does not find the charming village that her husband described, but rather a jumble of rundown buildings populated with people whose opinions offer

"nothing but gossip, trivial talk, spite, and prejudice," as Light related.

It was Lewis's satirical depiction of Americans as ignorant, hypocritical busy-bodies rather than as neighborly, hard-working people with high values that caused a sensation when *Main Street* was first published. "People argued either that it was a libel upon the village or that it was a revelation of the truths about American pettiness and hypocrisy," wrote Light. Many critics who held the latter opinion felt that this aspect of the novel is what makes it a significant contribution to American literature. C. E. Bechhofer, for one, wrote in his *The Literary Renaissance in America* that "the essential part of the book is its description of the clash between the culture of the more or less civilized Eastern American cities and the arid self-complacency of the Middle Western small towns. . . . The importance of *Main Street* lies in its merciless, sardonic study of Middle Western life." Writing in *Smart Set,* prominent critic and author H. L. Mencken similarly emphasized *Main Street*'s illustrative power. "It is an attempt, not to solve the American cultural problem, but simply to depict with great care a group of typical Americans. This attempt is extraordinarily successful." Part of the author's success is due to his frequently noted skills at mimicking colloquial language. "Mr. Lewis represents [American] speech vividly and accurately," praised Mencken.

But even though much attention has been given to Lewis's depiction of American life in *Main Street,* Carol Kennicott's story is not without significance. Sometimes compared to the character of Emma Bovary in Gustave Flaubert's *Madame Bovary,* Carol is plagued with a vague longing for a better, more enriching life. Disgusted by the drabness and lack of culture in Gopher Prairie, she "overcompensates with almost frenzied activity, gives silly but lively parties, and takes up and drops many useless projects," described *American Literature* critic Stephen S. Conroy. The townspeople, however, do not want their village changed and perceive Carol's actions to be motivated by a snobbish condescension toward them. Sensing their growing hostility and feeling suffocated by the town's inertia, she runs away to Washington, D.C. But Carol soon discovers that she cannot find fulfillment in the city, either, and becomes homesick for Gopher Prairie and her husband. She returns home to raise her child, adapting to and learning to love village life. In this way, people like Carol Kennicott are "inoculated with the 'village virus,' " revealed Stanton A. Coblentz in *Bookman,* ". . . [and] discover escape to be [as] meaningless as imprisonment, and in the end resign themselves to Gopher Prairie and to 'the humdrum inevitable tragedy of struggle against inertia.' "

A number of critics such as *Prairie Schooner* reviewer George H. Douglas found that despite the story's "inexplicable charm," *Main Street* was "a work of weak development and poor characterization." The rambling plot of the novel caused May Sinclair to complain in the *New York Times Book Review* that "the book lacks a certain concentration and unity." But Sinclair joined other reviewers in her opinion that with *Babbitt,* Lewis's next novel, the author "triumphs precisely where in 'Main Street' he failed. By fixing attention firmly on one superb central figure he has achieved an admirable effect of unity and concentration." "The plain truth is, indeed, that *Babbitt* is at least twice as good a novel as *Main Street,*" enthused Mencken in another *Smart Set* review.

Lewis's *Babbitt* was to become such an influential work that, as Light noted, "the word *babbit* [meaning a person who conforms to prevailing social and moral standards] has entered common parlance." *Babbitt* is set in Zenith, Winnemac, the fictional city and state that would later appear in a number of Lewis's other novels. In this urbanized version of Gopher Prairie, the author presents a memorable description of George F. Babbitt, a real estate agent with a passionate desire "to seize something more than motor cars and a house *before it's too late.*" According to Mark Schorer in *Landmarks of American Writing,* by following Babbitt in his daily activities Lewis gives the reader "an almost punctilious analysis of the sociology of American commercial culture and middle-class life." "Indeed," wrote Light, "the triumph of this book is that it brought before us an enduring perception of an American type . . . [and it] is the book, moreover, in which Lewis was most skillful in his satiric representation of American speech."

"Since the publication of *Babbitt,*" Schorer reflected, "everyone has learned that conformity is the great price that our predominantly commercial culture exacts of American life. But when *Babbitt* was published, this was its revelation to Americans, and this was likewise how the novel differed from all novels about business that had been published before it." Most such books portrayed larger-than-life tycoons, but Lewis's character is, as Mencken described him, "a sound business man, a faithful Booster, an assiduous Elk, a trustworthy Presbyterian, a good husband, a loving father, a successful and unchallenged fraud." Discontented with his conformity, Babbitt has a brief affair and dabbles in leftist politics to the point that he risks being ostracized by all his friends. His wife's sudden illness toward the end of the novel, however, provides "Babbitt and his clan a pretext for patching up their squabble," said Conroy. Soon, Babbitt is back to his old self, a conformist and member of the Good Citizen's League.

The story of Babbitt's discontentment, rebellion, and reassimilation has caused some critics to compare George Babbitt to Carol Kennicott, who goes through the same process in *Main Street.* "Freedom is, in fact, the main theme of Lewis' novels," revealed Anthony Channell Hilfer in his *The Revolt from the Village: 1915-1930,* later adding that "[as] far as the theme of freedom goes, *Babbitt* is a mere rewriting of *Main Street* though far superior in technique." In his analysis of these two works, Hilfer concludes that Lewis's protagonists fail to find their freedom because the "truth is that Lewis simply cannot imagine freedom within the social structure of America." *Men of Destiny* author Walter Lippmann, however, offered another explanation. Describing these novels along with Lewis's *Arrowsmith* as "stories of an individual who is trying to reform the world, or to find salvation by escaping it," Lippmann observed that Carol and Babbitt fail because they have no direction in their lives, "no religion available which they can embrace, and therefore, there is no salvation." Martin Arrowsmith, on the other hand, discovers salvation through his reverence for science.

Lewis conceptualized Arrowsmith as a heroic figure, a character who would embody the ideas of purity, hard work, and freedom that the author considered an integral part of the pioneer America whose spirit was being swallowed by the country's urbanization. Although in his earlier books Lewis also lamented the passing of the days of America's pioneers, he had not before focused on a character who could remain faithful to what the author saw as their way of life. *Arrowsmith* concerns the life of a medical doctor who devotes himself to research in bacteriology. Standing in the way of his search for scientific truths are, as T. K. Whipple cataloged in *New Republic,* "the commercialism of the medical school, the quackery which thrives in the country, the politics and fraud of a Department of Public Health in a small city, the more refined commercialism of a metropolitan clinic, and the social and financial temptations of a great institute for research."

After a series of struggles against all these overpowering forces, however, Arrowsmith manages to resist temptation by reasserting his faith in science and "finally takes refuge in the wilds of Vermont where he can pursue his researches undisturbed." "The chief importance of *Arrowsmith,* then," Whipple concluded, "is that it shows the extreme difficulty of pursuing the creative or theoretic life in the United States."

Arrowsmith, like *Main Street* and *Babbitt,* was an immense popular and critical success. Critics praised its characterization, unity of point-of-view, and compelling plot. "*Arrowsmith,*" declared Whipple in his *Spokesmen: Modern Writers in American Life,* ". . . is the final proof of [Lewis's] creative power." The American Academy of Arts and Letters felt that the novel deserved the Pulitzer Prize, but Lewis refused the honor, saying that it was an award given only to those who champion American wholesomeness. He also objected to the Academy's selection procedures and to the possibility that if the prize became too prestigious authors might strive to write less controversial books in order to win it. But Lewis revealed privately in a letter to his publisher and friend Alfred Harcourt—reprinted in the *Dictionary of Literary Biography Documentary Series*—"that ever since the *Main Street* burglary, I have planned that if they ever did award [the Pulitzer] to me, I would refuse it." Believing that *Main Street* deserved an award, Lewis "also felt that perhaps *Babbitt* had been neglected two years later," said Light, and this resentment helped to fuel his decision to reject the Pulitzer. Many American journalists, however, speculated that Lewis was just looking for publicity.

With the publication of *Elmer Gantry,* the novelist caused an even greater uproar. A satire of religion and the ministry in the United States, many critics thought that Lewis had gone too far in lambasting American religious practices. The novel was censured in Boston, denounced by clergymen of all faiths, and enraged several readers enough to threaten Lewis with bodily injury. Lippmann described *Elmer Gantry* as "the study of a fundamentalist clergyman in the United States, portrayed as utterly evil in order to injure the fundamentalists. The calumny is elaborate and deliberate. Mr. Lewis hates fundamentalists, and in his hatred he describes them as villains. This was, I believe, a most intolerant thing to do." Calling the novel "a horrible book," a *New Statesman* writer similarly asserted that the picture Lewis offers as an illustration of corruption of organized religion in America "must surely be overdrawn, for it is worse than the worst that we know of common human nature." In *The Last of the Provincials: The American Novel, 1915-1925,* author Maxwell Geismar concluded that if "the larger scene of *Elmer Gantry* presents a cross-section of religious activity in the United States, and if there are some witty descriptions of this activity, there is also remarkably little insight into the more fundamental aspects of religious motivation—either personal or cultural—or into that commercial exploitation of religion which is the ostensible theme of the novel."

If *Elmer Gantry* seemed like an unfair tract against fundamentalism, however, *Dodsworth* "once more assured Lewis' readers that he was a generous man," according to Schorer in his biography of the author. *Dodsworth* studies American culture by contrasting it with life in Europe as seen during the travels of Sam Dodsworth and his wife Fran. Portraying Dodsworth as a man possessing the most enviable virtues of middle-class America, Lewis chronicles the final days of his marriage to his shrewish wife and his realization that practical work and art can be combined to form a worthwhile career. Rather than directing any satire toward his main protagonist, the author this time directs his scorn at Fran, who is envious of the European aristocracy's display of wealth and surfeit of leisure time. She has several affairs with the shallow, ostentatious friends she makes until Dodsworth is compelled to ask for a divorce despite his undying love for her. Afterwards, Dodsworth learns from his relationship with Edith Cortright to appreciate the simpler lifestyles that Europe has to offer, such as that of the Italian peasants whom Edith admires. At the novel's conclusion, he returns home planning to become an architect of modern, artistically designed houses. Though some critics were more interested in Lewis's switch from satirizing Midwesterners to the simple criticism of Fran's snobbishness, others like *Nation* reviewer Carl Van Doren felt that the author's sympathetic portrayal of Dodsworth was more significant. The "sympathetic insight" and description of Dodsworth's hopeless, foolish love for Fran "gives him a dignity which no other character of Sinclair Lewis has ever had."

In 1930, Lewis won the Nobel Prize for Literature. The award, however, also marked a plateau in the novelist's career. Although many of his later works after *Dodsworth* sold well, it is generally maintained that he never again reached the same level of achievement that he had in the 1920s. Orville Prescott, author of *In My Opinion: An Inquiry into the Contemporary Novel,* attested that Lewis's later books "were either pale imitations of his earlier work or venomous outbursts of hatred and melodrama." His command of satiric mimicry that had been praised in the earlier books, Light also noted, became "almost a parody of itself" during the last years. Even during the 1920s, the author had written critical failures such as *Mantrap* and *The Man Who Knew Coolidge,* but he could no longer compensate with books equal to *Babbitt* or *Arrowsmith.*

The most notable novels that Lewis wrote during the last two decades of his life include such sensationalistic works as *It Can't Happen Here* and *Kingsblood Royal* and the one novel that many critics consider his best during this period, *Cass Timberlane: A Novel of Husbands and Wives. It Can't Happen Here,* published in 1935, describes a possible scenario in which America elects a man who becomes a fascist dictator; and *Kingsblood Royal* is Lewis's attempt to decry racism by describing its effects on a white man who discovers he has a distant black ancestor. *Ebony* magazine gave *Kingsblood Royal* an award in recognition of Lewis's attempt to dispel racial preconceptions, but Prescott wrote that in trying to denounce racists in *Kingsblood Royal* "Lewis protested much too much," making the characters "unreal and unrepresentative." Similarly, critics such as *Commonweal* contributor Geoffrey Stone considered *It Can't Happen Here* to be "poorly characterized and as hastily written as anything" by Lewis. Prescott also denounced novels like *Cass Timberlane* and *Kingsblood Royal* for their completely unsympathetic portrayal of Americans. "The two books were not only inferior as fiction," the critic protested, "they were cruelly unjust caricatures of American life." Nevertheless, *Cass Timberlane* is often recognized as one of the author's better novels during his later years. As Edward Weeks remarked in *Atlantic,* the book shows merit in that "it is written with more affection than his other [later] works"; and Light labeled it "Lewis's most successful effort after the Nobel Prize."

As early as 1935, Granville Hicks observed that Lewis was "losing those virtues" that he had previously displayed. Several literary analysts have hypothesized about the decline in Lewis's writing. "Lewis either ran out of or ran out on ideas about character and personality, and started basing his books on issues of a near-political nature, leaving matters of art for matters more properly the concern of the day's newspapers," suggested Anthony West in the *New Yorker.* Alfred Kazin offered in his *On Native Grounds: An Interpretation of Modern American Prose Literature*

that the novelist's satire lost its power "when . . . America lost its easy comfortable self-consciousness, [and] Lewis's nervous mimicry merely brushed off against it. . . . What these later works also signified, however, was not only Lewis's growing carelessness and fatigue, but an irritable formal recognition of his relation to American life." As a number of critics suggested, this recognition by the author marked his own acceptance of the village virus. In an obituary for Lewis, a London *Times* writer reflected how Lewis, once the rebel and critic of American values, had become respectable: "He became a member of the American Academy of Arts and Letters, which he had derided and denounced. His home town graciously forgave his insults, made him its favorite son. . . . Sinclair Lewis, Knocker, had turned into Sinclair Lewis, Booster." "When he abandoned satire," concluded Leo and Miriam Gurko in *College English,* "vitality drained away from his work, to which the succession of undistinguished novels of the 1930's bears witness."

Some critics have never considered Lewis to be a major writing talent, even during the peak of his career. In his *Spokesmen,* for example, Whipple also disparaged Lewis's characterization, and wrote that the author's "interest is in social types and classes rather than in individuals as human beings." This, along with his dependence on mimicry, research, and use of his own personal experience for material mark "a poverty of invention or imagination," according to Whipple. As *Nation* contributor Joseph Wood Krutch attested, Lewis "rarely if ever escaped the limitations of mimicry as an artistic device." Despite Lewis's limitations, however, critics like Light acknowledged that "he deserves more attention than he now receives."

"Lewis's reputation has rested," Lundquist wrote, "and most likely will continue to rest, on his notoriety as a polemicist—and he was a good one, deserving comparison to H. L. Mencken and perhaps even to Thomas Paine." "Lewis accomplished a great deal in his writing career," reflected Light in his book, *The Quixotic Vision of Sinclair Lewis.* "As America's first Nobel Prize winner in literature, he became for Europe the symbol of America's coming of age. He was a leader on best-seller lists in the United States; . . . he helped destroy one picture of the small town and substitute another." Today, many critics like *Mid-America* contributor David D. Anderson regard Lewis as "not a great writer. . . . But the best of his works, those that have added words to our language, those that give us greater insight into moral shortcomings of our times and ourselves, those that define the victimization of the individual in a world of mass vulgarity, deserve better of us than we have been willing to give."

BIOGRAPHICAL/CRITICAL SOURCES:

BOOKS

Bechhofer, C. E., *The Literary Renaissance in America,* William Heinemann, 1923.

Boynton, Percy, *More Contemporary Americans,* University of Chicago Press, 1927.

Cabell, James Branch, *Some of Us: An Essay in Epitaphs,* Robert M. McBride, 1930.

Cohen, Hennig, editor, *Landmarks of American Writing,* Basic Books, 1969.

Concise Dictionary of American Literary Biography: The Twenties, 1917-1929, Gale, 1989.

Dictionary of Literary Biography, Volume 9: *American Novelists, 1910-1945,* Gale, 1981.

Dictionary of Literary Biography Documentary Series, Volume 1, Gale, 1982.

Forster, E. M., *Abinger Harvest,* Harcourt, 1936.

Frank, Waldo, *Salvos: An Informal Book about Books and Plays,* Boni & Liveright, 1924.

Geismar, Maxwell, *The Last of the Provincials: The American Novel, 1915-1925,* Houghton, 1947.

Grebstein, Sheldon Norman, *Sinclair Lewis,* Twayne, 1962.

Hatcher, Harlan, *Creating the Modern American Novel,* Farrar & Rinehart, 1935.

Hicks, Granville, *The Great Tradition: An Interpretation of American Literature since the Civil War,* Macmillan, 1935.

Hilfer, Anthony Channell, *The Revolt from the Village: 1915-1930,* University of North Carolina Press, 1969.

Kazin, Alfred, *On Native Grounds: An Interpretation of Modern American Prose Literature,* Reynal & Hitchcock, 1942.

Lewis, Sinclair, *Babbitt,* Harcourt, 1922.

Lewis, Sinclair, *From Main Street to Stockholm: Letters of Sinclair Lewis, 1919-1930,* edited by Harrison Smith, Harcourt, 1952.

Lewis, Sinclair, *Main Street: The Story of Carol Kennicott,* New American Library, 1961.

Light, Martin, *The Quixotic Vision of Sinclair Lewis,* Purdue University Press, 1975.

Lippmann, Walter, *Men of Destiny,* Macmillan, 1927.

Lundquist, James, *Sinclair Lewis,* Ungar, 1973.

Mencken, H. L., *H. L. Mencken's "Smart Set" Criticism,* edited by William H. Nolte, Cornell University Press, 1968.

Prescott, Orville, *In My Opinion: An Inquiry into the Contemporary Novel,* Bobbs-Merrill, 1952.

Priestly, J. B., *Literature and Western Man,* Harper, 1960.

Rourke, Constance, *American Humor: A Study of the National Character,* Harcourt, 1931.

Rubin, Louis D., Jr., editor, *The Comic Imagination in American Literature,* Rutgers University Press, 1973.

Schorer, Mark, editor, *Sinclair Lewis: A Collection of Critical Essays,* Prentice-Hall, 1962.

Schorer, Mark, *Sinclair Lewis,* University of Minnesota Press, 1963.

Sherman, Stuart P., *The Significance of Sinclair Lewis,* Harcourt, 1922.

Spindler, Michael, *American Literature and Social Change: William Dean Howells to Arthur Miller,* Indiana University Press, 1983.

Stegner, Wallace, editor, *The American Novel: From James Fenimore Cooper to William Faulkner,* Basic Books, 1965.

Twentieth Century Literary Criticism, Gale, Volume 4, 1981, Volume 13, 1984, Volume 23, 1987.

Watkins, Floyd C., *In Time and Place: Some Origins of American Fiction,* University of Georgia Press, 1977.

Whipple, T. K., *Spokesmen: Modern Writers and American Life,* D. Appleton, 1928.

Woolf, Virginia, *The Moment and Other Essays,* Harcourt, 1948.

PERIODICALS

American Literature, November, 1970.

American Mercury, August, 1930.

Atlantic, October, 1945.

Bookman, January, 1921.

College English, February, 1943.

Commonweal, November 22, 1935; November 13, 1936; June 6, 1947.

MidAmerica, Volume 8, 1981.

Modern Fiction Studies, autumn, 1985.

Nation, March 12, 1914; November 10, 1920; April 3, 1929; February 24, 1951.

New Republic, March 24, 1917; December 1, 1920; April 15, 1925.

New Yorker, April 7, 1928; May 24, 1947; April 28, 1951.

New York Herald Tribune Books, March 8, 1925.

New York Times Book Review, November 14, 1920; May 29, 1921 (interview); September 24, 1922; October 1, 1961.

New York Times Magazine, February 5, 1950 (interview).

Outlook, May 2, 1914.

Prairie Schooner, winter, 1970-71.

Renascence, winter, 1966.

Saturday Review of Literature, August 1, 1925.

Scribner's Magazine, July, 1930.

Smart Set, January, 1921; October, 1922.

OBITUARIES:

PERIODICALS

Time, January 22, 1951.

—*Sketch by Kevin S. Hile*

*   *   *

LINDBERGH, Anne (Spencer) Morrow   1906-

PERSONAL: Born in 1906 in Englewood, N.J.; daughter of Dwight Whitney (formerly U.S. Ambassador to Mexico) and Elizabeth Reeve (Cutter) Morrow; married Charles Augustus Lindbergh, Jr. (aviator; first pilot to fly from New York to Paris), May 27, 1929 (died August 26, 1974); children: Charles Augustus III (died, 1932), Jon Morrow, Land Morrow, Anne Spencer, Reeve, Scott. *Education:* Smith College, B.A., 1928.

ADDRESSES: Home—Maui, Hawaii.

CAREER: Writer.

AWARDS, HONORS: Cross of Honor, U.S. Flag Association, 1933, for part in survey of trans-Atlantic air routes; Hubbard Medal of the National Geographic Society, 1934, for work as co-pilot and radio operator in flight of 40,000 miles over five continents; M.A., Smith College, 1935; LL.D., Amherst College, 1939; LL.D., University of Rochester, 1939; Christopher Award for *War Within and Without.*

WRITINGS:

North to the Orient, Harcourt, 1935.

Listen! The Wind, Harcourt, 1938.

The Wave of the Future, Harcourt, 1940.

The Steep Ascent, Harcourt, 1944.

Gift from the Sea (also see below), Pantheon, 1955, 20th anniversary edition, with an afterword by the author, Vintage Trade, 1975.

The Unicorn and Other Poems, 1935-1955, Pantheon, 1956.

Dearly Beloved, Harcourt, 1962.

Selections from "Gift from the Sea," Hallmark Editions, 1967.

Earth Shine, Harcourt, 1969.

Christmas in Mexico: 1972, Harcourt, 1971.

Bring Me a Unicorn: Diaries and Letters of Anne Morrow Lindbergh, Harcourt, 1972.

Hour of Gold, Hour of Lead: Diaries and Letters of Anne Morrow Lindbergh, 1929-1932, Harcourt, 1973.

Locked Rooms and Open Doors: Diaries and Letters of Anne Morrow Lindbergh, 1932-1935, Harcourt, 1974.

The Flower and the Nettle: Diaries and Letters of Anne Morrow Lindbergh, 1936-1939, Harcourt, 1976.

War Within and Without: Diaries and Letters of Anne Morrow Lindbergh, 1939-1944, Harcourt, 1980.

SIDELIGHTS: Anne Morrow Lindbergh is widely respected as an author of philosophical novels and essays. But she is even better known for having lived "a life that most scenario writers would hesitate to invent," observes Glendy Culligan in *Saturday Review*. The dramatic events of Lindbergh's life, including her marriage to aviation pioneer Charles A. Lindbergh, her participation in early experimental flights, and a successful career as an author, have made best sellers of her published diaries and letters.

Lindbergh was born into "what may have been the closest-knit nuclear family in modern history," writes Jane Howard in the *Washington Post Book World*. Her father, Dwight Morrow, was at various times a business partner (to banker J. P. Morgan), an ambassador, and a U.S. senator. Her mother, Elizabeth Cutter Morrow, was a poet, a trustee of Smith College, and a crusader for equal education for women. The Morrow's wealth and status ensured that their children, all daughters, were well educated and well traveled at an early age. It also produced a "haze of insulation which permeated our early years," an "indefinable sense of isolation from the world," notes Lindbergh in the introduction to the first volume of her diaries, *Bring Me a Unicorn*. She explains, "No matter what we read or where we traveled we were enclosed in the familial circle, confined, although also enriched, by the strong family bonds and strictly defined child-parent roles."

"Only in college did I begin to realize how much I resembled the 'sheltered Emelye' of Chaucer's Knight's Tale, enclosed in a walled garden," Lindbergh continues. Her years at Smith College were important for discovering the existence of a world beyond her sheltered circle, but her preoccupation with her family was still dominant. In 1927, she eagerly anticipated spending Christmas with her relatives in Mexico, where her father was then U.S. ambassador. When Anne heard that America's hero, Charles A. Lindbergh, would also be visiting the embassy as part of a good-will tour, she was unimpressed, admitting only "a little annoyance" at "all this public-hero stuff breaking into our family party." Meeting Charles swept away her indifference, however, and before the Christmas holiday was over, she admitted that she was hopelessly in love with him. He returned her feelings, and after several months, the couple announced their engagement. By that time, Anne realized that her fiance's celebrity status would forever rule out the secluded life she preferred, but it made no difference. "Don't wish me happiness," she wrote to a friend. "I don't expect to be happy, but it's gotten beyond that. . . . Wish me courage and strength and a sense of humor—I will need them all."

The first years of the Lindberghs' marriage are covered in the diary's second volume, *Hour of Gold, Hour of Lead*. Anne learned the skills necessary to serve as Charles' co-pilot, navigator, and radio operator, and the newlyweds spent most of the early days of their marriage in the air. The hysterical hero-worship that Charles had inspired since his solo New York-Paris flight in 1927 was only intensified by his marriage to Anne and their subsequent adventures together. "To millions around the world—reading of the Lindberghs flying everywhere in their own Lockheed Sirius seaplane, looking at photographs of the 'perfect'-looking couple ('the lone eagle and his mate') landing in Siberia, China, Japan—the Lindberghs seemed to enjoy the greatest possible good fortune that a young couple could have," writes Alfred Kazin in his *New York Times Book Review* article on *Hour of Gold, Hour of Lead*. The image of perfection was completed in 1930 by the birth of their first child, a son named Charles A. Lindbergh III. But on March 1, 1932, the illusion was shattered. That evening, when Anne went upstairs to check the child before retiring, she found his crib empty; the baby had been kidnapped.

Weeks passed in frantic investigations and negotiations. Over 12,000 people wrote to describe dreams envisioning the exact location of the missing child. Al Capone and other crime bosses offered their help. Reporters, photographers, and state troopers laid siege to the Lindberghs' New Jersey residence. Newspapers had extras ready at every hour, prepared to announce the baby's safe return. But on May 12, 1932, his body was found in a ditch not far from the Lindbergh home. "Rarely has a personal tragedy had such public reverberations and consequences," states Kazin. "A whole simplistic 'American' idea of life died with the Lindbergh baby."

The parents' anguish over the loss of their baby was exacerbated by the relentless public exposure to which they were subjected. "The contrast between the Lindbergh character and the Lindbergh case is painful and ominous in its interest," notes Kazin. "Both the Lindberghs have always been intensely private persons, with an austere, restrained, glowingly creative sense of life. Their laconic self-confidence (old American style) hardly prepared them for the hideous absurdity (contemporary American style) of their public anxiety and laceration. . . . Their natural sensitiveness was intensified, after the kidnapping, by armies of reporters, photographers, marauders, publicity seekers, vandals who drove by the house just long enough to kill a dog, shakedown artists of every kind who tried to cash in on the case."

Lindbergh's diary *Locked Rooms and Open Doors* details the family's recovery from their trauma. The diary depicts Charles as an invaluable source of support for Anne. He urged her to begin writing the story of their daring 1931 survey flight to the Orient via the Arctic Circle, and he later convinced her to assist him in a five-month flight exploring the Atlantic for commercial air routes. Although reluctant to leave her new baby, Jon, born in August, 1932, Anne welcomed the solitude of flight. "Flying was normal life for us," she explains in her introduction to *Locked Rooms*. "The project lifted us out of the aftermath of crime and turned the publicity that surrounded us to a constructive end—the advance of air travel. . . . For me, the trip was the nearest approximation to a life of our own than could then be found. . . . It meant more freedom, more privacy with my husband, and more contact with people in natural surroundings. . . . All these factors were restoring." Unfortunately, the serenity lasted only until the Lindberghs returned to the United States. Then the trial of the baby's kidnapper, Bruno Hauptmann, returned them to the unwelcome glare of world-wide publicity. Privacy and safety began to seem impossibilities in the U.S., so after the trial and the publication of Anne's book *North to the Orient*, the couple took their baby and fled to a self-imposed exile in England and Europe. Anne described these experiences in the diary later entitled *The Flower and the Nettle*.

They found a welcome peace in England. Charles again encouraged Anne to pursue her writing, and she began work on the story of their Atlantic flight, which was published as *Listen! The Wind*. Reviews of *North to the Orient* had been favorable, such as one by Edward Weeks in *Atlantic Bookshelf* that states, "One's first impression of the book is that Anne Lindbergh writes so well that she must not stop." Publication of *Listen! The Wind* solidified her reputation as critics emphasized that Lindbergh's elegant, graceful prose gives the book an importance that goes far beyond its historical significance. " 'Listen! The Wind' is a record of technical achievement, a record historically valuable; in Anne Lindbergh's hands it becomes literature," writes Katherine Woods in *the New York Times Book Review*. In *Books*, William Soskin calls her "one of the finest writers in America, [who has] emerged to an artistry which the most meticulous of critics cannot challenge."

After two years in England, punctuated by several flights and the birth of another son, the Lindberghs moved to France. World War II was brewing in Europe. Politically, Charles was an isolationist who believed for many reasons that the United States should not become involved in a foreign conflict. When the U.S. government asked him to quietly investigate the growth of the German air force, however, he willingly complied. The American press questioned his frequent, unexplained visits to Germany and began to paint a new picture of their former hero as a possible Nazi sympathizer. When Hitler invaded Czechoslovakia in 1939, the Lindberghs returned to the United States—and to a new public ordeal, described in the last published volume of Anne's diaries, *War Within and Without.*

With war fever mounting, isolationism was popularly considered tantamount to treason. The individualistic Charles was not ashamed of his stance, but it quickly earned him the titles of anti-Semite and pro-Nazi. Although Anne only partly agreed with his position, she felt obliged to support it. Her 1940 book *The Wave of the Future* was, according to Joseph P. Lash in the *New York Times Book Review,* Anne's "effort to build a bridge between her husband's position and her own. In it she argues for staying out of the war and concentrating on domestic reform because, among other reasons, Italy, Germany, and Russia, whatever their flaws, are symptoms of a new world struggling to be born." Anne's style was once again generally praised by critics such as Clare Boothe who, in *Current History and Forum,* deems it "clear, chiseled, cadenced—almost a classic." But, states Lash, "people [Lindbergh] cared about damned the widely-read book as a plea for appeasement and a condonation of totalitarianism, . . . a lyrical and silver-coated exposition of the views expressed by Charles."

Strangers threatened new disasters for the Lindbergh children as retribution for their parents' politics. Old friends, alienated by the isolationist issue, spoke publicly against them. When Charles offered his services to the Roosevelt administration he was turned down. He then offered his services to private companies involved in the war effort; of these, only the Ford Motor Company in Detroit was powerful enough to defy the Roosevelt administration's disapproval and accept Lindbergh's offer of help. "I have had three big things to fight against in my life," wrote Anne at the time. "The first was just sorrow (the kidnapping case), the second was fear (the flights), and the third is bitterness (the whole war struggle). And the third is the hardest."

However, the stress brought by wartime issues did not keep Anne from writing. Indeed, Charles "pressed her, almost fiercely, to write and was angry when household chores or children intervened. . . . To make sure she had a quiet place to work, he pitched a tent above the beach at Martha's Vineyard, set up a trailer behind their house outside Detroit," remarks *Washington Post Book World* contributor Katherine Winton Evans. "Almost all our quarrels," wrote Anne in 1941, "arise from this passionate desire to see me freed to fulfill what there is in me."

In 1941 Anne Lindbergh's first novel was published, entitled *The Steep Ascent,* and was well received by critics. "It would be a pity if those who were disturbed by Mrs. Lindbergh's last book [*The Wave of the Future*] were to ignore this one because of it," writes Amy Loveman in *Saturday Review.* "For they would lose in so doing one of the most beautifully written, sensitive, and lovely volumes which has appeared since those earlier ones which were akin to it, 'North to the Orient' and 'Listen! The Wind.' " Like those books, *The Steep Ascent* tells of a perilous flight made by a woman and her husband. "As always there is the exquisite deli-

cacy of expression, the talent for the right word, the right phrase, and the descriptions that are acute observations of the passing scene filtered through the screen of personality. . . . To the beauty which her earlier books had there is added excitement in this one," declares Loveman. "As an adventure story it is keen and exciting," affirms *New York Times Book Review* contributor Beatrice Sherman, "but it is much more than that. Its charm and grace are rooted in the fabric of the author's mind and in the fruit of her philosophy."

Following *The Steep Ascent* was what was to become one of Lindbergh's most enduring works, *Gift from the Sea,* a book that remains in print thirty years after its first edition. It is a collection of essays with the central theme of "the tremendous and ever-encroaching problem of how to maintain an inner serenity in the midst of the distractions of life, how to remain balanced, no matter what forces tend to pull one off center; how to be the still axis within the revolving wheel of relationships and activities," as Sara Henderson Hay writes in *Saturday Review.* Each essay takes the form of a meditation on a seashell, and Elizabeth Gray Vining writes in the *New York Times Book Review* that *Gift from the Sea* "is like a shell itself, in its small and perfect form, the delicate spiraling of its thought, the poetry of its color, and its rhythm from the sea, which tells of light and life and love and the security that lies at the heart of intermittency." And although it "deals with the essential needs, gifts, obligations and aspirations of woman as distinct from those of man, it is in no sense merely what is sometimes slightly called a woman's book. A sensitive, tensile, original mind probes delicately into questions of balance and relationship in the world today, and the result is a book for human beings who are mature or in search of maturity, whether men or women."

The Unicorn and Other Poems was Lindbergh's next published work. "There are many beautiful lyrics here," praises Robert Hillyer in the *New York Times Book Review.* "The reader will be well rewarded who joins the poet in this garden by the mortal sea whence, from time to time, rifts in the clouds show flashes from immortality." But *Saturday Review*'s poetry editor John Ciardi's review is in strong disagreement. "As a reviewer not of Mrs. Lindbergh but of her poems I have, in duty, nothing but contempt to offer," Ciardi writes. "I am compelled to believe that Mrs. Lindbergh has written an offensively bad book—inept, jingling, slovenly, illiterate even, and puffed up with the foolish afflatus of a stereotyped high-seriousness, that species of esthetic and human failure that will accept any shriek as a true high-C." A month after Ciardi's review appeared, *Saturday Review* editor Norman Cousins reported: "John Ciardi's review of Anne Morrow Lindbergh's 'The Unicorn and Other Poems' has produced the biggest storm of reader protest in the thirty-three-year history of *The Saturday Review.* Hundreds of readers have hastened to tell us of their pointed disapproval of Mr. Ciardi's review; four have written in his support. . . . There are few living authors who are using the English language more sensitively or with more genuine appeal [than Lindbergh]. There is in her books a respect for human responses to beauty and for the great connections between humankind and nature that gives her work rare distinction and that earns her the gratitude and loyalty of her readers, as the present episode makes clear."

Lindbergh's audience was considerably widened when publication of her diaries began in 1972. The public was eager to read the inside story on the celebrated couple, and the diaries sold briskly. Lindbergh had at first been reluctant to expose her personal papers. "William Jovanovich, who was my husband's publisher as well as mine, knew that I kept diaries and told me I should publish them," she explained in a *New York Times Book*

Review interview with Carol Lawson. "[But] I wrote them because I *had* to, not to get them published." An autobiography was considered as a means of preserving Lindbergh's sense of privacy, but it was finally decided that the original journals would be published. She explains her decision in the introduction to *Locked Rooms:* "When one has processed and packaged part of one's life in books, as I have, it is fair to ask, Why not leave it in that form? Why go back to the imperfect raw material of the diaries? Why publish the grimy minutiae of preparing for a trip; the tedium of long hours of work, the reluctant early risings; the exasperations of cold feet and dusty clothes; the irrational night terrors, lost tempers, and depressions? Because, after sixty, I think, one knows the ups and downs that life holds for everyone, and would like—a last chance—to see and present, truthfully and not glamorized, what happened."

Her decision to print the original journals and letters won the approval of readers and reviewers alike. According to Glendy Culligan of *Saturday Review,* the "letters and diaries [achieve] both spontaneity and art, thanks in part to her style, in part to a built-in plot and a soul-searching heroine worthy of a Bronte novel. In only one respect does Mrs. Lindbergh fail to meet her own standard of candor. When she introduces herself as 'this quite ordinary person' any reader with a long memory is bound to smile."

BIOGRAPHICAL/CRITICAL SOURCES:

BOOKS

Lindbergh, Anne Morrow, *North to the Orient,* Harcourt, 1935.
Lindbergh, Anne Morrow, *Listen! The Wind,* Harcourt, 1938.
Lindbergh, Anne Morrow, *Bring Me a Unicorn: Diaries and Letters of Anne Morrow Lindbergh,* Harcourt, 1972.
Lindbergh, Anne Morrow, *Hour of Gold, Hour of Lead: Diaries and Letters of Anne Morrow Lindbergh, 1929-1932,* Harcourt, 1973.
Lindbergh, Anne Morrow, *Locked Rooms and Open Doors: Diaries and Letters of Anne Morrow Lindbergh, 1932-1935,* Harcourt, 1974.
Lindbergh, Anne Morrow, *The Flower and the Nettle: Diaries and Letters of Anne Morrow Lindbergh, 1936-1939,* Harcourt, 1976.
Lindbergh, Anne Morrow, *War Within and Without: Diaries and Letters of Anne Morrow Lindbergh, 1939-1944,* Harcourt, 1980.

PERIODICALS

Atlantic Bookshelf, October, 1935.
Books, October 16, 1938.
Chicago Tribune, April 4, 1980.
Current History and Forum, November 7, 1940.
Newsweek, April 11, 1955.
New Yorker, March 21, 1974.
New York Times, September 9, 1956, October 12, 1969, February 21, 1970, April 20, 1974, April 29, 1980, August 2, 1980.
New York Times Book Review, October 16, 1938, November 3, 1940, March 19, 1944, March 20, 1955, September 9, 1956, June 10, 1962, February 27, 1972, March 4, 1973, March 24, 1974, April 20, 1980, June 15, 1980.
Saturday Review, October 15, 1938, March 18, 1944, February 2, 1955, January 12, 1957, February 16, 1957, June 9, 1962, March 4, 1972.
Time, September 17, 1956, June 8, 1962, March 11, 1974.
Times Literary Supplement, February 26, 1971, August 1, 1972.
Washington Post Book World, March 10, 1974, April 27, 1980.

LIPPMANN, Walter   1889-1974

PERSONAL: Born September 23, 1889, in New York, N.Y.; died December 14, 1974; son of Jacob (a clothing manufacturer) and Daisy (Baum) Lippmann; married Faye Albertson, May 24, 1917 (divorced, 1938); married Helen Byrne Armstrong, March 26, 1938. *Education:* Harvard University, A.B. (cum laude), 1909, graduate study, 1909-10. *Politics:* Independent.

ADDRESSES: Home—Hotel Lowell, 28 East 63rd St., New York, N.Y. 10021; and Southwest Harbor, Mount Desert, Me.

CAREER: Worked for *Everybody's Magazine* as Lincoln Steffens's secretary, 1910, became associate editor within a year; executive secretary to George R. Lunn, Socialist mayor of Schenectady, N.Y., during four months in 1912; with Herbert Croly, founded the *New Republic,* 1914, served as associate editor until 1917, returned to it in 1919; assistant to Secretary of War Newton D. Baker, 1917; secretary to a governmental organization, 1917, was one of the authors of President Woodrow Wilson's Fourteen Points; *The Inquiry,* secretary, 1917-18; editorial staff member of *New York World,* 1921-29, editor, 1929-31; columnist ("Today and Tomorrow") for *New York Herald Tribune,* 1931-62, column syndicated by *Washington Post* and *Los Angeles Times* syndicates, 1963-67; also syndicated in over 275 papers around the world; fortnightly columnist, *Newsweek,* beginning 1962. Member of board of overseers, Harvard University, 1933-39; member of board of directors, Fund for the Advancement of Education, beginning 1951. *Military service:* U.S. Army Military Intelligence, 1918-19; commissioned a captain; attached to General Pershing's headquarters.

MEMBER: National Institute of Arts and Letters, American Academy of Arts and Letters (fellow), National Press Club, Phi Beta Kappa (senator, 1934-40), Sigma Delta Chi (fellow, 1950); Cosmos Club, Metropolitan Club, Army-Navy Country Club (all Washington, D.C.); Century Club, River Club, Harvard Club, Coffee House Club (all New York); Harvard Club, Tavern Club (both Boston).

AWARDS, HONORS: Commander, Legion of Honor (France), 1946; Commander, Legion of Honor, Officer of Order of Leopold (Belgium), 1947; Knight's Cross of Order of St. Olav (Norway), 1950; Commander, Order of Orange Nassau (Netherlands), 1952; Overseas Press Club Award, 1953, 1955, and 1959; Pulitzer Prizes, 1958 and 1962; George Foster Peabody Award, 1962; Presidential Medal of Freedom, 1964, for "profound interpretation of his country and the affairs of the world"; Gold Medal, National Academy of Arts and Letters, 1965. LL.D., Wake Forest College, 1926, University of Wisconsin, 1927, University of California and Union College, 1933, Wesleyan University and University of Michigan, 1934, George Washington University and Amherst College, 1935, University of Rochester, 1936, College of William and Mary and Drake University, 1937, University of Chicago, 1955, New School for Social Research, 1959; Litt.D. from Dartmouth College and Columbia University, 1932, Oglethorpe College, 1934, Harvard University, 1944.

WRITINGS:

A Preface to Politics, Mitchell Kennerly, 1913.
Drift and Mastery: An Attempt to Diagnose the Current Unrest, Mitchell Kennerly, 1914, new edition with an introduction and notes by William E. Leuchtenberg, Prentice-Hall, 1961, reprinted, Greenwood Press, 1977.
The Stakes of Diplomacy, Holt, 1915, 2nd edition, 1917.
The World Conflict in Its Relation to American Democracy (originally published in *Annals of the American Academy of Po-*

litical Science, July, 1917), U.S. Government Printing Office, 1917.

The Political Scene: An Essay on the Victory of 1918, Holt, 1919.

Liberty and the News (portion originally published in *Atlantic*), Harcourt, 1920.

France and the European Settlement (pamphlet), Foreign Policy Association, 1922.

Public Opinion, Harcourt, 1922, reprinted, Free Press, 1965.

Mr. Kahn Would Like to Know (pamphlet; originally published in *New Republic,* July 4, 1923), Foreign Policy Association, 1923.

The Phantom Public, Harcourt, 1925, published as *The Phantom Public: A Sequel to "Public Opinion,"* Macmillan, 1930.

H. L. Mencken (pamphlet; originally published in *Saturday Review,* December 11, 1926), Knopf, 1926.

Men of Destiny, drawings by Rollin Kirby, Macmillan, 1927, reprinted with an introduction by Richard Lowitt, University of Washington Press, 1969.

American Inquisitors: A Commentary on Dayton and Chicago, Macmillan, 1928.

A Preface to Morals, Macmillan, 1929, published with a new introduction by Sidney Hook, Time, Inc., 1964.

Notes on the Crisis (pamphlet; originally published in *New York Herald Tribune,* September, 1931), John Day, 1931.

(With W. O. Scroggs and others) *The United States in World Affairs: An Account of American Foreign Relations, 1931,* Harper, Volume I, 1932, Volume II, 1933.

Interpretations, 1931-1932, edited by Allan Nevins, Macmillan, 1932.

A New Social Order (pamphlet), John Day, 1933.

The Method of Freedom, Macmillan, 1934.

(With G. D. H. Cole) *Self-Sufficiency: Some Random Reflections* [and] *Planning International Trade* (the former by Lippmann, the latter by Cole), Carnegie Endowment for International Peace, 1934.

The New Imperative (portions originally published in *Yale Review,* June, 1935), Macmillan, 1935.

Interpretations, 1933-1935, edited by Nevins, Macmillan, 1936.

(Editor with Nevins) *A Modern Reader: Essays on Present-day Life and Culture,* Heath, 1936, 2nd edition, 1946.

An Inquiry into the Principles of the Good Society, Little, Brown, 1937, new edition, 1943 (published in England as *The Good Society,* Allen & Unwin, 1938), reprinted, Greenwood Press, 1973.

The Supreme Court: Independent or Controlled?, Harper, 1937.

Some Notes on War and Peace, Macmillan, 1940.

U.S. Foreign Policy: Shield of the Republic, Little, Brown, 1943, reprinted, Johnson Reprint, 1972.

U.S. War Aims, Little, Brown, 1944, reprinted, Da Capo Press, 1976.

In the Service of Freedom (pamphlet), Freedom House, c. 1945.

The Cold War: A Study in U.S. Foreign Policy, Harper, 1947, reprinted, 1972.

Commentaries on American Far Eastern Policy (pamphlet), American Institute of Pacific Relations, 1950.

Isolation and Alliances: An American Speaks to the British, Little, Brown, 1952.

Public Opinion and Foreign Policy in the United States (lectures), Allen & Unwin, 1952.

Essays in the Public Philosophy, Little, Brown, 1955 (published in England as *The Public Philosophy,* Hamish Hamilton, 1955).

America in the World Today (lecture), University of Minnesota Press, 1957.

The Communist World and Ours, Little, Brown, 1959.

The Confrontation (originally published in column "Today and Tomorrow," September 17, 1959), Overbrook Press, 1959.

(With Clarence C. Little) *Speeches of Walter Lippmann and Clarence C. Little,* [Cambridge], 1960.

The Coming Tests with Russia, Little, Brown, 1961.

The Nuclear Era: A Profound Struggle (pamphlet), University of Chicago Press, 1962.

Western Unity and the Common Market, Little, Brown, 1962.

The Essential Lippmann: A Political Philosophy for Liberal Democracy, edited by Clinton Rossiter and James Lave, Random House, 1963.

(Author of introduction) *Fulbright of Arkansas: The Public Positions of a Private Thinker,* edited by Karl E. Meyer, Luce, 1963.

A Free Press (pamphlet), Berlingske Bogtrykkeri (Copenhagen), c. 1965.

Conversations with Walter Lippmann (CBS Reports television program), introduction by Edward Weeks, Little, Brown, 1965.

(Author of introduction) Carl Sandburg, *The Chicago Race Riots, July, 1919,* Harcourt, 1969.

Early Writings, introduction by Arthur Schlesinger, Jr., Liveright, 1971.

Public Persons, edited by Gilbert A. Harrison, Liveright, 1976.

Public Philosopher: Selected Letters of Walter Lippmann, edited by John Morton Blum, Ticknor & Fields, 1985.

Also author of *American Trade Policy* (originally published in *Sunday Times* [London]), 1943; editor of *The Poems of Paul Mariett,* 1913.

CONTRIBUTOR

Arno Lehman Bader, Theodore Hornberger, Sigmund K. Proctor, and Carlton Wells, editors, *Prose Patterns,* Harcourt, 1933.

Edward Simpson Noyes, editor, *Readings in the Modern Essay,* Houghton, 1933.

Albert Craig Baird, editor, *Essays and Addresses Toward a Liberal Education,* Ginn, 1934.

Joseph Bradley Hubbard and others, editors, *Current Economic Policies: Selected Discussions,* Holt, 1934.

Frank Howland McCloskey and Robert B. Dow, editors, *Pageant of Prose,* Harper, 1935.

Frank Luther Mott and Ralph D. Casey, editors, *Interpretations of Journalism: A Book of Readings,* F. S. Crofts, 1937.

Hillman M. Bishop and Samuel Hendel, editors, *Basic Issues of American Democracy: A Book of Readings,* Appleton, 1948, 6th edition, 1969.

William Ebenstein, editor, *Modern Political Thought: The Great Issues,* Rinehart, 1954, 2nd edition, 1960.

Robert U. Jamison, editor, *Essays Old and New,* Harcourt, 1955.

H. J. Rockel, editor, *Reflective Reader: Essays for Writing,* Holt, 1956.

Alan P. Grimes and Robert Horwitz, editors, *Modern Political Ideologues,* Oxford University Press, 1959.

C. Wright Mills, editor, *Images of Man,* Braziller, 1960.

Harry K. Girvetz, editor, *Contemporary Moral Issues,* Wadsworth, 1963.

Arthur A. Ekirch, editor, *Voices in Dissent: An Anthology of Individualistic Thought in the U.S.,* Citadel, 1964.

D. L. Larson, editor, *The Puritan Ethic in United States Foreign Policy,* Van Nostrand, 1966.

Anthologized in numerous volumes, including *Roots of Political Behavior,* edited by Richard Carlton Snyder and H. Herbert Wilson, American Book Co., 1949, *State of the Social Sciences,* edited by L. D. White, University of Chicago Press, 1956, *Conflict and Cooperation among the Nations,* edited by Ivo D. Duchacek and K. W. Thompson, Holt, 1960, and *Power and Civilization: Political Thought in the Twentieth Century,* edited by David Cooperman and E. V. Walter, Crowell, 1962. Contributor to many periodicals, including *Atlantic, Yale Review, New Republic, Life,* and *Harper's.*

SIDELIGHTS: "Anything that makes the world more humane and more rational is progress," Walter Lippmann once said. "That's the only measuring stick we can apply to it." This statement exemplifies the attitude that characterized Lippmann's career. Although he was always fully cognizant of the occurrences of the day, he also attempted to place these events in a larger perspective in his effort to make reason out of the chaos of political events. He once stated: "I have led two lives. One of books and one of newspapers. Each helps the other. The philosophy is the context in which I write my columns. The column is the laboratory or clinic in which I test the philosophy and keep it from becoming too abstract."

This objective viewing of current events as though they were already part of history made Lippmann unique. Norman Podhoretz, in *Doings and Undoings: The Fifties and After in American Writing,* recognized this quality in Lippmann, although he believed that it had its disadvantages. Podhoretz wrote in 1964: "His main fault, I think, is a tendency toward pomposity which showed itself even in his most youthful efforts and which, if anything, has been encouraged by the veneration that his advancing years . . . have brought upon him. Presidents come and go; Congressmen and Senators come, and even they eventually go; but Walter Lippmann stays on in Washington forever—the last articulate representative of the political ambience of an older America, our last remaining link to the ethos of the Federalist Papers. He is, apparently, heeded and feared in Washington in a way that no other writer is, for his judgment of a government official, or of a policy, or of a bill seems to carry with it all the authority of the basic intentions of the American political system. When he speaks, it is as though the true Constitution were speaking, or as though Jefferson and Madison and Hamilton were communicating a mystical consensus through him—so thoroughly has he steeped himself in their spirit, and with such authenticity is he capable of recapturing the accents of their intellectual style. This, I suspect, is the secret source of his unique power to make the mighty listen: Walter Lippmann's opinion is the closest they can ever come to the judgment of history upon them. Under these circumstances, it is no wonder that Lippmann should occasionally be given to delivering himself of portentous platitudes without being aware that platitudes are what they are. The wonder is that he should be capable of anything else at all."

Podhoretz's comparison of Lippmann to the founding fathers is characteristic of many other analyses of Lippmann's philosophy and writing. In *A Continuing Journey,* Archibald MacLeish described Lippmann's attitude toward freedom in a democracy as one which closely paralleled the idealism of the leaders of the American Revolution: "True freedom, to Mr. Lippmann, is not the freedom of the liberal democracies. True freedom was founded on the postulate that there was a universal order on which all reasonable men were agreed: within that public agreement on the fundamentals and on the ultimates, it was sage to permit, and it would be desirable to encourage, dissent and dispute. True freedom for Mr. Lippmann, in other words, is freedom to think as you please and say as you think provided what you say and think falls within the periphery of what all reasonable men agree to be fundamentally and ultimately true." For Lippmann rationality was not only the highest ideal, but the pos-

sible savior of modern society. He once said: "The world will go on somehow, and more crises will follow. It will go on best, however, if among us there are men who have stood apart, who refused to be anxious or too much concerned, who were cool and inquiring, and had their eyes on a longer past and longer future."

It was in the field of foreign affairs that Lippmann revealed the principles central to his view of man and the modern world. In a *New York Times Magazine* interview, Lippmann stated that U.S. foreign policy was most responsible for the political unrest and social crises of the 1960s: "I ascribe the essence of the failure [of the United States to solve its internal problems] to miscalculation, to misunderstanding our post-World War II position in the world. That has turned our energies away from our real problems. The error is not merely the trouble in Vietnam, but the error lies in the illusion that the position occupied in the world by the United States at the end of the war was a permanent arrangement of power in the world. It wasn't. The United States was victorious; but by then all the imperial structures which set the bounds of American power had been destroyed: the German Reich, the Japanese empire. The result is that we flowed forward beyond our natural limits and the cold war is the result of our meeting the Russians with no buffers between us. That miscalculation, which was made by my generation, has falsified all our other calculations—what our power was, what we could afford to do, what influence we had to exert in the world."

One of Lippmann's chief concerns was that lack of reasonable attitudes toward other nations and domestic dissenters would continue to lead to an illogical disregard for the truly significant issues with which U.S. leaders must deal. "You have only to look at the Senate of the United States," Lippmann wrote in 1912, "to see how that body is capable of turning itself into a court of preliminary hearings for the Last Judgment, wasting its time and our time and absorbing public enthusiasm and newspaper scareheads. For a hundred needs of the nation it has no thought, but about the precise morality of an historical transaction eight years old there is a meticulous interest . . . enough to start the Senate on a protracted man-hunt. Now if one half of the people is bent upon proving how wicked a man is and the other half is determined to show how good he is, neither half will think very much about the nation." Lippmann also applied this disparagement of emotional politics to the passionate anti-Communists: "The reactionary radicals, who would like to repeal the twentieth century, are, so they tell us, violently opposed to Communism. But Communism also belongs to the twentieth century and these reactionary radicals do not understand it and do not know how to resist it."

Lippmann believed that it was his ultimate role as a journalist to reveal the absurdity of these emotional diversions. With this goal he hoped to influence the people to accept his creed; he objectified events so that the populace could comprehend them. "If the country is to be governed with the consent of the governed, then the governed must arrive at opinions about what their governors want them to consent to. How do they do this? They do it by hearing on the radio and reading in the newspapers what the corps of correspondents tells them is going on in Washington and in the country at large and in the world. Here we perform an essential service . . . we do what every sovereign citizen is supposed to do, but has not the time or the interest to do for himself. This is our job. It is no mean calling, and we have a right to be proud of it."

Some of Lippmann's books have been translated into French, German, Italian, Spanish, and Chinese.

BIOGRAPHICAL/CRITICAL SOURCES:

BOOKS

Authors in the News, Volume 1, Gale, 1976.

Brown, John Mason, *Through These Men: Some Aspects of Our Passing History,* Harper, 1956.

Cary, F. C., *The Influence of Walter Lippmann, 1914-1944,* State Historical Society of Wisconsin, 1967.

Childs, Marquis, and James Reston, editors, *Walter Lippmann and His Times,* Harcourt, 1959.

Cohen, Felix S., *The Legal Conscience,* Yale University Press, 1960.

Commager, Henry Steele, *The American Mind,* Yale University Press, 1950.

Dictionary of Literary Biography, Volume 29: *American Newspaper Journalists, 1926-1950,* Gale, 1984.

Forcey, Charles B., *The Crossroads of Liberalism: Croly, Weyl, Lippmann, and the Progressive Era, 1900-1925,* Oxford University Press, 1961.

Forsee, Aylesa, *Headliners: Famous American Journalists,* Macrae, 1967.

Lerner, Max, *Actions and Passions: Notes on the Multiple Revolution of Our Time,* Simon & Schuster, 1949.

MacLeish, Archibald, *A Continuing Journey,* Houghton, 1967.

Morgenthau, Hans J., *The Restoration of American Politics,* University of Chicago Press, 1962.

Norman, Podhoretz, *Doings and Undoings: The Fifties and After in American Writing,* Farrar, Straus, 1964.

Schapsmeier, Edward L., and Frederick H. Schapsmeier, *Walter Lippmann: Philosopher, Journalist,* Public Affairs Press, 1969.

Schlesinger, Arthur, Jr., *The Politics of Hope,* Houghton, 1963.

Sevareid, Eric, *Conversations with Eric Sevareid,* Public Affairs Press, 1976.

Steel, Ronald, *Walter Lippmann and the American Century,* Atlantic/Little, Brown, 1980.

Stewart, Kenneth Norman, and John Tibbel, *Makers of Modern Journalism,* Prentice-Hall, 1952.

Syed, Anwar H., *Walter Lippmann's Philosophy of International Politics,* University of Pennsylvania Press, 1964.

Weingast, David E., *Walter Lippmann: A Study in Personal Journalism,* Rutgers University Press, 1949, reprinted, Greenwood Press, 1970.

Wellborn, Charles, *Twentieth Century Pilgrimage: Walter Lippmann and the Public Philosophy,* Louisiana State University Press, 1969.

PERIODICALS

Chicago Tribune Book World, December 22, 1985.
New York Times Magazine, September 14, 1969.

*   *   *

LITTLE, Malcolm 1925-1965
(El-Hajj Malik El-Shabazz, Malcolm X)

PERSONAL: Born May 19, 1925, in Omaha, Neb.; assassinated February 21, 1965, in New York, N.Y.; son of Earl (a minister and activist) and Louise Little; married wife, Betty (a student nurse), 1958; children: six daughters. *Religion:* Muslim.

CAREER: Activist. Worker in Lost-Found Nation of Islam (Black Muslims) religious sect, 1952-64, began as assistant minister of mosque in Detroit, Mich., then organized mosque in Philadelphia, Pa., became national minister, 1963; established Muslim Mosque, Inc., 1964; lecturer and writer. Founded Organization of Afro-American Unity in New York City, 1964.

WRITINGS:

UNDER NAME MALCOLM X

(With Alex Haley) *The Autobiography of Malcolm X,* introduction by M. S. Handler, epilogue by Haley, Grove, 1965, recent edition, Ballantine, 1990.

Malcolm X Speaks: Selected Speeches and Statements, edited and with prefatory notes by George Breitman, Merit Publishers, 1965.

Malcolm X on Afro-American History, Merit Publishers, 1967, expanded edition, Pathfinder Press, 1970.

The Speeches of Malcolm X at Harvard, edited and with an introductory essay by Archie Epps, Morrow, 1968.

Malcolm X Talks to Young People, Young Socialist Alliance, 1969.

Malcolm X and the Negro Revolution: The Speeches of Malcolm X, edited and with an introductory essay by Archie Epps, Owen, 1969.

Two Speeches by Malcolm X, Merit Publishers, 1969.

By Any Means Necessary: Speeches, Interviews, and a Letter by Malcolm X, edited by George Breitman, Pathfinder Press, 1970.

The End of White World Supremacy: Four Speeches, edited and with an introduction by Benjamin Goodman, Merlin House, 1971.

Malcolm X: The Last Speeches, Pathfinder Press, 1989.

Work represented in anthologies, including *100 and More Quotes by Garvey, Lumumba, and Malcolm X,* compiled by Shawna Maglangbayan, Third World Press, 1975.

Also speaker, with Bayard Rustin, on recording *A Choice of Two Roads,* Pacifica Archives.

SIDELIGHTS: Malcolm Little was a religious and sociopolitical activist who rose to prominence, and notoriety, in the mid-1950s under the name Malcolm X. A staunch, outspoken advocate of black separatism, he inspired many with his efforts on behalf of Elijah Muhammad's Black Muslim religion, which characterizes the black race as superior and the white race as inherently evil. For Malcolm X, the Western black's sole response to racism was total withdrawal from Western culture and society. These radical contentions, while uniting a portion of the American black community, alienated other members, including civil rights activists and pacifists. Eventually Malcolm X became disillusioned with Elijah Muhammad's antagonistic religion and left to start his own Muslim organization. This action, in turn, offended Elijah Muhammad and his followers, and in early 1965, while preparing to speak in a Harlem ballroom, Malcolm X was gunned down by men believed sympathetic to the Black Muslims.

As I. F. Stone noted in the *New York Review of Books,* "Malcolm X was born into Black Nationalism." Earl Little, Malcolm's father, was a Baptist minister who strongly supported separatist Marcus Garvey's back-to-Africa movement in the 1920s. For his actions on behalf of Garvey, Earl Little soon found himself the target of hostility while living in Omaha, Nebraska, where members of the racist Ku Klux Klan organization threatened his family because he was sparking dissension among the normally cooperative blacks. The Littles consequently left Omaha, but during the next few years they failed to find a hospitable community and thus moved often. In his autobiography, Malcolm X recalled a particularly harrowing experience in Lansing, Michigan, where his family home was torched by members of the Black Legion, an oddly named band of white supremacists. Shortly afterwards the corpse of Earl Little was found horribly butchered.

Following Earl Little's death, Louise Little and her eight children subsisted on welfare. Eventually, however, the severe strain overwhelmed her and she succumbed to mental illness. Louise Little was then placed in a mental institution and her children were sent separately to various foster homes. Despite this continued adversity and emotional hardship, Malcolm still held aspirations of assimilation in America's predominantly white society. But even those hopes faded after he confided to his high-school English teacher that he hoped to someday become a lawyer, whereupon the teacher urged him towards a vocation instead of a profession and told him to be "realistic about being a nigger."

A distinguished student, Malcolm was shattered by his teacher's racist counseling, and soon afterward he quit high school. Living with a sister in Boston, Malcolm found menial work and began associating with low-lifes and criminals. He became involved with illegal gambling, managed his own prostitution ring, and consorted with drug dealers. Eventually he also sold narcotics, to which he swiftly became addicted, and turned to robbery to sustain his drug habit. He developed a formidable reputation as an enterprising, quick-thinking hustler, becoming notorious in the Boston ghetto as "Detroit Red." With that notoriety, however, came increasing attention from the police, and in early 1946 Malcolm was arrested and charged with robbery. That February—three months before his twenty-first birthday—he was sentenced to ten years imprisonment.

In the penitentiary Malcolm continued his reckless ways, using drugs and presenting such an unsavory demeanor that his fellow inmates referred to him as "Satan." Because of his vicious behavior he was often held in solitary confinement. But he did manage to befriend another convicted burglar, Bimbi, who introduced him to the prison's extensive library. Through the library Malcolm broadened his education and familiarized himself with subjects ranging from philosophy to politics. He also began studying the tenets of the Black Muslims' Lost-Found Nation of Islam, a religion that extolled the superiority of the black race and denounced the white as evil and doomed to destruction. The Black Muslims' founder and leader, Elijah Muhammad, proclaimed himself divine messenger of the Muslim deity, Allah, and—like Marcus Garvey—counseled his followers to abjure white America in favor of an autonomous black society. Elijah Muhammad's doctrine of black pride exerted considerable appeal to Malcolm, who denounced his allegedly enslaving Christian surname and adopted the name Malcolm X.

While still in prison Malcolm X corresponded with Elijah Muhammad, who lived comfortably at Black Muslim headquarters in Chicago, and after obtaining freedom in 1952 he traveled there and commenced a brief tutelage under the Muslim leader. He then served briefly as an assistant minister at a Detroit mosque before becoming minister at Harlem's Mosque Number Seven. It was in Harlem that Malcolm X achieved impressive status as an articulate, mercurial spokesperson for the radical black perspective. From street corners, church pulpits, and college podiums he railed against racism and championed separatism and faith in Allah as the salvation of blacks. He claimed that civil rights, equal opportunity, and integration were all futile within a society that was determinedly racist. Even Christianity was reviled as a method of enslavement and was denounced as a historical distortion—Christ having been, according to Malcolm X, a black. He advised blacks to reject white society and unite under Elijah Muhammad and the Black Muslim faith, which held the true way to dignity for blacks.

Malcolm X proved an impressive representative for Elijah Muhammad, and as he enthusiastically proselytized for the Black

Muslims their membership increased significantly. Elijah Muhammad, acknowledging the impressive effectiveness of his acolyte, named him the religion's first national minister. As Malcolm X rose in status, however, he became increasingly critical of Elijah Muhammad's materialism, particularly his many expensive cars and business suits and his lavishly furnished estate in Chicago. In addition, he was dismayed when former secretaries claimed that Elijah Muhammad had seduced them and sired their children, thus violating the sect's tenet on sexual promiscuity. Elijah Muhammad, in turn, reportedly grew resentful of Malcolm X's growing prominence across the nation and thus his formidable influence within the Black Muslim organization.

Rivalry between the two men peaked in 1963 when Malcolm X violated Elijah Muhammad's commandment of silence regarding the November 22nd assassination of President Kennedy and termed it a case of "the chicken coming home to roost." Malcolm X, who later explained that his comment was meant to indicate that "the hate in white men . . . finally had struck down the President," was reprimanded by Elijah Muhammad for the potentially incendiary remark. "That was a very bad statement," Elijah Muhammad told him. "The country loved this man." He ordered Malcolm X to refrain from public comment for ninety days, and Malcolm complied.

Within days, however, Malcolm X learned that members of his sect were plotting his demise. His dissatisfaction with the Black Muslims mounted, and he decided to tour Mecca, birthplace of the Muslim prophet Muhammad. Once there, Malcolm X experienced a powerful conversion, one which left him with greater compassion for people of all races and nationalities. He renamed himself El-Hajj Malik El-Shabazz and vowed to promote greater harmony among all blacks, including non-Muslims and civil rights activists he had alienated earlier with his uncompromising positions. Once back in the United States he founded his own Muslim association, the Organization of Afro-American Unity, and began actively working to unite blacks throughout the world.

Once he began operating outside the Black Muslim sect, Malcolm X was apparently perceived as a threat to the organization. "Now I'm out," he stated. "And there's the fear [that] if my image isn't shattered, the Muslims in the movement will leave." He was informed that members within the organization were plotting to end his life, and in mid-February he told the *New York Times* that he was a "marked man." Around that time his home was firebombed. But he was undaunted and continued to speak on behalf of black unity and harmony. On February 21, 1965, he stepped to the podium in a Harlem ballroom and greeted the audience of four hundred that had gathered to hear him speak. Within seconds at least three men rose from their seats and began firing at Malcolm X with shotguns and pistols. Seven shots slammed him backwards while spectators scrambled for cover. As gunfire continued—more than thirty shots were reportedly heard—daring witnesses attacked and subdued the assassins. Three men—Talmadge Hayer and Black Muslims Norman 3X Butler and Thomas 15X Johnson—were eventually convicted of the killing, and it is widely believed the assassins intended to intimidate Malcolm X's followers into remaining within the Black Muslim fold.

In the years since his death Malcolm X has come to be recognized as a leading figure in the black struggle for recognition and equality. *The Autobiography of Malcolm X,* published the same year as his death, is highly regarded as a moving account of his own experiences with racism, his criminal past, and his years as an activist for both the Black Muslims and his own Afro-

American organization. During the remaining years of the 1960s Malcolm X's speeches and comments were collected and published in volumes such as *Malcolm X Speaks, Malcolm X on Afro-American History,* and *Malcolm X and the Negro Revolution.* Together with the autobiography, these books offer numerous insights into America's social climate from the mid-1950s to the mid-1960s and articulate the concerns of a significant portion of the black community in those years. Additionally, they serve as an imposing indication of Malcolm X's beliefs, his achievements, and his potential, which—like that of President Kennedy, Reverend Martin Luther King, Jr., and Senator Robert Kennedy—were violently rendered unrealized. As I. F. Stone noted in his essay-review for the *New York Review of Books:* "There are few places on earth where whites have not grown rich robbing [blacks]. It was Malcolm's great contribution to help make us aware of this." Stone called Malcolm X's murder "a loss to the country as well as to his race."

MEDIA ADAPTATIONS: James Baldwin adapted portions of *The Autobiography of Malcolm X* as *One Day, When I Was Lost: A Scenario,* Dial, 1973.

BIOGRAPHICAL/CRITICAL SOURCES:

BOOKS

Alexander, Rae Pace, *Young and Black in America,* Random House, 1973.
Breitman, George, *The Last Year of Malcolm X: The Evolution of a Revolutionary,* Merit Publications, 1967.
Clarke, John Henrik, editor and author of introduction, *Malcolm X: The Man and His Times,* Macmillan, 1969.
Curtis, Richard, *Life of Malcolm X,* Macrae Smith, 1971.
Darling, Edward, *When Sparks Fly Upward,* Washburn, 1970.
Goldman, Peter Louis, *Death and Life of Malcolm X,* University of Illinois Press, 1979.
Haskins, James, *Revolutionaries,* Lippincott, 1971.
Jamal, Hakin A., *From the Dead Level: Malcolm X and Me,* Random House, 1972.
Lomax, Louise E., *To Kill a Black Man,* Holloway House, 1968.
McKinley, James, *Assassination in America,* Harper, 1977.
Miah, Malik, editor and author of introduction, *Assassination of Malcolm X,* Pathfinder Press, 1976.
Paris, Peter J., *Black Leaders in Conflict: Joseph H. Jackson, Martin Luther King, Jr., Malcolm X, Adam Clayton Powell, Jr.,* Pilgrim Press, 1978.
Parks, Gordon, *Born Black,* Lippincott, 1971.
Playboy Interviews, Playboy Press, 1967.
Wolfenstein, Eugene Victor, *Victims of Democracy: Malcolm X and the Black Revolution,* University of California Press, 1981.

PERIODICALS

Catholic World, September, 1967.
Christian Century, April 7, 1965.
Ebony, October, 1965, June, 1969.
Encounter, September, 1973.
Harper's, June, 1964.
Life, March 20, 1964.
Journal of Black Studies, December, 1981.
Nation, March 8, 1965, November 8, 1965.
Negro Education Review, January, 1979.
New Statesman, June 12, 1964.
Newsweek, December 16, 1963, November 15, 1965, March 3, 1969, January 8, 1973, May 7, 1979.
New York Review of Books, November 11, 1965.
New York Times Book Review, September 11, 1966, April 13, 1969, May 16, 1971.
Saturday Review, November 20, 1965, July 30, 1966.
Spectator, February 26, 1965.
Time, March 5, 1965, February 23, 1970, June 12, 1972.
Times Literary Supplement, June 9, 1966, May 28, 1971.
Washington Post, May 20, 1989.
Yale Review, December, 1966.

OBITUARIES:

PERIODICALS

New York Times, February 22, 1965.

*   *   *

LITTLEWIT, Humphrey, Gent.
   See LOVECRAFT, H(oward) P(hillips)

*   *   *

LIVELY, Penelope (Margaret)   1933-

PERSONAL: Born March 17, 1933, in Cairo, Egypt; daughter of Roger Low (a bank manager) and Vera Greer; taken to England in 1945; married Jack Lively (a university teacher), June 27, 1957; children: Josephine, Adam. *Education:* St. Anne's College, Oxford, B.A., 1956.

ADDRESSES: Home and office—Duck End, Great Rollright, Chipping, Norton, Oxfordshire OX7 55B, England. *Agent*—Murray Pollinger, 4 Garrick St., London WC2E 9BH, England.

CAREER: Free-lance writer.

MEMBER: Society of Authors.

AWARDS, HONORS: Children's Spring Book Festival Award, *Book World,* 1973, for *The Driftway;* Carnegie Medal, 1973, and Hans Christian Anderson Award List, 1973, both for *The Ghost of Thomas Kempe;* Whitbread Award, 1976, for *A Stitch in Time;* named to Booker-McConnell Prize shortlist, 1977, for *The Road to Lichfield,* and 1984, for *According to Mark: A Novel;* Southern Arts Literary Prize, 1978, for *Nothing Missing but the Samovar and Other Stories;* Arts Council of Great Britain National Book Award, 1979, for *Treasures of Time;* Booker-McConnell Prize, 1987, for *Moon Tiger.*

WRITINGS:

FOR CHILDREN

Astercote, illustrated by Antony Maitland, Heinemann, 1970, Dutton, 1971.
The Whispering Knights, illustrated by Gareth Floyd, Heinemann, 1971, Dutton, 1976.
The Wild Hunt of Hagworthy, illustrated by Juliet Mozley, Heinemann, 1971, new edition illustrated by Robert Payne, Pan Books, 1975, published as *The Wild Hunt of the Ghost Hounds,* Dutton, 1972, new edition illustrated by Jeremy Ford, Puffin Books, 1984.
The Driftway, Heinemann, 1972, Dutton, 1973.
The Ghost of Thomas Kempe, illustrated by Maitland, Dutton, 1973.
The House in Norham Gardens, Dutton, 1974.
Boy without a Name, illustrated by Ann Dalton, Parnassus Press, 1975.
Going Back, Dutton, 1975.
A Stitch in Time, Dutton, 1976.
The Stained Glass Window, illustrated by Michael Pollard, Abelard-Schumann, 1976.

Fanny's Sister (also see below), illustrated by John Lawrence, Heinemann, 1976, new edition, illustrated by Anita Lobel, Dutton, 1980.

The Presence of the Past: An Introduction to Landscape History, Collins, 1976.

The Voyage of QV66, illustrated by Harold Jones, Heinemann, 1978, Dutton, 1979.

Fanny and the Monsters (also see below), illustrated by Lawrence, Heinemann, 1979, enlarged edition, 1983.

Fanny and the Battle of Potter's Piece (also see below), illustrated by Lawrence, Heinemann, 1980.

The Revenge of Samuel Stokes, Dutton, 1981.

Fanny and the Monsters and Other Stories (contains *Fanny's Sister, Fanny and the Monsters,* and *Fanny and the Battle of Potter's Piece*), Puffin Books, 1982.

Uninvited Ghosts and Other Stories, illustrated by Lawrence, Heinemann, 1984, Dutton, 1985.

Dragon Trouble, illustrated by Valerie Littlewood, Heinemann, 1984.

A House Inside Out, illustrated by David Parkins, Deutsch, 1987, Dutton, 1988.

FOR ADULTS

The Road to Lichfield, Heinemann, 1977, Penguin, 1983.

Nothing Missing but the Samovar and Other Stories, Heinemann, 1978.

Treasures of Time, Heinemann, 1979, Doubleday, 1980.

Judgement Day, Heinemann, 1980, Doubleday, 1981.

Next to Nature, Art, Heinemann, 1982, Penguin, 1984.

Perfect Happiness, Heinemann, 1983, Dial Press, 1984.

Corruption and Other Stories, Heinemann, 1984.

According to Mark: A Novel, Beaufort Books, 1984.

Pack of Cards (short stories, including "Nothing Missing but the Samovar" and "Corruption"), Heinemann, 1986, Penguin, 1988.

Moon Tiger, Deutsch, 1987, Grove, 1988.

Passing On (novel), Deutsch, 1989.

OTHER

Contributor to periodicals, including *Encounter.*

SIDELIGHTS: Penelope Lively has distinguished herself as a writer of both juvenile and adult books, winning such prestigious awards as the Booker-McConnell Prize and the Whitbread Award. *Publishers Weekly* contributor Amanda Smith remarks that "'Lively is one of England's finest writers," and adds that her novels are "characterized by intelligence, precision and wit." Sheila A. Egoff, author of *Thursday's Child: Trends and Patterns in Contemporary Children's Literature,* writes that Lively "has an uncannily accurate and honest recall of what it is like to be a child in a world made for adults." As to her adult fiction, a *Times Literary Supplement* reviewer comments that Lively conveys "a prose that is invariably as precise as it is unostentatious."

Born in Cairo, Egypt, Lively received no formal education until she was taken to England at the age of twelve and placed in a boarding school, one she was later to condemn in a *Dictionary of Literary Biography* article as a "barbaric institution." The school was "aimed at turning out competent hockey and lacrosse players and did not encourage other activities," writes Lively. Once, she was even reprimanded by her headmistress for reading *The Oxford Book of English Verse* on her own time. Despite this discouragement, her curiosity about the past, which had developed in Egypt, was nourished by England's historical richness. "I need to write with a very strong sense of topography and place," remarks Lively in a *Publishers Weekly* interview, and her

new home well satisfied this need. In the same article she recalls that her studies in modern history at St. Anne's College, where she received a B.A. in 1954, were "wonderful" compared to her earlier education. With her degree completed, the author "originally intended to write social history, but turned to stories for children as a convenient way of exploring her own particular interests," according to Alec Ellis, editor of *Chosen for Children: An Account of the Books Which Have Been Awarded the Library Association Carnegie Medal, 1936-1975.*

In a public speech that was revised to appear in *Horn Book,* Lively writes: "My particular preoccupation as a writer, is with memory. Both with memory in the wide historical sense and memory in the personal sense." Children's literature, with its strong element of imagination, has provided an appropriate means for her study of memory, since, in her view, there is a large amount of fantasy involved in the way people remember the past. Whether it is world history or our own personal history, "we like the past gutted and nicely cleaned up," says Lively; "then we know where we are with it." The relationship between our conceptions of the past and the actual past is a subject the author likes to explore "without presuming to come up with any answers."

Writing juvenile fiction, however, is also a type of mission for Lively that can provide enlightenment. In *A Sounding of Storytellers: New and Revised Essays on Contemporary Writers for Children,* John Rowe Townsend comments: "Penelope Lively sees a sense of continuity as essential to the life of the imagination. In an article in the *Horn Book* for August, 1973, she regretted that modern children were in danger of losing the personal memory that came from contact with the old ('the grandmother at the fireside')." She suggests in this article: "It may be that books attending to memory . . . are more important than ever before." While discussing *The Ghost of Thomas Kempe* in *Junior Bookshelf,* Lively notes that children are not aware of memory simply because they have not lived long enough to become well acquainted with it. It is hard for them to understand how people and their viewpoints change over time. "The point at which children extend this unimaginable truth" towards others, explains Lively, is "an important moment in the growing-up process." It is through her books, then, that she seeks to "introduce children to the art of memory so that they can observe its possibilities and effects and wonder about them," as the author does herself.

It is this process which Lively attempts to describe in *The Driftway.* The story follows Paul and his tag-along sister as he runs away from his stepmother and a charge of shoplifting. He comes across an old road which has been used for thousands of years by various travellers. They have left messages from the past which Paul is able to see and interpret with the help of a cart-driver named Bill. Margery Fisher, editor of *Growing Point,* explains that each "interlude reflects part of Paul's situation and brings him a step nearer to understanding himself and his family." The characters from the past make him aware that "there is more than one point of view to every story, and he takes the first steps away from the morbid self-absorption of childhood towards feeling sympathy for others," concludes a *Times Literary Supplement* reviewer. Some writers such as John Townsend feel that the point of the story is weakened because the book as a whole lacks a strong storyline—the reader never does find out what happens to Paul and his sister. However, *Junior Bookshelf* contributor Aneurin R. Williams expresses her belief that, overall, "Lively writes well, exceeding by far the style and effect of" her earlier work.

Lively's best-received juvenile book, *The Ghost of Thomas Kempe,* offers a much lighter approach to the coming-of-age theme. But, a *Times Literary Supplement* critic qualifies, "the gaiety and high spirits of Penelope Lively's story do not disguise its essentially sober wisdom." In this book the author uses one of her favorite devices: the ghost. The purpose of Thomas Kempe's character, explains Lively in *Junior Bookshelf,* is to explore "the memory of places and the memory of people, and the curious business that we are all of us not just what we are now but what we have been." Putting this another way, *Children's Literature in Education* contributor Judith Armstrong writes that this book "is concerned with different aspects of the same person, the person [James] might have been, or might still become, had he not encountered the ghost of his potential self." The story involves a boy's visitation by the spirit of a sorcerer from Stuart England. At first, the ghost seems only mischievous, but slowly becomes more and more menacing. James learns through the ghost what wickedness is, and is only able to put Kempe to rest by learning to recognize and cope with the wickedness within himself. Many critics agree that *The Ghost of Thomas Kempe* is a well written children's book. "The expert blend of humour and historical imagination is at once more mature and more skillful than anything Penelope Lively has so far written," claims Margery Fisher. David Rees, author of *The Marble in the Water: Essays on Contemporary Writers of Fiction for Children and Young Adults,* feels that the book is of such high quality because for the first time "the author is completely sure of her own abilities, and the writing has a positiveness that derives from the author's pleasure in her awareness of these abilities."

Rees has even higher praise for *A Stitch in Time,* Lively's Whitbread Award winner. "*A Stitch in Time* is probably Penelope Lively's most important and memorable book," he declares. "Not only is its exploration of the significance of history and memory more profound than in any other of her novels, but the unfolding of the story is very fine." As *Times Literary Supplement* reviewer Ann Thwait notes, the story does not have a great deal of plot action, since most of this action occurs unobtrusively within the mind of Marie, the main character. Marie, who is spending her vacation with her parents in an old Victorian house in Lyme Regis, discovers a sampler made in 1865 by a girl named Harriet. The sampler provides a link to the past which Marie senses through such things as the squeaking of a swing and the barking of a dog, neither of which exist near the house at the present; they are only echoes of the past. The tension in the story lies in Marie's suspicion that something tragic has happened to Harriet, a belief supported by the lack of any pictures in the house of Harriet as an adult. Though the mystery is eventually solved, the real message of the book is summarized by the owner of the old house when he sagely remarks: "Things always could have been otherwise. The fact of the matter is that they are not." This declaration, explains Terry Jones, a contributor to *Children's Literature in Education,* "finally ends Maria's 'vague imaginings' and completes one part of her education. . . . She leaves the Regency house determined to acquire 'some new wisdom about the way things are.' She grows, and the reader grows with her."

In the late 1970s, after writing children's books for almost a decade, Lively decided it was time for a change. "I began to feel that I was in danger of writing the same children's books over and over again," she says in *Publishers Weekly.* "More than that, I'd exhausted the ways in which I could explore my own preoccupations and interests within children's books.' " In writing for this new audience, the author has maintained her interest in the past and memory, but has followed a different approach. Her adult characters consider memory "in the context of a lifetime rather than in the context of history," explains Lively in *Horn Book.* These later works no longer deal with how the past can teach one to mature so much as how it can change one's perspective or philosophy of life.

Lively's first novel for adults, *The Road to Lichfield,* is a complex tale about what happens to a married history teacher named Anne Linton when her conceptions about her childhood family life are suddenly altered. While going through her dying father's papers, she discovers that he was involved in an affair similar to her own extramarital relationship. "As everything in her life swings and changes, her father dies, her love is choked off, and only the road [between her present life in Cuxing and her childhood memories of Lichfield] remains permanent," summarizes Jane Langton in the *Dictionary of Literary Biography.* "There is nothing very original about the plot [of *The Road to Lichfield*]," notes John Mellors of *Listener,* but the "book is lifted out of the ordinary by the author's treatment of her two main themes: continuity and memory." Lively "has an easy, unobtrusive style," adds Mellors, which "throws light from unexpected angles" upon questions like whether or not memory actually distorts or preserves the past.

History is not clouded by memory at all in Lively's more cynical book, *Judgement Day.* In this novel, the violent history of an ancient church nags at the thoughts of the main character, Clare, as she witnesses similarly senseless acts occuring in her own life. From the vicar of the church she receives only muddled, unsatisfactory answers to her doubts that a loving and omnipotent God could allow such atrocities. Her experiences in the book eventually compel her to believe "that we are quite fortuitously here, and that the world is a cruel and terrible place, but inexplicably and bewilderingly beautiful." Francis King of *Spectator* wonders if it is "presumptuous to assume that it is also Clare's creator who is speaking here." Stating her beliefs in a *Publishers Weekly* article, Lively appears to confirm King's suspicion: "Life is governed by Fate—Fate being another word for history—governed by outside forces over which one has no control. This is one of the things that most people find unacceptable about life and therefore try to camouflage." Although *Times Literary Supplement* contributor William Boyd questions the effectiveness of "fate's visitations" in *Judgement Day, Encounter* contributor Alan Brownjohn feels that Lively handles this premise well. *Listener* reviewer John Naughton asserts that this novel "is an impressive work, sharp and surefooted on the nuances of class and of personal conflict."

In Lively's Booker-McConnell Award-winning story *Moon Tiger,* a novel which presents a perspective on life similar to that of *Judgement Day,* the "true center is no less than history itself—the abiding backdrop across which mere human beings flutter," says Ann Tyler in the *New York Times Book Review.* It is "the transitoriness of all human happiness and indeed of all human life" which is the concern of a respected historian, Claudia Hampton, as she considers her life from the vantage point of her deathbed, explains Francis King in a *Spectator* article. In this book a complex interweaving of flashbacks takes the reader on a voyage through the dying historian's life, including a sojourn in World War II Egypt, where Claudia finds brief happiness with a tank commander, who is later killed in action. "Her image for their love," writes Richard Eder of the *Los Angeles Times Book Review,* "is the moon tiger—a spiral coil of punk that burns slowly through the night beside their bed to keep away mosquitos and that leaves only ash in the morning."

Parallel to this image are the last lines of the book in which Claudia passes away: "The sun sinks and the glittering tree is extinguished. The room darkens again. . . . And within the room a change has taken place. It is empty. Void. It has the stillness of a place in which there are only inanimate objects; metal, wood, glass, plastic. No Life." The denoument marks the end of, in Eder's words, Claudia's "long postponed search for herself." For some critics, like Martha Duffy of *Time* magazine, the flashbacks involved in her search become "overdrawn" after a while. However, many reviewers concur with *Times Literary Supplement* contributor J. K. L. Walker, who writes: "Penelope Lively's ingenious, historically informed handling of [the story] is a considerable achievement and Claudia Hampton herself a formidably reflective and articulate protagonist." It is a tale told from the most widely encompassing perspective possible for a human being, a study of one character's entire lifetime memory and how she regards it.

Although Lively bases most of *Moon Tiger* upon the memory of a single character, exploring this favorite subject in depth, the author admits to herself in *Horn Book*: "I don't imagine that I am ever going to find the answer to the questions prompted by the workings of memory; all I can do is pose these questions in fictional form and see what happens." Nevertheless, Penelope Lively has achieved "something unique" in her novels, according to David Rees, "a kind of book that is neither history nor fantasy but has something of both, and that cannot be labeled conveniently—a book . . . where 'history is now.' " Ultimately, the purpose of writing, explains Lively in *Horn Book,* is "to provide plunder for the reader's imagination." Books should give the reader "something to take away and mull over on his own and maybe develop and enlarge and breed from." In this way, Lively hopes her books will help illustrate "what it is like to be a human being."

BIOGRAPHICAL/CRITICAL SOURCES:

BOOKS

Children's Literature Review, Volume 7, Gale, 1984.
Contemporary Literary Criticism, Volume 32, Gale, 1985.
Dictionary of Literary Biography, Volume 14: *British Novelists Since 1960,* Gale, 1983.
Egoff, Sheila A., *Thursday's Child: Trends and Patterns in Contemporary Children's Literature,* American Library Association, 1981.
Ellis, Alec, and Marcus Crouch, editors, *Chosen for Children: An Account of the Books Which Have Been Awarded the Library Association Carnegie Medal, 1936-1975,* 3rd edition, American Library Association, 1977.
Rees, David, *The Marble in the Water: Essays on Contemporary Writers of Fiction for Children and Young Adults,* Horn Book, 1980.
Townsend, John Rowe, *A Sounding of Storytellers: New and Revised Essays on Contemporary Writers for Children,* Lippincott, 1979.

PERIODICALS

Chicago Tribune Book World, August 9, 1981, May 15, 1988.
Children's Literature in Education, summer, 1978, autumn, 1981.
Encounter, May, 1981.
Globe and Mail (Toronto), November 14, 1987.
Growing Point, July, 1972, July, 1973.
Horn Book, June, 1973, August, 1973, February, 1978, April, 1978.
Junior Bookshelf, September, 1972, June, 1974.

Listener, August 4, 1977.
Los Angeles Times Book Review, April 17, 1988.
New York Times Book Review, April 17, 1988.
Publishers Weekly, November 13, 1987, March 25, 1988.
Spectator, November 22, 1980, May 23, 1987.
Time, May 2, 1988.
Times (London), October 30, 1987.
Times Literary Supplement, July 14, 1972, April 6, 1973, July 16, 1976, November 21, 1980, May 23, 1986, May 15, 1987.
Washington Post Book World, August 2, 1981, September 13, 1988.

*   *   *

LIVESAY, Dorothy (Kathleen)   1909-

PERSONAL: Born October 12, 1909, in Winnipeg, Manitoba, Canada; daughter of John F. B. (general manager of Canadian Press) and Florence (a writer; maiden name, Randal) Livesay; married Duncan Cameron Macnair, August 14, 1937 (deceased); children: Peter, Marcia. *Education:* University of Toronto, Trinity College, B.A., 1931, attended School of Social Work, 1933-34; Sorbonne, University of Paris, Diplome d'Etudes Superieures, 1932; University of British Columbia, M.Ed., 1966. *Politics:* No affiliation. *Religion:* Unitarian Universalist.

*ADDRESSES: Home and office—*R.R. No. 1, Galiano, British Columbia, Canada V0N 1P0.

CAREER: Poet. Memorial House, Englewood, N.J., social worker, 1935-36; British Columbia Department of Social Welfare, Vancouver, social worker, 1936-39; *Toronto Daily Star,* Toronto, Ontario, correspondent, 1946-49; documentary scriptwriter, Canadian Broadcasting Corporation, 1950-55; Young Women's Christian Association, Vancouver, British Columbia, young adult director, 1953-55; University of British Columbia, Vancouver, lecturer in English, 1955-56; Vancouver (British Columbia) School Board, high school teacher, 1956-58; UNESCO English Specialist, program specialist in Paris, France, 1958-60, specialist in English-teacher training in Northern Rhodesia (now Zambia), 1960-63; University of British Columbia, lecturer in poetry, department of creative writing, 1965-66; University of New Brunswick, Fredericton, writer-in-residence, 1966-68; University of Alberta, Edmonton, associate professor of English, 1968-71; University of Victoria, Victoria, British Columbia, visiting lecturer in English, 1972-74; University of Manitoba, St. John's College, Winnipeg, writer-in-residence, 1974-75; University of Ottawa, Ottawa, Ontario, writer-in-residence, 1977; Simon Fraser University, Burnaby, British Columbia, writer-in-residence, 1980, associated with creative writing seminar, 1981; University of Toronto, New College, Toronto, writer-in-residence, 1983. Reader of poetry at universities and high schools throughout Canada, 1971-77.

MEMBER: League of Canadian Poets.

AWARDS, HONORS: Jardine Memorial prize, 1927, for poetry; Governor General's Literary Award in poetry, 1944, for *Day and Night,* and 1947, for *Poems for People;* Lorne Pierce Medal of Royal Society of Canada, 1947, for *Poems for People;* President's Medal of University of Western Ontario, 1954, for a single poem, "Lament"; Canada Council grants, 1958, 1975, and 1982; D.Litt., University of Waterloo, 1973; honorary fellow, St. John's College, University of Manitoba, 1976, and Trinity College, University of Toronto, 1983; honorary doctorate, Athabasca University, 1983.

WRITINGS:

POETRY, EXCEPT AS INDICATED

Green Pitcher (chapbook), Macmillan (Toronto), 1928.
Signpost, Macmillan, 1932.
Day and Night, Ryerson, 1944.
Poems for People, Ryerson, 1947.
(Editor) *The Collected Poems of Raymond Knister,* Ryerson, 1949.
Call My People Home (chapbook; also see below), Ryerson, 1951.
New Poems (chapbook), Emblem Press, 1955.
Selected Poems of Dorothy Livesay, 1926-1956, Ryerson, 1957.
The Colour of God's Face (chapbook), Vancouver Unitarian Service Committee, 1964.
The Unquiet Bed, Ryerson, 1967.
The Documentaries: Selected Longer Poems (poems and reminiscences), Ryerson, 1968.
Plainsongs (chapbook), Fiddlehead Press, 1969.
(Contributor) *How Do I Love Thee: Sixty Poets of Canada (and Quebec) Select and Introduce Their Favourite Poems from Their Own Work* (anthology), edited by John Robert Colombo, M. G. Hurtig (Edmonton), 1970.
(Contributor) *Contexts of Canadian Criticism,* edited by Eli Mandel, University of Chicago Press, 1971.
(Editor with Seymour Mayne) *Forty Women Poets of Canada* (anthology), Ingluvin (Montreal), 1971.
Collected Poems: The Two Seasons, McGraw (Toronto), 1972.
A Winnipeg Childhood (short stories), Peguis Press, 1973.
(Editor) *Woman's Eye: Twelve British Columbian Women Poets* (anthology), Air Publications, 1975.
Ice Age, Press Porcepic, 1975.
Right Hand Left Hand (autobiography), Press Porcepic, 1977.
The Woman I Am, Press Porcepic, 1978.
The Raw Edges, Turnstone Press, 1981.
The Phases of Love, Coach House Press, 1983.
Feeling the Worlds, Fiddlehead Press, 1984.
Beyond War: The Poetry, [Vancouver], 1985.
Selected Poems: The Self-Completing Tree, Press Porcepic, 1986.
The Husband (novella), Ragweed Press, 1990.

Also author of monographs and of "Call My People Home," a documentary drama about Japanese-Canadians, produced by Canadian Broadcasting Corp., 1950.

Contributor to anthologies, including *Book of Canadian Poetry,* Oxford University Press; *Oxford Book of Canadian Verse, Penguin Anthology of Canadian Poetry, Canadian Anthology,* W. J. Gage; *Anthology of Commonwealth Poetry,* 1966; *Poets between the Wars,* edited by Milton T. Wilson, McClelland & Stewart, 1967; *Fifteen Canadian Poets Plus Five,* edited by Gary Geddes, Oxford University Press, 1981; *Canadian Poetry,* Volume 1, edited by John David and Robert Lecker, ECW Press, 1982; and *New Oxford Book of Canadian Verse,* Oxford University Press, 1982.

Contributor to periodicals, including *Canadian Literature, Canadian Forum, Fiddlehead, Quarry, Tamarack Review, Queen's Quarterly, Dalhousie Review, Prison International, Canadian Dimension,* and *Journal of Canadian Fiction.* Editor-in-chief, *CV/II* (a quarterly of poetry criticism), 1975—.

WORK IN PROGRESS: Memoirs.

SIDELIGHTS: D. V. Smith writes that Dorothy Livesay "is a poet remarkable for her strong, pioneering personality. For me she is the spirit of Pound—steeped in literature, rugged, artistically and socially conscious. . . . She is probably a major poet of the English language of the 20th century. She is prolific as well as she is brilliant. At any rate, she is just that for me—a major poet."

"Dorothy Livesay believes in the human value of writing poetry, which is to say that she urges people—everyone—to write poems," writes Kent Thompson in discussing *The Unquiet Bed.* She "cannot be tied to any school of poets. . . . Miss Livesay's poems use what is necessary to their success. She is not afraid of rich metaphor, nor even of literary allusions. . . . Miss Livesay seems to have allowed the poems to make their own demands, and she has not imposed patterns on either her poetic craft or her eyesight, which is why, I think, the poems are so successful."

Mary Novik of the *Vancouver Sun* writes of *Ice Age:* "This volume reaffirms Livesay's presence as the most lyric of our older generation of modern poets. The personal voice runs through her work, always emotional, always immediate. Her love poems are the most frankly sensual of those written in Canada today. In fact, the title seems at first to be ironic, for old age is no ice age to Livesay, but a time of passion and fury." Zoe Huggins of the *Ottawa Citizen* surmises: "For more than 40 years, Dorothy Livesay's poetry has displayed her lively interests. She has an acute social conscience and a vibrant awareness of the changing world outside—and she explores the self honestly and with passion. *Ice Age,* her new collection is a characteristic blend of intensely personal poems and unabashedly public ones, linked by a concern with aging. Sometimes funny and often pathetic, the public poems describe the plight of the old in a society geared for the young. . . . Livesay dedicates this slim volume 'to my younger' because she has set out to introduce a young world to the perceptions and concerns of those not so young." Livesay told *CA:* "My work has been the evocation of the Canadian scene through the writing of lyrical and documentary poetry from 1928 to 1968. My range of interest as exemplified in the poetry is personal, sexual, social, educational and political. My chief passion is to encourage young poets in self-knowledge and self-expression."

Dorothy Livesay has traveled in the British Isles, Europe, and Central and East Africa. There is a manuscript collection of her work at the University of Alberta, Edmonton.

BIOGRAPHICAL/CRITICAL SOURCES:

BOOKS

Contemporary Literary Criticism, Gale, Volume 4, 1975, Volume 15, 1980.
Dictionary of Literary Biography, Volume 68: *Canadian Writers, 1920-1959, First Series,* Gale, 1988.
Mandel, Eli, editor, *Contexts of Canadian Literature,* University of Chicago Press, 1974.

PERIODICALS

Canadian Forum, April, 1969.
Canadian Literature, winter, 1971, autumn, 1973, spring, 1974.
Fiddlehead, summer, 1967, March-April, 1969.
Globe and Mail (Toronto), January 26, 1985, April 21, 1990.
The Human Voice, winter, 1967-68.
Queen's Quarterly 4, winter, 1969.

*   *   *

LLOSA, (Jorge) Mario (Pedro) Vargas
   See VARGAS LLOSA, (Jorge) Mario (Pedro)

LODGE, David (John) 1935-

PERSONAL: Born January 28, 1935, in England; son of William Frederick (a musician) and Rosalie (Murphy) Lodge; married Mary Frances Jacob, May 16, 1959; children: Julia, Stephen, Christopher. *Education:* University College, London, B.A. (with first class honors), 1955, M.A., 1959; University of Birmingham, Ph.D., 1967. *Religion:* Roman Catholic.

ADDRESSES: Home—14 Harrisons Rd., Edgbaston, Birmingham B15 3QP, England. *Office*—Department of English, University of Birmingham, Birmingham B15 2TT, England. *Agent*—Curtis Brown Ltd., 162-168 Regent St., London WlR 5TA, England.

CAREER: British Council, London, England, assistant, 1959-60; University of Birmingham, Birmingham, England, lecturer, 1960-71, senior lecturer, 1971-73, reader, 1973-76, professor of modern English literature, 1976-87, professor emeritus, 1987—. Visiting associate professor, University of California, Berkeley, 1969. *Military service:* British Army, 1955-57.

AWARDS, HONORS: Harkness Commonwealth fellowship, 1964-65, for study and travel in the United States; *Yorkshire Post* fiction prize and Hawthornden Prize, both 1975, both for *Changing Places;* Royal Society of Literature fellowship, 1976; Whitbread Award for fiction and for book of the year, 1980, for *Small World; Sunday Express* Book of the Year Award, 1988; *Nice Work* was shortlisted for a Booker Prize, 1988.

WRITINGS:

CRITICISM

The Language of Fiction, Columbia University Press, 1966.
Graham Greene, Columbia University Press, 1966.
The Novelist at the Crossroads and Other Essays on Fiction and Criticism, Cornell University Press, 1971.
Evelyn Waugh, Columbia University Press, 1971.
The Modes of Modern Writing: Metaphor, Metonymy and the Typology of Modern Literature, Cornell University Press, 1977.
Working with Structuralism: Essays and Reviews on Nineteenth- and Twentieth-Century Literature, Routledge & Kegan Paul, 1981.
Write On: Occasional Essays, Secker & Warburg, 1986.

Also author of *Modern Criticism and Theory,* Longman.

NOVELS

The Picturegoers, MacGibbon & Kee, 1960.
Ginger, You're Barmy, MacGibbon & Kee, 1962, Doubleday, 1965, reprinted, with a new introduction by the author, Secker & Warburg, 1982.
The British Museum Is Falling Down, MacGibbon & Kee, 1965, Holt, 1967, reprinted, with a new introduction by the author, Secker & Warburg, 1981.
Out of the Shelter, Macmillan, 1970, revised edition, Secker & Warburg, 1985.
Changing Places: A Tale of Two Campuses, Secker & Warburg, 1975, Penguin, 1979.
How Far Can You Go?, Secker & Warburg, 1980, published as *Souls and Bodies,* Morrow, 1982.
Small World: An Academic Romance, Secker & Warburg, 1984, Macmillan, 1985.
Nice Work, Secker & Warburg, 1988, Viking, 1989.

EDITOR

Jane Austen's "Emma": A Casebook, Macmillan, 1968.

(With James Kinsley; and author of introduction) Jane Austen, *Emma,* Oxford University Press, 1971.
Twentieth Century Literary Criticism: A Reader, Longman, 1972.
George Eliot, *Scenes of Clerical Life,* Penguin, 1973.
Thomas Hardy, *The Woodlanders,* Macmillan, 1974.

PLAYS

(With Malcolm Bradbury and James Duckett) "Between These Four Walls," produced in Birmingham, 1963.
(With Duckett and David Turner) "Slap in the Middle," produced in Birmingham, 1965.

OTHER

About Catholic Authors (juvenile), St. Paul Press, 1958.
(Contributor) Leonard Michaels and Christopher Ricks, editors, *The State of the Language,* University of California Press, 1980.
(Author of introduction) *The Best of Ring Lardner,* Dent, 1984.

Contributor of articles and reviews to *Critical Quarterly, Tablet, Times Literary Supplement, New Republic, New York Times Book Review,* and *Encounter.*

SIDELIGHTS: David Lodge's books of literary criticism *The Language of Fiction, The Modes of Modern Writing,* and *Working with Structuralism* are considered by many in the field to be important introductions to contemporary literary theory; however, he is better known to general readers as a novelist whose works, while often treating serious themes, are "exuberant" and "marvelously funny," in the words of *New York Times Book Review* contributor Michael Rosenthal. The settings and characters of Lodge's novels reflect his own life experiences, including a childhood in wartime London, a stint in the British Army, study as a graduate student, and work as a university professor. His Roman Catholic upbringing has profoundly influenced his fiction as well. "Most of his novels have at least some Catholic statement in them," notes Dennis Jackson in *Dictionary of Literary Biography,* and "one of the recurrent themes in Lodge's stories is the struggle of his Catholic characters to reconcile their spiritual and sensual desires."

Lodge began work on his first published novel while completing his service in the army. Published in 1960 as *The Picturegoers,* this book describes a group of Catholics living in a dingy London suburb and the changes they experience over the course of a year. The thoughts and dreams of more than a dozen characters are revealed through their reactions to the films they watch regularly in the crumbling local cinema, focusing most sharply on Michael Underwood, a thoughtful young literature student who has fallen away from the church. While finishing school, Michael boards with the Mallory family and becomes enamored of Clare Mallory, a former convent novice. As he attempts to seduce her, she attempts to reawaken his faith. In an ironic conclusion, Clare, having fallen in love with Michael, offers herself to him, but he rejects her to join the priesthood. Some reviewers fault the book as disconnected and overburdened with characters, but "for a first novel, *The Picturegoers* is eminently lively and readable," believes Jackson. Lodge's "alternation of diction, tone, and rhythm as he shifts from . . . the inner thoughts of one character to those of another seems particularly impressive." In addition, "a lot of it is quite funny," writes Maurice Richardson in *New Statesman.*

An "act of revenge" is Lodge's description of his next book, writes Jackson. *Ginger, You're Barmy* grew out of the author's years in the army, an experience he bitterly resented. The tedium, brutality, and dehumanizing atmosphere of life in the service are evoked with a "total recall" that is "unnerving," according to *New Statesman* contributor Christopher Ricks. The novel's tension is provided by the contrast between the narrator, Jonathan Browne, and his friend, Mike "Ginger" Brady. Jonathan is a cynical intellectual, a former university student who concentrates on living through his two-year hitch with as little trouble as possible. Mike, on the other hand, is a passionate, idealistic fighter who eventually becomes involved with the Irish Revolutionary Army. Ultimately, Jonathan betrays Mike, stealing his girlfriend and playing a key part in his arrest. Critics have noted similarities in style and subject matter between Lodge's novels and Graham Greene's, and Lodge later acknowledged that he had modeled *Ginger, You're Barmy* after Greene's *The Quiet American.*

Some reviewers, while conceding that Lodge has portrayed army life convincingly, feel that *Ginger, You're Barmy* is plagued by stereotypes and a predictable storyline. "The story has been told so often that merely to tell it again is not enough," maintains Chad Walsh in the *Washington Post Book World.* But Thomas P. McDonnell counters in a *Commonweal* review: "Some reviewers have passed off *Ginger, You're Barmy* as the same old thing about life in the army, but it is a much better book than they are readers. They are certainly unknowing in the ways of military life if they do not realize that extreme regimentation all but forces a reversion to types. . . . They have missed, certainly, that it is a beautifully written book, and that its marvelously controlled first-person orientation lifts it out of the mere melodrama that they were no doubt expecting to read in just another book about life in the army. . . . Mostly, I think, they have missed . . . a poignancy in crisis and denouement, no less, that you will be hard put to it to find anywhere in the reams of overblown nihilism which passes for fiction today."

Lodge followed *Ginger, You're Barmy* with *The British Museum Is Falling Down,* a book which "represented a real development in his career as a writer of fiction," according to Dennis Jackson. It was the first of the highly comic, satiric novels which were to become his trademark, and it embodies one of Lodge's recurring themes, that of the sincere Catholic struggling with the difficulties imposed on him by the rigid doctrines of his church—specifically, the complexities of the unreliable "rhythm" method of birth control, the only form of contraception permitted to Catholics. The novel details one day in the life of Adam Appleby, a harried graduate student who has already fathered three children while using the rhythm method. When Adam awakes that day, his wife Barbara confides that she may again be pregnant, sending Adam out into a day of pandemonium much like Leopold Bloom's in James Joyce's *Ulysses.* "Like Leopold Bloom, Adam—because of the domestic and academic pressures he is facing—becomes increasingly disoriented as his day progresses, and his perceptions of life around him become increasingly phantasmagoric," writes Jackson.

After a day of countless mishaps, hallucinations, and anxious telephone calls to Barbara, Adam returns home to make love to his wife. Immediately thereafter, their "day of alarm [is] clinched by the arrival of her period," notes *Commonweal* contributor Paul West. The book concludes with a long, one-sentence monologue by Barbara (patterned after Molly Bloom's in *Ulysses*). West reports that this "night-reverie . . . twists the preceding comedy by the tail, gives it a depth and resonance." Lodge's skillful blend of humor and thoughtful discourse is also praised by Jackson, who writes: "*The British Museum Is Falling Down* is unceasingly and vigorously funny. . . . Yet throughout the book serious undertones give emphasis and point to the author's

general levity. His comic and satiric treatment of the current Catholic indecision over family planning is not a frontal attack on the church itself but rather a good-natured tickling meant to evoke laughter and a serious new consideration of the effect of the Catholic ban on artificial contraception on couples such as the Applebys."

A strong Joycean influence is again evident in Lodge's fourth novel, *Out of the Shelter.* This story of a young man's maturation opens with a stream-of-consciousness narrative obviously inspired by the beginning of Joyce's *A Portrait of the Artist as a Young Man.* The plot follows Timothy Anderson through his childhood in London during the Blitzkrieg to his coming of age on a summer holiday in postwar Germany. Jackson judges this to be Lodge's least successful novel, pointing out that "the book lacks intensity; it has no sharply drawn conflict or dramatic tension, and, for most of the story, the only real suspense has to do with this question of how and when Timothy will learn about sex." Nevertheless, *Times Literary Supplement* critic Christopher Hawtree finds that "Timothy's development is chronicled with a fine sense of pace, the tone of the narrative reflecting his changing attitudes," and Philip Howard calls *Out of the Shelter* "a charming period piece, heavy with nostalgia for vanished childhood" in the London *Times.*

Immediately after finishing *Out of the Shelter* in 1969, Lodge and his family travelled to the United States, where the author was to be a visiting professor for two terms at the University of California in Berkeley. It was a time of unrest on campuses everywhere, and Lodge's American stay was punctuated by student strikes and sometimes bloody altercations between students and National Guardsmen. Although student protests were also occurring in England, they were of a much milder nature. Lodge's fascination with the differences between the two cultures led to his fifth novel, *Changing Places.* Eliciting positive responses from almost all reviewers, *Changing Places* won major prizes and boosted Lodge's popularity considerably.

A university exchange program provides the premise for *Changing Places.* Aggressive, flamboyant Morris Zapp leaves his post at the State University of Euphoria (a thinly-disguised Berkeley) to trade places with timid, unambitious Philip Swallow from the dreary University of Rummidge in the English Midlands. Eventually they exchange cars, homes, and wives as well. Prior to the switch, both Zapp and Swallow have suffered from failing marriages and stagnating careers, but each finds a new identity and flourishes in his new surroundings. Neil Hepburn writes in *Listener* that Zapp and Swallow's parallel stories provide "a series of reflections, both on and of the two worlds—reflections on symmetry, on the novel as a reflection of reality, on the way real troubles like Vietnam and the Prague Spring are reflected in unreal ones like student unrest, on narrative techniques and literary styles . . . and, finally, on America and England as reflections of each other. No funnier or more penetrating account of the special relationship is likely to come your way for a long time."

Zapp and Swallow appear again in *Small World,* another "campus novel"—and Lodge's best-selling book. In *Small World,* they are only two of the many characters who jet around the globe from one academic conference to another in search of glory, romantic trysts, and the UNESCO chair of literary criticism—a job with virtually no responsibilities and a $100,000 tax-free salary. Michael Rosenthal writes in the *New York Times Book Review:* "[This] exuberant, marvelously funny novel demonstrates [that] no one is better able to treat the peripatetic quality of current academic life than the British writer David Lodge. . . . Despite the novel's breathless pace, profusion of incident and geographic scope, Mr. Lodge never loses control of his material. His deliberately outrageous manipulation of character and event is entirely successful."

While *Changing Places* cemented Lodge's reputation as a poplar novelist in England, it was only the first of his books to attract much notice in the United States. Widespread attention in America did not come to Lodge until the publication of his sixth novel, *How Far Can You Go?*, which appeared in the United States under the title *Souls and Bodies.* Jackson believes that *How Far Can You Go?* represents a "circling back over thematic grounds covered in [Lodge's] earlier novels," now handled in a more accomplished fashion by the mature novelist. As in *The Picturegoers, The British Museum Is Falling Down,* and *Out of the Shelter,* the focus is on the sexual and religious evolution of a group of English Catholic characters, treated in a comic fashion. The changes that Lodge's characters experience over the book's twenty-year time span present "a panoramic view of the vast changes effected inside the church during the era spanning the 1950s up to Pope John Paul II's installation in the late 1970s," writes Jackson.

Lodge used a large cast of characters to illuminate the many aspects of a Catholic upbringing in *How Far Can You Go?* Some critics dislike what they see as a collection of stereotypes, but Le Anne Schreiber points out in the *New York Times:* "By drafting his characters . . . into service as prototypes of every variant of Catholic experience, the author does at times lose something vital, but, in recompense, we get a very thorough crash course in modern Catholicism, including an introduction to process theology, the charismatic movement and the debates over priestly celibacy and the ordination of women. . . . Mr. Lodge has written a book full of his own energy, intelligence, wit, compassion and anger."

To incorporate explications of Catholic doctrine, Lodge also used narrative asides and other unconventional fictional devices in *How Far Can You Go?* Some critics find these intrusive, such as Paul Theroux, whose *New York Times Book Review* article indicates that the book is best when Lodge "forgets he is a Professor of Modern English literature, ditches the arch tone and all the mannerisms and begins to believe in these characters." Others feel that Lodge's narrative musings give his book added depth and power. Nicholas Shrimpton explains in a *New Statesman* piece: "*How Far Can You Go?* is at its best at those moments when an intimate link is established between theological debate and personal life. The real hero of the novel is the pill, and Lodge's picture of these couples struggling to come to terms with it hovers delicately between tragedy and farce."

"Like his characters, Lodge is searching for faith and his religion," writes John Podhoretz in *New Republic.* "We have grown so accustomed to those highly praised novels in which adolescents discover sexual freedom, irrational violence wreaks its consequences on a wise but hapless hero, and the struggle of life is reduced to a battle between superego and id, that a good novel about a few people merely trying to get by may seem a rather small achievement. If so, then perhaps we have lost sight of the value and purpose of fiction. . . . The modern popular novel has devoted itself to the body alone; Lodge joins an honorable and great tradition by restoring the primacy of the soul in fiction."

MEDIA ADAPTATIONS: Small World has been adapted for television, 1988; *Nice Work* has been adapted for television, 1989.

BIOGRAPHICAL/CRITICAL SOURCES:

BOOKS

Bestsellers 90, Issue 1, Gale, 1990.
Contemporary Literary Criticism, Volume XXXVI, Gale, 1986.
Dictionary of Literary Biography, Volume XIV: *British Novelists since 1960,* Gale, 1983.
Lodge, David, *How Far Can You Go?,* Secker & Warburg, 1980, published as *Souls and Bodies,* Morrow, 1982.

PERIODICALS

Commonweal, November 26, 1965, September 30, 1966, June 16, 1967.
Detroit News, October 1, 1989.
Encounter, August-September, 1980.
Globe and Mail (Toronto), September 8, 1981, July 7, 1984, February 14, 1987.
Listener, February 27, 1975, May 1, 1980, March 29, 1984.
Los Angeles Times, November 22, 1989.
Modern Fiction Studies, summer, 1982.
Modern Language Review, October, 1972.
Month, February, 1970.
New Republic, April 7, 1982.
New Statesman, July 30, 1960, November 9, 1962, December 17, 1971, December 9, 1977, May 16, 1980, June 26, 1981, August 13, 1982.
Newsweek, December 28, 1981.
New York Herald Tribune, July 25, 1965.
New York Times, January 1, 1982, March 8, 1985, August 7, 1989, October 16, 1989.
New York Times Book Review, January 31, 1982, March 17, 1985, July 23, 1989.
Novel: A Forum on Fiction, winter, 1972.
Observer, March 18, 1984.
Publishers Weekly, August 18, 1989.
Punch, March 21, 1984.
Spectator, March 25, 1966, May 3, 1980, July 31, 1982, April 7, 1984.
Tablet, October 3, 1970.
Time, April 15, 1985, August 7, 1989.
Times (London), March 22, 1984, April 4, 1985, June 29, 1985.
Times Literary Supplement, February 14, 1975, May 2, 1980, June 26, 1981, March 23, 1984, May 31, 1985, September 23, 1988.
Tribune Books (Chicago), July 30, 1989.
Washington Post Book World, February 7, 1982, March 3, 1985, August 13, 1989.
Yale Review, December, 1966, December, 1977.

*   *   *

LOMBARD, Nap
See JOHNSON, Pamela Hansford

*   *   *

LONDON, Jack
See LONDON, John Griffith

*   *   *

LONDON, John Griffith 1876-1916
(Jack London)

PERSONAL: Original name cited in some sources as John Griffith Chaney; born January 12, 1876, in San Francisco, Calif.;

died of an overdose of morphine, November 22, 1916, in Glen Ellen (some sources say Santa Rosa), Calif.; buried in Jack London State Park, Valley of the Moon, Sonoma County, Calif.; son of William Henry Chaney (an itinerant astrologer; some sources list paternity as questionable) and Flora Wellman (a spiritualist and music teacher); adopted surname of stepfather, John London, c. 1876; married Bessie Mae Maddern (a tutor) April 7, 1900 (divorced, 1905); married Clara Charmian Kittredge, November 19, 1905; children: (first marriage) Joan, Bess; (second marriage) Joy (died, 1910). *Education:* Attended University of California, Berkeley, 1897-98.

ADDRESSES: Home—Jack London Ranch, Glen Ellen, Calif.

CAREER: Novelist, short story writer, and political essayist. Worked at a succession of odd jobs, including salmon canner, oyster pirate, patrol agent of San Francisco shore police, seal fisher, jute millworker, coal shoveler, and laundry worker, beginning c. 1890; joined Coxey's Army (a band of jobless men who marched to Washington, D.C.), and tramped throughout the United States and Canada, beginning in 1893; arrested for vagrancy and sentenced to one month in Erie County Penitentiary in New York, c. 1895; gold miner in the Yukon Territory, 1897-98; worked as a journalist and reported the Russo-Japanese War for the Hearst Newspapers, 1904; ran for mayor of Oakland, Calif., on the Socialist ticket, 1905; lecturer throughout the United States, 1905-06; reported the Mexican Revolution for *Collier's,* 1914.

WRITINGS:

UNDER NAME JACK LONDON

NOVELS

A Daughter of the Snows, illustrations by Frederick C. Yohn, Lippincott, 1902, reprinted, Panther Books, 1964.

The Cruise of the Dazzler, Century Co., 1902, reprinted, Amereon House, 1982.

(With Anna Strunsky) *The Kempton-Wace Letters* (1st edition printed anonymously), Macmillan, 1903, 2nd edition, 1903, reprinted, Haskill House, 1969.

The Call of the Wild (first published serially in the *Saturday Evening Post,* June 28-July 18, 1903), illustrations by Philip Goodwin and Charles Livingston Bull, Macmillan, 1903, reprinted, with photographs by Seymour Linden, Harmony Books, 1977.

The Sea-Wolf (first published serially in *Century,* January-November, 1904), illustrations by W. J. Aylward, Macmillan, 1904, reprinted, illustrations by John Thompson, Franklin Library, 1980.

The Game (first published serially in *Metropolitan,* April 19-26, 1905), illustrations by Henry Hutt and T. C. Lawrence, Macmillan, 1905, reprinted, Literature House, 1969.

White Fang (first published serially in *Outing,* May-October, 1906), Macmillan, 1906, reprinted, edited by Joseph W. Nash, Andor Publishing, 1976.

Before Adam (science fiction; first published serially in *Everybody's Magazine,* October, 1906-February, 1907), illustrations by Charles Livingston Bull, Macmillan, 1907, reprinted, introduction by Willy Ley, illustrations by Leonard Everett Fisher, epilogue by Loren Eiseley, 1962.

The Iron Heel (science fiction), Macmillan, 1908, revised edition, Lawrence Hill, 1980.

Martin Eden (first published serially in *Pacific Monthly,* September, 1908-September, 1909), Macmillan, 1909, reprinted, introduction by Andrew Sinclair, Penguin Books, 1984.

Burning Daylight (first published serially in the *New York Herald,* June-August, 1910), Macmillan, 1910, reprinted, Manor Books, 1973.

Adventure (first published serially in *Popular Magazine,* November 1, 1910-January 15, 1911), Macmillan, 1911, reprinted, Arcadia House, 1950.

Smoke Bellew (first published serially in *Cosmopolitan,* June, 1911-June, 1912), illustrations by P. J. Monahan, Century Co., 1912, revised edition, 1940 (published in England as *Smoke and Shorty,* Mills & Boon, 1920).

The Abysmal Brute, Century Co., 1913.

John Barleycorn (first published serially in the *Saturday Evening Post,* March 15-May 3, 1913) illustrations by H. T. Dunn, Century Co., 1913, reprinted, illustrations by Dunn, afterword by James B. Hall, Western Tanager Press, 1981 (published in England as *John Barleycorn; or, Alcoholic Memoirs,* Mills & Boon, 1914, reprinted, introduction by Arthur Calder-Marshall, Robert Bentley, 1978].

The Valley of the Moon (first published serially as "The Valley of the Moon, the Story of a Fight Against Odds for Love and a Home," in *Cosmopolitan,* April-December, 1913), Macmillan, 1913, reprinted, introduction by Russ Kingman, Peregrine Smith, 1975.

Mutiny of the Elsinore (first published serially as "The Sea Gangsters," in *Hearst's Magazine,* November, 1913-August, 1914), Macmillan, 1914, reprinted, edited and introduced by I. O. Evans, Arco, 1968.

The Scarlet Plague (science fiction; first printed serially in *London Magazine,* June, 1912), illustrations by Gordon Grant, Macmillan, 1915, reprinted, Arno, 1975.

The Star Rover (science fiction; first printed serially in the *Los Angeles Examiner, American Weekly Magazine,* February-October, 1915), Macmillan, 1915, reprinted, Valley Sun, 1983, revised edition, autobiographical introduction by Jack London, illustrations by Leonard Everett Fisher, epilogue by Gardner Murphy, Macmillan, 1963; also published in England as *The Jacket,* Mills & Boon, 1915, reprinted, Horizon Press, 1969.

The Little Lady of the Big House (first published serially in *Cosmopolitan,* April, 1915-January, 1916), Macmillan, 1916.

Jerry of the Islands (first published serially in *Cosmopolitan,* January-April, 1917), Macmillan, 1917.

Michael, Brother of Jerry, Macmillan, 1917, reprinted, Laurie, 1950.

The Assassination Bureau Ltd. (unfinished novel; completed by Robert L. Fisk from notes by London), McGraw, 1963.

Hearts of Three (science fiction), Mills & Boon, 1918, Macmillan, 1920, reprinted, edited by R. Reginald and Douglas Melville, Arno, 1978.

SHORT STORIES COLLECTIONS

The Son of the Wolf: Tales of the Far North (includes "An Odyssey of the North," "The Wife of a King," and "The White Silence"), Houghton, 1900, reprinted, Scholarly Press, 1978 (published in England as *An Odyssey of the North,* Mills & Boon, 1915; also published as *The Son of the Wolf: Stories of the Northland,* Star Rover, 1981).

The God of His Fathers, and Other Stories, McClure, Phillips, 1901 (published in England as *The God of His Fathers: Tales of the Klondyke,* Isbister, 1902), published as *The Man With the Gash and Other Stories,* illustrations by Peter Thorpe, Star Rover, 1981.

Children of the Frost, illustrations by Raphael M. Reay, Macmillan, 1902, reprinted, edited and introduced by I. O. Evans, Arco, 1963.

The Faith of Men, and Other Stories (includes "Batard" and "The Story of Jees Uck"), Macmillan, 1904, reprinted, Books for Libraries, 1970.

Tales of the Fish Patrol (includes "White and Yellow," "The Siege of the *Lancashire Queen*," "Demetrios Contos," "Yellow Handkerchief," and "A Raid on the Oyster Pirates"), illustrations by George Varian, Macmillan, 1905, reprinted, Star Rover, 1982.

Moon-Face, and Other Stories, Macmillan, 1906, reprinted, Star Rover, 1982.

The Apostate: A Parable of Child Labor, (first published in *Woman's Home Companion,* September, 1906), The Appeal to Reason, 1906.

Love of Life, and Other Stories, Macmillan, 1906, reprinted, Chatto & Windus, 1968.

The Road, Macmillan, 1907, reprinted, introduction by King Hendricks, Peregrine Publishers, 1970.

Lost Face (includes "To Build a Fire," "That Spot," and "Flush of Gold"), Macmillan, 1910.

When God Laughs, and Other Stories (includes "A Piece of Steak"), Macmillan, 1911.

South Sea Tales, Macmillan, 1911, reprinted, 1961, published as *The Seed of McCoy, and Other Stories: South Sea Tales,* Pyramid Books, 1925, reprinted, 1956.

The Strength of the Strong (science fiction), illustrations by Dan Sayre Groesheck, C. H. Kerr, 1911.

The House of Pride, and Other Stories, Macmillan, 1912.

A Son of the Sun, illustrations by A. O. Fischer and C. W. Ashley, Doubleday, Page, 1912, revised edition published as *The Adventures of Captain Grief,* World Publishing Co., 1954.

The Dream of the Debs (science fiction), C. H. Kerr, 1912.

The Night-Born, and also The Madness of John Harned, When the World Was Young, The Benefit of the Doubt, Winged Blackmail, Bunches of Knuckles, War, Under the Deck Awnings, To Kill a Man, The Mexican, Century Co., 1913.

The Strength of the Strong (science fiction), Macmillan, 1914.

The Turtles of Tasman, Macmillan, 1916 (published in England as *Turtles of Tasman, and Other Stories,* Mills & Boon, 1917).

The Human Drift, Macmillan, 1917.

The Red One (science fiction), Macmillan, 1918.

On the Makaloa Mat, Macmillan, 1919 (published in England as *Island Tales,* Mills & Boon, 1923).

Dutch Courage, and Other Stories, Macmillan, 1922.

Contributor of short stories such as "Morganson's Finish," "And Frisco Kid Came Back," "A Thousand Deaths," and numerous others to newspapers and periodicals, including the *Independent, Century, Smart Set, Lady's Realm, Pilgrim, Oakland Herald, Woman's Home Companion, Pittsburgh Leader, Los Angeles Tribune, Youth's Companion, Cosmopolitan, C. B. Fry's Magazine, Saturday Evening Post, Everybody's Magazine, Windsor Magazine,* and *International Socialist Review.*

PLAYS

"The Great Interrogation," first produced in San Francisco, Calif., in 1905.

Scorn of Women: In Three Acts, Macmillan, 1906.

Theft: A Play in Four Acts, Macmillan, 1910.

The Acorn-Planter: A California Forest Play Planned to Be Sung by Efficient Singers, Accompanied by a Capable Orchestra, Macmillan, 1916.

Daughters of the Rich, Holmes Book Co., 1971.

Gold: A Play, Holmes Book Co., 1972.

NONFICTION

The People of the Abyss, Macmillan, 1903, reprinted, illustrations by Peter Thorpe, Star Rover, 1982.

War of the Classes (includes "How I Became a Socialist"), Macmillan, 1905, reprinted, Star Rover, 1982.

Goliah, A Utopian Essay (first published in 1908), reprinted in *Revolution and Other Essays,* Macmillan, 1910 [see below], reprinted separately, Thorp Springs Press, 1973.

Revolution, and Other Essays (includes "Goliah"), Macmillan, 1910, reprinted, introduction by Robert Barltrop, Journeyman Press, 1979.

The Cruise of the Snark, Macmillan, 1911, published as *The Cruise of the Snark: A Pacific Voyage,* Odyssey Press, 1965.

Letters From Jack London: Containing an Unpublished Correspondence Between London and Sinclair Lewis, edited by King Hendricks and Irving Shepard, Odyssey Press, 1965.

The Letters of Jack London, three volumes, edited by Earle Labor, Stanford University Press, 1988.

Contributor of articles and social commentary to numerous newspapers and periodicals, including *Wilshire's Magazine, Saturday Evening Post, International Socialist Review, Century, Los Angeles Tribune, Everybody's Magazine, Collier's, San Francisco Examiner, New York Herald,* and *Oakland Herald.*

OTHER

Daddy Boy: A Series of Dedications to His First Wife by Jack London, Holt-Atherton Pacifica Center for Western Studies, 1976.

London's works have also appeared in dozens of omnibus volumes.

SIDELIGHTS: "The greatest story Jack London ever wrote," Alfred Kazin observed in *On Native Ground,* "was the story he lived." London is one of those writers whose lives seem to fascinate readers more than their art. His personal drama was the stuff of a Horatio Alger rags-to-riches story, a poor boy's rise to world fame and great wealth—but with the ironic ending that makes it a cautionary lesson in the price exacted for pursuing the "Bitch Goddess Success," as psychologist and philosopher William James called our national obsession. London's career constituted one of the darkest chronicles in our literary annals, wrote Maxwell Geismar, who agreed in *Rebels and Ancestors* that "the drama of his life, bold, sensational, tragic, has almost obscured the history of his writing, and his work has been ignored." This imbalance has been redressed somewhat since Geismar wrote these words in the 1950s—in subsequent years a number of significant scholarly studies of London's work have appeared—but in the writing about London since his death in 1916, biographical concern certainly has predominated over the critical. Probably the life of no American writer has been retold so often, although most studies on London rely heavily on biographical material for interpreting his art.

The facts of his life are, without question, fascinating. Born in San Francisco on January 2, 1876, the son of an itinerant astrologer father, William Henry Chaney, and a seance-conducting, spiritualist mother, Flora Wellman, Jack London grew up believing that he was the child of John London, the man who Flora subsequently married and who gave the child his name. When London, at twenty, discovered the truth and wrote to him, Chaney denied his paternity and refused to meet his son. This rebuff is often thought to account for the Oedipal struggles, open and covert, that appear in London's work. London's insecurity over his paternity, Irving Stone claimed in *Sailor on Horseback,* was "to torment and torture him to the end of his days."

London grew up in and around Oakland, California, in a family that was both poor and rootless: in one year they moved six times. John London was a decent but hapless man, unable to succeed in any line of work; Flora London, whose own family in Ohio had been wealthy and socially prominent, was pretentious, prejudiced, ambitious, and not very affectionate toward her son. A black woman, Virginia Prentiss, became the boy's nurse and surrogate mother. Except for her attentions, his childhood was one of loneliness, insecurity, and deprivation—or so he remembered it in later life. Recalling an incident when he stole food from a classmate, he wrote in an 1898 letter: "Hungry! Hungry! Hungry! From the time I stole the meat and knew no call above my belly, to now when the call is higher, it has been nothing but hunger." From other sources we know that London was exaggerating considerably here: in reality the Londons were never terribly poor. But the writer's memory—or pose—and not the reality is what matters most for understanding the psychological wounds he suffered as a child. He was starved, as Carolyn Johnston reported in *Jack London—An American Rebel?*, not for goods, but for attention and affection. Like many other sensitive and intelligent children who feel lonely and unloved, London found refuge in books and became an omnivorous reader. But he was hardly the typical bookworm. At sixteen this haunter of the Oakland Public Library borrowed the money to buy a fishing sloop and began a career as an oyster pirate, complete with mistress who came with the boat. Oyster pirating was an exciting, dangerous way for a boy to make a living and London was so good at it that he gained the title of "Prince of the Oyster Pirates." However, a brush with the law convinced him to change sides and pursue his former confederates as an agent of the shore police. These adventures later served as the material for one of his most popular juvenile works, *Tales of the Fish Patrol* (1905).

Tiring of this work, London signed aboard a sealing schooner in 1893 and spent seven months sailing the North Pacific, where he acquired both the nickname—"Sailor Jack"—that he used proudly in his hobo days and the knowledge of the brutality of seafaring that provided the background for one of his most famous novels, *The Sea-Wolf* (1904). The condition of his family necessitated, upon his return to San Francisco, that London find steady work, which he did, first in a salmon cannery, then in a power station shoveling coal for ten hours a day. He found this employment as a proletarian "wage slave" physically brutal and mentally debilitating, but—under the influence of the Horatio Alger myth so pervasive at the time—he was determined to stick to it until he could rise to the position of electrician. When he discovered, however, that because of his youthful strength and ambition he had been assigned the quota of two men, he quit his job and, at eighteen, joined the western contingent of Coxey's Army—a ragtag band of unemployed workingmen—for its bonus march on Washington, D.C. But even this wayward life proved too restrictive, and at Hannibal, Missouri, London deserted to ride the rails as a hobo and sometimes chicken thief. His adventures as a hobo are recounted with great verve and freshness in *The Road* (1907), perhaps the most immediately engaging of all London's works, termed "a brilliant little book" by George Orwell in *The Collected Essays, Journalism, and Letters of George Orwell.*

The buoyant sense of freedom and irresponsibility that London enjoyed while tramping collapsed, however, in Niagara Falls, New York, where he was arrested for vagrancy and sentenced to a month in the Erie County Penitentiary. This experience, London claimed in his crucial autobiographical essay "How I Became a Socialist" (1903), proved a turning point in his life and converted him to socialism. Before, he had been "an individualist

without knowing it," confident that his superior physical ability would allow him to make his way in the world. But on the road and in prison he encountered men who had once had as much physical ability as he but who nevertheless had sunk to the bottom of what he called the Social Pit. "I saw the picture of the Social Pit as vividly as though it were a concrete thing, and at the bottom of the Pit saw them, myself above them, not far, and hanging on to the slippery wall by main strength and sweat. And I confess a terror seized me. What when my strength failed? When I should be unable to work shoulder to shoulder with the strong men who were as yet babes unborn? And there and then I swore a great oath." He vowed, in short, to succeed in life not by his brawn as a workman, but by his brain as a writer. "I ran back to California," he concluded, "and opened the books."

Convinced now of the need for formal education, London entered Oakland High School to prepare himself for college exams, cramming with the same indefatigable energy that he had used shoveling coal. He also published his first stories in the school's literary magazine *The Aegis*. In addition, he joined the Socialist Labor party and threw himself into its activities, gaining a degree of notoriety as a street-corner orator, "the boy socialist of Oakland," as the newspapers styled him. He was arrested for violating a city ordinance against public street meetings, and his subsequent acquittal proved to be a successful challenge to the power structure, making him a hero to local radicals. The nature of London's socialism has proven enormously problematic, a source of controversy both in his own lifetime and ever since. In "How I Became a Socialist" he claimed that "my rampant individualism had pretty effectively been hammered out of me, and something else as effectively hammered in." That "something else" was a sense of class solidarity with all working men. Both these claims must be questioned. On the one hand, his rampant individualism clearly had not been hammered out of him and never would be; his desire to succeed as a writer was a desire to achieve personal distinction—personal fame and status and wealth. On the other hand, his resolution to do only "brain work" was the deliberate choice to separate himself from the proletariat: while he would work for them, he was determined never again to be of them. Thus London's involvement in socialist activities in the early years is sometimes presented as self-serving, primarily a vehicle for personal, intellectual, and social advancement. But such claims cannot explain why London remained a socialist for twenty years more—long after he was rich and famous—and willingly alienated large sections of his bourgeois readership by his militant advocacy of an unpopular cause.

Compressing years of study into a few months, London passed his college exams and entered the University of California at Berkeley in 1896. The experience proved disillusioning, however, and he remained there for only one semester. He began submitting his work—everything from light verse to sociological essays—to magazines, but with no success. His motive for writing was simple, as he explained to his friend Cloudesley Johns: "I am writing for money; if I can produce fame that means more money. . . . I shall always hate the task of getting money; everytime I sit down to write it is with great disgust." This was not a very exalted notion of his chosen vocation—and one probably intended to shock his literary friend—but it was a view he shared with English lexicographer and critic Samuel Johnson, who once claimed that only a blockhead wrote for any reason other than money. Since no one was buying what London wanted to sell, he was forced to violate his oath never to do manual labor again and took a job in a laundry, working six days a week for very long hours. This depressing period in his life is vividly recreated in the early chapters of his semi-autobiographical novel *Martin Eden* (1909).

London's ambition to get rich quick now took a new—and ultimately fortuitous—turn. He decided to join the Yukon gold rush and in July of 1897 embarked for Alaska. He remained in the Klondike for almost a year and struck no gold, but he did discover a rich vein of narrative material that he would mine lucratively in his soon-to-come leap to fame. Many of the ideas that later informed his writing began to crystallize for London during this period. The books that he carried with him to the Klondike indicate the direction in which his mind was developing: naturalist and evolutionist Charles Darwin's *Origin of Species* and socialist philosopher Karl Marx's *Das Kapital,* poet John Milton's *Paradise Lost*—it was Satan, not surprisingly, who intrigued the young rebel—and works of the materialistic philosophers Herbert Spencer and Ernst Haeckel. As Martin Jay observed in *Harvests of Change,* "Essentially, London wrote in a philosophical tradition rather than a literary one." Usually accounted a naturalist, London had, in fact, little affinity with Frank Norris or Stephen Crane or other writers of that movement. At a time when nineteenth-century American novelist Herman Melville was all but forgotten, Melville's classic *Moby Dick* was London's favorite novel, which he read again and again.

Otherwise, London showed little interest in literature, particularly the genteel literature of his day; instead, he read widely in and assimilated ideas from philosophy, economics, anthropology, psychology, and political theory. Ironically, a good case could be made that London, the proletarian autodidact and hard-living adventurer, was the most rigorously intellectual of all American writers. He particularly enjoyed reading the work of philosophers Friedrich Nietzsche and Herbert Spencer. Even more than Karl Marx—whose faith London professed, but little of whose work he read—these latter two writers seem to have been the major intellectual influences in his mental life. If prison had made him a socialist, Spencer made him a materialist and a "scientific" determinist. "We must conclude," London argued, "that there is no such thing as free will. Environment determines absolutely."

The environment of the Klondike—sketched chillingly in the opening pages of *White Fang* (1906) as brutal, relentless, destructive of everything soft or gentle—was for London the laboratory in which to test imaginatively his ideas about life. Here both nature and man appeared at their most elemental level, stripped of comforting illusions. On his return to Oakland in 1898, he thus had the subject matter for the works that would establish his fame. For two years he struggled in extreme poverty, working furiously day and night, to make his way as a writer. At first he accumulated only a drawer full of rejection notices, but slowly he began to sell his stories. Then, in 1900, the prestigious Boston publishing firm of Houghton, Mifflin brought out London's first collection of Alaskan tales, *The Son of the Wolf.* The writing in the best of London's early stories was, according to Maxwell Geismar in *Rebels and Ancestors,* "completely fresh in its time, offering a contrast to the sweetness and goodness of popular fiction of the 1900's. The cadence of this prose only became completely familiar to us, indeed, in the postwar generation of the 1920's." It was a prose lean, spare, and sinewy, suited to the often grim subject matter of the North. And, surprisingly perhaps for that period, both style and subject proved popular.

Following *The Son of the Wolf* London quickly published two other volumes of stories, *The God of His Fathers* (1901) and *Children of the Frost* (1902), as well as a first novel, *A Daughter of the Snows* (1902), which even its author deemed to be a failure.

But in 1903 he produced his acknowledged masterpiece, *The Call of the Wild.* This novella was conceived as a short story, a companion piece to London's first dog story "Batard," written a year earlier. "Batard" is, according to Earle Labor in a *Jack London Newsletter* essay, "an anatomy of hatred," an account of a struggle to the death between a diabolical dog—"hell's spawn"—and his equally diabolical master, Leclere. The innate evil of each is reinforced by his hatred of the other—and by the hardness of the Northland environment—but the dog proves ultimately the more cunning of the two and, in a grimly ironic ending, succeeds in hanging his tormenting master. *The Call of the Wild* was originally meant to be the antithesis of "Batard," a love story between man and dog; but it grew into something much greater than that. Joan London reports that her father considered his masterpiece "a purely fortuitous piece of work, a lucky shot in the dark that had unexpectedly found its mark"; when reviewers hailed it as a brilliant allegory, London pleaded "guilty": "But I was unconscious of it at the time. I did not mean to do it." Perhaps because what Geismar termed a "beautiful prose poem of the buried impulses" was so much the product of London's unconscious mind, it achieves a mythic resonance seldom found in his later works.

The Call of the Wild recounts the reversion of a civilized dog, Buck, to his primitive heritage. Kidnapped from a sunny California ranch, Buck, through a series of owners and adventures, moves ever farther North, ever closer to the sources of his true nature. In one owner, John Thornton, Buck finds the perfect master and serves him as the perfect sled dog: in this union London convincingly portrays the love between man and animal that was the novella's inspiration. But Thornton falls victim to the savage environment of the North, and Buck is free to fulfill his final destiny as the immortal Ghost Dog of Northland legend, incarnating, as Labor expressed it, "the eternal mystery and creation of life." In *The Call of the Wild* London wrote: "When the long winter nights come on and the wolves follow their meat into the lower valleys, he may be seen running at the head of the pack through the pale moonlight or glimmering borealis, leaping gigantic above his fellows, his great throat a-bellow as he sings a song of the younger world, which is the song of the pack."

Poet James Dickey in his introduction to a 1981 edition of *The Call of the Wild, White Fang, and Other Stories* suggests that London anthropomorphizes his wolf dogs, projecting himself through them: "The self-dramatizing Nietzschean is always very much present." In some sense, no doubt, Buck's saga is an autobiographical fantasy, revealing the deepest sources of London's imagination. His personal identification with the symbol of the wolf is well known—witness the name London gave to his grandiose Sonoma mansion, Wolf House—and in this symbolic animal he invests the virtues of courage, endurance, and nobility, as well as a primeval savagery, a sense of atavistic life-forces that lie beyond civilization's good and evil. In any case, *The Call of the Wild* remains a powerful and original work, and H. L. Mencken's 1921 judgment of London's achievement, published in *Prejudices: First Series,* still holds true: "No other popular writer of his time did any better writing than you will find in *The Call of the Wild. . . .* Here, indeed, are all the elements of sound fiction: clear thinking, sense of character, the dramatic instinct, and, above all, the adept putting together of words."

The Call of the Wild brought London worldwide fame, and he determined to follow its success with a companion book, but one that would "reverse the process. Instead of devolution or decivilization of a dog," he wrote to his publisher, "I'm going to give the evolution, the civilization of a dog—the development of domesticity, faithfulness, love, morality, and all the amenities and virtues." This book, *White Fang,* appeared in 1906 and, indeed, inverted the pattern of *The Call of the Wild:* moving its wolf dog protagonist from savagery to civilization, from brutal struggle for mere survival in the frozen wastes to a comfortable old age of dozing in the California sun. Though considered a lesser artistic achievement than its companion piece, it is no less serious a work—and one with a more palpable ideological intent. Here London presented his deterministic philosophy in action, demonstrating "the awful plasticity of life, . . . the marvelous power and influence of environment." If the specter of Nietzsche hovers over Buck, the spirit of Spencer shapes White Fang. Or, as Earle Labor noted: "*The Call of the Wild* is a mythic romance; *White Fang,* a sociological fable." As a fable celebrating the civilizing process, it has found less favor with critics, who seem to prefer adventure to security, danger to domestication. Why, asked Dickey, is *White Fang* inferior to its predecessor? "Largely, I think," Dickey continued, "because the events depicted in *The Call of the Wild* are closer to what one wants to see happen: because we desire the basic, the 'natural', the 'what is' to win [over] the world of streetcars and sentimentalism that we have made."

Throughout most of London's serious work, the dialectic established in these two dog fables continues to function in unresolved tension. On one side are those elements that might be called—loosely—Nietzschean; on the other, those that are—again, loosely—Spencerean. The Nietzschean elements include an admiration for the powerful individual, untrammeled by the narrow restraints of conventional society, the superman; a belief (implicit, at least) in the ability of genius to forge its own destiny; and a glorification of strength, savagery, and violence. The Spencerean elements include a faith in "scientific laws" that explain and determine all behavior and the attendant denial of freedom; a belief in a process of social evolution that will ultimately replace competition with cooperation (and capitalism with socialism); and a celebration of such ego-ideals of civilization as universal brotherhood and peace. A graphic illustration of the unstable mix in which these elements can be found in London's work is a fantasy that he wrote in 1908, "Goliah." Here the usual utopian ideals—brotherhood, cooperation, equality, and world peace—are brought about by a single scientific genius who destroys hundreds of thousands of lives with his secret death ray. Social sweetness and light result from megalomania and carnage—a formula typical in London's work.

Disturbing as "Goliah" is ideologically, it nevertheless epitomizes the internal conflict of values that marks some of London's most important works, particularly *The Sea-Wolf* and *Martin Eden.* Both of these books, London claimed, constituted attacks on individualism, on the Nietzschean ideal. "At the very beginning of my career," he wrote in a letter near the end of his life, "I attacked Nietzsche and his super-man idea. This was in *The Sea-Wolf.* Lots of people read *The Sea-Wolf;* no one discovered that it was an attack on the superman philosophy." Similarly of *Martin Eden* he said in 1910: "Written as an indictment of individualism it was accepted as an indictment of socialism." And in his last literary note written just before his death in 1916, London spoke of "Martin Eden and Sea Wolf, attacks on Nietzschean philosophy, which even the Socialists missed the point of." But London's maligned readers, whom he thought had consistently missed his point, were not entirely in error, for, as Geismar correctly suggested, "there was a certain ambiguity between the 'conscious' moral of the artist and the true emotional center of his work." Perhaps readers perceived in his fiction the paradox that London expressed to his publisher, George Brett: "I as you

know am in the opposite intellectual camp from that of Nietzsche. Yet no man in my own camp stirs me as does Nietzsche."

The Sea-Wolf clearly manifests that paradox. Published in 1904 and an immediate best-seller, the novel is the first-person narrative of Humphrey Van Weyden, a cultured literary aesthete who is rescued from drowning by the seal schooner *Ghost.* But it is the Nietzschean captain of the *Ghost,* Wolf Larsen, who looms as the towering figure in the novel. Powerful, brutal, amoral, and cynical, a self-taught genius utterly contemptuous of civilized conventions, Larsen tyrannizes the crew of his ship with a chillingly sadistic contempt for their lives and his own. Van Weyden is simultaneously repelled and intrigued by Larsen, not only by his powerful personality but also by his "terrible beauty." London details the development of the effete "sissy" into a self-reliant man: first, through subjugation to the brutal regimen of the *Ghost* and, second, through open challenge to Larsen's dominance. The second phase of Van Weyden's initiation opens with the rescue of another shipwreck victim, poetess Maud Brewster. In defense of her honor, Van Weyden stands up to Larsen, and escapes with her from the *Ghost* to an uninhabited island, where they maintain separate living quarters and their modesty. London's design is clear: the love and cooperation of Brewster and Van Weyden enable them to triumph not only over the harshness of nature, but over the sea wolf himself, who—blind, dying, and set adrift by his mutinous crew—turns up on their island. This second half of the book is generally considered a failure. Quoted in *Jack London: American Rebel,* Ambrose Bierce, London's acquaintance and fellow author, wrote that "the love element, with its absurd suppressions and impossible proprieties, is awful." Few modern readers would dissent from that view. The rhetoric of the lovers is so inflated and twittery that the effect becomes comic. Charles C. Walcutt, in his book *Jack London,* attributed this miscalculation to the influence of Charmian Kittredge, whom London was soon to marry and who served as the model for Maud Brewster: "Charmian's style invaded Jack's style, and it was never the same again."

If the critical reaction to the second part of the novel is almost universally negative, reaction to the first part—chiefly the depiction of Wolf Larsen—is more evenly divided. Lewis Mumford contended in *The Golden Day* that instead of a superior type, London created in Wolf only "a preposterous bully . . . the infantile dream of a barroom tough"; and Geismar deemed him "an empty and inflated figure." Other critics—such as Earle Labor and, writing in *The Novels of Jack London: A Reappraisal,* Charles N. Watson, Jr.—have identified Larsen as one of the major creations of American literature, akin to, if not quite the equal of, the character Captain Ahab in Melville's *Moby Dick.* Ironically, however, the more the sea wolf captures the reader's imagination, the more his demonic personality overpowers the pallid figures of Van Weyden and Brewster, the more he subverts the ostensible purpose of the novel as an attack on the superman philosophy.

Critical response to *Martin Eden* is likewise divided. London thought it was his best novel, and some critics have agreed; but others, like Charles C. Walcutt, have placed the novel among London's worst. Clearly an autobiographical character, Eden represents London's conception of what he would have become without his socialism: a self-styled superman who perished because of his separation, as London put it, from the People. "Had Martin Eden been a socialist," his creator avowed, "he would not have died." The socialist "message" of the novel, however, is highly attenuated, and its socialist characters are not a particularly compelling group. The imaginative core of the work is clearly Eden's individual struggle for success as a writer, not class struggle.

Martin Eden ought to have been one of the great American novels on one of the great themes: the cost and compromise necessitated by cutting away one's roots to rise in the world. And the first part of Eden's story is very promising—the story of an ignorant but intelligent young sailor, awakened to the possibilities of life and a thirst for knowledge, eager to enter the bourgeois world that seems to him to embody culture and beauty and finer sensibilities. His first clumsy efforts to learn correct grammar and proper table manners are at once amusing and entirely convincing: the reader feels embarrassment over his social gaffes with all the pain of recollected adolescence. Eden's hopelessly idealized love for the wealthy Ruth Morse is as believably impossible as that of Gatsby for Daisy Buchanan in F. Scott Fitzgerald's novel *The Great Gatsby;* but unlike Fitzgerald, London lacks proper distance from his characters and situations. He allows all his own social resentments to surface, and Eden's story becomes a wish-fulfillment of scores evened and grudges repaid, termed by Geismar one of the angriest books of American literature. As Eden rises, the novel declines. In argument, Eden crushes even the most erudite professors; in aesthetic appreciation, he is infallible; morally, he troops like a swan among crows; and intellectually, he towers as one of the great minds of the age. Martin Eden—and behind him London—as a deep-delving philosopher, however, strikes a false note and leads the book off into windy abstract speculations; even a sympathetic reader like Charles N. Watson, Jr. conceded that in the late chapters Eden surpasses even London's other supermanly figures "in his intellectual arrogance and sophomoric rant." When he finds his phenomenal literary success empty, Ruth Morse selfish and scheming, the world of bourgeois culture a sham, and his materialistic philosophy devoid of consolation or hope, the despairing Eden drowns himself. This ending has been criticized as arbitrary and unexpected, but London had written Eden into a dead end and there was no other way out. It would not spontaneously occur to many readers that Eden might have saved himself by turning socialist.

In the half dozen years between *The Call of the Wild* and *Martin Eden,* London published most of his other major works as well: *The People of the Abyss* (1903), a masterful piece of sociological reportage on life in the East End slums of London; his most important collection of essays on social issues, *War of the Classes* (1905); *The Game* (1906), an alternately toughly realistic and stickily sentimental boxing tale, among the earliest examples of sports fiction in American literature; *The Road* (1907), a crisp, trenchant, and often amusing account of young London's days as a hobo; *Before Adam* (1907), an "anthropological romance" of prehistoric times in which London anticipates a number of the insights of Jungian psychology; and *The Iron Heel* (1908), a futuristic dystopian vision of the development of capitalism into fascism, widely praised as a classic of socialist literature. When one considers that *White Fang, The Sea-Wolf* and several collections of short stories—which included such memorable works as "To Build a Fire" (1902) and "The Love of Life" (1905)—were also the products of these few years, London's industry and invention appear awe-inspiring. This was, without doubt, his peak creative period.

In addition, however, as America's most famous and best-selling author—the first, in fact, ever to become a millionaire by his pen—London had transformed himself into a public personality, like Mark Twain before him and Ernest Hemingway, for example, or Norman Mailer after. His lavish standard of living, complete with an oriental valet; his drinking binges and occasional barroom brawls—all were subject matter for the popular press,

which found London's exploits good copy. As much as he resented the often hostile attention of the press, London nevertheless increasingly offered up his own accounts of his private life for public consumption. In 1913 he published *John Barleycorn,* aptly subtitled an "Alcoholic Memoir." A candidly autobiographical account of his battle with alcohol, the book's fault, London claimed, was "that I did not dare put in the whole truth." Even earlier, in 1911, London treated his readers to a minutely detailed account of his disastrous attempt to sail his ill-fated yacht, the *Snark,* around the world. Built at enormous expense, the *Snark* was meant to give him back the freedom of his youth; instead, it gave him only headaches and heartache. Although the voyage was a complete fiasco, *The Cruise of the Snark* is an engagingly self-indulgent—even lighthearted—account of his nautical trials and tribulations. As Walcutt noted, London spoke directly and immediately to his readers, assuming "that the smallest detail of his life will be of interest" to them. Fame had made his private life an exploitable commodity.

Fame also had a deleterious effect, however, on London's art, which declined precipitously after about 1909. In the wake of the *Snark* fiasco London undertook an even more grandiose plan—the development of his 260-acre Beauty Ranch in the Sonoma Valley, with its baronial mansion, Wolf House, designed to "stand for a thousand years." Though his income was great by the standards of the day, his expenses were greater: and London's oft-repeated claim that he wrote only for money became ever truer. To pay for his ambitious agricultural ventures, Andrew Sinclair reported in *Jack: A Biography of Jack London,* London mortgaged his future as an author, "condemning himself to write the commercial at the expense of the good." He even resorted to buying story plots from struggling young writers like Sinclair Lewis and to imitating his own earlier successes. Thus, while the bulk of London's works appeared in the second half of his career—when he was averaging more than two books a year—none of them ever reached the level of his best early work, and, indeed, few of them have much literary merit at all. *The Scarlet Plague* (1915)—an end-of-civilization catastrophe tale and London's most accomplished venture into science fiction—is an exception, and the so-called Sonoma novels—*Burning Daylight* (1910), *The Valley of the Moon* (1913), and *The Little Lady of the Big House* (1916)—are at least serious in intent, if not very successful in execution. Their primitivist theme of salvation through a return to the land was an obvious projection of London's own hopes of fulfillment that his experiments at Beauty Ranch would bring; but even these hopes proved futile. Wolf House burned in 1913 just as it was completed, and was uninsured. The last of London's dreams seemed to die with it. *Little Lady* reflects his disillusion, ending with a suicide that now appears both symbolic and prophetic.

As the quality of London's work declined after 1909, so did the quality of his life, which was increasingly marked by personal tragedy and physical pain. In 1910 his and Charmian's daughter, Joy, died only a few days after her birth. Then in 1912 Charmian suffered a miscarriage, and London became convinced that they would never have the son that he wanted so desperately. His attempt at a reconciliation with his daughter Joan proved an embittering failure. And physically the body in whose strength and vigor London had always taken such pride started to fail him as well: his kidneys were seriously deteriorating by 1914, and he began to suffer from acute rheumatism as well as an assortment of other ills.

Still, in 1914 he undertook to cover the Mexican revolution as a war correspondent for *Collier's.* But in Mexico, London "no longer spoke as the compassionate revolutionary," Sinclair noted, "but as the racist and jingoist supporter of American oil interests." The authoritarian and even protofascist streak that critics like Orwell and Kazin perceived in London is pronounced in his *Collier's* articles, and his white-supremacist racism, always one of the most disfiguring features of his thought, becomes particularly shrill. Not surprisingly, his erstwhile allies among the socialists condemned his views; and in 1916, a few months before his death, London resigned from the Socialist party because, he said, "of its lack of fire and fight and its loss of emphasis on the class struggle." This charge, however, fits London himself as much as the party that had once served him as a surrogate religion.

Much of the period from 1915 to 1916 London spent in Hawaii, seeking to recuperate from his increasingly severe illnesses. Even then he continued to write prolifically, producing mostly hack work—very profitable hack work—including a frivolous movie script. But amidst the potboilers he produced one of his very best stories, "The Red One" (1918), a hauntingly evocative fantasy of an indecipherable message sent to earth from space; not highly regarded at the time, it is now accepted as one of the classics of science fiction and among the most powerful of London's fictions. In July, 1916, he returned to his ranch in California, in poor and deteriorating health. He had become dependent on a variety of pain-killing drugs, and on November 22, 1916— suffering an agonizing Intestinal attack—he took a fatal overdose of morphine. Whether his death was an accident or a suicide is an issue of much controversy among critics, dividing them about equally. On the death certificate London's family doctor gave the cause as an acute attack of a "gastro-intestinal type of uremia"—no mention of the drug overdose. London was forty years old, the author of more than fifty books, and America's most famous writer.

MEDIA ADAPTATIONS: Films—"A Piece of Steak" was adapted for film and released by Balboa Amusement Co., 1913. *The Sea-Wolf* was adapted for film seven times: it was adapted and released by the Balboa Amusement Co. and by Bosworth, Inc., both in 1913; it was released, with screenplay by Will M. Richey, produced and directed by George Melford, by Paramount-Artcraft, 1920; a film with a screenplay by J. Grubb Alexander, directed by Ralph W. Ince, was released by Producers Distribution, Corp., 1926; the work was adapted and released by Fox, November 29, 1930; Jack L. Warner and Hal B. Wallis produced a screenplay by Robert Rossen, directed by Michael Curtiz, starting Edward G. Robinson, Ida Lupino, John Garfield, Alexander Knox, Gene Lockhart, Barry Fitzgerald, and others, released by Warner Bros., March 22, 1941; a film with a screenplay adaptation by Jack DeWitt and Tunley Walker, produced by Lindsley Parsons, directed by Harman Jones, and starring Barry Sullivan, Peter Graves, Gita Hall, and others, was released under the title "Wolf Larsen" by Allied Artists, October 26, 1958. "To Kill a Man" was adapted for film and released by Balboa Amusement Co., 1913. *Burning Daylight* was adapted for film three times: it was adapted and released by Bosworth, Inc., September 14, 1914; a version directed by Edward Sloman, with scenario by A. S. LeVino, was released by Shurtleff, Inc., 1920; and an adaptation directed by Charles J. Brabin and Wid Gunning, starring Milton Sills, was released by Rowland Distributors, 1928. *John Barleycorn* was adapted for film and released by Bosworth, Inc., 1914. *Martin Eden* was adapted for film and released by Bosworth, Inc., 1914; it was also produced by B. P. Shulberg, with a screenplay adaptation by W. L. River, directed by M. W. Stoloff, starting Glenn Ford, Claire Trevor, Evelyn Keyes, Stuart Erwin, and others, and released under the title "The Adventures of Martin Eden" by Columbia, February 26,

1942. "An Odyssey of the North" and *Valley of the Moon* were adapted and released by Bosworth, Inc., both in 1914.

The Mutiny of the Elsinore was adapted for film by A. S. LeVino, directed by Edward Sloman, and released under the title "The Mutiny" by Shurtleff, Inc., 1920. *The Star Rover* was adapted for film by A. S. LeVino, directed by Edward Sloman, and released by Shurtleff, Inc., 1920. A film based on the novel *The Little Lady of the Big House* was directed by Philip E. Rosen and released under the title "The Little Fool" by Shurtleff, Inc., 1920. A film based on "The Story of Jees Uck" was directed by S. E. V. Taylor and released under the title "Mohican's Daughter" by P.T.B., Inc., 1922. A film based on the stories "The Son of the Wolf" and "Wife of a King" was adapted by W. Haywood, directed by Norman Dawn, and released by R-C under the title "The Son of the Wolf," 1922. Eight short films based on the stories in *Tales of the Fish Patrol* were released by Universal Film Manufacturing Co., under the series title "Jack London's Tales of the Fish Patrol," 1922-23. *The Call of the Wild* was adapted for film and directed by Fred Jackman, produced by Hal Roach, and released by Pathe, September 23, 1923; it was released, with screenplay by Gene Fowler and Leonard Praskin, produced by Darryl Zanuck, directed by William Wellman, starring Clark Gable, Loretta Young, Jack Oakie, and others, by United Artists, 1935. *The Abysmal Brute* was adapted for film, directed by Hobart Henley, and released by Universal, 1923; it was released with screenplay by Charles Logue and Walter Weems, directed by David Howard, produced by Trem Carr, starring John Wayne, Jean Rogers, Ward Bond, and others, under the title "Conflict," by Universal, 1936.

Adventure, screenplay by A. P. Young and L. G. Rigby, produced and directed by Victor Fleming, and starring Tom Moor, Pauline Starke, and Wallace Berry, was released by Paramount, 1925. *White Fang* was adapted for film by Jane Murtin and released by F.B.D., 1925; it was released, with screenplay by Gene Fowler, Hal Long, and S. G. Duncan, directed by David Butler, produced by Darryl F. Zanuck, and starring Michael Whalen, Jean Muir, Slim Sumerville, John Canadine, and others, by Twentieth Century-Fox, 1936. "Morganson's Finish" was adapted for film, directed by Fred Windermere, and released by Tiffany Productions, 1926. "White and Yellow" was adapted for film by E. Morton Haugh, directed by Forrest Sheldon, and released under the title "The Haunted Ship" by Tiffany-Stahl, 1927. "Demetrios Contos" was adapted by Robert Dillon, directed by John G. Adolphi, and released under the title "The Devil's Skipper" by Tiffany- Stahl, 1928. "The Siege of the *Lancashire Queen*" was adapted for film, directed by John G. Adolphi, and released under the title "Prowlers of the Sea" by Tiffany-Stahl, 1928. "Yellow Handkerchief" was adapted by Harry Ditmar, directed by Edgar Lewis, and released under the title "Stormy Waters" by Tiffany-Stahl, 1928. "A Raid on the Oyster Pirates" was adapted by Bennett Cohn, directed by Elmer Miller, and released under the title "Tropical Nights" by Tiffany-Stahl, 1928. *Smoke Bellew* was adapted for film, directed by Scott Dunlop, starring Conway Tearle, Barbara Bedford, Mark Hamilton, and others, and released by First Division, 1929. "The White Silence," adapted by Michael L. Simmons, directed by Charles Widor, and starring Charles Bickford, Jean Parker, Alan Bridges, and others, was released under the title "Romance of the Redwoods" by Columbia, March 30, 1939. "A Thousand Dollars," starring Lyle Talbot, was released under the title "Torture Ship" by Producers Releasing Corp., 1939. "Wolf Call," screenplay by Joseph West, directed by George Waggner, starring John Carroll, Novita, Peter George Lynn, and others, was released by Monogram, 1939.

"Queen of the Yukon," screenplay by Joseph West, directed by Phil Rosen, produced by Paul Malvern, starring Charles Bickford, Irene Rich, June Carlson, and others, was released by Monogram, August 26, 1940. "That Spot," screenplay by Elizabeth Hopkins and Edmund Kelso, directed by Howard Bretherton, produced by Paul Malvern, starring Michael Whalen, Grace Bradley, Mantan Mareland, Darryl Hickman, and others, was released under the title "Sign of the Wolf" by Monogram, March 25, 1941. "Flush of Gold," screenplay by George Wallace Sayre, Harrison Orkow, and Malcom Stuart Boyle, directed by George Archainbaud, produced by Lindsley Parsons, starring Kent Taylor, Margaret Lindsay, John Carradine, Dean Jagger, and others, was released under the title "Alaska" by Monogram, December 22, 1944.

"The Mexican," screenplay by Aben Kandel and H. Kline, directed by Herbert Kline, produced by Alex Gottlieb, starring Richard Conte, Vanessa Brown, Lee J. Cobb, and others, was released under the title "The Fighter" by United Artists-Gottlieb, 1952. "To Build a Fire" was adapted for film and released by Montana State College, 1963; it was released as a filmstrip by Educational Record Sales, 1972. "The Assassination Bureau Ltd.," was released by Paramount, 1969.

Recordings—"To Build a Fire," read by Robert Donly, Miller-Brody; Jack London Cassette Library, including "The Call of the Wild," "Martin Eden," and "The Sea-Wolf," read by Jack Dahlby, Listening Library; "The Call of the Wild" read by Arnold Moss, Miller-Brody.

Other—London's writings have been adapted and published as comic books. His works have also been adapted for the stage, radio, and television.

BIOGRAPHICAL/CRITICAL SOURCES:

BOOKS

Authors in the News, Volume 2, Gale, 1976.

Baltrop, Robert, *Jack London: The Man, the Writer, the Rebel,* Pluto, 1976.

Beauchamp, Gorman, *Jack London,* Starmount House, 1984.

Concise Dictionary of American Literary Biography: Realism, Naturalism, and Local Color, 1865-1917, Gale, 1988.

Dickson, Samuel, *Streets of San Francisco,* Stanford University Press, 1955.

Dictionary of Literary Biography, Gale, Volume 8: *Twentieth-Century American Science Fiction Writers,* 1981, Volume 12: *American Realists and Naturalists,* 1982, Volume 78: *American Short Story Writers, 1880-1910,* 1989.

Feied, Frederick, *No Pie in the Sky: The Hobo as American Cultural Hero in the Works of Jack London, John Dos Passos, and Jack Kerouac,* Citadel, 1964.

Foner, Philip, editor, *Jack London: American Rebel,* Citadel, revised edition, 1964.

Franchere, Ruth, *Jack London: The Pursuit of a Dream,* Crowell, 1962.

Garst, Shannon, *Jack London: Magnet for Adventure,* Wolf House, 1972.

Geismar, Maxwell, *Rebels and Ancestors: The American Novel,* Houghton, 1953.

Hedrick, Joan D., *Solitary Comrade: Jack London and His Work,* University of North Carolina Press, 1982.

Hendricks, King and Irving Shepard, editors, *Letters From Jack London: Containing an Unpublished Correspondence Between London and Sinclair Lewis,* Odyssey Press, 1965.

Jay, Martin, *Harvests of Change: American Literature, 1865-1914,* Prentice-Hall, 1967.

Johnston, Carolyn, *Jack London—An American Rebel?,* Greenwood Press, 1984.

Kazin, Alfred, *On Native Ground,* Harcourt, 1942.

Kingman, Russ, *A Pictorial Biography of Jack London,* Crown, 1979.

Labor, Earle, *Jack London,* Twayne, 1974.

London, Charmian Kittredge, *The Book of Jack London,* two volumes, Century, 1921.

London, Jack, *The Call of the Wild, White Fang, and Other Stories,* edited by Andrew Sinclair, introduction by James Dickey, Penguin, 1981.

London, Joan, *Jack London and His Times: An Unconventional Biography,* Doubleday, Doran, 1939.

Lynn, Kenneth S., *Dream of Success,* Little, Brown, 1955.

McClintock, James I., *White Logic: Jack London's Short Stories,* Wolf House, 1976.

Mencken, H. L., *Prejudices: First Series,* Knopf, 1921.

Mumford, Lewis, *The Golden Day: A Study in American Literature and Culture,* Boni & Liveright, 1926.

O'Connor, Richard, *Jack London: A Biography,* Little, Brown, 1964.

Orwell, George, *The Collected Essays, Journalism, and Letters of George Orwell,* Volume 4: *In Front of Your Nose,* edited by Sonia Orwell and Ian Ingus, Harcourt, 1968.

Ownby, Ray Wilson, editor, *Jack London: Essays in Criticism,* Peregrine Smith, 1978.

Sherman, Joan R., *Jack London: A Reference Guide,* G. K. Hall, 1977.

Sinclair, Andrew, *Jack: A Biography of Jack London,* Harper, 1977.

Stone, Irving, *Sailor on Horseback: The Biography of Jack London,* Houghton, 1938.

Tavernier-Corbin, Jacqueline, editor, *Critical Essays on Jack London,* G. K. Hall, 1983.

Twentieth-Century Literary Criticism, Gale, Volume 9, 1983, Volume 15, 1985.

Walcutt, Charles C., *American Literary Naturalism, A Divided Stream,* University of Minnesota Press, 1956.

Walcutt, Charles C., *Jack London,* University of Minnesota Press, 1966.

Walker, Dale L., editor, *The Fiction of Jack London: A Chronological Bibliography,* Texas Western Press, 1972.

Walker, Franklin, *Jack London and the Klondike: The Genesis of an American Writer,* Huntington Library, 1966.

Watson, Charles N., Jr., *The Novels of Jack London: A Reappraisal,* University of London Press, 1983.

Woodbridge, Hensley C., John London, and George H. Tweney, *Jack London: A Bibliography,* Talisman Press, 1966, revised and enlarged edition, Kraus, 1973.

PERIODICALS

American Literature, Number 38, 1966.

American Quarterly, Number 7, 1955.

American Studies, Number 16, 1975.

Jack London Newsletter, Number 1, 1967, Number 7, 1974, Number 12, 1979.

Los Angeles Times, July 30, 1988.

Modern Fiction Studies, spring, 1976.

Nineteenth-Century Fiction, Number 1, 1962.

Papers of the Michigan Academy of Science, Arts, and Letters, Number 24, 1938.

LOPEZ, Barry Holstun 1945-

PERSONAL: Born January 6, 1945, in Port Chester, N.Y.; son of Adrian Bernard and Mary (Holstun) Lopez; married Sandra Landers (a bookwright), June 10, 1967. *Education:* University of Notre Dame, A.B. (cum laude), 1966, M.A.T., 1968; University of Oregon, graduate study, 1969-70.

ADDRESSES: Agent—Peter Matson, Literistic Ltd., 264 Fifth Ave., New York, N.Y. 10001.

CAREER: Full-time writer, 1970—. Associate at Gannett Center for Media Studies, Columbia University, 1985—; Distinguished Visiting Writer, Eastern Washington University, 1985; Ida Beam Visiting Professor, University of Iowa, 1985; Distinguished Visiting Naturalist, Carleton College, 1986.

AWARDS, HONORS: John Burroughs Medal for distinguished natural history writing, Christopher Medal for humanitarian writing, and Pacific Northwest Booksellers award for excellence in nonfiction, all 1979, and American Book Award nomination, 1980, all for *Of Wolves and Men;* Distinguished Recognition Award, Friends of American Writers, 1981, for *Winter Count;* National Book Award in nonfiction (formerly American Book Award), Christopher Book Award, Pacific Northwest Booksellers award, National Book Critics Circle award nomination, *Los Angeles Times* book award nomination, American Library Association notable book citation, *New York Times Book Review* "Best Books" listing, and American Library Association "Best Books for Young Adults" citation, all 1986, and Francis Fuller Victor Award in nonfiction from Oregon Institute of Literary Arts, 1987, all for *Arctic Dreams: Imagination and Desire in a Northern Landscape;* Award in Literature from American Academy and Institute of Arts and Letters, 1986, for body of work; Guggenheim fellow, 1987.

WRITINGS:

Desert Notes: Reflections in the Eye of a Raven (fictional narratives), Andrews & McMeel, 1976.
Giving Birth to Thunder, Sleeping with His Daughter: Coyote Builds North America (native American trickster stories), Andrews & McMeel, 1978.
Of Wolves and Men (nonfiction), Scribner, 1978.
River Notes: The Dance of Herons (fictional narratives), Andrews & McMeel, 1979.
Desert Reservation (chapbook), Copper Canyon Press, 1980.
Winter Count (fiction), Scribner, 1981.
Arctic Dreams: Imagination and Desire in a Northern Landscape (nonfiction), Scribner, 1986.
Crossing Open Ground (essays), Scribner, 1988.

CONTRIBUTOR TO ANTHOLOGIES

Thomas Cooley, editor, *The Norton Sampler,* Norton, 1979, new edition, 1985.
Mary Van Derventer, editor, *Earthworks: Ten Years on the Environmental Front,* Friends of the Earth, 1980.
Dewitt Jones, editor, *Visions of Wilderness,* Graphic Arts Center, 1980.
Johnathan Cott and Mary Gimbel, editors, *Wonders: Writings and Drawings for the Child in Us All,* Rolling Stone Press, 1980.
Joseph Trimmer and Maxine Hairston, editors, *The Riverside Reader,* Houghton, new edition, 1985.
Charles Erdoes and Alfonso Ortiz, *American Indian Myths and Legends,* Pantheon, 1985.

James Hepworth and Gregory McNamee, editors, *Resist Much, Obey Little: Some Notes on Edward Abbey,* Dream Garden, 1985.
D. L. Emblen and Arnold Solkov, editors, *Before and After: The Shape and Shaping of Prose,* Random House, 1986.
A. M. Rosenthal, Arthur Gelb, and others, editors, *The Sophisticated Traveler: Enchanting Places and How to Find Them,* Villard Books, 1986.
Rich Ives, editor, *From Timberline to Tidepool: Contemporary Fiction from the Northwest,* Owl Creek Press, 1986.
Richard Haswell and others, editors, *The HBJ Reader,* Harcourt, 1987.
Daniel Halpern, editor, *On Nature,* North Point Press, 1987.
Alexander Blackburn, editor, *The Interior Country: Stories of the Modern West,* Swallow Press/Ohio University Press, 1987.
Robley Wilson, Jr., editor, *Four-Minute Fictions: Fifty Short-Short Stories from The North American Review,* Word Beat Press, 1987.

Also contributor to *Best American Essays 1987,* in press.

OTHER

Contributor of articles, essays, and short fiction to numerous periodicals including *Harper's, North American Review, New York Times, Orion Nature Quarterly, Antaeus, National Geographic,* and *Outside.* Contributing editor, *North American Review,* 1977—, and *Harper's,* 1981-82 and 1984—; guest editor of special section, "The American Indian Mind," for *Quest,* September/October, 1978; correspondent, *Outside,* 1982—; advisory editor, *Antaeus,* autumn, 1986.

WORK IN PROGRESS: A work of fiction, set on the northern plains in the eighteenth century; a work of nonfiction about landscapes remote from North America; essays, articles, and short fiction for magazines.

SIDELIGHTS: Barry Holstun Lopez's early magazine articles and books established his reputation as an authoritative writer on the subjects of natural history and the environment. He has been favorably compared to such distinguished naturalist authors as Edward Hoagland, Peter Matthiessen, Edward Abbey, Sally Carrighar, and Loren Eiseley. Lopez's more recent works are praised for their philosophical content as well, for in *Of Wolves and Men* and *Arctic Dreams: Imagination and Desire in a Northern Landscape,* the author uses natural history as a metaphor for discussing some larger moral issues. "A writer has a certain handful of questions," he explained to Nick O'Connell in a *Seattle Review* interview. "Mine seem to be the issues of tolerance and dignity. You can't sit down and write directly about those things, but if they are on your mind and if you're a writer, they're going to come out in one form or another. The form I feel most comfortable with, where I do a lot of reading and aimless thinking, is in natural history."

Lopez spent most of his first ten years in Southern California—"before it became a caricature of itself," he told *Western American Literature* interviewer Jim Aton. By the time the family moved back to Lopez's birthplace, New York, he had formed a strong emotional attachment to the West Coast, and so he returned to live there when he was twenty-three years old. His graduate studies in folklore led him to write his first book, a retelling of American Indian stories featuring the coyote as a trickster figure. It was published some time later as *Giving Birth to Thunder, Sleeping with His Daughter: Coyote Builds North America.* Deciding that life as a writer was preferable to life as a scholar, Lopez left the university in 1970, settled with his wife on the McKenzie River in western Oregon, and devoted himself to writing full time.

A 1974 magazine assignment for *Smithsonian* magazine led to Lopez's first major book, *Of Wolves and Men.* His research for that article "catalyzed a lot of thinking about human and animal relationships which had been going on in a vague way in my mind for several years," he said in a *CA* interview. "I realized that if I focused on this one animal, I might be able to say something sharp and clear." In his book, Lopez attempts to present a complete portrait of the wolf. He includes not only scientific information, but also wolf lore from aboriginal societies and an overview of the animal's role in literature, folklore, and superstition.

The result, say many critics, is a book that succeeds on several levels. First of all, Lopez has gathered "an extraordinary amount of material," writes a contributor to *The New York Review of Books,* making *Of Wolves and Men* one of the most comprehensive sources of information on these animals ever published. Secondly, in showing readers the many diverse images of the wolf, the author reveals how man "creates" animals by projecting aspects of his own personality on them. Thirdly, Lopez illustrates how undeserved is Western civilization's depiction of the wolf as a ruthless killer. His observations showed him that the Eskimos' conception of the wolf is much closer to the truth; among them, wolves are respected and emulated for their intelligence and strong sense of loyalty. What we think about the wolf may reveal something about ourselves, concludes Lopez, for while Western man has reviled the wolf as a wanton killer, he himself has brutally and pointlessly driven many animals to extinction. Whitley Streiber of the *Washington Post* believes that *Of Wolves and Men* is "a very important book by a man who has thought much on his subject. Above all he has listened to many people who claim to know about wolves. In coming to terms with the difference between what we know and what we imagine about the wolf, Lopez has shed light on some painful truths about the human experience. By laying no blame while facing the tragedy for what it is, he has made what we have done to the wolf a source of new knowledge about man."

Lopez found that he was strongly drawn to the Arctic even after *Of Wolves and Men* was completed. Over the next four years he made several more trips there, and in 1986 he published an account of his travels, entitled *Arctic Dreams: Imagination and Desire in a Northern Landscape.* While the book provides a wealth of factual information about the Arctic region, it is, says the *New York Times*'s Michiko Kakutani, "a book about the Arctic North in the way that 'Moby-Dick' is a novel about whales." Lopez in *Arctic Dreams* restates the deeper themes found in *Of Wolves and Men,* but while *Of Wolves and Men* focused tightly on man's relationship with a specific animal, *Arctic Dreams*'s scope is wider, exploring man's relationship with what Lopez refers to as "the landscape." He explained to Jim Aton, "By landscape I mean the complete lay of the land—the animals that are there, the trees, the vegetation, the quality of soils, the drainage pattern of water, the annual cycles of temperature, the kinds of precipitation, the sounds common to the region."

Arctic Dreams drew many favorable reviews, both for its vivid descriptions of the North and for the questions it raises about man's place in nature. "The writing, at times, is luminous, powerful and musical. Lopez infuses each sentence with grace," asserts George Tombs in the Toronto *Globe and Mail.* "It is a lyrical geography and natural history, an account of Eskimo life, and a history of northern explorations," finds *Los Angeles Times Book Review* contributor Richard Eder. "But mainly, it is a . . .

reflection about the meaning of mankind's encounter with the planet. . . . Its question, starting as ecology and working into metaphysics, is whether civilization can find a way of adapting itself to the natural world, before its predilection for adapting the natural world to itself destroys self and world, both." Lopez elaborated on the feelings that prompted him to write *Arctic Dreams* in his interview with Aton: "I think if you can really see the land, if you can lose your sense of wishing it to be what you want it to be, if you can strip yourself of the desire to order and to name and see the land entirely for itself, you see in the relationship of all its elements the face of God. And that's why I say the landscape has an authority."

Man's interactions with "the landscape" are often highlighted in Lopez's fiction as well as in his nonfiction. His short story collections are praised by many reviewers. For example, in a *Detroit News* review of *River Notes: The Dance of Herons,* David Graber writes: "Lopez delicately surveys the terrain of shared experience between a man and a place, in this case a river in the Pacific Northwest. . . . [The author] has an unsentimental naturalist's knowledge combined with profound love-of-land. . . . [His] writing has a dreamlike quality; the sensuality of his words, his . . . playful choice of simile serve as counterpoint to his precisely accurate portrayals of salmon spawning and herons fishing, of Douglas fir falling to the chainsaw and willow crowding the riverbank." Edith Hamilton of the *Miami Herald* says that in *River Notes* "Lopez transmogrifies the physical characteristics of the river—the bend, the falls, the shallows, the rapids—into human experience: the bend as a man seriously ill for a long time who suddenly, for no reason as the river bends for no reason, decides he will recover. The falls is a strangely gothic convolution of the original fall from grace, brought up to date by a vagabond with mythic yearnings who ends his search at the high brink of the river's falls. . . . Lopez's nice shallows become deep reflecting mirrors, their images multiplying beyond ease. . . . Not since Ken Kesey's drastically different novel, *Sometimes a Great Notion,* has a writer so caught and pinned the mossy melancholy of Oregon." In his *Progressive* review, David Miller makes the point that, despite the book's deceptively simple title, it is no mere study of herons. He writes that *River Notes* "is about a small world of relationships among people, herons, salmon, cottonwoods—and all creatures drawn to this rushing, tumbling, powerful, and endangered emblem of natural life, the river. . . . [The book] is a thing of beauty in itself, as tantalizingly real and yet as otherworldly as your own reflection on a river's surface. . . . It is a rare achievement; perhaps—I've never said this before and know that only time will tell—it is a work of genius."

Saturday Review writer Alan Cheuse believes that *Winter Count,* another collection of short fiction, is the book that will win for Lopez "recognition as a writer who like, say, Peter Matthiessen or Edward Hoagland, goes to the wilderness in order to clarify a great deal about civilization." Cheuse commends Lopez for weaving "a style reminiscent of some important contemporary Latin American magical realists" and for turning "the sentiments of a decade's worth of ecology lovers into a deeply felt and unnervingly powerful picture of reality." *Los Angeles Times* reviewer Elaine Kendall writes: "There's a boundary, no wider than a pinstripe, where fact and fiction barely touch. With so much room on either side and assorted areas where overlap is expected, few writers choose to confine themselves to that fine line where the two simply meet. Lopez is one of those few. He makes that delicate border his entire territory. *Winter Count* is a small and perfectly crafted collection of just such encounters between imagination and reality. . . . Lopez's observations are so acute the stories expand of their own accord, lingering in the mind the way intense light lingers on the retina." Finally, David Quammen, in *a New York Times Book Review* article, says that *Winter Count* is "full of solid, quiet, telling short works. Each of the stories . . . is as economical in design, as painstakingly crafted and as resonant as a good classical guitar." Quammen concludes that Lopez's fiction "is as spare, as pared down and elemental as the lives it describes, the values it celebrates. One of his characters says, 'I've thrown away everything that is no good,' and this perilously righteous algorithm seems a key part of the author's own epic."

Discussing his fiction work with Aton, Lopez commented: "My interest in a story is to illuminate a set of circumstances that bring some understanding of human life, enough at least so that a reader can identify with it and draw some vague sense of hope or sustenance or deep feeling and in some way be revived. . . . It's important to me . . . to go into a story with a capacity for wonder, where I know I can derive something 'wonder-full' and then bring this into the story so that a reader can feel it and say, 'I am an adult. I have a family, I pay bills, I live in a world of chicanery and subterfuge and atomic weaponry and inhumanity and round-heeled politicians and garrulous, insipid television personalities, but still I have wonder. I have been brought to a state of wonder by contact with something in a story.' "

Lopez's books have been translated into French, German, Swedish, Japanese, Dutch, Finnish, Spanish, Chinese, Norwegian, and Italian.

BIOGRAPHICAL/CRITICAL SOURCES:

BOOKS

Lopez, Barry, *Arctic Dreams: Imagination and Desire in a Northern Landscape* (nonfiction), Scribner, 1986.

PERIODICALS

Chicago Tribune, November 5, 1978, March 30, 1986, April 28, 1988.
Chicago Tribune Book World, November 23, 1979.
Christian Science Monitor, February 12, 1979.
Detroit News, November 4, 1979.
Globe and Mail (Toronto), May 31, 1986.
Harper's, December, 1984.
Los Angeles Times, November 12, 1978, May 9, 1981.
Los Angeles Times Book Review, March 2, 1986.
Miami Herald, September 30, 1979, March 29, 1986.
Nation, November 11, 1978.
New Republic, June 30, 1979.
Newsweek, October 16, 1978.
New Yorker, February 26, 1979, March 17, 1986.
New York Times, January 4, 1979, February 12, 1986, March 29, 1986.
New York Times Book Review, November 19, 1978, June 14, 1981, February 16, 1986.
Observer, June 24, 1979.
Pacific Northwest, March/April, 1980.
Progressive, May, 1980.
Saturday Review, April, 1981.
Seattle Review, fall, 1985.
Time, March 10, 1986.
Times Literary Supplement, December 7, 1979, August 8, 1986.
Washington Post, November 27, 1978, November 18, 1986, November 24, 1986.
Washington Post Book Review, March 9, 1986.
Western American Literature, spring, 1986.

LORCA, Federico Garcia
See GARCIA LORCA, Federico

*   *   *

LORDE, Audre (Geraldine) 1934-
(Rey Domini)

PERSONAL: Born February 18, 1934, in New York, N.Y.; daughter of Frederic Byron (a real estate broker) and Linda Gertrude (a homemaker; maiden name, Belmar) Lorde; married Edwin Ashley Rollins (an attorney), March 31, 1962 (divorced, 1972); children: Elizabeth, Jonathan. *Education:* Attended National University of Mexico, 1954; Hunter College (now Hunter College of the City University of New York), B.A., 1960; Columbia University, M.L.S., 1962. *Politics:* Radical. *Religion:* Quaker.

ADDRESSES: Home—A2 Judith's Fancy, Christiansted, St. Croix 00820, U.S. Virgin Islands. *Office*—Department of English, Hunter College of the City University of New York, 695 Park Ave., New York, N.Y. 10019. *Agent*—Charlotte Sheedy, 41 King St., New York, N.Y. 10014.

CAREER: Mount Vernon Public Library, Mount Vernon, N.Y., librarian, 1961-63; Town School Library, New York City, head librarian, 1966-68; City University of New York, New York City, lecturer in creative writing at City College, 1968, lecturer in education department at Herbert H. Lehman College, 1969-70, associate professor of English at John Jay College of Criminal Justice, beginning 1970, professor of English at Hunter College, 1980—, Thomas Hunter Professor, 1987—. Distinguished visiting professor, Atlanta University, 1968; poet in residence, Tougaloo College, 1968. Lecturer throughout the United States; has taught and lectured in Russia, Nigeria, Granada, Ghana, Mexico, Denmark, Germany, Holland, Switzerland, New Zealand, and Australia. Founding Mother of Kitchen Table: Women of Color Press and Sisterhood in Support of Sisters in South Africa.

MEMBER: American Association of University Professors, Harlem Writers Guild.

AWARDS, HONORS: National Endowment for the Arts grants, 1968 and 1981; Creative Artists Public Service grants, 1972 and 1976; National Book Award nominee for poetry, 1974, for *From a Land Where Other People Live;* American Library Association Gay Caucus Book Award, 1981, for *The Cancer Journals;* Borough of Manhattan President's Award for literary excellence, 1987; American Book Award, Before Columbus Foundation, 1989, for *A Burst of Light;* received honorary doctorates from Oberlin College and Haverford College, both 1989.

WRITINGS:

The Cancer Journals (nonfiction), Spinsters Ink, 1980.
Zami: A New Spelling of My Name (fiction), Crossing Press, 1982.
Sister Outsider (nonfiction), Crossing Press, 1984.
A Burst of Light (nonfiction), Firebrand Books, 1988.

POETRY

The First Cities, introduction by Diane di Prima, Poets Press, 1968.
Cables to Rage, Broadside Press, 1970.
From a Land Where Other People Live, Broadside Press, 1973.
The New York Head Shop and Museum, Broadside Press, 1974.
Coal, Norton, 1976.
Between Our Selves, Eidolon, 1976.
The Black Unicorn, Norton, 1978.

Chosen Poems Old and New, Norton, 1982.
Our Dead Behind Us, Norton, 1986.

CONTRIBUTOR OF POETRY TO ANTHOLOGIES

Langston Hughes, editor, *New Negro Poets,* USA, University of Indiana Press, 1962.

P. Breman, editor, *Sixes and Sevens,* Breman Ltd. (London), 1963.

R. Pool, editor, *Beyond the Blues,* Hand & Flower Press (Amsterdam), 1964.

G. Menarini, editor, *I Negri: Poesie E Canti,* Edizioni Academia (Rome), 1969.

C. Major, editor, *New Black Poetry,* International Press, 1969.

T. Wilentz, editor, *Natural Process,* Hill & Wang, 1970.

T. Cade, editor, *The Black Woman,* American Library Publishing, 1970.

Contributor of poetry to other anthologies, including *Soul-Script,* edited by J. Meyer, Simon & Schuster.

OTHER

Contributor of poetry to periodicals, including *Iowa Review, Black Scholar, Chrysalis, Black World, Journal of Black Poetry, Transatlantic Review, Massachusetts Review, Pound, Harlem Writers' Quarterly, Freedomways, Seventeen,* and *Women: A Journal of Liberation;* contributor of fiction, under pseudonym Rey Domini, to *Venture* magazine. Editor, *Pound* magazine (Tougaloo, Miss.), 1968; poetry editor, *Chrysalis* and *Amazon Quarterly.*

WORK IN PROGRESS: Poetry and collected essays.

SIDELIGHTS: Audre Lorde's poetry and "indeed all of her writing," according to contributor Joan Martin in *Black Women Writers (1950-1980): A Critical Evaluation,* "rings with passion, sincerity, perception, and depth of feeling." Her first poem to be published was accepted by *Seventeen* magazine when she was still in high school. The poem had been rejected by her school paper, Lorde explains in *Black Women Writers,* because her "English teachers . . . said [it] was much too romantic." Her mature poetry, published in volumes including *New York Head Shop and Museum, Coal,* and *The Black Unicorn,* is sometimes romantic also. Often dealing with her lesbian relationships, her love poems have nevertheless been judged accessible to all by many critics. In Martin's words, "one doesn't have to profess heterosexuality, homosexuality, or asexuality to react to her poems. . . . Anyone who has ever been in love can respond to the straightforward passion and pain sometimes one and the same, in Lorde's poems."

As Jerome Brooks reports in *Black Women Writers (1950-1980): A Critical Evaluation,* however, "Lorde' s poetry of anger is perhaps her best-known work." In her poem "The American Cancer Society Or There Is More Than One Way to Skin a Coon," she protests against white America thrusting its unnatural culture on blacks; in "The Brown Menace or Poem to the Survival of Roaches," she likens blacks to cockroaches, hated, feared, and poisoned by whites. *Poetry* critic Sandra M. Gilbert remarks that "it's not surprising that Lorde occasionally seems to be choking on her own anger . . . [and] when her fury vibrates through taut cables from head to heart to page, Lorde is capable of rare and, paradoxically, loving jeremiads." Her anger does not confine itself to racial injustice but extends to feminist issues as well, and occasionally she criticizes black men for their role in the perpetuating of sex discrimination: "As Black people, we cannot begin our dialogue by denying the oppressive nature of male privilege," Lorde states in *Black Women Writers.* "And if Black males

choose to assume that privilege, for whatever reason, raping, brutalizing, and killing women, then we cannot ignore Black male oppression. One oppression does not justify another."

Of her poetic beginnings Lorde comments in *Black Women Writers:* "I used to speak in poetry. I would read poems, and I would memorize them. People would say, well what do you think, Audre. What happened to you yesterday? And I would recite a poem and somewhere in that poem would be a line or a feeling I would be sharing. In other words, I literally communicated through poetry. And when I couldn't find the poems to express the things I was feeling, that's what started me writing poetry, and that was when I was twelve or thirteen." As an adult, her primary poetic goal is still communication. "I have a duty," she states later in the same publication, "to speak the truth as I see it and to share not just my triumphs, not just the things that felt good, but the pain, the intense, often unmitigating pain." As a mature poet, however, rather than relying solely on poetry as a means of self-expression Lorde often extracts poems from her personal journals. Explaining the genesis of "Power," a poem about the police shooting of a ten-year-old black child, Lorde discusses her feelings when she learned that the officer involved had been acquitted: "A kind of fury rose up in me; the sky turned red. I felt so sick. I felt as if I would drive this car into a wall, into the next person I saw. So I pulled over. I took out my journal just to air some of my fury, to get it out of my fingertips. Those expressed feelings are that poem."

In addition to race problems and love affairs, another important theme that runs through many of Lorde's volumes of poetry is the parent-child relationship. Brooks sees a deep concern with the image of her deceased father in Lorde's "Father, Son, and Holy Ghost" which carries over to poems dealing with Africa in *The Black Unicorn.* According to Brooks, "the contact with Africa is the contact with the father who is revealed in a wealth of mythological symbols. . . . The fundamental image of the unicorn indicates that the poet is aware that Africa is for her a fatherland, a phallic terrain." Martin, however, takes a different view: "Audre Lorde is a rare creature. . . . She is the Black Unicorn: magical and mysterious bearer of fantasy draped in truth and beauty." Further, Martin finds the poet's feelings about her mother to be more vital to an understanding of her works. In many of Lorde's poems, the figure of her mother is one of a woman who resents her daughter, tries to repress her child's unique personality so that she conforms with the rest of the world, and withholds the emotional nourishment of parental love. For example, Lorde tells us in *Coal*'s "Story Books on a Kitchen Table": "Out of her womb of pain my mother spat me / into her ill-fitting harness of despair / into her deceits / where anger reconceived me." In *The Black Unicorn*'s "From the House of Yemanja," the mother's efforts to shape the speaker into something she is not do not quench the speaker's desire for the mother's love: "Mother I need / mother I need / . . . I am / the sun and moon and forever hungry." "Ballad From Childhood" in *The New York Head Shop and Museum* is Lorde's depiction of the ways in which a child's hopes and dreams are crushed by a restrictive mother. After the mother has made withering replies to her child's queries about planting a tree to give some beauty to their wasteland surroundings, the child gives up in defeat, saying: "Please mommy do not beat me so! / yes I will learn to love the snow! / yes I want neither seed nor tree! / yes ice is quite enough for me! / who knows what trouble-leaves might grow!"

As Martin notes, however, Lorde's ambivalent feelings about her mother "did not make [her] bitter against her own children when circumstances changed her role from that of child to mother."

Coal includes the poem "Now That I Am Forever with Child," which discusses the birth of Lorde's daughter. "I bore you one morning just before spring," she recounts, "my legs were towers between which / A new world was passing. / Since then / I can only distinguish / one thread within runnings hours / You, flowing through selves / toward You."

Lorde is also famed for writing the courageous account of her agonizing struggle to overcome breast cancer and mastectomy, *The Cancer Journals.* Her first major prose work, the *Journals* discuss Lorde's feelings about facing the possibility of death. Beyond death, Martin asserts, Lorde feared "she should die without having said the things she as a woman and an artist needed to say in order that her pain and subsequent loss might not have occurred in vain." The book also explains Lorde's decision not to wear a prosthesis after her breast was removed. As Brooks points out, "she does not suggest [her decision] for others, but . . . she uses [it] to expose some of the hypocrisies of the medical profession." Lorde summarizes her attitude on the issue thus in the *Journals:* "Prosthesis offers the empty comfort of 'Nobody will know the difference.' But it is that very difference which I wish to affirm, because I have lived it, and survived it, and wish to share that strength with other women. If we are to translate the silence surrounding breast cancer into language and action against this scourge, then the first step is that women with mastectomies must become visible to each other." Martin concludes: "*The Cancer Journals* affords all women who wish to read it the opportunity to look at the life experience of one very brave woman who bared her wounds without shame, in order that we might gain some strength from sharing in her pain."

Lorde's 1982 novel, *Zami: A New Spelling of My Name,* is described by its publishers as a "biomythography, combining elements of history, biography and myth," and Rosemary Daniell, in the *New York Times Book Review,* considers the work "excellent and evocative. . . . Among the elements that make the book so good are its personal honesty and lack of pretentiousness, characteristics that shine through the writing, bespeaking the evolution of a strong and remarkable character." Daniell says that, throughout the book, Lorde's "experiences are painted with exquisite imagery. Indeed, her West Indian heritage shows through most clearly in her use of word pictures that are sensual, steamy, at times near-tropical, evoking the colors, smells—repeatedly, the smells—shapes, textures that are her life."

Lorde once commented: "I am a Black Woman intent on survival and telling the truth as I see it. I believe in a future for us all if we use our power for what we believe."

BIOGRAPHICAL/CRITICAL SOURCES:

BOOKS

Addison, Gayle, editor, *Black Expression,* Weybright & Talley, 1969.
Bigsby, C. W. E., editor, *The Black American Writer,* Penguin, 1969.
Christian, Barbara, editor, *Black Feminist Criticism: Perspectives on Black Women Writers,* Pergamon, 1985.
Contemporary Literary Criticism, Volume 18, Gale, 1981.
Dictionary of Literary Biography, Volume 41: *Afro-American Poets Since 1955,* Gale, 1985.
Evans, Mari, editor, *Black Women Writers (1950-1980): A Critical Evaluation,* Doubleday, 1984.
Lorde, Audre, *The New York Head Shop and Museum,* Broadside Press, 1974.
Lorde, Audre, *Coal,* Norton, 1976.
Lorde, Audre, *The Black Unicorn,* Norton, 1978.

Lorde, Audre, *The Cancer Journals,* Spinsters Ink, 1980.
Tate, Claudia, editor, *Black Women Writers at Work,* Continuum, 1984.

PERIODICALS

Callaloo, Volume 9, number 4, 1987.
Essence, January, 1988.
Ms., September, 1974.
Negro Digest, September, 1968.
New York Times Book Review, December 19, 1982.
Poetry, February, 1977.

*   *   *

LORENZ, Konrad Zacharias   1903-

PERSONAL: Born November 7, 1903, in Vienna, Austria; son of Adolf (an orthopedic surgeon) and Emma (Lecher) Lorenz; married Margarethe Gebhardt (a gynecologist), June 24, 1927; children: Thomas, Agnes (Lorenz von Cranach), Dagmar. *Education:* Attended Columbia University, 1922; University of Vienna, M.D., 1928, Ph.D. (zoology), 1933.

ADDRESSES: Home—Adolf-Lorenzgasse 2, A-3422 Altenberg, Austria. *Office*— Institut fuer Vergleichende Verhaltensforschung, Abt. 4 Tiersoziologie, Adolf-Lorenzgasse 2, A-3422 Altenberg, Austria.

CAREER: University of Vienna, Vienna, Austria, lecturer in comparative anatomy and animal psychology, 1937-40, university lecturer, 1940; University of Koenigsberg, Koenigsberg, Germany, professor and head of the department of general psychology, 1940-42; Institute of Comparative Ethology, Altenberg, Austria, director, 1949-51; Max Planck Society for the Advancement of Science, Institute for Marine Biology, head of research station for physiology of behavior in Buldern, Germany, 1951-58, Institute for Behavior Physiology, Seewiesen, Germany, co-founder, 1958, co-director, 1958-61, director, 1961-73; Austrian Academy of Science, Institute of Comparative Ethology, Vienna, director of department of animal sociology, 1973—. Honorary professor at University of Muenster, 1953, University of Munich, 1957, University of Vienna, 197 , and University of Salzburg, 1974—. Lecturer at numerous educational institutions worldwide, including University of Colorado, Denver. *Military service:* German Army, physician, 1942-44; captured in Russia and returned to Austria, 1948.

MEMBER: Pour le Merite for Arts and Science, Austrian Academy of Sciences, Bavarian Academy of Sciences, American Philosophical Society, Association for the Study of Animal Behaviour, American Ornithology Union, Deutsche Akademie der Naturforscher Leopoldina, Royal Society (foreign member), National Academy of Sciences (foreign associate).

AWARDS, HONORS: Gold Medal from Zoological Society of New York, 1955; City of Vienna Prize, 1959; Gold Boelsche Medal, 1962; Austrian Distinction for Science and Art, 1964; Prix Mondial, Cino de Duca, 1969; Kalinga Prize from UNESCO, 1970; Nobel Prize for Physiology or Medicine, 1973; Cervia Amniente Naturschutzpreis; Ehrenmedaille d. Katholischen Universitet Mailand, Bayer; Maximiliansorden. Honorary degrees from University of Leeds, 1962, University of Basel, 1966, Yale University, 1967, Oxford University, 1968, University of Chicago, 1970; University of Durham, 1972; University of Birmingham, 1974; Grosses Verdienstkreuz der Bundesrepublik Deutschland, 1974; Bayerischer Verdienstorden, 1974.

WRITINGS:

Er redete mit dem Vieh, den Voegeln, und den Fischen, Borotha-Schoeler (Vienna), 1949, 17th edition, 1958, U.S. edition, edited by Eva Schiffer, Scott, Foresman, 1968, translation by Marjorie Kerr Wilson, with illustrations by the author and foreword by Sir Julian Huxley, published as *King Solomon's Ring: New Light on Animal Ways,* Crowell, 1952, P. Smith, 1988.

So kam der Mensch auf den Hund, Borotha-Schoeler, 1950, translation by Wilson, with illustrations by the author and Annie Eisenmenger, published as *Man Meets Dog,* Methuen, 1954, Houghton, 1955, reprinted, Penguin, 1988.

(Contributor) Claire H. Schiller, editor and translator, *Instinctive Behavior: The Development of a Modern Concept,* International Universities Press, 1957.

Principles of Ethology, translated by Erich Klinghammer, Springer-Verlag, 1961.

Das sogenannte Boese: Zur Naturgeschichte der Aggression, Borotha-Schoeler, 1963, translation by Marjorie Latzke, with foreword by Sir Julian Huxley, published as *On Aggression,* Methuen, 1966, translation by Wilson published under same title, Harcourt, 1966.

Gestaltwahrnehmung als Quelle wissenschaftlicher Erkenntnis (title means "Gestalt Perception as a Source of Scientific Knowledge"), Wissenschaftlicher Buchgesellschaft (Darrnstadt), 1964.

Darwin hat recht gesehen (title means "Darwin Saw the Truth"), Neske (Pfullingen), 1965.

Ueber tieresches and menschliches Verhalten, R. Piper (Munich), 1965, selections published as *Vom Weltbild des Verhaiteniforschers,* Deutscher Tashenbuch-Verlag (Munich), 1968, translation of unabridged edition by Robert Martin published as *Studies in Animal and Human Behavior,* two volumes, Harvard University Press, 1970-71.

Evolution and Modification of Behavior, University of Chicago Press, 1965, reprinted, 1986.

Der Vogelflug (title means "Bird Flight"), Neske, 1965.

(With Paul Leyhausen) *Antriebe tierischen and menschlichen Verhaltens,* R. Piper, 1968, translation by B. A. Tonkin published as *Motivation of Human and Animal Behavior: An Ethological View,* Van Nostrand, 1973.

Die acht Todsuendender der zivilisierten Menschheit, R. Piper, 1973, translation by Wilson published as *Civilized Man's Eight Deadly Sins,* Harcourt, 1974.

Die Rueckseite des Spiegels: Versuch einer Naturgeschichte menschlichen Erkennens R. Piper, 1973, translation by Ronald Taylor published as *Behind the Mirror: A Search for a Natural History of Human Knowledge,* Harcourt, 1978.

(Editor) *Konstructionen Versus Positionen; Beitrage zur Wissenschaftstheoretischen Diskussion zum 60: Geburstag von Paul Lorensen,* two volumes, De Gryter, 1978.

The Waning of Humaneness, Little, Brown, 1987.

Also author of *The Year of the Graylag Goose,* 1980. Contributor of articles to numerous journals in his field. Co-editor of *Zeitschrift fuer Tierpsychologie* (occasional periodical of Deutsche Gesellschaft fuer Tierpsychologie), 1937—.

WORK IN PROGRESS: A continuation of *Die Rueckseite des Spiegels;* a book on basic ethology.

SIDELIGHTS: The acknowledged father of modern ethology, Konrad Zacharias Lorenz has contributed toward a greater understanding of human behavioral patterns through the study of animals in their natural environment. Working with Oskar Heinroth, he identified the early biological learning process of im-printing, which, although the cybernetics are not understood, has successfully applied in psychoanalysis and psychiatry.

Of his work, Maxine Kingston wrote: "Lorenz integrates poetry and science by describing animal behavior with accuracy and beauty. A zoologist who sometimes seems to take flight with his jackdaws, ravens, and greylag geese, Lorenz, perhaps believing his own delightful use of language merely 'scientific,' often uses the classical English poets and Goethe . . . to help him introduce chapters and to culminate both scientific and philosophical speculations."

The books are more controversial in the scientific community. In answer to the criticism that his work is speculative and anthropomorphic, Lorenz once said: "If in an octopus or a squid I find an eye, with lens, an iris, a nerve—I need not even observe the animal—I need only to state these formal analogies to know it is an eye, which has evolved to see with. It has the same formation as my eye, my vertebrate eye, which has evolved independently of the octopus eye, but a detailed similarity informs me it has the same function, and nobody balks at calling it an eye. . . . Construct a computer model of an animal being jealous—one system having a social relationship with another, resenting a third one doing the same, and interacting with both and trying to break up their relationship. This function would presuppose an enormous complication, much more so than the functioning of an eye. You can speak of jealousy with respect to dogs and ganders, certainly. Assertions that these are false analogies or anthropomorphizations betray a lack of understanding of functional conceptions. To call the animal jealous is just as legitimate as to call an octopus' eye an eye or a lobster's leg a leg."

BIOGRAPHICAL/CRITICAL SOURCES:

PERIODICALS

English Journal, January, 1973.
Harper's, May, 1968.
Newsweek, August 6, 1973, October 22, 1973.
New Yorker, March 8, 1969.
Psychology Today, November, 1974.
Science, November 2, 1973.
Time, October 22, 1973.
Zeitschrift fuer Tierpsychologie, 1963.

*   *   *

LOUIS, Father M.
See MERTON, Thomas

*   *   *

LOVECRAFT, H(oward) P(hillips)   1890-1937
(Lawrence Appleton, Houdini, John J. Jones, Humphrey Littlewit, Gent., Henry Paget-Lowe, Ward Phillips, Richard Raleigh, Ames Dorrance Rowley, Edgar Softly, Edward Softly, Augustus Swift, Lewis Theobald, Jr., Frederick Willie, Zoilus)

PERSONAL: Born August 20, 1890, in Providence, R.I.; died of cancer and Bright's disease, March 15, 1937, in Providence, R.I.; son of Winfield Scott (a traveling salesman) and Sarah (Phillips) Lovecraft; married Sonia H. Greene, 1924 (divorced, 1929). *Education:* Self-educated.

CAREER: Short story writer, novelist, poet, and essayist. Worked as a ghostwriter, revisionist, and amateur journalist; *Evening News,* Providence, R.I., astrology columnist, 1914-18; publisher of *The Conservative,* 1915-19 and 1923. President of United Amateur Press Association, 1917-18 and 1923.

WRITINGS:

FICTION

The Shadow Over Innsmouth, illustrated by Frank A. Utpatel, Visionary Publishing (Everett, Pa.), 1936.

The Outsider and Others, collected by August Derleth and Donald Wandrei, Arkham, 1939.

Beyond the Wall of Sleep (includes *The Dream Quest of Unknown Kadath* [also see below] and *The Case of Charles Dexter Ward* [also see below]), collected by Derleth and Wandrei, Arkham, 1943.

The Weird Shadow Over Innsmouth, and Other Stories of the Supernatural, Bartholomew House, 1944.

The Dunwich Horror, [New York], 1945.

(With Derleth) *The Lurker at the Threshold,* Arkham, 1945.

Best Supernatural Stories of H. P. Lovecraft, edited with introduction by Derleth, World Publishing Company, 1945.

The Lurking Fear, and Other Stories, Avon, 1948, published under title *Cry Horror!,* 1958, reprinted under original title, Ballantine, 1971.

Something About Cats, and Other Pieces, collected by Derleth, Arkham, 1949.

The Dream Quest of Unknown Kadath, introduction by George T. Wetzel, Shroud (Buffalo, N.Y.), 1955, reprinted, edited with new introduction by Lin Carter, Ballantine, 1970.

(With Derleth) *The Survivor and Others,* Arkham, 1957.

The Shuttered Room, and Other Pieces, collected by Derleth, Arkham, 1959.

Dreams and Fancies, Arkham, 1962.

(With Derleth) *The Shadow out of Space,* introduction by Sam Moskowitz, [New York], 1962.

The Dunwich Horror, and Others: The Best Supernatural Stories of H. P. Lovecraft, collected with introduction by Derleth, Arkham, 1963, revised edition, edited by S. T. Joshi, 1985.

At the Mountains of Madness, and Other Novels, collected with introduction by Derleth, Arkham, 1964, revised edition, edited by Joshi, introduction by James Turner, 1985.

Dagon, and Other Macabre Tales, collected with introduction by Derleth, Arkham, 1965, revised edition, edited by Joshi, 1987.

The Case of Charles Dexter Ward, complete edition, Belmont Books, 1965.

The Dark Brotherhood, and Other Pieces, Arkham, 1966.

Three Tales of Horror, illustrated by Lee Brown Coye, Arkham, 1967.

The Colour out of Space, and Others, Lancer Books, 1967.

(With Derleth) *The Shadow out of Time, and Other Tales of Horror,* Gollancz, 1968.

At the Mountains of Madness, and Other Tales of Terror, Panther, 1968, Beagle Books, 1971.

The Haunter of the Dark, and Other Tales of Horror, edited with introduction by Derleth, Gollancz, 1969.

(With others) *Tales of the Cthulhu Mythos,* collected by Derleth, Arkham, 1969.

The Tomb and Other Tales, collected by Derleth, Panther, 1969, Ballantine, 1970.

(With Derleth) *The Shuttered Room, and Other Tales of Horror,* Panther, 1970.

(With others) *The Horror in the Museum, and Other Revisions,* Arkham, 1970, 3rd revised and enlarged edition, edited by Joshi, 1989 (also see below).

The Doom That Came to Sarnath, edited with introduction by Lin Carter, Ballantine, 1971.

Nine Stories From "The Horror in the Museum and Other Revisions," Beagle Books, 1971.

(With others) *The Spawn of Cthulhu,* edited with introduction by Lin Carter, Ballantine, 1971.

(With Derleth) *The Watchers out of Time, and Others,* foreword by April Derleth, Arkham, 1974.

(With others) *The Horror in the Burying Ground, and Other Tales,* Panther, 1975.

Herbert West: Reanimator, edited by Marc A. Michaud, Necronomicon, 1977.

Writings in the Tryout, edited by Michaud, foreword by Joshi, Necronomicon, 1977.

(With others) *New Tales of the Cthulhu Mythos,* Arkham, 1980.

The Best of H. P. Lovecraft: Bloodcurdling Tales of Horror and the Macabre, introduction by Robert Bloch, Ballantine, 1982.

The Night Ocean, Necronomicon, 1986.

Author of about sixty stories—many of which were first published in magazines *Weird Tales,* beginning in 1923, *Amazing Stories,* and *Astounding Stories*—including "The White Ship," "The Silver Key," "The Rats in the Walls," "The Statement of Randolph Carter," "The Horror at Red Hook," "The Music of Erich Zann," "The Moon-Bog," "The Cats of Ulthar," "Through the Gates of the Silver Key," "Celephais," "The Unnameable," "The Picture in the House," "The Festival," "From Beyond," "The Dreams in the Witch-House," "The Thing on the Doorstep," "Pickman's Model," "The Shunned House," "The Nameless City," "The Call of the Cthulhu," and "The Whisperer in the Darkness."

Ghostwriter and revisionist under pseudonyms Lawrence Appleton, Houdini, John J. Jones, Humphrey Littlewit, Gent., Henry Paget-Lowe, Ward Phillips, Richard Raleigh, Ames Dorrance Rowley, Edgar Softly, Edward Softly, Augustus Swift, Lewis Theobald, Jr., Frederick Willie, and Zoilus.

Stories have been published in various multi-work volumes, including *Eleven Great Horror Stories,* 1969, *Ghosts,* 1971, *Summoned From the Tomb,* 1973, *Cries of Terror,* 1976, and *Feast of Fear,* 1977.

POETRY

Collected Poems, illustrated by Frank Utpatel, Arkham, 1963, published under title *Fungi From Yuggoth, and Other Poems,* Ballantine, 1971.

The Prose Poems of H. P. Lovecraft, 4 volumes, Roy Squires, 1969-70.

Four Prose Poems, Necronomicon, 1987.

Contributor of poetry to amateur publications.

OTHER

The Notes and Commonplace Book, Futile Press, 1938, reprinted, Necronomicon, 1978.

Marginalia, collected by Derleth and Wandrei, Arkham, 1944.

Supernatural Horror in Literature (essay), introduction by Derleth, Ben Abramson, 1945, reprinted with new introduction by E. F. Bleiler, Dover, 1973.

Autobiography: Some Notes on a Nonentity, annotated by Derleth, Arkham, 1963.

Selected Letters, Volume 1: *1911-1924,* Volume 2: *1925-29,* Volume 3: *1929-31,* Volume 4: *1932-34,* Volume 5: *1934-37,* Volumes 1-3 edited by Derleth and Wandrei, Volumes 4 and 5 edited by Derleth and J. Turner, Arkham, 1965-76.

(With Willis Conover) *Lovecraft at Last,* foreword by Harold Taylor, Carrollton, Clark, 1975.

The Conservative: Complete, 1915-1923, edited by Michaud, foreword by Frank Belknap Long, Necronomicon, 1976.

To Quebec and the Stars, edited by L. Sprague de Camp, D. M. Grant, 1976.

First Writings: Pawtuxet Valley Gleaner, 1906 (essays), edited by Michaud, foreword by Ramsey Campbell, Necronomicon, 1976.

A Winter Wish (essays and poetry), edited by Tom Collins, Whispers Press, 1977.

(With R. H. Barlow) *Collapsing Cosmoses,* Necronomicon, 1977.

Memoirs of an Inconsequential Scribbler, Necronomicon, 1977.

Uncollected Prose and Poetry, edited by Joshi and Michaud, Necronomicon, 1978.

(With J. F. Hartmann) *Science Versus Charlatanry: Essays on Astrology,* edited with introduction and notes by Joshi and Scott Connors, The Strange Company, 1979.

H. P. Lovecraft in "The Eyrie," edited by Joshi and Michaud, Necronomicon, 1979.

Juvenilia, 1897-1905, introduction by Joshi, Necronomicon, 1984.

Contributor of nonfiction to amateur publications.

MEDIA ADAPTATIONS: The Case of Charles Dexter Ward was adapted for a film titled "The Haunted Palace," directed by Roger Corman, 1963; "The Colour out of Space" was adapted for a film titled "Die, Monster, Die!," directed by Daniel Haller, 1965; "The Shuttered Room" was adapted for a film directed by David Greene, 1968; "The Dunwich Horror" was adapted for a film directed by Haller, 1970; *Herbert West: Reanimator* was adapted for a film titled "Re-Animator," directed by Stuart Gordon, 1985; "From Beyond" was adapted for a film directed by Gordon, 1986; "The Unnameable" was adapted for a film directed by Jean-Paul Ouellette, 1988.

SIDELIGHTS: H. P. Lovecraft is widely considered the twentieth century's most important writer of supernatural horror fiction. Forging a unique niche within the horror genre, he created what became known as "weird tales," stories containing a distinctive blend of dreamlike imagery, Gothic terror, and elaborate concocted mythology. During his lifetime Lovecraft's work appeared almost exclusively in pulp magazines, and only since his death in 1937 has it received a wide readership and critical analysis. While many disparage his writings as verbose, melodramatic, and inconsequential, others extol his precise narrative skills and capacity to instill the unsettling. He has been placed among the ranks of storytellers Lord Dunsany, Arthur Machen, and Edgar Allan Poe, but, as August Derleth pointed out in *H. P. L.: A Memoir,* "Lovecraft was an original in the Gothic tradition; he was a skilled writer of supernatural fiction, a master of the macabre who had no peer in the America of his time."

Born in 1890 in Providence, Rhode Island, Lovecraft grew up in the affluent and intellectual surroundings of his grandfather's Victorian mansion. Sickly as a child and only able to attend school sporadically, he read voluminously, fascinated by eighteenth-century history and Gothic horror stories. He was particularly interested in science and began to write about it at an early age. Following the death of his grandfather in 1904, Lovecraft and his mother moved from the family mansion to a nearby duplex. (His father, a virtual stranger to Lovecraft, had died some years earlier after spending the last years of his life in a sanitorium.) Lovecraft would later relate that, raised by a sensitive and overprotective mother, he grew up in relative isolation, believing he was unlike other people.

Chronic sickness as a teenager prevented Lovecraft from finishing high school or attending college. He continued his self-education and supported himself by working as a ghostwriter and revisionist—vocations that, though disliked by Lovecraft,

would financially sustain him throughout his life. An admirer of Poe, he had begun writing horror tales but, deeming them meager efforts, devoted himself to amateur journalism. In addition, he contributed nonfiction and poetry to magazines. In 1914 Lovecraft joined the United Amateur Press Association, a group of nonprofessional writers who produced a variety of publications and exchanged letters, and one year later he began publishing his own magazine, *The Conservative.* His numerous letters and essays written during this time focus on his deep respect for scientific truth, his love of the past, and his relative disdain for the present-day world populated by non-Anglo-Nordic citizens. Lovecraft developed the belief, divulged Darrell Schweitzer in *The Dream Quest of H. P. Lovecraft,* "that only by clinging to tradition could we make life worth living amidst the chaos of modern civilization."

Lovecraft resumed writing fiction in 1917 and, at the behest of friends, began submitting stories to *Weird Tales,* a pulp magazine that would serve as the major host to Lovecraft's writings during his lifetime. Critics note that many of his early tales are heavily influenced by Irish fantasist Lord Dunsany. Such stories as "Dagon," "The White Ship," "The Silver Key," "The Doom That Came to Sarnath," and "The Cats of Ulthar" stem from fairy tale tradition, exhibiting rich dreamlike descriptions and imaginary settings. "This early cycle culminated in the extraordinary short novel Lovecraft called *The Dream Quest of Unknown Kadath,*" stated Lin Carter in his introduction to Ballantine's edition of the work. The story of protagonist Randolph Carter's search for a magnificent city he once envisioned, *The Dream Quest of Unknown Kadath* depicts Carter's voyage into the world of his dreams, where wondrous landscape and fantastic creatures exist. "Few more magical novels of dream-fantasy exist than this phantasmagoric adventure," declared Carter. "[Never have] the fluid and changing landscapes, the twilit and mysterious silences, and the spire-thronged and opulent Oriental cities of the dreamworld been so lovingly explored."

Contrasting to these relatively innocuous stories of fantasy are Lovecraft's tales of horror, remarkable for their bizarre supernatural conceptions rooted in the realism of a New England setting. Lovecraft was captivated by what he considered the ideal beauty of New England's traditional landscape and architecture; the writer, though, was also intrigued by a perceived darker dimension. His stories "The Unnameable" and "The Picture in the House," for example, depict corruption and superstition that persist in secluded New England areas; "The Festival" illustrates unearthly rituals practiced in the picturesque town of Kingsport—a village Lovecraft modeled after Marblehead, Massachusetts; and "Pickman's Model" focuses on a group of ghouls inhabiting modern Boston. Similar to these stories is the novel *The Case of Charles Dexter Ward,* in which the title character engages in magic to resurrect a seventeenth-century ancestor named Curwen. A practitioner of the black arts in Salem, Curwen is determined to inflict his evil on modern Massachusetts and consequently takes over the identity of Ward, who is later saved by the family doctor.

The best known of Lovecraft's stories are his later ones centering on the "Cthulhu Mythos," a term critics use to describe a distinctive universe of landscape, legends, and mythology completely of Lovecraft's invention. Like his earlier tales, the "Cthulhu Mythos" works are inspired by New England locales, but their settings are extensively recast to form Arkham, Innsmouth, and Dunwich, fictional worlds overseen by Cthulhu, Yog-Sothoth, and other gods. These stories, explained Lovecraft as quoted by Derleth, "are based on the fundamental lore or legend that this world was inhabited at one time by another race who, in practising black magic, lost their foothold and were expelled, yet live on outside ever ready to take possession of this earth again." Tales governed by this principle include "The Nameless City," "The Call of the Cthulhu," "The Whisperer in the Darkness," and *At the Mountains of Madness.*

In addition to writing weird tales, Lovecraft maintained an extensive correspondence and continued to generate a number of essays. Through these nonfiction outlets, he expounded on the aesthetics of supernatural horror fiction and on such philosophies as "mechanistic materialism" and "cosmic indifferentism"—the idea that the universe is a purposeless mechanism wherein humankind is largely insignificant. Lovecraft also produced a relatively large body of poetry, mostly imitative of eighteenth-century masters. Though he wrote prolifically, only one book, 1936's *The Shadow Over Innsmouth,* realized publication during his lifetime. When Lovecraft died of intestinal cancer at the age of forty-six, the bulk of his writings remained either scattered in magazines or unpublished.

Later Lovecraft's friends and fellow writers August Derleth and Donald Wandrei brought his writings to a wide readership. Establishing the publishing house of Arkham expressly to bring Lovecraft's work into book form, Derleth and Wandrei edited such early collections as *The Outsiders and Others* in 1939 and *Beyond the Wall of Sleep* in 1943. Numerous volumes of the horror writer's work have been collected by Arkham and other publishers over subsequent decades, and this broader circulation has spawned an extensive and diverse body of analysis.

Admirers of Lovecraft point to several elements in his fiction that distinguish him as a master of supernatural horror. Foremost is his ability to evoke terror through the creation of an unseen and unearthly presence. Lovecraft once explained in his lengthy essay *Supernatural Horror in Literature* that in order for fiction to instill fear "a certain atmosphere of breathless and unexpected dread of outer, unknown forces must be present." Particularly impressed by Lovecraft's capacity to induce anxiety in this way was Angela Carter, who described in an essay appearing in George Hay's *The Necronomicon:* "The twisted shapes of the trees in the woods above Arkham are emanations of the menace they evoke—menace, anguish, perturbation, dread. The cities themselves, whether those of old New England or those that lie beyond the gates of dream, present the dreadful enigma of a maze, always labyrinthine and always, the Minotaur at the heart of this labyrinth, lies the unspeakable in some form or else in some especially vile state of formlessness—the unspeakable, a nameless and unnameable fear."

While some critics are satisfied that Lovecraft effectively arouses fear solely through developing a sense of imminent dread, others point to an extra element in his fiction that creates a more powerful terror. Donald Burleson explained in *H. P. Lovecraft: A Critical Study:* "The horror, ultimately, in a Lovecraft tale is not some gelatinous lurker in dark places, but rather the realization, by the characters involved, of their helplessness and their insignificance in the scheme of things—their terribly ironic predicament of being sufficiently well-developed organisms to perceive and feel the poignancy of their own motelike unimportance in a blind and chaotic universe which neither loves them nor even finds them worthy of notice, let alone hatred or hostility." Steven J. Mariconda writing in *Lovecraft Studies* concurred, calling Lovecraft's tales "cosmic horror . . ., the horror of unknowable forces or beings which sweep men aside as indifferently as men do ants."

Other uncommon components marking Lovecraft's work include his manner of combining sterile scientific facts with arcane mysticism. Lovecraft "was uniquely able to link the inner substance of former spiritual beliefs with the most recent scientific discoveries," explained Schweitzer. "He used a rational, mechanistic context to get his readers to the edge of the abyss—and then dropped them over. The result was an irrational horror grimmer than anything a Puritan could conjure up." Critics also admire Lovecraft's ability to agitate his readers by creating an atmosphere of chaos. Lovecraft's universe, according the Maurice Levy in *Lovecraft: A Study in the Fantastic,* is a place of "bizarre dimensions . . ., where time and space stretch or contract in incomprehensible ways." These various features of Lovecraft's fiction lead many reviewers to conclude, as Dirk Mosig did in *Whispers,* that "[Lovecraft's] *oeuvre*] is a work of genius, a cosmic-minded *oeuvre* embodying a mechanistic materialist's brilliant conception of the imaginary realms and frightful reality 'beyond the fields we know,' a literary rhapsody of the cosmos and man's laughable position therein. . . . The Lovecraft *oeuvre* can be regarded as a significant contribution to world literature."

Despite extensive praise, controversy exists over Lovecraft's position in American letters. "At his best, . . . [Lovecraft] was a superior literary technician," wrote Schweitzer. "At his worst, he was one of the more dreadful writers of this century who is still remembered." Other critics have been less gentle. Deeming Lovecraft "a totally untalented and unreadable writer" as well as "a hopeless and rather pitiful literary crank," Larry McMurtry writing in the *Washington Post* decried Lovecraft as "the master of the turgid and the inflated." Colin Wilson in his *Strength to Dream: Literature and the Imagination* further attacked the author's prose, claiming, "Lovecraft hurls in the adjectives ('monstrous,' 'slithering,' 'ghoulish,' 'thunder-crazed') until he seems to be a kind of literary dervish who gibbers with hysteria as he spins. . . . [It] must be admitted that Lovecraft is a very bad writer." Even more scornful was Ursula Le Guin, who announced in the *Times Literary Supplement* that "Lovecraft was an exceptionally, almost impeccably, bad writer. . . . Derivative, inept, and callow, his tales can satisfy only those who believe that a capital letter, some words, and a full stop make a sentence."

Lovecraft, though, made no pretensions of possessing great writing talent. "No one is more acutely conscious than I of the inadequacy of my work. . . . I am a self-confessed amateur and bungler, and have not much hope of improvement," the author confessed in "The Defense Reopens!," an article later collected in S. T. Joshi's *In Defense of Dagon.* He did, however, consider himself a serious artist, practitioner, and theorist. Lovecraft "demanded that the fantastic tale be treated as art, not just a frivolous parlor game or an easy way to make a buck," wrote Schweitzer. Placing himself among those whom he considered "imaginative artists," such as Poe, Dunsany, William Blake, and Ambrose Bierce, Lovecraft explained in "The Defense Reopens!": "The imaginative writer devotes himself to art in its most essential sense. . . . He is the painter of moods and mind-pictures—a capturer and amplifier of elusive dreams and fancies—a voyager into those unheard-of lands which are glimpsed through the veil of actuality but rarely, and only by the most sensitive. . . . Most persons do not understand what he says, and most of those who do understand object because his statements and pictures are not always pleasant and sometimes *quite impossible.* But he exists not for praise, nor thinks of his readers. His only [goal is] to paint the scenes that pass before his eyes."

BIOGRAPHICAL/CRITICAL SOURCES:

BOOKS

Burleson, Donald, *H. P. Lovecraft: A Critical Study,* Greenwood Press, 1983.

Carter, Lin, *Lovecraft: A Look Behind the "Cthulhu Mythos,"* Ballantine, 1972.

Carter, Paul A., *The Creation of Tomorrow: Fifty Years of Magazine Science Fiction,* Columbia University Press, 1977.

Davis, Sonia H., *The Private Life of H. P. Lovecraft,* Necronomicon, 1985.

de Camp, L. Sprague, *Lovecraft: A Biography,* Doubleday, 1975.

Derleth, August, *H. P. L.: A Memoir,* Ben Abramson, 1945.

Faig, Kenneth W., Jr., *H. P. Lovecraft: His Life, His Work,* Necronomicon, 1979.

Hay, George, editor, *The Necronomicon,* Neville Spearman, 1978.

Joshi, S. T., editor, *H. P. Lovecraft: Four Decades of Criticism,* Ohio University Press, 1980.

Joshi, S. T., *H. P. Lovecraft and Lovecraft Criticism: An Annotated Bibliography,* Kent State University Press, 1981.

Joshi, S. T., editor, *In Defense of Dagon,* Necronomicon, 1985.

Levy, Maurice, *Lovecraft: A Study in the Fantastic,* translated by Joshi, Wayne State University Press, 1988.

Long, Frank Belknap, *Howard Phillips Lovecraft: Dreamer on the Nightside,* Arkham, 1975.

Lovecraft, H. P., *Supernatural Horror in Literature,* introduction by August Derleth, Ben Abramson, 1945.

Lovecraft, H. P., *The Dream Quest of Unknown Kadath,* edited by Lin Carter, Ballantine, 1970.

Schweitzer, Darrell, *The Dream Quest of H. P. Lovecraft,* Borgo Press, 1978.

Schweitzer, Darrell, editor, *Discovering H. P. Lovecraft,* Starmont House, 1987.

Short Story Criticism, Gale, Volume 3, 1989.

Twentieth Century Literary Criticism, Gale, Volume 4, 1981, Volume 22, 1987.

Wilson, Colin, *The Strength to Dream: Literature and the Imagination,* Houghton, 1962.

PERIODICALS

Chicago Tribune, October 25, 1985.
Lovecraft Studies, spring, 1986.
Times Literary Supplement, March 26, 1976.
Village Voice, March 19, 1985.
Washington Post, February 17, 1975, October 25, 1985.
Whispers, December, 1976.

—*Sketch by Janice E. Drane*

*   *   *

LOVELACE, Earl   1935-

PERSONAL: Born in 1935 in Trinidad; married.

ADDRESSES: c/o Andre Deutsch, 105 Great Russel St., London WC1B 3LJ, England.

CAREER: Novelist, playwright, and short story writer. Has also worked as an agricultural assistant for the Jamaican Civil Service.

AWARDS, HONORS: British Petroleum Independence Award, 1965, for *While Gods Are Falling.*

WRITINGS:

While Gods Are Falling (novel), Collins, 1965, Regnery, 1966.
The Schoolmaster (novel), Regnery, 1968.

The Wine of Astonishment, Heinemann, 1982.
Jestina's Calypso and Other Plays, Heinemann, 1984.
The New Hardware Store (play), produced in the West End, March, 1985.
Brief Conversion and Other Stories, Heinemann, 1988.

Also author of *The Dragon Can't Dance,* 1979.

SIDELIGHTS: Earl Lovelace's *The Schoolmaster,* a novel about the building of a school in the remote Trinidad village of Kumaca, was reviewed by Martin Levin in the *New York Times Book Review:* "*The Schoolmaster* is a folk fable with the clean, elemental structure of Steinbeck's *The Pearl.* But unlike *The Pearl,* Mr. Lovelace tells his story from the inside looking out, using the unsophisticated accents of everyday speech to lead to a Homeric conclusion." Levin added that Lovelace is a "writer of elegant skills, with an infectious sensitivity to the heady Caribbean atmosphere."

BIOGRAPHICAL/CRITICAL SOURCES:

BOOKS

Contemporary Literary Criticism, Volume 51, Gale, 1989.

PERIODICALS

New Statesman, January 5, 1968.
New York Times Book Review, October 30, 1966, November 24, 1968.
Times (London), March 12, 1985.

*   *   *

LOVESEY, Peter (Harmer)   1936-
(Peter Lear)

PERSONAL: Born September 10, 1936, in Whitton, Middlesex, England; son of Richard Lear (a bank official) and Amy (Strank) Lovesey; married Jacqueline Ruth Lewis, May 30, 1959; children: Kathleen Ruth, Philip Lear. *Education:* University of Reading, B.A. (honors), 1958.

ADDRESSES: Agent—John Farquharson Ltd., 162-168 Regent St., London W1R 5TB, England.

CAREER: Thurrock Technical College, Grays, Essex, England, senior lecturer, 1961-69; Hammersmith College for Further Education, London, England, head of general education department, 1969-75; currently full-time writer. *Military service:* Royal Air Force, 1958-61; served as education officer; became flying officer.

MEMBER: Crime Writers' Association, Writers Guild, Detection Club.

AWARDS, HONORS: Macmillan/Panther First Crime Novel award, 1970, for *Wobble to Death;* Silver Dagger, 1979, and Gold Dagger, 1983, both from Crime Writers' Association; Grand Prix de Litterature Policiere, 1985; Prix du Roman d'Adventures, 1986; Veuve Clicquot/Crime Writers Association Short Story Award, 1986.

WRITINGS:

CRIME NOVELS

Wobble to Death (Sergeant Cribb mystery), Dodd, 1970.
The Detective Wore Silk Drawers (Sergeant Cribb mystery), Dodd, 1971.
Abracadaver (Sergeant Cribb mystery), Dodd, 1972.
Mad Hatter's Holiday: A Novel of Murder in Victorian Brighton (Sergeant Cribb mystery), Dodd, 1973.

Invitation to a Dynamite Party (Sergeant Cribb mystery), Macmillan, 1974, published as *The Tick of Death,* Dodd, 1974.
A Case of Spirits (Sergeant Cribb mystery), Dodd, 1975.
Swing, Swing Together (Sergeant Cribb mystery), Dodd, 1976.
Waxwork (Sergeant Cribb mystery), Pantheon, 1978.
The False Inspector Dew, Pantheon, 1982.
Keystone, Pantheon, 1983.
Rough Cider, Bodley Head, 1986, Mysterious Press, 1987.
Bertie and the Tinman, Mysterious Press, 1988.
On the Edge, Mysterious Press, 1989.

NONFICTION

The Kings of Distance: A Study of Five Great Runners, Eyre & Spottiswoode, 1968, published as *Five Kings of Distance,* St. Martin's Press, 1981.
(With Tom McNab) *The Guide to British Track and Field Literature 1275-1968,* Athletics Arena (London), 1969.
The Official Centenary History of the Amateur Athletic Association, Guinness Superlatives (London), 1979.

CONTRIBUTOR

Virginia Whitaker, editor, *Winter's Crimes 5,* St. Martin's Press, 1973.
Dilys Winn, editor, *Murder Ink: The Mystery Reader's Companion,* Workman, 1977.
Hilary Watson, editor, *Winter's Crimes 10,* St. Martin's Press, 1978.
John Waite, editor, *Mystery Guild Anthology,* Constable, 1980.
Edward D. Hoch, editor, *Best Detective Stories of the Year 1981,* Dutton, 1981.
Watson, editor, *Winter's Crimes 14,* St. Martin's Press, 1982.
Josh Pachter, editor, *Top Crime,* St. Martin's Press, 1983.
George Hardinge, editor, *Winter's Crimes 15,* St. Martin's Press, 1983.
Herbert Harris, editor, *John Creasey's Crime Collection, 1983,* St. Martin's Press, 1983.
Hardinge, editor, *Winter's Crimes 17,* St. Martin's Press, 1985.
Harris, editor, *John Creasey's Crime Collection, 1985,* St. Martin's Press, 1985.
Hardinge, editor, *The Best of Winter's Crimes,* St. Martin's Press, 1986.
Harris, editor, *John Creasey's Crime Collection, 1986,* St. Martin's Press, 1986.
Hoch, editor, *The Year's Best Mystery and Suspense Stories, 1986,* Walker, 1986.
Hilary Hale, editor, *Winter's Crimes 19,* St. Martin's Press, 1987.
Harris, editor, *John Creasey's Crime Collection, 1987,* St. Martin's Press, 1987.
Martin H. Greenberg and Carol-Lynn Waugh, editors, *The New Adventures of Sherlock Holmes,* Carroll & Graf, 1987.
Hale, editor, *Winter's Crimes 20,* St. Martin's Press, 1988.
Harris, editor, *John Creasey's Crime Collection, 1988,* St. Martin's Press, 1988.

OTHER

(Under pseudonym Peter Lear) *Goldengirl,* Cassell, 1977, Doubleday, 1978.
(Under pseudonym Peter Lear) *Spider Girl,* Viking, 1980.
Butchers and Other Stories of Crime (short stories), Macmillan (London), 1985, Mysterious Press, 1987.
(Under pseudonym Peter Lear) *The Secret of Spandau,* Michael Joseph, 1986.

Also author with wife, Jacqueline Ruth Lovesey, of "Sergeant Cribb" teleplays for Granada television and the Public Broadcasting Service's "Mystery!" program, including "The Last Trumpet," "Murder, Old Boy?," "Something Old, Something New," "The Horizontal Witness," and "The Choir That Wouldn't Sing." Contributor to periodicals, including *Armchair Detective, Ellery Queen's Mystery Magazine, Harper's,* and *Company.*

SIDELIGHTS: Peter Lovesey's interest in sport led him to write his prize-winning first Victorian crime novel *Wobble to Death.* He told Diana Cooper-Clark in the *Armchair Detective,* "At this time, I didn't regard myself as an authority or expert on the Victorian period. But I had become interested in Victorian sport as a school boy because I wasn't a very good athlete and would have liked to have been. I was flat-footed and butter-fingered and couldn't really perform very well in any team game, so I tried to take up the more individual sports, like high jumping." While researching the life of an American Indian athlete, he found a description of the Victorian "wobble," a walking endurance contest. Later, while "perusing the personals columns of the [London] *Times* as Sherlock Holmes used to do," he states, he discovered an advertisement for a crime novel contest. *Wobble to Death* was the result.

Wobble to Death is the first of a series of novels featuring Detective Sergeant Cribb and his assistant Constable Thackeray. Critics have praised these books for their authentic evocation of Victorian atmosphere and restrained characterization. Lovesey explains to Cooper-Clark: "I was looking in *Wobble to Death* for a realistic Victorian detective. I was conscious that the great detectives were super figures, the omniscient Sherlock Holmes, the sophisticated Lord Peter Wimsey, and even Hercule Poirot, with the little grey cells. These were not really for me. I wanted somebody who would have to struggle to solve a crime and have to work against the limitations of the period." Marcel Berlins of the London *Times* states: "Peter Lovesey has written eight [Sergeant Cribb] detective novels set in late Victorian times, and not one has fallen short on factual accuracy or ratiocinative skill. . . . Mr. Lovesey's strength is to place those subdued characters into a meticulously researched historical reality, and produce a supremely satisfying novel of detection." All eight novels featuring Cribb and Thackeray proved very popular. They were adapted and broadcast in America on the Public Broadcasting Service's "Mystery!" program, and Lovesey later collaborated with his wife Jacqueline to produce six new "Sergeant Cribb" stories for the series.

Besides his "Sergeant Cribb" novels Lovesey has written detective fiction set in a variety of other times and places. He left the Victorian period for *The False Inspector Dew,* bringing his evocative talents to a 1920s transatlantic cruise. A reviewer for the London *Times* reports, "Lovesey has researched his setting not merely just enough to have plenty of local colour to push in when there's some excuse, but so thoroughly that he had at his fingertips a dozen facts to choose from at any instant." This, along with a gripping story line, the reviewer adds, is part of "the charge that powers his book." Other stories include *Keystone,* a mystery set in Hollywood just before the First World War, which involves the Keystone Kops and many of the period's actors, and *Rough Cider,* a novel of psychological suspense.

More recently Lovesey has returned to the Victorian era with *Bertie and the Tinman.* This time the author features a rather unusual detective—Albert Edward, Prince of Wales, Queen Victoria's son and heir, who later became Edward VII of England. Bertie, as he is known to his intimates, tells the story of the apparent suicide of his favorite jockey Fred Archer, popularly known as the Tinman. Doubting that Archer was suicidal, the Prince becomes suspicious and launches a personal investigation that takes him all over Victorian London, from the coarsest fleshpots to the most elegant salons. "The rueful, candid voice [Lovesey] gives to the fleshy prince rings true," declares *Time* magazine contributor William A. Henry III, "the details of the horse-racing and music-hall worlds are vivid, and much of the tale is sweetly funny." "This is an affectionate look at Prince Albert, a likable chap even with his pomposities and one-sided view of life," reports Newgate Callendar in the *New York Times Book Review.* "And the race-track scenes and backgrounds crackle with authenticity. There is a great deal of humor in the book, even a strong dash of P. G. Wodehouse. 'Bertie and the Tinman' is a delightful romp."

MEDIA ADAPTATIONS: Peter Lovesey's *Goldengirl,* written under the pseudonym Peter Lear, was filmed by the Avco Embassy Pictures Corp. in 1979. It starred James Coburn as Dryden, the shrewd sports agent, and Susan Anton as Goldengirl, the woman bred to win three gold medals in track events at the 1980 Moscow Olympics. Lovesey's "Sergeant Cribb" novels were filmed for Granada Television and broadcast in America by the Public Broadcasting Service (PBS-TV) on its "Mystery!" program, 1980-82, featuring Alan Dobie as Sergeant Cribb and William Simons as Constable Thackeray.

BIOGRAPHICAL/CRITICAL SOURCES:

BOOKS

Barnes, Melvin, *Murder in Print: A Guide to Two Centuries of Crime Fiction,* Barn Owl Books, 1986.
Benstock, Bernard, editor, *Art in Crime Writing,* St. Martin's Press, 1983.
Burack, Sylvia K., *Writing Mystery and Crime Fiction,* The Writer, 1985.
Carr, John C., *The Craft of Crime: Conversations with Crime Writers,* Houghton, 1983.
Cooper-Clark, Diana, *Designs of Darkness: Interviews with Detective Novelists,* Bowling Green State University Popular Press, 1983.
Dove, George N., and Earl F. Bargainner, *Cops and Constables: American and British Fictional Policemen,* Bowling Green State University Popular Press, 1986.
Keating, H. R. F., *Crime and Mystery: The One Hundred Best Books,* Carroll & Graf, 1987.

PERIODICALS

Armchair Detective, summer, 1981.
New Republic, March 3, 1982.
Newsweek, July 3, 1978, April 5, 1982.
New York Times, June 15, 1979, October 14, 1983.
New York Times Book Review, October 25, 1970, October 15, 1972, February 15, 1976, May 28, 1978, October 3, 1982.
Publishers Weekly, October 25, 1985.
Saturday Review, October 28, 1972.
Spectator, March 28, 1970, April 10, 1982.
Times (London), March 1, 1980, March 18, 1982, December 31, 1987.
Times Literary Supplement, April 9, 1970, June 25, 1982.
Washington Post Book World, September 17, 1972, May 16, 1982, March 20, 1988.

*   *   *

LOWE, Henry Paget
  See LOVECRAFT, H(oward) P(hillips)

LOWELL, Robert (Traill Spence, Jr.) 1917-1977

PERSONAL: Born March 1, 1917, in Boston, Mass.; died of congestive heart failure, September 12, 1977, in New York, N.Y.; buried in Dumbarton, N.H.; son of Robert Traill Spence (a naval officer) and Charlotte (Winslow) Lowell; married Jean Stafford (a writer), April 2, 1940 (divorced June, 1948); married Elizabeth Hardwick (a writer), July 28, 1949 (divorced, 1972); married Caroline Blackwood (a writer), 1972; children: (second marriage) Harriet Winslow; (third marriage) Robert Sheridan. *Education:* Attended St. Marks School; attended Harvard University, 1935-37; Kenyon College, A.B. (summa cum laude), 1940; additional study at Louisiana State University, 1940-41.

ADDRESSES: Home—Neilgate Park, Bearsted, Maidstone, Kent, England.

CAREER: Poet, writer, and translator. Sheed & Ward, New York, N.Y., editorial assistant, 1941-42; Library of Congress, Washington, D.C., consultant in poetry, 1947-48. Taught at State University of Iowa (now Iowa State University), 1950 and 1953, Kenyon School of Letters, 1950 and 1953, Salzburg Seminar on American Studies (Salzburg, Austria), 1952, University of Cincinnati, 1954, Boston University, 1956, Harvard University, 1958, 1963-70, 1975, and 1977, New School for Social Research, 1961-62, University of Essex (Wivenhoe, Colchester, England), 1970-72, and Kent University (Canterbury, England), 1970-75. Writer in residence, Yale University, 1967. Visiting fellow, All Souls College, Oxford, 1970. *Wartime activity:* Conscientious objector, World War II; served a prison term as a result, 1943-44.

MEMBER: National Academy and Institute of Arts and Letters, American Academy of Arts and Letters, Phi Beta Kappa.

AWARDS, HONORS: National Institute of Arts and Letters Award, 1947; Guggenheim fellowship, 1947; Pulitzer Prize, 1947, for *Lord Weary's Castle;* Harriet Monroe Poetry Award, University of Chicago, 1952; Guinness Poetry Award (Ireland; shared with W. H. Auden, Edith Sitwell, and Edwin Muir), 1959, for "Skunk Hour"; National Book Award, 1960, for *Life Studies;* Boston Arts Festival Poet, 1960; Harriet Monroe Memorial Prize, *Poetry,* 1961; Bollingen Prize in Poetry for translation, Yale University Library, 1962, for *Imitations;* Levinson Prize, *Poetry,* 1963; Golden Rose Trophy, New England Poetry Club, 1964; Obie Award for best new play, *Village Voice,* 1965, for "The Old Glory"; Sarah Josepha Hale Award, Friends of the Richards Library, 1966; National Council on the Arts grant, 1967, to produce "Prometheus Bound"; Copernicus Award, Academy of American Poets, 1974; Pulitzer Prize, 1974, for *The Dolphin;* National Medal for Literature, National Academy and Institute of Arts and Letters, 1977; National Book Critics Circle Award, 1978, for *Day by Day,* and posthumous nomination (in criticism), 1987, for *Collected Prose;* Litt.D., Williams College, 1965, and Yale University, 1968; honorary degree, Columbia University, 1969.

WRITINGS:

POETRY

Land of Unlikeness, introduction by Allen Tate, Cummington Press (Cummington, Mass.), 1944, reprinted, University Microfilms (Ann Arbor, Mich.), 1971.
Lord Weary's Castle (also see below), Harcourt, 1946, reprinted, 1985.
Poems, 1938-1949, Faber, 1950, reprinted, 1987.
The Mills of the Kavanaughs (also see below), Harcourt, 1951.

Life Studies (also see below), Farrar, Straus & Cudahy, 1959, 2nd edition published with prose memoir "91 Revere Street," Faber, 1968.

Lord Weary's Castle [and] *The Mills of the Kavanaughs,* Meridian Books, 1961, reprinted, Harcourt, 1979.

For the Union Dead (also see below), Farrar, Straus, 1964.

Nathaniel Hawthorne, 1804-1864 (limited edition keepsake of centenary commemoration of Hawthorne's death), Ohio State University Press, 1964.

Selected Poems, Faber, 1965, reprinted, 1986.

The Achievement of Robert Lowell: A Comprehensive Selection of His Poems, edited and introduced by William J. Martz, Scott, Foresman, 1966.

Life Studies [and] *For the Union Dead,* Noonday, 1967.

Near the Ocean (also see below), drawings by Sidney Nolan, Farrar, Straus, 1967.

4, privately printed limited edition by Laurence Scott (Cambridge, Mass.), 1969.

R. F. K., 1925-1968, privately printed limited edition, 1969.

Notebook 1967-1968, Farrar, Straus, 1969, 3rd edition revised and expanded as *Notebook,* 1970.

Fuer die Toten der Union (English with German translations; contains poetry from *Life Studies, Near the Ocean,* and *For the Union Dead*), Suhrkamp (Frankfort on the Main), 1969.

Poems de Robert Lowell (English with Spanish translations), Editorial Sudamericana (Buenos Aires), 1969.

Poesie, 1940-1970 (English with Italian translations), Longanesi (Milan), 1972.

History (also see below), Farrar, Straus, 1973.

For Lizzie and Harriet (also see below), Farrar, Straus, 1973.

The Dolphin (also see below), Farrar, Straus, 1973.

Robert Lowell's Poems: A Selection, edited and introduced, with notes, by Jonathan Raban, Faber, 1974.

Selected Poems, Farrar, Straus, 1976, revised edition, Noonday, 1977.

Ein Fischnetz aus teerigem Garn zu knuepfen: Robert Lowell (English with German translations; contains poems from *Lord Weary's Castle, Life Studies, For the Union Dead, Near the Ocean, History, The Dolphin,* and *For Lizzie and Harriet*), Verlag Volk und Welt (Berlin), 1976.

Day by Day, Farrar, Straus, 1977.

A Poem, Menhaden Press (Vermillion, S.D.), 1980.

DRAMA

The Old Glory (trilogy; contains "Endecott and the Red Cross" [also see below] and "My Kinsman, Major Molineux," both based on short stories by Nathaniel Hawthorne, and "Benito Cereno" [also see below], based on a novella by Herman Melville; first produced Off-Broadway at the American Place Theatre, November 1, 1964), introduction by Robert Brustein, director's note by Jonathan Miller, Farrar, Straus, 1965, revised edition, 1968.

Prometheus Bound: Derived from Aeschylus (first produced by Yale School of Drama, May 9, 1967; produced Off-Broadway at Mermaid Theatre, June 24, 1971), Farrar, Straus, 1969, reprinted, 1987.

Endecott and the Red Cross (revised and expanded version of one-act play of the same title; first produced in New York City by the American Place Theatre at St. Clements Episcopal Church, May, 1968), American Place Theatre, 1968.

Benito Cereno (English with Italian translation), edited and introduced by Rolando Anzilotti, All'insegna del pesce d'oro (Milan), 1969.

TRANSLATOR

Eugenio Montale, *Poesie de Montale,* Laterna (Bologna), 1960.

(And editor) *Imitations* (versions of poems by Homer, Sappho, Rainer Maria Rilke, Francois Villon, Stephane Mallarme, Charles-Pierre Baudelaire, and others; mimeographed typescript entitled *Imitations: A Book of Free Translations by Robert Lowell for Elizabeth Bishop* privately circulated before publication, c. 1960), Farrar, Straus & Cudahy, 1961.

(With Jacques Barzun) Jean Baptiste Racine and Pierre Beaumarchais, *Phaedra and Figaro* (also see below; Beaumarchais's *Figaro* translated by Barzun; Racine's *Phaedra* translated by Lowell), Farrar, Straus & Cudahy, 1961.

Phaedra, Faber, 1963, Octagon Books, 1971.

The Voyage, and Other Versions of Poems by Baudelaire, illustrations by Sidney Nolan, Farrar, Straus, 1968.

The Oresteia of Aeschylus (contains "Agamemnon," "Orestes," and "The Furies"), Farrar, Straus, 1978.

OTHER

(Author of introduction) Nathaniel Hawthorne, *Pegasus, the Winged Horse,* Macmillan, 1963.

(Author of introductions with Kenneth Rexroth) Ford Madox Ford, *Buckshee* (poems), Pym-Randall Press, 1966.

(Author of appreciation) Randall Jarrell, *The Lost World,* Collier, 1966.

(Editor with Peter Taylor and Robert Penn Warren) *Randall Jarrell, 1914-1965* (essays), Farrar, Straus, 1967, reprinted, Noonday, 1985.

The Poetry of Robert Lowell (sound recording of reading at Y.M.-Y.W.H.A. Poetry Center in New York City, 1968), Jeffrey Norton, 1974.

Robert Lowell: A Reading (sound recording of reading at Poetry Center of the 92nd Street "Y" in New York City, December 8, 1976), Caedmon, 1978.

Robert Lowell Reading His Own Poems (sound recording of Twentieth-Century Poetry in English series), Library of Congress, 1978.

Collected Prose, edited and introduced by Robert Giroux, Farrar, Straus, 1987.

Contributor to numerous anthologies. Contributor to periodicals, including *Kenyon Review, New Republic, New World Writing, New York Review of Books, Observer, Partisan Review, Salmagundi,* and *Sewanee Review.*

SIDELIGHTS: Robert Lowell is best known for his volume *Life Studies,* but his true greatness as an American poet lies in the astonishing variety of his work. In the 1940s he wrote intricate and tightly patterned poems that incorporated traditional meter and rhyme; in the late 1950s when he published *Life Studies,* he began to write startlingly original personal or "confessional" poetry in much looser forms and meters; in the 1960s he wrote increasingly public poetry; and finally in the 1970s he created poems that incorporated and extended elements of all the earlier poetry. Meanwhile he also produced a volume of translations he called "imitations" and wrote or translated several plays. Lowell had a profound interest in history and politics; in his poetry he juxtaposed self and history in ways that illuminated both. His art and his life were inseparably intertwined, and he believed firmly in the identity of self and language.

In "After Enjoying Six or Seven Essays on Me," a 1977 *Salmagundi* essay, Lowell wrote that "looking over my *Selected Poems,* about thirty years of writing, my impression is that the thread that strings it together is my autobiography." His poetry and "91 Revere Street," the prose sketch that forms an important part of

Life Studies, give glimpse after glimpse into the world of his childhood. He was born on March 1, 1917, into a home dominated by the incessant tension between his ineffectual father and his imperious mother. His father was a member of the famous Lowell family of Massachusetts, and his mother's prominent family, the Winslows, dated, like the Lowells, back to the early days of New England. The young Lowell felt acutely the strains of his childhood, and both his immediate family and his Puritan forebears would figure largely in his poetry.

In "91 Revere Street," Lowell described his experiences at the Brimmer Street School in Boston; he later attended preparatory school at St. Mark's in Southborough, Massachusetts, and then, briefly, Harvard University. But while he was a student at Harvard in 1937, he had a fight with his father and left home, a rebellion that had serious consequences for his life and his poetry. Lowell went south to the Tennessee home of poet Allen Tate, who proved to be an important influence on the young writer; in a 1961 *Paris Review* interview with Frederick Seidel, Lowell gave this account of his arrival at the Tate home: "Mrs. Tate . . . had three guests and her own family, and was doing the cooking and writing a novel. And this young man arrived, quite ardent and eccentric. I think I suggested that maybe I'd stay with them. And they said, 'We really haven't any room, you'd have to pitch a tent on the lawn.' So I went to Sears Roebuck and got a tent and rigged it on their lawn. The Tates were too polite to tell me that what they'd said had been just a figure of speech. I stayed two months in my tent and ate with the Tates."

Lowell crammed much activity into the next few years. He followed Tate to Kenyon College in Ohio; received a degree in classics, summa cum laude; met Randall Jarrell and Peter Taylor, two writers who would remain his lifelong friends; converted to Roman Catholicism; married the fiction writer Jean Stafford; refused induction into the armed forces; and served five months in jail as a conscientious objector. And during all this time, Lowell was working on the poems that would be published in *Land of Unlikeness* and *Lord Weary's Castle.*

The title of *Land of Unlikeness,* as Jerome Mazzaro points out in *The Poetic Themes of Robert Lowell,* is taken from a quotation of Saint Bernard and refers to the human soul's unlikeness to God and unlikeness to its own past self. In this volume, according to Hugh B. Staples in *Robert Lowell: The First Twenty Years,* the poet "appears so horrified by the spectacle of contemporary chaos that he can scarcely bring himself to comment on it in realistic terms. Cut off from the sight of God, modern man wanders about in his Land of Unlikeness, driven by greed and cruelty." But, as Mazzaro shows, some images of salvation also operate in these poems, images usually based on the figure of Mary or related in some other way to Roman Catholic beliefs.

Many of the poems in *Land of Unlikeness* appear as well in Lowell's second volume, *Lord Weary's Castle,* and the two books address the same concerns. Staples says that in these poems "the conflicts . . . remain unresolved, and the theme of rebellion remains dominant." Randall Jarrell declares in an essay collected in *Poetry and the Age* that these poems "understand the world as a sort of conflict of opposites. In this struggle one opposite is that cake of custom in which all of us lie embedded. . . . Into this realm of necessity the poems push everything that is closed, turned inward, incestuous, that blinds or binds: the Old Law, imperialism, militarism, capitalism, Calvinism, Authority, the Father, the 'proper Bostonians,' the rich who will 'do everything for the poor except get off their backs.' But struggling within this like leaven, falling to it like light, is everything that is free or open, that grows or is willing to change: . . . this is the realm of freedom, of the Grace that has replaced the Law, of the perfect liberator whom the poet calls Christ."

Lord Weary's Castle, with its blending of oppositions to war, to the Puritan ethic, and to materialism and greed, is Lowell's finest early volume, one that earned him the Pulitzer Prize in 1947. But his next book, *The Mills of the Kavanaughs,* was less successful. By the time of its publication in 1951, Lowell had been divorced from Jean Stafford, had left the Roman Catholic church, had suffered the first serious attack of the manic-depressive illness that was to plague him throughout his life, and had married the writer Elizabeth Hardwick. *The Mills of the Kavanaughs,* which consists of a series of dramatic monologues, reflects, like the other volumes, the turbulence of its writer's life.

Between the publication of *The Mills of the Kavanaughs* and the publication in 1959 of *Life Studies,* Lowell taught at several universities and made a speaking tour of the west coast, where he encountered the thematically and stylistically revolutionary poetry of Allen Ginsberg and the other "Beat" writers. He continued the friendship he had earlier begun with the poet William Carlos Williams, who as an innovator in language and forms began to have an important influence on his work. Lowell and Hardwick lived primarily in Boston during this time; the poet taught for several years at Boston University, and their daughter Harriet was born in 1957. During this period, Lowell continued to suffer attacks of mania and depression, and for a while found it difficult to write. "When I was working on *Life Studies,*" he revealed in his *Salmagundi* essay, "I found I had no language or meter that would allow me to approximate what I saw or remembered. Yet in prose I had already found what I wanted, the conventional style of autobiography and reminiscence. So I wrote my autobiographical poetry in a style I thought I had discovered in [French novelist Gustave] Flaubert, one that used images and ironic or amusing particulars. I did all kinds of tricks with meter and the avoidance of meter. . . . I didn't have to bang words into rhyme and count."

In an essay appearing in *Next-to-Last Things: New Poems and Essays,* Stanley Kunitz has called *Life Studies,* which won the 1960 National Book Award, "perhaps the most influential book of modern verse since [T. S. Eliot's] *The Waste Land.*" There is no question but that its so-called "confessional" poetry was something radically new in American literature. As Marjorie Perloff declares in *The Poetic Art of Robert Lowell,* this new poetry "is informal and autobiographical; its diction is casual and colloquial, its sound patterns tend to be almost prosaic." Discussing the important poem "Skunk Hour," Perloff says that the "One dark night" of that poem—"the painful moment of terror and anxiety that leads to a renewal of self-insight and understanding—this is the central experience that Lowell's self undergoes." Some readers were troubled by the personal nature of many of the poems in this volume; several of the works deal with Lowell's reminiscences of childhood and include often unflattering portraits of his parents and grandparents, while others deal with his marriage, his illness, and other aspects of his adult life. But *Life Studies,* very different from both his own earlier work and most of the verse being written in English by anyone else, had an enormous influence on the future of poetry in the United States.

In 1960, Lowell moved to New York, where he was to live for the next ten years; beginning in 1963 he commuted on a more or less regular basis to Harvard, where he taught intermittently until his death in 1977. In 1961, Lowell published two volumes, a verse translation called *Phaedra* of Racine's tragedy, and *Imitations,* a collection of loose translations of poems by writers from Homer to the contemporary Italian, Eugenio Montale. Although these volumes might appear to be a radical change from the personal poetry of *Life Studies,* Irvin Ehrenpreis says in an essay appearing in *American Poetry* that in *Imitations* Lowell "is legitimizing his progeny, replacing the Lowells and Winslows by [the poets Charles-Pierre] Baudelaire, [Arthur] Rimbaud, and [Rainer Maria] Rilke. In drawing up such a genealogical tree, Lowell . . . implies that he has found his essential identity not in a social class or in a religious communion but in his character as a writer."

With the publication in the mid-1960s of *The Old Glory* and *For the Union Dead,* Lowell returned to a consideration of the individual's relation to history, both in its personal and in its public dimensions. *The Old Glory* consists of three plays: "Endecott and the Red Cross" and "My Kinsman, Major Molineux," both adapted from short stories by Nathaniel Hawthorne, and "Benito Cereno," adapted from a novella by Herman Melville. In his introduction to the plays, Robert Brustein says that "Mr. Lowell feels the past working in his very bones. And it is his subtle achievement not only to have evoked this past, but also to have superimposed the present upon it, so that the plays manage to look forward and backward at the same time." All the plays incorporate some aspect of conflict between individuals and authority and thus look back to Lowell's earlier poetry, as well as outward to the political turmoil of the 1960s.

In a *Salmagundi* essay Thomas Parkinson declares, "The person in history is the main subject" of *For the Union Dead,* "and it is good to see poetry treating the moment where person and history meet." In an essay collected in Jonathan Price's *Critics on Robert Lowell,* Richard Poirier agrees: "It is nearly impossible in Lowell's poetry to separate personal breakdown from the poet's visions of public or historical decline. . . . The assurance that the poet's most private experiences simply are of historical, even mythical, importance" gives this poetry "an extraordinary air of personal authority." Many of these poems are as personal as the works in *Life Studies,* but here they are anchored more firmly in the world outside the family, the world of history and myth. "More than any contemporary writer, poet or novelist," Poirier asserts, "Lowell has created the language, cool and violent all at once, of contemporary introspection. He is our truest historian."

Of *For the Union Dead,* Lowell said in "After Reading Six or Seven Essays on Me" that "free verse subjects seemed to melt away, and I found myself back in strict meter, yet tried to avoid the symbols and heroics of my first books." In his next collection, *Near the Ocean,* he wrote a long sequence in eight-line four-foot couplet stanzas, a form he borrowed from the seventeenth-century English poet Andrew Marvell; "God knows why, except that it seemed fit to handle national events," Lowell remarked in the same essay. The publication of *Near the Ocean* coincided with the period of Lowell's most active involvement in national events. He protested against United States involvement in Vietnam, and in fact appears as a character in Norman Mailer's *The Armies of the Night,* an account of the historic protest march on the Pentagon in 1967.

Besides his books of poetry, Lowell continued in the late 1960s to write for the theater. The revised edition of *The Old Glory* was published in 1968, with most of the revisions appearing in "Endecott and the Red Cross." "What I have added are mostly Indians," Lowell said, only partly in jest, in his note on the revised edition. "It has been lengthened to give it substance," and "innumerable lines have been 'improved' to be stronger, to be quieter, less in character, more in character." His translation of Aeschylus's *Prometheus Bound* also appeared during this period; Lowell's is a prose version of the myth of this famous rebel.

In 1969 Lowell also published the first of what would become a series of volumes of sonnets. "For six years I wrote unrhymed blank verse sonnets," he recalled in his *Salmagundi* essay. "They had the eloquence at best of iambic pentameter, and often the structure and climaxes of sonnets. . . . I had a chance such as I had never had before, or probably will again, to snatch up and verse the marvelous varieties of the moment." Lowell's plan, says Steven Gould Axelrod in *Robert Lowell: Life and Art,* was "to achieve the balance of freedom and order, discontinuity and continuity, that he observed in [Wallace] Stevens's late long poems and in John Berryman's *Dream Songs,* then nearing completion. He hoped that his form . . . would enable him 'to describe the immediate instant,' an instant in which political and personal happenings interacted with a lifetime's accumulation of memories, dreams, and knowledge. In his 'jagged' yet unified poem Lowell sought to create nothing less than an epic of his own consciousness."

In his "Afterthought" to *Notebook 1967-1968,* the first version of this epic, Lowell explained that "the poems in this book are written as one poem." The plot, he said, "rolls with the seasons": "The time is a summer, an autumn, a winter, a spring, another summer; here the poem ends, except for turned-back bits of fall and winter 1968. I have flashbacks to what I remember, and notes on old history." Axelrod, who sees Lowell's political activism as the "motive and thematic center" for this volume, suggests that the "real subject" of the volume is "the human lust for violence and the moral horror of violence, a polarity Lowell has long detected in his own character and which he now discerns on a massive scale throughout human history." In the course of the volume, Axelrod continues, Lowell "obsessively exposes the violent acts of 'the great,' among them Caligula, Mohammed, Henry VIII, Marie Antoinette, Napoleon, Frederick the Great, the Russian Czars, Lenin, Stalin, Mao, the Indian killers, Andrew Jackson, Truman, an unnamed 'leader of the left,' and the book's darkest villain, Adolf Hitler."

But these sonnets are full of personal history as well, and this history is equally bleak. Axelrod suggests that in the next volume of sonnets, *Notebook,* which consists largely of revised and rearranged versions of the poems in *Notebook 1967-1968,* "the theme of Lowell's increasingly troubled domestic life" comes to the fore, while the political emphasis is somewhat muted. He continues to juxtapose personal and public history, however, and jumbles together in the volume and in individual poems his friends, his family, historical figures, writers, artists, and characters from literature and myth. In the eight sonnets that make up the "Charles River" sequence, for example, he refers, among other subjects, to his parents, his first love, Massachusetts Institute of Technology, Harvard, industrial pollution, Milton's "Lycidas," the *Anschluss,* Nero, Christ, French painter Claude Lorrain, miscellaneous Greeks, aqueducts and arches, a snow-yellow knife with eleven blades, and plowshares beaten into swords. He conflates the particular and the general, the fresh and the hackneyed, the present and the past into an amalgam of poetry that ranges in quality from outstanding to outrageous.

In 1970 Lowell moved to England, where he spent most of his next six years; for two of these years he taught at Essex University, although he also returned to Harvard for one semester each year. The British had been favorably disposed to Lowell's poetry from the beginning; indeed, the British publisher Faber & Faber brought out editions of Lowell's poetry throughout his career, and in 1962 had published Staples's *Robert Lowell,* the first important critical book on the poet. Lowell's move to England was in part a result of continuing personal and domestic turmoil; in 1972 he divorced Elizabeth Hardwick and married British writer Caroline Blackwood, with whom he had a son, Robert Sheridan Lowell.

Among the three volumes of poetry published by Lowell in 1973, two are made up primarily of poems from *Notebook.* *For Lizzie and Harriet* is a slender volume reprinting *Notebook* sonnets that deal with Lowell's personal life, while *History,* as its title suggests, is more ambitious in scope. For *History,* Lowell added some new sonnets and revised and rearranged the old ones; the result is a much more coherent volume, arranged in the chronology of historical time. In this book, Axelrod says, Lowell downplays the once-dominant theme of political revolt and "expunges the theme of married love from the poem entirely. Instead, he expands upon two of the minor themes of the preceding volumes, making them central to his new conception"—the theme of death and the theme of art. "Art, the triumph of consciousness, counters death, the cessation of consciousness," Axelrod declares, but, as the critic notes, "Lowell suffers from no illusion that art affords immortality; rather he views art as proof of existence and means of creating identity. Throughout his career he has struggled to close the gap between life and artwork, and in *History* the two have finally joined." This volume, says Axelrod, "seeks to reveal not the truth of the past but the truth of Lowell's mind as it meditates upon the past in terms of its inmost concerns."

Although *The Dolphin,* the third volume of Lowell's poetry published in 1973, was like the others in that it consisted of a series of sonnets, these sonnets were all new. In *Robert Lowell: An Introduction to the Poetry,* Mark Rudman observes that this book "charts a year, from summer to summer. The plot, such as it is, revolves around the breakup with his wife, Elizabeth Hardwick, and his relationship with Caroline Blackwood." Calling the volume "half memoir" and "half fiction," Axelrod says that "it is a book of changes, not only of 'changing marriages' but of changing minds (Lowell's, Caroline's, Lizzie's) and changing lives. On this level *The Dolphin* is about human freedom and growth. And it is supremely a poem about love, love that makes freedom meaningful, love that allows for human growth. The figure of love in the poem is Caroline, the dolphin and mermaid. . . . In the largest sense Caroline as dolphin stands for Lowell's loving relationship to the universe. His opening himself to her represents his opening to the world outside himself; his physical and spiritual union with her represents his union with his world. His love for the dolphin brings him to earth and rescues his life."

Critical reception of *The Dolphin* was mixed, with some readers objecting strenuously to Lowell's use of language taken directly from the personal letters of Elizabeth Hardwick. But the volume is not simply a collection of poems about family turmoil; Axelrod finds a second subject of *The Dolphin* to be "the process of the poem itself. As Lowell tells his love story, he simultaneously meditates upon his consciousness, which through invention and intense perception becomes imagination, which in turn through inspired craft becomes art. On this level the poem explores the interrelationship of being, consciousness, and art." Although some critics found the poetry unsatisfying, *The Dolphin* was awarded the 1974 Pulitzer Prize for poetry.

After the flurry of sonnets that culminated in the publication of the three 1973 volumes, collections of Lowell's poems appeared in England (*Robert Lowell's Poems: A Selection*) and in the United States (*Selected Poems*). Lowell's translation of *The Oresteia of Aeschylus* would not be published until 1978, but his last

volume of new poetry, *Day by Day,* appeared shortly before he died on September 12, 1977. With this volume, Lowell abandoned the sonnet form and returned to free verse. He returned as well for a last look at many of the situations and people whom he had incorporated into his earlier poetry. *Day by Day,* which won the National Book Critics Circle Award in 1978, is an elegiac and deeply personal volume that discusses Lowell's family and friends, his wives and children, the horrors of his illness and the joys of his recoveries. As J. D. McClatchy observes in the *American Poetry Review,* the poems are like a series of snapshots—quick glimpses of past and present moments.

In a note prefacing his *Selected Poems,* Lowell remarked that "my verse autobiography sometimes fictionalizes plot and particular"; by labeling his poems "verse autobiography," he called attention to the inseparable relation between his life and his art. At the end of his life he left England and Caroline Blackwood and returned to the United States and Elizabeth Hardwick. After his death from congestive heart failure his funeral was held at the Episcopal Church of the Advent on Brimmer Street, in Boston, near where he had lived and gone to school as a child; he was buried in the cemetery where generations of his family had been buried. Thus he returned to his beginnings in his life as well as in his poetry.

Lowell said in the "Afterthought" to *Notebook 1967-1968* that "in truth I seem to have felt mostly the joys of living; in remembering, in recording, thanks to the gift of the Muse, it is the pain." A poetry of scrupulous self-examination, Lowell's work, as Vereen M. Bell declares in *Robert Lowell: Nihilist as Hero,* "is identifiable by nothing so much as its chronic and eventually systematic pessimism"; indeed, says Bell, "whatever spirit of affirmation that we think we perceive in Lowell's work we must always suspect ourselves of projecting upon it." Furthermore, in *Pity the Monsters: The Political Vision of Robert Lowell,* Alan Williamson observes that "Lowell's vision of civilization—being a product both of the man he is and of the time he lives in—is particular, painful, and dark. It is redeemed neither by . . . faith that an adequate, if authoritarian, utopia may have existed in the past, nor by a revolutionary's faith that one can be abstractly yet accurately designed for the future. Consequently, Lowell must necessarily leave more questions of value, of cause and responsibility, of fundamental 'human nature' open to poetic inquiry than did his nearest predecessors. But it is this very appalling fundamentalness of Lowell's questions, combined with his honesty about historical terror, that make him a modern epic poet."

Lowell was an epic poet as well in the scope and greatness of his poetry. He addressed large questions, and he used a multiplicity of forms and styles in his continuing quest, which his friend Peter Taylor describes in a 1979 *Ploughshares* essay as a search for "a oneness in himself and a oneness in the world." "This is how he must always be remembered," Taylor says, "one moment playful to the point of violent provocation, the next in profound contemplation of the great mystery: What does life mean? What is it all about?"

BIOGRAPHICAL/CRITICAL SOURCES:

BOOKS

Anzilotti, Rolando, editor, *Robert Lowell: A Tribute,* Nistri-Lischi Editori (Pisa), 1979.

Axelrod, Steven Gould, *Robert Lowell: Life and Art,* Princeton University Press, 1978.

Axelrod, and Helen Deese, editors, *Robert Lowell: A Reference Guide,* G. K. Hall, 1982.

Axelrod and Deese, editors, *Robert Lowell: Essays on the Poetry,* Cambridge University Press, 1986.

Bell, Vereen M., *Robert Lowell: Nihilist as Hero,* Harvard University Press, 1983.

Berryman, John, *The Freedom of the Poet,* Farrar, Straus, 1976.

Bogan, Louise, *Selected Criticism: Prose and Poetry,* Noonday, 1955.

Breslin, James E. B., *From Modern to Contemporary: American Poetry, 1945-1965,* University of Chicago Press, 1984.

Brooks, Cleanth, and Robert Penn Warren, editors, *Conversations on the Craft of Poetry,* Holt, 1961.

Brustein, Robert, *Seasons of Discontent: Dramatic Opinions, 1959-1965,* Simon & Schuster, 1967.

Cambon, Glauco, *The Inclusive Flame: Studies in Modern American Poetry,* Indiana University Press, 1963.

Clurman, Harold, *The Naked Image: Observations on the Modern Theatre,* Macmillan, 1966.

Contemporary Authors Bibliographical Series, Volume 2: *American Poets,* Gale, 1986.

Contemporary Literary Criticism, Gale, Volume 1, 1973, Volume 2, 1974, Volume 3, 1975, Volume 4, 1975, Volume 5, 1976, Volume 8, 1978, Volume 9, 1978, Volume 11, 1979, Volume 15, 1980, Volume 37, 1986.

Cooper, Philip, *The Autobiographical Myth of Robert Lowell,* University of North Carolina Press, 1970.

Cosgrave, Patrick, *The Public Poetry of Robert Lowell,* Gollancz, 1970, Taplinger, 1972.

Crick, John, *Robert Lowell,* Oliver & Boyd, 1974.

Deutsch, Babette, *Poetry in Our Time,* Holt, 1952, revised edition, Doubleday, 1963.

Dictionary of Literary Biography, Volume 5: *American Poets since World War II,* Gale, 1980.

Dillard, R. H. W., George Garrett, and John Rees Moore, editors, *The Sounder Few: Essays from the Hollins Critic,* University of Georgia Press, 1971.

Donoghue, Denis, *Connoisseurs of Chaos: Ideas of Order in American Poetry,* Macmillan, 1965.

Ehrenpreis, Irvin, editor, *American Poetry,* St. Martin's, 1965.

Fein, Richard J., *Robert Lowell,* Twayne, 1970, 2nd edition, 1979.

Frankenberg, Lloyd, *Pleasure Dome: On Reading Modern Poetry,* Houghton, 1949.

Hamilton, Ian, *Robert Lowell: A Biography,* Random House, 1982.

Hungerford, Edward, editor, *Poets in Progress,* Northwestern University Press, 1962, new edition, 1967.

Jarrell, Randall, *Poetry and the Age,* Knopf, 1953, reprinted, Vintage, 1959.

Jarrell, *The Third Book of Criticism,* Farrar, Straus, 1969.

Kalstone, David, *Five Temperaments: Elizabeth Bishop, Robert Lowell, James Merrill, Adrienne Rich, John Ashbery,* Oxford University Press, 1977.

Kazin, Alfred, *Contemporaries,* Little, Brown, 1962.

Kazin, *New York Jew,* Knopf, 1978.

Kostelanetz, Richard, *On Contemporary Literature: An Anthology of Critical Essays on the Major Movements and Writers of Contemporary Literature,* Avon, 1964.

Kunitz, Stanley, *Next-to-Last Things: New Poems and Essays,* Atlantic Monthly, 1985.

London, Michael, and Robert Boyars, editors, *Robert Lowell: A Portrait of the Artist in His Time,* David Lewis, 1970.

Lowell, Robert, *Land of Unlikeness,* Cummington Press, 1944, reprinted, University Microfilms, 1971.

Lowell, *Lord Weary's Castle,* Harcourt, 1946, reprinted, 1985.

Lowell, *The Mills of the Kavanaughs,* Harcourt, 1951.

Lowell, *Life Studies,* Farrar, Straus & Cudahy, 1959, 2nd edition, Faber, 1968.

Lowell, *For the Union Dead,* Farrar, Straus, 1964.

Lowell, *Selected Poems,* Faber, 1965, reprinted, 1986.

Lowell, *The Old Glory,* introduction by Robert Brustein, Farrar, Straus, 1965, revised edition, 1968.

Lowell, *Near the Ocean,* Farrar, Straus, 1967.

Lowell, *Notebook 1967-1968,* Farrar, Straus, 1969, 3rd edition revised and expanded as *Notebook,* 1970.

Lowell, *History,* Farrar, Straus, 1973.

Lowell, *For Lizzie and Harriet,* Farrar, Straus, 1973.

Lowell, *The Dolphin,* Farrar, Straus, 1973.

Lowell, *Robert Lowell's Poems: A Selection,* Faber, 1974.

Lowell, *Selected Poems,* Farrar, Straus, 1976, revised edition, 1977.

Lowell, *Day by Day,* Farrar, Straus, 1977.

Mailer, Norman, *The Armies of the Night,* New American Library, 1968.

Martin, Jay, *Robert Lowell,* University of Minnesota Press, 1970.

Mazzaro, Jerome, *The Achievement of Robert Lowell: 1939-1959,* University of Detroit Press, 1960.

Mazzaro, *The Poetic Themes of Robert Lowell,* University of Michigan Press, 1965.

Mazzaro, editor, *Profile of Robert Lowell,* Merrill, 1971.

Meiners, R. K., *Everything to Be Endured: An Essay on Robert Lowell and Modern Poetry,* University of Missouri Press, 1970.

Meyers, Jeffrey, editor, *Robert Lowell: Interviews and Memoirs,* University of Michigan Press, 1988.

Mills, Ralph J., *Cry of the Human: Essays on Contemporary Poetry,* University of Illinois Press, 1975.

Ostroff, Anthony, editor, *The Contemporary Poet as Artist and Critic,* Little, Brown, 1964.

Parkinson, Thomas Francis, editor, *Robert Lowell: A Collection of Critical Essays,* Prentice-Hall, 1968.

Perloff, Marjorie, *The Poetic Art of Robert Lowell,* Cornell University Press, 1973.

Plimpton, George, editor, *Writers at Work: "Paris Review" Interviews,* 2nd series, Viking, 1963.

Price, Jonathan, editor, *Critics on Robert Lowell,* University of Miami Press, 1972.

Procopiow, Norma, *Robert Lowell: The Poet and His Critics,* American Library Association, 1984.

Raffel, Burton, *Robert Lowell,* Ungar, 1981.

Rosenthal, M. L., *The Modern Poets: A Critical Introduction,* Oxford University Press, 1960.

Rosenthal, *The New Poets: American and British Poetry since World War II,* Oxford University Press, 1967.

Rudman, Mark, *Robert Lowell: An Introduction to the Poetry,* Columbia University Press, 1983.

Sexton, Anne, *Anne Sexton: A Self-Portrait in Letters,* edited by Linda Gray Sexton and Lois Ames, Houghton, 1977.

Simpson, Eileen, *Poets in Their Youth: A Memoir,* Random House, 1982.

Smith, Vivian, *The Poetry of Robert Lowell,* Sydney University Press, 1974.

Staples, Hugh B., *Robert Lowell: The First Twenty Years,* Faber, 1962, Farrar, Straus, 1962.

Stein, Jean, and George Plimpton, editors, *American Journey: The Times of Robert Kennedy,* Harcourt, 1970.

Steiner, George, *Language and Silence: Essays on Language, Literature, and the Inhuman,* Atheneum, 1967.

Stepanchev, Stephen, *American Poetry since 1945,* Harper, 1965.

Untermeyer, Louis, *Lives of the Poets: The Story of 1000 Years of English and American Poetry,* Simon & Schuster, 1959.

von Hallberg, Robert, *American Poetry and Culture: 1945-1980,* Harvard University Press, 1985.

Weatherhead, A. Kingsley, *The Edge of the Image,* University of Washington Press, 1967.

Williamson, Alan, *Pity the Monsters: The Political Vision of Robert Lowell,* Yale University Press, 1974.

Yenser, Stephen, *Circle to Circle: The Poetry of Robert Lowell,* University of California Press, 1975.

PERIODICALS

Agenda (special Lowell issue), autumn, 1980.
American Book Review, December, 1978-January, 1979.
American Literature, March, 1980.
American Poetry Review, Volume 7, number 5, 1978.
American Quarterly, fall, 1967, winter, 1970.
Antioch Review, spring, 1985.
Ariel, January, 1981.
Atlantic, January, 1952, July, 1959, July, 1982, June, 1983.
Book Week, October 11, 1964, February 20, 1966, January 29, 1967.
Book World, May 11, 1969.
Boundary 2, fall, 1972.
Christian Science Monitor, October 15, 1964, December 16, 1965, January 26, 1967, September 21, 1977.
Classical and Modern Literature, winter, 1981.
Commonweal, May 12, 1961, May 12, 1967, October 17, 1969.
Contemporary Literature, Volume 23, number 4, 1982.
Critic, April, 1966.
Criticism, winter, 1969.
Dissent, November/December, 1969.
Encounter, October, 1973, August, 1978, July, 1987.
English Language Notes, March, 1974.
English Literary History, winter, 1978.
Esquire, September, 1969.
Essays in Criticism, January, 1979.
Georgia Review, spring, 1971, summer, 1973.
Harvard Advocate (special Lowell issues), November, 1961, November, 1979.
Journal of Modern Literature, September, 1979.
Life, February 17, 1967.
Literary Review, spring, 1980.
London Review of Books, September 17, 1987.
Los Angeles Times Book Review, February 2, 1986.
Modern Drama, March, 1973.
Nation, January 18, 1947, September 19, 1959, October 26, 1964, January 24, 1966, December 23, 1968, July 7, 1969, May 19, 1979, April 11, 1987.
National Review, February 17, 1978, March 13, 1987, August 14, 1987.
New England Quarterly, March, 1971, December, 1972.
New Republic, June 8, 1959, October 17, 1964, July 7-14, 1973, July 17, 1976, November 20, 1976, November 26, 1977, June 30, 1979, March 30, 1987.
New Statesman, August 31, 1973, March 10, 1978, June 15, 1979.
Newsweek, October 12, 1964, September 6, 1976, September 5, 1977, April 27, 1987.
New York, July 7, 1969.
New Yorker, November 30, 1946, June 9, 1951.
New York Herald Tribune, February 7, 1966, February 9, 1966.
New York Herald Tribune Book Review, April 22, 1951, February 4, 1962.
New York Review of Books, November 23, 1967, October 28, 1976, October 27, 1977, February 9, 1978, March 8, 1979, March 3, 1988.

New York Times, November 3, 1946, April 22, 1951, May 3, 1959, April 4, 1976, July 18, 1976, July 7, 1987.
New York Times Book Review, May 28, 1961, October 4, 1964, January 15, 1967, September 3, 1967, June 15, 1969, April 4, 1971, July 18, 1976, August 14, 1977, October 16, 1977, December 3, 1978, April 8, 1979, July 12, 1987.
Observer, July 14, 1987.
Paris Review, Volume 25, 1961.
Partisan Review, fall, 1967, summer, 1968.
Philological Quarterly, spring, 1983.
Ploughshares, Volume 5, number 2, 1979.
PMLA, January, 1975.
Poetry, October, 1959, April, 1962, June, 1966, September, 1967, December, 1971, May, 1978.
Prose, Volume 6, 1973.
Review, Volume 20, 1969.
Salmagundi (special Lowell issues), fall/winter, 1966-1967, spring, 1977.
Saturday Review, September 2, 1967, May 3, 1969, September 6, 1969.
Saturday Review of Literature, November 16, 1946.
Sewanee Review, winter, 1978.
Spectator, July 18, 1987.
Texas Studies in Language and Literature, summer, 1973, winter, 1976.
Time, April 28, 1961, November 3, 1961, October 16, 1964, June 2, 1967, September 15, 1967, June 6, 1969, August 29, 1977.
Times (London), June 15, 1962, April 25, 1985.
Times Literary Supplement, August 3, 1967, December 25, 1970, August 10, 1973, January 25, 1980, July 10, 1987.
Tulane Drama Review, summer, 1967.
Twentieth Century Literature, October, 1971, spring, 1985.
Virginia Quarterly Review, summer, 1967, spring, 1968.
Washington Post Book World, January 28, 1979, August 2, 1987.
Weekly Book Review, November 24, 1946.
Yale Review, December, 1959, March, 1962, December, 1964, June, 1967, December, 1969.

OTHER

Lieberson, Goddard, *Benito Cereno by Robert Lowell* (recorded interview), Columbia Records, 1965.
Robert Lowell (filmed interview), National Educational Television, 1964.

OBITUARIES:

PERIODICALS

AB Bookman's Weekly, November 7, 1977.
New York Times, September 13-14, 1977.
Observer, September 18, 1977.
Washington Post, September 14, 1977.

* * *

LOWRY, (Clarence) Malcolm   1909-1957

PERSONAL: Born July 28, 1909, in Liscard, Cheshire, England; died of an overdose of barbiturates and alcohol, June 27, 1957, in London, England; buried in churchyard of St. John the Baptist, Ripe, East Sussex, England; son of Arthur Osborne (a cotton broker) and Evelyn (Boden) Lowry; married Jan Gabrial (an American writer), January 6, 1934 (divorced, 1940); married Margerie Bonner (an actress and secretary), December 2, 1940. *Education:* Received degree from Cambridge University, 1932.

CAREER: Writer. Deckhand on the British freighter *S.S. Pyrrhus,* 1927; lived and wrote in England, Spain, and Mexico during the late 1930s, and Canada throughout most of the 1940s and early 1950s.

WRITINGS:

Ultramarine (novel), J. Cape, 1933, revised, Lippincott, 1962.

Under the Volcano (novel), Reynal & Hitchcock, 1947, reprinted with an introduction by Stephen Spender, Lippincott, 1965, reprinted, Harper, 1984.

Hear Us O Lord From Heaven Thy Dwelling Place (short stories), Lippincott, 1961.

Selected Poems, edited by Earle Birney and Margerie Bonner Lowry, City Lights Books, 1962.

Selected Letters of Malcolm Lowry, edited by Harvey Breit and Margerie Bonner Lowry, Lippincott, 1965.

Dark As the Grave Wherein My Friend Is Laid (incomplete novel), edited by Douglas Day and Margerie Bonner Lowry, preface by Day, New American Library, 1968.

Lunar Caustic (novella), edited by Birney and Margerie Bonner Lowry, foreword by Conrad Knickbocker, J. Cape, 1968, World, 1970.

October Ferry to Gabriola (incomplete novel), edited by Margerie Bonner Lowry, World, 1970.

(With wife, Margerie Bonner Lowry) *Notes on a Screenplay for F. Scott Fitzgerald's Tender Is the Night,* introduction by Paul Tiessen, Bruccoli Clark, 1976.

Works also collected in other editions and represented in anthologies. Contributor to periodicals, including *Paris Review, Partisan Review,* and *Leys Fortnightly,*

SIDELIGHTS: Malcolm Lowry was an experimental English writer who produced a small but important body of writings. Influenced by the introspective, stream-of-consciousness literature of such authors as James Joyce, Lowry is remembered for his intense and highly personal brand of fiction. Only two of his works—the novels *Ultramarine* and *Under the Volcano*—reached publication before his death in 1957 at the age of forty-eight. Although several of the author's unfinished works have been edited and published posthumously, *Under the Volcano,* the largely autobiographical story of the final day in the life of an alcoholic, remains his crowning literary achievement.

Lowry was the youngest child born to an upper-class English family. Sent to a private boarding school at an early age, he failed to develop a close relationship with his parents and would later disregard his claims to the family cotton business. Lowry endured additional isolation for four of his preteen years, suffering a substantial loss of vision in both eyes due to ulcerations of his corneas. Following his recovery, however, he went on to become an avid and accomplished athlete. After a brief stint as a crew-hand aboard a British freighter—a diversion frowned upon by his father—Lowry placated his parents by agreeing to attend Cambridge University. Remaining remote and detached during his college years, he chose to cultivate his interest in literature and writing. During this time, Lowry's increasing reliance on alcohol began to surface. As Douglas Day noted in *Malcolm Lowry: A Biography,* alcohol served as "a source of spiritual strength, even of mystical insights [for the writer]. . . . He *liked* to drink." Lowry's drinking addiction would overshadow both his personal life and his fiction, and it would eventually lead to his death.

Biographers have described Lowry as a tormented and self-absorbed individual plagued by feelings of inadequacy, melancholia, detachment, and despair. Yet, in spite of the flaws in his character, the author is said to have possessed an unfailing charm: Day related that a barroom friend once said of Lowry,

"The very sight of the old bastard makes me happy for five days. No bloody fooling." Lowry's fiction mirrors his feelings of alienation, frustration, and internal turmoil. He intended to organize his writings under the general title "The Voyage That Never Ends," but the sequence never materialized as Lowry planned. His tendency to write and rewrite numerous drafts of each of his works resulted in the realization of few projects. The works that were edited and published after his death, then, must be viewed as unpolished representations of Lowry's literary vision.

Lowry's first full-length publication, *Ultramarine,* appeared in his native England in 1933. Written when the author was in his early twenties, *Ultramarine* concerns refined young sailor Dana Hilliot's psychological and social development while journeying to the Far East. An outcast among a crew of lower-class men, Hilliot undergoes a gradual assimilation into the ship's subculture, achieving the acceptance he craves. The story is reportedly based on Lowry's own experience as a restless youth aboard the *S.S. Pyrrhus* in late 1920s, although the author failed to realize the triumph of integration that the fictional Hilliot experienced.

Ultramarine received mixed reviews. Faulted mainly for its lack of cohesiveness, the novel has been described as the rough-edged work of a promising young voice in fiction. In a letter to his agent reprinted in *Selected Letters,* Lowry himself described *Ultramarine* as "an altogether unmentionable early novel . . . that I would like in every way to forget." But *Ultramarine* is now generally regarded as a preface to *Under the Volcano,* Lowry's most enduring work. As *New Republic* contributor J. M. Edelstein wrote, *Ultramarine* represents only "traces of the brilliance and the power which Malcolm Lowry possessed and which he used to create his masterpiece."

Shortly after completing *Ultramarine*—while traveling across Europe with such friends as American writer Conrad Aiken—Lowry met his first wife, American writer Jan Gabrial, whom he married after a brief courtship. Their years together were marred by alternating periods of disagreement and reconciliation. Lowry's drinking problem worsened during this time and eventually led to his two-week treatment at Bellevue Hospital's psychiatric ward in 1935.

Lowry began work on *Under the Volcano* the following year, while living with Gabrial in Cuernavaca, Mexico. They separated permanently in 1937 and were finally divorced three years later. Between 1937 and 1940, Lowry wrote three drafts of *Under the Volcano,* met his second wife, Margerie Bonner, and relocated to Vancouver, British Columbia. The couple was married in December of 1940, one month after Lowry's divorce from Gabrial was finalized. As noted in the *Atlantic* by Clarissa Lorenz, wife of Aiken, Lowry's marriage to Bonner seemed to provide him with the only joy he had ever known. As quoted by Lorenz, Lowry later referred to the relationship as "the only thing holding me to life and sanity."

Lowry and Bonner rented a squatter's shack at Dollarton on a harbor known as Burrard Inlet (near Vancouver), where they would live for the better part of the next fifteen years. There, Lowry worked for nearly four years completing the fourth draft of *Under the Volcano.* After the shack was destroyed in a 1944 fire, Lowry and his wife returned to Dollarton the next winter and, with the help of friends, rebuilt it.

Lowry began to drink heavily over the next year as he awaited word on *Under the Volcano* from publishers in New York and London. Several months passed before he heard from London publisher Jonathan Cape, who requested that Lowry condense and revise the novel extensively. In a thirty-one-page response, later printed in *Selected Letters of Malcolm Lowry,* Lowry advanced a detailed defense of the book: "I have tried . . . to conceal in the *Volcano* as well as possible the deformities of my own mind. . . . [The novel] can be regarded as a kind of symphony, or in another way as a kind of opera. . . . It is hot music, a poem, a song, a tragedy, a comedy, a farce. . . . It is superficial, profound, entertaining and boring, according to taste. . . . It is also I claim a work of art [that focuses on] the forces in man which force him to be terrified of himself. It is also concerned with the guilt of man, with his remorse, with the ceaseless struggling toward the light under the weight of the past."

Under the Volcano was published in New York by Reynal & Hitchcock and in London by Jonathan Cape in 1947. Set against the political unrest of 1938 Mexico, *Under the Volcano* is a dramatic account of one man's inevitable downfall. The novel chronicles the last twelve hours in the life of Geoffrey Firmin, a divorced alcoholic and former British Consul in Quauhnahuac, Mexico. Firmin's ex-wife, Yvonne, returns to him on the festive Day of the Dead to attempt a reconciliation; her efforts, though, are hampered by Firmin's continued abusiveness and drinking, combined with the presence in Mexico of two of her past lovers: Firmin's half-brother, Hugh, and longtime friend Jacques Laurelle, a film producer. Firmin spends his final hours in a bar—drinking and musing over his life as an outcast—and is shot to death by a Mexican fascist who mistakes him for a murderer and thief.

Day has suggested that Firmin's decline is the inexorable result of his "failure to experience love." The critic further noted that the character "never succeeds in escaping from what he calls 'this dreadful tyranny of self' enough to exist in any real way for others. . . . [Firmin] is in hell and the hell is himself." Lowry explained in his letter to Cape the significance of his character's destruction: "The drunkenness of the Consul is used on one plane to symbolize the universal drunkenness of mankind during the [Second World] war, or during the period immediately preceding it, . . . and what profundity and final meaning there is in his fate should be seen also in its universal relationship to the ultimate fate of mankind."

Some reviewers decried the erudite and overly introspective nature of the work. According to Denis Donoghue in the *New York Review of Books,* "*Under the Volcano,* remarkable as it is, gives the impression of being overwritten. After a few chapters we long for something casual, even a mistake, anything to relieve the pressure of deliberate significance." Other critics have deemed the novel a classic—the work of a genius. In a review of *Under the Volcano* for the *New York Herald Tribune Book Review,* Mark Schorer claimed that he knew of few other literary works "which convey so powerfully the agony of alienation, the internal suffering of disintegration." And H. R. Hays, writing in the *New York Times Book Review,* asserted: "It is cause for rejoicing when one encounters a novel which achieves a rich variety of meaning on many levels, which is written in a style both virile and poetic, which possesses profundity of insight, which is, in short, literature."

Having struggled eight years with *Under the Volcano,* Lowry seemed to have expended most of his creative energies. "Then," as Day put it, "he was finished, with ten years of life still left. What remained to him was only the inevitable deterioration of his art, and the analogous deterioration of his self." The frustrated writer's drinking increased in ensuing years, and in 1955 he underwent psychiatric treatment at Atkinson Morley's Hospital. Lowry spent the last year and a half of his life with his wife in the picturesque town of Ripe, Sussex. On the night of June 27,

1957—the culmination of a period of intense depression for the writer—Lowry and his wife argued. Fearing he might do her physical harm, she ran from their house, only to discover his corpse when she returned the next morning. A broken gin bottle was on the floor beside him, and a bottle of Bonner's sleeping tablets had been emptied.

In the first dozen or so years following Lowry's death, several of his works in progress were edited—by his wife and others—and published in the United States and England. *Hear Us O Lord From Heaven Thy Dwelling Place* is a collection of seven short stories that Lowry had started in the late 1940s. Phoebe-Lou Adams, writing in the *Atlantic,* suggested the pieces in this volume are not really stories, but "rather elaborations of mood and revelations of the workings of the author's disintegrating mind, with the intensity and egocentricity of lyric poetry." While five of the pieces in the collection garnered little attention, the remaining two—"Through the Panama" and "The Forest Path to the Spring"—are said to be among Lowry's finest compositions after *Under the Volcano.* "Through the Panama" traces a tormented writer's rise from the depths of self-consciousness. "The Forest Path to the Spring," the most poetic of the volume's stories, alludes to the psychic development Lowry experienced during his years with his wife at Dollarton. As a whole, *Hear Us O Lord From Heaven Thy Dwelling Place* presents a rare vision of change and even growth in Lowry's otherwise bleak canon.

Following the completion of *Under the Volcano,* Lowry returned to Mexico in an apparent attempt to recapture his past. Bonner had not experienced the Cuernavaca of the late 1930s, and, captivated by the country's intrigue and beauty, she wanted to explore the areas of Mexico that her husband had immortalized in his novel. Lowry was anxious to visit with Juan Fernando Marquez, a Mexican revolutionary and drinking companion who appears briefly in *Under the Volcano* as the character of Juan Cerillo. The author later learned, though, that his friend had been killed in a brawl more than five years earlier. Lowry then began writing a fictionalized account of his search for Marquez. Published more than a decade after the author's death, the novel *Dark As the Grave Wherein My Friend Is Laid* was compiled by Lowry's widow and Day from Lowry's notes. In the book, Lowry's protagonist Sigbjorn Wilderness, a reformed alcoholic, travels to Mexico in an attempt to put his past behind him. But as Day noted in a preface to *Dark As the Grave Wherein My Friend Is Laid,* "Sigbjorn learns that he really does not *want* to lay the ghosts, but to rejoin them—and this is what makes his descent into the Mexican hell truly perilous."

Because of its setting and subject matter, *Dark As the Grave Wherein My Friend Is Laid* generally drew comparisons to *Under the Volcano.* Elizabeth Janeway, writing in the *New York Times Book Review,* deemed the work "in itself an astounding performance," but several other critics faulted its loose structure, lack of action, and obscure language and allusions. Day defended Lowry's works against such criticism: "If there is no external action, there is almost a surfeit of movement internally; and there is enough tension within the mind of [one of Lowry's] protagonist[s] to render any other conflict superfluous. . . . Whenever he lets his protagonist think, Lowry becomes a great writer." Day went on to call *Dark As the Grave Wherein My Friend Is Laid* "a work of embryonic greatness," noting that although it exists in an "imperfect state," readers should "be glad to have it even as it is."

Another thinly veiled autobiography, the posthumously published *Lunar Caustic* is viewed as a partial record of the time Lowry spent in Bellevue in 1935. Lowry began writing *Lunar*

Caustic immediately after his release from Bellevue, and he revised the work many times over the last two decades of his life. The slim and unusual volume takes its title from a silver nitrate treatment for syphilis. (As a child, the impressionable Lowry developed an obsessive fear of contracting syphilis. According to Day, this fear may have stemmed from his religious upbringing, feelings of sexual inadequacy, and guilt.) Published for the first time in 1968, eleven years after Lowry's death, *Lunar Caustic* centers on disoriented alcoholic Bill Plantagenet, who one day finds himself confined to Bellevue's psychiatric wing. Plantagenet encounters three other patients in the ward. Although he eventually equates elements of their insanity with aspects of his own character, he realizes that he is not mad; he is instead a sane drunk.

Dale Edmonds, writing in *Tulane Studies in English,* theorized that "*Lunar Caustic* fails as a work of fiction because of Lowry's uncertainty of intention and inconsistency of style." But several other critics judged the work a striking and insightful study of nothingness, a frightening depiction of a psychic limbo, and a painful reminder of the horrors of earthly life. Day speculated that Lowry may have viewed his own alcoholic degeneration as a source of literary inspiration; in destroying himself, he was better able to fathom—and therefore articulate in his writings—the disintegration of the world. Assessed in these terms, *Lunar Caustic* is a success, since it offers a stunning view of human destruction and disillusionment.

Lowry's last published novel, *October Ferry to Gabriola,* was edited by Bonner Lowry for release in 1970. The story concerns a criminal lawyer who, reacting to apparent omens, moves with his family to British Columbia in search of peace and solitude. A thin and rather formless work, *October Ferry to Gabriola* is generally considered more valuable as an idea than as a fully developed piece of fiction.

In evaluating Lowry's contributions to modern English fiction, Richard Hauer Costa surmised that without *Under the Volcano,* "it would be easy to conclude that Lowry was incapable of transmuting vision into viable fiction." Day ascertained that "Lowry was . . . in no sense a 'natural' writer—compulsive, yes, but not natural," adding, "He was a writer not because words flowed effortlessly from him, but because he was damned if he were going to be anything else." "To Lowry," Day concluded, "not to write was unimaginable; not to write was death. Genius . . . was something which Lowry had to labor, often frantically, to attain. And attain it he did: for there is before us, after all, the monolithic and undeniable fact of *Under the Volcano.* . . . Such achievement transcends the realm of mere talent."

AVOCATIONAL INTERESTS: Jazz; playing ukulele.

MEDIA ADAPTATIONS: Portions of the novel *Under the Volcano* are recited in the documentary "Volcano," released by the National Film Board of Canada, 1976; *Under the Volcano* was adapted by Guy Gallo for a film of the same title, directed by John Huston, released by Universal Pictures, 1984.

BIOGRAPHICAL/CRITICAL SOURCES:

BOOKS

Bradbrook, M. C., *Malcolm Lowry: His Art and Early Life, A Study in Transformation,* Cambridge University Press, 1974.
Bradbury, Malcolm, *Possibilities: Essays on the State of the Novel,* Oxford University Press, 1973.
Cross, Richard K., *Malcolm Lowry: A Preface to His Fiction,* University of Chicago Press, 1980.

Day, Douglas, *Malcolm Lowry: A Biography,* Oxford University Press, 1973.
Dictionary of Literary Biography, Volume 15, *British Novelists, 1930-1959,* Gale, 1983.
Dodson, Daniel B., *Malcolm Lowry,* Columbia University Press, 1970.
Epstein, Perle S., *The Private Labyrinth of Malcolm Lowry: "Under the Volcano" and the Cabbala,* Holt, 1969.
Hauer Costa, Richard, *Malcolm Lowry,* Twayne, 1972.
Lowry, Malcolm, *Selected Letters of Malcolm Lowry,* edited by Harvey Breit and Margerie Bonner Lowry, Lippincott, 1965.
Lowry, Malcolm, *Under the Volcano,* introduction by Stephen Spender, Lippincott, 1965.
Lowry, Malcolm, *Dark As the Grave Wherein My Friend Is Laid,* edited by Douglas Day and Bonner Lowry, preface by Day, New American Library, 1968.
Lowry, Margerie, editor, *Malcolm Lowry: Psalms and Songs,* New American Library, 1975.
Markson, David, *Malcolm Lowry's "Volcano": Myth, Symbol, Meaning,* Times Books, 1978.
Twentieth-Century Literary Criticism, Volume 6, Gale, 1982.
Wood, Barry, editor, *Malcolm Lowry: The Writer and His Critics,* Tecumseh Press, 1980.
Woodcock, George, editor, *Malcolm Lowry: The Man and His Work,* University of British Columbia Press, 1971.

PERIODICALS

Atlantic, August, 1961, June, 1970.
Canadian Literature, spring, 1963, spring, 1971.
Modern Fiction Studies, summer, 1958.
New York Herald Tribune Book Review, February 23, 1947.
New York Review of Books, March 3, 1966.
New York Times Book Review, February 23, 1947, November 8, 1964, August 4, 1968, July 27, 1969.
Saturday Review, December 4, 1965, July 6, 1968.
Spectator, June 23, 1933.
Studies in the Novel, fall, 1974.
Times Literary Supplement, January 26, 1967, March 21, 1968, July 3, 1969.
Tulane Studies in English, Volume 15, 1967.

—*Sketch by Barbara Carlisle Bigelow*

*   *   *

LOXSMITH, John
    See BRUNNER, John (Kilian Houston)

*   *   *

LUCAS, Victoria
    See PLATH, Sylvia

*   *   *

LUCE, Henry R(obinson) 1898-1967

PERSONAL: Born April 3, 1898, in Tengchow (now P'englai), Shantung Province, China (American citizen born abroad); died February 28, 1967, in Phoenix, Arizona; son of Henry Winters (an American Presbyterian missionary) and Elizabeth Middleton (a missionary; maiden name, Root) Luce; married Lila Ross Hotz, December 22, 1923 (divorced, October 4, 1935); married Clare Boothe Brokaw (a writer and congresswoman), November 23, 1935; children: (first marriage) Henry III, Peter Paul. *Educa-*

tion: Yale University, B.A., 1920; attended Oxford University, 1920-21.

CAREER: Chicago Daily News, Chicago, Ill., cub reporter, 1921-22; *Baltimore News,* Baltimore, Md., reporter, 1922-23; co-founder and editor-in-chief of *Time* magazine, 1923-64; founder and editor-in-chief of *Fortune* magazine, 1930-64, *Life* magazine, 1936-64, and *Sports Illustrated* magazine, 1954-64; publisher of *Architectural Forum* magazine, 1932-64, and *House and Home* magazine, 1962-64; editorial chairman of *Time, Life, Fortune,* and *Sports Illustrated,* 1964-67; director of Time Inc. Organizer of United China Relief, 1940. Initiated Committee on Freedom of the Press, 1944. Director of Union Theological Seminary; trustee of American Heritage Foundation, China Institute in America, Metropolitan Museum of Art (New York), and Roosevelt Hospital (New York). *Military service:* U. S. Army Field Artillery, 1918; became second lieutenant.

MEMBER: United Board of Christian Higher Education in Asia, New York Chamber of Commerce, Phi Beta Kappa, Omicron Delta Kappa, Alpha Delta Phi.

AWARDS, HONORS: Chevalier of French Legion of Honor, 1937; Order of Auspicious Star, China, 1947; Henry Johnson Fisher Award from Magazine Publishers Association, 1965; Commander of Order of Orange-Nassau, the Netherlands; Commander of Order of Cedars of Lebanon; Commander of Royal Order of George I, Greece; Commander's Cross, Order of Danneborg, Denmark; Knight Commander's Cross, Order of Merit, Federal Republic of Germany. Honorary degrees: M.A. from Yale University, 1926; LL.D. from Rollins College, 1938, Grinnell College, 1942, Colgate University, 1948, Lafayette College, 1952, Occidental College, 1954, St. Louis University, 1955, Springfield College, 1961, Adelphi University, 1963, Williams College, 1965, Yale University, 1966, and Westminster College, 1967; Litt.D. from Boston University, 1941, Syracuse University, 1945, Rutgers University, 1949, and University of Arizona, 1961; L.H.D. from Hamilton College, 1942; H.H.D. from College of Idaho, 1951, and College of Wooster, 1962; Doctor of Journalism from Temple University, 1953.

WRITINGS:

The American Century, Time Inc., 1941, 2nd edition, with comments by Dorothy Thompson, John Chamberlain, Quincy Howe, Robert G. Spivak, and Robert E. Sherwood, Farrar & Rinehart, 1941.
The Place of Art in American Life, Time Inc., 1956.
Good Architecture Is Good Government, Time Inc., 1957.
The Dangerous Age of Abundance, Newcomen Society in North America, 1959.
The Rule of Law and the Administration of Justice, American Judicature Society, 1961.
Sight and Insight, University of Miami Press, 1961.
The Pursuit of Significance, College of Wooster (Ohio), 1966.
The Ideas of Henry Luce, edited by John K. Jessup, Atheneum, 1969.

SIDELIGHTS: Henry Luce once described himself as "a Protestant, a Republican, and a free-enterpriser, which means I am biased in favor of God, Eisenhower, and the stockholders of Time Inc." Others have variously called him an empire builder and an imperialist, a publishing genius, and a totalitarian editor, but most would agree that, as Joseph Epstein in *Commentary* simply put it, Luce was "a genuine force in American life."

The son of American missionaries in China, Luce developed an unshakable Protestant ethic and belief in America's superiority. Nym Wales, in the *New Republic,* explained: "[Luce] was an An-

glophile WASP—Ivy League and British-trained. . . . He received the British discipline intended to train empire-builders and administrators. . . . He had to be superhuman and a sophisticated Puritan. . . . He was an A Student at Hotchkiss in Connecticut and at Yale, with a postgraduate year at Oxford in England, essential for any American Cecil Rhodes tradition."

At Hotchkiss Luce met future publishing partner Briton Hadden. The two began their collaboration on the Hotchkiss school paper and then continued together on the Yale *Daily News.* Then in the early 1920's Luce and Hadden, believing that most Americans lacked the time to keep abreast of current events, conceived the idea of a weekly news magazine. They accumulated $86,000 from acquaintances and old school friends, and on March 3, 1923, the first issue of *Time* appeared. For four years the magazine ran at a loss, but by 1927 it was making a profit and, at the age of thirty, Luce was a self-made millionaire.

With the success of *Time* assured, the partners began work on a new magazine. They planned it, as stated in the prospectus, around the premise that "business is obviously the greatest single denominator of interest among the active leading citizens of the U.S.A. [It is a] distinctive expression of the American genius." When Hadden died suddenly in 1929, Luce assumed sole control of *Time* and carried on with the new magazine, *Fortune,* which appeared for the first time in January, 1930. Despite the stock market crash of 1929, *Fortune* was successful, and Time Inc.'s pattern of almost constant growth was established. "The March of Time," a radio broadcast presenting the news in dramatic form, came next; first aired on March 6, 1931, the program evolved into a newsreel series, first screened in February, 1935, and eventually seen thirteen times a year in over ten thousand movie theatres worldwide.

Venturing next into photojournalism, Luce brought out, on November 17, 1936, the first issue of *Life.* It has often been said that *Life* nearly died of success: advertising contracts were based on expected sales figures that were far below the number of copies actually sold. As a result, *Life* lost $3 million its first year. Once advertising rates were adjusted, the magazine recovered; its circulation at the time of Luce's death was seven and a half million. A fourth Luce magazine followed its successful predecessors; *Sports Illustrated* appeared on August 16, 1954, with an original circulation of over a half million, and it too grew steadily.

Luce experienced a few failures with magazines such as *Tide* and *Letters,* but they did not undermine his enormous business success. From the original investment of $86,000, he built a publishing empire with a market value at the time of his death of $690 million. (His own share was valued at $109,862,500.) In 1967, the combined circulation of his four major magazines exceeded fourteen million copies. Time Inc.'s expansion into other businesses, including book publishing and television and radio broadcasting, was consistently profitable.

In addition to his financial success, Luce was highly praised for his editorial acumen, his ability to personally control a huge journalistic staff, and his consistency of editorial style and content. He introduced a series of editorial innovations based on the idea that the news must entertain as well as inform. He himself once acknowledged: "I am all for titillating trivialities. I am all for the epic touch. I could almost say that everything in *Time* should be either titillating or epic or starkly, super-curtly factual." In fact, one of the fundamentals of *Time* editorial policy was to dramatize the news. A typical story began with a catchy lead, proceeded with an angle to a climax, and was brought to a neat conclusion. Epstein likened this approach to a B-movie: "As a B-movie contorts human experience, snuffing out its complexity and tidying up its loose ends for an audience which has, after all, come primarily to be entertained, so does *Time* magazine: the B-movie of current events and personality."

While *Time*'s content emphasized personalities, its style fostered anonymity of authorship. This resulted from Luce's pioneering use of group journalism, a technique through which stories are produced by teams of researchers, correspondents, and editors. Nevertheless, by offering excellent salaries, Luce was able to attract and retain outstanding individual talent, including at various times such notables as James Agee, Stephen Vincent Benet, John Kenneth Galbraith, John O'Hara, Alfred Kazin, Archibald MacLeish, and Theodore H. White.

The criticism most often leveled at Luce has concerned the absence of objectivity in his publications. Yet objectivity seems never to have been among Luce's goals—even the original prospectus for *Time* included six points of "Editorial Bias." Herbert Mayes, in the *Saturday Review,* recalled a conversation that exemplified Luce's editorial influence: When asked what the magazines would do if his editors decided to support candidate A for President when he was for candidate B, Luce responded, "That's simple. They will support candidate B."

The interpretive slant at Time Inc. was all Luce's own. "Every substantive stand that *Time* ever took was, above all, the stand of Henry Luce," Epstein declared. "In a way that applies to few other recent publishers, Luce turned his magazines into his personal diaries." As reflected in his magazines, Luce's beliefs emphasized a foreign policy that would extend American economic resources and technology to all nations that would support American ideology. Specifically, this was manifested in a distrust of such men as Franklin Roosevelt and Adlai Stevenson and support for such men as Dwight Eisenhower and Richard Nixon, as well as in his promotion of free enterprise and condemnation of Communism. As Nym Wales explained: "When the Luce group-journalism got through mastering 10,000 reports, the result was not objective. It was slanted toward building up stone by stone the so-called American neoimperialism in all of its unconsciousness and contradictoriness." On the subject of China, Luce's subjective influence was most distinguishable. He believed that America should maintain an adverserial role toward Communist China, and he continually presented in his magazines a picture of a country in chaos. Epstein remarked: "It is safe to say, then, that Henry Luce's magazines have done more than their share to contribute to the mystification and general hysteria about Communist China."

Although Luce's editorial bias was undeniable, some defended his proprietary approach to journalism. Mayes, a personal friend and former president of the McCall Corporation, maintained: "If I think that Henry Luce tempered the news now and then, I do not believe that he tampered with the facts, ever." Others defined Luce's methods in the context of a broader purpose; when Luce died, *Time* published a letter from the staff which in part read: "H. R. L. was no press lord in the tradition of Britain's Lord Beaverbrook or America's William Randolph Hearst. Power was not his passion—what burned in him was the search for truth and the desire to communicate it."

BIOGRAPHICAL/CRITICAL SOURCES:

BOOKS

Busch, Noel, *Briton Hadden: A Biography of the Co-Founder of Time,* Straus & Cudahy, 1949.
Cort, David, *The Sin of Henry Luce,* L. Stuart, 1974.
Jessup, John K., editor, *The Ideas of Henry Luce,* Atheneum, 1969.

Kubler, John, *Luce,* Doubleday, 1968.
Profiles from the New Yorker, Knopf, 1938.
Stewart, Kenneth and John Tebbel, *Makers of Modern Journalism,* Prentice-Hall, 1952.
Swanberg, W. A., *Luce and His Empire,* Scribner, 1972.

PERIODICALS

Commentary, November, 1967.
Esquire, September, 1967.
Fortune, April 1, 1967.
Life, March 10, 1967.
Nation, March 20, 1967.
New Republic, April 1, 1967.
Newsweek, March 13, 1967.
Saturday Review, March 18, 1967, April 29, 1967.
Time, March 10, 1967, March 17, 1967.
U.S. Camera, June, 1967.
U.S. News and World Report, March 13, 1967.

OBITUARIES:

PERIODICALS

National Review, March 21, 1967.
New Yorker, March 18, 1967.
New York Times, March 1, 1967.
Publishers Weekly, March 13, 1967.

*   *   *

LUDLUM, Robert 1927-
(Jonathan Ryder, Michael Shepherd)

PERSONAL: Born May 25, 1927, in New York, N.Y.; son of George Hartford (a businessman) and Margaret (Wadsworth) Ludlum; married Mary Ryducha (an actress), March 31, 1951; children: Michael, Jonathan, Glynis. *Education:* Wesleyan University, B.A., 1951. *Politics:* Independent.

ADDRESSES: Home—Hartford, Conn. *Agent*—Henry Morrison, Box 235, Bedford Hills, N.Y. 10507.

CAREER: Writer, 1971—. Actor on Broadway and on television, 1952-60; North Jersey Playhouse, Fort Lee, N.J., producer, 1957-60; producer in New York, N.Y., 1960-69; Playhouse-on-the-Mall, Paramus, N.J., producer, 1960-70. *Military service:* U.S. Marine Corps, 1944-46.

MEMBER: Authors League of America, American Federation of Television and Radio Artists, Screen Actors Guild.

AWARDS, HONORS: New England Professor of Drama Award, 1951; awards and grants from American National Theatre and Academy, 1959, and from Actors' Equity Association and William C. Whitney Foundation, 1960; Scroll of Achievement, American National Theatre and Academy, 1960.

WRITINGS:

The Scarlatti Inheritance (Book-of-the-Month Club alternate selection), World Publishing, 1971.
The Osterman Weekend, World Publishing, 1972.
The Matlock Paper, Dial, 1973.
(Under pseudonym Jonathan Ryder) *Trevayne,* Delacorte, 1973.
(Under pseudonym Jonathan Ryder) *The Cry of the Halidon,* Delacorte, 1974.
The Rhinemann Exchange, Dial, 1974.
(Under pseudonym Michael Shepherd) *The Road to Gandolfo,* Dial, 1975, reprinted under name Robert Ludlum, Bantam, 1982.
The Gemini Contenders, Dial, 1976.

The Chancellor Manuscript (Literary Guild selection), Dial, 1977.
The Holcroft Covenant, Richard Marek, 1978.
The Matarese Circle (Book-of-the-Month Club selection), Richard Marek, 1979.
The Bourne Identity, Richard Marek, 1980.
The Parsifal Mosaic, Random House, 1982.
The Aquitane Progression, Random House, 1984.
The Bourne Supremacy, Random House, 1986.
The Icarus Agenda, Random House, 1988.
The Bourne Ultimatum, Random House, 1990.

SIDELIGHTS: With some eighty million copies of his books in print, novelist Robert Ludlum dominates the field of espionage thrillers, outselling such popular spy writers as Len Deighton, John le Carre, and Ian Fleming. "Ludlum's awesome record of success," Susan Baxter and Mark Nichols report in *Maclean's,* "means that he is one of the most popular living authors in the English language." Since he began writing in 1971, Ludlum's novels of international conspiracy and suspense have regularly appeared on best-seller lists across the nation. In 1980, in fact, two of Ludlum's books topped the hardcover and paperback best-seller lists at the same time. "The fans of Robert Ludlum," Richard Freeman writes in the *New York Times Book Review,* "[are] as numerous as the leaves on the trees."

The typical Ludlum novel concerns a political conspiracy of some sort—usually masterminded by multinational corporations, ex-Nazis, secret terrorist groups, international bankers, or a combination of such plotters—which threatens the safety of the free world. War, assassination, financial manipulations, and blackmail are the tools of the conspirators, who can only be stopped by a single, determined individual. Ludlum's heroes, drawn into the fight for purely personal reasons, must undergo a series of rapid, boisterously-related dangers, chases, and escapes as they uncover and derail the secret conspiracy. Baxter and Nichols admit that "the improbable realm of [Ludlum's] imagination [is] a realm of spectacular evil and monstrous conspiracies, of casual brutality and gory death."

Ludlum's novels strike Thomas R. Edwards as being so similar to one another that he labels them a distinct genre: "ludlums." Writing in the *New York Review of Books,* Edwards defines a ludlum as "a long, turgidly written, and frantically overplotted novel. . . . Its subject is conspiracy. . . . Any reader of ludlums knows that no sensible reference to geopolitical reality is intended." Allan A. Ryan, Jr., in a review for the *Washington Post Book World,* speculates that Ludlum creates his plots "the way the rest of us play Scrabble. Ludlum has 25 tiles, with words on each—words like World War II, secret documents, Nazi war treasure, CIA, Vatican. . . . Each year Ludlum chooses half the tiles, face down, and turns them over, arranging them this way and that until some reasonably plausible sequence appears." But although Ryan finds that "Ludlum's thrillers tend to have a certain interchangeability," he asks, "but what of it? The prose fits and the plots are as convoluted as anyone could wish, with as many twists and turns as, well, as a chase through Geneva in a Maserati." John Leonard of the *New York Times* complains that Ludlum "finds his characters on the backs of cereal boxes, his prose in movie magazines, his sex in the want ads and his paranoia in our dental cavities. Nevertheless he pleases and seduces, telling his story like a man who must get it done before the house burns down around us. I sprained my wrist turning his pages."

The breathtaking dangers of Ludlum's fiction are not to be found in his personal life. He and his wife live quietly in Connecticut and have a condominium in Florida. Ludlum has never been, by his own admission to the *Chicago Tribune,* "a CIA agent, a retired general, an international lawyer, a Nazi spy or a member of the Mafia." For some two decades before becoming a writer, in fact, Ludlum was a professional actor and theatrical producer. Beginning in 1952 he appeared on Broadway, in regional theaters, and in over two hundred television programs, including "Kraft Television Theatre," "Studio One," "Omnibus," "Playhouse 90," and "Robert Montgomery Presents." "Usually I was cast as a lawyer or a homicidal maniac," Ludlum explains to Ron Base of the *Chicago Tribune Magazine.* By the late 1950s he had grown tired of acting and turned his talents to theatrical production instead, opening the Playhouse-on-the-Mall in Paramus, New Jersey, the country's first theater in a shopping center. The idea was a success. Ludlum staged revivals of classic Broadway staples, openings for Broadway-bound plays like "The Owl and the Pussycat," and premiered some more innovative works as well.

But by 1970 Ludlum was looking around for a new career. "I just got bored to death with the theater," he tells Base. He revived a decades-old dream of becoming a writer, dug out a story idea he had outlined years before, and fleshed it out into a novel entitled *The Scarlatti Inheritance.* When the book hit the best-seller lists and was picked up by a major book club, Ludlum was on his way. He credits his years in the theater with making his writing career possible. "The theater is a wonderful place to learn the architecture of scenes and conflict," he tells the *Chicago Tribune.*

The Scarlatti Inheritance set the pattern for all of Ludlum's later thrillers. The story of wealthy financiers who secretly bankrolled Adolf Hitler's Third Reich, *The Scarlatti Inheritance* is like "Saturday night at the old Bijou," according to J. R. Frakes of the *Chicago Tribune Book World.* The book, Frakes writes, pulsates "like a rusty bellows with high-level financial, international, familial, marital and governmental intrigue and [is] sparked with more stop-action cuts than a Pearl White serial." Patricia L. Skarda of the *Dictionary of Literary Biography Yearbook, 1982* allows that *The Scarlatti Inheritance* has a "somewhat erratic pace and occasionally melodramatic characterizations," but judges it "a thrilling, compelling tale."

Ludlum's next two novels, *The Osterman Weekend* and *The Matlock Paper,* are set closer to home. *The Osterman Weekend* tells of a New Jersey reporter who becomes entangled in a CIA plot to expose Omega, a group of international businessmen who manipulate the world's economy. "The tale is tautly told and the writing is vivid, the action gratifyingly rapid," William B. Hill remarks in *Best Sellers.* Skarda believes that *The Osterman Weekend* "exposes the inadequacies of American intelligence operations and our deepest fears that our friends cannot be trusted." *The Matlock Paper,* about a drug and prostitution ring at a New England college, "is a good thriller and well written," Kelly J. Fitzpatrick maintains in *Best Sellers.* "The basic situation," Newgate Callendar reports in the *New York Times Book Review,* "is unreal—indeed, it's unbelievable—but a good writer can make the reader suspend his disbelief, and Ludlum is a good writer."

In many of his books, Ludlum "returns again and again to interpretations of World War II history," Skarda maintains. *The Rhinemann Exchange, The Gemini Contenders,* and *The Holcroft Covenant* all revolve around Nazi quests to regain power with the help of unscrupulous corporations and bankers. *The Rhinemann Exchange,* the story of treasonous businessmen who illegally trade military and industrial products with the Nazis, is "a big and ambitious book," Callendar writes. "It is written in breathless, end-of-Armageddon prose that pants relentlessly along. But . . . a real storyteller is at work. You'll go along." Speaking of *The Holcroft Covenant,* in which Nazi war money is being used to finance a planned Fourth Reich, Christopher Lehmann-Haupt of the *New York Times* claims that "Ludlum stuffs more surprises into his novels . . . than any other six-pack of thriller writers combined, out on a narrative toot."

In *The Bourne Identity* and its sequels, *The Bourne Supremacy* and *The Bourne Ultimatum,* Ludlum writes of top assassin Jason Bourne, a man who, because of a head injury, begins the first book suffering from amnesia. While attempting to discover his identity and the purpose of his current undercover assignment, Bourne must fight off attacks on his life. Michael Demarest of *Time* calls *The Bourne Identity* "the most absorbing of Ludlum's . . . novels to date. His characters are complex and credible, his slight of plot as cunning as any terrorist conspiracy. And his minutiae, from the rituals of Swiss banking to the workings of a damaged brain, are always absorbing."

Jason Bourne returns in *The Bourne Supremacy,* in which a plot to cause war among China, the Soviet Union, and the United States must be stopped. Reluctant to leave his new position as a professor of Oriental studies to join the effort, Bourne is forced into action when his wife is kidnapped. Arnold R. Isaacs of the *Washington Post Book World* believes that the novel "delivers exactly what Ludlum's fans want and expect," although he also asks, "should it matter if a non-fan finds it bloated, witless and boring? Probably not." Lehmann-Haupt also has a mixed opinion, calling *The Bourne Supremacy* "Ludlum's most overwrought, speciously motivated, spuriously complicated story to date. . . . And yet—shameful to admit—one keeps reading. . . . The effect is like dessert after certain rich meals. It's too much. One shouldn't. One doesn't really feel like it. 'Oh, my God,' one gasps, contemplating the enormity of it. And promptly devours the entire concoction."

Ludlum was inspired to write *The Bourne Supremacy,* which is set in China, after reading of talks between England and China to return the city of Hong Kong to the Chinese. "I was fascinated by the Sino-British negotiations," Ludlum tells Lanny Sherwin of *Writer's Digest.* "So Mary [his wife] and I went there, went through China and the whole thing, and it simply confirmed everything I had thought: This is the setting for a hell of a book." As he does for each new book he researches, Ludlum took photographs of streets and buildings that caught his eye and incorporated the actual sites into his story. "Ludlum," Elizabeth Mehren explains in the *Los Angeles Times,* "still travels to each place he writes about; he researches fiendishly, as if every book were a documentary." Charles P. Wallace of the *Los Angeles Times Book Review* notes that Ludlum is especially "adept at recreating European locales."

When he is writing a new book, a process for which he usually allots eighteen months, Ludlum begins his work day at 4:15 in the morning and writes for five or six hours. By beginning early, he avoids being interrupted by telephone calls. To avoid distractions from passersby, his office is equipped with a one-way mirror-window. Ludlum can enjoy the view but cannot be seen from outside. His writing is done in longhand on legal pads with a Ticonderoga #2 pencil. "I always write with a Ticonderoga #2 pencil," he tells Sherwin. "I started out with it and I'll go to that Great Bookstore in the sky with one of those in my hands."

Not only is Ludlum a best-selling author in the United States, but his work has been translated into over thirty languages and published in twenty-seven foreign countries as well. Base avows that Ludlum is "one of the most popular pop novelists of the de-

cade. As achievements go, his is rather remarkable." Sherwin claims that Ludlum's work has "set the standard for suspense-thriller fiction." Baxter and Nichols explain that "Ludlum manages—by pumping suspense into every twist and turn in his tangled plots and by demanding sympathy for well-meaning protagonists afflicted by outrageous adversity—to keep millions of readers frantically turning his pages." Speaking to Mehren about his success as a writer, Ludlum admits: "It's not only satisfying, it's not only gratifying, but my God, they pay you for it."

MEDIA ADAPTATIONS: The Rhinemann Exchange was adapted as a television miniseries by the National Broadcasting Company in March, 1977; *The Osterman Weekend* was filmed by EMI in 1980; *The Scarlatti Inheritance* was filmed by Universal; and *The Bourne Identity* was adapted as a television miniseries in May, 1988.

BIOGRAPHICAL/CRITICAL SOURCES:

BOOKS

Bestsellers 89, Issue 1, Gale, 1989.
Bestsellers 90, Issue 3, Gale, 1990.
Contemporary Literary Criticism, Gale, Volume 22, 1982, Volume 43, 1987.
Dictionary of Literary Biography Yearbook, 1982, Gale, 1983.

PERIODICALS

Best Sellers, June 1, 1971, April, 1972, April, 1973, June, 1977.
Book World, March 21, 1971.
Chicago Sun-Times, March 7, 1982.
Chicago Tribune, May 11, 1986.
Chicago Tribune Book World, March 21, 1971, April 18, 1982.
Chicago Tribune Magazine, November 11, 1979.
Compass, March 14, 1982.
Connecticut Today, May 3, 1982.
Hollywood Reporter, April 8, 1982.
Los Angeles Times, April 15, 1982.
Los Angeles Times Book Review, March 11, 1984, March 23, 1986.
Maclean's, April 9, 1984, April 2, 1990.
New Leader, April 23, 1979.
New Republic, September 20-27, 1982.
Newsday, March 11, 1982.
New Statesman, June 27, 1980.
Newsweek, April 19, 1982.
New Yorker, October 14, 1974.
New York Review of Books, May 8, 1986.
New York Times, October 27, 1974, April 5, 1977, March 13, 1978, March 20, 1980, March 2, 1982, March 16, 1984, March 6, 1986.
New York Times Book Review, April 4, 1971, January 28, 1973, March 6, 1973, August 4, 1974, March 28, 1976, March 27, 1977, July 10, 1977, April 16, 1978, April 8, 1979, March 30, 1980, February 7, 1982, March 21, 1982, April 22, 1984, March 27, 1988.
New York Times Magazine, May 2, 1982.
Publishers Weekly, February 2, 1972, April 8, 1974, February 10, 1975.
San Francisco Chronicle, April 5, 1982.
Time, March 8, 1971, April 14, 1980, April 5, 1982, March 10, 1986.
Tribune Books (Chicago), February 28, 1988.
Washington Post Book World, March 19, 1978, March 18, 1979, March 23, 1980, March 9, 1986, February 21, 1988.
Writer's Digest, July, 1987.

LUKACS, Georg
  See LUKACS, Gyorgy (Szegedy von)

* * *

LUKACS, George
  See LUKACS, Gyorgy (Szegedy von)

* * *

LUKACS, Gyorgy (Szegedy von) 1885-1971
  (Georg Lukacs, George Lukacs)

PERSONAL: Given name sometimes transliterated as Georg or George; Born April 13, 1885, in Budapest, Hungary; died June 4, 1971, in Budapest, Hungary; son of a titled banker. *Education:* University of Budapest, Ph.D., 1906; attended University of Heidelberg and University of Berlin.

CAREER: Philosopher, writer, and critic. Minister of education during Bela Kun communist regime in Hungary, 1919; Marx-Engels Institute, Moscow, U.S.S.R., staff member, 1930; affiliated with Philosophical Institute of Academy of Sciences in U.S.S.R., c. 1933-45; University of Budapest, Budapest, Hungary, professor of philosophy, 1945-56; minister of culture during Imre Nagy regime in Hungary, 1956.

AWARDS, HONORS: Goethe Prize, 1970, for *Goethe and His Age.*

WRITINGS:

IN ENGLISH

Die Seele and die Formen (essays), E. Fleischel, 1911, translation by Anna Bostock published as *Soul and Form,* M.I.T. Press, 1974.

Die Theorie des Romans: Ein geschichtsphilosophischer Versuch ueber die Formen der grossen Epik, P. Cassirer, 1920, reprinted, Luchterhand, 1971, translation by Bostock published as *The Theory of the Novel: A Historico-Philosophical Essay on the Forms of Great Epic Literature,* M.I.T. Press, 1971.

Geschichte und Klassenbewusstsein: Studien ueber Marxistische Dialektik, Malik Verlag, 1923, reprinted, Luchterhand, 1968, translation by Rodney Livingstone published as *History and Class Consciousness: Studies in Marxist Dialectics,* M.I.T. Press, 1971.

Goethe und seine Zeit, A. Francke, 1947, translation by Robert Anchor published as *Goethe and His Age,* Merlin Press, 1968, Grosset & Dunlap, 1969.

Essays ueber Realismus, Aufbau Verlag, 1948, reprinted, Luchterhand, 1971, translation by Edith Bone published as *Studies in European Realism: A Sociological Survey of the Writings of Balzac, Stendhal, Zola, Tolstoy, Gorki, and Others,* Hillway, 1950, Grosset & Dunlap, 1964.

Der junge Hegel: Ueber die Beziehungen von Dialektik und Oekonomie, Europa Verlag, 1948, also published as *Der junge Hegel und die Probleme der kapitalistischen Gesellschaft,* Aufbau Verlag, 1954, translation by Livingstone published as *The Young Hegel: Studies in the Relations Between Dialectics and Economics,* Merlin Press, 1975, M.I.T. Press, 1976.

Thomas Mann, Aufbau Verlag, 1949, translation by Stanley Mitchell published as *Essays on Thomas Mann,* Merlin Press, 1964, Grosset & Dunlap, 1965.

Der historische Roman, Aufbau Verlag, 1955, translation by Hannah Mitchell and Stanley Mitchell published as *The Historical Novel,* Merlin Press, 1962, Humanities Press, 1965.

Wider den missverstandenen Realismus (2nd edition of original *Die Gegenwartsbedeutung des kritischen Realismus*), Claassen, 1958, translation by John Mander and Necke Mander published as *The Meaning of Contemporary Realism,* Merlin Press, 1963, published as *Realism in Our Time: Literature and the Class Struggle,* Harper, 1964.

Lenin: Studie ueber den Zusammenhang seiner Gedanken, Luchterhand, 1967, translation by Nicholas Jacobs published as *Lenin: A Study on the Unity of His Thought,* N.L.B. (England), 1970, M.I.T. Press, 1971.

(Contributor) Theo Pinkus, editor, *Gesprache mit Georg Lukacs, Hans Heinz Holz, Leo Kotler, Wolfgang Abendroth,* Rowolt, 1967, translation by David Fembach published as *Conversations With Lukacs,* Merlin Press, 1974, M.I.T. Press, 1975.

Solschenizyn, Luchterhand, 1970, translation by William David Graf published as *Solzhenitsyn,* Merlin Press, 1970, M.I.T. Press, 1971.

Writer and Critic, and Other Essays, translation from the original edited by Arthur D. Kahn, Grosset & Dunlap, 1971.

Political Writings, 1919-1929: The Question of Parliamentarianism and Other Essays, translated by Michael McColgan from the original *Taktika es Ethika,* N.L.B., 1972, published as *Tactics and Ethics: Political Essays, 1919-1929,* Harper, 1975.

Marxism and Human Liberation: Essays on History, Culture, and Revolution, translation from the original edited by E. San Juan, Jr., Dell, 1973.

Revolution und Gegenrevolution, Luchterhand, 1976, translation by Victor Zitta published as *Revolution and Revelation,* 1976.

IN GERMAN; ALL PUBLISHED BY AUFBAU VERLAG, UNLESS OTHERWISE NOTED

Alte und neue Kultur (title means "Old and New Culture"), Jungarbeiter Verlag, 1921, reprinted, 1970.

Deutsche Literatur im Zeitalter des Imperialismus: Ein Uebersicht ihrer Hauptstroemungen, 1945.

Gottfried Keller, 1946.

Fortschritt und Reaktion in der deutschen Literatur, 1947.

Karl Marx und Friedrich Engels als Literaturhistoriker, 1947.

Schicksalswende: Beitrage zu einer neuen deutschen Ideologie, 1948, 2nd edition, 1956.

Der russische Realismus in der Weltliteratur, 1949, 3rd edition, 1952.

Existentialismus oder Marxismus?, 1951.

Deutsche Realisten des 19. Jahrhunderts, 1951.

Skizze einer Geschichte der neuen deutschen Literatur (title means "An Outline of the History of Modern German Literature"), 1953.

Beitrage zur Geschichte der Aesthetik, 1954.

Die Zerstorung der Vernunft (title means "The Destruction of Reason"), 1954.

(Author of introduction) Georg Wilhelm Friedrich Hegel, *Aesthetik,* 1955.

(With Franz Mehring) *Friedrich Nietzsche,* 1957.

Tolstoi und die westliche Literatur, J. Fladung, c. 1959.

Schriften zur Literatursoziologie, Luchterhand, 1961.

Aesthetik, four volumes, Luchterhand, 1963.

Die Eigenart des Aesthetischen (title means "The Specific Nature of the Aesthetic"), Luchterhand, 1963.

Deutsche Literatur in zwei Jahrhunderten, Luchterhand, 1964.

Der junge Marx: Seine philosophische Entwicklung von 1840-1844, Neske, 1965.

Von Nietzsche bis Hitler; oder, Der Irrationalismus in der deutschen Politik, Fischer Bucherei, 1966.

Ueber die Besonderheit als Kategorie der Aesthetik, Luchterhand, 1967.

Schriften zur Ideologie und Politik, Luchterhand, 1967.

Die Grablegung des alten Deutschland: Essays zur deutschen Literatur des 19. Jahrhunderts, Rowolt, 1967.

Faust und Faustus: Vom Drama der Menschengattung zur Tragoedie der modernen Kunst, Rowolt, 1967.

Frueheschriften, Luchterhand, 1968.

Werke, fourteen volumes, Luchterhand, 1968-69.

Probleme der Aesthetik, Luchterhand, 1969.

Russische Literatur, russische Revolution: Puschkin, Tolstoi, Dostojewskij, Fadejew, Makarenko, Scholochow, Solschenizyn, Luchterhand, 1969.

(Author of afterword) Hegel, *Phaenomenologie des Geistes,* Ullstein, 1970.

Die ontologischen Grundlagen des menschlichen Denkens und Handelns, [Vienna], 1970.

Marxismus und Stalinismus, Rowohlt, 1970.

Zur Ontologie des gesellschaftlichen Seins (title means "The Ontology of Social Existence"; also see below), Luchterhand, 1971.

Die ontologischen Grundprinzipien von Marx (selection from *Zur Ontologie des gesellschaftlichen Seins*), Luchterhand, 1972.

Die Arbeit (selection from *Zur Ontologie des gesellschaftlichen Seins*), Luchterhand, 1973.

(Contributor) Ruediger Bubner, Konrad Cramer, and Reiner Wiehl, editors, *Ist eine philosophische Aesthetik moeglich?,* Vandenhoeck & Ruprecht, 1973.

(Contributor) Johann Wollgang von Goethe, *Die Leiden des jungen Werther,* Insel Verlag, 1973.

Fruehe Schriften zur Aesthetik, Luchterhand, Volume I: *Heidelberger Philosophie der Kunst, 1912-1914,* 1974, Volume II: *Heidelberger Aesthetik, 1916-1918,* 1975.

(With others) *Individuum und Praxis Positionen der budapester Schule,* Suhrkamp, 1975.

Politische Aufsatze, 1918, Luchterhand, 1975.

Kunst und obiektive Warheit: Essays zur Literaturtheorie und Geschichte, P. Reclam, 1977.

(With Arnold Hauser) *Im Gespraech mit Georg Lukacs,* Beck, 1978.

IN HUNGARIAN

A Modern Drama fejlodesenek tortenete: Kiadja a kisfaludytarsasag, two volumes, Franklin Tarsulet, 1911.

Kristorii realizma, [Hungary], 1939.

Irastudok felelossege, Idegennyelvii irodalmi kiado, 1944.

Irodalom es demokracia, Szikra, 1947.

A Polgari filozofia valsaga, [Hungary], 1947.

A Realizmus problemai: Nemet eredetibol forditotta, Atheneum (Budapest, Hungary), 1948.

Balzac, Stendhal, Zola, Hungaria eloszo, 1949.

Nagy orosz realistak, Szikra, 1949.

Az esz tronfosztasa: Az irracionalista ftlozofia kritikaja, Akademiai Kiado, 1956.

A Kulonosseg mint esztetika katagoria, Akademiai Kiado, 1957.

Istoriski roman, Kultura, 1958.

Prolegomena za marksisticku estetiku: Posebnost kao centralna kategorija estetike, Nolit, 1960.

Az esztetikum sajatossaga, Akademiai Kiado, 1965.

Lukacs Gyorgy valogatott muvei, Gondolat, 1968.

Muveszet es tarsadalom: Valogatott esztetikai tanulmanyok, Gondolat, 1968.

Vilagirodalom: Valogatott vilagirodalmi tanulmanyok, two volumes, Gondolat, 1969.

Magyar irodalom—magyar kultura: Valogatott tanulmanyok, Gondolat, 1970.

Utam Marxhoz: Valogatott filozofiai tanulmanyok, Magveto Konyvkiado, 1971.

Adalekok az esztetika tortenetenez, two volumes, Magveto Konyvkiado, 1972.

Ifjukori muvek, 1902-1918, Magveto Konyvkiado, 1977.

SIDELIGHTS: In *Language and Silence,* George Steiner extrapolated two principal beliefs from Lukacs's works: "First, that literary criticism is not a luxury, that it is not what the subtlest of American critics has called 'a discourse for amateurs.' But that it is, on the contrary, a central and militant force toward shaping men's lives. Secondly, Lukacs affirms that the work of the critic is neither subjective nor uncertain. The truth of judgment can be verified." With such a basis for his writings, Lukacs has been credited with three major contributions to modern philosophical thought, defined by Alden Whitman in the *New York Times:* "A defense of humanism in Communist letters; elaboration of Marx's theory of the alienation of man by industrial society; and formulation of a system of esthetics that repudiated political control of Socialist artists while emphasizing what Mr. Lukacs termed the 'class nature' of beauty."

Although Lukacs is, as Alfred Kazin wrote in the introduction to Lukacs's *Studies in European Realism,* "an individual thinker who is fascinated by and thoroughly committed to Marxism as a philosophy, and who uses it for the intellectual pleasure and moral satisfaction it gives him," he was throughout his life in conflict with the Communist International. From the appearance of *History and Class Consciousness* in 1923, he was forced in and out of political life by charges of "revisionism." Because in his theories he considered the classics and "bourgeois" writers of the eighteenth and nineteenth centuries, he came under frequent attack and was often compelled to publicly recant his own views. Still, he remained an opponent of the party line in literature and disparaged, as Whitman observed, "writers who were Socialists first and writers second."

After his university studies and travels in Italy, Lukacs lived in Heidelberg for a time, where he associated with Max Weber and his circle. Weber, Lukacs's former teacher, was a sociologist and historian in the tradition of Georg Wilhelm Friedrich Hegel, whose philosophical idealism, dialectical method, and concern with history were an early influence on both Lukacs and Marxism itself; Hegel's conception of the historical development of artistic form provided the basis of much of Lukacs's aesthetic.

In 1918 Lukacs joined the Communist party. With his international reputation as a literary critic already established with the appearance of *Soul and Form* in 1911, he was made Hungarian minister of culture and public education in the Communist regime of Bela Kun. Kun remained in power briefly, from March to August of 1919, and upon his overthrow, Lukacs went into hiding. Lukacs spent the next ten years in exile in Vienna, where he was granted asylum.

From Vienna, Lukacs carried on a struggle with Kun for control of the Hungarian underground movement. Official denunciation of Lukacs's writing settled the issue against him, but following statements of "self-criticism" he was granted refuge in the Soviet Union during Hitler's rise to power. When he returned to Budapest after World War II, ending a twenty-five-year period of exile, he joined the coalition government as a member of the National Assembly of Hungary. In 1949 the Communist party again took control, establishing the People's Republic of Hungary, which was overthrown in October, 1956, by an anti-Soviet revolt. As a leader of the insurrectionist Petofi circle and then minister of culture in Imre Nagy's regime, Lukacs was deported to Romania when Soviet troops returned the Communists to power. Allowed to return to Hungary in 1957, Lukacs retired from political activity and devoted his last years to teaching and writing.

Lukacs's early publications, which he renounced after joining the Communist party, strongly influenced existential thought. The neo-Kantian aesthetic of *Soul and Form* and *The Theory of the Novel* saw literature as an expression of man's inwardness. The former, for example, is concerned with the relationship between human life and absolute values. Lucien Goldmann pointed out in *TriQuarterly* that with *Soul and Form* Lukacs was "the first to pose in all its acuteness and force the problem of the relation between the individual, authenticity, and death, . . . affirming the absolute nonvalue of the social world." In *The Theory of the Novel,* on the other hand, Lukacs examined the epic genre as "the expression of complex and multiple relationships between the soul and the world."

Often considered his most important work, *History and Class Consciousness* is marked by a neo-Hegelian idealism, what George Lichtheim called a "belief in the possibility of objective insight into reality." To unify philosophical theory with political practice and to unite Marx's interpretation of history with Hegel's concept of totality, Lukacs here asserted, according to Lichtheim, "that the totality of history could be apprehended by adopting a particular 'class standpoint': that of the proletariat." Lukacs was moving away from his earlier, western humanist conception of literature toward his theory of the "great realism," from his portrayal of man as alienated and alone to his anticipation of a mankind freed from alienation by a consciousness of the historical process.

Although Lukacs eventually repudiated *History and Class Consciousness* along with his first two books, the work contains the seeds of his later orthodoxy, mainly in "its identification of 'true consciousness' with a particular doctrine and a particular class, and its faith in the party as the repository of the doctrine and the vanguard of the class," noted Steven Lukes in the *Washington Post.* Tibor Szamuely, moreover, saw *History and Class Consciousness* as "the best, the frankest, the most wide-ranging and powerful exposition of the philosophy of totalitarianism ever written."

Lukacs's subsequent critical work often ran counter to party position, however. His reading of literature took into account sociology, history, and politics, and he advocated realism as the highest mode of fiction while condemning formalism. But he distinguished realism both from psychological novels and from naturalism, which led him to praise Balzac, for example, and disparage Zola, in direct opposition to party line. Moreover, he valued the realism of such writers as Sir Walter Scott and Tolstoy as manifestations of the dialectical relationship between historical reality and literature. He was opposed, however, to "proletarian realism" and party control of the literary process. He contended, as Whitman explained, that in a Communist society, "noble art would emerge from the artist's interaction with his environment; but works of art could not be summoned forth in a predetermined pattern."

Although the occasion of Lukacs's death in 1971 was scarcely acknowledged in the eastern European Communist press, he was buried with customary party honors, having refrained from personal involvement in politics after 1957. It was only after his death that his works began to be widely available to English-speaking audiences. Despite the limited circulation of Lukacs's works, Lucien Goldmann, as early as 1967, deemed Lukacs to be "one of the most influential figures in the intellectual life of the 20th century."

BIOGRAPHICAL/CRITICAL SOURCES:

BOOKS

Bahr, Ehrhard, and Ruth Kunzer, *Georg Lukacs,* Ungar, 1972.
Georg Lukacs, Boorberg, 1973.
Lichtheim, George, *George Lukacs,* Viking, 1970.
Parkinson, G. H. R., editor, *Georg Lukacs: The Man, His Work, and His Ideas,* Random House, 1970.
Steiner, George, *Language and Silence,* Faber, 1967.
Ungar, Frederick, editor, *Handbook of Austrian Literature,* Ungar, 1973.

PERIODICALS

Books and Bookmen, September, 1969.
Canadian Forum, August, 1968.
Commonweal, November 27, 1970.
Contemporary Literature, summer, 1968, winter, 1968.
Encounter, May, 1963, April, 1965.
Listener, September 5, 1968.
Nation, July 14, 1969, December 27, 1971.
National Review, June 1, 1971.
New Statesman, December 17, 1971.
New York Times, June 11, 1968.
New York Times Book Review, May 10, 1964, July 18, 1971.
Saturday Review, June 13, 1964, November 6, 1965, December 4, 1971.
Times Literary Supplement, September 25, 1969, November 6, 1970, June 11, 1971
TriQuarterly, spring, 1967, spring, 1968.
Washington Post, July 24, 1971.

OBITUARIES:

PERIODICALS

Antiquarian Bookman, July 19-26, 1971.
New York Times, June 5, 1971.
Time, June 14, 1971.

*   *   *

LUKAS, J(ay) Anthony   1933-

PERSONAL: Born April 25, 1933, in New York, N.Y.; son of Edwin Jay (a lawyer) and Elizabeth (Schamberg) Lukas; married Linda Healey, September 18, 1982. *Education:* Harvard University, B.A. (magna cum laude), 1955; graduate study at Free University of Berlin, 1955-56.

ADDRESSES: Home—890 West End Ave., New York, N.Y. 10025.

CAREER: Baltimore Sun, Baltimore, Md., city hall correspondent, 1958-62; *New York Times,* New York City, member of Washington, D.C., and United Nations bureaus, 1962, correspondent in the Congo, 1962-65, and in India, 1965-67, member of metropolitan staff, 1967-68, roving national correspondent, 1969-70, staff writer for Sunday magazine, 1970-71; free-lance writer. Visiting lecturer at Yale University, 1973; adjunct professor, School of Public Communications, Boston University, 1977-78; visiting lecturer, Kennedy School of Government, Harvard University, 1979-80; faculty member of Wesleyan Writers Conference, 1986. Host of radio program "In Conversation," WOR, New York City. Member of Committee on Public Justice;

member of steering committee, Reporter's Committee on Freedom of the Press; member of executive board, New York Council for the Humanities. Consultant, Hastings Center. *Military service:* U.S. Army, news commentator and writer of propaganda, 1956-58.

MEMBER: PEN American Center (member of executive committee, 1977-83), Authors Guild (council member, 1987—), Signet Society, Phi Beta Kappa, Harvard Club (New York, N.Y.), Coffee House Club (New York City), St. Botolph Club (Boston, Mass.).

AWARDS, HONORS: Pulitzer Prize, 1968, for local reporting; George Polk Memorial Award from Long Island University, 1968; Mike Berger Award from Columbia University, 1968; Page One Award from New York Newspaper Guild; By-line Feature Award from Newspaper Reporters Association, 1968; Harvard University, Nieman fellow, 1968-69, and Institute of Politics fellow, 1976-77; Guggenheim fellow, 1978-79; judge for American Book Award in nonfiction, 1983 and 1986; American Book Award in nonfiction, 1985, and National Book Critics Circle Award in general nonfiction, Robert F. Kennedy Book Award, *Washington Monthly* Political Book of the Year, and Pulitzer Prize, all 1986, all five for *Common Ground: A Turbulent Decade in the Lives of Three American Families;* named Literary Lion by New York Public Library, 1986; honorary degrees from Northeastern University, 1986, and Colby College, 1987.

WRITINGS:

The Barnyard Epithet and Other Obscenities: Notes on the Chicago Conspiracy Trial, Harper, 1970.
Don't Shoot—We Are Your Children!, Random House, 1971.
Nightmare: The Underside of the Nixon Years, Viking, 1975.
(Contributor) *My Harvard, My Yale,* Random House, 1982.
Common Ground: A Turbulent Decade in the Lives of Three American Families, Knopf, 1985.

Contributor to magazines, including *Esquire, Harper's, Saturday Review, New Republic, Reader's Digest, Atlantic, Nation, Psychology Today, New Times,* and *American Scholar. MORE Journalism Review,* senior editor, 1972-77, associate editor, 1977-78; contributing editor, *New Times,* 1973-75.

SIDELIGHTS: Reporting on controversial issues and social unrest is the forte of J. Anthony Lukas, two-time Pulitzer Prize recipient and former correspondent for the *New York Times.* Throughout the 1970s Lukas produced several critically praised books, including *Don't Shoot—We Are Your Children!,* an examination of the alternative lifestyles of America's countercultural youth. The volume was an expansion of a newspaper article (which won the writer his first Pulitzer Prize) on the life and death of Linda Fitzpatrick, an upper-class Connecticut teenager who in 1967 was found beaten to death, along with her hippie boyfriend, in New York's Greenwich Village. *Don't Shoot—We Are Your Children!* profiles not only the murder victims but also eight other youths of various ethnic and economic backgrounds. And Ross Macdonald in a *New York Times Book Review* article points out that "an eleventh young American, a few years older than the others, comes to be known in these pages. Their author, Mr. Lukas. His eloquence as a writer, his tenacity in research, his respect for other human beings, have combined to give us a beautiful and important book which I think may become a classic."

Despite the success of *Don't Shoot—We Are Your Children!* and other volumes, Lukas felt dissatisfied after the books were published, according to Joseph Barbato in *Publishers Weekly.* "I don't disown them; I'm happy to have written them," the author

told Barbato, "but they weren't my best books. They grew haphazardly out of journalistic works." Thus in 1974 Lukas embarked on what many consider his best book to date, *Common Ground: A Turbulent Decade in the Lives of Three American Families.* The three families of the title, all residents of Boston, Mass., were the subjects of Lukas's exhaustive, seven-year research and writing project detailing the effects of court-ordered busing in the Boston public schools on the people whose lives were changed by the decision. The busing edict, handed down in the early 1970s, was an attempt to desegregate the city's school system, which had long been plagued by charges of racial discrimination and poor administration, particularly in the disadvantaged neighborhoods.

After screening dozens of families for possible use in the book, Lukas settled on three that he found to represent the socioeconomic spectrum of the city. The Divers were an affluent "Wasp" couple with two children. Colin Diver, a lawyer who had been offered a lucrative position in Washington, D.C., was so inspired by the Rev. Martin Luther King's ideals, and so shocked by King's assassination, that he moved his family from the suburbs into an old Victorian home in the South End section of Boston—one of the few multiracial communities left there. Just six blocks from the Divers lived the Twymons, headed by welfare mother Rachel (her husband had left her), a semi-invalid with six children. Her family was representative of the working-class blacks who populated the Roxbury district, and whose children were primarily the ones bused into the suburbs to integrate its mostly white schools. Finally, Lukas profiles a white counterpart to the Twymons, the McGoffs. Also headed by the mother (Alice McGoff was a widow), containing seven children, and living in a disadvantaged neighborhood, the McGoff family was part of the Irish Catholic minority of Boston, of which many, like Alice, were vehemently anti-busing.

The book begins with the 1968 assassination of Dr. King, and ends ten years later with the families coping with the many changes in their lives created in the wake of the 1970s. By the end of the book, for instance, Colin Diver moves his family back to the suburbs after an encounter with a mugger forces him and his wife to reconsider their liberal ways. Rachel Twymon sees one daughter become pregnant and a son face charges of rape. Lukas, while maintaining an objective stance during the years he studied the three families, nevertheless shared in their joys and sorrows. His professionalism was admired by his subjects. Rachel Twymon calls the author, in a *People* article, "a very, very compassionate man," while a McGoff daughter, in the same article, notes that "no matter what I said he never condemned me. . . . He really researched the story. He didn't do a half-hearted job."

Indeed, the author, known for his meticulous research methods, went to great lengths to study the historical backgrounds of his subjects. He traced the Twymon family to its slave days in Georgia, making several trips there and traced the Divers to their pre-Revolutionary War forebears. To examine the McGoff heritage Lukas visited Ireland. (As Barbato reports, the author actually spent four years chronicling another working-class family before deciding that "they were not working dramatically for the book" and abandoning them for the McGoffs.) "Ultimately," says Barbato, Lukas "found himself writing from about 555 taped interviews, among other materials, then reworking and cutting a manuscript that ran to 1400 pages."

As evidenced by the critical reaction to *Common Ground,* Lukas's extensive work was justified. "This is a book of such force and clarity that its just praise would require language long rendered empty by jacket blurbs," begins *Chicago Tribune Book World* reviewer Robert B. Parker. "To say that 'Common Ground' is about busing in Boston is a bit like saying that 'Moby Dick' is about whaling in New Bedford, but it's a start." Many critics agree that the force of the book lies far beyond its basic subject—busing—and that its true strength is in the drama behind the controversy. To *Los Angeles Times* writer David Holstrom, *Common Ground* "so thoroughly documents the nature and debilitating effects of entrenched bigotry that when I reached the last page I said, 'Could it be that there are only two sensible answers: leave Boston or start the city all over again?' "

Mark Zanger, in *Nation,* says that Lukas develops themes in the work, most notably "the power of class." All three families, Zanger continues, "debate their relationship to Boston's power elite, and all three discover mixed traditions in their histories. . . . How people respond when they are cheated, how their families are strained and how they, go on living and find new understanding are Lukas's themes."

Other reviewers see artistic merit in the author's reportage. "In many respects [*Common Ground*] belongs in the tradition of literary-documentary studies—the kind of work James Agee did upon returning from his stint in rural Alabama in the 1930s, or [George] Orwell did when he wrote of his experiences among England's coal miners in that same decade," as Robert Coles states in *Washington Post Book World.* "Their writing was suggestive rather than categorical—geared to an evocation of individual variation rather than the requirements of a universal standard. . . . Without question J. Anthony Lukas now belongs in their company—his book [is] well up to their high and idiosyncratic standards." Christopher Lehmann-Haupt compares Lukas's journalism to fiction, remarking that "a novelist would not have dared to make these families so neatly representative that their members run the gamut from Methodist churchgoers to muggers and rapists, from Irish street-gang rowdies to the head of a trust fund dispensing charity. Yet in the pages of 'Common Ground' they seem as real as the work of a naturalist," says the critic in a *New York Times* piece. "This is not a Studs Terkel approach to history—solely the related experience of participants," adds Holstrom, "—but a careful, dispassionate reconstruction of events by a writer who knows how to weave history, fact, anecdote, dialogue and description into an utterly compelling narrative."

While *Common Ground* enjoyed widespread success, winning a second Pulitzer Prize for its author, some reviewers had measured criticism for the work. Lehmann-Haupt, for example, is disconcerted by Lukas's penchant for "illustrating history with so many personal biographies: his chronology gets confusing at times, with events that seemed years in the past suddenly popping up again in the present." And to *Maclean's* writer Lenny Glynn, *Common Ground* "has several weaknesses. Adopting a coolly reportorial stance, [Lukas] draws few clear conclusions. In a brief epilogue, he updates the lives of his principal subjects but leaves the reader with few insights into the busing experiment, which continues in a shrunken Boston school system." But both reviewers add that such stylistic flaws do not deflate the power of the work's message—with Glynn stating that *Common Ground* is "the best book in years on any American city."

In a *New York Times Book Review* article, Lukas explains why he devoted some seven years to *Common Ground:* "I believe that what happened in Boston was not a random series of events but the acting out of the burden of American history." "It is a big book, and potential readers may fear that it will tell them more than they want to know about Boston," writes Jack Beatty in the

Atlantic. "And so it may. Still, just as novels about strikingly individual people contain glints of truth about all of our lives, so *Common Ground* lights up not only Boston's particular troubles but the generic troubles of the American city—poverty, racism, crime, decaying public housing, poor public schools, racial polarization, and the destruction of old neighborhoods by new money and those puissant forms of intervention of the federal bulldozer and the federal writ." In the view of *Time* critic William A. Henry III, Lukas "well knows Emerson's dictum that there is properly no history, only biography. When Colin Diver chases a mugger who battered a black woman outside his front door, when Alice McGoff debates with herself whether she can respect a Catholic priest who is a 'pro-buser,' when Rachel Twymon's sister hears rocks smash through her windows night after night, the story is larger than three families, and larger than Boston. As a narrative of people's repeated losses of faith, above all the faith that they can shape and control their lives, *Common Ground* explains what once seemed incomprehensible, and persuades the reader that to understand is indeed to forgive."

BIOGRAPHICAL/CRITICAL SOURCES:

PERIODICALS

Atlantic, September, 1985.
Chicago Tribune Book World, September 8, 1985.
Detroit News, October 13, 1985.
Los Angeles Times, October 16, 1985.
Maclean's, November 4, 1985.
Nation, October 5, 1985.
New Republic, May 29, 1971, March 20, 1976, October 14, 1985.
Newsweek, April 12, 1971, February 9, 1976, September 23, 1985.
New York Review of Books, June 24, 1976.
New York Times, October 30, 1970, February 11, 1976, September 12, 1985, September 30, 1985.
New York Times Book Review, November 8, 1970, April 25, 1971, January 25, 1976, September 15, 1985.
People, January 13, 1986.
Publishers Weekly, March 8, 1971, September 27, 1985.
Saturday Review, December 12, 1970, May 1, 1971.
Time, May 17, 1976, September 23, 1985.
U.S. News & World Report, April 28, 1986.
Washington Post Book World, May 2, 1971, September 8, 1985.

* * *

LURIA, Alexander R(omanovich) 1902-1977

PERSONAL: Name is sometimes transliterated as Aleksander Romanovich Luriya; born July 16, 1902, in Kazan, Russia (now U.S.S.R.); died August, 1977, in Moscow, U.S.S.R.; son of Roman A. (a physician) and Eugenia (Hasskin) Luria; married Lana P. Lipchina (a professor of biology), July 16, 1933; children: Helen A. *Education:* Studied at University of Kazan; University of Moscow, Dr. Phil., 1936, Dr. Med., 1943. *Religion:* None.

ADDRESSES: Home—13 Frunze St., Moscow G 19, U.S.S.R. *Office*—Department of Neuropsychology, University of Moscow, Moscow, U.S.S.R.

CAREER: Affiliated with N. K. Krupskaya Academy for Communistic Education, 1923-31; psychologist at psychology and neurology institutes in the U.S.S.R., 1923-45; University of Moscow, Moscow, U.S.S.R., professor of neuropsychology and head of department, 1945-77.

MEMBER: Soviet Psychological Society, Soviet Neurological Society, Academy of Pedagogical Sciences of the U.S.S.R., British Psychological Society (honorary fellow), American Academy of Arts and Sciences (foreign member), National Academy of Sciences (United States; foreign associate), American Academy of Education (foreign member), Columbian Psychological Society (honorary fellow), Swiss Psychological Society (honorary member), French Neurological Society (honorary member).

AWARDS, HONORS: Order of Lenin, 1955; Lomorossov Award, 1968; D.Sc. from University of Leicester, 1968, University of Nejmegen, 1969, University of Lublin, 1973, University of Brussels, 1975, and University of Tampere, 1975.

WRITINGS:

Rech i intellekt v razvitii rebenka (title means "Speech and Intellect in the Development of the Child"), Poligrafshkola imeni A. V. Lunacharskogo, 1927.

(With Lev Vygotsky) *Etiudy po istorii povedeniia* (title means "Studies in History of Behavior"), Goscizdat, 1930.

The Nature of Human Conflicts; or, Emotion, Conflict, and Will: An Objective Study of Disorganization and Control of Human Behavior, translation by W. Horsely Gantt, Liveright, 1932, reprinted, 1976.

Vnutreniaia kartina boleznei iatrogennye zabolevaniia (title means "An Integral Picture of Illnesses and Diseases"), Medgiz, 1944.

Travmaticheskaia afasiia: Klinika, semiotika, vosstanovitel'naia terapiia, Medical Academy Press (Moscow), 1947, translation by MacDonald Critchley published as *Traumatic Aphasia: Its Syndromes, Psychology and Treatment,* Mouton & Co., 1970.

Vosstanovlenie funktsii mozga posle voennoi travmy, Medical Academy Press, 1948, translation by Basil Haigh published as *The Restoration of Functions after Brain Injury,* edited by O. L. Zangwill, Pergamon, 1963.

Ocherki psikhofiziologii pisma (title means "Essays on the Psychophysiology of Writing"), Pedagogical Academy Press, 1950.

Rol'slova v formirovanii vremennykh sviazei v normal'nom i anomal'nom razvitii (detei), Pedagogical Academy Press, 1955, translation published as *The Role of Speech in the Regulation of Normal and Abnormal Behaviour,* edited by J. Tizard, Pergamon, 1961.

(With F. Ia Yudovich) *Rech'i razvitie psikhicheskikh professov u rebenka: Experimental'noe issledovanie,* Pedagogical Academy Press, 1956, translation by O. Kovasc and Joan Simon published as *Speech and the Development of Mental Processes in the Child: An Experimental Investigation,* edited by Simon, Staples, 1959, Humanities, 1966.

Problemy vysstei nervnoi deiatel'nosti normal'nego i anomal'nogo rebenka, (title means "Problems of Higher Nervous Activity in the Normal and Abnormal Child"), Pedagogical Academy Press, 2 volumes, 1956-58.

(Editor) *Umstvenno otstalyi rebionok,* Pedagogical Academy Press, 1960, translation by W. K. Robinson published as *The Mentally Retarded Child: Essays Based on a Study of the Peculiarities of the Higher Nervous Functioning of Child-doligophrenics,* edited by Brian Kerman, Pergamon, 1963.

Ob otbore detel'vo vspomogatel'nye shkoly: Metodicheskoe pis'mo dlia rabotnikov priemnykh komissii, Institut Defektologii, Akademiia Pedagogicheskikh nauk RSFSR, 1961.

Vysshiye korkovye funktsii cheloveka i ikh narusheniia pri lokal'nykh porazheniiakh mozga, Moscow University Press, 1962, 2nd edition, 1966, translation by Haigh published as *Higher Cortical Functions in Men,* Basic Books, 1966, 2nd edition, Consultants Bureau, 1980.

Mozg cheloveka i psikhicheskie protsessy, Pedagogical Academy Press, Volume 1, 1963, Volume 2, 1970, translation of Volume 1 by Haigh published as *Human Brain and Psychological Process,* Harper, 1966.

Metody issledovania detei pri otbore vo vspomogatel'nye shkoly (title means "Methods of Investigating Children During Selection for Auxiliary Schools"), Pzoveschenie Publishing House (Moscow), 1964.

(Editor) *Psychological Research in the U.S.S.R.,* Progress Publishers, 1966.

(Editor with E. D. Khomskaia) *Lobnye doli i reguliatsiia psikhicheskikh protsessov i neiropsikhologicheskie issledovaniia* (title means "Frontal Lobes and Regulation of Psychological Processes"), Moscow University Press, 1966.

(With Liubov S. Tsvetkova) *Neiropsikhologicheskii analiz resheniia zadach: Narusheniia protsessa resheniia zadach pri lokal'nykh porazheniiakh mozga* (title means "A Neuropsychological Analysis of Problem-Solving Disturbances of the Problem-Solving Process from Localized Injuries of the Brain"), Pzoveschenie Publishing House, 1966.

Malen'kaia knizhka o bol'shoi pamiati (Um mnemonista), Moscow University Press, 1968, translation by Lynn Solotaroff published as *The Mind of a Mnemonist: A Little Book about a Vast Memory,* foreword by Jerome S. Bruner, Basic Books, 1968.

(With others) *Rasstroistva pamiati v klinike anevrism perednei soedinitel'noi arterii* (title means "Memory Disorders in the Clinic from Aneurysms of the Frontal Connective Artery"), Moscow University Press, 1970.

Poteriannyi i vozvrashchennyi mir (Istoriia odnogo raneniia), Moscow University Press, 1971, translation by Solotaroff published as *The Man with a Shattered World: The History of a Brain Wound,* Basic Books, 1972.

Neiropsikhologiia pamiati, Pedagogical Academy Press, Volume 1, 1972, Volume 2, 1976, translation by Haigh published as *The Neuropsychology of Memory,* Scripta, 1976.

(With others) *Psikhologiia vospriiatiia (uchebnoe posobie),* (title means "The Psychology of Perception: A Textbook"), Moscow University Press, 1973.

Osnovy Neiropsychologii, Moscow University Press, 1973, translation by Haigh published as *The Working Brain: An Introduction to Neuropsychology,* Basic Books, 1973.

(Editor with K. Pribram) *Electrophysiology of the Frontal Lobes* (translation), Academic Press, 1973.

Ob istoricheskom razvitii poznavatel'nykh protsessov, Nauka, 1974, translation by Martin Lopez-Morillas and Solotaroff published as *Cognitive Development: Its Cultural and Social Foundations,* Harvard University Press, 1976.

Osnovnye problemy neirolingvistiki, Moscow University Press, 1975, translation by Haigh published as *Basic Problems of Neurolinguistics,* Mouton & Co., 1976.

(Contributor) *Mozg pamiat* (title means "Brain and Memory"), Moscow University Press, 1975.

Materialy k kursu lektsii po obshchei psikhologii (title means "Material for a Course of Lectures on Common Psychology"), Moscow University Press, 1975.

Neuropsychological Studies in Aphasia, Schwetz & Zeitlinger, 1977.

The Selected Writings of A. R. Luria, edited and with an introduction by Michael Cole, M. E. Sharpe, 1978.

The Making of Mind: A Personal Account of Soviet Psychology, edited by Michael and Sheila Cole, Harvard University Press, 1979.

Iazyk i soznanie, Izdatel'stvo MGU, 1979, translation published as *Language and Cognition,* edited by James V. Wertsch, J. Wiley, 1981.

Also author of *Man's Conscious Actions: Their Origin and Brain Organization,* Plenum, and *Yazyk mozg* (title means "Language and Brain"), Moscow University Press.

BIOGRAPHICAL/CRITICAL SOURCES:

BOOKS

Christensen, Anne-Lise, *Luria's Neuropsychological Investigation,* Spectrum, 1975.

PERIODICALS

Book World, March 10, 1968.
Observer Review, January 26, 1969.

OBITUARIES:

PERIODICALS

New York Times, August 17, 1977.

*   *   *

LURIE, Alison   1926-

PERSONAL: Born September 3, 1926, in Chicago, Ill.; daughter of Harry and Bernice (Stewart) Lurie; married Jonathan Peale Bishop (a professor), September 10, 1948 (divorced, 1985); children: John, Jeremy, Joshua. *Education:* Radcliffe College, A.B., 1947.

ADDRESSES: Office—Department of English, Cornell University, Ithaca, N.Y. 14850.

CAREER: Cornell University, Ithaca, N.Y., lecturer, 1969-73, associate professor, 1973-76, professor of English, 1976—. Has also worked as a ghostwriter and librarian.

MEMBER: American Academy and Institute of Arts and Letters.

AWARDS, HONORS: Yaddo Foundation fellow, 1963, 1964, 1966; Guggenheim grant, 1965-66; Rockefeller Foundation grant, 1967-68; New York State Cultural Council Foundation grant, 1972-73; American Academy of Arts and Letters award in literature, 1978; American Book Award nomination in fiction, 1984, National Book Critics Circle Award nomination for best work of fiction, 1984, and Pulitzer Prize in fiction, 1985, all for *Foreign Affairs.*

WRITINGS:

V. R. Lang: A Memoir, privately printed, 1959.
V. R. Lang: Poems and Plays, Random House, 1974.
The Heavenly Zoo (juvenile), Farrar, Straus, 1980.
Clever Gretchen and Other Forgotten Folk Tales (juvenile), Crowell, 1980.
Fabulous Beasts (juvenile), Farrar, Straus, 1981.
The Language of Clothes (nonfiction), Random House, 1981.
Don't Tell the Grown Ups: Subversive Children's Literature (nonfiction), Little, Brown, 1990.

NOVELS

Love and Friendship, Macmillan, 1962.
The Nowhere City, Coward, 1965.
Imaginary Friends, Coward, 1967.
Real People, Random House, 1969.
The War Between the Tates, Random House, 1974.
Only Children, Random House, 1979.

Foreign Affairs, Random House, 1984.
The Truth About Lorin Jones, Little, Brown, 1988.

OTHER

Also editor, with Justin G. Schiller, of "Classics of Children's Literature, 1631-1932" series, Garland Publishing. Contributor of articles and reviews to periodicals, including *New York Review of Books, New York Times Book Review, New Statesman,* and *New Review.*

SIDELIGHTS: Although she has written children's books and several works of nonfiction, Alison Lurie is best known for her novels, especially *The War Between the Tates* and *Foreign Affairs,* each one a finely structured comedy of manners about people from an academic milieu. As Sara Sanborn states in a *New York Times Book Review* critique of *The War Between the Tates,* from the beginning of her career Lurie "has regularly produced insightful and witty novels about The Way We Live Now, drawing on a large talent for social verisimilitude." Her work has been praised by a London *Times* reviewer as "formidably well made," while Christopher Lehmann-Haupt declares in the *New York Times* that Lurie "has quietly but surely established herself as one of this country's most able and witty novelists."

In the opinion of several critics, *The War Between the Tates* and Lurie's Pulitzer Prize-winning *Foreign Affairs* are examples of the author at her best. A London *Times* reviewer explains that *The War Between the Tates,* a comic novel about the marital difficulties of a professor and his wife in an era of campus unrest, "caught, just on the instant, the conflict between radical passions and more conventional moralities that raged like foreign wars in the early 1970s. It could now seem a period piece, its targets, with the hindsight of the 1980s and the new conservatism, almost too easy to pick off. But, reread, its toughness and satirical precision hold it together; its satirical object is not just the age but contradictory human nature." *Foreign Affairs,* the story of two American academics on sabbatical in England, "should help propel Alison Lurie into the forefront of American novelists, where she clearly belongs," according to William French in the Toronto *Globe and Mail.*

Lurie's characters are usually well-educated, sophisticated members of the upper middle class. Everett Wilkie and Josephine Helterman describe her in the *Dictionary of Literary Biography* as "a highly intelligent writer, perhaps too intelligent for popular tastes since much of her satire is of a cerebral sort aimed at persons in academic life, especially those in prestigious colleges." As Sanborn relates, "Miss Lurie's protagonists are always academics or writers, well-read and well-controlled, thoughtful and successful, people of good taste—and hence people especially susceptible to the Call of the Wild and the perfectly rational processes of self-deception. In each case, their carefully constructed lives and self images, glowing with conscious enlightenment, break up on the rocks of the irrational, to which they have been lured by the siren song of sheer sexual energy."

Extramarital sex is a recurring element in the tendency of Lurie's characters to depart from the carefully controlled, rational path; it figures prominently in almost every novel. *Love and Friendship* is a comedy set in academia that centers around the dissolution of a young couple's marriage, just as *The Nowhere City* contrasts the values of the northeastern United States with those of California against the backdrop of another marriage that is coming apart. In *Imaginary Friends,* described by the London *Times* reviewer as "a classic comedy about the desire to command knowledge," a sociologist becomes influenced by a millenarian cult he has infiltrated, while *Real People* satirizes Illyria, a pastoral artists' retreat. In each book, Sanborn writes, "the protagonists leave home and journey into the bizarre, where they learn their own mettle or come to terms with their lack of it. Thus each of these novels is marked to a greater or lesser degree by a certain laboriousness of invention, an intrusive quality of the special case."

In *The War Between the Tates,* however, Lurie raises "The Way We Live Now into the Human Comedy" with "the effortless grace of a real ironic gift," to use Sanborn's words. The book examines the midlife crisis of Brian Tate, a professor of political science at Corinth University who is just beginning to realize that he will never be a great man outside of his department. He becomes involved with a student whom he later impregnates, and this affair precipitates the rebellion of his wife, Erica, who experiments briefly with sex, drugs, and Eastern philosophy.

The Tates' marital difficulties and the student's pregnancy are not the only sources of discontent in the Tate household, however. Their best friends, Danielle and Leonard Zimmern, have just weathered their own divorce and are adopting radically different ways of life—Danielle is becoming an abrasive feminist, and Leonard is turning into an outspoken bachelor with an apartment in New York City—and Brian and Erica are forced to align themselves against one or the other. Furthermore, the much-glorified Tate children are growing into unpleasant, rebellious adults. Well into the novel Lurie draws an elaborate parallel between the war in Vietnam and the continuing battle between sexes and generations that is taking place in the Tate household. "This metaphor, of Miltonic grandeur and epic absurdity, ascends from the embattled Tate home and floats over the campus of Corinth University like a majestic balloon," Walter Clemons claims in *Newsweek.* The book climaxes with a feminist demonstration during which Brian Tate has to rescue a colleague from the wrath of his girlfriend and the other protesters.

Overall, reviewers have high praise for the novel. The book "represents a breakthrough into ease in the handling of the author's favorite themes," says Sanborn. Many of the incidents in the book are exaggerated or heightened for comic effect, with the plot often bordering on the preposterous, but unlike many of Lurie's earlier works, "no one goes anywhere; the Tates meet their destiny and the truth about themselves in their own back yard, on their daily rounds," Sanborn observes. "The whole plot unfolds, with the inevitability of a round dance once the first steps are taken in the college of Corinth."

Roger Sale adds in the *New York Review of Books* that Lurie "cheerfully takes on the standard plot—an ambitious professor, his well-educated wife, their domestic boredom and strain, a student mistress for the husband, futile attempts at retaliation and freedom by the wife, and whenever these figures and actions move into the surrounding community, we have clarity and brightness where others usually have managed murky expositions and cute tricks." In *The War Between the Tates,* agrees Doris Grumbach in the *Washington Post Book World,* Lurie "has taken a set of ordinary characters, or at least not exceptional ones, submitted them to the strains and battles of time, sex, legal alliances, generation gaps, politics and work: all the ingredients of a popular novel. But her sensibility and talent are so superior that she has given us an artistic work, which every one will read because it is 'common' to us all, but which some will perceive to have the crafted look and feel of a first-rate work."

Some reviewers criticize Lurie's tendency to distance herself from the characters in *The War Between the Tates,* finding various portraits overly satirical and unsympathetic. In general,

however, most regard the novel as a real accomplishment, primarily due to the author's familiarity with her subject matter. Lurie is a professor of children's literature at Cornell University, the campus that is the source of much of her inspiration, and as Sale sums up, Lurie creates a convincing fictional world "by means of her quickness, her efficiency, her lightness of touch, with lots of subjects that others manage only with ponderousness or self-regarding wit: The Department, The Book, The Cocktail Party, the Young, both children and students." Sanborn points out that the book is "a novel not only to read, but to reread for its cool and revealing mastery of a social epoch."

Only Children concerns itself with some of the same subjects as *The War Between the Tates,* most notably the conflict between the sexes and the generations, but whereas *The War Between the Tates* depicts children as rude interlopers, *Only Children* takes a more sympathetic view in that the story unfolds through the eyes and voices of two eight-year-old girls. The novel also reflects Lurie's interests in children's literature and gender discrimination, like her book *Clever Gretchen and Other Forgotten Folk Tales,* a collection of retold fairy tales that present women in a positive light.

Only Children relates the events of a Depression-era Fourth of July holiday that two couples and their daughters spend on a farm owned by the headmistress of the progressive school the girls attend. (Leonard Zimmern also appears in the story as the adolescent son from a previous marriage of one of the adults.) The author's preoccupation in *Only Children* is with sexual role dynamics and the flirtations that occur among the parents as observed and puzzled over by their daughters. In the process, notes *Time* critic John Skow, Lurie also depicts "the narrow range of adult female behavior that was on view to a girl of four decades ago." During the course of the long weekend, the adults' actions become more and more childish, while the girls' sensibilities take on a more mature awareness. Only the headmistress, independent and manless, but sexually experienced, remains an adult.

The book has garnered significant praise from reviewers. An *Atlantic* critic calls it Lurie's "gentlest, most sympathetic satire," while Mary Gordon describes it in the *New York Review of Books* as "the most interior of Lurie's novels, the most reflective, the most lyrical." And in the opinion of Ann Hulbert in the *New Republic,* "this novel about love and its disorderly ways in unexamined lives is a thoughtfully crafted and traditionally unified comic drama. In *Only Children* Lurie draws deftly from her academic literary discipline, without cramping her ironic and sympathetic imagination, which ranges as easily and fruitfully as ever."

Lurie's work "is triumphantly in the comic mode, and she knows its contours and idiosyncrasies and its meticulous pacing exceptionally well," agrees Joyce Carol Oates in a *New York Times Book Review* critique of the novel. The *Atlantic* reviewer adds that Lurie's "lovely evocations of the natural world nicely offset the minutely observed artificiality of her adult characters, and she deftly avoids the obvious pitfalls of writing about children."

Other critics also laud the author's descriptive abilities in *Only Children.* Gabriele Annan comments in the *Listener* that "Lurie is superb at describing nature, weather, interiors, sandwich cutting, stewing in a traffic jam, swimming in a sand-bottomed creek," while a *West Coast Review of Books* critic remarks that "one can almost feel the Unguentine as it spreads over a firecracker burn, or taste the homemade lemon-coconut cake (and later the baking soda for the indigestion), or smell the insides of the new DeSoto sedan, or see the designs made with the Gyro Art machine."

Some reviewers find the style of *Only Children* didactic and the work less fulfilling as a novel than *The War Between the Tates,* but still noteworthy. Gordon feels that the attempt to tell the story through the eyes of children is not always successful, but maintains that Lurie "is doing something different from what she has already done successfully, and has tried to go deeper." As Lynne Sharon Schwartz in *Saturday Review* indicates, "one must admire her willingness to risk this quite different and difficult conception." *Only Children* "is not so free-wheeling and inventive as 'The War between the Tates,' " Oates concludes, "but it is a highly satisfactory achievement and should be read with enthusiasm by Miss Lurie's many admirers."

Lurie's Pulitzer Prize-winning comedy of manners *Foreign Affairs* returns to more familiar subject matter for the author, as it "reassemble[s] her Corinth cast in a new setting," states James McGrath Morris in the *Washington Post.* Two members of the faculty of Corinth University's English department, fifty-four-year-old Vinnie Miner and young, handsome Fred Turner, "spend a semester in London and learn a great deal more about love than about their intended scholarly pursuits," says Morris.

As the book opens, Vinnie Miner has boarded the plane and is settling into her seat in preparation for an uneventful flight to England. Vinnie is a professor of children's literature, single, childless, and plain-looking, who is researching the difference between American and English playground rhymes for a forthcoming book. She is a selfish woman, but also afflicted with self-pity; she realizes that, though she has been married and has always had an active sex life, she has never really been loved, probably because she is not pretty, and now she is growing too old. Furthermore, her work, which is funded by a not-so-secure grant, has just been ridiculed in a national magazine by a critic she has never heard of (Leonard Zimmern from *The War Between the Tates* and *Only Children*). As Charles Champlin relates in the *Los Angeles Times Book Review,* "Vinnie Miner is accompanied by a small invisible dog that is the tangible embodiment of her self-pity (an allowable conceit in an imaginative 54-year-old academic, I expect, although I didn't so much accept it as admire Lurie's daring in making it almost credible)." Despite the fact that Vinnie feels sorry for herself, she is still excited about the trip, being an Anglophile with a wide circle of friends in London.

Seated next to Vinnie on the plane is Chuck Mumpson, a loud, retired waste disposal engineer from Tulsa, dressed cowboy-style and accompanied by a group of noisy tourists on a package tour. Though Vinnie initially finds Chuck annoying, he and Vinnie eventually become friends and passionate lovers. (Mumpson even develops an interest in researching his genealogy.) He dies of a heart attack before Vinnie figures out a way to make him fit in with her English friends and reconcile him with her career, but she gradually comes to the conclusion that, with Mumpson, she has finally loved and been loved in return.

Alternating chapters relate in counterpoint the experiences of youthful and handsome Fred Turner, who is an untenured member of Vinnie's faculty. Fred is in London researching John Gay, the eighteenth-century poet and playwright, and he's having a considerably worse time than Vinnie. Penniless between paychecks and recently separated from his feminist wife, Roo (Leonard Zimmern's daughter), he spends some of his time with a poor, complaining university couple who are having an equally miserable time in London. He has an affair with a spoiled, titled English actress who introduces him to her trendy friends, but it does not improve the quality of the time he spends in London wrapped up in his personal problems.

The book examines the differences between the English and the Americans while at the same time exploring a recurring theme in Lurie's novels, the line between illusion or appearance and reality. "For the real inspiration of Miss Lurie's entertaining fables is her fascination with levels of truth, with the war between fact and fantasy," says a *Times Literary Supplement* reviewer. According to William French in the Toronto *Globe and Mail,* "the characters in the novel of both nationalities simultaneously have their illusions shattered and prejudices confirmed, proving that generalizations about national traits are superficial and dangerous." And as French reports, Lurie "is sardonic, droll, intelligent and literary, in the best sense of that word, with a sure grasp of her characters and the social and cultural conditioning that has made them what they are."

The novel contains references to novelist Henry James and echoes of his work. And as Annan points out, even the fable itself is Jamesian: "Against a background of alluring, repellent London society a sophisticated American learns from an unsophisticated one that, contrary to appearances, true goodness exists and matters more than beauty, wit or grace." But Joel Conarroe adds in the *Washington Post Book World* that "although her plot is concerned with the confrontation of American naivete and European sophistication, a major Jamesian theme, she resists the temptation to explore various levels of ironic correspondence."

Foreign Affairs also has some elements of the fairy tale; *Voice Literary Supplement* writer Maureen Corrigan finds extensive borrowings from "The Frog Prince" in the love story of Vinnie and Chuck. A more direct theme of the narrative, though, is the extent to which it is assumed that only the young and the beautiful have sex lives. Although some reviewers believe that the author states this a little too forthrightly in the novel, and others regard the portrait of Chuck Mumpson as more of a caricature than a characterization, Dorothy Wickenden in the *New Republic* indicates that "Lurie is as deft as ever when she turns to the mortifications of romance. She is an uncannily accurate observer of the ambivalent emotions that enter into unconventional sexual alliances."

Another criticism of the novel is its busy, formulaic, and often incredible plot, as *Chicago Tribune Book World* reviewer Peter Collier describes it. Lurie's novels tend to be "programmatic," with the author relying upon "formal contrivances to heighten irony, to create startling juxtapositions, and to make a larger point about the individual's accommodations to the demands of society," says Wickenden, who considers *Foreign Affairs* to be an extreme case. And Anne Bernays in the *New York Times Book Review* would have preferred a less intrusive omniscient narrator. But Collier disagrees, claiming that "this narrative voice—by turns wicked and insightful, ironic and aloof—is the primary source of pleasure" in the novel. Wickenden also qualifies her criticism as she points out that when Lurie "abandons her gimmicky plot devices and moral posturing, *Foreign Affairs* is funny, touching, and even suspenseful."

In the opinion of some reviewers, the novel is perfectly constructed. "Besides amusing us with its story," Lehmann-Haupt writes, "[*Foreign Affairs*] is wonderfully stimulating for its sheer performance as a novel. Perhaps by stressing this I'm admitting nostalgia for a classical approach to literature, but as I read 'Foreign Affairs' I couldn't help visualizing a diagram with the rise of Vinnie's fortunes superimposed on the decline of Fred Turner's. There's something almost musical in the way the two plots interplay, like two bands marching toward each other playing consonant music." The book's construction "is so neat, so ingenious and satisfying, with no loose ends anywhere, that you barely notice its two stories operating on different levels of truth and entertainment," agrees Annan.

Writing in the *Times Literary Supplement,* Lorna Sage also refers to the novel's classical structure, indicating that *Foreign Affairs* is "warm, clever and funny—the kind of novel that elicits a conspiratorial glow from the start because it flatters the reader unmercifully. You're assumed to be witty and literate, you're told (indirectly, of course) how very wide awake you are, and you're congratulated for being (on the other hand and after all) so sensible as to prefer your metafiction in traditional form." The book is "one of those rare novels," remarks French, "in which the author's vision is perfectly realized, and the reader finishes it with a sense of shared triumph and generous benediction." According to Conarroe, "it also earns the gratitude of all of us who admire literacy, wit, and the underrated joys of ironic discourse." And as Anthony Thwaite declares in the *Observer,* "let no one suppose that [Lurie's] field of social observation is a restricted one, or in any way slight: she makes a world, commands it, and is a mistress not only of wit but of passion."

In her 1988 novel, *The Truth About Lorin Jones,* Lurie presents a familiar protagonist. Polly Alter is a well-educated, middle-aged art historian. Recently divorced from her husband, Polly struggles to adjust to raising her twelve-year-old son by herself. In addition, her career is suddenly flowering—she has been awarded a grant to write a biography of Lorin Jones, a painter who died in 1969. When her son leaves to spend the summer with his father, Polly experiments with her newfound freedom by having an affair with a lesbian friend. The affair turns sour, though, as Polly finds herself being manipulated by her friend—just as Polly's husband had manipulated her during their marriage. In addition to the turmoil in her personal life, Polly discovers that the life of her biographical subject is both mysterious and contradictory. Polly struggles to impose order on her subject's life, but eventually she realizes that she must accept and portray Lorin Jones as she really was, regardless of the confusion that will characterize her narrative. This professional discovery also leads to self-understanding, as Polly realizes that she must accept responsibility for the failures in her personal life. By the novel's end, Polly has matured significantly.

Reviews of the book, while not as laudatory as those for *Foreign Affairs,* are generally positive. Lehmann-Haupt, again writing in the *New York Times,* calls the novel "sparkling" and notes that Lurie, "as usual, plays charmingly with the medium, as if she were sprinkling confetti on a drama whose issues might in another century have attracted an Ibsen." Other reviewers state that Lurie fails to achieve the comic irony that marks her earlier novels. *Chicago Tribune* contributor Laurel Bauer, for instance, writes that "those who are expecting from Lurie her customary mordant take on our life and times may feel puzzled, because in her latest effort she seems to be placing an undue burden on the deadpan presentation of material." Toronto *Globe and Mail* reviewer Carol Shields registers a similar complaint, stating that the novel "lacks some of the comic bite of [*The War Between the Tates*]." Shields adds, however, that *The Truth About Lorin Jones* is able "to approach serious questions about the ineffable mystery of human personality, its artful disguises, its angles of accessibility and its occasional godly gusts of oxygen that produce the random acts of magic we call art."

Lurie's manuscripts are collected at Radcliffe College Library.

MEDIA ADAPTATIONS: The War Between the Tates was filmed for television.

BIOGRAPHICAL/CRITICAL SOURCES:

BOOKS

Contemporary Literary Criticism, Gale, Volume 4, 1975, Volume 5, 1976, Volume 18, 1980, Volume 39, 1986.
Dictionary of Literary Biography, Volume 2: *American Novelists since World War II,* Gale, 1978.

PERIODICALS

America, August 10, 1974, October 18, 1975.
Atlantic, September, 1974, May, 1979, December, 1981.
Best Sellers, March 1, 1966, November 15, 1967, September 1, 1974.
Book Week, January 23, 1966.
Books and Bookmen, April, 1970.
Book World, September 24, 1967, May 18, 1969.
Chicago Sunday Tribune, April 8, 1962.
Chicago Tribune, September 26, 1988.
Chicago Tribune Book World, November 4, 1984.
Christian Science Monitor, October 26, 1967, May 22, 1969, September 18, 1974, May 14, 1979, May 12, 1980.
Commentary, August, 1969, January, 1975.
Commonweal, January 12, 1968.
Encounter, August, 1979.
Globe and Mail (Toronto), September 15, 1984, September 17, 1988.
Harper's, July, 1979.
Hudson Review, spring, 1966, spring, 1975.
Life, November 24, 1967, May 23, 1969.
Listener, February 19, 1970, June 20, 1974, April 19, 1979, May 6, 1982.
London Magazine, December, 1974-January, 1975.
Los Angeles Times, October 21, 1988.
Los Angeles Times Book Review, October 21, 1984.
Nation, November 21, 1981.
National Review, December 7, 1979.
New Leader, September 2, 1974.
New Republic, August 10-17, 1974, December 21, 1974, May 12, 1979, December 7, 1979, December 23, 1981, October 8, 1984.
New Statesman, February 5, 1965, June 30, 1967, June 21, 1974, April 20, 1979.
Newsweek, January 10, 1966, November 6, 1967, May 26, 1969, August 5, 1974, December 30, 1974, April 23, 1979, September 24, 1984.
New Yorker, March 23, 1968, October 11, 1969, August 19, 1974, May 14, 1979, November 5, 1984.
New York Review of Books, February 3, 1966, December 7, 1967, August 8, 1974, June 14, 1979, April 15, 1982, October 11, 1984.
New York Times, May 27, 1969, November 18, 1981, September 13, 1984, September 12, 1988.
New York Times Book Review, April 1, 1962, January 16, 1966, October 15, 1967, May 25, 1969, July 28, 1974, April 22, 1979, April 27, 1980, July 13, 1980, January 17, 1982, June 6, 1982, November 7, 1982, September 16, 1984, September 4, 1988, March 11, 1990.
Observer, May 16, 1965, February 15, 1970, June 16, 1974, July 31, 1977, April 16, 1978, July 23, 1978, April 15, 1979, December 9, 1979, January 20, 1985.
Progressive, April, 1975, September, 1979.
Publishers Weekly, August 19, 1974.
Punch, February 17, 1965.
Saturday Review, January 29, 1966, June 9, 1979, November, 1981, November, 1984.

Spectator, July 7, 1967, February 21, 1970, June 29, 1974, April 21, 1979, January 26, 1985.

Time, March 4, 1966, June 6, 1969, July 29, 1974, June 11, 1979, November 30, 1981, October 15, 1984.

Times (London), May 27, 1982, January 19, 1985, January 31, 1985.

Times Literary Supplement, February 4, 1965, July 6, 1967, February 10, 1970, February 19, 1970, June 21, 1974, November 23, 1979, July 18, 1980, November 20, 1981, May 14, 1982, February 1, 1985, July 8, 1988.

Tribune Books (Chicago), March 4, 1990.

Village Voice, August 8, 1974.

Voice Literary Supplement, October, 1984.

Wall Street Journal, October 30, 1967.

Washington Post, April 25, 1985.

Washington Post Book World, August 11, 1974, September 7, 1975, April 29, 1979, July 13, 1980, November 29, 1981, September 30, 1984, September 4, 1988.

West Coast Review of Books, September, 1979.

Yale Review, October, 1979.

LYNCH, B. Suarez
    See BIOY CASARES, Adolfo and BORGES, Jorge Luis

*   *   *

LYNCH DAVIS, B.
    See BIOY CASARES, Adolfo and BORGES, Jorge Luis

*   *   *

LYNX
    See WEST, Rebecca

*   *   *

LYONS, Marcus
    See BLISH, James (Benjamin)

*   *   *

LYRE, Pinchbeck
    See SASSOON, Siegfried (Lorraine)

M

MacBETH, George (Mann) 1932-

PERSONAL: Born January 19, 1932, in Shotts, Scotland; son of George and Amelia Morton Mary (Mann) MacBeth; married Elizabeth Browell Robson, 1955 (marriage dissolved, 1975); married Lisa St. Aubin de Teran, 1982 (marriage dissolved, 1989); children: one. *Education:* New College, Oxford, Litt.Hum. (first class honors), 1955.

ADDRESSES: Home—Moyne Park, County Galway, Ireland. *Office*—44 Sheen Rd., Richmond, Surrey, England.

CAREER: British Broadcasting Corp., London, England, 1955-76, producer, Overseas Talks Department, 1957-58, producer, Talks Department, 1958-76; writer, 1976—.

AWARDS, HONORS: Co-recipient of Sir Geoffrey Faber Award, 1964; Cholmondeley Award, 1977.

WRITINGS:

POETRY

A Form of Words, Fantasy Press (England), 1954.
Lecture to the Trainees, Fantasy Press, 1962.
The Broken Places, Scorpion Press (England), 1963, Walker & Co., 1968.
The Calf: A Poem, Turret Books (London), 1965.
Missile Commander, Turret Books, 1965.
A Doomsday Book: Poems and Poem-Games, Scorpion Press, 1965.
The Twelve Hotels, Turret Books, 1965.
Noah's Journey (a long poem in four parts, for children), Viking, 1966.
The Castle, privately printed, 1966.
The Colour of Blood, Atheneum, 1967.
The Screens, Turret Books, 1967.
The Night of Stones, Macmillan, 1968, Atheneum, 1969.
A War Quartet, Macmillan, 1969.
Jonah and the Lord (long poem for children), Macmillan, 1969, Holt, 1970.
A Death, Sceptre Press, 1969.
Zoo's Who, privately printed, 1969.
The Burning Cone, Macmillan, 1970.
The Bamboo Nightingale, Sceptre Press, 1970.
Poems, Sceptre Press, 1970.
The Hiroshima Dream, Academy Editions, 1970.
Two Poems, Sceptre Press, 1970.

Collected Poems: 1958-70, Macmillan, 1971, Atheneum, 1972.
The Orlando Poems, Macmillan, 1971.
A Prayer, Against Revenge, Sceptre Press, 1971.
A Farewell, Sceptre Press, 1972.
Lusus: A Verse Lecture, Fuller d'Arch Smith, 1972.
A Litany, Sceptre Press, 1972.
Shrapnel, Macmillan, 1972.
Prayers, Aquila, 1973.
My Scotland: Fragments of a State of Mind (prose poems), Macmillan, 1973.
A Poet's Year, Gollancz, 1973.
The Vision, Sceptre Press, 1973.
Elegy for the Gas Dowsers, Sceptre Press, 1974.
Shrapnel, and A Poet's Year, Atheneum, 1974.
In the Hours Waiting for Blood to Come, Gollancz, 1975.
Buying a Heart, Atheneum, 1978.
Poems of Love and Death, Atheneum, 1980.
The Katana, Simon & Schuster, 1981.
Poems From Oby, Secker & Warburg, 1982, Atheneum, 1983.
The Long Darkness, Secker & Warburg, 1983, Atheneum, 1984.
The Cleaver Garden, Secker & Warburg, 1986.
Anatomy of a Divorce, Hutchinson, 1988.
Collected Poems 1958-1982, Hutchinson, 1989.

FICTION

Transformation, Gollancz, 1972.
Samurai, Harcourt, 1975.
The Survivor, Quartet, 1977, Harcourt, 1978.
The Seven Witches, Harcourt, 1978.
A Kind of Treason, Hodder & Stoughton, 1981.
The Born Losers, Warner, 1982.
Anna's Book, J. Cape, 1983, Holt, 1984.
The Lion of Pescara, J. Cape, 1984.
Dizzy's Woman, J. Cape, 1986.

OTHER

(Editor) *The Penguin Book of Sick Verse,* Penguin (London), 1963, Penguin (Baltimore), 1965.
(With Edward Lucie-Smith and Jack Clemo) *Penguin Modern Poets VI* (anthology), Penguin (London), 1964.
The Humming Birds: A Monodrama, Turret Books, 1965.
(Editor) *The Penguin Book of Animal Verse,* Penguin (London), 1965.
(Editor) *Poetry 1900-1965,* Longmans, Green, 1967.

(Editor) *The Penguin Book of Victorian Verse,* Penguin, 1968.
"The Doomsday Show" (play; first produced in London, 1964), published in *New English Dramatists 14,* Penguin, 1970.
(Editor) *The Falling Splendor: Poems of Alfred Lord Tennyson,* Macmillan, 1970.
The Scene-Machine (play; first produced in Kassel, Germany, 1971; produced in London, 1972), B. Schott's Soehne (Germany), 1971.
(Editor with Martin Booth) *The Book of Cats,* Secker & Warburg, 1976, Morrow, 1977.
The Rectory Mice (for children), Hutchinson, 1982.
A Child of War (autobiography), J. Cape, 1987.

Also author of children's book *The Story of Daniel,* 1986. Editor, *Poet's Voice,* 1958-65, *New Comment,* 1959-64, and *Poetry Now,* 1965-76.

SIDELIGHTS: D. M. Thomas writes: "George MacBeth's poems in *The Colour of Blood* move in the post-Einstein world where Time and the Ego are fluid, past slides and merges into present and future, mind slides into mind: the kind of neo-Christian world—all of us, in the space-time continuum, members of one body—that Lawrence Durrell symbolizes in the city Alexandria." Similarly, Peter Bland found a certain fluency in the poems composing *The Night of Stones* which, he said: "liberates the imagination . . . in an unusual and yet recognizable way. Recognizable, I think, because MacBeth's imagination is often cinematic." "MacBeth directs," Bland continues, a "constantly changing 'non-picture' with consummate skill, cutting back and forth between various states of mind and creating a world where normal oppositions between fantasy and reality cease to exist."

Several critics, however, agree with Thomas Kinsella, who notes that many of MacBeth's poems "suffer under their formal intricacies and a cumulative rhythmic dullness." MacBeth, writes Kinsella, "is chameleon poet only in his agile attempts to compensate for an essentially technical obscurity."

But many more critics, particularly the Americans who read MacBeth's poems for the first time in the Atheneum edition of *The Colour of Blood,* were favorably impressed. "*The Colour of Blood* gives us a poet in full stride," said a *Virginia Quarterly Review* writer, "seeing with a clear eye and commanding a language rich in metaphor and alive with sound. Dream poems and rituals, a bright and witty discourse on metre and even some amazing 'Chinese synopses,' all give this book a vitality and vibrancy that has so long been lacking in English poetry (although MacBeth *is* Scottish). Wit and violence, elegance and a grand lack of restraint, he has them all, can look at the blood that spills around us and find the strength and the wisdom to make his songs fly far and high. This is an exciting collection of poems."

While reviewing *A War Quartet,* Peter Porter writes: "George MacBeth is a poet who rarely writes without a consciously chosen and pursued form. For all his diversity of interests and many changes of style, he remains true to one aspect of his first collection—called appropriately *A Form of Words*—the ordering of feeling by means of rules and regulations. The principles of construction he uses are not merely the traditional ones of metre, rhyme and stanza pattern; they can also be instructions to the reader, rules of a game, mathematical divisions or patterns on the page. He is not a characteristic member of an avant-garde, though he likes a lot of its work. In a very real sense, MacBeth is a public poet. He can be obscure and recondite and yet every poem he writes is open to the audience. There is a direct appeal to the common reader—in this sense he is the opposite of a guild-poet like Graves; he doesn't want his washing taken in only by

other professionals. The pop side of the avant-garde has attracted him most, because they are the ones who are making it with the public. But he would never allow himself to be as rhapsodic or sloppy as they can be. Ever since *The Broken Places,* which is still his finest book, he has been seeking new ways of combining approachableness (the sine qua non of our poetic renaissance) with the lapidary skill of the Victorians he admires."

BIOGRAPHICAL/CRITICAL SOURCES:

BOOKS

Contemporary Literary Criticism, Gale, Volume 2, 1974, Volume 5, 1976, Volume 9, 1978.
Dictionary of Literary Biography, Volume 40: *Poets of Great Britain and Ireland Since 1960,* Gale, 1985.
MacBeth, George, *A Child of War,* J. Cape, 1987.

PERIODICALS

Book World, December 24, 1967, November 9, 1969.
Books and Bookmen, November, 1967.
Hudson Review, winter, 1967-68.
Kenyon Review, November, 1967.
Listener, July 6, 1967.
London Magazine, May, 1967, October, 1968, January, 1970.
Los Angeles Times Book Review, February 10, 1985, October 10, 1982.
New York Times Book Review, October 16, 1966, May 18, 1986.
Observer, May 4, 1967.
Poetry Review, summer, 1967.
Punch, July 5, 1967.
Times (London), November 3, 1983, February 16, 1984.
Times Literary Supplement, June 22, 1967, August 1, 1980, November 19, 1982, November 26, 1982, October 28, 1983, April 27, 1984, October 12, 1984, August 28, 1987, June 10, 1988, January 26, 1990.
Virginia Quarterly Review, winter, 1968, summer, 1969.
Washington Post, May 12, 1984.

*   *   *

MacDIARMID, Hugh
See GRIEVE, C(hristopher) M(urray)

*   *   *

MacDONALD, Anson
See HEINLEIN, Robert A(nson)

*   *   *

MACDONALD, John
See MILLAR, Kenneth

*   *   *

MacDONALD, John D(ann)   1916-1986

PERSONAL: Born July 24, 1916, in Sharon, PA; died of complications following heart surgery, December 28, 1986, in Milwaukee, WI; son of Eugene Andrew and Marguerite Grace (Dann) MacDonald; married Dorothy Mary Prentiss, July 3, 1937; children: Maynard John Prentiss. *Education:* Attended University of Pennsylvania, 1934-35; Syracuse University, B.S., 1938; Harvard University, M.B.A., 1939.

ADDRESSES: Home—100 Ocean Pl., Sarasota, FL 34242. *Agent*—George Diskart, 1033 Gayley Ave., Los Angeles, CA 90024.

CAREER: Author. Worked for a time in investment and insurance. *Military service:* U.S. Army, 1940-46; served in India and Asia with Office of Strategic Services; became lieutenant colonel.

MEMBER: Mystery Writers of America (president, 1962), P.E.N., Authors Guild.

AWARDS, HONORS: Benjamin Franklin Award, 1955, for best American short story; Gran Prix de Litterature Policiere, 1964, for French edition of *A Key to the Suite;* Pioneer Medal, Syracuse University, 1971; Grand Master Award, Mystery Writers of America, 1972; Popular Culture Association National Award for Excellence, 1978; D.H.L., Hobart and William Smith colleges, 1978, University of South Florida, 1980; American Book Award, 1980, for *The Green Ripper.*

WRITINGS:

FICTION

The Damned, Fawcett, 1952.
Cancel All Our Vows, Appleton, 1953.
Contrary Pleasure, Appleton, 1954.
The Deceivers, Dell, 1958.
Clemmie, Fawcett, 1958.
Please Write for Details, Simon & Schuster, 1959.
The Crossroads, Simon & Schuster, 1959.
Slam the Big Door, Fawcett, 1960.
A Key to the Suite, Fawcett, 1962.
A Flash of Green, Simon & Schuster, 1962.
I Could Go On Singing (novelization of a screenplay), Fawcett, 1963.
Condominium, Lippincott, 1977.
One More Sunday, Random House, 1984.
Barrier Island, Knopf, 1986.

MYSTERY FICTION

The Brass Cupcake, Fawcett, 1950.
Murder for the Bride, Fawcett, 1951.
Judge Me Not, Fawcett, 1951.
Weep for Me, Fawcett, 1951.
The Neon Jungle, Fawcett, 1953.
Dead Low Tide, Fawcett, 1953.
All These Condemned, Fawcett, 1954.
Area of Suspicion, Dell, 1954.
A Bullet for Cinderella, Dell, 1955, published as *On the Make,* 1960.
Cry Hard, Cry Fast, Popular Library, 1955.
You Live Once, Popular Library, 1955.
April Evil, Dell, 1956.
Border Town Girl, Popular Library, 1956.
Murder in the Wind, Dell, 1956.
Death Trap, Dell, 1957.
The Price of Murder, Dell, 1957.
The Empty Trap, Popular Library, 1957.
A Man of Affairs, Dell, 1957.
The Soft Touch, Dell, 1958.
The Executioners, Simon & Schuster, 1958, published as *Cape Fear,* Fawcett, 1962.
Deadly Welcome, Dell, 1959.
The Beach Girls, Fawcett, 1959.
The End of the Night, Simon & Schuster, 1960.
The Only Girl in the Game, Fawcett, 1960.
Where Is Janice Gantry?, Fawcett, 1961.
One Monday We Killed Them All, Fawcett, 1961.
On the Run, Fawcett, 1963.
The Drowner, Fawcett, 1963.
End of the Tiger and Other Stories, Fawcett, 1966.

The Last One Left, Doubleday, 1967.
S*E*V*E*N (short story collection), Fawcett, 1971.
The Good Old Stuff: 13 Early Stories, edited by Martin H. Greenberg and others, Harper, 1982.
More Good Old Stuff, Knopf, 1984.

"TRAVIS McGEE" NOVEL SERIES

The Deep Blue Good-By (also see below), Fawcett, 1964.
Nightmare in Pink (also see below), Fawcett, 1964.
A Purple Place for Dying (also see below), Fawcett, 1964.
The Quick Red Fox, Fawcett, 1964.
A Deadly Shade of Gold, Fawcett, 1965.
Bright Orange for the Shroud, Fawcett, 1965.
Darker than Amber, Fawcett, 1966.
One Fearful Yellow Eye, Fawcett, 1966.
Pale Gray for Guilt, Fawcett, 1968.
The Girl in the Plain Brown Wrapper, Fawcett, 1968.
Three for McGee (contains *The Deep Blue Good-By, Nightmare in Pink, A Purple Place for Dying*), Doubleday, 1968 (published in England as *McGee,* R. Hale, 1975).
Dress Her in Indigo, Fawcett, 1969.
The Long Lavender Look, Fawcett, 1970.
A Tan and Sandy Silence, Fawcett, 1972.
The Scarlet Ruse, Fawcett, 1973.
The Turquoise Lament, Lippincott, 1973.
The Dreadful Lemon Sky, Lippincott, 1975.
The Empty Copper Sea, Lippincott, 1978.
The Green Ripper, Lippincott, 1979.
Free Fall in Crimson, Harper, 1981.
Cinnamon Skin, Harper, 1982.
The Lonely Silver Rain, Knopf, 1985.
Five Complete Travis McGee Novels, Avenel Books, 1985.

Also author of *Shades of Travis McGee,* Doubleday.

SCIENCE FICTION

Wine of the Dreamers, Greenberg, 1951, published as *Planet of the Dreamers,* Pocket Library, 1953.
Ballroom of the Skies, Greenberg, 1952.
The Girl, the Gold Watch, and Everything, Fawcett, 1962.
Other Times, Other Worlds (short story collection), Fawcett, 1978.

OTHER

(Editor) *The Lethal Sex,* Dell, 1959.
(Editor) *Mystery Writers of America Anthology,* Dell, 1959.
The House Guests (nonfiction), Doubleday, 1965.
No Deadly Drug (nonfiction), Doubleday, 1968.
(With John Kilpack) *Nothing Can Go Wrong* (nonfiction), Harper, 1981.
(Author of introduction) Richard Riley, *The Gulf Coast of Florida,* Skyline Press, 1984.
A Friendship: The Letters of Dan Rowan and John D. MacDonald, 1967-1974, Knopf, 1986.
Reading for Survival, Library of Congress, 1988.

Contributor to anthologies. Also contributor of over five hundred short stories, some under house pseudonyms, to *Cosmopolitan, Collier's,* and other magazines.

WORK IN PROGRESS: Another Travis McGee novel.

SIDELIGHTS: "Most things seem a little chancy while this 20th Century ebbs away," wrote Nick B. Williams in the *Los Angeles Times Book Review,* "but of two things you may feel reasonably certain—(1) that a John D. MacDonald mystery thriller is destined to become a runaway best seller, and (2) that his protagonist, Travis McGee, will survive all bullets and all wild or wily women, remaining as fit as ever for whatever happens to him next."

Considered the heir apparent to such classic crime novelists as Dashiell Hammett and Raymond Chandler, John D. MacDonald enjoyed critical and commercial success as both the author of the Travis McGee series and as a serious novelist with such books as *Condominium, One More Sunday,* and *Barrier Island* to his credit. While best known for his mysteries, MacDonald produced books in a number of genres; his foray into science fiction, for instance, earned him praise from Raymond Carney, who remarked in the *Dictionary of Literary Biography* that in *Wine of the Dreamers* and *Ballroom of the Skies,* MacDonald "avoids entrapment by the various plots he creates. His writing depends on his ability to deploy and negotiate the intersecting technologies of law, bureaucracy, history, and memory more deftly and humanely than the best of his readers."

MacDonald began his career by writing mysteries for the "pulp" magazines popular in the 1940s and 1950s, and he soon graduated to paperback novels. Of the author's early days, Francis M. Nevins, Jr., related in *Clues:* "Several of MacDonald's earliest pulp crime stories were set in the China-Burma-India locales in which he had served during the war as an officer in the [Office of Strategic Services], but before long [his editor] persuaded him to take off his pith helmet and start writing about the United States. From then on the vast majority of his stories took place in postwar America. Indeed MacDonald portrayed more vividly and knowledgeably than any other crime writer the readjustment of American business from a war footing to a consumer-oriented peacetime economy which would soon be spewing out megatons of self-destructing plastic junk and incurring the wrath of the later MacDonald and his beach bum-philosopher-adventurer hero Travis McGee."

In 1962, after he had published a score of successful novels, MacDonald was approached by Fawcett Books senior editor Knox Burger to develop a new detective series. As the author told Toronto *Globe and Mail* writer Patrick Hynan, he wasn't thrilled by the idea "because I didn't want to be locked into something that I would find hard to get out of if I didn't like it." However, MacDonald agreed to write three novels featuring a character then called Dallas McGee. While writing the first McGee book, *The Deep Blue Good-By,* MacDonald learned of President John F. Kennedy's assassination. Convinced that "Dallas" had been given a bad resonance in the public subconscious by the slaying in that city, he changed McGee's first name to Travis, after the California air force base.

The immediate acceptance of the McGee books led to some twenty more—all distinguishable by their rainbow array of titles, from *Nightmare in Pink* to *The Green Ripper, The Scarlet Ruse,* and *Cinnamon Skin.* The McGee character has been embraced by literary scholars and mystery buffs alike. Described by the author as a knight-errant, and by the character himself as a "salvage expert," Travis McGee is a year-round resident of Florida, where he lives on his houseboat, *The Busted Flush,* which he won in a poker game. McGee rents himself out on occasion as a private detective, abetted by his friend Meyer, an economist by trade, who once had a houseboat, the *John Maynard Keynes,* named for the noted English economist.

In his adventures McGee is endangered by all manner of professional killers, amateur psychopaths, and everyday villains, but his fans rest assured that their hero will emerge unscathed. "Travis McGee can always *get* results, and that one ability probably sets him apart from most of us," found Wister Cook in a *Clues* article. "McGee's life is violent, simple and neat—in its broad outlines not one with which we can make much sympathetic identification. His nemeses do not return to haunt him another year, as ours do. For he survives beating, shooting, and bombing; he comes back to smash heads, terrorize and kill; he oversees the violent deaths of his principal antagonists. He calls himself a salvage man, and by the end of each novel he has indeed saved something important—a life, a reputation, a fortune, a friendship. Presiding over the action and ultimately controlling it, he achieves success—within the term as he defines it. He gets money, romance, self-esteem."

But his life is not always satisfying. For McGee is also a man tormented by what he sees as the decline of America in general, and his beloved Florida in particular. In his railings against the "junk" culture of fast food, bad television, and gross commercial overdevelopment, the detective is a stringent social critic, and MacDonald devoted much of each novel to chronicling modern ills as McGee sees them. "We cannot conclude just yet, however, that in his aversions Travis McGee is just like you and me," stated Cook. "We could, actually, make the case that McGee's concern for the general trashiness of everyday consumer life is merely window-dressing: it gives him a kind of spurious depth while filling the empty spaces between beatings, bombings, stabbings and shootings." But to *Clues* critic Edgar W. Hirschberg, McGee's musings serve a more important purpose. Although he acknowledged that the salvage expert's internal monologues often "stop the action dead," Hirschberg went on to say that "what these speculations do accomplish is to provide you with a much deeper and broader understanding of why McGee does what he does than you otherwise would have. Like his recent progenitors in the hard-boiled detective genre . . . he is a knight-errant riding into a crime-infested world, righting the few wrongs he can do anything about. But he does a lot more thinking about the people who commit them . . . than most fictional detectives do, and his penchant for speculations about the social evils which are the real reason why he never lacks employment adds substantial depth and significance to MacDonald's work, both as a teller of tales about violence and detection and as a serious novelist."

Women, as consorts, victims, and villains, play an important role in McGee's life. Scarcely a novel goes by without the detective involving himself with any number of obliging women; many of them, however, end up dead by story's end. In *Free Fall in Crimson,* drugs and pornography highlight the making of a film in Iowa, sending McGee to the Midwest and into an expected romantic foray. "The sex—steamy, but not unpleasantly graphic—and the violence and the violent death seem by now ritualistic, and in some perplexing way comforting in their predictability rather than arousing," declared *Los Angeles Times Book Review* critic Charles Champlin. John Leonard, writing in the *New York Times,* saw in this novel an opportunity for the author to allow his lady-killer hero "to raise his consciousness. Instead of the usual machismo rubbish of wounded bird and tender muscle and stifled sob, there are women in [*Free Fall in Crimson*] who might actually be able to cope with New York—two of them, only one of whom sleeps with McGee."

One critic who did not appreciate MacDonald's portrayal of female characters was Barbara Lawrence. In a *Clues* article, Lawrence decried McGee as "responsible for much of the suffering endured by the women, particularly psychological suffering. For McGee has such personal magnetism and attraction that women proposition him before the introductions are completed. An endless train of women bed down with McGee, and at first reading, it appears that this great lover truly admires and respects women. . . . But a closer examination of the novels belies this assumption and shows that he intensely dislikes successful women and has no use for any woman until she is totally submissive to him. He humiliates them and occasionally physically abuses them." In a letter to *CA,* MacDonald answered this charge by responding that McGee "does not dislike successful women intensely or to any other degree. He wants no woman totally submissive to him. He neither humiliates nor abuses women." Rather, MacDonald suggested, the misinterpretation lies with "readers who believe they see proof of their pre-prejudices in whatever they come upon."

But if violence toward women stood out to Lawrence, it was only one aspect of the total picture of McGee's savage world to other critics. Champlin pointed out that the detective "has been kicked, hammered, beaten, flayed, drugged, immersed, stabbed, jabbed, bent, thrown, and shot at so often he has more entry and exit signs than a shopping mall. He has spent more time unconscious than most men have spent waking." *Time*'s John Skow compared McGee to "a Robin Hood among chattel rustlers who steals loot back from thugs and swindlers and returns it, minus a 50% commission, to the widows and orphans from whom it was taken."

Most critics agreed that, the appeal of sex and violence notwithstanding, the real pleasure of a McGee mystery lies in MacDonald's crisp, hard-hitting prose style. In his study of the author, *John D. MacDonald,* David Geherin called his subject "a gifted storyteller. . . . Neither as byzantine as Ross Macdonald's nor as loose and desultory as Raymond Chandler's, MacDonald's plots are well-woven, artfully constructed arrangements of action sequences. They are neither needlessly complex nor do they exist simply to obscure the identity of the villain until the final chapter. A master at creating and sustaining mystery, suspense, tension, and drama, MacDonald understands all the tricks of readability; turning the pages in one of his novels is always a pleasure, never a duty."

In a review of *Cinnamon Skin, Washington Post* critic Jonathan Yardley said that one of MacDonald's "most admirable qualities as a novelist is that he almost unfailingly manages to deliver precisely the pleasure that his readers anticipate—a quality too-little noticed and remarked upon among writers whose principal business it is to entertain. But also as usual, MacDonald provides a good deal more than mere diversion. He is tinkerer in the grand old American tradition, a man who loves to learn how things work and a writer who loves to pass that knowledge along to his readers. . . . He also takes pleasure in tracking the continuing emotional adventures of Travis McGee, the loner who would love to be a husband and father except that he couldn't stand it." And Skow defended the author against the stereotype of mystery novels as empty escapism; in MacDonald's examinations of his hero's complex character, Skow remarked, "let no man say that this is escapist claptrap. MacDonald offers something far more profound, the claptrap of no way out."

In 1977 MacDonald took one of his ongoing Travis McGee themes and developed it into a non-mystery work that eventually attained best-seller status. *Condominium,* according to Stephen Zito, "is a brief against the rape of Florida." In a *Washington Post Book World* piece, Zito explained that the author "writes with outrage about what the developers and quick-buck artists have done to his adopted state where condominiums litter the white beaches, freeways cut across the wilderness, the air and water is fouled, and there is a cheapening and coarsening of life everywhere."

"Essentially a cautionary tale, *Condominium* is intimately concerned with the balance of nature and thus with death," noted literary agent Knox Burger in a *Village Voice* article. "The story concerns the developers and the inhabitants of a high-rise building designed for retired people. Badly designed. It is set on piles driven into the fragile subsurface of a sandy island just off the west coast of Florida. After numerous convincing portents, a hurricane blows in and washes everything away." The novel received mixed reviews, with the negative notices focusing on the contention that in this book MacDonald, as Michael Mewshaw put it in the *New York Times Book Review,* "seems to have lost sight of what he learned from the detective genre—economy, taut structure and pace." However, critic John Leonard, while not a fan of the Travis McGee series, did have praise for *Condominium.* "Those who know [MacDonald] only through the [mystery novels] are missing him at his story-telling best," stated Leonard in the *New York Times.* "Outside the series and its formulas, the wounded women and the macho rubbish, he breathes. His appetite [for issues] is enormous." "*Condominium* is, in many ways, a remarkable achievement," added Zito. "In a novel peopled by perhaps 25 major characters, MacDonald has structured a book which is compulsively readable and coherent, building from the small disturbances of domestic life to the hurricane which comes with the force of the Apocalypse."

The author took on religious hypocrisy with *One More Sunday.* A behind-the-scenes look at the corruption rampant in the popular Church of the Eternal Believer, *One More Sunday* was compared to a classic of the genre, *Elmer Gantry,* by Yardley in a *Washington Post* piece. MacDonald's work, in Yardley's opinion, "is no mere knee-jerk [criticism] of the evangelicals. He realizes that they can often be ruthlessly exploitive—'they rope in their supporters by playing on their fears and on their hatred and their loneliness'—but he is also quick to acknowledge that they seek, out of whatever motive, to fill a genuine longing among their followers."

Moving from evangelical corruption to white-collar crime, MacDonald produced *Barrier Island* in 1986 to praise from *Los Angeles Times Book Review* writer Stephen Vizinczey. Explaining that the story was about a "fraudulent deal in the making"—an unspoiled island off the coast of Mississippi is about to be purchased and resold to the government at an unfair profit—Vizinczey remarked that MacDonald "has the gift of moral vision, which is to say he portrays actions in the light of their consequences. This is an almost revolutionary approach in an age when every other book or film is romanticizing cruelty and unscrupulousness by concentrating on the charm of criminals rather than their crimes, and by making villains sympathetic and their victims repellant. In 'Barrier Island' there is never any doubt who hurts whom and how. Nor are readers conned into loving the sort of characters who endanger their survival."

With the acclaim for his non-mystery novels reflecting the acclaim for his Travis McGee series, MacDonald proved to Geherin that he was a writer of worth. As Geherin concluded in his *John D. MacDonald,* "Whether for the sake of convenience one categorizes his works as mysteries, adventures, or thrillers, it is clear that such labels are inadequate in conveying the full extent of his accomplishment. By creating a substantial body of thoughtful and provocative entertainment for an enormously diverse and widespread audience, MacDonald has justly earned for himself the right to be considered a serious American novelist worthy of the highest distinction."

MEDIA ADAPTATIONS: Film options to several of MacDonald's novels have been sold, with "Man Trap," based on the novelette "Taint of the Tiger," released by Paramount in 1961, and "Cape Fear," based on the novel *The Executioners,* released by Universal/International in 1962; some thirty MacDonald stories have been adapted for television, including "Condominium," released by Operation Prime Time TV in April, 1980, and "The Girl, the Gold Watch, and Everything," released by Operation Prime Time TV in May, 1980.

BIOGRAPHICAL/CRITICAL SOURCES:

BOOKS

Contemporary Literary Criticism, Gale, Volume 3, 1975, Volume 27, 1984, Volume 44, 1987.
Dictionary of Literary Biography, Volume 8: *Twentieth-Century American Science-Fiction Writers,* Gale, 1981.
Dictionary of Literary Biography Yearbook: 1986, Gale, 1987.
Geherin, David, *John D. MacDonald,* Unger, 1982.
MacDonald, John D., *One More Sunday,* Random House, 1984.

PERIODICALS

Chicago Tribune, November 5, 1986, January 14, 1987.
Chicago Tribune Book World, June 27, 1982, November 27, 1983.
Clues, spring, 1980, fall-winter, 1985.
Detroit News, June 7, 1981.
Globe and Mail (Toronto), February 25, 1984, May 5, 1984.
Los Angeles Times Book Review, May 4, 1980, April 19, 1981, July 4, 1982, March 4, 1984, April 28, 1985, June 1, 1986.
New Republic, June 26, 1975.
Newsweek, March 10, 1975, July 7, 1986.
New York Times, January 1, 1974, April 5, 1977, April 17, 1981, August 3, 1983, March 12, 1985.
New York Times Book Review, January 6, 1974, February 23, 1975, March 27, 1977, October 7, 1979, May 3, 1981, August 22, 1982, April 8, 1984, March 17, 1985.
Publishers Weekly, July 29, 1983.
Time, December 3, 1973, July 4, 1977, October 15, 1979, April 27, 1981.
Times (London), August 9, 1984.
Times Literary Supplement, May 28, 1976, February 10, 1978.
Village Voice, April 11, 1977, October 4, 1983.
Washington Post, June 23, 1982, July 15, 1983, March 14, 1984.
Washington Post Book World, March 27, 1977, September 10, 1978, May 17, 1981, September 9, 1984, March 24, 1985, January 17, 1988.

OBITUARIES:

PERIODICALS

Chicago Tribune, December 30, 1986.
Detroit Free Press, December 29, 1986.
Detroit News, December 29, 1986.
Los Angeles Times, December 29, 1986.
New York Times, December 29, 1986.
Publishers Weekly, January 9, 1987.
Time, January 12, 1987.
Times (London), January 2, 1987.
Washington Post, December 29, 1986.

*   *   *

MACDONALD, John Ross
See MILLAR, Kenneth

MACDONALD, Ross
See MILLAR, Kenneth

*   *   *

MacDOUGAL, John
See BLISH, James (Benjamin)

*   *   *

MacINNES, Colin   1914-1976

PERSONAL: Born 1914, in London, England; died of cancer April 22, 1976, in London; son of J. Campbell MacInnes and Angela Thirkell (a novelist). *Education:* Educated in Australia.

CAREER: Novelist and journalist. *Military service:* British Army Intelligence Corps, 1939-45; became sergeant.

AWARDS, HONORS: Book Find of the Month Award from the *Daily Sketch,* and Book Society recommendation, both 1950, for *To the Victors the Spoils.*

WRITINGS:

To the Victors the Spoils (novel), MacGibbon & Kee, 1950, reprinted, Schocken, 1986.
June in Her Spring (novel), MacGibbon & Kee, 1952, reprinted, Panther, 1974.
City of Spades (Part 1 of trilogy; also see below), MacGibbon & Kee, 1957, Macmillan, 1958.
Absolute Beginners (Part 2 of trilogy; also see below), MacGibbon & Kee, 1959, Macmillan, 1960.
Mr. Love and Justice (Part 3 of trilogy; also see below), MacGibbon & Kee, 1960, Dutton, 1961.
England, Half English (essays), MacGibbon & Kee, 1961, Random House, 1962.
(With Kenneth Clark and Bryan Robertson) *Sidney Nolan,* Thames & Hudson, 1961.
London: City of Any Dream, Thames & Hudson, 1962.
(Author of foreword) Ada Leverson, *The Little Ottleys,* MacGibbon & Kee, 1962.
(With editors of *Life*) *Australia and New Zealand,* Time-Life, 1964.
All Day Saturday, MacGibbon & Kee, 1966.
Sweet Saturday Night (novel), MacGibbon & Kee, 1967.
(Author of introduction) Tim Scott, *Sculpture 1961-67,* Whitechapel Gallery, 1967.
The London Novels (trilogy; including *City of Spades, Absolute Beginners,* and *Mr. Love and Justice*), Farrar, Straus, 1969 (published in England as *Visions of London,* MacGibbon & Kee, 1969).
Westward to Laughter, 1969, Farrar, Straus, 1970.
Three Years to Play, Farrar, Straus, 1970.
Out of the Garden (novel), Hart-Davis, MacGibbon, 1974.
Loving Them Both: A Study of Bisexuality and Bisexuals, Martin Brian & O'Keeffe, 1974.
"No Novel Reader" (on Rudyard Kipling), Martin Brian & O'Keeffe, 1975.
Out of the Way: Later Essays, Martin Brian & O'Keeffe, 1980.
Tony Gould, editor, *Absolute MacInnes,* Allison & Busby, 1985.

Works also collected in *The Colin MacInnes Omnibus,* 1986. Author of more than 1500 radio scripts, 1945-48. Contributor to *Encounter, Guardian, New Left Review, New Society, New Statesman, Observer, Partisan Review, Spectator, New York Times,* and other periodicals.

SIDELIGHTS: By the time he died of cancer at age 62 in 1976, Colin MacInnes had established himself as "a curious but possibly inevitable chronicler of a city in revolutionary change," according to *Los Angeles Times* critic Charles Champlin. That city was London, and the revolution occurred during the postwar years up to 1960, as a generation of young adults came of age questioning Britain's rigid class system. It was also the time immigrants from Africa and the West Indies challenged the country's white culture, sparking racial unrest.

That tumultuous era is characterized by three MacInnes novels: *City of Spades, Absolute Beginners,* and *Mr. Love and Justice*—which began receiving serious attention about a decade after they were first published, when the trilogy was rereleased under the banner titles of *The London Novels* in the United States and *Visions of London* in the United Kingdom. By the late 1960s, Britain and America were so firmly entrenched in social reform and youthful uprising that MacInnes's novels were seen as both a vanguard of the era to come and as an explanation of how the call for change came about. *City of Spades,* for instance, described by Mordecai Richler as "a penetrating and immensely good-hearted study of blackness and perplexed white liberals" in Richler's *Washington Post Book World* review, was in its subject matter a rarity on its initial release in 1959.

In portraying the life of Johnny Fortune, newly arrived in Britain from his native Lagos and facing the wide spectrum of racial bigotry, the author provided, in several critics' views, his best novel. *City of Spades* "captures the tempo and the texture not just of the language but of the lives of black men in postwar London," noted *Saturday Review* critic Eric Moon. In a *Dictionary of Literary Biography* article on MacInnes, Harriett Blodgett labeled *City of Spades* "by far the best novel [of the trilogy] because of its firmly controlled indignation over social injustice and its compelling characterization of a young Nigerian. . . . While it is a plea for brotherhood," she continues, "*City of Spades* nonetheless acknowledges the practical realities of the cultural clash between peoples so different as the Africans . . . and the English."

Blodgett also remarked that the Johnny Fortune character shared several traits with a real-life African immigrant, known as Hawton, with whom the author resided for a while during the 1950s. Indeed MacInnes was remembered in a 1969 *New Republic* article by Nat Hentoff as "one of the few white men I have met who lives racial equality as well as he preaches it and who is as totally accepted by black men as he totally accepts them."

Not every reviewer, however, was enthusiastic about the author's work. Kingsley Shorter, for one, saw MacInnes's book as an exercise in "pandering to our bourgeois romanticism, to wistful yearnings for a more colonial life." *City of Spades,* he continued in *New Leader,* "was less a contribution to interracial entente than an invitation to ethnic slumming—a painless round trip across the tracks to see how the other half lives." And while Hentoff admitted that MacInnes's writing is less than perfect—he had "an unfortunate tendency to give his characters facetious names"—and Richler noted "a sometimes irritating tendency to stop the action . . . to explain social attitudes," both reviewers found the stylistic flaws did not diminish the power of the author's message.

Absolute Beginners "is a celebration of the teenage thing," wrote Hentoff, "but there is about it none of that rosy tinted allure that always creeps in when middle-aged writers try vicariously to recapture their youth." Populated by a rogue's gallery of London's embryonic countercultural youth, including bikers and thugs, pimps and prostitutes, artists and models, the novel examines the relationship between such "absolute beginners" in society and the status quo they were up against. Again MacInnes's empathy

and sharp ear for language helped distinguish his storytelling. As a *Time* reviewer stated, the author's perception of the young people of that era was so acute that "years before anyone else had noticed, MacInnes [saw that English youth] were rocking out in accents more than half American. Years before the Beatles, he predicted [in an essay] exactly what the Beatles would sound like and be like."

Such attention to detail infuses *Absolute Beginners.* The author "lets his narrator instruct the reader in the dress, mores, preoccupations, and preferences of teenage culture and, as the sole point of view, saturate the reader in its locutions," according to Blodgett. The story culminates in the real-life race riots at London's Notting Hill, adding a different note of social unrest to the story. To Martin Green in *Kenyon Review, Absolute Beginners* is "the most American of [the trilogy]. There is much lyrical affirmation of life, and a total commitment to teen-agers."

Generally assumed to be the least significant of the London novels, *Mr. Love and Justice* was nonetheless praised by Hentoff as "the heavyweight of the trio." Described by the critic as a novel "about the refusal to betray and the prices exacted for that refusal," the narrative weaves together the lives of sailor-turned-pimp Frankie Love and rookie policeman Edward Justice. The two characters don't meet until the end of the book, when they become unlikely friends. "Cleverly constructed and successful in depicting its main characters, the novel is weakened by excessive set speeches and incredibly villainous minor characters," wrote Blodgett of *Mr. Love and Justice,* adding that she, like some other reviewers, appreciated MacInnes's atmospheric details.

The belated success of the London trilogy was a point Moon took up. He summarized that "what raises these novels far above many of today's excursions on the wild side is that they are not simply elemental explosions of anger or social protest. . . . [The books] reflect an insistent realization of the joy of life and the process of discovery that is its bloodstream, a trait that surfaces doggedly in MacInnes's characters even when they are struggling down there in the darker depths of adversity. The most surprising elements in stories set in such a milieu are their romanticism, their humor, and their warmth."

The remainder of the MacInnes collection includes a handful of novels, of which *Westward to Laughter* received perhaps the most widespread critical notice, and a half-dozen nonfiction books, including the posthumously published *Out of the Way: Later Essays. Westward to Laughter* was a departure for the author: a period comedy-drama set in the fictitious West Indies isle of St. Laughter in the mid-18th century. The events, including slave trade, pirating, and general cruelty, are seen through the eyes of young Alexander Nairn, a Scot who signs on as a shipmate to seek his fortune and winds up a slave himself. "Contrary to appearances, however, *Westward to Laughter* is not really an adventure story," noted Shorter. "Neither is it . . . an attempt to explore some of the background of the race situation in our own time. It is, rather, a skillful exercise in camp, a self-mocking comic-strip account of some purportedly serious matters." Guy Davenport, in a *National Review* article, added his view that, "like Voltaire, [MacInnes] describes injustice in a calm voice, never offering a word of disapproval, or so much as raising an eyebrow. This unruffled tidiness of narration makes its way through rapes, mayhem, torture and every degree of inhumanity, until his satiric voice has penetrated to the bone with its feigned indifference."

Some of the topics MacInnes covers in *Out of the Way,* published four years after his death, include gardening, the women's movement, and the cult of Gilbert & Sullivan. This essay collection "brings his talent into proper focus," as London *Times* writer Richard Holmes remarked. "It places him in a commanding position amidst the social and cultural debate of the Sixties, raising questions that are still with us fifteen or twenty years after, acute and unresolved. Principal among these are problems of racial misunderstanding and 'post-Colonial' attitudes; difficulties of class and social prejudice; crime and the practical administration of justice; and perhaps the most vital of all, the whole problem of national morale. MacInnes takes his stand on all these not really as a novelist at all, but as an essayist, as an impassioned liberal commentator on our life and times."

Blodgett, summing up MacInnes's career, said that while the author often used comedy to make his point, he "always wanted to be taken seriously. Throughout his career, his fiction was more in danger of overly earnest teaching and telling than of any other fictional failing. He had a regrettable urge to guide the general reader to truth by explaining what the reader might better have discovered unaided and to lecture where he could better have dramatized—or already had. Yet MacInnes also knew how to concoct a tale and phrase the speech issuing from an individual mouth in a specific setting. Once he discovered his flair for social consciousness, he wrote fictions which are largely, and sometimes wholly, acts of skillful imaginative apprehension of an impressively varied array of lives, illuminating areas most other serious novelists have ignored; and he did this in novels which are not repetitions of each other."

MEDIA ADAPTATIONS: Absolute Beginners was adapted into a movie musical and released in 1986.

BIOGRAPHICAL/CRITICAL SOURCES:

BOOKS

Burgess, Anthony, *The Novel Now: A Guide to Contemporary Fiction,* Norton, 1967.
Contemporary Literary Criticism, Gale, Volume 4, 1975, Volume 23, 1983.
Dictionary of Literary Biography, Volume 14: *British Novelists since 1960,* Gale, 1983.
MacInnes, Colin, *Out of the Way: Later Essays,* Martin Brian & O'Keeffe, 1980.
MacInnes, Graham, *Finding a Father,* Hamilton, 1967.
Urwin, G. G., editor, *A Taste for Living: Young People in the Modern Novel,* Faber & Faber, 1967.
West, Paul, *The Modern Novel,* Hutchinson, 1963.

PERIODICALS

Kenyon Review, Volume 31, no. 2, 1969.
Listener, June 4, 1970.
London Magazine, August, 1962.
Los Angeles Times, February 23, 1981.
National Review, February 10, 1970.
New Leader, April 6, 1970.
New Republic, February 15, 1969.
Newsweek, January 5, 1970.
New York Times, January 6, 1970.
New York Times Book Review, January 18, 1970.
Observer, April 5, 1970.
Saturday Review, February 8, 1969.
Spectator, May 1, 1976.
Time, May 16, 1969, February 23, 1970.
Times (London), April 10, 1980.
Times Literary Supplement, April 23, 1970, October 25, 1985.
Washington Post, February 1, 1969.
Washington Post Book World, January 26, 1969.

OBITUARIES:

PERIODICALS

New York Times, April 24, 1976.
Washington Post, April 25, 1976.

*　　*　　*

MacINNES, Helen (Clark) 1907-1985 (Helen Highet)

PERSONAL: Born October 7, 1907, in Glasgow, Scotland; died September 30, 1985, following a stroke, in New York, N.Y.; came to United States in 1937, naturalized in 1951; daughter of Donald and Jessica (McDiarmid) MacInnes; married Gilbert Highet (a scholar and critic), September 22, 1932 (died January 20, 1978); children: Keith. *Education:* Glasgow University, M.A., 1928; University College, London, diploma in Librarianship, 1931. *Religion:* Presbyterian.

ADDRESSES: Home—15 Jefferys Lane, East Hampton, N.Y. 11937.

CAREER: Acted with Oxford University Dramatic Society and with Experimental Theatre, both Oxford, England; writer, 1941-1985.

AWARDS, HONORS: Wallace Award, America-Scottish Foundation, 1973.

WRITINGS:

TRANSLATIONS FROM THE GERMAN

(With husband, Gilbert Highet; under name Helen Highet) Otto Kiefer, *Sexual Life in Ancient Rome,* Routledge & Kegan Paul, 1934, Dutton, 1935, reprinted, AMS Press, 1972.
(With G. Highet; under name Helen Highet) Gustav Mayer, *Friedrich Engels,* Chapman & Hall, 1936.

NOVELS

Above Suspicion (also see below), Little, Brown, 1941, reprinted, Fawcett, 1978.
Assignment in Brittany (also see below), Little, Brown, 1942, reprinted, Fawcett, 1978.
While Still We Live, Little, Brown, 1944 (published in England as *The Unconquerable,* Harrap, 1944), reprinted, Fawcett, 1964.
Horizon (also see below), Harrap, 1945, Little, Brown, 1946, reprinted, Fawcett, 1979.
Friends and Lovers, Little, Brown, 1947, reprinted, Fawcett, 1978.
Rest and Be Thankful, Little, Brown, 1949, reprinted, Fawcett, 1978.
Neither Five Nor Three, Harcourt, 1951, reprinted, Fawcett, 1978.
I and My True Love, Harcourt, 1953, reprinted, Fawcett, 1978.
Pray for a Brave Heart, Harcourt, 1955, reprinted, Fawcett, 1979.
North from Rome (also see below), Harcourt, 1958, reprinted, Fawcett, 1979.
Decision at Delphi, Harcourt, 1960.
Assignment: Suspense (contains *Above Suspicion, Horizon,* and *Assignment in Brittany*), Harcourt, 1961.
The Venetian Affair, Harcourt, 1963, reprinted, Fawcett, 1978.
Home Is the Hunter (two-act play), Harcourt, 1964.
The Double Image (also see below; Book-of-the-Month Club alternate selection), Harcourt, 1966.
The Salzburg Connection, Harcourt, 1968.

Message from Malaga, Harcourt, 1971.
Triple Threat (contains *Above Suspicion, North from Rome,* and *The Double Image),* Harcourt, 1973.
Snare of the Hunter, Harcourt, 1974.
Agent in Place, Harcourt, 1976.
Prelude to Terror, Harcourt, 1978.
The Hidden Target, Harcourt, 1980.
Cloak of Darkness, Harcourt, 1982.
Ride a Pale Horse, Harcourt, 1984.

SIDELIGHTS: Helen MacInnes's novels of international intrigue have long been regarded as among the most entertaining in the genre. As P. L. Buckley explains in the *National Review:* "In the long ago, before Ian Fleming's sex 'n' sadists and John Le Carre's weary professionals took over the espionage field, a young English woman carved herself out a following. . . . [Her] formula, a quarter of a century later, remains much the same, a couple of non-professionals inveigled into taking a hand from—hold your breath—patriotic motives with the good guys against the bad [and] the adventure taking place in some attractive foreign part." A *Christian Science Monitor* reviewer notes: "Novels that blot out our environment can hardly be measured by those that reveal it, but they have their place all the same. There is nothing quite like 'a good read' to take us out of all our waiting-rooms. In her mysteries, Helen MacInnes has hit on just the formula, carefully combining a European countryside, much suspense, a little romance, and any number of likable, sensible characters."

MacInnes once commented on the objectives of her writing: "I'm continually interested in the question of how an ordinary guy of intelligence and guts resists oppression. . . . My basic characters have a certain decency and honesty. They still believe in standards of human conduct, and they rise to the occasion without fear. . . . [In my stories,] suspense is not achieved by hiding things from the reader [who] . . . always would know who did it. The question is, when is the event going to take place and how can you stop it? A reader may know everything, but still be scared stiff by the situation."

MacInnes painstakingly researched her books, wanting them to be as accurate—and credible—as possible. A typical MacInnes novel, for example, begins with a kernel of truth, usually drawn from a brief newspaper clipping which has caught the author's eye and imagination. Around this seemingly insignificant fact, MacInnes would build her story, embellishing it with information discovered in the course of extensive reading (which she insisted was "the best training" for a would-be-writer) or from personal experience and observation (she visited and became thoroughly familiar with nearly every place she wrote about). To add even more authenticity to her novels, MacInnes made sure that such things as street names and directions were correct, though she occasionally invented a town or street for the purposes of plot. "Underlying everything," MacInnes once explained, "is the fact that I'm interested in international politics [and] in analyzing news, [for I try] to read newspapers both on and between the lines, to deduct and add, to utilize memory."

Some reviewers find the inclusion of such detail to be overwhelming at times; many of these same reviewers also criticize MacInnes for what they perceive as shallow and cliche-ridden characterization. A *National Observer* critic, though admitting that MacInnes is probably "second to none in her power to evoke and employ a setting," feels that her heroes and heroines "are rather flimsy stuff, curiously untouched by the deep drama in which the author involves them." In addition, the critic reports, "there is the matter of length, sometimes a difficulty with

MacInnes books. [*The Salzburg Connection,* for example,] could well have been about 100 pages shorter. Not that it seems padded—merely overanalytical, a bit too discursive: The lady tells us perhaps a bit *too* much." A reviewer for *Spectator* agrees with this evaluation: "[MacInnes's] plots are invariably as twisty and opaque as her heroes are broad-shouldered and thoroughly transparent. . . . After 380 pages the enemy are routed and [the hero] drives into the sun. . . . I found the novel far too long, but Miss MacInnes's fans will not be disappointed."

Anatole Broyard of the *New York Times* similarly comments that, unlike "the new suspense movies, in which nothing is explained; in which there are no transitions and the actors never change expressions," in a MacInnes book, "everything is slow—talk, talk, talk,—and the burden of [interpretation] is on you too." In addition, Broyard notes, "it would not be unreasonable to say that [she] . . . ought to avoid portraying desperate men who will stop at nothing. But her women are not much better. . . . [The author's] forte—her intimate evocation of the glamorous cities of Europe—is so overlaid with her characters' cliches that we see them as if through a chill rain. . . . Though [MacInnes] obviously knows these places well, we can't enjoy them in the company she has given us."

Joseph McLellen of *Book World,* however, is convinced that there is much more to admire in a Helen MacInnes novel than there is to criticize: "One reads Helen MacInnes for a good story well-told, of course, but also for reassurance that some things remain unchanged. . . . She has been writing her kind of novel for nearly 40 years, and her writing has reflected the realities of a changing world, but the basic approach has remained refreshingly the same. She writes of decent people in bad situations. There are certain truths to be learned, certain things awry to be set right, and her sympathetic characters go about what must be done, a bit clumsily and not without pain—but goodness wins out, and (a growing rarity in this kind of writing) it is recognizable as goodness. . . . Beyond the plot lie the values without which a good plot is merely a meaningless spinning of wheels. . . . [Her novels are] full of the things that make life worthwhile—not a perfectly mixed martini or an invigorating tumble in the hay, but works of art, dreams, the feelings of home, family, specially cherished places, friendship and (the only crime unthinkable in most suspense fiction) love. . . . Partly because she is a woman and much more because she is determinedly a bit old-fashioned, Helen MacInnes insists that [the good guys *do* differ from the bad guys] and that the difference is important."

MacInnes's novels have sold over twenty-three million copies in their various American editions and have been translated into twenty-two languages. Just before MacInnes's death in 1985, her novel *Ride a Pale Horse* appeared on the *New York Times* paperback bestseller list for the first time.

MEDIA ADAPTATIONS: Several of MacInnes's novels have been made into films, including *Above Suspicion,* 1943, *Assignment in Brittany,* 1943, and *The Venetian Affair,* 1967, all by Metro-Goldwyn-Mayer, Inc., and *The Salzburg Connection,* 1972, by Twentieth Century-Fox Film Corp.

AVOCATIONAL INTERESTS: The American West, travel, music.

BIOGRAPHICAL/CRITICAL SOURCES:

BOOKS

Breit, Harvey, *The Writer Observed,* World Publishing, 1956.
Contemporary Literary Criticism, Gale, Volume 27, 1984, Volume 39, 1986.

Dictionary of Literary Biography, Volume 87: *British Mystery and Thriller Writers Since 1940, First Series,* Gale, 1989.
Newquist, Roy, *Counterpoint,* Rand McNally, 1964.
Writer's Yearbook, Writer's Digest, 1967.

PERIODICALS

Atlantic Monthly, June, 1944.
Best Sellers, September 13, 1968.
Book World, September 21, 1978.
Chicago Tribune Magazine, May 4, 1980.
Christian Science Monitor, October 3, 1968, March 27, 1974, September 27, 1978.
Commonweal, August 8, 1941, May 26, 1944.
Cosmopolitan, January, 1967.
Harper's, December, 1968.
National Observer, November 11, 1968.
National Review, January 14, 1969.
New York Herald Tribune Book Review, August 7, 1949, October 30, 1960.
New York Herald Tribune Books, July 13, 1941, July 12, 1942, October 30, 1960.
New York Times, January 8, 1966, September 16, 1971, August 13, 1976, September 26, 1980, October 1, 1985.
New York Times Book Review, May 26, 1946, August 17, 1947, November 29, 1963, January 9, 1966, December 17, 1978, January 11, 1981, September 26, 1982, November 11, 1984.
Punch, March 5, 1969.
Saturday Review, February 14, 1953.
Spectator, February 21, 1969.
Times (London), October 2, 1985.
Times Literary Supplement, October 1, 1976.
Washington Post, October 20, 1963, February 9, 1969, October 12, 1984.

OBITUARIES:

PERIODICALS

Chicago Tribune, October 3, 1985.
Los Angeles Times, October 2, 1985.
New York Times, October 1, 1985.
Times (London), October 2, 1985.
Washington Post, October 2, 1985.

*   *   *

MacLAREN, James
See GRIEVE, C(hristopher) M(urray)

*   *   *

MacLEAN, Alistair (Stuart)   1922(?)-1987
(Ian Stuart)

PERSONAL: Born 1922 (some sources say 1923), in Glasgow, Scotland; died of heart failure following a stroke, February 2, 1987, in Munich, West Germany; married Gisela Hinrichsen (divorced, 1972); married Mary Marcelle Georgeus (a film production company executive), October 13, 1972 (divorced, 1977); children: Lachlan, Michael, and Alistair; Curtis (stepson). *Education:* University of Glasgow, M.A., 1953.

ADDRESSES: Office—c/o William Collins & Sons Ltd., 8 Grafton St., London W1X 3LA, England.

CAREER: Writer, 1955-87. Former teacher of English and history at Gallowflat Secondary School in Glasgow, Scotland. *Military service:* Royal Navy, 1941-46; served as torpedo man on convoy escorts.

WRITINGS:

NOVELS

H.M.S. Ulysses, Collins, 1955, Doubleday, 1956.
The Guns of Navarone (also see below), Doubleday, 1957.
South by Java Head, Doubleday, 1958.
The Secret Ways, Doubleday, 1959 (published in England as *The Last Frontier,* Collins, 1959).
Night without End, Doubleday, 1960.
Fear Is the Key, Doubleday, 1961.
The Golden Rendezvous (also see below), Doubleday, 1962.
Ice Station Zebra, Doubleday, 1963.
When Eight Bells Toll (also see below), Doubleday, 1966.
Where Eagles Dare (also see below; Companion Book Club and Readers' Book Club selections), Doubleday, 1967.
Force 10 from Navarone (also see below), Doubleday, 1968.
Puppet on a Chain (also see below), Doubleday, 1969.
Caravan to Vaccares (also see below), Doubleday, 1970.
Bear Island, Doubleday, 1971.
The Way to Dusty Death, Doubleday, 1973.
Breakheart Pass (also see below), Doubleday, 1974.
Circus, Doubleday, 1975.
The Golden Gate, Doubleday, 1976.
Seawitch, Doubleday, 1977.
Goodbye, California, Collins, 1977, Doubleday, 1978.
Athabasca, Doubleday, 1980.
River of Death, Collins, 1981, Doubleday, 1982.
Partisans, Collins, 1982, Doubleday, 1983.
Floodgate, Collins, 1983, Doubleday, 1984.
San Andreas, Collins, 1984, Doubleday, 1985.
Santorini, Collins, 1986, Doubleday, 1987.
(With Milton Bowser) *Mother Wore White, Mother Wore Black,* edited by Jeffrey Simmons and Merilee Annerau, Sitare, 1989.

OMNIBUS VOLUMES

Five War Stories, Collins, 1978.
Four Great Adventure Stories, Collins, 1981.

UNDER PSEUDONYM IAN STUART

The Black Shrike, Scribner, 1961 (published in England as *The Dark Crusader,* Collins, 1961, published under name Alistair MacLean, Collins, 1963).
The Satan Bug, Scribner, 1962.

SCREENPLAYS

"The Guns of Navarone" (based on novel of same title), Columbia, 1959.
"Where Eagles Dare" (based on novel of same title), Metro-Goldwyn-Mayer, 1969.
"When Eight Bells Toll" (based on novel of same title), Rank, 1971.
"Puppet on a Chain" (based on novel of same title), Scotia-Barber, 1971.
"Caravan to Vaccares" (based on novel of same title), Rank, 1974.
"Breakheart Pass" (based on novel of same title), United Artists, 1976.
"The Golden Rendezvous" (based on novel of same title), Rank, 1977.
"Force 10 from Navarone" (based on novel of same title), American-International, 1978.

Also author of "Deakin."

OTHER

Lawrence of Arabia (juvenile), Random House, 1962 (published in England as *All About Lawrence of Arabia,* W. H. Allen, 1962).

Captain Cook (nonfiction), Doubleday, 1972.

Alistair MacLean Introduces Scotland, McGraw-Hill, 1972.

(With John Denis) *Hostage Tower,* Fontana, 1980.

(With Denis) *Air Force One Is Down,* Fontana, 1981.

Night Falls on Ardnamuchan: The Twilight of a Scottish Crofting Family, David & Charles, 1984.

A MacDonald for the Prince, State Mutual Book, 1985.

The Lonely Sea (story collection), Collins, 1985, Doubleday, 1986.

Also author of *A Layman Looks at Cancer,* for the British Cancer Council.

SIDELIGHTS: Alistair MacLean once claimed that he wrote quickly—taking only thirty-five days to complete a novel—because he disliked writing and didn't want to spend much time at it. He also claimed never to re-read his work once it was finished or read reviews of his books. According to the *New York Post,* MacLean once explained: "I'm not a novelist, I'm a storyteller. There's no art in what I do, no mystique." Despite his disclaimers, MacLean's many adventure novels sold over 30 million copies and were translated into a score of languages. He was, Edwin McDowell noted in the *New York Times,* "one of the biggest-selling adventure writers in the world."

MacLean's first success as a writer came while he was teaching school in his native Glasgow, Scotland, in the mid-1950s. A local newspaper, the *Glasgow Herald,* sponsored a story contest and MacLean's entry about a fishing family in the West Highlands won first prize. The story attracted the interest of an editor at the publishing house of William Collins & Sons who noticed his wife crying over a short story in the local newspaper and asked to see it for himself. It was MacLean's winning entry. The editor, Ian Chapman, enjoyed the story so much that he called MacLean and suggested that he try his hand at a novel. MacLean agreed. Over the next three months he worked evenings on the novel, *H.M.S. Ulysses,* drawing upon his years as a torpedo man in the Royal Navy. The novel came out in September of 1955 and sold a record 250,000 copies in hardcover in its first six months. It was to be the first in a long string of best-selling novels.

H.M.S. Ulysses is based on MacLean's own experiences during World War II. For much of the war he worked on convoy ships delivering much-needed supplies to Britain, the Soviet Union, and other Allied nations. The work was perilous. MacLean was wounded twice by the Nazis and captured by the Japanese. The Japanese tortured him, pulling out his teeth "without benefit of anesthetic," as MacLean once remarked. The ordeal, Bob McKelvey noted in the *Detroit Free Press,* "left him bearing a grudge against the Japanese until his death."

The pain and hardship of the war at sea is evident in *H.M.S. Ulysses,* the story of a convoy in the North Atlantic which battles German submarines as well as the treacherous weather. "Even in his first novel," Robert A. Lee wrote in his *Alistair MacLean: The Key Is Fear,* "MacLean has an acute sense of plot and structure, and it is clear that he understands quite well the consequences of action as defined by the necessities of story-telling." Reviewers of the time found faults with MacLean's work, citing a melodramatic tendency, for example, but saw the novel as a forceful and realistic portrayal of the war at sea. E. B. Garside of the *New York Times* claimed that "this novel is a gripping thing. . . . Mr. MacLean, former torpedoman, now a Scottish schoolmaster, has caught the bitter heart of the matter." Writing in the *Saturday Review,* T. E. Cooney maintained that "Mr. MacLean's true achievement [is] that of setting down in print the image of war, so that any reader, regardless of his experience, can say, That is what it was like."

This "first and greatest work," as Martin Sieff of the *Washington Times* called *H.M.S. Ulysses,* was MacLean's personal favorite and the novel which he believed was his best work. It also set the pattern for many of his later novels. Its emphasis on men battling the elements as well as the immoral machinations of other men was to recur in all of MacLean's later books. Speaking of the clear demarcation between good and evil to be found in MacLean's work, Sieff explained that MacLean's "novels are imbued with a powerful, uncompromising moral vision—that there is wickedness in the world and that it must be recognized and fought to the death, come what may."

Despite the success of his first novel, MacLean was too cautious to leave his teaching job. He suspected that the book's success might prove to be only a fluke. It wasn't until his second novel, *The Guns of Navarone,* appeared in 1957 to popular acclaim that he became a full-time writer. This novel, telling of a mission to destroy an enemy gun installation during the Second World War, proved to be "MacLean's most famous and popular novel." as Lee observed. It is, William Hogan remarked in the *San Francisco Chronicle,* "a tense, compelling, extraordinarily readable adventure." The book sold some 400,000 copies in its first six months and is still a worldwide best-seller. In 1959, it was adapted as a successful motion picture starring Gregory Peck and David Niven and produced by Carl Forman.

After the success of *The Guns of Navarone,* MacLean moved to Switzerland, where he found the climate and tax laws to his liking. For a time he wrote one new novel every year. His usual writing schedule began early in the morning and lasted until early afternoon, working away on an IBM electric typewriter. "He never rewrote anything," Caroline Moorehead revealed in the London *Times,* "and resisted, with considerable stubbornness, even minor editorial changes proposed by [his publisher] Collins." MacLean's faith in his work proved to be justified. Once, after receiving the manuscript for a MacLean novel and judging it unsatisfactory, his publisher dispatched a representative to speak with MacLean about rewriting it. By the time the agent arrived in Switzerland, however, film rights to the book had already been sold and the rewrite idea was quietly shelved. "I don't write the first sentence," MacLean told Moorehead, "until I have the last in mind. . . . I don't even re-read. One draft and it's away." MacLean never kept copies of any of his books, preferring to give them away to friends and admirers. "I don't think any are very good," he explained to Moorehead. "I'm slightly dissatisfied with all of them. I'm pleased enough if at the end of the day I produce a saleable product—and that I do."

By the early 1970s, MacLean's books had sold over 20 million copies and had been made into several popular films. He was one of the top ten best-selling writers in the world and arguably the one whose books were most often adapted for the screen. MacLean made enough money from his writing that at one point in the 1960s he gave it up and went into business as a hotelier, buying the famous Jamaica Inn and three other hotels. But he found running a hotel chain boring. When a filmmaker offered him the chance to write a screenplay in 1967, MacLean accepted. The resulting work, *Where Eagles Dare,* was a bestseller and a successful film and MacLean returned to his book-a-year schedule again.

The enormous amount of money that his adventure novels earned him never seemed to alter MacLean's lifestyle. Several observers noted that he lived frugally, content with few of the luxuries one might associate with such a successful writer. MacLean's frugality was in part the result of his innate caution. He had been raised in poverty and was always aware that his wealth might prove to be transitory. And, as Moorehead noted, he always felt "that it is morally wrong to earn so much." A writer for the London *Times* claimed that MacLean's "vast wealth lay uncomfortably on his conscience." At the time of his death in 1987, MacLean was living in a modest apartment in Switzerland, where he bought his own food and prepared his own meals.

Evaluations of MacLean's career are often colored by the sheer popularity of his books, which moved some critics to see him as nothing more than a writer who catered to mass tastes. And MacLean's flippant dismissals of his work abet this view. One such critic is Reg Gadney. Writing in *London Magazine,* Gadney described a typical MacLean adventure as "a hero, a band of men, hostile climate, a ruthless enemy. . . . The pace of the narrative consists in keeping the hero or heroes struggling on in the face of adversity. There's little time for reflection upon anything which does not contribute to the race: no characterization, merely the odd caricature; no subtlety of ploy, anything other than a fatuous one would get in the way. So the refinements are discarded and the narrative is a sprint from start to finish."

Yet, at his best, MacLean moved other critics to praise his work. Tim Heald of the London *Times* called him the "Yarnspinner Laureate" and "one of the country's most distinguished old thriller writers." Heald affectionately explained that MacLean "is at his best on the bridge of an indomitable British craft fighting its way through stupendous seas. The crew—and part of the plot—will resemble one of those stories in which an Englishman, a Scotsman, an Irishman, and a Welshman say or do something incredibly characteristic. They will be united, not only against the appalling gale, but also against a number of perfectly filthy foreigners." According to Sieff, MacLean's strong points included his "unmatched narrative drive, his complex plots and his—in the earlier novels—powerfully compelling characters." Sieff maintained that MacLean "was also a master of black, biting wit—a quality for which he was seldom given credit."

Most reviewers did credit MacLean with writing absorbing adventure novels, a task he performed with particular skill in such books as *H.M.S. Ulysses, The Guns of Navarone, Ice Station Zebra,* and *Where Eagles Dare.* In a review of *Ice Station Zebra,* the story of a nuclear submarine in peril under the Arctic ice cap, a *Times Literary Supplement* critic maintained that "the story evolves in a succession of masterful puzzles as astonishing as they are convincing. . . . There is so much swift-moving action, so much clever innuendo and such a feeling for relevant detail that one cannot help but be fascinated by the mind at work here." Speaking of *Where Eagles Dare,* Anthony Boucher of the *New York Times Book Review* described it as "a real dazzler of a thriller, with vivid action, fine set pieces of suspense, and a virtuoso display of startling plot twists."

Despite such appreciation of his work, MacLean always dismissed the value of his accomplishment. According to McKelvey, the author once claimed: "I am just a journeyman. I blunder along from one book to the next, always hopeful that one day I will write something really good." This appraisal of his work was not shared by Sieff, who ranked MacLean's *H.M.S. Ulysses* with "Nicholas Montsarrat's 'The Cruel Sea' as the greatest novel to come out of the maritime war." Lee concluded

that "MacLean's books work best when he allies evil and the natural forces of violence, when he makes the structure of his novels an undulation of tension, release, and tension, when he manages to twist his plots in such a way as to reveal parts of the mystery bit by bit, until a final stunning denouement at the end. When all these elements mesh together in one harmonious whole, the result is adventure writing at its best." MacLean, according to Linda Bridges of the *National Review,* was "one of the best suspense writers around."

MEDIA ADAPTATIONS: South by Java Head was filmed by Twentieth Century-Fox, 1959; *The Secret Ways* was filmed by Universal, 1961; *The Satan Bug* was filmed by United Artists, 1964; *Ice Station Zebra* was filmed by Metro-Goldwyn-Mayer, 1968; *Fear Is the Key* was filmed by Metro-Goldwyn-Mayer—EMI, 1972. *H.M.S. Ulysses* and *Bear Island* were also adapted for film.

AVOCATIONAL INTERESTS: Science and astronomy.

BIOGRAPHICAL/CRITICAL SOURCES:

BOOKS

Contemporary Literary Criticism, Gale, Volume 3, 1975, Volume 13, 1980, Volume 50, 1988.
Lee, Robert A., *Alistair MacLean: The Key Is Fear,* Borgo Press, 1976.

PERIODICALS

Books and Bookmen, May, 1968, November, 1971.
Glasgow Herald, March 6, 1954, September 27, 1955.
Life, November 26, 1971.
London Magazine, December-January, 1972-73.
National Review, January 31, 1975.
New Statesman, February 20, 1976.
New York Times, January 15, 1956, March 2, 1984.
New York Times Book Review, December 31, 1967, March 12, 1978.
San Francisco Chronicle, February 3, 1957.
Saturday Review, January 14, 1956.
Spectator, January 22, 1977.
Times (London), September 8, 1983, December 13, 1984, October 7, 1985, December 4, 1986.
Times Literary Supplement, August 9, 1963, September 14, 1973.
Washington Post, March 6, 1982, March 12, 1984.

OBITUARIES:

PERIODICALS

AB Bookman's Weekly, February 23, 1987.
Chicago Sun-Times, February 3, 1987.
Chicago Tribune, February 3, 1987.
Detroit Free Press, February 3, 1987.
Los Angeles Times, February 3, 1987.
New York Post, February 3, 1987.
New York Times, February 3, 1987.
San Francisco Examiner, February 3, 1987.
Times (London), February 3, 1987.
Washington Post, February 3, 1987.
Washington Times, February 3, 1987.

*   *   *

MacLEISH, Archibald   1892-1982

PERSONAL: Born May 7, 1892, in Glencoe, Ill.; died April 20, 1982, in Boston, Mass.; son of Andrew (a partner in Chicago department store of Carson, Pirie, Scott & Co.) and Martha (Hillard) MacLeish; married Ada Hitchcock (a singer), June 21,

1916; children: Kenneth (deceased), Brewster Hitchcock (deceased), Mary Hillard, William Hitchcock. *Education:* Attended Hotchkiss School; Yale University, A.B., 1915; Harvard University, LL.B., 1919.

ADDRESSES: Home—Conway, Mass.

CAREER: Poet, dramatist. Harvard University, Cambridge, Mass., instructor in constitutional law, 1919; Choate, Hall & Stewart (law firm), Boston, Mass., staff member, 1920-23; freelance writer in France, 1923-28; *Fortune,* New York City, staff member, 1929-38; Harvard University, Cambridge, named first curator of Niemann Collection of Contemporary Journalism and adviser to Niemann fellows, 1938. Served as Librarian of Congress, 1939-44, director of Office of Facts and Figures, 1941-42, assistant director of Office of War Information, 1942-43, Assistant Secretary of State, 1944-45, American delegate to Conference of Allied Ministers of Education in London, 1944. Admitted to U.S. Supreme Court Bar, 1942. Served as chairman of U.S. delegation to London conference drafting UNESCO constitution, 1945, as first U.S. delegate to General Conference of UNESCO in Paris, 1946, and first U.S. member of Executive Council of UNESCO. Harvard University, Cambridge, Boylston Professor of Rhetoric and Oratory, 1949-62, Boylston Professor Emeritus, 1962-82. U.S. Department of State lecturer in Europe, 1957; Simpson Lecturer, Amherst College, 1963-67. Museum of Modern Art, New York City, trustee, beginning 1940; Sara Lawrence College, Bronxville, N.Y., trustee, beginning 1949. *Military service:* U.S. Army, Field Artillery, 1917-18; served in France; became captain.

MEMBER: American Academy of Arts and Letters (president, 1953-56), National Institute of Arts and Letters, Academy of American Poets (fellow, 1966), League of American Writers (chairman, 1937), National Committee for an Effective Congress Commission on Freedom of the Press, Phi Beta Kappa, Century Club (New York), Tavern Club and Somerset Club (Boston).

AWARDS, HONORS: John Reed Memorial prize, 1929; Shelley Memorial Award for Poetry, 1932; Pulitzer Prize in poetry for *Conquistador,* 1933; Golden Rose Trophy of New England Poetry Club, 1934; Levinson Prize for group of poems published in *Poetry,* 1941; Commander, Legion of Honor (France), 1946; Commander, el Sol del Peru, 1947; Bollingen Prize in Poetry of Yale University Library, 1952, Pulitzer Prize in poetry, 1953, and National Book Award in poetry, 1953, all for *Collected Poems: 1917-1952;* Boston Arts Festival poetry award, 1956; Sarah Josepha Hale Award, 1958; Chicago Poetry Day Poet, 1958; Antoinette Perry ("Tony") Award in drama, 1959, and Pulitzer Prize in drama, 1959, for *J. B.: A Play in Verse;* Academy Award (best screenplay), 1966, for *The Eleanor Roosevelt Story;* Presidential Medal of Freedom, 1977; National Medal for Literature, 1978; Gold Medal for Poetry, American Academy of Arts and Letters, 1979. M.A. from Tufts University, 1932; Litt.D. from Colby College, 1938, Wesleyan University, 1938, Yale University, 1939, University of Pennsylvania, 1941, University of Illinois, 1946, Washington University, 1948, Rockford College, 1953, Columbia University, 1954, Harvard University, 1955, University of Pittsburgh, 1959, Princeton University, 1965, University of Massachusetts, 1969, and Hampshire College, 1970; L.H.D. from Dartmouth University, 1940, and Williams College, 1942; D.C.L. from Union College, 1941, and University of Puerto Rico, 1953; LL.D. from Johns Hopkins University, 1941, University of California, 1943, Queen's University at Kingston, 1948, Carleton College, 1956, and Amherst College, 1963.

WRITINGS:

POETRY

Songs for a Summer's Day (sonnet cycle), Yale University Press, 1915.

Tower of Ivory, Yale University Press, 1917.

The Happy Marriage, and Other Poems, Houghton, 1924.

The Pot of Earth, Houghton, 1925.

Streets in the Moon, Houghton, 1926.

The Hamlet of A. MacLeish, Houghton, 1928.

Einstein, Black Sun Press, 1929.

New Found Land (limited edition), Black Sun Press, 1930, Houghton, 1930.

Conquistador (narrative poem), Houghton, 1932.

Before Match, Knopf, 1932.

Poems, 1924-1933, Houghton, 1933.

Frescoes for Mr. Rockefeller's City, Day, 1933, reprinted, Folcroft Library Editions (Folcroft, Pa.), 1971.

Poems, John Lane (London), 1935.

Public Speech, Farrar & Rinehart, 1936.

Land of the Free, Harcourt, 1938, reprinted, Da Capo Press, 1977.

America Was Promises, Duell, Sloan & Pearce, 1939.

Actfive and Other Poems, Random House, 1948.

Collected Poems, 1917-52, Houghton, 1952.

Songs for Eve, Houghton, 1954.

Collected Poems, Houghton, 1962.

The Collected Poems of Archibald MacLeish, Houghton, 1963.

The Wild Old Wicked Man and Other Poems, Houghton, 1968.

The Human Season: Selected Poems, 1926-72, Houghton, 1972.

New and Collected Poems, 1917-1976, Houghton, 1976.

New and Collected Poems, 1917-1984, Houghton, 1985.

PROSE

Housing America (articles from *Fortune*), Harcourt, 1932.

Jews in America (first published in *Fortune*), Random, 1936.

Libraries in the Contemporary Crisis, U.S. Government Printing Office, 1939.

Deposit of the Magna Carta in the Library of Congress on November 28, 1939, Library of Congress, 1939.

The American Experience, U.S. Government Printing Office, 1939.

The Irresponsibles, Duell, Sloan & Pearce, 1940.

The American Cause, Duell, Sloan & Pearce, 1941.

The Duty of Freedom, privately printed for the United Typothetae of America, 1941.

The Free Company Presents . . . The States Talking (radio broadcast, April 2, 1941), [New York], 1941.

The Next Harvard, Harvard University Press, 1941.

Prophets of Doom, University of Pennsylvania Press, 1941.

A Time to Speak, Houghton, 1941.

American Opinion and the War (Rede lecture at Cambridge University, Cambridge, England, 1942), Macmillan, 1942.

A Free Man's Books (limited edition of 200 copies), Peter Pauper, 1942.

In Honor of a Man and an Ideal . . . Three Talks on Freedom, by Archibald MacLeish, William S. Paley, Edward R. Murrow (radio broadcast, December 2, 1941), [New York], 1942.

Report to the Nation, U.S. Office of Facts and Figures, 1942.

A Time to Act, Houghton, 1943.

The American Story: Ten Broadcasts (presented on NBC Radio, 1944, and for which MacLeish served as commentator), Duell, Sloan & Pearce, 1944, 2nd edition, 1960.

Martha Hillard MacLeish, 1856-1947, privately printed, 1949.

Poetry and Opinion: The Pisan Cantos of Ezra Pound, University of Illinois Press, 1950, reprinted, Haskell House, 1974.

Freedom Is the Right to Choose: An Inquiry into the Battle for the American Future, Beacon, 1951.

Poetry and Journalism, University of Minnesota Press, 1958.

Poetry and Experience, Riverside Editions, 1960.

The Dialogues of Archibald MacLeish and Mark Van Doren (televised, 1962), Dutton, 1964.

A Continuing Journey, Houghton, 1968.

Champion of a Cause: Essays and Addresses on Librarianship, compiled by Eva M. Goldschmidt, American Library Association, 1971.

Riders on the Earth: Essays and Recollections, Houghton, 1978.

Letters of Archibald MacLeish, 1907 to 1982, edited by R. H. Winnick, Houghton, 1983.

Archibald MacLeish: Reflections, edited by Bernard A. Drabeck and Helen E. Ellis, University of Massachusetts Press, 1986.

DRAMA

Nobodaddy (verse play; also see below), Dunster House, 1926, reprinted, Norwood, 1974.

Panic: A Play in Verse (first produced on Broadway at Imperial Theater, March 14, 1935; also see below), Houghton, 1935.

The Fall of the City: A Verse Play for Radio (first presented on CBS Radio, 1937, and on CBS-TV, 1962; also see below), Farrar & Rinehart, 1937, cassette recording, All-Media Dramatic Workshop (Chicago), 1977.

Air Raid: A Verse Play for Radio (first presented on CBS Radio, 1938; also see below), Harcourt, 1938.

The Trojan Horse (verse play; first presented on BBC Radio, London, c. 1950; also see below), Houghton, 1952.

This Music Crept By Me upon the Waters (verse play; also see below), Harvard University Press, 1953.

J. B.: A Play in Verse (first produced at Yale School of Drama; produced on Broadway at ANTA Theater, December 11, 1958), Houghton, 1958, sound recording, Minnesota Public Radio, 1976.

Three Short Plays (includes *Air Raid, The Fall of the City,* and *The Secret of Freedom,* a television play, produced for Sunday Showcase, 1960), Dramatists Play Service, 1961.

The Eleanor Roosevelt Story (filmscript; first produced by Allied Artists, 1965), Houghton, 1965.

An Evening's Journey to Conway, Massachusetts (play; first produced for NET Playhouse, November 3, 1967), Gehenna Press, 1967.

Herakles (verse play; first produced, 1965), Houghton, 1967.

Scratch (based on short story by Stephen Vincent Benet, "The Devil and Daniel Webster"; first produced on Broadway at St. James Theatre, May 6, 1971), Houghton, 1971.

The Great American Fourth of July Parade: A Verse Play for Radio, University of Pittsburgh Press, 1975.

Six Plays (contains *Nobodaddy, Panic, The Fall of the City, Air Raid, The Trojan Horse,* and *The Music Crept by Me Upon the Waters*), Houghton, 1980.

(Contributor) Samuel Moon, editor, *One Act: Eleven Short Plays of the Modern Theater* (includes *This Music Crept by Me upon the Waters*), Grove, 1987.

OTHER

(Co-author with editors of *Fortune*) *Background of War,* Knopf, 1937.

(Author of foreword) William Meredith, *Love Letters from an Impossible Land,* Yale University Press, 1944.

(Author of introduction) St. John Perse (pseudonym for Alexis Saint-Leger Leger), *Eloges and Other Poems,* Norton, 1944.

(Editor) Gerald Fitzgerald, *The Wordless Flesh,* [Cambridge], 1960.

(Editor) Edwin Muir, *The Estate of Poetry,* Hogarth, 1962.

(Contributor) *Let Freedom Ring,* American Heritage, 1962.

(Editor with E. F. Prichard, Jr., and author of foreword), Felix Frankfurter, *Law and Politics: Occasional Papers, 1913-38,* Peter Smith, 1963.

(Editor) Leonard Baskin, *Figures of Dead Men,* University of Massachusetts Press, 1968.

(Author of introduction) *The Complete Poems of Carl Sandburg,* Harcourt, 1970.

(Adapter) William Shakespeare, *King Lear* (sound recording; recorded from the original CBS broadcast on July 10, 1937), Radio Yesteryear (Sandy Hook, Conn.), c. 1975.

The Nature of Poetry: Pulitzer Prize Poet Archibald MacLeish Discusses Poetry (cassette recording), interviewed by Walter Kerr, Center for Cassette Studies, c. 1975.

(Author of foreword) Anthony Piccione, *Anchor Dragging: Poems,* Boa Editions, 1977.

Also author of "The Son of Man," presented on CBS Radio, 1947. Librettist, with Nicolas Nabokoff, for "Union Pacific," a verse ballet, written for Federal Theatre Project (WPA), first produced on Broadway at St. James Theatre, April 25, 1934, later performed by Monte Carlo Ballet Russe in Philadelphia, Pa., 1934; librettist for "Magic Prison," 1967.

SIDELIGHTS: Archibald MacLeish's roots were firmly planted in both the new and the old worlds. His father, the son of a poor shopkeeper in Glasgow, Scotland, was born in 1837, the year of Victoria's coronation, and ran away first to London and then, at the age of eighteen, to Chicago. His mother was a Hillard, a family that, as *Dialogues of Archibald MacLeish and Mark Van Doren* reveals, MacLeish was fond of tracing back through its New England generations to Elder Brewster, the minister of the Mayflower. MacLeish was born in Glencoe, Illinois, in 1892, attended Hotchkiss School from 1907 to 1911, and from 1911 to 1915 studied at Yale where he edited and wrote for the *Yale Literary Magazine,* contributed to the *Yale Review,* and composed a sonnet sequence "Songs for a Summer's Day," which was chosen as the Yale University Prize Poem in 1915. He married Ada Hitchcock in 1916. In 1917, he saw service in France and published his first collection of poems, *Tower of Ivory.*

MacLeish viewed World War I as the ending of an old world and the beginning of a new one that was *sensed* rather than understood. His early poetry was his attempt to understand this new world; MacLeish would say later that his education regarding this world began not in his undergraduate years at Yale, but in years after the war at Harvard Law School. As he declared in *Riders on the Earth: Essays and Recollections,* Harvard sparked in him a sense of the human tradition, "the vision of mental time, of the interminable journey of the human mind, the great tradition of the intellectual past which knows the bearings of the future."

His personal dilemma, and the constant theme of his early writings, was the reconciliation of idealism with reality. This theme had run through his undergraduate short stories and through his first long poem, "Our Lady of Troy," which was published in *Tower of Ivory.* In his own life, he resolved this dilemma by turning from his promising career as a lawyer to pursue the vocation for which the law courts had left him little time—that of poet. In the summer of 1923, MacLeish announced his commitment to poetry by moving from Boston with his wife and two children, into a fourth floor flat on the Boulevard St. Michel in Paris.

The first major period of MacLeish's poetic career—some would say the only major one—thus began in the early 1920s, when he gave up the law and moved abroad, and closed in the later 1930s, when he took on a succession of "public" obligations. During these years, MacLeish's work was made up of nine longer poems or sequences of poems, accompanied by lyric meditations and statements in various forms on diverse but characteristic themes: doubt, loss, alienation, art, aging, the quest. The shorter poems, some of them very successful, have by anthologizing and other emphases become better known than the longer ones. MacLeish's collection, *New and Collected Poems, 1917-1984,* however, emphasizes the interrelation of his longer and shorter poems, as did his first major collection, *Poems, 1924-1933.*

The "other poems" of *The Happy Marriage, and Other Poems,* still late Victorian prentice-work, are often reminiscent of Edwin Arlington Robinson—whom MacLeish admired—and are justly forgotten. But the title poem, with its more complex, more contemporary subject, alternates skilled imitation of major predecessors with accents of personal authority. It could even be argued that this mixed transitional style fits, if only by chance, the protagonist's own confusion between trite attitudes and existential authenticity. By Part Four of "The Happy Marriage," the protagonist's recognition of marital reality has found its poetic voice, what Grover Smith called in *Archibald MacLeish* "conscious symbolism; witty, almost metaphysical strategies of argument; compressed and intense implications."

The Pot of Earth tells the very different story of a very different figure, a young woman deeply affected psychologically or culturally by archetypal myths of woman's fertility and its transformative powers as seen through "the figure of the dying god whose imaginative presence is at the core of cultural vitality," according to John B. Vickery in *The Literary Impact of the Golden Bough.* Obsessed by symbolic mythical images—excessively so in the unrevised version—she dies in childbirth, sought by or seeking a death dictated by myth, the unconscious, or simple biology. To tell her moving story, MacLeish interweaves narrative and lyric forms, regular and irregular verse of great eloquence that reinforces the pathos, irony, and mystery of her fate.

Besides marking the first publication of "Einstein," *Streets in the Moon* has some of MacLeish's best and best-known shorter poems. In "Memorial Rain" (directly) and in "The Silent Slain" (indirectly) MacLeish came to what terms he could with concerns identified in Paul Fussell's *The Great War and Modern Memory.* "The Farm" illustrates the search for New England roots that ran through MacLeish's career and his writings in prose and verse. Other poems reflect the varying expatriate moods that came together after a few years in "American Letter." And the too well-known, too often misunderstood "Ars Poetica" conveys in its images, imitative form, and self-contradictions MacLeish's permanent conviction that a poem should both mean and be.

In *Einstein,* published separately in 1929, MacLeish presented a day's meditation that recapitulates the major stages in Einstein's physical and metaphysical struggle to contain and comprehend the physical universe, from classical empiricism through romantic empathy to modern, introspective, analytic physics. In flexible, elaborate, evocative blank verse, with an epigrammatic literal-allegorical prose gloss, and in a rich texture of spatial imagery the poem "narrates" Einstein's quest for knowledge. To Frederick J. Hoffman in *The Twenties,* this quest is shown as "pathetic and futile," but to Lauriat Lane, Jr., in an *Ariel* essay, it is "potentially tragic" and an example of "modern, existential Man Thinking."

Citing *The Hamlet of A. MacLeish,* Leslie Fiedler in *Unfinished Business* identified four appeals of the story of Hamlet to the American imagination: 1) "anguish and melancholy," 2) "the notion of suicide," 3) "the inhibitory nature of conscience," and 4) "an oddly apt parable of our relationship to Europe." This poem, MacLeish's most complex and elaborate, addresses all four subjects. Combining and contrasting what Fiedler elsewhere called signature and archetype, autobiography and myth, the work, which contains fourteen sections and a Shakespearean gloss, juxtaposes dialectically *Hamlet,* MacLeish's personal and poetic autobiographical uncertainties, and two fulfilled quests—a medieval Grail romance and tribal migrations out of the *Anabase* of Saint-John Perse, whose fulfillment only intensifies the doubts and despairs of Hamlet/MacLeish. As he recorded in *A Reviewer's ABC,* Conrad Aiken, who had found *Einstein* "a long poem which any living poet might envy, as rich in thought as it is in color and movement," labeled *The Hamlet of A. MacLeish* "a kind of brilliant *pastiche,*" although "full of beautiful things." Aiken went on, however, to pose the unanswered question of "whether [MacLeish's] 'echoes' might not, by a future generation, be actually preferred to the things they echo." Often, in MacLeish's work, such "echoes" are a form of brilliant, purposeful parody, an additional stylistic power finally recognizable fifty postmodern years later for what it is.

As its title implies, MacLeish published *New Found Land* after he had returned to America for good. Less varied and experimental in form than the short poems of *Streets in the Moon,* the poems in the slender *New Found Land* share the moods and concerns of *The Hamlet of A. MacLeish.* Along with "American Letter," the book has one of MacLeish's most famous "international" poems, "You, Andrew Marvell," and one of his greatest regional ones, "Immortal Autumn." For Signi Falk in *Archibald MacLeish, New Found Land* reveals "a poet torn between the old world and the new."

Conquistador, too, combines the old world and the new, but by 1932, the year of the book's publication, the choice had become clear if often tragic in its outcome. In the conquerors of Central American native civilization MacLeish found a romantic, exotic history that could also serve as a myth, a metaphor, for closer, more familiar history and concerns. In Montezuma, Cortez, and Diaz, the poem offers three figures—god, hero, and man—who share the reader's attention and good will and who are examined in an ironic context of human blood and natural beauty, greed for gold and sun-worship, political intrigue and heroic quest. Seeing the poem wholly through its narrator, Diaz, Allen Tate praised the poem for its "finely sustained tone," its "clarity of sensuous reminiscence," its "technical perfection," but found in its sentimentality "one of the examples of our modern sensibility at its best; it has the defect of its qualities," as Tate recorded in *Essays of Four Decades.*

In their many interrelations, *The Pot of Earth, Einstein, The Hamlet of A. MacLeish,* and *Conquistador* form a tetralogy of four major high modernist poems. With "Elpenor," originally "1933," which appeared in *Poems, 1924-1933* and which has subsequently been republished under each title, MacLeish moved toward the "public speech" of the post-Depression, Rooseveltian 1930s. Both a vivid retelling and sequel to Homer and Dante, this compressed little epic populates a modern Hell in the manner of Ezra Pound's poetry and points "the way on," in MacLeish's characteristic symbolic topographical imagery, where its readers can "begin it again: start over."

Among the other new poems in *Poems, 1924-1933,* "Frescoes for Mr. Rockefeller's City" (also published separately in 1933) dealt with a public controversy and caused additional public excitement. Although praised by Cleanth Brooks in *Modern Poetry and the Tradition,* it has "not only ideological but functional problems," as Grover Smith declared; and some of its sections, like several of MacLeish's other public poems of the 1930s, reveal "the absence of arresting images and the slackness of the rhythm" that troubled David Luytens in *The Creative Encounter.* However, as recorded in *Literary Opinion in America,* Morton D. Zabel also found in these public poems "a signal of profitable intentions" and discovered "a very moving beauty" in the very unpublic set of lyrics, "The Woman on the Stair," in *Public Speech.*

The last of MacLeish's longer poems of the 1930s was *America Was Promises.* In an essay collected in *A Poet's Alphabet,* Louise Bogan attacked it as "MacLeish's saddest and most conglomerate attempt at 'public speech's' to date . . . political poetry, even a kind of official poetry," but Grover Smith later reassessed it as "the most eloquent of the 'public' poems . . . much better as a poem than as a message: for once, MacLeish's adaptation of St. J. Perse's geographic evocations seems precisely right." *America Was Promises* combines such "geographic evocations" with a quasi-allegorical populist history of Jefferson and Man, Adams and the Aristocracy, Paine and the People. For *The Human Season: Selected Poems, 1926-1972* MacLeish cut from *America Was Promises* almost all its "official" poetry and possibly made it a much better poem.

Looking back over these first two decades of MacLeish's poetry, Karl Shapiro declared in *Essay on Rime* "a special speech is born / Out of this searching, something absolute, . . . a linguistic dream . . . an influential dialect. . . ." In this poetry, said Hyatt H. Waggoner in *The Heel of Elohim,* "The will to believe is certainly present, but so also are the vacant lights, the bright void, the listening, idiot silence"; yet in *North American Review,* Mason Wade saw in the same poetry a "moving . . . intellectual anabasis," and in *Sewanee Review* Reed Whittemore praised some of it as "Democratic Pastoral."

In 1924 "The Happy Marriage" had explored the idea that out of the union of the ideal and the real must emerge a more mature sense of individual identity. This same theme carried through MacLeish's 1926 poetic drama, *Nobodaddy,* a verse play that uses the Adam and Eve story as "the dramatic situation which the condition of self-consciousness in an indifferent universe seems to me to present." MacLeish would affirm, a few years later, that the poet's role was "the restoration of man to his position of dignity and responsibility at the centre of his world." *Nobodaddy* provided its author with the opportunity to return to man's origins, to explore the human condition in terms of its myths and mysteries. To MacLeish, the work was a simple and forthright play of the beginnings of human consciousness.

In the resolution of his own sense of self-consciousness, symbolized by his move to Paris in 1923, MacLeish showed a certain kinship with his character Cain. Both had found the strength necessary to sever—in Cain's words—the thick vein "that knots me to the body of the earth," and to grab control of the centers of their own worlds. *Nobodaddy* is the story of man attempting to make sense of the chaos of his life. It can also be read as the *apologia* for its author. And its theme of a world in which man is bewildered and bored, a world in which his knowledge is not matched by his understanding, is one that would run through much of MacLeish's writing during the 1920s.

When MacLeish returned from Europe in 1928 and settled in Conway, Mass., he had obviously "re-viewed" America. The country's idealism, reflected especially in the philosophies of its founding father, supplied him with a sense of identity and place that existential *angst* had failed to engender. The questor had reached this personal goal only to find the obvious truth that each goal is a new beginning and that his search had been only his initiation into what would be a lengthy continuing journey. While the writer was now set to move in new directions, George Dangerfield asserted in a 1931 *Books* essay that "if [MacLeish] were never to write another word, he would still be a poet of definite importance."

MacLeish's first produced stage play, *Panic: A Play in Verse,* is a variation on the Cain story set against the background of the American Depression and a generation of capitalists he felt were in the process of leaving capitalism "intellectually defenseless and unarmed." The conflict of the play is between the will of a man (McGafferty, played in the original production by Orson Welles) and a fatalistic concept of human life (dialectical materialism). McGafferty surrenders to the delphic oracle of Marxist determinism and thus falls victim to it. As the Blind Man in the play observes, the financier fails because (unlike Cain) he will not trust his own freedom.

The play was MacLeish's attempt to comprehend the real sense of panic in a country where individualism had turned into individual greed and freedom had been replaced by a failing "free enterprise." American Communists found the play particularly frustrating, as MacLeish (who was on the editorial board of *Fortune*) refused to view what they took to be the imminence and inevitability of the Marxist revolution as anything more than a delphic prophecy that the crowd chorus was free to reject. Various other reviews of the production centered on the poet's attempt to create a verse line for the modern stage. Malcolm Cowley declared in a 1935 *New Republic* assessment that the play brought "a new intelligence to the theatre and [embodied] the results of the experiments made by modern poets."

In the late 1930s, speaking with the "public voice" that characterized his writings from the beginning of the decade, MacLeish wrote two verse plays for radio: *The Fall of the City,* broadcast on April 11, 1937, and *Air Raid,* broadcast on October 27, 1938. The first of these was the poet's exploration of his sense of a developing worldwide change in the commitment of human consciousness to human freedom. It was a change that MacLeish's own hero and friend, President Franklin D. Roosevelt, had addressed at his first inauguration: "We have nothing to fear but fear itself." *Air Raid* grew out of the German bombing of Guernica and Pablo Picasso's response to that slaughter through his painting, "Guernica." *Air Raid* is a play for voices dealing with the changes in the nature of war and with the alterations in the human spirit that had permitted such changes. MacLeish intended neither script to be primarily a political statement; he looked upon both as poems, as creations that explored what he perceived to be these changes rather than as attempts to persuade. Still, the closeness of MacLeish's sympathies to Roosevelt's has led Luytens to call MacLeish "the poet laureate of the New Deal."

The Trojan Horse, a verse drama first presented on the BBC in 1952, is in many ways a return to earlier decades and earlier characters. Helen of Troy had been earlier seen in a closet drama entitled "Our Lady of Troy" and collected in MacLeish's *Tower of Ivory.* She had later appeared in "The Happy Marriage" as the symbol of Beauty. The Blind Man, who earlier laid the future before McGafferty in *Panic,* has the same function here. Paul Brooks, in a note accompanying the first edition of *The Trojan Horse,* tied the play to the McCarthy era, but the script was intended more generally to explore in myth the sense of deception the poet had perceived in his own century. The poetic sense of awareness itself is presented in a 1953 play, *This Music Crept by Me upon the Waters,* where Elizabeth, as did Cain before her, experiences the discovery of her own place in the cosmos.

The public voice which found its way into MacLeish's poetry in the 1930s was a reflection of the sense of public responsibility he had come to accept on his return from Paris. Harriet Monroe in a 1931 issue of *Poetry,* wrote that she has "much faith in the ability of this poet to interpret his age: he has the thinking mind, the creative imagination, the artistic equipment of beautiful words and rhythms." This voice was heard most directly in the many articles and speeches MacLeish wrote on the role of the poet and, through the political chaos of the western world in the 1930s and 1940s, on the direction he felt America should be pursuing. Much of this material has been collected in *A Time to Speak, A Time to Act,* and *A Continuing Journey.* Also, as Falk points out, MacLeish committed himself to such public offices as Librarian of Congress from 1939 to 1944, Assistant Director of the Office of War Information in 1942, Assistant Secretary of State from 1944 to 1945, and Chairman of the American delegation to the founding conference of UNESCO in 1945.

MacLeish said several times that in the long poem "Actfive," published in *Actfive and Other Poems* in 1948, he tried to come to terms with his and the world's experiences in the immediately preceding years: the challenge and suffering of the war, the opportunities and failures of the peace, the loss of so many faiths. *Conquistador* had offered an implicit choice between god, hero, and man; "Actfive," in its three scenes, redefines and makes that choice. With the God gone, the King dethroned, and Man murdered—all in elegiac, characteristically despairing lines—the heroes of the age are then thrust forward in their emptiness through sardonically abrupt rhythms. They give way, in turn, to "the shapes of flesh and bone," in whose moving, subtly musical, indirect voices MacLeish's long involvement with Matthew Arnold (noted Arthur Mizener as early as 1938 in *Sewanee Review*) is fulfilled. The result is a poetic affirmation, "humanist and existentialist," according to Luytens, for an even darker, more confused, post-Arnoldian time.

"Actfive" was MacLeish's last poem to interweave lyric statement and emblematically condensed narrative within an extended structure of feeling and idea. In the ten years from 1944 to 1954, called by Grover Smith "his second renaissance," he published over eighty short poems, half of them, apparently, written in two very creative years after he began teaching poetry at Harvard, where he was Boylsten Professor from 1949 to 1962. In style these poems, having many forms and treating a great variety of subjects, might be called neo-modernist, embodying a riper, wiser Imagism, for example. But their combination of immediate, personal concern with impersonal form, image, and language is not easily labeled. Poets Hayden Carruth in *Effluences from the Sacred Cave,* Richard Eberhart in *Virginia Quarterly Review,* John Ciardi in *Atlantic,* and Kimon Friar in *New Republic* have all praised these poems.

The best of these short works succeed, not surprisingly, in the terms of MacLeish's *Poetry and Experience,* which defines the "means" by which and the "shapes" in which poetry finds its "end" meaning. In brief, MacLeish contended, poetry combines sounds, signs, images, and metaphor to give meaning to the private world (Emily Dickinson), the public world (William Butler Yeats), the anti-world (Arthur Rimbaud), and the arable world (John Keats).

Among the lyrics of the private world, which record recognizable and therefore meaningful experience spoken in a living, personal voice, are such fine love poems as "Ever Since," "Calypso's Island," "What Any Lover Learns," and such testaments of poetic and humanist faith as "A Man's Work," "The Two Priests," "The Infinite Reason," and "Reasons for Music," some of which also look outward to the public world. MacLeish's poetic statements of and for the world of public affairs are designed both "to lash out" and to try to "make *positive* sense of the public world," as he asserted in *Poetry and Experience.* "Brave New World," for example, "lashes out" in tight, cutting quatrains at the loss of Jefferson's vision of human freedom. "The Danger in the Air" and "The Sheep in the Ruins" move meditatively toward making some sense against the danger, amid the ruins. Very few of these short poems look toward Rimbaud's anti-world. For MacLeish, as for Rimbaud, the sea was the great image of the Unknown: over the sea in "Voyage West," beneath it in "The Reef Fisher." MacLeish declared in *Poetry and Experience* that "Rimbaud's anti-world was not a rejection of the *possibility* of the world"; nor were MacLeish's own few visions of that anti-world. Poems of the arable world try to make familiar yet tragic "truth of the passing-away of the world." In his *Dialogues* with Mark Van Doren, MacLeish testifies how much the arable world of Uphill Farm in Massachusetts meant to him, as do "The Two Trees," "The Snow Fall," and "The Old Men in the Leaf Smoke." From Caribbean Antigua, on the other hand, probably came "The Old Man to the Lizard" and "Vicissitudes of the Creator." And the truth of the passing-away of the world took another, more direct, even more moving form in "For the Anniversary of My Mother's Death" and "My Naked Aunt."

Several volumes of MacLeish's prose—*Poetry and Experience,* a section of *A Continuing Journey,* and *Poetry and Opinion: The Pisan Cantos of Ezra Pound,* on the controversy surrounding Ezra Pound's support for Mussolini during World War II—grew out of his teaching. His two earliest collections of literary and political statements were *A Time to Speak* and *A Time to Act*—"a couple of books of speeches," as he labeled them in *Letters of Archibald MacLeish, 1907 to 1982.* Some of these prose pieces, most notoriously "The Irresponsibles," strayed dangerously close to propaganda—admittedly in a time of great public danger—and were attacked for this failing by critics like Edmund Wilson in *Classics and Commercials* and Morton D. Zabel in *Partisan Review.* In still another vein, *Champion of a Cause: Essays and Addresses on Librarianship* reprinted MacLeish's deliberately nonprofessional, nontechnical "essays and addresses on librarianship."

MacLeish's prose, for the most part, bore public witness to familiar but important ideas and beliefs. The editors of *Ten Contemporary Thinkers* included four MacLeish essays that represent well the range of his prose: "The Writer and Revolution," "Humanism and the Belief in Man," "The Conquest of America," and "The Isolation of the American Artist"; his essays and books specifically on poetry and poets eloquently and even more significantly witness to the broadly-defined powers of poems to move their readers. And even the most topical of MacLeish's political essays keep their relevance. In 1949 he first published "The Conquest of America" on the dangers of mindless anti-Communism and failure to reaffirm the American "revolution of the individual." In 1980 the *Atlantic* felt obliged by events to reprint MacLeish's warning. To the end of his long life he continued, in prose and in poetry, to praise and to warn "the Republic."

Having left public life and moved to Harvard by the late 1940s, MacLeish refocused his attention from the social and political themes of the preceding two decades toward an earlier poetic interest: the place and value of man in the universe. In his longer postwar poetic works, he followed his own exhortation to invent the metaphor for the age. His series of poems collected as *Songs for Eve* returned again to the setting of *Nobodaddy* to emphasize once more the fundamental importance of self-consciousness in an indifferent universe. Despite his various attempts to find in Adam and Eve the metaphor for the age, the poet's most successful image of the human spirit appeared four years later on the stage of New York's ANTA Theatre in the character of J. B.

J. B.'s structure, in the acting edition of the play, differs substantially from the original version published by Houghton Mifflin in 1958, but the main characters remain basically the same. J. B. comes across both the footlights and the page not as a character in a morality play—for the play, despite its early scenes, is not a morality play—but as a flesh-and-blood common man beset by sufferings to which all flesh is heir. And in J. B.'s struggle and success against an inexplicable, brutal, and unjust universe, MacLeish presented what he hoped would be the metaphor for man's next era. Like Job, J. B. is not answered, yet his love for Sarah affirms, in the playwrights phrase, "the worth of life in spite of life." That worth is found in a love that paradoxically answers nothing but "becomes the ultimate human answer to the ultimate human question."

After receiving a Pulitzer Prize, his third, for *J. B.,* MacLeish returned to man's quarrels with the gods in *Herakles,* first produced in 1965 and published in 1967. During the first part of the play, Professor Hoadley is drawn to Greece, the *patria* of the intellectual life, in search of the spirit of Herakles, the half-man, half-god who dared to struggle with the unanswered questions of the universe. Balancing Hoadley's search for intellectual perfection is his wife's conviction that life is a concrete reality including the human imperfection her husband would transcend. In the second half of the play, a frustrated Herakles fails to receive a sign from Apollo and angrily ascends to the temple door threatening to answer his own oracle. But, despite the merits of his deeds, he is unable to perform the god-like act of pronouncing his own destiny. In the end, Hoadley's wife and Herakles's Megara refocus the human spirit where J. B. had earlier found it—on the day-to-day occupation of living, not in glorious myth, but in concrete reality.

If *J. B.* and *Herakles* raise still-unanswered questions, they also affirm that all questions need not be answered. MacLeish's last full-length play, *Scratch,* finds its source in "The Devil and Daniel Webster," Stephen Vincent Benet's treatment of the mythical American confrontation between man and the Devil. Alone of the final three plays, it explores questions that, because of their American roots, could move closer to resolution within the text. MacLeish felt there were three reasons that Benet's story had widened into myth: that the Republic had become full of men and women who had sold their souls "for its comforts and amenities"; that "belief in hell was reviving everywhere and that, if only love of life could be turned into contempt for living, hope into despair, the entire planet would dissolve into that cistern of self-pity where [Samuel Becket's] Godot never comes"; and that Daniel Webster's concern for Liberty and Union, or freedom and government, was as contemporary as it had ever been.

During the 1960s and 1970s, MacLeish also wrote three shorter scripts: a highly polemical television play, *The Secret of Freedom;* an "outdoor play" for the bicentennial of Conway entitled *An Evening's Journey to Conway, Massachusetts;* and *The Great American Fourth of July Parade,* a verse play for radio. All three works reflect their author's continual concern for the central values of America's founding fathers, as does his dramatic monologue, "Night Watch in the City of Boston."

In his last decades, MacLeish became not so much an elder statesman as an elder of various churches: the churches of friendship, of patriotism, of poetry, of love, of death. His talks, letters, essays, and poems, and his parable-play for radio, *The Great American Fourth of July Parade,* all voice the recurring, autumnal concerns of "the human season" in a quiet, personal, "elderly" voice. Almost ninety, MacLeish died on April 20, 1982, the day after Patriot's Day.

BIOGRAPHICAL/CRITICAL SOURCES:

BOOKS

Aarons, Daniel, *Writers on the Left,* Harcourt, 1961.

Aiken, Conrad, *A Reviewer's ABC,* Meridian Publishing, 1958.

Amend, Victor E., and Leo T. Hendrick, editors, *Ten Contemporary Thinkers,* Free Press of Glencoe (New York), 1964.

Benson, Frederick R., *Writers in Arms,* New York University Press, 1967.

Bogan, Louise, *A Poet's Alphabet,* McGraw, 1970.

Brenner, Rica, *Poets of Our Time,* Harcourt, 1941.

Brooks, Cleanth, *Modern Poetry and the Tradition,* Oxford University Press, 1965.

Bush, Warren V., editor, *Dialogues of Archibald MacLeish and Mark Van Doren,* Dutton, 1964.

Carruth, Hayden, *Effluences from the Sacred Caves,* University of Michigan Press, 1983.

Contemporary Literary Criticism, Gale, Volume 3, 1975, Volume 8, 1978, Volume 14, 1980.

Dictionary of Literary Biography, Gale, Volume 4: *American Writers in Paris, 1920-1939,* Volume 7: *Twentieth Century American Dramatists,* Volume 45: *American Poets, 1880-1945, First Series.*

Dictionary of Literary Biography Yearbook: 1982, Gale, 1983.

Donoghue, Denis, *The Third Voice,* Princeton University Press, 1959.

Falk, Signi, *Archibald MacLeish,* Twayne, 1965.

Fiedler, Leslie, *Unfinished Business,* Stein & Day, 1972.

Fussel, Paul, *The Great War and Modern Memory,* Oxford University Press, 1975.

Gassner, John, *Theatre at the Crossroads,* Holt, 1960.

Graff, Gerald, *Poetic Statement and Critical Dogma,* University of Chicago Press, 1970.

Hoffman, Frederick J., *The Twenties,* Viking, 1955.

Hone, Ralph E., editor, *The Voice out of the Whirlwind,* Chandler, 1960.

Literary Opinion in America, Harper, 1937.

Luytens, David Bulwer, *The Creative Encounter,* Secker & Warburg, 1960.

MacLeish, Archibald, *Six Plays,* Houghton, 1980.

Mullaly, Edward J., *Archibald MacLeish: A Checklist,* Kent State University Press, 1973.

Nemerov, Howard, *Poetry and Fiction,* Rutgers University Press, 1963.

Saltzman, Jack, editor, *Years of Protest,* Pegasus, 1967.

Saltzman, editor, *The Survival Years,* Pegasus, 1969.

Shapiro, Karl, *Essay on Rime,* Reynal & Hitchcock, 1945.

Slote, Bernice, editor, *Myth and Symbol,* University of Nebraska Press, 1963.

Smith, Grover, *Archibald MacLeish,* University of Minneapolis Press, 1971.

Tate, Allen, *Essays of Four Decades,* Oxford University Press, 1970.

Vickery, John B., *The Literary Impact of the Golden Bough,* Princeton University Press, 1973.

Waggoner, Hyatt H., *The Heel of Elohim,* University of Oklahoma Press, 1950.

Weiler, Gottfried, *Die Poetologische Lyrik Archibald MacLeishs,* Waag & Herchen (Frankfurt), 1977.

Wilson, Edmund, *Classics and Commercials,* Farrar, Straus, 1950.

Winnick, R. H., editor, *Letters of Archibald MacLeish,* Houghton, 1983.

Winters, Yvor, *Uncollected Essays and Reviews,* Swallow Press, 1973.

PERIODICALS

American Literature, Volume 15, 1943, Volume 35, 1963.
American Review, May, 1934.
Ariel, July, 1984.
Atlantic, May, 1953.
Books, January, 1931.
Boston Globe, April 22, 1982.
Canadian Review of American Studies, spring, 1983.
Chicago Tribune Book World, April 24, 1983.
Christian Science Monitor, November 21, 1968.
English Journal, June, 1935.
Harper's, December, 1971.
New Mexico Quarterly, May, 1934.
New Republic, March 27, 1935, December 15, 1952, July 22, 1967.
New York Times, March 2, 1971, May 16, 1971.
New York Times Book Review, August 6, 1967, January 28, 1968, July 9, 1978, January 2, 1983.
North American Review, summer, 1937.
Partisan Review, January, 1941, March, 1941.
Poetry, August, 1930, June, 1931, April, 1940.
Sewanee Review, October, 1938, July, 1940, April, 1943, October, 1953.
South Atlantic Quarterly, October, 1939.
University of Toronto Quarterly, October, 1940.
Variety, April 14, 1971.
Virginia Quarterly Review, autumn, 1958.
Washington Post Book World, January 21, 1968, November 3, 1968.
Yale Review, spring, 1934.

OBITUARIES:

PERIODICALS

Chicago Tribune, April 22, 1982.
Library Journal, June 1, 1982.
Newsweek, May 3, 1982.
New York Times, April 22, 1982.
Publishers Weekly, May 7, 1982.
Time, May 3, 1982.
Times (London), April 22, 1982.
Washington Post, April 22, 1982.

*   *   *

MacLENNAN, (John) Hugh   1907-

PERSONAL: Born March 20, 1907, in Glace Bay, Cape Breton Island, Nova Scotia; son of Samuel John (a doctor) and Katherine (MacQuarrie) MacLennan; married Dorothy Duncan, June 22, 1936 (died, 1957); married Frances Walker, May 15, 1959. *Education:* Dalhousie University, B.A., 1929; Oriel College, Oxford (Rhodes Scholar), B.S., 1932; Princeton University, M.A., Ph.D., 1935.

ADDRESSES: Office—Concordia University, Montreal, Quebec, Canada. *Agent*—Russell & Volkening, Inc., 551 Fifth Ave., New York, N.Y. 10017.

CAREER: Writer and teacher, 1935-62; teacher of English literature, McGill University, Montreal, Quebec, Canada, 1951-85.

MEMBER: Royal Society of Literature (United Kingdom), Royal Society of Canada (fellow), McGill Faculty Club, Montreal Indoor Tennis Club.

AWARDS, HONORS: Guggenheim fellowship, 1943; Governor General's Award in fiction for *Two Solitudes,* 1946, *The Precipice,* 1949, and *The Watch That Ends the Night,* 1959; Governor General's Literary Award in nonfiction for *Cross Country,* 1950, and *Thirty and Three,* 1955; Lorne Pierce Medal, 1952, for contributions to Canadian literature; Molson Award for services to literature and the nation, 1967; Canadian Authors Association Literary Award for fiction, 1982, for *Voices in Time.* Honorary degrees from many institutions of higher learning, including D.Litt. from University of Western Ontario, University of Manitoba, Waterloo Lutheran University, McMaster University, and Laurentian University; LL.D. from Dalhousie University, University of Saskatchewan, and University of Toronto; D.C.L. from Bishop's University.

WRITINGS:

Oxyrhynchus: An Economic and Social Study, Princeton University Press, 1935.
Barometer Rising (novel), Duell, Sloan & Pearce, 1941.
Two Solitudes (novel), Duell, Sloan & Pearce, 1945.
The Precipice (novel), Duell, Sloan & Pearce, 1948.
Cross Country (nonfiction), Collins, 1949.
Each Man's Son (novel), Little, 1951.
The Present World as Seen in Its Literature (address), University of New Brunswick, 1952.
Thirty and Three (essays), edited by Dorothy Duncan, Macmillan, 1954.
The Future of the Novel as an Art Form (lecture), University of Toronto Press, 1959.
The Watch That Ends the Night (novel), Scribner, 1959.
Scotchman's Return and Other Essays, Scribner, 1960, published in England as *Scotman's Return and Other Essays,* Heinemann, 1960.
(Editor) *McGill: The Story of a University,* Allen & Unwin, 1960.
Seven Rivers of Canada, Macmillan (Toronto), 1961, published as *The Rivers of Canada,* Scribner, 1962.
The History of Canadian-American Relations (lecture), Goddard College, 1963.
Return of the Sphinx (novel), Scribner, 1967.
The Colour of Canada, McClelland, 1967, Little, 1968, revised edition, 1978.
The Other Side of Hugh MacLennan: Selected Essays Old and New, edited by Elspeth Cameron, Macmillan (Toronto), 1978.
Quebec, photographs by Mia and Klaus, McClelland & Stewart, 1981.
Voices in Time (novel), Macmillan (Toronto), 1980, St. Martin's, 1981.
On Being a Maritime Writer, Mount Allison University, 1984.

Wrote monthly essay for *Montrealer,* 1951-57, and weekly column for Toronto Star syndicate, 1962-63; contributor to *Holiday, Saturday Review, Maclean's Magazine* and other periodicals.

SIDELIGHTS: To anyone who wants to understand Canada, Edmund Wilson, writing in *O Canada,* recommends a reading of the novels and essays of Hugh MacLennan. MacLennan, he writes, "is so special a figure that he requires some explanation. I should describe him as a Highlander first; a patriotic Nova Scotian second . . . ; a spokesman for Canada third; and—but simultaneously with all of these—a scholar of international culture and a man of the great world." *Dictionary of Literary Biography* contributor Elspeth Cameron explains that MacLennan "was the first Canadian novelist to attempt to set the local stage on which the nation's dramas might be played before an international audience." His essays and novels, especially *Barometer Rising* and *Two Solitudes,* she adds, have earned him a reputation as "the Grand Old Man of Canadian Letters."

Wilson remembers that he first became interested in MacLennan's work when he read the essays in *Scotchman's Return.* He found therein "a point of view surprisingly and agreeably different from anything else I knew in English. MacLennan writes . . . with much humor and shrewd intelligence about Canada, Scotland, England, the Soviet Union and the United States. I came to recognize that there did now exist a Canadian way of looking at things which had little in common with either the 'American' or the British colonial one and which has achieved a self-confident detachment in regard to the rest of the world."

Barometer Rising, MacLennan's first published novel, draws its story from the author's past. It climaxes with the cataclysmic collision between two ships—one of them carrying a load of TNT—in the harbor of Halifax, Nova Scotia, in 1917, an event that nearly levelled the town, and one that MacLennan had witnessed himself. "To Canadian readers," Cameron declares, "*Barometer Rising* seemed to express, as no Canadian novel had yet done, the nationalism that had blossomed gradually over the past two decades." When the novel first appeared in 1941, J. S. Southron wrote in the *New York Times:* "Unless you had been told you could not have known this to be a first novel. . . . Both in conception and workmanship it is first class." Wilson, writing more than twenty years later, says that *Barometer Rising* is the most sustained example of "how excellent Mr. MacLennan's writing can be when he is carried along by the sweep of one of his large descriptions or impassioned actions that are solidly realistic and yet never without their poetry. . . . It seems to me that *Barometer Rising* should not merely be accepted, as it is, as a landmark in Canadian writing but also, as an artistic success, be regarded as one of its authentic classics."

Two Solitudes, MacLennan's second novel, was also enthusiastically reviewed. It examines what Oakland Ross terms in the Toronto *Globe and Mail* as "the troubled psychic borderland between Canada's two cultures," the conflict between the Catholic, French-speaking heritage and the Protestant, English-speaking one. It was published (in New York, ironically) to great critical and popular acclaim. "This volume," L. L. Marchland wrote in the *Boston Globe,* "is definitely your passport to two evenings of rare literary delight." Its themes, says Ross, "continue to resonate for Canadians as insistently as they did when the book was first published." *Two Solitudes,* the reviewer concludes, marked "the beginning of something quite new, a Canadian novel that was essentially about Canada." MacLennan reexamined the problem—still a volatile subject in Canada—in *Return of the Sphinx.*

MacLennan's gift for eliciting understanding and appreciation of Canada and its people is in fact one of his most conspicuous talents. But his novels did not meet with unqualified acclaim; Wilson writes: "In an essay called 'The Story of a Novel,' in which he describes the writing of *The Watch That Ends the Night,* he explains that after putting down 'millions of words' and tearing up 'again and again . . . I refined my style and discovered new techniques I had previously known nothing about.' But when one comes to the novel, it is hard to see what he means

by 'new techniques,' except that the story is told partly, by now a pretty familiar device, in a series of flashbacks that alternate with the narrative of the later happenings. The one feature of MacLennan's novels that does seem to me new and interesting is his use of the geographical and the meteorological setting. He always shows us how the characters are situated—as they pursue their intrigues, undergo their ordeals or are driven by their desperate loves—in a vast expanse of land and water, the hardly inhabited spaces of the waste upper margins of a continent."

Therefore, even though the recent novels have been reviewed with some disappointment, MacLennan's place in contemporary letters is secure. As Dick Adler says in his *Book World* review of *Return of the Sphinx,* although this is "not so warm and richly woven a novel as . . . *The Watch That Ends the Night,* . . . MacLennan's talent and the personality behind that talent are more than enough to recommend the book most highly." Similarly, Peter Buitenhuis observes in the *New York Times Book Review* that the novel "seems disconnected"; but, he adds, "the parts themselves are written with great perception and grace and a rare command of social, professional and political milieux." This ability, in evidence throughout MacLennan's career, seems to be in no danger of fading.

AVOCATIONAL INTERESTS: Tennis and gardening.

BIOGRAPHICAL/CRITICAL SOURCES:

BOOKS

Buitenhuis, Peter, *Hugh MacLennan,* Forum House, 1969.
Cameron, Elspeth, *Hugh MacLennan: A Writer's Life,* University of Toronto Press, 1981.
Cameron, editor, *Hugh MacLennan 1982: Proceedings of the MacLennan Conference at University College,* University College Canada Studies Program, 1982.
Cockburn, Robert H., *The Novels of Hugh MacLennan,* Harvest House, 1971.
Contemporary Literary Criticism, Gale, Volume 2, 1974, Volume 14, 1980.
Dictionary of Literary Biography, Volume 68: *Canadian Writers, 1920-1959,* Gale, 1988.
Goetsch, Paul, editor, *Hugh MacLennan,* McGraw Hill Ryerson, 1973.
Lucas, Alex, *Hugh MacLennan,* McClelland & Stewart, 1970.
MacLulich, T. D., *Hugh MacLennan,* Twayne, 1983.
Morley, Patricia, *The Immoral Moralists: Hugh MacLennan and Leonard Cohen,* Clarke Irwin, 1972.
Wilson, Edmund, *O Canada,* Farrar, Straus, 1964.
Woodcock, George, *Hugh MacLennan,* Copp Clark, 1969.

PERIODICALS

Books, October 12, 1941.
Book World, November 5, 1967.
Boston Globe, January 17, 1945.
Canadian Forum, January, 1959.
Commonweal, October 1, 1948, April 20, 1951.
Globe and Mail (Toronto), May 18, 1985, April 18, 1987.
New York Times, October 5, 1941.
New York Times Book Review, August 20, 1967.

*   *   *

MacNEICE, (Frederick) Louis   1907-1963
(Louis Malone)

PERSONAL: Born September 12, 1907, in Belfast, Ireland; died of pneumonia, September 4, 1963, in London, England; son of

John Frederick (a Protestant bishop) and Elizabeth Margaret (Clesham) MacNeice; married Giovanna Marie Therese Babette Ezra, 1930 (divorced, 1936); married second wife, Hedli Anderson (a singer), April, 1942 (separated, 1960); children: (first marriage) Dan; (second marriage) Corinna. *Education:* Attended Merton College, Oxford University, 1926-30.

CAREER: University of Birmingham, Birmingham, England, lecturer in classics, 1930-36; University of London, Bedford College, London, England, lecturer in Greek, 1936-40; British Broadcasting Corp. (BBC), London, feature writer and producer, 1940-49 and 1950-63. Special lecturer in English, Cornell University, spring, 1940; director, British Institute, Athens, Greece, 1949-50, assistant representative, 1951.

AWARDS, HONORS: Commander of the Order of the British Empire, 1957.

WRITINGS:

POETRY

Blind Fireworks, Gollancz, 1929.
(Editor with Stephen Spender) *Oxford Poetry: 1929,* Oxford University Press, 1929.
Poems, Faber, 1935, Random House, 1937.
The Earth Compels: Poems, Faber, 1938.
Autumn Journal, Random House, 1939.
Poems 1925-1940, Random House, 1940.
Selected Poems, Faber, 1940.
The Last Ditch, Cuala Press (Dublin), 1940, reprinted, Irish University Press (Shannon), 1971.
Plant and Phantom, Faber, 1941.
Springboard: Poems, 1941-1944, Faber, 1944, Random House, 1949.
Holes in the Sky: Poems, 1944-1947, Faber, 1948, Random House, 1949.
Collected Poems, 1925-1948, Faber, 1949.
Ten Burnt Offerings, Faber, 1952.
Autumn Sequel: A Rhetorical Poem, Faber, 1954.
The Other Wing, Faber, 1954.
Visitations, Faber, 1957, Oxford University Press (New York), 1958.
Eighty-five Poems, Faber, 1959.
Solstices, Oxford University Press, 1961.
The Burning Perch, Faber, 1963.
Round the Corner, Faber, 1963.
Selected Poems, selected by W. H. Auden, Faber, 1964.
The Collected Poems of Louis MacNeice, edited by E. R. Dodds, Faber, 1966, Oxford University Press, 1967.
The Revenant: A Song Cycle for Hedli Anderson, Cuala Press, 1975.
Selected Poems, edited by Michael Longley, Faber, 1989.

PLAYS

(Translator) *The Agamemnon of Aeschylus* (first produced in London by the English Group Theatre, 1936), Faber, 1936, reprinted, 1967.
"Station Bell," first produced at Birmingham University, 1937.
Out of the Picture: A Play in Two Acts (first produced in London by the English Group Theatre), Faber, 1937, reprinted, 1956, Harcourt, 1938.
Christopher Columbus (produced October 12, 1942, on BBC-Radio), Faber, 1944.
"He Had a Date," produced June 28, 1944, on BBC-Radio.
"Sunbeams in His Hat" (also see below), produced July 16, 1944, on BBC-Radio.

"The Dark Tower" (also see below), music by Benjamin Britten, produced January 21, 1946, on BBC-Radio.
"Enter Caesar" (also see below), produced September 20, 1946, on BBC-Radio.
The Dark Tower and Other Radio Scripts (includes "The Dark Tower," "Sunbeams in His Hat," "The Nosebag," and "The March Hare Saga"), Faber, 1948, Random House, 1949.
"The Queen of Air and Darkness," produced March 28, 1949, on BBC-Radio.
(Translator with E. L. Stahl) *Goethe's Faust* (produced October 30, 1949, on BBC-Radio), Faber, 1951, Oxford University Press, 1953.
"Prisoner's Progress," produced April 27, 1954, on BBC-Radio.
"The Waves" (adapted from the novel by Virginia Woolf), produced March 18, 1955, on BBC-Radio.
"Traitors in Our Way," first produced at Lyric Theatre, Belfast, March, 1957.
"The March Hare Reigns," published in *The Smith,* 1959.
"East of the Sun and West of the Moon" (also see below), produced July 25, 1959, on BBC-Radio.
"They Met on Good Friday" (also see below), produced September 8, 1959, on BBC-Radio.
The Mad Islands [and] *The Administrator* (radio plays; "The Mad Islands" produced April 4, 1962, on BBC-Radio; "The Administrator" produced March 10, 1961, on BBC-Radio), Faber, 1964.
"Persons from Porlock" (also see below), produced August 30, 1963, on BBC-Radio.
One for the Grave: A Modern Morality Play (first produced at Abbey Theatre, Dublin, October, 1966), Faber, 1968, Oxford University Press, 1968.
Persons From Porlock and Other Plays for the Radio (includes "Persons from Porlock," "Enter Caesar," "East of the Sun and West of the Moon," and "They Met on Good Friday"), British Broadcasting Corp., 1969.

OTHER

(Under pseudonym Louis Malone) *Roundabout Way* (novel), Putnam, 1932.
(With W. H. Auden) *Letters From Iceland,* Random House, 1937, reprinted, 1969.
I Crossed the Minch, Longmans, Green, 1938.
Modern Poetry: A Personal Essay, Oxford University Press, 1938, reprinted, Haskell House (New York), 1969.
Zoo, M. Joseph, 1938.
The Poetry of W. B. Yeats, Oxford University Press, 1941, reprinted, 1969.
Meet the U.S. Army, Ministry of Information (London), 1943.
"Louis MacNeice Reading His Own Poetry" (sound recording with commentary), Harvard College Library, 1953.
"Collected Poems" (sound recording), Harvard College Library, 1953.
The Penny That Rolled Away, Putnam, 1954 (published in England as *The Sixpence That Rolled Away,* Faber, 1956).
Astrology, edited by Douglas Hill, Doubleday, 1964.
Varieties of Parable, Cambridge University Press, 1965.
The Strings Are False: An Unfinished Autobiography, Faber, 1965, Oxford University Press (New York), 1966.

Contributor to numerous periodicals, including *Spectator, New Statesman and Nation, London Mercury, Criterion, Times Literary Supplement,* and *New Verse.*

SIDELIGHTS: In the 1930s, Louis MacNeice was associated with the group of English poets that included W. H. Auden, Stephen Spender, and C. Day Lewis. Theirs was a Freudian Marxian verse that shared, in M. L. Rosenthal's words in *Chief Modern Poets of England and America,* "a sense of the historical moment that was sometimes as violent as a physical sensation." They also shared a discursive, allusive and, at the same time, pointed manner. Yet MacNeice is distinguished from these thirties poets: his tone was more colloquial than that of the others, his manner more casual. In addition, he refrained from following in his poetry the dictates of any political party. As Martin S. Day explained in *History of English Literature, 1837 to the Present,* MacNeice remained "the sensitive intellectual protesting the world's disorder but offering no panacea."

During the forties and fifties, MacNeice's youthful poetic energy lagged. In 1959, Anthony Thwaite wrote in *Contemporary English Poetry:* "His work is very readable, he is never boring, he is an excellent craftsman, and has many of the virtues of a good journalist—a 'reporter of experience' with sharp, vivid, precise phrases. But he seldom has much depth or penetration." Thus has MacNeice's reputation suffered, for it is only recently that critics have begun again to see his work and his attention to detail as more than poetic journalism.

Thomas Blackburn has insisted in *The Price of an Eye* that MacNeice was not a shallow writer. He "is always implicated in whatever he writes about. He is not the detached reporter . . . but a poet who writes with open heart and mind . . . [about] his own humanity." In *The Poetry of Louis MacNeice* Donald Best Moore has counted among the poet's gifts "an acute sensory, and especially visual, perception" that is an integral part of the emotional or intellectual feeling being poetically expressed: "Colour, shape, light and shade, sound, smell, touch and taste, lend to his verse an immediacy closely connected with time and place."

Furthermore, in *Louis MacNeice: Sceptical Vision,* Terence Brown has recognized MacNeice's maturity and assurance of voice: "His poetic contribution to our literature is the embodiment of a creative scepticism in a verse, and therefore in a voice, which is nearly always recognisably and maturely his own." John Press, writing in *Louis MacNeice,* has even ranked MacNeice with Shakespeare, Jenson, Herrick, Burns, Byron, Tennyson and Browning, the few poets who "have managed to make poetry out of the enjoyment which they have distilled from the minor pleasures of life."

Upon his death, MacNeice's other work—especially his translations of Horace and Goethe and his pioneering work in radio drama—were much praised along with the poetry. Walter Allen summed it up: "If his poetry was minor poetry it was of a kind we can never have too much of and that was particularly rare in our time. . . . His poetry was a poetry of comment, and the whole of his life, and the life of his times, was his subject matter."

BIOGRAPHICAL/CRITICAL SOURCES:

BOOKS

Blackburn, Thomas, *The Price of an Eye,* Longmans, Green, 1961.
Brown, Terence, *Louis MacNeice: Sceptical Vision,* Barnes & Noble, 1975.
Contemporary Literary Criticism, Gale, Volume 1, 1973, Volume 4, 1975, Volume 10, 1979, Volume 53, 1989.
David, Dan, *Closing Time,* Oxford University Press, 1975.
Day, Martin S., *History of English Literature, 1837 to the Present,* Doubleday, 1964.
Dictionary of Literary Biography, Gale, Volume 10: *Modern British Dramatists, 1900-1945,* 1982, Volume 20: *British Poets, 1914-1945,* 1983.

Moore, Donald Best, *The Poetry of Louis MacNeice,* Leicester University Press, 1972.
Press, John, *Louis MacNeice,* Longmans, Green, 1965.
Rosenthal, M. L., *Chief Modern Poets of England and America,* Volume 1, MacMillan, 1966.
Southworth, J., *Sowing the Spring,* Oxford University Press, 1940.
Stanford, Derek, *MacNeice, Spender, Day Lewis: The Pylon Poets,* Erdmans, 1969.
Thwaite, Anthony, *Contemporary English Poetry,* Heinemann, 1959.

PERIODICALS

Encounter, August, 1972.
New York Times, September 22, 1963.
Times Literary Supplement, October 28, 1949, January 6-12, 1989.

* * *

MADDEN, (Jerry) David 1933-

PERSONAL: Born July 25, 1933, in Knoxville, Tenn.; son of James Helvy and Emile (Merritt) Madden; married Roberta Margaret Young, September 6, 1956; children: Blake Dana. *Education:* Attended Iowa State Teachers College (now University of Northern Iowa), 1956; University of Tennessee, B.S., 1957; San Francisco State College (now University), M.A., 1958; attended Yale Drama School, 1959-60.

ADDRESSES: Home—614 Park Blvd., Baton Rouge, La. 70806. *Agent*—Georges Borchardt, Inc., 136 East 57th St., New York, N.Y. 10022.

CAREER: Appalachian State Teachers College (now Appalachian State University), Boone, N.C., instructor, 1958-59; Centre College of Kentucky, Danville, instructor in English, 1960-62; University of Louisville, Louisville, Ky., instructor in creative writing, 1962-64; Kenyon College, Gambier, Ohio, lecturer in creative writing and assistant editor of *Kenyon Review,* 1964-66; Ohio University, Athens, lecturer in creative writing, 1966-68; Louisiana State University, Baton Rouge, writer in residence, 1968—. Gives dramatic readings from his fiction. *Military service:* U.S. Army, 1955-56.

MEMBER: National Book Critics Circle, National Organization for Women, P.E.N., Authors Guild, Coordinating Council of Literary Magazines, Society for the Study of Southern Literature, Poets and Writers, Associated Writing Programs, Thomas Wolfe Society, People for the American Way, Citizens Opposed to Censorship, Tennessee Historical Society.

AWARDS, HONORS: Pearl Setzer Deal Award for best religious drama, 1959, for "From Rome to Damascus"; John Golden fellowship in playwriting at Yale University, 1959-60; six regional and national play contest awards; Rockefeller grant, 1969; National Endowment for the Arts fiction prize, 1970; Bread Loaf Writers Conference William Raney fellowship, 1972.

WRITINGS:

FICTION; NOVELS, EXCEPT AS NOTED

The Beautiful Greed, Random House, 1961.
Cassandra Singing, Crown, 1969.
The Shadow Knows (short stories), Louisiana State University Press, 1970.
Brothers in Confidence, Avon, 1972.
Bijou, Crown, 1974.
The Suicide's Wife, Bobbs-Merrill, 1978.

Pleasure-Dome, Bobbs-Merrill, 1979.
On the Big Wind: Being Seven Comic Episodes in the Fitful Rise of Big Bob Travis From Disc Jockey in a Small Eastern Kentucky Mountain Town to Network Television News Reporter, Holt, 1980.
The New Orleans of Possibilities (short stories), Louisiana State University Press, 1982.

NONFICTION

Wright Morris (literary study), Twayne, 1964.
The Poetic Image in Six Genres (essays), Southern Illinois University Press, 1969.
James M. Cain (literary study), Twayne, 1970.
Harlequin's Stick, Charlie's Cane: A Comparative Study of Commedia dell'arte and Silent Slapstick Comedy, Bowling Green University, 1975.
A Primer of the Novel, Scarecrow, 1979.
(With Richard Powers) *Writer's Revisions: An Annotated Bibliography of Articles and Books About Writers' Revisions and Their Comments on the Creative Process,* Scarecrow, 1981.
Cain's Craft, Scarecrow, 1985.
Revising Fiction: A Handbook for Writers, New American Library, 1988.

EDITOR

Tough Guy Writers of the Thirties, Southern Illinois University Press, 1968, 3rd edition, 1978.
Proletarian Writers of the Thirties, Southern Illinois University Press, 1968, 3rd edition, 1978.
American Dreams, American Nightmares, Southern Illinois University Press, 1970, 3rd edition, 1972.
Rediscoveries: Informal Essays in Which Well-known Novelists Rediscover Neglected Works of Fiction by One of Their Favorite Authors, Crown, 1971.
(With Ray B. Browne) *The Popular Cultural Explosion: Experiencing Mass Media,* William C. Brown, 1972.
Nathanael West: The Cheaters and the Cheated, Everett/Edwards, 1973.
(With Frank N. Magill) *The Contemporary Literary Scene, 1973,* Salem Press, 1974.
Remembering James Agee, Louisiana State University Press, 1974.
Creative Choices: A Spectrum of Quality and Technique in Fiction, Scott, Foresman, 1975.
(With Virgil Scott) *Studies in the Short Story,* Holt, 1975, 6th edition, 1984.
(With Peggy Bach) *Rediscoveries II: Important Writers Select Their Favorite Works of Neglected Fiction,* Carroll & Graf, 1988.

PLAYS

"Call Herman to Supper," first produced in Knoxville, Tenn., 1949.
"They Shall Endure," first produced in Knoxville, 1953.
"Cassandra Singing," first produced in Knoxville, 1955; expanded version produced in Albuquerque, N.M., 1964.
"From Rome to Damascus," first produced in Chapel Hill, N.C., 1959.
(With music by Robert Rogers and lyrics by Joseph Matthewson) "Casina," first produced in New Haven, Conn., 1960.
"Fugitive Masks," first produced in Abingdon, Va., 1966.
The Day the Flowers Came (first produced in Baton Rouge, La., 1974), Dramatic Publishing, 1975.

OTHER

Work represented in anthologies, including: *New Campus Writing,* Volume II, Putnam, 1957; *Best American Short Stories 1969,* edited by Martha Foley and David Burnett, Houghton, 1969; *Short Stories From the Little Magazines,* edited by Jarvis Thurston and Curt Johnson, Scott, Foresman, 1970; *Best American Short Stories 1971,* edited by Foley and Burnett, Houghton, 1971; *Playboy's Ribald Classics 3,* Playboy Press, 1972; *Scenes From American Life: Contemporary Short Fiction,* edited by Joyce Carol Oates, Random House, 1972; *The Bottege Obscure Reader,* edited by George Garrett and Katherine Garrison Biddle, Wesleyan University Press, 1974; *Stories of the Modern South,* edited by Benjamin Forkner and Patrick Samway, Jr., Bantam, 1978, revised edition, Penguin, 1981; *The Pushcart Prize V: Best of the Small Presses,* edited by Bill Henderson, Pushcart Press, 1980.

Contributor of plays, short stories, poems, essays, reviews, and critical articles to literary journals.

WORK IN PROGRESS: Sharpshooter, a novel set during the Civil War that examines the conflict between the historical figures William "Parson" Brownlow and J. G. M. Ramsey; *The Sunshine Man,* another sequel to *Bijou* that focuses on the little brother, Bucky; *The Loner,* a novel set in the army in 1953; *Cherokee Lyrics,* a book of poems; *Southern Photographs, Southern Fiction; Point of View in Life and Literature;* a biography of Nathan Bedford Forrest; a play about Tennessee Williams and Carson McCullers; a novel about the old London Bridge.

SIDELIGHTS: Although he has written more than half a dozen plays, "enough published poems to make a first volume," eleven books of literary criticism, and several screenplays, David Madden told *CA* that "I am known first as a writer of fiction." A native of Knoxville, Tennessee, Madden cites the Southern oral tradition, as well as various elements of folk and popular culture (mainly movies, radio plays, country music, and comics) as major influences on his novels and short stories.

The impact of the Southern oral tradition on Madden's development as a writer goes back to his early childhood, a time when he recalls being enchanted by the sound of his grandmother's voice as she told him stories and transported him into the "pleasure-dome" of the imagination. It was a skill for which the young boy soon displayed an unusual aptitude of his own; encouraged by his grandmother, he entertained his brothers and other playmates by spinning yarns for some eight years before writing one down at the age of eleven.

Madden readily professes to a lifelong fascination with the relationship between the storyteller and his audience, a relationship Thomas E. Dasher of the *Dictionary of Literary Biography* describes as a "bond of trust and deceit." As Madden himself explained to Dasher: "The relationship between the storyteller and the listener is like that between the con man and his mark, who charge each other through phantom circuits of the imagination; the storyteller uses many of the same techniques for capturing attention, holding it, and projecting the reader into a totally different world from the one he is living in." A man who thrives on interaction with his audience, Madden views the reader not as a passive receiver of material, but as "an emotional, imaginative, and intellectual collaborator," a person who helps him create and shape a work of fiction.

In addition to his passion for storytelling, Madden has always been infatuated with radio drama and Hollywood movies of the 1930s and 1940s. Basically, he regards them both as extensions of storytelling. In an interview with Shirley Williams of the Louisville *Courier-Journal,* Madden credits radio drama with developing his imagination "because the oral element of it was meant to evoke all kinds of pictures and images somewhat the way storytelling did. Without the presence of the storyteller, I had this disembodied voice, which emphasized even more the power of the imagination of the listener in the storytelling process, the necessity for the imagination of the listener to become engaged." Madden also feels that by obtaining some of his material from radio and movies, he makes his work more "accessible" than that of other serious writers, whose audiences are usually smaller and more specialized (i.e., academic). While he does not avoid incorporating a message into his stories, he never allows it to interfere with his goal of providing the reader with entertainment, for he is convinced that "people don't read stories to experience messages."

Despite his strong identification with the South, Madden does not consider himself to be a strictly regional writer. According to Dasher, Madden "sees the Southern experience as representative of the universal experience." Nevertheless, the critic goes on to point out, "even in [Madden's] non-Southern stories, the central character often faces the characteristic dilemma of Southern fiction: isolation—being cut off from the past, from place, family and community. Madden's autobiographical protagonists, . . . regardless of how they struggle to break away from the forces which shape them, always draw a certain strength and security from their sense of identity. Madden seems to suggest that when man is successful in severing his ties with tradition or has no tradition in which he can discover a place, he is cut off from vital sources which make the individual life part of a continuum rather than a separate fragment."

Judging by these various criteria, Madden's most "typical" works would seem to be the novels *Cassandra Singing, Bijou,* and *Pleasure-Dome.* Though the last two contain a great deal of autobiographical material, *Cassandra Singing* is one of Madden's least autobiographical pieces. Dasher contends that "Madden's primary education as a novelist was the writing of this novel," for it went through more than a dozen versions as either drama or fiction over a fifteen-year period before being published in 1969. *Cassandra Singing* is set in the poor coal-mining region of eastern Kentucky and focuses on the nearly incestuous relationship between a teenage brother and sister, Lone and Cassie McDaniel. Lone, the sole member of the family to show any ability or inclination to escape from his squalid life, almost ruins his chances by joining up with Boyd Weaver, a reckless motorcycle-riding ex-Marine with a penchant for black clothes, and Boyd's girlfriend, Gypsy. Cassie, bedridden ever since a childhood bout with rheumatic fever, spends her time singing folksongs and telling stories, living vicariously through the experiences of her brother and her own power to imagine the world outside her room. A turning point occurs in their relationship when Lone is sent to prison for looting a coal company store and Cassie is forced to leave her sickbed and attempt to lead her own life.

For the most part, Madden views the story of Lone and Cassie as an example of the tensions that exist between a life of action and a life of the imagination. "To live fully," he told Dasher, "one must balance the forces of action and imagination. Lone's life is an exaggeration of action, Cassie's an exaggeration of imagination." The *New York Times Book Review*'s Peter Wolfe looks at *Cassandra Singing* in a similar fashion, describing it as a successful combination of "crude animal vigor with intellectual force" and adding that it "takes us into a strange world and brings that world to life."

On the other hand, Joyce Carol Oates's interpretation of the story brings to mind Dasher's remarks on the extent to which Madden is indeed a Southern writer. Commenting in the *Southern Review,* she states that *Cassandra Singing* is a "haunting" and poetic portrayal of "a pastoral, ruined, mythic past, a world of perpetual childhood and perpetual struggle to break free of this childhood."

But Lawrence S. Thompson of the *Richmond News Leader* sees it in more universal terms as a "serious and deeply penetrating analysis" of what he identifies as "elemental human characteristics, sentiments and passions stripped of the veneer of urban life." The Louisville *Courier-Journal*'s Romulus Linney also regards *Cassandra Singing* as a novel with more than just a Southern scope. He writes: "The central characters are wonderful, stunning creations and the love-massacres into which they plunge reach a long way out of Eastern Kentucky. . . . This book is at its best, which is very beautiful, when we feel that agony by which the degraded survive their humiliation."

Whatever their interpretations of *Cassandra Singing,* though, reviewers almost unanimously praise Madden's storytelling skills. Gerald Locklin, writing in the Long Beach *Press-Telegram,* notes that "David Madden has the most important gift of a fiction writer: he can create the sense of life. The characters of this novel live; the place . . . lives. Their idiom—its wit and lyricism—rings true." Carter Brooke Jones of the *Washington Evening Star* says that despite a narrative that is "cluttered" with excessive dialogue, "I became so involved with the clan that I couldn't have put the book aside until I found out what happened to each member." And though the *New York Times*'s Thomas Lask thinks *Cassandra Singing* somewhat too long, that its symbolism is often quite obvious, and that several of its scenes are "squeezed out to their last cinematic moment," he concludes that "the sharpness of the writing, the distinctiveness of the characters and the genuine feel for the floundering dilemma of the boy puts this novel at least a couple of notches above the usual efforts in this genre."

Bijou and its sequel, *Pleasure-Dome,* grew out of what Madden refers to as "a kind of terrible nostalgia for the Bijou [Theater], for the place itself rather than the events which occurred there." The central character in *Bijou,* Lucius Hutchfield, is a thirteen-year-old boy growing up in the town of Cherokee, Tennessee, during the late 1940s. An usher at the Bijou Theater (as Madden himself had once been), he is obsessed with the world he sees in the movies. He reconstructs plots over and over again in his mind, fantasizes about what he has reconstructed, and even tries to write his own purple-prose-laden versions of his favorites, for what he dreams of most of all is one day becoming a rich and famous writer.

Because the characters and the plot so closely resemble people and events in Madden's own life, what might ordinarily be regarded as just another story of a Southern boyhood becomes, says Dasher, a novel "about the creative process at work—the ways in which even a very young artist absorbs and radiates. *Bijou* traces Lucius's development—emotionally, physically, and artistically—at school, at home, and mainly at the Bijou with his family, the other ushers, and his friends. . . . Madden takes himself and his reader on a pilgrimage into the past, not at all for sentimental reasons but to capture those moments, perhaps the moment, of an entire year frozen in time. This type of nostalgia allows for revelation not only of what the past might have been, but also of what people were at the moment. Rather than reveling in what has passed, we can then examine in all their complex facets the elements which made individuals and which, continuing into the present, make life and art a timeless reality transcending the past and the artist himself."

But some critics take issue with Madden's type of nostalgia. In the *New York Review of Books,* for instance, Roger Sale reports being "nervous" when he realizes "how much work one is doing for the author, how much supplying from one's own memory is going on, how blank it must all seem to an innocent reader, of a different place or time, who cannot do this work. . . . What makes the book so static, so long, so unresponsive and even irresponsible about itself, is the use of nostalgia, pure, unruffled nostalgia, as the impulse behind the entire creation."

Other reviewers, even many of those who basically like *Bijou,* believe that it too often becomes bogged down in repetitive, movie-oriented detail. The *New York Times Book Review*'s Sara Blackburn, though impressed by "a proud, tough sweetness about Lucius and his passage, and an intriguing authenticity to Madden's provincial Tennessee town of 30 years ago," nevertheless finds that the movie plot recitations are "immediately and unceasingly boring, and Lucius as a character is finally overwhelmed by them." The *New Yorker* critic agrees they have "a soporific effect on the reader," while Larry McMurtry, writing in the *Washington Post Book World,* declares that "Lucius grows dimmer and dimmer as the book progresses. . . . Madden seems to have let his own yen for pop culture swamp his artistic instincts."

Pleasure-Dome, the sequel to *Bijou,* is a two-part novel consisting of an only slightly altered version of *Brothers in Confidence* followed by mostly new material based on ideas Madden explored earlier in "Nothing Dies But Something Mourns." Though by no means devoid of *Bijou*'s preoccupation with old movies, *Pleasure-Dome* represents more of a thematic return to the conflict in *Cassandra Singing* between action and imagination. As in *Bijou,* however, the central character is Lucius Hutchfield, some six years older but still fascinated by the way in which fiction interacts with reality. The first half of the novel basically recounts one "good ole boy" adventure after another as Lucius employs his storytelling abilities to get his brother Bucky out of prison. After this is accomplished, the focus of the novel shifts to Lucius's experiences with an old woman who claims she was once seduced by Jesse James, a claim that inspires Lucius to weave a few more stories of his own (leading to more reckless adventures, as well as to some meditations on the responsibilities of a storyteller to his art—and to truth).

Shorter and more intense than *Bijou, Pleasure-Dome* is a veritable "writer's notebook of plot possibilities, social observations, narrative lines, character sketches and [Madden's] own sentiments about the meaning of his craft or art," according to Webster Schott of the *Washington Post Book World.* Calling the blend "exhilarating," Schott nevertheless admits that "one hundred pages into *Pleasure-Dome* I thought it was one of the few novels I couldn't force myself to finish. Madden seems incapable of controlling his impulses to collect scenes, a writer writing with nothing to say. But Madden's playfulness turns serious. . . . At exactly the right point . . . his novel becomes an elaborate, serio-comic commentary on U.S. middle-class trash culture, the crazy tyranny of families, and the marvel that human beings should make and take pleasure in art."

Lagniappe's W. Kenneth Holditch agrees that "entertaining though the picaresque plot may be, the more intriguing and valuable journey is that of the spirit. . . . As a result of his experiences, [Lucius] learns something of the duties and obligations of a man, something of the dangers of imagination directed into the wrong channels—or perhaps set loose to roam at will. . . . *Pleasure-Dome* is fun to read. . . . Finally, however, it must be re-

membered for what it is—a serious and significant commentary on life."

Some reviewers, though, do not appreciate the injection of a message into what they feel is an otherwise entertaining novel, recalling Madden's own pronouncement that people don't read stories to experience messages. The *Chicago Tribune*'s Larry Swindell, for example, describes *Pleasure-Dome* as "a charming but distinctly trivial thing" whose "ambitious design . . . does not quite work." Phil Thomas, commenting in the *Knoxville Journal,* believes the book "falters" in the second half, for "after the focus has been shifted [the narrative] clouds and it no longer is possible to tell the real from the unreal." Gary Dretzka of the *Los Angeles Herald Examiner* goes so far as to say that "the promise of an intriguing flimflam perpetrated by three colorful brothers is destroyed in the novel's final third by an introspective questioning of the moral consequences of the writer's art. . . . [*Pleasure-Dome*] falls apart in a wispy haze."

Yet Thomas Dasher concludes that *Pleasure-Dome,* like *Bijou,* depicts an important stage in Lucius's (and therefore in Madden's) ever-changing perception of himself as a storyteller and writer. In short, the critic explains, by the end of the novel "Lucius has moved beyond nostalgia for its own sake and beyond his curiosity into a realization that the artist must be more than the successful teller of stories. He must make of the pleasure-dome not a nightmare, but a dream of possibilities and beauty. The storyteller who only exploits others and himself to gather material is finally the man who has conned himself. Only when he transcends the factual and learns to cherish what has been and can be created—not to inform, but to enlighten—can the storyteller become the artist, mingling despair and guilt with joy and forgiveness."

Achieving a balance between truth and fiction, or between action and imagination, has long been one of David Madden's main concerns. Drawing on themes and images from his own youth and from Southern and American culture as a whole, he leads the unwary reader into the "pleasure-dome" of the imagination he himself knows and loves so well. The resulting piece of fiction, reviewer Schott admits, may be "troublesome, demanding and sometimes a bore. But at its height it is indeed a work of art. . . . David Madden is a novelist for the head as well as the heart."

BIOGRAPHICAL/CRITICAL SOURCES:

BOOKS

Contemporary Authors Autobiography Series, Volume 3, Gale, 1986.
Contemporary Literary Criticism, Gale, Volume 5, 1976, Volume 15, 1980.
Dictionary of Literary Biography, Volume 6: *American Novelists since World War II, Second Series,* Gale, 1980.

PERIODICALS

Best Sellers, February, 1979, December, 1979.
Boston Advertiser, April 21, 1974.
Boston Herald, November 12, 1978.
Chattanooga Times, January 18, 1970.
Chicago News, March 30, 1974.
Chicago Tribune Book World, November 11, 1979.
Courier-Journal (Louisville), July, 1961, January 4, 1970, November 5, 1978.
Courier-Journal Magazine (Louisville), January 28, 1979.
Critique: Studies in Modern Fiction, Volume XV, number 2, 1973.
Detroit Free Press, April 24, 1974.

Detroit News, May 5, 1974.
Examiner & Chronicle (San Francisco), March 31, 1974.
Gri-Gri, November 5, 1979.
Gyre, spring, 1972.
Knoxville Journal, December 14, 1979.
Lagniappe, December 8, 1979.
Los Angeles Herald Examiner, October 16, 1979.
Los Angeles Times, May 12, 1974.
Los Angeles Times Book Review, July 11, 1982.
Miami Herald, November 16, 1969.
New Orleans Review, Volume VI, number 4, 1979.
Newport News Daily Press New Dominion Magazine, March 15, 1970.
New Republic, March 30, 1974, October 7, 1978.
Newsday, July 10, 1971.
Newsweek, October 9, 1978.
New Yorker, May 27, 1974, December 4, 1978.
New York Review of Books, June 27, 1974.
New York Times, November 28, 1969.
New York Times Book Review, December 14, 1969, April 21, 1974, September 19, 1976, November 11, 1979.
Press-Telegram (Long Beach), April 8, 1970.
Richmond News Leader, March 4, 1970.
Southern Review, winter, 1971.
Sun-Times (Chicago), April 7, 1974.
Tennessean, November 12, 1978.
Time, October 30, 1978.
Virginia Quarterly Review, summer, 1968, spring, 1970.
Washington Evening Star, November 25, 1969.
Washington Post, April 1, 1974, October 30, 1980.
Washington Post Book World, November 5, 1978, January 6, 1980.
Washington Star-News, April 25, 1974.
West Coast Review of Books, November, 1979.

*　　　*　　　*

MADDERN, Al(an)
See ELLISON, Harlan

*　　　*　　　*

MAHFOUZ, Naguib (Abdel Aziz Al-Sabilgi)　1911(?)-
(Najib Mahfuz)

PERSONAL: Given name also transliterated as Nagib; born December 11, 1911 (some sources say 1912 or 1914), in Gamaliya, Cairo, Egypt; son of Abdel Aziz Ibrahim (a merchant) and Fatma Mostapha Mahfouz; married Attiya Allah (name also transliterated as Inayat Allah, Ateyate Ibrahim), September 27, 1954; children: Om Kolthoum, Fatima. *Education:* Received degree in philosophy from University of Cairo, 1934; post-graduate study in philosophy, 1935-36.

ADDRESSES: Home—172 Nile St., Al Agouza, Cairo, Egypt. *Office*—Al-Ahram, Al Galaa St., Cairo, Egypt. *Agent*—c/o Donald E. Herdeck, Three Continents Press, 1636 Connecticut Ave. N.W., Washington, D.C. 20009.

CAREER: Civil servant, journalist, and writer. University of Cairo, Cairo, Egypt, secretary, 1936-1938; Egyptian Government, Cairo, bureaucrat affiliated with the Ministry of Wakfs (also called Ministry of Islamic Affairs), 1939-1954, director of censorship for the Department of Art, 1954-59, director of Foundation for Support of the Cinema for the State Cinema Organization, 1959-69, consultant for cinema affairs to the Minis-

try of Culture, 1969-1971. Affiliated with Cairo newspaper *Al-Ahram.*

AWARDS, HONORS: Egyptian State Prize, 1956, for *Bayn al-qasrayn;* National Prize for Letters (Egypt), 1970; Collar of the Republic, 1972; Nobel Prize for literature from the Swedish Academy, 1988; named to Egyptian Order of Independence, and to Order of the Republic.

WRITINGS:

Hams al-junun, Maktabat Misr, 1939.
Abath al-aqdar, Maktabat Misr, 1939.
Radubis, Maktabat Misr, 1943.
Kiftah Tiba, Maktabat Misr, 1944.
Khan al-khalili, Maktabat Misr, c. 1945.
Al-Qahira al-jadida, Maktabat Misr, 1946.
Zuqaq al Midaqq (novel), Maktabat Misr, 1947, translation with introduction by Trevor Le Gassick published as *Midaq Alley* (also see below), Khayats, 1966, revised, Heinemann, 1975, reprinted, Three Continents, 1981.
Al-Sarab, Maktabat Misr, c. 1949.
Bidaya wa-nihaya, Maktabat Misr, 1949, translation by Ramses Awad published as *The Beginning and the End,* American University in Cairo Press, 1951, reprinted, edited by Mason Rossiter Smith, Doubleday, 1990.
Bayn al-qasrayn, Maktabat Misr, 1956, translation by William M. Hutchins and Olive E. Kenny published as *Palace Walk,* Doubleday, 1990.
Qasr al-shawq, Maktabat Misr, c. 1957.
Al Sukkariya, Maktabat Misr, 1957.
Al-Liss wa-al-kilab (novel), Maktabat Misr, 1961, translation by Le Gassick and Muhammad Mustafa Badawi published as *The Thief and the Dogs* (also see below), revised by John Rodenbeck, American University in Cairo Press, 1984.
Al-Summan wa-al-kharif, Maktabat Misr, 1962, translation by Roger Allen published as *Autumn Quail,* American University in Cairo Press, 1985.
Dunya Allah, Maktabat Misr, c. 1963.
Al-Tariq, 1964, translation by Mohamed Islam published as *The Search,* edited by Magdi Wahba, American University in Cairo Press, 1987.
Bayt sayyi al-sum'a, Maktabat Misr, 1965.
Al-Shahhadh, Maktabat Misr, 1965, translation by Kristin Walker Henry and Nariman Khales Naili al-Warraki published as *The Beggar,* American University in Cairo Press, 1986.
Tharthara fawqa al-Nil, Maktabat Misr, 1966.
Miramar (novel), Maktabat Misr, 1967, translation by Fatma Moussa-Mahmoud published as *Miramar* (also see below), edited and revised by Maged el Kommos and Rodenbeck, introduction by John Fowles, Heinemann, 1978, reprinted, Three Continents, 1983.
Awlad haratina, [Beirut], 1967, published in serialized form, 1969, translation by Philip Stewart published as *Children of Gebelawi,* Heinemann, Three Continents, 1981.
Tahta al-mizalla, Maktabat Misr, c. 1967.
Khammarat al-qitt al-aswad, Maktabat Misr, c. 1968.
Hikaya bi-la bidaya wa-la nihaya, Maktabat Misr, 1971.
Shahr al-asal, Maktabat Misr, 1971.
Al-Maraya, Maktabat Misr, 1972, translation by Allen published as *Mirrors,* Bibliotheca Islamica, 1977.
Al-Hubb tahta al-matar, Maktabat Misr, 1973.
Al-Jarima, Maktabat Misr, 1973.
God's World: An Anthology of Short Stories, translated with an introduction by Akef Abadir and Allen, Bibliotheca Islamica, 1973.

Al-Karnak, Maktabat Misr, 1974, reprinted in *Three Contemporary Egyptian Novels,* translated with a critical introduction by Saad El-Gabalawy, York Press, 1979.

Hikayat haratina, Maktabat Misr, 1975, translation by Soad Sobhy, Essam Fattouh, and James Kenneson published as *Fountain and Tomb,* Three Continents, 1988.

Qalb al-layl, Maktabat Misr, 1975.

Hadrat al-muhtaram, Maktabat Misr, 1975, translation by Rasheed El-Enany published as *Respected Sir,* Quartet, 1988.

(Contributor) *Modern Egyptian Short Stories,* translated with a critical introduction by El-Gabalawy, York Press, 1977.

Malhamat al harafish, Maktabat Misr, 1977.

Hubb fawqa hadabat al-haram, Maktabat Misr, 1979.

Shaytan ya'iz, Maktabat Misr, 1979.

Nagib Mahfuz-yatadhakkar (title means "Naguib Mahfouz Remembers"), edited by Gamal al-Gaytani, Al-Masirah, 1980.

Asr al-hubb, Maktabat Misr, 1980.

Afrah al-qubbah, Maktabat Misr, 1981, translation by Kenny published as *Wedding Song,* edited and revised by Mursi Saad El Din and Rodenbeck, introduction by Saad El Din, American University in Cairo Press, 1984.

Ra'aytu fima yara al-na'im, Maktabat Misr, 1982.

Baqi min al-zaman sa'ah, Maktabat Misr, 1982.

Layali alf laylah, Maktabat Misr, 1982.

Amam al-'arsh, Maktabat Misr, 1983.

Rihlat ibn Fattumah, Maktabat Misr, 1983.

Al-Tanzim al-sirri, Maktabat Misr, 1984.

Al-A'ish fi al-haqiqa, Maktabat Misr, 1985.

Yawm qutila al-za'im, Maktabat Misr, 1985.

Hadith al sabah wa-al-masa, Maktabat Misr, 1987.

Sabah al-ward, Maktabat Misr, 1987.

Qushtumor, [Cairo], 1989.

Midaq Alley, Miramar, [and] *The Thief and the Dog,* Quality Paperback Book Club, 1989.

Contributor to Arabic newspapers, including *Ar-Risala* and *Al-Hilal.*

SIDELIGHTS: Naguib Mahfouz is widely regarded as Egypt's finest writer. While his works were largely unknown in English-speaking countries for most of the twentieth century, the author has nevertheless been viewed by many critics outside the Middle East as the exemplar of Arabic literature. Mahfouz was suddenly cast into the limelight in the West on October 13, 1988, when he became the first Arab writer honored with the Nobel Prize for literature. Prior to his receiving the esteemed award, only a fraction of Mahfouz's more than fifty works had been translated into English; after weeks of negotiations in the fall of 1988, however, Doubleday acquired the English publishing rights to fourteen of the Nobel laureate's books, including four titles that had never before appeared in English.

Mahfouz is credited with popularizing the novel and short story as viable genres in the Arab literary world, where poetry has been the medium of choice among writers for generations. A native of the Gamaliya quarter of Cairo, the author recreates in his writings life on the streets of urban Egypt. His prose works—which have been compared in spirit, tone, and ambience to the raw social realism of nineteenth-century novelists Honore de Balzac and Charles Dickens—reflect Egypt's volatile political history and depict the distressing conditions under which the Arab poor live.

The author established his reputation in American literary circles with the 1981 release, in English translation, of *Midaq Alley,* a novel that he had originally penned in Arabic in 1947. An evocation of life in a Cairo ghetto, *Midaq Alley* centers on Hamida, a beautiful girl who escapes the poverty, filth, and contamination of her village by becoming a prostitute for wealthy Allied soldiers. Trevor Le Gassick noted in his introduction to the English edition of the book that "the universal problems of behaviour and morality [Mahfouz] examines remain . . . the same. . . . The aspirations and tragedies of [*Midaq Alley*'s] inhabitants are witnessed with total indifference by the Alley within which the circle of life and death is forever run again." Echoing Le Gassick's sentiments, P. J. Vatikiotis pointed to the timelessness of the work, stating in the *Times Literary Supplement* that the novel skillfully "portrays the tragic attraction of modernity" and "stresses the oppressiveness of an unjust order."

Mahfouz is best known in the Arab world for his critically acclaimed "Cairo Trilogy," which was written in 1956 and 1957. *Bayn al-qasrayn,* the first volume in the trilogy, was published in English as *Palace Walk* in 1990, and the other two volumes are expected to be published by Doubleday in 1991 and 1992. John Fowles, in his introduction to Mahfouz's *Miramar,* commented on the long delay in the release of the writer's books in translation for Western readers: "Of all the world's considerable contemporary literature, that in Arabic must easily be the least known. . . . It is far from easy to translate [the Arabic language] into a pragmatic, almost purely vernacular language like English. . . . [A] linguistic Iron Curtain has kept us miserably short of first-hand information about the very considerable changes that Egypt has undergone in this century."

Mahfouz's "Cairo Trilogy" chronicles these changes in its fifteen hundred pages, tracing three generations of a middle-class Cairo family through the onset and aftermath of the 1952 military coup that overthrew King Farouk—abolishing an Egyptian monarchy—and facilitated the eventual rise of Colonel Gamal Abdel Nasser to power. Roger Allen, quoted by William H. Honan in the *New York Times,* called the trilogy "a monumental work," and, in the same article, Sasson Somekh added that the author's masterpiece is also "symbolic . . . because through the development of its characters you can see the development of modern Egypt."

Palace Walk, the English translation of the first volume of the trilogy, takes place between the end of World War I and the beginning of the 1919 revolution against Britain and introduces the Egyptian family. Al-Sayyid Ahmad Abd al-Jawad, the father, is depicted as a complex, contradictory figure who is both a stern disciplinarian at home but a gregarious, lewd merchant outside the home. Amina, his submissive wife, lives to serve her husband and children, but disobeys her husband by visiting the local mosque. The oldest son, Yasin, is a clerk who, upon finding his father with another woman, admires his father's manliness. Other children include Fahmy, the idealistic middle son; Kamal, the youngest son; Khadija, the older and smarter daughter; and Aisha, the younger and more attractive daughter.

"Each character," wrote Taghi Modarressi in *Washington Post Book World,* "like a figure in an old-fashioned puppet show, represents a particular vice or virtue." Modarressi remarked that such characters weaken the book and reflect the author's "middle phase . . ., [when] he employed an exaggerated narrative style apparently borrowed from the Middle Eastern storytelling tradition." On the other hand, Joseph Coates in Chicago *Tribune Books* praised Mahfouz's characters: "It's a mark of Mahfouz's genius that we see the resemblances and differences among the family members without having to be told about them, and that, with amazing speed, we get to know these people as we know few people in our own lives." *New York Times Book Review* contributor Edward Hower agreed, saying Mahfouz's "characters, like [Balzac's and Dickens's], are drawn with absolute authority and acute psychological insight." Lauding *Palace Walk,* Hower reflected on the long-awaited translation of Mahfouz's masterwork and decided, "Now, finally, readers can see for themselves why Mr. Mahfouz has long been considered the finest Arab writer of modern times."

Mahfouz, though he had supported Nasser's revolution at its inception in the 1950s, became disillusioned with the colonel's social, educational, and land reforms. After seven years of silence, Mahfouz began to voice his frustrations in his writings, composing the pessimistic and allegorical *Children of Gebelawi* in 1967. In thinly veiled allusions to the three monotheistic religions, the narrative relates humanity's quest for religion, beginning with Adam and Eve and ending with the last prophet (represented as the modern man of science), who is inadvertently responsible for the death of Gebelawi (God). The 1969 serialization of the novel inflamed Islamic fundamentalists and led to the banning of the manuscript's publication in book form. M. M. Badawi, writing in the *Times Literary Supplement,* lauded the novel for its "keen awareness of social injustice and the evil perpetrated by man against man." In a review for *World Literature Today* Issa Peters suggested that *Children of Gebelawi* "marks a significant point of transition in Mahfouz's career," as the author moves "toward an introspective phase characterized by an increasing sense of personal futility and political disillusionment." Although it was published in Beirut, Lebanon, in 1967, the novel has not yet been published in Egypt.

The 1967 publication of Mahfouz's *Miramar,* a novel released in the United States in 1983, marked the culmination of the author's disenchantment with the Nasser revolution, a revolution that, according to Fowles, merely "redistributed" Egypt's "wealth and influence . . . among a new elite." Evaluated by some critics as an unabashed attack on Nasser's political policies, *Miramar* explores the clashing values in a changing Egypt. As a reaction to the 1952 revolution, continued Fowles, *Miramar* is haunted by "despair" over the "moral failure" that tainted the newly established republic.

Miramar focuses on a peasant girl named Zohra who, after fleeing from the country to escape an arranged marriage, takes a job as a maid at Miramar, a *pension* in Alexandria. Striving for independence, Zohra educates herself. Her beauty and modern ideas, however, incite intrigue, jealousy, and resentment in the residents of Miramar. Told from the points of view of five different fictional characters, the unusual narrative presents what Ivan Hill, writing in the *Times Literary Supplement,* termed "a microcosm of Egypt." Fowles asserted that Zohra "stands for Egypt itself," and pronounced the spirit of Alexandria that Mahfouz creates "languorous, subtle, perverse, eternally *fin de siecle.*"

Mahfouz's realistic accounts of Egypt's social and political history have earned him both acclaim and condemnation. The head of the Jordan League of Writers, as quoted in *Time,* deemed Mahfouz "a delinquent man" whose works are "plagued with sex and drugs." Philip Stewart, as cited by Fowles, recalled the author's own assessment of his works: "In relation to European literature, [Mahfouz] said they were 'probably, like the rest of modern Arabic literature, fourth or fifth rate.'" But according to a press release from Stockholm, Sweden, published in the *Chicago Tribune,* the Swedish Academy saw fit to honor Mahfouz as an author "who, through works rich in nuance—now clear-sightedly realistic, now evocatively ambiguous—has formed an Arabian narrative art that applies to all mankind."

MEDIA ADAPTATIONS: Sixteen of Mahfouz's novels, including *Miramar,* were adapted for films in Egypt.

BIOGRAPHICAL/CRITICAL SOURCES:

BOOKS

Allen, Roger, *The Arabic Novel: An Historical and Critical Introduction,* Syracuse University Press, 1982.
Brugman, J., *An Introduction to the History of Modern Arabic Literature in Egypt,* Brill, 1984.
Dictionary of Literary Biography Yearbook: 1988, Gale, 1989.
Kilpatrick, H., *The Modern Egyptian Novel,* Ithaca, 1983.
Mahfouz, Naguib, *Midaq Alley,* translated with introduction by Trevor Le Gassick, Three Continents, 1981.
Mahfouz, *Miramar,* translated by Fatma Moussa-Mahmoud, introduction by John Fowles, Three Continents, 1983.
Ostle, R. C., editor, *Studies in Modern Arabic Literature,* Aris & Phillips, 1975.
Sakkut, Hamdi, *The Egyptian Novel and Its Main Trends From 1913-1952,* American University in Cairo Press, 1971.
Somekh, Sasson, *The Changing Rhythm: A Study of Mahfuz's Novels,* Brill, 1973.

PERIODICALS

Chicago Tribune, October 14, 1988.
Listener, November 23, 1978.
Los Angeles Times, October 14, 1988.
Los Angeles Times Book Review, November 12, 1989.
Newsweek, October 24, 1988.
New York Times, October 14, 1988, November 23, 1988, December 8, 1988.
New York Times Book Review, January 31, 1988, December 10, 1989, February 4, 1990.
Time, October 24, 1988.
Times (London), March 31, 1990.
Times Literary Supplement, April 30, 1976, September 25, 1981, January 1, 1988.
Tribune Books, January 21, 1990.
Washington Post, October 14, 1988, May 4, 1989.
Washington Post Book World, February 4, 1990.
World Literature Today, autumn, 1978, autumn, 1979, spring, 1982, autumn, 1986.

*   *   *

MAHFUZ, Najib
    See MAHFOUZ, Naguib (Abdel Aziz Al-Sabilgi)

*   *   *

MAILER, Norman 1923-

PERSONAL: Born January 31, 1923, in Long Branch, N.J.; son of Isaac Barnett (an accountant) and Fanny (owner of a small business; maiden name, Schneider) Mailer; married Beatrice Silverman, 1944 (divorced, 1952); married Adele Morales (an artist), 1954 (divorced, 1962); married Lady Jeanne Campbell, 1962 (divorced, 1963); married Beverly Rentz Bentley (an actress), 1963 (divorced, 1980); married Carol Stevens, 1980 (divorced, 1980); married Norris Church (an artist), 1980; children: (first marriage) Susan; (second marriage) Danielle, Elizabeth Anne; (third marriage) Kate; (fourth marriage) Michael Burks, Stephen McLeod; (fifth marriage) Maggie Alexandra; (sixth marriage) John Buffalo. *Education:* Harvard University, S.B. (cum laude), 1943; graduate studies at Sorbonne, Paris, France, 1947-48. *Politics:* "Left Conservative."

ADDRESSES: Home—142 Columbia Heights, Brooklyn, N.Y.; and Provincetown, Mass. *Agent*—Scott Meredith, Inc., 580 5th Ave., New York, N.Y. 10022.

CAREER: Writer. Producer and director of and actor in films, including "Wild 90," 1967, and "Maidstone: A Mystery," 1968; producer, "Beyond the Law," 1967; actor, "Ragtime," 1981; director, "Tough Guys Don't Dance," 1987. Lecturer at colleges and universities, 1950-89; University of Pennsylvania Pappas Fellow, 1983. Candidate for democratic nomination in mayoral race, New York, N.Y., 1960 and 1969. Co-founding editor of *Village Voice;* founder, Fifth Estate (merged with Committee for Action Research on the Intelligence Community), 1973. *Military service:* U.S. Army, 1944-46, field artillery observer; became infantry rifleman serving in the Philippines and Japan.

MEMBER: PEN (president of American Center, 1984-86), American Academy and Institute of Arts and Letters.

AWARDS, HONORS: Story magazine college fiction prize, 1941, for "The Greatest Thing in the World"; National Institute and American Academy grant in literature, 1960; elected to National Institute of Arts and Letters, 1967; National Book Award nomination, 1967, for *Why Are We in Vietnam?;* National Book Award for nonfiction, 1968, for *Miami and the Siege of Chicago;* National Book Award for nonfiction, Pulitzer Prize in letters-general nonfiction, and George Polk Award, all 1969, all for *Armies of the Night;* Edward MacDowell Medal, MacDowell Colony, 1973, for outstanding service to arts; National Arts Club Gold Medal, 1976; National Book Critics Circle nomination, Notable Book citation from the American Library Association, and Pulitzer Prize in letters, all 1979, and American Book Award nomination, 1980, all for *The Executioner's Song;* Emmy nomination for best adaptation, for script for "The Executioner's Song"; Rose Award, Lord & Taylor, 1985, for public accomplishment; Emerson-Thoreau Medal for lifetime literary achievement from American Academy of Arts and Sciences, 1989.

WRITINGS:

NOVELS

The Naked and the Dead, Rinehart, 1948, recent edition, Holt, 1980.
Barbary Shore, Rinehart, 1951, reprinted, Fertig, 1980.
The Deer Park (also see below), Putnam, 1955, reprinted with preface and notes by Mailer, Berkley, 1976.
An American Dream (first written in serial form for *Esquire,* January-August, 1964), Dial, 1965, reprinted, Holt, 1987.
Why Are We in Vietnam?, Putnam, 1967, reprinted with preface by Mailer, 1977, recent edition, Holt, 1982.
A Transit to Narcissus: A Facsimile of the Original Typescript with an Introduction by the Author (limited edition of unpublished 1944 manuscript), Fertig, 1978.
The Executioner's Song (excerpted in *Playboy* in 1979; also see below), Little, Brown, 1979.
Ancient Evenings, Little, Brown, 1983.
Tough Guys Don't Dance (also see below), Random House, 1984, signed edition, Franklin Library, 1984.
Harlot's Ghost, Random House, 1991.

Also author of *No Percentage,* 1941.

NONFICTION NARRATIVES

The Armies of the Night: History as a Novel, the Novel as History, New American Library, 1968.
Miami and the Siege of Chicago, New American Library, 1968, reprinted, D. I. Fine, 1986 (published in England as *Miami and the Siege of Chicago: An Informal History of the American Political Conventions of 1968,* Weidenfeld & Nicolson, 1969).
Of a Fire on the Moon (first appeared in *Life* magazine), Little, Brown, 1970, reprinted, Grove, 1985 (published in England as *A Fire on the Moon,* Weidenfeld & Nicolson, 1970).
King of the Hill: On the Fight of the Century (also see below), New American Library, 1971.
St. George and the Godfather, New American Library, 1972.
The Fight, Little, Brown, 1975.

NONFICTION

The Bullfight: A Photographic Narrative with Text by Norman Mailer (with record of Mailer reading from text; also see below), CBS Legacy Collection/Macmillan, 1967.
The Prisoner of Sex (first published in *Harper's* magazine), Little, Brown, 1971, Primus, c. 1985.
Marilyn: A Biography, Grosset and Dunlap, 1973, reprinted with new chapter by Mailer, Warner, 1975.
The Faith of Graffiti (also see below), photographs by Jon Naar, Praeger, 1974 (published in England as *Watching My Name Go By,* Matthews Miller Dunbar, 1974).
(Editor and author of introductions) *Genius and Lust: A Journey Through the Major Writings of Henry Miller,* Grove, 1976.
Of a Small and Modest Malignancy, Wicked and Bristling with Dots (essay; also see below), limited edition, Lord John, 1980.
Huckleberry Finn: Alive at 100 (booklet; criticism), limited edition, Caliban Press, 1985.

SCREENPLAYS

"Wild 90" (adaptation of *The Deer Park;* 16mm film), Supreme Mix, 1967.
"Beyond the Law" (16mm film), Supreme Mix/Evergreen Films, 1968.
"Maidstone: A Mystery" (16mm film; also see below), Supreme Mix, 1971.
"The Executioner's Song," Film Communication Inc. Productions, 1982.
"Tough Guys Don't Dance," Zoetrope, 1987.

Also author of movie script for a modern version of King Lear.

COLLECTIONS

The White Negro: Superficial Reflections on the Hipster (essays; includes "Communications: Reflections on Hipsterism"; "The White Negro" first published in *Dissent* magazine, summer, 1957; also see below), City Lights, 1957.
Advertisements for Myself (short stories, verse, articles, and essays, with narrative; includes "The White Negro," "The Man Who Studied Yoga," and "The Time of Her Time"), Putnam, 1959, reprinted with preface by Mailer, Berkley, 1976.
The Presidential Papers (also see below), Putnam, 1963, reprinted with preface by Mailer, 1976.
Cannibals and Christians (also see below), Dial, 1966, abridged edition, Panther, 1979.
The Short Fiction of Norman Mailer (also see below), Dell, 1967, reprinted, Fertig, 1980.
The Idol and the Octopus: Political Writings on the Kennedy and Johnson Administrations (includes selections from *The Presidential Papers* and *Cannibals and Christians*), Dell, 1968.
The Long Patrol: 25 Years of Writing from the Work of Norman Mailer, edited by Robert F. Lucid, World, 1971.
Existential Errands (includes *The Bullfight: A Photographic Narrative with Text by Norman Mailer,* "A Course in Filmmak-

ing," and *King of the Hill;* also see below), Little, Brown, 1972.

Some Honorable Men: Political Conventions 1960-1972 (collection of previously published nonfiction narratives), Little, Brown, 1976.

The Essential Mailer (includes *The Short Fiction of Norman Mailer* and *Existential Errands*), New English Library, 1982.

Pieces and Pontifications (essays and interviews first appearing 1973-77; includes *The Faith of Graffiti* and *Of a Small and Modest Malignancy, Wicked and Bristling with Dots*), edited by Michael Lennon, Little, Brown, 1982, published as *Pieces,* 1982, published as *Pontifications: Interviews,* 1982.

OTHER

Deaths for the Ladies and Other Disasters: Being a Run of Poems, Short Poems, Very Short Poems, and Turns of Prose, Putnam, 1962, reprinted with introduction by Mailer, New American Library, 1971.

Gargoyle, Guignol, False Closets (booklet; first published in *Architectural Forum,* April, 1964), privately printed, 1964.

The Deer Park: A Play (two-act; adaptation of novel *The Deer Park;* first produced Off-Broadway at Theater De Lys, January 31, 1967), Dell, 1967.

The Pulitzer Prize for Fiction, Little, Brown, 1967, reprint, 1980.

Maidstone: A Mystery (film script; includes essay "A Course in Filmmaking"), New American Library, 1971.

Of Women and Their Elegance (fictional interview), photographs by Milton H. Greene, Simon & Schuster, 1980.

"The Executioner's Song" (two-part television movie), Film Communications Inc. Productions, 1982.

The Last Night: A Story (first published in "Esquire," 1962), limited, signed edition, Targ Editions, 1984.

"Strawhead" (play), first produced at Actors Studio, January 3, 1985.

CONTRIBUTOR

Writers at Work, Third Series, Viking, 1967.

Running Against the Machine: The Mailer-Breslin Campaign, edited by Peter Manso, Doubleday, 1969.

(Author of introduction and captions) *The 1974 Marilyn Monroe Datebook,* photographs by Eve Arnold and others, Simon & Schuster, 1973.

Writer's Choice, edited by Rust Hills, McKay, 1974.

(Author of preface) Hallie and Whit Burnett, *A Fiction Writer's Handbook,* Harper, 1975.

(Author of foreword) Eugene Kennedy, *St. Patrick's Day with Mayor Daley and Other Things Too Good to Miss,* Seabury, 1976.

(Author of introduction) Abbie Hoffman, *Soon To Be a Major Motion Picture,* Putnam, 1980.

Black Messiah, Vagabond, 1981.

(Author of introduction) Jack Henry Abbott, *In the Belly of the Beast: Letters from Prison,* Random House, 1981.

(Author of foreword) Harold Conrad, *Dear Muffo: 35 Years in the Fast Lane,* Stein & Day, 1982.

Also contributor to anthologies. Author of column for *Esquire,* "The Big Bite," 1962-63; columnist for *Village Voice,* January-May, 1946, and for *Commentary,* 1962-63. Contributor to numerous periodicals, including *Harper's, Rolling Stone, New Republic, Playboy, New York Times Book Review,* and *Parade.* Contributing editor of *Dissent,* 1953-69; co-founding editor of *Village Voice,* 1955.

WORK IN PROGRESS: A novel about the U.S. Central Intelligence Agency (CIA).

SIDELIGHTS: When *The Naked and the Dead,* drawing on Norman Mailer's experiences in the Pacific theater of World War II, was published in 1948, *New York Times* critic Orville Prescott called it "the most impressive novel about the Second World War that I have ever read." The large, ambitious book was number one on the *New York Times* bestseller list for eleven consecutive weeks and was the object of continuing critical admiration. The twenty-five-year-old literary novice was suddenly famous and at the dawn of a prolific career in which he would henceforth be forever a public figure and measured, by others as well as himself, against his precocious success. "I had the freak of luck to start high on the mountain, and go down sharp while others were passing me," wrote the author in *Advertisements for Myself,* in which he shows himself determined from the outset "to hit the longest ball ever to go up into the accelerated hurricane air of our American letters."

Mailer's second novel, *Barbary Shore,* centers on a young leftist, Michael Lovett, who lives in a Brooklyn Heights boarding house and who discovers revolutionary socialism as the only alternative to contemporary barbarism. Hilary Mills reports in *Mailer: A Biography* that the book was dismissed by Mailer's French mentor, Jean Malaquais, as "a political tract, not a novel"; and *Time* labeled it "paceless, tasteless and graceless." Still suffering from what he called in *Advertisements for Myself* "the peculiar megalomania of a young writer who is determined to become an important writer," Mailer was devastated by the novel's hostile reception and became more preoccupied than ever not only with attaining his grandiose literary goals but also with establishing himself as an important public figure.

Mailer became part of a circle of prominent cultural figures in New York and began conceiving an ambitious cycle of eight novels centering on a universal mythical hero named Sergius O'Shaugnessy. The short story "The Man Who Studied Yoga" was designed as a prologue to the series, and *The Deer Park,* published in 1955, was its first installment. Three years in the making, *The Deer Park,* which Mailer later adapted for theater, also proved to be the cycle's only volume. Primarily because of the work's overt sexuality, Rinehart, Mailer's original publisher, backed out of an agreement to publish the novel, a study in the powers of art, sex, and money in a hedonist resort in southern California. Several other houses rejected the manuscript before it was accepted by G. P. Putnam's. Reviews of *The Deer Park* were mixed, with Brendan Gill asserting in the *New Yorker:* "Only a writer of the greatest and most reckless talent could have flung it between covers."

Mailer continued recklessly throughout the 1950s, attempting to embody the values of "the hipster" as he defined them in a defiant essay "The White Negro": "energy, life, sex, force, the Yoga's *prana,* the Reichian's orgone, Lawrence's blood, Hemingway's 'good,' the Shavian life-force; 'It'; God; not the God of the churches but the unachievable whisper of the mystery within the sex." His own flirtations with the frontiers of sex, drugs, violence, and belligerency culminated in a boisterous party on the evening of November 19, 1960, at the conclusion of which the drunken author stabbed his wife Adele. Mailer was arrested, but, after Adele refused to press charges, he received a suspended sentence.

It took a decade after *The Deer Park* for Mailer to publish his next novel, *An American Dream,* in 1965. The book, about a prominent professor of existential psychology who murders his wealthy wife, was a great commercial success and the object of intense critical controversy. Elizabeth Hardwick described it in *Partisan Review* as "a very dirty book—dirty and extremely ugly," while John Adlridge's review in *Life* called the novel "a major creative breakthrough." The protagonist of *An American Dream,* Stephen Rojack, was loosely modeled after Mailer himself, and his strongest writing now included explicitly autobiographical elements. In *Advertisements for Myself,* he brashly anthologized a selection of his own writings and interpolated a running, and pugnacious, personal commentary. As co-founding editor of the *Village Voice* and as a regular contributor of nonfiction to it and to *Dissent* and *Esquire,* Mailer found an effective arena for his combative ego. It is arguably in his nonfiction writing, directly engaging contemporary issues in his own distinctive voice, that Mailer's special talents as antic public gadfly are most effectively exploited. His provocative self-portrait as philosophical "existentialist" and political "left conservative" ensured that his own personality would be a continuing stage for dramatic conflict.

Mailer cultivated the mystique of personal violence through a close friendship with professional boxer Jose Torres. As a writer and public figure, Mailer increasingly placed himself at the epicenter of contemporary trends and events—political campaigns, space exploration, feminist polemics, boxing, peace demonstrations. He became a familiar, notorious presence on television talk shows and, in 1969, a very unconventional candidate for the Democratic nomination for mayor of New York, advocating that the city secede from the state. He and his running mate the writer Jimmy Breslin finished fourth in a field of five. Mailer was also producer, director, writer, and star of three low-budget improvisational films that he and his friends made in rapid succession—"Wild 90," "Beyond the Law," and "Maidstone." His many marriages and progeny added to the publicity surrounding the author who in 1968 described himself as "a warrior, presumptive general, expolitical candidate, embattled enfant terrible of the literary world, wise father of six children, radical intellectual, existential philosopher, hard-working author, champion of obscenity, husband of four battling sweet wives, amiable bar drinker, and much exaggerated street fighter, party giver, hostess insulter. . . ." Though the number of wives and children would soon change, the summary accurately reflects his protean personality.

This self-portrait appears in *The Armies of the Night,* a literary triumph that redeemed Mailer in the eyes of critics who were convinced he had squandered his talents in playing the part of a national celebrity. In this book, a very personal account of a massive demonstration against the Vietnam War staged in front of the Pentagon on October 21, 1967, Mailer joined his artistic skills with his own compulsive involvement in the event to create a work that is more than just insightful reportage of a momentous phenomenon. Mailer's status as both participant and observer resulted in a night in jail and a book that won both the Pulitzer Prize and the National Book Award. *The Armies of the Night* comically inflates Mailer's role in the proceedings to create both a bracing portrait of individual orneriness in combat against the tyranny of modern mass society and a meditation on the relationship between the self and history. Subtitled *History as a Novel, the Novel as History,* the work is likely to be among the most enduring of many contemporary attempts to contest the boundaries between fiction and chronicle. Richard Gilman's review in the *New Republic* applauded "the central, rather wonderful achievement of the book, that in it history and personality confront each other with a new sense of liberation."

In *The Armies of the Night,* Mailer himself quotes Alfred Kazin's observation in *Bright Book of Life* "that Mailer was as fond of his style as an Italian tenor is fond of his vocal chords," and it is the congruence of the author's stylistic bravura with his acute perceptions of political realities that makes that "nonfiction novel" so compelling. *Miami and the Siege of Chicago* contains fresh observations of 1968, but lacks the rich conjunction of incident and personal style found in *The Armies of the Night.* Mailer's account of the 1972 national political conventions, *St. George and the Godfather,* was not nearly as successful as the earlier nonfiction novels. The whimsically titled novel *Why Are We in Vietnam?,* a disk jockey's violent, vulgar narrative of a bear hunt in Alaska, is an ostentatiously inventive allegory of American foreign policy.

Though he had received a bachelor's degree in engineering from Harvard, Mailer was notorious as a scourge of modern technology. Nevertheless, *Life* magazine commissioned him to write a book about the first moon landing in July, 1969. NASA was wary of Mailer's antibureaucratic attitudes, and he was denied access to the astronauts themselves. *Of a Fire on the Moon* is the product of months spent in Houston and Cape Canaveral and in technical research into the space program. Calling himself "Aquarius," Mailer characteristically writes of himself in the third person and as a central character at odds with the triumphant antisepsis of the technocrats. "I liked the book in a lot of ways," Mailer later told the *New York Times Book Review,* "but I didn't like my own person in it—I felt I was highly unnecessary." Depressed over the collapse of his marriage to actress Beverly Bentley (his fourth marriage), Aquarius confessed in *Of a Fire on the Moon,* "He was weary of his own voice, own face, person, persona, will, ideas, speeches, and general sense of importance." But it was to be only a transient weariness.

When Mailer found himself portrayed as the archetypal male chauvinist pig in Kate Millett's 1970 literary study *Sexual Politics,* he participated in a raucous debate on feminism at New York's Town Hall, and he wrote *The Prisoner of Sex,* which, when first published in *Harper's,* accounted for the widest sales of any issue in the magazine's history and for the departure of its editors because of a dispute with its publisher over the work's offensive language. The book was another chapter in Mailer's continuing obsession with the mysteries of sexuality, pursued later in his passionate meditations on Marilyn Monroe in *Marilyn* and *Of Women and Their Elegance.* Praising *The Prisoner of Sex* as "Mailer's best book," *New York Times* critic Anatole Broyard declared: "What Mailer has tried to do here is write a love poem." But Gore Vidal in the *New York Review of Books* found: "There has been from Henry Miller to Norman Mailer to Charles Manson a logical progression." The remark ignited a sensational public feud between rival novelists Mailer and Vidal. Mailer attracted further controversy when he successfully petitioned the Utah State Prison parole board to release Jack Henry Abbott, for whose book *In the Belly of the Beast* he had helped find a publisher. One month after leaving the penitentiary, Abbott, who had spent much of his life incarcerated, killed another man, and Mailer was again sparring with the press.

Mailer had met Abbott while conducting exhaustive research for *The Executioner's Song,* a self-described "true life novel" about the sad, bizarre life and death of Gary Gilmore, who, on January 17, 1977, became the first convict to be executed in the United States in more than a decade. What is most remarkable about this long and detailed narrative is the patient self-effacement of its author. Gone from *The Executioner's Song* are the familiar, patent Mailerisms—the baroque syntax, the hectoring tone, the outrageous epigrams, the startling bravura imagery, the political/metaphysical digressions, the self-conscious presence of the author in every line. Instead, from its first crisp, limpid sentence, Mailer's prose assumes the coloration of its huge cast of characters—lawyers, policemen, doctors, journalists, as well as relatives, friends, and victims of Gary Gilmore—and immerses the reader in the alarmingly ordinary world of its main character. *The Executioner's Song* was an extraordinary triumph, the second Mailer work to win a Pulitzer Prize and enormous success.

For all of his bestsellers, Mailer was, as a result of his many failed marriages, in dire financial straits, and it was only through lucrative but demanding multi-book contracts that he was able to remain solvent while supporting his large extended family. *The Executioner's Song* is, possibly, the big, important book that he had aspired to write throughout his career, but he wrote it, on assignment, in a mere fifteen months. Mailer was, meanwhile, planning a boldly immense fictional creation, a vast trilogy that would encompass the distant past, the future, and the present in each successive volume. After ten years of intermittent work on it, in 1983 he published the first installment, a seven hundred-page novel set in ancient Egypt. By turns dense, overwrought, self-indulgent, forbidding, daring, and brilliant, *Ancient Evenings* follows the four lives of the courtier Menenhetet through three reincarnations during the nineteenth and twentieth dynasties of Egypt. The book is rich in researched details about daily life, beliefs, and battles of the period. Mailer's intoxication with grandiose ideas, his delight in stylistic flourishes, and his preoccupation with sex and violence are again on ostentatious display, and *Ancient Evenings* once more polarized critics in their assessment of his achievement. George Stade in the *New Republic* called it "a new and permanent contribution to the possibilities of fiction and our communal efforts of self-discovery," while Benjamin DeMott dismissed it in the *New York Times Book Review* as "pitiably foolish in conception" and "a disaster." Mailer characteristically taunted his critics with a full-page advertisement for *Ancient Evenings* juxtaposing scathing reviews of his novel with similar attacks on Herman Melville's *Moby Dick,* Leo Tolstoy's *Anna Karenina,* Walt Whitman's *Leaves of Grass,* and Charles-Pierre Baudelaire's *Les Fleurs du mal.*

Mailer was critical of Little, Brown's limited zeal in marketing his ambitious book and was disappointed with their paperback and foreign sales of it. In 1983, he signed a $4 million contract with Random House to deliver four novels to them within nine years. His new publisher also took on an additional novel that Mailer had written, a short, seamy murder mystery called *Tough Guys Don't Dance.* He also returned to the cinema when he chose to write a screenplay for *Tough Guys Don't Dance* and to direct it himself. In 1981, Mailer had had some experience with mainstream commercial movie production when he was cast in the minor role of architect Stanford White in Milos Forman's adaptation of E. L. Doctorow's novel *Ragtime.* The film noir "Tough Guys Don't Dance," in contrast to "Wild 90," "Beyond the Law," and "Maidstone," received studio backing, and Mailer cast a bankable star, Ryan O'Neal, in the lead role of Tim Madden. "Tough Guys Don't Dance" was well received at the 1987 Cannes film festival.

In his sixties, Mailer was increasingly positioning himself in the role of elder statesman of American letters. The feistiness was still there, but the aging *enfant terrible* was growing perceptibly more mellow and even courtly. Active in the writers' organization PEN, he became president of its American center in 1984, in time to serve as host for the 1986 international PEN Congress in New York. The gathering of some seven hundred authors from throughout the world proved to be a tumultuous event, and while cherishing the role of executive conciliator, Mailer was again the lightning rod for public controversy. He assailed U.S. foreign policy, but he invited Secretary of State George Schultz to address the assembly of writers, a decision that provoked fierce opposition. President Mailer was also angrily attacked for

his alleged sexism in assigning men a dominant position in the program for the PEN meeting. The author who, in *Advertisements for Myself,* had declared, "I have been running for President these last ten years in the privacy of my mind," relished this very public and pugnacious presidency and the opportunity to do battle again with his literary rivals.

"The sour truth," wrote Mailer in the same book, "is that I am imprisoned with a perception which will settle for nothing less than a revolution in the consciousness of our time." Few American writers of his time have had such magisterial aspirations and such genuine claims to public attention. The self presented in *Advertisements for Myself* is "an actor, a quick-change artist, as if I believe I can trap the Prince of Truth in the act of switching a style." Thus, it is appropriate that one scholar of Mailer's protean career titled a collection of essays about her subject *Will the Real Norman Mailer Please Stand Up?*

Throughout all the artist's quick changes, the real Norman Mailer has been an author of enormous, agonistic energies and elaborate initiative. Though he finds much of Mailer's writing unreadable after it has lost the immediacy of the occasion, Harold Bloom, in *Norman Mailer,* characterizes him as "a historian of the moral consciousness of his era, and as the representative writer of his generation." A self-styled nice Jewish boy from Brooklyn who has lived for most of his life within close proximity to his adoring mother, Mailer has been animated by transgression. His career has thrived on risk and friction and has undergone as many incarnations as his Egyptian character Menenhetet. Fond of pugilistic metaphors for the writing life, as he is of boxing itself (as spectator and participant), Norman Mailer is the contemporary American author for whom a literary Golden Glove would be most fitting.

MEDIA ADAPTATIONS: The Naked and the Dead was made into a film by Warner Brothers in 1958; *An American Dream* was adapted for film as "See You in Hell, Darling," produced by Warner Brothers in 1966.

AVOCATIONAL INTERESTS: Skiing, sailing, hiking.

BIOGRAPHICAL/CRITICAL SOURCES:

BOOKS

Adams, Laura, *Norman Mailer: A Comprehensive Bibliography,* Scarecrow, 1974.

Adams, Laura, editor, *Will the Real Norman Mailer Please Stand Up?,* Kennikat Press, 1974.

Adams, Laura, *Existential Battles: The Growth of Norman Mailer,* Ohio University Press, 1976.

Authors in the News, Volume 2, Gale, 1976.

Bailey, Jennifer, *Norman Mailer: Quick-Change Artist,* Harper, 1979.

Begiebing, Robert J., *Acts of Regeneration: Allegory and Archetype in the Works of Norman Mailer,* University of Missouri Press, 1980.

Bloom, Harold, editor, *Norman Mailer,* Chelsea House, 1986.

Braudy, Leo Beal, editor, *Norman Mailer: A Collection of Critical Essays,* Prentice-Hall, 1972.

Bufithis, Philip H., *Norman Mailer,* Ungar, 1978.

Contemporary Authors Bibliographical Series, Volume 1: *American Novelists,* Gale, 1986.

Contemporary Literary Criticism, Gale, Volume 1, 1979, Volume 2, 1974, Volume 3, 1975, Volume 4, 1975, Volume 5, 1976, Volume 8, 1978, Volume 11, 1979, Volume 14, 1980, Volume 28, 1984, Volume 39, 1986.

Dictionary of Literary Biography, Gale, Volume 2: *American Novelists since World War II,* 1978, Volume 16: *The Beats:*

Literary Bohemians in Postwar America, 1983, Volume 28: *Twentieth-Century American-Jewish Fiction Writers,* 1984.

Dictionary of Literary Biography Documentary Series, Gale, Volume 3, 1983.

Dictionary of Literary Biography Yearbook:, Gale, *1980,* 1981, *1983, 1984.*

Ehrlich, Robert, *Norman Mailer: The Radical as Hipster,* Scarecrow Press, 1978.

Gordon, Andrew, *An American Dreamer: A Psychoanalytic Study of the Fiction of Norman Mailer,* Farleigh Dickinson University Press, 1980.

Gutman, Stanley T., *Mankind in Barbary: The Individual and Society in the Novels of Norman Mailer,* University Press of New England, 1975.

Jackson, Richard, *Norman Mailer,* University of Minnesota Press, 1968.

Kazin, Alfred, *Bright Book of Life: American Novelists and Storytellers from Hemingway to Mailer,* Little, Brown, 1973.

Kellman, Steven, G., *Loving Reading: Erotics of the Text,* Archon, 1985.

Leeds, Barry H., *The Structured Vision of Norman Mailer,* New York University Press, 1969.

Lennon, J. Michael, editor, *Critical Essays on Norman Mailer,* G. K. Hall, 1986.

Lucid, Robert F., editor, *Norman Mailer: The Man and His Work,* Little, Brown, 1971.

Mailer, Norman, *The White Negro: Superficial Reflections on the Hipster,* City Lights, 1957.

Mailer, Norman, *The Armies of the Night: History as a Novel, the Novel as History,* New American Library, 1968.

Mailer, Norman, *Advertisements for Myself,* Berkley, 1976.

Mailer, Norman, *Of a Fire on the Moon,* Grove, 1985.

Manso, Peter, *Mailer: His Life and Times,* Simon & Schuster, 1985.

Merrill, Robert, *Norman Mailer,* G. K. Hall, 1978.

Middlebrook, Jonathan, *Mailer and the Times of his Time,* Bay Books (San Francisco), 1976.

Millett, Kate, *Sexual Politics,* Doubleday, 1970.

Mills, Hilary, *Mailer: A Biography,* Empire, 1982.

Poirier, Richard, *Norman Mailer,* Viking, 1972.

Radford, Jean, *Norman Mailer: A Critical Study,* Harper, 1975.

Sokoloff, B. A., *A Biography of Norman Mailer,* Darby Books, 1969.

Solotaroff, Robert, *Down Mailer's Way,* University of Illinois Press, 1974.

Weatherby, William J., *Squaring Off: Mailer vs. Baldwin,* Mason/Charter, 1977.

PERIODICALS

Atlantic, July, 1971, September, 1984.

Chicago Tribune, December 20, 1982, September 21, 1987.

Chicago Tribune Book World, October 7, 1979, November 30, 1980, June 13, 1982, April 10, 1983, August 5, 1984, July 14, 1985.

Cosmopolitan, August, 1963.

Esquire, June, 1966, December, 1968, June, 1986.

Life, March 19, 1965, September 24, 1965, February 24, 1967, September 15, 1967.

Look, May, 1969.

Los Angeles Times, September 23, 1984.

Los Angeles Times Book Review, December 14, 1980, July 11, 1982, April 24, 1983, August 19, 1984.

Nation, May 27, 1968, June 25, 1983, September 15, 1984.

National Review, April 20, 1965.

New Republic, February 9, 1959, February 8, 1964, June 8, 1968, January 23, 1971, May 2, 1983, August 27, 1984.

New Statesman, September 29, 1961.

Newsweek, December 9, 1968, April 18, 1983, August 6, 1984.

New Yorker, October 23, 1948, October 22, 1955.

New York Review of Books, May 6, 1971, June 15, 1972.

New York Times, October 27, 1968, April 28, 1983, December 23, 1985.

New York Times Book Review, May 7, 1948, September 17, 1967, May 5, 1968, October 27, 1968, January 10, 1971, February 18, 1972, October 7, 1979, September 20, 1980, December 7, 1980, June 6, 1982, January 30, 1983, April 10, 1983, July 20, 1984, July 29, 1984, April 11, 1985.

New York Times Sunday Magazine, September, 1979.

Partisan Review, spring, 1965, fall, 1965, summer, 1967, July, 1980.

People, May 30, 1983, October 5, 1987.

Publishers Weekly, March 22, 1965, October 8, 1979.

Saturday Review, January, 1981.

Smart, September, 1989.

Time, May 28, 1951, June 28, 1982, April 18, 1983, January 27, 1986.

Times (London), June 10, 1983.

Times Literary Supplement, October 3, 1968, January 11, 1980, March 6, 1981, December 10, 1982, June 10, 1983, October 19, 1984.

Village Voice, February 18, 1965, January 21, 1971.

Washington Post, August 22, 1989.

Washington Post Book World, July 11, 1970, October 14, 1979, November 30, 1980, July 11, 1982, April 10, 1983, August 12, 1984, November 24, 1985.

*   *   *

MAIS, Roger   1905-1955

PERSONAL: Born August 11, 1905, in Kingston, Jamaica; died of cancer, June 21, 1955, in Kingston, Jamaica. *Education:* Attended public schools in the Blue Mountains, Jamaica.

CAREER: Writer. Worked variously as a civil servant, painter, farmer, photographer, and journalist for the Daily Gleaner and Public Opinion.

WRITINGS:

And Most of All Man (short stories and verse), City Printery (Kingston, Jamaica), 1939.

Face and Other Stories (short stories and verse), Universal Printery, 1942.

"The Potter's Field" (play), first published in *Public Opinion,* December 23, 1950.

Atalanta at Calydon (play), J. Cape, 1950.

Come Love, Come Death, Hutchinson, 1951.

The Hills Were Joyful Together (also see below), J. Cape, 1953, reprinted, with introduction by Daphne Morris, Heinemann, 1981.

(And illustrator) *Brother Man* (also see below), J. Cape, 1954, reprinted with introduction by Edward Brathwaite, Heinemann, 1974.

Black Lightning (also see below), J. Cape, 1955, reprinted with introduction by Jean D'Costa, Heinemann, 1983.

The Three Novels of Roger Mais (contains *The Hills Were Joyful Together, Brother Man,* and *Black Lightning*), introduction by Norman W. Manley, J. Cape, 1966.

Listen, The Wind, and Other Stories, Longman, c. 1986.

Also author of other plays, such as "Hurricane," "Masks and Paper Hats," and "The First Sacrifice."

WORK IN PROGRESS: A fourth novel.

SIDELIGHTS: Roger Mais, "the spokesman of emergent Jamaica," according to Jean D'Costa in her 1978 critique on Mais, is known primarily for his three novels of social protest. Among the first Jamaican novels to realistically examine that country's squalid urban conditions, *The Hills Were Joyful Together, Brother Man,* and *Black Lightning* greatly influenced the development of West Indian literature. Despite his middle-class upbringing in Jamaica's Blue Mountains, Mais empathized with the less fortunate urban slum dwellers and, as a writer, remained "fiercely dedicated to the exposure of social ills in [mid-twentieth-century] Jamaica," wrote D'Costa.

Of the three novels, *The Hills* provides the most explicit portrait of Caribbean slum life. Set in a ghetto in Kingston, Jamaica, *The Hills* examines the lives of three groups of black lower-class people. "Violence and misery is their common lot," observed reviewer Karina Williamson in the *Journal of Commonwealth Literature.* The Hills's subject matter disturbed many members of Jamaican society, according to Jean Creary, who explained in *The Islands in Between* that Mais's readers were "thrown straight into a world everyone in Jamaica knew existed, and yet which the middle classes were united in a conspiracy of silence to ignore and reject." She found, however, that "within and behind this human underworld lies beauty and pattern." In one particularly acclaimed passage, Williamson wrote, Mais describes the ghetto community's "common capacity for gaiety and goodwill" during a beach celebration. In other instances he depicts sympathy and loyalty between characters despite their misfortunes, indicating that personal integrity can withstand even the most hostile environment. "Mais's attitude . . . is ultimately neither cynical nor defeatist," Williamson explained, asserting that it is the author's balanced perspective that accounts for the novel's literary merit. "The book has its grave weaknesses," Creary admitted, citing wordiness and melodrama, but it succeeds because the author's "weaknesses come from the same source where lies his strength—from his innocent and yet potent awareness of himself and of his environment."

Mais's second novel, *Brother Man,* focuses on Rastafarianism, a Caribbean religious movement in which members seek a return of blacks to Africa. For some of their rituals, which include smoking marijuana—though shunning alcohol—and refusing to cut their hair, Rastafarians were "feared, despised, and rejected" during the 1940s and 1950s, explained Edward Brathwaite in his 1974 introduction to Mais's novel. The protagonist of *Brother Man* is a peaceful Rastafarian leader named John Power or "Bra Man," whose life resembles that of Jesus Christ. "In many ways," wrote Oscar R. Dathorne in *Studies in the Novel,* "the parallel between Christ and Bra Man is followed almost too carefully." Most critics agreed that the novel's credibility weakens whenever Bra Man becomes too Christ-like, healing the sick and teaching in parables, for example. Dathorne added, however, that "in spite of all this, Bra Man is convincing, not only as a messianic Christ-figure but as a person."

Reviewers praised Mais's refinement in *Brother Man* of a complex linguistic technique he had introduced in *The Hills.* Combining the figurative language of the King James Bible with the words and syntax of Jamaican Creole, Mais developed an elaborate writing style that enhanced his allegorical narratives. This style, according to Creary, is especially effective in descriptions of Bra Man, "Mais's vision of the reincarnate Christ. . . . This Gospel Presence fuses with Mais's writing in the rhythmical, Biblical prose." Dathorne agreed, explaining that "the language helps to identify Bra Man, and the rhythm of the Bible is reserved for him."

Black Lightning, Mais's third novel, is a biblical allegory like *Brother Man.* Unlike Mais's first two novels, however, *Black Lightning* skirts social issues, focusing instead on the solitary artist. Set in the Jamaican countryside, the novel follows the progress a sculptor, Jake, makes on a statue he is carving of the biblical hero Samson. "As it takes shape," Creary noted, "the figure of Samson becomes increasingly identified with Jake himself." Initially perceiving himself as strong and independent, the artist begins fashioning his work after his own self-image. After his wife leaves him, Jake becomes more aware of his dependence on her and begins molding his statue into the image of a weaker man. "The finished work Jake contemptuously reveals . . . is not Samson in his prime, but the blinded Samson, a figure of ruined strength leaning on a little boy," related Kenneth Ramchand in *The West Indian Novel and Its Background.* Like Samson, Jake is eventually blinded and, in despair, he kills himself.

Although Mais's first two novels received greater popular and critical acclaim upon their publication, Ramchand believes that the author's third book is his most powerful one. "The work has been virtually disregarded in the West Indies," the critic pointed out, "but I would like to contend that it is in *Black Lightning* that Mais's art and understanding are in greatest harmony, and that it is upon this . . . novel that his reputation must rest." Williamson also lauded *Black Lightning*'s artistic merit and its contribution to Caribbean literature: "*Black Lightning,* more than either of Mais's other novels, seems to me a landmark in the development of the West Indian novel."

A supporter of the Jamaican nationalist movement of the 1930s and 1940s, Mais was imprisoned in 1944 for an essay he wrote, titled "Now We Know," attacking English colonialism. Already the author of two short story collections, *And Most of All Man* and *Face and Other Stories,* Mais began writing his first novel during his six months in prison. Published nine years later, *The Hills Were Joyful Together* was quickly followed by *Brother Man* and *Black Lightning.* The author traveled to Europe in 1951 in search of a more accommodating artistic climate, but he returned to his homeland three years later, suffering from cancer. He died in Kingston in 1955, the year his third novel was published, leaving a fourth novel incomplete.

BIOGRAPHICAL/CRITICAL SOURCES:

BOOKS

D'Costa, Jean, *Roger Mais: "The Hills Were Joyful Together" and "Brother Man,"* Longman, 1978.

James, Louis, editor, *The Islands in Between: Essays on West Indian Literature,* Oxford University Press, 1968.

Mais, Roger, *Brother Man,* introduction by Edward Brathwaite, Heinemann, 1974.

Moore, Gerald, *The Chosen Tongue: English Writings in the Tropical World,* Harper, 1969.

Ramchand, Kenneth, *The West Indian Novel and Its Background,* Barnes & Noble, 1970.

Twentieth-Century Literary Criticism, Volume 8, Gale, 1982.

PERIODICALS

Black Images, summer, 1972.
Journal of Commonwealth Literature, December, 1966.
Studies in the Novel, summer, 1972.

MALABAILA, Damiano
See LEVI, Primo

* * *

MALAMUD, Bernard 1914-1986

PERSONAL: Born April 28, 1914, in Brooklyn, N.Y.; died of natural causes, March 18, 1986, in New York, N.Y.; son of Max (a grocery store manager) and Bertha (Fidelman) Malamud; married Ann de Chiara, November 6, 1945; children: Paul, Janna. *Education:* City College of New York (now City College of the City University of New York), B.A., 1936; Columbia University, M.A., 1942.

ADDRESSES: Home—New York, N.Y.; and Bennington, Vt. *Agent*—Russell & Volkening, 50 West 29th St., New York, N.Y. 10001.

CAREER: Worked for Bureau of Census, Washington, D.C., 1940; Erasmus Hall High School, New York, N.Y., evening instructor in English, beginning 1940; instructor in English, Harlem High School, 1948-49; Oregon State University, 1949-61, began as instructor, became associate professor of English; Bennington College, Bennington, Vt., Division of Language and Literature, member of faculty, 1961-86. Visiting lecturer, Harvard University, 1966-68. Honorary consultant in American letters, Library of Congress, 1972-75.

MEMBER: National Institute of Arts and Letters, American Academy of Arts and Sciences, PEN American Center (president, 1979).

AWARDS, HONORS: Partisan Review fellow in fiction, 1956-57; Richard and Hinda Rosenthal Foundation Award, and Daroff Memorial Award, both 1958, both for *The Assistant;* Rockefeller grant, 1958; National Book Award in fiction, 1959, for *The Magic Barrel,* and 1967, for *The Fixer;* Ford Foundation fellow in humanities and arts, 1959-61; Pulitzer Prize in fiction, 1967, for *The Fixer;* O. Henry Award, 1969, for "Man in the Drawer"; Jewish Heritage Award of the B'nai B'rith, 1976; Governor's Award, Vermont Council on the Arts, 1979, for excellence in the arts; American Library Association Notable Book citation, 1979, for *Dubin's Lives;* Brandeis University Creative Arts Award in fiction, 1981; Gold Medal for fiction, American Academy and Institute of Arts and Letters, 1983; Elmer Holmes Bobst Award for fiction, 1983; honorary degree from City College of the City University of New York.

WRITINGS:

NOVELS

The Natural, Harcourt, 1952, reprinted, Avon, 1980.
The Assistant, Farrar, Straus, 1957, reprinted, Avon, 1980.
A New Life, Farrar, Straus, 1961, reprinted, 1988.
The Fixer, Farrar, Straus, 1966, reprinted, Pocket Books, 1982.
Pictures of Fidelman: An Exhibition (includes "Last Mohican," "A Pimp's Revenge," and "Glass Blower of Venice"), Farrar, Straus, 1969, reprinted, New American Library, 1985.
The Tenants, Farrar, Straus, 1971, reprinted, 1988.
Dubin's Lives, Farrar, Straus, 1979.
God's Grace, Farrar, Straus, 1982.

SHORT STORIES

The Magic Barrel (includes "The Magic Barrel" and "The First Seven Years"), Farrar, Straus, 1958, reprinted, Avon, 1980.
Idiots First (includes "Idiots First" and "The Maid's Shoes"), Farrar, Straus, 1963.

Rembrandt's Hat (includes "The Silver Crown" and "Man in the Drawer"), Farrar, Straus, 1973.
The Stories of Bernard Malamud, Farrar, Straus, 1983.
The People, and Uncollected Stories, edited by Robert Giroux, Farrar, Straus, 1989.

OTHER

(Contributor) John Fisher and Robert B. Silvers, editors, *Writing in America,* Rutgers University Press, 1960.
A Malamud Reader, edited by Philip Rahv, Farrar, Straus, 1967.

Contributor of short stories to various magazines, including *American Preface, Atlantic, Commentary, Harper's, New Threshold,* and *New Yorker.* Contributor of articles to *New York Times* and *New York Times Book Review.* Manuscripts, typescripts, and proofs of *The Natural, The Assistant, A New Life, The Fixer, Pictures of Fidelman,* and various stories from *The Magic Barrel* and *Idiots First* are in the collection of the Library of Congress.

SIDELIGHTS: Novelist and short story writer Bernard Malamud often drew on the New York East Side where his Russian-Jewish immigrant parents worked in their grocery store sixteen hours a day. Malamud attended high school and college during the height of the Depression. His own and his family's experience is clearly echoed in his fiction, much of which chronicles, as Mervyn Rothstein declares in the *New York Times,* "simple people struggling to make their lives better in a world of bad luck." His writings also are strongly influenced by classic nineteenth-century American writers, especially Nathaniel Hawthorne, but also Henry David Thoreau, Herman Melville, and Henry James. In addition his works reflect a post-Holocaust consciousness in addressing Jewish concerns and employing literary conventions drawn from earlier Jewish literature.

The first major period of Malamud's work extended from 1949 to 1961 when he was teaching composition at Oregon State College. Producing three novels and a collection of short stories during this period, he won several fiction prizes, including the National Book Award. Each of the first three novels feature a schlemiel figure who tries to restore a Wasteland to a Paradise against a Jewish background. The setting varies in the novels, but in the short fiction is most often the East Side of New York. "The Prison" portrays a small New York grocery store based on that of Malamud's parents, in which a young Italian, Tommy Castelli, is trapped. Similarly "The Cost of Living"—a predecessor of *The Assistant*—and "The Bill" both present the grocery store as a sort of prison. As Leslie and Joyce Field observe in *Bernard Malamud: A Collection of Critical Essays,* "In Malamud's fictional world, there is always a prison," and in a 1973 interview with the Fields, Malamud said: "Necessity is the primary prison, though the bars are not visible to all." Beneath most Malamudian surfaces lie similar moral and allegorical meanings.

Malamud's first novel, *The Natural,* is, as Earl R. Wasserman declares in *Bernard Malamud and the Critics,* "the necessary reference text for a reading of his subsequent fiction." The work is a mythic novel, based on the Arthurian legends, in which the Parsifal figure, Roy (King) Hobbs, restores fertility to the Fisher King, Pop Fisher, the manager of a baseball team called The Knights. Pitcher Roy appears as an Arthurian Knight modeled in part on Babe Ruth, but his character also probably is drawn from Chretien de Troye's medieval tale, *Lancelot of the Cart,* featuring a Lancelot who is most often unhorsed and frequently humiliated. As Peter L. Hays has said in *The Fiction of Bernard Malamud,* "Like Lancelot, Malamud's heroes are cut to ribbons in their quests for love and fortune."

The novel's title is baseball slang for a player with natural talent, but it can also mean, as it did in the Middle Ages, an innocent fool. As Philip Roth has said in *Reading Myself and Others,* this is "not baseball as it is played in Yankee Stadium, but a wild, wacky game." Roy thinks of himself as "Sir Percy lancing Sir Maldemer, or the first son (with a rock in his paw) ranged against the primitive papa." Even more Freudian is Roy's lance-like bat, Wonderboy, which droops when its phallic hero goes into a slump and finally splits at the novel's conclusion.

In an echo of the Black Sox scandal of 1919, Roy is bribed to throw the pennant game by evil-eyed Gus Sands, whose Pot of Fire nightclub and chorus girls wielding pitchforks suggest hell itself. Though there are few obvious Jewish traces in *The Natural,* the prank Roy plays on Gus is a retelling of a Yiddish prank-ster tale, with the challenge by the prankster, the foil or victim's reaction, and the retort or prank—here Roy's pulling silver dol-lars out of Gus's ears and nose. Yet Roy's success is only tempo-rary. As Glenn Meeter notes in *Bernard Malamud and Philip Roth: A Critical Essay,* "From the grail legend also we know that Roy will fail; for the true grail seeker must understand the super-natural character of his quest, and Roy does not." In the end Roy, defeated, throws his bribe money in the face of Judge Ban-ner, who is a dispenser of "dark wisdom, parables and aphorisms which punctuate his conversation, making him seem a cynical Poor Richard," as Iska Alter remarks in *The Good Man's Di-lemma: Social Criticism in the Fiction of Bernard Malamud.* This dramatic scene, and others in Malamud's work, accord with his statement in a 1973 interview: "My novels are close to plays."

Other influences are also clearly at work in Malamud's first novel. *The Natural* has significant references to birds and flowers and steady reminders of the passage of the seasons. The simplic-ity of this pastoral style at its best allows the presentation of com-plex ideas in a natural way. A second influence, as Malamud ac-knowledged, is film technique. For example, there are quick movie-like changes of scene, called jump cuts, when Roy and Memo Paris are tricked into sleeping with each other. In addi-tion, the portrayal of Roy has a Chaplinesque quality of humor to it. Though Malamud would never again write non-Jewish fic-tion, *The Natural* was a treasure house of reusable motifs and methods for all his subsequent work.

In 1954 Malamud published one of his greatest short stories, "The Magic Barrel," which Sanford Pinsker, in *Bernard Mala-mud: A Collection of Critical Essays,* calls "a nearly perfect blend of form and content." In this story the matchmaker Pinye Salz-man, using cards listing eligible women and drawn from his magic barrel, tricks student rabbi Leo Finkle into a love match with Salzman's daughter, Stella, a streetwalker. In *Judaism,* Marcia Booher Gealy describes the structural essence of such Hasidic-influenced stories: (1) the inward journey; (2) the older man tutoring the younger; (3) the triumph of love; (4) the reality of evil; and (5) transformation through the tale itself. This struc-ture merges with another influence, that of nineteenth-century American romanticism, for Malamud often joins the Hasidic and Hawthornian in his fables. As Renee Winegarten comments in *Bernard Malamud: A Collection of Critical Essays,* "His magic barrels and silver crowns, whatever their seal, firmly belong in the moral, allegorical realm of scarlet letters, white whales and golden bowls."

Concerning Salzman, as Irving Howe has said in *World of Our Fathers,* "The matchmaker, or *shadkhn,* is a stereotypic Yiddish figure: slightly comic, slightly sad, at the edge of destitution." Such confidence men reappear in Malamud's fiction, in "The Sil-ver Crown," for example. And Salzman shows Malamud's early perfection of a Jewish-American speech, which is neither pure Yiddish dialect nor mere literary chat, but an imaginative combi-nation of both. Kathryn Hellerstein observes in *The State of the Language* that Yiddish speakers in Malamud's works are "el-derly, static, or declining" and concludes that for Malamud, Yiddish figures are "a spectral presence of the constraining, de-limited, stultified past."

What many critics have referred to as Malamud's finest novel, *The Assistant,* appeared in 1957. As Ihab Hassan has said in *The Fiction of Bernard Malamud,* "*The Assistant,* I believe, will prove a classic not only of Jewish but of American literature." Frank Alpine, "the assistant," suggests St. Francis of Assisi, whose biography, *The Little Flowers,* is Alpine's favorite book and whose stigmata he at one point seems to emulate. Like Roy in *The Natural,* Frank is the Parsifal figure who must bring fer-tility, or at least new life, to the Fisher King, here the grocery store owner Morris Bober. Some critics have contended that Bober may parallel philosopher Martin Buber, whose I-THOU philosophy of human relations Bober seems, however instinc-tively, to share, though Malamud himself denied any use of Buber in this novel.

When he stands under a "No Trust" sign, Bober also recalls Mel-ville's novel, *The Confidence Man.* Giving food to a drunk woman who will never pay, Morris teaches Frank to have com-passion for others. Yet Frank cannot control his passion for Morris's daughter, Helen. Thus when Frank saves Helen from an attempted rape, he fails the trial of the Perilous Bed, rapes her just as she is about to admit her love for him, and loses her.

Frank and Morris represent a familiar motif in Malamud's works, that of the father-son pair, the schlemiel-schlimazel twins. Malamud likes these doublings and there are three other father/son pairs in the novel. A favorite definition of these types is that the schlemiel spills his teacup, and the schlimazel is the one he spills it on. Norman Leer, thinking perhaps of Russian novelist Feodor Dostoevsky's *Crime and Punishment,* speaks in *Mosaic: A Journal for the Comparative Study of Literature and Ideas* of "the notion of the divided self, and the attraction of two characters who mirror a part of each other, and are thereby drawn together as doubles."

Another recurrent feature of Malamudian narrative, the Holo-caust, is never far from the surface, though it appears almost al-ways in an oblique way. Morris, in despair over his luckless gro-cery store/prison, turns on the gas to commit suicide, a reminder of the gas chambers of the Holocaust. And here Malamud intro-duces from the world of fantasy a professional arsonist who is like a figure from hell—recalling the night club women and their pitchforks in *The Natural.* In *The Assistant,* at Morris's funeral, Frank halts the ceremony by falling into the open grave while trying to see the rose Helen had thrown into it. The characters in Malamud's fiction frequently dream, and in Frank's dream, St. Francis successfully gives Frank's rose to Helen. Rachel Ertel declares in *Le Roman juif americain: Une Ecriture minoritaire,* "By going constantly from the real to the supernatural, Bernard Malamud deadens, nullifies the disbelief of the reader and gives himself elbow room to narrate the fables, the parables that make up his novels and short stories."

In 1958, with the publication of his first volume of short stories, *The Magic Barrel,* Malamud received national recognition and in 1959 won the National Book Award for the collection. All the stories in the volume display Malamud's continuing debt to Hawthorne; as Jackson J. Benson says in *The Fiction of Bernard Malamud,* the two writers "possess the ability to combine, with great skill, reality and the dream, the natural and supernatural."

Thus there is a kinship between Malamud's "Idiots First," "The Silver Crown," and "The Magic Barrel" and Hawthorne's short stories "My Kinsman, Major Molineux," "Young Goodman Brown," and "The Birthmark." Moreover, "The First Seven Years"—featuring Feld, a Polish immigrant shoemaker who refuses to speak Yiddish and who wants his daughter Miriam to marry a rising young suitor, Max, rather than his middle-aged but devoted helper, Sobel—is reminiscent of Hawthorne's "Ethan Brand," with its warning about "hardness of the heart." However, "The First Seven Years" is Hawthorne plus Holocaust, for Sobel had barely escaped Hitler's incinerators.

In the years from 1949 to 1961 Malamud slowly became "one of the foremost writers of moral fiction in America," as Jeffrey Helterman comments in *Understanding Bernard Malamud.* Of his last work in this first period, Sheldon J. Hershinow remarks in *Bernard Malamud:* "*A New Life* is Malamud's first attempt at social satire, and much of the novel is given over to it." Its hero, marginal Jew Sy Levin, shows the complexity behind the names of practically all major characters in Malamud. In *City of Words: American Fiction 1950-1970,* Tony Tanner explains that the name Levin means the east, or light; it is also associated with lightning. Tanner writes: "I have it direct from Mr. Malamud that by a pun on 'leaven' he is suggesting what the marginal Jew may bring in attitude to the American scene." Levin, whose fictional career resembles that of Malamud, is a former high school teacher who joins the faculty at Cascadia University in Easchester, Oregon, a name that suggests a castle of ease. According to Mark Goldman, in a *Critique* review, "Early in the novel, Levin is the tenderfoot Easterner, the academic sad sack, or schlimazel of Yiddish literature, invoking nature like a tenement Rousseau." Levin, then is the schlemiel as lecturer, who teaches his first class with his fly open, then bumbles his way into an affair with a coed, Nadalee, a lady of the lake who has written an essay on nude bathing. As Sandy Cohen says in *Bernard Malamud and the Trial by Love,* "Malamud's favorite method of portraying a protagonist's struggle to overcome his vanity is to symbolize it in terms of the Grail myth. Thus Levin's journey to meet Nadalee takes on certain aspects of the grail quest." Indeed, Levin journeys "in his trusty Hudson, his lance at his side."

Later Levin makes love in the woods to Pauline Gilley; in an echo of English novelist D. H. Lawrence's *Lady Chatterley's Lover,* Pauline also has an impotent husband, Gerald Gilley, future chairman of the English Department. Against this pastoral background, complete with the passage of the seasons, Levin is also the American Adam: as Hershinow observes, "Immersed in the writings of Emerson, Thoreau, and Whitman, Levin believes wholeheartedly the metaphors about America as a New-World Garden of Eden. By going west he feels he can recapture his lost innocence and escape the past—become the New-World Adam."

This major love affair is also Hawthornian: as Paul Witherington notes in *Western American Literature,* "Levin's affair with Pauline matures in Hawthorne fashion to an inner drama of the ambiguities of paradise." In fact, Levin sees himself as "Arthur Dimmesdale Levin, locked in stocks on a platform in the town square, a red A stapled on his chest." From Levin's point of view, Pauline, whose love earned him his scarlet letter A, is also the tantalizing *shiksa,* the Gentile temptress of so many Jewish-American novels, not only those of Malamud but also of Saul Bellow and Philip Roth among others. As Frederick Cople Jaher points out in the *American Quarterly,* to Jewish men, such women seem to be "exotic insiders" and so represent "tickets of admission into American society."

At the conclusion of the novel, Gilley asks Levin why he wants to take on two adopted children and Gilley's apparently barren wife. Levin replies, "Because I can, you son of a bitch." And Levin, defeated in academe, but having impregnated the barren Pauline, whose flat breasts are beginning to swell, drives away with his new family, having agreed with Gilley never again to teach in a university. This ending, as so often in Malamud, is ambiguous, for Levin is no longer in romantic love with Pauline. Here is what *Critique* contributor Ruth B. Mandel calls "ironic affirmation"—"The affirmation itself is ironic in that the state of grace is unaccompanied by paradise."

After Malamud's move back east to Bennington College, his second period (roughly 1961-1970) began, and both his stories and his next two novels took a more cosmopolitan and international direction. In *Bernard Malamud,* Sidney Richman perceptively observes that the title story in *Idiots First* is "a morality [play] a la Everyman in which the sense of a real world (if only the sense of it) is utterly absorbed by a dream-landscape, a never-never-land New York City through which an elderly Jew named Mendel wanders in search of comfort and aid." Mendel is indeed a Jewish Everyman, who tries to dodge the Angel of Death (here named Ginzburg) to arrange for the future of his handicapped son, Isaac.

Another short story, "The Maid's Shoes," reveals the new subject matter and style. Professor Orlando Krantz, who plays the part of the comparatively wealthy American as Everyman, tries to give a small gift to his poor Italian maid, Rosa, but it is a gift without the understanding that the impoverished European needs: "But though they shared the same roof, and even the same hot water bottle and bathtub, they almost never shared speech." Here, failures of the heart, common to the fiction of the first period, are extended to complete failures of empathy. Furthermore, the story is no longer fantastic, as in Malamud's first period, but realistic. Of Rosa, Malamud writes: "She was forty-five and looked older. Her face was worn but her hair was black, and her eyes and lips were pretty. She had few good teeth. When she laughed she was embarrassed around the mouth." Finally, the story has a single consistent point of view instead of the omniscient point of view of the earlier stories. Yet since that omniscient narration contained Malamud's often compassionate comments that are a part of his first period manner, these newer stories have a bleaker cast to them.

Next to *The Assistant* in critical reputation comes *The Fixer,* winner of the Pulitzer Prize and the National Book Award in 1967. In a search for a suffering Everyman plot, Malamud had thought of several subjects—the trial of Alfred Dreyfus and the Sacco-Vanzetti case, among others—before deciding on a story he had heard from his father as a boy, that of the trial of Mendel Beiliss for ritual bloodletting and murder in 1913 in Russia. Through this story, Malamud also tries to answer the question of how the death camps in Germany had been possible. Hero Yakov Bok's last name suggests a scapegoat, and also the goat mentioned in the song chanted for the end of the Passover Seder as a symbol of Jewish survival. As Malamud said in an interview with Christopher Lehmann-Haupt in the *New York Times Book Review,* it was necessary "to mythologize—that is, to make metaphors and symbols of the major events and characters."

The novel itself covers two years, spring 1911 to winter 1913, during which Bok is imprisoned after being falsely accused of the ritual murder of a Gentile boy. Without legal counsel Bok suffers betrayal, gangrene, poison, and freezing cold, and finally turns inward to develop a sense of freedom. In prison this Everyman fixer learns through suffering to overcome, at least in part, his initial agnosticism, and his doubts of what is meant by the Chosen People. He rejects both suicide and a pardon, and accepts his Jewishness. Finally, in a dream encounter with Tsar Nicholas II, Bok shoots the Tsar. As John F. Desmond writes in *Renascence: Essays on Values in Literature,* "Yakov has come to understand that no man is apolitical, especially a Jew; consequently, if his chance came, as it does in the imaginary meeting with the Tsar, he would not hesitate to kill the ruler as a beginning step towards purging that society of its agents of repression and injustice, and thus strike a blow for freedom and humanity." Bok, at least in his dream, is no longer the passive suffering servant of Isaiah, portrayed in many of Malamud's first period fictions, but one who seeks revenge. Has Bok lost more important values? The dream setting leaves the ending ambiguous, but Malamud's real subject is not so much Bok himself, as those, like the Germans, other Europeans, and Americans during the Holocaust, who either participate in, or passively observe, the treatment of Everyman as victim. As the Fields remark, Malamud repeatedly tried to make clear, especially in this second period, that Jewish victims are Everyman as victim, for history, sooner or later, treats all men as Jews.

The final major work of this second period was *Pictures of Fidelman: An Exhibition.* As Leslie A. Field has written in *Bernard Malamud: A Collection of Critical Essays,* "Of all the Malamud characters, early and late, one must return to Arthur Fidelman as the Malamud *schlemiel par excellence.*" The Fidelman stories appeared both separately in magazines and in two story collections from 1958 to 1969, and they were not originally thought of as a unit. But the last three stories are tightly linked, and as Robert Ducharme asserts in *Art and Idea in the Novels of Bernard Malamud: Toward "The Fixer,"* Malamud deliberately saved the last story for the book because he didn't want to let readers know the ending. Three genres merge in *Pictures of Fidelman,* that of the *Kunstlerroman* or artist novel, the *Bildungsroman* or education novel, and the *Huckleberry Finn*-like picaresque novel, in which the main character wanders through a series of adventures. Fidelman (faith man) encounters Susskind (sweet child) in the first story or chapter, "Last Mohican." Susskind is a Jewish folktale type, a *chnorrer,* or as Goldman terms him, "a beggar with style," who wants the second of Fidelman's two suits. Rebuffed, Susskind steals the first chapter of Fidelman's book on Italian artist Giotto di Bondone. Hershinow suggests that "Susskind becomes for Fidelman a kind of dybbuk (demon) who inhabits his conscience, destroying his peace of mind." As Cohen remarks, "So Fidelman begins an active search for Susskind who begins to take on the roles of alter-ego, superego, and symbol for Fidelman's true heritage and past." Here again is the familiar Malamud motif of the journey that changes a life.

In pursuit, Fidelman visits a synagogue, a Jewish ghetto, and a graveyard that contains victims of the Holocaust. Both at the cemetery and in his crazy pursuit of Susskind, Schlemiel Fidelman recalls Frank Alpine in *The Assistant,* for Fidelman too is linked to St. Francis. In a dream Fidelman sees Susskind, who shows him a Giotto fresco in which St. Francis gives his clothing to a poor knight. As Sidney Richman affirms in *Bernard Malamud and the Critics,* "In the same fashion as Frankie Alpine, Fidelman must discover that the way to the self is paradoxically through another; and the answer is heralded by a sudden alteration of the pursuit." At the end of this artistic pilgrim's progress, "against his will, Fidelman learns what the ancient rabbis taught and what Susskind has always known: Jews—that is, human beings, *menschen,* in Malamud's terms—are responsible

for each other. That is the essence of being human," Michael Brown relates in *Judaism.*

Fidelman must learn in the next stories what makes a great artist. For example, in the fourth story, "A Pimp's Revenge," Fidelman returns his mistress, Esmeralda, to prostitution to pay for his constantly repainted masterwork, a portrait of her, first as Mother and Son, then as Brother and Sister, and finally as Prostitute and Procurer. "The truth is I am afraid to paint, like I might find out something about myself," Fidelman says. Esmeralda knows the secret: "If I have my choice, I'll take life. If there's not that there's no art." Barbara Lefcowitz justly argues in *Literature and Psychology,* "Where Malamud excels is in his subtle and nearly always comical juxtaposition of a neurotic character against a deeper and wider moral and historical context." Fidelman finally produces a masterpiece, but, second-rate artist that he is, can't let it alone, and mars it. The genius knows when to stop, but Everyman does not, and Esmeralda calls him a murderer.

In the final story, "Glass Blower of Venice," Fidelman tries to play artist once more, under the reluctant teaching of his homosexual lover Beppo, but at last gives up art for craftsmanship and returns to America. Fidelman, the craftsman, no longer the inadequate artist, has finally achieved the goals toward which Susskind—and later Esmeralda—pointed him. Samuel I. Bellman argues in *Critique* that "more than any other Malamudian character Fidelman is constantly growing, realizing himself, transforming his unsatisfactory old life into a more satisfactory new one." In *Bernard Malamud: A Collection of Critical Essays,* Sheldon N. Grebstein praises the juxtaposition of "the coarsely sexual and the sublimely aesthetic." Indeed, no other work of Malamud shows so much appetite for life; as Helterman has argued: "[Fidelman] also seeks, and occasionally participates in, a richness of passion not typical of Malamud's urban heroes." The epigraph for *Pictures of Fidelman* is from Yeats: "The intellect of man is forced to choose Perfection of the life or of the work." However, the new Fidelman chooses "both."

The Tenants inaugurated Malamud's third and final period. In the works of this period the heroic structuring of the first period is gone, as are the Wandering Jews and the Everyman motifs of the second. Beneath differing surface plots, though, a new structural likeness appears. Before 1971 Malamud's typical Jewish characters tend to move towards responsibility rather than towards achievement; but from 1971 on, they become extraordinary achievers, or *machers.*

In *The Tenants* Harry Lesser, a minor Jewish novelist, is writing a novel about being unable to finish a novel, in a kind of infinite regression. He keeps on living in the apartment building that landlord Levenspiel (leaven game) wants to tear down; then a squatter, black writer Willie Spearmint (Willie Shakespeare), moves into the building. Willie and Harry are the kind of doubled pair (drawn from Edgar Allan Poe and Dostoevsky) that Malamud is fond of, for Harry's writing is all form, and Willie's is all vitality. Harry takes over Irene, Willie's Jewish girl; Willie burns Harry's manuscript; Harry axes Willie's typewriter; and in a final burst of overachievement, Willie brains Harry and Harry castrates Willie. *The Tenants* "ends in a scream of language," reports Malcolm Bradbury in *Encounter.* Though the novel hints at two other possible endings—by fire, or by Harry's marriage to Irene—Levenspiel has the last word, which is *Rachmones,* or mercy.

Though *The Tenants* did little for Malamud's reputation, he continued to place stories in top American magazines. Mervyn Rothstein reported in the *New York Times* that Malamud said at the end of his life, "With me, it's story, story, story." In Malamud's next-to-last collection, *Rembrandt's Hat,* only one story, "The Silver Crown," is predominantly Jewish, in sharp contrast to his first collection, while other stories are more reminiscent of Chekhov. There is even a visit to the Chekhov Museum in "Man in the Drawer," a story that shows the fascination with achievement so dominant in Malamud's final period. Howard Harvitz, an intellectual tourist in Russia and a marginal Jew, has changed his name from Harris back to Harvitz. Hardly a creative writer himself, he is doing a piece on museums. A Russian writer, Levitansky—also a marginal Jew, but a determined achiever in spite of official opposition—intends to smuggle his stories out of Russia. Harvitz at first doesn't want this charge, but discovers that four of the stories show heroes not taking responsibility. After reading them, Harvitz timorously takes the stories out of Russia.

Dubin's Lives took Malamud over five years to write, twice as long as any previous novel. Ralph Tyler in the *New York Times Book Review* reports that Malamud said *Dubin's Lives* was "his attempt at bigness, at summing up what he . . . learned over the long haul." In the novel, the biographer Dubin is an isolated achiever, no mere recorder of biographical facts but a creative, even fictionalizing biographer: "One must transcend autobiographical detail by inventing it after it is remembered." Dubin is trying to write a biography of D. H. Lawrence, a writer who made passion his religion, yet was impotent. There had been a glancing counterpointing of Lawrence's career in *A New Life,* but here this motif is much enlarged; as David Levin observes in *Virginia Quarterly Review,* "The complexities of Dubin's subsequent adventures often run parallel to events in Lawrence's life."

In the kind of psychomachia, or inner struggle, which some critics see as the essence of American fiction, Dubin, as Helterman notes, "loses his memory, his sexual powers, his ability to work, even his ability to relate to his family. At first, the only compensation for these losses is a kind of high-grade nostalgia brought about by a process called reverie." These reveries lead Dubin to a liaison with young Fanny Bick, whose first name comes from English novelist Jane Austen's heroine in *Mansfield Park,* Fanny Price; Fanny Bick is an Austen heroine with glands. Like a number of heroines in Malamud's fiction, she is significantly associated with wildflowers, fruit, and bird flights. Chiara Briganti remarks in *Studies in American Jewish Literature* that "all the female characters in Malamud's fiction share a common shallowness and common values: they all respect marriage and family life, and, whatever their past, they all seek fulfillment through a permanent relationship with a man." But Fanny breaks this stereotypical pattern, for at the end of *Dubin's Lives* she ambitiously intends to become a lawyer.

Dubin's affair in Venice, where the youthful Fanny almost immediately betrays him with their gondolier, is that of the schlemiel lover seen before in Frank Alpine and Sy Levin. Barbara Quart, in *Studies in American Jewish Literature,* has seen a further problem: "While Malamud's central characters try to break out of their solitude, they appear to fear love and women as much as they long for them." But dominant among familiar motifs is the character of Dubin as the isolated overachiever, who moves his study from his country house into the barn to devote all possible energy and space to his biography. Dubin even begrudges time wasted thinking about Fanny, with whom he is genuinely in love.

Malamud's last finished novel, *God's Grace,* treats both the original Holocaust and a new, imagined Holocaust of the future. In

Immigrant-Survivors: Post-Holocaust Consciousness in Recent Jewish-American Literature, Dorothy Seldman Bilik has pointed out that the question of why God permitted the Holocaust has been an issue in Malamud's fiction for thirty years; indeed, for Malamud the Holocaust has been the ultimate mark of inhumanity, and *God's Grace* treats the Holocaust not only as man's inhumanity to man, but as God's inhumanity to man. The novel is a wild, at times brilliant, at times confusing description of a second Noah's Flood. Calvin Cohn, a paleologist and the son of a rabbi-cantor, had been doing underseas research when the Djanks and the Druzhkies (Yanks and Russians) launched an atomic Holocaust and destroyed every other human. Calvin recalls many Biblical and literary figures: Parsifal, Romeo, Prospero, Robinson Crusoe, Gulliver, and Ahab. His Eve and Juliet is Mary Madelyn, a chimpanzee. An albino ape appears (possibly an oblique reference to Moby Dick) with other apes as Yahoos from Jonathan Swift's *Gulliver's Travels,* and the chimpanzee Buz serves as Cohn's Isaac, Caliban, and man Friday. There is even an Arthurian spear used to harpoon the albino ape.

On Cohn's Island Calvin turns into an overachiever, and even an un-Job-like defier of God, in spite of God's pillars of fire, showers of lemons, and occasional warning rocks. The foundation of *God's Grace* is Biblical in part, but also characteristically American, for it is the story of the Americanized—and reversed—Fortunate Fall. The idea conveyed by the Fortunate Fall is that Adam and Eve, driven from Paradise by eating of the tree of Knowledge, in fact obtained benefits from their fall, notably free will and a consciousness of good and evil. Cohn has treated the chimpanzees as his inferiors; as a schlemiel lecturer he has imposed his admonitions and teachings on them, rather than encouraging them to learn for themselves. He has promised but never given Mary Madelyn the marriage she has wanted, and he has prevented the marriage or mating of Buz and Mary Madelyn, which could have been just as desirable for the future gene stock as Cohn's half-chimpanzee child Rebekah. In short, overachieving Calvin Cohn has eaten from the tree of hubris, or sinful pride, rather than knowledge.

This complex novel baffled its first reviewers; for example, Joseph Epstein wrote in *Commentary:* "Much of the humor in the novel is of the kind known as faintly amusing, but the chimp humor, on the scale of wit, is roughly three full rungs down from transvestite jokes." Part of the difficulty in the novel is that *God's Grace* does not fall into a clear genre category; in a 1982 *Christian Science Monitor* article, Victor Howes called it "somewhat east of sci-fi, somewhat west of allegory." However, like much of Malamud's work, *God's Grace* not only reflects the Jewish Old Testament but also partakes of an American colonial genre, the Jeremiad, or warning of future disaster.

Malamud's final, but unfinished work, "The Tribe," concerns the adventures of a Russian Jewish peddlar, Yozip, among the western Indians. As Nan Robertson recounts in the *New York Times,* the schlemiel hero Yozip becomes a marshal, is kidnapped by a tribe of Indians, and has a dialogue with an Indian chief about obtaining his freedom.

Malamud gave few interviews, but those he did grant provided the best commentary on his work, as when he told Michiko Kakutani in the *New York Times:* "People say I write so much about misery, but you write about what you write best. As you are grooved, so you are grieved. And the grieving is that no matter how much happiness or success you collect, you cannot obliterate your early experience." Yet perhaps Malamud's contribution is clearest in his greatest invention, his Jewish-American dialect, comic even at the height of tragedy. For example, Calvin

Cohn, sacrificed by the chimpanzee Buz in a wild inversion of the story of Abraham and Isaac, reflects that God after all has let him live out his life; Cohn then asks himself—forgetting his educated speech and reverting to the Yiddish rhythms of his youth—"Maybe tomorrow the world to come?" In such comic-serious questioning, Malamud captures the voice of the past and gives it relevance to the present.

MEDIA ADAPTATIONS: The Fixer was filmed by John Frankenheimer for Metro-Goldwyn-Mayer and released in 1969. "The Angel Levine" starred Zero Mostel and Harry Belafonte and was adapted by William Gunn for United Artists in 1970. *A New Life* and *The Assistant* were both optioned in the early 1970s, and producer Sidney Glazier planned a filmscript based on "Black Is My Favorite Color." "The Natural," starring Robert Redford as Roy Hobbs, Robert Duvall as Max Mercy, Glenn Close as Iris Gaines, and Kim Basinger as Memo Paris, was directed by Barry Levinson for Tri-Star Pictures and released in 1984.

AVOCATIONAL INTERESTS: Reading, travel, music, walking.

BIOGRAPHICAL/CRITICAL SOURCES:

BOOKS

Alter, Iska, *The Good Man's Dilemma: Social Criticism in the Fiction of Bernard Malamud,* AMS Press, 1981.

Astro, Richard, and Jackson J. Benson, editors, *The Fiction of Bernard Malamud,* Oregon State University Press, 1977.

Avery, Evelyn G., *Rebels and Victims: The Fiction of Richard Wright and Bernard Malamud,* Kennikat, 1979.

Baumbach, Jonathan, *The Landscape of Nightmare: Studies in the Contemporary American Novel,* New York University Press, 1965.

Bilik, Dorothy Seldman, *Immigrant-Survivors: Post-Holocaust Consciousness in Recent Jewish-American Literature,* Wesleyan University Press, 1981.

Bloom, Harold, *Bernard Malamud,* Chelsea House, 1986.

Cohen, Sandy, *Bernard Malamud and the Trial by Love,* Rodopi (Amsterdam), 1974.

Concise Dictionary of American Literary Biography: The New Consciousness, 1941-1968, Gale, 1987.

Contemporary Authors Bibliographical Series, Volume 1: *American Novelists,* Gale, 1986.

Contemporary Literary Criticism, Gale, Volume 1, 1973, Volume 2, 1974, Volume 3, 1975, Volume 5, 1976, Volume 8, 1978, Volume 9, 1978, Volume 11, 1979, Volume 18, 1981, Volume 27, 1984, Volume 44, 1987.

Dictionary of Literary Biography, Gale, Volume 2: *American Novelists since World War II,* 1978, Volume 28: *Twentieth-Century American-Jewish Fiction Writers,* 1984.

Dictionary of Literary Biography Yearbook, Gale, *1980,* 1981, *1986,* 1987.

Ducharme, Robert, *Art and Idea in the Novels of Bernard Malamud: Toward "The Fixer,"* Mouton, 1974.

Ertel, Rachel, *Le Roman juif americain: Une Ecriture minoritaire,* Payot (Paris), 1980.

Fiedler, Leslie, *Love and Death in the American Novel,* Criterion, 1960.

Field, Leslie A., and Joyce W. Field, editors, *Bernard Malamud and the Critics,* New York University Press, 1970.

Field, Leslie A., and Joyce W. Field, editors, *Bernard Malamud: A Collection of Critical Essays,* Prentice-Hall, 1975.

Helterman, Jeffrey, *Understanding Bernard Malamud,* University of South Carolina Press, 1985.

Hershinow, Sheldon J., *Bernard Malamud,* Ungar, 1980.

Howe, Irving, *World of Our Fathers,* Harcourt, 1976.

Kosofsky, Rita Nathalie, *Bernard Malamud: An Annotated Checklist,* Kent State University Press, 1969.

Malamud, Bernard, *The Natural,* Harcourt, 1952, reprinted, Avon, 1980.

Malamud, Bernard, *A New Life,* Farrar, Straus, 1961, reprinted, 1988.

Malamud, Bernard, *Idiots First,* Farrar, Straus, 1963.

Malamud, Bernard, *Pictures of Fidelman: An Exhibition,* Farrar, Straus, 1969, reprinted, New American Library, 1985.

Malamud, Bernard, *Dubin's Lives,* Farrar, Straus, 1979.

Malamud, Bernard, *God's Grace,* Farrar, Straus, 1982.

Meeter, Glen, *Bernard Malamud and Philip Roth: A Critical Essay,* Eerdmans, 1968.

Michaels, Leonard, and Christopher Ricks, editors, *The State of the Language,* University of California Press, 1980.

Radical Innocence: Studies in the Contemporary American Novel, Princeton University Press, 1961.

Richman, Sidney, *Bernard Malamud,* Twayne, 1966.

Roth, Philip, *Reading Myself and Others,* Farrar, Straus, 1975.

The Schlemiel as Metaphor: Studies in the Yiddish and American Jewish Novel, Southern Illinois University Press, 1971.

Tanner, Tony, *City of Words: American Fiction 1950-1970,* Harper, 1971.

PERIODICALS

American Quarterly, Volume 35, number 5, 1983.

Centennial Review, Volume 9, 1965, Volume 13, 1969.

Chicago Tribune Book World, February 11, 1979, September 5, 1982, October 30, 1983.

Christian Science Monitor, September 10, 1982.

Commentary, October, 1982.

Commonweal, October 28, 1966.

Critique, winter, 1964/65.

Detroit News, December 25, 1983.

Encounter, Volume 45, number 1, 1975.

Judaism, winter, 1979, fall, 1980.

Linguistics in Literature, fall, 1977 (special Malamud number).

Literature and Psychology, Volume 20, number 3, 1970.

Los Angeles Times Book Review, September 12, 1982, December 25, 1983, November 26, 1989.

Mosaic: A Journal for the Comparative Study of Literature and Ideas, spring, 1971.

New Leader, May 26, 1969.

New Republic, September 20, 1982, September 27, 1982.

Newsweek, September 6, 1982, October 17, 1983.

New Yorker, November 8, 1982.

New York Review of Books, September 30, 1973.

New York Times, May 3, 1969, February 2, 1979, July 15, 1980, August 23, 1982, October 11, 1983, February 23, 1985, July 15, 1985, November 14, 1989.

New York Times Book Review, September 4, 1964, May 4, 1969, October 3, 1971, February 18, 1979, August 29, 1982, August 28, 1983, October 16, 1983, April 20, 1986, November 19, 1989.

Paris Review, spring, 1975.

Partisan Review, winter, 1962, summer, 1964.

Renascence: Essays on Values in Literature, winter, 1975.

Saturday Review, May 10, 1969.

Studies in American Jewish Literature, spring, 1978 (special Malamud number), number 3, 1983.

Time, May 9, 1969, September 13, 1982, October 17, 1983.

Times Literary Supplement, October 16, 1969, October 29, 1982, February 24, 1984, February 9, 1990.

Tribune Books (Chicago), November 26, 1989.

Virginia Quarterly Review, winter, 1980.
Washington Post, August 27, 1982.
Washington Post Book World, February 25, 1979, August 29, 1982, October 16, 1983, November 26, 1989.
Western American Literature, August, 1975.
Western Humanities Review, winter, 1968, winter, 1970.
Writer's Digest, July, 1972.

OBITUARIES:

PERIODICALS

Chicago Tribune, March 20, 1986.
Detroit News, March 23, 1986.
Los Angeles Times, March 19, 1986.
New Republic, May 12, 1986.
Newsweek, March 31, 1986.
New York Times, March 20, 1986.
Times (London), March 20, 1986.
Washington Post, March 20, 1986.

*   *   *

MALCOLM, Dan
See SILVERBERG, Robert

*   *   *

MALCOLM X
See LITTLE, Malcolm

*   *   *

MALLOWAN, Agatha Christie
See CHRISTIE, Agatha (Mary Clarissa)

*   *   *

MALONE, Louis
See MacNEICE, (Frederick) Louis

*   *   *

MALRAUX, (Georges-)Andre   1901-1976

PERSONAL: Born November 3, 1901, in Paris, France; died of a pulmonary embolism, November 23, 1976; son of Fernand-Georges (a businessman, from a seafaring family) and Berthe (Lanny) Malraux; married Clara Goldschmidt (an author), October 26, 1921 (divorced, 1930s); married Josette Clotis (a writer; killed in a rail accident during World War II); married Marie-Madeleine Lioux (a concert pianist; widow of his half-brother, Roland), March, 1948; children: (first marriage) Florence; (second marriage) Gautier and Vincent (both killed in an automobile accident, 1961); Alain (stepson). *Education:* Attended Lycee Condorcet, and Ecole des Langues Orientales, where he developed his interest in archaeology and oriental art.

ADDRESSES: Home—2, rue d'Estienne d'Orves, Verrieres-le-Buisson 91370, France.

CAREER: After leaving school worked for the bookseller Rene-Louis Doyon, and in the art department of the publisher Kra in Paris, France; in 1923, left, with wife, Clara Goldschmidt Malraux, for Indochina on an archaeological expedition sponsored by the French Government; was imprisoned on a charge of taking ancient sculptures, which were regarded as official property by the colonial regime; his wife returned to France in 1924 to or-

ganize a petition of writers (including Andre Gide), which led to his release; returned to France, but set off again for Indochina two months later; collaborated in Saigon with the nationalist "Jeune-Annam" movement on the newspaper *L'Indochine* (later became *L'Indochine enchainee*); joined the Kuomintang in Indochina and Canton; returned to France in 1927; in 1928, became art editor at the publishing firm Gallimard, for whom he continued to work—in between numerous archaeological expeditions, and other activities—both as literary editor and director of the series, "La Galerie de la Pleiade." Devoted the Prix Goncourt money to a trip in search of the lost city of the Queen of Sheba in Southern Arabia; spoke at the 1934 Writers' Congress in Moscow (where he was listed as a "Marxist humanist"), and at the June, 1935 Congress of Writers in Defence of Culture, Paris; was involved in the activities of anti-Fascist organizations, including the "Comite mondial antifasciste" and "La Ligue internationale contre l'anti-semitisme." Became Minister of Information in de Gaulle's government, November, 1945-46; was Minister of Culture in the de Gaulle cabinet, 1958-59. *Wartime activity:* In 1936, organized the foreign division of the Republican air-force in the Spanish Civil War; at the outbreak of World War II he joined the French Army; was wounded, imprisoned, then escaped; after further wounds and imprisonment, organized the Resistance in southwest France, heading the Alsace-Lorraine brigade in 1945, in which he was known as "Colonel Berger."

AWARDS, HONORS: Military: Officier de la Legion d'honneur, Compagnon de la Liberation, Medaille de la Resistance, Croix de guerre (1939-45), Distinguished Service Order. Civilian: Prix Goncourt, 1933, for *La Condition humaine;* Prix Louis-Delluc, 1945, for the film "L'Espoir"; Prix Nehru, 1974, for promoting international understanding; Alfonso Reyes Prize from the government of Mexico, 1976; honorary degrees from University of Sao Paulo, University of Benares, Oxford University, Jyvaeskylaen University (Finland), and Rajshahi University (Bangladesh).

WRITINGS:

FICTION

Lunes en papier (fantastic tale; also see below), Simon, 1921.
La Tentation de l'Occident (philosophical tale; also see below), Grasset, 1926, reprinted, Les Bibliophiles Comtois, 1962, translation and introduction by Robert Hollander published as *The Temptation of the West,* Vintage Books, 1961.
Les Conquerants (novel; also see below), Grasset, 1928, revised definitive edition (contains a "postface" by Malraux consisting of his March 5, 1948 speech in defense of Gaullism), 1949, reprinted, Gallimard, 1967, translation by Winifred Stephen Whale published as *The Conquerors,* Harcourt, 1929, revised edition (with "postface" translated by Jacques Le Clerq), Beacon Press, 1956.
Royaume farfelu (fantastic tale; also see below), Gallimard, 1928.
La Voie royale (novel; also see below), Grasset, 1930, reprinted, 1968, translation by Stuart Gilbert published as *The Royal Way,* Smith & Haus, 1935.
La Condition humaine (novel; also see below), Gallimard, 1933, revised edition, 1946, translation by Haakon M. Chevalier published as *Man's Fate,* Smith & Haus, 1934, reprinted, Random House, 1968, translation by Alistair Macdonald published as *Storm in Shanghai,* Methuen, 1934, published as *Man's Estate,* 1948, reprinted, Hamish Hamilton, 1968.
Le Temps du mepris (novel), Gallimard, 1935, translation by Chevalier, with a foreword by Waldo Frank, published as

Days of Wrath, Random House, 1936 (published in England as *Days of Contempt,* Gollancz, 1936).

L'Espoir (novel; also see below), Gallimard, 1937, reprinted, 1974, translation by Gilbert and Macdonald published as *Man's Hope,* Random House, 1938, reprinted, 1968 (published in England as *Days of Hope,* Routledge & Kegan Paul, 1938).

La Lutte avec l'ange (philosophical novel; part of a larger project, the rest of which was destroyed by the Gestapo), Editions du Haut Pays, 1943, published as *Les Noyers de l'Altenburg,* Gallimard, 1948, translation by A. W. Fielding published as *The Walnut Trees of Altenburg,* John Lehmann, 1952.

ART CRITICISM

Oeuvres gothico-bouddhiques du Pamir, Gallimard, 1930.

Esquisse d'une psychologie du cinema, Gallimard, 1946.

La Psychologie de l'art, Skira, Volume I: *Le Musee imaginaire,* 1947, Volume II: *La Creation artisque,* 1948, Volume III: *La Monnaie de l'absolu,* 1949, translation by Stuart Gilbert published as *The Psychology of Art,* Pantheon, Volume I: *Museum without Walls,* 1949, Volume II: *The Creative Act,* 1950, Volume III: *The Twilight of the Absolute,* 1951, revised and enlarged French edition published as *Les Voix du silence* (contains an additional section, "Les Metamorphoses d'Apollon"), Galerie de la Pleiade, Gallimard, 1951, translation by Gilbert published as *The Voices of Silence,* Doubleday, 1953, Volume I: *Museum without Walls,* Volume II: *The Metamorphoses of Apollo,* Volume III: *The Creative Process,* Volume IV: *The Aftermath of the Absolute.*

Saturne: Essai sur Goya, Skira, 1949, translation by C. W. Chilton published as *Saturn: An Essay on Goya,* Phaidon, 1957.

Tout Vermaer de Delft, Gallimard, c. 1950.

Le Musee imaginaire de la sculpture mondiale, Volume I, Gallimard, 1952, Volume II published as *Des bas-relief's aux grottes sacree,* Gallimard, 1954, Volume III published as *Le Monde chretien,* 1954.

Le Metamorphose des dieux (philosophy and religion in art), Gallimard, Volume I: *Le Surnaturel,* 1957, translation by Gilbert published as *The Metamorphosis of the Gods,* Doubleday, 1960, Volume II: *L'Ireel,* 1974, Volume III: *L'Intemporel,* 1976.

Le Triangle noir, Gallimard, 1970.

La Tete d'obsidienne, Gallimard, 1974, translation published as *Picasso's Mask,* Holt, 1976.

POLITICAL WRITINGS AND OFFICIAL SPEECHES

(In dialogue with James Burnham) *The Case for De Gaulle,* Random House, 1949.

Brasilia, la capitale de l'espoir (French text followed by Spanish and English translations), Presidencia de Republicia, Servico de Documentacao, 1959.

Discours, 1958-1965, Action Etudiante Gaullistes, 1966.

Oraisons funebres, Gallimard, 1970.

Paroles et ecrits politiques, 1947-1972, Plon, 1973.

AUTHOR OF PREFACE

D. H. Lawrence, *L'Amant de Lady Chatterley,* translation by Roger Cornaz, Gallimard, 1932, preface published as "Preface to Lady Chatterley's Lover," in *Yale French Studies,* Number 1, 1953.

William Faulkner, *Sanctuaire,* translation by R. M. Raimbault and Henri Delgove, Gallimard, 1933, preface published as "Preface to Faulkner's Sanctuary," in *Yale French Studies,* Number 10, 1952.

Andree Viollis, *Indochine S.O.S.,* Gallimard, 1935.

Goya: Dessins du Musee du Prado, Skira, 1947.

Manes Sperber, *Q'une larme dans l'ocean,* translation by author and Blanche Gidon, Calmann-Levy, 1952.

Tout l'oeuvre peint de Leonard de Vinci, Gallimard, 1952.

General P. E. Jacquot, *Essai de strategie occidentale,* Gallimard, 1953.

Albert Olivier, *Saint-Just et la force des choses,* Gallimard, 1954.

Izis Bidermanas, *Israel,* Clairefontaine, 1955.

Andre Parrot, *Sumer,* Gallimard, 1960.

Pierre Bockel, *L'Enfant du rire,* Grasset, 1973.

Maria Van Ryssellberghe, *Les Cahiers de la petite dame, 1918-1929,* Gallimard, 1973.

Georges Bernanos, *Journal d'un cure de campagne,* Plon, 1974.

Correspondance Romain Rolland-Jean Guehenno, Albin Michel, 1975.

AUTOBIOGRAPHY

Le Miroir des limbes, Gallimard, Volume I: *Antimemoires,* 1967, revised definitive edition, Schoenhof, 1976, Volume II: *La Corde et le souris,* 1976, translation of first volume by Terrence Kilmartin published as *Anti-memoirs,* Holt, 1968.

OMNIBUS VOLUMES

Oeuvres completes, Skira, 1945.

Scenes choisies, Gallimard, 1946.

Romans (contains *Les Conquerants, La Condition humaine,* and *L'Espoir*), Gallimard, 1947, reprinted, 1969.

Lectures choisies, edited by Anne Prioleau Jones, Macmillan, 1965.

Oeuvres (contains *Lunes en papier, Tentation de l'Occident, Les Conquerants, Royaume farfelu, La Voie royale, La Condition humaine, L'Espoir,* and *Antimemoires*) four volumes, Gallimard, 1970.

OTHER

Les Chenes qu'on abat . . . , Gallimard, 1970, translation by Irene Clephane published as *Fallen Oaks: Conversation with De Gaulle,* Hamish Hamilton, 1972, published as *Felled Oaks: Conversation with De Gaulle,* revised by Linda Asher, Holt, 1972.

Roi, je t'attends a Babylone, Skira, 1973.

Lazare, Gallimard, 1974, translation by T. Kilmartin published as *Lazarus,* Grove, 1978.

Hotes de passage, Gallimard, 1975.

Et sur la terre . . . , Illustrations by Marc Chagall, Maeght, 1977.

L'Homme precaire et la litterature (philosophical essay), Gallimard, 1977.

De Gaulle par Malraux, Le Club du Livre, 1979.

Also author of screenplay "Sierra de Teruel," 1938; author of "postface" titled "Neocritique," published in Martine de Courcel, *Malraux, etre et dire,* Plon, 1976. Contributor to *Action, L'Intransigeant, Commune, Les Conferences de l'Unesco, Liberte de l'esprit, Carrefour, Europe, Nouvelle Revue Francaise, L'Express,* and many other journals and publications. General editor of *The Arts of Mankind,* beginning in 1960.

SIDELIGHTS: W. M. Frohock wrote, "For Americans, Malraux has the special interest of being what America rarely produces, an artist who is also an intellectual." All of Malraux's major novels were strongly biographical—though not personal. Gaetan Picon suggested that "the events which provided the material for the work are directly lived through, but remain external. The encounter between Malraux and History becomes the history of Malraux himself." His experience in Indochina, wrote the *Times Saturday Review*, "turned Malraux from a dilettante into a revolutionary." Donald Schier continued: "*L'Espoir* makes it plain that by 1938 Malraux was finding it impossible to identify himself with the Communist Party, although he continued to share, rather suspiciously, in its struggle against Fascism. (*In Les Conquerants*, the forcing of other people into paths they would not otherwise have taken not by party discipline but by individual leadership) is the real justification for the hero's existence. Malraux sees himself as a hero." With respect to General de Gaulle, the *Times Saturday Review* commented how "Malraux has come to regard him not as a politician but as a 'mythe vivant.' "

In an interview with Roger Stephane, Malraux noted: "I couldn't say that man is what he does, because, to the question, what is man? would apply that we are the first civilization which says it doesn't know. We are the only civilization in which man has no purpose. Not that he cannot have one, but that we are still trying to find out what it is. All other civilizations have rested in the end on religion." In an age without faith, he accorded a supreme role to the artist: "Art lives because its function is to let men escape from their human condition, not by means of evasion, but through a possession. All art is a way of possessing destiny."

Malraux was described in the *Times Saturday Review* as "a slight, intense hollow-eyed man, a chain-smoker who looks like a character from a Malraux novel." Janet Flanner wrote: "No other French writer is so rapid, compulsive, fascinating and rewarding a monologist. As he walks, words and ideas rush from his brain and out of his mouth in extemporaneous creation, as though they were long quotations from books he had not yet written." Flanner continued: "He could work at his publishing job by day, and at his writing more than half the night at home. It was in these circumstances that he wrote *La Condition humaine*."

It is well known that Malraux was not prepared to discuss his personal life with the public. Flanner reported that, "if a question of a biographical nature is inadvertently asked in an interview, Malraux will reply by saying 'Vie Privee' and nothing more. In his own view, which is aloof, his *vie publique* lies in his books." His autobiography revealed the same attitude towards what he called "confessions": "What interests me in a man is the human condition . . . and some features which express less an individual character, than a particular relationship with the world. . . . I call this book *Antimemoires* because it replies to questions that memoirs do not put, and does not answer those they do." David Caute noted: "These *Antimemoires* break away entirely from the traditional biography or memoir form. Not only is orthodox chronology rejected: there is in addition no attempt to provide a factually coherent outline of the author's life." Schier added: "The various sections of the *Antimemoires* bear the titles of his books but he does not discuss them. Rather the *Antimemoires* provide variations on the novelistic themes: individual action versus party discipline, terrorism as a political technique, art as a surrogate for religion, *fraternite verile*." Malraux told Stephane: "My problem is this: what answer can life give to the basic question posed by death? This question was always subordinate in great religious cultures which preceded our culture. My intention is to answer it in a fundamental way. This has been made easier for me because my memoirs don't follow a chronological sequence. . . . Up to a point, we can say that memoirs are essentially novels about the education of the author's personality. But I am concerned with something different, and I have taken another title because of that."

As de Gaulle's minister of culture, Malraux was probably best known for organizing the cleaning of Paris buildings, creating what was alluded to in the *Times Saturday Review* as "Paris blanchi." In the same article, it was reported that *Antimemoires* sold a quarter of a million copies in the first two months of publication.

MEDIA ADAPTATIONS: There are a number of recordings of Malraux's work, including a reading by Malraux himself from *Les Voix du silence*, in the series "Auteurs du 20e Siecle," Philips. A film scenario of *L'Espoir* was made in Barcelona in 1938.

BIOGRAPHICAL/CRITICAL SOURCES:

BOOKS

Blend, Charles D., *Andre Malraux: Tragic Humanist*, Ohio State University Press, 1963.
Boak, Denis, *Andre Malraux*, Oxford University Press, 1968.
Contemporary Literary Criticism, Gale, Volume 1, 1973, Volume 4, 1975, Volume 9, 1978, Volume 13, 1980, Volume 15, 1980.
Cruickshank, John, editor, *The Novelist as Philosopher*, Oxford University Press, 1962.
Dictionary of Literary Biography, Volume 72: *French Novelists, 1930-1960*, Gale, 1988.
Flanner, Janet, *Men and Monuments*, Harper, 1957.
Frohock, W. M., *Andre Malraux and the Tragic Imagination*, Stanford University Press, 1952, revised edition, with new preface, 1967.
Greshoff, C. J., *An Introduction to the Novels of Andre Malraux*, Balkema, 1976.
Hartman, Geoffrey, *Andre Malraux*, Hillary, 1960.
Kline, T. J., *Andre Malraux and the Metamorphosis of Death*, Columbia University Press, 1973.
Lacouture, Jean, *Andre Malraux*, Editions du Seuil, 1973, translation by Alan Sheridan published under same title, Pantheon, 1975.
Langlois, Walter G., *The Indochina Adventure*, Praeger, 1966.
Lewis, R. W. B., editor, *Malraux: A Collection of Critical Essays*, Prentice-Hall, 1964.
Malraux, Andre, *Antimemoires*, Gallimard, 1967.
Malraux, Clara, *Le Bruit de nos pas*, Grasset, Volume I: *Apprendre a vivre*, 1963, Volume II: *Nos vingt ans*, 1966, translation by Patrick O'Brian published in a single volume as *Memoirs*, Bodley Head, 1967.
Payne, P. S. R., *A Portrait of Andre Malraux*, Prentice-Hall, 1970.
Picon, Gaetan, *Malraux par lui-meme* (with annotations by Malraux), Editions du Seuil, 1953.
Suares, Guy, *Malraux, Past, Present, Future*, translated by Derek Coltman, Little, Brown, 1974.

PERIODICALS

Burlington Magazine, December, 1954.
Carleton Miscellany, winter, 1969.
Encounter, Volume XXX, number 1, 1967.
Esprit (nearly entire issue devoted to Malraux), October, 1948.
Le Nouvel Observateur September 1, 1967.
Listener, January 25, 1968, October 31, 1968.
Melanges-Malraux-Miscellany, 1969—.
Modern Language Quarterly, June, 1953.
Newsweek, December 6, 1976.
New York Times, November 25, 1976.
Observer Weekend Review, April 5, 1964.
Times Literary Supplement, November 26, 1964.
Times Saturday Review, November 18, 1967.

University of Kansas City Review, Volume XXVIII, number 1, 1961.

*   *   *

MAMET, David (Alan) 1947-

PERSONAL: Surname is pronounced "*Mam*-it"; born November 30, 1947, in Chicago, Ill.; son of Bernard (an attorney) and Lenore (a teacher; maiden name, Silver) Mamet; married Lindsay Crouse (an actress), December 21, 1977. *Education:* Attended Neighborhood Playhouse School of the Theater, 1968-69; Goddard College, B.A., 1969. *Politics:* "The last refuge of the unimaginative." *Religion:* "The second-to-last."

ADDRESSES: Office—St. Nicholas Theater Company, 2851 North Halstead St., Chicago, Ill. 60657. *Agent*—Rosenstone/Wender, East 48th St., New York, N.Y. 10017.

CAREER: Playwright, director, and screenwriter. St. Nicholas Theater Company, Chicago, Ill., founder, 1973, artistic director, 1973-76, member of board of directors, beginning in 1973; Goodman Theater, Chicago, associate artistic director, 1978-79. Special lecturer in drama, Marlboro College, 1970; artist in residence in drama, Goddard College, 1971-73; faculty member, Illinois Arts Council, 1974; visiting lecturer in drama, University of Chicago, 1975-76 and 1979; teaching fellow, Yale University, 1976-77; guest lecturer, New York University, 1981; associate professor of film, Columbia University, 1988. Has also worked at a canning plant, a truck factory, a real estate agency, and as a window washer, office cleaner, and taxi driver.

MEMBER: Dramatists Guild, Writers Guild of America, Actors Equity Association, P.E.N., United Steelworkers of America, Randolph A. Hollister Association.

AWARDS, HONORS: Joseph Jefferson Award, 1975, for "Sexual Perversity in Chicago," and 1976, for "American Buffalo"; "Obie" Award from *Village Voice* for best new playwright, 1976, for "Sexual Perversity in Chicago" and "American Buffalo," and for best American play, 1983, for "Edmond"; Children's Theater grant, New York State Council on the Arts, 1976; Rockefeller grant, 1976; Columbia Broadcasting System fellowship in creative writing, 1976; New York Drama Critics' Circle Award for best American play, 1977, for "American Buffalo," and 1984, for "Glengarry Glen Ross"; Outer Critics Circle award for contributions to the American theater, 1978; Academy Award ("Oscar") nomination for best adapted screenplay, Academy of Motion Picture Arts and Sciences, 1983, for "The Verdict"; Pulitzer Prize in drama, 1984, for "Glengarry Glen Ross"; Antoinette Perry Award ("Tony") nominations, American Theater Wing, for best play, for "Glengarry Glen Ross," and for reproduction of a play, for "American Buffalo," both 1984, and for best play, 1988, for "Speed-the-Plow"; American Academy and Institute of Arts and Letters Award for Literature, 1986.

WRITINGS:

Warm and Cold (juvenile), illustrations by Donald Sultan, Solo Press, 1984.
(With wife, Lindsay Crouse) *The Owl,* Kipling Press, 1987.
Writing in Restaurants (essays, speeches, and articles), Penguin, 1987.
Some Freaks (essays), Viking, 1989.

PLAYS; PUBLISHED BY GROVE EXCEPT AS INDICATED

American Buffalo (two-act; first produced in Chicago at Goodman Theater Stage Two, October 23, 1975; produced Off-

Off-Broadway at St. Clements, January 23, 1976; produced on Broadway at Ethel Barrymore Theater, February 16, 1977), 1977.
Sexual Perversity in Chicago [and] *Duck Variations* ("Duck Variations" [one-act], first produced in Plainfield, Vt., at Goddard College, 1972; produced Off-Off-Broadway at St. Clements, May 27, 1975; "Sexual Perversity in Chicago" [one-act; also see below], first produced in Chicago by Organic Theater Company, 1974; produced Off-Off-Broadway at St. Clements, September 29, 1975; both produced Off-Broadway at Cherry Lane Theater, June 6, 1976), 1978.
A Life in the Theatre (one-act; first produced in Chicago at Goodman Theater Stage Two, February 3, 1977; produced Off-Broadway at Theater de Lys, October 20, 1977), 1978.
The Water Engine: An American Fable [and] *Mr. Happiness* ("The Water Engine" [two-act], first produced as a radio play on the program "Earplay" by Minnesota Public Radio, 1977; stage adaptation produced in Chicago by St. Nicholas Theater Company, May 1, 1977; produced Off-Broadway at New York Shakespeare Festival Public Theater, December 20, 1977; "Mr. Happiness," first produced with "The Water Engine" on Broadway at Plymouth Theater, March 6, 1978), 1978.
The Revenge of the Space Pandas; or, *Binky Rudich and the Two-Speed Clock* (one-act for children; first produced in New York City at Flushing Town Hall, 1977), Sergel, 1978.
The Woods (two-act; first produced in Chicago by St. Nicholas Theater Company, November 1, 1977; produced Off-Broadway at New York Shakespeare Festival Public Theater, April 25, 1979), 1979.
Reunion [and] *Dark Pony* ("Reunion" [one-act], first produced with "Sexual Perversity in Chicago" in Louisville at Actors' Theater of Louisville, October 12, 1976; "Dark Pony" [one-act], first produced with "Reunion" in New Haven, Conn. at Yale Repertory Theater, October 14, 1977; both produced Off-Broadway with "The Sanctity of Marriage" [also see below] at Circle Repertory Theater, October 18, 1979), 1979.
Lakeboat (one-act; first produced in Marlboro, Vt., at Marlboro Theater Workshop, 1970; revised version produced in Milwaukee at Milwaukee Repertory Theater, April 24, 1980), 1981.
Edmond (first produced in Chicago at Goodman Theater, June, 1982; produced Off-Broadway at Provincetown Playhouse, October 27, 1982), 1983.
Glengarry Glen Ross (two-act; first produced on the West End at National Theatre, October, 1983; produced in Chicago at Goodman Theater, January 27, 1984; produced on Broadway at John Golden Theater, March 25, 1984), 1984.
The Shawl [and] *Prairie du Chien* (one-act plays; first produced together at the Lincoln Center in December, 1985), 1985.
Vint (one-act; based on Anton Chekov's short story of the same name; first produced in New York with six other one-act plays based on Chekov's short works, under the collective title "Orchards"), published under same collective title, 1986.
(Adaptor) Chekov, *The Cherry Orchard,* 1987.
Speed-the-Plow (first produced on Broadway at the Royale Theatre, May, 1988), 1988.
(Adaptor) Chekov, *Uncle Vanya,* 1989.
Goldberg Street: Short Plays and Monologues, 1989.

UNPUBLISHED PLAYS

"Squirrels" (one-act), first produced in Chicago by St. Nicholas Theater Company, 1974.

"All Men Are Whores," first produced in New Haven at Yale Cabaret, 1977.

"Lone Canoe; or, the Explorer" (musical), music and lyrics by Alaric Jans, first produced in Chicago at Goodman Theater, May, 1979.

"The Sanctity of Marriage" (one-act), first produced Off-Broadway with "Reunion" and "Dark Pony" at Circle Repertory Theater, October 18, 1979.

"Shoeshine" (one-act), first produced Off-Off-Broadway at Ensemble Studio Theater, December 14, 1979.

"A Sermon" (one-act), first produced Off-Off-Broadway at Ensemble Studio Theater, May, 1981.

"Five Unrelated Pieces," first produced Off-Off-Broadway at Ensemble Studio Theater, May, 1983.

"The Disappearance of the Jews" (one-act), first produced in Chicago at Goodman Theater, June 14, 1983.

"The Water Engine," first produced in Hampstead, England, August, 1989.

"Bobby Gould in Hell," first produced in New York with "The Devil and Billy Markham," by Shel Silverstein, December, 1989.

SCREENPLAYS

"The Postman Always Rings Twice" (adaptation of novel of the same title by James M. Cain), Paramount, 1981.

"The Verdict" (adaptation of novel of the same title by Barry Reed), Columbia, 1982.

(And director) "House of Games," Orion, 1987.

"The Untouchables," Paramount, 1987.

(With Shel Silverstein; and director) "Things Change," Columbia Pictures, 1988.

"We're No Angels," Paramount, 1989.

Contributing editor, *Oui,* 1975-76.

SIDELIGHTS: David Mamet has acquired a great deal of critical recognition for his plays, each a microcosmic view of the American experience. "He's that rarity, a pure writer," notes Jack Kroll in *Newsweek,* "and the synthesis he appears to be making, with echoes from voices as diverse as Beckett, Pinter, and Hemingway, is unique and exciting." Since 1976, Mamet's plays have been widely produced in regional theaters and in New York. His most successful play, "Glengarry Glen Ross," earned the New York Drama Critics' Circle best American play citation and the Pulitzer Prize in drama, both in 1984. Critics have also praised Mamet's screenwriting; his adapted screenplay for the film "The Verdict" was nominated for an Oscar in 1983.

Mamet "has carved out a career as one of America's most creative young playwrights," observes Mel Gussow in the *New York Times,* "with a particular affinity for working-class characters." These characters and their language give Mamet's work its distinct flavor. Mamet is, according to Kroll, "that rare bird, an American playwright who's a language playwright." "Playwriting is simply showing how words influence actions and vice versa," Mamet told *People* contributor Linda Witt. "All my plays attempt to bring out the poetry in the plain, everyday language people use. That's the only way to put art back into the theater." Mamet has been accused of eavesdropping, simply recording the insignificant conversations of which everyone is aware; yet, many reviewers recognize the playwright's artistic intent. Jean M. White comments in the *Washington Post,* "Mamet has an ear for vernacular speech and uses cliche with telling effect." Furthermore, adds Jack Kroll, "Mamet is the first playwright to create a formal and moral shape out of the undeleted expletives of our foul-mouthed time."

In his personal and creative life, Mamet resists the lure of Broadway, its establishment, and its formulas for success. Chicago, where he was born and grew up and still lives part of the year, serves not only as inspiration for much of his work, but it also provides an accepting audience for Mamet's brand of drama. "Regional theaters are where the life is," he told Robin Reeves in *Us.* "They're the only new force in American theater since the 30s." He added, "Artistically and now commercially, regional theaters are taking over." Yet, despite Mamet's seeming indifference to Broadway and the fact that the language and subject matter of his plays make them of questionable commercial value, several of his plays have been featured on Broadway.

The first of David Mamet's plays to be commercially produced were "Sexual Perversity in Chicago" and "Duck Variations." "Sexual Perversity in Chicago" portrays the failed love affair of a young man and woman, each trying to leave behind a relationship with a homosexual roommate. The dialogue between the lovers and their same-sex roommates reveals how each gender can brutally characterize the other. Yet, "the play, itself is not another aspect of the so-called battle of the sexes," observes C. Gerald Fraser in the *New York Times.* "It concerns the confusion and emptiness of human relationships on a purely physical level." Edith Oliver adds, "The piece is written with grace," and she calls it "one of the saddest comedies I can remember." In "Duck Variations," two old Jewish men sit on a bench in Chicago looking out on Lake Michigan. Their observation of the nearby ducks leads them into discussions of several topics. "There is a marvelous ring of truth in the meandering, speculative talk of these old men," comments Oliver, "the comic, obsessive talk of men who spend most of their time alone, nurturing and indulging their preposterous notions." In the conversation of these men, writes T. E. Kalem in *Time,* "[Mamet] displays the Pinter trait of wearing word masks to shield feelings and of defying communication in the act of communicating." "Duck Variations" reveals, according to Oliver, that David Mamet is an "original writer, who cherishes words and, on the evidence at hand, cherishes character even more." "What emerges is a vivid sense of [the old men's] friendship, the fear of solitude, the inexorable toll of expiring lives," concludes Kalem.

Mamet emerged as a nationally acclaimed playwright with his two-act "American Buffalo." "America has few comedies in its repertory as ironic or as audacious as 'American Buffalo,'" notes John Lahr in the *Nation.* Set in a junk shop, the play features the shop's owner, an employee, and a friend engaged in plotting a theft; they hope to steal the coin collection of a customer who, earlier in the week, had bought an old nickel at the shop. When the employee fails to tail the mark to his home, the plot falls into disarray and "the play ends in confused weariness," writes Elizabeth Kastor in the *Washington Post.* Although little takes place, Oliver comments in the *New Yorker,* "What make [the play] fascinating are its characters and the sudden spurts of feeling and shifts of mood—the mounting tension under the seemingly aimless surface, which gives the play its momentum."

"American Buffalo" confirmed Mamet's standing as a language playwright. Reviewing the play in the *Nation,* Lahr writes, "Mamet's use of the sludge in American language is completely original. He hears panic and poetry in the convoluted syntax of his beleaguered characters." And, even though the language is uncultivated, David Richards notes in the *Washington Post,* "the dialogue [is] ripe with unsettling resonance." As Frank Rich of the *New York Times* observes, "Working with the tiniest imaginable vocabulary . . . Mr. Mamet creates a subterranean world with its own nonliterate comic beat, life-and-death struggles, pathos and even affection."

In this play, critics also see Mamet's vision of America, "a restless, rootless, insecure society which has no faith in the peace it seeks or the pleasure it finds," writes Lahr. *American Buffalo* superbly evokes this anxious and impoverished world." Its characters, though seemingly insignificant, reflect the inhabitants of this world and their way of life. "In these bumbling and inarticulate meatheads," observes Lahr, "Mamet has found a metaphor for the spiritual failure of entrepreneurial capitalism."

Since its first Chicago production in 1975, "American Buffalo" has been produced in several regional theaters and has had three New York productions. In Mamet's management of the elements of this play, *New York Times* reviewer Benedict Nightingale sees the key to its success: "Its idiom is precise enough to evoke a city, a class, a subculture; it is imprecise enough to allow variation of mood and feeling from production to production." Nightingale adds in another article, " '[American] Buffalo' is as accomplished as anything written for the American stage over . . . the last 20 years."

In 1979, Mamet was given the opportunity to write screenplays. As he told Don Shewey in the *New York Times,* working on the screenplay for the 1981 film version of James M. Cain's novel *The Postman Always Rings Twice* was a learning experience. "[Director Bob Rafelson] taught me that the purpose of a screenplay is to tell the story so the audience wants to know what happens next," Mamet said, "and to tell it in pictures." He added, "I always thought I had a talent for dialogue and not for plot, but it's a skill that can be learned. Writing for the movies is teaching me not to be so scared about plots." Mamet's screenplay for "The Postman Always Rings Twice" has received mixed reviews. Its critics often point out, as Gene Siskel does in the *Chicago Tribune,* Mamet's "ill-conceived editing of the book's original ending." Yet, except for the ending, notes Vincent Canby in the *New York Times,* "Mr. Mamet's screenplay is far more faithful to the novel than was the screenplay for Tay Garnett's 1946 version." Thus, Robert Hatch writes in the *Nation,* "Mamet and Rafelson recapture the prevailing insanity of the Depression, when steadiness of gaze was paying no bills and double or nothing was the game in vogue."

In the 1982 film "The Verdict," screenwriter Mamet and director Sydney Lumet "have dealt powerfully and unsentimentally with the shadowy state that ideas like good and evil find themselves in today," observes Jack Kroll in *Newsweek.* The film stars Paul Newman as a washed-up lawyer caught in a personal, legal, and moral battle. "David Mamet's terse screenplay for 'The Verdict' is . . . full of surprises," comments Janet Maslin in the *New York Times;* "Mamet has supplied twists and obstacles of all sorts." "Except for a few lapses of logic and some melodramatic moments in the courtroom," writes a *People* reviewer, "[this] script from Barry Reed's novel is unusually incisive." Kroll details the screenplay's strong points, calling it "strong on character, on sharp and edgy dialogue, on the detective-story suspense of a potent narrative." In a *New Republic* article, Stanley Kauffmann concludes, "It comes through when it absolutely must deliver: Newman's summation to the jury. This speech is terse and pungent: the powerful have the power to convert all the rest of us into victims and that condition probably cannot be changed, but must it always prevail?"

Mamet's Pulitzer Prize-winning play "Glengarry Glen Ross" is "so precise in its realism that it transcends itself," writes Robert Brustein in the *New Republic,* "and takes on reverberant ethical meanings. It is biting, . . . showing life stripped of all idealistic pretenses and liberal pieties." The play is set in and around a Chicago real estate office whose agents are embroiled in a competition to sell the most parcels in the Florida developments Glengarry Highlands and Glen Ross Farms. "Craftily constructed, so that there is laughter, as well as rage, in its dialogue, the play has a payoff in each scene and a cleverly plotted mystery that kicks in with a surprise hook at its ending," says Richard Christiansen in the *Chicago Tribune.*

As in Mamet's earlier plays, the characters and their language are very important to "Glengarry Glen Ross." In the *Nation,* Stephen Harvey comments on Mamet's ability to create characters who take on a life of their own within the framework of the play: "In *Glengarry,* . . . he adjusts his angle of vision to suit the contours of his characters, rather than using them to illustrate an idea." Mamet told Elizabeth Kastor of the *Washington Post,* "I think that people are generally more happy with a mystery than with an explanation. So the less that you say about a character the more interesting he becomes." Mamet uses language in a similar manner. Harvey notes, "The pungency of Glengarry's language comes from economy: if these characters have fifty-word vocabularies, Mamet makes sure that every monosyllable counts." And, Jack Kroll comments, "His antiphonal exchanges, which dwindle to single words or even fragments of words and then explode into a crossfire of scatological buckshot, make him the Aristophanes of the inarticulate." Mamet is, according to *New York Times* reviewer Benedict Nightingale, "the bard of modern-day barbarism, the laureate of the four-letter word."

For the real estate agents in "Glengarry Glen Ross," the bottom line is sales. And, as Robert Brustein notes, "Without a single tendentious line, without any polemical intention, without a trace of pity or sentiment, Mamet has launched an assault on the American way of making a living." Nightingale calls the play "as scathing a study of unscrupulous dealing as the American theater has ever produced." The Pulitzer Prize awarded to Mamet for "Glengarry Glen Ross" not only helped increase its critical standing, but it also helped to make the play a commercial success. However, unlike his real estate agents, Mamet is driven by more than money. He told Elizabeth Kastor, "In our interaction in our daily lives we tell stories to each other, we gossip, we complain to each other, we exhort. These are means of defining what our life is. The theater is a way of doing it continually, of sharing that experience, and it's absolutely essential."

In the latter half of the 1980s, Mamet published two collections of essays, *Writing in Restaurants* and *Some Freaks;* wrote stage adaptations for several fictional works by Anton Chekov; made his directorial debut with the 1987 film "House of Games" (for which he also wrote the screenplay), about a psychiatrist's involvement with a con man; penned popstress Madonna's Broadway debut "Speed-the-Plow"; and produced the script for director Brian De Palma's gangster epic "The Untouchables."

MEDIA ADAPTATIONS: The film "About Last Night . . .", released by Tri-Star Pictures in 1986, was based on Mamet's "Sexual Perversity in Chicago."

BIOGRAPHICAL/CRITICAL SOURCES:

BOOKS

Contemporary Literary Criticism, Gale, Volume 9, 1978, Volume 15, 1980, Volume 34, 1985, Volume 46, 1988.
Dictionary of Literary Biography, Volume 7: *Twentieth-Century American Dramatists,* Gale, 1981.

PERIODICALS

Chicago Tribune, October 11, 1987, May 4, 1988, February 19, 1989.
Harper's, May, 1978.
Los Angeles Times, November 27, 1979, June 25, 1984, July 7, 1987, October 11, 1987.
Nation, May 19, 1979, April 14, 1981, October 10, 1981, April 28, 1984.
Newsweek, February 28, 1977, March 23, 1981, November 8, 1982, December 6, 1982, April 9, 1984, October 19, 1987.
New Yorker, November 10, 1975, October 31, 1977, January 16, 1978, October 29, 1979, June 15, 1981, November 7, 1983.
New York Times, July 5, 1976, March 18, 1979, April 26, 1979, May 26, 1979, June 3, 1979, October 19, 1979, March 20, 1981, May 29, 1981, June 5, 1981, February 17, 1982, May 17, 1982, June 17, 1982, October 24, 1982, October 28, 1982, December 8, 1982, May 13, 1983, October 9, 1983, November 6, 1983, March 26, 1984, March 28, 1984, April 1, 1984, April 18, 1984, April 24, 1984, September 30, 1984, February 9, 1986, April 23, 1986, January 1, 1987, March 15, 1987, June 3, 1987, October 11, 1987, May 4, 1988, December 4, 1989.
People, November 12, 1979, December 20, 1982, May 4, 1987.
Saturday Review, April 2, 1977.
Time, July 12, 1976, April 9, 1984.
Times Literary Supplement, January 29, 1988.
Us, January 10, 1978.
Washington Post, May 4, 1988.

*   *   *

MANCHESTER, William (Raymond) 1922-

PERSONAL: Born April 1, 1922, in Attleboro, Mass.; son of William Raymond and Sallie (Thompson) Manchester; married Julia Brown Marshall, March 27, 1948; children: John Kennerly, Julie Thompson, Laurie. *Education:* Massachusetts State College (now University of Massachusetts), A.B., 1946; University of Missouri, A.M., 1947.

ADDRESSES: Office—Wesleyan University, 329 Wesleyan Station, Middletown, Conn. 06457. *Agent*—Don Congdon Associates, Inc., 156 Fifth Ave., Suite 625, New York, N.Y. 10010.

CAREER: Daily Oklahoman, Oklahoma City, Okla., reporter, 1945-46; *Baltimore Sun,* Baltimore, Md., reporter, Washington correspondent, and foreign correspondent in the Middle East, India, and Southeast Asia, 1947-54; Wesleyan University, Middletown, Conn., managing editor of Wesleyan University Publications, 1955-64, member of university faculty, 1968-69, member of faculty of East College, 1968—, writer in residence, 1975—, adjunct professor of history, 1979—. Friends of the University of Massachusetts Library, president of board of trustees, 1970-72, trustee, 1970-74. *Military service:* U.S. Marine Corps, 1942-45; became sergeant; awarded Purple Heart.

MEMBER: American Historical Association, Society of American Historians, Authors Guild, Authors League of America, Williams Club, Century Club.

AWARDS, HONORS: Guggenheim fellow, 1959-60; Wesleyan Center for Advanced Studies fellow, 1959-60; L.H.D., University of Massachusetts, 1965; Prix Dag Hammarskjoeld au merite litteraire, 1967; Overseas Press Club citation for best book on foreign affairs, 1968; University of Missouri honor award for distinguished service in journalism, 1969; Connecticut Book Award, 1975; L.H.D., University of New Haven, 1979; National Book Award nomination, 1980, for *American Caesar: Douglas MacArthur, 1880-1964;* ALA Notable Book citation, 1980, for *Goodbye, Darkness: A Memoir of the Pacific War;* President's Cabinet Award, University of Detroit, 1981; Frederick S. Troy Award, University of Massachusetts, 1981; McConnaughty Award, Wesleyan University, 1981; *Los Angeles Times* Biography Prize nomination, 1983, and Union League/Abraham Lincoln Literary Award, 1984, both for *The Last Lion: Winston Spencer Churchill,* Volume 1: *Visions of Glory: 1874-1932;* Connecticut Bar Association Distinguished Public Service Award, 1985.

WRITINGS:

Disturber of the Peace: The Life of H. L. Mencken (originally serialized in *Harper's,* July-August, 1950), Harper, 1951, 2nd edition edited by Stephen B. Oates and Paul Mariani, University of Massachusetts Press, 1986.
The City of Anger (novel), Ballantine, 1953, reprinted, Little, Brown, 1987.
Shadow of the Monsoon (novel), Doubleday, 1956.
Beard the Lion (novel), Morrow, 1958.
A Rockefeller Family Portrait: From John D. to Nelson, Little, Brown, 1959.
(Contributor) Bredemier and Toby, editors, *Social Problems in America,* Wiley, 1960.
The Long Gainer: A Novel, Little, Brown, 1961.
Portrait of a President: John F. Kennedy in Profile, Little, Brown, 1962, 2nd edition, 1967.
(Contributor) Don Congdon, editor, *Combat World War I,* Dial, 1964.
(Contributor) Poyntz Tyler, *Securities Exchanges and the SEC,* Wilson, 1965.
The Death of a President: November 20-November 25, 1963 (originally serialized in *Look,* January 24-March 7, 1967; Book-of-the-Month Club selection), Harper, 1967, published with revised introduction, Arbor House, 1985, published with new addition by the author, Harper, 1988.
The Arms of Krupp, 1587-1968 (originally serialized in *Holiday,* November, 1964-February, 1965; Literary Guild selection), Little, Brown, 1968.
The Glory and the Dream: A Narrative History of America, 1932-1972 (Literary Guild selection), Little, Brown, 1974, reprinted, Bantam, 1989.
Controversy and Other Essays in Journalism, Little, Brown, 1976.
American Caesar: Douglas MacArthur, 1880-1964 (Book-of-the-Month Club selection), Little, Brown, 1978.
Goodbye, Darkness: A Memoir of the Pacific War (Book-of-the-Month Club selection), Little, Brown, 1980.
One Brief Shining Moment: Remembering Kennedy (Book-of-the-Month Club selection), Little, Brown, 1983.
The Last Lion: Winston Spencer Churchill, Volume 1: *Visions of Glory: 1874-1932* (Book-of-the-Month Club selection), Little, Brown, 1983, Volume 2: *Alone: 1932-1940* (Book-of-the-Month Club selection), Little, Brown, 1987.
(Contributor) *A Sense of History: The Best Writing from the Pages of American Heritage,* American Heritage/Houghton, 1985.
(Contributor) Annie Dillard and Robert Atwan, editors, *Best American Essays 1988,* Ticknor & Fields, 1988.
(Author of text) *In Our Time: The World as Seen by Magnum Photographers,* Norton, 1989.

Also author of introduction for *Thimblerigger: The Law v. Governor Marvin Mandel.* Contributor to *Encyclopaedia Britannica.* Contributor to *Atlantic, Harper's, Reporter, Saturday Review, Holiday, Nation, Esquire,* and *Saturday Evening Post.*

WORK IN PROGRESS: The Last Lion: Winston Spencer Churchill, Volume 3: *Defender of the Realm: 1940-1965.*

SIDELIGHTS: William Manchester's oeuvre ranges from structured novels to massive biographies. But his books, the author tells Stefan Kanfer of *People* magazine, all share one common theme—the study of power: "What exactly is power? Where are its roots? How do some people get it and others miss it entirely?" Using what Kanfer calls the "Manchester trademarks: unflagging energy, hundreds of interviews, monuments of detail and pounds of manuscript," Manchester, states Kenneth Atchity in the *Los Angeles Times,* has made himself "the [James] Michener of biographers."

Manchester's first book focused on the power of words. He was first attracted to the writings of H. L. Mencken, the famous critic and literary curmudgeon, while an undergraduate in college. After serving with the Marines in World War II, Manchester entered the graduate school of the University of Missouri and completed a thesis on Mencken. The critic read the thesis, authorized Manchester's proposed biography, and invited the young writer to join the staff of the Baltimore *Evening Sun,* Mencken's newspaper.

Disturber of the Peace: The Life of H. L. Mencken helped establish Manchester's reputation as a talented writer. Although some reviewers felt that Manchester's devotion to Mencken interfered with the story, many praised the young biographer's effort. *Saturday Review* critic Charles Angoff declared that *Disturber of the Peace* "is probably the most fully documented" of all Mencken studies and added that some of Manchester's remarks "display a refreshing critical independence." George Genzmer, writing in *Nation,* called the book "a generally well-proportioned narrative that . . . portrays [Mencken's] charm, vigor, and humor with notable effect." Manchester, Genzmer continued, "is slapdash in handling some details and in brushing in the background, but, such matters aside, the story is authentic."

Manchester then turned to fiction, and wrote four novels over the next few years. Many of these deal with the use and abuse of power and are based on Manchester's reporting experiences; for instance, *The City of Anger* traces corruption in an East Coast city very much like Baltimore, while *The Long Gainer* examines an academic and political scandal resembling one that "rocked the University of Maryland some years ago," reports Wirt Williams in the *New York Times Book Review. Beard the Lion* is a thriller involving politics in the Near East in the late 1950s, while *Shadow of the Monsoon* tells of post-Raj India, where Manchester served as a foreign correspondent.

Although they were generally favorably received, Manchester's novels are perhaps most significant because of the way they prefigure stylistic elements of his later nonfiction. The publisher's note that introduces the 1985 edition of *The City of Anger* explains, "The reviewers of each [of Manchester's four novels] commented on his skillful command of detail—accurate detail, for his eye has always been a lens, not a prism." "His use of detail is both Manchester's strength and his weakness," the publisher's note continues. "Those who dislike it, particularly in his nonfiction, criticize him as a collector of trivia. But to Manchester the skills of narration grow out of the mastery of detail. It is a matter of taste."

Manchester returned to biography in 1959 with *A Rockefeller Family Portrait: From John D. to Nelson,* and in 1962 with *Portrait of a President: John F. Kennedy in Profile.* Although different in many ways, the two books share several features: both were originally published as magazine articles, both reiterate Manchester's interest in power in their subjects (the family of then-governor Nelson Rockefeller of New York and then-President Kennedy), and critics gave both mixed reviews while recognizing that the two volumes were highly approving of their subjects. "Those who are looking for material to criticize the Rockefeller family or its individual members," writes Leo Egan in the *New York Times* about *A Rockefeller Family Portrait,* "would be well advised to look somewhere else." Tom Wicker remarks in the *New York Times Book Review,* that *Portrait of a President* "is what its title says it is—a portrait, not dishonest, but smitten, one in which the dazzled artist has gazed upon the subject with loving eyes and found redeeming beauty in his every flaw."

Yet several critics admit that Manchester's depictions of the Rockefellers and of Kennedy are appealing; in *Saturday Review,* Cleveland Amory calls *A Rockefeller Family Portrait* "skillfully and carefully" composed, and adds, "At least the first three-quarters of this book is as capably written as anything that has passed this writer's desk in some time." "In sum," declares G. W. Johnson in the *New Republic,* "what Manchester gives us [in *Portrait of a President*] is a picture of a brave, honorable and resolute man struggling with problems that may well be beyond his, or any human capacity to solve."

It was partly on the basis of *Portrait of a President* that, early in 1964, Jacqueline Kennedy asked Manchester to write an account of President Kennedy's assassination, offering him exclusive interviews with family members. Manchester had met Kennedy shortly after World War II when both of them were disabled veterans living in Boston, and he had since become a family friend. He agreed to write the book, and signed an agreement with Senator Robert Kennedy providing that most of the volume's royalties would go to the new Kennedy Memorial Library, and that Senator Kennedy and the President's widow would have the right to review the manuscript. When Manchester finished the book after two years of exhaustive research and writing, however, both Kennedys felt unable to read it. They sent representatives to review the manuscript instead, and, after some changes, the representatives unanimously approved publication of *The Death of a President: November 20-November 25, 1963.*

Controversy followed close behind the book's approval. After *Look* magazine made a record-setting bid of $665,000 for serialization rights, Jacqueline Kennedy, on the advice of several associates, withdrew her permission to publish the story. Her action was based on fears that Manchester's representation of Johnson's government would damage Senator Kennedy's presidential aspirations in 1968. However, both Manchester's publishers, *Look* and Harper & Row, refused to stop publication and, in December of 1966, representatives of the Kennedy family filed suit. "We *couldn't* stop," Manchester told *CA.* "Contracts had been signed in 17 countries, [and] we (Bobby [Kennedy] and me) would have been sued into penury." The matter was settled out of court when the publishers' representatives persuaded Mrs. Kennedy to read the book for herself, and, after superficial changes, *The Death of a President* went to press early in 1967.

Although much of the media attention the book received centered on Mrs. Kennedy's suit rather than on its substance, reviewers noted several important characteristics of the work: Manchester's massive accumulation of facts, and his subjective treatment of the subject. "Had the Kennedy family merely wanted to set the record straight," states Margaret L. Coit in *Saturday Review,* "they should have approached some cut-and-dried academician who would have marshaled the facts with cold objectivity. Instead, their choice fell upon a highly emotional and subjective writer who identified himself with John F. Kennedy, his time, and his generation. They should have foreseen that the facts would not remain inert under his fingers, that the whole horror would blaze forth again with compounded intensity."

Manchester himself lends credibility to this interpretation of his work. In the introduction to the 1985 edition of *The Death of a President,* he writes: "Here . . . I have attempted to lead the reader back through historical events by recreating the sense of immediacy people felt at the time, so that he sees, feels, and hears what was seen, felt, and heard—mourns, rejoices, weeps, or loves with mourners, rejoicers, weepers, or lovers long since vanished: figures whose present has become our past." Finally, Manchester concludes, "*The Death of a President* was not written for Jackie or any of the others. I wrote it for the one Kennedy I had known well and deeply loved, the splendid man who had been cruelly slain at 12:30 p.m. Texas time on Friday, November 22, 1963."

After the furor surrounding *The Death of a President* died down, Manchester returned to the work he had abandoned for the Kennedy project: a history of the Krupp family, chief of the steel and munitions makers in Germany until 1967. Although Manchester's investigation begins in Renaissance Germany, the major portion of his study concentrates on the Krupps' role in Hitler's Third Reich. Alfried Krupp, who ran the business during the Second World War, was convicted at the Nuremburg trials of war crimes, including the exploitation of citizens of occupied countries and Jews as slave labor; he received a sentence of twelve years' imprisonment and the confiscation of all his property. However, Alfried served only three years of his term before the American High Commissioner in Germany released him and restored his property to him.

Many reviewers were impressed by the scope of *The Arms of Krupp.* "In this monumental study," declares *Saturday Review* commentator Henry C. Wolfe, "William Manchester has written a melodramatic, often macabre account of the Krupp empire that fascinates from beginning to ironical end." Christopher Lehmann-Haupt, writing in the *New York Times,* comments, "As research alone, the book is impressive. Manchester has unearthed material not known to the public before, and pieced it together in patterns that were not seen before." "The Krupps story, as Mr. Manchester tells it," states Geoffrey Barraclough in the *New York Review of Books,* "is a paradigm of German history."

Manchester chose an even broader range for his next book, *The Glory and the Dream: A Narrative History of America, 1932-1972.* Manchester follows the generation that grew up during the Depression, chronicling its triumphs and tragedies, telling of its heroes and struggles: the Second World War, the loss of FDR, General MacArthur's resignation, Frank Sinatra and the Beatles, and the Bomb. Writing in the *New York Times Book Review,* Alfred Kazin calls *The Glory and the Dream* a "fluent, likeable, can't-put-it-down narrative history of America" that is "popular history in our special tradition of literary merchandising." "Reading Manchester," Kazin continues, "you run with the Bonus Army, lift up your chin like Roosevelt, put up the flag at Iwo Jima, and nervously dismiss MacArthur. You are against Communism and the Cold War. You participate!" "There is no fiction that can compare with good, gossipy, anecdotal history—the 'inside story' of who said or did what in moments of great tension or crisis," reports Anatole Broyard in the *New York Times.* "I think you ought to read this history and weep, read it and laugh, read it and make sure you don't repeat it."

The biography *American Caesar: Douglas MacArthur, 1880-1964,* Manchester's next book, brought wide acclaim from critics for its authoritative evocation of one of the most powerful and controversial figures in modern American history. Although MacArthur's military expertise defeated the Japanese in World War II's South Pacific theater with a minimum of casualties, his repeated disobedience of orders forced President Truman to remove him from command during the Korean War. "The personality and charisma of MacArthur are so successfully recreated in Manchester's biography that it is easy to forget that the book, unlike the man, had an author," remarks Orville Schell in *Saturday Review.* "This is to Manchester's credit. . . . [He] has written a thorough and spellbinding book. It is a dramatic chronicle of one of America's last epic heroes." Manchester's *American Caesar* "is exquisitely ambivalent," declares Broyard in the *New York Times,* "not so much torn as balanced between the two MacArthurs, whom he calls 'noble and ignoble, arrogant and shy, the best of men and the worst of men, the most protean, most ridiculous, and most sublime.' "

The author's own South Pacific experiences as a sergeant of Marines in World War II are the subject of *Goodbye, Darkness: A Memoir of the Pacific War.* Recalling his combat service, Manchester wonders what made his lightly-wounded younger self leave the hospital and return to his unit, only to receive an almost fatal injury. He believes that his gesture was partly an act of solidarity with his men, partly a desire to uphold family tradition, and partly a pride of country—feelings that, Manchester believes, have atrophied in post-war America. While not all critics agree with the author's analysis of the situation, many extol the power of his book. "Those sections of the book that are about the war itself are very well done," declares Broyard in the *New York Times.* "Manchester's combat writing is one of his book's strengths and stands comparison with the best" of the genre, adds *New York Times Book Review* contributor Ted Morgan. Clay Blair, writing in the *Chicago Tribune Book World,* states, "The reviewer is hard put to describe this intelligent, beautifully crafted but complicated work in a nutshell."

Most recently Manchester has examined the life of another important figure of the Second World War, Winston Churchill. The first two volumes of the biography *The Last Lion: Winston Spencer Churchill* trace Churchill's personal and political career from his early years to the time he became Prime Minister of Great Britain. Since Manchester's volumes have been preceded by many other studies, including Martin Gilbert's official Churchill biography, which runs eight and a half million words, some reviewers, in the words of *New York Review of Books* contributor Norman Stone, "simply do not see any need for Manchester's book[s]." Others, however, recognize valuable elements in the author's work that sets his version of the Churchill epic apart from all others. Robert Conot writes in the *Chicago Tribune Book World* that "Churchill and Manchester were clearly made for each other." Manchester's "accumulated merits, of scrupulous research, sustained narrative lucidity, . . . [and] unabashed inquisitiveness, seem to me to outweigh most of the errors—of judgment, mainly—that [he] can be charged with," declares Alistair Cooke in the *New Yorker.* Finally, Cooke concludes, Manchester is able "to introduce us, by way of new and dramatic emphases, to many startling things we thought we knew."

MEDIA ADAPTATIONS: "The City of Anger," adapted from Manchester's novel of the same title, aired on NBC-TV in 1955. "American Caesar," a television miniseries based on Manchester's biography of Douglas MacArthur, was narrated by John Huston, produced by John McGreevey, aired on the Ted Turner cable network in 1985, and is presently available on videocassette.

BIOGRAPHICAL/CRITICAL SOURCES:

BOOKS

Authors in the News, Volume 1, Gale, 1976.
Corry, John, *The Manchester Affair,* Putnam, 1967.
Manchester, William, *The City of Anger* (novel), Ballantine, 1953, reprinted, Little, Brown, 1985.
Manchester, William, *The Death of a President: November 20-November 25, 1963,* revised edition, Arbor House, 1985.

PERIODICALS

Atlantic, May, 1967.
Boston Sunday Globe, October 23, 1988.
Chicago Tribune Book World, September 28, 1980, May 15, 1983, November 20, 1983.
Detroit Free Press, January 1, 1989.
Detroit News, June 26, 1983.
Los Angeles Times, November 6, 1983.
Los Angeles Times Book Review, May 8, 1983, November 27, 1983, December 11, 1988.
Nation, April 14, 1951, September 19, 1959, April 17, 1967.
National Review, May 30, 1967.
New Republic, October 8, 1962, April 22, 1967.
New Statesman, April 21, 1967.
Newsday, September 18, 1988, October 2, 1988.
Newsweek, November 25, 1974, September 11, 1978, December 12, 1988.
New Yorker, January 20, 1951, April 8, 1967, August 22, 1983.
New York Herald Tribune Book Review, January 7, 1951, July 19, 1953, August 2, 1959.
New York Review of Books, April 20, 1967, March 27, 1969, October 12, 1978, January 22, 1981, November 10, 1983.
New York Times, January 14, 1951, July 13, 1953, April 8, 1956, August 9, 1959, April 3, 1967, December 6, 1968, November 15, 1974, September 20, 1978, September 17, 1980, May 25, 1983.
New York Times Book Review, September 10, 1961, September 30, 1962, April 9, 1967, November 24, 1968, November 17, 1974, August 31, 1980, June 5, 1983, November 27, 1988.
People, November 27, 1978.
Saturday Review, July 11, 1959, January 21, 1967, April 15, 1967, December 21, 1968, January 11, 1975, October 14, 1978.
Saturday Review of Literature, January 6, 1951.
Time, January 8, 1951, December 20, 1968, November 18, 1974, September 11, 1978, October 31, 1988.
Times (London), November 24, 1988.
Times Literary Supplement, December 14, 1967, February 20, 1969, August 19, 1983.
Tribune Books (Chicago), September 18, 1988.
Washington Post Book World, October 30, 1983, November 10, 1985, October 16, 1988.

—*Sketch by Kenneth R. Shepherd*

*   *   *

MANN, Abel
  See CREASEY, John

MANN, (Paul) Thomas   1875-1955
(Paul Thomas)

PERSONAL: Born June 6, 1875, in Luebeck, Germany (now West Germany); voluntary exile in Switzerland, 1933; German citizenship revoked, 1936; naturalized Czech citizen, 1936; immigrated to United States, 1938; naturalized American citizen, 1944; immigrated to Switzerland, 1952; died of phlebitis, August 12, 1955, in Zurich, Switzerland; buried August 16, 1955, in Kilchberg, Switzerland; son of Thomas Johann Heinrich (government official and owner of a trading firm) and Julia (da Silva-Bruhns) Mann; married Katja Pringsheim, February 11, 1905; children: Erika, Klaus, Golo, Monika, Elisabeth, Michael. *Education:* Attended Technische Hochschule (Munich) during 1890s.

CAREER: Writer and lecturer. South German Fire Insurance Co., Munich, Germany (now West Germany), apprentice, 1894-95; *Simplizissimus* (periodical), Munich, reader and copyreader, 1898-1900; Princeton University, Princeton, N.J., lecturer in the humanities, 1938-c. 1940; Library of Congress, Washington, D.C., consultant in Germanic literature, 1942-44. Member of Munich Censorship Council, 1912-13; German correspondent for *Dial* during 1920s; author and presenter of radio talks for British Broadcasting Corporation. *Military service:* Royal Bavarian Infantry, 1900.

MEMBER: Prussian Academy of Arts (founding member of literary section, 1926), Union of German Writers (honorary chairman, 1949), Bavarian Academy of Fine Arts (honorary chairman, 1949), German Academy of Arts (honorary member), Schiller Society (East Germany; honorary member), German Academy of Language and Poetry (West Germany; honorary member), Gerhart Hauptmann Society (honorary member), Society of Those Persecuted by the Nazi Regime (honorary member), Accademia Lincei (Italy), Authors' League of America, American Academy of Arts and Letters, Phi Beta Kappa.

AWARDS, HONORS: Bauernfeld Prize, 1904; Nobel Prize in literature, 1929; Herder Prize for exiled writers from Czechoslovakia, 1937; Cardinal Newman Award, 1938; Goethe Prize from city of Frankfurt, West Germany, 1949; Goethe Prize from East Germany, 1949; Medal of Service from American Academy of Arts and Letters, 1949; Feltrinelli Prize from Accademia Nazionale dei Lincei (Italy), 1952; Officer's Cross of the French Legion of Honor, 1952; honorary citizen of Luebeck, West Germany, 1955; Cross of Orange-Nassau from the Netherlands, 1955; Order of Merit in the Sciences and Arts from West Germany, 1955. Honorary doctorates from numerous colleges and universities, including Bonn, 1919 (withdrawn, 1936, restored, 1947), Harvard, 1935, Columbia, 1938, Rutgers, 1939, Dubuque, 1939, California at Berkeley, 1941, Hebrew Union (Cincinnati, Ohio), 1945, Oxford, 1949, Lund, 1949, Cambridge, 1953, Friedrich Schiller (East Germany), 1955, and Technische Hochschule (Zurich, Switzerland), 1955.

WRITINGS:

NOVELS

Buddenbrooks: Verfall einer Familie, S. Fischer, 1901, translation by H. T. Lowe-Porter published as *Buddenbrooks: The Decline of a Family,* Knopf, 1924, recent edition, Vintage, 1984.
Koenigliche Hoheit, S. Fischer, 1909, translation by A. Cecil Curtis published as *Royal Highness: A Novel of German Court-Life,* Knopf, 1916, recent edition, Vintage, 1983.

Bekenntnisse des Hochstaplers Felix Krull, first fragmentary version, subtitled *Buch der Kindheit,* Rikola, 1922, enlarged, Querido, 1937, novel-length version, subtitled *Der Memoiren erster Teil,* S. Fischer, 1954; translation of final enlargement by Denver Lindley published as *Confessions of Felix Krull, Confidence Man: The Early Years,* Knopf, 1955 (published in England as *Confessions of Felix Krull, Confidence Man: Memoirs, Part I,* Secker & Warburg, 1955).

Der Zauberberg, S. Fischer, 1924, translation by H. T. Lowe-Porter published as *The Magic Mountain,* Knopf, 1927, recent edition, 1975.

Die Geschichten Jaakobs (first in the "Joseph und seine Brueder" ["Joseph and His Brothers"] series of novels), S. Fischer, 1933, translation by H. T. Lowe-Porter published as *Joseph and His Brothers,* Knopf, 1934 (published in England as *The Tales of Jacob,* Martin Secker, 1934).

Der junge Joseph (second in the "Joseph und seine Brueder" series of novels), S. Fischer, 1934, translation by H. T. Lowe-Porter published as *Young Joseph: Joseph and His Brothers II,* Knopf, 1935.

Joseph in Aegypten (third in the "Joseph und seine Brueder" series of novels), Bermann-Fischer, 1936, translation by H. T. Lowe-Porter published as *Joseph in Egypt: Joseph and His Brothers III,* Knopf, 1938.

Lotte in Weimar, Bermann-Fischer, 1939, translation by H. T. Lowe-Porter published as *The Beloved Returns,* Knopf, 1940, recent edition, Vintage, 1983 (translation published in England under original title, Secker & Warburg, 1940).

Die vertauschten Koepfe: Eine indische Legende, Bermann-Fischer, 1940, translation by H. T. Lowe-Porter published as *The Transposed Heads: A Legend of India,* Knopf, 1941, recent edition, Vintage, c. 1965.

Joseph der Ernaehrer (fourth in the "Joseph und seine Brueder" series of novels), Bermann-Fischer, 1943, translation by H. T. Lowe-Porter published as *Joseph the Provider: Joseph and His Brothers IV* (Book-of-the-Month Club selection), Knopf, 1944.

(And author of introduction) *Joseph and His Brothers* (complete series of novels; contains *The Tales of Jacob, Young Joseph, Joseph in Egypt,* and *Joseph the Provider;* also see above), translation by H. T. Lowe-Porter, Knopf, 1948, reprinted, 1983.

Doktor Faustus: Das Leben des deutschen Tonsetzers Adrian Leverkuehn, erzaehlt von einem Freunde, Bermann-Fischer, 1947, translation by H. T. Lowe-Porter published as *Doctor Faustus: The Life of the German Composer Adrian Leverkuehn as Told by a Friend* (Book-of-the-Month Club selection), Knopf, 1948, recent edition, Random House, 1971.

Der Erwaehlte, S. Fischer, 1951, translation by H. T. Lowe-Porter published as *The Holy Sinner* (Book-of-the-Month Club selection), Knopf, 1951, recent edition, Vintage, 1983.

SHORT FICTION

Der kleine Herr Friedemann (contains "Der kleine Herr Friedemann," "Der Tod," "Der Wille zum Glueck," "Enttaeuschung," "Der Bajazzo," "Tobias Mindernickel"), S. Fischer, 1898.

Tristan (contains "Der Weg zum Friedhof," "Tristan," "Der Kleiderschrank," "Luischen," "Gladius Dei," "Tonio Kroeger"), S. Fischer, 1903.

Fiorenza (three-act play; first performed in Frankfurt, Germany, at Schauspielhaus, May 11, 1907), S. Fischer, 1906, translation published in *Stories of Three Decades* (also see below).

Der kleine Herr Friedemann und andere Novellen (includes "Die Hungernden," "Das Eisenbahnunglueck"), S. Fischer, 1909.

Der Tod in Venedig (novella), Hyperionverlag Hans von Weber (Munich), 1912, translation by H. T. Lowe-Porter published as *Death in Venice,* Knopf, 1928, recent edition, Penguin, 1976 (also see below).

Das Wunderkind (contains "Das Wunderkind," "Schwere Stunde," "Beim Propheten," "Ein Glueck," "Wie Jappe und Do Escobar sich pruegelten"), S. Fischer, 1914.

Herr und Hund [novella; bound with] *Gesang vom Kindchen* (narrative poem), S. Fischer, 1919, translation of the former by Herman George Scheffauer published as *Bashan and I,* Holt, 1923, and as *A Man and His Dog,* Knopf, 1930.

Waelsungenblut (novella), Phantasus (Munich), 1921, translation published as "Blood of the Walsungs" in *Stories of Three Decades* (also see below).

Death in Venice and Other Stories (contains "Death in Venice," "Tristan," "Tonio Kroeger"), translation by Kenneth Burke, Knopf, 1925, translation by H. T. Lowe-Porter, Martin Secker, 1928.

Unordnung und fruehes Leid (novella; title means "Disorder and Early Sorrow"), S. Fischer, 1926, translation by Herman George Scheffauer published as *Early Sorrow,* Martin Secker, 1929, Knopf, 1930, translation by H. T. Lowe-Porter published as *Early Sorrow* [bound with] *Mario and the Magician,* Martin Secker, 1934, published as "Disorder and Early Sorrow" in *Stories of Three Decades* (also see below).

Children and Fools (contains "Disorder and Early Sorrow," "How Jappe Fought Do Escobar," "The Infant Prodigy," "Tobias Mindernickel," "The Path to the Cemetery," "At the Prophet's," "Little Louise," "Little Herr Friedemann"), translation by Herman George Scheffauer, Knopf, 1928, recent edition, Books for Libraries Press, 1970.

Mario und die Zauberer: Ein Tragisches Reiseerlebnis (novella), S. Fischer, 1930, translation by H. T. Lowe-Porter published as *Mario and the Magician,* Martin Secker, 1930, Knopf, 1931.

Tonio Kroeger, edited with introduction, notes, and vocabulary by John Alexander Kelly, F. S. Crofts, 1931, edited by Elizabeth M. Wilkinson, 2nd edition, Basil Blackwell, 1968.

(And author of introduction) *Stories of Three Decades* (contains "Little Herr Friedemann," "Disillusionment," "The Dilettante," "Tobias Mindernickel," "Little Lizzy," "The Wardrobe," "The Way to the Churchyard," "Tonio Kroeger," "Tristan," "The Hungry," "The Infant Prodigy," *"Gladius Dei,"* "Fiorenza," "A Gleam," "At the Prophet's," "A Weary Hour," "The Blood of the Walsungs," "Railway Accident," "The Fight Between Jappe and Do Escobar," "Felix Krull," "Death in Venice," "A Man and His Dog," "Disorder and Early Sorrow," "Mario and the Magician"), translation by H. T. Lowe-Porter, Knopf, 1936, recent edition, 1971.

Das Gesetz (novella), Pazifische Presse (Los Angeles), 1944, Bermann-Fischer, 1944, translation by H. T. Lowe-Porter published as *The Tables of the Law,* Knopf, 1945, recent edition, 1964.

Die Betrogene (novella), S. Fischer, 1953, translation by Willard R. Trask published as *The Black Swan,* Knopf, 1954, recent edition, Harcourt, 1980.

Erzaehlungen (collection; includes "Vision," "Gefallen," "Geraecht," "Anekdote"), S. Fischer, 1957.

Stories of a Lifetime, two volumes, Secker & Warburg, 1961, selected edition published as *Little Herr Friedemann and Other Stories,* Penguin, 1972.

Death in Venice, and Seven Other Stories (contains "Death in Venice," "Tonio Kroeger," "Mario and the Magician," "Disorder and Early Sorrow," "A Man and His Dog," "The Blood of the Walsungs," "Tristan," and "Felix Krull"), translation by H. T. Lowe-Porter, Vintage, 1964, reprinted, 1989.

Death in Venice and Other Stories, translation by David Luke, Bantam Books, 1988.

Short fiction represented in numerous other collections and anthologies.

NONFICTION; EXCEPT PERSONAL PAPERS

Friedrich und die grosse Koalition (essays; title means "Frederick the Great and the Grand Coalition"), S. Fischer, 1915.

Betrachtungen eines Unpolitischen (essay), S. Fischer, 1918, translation by William D. Morris published as *Reflections of a Nonpolitical Man,* Ungar, 1983.

Rede und Antwort: Gesammelte Abhandlungen und kleine Aufsaetze (essays), S. Fischer, 1922.

Goethe und Tolstoi (essay), Verlag "Die Kuppel" (Aachen), 1923, translation published as "Goethe and Tolstoi" in *Three Essays* and *Essays of Three Decades* (also see below).

Von Deutscher Republik (speech), S. Fischer, 1923, translation by H. T. Lowe-Porter published as "The German Republic" in *Order of the Day* (also see below).

Okkulte Erlebnisse (essay), Alf Haeger (Berlin), 1924, translation published as "An Experience in the Occult" in *Three Essays* (also see below).

Bemuehungen: Neue Folge der Gesammelten Abhandlungen und kleinen Aufsaetze (essays), S. Fischer, 1925.

Pariser Rechenschaft, S. Fischer, 1926.

Luebeck als geistige Lebensform (speech), Otto Quitzow (Luebeck), 1926, translation by Richard and Clara Winston published as "Luebeck as a Way of Life and Thought" in *Buddenbrooks,* Knopf, 1964.

Three Essays, translation by H. T. Lowe-Porter, Knopf, 1929.

Die Forderung des Tages: Reden und Aufsaetze aus den Jahren 1925-1929 (speeches and essays from 1925 to 1929), S. Fischer, 1930.

Lebensabriss, first published in *Die Neue Rundschau,* July 7, 1930, translation by H. T. Lowe-Porter published as *A Sketch of My Life,* Harrison (Paris), 1930, recent edition, Knopf, 1960.

Goethe als Repraesentant des buergerlichen Zeitalters (speech), S. Fischer, 1932, translation published as "Goethe as Representative of the Bourgeois Age" in *Essays of Three Decades* (also see below).

Goethe und Tolstoi; Zum Problem der Humanitaet: Neue und Veraenderte Ausgabe, S. Fischer, 1932.

Past Masters and Other Papers (essays), translation by H. T. Lowe-Porter, Knopf, 1933, recent edition, Books for Libraries Press, 1968.

Leiden und Groesse der Meister: Neue Aufsaetze (essays), S. Fischer, 1935.

Freud und die Zukunft (essay), Bermann-Fischer, 1936, translation published as "Freud and the Future" in *Freud, Goethe, Wagner* (also see below).

Freud, Goethe, Wagner (essays), translation by H. T. Lowe-Porter and Rita Matthias-Reil, Knopf, 1937.

Vom Zukuenftigen Sieg der Demokratie (speech), Europa Verlag Oprecht (Zurich), 1938, translation by Agnes E. Meyer published as *The Coming Victory of Democracy,* Knopf, 1938.

Achtung, Europa! Aufsaetze zur Zeit (essays), Longmans, Green, 1938.

Schopenhauer (essay), Bermann-Fischer, 1938, translation by H. T. Lowe-Porter published as introduction to *The Living Thoughts of Schopenhauer* (also see below).

Order of the Day: Political Essays and Speeches of Two Decades, translation by Agnes E. Meyer, Eric Sutton, and H. T. Lowe-Porter, Knopf, 1942, recent edition, Books for Libraries Press, 1969.

Deutsche Hoerer! 25 Radiosendungen nach Deutschland (speeches), Bermann-Fischer, 1942, translation published as *Listen Germany! 25 Radio Messages to the German People over the B.B.C.,* Knopf, 1943, enlarged edition published as *Deutsche Hoerer! 55 Radiosendungen nach Deutschland,* Bermann-Fischer, 1945.

Adel des Geistes: 17 Versuche zum Problem der Humanitaet (essays), Bermann-Fischer, 1945, translation by H. T. Lowe-Porter published as *Essays of Three Decades,* Knopf, 1947, recent edition, 1965.

Nietzsches Philosophie im Lichte unserer Erfahrung (essay), Suhrkamp/S. Fischer, 1948, translation published as "Nietzsche's Philosophy in Light of Recent History" in *Last Essays* (also see below).

Neue Studien (essays), Bermann-Fischer, 1948, Suhrkamp/S. Fischer, 1948.

Die Entstehung des Doktor Faustus: Roman eines Romans, Bermann-Fischer/Querido, 1949, translation by Richard and Clara Winston published as *The Story of a Novel: The Genesis of "Doctor Faustus,"* Knopf, 1961, published in England as *The Genesis of a Novel,* Secker, 1961.

Der Kuenstler und die Gesellschaft (speech), Wilhelm Frick (Vienna), 1953.

Gerhart Hauptmann (speech), C. Bertelsmann, 1953.

Altes und Neues: Kleine Prosa aus Fuenf Jahrzehnten (collected short prose pieces), S. Fischer, 1953.

Versuch ueber Schiller (essay), S. Fischer, 1955, translation published as "On Schiller" in *Last Essays* (also see below).

Nachlese: Prosa, 1951-1955 (collection), S. Fischer, 1956.

Leiden und Groesse der Meister (essays; not same as earlier collection with same title), S. Fischer, 1956.

Last Essays, translation by Richard and Clara Winston and Tania and James Stern, Knopf, 1958.

Addresses Delivered at the Library of Congress, 1942-1949 (includes "Germany and the Germans"), U.S. Library of Congress, 1963.

Wagner und unsere Zeit: Aufsaetze, Betrachtungen, Briefe (collected writings on Richard Wagner), edited by Erika Mann, S. Fischer, 1963, translation by Allan Blunden published as *Pro and Contra Wagner,* introduction by Erich Heller, University of Chicago Press, 1985.

Also author of introduction for numerous books, including Theodor Fontane, *Ausgewaehlte Werke,* Reclam, 1929; Martin Niemoeller, *"God is My Fuehrer": Being the Last 28 Sermons,* Philosophical Library and Alliance Book, 1941; *The Short Novels of Dostoevsky,* Dial Press, 1945; *Klaus Mann zum Gedaechtnis,* Querido, 1950; and Heinrich von Kleist, *Die Erzaehlungen,* S. Fischer, 1956.

Contributor of articles and reviews to numerous periodicals.

PERSONAL PAPERS; LETTERS, EXCEPT AS INDICATED

Leiden an Deutschland: Tagebuchblaetter aus den Jahren 1933 und 1934 (diaries), Pazifische Presse (Los Angeles), 1946.

Zeit und Werk: Tagebuecher, Reden, und Schriften zum Zeitgeschehen (collected diaries, speeches, and letters), Aufbau-Verlag (Berlin), 1956.

Briefe an Paul Amann, 1915-1952, edited by Herbert Waegner, Schmidt-Roemhild, 1959, translation by Richard and Clara Winston published as *Letters to Paul Amann,* Wesleyan University Press, 1960.

(With Karl Kerenyi) *Gespraech in Briefen,* edited by Kerenyi, Rhein-Verlag, 1960, translation by Alexander Gelley published as *Mythology and Humanism: The Correspondence of Thomas Mann and Karl Kerenyi,* Cornell University Press, 1975.

Thomas Mann an Ernst Bertram: Briefe aus den Jahren 1910-1955, edited by Inge Jens, Neske, 1960.

Briefe, 1899-1955, edited by Erika Mann, three volumes, S. Fischer, 1961-65.

(With Robert Faesi) *Briefwechsel,* edited by Faesi, Atlantis, 1962.

Letters of Thomas Mann, 1889-1955, translation by Richard and Clara Winston, two volumes, Knopf, 1970.

(With Heinrich Mann) *Briefwechsel, 1900-1949,* edited by Ulrich Dietzel, Aufbau-Verlag (Berlin), 1965, third edition, enlarged, 1975.

(With Heinrich Mann) *Briefwechsel, 1900-1949,* edited by Hans Wysling, S. Fischer, 1968, enlarged, 1984.

(With Hermann Hesse) *Briefwechsel,* edited by Anni Carlsson, S. Fischer, 1968, enlarged by Volker Michels, 1975, translation by Ralph Manheim published as *The Hesse-Mann Letters: The Correspondence of Hermann Hesse and Thomas Mann, 1910-1955,* Harper, 1975.

Thomas Mann und Hans Friedrich Blunck: Briefwechsel und Aufzeichnungen, edited by Walter Blunck, Troll-Verlag, c. 1969.

(With Erich Kahler) *Briefwechsel im Exil,* edited by Hans Wysling, Thomas Mann Gesellschaft, 1970, translation by Richard and Clara Winston published as *An Exceptional Friendship: The Correspondence of Thomas Mann and Erich Kahler,* Cornell University Press, 1975.

Briefwechsel mit seinem Verleger Gottfried Bermann Fischer, 1932-1955 (correspondence with his publisher, Gottfried Bermann Fischer), edited by Peter de Mendelssohn, S. Fischer, 1973.

Briefe an Otto Grautoff, 1894-1901, und Ida Boy-Ed, 1903-1928, edited by Peter de Mendelssohn, S. Fischer, 1975.

Thomas Mann, edited by Hans Wysling, Heimeran, 1975.

Die Briefe Thomas Manns (extracts and indexes), edited by Yvonne Schmidlin, Hans Buergin, and Hans-Otto Mayer, five volumes, S. Fischer, 1976-87.

(With Alfred Neumann) *Briefwechsel,* edited by Peter de Mendelssohn, Schneider, 1977.

Tagebuecher (diaries), edited by Peter de Mendelssohn, S. Fischer, *1933-1934,* 1977, *1935-1936,* 1978, *1918-1921,* 1979, *1937-1939,* 1980, *1940-1943,* 1982; selections from *1918-21* and *1933-39,* translation by Richard and Clara Winston, published as *Diaries, 1918-1939,* H. N. Winston, 1982.

Tagebuecher, 1944-1946 (diaries), edited by Inge Jens, S. Fischer, 1986.

Briefwechsel mit Autoren, S. Fischer, 1988.

OTHER

(Editor) E. von Mendelssohn, *Nacht und Tag* (novel), Verlag der Weissen Buecher, 1914.

(Editor and author of introduction) *The Living Thoughts of Schopenhauer,* Longmans, Green, 1939.

(Editor and author of introduction) *The Permanent Goethe,* Dial Press, 1948.

Gesammelte Werke (collected works), S. Fischer, 1980—.

Co-editor of the book series "Romane der Welt," for Knaur, beginning in 1927. Co-editor of periodicals, including (under name Paul Thomas) *Der Fruehlingssturm: Monatsschrift fuer Kunst, Litteratur, und Philosophie,* 1893, and *Mass und Wert: Zweimonatsschrift fuer freie deutsche Kultur,* beginning in 1937. Member of advisory committee of *Forum Deutscher Dichter,* for Bermann-Fischer, Allert de Lange (Amsterdam), and Querido, 1938-39.

SIDELIGHTS: Thomas Mann, winner of the 1929 Nobel Prize in literature, is considered one of the foremost German novelists of the twentieth century. Admirers have often ranked him, in the words of Alfred Kazin in *Contemporaries,* as "the creative peer . . . of great experimental novelists like [Marcel] Proust and [James] Joyce." Mann is renowned as a novelist of ideas, though commentators generally agree that he expounded no single philosophy and that his ideas changed over time. His accomplishment, admirers suggest, was to use fiction to conduct a lifelong exploration of philosophical issues, ranging from the role of a creative individual in society to the nature of Western culture. He wrote at a time when Europe was experiencing massive and shocking changes: new technology challenged traditional values and ways of life; mass social movements gained unprecedented importance; and Germany erupted with the horrors of Nazism. Reflecting in his work the doubts and fears of his era, Mann held the attention of millions of readers throughout the world.

"At bottom I am aware that my books are not written for Prague and New York, but for Germans," wrote Mann as he neared his sixtieth birthday, quoted by Richard and Clara Winston in *Letters of Thomas Mann, 1889-1955.* "The rest of the world has always been merely an 'extra.' " Though Mann gained a progressively broader understanding of the world outside Germany throughout his life, his work remained steeped in a German tradition that, observers believe, has made him difficult for many English-speaking readers to fully appreciate. Mann was born in 1875 in Luebeck, a German port on the Baltic Sea that was in economic decline throughout the nineteenth century. His diligent and well-respected father was forced to grapple with Luebeck's failing economy, both as head of the family trading firm and as an officer in the city government. The elder Mann chided sons Thomas and Heinrich for their lack of interest in commerce, for he hoped to groom them as his successors in the family business. Mann's mother, of mixed German and Brazilian parentage, seemed exotic by contrast with her business-oriented husband. Highly interested in music, she encouraged her sons' growing interest in the arts. To Mann, his parents embodied a common German view of European culture: a Germanic North, emotionally aloof but dutiful and productive, versus a Latin South, passionate and artistic but potentially irresponsible. In 1891, when Mann was sixteen, his father died at an untimely age and the trading firm was liquidated. The family relocated to Munich, widely regarded at the time as the leading city of German culture; Thomas and Heinrich soon became professional writers.

Nevertheless, as many biographers suggest, Mann often expressed a businessman's suspicion of the artist's role, fearing that self-expression could lapse into empty self-indulgence. As an established writer he paid tribute to the restraining influence of his father and hometown, most notably in the 1926 speech *Luebeck als geistige Lebensform* ("Luebeck as a Spiritual Concept of Life"). Heinrich and Thomas owed much to their mother's "blithe southern disposition," Mann said, quoted by the Winstons. "[But] our father endowed us with 'the serious conduct of life' . . . the ethical note that so strikingly coincides with the bourgeois temper." Mann's ideal bourgeois was not the grasping capitalist disdained by Marxism, but rather the German burgher of pre-industrial times. The lives of such merchants, wrote biographer R. Hinton Thomas, "signified an ideal humanism—freedom without licence, spirituality without extravagant subjectivism, practicality without philistinism."

When Mann prepared to become a writer in his teens and early twenties, he became acquainted with a wide variety of artists and thinkers. As biographer Henry Hatfield observed, his inspiration often came from beyond the world of fiction writing. While a teenager Mann became infatuated with the music of Richard Wagner, whose operas were known for their complexity, passion, and epic vision; but soon, Mann's love of Wagner became tinged with skepticism. As T. E. Apter explained in *Thomas Mann: The Devil's Advocate,* Wagner's strong appeal to the emotions "can appear as a disturbing attack" on rationality and social responsibility. In the opera "Tristan und Isolde," for instance, the composer pointedly mixes such powerful and contradictory feelings as the yearning for love and the fascination with death. R. Hinton Thomas observed that "the evil power of music," which could draw its listeners towards "escape from the restraints and commitments of practical existence," became "a major theme of Mann's work."

After discovering Wagner, Mann delved into the works of nineteenth-century German philosophers Arthur Schopenhauer and Friedrich Nietzsche. Both philosophers rejected the truths by which most Europeans, including Mann's burgher class, had directed their lives—that good would be rewarded and evil punished because the world was a rational place, presided over by a benevolent God or by human reason. Schopenhauer believed that life was fundamentally irrational, for all living things were driven by the force of will—an inborn, mindless striving that could never be satisfied. Human reason was only a tool created by this striving force in order to attain its desires, he maintained, and all people were condemned to unhappiness as their individual wills conflicted with each other. Though pessimistic about the human condition, Schopenhauer found limited consolation in the effort to transcend one's own will, either through charity to others, through art, or, possibly, by losing one's sense of self after death.

Nietzsche took Schopenhauer's premises to more audacious conclusions. He detected a clear purpose in the human force of will, which he labeled the "will to power." According to Nietzsche, every human being is driven to dominate their surroundings, including other people; much of human unhappiness comes from misdirecting this natural drive. Accordingly, he blasted Christianity for advocating guilt and submissiveness, finding its followers self-tortured and too weak to meet the demands of life. He also became dubious of Schopenhauer, whose subdued pessimism seemed as unhealthy as Christianity. Aware that modern science was undermining religious faith in the West, Nietzsche feared that disillusioned believers would lapse into nihilism, choosing death and destruction on the grounds that life had lost its purpose. Thus he advocated a new, more confident human being—the superman or overman—who would find a sense of purpose in the innate force of will.

Commentators suggest that Mann's diverse influences—from dutiful burghers to the flamboyant Nietzsche—do not form a unified philosophy, or even a succession of philosophies. For many of Mann's admirers, his ability to pursue several different modes of thought at once is key to his appeal. As Hatfield explained in *Modern German Literature:* "Mann's gift—or curse—of seeing both sides of almost everything and everyone was perhaps his most characteristic talent. It often made him irritating and unsatisfactory as a thinker, and particularly as a political essayist. But in the realm of fiction this 'dual perspective' on man gave his vision a stereoptic quality, and his characters a third dimension. His people are good *and* evil, perceptive *and* blind; they are extraordinarily real. . . . their very inconsistencies keep them alive and fascinating." Mann's double vision extends to his narrative style, which is well known for its irony. His narrators tend to remain aloof, undercutting characters with bemused skepticism. (Often, reviewers lament, the irony is conveyed by subtleties of the German language that are difficult to reproduce in translation.) In *Rede und Antwort* (1922), quoted by R. Hinton Thomas, Mann celebrated "the poetic charms and possibilities which arise out of doubt, out of faith called into question." The author asked: "What is poetry if not irony"?

Mann's early writing career was marked by sudden successes. At nineteen he was apprenticed to a Munich insurance firm, where he eluded work in order to write his first short story; its publication gained him an appreciative letter from Richard Dehmel, a prominent poet of the day. The short story made Mann determined to write professionally, so he quit his job after a few months in order to audit a broad range of courses at Munich's university. A few more short stories quickly led to Mann's first book—*Der kleine Herr Friedemann* ("Little Herr Friedemann"; 1898), a collection published by the distinguished literary firm of Samuel Fischer. By the time *Friedemann* was published Thomas was in Italy with his brother Heinrich, who was a great admirer of Italian culture. Thomas showed little interest in his surroundings, however: he was writing a novel about his German merchant ancestors, whom he thinly disguised as the Buddenbrook family. *Buddenbrooks* was a work with few precedents in German literature. It was patterned on the naturalistic novels of Western Europe and Scandinavia, which used lavish detail to create the portrait of an individual, a family, or a society. Many Luebeckers were soon filled with shock and outrage, for Mann had surveyed his hometown with unsettling detachment, as betrayed by his book's subtitle—*Verfall einer Familie* (*Decline of a Family*).

Buddenbrooks opens with a celebration, as Johann Buddenbrook, elderly head of a prosperous trading firm, entertains guests at his new mansion. Hatfield calls him "a type of the eighteenth century as popularly conceived—rationalistic, optimistic, skeptical, and of uncomplicated, single-minded energy." Johann soon dies, having virtually disinherited one son who married below the proper station; a dutiful and religious son, Jean, gains control of the family business. In the name of duty Jean persuades his tempestuous daughter Tony to boost the family finances through a loveless marriage, but the husband turns out to be a bankrupt swindler. As Tony careens through a succession of unhappy marriages, control of the firm falls to her brother Tom, a talented and honorable man slowly overwhelmed by his responsibilities. Tom draws solace from the writings of a pessimistic philosopher, reading that after death he will lose his individual identity; Mann later suggested that the philosopher was Schopenhauer. Tom dies while still in middle age, and his son Hanno represents the final generation of Buddenbrooks. Hanno, an artistic and sensitive child, fond of Wagner and devoid of will-power, dies at the age of fifteen. Financial success comes to other families, whose crass attitudes, critics suggest, signify the triumph of grasping modern capitalists over the more humane burghers of German tradition.

Buddenbrooks was massive, even by nineteenth-century standards. Fischer, fearful he could not sell a costly two-volume novel, unsuccessfully pressured Mann to condense the book. The first edition sold slowly, but when Fischer reissued the work in a single volume it became wildly popular, and Mann was suddenly celebrated throughout Germany. "Mann has given evidence of a capacity and ability that cannot be ignored," declared poet Rainer Maria Rilke. In a 1902 review, later quoted in Hatfield's *Thomas Mann: A Collection of Critical Essays,* Rilke hailed Mann as both "chronicler" and "poet," a master of detail and of vivid characterization. He praised the "particular subtlety" Mann uses to show how progressive self-absorption speeds the family's decline. Other German-speaking contemporaries praised Mann's skill and chided his wordiness, thus expressing opinions that would follow the author throughout his career. American reviewers had comparable reactions when *Buddenbrooks* appeared in English in the 1920s. "There is a beauty of decay as well as of growth, a charm of fading colors . . . as well as of the dawn," wrote Robert Morss Lovett in *New Republic.* "Of this beauty and this eloquence Thomas Mann is master."

Despite the popular success of *Buddenbrooks,* Mann never wrote such a highly realistic work again. Admirers stress that he continued to show a flair for realistic detail, including subtle insights into human psychology. Nevertheless, in analyzing most of Mann's fiction, commentators tend to view the characters as representations of ideas. In his study of Mann, Hatfield attempted to reconcile the contrasting views of Mann as philosopher and storyteller. Hatfield advised: "Whatever Mann's importance as a thinker—and many of his critics seem to discuss the 'philosophy' of his stories with a certain pontifical overseriousness—the works can best be read as literature; the artistic *how* is at least as interesting as the ideological *what.* With Mann one cannot afford to neglect either."

Commentators suggest that *Buddenbrooks,* for all its meticulous realism, is based on a philosophical issue: can successive generations of a family become so emotionally sensitive, so preoccupied with personal concerns, that they become unable to survive in life? In Mann's other early fiction, typically novellas and short stories, he applied such a question to his own situation as a fledgling writer, showing the conflict between life and art. The tone of these stories is often cold and pessimistic: as Hatfield observed, " 'life' and its healthy representatives are dull or brutal or both; but the antagonists to 'life,' the isolated and introspective protagonists, are sick, psychologically maladjusted, and frequently grotesque." "Der kleine Herr Friedemann" was the title story of Mann's first book. Friedemann is a hunchback who avoids human society in favor of literature and music. At a performance of Wagner, Friedemann observes a socialite with fascination; the two begin a tentative friendship, but he is soon rejected and attempts suicide. The title character of "Tobias Mindernickel" is a lonely misfit who is taunted by children as he walks the streets. He enjoys comforting his dog when it is weak, but when the dog becomes willful, Mindernickel kills it and weeps over the corpse. Soon after Mann's first short stories appeared, he spent about two years on the editorial staff of *Simplizissimus*—a Munich periodical noted for its strong satire.

In *Tonio Kroeger,* published shortly after *Buddenbrooks,* Mann made an explicit effort to resolve the controversy between art and life. Son of a North German merchant with a foreign-born wife, Tonio Kroeger invites comparison to Mann; his Italian-German name underscores his divided sympathies. As a child Kroeger realizes that he is too morbidly introspective to share the simple joys of his handsome, blond, outgoing schoolmates. He matures into a talented writer, but as he circulates among contrasting social settings—the middle class and the artists, northern and southern Europe—he continues to agonize about his relationship to other people. A girlfriend diagnoses him as a "lost burgher" and an artist "with a bad conscience." Finally, Kroeger finds a sense of purpose by accepting his ambiguous position in society. "It is precisely [Kroeger's] frustrated love for the Nordic-normal-bourgeois which gives him the inner tension that makes him creative," wrote Hatfield. "He will stand between [the art world and the middle class], a sympathetic if ironic mediator."

During the next several years Mann suffered a series of professional setbacks. "Fiorenza" (1906), his only play, was judged too slow-moving for the stage; *Koenigliche Hoheit (Royal Highness;* 1909), a novel based on his happy marriage, was found disappointingly shallow. He soon became stalled on his next novel, a projected multivolume saga titled *Bekenntnisse des Hochstaplers Felix Krull (Confessions of Felix Krull, Confidence Man;* 1922, 1937, and 1954). Lamenting his inability to write, Mann took his wife on a vacation to Venice. In the decaying Italian port, which largely survived by displaying its Renaissance art treasures to tourists, he met a series of exotic characters who gave him inspiration for a short story. Conceived as a diversion suitable for *Simplizissimus, Der Tod in Venedig (Death in Venice;* 1912) became known as one of the world's finest examples of short fiction.

Death in Venice begins in Munich, as the renowned writer Gustav Aschenbach struggles against the exhaustion of his creativity. Aschenbach is about fifty years old, unmarried, highly disciplined and repressed; he writes tales of spiritual struggle that reassert conservative values. Walking by a cemetery, Aschenbach is startled by an odd-looking traveler standing at the door of a crypt; the writer suddenly decides to leave Munich and refresh himself with a trip to southern Europe. The ominous stranger seems to appear twice more as Aschenbach travels to Venice: once as a decrepit homosexual whose face is rouged in a futile effort to look younger; again as a menacing gondolier who apparently operates without a license. In the city Aschenbach spots an adolescent Polish boy named Tadzio whom he finds strikingly beautiful; he begins following the boy and his family throughout Venice. The writer is alternately frightened and elated by his growing passion for Tadzio, and in a nightmare he joins animals and humans at an orgy in honor of a "stranger god." One day Aschenbach smells the sweet odor of disinfectant on the city's air, denoting an outbreak of cholera; however, he does nothing to save himself or the boy's family. Instead he asks a barber to rouge his face and redden his lips, then eats overripe strawberries that are apparently contaminated with the fatal disease. On the beach a few days later Aschenbach shouts to intervene when other boys beat Tadzio, and the boy then stands alone by the sea, returning the writer's gaze. Aschenbach rises from his beach chair, then collapses from illness. "By nightfall," the tale concludes, "a shocked and respectful world learned of his decease."

Unsettling and evocative, *Death in Venice* has been treated by commentators as a major work despite its modest size. Many reviewers have praised the carefully controlled tone of Mann's prose. Devoid of either harsh judgment or sympathy, the narration echoes the degeneration of Aschenbach's personality: the style is austere at the opening, then grows overwrought as the writer sinks into irrationality. Recurrent words and images create an oppressive, deathly atmosphere; reviewers liken the effect to repeated musical themes in Wagner's operas. The word "sweet," for instance, acquires a menacing tone as Mann uses it to describe the smell of overgrown plants, rotting fruit, and disinfectant. The recurring figure of a sinister stranger recalls the imagery of ancient myths, in which men are confronted by the figure of death. Mann, wrote Cyril Connolly in *The Condemned Playground,* has given Aschenbach's demise the impact of an ancient tragedy; the story, he wrote, "has the frozen completeness of a work of art."

Death in Venice has prompted a vast array of interpretations. Some critics have suggested that the work is based on Mann's own homosexual fantasies; by contrast, Mann suggests in his correspondence that the story was often viewed as an attack on homosexuality. D. H. Lawrence, who tried to portray the joys of sexuality in his works, blasted Mann's "sick vision": Lawrence did not object to the story's plot, which he considered largely symbolic, but to Mann's apparent inability to portray human sexuality in terms that were not repulsive. T. E. Apter, noting the story's focus on "death, passion and the debilitating effects of beauty," averred that Mann was repudiating the emotional excess he found in Wagner's work. Martin Swales, in *Thomas Mann: A Study,* pointed out that Aschenbach's widespread popularity as a writer makes him "the spokesman of a generation"; thus Aschenbach's swing between emotional extremes—from strident repression to unthinking frenzy—seems an ominous diagnosis of European society on the eve of World War I. Europe, relatively peaceful and productive for a century, greeted the war in 1914 with what Swales calls "waves of collective enthusiasm."

But as biographers suggest, Mann's perceptiveness as a writer of fiction did not always carry over into his personal life. For example, the year that the rather daring *Death in Venice* was published, Mann paradoxically joined the Munich Censorship Council; he soon withdrew after heated criticism from other writers. After World War I began, Heinrich became a pioneering advocate of peace, praising the more democratic society of Germany's opponent, France. But Thomas cast aside his fiction to write words of encouragement for the German war effort; in such missives, he echoed the nationalist position that Germany was an emerging power, entitled to take an aggressive stand against overbearing countries such as France and England. The Mann brothers began a painful political quarrel that, as many biographers observed, mirrored German society's debate about its future. In the closing years of the war Thomas summarized his view of Germany in a book that remains the most controversial part of his literary legacy—*Betrachtungen eines Unpolitischen* (*Reflections of a Nonpolitical Man;* 1918). Drawing a sharp contrast between Germany and France, the book suggests that French democracy, a product of intellectual theories rather than long-term experience with human nature, is by nature didactic and intolerant; whereas Germany's less political, more inward-looking culture is better attuned to the realities of human experience, including society's need for a well-established hierarchy. "To transform Germany into a middle-class democracy," summarized Carolly Erickson in the *Los Angeles Times Book Review,* "would reduce her rich spiritual complexity to something 'dull, shallow, stupid and un-German.' "

In light of Germany's subsequent plunge into Nazism, Mann's nationalist rhetoric seems at best naive; at worst, willfully blind. After World War I *Reflections* was embraced by German ultra-conservatives as a political tract, and for years thereafter Mann faced charges that he had encouraged incipient fascism. Mann's defenders, stressing the confused, tormented nature of the work, echo the view that Mann himself provided several years later in *Lebensabriss* (*A Sketch of My Life;* 1930). *Reflections,* Mann suggested, was an inner dialogue, the struggle of a burgherly German conservative to adjust to the changes sweeping Europe in the early twentieth century. For the rest of his life Mann was steadfast in his views about the fundamental differences between Germany and Western Europe, but he concluded that rational democracy was the salvation of the West and that Germany's culture had spurred the country's downfall.

In 1918 Germany surrendered and replaced its imperial government with a western-style democracy—events that seem to have left Mann temporarily baffled. He asked that *Reflections* be viewed as a novel, and penned a lengthy poem (*Gesang vom Kindchen;* 1919) about the birth of his youngest daughter. But by the 1920s Mann showed renewed interest in social issues, for he had begun what admirers call his education in democracy. He shocked conservatives with the speech *Von Deutscher Republik* ("The German Republic"; 1923), backing the new democratic government and attempting, somewhat awkwardly, to link democracy to German tradition. "My ideas have perhaps altered—not my intention," Mann declared in a preface to the printed work, quoted by Hamilton. "Thoughts are always—however sophistic this may sound—only a means to an end, a tool in the service of an intention." Mann declared that his main concern was "exactly the same as in *Reflections:* namely that of German humanity." The Mann brothers were reconciled in the 1920s, and Heinrich praised his brother's growth from a mere "observer" to a man "involved with his people." The fruit of Thomas Mann's new social consciousness—according to his brother and many literary critics—is his 1924 novel, *Der Zauberberg* (*The Magic Mountain*). Considered a landmark of world literature, *The Magic Mountain* depicts the conflicting cultural and political trends that sundered the Mann brothers and vexed all Europe in the opening decades of the twentieth century.

Set in the years preceding World War I, *The Magic Mountain* takes place on a Swiss mountaintop in a tuberculosis sanatorium. Mann had visited such a place in 1912, when his wife was recovering from the disease. Mann's fictional sanatorium serves as a symbolic gathering place for the nations of Europe, for its patients include wealthy patrons from throughout the continent. As guests undergo the prescribed "rest cure," they lose their sense of the passing of time, for they are removed from the struggles of ordinary existence and turn to pastimes that range from games to endless philosophical discussions. The staff systematically insulates the patients from their most pressing concern—death—by affecting a cheerful attitude and surreptitiously removing the bodies of the dead. The book opens as Hans Castorp, a newly graduated engineer, arrives to visit his sick cousin. When doctors find a trace of tuberculosis in Hans, he agrees to stay at the sanatorium for a few weeks; instead, he becomes captivated by the hospital's unworldly atmosphere and remains for seven years. As an open-minded, somewhat directionless young man, Hans becomes the central character in Mann's revival of the *Bildungsroman,* or "novel of education"—a classic German genre in which thoughtful role models aid a naive youth to become a productive member of society.

But unlike the typical hero of a novel of education, Hans never finds a trustworthy mentor. Instead, he learns moderation by confronting extremists—patients or doctors whose doctrinaire approaches to life are undercut by their self-contradictory personalities. Naphta, named for a flammable liquid, relishes strong emotions. An Eastern European Jew who saw his father crucified in a pogrom, he nonetheless became a Christian and joined the Jesuits, a religious order known for its zealous defense of Catholic doctrine. Now he praises communism as well as Catholicism, for both, he contends, are admirably authoritarian; to reform society, he advocates "anointed Terror." Naphta's opposite is the Italian Settembrini, a humanist whose strong faith in reason, which initially appeals to Hans, proves to be laced with intellectual arrogance. Settembrini relishes the destruction of his enemies much as Naphta does, but he cannot consciously accept the validity of human emotion. Trivializing insanity, Settembrini claims to have cured a madman by giving him a "rational" stare; he also dismisses Hans's pangs of love for a woman patient, prompting Hans to denounce him. Finally Settembrini and Naphta stage a duel that is considered Mann's satire on intellectual excess. Settembrini fires his gun in the air; Naphta, unable to comprehend such a gesture, shoots himself in the head. Hans also seeks out patients who are more comfortable with their physical nature, but his mentors once again prove to be flawed. Clavdia Chauchat, a languorous Russian woman, thrills Hans with sexual flirtation but prefers the company of Mynheer Peeperkorn, a charismatic Dutch planation owner who dominates and frightens her. Peeperkorn, though aggressive and inarticulate, draws the admiration of Hans and many others for his impassioned love of life. As the Dutchman approaches old age, however, he surrenders to despair, and shortly after arriving at the sanatorium he commits suicide. Hans's lessons in the need for moderation end abruptly, for as the book ends he is drafted into the German Army to serve in World War I. Mann last shows him facing enemy fire on a battlefield. Many reviewers surmise that he is killed.

As biographer Hamilton wrote, "*The Magic Mountain* restored [Mann] to his rightful standing: the master novelist of his age." The book received widespread attention in Germany and throughout the Western world, garnering praise from such notables as French novelist Andre Gide and American literary critic Joseph Wood Krutch. When the novel first appeared, Krutch proclaimed it comparable in stature to Proust's *Remembrance of Things Past.* Mann, wrote Krutch in *Nation,* had "[told] the whole story of the modern mind," creating a unique work about the interaction between ideas and individual character. Commentators have reiterated such views for decades. *The Magic Mountain* "is Thomas Mann's most complex creation," wrote T. J. Reed in *Thomas Mann: The Uses of Tradition,* "the summa of his life, thought, and technical achievement to the age of fifty." Reed called the work "spiritual autobiography . . . intricate allegory . . . historical novel, an analysis of Man and a declaration of principle for practical humanism." Five years after *The Magic Mountain* was published, the author received the Nobel Prize in literature.

Mann, biographers believe, hoped that postwar Germany would choose the course of sensible moderation embodied by Hans Castorp. Instead the nation became politically polarized, and when spokesmen of the increasingly fascist right branded Mann a traitor to their cause, he responded by endorsing socialism. While the Nazi Party consolidated its control of Germany after the 1933 elections, Mann and his wife were out of the country. To his dismay, he received warnings from his eldest daughter that it was unsafe to return, in part, presumably, because Mann's wife was Jewish. At first Mann avoided an open break with the Nazis, apparently hoping, along with the Jewish president of his publishing house, that prominent moderates could outlast the regime and encourage opposition. As a result Mann's work escaped the first wave of Nazi censorship campaigns, but he was compromised in the eyes of antifascist groups and came to view his forbearance as a mistake. In 1936 Mann issued a series of increasingly strong statements against the Nazi regime, and before the end of the year his German citizenship had been revoked. The University of Bonn promptly withdrew its honorary doctorate, and Mann replied with a blistering open letter that was read throughout the world. If the Nazis held sway, Mann warned,

quoted by Hamilton, the German people would become "an instrument of war . . . driven by a blind and fanatical ignorance." He declared: "Woe to the people which . . . seeks its way out through the abomination of war, hatred of God and man! Such a people will be lost. It will be so vanquished that it will never rise again." For the rest of the Nazi era, Mann was widely known for both his attacks on wayward Germany and his praise of democracy. Combined with his Nobel Prize-winning status, such activities made him—perhaps against his wishes—a leading representative of German progressives in the eyes of the public. After receiving a warm welcome on lecture tours of the United States, Mann took up residence there and became an American citizen in 1944.

In contrast to his speeches, Mann's reaction to Nazism in his fiction was at first indirect. His new series of biblical novels about the ancient history of the Jews, for instance, became a refutation of the Nazis' racist mythmaking. The novels focus on the story of Joseph, whose great-grandfather Abraham had initiated the special relationship between the Jews and God. Known collectively as *Joseph und Seine Brueder* (*Joseph and His Brothers*), the series comprises four books: *Die Geschichten Jaakobs* (*The Tales of Jacob;* 1933), *Der Junge Joseph* (*Young Joseph;* 1934), *Joseph in Aegypten* (*Joseph in Egypt;* 1936), and *Joseph der Ernaehrer* (*Joseph the Provider;* 1943). Joseph, supremely talented, confident in his abilities and in God's providence, is for R. J. Hollingdale a benevolent variation on Nietzsche's overman and the leading character in a "cheerful myth." Joseph survives his own egotism, the envy of his brothers, betrayal into slavery, and false imprisonment to become the savior of his Egyptian masters in time of famine. Mann's narrative, lightly irreverent, is a blend of mythology and psychology. The author wished, in Hatfield's words, "to reveal basic human archetypes as they occur in the myths of the gods, in legend, and in history"; to this end the characters often resemble each other or famous persons from history and fiction. At the same time, as Mann himself suggested, he wanted to show the emergence of individuality; accordingly, the characters acquire subtle motivations missing from the short biblical account. The series of Joseph novels drew regular praise from reviewers in the United States. "The whole," wrote J. F. Fullington in *Atlantic Monthly,* "constitutes a work which in encyclopedic scholarship, imaginative power, and magnitude of conception can hardly be approached by any other literary product of our time." But Hatfield observed that the books have also been accused of slow pacing, repetition, and pedantry; such problems could be symptoms, he observed, of "that decrease in intensity often characteristic of aging writers."

Upon completing the Joseph books, Mann began a novel he both dreaded and felt compelled to write—an explicit indictment of German culture and its role in fomenting the Nazi regime. Heinrich, one of Germany's first social satirists, had long viewed his native culture as if he were an outsider, but Thomas tended to identify strongly with German tradition: to indict German culture was to indict his own nature. Mann discussed his situation in the 1945 speech "Germany and the Germans," which he delivered at the U.S. Library of Congress just weeks after the fall of the Nazi regime. Here he rejected his public image as the representative of a "good Germany" that stood apart from the Nazis. There is only a single Germany, Hamilton quoted him, "which has turned its best by devilry into bad." Mann concluded: "It is . . . impossible for a German-born mind to disown the evil, guilt-laden Germany. . . . I have it also in me; I have experienced it in my own body."

To portray Germany's descent into evil, Mann revived the old German legend of Faust, a learned man who sold his soul to the devil in exchange for knowledge and supernatural power. Titling his work *Doktor Faustus* (*Doctor Faustus;* 1947), he made his lead character Adrian Leverkuehn, a fictional German composer who lives from 1885 to 1940. Adrian spends his childhood on a farm and in a small town, then studies religion at a university where his teachers show a morbid interest in the nature of evil. Soon he opts for a career in music, which remained for Mann a symbol of irrationality, as the author suggested in "Germany and the Germans." As a composer Adrian discovers a problem familiar to creative artists in the sophisticated twentieth century: he believes he has arrived on the world scene too late, and that all the original, expressive works of art have already been made. The complaint also recalls the German nationalist doctrines that Mann had once endorsed; Adrian's cry for an artistic "breakthrough" resembles Nazi rhetoric about overcoming Anglo-French domination. Using the technique he developed in the Joseph saga, Mann makes Adrian the embodiment of a menacing human archetype: the arrogant, overreaching German. Adrian's life particularly resembles that of Nietzsche, whose works Nazi propagandists falsely claimed as precursors of their own ideas about a master Germanic race. In his youth Adrian contracts syphilis in a brothel, as Nietzsche is alleged to have done, and thereafter his life is a similar mixture of daring creativity and growing madness. The composer becomes convinced that in Italy he conversed with the devil about music and traded his soul for the chance to write great new compositions. He soon becomes renowned as the inventor of twelve-tone music, a system that abjures the harmonies familiar to Western listeners (and that was actually the brainchild of Mann's fellow expatriate, Arnold Schoenberg). In 1930, as the Nazis rise to power, Adrian summons friends and reviewers to his home to introduce his new symphony, "The Lamentation of Doctor Faustus." Before playing parts of the work on his piano, Adrian gives a long, tormented speech that amounts to a confession of his pact with Satan. But his speech is so disordered, the language so archaic, that his auditors assume he is demented: they respond with a mixture of shock and mere embarrassment. As with Nietzsche, Adrian suddenly collapses in insanity and spends the last ten years of his life being tended by his mother. *Doctor Faustus* is narrated by Adrian's friend Serenus Zeitblom, a well-intentioned, burgherly German who is slow to comprehend the evil nature of the composer's genius. Zeitblom writes his reminiscences during the war years from 1943 to 1945, as Germany is driven to defeat. By the end of his account, Zeitblom is conscious of the parallel fates of his friend and his country.

Mann spoke of *Doctor Faustus* as one of the most important and daring works of his career, calling it his "wildest" novel, as biographer Ignace Feuerlicht noted. But even commentators who respected the author's effort often found the book flawed. Mann's characteristic weaknesses—a love of length and complexity, a preoccupation with philosophy—seemed, for many commentators, to have defeated his intention. "This book is a monster: one cannot love it," wrote Hollingdale, citing such problems. Nonetheless, he called the novel "a 'great' book, an enduring book . . . full of faults and yet worth ten thousand petty 'successes.'" "Among [Mann's] longer works," wrote Hatfield, *The Magic Mountain* "is formally more successful, and conveys a far greater sense of intellectual excitement," but *Doctor Faustus* is still much more than "an ambitious failure." Hatfield called the work an "end product"—a writer's final summation of his artistic vision. As with the "vast late works" of other authors, Hatfield averred, the novel is "only partially successful" but "contain[s] an enormous variety of riches."

Mann lived for a decade after World War II, and as a man of high public stature he was the object of both admiration and outrage. He received many prestigious awards throughout Europe, but he was blasted as a fraud by German writers who had lived under Hitler and were compromised by Nazism. At first reluctant to visit Germany at all, he finally insisted on touring the communist eastern half as well as the noncommunist west. Suddenly the man once denounced as a conservative ideologue was branded by the American right as a communist dupe, and he moved from the United States to Switzerland, expressing concern that America might be headed for fascism. Mann's last major work, begun a half-century earlier, was the completed first volume of *Felix Krull* (1954). The novel is of special interest to admirers of Mann as a burlesque of many ideas that appear in the rest of his writing. The title character, a confidence man, combines the moral blindness of Adrian Leverkuehn with the cheerful self-confidence of Joseph. For Felix Krull—who is seen as a mocking self-portrait of the author—fraud is both an art and a philosophy of life.

After Mann died in 1955, he was sometimes recalled as a friend of democracy and humanism—ignoring, perhaps, the complex and ambiguous nature of his work. "I once saw Thomas Mann plain," declared Alfred Kazin, contending that Mann used a "conservative social self" to mask "a mind so complex that his real opinions were always elusive." Hollingdale depicted Mann in Nietzschean terms, as the child of a Western civilization that had become unable to believe in God or anything else. In a world without values, Mann's novels were long because there was, in the critic's words, "no principle of selection." Mann preached no ideology because none was credible; irony was his "self-defence against the meaningless." For a world that "*really has no values,*" Hollingdale observed, Mann's "fictional world is a *true* mirror." He summarized Mann with a proverb: "As the mirror replied to the monster: 'There is nothing wrong with me, it is *you* who are distorted.'"

MEDIA ADAPTATIONS: Buddenbrooks was adapted for films of the same title, [Germany], 1923 and 1959, and for a television series of the same title, [Germany], 1982; *Tonio Kroeger* was adapted by Erika Mann and Ennio Flajano for the film "Tonio Kroger," [France and Germany], 1968; *Death in Venice* was adapted by Luchino Visconti and Niccolo Badalucco for a film of the same title, Warner, 1971; "Disorder and Early Sorrow" was adapted by Franz Seitz for the film "Disorder and Early Torment," Jugendfilm, 1977; *The Transposed Heads* was adapted for musical dramas of the same title by Peggy Glanville-Hicks, and by Julie Taymor and Sidney Goldfarb, 1984-86; *The Confessions of Felix Krull, Confidence Man* was adapted by Robert Thoeren and Erika Mann for the film "The Confessions of Felix Krull," Filmaufbau, 1957, and for a television series, [Germany], 1981.

BIOGRAPHICAL/CRITICAL SOURCES:

BOOKS

Apter, T. E., *Thomas Mann: The Devil's Advocate,* New York University Press, 1979.

Bauer, Arnold, *Thomas Mann,* translation by Alexander and Elizabeth Henderson, Ungar, 1971.

Bloom, Harold, editor, *Thomas Mann: Modern Critical Views,* Chelsea House, 1986.

Bloom, Harold, editor, *Thomas Mann's "The Magic Mountain,"* Chelsea House, 1986.

Brennan, Joseph Gerard, *Thomas Mann's World,* Russell & Russell, 1962.

Buergin, Hans, *Das Werk Thomas Manns: Eine Bibliographie,* S. Fischer, 1959.

Buergin, Hans and Hans-Otto Mayer, *Thomas Mann: A Chronicle of His Life,* translation by Eugene Dobson, University of Alabama Press, 1969.

Cather, Willa, *Not Under Forty,* Knopf, 1936.

Connolly, Cyril, *The Condemned Playground: Essays, 1927-1944,* Macmillan, 1946.

De Mendelssohn, Peter, *Der Zauberer: Das Leben des deutschen Schriftstellers Thomas Mann,* S. Fischer, 1975.

Dictionary of Literary Biography, Volume 66: *German Fiction Writers, 1885-1913,* Gale, 1988.

Domandi, Agnes Koerner, *Modern German Literature: A Library of Literary Criticism,* Ungar, 1972.

Feuerlicht, Ignace, *Thomas Mann,* Twayne, 1968.

Gray, Ronald, *The German Tradition in Literature, 1871-1945,* Cambridge University Press, 1965.

Hamilton, Nigel, *The Brothers Mann: The Lives of Heinrich and Thomas Mann, 1871-1950 and 1875-1955,* Yale University Press, 1979.

Hatfield, Henry, *Thomas Mann,* New Directions, 1951, revised, 1962.

Hatfield, Henry, editor, *Thomas Mann: A Collection of Critical Essays,* Prentice-Hall, 1964.

Hatfield, Henry, *From the Magic Mountain: Thomas Mann's Later Masterpieces,* Cornell University Press, 1979.

Heller, Erich, *Thomas Mann: The Ironic German,* Regnery/Gateway, 1979.

Hirschbach, Frank Donald, *The Arrow and the Lyre: A Study of Love in the Works of Thomas Mann,* Nijhoff, 1955.

Hollingdale, R. J., *Thomas Mann: A Critical Study,* Bucknell University Press, 1971.

Kaufmann, Fritz, *Thomas Mann: The World as Will and Representation,* Beacon Press, 1957.

Kazin, Alfred, *Contemporaries,* Little, Brown, 1962.

Lawrence, D. H., *Phoenix: The Posthumous Papers of D. H. Lawrence,* edited by Edward D. McDonald, Viking Penguin, 1936.

Mann, Erika and Klaus Mann, *Escape to Life,* Houghton, 1939.

Mann, Erika, *The Last Years of Thomas Mann,* Farrar, Straus & Cudahy, 1958.

Mann, Katja, *Unwritten Memories,* Knopf, 1975.

Mann, Klaus, *The Turning-Point: Thirty-Five Years in This Century,* S. Fischer, 1943.

Mann, Thomas, *A Sketch of My Life,* Knopf, 1960.

Mann, Thomas, *The Story of a Novel: The Genesis of "Doctor Faustus",* Knopf, 1961.

Mann, Thomas, *Letters of Thomas Mann, 1889-1955,* edited by Richard and Clara Winston, Vintage, 1975.

Neider, Charles, editor, *The Stature of Thomas Mann,* New Directions, 1948.

Nicholls, R. A., *Nietzsche in the Early Works of Thomas Mann,* University of California Press, 1955.

Reed, T. J., *Thomas Mann: The Uses of Tradition,* Oxford University Press, 1974.

Stern, J. P., *Thomas Mann,* Columbia University Press, 1967.

Swales, Martin, *Thomas Mann: A Study,* Heinemann, 1980.

Thomas, R. Hinton, *Thomas Mann: The Mediation of Art,* Oxford University Press, 1963.

Twentieth-Century Literary Criticism, Gale, Volume 2, 1979, Volume 8, 1982, Volume 14, 1984, Volume 21, 1986.

Von Gronicka, Andre, *Thomas Mann: Profile and Perspectives,* Random House, 1970.

Weigand, Hermann J., *"Der Zauberberg": A Study,* Appleton-Century, 1933.

Winston, Richard, *Thomas Mann: The Making of an Artist,* Knopf, 1981.

PERIODICALS

American Mercury, October, 1951.

American Scholar, summer, 1957.

Atlantic Monthly, September, 1944, June, 1975.

Dial, May, 1925, July, 1928.

Germanic Review, February, 1960.

Kenyon Review, winter, 1950.

Los Angeles Times Book Review, May 22, 1983.

Modern Fiction Studies, summer, 1965.

Nation, April 16, 1924, March 25, 1925, December 9, 1925, April 21, 1926, June 8, 1927, December 4, 1929, November 22, 1933, July 13, 1934, May 22, 1935, July 8, 1944, June 11, 1955, September 3, 1955, October 1, 1955.

New Republic, April 9, 1924, July 6, 1927, June 26, 1935, December 7, 1942, November 1, 1948, October 3, 1955.

New Statesman, November 7, 1936, November 5, 1955.

Newsweek, March 8, 1971.

New Yorker, August 31, 1940, July 22, 1944, October 30, 1948.

New York Times Book Review, November 4, 1923, February 17, 1924, February 22, 1925, May 8, 1927, December 8, 1929, July 12, 1931, December 10, 1933, July 10, 1934, April 28, 1935, June 7, 1936, August 8, 1937, June 15, 1947, October 31, 1948, August 8, 1965, February 22, 1971, July 20, 1975, May 15, 1983.

Partisan Review, spring, 1956.

Saturday Review, June 27, 1925, July 16, 1927, May 19, 1928, November 11, 1933, June 9, 1934, June 6, 1936, July 31, 1937, October 30, 1948, June 10, 1950, June 4, 1955, September 17, 1955, December, 1981.

Sewanee Review, fall, 1929, summer, 1933.

South Atlantic Quarterly, July, 1937.

Time, July 3, 1944, February 12, 1951.

Times Literary Supplement, August 9, 1923, October 2, 1924, July 7, 1927, June 14, 1934, February 25, 1983, August 5, 1983.

OBITUARIES:

PERIODICALS

Commonweal, September 16, 1955.

New York Times, August 13, 1955, August 17, 1955.

Saturday Review, September 17, 1955.

Times Literary Supplement, August 19, 1955.

—*Sketch by Thomas Kozikowski*

*   *   *

MANNING, Olivia   1915-1980

PERSONAL: Born in 1915, in Portsmouth, England; died July 23, 1980, in Isle of Wight, England; daughter of Oliver (a commander in Royal Navy) and Olivia (Morrow) Manning; married Reginald Donald Smith (a drama producer for British Broadcasting Corp.), August, 1939.

ADDRESSES: 36 Abbey Gardens, London NW8, England.

CAREER: Writer.

AWARDS, HONORS: Commander of the Order of the British Empire, 1976.

WRITINGS:

FICTION

The Wind Changes, Cape, 1937, Knopf, 1938.

Artist among the Missing, Heinemann, 1945, reprinted, 1975.

Growing Up: A Collection of Short Stories, Heinemann, 1948.

School for Love, Heinemann, 1951, reprinted, Penguin, 1982.

A Different Face, Heinemann, 1953, Abelard-Schuman, 1957, reprinted, Heinemann, 1975.

The Doves of Venus, Heinemann, 1955, Abelard-Schuman, 1956, published with a new introduction by Isobel English in an omnibus edition with Rosamond Lehmann's *The Weather in the Streets* and Antonia White's *Frost in May,* Virago, 1984,

My Husband Cartwright, illustrations by Len Deighton, Heinemann, 1956.

The Great Fortune (first novel in "Balkan" trilogy; also see below), Heinemann, 1960, Doubleday, 1961.

The Spoilt City (second novel in "Balkan" trilogy; also see below), Doubleday, 1962.

The Crimson Dawn, Merlin Press, 1963.

Friends and Heroes (third novel in "Balkan" trilogy; also see below), Heinemann, 1965, Doubleday, 1966.

A Romantic Hero and Other Stories, Heinemann, 1967.

The Camperlea Girls, Coward-McCann, 1969.

The Play Room, Heinemann, 1969, published with a new introduction by Isobel English, Virago, 1984.

The Rain Forest, Heinemann, 1974.

The Danger Tree (first novel in "Levant" trilogy; also see below), Atheneum, 1977.

The Battle Lost and Won (second novel in "Levant" trilogy; also see below), Weidenfeld & Nicolson, 1978, Atheneum, 1979.

The Sum of Things (third novel in "Levant" trilogy; also see below), Weidenfeld and Nicolson, 1980, Atheneum, 1981.

The Balkan Trilogy, Volume 1: *The Great Fortune,* Volume 2: *The Spoilt City,* Volume 3: *Friends and Heroes,* Penguin, 1981.

The Levant Trilogy, Volume 1: *The Danger Tree,* Volume 2: *The Battle Lost and Won,* Volume 3: *The Sum of Things,* Penguin, 1982.

Summer Companions, Leisure Books, 1982.

NONFICTION

The Reluctant Recluse: The Story of Stanley's Rescue of Emin Pasha from Equatorial Africa, Doubleday, 1947 (published in England as *The Remarkable Expedition: The Story of Stanley's Rescue of Emin Pasha from Equatorial Africa,* Heinemann, 1947), reprinted under English title, Atheneum, 1985.

The Dreaming Shore (travelogue of Ireland), Evans Brothers, 1950.

Extraordinary Cats, Joseph, 1967.

OTHER

(With Ken Annakin) "The Playroom" (screenplay; based on Manning's novel of same title), International Screen Production, 1970.

(Editor) *Romanian Short Stories,* Oxford University Press, 1971.

(Author of introduction and notes) Jane Austen, *Northanger Abbey,* Pan Books, 1979.

Also contributed to newspapers and periodicals, including *Horizon, Spectator, New Statesman, Punch, Observer,* and *Times* (London).

SIDELIGHTS: Olivia Manning, considered "one of the most gifted English writers of her generation" by Eve Auchincloss in *Book World,* was born at the outset of World War I to a British father and an Irish mother in Portsmouth, England. She spent much of her childhood in Northern Ireland; and when she mar-

ried at the outset of World War II, she travelled abroad with her husband, living in the Balkans before fleeing from the German invasion to Greece and then the Middle East. Despite an early ambition to become a painter, Manning "realized that her artistic tool should be the pen rather than the brush," according to a London *Times* contributor, and she believed that "the novel form seemed 'perfectly adapted to the expression of our bewildered and self-conscious civilization.' " Although she authored several books of fiction and nonfiction during a career that spanned more than forty years, Manning was perhaps best recognized for the six novels about the Second World War that comprise her Balkan and Levant trilogies, which focus upon what Peter Ackroyd described in the *Spectator* as "a world of war, of panic, of violence and isolation." And according to Auchincloss, "Nobody has written better about World War II—the feel of fighting it and its dislocating effects on ordinary, undistinguished lives."

The novels of the Balkan trilogy, *The Great Fortune, The Spoilt City,* and *Friends and Heroes,* recreate the period of impending war and its early years; its sequel, the Levant trilogy, is composed of *The Danger Tree, The Battle Lost and Won,* and *The Sum of Things,* and focuses upon the remaining years of the war. "Obviously rooted in personal experience, the trilogies, centered first in Bucharest, shift South in the face of the advancing Germans, anchor in Athens, decamp in Cairo, and—with stopovers in Beirut, Cairo, and Damascus—end up in Jerusalem," wrote Howard Moss in the *New York Review of Books.* Although Manning's characterizations of Harriet and Guy Pringle were autobiographically inspired, critics such as Auchincloss recognized "this restrained and civilized writer's ability to penetrate mentalities very unlike her own and to infuse a knowledge of circumstances she could never have participated in, or even observed, with an imaginative life that is vivid, rich and precise." In his *Continuance and Change: The Contemporary British Novel,* Robert K. Morris observed: "The series concerns itself neither with abstract or metaphysical theories of time, refashioned or shifting ideologies, nor various plays for power or status; but with the often bare, ironically conditioned facts of living in uncertainty—uncertainty not as accident, but as a constant of life—in a world over which hangs the certainty of ruin."

To Anthony Burgess in his *The Novel Now,* the Balkan trilogy seemed "one of the finest records we have of the impact of that war on Europe." Moreover, Burgess considered it a rarity to find "such a variety of gifts in one contemporary woman writer— humour, poetry, the power of the exact image, the ability to be both hard and compassionate, a sense of place, all the tricks of impersonation and, finally, a historical eye." As historical fiction, the novels are as "remarkable," assessed Walter Allen, suggesting in his *Tradition and Dream: The English and American Novel from the Twenties to Our Time* that "the place and the time, the corruption and the sense of doom, seem caught perfectly; and the characters . . . are drawn with delicacy and strength, so that they come alive on the page, often absurd, but even so always as suffering human beings." For against the larger canvas of the war itself, Manning depicted the problems confronted by ordinary individuals; and as a *Times Literary Supplement* reviewer of *The Great Fortune* stated, by "juxtaposing the personal, sometimes trivial, problems of individuals within the great European conflict which distantly threatens all their futures," Manning offers the reader "the consolation that the great fortune is indeed to have preserved life and hope; nothing else really matters." Noting in a *Christian Science Monitor* review of *The Battle Lost and Won* that the war's effect on manning's protagonists "is the paradigm of a dismal contradiction: that human labor and human affection exist in a universe which makes rather little of either," Edith Milton added that Manning "has a fine, tragic vision of the enormity of our littleness, and she defines that vision with force and with restraint. Her ironies are deep but understated; her prose is totally admirable in its chill clarity."

Manning was regularly praised for her mastery in creating authenticity of scene or sense of place. A *Times Literary Supplement* reviewer of *Friends and Heroes* found the Balkan trilogy "so full of intriguing minor characters . . ., so evocative of both place and mood, and so well proportioned the incidents that provide constant narrative pleasure . . . that one might extract from the trilogy all kinds of meanings and thereby lose the overlying quality, which is simply to have covered an amazingly full and colourful canvas with people and scenes so real and authoritatively recalled that it hardly seems like fiction." And regarding the Levant trilogy, John Mellors stated in the *Listener:* "Place and people are equally real in Olivia Manning's books. She could conjure up a city and a season with a few almost throwaway remarks." Virgilia Peterson indicated in the *New York Times Book Review* about *The Great Fortune* that "Bucharest . . . the way it looked and behaved, its expressions and its probable rumors and improbable characters in those last few months of freedom are boldly drawn." Maurice Richardson concurred in *New Statesman,* "You get such a detailed picture of Rumanian society, haphazard, frivolous, iniquitous and indefensible, that you acquire quite a strong taste for it and regret that you will know what it was like during the German occupation and the sovietisation that followed."

"One of Miss Manning's greatest talents is that she so cleverly conceals the intricate machinery which is needed in organizing so variegated and full a novel," according to a *Times Literary Supplement* reviewer of *The Spoilt City.* "Her often wise and witty comments on the futility of war as it touches ordinary people are always concealed in understatements of fact." Other critics commented about the way in which form complimented content in her work. For instance, in a *New York Times Book Review* assessment of the novel, Martin Levin called its intrigue "the bumbling loosely organized kind, approximating the real thing in those desperate days," adding that the novel's design is one "of a prelude to disaster, which the author's skill resurrects vividly." Describing the trilogies as "the work of a dispassionate moralist who is also an inimitable storyteller," Moss suggested that "Manning's giant six-volume effort is one of those combinations of soap opera and literature that are so rare you'd think it would meet the conditions of two kinds of audiences: those after what the trade calls 'a good read,' and those who want something more." Although finding Manning's prose "often pedestrian, and sometimes so bone-plain we wince a little," Moss nonetheless declared that "as the six novels of the two trilogies accumulate, one reinforcing the other, they ultimately have the effect of a strongly lit tableaux."

"Subtlety, asperity, vividness and ease of manner" distinguish the Levant trilogy, remarked a *Times Literary Supplement* contributor. And Manning was especially credited for the ability, despite her gender, to realistically render scenes of battle. Calling Manning "an adroit technician," Moss observed that "her depictions of desert warfare is chilling and exact; it has the quality of the fantastic that rises from the simultaneous conjunction of the incredibility and believability of fact." Ackroyd echoed this impression about *The Danger Tree:* "I haven't often read battle scenes which come so immediately and horrifyingly to life. And yet they are presented neutrally and even blandly, as if the world were always like this. It all fits very well within the pessimistic vision of the book, but the images which embody it are of an extraordinary power."

"She writes with blessed economy, evoking the sights and smells of the Middle East, the spring-green deserts and a mosque at dawn, with beautiful precision rather than purple passages," commented Charles Champlin in his *Los Angeles Time* review of Manning's final novel, *The Sum of Things.* Although praising Manning's "accurate, superbly economical writing," Jonah Jones felt in the London *Times* that her characterizations inspired little interest, and therefore considered the novel, "further evidence that the reputation she enjoyed during her life may have been inflated." Champlin maintained, however, that "there is in her work as well a calm judiciousness, a special combination of distance and sympathy, of passion described, not celebrated, and of violence serenely depicted, that may have stood in the way of wider sales, but that is individual and very satisfying."

Although loyal, Manning's audience was not large. Remarking that Manning "has been compared with Graham Greene and Anthony Powell," Champlin added that in the United States, she "remains bafflingly little-known . . ., and in England is less a cult figure than a quiet enthusiasm." Explaining that she was "a dedicated professional . . . with a reputation for shyness," the London *Times* contributor pointed out that she "never sought the attention of press or prizegivers." Allen suggested that from the beginning, Manning "possessed an exceedingly pure and exact style, together with what one thinks of as a painter's eye for the visible world, that . . . enabled her to render particularly well the sensual surface of landscapes and places. . . . It is a prose and an eye that seem accurately to take the measure of things." Manning ought to "rank among the very rare writers of our day whose gift of style and story is enlarged to importance by the dimensions of intelligence and moral purpose," said Milton. Victoria Glendinning suggested in the *Times Literary Supplement* that "the 'stray figures' of Olivia Manning's fiction won her a *succes d'estime.* A *succes d'estime* that survives an author's lifetime becomes something more."

MEDIA ADAPTATIONS: Manning's *The Balkan Trilogy* was adapted for British Broadcasting Corp. (BBC-Radio) and for the Public Television Service series, "Masterpiece Theatre."

AVOCATIONAL INTERESTS: Theatre-going, travel, and cats.

BIOGRAPHICAL/CRITICAL SOURCES:

BOOKS

Allen, Walter, *Tradition and Dream: The English and American Novel from the Twenties to Our Time,* J. M. Dent, 1964.
Burgess, Anthony, *The Novel Now,* Norton, 1967.
Contemporary Literary Criticism, Gale, Volume 5, 1976, Volume 19, 1981.
Morris, Robert K., *Continuance and Change: The Contemporary British Novel Sequence,* Southern Illinois University Press, 1972.

PERIODICALS

Book World, May 17, 1981.
Christian Science Monitor, April 9, 1979.
Guardian, February 23, 1960.
Listener, September 25, 1980.
Los Angeles Times, March 23, 1981.
New Statesman, January 30, 1960, November 5, 1965, November 17, 1978, September 26, 1980.
New York Herald Tribune Books, November 25, 1962.
New York Review of Books, April 25, 1985.

New York Times Book Review, July 16, 1961, November 11, 1962, August 28, 1966, October 9, 1977.
Saturday Review, January 22, 1961.
Spectator, January 29, 1960, August 20, 1977, November 25, 1978.
Times (London), July 24, 1980, October 2, 1980.
Times Literary Supplement, January 29, 1960, May 11, 1962, November 4, 1965, August 19, 1977, November 24, 1978, September 19, 1980, January 21, 1983, September 21, 1984.
Washington Post Book World, October 21, 1985.

OBITUARIES:

PERIODICALS

AB Bookman's Weekly, October 6, 1980.
Publishers Weekly, September 5, 1980.
Times (London), July 24, 1980.

*   *   *

MANTECON, Juan Jimenez
   See JIMENEZ (MANTECON), Juan Ramon

*   *   *

MANTON, Peter
   See CREASEY, John

*   *   *

MAO Tse-tung   1893-1976

PERSONAL: Born December 26, 1893, in Shao Shan, Hunan, China (now People's Republic of China); died September 9, 1976, in Peking, People's Republic of China; son of Mao Jensheng (a grain merchant) and Mao Wen; married Yang K'ai-hui, 1920 (died, 1927); married Ho Tze-cheng, 1928 (divorced); married Chiang Ch'ing (an actress), 1939; children: An-ying (died, 1950), Anch'ing, Li Na. *Education:* Teachers' Training College at Changsha, diploma, 1918.

CAREER: Founding member and chairman of Chinese Communist party (CPC); political writer and philosopher; poet. Organized New People's Society, 1917; library assistant at Peking University, 1918-19; primary school teacher in Hunan, 1919; founder, Hunan Reconstruction Alliance, 1919; teacher at First Normal School at Changsha, 1920-22; attended First Congress of CPC as one of twelve original delegates, 1921; organized labor unions in Hunan, China, 1921-27; member of Politburo of Third Central Committee of CPC, 1923; member of Kuomintang, 1923-27, and director of propaganda department, 1925; head of CPC peasants' department, 1926; president, All-China Peasants' Association, 1927; led Hunan peasants in abortive Autumn Harvest Uprising and fled to Chingkangshan, China, during Chiang Kai-shek's purge of Communists, 1927; established Fourth Workers' and Peasants' Red Army, 1928; chairman, China Workers and Revolutionary Committee, 1930; chair of Central Chinese Soviet Republic, 1931-34; on Long March to Shensi Province, China, October, 1934, to October, 1935; political commissar, Red First Front Army, 1935; headquartered in caves of Yenan, China, 1935-45, organizing peasant masses and building the Communist army to nine hundred thousand troops; chairman of politburo, CPC Seventh Central Committee, 1945; chairman, People's Revolutionary Military Council, 1945-56; fought Civil War with Chiang's Nationalists, 1946-49, defeating Chiang's forces and forcing them in political retreat to Taiwan;

elected Chairman of People's Government of People's Republic of China, October 1, 1949, served through 1954; instituted series of rectification campaigns during early 1950s; Chairman of People's Republic of China and National Defense Council, 1954-59, chairman of CPC eighth Central Committee and Standing Committee Politburo, 1956-59; launched "anti-rightist campaign" and Great Leap Forward program, 1957; directed Cultural Revolution, 1966-69; chairman of CPC central committee, 1967-76; chairman presidium, CPC ninth Congress, 1969; supreme commander, Whole Nation and Whole Army, 1970-76.

WRITINGS:

IN ENGLISH

(With others) *China, the March Toward Unity,* Workers Library Publishers, 1937, reprinted, AMS Press, 1978.
The New Stage, New China Information Committee, 1938.
China's "New Democracy," People's Publishing House (Bombay), 1944.
The Fight for a New China, New Century, 1945.
China's Strategy for Victory, People's Publishing House, 1945.
The Way Out of China's Civil War, People's Publishing House, 1946.
Aspects of China's Anti-Japanese Struggle, People's Publishing House, 1948.
Unbreakable China, translated by Hsia Zoh-tsung, Low Phay Hock (Singapore), 1949.
The Autobiography of Mao Tse-tung, transcribed by Edgar Snow, China Truth, 1949.
(With Liu Shao-chi) *Lessons of the Chinese Revolution,* People's Publishing House, 1950.
Strategic Problems of China's Revolutionary War, People's Publishing House, 1951.
On Contradiction, Foreign Languages Press (Peking), 1952.
Maoism: A Sourcebook, edited by H. Arthur Steiner, University of California at Los Angeles, 1952.
Mao's China: Party Reform Documents, 1942-44, translated by Boyd Compton, originally published in 1952, reprinted, Greenwood Press, 1982.
Report of an Investigation Into the Peasant Movement in Hunan, Foreign Languages Press, 1953.
Mind the Living Conditions of the Masses and Attend to the Methods of Work, Foreign Languages Press, 1953.
The Chinese Revolution and the Chinese Communist Party, Foreign Languages Press, 1954.
Strategic Problems in the Anti-Japanese Guerrilla War, Foreign Languages Press, 1954.
On the Protracted War, Foreign Languages Press, 1954.
Selected Works, four volumes, Lawrence & Wishart, 1954-56.
Selected Works, Volume I: *1926-1936,* Volume II: *1937-1938,* Volume III: *1939-1941,* Volume IV: *1941-1945,* Volume V: *1945-1949,* International Publishers, 1954-62.
On Coalition Government, Foreign Languages Press, 1955.
Our Study and the Current Situation, Foreign Languages Press, 1955.
Talks at the Yenan Forum on Art and Literature, Foreign Languages Press, 1956.
On the Correct Handling of Contradictions Among the People, Foreign Languages Press, 1957.
Nineteen Poems, Foreign Languages Press, 1958.
On Art and Literature, Foreign Languages Press, 1960.
Guerrilla Warfare in China, translated by Samuel B. Griffith, Marine Corps Institute, 1960.
On New Democracy, Foreign Languages Press, 1960.
On Guerrilla Warfare, translated by Samuel B. Griffith, Praeger, 1961.

Selected Works of Mao Tse-tung, five volumes, Foreign Languages Press, 1961-77.

Mao Tse-tung: An Anthology of His Writings, edited by Anne Fremantle, New American Library, 1962.

The Political Thought of Mao Tse-tung, edited by Stuart Schram, Praeger, 1963.

Selected Military Writings, Foreign Languages Press, 1963.

Statement Calling on the People of the World to Unite, Foreign Languages Press, 1964.

Poems, translated by Wong Man, Eastern Horizon Press (Hong Kong), 1966.

Four Essays on Philosophy, Foreign Languages Press, 1966.

Quotations from Chairman Mao Tse-tung, Foreign Languages Press, 1966.

Mao Tse-tung on War, English Book Depot (Dehra Dun, India), 1966.

Basic Tactics, translated by Samuel B. Griffith, Praeger, 1966.

Ten More Poems of Mao Tse-tung, Eastern Horizon Press, 1967.

The Thoughts of Chairman Mao, Gibbs, 1967.

On Practice, National Book Agency (Calcutta), 1967.

Selected Readings From the Works of Mao Tse-tung, Foreign Languages Press, 1967.

Why Is It That Red Power Can Exist in China?, Foreign Languages Press, 1968.

Five Articles: Serve the People, China Books, 1968.

The Wisdom of Mao Tse-tung, Philosophical Library, 1968.

On Revolution and War, edited by M. Rejai, Doubleday, 1969.

Supplement to Quotations from Chairman Mao, Chih Luen Press (Hong Kong), 1969.

Long Live Mao Tsetung Thought: A Collection of Statements, American Consulate General, 1969.

Mao Papers: Anthology and Bibliography, edited by Jerome Ch'en, Oxford University Press, 1970.

Talks and Writings, Joint Publications Research Service, 1970.

Six Essays on Military Affairs, Foreign Languages Press, 1971.

Four Essays on China and World Communism, Lancer Books, 1972.

Poems of Mao Tse-tung, translated by Hua-ling Nieh Engle and Paul Engle, Simon & Schuster, 1972.

Ten Poems and Lyrics by Mao Tse-tung, translated by Wang Hui-Ming, University of Massachusetts Press, 1975.

Unselected Works of Mao Tse-tung, 1957 (in English and Chinese), translated by Yang Tsung-han, Union Research Institute, 1976.

Mao Tsetung Poems (in English and Chinese), Foreign Languages Press, 1976.

A Critique of Soviet Economics, translated by Moss Roberts, Monthly Review Press, 1977.

Five Essays on Philosophy, Foreign Languages Press, 1977.

Mao Zedong Poems, translated by Zhao Zhentao, Hunan People's Publishing House, 1980.

Reverberations: A New Translation of Complete Poems of Mao Tse-tung, notes by Nancy T. Lin, Joint Publishing, 1980.

Maoism as It Really Is: Pronouncements of Mao Zedong, Some Already Known to the Public and Others Hitherto Not Published in the Chinese Press, edited by O. F. Vladimirov, translated from the Russian by Cynthia Carlile, Progress (Moscow), 1981.

The Writings of Mao Zedong, 1949-1976, edited by Michael Y. M. Kau and John K. Leung, M. E. Sharpe, 1986.

Snow Glistens on the Great Wall: A New Translation of the Complete Collection of Mao Tse-tung's Poetry With Notes and Historical Commentary, edited and translated by Ma Wen-Yee, Santa Barbara Press, 1986.

Also author of numerous pamphlets and speeches. Editor of *Xiang River Review,* 1919, *New Hunan,* 1919, *Popular Daily,* 1920-21, and *Political Weekly,* 1925.

SIDELIGHTS: "The Chinese people has stood up!" With these words, spoken on October 1, 1949, from a giant rostrum overlooking Tien An Men Square in Peking, Mao Tse-tung announced the beginning of the People's Republic of China. The radical transformation which followed would sweep from China virtually all traces of staid Confucian attributes of docility and resignation and metamorphose the new republic from "a devastated, underdeveloped satellite of the Soviet Union" into a growing, fiercely independent, almost self-sufficient world power governed, at least in spirit, by Mao's Promethian notion that "the human will can solve all problems." Mao himself, a lean and hunted bandit with a bounty of nearly two hundred fifty thousand silver dollars on his head in the 1930s, rose to become "a red and gold godhead of perfection seen on banners, posters, pins and family altars—the universal metonym of China, father image to more people than any national leader, and author of 'works' officially pushed into literally billions of copies in major and minor languages." Edgar Snow, who understood China and Mao better than any other Western journalist, wrote: "My first and lasting impression of Mao Tse-tung was of a man serenely convinced that he was destined to liberate and unify China; to restore its ancient greatness; to humble tyrants and bring into the lowliest peasant a new sense of self-reliance and self-respect; and to educate young people to become nobler beings. Mao was deeply touched by the age-old reformer's *hybris*—to remodel the inner man to perfection—and the vision never entirely left him."

A revolutionary even in his youth, Mao admittedly hated his father and later recalled the aftermath of an argument they had in his fourteenth year: "I reached the edge of a pond and threatened to jump in if my father came any nearer. My father insisted that I apologize and kowtow as a sign of submission. I agreed to give a one-knee kowtow if he would agree not to beat me. Thus the war ended, and from it I learned that when I demanded my rights by open rebellion, my father relented." Three years later, as Sun Yat-sen's republican forces plotted the overthrow of the Manchu dynasty, Mao led his first revolt: he and another student cut off their pigtails (symbols of submission to Manchu rulers) and forced eight others to cut theirs.

Mao made his way to Peking in autumn, 1918. The Great War in Europe had just ended and the architects of the Versailles Treaty, ignoring Chinese demands for the abolition of unequal treaties, granted Japan the former German concessions in China. Incensed by what he considered perfidious "Western bourgeois democracy," Mao, along with hundreds of other young nationalists, turned to Marxism. In 1921 Mao was one of the twelve founding delegates at the First Congress of the Chinese Communist party.

Returning to Hunan to organize labor unions, Mao at first followed Karl Marx's doctrine that the industrial proletariat would lead the Communist revolution, and he ignored the long-oppressed peasants, considering them "dirty" and "uncultivated." He soon discerned, however, that the peasants had reached their limits of endurance and were near revolt. In an essay considered highly unorthodox at the time, Mao argued that the key to the revolution was in organizing China's rural masses rather than mobilizing urban workers, and he urged the Communist party to harness the peasantry and place them in the vanguard of the revolution. "Several hundred million peasants," he predicted, would "rise like a tornado or tempest—a force so extraordinarily swift and violent that no power, however great, will be able to suppress it."

In 1927 the Chinese Communist party underwent a series of serious reversals. Nationalist Generalissimo Chiang Kai-shek of the Kuomintang (national people's party) launched a bloody purge of Communists. Communist structures in the cities were shattered. After failing to capture the capitol during the Autumn Harvest Uprising, Mao and his peasant army were forced to flee Hunan to a rural mountain base in the Chingkangshan region of south central China. Mao's sister and wife were executed by Chiang's troops.

For the next seven years Mao and his growing forces headquartered in Chingkangshan. At first harassed by mountain bandits, Mao shrewdly sent bandit leaders gifts and sought advice on guerrilla tactics. He developed his own highly successful formula of guerrilla warfare, summed up in one of his most quoted slogans: "The enemy advances, we retreat; the enemy camps, we harass; the enemy tires, we attack; the enemy retreats, we pursue." From Chingkangshan Mao announced his plan for a program of land reform combined with the creation of mass organizations, which succeeded in winning a large popular following for the Communist party. By the early 1930s Mao's army—now combined with the forces of Marshal Chu Teh—numbered more than sixty thousand men.

Chiang launched a "final extermination campaign" against the Communists in 1934, and in October the Chinese Red Army was forced to abandon their Chingkangshan base and begin the six-thousand-mile Long March to the rocky hillsides far to the north in Yenan. They were harassed and pursued by Kuomintang troops; their first three hundred miles were a disaster. Fighting nearly every step of the way, the Communists crossed eighteen major mountain ranges, twenty-five rivers, and ten provinces governed by hostile warlords. When they reached the Shensi province a year later, only a tenth of the one hundred thousand troops had survived. From these hardened survivors would emerge most of the men who would govern the People's Republic of China during its first decades.

Mao headquartered in Yenan for the next decade, and it was here, historians agree, that the myth began to overshadow the man. Living in conditions austere even to rural peasants—a cave furnished with an earthen bed, a broken wooden desk, a stool, and an urn—Mao raised his own tobacco and spent his nights studying and writing political essays. Dressed in a goat's hair jacket, he received visitors and continually chain-smoked cigarettes. By 1938 he was the recognized leader and theoretician of the Communist movement. From Yenan Mao organized peasant masses, set up mutual aid teams, and organized village elections. Within a few years the party's control extended over 100 million people, and Mao's program expanded to include expropriating land from wealthy landlords and urging peasants to "speak bitterness" to local tyrants. "Revolution is a drama of passion," Mao wrote later. "We did not win the people over by appealing to reason but by developing hope, trust, fraternity."

The Communist and Kuomintang armies formed a coalition with the outbreak of war with Japan in 1937. Cooperation soon ended after skirmishes between the two armies became as frequent as skirmishes with the Japanese. The Soviet Union viewed the success of the Chinese Communists with alarm; Joseph Stalin feared that if Mao remained in control he would not follow the lead of the U.S.S.R. Mao survived plots to subvert his leadership during the war, and by 1945 the Communist army numbered nearly a million troops and party control extended over 90 million miles. Fearing a Communist and Kuomintang civil war,

U.S. President Harry Truman dispatched General George C. Marshall to China in December, 1945. Marshall's efforts failed, and by 1946 civil war erupted. For the next three years Mao demonstrated that he had learned his guerrilla warfare lessons well. When the Communist army crossed the Yangtze River on April 21, 1949, the end was in sight. In the final months of the war Kuomintang cities "fell like ripe fruit," and Chiang's army retreated to Taiwan.

The centuries-old dream of a unified China was realized on October 1, 1949, as Mao declared "our nation will never again be an insulted nation." The formation of the People's Republic of China signaled the end of nearly a half century of chaos and bitter civil war.

The new chairman's first actions included organizing China's manpower to improve agricultural production, and the collectivizing of land. Kangaroo courts convicted wealthy landlords and former Kuomintang supporters of "crimes against the people," and at least one million people, sinologists agree, were executed for these "crimes." Intellectuals and "capitalist elements" were subjected to the long and usually painful process of *ssu-hsiang kaitsao* (thought reform) in which they purged themselves of "bourgeois, individualist" ideas. Millions were sent to re-education camps.

In December, 1949, Mao made his first trip to Moscow for nine weeks of hard bargaining with Stalin. He emerged with an alliance promising Russia strategic bases at Dairen and Port Arthur in exchange for $60 million in yearly aid. The death of Stalin in 1953 led Mao to a renegotiation of the Sino-Soviet Treaty of Alliance which succeeded in removing all traces of foreign domination in China.

The domestic front in China during the 1950s was marked by increased grain production and dramatic expansion of steel production due, in large part, to an infusion of loans and technology from the Soviets. Fearing an insurrection at home following the Hungarian uprising of 1956, Mao declared: "Let a hundred flowers blossom and a hundred schools of thought contend." The Hundred Flowers campaign caused such a huge wave of criticism from the country's intellectuals that in 1957 Mao launched an "anti-rightist campaign" and thousands of his critics were sent to *ssu-hsiang kaitsao* camps. The same year Mao journeyed to Moscow to declare "the east wind" was now stronger than "the west wind," and to ask for atomic bombs and military help in Taiwan. Russian leader Nikita Khrushchev flatly refused. Mao, convinced that a heroic collective action of the Chinese people was needed to transform the nation into a great power, declared the Great Leap Forward economic experiment. "Backyard steel furnaces," eighteen-hour work days, and rural communes combined with three years of bad weather to plunge China into national chaos. Economic experts, now calling it "the Great Slide Backward," predicted that China's economic progress was set back ten years. Faced with harsh party criticism, Mao asked that he not be reelected as chairman of the People's Republic and was replaced by Liu Shoa-chi on April 27, 1959. Though he later complained of being treated "like a father at his own funeral," Mao retained the real power in China as chairman of the Chinese Communist party.

For years Mao had warned of "blind obedience" to the Russian version of socialism, and in 1960 the first anti-Soviet attacks appeared in Chinese papers. Fearing that a technocratic elite class, already visible in Russia, could destroy China, Mao sharply criticized Soviet "revisionist" leaders and, critics proclaimed, permanently divided the world Communist movement. In November, 1965, Mao launched the Great Proletarian Cultural Revolution, the first of "an unending series of revolutions" he envisioned. When he urged China's youth to "learn revolution by making revolution," millions of Red Guards went on rampages, smashing temples and statues, arresting the "power holders taking the capitalist road," and following Mao's order to "bombard the party headquarters" by seizing ministries. The face of China—even the Great Wall itself—was plastered with slogans and posters calling for the removal of party officials. As the movement grew increasingly irrational, thousands were killed. The army was called in to quell the masses; Defense Minister Lin Piao, chosen by Mao in 1969 to be his successor, was accused of a plot to assassinate Mao and then allegedly died in a plane crash. It was at this time that Mao became nearly deified: his picture appeared on millions of posters and badges, and his "Little Red Book" became the focus of national veneration.

China entered a period of moderation following the Cultural Revolution. Chou En-lai was called to launch a policy of reconciliation with Japan and the United States and to try to reconstruct the internal government of China. In one of his boldest political moves, Mao opened the gates of China to U.S. President Richard Nixon for the Peking summit of 1972.

Politicians and leaders the world over joined in the sentiment of Japanese Prime Minister Takeo Miki when he announced on the occasion of Mao's death: "He left his great footprints on history."

BIOGRAPHICAL/CRITICAL SOURCES:

BOOKS

Ch'en, Jerome, *Mao and the Chinese Revolution,* Oxford University Press, 1965.
Ch'en, *Mao,* Prentice-Hall, 1969.
Chou, Eric, *Mao Tse-tung: The Man and the Myth,* Stein & Day, 1982.
Hollingworth, Clare, *Mao and the Men Against Him,* Cape, 1985.
Hsiao-Yu, *Mao Tse-tung and I Were Beggars,* Syracuse University Press, 1959.
Mao Tse-tung, *The Autobiography of Mao Tse-tung,* transcribed by Edgar Snow, China Truth, 1949.
Rule, Paul, *Mao Zedong,* University of Queensland Press, 1984.
Schram, Stuart, *Mao Tse-tung,* Simon & Schuster, 1966.
Schram, *Mao Zedong: A Preliminary Reassessment,* St. Martin's, 1983.
Schwartz, Benjamin, *Chinese Communism and the Rise of Mao,* Harvard University Press, 1951.
Snow, Edgar, *Red Star Over China,* Gollancz, 1937, Random House, 1938.
Snow, *The Other Side of the River,* Random House, 1962.
Watson, Andrew, *Mao Zedong and the Political Economy of the Border Region: A Translation of Mao's Economic and Financial Problems,* Cambridge University Press, 1980.
Womack, Brantly, *The Foundations of Mao Zedong's Political Thought, 1917-1935,* University Press of Hawaii, 1982.

PERIODICALS

Newsweek, February 3, 1975, May 31, 1976, June 28, 1976, September 20, 1976, September 27, 1976, October 18, 1976.
New York Times, September 10, 1976.
Time, October 7, 1974, December 22, 1975, September 20, 1976, September 27, 1976.*

MARA, Sally
See QUENEAU, Raymond

*　　*　　*

MARCEL, Gabriel Honore   1889-1973

PERSONAL: Born December 7, 1889, in Paris, France; died a heart attack, October 8, 1973, in Paris, France; son of Henri (a diplomat) and Laure (Meyer) Marcel; married Jacqueline Boegner; children: one. *Education:* University of Paris, Sorbonne, aggregation de philosophie, 1910. *Religion:* Roman Catholic.

ADDRESSES: Home—Paris, France.

CAREER: Writer. Teacher at lycees in Vendome, Condorcet, and Sens, France, 1911-23; reader at Grasset and Plon publishers and teacher at various schools, 1923-41; *Nouvelles Litteraires,* drama and music critic, 1945-73. Gifford lecturer at University of Aberdeen, 1949-50; William James lecturer at Harvard University, 1961. *Wartime service:* Served with the Red Cross during World War I.

MEMBER: Academie des Sciences Morales et Politiques.

AWARDS, HONORS: Grand prix de litterature from Academy Francaise, 1948; Goethe Hanseatic Prize from Hamburg University, 1956; Grand Prix National des Lettres, 1958; Frankfurt peace prize, 1964; European Erasmus Prize, 1969; West German Booksellers peace prize; named officer of Legion of Honor, commander of arts and letters, and commander des Palmes Academiques.

WRITINGS:

ALL PHILOSOPHY, EXCEPT AS NOTED

Journal metaphysique, Gallimard, 1927, 15th edition, 1958, translation by Bernard Wall published as *Metaphysical Journal,* Regnery, 1952.
Etre et avoir, Aubier, 1935, translation by Katharine Fatter published as *Being and Having,* Dacre Press, 1949, Beacon Press, 1951, also published as *Being and Having: An Existentialist Diary,* Harper, 1965.
Du refus a l'invocation, Gallimard, 1940, reprinted, 1964, also published as *Essai de philosophie concrete,* 1967, translation by Robert Rosthal published as *Creative Fidelity,* Farrar, Straus, 1964, recent edition, Crossroad, 1982.
Homo Viator: Prolegomenes a une metaphysique de l'esperance (addresses, essays, and lectures), Aubier, 1945, translation by Emma Craufurd published as *Homo Viator: Introduction to a Metaphysic of Hope,* Regnery, 1951.
La Metaphysique de Royce, Aubier, 1945 translation by Virginia Ringer and Gordon Ringer published as *Royce's Metaphysics,* Regnery, 1956.
(Editor and author of introduction) Marcelle de Jouvenel, *Au diapason du ciel,* Colombe, 1948.
The Philosophy of Existence, translated by Manya Harari, Harvill, 1948, Philosophical Library, 1949.
Position et approches concretes du mystere ontologique Nauwelaerts, 1949, 2nd revised edition, 1967.
(With others) *Recherche de la famille: Essai sur "l'etre familial,"* Editions Familiales de France, 1949.
Le Mystere de l'etre (lectures), Volume I: *Reflexion et mystere,* Volume II: *Foi et realite,* Auber, 1951, translation published as *The Mystery of Being,* Volume I: *Reflection and Mystery,* translated by G. S. Fraser, Volume II: *Faith and Reality,*

translated by Rene Hague, Regnery, 1960, recent edition, University Press of America, 1984.

Les Hommes contre l'humain, La Colombe, 1951, translation by Fraser published as *Man Against Mass Society,* Regnery, 1952, recent edition, University Press of America, 1985 (published in England as *Men Against Humanity,* Harvill, 1952).

Le Declin de la sagesse (addresses, essays, and lectures), Plon, 1954, translation by Harari published as *The Decline of Wisdom,* Harvill, 1954, Philosophical Library 1955.

L'Homme problematique, Aubier, 1955, translation by Brian Thompson published as *Problematic Man,* Herder, 1967.

The Influence of Psychic Phenomena on My Philosophy, Society for Psychical Research, 1956.

(Editor) *Un Changement d'esperance a la rencontre du rearmement moral: Des temoignages, des faits,* Plon, 1958, translation by Helen Hardinge published as *Fresh Hope for the World: Moral Re-armament in Action,* Longmans, 1960.

Presence et immortalite, Flammarion, 1959, translation by Michael A. Machado published as *Presence and Immortality,* Duquesne University Press, 1967.

Theatre et religion, E. Vitte, 1959.

L'Heure theatrale de Giraudoux a Jean-Paul Sartre (criticism), Plon, 1959.

Philosophy of Existentialism, translated by Harari, Citadel, 1961, 7th edition, 1966.

Fragments philosophiques 1909-1914, Nauwelaerts, 1961, translation by Lionel A. Blain published in *Philosophical Fragments: 1904-1914; and the Philosopher and Peace,* University of Notre Dame Press, 1965.

The Existential Background of Human Dignity (lectures), Harvard University Press, 1963.

Regards sur le theatre de Claudel, Beauchesne, 1964.

Auf der Suche nach Wahrheit und Gerechtikeit (lectures), J. Knecht, 1964, translation published as *Searchings,* Newman Press, 1967.

Der Philosoph und der Friede, J. Knecht, 1964.

Paix sur la terre: Deux Discours, une tragedie, Aubier, 1965.

Die Musik als Heimat der Seele (addresses, essays, and lectures), Festungs-Verlag, 1965.

Gabriel Marcel et les niveaux de l'experience, edited by Jeanne Parain-Vial, Seghers, 1966.

Pour une sagesse tragique et son au-dela (addresses, essays, and lectures), Plon, 1968, translation by Stephen Jolin and Peter McCormick published as *Tragic Wisdom and Beyond,* Northwestern University Press, 1973.

Martin Buber: L'Homme et le philosophe, l'Institut de Sociologie de l'Universite Libre de Bruxelles, 1968.

(Contributor) Andreas Resch, editor, *Im Kraftfeld des Christlichen Weltbildes,* Schoeningh, 1968.

Coleridge et Schilling (title means "Coleridge and Schilling"), Aubier-Montaigne, 1971.

En chemin, vers quel eveil?, Gallimard, 1971.

(With others) *Plus decisif que la violence* (addresses, essays, and lectures), Plon, 1971.

Percees vers un ailleurs, Fayard, 1973.

The Philosophy of Gabriel Marcel, edited by Paul A. Schilpp and Lewis E. Hahn, Open Court, 1984.

PLAYS

Le Seuil invisible (contains "La Grace" and "Le Palais de Sable"), Grasset, 1914.

Le Coeur des autres (three-act), Grasset, 1921.

"Le Regard neuf," 1922, published in *Trois Pieces* (see below).

L'Iconoclaste (four-act; title means "The Iconoclast"), Stock, 1923.

Un Homme de Dieu (four-act; first produced in Genoa, Italy, at Piccolo Teatro, May, 1946), Grasset, 1925.

La Table Ronde, 1957, translation published as "A Man of God" in *Three Plays* (see below).

La Chapelle ardente (three-act; first produced in Paris, France, at Theatre du Vieux-Colombier, September 25, 1925), L'Illustration, 1925, La Table Ronde, 1950, translation published as "The Funeral Pyre" in *Three Plays,* and as "The Votive Candle" in the revised edition of *Three Plays* (see below).

Le Quatuor en fa diese, Plon, 1929.

Trois Pieces (contains "Le Regard neuf," "Le Mort de demain," "La Chapelle ardente"), Plon, 1931.

Le Monde casse (four-act; title means "The Broken World"; first produced in Paris, 1930), Desclee de Brouwer, 1933, also published in *Cinq Pieces majeurs* (see below).

Le Fanal (one-act; title means "The Beacon"), Stock, 1936.

Le Secret dans les iles (first produced in Paris at Theatre des Arts, March 1, 1937), published in *Le Secret est dans les iles, theatre* (see below).

Le Dard (three-act; title means "The Dart"; produced in Paris at Theatre des Arts, March 1, 1937), Plon, 1938, also published in *Le Secret est dans les iles, theatre* (see below).

La Soif (three-act; title means "The Thirst"), Desclee de Brouwer, 1938, also published in *Cinq Pieces majeures* (see below), also published as *Les Coeurs avides* (title means "The Hungry Hearts"), La Table Ronde, 1952.

"Les Pointes sur les I" (one-act), published in *Les Oeuvres libres,* [Paris], 1938, also published in *Theatre comique* (see below).

"L'Emissaire" (title means "The Emissary"; first produced in 1945), published in *Le Secret est dans les iles, theatre* (see below).

L'Horizon (four-act; title means "The Horizon"), Editions aux Etudiants de France, 1945.

Theatre comique (contains "Colombyre, ou le brasier de la paix," "La Double expertise," "Les Points sur les I," and "Le Divertissement posthume"), A. Michel, 1947.

"La Fin des temps" (first produced by Radiodiffusion Francaise, June 17, 1950), published in *Le Secret est dans les iles, theatre* (see below).

Rome n'est plus dans Rome (five-act; title means "Rome Is No Longer in Rome"), La Table Ronde, 1951.

"Le Chemin de Crete" (first produced in Paris at Theatre du Vieux-Colombier, November 14, 1953), published in *Cinq Pieces majeures* (see below), translation published as "Ariadne" in *Three Plays* (see below).

Croissez et multipliez (four-act; title means "Increase and Multiply"), Plon, 1955.

Mon Temps n'est pas le votre (five-act; title means "My Time Is Not Yours"), Plon, 1955.

La Dimension florestan (three-act), Plon, 1958.

Three Plays: A Man of God, Ariadne, The Funeral Pyre, Hill & Wang, 1958, revised edition published as *Three Plays: A Man of God, Ariadne, The Votive Candle,* 1965.

Le Signe de la croix (three-act; title means "The Sign of the Cross"), Plon, 1961 (also see below).

Le Secret est dans les Iles, theatre (contains "Le Dard," "L'Emissaire," and "La Fon des temps"), Plon, 1967.

Cinq Pieces majeures (contains "Un Homme de Dieu," "Le Monde casse," "Le Chemin de Crete," "La Soif," and "Le Signe de la croix"), Plon, 1973.

Also author of "Le Palaise de sable" and "La Grace," both published in *Le Seuil invisible* (see above); "Le Mort de demain," published in *Trois Pieces* (see above); and "Le Divertissement posthume," "La Double expertise," and "Colombyre, ou le brasier de la paix," all published in *Theatre comique* (see above).

Contributor of articles to periodicals, including *L'Europe Nouvelle, Nouvelle Revue Francaise, Temps Present,* and *Vigile.*

SIDELIGHTS: According to Kenneth T. Gallagher, "nothing could be more uncustomary than the thought of Gabriel Marcel: there seems to be no direct precedent for it in the entire history of philosophy. Presenting elements of phenomenology, existentialism, idealism, and empiricism all consorting together in symbiotic bliss, it completely defies classification." Despite this, however, Marcel has been dubbed a "Christian existentialist," due to his deep commitment to Catholicism and the early influence of Soren Kierkegaard, the father of existentialism, on his philosophical thought. Marcel first introduced Kierkegaard's work to France in a 1925 article published by the *Revue de Metaphsique.* This article brought forth the philosophy of existentialism, which became a prevalent school of thought through the works of Jean-Paul Sartre. Unlike Sartre, though, Marcel was not a pessimistic atheist, but a devout and optimistic Roman Catholic. He himself preferred to be called a "neo-Socratic" or a "Socratic Christian."

In common with atheistic existentialists, Marcel rejected the validity of philosophical systems and the search for abstract, universal truths. His interest lay with the real, individual human being; his approach is phenomenological, stressing experiences as they are actually encountered. Thus Marcel also called his theory "concrete philosophy." He concerned himself with the increasing dehumanization of man in twentieth-century society and with the means by which a human being can overcome the resulting sense of alienation and absurdity in order to live an authentic, meaningful existence. On the other hand, Marcel is distinguished from atheistic existentialists by his fundamental idealism; buoyed by his strong faith in God, he rejected the idea of an absurd universe. In this sense, Marcel most differed from the existentialists, for he lacked, as Marjorie Grene pointed out, "the terrible realization of dread as the core of human life," the concept, according to Grene, that sets existentialism apart from other schools of thought. Nevertheless, Marcel does begin from what Grene called "the impassioned realization of the utter loneliness and dread of our being-in-the-world." A character in his play "Le Coeur des autres" commented that "there is only one suffering, it is to be alone"; and, in fact, Marcel himself described his plays as dramas "of the soul in exile." Perhaps as a result, Francis J. Lescoe speculated, of a solitary childhood "literally starved for friendship, companionship and other spiritual values," Marcel came to regard the concrete experience of love, a relationship between oneself and an "other," as the key to an authentic, meaningful existence.

Marcel grew up in a generally nonreligious atmosphere. His mother died when he was four years old and Marcel never talked about the event with his father. His agnostic parent and the liberal Protestant aunt who helped raise him largely ignored the subject of religion. Discussions concerning death and the possibility of an afterlife were forbidden. As a result of the absence of spiritualism in Marcel's upbringing, the author took up the study of philosophy in school and eventually graduated with a degree in the subject in 1910.

Marcel, however, still entertained nagging questions regarding death and obsessively reflected on the probability of the existence of immortality. His perplexity was exacerbated by the work he did during World War I. Exempted from armed combat because of frail health, Marcel worked with the Red Cross as a liaison officer dealing with the frantic relatives of soldiers missing in action. Often it was his duty to inform an unfortunate family of the death of their loved one. These wartime experiences left an indelible mark on Marcel's way of thinking. He became especially aware of the uselessness of abstract thought when one must confront human suffering. Marcel became convinced that man must be a participant in any philosophical theory and not a cold, objective observer.

The philosopher continued his quest for answers and began to record his thoughts in a diary that was published in 1927 as *Journal metaphysique.* Marcel experimented with Protestantism and other beliefs and attended seances, but gradually gravitated towards the Roman Catholic church. He was finally prompted to formally join the religion by the Catholic author Francois Mauriac, who in a letter asked, "Come, Marcel, why are you not one of us?" In 1929 Marcel converted to Catholicism at the age of thirty-nine, after which time, Lescoe noted, he "never wavered for a moment in his loyalty to the Catholic faith."

After his conversion, Marcel began to incorporate his previous thoughts and conclusions into his newly adopted religion. Thus he created the curious blend of spiritual elements that distinguished his philosophy. Marcel never sought to explain God or prove His existence. He found such proofs meaningless, believing that God could be known only through participation, not observation. Hence, in Marcel's philosophy, the relationship with another human being is all-important. Lescoe explained that Marcel "insists that to be genuine in our interpersonal relationships, we must be totally and unreservedly available to the other. We must sympathize with the afflicted, that we become the afflicted ones ourselves." Only through such concrete experiences, involving faith, love, and hope, Marcel proposed, could one know God.

Marcel felt his philosophy was especially important in view of the increasing alienation of modern man. Like Martin Buber and Karl Jaspers he was concerned with the "erosion of human values and human personality," which Marcel attributed to the denial of God's existence as well as to the growing importance of technology. The denial of God (and therefore of the existence of an afterlife) leaves man without hope and leading a meaningless existence while technology defines man purely in terms of his function, thus reducing him to an object and completely disregarding his human dignity. Only by being available to another human being and truly open to a genuine encounter can a person achieve freedom and identity. Through such an "I-Thou relationship," Lescoe asserted, Marcel thought one could find "authentic personhood."

The philosopher maintained that this "I-Thou" communion can then be expanded to communion with God. Faith in another will lead to a similar relationship with God. Conversely, it is faith in God that makes possible the relationship between two human beings. Lescoe reflected that "all true love of the other must ultimately be based on the love of God."

The majority of Marcel's books are not systematic explanations of his philosophy. Rather, the author recorded his thoughts unmethodically in either diary form or in collections of his talks and articles. Grene described Marcel's first book, *Journal metaphysique,* as "jotting of day-by-day reflections, sometimes interconnected, sometimes quite random." Consequently, his books did not receive great literary notice. His plays also did not enjoy much success as they were too heavily philosophical for the theatre. Dealing with alienation in some form, Marcel's plays study man "in his loneliness," noted Lescoe. "He examines man frustrated, alienated, bewildered and restless, when he cuts himself off from his fellow man and from God." The author summed up the philosopher's thought by disclosing that Marcel "underscores man's deepest longing for friendship, fidelity, interpersonal relationship and communion with others."

BIOGRAPHICAL/CRITICAL SOURCES:

BOOKS

Cain, Seymour, *Gabriel Marcel,* Regnery, 1979.
Contemporary Literary Criticism, Volume 15, Gale, 1980.
Gallagher, Kenneth T., *The Philosophy of Gabriel Marcel,* Fordham University Press, 1975.
Grene, Marjorie, *Introduction to Existentialism,* University of Chicago Press, 1959.
Keen, Samuel, *Gabriel Marcel,* John Knox, 1967.
Lapointe, Francois and Claire Lapointe, *Gabriel Marcel and His Critics: An International Bibliography,* Garland, 1977.
Lazaron, Hilda, *Gabriel Marcel the Dramatist,* Humanities, 1978.
Lescoe, Francis J., *Existentialism With or Without God,* Alba House, 1973.
McCowan, Joe, *Availability: Gabriel Marcel and the Phenomenology of Human Openness,* Scholars Press, 1978.
O'Malley, J. B., *The Fellowship of Being,* Hague, 1966.
Wall, Barbara, *Love and Death in the Philosophy of Gabriel Marcel,* University Press of America, 1977.

OBITUARIES:

PERIODICALS

Newsweek, October 22, 1973.
New York Times, October 9, 1973.
Time, October 22, 1973.

*　　　*　　　*

MARCHANT, Catherine
　　See COOKSON, Catherine (McMullen)

*　　　*　　　*

MARCHBANKS, Samuel
　　See DAVIES, (William) Robertson

*　　　*　　　*

MARCHI, Giacomo
　　See BASSANI, Giorgio

*　　　*　　　*

MARINER, Scott
　　See POHL, Frederik

*　　　*　　　*

MARION, Henry
　　See del REY, Lester

*　　　*　　　*

MARKHAM, Robert
　　See AMIS, Kingsley (William)

MARLOWE, Hugh
　　See PATTERSON, Harry

*　　　*　　　*

MARRIC, J. J.
　　See CREASEY, John

*　　　*　　　*

MARSDEN, James
　　See CREASEY, John

*　　　*　　　*

MARSH, (Edith) Ngaio　1899-1982

PERSONAL: Name is pronounced "*Nye*-o"; born April 23, 1899, in Christchurch, New Zealand; died February 18, 1982, in Christchurch; daughter of Henry Edmund and Rose Elizabeth (Seager) Marsh. *Education:* Attended St. Margaret's College, New Zealand, 1910-14, and Canterbury University College School of Art, 1915-20. *Religion:* Church of England.

ADDRESSES: Home—37 Valley Rd., Christchurch S.2, New Zealand. *Agent*—Harold Ober Associates, Inc., 40 East 49th St., New York, N.Y. 10017; and Hughes Massie Ltd., 69 Great Russell St., London WC1B 3DH, England.

CAREER: Actress with touring Shakespearean company in Australia and New Zealand 1920-23; theatrical producer, 1923-27; interior decorator in London, England, 1928-32; returned to New Zealand and lived there and in London, writing detective novels, 1933-82; D. D. O'Connor Theatre Management, producer, 1944-52; directed ten Shakespearean productions and many modern plays; director of first all-New Zealand Shakespearean company, Canterbury University College Student Players, 1946; also directed at Embassy Theatre, London, England, and on a professional tour of Australasia. Honorary lecturer in drama, Canterbury University College, 1948. *Wartime service:* Head section leader, Red Cross Transport Unit in New Zealand, 1939.

MEMBER: Royal Society of Arts (fellow), British Authors, Playwrights and Composers Society, PEN, Queen's Club (Christchurch).

AWARDS, HONORS: Officer, Order of the British Empire, 1948; D.Litt., University of Canterbury, 1963; Dame Commander, Order of the British Empire, 1966; Grand Master Award, Mystery Writers of America, 1977.

WRITINGS:

DETECTIVE NOVELS

A Man Lay Dead, Bles, 1934, Sheridan, 1942, reprinted, Aeonian Press, 1976.
Enter a Murderer, Bles, 1935, Sheridan, 1942, reprinted, Aeonian Press, 1976.
(With Henry Jellett) *The Nursing-Home Murder,* Bles, 1935, Sheridan, 1941, reprinted, Aeonian Press, 1976.
Death in Ecstasy, Bles, 1936, Sheridan, 1941, reprinted, Aeonian Press, 1976.
Vintage Murder, Bles, 1937, Sheridan, 1940, reprinted, Aeonian Press, 1976.
Artists in Crime, Furman, 1938, reprinted, Aeonian Press, 1976.
Death in a White Tie, Furman, 1938, reprinted, Aeonian Press, 1976.
Overture to Death, Furman, 1939, reprinted, Aeonian Press, 1976.

Death of a Peer, Little, Brown, 1940, reprinted, Aeonian Press, 1976 (published in England as *Surfeit of Lampreys* [also see below], Collins, 1941).

Death at the Bar, Little, Brown, 1940, reprinted, Aeonian Press, 1976.

Death and the Dancing Footman, Little, Brown, 1941, reprinted, Aeonian Press, 1976.

Colour Scheme, Little, Brown, 1943, reprinted, Aeonian Press, 1976.

Died in the Wool, Little, Brown, 1945, reprinted, Aeonian Press, 1976.

Final Curtain (originally serialized in *Saturday Evening Post,* March 8-April 12, 1947), Little, Brown, 1947, reprinted, Aeonian Press, 1976.

A Wreath for Rivera (also see below), Little, Brown, 1949, reprinted, Aeonian Press, 1976 (published in England as *Swing, Brother, Swing,* Collins, 1949).

Night at the Vulcan (also see below), Little, Brown, 1951, reprinted, Aeonian Press, 1976 (published in England as *Opening Night,* Collins, 1951).

Spinsters in Jeopardy (also see below), Little, Brown, 1953, reprinted, Aeonian Press, 1976.

Scales of Justice (also see below), Little, Brown, 1955, reprinted, Aeonian Press, 1976.

Death of a Fool, Little, Brown, 1956, reprinted, Aeonian Press, 1976 (published in England as *Off with His Head,* Collins, 1957).

Singing in the Shrouds (also see below), Little, Brown, 1958, reprinted, Aeonian Press, 1976 (bound with *A Stir of Echoes,* by Richard Matheson, and *The Malignant Heart,* by Celestine Sibley, Walter J. Black, 1958).

False Scent (also see below), Little, Brown, 1959, reprinted, Aeonian Press, 1976 (bound with *The Man Who Followed Women,* by Bert and Dolores Hitchens, and *Tiger on My Back,* by Gordon and Mildred Nixon Gordon, Walter J. Black, 1960).

Three-Act Special (contains *A Wreath for Rivera, Spinsters in Jeopardy,* and *Night at the Vulcan*), Little, Brown, 1960.

Another Three-Act Special (contains *False Scent, Scales of Justice,* and *Singing in the Shrouds*), Little, Brown, 1962.

Hand in Glove, Little, Brown, 1962, reprinted, Aeonian Press, 1976.

Dead Water, Little, Brown, 1963, reprinted, Aeonian Press, 1976.

Killer Dolphin, Little, Brown, 1966 (published in England as *Death at the Dolphin,* Collins, 1967).

Clutch of Constables, Collins, 1968, Little, Brown, 1969.

When in Rome, Collins, 1970, Little, Brown, 1971.

Tied Up in Tinsel, Little, Brown, 1972.

Black as He's Painted, Little, Brown, 1975.

Last Ditch, Little, Brown, 1978.

Grave Mistake, Little, Brown, 1978.

Photo Finish, Little, Brown, 1980.

Light Thickens, Little, Brown, 1982.

NONFICTION

(With Randal Matthew Burdon) *New Zealand,* Collins, 1942, reprinted, Aeonian Press, 1976.

(Contributor) Walter J. Turner, editor, *The British Commonwealth and Empire,* Collins, 1943.

A Play Toward: A Note on Play Production, Caxton Press, 1946.

Perspectives: The New Zealander and the Visual Arts, Auckland Gallery Associates, 1960.

Play Production, R. E. Owen, Government Printer (New Zealand), 1960.

New Zealand (juvenile), Macmillan, 1964.

Black Beech and Honeydew (autobiography), Little, Brown, 1965.

PLAYS

(With Owen B. Howell) "Surfeit of Lampreys" (based on Marsh's novel of same title), produced in London in 1950.

(With Eileen MacKay) "False Scent" (based on Marsh's novel of same title), produced in England in 1961.

The Christmas Tree (juvenile), Religious Drama Society of Great Britain, 1962.

"A Unicorn for Christmas," music by David Farquhar, produced in Australia in 1965.

"Murder Sails at Midnight" (based on *Singing in the Shrouds*), produced in England in 1972.

OTHER

The Collected Short Fiction of Ngaio Marsh, Fitzhenry & Whiteside, 1989.

Also author of television play, "Evil Liver." Contributor to anthologies, including *Queen's Awards 1946,* edited by Ellery Queen, Little, Brown, 1946, *Anthology 1969,* edited by Queen, Davis Publications, 1968, *Ellery Queen's Murdercade,* Random House, 1975, *Ellery Queen's Crime Wave,* Putnam, 1976. Contributor of short stories, travel articles, and reviews to periodicals.

WORK IN PROGRESS: Another detective novel.

SIDELIGHTS: Ngaio Marsh, a well-traveled mystery writer and theatrical producer, wrote detective stories which have been called the best of their kind. Her theatrical background and the wide variety of people and scenery she encountered in her travels provided a rich source of material for her novels, which have received world-wide recognition. A *Spectator* critic praised Marsh's "extraordinary gift for the drawing of characters just this side of eccentricity" as well as her "amazing sense of the visual: her atmospheres and scenic set pieces are always pure magic."

In her first novel, *A Man Lay Dead,* Marsh introduced Inspector Roderick Alleyn, a practical, charming detective who has captured readers' imaginations and contributed to Marsh's enduring popularity. A tall, lean man with dark hair, Alleyn belongs to the ranks of the socially privileged, yet eschews social snobbery. According to *New York Times* writer Thomas Lask, Alleyn has a "keen eye" and an "unflappable, cool style" which always uncovers the guilty person. Although Alleyn appears in a majority of her novels, Marsh once stated that she never grew tired of him: "It would be an affectation to say I'm sick of him. I'm not. I'm completely crazy about him."

Some of Marsh's novels are set in the theatre, and most of them make reference to Shakespeare's plays. *Killer Dolphin* (the title refers to a crumbling nineteenth-century London theatre where a murder is committed) contains a stage presentation of Shakespeare's life. In the *New York Times Book Review,* Anthony Boucher stated that Marsh "writes about the London theatrical scene delightfully, vividly and inimitably. [*Killer Dolphin*] is a joy absolute."

The 1980 publication of *Photo Finish* prompted *Washington Post Book World*'s Jean M. White to write: "It is good news, indeed, to report that the 81-year-old queen dowager of British mystery is the same stylish, witty and lively writer that she has been over a span of nearly five decades and some 30 novels. She hasn't lost her touch." Newgate Callendar of the *New York Times Book Re-*

view echoed White's opinion: "Marsh has been writing mystery stories since 1934, but you wouldn't know it from her prose. By some kind of miracle she has retained stylistic freshness. Characterizations are, as always, sharply drawn, and there is a great deal of quiet humor. *Photo Finish* is a book that should make all readers happy."

AVOCATIONAL INTERESTS: Art, Shakespeariana.

BIOGRAPHICAL/CRITICAL SOURCES:

BOOKS

Contemporary Literary Criticism, Gale, Volume 7, 1977, Volume 53, 1989.
Dictionary of Literary Biography, Volume 77: *British Mystery Writers, 1920-1939,* Gale, 1989.
Penzler, Otto, editor, *The Great Detectives,* Little, Brown, 1978.

PERIODICALS

Christian Science Monitor, November 2, 1965, December 4, 1978.
Detroit News, June 4, 1972.
National Observer, July 15, 1972.
Newsweek, June 13, 1960.
New York Times, July 22, 1972, January 26, 1979.
New York Times Book Review, June 5, 1960, September 25, 1966, April 7, 1971, January 18, 1981.
Saturday Evening Post, March 8, 1947.
Saturday Review, April 24, 1971.
Spectator, December 12, 1970, May 4, 1974.
Times Literary Supplement, June 29, 1967.
Washington Post Book World, November 16, 1980.
Wilson Library Bulletin, September, 1940.

OBITUARIES:

PERIODICALS

Chicago Tribune, February 19, 1982.
New York Times, February 19, 1982.
Publishers Weekly, March 5, 1982.
Times (London), February 19, 1982.
Washington Post, February 19, 1982.

*   *   *

MARSHALL, Paule 1929-

PERSONAL: Born April 9, 1929, in Brooklyn, N.Y.; daughter of Samuel and Ada (Clement) Burke; married Kenneth E. Marshall, 1950 (divorced, 1963); married Nourry Menard, July 30, 1970; children (first marriage): Evan. *Education:* Brooklyn College (now of the City University of New York), B.A. (cum laude), 1953; attended Hunter College (now of the City University of New York), 1955.

ADDRESSES: Home—407 Central Park West, New York, N.Y. 10025.

CAREER: Free-lance writer. Worked as librarian in New York Public Libraries; *Our World* magazine, New York, N.Y., staff writer, 1953-56. Lecturer on creative writing at Yale University, 1970—; lecturer on Black literature at colleges and universities including Oxford University, Columbia University, Michigan State University, Lake Forrest College, and Cornell University.

MEMBER: Harlem Writers Guild, Phi Beta Kappa.

AWARDS, HONORS: Guggenheim fellowship, 1960; Rosenthal Award from the National Institute of Arts and Letters, 1962, for

Soul Clap Hands and Sing; Ford Foundation grant, 1964-65; National Endowment for the Arts grant, 1967-68; Before Columbus Foundation American Book Award, 1984, for *Praisesong for the Widow.*

WRITINGS:

Brown Girl, Brownstones (novel), Random House, 1959, reprinted with an afterword by Mary Helen Washington, Feminist Press, 1981.
Soul Clap Hands and Sing (short stories), Atheneum, 1961, reprinted, Howard University Press, 1988.
The Chosen Place, The Timeless People, Harcourt, 1969, reprinted, Vintage Books, 1984.
Praisesong for the Widow (novel), Putnam, 1983.
Reena and Other Stories (includes novella "Merle," and short stories "The Valley Between," "Brooklyn," "Barbados," and "To Da-duh, in Memoriam"), with commentary by the author, Feminist Press, 1983, reprinted as *Merle: A Novella and Other Stories,* Virago Press, 1985.

Also author of a teleplay based on *Brown Girl, Brownstones,* 1960. Contributor of articles and short stories to periodicals.

SIDELIGHTS: "My work asks that you become involved, that you think," writer Paule Marshall once commented in the *Los Angeles Times.* "On the other hand, . . . I'm first trying to tell a story, because I'm always about telling a good story." Marshall received her first training in storytelling from her mother, a native of Barbados, and her mother's West Indian friends, all of whom gathered for daily talks in Marshall's home after a hard day of "scrubbing floor." Marshall pays tribute to these "poets in the kitchen" in a *New York Times Book Review* essay where she describes the women's gatherings as a form of inexpensive therapy and an outlet for their enormous creative energy. She writes: "They taught me my first lessons in the narrative art. They trained my ear. They set a standard of excellence. This is why the best of my work must be attributed to them; it stands as testimony to the rich legacy of language and culture they so freely passed on to me in the wordshop of the kitchen."

The standard of excellence set by these women has served Marshall well in her career as a writer. Her novels and stories have been lauded for their skillful rendering of West Indian/Afro-American dialogue and colorful Barbadian expressions. *Dictionary of Literary Biography* contributor Barbara T. Christian believes that Marshall's works "form a unique contribution to Afro-American literature because they capture in a lyrical, powerful language a culturally distinct and expansive world." This pursuit of excellence makes writing a time-consuming effort, according to Marshall. "One of the reasons it takes me such a long time to get a book done," she explained in the *Los Angeles Times,* "is that I'm not only struggling with my sense of reality, but I'm also struggling to find the style, the language, the tone that is in keeping with the material. It's in the process of writing that things get illuminated."

Marshall indicates, however, that her first novel *Brown Girl, Brownstones* was written at a faster pace. "I was so caught up in the need to get down on paper before it was lost the whole sense of a special kind of community, what I call Bajan (Barbardian) Brooklyn, because even as a child I sensed there was something special and powerful about it," she stated in the *Los Angeles Times.* When the novel was published in 1959 it was deemed an impressive literary debut, but because of the novel's frank depiction of a young black girl's search for identity and increasing sexual awareness, *Brown Girl, Brownstones* was largely ignored by readers. The novel was reprinted in 1981, and is now considered a classic in the female *bildungsroman* genre, along with Zora Neale Hurston's *Their Eyes Were Watching God* and Gwendolyn Brooks's *Maud Martha*.

The story has autobiographical overtones, for it concerns a young black Brooklyn girl, Selina, the daughter of Barbadian immigrants Silla and Deighton. Silla, her ambitious mother, desires most of all to save enough money to purchase the family's rented brownstone. Her father Deighton, on the other hand, is a charming spendthrift who'd like nothing better than to return to his homeland. When Deighton unexpectedly inherits some island land, he makes plans to return there and build a home. Silla meanwhile schemes to sell his inheritance and fulfill her own dream.

Selina is deeply affected by this marital conflict, but "emerges from it self-assured, in spite of her scars," writes Susan McHenry in *Ms.* Selina eventually leaves Brooklyn to attend college; later, realizing her need to become acquainted with her parents' homeland, she resolves to go to Barbados. McHenry writes: *"Brown Girl, Brownstones* is meticulously crafted and peopled with an array of characters, and the writing combines authority with grace. . . . Paule Marshall . . . should be more widely read and celebrated." Carol Field comments in the *New York Herald Tribune Book Review:* "[*Brown Girl, Brownstones*] is an unforgettable novel written with pride and anger, with rebellion and tears. Rich in content and in cadences of the King's and 'Bajan' English, it is the work of a highly gifted writer."

Marshall's most widely reviewed work to date is *Praisesong for the Widow,* winner of the Before Columbus American Book Award. The novel is thematically similar to *Brown Girl, Brownstones* in that it also involves a black woman's search for identity. This book, though, concerns an affluent widow in her sixties, Avatar (Avey) Johnson, who has lost touch with her West Indian-Afro-American roots. In the process of struggling to make their way in the white man's world, Avey and her husband Jerome (Jay) lost all of the qualities that made them unique. Novelist Anne Tyler remarks in the *New York Times Book Review,* "Secure in her middle class life, her civil service job, her house full of crystal and silver, Avey has become sealed away from her true self."

While on her annual luxury cruise through the West Indies however, Avey has several disturbing dreams about her father's great aunt whom she visited every summer on a South Carolina island. She remembers the spot on the island where the Ibo slaves, upon landing in America, supposedly took one look around at their new life and walked across the water back to Africa. Avey decides to try to escape the uneasiness by flying back to the security of her home. While in her hotel on Grenada awaiting the next flight to New York, Avey reminisces about the early years of her and Jay's marriage, when they used to dance to jazz records in their living room, and on Sundays listen to gospel music and recite poetry. Gradually though, in their drive for success they lost "the little private rituals and pleasures, the playfulness and wit of those early years, the host of feelings and passions that had defined them in a special way back then, and the music which had been their nourishment," writes Marshall in the novel.

In the morning, Avey becomes acquainted with a shopkeeper who urges her to accompany him and the other islanders on their annual excursion to Carriacou, the island of their ancestors. Still confused from the past day's events, she agrees. During the island celebration, Avey undergoes a spiritual rebirth and resolves to keep in close contact with the island and its people and to tell others about her experience.

Reviewers question if Avey's resolution is truly enough to compensate for all that she and Jay have lost, if "the changes she envisions in the flush of conversion commensurate with the awesome message of the resisting Ibos," to use *Village Voice Literary Supplement* reviewer Carol Ascher's words. "Her search for roots seems in a way the modern, acceptable equivalent of the straightened hair and white ways she is renouncing," writes *Times Literary Supplement* contributor Mary Kathleen Benet, who adds: "On the other hand there is not much else she can do, just as there was not much else Jerome Johnson could do. Paule Marshall respects herself enough as a writer to keep from overplaying her hand; her strength is that she raises questions that have no answers."

Los Angeles Times Book Review contributor Sharon Dirlam offers this view: "[Avey] has learned to stay her anger and to swallow her grief, making her day of reckoning all the more poignant. She has already missed the chance to apply what she belatedly learns, except for the most important lesson: What matters is today and tomorrow, and, oh yes, yesterday life, at age 30, age 60, the lesson is to live." Jonathan Yardley concludes in the *Washington Post Book World:* "*Praisesong for the Widow* . . . is a work of quiet passions book all the more powerful precisely because it is so quiet. It is also a work of exceptional wisdom, maturity and generosity, one in which the palpable humanity of its characters transcends any considerations of race or sex; that Avey Johnson is black and a woman is certainly important, but Paule Marshall understands that what really counts is the universality of her predicament."

MEDIA ADAPTATIONS: A television version of *Brown Girl, Brownstones* was produced as a CBS-TV Workshop Production, 1980.

BIOGRAPHICAL/CRITICAL SOURCES:

BOOKS

Bruck, Peter, and Wolfgang Karrer, editor, *The Afro-American Novel since 1960,* B. R. Gruener, 1982.
Christian, Barbara, *Black Women Novelists,* Greenwood Press, 1980.
Contemporary Literary Criticism, Volume 27, Gale, 1984.
Dictionary of Literary Biography, Volume 33: *Afro-American Fiction Writers after 1955,* Gale, 1984.
Evans, Mari, editor, *Black Women Writers, 1950-1980,* Anchor Press, 1984.
Marshall, Paule, *Brown Girl, Brownstones,* Random House, 1959, reprinted with an afterword by Mary Helen Washington, Feminist Press, 1981.
Marshall, *Praisesong for the Widow,* Putnam, 1983.

PERIODICALS

Black American Literature Forum, winter, 1986, spring/summer, 1987.
Black World, August, 1974.
Book World, December 28, 1969.
Callaloo, spring/summer, 1983.
Chicago Tribune Book World, May 15, 1983.
Christian Science Monitor, January 22, 1970, March 23, 1984.
CLA Journal, March, 1961, September, 1972.
Critical Quarterly, summer, 1971.
Essence, May, 1980.
Freedom Ways, 1970.
Journal of Black Studies, December, 1970.
London Review of Books, March 7, 1985.
Los Angeles Times, May 18, 1983.
Los Angeles Times Book Review, February 27, 1983.

Ms., November, 1981.
Nation, April 2, 1983.
Negro American Literature Forum, fall, 1975.
Negro Digest, January, 1970.
New Letters, autumn, 1973.
New Yorker, September 19, 1959.
New York Herald Tribune Book Review, August 16, 1959.
New York Review of Books, April 28, 1983.
New York Times, November 8, 1969, February 1, 1983.
New York Times Book Review, November 30, 1969, January 9, 1983, February 20, 1983.
Novel: A Forum on Fiction, winter, 1974.
Saturday Review, September 16, 1961.
Times Literary Supplement, September 16, 1983, April 5, 1985.
Village Voice, October 8, 1970, March 22, 1983, May 15, 1984.
Village Voice Literary Supplement, April, 1982.
Washington Post, February 17, 1984.
Washington Post Book World, January 30, 1983.

*   *   *

MARSTEN, Richard
   See HUNTER, Evan

*   *   *

MARTIN, Richard
   See CREASEY, John

*   *   *

MARTIN, Stella
   See HEYER, Georgette

*   *   *

MARTIN, Steve 1945-

PERSONAL: Born August, 1945 in Waco, Tex.; son of Glenn (a realtor) and Mary (Lee) Martin; married Victoria Tennant, 1986. *Education:* Attended Long Beach State College and University of California at Los Angeles.

ADDRESSES: Home—Beverly Hills, Calif. *Office*—P. O. Box 929, Beverly Hills, Calif. 90213. *Agent*—Marty Klein, Agency for the Performing Arts, 9000 Sunset Blvd., Suite 1200, Los Angeles, Calif. 90069; (public relations) Paul Bloch, Rogers & Cowan, 10000 Santa Monica Blvd., Los Angeles, Calif. 90067.

CAREER: Comedian, actor, and writer. Partner in the Aspen Film Society and 40 Share Productions. Worked at Disneyland and Knott's Berry Farm in the early 1960s; performer in coffeehouses, c. 1963; comedy writer for television programs, including "The Smothers Brothers Comedy Hour," 1968, "The John Denver Rocky Mountain Christmas Show," 1975, and "Van Dyke and Company," 1975, and for performers, including Glen Campbell, Ray Stevens, Pat Paulsen, John Denver, and Sonny and Cher; has made numerous guest appearances on television programs, including "The Tonight Show Starring Johnny Carson," "Dinah!," "The Merv Griffin Show," "The Dick Cavett Show," and "Saturday Night Live"; executive producer, "Domestic Life" (television series), Columbia Broadcasting System (CBS), 1984; actor in motion pictures, including "The Absent Minded Waiter," 1977, "The Jerk," 1979, "Pennies from Heaven," 1981, "Dead Men Don't Wear Plaid," 1982, "The Man with Two Brains," 1983, "The Lonely Guy," 1984, "All of

Me," 1984, "Little Shop of Horrors," 1986, "Three Amigos!," 1986, "Roxanne," 1987, "Planes, Trains, and Automobiles," 1987, "Dirty Rotten Scoundrels," 1988, and "Parenthood," 1989.

MEMBER: Screen Actors Guild, American Guild of Variety Artists, American Federation of Television and Radio Artists.

AWARDS, HONORS: Emmy Award, National Academy of Television Arts and Sciences, 1969, for best achievement in comedy, variety, or music for "The Smothers Brothers Comedy Hour"; Emmy Award nomination, 1975, for best writing in a comedy, variety, or music special for "Van Dyke and Company"; Georgie Award, American Guild of Variety Artists, 1977; Academy Award nomination, Academy of Motion Picture Arts and Sciences, 1977, for "The Absent-Minded Waiter"; Jack Benny Award, University of California at Los Angeles, 1978, for entertainment excellence; Grammy Award, National Academy of Recording Arts and Sciences, 1978, for "Let's Get Small," and 1979, for "A Wild and Crazy Guy"; National Society of Film Critics Award and New York Film Critics Circle Award, both 1984, both for role in "All of Me."

WRITINGS:

Cruel Shoes (humorous sketches; Literary Guild alternate selection; Playboy Book Club featured alternate), Press of the Pegacycle Lady, 1977, revised and enlarged edition, Putnam, 1979.
"The Absent-Minded Waiter" (screenplay), Paramount, 1977.
"Let's Get Small" (recording), Warner Bros., 1977.
"Steve Martin: A Wild and Crazy Guy" (television special), National Broadcasting Corp. (NBC), 1978.
"A Wild and Crazy Guy" (recording), Warner Bros., 1978.
"King Tut" (recording), Warner Bros., 1978.
"Comedy Is Not Pretty" (recording; also see below), Warner Bros., 1979.
(With Carl Reiner) "The Jerk" (screenplay), Universal, 1979.
"Comedy Is Not Pretty" (television special), NBC, 1980.
"Steve Martin's Best Show Ever" (television special), NBC, 1981.
"The Steve Martin Brothers" (recording), Warner Bros., 1982.
(With Reiner and George Gipe) "Dead Men Don't Wear Plaid" (screenplay), Universal, 1982.
(Co-writer) "The Man with Two Brains" (screenplay), Warner Bros., 1983.
(With Lorne Michaels and Randy Newman; and executive producer) "Three Amigos!" (screenplay), Orion, 1986.
(And executive producer) "Roxanne" (screenplay; based on "Cyrano de Bergerac" by Edmond Rostand), Columbia, 1987.

SIDELIGHTS: "Well, EXCUUUUSE MEEEE!!!" Steve Martin would roar during his stand-up comedy routine, his entire body shaking with indignation, and the audience, many sporting giant bunny ears or a fake arrow through the head, erupting with howls, cheers, and an ovation comparable to those heard at rock concerts. The bizarre incongruity of a junior-executive type wearing balloons on his head, latex nose and glasses, and a white, custom-tailored, three-piece suit struck the perfect chord with American audiences in the 1970s. Martin's sudden attacks of "happy feet" took him lurching across the stage; he twisted balloons into absurd shapes, then named them "Puppy dog! Venereal disease! The Sistine Chapel!"; he performed magic tricks that didn't quite work. But most of all, Martin parodied the whole idea of a comedian standing on stage telling jokes. Playing the part of a "wild and crazy guy," Martin became one of the hottest stand-up comics of the decade. His first two comedy albums won Grammy Awards and sold millions of copies; he scored a hit single with the absurd song "King Tut"; and the book *Cruel Shoes,* his collection of humorous sketches, was a national bestseller. By 1979 Martin had graduated to films, making the box office smash "The Jerk" and following with a string of other films throughout the 1980s. His performance in 1984's "All of Me" earned popular acclaim as well as awards from the National Society of Film Critics and the New York Film Critics Circle. "Roxanne" showed him capable of touching character portrayals, while "Planes, Trains and Automobiles" gave Martin the chance to play the straight man. Over the course of two decades, Martin has "evolved from a cooly absurdist stand-up comic to a fully formed, amazingly nimble comic actor," notes Janet Maslin in the *New York Times.*

Martin's fascination with the entertainment world stems back to his childhood. He was stagestruck at the age of three and grew up idolizing such comedians as Laurel and Hardy, Jerry Lewis, and Red Skelton. "The first day I saw a movie," he told *Newsweek*'s Tony Schwartz, "I knew that's what I wanted to do." By the age of five, he was memorizing Red Skelton's television skits and performing them at school show-and-tells. When his family moved to California, he hiked over to the new Disneyland amusement park and got a part-time job selling guidebooks, magic tricks, and Frontierland rodeo ropes. "I had mystical summer nights there," he recalls. "Fireworks, lights in the trees, a dance band playing music from the '40s."

During working hours he would sneak away to watch an old vaudevillian comic, Wally Boag, at Disneyland's Golden Horseshoe Revue. The comedian performed a routine of songs, jokes, and balloon tricks that Martin committed to memory. Soon he was performing the tricks he sold, twirling a lasso, playing the banjo, and appearing in a Boag production called "It's Vaudeville Again." After eight years at the Magic Kingdom, Martin left for nearby Knott's Berry Farm to act in melodrama at the Birdcage Theatre and perform his own fifteen-minute routines of comedy, magic, and banjo music.

Martin's budding career was cut short by his discovery of education. He fell in love with Stormy, an actress in the Birdcage company, who persuaded him to read Somerset Maugham's *The Razor's Edge.* "It was all about a person who questions life," Martin told Schwartz. "I read it and I can remember afterward sitting in a park and Stormy saying, 'Knowledge is the most important thing there is.'" Convinced, Martin enrolled at Long Beach State College where he studied philosophy for the next three years. But when he came across the arguments of Ludwig Wittgenstein concerning semantics, and the philosopher's contention that nothing was absolutely true, his interest in philosophy waned. Martin concluded that "the only logical thing was comedy because you don't have to explain it or justify it." He transferred to the University of California and changed his major to theatre.

Martin's first big break in show business came when he submitted some of his written material to Mason Williams, the headwriter for CBS-TV's "The Smothers Brothers Comedy Hour." At the time, Martin was broke, living in a maid's quarters in Bel Air, struggling as a performer at small clubs and coffeehouses, and studying television writing at UCLA. Williams invited him to join the writing staff of the show, one of the highest-rated shows on television at the time. "I didn't have any *idea* what I was doing there," he admits. "So young and inexperienced in such a big-league job. But I was too busy repressing it all to deal with it." CBS cancelled the show in 1968, but Martin and the show's other ten writers won an Emmy for their work. The

award tripled Martin's value as a writer, and he was soon making $1,500 a week writing for entertainers like Glen Campbell, Ray Stevens, Pat Paulsen, John Denver, and Sonny and Cher. Still, his ambition was to work onstage: "I decided to stop writing for other people and perform full-time again," he tells Kathy Lowry of *New Times.* "I was bored with writing all that formula stuff. I wanted to deal directly with the audience."

The early 1970s was a dismal period in Martin's career. He took his stand-up act on the road, playing every small club he could find and opening for rock groups whose drugged, impatient audiences shouted him off the stage. "Back then they didn't know what a comedian was," Martin tells Janet Coleman in *New York.* He later satirized the period in one of his routines: a marijuana-smoking hippie is watching Martin perform, nods slowly, then drawls, "These guys are *good.*" Coleman recounts that Martin is "still annoyed by the ritual sloppiness and inattention of the 'love generation' audience."

Success as a stand-up comedian came when Martin developed a distinctive stage persona. When doing his act, Martin became a parody of a comedian, a satire on the idea of a professional comic. His character was shallow and slick, desperate for acceptance, full of insincere show-business asides to the audience, and unaware of his own stupidity. Balloon gags, juggling, banjo playing, and rabbit ears were all used in a purposely hokey attempt to get laughs. Pauline Kael describes Martin's stand-up act in the *New Yorker:* "Onstage, he puts across the idea that he's going to do some cornball routine, and then when he does it it has quotation marks around it, and that's what makes it hilarious. He does the routine straight, yet he's totally facetious."

His usual performance began with Martin walking out in his six-hundred-dollar white suit, an expensive banjo slung over his shoulder, and announced: "Hi, I'm Steve Martin, and I'll be out in *just* a minute!" For a few moments, he goofed in the spotlight, hummed to himself, looked around aimlessly. He was "waiting for the drugs to take effect," he explained. Then, "Okay, you paid the money, you're expecting to see a professional show, so let's not waste any more time, here we go with Professional Show Business, let's go, hey!" He steps back, starts tuning the banjo, plucking one string then another, turning a peg or two, then moves up and smashes his nose into the microphone. "Okay, we're moving now, eh folks? Yes, these are the good times and we're having them, ah ha ha ha."

"I mean," David Felton wonders in *Rolling Stone,* "what *is* this shit? Here's one of the hottest comedians in the business . . . and he's standing up there like a *jerk,* an *idiot,* a f——ing *asshole!* And that's the whole point." Lowry explains: "Steve Martin just wants to get a laugh; he doesn't much care about being profound or pricking society's conscience." Tony Schwartz in *Newsweek* claims that "Martin's style is a pie in the faces of Lenny Bruce, Dick Gregory, Mort Sahl and all the iconoclastic comics who dominated the stand-up scene in the '60s." Martin agrees. Speaking to *U.S. News & World Report,* he reveals: "The '60s was a time of humorlessness in America. Everybody was so dead earnest. . . . During this time, the cheapest way to get a laugh was to make a political joke. . . . When I made my breakthrough in comedy in the early 1970s, politics was very much on everybody's mind. I saw it as my job to take it off their minds and so left politics out of my comedy. I think that was a big part of my success. There was no moralizing, no left, no right; it was just about a human being."

Martin transferred his stage persona to the screen in 1979's "The Jerk," a film that grossed over seventy million dollars at the box office. Playing the white son in a poor black family (obviously an adopted son, but Martin doesn't realize it), he goes on to win and lose a fortune with a crazy invention. Audiences loved the movie, but critics found it wanting, expecting it to be somehow more "relevant" or provocative. Martin's next few efforts were also met with critical coolness. Audience appeal was also limited. "Pennies from Heaven," a lush musical set in the Thirties, lost money; "Dead Men Don't Wear Plaid," a spoof of the hard-boiled detective genre which incorporated scenes from vintage movies, was a box office disappointment. As Martin tells Kenneth Turan in *Rolling Stone* of this period, "It was like a dog scratching around to find a place to sit, getting up and down, walking around five or six times, before finally settling somewhere. That's the way I kept walking, trying to find the right screen persona to sit in. Something I like playing. Something I can do again."

It was only with "All of Me," in which Martin co-starred with Lily Tomlin, that he discovered a comfortable screen character. Ironically for the comic who had made his reputation as a "wild man," Martin's new character was a normal fellow who is beset with unusual problems. In the film, Martin plays a lawyer who becomes possessed by the spirit of a dead woman. One side of his body is controlled by the woman, the other side by him. Martin's amazing ability to portray this absurd physical condition—half male and half female—drew widespread critical praise and won him two major film awards as well. "To see his physical contortions in *All of Me*," writes Turan, "to watch him trying to play both sexes simultaneously . . . is so boggling that audiences are often far too flabbergasted to laugh at all. Had he been born in another century, Martin might have been burned at the stake for witchcraft or demonic possession." In addition to the film's physical humor, Jack Barth writes in *Film Comment,* "All of Me* is Martin's first comedy to subjugate gags to story and characterization. . . . [It] is also the first Martin film to deliver a satisfying ending." The result pleased the filmgoing public as well as the critics. "All of Me," notes Turan, was "the Number One film in America, with reviews to match."

Martin further developed his new screen character in subsequent films, particularly in "Roxanne," a gentle, updated version of the classic "Cyrano de Bergerac." Martin plays a small town fireman with an absurdly long nose. Called upon to assist a friend woo the new woman in town, Martin falls in love with her himself. Writing in the *Chicago Tribune,* Dave Kehr calls the film "a romantic comedy of grace, buoyancy and surprising emotional depth, filled with civilized pleasures." Tom Shales in the *Washington Post* reports that "critics have adored the writing, but have also likened Martin's comedic agility onscreen to Charlie Chaplin's. There have been references to things like 'comic genius' bursting forth." In her review for the *Los Angeles Times,* Sheila Benson notes: "I can't think of a current movie in which every element is in such balance: Martin seems unfettered, expansive, utterly at ease, capable of any physical feat. . . . There's a tenderness to him that's magnetic." David Ansen in *Newsweek* concludes: " 'Roxanne' is a charmer. Sweet-spirited, relaxed, it's a sun-dappled romantic comedy. . . . This is the culmination of a long quest to exorcise [Martin's] stage persona as a wild and crazy guy."

By the late 1980s Martin had left his stand-up "wild and crazy" image behind him. He had become, in the words of Richard Corliss of *Time,* "this decade's most charming and resourceful comic actor." A wide variety of film comedy roles were suddenly available to him. In "Planes, Trains and Automobiles" Martin played the straight man to John Candy, in "Dirty Rotten Scoundrels" he played a conman with Michael Caine, and in "Parenthood"

he was a middle-class father. And all three films, in pleasant contrast to several earlier Martin efforts, were solid box office hits.

Although he is now one of comedy's most successful stars, Martin lives quietly in Beverly Hills. He avoids the film industry's nightlife, and he is known as an art collector, a vegetarian, and a man who cherishes his privacy. Speaking to *U.S. News & World Report,* Martin muses on the entertainment industry: "One thing about show business is that you only get what you earn. If Prince sells out a concert, it's not as though the money is coming from the government. He says, 'I'm going to charge $15 . . . to get in, and you don't have to come if you don't want to.' It's very capitalistic, democratic and fair."

AVOCATIONAL INTERESTS: Reading old magic books, art books, museum catalogs, and the *New Yorker* magazine; playing horseshoes; skiing.

BIOGRAPHICAL/CRITICAL SOURCES:

BOOKS

Contemporary Literary Criticism, Volume 30, Gale, 1984.
Lenburg, Greg, Randy Skretvedt and Jeff Lenburg, *Steve Martin: The Unauthorized Biography,* St. Martin's, 1980.

PERIODICALS

American Film, June, 1982, November, 1988, August, 1989.
Chicago Tribune, June 19, 1987, July 13, 1987.
Esquire, March 27, 1979.
Film Comment, January, 1979.
Films in Review, February, 1988.
Los Angeles Times, December 27, 1984, June 19, 1987, June 28, 1987, June 30, 1987.
Newsweek, January 31, 1977, April 3, 1978, June 22, 1987.
New Times, September 2, 1977.
New York, August 22, 1977.
New Yorker, June 27, 1983.
New York Times, January 14, 1980, May 21, 1982, June 19, 1987, July 12, 1987.
People, May 1, 1978, July 6, 1987.
Rolling Stone, December 1, 1977, July 27, 1978, November 30, 1978, April 5, 1979, November 8, 1984.
Time, October 31, 1977, June 15, 1987, August 24, 1987.
U. S. News & World Report, June 17, 1985.
Washington Post, September 15, 1977, June 3, 1979, June 23, 1979, June 19, 1987.

—*Sketch by Thomas Wiloch*

*   *   *

MARTIN, Webber
  See SILVERBERG, Robert

*   *   *

MARTINES, Julia
  See O'FAOLAIN, Julia

*   *   *

MARTINSEN, Martin
  See FOLLETT, Ken(neth Martin)

MARUT, Ret
   See TRAVEN, B.

*   *   *

MASEFIELD, John (Edward) 1878-1967

PERSONAL: Born June 1, 1878 (although this is his official birthday, he notes in his autobiography that "there is some doubt of the day"), in Ledbury, Herefordshire, England; died May 12, 1967; son of George Edward (a solicitor) and Carolyn (Parker) Masefield; raised by an uncle, William, after the death of his parents; married Constance de la Cherois-Crommelin, 1903 (died, 1960); children: Lewis (killed in action, 1942), Judith (illustrator of several of Masefield's books). *Education:* Briefly attended King's School, Warwick, England (ran away when he was about thirteen).

ADDRESSES: Home—Burcote Brook, Abingdon, Berkshire, England.

CAREER: Indentured to merchant ship *Conway* about 1892; apprenticed aboard a windjammer about a year and a half later and sailed around Cape Horn to Chile where he became ill and returned to England by steamer; shipped aboard the White Star liner *Adriatic* as sixth officer but left the ship when she docked in New York; lived in Greenwich Village, New York City, 1895-97 (except for an interval in which he traveled as a hobo to California and back), and worked in a bakery, in a livery stable, on the waterfront, and in the saloon of Luke O'Connor's Columbian Hotel; moved to Yonkers, New York, where he worked as a "mistake finder" in a carpet factory; returned to England in 1897 and became friendly with John Millington Synge in London, then spent one summer in Devonshire with William Butler Yeats; about 1900 he became literary editor of the *Speaker* and was subsequently recommended to the *Manchester Guardian* for which he wrote articles and organized a "Miscellany" feature (he served on the permanent staff of the *Guardian* for about six months); in 1930 King George appointed him Poet Laureate of England succeeding Robert Bridges. Appointed chairman of the committee acting on the awards of the King's medals for poetry, 1933; member of British Council's Books and Periodicals Committee; lectured in Turkey and other European countries for the British Council; frequent lecturer in the United States. *Military service:* During World War I served with the Red Cross in France and on the Gallipoli Peninsula.

MEMBER: Royal Society of Literature (member of academic committee, 1913; Companion, 1961), Incorporated Society of Authors, Playwrights and Composers (president, 1937-67).

AWARDS, HONORS: Polignac Prize for Poetry, 1912; D.Litt., Oxford University, 1922; LL.D., University of Aberdeen, 1922; Order of Merit, 1935; Hanseatic Shakespeare Prize, Hamburg University, 1938; William Foyle Prize, 1961, for *The Bluebells, and Other Verses.*

WRITINGS:

POETRY

Salt-Water Ballads, Grant Richards, 1902, Macmillan, 1913.
Ballads and Poems, Mathews, 1910.
The Everlasting Mercy, Sidgwick & Jackson, 1911.
The Story of a Round-House, Macmillan, 1912, revised edition, 1913.
The Widow in the Bye Street, Sidgwick & Jackson, 1912.
The Daffodil Fields, Macmillan, 1913.
Dauber: A Poem, Heinemann, 1913.

Philip the King, and Other Poems, Macmillan, 1914 (*Philip the King* published separately in England, Heinemann, 1927).
Good Friday: A Dramatic Poem, Macmillan, 1915, published with additional poems as *Good Friday, and Other Poems,* 1916.
Sonnets (from *Good Friday, and Other Poems*), Macmillan, 1916.
Sonnets and Poems (from *Good Friday, and Other Poems*), privately printed, 1916.
Salt-Water Poems and Ballads, Macmillan, 1916, published as *Salt-Water Ballads and Poems,* 1923.
Lollingdon Downs, and Other Poems, Macmillan, 1917.
The Cold Cotswolds, Express Printing Works, 1917.
Rosas, Macmillan, 1918.
Reynard the Fox, Macmillan, 1919, new edition, 1920.
Enslaved, Macmillan, 1920, published with additional poems as *Enslaved, and Other Poems,* 1923.
Right Royal, Macmillan, 1920.
King Cole, Macmillan, 1921.
The Dream, Macmillan, 1922, published with additional poems as *The Dream, and Other Poems,* 1923.
Sonnets of Good Cheer to the Lena Ashwell Players, From Their Well-Wisher, John Masefield, Mendip Press, 1926.
Midsummer Night, and Other Tales in Verse, Macmillan, 1928.
South and East, Macmillan, 1929.
The Wanderer of Liverpool, Macmillan, 1930.
Minnie Maylow's Story, and Other Tales and Scenes, Macmillan, 1931.
A Tale of Troy, Macmillan, 1932.
A Letter From Pontus, and Other Verse, Macmillan, 1936.
The Country Scene in Poems, Collins (London), 1937, Collins (New York), 1938.
Tribute to Ballet in Poems, Macmillan, 1938.
Some Verses to Some Germans, Macmillan, 1939.
Gautama the Enlightened, and Other Verse, Macmillan, 1941.
Generation Risen, Collins, 1942, Macmillan, 1943.
Land Workers, Heinemann, 1942, Macmillan, 1943.
Wonderings, Macmillan, 1943.
On the Hill, Macmillan, 1949.
The Bluebells, and Other Verses, Macmillan, 1961.
Old Raiger, and Other Verse, Heinemann, 1964, Macmillan, 1965.
In Glad Thanksgiving, Macmillan, 1967.

Also author of *Animula,* 1920.

NOVELS

Captain Margaret, Grant Richards, 1908, Macmillan, 1916, reprinted, Scholarly Press, 1972.
Multitude and Solitude, Grant Richards, 1909, Macmillan, 1916.
The Street of To-Day, Dutton, 1911.
Sard Harker, Macmillan, 1924, reprinted, Heinemann, 1956.
Odtaa, Macmillan, 1926, reprinted, Penguin, 1966.
The Midnight Folk, Macmillan, 1927, recent edition, Dell, 1985.
The Hawbucks, Macmillan, 1929.
The Bird of Dawning, Macmillan, 1933, reprinted, 1967.
The Taking of the Gry, Macmillan, 1934.
The Box of Delights, Macmillan, 1935, reprinted, Heinemann, 1957.
Victorious Troy; or, The Hurrying Angel, Macmillan, 1935.
Eggs and Baker, Macmillan, 1936.
The Square Peg; or, The Gun Fella, Macmillan, 1937.
Dead Ned, Macmillan, 1938, reprinted, Heinemann, 1970.
Live and Kicking Ned, Macmillan, 1939, reprinted, Heinemann, 1970.

SHORT STORIES

The Mainsail Haul, Mathews, 1905, revised edition, Macmillan, 1913.

A Tarpaulin Muster, B. W. Dodge, 1908, reprinted, Books for Libraries, 1970.

PLAYS

The Tragedy of Nan, Kennerley, 1909.

The Tragedy of Pompey the Great, Little, Brown, 1910, revised edition, Macmillan, 1914, reprinted, Sidgwick & Jackson, 1964.

The Faithful (three-act tragedy), Heinemann, 1915.

Good Friday: A Play in Verse, Garden City Press, 1916, reprinted, Heinemann, 1955.

The Locked Chest [and] *The Sweeps of Ninety-Eight* (prose plays), Macmillan, 1916.

Melloney Holtspur, Macmillan, 1922.

A King's Daughter (verse play), Macmillan, 1923.

The Trial of Jesus, Macmillan, 1925.

Tristan and Isolt (verse play), Heinemann, 1927.

The Coming of Christ, Macmillan, 1928.

Easter: A Play for Singers, Macmillan, 1929.

End and Beginning, Macmillan, 1933.

A Play of Saint George, Macmillan, 1948.

Also author of "The Campden Wonder," 1907.

JUVENILE

A Book of Discoveries, F. A. Stokes, 1910.

Lost Endeavor, Nelson, 1910.

Martin Hyde: The Duke's Messenger, Little, Brown, 1910.

Jim Davis, F. A. Stokes, 1912, reprinted, Penguin, 1966, published as *The Captive of the Smugglers,* Page, 1918.

ESSAYS AND STUDIES

Sea Life in Nelson's Time, Methuen, 1905, Macmillan, 1925, reprinted, Books for Libraries, 1969, 3rd edition, U.S. Naval Institute, 1971.

On the Spanish Main; or, Some English Forays on the Isthmus of Darien, Macmillan, 1906, new edition, Naval Institute Press, 1972.

William Shakespeare, Holt, 1911, reprinted, Fawcett, 1964, quartercentenary edition, Barnes & Noble, 1969.

John M. Synge, Macmillan, 1915, reprinted, Folcroft Press, 1970.

Gallipoli, Macmillan, 1916, 13th edition, 1925.

The Old Front Line; or, The Beginning of the Battle of the Somme, Macmillan, 1917, published as *The Battle of the Somme,* Heinemann, 1919, reprinted, C. Chivers, [Bath], 1968.

The War and the Future, Macmillan, 1918 (published in England as *St. George and the Dragon,* Heinemann, 1919).

John Ruskin, Yellowsands Press, 1920.

Shakespeare and Spiritual Life, Oxford University Press, 1924, reprinted, Folcroft Press, 1969.

With the Living Voice: An Address, Macmillan, 1925.

Chaucer, Macmillan, 1931.

Poetry, Heinemann, 1931, Macmillan, 1932.

The Conway: From Her Foundation to the Present Day, Macmillan, 1933.

The Nine Days Wonder (story of the Dunkirk retreat), Macmillan, 1941.

Conquer: A Tale of the Nika Rebellion in Byzantium, Macmillan, 1941.

Thanks Before Going: Notes on Some of the Original Poems of Dante Gabriel Rosetti, Heinemann, 1946, Macmillan, 1947, reissued as *Thanks Before Going, With Other Gratitude for Old Delight,* Heinemann, 1947.

Baden Parchments, Heinemann, 1947.

St. Katherine of Ledbury, and Other Ledbury Papers, Heinemann, 1951.

An Elizabethan Theatre in London, Oxford University, 1954.

The Western Hudson Shore, [New York], 1962.

The Twenty-five Days, Heinemann, 1972.

OTHER

The Taking of Helen, Macmillan, 1923, new edition with additional material published as *The Taking of Helen, and Other Prose Selections,* Macmillan, 1924.

Recent Prose, Heinemann, 1924, revised edition, 1932, Macmillan, 1933.

Prologue to a Book of Pictures of Adventure by Sea, [New York], 1925.

Any Dead to Any Living, [New Haven], 1928.

A Masque of Liverpool, Brown Brothers, 1930.

Lines on the Tercentenary of Harvard University, Macmillan, 1936.

Basilissa: A Tale of the Empress Theodore (fictional biography), Macmillan, 1930.

Some Memories of W. B. Yeats, Macmillan, 1940, reprinted, Irish University Press, 1971.

In the Mill (autobiography), Macmillan, 1941.

Shopping in Oxford, Heinemann, 1941.

Natalie Maisie and Pavilastukay, Macmillan, 1942.

I Want! I Want!, National Book League, 1944, Macmillan, 1945.

Macbeth Production, Heinemann, 1945, Macmillan, 1946.

New Chum, Macmillan, 1945.

Book of Both Sorts, Heinemann, 1947.

In Praise of Nurses, Heinemann, 1950.

A Book of Prose Selections, Heinemann, 1950.

The Ledbury Scene as I Have Used It in My Verse, Hereford, 1951.

So Long to Learn: Chapters of an Autobiography, Macmillan, 1952.

Grace Before Ploughing (autobiographical sketches), Macmillan, 1966.

CORRESPONDENCE

John Masefield: Letters to Reyna, edited by William Buchan, Buchan & Enright, 1984.

John Masefield's Letters From the Front, 1915-1917, edited by Peter Vansittart, Constable, 1984.

John Masefield: Letters to Margaret Bridges, 1915-1919, edited by Donald Stanford, Carcanet, 1984.

COLLECTIONS

The Everlasting Mercy [and] *The Widow in the Bye Street,* Macmillan, 1912, new edition, 1919.

Poems of John Masefield, Macmillan, 1917.

The Poems and Plays of John Masefield, Macmillan, 1918.

A Poem and Two Plays, Heinemann, 1919.

Dauber [and] *The Daffodil Fields,* Macmillan, 1923.

Selected Poems, Heinemann, 1922, Macmillan, 1923, 3rd edition, Heinemann, 1950, recent edition, Carcanet, 1984.

King Cole, The Dream, and Other Poems, Macmillan, 1923.

Philip the King, and Other Poems; Good Friday: A Play in Verse; Lollingdon Downs, and Other Poems, With Sonnets, Macmillan, 1923.

The Collected Poems of John Masefield, Heinemann, 1923, new edition, 1932, revised edition published as *Poems,* 1946.

Poems, two volumes, Macmillan, 1925, published in one volume, 1930, 3rd edition with new poems, 1958.

Prose Plays, Macmillan, 1925.

Verse Plays, Macmillan, 1925.

Plays, Heinemann, 1937.

Dead Ned [and] *Live and Kicking Ned,* Macmillan, 1941.

Dauber [and] *Reynard the Fox,* Heinemann, 1962, Macmillan, 1963.

EDITOR

(With wife, Constance Masefield) *Lyrists of the Restoration From Sir Edward Sherbourne to William Congreve,* Grant Richards, 1905.

W. Dampier, *Voyages,* Dutton, 1906.

A Sailor's Garland, Methuen, 1906, Macmillan, 1924, reprinted, Books for Libraries, 1969.

(With C. Masefield) *Essays, Moral and Polite, 1660-1714,* Grant Richards, 1906, reprinted, 1930, and Books for Libraries, 1971.

Defoe (selections), Macmillan, 1909.

(And translator) Jean Racine, *Esther* (play), Heinemann, 1922.

(And translator) Racine, *Berenice* (play), Macmillan, 1922.

My Favourite English Poems, Macmillan, 1950.

(And author of introductions) Shakespeare, *Three Tragedies,* Dodd, 1965.

(And author of introductions) Shakespeare, *Three Comedies,* Dodd, 1965.

(And author of introductions) Shakespeare, *Three Histories,* Dodd, 1966.

(And author of introductions) Shakespeare, *Tragedies II,* Dodd, 1966.

(And author of introductions) Shakespeare, *Commedies II,* Dodd, 1967.

Editor of several collections for Dent's "Everyman's Library" series.

AUTHOR OF INTRODUCTION

Chronicles of the Pilgrim Fathers, Dutton, 1910.

George Anson, *Voyage Round the World in the Years 1740-1744,* Dutton, 1911.

Richard Hakluyt, *Voyages,* Dutton, 1962.

SIDELIGHTS: In 1913 an *American Review of Reviews* writer noted that *The Daffodil Fields* "is filled with Masefield's own peculiar literary beauties that mark his passionate gift of simple utterance; the art to tell a simple tale and yet reflect all of heaven and earth within it as a pool of water reflects the sky." For over seventy years John Masefield told stories that excited his readers. His prosody was variously praised and deprecated, but his talent as a storyteller remains unquestioned. Nearly eighty years ago a *New York Times* reviewer wrote: "[Masefield's work] bears the stamp of verity wherever the scene may be, and holds one's attention breathlessly in every part, in spite of its simplicity." And in 1961 Donald Davie recognized Masefield's venerability: "For the most part Masefield's poems still belong to the world of the 'Come all ye,' the street-ballad and modern folk-lyric. . . . It's delightful to be reminded that we have with us still a professional improviser of this ancient sort. He is probably the last of his kind."

In the autobiographical sketch included in Schreiber's *Portraits and Self-Portraits,* Masefield described his earliest poetic inclination: "While living in Yonkers in 1896, I first became acquainted with the works of the English poet Chaucer. The reading of his poems turned me to a systematic study of the English poets and also made me determined to attempt to write poetry." Masefield later spoke of the three distinct eras that composed his long career as a poet. In the preface to the 1958 edition of his collected poems he noted that his first period was characterized by an intense desire for escape and freedom. Later he devoted himself to the composition of long tales in verse and finally turned to "dramatic production and verse-speaking." (For many years Masefield maintained a small theater in his home for the production of verse plays.)

Although his early work won far more acclaim than his later verse, Masefield's poems were rarely greeted with unqualified praise. In 1913 a *Saturday Review of Literature* writer noted: "In Mr. Masefield it is the rush of his lines, their momentum and energy, that makes his poem. Our only doubt, which often runs to certainty, is that this momentum is less the momentum of genius than the momentum of an extremely clever writer exploiting an amazing facility of style and emotion." But the later poems frequently exhibited only what John Malcolm Brinin called "tired competence." Anthony Thwaite wrote of one narrative poem, "It has a kind of stately flatness, which sometimes takes one step down into bathos." And Dudley Fitts deplored Masefield's increasing ineptitude as early as 1950: "No man living has served poetry longer and with more devotion than has the present Laureate, but the publication of this book of new poems [*On the Hill*] is regrettable. Whatever ardor, whatever creative energy Mr. Masefield has displayed in the past . . . is shown here either in sad dilution or in an unconscious and cruel kind of self-parody. There are occasional passages of beauty, and of course the essential sweetness of the man is apparent everywhere; but these are not enough to outweigh the appalling mediocrity of the verse, both in content and execution."

A few critics of the later work were willing to examine the poems apart from the context of contemporary poetry. Thomas Lask wrote: "Though he may have looked at the 20th-century world, it was with 19th-century eyes. The forms, the mold, the very rhythms carried with them old-fashioned comfort. 'Poets,' [Masefield] wrote, 'are great or little according to the nobleness of their endeavor to build a mansion for soul.' It is not only the didacticism of this sentiment but also the language in which it is couched that indicates his distance from the contemporary world." Margery Fisher added: "Over the years, Masefield has been defining imagination for us, by precept and example. I think he can never have been afraid of the tug between reality and fantasy that bedevils so many writers. He is a formidably straight and simple visionary."

Nevertheless, the modern critic is constantly aware that most of Masefield's verse is now "unfashionable." Paul Engle wrote: "There are many lines of great verbal attractiveness [in *The Bluebells, and Other Verses*] in which the traditional subjects are treated in the traditional manner. Nothing is here to startle or amaze. Conventional beauty is conventionally reported. Many fine lyrical passages occur, but the dominant tone is one of subdued mediation on bluebells, ships, farms—the usual substance of John Masefield's books. All of that world has tremendous attractiveness, and yet it is very hard to accept the result as poetry which has truly confronted this actual world." Robert Hillyer, on the other hand, saw a purer sort of beauty in this collection. "Age has renewed Masefield's laurels more richly than ever," he wrote. "Here is the delight in fine stanza forms—the couplet, the rime royal, the Spenserian stanza and several of his own invention—and here the well-modulated rise from realistic effects to the high apostrophes of rapture."

It is, however, the earliest poems with which Masefield's name will most readily be associated. More than fifty years ago an *American Review of Reviews* writer said prophetically of *Salt-Water Ballads,* "These ballads of the sea, torn freshly from his . . . recent experiences, will quite likely remain to the end of his life the freshest and purest of all the Masefield posey." Indeed, Masefield's *Sea Fever* was published in this 1902 collection and there are few today who do not recognize its opening statement: "I must go down to the seas again, to the lonely sea and the sky. And all I ask is a tall ship and a star to steer her by." According to one *Time* reviewer, "Masefield led English poetry out of its Victorian sententiousness and thus earned his modest place in the poets' pantheon." When he was awarded the Laureateship in 1930 he was already "safe from obscurity," continued the *Time* reviewer, "[and] thus turned out only occasionally the dutiful doggerel that has so often been the lot of poets laureate." Masefield himself wrote in one of his last books, "It is time now to pipe down and coil up."

In his novels, as in his poems, Masefield's achievement was his ability to tell a fresh and energetic tale in unpretentious language. His most famous novel is probably *Sard Harker,* but in 1924 P. A. Hutchinson wrote of this book: "*Sard Harker* will not live; it will not go down as a great novel, or even as a great romance. Masefield has drunk a little too freely of the milk of Paradise. But the yarn—yes, that will have to be the final designation—must not be missed. Assuredly it must not be missed." A *Times Literary Supplement* reviewer cited the "matter-of-fact precision" with which *Sard Harker* was composed. "You must have greatness of mind, and greatness of art as well," he wrote, "to be capable of telling a simple adventure story about simple people in simple sentences, and making of the whole a great heroic tale."

Dead Ned and its sequel, *Live and Kicking Ned,* were also praised as excellent stories, imaginatively conceived. The *Boston Transcript* reviewer wrote: "In a day when a goodly portion is patently written in exposition of a thesis, it is refreshing to pick up a book that has no social, economic or emotional problem, past or present, in need of interpretation. Adventure, pure and simple, is the stuff of which John Masefield's latest romance, *Dead Ned,* is compounded." The *Times Literary Supplement* writer stated that "Mr. Masefield's is the art of reflecting life in a double glass so as to capture a twice-faithful image. It with the lessons of philosophy learned by experience, full of gentle skepticism also." William Soskin, impressed with the originality shown in the Ned sequence, even implied that Masefield's prose showed more skill than his poems. "Masefield contrives to incorporate nuances of satirical and reflective meaning," Soskin wrote, "which suggests he would be more wholesomely occupied as a Homer of adventure than an official poet for his native little island."

Masefield's autobiographical pieces were among his last writings, and those who read them were impressed with his ability to recall the excitement of the many "bright festivals" in his past. Chinua Achebe, in his review of *Grace Before Ploughing,* recalled the entire achievement of Masefield's career: "[He] took me along and I saw with wide-eyed wonder the sights of his childhood and felt something of the terror planted in his young mind by protective, well-meaning adults. . . . Masefield's art astonishes by the simplicity of its line. I think it comes from a rare gift of sight that reveals to those who possess it 'the unutterable worth of humble things.' "

A memorial service for Masefield was held at Westminster Abbey on June 20, 1967; Robert Graves gave the address and C. Day Lewis read from Masefield's works.

BIOGRAPHICAL/CRITICAL SOURCES:

BOOKS

Contemporary Literary Criticism, Gale, Volume 11, 1979, Volume 47, 1988.
Dictionary of Literary Biography, Volume 10: *Modern British Dramatists, 1940-1945,* Gale, 1982.
Schreiber, Georges, editor, *Portraits and Self-Portraits,* Houghton, 1936.

PERIODICALS

American Review of Reviews, June, 1913, November, 1913.
Boston Transcript, November 5, 1938.
Chicago Sunday Tribune, October 1, 1961.
International Book Review, December, 1924.
Kenyon Review, March, 1967.
New Statesman, June 16, 1961, June 17, 1966.
Newsweek, May 22, 1967.
New Yorker, November 4, 1939.
New York Herald Tribune Books, November 12, 1939.
New York Times, April 16, 1913, March 12, 1950, May 13, 1967.
New York Times Book Review, October 15, 1961.
Publishers Weekly, April 10, 1967.
Saturday Review of Literature, November 8, 1913, November 4, 1961.
Spectator, June 9, 1961.
Time, May 19, 1967.
Times Literary Supplement, October 16, 1924, September 24, 1938, June 22, 1967, March 2, 1984, April 26, 1985.
Washington Post, February 2, 1979.
Washington Post Book World, January 12, 1986.

*   *   *

MASLOW, Abraham H. 1908-1970

PERSONAL: Born April 1, 1908, in New York, N.Y.; died June 8, 1970, in Menlo Park, Calif.; son of Samuel and Rose (Schilofsky) Maslow; married Bertha Goodman, December 31, 1928; children: Ann, Ellen. *Education:* University of Wisconsin, B.A., 1930, M.A., 1931, Ph.D., 1934.

ADDRESSES: Office—Brandeis University, Waltham, Mass.

CAREER: Columbia University, Teachers College, New York, N.Y., research fellow, 1935-37; Brooklyn College (now Brooklyn College of the City University of New York), Brooklyn, N.Y., 1937-51, began as instructor, became associate professor of psychology; Brandeis University, Waltham, Mass., 1951-70, began as associate professor, became Philip Meyers Professor of Psychology, chairman of department, 1951-61. Plant manager, Maslow Cooperage Corp., Pleasanton, Calif., 1945-47.

MEMBER: American Psychological Association (member of council, 1946-48, 1949-50, and 1953-56; president of division of personality, 1955; president of division of aesthetics, 1960; president, 1967-68), American Humanist Association, Society for the Psychological Study of Social Issues (member of council, 1947-49, 1951-55, and 1959-62), New England Psychological Association (president, 1962-63), Massachusetts Psychological Association (director, 1953-56; president, 1960-62).

AWARDS, HONORS: D.Let., Xavier University; American Humanist Association Humanist of the Year, 1967; Laughlin Foundation writing and research grant, 1969-70.

WRITINGS:

(Contributor) Ross Stagner, *Psychology of Personality,* McGraw, 1937.

(With Bela Mittelmann) *Principles of Abnormal Psychology,* Harper, 1941, revised edition, 1951.

Motivation and Personality, Harper, 1954, 2nd edition, 1970.

(Editor) *New Knowledge in Human Values,* Harper, 1959.

Toward a Psychology of Being, Van Nostrand, 1962, 2nd edition, 1968.

Religions, Values and Peak-Experiences, Ohio State University Press, 1964.

Eupsychian Management: A Journal, Irwin, 1965.

The Psychology of Science: A Reconnaissance, Harper, 1966.

(Editor with Hung-min Chiang) *The Healthy Personality,* Van Nostrand, 1969, 2nd edition, 1977.

New Knowledge in Human Values, Regnery, 1970.

The Farther Reaches of Human Nature, Viking, 1971.

Dominance, Self-Esteem, Self-Actualization: Germinal Papers of A. H. Maslow, edited by Richard J. Lowry, Brooks/Cole, 1973.

The Journals of A. H. Maslow, two volumes, Brooks/Cole, 1979.

Also author, with others, of *The S-I Inventory,* Stanford University Press. Contributor of more than one hundred articles to professional journals.

SIDELIGHTS: As a result of his pioneering work in what has come to be known as humanistic psychology, Abraham H. Maslow is considered to be the founder of the third major school of thought in the field of psychology, the other two being behaviorism, with its emphasis on the study of objective *evidence* of behavior rather than on subjective interpretations, and psychoanalysis (or Freudianism), with its emphasis on psychic phenomena and the importance of talking freely about one's dreams and childhood experiences. In general, Maslow felt that each of these other theories was basically too negativistic and scientifically oriented to accurately describe and explain human behavior. His ideas, more attuned to literature and the humanities, emphasize man's positive features and his capacity for personal growth and achievement.

Maslow perceived man as having two different sets of needs—basic needs, such as hunger, thirst, sex, and security, and metaneeds (or spiritual qualities), such as justice, goodness, beauty, order, and unity. For obvious reasons, basic needs take precedence over metaneeds; they must be adequately fulfilled before a person can concentrate on fulfilling the metaneeds.

Furthermore, he claimed, everyone feels an inherent desire to satisfy *both* types of needs in order to live up to his or her full potential (a process known as self-actualization). Frustration, unhappiness, and, in more extreme cases, mental illness can result when a person is unable to continue this spiritual growth due to external forces (such as an unfulfilled basic need).

Though first outlined in the 1940s, humanistic psychology continues to be the most rapidly developing of the three schools of thought. One of its more popular manifestations is encounter-group psychotherapy, widely practiced at rehabilitation centers and psychology institutes throughout the country.

BIOGRAPHICAL/CRITICAL SOURCES:

BOOKS

Abraham H. Maslow: A Memorial Volume, Brooks/Cole, 1972.

Frick, Willard B., *Humanistic Psychology: Interviews with Maslow, Murphy, and Rogers,* C. E. Merrill, 1971.

Goble, Frank, *The Third Force: The Psychology of Abraham Maslow,* Grossman, 1970.

Lowry, Richard A., *A. H. Maslow: An Intellectual Portrait,* Brooks/Cole, 1973.

Schultz, Duane, *Theories of Personality,* Brooks/Cole, 1976.

Wilson, Colin, *New Pathways in Psychology: Maslow and the Post-Freudian Revolution,* Gollancz, 1972.

*   *   *

MASON, Bobbie Ann 1940-

PERSONAL: Born May 1, 1940, in Mayfield, Ky.; daughter of Wilburn A. (a dairy farmer) and Christianna (Lee) Mason; married Roger B. Rawlings (a magazine editor and writer), April 12, 1969. *Education:* University of Kentucky, B.A., 1962; State University of New York at Binghamton, M.A., 1966; University of Connecticut, Ph.D., 1972.

ADDRESSES: Agent—Amanda Urban, International Creative Management, 40 West 57th St., New York, N.Y. 10019.

CAREER: Writer. *Mayfield Messenger,* Mayfield, Ky., writer, 1960; Ideal Publishing Co., New York, N.Y., writer for magazines, including *Movie Stars, Movie Life,* and *T.V. Star Parade,* 1962-63; Mansfield State College, Mansfield, Pa., assistant professor of English, 1972-79.

AWARDS, HONORS: National Book Critics Circle Award nomination and American Book Award nomination, both 1982, PEN-Faulkner Award for fiction nomination and Ernest Hemingway Foundation Award, both 1983, all for *Shiloh and Other Stories;* National Endowment for the Arts fellowship, 1983; Pennsylvania Arts Council grant, 1983; Guggenheim fellowship, 1984; American Academy and Institute for Arts and Letters award, 1984.

WRITINGS:

Nabokov's Garden: A Guide to Ada, Ardis, 1974.

The Girl Sleuth: A Feminist Guide to the Bobbsey Twins, Nancy Drew, and Their Sisters, Feminist Press, 1975.

Shiloh and Other Stories, Harper, 1982.

In Country (novel), Harper, 1985.

Spence + Lila (novel), Harper, 1988.

Love Life: Stories, Harper, 1989.

Also contributor of short stories to awards anthologies, including *Best American Short Stories,* 1981 and 1983, *The Pushcart Prize,* 1983, and *The O. Henry Awards,* 1986 and 1988. Contributor to numerous magazines, including *New Yorker, Atlantic,* and *Mother Jones;* frequent contributor to "The Talk of the Town" column, *New Yorker.*

WORK IN PROGRESS: Short stories and a novel; a television adaptation of *Spence + Lila.*

SIDELIGHTS: When Bobbie Ann Mason's first volume of fiction, *Shiloh and Other Stories,* was published in 1982, it established her reputation as a rising voice in Southern literature. "[But] to say that she is a 'new' writer is to give entirely the wrong impression, for there is nothing unformed or merely promising about her," emphasizes Anne Tyler in the *New Republic.* "She is a full-fledged master of the short story." Most of the sixteen works in *Shiloh* originally appeared in the *New Yorker, Atlantic,* or other national magazines, a fact surprising to several critics who, like Anatole Broyard in the *New York Times Book Review,* label Mason's work "a regional literature that describes people and places almost unimaginably different from ourselves and the big cities in which we live." Explains

David Quammen in another *New York Times Book Review* piece: "Miss Mason writes almost exclusively about working-class and farm people coping with their muted frustrations in western Kentucky (south of Paducah, not far from Kentucky Lake, if that helps you), and the gap to be bridged empathically between her readership and her characters [is] therefore formidable. But formidable also is Miss Mason's talent, and her craftsmanship."

Most critics attribute Mason's success to her vivid evocation of a region's physical and social geography. "As often as not," Gene Lyons reports in *Newsweek,* the author describes "a matter of town—paved roads, indoor plumbing, and above all, TV—having come to the boondocks with the force of an unannounced social revolution." While the language of Mason's characters reflects their rural background, her people do not fit the Hollywood stereotype of backwoods hillbillies content to let the rest of the world pass by. Tyler notes that "they have an earnest faith in progress; they are as quick to absorb new brand names as foreigners trying to learn the language of a strange country they've found themselves in. It is especially poignant," she adds, "that the characters are trying to deal with changes most of us already take for granted." Mason's Kentucky is, reviewers note, a world in transition, with the old South fast becoming the new. As Suzanne Freeman comments in the *Washington Post Book World:* "Mason's characters are just trying not to get lost in the shuffle."

Mason often explores intensely personal events that lead to the acceptance of something new or the rejection—or loss—of something old. These adjustments in the characters' lives reflect a general uneasiness that pervades the cultural landscape; the forces of change and alienation are no less frightening because they are universal or unavoidable. "Loss and deprivation, the disappointment of pathetically modest hopes, are the themes Bobbie Ann Mason works and reworks," states Quammen. "She portrays the disquieted lives of men and women not blessed with much money or education or luck, but cursed with enough sensitivity and imagination to suffer regrets." The characters in Mason's fiction are caught between isolation and transience, and this struggle is reflected in their relationships, which are often emotionally and intellectually distant. "Some people will stay at home and be content there," the author noted in a *People* interview. "Others are born to run. It's that conflict that fascinates me." As a result, writes *Time* critic R. Z. Sheppard, "Mason has an unwavering bead on the relationship between instincts and individual longings. Her women have ambitions but never get too far from the nest; her men have domestic moments but spend a lot of time on wheels." Mason's characters "exist in a psychological rather than a physical environment," Broyard similarly contends, "one that has been gutted—like an abandoned building—by the movement of American life. They fall between categories, occupy a place between nostalgia and apprehension. They live, without history or politics, a life more like a linoleum than a tapestry."

Other critics, while noting Mason's ability to evoke psychological states, emphasize her skill at depicting the material details of her "linoleum" world. Tyler points out that readers know precisely what dishes constitute the characters' meals, what clothes hang in their closets, and what craft projects fill their spare time. Mason intones the brand names that are infiltrating her characters' vocabularies, and the exact titles of soap operas and popular songs provide an aural backdrop for Mason's own emotional dramas. Likewise, her characters' voices, according to Tyler, "ring through our living rooms." Freeman, however, cites Mason's use of colloquialisms as one of the book's few problems. "A couple of the stories have promising starts and clunky, disappointing endings," she writes. "And, here and there throughout the stories, Mason has overdone the country talk." Yet in the

final analysis, the critic admits, "Mason has a vision and she makes us see it too—it is a glimpse straight into the heart of her characters' lives." "In true short-story tradition, [her] insights and epiphanies are spring-loaded," adds Sheppard. "Mason rarely says more than is necessary to convey what Hemingway called 'the real thing, the sequence of motion and fact which made the emotion.' "

In her first novel, *In Country,* "Mason returns to this same geographical and spiritual milieu" as her short fiction, notes *New York Times* critic Michiko Kakutani, "and she returns, too, to her earlier themes: the dislocations wrought on ordinary, blue-collar lives by recent history—in this case, recent history in the form of the Vietnam War." Seventeen-year-old Samantha Hughes doesn't remember the war, but it has profoundly affected her life: her father died in Vietnam and her uncle Emmett, with whom she lives, still bears the emotional and physical scars of his service. In the summer after her high school graduation, Sam struggles to understand the war and learn about her father; "ten years after the end of the Vietnam War," summarizes Richard Eder of the *Los Angeles Times Book Review,* "in the most prosaic and magical way possible, she stubbornly undertakes the exorcism of a ghost that almost everything in our everyday life manages to bury." In addition, Mason shows the same concern for particulars that distinguishes her short fiction, as *Christian Science Monitor* contributor Marilyn Gardner observes: "She displays an ear perfectly tuned to dialogue, an eye that catches every telling detail and quirky mannerism. Tiny, seemingly insignificant observations and revelations accumulate almost unnoticed until something trips them, turning them into literary grenades explosive with meaning."

Detroit Free Press writer Suzanne Yeager similarly believes that the author's details contribute to the authenticity of the novel. "Mason's narrative is so extraordinarily rich with the sounds, smells and colors of daily life in the '80s that Sam and her family and friends take on an almost eerie reality." As a result, the critic adds, *In Country* "becomes less a novel and more a diary of the unspoken observations of ordinary America." Jonathan Yardley, however, faults the novel for the "dreary familiarity" of its Vietnam themes; writing in the *Washington Post Book World,* he asserts that Mason "has failed to transform these essentially political questions into the stuff of fiction; none of her characters come to life, the novel's structure is awkward and its narrative herky-jerky, her prose wavers uncertainly between adult and teenaged voices." But other critics find Mason's work successful; *Chicago Tribune Book World* contributor Bruce Allen, for instance, says that the novel's "real triumph . . . is Mason's deep and honest portrayal of her two protagonists," especially Sam. "More than any other character in our recent fiction," the critic continues, Sam "is a real person who grows more and more real the better we come to know her—and the novel that affords us the opportunity to is, clearly, the year's most gratifying reading experience." "[Mason's] first novel, although it lacks the page-by-page abundance of her best stories," concludes Joel Conarroe in the *New York Times Book Review,* "is an exceptional achievement, at once humane, comic and moving."

Spence + Lila, Mason's second novel, "is a love story that explores both human love and a love for life," writes Jill McCorkle in the *Washington Post.* "It is a short novel with a simple plot, the limited space enriched by characters whose voices and situations are realistic and memorable." Spence and Lila are a Kentucky farm couple who have been married for over forty years; Lila's upcoming surgery is forcing them to face the prospect of being separated for the first time since World War II. "The chapters alternate between Spence's and Lila's point of view, and such resonances [in their thoughts] range freely through the past and present," describes *Los Angeles Times Book Review* contributor Nancy Mairs. Despite the potential for sentimentality in the story, Mason "manages to avoid the gooey and patronizing muck that is usually described as heartwarming," remarks a *Time* reviewer. "Her account is funny and deft, with plenty of gristle."

Newsweek writer Peter S. Prescott, however, finds *Spence + Lila* a "gently tedious" book saved only by Mason's skillful writing. But Kakutani, although she acknowledges that the book "suffers from a melodramatic predictability absent from Ms. Mason's earlier works," thinks that the author treats her subject "without ever becoming sentimental or cliched." The critic goes on to praise Mason's "lean stripped-down language" and "nearly pitch-perfect ear for the way her characters speak," and adds that "mainly, however, it's her sure-handed ability to evoke Spence and Lila's life together that lends their story such poignance and authenticity." *New York Times Book Review* contributor Frank Conroy likewise commends Mason's dialogue, but admits that "one wishes she had risked a bit more in this book, taking us under the surface of things instead of lingering there so lovingly and relentlessly." "Awkward silence in the face of ideas and feelings is a common frailty," elaborates Mairs, "but it represents a limitation in 'Spence + Lila,' constraining Mason to rush her story and keep to its surface. . . . If I perceive any defect in 'Spence + Lila,' " the critic continues, "it's that this is a short novel which could well have been long." "As soon as [Mason's] characters open their mouths, they come to life and move to center stage," McCorkle similarly concludes. "If there is a weakness it would be the reader's desire to prolong their talk and actions before moving to an ending that is both touching and satisfying."

Despite the author's success with *In Country* and *Spence+Lila*, "Mason's strongest form may be neither the novel nor the story, but the story *collection*," Lorrie Moore maintains in her *New York Times Book Review* assessment of *Love Life: Stories*. "It is there, picking up her pen every 20 pages to start anew, gathering layers through echo and overlap, that Ms. Mason depicts most richly a community of contemporary lives." Jack Fuller, however, believes that *Love Life* has a weakness: "Mason is a strong enough writer to make you believe her people, but she does not allow them any escape from the cliches that surround them," the Chicago *Tribune Books* writer notes, adding that her characters have "no exit" from their problems. While Kakutani likewise remarks that "few of Ms. Mason's characters ever resolve their dilemmas—or if they do, their decisions take place . . . beyond the knowledge of the reader," she asserts that the stories "are not simply minimalist 'slice-of-life' exercises, but finely crafted tales that manage to invest inarticulate, small-town lives with dignity and intimations of meaning." Mason's "stories work like parables, small in scale and very wise, tales wistfully told by a masterful stylist whose voice rises purely from the heart of the country," states Judith Freeman in the *Los Angeles Times Book Review*. As a *Chicago Tribune Book World* critic similarly concludes, "[Mason] is a writer of immense sensitivity, a true seer; technically, in terms of the making of sentences, she is a near virtuoso."

MEDIA ADAPTATIONS: In Country was made into a Warner Brothers film by director Norman Jewison in 1989.

BIOGRAPHICAL/CRITICAL SOURCES:

BOOKS

Contemporary Literary Criticism, Gale, Volume 28, 1984, Volume 43, 1987.
Dictionary of Literary Biography Yearbook: 1987, Gale, 1988.
Prenshaw, Peggy Whitman, editor, *Women Writers of the South,* University Press of Mississippi, 1984.

PERIODICALS

Chicago Tribune Book World, January 23, 1983, September 1, 1985.
Christian Science Monitor, September 6, 1985.
Detroit Free Press, October 13, 1985.
Globe and Mail (Toronto), November 9, 1985, July 30, 1988.
Los Angeles Times Book Review, September 22, 1985, June 19, 1988, March 19, 1989.
Louisville Courier-Journal Magazine, January 29, 1989.
Nation, January 18, 1986.
New Republic, November 1, 1982.
Newsweek, November 15, 1982, September 30, 1985, August 1, 1988.
New York Review of Books, November 7, 1985.
New York Times, November 23, 1982, September 4, 1985, June 11, 1988, March 3, 1989.
New York Times Book Review, November 21, 1982, December 19, 1982, September 15, 1985, June 26, 1988, March 12, 1989.
New York Times Magazine, May 15, 1988.
People, October 28, 1985.
Publishers Weekly, August 30, 1985.
Time, January 3, 1983, September 16, 1985, July 4, 1988.
Times (London), August 11, 1983, March 6, 1986.
Times Literary Supplement, August 12, 1983, April 18, 1986.
Tribune Books (Chicago), June 26, 1988, February 19, 1989.
Voice Literary Supplement, November, 1982, February, 1986.
Washington Post, February 5, 1976, July 1, 1988.
Washington Post Book World, October 31, 1982, September 8, 1985, March 26, 1989.

—*Sketch by Diane Telgen*

*   *   *

MASON, Ernst
   See POHL, Frederik

*   *   *

MASTERS, Edgar Lee   1868-1950
   (Lucius Atherton, Elmer Chubb, Webster Ford,
   Harley Prowler, Lute Puckett, Dexter Wallace)

PERSONAL: Born August 23, 1868, in Garnett, Kan.; died March 5, 1950, in Melrose Park, Penn.; buried in Petersburg, Ill.; son of Hardin Wallace (a grocer, schoolteacher, and lawyer) and Emma Jerusha (Dexter) Masters; married Helen M. Jenkins, June 21, 1898 (divorced, 1923); married Ellen F. Coyne (an English teacher), November 5, 1926; children: (first marriage) Hardin, Marcia, Madeline; (second marriage) Hilary. *Education:* Attended Knox College, Galesburg, Ill., 1889-90; read law in his father's law office, 1890-91. *Politics:* Democrat.

CAREER: Admitted to the Illinois Bar, 1891; practiced law in partnership with his father, 1891-92; practiced law in Chicago,

Ill., 1892-1920, in partnership with Clarence Darrow, 1903-11; writer, 1920-50.

AWARDS, HONORS: Levinson Prize, *Poetry* magazine, 1916; Mark Twain Medal, 1936; National Institute and American Academy of Arts and Letters Award in Literature, 1942; Poetry Society of America medal, 1942; Shelley Memorial Award, 1944; Academy of American Poets fellowship, 1946.

WRITINGS:

A Book of Verses, Way & Williams, 1898.
Maximilian: A Play In Five Acts, Badger, 1902.
The New Star Chamber and Other Essays, Hammersmark, 1904.
(Under pseudonym Dexter Wallace) *The Blood of the Prophets* (poetry), Rooks, 1905.
Althea: A Play in Four Acts, Rooks, 1907.
The Trifler: A Play, Rooks, 1908.
The Leaves of the Tree: A Play, Rooks, 1909.
Eileen: A Play in Three Acts, Rooks, 1910.
(Under pseudonym Webster Ford) *Songs and Sonnets,* Rooks, 1910.
The Locket: A Play in Three Acts, Rooks, 1910.
The Tread of Idleness: A Play in Four Acts, Rooks, 1911.
(Under pseudonym Webster Ford) *Songs and Sonnets: Second Series,* Rooks, 1912.
Spoon River Anthology (poetry; originally published in *Reedy's Mirror,* under pseudonym Webster Ford), Macmillan, 1915, enlarged edition, 1916, new edition, 1944.
Songs and Satires (poetry), Macmillan, 1916.
The Great Valley (poetry), Macmillan, 1916.
Toward the Gulf (poetry), Macmillan, 1918.
Starved Rock (poetry), Macmillan, 1919.
Mitch Miller (novel), Macmillan, 1920.
Domesday Book (long poem), Macmillan, 1920.
The Open Sea (poetry), Macmillan, 1921.
Children of the Market Place (novel), Macmillan, 1922.
Skeeters Kirby (novel), Macmillan, 1923.
The Nuptial Flight (novel), Boni & Liveright, 1923.
Mirage (novel), Boni & Liveright, 1924.
The New Spoon River (poetry), Boni & Liveright, 1924.
Selected Poems, Macmillan, 1925.
Lee: A Dramatic Poem, Macmillan, 1926.
Kit O'Brien (novel), Boni & Liveright, 1927.
Levy Mayer and the New Industrial Era (biography), Yale University Press, 1927.
Jack Kelso: A Dramatic Poem, Appleton, 1928.
The Fate of the Jury: An Epilogue to Domesday Book (long poem), Appleton, 1929.
Gettysburg, Manila, Acoma (three plays), Liveright, 1930.
Lichee Nuts (poetry), Liveright, 1930.
Lincoln: The Man (biography), Dodd, Mead, 1931.
Godbey: A Dramatic Poem, Dodd, Mead, 1931.
The Serpent in the Wilderness (poetry), Sheldon Dick, 1933.
The Tale of Chicago (history), Putnam, 1933.
Dramatic Duologues: Four Short Plays in Verse, Samuel French, 1934.
Richmond: A Dramatic Poem, Samuel French, 1934.
Invisible Landscapes (poetry), Macmillan, 1935.
Vachel Lindsay: A Poet in America (biography), Scribners, 1935.
Poems of People, Appleton-Century, 1936.
The Golden Fleece of California (poetry), Countryman, 1936.
Across Spoon River: An Autobiography, Farrar & Rinehart, 1936.
Whitman (biography), Scribners, 1937.
The Tide of Time (novel), Farrar & Rinehart, 1937.
The New World (poetry), Appleton-Century, 1937.

Hymn to the Unknown God, New Age Ministry of Religious Research, ca. 1937.
Mark Twain: A Portrait, Scribners, 1938.
More People (poetry), Appleton-Century, 1939.
(Editor and author of introduction) Ralph Waldo Emerson, *The Living Thoughts of Emerson,* Longmans, Green, 1940.
Illinois Poems, James A. Decker, 1941.
The Sangamon (novel), Farrar & Rinehart, 1942.
Along the Illinois (poetry), James A. Decker, 1942.
(Contributor) Hardin W. Masters, *Edgar Lee Masters: A Centenary Memoir-Anthology,* A. S. Barnes for the Poetry Society of America, 1972.
Poems, selected and edited by Denys Thompson, Chatto & Windus, 1972.
The Harmony of Deeper Music: Posthumous Poems of Edgar Lee Masters, edited by Frank K. Robinson, Humanities Research Center, University of Texas at Austin, 1976.

Also author of *The Constitution and Our Insular Possessions,* and *Browning as a Philosopher,* 1912. Contributor to magazines and newspapers under pseudonyms Lucius Atherton, Elmer Chubb, Webster Ford, Harley Prowler, Lute Puckett, and Dexter Wallace. Many of Masters's letters and papers are in the collection of the University of Texas at Austin. Other items are at the Newberry Library, Chicago, Ill., and the Regenstein Library of the University of Chicago.

SIDELIGHTS: Edgar Lee Masters is best remembered for his great collection *Spoon River Anthology,* a sequence of over two hundred free-verse epitaphs spoken from the cemetery of the town of Spoon River. When the collection first saw publication in 1915, it caused a great sensation because of its forthrightness about sex, moral decay, and hypocrisy; but its cynical view of Midwestern small town values, and influenced a whole generation of writers and their works. "The volume," said Herbert K. Russell in the *Concise Dictionary of American Literary Biography,* "became an international popular and critical success and introduced with a flourish what has since come to be known as the Chicago Renaissance"—a group of writers, including Masters, Carl Sandburg, Vachel Lindsay, and Theodore Dreiser, who disproved the commonly held notion that only on the East Coast of the U.S. were there writers capable of producing literature. "It is safe to say," declared Ernest Earnest in *Western Humanities Review,* "that no other volume of poetry except *The Waste Land* (1922) made such an impact during the first quarter of this century."

Born on the Kansas prairie and brought up in the small Illinois towns of Petersburg and Lewistown, Masters was firmly rooted in the Midwestern society he both praised and criticized in *Spoon River Anthology.* The central Illinois area in which Masters grew up was especially revered for its historic association with Abraham Lincoln; Russell commented that Masters's "hometown of Petersburg was but two miles from Lincoln's New Salem; he knew personally William Herndon (Lincoln's law partner), the Armstrong family (one of whom Lincoln had defended), and John McNamar (the man who jilted Ann Rutledge before her story became entwined with Lincoln's)."

Masters himself was trained for the law—he practiced as an attorney in Chicago for nearly thirty years, and for several years he was the law partner of Clarence Darrow, the lawyer later to become famous as the counsel for the defense at the 1925 Scopes trial—although he had long harbored literary ambitions. Using a variety of pseudonyms to avoid possible damage to his law practice, Masters began to publish poetry in magazines. By 1915 he had published four books of poetry, seven plays, and a collection of essays, but none of them had received much critical attention. Then, following the advice of *Reedy's Mirror* publisher William Marion Reedy, Masters began to experiment with poetic form, bringing to life the sort of people he had known in his boyhood. The result was a book that he called *Spoon River Anthology.*

Spoon River Anthology mixed classical forms with innovative ones to create a work that critics both praised and scorned. It followed the example of the *Greek Anthology,* a collection of some 4500 Greek poems written between about 500 B.C. and 1000 A.D. Many of these poems, like those in *Spoon River,* took the form of epigrams—laconic sayings that harbor (or seem to harbor) a truth—and others were expressed as confessional epitaphs, in which the dead commented on their lives. Unlike the ancient Greeks, however, Masters made his dead recite their speeches in free verse, a form of poetry that, although pioneered by Walt Whitman many years before, still had not gained popular acceptance; for instance, novelist William Dean Howells, writing in *Harper's,* regarded Masters's work as nothing but "shredded prose." Late nineteenth century literary fashion saw the small town as a bastion of American values, but Masters showed that this was not necessarily so—he portrayed the deceased citizens as fornicators, adulterers, prostitutes, thieves, victims of botched abortions—"a gallery," said Russell, "of many different types of people which ultimately served to universalize the people of Spoon River."

The citizens themselves are types rather than historical portraits, which may be one of the factors contributing to their universality. The soliloquy of "Lucinda Matlock," one of the sequence's best known poems, was based on Master's pioneering grandmother; yet it provides a picture of the common experience of the frontier wife and mother rather than outlining the life of a particular person. "The names I drew from both the Spoon river and the Sangamon river neighborhoods," wrote Masters in *American Mercury,* "combining first names here with surnames there, and taking some also from the constitutions and State papers of Illinois. Only in a few instances, such as those of Chase Henry, William H. Herndon and Anne Rutledge and two or three others, did I use anyone's name as a whole."

Uproar over the volume's blunt attitude toward sex and its commentary on the morals of small town life quickly spread outside the literary community. The book became a bestseller: it was, said Stanley Edgar Hyman in his *The Critic's Credentials: Essays and Reviews,* a "*succes de scandale*—it was the sex-shocker, the *Peyton Place* of its day. Knowing that childbirth would kill his wife, Henry Barker impregnated her out of hatred. The only feeling Benjamin Pantier inspired in his wife was sexual disgust. Old Henry Bennett died of overexertion in the bed of his young wife." "It was the scandal and not the poetry of *Spoon River,*" wrote Carl Van Doren in *Contemporary American Novelists: 1900-1920,* ". . . which particularly spread its fame."

Although many poets—including Amy Lowell, who said in her *Tendencies in Modern American Poetry,* "One wonders, if life in our little Western cities is as bad as this, why everyone does not commit suicide"—objected to Masters's work, others welcomed the new voice in their midst. "At last. At last America has discovered a poet," rejoiced fellow poet Ezra Pound in the *Egoist.* "At last the American West has produced a poet strong enough to weather the climate, capable of dealing with life directly, without circumlocution, without resonant meaningless phrases." "Once in a while a man comes along who writes a book that has his own heart-beats in it," wrote Carl Sandburg in the *Little Review.* "The people whose faces look out from the pages of the book are the people of life itself, each trait of them as plain or as mysterious as in the old home valley where the writer came from. Such a writer and book are realized here." Later critics also recognized the volume's importance: "The value of the *Spoon River* volume lies in its originality of design, its uniqueness, its effect upon its times," declared Fred Lewis Pattee in *The New American Literature: 1890-1930.* "Its colossal success started a choir of young poets. Whether we condemn or praise, we must accept it as a major episode in the history of the poetic movement in the second decade of the new century."

Although Masters published many more works, including novels, history and a sequel, *The New Spoon River,* he never succeeded in producing another volume to match his masterpiece. Part of the reason Masters's later efforts failed, suggested Russell, lay in his tendency to expound his political views in his work, and in his "willingness to publish as finished works books that were inartistically cluttered with his own highly subjective viewpoints." His biography *Lincoln: The Man* is especially flawed in this manner; Russell explained that "Masters, a Jeffersonian Democrat, was so unfair to his Republican subject that *Lincoln: The Man* drew some of the most hostile criticism ever leveled at an American biography." "With *Spoon River Anthology,*" wrote Louis Untermeyer in *American Poetry since 1900,* "Masters arrived—and left." He was, Russell concluded, "the victim of the success of his one enduring achievement, *Spoon River Anthology;* no matter what he published after it, he could never produce a rival to it, and so each ensuing volume represented a decline. *Spoon River Anthology* made him famous, but it also contributed to some of the sadness in his life, and it is (to borrow from it) his 'true epitaph, more lasting than stone.' "

BIOGRAPHICAL/CRITICAL SOURCES:

BOOKS

Concise Dictionary of American Literary Biography: Realism, Naturalism and Local Color, 1865-1917, Gale, 1988.

Dictionary of Literary Biography, Volume 54: *American Poets, 1880-1945,* Gale, 1987.

Flanagan, John T., *Edgar Lee Masters: The Spoon River Poet and His Critics,* Scarecrow Press, 1974.

Hartley, Lois Teal, *Spoon River Revisited,* Ball State University, 1963.

Hyman, Stanley Edgar, *The Critic's Credentials: Essays and Reviews,* edited by Phoebe Pettingell, Atheneum, 1978.

Lowell, Amy, *Tendencies in Modern American Poetry,* Macmillan, 1917.

Masters, Hardin W., *Edgar Lee Masters: A Biographical Sketchbook about a Famous American Author,* Fairleigh Dickinson University Press, 1978.

Masters, Hilary, *Last Stands: Notes from Memory,* David R. Godine, 1982.

Pattee, Fred Lewis, *The New American Literature: 1890-1930,* Appleton-Century, 1930.

Primeau, Ronald, *Beyond Spoon River: The Legacy of Edgar Lee Masters,* University of Texas Press, 1981.

Robinson, Frank K., *Edgar Lee Masters: An Exhibition in Commemoration of His Birth,* Humanities Research Center, University of Texas at Austin, 1970.

Twentieth-Century Literary Criticism, Gale, Volume 2, 1979, Volume 25, 1988.

Untermeyer, Louis, *American Poetry since 1900,* Holt, 1923.

Van Doren, Carl, *Contemporary American Novelists: 1900-1920,* Macmillan, 1922.

Wrenn, John H., and Margaret H. Wrenn, *Edgar Lee Masters,* Twayne, 1983.

PERIODICALS

American Mercury, January, 1933.
CEA Critic, January, 1977.
Century, August, 1925.
Egoist, January 1, 1915.
Essays in Literature, fall, 1977.
Harper's, September, 1915.
Journal of the Illinois State Historical Society, October, 1921-January, 1922.
Little Review, May, 3915.
MidAmerica, Volume 7, 1980.
New Republic, April 17, 1915.
New York Times, February 6, 1931.
New York Times Book Review, September 7, 1924, February 15, 1942.
New York Tribune, August 9, 1915.
Springfield Sunday Journal (Springfield, Ill.), January 1, 1922.
Western Humanities Review, winter, 1967.

—Sketch by Kenneth R. Shepherd

*　　*　　*

MATHE, Albert
   See CAMUS, Albert

*　　*　　*

MATTHESON, Rodney
   See CREASEY, John

*　　*　　*

MATTHEWS, Patricia (Anne) 1927-
   (P. A. Brisco, Patty Brisco; Laura Wylie, a pseudonym)

PERSONAL: Born July 1, 1927, in San Fernando, Calif.; daughter of Roy Oliver and Gladys (Gable) Ernst; married Marvin Owen Brisco, December 21, 1946 (divorced, 1961); married Clayton Hartley Matthews (a writer), November 3, 1972; children: (first marriage) Michael Arvie, David Roy. *Education:* Attended Pasadena Junior College, 1942-45, Mt. San Antonio Junior College, 1953, and Los Angeles State College of Applied Arts and Sciences (now California State University, Los Angeles), 1960.

ADDRESSES: Home and office—P.O. Box 277, Bonsall, Calif. 92003. *Agent*—Jay Garon, 415 Central Park W., New York, N.Y. 10025.

CAREER: Writer, 1957—; California State University, Los Angeles, 1959-77, began in accounting department, became office manager for Office of Associated Students.

MEMBER: Romance Writers of America, Mystery Writers of America.

AWARDS, HONORS: Porgie Awards, *West Coast Review of Books,* silver medal, 1979, for *The Night Visitor,* silver medal (with husband, Clayton Matthews), 1983, for *Empire,* and bronze medal, 1983, for *Flames of Glory;* Team Writing Award (with Clayton Matthews), *Romantic Times,* 1983.

WRITINGS:

JUVENILES

(With husband, Clayton Matthews; jointly written under name Patty Brisco) *Merry's Treasure,* Avalon Books, 1969.

(Under name Patty Brisco) *The Carnival Mystery,* Scholastic Book Services, 1974.
(Under name Patty Brisco) *The Campus Mystery,* Scholastic Book Services, 1977.
(Under name Patty Brisco) *Raging Rapids,* Bowman/Noble, 1978.
(Under name Patty Brisco) *Too Much in Love,* Scholastic Book Services, 1979.
Destruction at Dawn, David Lake, 1986.
Twister, David Lake, 1986.

WITH CLAYTON MATTHEWS; JOINTLY WRITTEN UNDER NAME PATTY BRISCO; GOTHIC NOVELS

Horror at Gull House, Belmont Tower, 1973.
House of Candles, Manor Publishing, 1973.
The Crystal Window, Avon, 1973.
Mist of Evil, Manor Publishing, 1976.

HISTORICAL ROMANCES

Love's Avenging Heart, Pinnacle Books, 1977.
Love's Wildest Promise, Pinnacle Books, 1977.
Love, Forever More, Pinnacle Books, 1977.
Love's Daring Dream, Pinnacle Books, 1978.
Love's Pagan Heart, Pinnacle Books, 1978.
Love's Magic Moment, Pinnacle Books, 1979.
Love's Golden Destiny, Pinnacle Books, 1979.
Love's Raging Tide, Pinnacle Books, 1980.
Love's Sweet Agony, Pinnacle Books, 1980.
Love's Bold Journey, Pinnacle Books, 1980.
Tides of Love, Bantam, 1981.
Embers of Dawn, Bantam, 1982.
Flames of Glory, Bantam, 1983.
Dancer of Dreams, Bantam, 1984.
Gambler in Love, Bantam, 1985.
Tame the Restless Heart, Bantam, 1986.
Enchanted, Worldwide Library, 1987.
Thursday and the Lady, Worldwide Library, 1987.
The Dreaming Tree, Harlequin, 1989.

WITH CLAYTON MATTHEWS; SUSPENSE NOVELS

Midnight Whispers, Bantam, 1981.
Empire, Bantam, 1982.
Midnight Lavender, Bantam, 1985.

OTHER NOVELS

(Under name P. A. Brisco) *The Other People* (fantasy), Powell Publications, 1970.
(Under pseudonym Laura Wylie) *The Night Visitor* (occult), Pinnacle Books, 1979, reprinted (under name Patricia Matthews), Severn House Publishers, 1988.
Mirrors (romantic suspense), Worldwide Library, 1988.
Oasis (general fiction), Worldwide Library, 1988.
Sapphire (general fiction), Harlequin, 1989.

OTHER

(Contributor) Dolly Hasinbiller, editor, *Action: The Strange Notion and Other Stories,* Scholastic Book Services, 1977.
Love's Many Faces (poetry), Pinnacle Books, 1979.
(Contributor) Isaac Asimov, Martin H. Greenberg, and Joseph D. Olander, editors, *Microcosmic Tales: One Hundred Wondrous Science Fiction Short-Stories,* Taplinger, 1980.
(Contributor) Asimov, Greenberg, and Olander, editors, *Miniature Mysteries: One Hundred Malicious Little Mystery Stories,* Taplinger, 1982.

Also contributor to *Escapade Annual,* 1960, *Alfred Hitchcock Anthology, Candlelight, Romance and You, Your First Romance, My First Romance,* and *Writing the Romance.* Contributor of short stories to periodicals, including *Alfred Hitchcock's Mystery Magazine, Dude, Ellery Queen's Mystery Magazine, Escapade, Magazine of Fantasy and Science Fiction, Mike Shayne Mystery Magazine, Motive,* and *Topper;* contributor of articles to *Los Angeles Times* and *Valley People;* contributor of poetry to *American Bard, Cosmopolitan, Ellery Queen's Mystery Magazine, Ladies' Home Journal, Oregonian,* and *Statement.*

SIDELIGHTS: Patricia Matthews has established herself as one of the most popular authors of historical romantic fiction, the genre made famous in the early 1970s by writers such as Rosemary Rogers and Jennifer Wilde. Beginning with *Love's Avenging Heart,* published in 1977, Matthews has produced a string of best-selling historical romances, a number of her books in the millions of copies. Typical of the genre, Matthews relates the romantic pursuits of her heroines and heroes in a variety of exotic locales, calling upon various historical details to evoke a particular time and place. And, as with other romances of their type, Matthews's novels depict passionate love scenes between characters who are embroiled in an atmosphere of adversity and struggle.

Matthews's particular brand of the historical romance features storylines that emphasize action—often a great deal of suspense—and characters who make decisions that significantly affect the outcome of their romantic pursuits. Matthews varies from the usual historical romance format in this respect, her novels opposite those where the heroine's dormant passions are unleashed through some form of rape. "Patricia Matthews writes chaste romances," comments a *West Coast Review of Books* contributor, clarifying that although forceful sex is present in Matthews's novels, it only occurs "after love has been declared" by the participants. Rape is also present in Matthews's novels, yet her characters eventually assert control over their lives. As a result, Matthews's novels have been praised for charting new territory in the genre. "Having read gobs of those historical romances where downtrodden heroines are raped and plundered only to end up with the hero and the right way of life at the end," writes another reviewer in the *West Coast Review of Books,* "it's a pleasure to find an author knowing when to follow the formula and when to deviate." The saga of a young woman in plantation-era Virginia who escapes the bonds of indentured prostitution, finally inheriting the estate of a rich and lonely widower, *Love's Avenging Heart* introduces a protagonist "far more designing than the roster of other heroines," continues the reviewer. Matthews provides "good reading overall for those who would like a faster-moving heroine who makes things happen, rather than those mooning maidens to whom things happen."

Although Matthews is best known for her romance novels, her experience as a writer was developed earlier in different genres. "I have been writing, off and on, since I was eleven; but only began to work at it seriously in 1957, when I made my first poetry sales," she told *CA.* "My first love was science fiction, and phantasy, and my first short story sales were made in this field, strangely enough, to the men's magazines—at the time, one of the few markets for this type of story. My first novel, *The Other People,* was also in this field." After the huge success of *Love's Avenging Heart,* Matthews left her job at California State University in Los Angeles and began writing full time. In addition to her historical romance novels, she has collaborated with her husband Clayton on a number of writing projects, including a juvenile book and several suspense and gothic novels. Both prolific authors—Clayton with over twenty-five books of his own

published—the Matthews' lives revolve around their writing careers. Both spend time traveling, in which they compile historical research for their novels. Matthews commented to *CA* on the personal importance of her work and its objectives: "I love writing, and receive much gratification from the creative process. Through my writing, I hope to communicate with, and to entertain, my readers." She adds: "When my readers write to tell me how much my work means to them, that I bring them pleasure and information, I am both pleased and proud. To bring pleasure and escape and mental stimulation to others is not an insignificant thing."

AVOCATIONAL INTERESTS: Reading, playing piano, songwriting, theatre, painting, swimming, Tai Chi Chuan, studying guitar.

BIOGRAPHICAL/CRITICAL SOURCES:

BOOKS

Falk, Kathryn, editor, *Love's Leading Ladies,* Pinnacle Books, 1982.

PERIODICALS

Best Sellers, July, 1981.
Los Angeles Times, February 12, 1987.
Publishers Weekly, November 21, 1986.
West Coast Review of Books, May, 1977, September, 1977, July, 1978, May, 1979.

*   *   *

MATTHIESSEN, Peter 1927-

PERSONAL: Surname is pronounced "*Math*-e-son"; born May 22, 1927, in New York, N.Y.; son of Erard A. (an architect) and Elizbeth C. Matthiessen; married Patricia Southgate, February 8, 1951 (divorced, 1958); married Deborah Love, May 16, 1963 (deceased, 1972); married Maria Eckhart, November 28, 1980; children: (first marriage) Lucas, Sara C.; (second marriage) Rue, Alexander. *Education:* Attended Sorbonne, University of Paris, 1948-49; Yale University, B.A., 1950.

ADDRESSES: Home—Bridge Lane, Sagaponack, Long Island, N.Y. 11962. *Agent*—Candida Donadio Associates, Inc., 231 West 22nd St., New York, N.Y. 10011.

CAREER: Writer, 1950—; *Paris Review,* New York City (originally Paris, France), co-founder, 1951, editor, 1951—. Former commercial fisherman; captain of deep-sea charter fishing boat, Montauk, Long Island, N.Y., 1954-56; member of expeditions to Alaska, Canadian Northwest Territories, Peru, Nepal, and East Africa, and of Harvard-Peabody Expedition to New Guinea, 1961; National Book Awards judge, 1970. *Military service:* U.S. Navy, 1945-47.

MEMBER: American Academy and Institute of Arts and Letters, New York Zoological Society (trustee, 1965-78).

AWARDS, HONORS: *Atlantic* Prize, 1950, for best first story; *Wildlife in America* is in the permanent library at the White House; National Institute/American Academy of Arts and Letters grant, 1963, for *The Cloud Forest: A Chronicle of the South American Wilderness and Under the Mountain Wall: A Chronicle of Two Seasons in the Stone Age;* National Book Award nomination, 1966, for *At Play in the Fields of the Lord;* Christopher Book Award, 1971, for *Sal si puedes: Cesar Chavez and the New American Revolution;* National Book Award nomination, 1972, for *The Tree Where Man Was Born;* "Editor's Choice" citation from *New York Times Book Review,* 1975, for *Far Tortuga;* National Book Award for contemporary thought, 1979, for *The Snow Leopard;* American Book Award, 1980, for paperback edition of *The Snow Leopard;* John Burroughs Medal and African Wildlife Leadership Foundation Award, both 1982, both for *Sand Rivers;* gold medal for distinction in natural history from the Academy of Natural Sciences, 1985.

WRITINGS:

NOVELS

Race Rock, Harper, 1954, reprinted, Heinemann, 1966.
Partisans, Viking, 1955.
Raditzer, Viking, 1961.
At Play in the Fields of the Lord, Random House, 1965.
Far Tortuga, Random House, 1975.
Midnight Turning Gray, Ampersand, 1984.
Killing Mister Watson, Random House, 1990.

NONFICTION

Wildlife in America, Viking, 1959, Penguin Books, 1977.
The Cloud Forest: A Chronicle of the South American Wilderness, Viking, 1961.
Under the Mountain Wall: A Chronicle of Two Seasons in the Stone Age, Viking, 1962.
Oomingmak: The Expedition to the Musk Ox Island in the Bering Sea, Hastings House, 1967.
(With Ralph S. Palmer and artist Robert Verity Clem) *The Shorebirds of North America,* edited by Gardner D. Stout, Viking, 1967.
Sal si puedes: Cesar Chavez and the New American Revolution, Random House, 1970.
Blue Meridian: The Search for the Great White Shark, Random House, 1971.
Everglades: With Selections from the Writings of Peter Matthiessen, edited by Paul Brooks, Sierra Club-Ballantine, 1971.
(Contributor) Alvin M. Josephy, editor, *The American Heritage Book of Natural Wonders,* American Heritage Press, 1972.
(With photographer Eliot Porter) *The Tree Where Man Was Born/ The African Experience* (Book-of-the-Month Club special fall selection), Dutton, 1972.
The Wind Birds, with drawings by Robert Gillmor, Viking, 1973.
The Snow Leopard, Viking, 1978.
Sand Rivers, with photographs by Hugo van Lawick, Viking, 1981.
In the Spirit of Crazy Horse, Viking, 1983.
Indian Country, Viking, 1984.
Men's Lives: The Surfmen and Baymen of the South Fork, Random House, 1986.
Nine-Headed Dragon River: Zen Journals, 1969-1982, Shambhala, 1986.

OTHER

Seal Pool (juvenile), illustrated by William Pene Du Bois, Doubleday, 1972 (published in England as *The Great Auk Escape,* Angus & Robertson, 1974).
On the River Styx, and Other Stories (collection), Random House, 1989.

Contributor of numerous short stories, articles, and essays to popular periodicals, including *Atlantic, Esquire, Harper's, New Yorker, Saturday Evening Post, Audubon, Newsweek,* and *New York Review of Books.*

WORK IN PROGRESS: A novel.

SIDELIGHTS: Peter Matthiessen is widely considered one of the most important wilderness writers of the twentieth century. In fiction and nonfiction alike, he explores endangered natural environments and human cultures threatened by encroaching technology. As Conrad Silvert notes in *Literary Quarterly,* Matthiessen "is a naturalist, an anthropologist and an explorer of geographies and the human condition. He is also a rhapsodist who writes with wisdom and warmth as he applies scientific knowledge to the peoples and places he investigates. Works of lasting literary value and moral import have resulted." Matthiessen also writes of inner explorations he has undertaken as a practitioner of Zen Buddhism. His National Book Award-winning work *The Snow Leopard* combines the account of a difficult Himalayan trek with spiritual autobiography and contemplations of mortality and transcendence. According to Terrance Des Pres in the *Washington Post Book World,* Matthiessen is "a visionary, but he is very hardminded as well, and his attention is wholly with abrupt detail. This allows him to render strangeness familiar, and much that is menial becomes strange, lustrous, otherworldly." *Dictionary of Literary Biography* contributor John L. Cobbs concludes: "In fiction and in nonfiction, Peter Matthiessen is one of the shamans of literature. He puts his audience in touch with worlds and forces which transcend common experience."

Matthiessen has journeyed through numerous exotic locales, including the far North, the Amazon rain forest, East Africa, the high country of Nepal, and the jungles of New Guinea. His works hardly conform to the standard notion of travelogue, however. Des Pres writes: "Matthiessen is not an adventurer, nor have his voyages been impelled by some silly man-against-the-elements ideal. His central thrust has been to celebrate the virtues of lost cultures, to praise the excellence of life apart from human life, to bear witness to creation vanishing. And in this pursuit he has been quietly obsessed with one of the uglier truths of our age: that nothing lasts, that no place, culture, bird or beast can survive in the path of Western—and now Eastern—greed." This theme pervades Matthiessen's fiction in *At Play in the Fields of the Lord* and *Far Tortuga* and forms the basis of a good portion of his nonfiction, including *Indian Country, Sand Rivers* and *Men's Lives: The Surfmen and Baymen of the South Fork.* "Anyone who has really read his nature writing knows that Matthiessen's attitude toward the natural world is hardly that of a fatuous admirer in his dotage," notes Cobbs. "He brings to his work a skeptical, wary professionalism, the uncompromising eye of a scientist, and an almost cynical and often bitter knowledge of the vulnerability of nature."

Critics contend that despite his pessimistic forecasts for the future of natural areas and their inhabitants, Matthiessen imbues his work with descriptive writing of high quality. According to Vernon Young in the *Hudson Review,* Matthiessen "combines the exhaustive knowledge of the naturalist . . . with a poet's response to far-out landscapes. . . . When he pauses to relate one marvel to another and senses the particular merging into the general, his command of color, sound and substance conjures the resonance of the vast continental space." *New York Times Book Review* contributor Jim Harrison feels that Matthiessen's prose has "a glistening, sculpted character to it. . . . The sense of beauty and mystery is indelible; not that you retain the specific information on natural history, but that you have had your brain, and perhaps the soul, prodded, urged, moved into a new dimension." Robert M. Adams offers a concurrent assessment in the *New York Review of Books.* Matthiessen, Adams writes, "has dealt frequently and knowingly with natural scenery and wild life; he can sketch a landscape in a few vivid, unsentimental words, capture the sensations of entering a wild, windy Nepalese mountain village, and convey richly the strange, whinnying behavior of a herd of wild sheep. His prose is crisp, yet strongly appealing to the senses; it combines instinct with the feeling of adventure."

Although Matthiessen was born in New York City, he spent most of his youth in rural New York State and in Connecticut, where he attended the Hotchkiss School. His father, an architect, was a trustee of the National Audubon Society, and Matthiessen took an early interest in the fascinations of the natural world. "I had always been interested in nature," he remembered in *Publishers Weekly.* "My brother and I started with a passion for snakes, and he went into marine biology, while I took courses in [zoology and ornithology] right up through college." After service in the U.S. Navy, Matthiessen attended Yale University, spending his junior year at the Sorbonne in Paris. Having realized that a writing vocation drew him strongly, he began authoring short stories, one of which won the prestigious *Atlantic* Prize in 1950. Matthiessen also received his degree in 1950, and after teaching creative writing for a year at Yale, he returned to Paris.

In Paris Matthiessen became acquainted with a number of expatriate American writers, including James Baldwin, Richard Wright, Terry Southern, and Irwin Shaw. Cobbs quotes Gay Talese, who described Matthiessen's apartment as "as much a meeting place for young American literati as was Gertude Stein's apartment in the Twenties." A discussion about the critical pretentiousness of little magazines led Matthiessen and Harold L. Humes to found the *Paris Review* in 1951, with an initial investment of three hundred dollars. Matthiessen still serves as an editor of the magazine, which has become one of the best known literary periodicals in English. While living in Paris Matthiessen also completed his first novel, *Race Rock,* a psychological study of four upper-middle-class Americans. When *Race Rock* was published in 1954, Matthiessen returned to the United States, where he continued to write while eking out a livelihood as a commercial fisherman on Long Island. Reflecting on the early stages of his writing career in the *Washington Post,* Matthiessen said: "I don't think could have done my writing without the fishing. I needed something physical, something non-intellectual." The friendships Matthiessen formed with Long Island's fishermen enabled him to chronicle their vanishing life-style in his book *Men's Lives: The Surfmen and Baymen of the South Fork.* Although tourism threatens the solitude of the far reaches of Long Island, Matthiessen still makes his home there when he is not travelling.

Matthiessen embarked on his first lengthy journey in 1956. Loading his Ford convertible with textbooks, a shotgun, and a sleeping bag, he set off to visit every wildlife refuge in the United States. Matthiessen admitted in *Publishers Weekly* that he brought more curiosity than expertise to his quest. "I'm what the 19th century would call a generalist," he said. "I have a lot of slack information, and for my work it's been extremely helpful. I've always been interested in wildlife and wild places and wild people. I wanted to see the places that are disappearing." Nearly three years of work went into Matthiessen's encyclopedic *Wildlife in America,* published in 1959 to high critical acclaim. A commercial success as well, *Wildlife in America* initiated the second phase of Matthiessen's career, a period of two decades during which he undertook numerous expeditions to the wild places that captured his curiosity. Since 1959, he has supported himself solely by writing.

The popularity of Matthiessen's nonfiction somewhat overshadows his equally well-received fiction. Three of his first four books

are novels, and critics have found them commendable and promising works. In a *New York Herald Tribune Book Review* piece about *Race Rock,* Gene Baro comments: "Mr. Matthiessen's absorbing first novel, apart from being a good, well-paced story, offers the reader some depth and breadth of insight. For one thing, 'Race Rock' is a vivid but complex study of evolving character; for another, it is a narrative of character set against a variously changed and changing social background. Mr. Matthiessen has succeeded in making from many strands of reality a close-textured book." *New York Times* contributor Sylvia Berkman contends that with *Race Rock,* Matthiessen "assumes immediate place as a writer of disciplined craft, perception, imaginative vigor and serious temperament. . . . He commands also a gift of flexible taut expression which takes wings at times into a lyricism beautifully modulated and controlled." Cobbs feels that although *Race Rock* "does not anticipate the experimental techniques or exotic subject matter of Matthiessen's later fiction, the novel shows the author's early concern with fundamental emotions and with the tension between primitive vitality and the veneer of civilization."

Partisans and *Raditzer,* Matthiessen's second and third novels, have garnered mixed reviews. According to M. L. Barrett in the *Library Journal,* the action in *Partisans,* "notable for its integrity and dramatic quality, is realized in real flesh-and-blood characters." *New York Times* contributor William Goyen conversely states: "The characters [in *Partisans*] seem only mouthpieces. They are not empowered by depth of dramatic conviction—or confusion. They do, however, impress one with this young author's thoughtful attempt to find answers to ancient and serious questions." Critics have been more impressed with the title character in *Raditzer,* a man Cobbs finds "both loathsome and believable." In the *Nation,* Terry Southern describes *Raditzer's* antihero as "a character distinct from those in literature, yet one who has somehow figured, if but hauntingly, in the lives of us all. It is, in certain ways, as though a whole novel had been devoted to one of [Nelson] Algren's sideline freaks, a grotesque and loathsome creature—yet seen ultimately, as sometimes happens in life, as but another human being." Cobbs concludes: "A skillful ear for dialect and an immediacy in sketching scenes of violence and depravity saved *Raditzer's* moral weightiness from being wearisome, and the novel proved Matthiessen's ability to project his imagination into worlds far removed from that of the intellectual upper-middle class."

At Play in the Fields of the Lord, Matthiessen's 1965 novel, enhanced the author's reputation as a fiction writer. Set in a remote jungle village in the Amazon region, the work is, in the words of *New York Times Book Review* contributor Anatole Broyard, "one of those rare novels that satisfy all sorts of literary and intellectual hungers while telling a story that pulls you along out of sheer human kinship." The story recounts the misguided efforts of four American missionaries and an American Indian mercenary to "save" the isolated Niaruna tribe. Cobbs suggests that the book shows "a virtuosity and richness that few traditional novels exhibit. There is immense stylistic facility in shifting from surreal dream and drug sequences to scrupulous realistic descriptions of tropical nature." *Nation* contributor J. Mitchell Morse voices some dissatisfaction with *At Play in the Fields of the Lord,* claiming that Matthiessen "obviously intended to write a serious novel, but . . . he has unconsciously condescended to cheapness." Conversely, Granville Hicks praises the work in the *Saturday Review:* "[Matthiessen's] evocation of the jungle is powerful, but no more remarkable than his insight into the people he portrays. He tells a fascinating story, and tells it well. . . . It is this firm but subtle evocation of strong feeling that gives Matthiessen's book its power over the imagination. Here, in an appallingly strange setting, he sets his drama of familiar aspirations and disappointments." In the *New York Times Book Review,* Emile Capouya concludes that the novel "is never less than a very superior adventure story, and often a good deal more than that. . . . Where it counts most, the story is well conceived and beautifully written—all in all, a most unusual novel."

Matthiessen's 1975 novel *Far Tortuga* presents a stylistic departure from his previous fictional works. As Cobbs describes it, "the deep penetration of character and psychology that characterized *At Play in the Fields of the Lord* yields to an almost disturbing objectivity in *Far Tortuga,* an absolute, realistic reproduction of surface phenomena—dialogue, noises, colors, shapes." In *Far Tortuga* Matthiessen creates a fictitious voyage of a Caribbean turtling schooner, using characters' conversations and spare descriptions of time, weather, and place. "The radical format of *Far Tortuga* makes the novel a structural tour de force and assured a range of critical reaction," Cobbs notes. Indeed, the novel's use of intermittent blank spaces, wavy lines, ink blots, and unattributed dialogue has elicited extreme critical response. *Saturday Review* contributor Bruce Allen calls the work an "adventurous failure. . . . It exudes a magnificent and paradoxical radiance; but beneath the beautiful surface [it lacks] anything that even remotely resembles a harmonious whole." Eliot Fremont-Smith likewise concludes in the *Village Voice* that *Far Tortuga* "is a tone-poem or dirge that can be called (inaccurately) 'deceptively' simple when it is in fact plain simple. . . . That the book is literarily skillful . . . gives rise to guilt at not being very moved. So it all becomes very admirable, but a little dumb, and not wrenching."

Most of *Far Tortuga's* reviewers express a far different opinion, however. *Newsweek's* Peter S. Prescott praises the book as "a beautiful and original piece of work, a resonant, symbolical story of nine doomed men who dream of an earthly paradise as the world winds down around them. . . . This is a moving, impressive book, a difficult yet successful undertaking." *New York Review of Books* contributor Thomas R. Edwards feels that the novel "turns out to be enthralling. Matthiessen uses his method not for self-display but for identifying and locating his characters. . . . What, despite appearances, does *not* happen in *Far Tortuga* is a straining by literary means to make more of an acutely observed life than it would make of itself." "Despite its Spartan structure, this tale of the sea has the wholeness and scope of a grand epic," writes Silvert. "*Far Tortuga* is a work of stark beauty and subtle, troubling undercurrents." As Robert Stone concludes in the *New York Times Book Review:* "Peter Matthiessen's fifth novel . . . is a singular experience, a series of moments captured whole and rendered with a clarity that quickens the blood. . . . 'Far Tortuga' is an important book, its pleasures are many and good for the soul. Peter Matthiessen is a unique and masterful visionary artist."

"To judge from references in his work," Des Pres writes, "there seems no place on earth Matthiessen has not at least passed through." The author's extensive travels are sometimes partially underwritten by the *New Yorker,* a magazine that regularly publishes Matthiessen's work. This funding has enabled him to spend extended periods of time in the environments he portrays, from that of the Caribbean turtle fishermen to the world of the Stone Age peoples of New Guinea's Kurelu tribe. Though critics such as *New Republic* contributor Paul Zweig contend that "no one writes more vividly about the complex sounds and sights of a world without man," human beings and their vagaries invariably figure in Matthiessen's works, no matter how far afield he travels. Zweig feels that in some of Matthiessen's books, the nat-

uralist "has also been an elegist, chronicling the decline of an older earth of sparse populations hunting and gathering, or planting according to modest needs, in a ritual of respect for the cycles of the year." Quite a few of Matthiessen's nonfiction books and essays address the prerogative of saving cultural groups whose livelihood derives from cultivation of land or sea. Often these human cultures are as endangered as the many species of animal and plant life Matthiessen illuminates in his writings. According to Robert Sherrill in the *Atlantic,* "Death and violence have often inspired [Matthiessen]; . . . victims have stirred him to some of his finest writing."

Human victims form the core of Matthiessen's most recent writings about the United States. In his 1970 title *Sal si puedes: Cesar Chavez and the New American Revolution,* Matthiessen chronicles the herculean efforts of migrant worker Cesar Chavez to organize farm laborers in California. In a review for the *Nation,* Roy Borngartz expresses the opinion that in *Sal si puedes* Matthiessen "brings a great deal of personal attachment to his account of Chavez and his fellow organizers. . . . He makes no pretense of taking any objective stand between the farm workers and the growers. . . . But he is a good and honest reporter, and as far as he was able to get the growers to talk to him, he gives them their say. Matthiessen is most skillful at bringing his people to life." A similar sympathy for oppressed cultures provides the emphasis in Matthiessen's *Indian Country,* published in 1983. Zweig notes that the author "has two subjects in *Indian Country:* the destruction of America's last open land by the grinding pressure of big industry, in particular the energy industry; and the tragic struggle of the last people on the land to preserve their shrinking territories, and even more, to preserve the holy balance of their traditions, linked to the complex, fragile ecology of the land." According to David Wagoner in the *New York Times Book Review,* what makes *Indian Country* "most unusual and most valuable is its effort to infuse the inevitable anger and sorrow with a sense of immediate urgency, with prophetic warnings. . . . Few people could have been better equipped than Mr. Matthiessen to face this formidable task. He has earned the right to be listened to seriously on the ways in which tribal cultures can teach us to know ourselves and the earth."

The Snow Leopard integrates many of Matthiessen's themes— the variety of wildlife, the fragility of the environment, the fascinations of a foreign culture—with contemplations of a more spiritual sort. The book is an autobiographical account of a journey Matthiessen took, in the company of wildlife biologist George Schaller, to a remote part of Nepal. *New York Times* columnist Anatole Broyard writes of Matthiessen: "On this voyage he travels to the outer limits of the world and the inner limits of the self. . . . When he looks in as well as outward, the two landscapes complement one another." Jim Harrison likewise notes in the *Nation:* "Running concurrent to the outward journey in *The Snow Leopard* is an equally torturous inward journey, and the two are balanced to the extent that neither overwhelms the other." As part of that "inward journey," Matthiessen remembers his second wife's death from cancer and opens himself to the spiritual nourishment of Zen. Des Pres suggests that as a result of these meditations, Matthiessen "has expressed, with uncommon candor and no prospect of relief, a longing which keeps the soul striving and alert in us all."

The Snow Leopard has elicited wide critical respect as well as a National Book Award and an American Book Award. In the *Saturday Review,* Zweig comments that the book "contains many . . . passages, in which the naturalist, the spiritual apprentice, and the writer converge simply and dramatically." *Atlantic* contributor Phoebe-Lou Adams concludes of the work: "It is as though [Matthiessen] looked simultaneously through a telescope and a microscope, and his great skill as a writer enables the reader to share this double vision of a strange and beautiful country." Harrison contends that the author "has written a magnificent book: a kind of lunar paradigm and map of the sacred for any man's journey." As a conclusion to his review, Des Pres calls *The Snow Leopard* "a book fiercely felt and magnificently written, in which timelessness and 'modern time' are made to touch and join."

Though Matthiessen writes about Zen in *The Snow Leopard* and his more recent *Nine-Headed Dragon River: Zen Journals, 1969-1982,* he still expresses reservations about offering his personal philosophies for public perusal. "One is always appalled by the idea of wearing your so-called religion on your sleeve," he told *Publishers Weekly.* "I never talked about Zen much. . . . If people come along and want to talk about Zen, that's wonderful, but I don't want to brandish it. It's just a quiet little practice, not a religion . . . just a way of seeing the world. . . . And find myself very comfortable with it." He elaborated briefly: "Zen is a synonym for life, that's all. Zen practice is life practice. If you can wake up and look around you, if you can knock yourself out of your customary way of thinking and simply see how really miraculous and extraordinary everything around you is, that's Zen."

In the same *Publishers Weekly* interview, Matthiessen discussed the future direction of his work: "I prefer writing fiction; I find it exhilarating. Your battery is constantly being recharged with the excitement of it. I find that with nonfiction, it may he extremely skillful, it may be cabinetwork rather than carpentry, but it's still assembled from facts, from research from other people's work. It may be well made or badly made, but it's still an assemblage." Matthiessen admitted he is working on a novel and is "extremely happy" to be doing so. "In a sense," he stated, "I've always thought of nonfiction as a livelihood, my way of making a living so I could write fiction."

Matthiessen may view his nonfiction as the means to a livelihood, the "cabinetwork" that allows him leisure for more imaginative pursuits, but his critics have a different conception of the stature of his factual works. In his *New York Times Book Review* piece, Harrison contends that the reading public "should feel indebted to this man who has taken the earth, of all things, as his literary territory. In a curious reversal of a century of modernist dogma, Mr. Matthiessen appears to think that what he writes about is more important than how he writes about it; he does not mine and re-mine the narcissistic mode that so long has provided the energy of modern literature." Author William Styron likewise holds a high opinion of Matthiessen. In *This Quiet Dust and Other Writings,* Styron states: "With . . . infusion of the ecological and the anthropological, with . . . unshrinking vision of man in mysterious and uneasy interplay with nature—books at once descriptive and analytical, scrupulous and vivid in detail, sometimes amusing, often meditative and mystical, Peter Matthiessen has created a unique body of work."

Joseph Kastner offers an analogy for Matthiessen's writing career in a *Washington Post Book World* review. Kastner records: "A famous photographer once remarked that, for him, the ideal camera would be a lens screwed into his forehead and focused by his brain so that he could take pictures without any intervention. In a sense, Matthiessen, the writer, is equipped with that ideal camera. The things he sees are captured with the click of a thought on his mind and later fixed and printed by a prose rich with specific imagery." With Peter Matthiessen, concludes

Styron, "we behold a writer of phenomenal scope and versatility."

MEDIA ADAPTATIONS: Metro-Goldwyn-Mayer has optioned *At Play in the Fields of the Lord.*

BIOGRAPHICAL/CRITICAL SOURCES:

BOOKS

Contemporary Literary Criticism, Gale, Volume V, 1976, Volume VII, 1977, Volume XI, 1979, Volume XXXII, 1985.
Dictionary of Literary Biography, Volume VI: *American Novelists since World War II,* Second Series, Gale, 1980.
Matthiessen, Peter, *The Snow Leopard,* Viking, 1978.
Matthiessen, Peter, *Nine-Headed Dragon River: Zen Journals, 1969-1982,* Shambhala, 1986.
Nicholas, D., *Peter Matthiessen: A Bibliography,* Orirana, 1980.
Parker, William, editor, *Men of Courage: Stories of Present-Day Adventures in Danger and Death,* Playboy Press, 1972.
Styron, William, *This Quiet Dust and Other Writings,* Random House, 1982.

PERIODICALS

Atlantic, June, 1954, March, 1971, November, 1972, June, 1975, September, 1978, March, 1983.
Book World, December 10, 1967, April 18, 1971.
Chicago Tribune, August 11, 1989.
Chicago Tribune Book World, April 5, 1981, March 13, 1983.
Christian Science Monitor, March 11, 1983.
Commonweal, October 28, 1955.
Critic, May-June, 1970.
Georgia Review, winter, 1981.
Globe and Mail (Toronto), July 28, 1984, September 2, 1989.
Hudson Review, winter, 1975-76, winter, 1981-82.
Library Journal, August, 1955.
Literary Quarterly, May 15, 1975.
Los Angeles Times, March 22, 1979.
Los Angeles Times Book Review, May 10, 1981, March 6, 1983, May 18, 1986, August 24, 1986, December 20, 1987.
Nation, February 25, 1961, December 13, 1965, June 1, 1970, May 31, 1975, September 16, 1978.
National Review, October 13, 1978.
Natural History, January, 1968.
New Leader, June 9, 1975.
New Republic, June 7, 1975, September 23, 1978, March 7, 1983, June 4, 1984.
Newsweek, April 26, 1971, May 19, 1975, September 11, 1978, December 17, 1979, April 27, 1981, March 28, 1983, August 11, 1986.
New Yorker, May 19, 1975, April 11, 1983, June 4, 1984.
New York Herald Tribune Book Review, April 4, 1954.
New York Review of Books, December 23, 1965, January 4, 1968, August 31, 1972, January 25, 1973, August 7, 1975, September 28, 1978, April 14, 1983, September 27, 1984.
New York Times, April 4, 1954, October 2, 1955, November 8, 1965, April 23, 1971, August 24, 1978, March 19, 1979, May 2, 1981, March 5, 1983, June 19, 1986, October 11, 1986, January 16, 1988, May 3, 1989.
New York Times Book Review, April 4, 1954, October 2, 1955, November 22, 1959, October 15, 1961, November 18, 1962, November 7, 1965, December 3, 1967, February 1, 1970, November 26, 1972, May 25, 1975, May 29, 1977, August 13, 1978, November 26, 1978, May 17, 1981, March 6, 1983, July 29, 1984, June 22, 1986, May 14, 1989.
Paris Review, winter, 1974.
Publishers Weekly, May 9, 1986.

San Francisco Chronicle, April 9, 1954, October 10, 1955.
Saturday Review, April 10, 1954, November 6, 1965, November 25, 1967, March 14, 1970, October 28, 1972, June 28, 1975, August, 1978, April, 1981.
Spectator, June 13, 1981.
Time, May 26, 1975, August 7, 1978, March 28, 1983, July 7, 1986.
Times Literary Supplement, October 23, 1981, March 21, 1986, July 17, 1987, August 19, 1988, September 22, 1989.
Village Voice, June 2, 1975.
Washington Post, December 13, 1978, March 24, 1989.
Washington Post Book World, August 20, 1978, April 19, 1981, March 27, 1983, May 20, 1984, June 29, 1986, September 13, 1987, June 24, 1990.
Wilson Library Bulletin, March, 1964.

*   *   *

MATUTE (AUSEJO), Ana Maria   1925-

PERSONAL: Born July 26, 1925 (some sources say 1926), in Barcelona, Spain; daughter of Facundo and Maria (Ausejo) Matute; married in 1952 (divorced in 1963); children: Juan-Pablo. *Education:* Attended Damas Negras French Nuns College.

ADDRESSES: Home—Provenza 84, Dcha A-3 deg., Barcelona 29, Spain.

CAREER: Writer. Visiting professor at Indiana University, Bloomington, 1965-66, and at University of Oklahoma, Norman, 1969. Writer in residence at University of Virginia, Charlottesville, 1978-79.

MEMBER: Hispanic Society of America, American Association of Teachers of Spanish and Portuguese (honorary fellow), Sigma Delta Pi (Hispanic chapter).

AWARDS, HONORS: Runner-up for Premio Nadal, 1947, for *Los abel;* Cafe Gijon Prize, 1952, for *Fiesta al noroeste;* Planeta Prize, 1954, for *Pequeno teatro;* Critics Prize and Premio Nacional de Literature, 1958, for *Los hijos muertos;* Premio Miguel Cervantes, 1959, for *Los hijos muertos;* Premio Nadal, 1960, for *Primera memoria;* Lazarillo Prize, 1965, for *El polizon del "Ulises";* Fastenrath Prize, 1969, for *Los soldados lloran de noche.*

WRITINGS:

Los abel (title means "The Abels") Destino, 1948.
Fiesta al noroeste, La ronda [and] *Los ninos buenos* (titles mean "Festival of the Northwest," "The Round," [and] "The Good Children"), A. Aguado, 1953.
Pequeno teatro (title means "Little Theater"), Planeta, 1954.
En esta tierra (title means "On This Land"), Exito, 1955.
Los cuentos, vagabundos (title means "The Stories, Vagabonds"), Ediciones G.P., 1956.
Los ninos tontos (title means "The Foolish Children"), Arion, 1956.
El pais de la pizarra (title means "The Country of the Blackboard"), Molino, 1957.
El tiempo (title means "The Time"), Mateu, 1957.
Los hijos muertos, Planeta, 1958, translation by Joan MacLean published as *The Lost Children,* Macmillan, 1965.
Los mercaderes (title means "The Merchants"), Destino, 1959.
Paulina, el mundo y las estrellas (title means "Pauline, the World and the Stars"), Garbo, 1960.
El saltamontes verde [y] *El aprendiz* (titles mean "The Green Grasshopper" [and] "The Apprentice"), Lumen, 1960.
Primera memoria, Destino, 1960, translation by Elaine Kerrigan published as *School of the Sun,* Pantheon, 1963 (translation

by James Holman Mason published in England as *Awakening,* Hutchinson, 1963).
Tres y un sueno (title means "Three and a Dream"), Destino, 1961.
A la mitad del camino (title means "In the Middle of the Road"), Rocas, 1961.
Historias de la Artamila, Destino, 1961, published as *Doce historias de la Artamila,* Harcourt, 1965.
El arrepentido (title means "The Repentant One"), Rocas, 1961.
Libro de juegos para los ninos de los otros (title means "Book of Games for the Children of Others"), Lumen, 1961.
Caballito loco [y] *Carnivalito* (titles mean "Crazy Little Horse" [and] "Little Carnival"), Lumen, 1962.
El rio (title means "The River"), Argos, 1963.
Los soldados lloran de noche (title means "The Soldiers Weep at Night"), Destino, 1964.
El polizon del "Ulises" (title means "The Draft of 'Ulysses' "), Lumen, 1965.
Algunos muchachos (title means "Some Children"), Destino, 1968.
La trampa (title means "The Trap"), Destino, 1969.
La torre vigia (title means "The Watch Tower"), Lumen, 1971.
Olvidado rey Gudu (title means "Forgotten King Gudu"), Lumen, 1980.
Diablo vuelve a casa (title means "Devil, Come Back Home"), Destino, 1980.
The Heliotrope Wall and Other Stories, Columbia University Press, 1989.

Also author of *La pequena vide* (title means "The Little Life"), Tecnos.

SIDELIGHTS: Ana Maria Matute was ten years old when the Spanish Civil War broke out; it disrupted her education and became a potent, permanent force in her life. As a child, she has said, she confronted the fact that the world is filled with much that is terrifying.

By the time she published her first story for Destino in 1942, Matute was using writing as a vehicle for expressing anger toward a cruel, unjust world. The civil war became a recurring theme in her work, sometimes merely as a backdrop (as in *Pequeno teatro*), but more often as her central concern. Nevertheless, unlike many post-war Spanish writers, Matute is not a political partisan: she conveys what Desmond MacNamara called "unpolitical Spanish pessimism," focusing not on party machinations but on the angst of her people, particularly the children.

Indeed, Matute "sees the world through the eyes of childhood [with a] quality of mystery, of magic, of fairy tale, combined in a unique mixture with the harsh and bitter realities of life," wrote George Wythe. Her children are introverted victims of an adult world whose cruelty they cannot understand; and they suffer the existential pains of alienation and despair one usually thinks of as reserved for adults.

Matute creates her hostile world by means of an imaginative, personal style characterized, J. Wesley Childers has noted, "by simile, metaphor, oxymoron, and the use of natural phenomena to reflect human frustrations." To Rafael Bosch, her language is "direct and wonderfully simple without ceasing to be tremendously creative and poetic."

Matute's manuscripts are housed at the Mugar Library of Boston University, which has organized the Ana Maria Matute Collection. Editions of her books have appeared in many languages, including Italian, French, German, Russian, Portuguese, Swedish, Polish, Japanese, Hebrew, Lithuanian, Bulgarian, and Esperanto.

BIOGRAPHICAL/CRITICAL SOURCES:

BOOKS

Contemporary Literary Criticism, Volume 11, Gale, 1979.
Diaz, Janet, *Ana Maria Matute,* Twayne, 1971.
Jones, Margaret E. W., *The Literary World of Ana Maria Matute,* University Press of Kentucky, 1970.

PERIODICALS

Books Abroad, winter, 1966, winter, 1970, summer, 1972.
Modern Language Journal, November, 1966, December, 1971.
New Statesman, October 27, 1967.
New Leader, July, 1965.
Times Literary Supplement, December 28, 1967, October 8, 1971, August 4, 1989.

*   *   *

MAUGHAM, W. S.
See MAUGHAM, William Somerset

*   *   *

MAUGHAM, W. Somerset
See MAUGHAM, William Somerset

*   *   *

MAUGHAM, William Somerset   1874-1965
(W. S. Maugham, W. Somerset Maugham)

PERSONAL: Surname is pronounced "Mawm"; born January 25, 1874, in Paris, France; died December 16, 1965; buried on the grounds of Canterbury Cathedral, Canterbury, Kent, England; son of Robert Ormond (solicitor to the British Embassy) and Edith Mary (Snell) Maugham; married Syrie Barnardo Wellcome, 1915 (divorced, 1927; died, 1955); children: Liza. *Education:* Attended University of Heidelberg, 1891-92; briefly studied accountancy in Kent, England; St. Thomas Hospital, M.R.C.S., L.R.C.P., 1897. *Religion:* Rationalist.

ADDRESSES: Home—Villa Mauresque, St. Jean-Cap Ferrat, A.M., France.

CAREER: After completing medical studies left for Spain to write full time; lived in Spain, London, England, and Paris, France; after a bout with tuberculosis, began in the 1920s to travel extensively; served with the British Ministry of Information in Paris during World War II; after the war, stayed for a time in Russia and the United States and remained unfavorably impressed by both countries; served as narrator in 1949 for "Quartet," a dramatization of four of his stories, in 1950 for "Trio," a film based on three of his stories, and for "Encore," based on four of his stories; in America in 1950 and 1951, hosted television series of dramatizations of his stories. *Wartime service:* Served with ambulance unit and as medical officer during World War I; served with British Secret Service in Switzerland.

MEMBER: Royal Society of Literature (fellow and companion), American Academy of Arts and Letters (honorary member), Garrick Club.

AWARDS, HONORS: Companion of Honour, 1954; C.Litt., 1961; named honorary senator of Heidelberg University, 1961; D. Litt., Oxford University and University of Toulouse; honorary fellow, Library of Congress, Washington, D.C.; Commander, Legion of Honour.

WRITINGS:

NOVELS; OFTEN PUBLISHED UNDER NAME W. SOMERSET MAUGHAM

Liza of Lambeth, Unwin, 1897, Doran, 1921, reprinted, Penguin Books, 1978.
The Making of a Saint, L. C. Page & Co., 1898, published as *The Making of a Saint: A Romance of Medieval Italy,* Farrar, Straus, 1966, reprinted, Arno, 1977.
The Hero, Hutchinson, 1901, reprinted, Arno, 1977.
Mrs. Craddock, Heinemann, 1902, Doran, 1920, reprinted, Penguin Books, 1979.
The Merry-Go-Round, Heinemann, 1905, reprinted, Penguin Books, 1978.
The Bishop's Apron: A Study in the Origins of a Great Family, Chapman & Hall, 1906, reprinted, Arno, 1977.
The Explorer, Heinemann, 1907, Baker & Taylor, 1909.
The Magician, Heinemann, 1908, Duffield & Co., 1909, reprinted, Penguin Books, 1978.
Of Human Bondage, Doran, 1915, reprinted, Penguin Books, 1978.
The Moon and Sixpence, Doran, 1919, reprinted, Arno, 1977.
The Painted Veil, Doran, 1925, reprinted, Penguin Books, 1979.
Cakes and Ale; or, The Skeleton in the Cupboard, Doubleday, Doran & Co., 1930, reprinted, Arno, 1977, published as *Cakes and Ale,* Modern Library, 1950.
The Book-Bag, G. Orioli, 1932.
The Narrow Corner, Doubleday, Doran & Co., 1932, reprinted, Pan, 1978.
Theatre, Doubleday, Doran & Co., 1937.
Christmas Holiday, Doubleday, Doran & Co., 1939, reprinted, Pan, 1978.
Up at the Villa, Doubleday, Doran & Co., 1941, reprinted, Penguin Books, 1978.
The Hour Before the Dawn, Doubleday, Doran & Co., 1942, reprinted, Arno, 1977.
The Razor's Edge, Doubleday, Doran & Co., 1944, reprinted, Penguin Books, 1978.
Then and Now, Doubleday, 1946, published as *Fools and Their Folly,* Avon, 1949, reprinted, Pan, 1979.
Catalina: A Romance, Doubleday, 1948, reprinted, Pan, 1978.
Selected Novels, three volumes, Heinemann, 1953.

SHORT STORIES; OFTEN PUBLISHED UNDER NAME W. SOMERSET MAUGHAM

Orientations, Unwin, 1899.
The Trembling of a Leaf: Little Stories of the South Sea Islands, Doran, 1921, reprinted, Arno, 1977, published as *Sadie Thompson and Other Stories of the South Seas,* Readers Library, 1928, published as *"Rain," and Other Stories,* Grosset, 1932.
The Casuarina Tree: Six Stories, Doran, 1926, reprinted, Arno, 1977, published as *The Letter: Stories of Crime,* Collins, 1930.
Ashenden; or, The British Agent, Doubleday, Doran & Co., 1928, reprinted, Penguin Books, 1977.
Six Stories Written in the First Person Singular, Doubleday, Doran & Co., 1931, reprinted, Arno, 1977.
Ah King, Doubleday, Doran & Co., 1933 (published in England as *Ah King: Six Stories,* Heinemann, 1933), reprinted, Arno, 1977.
East and West: The Collected Short Stories, Doubleday, Doran & Co., 1934 (published in England as *Altogether; Being the Collected Stories of W. Somerset Maugham,* Heinemann, 1934).

Judgment Seat, Centaur, 1934.

Cosmopolitans, Doubleday, Doran & Co., 1936, reprinted, Arno, 1977, published as *Cosmopolitans: Twenty-nine Short Stories,* Avon, 1943.

The Favorite Short Stories of W. Somerset Maugham, Doubleday, Doran & Co., 1937.

Princess September and the Nightingale (fairy tale; first published in *The Gentleman in the Parlour*), Oxford University Press, 1939, published as *Princess September,* Harcourt, 1969.

The Mixture as Before, Doubleday, Doran & Co., 1940, reprinted, Arno, 1977.

The Unconquered, House of Books, 1944.

"Ah King," and Other Romance Stories of the Tropics (contains selections from *Ah King*), Avon, 1944.

Creatures of Circumstance, Doubleday, 1947, reprinted, Arno, 1977.

Stories of Love and Intrigue From "The Mixture as Before," Avon, 1947.

East of Suez: Great Stories of the Tropics, Avon, 1948.

Here and There, Heinemann, 1948.

The Complete Short Stories, three volumes, Heinemann, 1951, Doubleday, 1952, published as *Collected Short Stories,* Pan, 1976.

The World Over: Stories of Manifold Places and People, Doubleday, 1952.

Best Short Stories, selected by John Beecroft, Modern Library, 1957.

Favorite Stories, Avon, 1960.

Collected Short Stories, Penguin Books, 1963.

Husbands and Wives: Nine Stories, edited by Richard A. Cordell, Pyramid, 1963.

The Sinners: Six Stories, edited by Richard A. Cordell, Pyramid, 1964.

A Maugham Twelve, selected by Angus Wilson, Heinemann, 1966.

The Complete Short Stories of W. Somerset Maugham, four volumes, Washington Square Press, 1967.

"The Kite," and Other Stories, introduction by Ian Serriallier, Heinemann Educational, 1968.

Maugham's Malaysian Stories, edited by Anthony Burgess, Heinemann, 1969.

Seventeen Lost Stories, edited by Craig V. Showalter, Doubleday, 1969.

A Baker's Dozen: Thirteen Short Stories, Heinemann, 1969.

Four Short Stories, illustrations by Henri Matisse, Hallmark Editions, 1970.

A Second Baker's Dozen: Thirteen Short Stories, Heinemann, 1970.

The Hairless Mexican [and] *The Traitor,* Heinemann Educational, 1974.

"Footprints in the Jungle" and Two Other Stories, edited by Rod Sinclair, Heinemann Educational, 1975.

Sixty-five Short Stories, Octopus Books, 1976.

A short story, "The Vessel of Wrath," was published by Dell as *The Beachcomber.*

PLAYS; OFTEN PUBLISHED UNDER NAME W. S. MAUGHAM

"Marriages Are Made in Heaven" (produced in Berlin as "Schiffbruechig," 1902), in *The Venture Annual of Art and Literature,* edited by Maugham and Laurence Housman, Baillie, 1903 (also see below).

A Man of Honour: A Tragedy in Four Acts (produced in Westminster, England, at Imperial Theatre, February 23, 1903), Dramatic Publishing, 1903.

"Mademoiselle Zampa," produced in London, 1904.

Penelope: A Comedy in Three Acts (produced in London, 1909), Dramatic Publishing, 1909.

Lady Frederick: A Comedy in Three Acts (first produced in London, 1907; produced in New York, 1908), Heinemann, 1911, Dramatic Publishing, 1912.

"A Trip to Brighton" (adaptation of a play by Abel Tarride), produced in London, 1911.

Jack Straw: A Farce in Three Acts (produced in London and New York, 1908), Heinemann, 1911, Dramatic Publishing, 1912.

The Explorer: A Melodrama in Four Acts (produced in London, 1908), Heinemann, 1912, Doran, 1920, reprinted, Arno, 1977.

Mrs. Dot: A Farce in Three Acts (produced in London, 1908), Dramatic Publishing, 1912.

Smith: A Comedy in Four Acts (first produced in London, 1909; produced in New York, 1910), Dramatic Publishing, 1913.

Landed Gentry: A Comedy in Four Acts (produced as "Grace" in London, 1910), Dramatic Publishing, 1913.

The Tenth Man: A Tragic Comedy in Three Acts (produced in London, 1910), Dramatic Publishing, 1913.

The Land of Promise: A Comedy in Four Acts (first produced in New York, 1913), Bickers & Son, 1913.

"Love in a Cottage," produced in London, 1918.

The Unknown: A Play in Three Acts (produced in London, 1920), Doran, 1920.

The Circle: A Comedy in Three Acts (produced in New York and London, 1921), Doran, 1921.

Caesar's Wife: A Comedy in Three Acts (produced in London, 1919), Heinemann, 1922, Doran, 1923.

East of Suez: A Play in Seven Scenes (produced in London, 1922), Doran, 1922, reprinted, Arno, 1977.

Loaves and Fishes: A Comedy in Four Acts (produced in London, 1911), Heinemann, 1923.

The Unattainable: A Farce in Three Acts (produced in New York and London, 1916), Heinemann, 1923.

Our Betters: A Comedy in Three Acts (first produced in New York, 1917), Heinemann, 1923, Doran, 1924.

Home and Beauty: A Farce in Three Acts (produced in New York and London, 1919; produced as "Too Many Husbands" in New York, 1919), Heinemann, 1923.

"The Camel's Back," produced in Worcester, Mass., 1923; produced in London, 1924.

The Letter: A Play in Three Acts (based on "The Casuarina Tree"; produced in London, 1927), Doran, 1925, reprinted, Arno, 1977.

The Constant Wife: A Comedy in Three Acts (first produced in New York, 1926), Doran, 1926.

The Sacred Flame: A Play in Three Acts (produced in New York, 1928), Doubleday, Doran & Co., 1928, reprinted, Arno, 1977.

The Bread-Winner: A Comedy in One Act (first produced in London, 1930; produced in New York, 1931), Heinemann, 1930, published as *The Breadwinner: A Comedy,* Doubleday, Doran & Co., 1931.

Plays, Heinemann, 1931, reprinted, 1966.

Dramatic Works, six volumes, Heinemann, 1931-34, published as *Collected Plays,* three volumes, 1952, published as *The Collected Plays of W. Somerset Maugham,* 1961.

For Services Rendered: A Play in Three Acts (produced in London, 1932), Heinemann, 1932, Doubleday, Doran & Co., 1933, reprinted, Arno, 1977.

Sheppey: A Play in Three Acts (produced in London, 1933), Heinemann, 1933, Baker, 1949, reprinted, Arno, 1977.

"The Mask and the Face" (adaptation of a play by Luigi Chiarelli), produced in Boston, 1933.

Six Comedies, Doubleday, Doran & Co., 1937, reprinted, Arno, 1977.

(With Guy Reginald Bolton) *Theatre: A Comedy in Three Acts,* French, 1942, reprinted, Arno, 1977.

The Noble Spaniard: A Comedy in Three Acts (adapted from Ernest Grenet-Dancourt's "Les gaites du veuvage"; produced in London, 1909), Evans, 1953.

"The Perfect Gentleman" (adaptation of a play by Moliere; produced in London, 1913), published in *Theatre Arts,* November, 1955.

Selected Plays, Penguin Books, 1963.

Three Dramas: "The Letter," "The Sacred Flame," "For Services Rendered," Washington Square Press, 1968.

Three Comedies: "The Circle," "Our Betters," "The Constant Wife," Washington Square Press, 1969.

Also author of "Mrs. Beamish," 1917; "The Keys to Heaven," 1917; "Not To-Night, Josephine!" (farce), 1919; "The Road Uphill," 1924; "The Force of Nature," 1928.

EDITOR; OFTEN UNDER NAME W. SOMERSET MAUGHAM

(With Laurence Housman) *The Venture Annual of Art and Literature,* Baillie, 1903.

(With Laurence Housman) *The Venture Annual of Art and Literature 1905,* Simpkin Marshall, 1904.

Charles Henry Hawtrey, *The Truth at Last,* Little, 1924.

Traveller's Library, Doubleday, Doran & Co., 1933, reissued as *Fifty Modern English Writers,* Doubleday, Doran & Co., 1933.

(With Joseph Frederick Green) *Wisdom of Life: An Anthology of Noble Thoughts,* Watts, 1938.

(With introduction) George Douglas, *The House With the Green Shutters,* Oxford University Press, 1938.

Tellers of Tales: One Hundred Short Stories From the United States, England, France, Russia and Germany, Doubleday, Doran & Co., 1939, published as *The Greatest Stories of All Times, Tellers of Tales,* Garden City Publishing, 1943.

Great Modern Reading: W. Somerset Maugham's Introduction to Modern English and American Literature, Doubleday, 1943.

Charles Dickens, *David Copperfield,* Winston, 1948.

Henry Fielding, *The History of Tom Jones, a Foundling,* Winston, 1948.

Jane Austen, *Pride and Prejudice,* Winston, 1949.

Honore de Balzac, *Old Man Goriot,* Winston, 1949.

Emily Bronte, *Wuthering Heights,* Winston, 1949.

Fyodor Dostoyevski, *The Brothers Karamazov,* Winston, 1949.

Gustave Flaubert, *Madame Bovary,* Winston, 1949.

Herman Melville, *Moby Dick,* Winston, 1949.

Stendhal, *The Red and the Black,* Winston, 1949.

Leo Tolstoy, *War and Peace,* Winston, 1949.

A Choice of Kipling's Prose, Macmillan, 1952, reprinted, Telegraph Books, 1981, published as *Maugham's Choice of Kipling's Best,* Doubleday, 1953.

OTHER

"The Artistic Temperament of Stephen Carey" (earliest manuscript for novel *Of Human Bondage*), c. 1900.

The Land of the Blessed Virgin: Sketches and Impressions in Andalusia (travel), Heinemann, 1905, Knopf, 1920.

On a Chinese Screen (travel), Doran, 1922, reprinted, Arno, 1977.

The Gentleman in the Parlour: A Record of a Journey from Rangoon to Haiphong, Doubleday, Doran & Co., 1930, reprinted, Arno, 1977.

The Non-Dramatic Works, twenty-eight volumes, Heinemann, 1934-69.

Don Fernando; or, Variations on Some Spanish Themes (travel), Doubleday, Doran & Co., 1935, reprinted, Arno, 1977, revised edition, Heinemann, 1961.

Works, collected edition, Heinemann, 1935.

My South Sea Island, privately printed, 1936.

The Summing Up (autobiography), Doubleday, Doran & Co., 1938, reprinted, Penguin Books, 1978.

Books and You, Doubleday, Doran & Co., 1940, reprinted, Arno, 1977.

France at War, Doubleday, Doran & Co., 1940, reprinted, Arno, 1977.

Strictly Personal, Doubleday, Doran & Co., 1941, reprinted, Arno, 1977.

The W. Somerset Maugham Sampler, edited by Jerome Weidman, Garden City Publishing Co., 1943, published as *The Somerset Maugham Pocket Book,* Pocket Books, 1944.

W. Somerset Maugham's Introduction to Modern English and American Literature, New Home Library, 1943.

Great Novelists and Their Novels: Essays on the Ten Greatest Novels of the World and the Men and Women Who Wrote Them, Winston, 1948, revised edition published as *Ten Novels and Their Authors,* Heinemann, 1954, published as *The Art of Fiction: An Introduction to Ten Novels and Their Authors,* Doubleday, 1955, published as *The World's Ten Greatest Novels,* Fawcett, 1956, published as *W. Somerset Maugham Selects the World's Ten Greatest Novels,* Fawcett, 1962.

Quartet: Stories by W. Somerset Maugham, Screen-Plays by R. C. Sheriff, Heinemann, 1948, Doubleday, 1949.

A Writer's Notebook, Doubleday, 1949, reprinted, Arno, 1977.

The Maugham Reader, introduction by Glenway Wescott, Doubleday, 1950.

Trio: Original Stories by W. Somerset Maugham; Screenplays by W. Somerset Maugham, R. C. Sherriff and Noel Langley, Doubleday, 1950.

Cakes and Ale, and Other Favorites, Pocket Books, 1951.

Encore: Original Stories by W. Somerset Maugham, Screenplays by T. E. B. Clarke, Arthur Macrae and Eric Ambler, Doubleday, 1952.

The Vagrant Mood: Six Essays, Heinemann, 1952, Doubleday, 1953.

The Partial View (contains *The Summing Up* and *A Writer's Notebook*), Heinemann, 1954.

Mr. Maugham Himself, selected by John Beecroft, Doubleday, 1954.

The Travel Books, Heinemann, 1955.

The Magician: A Novel, Together With A Fragment of Autobiography, Heinemann, 1956, published as *The Magician: Together With A Fragment of Autobiography,* Doubleday, 1957.

Points of View (essays), Heinemann, 1958, Doubleday, 1959.

Purely for My Pleasure, Doubleday, 1962.

Selected Prefaces and Introductions of W. Somerset Maugham, Doubleday, 1963.

Wit and Wisdom of Somerset Maugham, edited by Cecil Hewetson, Duckworth, 1966.

Essays on Literature, New American Library, 1967.

Cakes and Ale, and Twelve Short Stories, edited by Angus Wilson, Doubleday, 1967.

Man From Glasgow and Mackintosh, Heinemann Educational, 1973.

Selected Works, Heinemann, 1976.

The Works of Somerset Maugham, forty-seven volumes, Arno, 1977.

A Traveller in Romance: Uncollected Writings 1901-1964, edited by John Whitehead, C. N. Potter, 1985.

SIDELIGHTS: "Looking back upon my work in my old age," Maugham wrote, "I am disposed to regard it very modestly and to admit frankly some of its shortcomings. In my youth I had accepted the challenge of writing and literature to idealize them; in my age I see the magnitude of the attempt and wonder at my audacity."

He may have been audacious, but more often people called him cynical, cold, uncharitable. One publisher said, "Willie's been true to himself; he's had a bad word for everybody." His attitude toward humanity was likened by Malcolm Cowley to "the milk of human kindness half-soured." Maugham once commented, "I've always been interested in people, but I don't like them." In *The Summing Up* he wrote: "I have been called cynical. I have been accused of making men out worse than they are. I do not think I have done this. All I have done is to bring into prominence certain traits that many writers shut their eyes to. I think what has chiefly struck me in human beings is their lack of consistency. . . ." To be fair to him, he did display a certain affection for ordinary men and reserved his scorn for the nobility.

Maugham sometimes cynically agreed with his detractors who saw him as merely an entertainer who became one of the world's richest authors. (It was estimated that he earned more than $3 million from his writings, and his estate came to be valued at about $5 million.) Alan Pryce-Jones wrote: "Of his popular success there can be no question. In the history of literature there is nobody whose work has been more widely sold, translated and devoured—partly because of his real merit as a storyteller, partly because the functional simplicity of his writing made his books unusually accessible." His stories are not difficult to comprehend. He once said that he had "a clear and logical brain, but not a very subtle nor a very powerful one."

The position Maugham established through more than sixty years of writing was no mean accomplishment. He was a storyteller—"the most continuously readable storyteller of our lifetime," said Christopher Morley—one who believed a story should have a beginning, a middle, and an end, carefully delineated characters, a lucid plot, and employ clear, concise language. Maugham was, Walter Allen wrote, "the last survivor of a vanished age, an age which had not divorced, as ours has largely done, the idea of entertainment from the idea of art." The writer, for him, was a purveyor of pleasure, and what he wrote about was more important than how it was presented. He said: "With me the sense is more than the sound, the substance is more than the form, the moral significance is more than the rhetorical adornment. I am not indifferent to the art and music of words, but I habitually treat them as of secondary importance. . . . The fact remains that the four greatest novelists the world has ever known—Balzac, Dickens, Tolstoi and Dostoyevski—wrote their respective languages very badly. It proves that if you can tell stories, create characters, devise incidents, and have sincerity and passion, it doesn't matter a damn how you write." He added: "I wrote stories because it was a delight to write them."

Of Human Bondage, however, "was written in pain." Its principal character, Philip Carey, sensitive and plagued with a clubfoot, was so like the author, who was afflicted with a stutter, that Maugham was unable to read the book after it was published. Perhaps to avoid similar pain, Maugham chose to write about other people and found material for stories everywhere. He once said, "I am almost inclined to say that I could not spend an hour in anyone's company without getting the material to write at least a readable story about him." "In all my work," he said, "I have tried . . . to touch many classes of readers and many varieties of mind. I can be severely simple and chastely sensuous, classic and grotesque, subtle and passionate, passing with perfect mastery from love to dialectics, from the wail of a somber pessimism to the exaltation and rapture of a triumphant lover. I can even be humorous, too." Coherence was evident in Maugham's ideas, "for the main principles of my philosophy are so simple and so definite, that from my earliest writings to my last there is perfect unity." And always in his travels and sojourns he was an observer, dispassionate and systematic. As he wrote once, "I do not know a better training ground for a writer than to spend some years in the medical profession."

John Brophy called Maugham's writings "extroverted." The resultant artificiality and informality were well suited to certain media in which Maugham had achieved success, notably the stage (at one time he had four plays running simultaneously on London's West End) and the "magazine" story. Maugham had reproached those who favored the mood story characteristic of Anton Chekhov and had defended his own narratives: "Where the critics to my mind err is when they dismiss stories as magazine stories because they are well constructed, dramatic and have a surprise ending."

Of Human Bondage is still regarded as Maugham's best, though he always showed a preference for *Cakes and Ale.* He believed Graham Greene was the best British novelist, and he liked William Faulkner. Though critics attributed influences on Maugham to such authors as Dickens, Fielding, Defoe, and Trollope, Maugham said, "I follow no master, and acknowledge none."

"In my twenties," he wrote, "the critics said I was brutal. In my thirties they said I was flippant, in my forties they said I was cynical, in my fifties they said I was competent, and in my sixties they say I am superficial." By 1959 this compulsive writer was writing, he said, only for himself, and at the time of his death he was reportedly working on an autobiography that was to be published posthumously. A few years before his death he destroyed all of his old notebooks and unfinished manuscripts. Yet he continued to assert that "literature, or pure imaginative creation, was the highest goal toward which man could strive."

Maugham lived in a villa once owned by Leopold II, and replicas of a Moorish symbol surrounded him. He entertained the wealthy, royalty, and great wits and beauties. He observed them all for his stories. He once received over half a million pounds for his collection of paintings.

A Maugham archive is maintained by the Yale University Library.

MEDIA ADAPTATIONS: The following films were based on Maugham's works: "Smith," 1917; "The Land of Promise," Famous Players, 1917, as "The Canadian," Paramount, 1926; "The Divorcee," based on "Lady Frederick," Metro Pictures, 1919; "Jack Straw," Famous Players/Lasky, 1920; "The Circle," Metro-Goldwyn-Mayer, 1925, as "Strictly Unconventional," Metro-Goldwyn-Mayer, 1930; "Sadie Thompson," 1928, remade as "Rain," United Artists, 1932, as "Miss Sadie Thompson," Columbia, 1954; "Charming Sinners," based on "The Constant Wife," Paramount, 1929; "Our Betters," RKO, 1933; "Of Human Bondage," RKO, 1934, remakes by Warner Bros., 1946, Metro-Goldwyn-Mayer, 1964; "The Painted Veil," Metro-Goldwyn-Mayer, 1934; "The Tenth Man," Wardour Films, 1937; "The Beachcomber" (based on "The Vessel of Wrath"), Paramount, 1938; "Too Many Husbands," based on "Not To-

Night, Josephine!'' Columbia, 1940, remade as "Three for the Show," Columbia, 1955; "The Letter," Warner Bros., 1940; "The Moon and Sixpence," United Artists, 1943; "The Razor's Edge," Twentieth Century-Fox, 1947, and Columbia, 1984; "Quartet" (film version of "The Facts of Life," "The Alien Corn," "The Kite," and "The Colonel's Lady"), J. Arthur Rank, 1949; "Trio," Paramount, 1951; "Encore" (film version of "The Ant and the Grasshopper," "Winter Cruise," and "Gigolo and Gigolette"), J. Arthur Rank, 1952.

Plays based on Maugham's works: "Rain" (dramatization of "Miss Thompson"), by John B. Colton and Clemence Randolph, produced in New York, 1922, published by Boni & Liveright, 1923, S. French, 1948; "Sadie Thompson," musical adaptation, produced in New York, 1944; "Before the Party" (dramatization of a short story), by Rodney Ackland, S. French, 1950; "Larger Than Life" (based on the novel *Theatre*), by Guy Bolton, S. French, 1951; "Jane" (dramatization of a short story), by S. N. Behrman, produced in New York, 1952, published by Random, 1952.

AVOCATIONAL INTERESTS: Bridge, music, gardening, and collecting paintings.

BIOGRAPHICAL/CRITICAL SOURCES:

BOOKS

Brander, L., *Somerset Maugham,* Barnes & Noble, 1963.
Brophy, John, *Somerset Maugham,* Longmans, Green, 1952, revised edition, 1958.
Breit, Harvey, editor, *The Writer Observed,* World Publishing, 1956.
Contemporary Literary Criticism, Gale, Volume 1, 1973, Volume 11, 1979, Volume 15, 1980.
Cordell, Richard Albert, *Somerset Maugham: A Biography and Critical Study,* Indiana University Press, 1961.
Curtis, A., *Somerset Maugham,* Macmillan, 1977.
Dictionary of Literary Biography, Gale, Volume 10: *Modern British Dramatists, 1940-1945,* 1982, Volume 36: *British Novelists, 1890-1929: Modernists,* 1985, Volume 77: *British Mystery Writers, 1920-1939,* 1989.
MacCarthy, D., *William Somerset Maugham,* Norwood Editions, 1977.
Maugham, Robin, *Somerset and All the Maughams,* New American Library, 1966.
Maugham, Robin, *Conversations With Willie: Recollections of W. Somerset Maugham,* Simon & Schuster, 1978.
McIver, C. S., *William Somerset Maugham,* Richard West, 1978.
Menard, W., *The Two Worlds of Somerset Maugham,* Sherbourne, 1965.
Morgan, Ted, *Maugham,* Simon & Schuster, 1980.
Pfeiffer, Karl Graham, *W. Somerset Maugham: A Candid Portrait,* Norton, 1959.
Swinnerton, Frank, *The Saturday Review Gallery,* Simon & Schuster, 1959.

PERIODICALS

Chicago Tribune, April 30, 1980, October 19, 1984, May 6, 1987.
Christian Science Monitor, July 6, 1970.
Detroit News, February 17, 1985.
Listener, October 17, 1968.
Los Angeles Times, October 19, 1984.
Los Angeles Times Book Review, June 2, 1985.
Newsweek, January 27, 1958.
New York Times, February 18, 1986, February 21, 1986.
New York Times Magazine, January 25, 1959, June 2, 1968.

Playboy, January, 1966.
Punch, October 16, 1968.
Saturday Review, October 14, 1961, November 5, 1966.
Stage, June 4, 1970, June 18, 1970, July 2, 1970, July 23, 1970.
Time, April 20, 1962.
Times (London), March 28, 1988.
Times Literary Supplement, April 5, 1985.
Variety, July 8, 1970.
Washington Post, October 8, 1969, October 19, 1984.

OBITUARIES:

BOOKS

Current Biography, H. W. Wilson, 1966.

PERIODICALS

Books Abroad, spring, 1966.
New York Herald Tribune, December 17, 1965.
New York Times, December 16, 1965.
Publishers Weekly, December 27, 1965.
Reporter, December 30, 1965.

*   *   *

MAURIAC, Francois (Charles)   1885-1970
(Forez)

PERSONAL: Surname is pronounced Mo-*ryak;* born October 11, 1885, in Bordeaux, France; died September 1, 1970, in Paris, France; son of Jean-Paul (a businessman) and Marguerite (Coiffard) Mauriac; married Jeanne Lafont, June 3, 1913; children: Claude (a novelist and critic), Claire (widow of Prince Jean Wiazemsky), Luce (Mme. Alain Le Ray), Jean. *Education:* Attended church school at Cauderan; University of Bordeaux, Licence es Lettres, 1905; attended Ecole National des Chartes, Paris, 1908. *Religion:* Roman Catholic.

CAREER: Novelist, playwright, poet, essayist, scenarist, and journalist. Went to Paris, 1906; was a journalist for *Temps Present,* 1908, and *Lettres Francais,* 1940; regular contributor to *Figaro,* beginning 1944, and was a director until 1955; wrote "Bloc-Notes" column (political and literary commentary) for *L'Express,* 1954-61, then for *Figaro Litteraire,* 1961-70. *Wartime activity:* During World War I, he served for two years as a hospital orderly in the Balkan campaigns; returned to France, March, 1917, after contracting illness at Salonika. During World War II, he played an active part in the French resistance as a journalist, writing under the pseudonym Forez, and sending articles abroad.

MEMBER: Societe des Gens de Lettres (president, 1932-70), Academie Francaise, American Institute of Art and Letters, American Academy of Arts and Letters, L'Academie des Sciences, Lettres es Arts de Bordeaux, L'Academie du Vin de Bordeaux.

AWARDS, HONORS: Grand Prix du Roman de l'Academie Francaise, 1926, for *Le Desert de l'amour;* Nobel Prize for Literature, 1952; D.Litt., Oxford University; Grand Croix de la Legion d'Honneur, 1958, upon the personal recommendation of President Charles de Gaulle.

WRITINGS:

FICTION

L'Enfant charge de chaines, Grasset, 1913, translation by Gerard Hopkins published as *Young Man in Chains,* Farrar, Straus, 1963.

La Robe pretexte (also see below), Grasset, 1914, translation by Hopkins published as *The Stuff of Youth,* Eyre & Spottiswoode, 1960, original French edition published in *Les Chefs-d'oeuvre de Francois Mauriac,* 1967.

La Chair et la sang, Emile-Paul, 1920, translation by Hopkins published as *Flesh and Blood,* Farrar, Straus, 1955, original French edition reprinted, with a preface by Henriette Geux-Rolle, Cercle du Bibliophile, 1967.

Preseances, Emile-Paul, 1921, translation by Hopkins published as *Questions of Precedence,* Eyre & Spottiswoode, 1958, Farrar, Straus, 1959, original French edition reprinted, Flammarion, 1972.

Le Baiser au lepreux, Grasset, 1922, translation by James Whitall published as *The Kiss to the Leper,* Heinemann, 1923, translation by Hopkins published as *A Kiss for the Leper,* Eyre & Spottiswoode, 1950.

Le Fleuve defeu, Grasset, 1923, reprinted, 1970, translation by Hopkins published as *The River of Fire,* Eyre & Spottiswoode, 1954.

Genitrix (also see below), Grasset, 1923.

Le Desert de l'amour, Grasset, 1925, reprinted, 1970, translation by Samuel Putnam published as *The Desert of Love,* Covici, Friede, 1929, translation by Hopkins published as *The Desert of Love,* Pellegrini & Cudahy, 1951.

Therese Desqueyroux, Grasset, 1927, reprinted, Le Livre de Poche, 1974, translation by Eric Sutton published as *Therese,* Boni & Liveright, 1928. *Destins,* Grasset, 1928, reprinted, 1967, translation by Sutton published as *Destinies,* Covici, Friede, 1929, translation by Hopkins published as *Lines of Life,* Farrar, Straus, 1957.

La Nuit du borreau soimeme, Flammarion, 1929.

Trois recits, Grasset, 1929.

Ce qui eta it perdu (also see below), Grasset, 1930, translation by Harold F. Kynaston-Snell published as *Suspicion,* Nash & Grayson, 1931, translation by Hopkins published as *The Mask ofInnocence,* Farrar, Straus, 1953.

Le Noeud de viperes, Grasset, 1932, reprinted, Grasset, 1972, translation by Warre B. Wells published as *Viper's Tangle,* Sheed & Ward, 1933, translation by Hopkins published as *The Knot of Vipers,* Eyre & Spottiswoode, 1951.

Le Mystere Frontenac, Grasset, 1933, translation by Hopkins published as *The Frontenac Mystery,* Eyre & Spottiswoode, 1952, and as *The Frontenacs,* Farrar, Straus, 1961.

Le Drole (short story for children), Paul Hartmann, 1933, French language edition, edited by Isabelle H. Clarke, Heath, 1957, translation by Anne Carter published as *The Holy Terror,* J. Cape, 1964, Funk, 1967.

La Fin de la nuit (also see below), Grasset, 1935.

Le Mal (also see below), Grasset, 1935.

Les Anges noirs (also see below), Grasset, 1936.

Les Chemins de la mer, Grasset, 1939, translation by Hopkins published as *The Unknown Sea,* Holt, 1948.

La Pharisienne, Grasset, 1941, reprinted, 1971, translation by Hopkins published as *A Woman of the Pharisees,* Holt, 1946.

Le Sagouin, Palatine-Plon, 1951, Cercle du Livre de France (New York), c.1951, translation by Hopkins published as *The Little Misery,* Eyre & Spottiswoode, 1952.

Galigai, Flammarion, 1952, reprinted, 1972, translation and postscript by Hopkins published as *The Loved and the Unloved,* Pellegrini & Cudahy, 1952, reprinted, Eyre & Spottiswoode, 1971.

L'Agneau, Flammarion, 1954, reprinted, 1973, translation by Hopkins published as *The Lamb,* Farrar, Straus, 1955.

Un Adolescent d'autrefois, Flammarion, 1969, translation by Jean Stewart published as *Maltaverne,* Farrar, Straus, 1970.

PLAYS

Asmodee (first produced in Paris at Comedie Francaise, March 1, 1945), Grasset, 1938, translation by Basil Bartlett published as *Asmodee; or, The Intruder,* Secker & Warburg, 1939, translation by Beverly Thurman published as *Asmodee* (produced in New York at Theatre 74, March 25, 1958), Samuel French, 1957.

Les Mal aimes (first produced in Paris at Comedie Francaise), Grasset, 1945, reprinted, 1965.

Passage du malin (first produced in Paris at Theatre de la Madeleine, December 9, 1947), Editions de 1a Table Ronde, 1948.

Le Feu sur la terre (first produced in Paris at Theatre Hebertot, November 7, 1950), Grasset, 1951, French language edition, edited by Robert J. North, published as *Le Feu sur 1a terre; ou, Le Pays sans chemin,* Harrap, 1962.

FILMS

Le Pain vivant (scenario and dialogue), Flammarion, 1955.

(Co-author of scenario) "Therese" (based on *Therese Desqueyrous*), 1963.

POETRY

Les Mains Jointes, published at Mauriac's expense by Falque, 1909.

L'Adieu a l'adolescence, Stock, 1911, revised edition, 1970.

Orages, Champion, 1925.

Le Sang d'Atys, Grasset, 1940.

NONFICTION

De Quelques coeurs inquiets: Petits essais de psychologie, Societe Litteraire de France, 1920.

Le Jeune homme, Hachette, 1926.

Proust, M. Lesage, 1926.

La Province, Hachette, 1926.

Bordeaux, Emile-Paul, 1926.

La Vie de Jean Racine, Plon, 1928, reprinted as *La Vie de Racine,* Plon, 1962.

Le Roman, L'Artisan du Livre, 1928.

Dieu et Mammon, Editions du Capitole, 1929, translation by Barnard Wall and Barbara Wall published as *God and Mammon,* Sheed & Ward, 1936.

Mes plus lointains souvenirs, E.Hazan, 1929.

Trois grands hommes devant Dieu, Editions du Capitole, 1930.

Blaise Pascal et sa soeur Jacqueline, Hachette, 1931.

Le Jeudi-saint, Flammarion, 1931, translation by Kynaston Snell published as *Maundy Thursday,* Burns & Oates, 1932.

Souffrances et bonheur du chretien, Grasset, 1931, translation by Harold Evans published as *Anguish and Joy of the Christian Life,* Dimension, 1964.

Rene Bazin, F. Alcan, 1931.

Pelerins, Editions de France, 1932.

Commencements d'une vie, Grasset, 1932.

Petits essais de psychologie religieuse, L'Artisan du Livre, 1933.

Le Romancier et ses personnages, Correa, 1933, excerpts published as *L'Education des filles,* Correa, 1936, original edition reprinted, Buchet/Chastel, 1970.

Discours de reception a l'Academie Francaise et reponse de M. Andre Ch.' meix, Grasset, 1934.

Journal, Volume I, Grasset, 1934, Volume II, Grasset, 1937, Volume III, Grasset, 1940, Volume IV, Flammarion, 1950,

Volume V, Flammarion, 1953, excerpts published in *Malagar,* 1972 (see Omnibus volumes, below).

La Vie de Jesus, Flammarion, 1936, translation by Julie Kernan published as *Life of Jesus,* Longmans, Green, 1937.

L'Homme et le peche, Plon, 1938.

(With others) *Communism and Christians,* translated by J. F. Scanlan, Sands, 1938.

Les Maisons fugitives, Grasset, 1939.

Lacordaire et nous, Gallimard, 1940.

(Editor) *Les Pages immortelles de Pascal,* Correa, 1940, translation published as *Living Thoughts of Pascal,* Cassell, c.1940.

(Under pseudonym Forez) *Le Cahier noir,* published clandestinely by Editions de Minuit, 1943, published with parallel French and English texts as *Le Cahier noir: The Black Notebook,* Burrup, Mathieson, 1944.

La Nation francaise a une ame, published clandestinely, c.1944.

Nepas se renier, Editions de la Revue Fontaine (Algeria), 1944.

Coups de couteau, Editions Lumiere (Brussels), 1944.

The Eucharist: The Mystery of Holy Thursday, translated by Marie-Louise Dufrenoy, Longmans, Green (New York), 1944.

Sainte Marguerite de Cortone, Flammarion, 1945, translation by Bernard Fruchtman published as *Saint Margaret of Cortona,* Philosophical Library, 1948, translation by Barbara Wall published as *Margaret of Cortona,* Burns & Oates, 1948.

Pages de Journal, Editions du Rocher (Monaco), 1945.

La Rencontre avec Barres, Editions de 1a Table Ronde, 1945, published in *Ecrits in times,* 1953 (see Omnibus volumes, below).

Le Baillon denoue, apres quatre ans de silence (articles originally published in *Figaro,* August, 1944, to March, 1945), Grasset, 1945.

Reponse a Paul Claudel: Academie Francaise, seance du 13 mars 1947, Editions de la Table Ronde, 1947.

Du cote de chez Proust, Editions de 1a Table Ronde, 1947, translation by Elsie Pell published as *Proust's Way,* Philosophical Library, 1950.

Mes grands hommes, Editions du Rocher, 1949, translation by Pell published as *Men I Hold Great,* Philosophical Library, 1951 (published in England as *Great Men,* Rockliff, 1952), reprinted, Kennikat, 1971.

Terresfranciscaines, Plon, 1950.

La Pierre d'achoppement, Editions du Rocher, 1951, translation by Hopkins published as *The Stumbling Block,* Philosophical Library, 1952.

La Mort d'Andre Gide, Editions Estienne, 1952.

(With others) *Bordeaux: Porte ouverte sur le monde,* R. Picquot (Bordeaux), 1952.

Lettres ouvertes, Editions du Rocher, 1952, translation by Mario A. Pei published as *Letters on Art and Literature,* Philosophical Library, 1953, reprinted, Kennikat, 1970.

Mauriac par lui-meme (with notes by Mauriac), edited by Pierre Henri Simon, Editions de Seuil, 1953.

Paroles catholiques, Plon, 1954, translation by Edward H. Flannery published as *Words of Faith,* Philosophical Library, 1955.

Bloc-notes, 1952-1957 (articles originally published in *La Table Ronde* and *L'Express*), Flammarion, 1958.

(Contributor) *Trois ecrivains devant Lourdes,* Plon, 1958.

Le Fils de l'homme, Grasset, 1958, translation by Bernard Murchland published as *The Son of Man,* World Publishing, 1960.

Memoires interieures, Flammarion, 1959, translation by Hopkins published with original French title, Eyre & Spottiswoode,

1960, Farrar, Straus, 1961. *Rapport sur les prix de vertu* (paper read at a meeting of Institut de France, December 17, 1960), Firmin-Didiot, 1960.

Le Nouveau bloc-notes, 1958-1960, Flammarion, 1961.

Second Thoughts: Reflections on Literature and on Life, translated by Adrienne Foulke, World Publishing, 1961.

Ce queje crois, Grasset, 1962, translation with an introduction by Wallace Fowlie published as *What I Believe,* Farrar, Straus, 1963.

Cain, Where Is Your Brother?, Coward, 1962.

De Gaulle, Grasset, 1964, translation by Richard Howard published as *De Gaulle,* Doubleday, 1966.

Les Plus belles pages de Maurice et Eugenie Guerin, Mercure de France, 1965.

Nouveaux memoires interieures, Flammarion, 1965, translation by Herma Briffault published as *The Inner Presence: Recollections of My Spiritual Life,* Bobbs-Merrill, 1968.

D'Autres et moi, Grasset, 1966.

Memoires politiques, Grasset, 1967.

Le Nouveau bloc-notes, 1961-1964 (articles originally published in *L'Express* and *Figaro*), Flammarior, 1968.

Le Nouveau bloc-notes, 1965-1967, Flammarion, 1970.

Le Dernier bloc-notes, 1968-1970, Flammarion, 1971.

Correspondance Andre Gide-Francois Mauriac, 1912-1950, edited by Jacqueline Morton, Gallimard, 1971.

Francois Mauriac en verve (quotations), edited by Jean Touzot, P. Horay, 1974.

(With Keith Goesch) *Lacordaire,* French and European Publications, 1976.

Correspondance entre Francois Mauriac et Jacques-Emile Blanche, (1916-1942), edited by Georges-Paul Collet, Grasset, 1976.

Lettres d'une vie (1904-1969), edited by Caroline Mauriac, Grasset, 1981.

Lettres de Francois Mauriac a Robert Vallery-Radot, 1909-1931, Grasset, 1985.

OMNIBUS VOLUMES

The Family (contains "The Kiss to the Leper" and "Genitrix"), translations by Louis Galantiere, Covici, Friede, 1930.

Plongees (also see below; stories; contains "Therese chez le docteur," "Therese a l'hotel," "Insomnie," "Le Rang," and "Conte de Noel"), Grasset, 1938.

Therese: A Portrait in Four Parts (contains *The End of the Night,* "Therese and the Doctor," and "Therese at the Hotel"), translations by Hopkins, Holt, 1947, reprinted, Penguin, 1975.

Oeuvres completes, 12 volumes, Fayard, 1950-59.

That Which Was Lost [and] *The Dark Angels,* translated by J.H.F. McEwen and Hopkins, Eyre & Spottiswoode, 1951.

The Weakling [and] *The Enemy,* translations by Hopkins, Pellegrini & Cudahy, 1952.

Ecrits intimes (contains *Commencements d'une vie, La Rencontre avec Barres,* "Journal d'un homme de trente ans," and *Du cote de chez Proust*), Palatine, 1953.

Therese Desqueyroux [suivi de] *Therese chez le docteur, Therese a l'hotel* [et] *La Fin de 1a nuit,* Grasset, 1956.

Marc Alyn, editor, *Francois Mauriac* (selections and a study of Mauriac by the editor), Seghers, 1960.

Asmodee: Piece en cinq actes de Francois Mauriac [et] *Sur un banc: Comedie en un acte de Charles Mahieu,* [Paris], 1961.

Therese Desqueyroux [et] *La Fin de la nuit,* introduction by Pierre Henri Simon, Club des Amis du Livre, 1963.

Oeuvres romanesques, Flammarion, 1965.

Les Chefs d'oeuvre de Francois Mauriac (contains *La Robe pretexte, Le Baiser au lepreux, Le Fleuve defeu,* and *Plongees*), Cercle du Bibliophile, 1967.

A Mauriac Reader (contains *A Kiss for the Leper,* "Genetrix," *The Desert of Love, The Knot of Vipers,* and *A Woman of the Pharisees*), translations by Hopkins, introduction by Wallace Fowlie, Farrar, Straus, 1968.

Five Novels, translations by Hopkins, Eyre & Spottiswoode, 1969.

La Vie de Jesus, Le Jeudi-saint, Sainte Marguerite de Cortone, [et] *La Pierre d'achoppement,* Cercle du Bibliophile, 1970.

Malagar: Ma maison de champs (contains selections from *Memoires interieurs, Nouveaux memoires interieurs,* and *Journal*), Arcaehon, 1972.

Oeuvres romanesques et theatrales completes, 3 volumes, Gallimard, 1978-81.

OTHER

Contributor to many books; contributor to more than forty newspapers and periodicals, including *Le Figaro, La Table Ron de, L'Express, Lettres Francaises, Le Temps Present,* and *L'Echo de Paris.*

SIDELIGHTS: Described by Slava M. Kushnir in the *Dictionary of Literary Biography* as "one of the most important and prolific French authors of this century," Francois Mauriac was awarded a Nobel Prize for Literature in 1952. The author of novels, nonfiction religious works, poetry, and plays, Mauriac often wrote of his native Bordeaux. Rayner Hoppenstall in *The Double Image* wrote: "The deep seam of regionalism in the French novel runs right through Mauriac. Even when they are to be found upon the pavements of Paris, his characters invariably come from the Landes in the neighborhood of Bordeaux and most of his characters stay there." It was this environment which provided the special atmosphere of his novels; a *Books Abroad* reviewer commented that "the monotonous *landes . . .* with their extremes of rain and drought are the perfect reflection of solitary brooding temperaments struggling against barely repressed passions, and this creates an atmosphere of intensity, a kind of poetry that is very difficult to translate." According to Cecil Jenkins in his book *Mauriac,* the author constantly explored his own relationship with his native Bordeaux: "Sixty books have scarcely exhausted the love-hate relationship with this region which Mauriac abandoned almost as many years ago at the age of twenty-one. If Paris has been the privileged platform for the man of letters, the human reality behind the writings has never ceased to be Bordeaux."

Because of this constant searching of his own past, Mauriac's writing involved a continuing exercise of memory. Jenkins reported that, in an interview with Malcolm Cowley, Mauriac stated: "I don't observe and I don't describe: I rediscover. I rediscover the narrow Jansenist world of my devout, unhappy and introverted childhood." His method of working was instinctive, rather than based on conscious organization; Jenkins continued: "He describes himself today as an 'instinctive writer'. . . . He says that, if he was never horrified by what he wrote, he was often surprised. He wrote extremely fast—in some cases completing the draft of a novel in three weeks—and, as indeed some of his hasty endings suggest, he was never very concerned with the deliberate ordering of the structure of his work. . . . Control, in the Mauriac novel, is purely organic, and quality a function of the intensity of concentrating upon a theme."

A Roman Catholic, Mauriac incorporated his religious beliefs into his fiction. His characters often suffer from a fatal flaw in their moral nature which leads them into tragic circumstances.

They only recover their balance with a return to their faith. In *The Knot of Vipers,* for example, the elderly narrator recounts the many villainies he has committed and laments the lack of love in his life. When he does receive love, it spurs a near-miraculous conversion to the faith. As the *Books Abroad* writer noted, Mauriac was "closely identified with Roman Catholicism and mention of his name invariably provokes lengthy arguments about the role of the Catholic novelist." Mauriac himself, however, disputed the notion that he was a "Catholic novelist." He told Alden Whitman: "I am a novelist who is a Catholic. With the aid of a certain gift for creating atmosphere, I have tried to make the Catholic universe of evil palpable, tangible, odorous." Although Mauriac's fictional world was a place of much suffering, it was relieved by a faith in eventual redemption. William R. Mueller, writing in *Celebration of Life: Studies in Modern Fiction,* remarked that Mauriac "acknowledges his reputation as a writer who presents a museum of horrors and specializes in monsters. . . . He asks . . . that we look beyond its blackness to 'the light that penetrates it and burns there secretly.' "

In his nonfiction, Mauriac dealt more directly with his religious faith, writing biographies of saints, essays on ethical and moral questions, and accounts of his own religious conversion. Neil C. Arvin noted in the *Sewanee Review* that Mauriac was "an ardent, intransigent Christian." Arvin quoted Mauriac explaining in his *Journal:* "I must write, and my books must be a running commentary on my soul; in my books I must recognize my most secret self." This concern was found in all of his writings. Germaine Bree, writing in *The Vision Obscured: Perceptions of Some Twentieth-Century Catholic Novelists,* maintained that although Mauriac wrote "many kinds of books" in several different genres, "whole sentences and paragraphs could be shifted from one category to the other without causing the slightest disturbance in atmosphere."

Mauriac was described by Hoppenstall as "tall, thin, dark, nervous, a brilliant conversationalist, afflicted with melancholy." The French commentator, Jean-Francois Revel, who often disapproved of Mauriac's journalistic style—though not the causes he espoused—affirmed that Mauriac was "honest, almost always sincere, and highly intelligent." Walter Clemons, writing in the *New York Times,* called Mauriac "an artist, when he is at his best, of astonishing power."

Time reported that "Mauriac provided his own eulogy in a recording he made 20 years ago to be released after his death. It reflected a lifelong preoccupation with the possibilities of grace that he had explored in his essays, if not in his other work. 'I believe,' he said, 'as I did as a child, that life has meaning, a direction, a value; that no suffering is lost, that every tear counts, each drop of blood, that the secret of the world is to be found in St. John's "Deus caritas est"—"God is Love." ' "

BIOGRAPHICAL/CRITICAL SOURCES:

BOOKS

Alyn, Marc, *Francois Mauriac,* Seghers, 1960.

Avakian, Beatrice, editor, *Francois Mauriac: Souvénirs retrouves: Entretiens avec Jean Amrouche,* Fayard/Institut National de l'Audiovisuel, 1981.

Bendz, Ernst, *Francois Mauriac: Ebauche d'une figure,* Messageries du Livre, 1946.

Bichelberger, Roger, *Rencontre avec Mauriac,* Editions de l'Ecole, 1973.

Chocon, Bernard, *Francois Mauriac ou la passion de la terre,* Lettres Modernes, 1972.

Contemporary Literary Criticism, Gale, Volume 4, 1975, Volume 9, 1978, Volume 56, 1989.

Cormeau, Nelly, *L'Art de Francois Mauriac,* Grasset, 1951.

Dictionary of Literary Biography, Volume 65: *French Novelists, 1900-1930,* Gale, 1988.

The Double Image, Secker & Warburg, 1947.

Fernand Seguin rencontre Francois Mauriac, Editions de L'Homme (Montreal), 1969.

Fillion, Amelie, *Francois Mauriac,* Edgar Malfere, 1956.

Flower, J. E., *Intention and Achievement: An Essay on the Novels of Francois Mauriac,* Oxford University Press, 1969.

Friedman, Melvin J., editor, *The Vision Obscured: Perceptions of Some Twentieth-Century Catholic Novelists,* Fordham University Press, 1970.

Gaspary, A. M., compiler, *Francois Mauriac,* Herder, 1968.

Glenisson, Emile, *L'Amour dans les romans de Francois Mauriac, essai de critique psychanalytique,* Editions Universitaires, 1970.

Goesch, Keith, editor, *Les Paroles restent,* Grasset, 1985.

Goesch, Keith, *Francois Mauriac,* Editions de l'Herne, 1985.

Grall, Xavier, *Francois Mauriac, Journaliste,* Editions du Cerf, 1960.

Greene, Graham, *The Lost Childhood, and Other Essays,* Eyre & Spottiswoode, 1951.

Jarret-Kerr, Martin, *Francois Mauriac,* Yale University Press, 1954.

Jenkins, Cecil, *Mauriac,* Barnes & Noble, 1965.

Kushner, Eva, *Francois Mauriac,* Desclee de Brouwer, 1972.

Kushnir, Slava M., *Mauriac journaliste,* Lettres Modernes, 1979.

Lacouture, Jean, *Francois Mauriac,* Seuil, 1980.

Landry, Anne Gertrude, *Represented Discourse in the Novels of Francois Mauriac,* Catholic University of America Press, 1953.

Mauriac, Francois, *Second Thoughts: Reflections on Literature and on Life,* translated by Adrienne Foulke, World Publishing, 1961.

Mauriac, Francois, *Memoires interieures,* Flammarion, 1959, translation by Gerard Hopkins published under the French title, Farrar, Straus, 1961. Mauriac, Francois, *Journal,* five volumes, Grasset, 1934, 1937, 1940, Flammarion, 1950, 1953.

Moloney, Michael, *Francois Mauriac: A Critical Study,* Swallow, 1958.

Mueller, William R., *Celebration of Life: Studies in Modern Fiction,* Sheed & Ward, 1972.

North, Robert, *Le Catholicisme dans l'ouevre de Francois Mauriac,* Conquistidor, 1950.

North, Robert J., editor, *Le Feu sur la terre* (critical edition), Harrap, 1962.

Pell, Elsie, *Francois Mauriac: In Search of the Infinite,* Philosophical Library, 1947.

Roussel, Bernard, *Mauriac, le peche et la grace,* Editions du Centurion, 1964.

Scott, Malcolm, *Mauriac: The Politics of a Novelist,* Scottish Academic Press (Edinburgh), 1980.

Simon, Pierre-Henri, *Mauriac par lui-meme,* Editions du Seuil, 1953.

Smith, Maxwell A., *Francois Mauriac,* Twayne, 1970.

Speaight, Robert, *Francois Mauriac: A Study of the Writer and the Man,* Chatto & Windus, 1976.

Stratford, Philip, *Faith and Fiction: Creative Process in Greene and Mauriac,* University of Notre Dame Press, 1963.

Suffran, Michel, *Francois Mauriac,* Seghers, 1973.

Touzot, Jean, *Mauriac avant Mauriac, 1913-1922,* Flammarion, 1977.

Touzot, Jean, *La Planete Mauriac,* Klincksieck, 1985.

Touzot, Jean, editor, *Francois Mauriac,* Editions de l'Herne, 1985.

Turnell, Martin, *The Art of French Fiction: Prevost, Stendhal, Zola, Maupassant, Gide, Mauriac, Proust,* New Directions, 1959.

PERIODICALS

American Society Legion of Honor Magazine, winter, 1963.

Books Abroad, winter, 1967.

Christianity Today, August 8, 1975.

Commonweal, March 17, 1961, December 25, 1970, November 16, 1973.

Connaissance des Hommes (special issue on Mauriac), autumn, 1972.

Esquire, December, 1970.

L'Express, June 19, 1967.

Figaro Litteraire (special issues on Mauriac), November 15, 1952, September 7, 1970.

Illustrated London News, November 15, 1952.

Kenyon Review, fall, 1959.

Modern Language Review, October, 1963.

Nation, March 28, 1966.

New Yorker, June 21, 1958.

New York Times, July 15, 1970.

New York Times Book Review, June 28, 1970.

La Parisienne (special issue on Mauriac), May, 1956.

Paris Review, summer, 1953.

Sewanee Review, July-September, 1942.

La Table Ronde (special issue on Mauriac), January, 1953.

Time, August 12, 1957.

Washington Post, September 3, 1970.

Yale French Studies, April, 1964, March, 1965.

OBITUARIES:

PERIODICALS

New York Times, September 1, 1970.

Observer Review, September 6, 1970.

Publishers Weekly, September 14, 1970.

Time, September 14, 1970.

Washington Post, September 2, 1970.

*   *   *

MAUROIS, Andre 1885-1967
(E. Herzog)

PERSONAL: Original name, Emile Salomon Wilhelm Herzog; name legally changed in 1947; born July 26, 1885, in Elbeuf (Seine-Inferieure), France; died October 9, 1967; son of Ernest (a textile manufacturer) and Alice-Helene (Levy) Herzog; married Jeanne-Marie Wande de Szymkievicz, October 30, 1912 (died, 1924); married Simone de Caillavet, September 6, 1926; children: (first marriage) Michelle, Gerald, Oliver; (second marriage) Francoise (child of a previous marriage of his second wife; died, 1930). *Education:* Lycee Corneille, Rouen (Prix d'honneur de philosophie), 1897-1902, diplome; l'Universite de Caen, licence in philosophy, 1902.

ADDRESSES: Home—86 Boulevard Maurice Barres, Neuilly sur seine, France (winter); and Essendieras, Excideuil, Dordogne, France (summer).

CAREER: Industrial manager in family textile factory, 1904-14, 1919-26; made a lecture tour in the United States (his first visit to America), 1927; lectured in New York, Schenectady, Worcester, Ottawa, Montreal, and at Dartmouth College, Smith College, and Cornell University, 1927-32; Clark Lecturer, Trinity College, Cambridge University, 1928; held Meridith Howland Pyne chair of French literature, Princeton University, October, 1929, to February, 1931; elected to the French Academy, June 23, 1938; Lowell Lecturer, Harvard University, 1940; pleaded the cause of France and Marshal Henri Petain to the Americans in his writings and lectures, 1940-43; professor of French literature, Mills College, Oakland, California, summer, 1941; professor of French literature, University of Kansas City, 1945-46; after World War II, Maurois devoted full time to writing and lecturing. *Military service:* French Army, volunteered and served with the Seventh Division, Rouen, 1903-04; interpreter for the Ninth Scottish Division, then liaison officer to the British Army Headquarters, 1914-18, received Distinguished Conduct Medal; Bureau of Information, attached to British Headquarters, 1939-40; volunteered for service in North Africa, Corsica, Italy, captain, 1943-44; went to the United States under the orders of General Giraud to relate to the Americans the effects of the lend-lease program and the extent of the French military effort in Italy.

MEMBER: Association France-Etats-Unis (president), Societe des Gens de Lettres, Comite de Lecture de la Comedie-Francaise, Portuguese Academy, Brazilian Academy.

AWARDS, HONORS: Honorary degrees from Edinburgh University, 1928, Princeton University, 1933, Oxford University, 1934, University of Saint Andrews, 1934, University of Louisiana, and other institutions; Grand Officer of the Legion of Honor awarded by the French Ministry of Commerce and Industry, 1937; Knight of the Order of the British Empire, 1938; Commandeur des Arts et des Lettres; Commandeur du Merite Sportif; Prix des Ambassadeurs.

WRITINGS:

NOVELS

Les Silences du Colonel Bramble, Grasset, 1918, new edition edited by E. A. Phillips and E. G. Le Grand, Cambridge University Press, 1920, revised edition, Brentano's, 1943, translation by Thurfrida Wake and Wilfrid Jackson published as *The Silence of Colonel Bramble,* Lane, 1920, revised edition of translation, 1927.

Ni ange, ni bete, Grasset, 1919.

Le General Bramble, Grasset, 1920, translation by Jules Castier and Ronald Boswell published as *General Bramble,* Lane, 1921, enlarged edition published as *Les Discours du Docteur O'Grady,* Grasset, 1922, translation by Castier and Boswell published as *The Discourses of Doctor O'Grady* in one volume with the above translation of *The Silence of Colonel Bramble,* Bodley Head, 1965.

Le Hausse et la baisse, Les Oeuvres Libres, 1922, revised edition published as *Bernard Quesnay,* Gallimard, 1926, translation by Brian W. Downs published as *Bernard Quesnay,* Appleton, 1927.

Climats, Grasset, 1928, translation by Joseph Collins published as *Atmosphere of Love,* Appleton, 1929, translation by J. Collins published in England as *Whatever Gods May Be,* Cassell, 1929, translation by Violet Schiff and Esme Cook published in England as *The Climates of Love,* Barrie, 1957, reprinted, Dufour, 1987.

Le Cercle de famille, Grasset, 1932, recent edition, 1977, translation by Hamish Miles published as *The Family Circle,* Appleton, 1932.

L'Instinct du bonheur, Grasset, 1934, translation by Edith Johannsen published as *A Time for Silence,* Appleton, 1942.

Terre promise, Maison Francaise (New York), 1945, translation by Joan Charles published as *Woman without Love,* Harper, 1945.

Nouveaux Discours du Docteur O'Grady, Grasset, 1950, translation by Gerard Hopkins published as *The Return of Doctor O'Grady,* Bodley Head, 1951.

Les Roses de septembre, Flammarion, 1956, translation by Hopkins published as *September Roses,* Harper, 1958.

SHORT STORIES

Par la faute de Monsieur Balzac, Paillart (Amiens), 1923.

Meipe; ou, La Delivrance, Grasset, 1926, new edition, augmented with *Les Derniers Jours de Pompei* and published as *Les Mondes Imaginaires,* Grasset, 1929, translation of first edition, by Eric Sutton, published as *Mape: The World of Illusion,* Appleton, 1926.

Les Souffrances du jeunne Werther, Schiffrin, 1926.

Les Chapitre Suivant, Kra, 1927, translation by K. Paul published as *The Next Chapter: The War against the Moon,* Dutton, 1927.

Voyage au pays des Articoles, J. Schiffrin, 1927, translation by David Garnett published as *A Voyage to the Island of the Articoles,* Appleton, 1929.

Deux Fragments d'une histoire universelle 1922, Portiques, 1928.

Les Derniers Jours de Pompei, Lapina, 1928.

Le Peseur d'ames, Gallimard, 1931, translation by Hamish Miles published as *The Weigher of Souls* (includes *The Earth Dwellers* and an autobiographical introduction by the author), Macmillan, 1963.

L'Anglaise et d'autres femmes, Nouvelles Societes, 1932, translation by Miles published as *Ricochets: Miniature Tales of Human Life,* Harper, 1935.

Premiers Contes, Defontaine (Rouen), 1935.

La Machine a lire les pensees, Gallimard, 1937, translation by James Whitall published as *The Thought-Reading Machine,* Harper, 1938.

Toujours l'inattendu arrive (stories and novellas), Maison Francaise (New York), 1943.

La Campagne, Transfert, Love in Exile (three novellas), Maison Francaise (New York), 1945.

Tu ne commettras point d'adultere, A. Michel, 1946, translation included in *The Ten Commandments* (ten short stories by various authors), Simon & Schuster, 1944, also published as *Les Dix commandments,* Maison Francaise, 1944.

Les Mondes impossibles: Recits et nouvelles fantastiques (five short stories previously published), Gallimard, 1947.

La Malediction de l'or, France Illustration, 1948.

L'Amour en exile, Les Oeuvres Libres, 1950.

Le Diner sous les marronniers, Deux Rives, 1951.

Les Erophages, Passerelle, 1966.

The Collected Stories of Andre Maurois, Washington Square Press, 1967.

BIOGRAPHY

Ariel; ou, La Vie de Shelley, Grasset, 1923, translation by Ella d'Arcy published as *Ariel: The Life of Shelley,* Appleton, 1924, translation by E. d'Arcy published in England as *Ariel: A Shelley Romance,* Lane, 1924, recent edition, Penguin, 1985.

Portrait d'une actrice, Tremois, 1925.

Lord Byron et le Demon de la tendresse, Porte Etroite, 1925.

Un Essai sur Dickens, Grasset, 1927, published as *Dickens,* Ferenczi (Paris), 1935, translation by Miles published as *Dickens,* Lane, 1934, Harper, 1935.

La Vie de Disraeli, Gallimard, 1927, translation by Miles published as *Disraeli: A Picture of the Victorian Age,* Appleton, 1928.

La Vie de Joseph Smith, Champion, 1927.

Byron, two volumes, Grasset, 1930, translation by Miles published under same title, Appleton, 1930, new edition with preface by the author, Bodley Head, 1963, recent edition, Constable, 1984, published as *Don Juan; ou, La Vie de Byron,* Grasset, 1952.

Lyautey, Plon, 1931, abridged edition, 1935, translation by Miles published as *Lyautey,* Appleton, 1931, same translation published in England as *Marshall Lyautey,* Lane, 1931.

Tourgueniev, Grasset, 1931.

Voltaire, translation by Miles, P. Davies, 1932, published in French by Gallimard, 1935.

Edouard VII et son temps, Editions de France, 1933, new edition, Grasset, 1937, translation by Miles published as *The Edwardian Era,* Appleton, 1933, same translation published in England as *King Edward and His Times,* Cassell, 1933.

Byron et les femmes, Flammarion, 1934.

Chateaubriand, Grasset, 1938, translation by Vera Fraser published as *Chateaubriand: Poet, Statesman, Lover,* Harper, 1938, published as *Rene; ou, La Vie de Chateaubriand,* Grasset, 1956, recent edition, 1977.

A la recherche de Marcel Proust, Hachette, 1949, translation by Hopkins published as *Proust: Portrait of a Genius,* Harper, 1950, Carroll & Graf, 1984, same translation published in England as *The Quest for Proust,* Cape, 1950, published as *Proust: A Biography,* Meridian, 1960.

Destins exemplaires, Plon, 1952, translation by Helen Temple Patterson published in England as *Profiles of Great Men,* Tower Bridge, 1954.

Lelia; ou, La Vie de George Sand, Hachette, 1952, translation by Hopkins published as *Lelia: The Life of George Sand,* Harper, 1953.

La Vie de Cecil Rhodes, Les Oeuvres Libres, 1953, translation by Rohan Wadham published as *Cecil Rhodes,* Macmillan, 1953.

Alexandre Dumas: Great Life in Brief, translation by Jack Palmer White, Knopf, 1954.

Olympio; ou, La Vie de Victor Hugo, Hachette, 1954, translation by Hopkins published in England as *Victor Hugo,* J. Cape, 1956, same translation published as *Olympio: The Life of Victor Hugo,* Harper, 1956, recent edition, Carroll & Graf, 1986, translation by Oliver Bernard published as *Victor Hugo and His World,* Viking, 1966.

Louis XIV a Versailles, Hachette, 1955.

Robert et Elizabeth Browning: Portraits suivis de quelques autres, Grasset, 1955.

Les Troi Dumas, Hachette, 1957, translation by Hopkins published as *The Titans: A Three-Generation Biography of the Dumas,* Harper, 1957, same translation published in England as *Three Musketeers: A Study of the Dumas Family,* J. Cape, 1957.

La Vie de Sir Alexander Fleming, Hachette, 1959, translation by Hopkins published as *The Life of Sir Alexander Fleming, Discoverer of Penicillin,* Dutton, 1959, same translation published in England as *Fleming, the Man Who Cured Millions,* Methuen, 1961.

Adrienne; ou, La Vie de Madame de La Fayette, Hachette, 1961, translation by Hopkins published as *Adrienne: The Life of the Marquise de La Fayette,* McGraw, 1961.

(With others) *Beethoven,* Hachette, 1961.

Promethee; ou, La Vie de Balzac, Hachette, 1965, translation by Norman Denny published as *Prometheus: The Life of Balzac,* Harper, 1966, recent edition, Carroll & Graf, 1983.

LITERARY HISTORY AND CRITICISM

Essais sur la litterature anglaise, Le Livre, 1924.

Etudes anglaises, Grasset, 1927.

Quatre Etudes anglaises, Artisan du Livre, 1927 (this work subsumes *Etudes anglaises*).

Aspects de la biographie (lectures given at Cambridge University, 1928), Au Sans Pariel, 1928, translation by Sidney Castle Roberts published as *Aspects of Biography,* Appleton, 1929.

Le Roman et le romancier (lecture), Imprimerie de Monaco, 1929.

Supplement a melanges et pastiches de Marcel Proust, Trianon, 1929, published as *Le Cote de Chelsea,* Gallimard, 1932, translation by Miles published in England as *Chelsea Way,* Matthews & Marrot, 1930.

(With Luc Durtain, Victor Llona, and Bernard Fay) *Romanciers americains,* Denoel et Steele, 1931.

Introduction a la methode de Paul Valery, Editions Libres, 1933.

Magiciens et logiciens, Grasset, 1935, translation by Miles published as *Prophets and Poets,* Harper, 1935, same translation published in England as *Poets and Prophets,* Cassell, 1936.

Etudes litterairs, Maison Francaise (New York), Volume 1, 1941, Volume 2, 1944, published as *Grands ecrivains du demi-siecle,* Club du Livre du Mois, 1957.

Cinq Visages de l'amour (lectures given at Princeton, 1930-31), Didier (New York), 1942, new edition published as *Sept visages de l'amour,* 1942, translation by Haakon M. Chevalier published as *Seven Faces of Love,* Didier, 1944.

Etudes americaines, Maison Francaise, 1945.

Alain, Domat, 1949.

Biographie, Editions Estienne, 1957.

Lecture, mon doux plaisir, Fayard, 1957, translation by Hopkins of most of the essays published as *The Art of Writing,* Dutton, 1960, published in French as *De La Bruyere a Proust,* Fayard, 1964.

Le Monde de Marcel Proust, Hachette, 1960.

Choses vues, Gallimard, 1963.

De Proust a Camus, Perrin, 1963, translation by Carl Morse and Renaud Bruce published as *From Proust to Camus,* Doubleday, 1966.

De Gide a Sartre, Perrin, 1965.

HISTORY

Histoire d'Angleterre, Fayard, 1937, translation by Miles published as *The Miracle of England: An Account of Her Rise to Preeminence and Present Position,* Harper, 1937, revised edition of this translation, Garden City, 1940, translation by Miles published as *A History of England,* J. Cape, 1937, revised edition of this translation, Farrar, Straus, 1958, published in a condensed version as *An Illustrated History of England,* Bodley Head, 1963.

L'Empire francais, Hachette, 1939.

Les Origines de la guerre de 1939, Gallimard, 1939.

The Battle of France, translated by F. R. Ludman, Lane, 1940.

Tragedie en France, Maison Francaise, 1940, translation by Denver Lindley published as *Tragedy in France,* Harper, 1940, same translation published in England as *Why France Fell,* Lane, 1941.

Defense de la France, [Buenos Aires], 1941.

(With Christian Megret) *Petit Traite sur les politiques d'hier et les libertes de demain,* Maison Francaise, 1942.

Histoire des Etats-Unis, two volumes, Maison Francaise, 1943-44, translation by Denver Lindley and Jane Lindley published as *The Miracle of America,* Harper, 1944, same translation published in England as *A New History of the United States,* Lane, 1948, revised edition published as *Histoire des Etats-Unis, 1492-1954,* Michel, 1954, published as *Histoire de peuple americain: Etats-Unis,* two volumes, Editions Litteraires, 1955-56.

Histoire de la France, Wapler, 1947, translation by Henry Binsse published as *The Miracle of France,* Harper, 1948, same translation published in England as *A History of France,* J. Cape, 1950, revised edition, two volumes, Club du Livre Selectionne, 1957, translation by Binsse and Hopkins published as *A History of France,* Farrar, Straus, 1957, published in a condensed form as *An Illustrated History of France,* Viking, 1960.

Rouen devaste, [Rouen], 1947.

(With Louis Aragon) *L'Histoire parallele des Etats-Unis et de l'U.R.S.S., 1917-1960,* four volumes, Presses de la Cite, 1962, published as *Les Deux Geants,* three volumes, Pont Royal, 1962, Volume 1 published as *Histoire des Etats-Unis de 1917 a 1961,* 1963, translation by Patrick O'Brien published as *From the New Freedom to the New Frontier,* McKay, 1963, same translation published in England as *A History of the USA: From Wilson to Kennedy,* Weidenfeld & Nicolson, 1964.

(With Aragon) *Conversations avec quelques Americains eminents et apercus donnes par quelques Sovietiques eminents,* Presses de la Cite, 1963.

Histoire de l'Allemagne, Hachette, 1965, translation by Stephen Hardman published as *An Illustrated History of Germany,* Viking, 1966.

JUVENILE BOOKS

Le Pays de trente-six mille volontes, Portiques, 1928, translation by Pauline Fairbanks published as *The Country of Thirty-six Thousand Wishes,* Appleton, 1930.

Patapoufs et filifers, Hartmann, 1930, translation by Rosemary Benet published as *Fatapoufs and Thinifers,* Holt, 1940, translation by Norman Denny published in England as *Fattypuffs and Thinifers,* Lane, 1941, recent edition, Knopf, 1989.

Frederic Chopin, Brentano's, 1941, translation by Ruth Green Harris published as *Frederic Chopin,* Harper, 1942.

Eisenhower, Didier (New York), 1945, translation by Eileen Lane Kinney published as *Eisenhower, the Liberator,* Didier, 1945.

Franklin: La Vie d'un optimiste, Didier, 1945, translation by Haakon M. Chevalier published as *Franklin: The Life of an Optimist,* Didier, 1945.

Washington: The Life of a Patriot, translation by Henry C. Pitz, Didier, 1946.

Nico, le petit garcon change en chien, Calmann-Levy, 1955, translation published as *The French Boy,* Sterling, 1957.

Nico a New York, Calmann-Levy, 1958.

Napoleon, Hachette, 1964, translation by D. J. S. Thomson published as *Napoleon: A Pictorial Biography,* Viking, 1964.

AUTOBIOGRAPHY

Fragments d'un journal de vacances, Emile Hazan, 1929.

Relativisme, Kra, 1931.

Etats-Unis 39: Journal d'un voyage en Amerique, Editions de France, 1939, new edition, 1940.

Memoires, two volumes, Maison Francaise, 1942, revised edition, Flammarion, 1948, translation by Denver and Jane Lindley published as *I Remember, I Remember,* Harper, 1942, same translation published in England as *Call No Man Happy,* J. Cape, 1943.

Journal: Etats-Unis 1946, Bateau Ivre, 1946, translation, with additional material, by Joan Charles published as *From My Journal,* Harper, 1948, same translation published in England as *My American Journal,* Falcon, 1950.

Retour en France, Maison Francaise, 1947, translation by J. Charles included in *From My Journal,* Harper, 1948.

Souvenirs d'enfance et de jeunesse, Les Oeuvres Libres, 1947.

Journal d'un tour en Amerique Latine, Bateau Ivre, 1948, translation by Frank Jackson published in England as *My Latin-American Diary,* Falcon, 1953.

Journal d'un tour en Suisse, Portes de France, 1948.

Portrait d'un ami qui s'appelait moi, Wesmael-Charlier, 1959.

Memoirs, 1885-1967 (autobiography), translation by Denver Lindley, Harper, 1970.

OMNIBUS VOLUMES

J. H. Brown, editor, *Selections from Andre Maurois,* [London], 1928.

Gerard Le Grand, editor, *Morceaux choisis,* Cambridge University Press, 1931.

H. Miles, translator, *A Private Universe* (essays), Appleton, 1932.

Edouard Maynial, editor, *Textes choisis,* Grasset, 1936.

Louis Chaigne, editor, *Poesie et action: Choix de textes,* Le Roux, 1949.

The Maurois Reader, introduction by Anne Fremantle, Didier, 1949.

Oeuvres completes, sixteen volumes, Fayard, 1950-56.

L'Angleterre romantique (biographies), Gallimard, 1953.

Pour piano seul (nouvelles), Flammarion, 1960.

Romans (novels), Gallimard, 1961.

The Collected Stories of Andre Maurois, Washington Square Press, 1967.

TRANSLATOR

(With G. Richet under the name E. Herzog) Ian Hay, *Les Premiers Mille . . . ,* [Paris], 1917.

(With Jeanne Simone Bussy) David Garnett, *La Femme changee en renard,* Grasset, 1924.

(With Virginia Vernon) Laurence Housman, *Victoria Regina* (play), Plon, 1937.

Elizabeth Barrett Browning, *Sonnets a la Portugaise,* Brentano's, 1946.

OTHER WORKS

Les Bourgeois de Witzheim, Grasset, 1920.

Dialogues sur le commandement, Paillart (Abbeville), 1923, translation by John Lewis May published as *Captains and Kings,* Appleton, 1925.

Arabesques, Marcelle Lesage, 1925.

Anarchie, Editions de la Lampe d'Argile, 1926.

Une Carriere, La Cite des Livres, 1926.

Les Anglais (includes "Opinion sur les Francais," by L. Washburn, translation by Andre Maurois), Cahiers Libres, 1927.

Ce qu'on appelle charme: Pensees, Claude Aveline, 1927.

Conseils a un jeune francais partant pour l'Angleterre, Paillart, 1927.

La Conversation, Hachette, 1927, translation by Yvonne Dufour published as *Conversation,* Dutton, 1930.

Decors, Emile Paul, 1927.

Petite Histoire de l'espece humaine, Cahiers de Paris, 1927.

Rouen, Emile-Paul, 1927.

Contact, Stols, 1928.

L'Amerique inattendue, Mornay, 1931.

"Sur le vif": L'Eposition coloniale de Paris, 1931, Librairie Eos, 1931.

Chantiers americains, Gallimard, 1933.

En Amerique (contains of *Contact* and *L'Amerique inattendue*), Flammarion, 1933, published in French by American Book Co. (Cincinnati), 1936.

Mes Songes que voici, Grasset, 1933.

Sentiments et Coutumes (five lectures), Grasset, 1934.

Malte, Editions Alpina, 1935.

La Jeunesse devant notre temps, Flammarion, 1937.

Three Letters on the English, Chatto & Windus, 1938, Transatlantic, 1943.

Un Art de vivre, Plon, 1939, translation by James Whitall published as *The Art of Living,* Harper, 1940.

Chef-d'oeuvre des aquarellistes anglais: Turner et ses contemporains, Plon, 1939.

Espoirs et souvenirs (lecture), Maison Francaise, 1943.

The Role of Art in Life and Law (address), translation by Arthur Cowan, Brandeis Lawyers Society (Philadelphia), 1945.

Conseils a un jeune Francais partant pour les Etats-Unis, Jeune Parque, 1947.

Quand la France s'enrichissait, Les Oeuvres Libres, 1947.

Retour en France, Maison Francaise, 1947.

J.-L. David, Le Divan, 1948.

Can Our Civilization Be Saved?, Brandeis Lawyers Society, 1949.

Centenaire de la mort de Frederic Chopin, Firmin Didot, 1949.

Ce que je crois, Grasset, 1951, new edition augmented with objections made by some readers and replies to these objections, 1952.

Cours de bonheur conjugal (radio play), Hachette, 1951, translation by Crystal Herbert published as *The Art of Being Happily Married,* Harper, 1953.

La Divine Comtesse, Georges Blaizot, 1951.

Metamorphoses, Goossens (Brussels), 1951.

Paris, Nathan (Paris), 1951.

Lettres a l'inconnue, Jeune Parque, 1953, translation by John Buchanan-Brown published as *To an Unknown Lady,* Dutton, 1957, same translation published in England as *To the Fair Unknown,* Bodley Head, 1957.

Rio de Janeiro, Nathan, 1953.

Centenaire de la mort de Lamennais, Firmin Didot, 1954.

Femmes de Paris, Plon, 1954, translation by Norman Denny published as *The Women of Paris,* Bodley Head, 1954.

Le Poeme de Versailles (text for the performances of the Sound and Light Festival given at Versailles), Grasset, 1954, published as *Versailles aux lumieres,* Editions Tel, 1954, translation by A. S. Alexander published in France as *A Vision of Versailles,* Amelot (Brionne), 1955.

Aux innocents les mains pleines (play), La Table Ronde, 1955.

Hollande, Hachette, 1955.

Paris Capitale, Foret, 1955.

Perigord, Hachette, 1955.

Portrait de la France et des francais, Hachette, 1955.

La France change de visage, Gallimard, 1956.

Wit and Humor (lecture), 1958.

Dialogues des vivants, Fayard, 1959.

France, Foret, 1959.

Cent Cinquantenaire de Barbey d'Aurevilly a Saint-Sauveur-Le-Vicomte, Firmin Didot, 1959.

La Bibliotheque publique et sa mission, UNESCO, 1961, translation published in Paris as *Public Libraries and Their Mission,* UNESCO, 1961.

(With J. M. Gavin) *A Civil War Album of Paintings by the Prince de Joinville,* Atheneum, 1964, published as *Princely Service:*

Excerpts from the Civil War Album of Paintings by the Prince de Joinville, American Heritage, 1964.

Lettre ouverte a un jeune homme, sur la conduite de la vie, Albin Michel, 1966.

Illusions (lectures prepared just before his death, and never presented), Columbia University Press, 1966.

Contributor to numerous volumes, including *Hommage a Andre Gide,* Editions du Capitole, 1928; *Europe unie, 1949-1950: Etude pour la formation d'une conscience europeenne,* Alsatia, 1949; and various numbers of *Les Oeuvres libres: Nouvelle serie.* Contributor of numerous articles to periodicals, including *Atlantic, Harper's, New York Times,* and *Spectator.*

Editor and annotator of numerous works, including *Voltaire: Pages immortelles choisies et expliques par Andre Maurois,* Correa, 1938, translation by Barrows Mussey and Richard Aldington published as *Voltaire: Living Thoughts, Presented by Andre Maurois,* Longmans, Green (New York), 1939.

SIDELIGHTS: The scope and volume of Andre Maurois's writings are certainly two of the most striking features of his literary output. His versatility as a biographer, novelist, popular historian, literary critic, practical philosopher, and writer of fantastic tales, is all the more remarkable considering that he was thirty-three years of age when his first book was published and that he did not devote the major part of his time to writing until almost ten years later. Despite his superior achievements as a student, his childhood desire to be a writer, and his ambition to become a professor, Maurois, out of a deep sense of family loyalty, devoted the first ten years of his professional life to assisting his father and uncles with the management of their cloth factory. It was the first World War which catapulted him out of the humdrum routine of the small provincial town of Elbeuf, exposed him to the British character and customs, and inspired him to write *The Silence of Colonel Bramble.* This witty and penetrating commentary on warfare and the British character and prejudices was received with unexpected enthusiasm on both sides of the Channel and immediately ushered Maurois into literary circles. It was at this time that Emile Herzog adopted the pseudonym Andre Maurois, because he was an officer in the French Army when this book, which could have offended the English, was originally published. (Maurois is the name of a French village, and Herzog reportedly liked its somber sound.) It was the first of a series of works on the English and American cultures that brought Maurois the reputation of being the foremost intellectual link between France and the English-speaking world.

In an article written for the *Revue de Paris* (May, 1959), Maurois attributed the wide scope of his writings to his innate and universal curiosity, his desire to understand, and his need to explain. In a sense, writing had been for him a means of self-education, the fruits of which he offered to the public. Robert Kemp described him as being "above all, a great professor." The most profound influence on Maurois was Emile Chartier, one of the finest teachers of modern times, who wrote under the pseudonym Alain. Maurois studied under Alain at Rouen and it was to him, Maurois stated, that he owed "everything" and to him that Maurois consistently made references in his writings and interviews. Maurois related in his *Memories* that Alain encouraged him to pursue a non-academic vocation, following the examples of Balzac and Dickens, so that he could see men at work, experience life, and avoid writing before he was mature enough to write. Maurois was further influenced by the personality and writings of Charles Du Bos who, like himself, interpreted foreign thought and literature to the French nation. As a result of the success of his early writings, his travels, and the captivating charm of his person, Maurois also came into close contact with such writers as Andre Gide, Rudyard Kipling, Virginia Woolf, H. G. Wells, Maurice Baring, Anatole France, Paul Valery, and Francois Mauriac.

It was as a biographer that Maurois made his most significant contribution to literature, and in America his nonscholarly biographies have been more widely read than either his novels or essays. With his first two biographies, *Ariel: The Life of Shelley* and *Disraeli: A Picture of the Victorian Age,* Maurois was instrumental in revolutionizing the basic concept and content of biography as a literary media, lending to it the qualities of a good novel. Professor Le Sage commented that Maurois had a talent for "imparting to biography the illusion of living reality characteristic of fiction. . . . Facts in his hands change from statistics into vital indications of some real human being." Because of his superior gift of intuition and projection, "a vivid idea of the person behind the personage" emerges in his prose. The *Times Literary Supplement,* however, noted that his work on Napoleon contains "many misstatements of facts . . . [and] instances of sheer carelessness." In his *Aspects of Biography* Maurois clearly specified the essentials of this form of "novelized" or interpretive biography. Primarily, the form requires strict adherence to facts even though these may be objectionable to descendants of the subject or threatening to the subject's legendary image. No attempt should be made to present a morally exemplary life. Whereas older biographers insisted on the homogeneity of character, Maurois stressed the multiplicity of the personality, its contradictory extremes, and its interior struggles. However, transcending these diversities of character, every life, according to Maurois, possesses a fundamental harmony or unifying thread that the biographer must discover and reveal. By choosing subjects with whom he could personally identify, Maurois further transformed biography, as Georges Lemaitre has indicated, into a medium that could "serve the writer as a vehicle for the outpouring of his suppressed emotions and desires." The quality of his biographies, in Lemaitre's opinion, varies directly with the degree of his personal affinity with the subjects. Notwithstanding these standards, Maurois maintained that there exists no possible scientific truth in biography, but only a psychological or poetic truth, and he believed that it is impossible to achieve the kind of synthesis of a person's inner life that one often finds in novels.

Maurois's histories were largely based on secondary sources which were not necessarily the most recent ones. In his histories of England, America, France, and Germany, he made effective use of his ability to empathize with other times, individuals, and cultures. Michel Droit pointed out that Maurois saw the essence of man's history as the struggle of individuals. In portraying the changing characteristics of men and nations, it was Maurois's goal to reveal the permanent features of a people. Utilizing his discriminate and artful choice of the clever anecdote and quick quotation, he injected color and drama into his texts. There is in his histories a cool detachment and an absence of distortion.

Maurois's novels are most often set within the framework of French provincial life. Maurois was a novelist of the bourgeoisie, of marriage, and of the family. Many of his characters and circumstances are autobiographical but, as Lemaitre stated, it is not possible to draw an unbroken parallel between his own life and any of the lives he created. *Bernard Quesnay,* the story of a young man who aspires to a literary career but is tied to a family textile industry is the most obviously autobiographical. The theme of reconciliation of opposing interests runs throughout his novels. Maurois once said: "I have felt an acute need to describe certain conflicts and sentiments which have divided and troubled me." In *Bernard Quesnay* he described the conflict between the

properted and working classes, in *The Family Circle,* that of two generations, in *The Atmosphere of Love,* that of two lovers, in *The Silence of Colonel Bramble,* that of two cultures, and, in *The Return of Doctor O'Grady,* that of the deterministic materialist and the spiritualist. Although his protagonists often exhibit attitudes of acceptance and resignation in the face of the unchangeable, Maurois, as Droit commented, did not resolve the problems he posed or postulate any moral or political doctrines. Rather, he tacitly urged the reader to find his own resolution. He reserved the explication of theories for his essays.

The most subtle of Maurois's talents as a biographer are given free play in his novels. Commenting on *The Atmosphere of Love,* Elmer Davis said: "You must go back to Stendhal to find so painstaking an analysis of the causes and workings of love and jealousy." This statement would have pleased the author, for Maurois, like his preceptor, Alain, venerated Stendhal and Balzac above all other writers. Alain instructed Maurois to copy out, word for word, passages from *La Chartreuse de Parme* or *Le Rouge et le Noir* "in order to learn the technique of writing, as young painters copy the pictures of their masters." Maurois's admiration of Balzac prompted him to write a biography of the author of *The Human Comedy.* At one time Maurois stated, "I would have liked to write a *Human Comedy.*" Maurois's novels display a balance, a restrained dynamism, and a technical skill that is usually concentrated on the development of character and psychological analyses rather than on action. His biographies, however, are generally considered to be superior to his novels which, as Margaret Wallace judged to be the case with *The Family Circle,* do not always impart a vivid or lasting sensation of life. Henri Peyre stated that Maurois wrote family novels with only moderate success and that, in his opinion, the novels of Maurois will not survive as outstanding literary achievements.

Practically all of Maurois's writings are lauded for their clarity and precision; he is a thoroughly readable author no matter what his subject may be. His style of exposition is compressed, graceful, urbane—"exquisitely civilized." His irony and wit, charm and delight. His structure is neatly ordered and balanced; nothing is superfluous. Louis Chaigne said that Maurois "knows how to put silences between his sentences and in his sentences." One critic commented that he has "the gift of skimming lightly over the most difficult ground and so making everything seem extraordinarily easy and pleasant." One seldom gets the feeling that he is deeply immersed in the pathos of the human condition. Because of his detached restraint, his polished elegance, and his disinclination to offend, Maurois's works are often devoid of intensity and are reproached for their superficiality, pseudosophistication, and artificiality.

Despite the fact that Maurois's novels are more popular in France than in the United States, the French regard him primarily as an analyst and moralist, not as an exceptionally creative writer. In the late twenties the originality of his work was challenged in a series of articles in the *Mercure de France.* Lemaitre stated that "frequently it is possible to trace the essentials of his plots and characters to certain well-known and definite sources . . . [but Maurois] has in no case consciously adapted to his own use fragments of some other author's work." The full force of Maurois's imagination is seen best in his science fiction tales like *The Weigher of Souls* and *The Earth Dwellers* which hold the reader in a sustained state of suspense and almost force him to surrender his rational faculties. Maurois excelled as a storyteller and his *contes fantastiques* represent, according to Droit, an absolutely original genre in modern French literature.

In Maurois's own life one can discern a dichotomy between his artistic nature and his conservative bourgeois background and sympathies. As a spokesman of his social class he wrote that "a horror of disorder has always been one of my strongest emotions." Describing his own youth, he commented that he had been "Frivolous? Yes. Perhaps. But above all, a conformist, exactly the opposite of a rebel." Similarly, he saw man as a brutish animal that has been civilized only gradually by philosophers, priests, rituals, and by society in general. He therefore defended conventions in an age when they were being challenged, and believed that the rejection of traditional customs is tantamount to a return to savagery. This is not to say that Maurois opposed reform; but change, he contended, should come about slowly, in accordance with traditional roots, and under the aegis of a firm and just power. It follows that his criticism of present society and the bourgeoisie was muted. One sympathetic critic, Louis Chaigne, wrote that, in Maurois's works, "one would like a sharper, more vigorous reprobation of [middle class] conformism and prejudices."

Maurois neither subscribed to nor formulated any formal philosophic system. He was most frequently labeled an agnostic and, according to Michel Droit, he accepted only one absolute—that all truth is relative. Maurois nonetheless stated that he believed in "the existence in man of something which transcends man." "I am ready," he added, "to call this common conscience God, but my god is imminent not transcendent." The universe, he believed, is neither hostile nor moral. It does not determine man's destiny. The individual, rather, has the power to create his fate to the degree that he refuses to create his unhappiness. That is, if one accepts what cannot be altered and does not ask, in an Epicurean sense, too much of life, he will then be capable of reaching some level of happiness which Maurois thought was man's duty to do. He attributed his optimism and confidence to Alain, who taught him that "the human condition is such that if one does not adopt an attitude of invincible optimism, the blackest pessimism would at once be justified, because despair . . . engenders despair and failure."

Many of the particulars of Maurois's practical philosophy are contained in the essays which compose *The Art of Living*. These have been described by some critics as tolerant, urbane, and sensible, and by others as unreasonably reasonable, complacent, and opportunistic. Some critics also discounted him as a "literary factory," an allegation not altogether groundless. He told the *New York Times* a few months before his death at the age of eighty-two: "I get up at seven and am at my desk at eight and work all day long. I write every day except for Sunday. . . . The job of a writer is to write."

MEDIA ADAPTATIONS: The short story "Palace Hotel Thanatos" was adapted by Peter Halasz for the play "Ambition," first produced in New York City in 1987.

BIOGRAPHICAL/CRITICAL SOURCES:

BOOKS

Bakeless, John, *Andre Maurois,* Appleton, 1932.
Chaigne, Louis, *Vie et oeuvres d'ecrivains,* 1933.
Dictionary of Literary Biography, Volume 65: *French Novelists, 1900-1930,* 1988.
Droit, Michel, *Andre Maurois,* Editions Universitaires, 1953, revised edition, 1958.
Dupuis, Victor, *Un Ecrivain tonique: Andre Maurois,* Editions de l'Efficience (Lausanne), 1945.
Fillon, Amelie, *Andre Maurois, romancier,* [Paris], 1937.
Guery, Suzanne, *La Pensee d'Andre Maurois,* Deux Rives, 1951.

Larg, David G., *Andre Maurois,* Harold Shaylor (London), 1931.
Lemaitre, Georges, *Andre Maurois,* Stanford University Press, 1939.
Maurois, Andre, *Memoirs, 1885-1967,* translation by Denver Lindley, Harper, 1970.
Peyre, Henri, *The Contemporary French Novel,* Oxford University Press, 1955.
Roya, Maurice, *Andre Maurois,* Editions de la Caravelle, 1934.
Sauvenier, J., *Andre Maurois,* Editions de Belgique, 1932.
Suffel, Jacques, *Andre Maurois avec des remarques par Andre Maurois,* Flammarion, 1963.

PERIODICALS

Annales, May 15, 1928.
Biblio, June-July, 1965.
Le Correspondant, June 10, 1928.
Etudes, June 20, 1935, January 20, 1938.
Everyman, September 11, 1930, July 22, 1965.
Le Figaro Litteraire, June 3-9, 1965.
Hommes et Mondes, January, 1955.
Independent Review, December 17, 1927.
Life, January 19, 1948, October 4, 1954.
Living Age, July 3, 1926, July 12, 1926, April 15, 1928, July 5, 1928.
Manchester Guardian, July 26, 1965.
Mercure de France, March 1, 1928, April 1 and 15, 1928, May 1, 1928, June 1 and 15, 1928.
Newsweek, April 10, 1950.
New Yorker, January 26, 1963.
New York Herald Tribune Weekly Book Review, February 8, 1948.
New York Times, October 10, 1967.
New York Times Book Review, August 7, 1932, May 22, 1966, January 12, 1986.
La Nouvelle Critique, November, 1960.
Nouvelle Revue Francaise, September 1, 1937.
Paris-Soir, June 23, 1939.
Revue de Paris, February, 1958, May, 1959.
Saturday Review of Literature, September 6, 1919, July 21, 1928, September 7, 1929, April 24, 1937, September 5, 1953, May 5, 1956.
Sewanee Review, October, 1928.
Time, March 25, 1940, November 17, 1967.
Times (London), November 10, 1984.
Times Literary Supplement, April 21, 1932, December 2, 1960, August 13, 1964, September 27, 1985.
Washington Post Book World, September 9, 1984.

OBITUARIES:

PERIODICALS

Books Abroad, spring, 1968.
New York Times, October 10, 1967.
Publishers Weekly, October 23, 1967.
Time, October 20, 1967.
Times (London), October 10, 1967.

*   *   *

MAX

See DIOP, Birago (Ismael)

MAXWELL, Gavin   1914-1969

PERSONAL: Born July 15, 1914, in Mochrum, Scotland; died September 7, 1969, in Inverness, Scotland; son of Aymer Edward Maxwell (an Army officer) and Lady Mary Percy; married Lavinia Joan Lascelles, February 1, 1962 (divorced 1964). *Education:* Attended Stowe School, Buckinghamshire, England; Hertford College, Oxford University, M.A.

ADDRESSES: Home—Isle Ornsay Lighthouse, Isle of Skye; Kyleakin Lighthouse, by Kyle, Ross-shire, Scotland; and Sandaig, by Kyle of Lochalsh, Ross-shire, Scotland. *Agent*—Peter Janson-Smith, 2 Caxton St., London SW1, England.

CAREER: Portrait painter, 1949-52; writer, 1952—. Soay Shark Fisheries, owner, 1944-49. Member of advisory committee of Wildlife Youth Service of the World Wildlife Fund. Danilo Dolci Trust, trustee. *Military service:* Scots Guards, 1939-41, Special Operations Executive, 1941-44; invalided, 1944; became major.

MEMBER: Royal Society for Literature (fellow), Royal Geographic Society (fellow), Zoological Society (scientific fellow), American Geographic Society (fellow), P.E.N., Fauna Preservation Society, Wildfowl Trust (honorary life member), Special Forces Club, Guards Club, Puffin Club, Third Guards Club, Household Brigade Yacht Club.

AWARDS, HONORS: Heinemann Award of Royal Society for Literature for *A Reed Shaken by the Wind.*

WRITINGS:

Harpoon at a Venture, Hart-Davis, 1952, also issued as *Harpoon Venture,* Viking, 1952.
God Protect Me from My Friends, Longmans, Green, 1956, also issued as *Bandit,* Dutton, 1956.
A Reed Shaken by the Wind, Green, 1957, also issued as *People of the Reeds,* Dutton, 1957.
The Ten Pains of Death (Book Society selection), Longmans, Green, 1959.
Ring of Bright Water (Book Society and Book-of-the-Month Club selection), Dutton, 1960.
The Otter's Tale (adaptation for children of *Ring of Bright Water*), Dutton, 1962.
The Rocks Remain, Dutton, 1962.
(Contributor) J. Montgomery, editor, *The Pan Book of Animal Stories,* Pan Books, 1964.
The House of Elrig, Dutton. 1965.
Lords of the Atlas: The Rise and Fall of the House of Glaoua, 1893-1956, Dutton, 1966.
(With John Stidworthy and David Williams) *Seals of the World,* Constable, 1967, Houghton, 1968.
Raven Seek Thy Brother, Dutton, 1969.

Contributor to *New Statesman, Saturday Review, Twentieth Century, National Geographic, American Magazine of Natural History, Observer,* and other periodicals. Member of advisory panel, *Animals* Magazine.

WORK IN PROGRESS: Autobiography; anthologies.

SIDELIGHTS: Nora Magid says that "Gavin Maxwell wrote of himself that his nature was romantic, tinged with melancholy." And although his works have been labeled as melodramatic or as detective stories he is most often cited as a writer who studies and knows his subjects thoroughly. For instance, in order to write *Bandit,* as A. L. Fessler states, "the author has spent many months on [an] unhappy island, seeking the facts by resorting not only to published and unpublished sources, but by personally

visiting and getting to know many of the individuals involved." However, Maxwell's skill does not only lie in relating facts. Louis MacNeice says that *Harpoon Venture* "is a detailed factual record of something pregnant with symbols." And Kathleen Raine says he "writes as one who sees with the poetic eye of a naturalist." Peter Quennell concludes: "To each subject he has brought the same intelligence, the same love of natural beauty and the same gift of unfolding a lively and exciting tale."

Maxwell is competent in French and Italian.

MEDIA ADAPTATIONS: Ring of Bright Water was released as a film in 1969.

BIOGRAPHICAL/CRITICAL SOURCES:

PERIODICALS

Atlantic, August, 1968.
Best Sellers, March 1, 1969.
Book Week, January 30, 1966.
Books and Bookmen, December, 1967.
Christian Science Monitor, December 15, 1966.
Home, February, 1963.
Library Journal, March 15, 1956.
New Republic, June 16, 1952.
New Statesman and Nation, June 7, 1952.
Saturday Review, July 26, 1952.
Spectator, March 30, 1956.
Time, February 28, 1969.

OBITUARIES:

PERIODICALS

New York Times, September 9, 1969.
Publishers Weekly, October 13, 1969.
Times (London), September 8, 1969.

*   *   *

MAYO, Jim
See L'AMOUR, Louis (Dearborn)

*   *   *

McBAIN, Ed
See HUNTER, Evan

*   *   *

McCAFFREY, Anne (Inez)   1926-

PERSONAL: Born April 1, 1926, in Cambridge, Mass.; daughter of George Herbert (a city administrator and colonel, U.S. Army) and Anne D. (McElroy) McCaffrey; married H. Wright Johnson (in public relations), January 14, 1950 (divorced, 1970); children: Alec Anthony, Todd, Georgeanne. *Education:* Radcliffe College, B.A. (cum laude), 1947; graduate study in meteorology, University of City of Dublin; also studied voice for nine years. *Politics:* Democrat. *Religion:* Presbyterian.

ADDRESSES: Home—Dragonhold, Kilquade, Greystones, County Wicklow, Ireland. *Agent*—Virginia Kidd, Box 278, Milford, Pa. 18337.

CAREER: Liberty Music Shops, New York City, copywriter and layout designer, 1948-50; Helena Rubinstein, New York City, copywriter and secretary, 1950-52; author. Director of Fin

Film Productions, 1979—, and Dragonhold, Ltd. Former professional stage director for several groups in Wilmington, Del.

MEMBER: Science Fiction Writers of America (secretary-treasurer, 1968-70), Mystery Writers of America, Authors Guild, PEN (Ireland).

AWARDS, HONORS: Hugo Award, 1967, for *Dragonflight;* Nebula Award for best novella, Science Fiction Writers of America, 1968, for "Dragon Rider"; E. E. Smith Award for fantasy, 1975; American Library Association notable book citation, 1976, for *Dragonsong,* and 1977, for *Dragonsinger;* Hornbook Fanfare Citation, 1977, for *Dragonsong;* Ditmar Award (Australia), Gandalf Award, and Eurocon/Streso Award, all 1979, for *The White Dragon;* Balrog citation, 1980, for *Dragondrums;* Golden Pen Award, 1981; Science Fiction Book Club Award, 1986.

WRITINGS:

PUBLISHED BY BALLANTINE, EXCEPT AS NOTED

Restoree, 1967.
Dragonflight, 1968, hardcover edition, Walker & Co., 1969.
Decision at Doona, 1969.
The Ship Who Sang, Walker & Co., 1969.
(Editor) *Alchemy and Academe,* Doubleday, 1970.
Dragonquest: Being the Further Adventures of the Dragonriders of Pern, 1971.
The Mark of Merlin, Dell, 1971.
The Ring of Fear, Dell, 1971.
(Editor) *Cooking out of This World,* 1973.
To Ride Pegasus, 1973.
A Time When, Being a Tale of Young Lord Jaxom, His White Dragon, Ruth, and Various Fire-Lizards (short story), NESFA Press, 1975.
The Kilternan Legacy, Dell, 1975.
Dragonsong, Atheneum, 1976.
Get off the Unicorn (short stories), 1977.
Dragonsinger, Atheneum, 1977.
Dinosaur Planet, Futura, 1977, Ballantine, 1978.
The White Dragon, 1978.
Dragondrums, Atheneum, 1979.
The Dragonriders of Pern (contains *Dragonflight, Dragonquest,* and *The White Dragon*), Doubleday, 1978.
The Harper Hall of Pern (contains *Dragonsong, Dragonsinger,* and *Dragondrums*), Doubleday, 1979.
Crystal Singer, 1981.
The Worlds of Anne McCaffrey (stories), Deutsch, 1981.
The Coelura, Underwood-Miller, 1983.
Moreta: Dragonlady of Pern, Severn House, 1983, Brandywyne Books, 1984.
Dinosaur Planet Survivors, 1984.
Stitch in Snow, 1984.
Killashandra, 1985.
The Girl Who Heard Dragons, Cheap Street, 1985.
The Ireta Adventure (contains *Dinosaur Planet* and *Dinosaur Planet Survivors*), Doubleday, 1985.
Nerilka's Story, 1986.
The Year of the Lucy, Tor Books, 1986.
The Lady, 1987.
Dragonsdawn, 1988.
(Author of text) Robin Wood, *The People of Pern,* Donning, 1988.
Renegades of Pern, 1989.
(With Jody Nye) *The Dragonlover's Guide to Pern,* 1989.
Pegasus in Flight, Del Rey, 1990.

CONTRIBUTOR

Crime Prevention in the 30th Century, Walker & Co., 1969.
The Disappearing Future, Panther Books, 1970.
Infinity One, Lancer, 1970.
The Many Worlds of Science Fiction, Dutton, 1971.
Future Quest, Avon, 1973.
Ten Tomorrows, Fawcett, 1973.
Science Fiction Tales, Rand McNally, 1973.
Future Love, Bobbs-Merrill, 1977.
Cassandra Rising, Doubleday, 1978.
Visitors' Book, Poolbeg Press, 1980.

Contributor of fiction to magazines, including *Analog, Galaxy,* and *Magazine of Fantasy and Science Fiction.*

WORK IN PROGRESS: A book for Future.

SIDELIGHTS: Science-fiction's much-heralded "Dragon Lady," Anne McCaffrey, resides in Ireland in a home called Dragonhold, where she produces fantastic tales of the dragon-riders of Pern, a long-lost colony of Earth. In such novels as *Dragonflight, Dragonquest,* and *The White Dragon* McCaffrey presents Pern as a land in which "social structure, tensions, legends, and traditions are all based on the fundamental ecological battle and on the empathetic kinship between dragon and rider," Debra Rae Cohen comments in *Crawdaddy.*

Indeed, that kinship is not taken lightly. As described by *Washington Post* critic Joseph McLellan, "When the dragon eggs are ready to hatch on the planet Pern, it is a major social event with enduring, almost cosmic implications." In a form of permanent selection called "Impression," "each fledgling dragon struggles out of its shell, there is a predestined conjunction of souls; the dragon selects the young human who will be its lifemate, rushing to his or her side and bowling over anyone imprudent enough to stand in the way," McLellan indicates.

Many readers respond to McCaffrey's highly convincing use of scientific detail in her fables. The author in fact took supplementary courses in physics in order to create credible science fiction. But mostly it is the fanciful atmosphere of Pern, with its never-ending opportunity for adventure, that draws in fans. Not surprisingly, the dragons are the scene-stealers in McCaffrey's novels; they are described as large, multicolored, flying reptiles "who communicate telepathically with their riders and keep the land free from the vicious Threads, destructive spores that fall from a neighboring planet whenever its irregular orbit brings it close enough," according to Edra C. Bogle, writing in *Dictionary of Literary Biography.* In the same article, Bogle cites *Dragonquest,* the second volume of the Pern series, as "full of action and unexpected twists" and indicates that it "may well be the best of these books. The major theme of all the volumes, how to rediscover and preserve the past while maintaining flexibility, is well brought out here, but much of the action seems to be leading toward a resolution in the third book: the discovery that fire lizards [a close cousin of the dragons] were the ancestors of dragons and hints about their racial memory, the records discovered deep under the Weyr, the confusion of traditional class structures and sex roles, and the birth of a white dragon."

Behind these magical tales lies a serious social commentary, according to Bogle. "Most of McCaffrey's protagonists are women or children, whom she treats with understanding and sympathy," Bogle says. "The injustices imposed on these women and children by powerful men, aided by the social system, are at the heart of most of McCaffrey's books," and although McCaffrey doesn't explore these injustices directly, "the heroines do gain some independence," Bogle indicates, "and McCaffrey has brought delineations of active women into prominence in science fiction."

AVOCATIONAL INTERESTS: Singing, opera directing, riding and horse care.

BIOGRAPHICAL/CRITICAL SOURCES:

BOOKS

Authors in the News, Gale, 1976.
Bestsellers 89, Issue 2, Gale, 1989.
Contemporary Literary Criticism, Volume 17, Gale, 1981.
Dictionary of Literary Biography, Volume 8: *Twentieth-Century American Science Fiction Writers,* Gale, 1981.
Walker, Paul, *Speaking of Science Fiction: The Paul Walker Interviews,* Luna, 1978.

PERIODICALS

Crawdaddy, June, 1978.
Dallas News, March 25, 1976.
New York Times Book Review, August 29, 1982, January 8, 1984.
People, March 12, 1984.
Rigel, winter, 1982.
Science Fiction Review, fall, 1982.
Times Literary Supplement, March 14, 1975.
Washington Post, June 26, 1978.

*   *   *

McCANN, Arthur
     See CAMPBELL, John W(ood, Jr.)

*   *   *

McCANN, Edson
     See del REY, Lester and POHL, Frederik

*   *   *

McCARTHY, Mary (Therese)   1912-1989

PERSONAL: Born June 21, 1912, in Seattle, Wash.; died of cancer, October 25, 1989, in New York, N.Y.; daughter of Roy Winfield (a lawyer) and Therese (Preston) McCarthy; sister of the actor Kevin McCarthy; married Harold Johnsrud (an actor and playwright), June 21, 1933 (divorced August, 1936); married Edmund Wilson (a writer and critic), February, 1938 (divorced December, 1946); married Bowden Broadwater, December 6, 1946 (divorced, 1961); married James Raymond West (a U.S. State Department official), April 15, 1961; children: (second marriage) Reuel Kimball Wilson. *Education:* Vassar College, A.B., 1933. *Politics:* Libertarian socialist.

ADDRESSES: Home—141 rue de Rennes, Paris 6e, France; and Box 5, Castine, Me. 04421 (summer). *Agent*—A. M. Heath & Co. Ltd., 40-42 William IV St., London WC2N 4DD, England.

CAREER: Novelist, literary critic, and essayist. Founder while at Vassar, with Elizabeth Bishop, Muriel Rukeyser, and Eleanor Clark, of a literary magazine to protest the policies of the *Vassar Review* (the two magazines later merged). Book reviewer for the *Nation* and the *New Republic,* typist and editor for Benjamin Stolberg, and brochure writer for the proprietor of an art gallery, all New York, N.Y., 1933-36; Covici Friede (publishers), New York City, editor, 1936-37; ghostwriter for H. V. Kaltenborn, 1937; *Partisan Review,* New York City, editor, 1937-38, drama critic, 1937-62. Bard College, Annandale-on-Hudson, N.Y., in-

structor in literature, 1945-46, Stevenson Chair of Literature, 1986—; instructor in English, Sarah Lawrence College, Bronxville, N.Y., 1948; Northcliffe Lecturer, University College, University of London, 1980.

MEMBER: American Academy of Arts and Letters, Authors League of America, National Institute of Arts and Letters, Phi Beta Kappa.

AWARDS, HONORS: Horizon prize, 1949, for *The Oasis;* Guggenheim fellowship, 1949-50 and 1959-60; National Institute of Arts and Letters grant in literature, 1957; D.Litt., Syracuse University, 1973, University of Hull, 1974, Bard College, 1976, Bowdoin College, 1981, and University of Maine at Orono, 1982; LL.D., University of Aberdeen, 1979; President's Distinguished Visitor, Vassar, 1982; Edward MacDowell Medal, MacDowell Colony, 1984, for outstanding contributions to literature; National Medal for Literature, Harold K. Guinzburg Foundation, 1984, for a distinguished and continuing contribution to American letters; First Rochester Literary Award, 1985; nomination for book of the year award in criticism from National Book Critics Circle, 1986, for *Occasional Prose.*

WRITINGS:

FICTION

The Company She Keeps (novel), Simon & Schuster, 1942, reprinted, Avon, 1981, 2nd edition, Weidenfeld & Nicolson, 1957, reprinted, 1982.
The Oasis (novel; first published in *Horizon;* also see below), Random House, 1949, reprinted, Avon, 1981 (published in England as *A Source of Embarrassment,* Heinemann, 1950, reprinted, 1968).
Cast a Cold Eye (short stories; also see below), Harcourt, 1950, expanded edition published as *The Hounds of Summer and Other Stories: Mary McCarthy's Short Fiction,* Avon, 1981.
The Groves of Academe (novel), Harcourt, 1952, reprinted, Avon, 1981.
A Charmed Life (novel), Harcourt, 1955, reprinted, Avon, 1981.
The Group (novel), Harcourt, 1963, reprinted, Avon, 1980.
Winter Visitors (excerpt from *Birds of America;* also see below), Harcourt, 1970.
Birds of America (novel), Harcourt, 1971.
Cast a Cold Eye [and] *The Oasis,* New American Library, 1972.
Cannibals and Missionaries (novel), Harcourt, 1979.

NONFICTION

Sights and Spectacles, 1937-1956 (theater criticism), Farrar, Straus, 1956, augmented edition published as *Sights and Spectacles, 1937-1958,* Heinemann, 1959, augmented edition published as *Mary McCarthy's Theatre Chronicles, 1937-1962* (also see below), Farrar, Straus, 1963.
Venice Observed (also see below), Reynal, 1956, 2nd edition, 1957.
Memories of a Catholic Girlhood, Harcourt, 1957, reprinted, Penguin, 1975.
The Stones of Florence (also see below), Harcourt, 1959, reprinted, 1976.
On the Contrary (essays; also see below), Farrar, Straus, 1961, reprinted, Weidenfeld & Nicolson, 1980.
The Humanist in the Bathtub (selected essays from *Mary McCarthy's Theatre Chronicles, 1937-1962* and *On the Contrary*), New American Library, 1964.
Vietnam (reportage; also see below), Harcourt, 1967.
Hanoi (reportage; also see below), Harcourt, 1968.
The Writing on the Wall and Other Literary Essays, Harcourt, 1970.

Medina (reportage; also see below), Harcourt, 1972.

Venice Observed [and] *The Stones of Florence,* Penguin, 1972.

The Mask of State: Watergate Portraits (reportage), Harcourt, 1974.

The Seventeenth Degree (reportage; includes *Vietnam, Hanoi,* and *Medina*), Harcourt, 1974.

Ideas and the Novel (literary essays), Harcourt, 1980.

Occasional Prose (essays), Harcourt, 1985.

How I Grew (autobiography), Harcourt, 1987.

OTHER

(Translator) Simone Weil, *The Iliad; or, The Poem of Force,* Politics Pamphlets, 1947, reprinted, Stone Wall Press, 1973.

(Translator) Rachel Bespaloff, *On the Iliad,* Pantheon, 1948.

(Author of afterword) Jean-Francois Revel, *Without Marx or Jesus: The New American Revolution Has Begun,* Doubleday, 1971.

(Author of afterword) Neat Slavin, *Portugal,* Lustrum Press, 1971.

(Contributor) Giuseppe Verdi, *La Traviata,* Little, Brown, 1983.

Mary McCarthy's books have been translated into French, Spanish, Italian, Dutch, Finnish, Danish, Swedish, Romanian, Serbo-Croatian, Hebrew, Japanese, German, and Polish.

Contributor of essays to periodicals, including *New York Review of Books, New York Times Book Review, Observer, Partisan Review,* and *Sunday Times.*

SIDELIGHTS: As a novelist, literary critic, essayist, and autobiographer, Mary McCarthy seriously treated a wide range of topics, including the faults of the intellectual elite, the value of history and art, the need for political responsibility, the death of nature, and the fate of the novel. Whatever her subject, McCarthy confronted it with her characteristic critical sense, the cold eye and sharp tongue that earned her a position of prominence among American writers. "Her uniqueness," Doris Grumbach notes in *The Company She Kept: A Revealing Portrait of Mary McCarthy,* "lies partly in her readiness to do battle, her willingness to attack in every direction, without concern for the barriers of established reputation." The result of her approach, Paul Schlueter comments in *Contemporary American Novelists,* is that "she cuts beneath the layers of accumulated social pretense and hypocrisy, to the core of contemporary man and woman." Similarly, McCarthy's effort brought her to the heart of contemporary issues. "[This] need to strip away facades and to uncover what she considers to be the truth," Barbara McKenzie notes in her book *Mary McCarthy,* "is the result of the unusually high value she places on honesty."

With this honesty guiding her pen, McCarthy set out to restore to the individual the capacity for understanding. "All of us, she supposes, are engaged for a multitude of reasons in a conspiracy to escape reality, to tame and falsify it," writes Arthur Schlesinger, Jr., in the *New Republic.* In such a world, McCarthy explained in "Settling the Colonel's Hash" (collected in *On the Contrary*), "the writer must be, first of all, a listener and observer, who can pay attention to reality, like an obedient pupil, and who is willing, always, to be surprised by the messages reality is sending through to him." Armed with the lessons of reality, McCarthy exposed the falseness of what seems to be and illuminated, notes Schlesinger, the "reality [that] exists in the spontaneities and unpredictabilities of human experience."

As a student at Vassar during the early 1930s, McCarthy had studied Elizabethan literature with the hope of pursuing a career in the theater—the career that her brother Kevin would later make his own. Yet by the time of her graduation she was convinced that she was not an actress. She wrote in *Memories of a Catholic Girlhood:* "I had no talent. I gave up the dream that had been with me thirteen years. . . . I started to write instead, which did not interest me nearly so much, chiefly because it came easier." She began writing book reviews for the *Nation* and the *New Republic;* with these brief reviews, McCarthy quickly revealed her critical eye. The *Nation* enlisted her as co-author of a series of articles about the critics and book reviewers of several periodicals, including the *New York Herald Tribune,* the *New York Times,* and the *Saturday Review.* "Pointed sharply to the weaknesses, foolishness, and ineptitude of critics," Grumbach observes in *The Company She Kept,* these articles "suggested the very real injustices that stupid but compassionate critics committed against the public by recommending second-rate, weakminded pap and ignoring really excellent work."

Her work at the *Nation* earned McCarthy some recognition, but it was free-lance work. She found regular work as an editor for Covici Friede (John Steinbeck's publisher) from 1936 to 1937 and then joined the staff of *Partisan Review.* She worked as an editor for the magazine only until 1938, but she continued to contribute drama criticism in a column entitled "Theatre Chronicle" for several years. To this role of drama critic McCarthy would soon add that of short story writer, novelist, literary critic, and journalist.

Until she married her second husband, Edmund Wilson, in 1938, McCarthy had not given much consideration to the writing of fiction. But with Wilson's encouragement, she began to soon after their marriage. Rather than sacrifice her personal commitment to honesty in order to create fiction, McCarthy would develop a fiction style rooted in this honesty.

Her first novel came about when McCarthy noticed a relationship between several stories that she had originally written separately. She worked these stories into the same framework; the result was *The Company She Keeps.* The novel reveals Margaret Sargent, a young woman much like McCarthy herself, engaged in a quest for her one true identity. But more than this, observes Irvin Stock in *Fiction as Wisdom: From Goethe to Bellow, The Company She Keeps* conveys Sargent's moral dilemma, her "increasingly desperate struggle, against all the temptations to falsehood in the intellectual life of her time, to stop lying and to live by the truth." Because the novel parallels the life of its author, one might expect from it a measure of protective distortion; however, Stock notes, "The book is remarkable for the honesty of its self-exposure, an exposure which dares to include the ignoble and the humiliating and which shows a kind of reckless passion for the truth that is to remain an important element of [McCarthy's] talent."

By 1960 McCarthy had written three other novels, *The Oasis, The Groves of Academe,* and *A Charmed Life.* These novels established McCarthy as a writer with a keen critical sense, a social satirist whose eye focused on the intellectual elite. Together with *The Company She Keeps,* they received considerable attention in literary circles. Those critical of these novels cite too much autobiographical material within the fiction and a preoccupation with intellectuals and their ideas. McCarthy herself responded to the charge that her fiction is overly autobiographical in an interview with Elisabeth Niebuhr published in *Writers at Work: The "Paris Review" Interviews:* "What I really do is take real plums and put them in an imaginary cake. If you're interested in the cake, you get rather annoyed with people saying what species the real plum was." She elaborated, "I do try . . . to be as exact as possible about the essence of a person, to find the key that works the person both in real life and in the fiction." Commenting on McCarthy's portrayal of intellectuals and their ideas, Irvin Stock writes, "Though she has written mainly about her own class of American intellectuals, people who try to live by ideas or to give the appearance of doing so, and has, therefore, naturally admitted the play of ideas into her stories, her chief concerns have always been psychological, emotional, and above all, moral, the concerns of the novelist."

With the publication of *The Group,* her 1963 novel, McCarthy became known to a wider audience. This novel, which chronicles the lives of a group of Vassar graduates from the time of their graduation until seven years later, became a best-seller and was made into a motion picture starring Candice Bergen and Joan Hackett. Because the book details the lives of eight upper-middle-class women, their careers, loves, and sexual attitudes, it was accused by some reviewers of playing up to the women's magazine audience. Norman Mailer, writing in the *New York Review of Books,* calls the novel "good but not nearly good enough." Mailer recognizes the value of *The Group* as a sociological study, and he admits: "It is skillful, intricately knitted as a novel, its characters while not always distinguishable from one another are true in their reactions, or at least are true in the severe field of limitation she puts on their comings and goings, their paltry passions, their lack of grasp, their lack of desire to grasp." Even so, he faults McCarthy for not following through on her theme. He comments, "She failed out of profound timidity. . . . She is afraid to unloose the demons." He adds, "Nice girls live on the thin juiceless crust of the horror beneath, the screaming incest, the buried diabolisms of the grand and the would-be-grand. . . . Yet Mary is too weak to push through the crust and so cannot achieve a view of the world which has root." Stock agrees that *The Group* has its shortcomings, but in his opinion the book is a pleasure to read. He notes, "The pleasure comes from the characters (most of them), so pathetic and comic, so true, in their struggle to live up to their advanced ideas or to cling to reality amid the general falsenesses; from the continuous vivifying detail of their setting, appearance, tone, and gesture; and from the sheer quantity of people and experiences the story brings to life."

McCarthy's deeply felt personal concern for the fate of nature is the central issue of her sixth novel, *Birds of America.* The author told Jean-Francois Revel in an interview for the *New York Times Book Review:* "Nature for centuries has been the court of appeals. It will decide one way or another. Not always justly; but nevertheless . . . the appeal is always to this court, to Nature's court. And if this is gone, we're lost. And I think we're lost, I'm not an optimist." Irvin Stock discusses how *Birds of America* illustrates McCarthy's pessimism in his book *Fiction as Wisdom:* "The tragedy at the heart of her novel is not only that Nature is dead, but that it has been murdered by an ideal she also values, the ideal of Equality." Stock adds that the servant of equality, technology, has not only "replaced Nature . . . with life-reducing conveniences and abstractions, but, far worse, by giving man control over what once controlled and educated him, it has put our whole world at the mercy of the ego-driven human will."

Birds of Prey follows nineteen-year-old Peter Levi, student and bird watcher, from the coast of New England, where he and his mother are spending the summer, to Paris, the site of Peter's foreign studies. In New England Peter discovers that the great horned owl that had captivated him during a previous visit is dead. Gone also is the quaint old-fashioned atmosphere of the small town, replaced by the technology of the 1960s. Paris is no better; it is alien and as an environment, unnatural. When Peter retreats to a zoo upon learning of the bombing of North Vietnam, he is struck by a black swan. Later, having been rushed to

the hospital, Peter sees Kant appear in his hospital room. His mentor tells him, "Nature is dead, *mein kind.*" "The didacticism of Miss McCarthy's theme in no way blunts her wit," writes a *Times Literary Supplement* reviewer; "indeed, the challenge of the *philosophes* and the attempt to make her Candide a convincingly likable as well as serious fall-guy hero seem to have stimulated her into some of the funniest scenes she has ever written."

The critical debate surrounding *Birds of America* has often centered on the characters in the book. Some reviewers find Peter Levi and the others who populate his world inadequately developed and unbelievable. "No creature more devoid of existential reality ever lived than this so-carefully-documented Peter Levi," comments Helen Vendler in the *New York Times Book Review.* The weakness of the characters is due, in Hilton Kramer's opinion, to a flaw in their creator. Kramer writes in the *Washington Post Book World,* "She lacks the essential fictional gift: She cannot imagine *others.* . . . Missing from the powerful arsenal of her literary talents is some fundamental mimetic sympathy." The result, Vendler adds, is that "stereotypes take over where her own knowledge leaves off." John Thompson expresses a different opinion in his review in *Commentary.* "This mother and her son [are] two people liked very much and found completely credible." And of Peter Levi, Foster Hirsch writes in *Commonweal,* "At the beginning of the novel, his idealizing vision is truly innocent, at the end, it is open-eyed, alert to the world: that he retains his sense of the potential fineness of life is his (and the book's) special triumph."

As *Birds of America* reflects the social turbulence of the war in Vietnam, McCarthy's next novel, *Cannibals and Missionaries,* reflects the political unrest of the 1970s. McCarthy's novel "is pure pleasure," Doris Grumbach notes in the *Chicago Tribune Book World,* "a psychological thriller, a suspense story, a brilliant ideological parable, all wrapped in a strong coat of the kind of witty and intelligent talk she has always been capable of." While confronting one of the central issues of our time, terrorism and the psychology of terror, McCarthy also offered for scrutiny another older question, as Robert M. Adams puts it, "the value of major works of art, relative to human life." In examining these issues, Adams writes in the *New York Review of Books,* "McCarthy writes crisp, unsentimental prose, with a cruel eye for weakness and inauthenticity."

In *Cannibals and Missionaries,* a group of liberal politicians and concerned citizens are on their way to Iran to investigate accusations that the Shah's secret police are engaged in the torture of dissidents. On the same flight, in first class, is a group of wealthy art collectors. Terrorists hijack the airplane, hoping to use the liberals as bargaining chips, but in time they realize that the collectors are more valuable. A scheme is concocted to exchange the collectors for their most precious possessions; an irreplaceable work of art, the terrorists reason, will command a higher price than any human hostage. *Cannibals and Missionaries* captures the tension of the hijack situation, observes Anne Tyler in her *Washington Post Book World* review: "There are the psychological quirks that the hostages show under stress: unexpected examples of cowardice and bravery, comic adherences to the old 'normal' rituals, illogical urges to protect the terrorists from defeat."

As with *Birds of America, Cannibals and Missionaries* has been faulted by some reviewers because of McCarthy's manipulation of the elements of the novel. "As a work of fiction," writes an *Atlantic* reviewer, "*Cannibals and Missionaries* suffers from a lack of focus. The characters are maddeningly banal." "Her cast is so large," adds *Time* reviewer R. Z. Sheppard, "that

[McCarthy] is forced to try to bring them to life with unwieldy dossiers rather than with dialogue and action."

Other reviewers, however, regarded *Cannibals and Missionaries* in terms of its thematic concerns. In the *Times Literary Supplement,* for example, T. J. Binyon notes, "This is very much a novel of ideas." In presenting ideas, in confronting issues and uncovering their underlying implications, McCarthy challenged the reader. "A remorseless, powerful intellect has burst open the seams of the novelist's kid glove," writes Binyon. "No longer allowed to laze in the groves of fiction, we are forced to exercise our minds on a series of philosophic problems." *New York Times Book Review* contributor Mary Gordon believes "the most important achievement of *Cannibals and Missionaries* is McCarthy's understanding of the psychology of terrorism, the perception that terrorism is the product of despair." Gordon concludes, "In response to the truly frightful prospect of anarchic terrorism, Mary McCarthy has written one of the most shapely novels to have come out in recent years: a well-made book. It is delightful to observe her balancing, winnowing, fitting in the pieces of her plot."

Given her high regard for truthfulness, McCarthy's approach to writing fiction is not surprising. She wrote in "Settling the Colonel's Hash" from *On the Contrary:* "Every short story, at least for me, is a little act of discovery. A cluster of details presents itself to my scrutiny, like a mystery that I will understand in the course of writing or sometimes not fully until afterward, when, if I have been honest and listened to these details carefully, I will find that they are connected and that there is a coherent pattern. This pattern is *in* experience itself; you do not impose it from the outside and if you try to, you will find that the story is taking the wrong tack, dribbling away from you into artificiality or inconsequence."

But as McCarthy pointed out in the *New York Times Book Review,* the author needs more than an accepting and understanding eye; the author also needs faith. McCarthy commented: "In any novel (in my experience) there is a crisis of faith for the author. This generally occurs toward the end of Chapter Two, when the first impetus has gone; occasionally in Chapter Three. . . . The crisis can last a night or a few hours; with 'The Group' it lasted years, during which I put the manuscript aside, thinking I would never go back to it. There is no use going on till the crisis is resolved. A moment comes, though, about three-quarters of the way through the book, when you know you are going to finish it; this is the moment when it has gained your belief."

As an author capable of understanding the lessons of reality and faithful to the vision of that reality contained in her writing, McCarthy was able to offer readers poignant insights into the nature of modern humans. As Stock writes in *Fiction as Wisdom,* "Though Mary McCarthy's novels are not all equally successful, each has so much life and truth, and is written in a prose so spare, vigorous, and natural, and yet at the same time so witty, graceful, and, in a certain way, poetic, that it becomes a matter for wonder that she is not generally named among the finest American novelists of her period."

In the late 1960s McCarthy interrupted a novel in progress to take action against the war in Vietnam. "Though she had tried to hide behind a novelist's detachment . . . Vietnam [had] finally gotten inside her and produced an 'identity crisis,' " Lee Lockwood observes in the *Nation.* McCarthy visited Southeast Asia twice; she traveled to Saigon in 1967 and later, in 1968, she went to Hanoi. McCarthy wrote several essays based upon these trips. The essays first appeared in the *New York Review of Books;*

they were later collected in her books *Vietnam* and *Hanoi.* "Her moral sensibility . . . led her to Vietnam where she experienced the anguish of societies in war," writes Marcus Raskin in the *Partisan Review.* "She was not there as an adventurer or as a journalist. She was there as a committed person who happened to write. Her visit to Vietnam led her to believe that the American system itself was decaying."

McCarthy not only opposed the war, she rejected its purpose, an opinion upon which she expounded in an exchange with Diana Trilling published in the *New York Review of Books:* "Nor frankly do I think it admirable to try to stop Communism even by peaceful subversion. The alternatives to Communism offered by the Western countries are all ugly in their own ways and getting uglier. What I would hope for politically is an internal evolution in the Communist states toward greater freedom and plurality of choice." Her first trip, to a Saigon filled with the by-products of an American presence, prompted her to write in *Vietnam:* "The worst thing that could happen to our country would be to win this war." As she commented in her exchange with Trilling "On Withdrawing from Vietnam," "The imminent danger for America is not of being 'taken in.' by Communism . . . but of being taken in by itself. If I can interfere with that process, I will."

McCarthy's criticism of the American war effort that appeared in *Vietnam* was well received by reviewers. "This is tight and excellent writing, and constitutes perhaps the most piercing wound delivered to America's conception of itself since the war," writes Neal Ascherson in the *Listener.* From McCarthy's essays on Vietnam, a sort of literary journalism, emerges a truth that exceeds that obtained from the mere reporting of facts. Ascherson comments, "She is not the first to record the grotesque terminology of the war, but as a professional with words, her understanding of what these phrases actually mean, as well as of what they conceal, is unrivalled."

Her essays reveal the physical products of the war—the pollution of the jungle, the squalor of the refugee camp—as well as the malaise that accompanies its inefficiency and corruption. Yet, despite her preconceived mission to return from her trip with "material damaging to the American interest," she refrained from prescribing quick remedies. "McCarthy wisely does not offer a solution," observes George Woodstock in *Canadian Forum.* "That the war is too appalling, too materially destructive to the Vietnamese, too morally destructive to the Americans, for it to be continued; this is what she sets out to present." Woodstock concludes, "Her argument on this point is a model lesson in the need to keep great moral issues simple and sharp to the point."

McCarthy found a much different environment when she visited North Vietnam in 1968. Her essays published in *Hanoi* convey her view of the contrast between the North and the South. Moved by what she saw, McCarthy strengthened her demand for an American withdrawal. Tom Buckley finds in *Hanoi* evidence that McCarthy's experience affected her position as a dispassionate observer. He writes in the *Washington Post Book World,* "The clear voice has been muted, indeed almost strangled, by rage and shame over the bombing of North Vietnam and by the author's compassion and admiration for its people and its leaders." Buckley adds, "The author's protective attitude toward the North Vietnamese, her expressed concern to do or say nothing that might prove injurious to them, seem excessive." Similarly, Peter Shaw indicates in *Commentary* that McCarthy's bias distorts her image of the situation. "When, in Mary McCarthy's books, a corrupt, Americanized South Vietnam and its people is contrasted with a utopian, inspiriting North," Shaw notes, "it becomes impossible for the most sympathetic reader, if he has the slightest sensitivity to the truth, not to mistrust the reality of what is being described." Concludes Ward Just in the *Washington Post*, "This book is very shrill and very polemical, and as a result is almost useless as a guide to North Vietnam."

In 1971 McCarthy attended the trial of Captain Ernest L. Medina, Lieutenant William Calley's company commander in 1968 when South Vietnamese civilians were massacred at My Lai. The trial and Medina's acquittal furnished McCarthy with the material for her third book of essays on the Vietnam War. In *Medina,* comments Fredrica S. Friedman in the *Saturday Review,* McCarthy "uses the trial of Capt. Medina to comment on America's resolution of the issue of wartime guilt." She focused on the former soldiers who testified and on the proceedings more than she did on the defendant, offering in her literary journalism her vision of what happened. "The novelist's cold eye surveys the scene and in the language that made her famous, she freezes the protagonists in their failures and venalities and evasions," Stephen Koch writes in the *Nation*.

As Basil T. Paquet notes in the *New York Review of Books,* McCarthy's "keen moral sensibility" allows her to see not only what happened but also the underlying significance of this trial. From *Medina,* he observes, "what emerges is not a document that vilifies the rather shallow figures of the trial but a polemic that tries to pull us closer to recognition of the nature of our involvement in this action." Such is the value of this style of reporting indicates Friedman: "In her fine-drawn observations on the ineptness of the prosecution and, more importantly, on the country's psyche at that time, she adds to our understanding."

In a review of *The Seventeenth Degree* (a collection of the essays previously published in *Vietnam, Hanoi,* and *Medina*) and of *The Mask of State: Watergate Portraits,* Harold Rosenberg discusses how McCarthy's approach to journalism, founded upon her dedication to honesty, succeeded where others fail. During the war in Vietnam and the Senate Watergate hearings, Rosenberg believes, "The problem was not to gather the 'news' but to get behind it or see through it." He observes in the *New York Review of Books,* "The news media, applying their traditional techniques, could only present a mixture of data and distortion." McCarthy, by seeing through to the meaning behind the facts, succeeded in capturing the social impact of that period. "Her constantly sparking style makes historical events as tangible to her readers as they are to her, instead of pushing off these events into the dead space of the media," observes Rosenberg. Writing in the *New York Times Book Review,* Richard Goodwin calls McCarthy "one of America's finest journalists."

McCarthy's commitment to honesty—her intolerance of deception and distortion—served as the standard for her critical writing. McCarthy first found an opportunity to exercise her critical talents in the book reviews she wrote for the *Nation* and the *New Republic* and then more regularly in her "Theatre Chronicles" for *Partisan Review.* "Although a Trotskyist view of art's relationship to society provided a foundation for her remarks about current theatrical productions," Julian Symons points out in *Critical Occasions,* "it was her native wit and sharp perceptiveness that made these monthly chronicles the most notable dramatic criticism of the period." These essays were first collected and published in book form in 1956 as *Sights and Spectacles, 1937-1956.*

On the Contrary, which contains social commentary as well as literary criticism, appeared in 1961, but her first book devoted exclusively to literary criticism was *The Writing on the Wall and Other Literary Essays,* published in 1970. Reviewing this book in *Esquire,* Malcolm Muggeridge comments, "Like all her writing in this genre, [*The Writing on the Wall* is] extremely readable, if at times vaguely irritating; a characteristic blend of shrewd observations, imaginative insight and occasional lapses into naivete." In this collection of essays, McCarthy offered her views of a large selection of literary works and their authors—William Shakespeare, Gustave Flaubert, Hannah Arendt, William Burroughs, George Orwell, J. D. Salinger, and others. "She certainly locates that 'false and sentimental' element in Salinger but her attack on Orwell is patently unfair and sometimes silly," writes Derek Stanford in *Books and Bookmen.* "Orwell has been called 'the conscience of his generation,' " Stanford points out, "and one has the feeling that Miss McCarthy is revolting against that conscience when she writes the title essay of her book upon him."

McCarthy found more with which to identify in the writing of Ivy Compton-Burnett, a novelist whose works are essentially observations of upperclass life in pre-World War I England. McCarthy noted, "What flashes out of her work is a spirited, unpardoning sense of injustice, which becomes even sharper in her later books. In her own eccentric way, Compton-Burnett is a radical thinker, one of the rare modern heretics." McCarthy also viewed favorably the work of some of the experimental novelists of the twentieth century, including Nathalie Sarraute, Monique Wittig, and Vladimir Nabokov. "She calls Nabokov's 'Pale Fire' 'one of the very great works of this century' and, with awesome powers of explication, supported by scholarly resources, shows why," writes a *Newsweek* contributor.

Although there are reviewers who find fault with the opinions and conclusions McCarthy expressed in *The Writing on the Wall,* they agree for the most part that it is a valuable addition to critical literature. *New York Times* writer Christopher Lehmann-Haupt comments: "Her prose is economical without being austere, witty without extravagance, tense and dramatic in its development from sentence to paragraph, clean as a chime. . . . Her intelligence and learning are dazzling." Moreover, Diana Loercher observes in the *Christian Science Monitor,* "This group of essays would be interesting even if one had not read the authors, for Miss McCarthy is superb at provoking thought well beyond the ostensible subject." Loercher concludes, "McCarthy deserves credit for the rectitude of her criticism, for she clearly possesses the verbal skill to be captious and vicious, but she has chosen to style herself as a champion of truth rather than a dragoness of destruction."

Ideas and the Novel offers McCarthy's vision of the modern novel and its fate. She had long considered that the tendency of the modern novel is to minimize the role of the traditional elements: plot, character, and setting. These novels also show a low regard for facts. And finally, the central point of *Ideas and the Novel,* ideas are for the twentieth-century author "unsightly in a novel." McCarthy believed that the modern novelist, taking Henry James as a model, feels a duty "to free himself from the workload of commentary and simply, awesomely, to show: his creation is beyond paraphrase or reduction."

McCarthy felt that the followers of James have over-aestheticized the novel. As John Leonard points out in the *New York Times,* the novel has lost its sense of audience, its sense of place, and its sense of society. "What [McCarthy] mourns most," he says, "is a modern failure of curiosity, a missing texture. The details are what make life interesting; ideas are what makes the brain interesting; plot implies that something happens, and something always does."

To emphasize her dissatisfaction with the novel since James, McCarthy contrasted the twentieth-century novel with its nineteenth-century counterpart. For McCarthy, the novels of Dostoevsky and other nineteenth-century novelists reveal the "fascination of ideas." The vision of empire created by Napoleon permeates these novels, affecting them, and informing them. The authors of these books were highly regarded by their readers; she notes that at that time the author was considered "an authority on . . . medicine, religion, capital punishment, the right relations between the sexes."

Ideas and the Novel has received a mixed response. Loosely defined terms and too much devotion of space to plot summaries are cited as weak points by some reviewers. Others find the book self-indulgent or judgmental. Yet, notes Herbert Gold in the *Los Angeles Times Book Review,* "sometimes she has seemed malevolent in judgment . . . but at her best she is redeemed by wit, cogency, conviction." Moreover, reviewers admit McCarthy does remind the reader of the value of the traditional elements of the novel; she did much to restore the acceptability of a close relationship between the idea and the novel. She also expressed her feeling that "emergency strategies [are necessary] to disarm and disorient reviewers and teachers of literature, who as always," she wrote, "are the reader's main foe." Gold concludes, "It's a pleasure to praise this mind as it casts about elegantly in the desire to understand a matter congenial to her and important to all good readers and serious writers."

McCarthy wrote on a broad range of subjects in a number of different forms, and in each case she proved her ability to cut through the surface clutter to expose the underlying reality. As Mary Gordon writes, "McCarthy's voice has always been reliable; the stirring and disturbing tone of the born truth-teller is hers, whether she is writing essays or fiction." McCarthy died of cancer in 1989.

MEDIA ADAPTATIONS: The Group was filmed by United Artists in 1966.

BIOGRAPHICAL/CRITICAL SOURCES:

BOOKS

Brightman, Carol, *American Heretic: The Life, Work, and Times of Mary McCarthy,* Clarkson N. Potter, in press.
Contemporary Literary Criticism, Gale, Volume 1, 1973, Volume 3, 1975, Volume 5, 1976, Volume 14, 1980, Volume 24, 1983, Volume 39, 1986.
Dictionary of Literary Biography, Volume 2: *American Novelists Since World War II,* Gale, 1978.
Dictionary of Literary Biography Yearbook: 1981, Gale, 1982.
Gelderman, Carol W., *Mary McCarthy: A Life,* St. Martin's, 1988.
Grumbach, Doris, *The Company She Kept: A Revealing Portrait of Mary McCarthy,* Coward, 1976.
McCarthy, Mary, *Memories of a Catholic Girlhood,* Harcourt, 1957, reprinted, Penguin, 1975.
McCarthy, Mary, *On the Contrary,* Farrar, Straus, 1961, reprinted, Weidenfeld & Nicolson, 1980.
McCarthy, Mary, *How I Grew,* Harcourt, 1987.
McKenzie, Barbara, *Mary McCarthy,* Twayne, 1966.
Moore, Harry T., editor, *Contemporary American Novelists,* Southern Illinois University Press, 1964.
Stock, Irvin, *Fiction as Wisdom: From Goethe to Bellow,* Pennsylvania State University Press, 1980.
Stock, Irvin, *Mary McCarthy,* University of Minnesota Press, 1968.
Symons, Julian, *Critical Occasions,* Hamish Hamilton, 1966.
Writers at Work: The "Paris Review" Interviews, second series, Viking, 1963.

PERIODICALS

Atlantic, July, 1971, November, 1979.
Best Sellers, March 1, 1970, June 15, 1971.
Books and Bookmen, August, 1970.
Canadian Forum, February, 1968.
Chicago Tribune, March 30, 1980.
Chicago Tribune Book World, October 14, 1979.
Christian Science Monitor, March 12, 1970.
Commentary, July, 1969, June, 1970, October, 1971, May, 1981.
Commonweal, September 3, 1971, December 21, 1979.
Descant, fall, 1968.
Esquire, October, 1970.
Globe and Mail (Toronto), May 16, 1987.
Hudson Review, spring, 1972, spring, 1980, spring, 1981.
Life, May 21, 1971.
Listener, November 2, 1967.
Los Angeles Times, May 13, 1985.
Los Angeles Times Book Review, November 23, 1980, May 10, 1987.
Modern Fiction Studies, winter, 1981.
Nation, March 24, 1969, September 18, 1972, November 10, 1979, May 19, 1984.
National Review, October 8, 1971, May 16, 1980, August 8, 1980.
New Leader, January 20, 1969, March 2, 1970.
New Republic, October 9, 1961, February 28, 1970.
New Statesman, September 17, 1971, March 6, 1981.
Newsweek, February 16, 1970, October 8, 1979.
New York Review of Books, January 18, 1968, March 13, 1969, August 13, 1970, June 3, 1971, September 21, 1972, October 31, 1974, October 25, 1979.
New York Times, February 9, 1970, May 19, 1971, July 31, 1979, October 4, 1979, November 18, 1980, April 13, 1987, September 23, 1987.
New York Times Book Review, October 17, 1963, November 26, 1967, March 8, 1970, May 16, 1971, August 13, 1972, June 30, 1974, September 30, 1979, November 25, 1979, May 11, 1980, January 18, 1981, May 5, 1985, April 19, 1987.
New York Times Magazine, March 29, 1987.
Observer Review, May 24, 1970.
Partisan Review, winter, 1975.
People, November 12, 1979.
Saturday Review, May 8, 1971, July 15, 1972, December, 1979.
Spectator, November 15, 1968, May 23, 1970, November 3, 1979.
Time, October 1, 1979, April 15, 1985.
Times Literary Supplement, November 9, 1967, January 16, 1969, June 4, 1970, September 17, 1971, March 16, 1973, December 7, 1979, March 6, 1981, September 18, 1987.
Village Voice, February 11, 1981.
Washington Post, November 21, 1968, August 21, 1971.
Washington Post Book World, December 1, 1968, October 14, 1979, November 30, 1980, May 12, 1985, April 5, 1987.

OBITUARIES:

PERIODICALS

Chicago Tribune, October 26, 1989.
Detroit Free Press, October 26, 1989.
New York Times, October 26, 1989.
Washington Post, October 26, 1989.

McCORQUODALE, Barbara
  See CARTLAND, Barbara (Hamilton)

         *   *   *

McCREIGH, James
  See POHL, Frederik

         *   *   *

McCULLERS, (Lula) Carson (Smith) 1917-1967

PERSONAL: Born February 19, 1917, in Columbus, Ga.; died September 29, 1967, in Nyack, N.Y.; buried in Oak Hill Cemetery, Nyack, N.Y.; daughter of Lamar (a jeweler) and Marguerite (Waters) Smith; married Reeves McCullers, September 20, 1937 (divorced, 1940); remarried McCullers, March 19, 1945 (committed suicide, 1953). *Education:* Attended Columbia University and New York University, 1935-36.

CAREER: Writer; also held various jobs. "I was always fired," McCullers once said. "My record is perfect on that. I never quit a job in my life."

MEMBER: American Academy of Arts and Letters (fellow).

AWARDS, HONORS: Fiction fellowship, Houghton Mifflin, 1939; Guggenheim fellow, 1942 and 1946; National Institute of Arts and Letters grant in literature, 1943; New York Drama Critics Circle Award, two Donaldson Awards, and the Theatre Club, Inc. gold medal, all 1950, all for the stage adaptation of *The Member of the Wedding;* prize of the younger generation from German newspaper *Die Welt,* 1965, for *The Heart Is a Lonely Hunter.*

WRITINGS:

The Heart Is a Lonely Hunter (also see below), Houghton, 1940.
Reflections in a Golden Eye (also see below), Houghton, 1941.
The Member of the Wedding (also see below), Houghton, 1946.
(Librettist) *The Twisted Trinity,* [Philadelphia], 1946.
The Member of the Wedding: A Play (based on McCullers's novel of the same title; produced in New York at the Empire Theatre, January 5, 1950), New Directions, 1951.
The Ballad of the Sad Cafe: The Novels and Stories of Carson McCullers (includes *The Ballad of the Sad Cafe* [also see below; first published serially in *Harper's Bazaar,* 1943], *The Heart Is a Lonely Hunter, Reflections in a Golden Eye,* and *The Member of the Wedding*), Houghton, 1951, published as *The Ballad of the Sad Cafe and Other Stories,* Bantam, 1967, (published in England as *The Shorter Novels and Stories of Carson McCullers,* Barrie & Jenkins, 1972).
Collected Short Stories and the Novel, The Ballad of the Sad Cafe (also see below), Houghton, 1955.
The Square Root of Wonderful (produced in New York at the National Theatre, October 30, 1957), Houghton, 1958.
Clock Without Hands, Houghton, 1961.
(Author of narration) Edward Albee, adaptor, *The Ballad of the Sad Cafe* (based on McCullers's novel of the same title; produced on Broadway at the Martin Beck Theatre, October 30, 1963), Atheneum, 1963.
Sweet as a Pickle and Clean as a Pig (poems for children), Houghton, 1964.
The Mortgaged Heart: The Previously Uncollected Writings of Carson McCullers, edited by Margarita Smith, Houghton, 1971.
Collected Stories of Carson McCullers, Houghton, 1987.

Contributor to *O'Henry Memorial Prize Stories of 1942* and *Best Plays of 1949-1950.*

SIDELIGHTS: A prominent member of the Southern gothic school, Carson McCullers wrote of lonely, alienated, and sometimes grotesque characters who symbolize man's essential isolation and the failure of interpersonal communication. As McCullers explained in an essay in *The Mortgaged Heart: The Previously Uncollected Writings of Carson McCullers,* "spiritual isolation is the basis of most of my themes." Much of McCullers's fiction is autobiographical, reflecting her Southern upbringing, her chronic ill health, and her troubled marriage. Though her world is filled with "conflict, frustration, grief, pain, and fear . . ., the mood is seldom morbid or bitterly melancholy," Louise Y. Gossett wrote in *Violence in Southern Fiction.* Gossett saw love as the primary motif in McCullers's writings and emphasized McCullers's compassion for her characters: "The author is charitable toward the violence and grotesqueness which develops when the impulse to love goes astray, and she treats deviation more with mercy than with horror."

In *The Heart Is a Lonely Hunter, Reflections in a Golden Eye, The Ballad of the Sad Cafe,* and *The Member of the Wedding,* McCullers's unique and disturbing vision is most vividly expressed. These novels have assured her literary reputation as one of the outstanding Southern novelists of this century. Tennessee Williams told the *New York Times,* "I regarded her as the greatest living prose writer and the greatest prose writer that the South produced." In his *The Modern Novel,* Walter Allen gave his opinion that, "[William] Faulkner apart, the most remarkable novelist the South has produced seems to me Carson McCullers."

Born and raised in Georgia, McCullers spent her childhood in the small Southern town of Columbus. Her mother, convinced that Carson was a genius, encouraged her daughter to pursue her creative interests. This encouragement led McCullers to take piano lessons beginning at the age of five. She showed such promise that it was thought that she might pursue a music career. At the age of seventeen, she was sent to the Juilliard School of Music in New York City, but because of poor health she did not attend classes. She instead studied writing at Columbia University, taking night classes while working a variety of jobs during the day. One of her teachers, Whit Burnett, arranged to have her first story published in *Story* magazine. An autobiographical work entitled "Wunderkind," it tells of a fifteen-year-old girl's realization that she is not, after all, a musical prodigy. When she subsequently drops her music lessons, she finds that she loses her circle of musical friends and the special parental treatment she had enjoyed. The story's sense of adolescent loss and insecurity prefigures such later works as *The Heart Is a Lonely Hunter* and *The Member of the Wedding.*

At the age of twenty-three, McCullers had her first book published, a novel entitled *The Heart Is a Lonely Hunter.* Set in a small Southern town similar to the one in which she was raised, the novel is "filled with impressions out of [McCullers's] childhood," as Richard M. Cook wrote in *Carson McCullers.* "It creates," Cook continued, "a richly detailed, integrated vision of the private and public life of a small Georgian town." The novel tells the story of deaf-mute John Singer, who finds himself the confidant of four disparate townspeople—a radical, a black doctor, a restaurant owner, and an adolescent girl. Each one is dissatisfied with small town life and yearns for escape. Each, too, is estranged from and unable to communicate with other people. Singer's silence is reassuring to them. When they speak to him (Singer reads their lips), they believe that he understands and cares about them. But in truth Singer seldom understands what he is told. He listens to be polite. The four characters, Cook explained, are "desperate for understanding from those around them, and tragically incapable of rendering the kind of love and understanding each of the others need." When Singer's only friend, a mute named Antonapoulous, dies, Singer commits suicide. His death forces those who confided in him to continue their lives without the essential emotional outlet Singer unknowingly provided.

The adolescent girl of the novel, Mick Kelly, is based on McCullers, and her story is "a fable about inescapable loneliness," Robert F. Kiernan wrote in the *Dictionary of Literary Biography.* Mick has dreams of someday conducting an orchestra, but her family's poverty limits her opportunity to achieve this goal. When, to help support her family, Mick is obliged to leave school to take a job in a dime store, she knows that this step means the end of her dreams. She will never be able to leave the dime store job. "One feels that Mick, once a fascinating, bright youngster, will grow up an unhappy, neurotic woman," Cook commented, "and that the loss involved in such a growing up is tragic."

Mick's story is representative of the emptiness and failure of the novel's other characters. Jake Blount, the political radical, is frustrated by his inability to relieve the poverty he sees around him; the black doctor, Benedict Copeland, is unable to fulfill his dream of leading the struggle for racial reform; and restaurant owner Biff Brannon has grown increasingly passive and withdrawn since the death of his wife. "Each character," Kiernan observed, "is dominated by a fixed set of ideas that makes it impossible for them to reach communion with others. Indeed, the characters are convinced they are doomed to solitude, and, out of their frustration, they tend to make antisocial gestures that compound their isolation."

Most critics saw the characters in *The Heart Is a Lonely Hunter* as grotesques in the tradition of the Southern gothic school, "a school supposedly concerned with the grotesque and the abnormal [and] with an outlandish love for the morbid," as Jane Hart wrote in the *Georgia Review.* But Hart emphasized the "tenderness" of McCullers's presentation of her characters. "Her vision," Hart believed, "is a clear, compassionate one of people spiritually isolated each from the other. . . . If she has used the grotesque it is because the loneliest of all human souls is found in the abnormal and deformed, the outward and manifest symbol of human separateness." Louis D. Rubin, Jr., writing in the *Virginia Quarterly Review,* also saw the symbolic nature of McCullers's characters. They were not meant to be, Rubin wrote, "a commentary upon the complacent 'normality' of the community which would term them freakish, but as exemplars of the wretchedness of the human condition." Similarly, in his *The Ballad of Carson McCullers,* Oliver Evans held that McCullers made Singer a deaf-mute "because of his symbolic value." Through Singer, McCullers suggests "that what men see in other men whom they admire or love is not what is 'really' there but what they wish to find. . . . It ought to be obvious that the more grotesque and repulsive a character is who is yet capable of inspiring love in another, the more forcefully he illustrates this thesis," Evans wrote. In *The Mortgaged Heart,* McCullers clarified her symbolic intentions. "Love," she wrote, "and especially love of a person who is incapable of returning or receiving it, is at the heart of my selection of grotesque figures to write about—people whose physical incapacity is a symbol of their spiritual incapacity to love or receive love—their spiritual isolation." W. P. Clancy of *Commonweal* thought that critics who labeled McCullers's work as gothic missed "the essential point." Clancy saw McCullers as "the artist functioning at the very loftiest symbolic level, and if one must look for labels [one] should prefer to call her work 'metaphysical.' Behind the strange and horrible in her

world there are layed out the most sombre tragedies of the human spirit."

An acclaimed best seller, *The Heart Is a Lonely Hunter* established McCullers's literary reputation. B. R. Redman of the *Saturday Review of Literature* thought it "an extraordinary novel to have been written by a young woman of twenty-two; but the more important fact is that it is an extraordinary novel in its own right." Another contemporary reviewer, Rose Feld of the *New York Times,* found that McCullers wrote "with a sweep and certainty that are overwhelming. 'The Heart Is a Lonely Hunter' is a first novel. One anticipates the second with something like fear. So high is the standard she has set. It doesn't seem possible that she can reach it again." Later evaluations of the book placed it among the most important works of its time. Writing in *Twentieth Century Literature,* Joseph R. Millichap called the novel "an impressive achievement" and believed that it "provides a critical perspective for viewing Mrs. McCullers' other works, and perhaps for the whole expanse of modern Southern fiction." At the time of McCullers's death in 1967, Eliot Fremont-Smith of the *New York Times* called *The Heart Is a Lonely Hunter* a "remarkable, still powerful book."

Reflections in a Golden Eye, McCullers's second novel, did not meet many of the critical expectations raised by *The Heart Is a Lonely Hunter.* This disappointment was due in part to its scandalous subject matter. As Margaret Clark complained in the *Boston Transcript,* the book "is too preoccupied with the morbid and bizarre to be the important work everyone was expecting."

The story is set on a Southern army base in the 1930s and concerns, as McCullers wrote in the book, "two officers, a soldier, two women, a Filipino, and a horse." One officer, Captain Penderton, is impotent, bisexual, and a sadomasochist; the other, Major Langdon, is a charming womanizer who is having an affair with Penderton's wife. Langdon's own wife, so distraught over the death of their son that she has cut off her nipples with a garden shear, befriends the homosexual houseboy Anacleto. Private Williams, who takes his sexual pleasure with Mrs. Penderton's horse, Firebird, attracts the homosexual attention of Captain Penderton. But when Penderton finds that Williams spies on his wife as she sleeps, he murders Williams. "In almost any hands," the *Time* critic commented, "such material would yield a rank fruitcake of mere arty melodrama. But Carson McCullers tells her tale with simplicity, insight, and a rare gift of phrase."

As in her first novel, McCullers wrote in *Reflections in a Golden Eye* of "the utter alienation of individual nature and the absence of reciprocity in human relationships," Kiernan believed. McCullers's effort was met with a mixed critical reception, however. Basil Davenport, writing in the *Saturday Review of Literature,* for example, found the novel to be a "vipers'-nest of neurasthenic relationships among characters whom the author seems hardly to comprehend, and of whose perversions she can create nothing." In his review for the *New Yorker,* Clifton Fadiman also found shortcomings. "McCullers was herself in her first novel," Fadiman wrote. "In her second effort she seems to be borrowing from her reading of others. This mimicry gives an effect of falseness which is further strengthened by her too obvious desire to create people and situations that are strange and startling." But Dayton Kohler saw merit in *Reflections in a Golden Eye,* pointing out in *College English* that the book is more "restricted and intense" than its predecessor. This quality results in "speed and concentration, and the reader has a feeling of powerlessness before this swift unfolding of physical violence and psychological horrors. But *Reflections in a Golden Eye* is more than a simple chronicle of violence. The book is an example of the planned novel, with every detail and symbol deliberately created and plotted. Story, character, and setting exist as one great metaphor."

Reflections in a Golden Eye was written during a troubled period in McCullers's life. Her marriage to Reeves McCullers was on the brink of collapse. Reeves had taken a male lover; McCullers soon found a female lover. The book, Kiernan observed, "was McCullers' imaginative response to [the] disintegration [of her marriage]." The hopelessness of the novel, the feeling that the characters are "beyond redemption as valuable, living personalities," as Cook described it, comes from McCullers's own sense of despair at this time. In 1940, shortly after finishing the book, McCullers divorced her husband and moved to Brooklyn to live with George Davis, the editor of *Harper's Bazaar.*

McCullers also began work on a new novel in 1940, *The Member of the Wedding.* She was to work on this book intermittently until 1946. In 1943, taking a break from this work, McCullers completed her long novella *The Ballad of the Sad Cafe.* This was published serially in *Harper's Bazaar* that year and was published in book form in the 1951 omnibus volume *The Ballad of the Sad Cafe: The Novels and Stories of Carson McCullers.* Called by Irving Howe in the *New York Times Book Review* "one of the finest novels ever written by an American," *The Ballad of the Sad Cafe* is regarded by many as McCullers's most accomplished work. Evans maintained that it alone justified McCullers's "position among the half dozen or so who comprise the highest echelon of living American writers."

The Ballad of the Sad Cafe is the story of Amelia Evans, who falls in love with the hunchback Lymon and, inspired by this love, opens a cafe in her Southern town. The cafe flourishes, providing a much-needed meeting place for the townspeople. But when Amelia's husband, Marvin Macy, is released from prison and returns home, Lymon falls in love with him. This love triangle leads to a fist fight between Amelia and Marvin which only ends when Lymon joins in and the two men best Amelia. They then tear up her cafe before leaving town together. The loss of her lover and the destruction of the cafe cause Amelia to withdraw from the world.

Critics have pointed out that it is McCullers's style that allows *The Ballad of the Sad Cafe* to transcend its violent and sometimes bizarre story. "The bare incidents, stripped of the narrator's poetic presentation, are ugly, ludicrous, even repulsive; no paraphrase could ever begin to convey their significance, much less their beauty," Albert J. Griffith wrote in the *Georgia Review.* Griffith concluded that "in context, the grotesqueness remains but is turned towards a purpose, becomes part of a whole which is not grotesque, transcends the human and moves into the numinous." McCullers's use of a nameless narrator, Kiernan believed, "casts the aura of folklore over the tale: the characters become archetypes rather than grotesques, and their story becomes something elemental, mysterious, and suggestive." Robert Phillips, writing in *Southwest Review,* maintained that McCullers's writing style, "lyrical and colloquial, lucid and enigmatic, at one and the same time," presents the character of Amelia "like an image seen in a carnival mirror, an exaggerated, comically distorted, and yet somehow sadly accurate reflection of ourselves." This presentation, distancing and intimate at the same time, creates "an extraordinarily subtle relationship between character and reader," Phillips concluded.

Several critics hold *The Ballad of the Sad Cafe* in high esteem. Griffith concluded his analysis of the book by saying that McCullers had successfully "elevated her primitive characters and

their grotesque actions to the wild, extravagant, and beautiful level of myth." John McNally, writing in the *South Atlantic Bulletin,* judged the book to be "a beautifully sculptured piece of writing" and "a song of the human spirit." And writing in his introduction to *Reflections in a Golden Eye,* Tennessee Williams referred to *The Ballad of the Sad Cafe* as "assuredly among the masterpieces of our language."

In 1946, McCullers finished and published her novel *The Member of the Wedding.* It concerns Frankie Addams, an adolescent girl in a small Southern town who feels acutely isolated from other people. "Doesn't it strike you as strange that I am I, and you are you? . . ." Frankie asks the black maid Berenice at one point in the novel. "We can look at each other, and touch each other, and stay together year in and year out in the same room. Yet always I am I, and you are you. And I can't ever be anything else but me, and you can't ever be anything else but you." This feeling of isolation moves Frankie to fantasize that her older brother's upcoming wedding will also include her, joining her with the married couple, whom she calls "the we of me." But her attempt at the wedding to ride along in the newlyweds' car is stopped by her father, who pulls her away, and Frankie comes to realize that to be human is to be forever alone. *The Member of the Wedding,* Jerry Bryant wrote in *The Open Discussion,* "is descriptive, showing what occurs to people who happen to be born into life. There is nothing we can 'do' to modify that life in its basic characteristics and hence we must content ourselves with separateness and the peculiar freedom that accompanies that separateness."

In this novel, McCullers handles the question of loneliness, George Dangerfield noted in the *Saturday Review of Literature,* "in its most undifferentiated form; places it in this light and in that; looks at it savagely, gleefully, tenderly; seems almost to taste it and to roll it round her tongue; but never attempts to find an answer." This analysis of loneliness takes place during the extended kitchen conversations between Frankie, the black maid Berenice, and the sickly six-year old boy John Henry. As Berenice tries to dissuade Frankie from joining the married couple, the three characters discuss the loneliness that is the nature of life. "And this," Marguerite Young observed in *Kenyon Review,* "is almost all that ever happens in the book but enough to keep the sensitive reader appalled to hear meaning after meaning dissolve, while the old problems continue." Their discussion ends with the three of them crying together, each for his own private reasons: Frankie because she cannot join her brother and his wife; Berenice because she has no husband; and John Henry because he is soon to die. "The scene dramatizes the sad fact of human existence—the impossibility of ever filling up consciousness without turning it into something else, the necessity of remaining separate, and most important, the beauty of sharing these human deprivations," Bryant wrote. Although Frankie is not able to achieve the union she imagined, she has found in Berenice a friend who understands her problems, and so the novel offers some hope for her future.

The Member of the Wedding has been compared to *The Heart Is a Lonely Hunter* because both novels are chiefly concerned with human isolation and the efforts to overcome it. Whereas *The Heart Is a Lonely Hunter* relates this problem to the larger issues of politics and race, *The Member of the Wedding* "dramatizes the more personal, private problems arising out of isolation by examining its effect on the consciousness of a single individual, Frankie Addams," Cook stated. Because of this narrowed focus of concern, some critics have found the novel less satisfying than its predecessor and a retreat from the larger issues previously raised. But Frederic Carpenter, writing in the *English*

Journal, thought that *The Member of the Wedding* provided a better insight into its adolescent character than did *The Heart Is a Lonely Hunter,* relating her pain to that of the other characters in a more effective manner. Carpenter stated that "by contrast, *The Heart Is a Lonely Hunter* seems hardly to describe adolescence at all. The youthful Mick Kelly appears a background figure, observing and partly sharing the tragedies of the deaf-mutes, the Negroes, and the labor agitators."

As in previous books, McCullers used the characters in *The Member of the Wedding* in a symbolic manner to confront the issue of human isolation. Dangerfield described the book as "a serious, profound, and poetic masquerade" in which aspects of McCullers's own unconscious speak through the three primary characters. It is "a monologue furnished with figures," Dangerfield wrote, pointing out that McCullers "seems to invest the various sides of her personality with attributes skillfully collected from the outside world." Dangerfield concluded that *The Member of the Wedding* is "a marvelous piece of writing" and "a work which reveals a strong, courageous, and independent imagination." Young stressed that McCullers treated her characters with "dignity and revealing tenderness" and that the novel's deeper concerns flowed naturally from their actions. "The metaphysical," Young wrote, "grows out of the immediate and returns to it, made no less rich because its origin is known." Young described McCullers as a "poetic symbolist, a seeker after those luminous meanings which always do transcend the boundaries of the stereotype, the conventional, and the so-called normal."

The Member of the Wedding received critical and popular acclaim. Rumer Godden, writing in the *New York Herald Tribune Book Review,* called it "a masterpiece" and pointed out that it has become "universally popular." But it was McCullers's last acclaimed novel. After its publication in 1946, only her omnibus volume *The Ballad of the Sad Cafe: The Novels and Stories of Carson McCullers* and her stage adaptation of *The Member of the Wedding,* produced on Broadway in 1950, were successful. The stage play ran for 501 performances and won several prestigious drama awards, including the New York Drama Critics Circle Award and two Donaldson Awards. It also was included in the *Best Plays of 1949-1950.* It is, Kiernan wrote, "one of the outstanding adaptations of a novel in the history of the American theatre." But although this stage adaptation "established her reputation as a playwright," Sara Nalley noted in the *Dictionary of Literary Biography,* McCullers was to write only one other play. *The Square Root of Wonderful,* produced in New York in 1957 and published in 1958, was a failure. Her last novel, *Clock Without Hands,* received few favorable reviews when it appeared in 1961.

McCullers's deteriorating health and personal difficulties hampered her later career and contributed to the decline of her writing. Because of a series of strokes in 1947, she lost the vision in her right eye and was partially paralyzed. She had great difficulty walking and could type only with one hand, averaging one page per day. In 1948, despondent over her health, McCullers attempted suicide; the failure of this attempt cured her from ever trying again. But her husband Reeves, whom she had divorced in 1940 and remarried in 1945, became increasingly suicidal. Upset by their unstable marriage and his inability to find a suitable career, Reeves began suggesting a double suicide to McCullers while they were living in Europe in 1953. McCullers became so frightened by her husband's insistence on suicide that she fled back to the United States alone. A few weeks later Reeves killed himself in a Paris hotel with an overdose of sleeping pills. McCullers's life continued to be plagued by tragedy. Her mother, with whom she lived after her return to the United States, died

in 1955; and in 1961, McCullers underwent surgery for breast cancer. Following another stroke in 1967 McCullers died in Nyack, New York, at the age of fifty.

Rubin pointed out that *The Heart Is a Lonely Hunter, Reflections in a Golden Eye, The Ballad of the Sad Cafe,* and *The Member of the Wedding*—all written during her twenties—were McCullers's major works, and "a very impressive body of fiction indeed. Nothing that she wrote in the remaining two decades of her life adds much to her achievement." Her vision of human isolation as expressed in this relatively small body of work has insured McCullers's continuing reputation. Hers is "a vision seen with sympathy. McCullers transforms her isolated eccentrics and disturbed children into human beings who seem not all that different from us," Cook wrote. Writing in *Critical Occasions,* Julian Symons agreed. After noting McCullers's interest in the symbolic, Symons wrote: "It is her triumph that from her preoccupation with freaks and with human loneliness she makes fictions which touch and illuminate at many points the world to which all art makes, however obliquely, its final reference: the world of literal reality." Perhaps the most flattering evaluations of McCullers's work have come from other writers. Tennessee Williams wrote in his introduction to *Reflections in a Golden Eye,* for instance, that he had "found in her work such intensity and nobility of spirit as we have not had in our prose writing since Herman Melville." Gore Vidal, writing in the *Reporter,* concluded that McCullers's "genius for prose remains one of the few satisfying achievements of our second-rate culture."

MEDIA ADAPTATIONS: The Member of the Wedding was filmed by Columbia in 1952, *Reflections in a Golden Eye* by Seven Arts in 1967, and *The Heart Is a Lonely Hunter* by Warners-Seven Arts in 1968.

BIOGRAPHICAL/CRITICAL SOURCES:

BOOKS

Allen, Walter, *The Modern Novel,* Dutton, 1964.

Bryant, Jerry, *The Open Decision,* Free Press, 1970.

Carr, Virginia Spencer, *The Lonely Hunter: A Biography of Carson McCullers,* Doubleday, 1975.

Clurrnan, Harold, *Lies Like Truth,* Macmillan, 1958.

Contemporary Literary Criticism, Gale, Volume 1, 1973, Volume 4, 1975, Volume 10, 1979, Volume 12, 1980.

Cook, Richard M., *Carson McCullers,* Ungar, 1975.

Dictionary of Literary Biography, Gale, Volume 2: *American Novelists Since World War II,* 1978, Volume 7: *Twentieth-Century American Dramatists,* 1981.

Edmonds, Dale, *Carson McCullers,* Steck-Vaughn, 1969.

Eisenger, Chester E., *Fiction of the Forties,* University of Chicago Press, 1963.

Evans, Oliver, *The Ballad of Carson McCullers,* Coward, 1966.

Gossett, Louise Y., *Violence in Recent Southern Fiction,* Duke University Press, 1965.

Graver, Lawrence, *Carson McCullers,* University of Minnesota Press, 1969.

Hassan, Ihab, *Radical Innocence: Studies in the Contemporary American Novel,* Princeton University Press, 1961.

Kazin, Alfred, *Bright Book of Life: American Novelists and Storytellers From Hemingway to Mailer,* Little, Brown, 1973.

Kiernan, Robert F., *Katherine Anne Porter and Carson McCullers: A Reference Guide,* G. K. Hall, 1976.

Malin, Irving, *New American Gothic,* Southern Illinois University Press, 1962.

McCullers, Carson, *Reflections in a Golden Eye,* Houghton, 1941.

McCullers, Carson, *The Member of the Wedding,* Houghton, 1946.

McCullers, Carson, *The Mortgaged Heart: The Previously Uncollected Writings of Carson McCullers,* edited by Margarita Smith, Houghton, 1971.

McDowell, Margaret B., *Carson McCullers,* Twayne, 1980.

Moore, Harry T., editor, *Contemporary American Novelists,* Southern Illinois University Press, 1964.

Schorer, Mark, *The World We Imagine,* Farrar, Straus, 1969.

Seven American Women Writers of the Twentieth Century, University of Minnesota Press, 1977.

Symons, Julian, *Critical Occasions,* Hamish Hamilton, 1966.

Weales, Gerald, *American Drama Since World War II,* Harcourt, 1962.

PERIODICALS

Books, February 16, 1941.

Books Abroad, summer, 1968.

Boston Transcript, June 8, 1940, February 15, 1941.

Bucknell Review, spring, 1973.

Bulletin of Bibliography, April, 1959, September-December, 1964.

Christian Century, January 10, 1968.

College English, October, 1951.

Commonweal, May 24, 1946, June 15, 1951, October 13, 1961.

Dalhousie Review, autumn, 1974.

English Journal, September, 1957.

Georgia Review, spring, 1957, Number 12, 1958, Number 16, 1962, spring, 1967, winter, 1968, fall, 1973, spring, 1974.

Jahrbuch fuer Amerikastudien, Number 8, 1963.

Kenyon Review, winter, 1947.

Literature and Psychology, Number 17, 1967.

Los Angeles Times, August 21, 1987.

Mademoiselle, September, 1948.

Modern Fiction Studies, Number 5, 1959.

Nation, July 13, 1940.

New Republic, August 5, 1940.

New Statesman and Nation, August 2, 1952.

New Yorker, February 15, 1941, March 30, 1946.

New York Herald Tribune Book Review, June 23, 1940, September 17, 1961.

New York Times, June 16, 1940, March 2, 1941, January 6, 1950, July 14, 1987.

New York Times Book Review, March 2, 1941, June 10, 1951, November 7, 1971.

Reporter, September 28, 1961.

Saturday Review, November 13, 1971.

Saturday Review of Literature, June 8, 1940, February 22, 1941, March 30, 1946.

South Atlantic Bulletin, November, 1973.

South Atlantic Quarterly, Number 56, 1957.

Southern Literary Journal, fall, 1972, spring, 1977.

Southwest Review, winter, 1978.

Studies in Short Fiction, winter, 1973.

Time, February 17, 1941, April 1, 1946.

Tribune Books (Chicago), July 26, 1987.

Twentieth Century Literature, April, 1965, January, 1971, January, 1974.

Virginia Quarterly Review, spring, 1977.

Wisconsin Studies in Contemporary Literature, Number 1, 1960, fall, 1962.

Yale Review, autumn, 1940.

OBITUARIES:

PERIODICALS

Antiquarian Bookman, October 23, 1967.

Books Abroad, spring, 1968.

National Observer, October 2, 1967.

Newsweek, October 9, 1967.

New York Times, September 30, 1967.

Publishers Weekly, October 9, 1967.

Time, October 6, 1967.

*   *   *

McCULLOCH, John Tyler
See BURROUGHS, Edgar Rice

*   *   *

McCULLOUGH, Colleen   1938(?)-

PERSONAL: Born c. 1938 in Wellington, New South Wales, Australia; married Ric Robinson (a housepainter), April 13, 1984. *Education:* Attended University of Sydney.

ADDRESSES: Home—Norfolk Island, Australia. *Agent*—Frieda Fishbein Ltd., 353 West 57th St., New York, N.Y. 10019.

CAREER: Worked as a teacher, a library worker, and a bus driver in Australia's Outback; journalist; Yale University, School of Internal Medicine, New Haven, Conn., associate in research neurology department, 1967-76; writer, 1976—.

WRITINGS:

Tim (novel), Harper, 1974.
The Thorn Birds (novel; Literary Guild selection), Harper, 1977.
An Indecent Obsession (novel), Harper, 1981.
An Australian Cookbook, Harper, 1982.
A Creed for the Third Millennium (novel), Harper, 1985.
The Ladies of Missalonghi (novel), Harper, 1987.
The First Man in Rome (novel), Morrow, 1990.

Contributor to magazines.

WORK IN PROGRESS: A series of historical novels entitled "The First Man in Rome."

SIDELIGHTS: "I always write books with peculiar themes: I don't like writing about boy meets girl, boy loses girl, boy gets girl," best-selling author Colleen McCullough told Kay Cassill in a *Publishers Weekly* interview. The plots of McCullough's novels back her statement: in *Tim,* a middle-aged businesswoman becomes romantically linked with a twenty-five-year-old, mentally retarded man; *The Thorn Birds* turns on a frustrated love between a young woman and a Roman Catholic cardinal; *An Indecent Obsession*'s heroine, a war nurse to battle-fatigued soldiers, is tacitly engaged to one of her patients and sexually attracted to another. Such ingenious story lines, combined with a talent for what Christopher Lehmann-Haupt calls in the *New York Times* "good old-fashioned story telling," have made McCullough's books appeal to millions of readers.

McCullough, a native of Australia, first aspired to a career as a physician but could not afford the necessary tuition. She taught in the Outback, drove a school bus, worked as a librarian and finally qualified as a medical technician specializing in neurophysiology. It was in this position that she eventually came to work at Yale University. In the evenings, she wrote—but not with an eye toward publication. "I always wrote to please myself," she told Cassill. "I was a little snobby about it—that way I could write entirely as I wished. To write for publication, I thought, was to prostitute myself." Once McCullough decided to approach writing commercially, however, she did so very systematically. "I sat down with six girls who were working for me. They were very dissimilar types, and not especially avid readers. Yet, they were all mad about Erich Segal's *Love Story.* I thought it was bloody awful and couldn't see what girls so basically intelligent could love about it. I asked them what they wanted most out of a book. First, they liked the idea that *Love Story* was about ordinary people. They didn't want to read about what was going on in Hollywood and all that codswallow, and they wanted something with touches of humor. Yet they enjoyed books that made them cry. . . . If you didn't cry the book wasn't worth reading. . . . So, I said, 'That's it, mate. No matter what else you do in a book, don't forget the buckets of tears.' " McCullough had a story in mind that would conjure "buckets of tears," a grand romance set mostly on a sheep ranch. She knew, however, that this tale—which would eventually be published as *The Thorn Birds*—would be lengthy, and that "no one would publish such a long book as a first novel. So I wrote *Tim.*"

Tim is a "novel of awakenings," according to a *Publishers Weekly* writer, "a lovely and refreshing addition to tales of love." Its two central characters are Mary Horton and Tim Melville. In her climb from an orphanage to success as a mining executive, forty-five-year-old Mary has developed her discipline and self-sufficiency to a high degree but has ignored her emotions. Tim arrives at her home one day to do some yard work. He catches her eye, for he is strikingly handsome. Eventually she learns that this attractive young man is "without the full quid"—that is, he is mentally retarded. First Tim's beauty then his gentle innocence draw Mary to him, unsettling her rigidly ordered world. This unusual pair experience first love together. When Tim faces being left without a family to care for him, Mary realizes that marriage could be fulfilling and practical for both of them. She must then decide if she has the courage to take such an unconventional step.

Tim was well received by critics. A *New York Times Book Review* contributor praises the story's "delightful freshness," and Margaret Ferrari, writing in *America,* remarks upon McCullough's sensitive treatment of her subject matter: "There are many genuinely touching moments in the novel. . . . Its language is clear and direct, full of colorful Australian slang. McCullough's feeling for character, from major to minor, is compassionate yet concise. They are without exception well-rounded and believable. Her delicacy is perfectly suited to the story. . . . *Tim* is a warm book to read, reassuring about goodness in human nature and about the power of love to overcome worldly obstacles and to make us care more for another person's interests than for our own." A *Publishers Weekly* reviewer calls Colleen McCullough's "telling of the story . . . accomplished, sensitive, and wise." The author herself is less generous than most reviewers in describing her first novel. "It's an icky book," she told Cassill, "a saccharine-sweet book." In spite of this negative assessment, she was pleased by its success. "I made $50,000 out of *Tim,* which wasn't bad for a first novel, and I thought I'd always be a middle of the road, modest selling, respectable novelist," said McCullough to Phillipa Toomey in the London *Times.*

Having established herself as a good risk in the publishing world, she began to work intensely at getting that long novel she had already "written in her head" down on paper. It was *The Thorn Birds,* a multigenerational saga of the Cleary family and their life on an Australian sheep station named Drogheda. McCullough focuses on three Cleary women: Fiona, her daughter, Meggie,

and Meggie's daughter, Justine. Meggie is loved by Ralph de Bricassart, an ambitious Catholic priest who has known her since her childhood. When he leaves the Outback for the Vatican, Meggie enters into an unhappy marriage that produces one child, Justine. When Father Ralph visits Drogheda many years later, he and Meggie consummate their love. Her second child, a son named Dane, is born nine months later. Meggie keeps the knowledge that she has borne Ralph's son secret, but it makes the boy especially beloved to her. When the child grows up, he, like his father, becomes a priest and leaves Drogheda for Rome; Justine goes to England to become the toast of the London stage.

McCullough was still working full time at Yale while drafting this story and so had to confine her writing to the evenings. She spent such long hours sitting at the typewriter that her legs became swollen; she took to wearing elbow-length evening gloves to keep her fingers from blistering and her arms from chafing against her desk. These efforts paid off: she wrote the first two drafts of *The Thorn Birds* in three months, churning out 15,000-word blocks of prose nightly. After working at this pace for a year, the final draft was completed. It was 1,000 pages long and weighed ten pounds. McCullough felt that its hefty size was justified; in her interview with Cassill, she declared, "If an editor had seen *Thorn Birds* in manuscript and 'just loved it,' but suggested it would make a better book if I cut it to a nice 300-page story, I'd have simply said, 'Get stuffed, mate.' "

Her editors made no such suggestion. Sensing that *The Thorn Birds* had the potential to be a major best-seller, they prepared its release carefully and backed it with an extensive publicity campaign. By the time the book became available to the general public, the publishing industry was abuzz with excitement over its prospects; paperback rights had been sold for a then-record price of $1.9 million. This faith and investment in the book were well rewarded, for *The Thorn Birds* has sold over half a million copies in hardcover and more than seven million copies in paperback. The book was clearly a hit with the reading public.

Some reviewers quickly dismissed the popularity of *The Thorn Birds* as a tribute to marketing rather than a reflection of the book's worth. Amanda Heller denounces McCullough's novel as "awesomely bad" in *Atlantic Monthly.* "The writing is amateurish, all adjectives and exclamation points. The dialogue is leaden. . . . The characters are mechanical contrivances that permit the plot to grind along without encountering much resistance." And Paul Gray, while admitting in *Time* that "McCullough knows how to stage convincing droughts, floods and fires" declares that she "has not made literature. For a season or so, her book will make commercial history."

Alice K. Turner counters negative assessments of *The Thorn Birds* with praise for the novel's value as entertainment. "To expect *The Thorn Birds* to be a Great Book would be unfair," she suggests in the *Washington Post.* "There are things wrong with it, stock characters, plot contrivances and so forth. But to dismiss it would also be wrong. On its own terms, it is a fine, long, absorbing popular book. It offers the best heart-throb since Rhett Butler, plenty of exotic color, plenty of Tolstoyan unhappiness and a good deal of connivance and action. Of its kind, it's an honest book." Eliot Fremont-Smith further praises McCullough's engaging style in the *Village Voice:* "Her prose, even when stately, owes little to any formula; it is driven by a curiosity of mind, a caring for the subject, and some other great energy within the author that in turn, at one remove, spurs the reader on. *The Thorn Birds* didn't make me laugh and weep, and I could put it down. It is, after all, a romance, and very long. But then

I kept picking it up again, more times than can be accounted for by any sense of duty. A fine book."

Both Fremont-Smith and Turner express admiration for McCullough's vivid characterizations. "McCullough does make her characters and their concerns come alive," asserts Fremont-Smith. "She gives them (the leads particularly, and Ralph most of all) intelligence and complexity and dimension. Even the minor characters are not dull." Elaborating on the priest's role in the story, Turner writes, "Very few novels spotlight a Roman Catholic priest as a sex symbol, but Father Ralph's bravura performance in this one rivals the landscape for originality. Father Ralph is simply yummy. . . . And, of course, he is out of the running, which gives the author plenty of opportunity to dangle him as an erotic tease." "Actually, Ralph was supposed to be a minor character," explained McCullough in her *Publishers Weekly* interview. "Yet, when I was planning it in my head I was aware I didn't have a dominant male lead. The minute the priest walked into the book I said, 'Ah ha, this is it. This is the male character I've lacked!' But I had to keep him in the story and, logically, he didn't belong in it. The only way I could do it was to involve him emotionally with Meggie, the only woman available. It worked beautifully because again it made more interesting reading to have a love that couldn't be fulfilled. It kept the reader going."

The solid success of *The Thorn Birds* made it almost inevitable that McCullough's next books would be compared with it. "When you produce a book which is well loved—and people do love it—it's a very hard book to bury," noted the author in the London *Times*. Although she believes "a lot of writers keep feeding people the same book," McCullough stated in a *New York Times Book Review* interview with Edwin McDowell that she had "decided long ago . . . to have a bash at different kinds of books." Her third novel, *An Indecent Obsession,* certainly differs from its predecessor in many ways; while *The Thorn Birds* spanned three continents and most of a century, *An Indecent Obsession* is set entirely within the confines of a ward of a South Pacific army hospital near the end of World War II. The drama centers on the tension between Honour Langtry, Ward X's nurse, and her group of "troppo" patients—soldiers who have snapped under the strain of tropical jungle fighting. Many reviewers characterized *An Indecent Obsession* as a more serious work than *The Thorn Birds.*

Despite these differences, *Chicago Tribune Book World* reviewer Julia M. Ehresmann finds that *An Indecent Obsession* "has McCullough's fingerprints all over it." Comparing the themes of *Tim, The Thorn Birds,* and *An Indecent Obsession,* Ehresmann observes that "in these times when personal gratification is valued so highly, Colleen McCullough is writing about old-time moral dilemmas and largely discarded qualities: self-denial, self-control, and notions of duty, honor, and love as self-displacing virtues." Joanne Greenberg agrees in the *New York Times Book Review* that *An Indecent Obsession* is "a very old-fashioned novel, with its focus on the conflict between duty and love, a rare concern in contemporary fiction." McCullough's well-drawn characterizations and powerfully-evoked setting once again gained praise from many critics, with Greenberg crediting the author's "attention to detail" as the factor that "makes one feel the discomfort of the sweltering tropical nights as well as appreciate the awesome beauty of the sea, the torrential rains and the sunsets." Finally, in his *Washington Post Book World* article, William A. Nolen addresses "the question a lot of potential readers will want answered: Is *An Indecent Obsession* as good as McCullough's *The Thorn Birds?* The question can't be answered. It's like asking if a nice, ripe orange is as tasty as a nice, ripe apple; it depends on your mood and your taste buds. I enjoyed both books, but I thought *An Indecent Obsession* was more intriguing, more thought provoking, than was *The Thorn Birds.*"

Christopher Lehmann-Haupt, however, finds fault with the book in the *New York Times.* "We turn the pages," he acknowledges. "I do not mean to make light of Colleen McCullough's already best-selling successor to her gigantically successful 'The Thorn Birds'. . . . Miss McCullough is a natural storyteller, more than merely clever at getting up a head of emotional steam. . . . But if [she] expects to be taken seriously as a novelist—and, to judge from the improvement of this book over 'The Thorn Birds,' there's no reason why she shouldn't be—she's going to have to write just a little less slickly." McCullough's glibness, continues Lehmann-Haupt, "makes one want to say that 'An Indecent Obsession' is merely a gilded version of what I believe teen-age readers used to refer to as a nurse book. It isn't really. But far too often, its faults reduce it to medical soap opera."

McCullough responds to such criticism calmly. "Only time tells," she philosophized in her interview with Cassill. "If it lasts, it's good literature. If it dies, it's just another book. Very often the books the critics like today are gone tomorrow." She says that the greatest change that her phenomenal success has brought to her life has been a feeling of increased security and freedom. While working at Yale, she expected to "have to go home and look after mother when I was 50, and try to hold down a job at the same time—then at 70 I'd be living in a cold-water, walk-up apartment, just about able to afford a 60-watt light bulb." She now owns several homes, spending most of her time on tiny Norfolk Island, some 1,000 miles off the east coast of Australia. This South Pacific island is inhabited mostly by descendants of the *Bounty* mutineers. Life there suits McCullough perfectly. "It isn't what you are, it's who you are in a place like this," she told Phillipa Toomey in the London *Times.* "It's incredibly beautiful and peaceful and remote. . . . I get a heck of a lot of work done because there is nothing much else to do."

MEDIA ADAPTATIONS: Tim was released as a film starring Piper Laurie and Mel Gibson, directed and produced by Michael Pate, in 1981. *The Thorn Birds* was broadcast as a ten-hour miniseries on ABC-TV in March, 1983.

AVOCATIONAL INTERESTS: Photography, music, chess, embroidery, painting, and cooking.

BIOGRAPHICAL/CRITICAL SOURCES:

BOOKS

Contemporary Literary Criticism, Volume 27, Gale, 1984.

PERIODICALS

America, August 10, 1974.
Atlantic Monthly, June, 1977.
Best Sellers, May 15, 1974.
Chicago Tribune Book World, October 11, 1981.
Christian Century, March 31, 1982.
Los Angeles Times Book Review, October 25, 1981, July 21, 1985, June 21, 1987.
National Observer, June 20, 1977.
New Leader, July 4, 1977.
Newsweek, April 25, 1977.
New York Times, May 2, 1977, March 25, 1979, September 17, 1981, October 29, 1981, March 26, 1983, March 27, 1983.
New York Times Book Review, April 21, 1974, May 8, 1977, October 25, 1981, November 15, 1981, April 26, 1987.
People, May 7, 1984.

Publishers Weekly, March 7, 1977, February 22, 1980, February 18, 1984.
Saturday Review, April 16, 1977.
Time, May 9, 1977, May 20, 1985.
Times (London), November 30, 1981.
Times Literary Supplement, October 7, 1977, December 11, 1981.
Tribune Books (Chicago), April 12, 1987.
Village Voice, March 28, 1977.
Washington Post, April 24, 1977, November 26, 1981, March 27, 1983.
Washington Post Book World, October 11, 1981, January 20, 1985, April 28, 1985, May 26, 1987.
Writer's Digest, March, 1980.

*   *   *

McEWAN, Ian (Russell) 1948-

PERSONAL: Born June 21, 1948, in Aldershot, England; son of David (a soldier) and Rose (Moore) McEwan; married Penny Allen (a healer and astrologer), 1984; children: Polly, Alice, William. *Education:* University of Sussex, B.A. (with honors), 1970; University of East Anglia, M.A., 1971.

CAREER: Writer.

AWARDS, HONORS: Somerset Maugham Award, 1976, for *First Love, Last Rites;* Booker Prize finalist, 1981, for *The Comfort of Strangers; Evening Standard* Award for best screenplay, 1983, for "The Ploughman's Lunch"; Whitbread Award, 1987, for *The Child in Time.*

WRITINGS:

First Love, Last Rites (short stories), Random House, 1975.
Conversations with a Cupboardman (radio play), British Broadcasting Corp., 1975.
The Cement Garden (novel), Simon & Schuster, 1978.
In Between the Sheets (short stories), Simon & Schuster, 1978.
The Imitation Game, BBC, 1980.
The Imitation Game (teleplays; contains *Jack Flea's Celebration, Solid Geometry,* and *The Imitation Game*), Cape, 1981.
The Comfort of Strangers (novel), Simon & Schuster, 1981.
Or Shall We Die: An Oratorio (first produced at the Royal Festival Hall, February, 1983; produced at Carnegie Hall, 1985), J. Cape, 1982.
The Ploughman's Lunch (film), Greenpoint Films, 1982, Methuen, 1985.
(With Roberta Innocenti) *Rose Blanche,* J. Cape, 1985.
The Child in Time, Houghton, 1987.
Soursweet (film), 1989.
Strangers (play; based on his novel *The Comfort of Strangers*), produced in London at the Old Red Lion, 1989.
The Innocent, Doubleday, 1990.

Contributor to *Radio Times* and to literary journals in Europe and the United States, including *Transatlantic Review, American Review, New American Review, Tri-Quarterly,* and *New Review.*

SIDELIGHTS: Ian McEwan began writing seriously just before enrolling at the University of East Anglia. That school's faculty included Angus Wilson, a major novelist of the generation preceding McEwan's, to whom the younger writer has been compared. A collection of McEwan's stories, written as his master's thesis, became his first published work, *First Love, Last Rites.* Writing in the *New York Review of Books,* Robert Towers praises the collection as "possibly the most brilliantly perverse and sinister batch of short stories to come out of England since Angus

Wilson's *The Wrong Set."* Towers describes McEwan's England as a "flat, rubble-strewn wasteland, populated by freaks and monsters, most of them articulate enough to tell their own stories with mesmerizing narrative power and an unfaltering instinct for the perfect sickening detail." The "freaks" include an incestuous brother and sister, a man who lives in a cupboard, a child-slayer, and a man who keeps the penis of a nineteenth-century criminal preserved in a jar. "Such writing would be merely sensational if it were not, like [Franz] Kafka's, so pointed, so accurate, so incapable indeed of being appalled," writes John Fletcher in the *Dictionary of Literary Biography.* "In contemporary writing one has to turn to French literature to encounter a similar contrast between the elegance of the language and the disturbing quality of the material; in writing in English McEwan is wholly unique. No one else combines in quite the same way exactness of notation with a comedy so black that many readers may fail to see the funny side at all."

Reviewing *First Love, Last Rites* in *Encounter,* Jonathan Raban declares that the book "oozes with talent as wayward, original and firm in vision as anything since [Jean] Rhys's early novels." He attributes the author's success in handling his somewhat distasteful plots to the fact that McEwan's writing takes "nothing for granted, it is surprised by nothing and observant of everything . . . at its frequent best, it has a musical purity matched to music's deep indifference to the merely moral." Of the young author's debut, Raban concludes: "*First Love, Last Rites* is one of those rare books which strike out on a new direction in current English fiction. The most important question is what will McEwan do next? His abilities as a stylist and a storyteller are profuse, and these stories are only the first harvest."

McEwan's next venture, a novel entitled *The Cement Garden,* has been likened to William Golding's *Lord of the Flies.* It is the story of four children's regression into a feral state, possessing the "suspense and chilling impact" of Golding's book "but without the philosophy lessons," notes William McPherson in *Washington Post Book World.* The four children, Julie, Jack, Sue, and Tom, have been raised in a Victorian house that stands alone among the abandoned ruins of modern prefabricated houses. The children's father dies at the moment that Jack, the fifteen-year-old narrator, experiences his first orgasm. When their mother dies a short time later, Jack convinces his siblings that they must bury her secretly rather than be separated and put into foster homes. They carry out his plan, encasing the body in a trunk of wet cement and hiding it in the basement. Julie and Jack then unsuccessfully attempt to assume the parental roles. They lapse into filth and apathy; their youngest brother regresses to an infantile state; flies infest the house as food rots in the kitchen. Eventually the cement in the trunk cracks, filling the house with the scent of the mother's decaying body. In time, Julie's boyfriend, Derek, discovers the corpse; then he stumbles upon Jack and Julie, engaged in incest. The book ends with the orphans' closed world shattered as Derek summons the police to the scene.

Robert Towers describes *The Cement Garden* as "a shocking book, morbid, full of repellent imagery—and irresistibly readable, . . . the work of a writer in full control of his materials. As in the short stories, the effect achieved by McEwan's quiet, precise, and sensuous touch is that of magic realism—a transfiguration of the ordinary that has a far stronger retinal and visceral impact than the flabby surrealism of so many 'experimental' novels. The setting and events reinforce one another symbolically, but the symbolism never seems contrived or obtrusive." Fletcher also praises McEwan's style; however, he expresses reservations about this type of subject matter. "The novel would be rather silly if its tone were not so obsessive and sustained, and if the sharpness of detail and observation were not so intense," he states. "It is difficult to see how McEwan can develop much further this line in grotesque horror and black comedy, with a strong admixture of eroticism and perversion."

Anne Tyler, in the *New York Times Book Review,* states: "Ian McEwan is a skillful writer, absolutely in control of his material." But she goes on to question the validity of such a bleak tale: "What makes the book difficult is that these children are not—we trust—real people at all. They are so consistently unpleasant, unlikable and bitter that we can't believe in them and we certainly can't identify with them. Jack's eyes, through which we're viewing this story, have an uncanny ability to settle upon the one distasteful detail in every scene, and to dwell on it. . . . It seems weak-stomached to criticize a novel on these grounds, but if what we read makes us avert our gaze entirely, isn't the purpose defeated? Jack, we're being told, has been so damaged and crippled that there's no hope for him. But if it's a foregone conclusion that there's no hope whatsoever, we tend to lose hope in the book as well."

Other critics consider McEwan's ability to gain reader sympathy for these children to be one of the major strengths of his novel. Paul Gray writes in *Time* magazine: "Jack, 15, [is] unattractive in a manner that only adolescent males can fully achieve. . . . Without any redeeming charm, he is nonetheless capable of evoking sympathy. . . . Seen from the inside, the characters are simply beleaguered children trying to cope and, ultimately, failing. Outsiders find their degeneration criminal; the book shows the inadequacy of such a judgement." John Leonard, in the *New York Times,* finds, "The odd thing is that the reader comes to root for [the children] . . . and against Derek, the moneyed snooker player who would invade their dream with his rationality and the authority of his disgust." Leonard calls the novel "remarkable because it takes materials so familiar from recent literature as to amount to a kind of dross of modernism—the psychopathology of family life, sinister shifts in sex roles, infantile regression, libidinal politics, tribal mores—and transmutes them into something dark and glowing. . . . Just about everything of craft that can be done right is done right in *The Cement Garden,* from the cement at the beginning to the sledgehammer at the end. . . . Disquieting, I suppose, is the word for this novel, as well as 'accomplished' and 'astonishing.' Mr. McEwan sneaks up and stabs us in the heart."

McEwan's collection of short stories *In Between the Sheets* has also attracted a great deal of critical attention. Some reviewers praise the less sensational nature of this book, citing in particular "Psychopolis," "Two Fragments: March 199-," and the title story as examples of a new restraint on McEwan's part. However, *In Between the Sheets* does include stories about teenage lesbians, a romantic ape who laments the end of his affair with a woman writer, and a man who eats ground glass, washes it down with juice, and hurls himself under a train. "McEwan is experimenting more," writes V. S. Pritchett in the *New York Review of Books.* In this critic's view, the collection demonstrates McEwan's versatility and contains what he terms "two encouraging breaks with 'mean' writing. [These two stories] enlarge his scene." "Two Fragments: March 199-" takes its theme and style from George Orwell's *1984.* It describes a London that has been half-destroyed by a war or revolution; its inhabitants have been reduced to a life of scavenging. Pritchett feels that McEwan treats the theme of a future society well, with a "far greater sense of physical and emotional dissolution" than Orwell, and Terence Winch of the *Washington Post Book World* says that McEwan's prose, "like Orwell's, is as clear as a windowpane." He calls

McEwan "a gifted story-teller and possibly the best British writer to appear in a decade or more."

In contrast to his earlier works, McEwan's next novel, *The Comfort of Strangers,* features two well-groomed, respectable adults. Colin and Mary are on holiday in Venice when they are drawn into a web of horror that climaxes in sadomasochistic murder. Though continuing to praise McEwan's gifts as a storyteller—calling him "a black magician"—John Leonard finds the book's plot contrived and unbelievable. His review concludes: "This novel, by a writer of enormous talent, is definitely diseased." Stephen Koch, too, faults the plot while praising McEwan's craftsmanship. "McEwan proceeds through most of this sickly tale with subtlety and promise," Koch writes in the *Washington Post Book World.* "The difficulty is that all this skill is directed toward a climax which, even though it is duly horrific, is sapped by a certain thinness and plain banality at its core. After an impressive wind-up, the sado-masochistic fantasy animating *The Comfort of Strangers* is revealed as . . . a sado-masochistic fantasy. And not much more. . . . Yet *The Comfort of Strangers* has real interest as a novel. . . . In all his recent fiction, McEwan seems to be reaching toward some new imaginative accommodation to the sexual questions of innocence and adulthood, role and need that have defined, with such special intensity, his generation. . . . I honor him for his effort."

"As the best young writer on this island," writes Andrew Sinclair in the London *Times,* "McEwan's evocation of feeling and place and his analyses of mood and relationship remain haunting and compelling. Yet his obsession with the thin skin between life and death, his concentration on menace and perversion, narrow his vision. His plots are cautionary tales with compulsory deadly endings. . . . His promise has been in walking on brittle ice; his achievement will be in his treading on solid ground." Fletcher concludes: "One hopes that [McEwan] is not cultivating a contemporary form of Gothic to the point of self-indulgence. If he is not—if, in other words, he can develop and deepen an already formidable talent—then he is likely to become one of the greatest British writers of his generation."

BIOGRAPHICAL/CRITICAL SOURCES:

BOOKS

Contemporary Literary Criticism, Volume 13, Gale, 1980.
Dictionary of Literary Biography, Volume 14: *British Novelists since 1960,* Gale, 1983.

PERIODICALS

Chicago Tribune Book World, November 26, 1978; September 30, 1979; July 19, 1981.
Encounter, June, 1975; January, 1979.
Listener, April 12, 1979.
London Magazine, August/September, 1975; February, 1979.
Monthly Film Bulletin, June 1983.
New Review, autumn, 1978.
New York Review of Books, March 8, 1979; January 24, 1980.
New York Times, November 21, 1978; August 14, 1979; June 15, 1981.
New York Times Book Review, November 26, 1978; August 26, 1979; July 5, 1981.
Time, November 17, 1978.
Times (London), February 16, 1981; October 8, 1981.
Times Literary Supplement, January 20, 1978; September 29, 1978; October 9, 1981.
Virginia Quarterly Review, autumn, 1975.
Washington Post Book World, October 29, 1978; August 5, 1979; June 28, 1981.

McGAHERN, John 1934-

PERSONAL: Born November 12, 1934, in Dublin, Ireland; son of John (a police officer) and Susan (McManus) McGahern. *Education:* Attended Presentation College, Carrick-on-Shannon, Ireland, and University College, Dublin.

ADDRESSES: c/o Viking Press, Inc., 40 West 23rd St., New York, N.Y. 10010.

CAREER: Writer, 1963—. Teacher at St. John the Baptist Boys National School, 1956-63; O'Connor Professor of Literature, Colgate University, 1969, 1972, 1977, 1979, 1983; British Northern Arts Fellow at University of Newcastle and University of Durham, 1974-76. Visiting professor at numerous colleges in England and Ireland.

AWARDS, HONORS: A. E. Memorial Award, 1962, and Macauley fellowship, 1964, both for *The Barracks;* Society of Authors award, 1967; British Arts Council awards, 1968, 1970, 1973; American Irish Foundation Literary Award, 1985; Galway Festival Tenth Anniversary Award, 1987.

WRITINGS:

NOVELS

The Barracks, Faber, 1963, Macmillan, 1964.
The Dark, Faber, 1965, Knopf, 1966.
The Leavetaking, Faber, 1974, Little, Brown, 1975.
The Pornographer, Faber, 1979, Harper, 1980.

SHORT STORIES

Nightlines, Faber, 1970, Atlantic, 1971.
Getting Through, Faber, 1978, Harper, 1980.
High Ground, Faber, 1985, Viking, 1987.

OTHER

Also author of radio play, "Sinclair," 1971, and the television plays, "Swallows," 1975, and "The Rockingham Shoot," 1987.

SIDELIGHTS: John McGahern is a contemporary Irish fiction writer whose works explore the vagaries of life in his native land. *Saturday Review* contributor Robert Emmet Long includes McGahern among Ireland's finest living writers, calling him "sure-footed, elegiac, graceful when he moves in the confines of the land of his birth, his people speaking in accents of truth as they do." Long also describes McGahern as "an original voice, a writer who works without tricks within carefully controlled limits. . . . In . . . all of his best work, he examines the epiphanies in ordinary Irish lives." McGahern has been praised for his style, which some have compared to that of James Joyce, as well as for his controversial themes. Regardless of his topic, writes Patricia Craig in the *Times Literary Supplement,* McGahern "always writes well about the state of being Irish, its special deprivations and depravities." *Washington Post* correspondent John Breslin likewise concludes that McGahern "poignantly details the abrasions we inflict as well as the brief glimpses of delight we afford one another." According to Julian Moynahan in the *New York Times Book Review,* McGahern is quite simply "the most accomplished novelist of his generation."

The Ireland of McGahern's fiction is often dark and dour, a prison for the soul. His stories reveal the lives of the suffering poor, "human nature at its bitterest," to quote Long. *New York Times Book Review* contributor Joel Conarroe finds McGahern's characters "paralyzed by convention and habit, . . . unable to escape their parochial fates; their powerlessness suggests a central motif in James Joyce." Tom Pavlin elaborates in *Encounter:* "Running through McGahern's work is a fusion of sex, death and hopelessness. They are the presiding trinity of his imagination and are revealed in a series of epiphanies." Indeed, McGahern's work deals forthrightly with several taboo aspects of Irish social life—the Catholic church and its repressive tactics, sexuality, and family turmoil, Shaun O'Connell explains in the *Massachusetts Review.* "To stay within the circle of acceptability is, spiritually and sexually, to starve, but to range outside the province of the predictable in Ireland, particularly for sexual purposes, is to bring about retribution," writes O'Connell. ". . . Repression is the means by which community is sustained." An important theme in McGahern is how his characters overcome this community repression, or conversely, how they are destroyed by it.

In *The Irish Short Story,* Terence Brown notes that McGahern, "while confident and skilled in portraying the provincial world he knows, recognises a need for modern Irish fiction to meet more stringent demands. It must be attentive to the recent major social changes in the country, in an art that more appropriately reflects the complex psychological currents that stir in its turbulent waters. So McGahern is consciously experimental in his work, welcoming the resonance of image and symbol to the enclosed worlds of rural and small-town Ireland, taking his protagonists away from their childhood farms and fields to the confused cultural settings of modern Dublin and London." Much of McGahern's work rests on the strength of his style, a feeling for "things like the everyday ecstasies" to quote Craig. *Newsweek* columnist Peter S. Prescott observes that McGahern "means us to read slowly, to hear the sounds, feel the weight of his words." *Encounter* essayist Jonathan Raban compares McGahern to that other experimental and widely-travelled Irish writer, James Joyce. "McGahern's and Joyce's prose styles bleed imperceptibly into one another like the voices of kissing-cousins," writes Raban. ". . . At his best, McGahern writes so beautifully that he leaves one in no doubt of his equality with Joyce: the similarities between the two writers spring from a sense of tradition which is thoroughly and profoundly shared. And that is something which one is so unused to encountering in 20th-century literature that it is tempting to mistake what is really a glory for a shabby vice."

McGahern was a teacher at the St. John the Baptist Boys National school in Clontarf when his first novel, *The Barracks,* was published in 1963. The novel set the tone for the author's early fiction; it details the last months in the life of Elizabeth Reegan, a rural Irish housewife afflicted with terminal cancer. *Studies* essayist John Cronin writes of Elizabeth: "Life has set her on a collision course and McGahern enters her experience at a point where his philosophy gives him complete and convincing command of her destiny and her doom." Moynahan finds the book memorable "for its dark portrayal of vindictiveness in the hateful feuding of a policeman with his superior, for the unusual sensitivity and fullness with which a stepmother's domestic unhappiness and grave illness were rendered, and for its hell of tedium and of self- and mutual thwarting." In the *Dictionary of Literary Biography,* Patricia Boyle Haberstroh contends that the juxtaposition of life and death, "the need to find a way of getting through the mysterious cycle from birth to death, and the acceptance of life as a series of small deaths leading to the final mystery recur. The death that overshadows every life pervades McGahern's fiction." *The Barracks* won two of Ireland's most prestigious literary awards, the A. E. Memorial Award and the Macauley fellowship. McGahern was thereby enabled to take a leave of absence from his teaching post in order to write full time.

Public acclaim for McGahern's next novel, *The Dark,* came almost entirely from outside Ireland. The controversial book was banned by the Irish Censorship Board, and it ultimately cost Mc-Gahern his teaching job as well. A portrait of a confused Catholic adolescent and his abusive father, *The Dark* takes "a sombre, sufferingly malicious view of contemporary Ireland, [dwelling] with fond revulsion on the strange, brutal paradoxes that feed on and are fed by the 'Irish imagination,' " according to a reviewer for the *Times Literary Supplement.* The novel focuses on the young boy's dawning sexuality and his conflicting desire to become a priest. "We think at times we are reading a story of studious success or failure about which the author is excited," writes the *Times Literary Supplement* reviewer. "We discover we are reading grim and terrible farce. The writer who is capable of such a double take deserves esteem." McGahern's well-publicized battles with the Censorship Board and with the Catholic school hierarchy over *The Dark* made him anxious to leave Ireland. For several years he travelled through England and Europe, teaching at universities, lecturing, and writing.

Censorship and marriage outside the church, both experienced by McGahern, form the foundation of his novel *The Leavetaking,* published in London in 1974. In that work, the protagonist comes to know himself through his loss of his teaching job at a Catholic school and his marriage to an American woman. O'Connell suggests that in the novel, and his other recent works, McGahern "leads some of his characters through a door into the light, into a problematic freedom, out to an open field in which they first run free, but from which they eventually seek release, so some return to the familiar confines." McGahern's hero in *The Leavetaking* escapes; his central character in the 1979 book *The Pornographer* chooses to stay after examining his tawdry life and casual sexual encounters. In either case, notes Craig, "the gloom which permeated John McGahern's earlier novels is beginning to lift. It has been transformed into a reasonable despondency and flatness, tempered with irony—no longer a terrible Irish seediness and vacancy of spirit."

McGahern has also published several volumes of short stories. These, like his novels, "deal in love, frustrated or misplaced, and in intimations of mortality," to quote Michael Irwin in the *Times Literary Supplement.* Most of the fiction is set in Ireland, but *New York Times Book Review* contributor David Pryce-Jones finds it "free from the emerald sentiments that have been invested in [McGahern's] native land. He is his own master, and his stories owe nothing to anybody." Irwin feels that each tale "has resonance: some slight incident is made to disclose a mode of living and an attitude to experience." In the *London Review of Books,* Pat Rogers maintains that the author's short works "are unmistakably conservative: their freshness proceeds from close observation, a deep inwardness with the milieu, and a willingness to let events and description do their work unmolested by the urge to be wise about human affairs." Haberstroh concludes that an Irish sensibility informs McGahern's stories, "and the public and fictional history he creates from his personal life testifies to the degree to which art and life intertwine."

McGahern told the *New York Times Book Review:* "In my upbringing, there were very few books, and one would never have met a writer. But there was the pleasure of playing with words, and then you found that, almost without knowing it, you wanted to do this more than anything else." McGahern is widely praised for his prose fiction, and for refusing "the poet laureateship offered by the *status quo,*" according to Anthony C. West in *The Nation.* O'Connell claims that McGahern's "revised version of the Irish pastoral is edged in irony, weighted by expectation and sustained by compelling fictional energies." Raban feels that the author "has a genius—and that word does not overstate what he does—for mediating between the deep currents of feeling which

belong to myth and history and the exact texture of the moment, seen so freshly that it comes off the page in a vivid cluster of sensations." Irwin observes that McGahern "writes with unobtrusive concision. So much of his skill lies in selection, or rather in omission, that his terse narrative seems free and full. He has the Irish gift of being able to move fluently and unselfconsciously between a simple and a heightened style. . . . Pace and proportion seem effortlessly adjusted: there is no sense of expository strain." Perhaps the most compelling praise for McGahern's work comes from fellow writer John Updike. In *Hugging the Shore: Essays and Criticism,* Updike concludes that the artist "writes well, and for the usual reasons: he observes well, hears faithfully, and feels keenly."

BIOGRAPHICAL/CRITICAL SOURCES:

BOOKS

Contemporary Literary Criticism, Gale, Volume 5, 1976, Volume 9, 1978, Volume 48, 1988.
Dictionary of Literary Biography, Volume 14: *British Novelists since World War II,* Gale, 1982.
Dunn, Douglas, editor, *Two Decades of Irish Writing,* Carcanet Press, 1975.
Rafroidi, Patrick and Terence Brown, editors, *The Irish Short Story,* Colin Smythe, 1979.
Updike, John, *Hugging the Shore: Essays and Criticism,* Knopf, 1983.

PERIODICALS

Catholic World, January, 1968.
Censorship, spring, 1966.
Chicago Tribune, April 27, 1987.
Critique: Studies in Modern Fiction, Volume XIX, number 1, 1977, Volume XXI, number 1, 1979.
Detroit News, August 3, 1980.
Encounter, June, 1975, June, 1978.
Globe and Mail (Toronto), August 18, 1984.
London Review of Books, October 3, 1985.
Los Angeles Times, February 18, 1987.
Massachusetts Review, summer, 1984.
Nation, November 7, 1966.
New Leader, March 31, 1975.
New Republic, December 15, 1979.
Newsweek, February 17, 1975, November 5, 1979.
New Yorker, December 24, 1979.
New York Review of Books, May 1, 1980.
New York Times, July 12, 1980.
New York Times Book Review, March 6, 1966, February 7, 1971, February 2, 1975, December 2, 1979, July 13, 1980, February 8, 1987.
Saturday Review, May 1, 1971.
Spectator, January 11, 1975, June 17, 1978.
Studies, winter, 1969.
Times Literary Supplement, May 13, 1965, November 27, 1970, January 10, 1975, June 16, 1978, January 11, 1980, September 13, 1985.
Washington Post, March 23, 1987.
Washington Post Book World, December 23, 1979.

* * *

McGRATH, Thomas (Matthew) 1916-

PERSONAL: Born November 20, 1916, near Sheldon, N.D.; son of James Lang (a farmer) and Catherine (Shea) McGrath; married Marian Points, 1942; married Alice Greenfield, 1952; married Eugenia Johnson, February 13, 1960; children: Thomas Samuel Koan. *Education:* University of North Dakota, B.A., 1939; Louisiana State University, M.A., 1940; New College, Oxford University, additional study, 1947-48. *Politics:* Communist Party, U.S.A.

ADDRESSES: Home—911 22nd Ave. S., #160, Minneapolis, Minn. 55404.

CAREER: Poet and novelist. Colby College, Waterville, Me., instructor in English, 1940-41; Los Angeles State College of Applied Arts and Sciences (now California State College, Los Angeles), assistant professor of English, 1952-54; Sequoia School (private study center), Los Angeles, co-founder and teacher, 1954-55; C. W. Post College, Long Island, N.Y., assistant professor of English, 1960-61; North Dakota State University, Fargo, N.D., associate professor of English, 1962-67; Moorhead State University, Moorhead, Minn., associate professor of English, 1969-82. Welder at Federal Shipbuilding and Drydock Co., Kearney, N.J., 1942; woodcarver at Artform Wood Sculpturing Co., Los Angeles, 1955-57; free-lance writer in television and film industry, 1956-60. *Military service:* U.S. Army Air Forces, 1942-45.

MEMBER: Phi Beta Kappa.

AWARDS, HONORS: Rhodes Scholar, Oxford University, 1947-48; Alan Swallow Poetry Book Award, 1954, for *Figures from a Double World;* Amy Lowell travelling poetry fellowship, 1965-66; Guggenheim fellowship, 1967; Minnesota State Arts Council grant, 1973 and 1979; National Foundation for the Arts fellowship, 1974, 1982, and 1987; Bush Foundation fellowship, 1976, 1981; honorary doctorate, University of North Dakota, 1981; American Book Award, Before Columbus Foundation, 1985, for *Echoes Inside the Labyrinth.*

WRITINGS:

The Gates of Ivory, the Gates of Horn (novel), foreword by Charles Humboldt, Mainstream Publishers, 1957, reprinted, Another Chicago Press, 1987.
Clouds (juvenile), illustrations by Chris Jenkyns, Melmont Publishers (Los Angeles), 1959.
The Beautiful Things (juvenile), illustrations by Jenkyns, Vanguard, 1960.
This Coffin Has No Handles (novel), North Dakota Quarterly, 1985, hardcover edition published by Thunders Mouth Press, 1988.

POETRY

First Manifesto, A. Swallow (Baton Rouge, La.), 1940.
(Contributor of "The Dialectics of Love") Alan Swallow, editor, *Three Young Poets: Thomas McGrath, William Peterson, James Franklin Lewis,* Press of James A. Decker (Prairie City, Ill.), 1942.
To Walk a Crooked Mile, Swallow Press (New York), 1947.
Longshot O'Leary's Garland of Practical Poesie, International Publishers, 1949.
Witness to the Times!, privately printed, 1954.
Figures from a Double World, Alan Swallow (Denver), 1955.
Letter to an Imaginary Friend, Part I, Alan Swallow, 1962, published with Part II, Swallow Press (Chicago), 1970, Parts III and IV, Copper Canyon Press, 1985.
New and Selected Poems, Alan Swallow, 1964.
The Movie at the End of the World: Collected Poems, Swallow Press, 1972.
Poems for Little People, [Gloucester], c. 1973.

Voyages to the Inland Sea #3, Center for Contemporary Poetry, 1973.
Voices from Beyond the Wall, Territorial Press (Moorhead, Minn.), 1974.
A Sound of One Hand: Poems, Minnesota Writers Publishing House, 1975.
Open Songs: Sixty Short Poems, Uzzano (Mount Carroll, Ill.), 1977.
Letters to Tomasito, graphics by Randall W. Scholes, Holy Cow! (St. Paul, Minn.), 1977.
Trinc: Praises II; A Poem, Copper Canyon Press, 1979.
Waiting for the Angel, Uzzano (Menomonie, Wis.), 1979.
Passages toward the Dark, Copper Canyon Press, 1982.
Echoes inside the Labyrinth, Thunder's Mouth Press, 1983.
Longshot O'Leary Counsels Direct Action: Poems, West End Press, 1983.
Selected Poems, 1938-1988, Copper Canyon Press, 1988.

Also author of *9 Poems,* Mandrill Press.

CONTRIBUTOR OF POETRY TO ANTHOLOGIES

Ian M. Parsons, editor, *Poetry for Pleasure,* Doubleday, 1960.
Donald Hall, *New Poets of England and America,* Meridian, 1962.
Walter Lowenfels, editor, *Poets of Today: A New American Anthology,* International Publishers, 1964.
Lucien Stryk, editor, *Heartland: Poets of the Midwest,* Northern Illinois University Press, 1967.
Lowenfels, editor, *Where Is Vietnam?,* Doubleday, 1967.
Morris Sweetkind, editor, *Getting Into Poetry,* Rostan Holbrook Press, 1972.
Traveling America, Macmillan, 1977.
The Norton Introduction to Literature, 2nd edition, Norton, 1977.
Robert Bly, editor, *News of the Universe,* Sierra Club, 1980.
From A to Z: 200 Contemporary Poets, Swallow Press, 1981.

Also contributor to *The New Naked Poetry,* and *The Voice That Is Great within Us.*

OTHER

Also author of about twenty documentary film scripts, 1954-60, including "The Museum," "The Fury," "Genesis," and "To Fly," which is still screened at the Smithsonian Institution. Author of unpublished manuscript, "All But the Last." Contributor of poetry, criticism, and short stories to magazines, including *Kayak, Sixties,* and *Poetry.* Assistant editor and member of editorial board of *California Quarterly,* 1951-54; contributing editor, *Mainstream,* 1955-57; founder and editor, with Eugenia McGrath, *Crazy Horse,* 1960-61; member of editorial boards of other literary magazines.

WORK IN PROGRESS: New book of poems.

SIDELIGHTS: For fifty years, Thomas McGrath has produced a prolific array of titles, encompassing poetry, novels, books for children, and several documentary film scripts, including uncredited work on the eloquent and exhilarating Smithsonian film about the history of flight, "To Fly," for which he may even have garnered his largest audience. But McGrath is primarily a poet, and although "important contemporary poets . . . proclaim him as a major voice in American poetry in the last three or four decades," notes Frederick C. Stern in *Southwest Review,* McGrath's work has been critically neglected for years. "He's one of those poets who *should* be known but isn't, who is constantly being rediscovered as if he were some precocious teenager who just got into town," declares Mark Vinz in *North Dakota Quarterly.* "If he's been honored, even revered by a few, he's also been ignored by most." According to Terrence Des Pres in *TriQuarterly*, "Thomas McGrath has been writing remarkable poems of every size and form for nearly fifty years. In American poetry he is as close to Whitman as anyone since Whitman himself, a claim I make with care. McGrath is master of the long wide line (wide in diction, long in meter), the inclusive six-beat measure of America at large. The scene of his work is the whole of the continent east to west with its midpoint in the high-plains rim of the heartland. His diction, with its vast word-stock and multitude of language layers, is demotic to the core yet spiced with learned terms in Whitman's manner, a voice as richly American as any in our literature."

McGrath was once described by Gerard Previn Meyer in the *Saturday Review of Literature* as "a likable and ingenious young poet very largely under the sway of two established 'myths'—the Whitman-democratic and the Marxist-revolutionary." And according to Roger Mitchell in the *American Book Review,* "McGrath's career makes an interesting comment on the possibilities of a Marxist art in America." Noting that "there has never been a time when any but a sentimental leftism could make the slightest dent in our consciousness," Mitchell points out, "These are not the times, and have not been for forty years or more, to make us think that 'the generous wish' could become fact, but Thomas McGrath, more than any other poet of his time and place, and with greater skill and energy than we have yet recognized, has helped keep that wish alive." "It is a credit to McGrath's integrity and courage that he has not abated his radicalism," concludes Stern in *Southwest Review,* "even though it . . . has perhaps cost him wider recognition among America's contemporary poets."

"It is the other peoples' opinions which have kept [McGrath] from being as well known as he deserves," estimates Kenneth Rexroth in the *New York Times Book Review,* "for he is a most accomplished and committed poet." Considering McGrath "one of the best American poets extant," a *New Republic* contributor explains that because he "is of the wrong political and esthetic camp," he is "consistently neglected by our literary power brokers." Several critics concur that McGrath's leftist political views have denied him the recognition his work warrants, but they do not consider his politics to impede his art. McGrath's work is "powerful, original, absorbing, funny and uncompromisingly American in its resources, techniques and hopes," writes Reginald Gibbons in *TriQuarterly.* Calling him "the most important American poet who can lay claim to the title 'radical,' " Stern observes that the essence of his poetry lies in "the past as shaping force, death as personal and political fact, the horror and loneliness of living in an inhuman and dehumanizing society." In *North Dakota Quarterly,* Valery Kirilovich Shpak, a Soviet poet and educator who understands the "democratic traditions" in McGrath's work, observes that he "depicts the life and struggle of working people who face the necessity of remaking themselves within capitalist society." According to Hugh Gibb in the *New York Times,* "In the first place, when contemplating a harsh and chaotic world, he never allows his genuine pity for the oppressed to degenerate into self-pity; and secondly, he is never forced to retreat into a world of private fantasy and introspection. In consequence he has been able not only to sustain the tradition which would otherwise appear to be almost extinct, but has brought to it a new and vigorous honesty."

Son of Irish Catholic parents whose own parents were lured across the Atlantic by promises of paradise to homestead in North Dakota, McGrath was born and raised there in a farming community during an era identified by Diane Wakoski in the

American Book Review as "a politically exciting locus—the organization of poor farmers against bankers, grain merchants, and industrial interests." Unable to survive financially in the dust-bowl thirties and its Great Depression, however, his family, like many farmers before and after them, finally succumbed to the bankers. In the assessment of social historian E. P. Thompson in *TriQuarterly,* "McGrath's family experience was the whole cycle—from homesteading to generations working together to bust—in three generations." And in the opinion of Des Pres, "Every aspect of this heritage—the place, the hard times, the religious and political culture—informs his art in a multitude of ways."

Raised in an environment where shared labor and unity against outside influences were vital to the survival of a rapidly disintegrating farming community, McGrath was also introduced to the political philosophy of a few Wobblies (members of the Industrial Workers of the World) among the seasonal farm workers. Consequently, McGrath formulated his politics early; and, as Des Pres observed, "his politics led him into a world of experience that, in turn, backed up his political beliefs in concrete ways." McGrath spent much of his young adult life on the road or riding the rails, witnessing and experiencing economic disparity, and variously employed at odd jobs to subsidize his writing. During the 1940s, he worked as a labor organizer and briefly as a shipyard welder on the New York's Chelsea waterfront, where he also edited a rank-and-file union newspaper. "To be a Red on the waterfront was to be the natural prey of goon squads patrolling the docks for the bosses and the racketeers," noted Des Pres. "It was also to see the world of industrial work at firsthand." McGrath wrote *Longshot O'Leary's Garland of Practical Poesy* for a few "Jesuitical and cabalistic" people he had met while working on the docks—"waterfront radicals who'd come by, drink my coffee, interrupt my day's work, and instruct me how *poetry ought to be written,*" McGrath recalls in an interview with Des Pres and Gibbons in *TriQuarterly.* Noting how his waterfront acquaintances believed poetry ought to rhyme, McGrath adds, "I wrote *Longshot O'Leary* in part to show them that it could be written in rhyme, and yet could include in it, a poem, some kind of zinger, which they might have to think about or look up in the dictionary."

After serving in the Aleutian Islands with the U.S. Army Air Forces during the war, he attended Oxford University as a Rhodes Scholar, returning to New York in the late 1940s where he wrote reviews and poems for the leftist press. Influenced especially by writers of the thirties whose art derived from their politics, McGrath launched his own career at a time when many literary figures had forsaken leftist aspirations, and began what most critics agree is his most important work, *Letter to an Imaginary Friend,* during the postwar conservativism of the fifties. "The thirties were not just over in the fifties: they were devalidated . . .," explains Mitchell. "The loss of faith in the public life and in progress in general was wide and deep, and it provided a rich ground for the cultivation of conservative social and political ideas." Mitchell points out that "this broad reversal of direction or cancellation of hope in western culture comes more and more to seem like one of the primary facts of life in the twentieth century, and Thomas McGrath is one of the few writers who, in living through it, saw it and refused to give in to its compelling logic."

Unwilling to cooperate with the House Committee on Un-American Activities during the blacklisting fifties, for instance, McGrath told them, as recorded in *North Dakota Quarterly:* "A teacher who will tack and turn with every shift of the political wind cannot be a good teacher. I have never done this myself, nor will I ever." As a poet, he was unwilling to cooperate on "esthetic grounds." McGrath explained, "The view of life which we receive through the great works of art is a privileged one—it is a view of life according to probability or necessity, not subject to the chance and accident of our real world and therefore in a sense truer than the life we see lived all around us." Consequently, because of his political underpinnings, McGrath lost his teaching post at Los Angeles State College of Applied Arts and Sciences. And following a brief stint at the Sequoia School, a private study center he helped found, he returned to the plains of North Dakota where he began *Letter to an Imaginary Friend.*

Letter to an Imaginary Friend, which Stern deems one of the "few really outstanding book-length poems published by an American," is a long, ongoing, autobiographical poem that integrates personal experience with political concerns. It represents "a contrast between what I thought of as the old community and what I saw when I came back to North Dakota . . . to live in my family's old farmhouse," recalls McGrath in *North Dakota Quarterly.* Describing the work as "a medley of memory and observation," a reviewer for *Choice* comments that McGrath "ranges back and forth over past and present. Episodes of childhood, youth, today mingle with reflections on social and political events." As McGrath explains in *North Dakota Quarterly,* "All of us live twice at the same time—once uniquely and once representatively. I am interested in those moments when my unique personal life intersects with something bigger, when my small brief moment has a part in 'fabricating the legend.' " In *Poetry,* James Atlas observes that "throughout, the resonance of personal history is drowned out by the larger concerns of American life during the Depression and World War II," and calls the work "an incessant, grieving lyric, obsessive and polemical, euphoric and bereaved." Detecting an "elegiac" tone in the third and fourth parts of *Letter to an Imaginary Friend,* Stern suggests in *Western American Literature* that "McGrath here seems to see much more the end of things."

"For McGrath politics and poetry emerge from the same source, from the geography of his life and the history of his time," observes Joseph Butkin in *North Dakota Quarterly.* "Consequently, the *Letter to an Imaginary Friend* is not simply a poetic autobiography or a portrait of the artist; it is a history of the left during these past forty years and a record of the poet's formation within that history. As geography, the poem turns America inside out. North Dakota, the hidden interior, is the paradise lost to be regained." Although McGrath is hardly a regional poet, the landscape of North Dakota assumes universal significance in *Letter to an Imaginary Friend.* According to Fred Whitehead in *North Dakota Quarterly,* "McGrath is not concerned with . . . the Old Midwest . . . but with the frontier beyond that, with the high plains, with the West. There's a feral quality to him which is rarely found in the older, civilized zones." In "McGrath on McGrath" in *North Dakota Quarterly,* McGrath explains what makes the experience of the poet "out here on the edge . . . different from that of the city poet": "First there is the land itself. It has been disciplined by machines, but it is still not dominated. The plow that broke the plains is long gone . . . but the process of making a living is still a struggle and a gamble. . . . Weather, which is only a nuisance in the city, takes on the power of the gods here. . . . Here man can never think of himself, as he can in the city, as the master of nature . . . he has an heroic adversary that is no abstraction. At a level below immediate consciousness we respond to this, are less alien to our bodies, to human and natural time."

Commending the multiplicity of sources upon which the poet draws to make his "personal and political statement," a *Library*

Journal contributor praises as well the linguistic and thematic "risks" that McGrath takes throughout. McGrath's work is "powerful, original, absorbing, funny and uncompromisingly American in its resources, techniques and hopes," writes Gibbons in *TriQuarterly.* Regarding McGrath's language as "the most impressive, most astonishing, of any American poet of our time," Gibbons adds that "his vocabulary wraps all manner of speech and written language within it, from the bawdy to unearthed glossological wonders. It is especially lively when it gathers together slang, both rural and urban, and McGrath's neologistical and sometimes surreal coinages." As Wakoski concludes: "McGrath's language is florid, compelling when allowed breadth and depth, and his concerns are so truly those born in a changing society and his ability to chronicle the past so graphic that *Letter to an Imaginary Friend* could easily become the first great poem out of the heart of the American Midwest." Calling it, in *North Dakota Quarterly,* "above all a poem of endurance and growth through radical commitment," Rory Holscher believes that for those who "have made a commitment to the exploration of radical possibilities, *Letter* could well assume the importance that *Howl* once had; it could become to adults what *Howl* was to so many adolescents."

"When McGrath began publishing in the early forties," wrote Des Pres, "his work was shaped by the strain and agitation of the thirties." Finding his early work "hard, spare, and abstract in the distantly conversational tone," and reflective of an established tradition, Mitchell describes McGrath's later work, however, as "long, loose in structure, extravagantly witty, emotionally varied, far less embedded in intellectual categories, local and personal." Moreover, McGrath's "ability to turn in these directions" Mitchell maintains, is responsible for *Letter to an Imaginary Friend*—"one of the most unusual poems we have, a personalized history of 'the generous wish' of the far Left in our country, tender and raucous, damning and hoping, a poem written in an uncongenial time in which he writhes and rages to keep the hope of 'the solidarity/In the circle of hungry equals' alive." Considered as a whole, "these volumes make one of the most interesting and important—yes, one of the most enjoyable—of long poems written in recent years," says Stern, adding that *Letter to an Imaginary Friend* is "a fine, first-rate piece of work, by our single best radical poet, and without any qualifiers, by one of our best poets." Similarly, in *North Country Anvil,* James N. Naiden recommends the epic as "essential reading to anyone who wishes to understand one of the most significant long poems in recent American history, as well as the moving force—the personal ethos—of one of the most important poets now writing."

"What is obvious to any careful reader of McGrath's poetry is that *nothing is missing* from the man's range . . .," writes Alvarado Cardona-Hine in *North Dakota Quarterly.* "It is sage and innocent, canny, detailed and in flight, sensual, fulminating, apparent, immanent, sacred. . . . He is a true poet, not a propagandist, and his work will live because it resonates with a thousand surprising innuendoes of an inner life beyond politics, beyond experience itself. McGrath's work is real and thus his roots are in Dream." According to Sam Hamill in *North Dakota Quarterly,* "This gentle, dedicated worker in the Republic of Letters neither needs nor wants a modifier before the noun that names him: poet. Let us please dispense with qualifiers of all kinds. What McGrath is, first and foremost, is a poet. . . . He is a comic genius and a gentle revolutionary. He is a Rhodes Scholar grown up to be a road scholar, a true literatus who exemplifies the best of the literary tradition. . . . Maybe we would do well enough to call him a poet's poet, or, even better, a people's poet. But while honoring a grand man, a grand poet, let us first of all honor him for the problem he presents. Too few of our poets are dexterous enough to present us with modulations of the human soul as profound as those of McGrath. And for that I praise."

"McGrath's poetry will be remembered in one hundred years when many more fashionable voices have been forgotten," predicts Thompson. "Here is a poet addressing not poets only but speaking in a public voice to a public which has not yet learned to listen to him." Adding that "the achievement of his art has matched the achievement of his integrity" Thompson suggests that "McGrath's is an implacable alienation from all that has had anything fashionable going for it in the past four decades of American culture—and from a good deal of what has been offered as counterculture also." And to Des Pres and Gibbons, McGrath declares, "I don't think I've ever lost any sense at all of what I wanted: to try to get as much in the world as I could to move."

MEDIA ADAPTATIONS: Taped recordings have been made of McGrath's poetry readings in Los Angeles for KUSC-radio, 1958-59, and for KPFK-radio, February 18, 1960, in addition to readings at radio station WBAI in New York, and in English departments at several colleges and universities, including North Dakota State University, Moorhead State College, University of New Mexico, and University of California, Berkeley. A video tape of a poetry reading at St. Cloud State College was also recorded.

BIOGRAPHICAL/CRITICAL SOURCES:

BOOKS

Contemporary Literary Criticism, Volume 28, Gale, 1984.
Stern, Frederick C., *The Revolutionary Poet in the United States: The Poetry of Thomas McGrath,* University of Missouri Press, 1988.

PERIODICALS

American Book Review, July/August, 1980, May/June, 1983.
Antioch Review, fall-winter, 1970-71.
Choice, June, 1971.
Library Journal, August, 1970, September 1, 1985.
New Republic, April 21, 1973.
New York Times, March 7, 1948.
New York Times Book Review, February 21, 1965.
North Country Anvil, August/September, 1973.
North Dakota Quarterly, fall, 1982, fall, 1988.
Poetry, October, 1971.
Publishers Weekly, March 2, 1970.
Saturday Review of Literature, April 17, 1948.
Southwest Review, winter, 1980.
TriQuarterly, fall, 1987.
Western American Literature, fall, 1986.

*   *   *

McGUANE, Thomas (Francis III) 1939-

PERSONAL: Born December 11, 1939, in Wyandotte, Mich.; son of Thomas Francis (a manufacturer) and Alice (Torphy) McGuane; married Portia Rebecca Crockett, September 8, 1962 (divorced, 1975); married Margot Kidder (an actress), August, 1976 (divorced May, 1977); married Laurie Buffett, September 19, 1977; children: (first marriage) Thomas Francis IV; (second marriage) Maggie; (third marriage) Anne Buffett, Heather Hume McGuane (stepdaughter). *Education:* Attended University of Michigan and Olivet College; Michigan State University,

B.A., 1962; Yale University, M.F.A., 1965; additional study at Stanford University, 1966-67.

ADDRESSES: Home—Box 25, McLeod, Mont. 59052. *Agent*—John Hawkins Associates, 71 West 23rd St., Suite 1600, New York, N.Y. 10010.

CAREER: Rancher in McLeod, Mont.; writer.

AWARDS, HONORS: Wallace Stegner fellowship, Stanford University, 1966-67; Richard and Hinda Rosenthal Foundation Award in fiction from American Academy, 1971, for *The Bushwacked Piano;* National Book Award fiction nomination, 1974, for *Ninety-two in the Shade.*

WRITINGS:

NOVELS

The Sporting Club, Simon & Schuster, 1969, recent edition, Penguin, 1987.
The Bushwacked Piano, Simon & Schuster, 1971, recent edition, Random House, 1984.
Ninety-two in the Shade (also see below), Farrar, Straus, 1973, recent edition, Penguin, 1987.
Panama, Farrar, Straus, 1977, recent edition, Penguin, 1987.
Nobody's Angel, Random House, 1982.
Something to Be Desired, Random House, 1984.
Keep the Change, Houghton, 1989.

SCREENPLAYS

"Rancho Deluxe," United Artists, 1975.
(Also director) "Ninety-two in the Shade" (adapted from his novel of the same title), United Artists, 1975.
The Missouri Breaks (produced by United Artists, 1976), Ballantine, 1976.
(With Bud Shrake) "Tom Horn," Warner Brothers, 1980.

OTHER

(Author of introduction) Russell Chatham, *The Angler's Coast,* Clark City Press, 1976.
An Outside Chance: Essays on Sport, Farrar, Straus, 1980.
In the Crazies: Book and Portfolio (signed limited edition), Winn Books, 1984.
(Author of introduction) William A. Allard, *Vanishing Breed: Photographs of the Cowboy and the West,* Bullfinch Press, 1984.
To Skin a Cat (short stories), Dutton, 1986.

Special contributor to *Sports Illustrated,* 1969-73.

SIDELIGHTS: Thomas McGuane's first three novels established his reputation as a flamboyant stylist and satirist. *The Sporting Club, The Bushwacked Piano,* and *Ninety-two in the Shade* juxtapose the ugly materialism of modern America against the beauty and power of the natural world. According to *Detroit Free Press* writer Gregory Skwira, this trio of books perfectly captures "the hip disillusionment and general disorientation of the late 1960s." Although his early work had earned him high praise from the literary establishment, McGuane temporarily abandoned the novel in the early 1970s for work in the film industry. The personal chaos he experienced during that time is reflected in such later novels as *Panama* and *Something to Be Desired.* In these books, emotional depth and honesty take precedence over stylistic flamboyance, and many critics regard them as McGuane's finest.

McGuane grew up in an Irish family where storytelling was a natural art. When he announced his intention to become a writer, however, his parents disapproved of his ambition as hopelessly impractical. To counter their skepticism, McGuane devoted himself almost exclusively to his artistic efforts. While his university classmates enjoyed traditional college parties and diversions, McGuane wrote, read voraciously, studied the novel, or engaged in esoteric discussions with fellow students and contemporary novelists Jim Harrison and William Hjortsberg. McGuane's sober disposition earned him the nickname "The White Knight." His single-mindedness paid off: *The Sporting Club* was published when he was nearly thirty, and *The Bushwacked Piano* and *Ninety-two in the Shade* followed in quick succession.

The plots of these three novels are very different, but they are closely linked in style, theme, and tone. Each is written in what R. T. Smith calls in *American Book Review* "amphetamine-paced, acetylene-bright prose." "All present a picture of an America which has evolved into a 'declining snivelization' (from *Bushwacked*), a chrome-plated, chaotic landscape which threatens to lead right-thinking men to extremes of despair or utter frivolity," explains Larry McCaffrey in *Fiction International.* "Each of them presents main characters . . . who have recognized the defiled state of affairs around them, and who are desperately seeking out a set of values which allows them, as Skelton [the protagonist of *Ninety-two in the Shade*] puts it, 'to find a way of going on.' " In McCaffrey's estimation, the most remarkable thing about McGuane's writing is that with it, the author is "able to take the elements of this degraded condition and fashion from them shocking, energetic, and often beautiful works of prose—works which both mirror and comment upon our culture and which, yet, in their eloquence, transcend it."

McGuane's intense approach to his art was altered forever in 1972. Driving at 120 miles per hour on a trip from Montana to Key West, he lost control of his car and was involved in a serious accident. He walked away from it physically unharmed, but so profoundly shaken that he was unable to speak for some time thereafter. After this brush with death, his relentless concentration on writing seemed misguided to him. McCaffrey quotes McGuane in the *Dictionary of Literary Biography Yearbook:* "After the accident, I finally realized I could stop pedaling so intensely, get off the bike and walk around the neighborhood. . . . It was getting unthinkable to spend another year sequestered like that, writing, and I just dropped out." McGuane was also finding it increasingly difficult to support his family on a novelist's income; while his books had received critical acclaim, none had been best-sellers. Accordingly, when movie producer Elliot Kastner asked him if he would be interested in a film project, McGuane eagerly accepted. Over the next few years he wrote several screenplays, and directed the screen version of *Ninety-two in the Shade.*

Changes were not limited to the author's work; his personal life was undergoing a transformation as well. Together with the other members of "Club Mandible"—a loosely structured group of friends including singer Jimmy Buffett—McGuane began to enjoy a hedonistic lifestyle. He explained to Thomas Carney in *Esquire,* "I had paid my dues. . . . Enough was enough. In 1962 I had changed from a sociopath to a bookworm and now I just changed back. Buffett was in the same shape. We both heard voices telling us to do something." Accordingly, writes Carney, "McGuane the straight arrow who had spent years telling his friends how to live their lives while he lived his like a hermit became McGuane the boogie chieftain, rarely out of full dance regalia. The White Knight began staying out all night, enjoying drugs and drink in quantities. And women other than his wife."

McGuane's name began appearing in tabloids when he became romantically involved with actress Elizabeth Ashley during the shooting of his first film, "Rancho Deluxe." Ashley also starred in "Ninety-two in the Shade"; while still linked with her, McGuane began an affair with another cast member, Margot Kidder. When McGuane and his first wife, Becky, divorced, Becky married the male lead of "Ninety-two in the Shade," Peter Fonda, and McGuane married Margot Kidder, already the mother of his second child. McGuane and Kidder divorced several months later. The unexpected deaths of his father and sister compounded the confusion in McGuane's life. He told Skwira that the media depiction of his activities at that time was "overblown," but admitted, "I had a lot of fun drinking and punching people out for a short period of time."

The turmoil of that interval was clearly reflected in *Panama,* McGuane's first novel in four years. It is a first-person description of the disintegrating life of rock star Chester Hunnicutt Pomeroy, an overnight sensation who is burning out on his excessive lifestyle. In McCaffrey's words, *Panama* "in many ways appears to be a kind of heightened, surreal portrayal of McGuane's own suffering, self-delusion, and eventual self-understanding—a book which moves beyond his earlier novels' satiric and ironic stances." The book drew strong reactions, both favorable and unfavorable. Many reviewers who had unreservedly praised McGuane's earlier work received *Panama* coolly, with some implying that the author's screenwriting stint had ruined him as a novelist. A *Washington Post Book World* essay by Jonathan Yardley dismisses *Panama* as "a drearily self-indulgent little book, a contemplation of the price of celebrity that was, in point of fact, merely an exploitation of the author's new notoriety." Richard Elman complains in the *New York Times Book Review* that *Panama* "is all written up in a blowsy, first-person prose that goes in all directions and winds up being, basically, a *kvetch.*" He states that McGuane, "who was once upon a time wacky and droll [and who] is now sloppy and doleful," suffers from an inability to recognize "good" versus "bad" writing. "Everything of craft that must be done right is done wrong. . . . This book isn't written; it is hallucinated. The reader is asked to do the writer's work of imagining."

Other reviewers applaud *Panama* as the novel that finally joins McGuane's stylistic brilliance with an emotional intensity lacking in his earlier efforts. Susan Lardner suggests in a *New Yorker* review that McGuane's work as a director perhaps enriched the subsequent novel: "Maybe as a result of the experience, he has added to his store of apprehensions some dismal views of fame and the idea that life is a circus performance. . . . Whatever risk McGuane may have sensed in attempting a fourth novel with a simultaneous plunge into first person narration, the feat proves successful. The audience is left dazzled by the ingenuity of his turn, somewhat aghast at the swagger, hungry for more." Writing in the *Washington Post Book World,* Philip Caputo calls it McGuane's "most relentlessly honest novel. . . . Although *Panama* is as well written as its predecessors, its first-person point of view endows it with a greater directness; and the book not only gives us a look at the void, it takes us down into it. . . . *Panama* also contains some of the finest writing McGuane has done so far." *Village Voice* contributor Gary L. Fisketjon notes, "*Panama* is more ambitious if less slick than the earlier novels, which were restrained and protected by the net of a hotwired style and a consummate mockery; the humor here is not as harsh, and the objectivity is informed more by empathy than disdain. . . . Moving beyond satire, McGuane has achieved something difficult and strange, a wonderfully written novel that balances suffering and understanding." And in a Toronto *Globe & Mail* essay, Thad McIlroy deems *Panama* "one of the best books to have been published in the United States in the last 20 years.

It's minimal, mad, disjointed at times, and consistently brilliant, terrifying and exhilarating. McGuane's use of language, and his ever-precise ear for dialogue, raise the novel out of the actual and into the universal, the realm of our finest literature."

McGuane's life stabilized considerably after his 1977 marriage to Laurie Buffett, sister of his friend Jimmy Buffett. He told *CA:* "Laurie and I share everything. She deserves a lot of credit for my sanity and happiness." Living on his Montana ranch, the author perfected his riding and roping techniques and became a serious rodeo competitor. He commented to Carney in *Esquire,* "I've come to the point where art is no longer as important as life. Dropping six or seven good colts in the spring is just as satisfying as literature." McGuane's new down-to-earth attitude carried over to his prose style, as he explained to a *Detroit Free Press* interviewer: "I'm trying to remove the *tour de force* or superficially flashy side of my writing. I'm trying to write a cleaner, plainer kind of American English. . . . I feel I have considerably better balance than I have ever had in my life and I don't care to show off; I just want to get the job done." Christopher Lehmann-Haupt refers favorably to McGuane's new direction in his *New York Times* review of the novel *Nobody's Angel:* "Both the author's affection for his characters and the strength of his narrative seem to matter even more to him than his compulsion to be stylistically 'original.' "

While *Nobody's Angel* echoes the dark tone of *Panama,* McGuane's next novel marks the first time that one of his restless protagonists finds fulfillment. *Something to Be Desired* revolves around Lucien Taylor and his two loves, Emily and Suzanne. When Emily, the more seductive and mysterious of the two, drops Lucien to marry a doctor, Lucien marries the virtuous Suzanne. The newlyweds go to work in Central America, where Lucien finds himself unable to forget Emily. When he hears she has murdered her husband, he deserts his wife and child to bail her out. He moves to Emily's ranch and becomes her lover, but she soon jumps bail, leaving him the ranch. Lucien converts it into a resort and finds happiness in a reconciliation with his family. Ronald Varney comments in the *Wall Street Journal* that "the somewhat bizarre plot twists of Mr. McGuane's story occasionally seem implausible. . . . And yet Mr. McGuane manages to pull this story off rather well, giving it, as in his other novels, such a compressed dramatic style that the reader is constantly entertained and diverted." *New York Times Book Review* critic Robert Roper names McGuane's sixth novel "his best, a remarkable work of honest colors and fresh phrasings that deliver strong, earned emotional effects."

Thomas McGuane's work has drawn comparisons to many famous authors, including William Faulkner, Albert Camus, Thomas Pynchon, F. Scott Fitzgerald, and most especially to Ernest Hemingway. Both McGuane and Hemingway portray virile heroes and antiheroes vibrantly aware of their own masculinity; each author explores themes of men pitted against themselves and other men; each passionately loves game fishing and the outdoors. Discussing *Ninety-two in the Shade,* Thomas R. Edwards of the *New York Times Book Review* claims: "Clearly this is Hemingway country. Not just the he-man pleasures of McGuane's men but even the locales of the novels . . . recapitulate Hemingway's western-hemisphere life and works." McCaffrey concurs in a *Fiction International* piece: "If [the set of value-systems of McGuane's protagonists] sounds very familiar to Hemingway's notion of a 'code' devised to help one face up to an empty universe, it should; certainly McGuane's emphasis on male aggressions, his ritualized scenes involving fishing, . . . and even the locales (Key West, the upper Rockies, up in Michigan)

suggest something of Papa's influence, though with a distinctly contemporary, darkly humorous flavor."

When asked by Carter in *Fiction International* about the numerous Hemingway comparisons, McGuane replied: "I admire him, of course, and share a lot of similar interests, but I really don't write like him. . . . We have totally different styles. His world view was considerably more austere than mine. His insistence on his metaphysical closed system was fanatical. And he was a fanatic. But it gave him at his best moments a very beautiful prose style. And anyone who says otherwise is either stupid or is a lying sack of snake shit. We have few enough treasures in this twerp-ridden Republic to have to argue over Ernest Hemingway's greatness." To John Dorschner of the *Miami Herald* he speculated, "I can only agree that [my life and Hemingway's] appear to be similar, but that's all. What might be more pertinent is to think how my father was influenced by Hemingway. Places like the Keys and northern Michigan, those were places I was taken by my father."

Discussing his writing habits with Skwira in the *Detroit Free Press,* McGuane noted, "I find it to my advantage to show up for work in an extremely regular, quite uninterrupted way." He averages eight to ten hours of work a day, six or seven days a week. He credits his temperate lifestyle with giving him a keener awareness of his craft, admitting that in earlier years "I really didn't quite know how I was achieving the effects I was achieving in literature. . . . But I know exactly how [*Something to Be Desired*] was written: long hours and a sore a—, in a state of clarity. And at the end, I remembered how I did all of it. With that behind me, as I sit down to start again, I start with a sort of optimism, with some expectation of achieving a certain level of results. . . . The thing that's most exciting to me now is that I feel that, barring illness, I think I'm looking at a long stretch of time where I can concentrate longer and harder on what I do best, more so than I've ever done before. And feeling that in itself produces kind of a glow."

MEDIA ADAPTATIONS: The Sporting Club was adapted by Lorenzo Semple, Jr., for a full-length film released by Avco Embassy Pictures in 1971.

AVOCATIONAL INTERESTS: Fly-fishing, rodeo.

BIOGRAPHICAL/CRITICAL SOURCES:

BOOKS

Authors in the News, Volume 2, Gale, 1976.
Contemporary Literary Criticism, Gale, Volume 3, 1975, Volume 7, 1977, Volume 18, 1981, Volume 45, 1987.
Dictionary of Literary Biography, Volume 2: *American Novelists since World War II,* Gale, 1978.
Dictionary of Literary Biography Yearbook: 1980, Gale, 1981.
Klinkowitz, Jerome, *The New American Novel of Manners: The Fiction of Richard Yates, Dan Wakefield, and Thomas McGuane,* University of Georgia Press, 1986.

PERIODICALS

America, May 15, 1971.
American Book Review, May-June, 1983.
Atlantic, September, 1973.
Book World, May 2, 1971.
Chicago Tribune, November 5, 1978, April 12, 1985, November 3, 1986, October 9, 1989.
Chicago Tribune Book World, February 15, 1981.
Commonweal, October 26, 1973.
Crawdaddy, February, 1979.
Critique: Studies in Modern Fiction, August, 1975.

Detroit Free Press, January 27, 1985.

Detroit News, August 17, 1980, April 25, 1982, November 18, 1984.

Esquire, June 6, 1978.

Feature, February, 1979.

Fiction International, fall/winter, 1975.

Globe & Mail (Toronto), January 26, 1985, April 4, 1987, September 23, 1989.

Hudson Review, winter, 1973-74.

Los Angeles Times Book Review, September 17, 1989.

Miami Herald, October 13, 1974.

Nation, January 31, 1981, March 20, 1982.

New Mexico Humanities Review, fall, 1983.

New Republic, August 18, 1979.

Newsweek, April 19, 1971, July 23, 1973.

New Statesman, July 26, 1974.

New Yorker, September 11, 1971, June 23, 1973, April 19, 1979.

New York Review of Books, December 13, 1973.

New York Times, November 21, 1978, May 23, 1980, March 4, 1982, December 10, 1984, October 11, 1986, September 14, 1989.

New York Times Book Review, March 14, 1971, July 29, 1973, November 19, 1978, October 19, 1980, February 8, 1981, March 7, 1982, December 16, 1984, September 24, 1989.

Partisan Review, fall, 1972.

People, September 17, 1979, November 3, 1980.

Publishers Weekly, September 29, 1989.

Saturday Review, March 27, 1971.

Spectator, July 13, 1974.

Time, August 6, 1973, June 30, 1980.

Times Literary Supplement, May 24, 1985.

Tribune Books, September 17, 1989.

Village Voice, September 15, 1975, December 11, 1978.

Virginia Quarterly Review, spring, 1981.

Wall Street Journal, December 24, 1984.

Washington Post, December 30, 1980, October 2, 1986.

Washington Post Book World, November 19, 1978, February 28, 1982, December 16, 1984, September 3, 1989.

*   *   *

McINTYRE, Vonda N(eel) 1948-

PERSONAL: Born August 28, 1948, in Louisville, Ky.; daughter of H. Neel (an electrical engineer) and Vonda Keith (a volunteer worker) McIntyre. *Education:* University of Washington, Seattle, B.S., 1970, graduate study, 1970-71.

ADDRESSES: Home—P.O. Box 31041, Seattle, Wash. 98103-1041. *Agent*—Frances Collin, Marie Rodell-Frances Collin Literary Agency, 110 West 40th St., New York, N.Y. 10018.

CAREER: Writer, 1969—.

MEMBER: Authors Guild, Authors League of America, Science Fiction Writers of America, Planetary Society, Space Studies Institute, National Organization for Women, Cousteau Society.

AWARDS, HONORS: Nebula Award from Science Fiction Writers of America, 1974, for best science fiction novelette, "Of Mist, and Grass, and Sand"; Hugo Award from World Science Fiction Convention and Nebula Award, both 1979, both for best science fiction novel, *Dreamsnake;* American Book Award nomination for best paperback science fiction novel, 1980, for *Dreamsnake.*

WRITINGS:

The Exile Waiting (novel), Fawcett, 1975.

(Editor with Susan Janice Anderson) *Aurora: Beyond Equality,* Fawcett, 1976.

Dreamsnake (novel), Houghton, 1978.

Fireflood and Other Stories (includes novelettes "Of Mist, and Grass, and Sand" and "Aztecs"), Houghton, 1979.

(Contributor) Ursula K. Le Guin and Virginia Kidd, editors, *Interfaces* (short stories), Ace Books, 1980.

The Entropy Effect (novel), Timescape, 1981.

Star Trek II: The Wrath of Khan (novelization), Pocket Books, 1982.

Superluminal (novel), Houghton, 1983.

Star Trek III: The Search for Spock (novelization), Pocket Books, 1984.

Enterprise: The First Adventure (novel), Pocket Books, 1986.

Star Trek IV: The Voyage Home (novelization), Pocket Books, 1986.

Barbary (novel), Houghton, 1986.

Starfarers, Ace Books, 1989.

Screwtop (bound with *The Girl Who Was Plugged In* by James Triptree), Tor Books, 1989.

Contributor to science fiction magazines, including *Analog: Science Fiction/Science Fact.*

WORK IN PROGRESS: Three screenplays, "The Zero Level," "Raith," and "Dreamsnake."

SIDELIGHTS: Vonda N. McIntyre is the author of award-winning science fiction, including short stories, novelettes, and novels. Like Ursula Le Guin, to whom she has been favorably compared, McIntyre "portrays positively and optimistically the realization of individual human potential in a variety of characters," in the words of *Science Fiction and Fantasy Review* contributing critic Philip E. Smith II. In a letter to *CA,* McIntyre explains her fascination with the genre this way: "I write science fiction because its boundaries are the only ones wide enough for me to explore experiences people have not had—*yet;* and because it allows my characters to develop as far as their ability will take them, unlimited by the crippling demands and unambitious expectations our society puts on us."

McIntyre's commitment to the unlimited development of her mostly female characters has earned her the reputation of being a feminist writer. In her novelette "Of Mist, and Grass, and Sand," first published in *Analog: Science Fiction/Science Fact,* McIntyre portrays Snake, a healer who cures with venomous snakes. Two of her three snakes, Mist and Sand, are genetically modified to produce a healing venom when fed the proper drug. The bite of the third, an alien dreamsnake named Grass, delivers a peaceful death to the incurably ill. The story ends with Grass being killed by the frightened parents of a boy Snake is trying to heal. "Snake is as complex and sympathetic a character as SF has realized in some years: tough, tender, bitter, forgiving, afraid, daring, independent and loving," comments Bud Foote in the *Detroit News.* Carolyn Wendell concurs, declaring in *Extrapolation* that Snake is a departure from "the cliched science-fiction female who may feel, but only the gentler emotions, and who certainly never thinks."

In *Dreamsnake,* a continuation of the successful novelette, Snake quests for a new dreamsnake, without which she risks the loss of her self-respect and the disparagement of her peers. "This is a superbly crafted s.f. adventure story," writes Gerald Jonas in the *New York Times Book Review.* Jonas also observes that "everything about this world, from its wild animals to its people, is described with luminous clarity." Alex de Jonge in *Spectator* praises *Dreamsnake* as "a gentle, moving and feminine book in the good sense of that word."

Many of the writings in McIntyre's next book, *Fireflood and Other Stories,* illustrate her theme of unlimited human development by presenting individuals who have been biologically altered in unusual ways. Some fly, others breathe underwater, and still others burrow through the earth. *Village Voice* reviewer Eve Ottenberg believes McIntyre's preoccupation with biological change "comes from her feminism, her desire to show a future in which sex roles have been radically changed by evolution." Yet other critics claim that these biological changes result not in freedom for either sex, but in the alienation of people in general. McIntyre "describes people isolated on genetic islands of intellectual, physiological, and technical specialization, and the grotesque mistakes possible to mere humans trying to invent better humans," writes Carolyn F. Ruffin in the *Christian Science Monitor.* Ruffin's view is shared by *Washington Post Book World* contributor Joanna Russ, who declares, "Critics have noted McIntyre's feminism, but (at least in this collection) alienation—usually literal—is her real subject, and alien(ated) beings her heroes."

One such alien being, who appears in the novelette "Aztecs," is starship pilot Laenea Trevelyan. The pilots are set apart from the rest of their species, not only because they hold a highly respected position, but also because they have had their hearts replaced with electronic pumps. These pulseless hearts allow them to travel at velocities surpassing the speed of light. Unfortunately, they also make the pilots incompatible with normal humans, which Laenea discovers when she falls in love with Radu Dracul, a starship crew member. Since Laenea is unwilling to renounce her profession and be returned to her normal state, and Radu is ineligible to become a pilot, the two must part. Praising "Aztecs" and the collection as a whole in the *Magazine of Fantasy and Science Fiction,* Thomas M. Disch writes that McIntyre "seems to be moving from strength to strength. In the concluding novella, 'Aztecs,' she is able finally to write 'paid' to an emotional theme dealt with obsessively, but never quite successfully, in many of the other stories—the need to renounce a love that is in conflict with personal growth."

In *Superluminal,* an expansion of "Aztecs," the paths of Radu and Laenea cross again when Laenea is lost on her training flight and Radu sets out to find her. Although the two are eventually reunited, Radu decides to stay with Orca, the underwater inhabitant who helped him search for Laenea. In this novel, "McIntyre has several point-of-view characters and tries to establish individual perspectives and backgrounds for each, but not always successfully," writes Smith in *Science Fiction and Fantasy Review.* Some of the more successful characterizations are of Orca and the divers, according to *New York Times Book Review* contributing critic Gerald Jonas, who finds their adventures "much more vivid" than those of Laenea and the pilots. "Perhaps Miss McIntyre is simply more at home with cultures whose 'technology' is based on biology rather than physics," he observes. In a review published in *Analog: Science Fiction/Science Fact,* Tom Easton expresses a similar view, predicting that "any sequel to this book will dwell far more on the world of divers. . . . Wonders loom in their lives, unpreempted by cosmology." Despite his reservations about parts of the narrative, Easton concludes: "I enjoyed the book. McIntyre's characters live. Her vision enchants and intrigues. Her world beckons. Follow, and enjoy."

BIOGRAPHICAL/CRITICAL SOURCES:

BOOKS

Contemporary Literary Criticism, Volume 18, Gale, 1981.

PERIODICALS

Analog: Science Fiction/Science Fact, March, 1984.
Christian Science Monitor, January 23, 1980.
Detroit News, March 16, 1980.
Extrapolation, winter, 1979.
Magazine of Fantasy and Science Fiction, January, 1979, July, 1980.
New York Times Book Review, June 25, 1978, November 6, 1983.
Pacific Northwest Review of Books, June, 1978.
Science Fiction and Fantasy Review, March, 1984.
Spectator, August 26, 1978.
Village Voice, March 3, 1980.
Washington Post Book World, February 24, 1980.

*   *   *

McKAY, Claude
See McKAY, Festus Claudius

*   *   *

McKAY, Festus Claudius   1889-1948
(Claude McKay; Eli Edwards, pseudonym)

PERSONAL: Born September 15, 1889 (some sources say 1890) in Sunny Ville (some sources say Clarendon), Jamaica, British West Indies (now Jamaica); immigrated to the United States; naturalized U.S. citizen, 1940; died of heart failure, May 22, 1948, in Chicago, Ill.; buried at Calvary Cemetery, Woodside, N.Y.; son of Thomas Francis (a farmer) and Anne Elizabeth (a farmer; maiden name, Edwards) McKay; married Eulalie Imelda Edwards, July 30, 1914 (divorced); children: Ruth Hope. *Education:* Attended Tuskegee Normal & Industrial Institute, 1912, and Kansas State College, 1912-14. *Religion:* Roman Catholic.

ADDRESSES: Home—Chicago, Ill.

CAREER: Writer. Worked as cabinetmaker's apprentice and wheelwright; constable at Jamaican Constabulary, Kingston, 1909; longshoreman, porter, bartender, and waiter, 1910-14; restaurateur, 1914; writer for *Pearsons Magazine,* 1918, and *Workers' Dreadnought* in London, England, 1919; associate editor of *Liberator,* 1921; American Workers representative at Third International in Moscow, U.S.S.R., 1922; artist's model in mid-1920s; worked for Rex Ingram's film studio in France, c. 1926; shipyard worker, c. 1941.

AWARDS, HONORS: Medal from Jamaican Institute of Arts and Sciences, c. 1912; Harmon Foundation Award for distinguished literary achievement from the National Association for the Advancement of Colored People (NAACP), 1929, for *Harlem Shadows* and *Home to Harlem;* award from James Weldon Johnson Literary Guild, 1937.

WRITINGS:

UNDER NAME CLAUDE McKAY

Songs of Jamaica (poetry; also see below), introduction by Walter Gardner, 1912, reprinted, Mnemosyne Publications.
Constab Ballads (poetry; also see below), Watts, 1912.
Spring in New Hampshire, and Other Poems, Richards, 1920.
Harlem Shadows: The Poems of Claude McKay, introduction by Max Eastman, Harcourt, 1922.
Home to Harlem (novel), Harper, 1928, reprinted, Books, 1965.
Banjo, a Story without a Plot (novel), Harper, 1929, reprinted, Harcourt, 1970.
Gingertown (short stories), Harper, 1932.

Banana Bottom (novel), Harper, 1933, reprinted, Chatham, 1970.

A Long Way From Home (autobiography), Furman, 1937, reprinted, Arno Press, 1969.

Harlem: Negro Metropolis (nonfiction), Dutton, 1940, reprinted, Harcourt, 1968.

Selected Poems, introduction by John Dewey, biographical note by Eastman, Bookman, 1953.

The Passion of Claude McKay: Selected Poetry and Prose, 1912-1948, edited by Wayne F. Cooper, Schocken, 1973.

The Dialectic Poetry of Claude McKay (contains *Songs of Jamaica* and *Constab Ballads*), edited by Cooper, Books for Libraries Press, 1972.

Trial by Lynching: Stories about Negro Life in North America, re-translated into English from Russian-language version by Robert Winter, edited by Alan L. McLeod, preface by H. H. Anniah Gowda, Centre for Commonwealth Literature and Research, University of Mysore, 1977.

The Negroes in America, re-translated into English from Russian-language version by Winter, edited by McLeod, Kennikat, 1977.

Work represented in anthologies. Contributor to periodicals, including *Workers' Dreadnought, Negro World, Catholic Worker, Ebony, Epistle, Interracial Review, Jewish Frontier, Nation, Seven Arts* (under pseudonym Eli Edwards), *New York Herald Tribune Books,* and *Phylon.*

SIDELIGHTS: Claude McKay was a key figure in the Harlem Renaissance, a prominent literary movement of the 1920s. His work ranged from vernacular verse celebrating peasant life in Jamaica to fairly militant poems challenging white authority in America, and from generally straightforward tales of black life in both Jamaica and America to more philosophically ambitious fiction addressing instinctual/intellectual duality, which McKay found central to the black individual's efforts to cope in a racist society. Consistent in his various writings is his disdain for racism and the sense that bigotry's implicit stupidity renders its adherents pitiable as well as loathsome. As Arthur D. Drayton wrote in his essay "Claude McKay's Human Pity" (included by editor Ulli Beier in the volume *Introduction to African Literature*): "McKay does not seek to hide his bitterness. But having preserved his vision as poet and his status as a human being, he can transcend bitterness. In seeing . . . the significance of the Negro for mankind as a whole, he is at once protesting as a Negro and uttering a cry for the race of mankind as a member of that race. His human pity was the foundation that made all this possible."

McKay was born in Sunny Ville, Jamaica, in 1889. The son of peasant farmers, he was infused with racial pride and a great sense of black heritage. His early literary interests, though, were in English poetry. Under the tutelage of his brother, schoolteacher Uriah Theophilus McKay, and a neighboring Englishman, Walter Jekyll, McKay studied the British masters—including John Milton, Alexander Pope, and the later romantics—and European philosophers such as eminent pessimist Arthur Schopenhauer, whose works Jekyll was then translating from German into English. It was Jekyll who advised aspiring poet McKay to cease mimicking the English poets and begin producing verse in Jamaican dialect.

At age seventeen McKay departed from Sunny Ville to apprentice as a woodworker in Brown's Town. But he studied there only briefly before leaving to work as a constable in the Jamaican capital, Kingston. In Kingston he experienced and encountered extensive racism, probably for the first time in his life. His native

Sunny Ville was predominantly populated by blacks, but in substantially white Kingston blacks were considered inferior and capable of only menial tasks. McKay quickly grew disgusted with the city's bigoted society, and within one year he returned home to Sunny Ville.

During his brief stays in Brown's Town and Kingston McKay continued writing poetry, and once back in Sunny Ville, with Jekyll's encouragement, he published the verse collections *Songs of Jamaica* and *Constab Ballads* in London in 1912. In these two volumes McKay portrays opposing aspects of black life in Jamaica. *Songs of Jamaica* presents an almost celebratory portrait of peasant life, with poems addressing subjects such as the peaceful death of McKay's mother and the black people's ties to the Jamaican land. *Constab Ballads,* however, presents a substantially bleaker perspective on the plight of Jamaican blacks and contains several poems explicitly critical of life in urban Kingston. Writing in *The Negro Novel in America,* Robert Bone noted the differing sentiments of the two collections, but he also contended that the volumes share a sense of directness and refreshing candor. He wrote: "These first two volumes are already marked by a sharpness of vision, an inborn realism, and a freshness which provides a pleasing contrast with the conventionality which, at this time, prevails among the black poets of the United States."

For *Songs of Jamaica* McKay received an award and stipend from the Jamaican Institute of Arts and Sciences. He used the money to finance a trip to America, and in 1912 he arrived in South Carolina. He then traveled to Alabama and enrolled at the Tuskegee Institute, where he studied for approximately two months before transferring to Kansas State College. In 1914 he left school entirely for New York City and worked various menial jobs. As in Kingston, McKay encountered racism in New York City, and that racism compelled him to continue writing poetry.

In 1917, under the pseudonym Eli Edwards, McKay published two poems in the periodical *Seven Arts.* His verses were discovered by critic Frank Hattis, who then included some of McKay's other poems in *Pearson's Magazine.* Among McKay's most famous poems from this period is "To the White Fiends," a vitriolic challenge to white oppressors and bigots. A few years later McKay befriended Max Eastman, Communist sympathizer and editor of the magazine *Liberator.* McKay published more poems in Eastman's magazine, notably the inspirational "If We Must Die," which defended black rights and threatened retaliation for prejudice and abuse. "Like men we'll face the murderous, cowardly pack," McKay wrote, "Pressed to the wall, dying, but fighting back!" In *Black Poets of the United States,* Jean Wagner noted that "If We Must Die" transcends specifics of race and is widely prized as an inspiration to persecuted people throughout the world. "Along with the will to resistance of black Americans that it expresses," Wagner wrote, "it voices also the will of oppressed people of every age who, whatever their race and wherever their region, are fighting with their backs against the wall to win their freedom."

Upon publication of "If We Must Die" McKay commenced two years of travel and work abroad. He spent part of 1919 in Holland and Belgium, then moved to London and worked on the periodical *Workers' Dreadnought.* In 1920 he published his third verse collection, *Spring in New Hampshire,* which was notable for containing "Harlem Shadows," a poem about the plight of black prostitutes in the degrading urban environment. McKay used this poem, which symbolically presents the degradation of the entire black race, as the title for a subsequent collection.

McKay returned to the United States in 1921 and involved himself in various social causes. The next year he published *Harlem Shadows,* a collection from previous volumes and periodicals publications. This work contains many of his most acclaimed poems—including "If We Must Die"—and assured his stature as a leading member of the literary movement referred to as the Harlem Renaissance. He capitalized on his acclaim by redoubling his efforts on behalf of blacks and laborers: he became involved in the Universal Negro Improvement Association and produced several articles for its publication, *Negro World,* and he traveled to the Soviet Union which he had previously visited with Eastman, and attended the Communist party's Fourth Congress.

Eventually McKay went to Paris, where he developed a severe respiratory infection and supported himself intermittently by working as an artist's model. His infection eventually necessitated his hospitalization, but after recovering he resumed traveling, and for the next eleven years he toured Europe and portions of northern Africa. During this period he also published three novels and a short story collection. The first novel, *Home to Harlem,* may be his most recognized title. Published in 1928, it concerns a black soldier—Jake—who abruptly abandons his military duties and returns home to Harlem. Jake represents, in rather overt fashion, the instinctual aspect of the individual, and his ability to remain true to his feelings enables him to find happiness with a former prostitute, Felice. Juxtaposed with Jake's behavior is that of Ray, an aspiring writer burdened with despair. His sense of bleakness derives largely from his intellectualized perspective, and it eventually compels him to leave alien, racist America for his homeland of Haiti.

In *The Negro Novel in America,* Robert Bone wrote that the predominantly instinctual Jake and the intellectual Ray "represent different ways of rebelling against Western civilization." Bone added, however, that McKay was not entirely successful in articulating his protagonists' relationships in white society. He declared that *Home to Harlem* was "unable to develop its primary conflict" and thus "bogs down in the secondary contrast between Jake and Ray."

Despite thematic flaws, *Home to Harlem*—with its sordid, occasionally harrowing scenes of ghetto life—proved extremely popular, and it gained recognition as the first commercially successful novel by a black writer. McKay quickly followed it with *Banjo,* a novel about a black vagabond living in the French port of Marseilles. Like Jake from *Home to Harlem,* protagonist Banjo embodies the largely instinctual way of living, though he is considerably more enterprising and quick-witted than the earlier character. Ray, the intellectual from *Home to Harlem,* also appears in *Banjo.* His plight is that of many struggling artists who are compelled by social circumstances to support themselves with conventional employment. Both Banjo and Ray are perpetually dissatisfied and disturbed by their limited roles in white society, and by the end of the novel the men are prepared to depart from Marseilles.

Banjo failed to match the acclaim and commercial success of *Home to Harlem,* but it confirmed McKay's reputation as a serious, provocative artist. In his third novel, *Banana Bottom,* he presented a more incisive exploration of his principal theme, the black individual's quest for cultural identity in a white society. *Banana Bottom* recounts the experiences of a Jamaican peasant girl, Bita, who is rescued by white missionaries after suffering a rape. Bita's new providers try to impose their cultural values on her by introducing her to organized Christianity and the British educational system. Their actions culminate in a horribly bun-

gled attempt to arrange Bita's marriage to an aspiring minister. The prospective groom is exposed as a sexual aberrant, whereupon Bita flees white society. She eventually finds happiness and fulfillment among the black peasants.

Critics agree that *Banana Bottom* is McKay's most skillful delineation of the black individual's predicament in white society. Unfortunately, the novel's thematic worth was largely ignored when the book first appeared in 1933. Its positive reviews then were related to McKay's extraordinary evocation of the Jamaican tropics and his mastery of melodrama. In the ensuing years, though, *Banana Bottom* has gained increasing acknowledgement as McKay's finest fiction and the culmination of his efforts to articulate his own tension and unease through the novel.

McKay's other noteworthy publication during his final years abroad was *Gingertown,* a collection of twelve short stories. Six of the tales are devoted to Harlem life, and they reveal McKay's preoccupation with black exploitation and humiliation. Other tales are set in Jamaica and even in North Africa. McKay's last foreign home before he returned to the United States in the mid-1930s. Once back in Harlem he began an autobiographical work, *A Long Way From Home,* in which he related his own problems as a black individual in a white society.

By the late 1930s McKay had developed a keen interest in Catholicism. Through Ellen Tarry, who wrote children's books, he became active in Harlem's Friendship House. His new-found religious interest, together with his observations and experiences at the Friendship House, inspired his essay collection, *Harlem: Negro Metropolis.* Like *Banjo, Banana Bottom,* and *Gingertown, Harlem: Negro Metropolis* failed to spark much interest from a reading public that was a tiring of literature by and about blacks. With his reputation already waning, McKay moved to Chicago and worked as a teacher for a Catholic organization. By the mid-1940s his health had deteriorated. He endured several illnesses throughout his last years and eventually died of heart failure in May, 1948.

In the years immediately following his death McKay's reputation continued to decline as critics found him conventional and somewhat shallow. Recently, however, McKay has gained recognition for his intense commitment to expressing the predicament of his fellow blacks, and he is now admired for devoting his art and life to social protest. As Robert A. Smith wrote in his *Phylon* publication, "Claude McKay: An Essay in Criticism": "Although he was frequently concerned with the race problem, his style is basically lucid. One feels disinclined to believe that the medium which he chose was too small, or too large for his message. He has been heard."

BIOGRAPHICAL/CRITICAL SOURCES:

BOOKS

Barton, Rebecca Chalmers, *Witnesses for Freedom: Negro Americans in Autobiography,* Harper, 1948.

Beier, Ulli, editor, *Introduction to African Literature: An Anthology of Critical Writing from "Black Orpheus,"* Longmans, 1967.

Bone, Robert, *The Negro Novel in America,* Yale University Press, 1958.

Brawley, Benjamin, *The Negro Genius: A New Appraisal of the Achievement of the American Negro in Literature and the Fine Arts,* Dodd, 1937.

Bronze, Stephen, *Roots of Negro Consciousness, the 1920's: Three Harlem Renaissance Authors,* Libra, 1964.

Dictionary of Literary Biography, Gale, Volume 4: *American Writers in Paris, 1920-1939,* 1980, Volume 45: *American*

Poets, 1880-1945, First Series, 1986, Volume 51: *American Writers from the Harlem Renaissance to 1940,* 1987.

Emanuel, James A., and Theodore L. Gross, *Dark Symphony: Negro Literature in America,* Free Press, 1968.

Fullinwider, S. P., *The Mind and Mood of Black America: 20th Century Thought,* Dorsey, 1969.

Gayle, Addison, Jr., *Claude McKay: The Black Poet at War,* Broadside, 1972.

Giles, James R., *Claude McKay,* Hall, 1976.

Gloster, Hugh M., *Negro Voices in American Fiction,* University of North Carolina Press, 1948.

Huggins, Nathan, *Harlem Renaissance,* Oxford University Press, 1971.

Hughes, Carl Milton, *The Negro Novelist: 1940-1950,* Citadel, 1953.

Kent, George E., *Blackness and the Adventure of Western Culture,* Third World Press, 1972.

Ramchand, Kenneth, *The West Indian Novel and Its Background,* Barnes & Noble, 1970.

Twentieth-Century Literary Criticism, Volume 7, Gale, 1982.

Wagner, Jean, *Les Poetes negres des Etats-Unis,* Librairies Istra, 1962, translation by Kenneth Douglas published as *Black Poets of the United States: From Paul Laurence Dunbar to Langston Hughes,* University of Illinois Press, 1973.

PERIODICALS

America, July 3, 1943.

Black Orpheus, June, 1965.

Bookman, April, 1928, February, 1930.

CLA Journal, March, 1972, June, 1973, December, 1975, March, 1980.

Crisis, June, 1928.

Extension, September, 1946.

Phylon, fall, 1948, fall, 1964.

New York Post, May 22, 1937.

Race, July, 1967.

Studies in Black Literature, summer, 1972.

*　　*　　*

McKILLIP, Patricia A(nne) 1948-

PERSONAL: Born February 29, 1948, in Salem, Ore.; daughter of Wayne T. and Helen (Roth) McKillip. *Education:* California State University, San Jose (now San Jose State University), B.A., 1971, M.A., 1973.

ADDRESSES: Home—2661 California, No. 14, San Francisco, Calif. 94115.

CAREER: Writer.

AWARDS, HONORS: World Fantasy Award for best novel, 1975, for *The Forgotten Beasts of Eld;* Hugo Award nomination, 1979, for *Harpist in the Wind.*

WRITINGS:

Stepping From the Shadows (novel), Atheneum, 1982.
Fool's Run (science fiction novel), Warner, 1987.

FANTASY ADVENTURES

The House on Parchment Street, Atheneum, 1973.
The Throme of the Erril of Sherill, Atheneum, 1973.
The Forgotten Beasts of Eld, Atheneum, 1974.
The Night Gift, Atheneum, 1976.
The Riddle-Master of Hed (first book in trilogy; also see below), Atheneum, 1976.

Heir of Sea and Fire (second book in trilogy; also see below), Atheneum, 1977.
Harpist in the Wind (third book in trilogy; also see below), Atheneum, 1979.
Riddle of Stars (trilogy; contains *The Riddle-Master of Hed, Heir of Sea and Fire,* and *Harpist in the Wind*), Doubleday, 1979 (published in England as *Chronicles of Morgon, Prince of Hed,* Futura Publications, 1979).
Moon-Flash, Atheneum, 1984.
The Moon and the Face, Atheneum, 1985.
The Changeling Sea, Atheneum, 1988.

SIDELIGHTS: Patricia A. McKillip's fantasy novels are remarkable for their rich characterizations and what Michael E. Stamm calls in *Fantasy Review* the "quiet elegance of her style and the sureness of her storytelling." "Before I ever started writing, I was a storyteller," the author tells *CA.* "I was the second of six children, and the babysitting duties were pretty constant. I don't know how old I was when I started telling stories to my younger siblings to while away the boredom of sitting in a car waiting while our parents shopped." She continues the explanation of her development as a writer in a publicity release from Atheneum Publishers: "At the beginning of my fourteenth summer . . . moody, bored with reading [and] playing the piano, . . . I sat down and wrote a thirty-page fairy tale. . . . I never stopped writing after that. A grim, tongue-tied, rather puritanical teenager, I developed a secret and satisfying other life, writing anything and everything: plays, poetry, short stories, fairy tales, even novels of a swashbuckling, Ruritanian sort. I read everything I could get my hands on—from [J. R. R.] Tolkien (who was a revelation) to Gore Vidal (a revelation of another sort)."

McKillip entered college as a music major, but upon deciding that "wanting to be a concert pianist was a little unrealistic," she became determined to make her living as a writer instead. "I spent the next few years studying history and literature, trying to turn the facile scribbling of a teenager into something that resembled a style, and trying to get published," she notes in the Atheneum publicity release. McKillip achieved this goal at the age of twenty-five when she published a children's novel, *The House on Parchment Street. Library Journal* describes it as "an entirely plausible contemporary ghost story peopled with three-dimensional characters."

Characterization is what *New York Times Book Review* contributor Georgess M'Hargue praises most highly in McKillip's next book, *The Forgotten Beasts of Eld.* This fantasy features Sybel, a woman wizard, and Coren, a warrior. *The Forgotten Beasts of Eld* is heavily laden with the trappings of fantasy, including dragons, talking animals, doorless towers and glass mountains. Although M'Hargue finds McKillip's language and imagery somewhat flowery, she praises the underlying story. *The Forgotten Beasts of Eld,* she declares, "works best on the strictly human level. Trust, loneliness, love's responsibilities and the toxicity of fate are the themes that underlie" the fantasy love story. "When [Sybel and Coren] manage to save their love in the end it is through a growth of courage and understanding far more meaningful than surviving any number of exotic eternal perils. That is why, finally, 'The Forgotten Beasts of Eld' is a very good book," summarizes M'Hargue.

The Forgotten Beasts of Eld and McKillip's later fantasies are classified by booksellers as children's books, but McKillip herself stated in a letter to *CA:* "I never deliberately decided to write for children; I just found them particularly satisfying to write about, and *The House on Parchment Street* happened to be the first thing I sold. When I decided to pull out the stops and write what I considered an adult fantasy, I was amazed when [it was published] as a young adult novel. What I didn't realize then was that the genre of young adult novels itself was changing and growing up."

Among McKillip's most ambitious projects has been her trilogy, *Riddle of Stars.* It follows the fortunes of Morgon from his beginnings as ruler of Hed, a peaceful, sleepy kingdom, to his ultimate destiny as a trained "riddle-master." Several reviewers note that, as in *The Forgotten Beasts of Eld,* the trilogy's greatest appeal comes from McKillip's strong, believable characters. Even after surviving many trials and a final "mythical and archetypal purification," Morgon "manages to maintain his humanity, . . . a humanity that endears him to the reader," explains Roger C. Schlobin in *Science Fiction and Fantasy Book Review.*

Reviewing the trilogy's first book, *The Riddle-Master of Hed,* for the *New York Times Book Review,* Glenn Shea agrees that McKillip's insight is great: "She understands that we spend much of our time choosing, not between good and evil, but between the lesser of two ills." But while conceding that McKillip is a writer of real talent, Shea claims that *The Riddle-Master of Hed* is burdened with "a stylized, operatic-fantasy plot that demands genius, not talent." Schlobin, however, reserves high praise for the entire trilogy, believing that its publication means "the canon of excellent women fantasists must now be expanded to include another superb effort. . . . McKillip's series delves deeply into the rich earth of full and human characterization, and creates a world elaborate in both magic and mythology."

Publication of *Stepping From the Shadows* marked McKillip's departure from the genre in which she had established herself. It is "her first adult novel," writes Charles Champlin of the *Los Angeles Times,* "and it is a beautifully written, honest, frequently funny and self-unsparing chronicle, in eight chapters, of the growing up of [Frances], a young woman who cannot be different, in any significant spiritual way, from McKillip herself." Each chapter is set in a different time and place of Frances's life and could stand alone as a short story, notes Champlin. "Cumulatively, they become a picture not only of the hard process of coming of age in current American society but an interior account of the making of a fantasist." Readers first meet Frances as a painfully shy second-grader with a rich fantasy life shared only with an imaginary sister. As she matures, the girl "starts to write out her fantasies and to conduct ever more serious dialogues with the other Frances," explains Champlin. "McKillip has put an imaginary playmate on paper and the more sophisticated truth that we all have an outside view of ourselves as well as the inside view; we perceive ourselves as strangers. What is different is just that the division within Frances is so intense, the withdrawal of both her selves from other human contact so complete that you sense she is at the brink of serious emotional disorder, redeemed by writing it all out. . . . McKillip's memory of the coming of age of an author is rich, particular and extremely appealing."

AVOCATIONAL INTERESTS: Music.

BIOGRAPHICAL/CRITICAL SOURCES:

PERIODICALS

Analog, January, 1980.
Fantasy Review, November, 1985.
Library Journal, May 15, 1973.
Los Angeles Times, March 26, 1982.
New York Times Book Review, October 13, 1974, March 6, 1977.
Science Fiction and Fantasy Review, May, 1979.
Washington Post Book World, January 9, 1986.

McLOUGHLIN, R. B.
See MENCKEN, H(enry) L(ouis)

*   *   *

McLUHAN, (Herbert) Marshall   1911-1980

PERSONAL: Born July 21, 1911, in Edmonton, Alberta, Canada; died after a long illness, December 31, 1980, in Toronto, Ontario, Canada; son of Herbert Ernest (a real estate and insurance salesman) and Elsie Naomi (an actress and monologuist; maiden name, Hall) McLuhan; married Corinne Keller Lewis, August 4, 1939; children: Eric, Mary McLuhan Colton, Teresa, Stephanie, Elizabeth, Michael. *Education:* University of Manitoba, B.A., 1932, M.A., 1934; Cambridge University, B.A., 1936, M.A., 1939, Ph.D., 1942. *Religion:* Roman Catholic.

ADDRESSES: Home—3 Wychwood Park, Toronto, Ontario, Canada M6G 2V5.

CAREER: University of Wisconsin—Madison, instructor, 1936-37; St. Louis University, St. Louis, Mo., instructor in English, 1937-44; Assumption University, Windsor, Ontario, associate professor of English, 1944-46; University of Toronto, St. Michael's College, Toronto, Ontario, associate professor, 1946-52, professor of English, 1952-80, creator (by appointment) and director of Center for Culture and Technology, 1963-80. Lecturer at numerous universities, congresses, and symposia in the United States and Canada; Albert Schweitzer Professor of Humanities at Fordham University, 1967-68. Chairman of Ford Foundation seminar on culture and communications, 1953-55; director of media project for U.S. Office of Education and National Association of Educational Broadcasters, 1959-60. Appointed by Vatican as consultor of Pontifical Commission for Social Communications, 1973. Consultant to Johnson, McCormick & Johnson Ltd. (public relations agency), Toronto, 1966-80, and to Responsive Environments Corp., New York City, 1968-80.

MEMBER: Royal Society of Canada (fellow), Modern Language Association of America, American Association of University Professors.

AWARDS, HONORS: Governor General's Literary Award for critical prose, 1963, for *The Gutenberg Galaxy: The Making of Typographic Man;* Fordham University Communications Award, 1964; D.Litt. from University of Windsor, 1965, Assumption University, 1966, Grinnell College, 1967, Simon Fraser University, 1967, St. John Fisher College, 1969, University of Edmonton, 1972, and University of Western Ontario, 1972; Litt.D. from University of Manitoba, 1967; Molson Prize of Canada Council for outstanding achievement in the social sciences, 1967; Carl-Einstein-Preis, German Critics Association, 1967; Companion of the Order of Canada, 1970; Institute of Public Relations President's Award (Great Britain), 1970; LL.D. from University of Alberta, 1971; Christian Culture Award, Assumption University, 1971; Gold Medal Award, President of the Italian Republic, 1971, for original work as philosopher of the mass media; President's Cabinet Award, University of Detroit, 1972.

WRITINGS:

"Henry IV": A Mirror for Magistrates (originally published in *University of Toronto Quarterly*), [Toronto], 1948.
The Mechanical Bride: Folklore of Industrial Man, Vanguard, 1951, reprinted, Beacon Press, 1967.
Counterblast, privately printed, 1954, revised and enlarged edition, designed by Harley Parker, Harcourt, 1969.

(Editor and author of introduction) Alfred Lord Tennyson, *Selected Poetry,* Rinehart, 1956.

(Editor with Edmund Carpenter) *Explorations in Communication* (anthology), Beacon Press, 1960.

The Gutenberg Galaxy: The Making of Typographic Man, University of Toronto Press, 1962, New American Library, 1969.

Understanding Media: The Extensions of Man (originally written as a report to U.S. Office of Education, 1960), McGraw, 1964.

(Compiler and author of notes and commentary with Richard J. Schoeck) *Voices of Literature* (anthology), two volumes, Holt (Toronto), 1964-65, Volume 1 published as *Voices of Literature: Sounds, Masks, Roles,* 1969. (With Quentin Fiore) *The Medium Is the Massage: An Inventory of Effects* (advance excerpt published in *Publishers Weekly,* April 3, 1967), designed by Jerome P. Agel, Random House, 1967.

(With V. J. Papanek and others) *Verbi-Voco-Visual Explorations* (originally published as Number 8 of *Explorations*), Something Else Press, 1967.

(With Fiore) *War and Peace in the Global Village: An Inventory of Some of the Current Spastic Situations That Could Be Eliminated by More Feedforward* (excerpt entitled "Fashion: A Bore War?" published in *Saturday Evening Post,* July 27, 1968), McGraw, 1968.

(With Parker) *Through the Vanishing Point: Space in Poetry and Painting,* Harper, 1968.

The Interior Landscape: The Literary Criticism of Marshall McLuhan, 1943-1962, edited and compiled by Eugene McNamara, McGraw, 1969.

Culture Is Our Business, McGraw, 1970.

(With Wilfred Watson) *From Cliche to Archetype,* Viking, 1970.

(With Barrington Nevitt) *Executives—Die-Hards and Dropouts: Management Lore in the Global Village,* Harcourt, 1971.

(With Nevitt) *Take Today: The Executive as Dropout,* Harcourt, 1972.

(Author of introduction) Harold Adams Innis and Mary Quale, editors, *Empire and Communications,* University of Toronto Press, 1972.

(Author of foreword) Willy Blok Hanson, *The Pelvic Tilt: Master Your Body in Seven Days,* McClelland & Stewart, 1973.

(With Sorel Etrog) *Spiral,* Fitzhenry & Whiteside, 1976.

(With Robert Logan) *Libraries without Shelves,* Bowker, 1977.

(With son, Eric McLuhan, and Kathy Hutchon) *City as Classroom: Understanding Language and Media,* Book Society of Canada, 1977.

(With Pierre Babin) *Autre homme, autre chretien a l'age electronique,* Chalet, 1978.

(With E. McLuhan and Hutchon) *Media, Messages, and Language: The World as Your Classroom,* preface and introduction by David A. Sohn, National Textbook Co., 1980.

Letters of Marshall McLuhan, edited by Matie Molinaro, Corinne McLuhan, and William Toye, Oxford University Press, 1988.

(With E. McLuhan) *Laws of Media: The New Science,* University of Toronto Press, 1989.

Contributor of chapters to books, including *Mass Culture,* edited by Bernard Rosenberg and David Manning White, Free Press of Glencoe, 1957; *The Compleat "Neurotica," 1948-1951,* edited by G. Legman, Hacker Art Books, 1963; *The Electronic Revolution* (published as a special issue of *American Scholar,* spring, 1966), United Chapters of Phi Beta Kappa, 1966; *McLuhan— Hot and Cool: A Primer for the Understanding of and a Critical Symposium with a Rebuttal by McLuhan,* edited by Gerald Emanuel Stearn, Dial, 1967; *The Meaning of Commercial Televi-sion,* (University of Texas-Stanford University seminar held in Asilomar, Calif., 1966), University of Texas Press, 1967; *Beyond Left and Right: Radical Thoughts for Our Times,* edited by Richard Kostelanetz, Morrow, 1968; *Innovations,* edited by Bernard Bergonzi, Macmillan, 1968; *Exploration of the Ways, Means, and Values of Museum Communication with the Viewing Public* (seminar held at the Museum of the City of New York, October 9-10, 1967), Museum of the City of New York, 1969; and *Mutacoes em educacao Segundo McLuhan,* Editora Vozes, 1971.

Author of a multimedia bulletin, *The Marshall McLuhan Dew-Line Newsletter,* published monthly by Human Development Corp., beginning 1968. General editor, with Ernest Sirluck and Schoeck, of "Patterns of Literary Criticism" series, seven volumes, University of Chicago Press and University of Toronto Press, 1965-69. Contributor of articles and essays to numerous periodicals, including *Times Literary Supplement, Vogue, American Scholar, Kenyon Review, Sewanee Review, Family Circle, Encounter,* and *Daedalus. Explorations,* co-editor with Carpenter, 1954-59, editor, beginning 1964; member of editorial board, *Media and Methods,* beginning 1967.

SIDELIGHTS: "The medium is the message," quipped Marshall McLuhan, and the world took notice. Summarized in this aphorism, McLuhan's novel insights into the functions of mass media and their implications for the future of our technological culture earned him both international acclaim and vitriolic criticism. He was variously called a prophet, a promoter, a poet, a prankster, an intellectual mad-hatter, a guru of the boob tube, a communicator who could not communicate, and a genius on a level with Newton, Darwin, Freud, Einstein, and Pavlov. Considered the oracle of the electronic age by advertising, television, and business executives who often admitted not understanding much of what he said, McLuhan made pronouncements on a vast range of contemporary issues, including education, religion, science, the environment, politics, minority groups, war, violence, love, sex, clothing, jobs, music, computers, drugs, television, and automobiles; all these pronouncements, however, were based on his belief that human societies have always been shaped more by the nature of the media used to communicate than by the content of the communication. Though he expressed his ideas in an abstruse style that reflected a predilection for puns, in books that declared the book obsolete, his influence was, and is, unmistakable. "One must admit regardless of whether he agrees with McLuhanism," observes Richard Kostelanetz in *Master Minds,* that McLuhan was "among the great creative minds— 'artists'—of our time."

Contrary to his public image, McLuhan was by training a man of letters. At the University of Manitoba, he first studied engineering because of an avowed "interest in structure and design," notes Kostelanetz, but later changed his major to English literature and philosophy. After earning his first M.A. in 1934 with a thesis on "George Meredith as a Poet and Dramatic Parodist," McLuhan pursued medieval and Renaissance literature abroad at Cambridge University, ultimately producing a doctoral thesis on the rhetoric of Elizabethan writer Thomas Nashe. His writing career began with a critical study of Shakespeare's "Henry IV," and his contributions to professional journals included essays on T. S. Eliot, Gerard Manley Hopkins, John Dos Passos, and Alfred Lord Tennyson. Kostelanetz points out that even after McLuhan became known as a communications theorist, "academic circles regard[ed] him as 'one of the finest Tennyson critics.' "

A combination of circumstances, however, gradually led McLuhan to transcend his literary upbringing. The lectures of I. A.

Richards and F. R. Leavis at Cambridge initiated an interest in popular culture that blossomed when McLuhan, a Canadian whose first two teaching jobs were in the United States, found himself "confronted with young Americans I was incapable of understanding," he said in *Newsweek.* "I felt an urgent need to study their popular culture in order to get through."

McLuhan's first published exploration of the effects of mass culture on those engulfed in it was *The Mechanical Bride: Folklore of Industrial Man.* The book deals with "the pop creations of advertising and other word-and-picture promotions as ingredients of a magic potion, 'composed of sex and technology,' that [is] populating America with creatures half woman, half machine," writes Harold Rosenberg in the *New Yorker.* Exposing the effects of advertising on the unconscious, the book describes the "mechanical bride" herself as that peculiar mixture of sex and technology exemplified in attitudes toward the automobile.

Kostelanetz believes that although the book was "sparsely reviewed [in 1951] and quickly remaindered, *The Mechanical Bride* has come to seem in retrospect, a radical venture in the study of American mass culture. Previous to McLuhan, most American critics of integrity were disdainfully horrified at the growing proliferation of mass culture—the slick magazines, the comic books, the Hollywood movies, radio, television. . . . McLuhan, in contrast, was probably the first North American critic to inspect carefully the forms the stuff in the mass media took and then wonder precisely how these forms influenced people; and while he was still more scornful than not, one of his more spectacular insights identified formal similarities, rather than differences, between mass culture and elite art."

Specifically, McLuhan noticed the abrupt apposition of images, sounds, rhythms, and facts in modern poems, symphony, dance, and newspapers. Discontinuity, he concluded in *The Mechanical Bride,* is a central characteristic of the modern sensibility: "[It] is in different ways a basic concept of both quantum and relativity physics. It is the way in which a Toynbee looks at civilization, or a Margaret Mead at human cultures. Notoriously, it is the visual technique of a Picasso, the literary technique of James Joyce."

Following *The Mechanical Bride* and his promotion to full professor at St. Michael's College of the University of Toronto, McLuhan expanded his study of the relationship between culture and communication. From 1953 to 1955 he directed a Ford Foundation seminar on the subject and, with anthropologist Edmund Carpenter, founded a periodical called *Explorations* to give seminar members an additional forum for their ideas. By the late 1950s, his reputation as a communications specialist extended into the United States, earning him an appointment as director of a media project for the U.S. Office of Education and the National Association of Educational Broadcasters. The University of Toronto acknowledged his growing importance by naming him the first director of its Center for Culture and Technology, founded in 1963 to study the psychic and social consequences of technology and the media.

McLuhan's work during this period culminated in what many regard as his two major books, *The Gutenberg Galaxy: The Making of Typographic Man*—which in 1963 won Canada's highest literary honor, the Governor General's Award—and *Understanding Media: The Extensions of Man,* which eventually brought him worldwide renown. Drawing on his own impressive erudition, the analytical techniques of modern art criticism, and the theories of, among others, political economist Harold Adams Innis, McLuhan presented in these books his view of the history of mass media as central to the history of civilization in general.

Borrowing Buckminster Fuller's metaphor that a tool of man's is essentially an extension of man, McLuhan claimed that the media not only represent extensions of the human senses but that they, by their very nature as determinants of knowledge, dictate "the character of perception and through perception the structure of mind," summarizes James P. Carey in *McLuhan: Pro and Con.* "The medium"—more than the content—"is the message" because it shapes human perception, human knowledge, human society.

Thus, according to McLuhan in *The Gutenberg Galaxy,* the rise of the printing press revolutionized Western civilization. By placing an overemphasis on the eye, rather than the ear of oral cultures, print reshaped the sensibility of Western man. Human beings came to see life as they saw print—as linear, often with causal relationships. Print accounted for such phenomena as linear development in music, serial thinking in mathematics, the liberal tradition, nationalism, individualism, and Protestantism (the printed book encouraged thinking in isolation; hence, individual revelation). By giving man the power to separate thought from feeling, it enabled Western man to specialize and to mechanize, but it also led to alienation from the other senses and, thus, from other men and from nature itself.

The theme of alienation was "central to the argument of Innis," notes Carey, "[but McLuhan went] beyond this critique and argue[d] that the reunification of man, the end of his alienation, the restoration of the 'whole' man will result from autonomous developments in communications technology." The electronic media of the modern era—telegraph, radio, television, movies, telephones, computers—according to McLuhan in *Understanding Media,* are reshaping civilization by "moving us out of the age of the visual into the age of the aural and tactile." Because electronic media create a mosaic of information reaching us simultaneously through several senses, our sensibility is being radically transformed as evidenced, for example, by the revolution in modern art. This redistribution and heightening of sensory awareness signifies a return to our tribal roots, where communication was multisensory and immediate. United by electronic media, the world is rapidly becoming a "global village," where all ends of the earth are in immediate touch with one another.

From this view of history branded "informational technological determinism" by Kostelanetz, McLuhan extrapolated numerous ideas in *The Gutenberg Galaxy, Understanding Media,* and subsequent books about the effects of education (the book is passe; one needs to be "literate" in many media), the concept of childhood, the landscape of social organization, the problem of personal privacy, war and propaganda, moral relativism, "hot" and "cool" media (a "cool" medium requires more sensory and mental participation than a "hot" one), the generation gap, television (those who worry about the programs on TV—a "cool" medium—are missing its true significance), modern art, and other topics. "McLuhan's performance was breathtaking," writes John Leonard in the *New York Times.* "He ranged from physics to Cezanne, from Africa to advertising, from the Moebius strip to Milman Parry's treatise on the oral character of Yugoslav epic poetry. Euclidean space, chronological narrative, artistic perspective, Newtonian mechanics, and capitalist economics were all called into question. They were lies of the dislocating eye."

McLuhan's ideas, however, were not as neatly nor as modestly presented as this brief summary might suggest, for he considered his books "probes"—invitations to explore—rather than carefully articulated arguments. McLuhan, notes Kostelanetz, believed "more in probing and exaggerating—'making discoveries'—than in offering final definitions, as well as raising . . . critical discourse to a higher level of insight and subtlety. For this reason, he [would] in public conversation rarely defend any of his statements as absolute truths, although he [would] explain how he developed them. 'I don't agree or disagree with anything I say myself' [was] his characteristic rationale."

To further dramatize his "probes," McLuhan eschewed the traditional, print-age, linear, expository structure of introduction, development, elaboration, and conclusion, attempting instead "to imitate in his writing the form of the TV image, which he describe[d] as 'mosaic,'" says Rosenberg. A typical McLuhan book or paragraph, according to Kostelanetz, "tends to make a series of analytic statements, none of which become an explicitly encompassing thesis, though all of them approach the same body of phenomena from different angles or examples. These become a succession of exegetical glosses on a mysterious scriptural text, which is how McLuhan analogously regard[ed] the new electronic world. . . . This means that one should not necessarily read his books from start to finish—the archaic habit of printman. True, the preface and first chapter of *The Mechanical Bride* . . . really do *introduce* the themes and methods of the book; but beyond that, the chapters can be read in any order. The real introduction to *The Gutenberg Galaxy* is the final chapter, called 'The Galaxy Reconfigured'; even McLuhan advise[d] readers to start there; and the book itself is all but a galaxy of extensive printed quotations."

In addition to these stylistic features, McLuhan had a "predilection for positively blood-curdling puns," says a *New Republic* contributor, as well as a penchant for aphorisms. Deliberately punning on his famous dictum "The medium is the message," for example, McLuhan titled his 1967 photo-montage *The Medium Is the Massage: An Inventory of Effects* to convey his belief that instead of neutrally presenting content, "all media work us over completely. They are so pervasive in their personal, political, esthetic, psychological, moral, ethical, and social consequences that they leave no part of us untouched, unaffected, unaltered. The medium is the massage." He said the 1967 book was designed to clarify the ideas in *Understanding Media* by depicting "a collide-oscope of interfaced situations."

McLuhan's habitual, mosaic mixture of fact and theory, pun and picture, came to be characterized as "McLuhanese," which George P. Elliott describes in *McLuhan—Hot and Cool* as "deliberately antilogical: circular, repetitious, unqualified, gnomic, outrageous." The late Dwight Macdonald refers to "McLuhanese" in *Book Week* as "impure nonsense, nonsense adulterated by sense," and in another *Book Week* article Arthur M. Schlesinger, Jr., calls it "a chaotic combination of bland assertion, astute guesswork, fake analogy, dazzling insight, hopeless nonsense, shockmanship, showmanship, wisecracks, and oracular mystification, all mingling cockily and indiscriminately in an endless and random monologue . . ., [which] contains a deeply serious argument."

The novelty of McLuhan's ideas coupled with their unconventional presentation gave rise by the late 1960s "to an ideology . . . and a mass movement producing seminars, clubs, art exhibits, and conferences in his name," reports James P. Carey. One of the most frequently quoted intellectuals of his time, McLuhan became, in Carey's words, "a prophet, a phenomenon, a happening, a social movement." Advertising and television executives hailed him as the oracle of the electronic age, although as Alden Whitman states in the *New York Times,* "he did not think highly of the advertising business. 'The hullabaloo Madison Avenue creates couldn't condition a mouse,' he said." In 1965, avant-garde composer John Cage visited him in Toronto to discuss his

insights. Publisher William Jovanovich later invited him to collaborate on a study of the future of the book. McLuhanisms soon appeared everywhere, including the popular American television show "Rowan and Martin's Laugh-In." And in 1977, Woody Allen persuaded him to make a cameo appearance in the Oscar-winning film "Annie Hall" to defend his theories.

Despite winning a great deal of admiration, McLuhan was also feared and rejected, "especially . . . by journalists and television personalities who saw themselves threatened by his analyses because they did not understand either him or his equally important sources," says E. C. Wheeldon in the London *Times.* He was often denounced as a fakir, a charlatan, and—because he considered TV the most influential medium of the electronic age—a guru of the boob tube. Critics charged him with oversimplification, faulty reasoning, inconsistency, confusion of myth and reality, as well as undermining the entire humanist tradition, and these charges continue to be leveled.

John Simon, writing in *McLuhan: Pro and Con,* considers McLuhan's "worst failing" to be "the wholesale reinterpretation of texts to prove his preconceived argument," and others scoff at McLuhan's attempt to explain virtually every social and cultural phenomenon in terms of the media. "For McLuhan," writes Harold Rosenberg, "beliefs, moral qualities, social action, even material progress play a secondary role (if that) in determining the human condition. The drama of history is a crude pageant whose inner meaning is man's metamorphosis through the media. As a philosophy of cultural development, *Understanding Media* is on a par with theories that trace the invention of the submarine to conflicts in the libido."

In the *New York Review of Books,* D. W. Harding praises McLuhan's "probes" as maneuvers that try "to break free from self-inhibition and sterile dispute," yet he believes they are ultimately self-defeating: "How in the face of independent common sense could McLuhan get away with, for example, his claim that primitive cultures are oral and auditory and ours is visual? Questionable even in the limited context of the psychiatrist's article he bases it on, the notion as a generalization is wildly implausible. The American Indians' skill in tracking, the bedouins' astonishing capacity for reading camel spoor, these are ordinary instances of the familiar fact that in many habitats the survival of a primitive people depended on constant visual alertness, acute discrimination, and highly trained inference from visual data. . . . One is left with the truism that we read a lot and pre-literates don't. The implications of that fact are well worth exploring, but we get no help from stories of alteration in some physiologically and psychologically undefined 'sensory ratio.'"

"McLuhan is a monomaniac who happens to be hooked on something extremely important," concludes Tom Nairn in the *New Statesman,* "but the colossal evasiveness, the slipshod reasoning, and weak-kneed glibness accompanying the mania make him dangerous going. . . . Capable of the most brilliant and stimulating insight into relationships other historians and social theorists have ignored, he systematically fails to develop this insight critically. Consequently, his view of the connection between media and society is an unbelievable shambles: his dream-logic turns necessary conditions into sufficient conditions, half-truths into sure things, the possible into a *fait accompli.*"

The overriding source of irritation for many readers is McLuhan's intricate style. John Fowles, for example, finds *From Cliche to Archetype* "as elegant and as lucid as a barrel of tar." The book, according to Fowles in *Saturday Review,* "makes one wonder whether Marshall McLuhan's celebrated doubts over the print medium don't largely stem from a personal incapacity to handle it. Perhaps the graceless style, the barbarously obscuring jargon, the incoherent hopping from one unfinished argument into the middle of the next are all meant to be subtly humorous. But the general effect is about as subtle and humorous as a Nazi storm trooper hectoring the latest trainload of Jews. It is all barked fiat: off with your head if you dare to disagree."

David Myers suggests in *Book World* that, ultimately, it is "as a poet and only as a poet that McLuhan can be read without exasperation," and others seem to agree. Kenneth Burke maintains in the *New Republic* that McLuhan "transcends the distinction . . . between 'prove' and 'probe,' both from the Latin *probare.* 'Proof' requires a considerable sense of continuity; 'probing' can be done at random, with hit-and-run slogans or titles taking the place of sustained exposition. And in the medium of books, McLuhan with his 'probing' has 'perfected' a manner in which the non sequitur never had it so good." "Even at his worst," insists Tom Wolfe in *Book World,* "McLuhan inspires you to try to see and understand in a new way, and in the long run this may prove to be his great contribution."

The aim of McLuhan's "poetry," however, remains a matter of dispute. James P. Carey, who considers McLuhan "a poet of technology," claims his work "represents a secular prayer to technology, a magical incantation of the gods, designed to quell one's fears that, after all, the machines may be taking over. . . . McLuhan himself is a medium and that is his message." But McLuhan maintained that rather than predicting the future of our technological age, he was merely extrapolating current processes to their logical conclusions. "I don't approve of the global village," he once told a *Playboy* interviewer, "I say we live in it." Writing in *McLuhan: Pro and Con,* John Culkin supports the detachment of McLuhan's viewpoint: "Too many people are eager to write off Marshall McLuhan or to reduce him to the nearest and handiest platitude which explains him to them. He deserves better. . . . He didn't invent electricity or put kids in front of TV sets; he . . . merely [tried] to describe what's happening out there so that it can be dealt with intelligently. When someone warns you of an oncoming truck, it's frightfully impolite to accuse him of driving the thing."

Richard Kostelanetz, moreover, believes that McLuhan was "trenchantly a humanist." He quotes McLuhan as saying, "By knowing how technology shapes our environment, we can transcend its absolutely determining power. . . . My entire concern is to overcome the determination that results from people trying to ignore what is going on. Far from regarding technological change as inevitable, I insist that if we understand its components we can turn it off any time we choose. Short of turning it off, there are lots of moderate controls conceivable."

Whether McLuhan was a poet of technology, a detached observer, or a trenchant humanist, "what remain paramount are his global standpoint and his zest for the new," concludes Harold Rosenberg. "As an artist working in a mixed medium of direct experience and historical analogy, he [gave] a needed twist to the great debate on what is happening to man in this age of technological speedup. [Whereas] other observers . . . [repeated] criticisms of industrial society that were formulated a century ago, . . . McLuhan, for all his abstractness, . . . found positive, humanistic meaning and the color of life in supermarkets, stratospheric flight, the lights blinking on broadcasting towers. In respect to the maladies of de-individuation, he . . . dared to seek the cure in the disease, and his vision of going forward into primitive wholeness is a good enough reply to those who would go back to it."

MEDIA ADAPTATIONS: A happening entitled "McLuhan Megillah," based on *Understanding Media* and *The Gutenberg Galaxy* and combining dance, film, painting, poetry, sculpture, and other art forms, was produced at Al Hansen's Third Rail Time/Space Theatre in Greenwich Village in January of 1966. A McLuhan television special based on *The Medium Is the Massage* was produced on NBC-TV, March 19, 1967. In September of 1967, Columbia Records released a four-track LP based on *The Medium Is the Massage* and produced by Jerome P. Agel.

BIOGRAPHICAL/CRITICAL SOURCES:

BOOKS

Contemporary Literary Criticism, Volume 37, Gale, 1986.
Crosby, Harry H. and George R. Bond, compilers, *The McLuhan Explosion* (casebook on McLuhan and *Understanding Media*), American Book Co., 1968.
Duffy, Dennis, *Marshall McLuhan,* McClelland & Stewart, 1969.
Fekete, John, *The Critical Twilight: Explorations in the Ideology of Anglo-American Literary Theory from Eliot to McLuhan,* Routledge & Kegan Paul, 1978.
Finkelstein, Sidney Walter, *Sense and Nonsense of McLuhan,* International Publishers, 1968.
Fiore, Quentin and Marshall McLuhan, *The Medium Is the Massage: An Inventory of Effects,* Bantam, 1967.
Gross, Theodore L., *Representative Men,* Free Press, 1970.
Kostelanetz, Richard, *Master Minds: Portraits of Contemporary American Artists and Intellectuals,* Macmillan, 1969.
McLuhan, *The Mechanical Bride: Folklore of Industrial Man,* Vanguard, 1951.
McLuhan, *Understanding Media: The Extensions of Man,* McGraw, 1964.
McLuhan, *The Gutenberg Galaxy: The Making of Typographic Man,* University of Toronto Press, 1962.
Miller, Jonathan, *Marshall McLuhan,* Viking, 1971.
Rosenthal, Raymond, editor, *McLuhan: Pro and Con,* Funk, 1968.
Stearn, Gerald Emanuel, editor, *McLuhan—Hot and Cool: A Primer for the Understanding of and a Critical Symposium with a Rebuttal by McLuhan,* Dial, 1967.
Theall, Donald F., *The Medium Is the Rear View Mirror: Understanding McLuhan,* McGill-Queens University Press, 1971.

PERIODICALS

American Dialog, autumn, 1967.
Antioch Review, spring, 1967.
Books, September, 1965, January, 1967.
Books and Bookmen, March 1971.
Book Week, June 7, 1964, March 19, 1967.
Book World, October 29, 1967, September 15, 1968, July 27, 1969, November 30, 1969, December 6, 1970.
Canadian Forum, February, 1969.
Chicago Tribune, January 1, 1981.
Christian Science Monitor, May 17, 1972.
Commentary, January, 1965.
Commonweal, January 20, 1967, June 23, 1967.
Critic, August, 1967.
Esquire, August, 1966.
Globe and Mail (Toronto), December 24, 1988.
Harper's, November, 1965, June, 1967.
Kenyon Review, March, 1967.
L'Express, February 14-20, 1972.
Life, February 25, 1966.
Listener, September 28, 1967, October 19, 1967.
Maclean's Magazine, January 7, 1980, March 17, 1980.

Nation, October 5, 1964, May 15, 1967, December 4, 1967, December 8, 1969.

National Review, November 19, 1968.

New Republic, February 7, 1970, June 10, 1972.

New Statesman, December 11, 1964, September 22, 1967.

Newsweek, February 28, 1966, March 6, 1967, September 23, 1968, January 12, 1981.

New Yorker, February 27, 1965.

New York Review of Books, August 20, 1964, November 23, 1967, January 2, 1969.

New York Times, October 21, 1951, February 27, 1967, September 7, 1967, January 1, 1981.

New York Times Book Review, May 1, 1966, March 26, 1967, September 8, 1968, December 21, 1969, July 12, 1970, December 13, 1970, February 26, 1989.

New York Times Magazine, January 29, 1967.

Partisan Review, summer, 1968.

Playboy, March, 1969.

Publishers Weekly, January 23, 1981.

Saturday Night, February, 1967.

Saturday Review, November 26, 1966, March 11, 1967, May 9, 1970, November 21, 1970.

Sewanee Review, spring, 1969.

Time, July 3, 1964, March 3, 1967, January 12, 1981.

Times (London), January 2, 1981.

Times Literary Supplement, August 6, 1964, September 28, 1967, May 6, 1988, August 25, 1989.

Twentieth-Century Literature, July, 1970.

Village Voice, May 12, 1966, December 26, 1970.

Vogue, July, 1966.

Western Humanities Review, autumn, 1967.

OBITUARIES

AB Bookman's Weekly, January 19, 1981.

Chicago Tribune, January 1, 1981.

Newsweek, January 12, 1981.

New York Times, January 1, 1981.

Publishers Weekly, January 23, 1981.

Time, January 12, 1981.

Times (London), January 2, 1981.

*   *   *

McMURTRY, Larry (Jeff) 1936-

PERSONAL: Born June 3, 1936, in Wichita Falls, Tex.; son of William Jefferson (a rancher) and Hazel Ruth (McIver) McMurtry; married Josephine Ballard, July 15, 1959 (divorced, 1966); children: James Lawrence. *Education:* North Texas State College (now University), B.A., 1958; Rice University, M.A., 1960; additional study at Stanford University, 1960.

ADDRESSES: Office—Booked Up Book Store, 1214 31st St., N.W., Washington, D.C. 20007. *Agent*—Dorothea Oppenheimer, 435 East 79th St., Apt. 4M, New York, N.Y. 10021.

CAREER: Texas Christian University, Fort Worth, instructor, 1961-62; Rice University, Houston, Tex., lecturer in English and creative writing, 1963-69; Booked Up Book Store, Washington, D.C., co-owner, 1970—. Visiting professor at George Mason College, 1970, and at American University, 1970-71. Has worked as a rare book scout and dealer for book stores in Texas and California.

MEMBER: PEN American Center (president, 1989—), Texas Institute of Letters.

AWARDS, HONORS: Wallace Stegner fellowship, 1960; Jesse H. Jones Award from Texas Institute of Letters, 1962, for *Horse-*

man, Pass By; Guggenheim fellowship, 1964; Academy of Motion Picture Arts and Sciences Award (Oscar) for best screenplay based on material from another medium, 1972, for "The Last Picture Show"; Barbara McCombs/Lon Tinkle Award for continuing excellence in Texas letters from Texas Institute of Letters, 1986; Pulitzer Prize for fiction, Spur Award from Western Writers of America, and Texas Literary Award from Southwestern Booksellers Association, all 1986, all for *Lonesome Dove.*

WRITINGS:

Horseman, Pass By, Harper, 1961, reprinted, Texas A & M University Press, 1988, published as *Hud,* Popular Library, 1961.

Leaving Cheyenne, Harper, 1963, recent edition, Texas A & M University Press, 1986.

The Last Picture Show (also see below), Dial, 1966, recent edition, Simon & Schuster, 1989.

In a Narrow Grave: Essays on Texas, Encino Press, 1968, recent edition, Simon & Schuster, 1989.

Moving On, Simon & Schuster, 1970, recent edition, Pocket Books, 1988.

(With Peter Bogdanovich) *The Last Picture Show* (screenplay; based on his novel of same title; produced by Columbia Pictures, 1971), B.B.S. Productions, 1970.

All My Friends Are Going to Be Strangers, Simon & Schuster, 1972, recent edition, 1989.

Terms of Endearment, Simon & Schuster, 1975, recent edition, 1989.

Somebody's Darling, Simon & Schuster, 1978.

Cadillac Jack, Simon & Schuster, 1982.

The Desert Rose, Simon & Schuster, 1983.

Lonesome Dove, Simon & Schuster, 1985.

(Contributor) *Texas in Transition,* Lyndon Baines Johnson School of Public Affairs, 1986.

Film Flam: Essays on Hollywood, Simon & Schuster, 1987.

Texasville, Simon & Schuster, 1987.

Anything for Billy, Simon & Schuster, 1988.

Some Can Whistle, Simon & Schuster, 1989.

Buffalo Girls, Simon & Schuster, 1990.

Also author of numerous articles, essays, and book reviews for magazines and newspapers, including *American Film, Atlantic, Gentleman's Quarterly, New York Times, Saturday Review,* and *Washington Post.* Contributing editor of *American Film,* 1975—.

SIDELIGHTS: In the quarter century since he published his first novel, Larry McMurtry has emerged as one of Texas's most prominent fiction writers. Though he has lived outside Texas for more than fifteen years, McMurtry has drawn themes for many of his novels from the uneasy interaction between his native state's mythic past and its problematic, ongoing urbanization. His earliest works, such as the critically acclaimed *Horseman, Pass By* and *The Last Picture Show,* expose the bleak prospects for adolescents on the rural ranches or in the small towns of west Texas, while his novels written in the 1970s, including *Terms of Endearment,* trace Texas characters drawn into the urban milieus of Houston, Hollywood, and Washington, D.C. More recently, his 1986 Pulitzer Prize-winning novel *Lonesome Dove* has received high praise for its realistic detailing of a cattle drive from the last century, a transformation into fiction of a part of Texas's history the author previously approached in his essays on cowboys, ranching, and rodeos. As Si Dunn notes in the *Dallas News,* McMurtry's readers find him "a writer who has made living in Texas a literary experience."

As a spokesman for the status of modern Texas letters, McMurtry has been known to criticize some Texas writers for their tendency to overlook the potentially rich material to be found in the present-day experience of Texas's new industries and burgeoning urban areas. In a piece from *In a Narrow Grave: Essays on Texas,* he concludes: "Texas writers are sometimes so anxious to avoid the accusation of provincialism that they will hardly condescend to render the particularities of their own place, though it ought to be clear that literature thrives on particulars. The material is here, and it has barely been touched. If this is truly the era of the Absurd, then all the better for the Texas writer, for where else except California can one find a richer mixture of absurdities? Literature has coped fairly well with the physical circumstances of life in Texas, but our emotional experience remains largely unexplored, and therein lie the drama, poems, and novels."

In *The Ghost Country: A Study of the Novels of Larry McMurtry,* Raymond L. Neinstein expresses the belief that McMurtry "has journeyed from an old-fashioned regionalism to a kind of 'neo-regionalism,' his characters, and the novels themselves, turning from the land as the locus of their values to an imaginary, fictive 'place.' But they, characters and novels both, are finally not able to manage there, at least not comfortably. McMurtry clearly does not trust 'living in the head'; the pull of the old myth is still strong." McMurtry himself is aware of this dichotomy, as he writes in *Holiday:* "A part of my generation may keep something of the frontier spirit even though the frontier is lost. What they may keep is a sense of daring and independence, transferred from the life of action to the life of the mind."

In McMurtry's case, this description is particularly apt. The son and grandson of cattle ranchers, he grew up in sparsely populated Archer County, in north central Texas. From childhood onward he was more interested in reading than ranching, but the family stories he heard as a youth exerted an enormous influence on his sense of identity. He writes in *In a Narrow Grave:* "It is indeed a complex distance from those traildrivers who made my father and my uncles determined to be cowboys to the mechanical horse that helps convince my son that he is a cowboy, as he takes a vertical ride in front of a laundrymat." If he felt pride and nostalgia for the ranching way of life, which was vanishing even as he came of age, McMurtry was far less enthusiastic about tiny Archer City, where he attended high school as an honor student. McMurtry found little with which to nourish his imagination within the confines of the town, as he notes in *In a Narrow Grave:* "I grew up in a bookless town, in a bookless part of the state—when I stepped into a university library, at age eighteen, the whole of the world's literature lay before me unread, a country as vast, as promising, and, so far as I knew, as trackless as the West must have seemed to the first white men who looked upon it."

In creating his own fiction, however, McMurtry has drawn many of his themes from his "blood's country" of Texas. His early works portray a fictional town and countryside with a strong resemblance to Archer County. In *Horseman, Pass By,* his first novel, McMurtry introduces an adolescent narrator named Lonnie Bannon, who describes a series of tragic events that occur on his grandfather's ranch when an epidemic of hoof-and-mouth disease is discovered. Nearing manhood himself, the orphaned Lonnie is confronted with several role models whose behavior he must evaluate: his step-uncle Hud, an egotistic and ruthless hedonist; his grandfather's hired hand Jesse, a storytelling drifter; and his grandfather Homer, who, Peavy states, "epitomizes all the rugged virtues of a pioneer ethic." Lonnie's frustration is additionally fanned by the presence of Halmea, the black housekeeper who Peavy suggests is both "love object and mother surrogate" to the young man. John Gerlach notes in the *Dictionary*

of Literary Biography that the relationship between Lonnie and Halmea, based on "tenderness, lack of fulfillment, and separation due here to differences in age and race trace out the beginning of what becomes an essential theme in [McMurtry's] later works—people's needs do not match their circumstances. Peavy sees *Horseman, Pass By* as the first chronicle of another recurring McMurtry theme: "the initiation into manhood and its inevitable corollaries—loneliness and loss of innocence."

Horseman, Pass By was published in 1961, when its author was twenty-five. While not an immediate commercial success, it established a reputation for McMurtry among critics of Western literature. In an article in *Regional Perspectives: An Examination of America's Literary Heritage,* Larry Goodwyn calls McMurtry "one of the most interesting young novelists in the Southwest—and certainly the most embattled in terms of frontier heritage." While McMurtry claims in *In a Narrow Grave* that "the world quietly overlooked" *Horseman, Pass By,* and that he himself has come to consider it an immature work, the book was not only significant enough to warrant an Academy Award-winning movie adaptation, but also of sufficient literary merit to garner McMurtry a 1964 Guggenheim award for creative writing. Peavy quotes a letter that critic John Howard Griffin wrote to McMurtry's agent after reading *Horseman, Pass By:* "This is probably the starkest, most truthful, most terrible and yet beautiful treatment of [ranching country] I've seen. It will offend many, who prefer the glamour treatment—but it is a true portrait of the loneliness and pervading melancholy of cowboying; and of its compensations in nature, in human relationships."

Leaving Cheyenne, McMurtry's second novel, was published in 1963. Also set in ranching country, the story revolves around a character named Molly Taylor and the two men she loves throughout a lifetime, Gid, a rancher, and Johnny, a cowboy. Each of the three central characters narrates a section of the book; their intertwined lives are traced from youth to death. "McMurtry is psychologically precise in tracing this three-sided relationship," writes Walter Clemons in the *New York Times Book Review.* Clemons adds: "Odd as the roots of this friendship may seem, there's enduring consideration and feeling in it. The story takes so many years to tell because feelings that last a lifetime are the subject." Gerlach notes that *Leaving Cheyenne* explores a new aspect of the theme of "mismatching and the isolation it brings. . . . The expanded time scheme and number of narrators enrich the themes of the novel." Clemons, who calls McMurtry "one of the two best writers to come out of Texas in the [1960s]," claims that *Leaving Cheyenne* is "a rarity among second novels in its exhilarating ease, assurance and openness of feeling."

When evaluating McMurtry's early works, critics tend to group *Horseman, Pass By* and *Leaving Cheyenne* due to their similarities of setting and theme. In a 1974 *New York* magazine discussion of his writings, McMurtry himself analyzes the two novels together, with pointed remarks about his attitude concerning them: "It is perhaps worth pointing out that both [*Leaving Cheyenne*] and my first novel were written in the same year—my twenty-third. I revised around on both books for a while, but essentially both incorporate, at best, a 22-year-old's vision. . . . I don't want that vision back, nor am I overjoyed to see the literary results of it applauded." Others praise the young author's efforts. Goodwyn, for one, writes: "McMurtry's first two novels . . . were promising efforts to put the materials of frontier culture to serious literary use. . . . [Both books] are in-the-grain novels of people striving to live by the cultural values of the legend. . . . McMurtry speaks through a narrator who is frontiersman enough to move with ease through the tall-in-the-saddle milieu, but sensitive enough to note the ritualized energy and directionless fury surrounding him. . . . Relying . . . on the literary device of the provincial narrator, McMurtry found a voice that seemed to serve well as a strengthening connection between himself and his sources."

The fictional town of Thalia figures peripherally in both *Horseman, Pass By* and *Leaving Cheyenne.* In *The Last Picture Show,* McMurtry's third novel, Thalia becomes the primary setting and the debilitating monotony of small town life one of the primary themes. Thomas Lask in the *New York Times* describes McMurtry's rendering of Thalia: "A sorrier place would be hard to find. It is desiccated and shabby physically, mean and small-minded spiritually. Mr. McMurtry is expert in anatomizing its suffocating and dead-end character." The novel's action once again revolves around a group of late adolescents who are struggling to achieve adulthood in the town's confining atmosphere. Peavy writes of McMurtry: "He examines the town's inhabitants—the oil rich, the roughnecks, the religious fanatics, the high school football stars, the love-starved women—with an eye that is at once sociological and satiric. For the first time he abandons the first-person narrative in his fiction, and the result is a dispassionate, cold look at the sordidness and hypocrisy that characterize the town."

First published in 1966, *The Last Picture Show* raised some controversy in McMurtry's home town of Archer City and elsewhere for its graphic detailing of teenage sexuality—including exhibitionism, bestiality, petting, masturbation, and homosexuality. "On the surface," Peavy notes, "McMurtry's treatment of small-town sexuality may seem quite sensational; actually, it is accurate. In the cloying confines of Thalia, the only outlet for frustrations, loneliness, boredom, even hatred—for both adolescents and adults—is sex. . . . Some of McMurtry's sexual scenes are highly symbolic, all are important thematically, and none should be taken as sensationalism." W. T. Jack expresses the same opinion in the *New York Times Book Review:* "Offensive? Miraculously, no. McMurtry is an alchemist who converts the basest materials to gold. The sexual encounters are sad, funny, touching, sometimes horrifying, but always honest, always human." Peavy feels, in fact, that "neither Updike nor Salinger has been successful as McMurtry in describing the gnawing ache that accompanies adolescent sexuality."

Some critics have felt that the characterization in *The Last Picture Show* approaches stereotype in certain instances. Peavy states: "McMurtry has said that part of the concern of *The Last Picture Show* is to portray how the town is emotionally centered in high school—in adolescence. As a result, the protagonist of the book is somewhat inadequately developed." In an essay for *Colonial Times,* McMurtry admits that his approach to the material in *The Last Picture Show* was "too bitter." He writes that Archer City "had not been cruel to me, only honestly indifferent, and my handling of many of the characters in the book represented a failure of generosity for which I blame no one but myself."

According to Peavy, some of the difficulties in McMurtry's novel have been surmounted in the film script "The Last Picture Show" through the added perspective of Peter Bogdanovich. "The film script . . . is a much more sympathetic portrait of McMurtry's hometown than is the novel," Peavy suggests. "The combination of the two young writers [McMurtry and Bogdanovich] was fortunate." Filmed in black and white on location in Archer City, "The Last Picture Show" was a commercial and critical success. It won three Academy Awards from the Academy of Motion Picture Arts and Sciences, including an award

for best screenplay based on material from another medium. In an *Atlantic* review, David Denby states that the movie "reverses many of the sentimental assumptions about small towns that were prevalent in the movies of the forties, but it never becomes a cinematic expose. It's a tough-minded, humorous, and delicate film—a rare combination in an American movie." Writing for *Newsweek,* Paul D. Zimmerman calls the film "a masterpiece" with "a finely tuned screenplay." Zimmerman also claims that " 'The Last Picture Show' . . . is not merely the best American movie of a rather dreary year; it is the most impressive work by a young American director since 'Citizen Kane.' "

McMurtry followed *The Last Picture Show* with what some have called his "urban trilogy" of novels: *Moving On, All My Friends Are Going to Be Strangers,* and *Terms of Endearment.* The books represent a radical departure in setting and tone from the author's earlier works as they detail the lives of Houston urbanites, some of whom travel across the country in various, seemingly aimless pursuits. In her *Western American Literature* study on McMurtry's work, Janis P. Stout writes of *Moving On* and *All My Friends:* "None of the characters in these two novels has any sense of a usable past, and none is purposefully directed toward the future. They inhabit the burgeoning cities of Texas with no apparent means of orienting themselves and nothing to engage them but endless, unsatisfying motion—as the title *Moving On* well indicates." McMurtry uses a revolving set of characters as the cast for all three books. The supporting troupe in one novel may evolve to primary importance in another volume, as is the case with Emma Horton, who appears briefly in *Moving On* and *All My Friends* before becoming the protagonist in *Terms of Endearment.* R. C. Reynolds notes in the *Southwest Review:* "Though time sequences often fall out of order in the three novels, key events and characters are repeated often enough to maintain a continuous theme which, not surprisingly, has three parts: sex and its frustrations, academics and its frustrations, and something like culture and its frustrations which McMurtry has branded *Ecch-Texas.*"

Considered as a group, *Moving On, All My Friends,* and *Terms of Endearment* have not achieved the favorable critical response that followed McMurtry's earlier publications. Stout claims, for instance, that "the journey pattern so insistent in McMurtry's first three novels has in [*Moving On* and *All My Friends*] become dominant, as the characters drive endlessly and pointlessly around the country chiefly between Texas and California. Not surprisingly, novels so constituted lack cohesive form; or rather, their forms may be described as being imitative to a radical and destructive degree. Similarly, McMurtry's construction of novels by no apparent principle but random accretion appears to be a self-defeating enterprise. The pattern of transient involvement . . . is brilliantly indicative of the cultural shortcoming McMurtry indicts . . . ; unfortunately, this expressive form, by its very nature, is destructive of the overall novelistic structure and renders the work a chronicle of tedium." Goodwyn senses an ambiguity at work in the novels: "the frontier ethos, removed from the center of [McMurtry's] work, continues to hover around the edges—it surfaces in minor characters who move with purpose through novels that do not."

Reviewers have not been unanimously disappointed with McMurtry's efforts in the "urban trilogy," however. In a review of *Moving On* for the *New York Times,* John Leonard writes: "McMurtry has a good ear: [the characters] talk the way people actually talk in Houston, at rodeos, in Hollywood. Mr. McMurtry also has a marvelous eye for locale: the Southwest is superbly evoked. It is a pleasure . . . to escape claustrophobic novels that rely on the excitation of the verbal glands instead of the exploration of social reality." "It is difficult to characterize a talent as outsized as McMurtry's," suggests Jim Harrison in the *New York Times Book Review.* "Often his work seems disproportionately violent, but these qualities in 'All My Friends Are Going to Be Strangers' are tempered by his comic genius, his ability to render a sense of landscape and place, and an interior intellectual tension that resembles in intensity that of Saul Bellow's 'Mr. Sammler's Planet.' McMurtry . . . has a sense of construction and proper velocity that always saves him." A *Times Literary Supplement* reviewer likewise concludes: "There are few books one remembers with a real sense of affection, but *All My Friends* is indisputably one of them. Mr. McMurtry's talent for characterization and the evocation of place—together with his ability to blend them convincingly, so that they seem almost to interdepend—makes [the protagonist's] near-indefinable yearnings for a past which seems close enough to grab at wholly understandable."

Terms of Endearment, first published in 1975, has since become the most popular segment of the "urban trilogy." The story concerns Aurora Greenway, a New England-born widow who lives in Houston, and her married daughter, Emma. The greater portion of the novel deals with Aurora's relationship with her several "suitors," including a retired armored corps commander and an oil millionaire, but the final chapter in the book follows Emma through a deteriorating marriage to her ultimate death from cancer. *New York Times* critic Christopher Lehmann-Haupt observes that "maybe what keeps one entertained [with the book] is the sympathy with which Mr. McMurtry writes about these people. . . . One laughs at the slapstick, one weeps at the maudlin, and one likes all of Mr. McMurtry's characters, no matter how delicately or broadly they are drawn." Gerlach finds Aurora "loveable because she can turn a phrase. . . . Her story has endless permutations but no motion; she is timeless." Though some critics feel that the tragic ending strikes a jarring note, following as it does the light comic adventures of Aurora, they nonetheless find the section moving. Robert Towers notes: "The final scenes between the dying Emma and her stricken boys are the most affecting in the book."

At least one critical comment on the "urban trilogy" has been proven erroneous. In 1976, R. C. Reynolds claimed: "One cannot help but feel that McMurtry wrote all three novels with an eye toward Hollywood's acceptance of them for film . . . one must doubt the possibility of film adaptation for any of the three." Whether or not McMurtry intended to attract the attention of film producers, one of the books was eventually made into a highly successful movie. The film version of "Terms of Endearment" won the coveted Academy Award for best picture of the year in 1983. Though the film adaptation by James L. Brooks created a major character not found in the novel and eliminated numerous characters from the novel, its plot remained faithful to McMurtry's work. Calling the movie "a funny, touching, beautifully acted film," *New York Times* critic Janet Maslin has suggested that despite the changes from novel to screenplay, the finished product "does echo the book's arch dialogue and its considerable sprawl."

Terms of Endearment, according to McMurtry, marked a turning point in his fiction writing. "I was halfway through my sixth Texas novel," he explained in the *Atlantic,* "when I suddenly began to notice that where place was concerned, I was sucking air. The book is set in Houston, but none of the characters are Texans." Having himself moved from Houston to Washington, D.C. in 1970, McMurtry began to seek new regional settings for his novels. In 1976 he told the *Dallas News:* "I lived in Texas quite a while, and for my own creative purposes had kind of ex-

hausted it. Texas is not an inexhaustible region." He elaborated on this point in the *Atlantic,* concluding: "The move off the land is now virtually completed, and that was the great subject that Texas offered writers of my generation. The one basic subject it offers us now is loneliness, and one can only ring the changes on that so many times."

The three novels McMurtry published between 1978 and 1983 all have primary settings outside of Texas. *Somebody's Darling* centers on the Hollywood career of a young female film director, *Cadillac Jack* follows the cross-country ramblings of an aging antiques dealer, and *The Desert Rose* provides a fictional portrait of a goodhearted Las Vegas showgirl. Critical appraisals of these works concentrate on McMurtry's ability to create appealing characters who are independent of his traditional regional setting. In a *Dictionary of Literary Biography Yearbook* essay, Brooks Landon suggests that *Somebody's Darling* contains "two of [McMurtry's] most mature and most fully realized characters." *Washington Post Book World* contributor Jonathan Yardley similarly states of *Somebody's Darling:* "Mr. McMurtry's characters are real, believable and touching, his prose has life and immediacy and he is a very funny writer." Less successful, according to reviewers, is *Cadillac Jack,* a novel based in Washington, D.C. Peter Prince writes in the *Nation* that the principal character "is the man to squelch everything down to the level of his own deep ordinariness," while Yardley states in the *Washington Post* that "the city as it emerges in the novel is a mere caricature, like too many of the characters in it." Of the three books, *The Desert Rose* has received the most commendation for its sympathetic characterization. Yardley claims in the *Washington Post Book World:* "In her innocent, plucky, unaffected way [the protagonist] is as courageous a character as one could hope to meet." As Larry McCaffery observes in the *Los Angeles Times Book Review,* McMurtry "flirts with being unbearably cute . . . but his lack of condescension toward characters and situation makes his depictions ring true."

At least one critic, Walter Clemons for *Newsweek,* has noted the "perfect inconsistency" that led McMurtry to publish yet another novel about Texas after having consciously bypassed the region for five years. *Lonesome Dove,* McMurtry's eight-hundred-page 1985 release, not only returns to the author's native state for its setting but also concerns the brief cattle drive era that has proven the focus of much of the Western romantic mystique. McMurtry told the *New York Times Book Review* that the novel "grew out of my sense of having heard my uncles talk about the extraordinary days when the range was open," a subject the author had previously addressed only in his nonfiction. According to the reviewers, a strong advantage to the book is the author's objective presentation of frontier life. As George Garrett explains in the *Chicago Tribune Book World, Lonesome Dove* contains "the authority of exact authenticity. You can easily believe that this is how it really was to be there, to live, to suffer and rejoice, then and there. And thus, the reader is most subtly led to see where the literary conventions of the Western came from, how they came to be in the first place, and which are true and which are false." *New York Times Book Review* contributor Nicholas Lemann also writes of *Lonesome Dove:* "Everything about the book feels true; being anti-mythic is a great aid to accuracy about the lonely, ignorant, violent West." This anti-mythic foundation in the novel, according to Lemann, "works to reinforce the strength of the traditionally mythic parts . . . by making it far more credible than the old familiar horse operas."

Lonesome Dove achieved best-seller status within weeks of its release and was a critical success as well. "McMurtry is a storyteller who works hard to satisfy his audience's yearning for the familiar," states R. Z. Sheppard in *Time*. "What, after all, are legends made of? The secret of his success is embellishment, the odd detail or colorful phrase that keeps the tale from slipping into a rut." Clemons claims that the novel "shows, early on, just about every symptom of American Epic except pretentiousness." Clemons concludes: "It's a pleasure . . . to be able to recommend a big popular novel that's amply imagined and crisply, lovingly written. I haven't enjoyed a book more this year." "The aspects of cowboying that we have found stirring for so long are, inevitably, the aspects that are stirring when given full-dress treatment by a first-rate novelist," explains Lemann. *Lonesome Dove* was awarded the Pulitzer Prize for fiction in April of 1986. McMurtry soon followed *Lonesome Dove* with another historical novel, *Anything for Billy,* based on the life of gunslinger Billy the Kid. He also wrote sequels to two earlier novels: *Texasville* shows the characters of *The Last Picture Show* thirty years later, and *Some Can Whistle* continues the narrative of *All My Friends Are Going to Be Strangers.*

In addition to his writing, McMurtry divides his time between the Washington, D.C. book store he has owned since 1970, a ranch in Texas that he bought several years ago, and coast-to-coast driving trips behind the wheel of a Cadillac. In 1989 he was chosen president of PEN American Center, a prestigious writers' organization with affiliates around the world. He was the first non-New Yorker to head the American branch since Indiana's Booth Tarkington, who founded it in 1922.

Though McMurtry no longer wears the sweatshirt with "Minor Regional Novelist" emblazoned on its front, he still describes his approach to his craft in peculiarly Texan terms. Writing, he claims in the *Los Angeles Times,* is "the ultimate analogue to my herding tradition. I herd words, I herd them into sentences and then I herd them into paragraphs and then I herd these paragraphs into books." As Raymond Neinstein indicates, the region McMurtry has written about with such success is "a ghost country . . . a country of love and of blood-ties. When those ties break down, when the love is gone, when the inheritance or inheritability of that country is somehow thwarted and its traditions are no longer viable, then the poignancy of the country's neglected beauty, of the tradition's unusable force, and of the human life left to survive without that beauty, that tradition, that center, becomes the subject of McMurtry's powerful and nostalgic novels." These novels, McMurtry tells the *Los Angeles Times,* are not based on mere "notes of scandals of the neighborhood," but rather are built by essential flights of imagination. "I am more and more convinced," he says, "that the essential reward of writing fiction is in the delight of seeing what you can make out of the sole tools of your imagination and your experience."

MEDIA ADAPTATIONS: "Hud," based on *Horseman, Pass By,* was produced by Paramount in 1962, and won two Academy Awards from the Academy of Motion Picture Arts and Sciences. "Lovin' Molly," based on *Leaving Cheyenne,* was produced by Columbia Pictures in 1974. "Terms of Endearment," based on the novel of the same title, was produced by Paramount in 1983, and won four Golden Globe Awards, the "best picture" award from the New York Film Critics Circle, and five Academy Awards from the Academy of Motion Picture Arts and Sciences, including "best picture of the year." "Lonesome Dove," based on the novel of the same title, was produced as a television miniseries for Columbia Broadcasting System in 1989. Peter Bogdanovich is planning to direct a film version of *Texasville,* McMurtry's sequel to *The Last Picture Show.*

BIOGRAPHICAL/CRITICAL SOURCES:

BOOKS

Authors in the News, Volume 2, Gale, 1976.
Bennett, Patrick, *Talking with Texas Writers: Twelve Interviews,* Texas A & M University Press, 1980.
Bestsellers 89, Issue 2, Gale, 1989.
Burke, John Gordon, editor, *Regional Perspectives: An Examination of America's Literary Heritage,* American Library Association, 1971, reprinted, 1973.
Contemporary Literary Criticism, Gale, Volume 2, 1974, Volume 3, 1975, Volume 7, 1977, Volume 11, 1979, Volume 27, 1984, Volume 44, 1987.
Dictionary of Literary Biography, Volume II: *American Novelists since World War II,* Gale, 1978.
Dictionary of Literary Biography Yearbook, Gale, *1980,* 1981, *1987,* 1988.
Landess, Thomas, *Larry McMurtry,* Steck-Vaughn, 1969.
McCullough, David W., *People Books and Book People,* Harmony Books, 1981.
McMurtry, Larry, *In a Narrow Grave: Essays on Texas,* Encino Press, 1968, Simon & Schuster, 1971.
Neinstein, Raymond L., *The Ghost Country: A Study of the Novels of Larry McMurtry,* Creative Arts Book Company, 1976.
Pages: The World of Books, Writers, and Writing, Gale, 1976.
Peavy, Charles D., *Larry McMurtry,* Twayne, 1977.
Schmidt, Dorey, editor, *Larry McMurtry: Unredeemed Dreams,* School of Humanities, Pan American University, 1978.

PERIODICALS

America, March 5, 1983.
American Film, November, 1975, December, 1975, January-February, 1976, March, 1976, April, 1976, May, 1976, June, 1976.
Arlington Quarterly, winter, 1969-70.
Atlantic, December, 1971, March, 1975.
Best Sellers, July 1, 1970.
Books and Bookmen, November, 1973.
Book Week, October 23, 1966.
Book World, June 21, 1970.
Chicago Tribune, June 9, 1987, November 14, 1989.
Chicago Tribune Book World, October 17, 1982, December 25, 1983, June 9, 1985.
Christian Science Monitor, February 6, 1976.
Colonial Times, December 21-January 12, 1972.
Commentary, January, 1972.
Commonweal, November 5, 1971, October 20, 1972.
Daily Rag, October, 1972.
Dallas News, January 18, 1976.
Detroit Free Press, November 13, 1988.
Detroit News, February 27, 1972, April 26, 1987, November 13, 1988.
Film Quarterly, summer, 1964.
Forum, summer-fall, 1972.
Globe & Mail (Toronto), August 10, 1985, June 20, 1987.
Holiday, September, 1965.
Houston Post, October 30, 1966, August 23, 1968.
Literature/Film Quarterly, April, 1973.
Los Angeles Times, May 27, 1984, January 31, 1989, July 3, 1989.
Los Angeles Times Book Review, November 14, 1982, September 4, 1983, June 9, 1985, August 16, 1987, October 30, 1988, October 22, 1989.
Maclean's, December 25, 1978.
Nation, February 3, 1979, November 20, 1982.

National Review, November 26, 1982, November 25, 1983.

New Republic, October 16, 1971, April 1, 1972, November 29, 1975, September 2, 1985.

Newsweek, October 1, 1971, June 3, 1985, September 26, 1988.

New York, February 5, 1973, April 29, 1974, October 3, 1988.

New Yorker, October 9, 1971, June 14, 1976, August 26, 1985, November 11, 1985.

New York Times, December 3, 1966, June 10, 1970, October 22, 1975, December 20, 1978, December 28, 1981, January 23, 1983, June 3, 1985, April 8, 1987, June 27, 1987, September 28, 1988, November 1, 1988, October 16, 1989.

New York Times Book Review, November 13, 1966, July 26, 1970, August 15, 1971, March 19, 1972, October 19, 1975, November 19, 1978, November 21, 1982, October 23, 1983, June 2, 1985, June 9, 1985, September 15, 1985, April 19, 1987, May 31, 1987, October 16, 1988, October 22, 1989.

People, May 4, 1987.

Prairie Schooner, summer, 1979.

Re: Arts and Letters, fall, 1969.

Saturday Review, October 17, 1970, October 16, 1971, January 10, 1976.

South Dakota Review, summer, 1966, Volume XIII, number 2, 1975.

Southwest Review, winter, 1976.

Southwestern American Literature, January, 1971.

Texas Observer, February 26, 1971.

Time, October 11, 1971, June 10, 1985, April 20, 1987, October 24, 1988.

Times Literary Supplement, March 23, 1973, September 11, 1987, November 3, 1989.

Tribune Books, April 5, 1987, October 9, 1988, October 15, 1989.

Village Voice Literary Supplement, October, 1982.

Vogue, March, 1984.

Washington Post, December 2, 1971, March 4, 1972, June 23, 1974, October 13, 1982, February 5, 1989.

Washington Post Book World, November 12, 1978, August 28, 1983, June 9, 1985, April 12, 1987, July 26, 1987, October 9, 1988, October 22, 1989.

Washington Post Magazine, December 5, 1982.

Western American Literature, fall, 1967, fall, 1969, Number 7, 1972, spring, 1976, November, 1986.

Western Humanities Review, autumn, 1970, winter, 1975.

*   *   *

McPHEE, John (Angus) 1931-

PERSONAL: Born March 8, 1931, in Princeton, N.J.; son of Harry Roemer (a doctor) and Mary (Ziegler) McPhee; married Pryde Brown, March 16, 1957 (marriage ended); married Yolanda Whitman (a horticulturist), March 8, 1972; children: (first marriage) Laura, Sarah, Jenny, Martha; (stepchildren) Cole, Andrew, Katherine, Vanessa Harrop. *Education:* Princeton University, A.B., 1953; graduate study at Cambridge University, 1953-54.

ADDRESSES: Home—Drake's Corner Rd., Princeton, N.J. 08540. *Office*—c/o Farrar, Straus, 19 Union Square W., New York, N.Y. 10003.

CAREER: Playwright for "Robert Montgomery Presents" television show, 1955-57; *Time,* New York City, associate editor, 1957-64; *New Yorker,* New York City, staff writer, 1964—; Princeton University, Princeton, N.J., Ferris Professor of Journalism, 1975—.

MEMBER: Geological Society of America (fellow).

AWARDS, HONORS: Award in Literature, American Academy and Institute of Arts and Letters, 1977; Litt.D., Bates College, 1978, Colby College, 1978, Williams College, 1979, and University of Alaska, 1980; American Association of Petroleum Geologists Journalism Award, 1982, 1986; Woodrow Wilson Award, Princeton University, 1982; author of the year award from American Society of Journalists and Authors, 1986.

WRITINGS:

NONFICTION

A Sense of Where You Are, Farrar, Straus, 1965.

The Headmaster, Farrar, Straus, 1966.

Oranges, Farrar, Straus, 1967.

The Pine Barrens, Farrar, Straus, 1968.

A Roomful of Hovings and Other Profiles (collection), Farrar, Straus, 1969.

The Crofter and the Laird, Farrar, Straus, 1969.

Levels of the Game, Farrar, Straus, 1970.

Encounters with the Archdruid, Farrar, Straus, 1972.

Wimbledon: A Celebration, with photographs by Alfred Eisenstaedt, Viking, 1972.

The Deltoid Pumpkin Seed, Farrar, Straus, 1973.

The Curve of Binding Energy, Farrar, Straus, 1974.

Pieces of the Frame (collection), Farrar, Straus, 1975.

The Survival of the Bark Canoe, Farrar, Straus, 1975.

The John McPhee Reader (collection), edited by William Howarth, Farrar, Straus, 1977.

Coming into the Country, Farrar, Straus, 1977.

Giving Good Weight (collection), Farrar, Straus, 1979.

(With Rowell Galen) *Alaska: Images of the Country,* Sierra, 1981.

Basin and Range, Farrar, Straus, 1981 (also see below).

In Suspect Terrain, Farrar, Straus, 1983 (also see below).

Annals of the Former World, two volumes (contains *Basin and Range* and *In Suspect Terrain*), Farrar, Straus, 1984.

La Place de la Concorde Suisse, Farrar, Straus, 1984.

Table of Contents (collection), Farrar, Straus, 1985.

Rising from the Plains, Farrar, Straus, 1986.

The Control of Nature, Farrar, Straus, 1989.

Looking for a Ship, Farrar, Straus, 1990.

SIDELIGHTS: "John McPheeland is a small nation populated almost entirely by canoemakers, basketball players, inspired tinkerers, backyard inventors, restaurateurs, vegetable growers and geologists," writes *Detroit News* critic William Marvel. "In John McPheeland all these people still care about what they do, and they do it exceedingly well." Many critics agree that the appeal of McPhee's nonfiction books, mostly collections of his *New Yorker* articles, lies in their offbeat subject matter. "Sometimes it seems that McPhee deliberately chooses unpromising subjects, just to show what he can do with them," remarks *New Republic* reviewer Richard Horwich.

One of the author's early books, *Oranges,* illustrates Horwich's point. The volume delves entirely into the history, growth cycles, and manufacture of that one citrus fruit. Another work, *The Survival of the Bark Canoe,* is "the best book on bark canoes," according to a *Time* critic, who adds, "It is part shop manual, part history, and part unforgettable-character sketch." The book introduces canoemaker Henri Vaillencourt, and "by the time we enter [that man's] obsession, we are drawn irresistibly to the tapering of thwarts, the laminating of stempieces, the goring of bark," says Christopher Lehmann-Haupt in *New York Times.* "And so lucid, indeed so dramatic, are Mr. McPhee's descriptions of these arts, one wonders if he isn't the one who should be put in charge of translating the instructions that come with Japanese toys."

Indeed, McPhee is regarded as a gifted liaison between specialist and layman reader. The author shows a "pleasantly flexible technique, well-mannered and accommodating," as Michiko Kakutani sees it. "Elegant without being elaborate, casual but never flippant, the prose always serves the material at hand, and combined with an obsession for detail . . . it enables [the author] to translate for the layman the mysteries that preoccupy professionals, be they athletes or engineers. He can reveal character in the description of a basketball toss, discover literary metaphors in the movement of subatomic particles," writes Kakutani in a *New York Times Book Review* article.

In what many critics believe is McPhee's best book to date, *Coming into the Country,* the author presents an insider's view of one of America's last frontiers—Alaska. The volume consists of "three lengthy bulletins" about Alaska, according to *Time* critic Paul Gray. The first concerns "a canoe trip that McPhee and four companions took down an unspoiled river in the northwestern reaches of the state, well above the Arctic Circle. [In the] second, McPhee tells of a helicopter ride with a committee looking for a site on which to build a new state capital. The last and longest section covers some wintry months spent in Engle, a tiny settlement on the Yukon River."

Edward Hoagland, who had characterized McPhee as no "risktaker" in previous books, declares that in *Coming into the Country,* "he made his will, took the gambit; and in so doing, he introduced a new generosity of tempo to his work, a leisurely artfulness of organization he has not had before." Continuing in his *New York Times Book Review* piece, Hoagland notes that his "main objection to [McPhee's] other books has been that he was too aloof with the reader about himself—almost neurotically so—and not aloof enough about some of the subjects of his pieces, over-admiring them, taking them just at their word. Here he lets down his own hair a bit, and includes a running commentary from neighbors, enemies and friends about most of the people in the book."

While *Atlantic* critic Benjamin DeMott enjoys the author's self-portrait of "his own embarrassments as a city man ravished by the woods but still dependent upon comforts," the reviewer sees a greater merit in *Coming into the Country:* "Not the least achievement of [the book] is that, in eschewing formulas, it manages simultaneously to represent fairly the positions of the parties in conflict—developers, conservationists, renegade individualists—and to show forth the implications, for human society, of the loss of the ground on which the dream of 'lighting out for The Territory' has immemorially been based." What the reader gains from this work, concludes DeMott, is a sense that "what is really in view in *Coming into the Country* is a matter not usually met in works of reportage—nothing less than the nature of the human condition."

McPhee has also produced several books on American geology, including *Basin and Range* and *In Suspect Terrain. Basin and Range* begins with McPhee taking "a deceptively simple cross-country trip: Interstate 80," says *Los Angeles Times* critic Carolyn See. The author is accompanied by an accomplished geologist who points out the vast history of various western rock formations, and "the ideas do tumble out—ideas about how ranges and basins were formed, about the difference between old mountains and new ones, about how silver got deposited in those Nevada bonanzas and how the Great Salt Lakes came to be both salty and great," according to Lehmann-Haupt in another *New York Times* article. "These ideas are entertaining enough in

themselves and lend a wonderful variety to [the author's] report."

"The descriptions of geologists at work are sympathetic and convincing," writes C. Vita-Finzi in *Times Literary Supplement.* "The digressions into the language and jargon of the subject should prove chastening to its practitioners." Among the theories discussed in *Basin and Range* is one suggesting that moving segments of the earth, both on land and in the oceans, will eventually cause the west coast of America to break off into the Pacific, "thus making California an island," as Evan Connell elaborates in *Washington Post Book World.* "Metaphorically, of course, many people believe this already has happened." McPhee, he continues, "discusses such matters easily. His tone is affable, his meandering appropriate, and the tutorial intent of *Basin and Range* is commendable—for surely nobody could measure the width or depth of our ignorance."

In Suspect Terrain "takes its title from the geologists' phrase for country whose history, as recorded in the rocks, is ambiguous or obscure," Wallace Stegner writes in a *Los Angeles Times Book Review* piece. McPhee's follow-up to *Basin and Range* explores the geological relationships in urban areas, including a study of the geology of Brooklyn, New York. "A travelogue across country and through time, [*In Suspect Terrain*] is a most instructive book," finds Stegner. And while Kakutani feels that "the presence of a shaping, interpretive sensibility . . . would have infused [the book with] a measure of welcome warmth," *Detroit News* reviewer Lisa Schwarzbaum maintains that the author's "expertise brings us great chunks of information and explication about subjects not always immediately accessible or even fascinating, in a way that makes them both. . . . In journeying across America and into its earth, McPhee takes his lucky readers across and into human dimensions. *In Suspect Terrain* gives breath and voice to the very rocks."

Giving Good Weight is another McPhee collection notable for the inclusion of perhaps the author's most notorious *New Yorker* entry, "Brigade de Cuisine," about a chef so talented—and so publicity-shy—that he will not allow his name or the name of his rural bistro to be mentioned, for fear that his comfortable existence would be shattered by swarms of East Coast gourmands. "The piece brought chaos among the pheasant pate crowd in Manhattan when it appeared," reports *Chicago Tribune Book World* critic William Brashler, "first, because so many Lutece-crazed New Yorkers felt cheated that they hadn't ever eaten there, and second, because McPhee's Chef Otto, a pseudonym, had the audacity to dine at some of the best French restaurants in the city . . . and declare that the turbot was frozen. *Sacre bleu!*"

Although Brashler criticizes that entry and another, "pre-Three Mile Island chapter [about a nuclear power plant] written so blithely that it's embarrassing," the critic praises the title piece, "a wonderful, discursive tour of New York City's Greenmarkets, where East Coast farmers come into the city to sell produce. McPhee is right there weighing, selling, and describing the people and places as only he can. Here is McPhee's writing at its best: his awe and insight, his sense of texture and variety, his listing of things and processes which involve a reader and shortly have him planting, tasting, bickering, and being there."

McPhee may have won widespread acclaim for his nonfiction, but, in a *New York Times Book Review* interview with Stephen Singular, the author reveals that his early career interests included a variety of genres. "I wrote poems in college—rank imitations of Pope, Yeats, Housman, Eliot. My senior year I wrote a novel. . . . After college, I sat all day in a captain's chair up on 84th Street trying to write plays for live television." Discussing the inspiration for his articles, McPhee notes that "most of them originate when they strike an echo from my earlier experience, like 'The Survival of the Bark Canoe.' When I was quite young, my father took me to a summer camp [where] our canoe trips were a big thing, and I dearly loved them. What you hope is that some subject will interest you and then you will have to deal with it on its own terms." As for the critical reaction that his work does not include enough personal material, the author calls it "pointless. I'm not going to go out and write 'Remembrance of Things Past.' You can't be all things. There are limitations everywhere you look. Critics may think I should be doing things on a grander scale and maybe I should be writing theological novels in Urdu. But fundamentally, I'm a working journalist and I've got to go out and work."

BIOGRAPHICAL/CRITICAL SOURCES:

BOOKS

Contemporary Literary Criticism, Volume 36, Gale, 1986.

PERIODICALS

Atlantic, January, 1978.
Chicago Tribune, April 19, 1984, August 27, 1989.
Chicago Tribune Book World, January 6, 1980.
Detroit Free Press, September 3, 1989.
Detroit News, July 12, 1981, March 13, 1983, May 13, 1984.
Globe and Mail (Toronto), May 2, 1987, September 30, 1989.
Los Angeles Times, April 27, 1981, August 6, 1989.
Los Angeles Times Book Review, February 27, 1983, November 9, 1986, July 30, 1989.
Nation, January 14, 1978.
National Review, June 2, 1989.
New Republic, July 11, 1970, September 1, 1973, July 5, 1975, January 7, 1978.
New York Review of Books, March 23, 1978, May 14, 1981.
New York Times, March 8, 1967, November 2, 1969, July 13, 1973, July 9, 1974, June 18, 1975, November 27, 1975, November 25, 1977, November 17, 1979, May 8, 1981, January 24, 1983, April 30, 1984, September 27, 1985, August 3, 1989.
New York Times Book Review, June 23, 1974, June 22, 1975, November 27, 1977, November 18, 1979, May 17, 1981, January 30, 1983, May 6, 1984, October 13, 1985, November 23, 1986, August 6, 1989.
Saturday Review, January 22, 1977, April, 1981.
Time, June 10, 1974, December 15, 1975, December 5, 1977, January 31, 1983.
Times Literary Supplement, February 18, 1983, January 6, 1984, December 7, 1984.
Washington Post, December 18, 1979, July 31, 1989.
Washington Post Book World, August 15, 1971, January 22, 1978, April 19, 1981, January 30, 1983, March 13, 1983, April 8, 1984, October 13, 1985, November 9, 1986.

*　　*　　*

McPHERSON, James Alan 1943-

PERSONAL: Born September 16, 1943, in Savannah, Ga.; son of James Allen and Mable (Smalls) McPherson. *Education:* Attended Morgan State University, 1963-64; Morris Brown College, B.A., 1965; Harvard University, LL.B., 1968; University of Iowa, M.F.A., 1969.

*ADDRESSES: Office-*Department of English, University of Iowa, Iowa City, Iowa 52242.

CAREER: University of Iowa, Iowa City, instructor in writing at Law School, 1968-69, instructor in Afro-American literature, 1969; University of California, Santa Cruz, faculty member, 1969-7O; Morgan State University, Baltimore, Md., faculty member, 1975-76; University of Virginia, Charlottesville, faculty member, 1976-81; University of Iowa, Writers Workshop, Iowa City, professor, 1981—.

MEMBER: Authors League of America.

AWARDS, HONORS: First prize, *Atlantic* short story contest, 1965, for "Gold Coast"; grant from Atlantic Monthly Press and Little, Brown, 1969; National Institute of Arts and Letters award in literature, 197O; Guggenheim fellow, 1972-73; Pulitzer Prize, 1978, for *Elbow Room: Stories;* MacArthur fellowship, 1981.

WRITINGS:

Hue and Cry: Short Stories, Atlantic-Little, Brown, 1969.
(Editor with Miller Williams) *Railroad: Trains and Train People in American Culture,* Random House, 1976.
Elbow Room: Stories, Atlantic-Little, Brown, 1977.
(Author of foreword) Breece D'J Pancake, *The Stories of Breece D'J Pancake,* Atlantic-Little, Brown, 1983.

CONTRIBUTOR

J. Hicks, editor, *Cutting Edges,* Holt, 1973.
Nick A. Ford, editor, *Black Insights: Significant Literature by Afro-Americans, 176O to the Present,* Wiley, 1976.
Llewellyn Howland and Isabelle Storey, editors, *Book for Boston,* Godine, 1980.
Kimberly W. Benson, editor, *Speaking for You,* Howard University Press, 1987.
Alex Harris, *A World Unsuspected,* [Chapel Hill], 1987.

OTHER

Also contributor to *New Black Voices,* New American Library. Contributor to *Atlantic, Esquire, New York Times Magazine, Playboy, Reader's Digest,* and *Callaloo.* Contributing editor, *Atlantic,* 1969—; editor of special issue, *Iowa Review,* winter, 1984.

SIDELIGHTS: James Alan McPherson's stories of ordinary, working class people, though often concerning black characters, are noted for their ability to confront universal human problems. "His standpoint," Robie Macauley explains in the *New York Times Book Review,* "[is] that of a writer and a black, but not that of a black writer. [McPherson] refused to let his fiction fall into any color-code or ethnic code." Because of this stance, McPherson's characters are more fully rounded than are those of more racially-conscious writers. As Paul Bailey writes in the *Observer Review,* "the Negroes and whites [McPherson] describes always remain individual people—he never allows himself the luxury of turning them into Problems." Explaining his approach to the characters in his stories, McPherson is quoted by Patsy B. Perry of the *Dictionary of Literary Biography* as saying: "Certain of these people [his characters] happen to be black, and certain of them happen to be white; but I have tried to keep the color part of most of them far in the background, where these things should rightly be kept." McPherson has published two collections of short stories, *Hue and Cry: Short Stories* and *Elbow Room: Stories.* In 1978 he was awarded the Pulitzer Prize for fiction.

McPherson was born and raised in Savannah, Georgia, a city in which several cultures—including the French, Spanish, and Indian—have been uniquely blended. He cites this rich cultural heritage as a determining factor in his own ability to transcend racial barriers. The McPherson family also influenced his development of values. His father, at one time the only licensed black master electrician in Georgia, and his mother, a domestic in a white household, had important contacts in both the white and black communities. Through their efforts, McPherson obtained work as a grocery boy in a local supermarket and as a waiter on a train. These experiences have formed the basis for several later stories. McPherson's train employment also allowed him to travel across the country. Perry notes that McPherson "affirms the importance of both white and black communities in his development as an individual and as a writer of humanistic ideas."

McPherson's writing career began in the 1960s while he was still attending law school. His story "Gold Coast" won first prize in a contest sponsored by the *Atlantic* magazine and was later published in the magazine as well. The *Atlantic* was to play a pivotal role in McPherson's career. After earning a bachelor's degree, a law degree, and a master's degree in creative writing, McPherson became a contributing editor of the *Atlantic* in 1969. And the magazine, in conjunction with Little, Brown, also published his two collections of short stories.

McPherson's first collection, *Hue and Cry,* deals with characters whose lives are so desperate that they can only rage impotently against their situations. "The fact that these characters . . .," writes Perry, "know nothing else to do except to sink slowly into madness, scream unintelligibly, or seek refuge . . . provides reason enough for McPherson's hue and cry." The *Times Literary Supplement* critic points to the book's "mostly desperate, mostly black, mostly lost figures in the urban nightmare of violence, rage and bewilderment that is currently America."

Despite the grim nature of his stories, McPherson manages to depict the lives of his characters with sympathy and grace. Bailey allows that McPherson's "powers of observation and character-drawing are remarkable, displaying a mature novelist's understanding of the vagaries and inconsistencies of human affairs." Writing in *Harper's,* Irving Howe maintains that McPherson "possesses an ability some writers take decades to acquire, the ability to keep the right distance from the creatures of his imagination, not to get murkily involved and blot out his figures with vanity and fuss." Granville Hicks of *Saturday Review* notes that McPherson "is acutely aware of the misery and injustice in the world, and he sympathizes deeply with the victims whether they are black or white."

Among the most prominent admirers of *Hue and Cry* is novelist Ralph Ellison. In a statement he contributed to the book's dust jacket, Ellison speaks of the difference between McPherson's writing and that of most other black writers. "McPherson," Ellison claims, "promises to move right past those talented but misguided writers . . . who take being black as a privilege for being obscenely second-rate and who regard their social predicament as Negroes as exempting them from the necessity of mastering the craft and forms of fiction. . . . McPherson will never, as a writer, be an embarrassment to such people of excellence as Willie Mays, Duke Ellington, Leontyne Price—or, for that matter, Stephen Crane or F. Scott Fitzgerald."

Elbow Room, McPherson's second collection, won even more critical praise than its predecessor. Again concerned with characters in desperate situations, the stories of *Elbow Room* are nonetheless more optimistic than McPherson's earlier works, the characters more willing to struggle for some measure of success. They "engage in life's battles with integrity of mind and spirit," as Perry explains. This optimism is noted by several critics. Robert Phillips of *Commonweal,* for example, finds the stories in *Elbow Room* to be "difficult struggles for survival, yet [McPher-

son's] sense of humor allows him to dwell on moments which otherwise might prove unbearable." Writing in *Newsweek,* Margo Jefferson calls McPherson "an astute realist who knows how to turn the conflicts between individual personalities and the surrounding culture into artful and highly serious comedies of manners."

McPherson's ability to create believable characters, and his focus on the underlying humanity of all his characters, is praised by such critics as Phillips. McPherson's stories, Phillips believes, "ultimately become not so much about the black condition as the human condition. . . . *Elbow Room* is a book of singular achievement." Macauley explains that McPherson has been able "to look beneath skin color and cliches of attitude into the hearts of his characters. . . . This is a fairly rare ability in American fiction." The *New Yorker* reviewer lists several other characteristics of McPherson's stories that are worthy of attention, calling him "one of those rare writers who can tell a story, describe shadings of character, and make sociological observations with equal subtlety."

Speaking of the obstacles and opportunities facing black writers, McPherson writes in the *Atlantic:* "It seems to me much of our writing has been, and continues to be, sociological because black writers have been concerned with protesting black humanity and racial injustice to the larger society in those terms most easily understood by nonblack people. It also seems to me that we can correct this limitation either by defining and affirming the values and cultural institutions of our people for their education or by employing our own sense of reality and our own conception of what human life should be to explore, and perhaps help define, the cultural realities of contemporary American life."

BIOGRAPHICAL/CRITICAL SOURCES:

BOOKS

Contemporary Literary Criticism, Volume 19, Gale, 1981.
Dictionary of Literary Biography, Volume 38: *Afro-American Writers after 1955: Dramatists and Prose Writers,* Gale, 1985.

PERIODICALS

Antioch Review, winter, 1978.
Atlantic, December, 1970, February, 1977.
Chicago Tribune Book World, May 25, 1969.
Christian Science Monitor, July 31, 1969.
CLA Journal, June, 1979.
Commonweal, September 19, 1969, September 15, 1978.
Ebony, December, 1981.
Harper's, December, 1969.
Iowa Journal of Literary Studies, 1983.
Nation, December 16, 1978.
Negro Digest, October, 1969, November, 1969.
Newsweek, June 16, 1969, October 17, 1977.
New Yorker, November 21, 1977.
New York Review of Books, November 10, 1977.
New York Times Book Review, June 1, 1969, September 25, 1977, September 2, 1979, February 13, 1983, May 13, 1984.
Observer Review, December 7, 1969.
Saturday Review, May 24, 1969.
Spectator, November 22, 1969.
Studies in American Fiction, autumn, 1973.
Times Literary Supplement, December 25, 1969.
Washington Post Book World, October 30, 1977, March 6, 1983.

McPHERSON, James M(unro) 1936-

PERSONAL: Born October 11, 1936, in Valley City, N.D.; son of James Munro (a high school teacher) and Miriam (a teacher; maiden name, Osborn) McPherson; married Patricia A. Rasche, December 28, 1957; children: Joanna Erika. *Education:* Gustavus Adolphus College, B.A., 1958; Johns Hopkins University, Ph.D., 1963. *Politics:* Democratic. *Religion:* Presbyterian.

ADDRESSES: Home—15 Randall Rd., Princeton, N.J. 08540. *Office*—Department of History, Princeton University, Princeton, N.J. 08544.

CAREER: Princeton University, Princeton, N.J., instructor, 1962-65, assistant professor, 1965-66, associate professor, 1966-72, professor of history, 1972—, Edwards Professor of American History, 1982. Fellow, Behavioral Sciences Center, Stanford University, 1982-83. Consultant, Social Science program, Educational Research Council, Cleveland, Ohio; elder, Nassau Presbyterian Church, 1976-79.

MEMBER: American Historical Association, Association for the Study of Negro Life and History, Organization of American Historians, Southern Historical Association, Phi Beta Kappa.

AWARDS, HONORS: Danforth fellow, 1958-62; Proctor & Gamble faculty fellowship; Anisfield Wolff Award in Race Relations, 1965, for *The Struggle for Equality: Abolitionists and the Negro in the Civil War and Reconstruction;* Guggenheim fellow, 1967-68; National Endowment for the Humanities-Huntington fellowship, 1977-78; Huntington-Seaver Institute fellow, 1987-88; National Book Award nomination, 1988, National Book Critics Circle nomination, 1988, and Pulitzer Prize in history, 1989, all for *Battle Cry of Freedom: The Civil War Era.*

WRITINGS:

The Struggle for Equality: Abolitionists and the Negro in the Civil War and Reconstruction, Princeton University Press, 1964.

(Editor) *The Negro's Civil War: How American Negroes Felt and Acted in the War for the Union,* Pantheon, 1965, reprinted, University of Illinois Press, 1982.

(Contributor) Martin B. Duberman, editor, *The Anti-Slavery Vanguard: New Essays on Abolitionism,* Princeton University Press, 1965.

(Editor) *Marching Toward Freedom: The Negro in the Civil War, 1861-1865,* Knopf, 1968.

(Contributor) Barton J. Bernstein, editor, *Towards a New Past: Dissenting Essays in American History,* Pantheon, 1968.

(With others) *Blacks in America: Bibliographical Essays,* Doubleday, 1971.

The Abolitionist Legacy: From Reconstruction to the NAACP, Princeton University Press, 1976.

Ordeal by Fire: The Civil War and Reconstruction, Knopf, 1981.

(Editor with J. Morgan Kousser) *Region, Race, and Reconstruction: Essays in Honor of C. Vann Woodward,* Oxford University Press, 1982.

Battle Cry of Freedom: The Civil War Era (volume 6 of "The Oxford History of the United States"), Oxford University Press, 1988.

Abraham Lincoln and the Second American Revolution, Oxford University Press, 1991.

Contributor of articles to *American Historical Review, Journal of American History, Journal of Negro History, Caribbean Studies, Phylon, Mid America,* and other publications. Member of editorial board, *Civil War History.*

WORK IN PROGRESS: Abraham Lincoln and the Second American Revolution, a collection of essays.

SIDELIGHTS: When James M. McPherson's *Battle Cry of Freedom: The Civil War Era,* the sixth volume of the "Oxford History of the United States," appeared in 1988 it caused a sensation among reviewers and readers alike—Ballantine Books made a record-setting bid of $504,000 for the paperback rights, and the book appeared on the *New York Times* bestseller chart from March to July of 1988. Critics noted that the volume made few new revelations about the war: "The Civil War," declared Hugh Brogan in the *New York Times Book Review,* "is the most worked-over topic in United States history, one of the most written about in the history of the world"; and Peter S. Prescott, writing in *Newsweek,* stated that "the more than 50,000 books already written about the Civil War have left the field as thoroughly turned over as the ground was at Antietam." What they admired about the book was its expert synthesis of the period's history, incorporating political, social, economic, and military factors to present a portrait of this most central event in U.S. history.

Civil War historiography has a long and distinguished history of its own. Although critics have acclaimed other single-volume histories of the Civil War—among them Bruce Catton's *This Hallowed Ground* and McPherson's own *Ordeal by Fire: The Civil War and Reconstruction*—generally the most prominent works have been multi-volume efforts. One of the earliest interpretations of the war appeared in George Bancroft's *History of the United States from the Discovery of the American Continent to the Present Time.* Bancroft, considered by many contemporaries to be the preeminent nineteenth-century American historian, lived through the events leading up to the War, through the war itself, and through most of the period of Reconstruction that followed it. His ten-volume work presented one of the first attempts to understand the war as the triumph of Unionism (right) over Secessionism (wrong). James Ford Rhodes, writing his seven-volume *History of the United States from the Compromise of 1850* around the turn of the century, was among the first historians to emphasize the importance of race as an issue in nineteenth-century politics. Allan Nevins, writing after World War II, completed eight volumes on *The Ordeal of the Union,* in which he challenged the then-held view that the Civil War had been unnecessary, forced on the South by fanatical Northern abolitionists. More recently, Bruce Catton and Shelby Foote have published narrative histories describing the military conflict from Northern and Southern perspectives—Catton's "Army of the Potomac" and "Centennial History of the Civil War" trilogies, and Foote's *The Civil War: A Narrative.*

Critical opinion gives *Battle Cry of Freedom* a distinguished place among its precursors. Historian Thomas L. Connelly, writing in the *Washington Post Book World,* calls *Battle Cry* the "finest single volume on the [Civil] war and its background." *New York Review of Books* contributor Richard E. Beringer declares, "It is the only recent book I know of that effectively integrates in one volume social, political, and military events from the immediate aftermath of the Mexican War through the sectional strife of the 1850s, the secession movement, and the Civil War." In the *Los Angeles Times Book Review,* Huston Horn calls *Battle Cry* "the finest compression of that national paroxysm ever fitted between two covers." Brogan states that the book "is the best one-volume treatment of its subject that I have ever come across. It may actually be the best ever published. It is comprehensive yet succinct, scholarly without being pedantic, eloquent but unrhetorical. It is compellingly readable. I was swept away, feeling as if I had never heard the saga before."

McPherson also offers a reassessment of the outcome of the war, believing that the Union victory was by no means as preordained as some historians would have it. He examines three reasons often cited for the South's defeat: 1. the South was overwhelmed by superior numbers; 2. Southern soldiers lost the will to fight; and 3. Union leadership proved better able to manage the new industrial warfare. While acknowledging that each interpretation has its strengths, McPherson notes in his epilogue to *Battle Cry of Freedom* that "most attempts to explain southern defeat or northern victory lack the dimension of *contingency*—the recognition that at numerous critical points during the war things might have gone altogether differently." "Northern victory and southern defeat in the war," he concludes, "cannot be understood apart from the contingency that hung over every campaign, every battle, every election, every decision during the war." "This is historical writing of the highest order," Brogan states, "conveying perhaps the most important lesson of all: that we are not always masters of our fate, even when we most need to be."

Another of McPherson's major themes concerns the war's revolutionary nature. He sees the Civil War as a turning point in American history, as do many other historians: a point in which American society turned away from Southern agrarianism to Northern capitalism and industrialization. However, he writes, "until 1861, it was the North that was out of the mainstream, not the South. . . . The South more closely resembled a majority of the societies in the world than did the rapidly changing North during the antebellum generation." Many southerners, McPherson explains, viewed the new "competitive, egalitarian, free-labor capitalism" in the North with alarm, seeing in its power a threat to their traditional liberties and property rights. When the Republican party won the election of 1860, the South figured "that the northern majority had turned irrevocably toward this frightening, revolutionary future," and accordingly began what McPherson calls "a pre-emptive counterrevolution"—a term Beringer defines as "a revolution launched to prevent the real revolution from occurring."

The war wrought as well a profound change in the way Americans perceived themselves and their government. "Before 1861," McPherson explains, "the two words 'United States' were generally rendered as a plural noun: 'the United States *are* a republic.' The war marked a transition of the United States to a singular noun. The 'Union' also became the nation, and Americans now rarely speak of their Union except in an historical sense." McPherson points out that before the war, most citizens were unaffected by the federal government in their daily lives, except through the postal service. By the war's end, however, a U.S. citizen had to deal with a federal income tax, the Internal Revenue Service, the draft, a national paper currency, and the first national welfare system. "At the end" of the book, declares Prescott, McPherson ". . . demonstrates a point he made firmly at the start: this country went into the war a union and came out a nation. What that difference is, is what this book is about."

BIOGRAPHICAL/CRITICAL SOURCES:

BOOKS

Dictionary of Literary Biography, Gale, Volume 17: *Twentieth-Century American Historians,* 1983, Volume 30: *American Historians, 1607-1865,* 1984, Volume 47: *American Historians, 1866-1912,* 1986.
McPherson, James M., *Battle Cry of Freedom: The Civil War Era,* Oxford University Press, 1988.
Shaara, Michael, *The Killer Angels,* McKay, 1974.
Something about the Author, Volume 16, Gale, 1979.

PERIODICALS

Book World, May 5, 1968.
Chicago Tribune, March 20, 1988.
Chicago Tribune Book World, October 17, 1982.
Commonweal, May 24, 1968.
Los Angeles Times Book Review, March 20, 1988.
National Observer, November 4, 1968.
Newsweek, April 11, 1988.
New York Review of Books, June 2, 1988.
New York Times Book Review, February 14, 1988.
U.S. News & World Report, August 15, 1988.
Washington Post Book World, March 13, 1988.

—*Sketch by Kenneth R. Shepherd*

*　　*　　*

MEAD, Margaret　1901-1978

PERSONAL: Born December 16, 1901, in Philadelphia, Pa.; died after a year-long battle with cancer, November 15, 1978, in New York City; buried in Buckingham, Pa.; daughter of Edward S. and Emily (Fogg) Mead; married Luther Cressman (a minister), September, 1923 (divorced); married Reo Fortune (an anthropologist), October, 1928 (divorced); married Gregory Bateson (an anthropologist and biologist), March, 1936 (divorced, 1950); children: Mary Catherine Bateson Kassarjian. *Education:* Attended DePauw University, 1919-20; Barnard College, B.A., 1923; Columbia University, M.A., 1924, Ph.D., 1929. *Religion:* Episcopalian.

ADDRESSES: Home—211 Central Park West, New York, N.Y. 10024. *Office*—American Museum of Natural History, 79th St. and Central Park West, New York, N.Y.

CAREER: Anthropologist. American Museum of Natural History, New York City, assistant curator, 1926-42, associate curator, 1942-64, curator of ethnology, 1964-69, curator emeritus, 1969-78; Columbia University, New York City, adjunct professor of anthropology, 1954-78; Fordham University, Lincoln Center campus, New York City, professor of anthropology and chairman of Division of Social Sciences, 1968-70. Did field work in Samoa, 1925-26, New Guinea, 1928-29, 1931-33, 1938, 1953, 1964, 1965, 1967, 1971, 1973, 1975, Nebraska, 1930, and Bali, 1936-38, 1957-58. Jacob Gimbel Lecturer for Stanford University and University of California, 1946; Mason Lecturer, University of Birmingham, 1949; Inglis Lecturer, Harvard University, 1950; Jubilee Lecturer for New Education Fellowship, Australia, 1951; Philips Visitor, Haverford College, 1955; Terry Lecturer, Yale University, 1957; Sloan Professor, Menninger School of Psychiatry, 1959; Reynolds Lecturer, University of Colorado, 1960; Alumni Distinguished Lecturer, University of Rhode Island, 1970-71; Fogarty Scholar-in-Residence, National Institutes of Health, 1973. Visiting lecturer, Vassar College, 1939-41; visiting professor, University of Cincinnati, beginning 1957, Emory University, 1964, New York University, 1965-67, Yale University, 1966. Directed Wellesley School of Community Affairs, 1943; taught Harvard seminars on American civilization, Salzburg, Austria, 1947, and at the UNESCO Workshop on International Understanding, Sevres, France, 1947; conducted courses in connection with the American Museum's audio-visual program on culture and communication in collaboration with Columbia University's Teacher's College, 1947-51; directed Columbia University project, "Research in Contemporary Cultures," for the Office of Naval Research, 1948-50. Secretary of committee on food habits, National Research Council, 1942-45; former member of World Health Organization study group on the psychological development of the child, Hampton Institute board of trustees, Josiah H. Macy Conference on Group Processes, and Macy Conference on Problems of Consciousness; member and co-editor of Macy Conference on Cybernetics.

MEMBER: American Academy of Arts and Sciences, American Anthropological Association (fellow; past president), American Association for the Advancement of Science (past president; past chairman of board), Institute for Intercultural Studies (secretary), American Association of University Women, Society of Applied Anthropology (past president), American Ethnological Society, Society of Woman Geographers (fellow), American Orthopsychiatric Association (fellow), World Society of Ekistics (past president), Scientists Institute for Public Information (past president), Society for General Systems Research (past president), Institute for Intercultural Studies, World Federation of Mental Health (past president), American Council of Learned Societies (past vice-president), New York Academy of Science (fellow), Phi Beta Kappa, Delta Kappa Gamma, Sigma Xi.

AWARDS, HONORS: Honorary degrees from Wilson College, 1940, Rutgers University, 1941, Elmira College, 1947, Western College for Women, 1955, University of Leeds, 1957, Kalamazoo College, 1957, Skidmore College, 1958, Goucher College, 1960, Temple University, 1962, Lincoln University, 1963, Columbia University, 1964, and University of Cincinnati, 1965. National achievement award, Chi Omega, 1940; gold medal award, Society of Women Geographers, 1942; one of outstanding women of the year in science, Associated Press, 1949; Viking Medal in anthropology, 1958; medal of honor, Rice University, 1962; Women's Hall of Fame, Nationwide Women Editors, 1965; William Proctor Prize for Scientific Achievement, Scientific Research Society of America, 1969; Arches of Science Award, Pacific Science Center, 1971; Kalinga Prize, UNESCO and government of India, 1971; Wilder Penfield Award, Vanier Institute of the Family, 1972; Lehmann Award, New York Academy of Sciences, 1973; Omega Achievers Award for Education, 1977; Presidential Medal of Freedom, 1979.

WRITINGS:

An Inquiry into the Question of Cultural Stability in Polynesia (Ph.D. thesis), Columbia University Press, 1928, reprinted, AMS Press, 1969.

Coming of Age in Samoa (also see below), Morrow, 1928, reprinted, 1971.

Social Organization of Manua, Bernice P. Bishop Museum, 1930, 2nd edition, 1969.

Growing Up in New Guinea (also see below), Morrow, 1930, reprinted, 1976.

The Changing Culture of an Indian Tribe, Columbia University Press, 1932, reprinted, AMS Press, 1969.

Sex and Temperament in Three Primitive Societies (also see below), Morrow, 1935, reprinted, Dell, 1968.

(Co-author and editor) *Cooperation and Competition among Primitive Societies,* McGraw, 1937, reprinted, Beacon Press, 1966.

From the South Seas (collection; contains *Coming of Age in Samoa, Growing Up in New Guinea,* and *Sex and Temperament in Three Primitive Societies*), Morrow, 1939.

And Keep Your Powder Dry: An Anthropologist Looks at America, Morrow, 1942, expanded edition, Books for Libraries, 1971.

(With Gregory Bateson) *Balinese Character: A Photographic Analysis,* New York Academy of Sciences, 1942, reprinted, 1962.

Male and Female, Morrow, 1949, reprinted, Greenwood, 1977.

Soviet Attitudes toward Authority, McGraw, 1951, reprinted, Greenwood Press, 1979.

The School in American Culture, Harvard University Press, 1951.

(With Frances Cooke MacGregor) *Growth and Culture: A Photographic Study of Balinese Childhood* (based on photographs by Gregory Bateson), Putnam, 1951.

(Co-author and editor) *Cultural Patterns and Technical Changes,* UNESCO, 1953, reprinted, Greenwood Press, 1985.

(Editor with Rhoda Metraux) *The Study of Culture at a Distance,* University of Chicago Press, 1953, reprinted, 1966.

(Editor with Nicolas Calas) *Primitive Heritage: An Anthropological Anthology,* Random House, 1953.

(With Metraux) *Themes in French Culture,* Stanford University Press, 1954.

(Editor with Martha Wolfenstein) *Childhood in Contemporary Cultures,* University of Chicago Press, 1955, reprinted, 1970.

New Lives for Old, Morrow, 1956, reprinted, Greenwood Press, 1980.

(Editor) *An Anthropologist at Work: Writings of Ruth Benedict,* Houghton, 1959, reprinted, Greenwood Press, 1977.

People and Places (for young people), World Publishing, 1959.

(Editor with Ruth L. Bunzel) *The Golden Age of American Anthropology,* Braziller, 1960.

A Creative Life for Your Children (booklet), U.S. Department of Health, Education, and Welfare, 1962.

(With Junius B. Bird and Hans Himmelheber) *Technique and Personality,* Museum of Primitive Art (New York), 1963.

Food Habits Research: Problems of the 1960's (booklet), National Academy of Sciences-National Research Council, 1964.

Anthropology, A Human Science: Selected Papers, 1939-1960, Van Nostrand, 1964.

Continuities in Cultural Evolution, Yale University Press, 1964.

(With Ken Heyman) *Family,* Macmillan, 1965.

Anthropologists and What They Do, F. Watts, 1965.

(With Muriel Brown) *The Wagon and the Star: A Study of American Community Initiative,* Curriculum Resources, 1966.

(With Paul Byers) *The Small Conference: An Innovation in Communication,* Ecole Pratique des Hautes Etudes, 1966.

The Changing Cultural Patterns of Work and Leisure (booklet), U.S. Department of Labor, 1967.

(Editor with others) *Science and the Concept of Race,* Columbia University Press, 1968.

The Mountain Arapesh, three volumes, Natural History Press, 1968-71.

Culture and Commitment: A Study of the Generation Gap, Natural History Press, 1970, published as *Culture and Commitment: The New Relationships between the Generations in the 1970s,* Doubleday, 1978.

(Compiler) *Hunger* (booklet), Scientists' Institute for Public Information, 1970.

(With Metraux) *A Way of Seeing,* McCall, 1970.

(With James Baldwin) *A Rap on Race,* Lippincott, 1971.

Blackberry Winter: My Earlier Years (memoirs), Morrow, 1972.

Ruth Benedict (biography), Columbia University Press, 1974.

(With Heyman) *World Enough: Rethinking the Future,* Little, Brown, 1975.

Letters from the Field, 1925-1975, Harper, 1977.

(With Metraux) *An Interview with Santa Claus,* Walker & Co., 1978.

(With Metraux) *Aspects of the Present,* Morrow, 1980.

Also author of a documentary, "Margaret Mead's New Guinea Journal," National Educational Television, 1968. Editor of a manual on cultural patterns and technical change for UNESCO, World Federation for Mental Health, 1950. Prepared case materials for the International Seminar on Mental Health and Infant Development, Chichester, England, 1950. Author and narrator of soundtracks for series, "Films in Character Formation in Different Cultures," produced with Gregory Bateson for New York University Film Library, 1952. Contributor of numerous articles to scholarly and popular periodicals. Contributing editor, *Redbook,* 1961-78.

SIDELIGHTS: "Dr. Mead was not only an anthropologist and ethnologist of the first rank but also something of a national oracle on other subjects ranging from atomic politics to feminism," wrote Alan Whitman in the *New York Times* obituary. As a professional she altered the scope and approach of her science; as a human being she embodied passionate concern and sensible humanism; as a celebrity "she lent her support to dozens of causes," wrote Boyce Rensberger, "above all, to the cause of greater understanding and human harmony."

Margaret Mead was an authority on more than a dozen aspects of human science, any one of which would be sufficient to occupy the attention of most individuals. "She did many things simultaneously—but she did them all well," John Willey, Mead's editor at Morrow for thirty years, told *Publishers Weekly.* As *Newsweek*'s Elizabeth Peer noted, "the obsession that ruled such diversity was to learn how people cope with change." John Thompson of *Harper's* summed up Mead's career as a continual study of "man's cultural evolution, particularly as it is marked in the successive adaptations of generations." She was concerned not only with the "generation gap" but with gaps in general. She was an arbiter, a peacemaker, trying to defuse emotionally laden conflicts with facts and common sense. *Life* described her as "the cool anthropologist, rational grandmother, symbol of common sense to millions of Americans."

Mead has been credited with revolutionizing anthropology. Still a new science when she began her studies with Franz Boas, anthropology was based on statistical analysis. Mead "broadened the base of information on which social anthropology now rests, enriching it with insights borrowed from such previously excluded disciplines as psychology and economics," said Peer. Rensberger, writing in the *New York Times,* observed: "This broad-based approach is typical of the best anthropological work today. From a young woman traipsing about in what was a man's field half a century ago, however, it was not appreciated. From a woman who also dared to write her conclusions in a way that non-specialists could understand and who drew bold comparisons between American ways and those of very different cultures, it was heresy." There remains a group of professionals who accuse Mead of vague and unscientific thinking. "Most of all," *Time* noted, "anthropologists stand aghast at the way her powerful mind sometimes links facts and implications with little more than pure faith. . . . Nonetheless, she has been proved right so often that her critics have to take her seriously." At the time of Mead's death, Peer summarized: "While all applauded her towering work in anthropology, there was little consensus on exactly what she'd done. To science philosopher Jacob Bronowski, the 'splendidly sensible' Mead was a scholar of true 'intellectual depth.' To anthropology Prof. Marvin Harris of Columbia, her scattershot approach to field work made for 'few lasting theoretical contributions.' " Such controversy continued in the years after Mead died, particularly with the publication of *Margaret Mead and Samoa: The Making and Unmaking of an Anthropological Myth,* in which Derek Freeman criticized the anthropologist's methodology at considerable length.

Margaret Mead devoted much of her career to the study of the native people of the Pacific and in the process mastered seven primitive languages. She turned her attention to the problems of cultural stability, adolescence, sex differences, cooperation and competition, education and culture, the relationship between character structure and social forms, personality and culture, nutrition, mental health, family life, cross-national relationships, national character, studies of orientation to time, space and the strange in different cultures, ecology and ekistics. She studied modern cultures with the perspective gained from her knowledge of small, homogeneous and stable societies.

Her field work began in 1925 when, as a fellow of the National Research Council, she made a study of adolescent girls on the Samoan Islands. In 1928 and 1929, as a fellow of the Social Science Research Council, she studied the children of the Manus tribe of the Admiralty Islands of New Guinea, and in 1930 she observed an American Indian tribe, the Omaha. Between 1931 and 1933 her field work concentrated on the relationship between sex and temperament in the Arapesh, Mundugumor, and Tchambuli tribes of New Guinea. She made extensive ethnological investigations on the island of Bali and studied a fourth New Guinea tribe, the Iatmul of the Sepik River, from 1936 to 1939. She revisited the Admiralty Islands and Bali several times over the years to study the changes that had taken place as a primitive society coped with the problems of becoming a modern community. In addition to her published works and scientific papers on these studies, she produced voluminous field notes in her fifty years of observation of primitive cultures before their missionization. "She was one of the first anthropologists to use still and motion pictures to record the customs and habits of primitive societies. She was also one of the first to develop the subscience of semiotics, or the study of how men communicate by gestures," *Time* noted.

From the beginning, Mead's work was popular with the general public and with students. Her first book, *Coming of Age in Samoa,* was, and is, "one of the most widely read pieces of scholarship ever penned," noted the *Chicago Tribune.* "From the start," wrote Whitman, "it was enormously popular, especially among young people, some of whom were influenced by it to become anthropologists." One source of this popularity, as well as of controversy, was the book's suggestion "that there were things that Americans could learn from the Samoans about raising children that might mitigate the anxieties and tensions of adolescence in this society," said J. Y. Smith of the *Washington Post,* who continued: "It was a theme that she would expand on in infinite variations through the rest of her life. She saw mankind as a whole and she cherished the diversity of its parts. She had an ability to go from the particular to the general and back again."

The editor of *Redbook,* a magazine with which Mead was associated for seventeen years, wrote in her tribute: "Since [the publication of *Coming of Age in Samoa*] her books, her scientific papers, her popular writings, her speeches, her . . . contributions to the works of others have accumulated into a sizeable monument to her genius and a treasury for those who seek ways to appreciate and understand the human condition. . . . She cared about us all. She wanted us to care about each other."

BIOGRAPHICAL/CRITICAL SOURCES:

BOOKS

Authors in the News, Volume 1, Gale, 1976.
Contemporary Issues Criticism, Volume 1, Gale, 1982.
Contemporary Literary Criticism, Volume 37, Gale, 1986.

Freeman, Derek, *Margaret Mead and Samoa: The Making and Unmaking of an Anthropological Myth,* Harvard University Press, 1983.

Howard, Jane, *Margaret Mead: A Life,* Simon & Schuster, 1984.

Mead, Margaret, *Blackberry Winter: My Earlier Years,* Morrow, 1972.

Metraux, Rhoda, editor, *Margaret Mead: Some Personal Views,* Walker, 1979.

PERIODICALS

America, March 28, 1970, March 3, 1973.
American Anthropologist, August, 1971.
American Sociological Review, June, 1971.
Annals of the American Academy of Political and Social Science, September, 1970.
Atlantic, June, 1971.
Best Sellers, May 15, 1971.
Chicago Tribune, November 16, 1978, March 22, 1983.
Christian Century, April 1, 1970.
Christian Science Monitor, February 19, 1970.
Commentary, March, 1973.
Commonweal, December 15, 1972.
Critic, September, 1971.
Detroit Free Press, November 20, 1978.
Harper's, January, 1970, February, 1970.
Life, June 4, 1971.
Los Angeles Times, February 4, 1983.
Los Angeles Times Book Review, May 25, 1980, December 12, 1984.
Nation, March 30, 1970.
New Statesman, September 11, 1970, August 6, 1971.
Newsweek, November 10, 1969, January 19, 1970, May 24, 1971, November 13, 1972, November 27, 1978.
New Yorker, February 14, 1970, June 12, 1971.
New York Review of Books, December 2, 1971.
New York Times, January 8, 1970, September 23, 1970, May 21, 1971, November 16, 1978, January 31, 1983, February 1, 1983, February 6, 1983.
New York Times Book Review, March 8, 1970, June 27, 1971.
New York Times Magazine, April 26, 1970.
Publishers Weekly, November 27, 1978.
Redbook, February, 1979.
Saturday Review, July 4, 1970, October 2, 1971, November 25, 1972.
Science, April 26, 1974.
Time, March 21, 1969, November 27, 1972, November 27, 1978.
Times Literary Supplement, August 20, 1971.
Virginia Quarterly Review, spring, 1970, autumn, 1971.
Vogue, April 15, 1969, May, 1969.
Washington Post, November 26, 1969, January 13, 1970, November 16, 1978.

*   *   *

MEAKER, M. J.
   See MEAKER, Marijane (Agnes)

*   *   *

MEAKER, Marijane (Agnes) 1927-
   (M. J. Meaker; Ann Aldrich, M. E. Kerr, Vin Packer, pseudonyms)

PERSONAL: Born May 27, 1927, in Auburn, N.Y.; daughter of Ellis R. (a mayonnaise manufacturer) and Ida T. Meaker. *Education:* University of Missouri, B.A., 1949.

ADDRESSES: Home—12 Deep Six Dr., East Hampton, N.Y. 11937. *Agent*—Patricia Schartle Myrer, McIntosh & Otis, Inc., 475 Fifth Ave., New York, N.Y. 10017.

CAREER: Worked at several jobs, including assistant file clerk for D. P. Dutton (publisher), 1949-50; free-lance writer, 1949—. Volunteer writing teacher at Commercial Manhattan Central High, 1968.

AWARDS, HONORS: Dinky Hocker Shoots Smack! was an American Library Association (ALA) notable book, one of *School Library Journal*'s best books of the year, 1972, and winner of the Media and Methods Maxi Awards, 1974; *If I Love You, Am I Trapped Forever?* was chosen as an honor book in the Children's Spring Book Festival, 1973; *Is That You, Miss Blue?* was among ALA notable books for children and best books for young adults, 1975; book of the year awards from *School Library Journal,* 1977 and 1978; Christopher Award from The Christophers, 1978, for *Gentlehands;* Golden Kite Award for fiction from the Society of Children's Book Writers, 1981, for *Little, Little; Me, Me, Me, Me, Me: Not a Novel* was among ALA best books for young adults, 1983; *I Stay Near You* was among ALA best books for young adults, 1985; *Night Kites* won an ALA award, 1986.

WRITINGS:

(Under name M. J. Meaker) *Sudden Endings,* Doubleday, 1964.
(Under name M. J. Meaker) *Hometown,* Doubleday, 1967.
Game of Survival, New American Library, 1968.
Shockproof Sydney Skate, Little, Brown, 1972.
Take a Lesbian to Lunch, MacFadden-Bartell, 1972.

UNDER PSEUDONYM ANN ALDRICH

We Walk Alone, Gold Medal Books, 1955.
We Too Must Love, Gold Medal Books, 1958.
Carol, in a Thousand Cities, Gold Medal Books, 1960.
We Two Won't Last, Gold Medal Books, 1963.

FOR CHILDREN; UNDER PSEUDONYM M. E. KERR

Dinky Hocker Shoots Smack!, Harper, 1972.
If I Love You, Am I Trapped Forever?, Harper, 1973.
The Son of Someone Famous, Harper, 1974.
Is That You, Miss Blue?, Harper, 1975.
Love Is a Missing Person, Harper, 1975.
I'll Love You When You're More Like Me, Harper, 1977.
Gentlehands, Harper, 1978.
Little, Little, Harper, 1980.
What I Really Think of You, Harper, 1981.
Me, Me, Me, Me, Me: Not a Novel (autobiography), Harper, 1983.
Him She Loves?, Harper, 1984.
I Stay Near You, Harper, 1985.
Night Kites, Harper, 1986.
Fell, Harper, 1987.

UNDER PSEUDONYM VIN PACKER

Dark Intruder, Gold Medal Books, 1952.
Spring Fire, Gold Medal Books, 1952.
Look Back to Love, Gold Medal Books, 1953.
Come Destroy Me, Gold Medal Books, 1954.
Whisper His Sin, Gold Medal Books, 1954.
The Thrill Kids, Gold Medal Books, 1955.
Dark Don't Catch Me, Gold Medal Books, 1956.
The Young and Violent, Gold Medal Books, 1956.
Three-Day Terror, Gold Medal Books, 1957.
The Evil Friendship, Gold Medal Books, 1958.
5:45 to Suburbia, Gold Medal Books, 1958.

The Twisted Ones, Gold Medal Books, 1959.
The Damnation of Adam Blessing, Gold Medal Books, 1961.
The Girl on the Best Seller List, Gold Medal Books, 1961.
Something in the Shadows, Gold Medal Books, 1961.
Intimate Victims, Gold Medal Books, 1962.
Alone at Night, Gold Medal Books, 1963.
The Hare in March, New American Library, 1967.
Don't Rely on Gemini, Delacorte Press, 1969.

SIDELIGHTS: Mary Kingsbury wrote in *Horn Book* that the juvenile novels of M. E. Kerr are among the most outstanding being published today, for in each of them the author elucidates "some problem of the human family, some aspect of human behavior, some quality of the human heart or mind or conscience" with both "credibility and grace." It is this "willingness to confront serious issues," the critic continued, "coupled with [Kerr's] artistic abilities, [that] lifts her novels above the myriad problem-novels that have little to recommend them but their topicality."

According to Kingsbury, Kerr's novels are essentially about love—"its presence and, more commonly, its absence in the lives of her characters." In all her books, the author investigates man's inability to give and to receive love in the myriad relationships that love creates. She portrays adolescents who come to learn that the people they love will, "more often than not, fail to live up to their expectations." "In addition to this common theme," the critic appended, "the novels share a pattern of elements and literary devices. Each introduces at least one contemporary issue such as mental illness, drug addiction, anti-Semitism, alcoholism, and racism. Each portrays the development of adolescent sexuality, and several offer insight into adult sexuality as well. Adolescents in all the books begin to view their parents more realistically and with greater understanding. Sharply drawn characters abound in all the books; frequent use is made of irony, humor, and quotations from literary sources."

The grown-ups that Kerr creates for her books are quite different from the unsympathetic ones often portrayed in juvenile fiction, Kingsbury pointed out, and their presence is an "obvious strength" in the author's work. "A reader of the majority of books written for young adults learns what motivates the adolescent characters," the critic explained, "but seldom learns what makes the adult characters act as they do. The adult characters [in Kerr's novels] are so fully realized, however, that readers acquire some idea of the pressures on adults in American society. The books offer a series of 'possible futures' for their readers."

In Kerr's first juvenile novel, *Dinky Hocker Shoots Smack!,* the author tells the story of an overweight girl who goes to extraordinary measures to gain the love and attention of her parents. Dinky "shoots smack," or rather, pretends that she does in order to wrest her too-busy mother away from the junkies Mrs. Hocker is dedicated to rehabilitating. Dinky fights to make people understand that "you don't have to be a public loser to have private problems," Dale Carlson summarized in the *New York Times Book Review.*

A *Times Literary Supplement* reviewer found the character of Dinky Hocker "likable, credible, distinctive," and Carlson determined that Kerr's first novel was "superb." Carlson continued: "[Kerr] has an ear for catching the sound of real people talking and a heart for finding the center of real people's problems. . . . This is a brilliantly funny book that will make you cry. It is full of wit and wisdom and an astonishing immediacy that comes from spare, honest writing. Many writers try to characterize the peculiar poignancy and the terrible hilarity of adolescence. Few succeed as well as M. E. Kerr in this timely, compelling and entertaining novel."

Another book for young people, *The Son of Someone Famous,* introduces Adam Blessing, a boy whose reaction to his famous diplomat father is to become "a confirmed failure who's been kicked out of more elite schools than he can remember," Joyce Alpern noted in the *Washington Post Book World.* Adam goes to live with his drunk Uncle Charlie in a small Vermont town, where he befriends a local girl who feels like an outcast too. Their relationship and shared escapades begin to give them a sense of belonging; during his sojourn, Adam also encounters some new information about his "perfect" dad that makes him realize that those who love and direct him don't necessarily know what's best. "Kerr is . . . making the familiar point about learning to accept others and ourselves, faults and all," Alpern commented. "But she is wise enough to realize that life is more than an extended problem-solving session and adroit enough to entertain."

A *Times Literary Supplement* reviewer echoed Alpern's compliments, noting that "there is some good, amusing writing throughout [*The Son of Someone Famous*]," yet determined that "perhaps finally the impression is of something bright but rather vacuous." And Carlson, in a second *New York Times Book Review* article, concurred: "Kerr is a brilliant writer with an ear for the minute agonies and hilarity of adolescents and their relationship to themselves and each other. But unlike her first novel, *Dinky Hocker Shoots Smack!,* in this, her subject matter is slight and her insights too glib."

In *Is That You, Miss Blue?* Kerr relates the tale of Miss Blue, a fervently religious woman who teaches at Charles Boarding School. The story is narrated by a fifteen-year-old student named Flanders who observes how intense ridicule and forced isolation—dealt by both students and parents—is prompting Miss Blue to lose her mind. By the novel's end, the narrator comes to protest "the type of exile reserved for those who march to the beat of a different drummer," Alix Nelson remarked in the *New York Times Book Review.* "M. E. Kerr has used the familiar microcosm of boarding school to make several points which apply at large, and to make them with so much grace, charm, and poignancy that one closes the book with the feeling, 'this is the way life really is.' "

A fourth novel, *Gentlehands,* begins as the familiar story of a lower middle-class boy vying for the attentions of a wealthy young beauty. Sixteen-year-old Buddy Boyle manages to overcome the social and financial gulfs that separate him from his love, Skye Pennington, with earnestness, good humor, and good looks. He even impresses Skye with his charming and wealthy grandfather, a man with whom the boy becomes increasingly close. Yet this simple story evolves into a nightmare when a visiting investigative reporter exposes Buddy's grandfather as a brutal former Nazi concentration camp guard. By the novel's end, Buddy is just beginning to come to grips with the shattering revelation.

In a *Times Literary Supplement* review Nicholas Tucker pronounced *Gentlehands* "very readable" yet determined that the grandfather character is "unconvincing" and the plot turn "a modish and pretentious note on which to end." Richard Bradford of the *New York Times Book Review* expressed an opposing view, however, maintaining that the story's surprise turn is an arresting exposition of "the paradoxes that exist in the heart of man. . . . If [Kerr] fails to explain thoroughly the alarming enigma of Frank Trenker's double life, it is only because there is, finally, no explanation possible." The critic also applauded the author's "superb" ear for youthful dialogue and her understanding of youthful feelings or the lack of them. In addition, Bradford concluded, "Miss Kerr's book is important and useful as an introduction [for young people] to the grotesque character of the Nazi period."

MEDIA ADAPTATIONS: Dinky Hocker Shoots Smack! was broadcast as a television special.

BIOGRAPHICAL/CRITICAL SOURCES:

BOOKS

Contemporary Literary Criticism, Gale, Volume 12, 1980, Volume 35, 1985.
Something About the Author Autobiography Series, Volume 1, Gale, 1986.

PERIODICALS

Chicago Tribune Book World, March 2, 1986.
English Journal, December, 1975.
Horn Book, February, 1973, August, 1975, June, 1977.
Los Angeles Times, October 25, 1986, August 1, 1987.
New York Times Book Review, February 11, 1973, September 16, 1973, April 7, 1974, April 13, 1975, October 19, 1975, April 30, 1978, September 12, 1982, May 22, 1983, June 5, 1983, April 13, 1986.
Times Literary Supplement, November 23, 1973, September 19, 1975, December 1, 1978.
Washington Post Book World, May 19, 1974, May 10, 1981, July 11, 1982, April 10, 1983, May 12, 1985, May 11, 1986.

*   *   *

MEHTA, Ved (Parkash)   1934-

PERSONAL: Born March 21, 1934, in Lahore, India (now Pakistan); naturalized U.S. citizen, 1975; son of Amolak Ram (a doctor and health official) and Shanti (Mehra) Mehta; married Linn Cary (an assistant program officer at Ford Foundation), 1983; children: Sage, Natasha. *Education:* Pomona College, B.A., 1956; Balliol College, Oxford, B.A. (with honors), 1959; Harvard University, M.A., 1961.

ADDRESSES: Office—New Yorker, 25 West 43rd St., New York, N.Y. 10036. *Agent*—Georges Borchardt Inc., 136 East 57th St., New York, N.Y. 10022.

CAREER: New Yorker magazine, New York, N.Y., staff writer, 1961—. Bard College, Annandale-on-Hudson, N.Y., professor of literature, 1985 and 1986; Sarah Lawrence College, Bronxville, N.Y., professor of art and cultural history, 1988.

MEMBER: Phi Beta Kappa.

AWARDS, HONORS: Hazen fellowship, 1956-59; Secondary Education Board Annual Book Award, 1958; Harvard Prize fellowship, 1959-60; Ford Foundation travel and study grants, 1971-76; Guggenheim fellowships, 1971-72 and 1977-78; D.Litt., Pomona College, 1972, Bard College, 1982, and Williams College, 1986; Dupont Columbia Award for excellence in broadcast journalism, 1977-78, for documentary film "Chachaji, My Poor Relation"; Association of Indians in America Award, 1978; Ford Foundation Public Policy grant, 1979-82; John D. and Catherine T. MacArthur Foundation fellowship, 1982-87; Distinguished Service Award, Asian/Pacific Americans Liberty Association, 1986; New York City Mayor's Liberty Medal, 1986.

WRITINGS:

Face to Face: An Autobiography, Atlantic-Little, Brown, 1957.
Walking the Indian Streets (travel; first appeared in the *New Yorker*), Atlantic-Little, Brown, 1960, 3rd revised edition, Penguin (Middlesex), 1975.

Fly and the Fly-Bottle: Encounters with British Intellectuals (first appeared in the *New Yorker*), Atlantic-Little, Brown, 1963, 2nd edition, Columbia University Press, 1983.
The New Theologian (first appeared in the *New Yorker*), Harper, 1966.
Portrait of India, Farrar, Straus, 1970.
John Is Easy to Please: Encounters with the Written and the Spoken Word, Farrar, Straus, 1971.
Daddyji (autobiographical; also see below), Farrar, Straus, 1972.
Delinquent Chacha (novel; first appeared in the *New Yorker*), Harper, 1976.
Mahatma Gandhi and His Apostles (first appeared in the *New Yorker*), Viking, 1977.
The New India (first appeared in the *New Yorker*), Viking, 1978.
Mamaji (autobiographical; also see below), Oxford University Press, 1979.
The Photographs of Chachaji: The Making of a Documentary Film (first appeared in the *New Yorker*; also see below), Oxford University Press, 1980.
A Family Affair: India under Three Prime Ministers (sequel to *The New India;* first appeared in the *New Yorker*), Oxford University Press, 1982.
Vedi (autobiographical), Oxford University Press, 1982.
The Ledge between the Streams (autobiographical), Norton, 1984.
Daddyji/Mamaji (combined edition of *Daddyji* and *Mamaji*), Picador, Pan Books, 1984.
Sound-Shadows of the New World (autobiographical), Norton, 1986.
Three Stories of the Raj (fiction), Scolar, 1986.
The Stolen Light (autobiographical), Norton, 1989.

CONTRIBUTOR TO ANTHOLOGIES

Henry I. Christs and Herbert Potell, editors, *Adventures in Living,* Harcourt, 1962, 1968.
Leo Kneer, editor, *Perspectives,* Scott, Foresman, 1963.
K. L. Knickerbocker and H. W. Reninger, *Interpreting Literature,* Holt, 1965, 1969.
Norman Cousins, editor, *Profiles of Nehru,* Indian Book Company (Delhi), 1966.
George Arms, William M. Gibson, and Louis G. Locke, editors, *Readings for Liberal Education,* Holt, 1967.
Walter Havighurst, Arno Jewett, Josephine Lowery, and Philip McFarland, editors, *Exploring Literature,* Houghton, 1968.
Nicholas P. Barker, editor, *Purpose and Function in Prose,* Knopf, 1969.
Mary V. Gaver, editor, *Background Readings in Building Library Collections,* Scarecrow, 1969.
Cousins, editor, *Profiles of Gandhi,* Indian Book Company, 1969.
Jerome W. Archer and Joseph Schwartz, editors, *A Reader for Writers: A Critical Anthology of Prose Readings,* McGraw, 1971.
T. Sadasivan, editor, *Rajaji-93 Souvenir,* T. Sadasivan, 1971.
Margaret Cormack and Kiki Skagen, editors, *Voices from India,* Praeger, 1971.
John F. Savage, editor, *Linguistics for Teachers,* Science Research Associates, 1973.
Albert R. Kitzhaber, editor, *Style and Synthesis,* Holt, 1974.
Anne Fremantle, editor, *A Primer of Linguistics,* St. Martin's, 1974.
Donald J. Johnson and Jean E. Johnson, editors, *Through Indian Eyes,* Praeger, 1974.
Havighurst, Jewett, Lowrey, and McFarland, editors, *Houghton Mifflin Literature Series, Grade 8,* Houghton, 1978.

Robert E. Beck, editor, *Experiencing Biography,* Hayden Book, 1978.

Ganesh Bagchi, editor, *ISCE English Language Test Papers,* Oxford University Press (New Delhi), 1982.

Irving Kenneth Zola, editor, *Ordinary Lives,* Apple-Wood, 1983.

Dean W. Tuttle, editor, *Self-Esteem and Adjusting with Blindness: The Process of Responding to Life's Demands,* C. C Thomas, 1984.

1985 Medical and Health Annual, Encyclopaedia Britannica, 1984.

India: A Teacher's Guide, Asia Society, 1985.

OTHER

Writer and commentator of documentary film "Chachaji, My Poor Relation," the filming of which is recounted in his book *The Photographs of Chachaji: The Making of a Documentary Film.* Contributor of articles and stories to American, British, and Indian newspapers and magazines, including *Atlantic, Saturday Review, New York Times Book Review, Village Voice, World, Political Science Quarterly, Hindustan Times* (New Delhi), *Asian Post,* and *Debonaire* (Bombay).

SIDELIGHTS: Ved Mehta was born in India and returns there often in his writings. From his first book to his most recent, Mehta has made this country of contradictions his backdrop, whether his description is political or personal. According to Maureen Dowd in the *New York Times Magazine,* William Shawn, Mehta's editor at the *New Yorker* (where Mehta has been a longtime staff writer), believes that "more than any other writer Mehta has educated Americans about India, illuminating that country with an insider's sensibility and an outsider's objectivity."

As natives of Lahore, India, which is now Pakistan, Mehta's own parents typified the split in India between West and East, between new technology and ancient tradition. Mehta's father was educated in medicine in England and became an important figure in India's public health service. Mehta's mother, uneducated, is a woman of superstition, confident in the powers of faith healers. When Mehta lost his sight at age four from a bout with meningitis, his mother was convinced his blindness was only a temporary form of punishment and followed a Muslim's advice, applying antimony to Mehta's eyes and flogging him with twigs, among other things. Mehta's more progressive-minded father believed an education would be the only way for his son to avoid the typical life of a blind person in India—alms beggar or chair caner. At age five, Mehta was sent to Bombay's Dadar School for the Blind, an American mission school so lacking in sanitation that the once-healthy boy suffered from numerous infections, including ringworm, typhoid fever, malaria, and bronchitis. At age fifteen, after experiencing the upheaval that accompanied the 1947 partition of India, he traveled alone to the United States to study at the only American school that would accept him, the Arkansas School for the Blind in Little Rock. From there, Mehta went on to excel at Pomona College in California, at Balliol College in Oxford, England, and finally at Harvard University. In 1961, at the age of twenty-six, he became a staff writer for the *New Yorker* magazine. All but one of his books have appeared first in installments in the *New Yorker.*

Mehta's first book, *Face to Face: An Autobiography,* addresses his blindness, but most of his subsequent works skirt this topic. In fact, for a while Mehta demanded that his publishers avoid any reference to his blindness on his book jackets. Writing in the *New York Times Book Review* in 1960, Herbert L. Matthews noted that "Mehta plays an extraordinary trick on his prospective readers and on anyone who does not know about him or has not read his previous book, *Face to Face.* . . . He has written [*Walking the Indian Streets*] about his return to India after ten years' absence as if he had normal vision."

Many of Mehta's books contain elaborate visual imagery, and reviewers refer to him as the blind man who can see better than the rest of us. Carolyn See explains in the *Los Angeles Times:* "When Mehta shows us the building of a dam; hundreds of brightly clad peasants carrying just a few bricks at a time; when in 'Mahatma Gandhi and His Apostles,' Mehta conjures up the evenings when the movement was still young, when the fragrance of blossoms was everywhere and Gandhi's followers stayed up late, out of doors, laughing, rubbing each other's backs—a whole world is given to us, and of course the kicker in all this is that . . . Mehta is blind." It was not until *Daddyji,* Mehta's biography of his father, that Mehta made reference to his blindness once again, and it was not until a later autobiographical work, *Vedi,* that he wrote "from the perspective of total blindness," according to Janet Malcom in the *New York Review of Books.* "[*Vedi*] is entirely without visual descriptions. We follow the blind child into the orphanage, and, like him, we never learn what the place or any of the people in it looked like. We hear, we feel, but we see nothing. . . . As the child misses the familiar persons and things of home, so the reader misses the customary visual clues of literature. . . . Not the least of *Vedi*'s originality is this very stylistic denial, which amounts to an approximation of the experience of blindness."

Although Mehta has written nonfiction, a novel, essays, and even a documentary script, highest critical regard has been for his contributions to the autobiographical genre. *Face to Face,* written when Mehta was in his early twenties, chronicles Mehta's early life, from his childhood in India to his three-year stay at the Arkansas School for the Blind where, among other things, he first encountered racism—"I wondered how dark I was, how much I looked like a Negro," Peter Ackroyd quotes Mehta in the London *Times.* Commenting in the *New York Herald Tribune Book Review,* Gerald W. Johnson observes: "It is extraordinary when a man at twenty-three has the material for an autobiography that deserves the serious attention of the intelligent, and still more extraordinary when a man so young can present his material in an arresting fashion. . . . Mehta has both material and ability."

Three years after *Face to Face* came *Walking the Indian Streets,* Mehta's memoir of his month-long visit to India after a ten-year absence. Dowd records how Mehta had idealized his native country during those years by listening to Indian music and dreaming about an arranged marriage to a beautiful Punjabi girl. The India Mehta encountered, however, disturbed him and shattered his idealistic vision. "Everywhere I went, I was assaulted by putrid odors rising from the streets, by flies relentlessly swarming around my face, by the octopus-like hands of a hundred scabrous, deformed beggars clutching at my hands and feet. My time in the West had spoiled me and I could now hardly wait to get back," Mehta wrote of his experience, as Dowd reports.

While he wrote numerous books on the politics and culture of a changing India during the twelve years following the 1960 publication of *Walking the Indian Streets,* Mehta eventually turned once more to the autobiographical form and began disclosing his life in very small chunks, expanding the years of his earlier autobiography *Face to Face* into several volumes and then proceeding to cover new ground. Indeed, Mehta's biographical/autobiographical *Daddyji* and *Mamaji* describe many years in his parents' lives before he was even born. Both books are noted for their adept presentations of the middle-class family in India.

"[*Daddyji's*] value," writes P. K. Sundara Rajan in the *Saturday Review,* "lies in the fact that . . . Mehta transforms an individual experience into one that is universal." And in his *New York Times Book Review* assessment of *Mamaji,* Clark Blaise feels "family is the tidiest metaphor for the vastness of India. To understand its compelling and often terrible hold is to possess a special understanding of the culture. . . . Mehta patiently delivers that understanding and courageously presents it without interpretation, limiting even its expected 'warmth' in the service of a sharper clarity." It is also with these two books that "Mehta draws a sharp contrast between his rational, decisive, tough-minded, Western-educated, physician father and his superstitious, backward, uneducated, childish, tender-hearted mother," remarks Malcolm.

The author followed the portraits of his parents with *Vedi,* which begins with Mehta boarding a train for the Bombay school for the blind, located approximately a thousand miles from his home. Mehta recounts his years at the Dadar School from age five to nine. In a London *Times* article, Howard states that "without sentimentality or self-pity [Mehta] recreates that vanished and alien world in one of the richest works of memory of our century." Though Mehta was frequently fighting disease, reviewers comment on how effectively this well-to-do boy adapted to his slum-like surroundings. Blaise notes in the *New York Times Book Review* that *Vedi* "is clearly a mature work. . . . Readers of the two earlier volumes of family biography [*Daddyji* and *Mamaji*] will find less of the overt 'India experience' in 'Vedi,' and more of the dreamlike landscape of childhood. The touch and smell of parents, the test of wills, nightmares, pets."

"Now I want to proclaim this autobiography as nothing less than a literary masterpiece," declares *Times Literary Supplement* contributor R. K. Narayan of Mehta's memoir *The Ledge between the Streams.* London *Times* reviewer Howard says that in *The Ledge between the Streams* "nothing much happens; except the most important thing in the world, a child growing up to accept life and enjoy the world." *The Ledge between the Streams* encompasses Mehta's years from age nine to fifteen. *New York Times* critic Michiko Kakutani capsulizes the Mehta described in this memoir as a "clumsy blind boy, plucky but hopelessly gauche when it came to participating in . . . fun and games—flying kites, riding bicycles and ponies, playing hide-and-seek. . . . In any case, having spent the first half of 'The Ledge' documenting the innocent world of his youth, . . . Mehta then goes on to show how that world was destroyed by the 1947 partition of the Indian subcontinent into India and Pakistan," an event that "turned many families, including . . . Mehta's own, into political and religious refugees. It is this depiction of the partition, as filtered through the sensibility of a 12-year-old boy, that distinguishes 'The Ledge' as a memoir." What reviewers also find successful about *The Ledge between the Streams* is the fact that the reader forgets his author is blind, a condition which is precisely in line with Mehta's longtime philosophy.

Mehta moves into his adolescent years with *Sound-Shadows of the New World,* the account of his first three years in the United States at the Arkansas School for the Blind. According to Mary Lutyens in the *Spectator,* "the vivid, detailed descriptions of this homesick boy's gradual adaptation to an alien culture are uplifting and enthralling," while Ackroyd believes "the single most important quality of the young . . . Mehta was his courage; *Sound-Shadows of the New World* is a record of that courage." This autobiography reveals how the boy who did not know how to eat with a fork and knife when he first arrived in America eventually became president of the student senate and editor of the school newspaper, an experience that convinced him of his desire to become a journalist.

The next installment in Mehta's series of autobiographical works is *The Stolen Light.* Beginning when the author is eighteen years old, the book chronicles his years at college during the 1950s when he comes of age and launches himself as a writer. Blind and newly emigrated from India, Mehta "poignantly conveys the agony of wanting to fit into the rigidly coded world of a small American college," writes Susan Allen Toth in the *New York Times Book Review.* Praising the author's "self-deprecating honesty, scrupulous memory and finely honed perceptions," the reviewer finds *The Stolen Light* "awe-inspiring" and a "remarkable story of indefatigable energy and determination." More volumes of Mehta's memoirs are expected to appear, a prospect that pleases critics who find his works fascinating and dismays those who feel he has already written enough about himself. Yet as Philip Howard observes in the London *Times,* Mehta's "very special kind of autobiography . . . is clearly going to run for as long as he lives."

From 1970 to 1982, Mehta wrote four nonfiction books aimed at disclosing the social and political milieu of modern-day India. According to Dowd, Mehta's "reports include vivid descriptions of Indian politics, dinner parties given by the viceroy, the assault of the industrial revolution, the attempts at birth control. His work explores the conflict between East and West in the Indian culture and its mixture of grace and vulgarity." Dowd further records professor of modern Indian literature at Columbia University Robin Lewis's estimation that "in a very quiet way, . . . Mehta is breaking the Western stereotypes and getting America to look at India as something other than a grandiose stage setting. He's taking the raw material of his personal experience and combining it with some of the pains, crises and historical dislocations that India has gone through."

Mehta's *Portrait of India,* published in 1970, "seems as vast as India" to Stephen Spender in the *New York Times Book Review;* "it is immensely readable, and the reader not only has the sense of immersion in the sights, scents and sounds of India, he also meets representative people from high and low walks of life." While a *Times Literary Supplement* reviewer feels Mehta has failed to produce a portrait of his native land, the *New York Times*'s Thomas Lask believes that if the reader can get through the first seventy-five pages, "you will find yourself in a first-class book. . . . It is surprising how, by the end of the book, the Indian continent has managed to assume a knowledgeable shape and how the problems begin to make sense in terms of the people and the land."

Of Mehta's political books, his 1977 account entitled *Mahatma Gandhi and His Apostles* has received the most attention. Though reviewers stress that some four hundred biographies have been written about the "acclaimed father of India," Mehta's tactics have been singled out as unique. As Mehta states in the preface to his book, his desire is "both to demythologize Gandhi and to capture something of the nature of this influence on his followers and . . . their interpretations of his life on India." To do this, Mehta traveled to India and England to speak directly with a number of the remaining disciples of Gandhi, something no other biographer had thought to do. As *New York Times* contributor Paul Grimes remarks, "the interviews make it clear that Gandhi-ism did not survive with them. Some profess to be still propagating the Mahatma's cause, but it is obvious that over the years their interpretations of it have become warped if they ever were otherwise."

Grimes finds Mehta's account of Gandhi "much more than a biography" and "a remarkable examination of the life and work of a human being who has been extolled around the world as one of the greatest souls of all time." Other reviewers criticize Mehta for concentrating too heavily on Gandhi's personal life. *Times Literary Supplement* reviewer Eric Stokes feels that Mehta who is "busy destroying old myths . . . is silently weaving a new one of his own. . . . The ultimate distortion in Mehta's picture of the Mahatma is . . . that it allows almost no place for the politician." Leonard A. Gordon in the *Nation* likewise senses that "Mehta has spent so much time with the private Gandhi, fascinated like his subject with food, sex and hygiene, that we learn almost nothing about the man's great appeal and political skills." Nevertheless, Stokes believes "Mehta's highly readable book may mark the beginning of a phase when Gandhi is eventually rescued from the hagiographers and given a juster appraisal by his countrymen." In Dowd's interview with Mehta, Mehta mentions his hope that Mahatma's idealism be restored in his native country: "Gandhi had the right vision for a poor country. . . . What people in India need basically is fertilizer, clean water, good seed, good storage facilities . . . , and proper sanitation. Those are the priorities. That's what Gandhi taught."

While most of Mehta's books have been published in India, it is as a staff writer for the *New Yorker* that Mehta is best known in the United States and England. And though to some he may be an easy man to classify, he said to Dowd: "I don't belong to any single tradition. I am an amalgam of five cultures-Indian, British, American, blind and [the *New Yorker*]." *Publishers Weekly* contributor Stella Dong records Mehta's lifelong literary intentions: "I'm not just slavishly following a chronological framework or trying to interpret India or blindness or any of that. All I'm trying to do is to tell a story of not one life, but many lives and through those stories, to try to say something that's universal."

Several of Mehta's books have been translated into Dutch, Finnish, French, Greek, Gujarati, Hindi, Italian, Japanese, Marathi, Spanish, and Urdu.

BIOGRAPHICAL/CRITICAL SOURCES:

BOOKS

Contemporary Literary Criticism, Volume XXXVII, Gale, 1986.
Cousins, Norman, *Present Tense: An American Editor's Odyssey,* McGraw, 1967.
Mehta, Ved, *Face to Face: An Autobiography,* Atlantic-Little, Brown, 1957.
Mehta, Ved, *Daddyji,* Farrar, Straus, 1972.
Mehta, Ved, *Mahatma Gandhi and His Apostles,* Viking, 1977.
Mehta, Ved, *Mamaji,* Oxford University Press, 1979.
Mehta, Ved, *Vedi,* Oxford University Press, 1982.
Mehta, Ved, *The Ledge between the Streams,* Norton, 1984.
Mehta, Ved, *Sound-Shadows of the New World,* Norton, 1986.
Mehta, Ved, *The Stolen Light,* Norton, 1989.
Weeks, Edward, *In Friendly Candor,* Little, Brown, 1959 (published in England as *In Friendly Candour,* Hutchinson, 1960).

PERIODICALS

Atlantic, November, 1963.
Book World, May 10, 1970.
Chicago Tribune Book World, May 10, 1970.
Christian Century, December 14, 1966.
Christian Science Monitor, May 4, 1967, October 17, 1970.
Globe and Mail (Toronto), July 26, 1986.
Journal of Asian Studies, November, 1983.

Library Journal, September 1, 1966, April 1, 1967.
Listener, September 24, 1970, August 18, 1977.
Los Angeles Times, April 16, 1984, March 3, 1989.
Los Angeles Times Book Review, April 2, 1989.
Manchester Guardian Weekly, June 14, 1981.
Nation, February 6, 1967, July 2, 1977.
National Review, July 30, 1963.
New Leader, April 10, 1978.
New Republic, May 13, 1967, July 9, 1977.
New Statesman, February 24, 1967, September 25, 1970.
Newsweek, December 31, 1962, July 1, 1963, January 17, 1977, January 30, 1978.
New York Herald Tribune Book Review, August 18, 1957.
New York Herald Tribune Books, June 16, 1963.
New York Post, January 10, 1962.
New York Review of Books, June 29, 1967, October 7, 1982.
New York Times, April 6, 1967, April 25, 1970, May 8, 1972, September 3, 1973, March 30, 1977, June 11, 1978, October 21, 1979, December 20, 1979, May 1, 1984, February 27, 1986.
New York Times Book Review, August 21, 1960, August 18, 1963, November 13, 1966, April 5, 1970, January 29, 1978, October 21, 1979, October 17, 1982, May 6, 1984, March 9, 1986, August 30, 1987, March 12, 1989.
New York Times Magazine, June 10, 1984.
Observer, March 18, 1962.
Publishers Weekly, January 3, 1985.
Reporter, May 4, 1967.
Saturday Review, August 17, 1957, November 12, 1966, April 29, 1967, April 25, 1970, May 20, 1972, January 22, 1977.
Spectator, May 12, 1961, October 4, 1963, July 28, 1984, May 31, 1986.
Times (London), October 19, 1972, June 15, 1977, July 5, 1984, June 8, 1985, May 15, 1986, May 20, 1989.
Times Literary Supplement, December 8, 1966, December 4, 1970, November 19, 1971, August 5, 1977, July 4, 1980, May 29, 1981, July 6, 1984, May 30, 1986.
Washington Post, December 28, 1982.
Washington Post Book World, January 20, 1980, July 25, 1982, March 9, 1986.
World Literature Today, autumn, 1983.

*   *   *

MENCKEN, H(enry) L(ouis) 1880-1956
(Herbert Winslow Archer, Pierre d'Aubigny, W. L. D. Bell, Atwood C. Bellamy, James Drayham, William Fink, J. D. Gilray, Amelia Hatteras, F. C. Henderson, Janet Jefferson, R. B. McLoughlin, Harriet Morgan, George Weems Peregoy, James P. Ratcliffe, The Ringmaster, Francis Clegg Thompson, Raoul della Torre, W. H. Trimball, Marie de Verdi, Irving S. Watson, James Wharton, Robert W. Woodruff, pseudonyms; C. Farley Anderson, Owen Hatteras, joint pseudonyms)

PERSONAL: Born September 12, 1880, in Baltimore, Md.; died of heart failure, January 29, 1956, in Baltimore, Md.; son of August (a cigar manufacturer) and Anna (Abhau) Mencken; married Sara Powell Haardt (a writer), August 27, 1930 (died, 1935). *Education:* Attended Baltimore Polytechnic Institute, 1892-96.

ADDRESSES: Home and office—1524 Hollins St., Baltimore, Md. 21223.

CAREER: Herald, Baltimore, Md., reporter, 1899-1901, Sunday editor, 1901-03, city editor, 1903-05, editor in chief, 1906; *Eve-*

ning News, Baltimore, news editor, 1906; *Sunpapers,* Baltimore, Sunday editor, 1906-10, editor and columnist, 1910-16; *Evening Mail,* New York, N.Y., columnist, 1917-18; *Sunpapers,* Baltimore, editor, columnist, and political correspondent, 1919-41, political correspondent, 1948. Co-editor of *The Smart Set: A Magazine of Cleverness,* 1914-23; creator and co-editor of *Parisienne,* 1915, *Saucy Stories,* 1916, and *Black Mask,* 1920; founder and editor of *The American Mercury: A Monthly Review,* 1924-33.

MEMBER: Saturday Night Club (Baltimore).

AWARDS, HONORS: Gold medal from National Institute and American Academy of Arts and Letters, 1950, for essays and criticism; "H. L. Mencken Writing Award" established in author's memory by the *Sunpapers,* given annually "to the newspaper columnist who most exemplifies the spirit and social commentary of H. L. Mencken."

WRITINGS:

Ventures into Verse: Being Various Ballads, Bailades, Rondeaux, Triolets, Songs, Quatrains, Odes, and Roundels, All Rescued From the Potter's Field of the Old Files and Here Given Decent Burial (Peace to Their Ashes) by Henry Louis Mencken, with Illustrations & Other Things by Charles S. Gordon & John Siegel, Marshall, Beck & Gordon, 1903.

George Bernard Shaw: His Plays, Luce, 1905, Haskell House, 1976.

The Philosophy of Friedrich Nietzsche, Luce, 1908, R. West, 1978.

(Editor and author of introduction) Henrik Ibsen, *A Doll's House,* Luce, 1909.

(Editor and author of introduction) Ibsen, *Little Eyolf,* Luce, 1909.

(With Leonard Keene Hirshberg) *What You Ought To Know about Your Baby,* Butterick, 1910.

(Editor) *The Gist of Nietzsche,* Luce, 1910, Norwood Editions, 1977.

Men Versus the Man: A Correspondence Between Rives La Monte, Socialist, and H. L. Mencken, Individualist, Holt, 1910, Arno Press, 1972.

The Artist: A Drama Without Words (also see below), Luce, 1912, Folcroft Library, 1973.

(With George Jean Nathan and Willard Huntington Wright) *Europe After 8:15,* illustrations by Thomas H. Benton, John Lane, 1914.

A Book of Burlesques (includes *The Artist: A Drama Without Words*), John Lane, 1916, revised edition, Knopf, 1920, reprinted, Scholarly Press, 1971.

A Little Book in C Major (Opus 11), John Lane, 1916.

(With Nathan, under joint pseudonym Owen Haiteras) *Pistols for Two,* Knopf, 1917, Folcroft Library, 1977.

A Book of Prefaces (Opus 13), Knopf, 1917, Octagon, 1977.

(Author of introduction) Ibsen, *The Master Builder* [and] *Pillars of Society* [and] *Hedda Gahler,* Boni & Liveright, 1917.

Damn! A Book of Calumny, Philip Goodman, 1918, republished as *A Book of Calumny,* Knopf, 1918.

In Defense of Women, Philip Goodman, 1918, revised edition, Knopf, 1922, reprinted, Octagon, 1977.

The American Language: A Preliminary Inquiry Into the Development of English in the United States, Knopf, 1919, 4th edition, revised, corrected, and enlarged (Book-of-the-Month Club selection), 1936, reprinted, 1974, Supplement 1, 1945, reprinted, 1975, Supplement 2, 1948, reprinted, 1975.

Prejudices: First Series, Knopf, 1919, Octagon, 1977.

Prejudices: Second Series, Knopf, 1920, Octagon, 1977.

(Editor and author of introduction) Edwin Muir, *We Moderns: Enigmas and Guesses,* Knopf, 1920.

(Editor and author of introduction) Friedrich Wilhelm Nietzsche, *The Antichrist,* Knopf, 1920.

(With Nathan) *The American Credo: A Contribution Toward the Interpretation of the National Mind,* Knopf, 1920, Octagon, 1977.

(With Nathan) *Heliogabalus: A Buffoonery in Three Acts,* Knopf, 1920.

Prejudices: Third Series, Knopf, 1922, Octagon, 1977.

Prejudices: Fourth Series, Knopf, 1924, Octagon, 1977.

Prejudices, J. Cape, 1925.

(Editor) *Americana,* Knopf, 1925.

Notes on Democracy, Knopf, 1926, Octagon, 1977.

Prejudices: Fifth Series, Knopf, 1926, Octagon, 1977.

James Branch Cabell (also see below), McBride, 1927.

Prejudices: Sixth Series, Knopf, 1927, Octagon, 1977.

Selected Prejudices, Knopf, 1927.

Selected Prejudices: Second Series, J. Cape, 1927.

(Editor with Sara Powell Haardt) *Menckeniana: A Schimpflexikon,* Knopf, 1928, Octagon, 1977.

Treatise on the Gods, Knopf, 1930, 2nd revised edition, 1946, reprinted, Random House, 1963.

Making a President: A Footnote to the Saga of Democracy, Knopf, 1932.

Treatise on Right and Wrong, Knopf, 1934, Octagon, 1977.

(Editor and author of preface) Sara Powell Haardt, *Southern Album,* Doubleday, 1936.

(Editor and contributor) *The Sunpapers of Baltimore, 1837-1937,* Knopf, 1937.

Happy Days, 1880-1892 (also see below), Knopf, 1940.

Newspaper Days, 1899-1906 (also see below), Knopf, 1941.

(Editor) *A New Dictionary of Quotations on Historical Principles from Ancient and Modern Sources,* Knopf, 1942.

Heathen Days, 1890-1936 (also see below), Knopf, 1943.

Christmas Story, illustrations by Bill Crawford, Knopf, 1946.

(Author of introduction) Theodore Dreiser, *An American Tragedy,* World, 1946.

The Days of H. L. Mencken: Happy Days, Newspaper Days, Heathen Days, Knopf, 1947.

(Contributor) *Literary History of the United States,* Macmillan, 1948.

A Mencken Chrestomathy, Knopf, 1949, Franklin Library, 1980.

Alistair Cooke, editor, *The Vintage Mencken,* Vintage Books, 1955.

Malcolm Moos, editor, *A Carnival of Buncombe,* Johns Hopkins Press, 1956, reprinted, University of Chicago Press, 1984.

Minority Report: H. L. Mencken's Notebooks, Knopf, 1956.

Robert McHugh, editor, *A Bathtub Hoax and Other Blasts & Bravos from the Chicago Tribune,* Knopf, 1958, Octagon, 1977.

Prejudices; A Selection Made by James T. Farrell, and with an Introduction by Him, Vintage Books, 1958.

H. L. Mencken on Music: A Selection by Louis Cheslock, Knopf, 1961.

Guy J. Forgue, editor, *Letters of H. L. Mencken,* Knopf, 1961.

Huntington Cairns, editor, *The American Scene: A Reader,* Knopf, 1965.

William H. Nolte, editor, *H. L. Mencken's "Smart Set" Criticism,* Cornell University Press, 1968.

(Contributor) *James Branch Cabell: Three Essays in Criticism,* Kennikot, 1971.

Carl Bode, editor, *The Young Mencken: The Best of His Work,* Dial Press, 1973.

C. Merton Babcock, editor, *The Mating Game—And How to Play It,* illustrations by Charles Saxon, Hallmark, 1974.

John Dorsey, editor, *Mencken's Baltimore,* Sunpapers, 1974.

Fenwick Anderson, editor, *Quotations From Chairman Mencken; or, Poor Henry's Almanac,* University of Illinois Press, 1974.

Theo Lippman, Jr., editor, *A Gang of Pecksniffs: And Other Comments on Newspaper Publishers, Editors, and Writers,* Arlington House, 1975.

Bode, editor, *The New Mencken Letters,* Dial Press, 1976.

Joseph C. Goulden, editor, *Mencken's Last Campaign: H. L. Mencken on the 1948 Election,* New Republic Book Company, 1976.

Edward L. Galligan, editor, *A Choice of Days* (contains excerpts from *Happy Days, Newspaper Days,* and *Heathen Days*), Knopf, 1980.

John Dorsey, editor, *On Mencken,* Knopf, 1980.

P. E. Cleator, editor, *Letters From Baltimore: The Mencken-Cleator Correspondence,* Associated University Presses, 1982.

Thomas P. Riggio, editor, *Dreiser-Mencken Letters: The Correspondence of Theodore Dreiser and H. L. Mencken, 1907-1945,* University of Pennsylvania Press, 1986.

Marion Elizabeth Rodgers, editor, *Mencken & Sara: A Life in Letters,* McGraw-Hill, 1987.

Jon Winokur, editor, *The Portable Curmudgeon,* New American Library, 1987.

Peter W. Dowell, editor, *"Ich Kuss die Hand": The Letters of H. L. Mencken to Gretchen Hood,* University of Alabama Press, 1987.

Bode, editor, *The Editor, the Bluenose, and the Prostitute: H. L. Mencken's History of the "Hatrack" Censorship Case,* Roberts Rinehart, 1988.

Charles Fecher, editor, *The Diary of H. L. Mencken,* Knopf, 1989.

Contributor of essays and literary criticism, sometimes under various pseudonyms, to numerous periodicals, including *The Smart Set, Chicago Sunday Tribune, Atlantic Monthly, Bookman, Criterion, World Review, Vanity Fair, New Yorker, Nation, New Republic, Cosmopolitan, Virginia Quarterly Review, Yale Review, Esquire, Reader's Digest, Encore, Harper's,* and *Saturday Review.* Contributor of fiction to *Short Stories* and *The Bohemian.*

SIDELIGHTS: Journalist and critic H. L. Mencken exercised an enormous influence on life and letters in early twentieth-century America. Described by William Henry Chamberlain in a 1956 issue of *New Leader* as the "scourge of the boobs," Mencken lambasted such sacred national institutions as religion, marriage, democracy, popular literature, and mass movements; according to *Dictionary of Literary Biography* contributor Elton Miles, the jolly attacks "yanked the garment of delusion off mankind to expose naked pretension, quackery, and stupidity." During the height of his notoriety in the 1920s, Mencken was called "the most powerful private citizen in the United States" in a *New York Times* editorial, and fellow journalist Walter Lippman deemed him "the most powerful personal influence on this whole generation of educated people." Mencken's singular voice rose from the pages of numerous nonfiction books, from magazines such as *The Smart Set* and *The American Mercury,* and from his hometown newspaper, the *Baltimore Sun.* As William Manchester noted in *Disturber of the Peace: The Life of H. L. Mencken,* the author's stinging prose "rolled across the nation and broke with a tremendous roar, sending the self-appointed policemen of our moral and political standards scampering about to see what

was the matter." In a 1987 issue of *Reason,* correspondent Thomas W. Hazlett observed that even after more than three decades following his death, Mencken rests "alone at the top among the epoch's essayists and satirists. Mencken's pen savaged all that was Great and Bogus in America: the cads in Washington, the Babbitts on main street, the archmorons in the pulpits. . . . Mencken was charming and correct, a combination virtually unheard of in the annals of American Thought. Hence, his life was a gem."

"Mencken took aim upon politicians, bishops, Holy Rollers, Christian Scientists, Methodists, Baptists, Presbyterians, and evangelicals of high and low degree," wrote James J. Kilpatrick in *Menckeniana.* "He belabored [censors], chiropractors, prohibitionists, . . . charity mongers, drive managers, YMCA secretaries, executive secretaries, town boomers, Rotarians, Kiwanians, Boomers, and Elks. He scorned bank presidents, tin roofers, delicatessen dealers, retired bookkeepers, nose and throat specialists, railroad purchasing agents, and the National Association of Teachers of English. More broadly, the Mencken blunderbuss sprayed powder and shot upon fools, yokels, halfwits, ignoramuses, dunderheads, scoundrels, lunatics, morons, rogues, charlatans, mountebanks, imbeciles, barbarians, vagabonds, clowns, fanatics, idiots, bunglers, hacks, quacks, and wowsers." Mencken was neither willing nor able to ignore the foolish antics of many of his fellow Americans. A born individualist, he took a dim view of mass tastes and of any laws—civic or religious—that threatened the growth of a free personality. Hence, the era of the Ku Klux Klan, Prohibition, book censorship, and literal interpretation of the Bible found in Mencken its harshest and most unrelenting critic. In *H. L. Mencken: Iconoclast From Baltimore,* Douglas C. Stenerson claimed that the author "was moved to indignation by the discrepancy between the realities he observed about him and his vision of the kind of art, ethics, and personal behavior a society composed exclusively of truth-seekers and artists would produce." Mencken fought the prevailing American standards in a personal crusade of penned polemic, and in the process he helped to elevate the aims of American thought and literature and the quality of American prose.

Mencken's attacks on what he called the "booboisie" were given added emphasis because, as Kilpatrick put it, he "wrote with a twinkle in his eye." Whether he was reviewing a novel or covering a political convention, Mencken strove first to entertain his audience. In a biography entitled *Mencken,* Carl Bode declared that the critic's prose style "was one of the striking creations of his era, far more dynamic than his solidly conservative ideas. His genius for seizing the unexpected and amusing word, for making the irreverent comparison, and for creating a tone that was not acid but alkaline helped to make him the most readable of American essayists." A humorist in the tradition of Mark Twain and the frontier journalists of the nineteenth century, Mencken played on his readers' emotions by employing a prodigious and colorful vocabulary—and by stating his opinions bluntly. *New World Writing: Sixth Mentor Selection* contributor James T. Farrell contended that as a voice of the Roaring Twenties, Mencken "made revolt and protest fun. He was a great satirist and humorist. He lambasted right, left, and center, and everything fell before his original onslaught of words. Some of this is interesting today only because it is so well-written. . . . But practically everything he wrote is remarkable for its style. You will always come upon a neologism, a vivid phrase, a sharp sentence, a tirade of words which pour out and reveal an amazing capacity to handle the American language."

Henry Louis Mencken was born on September 12, 1880, in Baltimore, Maryland. His father and uncle jointly owned a cigar factory, so the family was prosperous enough to afford a comfortable rowhouse just outside the central business district. When Mencken was three, his parents moved to this home at 1524 Hollins Street, and there Mencken grew up, the oldest of four children. Education was stressed in the Mencken household—throughout the seventeenth and eighteenth centuries, Mencken ancestors had been noted scholars and theologians—so young Henry was sent to Professor Friedrich Knapp's Institute, a private school for children of German descent. He then attended Baltimore Polytechnic Institute, a public secondary school, and graduated at the top of his class when he was only sixteen. Mencken was expected to take a position in his father's business, and he did so reluctantly after high school. For many years he had been fascinated with writing, literature, and newspapers, and he wanted more than anything to be a reporter. While his father lived, however, he had to content himself with correspondence courses and a program of independent reading. In 1899, his father died suddenly of an acute kidney infection. Henry, free to make his own decisions at last, announced that he was going to seek newspaper work.

Although he was a year shy of twenty and had no prior journalistic experience, Mencken presented himself at the offices of the Baltimore *Herald* and asked for a job. He was promptly turned down, but the editor, sensing the youth's enthusiasm invited him to drop in from time to time in case some opening should occur. Mencken did drop in—every night. His persistence amused the staff. Finally, on a snowy evening, he was sent to the suburbs to report on a stolen horse. A few days later he was asked to rewrite some obituaries. For several months he worked for free, taking assignments as they came, and by summer he had earned a staff job with a salary of seven dollars per week. According to Philip Wagner in his pamphlet *H. L. Mencken,* the young reporter "soon demonstrated his ability and moved swiftly through every job in the office: police reporter, drama critic, Sunday editor, city editor, and by 1906 at the age of twenty-five actually the editor of the paper." Mencken worked eighteen hours a day and loved every minute of it. In his memoir *Newspaper Days, 1899-1906,* he wrote that the life of a cub reporter "was the maddest, gladdest, damndest existence ever enjoyed by mortal youth. At a time when the respectable bourgeois youngsters of my generation were college freshmen, oppressed by simian sophomores and affronted with balderdash daily and hourly by chalky pedagogues, I was at large in a wicked seaport of half a million people, with a front seat at every public show, as free of the night as of the day, and getting earfuls and eyefuls of instruction in a hundred giddy arcana, none of them taught in schools."

In 1906 the *Herald* folded, and its exuberant editor was hired by the Baltimore *Sun.* By that time Mencken was recognized as "in no way a common talent," to quote William H. Nolte in the *Dictionary of Literary Biography.* Wagner noted that the *Sun* "provided the real launching pad for [Mencken's] career as a national figure and in turn gained immeasurably from the relationship." There Mencken wrote theater reviews and anonymous editorials, chiefly for the Sunday edition. He also found time to write and publish the books *George Bernard Shaw: His Plays* and *The Philosophy of Friedrich Nietzsche.* Both were the first full-length treatments of Shaw and Nietzsche to appear in America; critics feel that their lasting value lies more in the way they demonstrate Mencken's developing mindset than in the way they explore the topics at hand. Neither book had much impact on the reading public, but they did draw the attention of the editor of *The Smart Set,* a magazine based in New York City. In 1908 Mencken

agreed to write a monthly book review column for *The Smart Set* in addition to his duties at the *Sun.* At the *Smart Set* offices Mencken met George Jean Nathan, the magazine's new theater critic. The two men struck up a friendship that eventually led to a partnership; though they came from different backgrounds they were united in their cynical view that American art had all the quality and lasting power of a carnival sideshow.

Shortly after Mencken's thirtieth birthday, the editors of the *Sun* approached him about writing a bylined column. Manchester described the assignment: "It might deal with any subject whatever, so long as it remain irresponsible and readable. It was a significant order. It marked Mencken's final departure from the world of anonymous opinion. . . . He had left, and for good, the army of unidentified writers who present a newspaper's daily information and commentary and had become a public personality, free to exploit his own name." Mencken called his column "The Free Lance," and his pieces "swiftly became the sort of thing that no one of consequence in Baltimore dared not to read," according to Wagner. With rollicking good humor, Mencken opposed everything respectable, defended prostitution, alcohol, and war, and attacked every example of city boosterism, political hypocrisy, and public posturing. Manchester suggested that these "lethal and highly subversive ideas were couched in a language designed to inflame the greatest possible number of readers." While the editors of the *Sun* ground their teeth, Mencken was denounced from pulpits and from City Hall, but many ordinary readers seemed to appreciate his irreverent tone. "The Free Lance" ran from 1911 until 1915 and was canceled because Mencken openly favored Germany in the escalating World War I. Manchester concluded, however, that long before "The Free Lance" was at last discontinued, "it had developed Mencken as one of the foremost polemical writers of his day. . . . It had, however, done more than that. In its columns of fine body type lay the blueprint of all his future books."

Mencken's penchant for "stirring up the animals" was not confined to Baltimore. Through the pages of *The Smart Set,* first as book critic and then, in 1914, as co-editor, he became one of the country's most influential literary critics. Wagner wrote that the flood of Mencken's criticism, published in *The Smart Set* and reprinted in his books, "swept away the deadening literary standards, and the deadly standard-bearers, of our early twentieth century and cleared the way for a tremendous flowering of new writing." In scathing essays such as "Puritanism as a Literary Force," published in *A Book of Prefaces,* Mencken took issue with the Puritan stress on morality in literature and art. American fiction, he felt, was being stifled by religious censorship; he called for an art that could question accepted axioms and standards and for writing that portrayed the cold realities of life. *New Republic* contributor Alfred Kazin called Mencken "the last literary critic in this country to inspire novelists more than professors." Indeed, Mencken was instrumental in discovering or promoting numerous acclaimed authors, including Theodore Dreiser, Sinclair Lewis, F. Scott Fitzgerald, James Joyce, and Eugene O'Neill. Nolte remarked: "H. L. Mencken is not generally remembered for his criticism of belles lettres. Still, the fact is that Mencken, more than any other writer, helped to create a sophisticated reading public and thereby pave the way for the literature that came into being in the years just before, during, and after World War I."

The years of that war were difficult ones for Mencken. The *Sun* closed its doors to him because of his pro-German sympathies, and *The Smart Set* offered little salary as he and George Jean Nathan struggled to edit and publish it on a shoestring budget. Bode noted, however, that the lack of a forum during the war "did nothing to reduce [Mencken's] vitality as a writer. It simply channeled that vitality into his books." Mencken finally found time to produce a work on the subject that fascinated him the most—the American language and its hardy independent evolution from its parent tongue, European English. In 1919, Mencken published *The American Language: A Preliminary Inquiry Into the Development of English in the United States.* Mencken and his publisher Alfred A. Knopf were both surprised and delighted by the interest in the lengthy volume. Its first printing sold out rapidly; Wagner contended that the impression it made "on the new college generation especially, by its style, its humor and its lightly worn scholarship, was tremendous." In *On Mencken,* Alistair Cooke described *The American Language* as "a prolonged demonstration of the fact that the Americans, in a three-hundred-year experience of a new language, new crops, new climates, a new society, and the melding of many immigrant languages and ways of life, had developed institutions, foods, habits, relationships that coined thousands of new nouns, adjectives, and—in their speech—even new syntactical forms. It was, in fact, a new dialect." The first edition of *The American Language* was hardly on the bookstore shelves before Mencken began to work on an expanded version. Throughout the rest of his life, he returned to this linguistic work regularly, constantly updating and revising his book. Bode concluded of *The American Language:* "The scholarship would become more and more specific, more and more monumental. . . . The acclaim of the work would grow with its size. . . . It would end as a classic, something few foresaw when it appeared in 1919."

Reception of the first edition of *The American Language* was a harbinger of things to come. In the 1920s, a new generation of disillusioned war veterans and sophisticated college students began to see Mencken, in Wagner's words, as "what the times needed: a clearinghouse for the cynicism and discontents of the postwar years and a lash for their excesses wielded with alternating scorn and high good humor." Gradually Mencken drifted away from literary criticism and became instead a critic of the mundane American scene. He found much to criticize: bungling politicians like Warren G. Harding, Bible-thumping zealots like William Jennings Bryan, unscrupulous businessmen, Southerners, censor boards, the Ku Klux Klan, and especially Prohibition. Wagner related: "The object was to make his victim a butt of ridicule. . . . By inference, his readers could never be identified with the bores, shams, and neanderthals whom he delighted to take apart. . . . Before going into battles, Mencken always saw to it that the cheering section—his reader—was in good heart and ready to back him. He was a master of this sort of rhetorical sleight of hand." In *On Native Grounds: An Interpretation of Modern American Prose Literature,* Kazin observed: "By prodigious skill [Mencken] managed to insult everyone except his readers. He flattered them by kindling a sense of disgust; his ferocious attacks on Babbitry implied that his readers were all Superior Citizens; his very recklessness was intoxicating." ("Babbitry" refers to American scholar and critic Irving Babbit who, with Paul Elmer More, founded the New Humanism Movement, which called for literary moderation and restraint in the manner of classical literature and traditions).

Mencken felt no need to present a balanced argument in his essays. He was content to express his opinion, with the humor serving as a warning not to take him too seriously. When he was serious, it was generally in defense of individual rights or intellectual freedom, as Farrell explained. "The key to Mencken's thought is to be found in his libertarianism," Farrell wrote. "He believed in complete liberty. . . . He saw encroachments on the liberty of the individual from all sides. The institutions of society in gen-

eral, and of democracy in particular, were threatening the liberty of the individual. And liberty meant, more than anything else, liberty of thought." Mencken also held that all people were *not* equal—especially intellectually—and that democracy, "the worship of jackals by jackasses," merely legislated the lowest mass tastes. Religion, as Mencken saw it, was just another tool used to bamboozle and manipulate the credulous masses, but it too served to stifle freedom through censorship and blue laws. Farrell concluded that Mencken "took the privilege of . . . liberty in his own writings. Like or dislike them, agree or disagree with them, one cannot fail but be struck by their honesty and vigor."

"Much of Mencken's genius lay in the drive and dexterity that allowed him to be a newspaperman at the same time that he was an author and editor," noted Bode. "One role is enough for an ordinary person. Mencken played all three to the hilt. He became, certainly during the 1920s, the most influential magazine editor in the country. And, within the sphere of the subjects he chose, he became the best-known writer." Mencken still considered himself first and foremost a newspaperman, and he began writing for the *Sun* again in 1920. In addition to covering such spectacles as political conventions and the 1924 Scopes trial in Dayton, Tennessee, that challenged the teaching of evolution, Mencken wrote weekly "Monday Articles" for the *Sun*'s editorial page. These "imprinted his particular brand of commentary on the psyche of America," according to *Dictionary of Literary Biography* contributor J. James McElveen. Bode likewise observed that the general record of the Monday Articles "was magnificent. Over a span of eighteen years, from 1920 to 1938, Mencken published more good writing, through these columns, than any other newspaperman of his era. The Free Lance made him famous locally but the Monday Articles helped to establish his national renown."

Simultaneously, Mencken and Nathan were becoming celebrities through their magazine work. Having kept *The Smart Set* afloat during the war—sometimes by writing most of the issue themselves under an array of pseudonyms—they watched as circulation rose steadily in the first years of the 1920s. Neither editor was entirely satisfied with *The Smart Set,* however, so in 1924 they founded a new magazine, *The American Mercury.* Within the year, Mencken became sole editor of *The American Mercury,* and as Manchester related, "it became a product of the peculiar maelstrom which he had created, and in which he now lived." McElveen described Mencken's product: "With its Paris-green cover, the magazine was simply designed by standards of later decades but was a superb typographical specimen in its day. It was not only a status symbol but a voice of critical significance during the wild, unabashed decade of prosperity and Prohibition. . . . Mencken was an imaginative editor, and his special writing style, along with his keen insight and trenchant wit, gave the *American Mercury* a lively and intellectually stimulating quality that appealed to sophisticated and perceptive readers." Manchester remarked that Mencken's "stupendous gift for invective had now reached heights so incredible, so breathtaking, so awe-inspiring, so terrible, that in its indictment of the national culture it wrung monthly gasps from sixty thousand readers and porcupined the hair of intellectuals, Army officers, bond salesmen, and garage mechanics in St. Paul, St. Louis, St. Joseph, and St. Cloud. How could so violent a hymn of hate be sung so jubilantly?" Bode concluded that *The American Mercury* "was more than a breath of fresh air; it was a gust that once or twice grew into a gale."

Mencken's literary output during the 1920s was prodigious. Corollary to his regular journalism, his collected articles appeared in a series of volumes entitled *Prejudices,* and his thoughts on politics appeared in *Notes on Democracy.* His work attracted praise from other writers and critics, as well as from the college students who so admired him. "In so far as [Mencken] has influenced the tone of public controversy he has elevated it," Lippman wrote in *Men of Destiny. New Republic* essayist Edmund Wilson likewise contended that Mencken "is the civilized consciousness of modern America, its learning, its intelligence and its taste, realizing the grossness of its manners and mind and crying out in horror and chagrin." According to Joseph Wood Krutch in *If You Don't Mind My Saying So . . . Essays on Man and Nature,* Mencken's was "the best prose written in America during the twentieth century. Those who deny that fact had better confine themselves to direct attack. They will be hard put to find a rival claimant." In *Bookman* F. Scott Fitzgerald concluded simply that Mencken "has done more for the national letters than any man alive."

Mencken's detractors were equally passionate. Many colorful diatribes against him emanated from the hinterland; Manchester quotes one of these, from a Reverend Doctor Charles E. Jones in *Gospel Call:* "If a buzzard had laid an egg in a dunghill and the sun had hatched a thing like Mencken, the buzzard would have been justly ashamed of its offspring." Other more objective critics also found fault with Mencken. "The total effect of his writing is nearer to intellectual vaudeville than to serious criticism," observed Irving Babbitt in *Modern Writers at Work,* encapsulating a commonly held belief that Mencken sacrificed discrimination for bombast. Stenerson wrote: "Despite the changes which transformed America during Mencken's lifetime, his basic attitudes remained much the same in his maturity as they had been in his youth. His wide-ranging interests, the soundness of his information on many issues, and the common sense with which he treated them, were offset, to a considerable extent, by his failure to see any need for modifying his premises. . . . His prejudices were the themes of his art, not the building blocks of a coherent system of thought." This was to be Mencken's downfall, as Upton Sinclair predicted in *The Bookman:* "The darling and idol of the young intelligenzia has no message to give them, except that they are free to do what they please—which they interpret to mean that they are to get drunk, and read elegant pornography, and mock at the stupidities and blunders of people with less expensive educations. . . . For the present, that is all that is required; that is the mood of the time. But some day the time spirit will change; America will realize that its problems really have to be solved."

The spirit did change, almost overnight, with the 1929 stock market crash. As Hilton Kramer noted in the *New York Times Book Review,* the "carnival atmosphere that had supported Mencken's outrageous rhetoric was, after all, the coefficient of a false prosperity, and the collapse of that prosperity left him stranded in a style remote from the needs of a new social reality." Mencken's humorous attacks on "Homo boobiens" no longer seemed funny as the depression deepened. Moreover, Mencken, the great individualist, opposed the New Deal programs and discounted the seriousness of Hitler's rise to power in Germany. "What were jesting matters for him were serious or painful for most, and he lost his audience," states Galbraith in the *Washington Post Book World.* Though he caused a stir by marrying writer Sara Powell Haardt in 1930, Mencken witnessed a precipitous decline in his popularity over the next several years. Two books for which he had high hopes, *Treatise on the Gods* and *Treatise on Right and Wrong* sold few copies and earned lackluster reviews. The power he continued to wield became more and more localized in Baltimore, where his Monday Articles still appeared in the *Sun.* "Ten years before," claims Manchester, "[Mencken]

had ridden in on a wave of disillusion and irresponsibility, the surprised beneficiary of a changed society. Now that society had changed again and he was riding out, as helplessly the victim of the public whim as he had once been its darling. . . . There was no room for a writer with nothing to say about the crisis gripping the world. There was no room for H. L. Mencken."

In one particular arena, however—political convention coverage—Mencken continued to dominate throughout the 1930s. "Mencken's political specialty . . . was the national conventions, occasions which accorded him not only the greatest scope for his talent but much personal pleasure as well," Galbraith contended in the *Washington Post Book World.* "And here he was ahead of his time; before anyone, he saw them as a triumph of banality over content. . . . Mencken, a full 40 years ago, learned what all but the television people now know: the convention is our greatest non-event." Through Mencken's cynical eye, the colorful conventions were quickly reduced to absurdities punctuated by vacuous speeches and the antics of hero-worshipping hayseeds. According to Joe Conason in the *Village Voice,* Mencken "could enliven the deadliest bore in politics—Coolidge, Hoover, Landon—long enough to elicit a hearty laugh, and dismiss him when the guffaws subsided. His comic view of politics enabled him to see its absurdity with a clarity that seems contemporary 60 years later." From 1920 to 1948, with the sole exception of 1944, Mencken covered every convention, Democratic, Republican, and third party. Even as his energies waned and the *Sun*'s deadlines grew tighter, he never tired of the quadrennial political spectacles.

In 1935, Mencken's wife Sara died. The era's most notorious confirmed bachelor had enjoyed his brief marriage, and he mourned his wife's loss for many years thereafter. Mencken was unable to face life alone in the apartment he and Sara had shared, so he returned to the home that had been his base almost his whole life—1524 Hollins Street. From there, beginning in the late 1930s, he began to write anecdotal essays about his childhood for the *New Yorker* magazine. Wagner noted of these stories: "Absolutely and literally true they certainly were not. . . . They were better than that: they caught and preserved the smells and flavor and temper of an era." The essays accumulated: Mencken's youth on Hollins Street, his cub reporter days at the *Herald,* his recollection of the Great Baltimore Fire of 1904, his early travels to New York. Eventually these were published in three popular volumes, *Happy Days, 1880-1892; Newspaper Days, 1899-1906,* and *Heathen Days, 1890-1936.* Bode declared that the tales "were too extended to be called anecdotes. They were too actual to be local-color fiction. They were too exuberant and personal to qualify as social history. Perhaps the best way to put it is that they constituted the human comedy of young Mencken in old Baltimore. The writing was supple and deft, avoiding quaintness, condescension, and sentimentality. And above all it had the apparent artlessness which concealed the skills and resources he drew on." Bode concluded that "the result was classic." The *Days* books introduced Mencken to a new generation of readers and revived his national reputation. Wagner felt these works to be "what he gave to our literature which time is least likely to tarnish or erode."

Mencken's last productive year was 1948. He spent it in characteristic ways—covering the political conventions, attacking segregation laws as "relics of Ku Kluxery," and defending civil rights and civil liberties. His last article for the *Sun* lambasted a rule that would not allow blacks and whites to play tennis together on a local court. Several days later he suffered a severe stroke, the lasting legacy of which was an inability to read, write, or speak clearly. William Manchester was one of the few people

Mencken continued to see after the stroke; in *Disturber of the Peace* Manchester described Mencken's condition: "The great tragedy of his situation was that everything which had given life meaning for him was gone. Since his boyhood days the pattern of his life had built around the reading of the written word and the expression of his reflections. For sixty years . . . the cultivation of that expression had been the moving purpose of his life, and he had developed it to an art unmatched in his time. Now that was impossible, and he was left to vegetate back to a robust physical health with the purposes of his very being withdrawn. It was a terrible blow, and he was the first to recognize its magnitude." Attended by his brother and visited only by his secretary and a few close friends, Mencken lived eight more years in his Hollins Street home. He died there, in his sleep, on January 29, 1956.

Most critics agree that Mencken's influence has survived his death. "If Mencken had never lived," Kazin observed in *On Native Grounds*, "it would have taken a whole army of assorted philosophers, monologists, editors, and patrons of the new writing to make up for him. As it was, he not only rallied all the young writers together and imposed his skepticism upon the new generation, but also brought a new and uproarious gift for high comedy into a literature that had never been too quick to laugh." Nor has time dimmed the pertinence of Mencken's message, according to McElveen. "Mencken's dissent—his way of demolishing society's hypocrisy, of smashing the idols of human folly—set him apart from other writers of his day," wrote McElveen. "His thought embraced the whole range of the twentieth century; and his writings have not aged, because mankind is subject to the same shortcomings and foibles that prevailed in his day." Indeed, much of Mencken's work remains in print, new volumes of collected correspondence are still appearing, and a thriving Mencken Society, based in Baltimore, keeps his memory alive. "Mencken's basic attitude at all times, disrespect for the powers of this earth, for everything seeking to make us more righteous and obedient at all costs, will always lead people back to his work," Kazin stated in the *New York Review of Books*. Ben Hecht, commenting on Mencken in *A Child of the Century*, concluded that the work penned by the famous "Sage of Baltimore" is "proof that brave words can still lift the soul of man."

In a note published in *The Letters of H. L. Mencken*, the author himself summed up his philosophy. "My notion is that all the larger human problems are insoluble, and that life is quite meaningless—a spectacle without purpose or moral," he wrote. "I detest all efforts to read a moral into it. I do not write because I want to make converts. . . . I write because the business amuses me. It is the best of sports."

MEDIA ADAPTATIONS: A character based on Mencken appears in the play *Inherit the Wind*, by Jerome Lawrence and Robert E. Lee; an Off-Broadway one-man show entitled "An Evening With H. L. Mencken" was performed at the Cherry Lane Theater in 1975.

AVOCATIONAL INTERESTS: Music, especially piano.

BIOGRAPHICAL/CRITICAL SOURCES:

BOOKS

Adler, Betty, *H. L. M.: The Mencken Bibliography*, Johns Hopkins Press, 1961, *Ten-Year Supplement, 1962-1971*, Enoch Pratt Free Library, 1971.

Angoff, Charles, *H. L. Mencken: A Portrait From Memory*, Thomas Yoseloff, 1956.

Babbitt, Irving, *Modern Writers at Work*, Macmillan, 1930.

Bode, Carl, *Mencken*, Southern Illinois University Press, 1969, Johns Hopkins University Press, 1986.

Bode, Carl, editor, *The New Mencken Letters*, Dial Press, 1976.

Boyd, Ernest, *H. L. Mencken*, McBride, 1925.

Brooks, Van Wyck, *The Confident Years: 1885-1915*, Dutton, 1952.

Cabell, James Branch, *Some of Us: An Essay in Epitaphs*, McBride, 1930.

Concise Dictionary of American Literary Biography: The Twenties, 1917-1929, Gale, 1989.

Cooke, Alistair, editor, *The Vintage Mencken*, Vintage Books, 1955.

Cooke, Alistair, *Six Men*, Knopf, 1977.

DeCasseres, Benjamin, *Mencken and Shaw: The Anatomy of America's Voltaire and England's Other John Bull*, Silas Newton, 1930.

Dictionary of Literary Biography, Gale, Volume 11: *American Humorists, 1800-1950*, 1982, Volume 25: *American Newspaper Journalists, 1901-1925*, 1984, Volume 63: *Modern American Critics, 1920-1955*, 1988.

Dolmetsch, Carl R., *The "Smart Set," a History and Anthology*, Dial Press, 1966.

Dorsey, John, editor, *On Mencken*, Knopf, 1980.

Douglas, George H., *H. L. Mencken: Critic of American Life*, Archon Books, 1978.

Farrell, James T., *New World Writing: Sixth Mentor Selection*, New American Library, 1954.

Farrell, James T., *Reflections at Fifty and Other Essays*, Vanguard, 1954.

Fecher, Charles A., *Mencken: A Study of His Thought*, Knopf, 1978.

Fecher, Charles A., editor, *The Diary of H. L. Mencken*, Knopf, 1989.

Fitzpatrick, Vincent, *H. L. M.: The Mencken Bibliography, Second Ten-Year Supplement*, Enoch Pratt Free Library, 1986.

Geismar, Maxwell, *The Last of the Provincials: The American Novel, 1915-1925*, Secker & Warburg, 1947.

Gingrich, Arnold, and L. Rust Hills, editors, *The Armchair "Esquire,"* Putnam, 1958.

Goldberg, Isaac, *The Man Mencken: A Biographical and Critical Survey*, Simon & Schuster, 1925.

Hecht, Ben, *A Child of the Century*, D. I. Fine, 1985.

Hobson, Fred C., *Serpent in Eden: H. L. Mencken and the South*, Louisiana State University Press, 1974.

Kazin, Alfred, *On Native Grounds: An Interpretation of Modern American Prose Literature*, Reynal & Hitchcock, 1942.

Kemler, Edgar, *The Irreverent Mr. Mencken*, Little, Brown, 1950.

Krutch, Joseph Wood, *If You Don't Mind My Saying So . . . Essays on Man and Nature*, Sloane, 1964.

Lewis, Wyndham, *Paleface: The Philosophy of the "Melting Pot,"* Chatto & Windus, 1929.

Lippmann, Walter, *Men of Destiny*, Macmillan, 1927.

Manchester, William, *Disturber of the Peace: The Life of H. L. Mencken*, Harper, 1950, 2nd edition, University of Massachusetts Press, 1986.

Martin, Edward A., *H. L. Mencken and the Debunkers*, University of Georgia Press, 1984.

Mayfield, Sara, *The Constant Circle: H. L. Mencken and His Friends*, Delacorte, 1968.

Mencken, H. L., and Sara Powell Haardt, editors, *Menckeniana: A Schimpflexikon*, Knopf, 1928, Octagon, 1977.

Mencken, H. L., *Happy Days, 1889-1892*, Knopf, 1940.

Mencken, H. L., *Newspaper Days, 1899-1906*, Knopf, 1941.

Mencken, H. L., *Heathen Days, 1890-1936*, Knopf, 1943.

Nathan, George Jean, *The Borzoi 1920: Being a Sort of Record of Five Years' Publishing,* Knopf, 1920.

Nathan, George Jean, *The World of George Jean Nathan,* Knopf, 1952.

Nolte, William H., *H. L. Mencken, Literary Critic,* Wesleyan University Press, 1966.

Riggio, Thomas P., editor, *Dreiser-Mencken Letters: The Correspondence of Theodore Dreiser and H. L. Mencken, 1907-1945,* University of Pennsylvania Press, 1986.

Rodgers, Marion Elizabeth, editor, *Mencken & Sara: A Life in Letters,* McGraw, 1987.

Scruggs, Charles, *The Sage in Harlem: H. L. Mencken and the Black Writers of the 1920s,* Johns Hopkins University Press, 1984.

Shivers, Frank R., *Maryland Wits & Baltimore Bards: A Literary History with Notes on Washington Writers,* Maclay & Associates, 1985.

Singleton, M. K., *H. L. Mencken and the "American Mercury" Adventure,* Duke University Press, 1962.

Smith, H. Allen, *The Best of H. Allen Smith,* Trident, 1972.

Stenerson, Douglas C., *H. L. Mencken: Iconoclast from Baltimore,* University of Chicago Press, 1971.

Twentieth-Century Literary Criticism, Volume 13, Gale, 1984.

Wagner, Philip, *H. L. Mencken,* University of Minnesota Press, 1966.

Williams, W. H. L., *H. L. Mencken,* Twayne, 1977.

Wright, Richard, *Black Boy: A Record of Childhood and Youth,* Harper, 1964.

PERIODICALS

Americana, September-October, 1980.

American Literature, May, 1965.

Atlantic, January, 1946, May, 1956.

Bookman, March, 1921, November, 1927.

Commentary, April, 1977.

Comparative Literature Studies, March, 1970.

Harper's, July, 1950, August, 1950.

Life, August 5, 1946.

Los Angeles Times, December 5, 1989, December 12, 1989.

Menckeniana, fall, 1981.

Nation, May 13, 1950, September 12, 1953, September 16, 1961, May 24, 1965.

New Leader, March 19, 1956.

New Republic, June 1, 1921, March 8, 1943, September 13, 1954, May 21, 1956, April 17, 1965, September 14, 1968, January 12, 1972, December 27, 1975, March 12, 1977, October 22, 1984.

Newsweek, April 5, 1948, September 18, 1961.

New Yorker, May 31, 1969.

New York Herald Tribune Books, April 30, 1930.

New York Review of Books, June 11, 1981, February 26, 1987.

New York Times, February 10, 1987, December 13, 1989.

New York Times Book Review, August 19, 1973, December 19, 1976, September 7, 1980, November 9, 1986.

Philadelphia Inquirer, February 27, 1987.

Reason, December, 1987.

Saturday Review, December 11, 1926, August 6, 1949, September 10, 1955, September 7, 1968.

Sewanee Review, summer, 1966.

South Atlantic Quarterly, spring, 1964.

Spectator, September 4, 1982.

Sun Magazine (Baltimore), September 7, 1980.

Times Literary Supplement, March 13, 1969, September 27, 1985, July 17, 1987.

Village Voice, November 6, 1984.

Washington Post, June 9, 1984, October 5, 1985, December 5, 1989, December 8, 1989, January 12, 1990.

Washington Post Book World, August 15, 1976, September 14, 1980, January 25, 1987.

OTHER

"Henry L. Mencken, Interviewed by Donald Howe Kirkley, Sr." (sound recording), Library of Congress Recording Library, 1948.

Mencken's collected papers and books are stored at the Enoch Pratt Free Library in Baltimore, Maryland. Collections of Mencken's correspondence can be found at numerous libraries and universities, including New York Public Library, Dartmouth College, Goucher College, Harvard University, Princeton University, and Yale University.

OBITUARIES:

PERIODICALS

Life, February 20, 1956.

New Leader, February 13, 1956.

Newsweek, February 6, 1956, February 20, 1956.

New York Times, January 30, 1956, January 31, 1956, February 1, 1956.

New York Times Book Review, March 11, 1956.

Saturday Review, February 11, 1956.

*   *   *

MENNINGER, Karl (Augustus) 1893-1990

PERSONAL: Born July 22, 1893, in Topeka, Kan.; died of cancer, July 18, 1990; son of Charles Frederick (a physician) and Flora Vesta (a teacher; maiden name, Knisely) Menninger; married Grace Gaines, September 9, 1916 (divorced, 1941); married Jeanetta Lyle (editor of *Bulletin of the Menninger Clinic*), September 8, 1941; children: (first marriage) Julia (Mrs. A. H. Gottesman), Martha (Mrs. William Nichols), Robert Gaines; (second marriage) Rosemary Jeanetta Karla. *Education:* Attended Washburn College (now Washburn University of Topeka), 1910-12, and Indiana University, summer, 1910; University of Wisconsin, Madison, A.B., 1914, B.S., 1915; Harvard Medical School, M.D. (cum laude), 1917. *Religion:* Presbyterian.

ADDRESSES: Home—1819 Westwood Circle, Topeka, Kan. 66604. *Office*—Menninger Foundation, Box 829, Topeka, Kan. 66601; Topeka Veterans Administration Hospital, Topeka, Kan.; and Washburn University, Topeka, Kan.

CAREER: The Menninger Foundation (formerly the Menninger Clinic), Topeka, Kan., partner with father, Charles Frederick Menninger, 1919-25, chief of staff, 1925-46, director of education, 1946-70, chairman of board of trustees, 1954-70, member of education committee, 1967-70. Kansas City General Hospital, Kansas City, Mo., intern, 1917-18; Harvard Medical School, Cambridge, Mass., instructor in neuropathology, 1918-20; Boston Psychopathic Hospital, Boston, Mass., assistant physician, 1918-20; Tufts Medical School, Medford, Mass., assistant in neurology, 1919-20; Christ's Hospital and St. Francis Hospital, Topeka, staff member, 1919-90; Winter Veterans Administration Hospital, Topeka, manager, 1945-48, chairman of dean's committee and senior consultant, 1948-55; Menninger School of Psychiatry, Topeka, founder, 1946, dean, 1946-70; University of Kansas City (now University of Missouri—Kansas City) Medical School, clinical professor of psychiatry, 1946-62; Topeka Institute of Psychoanalysis, Topeka, 1960-90; University of Kansas, Lawrence, professor of medicine, 1970-76, professor at large,

1976-90. Visiting professor, University of Cincinnati Medical School. Trustee, Albert Deutsch Memorial Foundation, 1961, and Aspen Institute for Humanistic Studies, 1961-64. Advisor to the Surgeon General, U.S. Army, 1945; consultant, Veteran Administration Hospital, Topeka, 1948-90; consultant in psychiatry to State of Illinois Department of Welfare, and Governor of Illinois, 1953-54; consultant, Office of Vocational Rehabilitation, Department of Health, Education, and Welfare, 1953-55; consultant, Bureau of Prisons, Department of Justice, 1956-90; consultant, Forbes Air Force Base Hospital and Stone-Brandel Center, 1958-90; member of advisory committee, International Survey of Correctional Research and Practice, California, 1960-90; consultant to various other institutes and associations.

MEMBER: International Association for Suicide Prevention, World Society of Ekistics, Masons, Central Neuropsychiatric Association (co-founder; secretary, 1922-32; president, 1932-33), Central Psychiatric Hospital Association, American Orthopsychiatric Association (secretary, 1926-27; president, 1927-28), American Psychiatric Association (life fellow; counselor, 1928-29, 1941-43), American Psychological Association, American Psychoanalytic Association (life member; president, 1941-43), American Academy of Psychiatry and Law, American Society of Criminology, American Justice Institute (member of advisory committee), American Civil Liberties Union (vice-chairman of national committee), American Medical Association (fellow), American College of Physicians (life fellow), American College of Psychiatrists, American Medical Writers Association (life member; 2nd vice-president, 1957-58; 1st vice-president, 1958-59), American Association for the Advancement of Science, American Association for Child Psychoanalysis, National Commission for the Prevention of Child Abuse (co-chairman of honorary board), American Association of Suicidology (honorary member), Medical Association for the Research of Nervous and Mental Diseases, Royal College of Psychiatrists (honorary fellow), Association of Clinical Pastoral Education, Association for Psychiatry Treatment Offenders, Sigmund Freud Archives, American Humanities Foundation, NAACP, National Congress of the American Indian, American Association of Botanical Gardens and Arboreta, American Horticultural Council, Friends of the Earth, Sierra Club, Save the Tallgrass Prairie Inc. (chairman of national honorary board), Kansas Medical Society, Illinois Academy of Criminology, Illinois Committee on Family Law, Aspen Institute for Humanistic Studies (former trustee; currently honorary trustee), Chicago Psychoanalytic Association, American Indian Center (Chicago grand council), Chicago Orchestral Association (governor), Sigmund Freud Society (Vienna), University Presbyterian Club (Chicago), Country Lodge Presbyterian Club (Topeka, Kan.).

AWARDS, HONORS: D.Sc., Washburn University, 1949, University of Wisconsin, 1965, Oklahoma City University, 1966; L.H.D., Park College, 1955, St. Benedict College, 1963, Loyola University, 1972, DePaul University, 1974; LL.D., Jefferson Medical College of Philadelphia, 1956, Parsons College, 1960, Kansas State University, 1962, Baker University, 1965, Pepperdine University, 1974, John Jay College of Criminal Justice, 1978; Isaac Ray Award, 1962, First Distinguished Service Award, 1965, and First Founders Award, 1977, all from American Psychiatric Association; T. W. Salmon award, New York Academy of Medicine, 1967; Good Samaritan award, Eagles Lodge, 1968, 1969; Annual Service award, John Howard Association, 1969; Good Shepherd award, The Lambs (Chicago), 1969; American Academy of Psychiatry and Law award, 1974; Roscoe Pound award, National Council of Crime and Delinquency, 1975; Kansas Department of Corrections special award, 1976;

Sheen award, American Medical Association, 1978; Presidential Medal of Freedom, 1981; numerous other awards.

WRITINGS:

The Human Mind, Knopf, 1930, 2nd edition, 1945.
Man against Himself, Harcourt, 1938, reprinted, 1985.
(With wife, Jeanetta Menninger) *Love against Hate,* Harcourt, 1942.
(With G. Devereux) *A Guide to Psychiatric Books,* Grune & Stratton, 1950, 3rd revised edition, 1972.
A Manual for Psychiatric Case Study, Grune & Stratton, 1952, revised edition, 1962.
Theory of Psychoanalytic Technique, Basic Books, 1958, revised edition with Philip Holzman, 1973.
A Psychiatrists World (selected papers), Viking, 1959.
The Vital Balance: The Life Process in Mental Health and Illness, Viking, 1963, reprinted, Peter Smith, 1983.
The Crime of Punishment, Viking, 1968.
Sparks, edited by Lucy Freeman, Crowell, 1973.
A Celebration Issue Honoring Karl Menninger on His 80th Birthday: A Selection of His Previously Published Papers, Menninger Foundation, 1973.
Whatever Became of Sin?, Hawthorn, 1973, reprinted, Bantam, 1988.
The Human Mind Revisited, International University Press, 1978.
(With Sarah R. Haavik) *Sexuality, Law, and the Developmentally Disabled Person: Legal and Clinical Aspects of Marriage, Parenthood, and Sterilization,* Paul Brookes, 1981.
The Selected Correspondence of Karl A. Menninger, 1919-1945, edited by Howard J. Faulkner and Virginia D. Pruitt, Yale University Press, 1989.

Also author with others of *Why Men Fail,* 1918, *The Healthy-Minded Child,* 1930, and *America Now,* 1938. Editor in chief, *Bulletin of the Menninger Clinic,* 1936-90; member of editorial board, *Archives of Criminal Psychodynamics, Psychoanalytic Quarterly, Excerpta Criminologica,* and *Academic Achievement.*

WORK IN PROGRESS: The Suicidal Intention of Nuclear Armament Manufacture and Storage.

SIDELIGHTS: With his father Charles and brother William, Karl Menninger founded the famous Menninger Clinic in 1919, which later became the Menninger Foundation. The importance of the clinic was noted in the citation of the Albert Lasker Group Award for 1955: "The Menninger Foundation and Clinic, headed by Drs. Karl and William Menninger, has provided a sustained and highly productive attack against mental disease for many years. Inspired by their father, Dr. Charles Frederick Menninger, these brothers have developed an outstanding institution which has served as an example for other mental disease hospitals. . . . The influence of the Menninger Foundation and Clinic in increasing professional and public interest in the care of the mentally ill cannot be measured, but it is indelibly recorded as a great service to mankind."

BIOGRAPHICAL/CRITICAL SOURCES:

BOOKS

Chandler, Caroline A., *Famous Modern Men of Medicine,* Dodd, 1965.
Davis, Elizabeth L., *Fathers of America,* Revell, 1958.

PERIODICALS

Chicago Tribune, June 16, 1979.
Look, September 30, 1958.

Los Angeles Times, September 18, 1983.
New York Times, November 6, 1955.
New York Times Book Review, December 29, 1964, March 19, 1989.
Saturday Evening Post, April 7, 1962.
Saturday Review, January 25, 1964.

*   *   *

MERCER, David 1928-1980

PERSONAL: Born June 27, 1928, in Wakefield, Yorkshire, England; died of a heart attack, August 8, 1980, in Haifa, Israel; son of Edward (an engine driver) and Helen (Steadman) Mercer; married; wife's name Dafna; children: Rebecca. *Education:* University of Durham, B.A. (honors), 1953.

ADDRESSES: Home—37 Hamilton Gardens, London N.W. 8, England. *Agent*—Margaret Ramsay Ltd., 14 Goodwin Court London W.C.2, England.

CAREER: Technician in pathological laboratory in England, 1943-48; teacher of general subjects, 1956-61; writer of television plays, stage plays, and screenplays.

MEMBER: Screenwriters Guild.

AWARDS, HONORS: Screenwriters Guild Award for best teleplay, 1962, for "A Suitable Case for Treatment"; *Evening Standard* award for most promising playwright, 1965; British Film Academy award for best screenplay, 1966, for "Morgan!"; best British original teleplay award, Writers Guild, 1967, for "In Two Minds"; best British original teleplay award, Writers Guild, 1969, for "Let's Murder Vivaldi"; French Film Academy award, 1977, for "Providence"; International Emmy for best drama of the season, for "A Rod of Iron."

WRITINGS:

PLAYS

"Where the Difference Begins" (first play in trilogy; also see below), broadcast by British Broadcasting Corp. (BBC-TV), 1961; stage adaptation first produced at Hull Arts Centre, May 19, 1970.
"A Climate of Fear" (second play in trilogy; also see below), broadcast by BBC-TV, 1962.
"A Suitable Case for Treatment" (also see below), broadcast by BBC-TV, 1962.
"The Buried Man," first produced at Manchester Library Theatre, 1962; broadcast by Associated Television, 1963.
"A Way of Living," broadcast by ABC-TV (England), 1963.
"The Birth of a Private Man" (third play in trilogy; also see below), broadcast by BBC-TV, 1963.
"For Tea on Sunday" (also see below), broadcast by BBC-TV, 1963.
"And Did Those Feet" (also see below), broadcast by BBC-TV, 1965.
Ride a Cock Horse (first produced on West End at Picadilly Theatre, 1965), Hill & Wang, 1966.
The Governor's Lady (first produced on West End at Aldwych Theatre, 1965), Methuen, 1968.
Belcher's Luck (first produced at Aldwych Theatre, 1966), Hill & Wang, 1967.
"In Two Minds" (also see below), broadcast by BBC-TV, 1967; stage adaptation first produced in London, 1973.
"The Parachute" (also see below), broadcast by BBC-TV, 1968.
"Let's Murder Vivaldi" (also see below), broadcast by BBC-TV, 1968; stage adaptation first produced in London at King's Head Theatre Club, 1972.

"On the Eve of Publication" (also see below), broadcast by BBC-TV, 1968.
(Contributor) Kenneth Tynan, *Oh! Calcutta!* (revue; first produced Off-Broadway at Eden Theatre, June 17, 1969; produced in London at Roundhouse Theatre, July 29, 1970), Grove, 1969.
After Haggerty (two-act; first produced at Aldwych Theatre, February 26, 1970), Methuen, 1970.
"The Cellar and the Almond Tree" (also see below), broadcast by BBC-TV, 1970.
"Emma's Time" (also see below), broadcast by BBC-TV, May 13, 1970.
Flint (two-act comedy; first produced on West End at Criterion Theatre, May 5, 1970; produced in Buffalo, N.Y., 1974), Methuen, 1970.
"White Poem," first produced in London at Institute of Contemporary Arts, 1970.
"Blood on the Table," first produced in London, 1971.
"The Bankrupt" (also see below), broadcast by BBC-TV, November 27, 1972.
"The Arcata Promise" (also see below), broadcast by Yorkshire Television, 1974.
Duck Song (first produced at Aldwych Theatre, February 5, 1974), Methuen, 1974.
"Huggy Bear" (also see below), broadcast by Yorkshire Television, 1976.
Cousin Vladimir [and] *Shooting the Chandelier* ("Cousin Vladimir" first produced at Aldwych Theatre, September 22, 1978), Methuen, 1978.
The Monster of Karlovy Vary [and] *Then and Now* ("Then and Now" first produced at Hampstead Theatre, London, May 21, 1979), Methuen, 1979.
"A Rod of Iron," broadcast by Yorkshire Television, 1980.
No Limits to Love (first produced in London at Warehouse Theatre, October 2, 1980, produced in New York at New Theater of Brooklyn, May, 1989), Methuen, 1981.

Also author of stage play "The Long Crawl through Time," 1965, and of television plays "You and Me and Him," "An Afternoon at the Festival," and "Barbara of the House of Grebe," all broadcast in 1973, and "Find Me," broadcast in 1974.

COLLECTED PLAYS

The Generations: A Trilogy of Plays (contains "Where the Difference Begins," "A Climate of Fear," and "The Birth of a Private Man"), J. Calder, 1964.
Three TV Comedies (contains "A Suitable Case for Treatment," "For Tea on Sunday," and "And Did Those Feet"), Calder & Boyars, 1966.
The Parachute and Two More TV Plays (contains "The Parachute," "Let's Murder Vivaldi," and "In Two Minds"), Calder & Boyars, 1967.
On the Eve of Publication and Other Plays, (contains "On the Eve of Publication," "Emma's Time," and "The Cellar and the Almond Tree"), Methuen, 1970.
The Bankrupt and Other Plays (contains "The Bankrupt," "You and Me and Him," "An Afternoon at the Festival," and "Find Me"), Methuen, 1974.
Huggy Bear and Other Plays (contains "Huggy Bear," "The Arcata Promise," and "A Superstition"), Methuen, 1977.
Collected TV Plays, Volume I (contains "Where the Difference Begins," "A Climate of Fear," "The Birth of a Private Man"), Volume II (contains "A Suitable Case for Treatment," "For Tea on Sunday," "And Did Those Feet," "Let's Murder Vivaldi," "In Two Minds," "The Parachute"), Riverrun Press, 1981.

SCREENPLAYS

"Morgan!" (based on his television play "A Suitable Case for Treatment"), Cinema V, 1966.

"Family Life" (based on his television play "In Two Minds"), Kestrel Films, 1971, released in America as "Wednesday's Child".

"A Doll's House" (based on the play by Henrik Ibsen), Reindeer Productions, 1972.

"Providence," Action Films, 1977, published as *Providence: Un film pour Alain Resnais,* translated by Claude Roy, Gallimard, 1977.

Also author of "Ninety Degrees in the Shade," 1965.

OTHER

(Contributor) *New Writers 3,* Calder, 1965.

(Author of introduction) *Leon Kossoff: Recent Paintings,* Whitechapel Art Gallery (London), 1972.

(Author of text) *Portrait of Adelaide,* drawings by Cedric Emanuel, Rigby, 1975.

Also author of a radio play, "Folie a Deux," 1974.

SIDELIGHTS: David Mercer was a prolific dramatist who wrote for theatre, film, and television. He was best known for his daring and original teleplays, which garnered him a reputation as a pioneering force in British television. Paul Madden observed in *Sight and Sound:* "[Mercer's] stage work may have enhanced his cultural respectability, but undoubtedly a larger part of his reputation must rest on his television plays, in their time startling and innovatory. . . . Through them it is possible to trace not only Mercer's growing stature as a (television) dramatist but also in microcosm a history of a particularly fertile period of British television drama, when taking risks was a *modus operandi,* elevated into an artistic principle."

Mercer's plays frequently are concerned with the effects of psychological and political disorientation. Mercer himself suffered a nervous breakdown in 1957, and began writing plays while receiving treatment at the British Institute for Psychoanalysis. Mercer's teleplay "A Suitable Case for Treatment" clearly reflects this period of his life, according to *Dictionary of Literary Biography* contributor Marianna Deeken. "Deeply rooted in Mercer's own past, the play expresses the conflict he felt between his political ideologies and his perceptions about the course of world affairs at the time of his own nervous breakdown, when the head of the British Institute for Psychoanalysis had pronounced him 'a suitable case for treatment.' " The teleplay is also viewed as evidence of Mercer's creative foresight. "In 'A Suitable Case for Treatment'. . .," wrote Madden, "Mercer was already looking forward to a TV drama that enjoyed the fluidity and freedom of film." "A Suitable Case for Treatment" won the Screenwriters Guild Award for best teleplay of 1962, and was adapted by Mercer into a film entitled "Morgan!," which won the British Film Academy award for best screenplay.

Mercer explores similar themes in his teleplay "In Two Minds," the story of a young girl's battle with schizophrenia. The teleplay represents the philosophy of psychiatrist R. D. Laing, who acted as consultant to the work. Mercer was impressed with the Laingian approach to therapy, and believed that Laing's assistance would help give the play the credibility and realism that Mercer demanded of his work. Like "A Suitable Case for Treatment," "In Two Minds" was named the best British teleplay of the year, and was also made into the film, "Family Life," for which Mercer wrote the screenplay.

In later years, Mercer's plays were "less stylistically adventurous," according to Deeken, "but he continued to explore the mind of man and his efforts to deal with the world and the people around him." Assessing Mercer's literary career, a London *Times* writer concluded: "Though [Mercer] could come through more surely in the relative freedom of television, his principal stage plays had often a pounding eloquence, as if wave upon wave were endeavoring—may be with less momentum in later life—to penetrate a barrier reef. . . . How they may appear to later generations is problematical; but Mercer during the 1960s and 1970s was certainly one of the powerful minds of his day."

BIOGRAPHICAL/CRITICAL SOURCES:

BOOKS

Contemporary Literary Criticism, Volume V, Gale, 1976.

Dictionary of Literary Biography, Volume XIII: *British Dramatists since World War II,* Gale, 1982.

Jarman, Francis, editor, *The Quality of Mercer: Bibliography of Writings by and about the Playwright Mercer,* Smoothie Publications (Brighton, England), 1974.

PERIODICALS

Christian Science Monitor, May 20, 1970, February 26, 1971.

Dun's Review, summer, 1970, autumn, 1977, January, 1980, winter, 1981.

Listener, December 19, 1968.

London Magazine, September, 1970.

Nation, July 6, 1970.

New Statesman, March 6, 1970.

New York Times, May 4, 1970, November 16, 1977, March 19, 1979, June 4, 1982, May 4, 1989.

Plays and Players, June, 1970.

Sight and Sound, autumn, 1981.

Spectator, May 16, 1970.

Times Literary Supplement, January 15, 1970, June 25, 1970, September 25, 1970.

Transatlantic Review, spring, summer, 1968.

Variety, March 11, 1970, February 24, 1971.

OBITUARIES:

PERIODICALS

New York Times, August 22, 1980.

Times (London), August 9, 1980.

*   *   *

MERCHANT, Paul
    See ELLISON, Harlan

*   *   *

MERLIN, Arthur
    See BLISH, James (Benjamin)

*   *   *

MERRIL, Judith 1923-
    (Ernest Hamilton, Rose Sharon, Eric Thorstein; Cyril Judd, a joint pseudonym)

PERSONAL: Name originally Josephine Judith Grossman; born January 21, 1923, in New York, N.Y.; daughter of Schlomo S. and Ethel (Hurwitch) Grossman; children: (first marriage) Merril Zissman (Mrs. Howard MacDonald); (second marriage) Ann

Pohl. *Education:* Attended City College (now City College of the City University of New York), 1939-40. *Politics:* "Favor world government." *Religion:* Jewish.

ADDRESSES: Office—c/o Toronto Public Libraries, 40 St. George St., Toronto, Ontario, Canada M55 2E4. *Agent*—Virginia Kidd, Box 278, Milford, Pa. 18337.

CAREER: Research assistant and ghostwriter, 1943-47; Bantam Books, New York, N.Y., editor, 1947-49; free-lance writer and editor, specializing in science fiction, 1949-68; free-lance writer, lecturer, broadcaster, and radio documentarist, 1971—. Teacher of professional fiction writing, Port Jervis (N.Y.) Adult Education Program, 1963-64; consultant, Rochdale College, 1968-69, Spaced Out Library (Toronto), 1970-73; lecturer in science fiction, University of Toronto, 1971-72; associate of department of humanities of science at Sir George Williams University, 1972—; visiting professor, Trent University, 1983; director or participant in a number of science fiction writers' workshops and conferences.

MEMBER: Science Fiction Research Association (founding member), Writers Union of Canada, Institute for 21st Century Studies (member of editorial board), Association of Canadian Television and Radio Actors, Voice of Women, Mensa, Hydra Club (founding member), 21 McGill Women's Club (Toronto; founding member), Elves, Gnomes and Little Men Chowder & Marching Society (honorary member), Witchdoctors' Club (New York; member of Witch's Auxiliary).

AWARDS, HONORS: B.A., Rochdale College, 1970; Canadian Science Fiction and Fantasy Award, 1983; Canada Council senior arts grant, 1984-85.

WRITINGS:

Shadow on the Hearth (novel), Doubleday, 1950.
(With others) *The Petrified Planet* (three short novels), Twayne, 1953.
The Tomorrow People (novel), Pyramid Books, 1960.
Out of Bounds (short stories), Pyramid Books, 1960.
(With others) *Six Great Short Science Fiction Novels,* Dell, 1960.
Daughters of Earth (three novellas), Gollancz, 1968, Doubleday, 1969.
(Author of introduction) *Path into the Unknown: The Best of Soviet Science Fiction,* Delacorte, 1968.
(Author of introduction) E. L. Ferman, editor, *Once and Future Tales: From the "Magazine of Fantasy and Science Fiction,"* Delphi Press, 1968.
Survival Ship and Other Stories, Kakabeka, 1973.
The Best of Judith Merril, Warner Books, 1976.
Daughters of the Earth, and Other Stories, McClelland & Stewart, 1986.

EDITOR

Shot in the Dark, Bantam, 1950.
Beyond Human Ken, Random House, 1952.
Human?, Lion Press, 1952.
Beyond the Barriers of Space and Time, Random House, 1954.
Galaxy of Ghouls, Lion Press, 1955, published as *Off the Beaten Orbit,* Pyramid Books, 1958.
The Year's Best Science Fiction, Volumes I-IV, Gnome Press, 1956-59, Volumes V-IX, Simon & Schuster, 1960-64, Volumes X-XII, Delacorte, 1965-68.
SF: The Best of the Best, Delacorte, 1967.
England Swings SF: Stories of Speculative Fiction, Doubleday, 1968 (published in England as *Space-Time Journal,* Granada, 1972).

Tesseracts, Press Porcepic, 1985.

Also editor of *Science Fiction Sukiyaki,* Bantam.

RADIO DOCUMENTARIES

"How to Think Science Fiction," 1971-72.
"Women of Japan," 1972.
"What Limits?," 1973.
"Growing Up in Japan," 1973.
"How to Face Doomsday without Really Dying," 1974.

WITH C. M. KORNBLUTH, UNDER JOINT PSEUDONYM CYRIL JUDD

Outpost Mars, Abelard, 1952, published as *Sin in Space,* Beacon, 1961 (first published in serial form as "Mars Child" in *Galaxy Science Fiction,* 1951).
Gunner Cade, Simon & Schuster, 1952 (serialized in *Astounding Science Fiction,* 1952).

OTHER

Work appears in over 20 anthologies. Short stories have appeared in sports, western, and detective magazines under pseudonyms Ernest Hamilton, Rose Sharon, and Eric Thorstein, in sixteen science fiction magazines in America, and in periodicals published in England, France, Mexico, Japan, and other countries; also translator of science fiction short stories from the Japanese. Contributor of short stories to *Toronto Star* and *New York Post.* Book editor and reviewer for *Magazine of Fantasy and Science Fiction,* 1959-69.

WORK IN PROGRESS: The Testaments, a novel.

SIDELIGHTS: Judith Merril's importance in the field of science fiction has as much to do with her prolific activities as an anthologist as it does with her own forward-looking short stories and novels. Beginning in 1950, Merril edited a wide-ranging series of collections, including a twelve-volume "best-of-the-year" annual starting in 1956. In an article on the author's *Beyond the Barriers of Space and Time* collection, *New York Times* critic J. Francis McComas asserts that Merril is a "peerless anthologist."

Merril's fiction has also drawn praise from critics, and she has been given credit for bringing realistic female characters and issues of concern to women into science fiction at a time when both were uncommon. Her collection of three brief novels, entitled *Daughters of Earth,* is described by Mary K. Chelton in *Library Journal* as "absorbing, well-structured science-fiction fare . . . unique because of [its] feminine focus." Merril explained that she settled on the science fiction genre because "it is closely concerned with the essential relationship between modern man and the modern environment." Writing in the Toronto *Globe and Mail,* Douglas Hill calls Merril "one of Canada's national resources" and describes *Daughters of the Earth, and Other Stories* as "an excellent introduction to a writer whose international reputation is high."

MEDIA ADAPTATIONS: Shadow on the Hearth was televised as "Atomic Attack" on "Motorola Playhouse," and the short story "Whoever You Are" was dramatized on CBC-Radio.

BIOGRAPHICAL/CRITICAL SOURCES:

PERIODICALS

Globe and Mail (Toronto), October 19, 1985, January 11, 1986, February 8, 1986.
Library Journal, October 15, 1969.
New York Times, September 7, 1952, October 12, 1952, December 12, 1952, December 21, 1954.

MERRILL, James (Ingram) 1926-

PERSONAL: Born March 3, 1926, in New York, N.Y.; son of Charles Edward (a stockbroker) and Hellen (Ingram) Merrill. *Education:* Amherst College, B.A., 1947.

ADDRESSES: Home—107 Water St., Stonington, Conn. 06378.

CAREER: Poet, novelist, and playwright. *Military service:* U.S. Army, 1944-45.

MEMBER: National Institute of Arts and Letters.

AWARDS, HONORS: Oscar Blumenthal Prize, 1947; *Poetry* magazine's Levinson Prize, 1949, and Harriet Monroe Memorial Prize, 1951; Morton Dauwen Zabel Memorial Prize, 1965, for "From the Cupola"; National Book Award in poetry, 1967, for *Nights and Days,* and 1979, for *Mirabell: Books of Number;* D.Litt., Amherst College, 1968; Bollingen Prize in Poetry, 1973; Pulitzer Prize, 1976, for *Divine Comedies;* nomination for National Book Critics Circle Award in poetry, 1980, for *Scripts for the Pageant;* National Book Critics Circle Award in poetry, and *Los Angeles Times* Book Award in poetry, both 1984, both for *The Changing Light at Sandover;* nomination for National Book Critics Circle Award in poetry, 1986, for *Late Settings;* named first Poet Laureate of Connecticut; Medal of Honor for Literature, National Arts Club, 1989.

WRITINGS:

POEMS

The Black Swan and Other Poems, Icarus (Athens), 1946.
First Poems, Knopf, 1951.
Short Stories (poems), Banyan Press (Pawlet, Vt.), 1954.
A Birthday Cake for David, Banyan Press, 1955.
The Country of a Thousand Years of Peace, Knopf, 1959, revised edition, Atheneum, 1970.
Selected Poems, Chatto & Windus, 1961.
Water Street, Atheneum, 1962.
Violent Pastoral, privately printed, 1965.
Nights and Days, Atheneum, 1966.
The Fire Screen, Atheneum, 1969.
Braving the Elements, Atheneum, 1972.
Two Poems: From the Cupola and the Summer People, Chatto & Windus, 1972.
Yannina, Phoenix Book Shop (New York), 1973.
The Yellow Pages: 59 Poems, Temple Bar Bookshop (Cambridge, Mass.), 1974.
Divine Comedies (includes "The Book of Ephraim"; also see below), Atheneum, 1976.
Metamorphosis of 741, Banyan Press, 1977.
Mirabell: Books of Number (published as "Mirabell's Books of Number" in *The Changing Light at Sandover;* also see below), Atheneum, 1978.
Ideas, etc., Jordan Davies, 1980.
Scripts for the Pageant (also see below), Atheneum, 1980.
The Changing Light at Sandover (contains "The Book of Ephraim," "Mirabell's Books of Number," "Scripts for the Pageant," and a new coda), Atheneum, 1982.
Marbled Paper, Seluzicki (Salem, Ore.), 1982.
Santorini: Stopping the Leak, Metacom Press (Worcester, Mass.), 1982.
From the First Nine: Poems 1946-1976, Atheneum, 1982.
Souvenirs, Nadja, 1984.
Bronze, Nadja, 1984.
Late Settings, Atheneum, 1985.
The Inner Room: Poems, Knopf, 1988.

CONTRIBUTOR TO ANTHOLOGIES

Poetry for Pleasure, edited by I. M. Parson, Doubleday, 1960.
Contemporary American Poetry, edited by Donald Hall, Penguin, 1962.
New Poets of England and America, edited by Hall, Meridian, 1962.
Poet's Choice, edited by Paul Engle and J. T. Langland, Dial, 1962.
Modern Poets, edited by J. M. Brinnin and Bill Read, McGraw, 1963.
Poems on Poetry, edited by Robert Wallace and J. G. Taaffe, Dutton, 1965.
Poems of Our Moment, edited by John Hollander, Pegasus, 1968.
New Yorker Book of Poems, Viking, 1970.

OTHER

Jim's Book: A Collection of Poems and Short Stories, privately printed, 1942.
"The Bait," produced in New York, 1953, published in *Artists Theatre: Four Plays,* edited by Herbert Machiz, Grove, 1960.
"The Immortal Husband," produced in New York, 1955, published in *Playbook: Plays for a New Theatre,* New Directions, 1956.
The Seraglio (novel), Knopf, 1957.
The (Diblos) Notebook (novel), Atheneum, 1965.
Recitative: Prose, North Point Press, 1988.

Contributor to periodicals, including *Hudson Review* and *Poetry.* Some of Merrill's poetry has been translated into Greek. Merrill's manuscripts are collected at Washington University in St. Louis.

SIDELIGHTS: Since his work first surfaced in 1951, James Merrill has been recognized as a master of poetic forms. He once explained in the *New York Review of Books* how he took "instinctively to quatrains, to octaves and sestets, when I began to write poems." His earliest works reflect the gentility of his upbringing as well as his eloquence and wit. But for all their technical virtuosity, the verses of *The Black Swan and Other Poems* (1946) and *First Poems* (1951) are largely static works, more concerned with objects than people. It was not until his themes became more dramatic and personal that he began to win serious attention and literary acclaim. Merrill received his first National Book Award for *Nights and Days* (1967), his second for *Mirabell: Books of Number* (1979). In the interim he won both the Bollingen Prize in Poetry (1973) and the Pulitzer Prize (1977), the latter for a book of occult poetry called *Divine Comedies.* Since then, he has also won the National Book Critics Circle Award for his visionary collection *The Changing Light of Sandover* (1982). Such critical recognition, however, has not insured his popular appeal. Frequently, those who recognize his name at all know him only as "the Ouija poet"—one who composes with assistance from the spirit world.

Born into a wealthy New York family, James Merrill was privately educated in schools that placed a good deal of emphasis on poetry. His interest in language was also fired by his governess—a Prussian/English widow called Mademoiselle who was fluent in both German and French. She taught young James that English was merely one way of expressing things, while his parents encouraged his early efforts at verse. (His first book of poems was privately printed by his father—co-founder of the famous stockbrokerage known as Merrill Lynch—during James's senior year at Lawrenceville.) When he was twelve, his parents divorced, his governess was discharged, and James was sent to boarding school. The diary he kept during a subsequent vacation to Silver Springs, Florida, included what, in retrospect, would prove to be a revealing entry: "Silver Springs—heavenly colors and swell fish."

Years later, in the *New York Review of Books,* Merrill explained how that statement reflected his feelings of loss and foreshadowed a major theme in his poetry. " 'Heavenly colors and swell fish.' What is that phrase but an attempt to bring my parents together, to remarry on the page their characteristic inflections—the ladylike gush and the regular-guy terseness? In reality my parents have tones more personal and complex than these, but the time is still far off when I can dream of echoing them. To do so, I see in retrospect, will involve a search for magical places real or invented, like Silver Springs or Sandover [an imaginary setting in his mystical trilogy *The Changing Light at Sandover*]. . . . By then, too, surrogate parents will enter the scene, figures more articulate than Mademoiselle but not unlike her, either, in the safe ease and mystery of their influence: Proust and Elizabeth Bishop; Maria [an old Athenian friend] and Auden in the Sandover books. The unities of home and world, and world and page, will be observed through the very act of transition from one to the other."

Such fusion of autobiography and archetype has become a hallmark of Merrill's verse, according to Andrew V. Ettin who writes in the *Perspective,* "The transformation of the natural, autobiographical, narrative events and tone into the magical, universal, sonorous, eternal is one of the principal characteristics of Merrill's poetry, perhaps the main source of its splendid and moving qualities." *Dictionary of Literary Biography* contributor William Spiegelman credits Merrill with discovering "what most lyric poets . . . have yet to find: a context for a life, a pattern for presenting autobiography in lyric verse through the mediation of myth and fable."

Influenced not only by events, but also by the act of writing, Merrill, "with increasing awareness, courage and delight, has been developing an autobiography: 'developing' as from a photographic negative which becomes increasingly clear," David Kalstone explains in the *Times Literary Supplement.* "He has not led the kind of outwardly dramatic life which would make external changes the centre of his poetry. Instead, poetry itself has been one of the changes, something which continually happens to him, and Merrill's subject proves to be the subject of the great Romantics: the constant revisions of the self that come through writing verse. Each book seems more spacious because of the one which has come before."

While Merrill's verse abounds with details from daily life, Joseph Parisi notes in *Poetry* that it "never reeks of ego." Or, as Helen Vendler puts it in the *New York Times Book Review,* the best of Merrill's poems "are autobiographical without being 'confessional': they show none of that urgency to reveal the untellable or unspeakable that we associate with the poetry we call 'confessional'. . . . It is as though a curtain had been drawn aside, and we are permitted a glimpse of . . . a life that goes on unconscious of us, with the narrator so perfectly an actor in his own drama that his presence as narrator is rendered transparent, invisible."

One of the ways Merrill achieves this stance is through the manipulation of meter and rhyme. "His mastery of forms, whether old or new, keeps his self revelatory poems (and some of them are painful) from the worst lapses of recent poets of the confessional school," X. J. Kennedy observes in the *Atlantic Monthly.* "Merrill never sprawls, never flails about, never strikes postures. Intuitively he knows that, as Yeats once pointed out, in poetry, 'all that is personal soon rots; it must be packed in ice or salt.' "

Because they both wrote mystical poems, Yeats and Merrill have often been compared. Like Yeats, whose wife was a medium, Merrill receives inspiration from the world beyond. His *Divine Comedies* features an affable ghost named Ephraim who instructs the poet, while Yeats's "A Vision" features the spirit Leo Africanus in a similar role. Critics find other influences at work in Merrill's poems as well, drawing parallels between his writing and the work of Dante (whose *Divine Comedy* was the inspiration for Merrill's title), W. H. Auden (who, like Merrill, believed that poems are constructed of words, not emotions), and Marcel Proust (who was also dismissed as a mere aesthete early in his career).

In a *Times Literary Supplement* review, David Kalstone further explains how Proust's vision colors Merrill's world. "When he turned to narrative and social comedy, it was always with the sense—Proust's sense—that the world discerned is not quite real, that in its flashing action he might catch glimpses of patterns activated by charged moments of his life." Spiegelman believes that as "an heir to Proust, Merrill achieves a scope in poetry comparable to that of the major novelists: his great themes are the recovery of time (in spite of loss) through willed or automatic memory, and the alternating erosions and bequests of erotic experience. He focuses on what is taken, what abides, in love and time, and considers how to handle them."

But in his early poems, these concerns seldom surface. The verse of *First Poems* and *The Country of a Thousand Years of Peace and Other Poems* (1959) strikes reviewers as needlessly obscure, devoid of human passion, and removed from actual life. In his *Babel to Byzantium,* James Dickey writes that to read such poems is "to enter a realm of connoisseurish aesthetic contemplation, where there are no things more serious than gardens (usually formal), dolls, swans, statues, works of art, operas, delightful places in Europe, the ancient gods in tasteful and thought-provoking array, more statues, many birds and public parks, and, always, 'the lovers,' wandering through it all as if they surely lived." Writing of this kind, continues Dickey, "has enough of [Henry] James's insistence upon manners and decorum to evoke a limited admiration for the taste, wit, and eloquence that such an attitude makes possible, and also enough to drive you mad over the needless artificiality, prim finickiness, and determined inconsequence of it all."

In 1959, when Merrill began spending six months of each year in Athens, his poetry took on some of the warmth and intimacy of the old Greek culture. And, as the poems became more personal, they also became more accessible, although their appeal was still limited, as Ian Hamilton explains. "Even though (with *Water Street* in 1962) he had toughened and colloquialized his verse line and eliminated much of the wan artifice that marked his very early work, there was still—in his usual persona—a delicate strain of yearning otherworldliness, a delicate discomfiture which was neither neurotic nor ideological. His was a poetry of, and for, the few—the few kindred spirits," Hamilton writes in the *Washington Post Book World.*

With each step he took away from rigid formalism, Merrill gained critical ground. Unwilling to restrict his choice and assembly of language, he nevertheless progressed toward a more conversational verse reminiscent of the structure of prose. "The flashes and glimpses of 'plot' in some of the lyrics—especially the longer poems—reminded Merrill's readers that he wanted more than the usual proportion of dailiness and detail in his lyrics, while preserving a language far from the plainness of journalistic poetry, a language full of arabesques, fancifulness, play of wit, and oblique metaphor," writes Helen Vendler in the *New York*

Review of Books. In fact, Merrill tried his hand at both plays and novels and considered writing his epic poem "The Book of Ephraim" as a prose narrative. He abandoned the idea, for reasons that he explains in the poem: "The more I struggled to be plain, the more / Mannerism hobbled me. What for? / Since it had never truly fit, why wear / The shoe of prose? In verse the feet went bare."

It was "The Book of Ephraim"—which appeared in *Divine Comedies*—that prompted many critics to reevaluate the poet. Among them was Harold Bloom, who wrote in the *New Republic:* "James Merrill . . . has convinced many discerning readers of a greatness, or something like it, in his first six volumes of verse, but until this year I remained a stubborn holdout. The publication of *Divine Comedies* . . . converts me, absolutely if belatedly, to Merrill. . . . The book's eight shorter poems surpass nearly all the earlier Merrill, but its apocalypse (a lesser word won't do) is a 100-page verse-tale, 'The Book of Ephraim,' an occult splendor in which Merrill rivals Yeats' 'A Vision,' . . . and even some aspects of Proust."

William Spiegelman agrees. Describing *Divine Comedies* as "Merrill's supreme fiction, a self-mythologizing within an epic program," he observes in the *Dictionary of Literary Biography:* "At last Merrill's masters combine with graceful fluency in a confection entirely his own: the reader finds Proust's social world, his analysis of the human heart and the artist's growth; Dante's encyclopedia of a vast universal organization; and Yeats's spiritualism, for which the hints in the earlier volumes gave only small promise. Added to these are the offhand humor of Lord Byron and W. H. Auden, a Neoplatonic theory of reincarnation, a self-reflexiveness about the process of composition, and a virtual handbook of poetic technique. 'The Book of Ephraim,' the volume's long poem, is chapter one of Merrill's central statement."

The two volumes that follow—*Mirabell: Books of Number* (1978) and *Scripts for the Pageant* (1980)—continue the narrative that "The Book of Ephraim" begins. Together these three poems form a trilogy that was published with a new coda in *The Changing Light at Sandover* (1983). This unprecedented 560-page epic records the Ouija board sessions that Merrill and David Jackson, his lifelong companion, conducted with spirits from the other world.

Appropriately, Merrill has organized each section of the trilogy to reflect a different component of their homemade Ouija board. The twenty-six sections of "The Book of Ephraim" correspond to the board's A to Z alphabet, the ten sections of *Mirabell: Books of Number* correspond to the board's numberings from 0 to 9, and the three sections of *Scripts for the Pageant* ("Yes," "&," and "No") correspond to the board's Yes & No. The progression of poems also represents a kind of celestial hierarchy, with each book representing communication with a higher order of spirits than the one before. (Humans in the poem are identified by their initials—DJ and JM; spirits speak in all capitals.) By the time Merrill transcribes the lessons of the archangels in book three, he has been offered nothing less than a model of the universe. "Were such information conveyed to us by a carnival 'spiritual adviser,' we could dismiss it as mere nonsense," observes Fred Moramarco in the *Los Angeles Times Book Review,* "but as it comes from a poet of Merrill's extraordinary poetic and intellectual gifts, we sit up and take notice."

In the first book, Merrill's guide is Ephraim, "a Greek Jew Born AD 8 at XANTHOS," later identified as "Our Familiar Spirit." Over a period of twenty years and in a variety of settings, Ephraim alerts DJ and JM to certain cosmic truths, including

the fact that "on Earth / We're each the REPRESENTATIVE of a PATRON" who guides our souls through the nine stages of being until we become patrons for other souls. Witty, refined, full of gossip, Ephraim is "a clear cousin to Merrill's poetic voice," Kalstone says in the *Times Literary Supplement.*

Other spirits also appear in the poem, many of them family members or old friends who have died: Merrill's mother and father, the young poet Hans Lodeizen (whose death Merrill addressed in *The Country of a Thousand Years of Peace*), the Athenian Maria Mitsotaki (a green-thumbed gardener who died of cancer), as well as literary figures such as W. H. Auden and Plato. They form a community, according to Ephraim, "WITHIN SIGHT OF & ALL CONNECTED TO EACH OTHER DEAD OR ALIVE NOW DO YOU UNDERSTAND WHAT HEAVEN IS IT IS THE SURROUND OF THE LIVING." As Helen Vendler explains in the *New York Review of Books,* "The host receives his visible and invisible guests, convinced that . . . the poet's paradise is nothing other than all those beings whom he has known and has imagined." For this reason, Vendler maintains that "The Book of Ephraim" is "centrally a hymn to history and a meditation on memory—personal history and personal memory, which are, for this poet at least, the muse's materials."

Aware of the incredulity his spiritualism will provoke, Merrill addresses this issue early in book one: "The question / Of who or what we took Ephraim to be / And of what truths (if any) we considered / Him spokesman, had arisen from the start." Indeed, Vendler says, "for rationalists reading the poem, Merrill includes a good deal of self-protective irony, even incorporating in the tale a visit to his ex-shrink, who proclaims the evocation of Ephraim and the other Ouija 'guests' from the other world a *folie a deux* [mutual madness] between Merrill and his friend David Jackson."

In a *Poetry* review, Joseph Parisi suggests that Merrill uses "his own doubt and hesitation to undercut and simultaneously to underscore his seriousness in recounting his fabulous . . . message. Anticipating the incredulity of 'sophisticated' and even cynical readers, the poet portrays his own apparent skepticism at these tales from the spirit world to preempt and disarm the attacks, while making the reader feel he is learning the quasi-occult truths . . . along with the poet."

As the experience proceeds, Merrill's skepticism declines. And while the reader's may not, Judith Moffett suggests in the *American Poetry Review* that disbelief is not the issue: "Surely any literary work ought to be judged not on its matter but on the way the matter is presented and treated. . . . The critical question, then, should be not *Is this the story he ought to have told?* but *How well has he told* this *story?*" Moffett, as well as numerous other critics, believes Merrill has told it very well: "'The Book of Ephraim' is a genuinely great poem—a phrase no one should use lightly—and very possibly the most impressive poetic endeavor in English in this century."

In book two, Ephraim is overshadowed by a band of bat-like creatures who "SPEAK FROM WITHIN THE ATOM," demanding "POEMS OF SCIENCE" from JM. These are the fallen angels whose task is now to mind the machinery put in motion by God Biology, whose enemy is Chaos. Their request appears on the board: "FIND US BETTER PHRASES FOR THESE HISTORIES WE POUR FORTH HOPING AGAINST HOPE THAT MAN WILL LOVE HIS MIND & LANGUAGE." As poet, Merrill serves as a vehicle for divine revelation, and, by tapping his "word bank," the bats can combat Chaos. They explain: "THE SCRIBE SHALL / SUPPLANT

RELIGION, & THE ENTIRE APPARATUS / DEVELOP THE WAY TO PARADISE." (At another point, Merrill learns that he was chosen to receive this vision in part because of his homosexuality: he will devote his energies not to children, but to art.)

God Biology's chief messenger is a spirit initially identified as 741, who Merrill names Mirabell. Mirabell warns of the two major threats to man's existence: overpopulation and nuclear power. In passages that almost all critics consider elitist, Mirabell explains that there are only two million enlightened souls in the world. The rest are inferior animal souls who reproduce prolifically and into whose hands atomic weaponry now threatens to fall. Too little given to reason and restraint, these souls allow Chaos to gain ground.

While acknowledging that "one can see the intricate rationale of such statements in the context of *Mirabell*'s general themes," Joseph Parisi maintains that readers "may be uncomfortable with the elitism which is implicit, and ultimately counterproductive, if indeed the poem pretends to enlighten and to teach. . . . For all the charm of *Mirabell*'s small circle of friends, some may be put off by their blithe air of superiority, as others may be by the High Tea (not to mention Camp) atmosphere of the Heavenly get-togethers." Stephen Spender agrees, pointing out in the *New York Review of Books* that "this reader sometimes feels that Merrill's heaven is a tea party to which he is not likely to be invited because he will not understand the 'in' jokes." Remarks Moffett: "By portraying intelligent poetic and musical gays as the evolutionary creme de la creme, Merrill makes himself vulnerable to charges of narcissism; the same could be said of passages in which heaven lavishes praise upon its spokesmen." But, "to be fair," says Edmund White, "I should point out that the fault lies not in Merrill, but in his bats; they are the ones who portray the hierarchical system. He is merely their scribe."

One of the duties of the bats, Merrill explains in the *Kenyon Review,* is to prepare him and David for "a seminar with the angels—whose 25 lessons are in fact the marrow of the third volume." While the poet here confronts essential questions about the mystery of creation, the structure of the universe, and the fate of man, some critics find the final message of *Scripts for the Pageant* in its organizing principle, "Yes & No." Charles Molesworth explains in the *New Republic* that "taken serially, these three words form irreducible language acts, namely assertion, qualification, and denial. Taken all together, they form the essence of equivocation, which can be seen as either the fullest sort of language act or the very subversion of language." By characterizing his acceptance of the spirits' wisdom in terms of "Yes & No," Merrill "transforms the poem into a hymn celebrating, among other things, 'resistance' as 'Nature's gift to man,' " Mary Jo Salter writes in the *Atlantic Monthly.* As the myth is reappraised and corrected by the characters who are themselves a part of it, Salter believes that " 'Yes & No' becomes an answer to every question: not an equivocation of authorial (or divine) responsibility, but an acknowledgement that 'fact is fable,' that the question of man's future, if any, is one he must answer for himself."

By the time *Scripts for the Pageant* ends, Merrill has made clear his vision of the self as a story that unfolds over time. During one lesson, the angels discuss two previous races of creatures who were destroyed. Afterwards, Merrill, to use Molesworth's words, "advances a set of parallels between the account of the two earlier races and his own childhood, as he was preceded by two siblings and his parents divorced while he was still a child. Autobi-

ography and creation myth: by hinting they're the same Merrill deals with a key modernist, and a key American theme."

Molesworth concludes that "five years ago, Merrill hoped to be measured by Auden and Stevens; now his work asks comparison with that of Yeats and Blake, if not Milton and Dante. But the clearest analogue may be that of Byron, who, desiring a scale both intimate and grand, yet wanting a hero, decided to fill the role himself."

MEDIA ADAPTATIONS: The Changing Light at Sandover was adapted into a dramatic poetry reading entitled "Voices from Sandover," first staged at Harvard's Hasty Pudding Theater, with later performances at UCLA's Schoenberg Hall and the Guggenheim Museum in New York.

BIOGRAPHICAL/CRITICAL SOURCES:

BOOKS

Contemporary Literary Criticism, Gale, Volume 2, 1974, Volume 3, 1975, Volume 6, 1976, Volume 8, 1978, Volume 13, 1980, Volume 18, 1981, Volume 34, 1985.
Contemporary Poets, St. James Press/St. Martin's, 1985.
Dickey, James, *Babel to Byzantium,* Farrar, Straus, 1968.
Dictionary of Literary Biography, Volume 5: *American Poets Since World War II,* Gale, 1980.
Dictionary of Literary Biography Yearbook: 1985, Gale, 1986.
Kalstone, David, *Five Temperaments: Elizabeth Bishop, Robert Lowell, James Merrill, Adrienne Rich, John Ashbery,* Oxford University Press, 1977.
Lehman, David and Charles Berger, editors, *James Merrill: Essays in Criticism,* Cornell University Press, 1982.
Merrill, James, *The Changing Light at Sandover,* Atheneum, 1982.

PERIODICALS

American Book Collector, November-December, 1983.
American Poetry Review, September-October, 1979.
Atlantic Monthly, March, 1973, October, 1980.
Chicago Tribune Book World, December 17, 1978, April 24, 1983.
Georgia Review, fall, 1979.
Los Angeles Times Book Review, February 13, 1983, October 25, 1987.
New Leader, December 4, 1978.
New Republic, June 5, 1976, November 20, 1976, July 26, 1980.
Newsweek, February 28, 1983, August 26, 1985.
New York Review of Books, May 6, 1971, September 20, 1973, March 18, 1976, December 21, 1978, May 3, 1979, February 21, 1982.
New York Times, January 29, 1983, May 29, 1985.
New York Times Book Review, September 24, 1972, March 21, 1976, April 4, 1976, April 29, 1979, June 15, 1980, March 13, 1983, November 12, 1989.
Partisan Review, winter, 1967.
Perspective, spring, 1967.
Poetry, June, 1973, October, 1976, December 1979.
Saturday Review, December 2, 1972.
Shenandoah, summer, 1976, fall, 1976.
Time, April 26, 1976, June 25, 1979.
Times Literary Supplement, September 29, 1972, October 28, 1977, January 18, 1980, February 7, 1986.
Voice Literary Supplement, March, 1983.
Washington Post, November 18, 1986.
Washington Post Book World, July 6, 1980, March 27, 1983, July 28, 1985.
Yale Review, winter, 1971, spring, 1975.

MERRIMAN, Alex
　See SILVERBERG, Robert

*　　*　　*

MERTON, Thomas   1915-1968
　(Father M. Louis)

PERSONAL: One source cites name as Tom Feverel Merton; born January 31, 1915, in Prades, Pyrennes-Orientales, France; brought to United States, 1916; returned to France, 1925; came to United States, 1939; naturalized, 1951; accidentally electrocuted in Bangkok, Thailand, December 10, 1968; buried in monastic cemetery at Abbey of Our Lady of Gethsemani, near Bardstown, Ky.; son of Owen Heathcote (an artist) and Ruth (an artist; maiden name, Jenkins) Merton. *Education:* Attended Clare College, Cambridge, 1933-34; Columbia University, B.A., 1938, M.A., 1939. *Politics:* "No party; generally liberal." *Religion:* Roman Catholic.

ADDRESSES: Home—Abbey of Our Lady of Gethsemani, Trappist, Ky. 40073.

CAREER: Roman Catholic monk of Cistercians of the Strict Observance (Trappists); name in religion, Father M. Louis; Abbey of Our Lady of Gethsemani, near Bardstown, Ky., 1941-68, ordained priest, 1949, master of scholastics, 1951-55, monastic forester, beginning 1951, novice master, 1955-65, lived as a hermit on grounds of monastery, 1965-68. Instructor in English, Columbia University Extension Division, New York, N.Y., 1938-39; instructor in English, St. Bonaventure University, Allegany, N.Y., 1939-41. Drawings have been exhibited in Louisville, Ky., St. Louis, Mo., New Orleans, La., Milwaukee, Wis., and Santa Barbara, Calif., 1964-65.

MEMBER: Fellowship of Reconciliation.

AWARDS, HONORS: Mariana Griswold Van Rensselaer Award, 1939; citation from Literary Awards Committee of the Catholic Press Association of the United States, 1948, for *Figures for an Apocalypse;* Catholic Literary Award from the Gallery of Living Catholic Authors, 1949, for *The Seven Storey Mountain;* Catholic Writers Guild Golden Book Award for the best spiritual book by an American writer, 1951, for *The Ascent to Truth;* Columbia University Medal for Excellence, 1961; LL.D., University of Kentucky, 1963; Pax Medal, 1963.

WRITINGS:

POETRY

Thirty Poems (also see below), New Directions, 1944.
A Man in the Divided Sea (includes poems from *Thirty Poems*), New Directions, 1946.
Figures for an Apocalypse (also contains an essay), New Directions, 1948.
The Tears of Blind Lions, New Directions, 1949.
Selected Poems of Thomas Merton, Hollis & Carter (London), 1950.
The Strange Islands: Poems (includes "The Tower of Babel" [also see below]), New Directions, 1957.
Selected Poems of Thomas Merton, New Directions, 1959, revised edition, 1967.
Emblems of a Season of Fury (also contains some prose and Merton's translations of other poets), New Directions, 1963.
Cables to the Ace; or, Familiar Liturgies of Misunderstanding, New Directions, 1968, reprinted, Unicorn Press (Greensboro, N.C.), 1986.
Landscape, Prophet and Wild-Dog, [Syracuse, N.Y.], 1968.
The Geography of Lograire, New Directions, 1969.

Early Poems: 1940-42, Anvil Press (Lexington, Ky.), 1972.
He Is Risen: Selections from Thomas Merton, Argus Communications, 1975.
The Collected Poems of Thomas Merton, New Directions, 1977.

ESSAYS

What Is Contemplation? (also see below), Saint Mary's College, Notre Dame (Holy Cross, Ind.), 1948, revised edition, Templegate (Springfield, Ill.), 1981.
Seeds of Contemplation, New Directions, 1949, revised edition, 1949, reprinted, 1986, revised and expanded edition published as *New Seeds of Contemplation,* 1962.
The Ascent to the Truth, Harcourt, 1951, reprinted, 1981.
Bread in the Wilderness, New Directions, 1953, reprinted, Fortress Press (Philadelphia, Pa.), 1986.
No Man Is an Island, Harcourt, 1955, reprinted, Octagon Books, 1983.
The Living Bread, Farrar, Straus, 1956, reprinted, 1980.
Praying the Psalms, Liturgical Press (Collegeville, Minn.), 1956, published as *The Psalms Are Our Prayer,* Burns & Oates, 1957, published as *Thomas Merton on the Psalms,* Sheldon Press (London), 1970.
The Silent Life, Farrar, Straus, 1957, reprinted, Peter Smith, 1983.
Thoughts in Solitude, Farrar, Straus, 1958, reprinted, Peter Smith, 1983.
The Christmas Sermons of Bl. Guerric of Igny (essay), Abbey of Our Lady of Gethsemani, 1959.
Spiritual Direction and Meditation [also see below], Liturgical Press, 1960.
Disputed Questions (also see below), Farrar, Straus, 1960, reprinted, Harcourt, 1985.
The Behavior of Titans (also includes prose poems and "Prometheus: A Meditation" [also see below]), New Directions, 1961.
The New Man, Farrar, Straus, 1962, reprinted, Peter Smith, 1983.
Life and Holiness, Herder & Herder, 1963.
Seeds of Destruction (also includes several letters), Farrar, Straus, 1964, reprinted, Peter Smith, 1983, abridged edition published as *Redeeming the Time,* Burns & Oates, 1966.
Seasons of Celebration, Farrar, Straus, 1965, reprinted, Peter Smith, 1983, published as *Meditations on Liturgy,* Mowbrays (London), 1976.
Mystics and Zen Masters (includes "The Ox Mountain Parable of Meng Tzu" [also see below]), Farrar, Straus, 1967.
Zen and the Birds of Appetite, New Directions, 1968.
Faith and Violence: Christian Teaching and Christian Practice, University of Notre Dame Press, 1968.
The Climate of Monastic Prayer, Cistercian Publications, 1969, published as *Contemplative Prayer,* Herder & Herder, 1969.
True Solitude: Selections from the Writings of Thomas Merton, Hallmark Editions (Kansas City, Mo.), 1969.
Three Essays, Unicorn Press, 1969.
Opening the Bible, Liturgical Press, 1970, revised edition, 1983.
Contemplation in a World of Action, Doubleday, 1971.
The Zen Revival, Buddhist Society (London), 1971.
Thomas Merton on Peace, McCall Publishing Co., 1971, revised edition published as *The Nonviolent Alternative,* edited and with an introduction by Gordon C. Zahn, Farrar, Straus, 1980.
Spiritual Direction and Meditation; and, What Is Contemplation?, A. Clarke (Westhampstead), 1975.
Thomas Merton on Zen, Sheldon Press (London), 1976.

The Power and Meaning of Love (includes six essays originally published in *Disputed Questions*), Sheldon Press, 1976.

Ishi Means Man: Essays on Native Americans, foreword by Dorothy Day, Unicorn Press, 1976.

The Monastic Journey, edited by Patrick Hart, Sheed, Andrews & McMeel, 1977.

Love and Living, edited by Naomi Burton Stone and Patrick Hart, Farrar, Straus, 1979.

Thomas Merton on St. Bernard, Cistercian Publications, 1980.

The Literary Essays of Thomas Merton, edited by Patrick Hart, New Directions, 1981.

AUTOBIOGRAPHIES

The Seven Storey Mountain, Harcourt, 1948, reprinted, Walker, 1985, abridged edition published as *Elected Silence: The Autobiography of Thomas Merton,* with introduction by Evelyn Waugh, Hollis & Carter, 1949.

The Sign of Jonas (journal), Harcourt, 1953, reprinted, Octagon Books, 1983.

The Secular Journal of Thomas Merton, Farrar, Straus, 1959, reprinted, Peter Smith, 1983.

Conjectures of a Guilty Bystander (journal), Doubleday, 1966, 2nd edition, Sheldon Press (London), 1977.

The Asian Journal of Thomas Merton, edited by Naomi Burton Stone, Patrick Hart, and James Laughlin, New Directions, 1973.

Woods, Shore, Desert: A Notebook, May, 1968, with photographs by Merton, Museum of New Mexico Press, 1982.

BIOGRAPHIES

Exile Ends in Glory: The Life of a Trappistine, Mother M. Berchmans, O.C.S.O., Bruce (Milwaukee), 1948.

What Are These Wounds?: The Life of a Cistercian Mystic, Saint Lutgarde of Aywieres, Clonmore & Reynolds (Dublin), 1949, Bruce, 1950.

The Last of the Fathers: Saint Bernard of Clairvaux and the Encyclical Letter "Doctor Mellifluus," Harcourt, 1954, reprinted, 1981.

LETTERS

Six Letters: Boris Pasternak, Thomas Merton, edited by Naomi Burton Stone, King Library Press, University of Kentucky, 1973.

(With Robert Lax) *A Catch of Anti-Letters,* Sheed, Andrews & McMeel, 1978.

Letters from Tom: A Selection of Letters from Father Thomas Merton, Monk of Gethsemani to W. H. Ferry, 1961-1968, edited by W. H. Ferry, Fort Hill Press (Scarsdale, N.Y.), 1983.

The Hidden Ground of Love: The Letters of Thomas Merton on Religious Experience and Social Concerns, selected and edited by William H. Shannon, Farrar, Straus, 1985.

LYRICIST

Four Freedom Songs, G.I.A. Publications (Chicago), 1968.

The Niles-Merton Songs: Opus 171 and 172, Mark Foster Museum, 1981.

EDITOR

What Ought I Do?: Sayings of the Desert Fathers, Stamperia del Santuccio (Lexington, Ky.), 1959, revised and expanded edition published as *The Wisdom of the Desert Fathers of the Fourth Century,* New Directions, 1961.

The Ox Mountain Parable of Meng Tzu, Stamperia del Santuccio, 1960.

(And contributor and author of introduction) *Break-through to Peace: Twelve Views on the Threat of Thermonuclear Extermination,* New Directions, 1962.

(And author of introduction) Mohandas Gandhi, *Gandhi on Non-violence: Selected Texts from Gandhi's "Non-violence in Peace and War,"* New Directions, 1965.

(And author of introductory essays) *The Way of Chuang Tzu,* New Directions, 1965.

(And author of introduction and commentary) Albert Camus, *The Plague,* Seabury Press, 1968.

TRANSLATOR

(From the French) Jean-Baptiste Chautard, *The Soul of the Apostolate,* Abbey of Our Lady of Gethsemani, 1946, new edition with introduction by Merton, Image Books, 1961.

(From the French) Saint John Eudes, *The Life and the Kingdom of Jesus in Christian Souls for the Use by Clergy or Laity,* P. J. Kennedy & Sons, 1946.

(And author of commentary) *The Spirit of Simplicity Characteristic of the Cistercian Order: An Official Report, Demanded and Approved by the General Chapter Together with Texts from St. Bernard Clairvaux on Interior Simplicity,* Abbey of Our Lady of Gethsemani, 1948.

(And author of preface) Cassiodorus, *A Prayer from the Treatise 'De anima,'* Stanbrook Abbey Press (Worcester, England), 1956.

(And author of explanatory essay) Clement of Alexandria, *Selections from the Protreptikos,* New Directions, 1963.

(From the Latin and author of introduction) Guigo I, *The Solitary Life: A Letter from Guigo,* Stanbrook Abbey Press, 1963, published as *On the Solitary Life,* Banyan Press (Pawlet, Vt.), 1977.

(From the Spanish with others) Nicanor Parra, *Poems and Antipoems,* edited by Miller Williams, New Directions, 1967.

Pablo Antonio Cuadra, *El jaguar y la luna/The Jaguar and the Moon* (bilingual edition), Unicorn Press (Greensboro, N.C.), 1974.

ILLUSTRATOR

A Hidden Wholeness: The Visual World of Thomas Merton, edited by John Howard Griffin, Houghton, 1970.

Geography of Holiness: The Photography of Thomas Merton, edited by Deba Prasad Patnaik, Pilgrim Press, 1980.

CONTRIBUTOR

Selden Rodman, editor, *New Anthology of Modern Poetry,* revised edition, Modern Library, 1946.

James E. Tobin, compiler, *The Happy Crusaders,* McMullen Books, 1952.

Fallon Evans, compiler, *J. F. Powers,* Herder & Herder, 1968.

OTHER

Cistercian Contemplatives: Monks of the Strict Observance at Our Lady of Gethsemani, Kentucky, Our Lady of the Holy Ghost, Georgia, Our Lady of the Holy Trinity, Utah—A Guide to the Trappist Life, Abbey of Our Lady of Gethsemani, 1948.

Gethsemani Magnificat: Centenary of Gethsemani Abbey, Abbey of Our Lady of Gethsemani, 1949.

The Waters of Siloe (history), Harcourt, 1949, reprinted, 1979, revised edition published as *The Waters of Silence,* Hollis & Carter, 1950, deluxe limited edition, Theodore Brun Limited, 1950.

Silence in Heaven: A Book of the Monastic Life, Studio Publications and Crowell, 1956.

The Tower of Babel (a morality play in two acts), [Hamburg], 1957, New Directions, 1958.

Monastic Peace, Abbey of Our Lady of Gethsemani, 1958.

Hagia Sophia (prose poems), Stamperia del Santuccio, 1962.

A Thomas Merton Reader, edited by Thomas P. McDonnell, Harcourt, 1962, revised and enlarged edition, Image Books, 1974.

Original Child Bomb: Points for Meditation to Be Scratched on the Walls of a Cave (prose poem), New Directions, 1962, reprinted, Unicorn Press, 1983.

Come to the Mountain: New Ways and Living Traditions in the Monastic Life, Saint Benedict's Cistercian Monastery (Snowmass, Colo.), 1964.

The Poorer Means: A Meditation on Ways to Unity, Abbey of Our Lady of Gethsemani, 1965.

Gethsemani: A Life of Praise, Abbey of Our Lady of Gethsemani, 1966.

(Author of introductory essay) George A. Panichas, editor, *Mansions of the Spirit: Essays in Religion and Literature,* Hawthorn, 1967.

Christ in the Desert, Monastery of Christ in the Desert (Abiquiu, N.M.), 1968.

My Argument with the Gestapo: A Macaronic Journal (novel), Doubleday, 1969.

Cistercian Life, Cistercian Book Service (Spenser, Mass.), 1974.

Introductions East and West: The Foreign Prefaces of Thomas Merton, edited by Robert E. Daggy, Unicorn Press, 1981.

Blaze of Recognition: Through the Year with Thomas Merton; Daily Meditations, selected and edited by Thomas P. McDonnell, with illustrations by Merton, Doubleday, 1983, published as *Through the Year with Thomas Merton: Daily Meditations from His Writings,* Image Books, 1985.

Also author of numerous shorter works and pamphlets, including "A Balanced Life of Prayer," 1951, "Basic Principles of Monastic Spirituality," 1957, "Prometheus: A Meditation," 1958, "Nativity Kerygma," 1958, "Monastic Vocation and the Background of Modern Secular Thought," 1964, and "Notes on the Future of Monasticism," 1968. Contributor of book reviews, articles, and poetry to the *New York Herald Tribune, New York Times Book Review, Commonweal, Catholic World,* and *Catholic Worker.* Editor, *Monks Pond* (quarterly), 1968.

SIDELIGHTS: An exact definition of who Thomas Merton was and what the significance of his work is seems elusive. In *The Seven Mountains of Thomas Merton,* Michael Mott called Merton a "poet, writer, activist, contemplative, . . . reformer of monastic life, artist, [and] bridge between Western and Eastern religious thought." In the *New York Times Book Review,* however, Mott admitted to D. J. R. Brucker that he "was never able to categorize [Merton]. The breadth and freshness of his interests [were] simply amazing."

Paradox is perhaps the word that best summarizes Merton's life and works. In a *Publishers Weekly* interview with Ellen Mangin, for example, Mott noted that although Merton had been a contemplative who led a life dedicated to meditation, Mott was able to write a nearly 600-page biography on him. Not only was Merton a contemplative, but he was also a Trappist, a member of a branch of Roman Catholic monks known for their severely simple living conditions and their vow of silence in which all conversation is forbidden. Merton's accomplishments as an author were even more amazing considering that when he entered the Trappist monastery in Kentucky in 1941, the monks were allowed to write only two half-page letters four times a year and nothing more.

In the *Dictionary of Literary Biography,* Victor A. Kramer also commented on the contradictory aspects of Merton's life and work, observing that "Merton's dual career as a cloistered monk and prolific writer, a career of silence yet one which allowed him to speak to thousands of readers world wide, was a paradox." The significance of this ambivalent need in Merton for both silence and fellowship with the people outside the monastery walls "was a source of anxiety to Merton himself," stated Ross Labrie in the *Dictionary of Literary Biography Yearbook.* But according to Labrie, "it is one of the strongest centers of excitement in approaching his work as well as being one of the clearest ways to see his role in twentieth-century letters." James Thomas Baker agreed that the dichotomy of monk/writer in Merton's personality was an essential ingredient in his writing. As Baker stated in *Thomas Merton: Social Critic,* "There was . . . an oriental paradox about his life and thought, the paradox of a monk speaking to the world, which gave it the quality that was uniquely Merton, and any other career would have robbed his work of that quality."

Due to the abundant autobiographical material Merton produced (at his death, he left 800,000 words of unpublished writings—mainly journals and letters), we know a great deal about how Merton dealt with the anxiety produced by his paradoxical desire to be both a contemplative and a social activist. Mott's research revealed that by 1940 Merton was actually keeping two sets of journals, private journals handwritten in bound notebooks and edited typewritten journals that he showed to others. Although not a journal, *The Seven Storey Mountain,* an autobiography Merton published in 1948 when he was only thirty-three years old, is probably the book for which he is best remembered. It was an instant success, selling 6,000 copies in the first month of publication and nearly 300,000 copies the first year.

Even before its publication, *The Seven Storey Mountain* had caused considerable excitement for its publisher. Looking for recommendations to print on the book's jacket, Robert Giroux (Merton's editor) sent galley proofs to Evelyn Waugh, Graham Greene, and Clare Boothe Luce for their opinions. According to Mott, Waugh said *The Seven Storey Mountain* "may well prove to be of permanent interest in the history of religious experience." Greene wrote that the autobiography had "a pattern and meaning valid for all of us." And Clare Boothe Luce declared, "It is to a book like this that men will turn a hundred years from now to find out what went on in the heart of men in this cruel century." These enthusiastic replies led Harcourt, Brace & Co. to increase the first printing order from five thousand to twenty thousand copies and then order a second printing even before the official publication date.

Post-publication reviewers admired *The Seven Storey Mountain* as well. In *Catholic World,* F. X. Connolly noted: "The book is bracing in its realism, sincere, direct and challenging. . . . *The Seven Storey Mountain* is a prolonged prayer as well as a great book." Commenting in the *New York Herald Tribune Weekly Book Review,* George Shuster wrote: "The fervor of [Merton's] progress to the monastery of Gethsemani is deeply moving. It is a difficult matter to write about, but I think there will be many who, however alien the experience may remain to them personally, will put the narrative down with wonder and respect." George Miles observed in a *Commonweal* review that "the book is written simply; the sensory images of boyhood are wonderful, and the incisive quality of his criticism, that tartness of his humor have not been sentimentalized by Merton's entry into a monastery. . . . 'The Seven Storey Mountain' is a book that deeply impresses the mind and the heart for days. It fills one with love and hope."

Reviewers and readers were moved by the intriguing story of Merton's undisciplined youth, conversion to Catholicism, and subsequent entry into the Trappist monastery. "With publication of his autobiography," noted Kenneth L. Woodward in *Newsweek,* "Merton became a cult figure among pious Catholics." According to Edward Rice in his biography of Merton, *The Man in the Sycamore Tree: The Good Times and Hard Life of Thomas Merton, An Entertainment,* "[the book] was forceful enough to cause a quiet revolution among American Catholics, and then among people of many beliefs throughout the world." A *Time* writer reported that "under its spell disillusioned veterans, students, even teen-agers flocked to monasteries across the country either to stay or visit as retreatants." As Richard Kostelanetz observed in the *New York Times Book Review,* "[Merton's] example made credible an extreme religious option that would strike many as unthinkable."

Rice theorized that the success of *The Seven Storey Mountain* was not only due to interest in Merton's story but also to the way the events in his life reflected the feelings of a whole society recovering from the shock of a world war. Explained Rice: "What [made *The Seven Storey Mountain*] different from [other books like it was] its great evocation of a young man in an age when the soul of mankind had been laid open as never before during world depression and unrest and the rise of both Communism and Fascism. . . . It became a symbol and a guide to the plight of the contemporary world, touching Catholics and non-Catholics alike in their deep, alienated unconsciousness."

The popularity of the book brought money to the Abbey of Gethsemani that was used for much-needed improvements and expansion. As Rice noted, however, it also "catapulted Merton into the eyes of the world," making a celebrity of a man who wanted to live in solitude. Mott wrote: "Without the publication of this . . . autobiography . . . it is just possible . . . that Thomas Merton might have achieved . . . obscurity and oblivion." It was not to be; for the rest of his life Merton was to deal with the consequences of having written such a popular book.

Mott felt that Merton's extensive journals were an answer to those who, after reading his autobiography, might want to portray Merton as a modern saint. Mott explained: "The journals would speak of him without editing, crossing-out, polishing a place where the narrow-minded, or those who made a cult of him, would flounder and where the seekers of truth without pretense would find him."

In an interview with Thomas P. McDonnell that appeared in *Motive* in 1967, Merton commented on being an author of a bestseller. "I left [*The Seven Storey Mountain*] behind many years ago. Certainly, it was a book I had to write, and it says a great deal of what I have to say; but if I had to write it over again, it would be handled in a very different way. . . . Unfortunately, the book was a best-seller, and it has become a kind of edifying legend or something. . . . I am doing my best to live it down. The legend is stronger than I am."

Merton's love of writing started early in his life, as Israel Shenker noted in the *New York Times.* "He wrote his first book at the age of ten," wrote Shenker, "and followed it with ten more unpublished novels." (One of these early novels was published posthumously as *My Argument with the Gestapo.*) By 1939, when Merton was teaching university extension classes at night, writing and re-writing novels and articles occupied most of his days. That same year, according to Mott, Merton also "wrote the first poem that would continue to mean something to him." Although Merton had already written quite a few poems, he explained in *The Seven Storey Mountain,* "I had never been able

to write verse before I became a Catholic [in 1938]. I had tried, but I had never really succeeded, and it was impossible to keep alive enough ambition to go on trying."

Merton became well known as a poet during his first years in the monastery. His first book of poetry, *Thirty Poems,* was published in 1944. It included poems he composed before and after entering the abbey. According to Baker, Merton felt "that the poetry which he wrote at that time was the best of his career." The book received favorable reviews, including one written by poet Robert Lowell for *Commonweal* in which the critic called Merton "easily the most promising of our American Catholic poets."

Merton's next book of poems included all the poems from his first book plus fifty-six more written during the same period. This book, *A Man in the Divided Sea,* was equally praised by critics. Calling it "brilliant" and "provocative" in *Poetry,* John Nerber commented, "It is, without doubt, one of the important books of the year." In the *New Yorker* Louise Bogan wrote that although Merton "has not yet developed a real synthesis between his poetic gifts and his religious ones . . . the possibility of his becoming a religious poet of stature is evident."

Merton was not able to write poems in such quantities again until the 1960s. After his appointment in 1951 as master of scholastics, many of his works such as *The Living Bread, No Man Is an Island,* and *The Silent Life* expanded on ideas expressed in the monastery classes he conducted for the young monks studying for the priesthood. Several critics, including Kramer and Baker, noted a change in Merton's writing style sometime between the end of the 1950s and the early 1960s. Whereas Merton previously appeared to advocate isolation from society as the answer to the question of how a Christian should respond to the unspirituality of the world, his writing began to suggest the need to deal with social injustice through social activism. Baker explained, "By the mid-1960s [Merton's] attitude toward the world had changed so dramatically that Merton-watchers were speaking of the 'early Merton' and the 'later Merton' to distinguish between his two careers, the one as a silent mystic who celebrated the virtues of monastic life in glowing prose and poetry, the other as a social commentator."

Kramer chose three Merton books to demonstrate "the significant changes in awareness" in Merton's writing. The first of these books, *Seeds of Contemplation,* published in 1949, was entirely spiritual in focus. *New Seeds of Contemplation,* published in 1961, was a revised version of the same book, and it reflected what Kramer called Merton's "greater concern for the problems of living in the world." The third book Kramer mentioned, *Seeds of Destruction,* published in 1964, was a collection of essays on world problems, including racism. According to Kramer, the changing themes illustrated in these three books reflect Merton's movement from solitary monk in a monastery cell to social activist. While unable to join the sit-ins and protest marches of the 1960s, Merton was able to express his support for such activities with his writing.

Mott explained the change in Merton's style by noting that at the end of the 1950s, "after sixteen years of isolation from social issues, Merton was beginning to feel cut off from what he needed to know." Since radios, televisions, and newspapers were forbidden in the monastery, only chance readings of magazines and books brought to the abbey by Merton's friends enabled him to keep up with world events. Belatedly, he found out about the suffering caused by the U.S. atomic bomb attacks on Japan and the horrors of Nazi concentration camps. He found out about social injustice in Latin America by reading Latin American poets, including Nicaraguan Ernesto Cardenal who spent some time at the Abbey of Gethsemani himself in the late 1950s. Mott continued: "[Merton] was unsure of himself, certain only that the time had come to move from the role of bystander . . . to that of declared witness." His poetic works *Original Child Bomb: Points for Meditation to be Scratched on the Walls of a Cave* (about the atomic bomb) and "Chants to be Used in Processions around a Site with Furnaces" (about the ovens of the Nazi extermination camps) were products of his awakening social conscience.

Merton's increasing concern with racial injustice, the immorality of war—particularly of the Vietnam conflict—and the plight of the world's poor caused more and more censorship problems. Actually, he had had problems with monastic censors throughout his stay at Gethsemani. When originally confronted with the manuscript version of *The Seven Storey Mountain,* for instance, the censors rejected it because of the numerous references to sex and drinking it contained. In a section of Merton's journal published as *The Sign of Jonas* the monk complained that one of the censors even "held [that Merton was] incapable of writing an autobiography 'with his present literary equipment' and . . . advised [Merton] to take a correspondence course in English grammar." Although the debate over *The Seven Storey Mountain* was eventually resolved, censors became even more concerned about Merton's writings on war and peace. Frustrated, Merton circulated some of his work in mimeographed form. These came to be known as "The Cold War Letters."

In 1962, Merton was forbidden by his superiors to write about war, but he could write about peace. Mott quoted a letter Merton wrote that year: "Did I tell you that the decision of the higher ups has become final and conclusive? . . . Too controversial, doesn't give a nice image of monk. Monk concerned with peace. Bad image."

Despite censorship and isolation Merton became, according to Kenneth L. Woodward in *Newsweek,* "a prophet to the peace movement [and] a conscience to the counterculture." At the height of the escalation of the Vietnam War, he welcomed a Vietnamese Buddhist monk to speak at the abbey, he met with peace activist Joan Baez, he corresponded with Daniel Berrigan (a Catholic priest arrested for burning draft cards), and he planned a retreat for Dr. Martin Luther King, a plan abruptly halted by King's assassination. Controversial comedian Lenny Bruce often closed his nightclub act reading from an essay Merton wrote about German Nazi leader Adolf Eichmann in which Merton questioned the sanity of the world.

Much of this activity occurred after Merton began living as a hermit in a cabin located in the woods on the monastery grounds. Just as his desire to be removed from the world became greatest, so did his need to speak out on social problems. In his writings, he attempted to explain this paradox as much to himself as to others.

In *Best Sellers,* Sister Joseph Marie Anderson wrote that in Merton's *Contemplation in a World of Action* the monk stressed "that the contemplative is not exempt from the problem of the world nor is the monastic life an escape from reality." In a review of Merton's *The Climate of Monastic Prayer,* a *Times Literary Supplement* critic noted, "Merton came to see that the monk is not exempt from the agonies of the world outside his walls: he is involved at another level." The reviewer offered this quote from Merton's book: "The monk searches not only his own heart: he plunges deep into the heart of that world of which he remains a part although he seems to have 'left' it. In reality the monk abandons the world only in order to listen more intently to the deepest and most neglected voices that proceed from the inner depth."

Along with social activism, Merton became increasingly interested in the study of other religions, particularly Zen Buddhism. His books *Mystics and Zen Masters* and *Zen and the Birds of Appetite* acknowledged his love for Eastern thought. In the *New York Times Book Review* Nancy Wilson Ross wrote, "In 'Mystics and Zen Masters' . . . Merton . . . has made a vital, sensitive and timely contribution to the growing worldwide effort . . . to shed new light on mankind's common spiritual heritage." She added: "Merton's reasons for writing this [book] . . . might be summed up in a single quotation: 'If the West continues to underestimate and to neglect the spiritual heritage of the East, it may well hasten the tragedy that threatens man and his civilization.' "

In the *New York Times Book Review* Edward Rice explained further: "Merton's first notion was to pluck whatever 'Christian' gems he could out of the East that might fit into the Catholic theological structure. Later he abandoned this attempt and accepted Buddhism, Hinduism and Islam on their own equally valid terms . . . without compromising his own Christianity." Merton died in 1968 while hoping to expand his understanding of Eastern thought at an ecumenical conference in Bangkok, Thailand, his first extended journey outside the monastery walls since his entry in 1941.

Merton's writings on peace, war, social injustice, and Eastern thought created controversy both inside the abbey and outside it, among his readers. In the revised edition of *Thomas Merton: Monk,* Daniel Berrigan noted that many people refused to accept the work of the "new" Merton and that they preferred "rather a Merton in their own image, a Merton who [was] safe, and cornered, contemplative in a terribly wrong sense, and therefore manageable." However, as J. M. Cameron remarked in the *New York Review of Books,* it is most likely these later writings that will stand out as Merton's most important work. According to Cameron, "Merton will be remembered for two things: his place . . . in the thinking about the morality of war . . . ; and his partially successful attempt to bring out, through study and personal encounter, what is common to Asian and West monasticism and . . . contemplative life." Rice agreed with this observation, noting in *The Man in the Sycamore Tree,* "It [was] the later writings on war and peace, nonviolence, race, . . . and above all on Buddhism, that show Merton at his best and most creative."

Thomas Merton was, as William H. Shannon noted in *Commonweal,* "one of those persons people instinctively like[d]" and, it appears, Merton's personal attraction is still felt more than two decades after his death. His works and life seem to have relevance to a new generation of Catholics and non-Catholics. "His influence," wrote Mitch Finley in *Our Sunday Visitor,* a national Catholic weekly, "is, if anything, on the increase." His ideas on war and peace contained in his writing from the 1960s were echoed in the U.S. Catholic bishops' statement on nuclear war published in the 1980s. His life, too, continues to reveal, Monica Furlong noted in *Merton: A Biography,* "much about the twentieth century and, in particular, the role of religion in it."

The largest collection of Merton's manuscripts is at the Thomas Merton Studies Center, Bellarmine College, Louisville, Kentucky.

MEDIA ADAPTATIONS: The Tower of Babel, condensed and adapted by Richard J. Walsh, was shown on the National Broadcast Corporation (NBC-TV) in 1957.

AVOCATIONAL INTERESTS: Merton reportedly told his publishers: "Zen. Indians. Wood. Birds. Beer. Anglican friends. Subversive tape recordings for nuns. Tea. Bob Dylan."

BIOGRAPHICAL/CRITICAL SOURCES:

BOOKS

Adams, Daniel J., *Thomas Merton's Shared Contemplation: A Protestant Perspective,* edited by Teresa A. Doyle, Cistercian Publications, 1979.

Baker, James Thomas, *Thomas Merton: Social Critic,* University of Kentucky, 1971.

Contemporary Literary Criticism, Gale, Volume I, 1973, Volume III, 1975, Volume XI, 1979, Volume XXXIV, 1985.

Dictionary of Literary Biography, Volume XLVIII: *American Poets, 1880-1945, Second Series,* Gale, 1986.

Dictionary of Literary Biography Yearbook: 1981, Gale, 1982.

Finley, James, *Merton's Palace of Nowhere,* Ave Maria Press, 1978.

Forest, James, *Thomas Merton: A Pictorial Biography,* Paulist Press, 1980.

Furlong, Monica, *Merton: A Biography,* Harper, 1980.

Grayston, Donald, *Thomas Merton: The Development of a Spiritual Theologian,* Edwin Mellon Press, 1985.

Hart, Patrick, *Thomas Merton: Monk,* Sheed & Ward, 1974, revised and enlarged edition, Cistercian Publications, 1983.

Hart, Patrick, editor, *The Message of Thomas Merton,* Cistercian Publications, 1981.

Hart, Patrick, editor, *The Legacy of Thomas Merton,* Cistercian Publications, 1985.

Kramer, Victor A., *Thomas Merton,* Twayne, 1984.

Labrie, Ross, *The Art of Thomas Merton,* Texas Christian University Press, 1979.

Lentfoehr, Therese, *Words and Silence: On the Poetry of Thomas Merton,* New Directions, 1979.

Lipski, Alexander, *Thomas Merton and Asia: His Quest for Utopia,* Cistercian Publications, 1983.

Maltis, Elena, *The Solitary Explorer: Thomas Merton's Transforming Journey,* Harper, 1980.

McInery, Dennis Q., *Thomas Merton: The Man and His Work,* Cistercian Publications, 1974.

Merton, Thomas, *The Seven Storey Mountain,* Harcourt, 1948.

Merton, Thomas, *The Sign of Jonas,* Harcourt, 1953.

Merton, Thomas, *Letters from Tom: A Selection of Letters from Father Thomas Merton, Monk of Gethsemani,* edited by W. H. Ferry, Fort Hill Press, 1983.

Mott, Michael, *The Seven Mountains of Thomas Merton,* Houghton Mifflin, 1984.

Mulhearn, Timothy, editor, *Getting It All Together: The Heritage of Thomas Merton,* M. Glazier, 1984.

Nouwen, Henri J. M., *Pray to Live; Thomas Merton: A Contemplative Critic,* Fides Publishers (Notre Dame, Ind.), 1972.

Rice, Edward, *The Man in the Sycamore Tree: The Good Times and Hard Life of Thomas Merton, An Entertainment,* Doubleday, 1970.

Shannon, William H., *Thomas Merton's Dark Path: The Inner Experience of a Contemplative,* Farrar, Straus, 1981, revised edition, 1986.

Sussman, Cornelia and Irving Sussman, *Thomas Merton,* Doubleday, 1980.

Woodcock, George, *Thomas Merton: Monk and Poet,* Farrar, Straus, 1978.

PERIODICALS

America, October 25, 1969, November 24, 1984.

Atlantic Monthly, May, 1949.

Best Sellers, November 15, 1970, April 15, 1971, August 15, 1973.

Boston Review, February, 1985.

Catholic World, October, 1948, November, 1948, October, 1949, December, 1949, June, 1950, November, 1951, March, 1953, June, 1955, February, 1957, July, 1958, November, 1960, August, 1961, April, 1962.

Chicago Tribune, January 27, 1985.

Commentary, April, 1965.

Commonweal, June 22, 1945, December 27, 1946, August 13, 1948, April 15, 1949, October 14, 1949, October 26, 1951, February 27, 1953, July 6, 1956, June 9, 1961, March 16, 1962, April 19, 1963, March 12, 1965, January 10, 1969, October 17, 1969, February 27, 1970, January 22, 1971, October 12, 1973, February 3, 1978, October 19, 1984, February 28, 1986.

Contemporary Literature, winter, 1973.

Critic, April, 1963, February, 1966, January, 1970, May, 1971, February 15, 1981.

Detroit Free Press, February 11, 1969.

Hudson Review, summer, 1978.

Los Angeles Times Book Review, December 14, 1980, December 30, 1984, October 13, 1985.

Motive, October, 1967.

Nation, November 6, 1948.

Negro Digest, December, 1967.

New Republic, October 4, 1948, September 12, 1949.

Newsweek, December 10, 1984.

New Yorker, October 5, 1946, October 9, 1948, October 8, 1949.

New York Herald Tribune Weekly Book Review, October 24, 1948.

New York Review of Books, February 11, 1965, April 10, 1969, September 27, 1979.

New York Times, March 18, 1945, October 3, 1948, March 20, 1949, September 18, 1949, March 26, 1950, September 23, 1951, February 8, 1953, March 27, 1955, March 11, 1956, July 10, 1969, December 10, 1984, December 20, 1984.

New York Times Book Review, February 14, 1965, April 17, 1966, July 2, 1967, March 30, 1969, March 15, 1970, March 14, 1971, July 8, 1973, February 5, 1978, May 23, 1982, December 23, 1984.

Our Sunday Visitor, January 25, 1987.

Poetry, February, 1945, December, 1946, October, 1948, July, 1950.

Publishers Weekly, December 7, 1984.

Renascence, winter, 1974, spring, 1978.

Saturday Review of Literature, October 9, 1948, April 16, 1949, September 17, 1949, February 11, 1950.

Sewanee Review, summer, 1969, winter, 1973, autumn, 1973.

Thought, September, 1974.

Time, January 24, 1968, December 31, 1984.

Times Literary Supplement, December 23, 1949, May 22, 1959, February 12, 1970, May 5, 1972.

Virginia Quarterly Review, summer, 1968.

Washington Post, September 4, 1969.

Washington Post Book World, December 16, 1984, June 30, 1985.

OBITUARIES:

PERIODICALS

Antiquarian Bookman, December 23-30, 1968.

Books Abroad, spring, 1969.

Detroit Free Press, December 11, 1968.

Newsweek, December 23, 1968.

New York Times, December 11, 1968.

Publishers Weekly, December 30, 1968.

Time, December 20, 1968.

Times (London), December 12, 1968.

Washington Post, December 12, 1968.

*   *   *

MERWIN, W(illiam) S(tanley) 1927-

PERSONAL: Born September 30, 1927, in New York, N.Y.; son of William (a Presbyterian minister) and Ann (Jaynes) Merwin; grew up in Union City, N.J., and Scranton, Pa.; married Diana Whalley, 1954 (marriage ended); married second wife, Paula. *Education:* Princeton University, A.B., 1947, one year of graduate study in modern languages.

ADDRESSES: Home—Haiku, Hawaii.

CAREER: Poet. Tutor in France and Portugal, 1949; tutor of Robert Graves's son in Majorca, 1950; lived in London, England, 1951-54, supporting himself largely by translating Spanish and French classics for the British Broadcasting Corporation Third Programme; returned to America in 1956 to write plays for the Poets' Theatre, Cambridge, Mass.; lived in New York, N.Y., 1961-63; associated with Roger Planchon's Theatre de la Cite, Lyon, France, 1964-65. *Military service:* U.S. Navy Air Corps.

MEMBER: National Institute of Arts and Letters, Academy of American Poets (elected member of the board of chancellors).

AWARDS, HONORS: Kenyon Review fellowship in poetry, 1954; Rockefeller fellowship, 1956; National Institute of Arts and Letters grant, 1957; Arts Council of Great Britain playwriting bursary, 1957; Rabinowitz Foundation grant, 1961; Bess Hokin Prize, *Poetry* magazine, 1962; Ford Foundation grant, 1964-65; fellowship from Chapelbrook Foundation, 1966; Harriet Monroe Memorial Prize, *Poetry,* 1967; P.E.N. Translation Prize, 1969, for *W. S. Merwin: Selected Translations, 1948-1968;* Rockefeller Foundation grant, 1969; Pulitzer Prize for poetry for *The Carrier of Ladders,* 1971 (refused); fellowship from the Academy of American Poets, 1973; Guggenheim fellowship, 1973 and 1983; Shelley Memorial Award, 1974; Bollingen Prize for poetry, Yale University Library, 1979.

WRITINGS:

POETRY, EXCEPT AS INDICATED

A Mask for Janus (also see below), Yale University Press, 1952.
The Dancing Bears (also see below), Yale University Press, 1954.
Green with Beasts (also see below), Knopf, 1956.
The Drunk in the Furnace (also see below), Macmillan, 1960.
(Editor) *West Wind: Supplement of American Poetry,* Poetry Book Society (London), 1961.
The Moving Target, Atheneum, 1963.
Collected Poems, Atheneum, 1966.
The Lice, Atheneum, 1969.
Animae, Kayak, 1969.
The Miner's Pale Children (prose), Atheneum, 1970.
The Carrier of Ladders, Atheneum, 1970.
(With A. D. Moore) *Signs,* Stone Wall Press, 1970.
(With Keith Wilson) *Broadsides,* Solo Press, 1972.
Asian Figures, Atheneum, 1973.
Writings to an Unfinished Accompaniment, Atheneum, 1973.
The First Four Books of Poems (contains *A Mask for Janus, The Dancing Bears, Green with Beasts,* and *The Drunk in the Furnace*), Atheneum, 1975.
The Compass Flower, Atheneum, 1977.
Houses and Travellers (prose), Atheneum, 1977.
Feathers from the Hill, Windhover, 1978.
Unframed Originals: Recollections (prose), Atheneum, 1982.
Finding the Islands, North Point Press, 1982.

Opening the Hand, Atheneum, 1983.
Regions of Memory: Uncollected Prose, 1949-1982, edited by Ed Folsom and Cary Nelson, Illinois University Press, 1987.
The Rain in the Trees, Knopf, 1988.
Selected Poems, Atheneum, 1988.

Contributor to numerous anthologies.

TRANSLATOR

The Poem of the Cid, Dent, 1959, New American Library, 1962.
(Contributor) Eric Bentley, editor, *The Classic Theatre,* Doubleday, 1961.
The Satires of Persius, Indiana University Press, 1961.
Some Spanish Ballads, Abelard, 1961, also published as *Spanish Ballads,* Doubleday Anchor, 1961.
The Life of Lazarillo de Tormes: His Fortunes and Adversities, Doubleday Anchor, 1962.
(Contributor) *Medieval Epics,* Modern Library, 1963.
(With Denise Levertov, William Carlos Williams, and others) Nicanor Parra, *Poems and Antipoems,* New Directions, 1968.
Jean Follain, *Transparence of the World,* Atheneum, 1969.
W. S. Merwin: Selected Translations, 1948-1968, Atheneum, 1969.
(And author of introduction) S. Chamfort, *Products of the Perfected Civilization: Selected Writings of Chamfort,* Macmillan, 1969.
Antonio Porchia, *Voices: Selected Writings of Antonio Porchia,* Follett, 1969.
Pablo Neruda, *Twenty Poems and a Song of Despair,* Cape, 1969.
The Song of Roland, Random House, 1970.
(With others) Pablo Neruda, *Selected Poems,* Dell, 1970.
(With Clarence Brown) Osip Mandelstam, *Selected Poems,* Oxford University Press, 1973, Atheneum, 1974.
(With J. Moussaieff Mason) *Sanskrit Love Poetry,* Columbia University Press, 1977, published as *The Peacock's Egg: Love Poems from Ancient India,* North Point Press, 1981.
Roberto Juarroz, *Vertical Poems,* Kayak, 1977.
(With George E. Dimock, Jr.) Euripides, *Iphigenia at Aulius,* Oxford University Press, 1978.
Selected Translations, 1968-1978, Atheneum, 1979.
Robert the Devil, Windhover, 1981.
Four French Plays, Atheneum, 1984.
From the Spanish Morning, Atheneum, 1984.
(With Soiku Shigematsu) Muso Soseki, *Sun at Midnight: Poems and Sermons,* North Point Press, 1989.

Also translator of Lope de Rueda, "Eufemia," in *Tulane Drama Review,* December, 1958; Lesage, "Crispin," in *Tulane Drama Review;* Lope Felix de Vega Carpio, *Punishment without Vengeance,* 1958; and Garcia Lorca, "Yerma," 1969.

OTHER

(With Dido Milroy) "Darkling Child" (play), produced in 1956.
"Favor Island" (play), produced at Poets' Theatre, Cambridge, Mass., in 1957, and on British Broadcasting Corporation Third Programme in 1958.
"The Gilded West" (play), produced at Belgrade Theatre, Coventry, England, in 1961.

Contributor to magazines, including *Nation, Harper's, Poetry, New Yorker, Atlantic, Kenyon Review,* and *Evergreen Review.* Poetry editor, *Nation,* 1962.

SIDELIGHTS: W. S. Merwin is a major American writer whose poetry, translations, and prose have won praise from literary critics since the publication of his first book. The spare, hard verse comprising the body of Merwin's work has been characterized by many as very difficult reading. However, it is generally agreed that this poetry is worth whatever extra effort may be required to appreciate it. In a *Yale Review* article, Laurence Lieberman states, "This poetry, at its best—and at our best as readers—is able to meet us and engage our wills as never before in the thresholds between waking and sleeping, past and future, self and anti-self, men and gods, the living and the dead." Although Merwin's writing has undergone many stylistic changes through the course of his career, it is unified by the recurring theme of man's separation from nature. The poet sees the consequences of that alienation as disastrous, both for the human race and for the rest of the world.

In an interview with *CA,* Merwin affirmed his strong feelings about ecological issues, saying, "It makes me angry to feel that the natural world is taken to have so little importance." He gave an example from his own life: "The Pennsylvania that I grew up in and loved as a child isn't there . . . it's been strip-mined: it really is literally not there. This happens to a lot of people, but I don't see why one has to express indifference about it. It matters. . . . It's like being told that you can't possibly be mentally healthy." Merwin's despair over the desecration of nature is strongly expressed in his collection *The Lice.* "If there is any book today that has perfectly captured the peculiar spiritual agony of our time, the agony of a generation which knows itself to be the last, and has transformed that agony into great art, it is W. S. Merwin's *The Lice,*" writes Lieberman. "To read these poems is an act of self-purification. Every poem in the book pronounces a judgment against modern men—the gravest sentence the poetic imagination can conceive for man's withered and wasted conscience: our sweep of history adds up to one thing only, a moral vacuity that is absolute and irrevocable. This book is a testament of betrayals; we have betrayed all beings that had power to save us: the forest, the animals, the gods, the dead, the spirit in us, the words. Now, in our last moments alive, they return to haunt us."

Merwin's obsession with the meaning of America and its values makes him like the great nineteenth-century poet Walt Whitman, writes L. Edwin Folsom in *Shenandoah.* "His poetry . . . often implicitly and often explicitly responds to Whitman; his twentieth century sparsity and soberness—his doubts about the value of America—answer, temper, Whitman's nineteenth century expansiveness and exuberance—his enthusiasm over the American creation." Folsom elaborates: "Merwin's answer to Whitman is begun in *The Lice,* an anti-song of the self. Here, instead of the Whitmanian self expanding and absorbing everything, naming it in an ecstasy of union, we find a self stripped of meaning, unable to expand, in a landscape that refuses to unite with the self, refuses to be assimilated, in a place alien and unnameable. . . . Instead of expanding his senses, like Whitman, and intensifying his touch, sight, hearing, so that he could contain the multitudes around him, Merwin's senses . . . crumble and fade, become useless. . . . All that is left is silence. . . . The self is dying, its head returning to 'ash' in the withering flames of the twentieth century. . . . Whitman's self sought to contain all, to embody past, present, and future; Merwin's self seeks to contain nothing, to empty itself of a dead past. . . . [Having taken a journey in the past,] Merwin does not return to the present replenished with the native ways: he returns only with an affirmation of man's stupidity and inhumanity, and of an irreplaceable emptiness lying beneath this continent. Having re-taken the Whitmanesque American journey, having relived the creation of the country via the medium of poetry, Merwin finds the American creation not to be a creation at all, but a de-

struction, an imposed obliteration that he believes will be repaid in kind."

The poetic forms of many eras and societies are the foundation for a great deal of Merwin's poetry. His first books contained many pieces inspired by classical models. According to Vernon Young in *American Poetry Review,* the poems are traceable to "Biblical tales, Classical myth, love songs from the Age of Chivalry, Renaissance retellings; they comprise carols, roundels, odes, ballads, sestinas, and they contrive golden equivalents of emblematic models: the masque, the Zodiac, the Dance of Death." Merwin's versions are so perfectly rendered, says Young, that "were you to redistribute these poems, unsigned, among collections of translated material or of English Poetry Down the Ages, any but the most erudite reader would heedlessly accept them as renderings of Theocritus, Catullus, Ronsard. . . . One thing is certain. Before embarking on the narratives published in 1956 and after, Merwin was in secure formal command. Shape and duration, melody, vocal inflection, were under superb control. No stanzaic model was alien to him; no line length was beyond his dexterity." Eric Hartley also comments on the importance of Merwin's background in *Dictionary of Literary Biography:* "From the first of his career as a poet, Merwin has steeped himself in other cultures and other literary traditions, and he has been praised as a translator. This eclectic background has given him a sense of the presence of the past, of timelessness in time, that comes across emphatically in his poetry. Without some understanding of this background the reader cannot fully appreciate Merwin's poetry. Moreover, without such appreciation one cannot comprehend the thrust of Merwin's poetic and philosophical development."

However, John Vernon points out in a *Western Humanities Review* article that Merwin's poems are not difficult in a scholarly sense. The problem is the jaded ear of the modern reader. "These are some of the most unacademic poems I have ever read, in the sense that they could never be discussed in a university classroom, since they have no 'meaning' in any usual sense. . . . I think of what Samuel Beckett said about *Finnegans Wake:* we are too decadent to read this. That is, we are so used to a language that is flattened out and hollowed out, that is slavishly descriptive, that when we encounter a language as delicately modulated and as finely sensual as this, it is like trying to read braille with boxing gloves on."

Some literary critics have identified Merwin with the group known as the oracular poets, but Merwin himself told *CA,* "I have not evolved an abstract aesthetic theory and am not aware of belonging to any particular group of writers. I neither read nor write much criticism, and think of its current vast proliferation chiefly as a symptom, inseparable from other technological substitutions. . . . I imagine that a society whose triumphs one after the other emerge as new symbols of death, and that feeds itself by poisoning the earth, may be expected, even while it grows in strength and statistics, to soothe its fears with trumpery hopes, refer to nihilism as progress, dismiss the private authority of the senses as it has cashiered belief, and of course find the arts exploitable but unsatisfying."

Of his development as a writer, Merwin said, "I started writing hymns for my father almost as soon as I could write at all, illustrating them. I recall some rather stern little pieces addressed, in a manner I was familiar with, to backsliders, but I can remember too wondering whether there might not be some more liberating mode. In Scranton there was an anthology of *Best Loved Poems of the American People* in the house, which seemed for a time to afford some clues. But the first real writers that held me were not poets: Conrad first, and then Tolstoy, and it was not until I had received a scholarship and gone away to the university that I began to read poetry steadily and try incessantly, and with abiding desperation, to write it. I was not a satisfactory student; . . . I spent most of my time either in the university library, or riding in the country: I had discovered that the polo and ROTC stables were full of horses with no one to exercise them. I believe I was not noticeably respectful either of the curriculum and its evident purposes, nor of several of its professors, and I was saved from the thoroughly justified impatience of the administration, as I later learned, by the intercessions of R. P. Blackmur, who thought I needed a few years at the place to pick up what education I might be capable of assimilating, and I did in fact gain a limited but invaluable acquaintance with a few modern languages. While I was there, John Berryman, Herman Broch, and Blackmur himself helped me, by example as much as by design, to find out some things about writing; of course it was years before I began to realize just what I had learned, and from whom."

He concluded: "Writing is something I know little about; less at some times than at others. I think, though, that so far as it is poetry it is a matter of correspondences: one glimpses them, pieces of an order, or thinks one does, and tries to convey the sense of what one has seen to those to whom it may matter, including, if possible, one's self." The success of Merwin's attempts to convey his vision is summed up by Stephen Spender in the *New York Review of Books:* "These poems communicate a sense of someone watching and waiting, surrounding himself with silence, so that he can see minute particles, listen to infinitesimal sounds, with a passivity of attention, a refusal to disturb with his own observing consciousness the object observed. It is as though things write their own poems through Merwin. At their best they are poems of total attention and as such they protest against our world of total distraction."

The W. S. Merwin Archive in the Rare Book Room of the University Library of the University of Illinois at Urbana-Champaign contains notes, drafts, and manuscripts of published and unpublished work by Merwin from the mid-1940s to the early 1980s.

BIOGRAPHICAL/CRITICAL SOURCES:

BOOKS

Contemporary Literary Criticism, Gale, Volume 1, 1973, Volume 2, 1974, Volume 3, 1975, Volume 5, 1976, Volume 8, 1978, Volume 13, 1980, Volume 18, 1981, Volume 45, 1987.

Dickey, James, *Babel to Byzantium,* Farrar, Straus, 1968.

Dictionary of Literary Biography, Volume 5: *American Poets since World War II,* Gale, 1980.

Howard, Richard, *Alone with America: Essays on the Art of Poetry in the United States since 1950,* Atheneum, 1969.

Hungerford, Edward, *Poets in Progress,* Northwestern University Press, 1962.

Nelson, Cary and Ed Folsom, editors, *W. S. Merwin: Essays on the Poetry,* Illinois University Press, 1987.

Rexroth, Kenneth, *With Eye and Ear,* Herder, 1970.

Rexroth, Kenneth, *American Poetry in the Twentieth Century,* Herder, 1971.

Rosenthal, M. L., *The Modern Poets: A Critical Introduction,* Oxford University Press, 1960.

Shaw, Robert B., editor, *American Poetry since 1960: Some Critical Perspectives,* Dufour, 1974.

Stepanchev, Stephen, *American Poetry since 1945,* Harper, 1965.

PERIODICALS

American Poetry Review, January-February, 1978.
Chicago Tribune Book World, December 26, 1982.
Concerning Poetry, spring, 1975.
Furioso, spring, 1953.
Hudson Review, winter, 1967-68, summer, 1973.
Los Angeles Times, August 21, 1983.
Los Angeles Times Book Review, August 21, 1983, March 27, 1988.
Modern Poetry Studies, winter, 1975.
Nation, December 14, 1970.
New Mexico Quarterly, autumn, 1964.
New York Review of Books, May 6, 1971, September 20, 1973.
New York Times Book Review, October 18, 1970, June 19, 1977, August 1, 1982, October 9, 1983, July 31, 1988.
Ontario Review, fall-winter, 1977-78.
Partisan Review, summer, 1958, winter, 1971-72.
Poetry, May, 1953, May, 1961, February, 1963, June, 1964, August, 1974.
Prairie Schooner, fall, 1957, fall, 1962, winter, 1962-63, fall, 1968, winter, 1971-72.
Sewanee Review, spring, 1974.
Shenandoah, spring, 1968, winter, 1970, spring, 1978.
Southern Review, April, 1980.
Times Literary Supplement, January 22, 1988.
Village Voice, July 4, 1974.
Virginia Quarterly Review, summer, 1973.
Voices, January-April, 1953, May-August, 1957, September-December, 1961.
Washington Post Book World, August 31, 1975, September 18, 1977, August 15, 1982, June 3, 1984.
Western Humanities Review, spring, 1970, spring, 1971.
Western Review, spring, 1955.
Yale Review, summer, 1961, summer, 1968, summer, 1973.

*　　*　　*

METCALF, Suzanne
  See BAUM, L(yman) Frank

*　　*　　*

METESKY, George
  See HOFFMAN, Abbie

*　　*　　*

MEYER, June
  See JORDAN, June

*　　*　　*

MICHAELS, Leonard 1933-

PERSONAL: Born January 2, 1933, in New York, N.Y.; son of Leon (a barber) and Anna (Czeskies) Michaels; married former wife, Priscilla Older, June 30, 1966; married third wife, Brenda Lynn Hillman (a poet), August 10, 1977; children: (first marriage) Ethan, Jesse; (third marriage) Louisa. *Education:* New York University, B.A., 1953; University of Michigan, M.A., 1956, Ph.D., 1966.

ADDRESSES: Home—409 Boynton Ave., Kensington, CA 94707. *Office*— Department of English, University of California,

Berkeley, CA 94720. *Agent*—Lynn Nesbit, International Creative Management, 40 West 57th St., New York, NY 10019.

CAREER: Paterson State College (now William Paterson State College of New Jersey), Wayne, instructor, 1961-62; University of California, Davis, assistant professor of English, 1966-69; University of California, Berkeley, professor of English, 1970—, editor of *University Publishing* review, 1977—. Visiting professor at many universities, including Johns Hopkins University and University of Alabama. Guest lecturer in institutions in the United States and abroad.

AWARDS, HONORS: Quill Award, Massachusetts Review, 1964, for "Sticks and Stones" (short story), and 1966, for "The Deal" (short story); National Book Award nomination, 1969, for *Going Places;* Guggenheim fellow, 1969; National Endowment for the Humanities fellow, 1970; American Academy Award in Literature, National Institute of Arts and Letters, 1971, for published work of distinction; *New York Times Book Review* Editor's Choice Award, 1975, for *I Would Have Saved Them If I Could;* American Book Award nomination and National Book Critics Circle Award nomination, both in 1982, for *The Men's Club;* National Foundation on the Arts and Humanities prize, for short story in *Transatlantic.*

WRITINGS:

Going Places (short stories; also see below), Farrar, Straus, 1969.
I Would Have Saved Them If I Could (short stories; also see below), Farrar, Straus, 1975.
(Contributor) Theodore Solotaroff, editor, *American Review 26,* Bantam, 1977.
(Contributor) William Abrahams, editor, *Prize Stories, 1980: The O. Henry Awards,* Doubleday, 1980.
(Editor with Christopher Ricks) *The State of the Language,* University of California Press, 1980.
The Men's Club (novel; also see below), Farrar, Straus, 1981.
"City Boy" (play adapted from short stories in *Going Places* and *I Would Have Saved Them If I Could*), produced in New York City at The Jewish Repertory Theater, 1985.
"The Men's Club" (screenplay based on his novel of the same title), Atlantic Releasing Corporation, 1986.
(Editor with Raquel Sheer and David Reid) *West of the West: Imagining California* (essays), North Point Press, 1989.
(Editor with Ricks) *The State of the Language* (new essays on English), University of California Press, 1990.

Short stories also appear in *The American Literary Anthology/One,* sponsored by the National Endowment for the Arts. Contributor of short stories to numerous literary journals and popular magazines, including *Esquire, Paris Review, Evergreen Review, Partisan Review,* and *Tri-Quarterly.* Contributing editor, *Threepenny Review,* 1980; corresponding editor, *Partisan Review.*

WORK IN PROGRESS: A collection of essays and stories; an autobiographical novel.

SIDELIGHTS: With several award-winning short stories placed in prestigious literary magazines, Leonard Michaels became known as an impressive writer—a reputation that was extended when *Going Places,* his first book-length collection, was nominated for the National Book Award in 1969. Reviews of his second collection, *I Would Have Saved Them If I Could,* named Michaels a master of short fiction forms. "The hallmarks of these stories," David Reid summarizes in the *Threepenny Review,* "are an amazing rapidity of image, incident, and idea and a deftness of rhythm and phrasing that, quite simply, confirm, sentence by sentence, his status as one of the most original, intelligent, and stylistically gifted writers of his generation." Critics praise the blend of horror and humor in the stories which are unified by their New York settings, often noting that Michaels's descriptions of urban brutality strike the reader with an almost physical impact. After *I Would Have Saved Them If I Could* was named by the *New York Times Book Review* staff as one of the six outstanding works of fiction published in 1975, Michaels co-edited three popular essay collections (*The State of the Language,* a six-hundred-page anthology of essays and poems; a second tome on the English language also entitled *The State of the Language;* and *West of the West: Imagining California,* about California's unique role in history as "the New World's New World") and wrote the controversial novel *The Men's Club.* Though not prolific, Michaels sustains critical favor by pressing on to new territory and larger forms, while reducing his use of literary allusions.

Michaels grew up in the Lower East Side of New York City, the son of immigrant Polish Jews. "I spoke only Yiddish until I was about five or six years old," he tells *Washington Post* contributor Curt Suplee. At that time, his mother bought a complete set of Charles Dickens, providing Michaels's introduction to English prose: "If you can imagine a little boy . . . listening to his mother, who can hardly speak English, reading Dickens hour after hour in the most extraordinary accent, it might help to account for my peculiar ear." Interested in literature, but feeling that his heritage placed him outside "The Tradition" as defined by T. S. Eliot, Michaels studied painting in high school and then entered New York University as a premed student. There he met and became the protege of Austin Warren, a respected critic who encouraged Michaels to cultivate his literary interests.

While under Warren's tutelage at the University of Michigan, Michaels earned a Ph.D. in romantic poetry and wrote two novels that were never published. Though he eventually reshaped the second novel into the series of stories in *I Would Have Saved Them If I Could,* he incinerated the first one, Helen Benedict reports in the *New York Times Book Review,* "because of the 'severe' ideas he then held about the writer's obligation to art." "It's true," Michaels told *Threepenny Review* contributor Mona Simpson, "I wrote it in a very short period of time and I threw it into the incinerator. It was absolutely horrible. I wrote it . . . to show I could write a novel any time I wanted to, even in two weeks. But I wasn't about to really *do* anything like that. . . . I was more interested in forms of writing that seemed to me closer to the high ideals of art." Michaels found the short story form more demanding and better suited to his artistic ideals. He was twenty-nine when *Playboy* magazine bought the first story he sent them for three thousand dollars, making him, as Suplee remarks, "an instant success." This assessment of Michaels's talent proved to be no exaggeration when stories published in literary journals such as the *Massachusetts Review* brought him two Quill Awards, the O. Henry Prize, and a National Foundation on the Arts and Humanities prize.

Going Places contains several of the prize winners. "The key events in [these] stories—usually holocausts in the lives of his protagonists—are indistinguishable from the settings in which they occur," Laurence Lieberman notes in the *Atlantic.* They are set in New York City, which is itself "a crucial protagonist in each story," according to *Village Voice* contributor Stephan Taylor. Taylor sees the city in these stories as a "laboratory" in which "human beings are the only remaining manifestations of nature," a condition that makes their relationships more intense, more sexual, and more prone to culminate in violence. More imposing than the city's skyline, the urban population is presented as a "monster" that brutally rapes or beats its victims. In "The Deal," an attractive woman's trip across the street to buy cigarettes puts her into a confrontation with "twenty Puerto Rican boys congregated into the shape of a great bird of prey on a banistered front stoop in Spanish Harlem," Lieberman notes; and in the title story, an aimless cab driver's fares beat him with such force that it leaves him near death, and—for the first time in his life—conscious of his will to live. In "Crossbones," an unmarried couple fight and maim each other in the tension provoked by an impending visit from the girl's father, making it clear to Taylor that "while we've controlled natural disasters like plague and drought and famine in our cities, we may simply have freed people to perpetrate personal disasters that are just as harrowing." This view is shared by Christopher Lehmann-Haupt of the *New York Times:* "Mr. Michaels creates a hostile, violent, and absurd world in which people grope for each other longingly, yet can only touch one another by inflicting damage."

Horrors such as "orgies, rapes, mayhem and suicide in city scenes and subwayscapes" keep the reader's attention while Michaels explores the familiar themes of love and death, Lore Segal remarks in a *New Republic* review. Segal believes the author "makes these horrors horrible again and funny." For instance, in "City Boy," Phillip and his girlfriend are caught in a carnal embrace on the girl's living room floor by her father. Phillip escapes into the street without his clothes, and tries to disguise his nakedness by walking on his hands. The nude Phillip fails to establish enough trust with the subway conductor to secure his ride home. As he leaves the subway station, his girlfriend greets him with his clothing and the news that her father has suffered a heart attack.

Taylor concedes that the stories are comic, "not funny," since "their comedy takes place on a tightrope, a high wire beneath which there's broken glass instead of nets. And the laughter, ranging everywhere from booming to tittery, is flung in the teeth of despair." "The balance between the plaintively humorous and the grotesquely sad is what gives full dimension to Michaels's fiction," Ronald Christ suggests in a *Commonweal* review. Segal summarizes, "If [*Going Places*] poses that old chestnut of a question, How is it possible to read about what is bleak and hideous and be reading something hilarious and beautiful and pleasurable, the answer is the old one: It is at the miraculous point where this transformation happens that literature has occurred."

Michaels's second collection of stories, *I Would Have Saved Them If I Could,* "is a useful reminder that the rich complexity of a successful novel can, in the hands of a master, be achieved within the limitations of smaller forms," Thomas R. Edwards comments in the *New York Times Book Review,* adding that he considers the book "an important literary event." These stories trace Phillip Liebowitz's social and sexual development as a second-generation Jew during the fifties. In one story, the adolescent Phillip and his friends climb a water tower from which they have an unobstructed view of their young rabbi enjoying sex with his voluptuous wife, until the youngest boy falls to his death. In this, as in the other stories, Edwards notes that Phillip "finds his sexuality a source of continuous humiliation and self-betrayal, and the fine comic flair of these stories doesn't obscure their gloomy appraisal of past postrevolutionary life." The book measures the development of Phillip's mind as well as his body. Edwards concludes, "I know of few writers who can so firmly articulate intensity of feeling with the musculature of cool and difficult thinking, and 'I Would Have Saved Them If I Could'. . . should be read by anyone who hopes that fiction can still be a powerful and intelligent art."

Michaels discusses the relationship between creativity and death through his character Phillip in the title story, which "identifies the personal history of the narrator with the history of modern European Jewry," Lehmann-Haupt writes in the *New York Times.* He feels that the story raises the question, "By what right do we go on living and creating when our forefathers have been slaughtered?" Phillip's reflections include a quote from Wallace Stevens (" 'Death is the mother of beauty' "), and an extended quote from Lord Byron. In a letter describing the execution of three robbers in Rome, Byron admits that, after the first decapitation, the next two failed to move him as horrors, though he would have rescued them if he could. Lehmann-Haupt paraphrases Byron to put the story's thesis, as he sees it, into simple terms: "I would have saved them if I could. But I couldn't, so I rescued art from them." Moreover, the reviewer concludes, "This is Mr. Michaels's achievement. . . . He has rescued art from the horror."

"Leonard Michaels's stories established him as a master phenomenologist of dread and desire. *The Men's Club* will confirm and enlarge that reputation," Dave Reid comments in the *Threepenny Review.* In the novel, a group of men assemble in the Berkeley home of a psychiatrist to form a club. The club's purpose, they discover, is "to make women cry," and to tell their life stories—tales of sexual conquest, marital frustration, and insatiable appetite. "It is a little as if Golding's *Lord of the Flies* had been transposed to middle-class, middle-aging California," Carol Rumens remarks in the *Times Literary Supplement.* "As the night progresses," David Evanier summarizes in his *National Review* article, "the men fight, throw knives, destroy furniture, and howl together in unison." At that point, the host's wife returns to find the feast she had prepared for her women's group devoured and her home demolished. While she gives her husband a serious head injury with an iron frying pan, his guests escape into the early morning, offering no answer when one of them shouts "Where are we going?" Evanier remarks that "on its own terms it is a considerable novel. Nothing in Michaels's two previous books of short stories . . . prepared me for the relentlessly dark and brilliant strength of these pages. Here is a middle-aged predatory Berkeley inferno of loss and chaos."

Some critics view *The Men's Club* as an antifeminist novel; others contend it is feminist. A review in the *New Yorker* claims that the men in the novel amount to "one married misogynist split seven ways." Robert Towers concedes, "*The Men's Club* might at first glance seem to be part of an anti-feminist backlash, to draw its energies from male fantasies of revenge against the whole monstrous regiment of women. As an ostensible *cri de coeur* from a small herd of male chauvinist pigs, it will thrive upon the outrage it provokes and the rueful yearnings it indulges." Nonetheless, Towers suggests, the book's subtler implications become apparent during a more careful reading. *Newsweek* magazine contributor Peter S. Prescott believes that since the men reveal themselves to be at fault in their failed relationships, the book takes on "a distinctly feminist cast that is far more appealing than what we find in most novels written by angry women today." Michaels is surprised by both interpretations. He tells Suplee, "[*The Men's Club*] is not in any sense propaganda, pro or con feminism, pro or con male sensibility. . . . It is, I hope, believe it or not, a description of reality."

Another debate among critics is the attempt to link Michaels with literary influences. "From [Franz] Kafka and [Jorge Luis] Borges . . . and more immediately [Donald] Barthelme, Michaels has learned how to dissolve the conventions of 'rational' narrative, replacing continuity with a collage of intensely rendered moments, so that reading feels like taking a number of hard blows to the head and groin," Edwards remarks in his review of Michaels's second book. A *Chicago Tribune Book World* review by Joyce Carol Oates and a review in *Atlantic* also name Barthelme as an influence and add Philip Roth. However, Larry Woiwode argues in the *Partisan Review* that Michaels's works were completed before Roth's; and, regarding the Barthelme connection, Woiwode maintains, "In terms of influence, it seems surely possible that Michaels has touched on Barthelme as much as Barthelme on Michaels, especially since Barthelme didn't really delve deeply into anguish, Michaels's prime subject, until *The Dead Father* [published in 1975]." Rather, the major influences on Michaels, Woiwode believes, are not his contemporaries: "[Isaac] Babel is obviously Michaels's literary mentor, but it often seems that [Ernest] Hemingway is a favorite sounding board, the Americanized side of Michaels's fascination with violence, suicide, and death (which has 'eat' at its center), and perhaps a bit of patriarchal scourge, being anti-intellectual, a tyrant in most matters, and a fellow practitioner of the short sentence with the kick-back of a pistol-shot."

Allusions to Michaels's favorite writers appear often in the stories, which Towers believes are "excessively literary in their inspiration." An *Atlantic* contributor muses that "One piece [in the second book] pays homage to Borges so efficiently that there is hardly any Michaels in it." In the novel, Michaels deliberately adopts a different approach. "I think of *The Men's Club* as a descent into the human," the author told Simpson. In another interview, he told Benedict, "By that I mean the considerations of literary art in this book are supposed to seem minimal. Everything I talk about, I try to talk about in regard to human reality, which is a much sloppier thing than art." Towers's comment on the novel indicates that Michaels succeeds: "The literary influences so evident in the stories have now been largely assimilated. Leonard Michaels has become his own man, with his own voice and a subject substantial enough to grant his talents the scope they have needed all along."

In 1985, Michaels worked with director Edward M. Cohen to produce several of the Phillip Liebowitz stories as a play. "Leonard writes splendid dialogue," Cohen told *New York Times* contributor Samuel G. Freedman. "He writes short, concise stories. So there is a dramatic compression already there." Speaking to Freedman, Michaels described the experience of working with other artists to adapt the stories for theater as "wrenching," "frightening," and "exhilarating." Michaels also wrote the screenplay for the film based on *The Men's Club,* condensing its long monologues and adding a new ending in which the men finish their evening out with prostitutes instead of breakfast. Janet Maslin's review in the *New York Times* states that "the lengthy whorehouse sequence" which makes up the film's second half "wasn't in Mr. Michaels's book and didn't need to be." A *Los Angeles Times* review concurs that the film's "porno ambiance is doubly unfortunate," and adds that the film does not reach the potential promised in the "stinging, smart, abrasive dialogue from scenarist Leonard Michaels." But whatever the outcome, the author's foray into yet another genre sustantiates Evanier's observation that "Leonard Michaels breaks new ground, in the tradition of the artist who does not stand still."

BIOGRAPHICAL/CRITICAL SOURCES:

BOOKS

Contemporary Literary Criticism, Gale, Volume 6, 1976, Volume 25, 1983.
Michaels, Leonard, *Going Places,* Farrar, Straus, 1969.
Michaels, *I Would Have Saved Them If I Could,* Farrar, Straus, 1975.
Michaels, *The Men's Club,* Farrar, Straus, 1981.

PERIODICALS

Antaeus, summer, 1979.
Atlantic, April, 1969.
Chicago Tribune, January 31, 1990.
Chicago Tribune Book World, March 30, 1969.
Commonweal, September 19, 1969, July 11, 1975.
Contemporary Review, April, 1980.
Esquire, May, 1981.
Harper's, September, 1975.
Hudson Review, autumn, 1981.
Kenyon Review, Volume 31, number 3, 1969.
Los Angeles Times, May 10, 1981, May 28, 1981, September 22, 1986, January 18, 1990.
Los Angeles Times Book Review, November 26, 1989.
Nation, November 15, 1975.
National Review, September 18, 1981.
New Republic, July 19, 1969, August, 1978, May 2, 1981.
Newsweek, March 2, 1970, April 27, 1981.
New Yorker, May 4, 1981.
New York Review of Books, July 10, 1969, November 11, 1975, July 16, 1981.
New York Times, April 14, 1969, July 30, 1975, April 7, 1981, February 8, 1985, September 21, 1986, September 28, 1986.
New York Times Book Review, May 25, 1969, August 3, 1975, January 6, 1980, April 12, 1981.
Observer, January 27, 1980.
Partisan Review, winter, 1977.
Publishers Weekly, March 13, 1981.
Saturday Review, August 2, 1969, April, 1981.
Spectator, February 16, 1980.
Threepenny Review, summer, 1981.
Time, April 27, 1981.
Times Literary Supplement, April 23, 1970, February 22, 1980, October 16, 1981, October 18, 1985, February 2, 1990.
Village Voice, February 19, 1970, October 20, 1975, March 10, 1980, April 8, 1981.
Washington Post, May 26, 1981, October 3, 1989.
Washington Post Book World, February 17, 1980, April 26, 1981, February 25, 1990.

*   *   *

MICHENER, James A(lbert) 1907(?)-

PERSONAL: Actual date and place of birth unknown, although his passport notes that he was born February 3, 1907, in New York, N.Y.; raised by Mabel (Haddock) Michener in Bucks County, Pa.; married Patti Koon, July 27, 1935 (divorced); married Vange Nord, September 2, 1948 (divorced); married Mari Yoriko Sabusawa, October 23, 1955. *Education:* Swarthmore College, A.B. (summa cum laude), 1929; Colorado State College of Education (now University of Northern Colorado), A.M., 1936; research study at the University of Pennsylvania, University of Virginia, Ohio State University, Harvard University, University of St. Andrews (Scotland), University of Siena (Italy), British Museum (Lippincott Traveling fellowship). *Politics:* Democrat. *Religion:* Society of Friends (Quakers).

ADDRESSES: Home and office—P.O. Box 250, Pipersville, Pa. 18947.

CAREER: Held many odd jobs in his youth, including that of being a leading man opposite Drew Pearson's sister in a traveling show; was a sports columnist at the age of fifteen; George School, Pennsylvania, teacher, 1933-36; Colorado State College of Education (now University of Northern Colorado), Greeley, associate professor, 1936-41; Macmillan Co., New York, N.Y., associate editor, 1941-49; freelance writer, 1949—; creator of "Adventures in Paradise" television series, 1959. Visiting professor, Harvard University, 1940-41, and University of Texas at Austin, 1983. Member of Board of International Broadcasting, 1984—. Chairman of President Kennedy's Food for Peace Program, 1961; congressional candidate from Pennsylvania's Eighth District, 1962; secretary of Pennsylvania Constitutional Convention, 1967-68. Member of advisory committee on the arts, U.S. State Department, 1957; member of U.S. advisory commission on information, 1971—; member of advisory council of the National Aeronautics and Space Administration, beginning 1979. *Military service:* U.S. Naval Reserve, 1944-45; became lieutenant commander; naval historian in the South Pacific.

MEMBER: Phi Beta Kappa.

AWARDS, HONORS: Pulitzer Prize for fiction, 1948, for *Tales of the South Pacific;* D.H.L., Rider College, 1950, Swarthmore College, 1954; National Association of Independent Schools Award, 1954, 1958; L.L.D., Temple University, 1957; Litt.D., American International College, 1957; Einstein Award, 1967; Litt.D., Washington University, St. Louis, 1967; Bestsellers Paperback of the Year Award, 1968, for *The Source;* George Washington Award, Hungarian Studies Foundation, 1970; Franklin Award for Distinguished Service, Printing Industries of Metropolitan New York, 1980; cited by the President's Committee on the Arts and the Humanities, 1983, for his long-standing support of the Iowa Workshop writer's project at the University of Iowa.

WRITINGS:

(Editor) *The Future of the Social Studies* (nonfiction), National Council for the Social Studies, 1939.
(With Harold Long) *The Unit in the Social Studies* (nonfiction), Harvard University Press, 1940.
Tales of the South Pacific (fiction), Macmillan, 1947, reprinted, Fawcett, 1984.
The Fires of Spring (novel), Random House, 1949, reprinted, Fawcett, 1984.
Voice of Asia (nonfiction), Random House, 1951.
Return to Paradise (short stories and travel sketches), Random House, 1951, reprinted, Fawcett, 1978.
The Bridges at Toko-Ri (novel; first published in *Life,* July 6, 1953), Random House, 1953, reprinted, Fawcett, 1984.
Sayonara (novel), Random House, 1954, reprinted, Fawcett, 1986.
The Floating World (nonfiction), Random House, 1954, reprinted, University of Hawaii Press, 1983.
Selected Writings, Modern Library, 1957.
(With A. Grove Day) *Rascals in Paradise* (biographical studies), Random House, 1957, reprinted, Fawcett, 1979.
The Bridge at Andau (nonfiction), Random House, 1957, reprinted, Corgi Books, 1984.
(Editor) *Hokusai Sketchbooks* (art selections), Tuttle, 1958.
Hawaii (novel; first section originally published in *Life*), Random House, 1959, reprinted, Fawcett, 1986.
Japanese Prints: From the Early Masters to the Modern (art selections), Tuttle, 1959.
Report of the County Chairman (nonfiction), Random House, 1961.
Caravans (novel), Random House, 1963, reprinted, Fawcett, 1986.
The Source (novel), Random House, 1965, Fawcett, 1984.
The Modern Japanese Print: An Appreciation, Tuttle, 1968.
Iberia: Spanish Travels and Reflections (nonfiction), Random House, 1968, reprinted, Fawcett, 1985.

Australia (Finnish adaptation of segment of *Return to Paradise*), Otava, 1968.
America vs. America: The Revolution in Middle-Class Values (nonfiction), New American Library, 1969.
Presidential Lottery: The Reckless Gamble in Our Electoral System (nonfiction; also see below), Random House, 1969.
The Quality of Life (essays; also see below), Random House, 1969.
Facing East: A Study of the Art of Jack Levine, Random House, 1970.
The Drifters (novel), Random House, 1971, reprinted, Fawcett, 1986.
Kent State: What Happened and Why (nonfiction), Random House, 1971.
A Michener Miscellany, 1950-1970, edited by Ben Hibbs, Random House, 1973.
(Editor) *Firstfruits: A Harvest of 25 Years of Israeli Writing* (collection of fiction), Jewish Publication Society of America, 1973.
Centennial (novel), Random House, 1974.
About "Centennial": Some Notes on the Novel, Random House, 1974.
Sports in America (nonfiction), Random House, 1976, revised edition published as *Michener on Sport,* Transworld, 1977, reprinted under original title, Fawcett, 1983.
Chesapeake (novel), Random House, 1978.
The Watermen (illustrated selections from *Chesapeake*), Random House, 1979.
The Quality of Life, Including Presidential Lottery, Transworld, 1980.
The Covenant (novel), Random House, 1980.
(Contributor and author of foreword) Peter Chaitin, editor, *James Michener's U.S.A.* (nonfiction), Crown, 1981.
Space (novel), Random House, 1982.
Poland (novel), Random House, 1983.
Texas (novel), Random House, 1985, published in two volumes, University of Texas Press, 1986.
Legacy, Random House, 1987.
Alaska, Random House, 1988.
Journey, Random House, 1989.
Caribbean, Random House, 1989.
Pilgrimage: A Memoir of Poland and Rome, Rodale, 1990.

Many of James A. Michener's works have been translated into foreign languages. Collections of his books and manuscripts are kept at the Swarthmore College and University of Hawaii libraries; the Library of Congress also has a large collection of his papers.

SIDELIGHTS: "As a literary craftsman [James] Michener has labored to entertain," says A. Grove Day in the *Dictionary of Literary Biography.* He "is the literary world's Cecil B. DeMille," according to Arthur Cooper in *Newsweek,* while *Time* reviewer Lance Morrow remarks that "practically entire forests have been felled to produce such trunk-sized novels as *Hawaii* and *The Source.*" In *Centennial,* a novel that fictionalizes the history of Colorado from the beginning of time up to 1974, the author "begins with the first faint primordial stirrings on the face of the deep and slogs onward through the ages until he hits the day before yesterday," says Morrow. "He is the Will Durant of novelists, less an artist than a kind of historical compacter."

More specifically, Cooper characterizes Michener as "a popular novelist with an awesome audience for his epic narratives, an unpretentious, solid craftsman." Day adds, though, that many of Michener's books "also appeal to the thoughtful reader and are laden with details that reveal Michener's academic training and bestow information as well as enlightenment." As Day indicates, "he is a master reporter of his generation, and his wide and frequent travels have given him material for colorful evocation of the lives of many characters in international settings in periods going back to earlier millennia." As Webster Schott summarizes in the *New York Times Book Review,* Michener "has found a formula. It delivers everywhere—Hawaii, Africa, Afghanistan, America, Israel, even outer space. The formula calls for experts, vast research, travel to faraway places and fraternizing with locals. And it calls for good guys and bad guys (both real and imagined) to hold the whole works together. It's a formula millions love. Mr. Michener gratifies their curiosity and is a pleasure to read."

Raised near Doylestown, Pennsylvania, by Mabel Michener, a widow he refers to as his foster mother, James Michener has never known when or where he was born or anything about his actual family background. The Micheners were far from wealthy, and the author told Bill Hutchinson in the *Miami Herald* that he had "a hell of a youth until I was 14 or 15 and discovered athletics, fell into the All-America pattern."

Michener became curious about the world outside of Doylestown at a young age, although he was keenly aware that he would have to make his own way. At the age of fourteen he hitchhiked for several months through forty-five American states. After he returned home, he delivered newspapers, excelled in sports, and wrote a sports column for the local paper. He won a sports scholarship to Swarthmore College, and during one summer vacation he traveled with a Chautauqua tent show. (Michener incorporated some of these experiences in his second novel, the semiautobiographical *The Fires of Spring.*) After graduation, he began teaching at a local school and won a traveling scholarship to Europe, where he enrolled at St. Andrews University in Scotland, collected folk stories in the Hebrides Islands, studied art in London and Siena, Italy, toured northern Spain with a troupe of bullfighters, and even worked on a Mediterranean cargo vessel.

After his return to the United States during the Depression Michener taught, earned his master's degree, and served as associate professor at the Colorado State College of Education from 1936 through 1939. He published about fifteen scholarly articles on the teaching of social studies, became a visiting professor at Harvard University, and in 1941 was asked to accept an editorship with the Macmillan Company in New York. According to Day in his book *James A. Michener,* the author once told a college group that "no aspirant can avoid an apprenticeship to his literary craft. 'I *did* serve an apprenticeship,' he affirms, 'and a very intense one, and learned what a great many people never learn. I learned how to write a sentence and how to write a paragraph. . . . The English language is so complex, so magnificent in its structure that I have very little patience with people who won't put themselves through an apprenticeship.' "

Michener didn't publish his first work of fiction until around the age of forty, however, a fact he attributes to his disinclination to take risks, particularly during the Depression. And it was not until he volunteered for service in the U.S. Navy in 1942 that he began to collect experiences he could visualize as marketable fiction. His first assignment as a lieutenant was at a post in the South Pacific. From 1944 to 1946, he served as a naval historian in that region. During this tour of duty, Michener had the occasion to visit some fifty islands, and "as the war wound down," explains Day in the *Dictionary of Literary Biography,* "he retreated to a jungle shack and began writing the stories that were

to appear as his first novel, *Tales of the South Pacific,*" which won the Pulitzer Prize in 1948.

According to Day, "although *Tales of the South Pacific* is sometimes considered a collection of short stories and several chapters have been separately published in anthologies, Michener has always thought of it as a novel because of its strong theme and largely unified setting; several characters recur throughout the book, and the chapters are united through the characters' participation in a single cause—the giant anti-Japanese operation called 'Alligator.' The beauties and terrors of the South Seas form the background for the actions of members of almost every section of the American armed forces in the Pacific war—army, navy, air force, doctors and nurses, Construction Battalion workers, and radio operators." In Day's opinion, *Tales of the South Pacific* "is one of the best novels about Americans in the Pacific theatre in World War II."

New York Herald Tribune Weekly Book Review writer P. J. Searles agrees, stating, "Romantic, nostalgic, tragic—call it what you will—this book seems to me the finest piece of fiction to come out of the South Pacific war." Michener "is a born story teller," *New York Times* writer David Dempsey adds, "but, paradoxically, this ability results in the book's only real weakness—the interminable length of some of the tales. Mr. Michener saw so much, and his material is so rich, that he simply could not leave anything out." When the book was published in 1947, Orville Prescott in the *Yale Review* described Michener as "certainly one of the ablest and one of the most original writers to appear on the American literary scene in a long time."

After his discharge, Michener returned to Macmillan as a textbook editor. In 1949, Richard Rodgers and Oscar Hammerstein II adapted *Tales of the South Pacific* into the successful musical "South Pacific"; a share of the royalties from the play—later to become a film—enabled Michener to become a full-time writer. In his book *James A. Michener,* Day reports that the author once told him that "I have only one bit of advice to the beginning writer: be sure your novel is read by Rodgers and Hammerstein." As for the Pulitzer, Michener once commented to Roy Newquist in *Conversations:* "There were editorials that declared it was the least-deserving book in recent years to win the Pulitzer; it was by no means the popular choice. In fact, it was an insulting choice to many. At least two other books had been definitely favored to win. . . . I had no occasion to develop a swelled head."

Throughout the 1950s and early 1960s, Michener continued to set much of his work in the South Pacific and Far East. He was assigned by *Holiday* magazine to write some feature articles about various places in the Pacific, so at the same time he wrote *Return to Paradise,* a collection of short stories and travel sketches. He then wrote some works of nonfiction about the area, *The Voice of Asia* and *The Floating World.* Several novels, including *The Bridges at Toko-Ri, Sayonara, Hawaii,* and *Caravans,* also date from this period in Michener's career.

It was with his novel *Hawaii,* though, that Michener established the format that would see him through several subsequent novels and make him a best-selling author. Although *Tales of the South Pacific* won the 1948 Pulitzer Prize, it was not a best-seller, and as *New York Times Magazine* writer Caryn James explains, it was "only when he moved from small stories of people to monolithic tales of places—beginning with the fictionalized history of 'Hawaii' in 1959 through Israel in 'The Source,' South Africa in 'The Covenant,' 'Poland,' 'Chesapeake' and 'Space'—did he become the kind of brand-name author whose books hit the best-seller lists before they reach the bookstores."

James notes that "the Michener formula might seem an unlikely one for the media age: big, old-fashioned narratives weaving generations of fictional families through densely documented factual events, celebrating the All-American virtues of common sense, frugality, patriotism. Yet these straitlaced, educational stories are so episodic that they are perfectly suited to the movie and television adaptations that have propelled Michener's success."

In his book *James A. Michener,* Day describes *Hawaii* as "the best novel ever written about Hawaii." It was published a few months after Hawaii was granted statehood in August, 1959. According to Day, the book "is founded on truth but not on fact." Michener drew from his own experiences in the Pacific region to develop *Hawaii* and also consulted a variety of other sources, including missionary accounts. As the author stated in his book *Report of the County Chairman,* his goal was to portray "the enviable manner in which Hawaii had been able to assimilate men and women from many different races."

Writing in the *New York Times Book Review,* Maxwell Geismar praises the book as "a brilliant panoramic novel about Hawaii from its volcanic origins to its recent statehood. It is a complex and fascinating subject, and it is rendered here with a wealth of scholarship, of literary imagination and of narrative skill, so that the large and diverse story is continually interesting." Day reports, "This is not a historical novel in the usual sense, for not one actual name or event is given; rather, it is a pageant of the coming of settlers from many regions; and the main theme might well be: Paradise is not a goal to attain, but a stage to which people of many colors and creeds may bring their traditional cultures to mingle with those of the others and create what may truly be an Eden at the crossroads of a hitherto empty ocean."

Fanny Butcher characterizes *Hawaii* as "one of the most enlightening books ever written, either of fact or fiction, about the integration of divergent peoples into a composite society." She continues in the *Chicago Sunday Tribune* that it is "even more thrilling than the reliving of events, exciting, tense, often stupendous as many of them were. What makes the novel unforgettable is not only the deep understanding of national dreams and ways of life, not only the exciting panorama of events, but the human beings who were the motivators and the movers in the creation of today's Hawaii."

Some of the praise was qualified. A *Times Literary Supplement* writer indicates that "Mr. Michener's zestful, knowledgeable progress through the millenia is absorbing. He cannot, of course, with such enormous slabs of raw material to handle and shape, go anywhere deeply below the surface, but there are some splendid sustained passages in his book." William Hogan writes in the *San Francisco Chronicle* that "as he has adjusted details in Hawaii's history to suit his fiction, the author is forced to adapt characters to fit into the big historical picture. And that is the book's main weakness." Although *Saturday Review* critic Horace Sutton is of a similar opinion, he maintains that *Hawaii* "is still a masterful job of research, an absorbing performance of storytelling, and a monumental account of the islands from geologic birth to sociological emergence as the newest, and perhaps the most interesting of the United States."

After publishing *Hawaii,* Michener became involved in national politics. He actively campaigned for John F. Kennedy and wrote a work of political nonfiction, *Report of the County Chairman,* in which he chronicles that involvement. (A later Michener study, *Presidential Lottery,* presents an argument for reform in the method Americans use to select their president.) He was also an unsuccessful candidate for the House of Representatives from Pennsylvania's Eighth District.

In 1963, however, Michener returned to fiction with *The Source,* a book researched while he was living in Israel, and described by Day as another best-selling "mammoth volume." In this novel, Michener describes the archaeological excavation of Makor Tell, a mound that contains the remnants of various settlements built over the course of many centuries. As Day explains, "artifacts found in the various layers introduce chapters dealing with events in the Holy Land during the period in which the articles were made. . . . Prominent families of several nationalities are followed through the ages; the setting is limited to the invented tell of Makor, the surrounding countryside, and the shores of the Sea of Galilee." Day claims that *The Source* is "one of the longest of Michener's books, and the best in the opinion of many readers. Although it may lack a clear general theme, its leading topic is certainly the various facets of religion."

Michener's nonfictional account of the Spanish peninsula, *Iberia: Spanish Travels and Reflections* was followed by *The Drifters,* published the same year as his report on the Kent State University shootings. *The Drifters* is a novelistic account that follows the adventures of six young members of the counterculture as they wander through Spain, Portugal, and parts of Africa. The story is narrated by a sixty-one-year-old man and reflects the author's own interest in modern times and contemporary issues. *Saturday Review* writer David W. McCullough points out that *The Drifters* is also "something of a guidebook loosely dressed up as fiction: a guide to quaint and colorful places especially on the Iberian peninsula, and to the life-styles of the rebellious young." According to Peter Sourian in the *New York Times Book Review, The Drifters* "is an interesting trip and Michener is an entertaining as well as a knowledgeable guide. The novel has a more serious purpose, however, which is exhaustively to examine the 'youth revolution.' Michener brings to this task narrative skill and a nicely adequate socio-psychological sophistication." And Thomas Lask of the *New York Times* claims that "those interested in knowing how a sympathetic member of the older generation views some of the shenanigans of the younger will find 'The Drifters' a tolerable interlude, especially as it is spiced with travelogue evocations of foreign climes. Dozens of readers will be making notes of the places they too will want to visit."

Michener returned to his historical panoramas with *Centennial,* which fictionalizes the history of Colorado from the beginning of time up until 1974. The book is narrated by Dr. Lewis Vernor, who is writing a report on the village of Centennial. The first eighty or so pages of the book cover the area's early geology, archaeology, and ecology before humans even appear. And then, according to Day, *Centennial* introduces some "seventy named characters—. . . not including Indians, fur traders, trappers, cattle drivers, miners, ranchers, dry farmers, real estate salesmen, and assorted townspeople. Again national and ethnic interminglings in a limited region are recorded through many years, and little is omitted from the panorama of the developing American West."

The novel has few all-encompassing themes. As James R. Frakes writes in the *New York Times Book Review,* "denying himself the luxury of 'flossy conclusions' and dogmatic theorizing, the author allows himself only a very few unqualified extrapolations from the text: the determining endurance of the land, for instance; the interdependence of man, animal, earth, and water; the possibility that white survival in some areas may require a return to the permanent values of the Indian."

In Michener's book, *Chesapeake,* according to Christopher Lehmann-Haupt in the *New York Times,* Michener "does for Maryland's Eastern Shore what he did for Colorado in 'Centennial.' By telling the story of dozens of fictional characters who live in a partly imaginary locale, he tries to capture the real history of the area—in the case of the Chesapeake Bay, from the time in the 6th century when Indians and crabs were its chief inhabitants, down to a present when developers and pollutants have taken over."

Michener applies this same pattern to explore the history of South Africa in *The Covenant.* In this book, says William McWhirter in *Time,* the author "manages to cover 15,000 years of African history, from the ritual-haunted tribes of Bushmen to present-day Afrikaners obstinately jeering at appeals for 'human rights.'" Michener was criticized for his attempt in *The Covenant* to combine fiction with nonfiction. As Andre Brink notes in the *Washington Post Book World,* "in his portrayal of history the author adapts a curious method also characteristic of his earlier novel, *The Source:* even though well-known historical figures appear in it—the Trek leader Piet Retief, the Boer general De Wet, Prime Minister Daniel Malan and a host of others—many of their major exploits are attributed to fictitious characters appearing alongside of them. Imagine a novel prominently featuring Abraham Lincoln but attributing the Gettysburg Address to a fictitious minor character." However, according to John F. Bums in the *New York Times Book Review,* "the book's accomplishment may be to offer a public inured to stereotypes a sense of the flesh and blood of the Afrikaners, the settlers who grew from harsh beginnings to a white tribe now nearing three million, commanding the most powerful economy and armed forces in Africa."

Writing in the *New York Times,* Stephen Farber describes Michener's *Space* as a "fictional rendering of the development of the space program from World War II to the present." Michael L. Smith reports in the *Nation* that "real participants make occasional appearances, but Michener relies primarily on fictional approximations." In fact, says Smith, *Space* "is less a historical novel than a tract. In part, it is a celebration of space exploration as a glorious blend of science, American frontiersmanship and human curiosity. But more than that, it's an impassioned denunciation of what Michener considers one of the gravest dangers facing post-Vietnam America: the proliferation of an 'anti-science movement.'" Ben Bova in the *Washington Post Book World* adds that the book "contrasts several varieties of faith, from the simplistic faith of the German rocket engineer who believes that technology can solve any problem, to the faith of the astronauts who believe that flying farther and faster is the greatest good in the world."

Michener began *Poland* in 1977 with the belief that the country would become a focal point within the decade. To write the book, explains Ursula Hegi in the *Los Angeles Times Book Review,* Michener "visited Poland eight times and traveled throughout the country. He talked to people of different backgrounds and enjoyed the assistance of 15 Polish scholars." The result is a novelization of the last 700 years of the country's history, including several invasions and partitionings, the Nazi occupation during World War II, and a modern struggle of farmers attempting to form a labor union. As Bill Kurtis reports in the *Chicago Tribune Book World,* "by now, Michener's form is familiar. History is seen through the lives of three fictional families: the nobility of the wealthy Counts Lubonski; the gentry or petty nobility of the Bukowskis; and the peasant heart of Poland, the family Buk. Around them, Michener wraps a detailed historical panorama; he combines fact and fiction to breathe life into nearly 1,000 years of battles, with far more Polish defeats than victories. If

recited as dates and incidents, these would otherwise be dry as dust."

The book received qualified praise. Hegi claims that "though Michener captures Poland's struggle and development, he presents the reader with too many names and personal histories, making it difficult to keep track of more than a few characters." Other critics cite omissions, historical inaccuracies, and oversimplifications in Michener's research. And Patricia Blake reports in *Time* that the work glosses over Polish anti-Semitism. However, *Washington Post* reviewer Peter Osnos describes Poland as "James Michener at his best, prodigiously researched, topically relevant and shamelessly intended for readers with neither will nor patience for more scholarly treatments." And, adds Hegi, his "descriptions of the country—blooms covering the hillsides, the swift flow of the rivers, splendid groves of beech trees—are as detailed as his depictions of weapons, castles and costumes."

Texas was written when a former governor of the state, William Clements, invited Michener to create a book that would be timed to appear for the Texas Sesquicentennial in 1986. According to Hughes Rudd in the *New York Times Book Review, Texas,* "at almost 1,000 pages, contains enough paper to cover several New England counties. The novel is so heavy you could probably leave it on a Lubbock, Tex., coffee table in a tornado and find it there when everything else was still in the air over Kansas City, Kan." The frame for *Texas* concerns a committee appointed by a Texas Governor to investigate the state's history and recommend what students should be taught about their state. The story begins early in the sixteenth century when the state was still an unexplored part of Mexico.

Texas received many of the criticisms that are frequently accorded Michener's work. According to Nicholas Lemann in the *Washington Post Book World,* none of the characters "stays in mind as embodying the complexity of real life. The reason is not exactly a lack of art on Michener's part; it's more that the form dictates that everything novelistic must be in the service of delivering history. Nothing ever happens that doesn't embody an important trend." For example, Lemann writes, "when it's time to recount the story of the battle of the Alamo, [Michener] invents a handful of characters on both sides and has them engaging in dialogue with Jim Bowie, Davy Crockett, and General Santa Anna."

Michener's public seems not to have heeded the criticism, perhaps because his works so closely reflect his own personality. "A Michener novel is a tribute to the industriousness of both author and reader," says James, "and, in addition to the easy-to-swallow data, it contains a morality tale about the heroism of hard work and guts. His thick, fact-filled books seem thoroughly impersonal, but several days in Michener's company show the novels to be perfect expressions of their author's anomalies—moral without being stern, methodical yet digressive, insistently modest yet bursting with ambition, full of social conscience yet grasping at facts as a way to avoid emotion."

Michiko Kakutani comments similarly in the *New York Times* that Michener's books contain many "bits of knowledge," which "served up in the author's utilitarian prose, are part of Mr. Michener's wide popular appeal: readers feel they're learning something, even while they're being entertained, and they're also able to absorb all these facts within a pleasant moral context: a liberal and a humanitarian, Mr. Michener argues for religious and racial tolerance, celebrates the old pioneer ethic of hard work and self-reliance, and offers such incontestable, if obvious, observations as 'war forces men to make moral choices.'"

James quotes literary critic Leslie Fiedler as commenting that Michener "puts a book together in a perfectly lucid, undisturbing way, so that even potentially troublesome issues don't seem so. 'Hawaii' is about the problem of imperialism, yet one never senses that. 'The Source' is about the Middle East, one of the most troublesome political issues in the world, but he's forgotten all the ambiguities. His approach is that if you knew all the facts, everything would straighten out, so it's soothing and reassuring to read him."

Such an approach has its flaws. *New York Times* critic Thomas Lask explains that Michener "likes to have his characters perform against the background or in accordance with the events of history. The quirks of personality, the oddities of character, the unpredictable Brownian motions of human psychology appear to interest him little. He prefers to represent a history in action." A *Time* reviewer sums up that Michener's "virtue is a powerful sense of place and the ability to convey great sweeps of time. His weakness is an insistence on covering murals with so much background and foreground that he has learned only a few ways of doing faces."

Other reviewers find the amount of detail Michener typically includes in his novels to be overwhelming. He is "one of the most didactic of novelists, cramming his books full of lessons of geology, anthropology, history, and sociology," comments Cooper. Julian Barnes reports in the *Times Literary Supplement* that "at the gentlest prompt, the characters will perorate with cramming detail on . . . irrigation, dry-land farming, or anything else you care to mention." And in the opinion of Peter LaSalle of the *Los Angeles Times,* "Michener's novels don't really have plots, but rather strategies to convey the mounds of information on the subject."

As Jonathan Yardley reports in the *New York Times Book Review,* though, Michener "deserves more respect than he usually gets. Granted that he is not a stylist and that he smothers his stories under layers of historical and ecological trivia, nonetheless he has earned his enormous popularity honorably. Unlike many other authors whose books automatically rise to the upper reaches of the best-seller lists, he does not get there by exploiting the lives of the famous or the notorious; he does not treat sex cynically or pruriently; he does not write trash. His purposes are entirely serious: he wants to instruct, to take his readers through history in an entertaining fashion, to introduce them to lands and peoples they do not know." In Day's words, "as a scholarly novelist, Michener has won wide popularity without stooping to cheap melodrama."

Schott concludes that "while the arbiters of letters try to figure out what James A. Michener's fat books are . . . Mr. Michener goes on writing them as if his life depended on it." As Michener told James, "I don't think the way I write books is the best or even the second-best. The really great writers are people like Emily Bronte who sit in a room and write out of their limited experience and unlimited imagination. But people in my position also do some very good work. I'm not a stylist like Updike or Bellow, and don't aspire to be. I'm not interested in plot or pyrotechnics, but I sure work to get a steady flow. If I try to describe a chair, I can describe it so that a person will read it to the end. The way the words flow, trying to maintain a point of view and a certain persuasiveness—that I can do." And he still has plenty of ideas for future development, he told *Insight* reporter Harvey Hagman in 1986. "I am able to work, and I love it. I have entered a profession which allows you to keep working at top energy. It's a wonderful job I have."

MEDIA ADAPTATIONS: Tales of the South Pacific was adapted by Richard Rodgers and Oscar Hammerstein II and produced as the musical "South Pacific."; a film was adapted from the play in 1958. *Return to Paradise, The Bridges of Toko-Ri,* and *Sayonara* were all made into films, as were the short stories "Until They Sail," and "Mr. Morgan," both from the book *Return to Paradise;* the film "Men of the Fighting Lady," 1954, was based on a Michener work entitled "Forgotten Heroes of Korea." The novel *Hawaii* was adapted into two films, "Hawaii," 1966, and "The Hawaiians," 1970, both released by United Artists in 1970. A television adaptation of *Centennial* was broadcast during the 1978-79 season; *Space* was adapted into a television mini-series in 1985.

BIOGRAPHICAL/CRITICAL SOURCES:

BOOKS

Authors in the News, Volume 1, Gale, 1976.
Becker, G. J., *James A. Michener,* Ungar, 1983.
Contemporary Literary Criticism, Gale, Volume 1, 1973, Volume 5, 1976, Volume 11, 1979, Volume 29, 1984.
Conversations with Writers, Gale, 1978.
Day, A. Grove, *James A. Michener,* Twayne, 1964.
Dictionary of Literary Biography, Volume 6: *American Novelists since World War II,* Second Series, Gale, 1980.
Hayes, J. P., *James A. Michener,* Bobbs-Merrill, 1984.
Kings, J., *In Search of Centennial,* Random House, 1978.
Michener, James A., *Report of the County Chairman,* Random House, 1961.
Michener, James A., *Iberia: Spanish Travels and Reflections,* Random House, 1968, reprinted, Fawcett, 1985.
Michener, James A., *About "Centennial": Some Notes on the Novel,* Random House, 1974.
Murrow, Edward Roscoe, *This I Believe,* Volume 2, Simon & Schuster, 1954.
Newquist, Roy, *Conversations,* Rand McNally, 1967.
Prescott, Orville, *In My Opinion: An Inquiry into the Contemporary Novel,* Bobbs, 1952.
Stuckey, W. J., *The Pulitzer Prize Novels,* University of Oklahoma Press, 1966.
Warfel, Harry Redcay, *American Novelists of Today,* American Book, 1951.

PERIODICALS

America, August 31, 1963, September 23, 1978, January 24, 1981.
Antioch Review, fall-winter, 1970-71.
Art America, November, 1969.
Atlantic, March, 1949, July, 1951, September, 1953, April, 1957, October, 1958, September, 1963, May, 1968, June, 1971, November, 1974.
Best Sellers, September 1, 1963, June 15, 1965, July 1, 1968, December 15, 1970, June 15, 1971, November, 1976, September, 1978.
Bookmark, June, 1951.
Books, October, 1971.
Books and Bookmen, December, 1971.
Book Week, May 30, 1965.
Book World, May 5, 1968, June 1, 1969, November 9, 1969, July 4, 1971, July 18, 1971.
Catholic World, June, 1960.
Chicago Sun, February 9, 1949.
Chicago Sunday Tribune, May 6, 1951, November 25, 1951, July 12, 1953, January 31, 1954, December 26, 1954, March 3, 1957, November 22, 1959, May 7, 1961.

Chicago Tribune, January 17, 1982, September 29, 1983, June 27, 1985, October 17, 1985.

Chicago Tribune Book World, October 3, 1982, September 4, 1983, October 13, 1985.

Children's Book World, November 5, 1967.

Christian Science Monitor, February 5, 1949, May 1, 1951, July 9, 1953, December 23, 1954, February 28, 1957, September 11, 1958, June 3, 1965, May 9, 1968, June 17, 1970, September 18, 1978, November 10, 1980, October 6, 1982.

College English, October, 1952.

Commentary, April, 1981.

Commonweal, April 27, 1951, February 12, 1953, July 31, 1953, April 12, 1957.

Congress Bi-Weekly, June 14, 1965.

Detroit News, October 3, 1982, September 18, 1983, October 27, 1985.

Esquire, December, 1970, June, 1971.

Good Housekeeping, February, 1960.

Guardian, November 10, 1961.

Harper's, January, 1961.

Insight, September 1, 1986.

Library Journal, October 7, 1970.

Life, November 7, 1955, June 4, 1971.

Los Angeles Times, November 21, 1985.

Los Angeles Times Book Review, December 7, 1980, October 3, 1982, July 31, 1983, September 4, 1983.

Nation, February 12, 1949, May 12, 1951, April 20, 1957, January 31, 1959, December 12, 1959, July 19, 1971, March 5, 1983.

National Observer, May 27, 1968, June 7, 1971.

National Review, June 29, 1971, June 29, 1974, November 22, 1974, August 7 and 14, 1976, September 15, 1978, May 27, 1983, November 11, 1983.

New Republic, May 14, 1951, August 17, 1953, May 29, 1961, September 21, 1974, August 7-14, 1976.

New Statesman, June 25, 1960, November 29, 1974.

Newsweek, January 25, 1954, May 14, 1962, August 12, 1963, May 24, 1965, May 6, 1968, September 16, 1974, July 24, 1978, November 24, 1980, January 16, 1984, September 23, 1985.

New Yorker, February 19, 1949, May 3, 1951, January 23, 1954, March 16, 1957, August 14, 1978.

New York Herald Tribune, May 28, 1961.

New York Herald Tribune Book Review, February 2, 1947, February 13, 1949, April 22, 1951, May 20, 1951, October 7, 1951, July 12, 1953, July 19, 1953, January 24, 1954, December 12, 1954, March 3, 1957, August 10, 1958, November 22, 1959, December 20, 1959, August 11, 1963.

New York Magazine, September 2, 1974.

New York Review of Books, December 19, 1968, August 17, 1978.

New York Times, February 2, 1947, February 3, 1947, February 6, 1949, February 7, 1949, April 22, 1951, April 23, 1951, October 30, 1951, July 12, 1953, January 24, 1954, December 12, 1954, March 3, 1957, August 3, 1958, May 1, 1968, June 10, 1971, September 27, 1974, July 1, 1976, August 1, 1978, November 14, 1980, September 29, 1982, September 3, 1983, February 20, 1984, September 25, 1984, October 9, 1985, October 31, 1985.

New York Times Book Review, May 16, 1948, May 22, 1949, July 12, 1953, March 3, 1957, November 8, 1959, November 22, 1959, June 18, 1961, August 11, 1963, May 23, 1965, July 24, 1966, May 12, 1968, May 25, 1969, June 6, 1971, June 27, 1971, September 30, 1973, February 10, 1974, September 8, 1974, June 27, 1976, July 23, 1978, November 26, 1978, July 15, 1979, November 23, 1980, September 19,

1982, June 12, 1983, September 4, 1983, November 20, 1983, October 13, 1985.

New York Times Magazine, September 8, 1985.

Palm Springs Life, October, 1974.

Paradise of the Pacific, September-October, 1963.

Philadelphia Bulletin, September 13, 1974.

Playboy, June, 1969.

Reader's Digest, April, 1954.

San Francisco Chronicle, February 4, 1949, May 6, 1951, July 12, 1953, January 29, 1954, December 19, 1954, February 28, 1957, August 17, 1958, November 24, 1959, November 25, 1959, May 3, 1961.

Saturday Evening Post, January, 1976.

Saturday Review, April 28, 1951, July 1, 1953, February 6, 1954, January 1, 1955, March 2, 1957, November 21, 1959, June 10, 1961, September 7, 1963, May 29, 1965, May 4, 1968, April 12, 1969, May 1, 1971, September 18, 1971, June 26, 1976, June, 1980, November, 1980.

Saturday Review of Literature, February 12, 1949, April 28, 1951.

Spectator, June 25, 1954, September 15, 1955, November 10, 1961.

Sports Illustrated, May 12, 1980.

This Week, December 4, 1966.

Time, February 14, 1949, April 23, 1951, July 13, 1953, January 25, 1954, March 4, 1957, November 23, 1959, August 9, 1963, May 28, 1965, May 17, 1968, May 3, 1971, September 23, 1974, June 28, 1976, July 10, 1978, February 9, 1981, October 3, 1983, October 28, 1985.

Times Literary Supplement, October 26, 1951, July 9, 1954, May 17, 1957, February 19, 1960, June 17, 1960, November 17, 1961, October 14, 1965, November 7, 1968, July 23, 1971, November 22, 1974, July 22, 1977.

U.S. News, February 4, 1980.

U.S. Quarterly Book Review, June, 1947, September, 1951, September, 1955.

Variety, June 22, 1970, November 8, 1972.

Vital Speeches, July 15, 1979.

Vogue, November 1, 1966.

Washington Post, September 2, 1983.

Washington Post Book World, June 4, 1972, September 1, 1974, July 9, 1978, September 30, 1979, November 2, 1980, December 6, 1981, September 12, 1982, September 29, 1985.

Writer's Digest, April 1972, May, 1972.

Yale Review, spring, 1947, spring, 1949.

* * *

MILITANT
See SANDBURG, Carl (August)

* * *

MILLAR, Kenneth 1915-1983
(John Macdonald, John Ross Macdonald, Ross Macdonald)

PERSONAL: Surname is pronounced Miller; born December 13, 1915, in Los Gatos, Calif.; died of complications from Alzheimer's disease, July 11, 1983, in Santa Barbara, Calif.; cremated, with ashes scattered in Santa Barbara Channel; son of John Macdonald (a newspaper editor) and Anne (Moyer) Millar; married Margaret Ellis Sturm (a mystery writer), June 2, 1938; children: Linda Jane (Mrs. Joseph J. Pagnusat; deceased). *Education:* University of Western Ontario, B.A., 1938; University of

Toronto, graduate study, 1938-39; University of Michigan, M.A., 1943, Ph.D., 1951. *Politics:* Democrat.

CAREER: Mystery writer. Kitchener Collegiate Institute, Kitchener, Ontario, Canada, teacher of English and history, 1939-41; University of Michigan, Ann Arbor, teaching fellow, 1942-44, 1948-49; teacher of writing in adult education program, Santa Barbara, Calif., 1957-59. Trustee, Santa Barbara Natural History Museum, beginning 1970. *Military service:* U.S. Naval Reserve, 1944-46; became lieutenant junior grade.

MEMBER: Mystery Writers of America (member of board of directors, 1960-61, and 1964-65; president, 1965), American Civil Liberties Union, Authors League of America, Crime Writers Association, Writers Guild of America West, Sierra Club, National Audubon Society, Santa Barbara Audubon Society (publicity chairman, 1965-66), Coral Casino.

AWARDS, HONORS: Edgar Allan Poe Award, Mystery Writers of America, 1962, for *The Wycherly Woman,* and 1963, for *The Zebra-Striped Hearse;* Crime Writers Association, Silver Dagger, 1965, for *The Chill,* and Gold Dagger, 1966, for *The Far Side of the Dollar;* University of Michigan Outstanding Achievement Award, 1972; Grand Master Award, Mystery Writers of America, 1973; Popular Culture Association Award of Excellence, 1973; Robert Kirsch Award, *Los Angeles Times,* 1982; the Kenneth Millar Memorial Fund was established in 1983 by the Foundation for Santa Barbara City College.

WRITINGS:

The Dark Tunnel, Dodd, 1944, reprinted under pseudonym Ross Macdonald, Gregg, 1980, published as *I Die Slowly,* Lion, 1955.
Trouble Follows Me, Dodd, 1946, published as *Night Train,* Lion, 1955.
Blue City, Knopf, 1947, reprinted under pseudonym Ross Macdonald, Hill & Co., 1987.
The Three Roads, Knopf, 1948.

UNDER PSEUDONYM JOHN MACDONALD

The Moving Target (also see below), Knopf, 1949, reprinted under pseudonym Ross Macdonald, Gregg, 1979, published as *Harper,* Pocket Books, 1966.

UNDER PSEUDONYM JOHN ROSS MACDONALD

The Drowning Pool, Knopf, 1950, reprinted under pseudonym Ross Macdonald, Garland Publishing, 1976.
The Way Some People Die (also see below), Knopf, 1951, reprinted under pseudonym Ross Macdonald, State Mutual Book, 1982.
The Ivory Grin, Knopf, 1952, reprinted under pseudonym Ross Macdonald, Bantam, 1988, published as *Marked for Murder,* Pocket Books, 1953.
Meet Me at the Morgue, Knopf, 1953 (published in England as *Experience with Evil,* Cassell, 1954).
Find a Victim, Knopf, 1954.
The Name Is Archer (story collection), Bantam, 1955.

UNDER PSEUDONYM ROSS MACDONALD; MYSTERIES

The Barbarous Coast (also see below), Knopf, 1956.
The Doomsters (also see below), Knopf, 1958.
The Galton Case (also see below), Knopf, 1959, reprinted, Bantam, 1980.
The Ferguson Affair, Knopf, 1960, reprinted, Bantam, 1980.
The Wycherly Woman, Knopf, 1961, reprinted, Bantam, 1984.
The Zebra-Striped Hearse (also see below), Knopf, 1962, reprinted, Bantam, 1984.

The Chill (also see below), Knopf, 1964.
The Far Side of the Dollar, Knopf, 1965, reprinted, Bruccoli Clark, 1982.
Black Money (also see below), Knopf, 1966, reprinted, Bantam, 1988.
Archer in Hollywood (contains *The Moving Target, The Way Some People Die,* and *The Barbarous Coast*), Knopf, 1967.
The Instant Enemy (also see below), Knopf, 1968.
The Goodbye Look, Knopf, 1969.
Archer at Large (contains *The Galton Case, The Chill,* and *Black Money*), Knopf, 1970.
The Underground Man, Knopf, 1971.
Sleeping Beauty, Knopf, 1973.
The Blue Hammer, Knopf, 1976.
Lew Archer, Private Investigator (story collection), Mysterious Press, 1977.
Archer in Jeopardy (contains *The Doomsters, The Zebra-Striped Hearse,* and *The Instant Enemy*), Knopf, 1979.

UNDER PSEUDONYM ROSS MACDONALD; EDITOR

William F. Nolan, *Dashiell Hammett: A Casebook,* McNally & Loftin, 1969.
The Santa Barbara Declaration of Environmental Rights, January 28 Committee (Santa Barbara), 1969.
Great Stories of Suspense, Knopf, 1974.

UNDER PSEUDONYM ROSS MACDONALD; NONFICTION

(Author of introduction) Matthew J. Bruccoli, compiler, *Kenneth Millar/Ross Macdonald: A Checklist,* Gale, 1971.
On Crime Writing, Capra, 1973.
A Collection of Reviews, Lord John, 1980.
Self-Portrait: Ceaselessly into the Past, edited by Ralph Sipper, Capra, 1981, reprinted as *Inward Journey,* Mysterious Press, 1987.

UNDER PSEUDONYM ROSS MACDONALD; CONTRIBUTOR

Dorothy Salisbury Davis, editor, *A Choice of Murders,* Scribner, 1958.
Brett Halliday, editor, *Best Detective Stories of the Year,* Dutton, 1962.
Anthony Boucher, editor, *Best Detective Stories of the Year,* Dutton, 1966.
R. W. Lid, editor, *Essays Classic and Contemporary,* Lippincott, 1967.
Thomas McCormack, editor, *Afterwords,* Harper, 1969.
J. Francis McComas, editor, *Crimes and Misfortunes,* Random House, 1970.

CONTRIBUTOR

Ellery Queen, editor, *The Queen's Awards, 1946,* Little, Brown, 1946.
Queen, editor, *Murder by Experts,* Ziff-Davis, 1947.
(Under pseudonym John Ross Macdonald) John Dickson Carr, editor, *Maiden Murders,* Harper, 1952.
(Under pseudonym John Ross Macdonald) Queen, editor, *Ellery Queen's Awards: Ninth Series,* Little, Brown, 1954.

OTHER

Contributor to *Ellery Queen's Mystery Magazine, Cosmopolitan, Esquire, Argosy, Sports Illustrated, Saturday Night,* and *San Francisco Chronicle.*

SIDELIGHTS: The late Kenneth Millar, better known under his pseudonym Ross Macdonald, won recognition for his mystery novels featuring private detective Lew Archer. The Archer books, William Goldman maintained in the *New York Times*

Book Review, are "the finest series of detective novels ever written by an American." Macdonald was considered, along with his predecessors Dashiell Hammett and Raymond Chandler, to comprise "the big three . . . of the American hard-boiled detective novel," as Matthew J. Bruccoli wrote in the *Dictionary of Literary Biography Yearbook: 1983.* Hammett and Chandler had a tremendous influence on Macdonald's early writings. The hard-boiled detective genre the two men helped to create struck Macdonald as being "a popular and democratic literature . . .," he wrote in his introduction to *Kenneth Millar/Ross Macdonald: A Checklist.* "[Hammett and Chandler's] heroes seemed to continue in highly complicated urban environments the masculine and egalitarian frontier traditions of Natty Bumppo. . . . Their abrupt and striking scenes seemed to reflect the disjunctions of an atomized society. Their style, terse and highly figured, seemed not quite to have reached the end of its development." Macdonald was so impressed with Hammett's work in particular that he named Lew Archer in honor of Miles Archer, a character in Hammett's classic detective novel *The Maltese Falcon.*

Although Macdonald wrote detective novels in the hard-boiled tradition of Hammett and Chandler, beginning with *The Galton Case* he took the genre into new territory, exploring its psychological dimensions. His novels after *The Galton Case* were concerned with a recurring theme: the resolution of family conflicts through a psychological search of the past. The typical Macdonald novel begins with Lew Archer being hired to find a missing family member. Sometimes the person seems to have been kidnapped, other times they are runaways. Archer's investigation soon becomes a search into the family's past to determine the reasons for the disappearance. Archer discovers that an old crime—usually a murder—is the hidden cause of the present trouble. This discovery leads to new violence in the present. "The origins of present crime, of present distress," Charles Champlin wrote in the *Los Angeles Times Book Review,* "are found to be a generation or more in the past, in a tangle of greeds, fears, hatreds and betrayals that will not stay buried." Archer grows obsessed with the case as it unfolds, even seeming to relive past events himself. "As other people's pasts and plots metamorphose into Archer's," George Grella stated in the *New Republic,* "he becomes a participant in the sequence of events, its victim, even its perpetrator." When Archer ultimately solves the crime, it is often "by some flash of irrational and illogical thought, by intuition or dream," Grella wrote.

The similarity of this theme to psychoanalysis has been noted by several observers. Writing in the *Armchair Detective,* Zahava K. Dorinson noted that the model for the Lew Archer stories "is psychoanalytic therapy in which the patient's symptoms are a 'problem' which cannot be solved without uncovering a hidden past, mysterious because it is hidden, unknown. To discover the truth about the unknown is to cure the patient." Dorinson concluded that each Archer "adventure finds the sensitive hero involved in a case rooted in the past of a family constellation, and the denouement of which is simultaneously the resolution of an intellectual problem, the uncovering of truth about mysterious events and the curing of a sickness which afflicts at least one of the actors." Macdonald had, Clifford A. Ridley summed up in the *Detroit News,* "an intensely Freudian view of the human condition that traced the crimes of the present into a long-repressed past."

Macdonald's obsession with this theme had its roots in his own troubled childhood. His father abandoned his mother when Macdonald was four years old, and he was forced to live with a series of relatives across Canada. By the time he was sixteen, he once recalled, he had lived in some fifty different rooms. Mac-

donald was unable to write of his childhood for many years. An early attempt at an autobiographical novel, he wrote in *Kenneth Millar/Ross Macdonald: A Checklist,* "turned out so badly that I never showed it to my publisher." But following psychotherapy in the middle 1950s Macdonald was finally able to deal with this material in *The Galton Case,* a novel in which a woman hires Archer to find her long-lost son. The trail Archer follows leads back to Canada and to many of the sites of Macdonald's own childhood. The book takes the autobiographical material Macdonald could not handle earlier and successfully reworks it into the form of a detective novel. *The Galton Case* "was a watershed book," Joe Gores wrote in the *Dictionary of Literary Biography Yearbook: 1983,* "the one in which [Macdonald] shook free of the Chandler influence and began to speak in his own unique voice." "It marks," Champlin believed, "a new dimension in the Ross Macdonald body of work."

In subsequent novels Macdonald continued to explore his childhood and Lew Archer became, Champlin stated, "more a surrogate for the author." Macdonald once described Archer as "a welder's mask enabling us to handle dangerously hot material," as John Leonard quoted him in the *New York Times Book Review.* Archer plays the pivotal role in these later novels. He asks the questions that reveal, in bits and pieces, the hidden events of the past. He then fuses these events into a coherent whole, revealing not only the solution to the mystery but the truth about the family past as well. Archer, Champlin quoted Macdonald as explaining, is "less a doer than a questioner, a consciousness in which the meanings of other lives emerge." Archer's investigations, John Vermillion maintained in the *Dictionary of Literary Biography,* "force people to examine themselves and their links to the past, and to recognize that they are bound by past events which have fashioned their lives and will fashion their futures."

Ironically, it was Archer's own lack of a private life that allowed him to uncover the private lives of others. Divorced and with few friends, Archer had the time to devote himself to his work. Michael Wood, writing in the *New York Times Book Review,* found Archer to be "a wise, tired, divorced, and lonely private eye." "He is very much his own man," Vermillion once pointed out, "a man who has come to grips with his own deficiencies, a man for whom life is lonely and frequently painful, but nonetheless strangely satisfying." Noting that Archer evolves over the course of the book series, Eudora Welty wrote in the *New York Times Book Review* that Archer "matured and deepened in substance. Possessed even when young of an endless backlog of stored information, most of it sad, on human nature, he tended once to be a bit cynical. Now he is something much more, he is vulnerable. . . . He cares. And good and evil both are real to him." Unlike the hard-boiled detectives of Hammett and Chandler, Archer is "the sensitive observer, watching the human tragedy, grieving for the victims," Champlin believed. Lew Archer was judged to be "a masterful creation" by Bruce Cook in *Catholic World* and a "distinguished creation" by Welty.

Because the Archer books always involved a similar search in the past, several critics were moved to question their value. Cook thought Macdonald was "rewriting the same novel over and over again. . . . As his plots continue to move backward in time and through the generations, they have also become rather baroque in their development—terribly involuted and complicated." Jean White of the *Washington Post Book World* also noted the repetition of plot to be found in the Archer books. "Perhaps," White mused, "Archer is a trifle weary himself as case after case leads him to some terrible crime from the past that explodes to shatter a family a generation or two later. By now, you pick up a new Lew Archer novel and immediately begin trying to piece together tangled kinships and hidden family secrets." But White found that despite the familiarity of the pattern, Macdonald's books were still satisfying: "Macdonald does it well, if again and again. He is an honest writer, a talented craftsman. He adds a psychological and social dimension to mystery writing."

Like Hammett and Chandler before him, Macdonald set his novels in California, and his ability to evoke the contemporary California scene was especially praised by several critics. "Nobody," Goldman asserted, "writes southern California like Macdonald writes it." Lew Archer's cases take him from his modest two-room office into the wealthy suburbs and the dangerous underworld of Los Angeles. "The setting is always California," Julian Symons wrote in *Mortal Consequences: A History—From the Detective Story to the Crime Novel,* "sometimes its rich face and often its dirty backside." Archer's southern California, White believed, is "the land of the new rich with their houses and egos clinging precariously to the hillsides; the land of restless, rootless human beings lost in a technological society. Macdonald's crime novels give a better feel for this life and the people than a lot of serious fiction." A deep concern for the environment is evident in much of Macdonald's work. In private life, he picketed on behalf of environmental groups against industrial polluters. He was also active in efforts to save the California condor from extinction. In such novels as *Sleeping Beauty,* in which the Santa Barbara oil spill of 1969 is prominently featured, Macdonald made clear his "view of California as a place of immense beauty made ugly by man," Symons noted.

Although he was born in California, Macdonald did not return there until the Second World War when, serving in the U.S. Navy, he was stationed in San Diego. In 1945 his wife, Margaret Millar, visited him. On her way back to Toronto, her train passed through nearby Santa Barbara. She fell in love with the city from her window. She got off at the next station and bought a house the following day. The couple never regretted it.

Macdonald's wife was a major impetus at the beginning of his writing career. Confined to bed for six months with a heart ailment, Margaret Millar began to read mystery novels and, eventually, to write one of her own. The book was published and she began a writing career. Her success led Macdonald to try his hand at writing. His first few efforts were published under his real name, but to avoid confusion with his wife, he adopted the pseudonym John Macdonald, derived from his father's name. Confusion with John D. Macdonald, the author of the Travis McGee mystery novels, then led him to use John Ross Macdonald and, finally, to use Ross Macdonald. Speaking of his wife's influence on his early career, Macdonald once recounted: "By going on ahead and breaking trail, she helped to make it possible for me to become a novelist, as perhaps her life with me had helped to make it possible for her." In tribute to his wife, Macdonald made the day of their wedding—June 2nd—Lew Archer's birthday.

Macdonald's standing as a detective novelist, Frank MacShane wrote in the *New York Times Book Review,* "lay in the psychological insights he added to the tradition that had been handed down to him by Hammett and Chandler." Outside of the detective genre, MacShane believed, Macdonald ranked as "one of the best writers of his generation." Similarly, Bruccoli made the distinction that "an attempt to assess [Macdonald's] career properly must judge him as a novelist who wrote mysteries, not as a mystery writer—that is, against the whole field of American fiction." William McPherson, writing in the *Washington Post Book World,* compared Macdonald with a respected American writer of the nineteenth century. "Macdonald resembles," McPherson

wrote, "another artist obsessed with guilt and retribution: Nathaniel Hawthorne, moved ahead a century and waking up in California, there to unravel the tangled past in the hope of exorcising it."

MEDIA ADAPTATIONS: The Moving Target was filmed as "Harper" by Warner Bros. in 1966; *The Underground Man* was filmed for television by Paramount in 1974; *The Drowning Pool* was filmed by Warner Bros. in 1975; "Archer," a National Broadcasting Company television series in 1975, was based on several of Macdonald's short stories featuring private detective Lew Archer.

BIOGRAPHICAL/CRITICAL SOURCES:

BOOKS

Bruccoli, Matthew J., compiler, *Kenneth Millar/Ross Macdonald: A Checklist,* Gale, 1971.
Bruccoli, Matthew J., *Kenneth Millar/Ross Macdonald: A Descriptive Bibliography,* University of Pittsburgh Press, 1983.
Bruccoli, Matthew J., *Ross Macdonald,* Harcourt, 1984.
Contemporary Literary Criticism, Gale, Volume 1, 1973, Volume 2, 1974, Volume 3, 1975, Volume 14, 1980, Volume 34, 1985, Volume 41, 1987.
Dictionary of Literary Biography, Volume 2: *American Novelists since World War II,* Gale, 1978.
Dictionary of Literary Biography Documentary Series, Volume 6, Gale, 1989.
Dictionary of Literary Biography Yearbook: 1983, Gale, 1984.
Macdonald, Ross, *Self-Portrait: Ceaselessly into the Past,* edited by Ralph Sipper, Capra, 1981.
Symons, Julian, *Mortal Consequences: A History—From the Detective Story to the Crime Novel,* Harper, 1972.
Wolfe, Peter, *Dreamers Who Live Their Dreams: The World of Ross Macdonald's Novels,* Bowling Green University, 1977.

PERIODICALS

Armchair Detective, August, 1973, January, 1977.
Books & Bookmen, October, 1968.
Catholic World, October, 1971.
Commentary, September, 1971.
Esquire, June, 1972, August, 1975.
Hudson Review, spring, 1966.
John O'London's Books of the Month, November, 1964.
London Magazine, June-July, 1972.
Los Angeles Magazine, March, 1963.
Los Angeles Times, July 31, 1983.
Los Angeles Times Book Review, September 6, 1981, November 21, 1982.
National Observer, September 15, 1969, January 5, 1970.
New Republic, July 26, 1975.
Newsweek, July 28, 1969, March 22, 1971.
New York Post, November 27, 1960, May 9, 1965.
New York Review of Books, May 18, 1972.
New York Times, July 6, 1986, February 19, 1971.
New York Times Book Review, March 3, 1968, June 1, 1969, February 14, 1971, May 20, 1973, June 13, 1976, December 18, 1977, September 11, 1983.
Seattle Times, August 17, 1968.
Time, August 15, 1967.
Times Literary Supplement, April 2, 1982.
Washington Post, April 21, 1971.
Washington Post Book World, February 2, 1967, May 20, 1973, June 27, 1976.
West, December 10, 1967.

OBITUARIES:

PERIODICALS

Chicago Tribune, July 14, 1983.
Detroit News, July 13, 1983.
Newsweek, July 25, 1983.
New York Times, July 13, 1983.
Publishers Weekly, July 29, 1983.
Rolling Stone, September 1, 1983.
Time, July 25, 1983.
Times (London), July 14, 1983.
Washington Post, July 13, 1983.

*　　*　　*

MILLAY, E. Vincent
See MILLAY, Edna St. Vincent

*　　*　　*

MILLAY, Edna St. Vincent   1892-1950
(E. Vincent Millay; Nancy Boyd, a pseudonym)

PERSONAL: Born February 22, 1892, in Rockland, Me.; died of a heart attack, October 19, 1950, at Steepletop, Austerlitz, N.Y.; daughter of Henry Tolman (a school principal and superintendent) and Cora Buzzelle (a singer and a practical nurse) Millay; married Eugen Jan Boissevain (in business), July 18, 1923 (died August 30, 1949). *Education:* Attended Barnard College, 1913; Vassar College, A.B., 1917.

CAREER: Poet, dramatist, lyricist, lecturer, translator, and short story writer. Acted with Provincetown Players, 1917-19; free-lance writer for periodicals, 1919-20; traveled in Europe, 1921-23; toured the Orient, 1924; gave reading tours, beginning in 1925, and national radio broadcasts, 1932-33; Prix Femina Committee, president and presenter, c. early 1930s; produced propaganda verse for Writers' War Board during early 1940s.

AWARDS, HONORS: Prize from *Poetry,* 1920, for "The Beanstalk"; Pulitzer Prize for poetry, 1923, for *The Ballad of the Harp-Weaver, A Few Figs From Thistles,* and eight sonnets in *American Poetry: A Miscellany;* Litt.D. from Tufts College, 1925, University of Wisconsin, 1933, Russell Sage College, 1933, and Colby College, 1937; Helen Haire Levinson Prize, 1931, for sonnets in *Poetry;* laureate of General Federation of Women's Clubs, 1933; L.H.D. from New York University, 1937; Gold Medal of the Poetry Society of America, 1943.

WRITINGS:

Renascence, and Other Poems (title poem first published under name E. Vincent Millay in *The Lyric Year,* 1912), M. Kennerley, 1917, reprinted, Books for Libraries Press, 1972.
A Few Figs From Thistles: Poems and Four Sonnets, F. Shay, 1920, enlarged edition published as *A Few Figs From Thistles: Poems and Sonnets,* F. Shay, 1921.
Second April (poems; includes "Spring," "Ode to Silence," and "The Beanstalk"), M. Kennerley, 1921, reprinted, Harper, 1935 (also see below).
(And director) *Aria da capo* (one-act play in verse; first produced in Greenwich Village, N.Y., December 5, 1919), M. Kennerley, 1921 (also see below).
The Lamp and the Bell (five-act play; first produced June 18, 1921), F. Shay, 1921 (also see below).
Two Slatterns and a King: A Moral Interlude (play), Stewart Kidd, 1921 (also see below).
The Ballad of the Harp-Weaver, F. Shay, 1922, reprinted as "The Harp-Weaver," in *The Harp-Weaver, and Other Poems* (in-

cludes "The Concert" and "Euclid alone has looked on Beauty bare"), Harper, 1923.
Poems, M. Secker, 1923.
(Under pseudonym Nancy Boyd) *Distressing Dialogues,* preface by Edna St. Vincent Millay, Harper, 1924.
Three Plays (contains "Two Slatterns and a King," "Aria da capo," and "The Lamp and the Bell"), Harper, 1926.
(Author of libretto) *The King's Henchman* (three-act play; first produced in New York, February 17, 1927), Harper, 1927.
The Buck in the Snow, and Other Poems (includes "The Buck in the Snow" [also see below] and "On Hearing a Symphony of Beethoven"), Harper, 1928.
Fatal Interview (sonnets), Harper, 1931.
The Princess Marries the Page (one-act play), Harper, 1932.
Wine From These Grapes (poems; includes "Epitaph for the Race of Man" and "In the Grave No Flower"), Harper, 1934.
(Translator with George Dillon; and author of introduction) Charles Baudelaire, *Flowers of Evil,* Harper, 1936.
Conversation at Midnight (narrative poem), Harper, 1937.
Huntsman, What Quarry? (poems), Harper, 1939.
"There Are No Islands, Any More": Lines Written in Passion and in Deep Concern for England, France, and My Own Country, Harper, 1940.
Make Bright the Arrows: 1940 Notebook (poems), Harper, 1940.
The Murder of Lidice (poem), Harper, 1942.
Second April [and] *The Buck in the Snow,* introduction by William Ross Benet, Harper, 1950.
Letters of Edna St. Vincent Millay, edited by Allan Ross Macdougall, Harper, 1952.
Mine the Harvest (poems), edited by Norma Millay, Harper, 1954.
Take Up the Song, Harper, 1986.

Works also published in various collections, including *Collected Poems,* edited by Norma Millay, Harper, 1956; *Collected Lyrics of Edna St. Vincent Millay,* Harper, 1967; and *Collected Sonnets of Edna St. Vincent Millay,* Perennial Library, 1988; works represented in *American Poetry: A Miscellany.*

Also author of "Fear," originally published in *Outlook* in 1927; *Invocation to the Muses; Poem and Prayer for an Invading Army;* and of lyrics for songs and operas. Contributor to numerous periodicals, including *St. Nicholas, Current Opinion, The Lyric Year, Ainslee's, Poetry, Reedy's Mirror, Metropolitan, Forum, The Smart Set, Vanity Fair, Century, Dial, Nation, New Republic, Chapbook, Yale Review, Vassar Miscellany Monthly, Liberator, Harper's, Saturday Review of Literature, Outlook, Saturday Evening Post, Ladies' Home Journal, St. Louis Post-Dispatch, New York Herald-Tribune Magazine,* and *New York Times Magazine.*

SIDELIGHTS: Throughout much of her career, Pulitzer Prizewinner Edna St. Vincent Millay was one of the most successful and respected poets in America. She is noted for both her dramatic works, including *Aria da capo, The Lamp and the Bell,* and the libretto composed for an opera, *The King's Henchman,* and for such lyric verses as "Renascence" and the poems found in the collections *A Few Figs From Thistles, Second April,* and *The Ballad of the Harp-Weaver.* Like her contemporary Robert Frost, Millay was one of the most skillful writers of sonnets in the twentieth century, and also like Frost she was able to combine modernist attitudes with traditional forms creating a unique American poetry.

From the age of eight Millay was reared by her strong, independent mother, who divorced the frivolous Henry Millay and became a practical nurse in order to support herself and her three daughters. Though the family was poor, Cora Millay strongly promoted the cultural development of her children through exposure to varied reading materials and music lessons, and she provided constant encouragement to excel. Millay recalled her mother's support in an entry included in *Letters of Edna St. Vincent Millay:* "I cannot remember once in the life when you were not interested in what I was working on, or even suggested that I should put it aside for something else." Millay initially hoped to become a concert pianist, but because her teacher insisted that her hands were too small, she directed her energies to writing. From 1906 to 1910 her poems appeared in the famous children's magazine *St. Nicholas,* and one of her prize poems was reprinted in a 1907 issue of *Current Opinion.* As for her reading, she reported in a 1912 letter that she was "very well acquainted" with William Shakespeare, John Milton, William Wordsworth, Alfred Tennyson, Charles Dickens, Walter Scott, George Eliot, and Henrik Ibsen, and she also mentioned some fifty other authors. New England traditions of self-reliance and respect for education, the Penobscot Bay environment, and the spirit and example of her mother helped to make Millay the poet she became.

Only through fortunate chance was Millay brought to public notice. Her mother happened on an announcement of a poetry contest sponsored by *The Lyric Year,* a proposed annual anthology. Millay submitted some poems, among them her "Renascence." Ferdinand Earle, the editor, liked the poem so well that he wrote to "E. Vincent Millay," as she styled herself, expressing confidence that it would be awarded the first prize. Because the other judges disagreed, "Renascence" won no prize, but it received great praise when *The Lyric Year* appeared in November, 1912. Meanwhile, Caroline B. Dow, a school director who heard Millay recite her poetry and play her own compositions for piano, determined that the talented young woman should go to college. Encouraged by Miss Dow's promise to contribute to her expenses, Millay applied for scholarships to attend Vassar. After taking several courses at Barnard College in the spring of 1913, Millay enrolled at Vassar, where she received the education that developed her into a cultured and learned poet.

Millay went to New York in the fall of 1917, gave some poetry readings, and refused an offer of a comfortable job as secretary to a wealthy woman. Kennerley published her first book, *Renascence, and Other Poems,* and in December she secured a part in socialist Floyd Dell's play *The Angel Intrudes,* which was being presented by the Provincetown Players in Greenwich Village. Millay was soon involved with Dell in a love affair, one that continued intermittently until late 1918, when he was charged with obstructing the war effort. Millay engaged in affairs with several different men, and her relationship with Dell disintegrated. Although sympathetic with socialist hopes "of a free and equal society," as she told Grace Hamilton King in an interview included in *The Development of the Social Consciousness of Edna St. Vincent Millay As Manifested in Her Poetry,* Millay never became a Communist. However, her works reflect the spirit of nonconformity that imbued her Greenwich Village milieu.

In February of 1918, poet Arthur Davison Ficke, a friend of Dell and correspondent of Millay, stopped off in New York. At the time Ficke was a U.S. Army major bearing military dispatches to France. When he met Millay, they fell in love and had a brief but intense affair that affected them for the rest of their lives and about which both wrote idealizing sonnets. Millay's were published in 1920 issues of *Reedy's Mirror* and then collected in *Second April* (1921). Though Millay wore "the red heart crumpled in the side," she believed that love could not endure, that ultimately the grave would have her lover, a sentiment expressed in the line, "And you as well must die, beloved dust." She suggested that lovers should suffer and that they should then sublimate their feelings by pouring them "into the golden vessel of great song." Fearful of being possessed and dominated, the poet disparaged human passion and dedicated her soul to poetry. Millay thus maintained a dichotomy between soul and body that is evident in many of her works.

Millay had made a connection with W. Adolphe Roberts, editor of *Ainslee's,* a pulp magazine, through a Nicaraguan poet and friend, Salomon de la Selva. Roberts published her poems but suggested that she adopt a pseudonym and write short stories, for which she would receive more money. Under the pen name Nancy Boyd, she produced eight stories for *Ainslee's* and one for *Metropolitan.* These "Nancy Boyd" stories, cut to the patterns of popular magazine fiction, mainly concern writers and artists who have adopted Greenwich Village attitudes: antimaterialism, approval of nude bathing, general flouting of conventions, and a Jazz Age spirit of mad gaiety. For the heroines the question of love and marriage versus career is significant. They espouse the view that bodily passions are unimportant compared to the demands of art. Some critics consider the stories footnotes to Millay's poetry.

During 1919 Millay worked mainly on her "Ode to Silence" and on her most experimental play, *Aria da capo.* Millay's one-act *Aria* portrays a symbolic playhouse where the play is grotesquely shifted into reality: those who were initially "acting" are ultimately murdered because of greed and suspicion. Moreover, the action will go on endlessly—*da capo.* Most critics called it an anti-war play; but it also expresses the representative and everlasting like the Medieval morality play *Everyman* and the biblical story of Cain and Abel. For Millay, *Aria da capo* represented a considerable achievement. She remained proud of *Aria;* "to see it well played is an unforgettable experience," she wrote her publisher in one of her collected letters. Since its first production it has remained a popular staple of the poetic drama.

In 1920 Millay's poems began to appear in *Vanity Fair,* a magazine that struck a note of sophistication. Two of its editors, John Peale Bishop and Edmund Wilson, became Millay's suitors, and in August Wilson formally proposed marriage. Unwilling to subside into a domesticity that would curtail her career, she put him off. In *The Shores of Light,* Wilson noted the intensity with which she responded to every experience of life. That intensity used up her physical resources, and as the year went on, she suffered increasing fatigue and fell victim to a number of illnesses culminating in what she described in one of her letters as a "small nervous breakdown." Frank Crowninshield, an editor of *Vanity Fair,* offered to let her go to Europe on a regular salary and write as she pleased under either her own name or as Nancy Boyd, and she sailed for France on January 4, 1921.

Millay wrote comparatively little poetry in Europe, but she completed some significant projects and, as Nancy Boyd, regularly sent satirical sketches to *Vanity Fair.* In March she finished *The Lamp and the Bell,* a five-act play commissioned by the Vassar College Alumnae Association for its fiftieth anniversary celebration on June 18, 1921. Based on the fairy tale *Rose White and Rose Red, The Lamp and the Bell* was a poetic drama shrewdly calculated for the occasion: an outdoor production with a large cast, much spectacle, and colorful costumes of the medieval period. The play's theme is friendship crossed by love. In the end integrity and unselfish love are vindicated. Though she was aware that the play echoed Elizabethan drama, Millay considered it well constructed, but as she later observed in an October, 1947, letter, its blank verse "seldom rises above the merely competent."

Millay spent the early 1920s cultivating her lyrical works, which by 1923 included four volumes. *A Few Figs From Thistles,* published in 1920, caused consternation among some of her critics and provided the basis for the so-called "Millay legend" of madcap youth and rebellion. Whereas the earlier "Renascence" portrays the transformation of a soul that has taken on the omniscience of God, concluding that the dimensions of one's life are determined by sympathy of heart and elevation of soul, the poems in *A Few Figs From Thistles* negate this philosophic idealism with flippancy, cynicism, and frankness.

As a humorist and satirist, Millay expressed in *Figs* the postwar feelings of young people, their rebellion against tradition, and their mood of freedom symbolized for many women by bobbed hair. These sentiments found expression in the opening poem of the collection, "First Fig," beginning playfully with the line, "My candle burns at both ends." Prudence, respectability, and constancy were denigrated in other poems of the volume. The cavalier attitude revealed in sonnets through lines like "Oh, think not I am faithful to a vow!" and "I shall forget you presently, my dear" was new, presenting the woman as player in the love game no less than the man and frankly accepting biological impulses in love affairs. "Rarely since [ancient Greek lyric poet] Sappho," wrote Carl Van Doren in *Many Minds,* had a woman "written as outspokenly as Millay."

Figs, with its wit and naughtiness, represents only one facet of Millay's versatility. Her strengths as a poet are more fully demonstrated by her strongly elegiac 1921 volume *Second April.* Containing both free verse and the impassioned sonnets she had written to Ficke, the collection celebrates the rapture of beauty and laments its inevitable passing. "Beauty is not enough," Millay says in "Spring," her first free-verse poem. April brings renewal of life, but "Life in itself / Is nothing, / An empty cup, a flight of uncarpeted stairs." Despair and disillusionment appear in many poems of the volume. "Ode to Silence," expressing dissatisfaction with the noisy city, is an impressive achievement in the long tradition of the free ode. With "The Beanstalk," brash and lively, she asserts the value of poetic imagination in a harsh world by describing the danger and exhilaration of climbing the beanstalk to the sky and claiming equality with the giant.

The Harp-Weaver, and Other Poems, Millay's collection of 1923, was dedicated to her mother: "How the sacrificing mother haunts her," Dorothy Thompson observed in *The Courage to Be Happy.* A carefully constructed mixture of ballad and nursery rhyme, the title poem tells a story of a penniless, self-sacrificing mother who spends Christmas Eve weaving for her son "wonderful things" on the strings of a harp, "the clothes of a king's son." Millay thus paid tribute to her mother's sacrifices that enabled the young girl to have gifts of music, poetry, and culture—the all-important clothing of mind and heart. Some of these poems speak out for the independence of women; in several, The Girl speaks, revealing an inner life in great contrast to outward appearances. Feminine independence is also dramatized in "The Concert," and the superior woman's exasperation at being patronized, in Sonnet 8: "Oh, oh, you will be sorry for that word!" Many other sonnets are notable. Sonnet 18, "I, being born a woman and distressed," is a frank, feminist poem acknowledging her biological needs as a woman that leave her "once again undone, possessed"; but thinking as usual in terms of a dichotomy between body and mind, she finds "this frenzy insufficient reason / For conversation when we meet again." The finest sonnet in the collection is the much-praised and frequently anthologized "Euclid alone has looked on Beauty bare," which like Percy Bysshe Shelley's "Hymn to Intellectual Beauty" exhibits an ide-

alism. By way of Euclid, the father of geometry, Millay pays honor to the perfect intellectual pattern of beauty that governs every physical manifestation of it. Also in the volume are seventeen "Sonnets from an Ungrafted Tree," telling of a New England farm woman who returns in winter to the house of an unloved, commonplace husband to care for him during the ordeal of his last days. Critics regarded the physical and psychological realism of this sequence as truly striking. The poems abound in accurate details of country life set down with startling precision of diction and imagery.

By 1924 Millay's poetry had received many favorable appraisals, though some reviewers voiced reservations. Mark Van Doren recorded in the *Nation* that Millay had made remarkable improvement from 1917 to 1921, and Pierre Loving in the *Greenwich Villager* regarded her as the finest living American lyric poet. Harold Lewis Cook said in the introduction to Karl Yost's Millay bibliography that the *Harp-Weaver* sonnets "mark a milestone in the conquest of prejudice and evasion." Critical commentary indicates that for many women readers, *Harp-Weaver* was perhaps more important than *Figs* for expressing the new woman. Harriet Monroe in her *Poetry* review of *Harp-Weaver* wrote appreciatively, "How neatly she upsets the carefully built walls of convention which men have set up around their Ideal Woman . . . !" Monroe further suggested that Millay might "perhaps be the greatest woman poet since Sappho."

In 1922, in the midst of her development as a lyric poet, Millay and her mother went to the south of France, where Millay was supposed to complete "Hardigut," a satiric and allegorical philosophical novel for which she had received an advance from her publisher. But weakened by illnesses, she did not finish the work, and the Millays returned to New York in February, 1923. Refusing the marriage proposals of three of her literary contemporaries, Millay wed Eugen Jan Boissevain in July of 1923. The forty-three-year-old son of a Dutch newspaper owner, Boissevain was a businessman with no literary pretensions. Handsome, robust, and sanguine, he was a widower, once married to feminist Inez Milholland. He did not expect domesticity of his wife but was willing to devote himself to the development of her talents and career. In addition, he assumed full responsibility for the medical care the poet needed and took her to New York for an operation the very day they were married.

Early in 1925 the Metropolitan Opera commissioned Deems Taylor to compose music for an opera to be sung in English, and he asked Millay, whom he had met in Paris, to write a libretto. She agreed to do so. Because she and her husband had decided to leave New York for the country, Boissevain gave up his import business, and in May he purchased a run-down, seven-hundred-acre farm in the Berkshire foothills near the village of Austerlitz, New York. During this period Millay suffered severe headaches and altered vision. She nevertheless began writing a blank verse libretto set in tenth-century England. The work was eventually produced and published as *The King's Henchman.*

According to the *New Yorker,* Taylor completed the orchestration of most of the opera in Paris and delivered the whole work on December 24, 1926. Both Elinor Wylie, in *New York Herald Tribune Books,* and Wilson praised the work for its celebration of youthful first love. Monroe found it an acceptable opera libretto, yet "merely picturesque period decoration" much inferior to *Aria da capo,* "a modern work of art of heroic significance." But in the second volume of *A History of American Drama,* Arthur Hobson Quinn gave *The King's Henchman* credit for passion, dramatic effectiveness, and "stark directness and simplicity." Successful in New York and on tour, the opera also sold well as a book, having eighteen printings in ten months. With its publication and performance, Millay had climbed to another pinnacle of success.

The years between 1923 and 1927 were largely devoted to marriage, travel, the move to the old farm Millay called Steepletop, and the composition of her libretto. In August of 1927, however, Millay became involved in the Nicola Sacco and Bartolomeo Vanzetti case. On August 22, she was arrested, with many others, for picketing the State House in Boston, protesting the execution of the Italian anarchists convicted of murder. Convinced, like thousands of others, of a miscarriage of justice, and frustrated at being unable to move Governor Fuller to exercise mercy, Millay later said that the case focused her social consciousness. In a 1941 interview with King she asserted that the Sacco-Vanzetti case made her "more aware of the underground workings of forces alien to true democracy." The experience increased her political disillusionment, bitterness, and suspicion, and it resulted in her article "Fear," published in *Outlook* on November 9, 1927. In "Fear" she vehemently lashed out against the callousness of mankind and the "unkindness, hypocrisy, and greed" of the elders; she was appalled by "the ugliness of man, his cruelty, his greed, his lying face." Her bitterness appeared in some of the poems of her next volume, *The Buck in the Snow, and Other Poems,* which was received with enthusiastic approbation in England, where all of her books were popular. "In these experiments the poet's instinct never fails her," summarized Monroe.

Millay began to go on reading tours in the 1920s. Afflicted by neuroses and a basic shyness, she thought of these tours—arranged by her husband—as ordeals. Nonetheless, she continued the readings for many years, and for many in her audiences her appearances were memorable. Ralph McGill recalled in *The South and the Southerner* the striking impression Millay made during a performance in Nashville: "She wore the first shimmering gold-metal cloth dress I'd ever seen and she was, to me, one of the most fey and beautiful persons I'd ever met." When she read at the University of Chicago in late 1928, she had much the same effect on George Dillon. Dillon was the man who inspired the love sonnets of the 1931 collection *Fatal Interview.* If Millay and Dillon's affair conformed to the pattern of *Fatal Interview,* it probably flourished during 1929 and early 1930 and then diminished, but continued sporadically. Fanny Butcher reported in *Many Lives: One Love* that after Dillon's death a copy of *Fatal Interview* in his library was found to contain a sheet of paper with a note by Millay: "These are all for you, my darling."

Fatal Interview is similar to a Shakespearean/Elizabethan sonnet sequence, but expresses a woman's point of view. A reviewer for the London *Morning Post* wrote, "Without discarding the forms of an older convention, she speaks the thoughts of a new age." American poet and critic Allen Tate also pointed out in the *New Republic* that Millay used a nineteenth-century vocabulary to convey twentieth-century emotion: "She has been from the beginning the one poet of our time who has successfully stood athwart two ages." And Patricia A. Klemans commented in the *Colby Library Quarterly* that Millay achieved universality "by interweaving the woman's experience with classical myth, traditional love literature, and nature." Several reviewers called the sequence great, praising both the remarkable technique of the sonnets and their meticulously accurate diction.

Millay's next collection, *Wine From These Grapes* (1934), though it had no personal love poems, contained a notable eighteen-sonnet sequence, "Epitaph for the Race of Man." The *St. Louis Post-Dispatch* had published ten of the poems under that title in 1928; Millay added others and made decisions regarding the organization of the sequence, which has a panoramic scope. The first five sonnets prophesy man's disappearance and indicate points in geological and evolutionary history from far past to distant future. The second set reveals man's activities and capacity for heroism, but is followed by two sonnets demonstrating human intolerance and alienation from nature. In the sequence's final sonnets, the eventual extinction of humanity is prophesied, with will and appetite dominating. The poet did not intend the "Epitaph" as a gloomy prediction but, rather, as a "challenge" to mankind, or as she told King in 1941, a "heartfelt tribute to the magnificence of man." Walter S. Minot in his University of Nebraska dissertation concluded: "By continually balancing man's greatness against his weakness, Millay has conjured up a miniature tragedy in which man, the tragic hero, is seen failing because of the fatal flaw within him."

During winter and spring of 1936, Millay worked on *Conversation at Midnight,* which she had been planning for several years. But soon after reaching a hotel on Sanibel Island, Florida, she saw the building in flames and knew her manuscript had been destroyed. Upon her return to Steepletop, she began to call up the material from memory and write it down. Other misfortunes followed. In the summer of 1936, when the door of Millay and Boissevain's station wagon flew open, Millay was thrown into a gully, injuring her arm and back. As time passed the pain from this injury worsened. She endured hospitalizations, operations, and treatment with addictive drugs, and she suffered neurotic fears. Witter Bynner noted in a June 29, 1939, journal entry, published in his *Selected Letters,* that at this time, Millay appeared "a mime now with a lost face. . . . She thinks immediately of going home, of escape. . . . [Her] . . . face sagging, eyes blearily absent, even the shoulders looking like yesterday's vegetables." Two days later she seemed more normal. By March 10, 1941, she reported in a letter, her pain was much less; but her husband had "lost everything" because of the war. Despite Millay and Boissevain's troubles, Christmas of 1941 found her "really cured."

Even through these years she continued to compose. *Huntsman, What Quarry?,* her last volume before World War II, came out in May, 1939, and within the month sixty-thousand copies had been sold. The uneven volume is a collection of poems written from 1927 to 1938. A few of these works reflect European events. Others are descriptive and philosophical poems—poems dealing with love and sex—and personal poems—some defiant, others pervaded by feelings of regret and loss. Millay's frank feminism also persists in the collection. The distinguished writers who reviewed the volume disagreed about its quality; but they generally felt, as did Paul Rosenfeld in *Poetry,* that it was an autumnal book in which a middle-aged woman looked back into her memories with a sense of loss.

The 1930s were trying years for Millay. Until the advent of Adolf Hitler's Third Reich in 1933 she had remained a fervent pacifist. But the attacks of the Japanese, the Nazis, and the Italians upon their neighbors, together with both the German-Russian treaty of August 23, 1939, and the start of World War II, combined to change her views. On October 24, 1939, she appeared at the *Herald Tribune* Forum to advocate American preparedness. After the Nazis defeated the Low Countries and France in May and June of 1940, she began writing propaganda verse. With what Millay herself described in her collected letters as "acres of bad poetry" collected in *Make Bright the Arrows: 1940 Notebook,* she hoped to rouse the nation. However, as Ficke noted in his personal copy of Millay's *Collected Sonnets* (1941), her efforts were not effective, "being so largely hysterical and vituperative."

After the Japanese attack on Pearl Harbor she produced propaganda verse upon assignment for the Writers' War Board. Chief among these writings is *The Murder of Lidice* (1942), a trite ballad on a Nazi atrocity, the destroying of the Czech village of Lidice.

The strain of composing, against deadlines, "hastily written and hot-headed pieces"—as she labeled them in a January, 1946, letter—led to a nervous breakdown in 1944, and for a long time she was unable to write. Friends who visited Steepletop thought Millay's husband babied her too much; but Joan Dash contended in *A Life of One's Own* that only Boissevain's solicitude and encouragement enabled Millay to enjoy creative satisfaction again. After her husband's death from a stroke in 1949 following the removal of a lung, Millay suffered greatly, drank recklessly, and had to be hospitalized. But a month later she was back at Steepletop, where she stoically passed a lonely year working on a new book of poems. The volume, *Mine the Harvest* (1954), did not appear, however, until four years after her death from a heart attack in 1950.

From almost universal acclaim in the 1920s, Millay's poetic reputation declined in the 1930s. Few critics thought she had spent her time well in translating Baudelaire with Dillon or in writing the discursive *Conversation at Midnight* (1937). Her directness came to seem old-fashioned as the intellectual poetry of international Modernism came into vogue. In 1931 Millay told Elizabeth Breuer in *Pictorial Review* that readers liked her work because it was on age-old themes such as love, death, and nature. When Winfield Townley Scott reviewed *Collected Sonnets* and *Collected Lyrics* in *Poetry,* he said the "literati" had rejected Millay for "glibness and popularity."

By the 1960s the Modernism espoused by T. S. Eliot, Ezra Pound, William Carlos Williams, and W. H. Auden had assumed great importance, and the romantic poetry of Millay and the other women poets of her generation was largely ignored. But the growing spread of feminism eventually revived an interest in her writings, and she regained recognition as a highly gifted writer—one who created many fine poems and spoke her mind freely in the best American tradition, upholding freedom and individualism; championing radical, idealistic humanist tenets; and holding broad sympathies and a deep reverence for life.

BIOGRAPHICAL/CRITICAL SOURCES:

BOOKS

Beach, Joseph Warren, *Obsessive Images: Symbolism in Poetry of the 1930s and 1940s,* University of Minnesota Press, 1960.

Bogan, Louise, *Achievement in American Poetry: 1900-1950,* Regnery, 1951.

Brittin, Norman A., *Edna St. Vincent Millay,* Twayne, 1967, revised edition, G. K. Hall, 1982.

Butcher, Fanny, *Many Lives: One Love,* Harper, 1972.

Bynner, Witter, *The Works of Witter Bynner: Selected Letters,* edited by James Kraft, Farrar, Straus, 1981.

Collins, Joseph P., *Taking the Literary Pulse,* Doran, 1924.

Cowley, Malcolm, editor, *After the Genteel Tradition: American Writers Since 1910,* Norton, 1937.

Dash, Joan, *A Life of One's Own: Three Gifted Women and the Men They Married,* Harper, 1973.

Dictionary of Literary Biography, Volume 45: *American Poets, 1880-1945, First Series,* Gale, 1986.

Eastman, Max, *Great Companions: Critical Memoirs of Some Famous Friends,* Farrar, Straus, 1959.

Gould, Jean, *The Poet and Her Book: A Biography of Edna St. Vincent Millay,* Dodd, Mead, 1969.

Gurko, Miriam, *Restless Spirit: The Life of Edna St. Vincent Millay,* Crowell, 1962.

King, Grace Hamilton, *The Development of the Social Consciousness of Edna St. Vincent Millay As Manifested in Her Poetry* (dissertation), [New York University], 1943.

Kreymborg, Alfred, *Our Singing Strength,* Coward, McCann, 1929.

Madeleva, Sister M., *Chaucer's Nuns and Other Essays,* Appleton, 1925.

McGill, Ralph, *The South and the Southerner,* Little, Brown, 1963.

Millay, Edna St. Vincent, *A Few Figs From Thistles: Poems and Sonnets,* F. Shay, 1921.

Millay, Edna St. Vincent, *The Harp-Weaver, and Other Poems,* Harper, 1923.

Millay, Edna St. Vincent, *Letters of Edna St. Vincent Millay,* edited by Allan Ross MacDougall, Harper, 1952.

Millay, Edna St. Vincent, *Second April,* M. Kennerley, 1921.

Minot, Walter, S., *Edna St. Vincent Millay: A Critical Revaluation* (dissertation), [University of Nebraska], 1972.

Nierman, Judith, *Edna St. Vincent Millay: A Reference Guide,* G. K. Hall, 1977.

Ostriker, Alicia Suskin, *Stealing the Language: The Emergence of Women's Poetry in America,* Beacon Press, 1986.

Quinn, Arthur Hobson, *A History of American Drama From the Civil War to the Present Day,* Volume 2, revised edition, Crofts, 1937.

Sheehan, Vincent, *The Indigo Bunting: A Memoir of Edna St. Vincent Millay,* Harper, 1951.

Thompson, Dorothy, *The Courage to Be Happy,* Houghton, 1957.

Twentieth-Century Literary Criticism, Volume 4, Gale, 1981.

Untermeyer, Louis, *American Poetry Since 1900,* Harcourt, 1923.

Van Doren, Carl, *Many Minds,* Knopf, 1924.

Wilson, Edmund, *The Shores of Light: A Literary Chronicle of the Twenties and Thirties,* Farrar, Straus, 1952.

Yost, Karl, *A Bibliography of the Works of Edna St. Vincent Millay,* with an essay in appreciation by Harold Lewis Cook, Harper, 1937.

PERIODICALS

Book Review, January, 1924.

Colby Library Quarterly, March, 1979.

Greenwich Villager, August 3, 1921.

Literary Digest, June 9, 1923.

Mark Twain Journal, spring, 1964.

Measure, April, 1924.

Modern American Poetry, October 13, 1928.

Morning Post, (London), November 10, 1931.

Nation, October 26, 1921, November 14, 1934.

New England Quarterly, June, 1975.

New Republic, December 10, 1924, May 6, 1931.

New Yorker, February 19, 1927.

New York Herald Tribune Books, February 20, 1927, November 11, 1934.

New York Times, December 14, 1919.

Outlook, November 9, 1927.

Outlook and Independent, April 29, 1931.

Pictorial Review, November, 1931.

Poetry, August, 1924, April, 1927, February, 1935, October, 1939, March, 1944.

Quarterly Journal of the University of North Dakota, summer, 1931.
Saturday Review of Literature, November 10, 1934.
Sewanee Review, January-March, 1930.
Southwest Review, January, 1935.

OBITUARIES:

PERIODICALS

Life, October 30, 1950.
Nation, December 20, 1950.
New York Times, October 20, 1950.
Saturday Evening Post, November 25, 1950.
Time, October 30, 1950.

* * *

MILLER, Arthur   1915-

PERSONAL: Born October 17, 1915, in New York, N.Y.; son of Isidore (a manufacturer) and Augusta (Barnett) Miller; married Mary Grace Slattery, 1940 (divorced, 1956); married Marilyn Monroe (an actress), June, 1956 (divorced, 1961); married Ingeborg Morath (a photojournalist), 1962; children: (first marriage) Jane Ellen, Robert Arthur; (third marriage) Rebecca Augusta, Daniel. *Education:* University of Michigan, A.B., 1938.

ADDRESSES: Agent—International Creative Management, 40 West 57th St., New York, N.Y. 10019.

CAREER: Writer, 1938—. Associate of Federal Theater Project, 1938; author of radio plays, 1939-44; dramatist and essayist, 1944—. Also worked in an automobile parts warehouse, the Brooklyn Navy Yard, and a box factory. Resident lecturer, University of Michigan, 1973-74.

MEMBER: Dramatists Guild, Authors League of America, National Institute of Arts and Letters, PEN (international president, 1965-69).

AWARDS, HONORS: Avery Hopwood Awards from the University of Michigan, 1936, for "Honors at Dawn," and 1937, for "No Villain: They Too Arise"; Bureau of New Plays Prize from Theatre Guild of New York, 1938; Theatre Guild National Prize, 1944, for *The Man Who Had All the Luck;* Drama Critics Circle Awards, 1947, for *All My Sons,* and 1949, for *Death of a Salesman;* Antoinette Perry Awards, 1947, for *All My Sons,* 1949, for *Death of a Salesman,* and 1953, for *The Crucible;* Donaldson Awards, 1947, for *All My Sons,* 1949, for *Death of a Salesman,* and 1953, for *The Crucible;* Pulitzer Prize for drama, 1949, for *Death of a Salesman;* National Association of Independent Schools award, 1954; L.H.D. from University of Michigan, 1956, and Carnegie-Mellon University, 1970; Obie Award from *Village Voice,* 1958, for *The Crucible;* American Academy of Arts and Letters gold medal, 1959; Anglo-American Award, 1966; Emmy Award, National Academy of Television Arts and Sciences, 1967, for *Death of a Salesman;* Brandeis University creative arts award, 1969; George Foster Peabody Award, 1981, for *Playing for Time;* John F. Kennedy Award for Lifetime Achievement, 1984.

WRITINGS:

PLAYS

"Honors at Dawn," produced in Ann Arbor, Mich., 1936.
"No Villain: They Too Arise," produced in Ann Arbor, Mich., 1937.
"The Man Who Had All the Luck," produced on Broadway at Forest Theatre, November 23, 1944.

All My Sons (three-act; produced on Broadway at Coronet Theatre, January 29, 1947; also see below), Reynal, 1947, reprinted, Chelsea House, 1987.
Death of a Salesman (two-act; produced on Broadway at Morosco Theatre, February 10, 1949; also see below), Viking, 1949, reprinted, Chelsea House, 1987, published as *Death of a Salesman: Text and Criticism,* edited by Gerald Weales, Penguin, 1977.
(Adaptor) Henrik Ibsen, *An Enemy of the People* (produced on Broadway at Broadhurst Theatre, December 28, 1950), Viking, 1951.
The Crucible (four-act; produced on Broadway at Martin Beck Theatre, January 22, 1953), Viking, 1953, published as *The Crucible: Text and Criticism,* edited by Weales, Viking, 1977.
A View from the Bridge, [and] *A Memory of Two Mondays* (produced together on Broadway at Coronet Theatre, September 29, 1955; also see below), Viking 1955, published separately, Dramatists Play Service, 1956, revised version of *A View from the Bridge* (produced Off-Broadway at Sheridan Square Playhouse, January 28, 1965; also see below), Cresset, 1956, reprinted, Penguin, 1977.
After the Fall (produced on Broadway at American National Theatre and Academy, January 23, 1964), Viking, 1964, reprinted, Penguin, 1980.
Incident at Vichy (produced on Broadway at American National Theatre and Academy, December 3, 1964), Viking, 1965.
The Price (produced on Broadway at Morosco Theatre, February 7, 1968; also see below), Viking, 1968, reprinted, Penguin, 1985.
The Creation of the World and Other Business (produced on Broadway at Shubert Theatre, November 30, 1972), Viking, 1972.
Up from Paradise, with music by Stanley Silverman (musical version of *The Creation of the World and Other Business;* first produced in Ann Arbor, Mich. at Trueblood Theatre, directed and narrated by Miller, April, 1974; produced Off-Broadway at Jewish Repertory Theater, October 25, 1983), Viking, 1978.
The Archbishop's Ceiling (produced in Washington, D.C., at Eisenhower Theatre, Kennedy Center for the Performing Arts, April 30, 1977), Dramatists Play Service, 1976.
The American Clock (first produced in Charleston, S.C., at Dock Street Theatre, 1980; produced on Broadway at Harold Clurman Theatre, 1980), Viking, 1980.
Elegy for a Lady [and] *Some Kind of Love Story* (one-acts; produced together under title "Two-Way Mirror" in New Haven, Conn., at Long Wharf Theatre, 1983), published separately by Dramatists Play Service, 1984.
Playing for Time (stage adaptation of screenplay; produced in England at Netherbow Art Centre, August, 1986; also see below), Dramatic Publishing, 1985.
Danger: Memory! Two Plays: "I Can't Remember Anything" and "Clara" (one-acts; produced on Broadway at Mitzi E. Newhouse Theatre, Lincoln Center for the Performing Arts, February 8, 1987), Grove, 1987.

SCREENPLAYS

(With others) "The Story of G.I. Joe," produced by United Artists, 1945.
"The Witches of Salem," produced by Kingsley-International, 1958.
The Misfits (produced by United Artists, 1961; also see below), published as *The Misfits: An Original Screenplay Directed*

by John Huston, edited by George P. Garrett, Irvington, 1982.
"The Price" (based on play of same title), produced by United Artists, 1969.
"The Hook," produced by MCA, 1975.
Fame (also see below), produced by National Broadcasting Company (NBC-TV), 1978.
"Playing for Time," produced by Columbia Broadcasting System (CBS-TV), 1980.

FICTION

Focus (novel), Reynal, 1945, reprinted with introduction by the author, Arbor House, 1984.
The Misfits (novella; also see below), Viking, 1961.
Jane's Blanket (juvenile), Collier, 1963.
I Don't Need You Anymore (stories), Viking, 1967.
"The Misfits" and Other Stories, Scribner, 1987.

NONFICTION

Situation Normal (reportage on the army), Reynal, 1944.
In Russia, with photographs by wife, Inge Morath, Viking, 1969.
In the Country, with photographs by Morath, Viking, 1977.
Robert A. Martin, editor, *The Theatre Essays of Arthur Miller,* Viking, 1978.
Chinese Encounters, with photographs by Morath, Farrar, Straus, 1979.
Salesman in Beijing, with photographs by Morath, Viking, 1984.
Timebends: A Life (autobiography), Grove, 1987.

OMNIBUS VOLUMES

(Also author of introduction) *Arthur Miller's Collected Plays* (contains "All My Sons," "Death of a Salesman," "The Crucible," "A Memory of Two Mondays," and "A View from the Bridge"), Viking, 1957.
Harold Clurman, editor, *The Portable Arthur Miller* (includes "Death of a Salesman," "The Crucible," "Incident at Vichy," "The Price," "The Misfits," "Fame," and "In Russia"), Viking, 1971.
(Also author of introduction) *Collected Plays, Volume II,* Viking, 1980.

CONTRIBUTOR

William Kozlendko, compiler, *One-hundred Non-Royalty Radio Plays,* Greenberg, 1941.
Edwin Seaver, editor, *Cross-Section 1944,* Fischer, 1944.
Erik Barnous, editor, *Radio Drama in Action,* Farrar & Rinehart, 1945.
Margaret Mayorga, editor, *The Best One-Act Plays of 1944,* Dodd, 1945.
Joseph Liss, editor, *Radio's Best Plays,* Greenberg, 1947.
H. William Fitelson, editor, *Theatre Guild on the Air,* Rinehart, 1947.
One-Act: Eleven Short Plays of the Modern Theatre, Grove, 1961.
Six Great Modern Plays, Dell, 1964.
Poetry and Film: Two Symposiums, Gotham, 1973.

OTHER

Contributor of essays, commentary, and short stories to periodicals, including *Collier's, New York Times, Theatre Arts, Holiday, Nation, Esquire,* and *Atlantic.* The University of Michigan at Ann Arbor, the University of Texas at Austin, and the New York Public Library have collections of Miller's papers.

SIDELIGHTS: Arthur Miller is widely recognized as a preeminent playwright of the modern American theatre. Miller's realis-

tic dramas explore the complex psychological and social issues that plague humankind in the wake of the Second World War: the dangers of rampant materialism, the struggle for dignity in a dehumanizing world, the erosion of the family structure, and the perils besetting human rights. In an era marked by theatrical experimentation, much of it at the expense of theme and message, Miller has concentrated on portraying life as it is lived and on proving, in his own words, that "we are made and yet are more than what made us."

Although none of Miller's theatre work is specifically autobiographical, it has been strongly influenced by his particular life experiences. An early influential event was the Great Depression of the 1930s. Miller was born in New York City in 1915, and until 1929 he lived the comfortable life of an upper middle class businessman's son. Then the stock market collapsed, and his father, a coat manufacturer, was forced out of work. First his parents sold their luxury items, one by one, to pay the bills. Later the family had to move from the spacious Harlem apartment of Miller's youth to a tiny house in Brooklyn. Miller told the *New York Times* that the Depression "occurred during a particularly sensitive moment" for him. "I was turning 14 or 15 and I was without leaders," he said. "This was symptomatic not just of me but of that whole generation. It made you want to search for ultimate values, for things that would not fall apart under pressure."

Lacking funds for college tuition, and not having earned the grades to merit a scholarship, Miller determined to work until he could afford to enter a university. His job at a Manhattan auto parts warehouse exposed him to yet another troubling social conundrum: anti-Semitism. Being Jewish, he was hired only reluctantly, and occasional comments by his fellow employees let him know that his faith was held against him. Eventually he overcame the prejudice and made friends at the warehouse, but the experience enhanced his desire to change some of society's damaging attitudes.

In the midst of the Depression Miller entered the University of Michigan where, to quote Nelson, "the atmosphere was one of challenge rather than despairing finality." An undistinguished high school student, Miller had to prove himself capable of college work in his first year. That accomplished, he matured into a good scholar who spent his spare hours writing for the college newspaper and working as a custodian in a research laboratory that housed several hundred mice. During a mid-semester break in his sophomore year, he turned his hand to playwrighting in hopes of winning a prestigious (and lucrative) Avery Hopwood Award from the university. His first play, "Honors at Dawn," won the award in 1936. The next year he won again with "No Villain: They Too Arise." Both dramas tackled themes that would later fuel his major works: the sins committed in the name of "free enterprise," sibling rivalry, and moral responsibility to family and community.

The Hopwood Awards and a Bureau of New Plays Prize from the Theatre Guild of New York enabled Miller to find writing jobs right out of college. In 1938 he worked briefly for the Federal Theater Project, then he began to turn out radio dramas. Although radio work paid well, Miller yearned to do plays for the stage. He got his chance in 1944, when his work "The Man Who Had All the Luck" had its Broadway premier. An investigation of man's ability to determine his own fate, the play serves as "a kind of simple alphabet of ideas that will be developed later," according to Sheila Huftel in *Arthur Miller: The Burning Glass.* "The Man Who Had All the Luck" folded shortly after its opening, and Miller went on to other non-theatrical projects. One of these, a nonfiction book entitled *Situation Normal,* examined the lives and attitudes of ordinary soldiers going to battle in World War II. The other, a novel called *Focus,* explored the irrationality of anti-Semitism. *Focus* was a modest success on the book market; Huftel observes that the work "is a dramatist's novel: tense in construction and dynamic in climax. The reader is driven by it as tragedy commands an audience, partly by technique but mainly by intensity." Despite the lackluster showing of his first Broadway play and the success of his novel, Miller felt drawn back to the theatre. By 1947 he had crafted a major play from the bare bones of a true wartime incident.

All My Sons is Miller's first successful "drama of accountability." In the play, an aging businessman comes to the anguished recognition that his responsibility extends beyond his immediate family to the wider world of humankind. Having sold defective merchandise to the army, and having lied to protect his business when the merchandise caused war planes to crash in battle, the businessman learns that he has in fact caused the death of one of his own sons. His other son, also a war veteran, savagely rebukes him for his warped sense of morality. In *Arthur Miller: A Collection of Critical Essays,* Gerald Weales notes that the businessman, Joe Keller, is "an image of American success, who is destroyed when he is forced to see that image in another context—through the eyes of his idealist son." The son, Chris, has learned from his war experiences that relatedness is not particular but universal; he is shocked by his father's unscrupulous renunciation of that knowledge. Huftel writes that in *All My Sons,* "Miller is concerned with consciousness, not crime, and with bringing a man face to face with the consequences he has caused, forcing him to share in the results of his creation." In his introduction to *Arthur Miller's Collected Plays,* the author himself suggests that the play lays siege to "the fortress of unrelatedness. It is an assertion not so much of a morality in terms of right and wrong, but of a moral world's being such because men cannot walk away from certain of their deeds."

With the box office proceeds from *All My Sons* Miller bought a farm in rural Connecticut. There he built himself a studio and began to work on another drama. It was produced in 1949 under the title *Death of a Salesman,* and it received overwhelming critical and public acclaim. The play centers on the emotional deterioration of Willy Loman, an aging and not too successful salesman who can hardly distinguish between his memories of a brighter past and his setbacks in the dismal present. In the course of the play Willy grapples with the loss of his job and the failure of his two grown sons to achieve wealth, and with it, presumably, happiness. Nelson writes of Willy: "Shot through with weaknesses and faults, he is almost a personification of self-delusion and waste, the apotheosis of the modern man in an age too vast, demanding and complex for him. . . . He personifies the human being's desire, for all his flaws, to force apart the steel pincers of necessity and partake of magnificence." Willy does aspire to greatness for himself and his sons, but he champions a success ethic that is both shallow and contradictory—the cult of popularity, good looks, and a winning personality. "From the conflicting success images that wander through his troubled brain comes Willy's double ambition—to be rich and to be loved," notes Weales. Facing ruin, Willy still cannot relinquish his skewed values, and he becomes a martyr to them. His sons must come to terms with their father's splintered legacy and determine the essence of his ultimate worth. *New York Times* contributor Frank Rich observes that *Death of a Salesman* "is most of all about fathers and sons . . . . The drama's tidal pull comes from the sons' tortured attempts to reconcile themselves to their father's dreams."

Most critics agree that *Death of a Salesman* is one of the significant accomplishments of modern American letters. In *The Forties: Fiction, Poetry, Drama,* Lois Gordon calls it "the major American drama of the 1940s" and adds that it "remains unequalled in its brilliant and original fusion of realistic and poetic techniques, its richness of visual and verbal texture, and its wide range of emotional impact." *New York Times* columnist Frank Rich concludes that *Death of a Salesman* "is one of a handful of American plays that appear destined to outlast the 20th century. In Willy Loman, that insignificant salesman who has lost the magic touch along with the shine on his shoes after a lifetime on the road, Miller created an enduring image of our unslaked thirst for popularity and success." According to John Gassner in the *Quarterly Journal of Speech,* Miller "has accomplished the feat of writing a drama critical of wrong values that virtually every member of our middle-class can accept as valid. It stabs itself into a playgoer's consciousness to a degree that may well lead him to review his own life and the lives of those who are closest to him. The conviction of the writing is, besides, strengthened by a quality of compassion rarely experienced in our theatre."

Miller rose to prominence during a particularly tense time in American politics. In the early 1950s many national leaders perceived a threat of communist domination even within the borders of the United States, and public figures from all walks of life fell under suspicion of conspiring to overthrow the government. Miller and several of his theatre associates became targets for persecution, and in that climate the playwright conceived *The Crucible.* First produced in 1953, *The Crucible* chronicles the hysterical witch-hunt in seventeenth-century Salem, Massachusetts, through the deeds of one courageous dissenter, John Proctor. As John Gassner notes in *Twentieth Century Interpretations of "The Crucible,"* Miller's motivation "plainly included taking a public stand against authoritarian inquisitions and mass hysteria. . . . It is one of Miller's distinctions that he was one of the very few writers of the period to speak out unequivocally for reason and justice." If Miller began his researches into the Salem witch trials with the communist-hunting trials in mind, he soon uncovered a deeper level for his prospective drama. In his autobiography, *Timebends: A Life,* Miller writes: "The political question . . . of whether witches and Communists could be equated was no longer to the point. What was manifestly parallel was the guilt, two centuries apart, of holding illicit, suppressed feelings of alienation and hostility toward standard, daylight society as defined by its most orthodox proponents." What Miller reveals in *The Crucible,* to quote *University College Quarterly* essayist John H. Ferres, is the tenet that "life is not worth living when lies must be told to one's self and one's friends to preserve it."

Early reviewers of *The Crucible* saw the play—and often denounced it—as an allegory for the McCarthy hearings on communism. That view has been revised significantly in the wake of the work's continuing popularity. "For a play that was often dismissed as a political tract for the times, *The Crucible* has survived uncommonly well," states Ferres. Robert A. Martin offers a similar opinion in *Modern Drama.* The play, writes Martin, "has endured beyond the immediate events of its own time. . . . As one of the most frequently produced plays in the American theater, *The Crucible* has attained a life of its own; one that both interprets and defines the cultural and historical background of American society. Given the general lack of plays in the American theater that have seriously undertaken to explore the meaning and significance of the American past in relation to the present, *The Crucible* stands virtually alone as a dramatically coherent rendition of one of the most terrifying chapters in American history." In *Twentieth Century Interpretations of "The Crucible,"* Phillip G. Hill speaks to the play's pertinence. To quote Hill, the work remains "a powerful indictment of bigotry, narrow-mindedness, hypocrisy, and violation of due process of law, from whatever source these evils spring." Edward Murray concludes in *Arthur Miller, Dramatist* that *The Crucible* "remains one of Miller's best plays and one of the most impressive achievements of the American theater."

The eight-year period following the first production of *The Crucible* was extremely hectic and ultimately dispiriting for Miller. In 1955 he divorced his first wife, and the following year he married actress Marilyn Monroe. At the same time, his supposed communist sympathies caused his expulsion from a scriptwriting project based on New York City's Youth Board, and he was denied a passport renewal by the State Department. Shortly after his celebrated second marriage, Miller was subpoenaed to appear before the House Un-American Activities Committee, where he was queried about his political beliefs. Miller admitted to the Committee that he had attended a few informal Communist Party meetings many years earlier, but he refused to name others who had attended the meetings even when the Committee insisted he do so. He was consequently charged with contempt of Congress and was tried and convicted in 1957. His conviction was overturned on appeal the next year.

Just before Miller's political problems began in earnest, he brought another production to Broadway. It consisted of two one-act plays, *A Memory of Two Mondays* and *A View from the Bridge.* Both are set in working-class Manhattan; *A Memory of Two Mondays* dramatizes a young man's escape from the crushing boredom of work in a warehouse, and *A View from the Bridge* chronicles the death of a misguided Italian longshoreman. Of the two, *A View from the Bridge* has had a longer and more varied theatrical life. After critics found the one-act version lacking in motive and detail, Miller expanded the work to two acts. The longer production had a successful run in London and has been revived several times in New York. In *A View from the Bridge,* writes Helterman, Miller "creates his contemporary classical tragedy." Eddie Carbone, the hero, accepts two illegal immigrants into the home he shares with his wife and his young niece. When one of the immigrants falls in love with the niece, Eddie reacts with irrational anger. Only he cannot see that his protectiveness towards the girl is a form of jealousy born of his own submerged sexual feelings for her. Eventually Eddie breaks the most important unwritten law of his ethnic community—he turns the immigrants over to the authorities for deportation. The decision marks Eddie for inglorious death, a high price for lack of self-knowledge.

Marriage to one of Hollywood's biggest stars brought Miller numerous unforeseen problems. The couple found themselves hounded by reporters at every turn, and Monroe relied on Miller to help her make business and artistic decisions. Helterman observes: "Despite her deference to his work habits, Miller soon fell into Monroe's orbit rather than vice versa." This difficulty was compounded by Monroe's deep-seated emotional problems and her barbiturate dependency, both of which predated her marriage to Miller. Still Miller found many admirable and poignant qualities in his famous wife, and he wrote a movie script, *The Misfits,* that reflected some of those qualities. Filmed in 1961, *The Misfits* gave Monroe a chance to perform a role with depth. It explores the last breaths of the wild West cowboy myth through three luckless drifters and an anguished divorcee who search for permanence in a world of purposeless flux. "Threatened with isolation, personal and social, these people and this way to life define instability," notes Sheila Huftel. "This film

script is like a city built on shifting sand; through it a search is going on for something stable in the face of change, for a way to live, and for a way out of chaos." Shortly after *The Misfits* finished shooting, Monroe filed for divorce, and Miller was plunged back into the relative obscurity he needed in order to write plays.

The Misfits and subsequent works such as *After the Fall* and *Incident at Vichy* introduced a new theme in Miller's work—man's hopeless alienation from himself and others. *Critical Quarterly* contributor Kerry McSweeney maintains that the horrors of World War II as well as his more personal problems caused Miller to reject his vision of possible social harmony among humankind. "His characters now grope alone for values to sustain their dissipating lives and each value, once discovered, slips again into ambiguity," writes McSweeney. "Most frightening of all is the realization that human corruption, once attributed to conscious deviation from recognizable moral norms, is now seen as an irresistible impulse in the heart of man. The theme of universal guilt becomes increasingly and despairingly affirmed." Also affirmed, however, is the possibility of redemption through an understanding of self and an abrogation of destructive impulses—a realization achieved with great difficulty. According to Clurman, the proposition that people can still relate one to another "takes on a new meaning; a new light is shed on the injunction of human responsibility. Each of us is separate and in our separateness we must assume responsibility even in full awareness of that separateness." Quentin, the protagonist of *After the Fall,* is the first Miller character to tackle these issues.

"*After the Fall* is the testimony of a life—a mind made visual," observes Huftel. The drama consists of a series of recollections from the mind of Quentin, an attorney facing the consequences of his actions for the first time. To quote Helterman, the play's action "is expressionistic throughout, using an open space in which various people and events come and go, always confronting Quentin's judging mind. In this episodic structure the recurrent matter to be resolved is the nature of guilt, the limits of personal responsibility for the lives of others, and the means of expiation for crimes real or imagined. Three crises in Quentin's life are vividly presented: Nazi death camps, the suicide of Quentin's beautiful but neurotic wife, Maggie, and Quentin's confrontation with the anti-Communist House Committee on Un-American Activities." Confessional in nature, *After the Fall* "resolved many of the problems which had vexed Miller throughout his writing career," according to C. W. E. Bigsby in *Twentieth Century Literature.* "It served to exorcise his personal sense of guilt but, more significantly, provided evidence that he had finally evolved a consistent concept of the relation between human freedom and human limitations."

When *After the Fall* was first produced in 1964, it met with round condemnation from the critics. Many of them felt that the play unfairly exploited Miller's relationship with Marilyn Monroe, and her subsequent suicide, for the purpose of high drama. Nelson calls the attacks on the play "blatantly unfair" and adds that by concentrating on the work's parallels to Miller's actual life "many critics and viewers wholly missed the genuine stature of the finest play Miller had written since *The Crucible.*" Robert Hogan likewise contends in *Arthur Miller* that *After the Fall* "was so obviously based on Miller's life that its true merits were at first difficult to see. . . . At any rate, *After the Fall* is Miller's most intellectually probing play."

Nazi atrocities continued to dominate Miller's thematics in his next play, *Incident at Vichy.* Returning to stark realism, the work explores human reactions to irrational and unavoidable sadism. Nelson suggests that the drama exposes "not the villainy of the Nazis—which is scarcely worth reiterating—but the involvement of human beings with justice and injustice, self-preservation and commitment to others, which make for some of the conditions responsible for Nazism's growth and, by strong implication, for its possible resurrection." *Incident at Vichy* highlights one man's sacrificial gesture to save the life of a Jewish doctor otherwise destined for the extermination camps. In the core of the work, Nelson notes, Miller "is grappling with *complicity,* not *equality,* in evil. . . . He is not claiming that we are all equally guilty of injustice in the world, but rather that very few of us, for all our avowed decency, are wholly innocent." *Incident at Vichy* is another of Miller's plays that has been revived and restaged many times in New York and elsewhere. In a *New York Times* review, Richard F. Shepard concludes: "This is Arthur Miller at his most searching and provocative, peeling the leaves of motivation as though they were coming off of an artichoke, always more remaining to shroud the core. It is a play that makes you think."

In 1969 Miller wrote *The Price,* one of his most successful Broadway plays. The work reprises his family dramas, this time with two middle-aged brothers who meet in an attic to dispose of their deceased parents' furniture. Old jealousies and self-righteous alibis flare as the brothers compare lives and bemoan lost opportunities. Speaking to the play's power to move viewers, *Modern Drama* correspondent Orm Oeverland writes: "Two hours in an attic with old furniture and four people—and the experience in the theater is of something organic, something that comes alive and evolves before us on the stage." Nelson likewise calls *The Price* a "powerful and provocative" work and concludes that it is "a play of the heart and for the heart, and although it advocates very few truths, it unmistakably and hauntingly has caught many."

Miller's more recent stage works have enjoyed longer runs in England than in the United States. *The American Clock,* Miller's 1980 portrait of the Great Depression, is one production that fared better in London than it did in New York. During the show's pre-Broadway run Miller tinkered with it endlessly, endeavoring to satisfy the demands of directors and producers. Still the show failed. The London production returned faithfully to Miller's original concept, and the play was a hit. Watching it in London, Miller writes in *Timebends,* he "felt the happy sadness of knowing that my original impulse had been correct in this work; but as had happened more than once before, in the American production I had not had the luck to fall in with people sufficiently at ease with psychopolitical themes. . . . I had hopelessly given way and reshaped a play for what I had come to think of as the Frightened Theatre." Several other Miller plays, including *Danger, Memory!* and *The Archbishop's Ceiling* have met with similar fates.

Miller has done relatively little work for movies or television, principally because he likes to maintain artistic control over his scripts. When he does write for the mass media, such as in his teleplay "Playing for Time," he invests the production with the same seriousness to be found in his stage dramas. "Playing for Time," first aired in 1980, tells the true story of Fania Fenelon, an inmate of Auschwitz whose position in the camp orchestra saves her from death. According to Helterman, the "portrayal of individual courage in the face of brutal dehumanization is even more searing than in *Incident at Vichy.* . . . That his heroine is able to unify multiple attitudes and that she has in fact survived to tell her story marks a decidedly positive conclusion to this most harrowing of scripts." *New York Times* reviewer John J. O'Connor writes: " 'Playing for Time' is totally uncompromising in its depictions of hope and despair, of generosity and vi-

ciousness, of death and survival in the bizarre, nightmare world of a concentration camp. . . . This is a powerful production featuring the best script Mr. Miller has written in years. . . . Perhaps the program itself can be watched for a glimmering of the truth, a truth that may be denied to those of us who did not directly experience the monumental inhumanity of an aspiring 'master race.' "

Ever active and energetic, Miller has become an international traveller and spokesman for human rights and artistic freedom. As the first international president of PEN he opened the Soviet Bloc nations to that organization and offered its support to imprisoned and persecuted writers. *New York Times Book Review* contributor Roger Shattuck observes that Miller "was the only American famous enough and courageous enough in 1966 to inject new vitality into PEN International." Indeed, Miller resuscitated the dwindling organization and has seen it grow in prominence and power. He has also seen his best-known plays produced in such unlikely locales as Moscow and Bejing, where *Death of a Salesman* was one of the first American dramas to be performed. Miller claims in *Timebends* that the Chinese reaction to *Death of a Salesman* confirmed "what had become more and more obvious over the decades in the play's hundreds of productions throughout the world: Willy was representative everywhere, in every kind of system, of ourselves in this time . . . not simply as a type but because of what he wanted. Which was to excel, to win out over anonymity and meaninglessness, to love and be loved, and above all, perhaps, to *count.* "

MEDIA ADAPTATIONS: All My Sons was filmed as a movie by Universal in 1948 and as a television special by the Corporation for Public Broadcasting in 1987; *Death of a Salesman* was filmed as a movie by Columbia in 1951 and as a television special by CBS-TV in 1985; *The Crucible* was filmed in France by Kingsley-International in 1958; *A View from the Bridge* was filmed by Continental in 1962; *After the Fall* was filmed as a television special by NBC-TV in 1969.

AVOCATIONAL INTERESTS: Carpentry, farming.

BIOGRAPHICAL/CRITICAL SOURCES:

BOOKS

Authors in the News, Volume 1, Gale, 1976.
Bhatia, S. K., *Arthur Miller,* Heinemann, 1985.
Bigsby, C. W. E., *Confrontation and Commitment: A Study of Contemporary American Drama, 1959-66,* University of Missouri Press, 1968.
Bigsby, C. W. E., *A Critical Introduction to Twentieth-Century American Drama,* Cambridge University Press, 1984.
Bogard, Travis, and William I. Oliver, editors, *Modern Drama,* Oxford University Press, 1965.
Brown, John Russell and Bernard Harris, editors, *American Theatre,* Edward Arnold, 1967.
Brustein, Robert, *The Third Theatre,* Knopf, 1969.
Carson, Neil, *Arthur Miller,* Grove, 1982.
Cohn, Ruby, *Dialogue in American Drama,* Indiana University Press, 1971.
Cole, Toby, editor, *Playwrights on Playwrighting,* Hill & Wang, 1961.
Contemporary Literary Criticism, Gale, Volume 1, 1973, Volume 2, 1974, Volume 6, 1976, Volume 10, 1979, Volume 15, 1980, Volume 26, 1983.
Corrigan, Robert W., editor, *Arthur Miller: A Collection of Critical Essays,* Prentice-Hall, 1969.
Dekle, Bernard, *Profiles of Modern American Authors,* Charles E. Tuttle, 1969.

Dictionary of Literary Biography, Volume 7: *Twentieth-Century American Dramatists,* Gale, 1981.

Downer, Alan S., editor, *The American Theatre Today,* Basic Books, 1967.

Duprey, Richard A., *Just off the Aisle: The Ramblings of a Catholic Critic,* Newman Press, 1962.

Evans, Richard, *Psychology and Arthur Miller,* Dutton, 1969.

Ferres, John H., editor, *Twentieth Century Interpretations of "The Crucible,"* Prentice-Hall, 1972.

French, Warren, editor, *The Forties: Fiction, Poetry, Drama,* Everett/Edwards, 1969.

Gardner, R. H., *The Splintered Stage: The Decline of the American Theater,* Macmillan, 1965.

Gassner, John, *Dramatic Soundings: Evaluations and Retractions Culled from 30 Years of Dramatic Criticism,* Crown, 1968.

Gilman, Richard, *Common and Uncommon Masks: Writings on Theatre 1961-1970,* Random House, 1971.

Gould, Jean, *Modern American Playwrights,* Dodd, 1966.

Hayashi, T., *Arthur Miller and Tennessee Williams,* McFarland, 1983.

Hogan, Robert, *Arthur Miller,* University of Minnesota Press, 1964.

Huftel, Sheila, *Arthur Miller: The Burning Glass,* Citadel, 1965.

Hurrell, John D., editor, *Two Modern American Tragedies: Reviews and Criticism of "Death of a Salesman" and "A Streetcar Named Desire,"* Scribner, 1961.

Lewis, Allan, *American Plays and Playwrights of the Contemporary Theatre,* Crown Publishers, 1970.

Madden, David, editor, *American Dreams, American Nightmares,* Southern Illinois University Press, 1970.

Martin, Robert, editor, *Arthur Miller: New Perspectives,* Prentice-Hall, 1982.

Martine, James J., editor, *Critical Essays on Arthur Miller,* G. K. Hall, 1979.

Miller, Arthur, *Arthur Miller's Collected Plays,* Viking, 1957.

Miller, Arthur, *Collected Plays, Volume II,* Viking, 1980.

Miller, Arthur, *Timebends: A Life,* Grove, 1987.

Moss, Leonard, *Arthur Miller,* Twayne, 1967.

Murray, Edward, *Arthur Miller, Dramatist,* Ungar, 1967.

Murray, Edward, *The Cinematic Imagination: Writers and the Motion Pictures,* Ungar, 1972.

Nelson, Benjamin, *Arthur Miller: Portrait of a Playwright,* McKay, 1970.

The New Consciousness, 1941-1968, Gale, 1987.

Porter, Thomas, *Myth and Modern American Drama,* Wayne State University Press, 1969.

Rahv, Philip, *The Myth and the Powerhouse,* Farrar, Straus, 1965.

Sheed, Wilfrid, *The Morning After,* Farrar, Straus, 1971.

Twentieth Century Interpretations of "Death of a Salesman," Prentice-Hall, 1983.

Tynan, Kenneth, *Curtains,* Atheneum, 1961.

Vogel, Dan, *The Three Masks of American Tragedy,* Louisiana State University Press, 1974.

Wager, Walter, editor, *The Playwrights Speak,* Delacorte, 1967.

Warshow, Robert, *The Immediate Experience: Movies, Comics, Theatre and Other Aspects of Popular Culture,* Doubleday, 1962.

Weales, Gerald, *American Drama since World War II,* Harcourt, 1962.

Weber, Alfred and Siegfried Neuweiler, editors, *Amerikanisches Drama und Theater im 20. Jahrhundert: American Drama and Theater in the 20th Century,* Vandenhoeck & Ruprecht, 1975.

Welland, Dennis, *Arthur Miller,* Grove, 1961, revised edition published as *Miller: The Playwright,* Methuen, 1979, reprinted, 1983.

White, Sidney, *Guide to Arthur Miller,* Merrill, 1970.

PERIODICALS

American Theatre, May, 1986.

Atlantic, April, 1956.

Book Week, March 8, 1964.

Catholic World, May, 1950.

Chicago Tribune, September 30, 1980, April 20, 1983, February 17, 1984, April 30, 1985, November 27, 1987.

Chicago Tribune Books, November 15, 1987.

College English, November, 1964.

Commentary, February, 1973.

Commonweal, February 19, 1965.

Critical Quarterly, summer, 1959.

Criticism, fall, 1967.

Dalhousie Review, Volume XL, 1960.

Detroit Free Press, March 5, 1967.

Detroit News, November 25, 1973.

Educational Theatre Journal, October, 1958, October, 1969.

Emory University Quarterly, Volume XVI, 1960.

Encounter, May, 1957, July, 1959, November, 1971.

Esquire, October, 1959, March, 1961.

Globe & Mail (Toronto), May 19, 1984.

Harper's, November, 1960.

Horizon, December, 1984.

Hudson Review, September, 1965, summer, 1968.

Life, December 22, 1958.

Listener, September 27, 1979.

Literary Criterion, summer, 1974.

Los Angeles Times, April 10, 1981, November 27, 1982, March 26, 1983, June 10, 1984, June 15, 1984, May 26, 1986, February 14, 1987, November 15, 1987.

Los Angeles Times Book Review, November 8, 1987.

Maclean's, September 16, 1985.

Michigan Quarterly Review, summer, 1967, fall, 1974, spring, 1977, summer, 1985.

Modern Drama, March, 1975, December, 1976, September, 1977, September, 1984.

Nation, July 19, 1975.

New Leader, November 3, 1980.

New Republic, May 27, 1972, July 19, 1975, May 6, 1978.

New Statesman, February 4, 1966.

Newsweek, February 3, 1964, December 11, 1972, July 7, 1975, November 16, 1987.

New York, May 15, 1972, July 7, 1975.

New Yorker, July 7, 1975.

New York Herald Tribune, September 27, 1965.

New York Review of Books, March 5, 1964, January 14, 1965.

New York Times, February 27, 1949, October 9, 1955, July 6, 1965, June 17, 1979, May 27, 1980, September 30, 1980, November 16, 1980, June 12, 1981, January 30, 1983, February 4, 1983, February 10, 1983, February 13, 1983, October 23, 1983, October 26, 1983, March 30, 1984, May 9, 1984, October 5, 1984, September 15, 1985, February 9, 1986, February 16, 1986, February 1, 1987, February 9, 1987, November 2, 1987.

New York Times Book Review, October 14, 1979, June 24, 1984, November 8, 1987.

New York Times Magazine, February 13, 1972.

Observer, March 2, 1969.

Paris Review, summer, 1966, summer, 1968.

Plays and Players, July, 1986.

Publishers Weekly, November 6, 1987.
Quarterly Journal of Speech, October, 1949.
Renascence, fall, 1978.
Saturday Review, January 31, 1953, June 4, 1966, July 25, 1970.
Sewanee Review, winter, 1960.
Studies in Short Fiction, fall, 1976.
Theatre Arts, June, 1947, April, 1953, October, 1953.
Theatre Journal, May, 1980.
Time, December 6, 1976, October 15, 1984, August 18, 1986, May 4, 1987, November 23, 1987.
Times (London), April 21, 1983, April 3, 1984, July 4, 1984, July 5, 1984, September 5, 1984, April 19, 1985, August 8, 1986, August 28, 1986, October 31, 1986, December 20, 1986, February 14, 1987, February 19, 1987, March 5, 1987.
Times Literary Supplement, December 25-31, 1987.
Tulane Drama Review, May, 1958, Volume IV, number 4, 1960.
Twentieth Century Literature, January, 1970.
University College Quarterly, May, 1972.
Virginia Quarterly Review, summer, 1964.
Washington Post, October 26, 1969, October 1, 1979, October 16, 1980, October 26, 1980, December 15, 1980, February 13, 1983, February 19, 1984, February 27, 1984, March 2, 1984, February 22, 1987, November 23, 1987.
Wilson Library Bulletin, May, 1965.

—*Sketch by Anne Janette Johnson*

*   *   *

MILLER, Henry (Valentine)   1891-1980

PERSONAL: Born December 26, 1891, in New York, N.Y.; died June 7, 1980, in Pacific Palisades, Calif.; married Beatrice Sylvas Wickens (a pianist), 1917 (divorced, 1924); married June Smith Mansfield, June 1, 1924 (divorced, 1934); married Janina Martha Lepska, December 18, 1944 (divorced, 1952); married Eve McClure, December 29, 1953 (divorced, 1962); married Hoki Tokuda (a jazz pianist and singer), September 10, 1967 (divorced, 1978); children: (first marriage) Barbara; (third marriage) Valentine (daughter), Tony. *Education:* Attended College of the City of New York (now City College of the City University of New York), 1909. *Religion:* Called himself religious, although he did not espouse any religion: "That means simply having a reverence for life, being on the side of life instead of death."

ADDRESSES: Home—Pacific Palisades, Calif.

CAREER: Writer, 1933-80. Worked for Atlas Portland Cement Co., New York City, 1909-11; traveled throughout the western United States working at odd jobs, 1913; worked with father in tailor shop in New York City, 1914; mail sorter with U.S. Government War Department, 1917; worked for Bureau of Economic Research, 1919; Western Union Telegraph Co., New York City, 1920-24, began as messenger, became employment manager; sold prose-poems from door to door, 1925; opened speakeasy in Greenwich Village, 1927; toured Europe, 1928; returned to New York, 1929, and then to Europe, 1930; lived in Paris, France, until 1939; *Chicago Tribune,* Paris edition, proofreader, 1932; Lycee Carnot, Dijon, France, English teacher, 1932; *Booster* (later, *Delta*), Paris, co-editor, 1937-38; *Phoenix,* Woodstock, N.Y., European editor, 1938-39; *Volontes,* Paris, continental editor, 1938-39; lived in Greece, 1939; toured the United States, 1940-41; practiced psychoanalysis in New York City. Painted and exhibited water colors at Santa Barbara Museum of Art, Calif., and in London, 1944; painted and exhibited water colors under auspices of Westwood Art Association, Los

Angeles, Calif., 1966, and at the Daniel Garvis Gallery in the Rue du Bac, Paris, 1967.

MEMBER: National Institute of Arts and Letters.

AWARDS, HONORS: Special citation from the Formentor Prize Committee, 1961, as "one of the most important literary figures of the twentieth century"; Commander of the Order of Arts and Letters, France, 1975.

WRITINGS:

Tropic of Cancer (autobiographical narrative; also see below), preface by Anais Nin, Obelisk (Paris), 1934, Medusa (New York City), 1940, reprinted with an introduction by Karl Shapiro, Grove, 1961, reprinted, 1987.
Aller Retour New York, Obelisk, 1935, American edition privately printed, 1945.
What Are You Going to Do about Alf?: An Open Letter to All and Sundry (pamphlet), Lecram-Servant (Paris), 1935, Bern Porter, 1944, 4th edition, 1972.
Black Spring (also see below; autobiographical narrative), Obelisk, 1936, Grove, 1963, reprinted, 1989.
Scenario: A Film with Sound (based on "The House of Incest" by Anais Nin), Obelisk, 1937.
Un Etre etoilique (also see below), privately printed, 1937.
Money and How It Gets That Way (broadside), Booster Publications (Paris), 1938, Bern Porter, 1945, 2nd edition, 1946.
Max and the White Phagocytes (also see below; contains *The Cosmological Eye,* "Glittering Pie," "Scenario," "The Universe of Death," "Max," "Reflections on 'Extase,'" four letters from "Hamlet," "The Golden Age," "Via Dieppe-Newhaven," "The Eye of Paris," "An Open Letter to Surrealists Everywhere," and *Un Etre etoilique*), Obelisk, 1938.
Tropic of Capricorn (also see below; autobiographical narrative), Obelisk, 1939, Grove, 1961, reprinted, 1987.
The Cosmological Eye (contains selections from *Max and the White Phagocytes, Black Spring,* and other unpublished material), New Directions, 1939, reprinted, 1973.
(With Michael Fraenkel) *Hamlet,* Carrefour, Volume 1, 1939, 2nd enlarged edition, 1943, Volume 2, 1941, Volumes 1-2 reissued and enlarged as *The Michael Fraenkel-Henry Miller Correspondence Called Hamlet,* Edition du Laurier/Carrefour (London), 1962.
The World of Sex (also see below), Argus Book Shop (Chicago), 1940, revised edition, Olympia (Paris), 1957, Grove, 1965.
The Wisdom of the Heart (short stories and essays), New Directions, 1941.
The Colossus of Maroussi; or, The Spirit of Greece, Colt Press, 1941, reprinted, Penguin Books, 1963.
Sunday after the War (contains "Reunion in Brooklyn," selections from "Sexus," and other prose pieces from then unpublished writings), New Directions, 1944.
(And illustrator) *The Plight of the Creative Artist in the United States of America,* Bern Porter, 1944, 2nd edition, 1969.
Varda: The Master Builder (pamphlet), privately printed, 1944, George Leite (Berkeley), 1947, revised edition, Bern Porter, 1972.
Semblance of a Devoted Past (also see below; selected letters from Miller to Emil Schnellock), Bern Porter, 1944, unexpurgated edition, David Grossman, 1968.
The Angel is My Watermark! (essay; also see below), Holve-Barrows (Fullerton), 1944, reprinted, Capra Press, 1972.
Murder the Murderer (an excursus on war from *The Air-Conditioned Nightmare*), Bern Porter, 1944, 2nd edition, 1972.

The Air-Conditioned Nightmare (stories and essays on Miller's impressions of the United States), New Directions, Volume 1, 1945, Volume 2: *Remember to Remember*, 1947, Volumes 1-2 reprinted, 1970.

(With Hilaire Hiler and William Saroyan) *Why Abstract?* (discussion on modern painting), New Directions, 1945, revised edition, Wittenborn, 1964 (published in England as *A Letter*, Falcon Press, 1948).

(And illustrator) *Henry Miller Miscellanea*, edited by Bernard H. Porter, Bern Porter, 1945.

(And illustrator) *Echolalia: Reproduction of Water Colors by Henry Miller*, Bern Porter, 1945.

Obscenity and the Law of Reflection, Alicat Book Shop (Yonkers), 1945.

The Amazing and Invariable Beauford Delaney, (fragment from *The Air-Conditioned Nightmare*, Volume 2), Alicat Book Shop, 1945.

(And illustrator) *Maurizius Forever* (essay), Colt Press, 1946, revised edition, Capra Press, 1973.

Patchen: Man of Anger and Light, with a Letter to God by Kenneth Patchen, Padell, 1946.

Into the Night Life, illustrated and designed by Bezalel Schatz, privately printed, 1947.

(With others) *Of, By and About Henry Miller: A Collection of Pieces by Miller, Herbert Read, and Others*, Alicat Book Shop, 1947.

The Smile at the Foot of the Ladder (bound with *About Henry Miller* by Edwin Corle), Duell, Sloan & Pearce, 1948, the former also published separately by New Directions, 1959, reprinted, 1975.

The Rosy Crucifixion (trilogy of autobiographical narratives), Book 1: *Sexus*, two volumes, Obelisk, 1949, Grove, 1965, reprinted, 1987, Book 2: *Plexus* (originally published in French), two volumes, translation by Elisabeth Guertic, Olympia, 1953, Grove, 1965, reprinted, 1987, Book 3: *Nexus*, Part 1, Obelisk, 1960, Grove, 1965, reprinted, 1987.

The Waters Reglitterized: The Subject of Water Colour in Some of Its More Liquid Phases (also see below), John Kidis (San Jose, Calif.), 1950, reprinted limited edition, Capra, 1973.

Blase Cendrars, Denoel (Paris), 1951.

The Books in My Life, New Directions, 1952, reprinted, 1969.

Rimbaud (two essays; written in English but originally published in French), translation by F. Roger Cornaz, Mermod (Lausanne), 1952, published in the United States as *The Time of the Assassins: A Study of Rimbaud*, New Directions, 1956, reprinted, Pocket Books, 1975.

Nights of Love and Laughter, (short stories), introduction by Kenneth Rexroth, New American Library, 1955.

Quiet Days in Clichy (also see below; two autobiographical narratives), includes photographs by Brassai, Olympia, 1956, Grove, 1965, reprinted, 1987.

The Hour of Man (originally published in *Chicago Review*, fall, 1956), [Chicago], c. 1956.

A Devil in Paradise: The Story of Conrad Moricand, Born Paris, 7 or 7:15 P.M., January 17, 1887, Died Paris, 10:30 P.M., August 31, 1954 (also see below; Part 3 of "Big Sur and the Oranges of Hieronymus Bosch"), New American Library, 1956.

Big Sur and the Oranges of Hieronymus Bosch (reminiscences), New Directions, 1957.

(With Bezalel Schatz) *Twelve Illustrations to Henry Miller* (illustrations by Schatz for Hebrew edition of selected writings by Miller, entitled "Half Past Midnight"), [Jerusalem], 1957.

First Letter to Trygve Hirsch (pamphlet), Henry Miller Literary Society (Minneapolis), 1957.

(With D. H. Lawrence) *Pornography and Obscenity: Handbook for Censors* (two essays) Fridtjog-Karla Publications, 1958.

The Red Notebook (autograph notes and sketches; contains Miller's horoscope), Jargon, 1958.

The Last of the Grenadiers; or, Anything You Like (catalog of an exhibition of Michonze paintings held at Adams Gallery, London, June-July, 1959), Favil Press (London), 1959,

(Contributor) Lawrence Durrell and Alfred Perles, *Art and Outrage: A Correspondence about Henry Miller between Alfred Perles and Lawrence Durrell, with an Intermission by Henry Miller* (correspondence about Miller between Perles and Durrell), Putnam (London), 1959, Dutton, 1961.

Reunion in Barcelona (letter to Perles, from *Aller Retour New York*), Scorpion Press, 1959.

The Henry Miller Reader, edited by Durrell, New Directions, 1959 (published in England as *The Best of Henry Miller*, Heinemann, 1960).

The Intimate Henry Miller (collection of stories, essays, and autobiographical sketches), includes introduction by Lawrence Clark Powell, New American Library, 1959.

Defence of the Freedom to Read: A Letter to the Supreme Court of Norway, in Connection with the Ban on "Sexus"/Forsvar for lesefrichetera: Brev til Norges Hoeyeste Domstol anledning av beslagleggelsen av "Sexus", bilingual edition, Forlag J. W. Cappelens (Oslo), 1959.

La Table Ronde, [Paris], 1960.

To Paint Is to Love Again, Cambria Books, 1960, revised edition published with the text of *Semblance of a Devoted Past*, Grossman, 1968.

Stand Still Like the Hummingbird (essays), New Directions, 1962.

(With Brassai, Durrell, and Bissiere) *Hans Reichel, 1892-1958*, J. Bucher (Paris), 1962.

(With others) *Joseph Delteil: Essays in Tribute*, St. Albert's Press (London), 1962.

Henry Miller: Watercolors, Drawings, and His Essay, "The Angel is My Watermark!", Abrams, 1962.

Just Wild about Harry: A Melo-Melo in Seven Scenes (play; first produced in Spoleto, 1968), New Directions, 1963, reprinted, 1979.

Henry Miller Trilogy (consists of *Tropic of Cancer, Tropic of Capricorn*, and *Black Spring*), Grove, 1963.

(With Jacques den Haan) *Milleriana* (articles on Miller's work and correspondence between den Haan and Miller), De Bestge Bij (Amsterdam), 1963.

(With Durrell) *Lawrence Durrell and Henry Miller: A Private Correspondence*, edited by George Wickes, Dutton, 1963.

Books Tangent to Circle: Reviews, Bern Porter, 1963, 2nd edition, 1971.

Greece, drawings by Anne Poor, Viking, 1964.

Henry Miller on Writing (selections from published and unpublished works), edited by Thomas H. Moore, New Directions, 1964.

Letters to Anais Nin, edited and with an introduction by Gunther Stuhlmann, Putnam, 1965, reprinted, Paragon House, 1988.

Selected Prose, two volumes, MacGibbon & Kee, 1965.

Order and Chaos chez Hans Reichel, includes introduction by Durrell, Loujon Press (Tucson), 1966.

(With Helmut Lander) *Torsi* (text by Miller), Verlag der Europaeischen Buecherei Hieronomi (Bonn), 1966.

(With Will Slotnikoff) *The First Time I Live: A Romantic Book about the Writing of a Book and the Birth of a Writer* (includes introduction by Miller and an exchange of letters between Slotnikoff and Miller), Manchester Lane Editions (Washington), 1966.

Lawrence Clark Powell: Two Tributes, Goliard Press, 1966.

(With William A. Gordon) *Writer and Critic: A Correspondence with Henry Miller,* Louisiana State University Press, 1968.

(With J. Rives Childs) *Collector's Quest: The Correspondence of Henry Miller and J. Rives Childs, 1947-1965,* edited and introduced by Richard Clement Wood, published by University Press of Virginia for Randolph-Macon College, 1968.

The World of Sex [and] *Max and the White Phagocytes,* Calder & Boyars, 1970.

Insomnia; or, The Devil at Large, Loujon Press, 1970.

(With Georges Belmont) *Entretiens de Paris,* Stock, 1970, translation by Antony Mcnabb and Harry Scott published as *Face to Face with Henry Miller: Conversations with Georges Belmont,* Sidgwick & Jackson, 1971, published in the United States as *In Conversation,* Quadrangle, 1972.

My Life and Times (autobiography), edited by Bradley Smith, Playboy Press, 1971, abridged edition, 1973.

Reflections on the Death of Mishima (also see below), Capra Press, 1972.

Journey to an Antique Land (also see below), illustrated by Bob Nash, Ben Ben Press (Big Sur), 1972.

On Turning Eighty (also see below; chapbook; includes *Journey to an Antique Land* and preface to *The Angel is My Watermark*), illustrated by Nash, Capra Press, 1972.

First Impressions of Greece (also see below), Village Press, 1973.

Reflections on the Maurizius Case: A Humble Appraisal of a Great Book, Capra Press, 1974.

(With Wallace Fowlie) *Letters of Henry Miller and Wallace Fowlie, 1943-1972,* introduction by Fowlie, Grove, 1975.

The Nightmare Notebook, New Directions, 1975.

Encounter with Henry Miller: A Giant of Literary Realism Explores His World and Art (cassette recording), Center for Cassette Studies, c. 1975.

Genius and Lust: A Journey through the Major Writings of Henry Miller (contains excerpts from *Tropic of Cancer, Black Spring, Tropic of Capricorn, Sexus, Plexus, Nexus, The Colossus of Maroussi; or, The Spirit of Greece, The Air-Conditioned Nightmare, Big Sur and the Oranges of Hieronymous Bosch*), compiled by Norman Mailer, Grove, 1976.

J'suis pas plus con qu'un autre, Buchet/Chastel, 1976, reprinted as *Je ne suis pas plus con qu'un autre,* Stanke (Montreal), 1980.

Flash Back: Entretiens a Pacific Palisades avec Christian de Bartillat (title means "Flash Back: Interviews in Pacific Palisades with Christian de Bartillat"), Stock, 1976.

(Author of comments with Anais Nin) Herta Hilscher-Wittgenstein, *The Ineffable Frances Steloff: A Photographic Visit,* Swallow Press, 1976.

Henry Miller's Book of Friends: A Tribute to Friends of Long Ago, photographs by Jim Lazarus, Capra Press, 1976, reprinted as *A Book of Friends: A Trilogy,* 1987.

Mother, China, and the World Beyond (also see below), Capra Press, 1977.

Sextet (contains *On Turning Eighty, Reflections on the Death of Mishima, First Impressions of Greece, The Waters Reglitterized: The Subject of Water Colour in Some of Its More Liquid Phases, Reflections on the Maurizius Case: A Humble Appraisal of a Great Book,* and *Mother, Child and the World Beyond*), Capra Press, 1977.

Gliding into the Everglades: And Other Essays, Lost Pleiade, 1977.

(With Elmer Gertz) *Henry Miller: Years of Trail and Triumph, 1962-1964: The Correspondence of Henry Miller and Elmer Gertz,* edited by Gertz and Felice Flanery Lewis, Southern Illinois University Press, 1978.

Quiet Days in Clichy and The World of Sex: Two Books, Grove, 1978.

My Bike and Other Friends, Capra Press, 1978.

An Open Letter to Stroker! Inspired by the Writings and Art Work of Tommy Trantino, edited by Irving Stettner, Stroker, 1978.

The Theatre and Other Pieces, Stroker, 1979.

Joey: A Loving Portrait of Alfred Perles, Together with Some Bizarre Episodes Relating to the Other Sex, limited edition, Capra Press, 1979.

(Contributor) Noel Young, editor, *The Capra Chapbooks Anthology,* Capra Press, 1979.

Notes on "Aaron's Rod" and Other Notes on Lawrence from the Paris Notebooks, edited by Seamus Cooney, Black Sparrow Press, 1980.

The World of Lawrence: A Passionate Appreciation, edited with an introduction and notes by Evelyn J. Hinz and John J. Teunissen, Capra Press, 1980.

Reflections: Henry Miller, edited by Twinka Thiebaud, Capra Press, 1981.

The Paintings of Henry Miller: Paint As You Like and Die Happy, with Collected Essays by Henry Miller on the Art of Watercolor, edited by Noel Young, foreword by Durrell, Capra Press, 1982.

The Letters of Henry Miller, Morning Star Press (Haydenville, Mass.), 1982.

Opus Pistorum, Grove, 1983, reprinted as *Under the Roofs of Paris,* 1985.

From Your Capricorn Friend: Henry Miller and the Stroker, 1978-1980 (letters), New Directions, 1984.

(With Brenda Venus) *Dear, Dear Brenda: The Love Letters of Henry Miller to Brenda Venus,* edited by Gerald Seth Sindell, Morrow, 1986.

Letters from Henry Miller to Hoki Tokuda Miller, edited by Joyce Howard, Freundlich Books, 1986.

A Literary Passion: Letters of Anais Nin and Henry Miller, 1932-1953, edited and with introduction by Stuhlmann, Harcourt, 1987.

The Durrell-Miller Letters, 1935-1980, edited by Ian S. MacNiven, New Directions, 1988.

(And author of preface) *Henry Miller's Hamlet Letters,* edited and with introduction by Michael Hargraves, Capra Press, 1988.

(With Schnellock) *Letters to Emil,* edited by Wickes, New Directions, 1989.

AUTHOR OF PREFACE

Michael Fraenkel, *Bastard Death: The Autobiography of an Idea,* Carrefour, 1936.

Alfred Perles, *The Renegade,* George Allen, 1943.

James Hanley, *No Directions,* Faber, 1943.

Parker Tyler, *Hollywood's Hallucination,* McClelland, 1944.

Henry David Thoreau, *Life without Principle* (three essays), Delkin, 1946.

Arthur Rimbaud, *Les Illuminations,* Editions des Gaules, 1949.

Brassai, *Histoire de Marie,* Editions de Point du Jour, 1949.

Lillian Bos Ross, *Big Sur,* Denoel, 1949.

Mezz Mezzrow and Bernhard Wolfe, *La Rage de vivre,* Correa, 1950.

Claude Houghton, *Je suis Jonathan Scrivener,* Correa, 1954.

Harold Maine, *Quand un homme est fou,* Correa, 1954.

W. R. Harding, editor, *Thoreau: A Century of Criticism,* Southern Methodist University Press, 1954.

Wallace Fowlie, *La Graal du clown,* [France], 1955.

Albert Maillet, *Le Christ dans l'oeuvre d'Andre Gide,* Le Cercle du Livre, 1955.

Perles, *My Friend Henry Miller: An Intimate Biography,* Neville Spearman, 1955.

T. Lobsang Rampa, *The Third Eye,* privately printed, 1957.

Blaise Cendrars, *A l'aventure,* Denoel, 1958.

Eric Barker, *In Easy Dark,* privately printed, 1958.

Jack Kerouac, *The Subterraneans,* Grove, 1958.

Cendrars, *Edition complete des oeuvres de Blase Cendrars,* Volume 5: *L'Homme foudroye [et] La Main coupee,* [Paris], 1960.

Junichiro Tanizaki, *Deux amours cruelles,* Stock, 1960.

Durrell, *Justine,* Buchet/Chastel, 1960.

Andreas Feininger, *Frauen und Goettinnen von der Steinzeit bis zu Picasso,* M. DuMont Schauberg, 1960.

(And author of postscript) Sydney Omarr, *Henry Miller: His World of Urania,* Ninth House Publishing, 1960.

Tanizaki, *The Key,* Knopf, 1961.

Bufano: Sculpture, Mosaics, Drawings (of Beniaminono Bufano), J. Weatherhill, 1968.

Herbert Ernest Bates, *Seven by Five: A Collection of Stories, 1926-61,* Penguin Books, 1972.

Eric Graham Howe, *The Mind of the Druid,* Samuel Weiser, 1973.

Haniel Long, *The Marvelous Adventure of Cabeza de Vaca,* Ballantine, 1973.

Jacqueline Langmann, *Henry Miller et son destin,* Stock, 1974.

Powell, *Le Train bleu/The Blue Train* (in French and English), French translation by Anne Joba, Buchet/Chastel, 1978.

OTHER

Author of four unpublished novels, still in manuscript form, written in the 1920's: "Clipped Wings," the story of twelve Western Union messengers, "Moloch," "Crazy Cock," and "This Gentile World"; author of pamphlet *The Story of George Dibbern's "Quest,"* 1958, and of short story collection, *Mezzotints.* Editor of "Villa Seurat" series during the 1930's. Contributor of essays, short stories, and sketches to *Crisis, New York Herald* (Paris), *New English Weekly* (London), *Criterion, The Booster, T'ien, Hsia Monthly* (Shanghai), *Cahiers du Sud* (Marseilles), *Volontes* (Paris), *Transition, New Republic, Phoenix, Partisan Review, Experimental Review, Story, Horizon* (London), *Nation, Town and Country, Athene, Poetry-London, Interim, Harper's Bazaar, Rocky Mountain Review, London Magazine, Mademoiselle, Evergreen Review,* and other periodicals.

WORK IN PROGRESS: The second part of *Nexus,* (Miller once told *CA:* "Volume 2 will probably never be written. Have about decided to leave *The Rosy Crucifixion* an 'unfinished symphony' "); seven new lithographs and nine etchings, produced in Japan by S. Kubo; a collection of new short stories.

SIDELIGHTS: Henry Miller is best remembered as the author of *Tropic of Cancer, Tropic of Capricorn,* and *Black Spring,* books about his expatriate days in Paris. Although these works were first published in France in the 1930s, it was not until 1961 that Miller was able to bypass censorship of his work in his native United States with the publication of *Tropic of Cancer* by Grove Press. Critics found the sexual passages in *Tropic of Cancer* obscene and the author was forced to go to court to lift the ban on his book. "That case brought in a new era of publishing," said Grove Press president Barney Rossett in Miller's *Chicago Tribune* obituary, and "there haven't been many cases of book censorship since." The sensationalism of this trial and the interest the ban on Miller's work created helped to make *Tropic of Cancer* an instant best seller in the United States. Critics, however, debated whether Miller's writings had any true literary merit. While some revered Miller for his ground-breaking efforts to frankly portray life's seamier side, others condemned him as being unartistic. In support of Miller's writing, Norman Mailer called the writer "our only Old Master," as Jack Kroll pointed out in a *Newsweek* obituary; others, like *Virginia Quarterly Review* critic John Williams, complained that Miller was "incapable of constructing dramatic sense" and had "no sense of character—except his own." "The truth about Henry Miller," wrote *Henry Miller* author Kingsley Widmer, one of the first serious critics of the writer's books, "is that he is neither 'the great living author' . . . nor the 'foulest writer of meaningless nonsense.' " However, he did make an important contribution "to the increasingly dominant and major poetic-naturalistic American styles."

The books Miller wrote were neither novels in the traditional sense, nor nonfiction, but autobiographical novels based largely on his experiences in Paris and other parts of the world. Although he had wanted to become an author of notoriety since his youth, a troubled and turbulent life during which he worked several unsatisfying jobs and had an unstable family life kept him from composing a book-length work until he reached middle age. Problems in his second marriage persuaded Miller to move to Paris alone in 1930, but this decision left him with no financial resources. He survived only with the help and encouragement of friends such as Lawrence Durrell and Alfred Perles, with whom he co-edited the magazine *Booster,* and author Anais Nin. These difficult times as an expatriate influenced Miller in his choice of genre, he once explained. A *Washington Post* article by J. Y. Smith quoted Miller: "I wrote all these auto[bio]graphical books not because I think myself such an important person but . . . because I thought when I began that I was telling the story of the most tragic suffering any man had endured. As I got on with it I realized that I was only an amateur at suffering."

The seamier side of Paris life was what Miller knew best, and part of that world involved the sex and prostitution one found on the streets. Miller continued in Smith's article: "I wrote about sex because it was such a big part of my life. Sex was always the dominant thing. People have said that I threw in juicy passages just to keep the reader awake. That is not true. My everyday life was full of this objectionable or questionable material." Nevertheless, a number of critics condemned Miller's writing as pornographic. One of the author's most vehement denouncers, Kate Millett, interpreted Miller's love scenes in her book *Sexual Politics* as portraying the sexes as "two warring camps between whom understanding is impossible since one [the male] is human and animal (according to Miller's perception, intellectual and sexual)—the other simply animal."

Responding to Millett's attack in a *London Magazine* article, James Campbell commented that her interpretation "is not the whole story." Sex is important in Miller's books "both as a means of subversion and as a metaphor of birth. The female sex organ is 'a symbol for the connection of all things,' " Campbell continued, quoting Miller, ". . . and [represents] the movement . . . away from all that is redolent of the real obscenity of hypocrisy and away from the" industrialized world. As for the other symbolic aspect of sexuality in the author's work, Campbell pointed out that Miller's writings "begin from the station of failure and that their whole movement is towards a vantage point beyond death. In this respect, too, sex is primary since the purpose of sex is to augment life."

Miller's philosophy was that life should be revered over all other considerations. Freedom was more important than materialism; individuality took precedence over social conformity. These ideas, as critics like Wallace Fowlie expressed in *Concise Dictionary of Literary Biography: The Age of Maturity, 1929-1941,* are best expressed in *Tropic of Cancer,* which "is largely concerned with the physiological and psychic aspects of sexuality. The sexual drive in man is, for Miller, a means of self-expression. This drive becomes uppermost when man is enslaved to a mechanistic society." In *American Dreams, American Nightmares,* Alan Trachtenberg commented that this idea is continued in *Black Spring.* "*Black Spring,* the most successful of his [books, evokes] both the suffocation and the frenzy of release. . . . The solution is to destroy the old American world in himself, the world of fraus, materialism, gadgetry, the dream turned nightmare, and to die into a new, free being." For the author, this theme of self-expression also applies to his own personal self-liberation, and in *Tropic of Cancer* it marked for Miller "a new beginning, a celebration of personal rebirth in a dying world."

In using the term "cancer" for his book, Miller was referring to the "sick reality that characterizes a society of one dimensional people whose lives are monotones and who live in a dead world beneath the earth's surface," explained Lawrence J. Shifreen in *Studies in Short Fiction.* Influenced as he was by such writers as D. H. Lawrence, Arthur Rimbaud, and American transcendentalists Ralph Waldo Emerson and Henry David Thoreau, the philosophical aspects of Miller's writing most strongly resemble those of American poet Walt Whitman. In fact, J. D. Brown noted in the 1980 *Dictionary of Literary Biography Yearbook* that the "formal model for *Tropic of Cancer* was Whitman's *Song of Myself.*" Miller believed that the United States was on the verge of collapse, just as Whitman had in his *Democratic Vistas,* and he denounced American society in such books as *Hamlet* and *The Air-Conditioned Nightmare.*

Far from being an occasion for despair, however, the "prospect of the decline and fall of America was to Miller something to be regarded with great joy," according to *American Quarterly* critic Harold T. McCarthy, "for only in its suffering and death could America be reborn." Miller was against the democratic form of government "because it reduces men as individuals 'to the least common denominator of intelligibility.' " Some critics, such as *Arizona Quarterly* reviewer Peter L. Hays, felt that this philosophy was "dangerous." The "sexual portions of Miller do not disturb me as much as his anarchy does, his celebration of life, energy, passion, ecstasy, and his condemnation of anything that restricts free enjoyment." "He wants to recreate life as he lived it, with no moral judgments," Hays also commented. "I disagree: I think an author should indicate, if only by negation, how life should by lived."

Philosophical considerations aside, once Miller's *Tropics* books and *Black Spring* were released in the United States they became immediate best sellers. Reactions among critics, however, were mixed when regarding the books' literary merits. The antiartistic style of his prose (Miller was not interested in conventional uses of plotting and characterization) disturbed some reviewers who felt that the lack of form in the writer's work was a sign of poor craftsmanship. In her *Don't Never Forget: Collected Views and Reviews,* for instance, Brigid Brophy attested, "What makes Henry Miller not a mere neutral but an enemy of art is that he disdains the skill and yet screams unskillfully that he has succeeded in becoming a great writer without really trying." Others, however, praised the surrealistic imagery and descriptions of Paris that the author employed. Mailer asserted in *American Review* that "no French writer no matter how great,

not Rabelais, nor Proust, not De Maupassant, Hugo, Huysmans, Zola, or even Balzac, not even Celine, has made Paris more vivid to us. . . . For in *Tropic of Cancer* Miller succeeded in performing one high literary act: he created a tone in prose which caught the tone of a period and a place." *Henry Miller* author George Wickes regarded Miller as "certainly the best surrealist writer America has produced. And while it is hard to imagine that the *Tropics* will ever be taught in the schools, several of his books should occupy a lasting place in American literature."

With the increasingly dangerous situation that was brewing in Europe in 1939, Miller left Paris for Greece. Here, he felt he had found the kind of life for which he was looking. "That voyage . . . was the apex of my happiness, my joy, a very great eye-opener," Smith quoted the author as having once said. "What one admires there is a poor people who are happy, compared to us who are miserable with our riches." About his sojourn in Greece, Miller wrote *The Colossus of Maroussi; or, The Spirit of Greece.* Brown described this book in the *Dictionary of Literary Biography* as "Miller's account of his quest for spiritual illumination in Greece while a guest of Lawrence Durrell. Miller and others later judged it his finest work, but it is a far lesser work than *Tropic of Cancer.* The narrative constantly promises spiritual revelations which it fails to deliver convincingly. As a work of art, and often of bombast, *Colossus* fails to plumb the deeper reservoirs of feeling and symbol which Miller tapped in his early Paris years. A falling off in Miller's power as an autobiographical artist is apparent in the forties, even in the late thirties."

This "falling off " was readily apparent to many critics upon reading Miller's *Quiet Days in Clichy* and *The Rosy Crucifixion,* a trilogy comprised of *Sexus, Plexus,* and *Nexus* that was the author's attempt to compose an expanded version of *Tropic of Capricorn.* "*Quiet Days in Clichy* repeats episodes from *Tropic of Cancer,* and *Tropic of Capricorn* is regurgitated *ad infinitum* and *ad nauseum* in *The Rosy Crucifixion,*" complained Hays. Even Durrell, the author's close friend and admirer, worried that all the " 'new mystical outlines' of Miller's art after 1940 were 'lost,' " according to Brown. As Wickes observed in the *New York Times Book Review,* the man who wrote *Quiet Days in Clichy* was not the same one who wrote *Tropic of Cancer.* "What is lacking is the vehemence and the anarchy which made the earlier book a cry of passionate protest. . . . In the thirties Miller's writing was always airborne; in the forties and fifties, his prose became more pedestrian."

By this time, Miller had returned to the United States and was living in California. His reputation as a ribald and scandalous writer had proceeded him and he soon had something he had never before experienced: an audience. Wickes surmised in his article, that this fact had a significant impact on Miller's writing. When he moved to Big Sur in 1944, related Fowlie, the city soon became "almost an artists' colony with Henry Miller as its leading prophet." The publication of *Big Sur and the Oranges of Hieronymus Bosch,* a rambling narrative detailing Miller's thoughts about his new life in California, "encouraged more pilgrims than ever to call on Miller. They saw him now as a kind of guru and often made impossible demands" on him. "By 1957," Wickes wrote, "Miller was a different man; he had assumed his Big Sur mantle and was addressing an audience. In 1940, he was merely trying to clarify some of his ideas and did not care if no one listened." Because of this change, Wickes suggested, Miller began to revise his works. The result was that in books like *The World of Sex* such alterations took "the bite out of incisive passages."

The Miller books that were published during the 1950s, '60s, and '70s were largely essay collections and volumes of correspondences with his friends. In a *New York Times Book Review* article by the author, he writes: "Now that writing has become like second nature to me the desire to write is weakening. Why bother? I say to myself over and over again. Coupled with that goes another more crippling thought, to wit, that nothing is as important as one imagines it to be." Settling down in California, Miller concentrated more on his other two passions: water color painting and Ping-Pong. Steadily painting about one hundred and fifty water colors a year, Miller exhibited his work in California and on occasional trips to Europe. But even after painting for several years, Miller considered himself "a beginner," according to *New York Times* contributor Peter Bart, who quoted the artist as saying: "That's what fascinates me about [painting]. As a writer I know I can do what I want to do. As a painter I'm still going. there's more of a challenge."

Today, many critics consider the philosophy that Miller expressed in his writings to be of more enduring importance than his actual skills as a writer. Miller's "message is precisely that of Whitman, of Rimbaud, of Rilke," concluded Karl Shapiro in his *In Defense of Ignorance:* " 'Everything we are taught is false'; and 'Change your life.' As a writer Miller may be second- or third-rate or of no rating at all; as a spiritual example he stands among the great men of our age." A bohemian since his expatriate days in Paris, Miller "is the true ancestor of all the beatniks and hippies, except that he is a most immensely learned, intensely cultivated writer of major stature," wrote *American Dreams, American Nightmares* contributor Maxwell Geismer. Brown listed such works as Jack Kerouac's *On the Road* and books by Allen Ginsberg, Richard Brautigan, and Hunter Thompson as being "rather direct extensions" of Miller's autobiographical novels. A *Times* obituary summarized: "He was above all the writer who stood up for private life against the bullying social pressures and the absurd encroachments of the political, commercial and military spheres on the individual life of sexual love and the arts, the spheres of men at their finest and freest." "[My] ideal is to be free of ideals," Miller reflected in *On Turning Eighty,* "free of principles, free of isms and ideologies. I want to take to the ocean of life like a fish takes to the sea."

A Miller archives, founded by Lawrence Clark Powell, is maintained at the University of California, Los Angeles. There is also a Miller collection at the library of Randolph-Macon College in Ashland, Va.

MEDIA ADAPTATIONS: In 1957 Riverside Records released a recording entitled "Henry Miller Recalls and Reflects." Robert Snyder produced the documentary "The Henry Miller Odyssey" in 1968. A motion picture of *Quiet Days in Clichy* was filmed by SBA-ABC Productions (Denmark) in 1969, released in the United States as "Henry Miller's Not So Quiet Days"; the book was again adapted for film in 1989 by French director Claude Chabrol. In 1969 Joseph Strick produced and directed a feature film of *Tropic of Cancer* for Paramount. Snyder also produced two National Educational Television specials on Miller in 1970: "Encounter: Buckminster Fuller and Henry Miller" and "Henry Miller Reads and Muses." In 1973 Tom Schiller filmed a movie of Miller in his bathroom. Playboy Enterprises, Inc., produced a recording of Henry Miller talking with Bradley Smith in 1973.

AVOCATIONAL INTERESTS: Ping-Pong, watercolor painting.

BIOGRAPHICAL/CRITICAL SOURCES:

BOOKS

Allen, Walter, *The Modern Novel,* Dutton, 1964.

Baxter, Annette Kar, *Henry Miller, Expatriate,* University of Pittsburgh Press, 1961.

Booth, Wayne C., *The Rhetoric of Fiction,* University of Chicago Press, 1961.

Brophy, Brigid, *Don't Never Forget: Collected Views and Reviews,* Holt, 1966.

Chapsal, Madeleine, *Quinze Ecrivains,* Julliard, 1963.

Concise Dictionary of American Literary Biography: The Age of Maturity, 1929-1941, Gale, 1989.

Contemporary Literary Criticism, Gale, Volume 1, 1973, Volume 2, 1974, Volume 4, 1975, Volume 9, 1978, Volume 14, 1980, Volume 43, 1987.

Dick, Kenneth C., *Henry Miller: Colossus of One,* E. M. Reynolds, 1967.

Dictionary of Literary Biography, Gale, Volume 4: *American Writers in Paris, 1920-1939,* 1980, Volume 9: *American Novelists, 1910-1945,* Gale, 1981.

Dictionary of Literary Biography Yearbook: 1980, Gale, 1981.

Fiedler, Leslie A., *Waiting for the End,* Stein & Day, 1964.

Fraenkel, Michael, *Genesis of the Tropic of Cancer,* Bern Porter, 1944.

Gordon, William A., *The Mind and Art of Henry Miller,* J. Cape, 1968.

The Happy Rock: A Book about Henry Miller, Bern Porter, 1945.

Harrison, Gilbert A., editor, *The Critic as Artist: Essays on Books 1920-1970,* Liveright, 1972.

Hassan, Ihab Habib, *The Literature of Silence: Henry Miller and Samuel Beckett,* Knopf, 1967.

Henry Miller: A Chronology and Bibliography, Bern Porter, 1945.

Hutchison, E. R., *Tropic of Cancer on Trial: A Case History of Censorship,* Grove, 1968.

Kermode, Frank, *Continuities,* Random House, 1968.

Littlejohn, David, *Interruptions,* Grossman, 1970.

Madden, David, editor, *American Dreams, American Nightmares,* Southern Illinois University Press, 1970.

Mailer, Norman, *A Journey through the Major Writings of Henry Miller,* Grove, 1976.

Martin, Jay, *Always Merry and Bright: The Life of Henry Miller,* Capra Press, 1979.

Mauriac, Claude, *The New Literature,* Braziller, 1959.

Miller, Henry, *On Turning Eighty,* Capra Press, 1972.

Millett, Kate, *Sexual Politics,* Doubleday, 1970.

Moore, Nicholas, *Henry Miller,* Opus Press, 1943.

Moore, Thomas H., editor, *Bibliography of Henry Miller,* Henry Miller Literary Society, 1961.

Nelson, Jane A., *Form and Image in the Fiction of Henry Miller,* Wayne State University Press, 1970.

Omarr, Sydney, *Henry Miller: His World of Urania,* 9th House, 1960.

Orwell, George, *Inside the Whale, and Other Essays,* Gollancz, 1940.

Perles, Alfred, *Reunion in Big Sur: A Letter to Henry Miller in Reply to His "Reunion in Barcelona,"* Scorpion Press, 1959.

Powell, Lawrence Clark, *Books in My Baggage,* World Publishing, 1960.

Rembar, Charles, *The End of Obscenity: The Trials of Lady Chatterley, Tropic of Cancer, and Fanny Hill,* Harper, 1986.

Renken, Maxine, *A Bibliography of Henry Miller, 1945-1961,* Alan Swallow, 1962.

Rexroth, Kenneth, *Bird in the Bush: Obvious Essays,* New Directions, 1959.

Shapiro, Karl, *In Defense of Ignorance,* Random House, 1960.

Solotaroff, Theodore, *The Red Hot Vacuum and Other Pieces on the Writing of the Sixties,* Atheneum, 1970.

Southern, Terry, Richard Seaver, and Alexander Trocchi, editors, *Writers in Revolt,* Berkley, 1963.

Symons, Julian, *Critical Occasions,* Hamish Hamilton, 1966.

Vidal, Gore, *Reflections Upon a Sinking Ship,* Little, Brown, 1969.

Whitbread, Thomas B., *Seven Contemporary Authors,* University of Texas Press, 1966.

White, Emil, editor, *Henry Miller—Between Heaven and Hell: A Symposium,* privately printed, 1961.

Wickes, George, editor, *Henry Miller and the Critics,* Southern Illinois University Press, 1963.

Wickes, George, *Henry Miller,* University of Minnesota Press, 1966.

Widmer, Kingsley, *Henry Miller,* Twayne, 1963.

Writers at Work: The Paris Review Interviews, 2nd series, Viking, 1963.

PERIODICALS

American Literature, May, 1971.

American Quarterly, May, 1971.

American Review, April, 1976.

Arizona Quarterly, autumn, 1971.

Best Sellers, November, 1983.

Books and Bookmen, February, 1960, March, 1960, June, 1972.

Chicago Tribune, January 7, 1979.

Critique, spring-summer, 1965, Volume 20, number 3, 1979.

Globe and Mail (Toronto), April 16, 1988.

Life, July 6, 1959.

London Magazine, February, 1979, October, 1980.

Los Angeles Times Book Review, September 18, 1983, February 26, 1984, February 2, 1986.

New Republic, March 7, 1970.

Newsweek, February 18, 1963, March 2, 1970, November 15, 1976.

New York Review of Books, October 14, 1965.

New York Times, March 23, 1966, June 7, 1983, December 20, 1985, August 9, 1989.

New York Times Book Review, June 18, 1961, June 27, 1965, August 8, 1965, January 2, 1972, September 14, 1975, October 24, 1976, February 25, 1979, November 23, 1980, May 9, 1982, April 1, 1984, May 24, 1987, November 20, 1988.

Observer Review, September 24, 1967.

Partisan Review, Volume 44, number 4, 1977.

Playboy, September, 1964 (interview), November, 1971.

Prairie Schooner, summer, 1959.

Punch, October 7, 1970.

Saturday Review, June 19, 1965, December 11, 1971.

Show, July 9, 1970.

South Atlantic Quarterly, summer, 1966.

Spectator, August 25, 1984.

Studies in Short Fiction, winter, 1979.

Time, March 1, 1963.

Times (London), April 26, 1984.

Times Literary Supplement, February 11, 1965, December 16, 1965, June 16, 1966, November 10, 1966, July 10, 1969, October 10, 1980, October 5, 1984, October 18, 1985.

Tribune Books (Chicago), July 19, 1987.

Under the Sign of Pisces, fall, 1980.

Variety, March 4, 1970, March 10, 1971.

Village Voice, December 6, 1983.

Virginia Quarterly Review, spring, 1968, spring, 1975.

Washington Post, February 18, 1970.

Washington Post Book World, August 29, 1976, February 4, 1979, March 30, 1986.

Western Humanities Review, summer, 1970.

OBITUARIES:

PERIODICALS

Chicago Tribune, June 9, 1980.

Newsweek, June 23, 1980.

New York Times, June 9, 1980.

Publishers Weekly, June 20, 1980.

Time, June 16, 1980.

Times (London), June 9, 1980.

Washington Post, June 9, 1980.

—*Sketch by Kevin S. Hile*

* * *

MILLETT, Kate 1934-

PERSONAL: Given name Katherine Murray Millett; born September 14, 1934, in St. Paul, Minn.; daughter of James Albert (an engineer) and Helen (a teacher; maiden name, Feely) Millett; married Fumio Yoshimura (a sculptor), 1965 (divorced, 1985). *Education:* University of Minnesota, B.A. (magna cum laude), 1956; St. Hilda's College, Oxford University, M.A. (first class honors), 1958; Columbia University, Ph.D. (with distinction), 1970. *Politics:* "Left, feminist, liberationist."

ADDRESSES: Home—295 Bowery St., New York, N.Y. 10003. *Agent*—Georges Borchardt, 136 East 57th St., New York, N.Y.

CAREER: Sculptor, photographer, and painter, 1959—, with numerous exhibitions, including Minami Gallery, Tokyo, Japan, 1963, Judson Gallery, Greenwich Village, N.Y., 1967, and Los Angeles Women's Building, Los Angeles, Calif., 1977; writer, 1970—. Professor of English at University of North Carolina at Greensboro, 1958; kindergarten teacher in Harlem, N.Y., 1960-61; English teacher at Waseda University, Tokyo, 1961-63; professor of English and philosophy at Barnard College, New York, N.Y., 1964-69; professor of sociology, Bryn Mawr College, 1971; distinguished visiting professor at State College of Sacramento, 1973—.

MEMBER: National Organization of Women (chairperson of education committee, 1965-68), Congress of Racial Equality, Phi Beta Kappa.

WRITINGS:

Sexual Politics, Doubleday, 1970.

Prostitution Papers, Banc Books, 1971.

(And director) "Three Lives" (documentary film strip), released by Impact Films, 1971.

Flying (autobiography), Knopf, 1974.

Sita (autobiography), Farrar, Straus, 1977.

(Contributor) *Caterpillars: Journal Entries by 11 Women,* Epona, 1977.

The Basement, Simon & Schuster, 1980.

Going to Iran, Coward, McCann, 1981.

Contributor of essays to numerous magazines, including *Ms.*

SIDELIGHTS: Author-artist Kate Millett has been an acknowledged leader of the women's liberation movement since 1970, when her book *Sexual Politics* became a manifesto on the inequity of gender distinctions in Western culture. Millett, who has described herself as an "unknown sculptor" who was transformed into a "media nut in a matter of weeks," has approached the topics of feminism and homosexuality from scholarly, personal, and artistic perspectives. Her books, including *Flying, Sita,* and *The Basement,* explore the dilemmas and dangers of growing up female in America. According to Susan Paynter in the *Seattle Post-Intelligencer,* "National Leader" is a label that has stuck with Millett since *Sexual Politics* "won her a Ph.D. at Columbia University and the wrath of much of the nation." Paynter adds, however, that "overall social, not just sexual, change is Millett's concern, and she uses her teaching, writing and speaking talents to make her contribution."

Millett was born Katherine Murray Millett in St. Paul, Minnesota in 1934. When she was fourteen, her father left the family, and her mother was forced to look for work in order to support the household. Millett recalled in the New York *Post* that despite a college degree, her mother faced nearly insurmountable odds in the postwar job market, eventually finding only commission work selling insurance. "We went hungry," Millett said. "We lived on fear largely." Her family's difficult circumstances notwithstanding, Millett was able to attend the University of Minnesota, where she graduated in 1956 with *magna cum laude* and Phi Beta Kappa distinctions. She then went to Oxford University for two years of graduate study, earning honors grades there as well. A rebellious young woman who enjoyed flouting convention, Millett decided in 1959 that she wanted to pursue painting and sculpting. Supporting herself by teaching kindergarten in Harlem, New York, she went to work crafting art in a Bowery studio. In 1961 she went to Japan, where she taught English at Waseda University and studied sculpting. Her first show was in Tokyo at the Minami Gallery in 1963. While in Japan she met her future husband, Fumio Yoshimura, also a sculptor.

Returning to the United States in 1963, Millett became a lecturer in English at Barnard College, a division of Columbia University. She also became passionately involved with the burgeoning civil rights movement. First she joined the Congress of Racial Equality; then, in 1965, the National Organization for Women, where she served as chairman of the education committee. Her fiery speeches on women's liberation, abortion reform, and other progressive causes did not endear her to the administration of Barnard, and she was relieved of her duties in 1968. When she returned to teaching in 1969, she was hard at work on a doctoral thesis aimed at dissecting the way literature and political philosophy subtly conspire against sexual equality. The thesis, *Sexual Politics,* won her a Ph.D. "with distinction" from Columbia in 1970.

Few doctoral dissertations see publication outside of the academic community. Fewer still become bestsellers. Millett's *Sexual Politics* was just such a success, going through seven printings and selling 80,000 copies in its first year on the market. *New York Times Book Review* correspondent Jane Wilson describes the work as "an original and useful book . . . that imposed a moratorium on reiterated, dead-end feminist complaint against the male chauvinist pig in the street. Millett's oblique approach to the problem of women's liberation—concentrating on the incidence of sexism in literature, as opposed to life—made cooler and somewhat more productive discussion possible." The critic explains that *Sexual Politics* "also dramatically increased the number of potential participants in the ongoing seminar. Where once personal experience of sexist discrimination had been the paramount credential, it was now possible to enter the fray armed only with a working knowledge of the perfidy of D. H. Lawrence or Norman Mailer." Although some reviews of *Sexual Politics* have been decidedly hostile, most critics have found the book a reasonable and scholarly political analysis of the sex war. In the *Saturday Review,* Muriel Haynes writes: "[*Sexual Politics*] is an impressively informed, controlled polemic against the patriarchal order, launched in dead seriousness and high spirits, the expression of a young radical sensibility, nurtured by intellectual and social developments that could barely be glimpsed even

twenty years ago. . . . *Sexual Politics* speaks in the newly emerging voice of the modern temper: self-realization lies in the embrace of process, the constant testing of creeds and social structures for their logic and their spiritually liberating content. Beyond patriarchy we can glimpse a world where the richness of human variety and choice among genuine alternatives will replace confinement by cultural stereotypes and institutions already put in question by the manifest problems and promise of the future. If men can read Kate Millett's book without prejudice, and it won't be easy, they will understand she is offering deliverance for them no less than for women."

Sexual Politics lifted Millett from the anonymity of the New York art world and ensconced her as a widely-interviewed spokesperson for the women's movement. Within months, Wilson observes, the author "came up hard against the fact that she could not control the image of herself that was projected by the press and on television. This being the case, and finding herself constitutionally unsuited to life as a talk-show exhibit, . . . why did she not simply quit the scene? Once recognized as an articulate member of the movement, she somehow ceased to be a free agent. In her uncomfortable new spokeswoman status she was urged on by her sisters to do her duty in speaking out on their behalf, while also being browbeaten and harassed for her arrogance and 'elitism' in presuming to do so." Millett's book *Flying,* published in 1974, details her struggle to remain self-aware, personally happy, and productive in the face of all the publicity. The central theme of that work, as well as that of her 1977 memoir *Sita,* is her avowed lesbianism and the effect her forthright admission had on her public and private roles. "The publicity that has attached to figures such as Kate Millett in America is unimaginable," notes Emma Tennant in the *Times Literary Supplement.* "Her greatest desire . . . was to reconstruct some sort of personality for herself after the glare of the cameras had begun to fade."

With the two biographical works behind her, Millett turned to a topic that had haunted her for over ten years—the brutal torture-death of an Indianapolis teenager named Sylvia Likens. *The Basement,* released in 1980, offers a chilling chronology of Sylvia's last months, from her point of view as well as her killers'. A *Ms.* reviewer contends that the book combines reporting, the various consciousnesses of those involved in the crime, and a feminist analysis of power "to follow human realities wherever they might lead." What emerges is "not just a story of an isolated incident, but of the powerlessness of children, the imposition of sexual shame on adolescent girls, [and] the ways in which a woman is used to break the spirit and the body of younger women." In the *New Republic,* Anne Tyler suggests that the fourteen years Millett spent pondering Sylvia's fate and how to write about it clearly enhance the book's value. "The writing is fully ripened, rich and dense, sometimes spilling out in torrents," Tyler states. "[*The Basement*] can stand alone, quite apart from any feminist polemics. It is an important study of the problems of cruelty and submission, intensely felt and movingly written."

Millett now divides her time between her art studio in New York City and a seventy-five acre Christmas tree farm she owns north of Poughkeepsie. The farm also serves as a summer retreat for artists—Millett has described it in *Ms.* as "26,000 trees and the company of good women." Millett and her guests farm the land in the morning and spend the afternoon hours making prints, paintings, and sculptures, and writing. "For three years now," she writes, "the plan has worked splendidly. At last we are artists from one in the afternoon until dinner, seven solid hours to do our own work. I adore this arrangement because I have seven hours to print my silkscreen pictures every day. And these prints are, like the trees, a way to support the colony." Reflecting on her hectic years as a crusader for women's rights, Millett told *Life* magazine: "I hope I pointed out to men how truly inhuman it is for them to think of women the way they do, to treat them that way, to act that way toward them. All I was trying to say was, look, brother, I'm human."

BIOGRAPHICAL/CRITICAL SOURCES:

BOOKS

Authors in the News, Volume 1, Gale, 1976.
Millett, Kate, *Flying,* Knopf, 1974.
Millett, Kate, *Sita,* Farrar, Straus, 1977.
Smith, Sharon, *Women Who Make Movies,* Hopkinson & Blake, 1975.

PERIODICALS

Books and Bookmen, June, 1971.
Book World, November 22, 1970.
Canadian Forum, November/December, 1970.
Kirkus Reviews, March 1, 1977.
Life, September 4, 1970.
Los Angeles Times Book Review, September 16, 1979.
Mademoiselle, February, 1971.
Ms., February, 1981, May, 1988.
Nation, April 17, 1982.
National Review, August 30, 1974.
New Leader, December 14, 1970.
New Republic, August 1, 1970, July 6-13, 1974, July 7-14, 1979.
Newsweek, July 27, 1970, July 15, 1974.
New Yorker, August 9, 1974.
New York Times, July 20, 1970, August 5, 1970, August 6, 1970, August 27, 1970, September 6, 1970, December 18, 1970, November 5, 1971, May 13, 1977.
New York Times Book Review, September 6, 1970, June 23, 1974, May 29, 1977, September 9, 1979, May 16, 1982.
People, April 2, 1979.
Post (New York), August 1, 1970.
Ramparts, November, 1970.
Saturday Review, August 29, 1970, June 15, 1974, May 28, 1977.
Seattle Post-Intelligencer, March 4, 1973.
Time, August 31, 1970, December 14, 1970, July 26, 1971, July 1, 1974, May 9, 1977.
Times Literary Supplement, April 9, 1971, October 7, 1977.
Washington Post, July 30, 1970.
Washington Post Book World, January 8, 1978.

—*Sketch by Anne Janette Johnson*

*   *   *

MILLIGAN, Spike
See MILLIGAN, Terence Alan

*   *   *

MILLIGAN, Terence Alan   1918-
(Spike Milligan)

PERSONAL: Born April 16, 1918, in India; son of Leo Alphonso (an Army officer) and Florence Winifred (Kettleband) Milligan; married Margaret Patricia Ridgeway (died, 1978); children: one son, three daughters. *Religion:* Catholic. *Avocational interests:* Restoration of antiques, oil painting, watercolors, gardening, eating, drinking, talking, wine, and jazz.

ADDRESSES: Office—Spike Milligan Productions Ltd., 9 Orme Court, London W.2, England.

CAREER: Writer, actor, and artist. Originator of and writer for the radio program "The Goon Show," British Broadcasting Corp., 1951-60; appeared in British television programs "Show Called Fred," "World of Beachcomber," "Q5," "Curry and Chips," "Oh in Colour," "A Milligan for All Seasons," "There's a Lot of It About," and "Last Laugh before TV-AM"; has appeared in over 25 movies, including "The Running, Jumping, and Standing Still Film," "The Magic Christian," "The Three Musketeers," and "The Life of Brian"; has appeared in plays, including "Treasure Island" and "The Bedsitting Room." *Military service:* Served in the British Army during World War II.

AWARDS, HONORS: TV Writer of the Year Award, 1956.

WRITINGS:

ALL UNDER NAME SPIKE MILLIGAN

Silly Verse for Kids, Dobson, 1959.
(Self-illustrated) *A Dustbin of Milligan,* Dobson, 1961.
The Little Pot Boiler: A Book Based Freely on His Seasonal Overdraft, Dobson, 1963.
Puckoon (novel), Anthony Blond, 1963.
(With John Antrobus) *The Bedsitting Room* (play; first produced on West End at Mermaid Theatre, January, 1963), Hobbs, 1970.
A Book of Bits; or, A Bit of a Book, Dobson, 1965.
(With Carol Baker) *The Bald Twit Lion* (juvenile), Dobson, 1968.
(Self-illustrated) *A Book of Milliganimals* (juvenile), Dobson, 1968.
The Bedside Milligan; or, Read Your Way to Insomnia, Hobbs, 1969.
Values (poetry), Offcut Press, 1969.
(Editor with Jack Hobbs) *Milligan's Ark,* Hobbs, 1971.
The Goon Show Scripts, Woburn Press, 1972, St. Martin's, 1973.
More Goon Show Scripts, Woburn Press, 1973.
Adolf Hitler: My Part in His Downfall, M. Joseph, 1971.
Badjelly the Witch (juvenile), M. Joseph, 1971.
Small Dream of a Scorpion (poetry), M. Joseph, 1972.
Rommel: Gunner Who?, M. Joseph, 1974.
Dip the Puppy (juvenile), M. Joseph, 1974.
(With Joseph McGrath) *The Great McGonagall* (screenplay), Daritan Productions, 1974.
(Contributor) *Cricket's Choice,* Open Court, 1974.
(With Hobbs) *The Great McGonagall Scrapbook,* M. Joseph, 1975.
The Milligan Book of Records, Games, Cartoons, and Commercials, M. Joseph, 1975.
Transport of Delight, Penguin, 1975.
(With others) *The Book of the Goons,* Corgi Books, 1975.
Monty: His Part in My Victory, M. Joseph, 1976.
(With Hobbs) *William McGonagall: The Truth at Last,* M. Joseph, 1976.
(Narrator and co-author) *The Snow Goose* (recording; based on the novel by Paul Gallico), RCA Records, 1976.
The Spike Milligan Letters, edited by Norma Farnes, M. Joseph, 1977.
Mussolini: His Part in My Downfall, M. Joseph, 1978.
A Book of Goblins (juvenile), Hutchinson, 1978.
The Q Annual, M. Joseph, 1979.
Open Heart University (poetry), M. Joseph, 1979.
Get in the Q Annual, Hobbs, 1980.
(Narrator) *Adolf Hitler: My Part in His Downfall* (recording), Columbia Records, 1981.
Indefinite Articles and Scunthorpe, M. Joseph, 1981.

(Self-illustrated) *Unspun Socks from a Chicken's Laundry* (juvenile), M. Joseph, 1981.
Sir Nobunk and the Terrible, Awful, Dreadful, Naughty, Nasty Dragon (juvenile), M. Joseph, 1982.
Goon Cartoons, M. Joseph, 1982.
More Goon Cartoons, M. Joseph, 1983.
There's a Lot of It About, M. Joseph, 1983.
Melting Pot, Robson Books, 1983.
More Milligan Letters, edited by Farnes, M. Joseph, 1984.
Floored Masterpieces and Worse Verse, MacMillan, 1985.
Where Have All the Bullets Gone?, Penguin, 1986.
Further Transports of Delight, Penguin, 1986.
Goodbye Soldier, M. Joseph, 1986.
The Looney: An Irish Fantasy, M. Joseph, 1987.
The Lost Goon Shows, Robson Books, 1987.
Mirror Running, M. Joseph, 1987.
One Hundred and One Best and Only Limericks of Spike Milligan, Penguin, 1988.
Milligan's War: The Selected War Memoirs of Spike Milligan, M. Joseph, 1988.
(With Hobbs) *William McGonagall Meets George Gershwin,* M. Joseph, 1988.
That's Amazing, Ladybird Books, 1988.

OTHER

Also author of the plays *Oblomov* and *Son of Oblomov,* and of radio and television scripts.

MEDIA ADAPTATIONS: The Bedsitting Room was filmed in 1969; *Adolf Hitler: My Part in His Downfall* was filmed in 1972.

SIDELIGHTS: Spike Milligan is best known for "The Goon Show," a radio program that he, Peter Sellers, and Harry Secombe did for the British Broadcasting Corporation in the 1950's. "The Goon Show," a blend of satire, traditional radio comedy, and surrealist absurdity, was instantly popular and enjoyed a long run on the British airwaves. Involving the adventures of the Goons in their constant defense of the British Empire from nefarious threats, the show satirized many traditional British ideas and served as inspiration for a generation of British comedians. "Milligan created not simply a zany comedy format," L. E. Sissman writes in the *New Yorker,* "but a band of sturdy anti-heroes and a whole cycle of anti-epics, a series of audio Eddas, for them to star in. Typically, these sagas borrowed from the literature of Imperial Britain and turned it inside out." John Lennon, writing in the *New York Times Book Review,* remembers "The Goon Show" as "hipper than the Hippest and madder than 'Mad,' a conspiracy against reality. A 'coup d'etat' of the mind." Richard Ingrams of *Books & Bookmen* calls Milligan "one of the few really original comic geniuses of our time." Reviewing the book *The Goon Show Scripts,* John Wells writes in *New Statesman,* "If anyone has any doubt about the original genius of Milligan and his fellow performers [Peter] Sellers and [Harry] Secombe, or the extent to which they have dominated and inspired British jokes . . . I seriously urge them to buy [*The Goon Show Scripts*]."

BIOGRAPHICAL/CRITICAL SOURCES:

BOOKS

Farnes, Norma, editor, *The Spike Milligan Letters,* M. Joseph, 1977.

PERIODICALS

Antioch Review, fall, 1975.
Books & Bookmen, January, 1978.
Bookseller, May 15, 1971.

Film Quarterly, winter, 1971-1972.
Listener, August 8, 1968; December 7, 1978.
New Statesman, November 24, 1972.
New Yorker, December 24, 1973.
New York Times Book Review, September 30, 1973.
Observer, June 20, 1971; December 14, 1975; December 10, 1978.
Times Literary Supplement, November 24, 1972.
Village Voice, October 16, 1969.

*   *   *

MILNE, A(lan) A(lexander)   1882-1956

PERSONAL: Born January 18, 1882, in London, England; died January 31, 1956, in Hartfield, Sussex, England; son of John Vire (a headmaster at Henley House school) and Sarah Maria (Heginbotham) Milne; married Dorothy de Selincourt (a writer), 1913; children: Christopher Robin. *Education:* Trinity College, Cambridge, B.A. (mathematics), 1903.

ADDRESSES: Home—Cotchford Farm, Hartfield, Sussex, England.

CAREER: Free-lance journalist in London, England, 1903-06; *Punch* magazine, London, assistant editor, 1906-14; essayist, dramatist, novelist, and writer for children. *Military service:* British Army, Royal Warwickshire Regiment, 1914-18.

AWARDS, HONORS: Lewis Carroll Shelf Awards, 1960, for *The World of Pooh,* and 1962, for *The World of Christopher Robin.*

WRITINGS:

PLAYS

Wurzel-Flummery (first produced at New Theatre, London, April 7, 1917; also see below), Samuel French, 1922.
Belinda: An April Folly (first produced at New Theatre, April 8, 1918; also see below), Rosenfield, 1918.
The Boy Comes Home (first produced at Victoria Palace, London, September 9, 1918; also produced as "Hallo, America"; also see below), Samuel French, 1926.
"The Camberley Triangle" (also see below), first produced at London Coliseum, London, September 8, 1919.
First Plays (includes "Wurzel-Flummery," "The Lucky One" [also see below], "The Boy Comes Home," "Belinda: An April Folly," and "The Red Feathers" [also see below]), Chatto & Windus, 1919, Knopf, 1930.
Mr. Pim Passes By (first produced at Gaity Theatre, Manchester, December 1, 1919; produced at New Theatre, January 5, 1920; also see below), Samuel French, 1921.
The Romantic Age (first produced at Comedy Theatre, London, October 18, 1920; also see below), Samuel French, 1922.
"The Stepmother" (also see below), first produced at Alhambra, London, November 16, 1920.
"The Red Feathers," first produced at Everyman Theatre, London, May 26, 1921.
Second Plays (includes "Make Believe," "Mr. Pim Passes By," "The Camberley Triangle," "The Romantic Age," and "The Stepmother"), Chatto & Windus, 1921, Knopf, 1922.
"The Great Broxopp: Four Chapters in Her Life" (also see below), first produced at Punch and Judy Theatre, New York, November 15, 1921.
The Truth about Blayds (first produced at Globe Theatre, London, December 20, 1921; also see below), Samuel French, 1923.
The Dover Road (first produced at Bijou Theatre, New York, December 23, 1921; also see below), Samuel French, 1923.

Three Plays (includes "The Dover Road," "The Truth about Blayds," and "The Great Broxopp"), Putnam, 1922.

"Berlud, Unlimited," first produced at Theatrical Garden Party, Chelsea, June 23, 1922.

"The Lucky One," first produced at Garrick Theatre, New York, November 20, 1922; produced under title "Let's All Talk about Gerald" at Arts Theatre, London, May 11, 1928.

Success (first produced at Haymarket Theatre, June 21, 1923; produced under title "Give Me Yesterday" at Charles Hopkins Theatre, New York, March 4, 1931; also see below), Chatto & Windus, 1923, Samuel French, 1924.

The Artist: A Duologue, Samuel French, 1923.

To Have the Honour (first produced at Wyndham's Theatre, London, April 22, 1924 [also see below]; also produced in America under title "To Meet the Prince"), Samuel French, 1925.

"Ariadne; or, Business First" (also see below), first produced at Garrick Theatre, New York, February 23, 1925.

"Portrait of a Gentleman in Slippers: A Fairy Tale" (also see below), first produced at Playhouse, Liverpool, September 4, 1926; produced at Royal Academy of Dramatic Arts, London, June 19, 1927.

Four Plays (includes "To Have the Honour," "Ariadne; or, Business First," "Portrait of a Gentleman in Slippers: A Fairy Tale," and "Success"), Chatto & Windus, 1926.

Miss Marlowe at Play (first produced at London Coliseum, April 27, 1927), Samuel French, 1936.

The Ivory Door: A Legend (first produced at Charles Hopkins Theatre, New York, October 18, 1927; also see below), Putnam, 1928.

The Fourth Wall: A Detective Story (first produced at Haymarket Theatre, February 29, 1928 [also see below]; produced under title "The Perfect Alibi" at Charles Hopkins Theatre, New York, November 27, 1928), Samuel French, 1929.

Michael and Mary (first produced at Charles Hopkins Theatre, New York, December 3, 1929; also see below), Samuel French, 1930.

Four Plays (includes "Michael and Mary," "To Meet the Prince," "The Perfect Alibi," and "Portrait of a Gentleman in Slippers"), Putnam, 1932.

Other People's Lives (first produced in New York under title "They Don't Mean Any Harm," February 23, 1932; revised version produced under title "Other People's Lives" at Arts Theatre, London, November 6, 1932), Samuel French, 1935.

Other Plays (includes "The Ivory Door: A Legend," "The Fourth Wall: A Detective Story," and "Other People's Lives" [also see below]), Samuel French, 1935.

Miss Elizabeth Bennet (based on Jane Austen's *Pride and Prejudice;* first produced at People's Palace, London, February 3, 1938), Chatto & Windus, 1936.

Sarah Simple (first produced at Garrick Theatre, London, May 4, 1937), Samuel French, 1939.

"Gentleman Unknown," first produced at St. James's Theatre, November 16, 1938.

Before the Flood, Samuel French, 1951.

Also author of screenplays "The Bump," "Five Pounds Reward," "Bookworms," "Twice Two," all 1920, and, with Basil Dean, of "Birds of Prey" (also released under title "The Perfect Alibi"), 1930.

FOR CHILDREN

Once on a Time (novel; adapted from an earlier play), illustrated by H. M. Brock, Hodder & Stoughton, 1917, Putnam, 1922.

Make Believe (one-act play; first produced December 24, 1918, at Lyric Theatre, Hammersmith; also see below), revised edition in three acts, with music by Georges Dorlay and lyrics by C. E. Burton, Samuel French, 1925.

The Man in the Bowler Hat: A Terribly Exciting Affair (play; first produced in New York, 1924), Samuel French, 1923.

When We Were Very Young (poetry; also see below), illustrated by Ernest H. Shepard, Dutton, 1924, new edition, Methuen, 1934, Dutton, 1935, edition with foreword by Sir James Pittman, Dutton, 1966.

A Gallery of Children, illustrated by "Saida" (pseudonym of H. Willebeek LeMair), David McKay, 1925, new edition, illustrated by A. H. Wilson, 1939.

The King's Breakfast (also see below), music by Harold Fraser-Simson, Dutton, 1925.

Fourteen Songs from "When We Were Very Young" (also see below), music by H. Fraser-Simson, Dutton, 1925.

Teddy Bear, and Other Songs from "When We Were Very Young," Dutton, 1926.

"King Hilary and the Beggarman" (play), produced in London, 1926.

Winnie-the-Pooh (short stories; also see below), illustrated by E. H. Shepard, Dutton, 1926, new edition, Methuen, 1934, Dutton, 1935, edition with foreword by Sir James Pittman, Dutton, 1966, full-color edition, Methuen, 1973, Dutton, 1974.

Now We Are Six (poetry; also see below) illustrated by E. H. Shepard, Dutton, 1927, new edition, 1934, revised edition, 1961.

The House at Pooh Corner (short stories; also see below), illustrated by E. H. Shepard, Dutton, 1928, new edition, Methuen, 1934, Dutton, 1935, revised edition, Dutton, 1961, full-color edition, Methuen, 1974.

The Hums of Pooh (verses by Milne set to music by H. Fraser-Simson; also see below), Methuen, 1929, revised edition, 1972.

Toad of Toad Hall (play; adapted from Kenneth Grahame's *Wind in the Willows;* first produced December 21, 1929, at Playhouse, Liverpool), music by H. Fraser-Simson, Scribner, 1929, reprinted, 1965, acting edition, Samuel French, 1932.

The Christopher Robin Story Book (selections from *When We Were Very Young, Now We Are Six, Winnie-the-Pooh,* and *The House at Pooh Corner*), illustrated by E. H. Shepard, Dutton, 1929, reprinted as *The Christopher Robin Reader,* 1929.

The Tales of Pooh (selections from *Winnie-the-Pooh* and *The House at Pooh Corner*), illustrated by E. H. Shepard, Methuen, 1930.

The Christopher Robin Birthday Book, illustrated by E. H. Shepard, Methuen, 1930, Dutton, 1931.

The Christopher Robin Verses (selections from *When We Were Very Young* and *Now We Are Six*), illustrated by E. H. Shepard, Dutton, 1932, published as *The Christopher Robin Book of Verse,* Dutton, 1967 (published in England as *The Christopher Robin Verse Book,* Methuen, 1969).

Songs from "Now We Are Six," illustrated by E. H. Shepard, Dutton, 1935.

The Magic Hill and Other Stories, illustrated by Helen Sewell, Grosset & Dunlap, 1937.

More "Very Young" Songs, Dunnton, 1937.

The Princess and the Apple Tree and Other Stories, illustrated by Sewell, Grosset & Dunlap, 1937.

The Ugly Duckling (one-act play), Samuel French, 1941.

Introducing Winnie-the-Pooh and Other Selections, illustrated by E. H. Shepard, Dutton, 1947.

The King's Breakfast and Other Selections, illustrated by E. H. Shepard, Dutton, 1947.

The Old Sailor and Other Selections, illustrated by E. H. Shepard, Dutton, 1947.

Sneezles and Other Selections, illustrated by E. H. Shepard, Dutton, 1947.

The World of Pooh (includes *Winnie-the-Pooh* and *The House at Pooh Corner*), illustrated by E. H. Shepard, Dutton, 1957.

The World of Christopher Robin (includes *When We Were Very Young* and *Now We Are Six*), illustrated by E. H. Shepard, Dutton, 1958.

The Pooh Song Book (includes *The Hums of Pooh, The King's Breakfast,* and *Fourteen Songs from "When We Were Very Young"*), music by H. Fraser-Simson, Dutton, 1961.

Prince Rabbit, and The Princess Who Could Not Laugh, illustrated by Mary Shepard, Dutton, 1966.

Milne's "Winnie-the-Pooh" stories and verses have also been presented in many other editions and selections. The manuscripts of the "Pooh" books are held at Trinity College, Cambridge.

OTHER

Lovers in London, Rivers, 1905.

The Day's Play (sketches from *Punch;* also see below), Methuen, 1910, Dutton, 1925.

The Holiday Round (sketches from *Punch;* also see below), Methuen, 1912, Dutton, 1925.

Once a Week (sketches from *Punch;* also see below), Methuen, 1914, Dutton, 1925.

Happy Days (sketches from *Punch*), G. H. Doran, 1915.

Not That It Matters (essays), Methuen, 1919, Dutton, 1920.

If I May (essays), Methuen, 1920, Dutton, 1921.

Mr. Pim (novel; adapted from his play, "Mr. Pim Passes By"), Hodder & Stoughton, 1921, G. H. Doran, 1922, published as *Mr. Pim Passes By,* Methuen, 1929.

The Sunny Side (essays; also see below), Methuen, 1921, Dutton, 1922.

The Red House Mystery (novel), Dutton, 1922, new edition, 1936.

For the Luncheon Interval: Cricket and Other Verses (poetry), Methuen, 1925.

Selected Works, seven volumes, Library Press, 1926.

The Ascent of Man, Benn, 1928.

The Secret and Other Stories, Fountain Press, 1929.

Those Were the Days (includes *The Day's Play, The Holiday Round, Once a Week,* and *The Sunny Side;* also see below), Dutton, 1929.

By Way of Introduction (essays), Dutton, 1929.

When I Was Very Young (autobiography), illustrated by E. H. Shepard, Fountain Press, 1930.

Two People (novel), Dutton, 1931.

A. A. Milne: An Anthology of His Humorous Work, edited by E. V. Knox, Methuen, 1933.

Four Days' Wonder (novel), Dutton, 1933.

Peace with Honour: An Enquiry into the War Convention, Dutton, 1934, new edition, Garland Publishing, 1972.

Autobiography, Dutton, 1939 (published in England as *It's Too Late Now: The Autobiography of a Writer,* Methuen, 1939).

Behind the Lines (poetry), Dutton, 1940.

War with Honour, Macmillan, 1940.

The Pocket Milne (selections from *Those Were the Days*), Dutton, 1941.

War Aims Unlimited, Methuen, 1941.

(Contributor) Edward C. Wagenknecht, editor, *When I Was a Child: An Anthology,* introduction by Walter de la Mare, Dutton, 1946.

Chloe Marr (novel), Dutton, 1946.

Going Abroad?, Council for Education in World Citizenship, 1947.

Books for Children: A Reader's Guide, Cambridge University Press, 1948.

The Birthday Party and Other Stories, Dutton, 1948.

The Norman Church (poetry), Methuen, 1948.

A Table near the Band (short stories), Dutton, 1950.

Year In, Year Out (essays), illustrated by E. H. Shepard, Dutton, 1952.

Contributor of essays, stories, and verse to various periodicals, including *Punch, Merry-Go-Round, Nation, Spectator, Country Life, Living Age,* and *Saturday Review.* Editor, *The Granta* (undergraduate paper of Trinity College, Cambridge), 1902.

SIDELIGHTS: Although best known today as the author of *Winnie-the-Pooh,* A. A. Milne established his reputation as a writer of comic essays and plays. He began his career with the British magazine *Punch,* writing humorous essays on subjects such as golf, croquet, parties, and cricket. Later, while serving in the Signal Corps during World War I, he began writing plays as a diversion. "After coming out of the army," writes Michael J. Mendelsohn in the *Dictionary of Literary Biography,* "Milne began his dramatic career in earnest, and the plays he wrote during the first decade after the war are his best by far." He scripted many successful whimsical comedies that ran on London and New York stages during the 1920s. Indeed, most of Milne's plays and many of his stories and novels are characterized by writing that focuses on fantastic or fanciful situations.

Wurzel-Flummery, Milne's first play, demonstrates this quality. It tells the story of two politicians who are to inherit a large sum of money provided they jointly change their last names to "Wurzel-Flummery." "The fun in this idea," explains Mendelsohn, "derives from the squirming that goes on before both politicians inevitably decide that progress, justice, and British government can be well served by their agreeing to such a change." *Mr. Pim Passes By,* a work that Mendelsohn regards as Milne's "one unqualified stage success and a genuinely warm, witty play," depicts the confusion that arises when a certain Mr. Pim visits George and Olivia Marden with the news that Olivia's ex-husband, believed dead, is in fact alive and living in Australia. Both plays are examples of drawing-room comedy, in which the humor arises from the awkward situations in which people are caught while trying to move in high society.

Milne's plays are part of a tradition of British comic theater dating from the eighteenth and nineteenth centuries. James M. Barrie, the author of "Peter Pan," who befriended the young playwright after reading some of his essays for *Punch,* and Dion Boucicault, an actor and producer who not only performed the title role in the original production of *Mr. Pim Passes By,* but also produced it, may have influenced his work. "Like Oscar Wilde," wrote Thomas Burnett Swann in *A. A. Milne,* "Milne satirized society and loved what he satirized. But, unlike Wilde, Milne as a dramatist has gathered dust along with his drawing rooms." Milne's works are rarely, if ever, performed today; according to Mendelsohn, few of his works after *Mr. Pim Passes By* were critically or financially successful. "Milne was writing drawing-room comedy at a time when the younger generation found drawing-room society old-fashioned," said Mendelsohn, "but his work was pleasant, rarely abrasive, often amusing, and at best witty."

Milne later adapted *Mr. Pim Passes By* into a novel that proved fully as successful as the play had. His best known novel, however, is his *Red House Mystery,* which Raymond Chandler in his book *The Simple Art of Murder* called "one of the glories of the literature, an acknowledged masterpiece of the art of fooling the reader without cheating him." Like Milne's plays, it has a rather fanciful plot—Mark Ablett, owner of the Red House, plans an impersonation of his long-lost brother Robert to fool his houseguests—but, as LeRoy Panek explains in the *Dictionary of Literary Biography,* "*The Red House Mystery* is important both because in it Milne attempted something new to meet the needs of sophisticated mystery fans who wanted witty books and wanted to take part in the detection, and because his popularity as a writer insured the book a wide audience."

It was, however, Milne's venture into children's fiction and poetry that earned him international recognition—and a reputation he later tried to renounce. *When We Were Very Young,* his first book of verses for children, started out as a break between writing plays. "Rose Fyleman [a British children's poet] was starting a magazine for children," Milne recalled in his *Autobiography.* "She asked me, I have no idea why, to write some verses for it." Although initially not interested, Milne mulled the idea over and, during a holiday in Wales, found himself at loose ends. "So there I was with an exercise-book and a pencil, and a fixed determination not to leave the heavenly solitude of that summerhouse until it stopped raining . . . and there in London were two people telling me what to write . . . and there on the other side of the lawn was a child with whom I had lived for three years . . . and here within me unforgettable memories of my own childhood . . . what was I writing? A child's book of verses obviously. Not a whole book, of course; but to write a few would be fun—until I was tired of it."

When We Were Very Young proved very popular; Helen Cady Forbes labeled it "the very music of childhood" in her *New York Herald Tribune Books* review. Some of these poems, Milne implied, were based on his son's activities, but others he drew from memories of his own childhood. Christopher Milne writes in his autobiography *The Enchanted Places,* "The Christopher Robin who appears in so many of the poems is not always me. For this was where my name, so totally useless to me personally, came into its own; it was a wonderful name for writing poetry round. So sometimes my father is using it to describe something I did, and sometimes he is using it to describe something he did as a child, and sometimes he is using it to describe something that any child might have done. 'At the Zoo,' for example, is about me. 'The Engineer' is not. 'Lines and Squares' and 'Hoppity' are games that every small child must have played."

In the same vein as *When We Were Very Young* Milne produced another book of poems, *Now We Are Six,* and two books of short stories, *Winnie-the-Pooh* and *The House at Pooh Corner.* These four books are Milne's best known, and are praised by critics both for their charming illustrations by Ernest Shepard and the technical expertise and lighthearted approach to childhood in their texts. "Milne was a most accomplished professional writer," declares John Rowe Townsend in *Written for Children: An Outline of English Language Children's Literature.* "He knew and accepted that he was a happy light-weight, and used to say merely that he had the good fortune to *be* like that. In children's as in adult literature, the light-weight of true quality is a rare and welcome phenomenon."

Some contemporary reviewers, however, saw these books as taking a sentimental attitude toward childhood. Milne felt they missed the point; he indicated in his *Autobiography* that "senti-

mental" was one thing children and childhood were not. "A pen-picture of a child which showed it as loving, grateful, and full of thought for others would be false to the truth; but equally false would be a picture which insisted on the brutal egotism of the child, and ignored the physical beauty which softens it," he wrote. "Equally false and equally sentimental, for sentimentality is merely an appeal to emotions not warranted by the facts." He continued, "When, for instance, Dorothy Parker, as 'Constant Reader' in *The New Yorker,* delights the sophisticated by announcing that at page five of *The House at Pooh Corner* 'Tonstant Weader fwowed up' (sic, if I may), she leaves the book, oddly enough, much where it was."

Despite Parker's witticisms, the Pooh stories have attained classic status and are recognized the world over as great children's literature. Writing in the *Times Literary Supplement,* Peter Green declares, "By mythicizing his own social world in terms of a small boy and a group of nursery animals, Milne at last broke through the restrictions of his own social class, age, and country, to achieve the immortality which his 'adult' writing always missed." Swann explains, "Lewis Carroll had caught the sensible nonsense of childhood; Barrie, the wonder and the wounding sadness. Kenneth Grahame had detailed the forests and fields, the rivers and islands of the English countryside with the accuracy of a naturalist and the language of a poet. But Milne captured, incomparably and enduringly, the frolic and indolence, the sweetness and foolishness, of animals which are also people."

Unfortunately, Milne tired of the genre long before his audience did. He wrote in his *Autobiography,* "It has been my good fortune as a writer that what I have wanted to write has for the most part proved to be saleable. It has been my misfortune as a business man that, when it has proved to be extremely saleable, then I have not wanted to write it any more." "It is easier in England to make a reputation than to lose one," Milne explained. "I wrote four 'children's books,' containing altogether, I suppose, 70,000 words—the number of words in the average-length novel. Having said good-bye to all that in 70,000 words, knowing that as far as I was concerned the mode was outmoded, I gave up writing children's books. I wanted to escape from them as I had once wanted to escape from *Punch;* as I have always wanted to escape. In vain. England expects the writer, like the cobbler, to stick to his last."

Although Milne's four children's books seem to be drawn from participating in his son's adventures, Christopher Milne indicates that this was not always the case. He explains, "My father was a creative writer and so it was precisely because he was *not* able to play with his small son that his longings sought and found satisfaction in another direction. He wrote about him instead." Many of the poems came from Milne's firsthand experience; he never lost his own sense of what it was to be a child. Christopher Milne continues, "My father's relationships were always between equals, however old or young, distinguished or undistinguished the other person. Once, when I was quite little, he came up to the nursery while I was having my lunch. And while he was talking I paused between mouthfuls, resting my hands on the table, knife and fork pointing upwards. 'You really oughtn't to sit like that,' he said, gently. 'Why not?' I asked, surprised. 'Well . . .' He hunted around for a reason he could give. Because it's considered bad manners? Because you mustn't? Because . . . 'Well,' he said, looking in the direction that my fork was pointing, 'Suppose somebody suddenly fell through the ceiling. They might land on your fork and that would be very painful.' 'I see,' I said, though I didn't really. . . . He could never bear to be dogmatic, never bring himself to say (in effect): This is so because I say it is, and I am older than you and must know better. How much easier, how much nicer to escape into the world of fantasy in which he felt himself so happily at home."

This "world of fantasy" and desire to revisit his childhood, Christopher Milne continues, characterized much of Milne's later work: "He wrote his autobiography because it gave him an opportunity to return to his boyhood—a boyhood from which all his inspiration sprang." The "we" in *When We Were Very Young* and *Now We Are Six*, Christopher Milne continues, was not a condescending "we" addressed to children, nor the universal "we" that refers to the childhood everyone has shared, but was intended "for just two people: himself and his son. . . . When I was three he was three. When I was six he was six. We grew up side by side and as we grew so the books were written." Christopher Milne concludes, "He needed me to escape from being fifty."

MEDIA ADAPTATIONS: Films made from Milne's works include "The Perfect Alibi" (based on the play of the same title), RKO Radio Pictures, 1931; "Michael and Mary" (based on the play of the same title), Gainsborough Pictures, 1932; "Mr. Shepard and Mr. Milne" (29-minute movie with selected readings by Christopher Milne), Weston Woods; stage adaptation of *The Red House Mystery* by Ruth Sergel, Dramatic Publishing, 1956. Motion picture adaptations from Walt Disney Productions include "Winnie-the-Pooh and the Honey Tree," released February 4, 1966; "Winnie-the-Pooh and the Blustery Day," December 20, 1968; "Winnie-the-Pooh and Tigger Too," December 20, 1974; "The Many Adventures of Winnie-the-Pooh" (compilation of "Honey Tree," "Blustery Day," and "Tigger Too"), March 11, 1977; "Winnie-the-Pooh Discovers the Seasons" (educational featurette), 1981; "Winnie-the-Pooh and a Day for Eeyore," March 11, 1983. All theatrical releases have also appeared on home video. "Welcome to Pooh Corner," a costume drama based on the Disney character concepts, premiered on the Disney Channel, April, 1983. "The New Adventures of Winnie the Pooh," an animated television program, premiered on the Disney Channel, January 10, 1988, and moved to ABC, September 10, 1988; "Disney Gummi Bears/Winnie the Pooh Hour" premiered on ABC, September 9, 1989. Recordings of "Winnie-the-Pooh" include material read and sung by Carol Channing, with music by H. Fraser-Simson and Julian Slade, Caedmon Records, 1972, and "When We Were Very Young," Caedmon. "Prince Rabbit," read by Tammy Grimes, has been recorded for Caedmon.

BIOGRAPHICAL/CRITICAL SOURCES:

BOOKS

Chandler, Raymond, *The Simple Art of Murder,* Houghton, 1950.
Children's Literature Review, Volume 1, Gale, 1976.
Dictionary of Literary Biography, Gale, Volume 10, *Modern British Dramatists, 1900-1945,* 1982, Volume 77: *British Mystery Writers, 1920-1939,* 1989.
Milne, A. A., *Autobiography,* Dutton, 1939.
Milne, Christopher, *The Enchanted Places,* Dutton, 1975.
Sutton, Graham, *Some Contemporary Dramatists,* Kennikat Press, 1925.
Swann, Thomas Burnett, *A. A. Milne,* Twayne, 1971.
Townsend, John Rowe, *Written for Children: An Outline of English Language Children's Literature,* Lippincott, 1974.
Twentieth-Century Literary Criticism, Volume 6, Gale, 1982.

PERIODICALS

Life, February 27, 1956.

McCall's, August, 1970.
New York Herald Tribune Books, December 14, 1924.
New York Herald Tribune Book Review, November 16, 1952, May 13, 1956.
New York Times Book Review, March 18, 1956.
Times Literary Supplement, April 4, 1975.

—*Sketch by Kenneth R. Shepherd*

*   *   *

MILNER, Ron(ald) 1938-

PERSONAL: Born May 29, 1938, in Detroit, Mich. *Education:* Attended Columbia University.

ADDRESSES: c/o New American Library, 1301 Sixth Ave., New York, N.Y. 10019.

CAREER: Playwright. Writer in residence, Lincoln University, 1966-67; teacher, Michigan State University, 1971-72; founder and director, Spirit of Shango theater company; director, "Don't Get God Started," 1986; led play writing workshop, Wayne State University.

AWARDS, HONORS: Rockefeller grant; John Hay Whitney fellowship.

WRITINGS:

PLAYS

"Who's Got His Own" (three-act; also see below), first produced Off-Broadway at American Place Theatre, October 12, 1966.
"The Warning—A Theme for Linda" (one-act; first produced in New York with other plays as "A Black Quartet" at Chelsea Theatre Center, Brooklyn Academy of Music, April 25, 1969), published in *A Black Quartet: Four New Black Plays,* edited by Ben Caldwell and others, New American Library, 1970.
"The Monster" (one-act; first produced in Chicago at Louis Theatre Center, October, 1969), published in Drama Review, summer, 1968.
"M(ego) and the Green Ball of Freedom" (one-act; first produced in Detroit at Shango Theatre, 1971), published in *Black World,* April, 1971.
(Editor, author of introduction with Woodie King, Jr., and contributor) *Black Drama Anthology* (includes "Who's Got His Own"), New American Library, 1971.
What the Wine Sellers Buy (first produced in New York at New Federal Theatre, May 17, 1973), Samuel French, 1974.
"These Three," first produced in Detroit at Concept East Theater, 1974.
"Season's Reasons," first produced in Detroit at Langston Hughes Theatre, 1976.
"Work," first produced for Detroit Public Schools, January, 1978.
"Jazz-set," first produced in Los Angeles at Mark Taper Forum, 1980.
"Crack Steppin'," first produced in Detroit at Music Hall, November, 1981.
"Checkmates," produced in Los Angeles at Westwood Playhouse, July 17, 1987.
"Don't Get God Started," first produced on Broadway at Longacre Theatre, October, 1987.

Also author of "Life Agony" (one-act), first produced in Detroit at the Unstable Theatre and "The Greatest Gift," produced by Detroit Public Schools.

CONTRIBUTOR

Langston Hughes, editor, *Best Short Stories by Negro Writers,*
Little, Brown, 1967.

Ahmed Alhamisi and Harun Kofi Wangara, editors, *Black Arts:
An Anthology of Black Creations,* Black Arts, 1969.

Donald B. Gibson, editor, *Five Black Writers,* New York University Press, 1970.

Addison Gayle, Jr., editor, *The Black Aesthetic,* Doubleday,
1971.

William R. Robinson, editor, *Nommo: An Anthology of Modern
Black African and Black American Literature,* Macmillan,
1972.

King, editor, *Black Short Story Anthology,* Columbia University
Press, 1972.

Also contributor to *Black Poets and Prophets,* edited by King
and Earl Anthony, New American Library.

OTHER

Contributor to *Negro Digest, Drama Review, Black World,* and
other periodicals.

SIDELIGHTS: Ron Milner is "a pioneering force in the contemporary Afro-American theater," writes Beunyce Rayford Cunningham in the *Dictionary of Literary Biography.* Much of his
work has involved growing beyond the theatre of the 1960s,
where, as Milner told *Detroit News* reporter Bill Gray, "There
used to be a lot of screaming and hate. . . . It was reacting to
white racism and the themes were defiant directives at the white
community." He continued, "We're no longer dealing with 'I am
somebody' but more of who that 'somebody' really is." While not
rejecting the revolutionary movements in black theatre, Milner
represents a change in approach: a shift from combative performances to quieter dramas that still make a point. Comments Geneva Smitherman in *Black World,* "Those of us who were patient
with our writers—as they lingered for what seems like an eternity in the catharsis/ screaming stage—applaud this natural
change in the course of theatrical events." Adds Cunningham,
"Ron Milner's is essentially a theatre of intense, often lyrical, retrospection devoted primarily to illuminating the past events,
personalities, and values which have shaped his struggling people."

Milner grew up in Detroit, on Hastings Street, also known as
" 'The Valley'—with the Muslims on one corner, hustlers and
pimps on another, winos on one, and Aretha Franklin singing
from her father's church on the other," reports Smitherman. It
"was pretty infamous and supposedly criminal," Milner told
David Richards of the *Washington Star-News.* But, he continued, "The more I read in high school, the more I realized that
some tremendous, phenomenal things were happening around
me. What happened in a Faulkner novel happened four times a
day on Hastings Street. I thought why should these crazy people
Faulkner writes about seem more important than my mother or
my father or the dude down the street. Only because they had
someone to write about them. So I became a writer."

Milner's work contains the constant appeal for stronger black
families and tighter communities. According to Larry Neal in
The Black American Writer, "Milner's main thrust is directed toward unifying the family around basic moral principles, toward
bridging the 'generation gap.' " This has led some critics to label
him a "preacher" and his dramas "morality plays." Not daunted
by criticism, Milner told Betty DeRamus in the *Detroit Free
Press* that art "has to educate as well as entertain. When people
call me a preacher, I consider it a compliment . . . when you get
an emotional response it's easier to involve the mind."

One of Milner's "morality plays" was very successful, both with
the critics and with black audiences. *What the Wine Sellers Buy*
centers on the tempting of seventeen-year-old Steve by Rico, a
pimp. Rico suggests that turning Steve's girlfriend into a prostitute is the easy way to make money. While Steve resists, future
trials lay ahead. According to Cunningham, the play contains
"many of the elements of Milner's previous family dramas: a
young, innocent person forced to make a conscious decision
about the direction of his or her life; a mother who retreats into
the church; the figure of a male savior—this time a man of the
church who befriends the mother and is determined to save her
son. What is new here is the Faustian framework in which the
menace to be dealt with is the seductions of street life represented
by the pimp."

"As in all morality plays, good and the power of love" triumph,
DeRamus notes, but adds, "what makes 'Wine Sellers' different
is that the villain, Rico, is no cardboard figure who is easily
knocked down. He is, in fact, so persuasive and logical that he
seduces audiences as well as Steve." DeRamus reports that Milner patterned Rico after "the typical American businessman,"
and quotes Milner's comment that when Rico "talks about everything for profit, trading everything for money, he's talking
about society. What he says about society is correct, but he is
wrong in what he decides to trade. If you trade life, what do you
buy?" In Rico, Milner did not create "simply the stereo-typical
Black pimp," writes Smitherman. "Rather, Rico is the devious
Seducer in our lives, moving to and fro, enticing us to compromise our morality, our politics and even our very souls." Still,
the play leaves critics with a positive impression, as it focuses on
young Steve triumphing over Rico's corruption. Edwin Wilson
in the *Wall Street Journal* applauds the play's outlook: "the emphasis is not on past grievances and injustices, but on the future—on the problems and perils young people face growing up
in broken homes and a hostile environment, and their determination to overcome these forces. . . . The play gives further evidence that black playwrights today . . . are determined to find
their own way."

Much of Milner's energy in the 1970s was directed to defining
and establishing a unique black theatre. "American theater was
(and still is) the nut that few blacks are able to crack," Milner
and his co-editor, Woodie King, Jr., observe in the introduction
to *Black Drama Anthology.* They continue that "Black theater
is, in fact, about the destruction of tradition, the traditional role
of Negroes in white theater. . . . We say that if this theater is
to be, it must—psychically, mentally, aesthetically, and physically—go home." By "going home," Milner and King mean returning to the experiences that have given blacks their identity.
Added Milner to Smitherman, " 'Theater' and 'play' have always meant going to see somebody else's culture and seeing how
you could translate it into your own terms. People always felt
they were going to a foreign place for some foreign reason. But
now there's a theater written to them, of them, for them and
about them."

Milner believes that a local theatre can also help to unify the
community. "Theater lifts a community in more ways than one,"
he said to Smitherman. "The idea of seeing yourself magnified
and dramatized on stage gives you a whole perspective on who
you are and where you are. You can isolate your emotions and
thoughts and bring them to a place and ritualize them in an audience of people who empathize with you." Milner stresses the
need for local theatre to communicate something valuable to its
audience; he disapproves of creating art only for aesthetic reasons. "Theater for theater's sake is incest," he told Richards. "It
gets thinner and thinner each time and drifts off into abstraction.

But when it's directly involved in life, even when its badly done, it can cause people to argue, discuss, grow, or at least clarify where they stand. It's true, the aesthetic side can do something for you spiritually. But you can't let that prevent you from communicating on a basic level."

The play that "could thrust [Milner] into the role of the theater's primary chronicler of the contemporary black middle class," is "Checkmates," writes Don Shirley for the *Los Angeles Times.* "Checkmates," produced in 1987, examines the lives of an upwardly mobile couple in their thirties, who are coping with the stresses of marriage, two careers, and urban life. The pair is complemented by their landlords, an older couple with simpler lives, who remember the days when blacks worked in the fields, not offices. The landlords, despite their lack of sophistication, possess a steadiness that the younger, financially successful couple lack. Milner told Shirley, "It's dangerous to identify with [the younger couple], because you can't tell what they might say or do next. They aren't fixed. They can't say, 'These are the values I stand for.' The point of the older couple's lives was to build for the future. Now here is the future, and there are no rules left for the younger couple." Dan Sullivan, also writing for the *Los Angeles Times,* enjoys the play's humor: Milner "knows his people so well that an equally big laugh will come on a quite ordinary remark, revealing more about the speaker than he or she realizes." But he also notes the underlying message. " 'Checkmates' gives us a specific sense of today's corporate jungle and its particular risks for blacks, however hip, however educated."

While Milner finds the idea of the middle class "one-dimensional," he is not hostile to the idea of writing to such an audience. "I was never a writer who said the middle class should be lined up against a wall and shot," he told Shirley. As different as it may seem from his previous work, "Checkmates" still falls in with Milner's basic philosophy toward black theatre, as he told Richards: "For a long time, black writers dwelled on our negative history. They could never see any real victory. For them, the only victory lay in the ability to endure defeat. I was consciously trying to break that. I function a great deal on what I intuitively feel are the needs of the time. And the needs of the time are for the positive."

BIOGRAPHICAL/CRITICAL SOURCES:

BOOKS

Alhamisi, Ahmed and Harun Kofi Wangara, editors, *Black Arts: An Anthology of Black Creations,* Black Arts, 1969.
Authors in the News, Volume 1, Gale, 1976.
Bigsby, C. W. E., editor, *The Black American Writer,* Volume 2: *Poetry and Drama,* Penguin Books, 1969.
Contemporary Literary Criticism, Volume 56, Gale, 1989.
Dictionary of Literary Biography, Volume 38: *Afro-American Writers after 1955: Dramatists and Prose Writers,* Gale, 1985.
Hill, Errol, editor, *The Theater of Black Americans,* Volume 1: *Roots and Rituals: The Search for Identity* [and] *The Image Makers: Plays and Playwrights,* Prentice-Hall, 1980.
King, Woodie, Jr., editor, *Black Short Story Anthology,* Columbia University Press, 1972.
King, Woodie, Jr., and Ron Milner, editors, *Black Drama Anthology,* Columbia University Press, 1972.
Robinson, William R., editor, *Nommo: An Anthology of Black African and Black American Literature,* Macmillan, 1972.

PERIODICALS

Black World, April, 1971, April, 1976.
Detroit Free Press, January 5, 1975.
Detroit Free Press Magazine, June 24, 1979.
Detroit News, October 20, 1974.
Drama Review, summer, 1968.
Los Angeles Times, March 19, 1980, September 3, 1986, July 12, 1987, July 20, 1987.
New Yorker, November 9, 1987.
New York Times, July 21, 1982, October 31, 1987.
Wall Street Journal, February 21, 1974.
Washington Star-News, January 5, 1975.

*   *   *

MILOSZ, Czeslaw 1911-
(J. Syruc)

PERSONAL: Surname is pronounced "*Mee*-wosh"; born June 30, 1911, in Szetejnie, Lithuania; defected to the West, 1951; immigrated to the United States, 1960, naturalized citizen, 1970; son of Aleksander (a civil engineer) and Weronika (Kunat) Milosz. *Education:* University of Stephan Batory (some sources say University of Wilno), M. Juris, 1934.

ADDRESSES: Office—Department of Slavic Languages and Literatures, University of California, 5416 Dwinelle Hall, Berkeley, Calif. 94720.

CAREER: Poet, critic, essayist, novelist, and translator. Programmer with Polish National Radio, 1935-39; worked for the Polish Resistance during World War II; cultural attache with the Polish Embassy in Paris, France, 1946-50; free-lance writer in Paris, 1951-60; University of California, Berkeley, visiting lecturer, 1960-61, professor of Slavic languages and literature, 1961-78, professor emeritus, 1978—.

MEMBER: American Association for the Advancement of Slavic Studies, American Academy and Institute of Arts and Letters, PEN.

AWARDS, HONORS: Prix Litteraire Europeen, 1953, for novel *La Prise du pouvoir;* Marian Kister Literary Award, 1967; Jurzykowski Foundation award for creative work, 1968; Institute for Creative Arts fellow, 1968; Polish PEN award for poetry translation, 1974; Guggenheim fellow, 1976; Litt.D., University of Michigan, 1977; Neustadt International Literary Prize for Literature, 1978; University Citation, University of California, 1978; Nobel Prize for literature, 1980; honorary doctorate, Catholic University, Lublin, 1981; honorary doctorate, Brandeis University, 1983; Bay Area Book Reviewers Association Poetry Prize, 1986, for *The Separate Notebooks;* honorary degree, University of Krakow, 1989; National Medal of Arts from President George Bush, 1989.

WRITINGS:

Zniewolony umysl (essays), Instytut Literacki (Paris), 1953, translation by Jane Zielonko published as *The Captive Mind,* Knopf, 1953, reprinted, Octagon, 1981.
Rodzinna Europa (essays), Instytut Literacki, 1959, translation by Catherine S. Leach published as *Native Realm: A Search for Self-Definition,* Doubleday, 1968.
Czlowiek wsrod skorpionow: Studium o Stanislawie Brzozowskim (title means "A Man Among Scorpions: A Study of St. Brzozowski"), Instytut Literacki, 1962.
The History of Polish Literature, Macmillan, 1969, revised edition, University of California Press, 1983.
Widzenia nad Zatoka San Francisco, Instytut Literacki, 1969, translation by Richard Lourie published as *Visions From San Francisco Bay,* Farrar, Straus, 1982.

Prywatne obowiazki (essays; title means "Private Obligations"), Instytut Literacki, 1972.

Moj wiek: Pamietnik nowiony (interview with Alexander Wat; title means "My Century: An Oral Diary"), edited by Lidia Ciolkoszowa, two volumes, Polonia Book Fund (London), 1977.

Emperor of the Earth: Modes of Eccentric Vision, University of California Press, 1977.

Ziemia Ulro, Instytut Literacki, 1977, translation by Louis Iribarne published as *The Land of Ulro,* Farrar, Straus, 1984.

Ogrod nauk (title means "The Garden of Knowledge"), Instytut Literacki, 1980.

Dziela zbiorowe (title means "Collected Works"), Instytut Literacki, 1980—.

Nobel Lecture, Farrar, Straus, 1981.

The Witness of Poetry (lectures), Harvard University Press, 1983.

The Rising of the Sun, Arion Press, 1985.

Unattainable Earth, translation from the Polish manuscript by Milosz and Robert Hass, Ecco Press, 1986.

POEMS

Poemat o czasie zastyglym (title means "Poem of the Frozen Time"), [Vilnius, Lithuania], 1933.

Trzy zimy (title means "Three Winters"), Union of Polish Writers, 1936.

(Under pseudonym J. Syruc) *Wiersze* (title means "Poems"), published by the Resistance in Warsaw, Poland, 1940.

Ocalenie (title means "Salvage"), Czytelnik, 1945.

Swiatlo dzienne (title means "Daylight"), Instytut Literacki, 1953.

Trak tat poetycki (title means "Treatise on Poetry"), Instytut Literacki, 1957.

Kontynenty (title means "Continents"), Instytut Literacki, 1958.

Krol Popiel i inne wiersze (title means "King Popiel and Other Poems"), Instytut Literacki, 1962.

Gucio zaczarowany (title means "Bobo's Metamorphosis"), Instytut Literacki, 1965.

Lied vom Weltende (title means "A Song for the End of the World"), Kiepenheuer & Witsch, 1967.

Wiersze (title means "Poems"), Oficyna Poetow i Malarzy (London), 1969.

Miasto bez imienia (title means "City without a Name"), Instytut Literacki, 1969.

Selected Poems, Seabury, 1973, revised edition published as *Selected Poems: Revised,* Ecco Press, 1981.

Gdzie wschodzi slonce i kedy zapada (title means "From Where the Sun Rises to Where It Sets"), Instytut Literacki, 1974.

Utwory poetyckie (title means "Selected Poems"), Michigan Slavic Publications, 1976.

The Bells in Winter, translation by Milosz and Lillian Vallee, Ecco Press, 1978.

Hymn O Perle (title means "Hymn to the Pearl"), Michigan Slavic Publications, 1982.

The Separate Notebooks, translation by Hass and Robert Pinsky, Ecco Press, 1984.

The Collected Poems, 1931-1987, translation by Hass, Iribarne, and Peter Dale Scott, Ecco Press, 1987.

NOVELS

La Prise du pouvoir, translation from the Polish manuscript by Jeanne Hersch, Gallimard (Paris), 1953, original Polish edition published as *Zdobycie wladzy,* Instytut Literacki, 1955, translation by Celina Wieniewska published as *The Seizure of Power,* Criterion, 1955 (published in England as *The Usurpers,* Faber, 1955).

Dolina Issy, Instytut Literacki, 1955, translation by Iribarne published as *The Issa Valley,* Farrar, Straus, 1981.

EDITOR

(With Zbigniew Folejewski) *Antologia poezji spolecznej* (title means "Anthology of Social Poetry"), [Vilnius], 1933.

Piesn niepodlegla (Resistance poetry; title means "Invincible Song"), Oficyna, 1942, reprinted, Michigan Slavic Publications, 1981.

(And translator) Jacques Maritain, *Drogami Kleski,* [Warsaw], 1942.

(And translator) Daniel Bell, *Praca i jej gorycze* (title means "Work and Its Discontents"), Instytut Literacki, 1957.

(And translator) Simone Weil, *Wybor pism* (title means "Selected Works"), Instytut Literacki, 1958.

(And translator) *Kultura masowa* (title means "Mass Culture"), Instytut Literacki, 1959.

(And translator) *Wegry* (title means "Hungary"), Instytut Literacki, 1960.

(And translator) *Postwar Polish Poetry: An Anthology,* Doubleday, 1965, revised edition, University of California Press, 1983.

Lettres inedites de O. V. de L. Milosz a Christian Gauss (correspondence of Milosz's uncle, the French poet Oscar Milosz), Silvaire, 1976.

Founder and editor, *Zagary* (literary periodical), 1931.

TRANSLATOR

(With Peter Dale Scott) Zbigniew Herbert, *Selected Poems,* Penguin, 1968.

Alexander Wat, *Mediterranean Poems,* Ardi, 1977.

Ewangelia wedlug sw. Marka (title means "The Gospel According to St. Mark"), Znak, 1978.

Ksiega Hioba (title means "The Book of Job"), Dialogue (Paris), 1980.

(With Leonard Nathan) Anna Swir, *Happy as a Dog's Tail,* Harcourt, 1985.

(With Nathan) Aleksander Wat, *With the Skin: The Poems of Aleksander Wat,* Ecco Press, 1988.

SIDELIGHTS: One of the most respected figures in twentieth-century Polish literature, Czeslaw Milosz was awarded the Nobel Prize for literature in 1980. Born in Lithuania and raised in Poland, Milosz has lived in the United States since 1960. His poems, novels, essays, and other works are written in his native Polish and translated by the author and others into English. Having lived under the two great totalitarian systems of modern history, National Socialism and Communism, Milosz writes of the past in a tragic, ironic style that nonetheless affirms the value of human life. Terrence Des Pres, writing in the *Nation,* states that "political catastrophe has defined the nature of our century, and the result—the collision of personal and public realms—has produced a new kind of writer. Czeslaw Milosz is the perfect example. In exile from a world which no longer exists, a witness to the Nazi devastation of Poland and the Soviet takeover of Eastern Europe, Milosz deals in his poetry with the central issues of our time: the impact of history upon moral being, the search for ways to survive spiritual ruin in a ruined world." Although Milosz writes in several genres, it is his poetry that has attracted the most critical acclaim. Several observers, Harold B. Segel writes in the *Washington Post Book World,* consider Milosz to be "the foremost Polish poet of this century." Similarly, Paul Zweig of the *New York Times Book Review* claims that Milosz "is considered by many to be the greatest living Polish poet." But Joseph Brodsky goes further in his praise for Milosz. Writing in

World Literature Today, Brodsky asserts: "I have no hesitation whatsoever in stating that Czeslaw Milosz is one of the greatest poets of our time, perhaps the greatest."

Born in Lithuania in 1911, Milosz spent much of his childhood in Czarist Russia, where his father worked as a civil engineer. After World War I the family returned to their hometown, which had become a part of the new Polish state, and Milosz attended local Catholic schools. He published his first collection of poems, *Poemat o czasie zastyglym* ("Poem of the Frozen Time"), at the age of twenty-one. Milosz was associated with the catastrophist school of poets during the 1930s. Catastrophism concerns "the inevitable annihilation of the highest values, especially the values essential to a given cultural system. . . . But it proclaims . . . only the annihilation of certain values, not values in general, and the destruction of a certain historical formation, but not of all mankind," Aleksander Fiut explains in *World Literature Today.* The writings of this group of poets ominously foreshadowed the Second World War.

When the war began in 1939, and Poland was invaded by Nazi Germany and Soviet Russia, Milosz worked with the underground Resistance movement in Warsaw, writing and editing several books published clandestinely during the occupation. One of these books, a collection entitled *Wiersze* ("Poems") was published under the pseudonym of J. Syruc. Following the war, Milosz became a member of the new communist government's diplomatic service and was stationed in Paris, France, as a cultural attache. In 1951, he left this post and defected to the West.

The Captive Mind explains Milosz's reasons for defecting and examines the life of the artist under a communist regime. It is, Steve Wasserman maintains in the *Los Angeles Times Book Review,* a "brilliant and original study of the totalitarian mentality." Karl Jaspers, in an article for the *Saturday Review,* describes *The Captive Mind* as "a significant historical document and analysis of the highest order. . . . In astonishing gradations Milosz shows what happens to men subjected simultaneously to constant threat of annihilation and to the promptings of faith in a historical necessity which exerts apparently irresistible force and achieves enormous success. We are presented with a vivid picture of the forms of concealment, of inner transformation, of the sudden bolt to conversion, of the cleavage of man into two."

Milosz's defection came about when he was recalled to Poland from his position at the Polish embassy. He refused to leave. Joseph McLellan of the *Washington Post* quotes Milosz explaining: "I knew perfectly well that my country was becoming the province of an empire." In a speech before the Congress for Cultural Freedom, quoted by James Atlas of the *New York Times,* Milosz declares: "I have rejected the new faith because the practice of the lie is one of its principal commandments and socialist realism is nothing more than a different name for a lie." After his defection Milosz lived in Paris, where he worked as a translator and free-lance writer. In 1960 the University of California at Berkeley offered him a teaching position, which he accepted. He became an American citizen in 1970.

In *The Seizure of Power,* first published as *La Prise du pouvoir* in 1953, Milosz renders as fiction much of the same material found in *The Captive Mind.* The book is an autobiographical novel that begins with the Russian occupation of Warsaw at the close of the Second World War. That occupation is still a matter of controversy in Poland. As the Russian army approached the Nazi-held city, the Polish Resistance movement rose against the German occupation troops. They had been assured that the Russian army would join the fight the day after their uprising began. But instead the Russians stood by a few miles outside of the city,

allowing the Nazis to crush the revolt unhindered. When the uprising was over, the Russian army occupied Warsaw and installed a communist regime. The novel ends with the disillusioned protagonist, a political education officer for the communists, emigrating to the West.

The Seizure of Power "is a novel on how to live when power changes hands," Andrew Sinclair explains in the London *Times.* Granville Hicks, in an article for the *New York Times Book Review,* sees a similarity between *The Captive Mind* and *The Seizure of Power.* In both books, "Milosz appeals to the West to try to understand the people of Eastern Europe," Hicks maintains. Told in a series of disjointed scenes meant to suggest the chaos and violence of postwar Poland, *The Seizure of Power* is "a novel of ineffable sadness, and a muffled sob for Poland's fate," Wasserman writes. Michael Harrington, in a review for *Commonweal,* calls *The Seizure of Power* "a sensitive, probing work, far better than most political novels, of somewhat imperfect realization but of significant intention and worth."

After living in the United States for a time, Milosz began to write of his new home. In *Native Realm: A Search for Self-Definition and Visions From San Francisco Bay,* Milosz compares and contrasts the West with his native Poland. *Native Realm,* Richard Holmes writes in the London *Times,* is "a political and social autobiography, shorn of polemic intent, deeply self-questioning, and dominated by the sense that neither historically nor metaphysically are most Westerners in a position to grasp the true nature of the East European experience since the First War." A series of personal essays examining events in Milosz's life, *Native Realm* provides "a set of commentaries upon his improbable career," as Michael Irwin maintains in the *Times Literary Supplement.* Milosz "has written a self-effacing remembrance composed of shards from a shattered life," Wasserman believes. "He tells his story with the humility of a man who has experienced tragedy and who believes in fate and in destiny. It is a work that reflects the stubborn optimism of his heart, even as it dwells on the pessimism of his intellect." Irving Howe, writing in the *New York Times Book Review,* finds *Native Realm* "beautifully written." Milosz, Howe continues, "tries to find in the chaos of his life some glimmers of meaning."

In *Visions From San Francisco Bay,* Milosz examines his life in contemporary California, a place far removed in distance and temperament from the scenes of his earlier life. His observations are often sardonic, and yet he is also content with his new home. Milosz "sounds like a man who has climbed up, hand over hand, right out of history, and who is both amazed and grateful to find that he can breathe the ahistorical atmosphere of California," Anatole Broyard states in the *New York Times.* The opening words of the book are "I am here," and from that starting point Milosz describes the society around him. "The intention," Julian Symons notes in the *Times Literary Supplement,* "is to understand himself, to understand the United States, to communicate something singular to Czeslaw Milosz." Broyard takes this idea even further, arguing that Milosz "expresses surprise at 'being here,' taking this phrase in its ordinary sense of being in America and in its other, Heideggerian sense of being-in-the-world."

Although Milosz's comments about life in California are "curiously oblique, deeply shadowed by European experience, allusive, sometimes arch and frequently disillusioned," as Holmes points out, he ultimately embraces his adopted home. "Underlying all his meditations," Leon Edel comments in the *New York Times Book Review,* "is his constant 'amazement' that America should exist in this world—and his gratitude that it does exist." "He is fascinated," Symons explains, "by the contradictions of a society with enormous economic power, derived in part from literally non-human technical achievement, which also contains a large group that continually and passionately indicts the society by which it is maintained." Milosz, P. I. Kavanagh remarks in the *Spectator,* looks at his adopted country with "a kind of detached glee at awfulness; an ungloomy recognition that we cannot go on as we are in any direction. He holds up a mirror and shows us ourselves, without blame and with no suggestions either, and in the mirror he himself is also reflected." Edel believes that Milosz's visions "have authority: the authority of an individual who reminds us that only someone like himself who has known tyranny . . . can truly prize democracy."

The story of Milosz's odyssey from tyranny to democracy—from East to West—is also recounted in his poetry. Milosz's "entire effort," Jonathan Galassi explains in the *New York Times Book Review,* "is directed toward a confrontation with experience— and not with personal experience alone, but with history in all its paradoxical horror and wonder." Speaking of his poetry in the essay collection *The Witness of Poetry,* Milosz stresses the importance of his nation's cultural heritage and history in shaping his work. "My corner of Europe," he states, "owing to the extraordinary and lethal events that have been occurring there, comparable only to violent earthquakes, affords a peculiar perspective. As a result, all of us who come from those parts appraise poetry slightly differently than do the majority of my audience, for we tend to view it as a witness and participant in one of mankind's major transformations." "For Milosz," Helen Vendler explains in the *New Yorker,* "the person is irrevocably a person in history, and the interchange between external event and the individual life is the matrix of poetry." Writing in *Tri-Quarterly,* Reginald Gibbons states that Milosz "seems to wonder how good work can be written, no matter how private its subject matter, without the poet having been aware of the pain and threat of the human predicament."

Milosz sees a fundamental difference in the role of poetry in the democratic West and the communist East. Western poetry, as Alfred Kazin of the *New York Times Book Review* writes, is " 'alienated' poetry, full of introspective anxiety." But because of the dictatorial nature of communist government, poets in the East cannot afford to be preoccupied with themselves. They are drawn to write of the larger problems of their society. "A peculiar fusion of the individual and the historical took place," Milosz writes in *The Witness of Poetry,* "which means that events burdening a whole community are perceived by a poet as touching him in a most personal manner. Then poetry is no longer alienated."

For many years Milosz's poetry was little noticed in the United States, though he was highly regarded in Poland. Recognition in Poland came in defiance of official government resistance to Milosz's work. The Communist regime refused to publish the books of a defector, and so for many years only underground editions of his poems were secretly printed and circulated in Poland. But in 1980, when Milosz was awarded the Nobel Prize for Literature, the Communist government was forced to relent. A government-authorized edition of Milosz's poems was issued. It sold a phenomenal 200,000 copies. One sign of Milosz's widespread popularity in Poland occurred when Polish workers in Gdansk unveiled a monument to their comrades who were shot down by the Communist police. Two quotations were inscribed on the monument: one was taken from the Bible; the other was taken from a poem by Milosz. The quotation, which is from a poem reprinted in *The Collected Poems, 1931-1987,* reads: "You who wronged a simple man / Bursting into laughter at the crime, / Do not feel safe. The poet remembers. / You can kill one, but

another is born. / The words are written down, the deed, the date."

The Nobel Prize also brought Milosz to the attention of a wider audience in the United States. Since 1980 a number of his earlier works have been translated into English and released in this country, while his new books have received widespread critical attention. Some of this critical attention has focused less on Milosz's work as poetry than "as the work of a thinker and political figure; the poems tend to be considered en masse, in relation either to the condition of Poland, or to the suppression of dissident literature under Communist rule, or to the larger topic of European intellectual history," as Vendler maintains. But most reviewers comment on Milosz's ability to speak in a personal voice that carries with it the echoes of his people's history. Zweig explains that Milosz "offers a modest voice, speaking an old language. But this language contains the resources of centuries. Speaking it, one speaks with a voice more than personal. . . . Milosz's power lies in his ability to speak with this larger voice without diminishing the urgency that drives his words."

This interweaving of the historical and personal is found in all of Milosz's poems. His early works focus on the Lithuania of his childhood and speak of the scenes and people from his own life; Milosz's later poems combine his memories of Europe with the images of his present life in the United States. "Milosz," Harlow Robinson writes in the *Nation,* "has rejected nothing of his long odyssey from the pagan green valleys of Lithuania to the emptying cafes of wartime Europe to the desolate concrete freeways of California." Clarence Brown of the *Village Voice* notes that when reading Milosz, "one has the impression that all his life experience is constantly available to him. . . . [His poetry] fuses the last waking thought with shards of distant or buried experience, foreshortens and warps the space-time of the poem, resulting in a sort of meta-tense, the everlasting now that came into being with Milosz (and thanks to these poems will outlast him)." This synthesis of personal and public, of past and present, is reflected in Milosz's combination of traditional poetic forms with a modern, individual sensibility. Louis Iribarne writes in the *Times Literary Supplement* that "the blending of private and public voices, the imaging of lyrical response to historical events, set off by a distinctly modern irony and a classical strictness of form, established the Milosz style."

Because he has lived through many of the great upheavals of recent history, and because his poetry fuses his own experiences with the larger events in his society, many of Milosz's poems concern loss, destruction, and despair. "There is a very dark vision of the world in my work," he tells Lynn Darling of the *Washington Post.* And yet Milosz goes on to say that he is "a great partisan of human hope." This essential optimism comes from his religious convictions. Milosz believes that one of the major problems of contemporary society—in both the East and the West—is its lack of a moral foundation. Writing in *The Land of Ulro,* Milosz finds that twentieth-century man has only "the starry sky above, and no moral law within." Speaking to Judy Stone of the *New York Times Book Review,* Milosz states: "I am searching for an answer as to what will result from an internal erosion of religious beliefs." Michiko Kakutani, reviewing *The Land of Ulro* for the *New York Times,* finds that "Milosz is eloquent in his call for a literature grounded in moral, as well as esthetic, values. Indeed, when compared with his own poetry, the work of many Westerners from the neurotic rantings of the Romantics to the cerebral mind games of the avant-gardists seems unserious and self-indulgent."

Because of his moral vision Milosz's writings make strong statements, some of which are inherently political in their implications. "The act of writing a poem is an act of faith," Milosz claims in *The History of Polish Literature,* "yet if the screams of the tortured are audible in the poet's room, is not his activity an offense to human suffering?" His awareness of suffering, Joseph C. Thackery of the *Hollins Critic* writes, makes Milosz a "spokesman of the millions of dead of the Holocaust, the Gulags, the Polish and Czech uprisings, and the added millions of those who will go on dying in an imperfect world."

But Milosz also warns of the dangers of political writing. In a PEN Congress talk reprinted in the *Partisan Review,* he states: "In this century a basic stance of writers . . . seems to be an acute awareness of suffering inflicted upon human beings by unjust structures of society. . . . This awareness of suffering makes a writer open to the idea of radical change, whichever of many recipes he chooses. . . . Innumerable millions of human beings were killed in this century in the name of utopia either progressive or reactionary, and always there were writers who provided convincing justifications for massacre."

In *The Witness of Poetry* Milosz argues that true poetry is "the passionate pursuit of the Real." He condemns those writers who favor art for art's sake or who think of themselves as alienated. Milosz suggests, as Adam Gussow writes in the *Saturday Review,* that poets may have "grown afraid of reality, afraid to see it clearly and speak about it in words we can all comprehend." What is needed in "today's unsettled world," Gussow explains, are poets who, "like Homer, Dante, and Shakespeare, will speak for rather than against the enduring values of their communities."

This concern for a poetry that confronts reality is noted by Thackery, who sees Milosz searching "for a poetry that will be at once harsh and mollifying, that will enable men to understand, if not to rationalize, the debasement of the human spirit by warfare and psychic dismemberment, while simultaneously establishing a personal *modus vivendi* and a psychology of aesthetic necessity." Des Pres also sees this unifying quality in Milosz's poetry, a trait he believes Milosz shares with T. S. Eliot. "The aim of both Milosz and Eliot," Des Pres states, "is identical: to go back and work through the detritus of one's own time on earth, to gather up the worst along with the best, integrate past and present into a culminating moment which transcends both, which embraces pain and joy together, the whole of a life and a world redeemed through memory and art, a final restoration in spirit of that which in historical fact has been forever lost." Vendler believes that "the work of Milosz reminds us of the great power that poetry gains from bearing within itself an unforced, natural, and long-ranging memory of past customs; a sense of the strata of ancient and modern history; wide visual experience; and a knowledge of many languages and literatures. . . . The living and tormented revoicing of the past makes Milosz a historical poet of bleak illumination."

Upon receiving the Nobel Prize in 1980, Milosz hoped to "continue with my very private and strange occupation," as McLellan quotes him. He has continued to publish books—some new titles and some older books appearing in English for the first time—and has spoken out at meetings of PEN, the international writers' organization, on such topics as censorship and totalitarianism. Darling explains that Milosz lives in Berkeley and writes "under the benevolent light of the California sun, in a country of easy consummation and temporary passion, poems about the past, about horror, about life in the abyss of the 20th century."

Milosz's place in Polish literature is secure, while his influence and reputation in other nations continues to grow. As Galassi writes, "Few other living poets have argued as convincingly for the nobility and value of the poet's calling. Whatever its importance to Polish letters, Mr. Milosz's work, as poetry in English, presents a challenge to American poetry to exit from the labyrinth of the self and begin to grapple again with the larger problems of being in the world." "Milosz has lived through, and participated in, some of the crucial political happenings of our century," Michael Irwin comments in the *Times Literary Supplement.* "If he had never written a line he would be an intriguing figure merely by virtue of his survival. Since he in fact brought to bear upon his experiences a refined and resilient analytical intelligence, unusually combined with a poet's sensibility, his testimony is of unique importance. Attention must be paid to such a man."

Because Milosz writes of recent Polish history, and decries the nation's political tragedies of the past thirty-five years, his work embodies a spirit of freedom that speaks powerfully to his countrymen as well as to others. "Polish independence exists in this poet's voice," Brodsky maintains in the *New York Times.* "This, at least, is one way to account for the intensity that has made him perhaps the greatest poet of our time." Milosz is one of three Poles who have come to international prominence during the 1980s, Norman Davies notes in the *New York Times Book Review.* Milosz, Pope John Paul II, and Lech Walesa, the leader of the Solidarity trade union challenging the Polish communist government, have "each served in different ways to illuminate the depth and richness of their native Polish culture," Davies writes. In 1981, during his first visit to Poland in thirty years, Milosz met with Walesa and the two men acknowledged their mutual indebtedness. "I told him that I considered him my leader," Milosz recounts to Darling. "He said that he had gone to jail because of my poetry."

BIOGRAPHICAL/CRITICAL SOURCES:

BOOKS

Contemporary Literary Criticism, Gale, Volume 5, 1976, Volume 11, 1979, Volume 22, 1982, Volume 31, 1985.
Czarnecha, Ewe, *Prdrozny swiata: Rosmowy z Czeslawem Miloszem, Komentane,* Bicentennial, 1983.
Fiut, Aleksander, *Rozmowy z Czeslawem Miloszem,* Wydawnictwo Literackie (Krakow), 1981.
Gillon, A. and L. Krzyzanowski, editors, *Introduction to Modern Polish Literature,* Twayne, 1964.
Goemoeri, G., *Polish and Hungarian Poetry, 1945 to 1956,* Oxford University Press, 1966.
Hass, Robert, *Twentieth Century Pleasures: Prose on Poetry,* Ecco Press, 1984.
Milosz, Czeslaw, *The Captive Mind,* Knopf, 1953.
Milosz, Czeslaw, *The History of Polish Literature,* Macmillan, 1969, revised edition, University of California Press, 1983.
Milosz, Czeslaw, *The Witness of Poetry,* Harvard University Press, 1983.
Milosz, Czeslaw, *The Land of Ulro,* Farrar, Straus, 1984.
Milosz, Czeslaw, *The Collected Poems, 1931-1987,* translation by Robert Hass, Louis Iribarne, and Peter Dale Scott, Ecco Press, 1987.

PERIODICALS

America, December 18, 1982.
American Poetry Review, January, 1977.
Books Abroad, winter, 1969, spring, 1970, winter, 1973, winter, 1975.

Book Week, May 9, 1965.
Book World, September 29, 1968.
Chicago Tribune, October 10, 1980.
Chicago Tribune Book World, May 31, 1981.
Commonweal, July 8, 1955.
Denver Quarterly, summer, 1976.
Eastern European Poetry, April, 1967.
Globe and Mail (Toronto), March 16, 1985, August 27, 1988.
Hollins Critic, April, 1982.
Ironwood, Number 18, 1981.
Los Angeles Times, January 14, 1987.
Los Angeles Times Book Review, May 10, 1981, August 22, 1982, June 5, 1983, August 24, 1984.
Nation, December 30, 1978, June 13, 1981.
New Republic, May 16, 1955, August 1, 1983.
New Statesman, October 24, 1980, December 17-24, 1982.
Newsweek, June 15, 1981, October 4, 1982.
New Yorker, November 7, 1953, March 19, 1984.
New York Review of Books, April 4, 1974, June 25, 1981.
New York Times, June 25, 1968, October 10, 1980, September 4, 1982, August 24, 1984, July 26, 1987, September 12, 1988, June 22, 1989.
New York Times Book Review, April 17, 1955, July 7, 1974, March 11, 1979, February 1, 1981, June 28, 1981, October 17, 1982, May 1, 1983, September 2, 1984, July 6, 1986, June 19, 1988.
Partisan Review, November, 1953, spring, 1977, Volume 53, number 2, 1986.
Poetry, April, 1980.
Publishers Weekly, October 24, 1980.
Saturday Review, June 6, 1953, May-June, 1983.
Spectator, December 4, 1982.
Theology Today, January, 1984.
Times (London), July 16, 1981, January 6, 1983, May 19, 1983, February 9, 1985, May 27, 1987.
Times Literary Supplement, December 2, 1977, August 25, 1978, July 24, 1981, December 24, 1982, September 9, 1983, September 2, 1988.
TriQuarterly, fall, 1983.
Village Voice, May 2, 1974.
Virginia Quarterly Review, spring, 1975.
Washington Post, October 10, 1980, April 29, 1982, September 20, 1989.
Washington Post Book World, June 14, 1981.
World Literature Today, winter, 1978, spring, 1978.

*   *   *

MIRANDA, Javier
See BIOY CASARES, Adolfo

*   *   *

MISHIMA, Yukio
See HIRAOKA, Kimitake

*   *   *

MISTRAL, Gabriela
See GODOY ALCAYAGA, Lucila

*   *   *

MITCHELL, Clyde
See ELLISON, Harlan and SILVERBERG, Robert

MITCHELL, Margaret (Munnerlyn)   1900-1949
(Peggy Mitchell, Margaret Mitchell Upshaw;
Elizabeth Bennett, a pseudonym)

PERSONAL: Born November 8, 1900, in Atlanta, GA; died from brain injuries sustained when struck by an automobile, August 16, 1949, in Atlanta, GA; buried in Oakland Cemetery, Atlanta, GA; daughter of Eugene Muse (an attorney) and Maybelle (a women's suffrage activist; maiden name, Stephens) Mitchell; married Berrien Kinnard Upshaw, September 2, 1922 (annulled, October 16, 1924; died January 10, 1949); married John Robert Marsh (in public relations), July 4, 1925 (died May 5, 1952). *Education:* Attended Smith College, 1918-19.

ADDRESSES: Home—1268 Piedmont Ave., Atlanta, GA.

CAREER: Atlanta Journal, Atlanta, GA, feature writer, 1922-26, free-lance columnist, 1926; novelist, 1926-36; homemaker, 1936-49. Volunteer selling war bonds during World War II; volunteer for the American Red Cross in the 1940s.

AWARDS, HONORS: Pulitzer Prize from Columbia University Graduate School of Journalism, 1937, for *Gone With the Wind;* M.A. from Smith College, 1939; named honorary citizen of Vimoutiers, France, 1949, for helping the city obtain American aid after World War II.

WRITINGS:

Gone With the Wind, Macmillan, 1936.
Margaret Mitchell's "Gone With the Wind" Letters, edited by Richard Harwell, Macmillan, c. 1976.
A Dynamo Going to Waste: Letters to Allen Edee, 1919-1921, edited by Jane Bonner Peacock, Peachtree Publications, 1985.

Also author, under names Peggy Mitchell and Margaret Mitchell Upshaw, of numerous feature stories, and, under pseudonym Elizabeth Bennett, of column "Elizabeth Bennett's Gossip," all for the *Atlanta Journal.* Author of unpublished short stories, plays, and the novella "'Ropa Carmagin."

MEDIA ADAPTATIONS: A film version of *Gone With the Wind* was released, starring Clark Gable, Vivien Leigh, Leslie Howard, and Olivia De Havilland, by Metro-Goldwyn-Mayer in 1939.

SIDELIGHTS: In 1936 Margaret Mitchell completed what was to become a lasting part of American culture—her novel, *Gone With the Wind.* After selling a record-breaking one million copies in six months, *Gone With the Wind* went on to become the largest-selling book in history with the exception of the Bible. By 1976 the work had been translated into twenty-seven languages in thirty-seven countries, and as Anne Edwards reported in her biography of Mitchell, *Road to Tara,* by 1983 the novel had "sold six million hardcover copies in the United States; one million copies in England; and nine million copies in foreign translation." Approximately 250,000 paperback copies of the book are sold annually in the United States.

Gone With the Wind's sales, however, are only a partial measure of Mitchell's importance as an author. Through her novel and the 1939 film of the same title, Mitchell's characters, especially Scarlett O'Hara and Rhett Butler, have become household names. As Edwards put it, "who can now think of the South before, during, and after the Civil War without images drawn from the pages of *Gone With the Wind?* Scarlett seated under the shade of a huge oak, surrounded by beaus . . . [and] defying convention and dancing in her widow's weeds with the dashing scoundrel, Rhett Butler; the hundreds of wounded lying in the pitiless sun, . . . the burning of Atlanta, . . . the moment when

Scarlett claws the earth to take from it a radish root to stave her hunger, . . . and—oh, yes—Scarlett O'Hara crying 'What shall I do?' . . . and Rhett's reply, 'My dear, I don't give a damn.' "

The woman who created these scenes was born into a middle-class Atlanta family in 1900. As a small child she heard stories of the Civil War told by relatives who had experienced the conflict, and her maternal grandmother, Annie Fitzgerald Stephens, showed her where Confederate forces had dug trenches in her back yard. Mitchell would tell the stories she heard, and stories she had herself made up, to her brother, Stephens, and his friends. She grew up knowing almost everything there was to know about the Civil War—except that the South had lost. This fact she finally learned at the age of ten from the black field workers of a relative's farm where she was spending a summer.

History was not the only thing Mitchell learned during childhood that would appear in her famous novel. From witnessing the different levels of prosperity apparent less than fifty years after the Civil War, she learned that some people were able to rebuild after the conflict's devastation but others were not, the difference being a matter of character and intelligence. From one of her great aunts she received the buckwheat analogy that Grandma Fontaine uses in *Gone With the Wind* to comfort Scarlett: "We're not wheat, we're buckwheat! When a storm comes along it flattens ripe wheat because it's dry and can't bend with the wind. But ripe buckwheat's got sap in it and it bends. And when the wind has passed, it springs up almost as straight and strong as before."

Mitchell's mother, Maybelle, who was active in the women's suffrage movement, used a more literal example to instill values in her daughter. According to Edwards, when Mitchell came home from school one day complaining that "she hated arithmetic and did not want to go back," her mother first spanked her and then took her in their horse-drawn carriage southward toward Jonesboro. The mother pointed out derelict plantations to her daughter, telling her that the people who had inhabited them had once been "fine and wealthy." Maybelle explained to Mitchell that some of the houses had been destroyed by Northern troops, but that others had decayed more gradually as their owners grew increasingly poorer during Reconstruction. Some houses were still well tended, however, and Maybelle reportedly told her daughter, "Now, those folk stood as staunchly as their houses did. . . . The world those people lived in was a secure world, just like yours is now. But theirs exploded right from underneath them. Your world will do that to you one day, too, and God help you, child, if you don't have some weapon to meet that new world. Education! . . . For all you're going to be left with after your world upends will be what you do with your hands and what you have in your head." Mitchell's mother concluded by telling the girl that she would go back to school the next day and "conquer arithmetic." In addition to determination, Scarlett is able to save herself and her family from starvation because of her "good head for figures."

When Mitchell was eleven years old her family moved from the Jackson Hill area of Atlanta to the more prestigious Peachtree Street. Her mother's work for the women's movement and her Catholicism tended to separate Mitchell from the rest of the neighborhood children, whose parents were generally conservative and Protestant. Her tomboyish early childhood did not help either; as Edwards observed, "Margaret was not accepted by the young residents of Peachtree Street, who had been learning the social niceties of Southern society while she had been sliding into first, second, or third base." Meanwhile, her brother had turned seventeen and was too old to let his young sister follow him

around. Increasingly, then, Mitchell turned to writing to fill her hours. She continued penning adventures, mostly in the form of plays, filling notebooks with titles like "Phil Kelly: Detective," "A Darktown Tragedy," and "The Fall of Roger Rover." When she wasn't actually writing, she was making plans for stories.

Mitchell's writing continued through her years at Washington Seminary, a private girls' school near her home which she began attending at the age of fourteen. Though she was unhappy with being expected to act like a lady by her peers as well as by her teachers of manners and deportment, she preferred Washington to the alternative—being sent to a convent school as the women on her mother's side of the family traditionally were. Mitchell did find encouragement for her writing at the school, however. A sympathetic English teacher, Eva Paisley, commented extensively on her papers, helping her toward the goals of unity, coherence, and simplicity. Paisley often read Mitchell's papers aloud in class, and it was while she was Paisley's pupil that Mitchell made her first attempt at a novel. Titled "The Big Four," it concerned four friends in a girls' boarding school. The heroine, named Margaret, engaged in valiant exploits such as leading her classmates through a fire and destroying incriminating documents that would have ruined a friend's family. Though she managed to finish the story, which amounted to fourteen chapters and four hundred copybook pages in cursive writing, she was not pleased with it after rereading it. According to Edwards, Mitchell inscribed on the inside of its back cover: "There are authors and authors but a *true* writer is born and not made. Born writers make their characters real, living people, while 'made writers' have merely stuffed figures who dance when the strings are pulled—that's how I know I'm a 'made' writer." Though she considered herself a failure as a novelist, she continued to write shorter pieces of fiction.

After graduating from Washington Seminary in 1918 Mitchell planned to enter Smith College, telling her family that she would eventually become a doctor. She had read Sigmund Freud and thought she might specialize in psychiatry. Maybelle Mitchell, in keeping with her suffragette activities, encouraged her daughter to be more than a housewife. Mitchell also confided her ambitions to one of the soldiers stationed in Atlanta that summer, Lieutenant Clifford Henry. She met him at a party and was attracted to his knowledge of literature, his seriousness, and his fair good looks. In spite of what Edwards labeled "his homosexual tendencies," Henry was attracted to Mitchell as well. When he learned in August that he would be transferred to the European front, they became engaged and corresponded frequently. Rather than being declarative of passion, Mitchell's letters were full of hopes for her academic and professional future. Henry's were filled with his feelings of disillusionment about the war.

At Smith College Mitchell was not nearly as successful as she wanted to be. In most of her classes she barely met the average standard. Though she admitted her doubts to no one, it became increasingly clear that she would be unable to become a psychiatrist. In one subject, however, she excelled—English composition. According to Edwards, her professor declared Mitchell "a youthful genius." But this praise did not buoy her spirits. She felt that the piece that led her instructor to make the pronouncement was bad, and that he lacked the discernment of her high school teacher, Paisley.

In September of 1918 Mitchell's fiance was seriously wounded at the battle of Saint-Mihiel in France. Henry died of his wounds in mid-October. Mitchell was said to grieve deeply, and she later declared that Henry had been the one great love in her life. This statement, along with the evidence of Henry's character traits, led Edwards to conjecture that he was the model for Ashley Wilkes, the idealistic but weak married man whom Scarlett O'Hara pursues throughout *Gone With the Wind*. Mitchell faced another emotional setback the following January when her mother fell desperately ill, a victim of the influenza epidemic that had swept the nation. Her father had been stricken by the flu earlier but had already convalesced. Maybelle developed pneumonia in one lung, and by the time Mitchell arrived home, summoned by the news that her mother had slipped into a coma, she was dead.

With her mother dead, Mitchell's motivation to do well at Smith and become a psychiatrist failed her. After she finished her first year she returned to Atlanta to run the household for her father and brother. Having been away for a time, and never having had many friends in her home town, she had virtually no social life. Fearing his daughter might become a lonely spinster if left to her own devices, Eugene Mitchell urged her to apply for membership in Atlanta's prestigious Debutante Club. Mitchell acquiesced, and by January of 1920 she was approved for membership. At one of the many gatherings she attended as a member, she met Berrien Kinnard Upshaw, nicknamed Red by his friends. Though her family and debutante friends found Red rough, rude, and thoroughly unsuitable for Mitchell, Edwards reported that "there was a certain mystery surrounding Upshaw that intrigued [her]; he had an aura of glamour that made him a topic of discussion among her peers and their families. It was known that he was the eldest son of a respectable old Georgia family now living in North Carolina, but there were also whisperings of scandal—although no one seemed to know any of the details."

After causing a minor scene by doing a sensual Apache dance in a suggestively slitted costume for a debutante charity function, Mitchell was passed over for membership in Atlanta's Junior League, the expected next step for debutantes. Mitchell was hurt and angry, but she was now also free of all restraints on her behavior except those imposed by her family. Her relationship with Upshaw deepened, and in his company she joined the Peachtree Yacht Club—in Edwards's words, "a drinking club that had nothing at all to do with boats." With the club members, Mitchell could indulge her taste for liquor, cigarettes, and risque jokes without censure. She wrote short humorous plays to entertain her new friends; these were performed at the family house until her disapproving father put a stop to them. At this time she also became friends with Red Upshaw's roommate, John Marsh. Totally opposite in personality to Upshaw, Marsh discussed literature with Mitchell and critiqued her short stories. Eventually both men declared their love for her. Though her father and brother showed a decided preference for Marsh as a more stable and respectable man, Mitchell was excited by Upshaw, who, according to Edwards, "claimed to have played a secret, dashing role in [World War I], something to do with espionage and being behind enemy lines," and was a liquor bootlegger during the days of Prohibition when alcoholic beverages were illegal. Noting similarities between Red Upshaw and Mitchell's fictional creation Rhett Butler, Edwards asserted: "Both were 'masterful,' 'scoundrelly,' and of 'low morals,' and both had been expelled from service academies—Rhett, from West Point; Red, from Annapolis. Both had been profiteers, Rhett using the war for profit; Red, Prohibition. . . . And both were Southerners, but not Atlantans. But it was the volatile spirits of the two men that were most synonymous—the inner violence, the strong passions, the brilliant minds always so self-serving, and the animal magnetism."

On September 2, 1922, Mitchell married Upshaw, with John Marsh serving as best man. By the following December the cou-

ple had separated, Upshaw leaving Atlanta for Asheville, North Carolina. Reportedly he told Mitchell she could get a divorce if she wished because he was never going to return. He did, however, in July of 1923 after Marsh had persuaded Mitchell to obtain a job as a feature writer for the *Atlanta Journal*. Mitchell asked him to come into the family house; no one else but the maid was there. In a deposition for their subsequent divorce, Edwards reported, Mitchell testified that Upshaw attempted to rape her. She struggled to get away, and her screams brought the family servant to investigate just as Upshaw decided to flee. He had beaten Mitchell so severely that she had to be hospitalized, and she was badly bruised. According to Edwards, Mitchell later "conceded that she never should have discussed her romantic feelings for Clifford Henry" during her honeymoon with Upshaw, "nor sent [Henry's parents] a postcard."

By October of 1924 Mitchell was granted an annulment of her marriage to Upshaw, and on July 4, 1925, she married John Marsh, on whom she had come to depend during her trials with Red. Throughout these changes in her personal life, Mitchell continued as a feature writer for the *Atlanta Journal*. She had her first byline feature printed in the paper, a story about an Atlanta plant expert, in early January, 1923. By the time she left the paper's employment, Edwards reported, Mitchell had written "139 by-lined features and 85 news stories, assisted in the writing of a personal advice column and a film column, and wrote a chapter for one of the *Journal*'s weekly serials when parts of a manuscript were lost." Her earlier assignments, however, usually dealt with light and humorous subjects. Dissatisfied with these topics, she requested that she be allowed to develop a more serious set of articles on eminent women in Georgia history. Though her editors had misgivings, Mitchell won permission to do a four-part series. Her first feature discussed four women: Rebecca Latimer Felton, who became the first woman United States senator though appointed to the post upon the death of her husband rather than elected; Lucy Mathilde Kenney, who disguised herself as a man to fight alongside her husband in the Civil War; Mary Musgrove, a native American woman who was named the empress of the Creek tribe despite having had three white husbands; and Nancy Hart, who took prisoner an entire troop of British soldiers when they attempted to gain entrance to her kitchen during the American Revolution. As Edwards pointed out, "the only one who fitted the ladylike stereotype of the Southern heroine was Rebecca Latimer Felton," and the article drew a large amount of negative response from the paper's readership. Because Mitchell had favorably depicted strong women who did not fit contemporary standards for femininity, "she [was] accused of everything from defaming Georgian womanhood to bastardizing history in order to sell newspapers." The rest of the series was canceled, and Mitchell, deeply hurt by the criticism she had received, limited herself to mostly lighter features such as an interview with film star Rudolph Valentino and articles which asked questions like "Should Husbands Spank Their Wives?"

A few months after marrying Marsh, however, Mitchell was asked to do a series of articles for the *Atlanta Journal* on the five Confederate generals selected to represent Georgia on the Stone Mountain Memorial, on which construction would soon begin. Because of her enthusiasm for Confederate history, Mitchell put much energy into the research and writing of the first article, which discussed generals John B. Gordon and Pierce M. Butler Young. Readers were so pleased with the feature that Mitchell's editor decided to stretch the series over the next three weeks so that she could compose an article about each of the remaining generals. These, too, were well received, but their importance went beyond their immediate reception. As Mitchell examined sources for her piece on General Henry Benning, "she found herself almost more caught up in the story of his wife," noted Edwards. Benning's wife had heroically struggled during the Civil War to keep the family plantation in operation, cared for her elderly parents and for her brother's widow, and nursed wounded Confederate soldiers. Edwards conjectured that Mitchell's interest in this woman's experiences and her desire to write the features on prominent women in Georgia foreshadowed her portrayal of the Civil War from the point of view of the women left behind by the men who went to battle in *Gone With the Wind.*

When Mitchell's husband, who was never completely happy about her working outside the home, received a raise in salary from the public relations department of the Georgia Power and Light Company in 1926, he urged her to leave her post at the *Atlanta Journal.* She did so, though she continued to write a freelance column for the *Journal* called "Elizabeth Bennett's Gossip," which was more a compilation of historical anecdotes than of gossip, until she injured her ankle in an automobile accident and could not sit at the typewriter. By the time Mitchell had completely given up newspaper work, however, she had already ceased to find it sufficiently challenging as a writer. With Marsh's encouragement she began working on her fiction again. Mitchell started a Jazz Age novel with a heroine named Pansy Hamilton. As Edwards asserted, "the young men and women in Pansy's circle all bore a strong resemblance to the group that belonged to the [Peachtree] Yacht Club," and the hero "closely resembled Red Upshaw." Mitchell apparently found the similarity between truth and fiction too unpleasant to continue her story after the first thirty pages. She next attempted a novel set during the 1880s in Georgia's Clayton county, where her ancestors once owned a plantation. It became the unpublished novella "'Ropa Carmagin," the tale of the daughter of a once-great antebellum plantation family now declining and her mulatto lover, the son of one of the family's slaves. A tragedy, the story ends with the hero being killed and 'Ropa being driven from her ancestral home by hostile neighbors.

Mitchell's late 1926 accident and ankle injury required her to spend three weeks in a cast and then several more weeks in bed. During her convalescence Marsh brought her many books from the library to read. As Edwards reported, "The day [Mitchell] graduated to crutches, early in 1927, [Marsh] came home from work with a stack of copy paper and told her that there was hardly a book left in the library that she would enjoy." Her husband said she would have to write a book herself if she was to have anything to read. Feeling as though she had been challenged, the next day she sat down at her typewriter and began the best selling novel in history. She started with the last chapter, but afterward worked more or less in chronological order.

Mitchell spent long hours in the basement of the Atlanta public library poring over old Atlanta newspapers to check the accuracy of her novel's historical details. As she worked on the Civil War epic, Mitchell called it "Tomorrow Is Another Day," from Scarlett's famous last lines after Rhett's departure: "I'll think of it all tomorrow, at Tara. I can stand it then. Tomorrow, I'll think of some way to get him back. After all, tomorrow is another day." Also, throughout the writing of the novel, the heroine's name was Pansy rather than Scarlett, while the name of the O'Hara plantation was initially Fontenoy Hall rather than Tara.

Pointing out that Pansy was also the name of the heroine in Mitchell's aborted Jazz Age novel, Edwards noted the many similarities between Pansy (later Scarlett) O'Hara and her creator: "Both were mavericks, constantly flouting convention and

society, and both suffered identity problems caused by strong, righteous, Catholic mothers. Both had to care for their fathers after their mothers' deaths. Both were flirts and teases. . . . Both turned their backs on the Catholic church. Both were women who drank in a society that frowned on such 'unladylike' behavior, and both had set society against them. Both had had romanticized, unfulfilled first loves, [and] a violent marriage." Edwards also revealed the correspondences between Pansy and Mitchell's maternal grandmother: "The O'Hara family had much in common with the Fitzgeralds, and had settled in Clayton County at about the same time. And, like Pansy O'Hara, Annie Fitzgerald Stephens had remained in Atlanta until the fire, had nursed the injured soldiers who had fallen or been brought there, had taken her firstborn infant back to Jonesboro alone just after the fire, and had remained there, fighting starvation and carpetbaggers, until the men returned from the war. Also, like Pansy, Annie was just a few years younger than the city of Atlanta." This likeness between Pansy and Mitchell's grandmother, coupled with the resemblances between Rhett Butler and Red Upshaw, and Ashley Wilkes and Clifford Henry, made Mitchell hesitant about ever submitting the novel for publication.

Despite her hesitation, Mitchell worked fairly steadily on the novel from 1926 to 1934 except for a few periods of discouragement. The first of these came in the spring of 1927, when, Edwards reported, Mitchell read James Boyd's Civil War novel, *Marching On.* She was apparently intimidated by the superiority of Boyd's writing. Edwards observed: "She [felt that she] did not write with the intellectual power of Boyd, nor did she understand the Confederate strategy or the Union aims as well as he did. She was writing a book about the great war without taking any of her characters into battle, and she was convinced that it was cowardly for her to avoid such scenes, that it only proved how inadequate she was for the job she was attempting." Mitchell did not touch her manuscript for three months. Another three-month break in the writing came after Mitchell read Stephen Vincent Benet's epic poem on the Civil War, *John Brown's Body.* She had much of the novel on paper, however, though disorganized and in a rough state, when another automobile accident in 1934 forced her to wear a brace that made composing at the typewriter difficult. Again, she stopped work on the book.

According to Edwards, Mitchell had just been told she would be able to do without the brace in a week's time when Macmillan acquisitions editor Harold Latham arrived in Atlanta looking for publishable manuscripts in April, 1935. Mitchell was enlisted by one of her former newspaper colleagues to entertain the visiting editor and help him in his search. Though she mentioned various friends and acquaintances who were working on novels, she did not tell him of her own project. Mitchell's friend Lois Cole worked for Macmillan, however, and though she had by that time moved to their New York offices, she remembered that Mitchell was writing a book and mentioned it to Latham. Latham, entranced by Mitchell's storytelling ability as she showed him the sights of her native city, inquired about her novel, but she denied she was writing one.

The night before Latham was to return to New York, however, Mitchell appeared at his hotel room accompanied by huge piles of manila envelopes. Apparently, derisive remarks from a friend about her lack of ambition and talent made her angry enough to show her manuscript to the Macmillan editor. On the train home, Latham examined what Mitchell had brought him and was nearly discouraged by what Edwards termed "the worst-looking manuscript he had ever been given in his long career in publishing." But when he started reading, in Edwards's words, "like all future readers of this book, whose numbers were to be in the millions, Harold Latham was hooked." Despite the fact that there was no real first chapter, several versions of other chapters, and missing bridges between the various incidents in the novel, Latham sent Mitchell a telegram saying that her book had great potential.

Eventually Macmillan purchased the book, and after an extensive revision, a name change for the heroine—Pansy became Scarlett because "pansy" was a slang term for a male homosexual in the North and Latham wished to avoid any negative connotations—and a search for a new title (because, as Cole explained, "there were thirteen books in print with titles beginning [with] 'Tomorrow . . .'"), it became the 1037-page opus *Gone With the Wind.*

Gone With the Wind was an immediate success. Before it was even published it was chosen as a Book-of-the-Month Club main selection; shortly after its publication the motion picture rights were purchased for fifty thousand dollars—a high sum in 1936—by Selznick-International Pictures. Even at three dollars a copy, expensive for the Great Depression, Mitchell's book was quickly on its way to becoming the best-selling work of fiction of all time. Indeed, Finis Farr, in *Margaret Mitchell of Atlanta: The Author of "Gone With the Wind,"* credited Mitchell with doing a great deal for the ailing American economy. "Benefits flowed through The Macmillan Company from top to bottom," he reported. "In December, Christmas bonuses appeared for the first time in recent memory." This prosperity spread throughout the bookselling industry as well. "The million copies of *Gone With the Wind* the public bought by Christmas of 1936 caused $3,000,000 to go through the retailers' cash registers," Farr added. Mitchell became an overnight celebrity, receiving countless pieces of fan mail, most of which she felt it her duty to answer personally. Her phone, which remained listed in the Atlanta directory, rang constantly; as Edwards revealed, one of the early callers was Red Upshaw. He reportedly told Mitchell that he figured she still loved him, because "Rhett Butler is obviously modeled after [him]." When Mitchell asked him what he wanted, he said he would "tell her someday in person" and hung up.

Hearing from Upshaw, coupled with her sudden phenomenal fame, made Mitchell fear that much of her private life would be exposed. But she was also flattered by the attention her book received, though she was baffled by it. In a letter to Herschel Brickell, one of *Gone With the Wind*'s early reviewers, dated October 9, 1936, Mitchell described her lack of ability to understand her novel's popularity. "I sit down and pull the story apart in my mind and try to figure it all out," she wrote. "Despite its length and many details it is basically just a simple yarn of fairly simple people. There's no fine writing, there are no grandiose thoughts, there are no hidden meanings, no symbolism, nothing sensational—nothing, nothing at all." Nevertheless, as she told Brickell, "the bench and bar like it, judges write me letters about it. The medical profession . . . like it. . . . The psychiatrists especially like it. . . . File clerks, elevator operators, sales girls in department stores, telephone operators, stenographers, garage mechanics, clerks in Helpsy-Selfsy stores, school teachers—oh, Heavens, I could go on and on!—like it. What is more puzzling, they buy copies. . . . The Sons of Confederate Veterans crashed through with a grand endorsement. . . . The debutantes and dowagers read it. Catholic nuns like it." Critics, though, were not as mystified as the author, generally explaining the novel's success by linking Scarlett's struggle to overcome poverty and Reconstruction to the struggles of the average American during the Great Depression—Scarlett's determination made her a character readers could admire and identify with in spite of her negative qualities.

Mitchell became so famous, even winning the 1937 Pulitzer Prize for *Gone With the Wind,* that women began impersonating her for their own ends. Edwards reported that "impostors were appearing in California, Mexico, and New York who claimed to be Margaret Mitchell, gave statements to the press and, in one case, tried to use her name to establish financial credit." Mitchell was also plagued by false rumors which circulated about her, including, according to Farr and Edwards, ones which claimed she was insane, that she had a wooden leg, that her husband John had really written *Gone With the Wind,* that she had paid author Sinclair Lewis to write the book for her, that she was dying of leukemia, and that she was going blind.

Critics discussed *Gone With the Wind* almost as avidly as the rest of the American public. Most were unanimous in their praise of its ability to hold a reader's attention; author Stephen Vincent Benet, reviewing the novel in the *Saturday Review of Literature,* avowed that "in spite of its length, the book moves swiftly and smoothly—a three-decker with all sails set." The best-seller's literary merit was less easily decided upon. Poet John Peale Bishop dismissed *Gone With the Wind* in the *New Republic* as "one of those thousand-page novels, competent but neither very good nor very sound"; Bernard DeVoto in the *Saturday Review of Literature* labeled Mitchell's work "wish-fulfillment literature" and complained that "its sentiments" were "commonplace and frequently cheap." On the other hand, reviewer Malcolm Cowley asserted that *Gone With the Wind* "has a simple-minded courage that suggests the great novelists of the past." Belle Rosenbaum, critiquing in *Scribner's Magazine,* pointed out that "Scarlett O'Hara and Rhett Butler retained a touch of [authors James] Joyce, [Ernest] Hemingway, [and F. Scott] Fitzgerald, and the aftermath of the Civil War was interpreted in modern terms with Scarlett O'Hara emerging as the modern prototype of [author William Makepeace] Thackeray's immortal [character] Becky Sharp." And, though Mitchell was criticized for her glorification of a society that practiced slavery, she was also lauded for her careful attention to historical detail.

Despite several changes of screenwriters, a change of directors, and casting difficulties, the film version of *Gone With the Wind* won ten Academy Awards, including one for best picture. Starring Clark Gable as Rhett, British actress Vivien Leigh as Scarlett, Leslie Howard as Ashley, and Olivia De Havilland as Ashley's wife Melanie, the film finally premiered in Mitchell's hometown Atlanta in December, 1939. The premiere was a huge event, with Mitchell and most of the film's major stars in attendance at Atlanta's Loew's Grand Theatre. After the film, nearly four hours in length, was shown and had received a standing ovation, Mitchell addressed the crowd. Edwards concluded: "It seemed doubtful that anything further could occur in her life that would equal the sense of accomplishment she had felt as she stepped out of the Selznick limousine before the Loew's Grand Theatre, unless it had been the moment when she had stood alone, front and center of the Grand's stage, waiting for the ovation that was being given her to subside."

After the release of "Gone With the Wind," most of the publicity Mitchell had been receiving died down. Her best-selling novel had changed her life irrevocably, however; she spent the rest of her life answering fan letters, and most critics assume that she was too intimidated by the amazing success of her first published work to ever seriously attempt another novel, though she sometimes joked about writing a sequel to be titled "Back With the Breeze." When the United States entered World War II, Mitchell busied herself in the war effort, serving as a volunteer in the American Red Cross, selling war bonds, corresponding with American servicemen overseas, and even christening the ill-fated cruiser the U.S.S. *Atlanta,* later sunk in battle. After the war she sent packages of food and supplies to Europe, eventually being named an honorary citizen of Vimoutiers, France, for her relief efforts. According to Edwards, Mitchell seemed proud of the fact that *Gone With the Wind* had been banned in Nazi-occupied Europe during the war and black market copies had sold for high prices among the rebellious citizens of occupied France, who identified heavily with her portrayal of the conquered but un-bowed Southerners. Though she had been accused of racism by many of her novel's reviewers, she involved herself in a charitable campaign to build a paying hospital for blacks in Atlanta, who at that time were segregated to charity hospitals whose facilities were often inferior. Also, many of Mitchell's black acquaintances had complained to her of their shame at having to take charity in order to receive medical care.

Mitchell was troubled at this time, however, by worries about her husband John's health (he suffered a heart attack in December, 1945, which left him a semi-invalid), and by premonitions that she would die a violent death. In a 1945 letter to friend and reviewer Edwin Granberry, Edwards reported, she wrote: "I'm going to die in a car-crash. I feel very certain of this." Also, in January, 1949, Mitchell's personal secretary brought her an obituary stating that her first husband, Red Upshaw, had died in a fall from the fifth-story fire escape of a Galveston, Texas, hotel; his death had been ruled a suicide.

On August 11, 1949, Mitchell and her husband decided to view a film at a local theater. As Mitchell helped John across the street, a speeding car came at them from around a corner. Mitchell panicked, released her husband's arm, and started running back to the curb. The car, having initially swerved to avoid the couple, hit her; the driver was intoxicated. Mitchell died of brain injuries five days later. While she lay unconscious many calls about her condition were made to the hospital, including one from U.S. President Harry S. Truman. So many people wished to attend Mitchell's funeral that tickets had to be distributed. Farr quoted from Mitchell's brother Stephens's account of her burial in Atlanta's Oakland Cemetery: "There was a crowd there for two or three days. She had said something to her people and they had answered."

BIOGRAPHICAL/CRITICAL SOURCES:

BOOKS

Dictionary of Literary Biography, Volume 9: *American Novelists, 1910-1945,* Gale, 1981.
Edwards, Anne, *Road to Tara: The Life of Margaret Mitchell,* Ticknor & Fields, 1983.
Farr, Finis, *Margaret Mitchell of Atlanta: The Author of "Gone With the Wind,"* Morrow, 1965.
Fiedler, Leslie A., *The Inadvertent Epic: From "Uncle Tom's Cabin" to "Roots,"* Simon & Schuster, 1979.
Mitchell, Margaret, *Gone With the Wind,* Macmillan, 1936.
Mitchell, *Margaret Mitchell's "Gone With the Wind" Letters,* edited by Richard Harwell, Macmillan, c. 1976.
Stuckey, W. J., *The Pulitzer Prize Novels: A Critical Backward Look,* University of Oklahoma Press, 1966.
Twentieth-Century Literary Criticism, Volume 11, Gale, 1983.

PERIODICALS

American Quarterly, fall, 1981.
Chicago Tribune, June 26, 1986, February 7, 1988.
Detroit Free Press, May 19, 1988.

Georgia Review, summer, 1958, spring, 1974.
Life, May, 1988.
Los Angeles Times, April 21, 1988.
New Republic, July 15, 1936, September 16, 1936.
Newsweek, June 30, 1986.
New York Times, June 24, 1986, July 3, 1986, July 6, 1986, April 26, 1988.
New York Times Book Review, June 25, 1961.
Photoplay, March, 1938.
Saturday Review of Literature, July 4, 1936, January 8, 1938.
Scribner's Magazine, August, 1937.
Southern Literary Journal, spring, 1970, fall, 1980.
Washington Post, December 28, 1987.
Washington Post Book World, June 29, 1986.

*   *   *

MITCHELL, Peggy
See MITCHELL, Margaret (Munnerlyn)

*   *   *

MO, Timothy (Peter) 1950(?)-

PERSONAL: Born December 30, 1950 (some sources list 1953), in Hong Kong; son of Peter Mo Wan Lung and Barbara Helena Falkingham. *Education:* Received B.A. from St. John's College, Oxford University.

ADDRESSES: Office—c/o Andre Deutsch Ltd., 105 Great Russell St., London WC1B 3LJ, England.

CAREER: Writer.

AWARDS, HONORS: Shortlisted for the Booker McConnell Prize for fiction, 1982, for novel *Sour Sweet,* and 1986, for *An Insular Possession;* Hawthornden Prize from Society of Authors, 1983, for *Sour Sweet.*

WRITINGS:

The Monkey King (novel), Deutsch, 1978.
Sour Sweet (novel), Deutsch, 1982.
An Insular Possession, Chatto & Windus, 1986, Random House, 1987.

Contributor of reviews to periodicals, including *New Statesman.*

MEDIA ADAPTATIONS: Sour Sweet was adapted for film in 1989.

SIDELIGHTS: Timothy Mo's novel *The Monkey King* was hailed by critics as an expatriate's portrait of Hong Kong culture, evocative of author V. S. Naipaul's masterful description of Asian society in Trinidad. *Sour Sweet,* Mo's second novel, was as fulsomely praised for its subtle depiction of the immigrant experience from the viewpoint of a Chinese family in London, and achieved the distinction of being nominated for the 1982 Booker McConnell Prize, Britain's most prestigious literary award. A principal theme in both novels, according to critics, is the cultural clash of East and West, viewed with a keen eye for comic incongruities and sympathetic respect for the courage and resilience people display coping with unfamiliar social milieu.

The Monkey King, noted Michael Neve in the *Times Literary Supplement,* "breaks new ground" for novels set in Hong Kong by creating an authentic urban ambiance that is more than simply an exotic background for the characters. The narrative follows the career of Wallace Nolasco, a Chinese-Portuguese youth from Macao who reluctantly agrees to a marriage with a daughter of his father's Hong Kong partner, the shady merchant Mr. Poon. Wallace and his dim-witted bride, May-Ling, live with the rest of the extended Poon family in a ramshackle mansion where mutual suspicion thrives as the various in-laws maneuver for a share of the family fortune. "The book captures the sense of familial claustrophobia well," observed Michael Neve. The Poons resent Wallace as an interloper and cultural outsider, and Wallace in turn is generally disparaging of the Hong Kong Chinese, despite his own ethnic affinities. This frequently results in comic clashes, yet "the comedy is never farce, the characters are never caricatures; all are uniquely Hong Kong," opined John Marney in *World Literature Today.* "The dialogue is in that inimitable and hilarious compost of obsolete and misspoken English idiom that uniquely and indelibly identifies Hong King Chinglish."

After years of unsuccessful struggle for a place in Mr. Poon's commercial empire, Wallace is exiled to manage one of his father-in-law's estates in the New Territories on the Chinese mainland. There he is immersed in traditional Chinese culture, arbitrating such matters as a local dispute over the siting of shrines and draining of paddy fields. He acquits himself successfully, and eventually gains the confidence of Mr. Poon, who on his deathbed summons Wallace back to Hong Kong to make him the leader of the family dynasty. By making the cultural compromise that enables him to survive and prosper, Wallace symbolically fulfills the title role of the mythical Chinese monkey king, who defeats his rivals by sharp-wittedness alone.

Mo also explores the clash of cultures in *Sour Sweet,* which *New Statesman* critic Mike Poole termed "a brilliantly observed study in the first-generation immigrant experience." The novel marks an original departure from past fictional treatment of the cross-cultural theme, noted Jonathan Yardley in the *Washington Post Book World,* by shifting the narrative point of view from Westerners in the exotic East to a recently settled Hong Kong Chinese immigrant family in England. Mo "has turned a witty, imaginative, and wholly successful twist on what has become a familiar 20th-century genre," Yardley declared. "*Sour Sweet* is, on every level that really matters, a work filled with wonders, surprises and rewards—a novel that, at the risk of using a word cheapened by familiarity and abuse, can only be described as enchanting."

The novel's main narrative strand follows the Chen family's gradual and somewhat reluctant accommodation to English society, in the process discovering much about themselves and each other. For several years, Chen, his wife Lily, their small son Man Kee, and Lily's sister Mui live largely within London's virtually autonomous Chinese subculture, with few links to the outside world. Chen works as a waiter in a Chinese restaurant, learning only enough English to haltingly communicate the menu, and the two women spend almost all their time in the small flat, caring for Man Kee and waiting Chen's return, the high point of the day.

"Mo marvelously evokes the cocooned self-sufficiency of the Chens' home life," remarked critic Michael Leapman in the *New York Times Book Review.* Strong-willed and irrepressible, Lily offers a sharp contrast in temperament to the stolid Chen, while Mui refuses to budge from a maddening lethargy, planted in front of the television set. The author "depicts the family relationships and tensions with a delicate balance between comic distance and emotional involvement," observed Peter Lewis in the *Times Literary Supplement.* "He has a very sharp eye indeed for the nuances of behaviour in close-knit social units."

The Chens' world begins to change when they open a Chinese take-out restaurant and expand their contacts with the English, resulting in numerous comic cultural collisions. The staple of their menu—carefully researched to accommodate English tastes—is sweet-and-sour pork served with pineapple chunks in a lurid orange sauce, which the Chens themselves refuse to eat, preferring such genuine Chinese cuisine as "white, bloody chicken and yellow duck's feet." Reversing a Western ethnic cliche, Lily finds it impossible to distinguish among the restaurant's English patrons. "They all looked the same to her. . . . How few types of face there were compared to the almost infinite variety of interesting Cantonese physiognomies."

Mui fares somewhat better, breaking out of her isolation in a radical metamorphosis to become the family's main go-between with their truck driving clientele. In the process of cultural adjustment and close cooperation in the business, all three adults gradually deepen their understanding of each other as "their lives unfold in ways that are often unpredictable but always illuminating," observed Jonathan Yardley. Mo "has given them qualities that are distinctly Chinese, and qualities that are distinctly human, and what he has to tell us is that the two are exuberantly the same."

Running parallel to the Chen family saga in *Sour Sweet* is a dark narrative of the Chinese criminal underworld organized in the secret Triad Societies that flourished in London in the early 1960's. Chen has the misfortune of once doing business with a Triad gang, and, though innocent of any wrong-doing, is subsequently murdered by the organization. He vanishes one day and never returns home, but to cover up the crime, the Triad Society sends his wife an anonymous monthly stipend. Lily consequently rationalizes that Chen has taken a job abroad to help the family with extra income, and she slowly adjusts to life without him while refusing to abandon hope that he will return. The family fortunes have indeed turned "sour sweet" and "the book thus ends on a note of serenity and optimism," appraised Leapman.

BIOGRAPHICAL/CRITICAL SOURCES:

BOOKS

Contemporary Literary Criticism, Volume 46, Gale, 1988.

PERIODICALS

Asiaweek, December 21, 1986.
Globe and Mail (Toronto), June 20, 1987.
Los Angeles Times, April 2, 1987.
Los Angeles Times Book Review, July 5, 1987.
New Statesman, July 14, 1978, April 23, 1982.
New York Times Book Review, March 31, 1985, April 19, 1987.
Times (London), May 8, 1986.
Times Literary Supplement, July 7, 1978, May 7, 1982, May 9, 1986.
Washington Post Book World, March 31, 1985, April 26, 1987.
World Literature Today, autumn, 1979, summer, 1981.

* * *

MOMADAY, N(avarre) Scott 1934-

PERSONAL: Surname is pronounced *Ma*-ma-day; born February 27, 1934, in Lawton, Okla.; son of Alfred Morris (a painter and teacher of art) and Mayme Natachee (a teacher and writer; maiden name, Scott) Momaday; married Gaye Mangold, September 5, 1959; married Regina Heitzer, July 21, 1978; children: (first marriage) Cael, Jill, Brit (all daughters); (second marriage) Lore (daughter). *Education:* Attended Augusta Military Academy; University of New Mexico, A.B., 1958; Stanford University, M.A., 1960, Ph.D., 1963.

ADDRESSES: Home—1041 West Roller Coaster Rd., Tucson, Ariz. 85704. *Office*—Department of English, University of Arizona, Tucson, Ariz. 85721.

CAREER: University of California, Santa Barbara, assistant professor, 1963-65, associate professor of English, 1968-69; University of California, Berkeley, associate professor of English and comparative literature, 1969-73; Stanford University, Stanford, Calif., professor of English, 1973-82; University of Arizona, Tucson, professor of English, 1982—. Artist; has exhibited his drawings and paintings in galleries. Trustee, Museum of American Indian, Heye Foundation, New York City, 1978—. Consultant, National Endowment for the Humanities, National Endowment for the Arts, 1970—.

MEMBER: Modern Language Association of America, American Studies Association, Gourd Dance Society of the Kiowa Tribe.

AWARDS, HONORS: Academy of American Poets prize, 1962, for poem "The Bear"; Guggenheim fellowship, 1966-67; Pulitzer Prize for fiction, 1969, for *House Made of Dawn;* National Institute of Arts and Letters grant, 1970; shared Western Heritage Award with David Muench, 1974, for nonfiction book *Colorado, Summer/Fall/Winter/Spring;* Premio Letterario Internazionale Mondelo, Italy, 1979.

WRITINGS:

(Editor) *The Complete Poems of Frederick Goddard Tuckerman,* Oxford University Press, 1965.

The Journey of Tai-me (retold Kiowa Indian folktales), with original etchings by Bruce S. McCurdy, limited edition, University of California, Santa Barbara, 1967, enlarged edition published as *The Way to Rainy Mountain,* illustrated by father, Alfred Momaday, University of New Mexico Press, 1969.

House Made of Dawn (novel), Harper, 1968, reprinted, 1989.

Colorado, Summer/Fall/Winter/Spring, illustrated with photographs by David Muench, Rand McNally, 1973.

Angle of Geese and Other Poems, David Godine, 1974.

The Gourd Dancer (poems), illustrated by the author, Harper, 1976.

The Names: A Memoir, Harper, 1976.

(Author of foreword) *A Coyote in the Garden: An Painter,* Confluence, 1988.

The Ancient Child (novel), Doubleday, 1989.

Also author of film script of Frank Water's novel, *The Man Who Killed the Deer.* Contributor of articles and poems to periodicals; a frequent reviewer on Indian subjects for *New York Times Book Review.*

WORK IN PROGRESS: A study of American poetry in the middle period, *The Furrow and the Glow: Science and Literature in America, 1836-1866* (tentative title), for Oxford University Press; a book on storytelling, for Oxford University Press.

SIDELIGHTS: N. Scott Momaday's poetry and prose reflect his Kiowa Indian heritage in structure and theme, as well as in subject matter. "When I was growing up on the reservations of the Southwest," he told Joseph Bruchac in *American Poetry Review,* "I saw people who were deeply involved in their traditional life, in the memories of their blood. They had, as far as I could see, a certain strength and beauty that I find missing in the modern world at large. I like to celebrate that involvement in my writing." Roger Dickinson-Brown indicates in the *Southern Review* that Momaday has long "maintained a quiet reputation in American Indian affairs and among distinguished *literati*" for his brilliance and range, "his fusion of alien cultures, and his extraordinary experiments in different literary forms." Momaday believes that his poetry, in particular, grows from and sustains the Indian oral tradition, he commented to Bruchac. And his Pulitzer Prize-winning novel *House Made of Dawn* is described by Baine Kerr in *Southwest Review* as an attempt to "transliterate Indian culture, myth, and sensibility into an alien art form without loss." *The Way to Rainy Mountain* melds myth, history, and personal recollection into a narrative about the Kiowa tribe, while Momaday's *The Names: A Memoir* explores the author's heritage in autobiographical form.

The Names is composed of tribal tales, boyhood memories, and genealogy, reports *New York Times Book Review* critic Wallace Stegner. Momaday's quest for his roots, writes Edward Abbey in *Harper's,* "takes him back to the hills of Kentucky and north to the high plains of Wyoming, and from there, in memory and imagination, back to the Bering Straits." Stegner describes it as "an Indian book, but not a book about wrongs done to Indians. It is a search and a celebration, a book of identities and sources. Momaday is the son of parents who successfully bridged the gulf between Indian and white ways, but remain Indian," he explains. "In boyhood Momaday made the same choice, and in making it gave himself the task of discovering and in some degree inventing the tradition and history in which he finds his most profound sense of himself." *New York Review of Books* critic Diane Johnson agrees that "Momaday does not appear to feel, or does not discuss, any conflict of the Kiowa and white traditions; he is their product, an artist, heir of the experiences of his ancestors and conscious of the benignity of their influence."

Momaday is only half Kiowa. His mother, Mayme Natachee Scott, is descended from early American pioneers, although her middle name is taken from a Cherokee great-grandmother. Momaday's memoir also includes anecdotes of such Anglo-American ancestors as his grandfather, Theodore Scott, a Kentucky sheriff. His mother, however, preferred to identify in her imagination with her Indian heritage, adopting the name Little Moon when she was younger and dressing Indian style. She attended Haskell Institute, an Indian school in Kansas, where she met several members of the Kiowa tribe; eventually she married Momaday's father, also a Kiowa. The author grew up in New Mexico, where his mother, a teacher and writer, and his father, an artist and art teacher, found work among the Jemez Indians in the state's high canyon and mountain country, but he was originally raised among the Kiowas on a family farm in Oklahoma. Although Momaday covers his Anglo-American heritage in the memoir, he prefers, like his mother, "to imagine himself *all* Indian, and to 'imagine himself' back into the life, the emotions, the spirit of his Kiowa forebears," comments Abbey. He uses English, his mother's language, according to Abbey, to tell "his story in the manner of his father's people; moving freely back and forth in time and space, interweaving legend, myth, and history."

Momaday doesn't actually speak Kiowa, but, in his work, he reveals the language as not only a reflection of the physical environment, but also a means of shaping it. The title of *The Names,* reports Richard Nicholls in *Best Sellers,* refers to all "the names given by Scott Momaday's people, the Kiowa Indians, to the objects, forms, and features of their land, the southwestern plains, and to its animals and birds." When he was less than a year old, Momaday was given the name Tsoai-talee or "Rock-Tree-Boy" by a paternal relative, after the 200-foot volcanic butte in Wyoming, which is sacred to the Kiowas and is known to Anglo-Americans as Devil's Tower. "For the Kiowas it was a place of high significance," points out Abbey. "To be named after that mysterious and mythic rock was, for the boy, a high honor and a compelling one. For among the Indians a name was never merely an identifying tag but something much more important, a kind of emblem and ideal, the determining source of a man or woman's character and course of life."

The Indian perception of man's relationship to the earth is a central concern in Momaday's writing; he told Bruchac: "I believe that the Indian has an understanding of the physical world and of the earth as a spiritual entity that is his, very much his own. The non-Indian can benefit a good deal by having that perception revealed to him." And, he explained, his own particular "growing up" within the Indian culture was a "fortunate" upbringing. "On the basis of my experience, trusting my own perceptions, I don't see any validity in the separation of man and landscape. Oh, I know that the notion of alienation is very widespread, in a sense very popular. But I think it's an unfortunate point of view and a false one, where the relationship between man and the earth is concerned. Certainly it is one of the great afflictions of our time, this conviction of alienation, separation, isolation. And it is certainly an affliction in the Indian world. But there it has the least chance of taking hold, I believe, for there it is opposed by very strong forces. The whole world view of the Indian is predicated upon the principle of harmony in the universe. You can't tinker much with that; it has the look of an absolute."

This view does not preclude conflict, however. Momaday's theme in his poem "Rainy Mountain Cemetery," Dickinson-Brown points out, "is as old as our civilization: the tension, the gorgeous hostility between the human and the wild—a tension always finally relaxed in death." And, ultimately, even the violent, discontinuous sequence of events in *House Made of Dawn* conveys what Vernon E. Lattin calls in an *American Literature* review "a new romanticism, with a reverence for the land, a transcendent optimism, and a sense of mythic wholeness." Momaday's "reverence for the land," according to Lattin, is comparable "to the pastoral vision found in most mainstream American literature," but with "essential differences." Dickinson-Brown argues that Momaday's use of landscape in *House Made of Dawn* "is peculiar to him and to his Indian culture. It is a landscape and a way of living nowhere else available." In Kerr's words, here, Momaday "may in fact be seeking to make the modern Anglo novel a vehicle for a sacred text."

House Made of Dawn tells "the old story of the problem of mixing Indians and Anglos," reports *New York Times Book Review* critic Marshall Sprague. "But there is a quality of revelation here as the author presents the heart-breaking effort of his hero to live in two worlds." In the novel's fractured narrative, the main character, Abel, returns to the prehistoric landscape and culture surrounding his reservation pueblo after his tour of duty in the Army during World War II. Back home, he kills an albino. He serves a prison term and is paroled, unrepentant, to a Los Angeles relocation center. Once in the city, he attempts to adjust to his factory job, like his even-tempered roommate, Ben, a modern Indian, who narrates parts of the novel. During his free time, Abel drinks and attends adulterated religious and peyote-eating ceremonies. He can't cope with his job; and, "because of his contempt," Sprague indicates that he's brutally beaten by a Los Angeles policeman, but returns again to the reservation "in time to carry on tradition for his dying grandfather," Francisco. The novel culminates in Abel's running in the ancient ritual dawn race against evil and death.

According to Kerr, the book is "a creation myth—rife with fabulous imagery, ending with Abel's rebirth in the old ways at the old man's death—but an ironic one, suffused with violence and telling a story of culture loss." The grandfather, he maintains, "heroic, crippled, resonant with the old ways, impotent in the new—acts as a lodestone to the novel's conflicting energies. His incantatory dying delirium in Spanish flexes Momaday's symbolic compass . . ., and around his dying the book shapes its proportions." Francisco is "the alembic that transmutes the novel's confusions," he comments. "His retrospection marks off the book's boundaries, points of reference, and focal themes: the great organic calendar of the black mesa—the house of the sun (which locates the title)—as a central Rosetta stone integrating the ceremonies rendered in Part One, and the source place by which Abel and [his brother] could 'reckon where they were, where all things were, in time.' "

Momaday meets with difficulties in his attempt to convey Indian sensibility in novelistic form, Kerr relates. The fractured narrative is open to criticism, in Kerr's opinion, and the "plot of *House Made of Dawn* actually seems propelled by withheld information, that besetting literary error," he writes. Of the novel's structure, Dickinson-Brown writes that the sequence of events "is without fixed order. The parts can he rearranged, no doubt with change of effect, but not always with recognizable difference. The fragments thus presented are the subject. The result is a successful depiction but not an understanding of what is depicted: a reflection, not a novel in the comprehensive sense of the word." Kerr also objects to the author's overuse of "quiet, weak constructions" in the opening paragraph and indicates that "repetition, polysyndeton, and *there* as subject continue to deaden the narrative's force well into the book." *Commonweal* reviewer William James Smith agrees that "Mr. Momaday observes and renders accurately, but the material seems to have sunken slightly beneath the surface of the beautiful prose." Lattin maintains, however, that the novel should also be regarded as "a return to the sacred art of storytelling and myth-making that is part of Indian oral tradition," as well as an attempt "to push the secular mode of modern fiction into the sacred mode, a faith and recognition in the power of the word." And a *Times Literary Supplement* critic points out Momaday's "considerable descriptive power," citing "a section in which Tosamah [a Los Angeles medicine man/priest] rehearses the ancient trampled history of the Kiowas in trance-like visionary prose that has moments of splendour."

John "Big Bluff" Tosamah, Kerr argues, "in his two magnificent 'sermons,' is really an incarnation of the author, Momaday's mouthpiece, giving us what we've been denied: interpretation of Indian consciousness, expatiation on themes." According to Lattin, he is "a more complex religious figure" than his thoroughly Christian counterpart, Father Olguin, the Mexican priest who works on the reservation. "In the first sermon, 'The Gospel According to St. John,' Tosamah perceives the Book of John as an overwrought creation myth, applies the lightning bolt concept of the Word to the Kiowa myth of Tai-me, and apotheosizes the Indian gift of the human need for a felt awe of creation," Kerr relates. Tosamah, he indicates, "is an intriguing, well-crafted interlocutor, but also a slightly caricatured self-portrait—like Momaday a Kiowa, a man of words, an interpreter of Indian sensibility."

Tosamah's sermon on Kiowa tribal history appears in a slightly altered form in Momaday's *The Way to Rainy Mountain,* and in a review of that book, *Southern Review* critic Kenneth Fields points out that Momaday's writing exemplifies a "paradox about language which is often expressed in American Indian literature." Momaday himself has written that "by means of words can a man deal with the world on equal terms. And the word is sacred," comments Fields. "On the other hand . . . the Indians took for their subject matter those elusive perceptions that resist formulation, never entirely apprehensible, but just beyond the ends of the nerves." In a similar vein, Dickinson-Brown maintains that Momaday's poem "Angle of Geese" "presents, better than any other work I know . . . perhaps the most important subject of our age: the tragic conflict between what we have felt in wilderness and what our language means." That Momaday must articulate in *The Way to Rainy Mountain,* Fields argues, is "racial memory," or "the ghostly heritage of [his] Kiowa ancestors," and "what it means to feel himself a Kiowa in the modern American culture that displaced his ancestors."

Described by Fields as "far and away [Momaday's] best book," *The Way to Rainy Mountain* relates the story of the Kiowas journey 300 years ago from Yellowstone down onto the plains, where they acquired horses, and, in the words of John R. Milton in *Saturday Review,* "they became a lordly society of sun priests, fighters, hunters, and thieves, maintaining this position for 100 years, to the mid-nineteenth century," when they were all but destroyed by the U.S. Cavalry in Oklahoma. And when the sacred buffalo began to disappear, Fields indicates, "the Kiowas lost the sustaining illumination of the sun god," since, as Momaday explains, the buffalo was viewed as "the animal representation of the sun, the essential and sacrificial victim of the Sun Dance." "Momaday's own grandmother, who had actually been present at the last and abortive Kiowa Sun Dance in 1887, is for him the last of the Kiowas," relates Fields.

Here, Momaday uses form to help him convey a reality that has largely been lost. His text is made up of twenty-four numbered sections grouped into three parts, The Setting Out, The Going On, and The Closing In. These parts are in turn divided into three different passages, each of which is set in a different style type face. The first passage in each part is composed of Kiowa myths and legends, the second is made up of historical accounts of the tribe, and the third passage is a personal autobiographical rendering of Momaday's rediscovery of his Kiowa homeland and roots. "In form," points out Fields, "it resembles those ancient texts with subsequent commentaries which, taken altogether, present strange complexes of intelligence; not only the author's, but with it that of the man in whose mind the author was able to live again."

By the end of the last part, however, writes Nicholas, the three passages begin to blend with one another, and "the mythic passages are no longer mythic in the traditional sense, that is Momaday is creating myth out of his memories of his ancestors rather than passing on already established and socially sanctioned tales. Nor are the historical passages strictly historical, presumably objective, accounts of the Kiowas and their culture. Instead they are carefully selected and imaginatively rendered memories of his family. And, finally, the personal passages have become prose poems containing symbols which link them thematically to the other two, suggesting that all three journeys are products of the imagination, that all have become interfused in a single memory and reflect a single idea." Dickinson-Brown considers the book's shape a well-controlled "associational structure," distinctively adapted to the author's purpose. The form, according to Fields, forces Momaday "to relate the subjective to the more objective historical sensibility. The writing of the book itself, one feels, enables him to gain both freedom and possession. It is therefore a work of discovery as well as renunciation, of finding but also of letting go."

Concentrating his efforts mostly on the writing of nonfiction and poetry, Momaday did not write another novel for twenty years after *House Made of Dawn.* "I don't think of myself as a novelist. I'm a poet," he told *Los Angeles Times* interviewer Edward Iwata. In 1989, however, the poet completed his second novel, *The Ancient Child.* Building this book around the legend behind his Indian name, Tsoailee, Momaday uses the myth to develop the story of a modern Indian artist searching for his identity. A number of reviewers have lauded the new novel. Craig Lesley, for one, says in the *Washington Post* that *The Ancient Child* "is an intriguing combination of myth, fiction and storytelling that demonstrates the continuing power and range of Momaday's creative vision." A "largely autobiographical novel," according to Iwata, *The Ancient Child* expresses the author's belief that "dreams and visions are pathways to one's blood ancestry and racial memory."

Momaday views his heritage objectively and in a positive light. He explained to Bruchac: "The Indian has the advantage of a very rich spiritual experience. As much can be said, certainly, of some non-Indian writers. But the non-Indian writers of today are culturally deprived, I think, in the sense that they don't have the same sense of heritage that the Indian has. I'm told this time and time again by my students, who say, 'Oh, I wish I knew more about my grandparents; I wish I knew more about my ancestors and where they came from and what they did.' I've come to believe them. It seems to me that the Indian writer ought to make use of that advantage. One of his subjects ought certainly to be his cultural investment in the world. It is a unique and complete experience, and it is a great subject in itself."

BIOGRAPHICAL/CRITICAL SOURCES:

BOOKS

Contemporary Literary Criticism, Gale, Volume 2, 1974, Volume 19, 1981.
Gridley, Marion E., editor, *Indians of Today,* I.C.F.P., 1971.
Gridley, Marion E., *Contemporary American Indian Leaders,* Dodd, 1972.
Momaday, N. Scott, *The Way to Rainy Mountain,* University of New Mexico Press, 1969.
Momaday, N. Scott, *The Names: A Memoir,* Harper, 1976.

PERIODICALS

American Indian Quarterly, May, 1978.
American Literature, January, 1979.
American Poetry Review, July/August, 1984.
Atlantic, January, 1977.
Best Sellers, June 15, 1968, April, 1977.
Commonweal, September 20, 1968.
Harper's, February, 1977.
Listener, May 15, 1969.
Los Angeles Times, November 20, 1989.
Nation, August 5, 1968.
New York Review of Books, February 3, 1977.
New York Times, May 16, 1969, June 3, 1970; New Yorker, May 17, 1969.
New York Times Book Review, June 9, 1968, June 16, 1974, March 6, 1977, December 31, 1989.
Observer, May 25, 1969.
Saturday Review, June 21, 1969.
Sewanee Review, summer, 1977.
South Dakota Review, winter, 1975-76.
Southern Review, winter, 1970, January, 1978, April, 1978.
Southwest Review, summer, 1969, spring, 1978.
Spectator, May 23, 1969.
Times Literary Supplement, May 22, 1969.
Tribune Books (Chicago), October 1, 1989.

Washington Post, November 21, 1969, November 28, 1989.
World Literature Today, summer, 1977.

*   *   *

MONROE, Lyle
See HEINLEIN, Robert A(nson)

*   *   *

MONTAGUE, John (Patrick) 1929-

PERSONAL: Born February 28, 1929, in Brooklyn, N.Y.; son of James Terence and Mary (Carney) Montague; married Madeleine de Brauer, October 18, 1956 (divorced, 1972); married Evelyn Robson, 1973; children: (second marriage) Oonogh, Silylle (daughters). *Education:* University College, Dublin, B.A., 1949, M.A., 1953; Yale University, postgraduate studies, 1953-54; University of Iowa, M.F.A., 1955.

ADDRESSES: Office—Department of English, University College, National University of Ireland, Cork, Ireland. *Agent*—A. D. Peters & Co., 10 Buckingham St., Adelphi, London WC2N 6BU, England.

CAREER: Author, poet, editor, and translator. *Standard* (newspaper), Dublin, Ireland, film critic, 1949-52; Bord Failte (Irish tourist board), Dublin, executive, 1956-59; *Irish Times,* Paris correspondent, 1961-64; currently lecturer in poetry, University College, University of Dublin. Visiting lecturer at University of California, Berkeley, 1964 and 1965, University of Dublin, 1967 and 1968, and University of Vincennes, 1968.

MEMBER: Irish Academy of Letters.

AWARDS, HONORS: Fulbright fellowship, 1953-54; May Morton Memorial Award for poetry, 1960; Arts Council of Northern Ireland grant, 1970; Irish American Cultural Institute prize, 1976; Marten Toonder Award, 1977; Alice Hunt Bartlett Memorial Award, 1979; Guggenheim fellowship, 1979.

WRITINGS:

Forms of Exile (poetry), Dolmen Press, 1958.
The Old People (poetry), Dolmen Press, 1960.
Poisoned Lands and Other Poems, MacGibbon & Kee, 1961, Dufour, 1963, revised edition, Humanities, 1977.
(With Thomas Kinsella and Richard Murphy) *Three Irish Poets* (pamphlet), Dolmen Press, 1961.
(Editor with Kinsella; also contributor) *The Dolmen Miscellany of Irish Writing,* Dolmen Press, 1962.
Death of a Chieftain and Other Stories, MacGibbon & Kee, 1964, Dufour, 1968.
Old Mythologies: A Poem, privately printed, c. 1965.
All Legendary Obstacles (poetry), Oxford University Press, 1966.
Patriotic Suite (poetry), Dufour, 1966.
(Editor with Liam Miller) *A Tribute to Austin Clarke on His Seventieth Birthday, 9 May 1966,* Dufour, 1966.
A Chosen Light (poetry), MacGibbon & Kee, 1967, Swallow Press, 1969.
Home Again, Festival Publications (Belfast), 1967.
Hymn to the New Omagh Road (poetry), Dolmen Press, 1968.
The Bread God: A Lecture, With Illustrations in Verse (pamphlet), Dolmen Press, 1968.
(With Seamus Heaney) *The Northern Muse* (recording), Claddagh, 1968.
A New Siege (poetry), Dolmen Press, 1969.
(With John Hewitt) *The Planter and the Gael,* Arts Council of Northern Ireland, 1970.

Tides (poetry), Dolmen Press, 1970, Swallow Press, 1971.
The Rough Field (poetry), Dolmen Press, 1971, Swallow Press, 1972, revised edition, Wake Forest University Press, 1979.
(Editor and translator) *The Faber Book of Irish Verse,* Faber, 1972, published as *The Book of Irish Verse,* Macmillan, 1974.
Small Secrets (poetry), Poem-of-the-Month Club, 1972.
(Contributor) *Irish Poets in English,* edited by Sean Lucy, Mercier Press, 1972.
(Translator) *A Fair House: Versions of Irish Poetry,* Cuala Press, 1973.
The Cave of Night (poetry), Stone Press, 1974.
(Contributor) *Time Was Away: The World of Louis MacNeice,* edited by Terence Brown and Alec Reid, Dolmen Press, 1974.
A Slow Dance (poetry), Wake Forest University Press, 1975.
O'Riada's Farewell (poetry), Golden Stone Press, 1975.
(Translator with wife Evelyn Robson) Andre Frenaud, *November,* Golden Stone Press, 1977.
The Great Cloak (poetry), Wake Forest University Press, 1978.
The Leap (poetry), Deerfield Press, 1979.
Selected Poems, Wake Forest University Press, 1982.
The Dead Kingdom (poetry), Wake Forest University Press, 1984.
Lost Notebook, Dufour, 1987.
The Figure in the Cave and Other Essays, Syracuse University Press, 1989.

Also author of forthcoming *Bitter Harvest,* Macmillan, and *Mount Eagle,* Wake Forest University Press. Also author of dramatization, "The Rough Field," produced in London, 1973. Contributor to journals and newspapers.

SIDELIGHTS: Although John Montague was born in Brooklyn, New York, he has lived most of his life in Ireland. His parents, strict Catholics, were born and raised in Northern Ireland. In 1920 Montague's father, James Terence Montague, came to the United States seeking a better life for himself and his family. Eight years later he sent for his wife, Mary, and their two sons. A year later, John was born. Mary Montague had a difficult time adjusting to her new home in America and, since times were very hard during this period in the United States, the three boys were sent to Northern Ireland to live with relatives. While his older brothers were raised by their maternal grandmother, Montague lived with his two maiden aunts on the family farm in rural Garvaghey.

It has been suggested that it was this early and traumatic separation from his parents and his brothers, coupled with a boyhood in rural Northern Ireland, that has most influenced Montague's writing. As a result, the attempt and pains of loving, political and religious dilemmas, and the vanishing simple country life are recurring themes in many of his works, especially his poetry. For example, in 1976 a reviewer for the *New York Times Book Review* comments that Montague for some time has "been working with large sequences that relate his personal life and psyche to his family's background in rural Ulster and to the whole of Ireland's catastrophic history."

Writing in the *Malahat Review,* Derek Mahon describes Montague as "the best Irish poet of his generation. . . . Montague is not a metaphysician: he is a historian and autobiographer." Montague has long been appreciated and admired for his deep feeling for Ireland—the people and the landscape—and his ability to reflect these emotions in his poetry. A reviewer for *Choice* points out that Montague's "best poems have always been those poems about himself, full of the intensity of feeling, the power of experience."

These intense feelings that Montague mirrors in his writings are especially evident in his collection *The Rough Field.* For example, in his review published in *Hollins Critic,* Benedict Kiely writes that this is Montague's most remarkable book and "one of the most interesting statements made in this century about Ireland past and present. . . . It is a unity, a movement and sequence of poems as strong and steady as the mountain stream descending on the lowlands to define a world, taking with it the past and present of that one small backward place, but a place over-burdened with history. . . . Family history and his own personal agony, and the history of the place over three and a half centuries . . . are all twisted together, strands in a strong rope." And M. L. Rosenthal points out in *Nation* that Montague's "poems come out of a deeply human speaking personality for whom language and reality are more than just a source of a plastic design of nuances. . . . [The author] tells a story, paints a picture, evokes an atmosphere, suggests the complexities and torments of adult love and marriage all in the most direct, concrete, involving way."

Montague's editing of the anthology *The Book of Irish Verse* is another example of his commitment to Ireland and his involvement in its heritage. Victor Howes remarks in the *Christian Science Monitor* that this collection of poetry written by other Irish authors "is rich in its translations of mythological early poems. It is similarly rich in its presentation of the 20th-century poets. [The] anthology conveys the sense that Irish poets are again finding a voice that is national, unique and as significant as it was in the days of 'Eire of high recital / Recital skillfully done,' the days of an Ireland known for its 'Kings and queens and poets a-many.' " And a critic writes in *Choice* that Montague's "winnowing results in an anthology having the vibrancy and understated qualities of fineness that mark all that is best in the Irish tradition."

Despite his interest in Ireland's heritage, Montague is a very contemporary Irish poet in that he writes about current issues and topics. However, not everyone feels Montague performs a service to his homeland by publicizing some of Ireland's troubles and problems. Derek Mahon writes in the *Malahat Review* that "Montague has been criticized for 'using' the present crisis in Ulster as raw material for his poetry. (His critics do not, however, accuse Yeats of doing the same thing at an earlier period.) The criticism seems to me at best an injustice founded in misunderstanding—at worst a cheap jibe. The implication, an essentially philistine one, is that something as frivolous as poetry has no business concerning itself with something as serious as human suffering. . . . Ireland is central to Montague's myth, and has been since his first booklet . . . was published."

Still another respected and admired feature of Montague's work is his craftsmanship. "Montague has always been a fastidious craftsman," W. J. McCormack writes in the *Times Literary Supplement.* And M. L. Rosenthal explains in *Nation* that "Montague does have a highly developed sense of the craft; he is a real poet, who works at his desk and drinks of the tradition. But he brings all his engagement with his art directly to bear on the world of our common life . . . and thus makes immediate contact with his readers. He thinks and talks like a grown-up man, and that fact alone makes him better literary company than most of his poetic contemporaries."

BIOGRAPHICAL/CRITICAL SOURCES:

BOOKS

Contemporary Literary Criticism, Gale, Volume 13, 1980, Volume 46, 1988.
Contemporary Poets, St. James Press/St. Martin's, 1985.
Dictionary of Literary Biography, Volume 40: *Poets of Great Britain and Ireland Since 1960,* Gale, 1985.
Ford, Boris, editor, *The Present,* Penguin, 1983.
Kersnowski, Frank, *John Montague,* Bucknell University Press, 1975.

PERIODICALS

Choice, May, 1977, December, 1978.
Christian Science Monitor, June 9, 1977.
Hollins Critic, December, 1978.
Library Journal, June 1, 1968, August, 1970, July, 1977.
Malahat Review, July, 1973.
Nation, May 17, 1971.
New Statesman, August 18, 1967.
New York Times, March 23, 1968.
New York Times Book Review, September 19, 1976.
Punch, January 3, 1968.
Spectator, December 5, 1970.
Stand, Volume 20, number 1, 1978-79.
Times Literary Supplement, January 5, 1967, November 9, 1967, March 19, 1976, August 11, 1978, July 16, 1982.
Voice Literary Supplement, February, 1983.

*   *   *

MONTALE, Eugenio   1896-1981

PERSONAL: Born October 12, 1896, in Genoa, Italy; died September 12, 1981, of heart failure in Milan, Italy; son of Domenico (a manufacturer of marine products) and Giuseppina (Ricci) Montale; married Drusilla "la Mosca" Tanzi, 1958 (died, 1963). *Education:* Attended schools in Genoa, Italy.

ADDRESSES: Home—Via Bigli, 15, Milan, Italy (winters); Forte dei Marmi, Italy (summers).

CAREER: Free-lance poet and critic in Genoa, Italy, 1922-26; Bemporad (publishing house), member of editorial staff, Florence, Italy, 1927-28; Gabinetto Vieusseux Library, Florence, curator, 1928-38; free-lance writer in Milan, Italy, 1938-48; *Corriere della Sera,* Milan, literary editor, 1948-73, and music critic, 1955-81. *Military service:* Italian Army, 1915-18, became lieutenant.

AWARDS, HONORS: Premio dell'Antico Fattore, 1932, for *La casa dei doganieri e altri versi;* Premio Manzotto, 1956, for *La bufera e altro;* Dante Medal (Italy), 1959; Feltrinelli prize of the Accademia dei Lincei, 1963, 1964; named Senator of the Republic, 1967; Calouite Bulbenkian Prize (Paris), 1971; Nobel Prize in Literature, 1975; honorary degrees from University of Milan, University of Rome, Cambridge University, Basel University, and Nice University.

WRITINGS:

POETRY

Ossi di seppia (also see below), Gobetti (Turin), 1925, reprinted, Mondadori, 1983, translation by Antonio Mazza published as *The Bones of Cuttlefish,* Mosaic Press, 1983.
La casa dei doganieri e altri versi (title means "The Customs House and Other Poems"; also see below), Antico Fattore (Florence), 1932.

Le occasioni (includes poems originally published in *La casa dei doganieri e altri versi;* also see below), Einaudi (Turin), 1939, reprinted, Mondadori, 1970, translation by William Arrowsmith published as *The Occasions,* Norton, 1987.

Finisterre (also see below), Collana di Lugano (Lugano), 1943.

Poesie, Mondadori, Volume I: *Ossi di seppia,* 1948, reprinted, 1968, Volume II: *Le occasioni,* 1949, Volume III: *La bufera e altro* (also see below), 1957.

La bufera e altro (includes poems published in *Finisterre*), Neri Pozza (Venice), 1956, translation by Charles Wright published as *The Storm and Other Poems,* Oberlin College, 1978, translation by Arrowsmith published as *The Storm and Other Things,* Norton, 1986.

Poems, translation by Edwin Morgan, School of Art, University of Reading (England), 1959.

Poesie di Montale (bilingual edition), with English adaptations of Montale's poems by Robert Lowell, Lanterna (Bologna), 1960.

Accordi e pastelli, Strenna per gli Amici, 1962.

Satura (collection of five poems), [Verona], 1963, translation by Donald Sheehan and David Keller published as *Satura: Five Poems,* Francesco, 1969, revised Italian edition published with "Xenia"(sequence of poems; also see below) as *Satura: 1962-1970* (also see below), Mondadori, 1971.

Poesie: Poems (bilingual edition), translation and introduction by George Kay, Edinburgh University Press, 1964, published as *Selected Poems of Eugenio Montale,* Penguin, 1969.

Selected Poems (bilingual edition), intoduction by Glauco Cambon, New Directions, 1965.

Il colpevole, V. Scheiwiller (Milan), 1966.

Provisional Conclusions: A Selection of the Poetry of Eugenio Montale, 1920-1970 (bilingual edition), translation by Edith Farnsworth, Regenery, 1970.

Xenia, translation by Ghan Singh, Black Sparrow Press, 1970.

Trentadue variazioni, G. Lucini, 1973.

Diario del '71 e del '72 (also see below), Mondadori, 1973.

Motetti: The Motets of Eugenio Montale (bilingual edition; poems originally included in *Le occasioni*), translation by Lawrence Kart, Grabhorn Hoyem Press, 1973.

Selected Poems (Italian text), edited with English introduction, notes, and vocabulary by Singh, with a preface by the author, Manchester University Press, 1975.

New Poems (selections from *Satura: 1962-1970* and *Diario del '71 e del '72*), translation and introduction by Singh, with an essay by F. R. Leavis, New Directions, 1976.

Xenia and Motets (bilingual edition), translation by Kate Hughes, Agenda Editions; 1977.

Tutte le poesie (title means "All the Poems"), Mondadori, 1977, revised edition, 1984.

L'opera in versi (title means "Poetical Works"; two volumes), edited by Rosanna Bettarini and Gianfranco Contini, Einaudi, 1980.

It Depends: A Poet's Notebook (bilingual edition), translation of *Quaderno di quattro anni* (also see below) and introduction by Singh, New Directions, 1980.

Altre versi e poesie disperse (anthology), Mondadori, 1981, translation by Jonathan Galassi published as *Otherwise: Last and First Poems of Eugenio Montale* (bilingual edition), Random House, 1984.

Also author of *Quaderno di quattro anni* (title means "Notebook of Four Years"), 1977.

PROSE

La solitudine dell'artista, Associazione Italiana per la Liberta della Cultura (Rome), 1952.

La farfalla di Dinard (short articles, prose poems, and memoirs), Neri Pozza, 1956, expanded edition, Mondadori, 1960, translation by Singh published as *The Butterfly of Dinard,* London Magazine Editions, 1970, University Press of Kentucky, 1971.

Eugenio Montale/Italo Svevo: Lettere, con gli scritti de Montale su Svevo (title means "Eugenio Montale/Italo Svevo: Letters, with Montale's Writings on Svevo"), De Donato, 1966, published as *Italo Svevo-Eugenio Montale: Carteggio* (title means "Italo Svevo-Eugenio Montale: Correspondence"), Mondadori, 1976.

Auto da fe: Cronache in due tempi (title means "Act of Faith: Chronicles from Two Periods"), Il Saggiatore (Milan), 1966.

Fuori di case (title means "Away from Home"; travel pieces), R. Riccardi (Milan), 1969.

La poesia non esiste (title means "Poetry Does not Exist"), All'insegna del Pesce d'Oro (Milan), 1971.

Nel nostro tempo, Rizzoli (Milan), 1972, translation by Alastair Hamilton published as *Poet in Our Time,* Urizen Books, 1976.

Sulla poesia (title means "On Poetry"), edited by Giorgio Zampa, Mondadori, 1976.

Selected Essays, translation and introduction by Singh, with foreword by the author, Carcanet New Press, 1978.

Montale comenta Montale (title means "Montale Speaks on Montale"), edited by Lorenzo Greco, Pratiche (Parma), 1980.

Prime alla Scala (title means "Openings at the Scala"; collected writings on music), Mondadori, 1981.

Lettere a Salvatore Quasimodo (correspondence), Bompiani, 1981.

I miei scritti sul 'Mondo': Da Bonsanti a Pannunzio, edited by Giovanni Spadolini, Le Monnier (Florence), 1981.

The Second Life of Art: Selected Essays of Eugenio Montale, translation, introduction, and notes by Galassi, Ecco Press, 1982.

Quaderno genovese (title means "Genoan Diary"; memoirs), Mondadori, 1983.

TRANSLATOR INTO ITALIAN

Herman Meville, *La storia di Billy Budd,* [Milan], 1942.

Eugene O'Neill, *Strano interludio,* Edizione Teatro dell'Universita (Rome), 1943.

Quaderno di traduzioni (translations of Shakespeare, T. S. Eliot, Gerard Manley Hopkins, and others), Edizioni della Meridiana, 1948.

Shakespeare, *Amleto, principe di Danimarca,* Cederna (Milan), 1949.

John Steinbeck, *Al dio sconosciuto,* [Milan], 1954.

Troilo e Cressida: Opera in tre atti (translation of Christopher Hassall's libretto), Carisch (Milan), 1956.

Angus Wilson, *La cicuta e dopo,* [Milan], 1956.

Jorge Guillen, *Jorge Guillen: Tradotto da Eugenio Montale,* All'insegna del Pesce d'Oro, 1958.

Also translator of *La battaglia,* by Steinbeck, 1940, *Il mio mundo e qui,* by Dorothy Parker, 1943, Shakespeare's *La commedia degli errori, Racconto d'inverno,* and *Timone d'Atene,* three volumes, 1947, *La tragica storia del dottor Faust,* by Christopher Marlowe, 1951, and *Proserpina e lo straniero,* by Omar Del Carlo, 1952.

CONTRIBUTOR

Mario Praz, editor, *Teatro,* [Milan], 1942.

A. Obertello, editor, *Teatro elizabettiano,* [Milan], 1951.

E. F. Accorocca, editor, *Ritratti su misura,* Socalizio del libro (Venice), 1960.

G. Macchia, editor, *Teatro francese del grande secolo,* [Turin], 1960.

Gianandrea Gavazzeni, editor, *I nemici della musica,* All'insegna del Pesce d'Oro, 1965.

OTHER

(Author of preface) Camillo Sbarbaro, *Poesia e prosa,* Mondadori, 1979.

Contributor to numerous anthologies. Also contributor of essays, critical pieces, and other articles and reviews to many literary journals, magazines, and newspapers, such as *Solaria* (Florence), *Botteghe Oscure* (Rome), *Gazetta del Popolo* (Turin), and to several foreign publications. Co-founder and literary critic for *Primo Tempo* (literary magazine; Turin), beginning 1921.

SIDELIGHTS: Despite the fact that Eugenio Montale produced only five volumes of poetry in his first fifty years as a writer, when the Swedish Academy awarded the Italian poet and critic the 1975 Nobel Prize for Literature they called him "one of the most important poets of the contemporary West," according to a *Publishers Weekly* report. One of Montale's translators, Jonathan Galassi, echoed the enthusiastic terms of the Academy in his introduction to *The Second Life of Art: Selected Essays of Eugenio Montale* in which he referred to Montale as "one of the great artistic sensibilities of our time." In a short summary of critical opinion on Montale's work, Galassi continued: "Eugenio Montale has been widely acknowledged as the greatest Italian poet since [Giacomo] Leopardi and his work has won an admiring readership throughout the world. His . . . books of poems have, for thousands of readers, expressed something essential about our age."

Montale began writing poetry while a teenager, at the beginning of what was to be an upheaval in Italian lyric tradition. Describing the artistic milieu in which Montale began his life's work, D. S. Carne-Ross noted in the *New York Review of Books:* "The Italian who set out to write poetry in the second decade of the century had perhaps no harder task than his colleagues in France or America, but it was a different task. The problem was how to lower one's voice without being trivial or shapeless, how to raise it without repeating the gestures of an incommodious rhetoric. Italian was an intractable medium. Inveterately mandarin, weighed down by the almost Chinese burden of a six-hundred-year-old literary tradition, it was not a modern language." Not only did Italian writers of the period have to contend with the legacy of their rich cultural heritage, but they also had to deal with a more recent phenomenon in their literature: the influence of the prolific Italian poet, novelist, and dramatist, Gabriele D'Annunzio, whose highly embellished style seemed to have become the only legitimate mode of writing available to them. "Montale's radical renovation of Italian poetry," according to Galassi, "was motivated by a desire to 'come closer' to his own experience than the prevailing poetic language allowed him."

Montale explained his effort to cope with the poetic language of the day and the final outcome of this struggle in his widely-quoted essay, "Intentions (Imaginary Interview)," included in *The Second Life of Art.* "I wanted my words to come closer than those of the other poets I'd read," Montale noted. "Closer to what? I seemed to be living under a bell jar, and yet I felt I was close to something essential. A subtle veil, a thread, barely separated me from the definitive *quid.* Absolute expression would have meant breaking that veil, that thread: an explosion, the end of the illusion of the world as representation. But this remained

an unreachable goal. And my wish to come close remained musical, instinctive, unprogrammatic. I wanted to wring the neck of the eloquence of our old aulic language, even at the risk of a counter-eloquence."

For Montale coming close meant a private focus in his poetry that caused many critics to label his work as obscure or hermetic. He is often named along with Giuseppe Ungaretti and Salvatore Quasimodo as one of the founders of the poetic school known as hermeticism, an Italian variant of the French symbolist movement. Montale himself denied any membership in such a group, and observed in his essay "Let's Talk about Hermeticism" (also included in Galassi's anthology): "I have never purposely tried to be obscure and therefore do not feel very well qualified to talk about a supposed Italian hermeticism, assuming (as I very much doubt) that there is a group of writers in Italy who have a systematic non-communication as their objective."

Whether hermetic or not, Montale's poetry is difficult. Noting the demanding quality of Montale's work, Soviet poet and critic Joseph Brodsky stated in a *New York Review of Books* essay that the "voice of a man speaking—often muttering—to himself is generally the most conspicuous characteristic of Montale's poetry." Many of Montale's poems are undiscernible to most casual readers, just as the meaning of the words of a man talking to himself is difficult for another to grasp. Problems in comprehension arise because Montale, in an effort to eliminate in his verse what *Parnassus: Poetry in Review* contributor Alfred Corn called "the merely expository element in poetry," sought not to talk about an occurrence in his poems but to simply express the feelings associated with the event. According to Corn, "this approach to poetic form allows for great condensation and therefore great power; but the poems are undeniably difficult." Montale's chief interpreter in recent years, Ghan Singh, examined Montale's poetic complexities in *Eugenio Montale: A Critical Study of His Poetry, Prose, and Criticism,* remarking: "Of all the important twentieth-century Italian poets Montale is the one in whose case it is most difficult to proceed by explicating, through definite formulations and statements, what a particular poem is about. In other words, what comes out through the reading of the poem and what was in the poet's mind when he wrote it, seldom lend themselves to a condensed summary."

In *Three Modern Poets: Saba, Ungaretti, Montale,* Joseph Cary echoed the thoughts of other critics on Montale's verse in general while pointing in particular to the obscurity of Montale's *The Occasions.* "As Montale himself has written," Cary observed, "it is a short step from the intense poem to the obscure one. We are not talking of any grammatical-syntactical ellipsis here but of the nature of the poet's dramatic methods, his procedural assumptions. To be plunged, with minimal or no preparation, *in medias res,* which is to say, into the midst of an occasion dense with its own particular history, cross-currents, associations and emotional resonances, seems to me to be a fair description of the difficulties typically encountered in certain of the *Occasioni* poems."

Corn and Carne-Ross regard Montale's group of twenty brief poems, "Motets" (originally included in the collection, *The Occasions*), as a leading example of Montale's condensed form of poetry. "Even a hasty reading," wrote Carne-Ross, "reveals their singular formal mastery (they have been compared to Mallarme's octosyllabic sonnets); even a prolonged reading is often baffled by these impenetrable little poems. The images are always sensuously lucid . . . , but they often point back to some 'occasion' which it is impossible to reconstruct, and as a result we do not know how to relate the images to each other or to the poem as a whole." Montale's technique in "Motets" is comparable to that used in the poetic sequence "Xenia" (included in the English translation of *Satura: 1962-1970*), written after the death of the poet's wife in 1963. Brodsky contended that in these later poems "the personal note is enforced by the fact that the poet's persona is talking about things only he and [his wife] had knowledge of—shoehorns, suitcases, the names of hotels where they used to stay, mutual acquaintances, books they had both read. Out of this sort of *realia,* and out of the inertia of intimate speech, emerges a private mythology which gradually acquires all the traits appropriate to any mythology, including surrealistic visions, metamorphoses, and the like."

The image of a man talking to himself can be used not only to allude to the opaque quality of Montale's verse but also to refer to what, according to critics, is a dominant characteristic of his poetry, that of the poet talking to an absent other. So frequently did Montale address his poems to a female—named or unnamed—that John Ahern observed in the *New York Times Book Review* that the reader could "surmise that for Montale life, like art, was quintessentially speech to a woman." "Motets" and "Xenia," for example, are addressed to absent lovers; the first to Clizia, the second to his dead wife, known as "la Mosca." Glauco Cambon studied the similarities and differences between the two sequences of poems in his *Books Abroad* essay on Montale in which Cambon referred to "one central feature of Montale's style, the use of a sometimes unspecifiable Thou to elicit self-revelation on the part of the lyrical persona." Elsewhere in the same piece Cambon commented: "Obviously la Mosca fulfills in *Xenia* a function analogous to that of Clizia in 'Motets' and in various other poems from *Le Occasioni* and *La Bufera:* to provide a focal Thou that draws the persona out, to conquer his reticence about what really matters, to embody the unseizable reality of what is personal. Distance, absence, memory are a prerequisite of such polar tension, as they were for Dante and Petrarch. In Clizia's case distance is geographic, while in la Mosca's case it is metaphysical, being provided by death."

Cambon is only one of many critics who made a comparison between Montale and the great early fourteenth-century Italian poet, Dante. Singh, for example, observed "Montale's use of Dante's vocabulary, style, and imagery," but also noted that "if while deliberately using a distinctly Dantesque word or phrase, Montale succeeds in making it do something quite different, it is because his thought and sensibility, his mode of analyzing and assessing his own experience, and the nature of his explorations into reality are as profoundly different from Dante's as they are characteristically modern." Both Arshi Pipa, who wrote a book-length study of Montale's resemblance to Dante entitled *Montale and Dante,* and Galassi concluded that one of the ways Montale was able to break with tradition and renovate Italian literature was by actually paying homage to that same tradition. "Montale's solution to the problem of tradition, certainly one of the most successful solutions achieved by a poet in our century," Galassi explained, "involved an innovative appropriation of the Italian literary past to serve his own very personal contemporary purposes. To Pipa, who sees Montale's relationship to Dante as the central issue in understanding this aspect of Montale's achievement in renewing Italian literature, 'he has continued tradition in poetry by recreating it, and this he has done by going back to its origin, where he has established contact with one who may well be called the father of the nation.' "

When parallels are drawn between Montale and writers outside the Italian tradition, they are most often between Montale and T. S. Eliot. "Comparison between the two poets is inevitable," according to Galassi, "for both turn to a re-evaluation of tradition in their search for an authentic means of giving voice to the existential anxiousness of twentieth-century man." A London *Times* writer observed that both poets possessed similar styles and "a common predilection for dry, desolate, cruel landscapes." This tendency is evident in the poem, "Arsenio" from *The Bones of Cuttlefish,* for example, which Carne-Ross called "in a real sense Montale's *Waste Land,*" referring to one of Eliot's best-known poems. "Arsenio," like much of Montale's early work, depicts the rugged, tormented Ligurian coastline of Cinque Terre, the part of the Italian Riviera where Montale was born and to which he returned every summer of his youth. The starkness of the area can be seen in Mario Praz's translation of the first lines of "Arsenio," which appears in *The Poem Itself:* "The whirlwinds lift the dust/ over the roofs, in eddies, and over the open spaces/ deserted, where the hooded horses/ sniff the ground, motionless in front/ of the glistening windows of the hotel." Praz maintained that the book's suggested "the dry, desolate purity of [Montale's] early inspiration: white cuttlefish bones stranded on the margin of the beach, where the sea casts up all its drift and wreckage. The white cuttlefish bones lie helpless among the sand and weeds; a wave every now and then disturbs and displaces them, giving them a semblance of motion and life." In this description of perceived motion or life amidst symbols of death critics find another relationship between "Arsenio" and "The Waste Land." While both poems are filled with desolate description, they both also embrace a desire for redemption or rebirth.

Other critics, such as Singh and Wallace Craft, see more differences between the two poets than similarities. In a *Books Abroad* essay on Montale published shortly after the poet won the Nobel Prize, Craft recognized that with similar intent Montale and Eliot both described nature as a series of fragmented images. The critic then went on to examine the dissimilarities between the two writers. "Both Eliot and Montale explored this fragmented world," observed Craft, "in order to fathom the mystery of human life. It must be pointed out, however, that Eliot emerges from his existential wilderness or wasteland to find resolution in the framework of Christianity. Montale's quest, on the other hand, never leads to final answers. The fundamental questions regarding life, death and human fate posed in the early poetry are deepened, repeated but not resolved in later verse."

Although his poetry was largely responsible for Montale's worldwide fame, he received considerable critical attention in the United States with the posthumous publication of Galassi's translation of a compilation of his essays, *The Second Life of Art: Selected Essays of Eugenio Montale.* Even though in the last three decades of his life Montale came to be regarded—mainly due to his position as literary editor for Milan's *Corriere della Sera*—"as the Grand Old Man of Italian criticism," according to a London *Times* writer, this book of essays was one of the first collections of the Italian's critical prose to appear in English. Galassi saw theses essays as both "selections from an unwritten intellectual autobiography" of Montale and "the rudiments of a context in which to view Montale's greatest work, his poetry."

BIOGRAPHICAL/CRITICAL SOURCES:

BOOKS

Almansi, Guido and Bruce Merry, *Eugenio Montale,* Edinburgh University Press, 1978.
Burnshaw, Stanley, editor, *The Poem Itself,* Horizen Press, 1981.
Cambon, Glauco, *Eugenio Montale,* Columbia University Press, 1972.
Cary, Joseph, *Three Modern Poets: Saba, Ungaretti, Montale,* New York University Press, 1969.

Contemporary Literary Criticism, Gale, Volume 7, 1977, Volume
    9, 1978, Volume 18, 1981.
Montale, Eugenio, *The Second Life of Art: Selected Essays of Eu-
    genio Montale,* edited and with an introduction by Jonathan
    Galassi, Ecco Press, 1982.
Pipa, Arshi, *Montale and Dante,* University of Minnesota Press,
    1968.
Singh, Ghan, *Eugenio Montale: A Critical Study of His Poetry,
    Prose, and Criticism,* Yale University Press, 1973.
West, Rebecca J., *Eugenio Montale: Poet on the Edge,* Harvard
    University Press, 1981.

PERIODICALS

Books Abroad, winter, 1947, summer, 1957, winter, 1967, au-
    tumn, 1971, winter, 1976.
Los Angeles Times Book Review, February 24, 1985.
Nation, October 9, 1976.
New Republic, July 17, 1976, February 25, 1985.
New York Review of Books, October 20, 1966, June 1, 1972, June
    9, 1977, February 17, 1983.
New York Times Book Review, May 30, 1976, November 14,
    1982, November 18, 1984, February 23, 1986.
Parnassus: Poetry in Review, spring-summer, 1977.
Saturday Review of Literature, July 18, 1936.
Times Literary Supplement, January 27, 1978, September 4,
    1981, October 16, 1981, January 8, 1982, November 8,
    1982, August 5, 1983.
Village Voice, November 10, 1975.
Washington Post Book World, January 2, 1983.
World Literature Today, autumn, 1981, spring, 1984.

OBITUARIES:

PERIODICALS

AB Bookman's Weekly, October 19, 1981.
Newsweek, September 28, 1981.
New York Times, September 14, 1981.
Publishers Weekly, September 25, 1981.
Time, September 28, 1981.
Times (London), September 14, 1981.
Washington Post, September 14, 1981.

*   *   *

MONTHERLANT, Henry (Milon) de   1896-1972

PERSONAL: Born April 21, 1896, in Paris, France; committed
suicide, September 21, 1972, in Paris; son of Joseph Milon and
Marguerite Camuset (de Riancey) de Montherlant. *Education:*
Attended Ecole Sainte-Croix de Neuilly.

ADDRESSES: Home—Paris, France.

CAREER: Sportsman, bullfighter, novelist, and playwright. Secretary of construction fund for Douaumont Cemetery honoring
the war dead, 1921-24; traveled and lived in Italy, Spain, and
North Africa, 1925-32; war correspondent for right-wing
weekly, *Marianne,* c. 1940. *Military service:* French Army,
1914-18; war correspondent with French infantry, 1930-40;
worked with Swiss Red Cross, 1942-45; received Croix de
Guerre and Medaille des Combattants Volontaires.

AWARDS, HONORS: Grand Prix de Litterature of the Academie Francaise, 1934, for *Les Celibataires;* elected to the Academie Francaise, 1960.

WRITINGS:

NOVELS

Le Songe, Grasset, 1922, translation by Terence Kilmartin pub-
    lished as *The Dream,* Weidenfeld & Nicholson, 1962, Mac-
    millan, 1963.
Les Bestiaires, Grasset, 1926, revised edition, Plon, 1929, transla-
    tion by Peter Wiles published as *The Matador,* Elek, 1957,
    reprinted French edition, Gallimard, 1972.
Les Celibataires, Grasset, 1934, reprinted, Gallimard, 1967,
    translation by Thomas McGreevy published as *Lament for
    the Death of an Upper Class,* J. Miles, 1935, and as *Perish
    in Their Pride,* Knopf, 1936, translation by Kilmartin pub-
    lished as *The Bachelors,* Macmillan, 1960, reprinted, Green-
    wood Press, 1977.
Les Jeunes Filles (first volume in tetralogy; also see below), Gras-
    set, 1936, translation by McGreevy published as *Young
    Girls* in *Pity for Women* (also see below).
Pitie pour les femmes (second volume in tetralogy; also see
    below), Grasset, 1936, translation by John Rodker pub-
    lished as *Pity for Women* in *Pity for Women* (also see below).
Pity for Women (contains *Young Girls* and *Pity for Women*),
    translated by McGreevy and Rodker, respectively, G.
    Routledge, 1937, Knopf, 1938.
Le Demon du bien (third volume in tetralogy; also see below),
    Grasset, 1937, translation by Rodker published as *The
    Demon of Good* in *Costals and the Hippogriff* (also see
    below).
Les Lepreuses (fourth volume in tetralogy; also see below), Gras-
    set, 1939, translation by Rodker published as *The Lepers* in
    Costals and the Hippogriff (also see below).
Costals and the Hippogriff (contains *The Demon of Good* and *The
    Lepers*), translated by Rodker, Knopf, 1940, published in
    England as *The Lepers,* G. Routledge, 1940.
Les Jeunes Filles (tetralogy; contains *Les Jeunes Filles, Pitie pour
    les femmes, Le Demon du bien,* and *Les Lepreuses*), Galli-
    mard, 1943, reprinted, Club des Libraires de France, 1961,
    translation by Kilmartin published as *The Girls,* two vol-
    umes, Harper, 1968.
L'Histoire d'amour de la "Rose de sable" (incomplete novel first
    published as a novelette), Plon, 1954, translation by Alec
    Brown published as *Desert Love,* Noonday, 1957.
Le Chaos et la nuit, Gallimard, 1963, translation by Kilmartin
    published as *Chaos and Night,* Macmillan, 1964.
La Rose de sable (completed version of *L'Histoire d'amour de la
    "Rose de sable";* title means "The Sand Rose"), Gallimard,
    1968.
Les Garcons, Gallimard, 1969, translation by Kilmartin pub-
    lished as *The Boys,* Weidenfeld & Nicholson, 1974.
Moustique (incomplete novel; title means "Mosquito"), Galli-
    mard, 1986.

OTHER FICTION

Histoire de la petite 19, Grasset, 1924.
La Peri, A. Rey, 1930.
Serge Sandrier, Droin, 1948.
Pages d'amour de "La Rose de sable," Laffont, 1949.
La Cueilleuse de branches, Horay, 1951.
Une aventure au Sahara, Archant, 1951.
Les Auligny (extracts from *La Rose de sable;* see above), Amiot-
    Dumont, 1956.

PLAYS

L'Exil (three-act; title means "The Exile"), Editions du Capitole,
    1929.

Pasiphae (one-act; first produced in Paris at Theatre Pigalle, December 6, 1938), Editions des Cahiers de Barbarie, 1936 (also see below).

La Reine morte; Ou, Comment on tue les femmes (three-act; first produced in Paris at Comedie-Francaise, December 8, 1942), Gallimard, 1942, revised edition published as *La Reine morte,* 1947, published under same title with introduction by H. R. Lenormand, Macmillan, 1951, reprinted, Gallimard, 1971, translation by Jonathan Griffin published as *Queen After Death* in *The Master of Santiago, and Four Other Plays* (also see below).

Fils de personne; ou, Plus que le sang (four-act; first produced in Paris at Theatre Saint-Georges, December 18, 1943), Laffont, 1943, reprinted, Gallimard, 1973, translation by Griffin published as *No Man's Son* in *The Master of Santiago, and Four Other Plays* (also see below).

Un incompris (one-act; title means "Misunderstood"; first produced in Paris at Theatre Saint-Georges, December 18, 1943), Gallimard, 1944.

Fils de personne [and] *Fils des autres* [and] *Un incompris,* Gallimard, 1944.

Malatesta (four-act; first produced in Paris at Theatre Marigny, December 19, 1950), Marguerat, 1946, reprinted, Gallimard, 1966, translation by Griffin published under same title in *The Master of Santiago, and Four Other Plays* (also see below), published in England separately, Routledge & Kegan Paul, 1962.

Le Maitre de Santiago (three-act; first produced in Paris at Theatre Hebertot, May 9, 1949), Gallimard, 1947, new edition edited by Lucille Becker and Alba della Fazia, Heath, 1965, new edition edited by J. Marks, G. G. Harrap (England), 1960, translation by Griffin published as *The Master of Santiago,* published in *The Master of Santiago, and Four Other Plays* (also see below), published in England separately, Routledge & Kegan Paul, 1962.

Demain il fera jour [and] *Pasiphae* (former in three acts; first produced in Paris at Theatre Hebertot, May 9, 1949), Gallimard, 1949, translation of former by Griffin published as *Tomorrow the Dawn* in *The Master of Santiago, and Four Other Plays* (also see below).

Celles qu'on prend dans ses bras (three-act; first produced in Paris at Theatre de la Madeleine, October 20, 1950; title means "Women One Takes in One's Arms"), Wapler, 1949, revised edition, Editions de Paris, 1957.

The Master of Santiago, and Four Other Plays (contains *Queen After Death, No Man's Son, Malatesta, The Master of Santiago,* and *Tomorrow the Dawn*), translated by Griffin, Knopf, 1951.

La Ville dont le prince est un enfant (three-act; title means "The City Whose Prince Is a Child"), Gallimard, 1951, revised edition, 1957, reprinted, 1973, translation by Vivian Cox and Bernard Miles published as *The Fire That Consumes,* Ritchie (San Francisco), 1980.

Port-Royal (one-act; first produced in Paris at Comedie-Francaise, December 8, 1942), Lefebvre, 1954, critical edition with notes in English by Richard Griffiths, Blackwell, 1976 (also see below).

Broceliande (three-act; first produced in Paris at Comedie-Francaise, October 24, 1956), Gallimard, 1956.

Don Juan (three-act; first produced in Paris at Theatre de l'Athenee, November 4, 1958), Gallimard, 1958, revised edition published as *La Mort qui fait le trottoir,* 1972.

Le Cardinal d'Espagne (three-act; title means "The Cardinal of Spain"; first produced in Paris in 1960), Gallimard, 1960, edition published under same title edited by Robert B. Johnson and Patricia J. Johnson, Houghton, 1972.

La Guerre civile (three-act; title means "The Civil War"), Gallimard, 1965.

ESSAYS

La Releve du matin (title means "Morning Exaltation"), Societe Litteraire, 1920, revised edition, Grasset, 1933, reprinted, Gallimard, 1972.

Premiere Olympique: Le Paradis a l'ombre des epees, Grasset, 1924 (also see below).

Deuxieme Olympique: Les Onze devant la porte doree, Grasset, 1924 (also see below).

Les Olympiques (contains *Premiere Olympique: Le Paradis a l'ombre des epees* and *Deuxieme Olympique: Les Onze devant la porte daree*), Gres, 1926, revised edition, Grasset, 1938, reprinted, Gallimard, 1965.

Aux fontaines du desir (title means "At the Fountains of Desire"), Grasset, 1927.

Chant funebre pour les morts de Verdun, Grasset, 1924.

Earinus, E. Hazan, 1929.

Hispano-Moresque, Emile-Paul Freres, 1929.

Pour une vierge noire, Editions du Cadran, 1930.

Mors et vita, Grasset, 1932.

Service inutile (title means "Useless Service"), Grasset, 1935, reprinted, Gallimard, 1973.

La Possession de soi-meme, Flammarion, 1938.

L'Equinoxe de septembre, Grasset, 1938.

Paysage des "Olympiques," photographs by Karel Egermeier, Grasset, 1940.

Le Solstice de juin, Grasset, 1941.

La Paix dans la guerre, Ides et Calendes, 1941.

Savoir dire non, Lardanchet, 1941.

Sur les femmes, Sagittaire, 1942.

D'aujourd'hui et de toujours, Hachette, 1944.

Croire aux ames, Vigneau, 1944.

Un Voyageur solitaire est un diable, Lefebvre, 1946.

La Deesse Cypris, Colas et Rousseau, 1946.

L'Eventail de fer, Flammarion, 1944.

L'Art et la vie, Denoel, 1947.

L'Etoile du soir, Lefebvre, 1949.

Notes sur mon theatre (contains "Notes de theatre," "La Reine morte," "Malatesta," and "Fils de personne"), L'Arche, 1950.

Coups de soleil, La Palantine, 1950, reprinted, Gallimard, 1976.

Espana sagrada, Wapler, 1951.

Le Fichier parisien, Plon, 1952, second revised edition, Gallimard, 1974. *Le Plaisir et la peur,* Chez l'Artiste, 1952.

Textes sous une occupation (1940-1944), Gallimard, 1953.

La Redemption par les betes, Fequet and Bandier, 1959.

Peter Quennell, editor, *Selected Essays,* translated by John Weightman, Weidenfeld & Nicolson, 1960, Macmillan, 1961.

Le Treizieme Cesar, Gallimard, 1970.

NOTEBOOKS

Carnets XXIX a XXXV, du 19 fevrier 1935 au 11 janvier 1939, La Table Ronde, 1947.

Carnets XLII a XLIII, du 1 janvier 1942 au 31 decembre 1943, La Table Ronde 1948.

Carnets XXII a XXVIII, du 24 avril 1932 au 22 novembre 1934, La Table Ronde, 1955.

Carnets XIX a XXI, du 19 septembre 1930 au 26 avril 1932, La Table Ronde, 1956.

Carnets, annees 1930 a 1944, Gallimard, 1957.

Va jouer avec cette poussiere (carnets, 1958-1964), Gallimard, 1966.

La Maree du soir (carnets, 1968-1971), Gallimard, 1972.

Tous feux eteints: Carnets 1965, 1966, 1977, carnets sans dates, carnets 1972, Gallimard, 1975.

OTHER

La Lecon de football dans an parc, Grasset, 1924.

Lettre sur le serviteur chatie, Editions des Cahiers Libres, 1927.

La Mort de Peregrinos, E. Hazan, 1927.

Sans remede, M. P. Tremois, 1927.

Barres s'eloigne, Grasset, 1927.

Pour le delassement de l'auteur, E. Hazan, 1928.

Un Desir frustre mime l'amour, Lapina, 1928.

Pages de tendresse, Grasset, 1928.

La Petite Infante de Castille (short story), Grasset, 1929, reprinted, Gallimard, 1973.

Les Iles de la felicite, Grasset, 1929.

Le Genie et les fumisteries du divin, Societe Nouvelle des Editions, 1929.

Sous les drapeaus morts, Editions du Capitole, 1929.

Le Chant des amazones, Govone, 1931.

Histoire naturelle imaginaire, Trianon, 1933.

Encore an instant de bonheur (poetry; title means "Still a Moment of Happiness"), Grasset, 1934, revised edition, 1938.

Il y a encore des paradis: Images d'Alger, 1928-1931, P. & G. Soubiron, 1935.

Mariette Lydis, Editions des Artistes D'aujourd'hui, 1938.

Les Nouvelles Chevaleries, Jean Vigneau, 1942.

La Vie en forme de proue, Grasset, 1942.

Le Meme, Nouvelle Revue Francaise, 1944.

Notes de la guerre seche: Somee-oise, mai-juin 1944, Editions Litteraires, 1944.

La Vie amoureuse de M. de Guiscart, Les Presses de la Cite, 1946.

Trois Romans, Grasset, 1946.

Marya Katerska, compiler, *Pages catholiques,* Plon, 1947.

Saint-Simon, L'Originale, 1948.

L'Infini est du cote de Malatesta, Gallimard, 1951.

Theatre choisi, Hachette, 1953.

Montherlant par lui-meme, Editions du Seuil, 1953.

Monuments et memories, Gallimard, 1956.

La Muse libertine, Editions de Paris, 1957.

Discours de reception a l'Academie francaise et reponse de M. le duc de Levis Mirepaix (speech), Gallimard, 1963.

Un assassin est mon maitre (title means "An Assassin Is My Master"), Gallimard, 1971.

La Tragedie sans masque: Notes de theatre, Gallimard, 1972.

Mais aimons-nous ceux que nous aimons?, Gallimard, 1973.

Romans II, Gallimard, 1982.

OMNIBUS VOLUMES

Le Chant de Minos [and] *Pasiphae,* M. Fabianc, 1944, reprinted, Editions L.C.L., 1967.

Fils de personne; au, Plus que le sang [and] *Un incompris,* Gallimard, 1944, reprinted, 1973.

L'Exil [and] *Pasiphae,* La Table Ronde, 1946.

Le Theatre complet [de Montherlant] (contains *Malatesta, La Reine morte, Fils de personne, Un Incompris, Le Maitre de Santiago, Demain il fera jour, Pasiphae,* and *Celles qu'on prend dans ses bras*), five volumes, Ides et calendes, 1950.

Aux fontaines du desir [and] *La Petite Infante de Castille,* Gallimard, 1954.

Mars et vita [and] *Service inutile,* Gallimard, 1954.

Port-Royal [and] *Notes de theatre,* Gallimard, 1954.

Theatre, preface by J. De Laprade, Gallimard, 1955, enlarged edition, 1965, new edition published as *Theatre [de] Montherlant,* 1968.

Broceliande [and] *L'Art et la vie,* Gallimard, 1956.

Romans et oeuvres de fiction non theatrales, preface by R. Secretain, Gallimard, 1959.

Essais, Gallimard, 1963.

Oeuvre romanesque, Editions Lidis, Volume I: *Le Sange,* 1963, Volume II: *Les Olympiques,* 1963, Volume III: *Les Bestiaires,* 1964, Volume IV: *La Petite Infante de Castille* [and] *Encore an instant de bonheur,* 1964, Volume V: *Les Celibataires,* 1964, Volume VI: *Les Jeanes Filles* [and] *Pitie pour les femmes,* 1963, Volume VII: *Le Demon du bien,* 1964, Volume VIII: *Le Chaos et la nuit,* 1964.

Theatre, Editions Lidis, 1965.

Works also published together in other multititled volumes.

CONTRIBUTOR

(Author of preface) Henri-Louis Dubly, *Les Mains tendues,* [Paris], 1926.

(Author of preface) Edouard Des Courrieres, *Physionomie de la baxe,* Editions de Paris, 1929.

F. Masereel, editor, *Juin 1940,* Somogny, 1942.

(Author of preface) Arlette Davids, *Rock Plants,* Hyperion Press, 1948.

(Editor) *Dictionnaire encyclopedique Lidis,* Lidis, 1971.

SIDELIGHTS: Despite the often controversial attitudes displayed in Henry de Montherlant's writings, many critics and several distinguished men of letters have praised his works. In 1961, Justin O'Brien wrote: "Many articulate Frenchmen had seen him as the greatest living writer of France. Andre Gide had spoken of his 'undeniable authenticity,' and Albert Camus had been stirred by his essays. Romain Rolland and Louis Aragon, both Marxists, declared him to be as thoroughly French as one could possibly be; and Andre Malraux saw him as reflecting the same heroic tradition that he himself embodied." In 1964, O'Brien added: "However much he feels himself to be out of harmony with our time, Henry de Montherlant will live as one of the outstanding writers of the century."

Montherlant began his writing career at an early age, having already written a book on the life of Scipio by the time he was ten years old. Judith Greenberg declared that his early essays contained in *Coups de soleil* "are so well written, so perfectly put, that it is hard to refrain from quoting nearly every page." Many of his first novels, such as *Le Songe* and *Les Bestiaires,* dealt with war, bullfighting, and sports, all of which played an important part in his life. His novels on these topics exalted the masculine qualities of virility, violence, and sensual enjoyment, and Lucille Becker noted that "they reflect, as a whole, the basic *joie de vivre* of youth, which sees before it infinite possibilities for self-fulfillment. They transcribe the author's passion for life and his confidence in the joys it will afford him."

After enlisting in the army during World War I, Montherlant was seriously wounded. Then after the war, when he returned to the bullfighting he had enjoyed since the age of fifteen, he was gored by a bull. In addition to these injuries, Montherlant contracted typhoid fever and had two attacks of pneumonia, all within two years. "In *Service inutile,* the reader will find not more than five or six pages dating from the years 1925-27," he wrote. "I was too preoccupied with myself, too busy worrying and trying to save myself from despair, to give much attention to anything else."

Even after his illness and injuries, Montherlant's writings maintained a generally optimistic view of life. Martin Turnell, however, believed that "in spite of the emphasis that [Montherlant] places on life, happiness and pleasure in his essays and *Notebooks* . . . neither his style nor his psychological acumen can blind us to the profoundly destructive attitude which underlies an apparently positive approach to experience." His later plays, notebooks, and the novel *Le Chaos et la nuit* most noticeably demonstrate Montherlant's cynicism, his rejection of unmanly qualities such as pity, sentimentality, tenderness, or mediocrity, his belief in the bitterness of useless service, and his nihilistic tendencies.

Though Montherlant served in the French army, he also adulated the enemy during World War II and welcomed the swastika as heralding a new era of grandeur. This caused him to be placed on a list of writers who had allegedly betrayed France. The case against him was based mainly on comments contained in *L'Equinoxe de septembre* and *Le Solstice de juin.*

In his *Carnets XLII a XLIII* Montherlant remarked, "I have never written anything without, at some time or other, feeling the urge to write the opposite." He often succumbed to this urge, leaving the reader with contrasting and paradoxical views of the author. Greenberg summarized this attitude: "Montherlant celebrates and identifies with all he finds: various dualities, *alternance* and *syncretisme,* innocence and sensuality, discipline and liberty, openness, honesty and the possible hypocrisy of 'truth,' gravity and humor, and always passion." Turnell agreed that Montherlant "is a man of contradictions: Catholic and pagan; a soldier who now detests modern warfare; a patriot who enjoys belaboring the fatherland; and—most important of all for an understanding of his work—a womaniser who at bottom hates women."

Montherlant never married. In his foreword to *Service inutile* he explained that if he married, "either my wife would be neglected and would suffer, or the deepest part of myself—my soul—would be ruined, or more probably still both would be seriously damaged. . . . And once married (given my ideas, I could obviously only marry someone poor) I should be lost; by 'lost' I mean, obliged to earn money." This he believed would not allow him the freedom to be open to new adventures.

Ben Ray Redman described Montherlant's attitude toward women: "Their only excuse for their inferior existence is that they are essential to what he likes to call The Act." Some critics believe that *Les Jeunes Filles* (*The Girls*), expresses most eloquently Montherlant's view of the opposite sex. Costals, the main character of this tetralogy, studiously avoids entanglements with women. He thinks men are embarrassed and ashamed at the passive role a man who is loved must play. "For a man to allow himself to be embraced, caressed, held hands with, looked at with swimming eyes—ugh! . . . A man who is loved is a prisoner."

Another work, *L'Histoire d'amour de la "Rose de sable,"* (*Desert Love*), also contains interesting observations on male/female relationships. One character, Guiscart, was an artist who devoted his whole life to chasing women: "In his room or his studio it was a rare hour, the sixty minutes of which could get by without the explosive prompting, jerking him to his feet, to hurry to the window and, at sight of the first skirt passing by, storm at himself: 'There goes another little dollop of love and I'm missing it.' " Yet Guiscart played by certain rules. He coveted only women whose conquest seemed doubtful, refusing to bother with any who made the first advance. He did not care about keeping the women, but rather found discarding them as pleasing as taking them on. Guiscart "had never taken anything seriously

which had originated in a women's mind or a woman's heart" and declared that "there was nothing to know [about women] and that if by any chance there were, it was not worth a man's understanding."

While these views reveal some insight into the author's mind, it is not to be automatically assumed that Montherlant believed as his characters do. In the foreword to *The Girls* he pointed out that "in Costals he has deliberately painted a character whom he intended to be disquieting and even, at times, odious; and that this character's words and actions cannot in fairness be attributed to its creator. . . . One might well wonder whether the critics and the public, on reading *La Rose de sable,* would attribute to the author the same abundance of virtues as they attributed to him of vices after reading *The Girls.*"

Montherlant's writings touch upon various other aspects of sexuality in addition to man/woman relationships. The play *Pasiphae* is a dramatic representation of Pasiphae, a character in Greek mythology, describing her vacillating emotions of passion and shame just before having sexual relations with a bull, an act which resulted in the birth of the Minotaur. Another play, *La Ville dont le prince est an enfant,* deals with the intimate friendship of two boys, Servrais and Soubrier, at a Catholic secondary school, and the jealousy of the school's Abbe, who is also passionately attached to Soubrier.

Reflecting upon his personal life, Montherlant once wrote: "I believe that very few contemporary French authors avoid the limelight more than I do, or are keener to remain in the background. I claim no credit for this; it is a matter of taste." He had no concern with the usual social amenities and accepted visitors so seldom that he was considered a recluse. This did not affect his writing career, however. In fact, he was elected to the Academie Francaise "without his making a single, traditional visit to the voting members and . . . [had] the unique privilege of giving his acceptance speech before a regular, private session of the members rather than in public, beneath the famous *Coupale,*" noted Henri Kops.

Although he began his career as a novelist, Montherlant achieved his greatest success as a playwright. His first play, *La Reine morte,* was an immediate success and ran for 825 performances. His other plays were also well received in Paris except for *Broceliande, Don Juan,* and *Le Cardinal d'Espagne.* Most of his plays are psychological studies, often with historical and religious themes, reminiscent of the classical tradition of Racine and Corneille. *Le Maitre de Santiago,* declared Lucille Becker, "is the closest to French classical tragedy, not only by reason of the purity and sobriety of the dramatic line, but also because all of the action takes place within the characters." Henri Peyre remarked that "it is unlikely that Montherlant's plays will ever be performed on Broadway . . . [because] they deride with haughty sarcasm not only the materialistic values of money and success, but also the religious delusions, the democratic consolations, the effeminacy of the modern world."

Suicide was a prominent theme in Montherlant's writings, especially in his notebooks of 1958 to 1964, titled *Va jouer avec cette poussiere.* A *Times Literary Supplement* reviewer observed that in *Le Treizieme Cesar* "Montherlant pleads for a greater understanding of suicide and of those who take their own lives. He sympathizes with suicide promoted by fear of suffering or old age, as well as with suicide as an alternative to the compromising of one's principles." Montherlant regarded suicide as "the last act by which a man can show that he dominated life and was not dominated by it."

In 1972, the seventy-six year old author had been blind in the left eye for four years, had recently suffered a heart attack, and had been in generally bad health for several years. It is not surprising under these circumstances that Montherlant took his own life. *New York Times* reporter Andreas Freund noted that Montherlant had hinted to friends about his suicide. He was found in his favorite chair at home where he had shot himself in the throat. Even the date of his death seemed to have been deliberately chosen by the novelist. A *Times Literary Supplement* critic commented, "He committed suicide on September 21, 1972, and we know that *L'Equinoxe de september*—the title of a collection of essays published in 1938—had a special place in his private mythology." Montherlant's foreword to *Service inutile* contains an ominous prediction of his fate: "Aedificabo et destruam; I shall build, and then I shall destroy that which I have built. There we have an epigraph for this book—an epigraph for my life."

BIOGRAPHICAL/CRITICAL SOURCES:

BOOKS

Batchelor, John, *Existence and Imagination: The Theatre of Henry de Montherlant,* University of Queensland Press, 1967.

Becker, Lucille, *Henry de Montherlant: A Critical Biography,* preface by Harry T. Moore, Southern Illinois University Press, 1970.

Contemporary Literary Criticism, Gale, Volume 8, 1978, Volume 19, 1981.

Cruickshank, John, *Montherlant,* Oliver & Boyd, 1964.

Dictionary of Literary Biography, Volume 72: *French Novelists, 1930-1960,* Gale, 1988.

Lemley, Friedrich, editor, *Trends in Twentieth Century Drama,* Barrie & Rockliff, 1960.

Montherlant, Henry de, *Service inutile,* Grasset, 1935.

Montherlant, Henry de, *Carnets XXIX a XXXV, du 19 fevrier 1935 au 11 janvier 1939,* La Table Ronde, 1947.

Montherlant, Henry de, *Carnets XLII a XLIII, du 1 janvier 1942 au 31 decembre 1943,* La Table Ronde, 1948.

Montherlant, Henry de, *Desert Love,* translated by Alec Brown, Noonday Press, 1957.

Montherlant, Henry de, *Va jouer avec cette poussiere (carnets, 1958-1964),* Gallimard, 1966.

Montherlant, Henry de, *The Girls,* translated by Terence Kilmartin, introduction by Peter Quennell, Harper, 1968.

Perruchot, Henri, *Montherlant,* Gallimard, 1959.

PERIODICALS

Books Abroad, spring, 1967, summer, 1968, summer, 1969, spring, 1970, winter, 1974.

Books and Bookmen, October, 1968.

Book World, January 26, 1969.

Commonweal, May 12, 1961.

Listener, January 11, 1968, August 15, 1968.

Nation, March 31, 1969.

National Review, February 11, 1969.

New Republic, February 8, 1969.

New York Review of Books, January 14, 1965.

New York Times, October 20, 1940.

New York Times Book Review, November 8, 1964, January 19, 1969.

Plays: Players, March, 1971.

Punch, April 2, 1969.

Reporter, September 14, 1961.

Saturday Review, October 12, 1940, September 29, 1951, August 26, 1961.

Spectator, April 20, 1974.

Stage, April 1, 1971.

Time, February 7, 1969.

Times Literary Supplement, September 25, 1970, May 25, 1973, October 4, 1974, September 3, 1976, May 6, 1977.

World Literature Today, summer, 1977.

OBITUARIES:

PERIODICALS

Antiquarian Bookman, October 16, 1972.

L'Express, September 25-October 1, 1972.

Newsweek, October 2, 1972.

New York Times, September 23, 1972.

Times Literary Supplement, September 5, 1986.

*   *   *

MOORCOCK, Michael (John) 1939-
(Bill Barclay, William Ewert Barclay, Edward P. Bradbury, James Colvin; Michael Barrington and Philip James, joint pseudonyms; Desmond Reid, house pseudonym)

PERSONAL: Born December 18, 1939, in Mitcham, Surrey, England; son of Arthur and June (Taylor) Moorcock; married Hilary Bailey (a writer), September, 1962 (divorced April, 1978); married Jill Riches, 1978 (divorced); married Linda Mullens Steele, September, 1983; children: (first marriage) Sophie, Katherine, Max.

ADDRESSES: Home—c/o Sheil, 43 Doughty St., London WC1, England. *Agent*—Wallace & Sheil, 177 East 70th St., New York, N.Y. 20021.

CAREER: Writer. Has worked as an office junior, singer-guitarist, and farm worker; editor, *Tarzan Adventures* (juvenile magazine), 1956-58; Amalgamated Press, London, England, editor and writer for the Sexton Blake Library and for comic strips and children's annuals, 1959-61; editor and pamphleteer, Liberal Party, 1962; *New Worlds* (science fiction magazine), London, England, editor and publisher, 1964-78; works with rock and roll band Hawkwind; member of rock and roll band Michael Moorcock and the Deep Fix.

MEMBER: Authors Guild.

AWARDS, HONORS: Nebula Award, Science Fiction Writers of America, 1967, for *Behold the Man;* British Science Fiction Association award and Arts Council of Great Britain award, both 1967, both for *New Worlds;* August Derleth Award, British Fantasy Society, 1972, for *The Knight of the Swords,* 1973, for *The King of the Swords,* 1974, for *The Jade Man's Eyes,* 1975, for *The Sword and the Stallion,* and 1976, for *The Hollow Lands;* International Fantasy Award, 1972 and 1973, for fantasy novels; Guardian Literary Prize, 1977, for *The Condition of Muzak;* John W. Campbell Memorial Award, 1978, and World Fantasy Award, World Fantasy Convention, 1979, both for *Gloriana; or, The Unfulfilled Queen.*

WRITINGS:

(With James Cawthorn, under house pseudonym Desmond Reid) *Caribbean Crisis,* Sexton Blake Library, 1962.

The Sundered Worlds, Compact Books, 1965, Paperback Library, 1966, published as *The Blood Red Game,* Sphere Books, 1970.

The Fireclown, Compact Books, 1965, Paperback Library, 1966, published as *The Winds of Limbo,* Sphere Books, 1970.

(Under pseudonym James Colvin) *The Deep Fix,* Compact Books, 1966.

The Wrecks of Time (bound with *Tramontane* by Emil Petaja), Ace Books, 1966 (revised edition published separately in England as *The Rituals of Infinity,* Arrow Books, 1971).

The Twilight Man, Compact Books, 1966, Berkley Publishing, 1970 (published in England as *The Shores of Death,* Sphere Books, 1970).

(Under pseudonym Bill Barclay) *Printer's Devil,* Compact Books, 1966, published under name Michael Moorcock as *The Russian Intelligence,* Savoy Books, 1980.

(Under pseudonym Bill Barclay) *Somewhere in the Night,* Compact Books, 1966, revised edition published under name Michael Moorcock as *The Chinese Agent,* Macmillan, 1970.

(Ghostwriter) Roger Harris, *The LSD Dossier,* Compact Books, 1966.

The Ice Schooner, Sphere Books, 1968, Berkley Publishing, 1969, revised edition, Harrap, 1985.

(With wife Hilary Bailey) *The Black Corridor,* Ace Books, 1969.

The Time Dweller, Hart-Davis, 1969, Berkley Publishing, 1971.

(With James Cawthorn under joint pseudonym Philip James) *The Distant Suns,* Unicorn Bookshop, 1975.

Moorcock's Book of Martyrs, Quartet Books, 1976, published as *Dying for Tomorrow,* DAW Books, 1978.

(With Michael Butterworth) *The Time of the Hawklords,* A. Ellis, 1976.

Sojan (juvenile), Savoy Books, 1977.

Epic Pooh, British Fantasy Society, 1978.

Gloriana; or, The Unfulfilled Queen, Allison & Busby, 1978, Avon, 1979.

The Real Life Mr. Newman, A. J. Callow, 1979.

The Golden Barge, DAW Books, 1980.

My Experiences in the Third World War, Savoy Books, 1980.

The Retreat from Liberty: The Erosion of Democracy in Today's Britain, Zomba Books, 1983.

Letters from Hollywood, Harrap, 1986.

(With James Cawthorn) *Fantasy: The One Hundred Best Books,* Carroll & Graf, 1988.

Mother London, Crown, 1989.

Wizardry and Wild Romance: A Study of Heroic Fantasy, Gollancz, 1989.

"ELRIC" SERIES; "ETERNAL CHAMPION" BOOKS

The Stealer of Souls, and Other Stories (also see below), Neville Spearman, 1963, Lancer Books, 1967.

Stormbringer, Jenkins, 1965, Lancer Books, 1967.

The Singing Citadel (also see below), Berkley Publishing, 1970.

The Sleeping Sorceress, New English Library, 1971, Lancer Books, 1972, published as *The Vanishing Tower,* DAW Books, 1977.

The Dreaming City, Lancer Books, 1972 (revised edition published in England as *Elric of Melnibone,* Hutchinson, 1972).

The Jade Man's Eyes, Unicorn Bookshop, 1973.

Elric: The Return to Melnibone, Unicorn Bookshop, 1973.

The Sailor on the Seas of Fate, DAW Books, 1976.

The Bane of the Black Sword, DAW Books, 1977.

The Weird of the White Wolf (contains some material from *The Stealer of Souls, and Other Stories* and *The Singing Citadel*), DAW Books, 1977.

Elric at the End of Time, DAW Books, 1985.

The Fortress of the Pearl, Ace Books, 1989.

"MICHAEL KANE" SERIES; UNDER PSEUDONYM EDWARD P. BRADBURY

Warriors of Mars (also see below), Compact Books, 1965, published under name Michael Moorcock as *The City of the Beast,* Lancer Books, 1970.

Blades of Mars (also see below), Compact Books, 1965, published under name Michael Moorcock as *The Lord of the Spiders,* Lancer Books, 1971.

The Barbarians of Mars (also see below), Compact Books, 1965, published under name Michael Moorcock as *The Masters of the Pit,* Lancer Books, 1971.

Warrior of Mars (contains *Warriors of Mars, Blades of Mars,* and *The Barbarians of Mars*), New English Library, 1981.

"THE HISTORY OF THE RUNESTAFF" SERIES; "ETERNAL CHAMPION" BOOKS

The Jewel in the Skull (also see below), Lancer Books, 1967.

Sorcerer's Amulet (also see below), Lancer Books, 1968 (published in England as *The Mad God's Amulet,* Mayflower Books, 1969).

Sword of the Dawn (also see below), Lancer Books, 1968.

The Secret of the Runestaff (also see below), Lancer Books, 1969 (published in England as *The Runestaff,* Mayflower Books, 1969).

The History of the Runestaff (contains *The Jewel in the Skull, Sorcerer's Amulet, Sword of the Dawn,* and *The Secret of the Runestaff*), Granada, 1979.

"JERRY CORNELIUS" SERIES

The Final Programme (also see below), Avon, 1968, revised edition, Allison & Busby, 1969.

A Cure for Cancer (also see below), Holt, 1971.

The English Assassin (also see below), Allison & Busby, 1972.

The Lives and Times of Jerry Cornelius (also see below), Allison & Busby, 1976.

The Adventures of Una Persson and Catherine Cornelius in the Twentieth Century (also see below), Quartet Books, 1976.

The Condition of Muzak (also see below), Allison & Busby, 1977, Gregg, 1978.

The Cornelius Chronicles (contains *The Final Programme, A Cure for Cancer, The English Assassin,* and *The Condition of Muzak*), Avon, 1977.

The Great Rock n' Roll Swindle, Virgin Books, 1980.

The Entropy Tango (also see below), New English Library, 1981.

The Opium General (also see below), Harrap, 1985.

The Cornelius Chronicles, Volume 2 (contains *The Lives and Times of Jerry Cornelius* and *The Entropy Tango*), Avon, 1986.

The Cornelius Chronicles, Volume 3 (contains *The Adventures of Una Persson and Catherine Cornelius in the Twentieth Century* and *The Opium General*), Avon, 1987.

"KARL GLOGAUER" SERIES

Behold the Man, Allison & Busby, 1969, Avon, 1970.

Breakfast in the Ruins: A Novel of Inhumanity, New English Library, 1972, Random House, 1974.

"CORUM" SERIES; "ETERNAL CHAMPION" BOOKS

The Knight of the Swords (also see below), Mayflower Books, 1970, Berkley Publishing, 1971.

The Queen of the Swords (also see below), Berkley Publishing, 1971.

The King of the Swords (also see below), Berkley Publishing, 1971.

The Bull and the Spear (also see below), Berkley Publishing, 1973.

The Oak and the Ram (also see below), Berkley Publishing, 1973.

The Sword and the Stallion (also see below), Berkley Publishing, 1974.

The Swords Trilogy (contains *The Knight of the Swords, The Queen of the Swords,* and *The King of the Swords*), Berkley Publishing, 1977.

The Chronicles of Corum (contains *The Bull and the Spear, The Oak and the Ram,* and *The Sword and the Stallion*), Berkley Publishing, 1978.

"JOHN DAKER" SERIES; "ETERNAL CHAMPION" BOOKS

The Eternal Champion, Dell, 1970, revised edition, Harper, 1978.

Phoenix in Obsidian, Mayflower Books, 1970, published as *The Silver Warriors,* Dell, 1973.

The Dragon in the Sword, Granada, 1986.

"OSWALD BASTABLE" SERIES

The Warlord of the Air (also see below), Ace Books, 1971.

The Land Leviathan (also see below), Quartet Books, 1974.

The Steel Tsar (also see below), DAW Books, 1983.

The Nomad of Time (contains *The Warlord of the Air, The Land Leviathan,* and *The Steel Tsar*), Granada, 1984.

"THE DANCERS AT THE END OF TIME" SERIES

An Alien Heat (also see below), Harper, 1972.

The Hollow Lands (also see below), Harper, 1974.

The End of All Songs (also see below), Harper, 1976.

Legends from the End of Time, Harper, 1976.

The Transformations of Miss Mavis Ming, W. H. Allen, 1977, published as *A Messiah at the End of Time,* DAW Books, 1978.

The Dancers at the End of Time (contains *An Alien Heat, The Hollow Lands,* and *The End of All Songs*), Granada, 1981.

"CASTLE BRASS" SERIES; "ETERNAL CHAMPION" BOOKS

Count Brass (also see below), Mayflower Books, 1973.

The Champion of Garathorm (also see below), Mayflower Books, 1973.

The Quest for Tanelorn (also see below), Mayflower Books, 1975, Dell, 1976.

The Chronicles of Castle Brass (contains *Castle Brass, The Champion of Garathorm,* and *The Quest for Tanelorn*), Granada, 1985.

"VON BEK FAMILY" SERIES

The War Hound and the World's Pain, Timescape, 1981.

The Brothel in Rosenstrasse, New English Library, 1982, Tigerseye Press, 1986.

The City in the Autumn Stars, Ace Books, 1986.

"COLONEL PYAT" SERIES

Byzantium Endures, Secker & Warburg, 1981, Random House, 1982.

The Laughter of Carthage, Random House, 1984.

SCREENPLAYS

"The Final Programme" (based on his novel of the same title; removed name from credits after dispute with director), EMI, 1973.

"The Land That Time Forgot," British Lion, 1975.

EDITOR

(And contributor under name Michael Moorcock and under pseudonym James Colvin) *The Best of "New Worlds,"* Compact Books, 1965.

Best SF Stories from "New Worlds," Panther Books, 1967, Berkley Publishing, 1968.

The Traps of Time, Rapp & Whiting, 1968.

(And contributor under pseudonym James Colvin) *The Best SF Stories from "New Worlds" 2,* Panther Books, 1968, Berkley Publishing, 1969.

(And contributor under pseudonym James Colvin) *The Best SF Stories from "New Worlds" 3,* Panther Books, 1968, Berkley Publishing, 1969.

The Best SF Stories from "New Worlds" 4, Panther Books, 1969, Berkley Publishing, 1971.

The Best SF Stories from "New Worlds" 5, Panther Books, 1969, Berkley Publishing, 1971.

(And contributor) *The Best SF Stories from "New Worlds" 6,* Panther Books, 1970, Berkley Publishing, 1971.

The Best SF Stories from "New Worlds" 7, Panther Books, 1971.

New Worlds Quarterly 1, Berkley Publishing, 1971.

New Worlds Quarterly 2, Berkley Publishing, 1971.

New Worlds Quarterly 3, Sphere Books, 1971.

(With Langdon Jones and contributor) *The Nature of the Catastrophe,* Hutchinson, 1971.

New Worlds Quarterly 4, Berkley Publishing, 1972.

New Worlds Quarterly 5, Sphere Books, 1973.

New Worlds Quarterly 6, Avon, 1973.

Before Armageddon: An Anthology of Victorian and Edwardian Imaginative Fiction Published before 1914, W. H. Allen, 1975.

England Invaded: A Collection of Fantasy Fiction, Ultramarine, 1977.

New Worlds: An Anthology, Fontana, 1983.

RECORDINGS; UNDER NAME "MICHAEL MOORCOCK AND THE DEEP FIX"

"The New Worlds Fair," United Artists, 1975.

"Dodgem Dude/Starcruiser" (single), Flicknife, 1980.

"The Brothel in Rosenstrasse/Time Centre" (single), Flicknife, 1982.

(With others) "Hawkwind Friends and Relations," Flicknife, 1982.

(With others) "Hawkwind & Co.," Flicknife, 1983.

Also composer of songs recorded by others, including "Sonic Attack," "The Black Corridor," "The Wizard Blew His Horn," "Standing at the Edge," "Warriors," "Kings of Speed," "Warrior at the End of Time," "Psychosonia," "Coded Languages," "Lost Chances," "Choose Your Masks," and "Arrival in Utopia," all recorded by Hawkwind; "The Great Sun Jester," "Black Blade," and "Veteran of the Psychic Wars," all recorded by Blue Oyster Cult.

OTHER

Contributor, sometimes under pseudonyms, to *Guardian, Punch, Ambit,* London *Times,* and other publications. Writer of comic strips in early 1960s.

SIDELIGHTS: Michael Moorcock was associated with the New Wave, an avant-garde science fiction of the 1960s which introduced a wider range of subject matter and style to the science fiction field. As editor of *New Worlds,* the most prominent of the New Wave publications, Moorcock promoted the movement and provided a showcase for its writing.

The New Wave, Donald A. Wollheim writes in *The Universe Makers,* was an "effort to merge science fiction into the mainstream of literature. . . . The charges brought against oldline science fiction were on the basis of both structure and content. Structurally, the charge was made that too much of the writing retained the flavor of the pulps [and] that science fiction writers were not keeping up with the experimental avant-garde. . . . Internally, the charge was made that science fiction actually was dead—because the future was no longer credible. The crises of the twentieth century . . . were obviously insurmountable. We would all never make it into the twenty-first century." In an interview with Ian Covell of *Science Fiction Review,* Moorcock says of the New Wave: "We were a generation of writers who had no nostalgic love of the pulp magazines, who had come to SF as a possible alternative to mainstream literature and had taken SF seriously. . . . We were trying to find a viable literature for our time. A literature which took account of science, of modern social trends, and which was written not according to genre conventions but according to the personal requirements of the individuals who produced it."

Moorcock's own writing covers a wide range of science fiction and fantasy genres. He has written science fiction adventures in the style of Edgar Rice Burroughs's Mars novels, sword and sorcery novels, comic and satirical science fiction, and time-traveling science fiction. Some of these books, Moorcock admits, were written for the money. *New Worlds* was an influential magazine in the science fiction field, but it was never a financial success. When creditors needed to be paid it was Moorcock, as editor and publisher, who was held responsible. He was often forced to write a quick novel to pay the bills. Even so, Charles Platt recounts in his *Dream Makers: The Uncommon People Who Write Science Fiction,* "it was not unusual for the magazine's staff to be found cowering on the floor with the lights out, pretending not to be home, while some creditor rang the bell and called hopefully through the mail slot in the front door—to no avail."

The genre books that brought Moorcock to critical attention, and those that he considers among his most important, combine standard science fiction trappings with experimental narrative structures. His *Breakfast in the Ruins: A Novel of Inhumanity,* for instance, contains a number of historical vignettes featuring the protagonist Karl Glogauer. In each of these, Karl is a different person in a different time, participating in such examples of political violence as the French Revolution, the Paris Commune, a Nazi concentration camp, and a My Lai-style massacre. Interwoven with these vignettes is a homosexual love scene, involving Karl and a black Nigerian, that takes on a mystical connotation as the two lovers seem to merge into each other's identities. Helen Rogan of *Time* describes the book as "by turns puzzling, funny, and shocking" and Moorcock as "both bizarrely inventive and highly disciplined." Writing in the *New York Times Book Review,* John Deck calls the book "a dazzling historical fantasy."

In the books and stories featuring Jerry Cornelius, Moorcock has experimented with character as well as with narrative structure. Cornelius has no consistent character or appearance. He is, as Nick Totton writes in *Spectator,* "a nomad of the territories of personality; even his skin color and gender are as labile as his accomplishments." Cornelius's world is just as flexible, containing a multitude of alternative histories, all contradictory, and peopled with characters who die and resurrect as a matter of course. Within this mutable landscape, Cornelius travels from one inconclusive adventure to another, trapped in an endless existence. As Colin Greenland maintains in the *Dictionary of Literary Biography,* Cornelius is "an entirely new kind of fictional character,

a dubious hero whose significance is always oblique and rarely stable, equipped to tackle all the challenges of his time yet unable to find a satisfactory solution to any of them."

The Condition of Muzak, completing the initial Jerry Cornelius tetralogy, won the Guardian Literary Prize in 1977, bringing Moorcock acceptance by a wider literary world. At the time of the award, W. L. Webb of the *Guardian* wrote: "Michael Moorcock, rejecting the demarcation disputes that have reduced the novel to a muddle of warring sub-genres, recovers in these four books a protean vitality and inclusiveness that one might call Dickensian if their consciousness were not so entirely of our own volatile times." Moorcock, according to Angus Wilson in the *Washington Post Book World,* "is emerging as one of the most serious literary lights of our time. . . . For me his Jerry Cornelius quartet [of novels] assured the durability of his reputation."

Moorcock's literary standing has been substantially enhanced with the publication of *Byzantium Endures* and *The Laughter of Carthage.* These two novels are the closest Moorcock has come to conventional literary fiction, being the autobiography of Russian emigre Colonel Pyat. Pyat was born on January 1, 1900, and so the story of his life is a history of the twentieth century. Pyat survived the Russian revolution, traveled throughout Europe and America, and participated in a number of important historical events. But he is a megalomaniac who imagines himself to be both a great inventor, the equal of Thomas Edison, and a major figure on the stage of world history. He is also an anti-Semite who sees true Christianity, as embodied in the Russian Orthodox Church, in a battle against the Jews, Orientals, Bolsheviks, and other destroyers of order. He likens Western Christianity to Byzantium, his enemies to Carthage. Naturally, Pyat's account of his life is self-aggrandizing and inaccurate.

Byzantium Endures focuses on the first twenty years of Pyat's life, telling of his opportunistic role in the Russian revolution. Pyat survives the upheaval of the revolution and the subsequent civil war by working first for one side and then another. As Frederic Morton writes in the *New York Times Book Review,* his mechanical skills are put to good use "repairing the rifles of anarchist guerrillas, fixing the treads of White Army tanks [and] doctoring the engine in one of Trotsky's armed trains." Pyat claims to have invented the laser gun on behalf of Ukrainian nationalists fighting against the Red Army, but when the electrical power failed, so did his gun. "Pyat's self-serving recollections," Bart Mills states in the *Los Angeles Times Book Review,* "contain a vivid picture of the events of 1917-1920, down to menus, street names and the color of people's moustaches." The novel, writes Robert Onopa in the *Chicago Tribune Book World,* is "utterly engrossing as narrative, historically pertinent, and told through characters so alive and detail so dense that it puts to shame all but a few writers who have been doing this kind of work all along."

The Laughter of Carthage covers Pyat's life from 1920 to 1924, detailing his escape from Communist Russia and subsequent travels in Europe and America. His activities are sometimes unlawful, requiring him to change his residence and name frequently. He meets everyone from Dylan Thomas to Tom Mix and lives everywhere from Constantinople to Hollywood. Because of the scope of Pyat's adventures, *The Laughter of Carthage* is a sweeping picture of the world during the 1920s. "Moorcock provides an exotic itinerary, a robust cast of opportunists and scoundrels, and a series of dangerous adventures and sexual escapades," notes R. Z. Sheppard of *Time.* "This is epic writing," Valentine Cunningham of the *Times Literary Supplement* writes. "As [D. W.] Griffith stuffed his movies with vast throngs and Promethean matter so Pyat's narration feeds hugely on the numerous people he claims to have met, the history he makes believe he has helped to shape, the many places his traveller's tales take him to."

Pyat's narration, because it is colored by his eccentric, offensive views and his distorted sense of self-importance, gives a fantastic sheen to the familiar historical events he relates. "This is Moorcock's achievement: he has rewritten modern history by seeing it in the distorting mirror of one man's perceptions so that the novel has the imaginative grasp of fantasy while remaining solidly based upon recognizable facts," Peter Ackroyd writes in the London *Times*. "Moorcock has here created a fiction," Nigel Andrew writes in the same paper, "that is seething with detailed life at every level—in the headlong narrative, in the bravura passages of scene-setting description, and, particularly, in the rendering of Pyat's vision of the world." Although Richard Eder of the *Los Angeles Times* finds Pyat's narrative an "extremely long-winded unpleasantness" because of his political views, the *New York Times Book Review*'s Thaddeus Rutkowski forgives the "sometimes tedious" nature of Pyat's narration. "Most often," he finds, "Pyat's tirades are beguiling. They are the pronouncements of a singularly innocent intelligence gone awry."

Moorcock's move from science fiction to mainstream fiction is welcomed by several critics. Observes Gregory Sandow in the *Village Voice:* "It's wonderful to see Moorcock grow from a genre writer into, simply, a writer. . . . A mainstream novel gives him far more scope to nourish the obsessions (and also the passion, zaniness, and eye for detail) that made his science fiction both fun and worthwhile." Moorcock, Andrew allows, "has had to come the long way to literary recognition. But now, with *The Laughter of Carthage*, he can surely no longer be denied his due; this enormous book—with its forerunner, *Byzantium Endures*—must establish him in the front rank of practising English novelists."

Speaking of his writing, Moorcock told *CA:* "Most of my work recently has been in terms of a moral and psychological investigation of Imperialism (Western and Eastern) seen in terms of fiction. Even my fantasy novels are inclined to deal with moral problems rather than magical ones. I'm turning more and more away from SF and fantasy and more towards a form of realism used in the context of what you might call an imaginative framework. Late Dickens would be the model I'd most like to emulate."

Moorcock also continues his work with English rock and roll band Hawkwind, specializing in science fiction-oriented music. The band took its name from a character in one of his novels. He has also formed his own band, Michael Moorcock and the Deep Fix, and has made several recordings. The League of Temporal Adventurers, based in Memphis, Tennessee, is the official Michael Moorcock fan society.

MEDIA ADAPTATIONS: The character Elric is featured in role-playing games from the Avalon Hill Game Company and from Chaosium, in comic books published by Pacific Comics and by Star Reach Productions, and in miniature figures marketed by Citadel Miniatures; the character Oswald Bastable is featured in a computer game.

BIOGRAPHICAL/CRITICAL SOURCES:

BOOKS

Bilyeu, R., *Tanelorn Archives*, Pandora's Books, 1979.
Callow, A. J., compiler, *The Chronicles of Moorcock*, A. J. Callow, 1978.

Carter, Lin, *Imaginary Worlds*, Ballantine, 1973.
Contemporary Authors Autobiography Series, Volume 5, Gale, 1987.
Contemporary Literary Criticism, Gale, Volume 5, 1976, Volume 27, 1984.
Dictionary of Literary Biography, Volume 14: *British Novelists since 1960*, Gale, 1983.
Greenland, Colin, *The Entropy Exhibition: Michael Moorcock and the British "New Wave" in Science Fiction*, Routledge & Kegan Paul, 1983.
Harper, Andrew and George McAulay, *Michael Moorcock: A Bibliography*, T-K Graphics, 1976.
Platt, Charles, *Dream Makers: The Uncommon People Who Write Science Fiction*, Berkley Publishing, 1980.
Walker, Paul, editor, *Speaking of Science Fiction: The Paul Walker Interviews*, Luna Publications, 1978.
Wollheim, Donald A., *The Universe Makers*, Harper, 1971.

PERIODICALS

Amazing Stories, May, 1971.
Analog, February, 1970.
Books and Bookmen, June, 1971, September, 1971, October, 1972, May, 1974, August, 1978.
Chicago Tribune Book World, January 31, 1982.
Commonweal, August 1, 1975.
Detroit News, February 24, 1985.
Encounter, November, 1981.
Guardian Weekly, April 10, 1969.
Harper's Bazaar (British edition), December, 1969.
Ink, August, 1971.
Kensington News, April 18, 1969.
Kensington Post, April 4, 1969.
Los Angeles Times, January 9, 1985, November 10, 1987.
Los Angeles Times Book Review, March 7, 1982, February 7, 1988.
Luna Monthly, November, 1975.
New Republic, June 15, 1974.
New Statesman, April 4, 1969, May 18, 1973, June 18, 1976, April 15, 1977.
New Worlds, March, 1969.
New York Times Book Review, April 5, 1970, May 19, 1974, April 25, 1976, February 21, 1982, February 10, 1985, November 23, 1986.
Observer, April 4, 1976.
Punch, January 16, 1985.
Saturday Review, April 25, 1970.
Science Fiction Monthly, February, 1975.
Science Fiction Review, January, 1971, January, 1979.
Spectator, April 1, 1969, August 10, 1974, November 20, 1976, April 9, 1977, December 24, 1977, June 27, 1981, February 9, 1985.
Speculation, May, 1970, August, 1970.
Time, August 5, 1974, January 28, 1985.
Time Out, September 17, 1971.
Times (London), September 6, 1984, November 25, 1984.
Times Literary Supplement, October 27, 1972, November 9, 1973, May 31, 1974, May 7, 1976, June 30, 1978, July 3, 1981, September 7, 1984, July 1, 1988.
Tribune Books (Chicago), March 26, 1989.
Village Voice, March 2, 1982.
Virginia Quarterly Review, spring, 1975.
Washington Post Book World, March 21, 1982, December 23, 1984, September 28, 1986, May 14, 1989.

MOORE, Alice Ruth
See NELSON, Alice Ruth Moore Dunbar

* * *

MOORE, Brian 1921-

PERSONAL: Born August 25, 1921, in Belfast, Northern Ireland; emigrated to Canada, 1948; Canadian citizen; son of James Brian (a surgeon) and Eileen (McFadden) Moore; married Jean Denney, October, 1967; children: Michael. *Education:* Graduated from St. Malachy's College, 1939.

ADDRESSES: Home—33958 Pacific Coast Hwy., Malibu, Calif. 90265. *Agent*—Curtis Brown Ltd., 10 Astor Place, New York, N.Y. 10003.

CAREER: Montreal Gazette, Montreal, Quebec, proofreader, reporter, and rewrite man, 1948-52; writer, 1952—. *Military service:* Served with British Ministry of War Transport in North Africa, Italy, and France during World War II.

AWARDS, HONORS: Author's Club first novel award, 1956; Quebec Literary Prize, 1958; Guggenheim fellowship, 1959; Governor General's Award for Fiction, 1960, for *The Luck of Ginger Coffey,* and 1975, for *The Great Victorian Collection;* National Institute of Arts and Letters fiction grant, 1961; Canada Council fellowship for travel in Europe, 1962; W. H. Smith Prize, 1972, for *Catholics;* James Tait Black Memorial Award, 1975, for *The Great Victorian Collection;* Neill Gunn International Fellowship from the Scottish Arts Council, 1983; "ten best books of 1983" citation from *Newsweek,* 1983, for *Cold Heaven;* Heinemann Award from the Royal Society of Literature, 1986, for *Black Robe;* Booker Prize shortlist citation, 1987, and *Sunday Express* Book of the Year Prize, 1988, both for *The Color of Blood.*

WRITINGS:

NOVELS

Judith Hearne, A. Deutsch, 1955, published as *The Lonely Passion of Judith Hearne,* Little, Brown, 1956.
The Feast of Lupercal, Little, Brown, 1957.
The Luck of Ginger Coffey (also see below), Little, Brown, 1960.
An Answer from Limbo (also see below), Little, Brown, 1962.
The Emperor of Ice-Cream, Viking, 1965.
I Am Mary Dunne, Viking, 1968.
Fergus, Holt, 1970.
The Revolution Script, Holt, 1971.
Catholics (also see below), J. Cape, 1972, Harcourt, 1973.
The Great Victorian Collection, Farrar, Straus, 1975.
The Doctor's Wife, Farrar, Straus, 1976.
The Mangan Inheritance, Farrar, Straus, 1979.
The Temptation of Eileen Hughes, Farrar, Straus, 1981.
Cold Heaven, Holt, 1983.
Black Robe, Dutton, 1985.
The Color of Blood, Dutton, 1987.

OTHER

(With others) *Canada* (travel book), Time-Life, 1963.
"The Luck of Ginger Coffey" (screenplay; based on his novel of same title), Continental, 1964.
"Torn Curtain" (screenplay), Universal, 1966.
"Catholics" (television script; based on his novel of same title), Columbia Broadcasting System, 1973.
Easter in Us, Meyer Stone, 1989.

Also author of screenplays "The Slave" (based on his novel *An Answer from Limbo*), 1967, "The Blood of Others," 1984, "Brainwash," 1985, "Black Robe" (based on his novel of same title), 1987, and "Gabrielle Chanel," 1988. Author of detective novels under pseudonyms Michael Bryan and Bernard Marrow. Contributor of articles and short stories to *Spectator, Holiday, Atlantic,* and other periodicals.

SIDELIGHTS: Brian Moore is a Canadian citizen of Irish origin currently living in the United States. He is also a novelist who "has gradually won the recognition his stubborn artistry deserves," to quote Walter Clemons in *Newsweek.* For more than thirty years Moore has been publishing fiction that reflects his multinational wanderings, his fascination with Catholicism's influence on modern life, and his insight into strained interpersonal relationships. "Book by book," writes Bruce Cook in *New Republic,* "Brian Moore has been building a body of work that is, in its quietly impressive way, about as good as that of any novelist writing today in English." Cook adds: "If Moore lacks the fame he deserves, he nevertheless has an excellent reputation. He is a writer's writer. His special virtues—his deft presentation of his characters, whether they be Irish, Canadian, or American, and the limpid simplicity of his style—are those that other writers most admire."

Many of Moore's plots are conventional in their inception, but typically the author brings additional depth of characterization to his stories so that they transcend genre classifications. As Joyce Carol Oates observes in the *New York Times Book Review,* Moore has written "a number of novels prized for their storytelling qualities and for a wonderfully graceful synthesis of the funny, the sardonic, and the near tragic; his reputation as a supremely entertaining 'serious' writer is secure." In *Saturday Night,* Christina Newman notes that Moore has a growing readership which has come to expect "what he unfailingly delivers: lucidity, great craftsmanship, and perceptions that evoke our fears, dreams, and shameful absurdities." *New York Times Book Review* contributor Julian Moynahan calls Moore "one of the most intelligent and accessible novelists now working. . . . He seems to have no crochets to hook or axes to grind and is adept at reworking his personal experience for the fiction public on both sides of the Atlantic." Oates feels that the author's works "succeed most compellingly on an immediate level: rich with convincing detail, communicating the admixture of drollery and sorrow that characterizes 'real' life, populated with individuals who speak and act and dream and breathe as if altogether innocent of the fact that they are mere fictitious characters."

In the *Spectator,* Francis King explains how Moore constructs his stories: "His sentences are unelaborate and his vocabulary narrow. . . . But, mysteriously, beneath this surface flatness, strange creatures thresh, slither and collide with each other. Many sentences may seem bare, some may even seem banal; but the cumulative impression left by a sequence of them is one of complexity and originality." *Village Voice* reviewer Alan Hislop similarly contends that Moore's prose "is disarming and seductive: you are led, nay drawn, into alarming stories . . . so polite that you never suspect there might be a trap door in the scrupulously polished floor." Beneath that "trap door" is a view of the dark side of human events; temptation, guilt, disillusionment, and dissatisfaction often play primary roles in Moore's characters' lives. In the *Washington Post Book World,* Alan Ryan states that it is this skillful exploration of human failings that makes Moore's work such thoughtful entertainment. "In most of Brian Moore's writing," the critic concludes, "one is always aware of larger, and darker, worlds lurking just out of view."

"Brian Moore comes from the middle-class sector of the submerged and currently beleaguered Catholic minority of Belfast in Ulster," writes Moynahan. "Like many Irish writers before him, he has followed the path of voluntary exile in managing a successful career as a novelist and is the only writer I know of who has lived and worked, and collected a number of impressive literary prizes, in no less than four English-speaking countries—Ireland, England, Canada and the United States." Moore left his native land and rejected his Catholic upbringing at an early age. Shortly after completing war-time service he emigrated to Canada, and from there he began to write about the Belfast he knew as a youth. According to Christopher Hawtree in the *Spectator,* this transatlantic stance "has yielded some sharp views both of his native Ireland and of Canada and America." *Time* contributor Patricia Blake likewise feels that Moore's expatriation has produced "a special talent for pungent portraiture of those Irish men and women who are, as James Joyce put it, 'outcast from life's feast': desperate spinsters, failed priests, drunken poets." Other critics note that the very process of moving from place to place fuels Moore's fiction. In *Critique: Studies in Modern Fiction,* John Wilson Foster contends that Moore's novels as a group "trace the growing fortunes in a new continent of one hypothetical immigrant who has escaped Belfast's lower middle-class tedium." London *Times* correspondent Chris Petit also concludes that absence is important to Moore's writing. "The stories have an air of cosmopolitan restlessness, often cross borders, and can be summarized as a series of departures," Petit states.

Eventually Moore moved to the United States—first to New York and then to Malibu, California. As Kerry McSweeney notes in *Critical Quarterly,* while the author retains Canadian citizenship, and Canada "was the halfway house which mediated his passage from the old world to the new, it has not stimulated his imagination in the way that America has done." Paul Binding elaborates in *Books and Bookmen:* "It is America, with its vigorous non-realistic, especially Gothic literary tradition, which would seem to have supplied Brian Moore with the fictional forms that he needed, that can express—with their violent epiphanies and their distortions and eruptions of the irrational—the anguishes of the uprooted and spiritually homeless, and the baffling diversities of Western society which can contain both puritan, taboo-ridden, pleasure-fearing Belfast and hedonistic, lost, restless California." In *Nation,* Jack Ludwig writes: "Moore is, like Joyce, essentially a city writer and, again like Joyce, someone who reacts to the city with lyric double awareness—the ugliness is there, but also the vigor. . . . The paralysis, hopelessness, colorlessness of Moore's first two novels is, I think, a dramatic equivalent of his Belfast. And it is not Europe which stands opposed to Belfast. It is New York."

Moore's early novels, *The Lonely Passion of Judith Hearne, The Feast of Lupercal, The Luck of Ginger Coffey,* and *The Emperor of Ice-Cream,* are character studies in which the protagonists rebel—sometimes unsuccessfully—against the essentially closed society of Northern Ireland. McSweeney suggests that the works "are studies of losers, whose fates are determined by the claustrophobic gentility of Belfast and the suffocating weight of Irish Catholicism. [They] illustrate one of the quintessential *donnees* of Moore's fiction: that (in his own words) 'failure is a more interesting condition than success. Success changes people: it makes them something they were not and dehumanizes them in a way, whereas failure leaves you with a more intense distillation of that self you are.' " In *Critique,* Hallvard Dahlie examines Moore's predilection for characters enmired in hopelessness: "Moore [chooses] for his central figures people in their late thirties or early forties who [are] failures of one sort or another, and [have] been failures for some time. In his first four novels, Moore ex-

ploited the constituents of failure so skillfully and sensitively that the characters achieve much more stature than many triumphant heroes of less gifted writers. But with none of these earlier characters do we sense the likelihood of any lasting triumph over their limitations or obstacles." *Chicago Tribune Book World* reviewer Eugene Kennedy finds these novels "a look beneath the aspects of Irish culture that, with a terrible mixture of repression and misuse of its religious heritage, can create pitiable monsters fated to groan eternally beneath the facades of their hypocritical adjustments."

The Lonely Passion of Judith Hearne, Moore's first and best-known novel, is, to quote *Los Angeles Times* reviewer Leonard Klady, "an acclaimed work about an aging woman's struggle to find her identity as the secure elements in her life start to disintegrate." Set in Belfast, the story—which has never been out of print since 1955—revolves around Judith Hearne's desperate and futile attempts to gain the affection of a paunchy and unscrupulous suitor. *New York Times Book Review* contributor Frances Taliaferro notes that the Irish setting gives "a special poignancy to this portrait of a sad middle class spinster resolutely slipping into emotional destitution." In *Commonweal,* William Clancy observes that in the novel, Moore "has taken an Irish city and laid bare its most secret soul through characters who could not have been born elsewhere. . . . In its relentless pursuit of this woman's sorrow, in its refusal to sentimentalize or easily alleviate her plight, the book achieves a kind of vision, and it is a tragic vision. As she accepts, finally, the end of all her hopes, Judith Hearne attains . . . a certain grandeur." *Saturday Review* essayist Granville Hicks is among the critics who have praised *The Lonely Passion of Judith Hearne.* "As a book by a young man about a middle-aged woman," Hicks writes, "it [is] a remarkable tour de force, but it [is] more than that, for in it one [feels] the terrible pathos of life as it is often led."

A fascination with Catholicism is central to much of Moore's work. He told the *Los Angeles Times:* "I am not a religious person, but I come from a very religious background. Always in the back of my mind, I've wondered what if all this stuff was true and you didn't want it to be true and it was happening in the worst possible way?" According to Paul Gray in *Time,* a refrain common to all of Moore's novels is this: "When beliefs can no longer comfort, they turn destructive." Such is the case in a variety of Moore's works, from *The Lonely Passion of Judith Hearne* to the more recent *Cold Heaven, Black Robe, Catholics,* and *The Color of Blood.* Craig writes: "Someone who is heading for the moment of apostasy . . . is almost statutory in a Moore novel. . . . A frightening emptiness takes the place of whatever ideology had kept the character going." The opposite may also apply in some of Moore's tales; occasionally non-believing characters are forced to pay heed to the deity through extreme means. "Mr. Moore's later novels show the vestigial religious conscience straining to give depth to North American life," observes a *Times Literary Supplement* reviewer. "Faith itself is unacceptable, making unreasonable demands on the behaviour of anyone who is sporadically forced to be honest with himself. Yet bourbon, bedrooms and success do not content the soul: in this, at least, the priests were always right." Craig concludes that Moore is "an author who in the past has used the emblems of Catholicism with conspicuous success. . . . No one has examined with greater acuity the moral deficiencies inherent in a Belfast Catholic upbringing."

Several of Moore's novels—*Fergus, The Great Victorian Collection,* and *Cold Heaven*—make use of miracles and the supernatural to advance the stories. In *The Great Victorian Collection,* for instance, a college professor finds his vivid dream about an exhibit of Victorian memorabilia transformed into reality in a hotel parking lot. Binding suggests that in these works Moore "has tried to explore the complexities of American/Californian life while coming to further terms with the ghosts of his Irish past." These miracles and ghostly visitations do not comfort or sustain; Moore's vision of the supernatural "is terrifying: a brutal energy that mocks our pretensions and transcends our ideas of good and evil," to quote Mark Abley in *Books in Canada*. Peter S. Prescott likewise notes in *Newsweek* that Moore is "concerned with a secular sensibility confronting the more alien aspects of Roman Catholic tradition. . . . He warns us of the ambiguities of miracles in a world that is darker, more dangerous and above all more portentous than we think." Such plot devices can strain verisimilitude, but according to David MacFarlane in *Maclean's,* the author's strength "is his ability to make tangible the unbelievable and the miraculous." MacFarlane adds: "His consistently fine prose and the precision of his narrative create a reality in which characters and readers alike are forced to believe the improbable. Moore inhabits a world which is partly that of a religious visionary and partly that of a thriller writer."

"Mr. Moore is not only the laureate of Irish drabness but also a psychological writer with some interest in the quirkier aspects of profane love," writes Taliaferro. "Throughout his career, one has been able to rely on Mr. Moore for narrative competence and psychological interest." Through novels such as *I Am Mary Dunne, The Doctor's Wife,* and *The Temptation of Eileen Hughes,* Moore has attained a reputation for uncovering the pitfalls in modern emotional entanglements, especially from the female point of view. In *Nation,* Richard B. Sale comments that the author "has never avoided the silliness, selfishness and sexuality that constitute most people's waking and dreaming thoughts. . . . He can extend the embarrassing scene beyond the point where the ordinary naturalistic novelist would lower the curtain." *Times Literary Supplement* reviewer Paul Bailey notes that it is "typical of Brian Moore's honesty that he should acknowledge that, superficially at least, there are certain liaisons which bear a shocking resemblance to those described in the pages of women's magazines: life, unfortunately, has a nasty habit of imitating pulp fiction." However, *Spectator* correspondent Paul Ableman points out that Moore's characters "are not formula figures, whose responses to any situation are predictable, but rather fictional beings that behave like people in the world, generally consistent or revealing a thread of continuity, but always quirky, volatile and sometimes irrational." Bailey also admits that it is "a hallmark of Brian Moore's art that it respects and acknowledges a state of unhappiness as raw and as ugly as an open wound."

Prescott characterizes Moore as a novelist who "enjoys playing with his readers' expectations. Aha, he seems to say, you thought I was writing about this; now don't you feel a little foolish to discover that I was really up to something else—something more innocent and yet more terrible—all along?" Moore himself echoes this sentiment in the *Los Angeles Times:* "I find it interesting to lull the reader into a sense that he's reading a certain kind of book and then jolt the reader about halfway through to make him realize that it's a different kind of book. That is not a recipe for best sellerdom; it's the opposite." Even the thriller format in such works as *Black Robe* and *The Color of Blood* becomes "a vehicle to explore serious political and theological issues," to quote Anne-Marie Conway in the *Times Literary Supplement*. It is this willingness to explore and experiment that contributes to Moore's novelistic originality, according to critics. McSweeney writes: "One of the most impressive features of Moore's canon has been his ability to keep from repeating himself. Over

and over again he has found fresh inventions which have developed his novelistic skills and enabled him to explore his obsessive themes and preoccupations in ways that have made for an increasingly complex continuity between old and new." Moreover, while the author's critical reputation is high, he is not particularly well-known to American readers—a state of affairs he welcomes. "I have never had to deal with the problem of a public persona becoming more important than the fiction," he said in the *Los Angeles Times*. "I've had a life where I've been able to write without having had some enormous success that I have to live up to."

Moore's success may not be enormous, but it is substantial in Canada and Great Britain. Cook claims that the author's retiring personality affects the tenor of his work for the better. "In a way," Cook concludes in *Commonweal*, "the sort of writer [Moore] is—private, devoted to writing as an end in itself—is the only sort who could write the intensely felt, personal, and close novels he has. The style, once again, is the man." Bailey writes: "It isn't fashionable to praise novelists for their tact, but it is that very quality in Brian Moore's writing that deserves to be saluted. It is a measure of his intelligence and his humanity that he refuses to sit in judgment on his characters. It is, as far as I am concerned, an honourable and a considerable measure." Perhaps the best summation of Moore's authorial talents comes from *Washington Post Book World* reviewer Jack Beatty, who says of the writer: "Pick him up expecting high talent in the service of a small design, go to him anticipating economy of style, characterization and description, as well as the pleasure of a plot that keeps you reading until the last page, and I can assure that your expectations will get along splendidly with his abilities."

MEDIA ADAPTATIONS: The Lonely Passion of Judith Hearne was produced as a feature film by Island Pictures in 1988; *The Temptation of Eileen Hughes* was produced for television by the British Broadcasting Corp. in 1988.

BIOGRAPHICAL/CRITICAL SOURCES:

BOOKS

Contemporary Literary Criticism, Gale, Volume 1, 1973, Volume 3, 1975, Volume 5, 1976, Volume 7, 1977, Volume 8, 1978, Volume 19, 1981, Volume 32, 1985.
Dahlie, Hallvard, *Brian Moore,* Copp, 1969.
Flood, Jeanne, *Brian Moore,* Bucknell University Press, 1974.
Raban, Jonathan, *The Techniques of Modern Fiction,* Edward Arnold, 1968.

PERIODICALS

Books & Bookmen, December, 1968, February, 1980.
Books in Canada, October, 1979, November, 1983.
Chicago Tribune, November 2, 1987.
Chicago Tribune Book World, July 12, 1981, October 30, 1983, May 19, 1985.
Commonweal, August 3, 1956, July 12, 1957, September 27, 1968, August 23, 1974.
Critical Quarterly, summer, 1976.
Critique: Studies in Modern Fiction, Volume 9, number 1, 1966, Volume 13, number 1, 1971.
Detroit News, October 14, 1979, May 19, 1985.
Globe & Mail (Toronto), March 30, 1985, September 5, 1987.
Harper's, October, 1965.
Life, June 18, 1968, December 3, 1972.
Los Angeles Times, September 14, 1983, July 2, 1987, September 15, 1987, December 23, 1987, January 1, 1988, April 10, 1988.

Los Angeles Times Book Review, September 11, 1983, April 7, 1985.

Maclean's, September 17, 1979, September 5, 1983.

Nation, March 15, 1965, June 24, 1968, October 12, 1970.

New Republic, August 17, 1968, June 9, 1973, October 24, 1983.

New Statesman, February 18, 1966, October 17, 1975, November 25, 1983.

Newsweek, June 2, 1975, September 20, 1976, October 15, 1979, July 20, 1981, September 5, 1983, March 18, 1985.

New Yorker, May 11, 1957, August 4, 1975, October 3, 1983, July 8, 1985.

New York Times, October 1, 1976, September 12, 1979, July 3, 1981, September 14, 1983, January 15, 1984, March 25, 1985, September 1, 1987, December 23, 1987, December 25, 1987.

New York Times Book Review, October 24, 1965, December 5, 1965, June 23, 1968, September 27, 1970, November 28, 1971, March 18, 1973, June 29, 1975, September 26, 1976, September 9, 1979, August 2, 1981, September 18, 1983, March 31, 1985, September 27, 1987.

People, October 12, 1987.

Saturday Night, September, 1968, November, 1970, July-August, 1975, October, 1976.

Saturday Review, October 13, 1962, September 18, 1965, June 15, 1968, February 12, 1972, July 26, 1975, September 18, 1976.

Spectator, November 1, 1975, November 10, 1979, October 10, 1981, November 12, 1983, July 13, 1985.

Time, June 18, 1956, June 21, 1968, October 12, 1970, July 14, 1975, September 6, 1976, September 19, 1983, March 18, 1985.

Times (London), October 1, 1981, November 3, 1983, June 13, 1985, September 24, 1987.

Times Literary Supplement, February 3, 1966, October 24, 1966, April 9, 1971, January 21, 1972, November 10, 1972, October 17, 1975, November 23, 1979, October 9, 1981, October 28, 1983, June 7, 1985, October 2, 1987.

Village Voice, June 30, 1957, October 22, 1979.

Washington Post, January 22, 1988.

Washington Post Book World, April 8, 1973, June 1, 1975, October 17, 1976, September 23, 1979, December 9, 1979, June 21, 1981, September 11, 1983, March 31, 1985, September 6, 1987, February 14, 1988.

*   *   *

MOORE, Marianne (Craig) 1887-1972

PERSONAL: Born November 15, 1887, in Kirkwood, Mo; died February 5, 1972; daughter of John Milton and Mary (Warner) Moore. *Education:* Bryn Mawr College, A.B., 1909; Carlisle Commercial College, graduate, 1910. *Religion:* Presbyterian.

ADDRESSES: Home—New York, N.Y.

CAREER: Author and poet. United States Indian School, Carlisle, Pa., teacher, 1911-15; New York Public Library, New York, N.Y., assistant, 1921-25.

MEMBER: National Institute of Arts and Letters, American Academy of Arts and Letters, Bryn Mawr Club.

AWARDS, HONORS: Dial Award, 1924; Helen Haire Levinson Prize, 1932; Ernest Hartsock Memorial Prize, 1935; Shelley Memorial Award, 1941; Contemporary Poetry's Patrons Prize, 1944; Harriet Monroe Poetry Award, 1944; Guggenheim Memorial fellowship, 1945; National Institute of Arts and Letters, grant in literature, 1946, gold medal, 1953; National Book Award for poetry and Pulitzer Prize in poetry, 1952, for *Collected Poems;* Bollingen Prize in poetry, Yale University, 1953, for *Collected Poems;* M. Carey Thomas Award, 1953; Poetry Society of America gold medal award, 1960, 1967; Brandeis Award for Poetry, 1963; Academy of American Poets fellowship, 1965, for distinguished poetic achievement over a period of more than four decades; MacDowell medal, 1967; named chevalier of the Legion of Honor, Order of Arts and Letters; named woman of achievement, American Association of University Women, 1968. Honorary degrees: Litt.D. from Wilson College, 1949, Mount Holyoke College, 1950, University of Rochester, 1951, Dickinson College, 1952, Long Island University, 1953, New York University, 1967, St. John's University, 1968, and Princeton University, 1968; L.H.D. from Rutgers University, 1955, Smith College, 1955, and Pratt Institute, 1958.

WRITINGS:

POETRY

Poems, Egoist Press, 1921, published with additions as *Observations,* Dial, 1924.

Selected Poems, introduction by T. S. Eliot, Macmillan, 1935.

Pangolin, and Other Verse: Five Poems, Brendin, 1936.

What Are Years and Other Poems, Macmillan, 1941.

Nevertheless, Macmillan, 1944.

Collected Poems, Macmillan, 1951.

Like a Bulwark, Viking, 1956.

O to Be a Dragon, Viking, 1959.

A Marianne Moore Reader, Viking, 1961.

The Arctic Ox, Faber, 1964.

A Talisman, Adams House, 1965.

Tell Me, Tell Me: Granite, Steel, and Other Topics (poetry and prose), Viking, 1966.

The Complete Poems of Marianne Moore, Macmillan, 1967, Penguin, 1987.

Selected Poems, Faber, 1969.

Unfinished Poems, P. H. and A.S.W. Rosenbach Foundation, 1972.

POETRY; PUBLISHED IN LIMITED EDITIONS

Eight Poems, illustrations by Robert Andrew Parker, New York Museum of Modern Art, 1962.

Occasionem cognosce, Stinehour Press, 1963.

Dress and Kindred Subjects, Ibex Press, 1965.

Le mariage . . . , Ibex Press, 1965.

Poetry and Criticism, privately printed, 1965.

Silence, L. H. Scott, 1965.

Tippoo's Tiger, Phoenix Book Shop, 1967.

OTHER

(Co-translator) A. Stifter, *Rock Crystal,* Pantheon, 1945.

(Translator) *Selected Fables of La Fontaine,* Faber, 1955, revised edition, Viking, 1964.

Predilections (essays and reviews), Viking, 1955.

Letters from and to the Ford Motor Company, Pierpont Morgan Library, 1958 (first appeared in *New Yorker,* April 13, 1957).

(Compiler with others) *Riverside Poetry Three: An Anthology of Student Poetry,* Twayne, 1958.

Idiosyncrasy and Technique: Two Lectures, University of California Press, 1958.

The Absentee: A Comedy in Four Acts (play based on Maria Edgeworth's novel of the same name), House of Books, 1962.

(Contributor) *Poetry in Crystal,* Spiral Press, 1963.

Puss in Boots, The Sleeping Beauty, and Cinderella (retelling of three fairy tales based on the French tales of Charles Perrault), illustrated by Eugene Karlin, Macmillan, 1963.

(Contributor) A. K. Weatherhead, *The Edge of the Image,* University of Washington Press, 1968.

The Accented Syllable, Albondocani Press, 1969 (first appeared in *Egoist,* October, 1916).

(Contributor) *Homage to Henry James,* Appel, 1971.

The Complete Prose of Marianne Moore, edited by Patricia C. Willis, Penguin, 1986.

Contributor of articles, essays, and verse to numerous magazines. *Dial,* acting editor, 1926-29, editor, 1929.

SIDELIGHTS: Marianne Moore once told an interviewer for the *New York Times:* "Poetry. I, too, dislike it: There are things that are important beyond all this fiddle. [But,] if you demand on the one hand/the raw material of poetry in/all its rawness and/that which is on the other hand/genuine, then you are interested in poetry."

Moore continued: "I don't call anything I have ever written poetry. In fact, the only reason I know for calling my work poetry at all is that there is no other category in which to put it. I'm a happy hack as a writer. . . . I never knew anyone with a passion for words who had as much difficulty in saying things as I do. I seldom say them in a manner I like. Each poem I think will be the last. But something always comes up and catches my fancy."

In spite of Moore's rather humble thoughts, many critics believe in the significance of her poetry. For example, John Ashbery glowed: "I am tempted simply to call her our greatest modern poet. This despite the obvious grandeur of her chief competitors, including Wallace Stevens and William Carlos Williams. It seems we can never remind ourselves too often that universality and depth are not the same thing. Marianne Moore has no 'Arma virumque cano' prefacing her work: She even avoids formal beginnings altogether by running the first line in as a continuation of the title. But her work will, I think, continue to be read as poetry when much of the major poetry of our time has become part of the history of literature."

Ashbery isn't alone in his praise of Moore's poetry. James Dickey wrote: "Each of her poems employs items that Ms. Moore similarly encountered and to which she gave a new, Mooreian existence in a new cosmos of consequential relationships. What seems to me to be the most valuable point about Ms. Moore is that such receptivity as hers . . . is not Ms. Moore's exclusive property. Every poem of hers lifts us toward our own discovery-prone lives. It does not state, in effect, that I am more intelligent than you, more creative because I found this item and used it and you didn't. It seems to say, rather, I found this, and what did you find? Or, a better, what can you find?"

Nation critic Sandra Hochman agreed: "The art of Marianne Moore is not just the valuable art of observation. She is magical. Her poems do have riddles. They can irk us. But they finally carry us forward by the strength of language and, in her own words, the poet's 'burning desire to be explicit.' Nothing is wasted. All is transformed."

It is this desire that underlies Moore's poetry. James Dickey explained that "Ms. Moore tells us that facts make her feel 'profoundly grateful.' This is because knowledge, for her, is not power but love, and in loving it is important to know what you love, as widely and as deeply and as well as possible. In paying so very much attention to the things of this earth that she encounters, or that encounter her, Ms. Moore urges us to do the same, and thus gives us back, in strict syllables, the selves that we had contrived to lose. She persuades us that the human mind is nothing more than an organ for loving things in both complicated and blindingly simple ways, and is organized so as to be able to love in an unlimited number of fashions and for an unlimited number of reasons. This seems to me to constitute the correct poetic attitude, which is essentially a life-attitude, for it stands forever against the notion that the earth is an apathetic limbo lost in space." As Ms. Moore herself explained to Howard Nemerov: "I am . . . much aware of the world's dilemma. People's effect on other people results, it seems to me, in an enforced sense of responsibility—a compulsory obligation to participate in others' problems."

Marianne Moore is almost as famous for her practice of rewriting her previously published poems as for her poetry itself. This practice has often disturbed many of her followers. Jean Garrigrie explained: "Poets who revise their poems are apt to incur surprise or weak query (a guise of protest) from those who have long ago fallen in love with that 'one and only,' the original. The poet, patient about perfection, has a right to be impatient with such resistance. But there it is. And a good deal is involved. A line taken out of a poem sparingly built in the first place, that line's removal subtly alters the whole in tone. An 'excess' excised—a qualifying extension or elaboration—complicated one's responses, for one is busy dismissing and it takes time to adjust to the revision. What is being felt is the absence, almost as much as the new presence."

And Anthony Hecht once wrote that as "an admiring reader I feel that I have some rights in [this] matter. Her poems are partly mine, now, and I delight in them because they exhibit a mind of great fastidiousness, a delicate and cunning moral sensibility, a tact, a decorum, a rectitude, and finally and most movingly, a capacity for pure praise that has absolutely biblical awe in it. She (and Mr. Auden, too, as it will appear) however much I may wish to take exception to the changes they have made, have provided a field day for Ph.D. candidates for years to come, who can collate versions and come up with theories about why the changes were made."

AVOCATIONAL INTERESTS: Baseball.

BIOGRAPHICAL/CRITICAL SOURCES:

BOOKS

Contemporary Literary Criticism, Gale, Volume I, 1973, Volume II, 1974, Volume IV, 1975, Volume VIII, 1977, Volume X, 1979, Volume XIII, 1980, Volume XIX, 1981, Volume XLVII, 1988.

Dictionary of Literary Biography, Volume XLV: *American Poets, 1880-1945, First Series,* Gale, 1986.

Engel, Bernard F., *Marianne Moore,* Twayne, 1964.

Hadas, P. W., *Marianne Moore: Poet of Affection,* Syracuse University Press, 1977.

Jarrell, Randall, *Poetry and the Age,* Knopf, 1953.

Nemerov, Howard, *Poets on Poetry,* Basic Books, 1966.

Rosenthal, M. L., *The Modern Poets,* Oxford University Press, 1965.

Stapleton, L., *Marianne Moore,* Princeton University Press, 1978.

PERIODICALS

Atlantic, February, 1962.

Detroit News, February 6, 1972.

Esquire, July, 1962.

Harper's, May, 1977.

Hudson Review, spring, 1968.

Life, January 13, 1967.

McCall's, December, 1965.

Nation, May 8, 1967.

New Leader, December 4, 1967.

New Republic, January 4, 1960, February 24, 1968.

Newsweek, January 2, 1967.

New Yorker, February 16, 1957, April 13, 1957, November 28, 1959, January 29, 1966, October 16, 1978.

New York Times, June 3, 1965, July 13, 1965, February 6, 1972, February 21, 1981, February 8, 1987, October 14, 1987.

New York Times Book Review, May 16, 1954, October 4, 1959, December 3, 1961, December 25, 1966, March 14, 1967, November 26, 1967.

Poetry, April, 1925, May, 1960.

Publishers Weekly, February 14, 1972.

Times (London), February 5, 1987.

Washington Post, March 16, 1968, February 7, 1972, January 19, 1988.

*   *   *

MORANTE, Elsa   1918-1985

PERSONAL: Born August 18, 1918, in Rome, Italy; died of a heart attack, November 25, 1985, in Rome, Italy; daughter of a schoolteacher; married Alberto Moravia (a writer), 1941 (marriage ended, c. 1963).

ADDRESSES: Home—Rome, Italy. *Agent*—c/o Alfred A. Knopf, Inc., 201 East 50th St., New York, N.Y. 10022.

CAREER: Writer.

AWARDS, HONORS: Viareggio Prize, 1948, for *Menzogne e sortilegio;* Strega Prize, 1966, for *L'isola di Arturo;* Prix Medicis Etranger, 1985, for *Aracoeli.*

WRITINGS:

Le bellisime avventure di cateri dalla trecciolina (self-illustrated children's story; title means "The Marvelous Adventures of Cathy Pigtail"), first published c. 1941, revised and expanded edition published as *Le straordinarie avventure di Caterina,* Einaudi, 1959.

(Translator) *Il libro degli appunti,* Rizzoli, 1945.

Menzogne e sortilegio, Einaudi, 1948, abridged translation by Adrienne Foulke published as *House of Liars,* Harcourt, 1951.

L'isola di Arturo, Einaudi, 1957, translation by Isabel Quigly published as *Arturo's Island,* Knopf, 1959.

Alibi (poems), Longanesi 1958.

Lo scialle andaluso (stories; title means "The Andalusian Shawl"), Einaudi, 1963.

Il monce salvato dai ragazzini e altri poemi (stories; title means "The World Saved by Little Children"), Einaudi, 1968.

La storia, Einaudi, 1974, translation by William Weaver published as *History: A Novel,* Knopf, 1977.

Aracoeli, Gallimard, 1982, translation by Weaver published under the same title, Random House, 1984.

Also author of *Il gioco segreto* (essays; title means "The Secret Game"), 1941, and *Botteghe oscure,* 1958. Translator of *Il meglio di Katherine Mansfield,* 1957. Work anthologized in *Modern Italian Stories,* 1955, and *Wake,* Volume 12.

SIDELIGHTS: Elsa Morante's first novel, *House of Liars,* though published in the United States only in an abridged version, is considered by some critics to be one of the great twenti-

eth-century Italian novels. It is the story of a woman, Elisa, and her attempts to discover the history of her parents and grandparents. "At first glance," wrote Serge Hughes, "the novel would appear to be a belated realistic novel of the late nineteenth century. But it does not require much reading to become aware that the psychology which motivates the characters is completely, darkly modern, and that in using a somewhat dated setting and technique, the author has achieved a horror effect." Frances Keene called *House of Liars* "a cross between a Gothic tale and a picaresque novel," but also felt that Morante had overextended herself in combining the two styles. She noted that "Morante is writing out of her epoch." Still, Paolo Milano found Morante to be a "visionary teller" and Keene declared, "The writer is an observant, stick-to-itive young woman: nothing escapes her."

Arturo's Island is similar to *House of Liars.* The main character, Arturo, recalls his childhood of being raised by a friend of his father. Arturo, who worships his father although he sees him only infrequently, discovers that his father has remarried. He transfers his adoration for his father to his stepmother. Eventually, Arturo leaves both the island and his past behind. Pamela Hansford Johnson deemed *Arturo's Island* "a poetic story, with all the charm the improbable has when it is told in the tone of probability." Johnson believed that the "theme of the book is remoteness; the remoteness of the island from the world of politics and war, the remoteness of the child from the parent." Granville Hicks found many similarities between *Arturo's Island* and *Huckleberry Finn.* He discovered that both books shared a penchant for "idyllic passages" but also noted, "Both boys are exposed to evil in varied and terrible forms, but Arturo is profoundly changed, whereas Huck isn't."

Frederic Morton claimed that *Arturo's Island* was "a much more successful creation" than *House of Liars.* Although he thought that both novels had "an impressionistic rather than a dramatic style, as well as a theme dealing with the fraying-away of human ties," he also found Morante's style in the earlier novel "too cluttered with tiny virtuosities."

Morante's novel *History* is the result of six years of work. It covers the lives of several people in Europe during the 1940s. "The plot is a progress of disasters," assessed Robert Alter. He added that "Morante's compassion . . . frequently spills over into pathetic excess, and her tough realism breaks down into a tediously proliferated series of disasters rigged by the novelist against her own creations." Because of the "pathetic excess," Alter decided that *History* "does not really support the weight of all its encrusted details, though if it fails as a whole, it nevertheless has a good many arresting moments." Paul Gray commented, "Morante continually makes old tricks fresh—not as a paring down of life's complexity but as short cuts into the absurdities of conflict and the urgencies of peace."

Stephen Spender felt that *History* succeeded in presenting an ideological viewpoint. "The tragedy of politics, as seen in *History*," wrote Spender, "is the inability of men to make politics human." He also noted, "The tragic end is of course inevitable, imposed by Elsa Morante's view of History and perhaps also by the nineteenth-century form she has chosen. The great virtue of her novel however is that although the reader accepts the inevitable ending, the life conveyed works as much against tragedy as for it."

Washington Post Book World contributor Thomas M. Disch decided that *Aracoeli,* Morante's subsequent novel (translated into English in 1985, the year she died), and *History* "correspond so closely in theme and treatment as to seem like two paintings of the same subject by the same hand rather than like separate novels." This tragedy concerns Aracoeli, a Spanish peasant girl who marries a wealthy Italian naval officer. He brings her back to Rome and they have a son, Emmanuele (who narrates the story), and a daughter. After the infant's death, however, the doting mother degenerates into a nymphomaniac and forces herself on numerous men, in front of her appalled seven year old son. She soon dies of a brain tumor, her husband becomes an alcoholic, and Emmanuele leads an emotionally and sexually unfulfilled life. Never accepting his mother's death, Emmanuele returns to her native village in a futile attempt to recapture the essence of his mother's lost innocence.

"Not since Celine has there been so violent a protest against life's conditions, such outrage at the thought of death, so relentless an assault on the bare physical facts of human existence," Raymond Rosenthal stated in a *New York Times Book Review* critique of *Aracoeli*. *Chicago Tribune* reviewer John Fludas was also moved by the novel. "Like its predecessors," he wrote, "it is a major creative achievement."

BIOGRAPHICAL/CRITICAL SOURCES:

BOOKS

Contemporary Literary Criticism, Gale, Volume 8, 1978, Volume 47, 1988.

PERIODICALS

Chicago Tribune, March 31, 1985.
Los Angeles Times, January 2, 1985.
Nation, October 27, 1951.
New Statesman and Nation, May 23, 1959.
New York Review of Books, April 28, 1977.
New York Times, October 7, 1951, August 16, 1959.
New York Times Book Review, April 24, 1977, January 13, 1985.
Saturday Review, October 20, 1951, August 15, 1959.
Time, May 2, 1977.
Washington Post Book World, February 10, 1985.

OBITUARIES:

PERIODICALS

Chicago Tribune, November 17, 1985.
Detroit Free Press, November 27, 1985.
Los Angeles Times, November 29, 1985.
New York Times, November 26, 1985.
Times (London), November 26, 1985.

*   *   *

MORAVIA, Alberto
See PINCHERLE, Alberto

*   *   *

MORGAN, Claire
See HIGHSMITH, (Mary) Patricia

*   *   *

MORGAN, Harriet
See MENCKEN, H(enry) L(ouis)

*   *   *

MORGAN, Robin   1941-

PERSONAL: Born January 29, 1941, in Lake Worth, Fla.; daughter of Faith Berkeley Morgan; married Kenneth Pitchford

(a poet, novelist and playwright), September 19, 1962; children: Blake Ariel Morgan-Pitchford. *Education:* Attended Columbia University. *Politics:* "Radical Feminist." *Religion:* "Wiccean Atheist."

ADDRESSES: Home—New York, N.Y. *Office*—c/o *Ms.,* 119 West 40th St., New York, N.Y. 10018. *Agent*—Georges Borchardt, Inc., 145 East 52nd St., New York, N.Y. 10022.

CAREER: Curtis Brown, Ltd., New York, N.Y., associate literary agent, 1960-62; free-lance editor, 1964-70; writer, 1970—; contributing editor, *Ms.* magazine, 1977—. International lecturer on feminism, 1970-76; guest professor at New College, Sarasota, Fla., 1972; has given poetry readings all over the United States. Member of board of directors, Women's Law Center, Feminist Self-Help Clinics, Battered Women's Refuge, Women's Institute Freedom Press, and National Alliance of Rape Crisis Centers.

MEMBER: Women's International Terrorist Conspiracy from Hell (founding member), Authors Guild, Authors League of America, Women's Anti-Defamation League, Susan B. Anthony National Memorial Association, Poetry Society of America, National Women's Political Caucus, Women Against Pornography (founding member), Feminist Writers Guild (founding member), New York Radical Women (founding member).

WRITINGS:

(Editor with Charlotte Bunch-Weeks and Joanne Cooke) *The New Women: A Motive Anthology on Women's Liberation,* Bobbs-Merrill, 1970.
(Editor) *Sisterhood Is Powerful: An Anthology of Writings from the Women's Liberation Movement,* Random House, 1970.
Monster: Poems, Random House, 1972.
Lady of the Beasts: Poems, Random House, 1976.
Going Too Far: The Personal Chronicle of a Feminist, Random House, 1977.
Depth Perception: New Poems and a Masque, Anchor/Doubleday, 1982.
The Anatomy of Freedom: Feminism, Physics, and Global Politics, Anchor/Doubleday, 1982.
(Contributor) Karen Payne, editor, *Between Ourselves: Letters between Mothers and Daughters,* Houghton, 1984.
(Contributing editor) *Sisterhood Is Global: The International Women's Movement Anthology,* Anchor, 1985.
Dry Your Smile (novel), Doubleday, 1987.
The Demon Lover: On the Sexuality of Terrorism, Norton, 1989.
Upstairs in the Garden: Selected and New Poems, Norton, 1990.

OTHER

"Our Creations Are in the First Place Ourselves" (in two cassettes), Iowa State University of Science and Technology, 1974.

Also author of "Their Own Country," a play, 1961. Works represented in many anthologies, including *No More Masks!,* edited by Howe and Bass, for Doubleday; *The Young American Writers,* edited by Kostelanetz, for Funk; and *Campfires of the Resistance,* edited by Gitlin, for Bobbs-Merrill. Contributor of articles and poems to about a hundred literary and political journals, including *Atlantic, New York Times, Hudson Review,* and *Feminist Art Journal.*

WORK IN PROGRESS: Tales of the Witches, historical fiction; a book of poems; a cycle of verse plays.

SIDELIGHTS: "One discovery of this decade has been a hitherto unplumbed, forbidden, inexpressible depth of female rage.

Robin Morgan—one of the most honestly angry women since Antigone—has rightly become a feminist heroine for her expression of it," notes Alicia Ostriker in the *Partisan Review*. Indeed, for more than twenty years, Morgan has been known as both an active leader in the international feminist movement and an accomplished poet. "I am an artist and a political being as well," Morgan once told *CA*. "My aim has been to forge these two concerns into an integrity which affirms language, art, craft, form, beauty, tragedy, and audacity with the needs and visions of women, as part of an emerging new culture which could enrich us all."

Morgan is best known for having edited "one of the first of the good anthologies of the women's movement, *Sisterhood Is Powerful* [*: An Anthology of Writings from the Women's Liberation Movement*]," notes Kathleen Wiegner in the *American Poetry Review*. Published soon after Kate Millet's *Sexual Politics*, Morgan's feminist reader has "profoundly affected the way that many of us think about women and the relations between the sexes," Paul Robinson says in a *Psychology Today* article. Reviewers concur with Jean Gardner of the *New York Times Book Review* that the collection maintains a distinctly anti-male tone; in fact, a *New Leader* contributor expressed a fear that its strident cast might eclipse "some basic truths: that women have indeed been discriminated against, their talents wasted or misused, by many institutions and many men for a very long time, and that an end to this inequality is still not in sight." Particularly hazardous are the book's dogmatic features, such as "The Drop Dead List of Books to Watch Out For," Gardner suggests. *Commonweal* contributor Kathy Mulherin sees these hazards as well, but recommends *Sisterhood Is Powerful* nonetheless because it relates "to the real conditions of women and is worth looking into."

She argues, "The worst aspects of the book can't really be helped; they are also the worst aspects of the women's liberation movement," which at that time was just beginning to address the concerns of women outside white middle-class status. Writing in the *Nation*, Muriel Haynes also defends the essays: "This is good personal journalism, some of it flecked with wit, though it is rarely amusing."

Morgan's next anthology, *Sisterhood Is Global: The International Women's Movement Anthology*, "clearly demonstrates that there is a vital international women's movement," observes *Choice* contributor S. E. Jacobs, who deems it, therefore, "one of the most important books to appear in the past decade." Reviewers such as Andrew Hacker question the validity and accuracy of certain statistics in the book; at the same time, Hacker, writing in the *New York Times Book Review*, admires the book's range: "By temperament, the editor and almost all the contributors veer toward the left. Yet, as Simone de Beauvoir points out in her article on France, if that side of the spectrum has been 'the chosen friend' of militant women, it has also been their 'worst enemy.'. . . Virtually every left-leaning regime has put women's issues on the back burner or ignored them altogether." The collection's other successes include "the reports from feminists perhaps many of us did not know existed—Senegalese, Tahitian, Nepalese—who describe working, sexual, marital, political and economic life in their respective countries," remarks Vivienne Walt in the *Nation*.

Contributors to the anthology met with Morgan in New York City in 1984 to define a strategy for the Sisterhood Is Global Institute. Members of the institute plan to "address the problems of women everywhere, including illiteracy; the care of the elderly; refugee populations and war victims; the crisis of world population; [and] the welfare, health, rights, and education of children," one participant told Marilyn Hoffman for a *Los Angeles Times* article. It also aims to translate books by women's rights activists; to investigate and impede the practice of sex tourism; and to expose religious groups they have identified "as being particularly adverse to women," Hoffman reports. Morgan, together with leaders from Greece, Portugal, New Zealand and Palestine, is one of the institute's founders.

"Morgan is a feminist, to be sure; she is also an accomplished and original poet," Jay Parini observes in a *Poetry* review. Because Morgan's political concerns are foremost, she sometimes deliberately relaxes her attention to poetic technique. As a result, says May Swenson in the *New York Times Book Review*, Morgan's first book of poems, *Monster*, offers some poems that are "strongly wrought" among others that are "polemical" and "formless." David Lehman, writing in *Poetry*, echoes this assessment, praising the poems that "attain an anger purer than prejudice, stereotype, or slogan." Particularly effective is the title poem, which records Morgan's reflections on the demands of political activism and in which she accepts the darker aspects of that role. "At her best," says Annette Niemtzow in the *Los Angeles Times*, Morgan possesses "a voice of passion, a gift of rhetoric and commitment, a verbal gesture which moves toward prophecy." Adrienne Rich, writing in the *Washington Post Book World*, values Morgan's "acute, devouring sense of her own potential, of the energy she and all women in patriarchal society expend in simply countering opposition—and of what that energy might achieve if it could be released from combat (and self-punishment) into creation."

Reviewing Morgan's second volume of poems, Wiegner comments, "*Monster* . . . dealt with female consciousness as an emerging political issue. Now, in *Lady of the Beasts* . . . she melds this consciousness with the Jungian theory of archetypes to present women in their mythic roles as mother, consort, sister, and finally, divine. . . . Her work appears to give power to women by showing the reader how, in some historic or mythic past, women held power through roles which have, in recent times, fallen into disrepute. *Lady of the Beasts* surpasses *Monster* while it contains more "engage poetry, the most difficult of . . . modes," Parini notes. In all of the poems, he goes on, "Morgan commands a wealth of technical resources," but her skill, he feels, is most evident in the poems "Voices from Six Tapestries" and "The Network of the Imaginary Mother."

Both poems are ambitious, reviewers explain. " 'Voices . . .' interprets the fifteenth-century *Lady with the Unicorn* tapestries, which hang in the Musee de Cluny in Paris, as the expression of a woman-centered pre-Christian religious system. It is also a moving, sustained love poem," Ostriker states. "The Network of the Imaginary Mother," notes Parini, is an "intricate long poem" that looks at Morgan's relationships with her mother, husband, woman lover, son, and self. Ostriker observes that this "descent into self has brought her to the sea floor where autobiography meets mythology." For example, its five sections "are laced together with horrifying lists of murdered prototypes of the women's liberation movement"—female veterinarians, herbalists, mystics, and others accused of witchcraft, Parini reports. These lists, he says, draw "taut the stitches between the concrete particulars of one life and their mythic potential." Though reviewers disagree about how well these poems serve the poet's intent, even those who see room for improvement find the poems successful on the emotional level. Ostriker, for example, comments, "I do not quarrel with Morgan's seriousness, her sense of the issues, or her conviction that poetry can make things happen. I have been touched and changed by her work, and presume that other contemporary women, and men, will be so also."

Morgan's later books place her continuing commitment to women's rights into context against a wider field of vision. *Depth Perception: New Poems and a Masque,* her third book of poems, takes her farther from "the unassimilated feminism of her first collection, *Monster,* and has gradually absorbed its ideas and concerns into an eloquent and forceful lyricism," says Parini in the *New York Times Book Review.* Essays in *Anatomy of Freedom: Feminism, Physics and Global Politics* claim a basis for human freedom in quantum physics, where particles in motion sometimes behave erratically. *Dry Your Smile,* a first novel, treats some of the same concerns in a fictional account of one woman writer's feelings as she writes her first novel. *Going Too Far: The Personal Chronicle of a Feminist* contains autobiographical nonfiction giving insight into the range of her opinions from 1962 to 1977. Critics comment on the unevenness in this selection, even though Morgan had explained in a *Ms.* "Forum" article that she meant to honestly represent her development by including some weaker pieces: "Ten years ago my poems quietly began muttering something about my personal pain as a woman—unconnected, of course, to anyone else, since I saw this merely as my own inadequacy, my own battle. I think a lot these days about the intervening decade and the startling changes it brought about, especially since the current book I'm working on [*Going Too Far*] is an assemblage of my own essays on feminism, dating back to the early 1960s: a graph of slow growth, defensiveness, struggle, painful new consciousness, and gradual affirmation. My decision to leave each piece 'as it was'—warts and all—has necessitated an editorial process redolent with a nostalgia punctuated by fits of embarrassed nausea."

Like other women writers who share her political concerns, Morgan has received "slings and arrows from all sides," she said in a later interview for the *Women's Review of Books.* She concluded, "Somehow there has to be more support for these women. In a country where the written word is not particularly esteemed, and where the message of feminism is complex and vast and not monolithic—and threatening—part of the problems that we're all of us having, well, they just come with the territory. And we have to keep fighting. There are no simple solutions. We chose this."

BIOGRAPHICAL/CRITICAL SOURCES:

BOOKS

Contemporary Literary Criticism, Volume 2, Gale, 1974.
Morgan, Robin, *Going Too Far: The Personal Chronicle of a Feminist,* Random House, 1977.
Payne, Karen, editor, *Between Ourselves: Letters between Mothers and Daughters, 1750-1982,* Houghton, 1984.

PERIODICALS

America, February 17, 1973.
American Book Review, March, 1983.
American Poetry Review, January, 1977.
Black World, August, 1971.
Choice, May, 1985.
Christian Century, March 31, 1971.
Christian Science Monitor, May 29, 1971, January 15, 1973.
Commonweal, April 2, 1971, January 15, 1973.
Library Journal, December 1, 1970.
Los Angeles Times, December 21, 1982, November 23, 1984.
Motive, March 4, 1969.
Ms., September, 1975, March, 1977.
Nation, December 14, 1970, March 2, 1985.

New Leader, December 14, 1970.
New Pages, spring, 1987.
New York Times, October 29, 1970.
New York Times Book Review, November 22, 1970, February 21, 1971, November 19, 1972, January 27, 1985, September 27, 1987.
Partisan Review, January 10, 1980.
Poetry, December, 1973, August, 1975, August, 1977.
Progressive, January, 1977, August, 1977.
Psychology Today, January, 1983.
San Francisco Review of Books, January, 1983.
Times Educational Supplement, January 10, 1987.
Times Literary Supplement, November 12, 1982.
Virginia Quarterly Review, spring, 1971.
Washington Post Book World, November 19, 1972, December 31, 1972, June 12, 1977.
Women's Review of Books, July 8, 1987.

*   *   *

MORRIS, Desmond (John) 1928-

PERSONAL: Born January 24, 1928, in Purton, Wiltshire, England; son of Harry Howe (a writer) and Dorothy Marjorie Fuller (Hunt) Morris; married Ramona Baulch (a writer), July 30, 1952; children: Jason. *Education:* Birmingham University, B.Sc., 1951; Magdalen College, Oxford, D.Phil., 1954. *Politics:* None. *Religion:* None. *Avocational interests:* Painting, archaeology.

ADDRESSES: Agent—c/o Jonathan Cape, 32 Bedford Sq., London WC1B 3EL, England.

CAREER: Oxford University, Oxford, England, researcher in animal behavior in department of zoology, 1954-56; Zoological Society of London, London, England, head of Granada TV and Film Unit, 1956-59, curator of mammals, 1959-67; Institute of Contemporary Arts, London, director, 1967-68; full-time writer, 1968—. Oxford University, research fellow at Wolfson College, 1973-81. Paintings exhibited in England, first in one-man show, London, 1950. Former host of "Zootime" television series, British Broadcasting Corp.

MEMBER: Zoological Society of London (scientific fellow).

AWARDS, HONORS: Statuette with Pedestal from World Organization for Human Potential, 1971, for *The Naked Ape* and *The Human Zoo.*

WRITINGS:

The Reproductive Behaviour of the Ten-Spined Stickleback, E. J. Brill, 1958.
(Editor with Caroline Jarvis) *The International Zoo Yearbook,* Zoological Society of London, Volume I, 1959-60, Volume II, 1960-61, Volume III, 1961-62, Volume IV, 1962-63.
Introducing Curious Creatures, Spring Books, 1961.
The Biology of Art: A Study of the Picture-Making Behaviour of the Great Apes and Its Relationship to Human Art, Knopf, 1962.
(With wife, Ramona Morris) *Men and Snakes,* McGraw, 1965.
The Mammals: A Guide to the Living Species, Harper, 1965.
(With R. Morris) *Men and Apes,* McGraw, 1966.
(With R. Morris) *Men and Pandas,* Hutchinson, 1966, McGraw, 1967, revised edition published as *The Giant Panda,* Penguin, 1981.
(Editor) *Primate Ethology,* Aldine, 1967.
The Naked Ape: A Zoologist's Study of the Human Animal (Book-of-the-Month Club selection), Cape, 1967, McGraw,

1968, revised edition published as *The Illustrated Naked Ape,* Cape, 1986.

The Human Zoo (Book-of-the-Month Club selection), McGraw, 1969.

Patterns of Reproductive Behaviour: Collected Papers (all previously published in journals), Cape, 1970, McGraw, 1971.

Intimate Behavior, Cape, 1971, Random House, 1972.

Manwatching: A Field Guide to Human Behavior, Abrams, 1977.

(With Peter Collett, Peter Marsh, and Marie O'Shaughnessy) *Gestures: Their Origins and Distributions,* Stein & Day, 1979.

Animal Days (Literary Guild alternate selection), Perigord Press, 1979.

The Soccer Tribe, Cape, 1981.

Inrock (fiction), Cape, 1983.

The Book of Ages, Viking, 1983.

The Art of Ancient Cyprus, Phaidon, 1985.

Bodywatching: A Field Guide to the Human Species, Cape, 1985.

Dogwatching, Cape, 1986, Crown, 1987.

Catwatching, Crown, 1987.

The Secret Surrealist: The Paintings of Desmond Morris, Salem House, 1987.

Catlore, Crown, 1988.

(With the Roadshow Team) *The Animals Roadshow,* Cape, 1988.

Horsewatching, Crown, 1988.

Animalwatching: A New Guide to the Animal World, Crown, 1990.

FOR CHILDREN

The Story of Congo, Batsford, 1958.

Apes and Monkeys, Bodley Head, 1964, McGraw, 1965.

The Big Cats, McGraw, 1965.

Zoo Time, Hart-Davis, 1966.

OTHER

Author of *The Human Nestbuilders,* 1988. Contributor to journals, including *Behavior, British Birds, New Scientist,* and *Zoo Life.*

MEDIA ADAPTATIONS: The Naked Ape was filmed by Universal and released in 1973.

WORK IN PROGRESS: Research in human ethology; planning another exhibit of his paintings.

SIDELIGHTS: Desmond Morris came to public attention as the host of "Zootime," a British Broadcasting Corporation television series featuring the animals of the London Zoo, and as the author of *The Naked Ape,* in which he examines man from a zoologist's perspective. Morris's fascination with animals began in early childhood, when he spent hours at a time in close observation of worms and beetles near his home. As a student, he was drawn to the science of ethology—the study of animals in the wild. His teachers were some of the founders of this young science, including Konrad Lorenz and Niko Tinbergen. Morris's research in this discipline uncovered such phenomena as homosexuality among the ten-spined stickleback fish and the "divorce" of mated pairs of zebra finches.

His work won him the respect of his peers, but when the opportunity came to trade his academic career for a stint as a television-show host, Morris accepted. "Zootime" was shown live, and its animal stars were known for their unpredictable—often embarrassing—antics. Morris's own popularity was built largely upon his deft, humorous handling of his misbehaving costars. In his book *Animal Days,* Morris explains the appeal that a public

role holds for him. He was a very shy child and admits that upon entering boarding school, "I often overcompensated and became almost painfully extroverted, as if determined to obliterate my inner relish for privacy. I became a joker, an entertainer. If I am honest, it is a struggle I have never fully resolved, the 'ham' and the academic in me doing battle with one another, with first one, then the other getting the upper hand." When the program ended, Morris resumed academic respectability by becoming the curator of mammals at the London Zoo and holding that post for eight years. He resigned when publication of *The Naked Ape* made him wealthy.

In *The Naked Ape,* Morris brings the methods of observation he learned as an ethologist to bear upon his fellow man. He states that man is merely one of many variations within the ape family. Proceeding from this premise, the author attempts to explain man's complex behavior by relating it to that of the lesser apes. The result proved fascinating to the general public; the book quickly became a best-seller. Many scientists, however, particularly anthropologists (whose domain is specifically the study of man), reserve harsh criticism for Morris and *The Naked Ape.*

Morton Fried, for example, believes that Morris is unqualified to write a book on human behavior. Discussing *The Naked Ape* in *Saturday Review,* Fried says: "This is the kind of book that makes an anthropologist—at least *this* anthropologist—run into a colleague's office crying, with hilarity or incredulity or at times even rage, 'Listen to this!' Although the publisher would like to believe this evidences the provocative and controversial nature of *The Naked Ape,* none of these reactions flatters the author, zoologist Desmond Morris, who has simply given us a naive and scientifically reactionary book. . . . Leaving to his zoological peers the task of criticizing the author's handling of the materials in his own discipline, I must comment on Morris's anthropology. Clearly, he never took even a freshman course in the subject, or he flunked it."

J. Z. Young, contributor to the *New York Review of Books,* suggests that Morris has deliberately emphasized the most provocative aspects of his subject in order to ensure his book's popularity. He points out that while more than one-fourth of *The Naked Ape* describes man's sexual habits, there is no mention whatsoever of language or learning. "It would be easy to criticize this book on many points of style, taste, and fact," notes Young. "The author tries to disarm with his claim that he is a zoologist, man is an animal and therefore 'fair game for my pen.' But it is not fair for any biologist to describe only those aspects of an animal that interest him and titillate his readers, especially if the ones omitted are the essential biological foundations of the success of the species."

Other reviewers praise Morris for making scientific material accessible to a wide audience. Peter Williams applauds *The Naked Ape* in *Natural History* for its "brilliant insights" and a *Times Literary Supplement* critic calls it "not only a thoughtful and stimulating book, but also an extremely interesting one." *The Naked Ape* was eventually published in twenty-three countries and sold over eight million copies. Morris continued its theme in several later works.

Publication of *Animal Days* marked a change in tone. "This time, Morris doesn't try to shock or titillate with . . . theories," notes Peter Gwynne of *Newsweek.* "[*Animal Days*] is a straightforward, unpretentious memoir of his encounters with animals and fellow scientists. And it is a delightful book." Writing in the *New York Times,* Christopher Lehmann-Haupt praises the book for its "gallery of arresting portraits of Mr. Morris's fellow animal behaviorists—the first great generation of them, really."

And a *New York Times Book Review* critic describes *Animal Days* as "a visit with an engaging raconteur who has spent his life in a fascinating field."

Morris's other books encompass a variety of subjects, from art to soccer. His wide range of interests prompts Gwynne to write of him, "Zoologist Desmond Morris is the epitome of the scholar with interests too lively to hide under an academic bushel." Of himself, Morris told William Overend of the *Los Angeles Times:* "I describe myself as a senile 14-year-old. . . . I get more foolish and frivolous each year. I confess to cultivating immaturity. I don't aspire to maturity because it's so often connected with rigid thought. . . . I really don't want to ever take things too seriously, least of all myself."

BIOGRAPHICAL/CRITICAL SOURCES:

BOOKS

Morris, Desmond, *Animal Days,* Perigord Press, 1979.

PERIODICALS

Best Sellers, December 15, 1969.
Book World, October 12, 1969, February 27, 1972.
Chicago Tribune, January 9, 1986.
Los Angeles Times, March 9, 1984, May 21, 1984.
Los Angeles Times Book Review, June 24, 1979, May 31, 1987.
Natural History, February, 1968, January, 1970.
Newsweek, August 4, 1980.
New York Review of Books, March 14, 1968.
New York Times, July 18, 1980.
New York Times Book Review, February 4, 1968, November 30, 1969, March 5, 1972, November 13, 1977, December 30, 1979, August 10, 1980.
Saturday Review, February 17, 1968, March 4, 1972, July, 1980.
Spectator, October 16, 1971, November 5, 1977.
Time, January 26, 1968, March 13, 1972, January 16, 1978, December 9, 1985.
Times Literary Supplement, November 9, 1967, October 30, 1969, December 7, 1979.
Washington Post, December 8, 1981, March 20, 1984.
Washington Post Book World, August 12, 1979.
Yale Review, summer, 1968.

*   *   *

MORRIS, James (Humphrey)
See MORRIS, Jan

*   *   *

MORRIS, Jan 1926-
(James [Humphrey] Morris)

PERSONAL: Formerly James Humphrey Morris; name changed to Jan Morris after sex change, 1972; born October 2, 1926, in Clevedon, Somerset, England; child of Walter and Enid (Payne) Morris; wife's name, Elizabeth (divorced); five children. *Education:* Christ Church, Oxford, B.A. (second class honors), 1951, M.A., 1961.

ADDRESSES: Home—Trefan Morys, Llanystumdwy, Gwynedd, Wales.

CAREER: Western Daily Press, Bristol, England, member of editorial staff, 1944; Arab News Agency, Cairo, Egypt, member of editorial staff, 1947-48; *Times,* London, England, member of editorial staff, 1951-56, and special correspondent in Egypt, Scandinavia, the Netherlands, India, and the United States; *Guardian,* Manchester, England, member of editorial staff, 1956-61; freelance writer, 1961—. *Military service:* British Army, Ninth Lancers, 1943-47; became lieutenant.

MEMBER: Royal Society of Literature (fellow).

AWARDS, HONORS: Commonwealth Fund fellow, 1953; Cafe Royal Prize, 1957, for *Coast to Coast;* George Polk Memorial Award, 1960; Heinemann Award, Royal Society of Literature, 1961, for *Venice.*

WRITINGS:

UNDER NAME JAMES MORRIS

As I Saw the U.S.A., Pantheon, 1956 (published in England as *Coast to Coast,* Faber, 1956, 2nd edition, 1962).
Islam Inflamed: A Middle East Picture, Pantheon, 1957 (published in England as *The Market of Seleukia,* Faber, 1957).
Sultan in Oman: Venture into the Middle East, Pantheon, 1957.
Coronation Everest, Dutton, 1958.
South African Winter, Pantheon, 1958.
The Hashemite Kings, Pantheon, 1959.
The World of Venice, Pantheon, 1960, revised edition, 1974 (published in England as *Venice,* Faber, 1960, revised edition, 1974).
The Upstairs Donkey, and Other Stolen Stories (juvenile), Pantheon, 1961.
South America, Manchester Guardian and Evening News Ltd., 1961.
The Road to Huddersfield: A Journey to Five Continents (Book-of-the-Month Club selection), Pantheon, 1963 (published in England as *The World Bank: A Prospect,* Faber, 1963).
Cities, Faber, 1963, Harcourt, 1964.
The Outriders: A Liberal View of Britain, Faber, 1963.
The Presence of Spain, Harcourt, 1964, published as *Spain,* Faber, 1970.
Oxford, Harcourt, 1965, 3rd edition, Oxford University Press, 1988.
Pax Britannica: The Climax of an Empire (first book of trilogy), Harcourt, 1968.
The Great Port: A Passage through New York, Harcourt, 1969, reprinted, Oxford University Press, 1985.
(Author of introduction) Roger Wood, *Persia,* Thames & Hudson, 1969, Universe Books, 1970.
Places, Faber, 1972, Harcourt, 1973.
Heaven's Command: An Imperial Progress (second book of trilogy), Harcourt, 1973.
Farewell the Trumpets: An Imperial Retreat (third book of trilogy), Harcourt, 1978.

UNDER NAME JAN MORRIS

Conundrum (autobiography), Harcourt, 1974.
Travels, Harcourt, 1976.
(Editor) *The Oxford Book of Oxford,* Oxford University Press, 1978.
Destinations: Essays from Rolling Stone, Oxford University Press, 1980.
(Compiler) *Wales,* Oxford University Press, 1982.
Stones of Empire: The Buildings of the Raj, Oxford University Press, 1984.
Among the Cities, Oxford University Press, 1985.
Journeys, Oxford University Press, 1985.
Last Letters from Hav: Notes from a Lost City (novel), Random House, 1985.
The Matter of Wales: Epic Views of a Small Country, Oxford University Press, 1985.

Scotland: The Place of Journeys, Crown, 1986.

(With others) *Architecture of the British Empire,* Vendome, 1986.

Manhattan, '45, Oxford University Press, 1987.

Hong Kong, Random House, 1988 (published in England as *Hong Kong: Xianggang,* Viking, 1988).

(Author of introduction) John Ruskin, *The Stones of Venice,* Moyer Bell Limited, 1989.

Pleasures of a Tangled Life (autobiography), Random House, 1989.

SIDELIGHTS: A critically acclaimed journalist and travel essayist, Jan Morris has written numerous books on travels and adventures around the world. Formerly known as leading British journalist James Morris—who changed genders in a sex-change operation—Jan Morris "is a traveler whose journeys have been both physical and philosophical, a writer who has written of the clash of armies and the history of empires, a former soldier and foreign correspondent," writes Lynn Darling in the *Washington Post.* As a reporter for the London *Times* in the 1950s, Morris gained fame for covering the Mt. Everest climbing expedition of Sir Edmund Hillary. From 22,000 feet up the mountain and through an ingeniously organized communications system, Morris "scooped the world with the news of Hillary's . . . triumph," reports John Richardson. Morris later recounted the landmark event in the 1958 book *Coronation Everest.* Following her career as a journalist, Morris traveled around the world, reporting on wars and rebellions, while writing numerous history and travel books.

Among Morris's most acclaimed works are her travel accounts, which are praised for their original and readable look at different places and cultures around the world. "Her travel books are oddly reassuring, showing us that there are more ways of experiencing cultures than most of us supposed," writes Anatole Broyard in the *New York Times.* "In her wanderlust, she is like a lover looking for consummation—and she finds it in the most unlikely places." Broyard also remarks that *Destinations: Essays from Rolling Stone,* "is a book about great cities, their moods, their manners and their response to time. Jan Morris is a connoisseur of cities, someone who approaches them, as almost none of their inhabitants do, as places simply to *be.* She submits herself to cities and then tells us what they do to her, say to her."

In addition to her travel books, Morris has written about her personal history. In the autobiographical *Conundrum,* she relates, "I was 3 or perhaps 4 years old when I realized that I had been born into the wrong body, and should really be a girl." In 1964, Morris began the transformation into the female Jan Morris by taking hormone pills; in 1972, the process was completed through surgery. A *Newsweek* writer calls *Conundrum* "certainly the best first-hand account ever written by a traveler across the boundaries of sex. That journey is perhaps the ultimate adventure for a human being, but although it has been the subject of myth and speculation since ancient times, it is an authentically modern experience." Regarding being a transsexual, Morris told Lorraine Kisly: "No one has ever been able to convince a real transsexual that his convictions about his true nature were wrong. No doctor or scientist can say where the conviction comes from, and for me it is a spiritual question, a matter of my soul, much deeper and broader than sexual preference or mode." The *Newsweek* writer comments that "Morris can offer no real answer to the central mystery; neither she nor the scientists of this era can explain with any certainty why a transsexual's mind and body are at odds with each other. What Jan Morris does offer, through her life and her work, is a window on the wondrous possibilities of humankind." Morris followed *Conundrum*

with a second autobiographical book, *Pleasures of a Tangled Life,* which, as William French remarks in the Toronto *Globe and Mail,* "emphasiz[es] the happy side of her life and the sources of her pleasures." French calls the book "a relaxed, unstructured series of reminiscences."

BIOGRAPHICAL/CRITICAL SOURCES:

BOOKS

Morris, Jan, *Conundrum,* Harcourt, 1974.
Morris, Jan, *Pleasures of a Tangled Life,* Random House, 1989.

PERIODICALS

Book World, January 12, 1969.
Chicago Tribune, December 16, 1988, January 22, 1989.
Christian Science Monitor, October 13, 1959.
Globe and Mail (Toronto), October 20, 1984, November 25, 1989.
Harper's, August, 1974.
Los Angeles Times, July 18, 1984, June 17, 1985.
Los Angeles Times Book Review, January 15, 1989.
Manchester Guardian, August 19, 1960.
New Statesman, December 5, 1959, October 25, 1968.
Newsweek, August 5, 1963, April 8, 1974.
New York Review of Books, May 2, 1974.
New York Times, May 17, 1980, May 31, 1984, March 1, 1985, March 19, 1987, May 22, 1987, January 3, 1989.
New York Times Book Review, April 14, 1974, November 19, 1978, January 29, 1989, November 12, 1989.
New York Times Magazine, March 17, 1974.
Saturday Evening Post, July 3, 1965.
Time, April 3, 1987.
Times (London), August 14, 1980, November 17, 1983, November 29, 1984, October 10, 1985, October 22, 1988.
Times Literary Supplement, October 7-13, 1988, December 8-14, 1989.
Tribune Books (Chicago), October 29, 1989.
Washington Post, July 3, 1980, January 4, 1987, March 25, 1987.
Washington Post Book World, October 15, 1989.

*   *   *

MORRIS, John
  See HEARNE, John (Edgar Caulwell)

*   *   *

MORRIS, Julian
  See WEST, Morris L(anglo)

*   *   *

MORRIS, Wright   1910-

PERSONAL: Born January 6, 1910, in Central City, Neb.; son of William Henry and Ethel Grace (Osborn) Morris; married Mary Ellen Finfrock, December 21, 1934 (divorced, 1961); married Josephine Mary Kantor, 1961. *Education:* Attended Crane College, 1929, and Pomona College, 1930-33.

ADDRESSES: Home—341 Laurel Way, Mill Valley, Calif. 94941.

CAREER: Writer. Lecturer at Haverford College, Princeton University, Sarah Lawrence College, Swarthmore College, University of Utah, and other institutions; California State University, San Francisco, professor, 1962-75.

MEMBER: National Institute of Arts and Letters, Modern Language Association of America (honorary fellow, 1975).

AWARDS, HONORS: Guggenheim fellowships in photography, 1942 and 1946, and in literature, 1954; National Book Award, 1957, for *The Field of Vision;* National Institute Grant in literature, 1960; honorary degrees from Westminster College and University of Nebraska, 1968, and from Pomona College, 1973; National Book Awards fiction judge, 1969; Distinguished Achievement Award, Western Literature Association, 1979; *Library Journal* and the American Library Association both named *Plains Song* a notable book, 1980; American Book Award, 1981, for *Plains Song;* Robert Kirsch Award, *Los Angeles Times,* 1981, for body of work; Common Wealth Award, Modern Language Association of America, 1982, for distinguished service in literature; Whiting Writers Award, the Whiting Foundation, 1985; Senior Fellowship, National Endowment for the Humanities, 1976, and National Endowment for the Arts, 1986.

WRITINGS:

NOVELS

My Uncle Dudley, Harcourt, 1942, reprinted, Greenwood Press, 1970.
The Man Who Was There, Scribner, 1945, reprinted, University of Nebraska Press, 1977.
The Home Place (fiction and photographs), Scribner, 1948, reprinted, University of Nebraska Press, 1968.
The World in the Attic, Scribner, 1949, reprinted, University of Nebraska Press, 1971.
Man and Boy, Knopf, 1951, reprinted, University of Nebraska Press, 1974.
The Works of Love (also see below), Knopf, 1952, reprinted, University of Nebraska Press, 1972.
The Deep Sleep, Scribner, 1953, reprinted, University of Nebraska Press, 1975.
The Huge Season: A Novel, Viking, 1954, reprinted, University of Nebraska Press, 1975.
The Field of Vision (also see below), Harcourt, 1956, reprinted, University of Nebraska Press, 1974.
Love among the Cannibals, Harcourt, 1957, reprinted, University of Nebraska Press, 1977.
Ceremony in Lone Tree, Atheneum, 1960.
What a Way to Go, Atheneum, 1962, reprinted, University of Nebraska Press, 1979.
Cause for Wonder, Atheneum, 1963, reprinted, University of Nebraska Press, 1978.
One Day, Atheneum, 1965.
In Orbit, New American Library, 1969.
Fire Sermon, Harper, 1971.
War Games, Black Sparrow Press, 1972.
A Life, Harper, 1973.
The Fork River Space Project: A Novel, Harper, 1977.
Plains Song: For Female Voices, Harper, 1980.

SHORT STORIES

Green Grass, Blue Sky, White House, Black Sparrow Press, 1970.
Here Is Einbaum, Black Sparrow Press, 1973.
The Cat's Meow, Black Sparrow Press, 1975.
Real Losses, Imaginary Gains, Harper, 1976.
Collected Stories, 1948-1986, Harper, 1986.

AUTOBIOGRAPHY

Will's Boy: A Memoir, Harper, 1981.
Solo: An American Dreamer in Europe, 1933-34, Harper, 1983.
The Cloak of Light: Writing My Life, Harper, 1985.

ESSAYS

(Contributor) Granville Hicks, editor, *The Living Novel: A Symposium,* Macmillan, 1957.
New World Writing, Volume XIII, New American Library, 1958.
The Territory Ahead, Harcourt, 1958, reissued as *The Territory Ahead: Critical Interpretations in American Literature,* Atheneum, 1963, reprinted, University of Nebraska Press, 1978.
(Contributor) A. Walton Litz, editor, *Modern American Fiction: Essays in Criticism,* Oxford University Press, 1963.
(Author of afterword) Richard H. Dana, *Two Years before the Mast,* New American Library, 1964.
(Author of introduction) Sherwood Anderson, *Windy McPherson's Son,* University of Chicago Press, 1965.
(Contributor) James E. Miller and Paul D. Herring, editors, *Arts and the Public,* University of Chicago Press, 1967.
A Bill of Rites, A Bill of Wrongs, A Bill of Goods, New American Library, 1968, reprinted, University of Nebraska Press, 1980.
(Contributor) Frank N. Magill, *The Contemporary Literary Scene, 1973,* Salem Press, 1974.
About Fiction: Reverent Reflections on the Nature of Fiction with Irreverent Observations on Writers, Readers, and Other Abuses, Harper, 1975.
Conversations with Wright Morris: Critical Views and Responses, edited and with introduction by Robert E. Knoll, University of Nebraska Press, 1977.
Earthly Delights, Unearthly Adornments: American Writers as Image Makers, Harper, 1978.

PHOTO TEXTS

(Contributor) James Laughlin, editor, *New Directions in Prose and Poetry,* New Directions Press, 1940.
(Contributor) Laughlin, editor, *New Directions in Prose and Poetry, 1941,* New Directions Press, 1941.
The Inhabitants (reminiscences), Scribner, 1946, 2nd edition, Da Capo, 1972.
(Contributor) *Spearhead: Ten Years of Experimental Writing in America,* New Directions Press, 1947.
God's Country and My People (reminiscences), Harper, 1968, reprinted, University of Nebraska Press, 1981.
Love Affair—A Venetian Journal, Harper, 1972.
Photographs and Words, edited and with introduction by James Alinder, Friends of Photography, in association with Publications, 1982.

OTHER

(Editor) *The Mississippi River Reader,* Doubleday-Anchor, 1962.
(Editor and author of foreword) Samuel L. Clemens, *The Tragedy of Puddn'head Wilson,* New American Library, 1964.
(Contributor) Thomas McCormack, editor, *Afterwords: Novelists on Their Novels,* Harper, 1969.
Wright Morris: A Reader (novels, short stories, and criticism; includes *The Works of Love* and *The Field of Vision*), with introduction by Granville Hicks, Harper, 1970.
(Contributor) Jonathan Baumbach, editor, *Writers as Teachers/ Teachers as Writers,* Holt, 1970.
(With an introduction by Norman A. Geske) *Wright Morris: Structures and Artifacts, Photographs 1933-54,* Sheldon Memorial Art Gallery, University of Nebraska, 1975.
The Wright Morris Portfolio, Witkin-Berley, 1981.
Picture America, with photographs by Alinder and an introduction by Ansel Adams, Little, Brown, 1982.

Time Pieces: The Photographs and Words of Wright Morris, March 16-May 15, 1983, The Corcoran Gallery of Art, Washington, D.C., The Gallery, 1983.

Contributor to *Harper's Bazaar, New York Times Magazine, Atlantic, Vogue, Esquire,* and other publications.

SIDELIGHTS: Wright Morris is often referred to as one of America's finest and most neglected living writers. Born near the geographical center of the nation, Morris has explored and defined what it means to be American in more than forty works of fiction, photography, and criticism since 1942. Though these works have received "the general indifference of the reading public," as Jonathan Yardley notes in the *Washington Post Book World,* Morris has garnered substantial critical acclaim and a number of coveted awards, not only for individual novels such as *The Field of Vision* and *Plains Song: For Female Voices,* but also for his life's work. *New York Times Book Review* contributor Edward Abbey names Morris a "writer's writer" who has also won an honor "more important than such prizes, the high esteem of his fellow authors here and abroad."

Although Morris's critical reputation was slow to develop, as Michael Adams observes in the *Dictionary of Literary Biography: American Novelists since World War II,* it is founded on thirty years of praise. In 1957, looking back on the nine novels Morris had then published, *New York Times* reviewer John W. Aldridge wrote, "It would in fact be hard to call to mind another novelist of Mr. Morris's generation who has been able to sustain through such a large body of work so clear a vision of the essence of the American experience, and to project it over and over again without tricks, without cheating and without once being tempted to afford his readers the kind of easy comfort that pays off in popular reputation." In the 1960s, Walter Allen named Morris "one of the liveliest talents in the American novel today" in *The Modern Novel in Britain and the United States,* and Leslie Fiedler wrote in *Love and Death in the American Novel* that Morris "expresses a kind of hopelessly American anti-Americanism unparalleled since Mark Twain." Six novels, a second major book award, and fifteen years later, Bruce Cook, a contributor to the *Detroit News,* wrote of Morris, "Here is a novelist who cannot write badly, whose most inconsequential work . . . is so far beyond the range of most of today's younger writers that to them it might as well be 'Moby Dick.' "

"Few American novelists have written so well in the late stages of their careers, and few have been so American in their work," Adams maintains. The Nebraska landscape is a major presence in the novels; though some are set in Mexico and Europe, the plains appear through the memories and manners of characters who have left Nebraska but remain haunted or marked by the plains experience. In his introduction to *Wright Morris: A Reader,* Granville Hicks quotes an explanation Morris had made in 1955: "I am not a regional writer, but the characteristics of this region have conditioned what I see, what I look for, and what I find in the world to write about." The novels recreate the frontier spirit and explore how ordinary people respond to its death—some with nostalgia, some with relief. As Leon Howard notes in *Wright Morris,* "the relationship between the identifiable past and the unknown future" has been Morris's "constant concern."

"The pioneer roots Morris uncovers are his own," Robert Dahlin remarks in *Publishers Weekly.* Morris was born in Central City, Nebraska, a town once known as Lone Tree, in 1910. Six days later, his mother died, leaving him "half an orphan" in the custody of his father, Will Morris. Will's efforts to find a new mother for Morris and to make a fortune in the egg business were rewarded with only intermittent success. Between 1925 and 1930, Morris worked a hard-scrabble farm in Texas with his uncle, crossed the country in several run-down cars, and lived in Chicago with his father, whose ill-fated enterprises encouraged Morris's early financial and emotional independence. In time, Morris came to see these "real losses" as "imaginary gains," since they had propelled him into his long and productive career. "Before coming of age, . . . " Morris writes in *The Territory Ahead,* "I had led, or rather been led by, half a dozen separate lives. Each life had its own scene, its own milieu; it frequently appeared to have its own beginning and ending, the only connecting tissue being the narrow thread of my *self.* I had been *there,* but that, indeed, explained nothing." Thereby challenged to create coherence from an oversupply of fragmented experiences, Morris began writing. The author tells Dahlin, "My raw material was the first thirty years of my life, and had to learn to organize it in fictional terms. That fact explains the number, the very nature of my books."

In 1933 Morris went to Europe "with a minor local infection of the writer's virus which I took along . . . for a period of incubation," he discloses in the *New York Times Book Review.* Though he returned "full of the adventures writers leave home in search of," the subject of his early writings was the boyhood he had "lost track of " in Chicago: "As a writer, I found I had access to it, and began to repossess it in short prose fragments." In *My Uncle Dudley,* published in 1942, a young boy and his uncle make a cross-country journey reminiscent of Morris's trips with his father. The hero of the next novel, a painter, is like Morris in that he tries to understand and identify with America, as Chester E. Eisinger, writing in *Fiction of the Forties,* sees it. In *The Man Who Was There,* Agee Ward leaves America to gain perspective and returns with a keen vision for the barrenness of life on the plains and "the almost conscious yearning toward the East which signalizes the bankruptcy of the myth of the frontier," Eisinger observes. As Ward rediscovers Nebraska and puts it behind him by coming to understand it, Eisinger believes the character accomplishes "what Morris himself had to do, and continues to do in subsequent books."

In the next two novels, *The Home Place* and *The World in the Attic,* Clyde Muncy, a son of the plains who is tired of living in New York, returns to his childhood home to find "that the frontier spirit has virtually vanished," Adams reports. "The dream of the frontier has collided with the brave new world of Sears, Roebuck. The positive, life-giving aspects of the past have not been retained. All that remains is nausea." Morris discovers that pursuit of the past is self-defeating, Marcus Klein, the author of *After Alienation: American Novels in Mid-Century,* believes: "Characters in the subsequent novels will be impaled on a moment of the past. They will squirm, when they are aware, to be free of it, to find a connection with the immediate present."

This challenge confronts the characters in Morris's first National Book Award winner, *The Field of Vision.* Five people who share the same Nebraska past assemble to witness a bullfight in Mexico, but each one views the event through a field of vision that has been narrowed by some event in his or her past. Boyd, the main character, is reminded of his attempt to walk on water—a failure that has limited his vision ever since; the elder Scanlon recalls the violence he witnessed when Nebraska was still truly a frontier; and Lois, his daughter, remembers how Boyd had once aggressively kissed her—an event that had hastened her marriage to the more passive Walter McKee, and had rendered it unsatisfying by comparison. The characters narrate the bullfight and the associations it calls up from inside them in their own voices, revealing, according to Adams, that they are "trapped in the past, retarded by their conceptions of what life offered them and how they turned it down." Boyd finds his connection with the present by the end of the novel, but the other characters are not liberated from the past until they reassemble in the novel *Ceremony in Lone Tree* to celebrate Scanlon's ninetieth birthday.

At about this time in his career, as Leon Howard notes in *Wright Morris,* it was appropriate that Morris should write *The Territory Ahead,* "a book of criticism explicitly concerned with the uses and abuses of the past in light of the immediate present." In his introduction to *Wright Morris: A Reader,* Granville Hicks identifies Morris's thesis in the phrase, "nostalgia has been the curse of American literature." With this assertion, according to Hicks, Morris expresses rebellion against his own enslavement to the past. *The Territory Ahead* marks a major turning point for Morris; though characters from previous novels and the familiar Nebraska setting are to reappear in later works, it will be to transcend nostalgia and to "make imaginative use of the past in the present." Morris confirms this estimate when he tells Dahlin, "For me it's not an effort to go back. I don't want to be back there. My effort is to possess what has escaped, to salvage from time that over which time has triumphed."

In another interview for *Accent* magazine, Morris tells Sam Bleufarb that, over the space of eight novels, the past which had dominated at first was called into question, and then "was compelled to recede." The novels that follow *The Territory Ahead* confront the immediate present. In *Love among the Cannibals,* the story of the romantic adventures of two Hollywood songwriters in Acapulco, the past is not mentioned at all. In *In Orbit,* a small Indiana town is struck by two disasters: a tornado and a delinquent draft-dodger, Jubal Gainer. Gainer rides into town on a stolen motorcycle, attempts to rape a half-witted woman, and stabs a store owner—not intentionally, Adams observes, but because "people just keep getting in his way." Gainer is aimless and prone to acts of spontaneous violence. According to Howard, Gainer embodies the role of the contemporary American artist, while Adams believes that "Gainer *is* the immediate present."

"But Morris is still not finished with the past," Adams notes. His objective is not to escape the past, but to gain control over it, David Madden explains in the *New Republic.* In *Fire Sermon,* the past gives way to the present in several forms: a young orphan boy transfers his allegiance from his aged uncle to a hippie couple they have met on the road, and a house full of artifacts bequeathed to the old man accidentally burns to the ground. Morris "sheds no tears" when the house is destroyed, and Uncle Floyd shows no "real grief, though the holocaust completes his alienation by wiping out his last link with the past," which proves, as Hicks concludes in the *New York Times Book Review,* that Morris "has said good-bye to nostalgia." A similar demolition befalls the homestead of Cora Atkins in *Plains Song: For Female Voices,* Morris's twenty-first novel and second major book award winner.

The core of *Plains Song* "is its tactful rendering of the emotional history of several women, but woven in with this is the social history of a particular part of the country," Larry McMurtry observes in the *New York Times Book Review.* Cora Atkins represents the first of four generations of Nebraska women who appear in the book. Brought to the plains after marrying a homesteader who had come to Ohio for supplies, Cora finds sex such a horror that she bites her hand through to the bone on her wedding night. A tireless worker, satisfied to make gradual improvements on the farm that becomes her domain, Cora feels guilty when she feels content. Her daughter Madge is fond of sex,

but embarrassed to admit it; like Cora, she sees no other role for herself beyond wife and mother. In contrast, Sharon Rose, Madge's cousin who was raised as her sister, rejects life on the plains and traditional roles. Sharon Rose finds a career in Chicago as a music teacher and an independence so complete that it borders on isolation, which she comes to recognize is her link to Cora. When Cora dies and the farmhouse is razed, Madge's feminist daughters celebrate their freedom from the past; but Sharon Rose, who has returned for Cora's funeral, is first troubled by nostalgia, then becomes reconciled to her past and accepts her future. As Lynne Waldeland writes in *Critique,* "[Sharon Rose] continues to feel the pull of the lives, especially Cora's, spent and spilled on the Plains and finally understands and values the dignity if not the sacrifice implicit in those lives. *Plains Song* is a great hymn to the pioneer spirit and particularly to women in whom, Morris believes, that spirit lives most powerfully."

Since winning the American Book Award for *Plains Song* in 1981, Morris has garnered admiration for a more direct treatment of his past. *Will's Boy: A Memoir* contains memories from the first nineteen years of his life, interspersed with sections from the novels which had drawn heavily on those raw materials. The second memoir, *Solo: An American Dreamer in Europe, 1933-34,* follows the fledgling writer through the bizarre experiences and disillusionments of his *Wanderjahr.* In *A Cloak of Light: Writing My Life,* Morris covers the development of his writing career beginning with his return from Europe. In this third memoir, Morris "concentrates on the essential self-shaping of his life, with quotations from his many novels and essays serving as commentary on the personal history," Abbey notes in the *New York Times Book Review.* James Idema of the *Chicago Tribune* believes "it is the clear way [Morris] observes the interplay between the events of his long life and the art that produced the books and stories that makes these memoirs such an impressive achievement."

"No writer in America is more honored and less read than Wright Morris," Stephen Goodwin declares in the *Washington Post Book World.* In 1982, Morris received the Common Wealth Award for distinguished service in literature; in 1985, he won the Whiting Writers Award, and in 1986, a senior fellowship from the National Endowment for the Arts—"nearly every award worth having," according to Goodwin. But Morris's characters may be too ordinary to attract readers, Goodwin speculates. Other critics point to a prejudice similar to the attitude H. L. Mencken had expressed about another plains writer, Willa Cather: "I don't care how well she writes, I don't give a damn what happens in Nebraska." Morris gives his own explanation to Edwin McDowell in the *New York Times:* "I'm a spokesman for people who don't want to be spoken for and who don't particularly want to read about themselves."

Adams reports in the *Dictionary of Literary Biography Yearbook: 1981* that Morris has not found the neglect regrettable; instead, he "believes that his lack of fame keeps him from being distracted from his aesthetic objectives and helps maintain the consistent quality of his work, a quality which must eventually be recognized more widely." Though writing has not made Morris wealthy, he tells McDowell, "writing has made me rich—not in money, but in a couple of hundred characters out there, whose pursuits and anguish and triumphs I've shared. I am unspeakably grateful at the life I have come to lead." As Susan Fromberg Schaeffer sees it, those who never read Morris may have more cause for regret. "He is a writer of truly astonishing beauty and power," she writes in the *Chicago Tribune Book World.* Schaeffer concludes, "Not to know Wright Morris is not to know the silent, often lovely, stretches of ourselves. In these trackless, silent landscapes of the mind, we could have no better guide than Wright Morris. He may be the only guide we have."

BIOGRAPHICAL/CRITICAL SOURCES:

BOOKS

Allen, Walter, *The Modern Novel in Britain and the United States,* Dutton, 1964.

Baumbach, Jonathan, *The Landscape of Nightmare: Studies in the Contemporary American Novel,* New York University Press, 1965.

Contemporary Literary Criticism, Gale, Volume I, 1973, Volume III, 1975, Volume VII, 1977, Volume XVIII, 1981, Volume XXXVII, 1986.

Crump, G. B., *The Novels of Wright Morris: A Critical Interpretation,* University of Nebraska Press, 1978.

Dictionary of Literary Biography, Volume II: *American Novelists since World War II,* Gale, 1978.

Dictionary of Literary Biography Yearbook: 1981, Gale, 1982.

Eisinger, Chester E., *Fiction of the Forties,* University of Chicago Press, 1963.

Fiedler, Leslie, *Love and Death in the American Novel,* Criterion Books, 1960.

Hicks, Granville, *Literary Horizons: A Quarter Century of American Fiction,* New York University Press, 1970.

Howard, Leon, *Literature and the American Tradition,* Doubleday, 1960.

Howard, Leon, *Wright Morris,* University of Minnesota Press, 1968.

Klein, Marcus, *After Alienation: American Novels in Mid-Century,* World Publishing, 1964.

Knoll, Robert E., editor, *Conversations with Wright Morris: Critical Views and Reviews,* University of Nebraska Press, 1977.

Kuehl, John, editor, *Creative Writing and Rewriting,* Appleton-Century-Crofts, 1967.

Madden, David, *Wright Morris,* Twayne, 1964.

Madden, David, *The Poetic Image in Six Genres,* Southern Illinois University Press, 1969.

McCormack, Thomas, *Afterwords: Novelists on Their Novels,* Harper, 1968.

Morris, Wright, *The Territory Ahead,* Harcourt, 1958.

Morris, Wright, *Wright Morris: A Reader,* with an introduction by Granville Hicks, Harper, 1970.

Morris, Wright, *Will's Boy: A Memoir,* Harper, 1981.

Morris, Wright, *Solo: An American Dreamer in Europe, 1933-34,* Harper, 1983.

Morris, Wright, *The Cloak of Light: Writing My Life,* Harper, 1985.

PERIODICALS

Accent, winter, 1959.
America, November 14, 1981.
Art in America, May, 1983.
Atlantic, October, 1962, September 1971, September, 1973.
Book Week, February 19, 1967.
Camera, April, 1966.
Chicago Tribune, October 7, 1962, March 3, 1985.
Chicago Tribune Book World, October 29, 1978, January 13, 1980, July 17, 1983.
Christian Science Monitor, September 20, 1962, March 19, 1970, July 29, 1981, February 28, 1985.
Commonweal, April 7, 1967.
Critic, April, 1965, January 15, 1979.
Critique, winter, 1961-62, spring, 1962, fall, 1982.
Detroit News, February 3, 1980, July 26, 1981.

Life, August 27, 1971.
Los Angeles Times Book Review, February 24, 1980, June 26, 1983, February 28, 1985.
Modern Fiction Studies, summer, 1980, winter, 1983, winter, 1985.
Nation, March 23, 1970.
National Observer, March 20, 1967.
New Republic, January 10, 1970, October 30, 1971, April 5 1975, February 9, 1980.
Newsweek, January 12, 1970, October 25, 1971, July 13, 1981, June 13, 1983.
New Yorker, October 18, 1969, April 14, 1975, August 10, 1981, September 12, 1983.
New York Herald Tribune Books, October 14, 1962.
New York Times, September 30, 1957, February 23, 1967, January 5, 1970, August 23, 1973, August 19, 1976, December 28, 1979, January 18, 1980, October 23, 1982, May 31, 1983.
New York Times Book Review, August 28, 1949, June 10, 1951, September 23, 1962, March 7, 1965, February 5, 1967, January 11, 1970, September 26, 1971, August 26, 1973, July 25, 1976, November 12, 1978, December 30, 1979, August 16, 1981, April 10, 1983, June 5, 1983, February 17, 1985.
Partisan Review, winter, 1968.
Prairie Schooner, summer, 1975.
Publishers Weekly, February 22, 1981.
Reporter, April 8, 1965.
Saturday Review, October 25, 1958, July 9, 1960, September 22, 1962, February 20, 1965, February 18, 1967, November 30, 1968, August 21, 1971, November 27, 1971.
Sewanee Review, summer, 1957, winter, 1977.
Time, September 21, 1962, October 18, 1971.
Washington Post Book World, January 20, 1980, July 19, 1981, June 1, 1983, February 3, 1985.
Western American Literature, spring, 1984, winter, 1986.

[Sketch reviewed by wife, Josephine Morris]

*   *   *

MORRISON, Toni   1931-

PERSONAL: Born Chloe Anthony Wofford, February 18, 1931, in Lorain, Ohio; daughter of George and Ramah (Willis) Wofford; married Harold Morrison, 1958 (divorced, 1964); children: Harold Ford, Slade Kevin. *Education:* Howard University, B.A., 1953; Cornell University, M.A., 1955.

ADDRESSES: Office—Random House, 201 East 50th St., New York, NY 10022. *Agent*—Lynn Nesbit, International Creative Management, 40 West 57th St., New York, NY 10019.

CAREER: Texas Southern University, Houston, instructor in English, 1955-57; Howard University, Washington, D.C., instructor in English, 1957-64; Random House, New York, N.Y., senior editor, 1965—; State University of New York at Purchase, associate professor of English, 1971-72; State University of New York at Albany, Schweitzer Professor of the Humanities, 1984-89; Princeton University, Princeton, N.J., Robert F. Goheen Professor of the Humanities, 1989—. Visiting lecturer, Yale University, 1976-77, and Bard College, 1986-88.

MEMBER: American Academy and Institute of Arts and Letters, National Council on the Arts, Authors Guild (council), Authors League of America.

AWARDS, HONORS: National Book Award nomination and Ohioana Book Award, both 1975, both for *Sula;* National Book

Critics Circle Award and American Academy and Institute of Arts and Letters Award, both 1977, both for *Song of Solomon;* New York State Governor's Art Award, 1986; National Book Award nomination and National Book Critics Circle Award nomination, both 1987, and Pulitzer Prize for fiction and Robert F. Kennedy Award, both 1988, all for *Beloved;* Elizabeth Cady Stanton Award from the National Organization of Women.

WRITINGS:

The Bluest Eye (novel), Holt, 1969.
Sula (novel), Knopf, 1973.
(Editor) *The Black Book* (anthology), Random House, 1974.
Song of Solomon (novel; Book-of-the-Month Club selection), Knopf, 1977.
Tar Baby (novel), Knopf, 1981.
"Dreaming Emmett" (play), first produced in Albany, New York, January 4, 1986.
Beloved (novel), Knopf, 1987.

Contributor of essays and reviews to numerous periodicals, including *New York Times Magazine.*

WORK IN PROGRESS: A sequel to *Beloved.*

SIDELIGHTS: Toni Morrison might best be described as the high priestess of village literature. Her award-winning novels chronicle small-town black American life, employing "an artistic vision that encompasses both a private and a national heritage," to quote *Time* magazine contributor Angela Wigan. Through works such as *The Bluest Eye, Song of Solomon* and *Beloved,* Morrison has earned a reputation as a gifted storyteller whose troubled characters seek to find themselves and their cultural riches in a society that warps or impedes such essential growth. According to Charles Larson in the *Chicago Tribune Book World,* each of Morrison's novels "is as original as anything that has appeared in our literature in the last 20 years. The contemporaneity that unites them—the troubling persistence of racism in America—is infused with an urgency that only a black writer can have about our society." Morrison's artistry has attracted critical acclaim as well as commercial success; *Dictionary of Literary Biography* contributor Susan L. Blake calls the author "an anomaly in two respects" because "she is a black writer who has achieved national prominence and popularity, and she is a popular writer who is taken seriously." Indeed, Morrison has won two of modern literature's most prestigious citations, the 1977 National Book Critics Circle Award for *Song of Solomon* and the 1988 Pulitzer Prize for *Beloved. Atlantic* correspondent Wilfrid Sheed notes: "Most black writers are privy, like the rest of us, to bits and pieces of the secret, the dark side of their group experience, but Toni Morrison uniquely seems to have all the keys on her chain, like a house detective. . . . She [uses] the run of the whole place, from ghetto to small town to ramshackle farmhouse, to bring back a panorama of black myth and reality that [dazzles] the senses."

"It seems somehow both constricting and inadequate to describe Toni Morrison as the country's preeminent black novelist, since in both gifts and accomplishments she transcends categorization," writes Jonathan Yardley in the *Washington Post Book World,* "yet the characterization is inescapable not merely because it is true but because the very nature of Morrison's work dictates it. Not merely has black American life been the central preoccupation of her . . . novels . . . but as she has matured she has concentrated on distilling all of black experience into her books; quite purposefully, it seems, she is striving not for the particular but for the universal." In her work Morrison strives to lay bare the injustice inherent in the black condition and blacks'

efforts, individually and collectively, to transcend society's unjust boundaries. Blake notes that Morrison's novels explore "the difference between black humanity and white cultural values. This opposition produces the negative theme of the seduction and betrayal of black people by white culture . . . and the positive theme of the quest for cultural identity." *Newsweek* contributor Jean Strouse observes: "Like all the best stories, [Morrison's] are driven by an abiding moral vision. Implicit in all her characters' grapplings with who they are is a large sense of human nature and love—and a reach for understanding of something larger than the moment."

Quest for self is a motivating and organizing device in Morrison's fiction, as is the role of family and community in nurturing or challenging the individual. In the *Times Literary Supplement,* Jennifer Uglow suggests that Morrison's novels "explore in particular the process of growing up black, female and poor. Avoiding generalities, Toni Morrison concentrates on the relation between the pressures of the community, patterns established within families, . . . and the developing sense of self." According to Dorothy H. Lee in *Black Women Writers (1950-1980): A Critical Evaluation,* Morrison is preoccupied "with the effect of the community on the individual's achievement and retention of an integrated, acceptable self. In treating this subject, she draws recurrently on myth and legend for story pattern and characters, returning repeatedly to the theory of *quest.* . . . The goals her characters seek to achieve are similar in their deepest implications, and yet the degree to which they attain them varies radically because each novel is cast in unique human terms." In Morrison's books, blacks must confront the notion that all understanding is accompanied by pain, just as all comprehension of national history must include the humiliations of slavery. She tempers this hard lesson by preserving "the richness of communal life against an outer world that denies its value" and by turning to "a heritage of folklore, not only to disclose patterns of living but also to close wounds," in the words of *Nation* contributor Brina Caplan.

Although Morrison herself told the *Chicago Tribune* that there is "epiphany and triumph" in every book she writes, some critics find her work nihilistic and her vision bleak. "The picture given by . . . Morrison of the plight of the decent, aspiring individual in the black family and community is more painful than the gloomiest impressions encouraged by either stereotype or sociology," observes Diane Johnson in the *New York Review of Books.* Johnson continues, "Undoubtedly white society is the ultimate oppressor, and not just of blacks, but, as Morrison [shows,] . . . the black person must first deal with the oppressor in the next room, or in the same bed, or no farther away than across the street." Morrison is a pioneer in the depiction of the hurt inflicted by blacks on blacks; for instance, her characters rarely achieve harmonious heterosexual relationships but are instead divided by futurelessness and the anguish of stifled existence. Uglow writes: "We have become attuned to novels . . . which locate oppression in the conflicts of blacks (usually men) trying to make it in a white world. By concentrating on the sense of violation experienced within black neighborhoods, even within families, Toni Morrison deprives us of stock responses and creates a more demanding and uncomfortable literature." *Village Voice* correspondent Vivian Gornick contends that the world Morrison creates "is thick with an atmosphere through which her characters move slowly, in pain, ignorance, and hunger. And to a very large degree Morrison has the compelling ability to make one believe that all of us (Morrison, the characters, the reader) are penetrating that dark and hurtful terrain—the feel of a human life—simultaneously." Uglow concludes that even the laughter of Morrison's characters "disguises pain, deprivation and violation. It is laughter at a series of bad, cruel jokes. . . . Nothing is what it seems; no appearance, no relationship can be trusted to endure."

Other critics detect a deeper undercurrent to Morrison's work that contains just the sort of epiphany for which she strives. "From book to book, Morrison's larger project grows clear," declares Ann Snitow in the *Voice Literary Supplement.* "First, she insists that every character bear the weight of responsibility for his or her own life. After she's measured out each one's private pain, she adds on to that the shared burden of what the whites did. Then, at last, she tries to find the place where her stories can lighten her readers' load, lift them up from their own and others' guilt, carry them to glory. . . . Her characters suffer—from their own limitations and the world's—but their inner life miraculously expands beyond the narrow law of cause and effect." *Harvard Advocate* essayist Faith Davis writes that despite the mundane boundaries of Morrison's characters' lives, the author "illuminates the complexity of their attitudes toward life. Having reached a quiet and extensive understanding of their situation, they can endure life's calamities. . . . Morrison never allows us to become indifferent to these people. . . . Her citizens . . . jump up from the pages vital and strong because she has made us care about the pain in their lives." In *Ms.,* Margo Jefferson concludes that Morrison's books "are filled with loss—lost friendship, lost love, lost customs, lost possibilities. And yet there is so much life in the smallest acts and gestures . . . that they are as much celebrations as elegies."

Morrison sees language as an expression of black experience, and her novels are characterized by vivid narration and dialogue. *Village Voice* essayist Susan Lydon observes that the author "works her magic charm above all with a love of language. Her soaring . . . style carries you like a river, sweeping doubt and disbelief away, and it is only gradually that one realizes her deadly serious intent." In the *Spectator,* Caroline Moorehead likewise notes that Morrison "writes energetically and richly, using words in a way very much her own. The effect is one of exoticism, an exciting curiousness in the language, a balanced sense of the possible that stops, always, short of the absurd." Although Morrison does not like to be called a poetic writer, critics often comment on the lyrical quality of her prose. "Morrison's style has always moved fluidly between tough-minded realism and lyric descriptiveness," notes Margo Jefferson in *Newsweek.* "Vivid dialogue, capturing the drama and extravagance of black speech, gives way to an impressionistic evocation of physical pain or an ironic, essay-like analysis of the varieties of religious hypocrisy." Uglow writes: "The word 'elegant' is often applied to Toni Morrison's writing; it employs sophisticated narrative devices, shifting perspectives and resonant images and displays an obvious delight in the potential of language." *Nation* contributor Earl Frederick concludes that Morrison, "with an ear as sharp as glass . . . has listened to the music of black talk and deftly uses it as the palette knife to create black lives and to provide some of the best fictional dialogue around today."

According to Jean Strouse, Morrison "comes from a long line of people who did what they had to do to survive. It is their stories she tells in her novels—tales of the suffering and richness, the eloquence and tragedies of the black American experience." Morrison was born Chloe Anthony Wofford in Lorain, Ohio, a small town near the shores of Lake Erie. *New York Review of Books* correspondent Darryl Pinckney describes her particular community as "close enough to the Ohio River for the people who lived [there] to feel the torpor of the South, the nostalgia for its folkways, to sense the old Underground Railroad under-

foot like a hidden stream." While never explicitly autobiographical, Morrison's fictions draw upon her youthful experiences in Ohio. In an essay for *Black Women Writers at Work* she claims: "I am from the Midwest so I have a special affection for it. My beginnings are always there. . . . No matter what I write, I begin there. . . . It's the matrix for me. . . . Ohio also offers an escape from stereotyped black settings. It is neither plantation nor ghetto."

Two important aspects of Chloe Wofford's childhood—community spirit and the supernatural—inform Toni Morrison's mature writing. In a *Publishers Weekly* interview, Morrison suggests ways in which her community influenced her. "There is this town which is both a support system and a hammer at the same time," she notes. ". . . Approval was not the acquisition of things; approval was given for the maturity and the dignity with which one handled oneself. Most black people in particular were, and still are, very fastidious about manners, very careful about behavior and the rules that operate within the community. The sense of organized activity, what I thought at that time was burdensome, turns out now to have within it a gift—which is, I never had to be taught how to hold a job, how to make it work, how to handle my time." On several levels the pariah—a unique and sometimes eccentric individual—figures in Morrison's fictional reconstruction of black community life. "There is always an elder there," she notes of her work in *Black Women Writers: A Critical Evaluation.* "And these ancestors are not just parents, they are sort of timeless people whose relationships to the characters are benevolent, instructive, and protective, and they provide a certain kind of wisdom." Sometimes this figure imparts his or her wisdom from beyond the grave; from an early age Morrison absorbed the folklore and beliefs of a culture for which the supernatural holds power and portent. Strouse notes that Morrison's world, both within and outside her fiction, is "filled with signs, visitations, ways of knowing that [reach] beyond the five senses."

Lorain, Ohio, is in fact the setting of *The Bluest Eye,* published in 1969. Morrison's first novel portrays "in poignant terms the tragic condition of blacks in a racist America," to quote Chikwenye Okonjo Ogunyemi in *Critique: Studies in Modern Fiction.* In *The Bluest Eye,* Morrison depicts the onset of black self-hatred as occasioned by white American ideals such as "Dick and Jane" primers and Shirley Temple movies. The principal character, Pecola Breedlove, is literally maddened by the disparity between her existence and the pictures of beauty and gentility disseminated by the dominant white culture. As Phyllis R. Klotman notes in the *Black American Literature Forum,* Morrison "uses the contrast between Shirley Temple and Pecola . . . to underscore the irony of black experience. Whether one learns acceptability from the formal educational experience or from cultural symbols, the effect is the same: self-hatred." Darwin T. Turner elaborates on the novel's intentions in *Black Women Writers: A Critical Evaluation.* Morrison's fictional milieu, writes Turner, is "a world of grotesques—individuals whose psyches have been deformed by their efforts to assume false identities, their failures to achieve meaningful identities, or simply their inability to retain and communicate love."

Blake characterizes *The Bluest Eye* as a novel of initiation, exploring that common theme in American literature from a minority viewpoint. Ogunyemi likewise contends that, in essence, Morrison presents "old problems in a fresh language and with a fresh perspective. A central force of the work derives from her power to draw vignettes and her ability to portray emotions, seeing the world through the eyes of adolescent girls." Klotman, who calls the book "a novel of growing up, of growing up young and black and female in America," concludes her review with the comment that the "rite of passage, initiating the young into womanhood at first tenuous and uncertain, is sensitively depicted. . . . *The Bluest Eye* is an extraordinarily passionate yet gentle work, the language lyrical yet precise—it is a novel for all seasons."

In *Sula,* Morrison's 1973 novel, the author once again presents a pair of black women who must come to terms with their lives. Set in a Midwestern black community called The Bottom, the story follows two friends, Sula and Nel, from childhood to old age and death. Snitow claims that through Sula, Morrison has discovered "a way to offer her people an insight and sense of recovered self so dignified and glowing that no worldly pain could dull the final light." Indeed, *Sula* is a tale of rebel and conformist in which the conformity is dictated by the solid inhabitants of The Bottom and even the rebellion gains strength from the community's disapproval. *New York Times Book Review* contributor Sara Blackburn contends, however, that the book is "too vital and rich" to be consigned to the category of allegory. Morrison's "extravagantly beautiful, doomed characters are locked in a world where hope for the future is a foreign commodity, yet they are enormously, achingly alive," writes Blackburn. "And this book about them—and about how their beauty is drained back and frozen—is a howl of love and rage, playful and funny as well as hard and bitter." In the words of *American Literature* essayist Jane S. Bakerman, Morrison "uses the maturation story of Sula and Nel as the core of a host of other stories, but it is the chief unification device for the novel and achieves its own unity, again, through the clever manipulation of the themes of sex, race, and love. Morrison has undertaken a . . . difficult task in *Sula.* Unquestionably, she has succeeded."

Other critics have echoed Bakerman's sentiments about *Sula.* Yardley declares: "What gives this terse, imaginative novel its genuine distinction is the quality of Toni Morrison's prose. *Sula* is admirable enough as a study of its title character, . . . but its real strength lies in Morrison's writing, which at times has the resonance of poetry and is precise, vivid and controlled throughout." Turner also claims that in *Sula* "Morrison evokes her verbal magic occasionally by lyric descriptions that carry the reader deep into the soul of the character. . . . Equally effective, however, is her art of narrating action in a lean prose that uses adjectives cautiously while creating memorable vivid images." In her review, Davis concludes that a "beautiful and haunting atmosphere emerges out of the wreck of these folks' lives, a quality that is absolutely convincing and absolutely precise." *Sula* was nominated for a National Book Award in 1974.

From the insular lives she depicted in her first two novels, Morrison moved in *Song of Solomon* to a national and historical perspective on black American life. "Here the depths of the younger work are still evident," contends Reynolds Price in the *New York Times Book Review,* "but now they thrust outward, into wider fields, for longer intervals, encompassing many more lives. The result is a long prose tale that surveys nearly a century of American history as it impinges upon a single family." With an intermixture of the fantastic and the realistic, *Song of Solomon* relates the journey of a character named Milkman Dead into an understanding of his family heritage and hence, himself. Lee writes: "Figuratively, [Milkman] travels from innocence to awareness, i.e., from ignorance of origins, heritage, identity, and communal responsibility to knowledge and acceptance. He moves from selfish and materialistic dilettantism to an understanding of brotherhood. With his release of personal ego, he is able to find a place in the whole. There is, then, a universal—indeed mythic—pattern here. He journeys from spiritual death to rebirth, a direc-

tion symbolized by his discovery of the secret power of flight. Mythically, liberation and transcendence follow the discovery of self." Blake suggests that the connection Milkman discovers with his family's past helps him to connect meaningfully with his contemporaries; *Song of Solomon,* Blake notes, "dramatizes dialectical approaches to the challenges of black life." According to Anne Z. Mickelson in *Reaching Out: Sensitivity and Order in Recent American Fiction by Women,* history itself "becomes a choral symphony to Milkman, in which each individual voice has a chance to speak and contribute to his growing sense of well-being."

Mickelson also observes that *Song of Solomon* represents for blacks "a break out of the confining life into the realm of possibility." Charles Larson comments on this theme in a *Washington Post Book World* review. The novel's subject matter, Larson explains, is "the origins of black consciousness in America, and the individual's relationship to that heritage." However, Larson adds, "skilled writer that she is, Morrison has transcended this theme so that the reader rarely feels that this is simply another novel about ethnic identity. So marvelously orchestrated is Morrison's narrative that it not only excels on all of its respective levels, not only works for all of its interlocking components, but also—in the end—says something about life (and death) for all of us. Milkman's epic journey . . . is a profound examination of the individual's understanding of, and, perhaps, even transcendence of the inevitable fate of his life." Gornick concludes: "There are so many individual moments of power and beauty in *Song of Solomon* that, ultimately, one closes the book warmed through by the richness of its sympathy, and by its breathtaking feel for the nature of sexual sorrow."

Song of Solomon won the National Book Critics Circle Award in 1977. It was also the first novel by a black writer to become a Book-of-the-Month Club selection since Richard Wright's *Native Son* was published in 1940. *World Literature Today* reviewer Richard K. Barksdale calls the work "a book that will not only withstand the test of time but endure a second and third reading by those conscientious readers who love a well-wrought piece of fiction." Describing the novel as "a stunningly beautiful book" in her *Washington Post Book World* piece, Anne Tyler adds: "I would call the book poetry, but that would seem to be denying its considerable power as a story. Whatever name you give it, it's full of magnificent people, each of them complex and multilayered, even the narrowest of them narrow in extravagant ways." Price deems *Song of Solomon* "a long story, . . . and better than good. Toni Morrison has earned attention and praise. Few Americans know, and can say, more than she has in this wise and spacious novel."

Morrison's 1981 book *Tar Baby* remained on bestseller lists for four months. A novel of ideas, the work dramatizes the fact that complexion is a far more subtle issue than the simple polarization of black and white. Set on a lush Caribbean Island, *Tar Baby* explores the passionate love affair of Jadine, a Sorbonne-educated black model, and Son, a handsome knockabout with a strong aversion to white culture. According to Caplan, Morrison's concerns "are race, class, culture and the effects of late capitalism—heavy freight for any narrative. . . . She is attempting to stabilize complex visions of society—that is, to examine competitive ideas. . . . Because the primary function of Morrison's characters is to voice representative opinions, they arrive on stage vocal and highly conscious, their histories symbolically indicated or merely sketched. Her brief sketches, however, are clearly the work of an artist who can, when she chooses, model the mind in depth and detail." In a *Dictionary of Literary Biography Yearbook* essay, Elizabeth B. House outlines *Tar Baby's* major themes; namely, "the difficulty of settling conflicting claims between one's past and present and the destruction which abuse of power can bring. As Morrison examines these problems in *Tar Baby,* she suggests no easy way to understand what one's link to a heritage should be, nor does she offer infallible methods for dealing with power. Rather, with an astonishing insight and grace, she demonstrates the pervasiveness of such dilemmas and the degree to which they affect human beings, both black and white."

Tar Baby uncovers racial and sexual conflicts without offering solutions, but most critics agree that Morrison indicts all of her characters—black and white—for their thoughtless devaluations of others. *New York Times Book Review* correspondent John Irving claims: "What's so powerful, and subtle, about Miss Morrison's presentation of the tension between blacks and whites is that she conveys it almost entirely through the suspicions and prejudices of her black characters. . . . Miss Morrison uncovers all the stereotypical racial fears felt by whites and blacks alike. Like any ambitious writer, she's unafraid to employ these stereotypes—she embraces the representative qualities of her characters without embarrassment, then proceeds to make them individuals too." *New Yorker* essayist Susan Lardner praises Morrison for her "power to be absolutely persuasive against her own preferences, suspicions, and convictions, implied or plainly expressed," and Strouse likewise contends that the author "has produced that rare commodity, a truly public novel about the condition of society, examining the relations between blacks and whites, men and women, civilization and nature. . . . It wraps its messages in a highly potent love story." Irving suggests that Morrison's greatest accomplishment "is that she has raised her novel above the social realism that too many black novels and women's novels are trapped in. She has succeeded in writing about race and women symbolically."

Reviewers have praised *Tar Baby* for its provocative themes and for its evocative narration. *Los Angeles Times* contributor Elaine Kendall calls the book "an intricate and orderly novel, moving from a realistic and orderly beginning to a mystical and ambiguous end. Morrison has taken classically simple story elements and realigned them so artfully that we perceive the old pattern in a startlingly different way. Although this territory has been explored by dozens of novelists, Morrison depicts it with such vitality that it seems newly discovered." In the *Washington Post Book World,* Webster Schott claims: "There is so much that is good, sometimes dazzling, about *Tar Baby*—poetic language, . . . arresting images, fierce intelligence—that . . . one becomes entranced by Toni Morrison's story. The settings are so vivid the characters must be alive. The emotions they feel are so intense they must be real people." Maureen Howard states in *New Republic* that the work "is as carefully patterned as a well-written poem. . . . *Tar Baby* is a good American novel in which we can discern a new lightness and brilliance in Toni Morrison's enchantment with language and in her curiously polyphonic stories that echo life." Schott concludes: "One of fiction's pleasures is to have your mind scratched and your intellectual habits challenged. While *Tar Baby* has shortcomings, lack of provocation isn't one of them. Morrison owns a powerful intelligence. It's run by courage. She calls to account conventional wisdom and accepted attitude at nearly every turn."

In addition to her own writing, Morrison has served as an editor at Random House and has helped to publish the work of other noted black Americans, including Toni Cade Bambara, Gayle Jones, Angela Davis, and Muhammed Ali. Discussing her aims as an editor in a quotation printed in the *Dictionary of Literary Biography,* Morrison said: "I look very hard for black fiction be-

cause I want to participate in developing a canon of black work. We've had the first rush of black entertainment, where blacks were writing for whites, and whites were encouraging this kind of self-flagellation. Now we can get down to the craft of writing, where black people are talking to black people." One of Morrison's important projects for Random House was *The Black Book,* an anthology of items that illustrate the history of black Americans. *Ms.* magazine correspondent Dorothy Eugenia Robinson describes the work: "*The Black Book* is the pain and pride of rediscovering the collective black experience. It is finding the essence of ourselves and holding on. *The Black Book* is a kind of scrapbook of patiently assembled samplings of black history and culture. What has evolved is a pictorial folk journey of black people, places, events, handcrafts, inventions, songs, and folklore. . . . *The Black Book* informs, disturbs, maybe even shocks. It unsettles complacency and demands confrontation with raw reality. It is by no means an easy book to experience, but it's a necessary one."

While preparing *The Black Book* for publication, Morrison uncovered the true and shocking story of a runaway slave who, at the point of recapture, murdered her infant child so it would not be doomed to a lifetime of slavery. For Morrison the story encapsulated the fierce psychic cruelty of an institutionalized system that sought to destroy the basic emotional bonds between men and women, and worse, between parent and child. "I certainly thought I knew as much about slavery as anybody," Morrison told the *Los Angeles Times.* "But it was the interior life I needed to find out about." It is this "interior life" in the throes of slavery that constitutes the theme of Morrison's Pulitzer Prize-winning novel *Beloved.* Set in Reconstruction-era Cincinnati, the book centers on characters who struggle fruitlessly to keep their painful recollections of the past at bay. They are haunted, both physically and spiritually, by the legacies slavery has bequeathed to them. According to Snitow, *Beloved* "staggers under the terror of its material—as so much holocaust writing does and must."

In *People* magazine, V. R. Peterson describes *Beloved* as "a brutally powerful, mesmerizing story about the inescapable, excruciating legacy of slavery. Behind each new event and each new character lies another event and another story until finally the reader meets a community of proud, daring people, inextricably bound by culture and experience." Through the lives of ex-slaves Sethe and her would-be lover Paul D., readers "experience American slavery as it was lived by those who were its objects of exchange, both at its best—which wasn't very good—and at its worst, which was as bad as can be imagined," writes Margaret Atwood in the *New York Times Book Review.* "Above all, it is seen as one of the most viciously antifamily institutions human beings have ever devised. The slaves are motherless, fatherless, deprived of their mates, their children, their kin. It is a world in which people suddenly vanish and are never seen again, not through accident or covert operation or terrorism, but as a matter of everyday legal policy." *New York Times* columnist Michiko Kakutani contends that *Beloved* "possesses the heightened power and resonance of myth—its characters, like those in opera or Greek drama, seem larger than life and their actions, too, tend to strike us as enactments of ancient rituals and passions. To describe 'Beloved' only in these terms, however, is to diminish its immediacy, for the novel also remains precisely grounded in American reality—the reality of Black history as experienced in the wake of the Civil War."

Acclaim for *Beloved* has come from both sides of the Atlantic. In his *Chicago Tribune* piece, Larson claims that the work "is the context out of which all of Morrison's earlier novels were written. In her darkest and most probing novel, Toni Morrison has demonstrated once again the stunning powers that place her in the first ranks of our living novelists." *Los Angeles Times Book Review* contributor John Leonard likewise expresses the opinion that the novel "belongs on the highest shelf of American literature, even if half a dozen canonized white boys have to be elbowed off. . . . Without 'Beloved' our imagination of the nation's self has a hole in it big enough to die from." Atwood states: "Ms. Morrison's versatility and technical and emotional range appear to know no bounds. If there were any doubts about her stature as a pre-eminent American novelist, of her own or any other generation, 'Beloved' will put them to rest." London *Times* reviewer Nicholas Shakespeare concludes that *Beloved* "is a novel propelled by the cadences of . . . songs—the first singing of a people hardened by their suffering, people who have been hanged and whipped and mortgaged at the hands of whitepeople—the men without skin. From Toni Morrison's pen it is a sound that breaks the back of words, making *Beloved* a great novel."

Morrison is an author who labors contentedly under the labels bestowed by pigeonholing critics. She has no objection to being called a black woman writer, because, as she told the *New York Times,* "I really think the range of emotions and perceptions I have had access to as a black person and a female person are greater than those of people who are neither. . . . My world did not shrink because I was a black female writer. It just got bigger." Nor does she strive for that much-vaunted universality that purports to be a hallmark of fine fiction. "I never asked Tolstoy to write for me, a little colored girl in Lorain, Ohio," she told the *New Republic.* "I never asked [James] Joyce not to mention Catholicism or the world of Dublin. Never. And I don't know why I should be asked to explain your life to you. We have splendid writers to do that, but I am not one of them. It is that business of being universal, a word hopelessly stripped of meaning for me. [William] Faulkner wrote what I suppose could be called regional literature and had it published all over the world. That's what I wish to do. If I tried to write a universal novel, it would be water. Behind this question is the suggestion that to write for black people is somehow to diminish the writing. From my perspective there are only black people. When I say 'people,' that's what I mean."

Black woman writer or simply American novelist, Toni Morrison is a prominent and respected figure in modern letters. In the *Detroit News,* Larson suggests that hers has been "among the most exciting literary careers of the last decade" and that each of her books "has made a quantum jump forward." Ironically, Elizabeth House commends Morrison for the universal nature of her work. "Unquestionably," House writes, "Toni Morrison is an important novelist who continues to develop her talent. Part of her appeal, of course, lies in her extraordinary ability to create beautiful language and striking characters. However, Morrison's most important gift, the one which gives her a major author's universality, is the insight with which she writes of problems all humans face. . . . At the core of all her novels is a penetrating view of the unyielding, heartbreaking dilemmas which torment people of all races." Snitow notes that the author "wants to tend the imagination, search for an expansion of the possible, nurture a spiritual richness in the black tradition even after 300 years in the white desert." Dorothy Lee concludes of Morrison's accomplishments: "Though there are unifying aspects in her novels, there is not a dully repetitive sameness. Each casts the problems in specific, imaginative terms, and the exquisite, poetic language awakens our senses as she communicates an often ironic vision with moving imagery. Each novel reveals the acuity of her perception of psychological motivation of the female especially, of the Black particularly, and of the human generally."

"The problem I face as a writer is to make my stories mean something," Morrison states in *Black Women Writers at Work.* "You can have wonderful, interesting people, a fascinating story, but it's not about anything. It has no real substance. I want my books to always be about something that is important to me, and the subjects that are important in the world are the same ones that have always been important." In *Black Women Writers: A Critical Evaluation,* she elaborates on this idea. Fiction, she writes, "should be beautiful, and powerful, but it should also work. It should have something in it that enlightens; something in it that opens the door and points the way. Something in it that suggests what the conflicts are, what the problems are. But it need not solve those problems because it is not a case study, it is not a recipe." The author who has said that writing "is discovery; it's talking deep within myself" told the *New York Times Book Review* that the essential theme in her growing body of fiction is "how and why we learn to live this life intensely and well."

BIOGRAPHICAL/CRITICAL SOURCES:

BOOKS

Bell, Roseann P., editor, *Sturdy Black Bridges: Visions of Black Women in Literature,* Doubleday, 1979.
Christian, Barbara, *Black Women Novelists: The Development of a Tradition, 1892-1976,* Greenwood Press, 1980.
Contemporary Literary Criticism, Gale, Volume 4, 1975, Volume 10, 1979, Volume 22, 1982, Volume 55, 1989.
Cooper-Clark, Diana, *Interviews with Contemporary Novelists,* St. Martin's, 1986.
Dictionary of Literary Biography, Gale, Volume 6: *American Novelists since World War II,* 1980, Volume 33: *Afro-American Fiction Writers after 1955,* 1984.
Dictionary of Literary Biography Yearbook: 1981, Gale, 1982.
Evans, Mari, editor, *Black Women Writers (1950-1980): A Critical Evaluation,* Doubleday, 1984.
Mekkawi, Mod, *Toni Morrison: A Bibliography,* Howard University Library, 1986.
Mickelson, Anne Z., *Reaching Out: Sensitivity and Order in Recent American Fiction by Women,* Scarecrow Press, 1979.
Ruas, Charles, *Conversations with American Writers,* Knopf, 1985.
Tate, Claudia, editor, *Black Women Writers at Work,* Continuum, 1986.

PERIODICALS

American Literature, January, 1981.
Atlantic, April, 1981.
Black American Literature Forum, summer, 1978, winter, 1979.
Black Scholar, March, 1978.
Black World, June, 1974.
Callaloo, October-February, 1981.
Chicago Tribune, October 27, 1987.
Chicago Tribune Books, August 30, 1988.
Chicago Tribune Book World, March 8, 1981.
CLA Journal, June, 1979, June, 1981.
Commentary, August, 1981.
Contemporary Literature, winter, 1983.
Critique: Studies in Modern Fiction, Volume 19, number 1, 1977.
Detroit News, March 29, 1981.
Essence, July, 1981, June, 1983, October, 1987.
First World, winter, 1977.
Harper's Bazaar, March, 1983.
Harvard Advocate, Volume 107, number 4, 1974.

Hudson Review, spring, 1978.
Los Angeles Times, March 31, 1981, October 14, 1987.
Los Angeles Times Book Review, August 30, 1987.
Massachusetts Review, autumn, 1977.
MELUS, fall, 1980.
Ms., June, 1974, December, 1974, August, 1987.
Nation, July 6, 1974, November 19, 1977, May 2, 1981.
New Republic, December 3, 1977, March 21, 1981.
Newsweek, November 30, 1970, January 7, 1974, September 12, 1977, March 30, 1981.
New York, April 13, 1981.
New Yorker, November 7, 1977, June 15, 1981.
New York Post, January 26, 1974.
New York Review of Books, November 10, 1977, April 30, 1981.
New York Times, November 13, 1970, September 6, 1977, March 21, 1981, August 26, 1987, September 2, 1987.
New York Times Book Review, November 1, 1970, December 30, 1973, June 2, 1974, September 11, 1977, March 29, 1981, September 13, 1987.
New York Times Magazine, August 22, 1971, August 11, 1974, July 4, 1976, May 20, 1979.
Obsidian, spring/summer, 1979.
People, July 29, 1974, November 30, 1987.
Philadelphia Inquirer, April 1, 1988.
Publishers Weekly, August 21, 1987.
Saturday Review, September 17, 1977.
Spectator, December 9, 1978, February 2, 1980, December 19, 1981.
Studies in Black Literature, Volume 6, 1976.
Time, September 12, 1977, March 16, 1981, September 21, 1987.
Times (London), October 15, 1987.
Times Literary Supplement, October 4, 1974, November 24, 1978, February 8, 1980, December 19, 1980, October 30, 1981, October 16-22, 1987.
U.S. News and World Report, October 19, 1987.
Village Voice, August 29, 1977, July 1-7, 1981.
Vogue, April, 1981, January, 1986.
Voice Literary Supplement, September, 1987.
Washington Post, February 3, 1974, March 6, 1974, September 30, 1977, April 8, 1981, Februrary 9, 1983, October 5, 1987.
Washington Post Book World, February 3, 1974. September 4, 1977, December 4, 1977, March 22, 1981, September 6, 1987.
World Literature Today, summer, 1978.

* * *

MORTIMER, John (Clifford) 1923-

PERSONAL: Born April 21, 1923, in London, England; son of Clifford (a barrister) and Kathleen May (Smith) Mortimer; married Penelope Ruth Fletcher (a writer), 1949 (divorced, 1972); married Penelope Gollop, 1972; children: (first marriage) Sally, Jeremy; (second marriage) Rosamond; stepchildren: Madelon Lee Mortimer Howard, Caroline, Julia Mortimer Mankowitz, Deborah Mortimer Rogers. *Education:* Attended Brasenose College, Oxford.

ADDRESSES: Home—Turville Heath Cottage, Henley-on-Thames, Oxfordshire RG9 6JY, England. *Agent*—A. D. Peters, 10 Buckingham St., Adelphi, London WC2N 6BU, England.

CAREER: Barrister-at-law, London, England, 1948—. Named to Queen's Council, 1966. Novelist, screenwriter, and playwright.

MEMBER: Garrick Club.

AWARDS, HONORS: Italia Prize, 1957, for play, "The Dock Brief"; Writers Guild of Great Britain award for best original teleplay, 1969, for "A Voyage round My Father"; Golden Globe award nomination, 1970, for screenplay "John and Mary"; writer of the year, British Film and Television Academy, 1980; Commander of the British Empire, 1986; honorary doctorate in law, Exeter University, 1986; D.Litt., Susquehanna University and St. Andrews University.

WRITINGS:

Charade (novel), Lane, 1948, reprinted, Viking, 1986.
Rumming Park (novel), Lane, 1949.
Answer Yes or No (novel), Lane, 1950, published as *Silver Hook,* Morrow, 1950.
Like Men Betrayed (novel), Collins, 1953, Lippincott, 1954, Viking, 1989.
Three Winters (novel), Collins, 1956.
The Narrowing Stream (novel), Collins, 1956, Viking, 1989.
(With first wife, Penelope Ruth Mortimer) *With Love and Lizards* (travel), M. Joseph, 1957.
Will Shakespeare (stories), Hodder & Stoughton, 1977.
Rumpole of the Bailey (stories), Penguin, 1978.
Clinging to the Wreakage: A Part of Life (autobiography), Weidenfeld & Nicolson, 1982.
Rumpole's Return (stories), Penguin, 1982.
Trials of Rumpole (stories), Penguin, 1982.
In Character (interviews), Allen Lane, 1983.
Rumpole and the Golden Thread, Penguin, 1984.
Rumpole for the Defence, Penguin, 1984.
A Rumpole Omnibus, Penguin, 1984.
Paradise Postponed (also see below), Viking, 1985.
Character Parts (interviews; originally published in *Sunday Times*), Penguin, 1987.
Summer's Lease, Viking, 1988.

Also author of *Regina vs. Rumpole,* 1981.

PLAYS

Three Plays: The Dock Brief; What Shall We Tell Caroline?; [and] I Spy (also see below), Elek, 1958, Grove, 1962.
The Wrong Side of the Park (three-act), Heinemann, 1960.
Lunch Hour, and Other Plays (contains "Collect Your Hand Baggage," "David and Broccoli," and "Call Me a Liar"), Methuen, 1960.
Lunch Hour (one-act), Samuel French, 1960.
What Shall We Tell Caroline? (three-act), Heinemann, 1960.
Collect Your Hand Baggage (one-act), Samuel French, 1960.
I Spy, Samuel French, 1960.
Two Stars for Comfort, Methuen, 1962.
The Judge (first produced in London at Cambridge Theatre, March 1, 1967), Methuen, 1967.
(Translator) Georges Feydeau, *A Flea in Her Ear: A Farce* (first produced in London at Old Vic Theatre, February 8, 1966; also see below), Samuel French, 1968.
(Translator) Georges Feydeau, *Cat among the Pigeons* (three-act; first produced in Milwaukee at Milwaukee Repertory Theatre, November, 1971), Samuel French, 1970.
Five Plays (contains "The Dock Brief," "What Shall We Tell Caroline?," "I Spy," "Lunch Hour," and "Collect Your Hand Baggage"), Methuen, 1970.
Come As You Are! (contains four one-act comedies, "Mill Hill," "Bermondsey," "Gloucester Road," and "Marble Arch"; first produced, under combined title, in London at New Theatre, January 27, 1970), Methuen, 1971.

A Voyage round My Father (first produced in New York at Greenwich Theatre, November 24, 1970; also see below), Methuen, 1971.

(Translator) Carl Zuckmayer, *The Captain of Koepenick* (first produced in London at Old Vic Theatre, March 9, 1971), Methuen, 1971.

"I, Claudius" (two-act; adapted from Robert Graves's novels *I, Claudius* and *Claudius the God*), first produced in London at Queen's Theatre, July 11, 1972.

Knightsbridge, Samuel French, 1973.

"Collaborators" (two-act), first produced in London at Duchess Theatre, April 17, 1973.

"Heaven and Hell" (includes one-act plays "The Fear of Heaven" and "The Prince of Darkness"), first produced in London at Greenwich Theatre, May 27, 1976.

(Translator) Georges Feydeau, *The Lady from Maxim's* (first produced in London at Lyttleton Theatre, October 18, 1977), Heinemann, 1977.

"The Bells of Hell" (full-length version of "The Prince of Darkness"; first produced in London at Garrick Theatre, July 27, 1977), published as *The Bells of Hell: A Divine Comedy,* Samuel French, 1978.

The Fear of Heaven, Samuel French, 1978.

"John Mortimer's Casebook" (collected plays including "The Dock Brief," "The Prince of Darkness," and "Interlude"), first produced in London at Young Vic, January 6, 1982.

"When That Was," first produced in Ottawa, Ontario at Arts Centre, February 16, 1982.

Contributor to anthologies, including *English One-Act Plays of Today,* edited by Donald Fitzjohn, Oxford University Press, 1962.

RADIO SCRIPTS; PRODUCED BY BRITISH BROADCASTING CORP. (BBC)

"Like Men Betrayed," 1955.
"No Hero," 1955.
"The Dock Brief," 1957.
"Three Winters," 1958.
"Call Me a Liar," 1958.
"Personality Split," 1964.
"Education of an Englishman," 1964.
"A Rare Device," 1965.
"Mr. Luby's Fear of Heaven," 1976.

TELEVISION PLAYS AND SERIES

"David and Broccoli," British Broadcasting Corp. (BBC-TV), 1960.
"The Encyclopaedist," BBC-TV, 1961.
"The Choice of Kings," Associated Rediffusion, 1966.
"The Exploding Azalea," Thames Television, 1966.
"The Head Waiter," BBC-TV, 1966.
"The Other Side," BBC-TV, 1967.
"Desmond," BBC-TV, 1968.
"Infidelity Took Place," BBC-TV, 1968.
"Married Alive," Columbia Broadcasting System (CBS-TV), January 23, 1970.
"Only Three Can Play," Independent Broadcasting Authority, June 6, 1970.
"Alcock and Gander," Thames Television, June 5, 1972.
"Swiss Cottage," BBC-TV, 1972.
"Knightsbridge," BBC-TV, 1972.
"Rumpole of the Bailey" (two series), BBC-TV, 1975 and 1978.
"Will Shakespeare," ATV, 1977.
"Unity," BBC-TV, 1978.
"A Voyage round my Father," Thames Television, 1980.

(Adaptor) "Brideshead Revisited," based on the novel by Evelyn Waugh, Granada, 1981.
"Paradise Postponed," Thames Television, 1986.

Also adapted several Graham Greene stories for Thames Television, 1976. Author of "Summer's Lease," 1989.

FILM SCRIPTS

"Bunny Lake is Missing," Columbia Pictures, 1965.
"A Flea in Her Ear," Twentieth Century-Fox, 1968.
"John and Mary," Twentieth Century-Fox, 1969.

OTHER

Also author of a scenario for ballet, "Home," 1968. Contributor to periodicals.

WORK IN PROGRESS: More scripts for "Rumpole of the Bailey."

SIDELIGHTS: John Mortimer's fiction has been compared to that of Charles Dickens for its eccentric characters and that of Evelyn Waugh for its portrayal of class consciousness. Best known in America for his television work, including creating "Rumpole of the Bailey" and adapting Waugh's *Brideshead Revisited* as a series, Mortimer is renowned in his native England as both a barrister and a playwright/author. Accordingly, these two professions have intermingled in much of Mortimer's writings. From the tippling, cynical Rumpole to Morgenhall, the failed hero of "The Dock Brief," to the autobiographical young protagonist of "A Voyage round My Father," writers and lawyers have played major roles in the author's work. He also has a talent for farce as an adaptor of Georges Feydeau's plays and author of his own "Come As You Are!"

The son of a barrister, Mortimer was himself called to the bar in 1948, about the same time his first novel, *Charade,* was published. He has been viewed as a controversial figure in both fields. In a celebrated 1970 case, Mortimer, the barrister, successfully defended the publishers of a magazine, *Oz,* against charges of pornography; the author has often been criticized for treading past the bounds of propriety in his own work. Mortimer's plays, in fact, run the gamut of style; as Ronald Hayman writes in his book *British Theatre since 1955: A Reassessment,* the author "has oscillated between writing safe plays, catering for the West End audience, and dangerously serious plays which might have alienated the public [he] had won."

"Indicative more of his versatility than of his limitations," continues Gerald H. Strauss in a *Dictionary of Literary Biography* article, "this ambivalence is shared by Mortimer with a number of his contemporaries. He can be praised for clever conception and deft management of situations, characters that are believable even when they are largely stereotypes, and dialogue that abounds with witticisms; and all of his plays, not just his ambitious ones, . . . are the work of a perceptive social conscience."

To be sure, socially conscious plays thrived during the mid-1950s, when Mortimer's work began receiving serious attention. What separates the author from such peers as John Osborne and Harold Pinter is that Mortimer "applies his exploratory techniques to the middle classes in decline rather than the working classes ascendent," according to John Russell Taylor in his book *Anger and After.* As Taylor goes on to say, in Mortimer's plays "there are no ready-made villains on whom the blame can be put; . . . instead, the seedy and downtrodden are accepted on their own terms, as human beings, mixtures inevitably of good and bad qualities, and then without glossing over or minimizing the bad qualities, Mortimer gradually unfolds the good for our inspection."

In his book *The Theatre of Protest and Paradox: Developments in the Avant-Garde Drama,* George Wellwarth finds another kind of nemesis in Mortimer's stories: "The efficient compromisers are the villains of Mortimer's plays, even though they do not appear in them personally." Wellwarth points out that in a typical example of Mortimer drama, the author presents "the glorification of the failure." A failure, Wellwarth adds, "is hardly a heroic figure. Mortimer's failures receive their stature by analogy: they are the antithesis of the organization men. . . . [The author] has no use for the survival-of-the-fittest doctrine, since, as he sees it, the terms of the survival are dictated by those who know they will triumph under those terms."

One play that illustrates Wellwarth's theory is "The Dock Brief," a study of how harsh reality intrudes on pleasant fantasy. Morgenhall is a small-time barrister who gets the chance to defend a murder suspect in a case that could turn his dismal career around. But instead of working diligently on the case, Morgenhall drifts into an elaborate fantasy of success, playing the roles of judge and jury himself, and subsequently ruins his own sense of reality. At the same time the accused, Fowle, is so caught up in his lawyer's illusions that he to adopts a fantasy perspective on his fate. Thus, even after a mistrial is called on account of the barrister's incompetence, the characters exit "with enough illusions to continue living," as Taylor puts it. The character of Morgenhall, the author adds, "might well have stepped straight from the pages of [Nikolai] Gogol—his seediness and unreliability, his proliferating fantasy life and his impotence in the world of action at once proclaim his kinship with many of the characters in *Dead Souls.*"

While he has been an active and prolific writer for three decades, Mortimer's greatest commercial successes perhaps came in the late 1970s and early 1980s. During that period he completed his television series for "Rumpole" and *Brideshead Revisited,* published an autobiography, *Clinging to the Wreakage: A Part of Life,* to accompany his autobiographical play "A Voyage round My Father," and produced two versions of *Paradise Postponed,* written concurrently as a novel and a television series. "A Voyage round My Father" is highly regarded by Tom Shales, who reviewed a television adaptation: the portrait of a father and son at odds, says the *Washington Post* columnist, reveals "bonds so deep that words cannot begin to express them, and that is part of what this sublimely lovely play is about." Less impressed is *New York Times* critic Clive Barnes, who feels that in this piece the character of Mortimer's blind, disagreeable father "remains a caricature blandly begging for kindness."

While "Voyage" is a fictional telling of the author's early life, *Clinging to the Wreakage* is pure autobiography, a book described by London *Times* critic Michael Ratcliffe as an "exceptionally touching and funny memoir[,] rich in remarkable occasions and disconcerting surprises." Like the play, the volume "is a moving but by no means always affectionate account of [Mortimer's] relationship with his father, [who wrote] a standard reference on probate law and who was blind for much of his career. He had an ungovernable temper . . . and a flair for courtroom dramatics that could make strong men quail," as Charles Champlin writes in a *Los Angeles Times* review. Champlin adds that the author "never really doubted [his father's] love; gaining his respect was a difficult, slow process. The autobiography, beautifully written, has the strength and sensitivity of a carefully observed novel."

"A witty chronicle of rural English life as it reflects national fads and preoccupations from 1945 to the present day" is how *Times* critic Stuart Evans characterizes *Paradise Postponed.* The novel and television series concern the Reverend Simeon Simcox, "one of those beaming, affluent, Christian Socialist crusaders," notes Evans. Simcox perplexes his parish by leaving a fortune not to his family, "but to a maladroit, opportunist local lad who has soared out of the lower middle-class into the rarefied air of the Conservative Cabinet of the present day." The inevitable clash of cultures and politics fuels the tale.

"To a considerable extent the story reflects the prejudices and regrets of the author, and some good times and redeeming optimism, too," finds *New York Times* reviewer Francis X. Clines; Mortimer, like Simcox, established himself as a socialist in the classic Bernard Shaw mold, one who maintains that "the idea that you should feel compassion for the less fortunate [should] be your dominant political feeling," as Mortimer states in Clines's article. And, like his protagonist, the author finds himself at a stage in history when Margaret Thatcher's Britain perpetuates "Conservatives, class distinctions, unemployment. It's where we started." What he wanted to emphasize in the book, Mortimer tells Elizabeth Neuffer in the *Washington Post,* "is that whether [paradise] fails or not, it's better to have believed in it than taken the other view."

In Wellwarth's study, Mortimer is quoted as saying near the beginning of his career: "There may, for all I know, be great and funny plays to be written about successful lawyers, brilliant criminals, wise schoolmasters, or families where the children can grow up without silence and without regret. There are many plays that show that the law is always majestic or that family life is simple and easy to endure. Speaking for myself I am not on the side of such plays and a writer of comedy must choose his side with particular care. He cannot afford to aim at the [defenseless], nor can he, like the more serious writer, treat any character with contempt."

BIOGRAPHICAL/CRITICAL SOURCES:

BOOKS

Contemporary Literary Criticism, Gale, Volume 28, 1984, Volume 43, 1987.

Dictionary of Literary Biography, Volume 13: *British Dramatists since World War II,* Gale, 1982.

Hayman, Ronald, *British Theatre since 1955: A Reassessment,* Oxford University Press, 1979.

Taylor, John Russell, *Anger and After,* Methuen, 1962.

Taylor, John Russell, *The Angry Theatre: New British Drama,* Hill & Wang, 1962, revised edition, 1969.

Wellwarth, George, *Theatre of Protest and Paradox: Developments in Avant-Garde Drama,* New York University Press, 1964.

PERIODICALS

Chicago Tribune, January 3, 1990.

Los Angeles Times, September 28, 1982, August 19, 1988.

Los Angeles Times Book Review, March 29, 1987, March 26, 1989.

Listener, December 17, 1981.

New Statesman, January 1, 1982.

New Yorker, October 25, 1982.

New York Times, November 22, 1961, August 27, 1971, November 20, 1982, October 19, 1986, January 23, 1987, July 27, 1988.

New York Times Book Review, March 28, 1954, March 8, 1987, July 31, 1988, October 15, 1989.

Publishers Weekly, November 5, 1982.
Punch, December 9, 1981.
Times (London), April 1, 1982, September 19, 1985, September 12, 1986.
Times Literary Supplement, June 23, 1950, July 3, 1953, September 25, 1970, April 29, 1988.
Tribune Books (Chicago), July 24, 1988, November 26, 1989.
Washington Post, February 15, 1989.
Washington Post Book World, March 1, 1987, July 24, 1988.

*   *   *

MORTON, Anthony
See CREASEY, John

*   *   *

MOWAT, Farley (McGill) 1921-

PERSONAL: Born May 12, 1921, in Belleville, Ontario, Canada; son of Angus McGill and Helen (Thomson) Mowat; married Frances Elizabeth Thornhill, December 21, 1947 (marriage ended); married Claire Angel Wheeler (a writer), 1965; children: (previous marriage) Robert Alexander, David Peter. *Education:* University of Toronto, B.A., 1949.

ADDRESSES: c/o McClelland & Stewart, 481 University Ave., Toronto, Ontario, Canada M5G 2E9; c/o Writers Union of Canada, 24 Ryerson Ave., Toronto, Ontario, Canada M4T 2P3.

CAREER: Self-employed author. *Military service:* Canadian Army, Infantry, 1939-45; became captain.

AWARDS, HONORS: President's Medal, University of Western Ontario, 1952, for best Canadian short story of 1952; Anisfield-Wolfe Award for contribution to interracial relations, 1954, for *People of the Deer;* Governor General's Medal, 1957, and Book of the Year Award, Canadian Association of Children's Librarians, both for *Lost in the Barrens;* Canadian Women's Clubs Award, 1958, for *The Dog Who Wouldn't Be;* Hans Christian Andersen International Award, 1958; Boys' Clubs of America Junior Book Award, 1962, for *Owls in the Family;* National Association of Independent Schools Award, 1963, for juvenile books; Hans Christian Andersen Honours List, 1965, for juvenile books; Canadian Centennial Medal, 1967; Leacock Medal, 1970, and L'Etoile de la Mer Honours List, 1972, both for *The Boat Who Wouldn't Float;* D.Lit., Laurentian University, 1970; Vicky Metcalf Award, 1970; Mark Twain Award, 1971; Doctor of Law from Lethbridge University, 1973, University of Toronto, 1973, and University of Prince Edward Island, 1979; Curran Award, 1977, for "contributions to understanding wolves"; Queen Elizabeth II Jubilee Medal, 1978; Knight of Mark Twain, 1980; Officer, Order of Canada, 1981; Doctor of Literature, University of Victoria, 1982, and Lakehead University, 1986.

WRITINGS:

NONFICTION

People of the Deer, Atlantic-Little, Brown, 1952, revised edition, McClelland & Stewart, 1975.
The Regiment, McClelland & Stewart, 1955, revised edition, 1973.
The Dog Who Wouldn't Be, Atlantic-Little, Brown, 1957.
(Editor) Samuel Hearne, *Coppermine Journey: An Account of a Great Adventure,* Atlantic-Little, Brown, 1958.
The Grey Seas Under, Atlantic-Little, Brown, 1958.
The Desperate People, Atlantic-Little, Brown, 1959.
(Editor) *Ordeal by Ice* (also see below), McClelland & Stewart, 1960.

The Serpent's Coil, McClelland & Stewart, 1961.
Owls in the Family (American Library Association Notable Book), Atlantic-Little, Brown, 1961.
Never Cry Wolf, Atlantic-Little, Brown, 1963, revised edition, McClelland & Stewart, 1973.
Westviking: The Ancient Norse in Greenland and North America, Atlantic-Little, Brown, 1965.
(Editor) *The Polar Passion: The Quest for the North Pole* (also see below), McClelland & Stewart, 1967, revised edition, McClelland & Stewart, 1973.
Canada North, Atlantic-Little, Brown, 1967.
(With John de Visser) *This Rock within the Sea: A Heritage Lost,* Atlantic-Little, Brown, 1969, new edition, McClelland & Stewart, 1976.
The Boat Who Wouldn't Float, McClelland & Stewart, 1969, Atlantic-Little, Brown, 1970.
The Siberians, Atlantic-Little, Brown, 1970 (published in Canada as *Sibir: My Discovery of Siberia,* McClelland & Stewart, 1970, revised edition, 1973).
A Whale for the Killing, Atlantic-Little, Brown, 1972.
(With David Blackwood) *Wake of the Great Sealers,* Atlantic-Little, Brown, 1973.
(Editor) *Tundra: Selections from the Great Accounts of Arctic Land Voyages* (also see below), McClelland & Stewart, 1973, Peregrine Smith, 1990.
Top of the World Trilogy (includes *Ordeal by Ice, The Polar Passion: The Quest for the North Pole,* and *Tundra: Selections from the Great Accounts of Arctic Land Voyages*), McClelland & Stewart, 1976.
The Great Betrayal: Arctic Canada Now, Atlantic-Little, Brown, 1976 (published in Canada as *Canada North Now: The Great Betrayal,* McClelland & Stewart, 1976).
And No Birds Sang (memoir), Atlantic-Little, Brown, 1979.
The World of Farley Mowat: A Selection from His Works, edited by Peter Davison, Atlantic-Little, Brown, 1980.
Sea of Slaughter, Atlantic Monthly Press, 1984.
My Discovery of America, McClelland & Stewart, 1985.
Woman in the Mists: The Story of Dian Fossey and the Mountain Gorillas of Africa, Warner Books, 1987.
The New Founde Land: A Personal Voyage of Discovery, McClelland & Stewart, 1989.

FICTION

Lost in the Barrens (juvenile novel), Atlantic-Little, Brown, 1956.
The Black Joke (juvenile novel), McClelland & Stewart, 1962.
The Curse of the Viking Grave (juvenile novel), Atlantic-Little, Brown, 1966.
The Snow Walker (short story collection), Atlantic-Little, Brown, 1975.

OTHER

Also author of television screenplays "Sea Fare" and "Diary of a Boy on Vacation," both 1964. Contributor to magazines. A collection of Mowat's manuscripts is housed at McMaster University.

WORK IN PROGRESS: Two feature films; an autobiography.

SIDELIGHTS: Farley Mowat is Canada's most internationally recognized living writer. He has published more than twenty-nine books, both fiction and nonfiction, many of which have been widely translated. Although he is frequently categorized as a nature writer, Mowat wishes to be considered a storyteller or "saga man" who is concerned about the preservation of all forms of life. Mowat's reputation is that of an outspoken advocate with an irreverent attitude toward bureaucracy and a love of the far Canadian North. He has aroused the ire of government officials many times in the course of his career with his harsh indictments of their treatment of endangered races of people and endangered species of animal life. With characteristic bluntness, Mowat once remarked in *Newsweek:* "Modern man is such an arrogant cement head to believe that he can take without paying."

Mowat first became aware of humanity's outrages against nature in the late 1940s when he accepted a position as a government biologist in the Barren Lands of northern Canada. He had accepted the assignment in part because it offered him a respite from civilization, since he had recently returned from serving in the Canadian Army where he had witnessed many injustices against his fellow man. "I came back from the war rejecting my species," he told Cheryl McCall in *People* magazine. "I hated what had been done to me and what I had done and what man did to man."

Mowat's assignment in the Barrens was to study the area's wolves and their diet. The Canadian government suspected that the wolves were responsible for the dwindling caribou population, and they wanted evidence to corroborate their suspicions. After observing a wolf couple he named George and Angeline, however, Mowat found the wolves to be intelligent creatures who ate only what they needed. He learned that their diet consisted primarily of field mice and an occasional sickly caribou, and that by choosing the weak caribou, the wolves actually helped strengthen the herd.

Mowat fashioned his findings into an entertaining tale, *Never Cry Wolf,* where he also noted that his findings were "not kindly received by ordained authority." A *Chicago Tribune Book World* reviewer calls Mowat's discovery "a perfect example of the bureaucrats getting more than they bargained for." According to an *Atlantic* reviewer, "the Canadian government . . . has never paid any discernible attention to the information it hired Mr. Mowat to assemble."

The book's message was heeded by the reading public and by the governments of other countries, including Russia. Shortly after a translation of *Never Cry Wolf* appeared in Russian, government officials there banned the slaughter of wolves, whom they had previously thought to be arbitrary killers. In addition, *Los Angeles Time Book Review* contributor David Graber believes that "by writing 'Never Cry Wolf,' [Mowat] almost single-handedly reversed the public's image of the wolf, from feared vermin to romantic symbol of the wilderness."

Never Cry Wolf was welcomed by critics as well. *Christian Science Monitor* reviewer Harry C. Kenney notes that the book "delightfully and instructively lifts one into a captivating animal kingdom," and Gavin Maxwell writes in *Book Week:* "This is a fascinating and captivating book, and a tragic one, too, for it carries a bleak, dead-pan obituary of the wolf family that Mr. Mowat had learned to love and respect. It is an epilogue that will not endear the Canadian Wildlife Service to readers. . . . Once more it is man who displays the qualities with which he has tried to damn the wolf."

While in the Barrens, Mowat also befriended an Eskimo tribe called the Ihalmiut, nicknamed the People of the Deer because they depend almost solely on caribou for food, clothing, and shelter. While conversing with the Ihalmiut in a simplified form of their language that they had taught him, Mowat learned that the tribe had been dwindling for a number of years due to the decreasing availability of caribou. Mowat, enraged at the government's apathy toward preserving the tribe, began to write scath-

ing letters to government officials, eventually losing his position as a result. He then decided to write a book entitled *People of the Deer* to help publicize the tribe's plight. *Saturday Review* contributor Ivan T. Sanderson observes: "What [Mowat] learned by living with the pathetic remnants of this wonderful little race of Nature's most perfected gentlemen, learning their language and their history, and fighting the terrifying northern elements at their side, so enraged him that when he came to set down the record, he contrived the most damning indictment of his own government and country, the so-called white race and its Anglo-Saxon branch in particular, the Christian religion, and civilization as a whole, that had ever been written."

Others express a similar admiration for *People of the Deer.* A *Times Literary Supplement* reviewer writes: "The author traces with a beautiful clarity the material and spiritual bonds between land, deer and people, and the precarious ecological balance which had been struck between the forefathers of this handful of men and the antlered multitude." Observes Albert Hubbell in the *New Yorker:* "It is not often that a writer finds himself the sole chronicler of a whole human society, even of a microcosmic one like the Ihalmiut, and Mowat has done marvellously well at the job, despite a stylistic looseness and a tendency to formlessness. Also, his justifiable anger at the Canadian government's neglect of the Ihalmiut, who are its wards, intrudes in places where it doesn't belong, but then, as I said, Mowat is something of a fanatic on this subject. His book, just the same, is a fine one." T. Morris Longstreth concludes in *Christian Science Monitor:* "Mr. Mowat says of his book, 'This is a labor of love, and a small repayment to a race that gave me renewed faith in myself and in all men.' It will widen the horizons of many who are at the same time thankful that this explorer did the widening for them."

Mowat's most bitter account of man's abuse of nonhuman life is *Sea of Slaughter,* published in 1984. "Built of the accumulated fury of a lifetime," according to *Los Angeles Times Book Review* contributor David Graber, *Sea of Slaughter* is viewed by several critics to be his most important work to date. Tracy Kidder notes in the *Washington Post Book World* that compared to his earlier work *Never Cry Wolf,* this book "is an out and out tirade." The book's title refers to the extinction and near-extinction of sea and land animals along the Atlantic seaboard of North America, extending from Cape Cod to Labrador. Mowat traces the area's history back to the sixteenth century when the waters teemed with fish, whales, walruses, and seals, and the shores abounded with bison, white bears (now known as polar bears because of their gradual trek northward), and other fur-bearing mammals. Currently, many of these species have been either greatly diminished or extinguished because of "pollution, gross overhunting . . ., loss of habitat, destruction of food supplies, poachings and officially sanctioned 'cullings,' " writes Kidder.

The stark contrast between past and present is tremendously affecting, reviewers note. *Detroit News* contributor Lewis Regenstein, for example, writes that the book has several shortcomings, including some inaccuracies and a lack of footnoting, but claims that these "shortcomings pale in comparison to the importance of its message: We are not only destroying our wildlife but also the earth's ability to support a variety of life forms, including humans. As Mowat bluntly puts it, 'The living world is dying in our time.' " *Los Angeles Times Book Review* contributor David Graber believes that "the grandest anguish comes from Mowat's unrelenting historical accounts of the sheer *numbers* of whales, bears, salmon, lynx, wolves, bison, sea birds; numbers that sear because they proclaim what we have lost, what we have thrown away." Ian Darragh writes in *Quill & Quire:* "Mowat's description of the slaughter of millions of shorebirds for sport, for example, is appalling for what it implies about the aggression and violence apparently programmed into man's genetic code. There is little room for humour or Mowat's personal anecdotes in this epitaph for Atlantic Canada's once bountiful fish and wildlife." Concludes *Commonweal* critic Tom O'Brien: "*Sea of Slaughter* provides some heavier reading [than Mowat's other books]; the weight in the progression of chapters starts to build through the book like a dirge. Nevertheless, it may help to focus the burgeoning animal rights movement in this country and abroad. The cause has no more eloquent spokesperson."

Sea of Slaughter received some unintended but nevertheless welcome publicity in 1984 when Mowat was refused entrance into the United States, where he was planning to publicize the book. While boarding a plane at a Toronto airport, Mowat was detained by officials from the United States Immigration and Naturalization Service (INS) who acted on the information that Mowat's name appeared in the *Lookout Book*, a government document that lists the names of those individuals who represent a danger to the security of the United States.

Mowat later speculated in the *Chicago Tribune* about some possible reasons for his exclusion: "At first, . . . the assumption was that I was excluded because of the two trips I made to the Soviet Union [in the late 1960s]. . . . Then some guy at the INS supposedly said I was kept out because I'd threatened the U.S. Armed Forces by threatening to shoot down American aircraft with a .22 caliber rifle. The fact is the Ottawa Citizen [where the story supposedly appeared in 1968] can't find any record of it, but that doesn't matter. I admit it, happily." Mowat added that more recently the suggestion has been that the "gun lobby and anti-environmentalists" might have wanted to prevent his publicizing *Sea of Slaughter.*

Although the United States Immigration and Naturalization Service later granted Mowat a month-long admittance for business purposes, Mowat refused the offer, demanding an as-yet undelivered apology. Instead, Mowat used the time he would have spent traveling to write *My Discovery of America*, where he describes in detail his attempts to determine why he was not allowed entry into the United States. *Los Angeles Times* contributor David Graber writes: " 'My Discovery of America' is an entertaining chronicle offering useful and provocative insights about the American body politic, but it shouldn't be a book. Shame on Farley Mowat, customarily an economical wordsmith. Shame on Atlantic Monthly, which has a perfectly good outlet for the longish essay that this should have been."

The excitement caused by Mowat's experience and the subsequent book earned Mowat as much, or perhaps more, notoriety than he would have received in his scheduled tour. Mowat, delighted by rising sales of *Sea of Slaughter*, told Jane Cawley in the *Chicago Tribune*: "I'm going to send a bouquet of roses to the INS . . . guy who stopped me, along with a note that says, 'Thanks for the publicity.' "

Mowat departs from his usual subject matter in *And No Birds Sang*, a memoir describing his experiences in the Canadian Army Infantry during World War II. The memoir, penned thirty years after Mowat's return from duty, was written in part to help refute the notion that it is sweet and honorable to die in service to one's country, a statement Mowat had seen gaining ground in the late 1970s. *And No Birds Sang* chronicles Mowat's initial enthusiasm and determination to fight and his gradual surrender to despair and a horrifying fear of warfare, a fear Mowat calls "The Worm That Never Dies." Contrary to the popular belief that each battle becomes increasingly easier, Mowat found that

each attack on the enemy became more difficult as "The Worm" became more insidious. Christopher Lehmann-Haupt writes in the *New York Times:* "Bit by bit we begin to notice Mr. Mowat's growing preoccupation with what he will eventually name the Worm That Never Dies—gut-twisting fear. It doesn't bother him much at first, during a night landing on the southeast tip of Sicily, or during his platoon's initial victorious skirmishing with remnants of the German Army rapidly retreating to the north. But images of death accumulate in Mr. Mowat's mind—men cut in half, decapitated, blown to bits, or just driven mad—and the desire to fight steadily drains out of him."

Several reviewers believe that *And No Birds Sang* is a valuable addition to the literature of World War II. *Washington Post Book World* contributor Robert W. Smith calls the book "a powerful chunk of autobiography and a valuable contribution to war literature." *Time* critic R. Z. Sheppard writes: "*And No Birds Sang* needs no rhetoric. It can fall in with the best memoirs of World War II, a classic example of how unexploded emotions can be artfully defused."

Although other reviewers express reservations about the familiar nature of Mowat's theme, they add that Mowat nevertheless manages to bring a fresh perspective to the adage, "War is hell." David Weinberger remarks in *Macleans:* "Everybody knows that war is hell; it is the author's task to transform that knowledge into understanding. At times Mowat succeeds, at times the writing bogs down in adjectives and ellipsis." He adds, however, that "it takes a writer of stature—both as an author and as a moral, sensitive person—to make the attempt as valiantly as Mowat has." A similar opinion is expressed by Jean Strouse in *Newsweek:* "That war is hell is not news, but a story told this well serves, particularly in these precarious, saber-rattling days, as a vivid reminder."

In addition to his own memoirs, Mowat has authored a biography of the famed primatologist Dian Fossey. Shortly after Fossey was brutally murdered in 1985, Mowat was approached by Warner Books to write her biography. Although he initially refused—simply because he had never written a commissioned book—Mowat later accepted the offer after reading one of Fossey's *National Geographic* articles. Moved by "her empathy with the animal world, the impression that she had penetrated the barrier humans have erected," writes Beverly Slopen in *Publishers Weekly*, Mowat also thought "he could use her story as a vehicle for his message." Mowat told Slopen that while reading Fossey's letters and journals, though, "I began to realize that the importance of the book was her message, not my message. . . . I really became her collaborator. It was the journals that did it. They weren't long, discursive accounts. They were short, raw cries from the heart."

The biography, *Woman in the Mists: The Story of Dian Fossey and the Mountain Gorillas of Africa*, was published in 1987. As Mowat indicated, the work relies heavily on Fossey's journal entries and letters to tell the story of her life. Fossey, originally a physical therapist, was invited by anthropologist Louis Leakey in 1967 to study primates in the Congo (now Zaire). Shortly thereafter Fossey's work was halted by political uprising, but the indomitable Fossey escaped armed soldiers to cross the border into Uganda. She established a research center on the Rwandan side of the Virunga Mountains, near the Parc National des Volcans, where she remained until her death.

Although the murder has not yet been solved, and thus Mowat is not able to say who killed Fossey, the book nevertheless "goes a long way toward revealing what it was about her that made a violent death seem inevitable," writes Eugene Linden in the *New*

York Times Book Review. Fossey was known to stalk gorilla poachers, and she lived by the motto "An eye for an eye." When a man who had stoned her dog Cindy was captured, Fossey and her associates likewise stoned him. She also angered government officials by opposing "gorilla tourism" and the development of park land for agrarian purposes.

Some critics view Fossey's protective stance toward the apes as evidence of her misanthropy. Indeed, Stefan Kanfer relates in *Time* that Fossey once declared, "I feel more comfortable with gorillas than people. I can anticipate what a gorilla's going to do." *Washington Post Book World* contributor Mary Battiata writes: "Forced to choose between the needs of people and the survival of a threatened gorilla population, Fossey chose gorillas every time." Linden, on the other hand, maintains that "the diaries reveal a woman whose self-righteousness and sense of mission justified the kind of behavior that borders on madness."

Mowat's biography also reveals a side of Fossey that was generous, kind, witty, and romantic. She had a succession of affairs throughout her lifetime, including one with Louis Leakey, and longed for a stable, monogamous relationship. Thus Mowat, Battiata believes, "puts to rest—forever one hopes—the shopworn notion of Fossey as a misanthrope who preferred animals to her own species."

Several reviewers feel that more commentary from Mowat is needed in order to make sense of Fossey's controversial life and death. Mowat's self-appointed role as a "collaborator" rather than a biographer makes Battiata "uneasy," and she explains: "Though Mowat offers an intriguing and credible solution to the mystery of Fossey's unsolved murder, there is little else that is genuinely new here. . . . Mowat never really gets around to a clear-eyed evaluation of Fossey's scientific contributions or her conservation efforts. By failing to do so, he leaves a thin veil of romance over a life strong enough to stand unadorned." *Chicago Tribune* contributor Anita Susan Grossman similarly observes: "Farley Mowat has declined to do any serious analysis of his controversial subject. Instead, he limits himself to presenting excerpts from Fossey's own writings, strung together with the barest of factual narration. As a result, the central drama of Fossey's life remains as murky as the circumstances of her death. One awaits other, more comprehensive accounts of this extraordinary woman." Although Linden concurs that *Woman in the Mists* does have several problems, including a lack of footnotes, Mowat's "pedestrian" prose, and "interlocutory words [that] add little to our understanding of Fossey or her world," he adds: "Despite these problems, this is a rare, gripping look at the tragically mingled destinies of a heroic, flawed woman and her beloved mountain gorillas amid the high mists of the Parc des Volcans."

Critical appraisal aside, Mowat states that the writing of Fossey's biography had a profound, sobering effect on him and that he will not undertake another biography. "It was a disturbing experience," he told Slopen. "It's almost as though I were possessed. I wasn't the master. I fought for mastery and I didn't win. It really was a transcendental experience and I'm uncomfortable with it."

Although Mowat has spent nearly a lifetime trying to convince humanity that we cannot continue to abuse nature without serious and sometimes irreversible repercussions, he believes that "in the end, my crusades have accomplished nothing." Mowat continues in *People* magazine: "I haven't saved the wolf, the whales, the seals, primitive man or the outport people. All I've done is to document the suicidal tendencies of modern man. I'm sure I haven't altered the course of human events one iota.

Things will change inevitably, but it's strictly a matter of the lottery of fate. It has nothing to do with man's intentions."

MEDIA ADAPTATIONS: A *Whale for the Killing* was made into a movie and shown on ABC-TV in March, 1980; *Never Cry Wolf* was made into a film of the same title and released by Buena Vista in 1983. The National Film Board of Canada released a biographical film, "In Search of Farley Mowat," in May, 1981.

BIOGRAPHICAL/CRITICAL SOURCES:

BOOKS

Authors and Artists for Young Adults, Volume 1, Gale, 1988.
Contemporary Literary Criticism, Volume 26, Gale, 1983.
Dictionary of Literary Biography, Volume 68: *Canadian Writers, 1920-1959, First Series,* Gale, 1988.
Egoff, Sheila, *The Republic of Childhood: A Critical Guide to Canadian Children's Literature in English,* Oxford University Press, 1975.
Mowat, Farley, *And No Birds Sang* (memoir), Atlantic-Little, Brown, 1979.

PERIODICALS

Atlantic, November, 1963.
Audubon, January, 1973.
Best Sellers, February, 1986.
Books in Canada, March, 1985, November, 1985.
Books of the Times, April, 1980.
Book Week, November 24, 1963.
Book World, December 31, 1972.
Canadian Children's Literature, Numbers 5 and 6, 1976.
Canadian Forum, July, 1974, March, 1976.
Canadian Geographical Journal, June, 1974.
Canadian Literature, spring, 1978.
Chicago Tribune, October 29, 1980, December 23, 1983, May 6, 1985, October 22, 1987.
Chicago Tribune Book World, November 13, 1983.
Christian Science Monitor, May 1, 1952, October 3, 1963, May 15, 1969, May 10, 1970, April 15, 1971, March 6, 1974.
Commonweal, September 6, 1985.
Contemporary Review, February, 1978.
Detroit News, April 21, 1985.
Economist, January 15, 1972.
Globe and Mail (Toronto), November 25, 1989.
Illustrated London News, September 20, 1952.
Los Angeles Times, December 13, 1985.
Los Angeles Times Book Review, March 16, 1980, April 28, 1985.
Macleans, October 8, 1979.
Nation, June 10, 1968.
New Republic, March 8, 1980.
Newsweek, February 18, 1980, September 30, 1985.
New Yorker, April 26, 1952, May 11, 1968, March 17, 1980.
New York Times, December 13, 1965, February 19, 1980.
New York Times Book Review, February 11, 1968, June 14, 1970, February 22, 1976, November 6, 1977, February 24, 1980, December 22, 1985, October 25, 1987.
Observer, March 4, 1973.
People, March 31, 1980.
Publishers Weekly, October 2, 1987.
Quill & Quire, December, 1984.
Saturday Evening Post, July 29, 1950, April 13, 1957.
Saturday Night, October 18, 1952, October 25, 1952, November, 1975.
Saturday Review, June 28, 1952, April 26, 1969, October 21, 1972.
Scientific American, March, 1964.

Sierra, September, 1978.

Spectator, November 21, 1952.

Time, February 18, 1980, May 6, 1985, October 26, 1987.

Times Literary Supplement, September 12, 1952, March 19, 1971, February 16, 1973.

Washington Post, October 9, 1983, April 25, 1985, October 25, 1985.

Washington Post Book World, February 24, 1980, May 12, 1985, October 25, 1987.

* * *

MROZEK, Slawomir 1930-

PERSONAL: Born June 26, 1930, in Borzecin, Poland; son of Antoni (a post office clerk) and Zofia (Kedzior) Mrozek; married Maria Obremba, 1959. *Education:* Studied architecture, oriental culture, and painting, in Krakow, Poland.

ADDRESSES: Home—5, Avenue Franco-Russe, 75007 Paris, France. *Agent*—Tessa Sayle, 11 Jubilee Place, London SW3 3TE, England.

CAREER: Worked as a caricaturist for various newspapers and magazines, and as a journalist, in Krakow, Poland. Director, editor, and producer of films, S. D. R., Stuttgart, West Germany, 1977 and 1979. Full-time writer.

AWARDS, HONORS: Prix de l'Humeur Noir, 1964.

WRITINGS:

FICTION

Opowiadania z Trzmielowej Gory (short stories; title means "Stories from Buble Bee Hill"), [Warsaw, Poland], 1953.

Polpancerze praktyczne (short stories; title means "Practical Half-Armours"), [Krakow, Poland], 1953.

Malenkie lato (satirical novel; title means "The Small Summer"; originally published in *Dziennik Polski,* 1955-56), Wydawnictwo Literackie (Krakow), 1956.

Slon (short stories; title means "The Elephant"), illustrations by Daniel Mroz, Wydawnictwo Literackie, 1957, translation from the Polish by Konrad Syrop published as *The Elephant,* Grove Press, 1963.

Wesele w Atomicach (short stories; title means "A Wedding at Atomville"), Wydawnictwo Literackie, 1959.

Deszcz (satire; title means "Rain"), Wydawnictwo Literackie, 1962.

Opowiadania (short stories), Wydawnictwo Literackie, 1964.

The Urgupu Bird (short stories), translation from the Polish by Syrop, Macdonald & Co., 1968.

Dwa listy i inne opowiadania (short stories; title means "Two Letters and Other Stories"; also see below), Instytut Literacki (Paris), 1970.

Dwa listy (short story), Wydawnictwo Literackie, 1974.

Opowiadania (short stories), Wydawnictwo Literackie, 1974.

Moniza Clavier (short story; originally published in *Tworczosc,* number 6, 1967), Wydawnictwo Literackie, 1983.

PLAYS

Meczenstwo Piotra Oheya (three-act; title means "The Ordeal of Peter Ohey"; first produced in Krakow, at the Groteska Theatre, 1959; also see below), *Dialog,* number 6, 1959.

Indyk (two-act; title means "The Turkey"; first produced in Krakow at Stary Theatre, 1960), *Dialog,* number 10, 1960.

Karol (first produced in Zakopane, Poland, at the Modrzejewska Theatre, 1961; also see below), *Dialog,* number 3, 1961.

The Policemen (originally published as *Policja* in *Dialog,* number 6, 1958; first produced in Warsaw at Dramatyczny Theatre,

1958; translation from the Polish by Edmund Ordon produced Off-Broadway at Phoenix Theatre, November, 1961; also see below), Hart Stenographic Bureau, 1961.

Na pelnym morzu (title means "On the Open Sea"; first produced in Zakopane at the Modrzejewska Theatre, 1961; translation from the Polish by Mai Rodman produced as "At Sea" Off-Broadway at Mermaid Theatre, January, 1962; also see below), *Dialog,* number 2, 1961.

Striptease (first produced in Zakopane at the Modrzejewska Theatre, 1961; also see below), *Dialog,* number 6, 1961.

Kynolog w rozterce (title means "A Dog Fancier in a Quandary"; first produced in Krakow at the Muzyczny Theatre, 1967), *Dialog,* number 11, 1962.

Zabawa (title means "Having a Ball"; first produced in Wroclaw, Poland, at Dramatyczny Theatre, 1963; also see below), *Dialog,* number 10, 1962.

Czarowna noc (title means "An Enchanting Evening"; first produced in Krakow at Groteska Theatre, 1963; also see below), *Dialog,* number 3, 1963.

Smierc porucznika (one-act with prologue and epilogue; title means "Death of the Lieutenant"; first produced in Warsaw at Dramatyczny Theatre, 1963), *Dialog,* number 5, 1963.

Utwory sceniczne (collection; title means "Stage Plays"), Wydawnictwo Literackie, 1963.

Dom na granicy (title means "The House on the Frontier"; first produced in Krakow at Groteska Lalka i Maski Theatre, 1968), *Dialog,* number 5, 1967.

Poczworka (title means "The Quarternion"; first produced in Gdansk, Poland, at the Wybrzeze Theatre, 1967), *Dialog,* number 1, 1967.

Testarium, published in *Dialog,* number 11, 1967.

Six Plays (contains *The Police, The Martyrdom of Peter Ohey, Out at Sea, Charlie, The Party,* and *An Enchanted Night*), translation from the Polish by Nicholas Bethell, Grove Press, 1967.

Drugie danie (title means "Main Course"; first produced in Lodz, Poland, at Nowy Theatre, 1979), *Dialog,* number 5, 1968.

Tango: A Play in Three Acts (originally published in *Dialog,* number 11, 1964; first produced in Warsaw at the Wspolczesny Theatre, 1964; produced on the West End at Aldwych Theatre, 1966; produced Off-Broadway at Pocket Theater, January, 1969; also see below), translation from the Polish by Ralph Manheim and Teresa Dzieduscycka, Grove Press, 1968, reprinted, Polska Macierz Skolna, [London], 1983.

Vatzlav: A Play in 77 Scenes (first produced in Stratford, Ontario, Canada, at the Festival Theatre, August, 1970; produced in New York City at the Quaigh, February, 1982; also see below), translation from the Polish by Manheim, Grove Press, 1970, reprinted, Applause Theatre Book Publications, 1986.

Striptease, Repeat Performance, and The Prophets: Three Plays, translations from the Polish by Dzieduscycka, Lola Gruenthal, and Manheim, Grove Press, 1972.

Utwory sceniczne (collection), Wydawnictwo Literackie, 1973.

Szczesliwe wydarzenie (title means "A Happy Event"; first produced in Warsaw at Wspolczesny Theatre, 1973), *Dialog,* number 4, 1973.

Rzeznia (radio play; title means "The Abattoir"; first produced in Warsaw at Dramatyczny Theatre, 1975), *Dialog,* number 9, 1973.

Utwory sceniczne nowe (collection; title means "New Stage Plays"), Wydawnictwo Literackie, 1975.

Garbus (title means "The Hunchback"; first produced in Krakow at Stary Theatre, 1975; also see below), *Dialog,* number 9, 1975.

Wyspa roz (teleplay; title means "Island of Roses"), *Dialog,* number 5, 1975.

Serenada (title means "Serenade"; first produced in Zabrze, Poland, at the Nowy Theatre, 1977; also see below), *Dialog,* number 2, 1977.

Lis filozof (title means "The Philosopher Fox"; first produced in Zabrze at the Nowy Theatre, 1977; also see below), *Dialog,* number 3, 1977.

Polowanie na lisa (title means "The Fox Hunt"; first produced in Zabrze at Nowy Theatre, 1977; also see below), *Dialog,* number 5, 1977.

Krawiec (title means "The Tailor"; first produced in Szczecin, Poland, at Wspolczesny Theatre, 1978; also see below), *Dialog,* number 11, 1977.

Lis aspirant (title means "Fox the Aspirant"; also see below), *Dialog,* number 7, 1978.

Amor (teleplay; originally published in *Dialog,* number 3, 1978; contains *Amor, The Tailor, The Hunchback, The Fox Hunt, Serenade, The Philosopher Fox,* and *Fox the Aspirant*), Wydawnictwo Literackie, 1979.

Striptease, Tango, Vatzlav: Three Plays, translations from the Polish by Gruenthal and others, Grove Press, 1981.

Pieszo, Czytelnik (Warsaw), 1983.

The Emigrants (originally published as *Emigranci* in *Dialog,* number 8, 1974; first produced in Warsaw at Wspolczesny Theatre, 1975; translation from the Polish by Maciej Wrona, Teresa Wrona, and Robert Holman produced Off-Broadway at the Brooklyn Academy of Music, 1979), translation from the Polish by Henry Beissel, S. French, 1984. 'The Ambassador,' first produced by the Vietnam Veterans Ensemble Theater Company, 1989.

Also author of "Jelen" (title means "The Stag"), 1963. Author and director of teleplay "Return."

CONTRIBUTOR TO ANTHOLOGIES

John Lahr, editor, *Grove Press Modern Drama,* Grove Press, 1975.

Wybor dramatow i opowiadan, Wydawnictwo Literackie, 1975.

OTHER

Polska w obrazach (satirical drawings; title means "Poland in Pictures"), [Krakow], 1957.

Postepowiec: Organ Slawomira Mrozka (satirical drawings; title means "The Progressive: Organ of Slawomir Mrozek"), Iskry, 1960.

Ucieczka na poludnie (comic book; title means "Flight to the South"), Iskry (Warsaw), 1961.

Przez okulary Slawomira Mrozka (humorous drawings; title means "Through Slawomir Mrozek's Eyeglasses"), Iskry, 1968.

Male listy (feuilletons), Wydawnictwo Literackie, 1982.

Rysunki, Iskry, 1982.

Donosy, Puls (London), 1983.

Alfa, Instytut Literacki, 1984.

Also contributor to *Dziennik Polski* (Krakow), 1955, and of cartoons to the weekly periodical *Przekroj.*

WORK IN PROGRESS: Short stories and plays.

SIDELIGHTS: Polish playwright and satirist Slawomir Mrozek has lived in exile since the Polish government withdrew his passport for having criticized its role in the Soviet occupation of Czechoslovakia. He began his career as a journalist, and then drew satirical cartoons before becoming a playwright and author of numerous short stories. Recognized primarily for his plays, several of which have been staged worldwide, Mrozek is fluent in English, French, and Italian, and his work has been published in several countries outside Poland and the United States, including Czechoslovakia, Denmark, West Germany, Finland, France, Great Britain, Greece, Holland, Hungary, Italy, Japan, Portugal, Rumania, Spain, Switzerland, the Soviet Union, and Yugoslavia. And although Mrozek is not well known in the United States, a few of his plays have been produced Off-Broadway.

Of his many plays, Mrozek is perhaps best known for "Tango," which according to Clive Barnes in the *New York Times,* "is a fascinating piece" and "created a sensation" when it was first performed and later banned in Poland. Walter Kerr describes the plot in the *New York Times:* "A family that discovered every kind of personal freedom for itself—freedom in art, freedom from religion—along about 1914 is now living contentedly in a house gone thoroughly to seed. . . . But, in however slovenly a way, these people are quite happy. Except for the son of the house . . . [who] would very much like to restore the conventions that were abandoned when his parents so courageously took to doing the tango. . . . Unfortunately, as he tries to bring the new/old order into being he discovers that it is empty. A convention cannot be restored simply because it is a convention; it must have an impulse, an idea, inside it, if it is going to work." In another *New York Times* piece, Barnes considered "Tango" to be "one of the most rewarding plays to come out of Eastern Europe in many years."

Remarking on the complexity of "Tango," Martin Esslin writes in his *The Theatre of the Absurd:* "It has been described as a parody or paraphrase of *Hamlet* in that it shows a young man horrified by the behaviour of his parents, deeply ashamed by his mother's promiscuity and his father's complacency. It is also, clearly, a bitter attack by a young man on the previous generation which has plunged his country into war, occupation and devastation." As such, Esslin suggests that the play has relevance for the West as well; Barnes concurs: "Like, Chekhov's 'The Cherry Orchard,' Mr. Mrozek's play is based on a family household that is intended to serve as a microcosm to the outside world. Indeed Mr. Mrozek is intentionally allegorical, and his play is intended to describe the decline of the West, postulating that our present laissez faire, hedonistically materialist society will . . . give way first to intellectual authoritarianism, and finally to the chaos of rule by brute force."

Praising Mrozek's "sharp, almost unerring ability to show things in a new perspective," Marketa Goetz Stankiewicz comments in *Contemporary Literature* that the reason Mrozek's play speaks especially to the Western world "lies in his ability to fuse three currents of contemporary drama . . . into a single medium of expression: first, the artist's acute sense of disaster evoked by the historical events of this century; second, the sensitivity to the false values and stultifying effects of a variety of social systems and man's subsequent change . . . to a vegetating weed without conscience or consciousness; third, the desire to recreate forms of the pre-literary theater expressing inexplicable and indefinable fears and hopes." Suggesting that Mrozek is writing within the tradition of the theatre of the absurd, Mardi Valgemae notes in *Contemporary Drama* that "Tango" exemplifies "a particular type of East European theatre of the absurd that differs somewhat from the French school of Beckett and his colleagues. For most French absurdists tend to concentrate on basic metaphysical issues, whereas many East European playwrights simply use absurd images in order to create social and political allegories."

In *Mrozek,* however, Jan Klossowicz disagrees with the tendency to categorize Mrozek within the absurdist tradition, offering instead the assessment that his plays must be "viewed within the framework of the tradition from which they sprang and of the experience by which they were determined." Klossowicz maintains that although Mrozek's plays employ devices of the absurdist theatre of the fifties, such as "emotional ambivalence, the grotesque technique, a mixture of the tragic and the comic, disregard for conventional plot and psychological motivation, ahistorical action, creation of a stage metareality, a new approach to the time of action and the duration of the play on stage," he is rather responding to the tradition of Polish Romanticism which, as Klossowicz explains, "stands for the tendency to proclaim political and social ideas in art (the struggle for freedom and criticism of the existing social structure), it stands for patriotism, exaltation, coupled with fantasy, sentimentalism and the professed superiority of 'emotion to mind.'" And according to Klossowicz, "Mrozek's works are a virtually ideal example of the anti-Romantic stance."

"Parody and imitation of the Romantic style is dominant in his writing," adds Klossowicz, who contends that "Mrozek's works as a whole may best be described by the term parabolic. His plays and most of his short stories are allegories. The characters are symbolic representation while situations illustrate theses." Klossowicz indicates that "instead of transcribing political or philosophical discourses into dialogue, Mrozek writes parables that illustrate the theses of these discourses, instead of devoting himself to the reconstruction of historical events, he writes fables where he narrates these events in the form of a metaphor." Klossowicz believes that Mrozek's work springs not from "the conviction of the absurdity of life and of the world, but a conviction of the absurdity of certain phenomena." As a satirist, Mrozek "scoffed at the surrounding world in the name of a laudable goal, and he remained faithful to this concept of literature later in life as well," observes Klossowicz, indicating that "the singular charm and originality" in his work rests in its "reflection of a specific social and historical situation."

BIOGRAPHICAL/CRITICAL SOURCES:

BOOKS

Contemporary Literary Criticism, Gale, Volume 3, 1975, Volume 13, 1980.
Esslin, Martin, *The Theatre of the Absurd,* revised edition, Doubleday, 1969.
Klossomicz, Jan, *Mrozek,* translation from the Polish by Christina Cenkalski, Authors Agency and Czytelnik (Warsaw), 1980.

PERIODICALS

Comparative Drama, spring, 1971.
Contemporary Literature, spring, 1971.
Nation, August 2, 1975.
New Statesman, July 9, 1976.
New York Times, November, 22, 1961, April 24, 1962, January 1, 1968, January 20, 1969, February 9, 1969, August 23, 1970, October 29, 1979, February 7, 1982.
Times Literary Supplement, April 20, 1967, March 21, 1968.
Virginia Quarterly Review, summer, 1973.
Washington Post, February 3, 1982.

MUGGERIDGE, Malcolm (Thomas) 1903-

PERSONAL: Born March 24, 1903, in Sanderstead, Surrey, England; son of Henry Thomas (a member of Parliament) and Annie (Booler) Muggeridge; married Katherine Dobbs, September, 1927; children: three sons, one daughter. *Education:* Selwyn College, Cambridge, M.A., 1923. *Religion:* Roman Catholic.

ADDRESSES: Home—Park Cottage, Robertsbridge, East Sussex, England.

CAREER: Union Christian College, South India, teacher, 1924-27; teacher in Minia, Egypt, 1927; Egyptian University, Cairo, Egypt, lecturer, 1927-30; *Manchester Guardian,* Manchester, England, editorial staff member, 1930-32, correspondent in Moscow, 1932-33; affiliated with International Labor Office, Geneva, Switzerland, 1933-34; *Calcutta Statesman,* Calcutta, India, assistant editor, 1934-35; *Evening Standard,* London, England, editorial staff member, 1935-36; *Daily Telegraph,* London, correspondent in Washington, D.C., 1946-47, deputy editor, 1950-52; television interviewer for "Panorama," 1951; *Punch,* London, editor, 1953-57; University of Edinburgh, Edinburgh, Scotland, rector, 1967-68. *Military service:* British Army, 1939-45, served in Intelligence Corps; became major; received Legion of Honor, Croix de Guerre with Palm, and Medaille de la Reconnaissance Francaise.

AWARDS, HONORS: Christopher Book Award, 1972, for *Something Beautiful for God,* and 1979, for *A Twentieth Century Testimony.*

WRITINGS:

Autumnal Faces (novel), Putnam, 1931.
Three Flats (three-act play), Putnam, 1931.
Winter in Moscow (novel), Little, Brown, 1934, new edition, Eerdmans, 1988.
(Translator) Maurice Bedel, *New Arcadia,* J. Cape, 1935.
The Earnest Atheist: A Study of Samuel Butler, Eyre & Spottiswoode, 1936, published as *A Study of Samuel Butler: The Earnest Atheist,* Putnam, 1937.
(With Hugh Kingsmill) *Brave Old World,* Eyre & Spottiswoode, 1936.
(With Kingsmill) *A Preview of Next Year's News,* Eyre & Spottiswoode, 1937.
In a Valley of This Restless Mind, Routledge & Kegan Paul, 1938.
The Sun Never Sets: The Story of England in the Nineteen Thirties, Random House, 1940, published in England as *The Thirties: 1930-1940 in Great Britain,* Hamish Hamilton, 1940, reprinted, Weidenfeld & Nicolson, 1989.
(Editor) Galeazzo Ciano, *Ciano's Diary, 1939-1943,* Heinemann, 1947.
(Editor) Ciano, *Ciano's Diplomatic Papers: Being a Record of Nearly 200 Conversations Held During the Years 1936-42 with Hitler,* Odhams, 1948.
Affairs of the Heart, Hamish Hamilton, 1949.
(With Hesketh Pearson) *About Kingsmill,* Methuen, 1951.
(Author of introduction) Ciano, *Diary, 1937-38,* Methuen, 1952, published as *Hidden Diary, 1937,* Dutton, 1953.
(Author of introduction) *Esquire's World of Humor,* Arthur Barker, 1965.
The Most of Malcolm Muggeridge, Simon & Schuster, 1966.
Tread Softly, for You Tread on My Jokes, Collins, 1966.
London a la Mode, Hill & Wang, 1966.
Muggeridge Through the Microphone: BBC Radio and Television, British Broadcasting Corp., 1967.
Jesus Rediscovered, Doubleday, 1969.

(With others) *What They Believe,* Hodder & Stoughton, 1969.

Something Beautiful for God: Mother Teresa of Calcutta, Harper, 1971.

(With Alec Vidler) *Paul: Envoy Extraordinary,* Harper, 1972.

Malcolm's Choice: A Collection of Cartoons, Mowbrays, 1972.

Chronicles of Wasted Time (autobiography), Morrow, Volume I: *The Green Stick,* 1973, Volume II: *The Infernal Grove,* 1974.

Jesus: The Man Who Lives, Harper, 1975.

A Third Testament, Little, Brown, 1976.

Christ and the Media, Eerdmans, 1977.

Things Past, Collins, 1978, Morrow, 1979.

A Twentieth Century Testimony, Collins, 1979.

The End of Christendom, Eerdmans, 1980.

Like It Was (diaries), edited by John Bright-Holmes, Collins, 1981.

(With others) *Christian Married Love,* Ignatius Press, 1981.

(With William Douglas-Home) *P. G. Woodhouse: Three Talks and a Few Words at a Festive Occasion,* Heineman, 1983.

My Life in Pictures (autobiographical text with photographs), Morrow, 1987.

Picture Palace (novel), Weidenfeld & Nicolson, 1987.

Confessions of a Twentieth-Century Pilgrim, Harper, 1988.

Conversion: A Spiritual Journey, Collins, 1988.

Contributor to magazines and newspapers, including *Ladies' Home Journal, Esquire, Horizon, Christianity Today, Reader's Digest,* and *Observer Review.*

SIDELIGHTS: Malcolm Muggeridge has been a journalist, a magazine editor, a university rector, a novelist, and a familiar figure on British television. In all his roles, he has been an outspoken, articulate, and controversial figure. As David Lodge notes in the *New York Times Book Review,* "Malcolm Muggeridge is famous for being Malcolm Muggeridge, scourge of liberalism, sardonic iconoclast, spiritual pilgrim." A socialist in his younger days, Muggeridge at one time was an avowed atheist. After a revelatory stint in Stalinist Moscow, however, he was to eschew socialism and find God. In some thirty books, Muggeridge has displayed a talent for stinging satire, controversial opinions, and elegant prose.

Muggeridge first desired to become a writer while he was attending Selwyn College, Cambridge. After a few years teaching in India and Egypt, he launched his career in journalism with the *Manchester Guardian,* serving initially as the newspaper's Cairo correspondent. Appointed the *Guardian*'s Moscow correspondent in 1932, Muggeridge and his wife went to the city with the intention of settling down in the Soviet Union, then considered by many leftists as a utopia in the making. They even spoke of becoming citizens. Muggeridge's father had been an outspoken socialist, while his wife was the niece of prominent Fabian Socialists Beatrice and Sidney Webb. The couple arrived in Moscow with high hopes, but their experience was a bitter one. Life for the average Soviet citizen was intolerable. Food shortages, police surveillance, and the brutal policies of the regime disillusioned Muggeridge with communist utopianism. He also became disillusioned with the Western correspondents based in the Soviet Union, whom he felt were whitewashing the truth. Many of the journalists were, Muggeridge found, more than eager to submit to Soviet censorship in exchange for the regime's special privileges.

When his editor at the *Manchester Guardian* refused to run an exclusive story on the Russian famine of the early 1930s—a famine deliberately caused by Soviet dictator Joseph Stalin to punish the rebellious Ukraine, claiming over 14 million lives—

Muggeridge angrily resigned his post. He then set about documenting the atrocity in his satirical novel, *Winter in Moscow.* A critic for the *Saturday Review of Literature* found Muggeridge's account to be refreshing: "There is such a thing as wholesome indignation, and there has been so much leaning over backward to be fair to Russia's present dictators, so much pussy-footing and 'on-the-other-hand' stuff, let alone downright misrepresentation, that it is refreshing to come across an intelligent observer who is just plain disgusted all through and doesn't give a hoot who knows it." Reviewing the book for *National Review* in 1988, William F. Buckley, Jr., finds it "mordant satire, to be sure, written out of an abyss of desolate cynicism, but Muggeridge renders it all with a vividness that is constantly believable." Buckley concludes, "An angrier book has never been written, nor one whose fury was so richly justified by its contents."

Another novel written at this time, *Picture Palace,* was meant as a satirical attack on the *Manchester Guardian* and what Muggeridge saw as that newspaper's acquiescence to Soviet tyranny. He also satirized the hypocritical liberalism of the newspaper's editor, C. P. Scott. The *Guardian* threatened legal action if the book were published, and Muggeridge's publisher suppressed the manuscript. *Picture Palace* was only published in 1987. Reviewing the book for the Toronto *Globe and Mail,* David Twiston Davies remarks that "the book's place in legend is due to the dramatic story of its suppression, rather than its quality, which has been hidden until now." Davies notes that Muggeridge's "picture of the domineering, self-deluding editor-proprietor, old Savoury [C. P. Scott], is worthy of hanging alongside [Evelyn] Waugh's Lord Copper."

After leaving the Soviet Union, Muggeridge worked for a time on the staffs of the *Calcutta Statesman* and the London *Evening Standard.* He also turned out a steady stream of books, including a study of Samuel Butler and a history of Great Britain in the 1930's. His biography of Butler, *The Earnest Atheist: A Study of Samuel Butler,* provided a new perspective on that author, but many critics were dismayed by Muggeridge's lack of objectivity. " 'The Earnest Atheist' is written from a depth of loathing and horror. As a result it is less objective than a study has a right to be. Allowing for the prejudice, however, it must be admitted that Mr. Muggeridge has succeeded in building up a strong case to prove that far from being the Anti-Victorian a future generation believed him to be, Butler was the Ultimate Victorian," Frances Winwar noted in the *New York Times.* Muggeridge's survey of England in the 1930's, *The Sun Never Sets,* makes no attempt at impartiality, either. "The book crackles with wit, it outdoes earlier only-yesterday studies with its cutting, flashing style, its glittering satire. Its epigrams fairly cry for quotations," observed R. H. Phelps. However, R. H. S. Crossman cautioned that "judged . . . as entertainment, [the book] is to be recommended; judged as a serious estimate of our age, it is clever, hysterical and defeatist, sacrificing truth for the sake of an epigram."

When World War II broke out, Muggeridge joined the Intelligence Corps, serving in East Africa, Italy, and France. During this time he became acquainted with Graham Greene and double agent Kim Philby. Although Muggeridge respected some of the British intelligence operations, by and large he felt that spying was a mockery. At one time he was so depressed by his espionage activities that he considered suicide. This period of his life is discussed in volume two of his autobiography, *The Infernal Grove.* In this book Muggeridge aims his lethal wit at the cult of intelligence, concluding that "diplomats and intelligence agents, in my experience, are even bigger liars than journalists."

Following a stint as Washington correspondent and deputy editor for the *Daily Telegraph,* Muggeridge was appointed editor of *Punch,* Britain's oldest humor magazine. From 1953-57 he worked as editor of *Punch,* encouraging such writers as Noel Coward, Lord Dunsany, Joyce Cary, J. B. Priestley, and Dorothy L. Sayers to contribute to the magazine. His acerbic editorials and clever parodies usually took aim at postwar England's Labor government, the strict food rationing then enforced (a carryover from the war), and other popular targets. A series of parodies of other magazines also proved popular. London's *World's Press News* cited him for putting "new life and new bite into this famous weekly magazine, [and] for courageously publishing some of the most controversial cartoons of the year." Perhaps the most controversial cartoon was a depiction of Winston Churchill as a blind man, which drew particularly heavy fire.

In the 1950's Muggeridge also became a familiar figure to the British television audience, conducting interviews with notable personalities, hosting travel documentaries on India, Israel, and the Soviet Union, as well as appearing on a number of special programs for BBC-TV. Critics compare his television writing to the best of his printed work. Here, too, however, Muggeridge could not avoid controversy. In the mid-1960s his remarks about the British monarchy, particularly the queen, almost cost him his broadcasting career. His televised attack on heart transplant pioneer Dr. Christiaan Barnard caused him to be banned from South African television. Yet, viewers have consistently enjoyed his work. In 1981 the BBC ran "Muggeridge Revisited," a series featuring the best of his three decades of television interviews, while some of his television commentaries have been collected in *Muggeridge Through the Microphone: BBC Radio and Television.*

Although Muggeridge frequently appears on the screen, he has often inveighed against television and the media. In 1953 he called for an end to the BBC monopoly of British television, warning in a *Time* article that those who appear on BBC "must be prepared to blow their trumpets or sound their cymbals or scratch their violins in accordance with the Corporation's baton." In an article for the *Observer Review,* he writes: "I see the camera, far more than even nuclear weapons, as the great destructive force of our time; the great falsifier. McLuhan is right; it's replaced the written and spoken word, captured the whole field of art and literature." Nonetheless, Muggeridge went on, he appears on television because "I may find an opportunity to say something, or convey something, which is worth while. . . . Supposing one was a pianist in a whorehouse—one might be able to persuade oneself that occasionally including a hymn like 'Abide with Me' in one's repertoire would have a beneficial influence on the inmates."

Muggeridge credits two programs that he did for the BBC with pushing him to convert to Christianity. In 1967 he filmed a program at a Cistercian abbey in Nunraw, Scotland. Reflecting on the time spent at the monastery, he penned these lines: "No heavenly visitation befell me, there was no Damascus Road grace; and yet, I know, life will never be quite the same after my three weeks with the Cistercians at Nunraw." Not long afterwards Muggeridge traveled to the Holy Land to film a documentary for the BBC, and it was there that a heavenly vision did befall him. Later he discussed his revelation: "I realized, in the first place, that many shrines, and the legends associated with them, were, for the most part, from my point of view, as fraudulent as the bones of St. Peter, the fragments of the True Cross, and other relics revered by the pious. Then, seeing a party of Christian pilgrims at one of these shrines, their faces so bright with faith, their voices, as they sang, so evidently and joyously aware of their Sav-

iour's nearness, I understood that for them the shrine was authentic. Their faith made it so. Similarly, I, too, became aware that there really had been a man, Jesus, who was also God; I was conscious of his presence."

Of course, a long series of events had led up to Muggeridge's conversion to Christianity. These events are recounted in his book, *Jesus Rediscovered.* He first learned about religion from his father, an agnostic whose religion was socialism. When Muggeridge lost faith in socialism in the early 1930's, he also lost any faith that man could make a heaven on earth. Reading the works of such religious figures as St. Augustine, John Bunyan, Pascal, and Tolstoi gave him valuable insights into Christianity. In many ways Muggeridge is far from an orthodox Christian. As he explains in *Jesus Rediscovered,* he believes that Christ is a living force, but he does not believe in the Resurrection. He has no interest in dogma and dislikes institutional religion. He also excoriates church leaders who concentrate on social issues rather than the teachings of Jesus.

Critics generally considered *Jesus Rediscovered* to be a significant book on religion. "This will be one of the widely read books of the religious year. . . . You will be satisfied that your time was well spent with some of the major issues that govern the last part of the 20th century," David Poling remarked. Similarly, Michael Novak observed: "This is an important book for Christianity. It sounds a deep, true note that has been missing from the chorus, a note without which everything else is off." Although Jeffrey Hart found Muggeridge's sense of Christ "convincing and moving," Harvey Cox perceived some un-Christian attitudes in the book: "It is lacking in love, short on hope, and almost completely devoid of charity. The Jesus he has rediscovered is not one I want to follow. Yet Muggeridge himself remains an irresistible old codger."

In the first two volumes of *Chronicles of Wasted Time,* a projected three-volume autobiography, Muggeridge has outlined the course of his early life. Critical reaction to the books has been generally favorable, with M. D. Aeschliman in *National Review* claiming that Muggeridge's "autobiographical writings contain some of the greatest and sanest writing in English in our time." Writing in the *New York Times Book Review,* Paul Johnson finds that "next to the late Evelyn Waugh, [Muggeridge] is, in my view, the finest writer of English prose of his generation." Muggeridge's published diaries have also brought his personal life into the public arena, giving his readers a glimpse into how he changed from a socialist atheist to a conservative Christian. Lodge notes that "one thing these diaries do is to scotch any suggestion that Malcolm Muggeridge's commitment to Christian asceticism is an old man's conversion. His yearning for spiritual peace, his effort to deny worldly desires in order to attain the serenity of the mystics, is a motif that runs through the pages."

Living quietly in the English countryside with his wife of sixty years, Muggeridge is working on the third volume of his autobiography. When Alan Watkins of the London *Times* visited Muggeridge in 1983, he noted that the author "loves talk for its own sake, as a good in itself " and enjoys telling anecdotes from his long and varied career. In a piece for the London *Times,* Muggeridge observed: "Human life, I have come to feel, in all its public or collective manifestations, is only theatre, and mostly cheap melodrama at that. There is nothing serious under the sun except love; of fellow-mortals and of God."

BIOGRAPHICAL/CRITICAL SOURCES:

BOOKS

Authors in the News, Volume 1, Gale, 1976.

Hunter, Ian, *Malcolm Muggeridge: A Life,* Nelson, 1980.

Mortimer, John Clifford, *In Character,* Penguin, 1984.

Muggeridge, Malcolm, *Chronicles of Wasted Time,* Morrow, Volume I: *The Green Stick,* 1973, Volume II: *The Infernal Grove,* 1974.

Muggeridge, Malcolm, *My Life in Pictures,* Morrow, 1987.

PERIODICALS

America, November 6, 1971, March 4, 1978.

Best Sellers, July 1, 1966, October 1, 1969, November 1, 1971.

Books and Bookmen, June, 1971.

Book Week, July 3, 1966.

Boston Transcript, May 11, 1940.

Christian Century, October 22, 1969, November 24, 1971.

Christian Science Monitor, September 26, 1934, April 7, 1937, June 29, 1940, August 2, 1966.

Economist, September 22, 1973.

Globe and Mail (Toronto), August 29, 1987, July 9, 1988.

Listener, December 7, 1967.

Nation, April 3, 1937.

National Review, December 2, 1969, December 19, 1975, February 19, 1988, March 4, 1988, September 30, 1988.

New Republic, May 5, 1937, May 27, 1940, October 27, 1973, August 23, 1974, July 18-25, 1983.

New Statesman and Nation, December 12, 1931, August 29, 1936, March 9, 1940, September 29, 1972, September 21, 1973, October 17, 1975.

Newsweek, September 9, 1957, July 19, 1965, January 29, 1968, September 8, 1969, July 22, 1974.

New York Herald Tribune Books, October 30, 1932, March 14, 1937.

New York Post, May 12, 1934.

New York Review of Books, December 29, 1966.

New York Times, September 11, 1932, March 14, 1937, June 16, 1940.

New York Times Book Review, March 5, 1961, September 7, 1969, November 14, 1971, May 7, 1972, September 30, 1973, July 14, 1974, February 21, 1982.

New York Times Magazine, April 29, 1956.

Observer Review, August 20, 1967, December 15, 1968.

Saturday Review, May 24, 1934, August 30, 1969.

Saturday Review of Literature, June 9, 1934, May 4, 1940.

Spectator, December 12, 1931, March 9, 1934, September 11, 1936.

Time, March 8, 1937, August 3, 1953, January 6, 1967, January 26, 1968, September 26, 1969, August 5, 1974.

Times (London), March 21, 1983.

Times Literary Supplement, December 10, 1931, March 15, 1934, September 5, 1936, March 9, 1940, July 24, 1969, March 31, 1972, September 29, 1972, September 28, 1973, September 12, 1975, May 1, 1981.

Variety, September 3, 1969.

Washington Post Book World, October 12, 1969, December 26, 1971.

Washington Star-News, February 18, 1975.

World's Press News (London), December 31, 1954.

—Sketch by Thomas Wiloch

*   *   *

MUKHERJEE, Bharati 1940-

PERSONAL: Born July 27, 1940, in Calcutta, India; immigrated to United States, 1961; immigrated to Canada, 1968, naturalized citizen, 1972; immigrated to United States, 1980, naturalized citizen; daughter of Sudhir Lal (a chemist) and Bina (Banerjee) Mukherjee; married Clark Blaise (a writer and professor), September 19, 1963; children: Bart, Bernard. *Education:* University of Calcutta, B.A., 1959; University of Baroda, M.A., 1961; University of Iowa, M.F.A., 1963, Ph.D., 1969. *Religion:* Hindu.

ADDRESSES: Home and office—115 Circular St., Saratoga Springs, N.Y. 12866. *Agent*—Timothy Seldes, Russell & Volkening, Inc., 551 Fifth Ave., New York, N.Y. 10017.

CAREER: Marquette University, Milwaukee, Wis., instructor in English, 1964-65; University of Wisconsin (now University of Wisconsin—Madison), Madison, instructor, 1965; McGill University, Montreal, Quebec, lecturer, 1966-69, assistant professor, 1969-73, associate professor, 1973-78, professor, 1978; Skidmore College, Saratoga Springs, N.Y., professor of English, beginning in 1979; affiliated with Montclair State College, Queens College, and Columbia University.

AWARDS, HONORS: Grants from McGill University, 1968 and 1970, Canada Arts Council, 1973-74 and 1977, Shastri Indo-Canadian Institute, 1976-77, Guggenheim Foundation, 1978-79, and Canadian Government, 1982; first prize from Periodical Distribution Association, 1980, for short story "Isolated Incidents"; National Magazine Awards second prize, 1981, for essay "An Invisible Woman"; National Book Critics Circle award for best fiction, 1988, for *The Middleman and Other Stories.*

WRITINGS:

The Tiger's Daughter (novel), Houghton, 1972.

Wife (novel), Houghton, 1975.

Kautilya's Concept of Diplomacy: A New Interpretation, Minerva, 1976.

(With husband, Clark Blaise) *Days and Nights in Calcutta* (nonfiction), Doubleday, 1977.

Darkness (short stories), Penguin, 1985.

(With Blaise) *The Sorrow and the Terror: The Haunting Legacy of the Air India Tragedy* (nonfiction), Viking, 1987.

The Middleman and Other Stories, Grove, 1988.

Jasmine (novel), Grove, 1989.

Contributor to periodicals, including *Saturday Night.*

SIDELIGHTS: Bharati Mukherjee's writings largely reflect her personal experiences. In *The Tiger's Daughter,* the author creates a heroine who, like herself, returns to India after several years in the West to discover a country quite unlike the one she remembered. Memories of a genteel Brahmin lifestyle are usurped by new impressions of poverty, hungry children, and political unrest. "In other words," a *Times Literary Supplement* reviewer noted, "Tara's westernization has opened her eyes to the gulf between two worlds that still makes India the despair of those who govern it."

"Miss Mukherjee writes entertainingly and with a sort of fluid prose that is very good to read," Roger Baker wrote in *Books and Bookmen.* "She can make her characters spring to life with a word and has what seems to be an acute ear for dialogue." The *Times Literary Supplement* critic held that Mukherjee's "elegant first novel" is skillfully wrought, with lively dialogue and full, descriptive passages. Yet he found the novel's heroine oddly lacking: "Because [Mukherjee] controls her emotions with such a skilled balance of irony and colorful nostalgia her novel is charming and intelligent—and curiously unmoving. . . . Tara herself remains so ineffectual a focus . . . it is hard to care whether or not she will be able to return."

A second novel, *Wife,* is the story of a young Indian woman, Dimple, who attempts to reconcile the Bengali ideal of the perfect passive wife with the demands of real life. Dimple's arranged marriage to an engineer is followed by their immigration to a New York City neighborhood. There she "watches television, sleeps, studies *Better Homes and Gardens,* and timorously meets people," Rosanne Klass detailed in *Ms.* "She is afraid to go out alone, and well she might be, since nobody—on TV or off—seems to talk about anything but murders and muggings." This alien environment, along with Dimple's inherent instability, prompts her to contemplate suicide or murder (she eventually chooses the latter, killing her husband). "Underneath the passivity lives rage which the heroine is hardly conscious of until it fully extends itself from fantasy to reality," Willa Swanson remarked in the *Antioch Review.*

Swanson found *Wife* a moving study of an individual whose society sees her as a trivial object. She related, "There is much wit, a good ear for dialogue, and above all the creation of a character that gives an insight into the sudden, seemingly inexplicable, explosion of a docile, passive person into violence." Yet other reviewers were not so comfortable with the motives behind Dimple's violent outburst. Klass noted that "possibly Dimple is supposed to be schizophrenic, but . . . it isn't indicated. The book seems to suggest that she goes bonkers from . . . a surfeit of . . . liberated women, Americanized men, and wilting houseplants. I have known a few Indian women in New York. Many had adjustment problems, . . . but none . . . felt that knifing their husbands would really help." And Martin Levin of the *New York Times Book Review* reiterated this sentiment: "The title and the drift of the book imply that the protagonist is in some way a victim of her social status. . . . However oppressed Dimple may be, she is also very crazy, a fact about which the author is amusing but ambiguous. You could raise Dimple's consciousness by ninety degrees and still have a zombie."

Mukherjee and her Canadian husband, Clark Blaise, collaborated on *Days and Nights in Calcutta,* a journal of their visit to India. After a ten-year sojourn in Canada, Mukherjee returned to her native country in 1973, accompanied by Blaise, who was visiting for the first time and eager to embrace his wife's native culture. Both encountered an India that neither anticipated: she found a world far less innocent than the one she remembered, and he met a people more enigmatic than he had ever imagined.

James Sloan Allen wrote in the *Saturday Review* of the couple's polar reactions: "Blaise, at first blinded by the squalor and the terrors, discovers a magic that enfolds reality in myth and ennobles Bengali life through a love of culture. His journal glows with the enthusiasm of discovery . . . and he turns against 'the whole bloated, dropsical giant called the West.' Mukherjee, by contrast, becomes angry and sad. For her fondly recalled traditions now mask fear and oppression—especially of women." Rather than examine the culture broadly, as her foreign husband can do, Mukherjee cannot help but see individuals, particularly those upper class women with whom she grew up and who she would have become. Her visit is filled with love and hate, sympathy and an unwillingness to forgive; she is in exile by choice but, in her words, "while changing citizenship is easy, swapping cultures is not." "It is that sort of honesty, turned by Mukherjee and Blaise upon themselves and their surroundings, that makes this book so distinctive and affecting a chronicle of voyages and discoveries," Margo Jefferson of *Newsweek* concluded.

In the 1980s Mukherjee wrote two short story collections, *Darkness* and *The Middleman and Other Stories,* and the novel *Jasmine.* In *Darkness* Mukherjee explores the Canadian prejudice against Indians that forced her to seek more tolerant society in America. In *Jasmine* she focuses on an Indian immigrant and the effect she has on various Americans she meets in Florida, New York, Iowa, and California. Mukherjee won the National Book Critics Circle award for best fiction for 1988 with *The Middleman,* a collection of tales also featuring Indian, Trinidadian, and Afghan immigrants who are struggling to understand their newly adopted cultures in the United States, Canada, and West Germany.

Bharati Mukherjee commented: "I left Canada after fifteen years due to the persistent effects of racial prejudice against people of my national origin. The history of this particular upheaval is found in my *Saturday Night* article, 'An Invisible Woman.' "

BIOGRAPHICAL/CRITICAL SOURCES:

BOOKS

Bestsellers 89, Issue 2, Gale, 1989.
Contemporary Literary Criticism, Volume 53, Gale, 1989.
Dictionary of Literary Biography, Volume 60: *Canadian Writers Since 1960, First Series,* Gale, 1986.

PERIODICALS

Antioch Review, spring, 1976.
Books and Bookmen, November, 1973.
Christian Science Monitor, February 2, 1977.
Detroit Free Press, February 22, 1989.
Globe and Mail (Toronto), May 9, 1987, October 14, 1989.
Los Angeles Times, July 19, 1988, November 12, 1989.
Los Angeles Times Book Review, September 17, 1989.
Maclean's, May 25, 1987, August 29, 1988.
Mother Jones, May, 1988.
Ms., October, 1975.
New Republic, April 14, 1986.
Newsweek, February 7, 1977.
New York, January 30, 1989.
New York Times, January 25, 1977, September 19, 1989.
New York Times Book Review, June 8, 1975, January 12, 1986, June 19, 1988, September 10, 1989.
Publishers Weekly, August 25, 1989.
Saturday Night, March, 1981.
Saturday Review, February 5, 1977.
Time, September 11, 1989.
Times Literary Supplement, June 29, 1973, July 21, 1989.
Tribune Books, July 17, 1988, September 10, 1989.
Voice Literary Supplement, June, 1988.
Washington Post Book World, August 27, 1989.

*   *   *

MUNRO, Alice 1931-

PERSONAL: Born July 10, 1931, in Wingham, Ontario, Canada; daughter of Robert Eric (a farmer) and Ann (Chamney) Laidlaw; married James Munro (a bookseller), December 29, 1951 (divorced, 1976); married Gerald Fremlin (a geographer), 1976; children: (first marriage) Sheila, Jenny, Andrea. *Education:* University of Western Ontario, B.A., 1952. *Politics:* New Democratic Party. *Religion:* Unitarian Universalist.

ADDRESSES: Home—Clinton, Ontario, Canada.

CAREER: Writer. Artist-in-residence, University of Western Ontario, 1974-75, and University of British Columbia, 1980.

MEMBER: Writers Union of Canada.

AWARDS, HONORS: Governor General's Literary Award, 1969, for *Dance of the Happy Shades,* and 1986, for *The Progress of Love;* Canadian Bookseller's Award, 1972, for *Lives of Girls and Women;* Canada-Australia Literary Prize, 1974; D.Litt., University of Western Ontario, 1976.

WRITINGS:

Dance of the Happy Shades (short stories), Ryerson, 1968.
Lives of Girls and Women (novel), McGraw, 1971.
Something I've Been Meaning to Tell You (short stories), McGraw, 1974.
Who Do You Think You Are?, Macmillan (Toronto), 1978, published as *The Beggar Maid: Stories of Flo and Rose,* Penguin, 1984.
The Moons of Jupiter, Macmillan (Toronto), 1982, Knopf, 1983.
The Progress of Love, McClelland & Stewart, 1986.

TELEVISION SCRIPTS

"A Trip to the Coast," Canadian Broadcasting Corp. (CBC), 1973.
"Thanks for the Ride," CBC, 1973.
"How I Met My Husband," CBC, 1974.
"1847: The Irish," CBC, 1978.

CONTRIBUTOR

Canadian Short Stories, second series, Oxford University Press, 1968.
Sixteen by Twelve: Short Stories by Canadian Writers, Ryerson, 1970.
The Narrative Voice: Stories and Reflections by Canadian Authors, McGraw, 1972.
74: New Canadian Stories, Oberon, 1974.
The Play's the Thing, Macmillan (Toronto), 1976.
Here and Now, Oberon, 1977.
Personal Fictions, Oxford University Press, 1977.
Night Light: Stories of Aging, Oxford University Press, 1986.

Contributor to *Canadian Forum, Queen's Quarterly, Chatelaine, Grand Street, New Yorker,* and other publications.

SIDELIGHTS: Usually concerned with characters living in the small towns of southwestern Ontario, the stories of Alice Munro present "ordinary experiences so that they appear extraordinary, invested with a kind of magic," according to Catherine Sheldrick Ross in the *Dictionary of Literary Biography.* "Few people writing today," Beverley Slopen claims in *Publishers Weekly,* "can bring a character, a mood or a scene to life with such economy. And she has an exhilarating ability to make the reader see the familiar with fresh insight and compassion."

In a review of *Dance of the Happy Shades,* Martin Levin writes that "the short story is alive and well in Canada, where most of the fifteen tales originate like fresh winds from the North. Alice Munro," he continues, "creates a solid habitat for her fiction—southwestern Ontario, a generation or more in the past—and is in sympathetic vibration with the farmers and townspeople who live there." Peter Prince calls the stories in this collection "beautifully controlled and precise. And always this precision appears unstrained. The proportions so exactly fit the writer's thematic aims that in almost every case it seems that really no other words could have been used, certainly no more or less." Ronald Blythe believes that "the stories are all to do with discovering personal freedom within an accepted curtailment. There is no intentional nostalgia although, strangely enough, one frequently finds oneself rather wistfully caught up in some of the scenes so perfectly evoked; and there is no distortion in the characterisation."

Reviewing *Something I've Been Meaning to Tell You,* Kildare Dobbs writes: "Readers who enjoyed the earlier books because they confirmed the reality of the Canadian small town experi-

ence for a certain generation, or because they seemed to reinforce some of the ideology of the women's movement, will find more of the same. But they will find something else, too. There is a hint at hermetic concerns in the first story, ironic suggestions of a quest for the grail. . . . All the stories are told with the skill which the author has perfected over the years, narrated with meticulous precision in a voice that is unmistakeably Ontarian in its lack of emphasis, its sly humour and willingness to live with a mystery." Joyce Carol Oates finds that the reader will be "most impressed by the feeling behind [Alice Munro's] stories—the evocation of emotions, ranging from bitter hatred to love, from bewilderment and resentment to awe. In all her work there is an effortless, almost conversational tone, and we know we are in the presence of an art that works to conceal itself, in order to celebrate its subject."

Speaking to Mervyn Rothstein of the *New York Times,* Munro explains: "I never intended to be a short-story writer. . . . I started writing them because I didn't have time to write anything else—I had three children. And then I got used to writing stories, so I saw my material that way, and now I don't think I'll ever write a novel."

BIOGRAPHICAL/CRITICAL SOURCES:

BOOKS

Authors in the News, Volume 2, Gale, 1976.
Contemporary Literary Criticism, Gale, Volume 6, 1976, Volume 10, 1979, Volume 1981, Volume 50, 1988.
Dahlie, Hallvard, *Alice Munro and Her Works,* ECW Press, 1985.
Dictionary of Literary Biography, Volume 53: *Canadian Writers since 1960,* Gale, 1986.
MacKendrick, Louis K., editor, *Probable Fictions: Alice Munro's Narrative Acts,* ECW Press, 1984.
Martin, W. R., *Alice Munro,* University of Alberta Press, 1987.

PERIODICALS

Canadian Forum, February, 1969.
Listener, June 13, 1974.
Maclean's, September 22, 1986.
New Statesman, May 3, 1974.
New York Times, November 10, 1986.
New York Times Book Review, September 23, 1973.
Ontario Review, fall, 1974.
Publishers Weekly, August 22, 1986.
Saturday Night, July, 1974.
Time, January 15, 1973.

*   *   *

MUNRO, H(ector) H(ugh)   1870-1916 (Saki)

PERSONAL: Born December 18, 1870, in Akyab, Burma; killed in action during World War I, November 14 (some sources say 13), 1916, in Beaumont-Hamel, France; son of Charles Augustus (a military police officer) and Mary Frances (Mercer) Munro. *Education:* Attended Bedford Grammar School, c. 1885-1887.

CAREER: Policeman in Burma, 1893-1894; political satirist for the *Westminster Gazette,* 1896-1902; foreign correspondent for the *Morning Post,* 1902-1908; full-time writer near London, England, 1909-1914. *Wartime service:* British Army, 1914-1916; served in the calvary and infantry during World War I; refused several officer commissions; killed in action.

WRITINGS:

UNDER THE PSEUDONYM SAKI

The Westminster Alice (political satire), illustrations by F. Carruthers Gould, Westminster Gazette, 1902, Viking Press, 1929 (also see below).

Reginald (short story collection), Methuen, 1904 (also see below).

Reginald in Russia, and Other Sketches (short story collection; includes "Reginald in Russia," "The Saint and the Goblin," "The Bag," and "Gabriel-Ernest"), Methuen, 1910 (also see below).

The Chronicles of Clovis (short story collection; includes "The Unrest Cure," "Tobermory," and "Sredni Vashtar"), John Lane, 1912, reprinted, Penguin Books, 1948 (also see below).

The Unbearable Bassington (novel), John Lane, 1912 (also see below).

Beasts and Super-Beasts (short story collection; includes "The Open Window"), John Lane, 1914 (also see below).

When William Came: A Story of London Under the Hohenzollerns (novel), John Lane, 1914 (also see below).

POSTHUMOUSLY PUBLISHED COLLECTIONS, UNDER THE PSEUDONYM SAKI

The Toys of Peace, and Other Papers, portrait and memoir by Rothay Reynolds, John Lane, 1919 (also see below).

The Square Egg, and Other Sketches, With Three Plays (contains the plays "The Death Trap," "Karl-Ludvig's Window," and "The Watched Pot"), biography by sister, Ethel M. Munro, John Lane, 1924 (also see below).

The Works of "Saki" (H. H. Munro), eight volumes (contains *The Chronicles of Clovis,* introduction by A. A. Milne, 1927; *The Unbearable Bassington,* introduction by M. Baring, 1927; *Beasts and Super-Beasts,* introduction by H. W. Nevinson, 1928; *Reginald* [and] *Reginald in Russia, and Other Sketches,* introduction by Hugh Walpole, 1928; *The Toys of Peace, and Other Papers,* introduction by G. K. Chesterton, 1928; *The Square Egg, and Other Sketches, With Three Plays,* introduction by J. C. Squire, 1929; *When William Came: A Story of London Under the Hohenzollerns,* introduction by Lord Charnwood, 1929; and *The Westminster Alice,* foreword by J. A. Spender, 1929), Viking Press, 1927-29 (also see above).

The Short Stories of Saki (H. H. Munro) Complete, introduction by Christopher Morley, Viking Press, 1930, reprinted, Modern Library, 1958.

The Novels and Plays of Saki (H. H. Munro) Complete in One Volume, Viking Press, 1933, reprinted, Scholarly Press, 1971.

The Best of Saki, selection and introduction by Graham Greene, Viking Press, 1961.

The Complete Works of Saki, introduction by Noel Coward, Doubleday, 1976.

OTHER

(Under name Hector H. Munro) *The Rise of the Russian Empire* (nonfiction), Grant Richards, 1900.

"The Miracle-Merchant" (play), published in *One-Act Plays for Stage and Study,* eighth series, preface by Alice Gerstenberg, Samuel French, 1934.

"Two New Stories by 'Saki' (H. H. Munro)" (contains "The Holy War" and "A Sacrifice to Necessity"), edited by James R. Thrane, published in *Modern Fiction Studies,* Volume 19, 1951.

Also author of *Not So Stories,* illustrations by F. Carruthers Gould, published anonymously, 1902. Contributor to the *Bystander* and *Daily Express.*

SIDELIGHTS: The reputation of British writer H. H. Munro (Saki) rests primarily on his short stories conveying whimsical humor, fascination with the odd and eerie, and worldly disillusionment with hypocrisy and banality. Written between the very end of Queen Victoria's reign and the beginning of World War I, Saki's works memorialize a comfortable world of upper-class town houses, tea parties, and weekends in the country that his characters may deride but never completely lose faith in. The stories present characters who, through capriciousness or eccentric behavior, get into odd situations from which they usually escape by means of their quick wits. Owing something to the witty paradoxes of Irish playwright and poet Oscar Wilde, the clever remarks and cynical views of Saki's characters expose the arbitrariness and artificiality of their society. Like the fiction of American short-story writer William Sydney Porter (O. Henry), Saki's narratives often employ surprise endings, but his accounts of children battling adults and of strangely human animals go beyond O. Henry's relatively straightforward realism into the slightly bizarre and obsessive. With Rudyard Kipling, another popular British writer of his time, Saki clung to an orderly, even staid view of the world, despite the flaws he saw in it; but while Kipling promoted the values underlying that world, Saki enjoyed teasing them.

Like Kipling, H. H. Munro was born in the Far East to well-to-do parents. His father, Colonel Charles Augustus Munro, was an officer in the British military police in Burma; his mother, Mary Frances Mercer, was the daughter of a Rear Admiral in the British Navy. The Munros' third child in as many years, Hector Hugh, was born in 1870. When Mrs. Munro was soon again pregnant, the family returned to England, where in 1872 she died suddenly before the baby was born. Colonel Munro sent his surviving children—Ethel, Charles, and Hector—to Pilton, a small village in Devon near Barnstaple, to live with his two sisters and his mother; then he returned to his post in Burma.

The aunts, Charlotte and Augusta (called Aunt Tom), squabbled endlessly over trivialities, involved the children in their petty jealousies, and enforced on their young charges a strict Victorian regimen that included permanently closed windows and little outside play. Hector, being the youngest, slight of build, delicate, and pale, escaped the worst of the aunts' tyranny, and he soon became adept at devising ways to bend their inflexible and contradictory rules. Ethel, two-and-a-half years older than Hector, assumed roles she would play throughout his life, becoming both a protector and an admiring audience for his antics. Reginald, Clovis Sangrail, and Comus Bassington, Saki's witty and self-absorbed comic heroes, clearly developed from Munro's own experience of being the unwilling captive of stern, idiosyncratic older women whose rules had ostensibly to be obeyed but not believed in for a minute.

After some casual tutoring at home, ten-year-old Hector was sent off to a nearby school, Pencarwick, and four years later he entered Bedford Grammar School, a public school that attracted the sons of British Indian Army officers. In 1887, Colonel Munro retired and returned to England to look after his nearly full-grown children. Over the next few years, he completed their education by traveling with them on the Continent: first the seaside in Normandy, then a "grand tour" of Germany, eastern Europe, Austria, and Switzerland that included months-long stays in Dresden and Davos, a newly fashionable Alpine resort in Switzerland.

Because Hector was still undecided on a career at twenty-three, his father arranged a position for him with the police in Burma. Though the fastidious young Munro disliked the heat and filth of the East, he loved the plants and animals, going so far as to keep a tiger cub for a pet. Munro's love of animals, wild or tame, was a constant in his life, and he wrote many stories in which humans and animals exchange characteristics: a cat talks; a man begins to resemble his pets—a parrot, a monkey, and finally a turtle; a ferret grants the fervent wish of a sick boy that he be rid of his spiteful elderly guardian. After about a year in Burma, Munro caught malaria and was sent home to Devon to recuperate with his family.

By 1894, Munro had determined to become a writer and, subsidized by his father, went off to London. He installed himself in the British Museum and, except for one short story, "Dogged," published nothing until 1900, when Grant Richards brought out Munro's *The Rise of the Russian Empire.* A young, enterprising publisher willing to gamble on new talent, Richards would later take a similar risk with James Joyce's *Dubliners* in 1906 but then delay publication of the work until 1914 because his printers objected to Joyce's material. Munro's first book, a well-researched history of Russia up to the early seventeenth century, was widely reviewed on both sides of the Atlantic. An anonymous critic in the *Nation* credited Munro with bringing early Russian history to life but also said that he approached "perilously near flippancy at times when the dignity of the occasion and of history demands a certain gravity of statement." In general, *The Rise of the Russian Empire* failed either to earn the respect of academic historians or to capture the interest of the reading public.

Munro's next writing venture was a collaboration with a popular cartoonist, Francis Carruthers Gould, whose work appeared regularly in the *Westminster Gazette,* an influential, liberal London daily newspaper. Gould and Munro conceived the idea of producing a series of cartoons using figures from Lewis Carroll's *Alice's Adventures in Wonderland* to satirize current political events, including the increasingly confused situation surrounding the Boer War in South Africa. Like the United States's Vietnam War some sixty years later, the Boer War was not supposed to cause real problems at home, but as it dragged on, its reason for being grew less and less clear. Gould drew caricatures of the lethargic Prime Minister Arthur Balfour as the Cheshire Cat, the Archbishop of Canterbury as the Caterpillar, the Secretary of War as the White Knight, and Alfred Austin, the Poet Laureate, as the White Rabbit. Devising seemingly innocent questions for Alice to ask the politicians and dignitaries, Munro planted hilariously absurd answers in their mouths. The cartoons by Gould and the comic sketches written under Munro's pseudonym, Saki, were an immediate success ("Saki," the name of the cupbearer to the gods, was borrowed from Edward Fitzgerald's *Rubaiyat of Omar Khayyam*). Under the pen name, Munro achieved public recognition and approval for his work. In 1902 the cartoons were published in book form as *The Westminster Alice.*

In 1901 Munro began contributing short sketches to the *Westminster Gazette* about the adventures of a witty, acerbic young man, Reginald, in fashionable drawing rooms, and at garden parties, the theater, art museums, and country house weekends. These sketches, narrated either by Reginald himself or by an older friend called "the Other," reveal Reginald to be a humorous observer of upper-class manners and mores as well as a somewhat dandified self-admirer. Reginald is fond of turning his opinions and attitudes into categorical pronouncements; he creates outrageous stories from the amusing eccentricities of his elderly aunts; he takes pride in dressing well and in being the confidant of a duchess. Reginald is a type of affable young man

of expensive tastes, no visible source of income, and an inexhaustible supply of clever jokes and deadpan comments that had entertained London theatergoers in Wilde's plays during the early 1890s, but who had not been heard from since.

Trying to repeat the success of the Alice sketches, Munro and Gould in 1902 parodied Kipling's *The Jungle Book* and *Just So Stories* in the "The Political Jungle Book" and "Not So Stories" for the *Westminster Gazette,* but these political satires were not nearly so popular as the Alice series. Munro then decided to widen his horizons by becoming a foreign correspondent in the Balkans for the *Morning Post,* a conservative newspaper. At the turn of the century, the Bulgarians and the Turks were fighting over Macedonia, the Ottoman Turks' last foothold in Europe. The *Morning Post* sent Munro to the area to cover the protracted guerrilla war, which had the potential for involving Russia on the side of Bulgaria and thus could incite a wider conflict. Since the fighting was sporadic, Munro sent pieces back to London on local political figures and local life as well as the war. Returning to London for a short break in 1903, Munro continued writing Reginald stories. In early 1904 he returned to the Balkans and then worked his way slowly north through Europe, reporting from Vienna, Warsaw, and finally St. Petersburg in Russia.

Munro's first collection of stories, titled simply *Reginald,* was published in 1904 while he was reporting on the increasing tension in St. Petersburg between the Czar's government and the people. Ethel Munro arrived for a visit in January 1905, in time to witness with her brother a bloody riot by striking workers in front of the Winter Palace. As he had done in his reporting from the Balkans, Munro used his dispatches to analyze the politics of the situation and to speculate on the Russian national character. Munro remained in St. Petersburg through 1906, covering the Czar's convening of the Duma, the Russian Parliament, in an attempt to quell the unrest.

From 1907 to 1909, Munro was based in Paris, writing reviews of plays, operas, and art shows, and sending home short feature articles on life in Paris. His father died in 1907, leaving an inheritance sufficient for Munro to consider abandoning journalism for full-time fiction writing. In 1909, Munro bought a cottage outside London in Surrey, moved Ethel in, and settled down to write; for relaxation he kept an apartment in London and joined several clubs there.

As A. J. Langguth has pointed out in *Saki: A Life of Hector Hugh Munro, With Six Short Stories Never Before Collected,* some of Munro's efforts reflect the influence of the master of the trick ending, O. Henry. However, Saki's stories are not innocent or sentimental like O. Henry's, but mix wit with outrageousness, humor with seemingly justified malice. In 1910, Munro's second collection of short fiction was published, misleadingly titled *Reginald in Russia* even though only the title story concerns Reginald. The rest venture into fable-like lessons, like "The Saint and the Goblin," or continue Saki's satiric examination of upper-class country life, like "The Bag," in which a fox mistakenly killed by a Russian weekend guest turns out to be a polecat. "Gabriel-Ernest" tells the macabre story of a retiring man living in the country who thinks that a boy he has found may be a werewolf. The man's aunt, knowing nothing of the boy's being also a wolf, decides he should be taken to her Sunday School class. Entrusted with walking a young child home, "Gabriel-Ernest," as she has named him, devours the child and disappears, only his discoverer suspecting the truth. Like many other Saki heroes, Gabriel-Ernest manages both to get his way and to preserve his spotless reputation in spite of his actions. Of stories like this one, V. S. Pritchett, in a 1957 *New Statesman* review, made a shrewd point: "Saki writes like an enemy. Society has bored him to the point of murder. Our laughter is only a note or two short of a scream of fear."

This successful collection was followed in 1912 by *The Chronicles of Clovis,* which introduced two new main characters, Clovis Sangrail and Bertie Van Tahn. Although both characters are akin to Reginald, Clovis is more likeable than either Reginald or Bertie; while he delights in absurd situations and in deflating the pretensions of others, he often has sympathy for those in real trouble. By contrast, the perpetually adolescent Bertie fails to see when humor at the expense of others turns into cruelty. Clovis is a shrewd practical joker, as were Munro and his sister Ethel in life, and in "The Unrest Cure," he shakes up a torpid middle-aged man and his equally staid sister by appearing at their house one day and announcing the imminent arrival of their bishop and a Colonel Alberti for lunch. Clovis concocts an afternoon of secret meetings in the study between the bishop and the colonel, who supposedly plan to massacre all the Jews in the area. Having panicked not only the man and his sister but the entire neighborhood, Clovis secretly leaves the house, knowing he has shaken dull lives out of their routines. One of Saki's short story masterpieces in the collection, "Tobermory," puts Clovis in the background. Tobermory is an utterly self-possessed talking cat that completely unnerves a weekend party in the country by threatening to reveal the guests' secrets he has overheard. In his introduction to the short stories of Saki, Christopher Morley characterizes the mixture of humor and almost evil intent of these stories: "Delicate, airy, lucid, precise, with the inconspicuous agility of perfect style, [Saki] can pass into the uncanny, the tragic, into mocking fairy-tales grimmer than Grimm."

Another animal story shows how some of Saki's stories appeal to his readers' unfulfilled childhood fantasies of revenge. In "Sredni Vashtar," the sickly, ten-year-old Conradin develops an attachment to a Houdan hen and a ferret, both of whom live in an unused toolshed the boy has turned into a secret playhouse. Conradin develops a cult around the ferret, whom he worships as a god in defiance of the religion his guardian cousin, Mrs. De Ropp, forces on him. When Mrs. De Ropp, who enjoys pressuring the boy to do things "for his own good," decides to stop Conradin from spending so much time in his hideaway, she sells the hen and vows to clean out the guinea pigs she believes attracts him to the place. While she is investigating the toolshed, Conradin prays fervently to his god Sredni Vashtar, chanting: "Sredni Vashtar went forth, / His thoughts were red thoughts and his teeth were white. / His enemies called for peace, but he brought them death. / Sredni Vashtar the beautiful." The ferret emerges from the toolshed with "dark wet stains around the fur of jaws and throat." While Mrs. De Ropp's maid screams hysterically and others wonder, "Whoever will break it to the poor child," Conradin calmly enjoys his supper. Saki's stories of pompous, self-righteous adults being tricked into their own destruction have led the British novelist Graham Greene to locate the source of Saki's imaginative energy in his recollection of childhood. In his introduction to a selection of stories, *The Best of Saki* (1961), Greene has written, "Unhappiness wonderfully aids the memory, and the best stories of Munro are all of childhood, its humor and its comedy as well its cruelty and unhappiness."

After these successes as a comic short story writer, Munro tried his hand at a novel. *The Unbearable Bassington,* published in 1912, is an extended Saki short story but one that contains a more serious tone than is usual in Munro's fiction. Its hero, Comus Bassington, is another version of Reginald, but this time Munro makes him almost completely unlikable by giving him a clear mean streak. It may be, as Langguth has suggested, that as he reached middle age, Munro came to feel that the antics of a good-looking, cynical, witty young man were no longer so funny and used the novel to turn against his creation. Readers may feel that Comus best describes himself at the end of the novel; Munro has sent him off alone to Africa, away from the whirl of London society of which he makes such fun and the attention of which he secretly craves: "Comus Bassington, the boy who went away. He had loved himself very well and never troubled greatly whether any one else really loved him, and now he realized what he had made of his life. And at the same time he knew that if his chance were to come again he would throw it away just as surely, just as perversely." This despondency may be a reflection of Munro's sadness over his departing youth, but the author's treatment of Comus also shows him struggling to get beyond the comic creation that gave him his early success, call him Reginald, Bertie Van Tahn, Clovis Sangrail, or Comus Bassington. Significantly, Munro leaves Comus to die alone in Africa.

Munro also continued writing stories for newspapers, and these works were collected in *Beasts and Super-Beasts* (1914). As the title suggests, animal stories take up a large part of the collection, but Munro also introduced a new main character, Vera, whose name, suggesting truthfulness, is at odds with her role in the stories. She is a practical joker like Clovis, and perhaps her best moment occurs in "The Open Window." She tells a guest, Framton Nuttel, that her mother is in the habit of leaving a French window open in the belief that her husband and brothers, who supposedly were lost in a bog while hunting three years ago to the day, will at any moment return through that window. Later the older woman enters and seems to confirm Vera's story by explaining to Mr. Nuttel that the window is open since she expects the hunting party momentarily. When the men are seen approaching, Nuttel runs madly from the house, leaving the reader to realize that he has been the victim of Vera's superbly told ghost story.

Munro's second novel, *When William Came* (1914), marks a definite advance in his development as a writer. Drawing upon his own and his family's military experience, an aspect of Munro's life that previously had been suppressed in his fiction, and tapping his familiarity with European politics gained during Munro's years as a foreign correspondent, the novel treats the approaching war that would involve all of Europe. *When William Came* is a fantasy about life in England under German occupation after a very short struggle in which superior German forces quickly overpower the English. "William" is Kaiser Wilhelm, and in the novel, Munro imagines the reaction of English society to being an appendage of a German empire. The main character, Murrey Yeovil, who is off hunting in Siberia when the war occurs, returns to England to find people in varying states of resignation to the apparently inevitable. He, almost alone, is indignant over what has happened and with the failure of nearly everyone to object to the occupation. Murrey's attempts to discover exactly what caused England's capitulation provide Munro with an opportunity to examine English society and to criticize qualities that he had earlier treated flippantly. The self-righteousness of the working classes is taken to task, as is the self-indulgence of aesthetic young men or "lounge lizards." In what Langguth has seen rightly as a striking reversal of Saki's usual values, the fortitude and determination of civic-minded, elderly women are extolled. After searching for grounds for sincere patriotism and reasons to affirm the best of English society, the novel ends ambiguously as Londoners assemble at Hyde Park for a march by Boy Scouts, who mysteriously never appear.

This novel shows what direction Munro's fiction might have taken had he lived longer; it reveals, too, that the writer had firmly planted himself in a world already fading into memory— the Victorian and Edwardian era, which allowed society's values to be laughed at but also vigorously defended these values when they were under serious attack. In this regard, the earnestness of *When William Came* can be linked to the comedy in Saki's stories. In his introduction to *The Complete Works of Saki* (1976), Noel Coward pointed out that Saki's "satire was based primarily on the assumption of a fixed social status quo which, although at the time he was writing may have been wobbling a bit, outwardly at least, betrayed few signs of imminent collapse." When it became possible for Saki to imagine a collapse of that fixed status quo, the moral indignation of the satirist rose to the surface and appeared without the disguising mask of comic intent.

Perhaps responding to this strain of seriousness in Saki, the English critic J. W. Lambert, in a 1956 essay in the *Listener,* noted Saki's affinities to Kipling and to two other English writers, William Makepeace Thackeray and, surprisingly, George Orwell: "All four had Anglo-Indian backgrounds and divided childhoods. They were all fascinated by the social display and organization of life 'at home'; their works [express] the colonial mentality, a little disappointed, sometimes more than a little embittered. Thackeray's self-conscious moralizing bubbled up often in Saki; so did Kipling's emotional afflatus. . . . The same feelings, in different generations, drove Orwell to prodigies of bleak panache and turned his snobberies upside down, and drove Saki in 1914 not only to join the Army when well over age but consistently to refuse a commission."

When William Came was well received, and Munro continued to raise his ambitions. In 1914, he wrote a play, "The Watched Pot." A comedy of manners set in a drawing room like that in many of Saki's stories, the play concerns the efforts of several young women to marry a wealthy man whose aunt resists their attempts to displace her as ruler of her nephew's household. "The Watched Pot" tries to translate the epigrammatic wit of Saki's stories to the theater. Never reaching the stage in Munro's lifetime, the play was eventually produced during World War II as an example of an Edwardian drawing-room comedy.

Less than a month after war was declared in early August 1914, Munro enlisted in the cavalry as an ordinary soldier. Though he was well past the age when social pressure stemming from war hysteria might influence him to join up, Munro shared the feelings of thousands of younger men who experienced the declaration of war as a chance to act nobly and heroically in an unquestionably good cause. Hoping to get into the fighting more quickly, Munro transferred into the infantry, joining the Royal Fusiliers. He enjoyed the life of a soldier, hiking for miles with heavy backpacks, serving long hours as camp orderly, and expressing contempt for those who had not enlisted. Proud of his ability to keep up with much younger men, Munro rose to the rank of corporal and eventually lance sergeant, but he refused offers of a commission as an officer, content to be a simple soldier among his comrades.

He was shipped off to France in 1915, and his wit and macabre sense of humor survived the horrific conditions he found on the battlefield. In her "Biography of Saki," which first appeared in the 1924 collection *The Square Egg,* Ethel Munro recalled that at Christmas 1915 her brother sent her this version of a carol: "While Shepherds watched their flocks by night / All seated on the ground / A high-explosive shell came down / And mutton rained around." Moreover, Munro once wrote home that a fel-

low soldier had found "a perfectly good ear," which, he said, was "no use to me so I threw it over the parapet to the rats, remembering that rats were traditionally very fond of ears." Along with several other men, Munro formed an eating club, whose members were to pool their food and always act as gentlemen. Though Munro loved the life of a soldier, one wonders whether, had he lived through two more years of the war in the trenches, he would have become disillusioned and embittered, as did many other soldier-writers in World War I.

In June 1916, Munro spent a short leave in London with his sister and brother, during which he decided to buy land in Siberia to farm and hunt after the war, plans made, of course, before the Bolshevik revolution of 1917. Munro returned to the front to fight in several battles, suffering a return of his old malaria, and, on November 14, receiving a fatal wound in no man's land during a night march. Langguth reports that when two officers stopped to talk, the men took cover where they could. Near Munro, who had crouched at a shell crater, a soldier lit a cigarette. Fearing the light would be seen, Munro barked, "Put that bloody cigarette out!" Almost immediately, a German sniper's bullet hit and killed him.

Two collections of Munro's stories appeared posthumously, *The Toys of Peace* (1919) and *The Square Egg* (1924). Various groupings of his stories have been in print almost continuously since then, and in 1976 *The Complete Works of Saki* was published with an introduction by Coward, a writer whose love of Saki's wit and style is reflected in Coward's own plays. In 1981, Langguth, who drew on letters and materials held by the family, produced the first full-length, well-researched biography of Munro.

Popular and respected as a master of the short story during his lifetime, throughout the twentieth century Saki has been ranked with the Frenchman Guy de Maupassant and the American O. Henry as a craftsman of the first order. Funny, original, sometimes bizarre, and at times creepily frightening, Saki's work clearly has left its mark on the British writer P. G. Wodehouse, whose farcical stories of well-heeled, empty-headed young men about town are reminiscent of the Reginald stories. The world of Wodehouse's characters Bertie and Jeeves is essentially the same as that of Reginald and Clovis. In these worlds, it is always about the turn of the century; England is the unquestioned center of the universe; life has been made comfortable for one by others; and a young man need only think about his social life, the quality of the food, drink, and entertainment provided, and the fun he can dream up.

Significantly, women in Saki and Wodehouse are usually hateful guardian aunts or elderly duchesses; they only rarely are young attractive girls of sexual interest to the main characters. Munro remained a bachelor throughout his life, and this fact plus some suggestiveness in his work has led modern readers to conclude he was homosexual; moreover, rumors of Munro's homosexuality were whispered in publishing circles during his lifetime. Sex is very far below the surface in Saki's work, and it seems to have been so in Munro's life as well. While the artist in Munro learned much from Wilde's writing, he also may have learned from Wilde's experience of a notorious trial and imprisonment what kind of public behavior would not be tolerated by English society, even in the relatively relaxed Edwardian years.

Readers and critics often mention the apparent cruelty and heartlessness in Saki's stories. Writing in 1940 in the *Atlantic Monthly,* Elizabeth Drew explained and justified this lack of fellow feeling: "The cruelty is certainly there, but it has nothing perverted or pathological about it. . . . It is the genial heartlessness of the normal child, whose fantasies take no account of adult standards of human behaviour, and to whom the eating of a gypsy by a hyena is no more terrible than the eating of Red Ridinghood's grandmother by a wolf. The standards of these gruesome tales are those of the fairy tale; their grimness is the grimness of Grimm." To see the cruelty in Saki as fantasy, and to set it next to the unsparing details of nursery rhymes and fairy tales, is to understand that even though in Saki's stories terribly unfair things happen, he provides a satisfying sense of justice done and human decency restored that can appeal to children and adults alike.

Some literary critics in the 1960s and 1970s argued that there is a serious side to Saki that goes beyond mere entertainment to explore weighty moral issues. Certainly Munro was trying to be taken in this way as a writer in his novels, and some of his stories can be analyzed to discover serious concerns. But it would be misleading to maintain that Saki's greatness rests on the breadth of his moral imagination. For better or worse, his genius resides in his stories, in which the qualities defined by Coward as "the verbal adroitness of Saki's dialogue and the brilliance of his wit" shine most brightly.

BIOGRAPHICAL/CRITICAL SOURCES:

BOOKS

Dictionary of Literary Biography, Volume 34: *British Novelists, 1890-1929: Traditionalists,* Gale, 1985.
Gillen, Charles H., *H. H. Munro (Saki),* Twayne, 1969.
Langguth, A. J., *Saki: A Life of Hector Hugh Munro, With Six Short Stories Never Before Collected,* Simon & Schuster, 1981.
Saki, *The Square Egg, and Other Sketches, With Three Plays,* biography by sister, Ethel M. Munro, John Lane, 1924.
Saki, *The Short Stories of Saki (H. H. Munro) Complete,* introduction by Christopher Morley, Viking Press, 1930, reprinted, Modern Library, 1958.
Saki, *The Best of Saki,* selected and introduction by Graham Greene, Viking Press, 1961.
Saki, *The Complete Works of Saki,* introduction by Noel Coward, Doubleday, 1976.
Spears, G. J., *The Satire of Saki,* Exposition, 1963.
Twentieth-Century Literary Criticism, Volume 3, Gale, 1980.

PERIODICALS

Atlantic Monthly, July, 1940.
Bookman, January, 1927.
English Fiction in Transition, Volume 5, number 1, 1962.
English Literature in Transition, Volume 9, number 1, 1966, Volume 11, number 1, 1968.
English Studies, Volume 47, number 6, 1966.
Listener, February 9, 1956.
Modern British Literature, Volume 4, 1979.
Nation, March 7, 1901.
New Statesman, January 5, 1957, November 1, 1963.
New York Times, August 25, 1981.
Spectator, May 30, 1952, December 21, 1956.
Times Literary Supplement, November 21, 1963, May 13, 1989.

*　　*　　*

MURDOCH, (Jean) Iris 1919-

PERSONAL: Born July 15, 1919, in Dublin, Ireland; daughter of Wills John Hughes and Irene Alice (Richardson) Murdoch; married John Oliver Bayley (a novelist, poet, critic), 1956. *Education:* Somerville College, Oxford, B.A., 1942; Newnham College, Cambridge, Sarah Smithson studentship in philosophy, 1947-48.

ADDRESSES: Home—Cedar Lodge, Steeple Aston, Oxfordshire, England.

CAREER: Writer. British Treasury, London, England, assistant principal, 1942-44; United Nations Relief and Rehabilitation Administration (UNRRA), administrative officer in London, Belgium, and Austria, 1944-46; Oxford University, St. Anne's College, Oxford, England, fellow and university lecturer in philosophy, 1948-63, honorary fellow, 1963—; Royal College of Art, London, lecturer, 1963-67. Member of Formentor Prize Committee.

AWARDS, HONORS: Yorkshire Post Book of the Year Award, 1969, for *Bruno's Dream;* Whitehead Literary Award, 1974, for fiction; Whitbread Literary Award, 1974, for *The Sacred and Profane Love Machine;* James Tait Black Memorial Prize, 1974, for *The Black Prince;* Order of the British Empire, Commander, 1976, Dame Commander, 1986; Booker Prize, 1978, for *The Sea, The Sea.*

WRITINGS:

NOVELS

Under the Net, Viking, 1954, published with introduction and notes by Dorothy Jones, Longmans, Green, 1966, Penguin, 1977.
The Flight from the Enchanter, Viking, 1956, Penguin, 1987.
The Sandcastle, Viking, 1957, Penguin, 1978.
The Bell, Viking, 1958, Penguin, 1987.
A Severed Head, Viking, 1961.
An Unofficial Rose, Viking, 1962, Penguin, 1987.
The Unicorn, Viking, 1963, Penguin, 1987.
The Italian Girl, Viking, 1964.
The Red and the Green, Viking, 1965, Penguin, 1988.
The Time of the Angels, Viking, 1966, Penguin, 1988.
The Nice and the Good, Viking, 1968.
Bruno's Dream, Viking, 1969.
A Fairly Honourable Defeat, Viking, 1970.
An Accidental Man, Viking, 1971.
The Black Prince, Viking, 1973.
The Sacred and Profane Love Machine, Viking, 1974.
A Word Child, Viking, 1975.
Henry and Cato, Viking, 1977.
The Sea, The Sea, Viking, 1978.
Nuns and Soldiers, Viking, 1980.
The Philosopher's Pupil, Viking, 1983.
The Good Apprentice, Chatto & Windus, 1985, Viking, 1986.
The Book and the Brotherhood, Chatto & Windus, 1987, Viking, 1988.
The Message to the Planet, Chatto & Windus, 1989, Viking, 1990.

NONFICTION

Sartre: Romantic Rationalist, Yale University Press, 1953, 2nd edition, Barnes & Noble, 1980 (published in England as *Sartre: Romantic Realist,* Harvester Press, 1980).
(Contributor) *The Nature of Metaphysics,* Macmillan, 1957.
(Author of foreword) Wendy Campbell-Purdie and Fenner Brockaway, *Woman against the Desert,* Gollancz, 1964.
The Sovereignty of Good over other Concepts (Leslie Stephen lecture, 1967), Cambridge University Press, 1967, published with other essays as *The Sovereignty of Good,* Routledge & Kegan Paul, 1970, Schocken, 1971.

The Fire and the Sun: Why Plato Banned the Artists (based on the Romanes lecture, 1976), Clarendon Press, 1977.

Reynolds Stone, Warren, 1981.

Acastos: Two Platonic Dialogues, Chatto & Windus, 1986, Penguin, 1987.

PLAYS

(With J. B. Priestley) *A Severed Head* (three-act; based on her novel of the same title; first produced in London at Royale Theatre, October 28, 1964; produced in New York, 1964), Chatto & Windus, 1964, acting edition, Samuel French, 1964.

(With James Saunders) *The Italian Girl* (based on her novel of the same title; first produced at Bristol Old Vic, December, 1967), Samuel French, 1968.

The Three Arrows [and] *The Servants and the Snow* (both original plays; *The Servants and the Snow* first produced in London at Greenwich Theatre, September 29, 1970; *The Three Arrows* first produced in Cambridge at Arts Theatre, October 17, 1972), Chatto & Windus, 1973, Viking, 1974.

"Art and Eros," produced in London, 1980.

"The Servants" (opera libretto; adapted from her play "The Servants and the Snow"), produced in Cardiff, Wales, 1980.

"The Black Prince" (based on her novel of the same title), produced in London at Aldwych Theatre, 1989.

OTHER

A Year of Birds (poems), Compton Press (Tisbury, England), 1978.

Contributor to periodicals in United States and Great Britain, including *Listener, Yale Review, Chicago Review, Encounter, New Statesman, Nation,* and *Partisan Review.*

SIDELIGHTS: Described by *Commonweal*'s Linda Kuehl as "a philosopher by trade and temperament," Irish-born Iris Murdoch is better known as a serious and witty novelist. She began her writing career in 1953 with a well-received study of the French existentialist Jean-Paul Sartre, then launched into fiction with a picaresque novel, *Under the Net,* the following year. Since then she has continued to produce, at a remarkable rate, what critics refer to as "novels of ideas."

Murdoch's allegiance to the Existentialist movement may have been relatively short-lived, as *Publishers Weekly* reports; nonetheless this philosophy had a lasting influence upon her work. Like Sartre, writes William Van O'Connor in *The New University Wits and the End of Modernism,* Murdoch views man as a "lonely creature in an absurd world . . . impelled to make moral decisions, the consequences of which are uncertain." Like Sartre, says Warner Berthoff in *Fictions and Events,* Murdoch believes that writing is "above all else a collaboration of author and reader in an act of freedom." And, continues Berthoff, "following Sartre she has spoken pointedly of the making of works of art as not only a 'struggle for freedom' but as 'a task which does not come to an end.'"

Despite these similarities, critics note some important differences between the two philosophers. Gail Kmetz writes in *Ms.* that Murdoch "rejected Sartre's emphasis on the isolation and anguish of the individual in a meaningless world . . . because she felt it resulted in a sterile and futile solipsism[, a belief that the self is the only existent thing]. She considers the individual always as a part of society, responsible to others as well as to herself or himself; and insists that freedom means respecting the independent being of others, and that subordinating others' freedom to one's own is a denial of freedom itself. Unlike Sartre,

Murdoch sees the claims of freedom and love as identical: love is real only when one accepts the 'otherness' of other people, and only when one is capable of love is one free."

Kmetz postulates that this philosophical position is close to that of the religious existentialists—"without the theological element. . . . [Murdoch] calls herself a 'Christian fellow-traveler,' [but] feels we must act as if humanity were alone in the universe, without guidance from some realm 'beyond.'" For Murdoch, Kmetz continues, "morality is not a divinely given truth, but a process which occurs when we respect the reality of other people."

How best to respect the "reality" of others, i.e., how best to live "morally," is an issue that emerges in Murdoch's fiction again and again. Together with questions of "love" and "freedom," it comprises her major concern. "Miss Murdoch's pervasive theme has been the quest for a passion beyond any center of self," explains *New York Times Book Review* critic David Bromwich. "What her characters seek may go by the name of Love or God or the Good: mere physical love is the perilous and always tempting idol that can become a destroyer." "The basic idea," says Joyce Carol Oates writing in the *New Republic,* "seems to be that centuries of humanism have nourished an unrealistic conception of the powers of the will: we have gradually lost the vision of a reality separate from ourselves. . . . Twentieth-century obsessions with the authority of the individual, the 'existential' significance of subjectivity, are surely misguided, for the individual cannot be (as he thinks of himself, proudly) a detached observer, free to invent or reimagine his life." The consequences of trying to do so are repeatedly explored in Murdoch's fiction, beginning with her first published novel, *Under the Net.*

Drawn on Austrian philosopher Ludwig Wittgenstein's idea that we each build our own "net" or system for structuring our lives, *Under the Net* describes the wanderings of bohemian Jake Donaghue as he attempts to structure his. But, observes James Gindin in *Postwar British Fiction,* "planned ways of life are . . . traps, no matter how carefully or rationally the net is woven, and Jake discovers that none of these narrow paths really works." Only after a series of comic misadventures (which change his attitude rather than his circumstances) is Jake able to accept the contingencies of life and the reality of other people. He throws off the net, an act which takes great courage according to Kmetz, "for nothing is more terrifying than freedom."

Though situations vary from book to book, the protagonists in Murdoch's novels generally fashion a "net" of some kind. "It may be a set of rules such as those adhered to by the community members in *The Bell:* always cover your head in church; no personal decorations in one's room; we never ask each other about our past lives," writes Kmetz. "It may be an ideology or a huge impersonal bureaucracy, like the Special European Labor Immigration Board in *The Flight from the Enchanter.* Or a role: loving wife, martyr, rake."

For Hilary Burde, protagonist of *A Word Child,* the net is a fixed routine. An unloved, illegitimate child, Hilary as a boy is a violent delinquent. Then, befriended by a teacher, he learns that he possesses a remarkable skill with words. In the rigid structure of grammar he seeks shelter from life's randomness. He is awarded a scholarship to Oxford and begins what should be a successful career. "But," as *New York Times* critic Bromwich explains, "the structure of things can bear only so much ordering: his university job ends disastrously with an adulterous love affair that is indirectly responsible for two deaths." The story opens twenty years later, when Gunnar—the husband of Hilary's former lover—appears in the government office where Hilary holds a menial job. "The novel's subject," explains Lynne Sharon Schwartz in *Nation,* "is what Hilary will do about his humiliation, his tormenting guilt and his need for forgiveness."

What he does, according to Schwartz, is the worst possible thing. "He attempts to order his friends and his days into the kind of strict system he loves in grammar," she says. "This rigid life is not only penance but protection as well, against chaos, empty time, and the unpredictable impulses of the self. The novel shows the breakdown of the system: people turn up on unexpected days, they refuse—sometimes comically—to act the roles assigned them, and Hilary's dangerous impulses do come forth and insist on playing themselves out." The tragedy of Hilary's early days is repeated. He falls in love with Gunnar's second wife; they meet in secret and are discovered. Once more by accident Hilary commits his original crime.

"At the novel's conclusion," writes *Saturday Review*'s Bruce Allen, "we must consider which is the illusion: the optimist's belief that we can atone for our crimes and outlive them or the nihilist's certainty (Hilary expresses it) that people are doomed, despite their good intentions, to whirl eternally in a muddle of 'penitence, remorse, resentment, violence, and hate.'" David Bromwich interprets the moral issue somewhat differently. "Hilary, the artist-figure without an art," he says, "wants to make the world (word) conform to his every design, and is being guided to the awareness that its resistance to him is a lucky thing. . . . Like the novelist in *The Black Prince* and the poet in *Bruno's Dream,* Hilary must consent at last to the arbitrariness of an order imposed on him."

Learning to accept the chaos of life without the aid of patterns or categories is a constant struggle for Murdoch's characters. In her novels it is artists who, in Bromwich's words, are "trying daily by their disinterestedness to create a world outside themselves," who most nearly succeed. The importance of their role in her novels reflects Murdoch's belief in the importance of art, as *Midwest Quarterly*'s Sohreh Tawakuli Sullivan explains. "If the sickness of the age, as Murdoch contends, is solipsism, lovelessness, neurosis, a fear of history, . . . she would hold that its manifestation in philosophy and art, for example, could be cured by a therapy of perception, a rebirth of imagination. The need to perceive the unique particularity of the other is for Murdoch a measure not only of virtue and love, but of the creative imagination." For Murdoch, writes Joyce Carol Oates in the *New Republic,* the highest art is "that which reveals and honors the minute, 'random' detail of the world, and reveals it together with a sense of its integrity, its unity and form."

The creation of art, Murdoch told *Publishers Weekly,* should be the novelist's goal. "I don't think a novel should be a committed statement of political and social criticism," she said in that interview. "Novelists do enlighten people, they are great sources of education, but that's just incidental. They should aim at being beautiful. The most important thing about art is that it tells you what nature is really like, as opposed to what people in their fantasy-ridden way vaguely imagine it's like. Art holds a mirror to nature, and I think it's a very difficult thing to do."

The way Murdoch mirrors nature is by creating what she calls "real characters"—in other words, says Warner Berthoff in *Fictions and Events,* "personages who will be 'more than puppets' and at the same time other than oneself." In Murdoch's novels, the emphasis is not on form, but on character, as Linda Kuehl writing in *Modern Fiction Studies* explains: "Form, Iris Murdoch warns, is the artist's consolation and his temptation: he is tempted to sacrifice the eccentric, contingent individual while he consoles himself with the secure boundaries of structure. As

[Murdoch] sees it, this constitutes a crisis since the contemporary novelist tends to produce fiction in the shape of tiny, self-contained crystal-like objects. Diagnosing the tyranny of form as an ill that must be cured, she postulates a return to the novel of character as it is manifested in the works of [Sir Walter] Scott, Jane Austen, George Eliot and [Leo] Tolstoy, for these nineteenth century writers were so capable of charity that they gave their people an independent existence in an external world."

Unfortunately, continues Kuehl, Murdoch fails in her attempt: "Miss Murdoch's enthusiasm for nineteenth century characters prompts her desire to give 'a lot of people' an existence separate from herself and to permit them to roam freely and cheerfully throughout her pages. [But,] she seems unable to do this, for in each successive novel there emerges a pattern of predictable and predetermined types. These include the enchanter or enchantress—occult, godly, foreign, ancient—who is torn between exhibitionism and introspection, egotism and generosity, cruelty and pity; the observer, trapped between love and fear of the enchanter, who thinks in terms of ghosts, spells, demons and destiny, and imparts an obfuscated view of life; and the accomplice, a peculiar mixture of diabolical intention and bemused charm, who has dealings with the enchanters and power over the observers. . . . All three groups—enchanters, observers and accomplices—make up a scheme symptomatic of the author's failure to break away from the tyranny of form. Though she produces many people, each is tightly controlled in a super-imposed design, each is rigidly cast in a classical Murdochian role."

Lawrence Graver, writing in the *New York Times Book Review,* expresses a similar view. Notwithstanding her theory of fiction, he says, "in practice, the more she talked about freedom and opaqueness the more over-determined and transparent her novels seemed to become. Thinking back now on books like *The Unicorn, The Red and the Green, A Fairly Honorable Defeat,* or *An Accidental Man,* one is likely to remember situations not characters, mechanisms not worlds. Despite the inventiveness of the situations and the brilliance of the design, Miss Murdoch's philosophy has recently seemed to do little more than make her people *theoretically* interesting."

The problem, says Oates, is that her novels are "structures in which ideas, not things, and certainly not human beings flourish." In *The Novel Now,* Anthony Burgess compares Murdoch to a puppeteer who exerts complete control: "[Murdoch's] characters dress, talk, act like ourselves, but they are caught up in a purely intellectual pattern, a sort of contrived sexual dance in which partners are always changing. They seem to be incapable of free choice; they are totally in the . . . hands of their creatrix." Because she creates symbols rather than personalities, few, if any, of her characters, says *Saturday Review/World*'s Barbara Harrison, "resonate in the mind." In the intellectual game she plays, observes William Van O'Connor, the real communication is "between Miss Murdoch and her reader, not between the reader and the characters." This is both her strength and her limitation from his point of view.

Despite the prodigious response her novels generate, Murdoch refuses to read her critics: "One never learns anything one doesn't know already from them," she told *Publishers Weekly.* "Any novelist worth her salt knows very clearly what is wrong with her work before it is ever published. Why else would she be writing her next novel except to try to correct in it the mistakes of her last?"

Despite Murdoch's implication that there is room for improvement in her work, many reviewers praise the writing she has done. "She wears her formidable intelligence with a careless swagger," writes *Encounter*'s Jonathan Raban, "and her astonishingly fecund, playful imagination looks as fresh and effortless as ever. . . . Part of the joy of reading Iris Murdoch is the implicit assurance that there will be more to come, that the book in hand is an installment in a continuing work which grows more and more important as each new novel is added to it." Concludes Raban, "At a time when fiction seems hard and harder to write with any confidence, Miss Murdoch makes it look as easy and natural as breathing."

MEDIA ADAPTATIONS: "A Severed Head" (based on her novel and play) was filmed by Columbia Pictures, 1971; the film rights to *A Fairly Honourable Defeat* were sold in 1972.

BIOGRAPHICAL/CRITICAL SOURCES:

BOOKS

Allsop, Kenneth, *The Angry Decade,* P. Owen, 1958.
Berthoff, Warner, *Fictions and Events: Essays in Criticism and Literary History,* Dutton, 1971.
Bradbury, Malcolm, *Possibilities: Essays on the State of the Novel,* Oxford University Press, 1973.
Burgess, Anthony, *The Novel Now: A Guide to Contemporary Fiction,* Norton, 1967.
Byatt, A. S. D., *Degrees of Freedom,* Barnes & Noble, 1965.
Conradi, P. J., *Iris Murdoch: Work for the Spirit,* Macmillan, 1985.
Contemporary Literary Criticism, Gale, Volume I, 1973, Volume II, 1974, Volume III, 1975, Volume IV, 1975, Volume VI, 1976, Volume VIII, 1978, Volume XI, 1979, Volume XV, 1980, Volume XXII, 1982, Volume XXXI, 1985, Volume LI, 1989.
Dictionary of Literary Biography, Volume XIV: *British Novelists Since 1960,* Gale, 1982.
Dipple, Elizabeth, *Iris Murdoch: Work for the Spirit,* University of Chicago Press, 1981.
Gindin, James, *Postwar British Fiction,* University of California Press, 1962.
O'Connor, William Van, *The New University Wits, and the End of Modernism,* Southern Illinois University Press, 1963.
Rabinowitz, Rubin, *Iris Murdoch,* Columbia University Press, 1968.
Todd, Richard, *Iris Murdoch,* Methuen, 1984.
Ward, A. C., *Twentieth-Century English Literature, 1901-1960,* Methuen-University Paperbacks, 1964.

Wolfe, Peter, *The Disciplined Heart,* University of Missouri Press, 1966.

PERIODICALS

Atlantic Monthly, March, 1981.
Commonweal, March 28, 1969.
Critique, Volume X, number 1, and spring, 1964.
Encounter, July, 1974.
Globe and Mail (Toronto), October 28, 1989.
Harper's, October, 1964.
Listener, April 4, 1968.
Los Angeles Times, November 13, 1983.
Los Angeles Times Book Review, February 21, 1988.
Midwest Quarterly, spring, 1975.
Modern Fiction Studies, Volume XV, number 3, 1969.
Ms., July, 1976.
Nation, March 29, 1975, October 11, 1975.
New Republic, November 18, 1978.
New Yorker, March 23, 1981.
New York Times, January 6, 1981, June 29, 1983, January 9, 1986, January 27, 1988.
New York Times Book Review, September 13, 1964, February 8, 1970, August 24, 1975, November 20, 1977, December 17, 1978, August 10, 1980, January 4, 1981, March 7, 1982.
Publishers Weekly, December 13, 1976.
Saturday Review, February 7, 1970, August 9, 1975, January 6, 1979.
Saturday Review/World, October 5, 1974.
Shenandoah, winter, 1968.
Time, June 27, 1983, February 8, 1988.
Times (London), April 25, 1983, April 28, 1983, September 26, 1985, September 10, 1987, January 23, 1988, April 27, 1989, May 13, 1989.
Times Literary Supplement, September 10, 1964, November 25, 1977, September 5, 1980, October 20, 1989.
Tribune Books (Chicago), February 7, 1988.
Washington Post, December 21, 1980.
Washington Post Book World, February 7, 1988.
World Literature Today, summer, 1981.

* * *

MYLES, Symon
See FOLLETT, Ken(neth Martin)

N

NABOKOV, Vladimir (Vladimirovich) 1899-1977
(V. Sirin)

PERSONAL: Name pronounced "Vla-*dee*-meer Nah-*boak*-off";
born April 23, 1899, in St. Petersburg, Russia (now Leningrad,
U.S.S.R.); came to United States, 1940; became U.S. citizen,
1945; died of a virus infection, July 2, 1977, at the Palace Hotel
in Montreux, Switzerland; son of Vladimir Dmitrievich (a jurist
and statesman) and Elena Ivanovna (Rukavishnikov) Nabokov;
married Vera (Evseevna) Slonim (his amanuensis, aide, chauffeur, and general helpmate), April 15, 1925; children: Dmitri.
Education: Attended Prince Tenishev School, St. Petersburg,
1910-17; Trinity College, Cambridge, B.A. (with honors), 1922.
Religion: "Non-churchgoing Greek Catholic."

ADDRESSES: Home—Palace Hotel, Montreux, Switzerland.

CAREER: Novelist, poet, dramatist, literary critic, translator,
essayist, lepidopterist. Left Russia with his family in 1919; lived
in Berlin, Germany, writing, teaching English and tennis, and
composing crossword puzzles (the first such puzzles in Russian)
for the daily emigre newspaper, *Rul* ("Rudder"), 1922-37; lived
in Paris, France, 1937-40; Stanford University, Palo Alto, Calif.,
instructor in Russian literature and creative writing, summer,
1941; Wellesley College, Wellesley, Mass., resident lecturer in
comparative literature and instructor in Russian, 1941-48; Harvard University, Museum of Comparative Zoology, Cambridge,
Mass., research fellow in entomology, 1942-48; Cornell University, Ithaca, N.Y., 1948-59, became professor of Russian literature. Visiting lecturer, Harvard University, 1952.

MEMBER: Writers Guild (Los Angeles).

AWARDS, HONORS: Guggenheim fellowships for creative
writing, 1943 and 1952; National Institute of Arts and Letters
grant in literature, 1951; prize for literary achievement from
Brandeis University, 1964; Medal of Merit, American Academy
of Arts and Letters, 1969; National Medal for Literature, 1973;
Lectures on Literature was nominated for a National Book Critics Circle Award, 1980.

WRITINGS:

*NOVELS; RUSSIAN WORKS UNDER PSEUDONYM V. SIRIN
UNTIL 1940*

Mashen'ka, Slovo (Berlin), 1926, translation by the author and
Michael Glenny published as *Mary,* McGraw, 1970, reprinted, Ardis, 1985.
Korol', dama, valet, Slovo, 1928, reprinted, Ardis, 1979, revised
translation by son Dimitri Nabokov in collaboration with
the author published as *King, Queen, Knave,* McGraw,
1968.
Zashchita Luzhina, Slovo, 1930, reprinted, Ardis, 1979, translation by the author and Michael Scammell published as *The
Defense,* Putnam, 1964.
Podvig, first published in *Sovremennye Zapiski* (a Russian emigre
journal in Paris), 1932, reprinted, Ardis, 1979, English
translation by D. Nabokov in collaboration with the author
published as *Glory,* McGraw, 1971.
Kamera Obskura, first published in *Sovremennye Zapiski,* 1932,
reprinted, Ardis, 1978, English translation by W. Roy published as *Camera Obscura,* J. Long, 1936, translation by the
author published as *Laughter in the Dark,* Bobbs-Merrill,
1938, revised edition, New Directions, 1960.
Otchayanie, first published serially in *Sovremennye Zapiski,*
1934, published as a book, Petropolis (Berlin), 1936, reprinted, Ardis, 1978, English translation by the author published as *Despair,* J. Long, 1937, revised edition, Putnam,
1966.
Dar, first published serially in *Sovremennye Zapiski,* 1937-38,
published as a book, Izdatelstvo Imeni Chekhova (New
York), 1952, English translation by D. Nabokov and Scammell in collaboration with the author published as *The Gift,*
Putnam, 1963.
Priglashenie na Kazn', Dom Knigi (Paris), 1938, reprinted,
Ardis, 1979, English translation by D. Nabokov in collaboration with the author, published as *Invitation to a Beheading,* Putnam, 1959.
Soglyadatay, Russkiya Zapiski (Paris), 1938, reprinted, Ardis,
1978, English translation by D. Nabokov in collaboration
with the author published as *The Eye,* Phaedra, 1965.
The Real Life of Sebastian Knight, New Directions, 1941, reprinted, Penguin, 1964.
Bend Sinister, Holt, 1947, reprinted with a new introduction by
the author, Time-Life, 1981.

Lolita, Olympia Press (Paris), 1955, Putnam, 1958, reprinted, Berkley Publishing, 1984, Russian translation by the author, Phaedra, 1966, annotated edition, edited with a preface, introduction, and notes by Alfred Appel, Jr., published as *The Annotated Lolita,* McGraw, 1970.

Pnin, Doubleday, 1957, reprinted, R. Bentley, 1982.

Pale Fire, Putnam, 1962, reprinted, Perigee Books, 1980, 2nd edition, Lancer Books, 1966.

Ada or Ardor: A Family Chronicle, McGraw, 1969.

Transparent Things, McGraw, 1972.

Look at the Harlequins, McGraw, 1974.

Five Novels, with an introduction by Peter Quennell, Collins, 1979.

Also author of *Solus Rex,* an unfinished novel partially published in *Sovremennye Zapiski,* 1940, and, under the title *Ultima Thule,* in *Novy Zhurnal* (New York), 1942.

STORIES; RUSSIAN WORKS UNDER PSEUDONYM V. SIRIN UNTIL 1940

Vozurashchenie Chorba, Slovo, 1929, reprinted, Ardis, 1983.

Nine Stories, New Directions, 1947.

Vesna v Fial'te, Drugie Rasskazy, Izdatelstvo Imeni Chekhova, 1956, published as *Vesna Fiualte: Spring in Fialte,* Ardis, c. 1978.

Nabokov's Dozen: A Collection of Thirteen Stories, Doubleday, 1958, reprinted, Anchor Press/Doubleday, 1984, published in paperback as *Spring in Fialta,* Popular Library, 1959 (published in England as *Nabokov's Dozen: Thirteen Stories,* Penguin, 1971).

Nabokov's Quartet, Phaedra, 1966.

A Russian Beauty and Other Stories, translated from the Russian by D. Nabokov and Simon Karlinsky in collaboration with the author, McGraw, 1973.

Tyrants Destroyed and Other Stories, translated from the Russian by D. Nabokov in collaboration with the author, McGraw, 1975.

Details of a Sunset and Other Stories, McGraw, 1976.

The Enchanter, translated by D. Nabokov from original unpublished Russian manuscript, Putnam, 1986.

POETRY; RUSSIAN WORKS UNDER PSEUDONYM V. SIRIN UNTIL 1940

Poems (in Russian), privately printed (St. Petersburg), 1916.

(With Andrei Balashov) *Two Paths,* privately printed (Petrograd), 1918.

Gorny Put', Grani (Berlin), 1923.

Grozd', Gamayun (Berlin), 1923, [Jerusalem], 1981.

Stikhotvoreniya, 1920-1951, Rifma (Paris), 1952.

Poems, Doubleday, 1959.

Poems and Problems, McGraw, 1970.

Stikhi, Ardis, 1979.

PLAYS; RUSSIAN WORKS UNDER PSEUDONYM V. SIRIN UNTIL 1940

"Smerti" (verse play), published in *Rul,* 1923.

"Dedushka" (verse play), published in *Rul,* 1923.

"Polius" (verse play), published in *Rul,* 1924.

"Tragedia gospodina Morna," excerpts published in *Rul,* 1925.

"Tshelovek iz SSSR" (five-act play), first produced in Berlin, 1926, excerpts published in *Rul,* 1927.

"Sobytie" (three-act comedy), first performed in Paris, 1938, performed in New York, 1941, published in *Russkiya Zapiski,* 1938.

"Izobretenie Val'sa," published in *Russkiya Zapiski,* 1938, English translation by D. Nabokov in collaboration with the

author published as *The Waltz Invention* (three-act, first produced by Hartford Stage Co., Hartford, Conn., January, 1969), Phaedra, 1966.

The Man from the U.S.S.R. and Other Plays, translated from the Russian by D. Nabokov, Harcourt/Bruccoli Clark, 1984.

P'esy (collected plays), Ardis, 1987.

Also author of "Skital'tsy," a pretended translation of the first act of a nonexistent eighteenth-century English play, 1923, and of "Agasfer," the poetic accompaniment to a symphony, c. 1923.

NONFICTION

Nikolai Gogol (critical biography), New Directions, 1944, corrected edition, 1961.

Notes on Prosody: From the Commentary to His Translation of Pushkin's "Eugene Onegin," Bollingen Foundation, 1963, published as *Notes on Prosody and Abram Gannibal: From the Commentary to the Author's Translation of Pushkin's "Eugene Onegin,"* Princeton University Press, 1964.

Strong Opinions (essays), McGraw, 1973.

Letters from Terra: Vladimir Nabokov zu Ehren, edited by Uwe Friesel, Rowohlt, 1977.

The Nabokov-Wilson Letters: Correspondence between Vladimir Nabokov and Edmund Wilson, 1940-1971, edited, annotated and with an introductory essay by Karlinsky, Harper, 1979.

Lectures on Literature, edited by Fredson Bowers, with an introduction by John Updike, Harcourt/Bruccoli Clark, 1980.

Lectures on Ulysses: Facsimile of the Manuscript, with a foreword by A. Walton Litz, Bruccoli Clark, 1980.

Lectures on Russian Literature, edited and with an introduction by Bowers, Harcourt/Bruccoli Clark, 1980.

(With others) *Nabokov's Fifth Arc: Nabokov and Others on His Life Work,* edited by J. E. Rivers and Charles Nicol, University of Texas Press, 1982.

Lectures on Don Quixote, edited by Bowers, Harcourt/Bruccoli Clark, 1983.

Perepiska s sestrol (correspondence), Ardis, 1985.

TRANSLATOR INTO ENGLISH

Three Russian Poets: Selections From Pushkin, Lermontov, Tyutchev, New Directions, 1945, reprinted, Folcroft Press, 1969.

(And author of introduction and commentary) *The Song of Igor's Campaign: An Epic of the Twelfth Century,* Vintage, 1960, reprinted, McGraw, 1975.

(And editor and author of commentary) Alexander Pushkin, *Eugene Onegin: A Novel in Verse,* four volumes, Bollingen, 1964, revised edition, 1975.

TRANSLATOR INTO RUSSIAN; UNDER PSEUDONYM V. SIRIN

Romain Rolland, *Nikolka Persik,* Slovo, 1922.

Lewis Carroll, *Anya v Strane Chudes,* Gamaiun (Berlin), 1923, reprinted, Ardis, 1982.

AUTOBIOGRAPHY

Conclusive Evidence: A Memoir, Harper, 1951 (published in England as *Speak Memory: Memoir,* Gollancz, 1951), revised edition by the author published in Russian as *Drugiye Berega,* Izdatelstvo Imeni Chekhova, 1954, reprinted, Ardis, 1978, expanded English language edition published as *Speak Memory: An Autobiography Revisited* (Book-of-the-Month Club selection), Putnam, 1966.

OTHER

(Author of introduction and notes) Mikhail Lermontov, *Hero in Our Time,* translation by D. Nabokov, Doubleday, 1958, reprinted, 1982.

Lolita: A Screenplay (produced by Metro-Goldwyn-Mayer, 1962), McGraw, 1961.

Nabokov's Congeries (reader), edited by Page Stegner, Viking, 1968.

The Portable Nabokov, selected and with a critical introduction by Stegner, Viking, 1968.

Vladimir Nabokov: Selected Letters, 1940-1977, edited by D. Nabokov and Matthew J. Bruccoli, Harcourt, 1989.

Multivolume collected works published by Ardis as *Sobranie sochinenii.*

Also author of *Vozvrashchenie Chorba,* 1930, and of a sound recording, *Vladimir Nabokov: An Intimate Self Portrait of a Great Writer,* Center for Cassette Studies. Contributor to Russian emigre journals in Berlin, Paris, and New York, and to English periodicals; contributor of papers on lepidoptera to such scientific journals as the *Bulletin of the Museum of Comparative Zoology,* Harvard.

WORK IN PROGRESS: Original of Laura, a novel; an illustrated history of the butterfly in art.

SIDELIGHTS: Vladimir Nabokov, a White Russian emigre who began writing in English in middle age, is considered one of the most brilliant and deceptive writers of the twentieth century. A trilingual author, equally competent in Russian, English and French, Nabokov wrote prodigiously in many genres, including fiction, drama, autobiography, translations, essays, literary criticism, and even, on occasion, scientific studies of butterflies and collections of chess problems. His writing remains so distinctive that several critics deem him not part of any family but a species unto himself, and often cite *Lolita,* his best-known work, as a prime example of truly original invention. "He is a major force in the contemporary novel" fictionist Anthony Burgess asserts in *The Novel Now: A Guide to Contemporary Fiction.* John Updike, another novelist who acknowledges Nabokov's tremendous impact on twentieth-century literature, deems him, in a *New Republic* article, one of the few writers "whose books, considered as a whole, give the happy impression of an *oeuvre,* of a continuous task carried forward variously, of a solid personality, of a plenitude of gifts exploited knowingly. His works are an edifice whose every corner rewards inspection. Each . . . yields delight and presents to the aesthetic sense the peculiar hardness of a finished, fully meant thing. His sentences are beautiful out of context and doubly beautiful in it. He writes prose the only way it should be written—that is ecstatically. In the intensity of its intelligence and reflective joy, his fiction is unique in this decade and scarcely precedented in American literature."

Despite an awareness of his technical brilliance and verbal facility, readers have sometimes been bewildered by the complexity of Nabokov's writing. "Virtually all of the foremost literary critics in the United States and England have written about Nabokov, with enthusiasm often bordering on awe," notes Andrew Field in *Nabokov: His Life in Art.* "But their eloquence, where one wants and would expect explication, betrays the fact that they are at least as ill at ease with Nabokov as they are fascinated by him." The critic Alfred Kazin, for instance, after reading *Ada or Ardor: A Family Chronicle,* wrote, "For some weeks now I have been floundering and traveling in the mind of that American genius Vladimir Vladimirovich Nabokov," according to the *New York Times.* In that novel, as in almost all his works, Nabo-

kov intentionally laced the narrative with obscure literary allusions and trilingual puns that pivot on an understanding of Russian, and to a lesser degree French, language and culture. Though helpful, even a broad knowledge of European literature would not make Nabokov's creations entirely clear for, as an artist, he enjoyed playing tricks on his readers.

A consummate gamesman, Nabokov reveled in what Field calls "artistic duplicity" and apparently conceived of writing as an elaborate interplay between author and reader. In the literature courses he taught at Cornell, reprinted in *Lectures on Literature,* Nabokov instructed his students "to read books for the sake of their form, their visions, their art" and cautioned them "to share not the emotions of the people in the book but the emotions of its author—the joys and difficulties of creation." Projected into almost all his narratives—including those, like *Lolita* which seem to revolve around a traditional plot—are "thinly disguised bits of literary criticism and . . . a variety of literary games involving allusion to and parody and citation of other men's writings," notes *New York Times Book Review* contributor Simon Karlinsky. Nabokovian scholar Alfred Appel, also writing in the *New York Times Book Review,* describes Nabokov as "the most allusive and linguistically playful writer in English since [James] Joyce," while *Hollins Critic* contributor R. H. W. Dillard cautions that Nabokov "is clearly and always the . . . serious and deceptive artist with whom we must play the game."

In addition to the difficulties presented by Nabokov's artistic deceptions, the circumstances of his checkered past further cloud his writing. Long after Nabokov had adopted English as his chosen language, his early writing remained untranslated and thus available only in its original Russian form. These early poems, reviews, essays, and fictions were published in Russian emigre newspapers first in Berlin and, later, in Paris, when that city became the center of emigre culture. While it was theoretically possible for displaced Russians to follow both the Berlin and Paris journals, few in practice did. The difficulties for American readers were further compounded, for without easy access to either source, they had no real context in which to place his work. "None of my American friends have read my Russian books and thus every appraisal on the strength of my English ones is bound to be out of focus," Nabokov wrote, in a passage reprinted by Field. Field himself postulates that "if the substantial body of Nabokov's Russian writing and the best critical articles about him had been translated before 1950, it is extremely unlikely that *Lolita* or *Pale Fire* would have been nearly as misunderstood as they were." In later years, Nabokov partially remedied the problem by working in close cooperation with his son Dmitri to translate his books.

Before the Bolshevik revolution, which precipitated his family's flight, Nabokov led a charmed life in one of Russia's noble families. His father was a distinguished lawyer and one of the country's few political liberals, opposed to both Tsarist absolutism and the revolutionary Bolsheviks. It was the elder statesman's custom to take a daily bath in a portable rubber tub, and this habit was adopted by his favorite son, who considered the warm water a catalyst of creative inspiration. From his father, Vladimir also seems to have inherited his belief in patrician democracy ("My father was an old-fashioned liberal, and I do not mind being labeled an old-fashioned liberal, too," he said in a *Paris Review* interview), an interest in the criminal mind, a capacity for sustained work, and a passionate love of butterflies. Because his father wrote under the name Vladimir Nabokov, young Vladimir adopted the pseudonym V. Sirin. His mother, "equally aristocratic" according to Samuel Schuman in *Vladimir Nabokov: A Reference Guide,* "was most distinguished in her son's memory by a finely developed and artistic sensitivity, sharing many of the novelist's acute reactions to sense impressions, especially reactions to color and sound." Nabokov records these impressions in *Speak Memory,* considered one of the finest autobiographies in the English language.

Vladimir was the eldest and, by all accounts, the most precocious of the five Nabokov children. He was adored by his parents, and they considered his education a matter of utmost concern. During his early childhood, which was divided between St. Petersburg and Vyra, the family's country estate, he was privately tutored by a governess. She taught him to speak English, the first language he learned. When he was twelve, Nabokov enrolled in the liberal Tenishev Academy in St. Petersburg, and there, during his six-year stay, he privately printed two books of poetry. In 1916, the same year his first chapbook *Poems* appeared, Nabokov inherited an estate worth several million dollars from his "Uncle Ruka."

Unfortunately, this prosperity would be short-lived. Just three years later the entire Nabokov family was forced to abandon their home and take refuge in the southern portion of Russia known as the Crimea. As they waited for the restoration of political order and the opportunity to return, unrest spread and the family again decamped, hurriedly boarding a boat bound for England. "The flight into exile resulted in the loss of most of the Nabokov fortune and, much more importantly for Vladimir, the loss of a homeland, a culture, and a language," Schuman reports, arguing that "that set of losses was perhaps the single most crucial event in the artist's lifetime—the role of the exile and the vitality of memory remained dominant motifs in Nabokov's work for the next half-century." Field reports in *Vladimir Nabokov: His Life in Part* that one of the author's 1920 poems "refers to that trip into exile of the previous year as *sailing to nowhere.*"

Nabokov spent the years from 1919 to 1922 studying Romance and Slavic languages at Cambridge and writing Russian poetry. He was an indifferent scholar who never once entered the university library, but after his father was assassinated at a political rally in Berlin in March 1922, "he returned for his last term with the determination to do well and took his degree with honors," according to Donald E. Morton in his book *Vladimir Nabokov.* After graduation, Nabokov moved to Berlin, the heart of the emigre community, and began contributing poems and prose to *Rul* ("Rudder"), a Russian-language daily his father had helped to found. For many years Nabokov entertained hopes of returning to Russia and continued to write primarily in Russian, a choice "made easier by the fact that I lived in a closed emigre circle of Russian friends and read exclusively Russian newspapers, magazines and books," Nabokov reports in *Strong Opinions.* In 1925, he married Vera Evseevna Slonim, who became his lifelong companion and literary assistant, and in 1926 his first novel, *Mashen'ka* (later translated as *Mary*) appeared.

The original Russian version of the book received little attention, but after Nabokov's reputation burgeoned and the work was translated into English, *Mary* received closer scrutiny. "In it," notes a *Virginia Quarterly Review* contributor, "we find some pleasing confirmations of what we have assumed to be Nabokov's themes." A nostalgic tale of a young emigre's longing for the love he left behind in Russia, *Mary* details what life was like for the residents of a Berlin pension in the early 1920s. As the story opens, the protagonist Ganin meets a fellow boarder in a stalled elevator and learns that the man is anticipating the arrival of his Russian wife in six days. Halfway through the novel, Ganin realizes that his friend's wife is none other than his beloved *Mary.* He plots to interrupt the marital liaison and meet

her in her husband's stead. At the last moment, however, he realizes that she will not be the same girl he remembers, and he departs, leaving her waiting alone at the station.

According to *New York Times* reviewer John Leonard, "the heroine would appear to be as much Mother Russia as the girl *Mary;* they are coextensive," and Morton expresses a similar view, noting that "the absent girl is a symbol of the exiles' longing for their lost homeland." Guy Davenport, in a *National Review* article maintains that "like all of Nabokov's novels [*Mary*] is about a man who has two minds, one containing an imaginary world, the other well-focused on reality. The characters, except for the lovely (and unseen) Mary, are all Nabokovian marginal people inhabiting interims and delusions. Practically all of the later themes are here." Writing in the *New York Times Book Review,* Mark Slonim identifies two of those themes as "the powers of memory and imagination" and goes on to suggest that, for Nabokov, these attitudes are "the lifegiving source of all creative acts and . . . the very foundations of art. Of course, Nabokov has traveled a long road and changed greatly since his twenties when he wrote 'Mary,' but throughout his work he has never failed to assert the basic truth that forms the core of his first novel."

In addition to their contributions to his thematic development, the early fictions also shaped Nabokov's literary technique. "It was in his Russian novels . . . that he developed his art of incorporating literary allusion and reference as an inherent device of fictional narration," writes Karlinsky. Nabokov's second novel, *Korol', dama, valet* (translated as *King, Queen, Knave*), marks the first appearance of this device. "It is . . . the first of his novels to have a plot and character serve as vehicles for the real subject, which is form, style and the strategies of total creation," writes Eliot Fremont-Smith in the *New York Times.* In this story, merely one of several Nabokovian variations on the eternal love triangle, a vain and selfish woman named Martha diabolically plots with her bumbling young lover, Franz, to kill her unsuspecting husband and Franz's uncle, Dreyer.

Field has traced the inspiration for this story to an obscure Hans Christian Andersen tale of the same name, in which a pack of cards fights a revolution. "While Nabokov's story apparently has little to do with Andersen's, it is presumably no accident that the novel has thirteen chapters, the number of cards in a suit. The characters are two dimensional, like cards, and the variations on a conventional plot suggest that the novel is one permutation of dealing a hand," writes Charles Nicol in the *Atlantic.* Another acknowledged literary source for the novel is Gustave Flaubert's *Madame Bovary,* which *King, Queen, Knave* burlesques. *New York Times Book Review* contributor Philip Toynbee notes that "with both women one has the same oppressive sense of fate hanging heavily over their heads."

The force controlling Martha's fate is, of course, the author, and Nabokov uses this power to manipulate the narrative in unexpected ways. Although he is patterning his tale on a situation readers will certainly have encountered in many other novels, "nothing ends as it's supposed to," according to *Washington Post* reviewer Geoffrey Wolff, who thinks the novel "abounds in comic incongruities: Martha is cold, selfish, aloof and beautiful, yet Nabokov has her slip into passionate love with a bumbling, graceless post-adolescent hayseed. Their rendezvous are made in a grubby comic-opera parody of a clerk's garret as it might be imagined in a nineteenth-century Russian novel."

With each new novel published, Nabokov garnered increased attention within the emigre community, but he remained unknown to the public at large and was forced to supplement his writing income with outside work. Between 1922 and 1937, he earned a living by tutoring, translating, performing as an extra in movies, and—as his reputation spread—by giving literary readings of his poems and prose. Still, the Berlin years were a time of material impoverishment, as Field notes in *Vladimir Nabokov: His Life in Part*: "In September 1935 after Nabokov was praised in print for the first time in the United States . . ., Nabokov wrote to his mother:—'In *The New York Times* they write "our age has been enriched by the appearance of a great writer," but I don't have a decent pair of trousers, and I quite don't know what I shall wear to Belgium where PEN has invited me to read.' "

Further hardships followed. In 1937 Nabokov left Berlin for Paris, accompanied by his wife Vera, who was Jewish, and Dmitri, his only child. In escaping the hostile political climate of Nazi Germany, Nabokov was also shifting to what appeared to be a more stimulating ambience, for Paris had superseded Berlin as the emigre lodestar. Despite its status as a Russian cultural center, Paris was disappointing, for even here emigre writing seemed ingrown and stale. Increasingly, Nabokov found himself without a proper audience for his Russian work. Writing of emigre Paris in the late 1930s, Field describes this decline: "The literature existed, but it had no resonance, or at best one so circumscribed that it could be calculated not even in thousands but in hundreds of readers. The old combinations by which a livelihood might be put together in ways more or less directly connected with literature were less possible now."

Around this time, Nabokov began to experiment with English, translating his Russian novel *Otchayanie* into the English *Despair* in 1937. Initially hesitant about his command of the language, Nabokov requested the assistance of a professional to proofread his work. H. G. Wells was recommended, but never materialized; a second candidate bowed out, declaring himself unsuited to the work. Finally, an English woman agreed to make corrections, but when her list of recommendations was completed, Nabokov found it spurious. "All of this stuff is completely insignificant, for any Russian reader can find just as many birthmarks on any page of any of my Russian novels, and any good English writer commits just as many grammatical imprecisions," he wrote in a letter to Vera, quoted in *Vladimir Nabokov: His Life in Part*. The book was published exactly as he wrote it, an event that "is important in Nabokov's biography," according to Field, "because it is part of that process of metamorphosis which was in a few years to . . . make him an English writer. After he had done that translation, he knew he could do it." Indeed, his very next book, *The Real Life of Sebastian Knight*, was written in English and marks the demise of the pseudonymous V. Sirin and the emergence of Vladimir Nabokov, an American writer.

Regarded as one of Nabokov's lesser accomplishments, *The Real Life of Sebastian Knight* strikes Conrad Brenner as "the most perverse novel you are ever likely to encounter. This book is quite openly a literary trick, astounding in [its] sleek deceitful contours," he writes in a *New Republic* article. Filled with autobiographical tidbits and typically Nabokovian allusions to chess, *The Real Life of Sebastian Knight* chronicles the narrator's search for the "essence" of his half-brother, the titular Sebastian Knight—a Russian emigre writer who died an early death in relative obscurity. The brothers had been out of touch for years, but V. (as the narrator is called) remains convinced of Sebastian's genius and sets out to write a biography that will insure his brother's critical stature and refute a second-rate biography that Sebastian's former secretary has published. Rather than clarifying the details of Sebastian's life, however, V.'s search only raises more questions. The book draws to a close with V. retrospec-

tively visiting Sebastian on his death bed and wondering if perhaps he himself is Sebastian Knight or if he might be a third person unknown to them both.

While composed largely in the sunlit bathroom of his Paris flat, *Sebastian Knight* was published in the United States in 1941, a year after Nabokov and his family arrived in New York in flight from Hitler's terror. During these first years of his American residency, Nabokov worked in obscurity at several part-time jobs. His knowledge of butterflies won him a coveted position as a research fellow at Harvard's Museum of Comparative Zoology, and he also received a guest lectureship at Wellesley College (though he was never offered tenure, partly because his anti-Soviet sentiments were suspect during the Russo-American alliance of World War II). Nabokov lived in rented quarters and never purchased his own home, but, eventually settled at Cornell University in Ithaca, N.Y., where he is remembered as an inspiring if somewhat eccentric teacher. He delivered his lectures from carefully prepared diagrams and notes, many of which have been published posthumously in *Lectures on Literature*.

Nabokov might have continued quietly lecturing to what he called, in *Playboy*, "the great fraternity of C-minus, backbone of the nation," but for the publication of a novel that would make his name an unpronounceable household word. "The first little throb of *Lolita* went through me late in 1939 or early in 1940 in Paris, at a time when I was laid up with a severe attack of intercostal neuralgia," Nabokov wrote in an appendix to the novel. The inspiration was a newspaper story about the first ape to have produced a drawing, a pathetic sketch of the bars of his cage. The text had no direct connection to the story that followed, but nonetheless resulted in what Nabokov called "a prototype" of *Lolita*—namely a Russian tale of fifty typewritten pages. Unhappy with the story, Nabokov abandoned the work (later rediscovered, translated, and posthumously published as *The Enchanter*), but "around 1949, in Ithaca, upstate New York, the throbbing, which had never quite ceased, began to plague me again." By then, however, "the thing was new and had grown in secret the claws and wings of a novel." Within a few years, Nabokov had completed *Lolita*.

First published in Paris by the Olympia Press because of its questionable subject matter, *Lolita* was later brought out in the United States by the respectable G. P. Putnam & Sons and ascended to the ranks of best-sellerdom. The novel purports to be the true confession of a middle-aged debaucher who chooses the pseudonym Humbert Humbert because it "expresses the nastiness best." Jailed for the murder of his rival, Humbert seeks to purge himself by recounting his tale, though the reader is warned in a mock preface by an obtuse Freudian psychiatrist that Humbert can never be absolved. Nor is his tone "the characteristic whine of the penitent," but rather, as *New Yorker* contributor Donald Malcolm observes, "an artful modulation of lyricism and jocularity that quickly seduces the reader into something very like willing complicity." In eloquent detail, Humbert describes his lust for that species of prepubescent girls he calls "nymphets" and for twelve-year-old Dolores Haze in particular. In order to be near his beloved Lolita, as Dolores is called, Humbert marries her mother, then finds his polluted dream fulfilled when she dies in an auto accident, leaving him the child's guardian. He is somewhat chagrined to discover, on their first night alone, that Lolita is a more experienced lover than he. "Their weird affair—which carries them on a frenzied motel-hopping trek around the American continent—is climaxed by Lolita's escape with a playwright and Humbert's eventual revenge on his rival," Charles Rolo concludes in the *Atlantic*.

With its theme of perversion, *Lolita* provoked a moralistic outcry from some of the more conservative critics, such as the *Catholic World* reviewer who believes the "very subject matter makes it a book to which grave objection must be raised." But for every critic who attacked the book, there were dozens who applauded, among them the editor of *The Annotated Lolita,* Alfred Appel, Jr., who considers *Lolita* "one of the few supremely original novels of the century"; *San Francisco Chronicle* contributor Lewis Vogler, who deems it "an authentic work of art which compels our immediate response"; and Conrad Brenner, who calls it "a work clearly foreshadowed in the body of [Nabokov's] prose, and the high water mark of his career as *agent provocateur.*"

While Nabokov paid little notice to most interpretations of *Lolita,* he reacted strongly against readers who envisioned the story as a satiric criticism of his adopted land. "Whether or not critics think that in *Lolita* I am ridiculing human folly leaves me supremely indifferent. But I am annoyed when the glad news is spread that I am ridiculing America," he told Alvin Toffler in *Playboy.* In another interview excerpted in the *Washington Post,* Nabokov asserted that "America is the only country where I feel emotionally and mentally at home." Nonetheless, with the proceeds from *Lolita,* Nabokov moved to the Palace Hotel in Switzerland, abandoning his teaching completely and devoting his time to writing and butterflies. His reasons, he told Toffler, were "purely private"—for one thing, most of his family remained in Europe, for another, he was comfortable with the ambience there.

In Montreux, the sixty-year-old Nabokov continued to write, often standing at a lectern in his room and recording his thoughts in longhand on specially ordered index cards. One of his first projects was to resume work on a novel (originally entitled *Solus Rex*) that had been interrupted by the war. Entitled *Pale Fire,* this difficult work demonstrates the increased emphasis on form and structure that dominates Nabokov's later fiction. "More than any other of his books *Pale Fire* lives up to his dictum that 'Art is never simple. . . . Because, of course, art at its greatest is fantastically deceitful and complex,' " John Hagopian reports in the *Dictionary of Literary Biography.* This complexity frustrated many would-be readers and led *New York Times Book Review* contributor George Cloyne to dismiss *Pale Fire* as a "curiosity . . . one more proof of Mr. Nabokov's rare vitality. Unluckily it is not much more than that." *Christian Science Monitor* contributor Roderick Nordell is less circumspect, judging the book "a prodigal waste of its author's gifts."

Pale Fire consists of a 999-line poem in four cantos, composed by the late John Shade, an American poet recently assassinated by a madman's bullet, and a foreword, commentary, and index, contributed by Dr. Charles Kinbote, an emigre scholar of dubious sanity. Since Kinbote's footnotes are keyed to various lines in the poem, the reader cannot simply read the book from cover to cover, but must continually flip back and forth from the commentary to the verse. "This is not the drudgery it may sound, for every vibration of the pages carries the reader to a fresh illumination, a further delight," writes Donald Malcolm in the *New Yorker.* "But on the other hand, it is not reading in the ordinary sense. It more nearly resembles the manipulation of a pencil along a course of numbered dots until the hidden picture stands forth, compact, single, and astonishing." Notes Mary McCarthy in the *New Republic,* "When the separate parts are assembled, according to the manufacturer's directions, and fitted together with the help of clues and cross-references, which must be hunted down as in a paperchase, a novel on several levels is revealed."

For some critics, this elaborate mechanism tends to overshadow the story. "Indeed the structure is so witty, and so obtrusive, that it threatens constantly to become its own end; and we are made to attend so closely to it that the novel itself seems wholly subordinate to its mode of enclosure," *Nation* contributor Saul Madoff concludes. Faced with the same material, however, Mary McCarthy reaches a very different conclusion. She calls *Pale Fire* "a Jack-in-the-box, a Faberge gem, a clockwork toy, a chess problem, an infernal machine, a trap to catch reviewers, a cat-and-mouse game, a do-it-yourself novel. . . . This centaur-work of Nabokov's, half poem, half prose, this merman of the deep, is a creation of perfect beauty, symmetry, strangeness, originality, and moral truth. Pretending to be a curio, it cannot disguise the fact that it is one of the very great works of art of this century, the modern novel that everyone thought dead and that was only playing possum."

In his seventieth year, Nabokov produced his last major work, *Ada or Ardor: A Family Chronicle,* a sexually explicit tale of incest, twice as long as any other novel he had written and, according to the *New York Times*'s John Leonard, "fourteen times as complicated." An immediate best-seller, *Ada* evoked a wide array of critical response, ranging from strong objections to the highest praise. While the value of the novel was debated, *Ada* was universally acknowledged as a work of enormous ambition that represented the culmination of all that Nabokov had attempted to accomplish in his writing over the years. "*Ada* is the fullest realization of the program for the novel articulated in 1941 in Nabokov's first English book, *The Real Life of Sebastian Knight,*" explains Robert Alter in *Commentary.* Like the character Sebastian who described his attempt to "use parody as a kind of springboard for leaping into the highest region of serious emotion," Nabokov, through his bristling word play, attempted to illuminate "in new depth and breadth the relation between art, reality, and the evanescent ever-never presence of time past," Alter believes.

On the surface, Ada chronicles the incestuous love affair between Van Veen and his cousin (soon revealed to be his sister) Ada, who fall in love as adolescents, embark upon a blissful sexual odyssey, are pulled apart by social taboo and circumstance, only to be reunited in late middle age, at which time they prosper together until both are in their nineties. "Nabokov sums up these amorous doings in a mock dust-jacket blurb that closes *Ada* by describing only the book's most superficial aspects," writes a *Time* reviewer. "Long before he gets around to that, though, a suspicion has set in that the surface love story is as different from the real Ada as a bicycle reflector is from a faceted ruby." Van's memoir of his love affair with Ada, ostensibly "Van's book," is actually an anagram for "Nabokov's," and "once the creator's name has been uttered, *Ada*'s profoundest purpose comes into view. . . . Ada is the supreme fictional embodiment of Nabokov's lifelong, bittersweet preoccupation with time and memory," the *Time* reviewer concludes.

Nabokov continued writing well into the 1970s, though his last books are considered minor additions to his oeuvre. Upon his death at seventy-eight, *New York Times* contributor Alden Whitman concluded his obituary with these words: "Anyone so bold as to venture explanations might attempt to show how Mr. Nabokov's fiction was the refinement through memory and art of his own experience as a man who lost both father and fatherland to violent revolution, who adopted another culture, who mastered its language as few of its own have mastered it and who never forgot his origins. But one hesitates to undertake such explorations. Mr. Nabokov always forbade intrusions into his privacy; he hated psychologists; and he would scoff at such extra-esthetic adventures. . . . But as long as Western civilization survives, his reputation is safe. Indeed, he will probably emerge as one of the greatest artists our century has produced."

MEDIA ADAPTATIONS: Laughter in the Dark, screenplay by Edward Bond, was filmed by Woodfall Films, 1969; *King, Queen, Knave* was filmed by David Wolper-Maran Productions, 1972; *Invitation to a Beheading* was dramatized by Russell McGrath and performed in New York for the Shakespeare Festival, at the New York Public Theatre, March 8-May 4, 1969; "Lolita, My Love," a musical play based on Nabokov's novel *Lolita* was performed on Broadway at the Mark Hellinger Theatre, March, 1971.

BIOGRAPHICAL/CRITICAL SOURCES:

BOOKS

Appel, Alfred, Jr., editor, *The Annotated Lolita,* McGraw, 1970.
Burgess, Anthony, *The Novel Now: A Guide to Contemporary Fiction,* Norton, 1967.
Concise Dictionary of American Literary Biography: The New Consciousness, 1941-1968, Gale, 1987.
Contemporary Literary Criticism, Gale, Volume 1, 1973, Volume 2, 1974, Volume 3, 1975, Volume 6, 1976, Volume 8, 1978, Volume 11, 1979, Volume 15, 1980, Volume, 23, 1983, Volume 44, 1987, Volume 46, 1988.
Dictionary of Literary Biography, Volume 2: *American Novelists Since World War II,* Gale, 1978.
Dictionary of Literary Biography Documentary Series, Volume 3, Gale, 1983.
Dictionary of Literary Biography Yearbook: 1980, Gale, 1981.
Field, Andrew, *Nabokov: His Life in Art,* Little, Brown, 1967.
Field, Andrew, *Nabokov: His Life in Part,* Viking, 1977.
Field, Andrew, *V. N.: The Life and Art of Vladimir Nabokov,* Crown, 1986.
Morton, Donald E., *Vladimir Nabokov,* Ungar, 1974.
Nabokov, Vladimir, *Lolita,* Putnam, 1958.
Nabokov, Vladimir, *King, Queen, Knave,* McGraw, 1968.
Nabokov, Vladimir, *Strong Opinions,* McGraw, 1973.
Nabokov, Vladimir, *Ada or Ardor: A Family Chronicle,* McGraw, 1969.
Nabokov, Vladimir, *Lectures on Literature,* edited by Fredson Bowers, with an introduction by John Updike, Harcourt/Bruccoli Clark, 1980.
Schuman, Samuel, *Vladimir Nabokov: A Reference Guide,* G. K. Hall, 1979.

PERIODICALS

Atlantic, September, 1958, June, 1968, June, 1969.
Catholic World, October, 1958.
Christian Science Monitor, May 31, 1962, May 8, 1969.
Commentary, August, 1969.
Encounter, February 1959, January, 1965, February 1966.
Hollins Critic, June, 1966.
Nation, August 30, 1958, June 16, 1962, January 17, 1966.
National Review, July 15, 1969, November 17, 1970.
New Republic, June 23, 1958, June 4, 1962, September 26, 1964, April 3, 1965, January 20, 1968, June 28, 1969.
New Yorker, November 8, 1958, September 22, 1962, August 2, 1969.
New York Times, January 12, 1968, May 13, 1968, May 1, 1969, October 7, 1970, August 24, 1989, October 5, 1989.
New York Times Book Review, May 27, 1962, May 15, 1966, January 15, 1967, July 2, 1967, May 12, 1968, May 4, 1969, June 14, 1970, October 25, 1970, April 18, 1971, October 1, 1989.
Paris Review, summer/fall, 1967.
Playboy, January, 1964.
San Francisco Chronicle, August 24, 1958.
Saturday Review, August 16, 1958, May 26, 1962, January 7, 1967, January 28, 1967.
Time, July 28, 1967, May 17, 1968, May 23, 1969, November 2, 1970, December 21, 1970.
Tribune Books (Chicago), September 24, 1989.
Virginia Quarterly Review, winter, 1971.

OBITUARIES:

PERIODICALS

Detroit Free Press, July 5, 1977.
Newsweek, July 18, 1977.
New York Times, July 5, 1977.
Publishers Weekly, July 18, 1977.
Time, July 18, 1977.
Washington Post, July 5, 1977.

*   *   *

NAIPAUL, Shiva(dhar Srinivasa)   1945-1985

PERSONAL: Born February 25, 1945, in Port of Spain, Trinidad (now Republic of Trinidad and Tobago), West Indies; died of a heart attack, August 13, 1985, in London, England; son of Seepersad and Dropatie Naipaul; married wife, Virginia Margaret Stuart, 1967; children: one. *Education:* Attended University College, Oxford, 1964-68.

ADDRESSES: Agent—Gillon Aitken, 17 South Eaton Pl., London SW1, England.

CAREER: Writer. Lecturer at Aarhus University, Aarhus, Denmark, 1972.

MEMBER: Royal Society of Literature (fellow).

AWARDS, HONORS: John Llewelyn Rhys Memorial Prize and Winifred Holtby Memorial Prize, both 1970, and Jock Campbell New Statesman Award, 1971, all for *Fireflies;* Whitbread Literary Award, 1973, for *The Chip-Chip Gatherers.*

WRITINGS:

Fireflies (novel), Deutsch, 1970, Knopf, 1971.
The Chip-Chip Gatherers (novel), Knopf, 1973.
North of South: An African Journey (nonfiction), Simon & Schuster, 1978.
Black and White (nonfiction), Hamish Hamilton, 1980, published as *Journey to Nowhere: A New World Tragedy,* Simon & Schuster, 1981.
A Hot Country (novel), Hamish Hamilton, 1983, published as *Love and Death in a Hot Country,* Viking, 1984.
Beyond the Dragon's Mouth (stories), Viking, 1985.
An Unfinished Journey (nonfiction), Viking, 1987.

Contributor of short stories to anthologies, including *Penguin Modern Stories 4,* Penguin, 1970, and *Winter's Tales 20,* Macmillan (London), 1974. Contributor of articles to *Times Literary Supplement, London Magazine, New Statesman,* and *Spectator.*

WORK IN PROGRESS: A book about Australia, unfinished at time of death.

SIDELIGHTS: The younger brother of writer V. S. Naipaul, Shiva Naipaul, an Indian born in Trinidad, established himself as a critically acclaimed author with his first novel, *Fireflies.* Set in a Trinidadian Hindu community, *Fireflies* describes the demise of that community's leaders, the Khoja family, who lose their elevated stature as a result of intrafamily squabbles, arranged and loveless marriages, poor education, and undisciplined and futile attempts to reach goals beyond their grasp. "There is unusually little in Shiva Naipaul's *Fireflies* to lead one to suppose that it is his first novel," wrote Stephen Wall in the *Observer*. "It is hard to wish any particular episode away once it has been read." In the *New York Times Book Review,* critic Annette Grant deemed *Fireflies* "a remarkable and vivid portrait of an exotic, highly special tribe, the Hindus of Trinidad—who, like most people, are fundamentally unremarkable, but who under examination, exhibit a full and rich spectrum of human possibilities." "That the details *do* fascinate," Grant added, "is a tribute both to the author's invention and to his subject."

Like *Fireflies,* Naipaul's second novel, *The Chip-Chip Gatherers,* is set in Trinidad and examines family relationships, this time between two very different families, the affluent Ramsarans and the less prestigious Bholais. Although brought together by marriage, the clans are never able to put aside their differences and work together for their common good. Therefore their association serves no purpose; it is as futile as the work of the village peasants who comb the beach to find the tiny shellfish chip-chip, a bucket of which might provide only a mouthful of meat.

Finding *The Chip-Chip Gatherers* "compelling," A. L. Hendricks in a *Christian Science Monitor* review judged Naipaul to be "a skillful storyteller" who "wastes no words on elaborate descriptions or philosophizing, but lets his characters make his point. He draws them sympathetically and yet never loses his artistic detachment." In his *New Statesman* critique Martin Amis predicted that Naipaul's "next novels will establish him as one of the most accomplished, and most accessible, writers of his generation."

Naipaul's six-month trek through Kenya, Tanzania, and Zambia inspired his next book, *North of South: An African Journey.* In this volume the author recorded his day-to-day observations of Africa in what critic John Darnton in the *New York Times Book Review* dubbed "the genre of travelogue *cum* essay." Naipaul relates his experiences of African life as he viewed it in cafes and buses, schools and homes, and through encounters with merchants, farmers, educators, and others. What impressed him most during his stay in Africa was the extent of European influence on African mores and customs.

Critics found *North of South* to be an interesting and well-written account of African ways, but not necessarily an unbiased and accurate observation. Darnton noted some "striking inaccuracies" and wrote that the citizens Naipaul profiles "are hardly the defining personalities in Africa today." Darnton nevertheless opined that *North of South* is "superbly written." Critic Roland Oliver also found *North of South* lacking in some areas. In his *New Statesman* review Oliver called Naipaul's effort "a witty but not wise book" that "is more informative about touts and tourists, pimps and prostitutes, than about national and international politics of the East African countries." "All this is told with a great deal of novelist's sparkle, a power of vivid description and of characterisation through reported dialogue, which will not endear Mr. Naipaul to his many acquaintances when his book comes into their hands."

Further comments about *North of South* came from Lewis Nkosi, who in the *Times Literary Supplement* noted Naipaul's "elegance of style," but concurred with the other critics that "it is not that the picture Naipaul paints of Africa is totally unrecognizable; the question is one of perspective and standards used." And Jim Hoagland, writing in the *Washington Post Book World,*

deemed *North of South* "ultimately one-dimensional," but judged it a "rare quick good read for the Africa shelf."

Naipaul followed *North of South* with *Journey to Nowhere: A New World Tragedy,* in which he seeks to explain and document the bizarre circumstances and events that precipitated the Jonestown Massacre, when more than nine hundred men, women, and children, all members of a cult known as the People's Temple, committed suicide at the command of the sect's leader, Jim Jones. The mass suicide occurred in 1978 in Guyana, where Jones had moved his cult after investigating journalists and concerned family members of the cultists interfered with the group's operation in San Francisco, California. Before instructing his followers to drink the cyanide-laced soft drink he offered them, Jones explained that their suicide was "an act . . . protesting the conditions of an inhuman world." Related deaths included California congressman Leo Ryan and several others who were gunned down on a Guyana airstrip by People's Temple members. Ryan and his entourage were on a mission to investigate the cult and free several members being held against their will.

Naipaul's account of the massacre was applauded by many reviewers, among them D. J. Enright, who wrote in the *Times Literary Supplement* that *Journey to Nowhere* is "a saddening, alarming, depressing book" that is "in part, a tribute to its author's assiduity, fortitude and powers of expression. . . . Only if the author had lived there could he have hoped to be more exhaustive and certain; and then he would not have lived to tell the tale at all." In the *New York Times Book Review* Peter L. Berger regarded Naipaul as "a masterful writer" and found *Journey to Nowhere* a "lively and readable" book. "Mr. Naipaul's is a harsh perspective," Berger opined. "It is also a very persuasive one. To be sure, a less idiosyncratic writer would have softened his interpretation, introduced more nuances, perhaps shown more compassion. One strength of the book is that Mr. Naipaul does none of these things, letting the reader make his own modifications if he is so inclined."

Peter Schrag also offered praise for *Journey to Nowhere* in his *Nation* review, calling Naipaul's book "a tough, intelligent, beautifully written account of how Californian and Third World illusions fused to set the stage for the disaster in Guyana." Schrag added that Naipaul "has a flawless ear for the gobbledygook of Third World pretenders, encounter-group gurus, esties, obfuscating politicians and the various other manipulators of rhetoric who populated the world of Pastor Jones." And critic John Coleman, in the *New Statesman,* wrote of *Journey to Nowhere:* "It is one man's view and helps to make hideous sense of that flight to a Guyanan graveyard. Naipaul writes as ever with an ice-tipped pen, elegantly summoning laughter that rings like anger."

Naipaul's third novel, *A Hot Country,* is set in the fictional South African state of Cuyama, a depressed region where politics have become "banditry, cynicism and lies," and where the land has been ravaged, leaving "the foundations of vanished houses," and "archways leading nowhere." Its people, too, are bleak, frustrated, and hopeless as a result of the poverty and hunger that prevail in Cuyama. In a London *Times* review, critic Andrew Sinclair felt Naipaul's "regressive view . . . leaves the readers in the doldrums, with hardly enough energy to turn these pages of fine prose without the least spark of life." And "there is much voluptuous self-surrender to pessimism by the author, who closes off all avenues of hope," wrote Nicholas Rankin in *Times Literary Supplement.* "Yet it does not mask Shiva Naipaul's other considerable talents as a novelist. He deftly captures place, mood and character, and has not lost his eye and ear for embarrassment and discomfiture. . . . *A Hot Country* is a sad book about waste, but a work of art that delights with its craft as it dismays with its vision."

BIOGRAPHICAL/CRITICAL SOURCES:

BOOKS

Contemporary Literary Criticism, Gale, Volume 32, 1985, Volume 39, 1986.
Dictionary of Literary Biography Yearbook: 1985, Gale, 1986.

PERIODICALS

Choice, January, 1972, October, 1973, October, 1981.
Christian Science Monitor, June 20, 1973.
Nation, May 2, 1981.
National Review, September 28, 1979, October 2, 1981.
New Republic, June 9, 1979, June 16, 1979.
New York Times, April 21, 1979, March 13, 1987.
New York Times Book Review, February 7, 1971, May 6, 1979, June 29, 1980, July 5, 1981, July 4, 1982, August 12, 1984, March 24, 1985, March 22, 1987.
New Yorker, August 6, 1973, July 2, 1979, May 25, 1981.
New Statesman, April 20, 1973, July 28, 1978, October 31, 1980.
Newsweek, May 21, 1979, June 1, 1979, May 14, 1984.
Observer, November 15, 1970, April 15, 1973, April 25, 1976, July 30, 1978, November 2, 1980.
Spectator, October 30, 1970, April 21, 1973, October 14, 1978, February 7, 1981.
Times Literary Supplement, December 11, 1970, April 13, 1973, September 29, 1978, October 31, 1980, August 30, 1983.
Times (London), August 28, 1983.
Times Literary Supplement, September 12, 1986.
Washington Post Book World, July 1, 1979, April 5, 1981, April 25, 1984, March 24, 1985, April 19, 1987.

OBITUARIES:

PERIODICALS

Los Angeles Times, August 25, 1985.
Newsweek, August 26, 1985.
New York Times, August 16, 1985.
Time, August 26, 1985.
Times (London), August 16, 1985, August 21, 1985.
Washington Post, August 17, 1985.

*   *   *

NAIPAUL, V(idiadhar) S(urajprasad) 1932-

PERSONAL: Born August 17, 1932, in Trinidad; married Patricia Ann Hale, 1955. *Education:* Attended Queen's Royal College, Trinidad and University College, Oxford.

ADDRESSES: Agent—c/o Aitken & Stone Ltd., 29 Fernshaw Rd., London SW10, England.

CAREER: Free-lance broadcaster for the British Broadcasting Corp., two years; writer.

MEMBER: Society of Authors, Royal Society of Literature (fellow).

AWARDS, HONORS: John Llewellyn Rhys Memorial Prize, 1958, for *The Mystic Masseur;* grant from government of Trinidad for travel in Caribbean, 1960-61; Somerset Maugham Award, 1961, for *Miguel Street;* Phoenix Trust Award, 1963; Hawthornden Prize, 1964, for *Mr. Stone and the Knights Companion;* W. H. Smith Award, 1968, for *The Mimic Men;* Booker Prize, 1971, for *In a Free State;* Bennett Award from *Hudson Review,* 1980; Hon.D. from Columbia University, 1981; Hon.Litt.

from Cambridge University, 1983; T. S. Eliot Award for Creative Writing from Ingersoll Foundation, 1986.

WRITINGS:

The Mystic Masseur, Deutsch, 1957, Vanguard, 1959, reprinted, Penguin, 1977.
The Suffrage of Elvira, Deutsch, 1958.
Miguel Street, Deutsch, 1959, Vanguard, 1960, reprinted, Penguin, 1977.
A House for Mr. Biswas, Deutsch, 1961, McGraw, 1962.
The Middle Passage: Impressions of Five Societies—British, French and Dutch in the West Indies and South America (nonfiction), Deutsch, 1962, Macmillan, 1963, reprinted, Penguin, 1978.
Mr. Stone and the Knights Companion, Deutsch, 1963, Macmillan, 1964.
An Area of Darkness (nonfiction), Deutsch, 1964, Macmillan, 1965.
The Mimic Men, Macmillan, 1967.
A Flag on the Island (short story collection), Macmillan, 1967.
The Loss of El Dorado: A History (nonfiction), Deutsch, 1969, Knopf, 1970.
(Contributor) Andrew Salkey, editor, *Island Voices: Stories from the West Indies,* new edition, Liveright, 1970.
In a Free State, Knopf, 1971.
The Overcrowded Barracoon and Other Articles, Deutsch, 1972, Knopf, 1973.
Guerrillas, Knopf, 1975.
India: A Wounded Civilization (nonfIction), Knopf, 1977.
A Bend in the River, Knopf, 1979.
The Return of Eva Peron (nonfiction), Knopf, 1980.
Among the Believers, Knopf, 1981.
Finding the Center, Vintage Books, 1986.
The Enigma of Arrival, 1987.
A Turn in the South, Viking, 1989.
A Million Mutinies Now, Penguin, 1991.

Contributor to *New York Review of Books, New Statesman,* and other periodicals. Fiction reviewer, *New Statesman,* 1958-61.

SIDELIGHTS: Born in Trinidad to the descendants of Hindu immigrants from northern India and educated at England's Oxford University, V. S. Naipaul is considered to be one of the world's most gifted novelists. As a *New York Times Book Review* critic writes: "For sheer abundance of talent there can hardly be a writer alive who surpasses V. S. Naipaul. Whatever we may want in a novelist is to be found in his books: an almost Conradian gift for tensing a story, a serious involvement with human issues, a supple English prose, a hard-edged wit, a personal vision of things. Best of all, he is a novelist unafraid of using his brains. . . . His novels are packed with thought, not as lumps of abstraction but as one fictional element among others, fluid in the stream of narrative. . . . [He is] the world's writer, a master of language and perception, our sardonic blessing."

This ability to regard Naipaul as "the world's writer" is in large measure due to the author's self-proclaimed rootlessness. Unhappy with the cultural and spiritual poverty of Trinidad, distanced from India, and unable to relate to and share in the heritage of each country's former imperial ruler (England), Naipaul describes himself as "content to be a colonial, without a past, without ancestors." As a result of these strong feelings of nonattachment to any particular region or set of traditions, most of his work deals with people who, like himself, are estranged from the societies they are supposedly a part of and who are desperately seeking to find a way to belong or to "be someone." The locales Naipaul chooses for his stories represent an extension of this same theme, for most take place in emerging Third World countries in the throes of creating a new "national" identity from the tangled remnants of native and colonial cultures.

Naipaul's early work explored these themes via a West Indian variation of the comedy of manners—that is, an almost farcical portrayal of the comic aspects of an illiterate and divided society's shift from a colonial to an independent status, with an emphasis on multiracial misunderstandings and rivalries and the various ironies resulting from the sudden introduction of such democratic processes as elections. In *The Mystic Masseur, The Suffrage of Elvira,* and *Miguel Street,* Naipaul essentially holds a mirror up to Trinidadian society in order to expose its follies and absurdities; his tone is detached, yet sympathetic, as if he is looking back at a distant past of which he is no longer a part. The tragic aspects of the situation are not examined, nor is there any attempt to involve the reader in the plight of the characters. Michael Thorpe describes the prevailing tone of these early books as "that of the ironist who points up the comedy, futility and absurdity that fill the gap between aspiration and achievement, between the public image desired and the individual's inadequacies, to recognize which may be called the education of the narrator: 'I had grown up and looked critically at the people around me.'"

A House for Mr. Biswas marks an important turning point in Naipaul's work; his increasing attention to subject and theme via a blend of psychological and social realism and certain symbolic overtones foreshadows the intensive character studies of his later works. In addition, *A House for Mr. Biswas* has a universality of theme that the author's earlier books lacked for the most part due to their emphasis on strictly local-color elements. The cumulative effect of these "improvements" has led many critics to regard *A House for Mr. Biswas* as Naipaul's masterpiece. As Robert D. Hamner writes: "With the appearance in 1961 of *A House for Mr. Biswas,* Naipaul may have published his best fiction. It is even possible that this book is the best novel yet to emerge from the Caribbean. It is a vital embodiment of authentic West Indian life, but more than that, it transcends national boundaries and evokes universal human experiences. Mr. Biswas' desire to own his own house is essentially a struggle to assert personal identity and to attain security—thoroughly human needs."

The *New York Herald Tribune Books* reviewer notes that "Naipaul has a wry wit and an engaging sense of humor, as well as a delicate understanding of sadness and futility and a profound but unobtrusive sense of the tragi-comedy of ordinary living. . . . His style is precise and assured. In short, he gives every indication of being an important addition to the international literary scene. [*A House for Mr. Biswas*] is funny, it is compassionate. It has more than 500 pages and not one of them is superfluous."

Paul Theroux of the *New York Times Book Review* admits that "it is hard for the reviewer of a wonderful author to keep the obituarist's assured hyperbole in check, but let me say that if the stilting-up of the Thames coincided with a freak monsoon, causing massive flooding in all parts of South London, the first book I would rescue from my library would be *A House for Mr. Biswas.*"

Michael Thorpe agrees that the novel is "a work of rare distinction; . . . [it is] a 'novelist's novel,' a model work. . . . The book's popularity must be largely due to its universality of subject and theme, the struggle of one ordinary man to climb—or cling on to—the ladder of life; the ordinariness lies in his ambitions for home, security, status, his desire to live through his son, yet he remains an individual. . . . At first sight Mr. Biswas

seems an abrupt departure from Naipaul's previous fiction: in its concentration upon the life history of a single protagonist it goes far deeper than *The Mystic Masseur* and the mood is predominantly 'serious,' the still pervasive comedy being subordinated to that mood. Yet on further consideration we can see *Mr. Biswas* as the natural and consummate development of themes that ran through the first three books: the perplexing relation of the individual to society, his struggle to impress himself upon it through achievement—or defy its pressures with a transforming fantasy that puts a gloss upon life and extracts order from the rude chaos of everyday existence. . . . We should not doubt that the narrative is to be heroic, the quest for the house—however flawed in its realization—a victory over the chaos and anonymity into which the hero was born. The novel is such a man's celebration, his witness, the answer to the dismal refrain, 'There was nothing to speak of him.'" In short, Thorpe concludes, "for West Indian literature *A House for Mr. Biswas* forged [the] connexion [between literature and life] with unbreakable strength and set up a model for emulation which no other 'Third World' literature in English has yet equalled."

After his success with *A House for Mr. Biswas,* Naipaul turned away from exclusively West Indian locales in order to "test" his themes in a broader geographic and nationalistic landscape. At the same time, his earlier light-hearted tone gradually faded as he explored the more tragic consequences of alienation and rootlessness in the world at large through the eyes of various "universal wanderers." As Thomas Lask reports in the *New York Times* on Naipaul's *In a Free State:* "V. S. Naipaul's writings about his native Trinidad have often enough been touched with tolerant amusement. His is an attitude that is affectionate without being overly kind. . . . On his own, Mr. Naipaul [has] made no secret of his alienation from his native island. . . . [*In a Free State*] takes the story one step further. How does the expatriate fare after he leaves the island? . . . [The author] lifts the argument above and beyond material success and social position. These new stories focus on the failure of heart, on the animallike cruelty man exhibits to other men and on the avarice that . . . is the root of all evil. . . . What the author is saying is that neither customs nor color nor culture seems able to quiet that impulse to destruction, that murderous wantonness that is so much part of our make-up. . . . Mr. Naipaul's style in these stories seems leaner than in the past and much more somber. There is virtually none of the earlier playfulness. He appears to have settled for precision over abundance. Each detail and each incident is made to carry its weight in the narrative. The effect is not small-scaled, for in the title story he has created an entire country. He has not tidied up every loose strand. . . . But there is nothing unfinished in these polished novellas."

Paul Theroux calls *In a Free State* "Naipaul's most ambitious work, a story-sequence brilliant in conception, masterly in execution, and terrifying in effect—the chronicles of a half-a-dozen self-exiled people who have become lost souls. Having abandoned their own countries (countries they were scarcely aware of belonging to), they have found themselves in strange places, without friends, with few loyalties, and with the feeling that they are trespassing. Worse, their lives have been totally altered; for them there is no going back; they have fled, each to his separate limbo, and their existence is like that of souls in a classical underworld. . . . The subject of displacement is one few writers have touched upon. Camus has written of it. But Naipaul is much superior to Camus, and his achievement—a steady advance through eleven volumes—is as disturbing as it is original. *In a Free State* is a masterpiece in the fiction of rootlessness."

Alfred Kazin of the *New York Review of Books* claims that "Naipaul writes about the many psychic realities of exile in our contemporary world with far more bite and dramatic havoc than Joyce. . . . No one else around today, not even Nabokov, seems able to employ prose fiction so deeply as the very choice of exile. . . . What makes Naipaul hurt so much more than other novelists of contemporary exodus is his major image—the tenuousness of man's hold on the earth. The doubly unsettling effect he creates—for the prose is British-chatty, proper yet bitter—also comes from the many characters in a book like [*In a Free State*] who don't 'belong' in the countries they are touring or working in, who wouldn't 'belong' any longer in the countries they come from, and from the endless moving about of contemporary life have acquired a feeling of their own unreality in the 'free state' of endlessly moving about. . . . Naipaul has never encompassed so much, and with such brilliant economy, with such a patent though lighthanded ominousness of manner, as in [*In a Free State*]. The volume of detail is extraordinary. . . . I suppose one criticism of Naipaul might well be that he covers too much ground, has too many representative types, and that he has an obvious desolation about homelessness, migration, the final placelessness of those who have seen too much, which he tends to turn into a mysterious accusation. Though he is a marvelous technician, there is something finally modest, personal, openly committed about his fiction, a frankness of personal reference, that removes him from the godlike impersonality of the novelist. . . . Naipaul belongs to a different generation, to a more openly tragic outlook for humanity itself. He does not want to play God, even in a novel."

A *New Statesman* critic, on the other hand, is not quite convinced that Naipaul's outlook is completely tragic. He writes: "Each piece [of *In a Free State*] is a tour de force. . . . I don't know any writer since Conrad who's exposed the otherness of Africa so starkly, and Naipaul leaves his readers freer by his massacre of obstinate illusions. But his vision excludes elements of growth and hope which are, palpably, there. . . . Naipaulia remains a kingdom of cryptic anti-climax. I wonder, though, if the 'cryptic' final section is nudging away from pessimism."

With the publication of *Guerrillas,* however, the first of Naipaul's novels to make his name widely known in the United States, more and more reviewers became convinced that his outlook is indeed grim. Notes Theroux: "*Guerrillas* is a violent book in which little violence is explicit. . . . It is a novel, not of revolt, but of the play-acting that is frequently called revolt, that queer situation of scabrous glamour which Naipaul sees as a throwback to the days of slavery. . . . *Guerrillas* is one of Naipaul's most complex books; it is certainly his most suspenseful, a series of shocks, like a shroud slowly unwound from a bloody corpse, showing the damaged—and familiar—face last. . . . This is a novel without a villain, and there is not a character for whom the reader does not at some point feel deep sympathy and keen understanding, no matter how villainous or futile he may seem. *Guerrillas* is a brilliant novel in every way, and it shimmers with artistic certainty. It is scarifying in the opposite way from a nightmare. One can shrug at fantasy, but *Guerrillas*—in a phrase Naipaul himself once used—is, like the finest novels, 'indistinguishable from truth.' "

Paul Gray of *Time* believes that *Guerrillas* "proves [Naipaul] the laureate of the West Indies. . . . [He] is a native expatriate with a fine distaste for patriotic rhetoric. . . . [The novel] is thus conspicuously short of heroes. . . . The native politicians are corrupt, the foreign businessmen avaricious, and the people either lethargic or criminal. When an uprising does flare, it is nasty and inept. Perhaps no one but Naipaul has the inside and outside

knowledge to have turned such a dispirited tale into so gripping a book. His island is built entirely of vivid descriptions and off-hand dialogue. At the end, it has assumed a political and economic history, a geography and a population of doomed, selfish souls. . . . *Guerrillas* is not a polemic (polemicists will be annoyed) but a Conradian vision of fallibility and frailty. With economy and compassion, Naipaul draws the heart of darkness from a sun-struck land."

Noting that Naipaul takes a "hackneyed" theme ("incipient Black Power") and manages to produce "a more significant treatment of it than most of his contemporaries with similar concerns," Charles R. Larson of the *Nation* writes that *Guerrillas* "builds so slowly and so skillfully that until the final scene bursts upon us, we are hardly aware of the necessary outcome of the events; it is only in retrospect that we see that the desultory action has in fact been charged with fate. . . . No one writes better about politics in the West Indies than V. S. Naipaul. Nor is there anyone who writes more profoundly about exiles, would-be revolutionaries and their assorted camp followers. Written in a deliberately flat style, *Guerrillas* is a deeply pessimistic novel, telling us that we have seen about as much political change in the West Indian island republics as we are likely to see."

In *A Bend in the River,* Naipaul returns to Africa as a locale (the scene of *In a Free State*), confirming his basic pessimism in the process. Comments John Leonard in the *New York Times:* "This is not an exotic Africa [in *A Bend in the River*]. . . . [The author] despises nostalgia for the colonial past, while at the same time heartlessly parodying . . . the African future. . . . *A Bend in the River* is a brilliant and depressing novel. It is no secret by now, certainly not since *Guerrillas* . . . , that V. S. Naipaul is one of the handful of living writers of whom the English language can be proud, if, still, profoundly uneasy. There is no consolation from him, any more than there is sentiment. His wit has grown hard and fierce; he isn't seeking to amuse, but to scourge."

John Updike, writing in the *New Yorker,* asserts that *A Bend in the River* "proves once more that Naipaul is incomparably well situated and equipped to bring us news of one of the contemporary world's great subjects—the mingling of its peoples. *A Bend in the River* struck me as an advance—broader, warmer, less jaded and kinky—over the much-praised *Guerrillas,* though not quite as vivid and revelatory as the fiction of *In a Free State. A Bend in the River* is carved from the same territory [as *In a Free State*]—an Africa of withering colonial vestiges, terrifyingly murky politics, defeated pretensions omnivorous rot, and the implacable undermining of all that would sustain reason and safety. . . . Rage . . . is perhaps the deepest and darkest fact Naipaul has to report about the Third World, and in this novel his understanding of it goes beyond that shown in *Guerrillas.* . . . In *A Bend in the River,* the alien observer—white bureaucrat or Asian trader—is drawn closer into the rationale of the riots and wars that seethe in the slums or the bush beyond his enclave. The novel might be faulted for savoring a bit of the visiting journalist's worked-up notes: its episodes do not hang together with full organic snugness; there are a few too many clever geopolitical conversations and scenically detailed car rides. . . . [But] the author's embrace of his tangled and tragic African scene seems relatively hearty as well as immensely knowledgeable. Always a master of fictional landscape, Naipaul here shows, in his variety of human examples and in his search for underlying social causes, a Tolstoyan spirit, generous if not genial."

Walter Clemons of *Newsweek* calls *A Bend in the River* "a hurtful, claustrophobic novel, very hard on the nerves, played out

under a vast African sky in an open space that is made to fee]
stifling. . . . Naipaul's is a political novel of a subtle and unusual kind. . . . [It] is about tremors of expectation, shifts in
personal loyalty, manners in dire emergency. . . . As an evocation of place, [the novel] succeeds brilliantly. . . . *A Bend in the
River* is by no means a perfected work. . . . But this imperfect,
enormously disturbing book confirms Naipaul's position as one
of the best writers now at work."

And Irving Howe wrote in the *New York Times Book Review:*
"On the surface, *A Bend in the River* emerges mostly as a web
of caustic observation, less exciting than its predecessor, *Guerrillas;* but it is a much better and deeper novel, for Naipaul has mastered the gift of creating an aura of psychic and moral tension
even as, seemingly, very little happens. . . . [But in the end,]
Naipaul offers no intimations of hope or signals of perspective.
It may be that the reality he grapples with allows him nothing
but grimness of voice. . . . A novelist has to be faithful to what
he sees, and few see as well as Naipaul; yet one may wonder
whether, in some final reckoning, a serious writer can simply
allow the wretchedness of his depicted scene to become the limit
of his vision. . . . Naipaul seems right now to be a writer beleaguered by his own truths, unable to get past them. That is surely
an honorable difficulty, far better than indulging in sentimental
or ideological uplift; but it exacts a price. . . . Perhaps we ought
simply to be content that, in his austere and brilliant way, he
holds fast to the bitterness before his eyes."

Subsequent works, notably *The Enigma of Arrival* and *A Turn
in the South,* have served to confirm Naipaul's status as one of
the English language's most distinguished and perceptive contemporary writers. In his 1976 study of Naipaul, Michael
Thorpe offers this overview of the novelist's accomplishments:
"While Naipaul is by no means alone in coming from a makeshift
colonial society and using the 'metropolitan' language with a native surety, these origins have helped him more than any of his
contemporaries from the Commonwealth to develop an inclusive
view of many facets of the larger world, a view focussed by his
intense sense of displacement from society, race or creed. . . .
He has gone beyond local conflicts, isolated instances of the colonial experience, to attempt something approaching a world
view. . . . His insights and his manner of conveying them carry
a persuasive truth."

As a result, continues Thorpe, "Naipaul has spoken from and to
more points within that world [of imperial or social oppression]
than any English writer—but his is not a comforting or hopeful
voice. . . . Asked if he were an optimist [Naipaul] replied: 'I'm
not sure. I think I do look for the seeds of regeneration in a situation; I long to find what is good and hopeful and really do hope
that by the most brutal sort of analysis one is possibly opening
up the situation to some sort of action; an action which is not
based on self-deception.'. . . [But] he supplies none of the props
even realists let us lean upon in the end: there are no consolations—no religious belief, no humanistic faith in man's future,
not even the personal supports of friendship or love. . . . [Thus]
Naipaul's is one of the bleakest visions any imaginative observer
alive has given us. . . . [He] refuses to leap to positive attitudes
he cannot justify. Naipaul would be the last to claim for his work
that it represents a final or adequate vision; it is the record of one
man's impressions of the world and it does not pretend to be the
whole truth about it. . . . Yet Naipaul insists that he is hopeful:
as one who has not flinched from harsh reality, he has earned
the right to our reciprocal hope that he may yet find a way beyond despair."

BIOGRAPHICAL/CRITICAL SOURCES:

BOOKS

Contemporary Literary Criticism, Gale, Volume 4, 1975, Volume
     7, 1977, Volume 9, 1978, Volume 13, 1980, Volume 18,
     1981, Volume 37, 1986.
Dictionary of Literary Biography Yearbook: 1985, Gale, 1986.
Hamner, Robert D., *V. S. Naipaul,* Twayne, 1973.
Thorpe, Michael, *V. S. Naipaul,* Longmans, 1976.

PERIODICALS

Atlantic, May, 1970, January, 1976, July, 1977, June, 1979.
Best Sellers, April 15, 1968.
Books and Bookmen, October, 1967.
Books Abroad, winter, 1968, winter, 1969.
Chicago Sunday Tribune, July 12, 1959.
Chicago Tribune Book World, May 13, 1979, April 20, 1980.
Choice, June, 1973.
Christian Science Monitor, July 19, 1962, March 29, 1968, May
     28, 1970.
Contemporary Literature, winter, 1968.
Economist, July 16, 1977.
Illustrated London News, May 20, 1967.
Kenyon Review, November, 1967.
Listener, May 25, 1967, September 28, 1967, May 23, 1968.
London Magazine, May, 1967.
Los Angeles Times, May 9, 1980, March 15, 1989.
Los Angeles Times Book Review, June 24, 1979.
Nation, October 9, 1967, October 5, 1970, December 13, 1975,
     July 2, 1977, June 30, 1979.
National Review, October 6, 1970.
New York Herald Tribune Books, June 24, 1962.
New Yorker, August 4, 1962, August 8, 1970, June 6, 1977, May
     21, 1979.
New York Review of Books, October 26, 1967, April 11, 1968,
     December 30, 1971, May 31, 1979.
New York Times, December 16, 1967, December 25, 1971, Au-
     gust 17, 1977, May 14, 1979, March 13, 1980.
New Statesman, May 5, 1967, September 15, 1967, November 7,
     1969, October 8, 1971, June 17, 1977.
New Republic, July 9, 1977, June 9, 1979.
New York Times Book Review, October 15, 1967, April 7, 1968,
     May 24, 1970, October 17, 1971, November 16, 1975, De-
     cember 28, 1975, May 1, 1977, June 12, 1977, May 13, 1979.
Newsweek, December 1, 1975, June 6, 1977, May 21, 1979.
Observer Review, April 30, 1967, September 10, 1967, October
     26, 1969.
Punch, May 10, 1967.
Saturday Review, July 2, 1960, October 23, 1971, November 15,
     1975.
Spectator, September 22, 1967, November 8, 1969.
Time, May 25, 1970, December 1, 1975, June 20, 1977, May 21,
     1979.
Times Literary Supplement, May 31, 1963, April 27, 1967, Sep-
     tember 14, 1967, December 25, 1969, July 30, 1971, No-
     vember 17, 1972.
Transition, December, 1971.
Washington Post Book World, April 19, 1970, December 5, 1971,
     November 28, 1976, June 19, 1977, July 1, 1979.

*   *   *

NARAYAN, R(asipuram) K(rishnaswami) 1906-

PERSONAL: Born October 10, 1906, in Madras, India. *Education:* Maharaja's College (now University of Mysore), received
degree, 1930.

ADDRESSES: Agent—Anthony Sheil Associates, 2-3 Maxwell St., London WC1B 3AR, England.

CAREER: Writer. Owner of Indian Thought Publications in Mysore, India.

AWARDS, HONORS: National Prize of the Indian Literary Academy, 1958; Padma Bhushan, India, 1964; National Association of Independent Schools award, 1965; D.Litt. from University of Leeds, 1967; English-Speaking Union Book Award for *My Days: A Memoir,* 1975; American Academy and Institute of Arts and Letters citation, 1982.

MEMBER: American Academy and Institute of Arts and Letters (honorary member).

WRITINGS:

Swami and Friends: A Novel of Malgudi, Hamish Hamilton, 1935, Fawcett, 1970, published with *The Bachelor of Arts: A Novel,* Michigan State College Press, 1954.
The Bachelor of Arts: A Novel, Thomas Nelson, 1937.
The Dark Room: A Novel, Macmillan, 1938.
Malgudi Days (short stories), Indian Thought Publications, 1941.
Dodu and Other Stories, Indian Thought Publications, 1943.
Cyclone and Other Stories, Indian Thought Publications, 1944.
Mysore, Indian Thought Publications, 1944.
The English Teacher (novel), Eyre & Spottiswoode, 1945, published as *Grateful to Life and Death,* Michigan State College Press, 1953.
An Astrologer's Day and Other Stories, Eyre & Spottiswoode, 1947.
Mr. Sampath (novel), Eyre & Spottiswoode, 1949, published as *The Printer of Malgudi,* Michigan State College Press, 1957.
The Financial Expert: A Novel, Metheun, 1952, Michigan State College Press, 1953.
Waiting for the Mahatma: A Novel, Michigan State College Press, 1955.
Lawley Road: Thirty-Two Short Stories, Indian Thought Publications, 1956.
The Guide (novel), Viking, 1958.
Next Sunday: Sketches and Essays, Pearl Publications, 1960.
My Dateless Diary (essays), Indian Thought Publications, 1960.
The Man-Eater of Malgudi (novel), Viking, 1961.
Gods, Demons and Others (short stories), Viking, 1965.
The Vendor of Sweets (novel), Viking, 1967 (published in England as *The Sweet-Vendor,* Bodley Head, 1967).
A Horse and Two Goats and Other Stories, Viking, 1970.
(Translator) *The Ramayana: A Shortened Modern Prose Version of the Indian Epic,* Viking, 1972.
My Days: A Memoir, Viking, 1974.
The Reluctant Guru, Hind Pocket Books, 1974.
The Painter of Signs, Viking, 1976.
(Translator) *The Mahabharata: A Shortened Prose Version of the Indian Epic,* Viking, 1978.
The Emerald Route, Ind-US Inc., 1980.
A Tiger for Malgudi, Viking, 1983.
Under the Banyan Tree and Other Stories, Viking, 1985.
Talkative Man, Viking, 1987.
A Writer's Nightmare: Selected Essays, 1958-1988, Penguin, 1989.

Contributor of short stories to *New Yorker.*

SIDELIGHTS: R. K. Narayan is perhaps the best-known Indian writing in English today. His works have met with uniformly favorable criticism, and his books have such a popular appeal that, as Narayan himself noted in a *Books Abroad* interview, they "have been translated into all European languages and Hebrew." Critics have appreciated Narayan's mythical village of Malgudi, a fictional microcosm as universal in scope as Faulkner's Yoknapatawpha County. His ability to present his characters sympathetically and realistically has been likened to that of such writers as Chekhov and Isaac Bashevis Singer.

In a British Broadcasting Corporation radio interview, Narayan spoke to William Walsh of his use of the English language: "English has been with us [in India] for over a century and a half. I am particularly fond of the language. I was never aware that I was using a different, a foreign, language when I wrote in English, because it came to me very easily. I can't explain how. English is a very adaptable language. And it's so transparent it can take on the tint of any country." Walsh added that Narayan's English "is limpid, simple, calm and unaffected, natural in its run and tone, and beautifully measured" in a unique fashion which takes on an Indian flavor by avoiding "the American purr of the combustion engine . . . [and] the thick marmalade quality of British English."

Other critics have noted the rhythms of Narayan's style and the richness of his narrative. Melvin J. Friedman suggested in a comparison with Isaac Bashevis Singer that "both seem part of an oral tradition in which the 'spoken' triumphs over the 'written,' " and theorized that the similarities between Narayan's fiction and the Indian epics echo "Singer's prose" and its "rhythm of the Old Testament." Eve Auchincloss noted that the translation-like quality of the language "adds curious, pleasing flavor."

Narayan's fictional setting is Malgudi, a village very similar to the village of his childhood, Mysore. In Malgudi every sort of human condition indigenous not only to India but to life everywhere is represented. Malgudi has been compared with William Faulkner's Yoknapatawpha County. "Narayan might . . . be called Faulknerian," wrote Warren French, "because against the background of a squalid community he creates characters with a rare quality that can only be called 'compassionate disenchantment.' " French also noted that both Narayan and Faulkner write frequently of "an unending conflict between individuality and the demands of tradition," typifying their respective geographical settings in such a way as to become universal by extension. Charles R. Larson demonstrated similar parallels but reflected that "while Faulkner's vision remains essentially grotesque, Narayan's has been predominantly comic, reflecting with humor the struggle of the individual consciousness to find peace within the framework of public life." Walsh stressed the universal quality of Malgudi: "Whatever happens in India happens in Malgudi, and whatever happens in Malgudi happens everywhere."

In Narayan's novels and short stories are characters who experience some kind of growth or change, or who gain knowledge through the experiences they undergo. As Walsh observed, Narayan most often focuses on the middle class and its representative occupations, many of which provide Narayan with titles for his books: *The Bachelor of Arts, The English Teacher, The Financial Expert, The Guide, The Sweet-Vendor.* Walsh explained Narayan's typical structural pattern in terms of concentric circles, whereby the village represents the outer circle, the family is the inner circle, and the hero, the focus of each novel, stands at the hub. "His hero is usually modest, sensitive, ardent, wry about himself," wrote Walsh, "and sufficiently conscious to have an active inner life and to grope towards some existence independent of the family." Walsh further observed that the typical progress of a Narayan hero involves "the rebirth of self and the progress of its pregnancy or education," thereby suggesting the Indian concept of reincarnation. "Again and again Narayan gives us the account of an evolving consciousness," wrote Larson, "beginning in isolation and confusion and ending in wholeness (peace within the traditional Hindu faith)" while maintaining a unique freshness of presentation.

Closely related to Narayan's gift for characterization is his ability to present his material in such a sympathetic manner that many critics have written at length of his comic vision in his treatment of his characters' failures and disappointments. French declared: "Although he satirizes the foibles of his characters, he never condescends to them or makes them targets for abuse. . . . Narayan is too sophisticated an artist to rail at people for being what they have to be." Walsh wrote of Narayan's "forgiving kindness" and labeled his novels "comedies of sadness . . . lighted with the glint of mockery of both self and others." Paul Zimmerman focused on the "affectionate amusement" with which Narayan treats his heroes, and Anthony Thwaite stated that "R. K. Narayan has achieved . . . an observation that is always acute, a humor that is never condescending, and a delicate sympathy that never becomes whimsical."

Herbert Lomas paraphrased Graham Greene's assessment that "R. K. Narayan [is] one of the glories of English Literature . . . a sage if ever there was one." John Updike wrote that, through Narayan's remarkable gifts, "the fabled Indian gentleness still permeates the atmosphere evoked by this venerable cherisher of human behavior," and Eve Auchincloss stated that "[So] poised, so balanced a writer is Narayan, his sympathy and amusement so large, that even God's design for an overpopulated India seems defensible."

MEDIA ADAPTATIONS: Narayan's *The Guide,* was adapted for the stage by Harvey Breit and Patricia Rinehart and produced Off-Broadway in New York City at the Hudson Theatre, March, 1968.

BIOGRAPHICAL/CRITICAL SOURCES:

BOOKS

Contemporary Literary Criticism, Gale, Volume 7, 1977, Volume 28, 1984, Volume 47, 1988.
Season of Promise: Spring Fiction, University of Missouri, 1967.
Walsh, William, *R. K. Narayan,* Longman, 1971.

PERIODICALS

Banasthali Patrika, January 12, 1969, July 13, 1969.
Book World, July 11, 1976, December 5, 1976.
Books Abroad, summer, 1965, spring, 1971, spring, 1976.
Christian Science Monitor, February 19, 1970.
Encounter, October, 1964.
Harper's, April, 1965.
Journal of Commonwealth Literature, Number 2, December, 1966.
Listener, March 1, 1962.
Literary Criterion, winter, 1968.
London Magazine, September, 1970.
Nation, June 28, 1975.
New Republic, May 13, 1967.
New Statesman, June 2, 1967.
Newsweek, July 4, 1976.
New Yorker, October 14, 1967, March 16, 1968, July 5, 1976.
New York Review of Books, June 29, 1967.
New York Times, August 1, 1965.
New York Times Book Review, May 14, 1967, June 20, 1976.
Osmania Journal of English Studies, Volume VII, number 1, 1970.

Sewanee Review, winter, 1975.
Times Literary Supplement, May 18, 1967.
Washington Post, April 14, 1970.

*   *   *

NASH, (Frediric) Ogden   1902-1971

PERSONAL: Born August 19, 1902, in Rye, N.Y.; died of heart failure, May 19, 1971, in Baltimore, Md.; buried in Little River Cemetery, North Hampton, N.H.; son of Edmund Strudwick and Mattie (Chenault) Nash; married Frances Rider Leonard, June 6, 1931; children: Linell Chenault (Mrs. J. Marshall Smith), Isabel Jackson (Mrs. Frederick Eberstadt). *Education:* Attended Harvard University, 1920-21.

CAREER: Poet, author; began writing light verse about 1925. Taught one year at St. George's School, Providence, R.I.; was a bond salesman on Wall Street, briefly in the mid-1920s; worked in the copy department of Barron Collier, writing streetcar ads; worked in the editorial and publicity departments of Doubleday, Doran & Co., 1925; member of *New Yorker* editorial staff, 1932; became full-time writer. Gave frequent lectures and readings; appeared on radio shows, including "Information, Please!," and the Bing Crosby and Rudy Vallee hours, and on television panel shows, including "Masquerade Party."

MEMBER: American Academy of Arts and Sciences, National Institute of Arts and Letters.

AWARDS, HONORS: Sarah Josepha Hale Award, 1964.

WRITINGS:

(With Joseph Alger) *Cricket of Carador,* Doubleday, 1925.
(With Christopher Morley, Cleon Throckmorton, and others) *Born in a Beer Garden; or, She Troupes to Conquer,* Rudge, 1930.
Free Wheeling (also see below) Simon & Schuster, 1931.
Hard Lines, Simon & Schuster, 1931, enlarged edition with selections from *Free Wheeling* published as *Hard Lines, and Others,* Duckworth, 1932.
(Editor) P. G. Wodehouse, *Nothing but Wodehouse,* Doubleday, 1932.
Happy Days, Simon & Schuster, 1933.
Four Prominent So and So's (music by Robert Armbruster), Simon & Schuster, 1934.
The Primrose Path, Simon & Schuster, 1935.
The Bad Parents' Garden of Verse, Simon & Schuster, 1936.
"The Firefly" (screenplay; adapted from Otto A. Harbach's play), Metro-Goldwyn-Mayer (MGM), 1937.
(With Jane Murfin) "The Shining Hair" (screenplay), MGM, 1938.
I'm a Stranger Here Myself, Little, Brown, 1938.
The Face is Familiar: The Selected Verse of Ogden Nash, Little, Brown, 1940, revised edition, Dent, 1954.
(With George Oppenheimer and Edmund L. Hartmann) "The Feminine Touch" (screenplay), MGM, 1941.
Good Intentions, Little, Brown, 1942, revised edition, Dent, 1956.
(Author of book with S. J. Perelman, and of lyrics) *One Touch of Venus* (musical; music by Kurt Weill; first produced on Broadway, 1943), Little, Brown, 1944.
The Ogden Nash Pocket Book, Blakiston, 1944.
Many Long Years Ago, Little, Brown, 1945.
The Selected Verse of Ogden Nash, Modern Library, 1946.
Ogden Nash's Musical Zoo (music by Vernon Duke), Little, Brown, 1947.
Versus, Little, Brown, 1949.

Family Reunion, Little, Brown, 1950.

Parents Keep Out: Elderly Poems for Youngerly Readers, Little, Brown, 1951, enlarged edition, Dent, 1962.

The Private Dining Room, and Other New Verses, Little, Brown, 1953.

(Editor) *The Moon Is Shining Bright as Day: An Anthology of Good-Humored Verse,* Lippincott, 1953.

The Pocket Book of Ogden Nash, Pocket Books, 1954.

You Can't Get There from Here, Little, Brown, 1957.

The Boy Who Laughed at Santa Claus (keepsake edition), Cooper & Beatty Ltd. (London), 1957.

The Christmas That Almost Wasn't, Little, Brown, 1957.

(Editor) *I Couldn't Help Laughing: Stories Selected and Introduced by Ogden Nash,* Lippincott, 1957.

Verses from 1929 On, Little, Brown, 1959 (published in England as *Collected Verse from 1929 On,* Dent, 1961).

Custard the Dragon, Little, Brown, 1959.

Beastly Poetry, Hallmark Editions, 1960.

A Boy Is a Boy: The Fun of Being a Boy, Watts, 1960.

Scrooge Rides Again, Hart, 1960.

(Editor) *Everybody Ought to Know: Verses Selected and Introduced by Ogden Nash,* Lippincott, 1961.

Custard the Dragon and the Wicked Knight, Little, Brown, 1961.

The New Nutcracker Suite, and Other Innocent Verses, Little, Brown, 1962.

Girls Are Silly, Watts, 1962.

Everyone but Thee and Me, Little, Brown, 1962.

A Boy and His Room, Watts, 1963.

The Adventures of Isabel, Little, Brown, 1963.

The Untold Adventures of Santa Claus, Little, Brown, 1964.

An Ogden Nash Bonanza (five-volume omnibus), Little, Brown, 1964.

Marriage Lines: Notes of a Student Husband, Little, Brown, 1964 (published in England as *Notes of a Student Husband,* Dent, 1964).

The Untold Adventures of Santa Claus, Little, Brown, 1964.

The Animal Garden, Evans, 1965.

The Mysterious Ouphe, Spadea Press, 1965.

Santa Go Home: A Case History for Parents, Little, Brown, 1967.

The Cruise of the Aardvark, M. Evans, 1967.

There's Always Another Windmill, Little, Brown, 1968.

Funniest Verses of Ogden Nash: Light Lyrics by One of America's Favorite Humorists, selected by Dorothy Price, Hallmark Editions, 1968.

(With Edward Lear) *The Scroobious Pip,* Harper, 1968.

(With others) *New Comic Limericks: Laughable Poems,* Compiled by Ivanette Dennis, Roger Schlesinger, 1969.

Bed Riddance: A Posy for the Indisposed, Little, Brown, 1970.

The Old Dog Barks Backwards, Little, Brown, 1972.

I Wouldn't Have Missed It: Selected Poems of Ogden Nash, selected by Linnel Smith and Isabel Eberstadt, Little, Brown, 1972.

Custard and Company, Little, Brown, 1980.

A Penny Saved Is Impossible, Little, Brown, 1981.

Ogden Nash's Zoo, edited by Roy Finamore, Stewart, Tabori, 1986.

Ogden Nash's Food, Stewart, Tabori, 1989.

Loving Letters From Ogden Nash: A Family Album, Little, Brown, 1990.

Wrote lyrics for Off-Broadway production "The Littlest Revue" and for television show "Art Carney Meets Peter and the Wolf." Wrote new verses to Saint-Saens's "Carnival of the Animals," narrated by Noel Coward, for Columbia; author of verses set to Prokofiev's "Peter and the Wolf" and Dukas's "Sorcerer's Apprentice." Contributor of verse to periodicals, including *New Yorker, Life, Saturday Evening Post, Holiday, Saturday Review, Harper's, Atlantic, Vogue, McCall's,* and *New Republic.*

SIDELIGHTS: Ogden Nash was probably America's most popular and most frequently quoted contemporary poet, drawing large and receptive audiences to his lectures and readings. Known for such lines as "Candy / Is dandy, / But liquor / Is quicker" and "If called by a panther / Don't anther," Nash was "secure in his possession of all the best and worst rhymes outside of the rhyming dictionaries," according to P. M. Jack. He called himself a "worsifier," and his "worses" bear the mark of a unique style—whimsical, offbeat, yet sophisticated—which he called "my individual method for concealing my illiteracy." He freely admitted to having "intentionally maltreated and manhandled every known rule of grammar, prosody, and spelling," yet the result, suggests Albin Krebs in a *New York Times* obituary, on closer examination reveals "a carefully thought-out metrical scheme and a kind of relentless logic." "I like the style because it gives me a mask," Nash told an interviewer for *Holiday,* a "front behind which I can hide. I can't go straight to the point about anything emotionally valid; that's one of my faults, I get ponderous. By backing off I can make the point without belaboring it."

Looking back on his writing career, Nash once remarked: "The only lines I've ever written which I think have any chance of surviving me were lines written in my unregenerate youth." Contrary to his modest estimate, Nash is widely recognized as having had few peers, especially when it came to exposing human frailties and absurdities. As St. George Tucker Arnold, Jr., claimed in his *Dictionary of Literary Biography* essay, "During his lifetime, Ogden Nash was the most widely known, appreciated, and imitated American creator of light verse. . . . [And his] reputation has grown still further in the years since his death." The poet was, in Eliot Fremont-Smith's words, "a master of a kind of civility in exposing silliness that has not been much nurtured in recent decades," retaining the possibility of "a wit expressed through a friendly wink or poke." Although some of his verse was quite serious, Nash characterized the body of his work as "fortunately slightly goofy and cheerfully sour." One critic described him as a "philosopher, albeit a laughing one," expressing "the vicissitudes and eccentricitudes of domestic life as they affected an apparently gentle, somewhat bewildered man." Nash's death in 1971 inspired numerous tributes patterned after his own work, such as one by poet Morris Bishop, quoted in *Time:* "Free from flashiness, free from trashiness / Is the essence of ogdenashiness. / Rich, original, rash and rational / Stands the monument ogdenational."

BIOGRAPHICAL/CRITICAL SOURCES:

BOOKS

Axford, L. B., *An Index to the Poems of Ogden Nash,* Scarecrow, 1972.

Benet, Laura, *Famous American Humorists,* Dodd, 1959.

Contemporary Literary Criticism, Volume 23, Gale, 1983.

Dictionary of Literary Biography, Volume 11: *American Humorists, 1800-1950,* Gale, 1982.

Newquist, Roy, *Conversations,* Rand McNally, 1967.

PERIODICALS

Holiday, August, 1967.

Life, December 13, 1968.

New York Herald Tribune Book Review, July 14, 1957.

Seventeen, January, 1963.

OBITUARIES:

PERIODICALS

New York Times, May 20, 1971.
Publishers Weekly, May 31, 1971.
Time, May 31, 1971.
Washington Post, May 21, 1971.

*   *   *

NATHAN, Daniel
See DANNAY, Frederic

*   *   *

NAUGHTON, Bill 1910-

PERSONAL: Born June 12, 1910, in Ballyhaunis, County Mayo, Ireland; son of Thomas (a coal miner) and Maria (Fleming) Naughton; married Ernestine Pirolt. *Education:* Educated in England.

ADDRESSES: Home—Kempis, Ortisdale Rd., Ballasalla, Isle of Man, England. *Agent*—Dr. Jan Van Loewen, Ltd., 81-83 Shaftesburg Ave., London W1V 8BX, England.

CAREER: Writer and playwright. Worked as laborer, lorry driver, weaver, coalbagger, and bleacher. *Wartime service:* Civil Defense driver in London, England.

AWARDS, HONORS: Screenwriters Guild Awards, 1967 and 1968; Prix Italia, 1974, for *The Mystery;* Other Award from Children's Rights Workshop, 1978, for *The Goalkeeper's Revenge.*

WRITINGS:

A Roof Over Your Head (autobiography), Pilot Press, 1945, revised edition edited by Vincent Whitcombe, Blackie & Son, 1967.
Pony Boy (juvenile novel), Pilot Press, 1946, revised edition, Hattap, 1966.
Rafe Granite (novel), Pilot Press, 1947.
One Small Boy (novel), MacKibbon & Kee, 1957, revised edition edited by David Grant, Hattap, 1970.
Late Night on Watling Street, and Other Stories (also see below), MacGibbon & Kee, 1959, Ballantine, 1967, revised edition, Longmans, Green, 1969.
The Goalkeeper's Revenge and Other Stories (also see below), Harrap, 1961.
Alfie (novel; also see below), Ballantine, 1966.
Alfie Darling (novel), Simon & Schuster, 1970.
The Goalkeeper's Revenge [and] *Spit Nolan* (*Spit Nolan* published separately, Creative Education, Inc., 1987), Macmillan, 1974.
The Bees Have Stopped Working, and Other Stories, Wheaton & Co., 1976.
A Dog Called Nelson (juvenile), Dent, 1976.
My Pal Spadger (juvenile), Dent, 1977.
On the Pig's Back: An Autobiographical Excursion, Oxford University Press, 1987.
Saintly Billy: A Catholic Boyhood (autobiography), Oxford University Press, 1988.

PLAYS

My Flesh, My Blood (two-act comedy; first broadcast in 1957; revised version first produced as *Spring and Port Wine* in Birmingham, England, 1964, and on the West End, 1965; also produced as *Keep It in the Family* on Broadway at Plym-

outh Theatre, September 27, 1967), Samuel French, 1959, published as *Spring and Port Wine,* 1967.
June Evening (first broadcast in 1958; produced in Birmingham, England, 1966), Samuel French, 1973.
Alfie (three-act; first broadcast as *Alfie Elkins and His Little Life,* 1962; produced as *Alfie* in London, 1963), Samuel French, 1963.
All in Good Time (comedy; first produced in London, 1963; produced in New York City, 1965; televised as *Honeymoon Postponed,* 1961), Samuel French, 1964.
He Was Gone When We Got There, music by Leonard Salzedo, first produced in London, 1966.
Annie and Fanny, first produced in Bolton, Lancashire, England, at Octagon Theatre, 1967.
Lighthearted Intercourse, first produced in Liverpool, England, at Liverpool Playhouse, December 1, 1971.

OTHER

(Contributor) *Worth a Hearing: A Collection of Radio Plays* (contains *She'll Make Trouble,* first broadcast, 1958), edited by Alfred Bradley, Blackie & Son, 1967.

Author of other radio plays, including *Timothy,* 1956; *Late Night on Watling Street,* 1959; *The Long Carry,* 1959; *Seeing a Beauty Queen Home,* 1960; *On the Run,* 1960; *Wigan to Rome,* 1960; *'30-'60,* 1960; *Jackie Crowe,* 1962; *November Day,* 1963; *The Mystery,* 1973; *A Special Occasion,* 1982. Author of television plays, including *Nathaniel Titlark* series, 1957; *Jim Batty,* 1957; *Starr and Company* series, 1958; (with Alan Prior) *Yorky* series, 1960; *Somewhere for the Night,* 1962; *Looking for Frankie,* 1963; *It's Your Move,* 1967.

MEDIA ADAPTATIONS: Alfie, a comedy-drama starring Shelley Winters and Michael Caine, was produced in 1966 by Paramount; *All in Good Time* was released as "The Family Way" by Warner Bros. in 1967; *Spring and Port Wine* was released by Warner-Pathe in 1970.

WORK IN PROGRESS: The Dream Mind, a book about the author's theories on dreams and sleep; another autobiographical book.

SIDELIGHTS: A prolific writer of books and plays for the stage, radio, and television, Bill Naughton grew up in the coal-mining county of Lancashire, England. His first book, *A Roof Over Your Head,* is a semi-autobiographical volume that describes the typical life of poverty and hardship in Lancashire during the twenties. Lancashire is also the setting for many of Naughton's subsequent books and plays, including two of his most successful scripts, *Spring and Port Wine* and *All in Good Time.*

As in a number of Naughton's writings, family life is the subject of *Spring and Port Wine.* In this critically acclaimed play, Naughton relates a series of episodes that take place in a household during a spring weekend, with special attention paid to a young daughter who overindulges in port wine. *All in Good Time* deals with newlywed couples of Lancashire as they nervously face their wedding nights. One of Naughton's most popular radio plays, however, involves the adventures of a bachelor. *Alfie Elkins and His Little Life,* which was later revised as a stage play and novel entitled *Alfie,* concerns the love life of a cockney Don Juan. While often humorous, the play has also been praised for the author's ability to reveal his character's inner loneliness.

Since the mid-1970s, Naughton has retreated to a seaside bungalow on the Isle of Man because of what he felt was a "need to escape the 'idle life' of writing plays and get back to his real writing," according to a London *Times* writer. His work has focused on condensing his personal journal—which he has kept for over two decades—into three publishable volumes. Two of these books, *On the Pig's Back: An Autobiographical Excursion* and *Saintly Billy: A Catholic Boyhood,* have already appeared in book stores.

BIOGRAPHICAL/CRITICAL SOURCES:

BOOKS

Dictionary of Literary Biography, Volume 13: *British Dramatists since World War II,* Gale, 1982.

PERIODICALS

Newsweek, January 4, 1965, March 1 1965, October 9, 1967.
New Yorker, January 2, 1965.
Time, December 25, 1964.
Times (London), July 15, 1985.
Times Literary Supplement, April 1, 1988.

*   *   *

NAYLOR, Gloria   1950-

PERSONAL: Born January 25, 1950, in New York, N.Y.; daughter of Roosevelt (a transit worker) and Alberta (a telephone operator; maiden name, McAlpin) Naylor. *Education:* Brooklyn College of the City University of New York, B.A., 1981; Yale University, M.A., 1983.

ADDRESSES: Agent—Sterling Lord, One Madison Ave., New York, N.Y. 10010.

CAREER: Missionary for Jehovah's Witnesses in New York, North Carolina, and Florida, 1968-75; worked for various hotels in New York, N.Y., including Sheraton City Squire, as telephone operator, 1975-81; writer, 1981—. Writer in residence, Cummington Community of the Arts, 1983; visiting lecturer, George Washington University, 1983-84, and Princeton University, 1986-87; cultural exchange lecturer, United States Information Agency, India, 1985; scholar in residence, University of Pennsylvania, 1986; visiting professor, New York University, 1986, and Boston University, 1987; Fannie Hurst Visiting Professor, Brandeis University, 1988. Senior fellow, Society for the Humanities, Cornell University, 1988.

AWARDS, HONORS: American Book Award for best first novel, 1983, for *The Women of Brewster Place;* Distinguished Writer Award, Mid-Atlantic Writers Association, 1983; National Endowment for the Arts fellowship, 1985; Candace Award, National Coalition of 100 Black Women, 1986; Guggenheim fellowship, 1988.

WRITINGS:

FICTION

The Women of Brewster Place, Viking, 1982.
Linden Hills, Ticknor & Fields, 1985.
Mama Day, Ticknor & Fields, 1988.

NONFICTION

Centennial, Pindar Press, 1986.

Also author of unproduced screenplay adaptation of *The Women of Brewster Place,* for American Playhouse, 1984, and of an unproduced original screenplay for Public Broadcasting System's "In Our Own Words," 1985. Contributor of essays and articles to periodicals, including *Southern Review, Essence, Ms., Life, Ontario Review,* and *People.* Contributing editor, *Callaloo,* 1984—. "Hers" columnist for *New York Times,* 1986.

WORK IN PROGRESS: A novel dealing with "whores, language, and music"; a screenplay for Zenith Productions, London.

SIDELIGHTS: "I wanted to become a writer because I felt that my presence as a black woman and my perspective as a woman in general had been underrepresented in American literature," Gloria Naylor commented. Her first novel, *The Women of Brewster Place,* which features a cast of seven strong-willed black women, won the American Book Award for best first fiction in 1983. Naylor has continued her exploration of the black female experience in two subsequent novels that remain focused on women while also expanding her fictional realm. In *Linden Hills,* for example, Naylor uses the structure of Dante Alighieri's *Inferno* to create a contemporary allegory about the perils of black materialism and the ways in which denying one's heritage can endanger the soul. Naylor's third novel, *Mama Day,* draws on another literary masterpiece—William Shakespeare's play *The Tempest*—and artfully combines Shakespearean elements with black folkloric strains. By drawing on traditional western sources, Naylor places herself firmly in the literary mainstream, broadening her base from ethnic to American writing. Unhappy with what she calls the "historical tendency to look upon the output of black writers as not really American literature," Naylor told *Publishers Weekly* interviewer William Goldstein that her work attempts to "articulate experiences that want articulating—for those readers who reflect the subject matter, black readers, and for those who don't—basically white middle class readers."

Naylor's first novel grew out of a desire to reflect the diversity of the black experience—a diversity that she feels neither the black nor the white critical establishment has recognized. "There has been a tendency on the part of both," she commented, "to assume that a black writer's work should be 'definitive' of black experience. This type of critical stance denies the vast complexity of black existence, even if we were to limit that existence solely to America. While *The Women of Brewster Place* is about the black woman's condition in America, I had to deal with the fact that one composite picture couldn't do justice to the complexity of the black female experience. So I tried to solve this problem by creating a microcosm on a dead-end street and devoting each chapter to a different woman's life. These women vary in age, personal background, political consciousness, and sexual preference. What they do share is a common oppression and, more importantly, a spiritual strength and sense of female communion that I believe all women have employed historically for their psychic health and survival."

Reviewing *The Women of Brewster Place* in the *Washington Post,* Deirdre Donahue writes: "Naylor is not afraid to grapple with life's big subjects: sex, birth, love, death, grief. Her women feel deeply, and she unflinchingly transcribes their emotions. . . . Naylor's potency wells up from her language. With prose as rich as poetry, a passage will suddenly take off and sing like a spiritual. . . . Vibrating with undisguised emotion, 'The Women of Brewster Place' springs from the same roots that produced the blues. Like them, her book sings of sorrows proudly borne by black women in America."

To date, Naylor has linked her novels by carrying over characters from one narrative to another. In *The Women of Brewster Place,* one of the young residents is a refugee from Linden Hills, an exclusive black suburb. Naylor's second novel spotlights that affluent community, revealing the material corruption and moral decay that would prompt an idealistic young woman to abandon her home for a derelict urban neighborhood. Though

Linden Hills, as the book is called, approaches the Afro-American experience from the upper end of the socioeconomic spectrum, it is also a black microcosm. This book "forms the second panel of that picture of contemporary urban black life which Naylor started with in *Women of Brewster Place,*" writes *Times Literary Supplement* contributor Roz Kaveney. "Where that book described the faults, passions, and culture of the good poor, this shows the nullity of black lives that are led in imitation of suburban whites."

In addition to shifting her focus, Naylor has also raised her literary sights in her second novel. *Linden Hills,* which has been described as a contemporary allegory with gothic overtones, is an ambitious undertaking structurally modeled after Dante's *Inferno.* Among its many accomplishments, Dante's Italian masterpiece describes the nine circles of hell, Satan's imprisonment in their depths, and the lost souls condemned to suffer with him. In Naylor's modern version, "souls are damned not because they have offended God or have violated a religious system but because they have offended themselves. In their single-minded pursuit of upward mobility, the inhabitants of Linden Hill, a black, middle-class suburb, have turned away from their past and from their deepest sense of who they are," writes Catherine C. Ward in *Contemporary Literature.* To correspond to Dante's circles, Naylor uses a series of crescent-shaped drives that ring the suburban development. Her heroes are two young street poets—outsiders from a neighboring community who hire themselves out to do odd jobs so they can earn Christmas money. "As they move down the hill, what they encounter are people who have 'moved up' in American society . . . until eventually they will hit the center of their community and the home of my equivalent of Satan," Naylor told Goldstein. Naylor's Satan is one Luther Needed, a combination mortician and real estate tycoon, who preys on the residents' baser ambitions to keep them in his sway.

Though *Women's Review of Books* contributor Jewelle Gomez argues that "the Inferno motif . . . often feels like a literary exercise rather than a groundbreaking adaptation," most critics commend Naylor's bold experiment. *San Francisco Review of Books* contributor Claudia Tate, for instance, praises "Naylor's skill in linking together complicated stories in a highly structured but unobtrusive narrative form. In combining elements of realism and fantasy with a sequence of ironic reversals, she sets into motion a series of symbols which become interlinked, producing complex social commentary. For example, the single ambition for residents of Linden Hills is to advance economically, but in order to achieve this end they must sacrifice the possibility of emotional and personal fulfillment. When the goal is attained, they measure their success by reversing the expected movement in social climbing."

Even those who find the execution flawed endorse Naylor's daring. Says *New York Times Book Review* contributor Mel Watkins: "Although Miss Naylor has not been completely successful in adapting the 'Inferno' to the world of the black middle class, in 'Linden Hills' she has shown a willingness to expand her fictional realm and to take risks. Its flaws notwithstanding, the novel's ominous atmosphere and inspired set pieces . . . make it a fascinating departure for Miss Naylor, as well as a provocative, iconoclastic novel about a seldom-addressed subject." Concludes the *Ms.* reviewer, "In this second novel, Naylor serves notice that she is a mature literary talent of formidable skill."

Naylor's third novel, *Mama Day,* is named for its main character—a wise old woman with magical powers whose name is Miranda Day, but whom everyone refers to as Mama Day. This ninety-year-old conjurer made a walk-on appearance in *Linden Hills* as the illiterate, toothless aunt who hauls about cheap cardboard suitcases and leaky jars of preserves. But it is in *Mama Day* that this "caster of hoodoo spells . . . comes into her own," according to *New York Times Book Review* contributor Bharati Mukherjee. "The portrait of Mama Day is magnificent," she declares.

Mama Day lives on Willow Springs, a wondrous island off the coast of Georgia and South Carolina that has been owned by her family since before the Civil War. The fact that slaves are portrayed as property owners demonstrates one of the ways that Naylor turns the world upside down, according to Rita Mae Brown. Another, continues Brown in the *Los Angeles Times Book Review,* is "that the women possess the real power, and are acknowledged as having it." When Mama Day's grandniece Cocoa brings George, her citified new husband, to Willow Springs, he learns the importance of accepting mystery. "George is the linchpin of 'Mama Day,'" Brown says. "His rational mind allows the reader to experience the island as George experiences it. Mama Day and Cocoa are of the island and therefore less immediately accessible to the reader. The turning point comes when George is asked not only to believe in Mama Day's power but to act on it. Cocoa is desperately ill. A hurricane has washed out the bridge so that no mainland doctor can be summoned." Only Mama Day has the power to help George save her life. She gives him a task, which he bungles because he is still limited by purely rational thinking. Ultimately, George is able to save Cocoa, but only by great personal sacrifice.

The plot twists and thematic concerns of *Mama Day* have led several reviewers to compare the work to Shakespeare. "Whereas 'Linden Hills' was Dantesque, 'Mama Day' is Shakespearean, with allusions, however oblique and tangential, to 'Hamlet,' 'King Lear,' and, especially, 'The Tempest,'" writes Chicago *Tribune Books* critic John Blades. "Like Shakespeare's fantasy, Naylor's book takes place on an enchanted island. . . . Naylor reinforces her Shakespearean connection by naming her heroine Miranda." Mukherjee also believes that *Mama Day* "has its roots in 'The Tempest.' The theme is reconciliation, the title character is Miranda (also the name of Prospero's daughter), and Willow Springs is an isolated island where, as on Prospero's isle, magical and mysterious events come to pass."

Naylor's ambitious attempt to elevate a modern love story to Shakespearean heights "is more bewildering than bewitching," according to Blades. "Naylor has populated her magic kingdom with some appealingly offbeat characters, Mama Day foremost among them. But she's failed to give them anything very original or interesting to do." Mukherjee also acknowledges the shortcomings of Naylor's mythical love story, but asserts, "I'd rather dwell on *Mama Day*'s strengths. Gloria Naylor has written a big, strong, dense, admirable novel; spacious, sometimes a little drafty like all public monuments, designed to last and intended for many levels of use."

MEDIA ADAPTATIONS: The Women of Brewster was adapted into a miniseries, produced by Oprah Winfrey and Carole Isenberg, and broadcast by American Broadcasting Co. (ABC-TV) in 1989; it became a weekly ABC series in 1990, produced by Winfrey, Earl Hamner, and Donald Sipes.

BIOGRAPHICAL/CRITICAL SOURCES:

BOOKS

Contemporary Literary Criticism, Gale, Volume 28, 1984, Volume 52, 1989.

PERIODICALS

Chicago Tribune Book World, February 23, 1983.
Christian Science Monitor, March 1, 1985.
Commonweal, May 3, 1985.
Contemporary Literature, Volume 28, number 1, 1987.
Detroit News, March 3, 1985, February 21, 1988.
Los Angeles Times, December 2, 1982.
Los Angeles Times Book Review, February 24, 1985, March 6, 1988.
London Review of Books, August 1, 1985.
Ms., June, 1985.
New Republic, September 6, 1982.
New York Times, February 9, 1985, May 1, 1990.
New York Times Book Review, August 22, 1982, March 3, 1985, February 21, 1988.
Publishers Weekly, September 9, 1983.
San Francisco Review of Books, May, 1985.
Times (London), April 21, 1983.
Times Literary Supplement, May 24, 1985.
Tribune Books (Chicago), January 31, 1988.
Washington Post, October 21, 1983, May 1, 1990.
Washington Post Book World, March 24, 1985, February 28, 1988.
Women's Review of Books, August, 1985.

* * *

NEHRU, Jawaharlal 1889-1964

PERSONAL: Name pronounced *Jawahar*lal Nay*roo;* born November 14, 1889, in Allahabad, India; died May 27, 1964, in New Delhi, India, of a heart attack; son of Motilal (a lawyer) and Swarup Rani Nehru; married Kamala Kaul, March, 1916 (died, 1936); children: Indira Nehru Gandhi (former Prime Minister of India; assassinated, 1984). *Education:* Trinity College, Cambridge, earned degree (second class honours), 1910; Inner Temple, London, law degree, 1912.

CAREER: Admitted to Bar of Inner Temple, England, 1912; barrister in high court of Allahabad, India; member of all-India congress, 1918-64; joined Mahatma Gandhi's non-violence movement, 1920; Government of India, president of national congress, 1929, 1936, 1937, 1946, 1951-54, minister of external affairs, 1946-64, first prime minister of independent India, 1947-64. Delegate of Bankepore Congress, 1912.

AWARDS, HONORS: Doctor of Laws, Osmania University (Hyderabad, India), 1948.

WRITINGS:

Statements, Speeches, and Writings, [Allahabad], 1929.
Principal R. Dwivedi, editor, *The Life and Speeches of Pandit Jawaharlal Nehru,* National Publishing (Delhi, India), c. 1930.
Glimpses of World History (also see below; juvenile), two volumes, Kitabistan (Bangladesh), 1934-35, reprinted, Oxford University Press, 1990.
India and the World (essays), Allen & Unwin, 1936.
Jawaharlal Nehru, John Lane, 1936, enlarged edition, Bodley Head, 1955, published as *Toward Freedom* (also see below), John Day, 1941.
Recent Essays and Writings on the Future of Indian Communalism, Labour and Other Subjects, Kitabistan, 1937.
Letters from a Father to His Daughter (for children), Kitabistan, 1938.
Nehru-Jinnah Correspondence, J. B. Kripalani, 1938.
Eighteen Months in India, 1936-1937, Kitabistan, 1938.

The Parting of the Ways and the Viceroy-Gandhi Correspondence, Lindsay Drummond for India League, 1940.
The Quintessence of Nehru, introduction by K. T. Narasimha Char, Allen & Unwin, 1941.
Points of View (extracts from *Toward Freedom*), John Day, 1941.
The Unity of India: Collected Writings 1937-1940, edited by V. K. Krishna Menon, Lindsay Drummond, 1941.
Nehru Flings a Challenge, Edited by "A Student," general editor, J. P. Gupta, foreword by P. S. Wadia, Hamara Hindustan Publications, 1943.
Prison Humours, New Literature, 1944.
Important Speeches: Being a Collection of Most Significant Speeches Delivered from 1922 to 1945, edited by Jagat S. Bright, Indian Printing Works, 1945.
The Discovery of India, John Day, 1946, reprinted, Oxford University Press, 1990.
India on the March, edited by Bright, Indian Printing Works, 1946, published as *Selected Writings,* Indian Printing Works, 1960.
(Contributor) *India: Constituent Assembly,* [New Delhi], 1947.
New India Speaks, compiled by D. R. Bose, A. Mukherjee, 1947.
Nehru on Gandhi, John Day, 1948.
Sri Ramakrishna and Swami Vivekananda, Advarta Ashrama, 1949.
Mahatma Gandhi, Signet Press, 1949.
Independence and After: A Collection of Speeches, 1946-49 (also see below), John Day, 1950.
Before and after Independence, edited and selected by Bright, Indian Printing Works, 1950.
Inside America: A Voyage of Discovery, National Book Stall, c. 1950.
Visit to America, John Day, 1950.
Talks With Nehru: India's Prime Minister Speaks Out on the Issues of Our Time, John Day, 1951.
The Story of the World (for children), sketches by Richard Albany, John Day, 1951.
Speeches, 1949-1953 (also see below), Ministry of Information and Broadcasting, Government of India, 1954
India and the Arab World, [Bombay], 1955.
(Author of introduction), Kanaiyalal Maneklal Munshi, *Indian Temple Sculpture,* A. Goswami, 1956.
Selections from Jawaharlal Nehru, edited by S. K. Narain, Oxford University Press, 1956.
Planning and Development: Speeches of Jawaharlal Nehru (1952-56), Ministry of Information and Broadcasting, 1956.
Towards a Socialistic Order, revised edition, All Congress Committee, 1956.
Speeches in Parliament, November 16-December 7, 1956, Information Service of India, c. 1957.
Speeches, Ministry of Information and Broadcasting, Government of India, 1957, Volume 1: *Independence and After: A Collection of Speeches, 1946-49,* Volume 2: *Speeches: 1949-1953,* Volume 3: *1953-57.*
A Bunch of Old Letters, Written Mostly to Jawaharlal Nehru and Some Written by Him, Asia, 1958.
Etam aura Nehru, edited by Basant Kumar Chatterjee, [India], 1958.
On Community Development, Ministry of Information and Broadcasting, Government of India, 1958.
(Contributor) *Official Correspondence between the Central Government of the People's Republic of China and the Government of India,* Foreign Languages Press (Peking), 1959.
Social Welfare in India, revised and abridged edition, Planning Commission, 1960.

The Wit and Wisdom of Gandhi, New Book Society of India, 1960.

Documents on the Sino-Indian Boundary Question, Foreign Languages Press, 1960.

Itihasa ke mahapuruba (in Hindi), [India], 1960.

Freedom from Fear: Reflections on the Personality and Teachings of Gandhi, edited by T. K. Mahadevan, Gandhi Smarak Nidhi, 1960.

Wit and Wisdom, edited by N. B. Sen, New Book Society of India, 1960.

The Mind of Mr. Nehru, interview by R. K. Karanjia, foreword by Radhakrishnan, Allen & Unwin, 1960.

India's Spokesman: From Speeches and Addresses, edited by C. D. Narasimhaiah, Macmillan, (Madras, India), 1960.

India Today and Tomorrow, Indian Council for Cultural Relations, Orient Longman, 1960.

The Quintessence of Nehru, Allen & Unwin, 1961.

(With Lopez Mateos) *Mexico y la Indio* (in Spanish), Editorial "La Justicia," 1961.

Prime Minister Nehru's Visit to U.S.A., [New Delhi], c. 1961.

The Prime Minister Comes to America, Information Service of India (Washington, D.C.), 1961.

India's Foreign Policy: Selected Speeches, September 1946-April 1961, Ministry of Information and Broadcasting, Government of India, 1961, reprinted, Asia, 1985.

Ardishah hayi Nihru, [India], c. 1961.

Prime Minister on Sino-Indian Relations, four parts, Ministry of External Affairs, Government of India, 1961-62.

Jawaharlal Nehru on Co-operation, Ministry of Information and Broadcasting, 1962.

Nehru Writes to Heads of States, [New Delhi], 1962.

Synopsis of the Nehru-Fateh Singh Talks, [Amritsar, India], 1962.

Nehru's Letter to Cho-En-Lai, November 14, 1962, [New Delhi], 1962.

Prime Minister of Goa, Ministry of External Affairs, 1962.

India's Freedom, Barnes & Noble, 1962.

Jawaharlal Nehru: Speeches, five volumes, Ministry of Information and Broadcasting, 1963.

Prime Minister on Chinese Aggression, Ministry of External Affairs, 1963.

Al-Udwan al-Sini fi alharb wa-al-silm (title means "Sino-Indian Border Dispute"), [India], 1963.

India's Quest, Being Letters on Indian History (excerpts from *Glimpses of World History*), Asia, 1963.

Nehru Souvenir, Review Publications (Meerut, India), 1964.

Tibbataye Bauddha manava samharaya, compiled by Jastin Vijayavardhana, [India], 1964.

Nehru on Socialism, Perspective Publication, 1964.

Nehru and Africa: Extracts from Jawaharlal Nehru's Speeches on Africa, 1946-1963, Indian Council for Africa, 1964.

Nehru, in His Own Words, edited by Ramnarayan Chandhary, Navajivan Publishing House, 1964.

Zindah dil Javahir (in Urdu), [India], 1964.

Jawaharlal Nehru: Excerpts from His Writings and Speeches, Ministry of Information and Broadcasting, 1964.

Glorious Thoughts of Nehru, edited by Sen, New Book Society of India, 1964, revised and enlarged edition, 1968.

Azadi de satraha kadama (in Hindi), [India], 1964.

Nehru on Society, Education and Culture, edited and compiled by Sita Ram Jayaswal, foreword by Radhakamal Mukerjee, Vinod Pustak Maudir, 1965.

Nehru, the First Sixty Years, edited with commentary by Dorothy Norman, two volumes, John Day, 1965.

Letters from Late Prime Minister Mr. Jawaharlal Nehru and Other Statesmen on National Issues, compiled by S. Chellaswamy, [Madras], 1965.

Vneshniaia politika Indii: izbrannye rechi i vystupleniia, 1946-1964, Progress, 1965.

Nehru on Communalism, edited by N. L. Gupta, Sampradayikta Virodhi Committee, 1965.

Nehru on Society, Education and Culture, edited and compiled by Sita Ram Jayaswal, foreword by Radhakamal Mukerjee, Vinod Pustak Maudir, 1965.

Congressman's Primer for Socialism, edited by H. D. Malaviya, foreword by daughter Indira Gandhi, introduction by Gulzari Lal Nanda, Socialist Congressman, 1965.

Mahatma Gandhi, Asia, 1966.

The Philosophy of Mr. Nehru, foreword by Zakir Husain, Allen & Unwin, 1966.

Nehrusuktislu (in Telugu), edited by K. Rames, [India], 1966.

Nehru on Police, compiled by B. N. Mullik, Dehra Dun, Palit & Dutt, 1970.

Selected Works of Jawaharlal Nehru, edited by S. Gopal, South Asia Books, Volumes 1-6, 1972-73, Volume 7, 1975, Volume 8, 1976, Volumes 9 and 10, 1977, Volume 11, 1978.

Jawaharlal Nehru: An Anthology, edited by Gopal, Oxford University Press, 1980.

India's Independence and Social Revolution: Speeches, Advent, 1984.

Selected Works of Jawaharlal Nehru, Second Series, seven volumes, edited by Gopal, Oxford University Press, 1984-1989.

Letters to Chief Ministers, 1947 to 1964, edited by G. Parthasarathi, Oxford University Press, Volume 1: *1947-1949,* Volume 2: *1950-1952,* Volume 3: *1952-1954,* 1987-88.

Also author of *Thoughts from Nehru,* Allied Publishers (Bombay). Also author of numerous booklets on political issues.

SIDELIGHTS: For thirty-one years, Jawaharlal Nehru was in the forefront of India's nationalist movement as the principal protege of spiritual leader Mohandes (Mahatma) Gandhi. From 1947 until his death, he served as the first prime minister of independent India, the largest democracy in the world.

It was surprising that two men as diverse as Nehru and Gandhi fought together so long for the same cause: freeing India from British supremacy. While both Nehru and Gandhi were considered "practical idealists," as Nehru once termed it, and both believed in reaching political goals via passive resistance, the basic ideology of the two men clashed. Nehru was an avid proponent of democracy while Gandhi believed in a single ruler as long as he or she was "spiritually emancipated," noted P. N. Pandy. In addition, Gandhi was adamantly against industrialization just as Nehru was fervently for it.

Nehru was "the epitome of modern man," wrote his sister, Krishna Nehru Hutheesing. Committed to developing India into a self-sufficient world power, he ardently supported science and technology, certain that research in these areas could mitigate "the harsh circumstances of the natural environment and triumph over illness, hunger and war," in Hutheesing's words. Acting toward the industrial development of India, Nehru established numerous institutes to study a wide-range of fields, including agriculture, medicine, the causes of cancer, nutrition, fuel, and textiles. Through his endeavors, national scientific laboratories were set up in several of India's major cities. In addition, he brought India into the atomic age by creating a national atomic energy commission with institutes in Bombay and Calcutta. He himself headed the ministry of atomic energy.

Nehru "envisioned a world of equal opportunity, education, and living standards for all mankind, made safe and just by an enlightened government operating on socialistic principles," Hutheesing pointed out. With these ends in mind, he first undertook the formidable task of unifying a country diverse in religious belief, language, and custom. In September of 1926, Nehru declared that "religion as practiced in India has become the old man of the sea for us and it has not only broken our backs but stunted and almost killed all originality of thought and mind. Like Sinbad the Sailor we must get rid of this terrible burden before we can aspire to breathe freely or do anything useful." Nehru also believed that of the fourteen languages spoken in India, one should be chosen as the country's official tongue. It was he who directed the gradual transition to Hindi.

As India's prime minister, Nehru brought about radical social and economic changes. He fought the iniquities of the Hindu caste system by promulgating the Untouchability Act of 1955, forbidding the practice of untouchability. In addition, he prohibited the custom of bigamy and gave widows the right of inheritance.

Profoundly influenced by his 1926 and 1938 visits to Europe, Nehru's nationalistic political stance grew to include a strong feeling of internationalism as well. In leading India, Nehru sought peaceful co-existence between his country and the rest of the world. In December, 1952, he stated, "As in the world today, so also in our country, the philosophy of force can no longer pay and our progress must be used on peaceful co-operation and tolerance of each other." He was the first of any Asian or African leader to espouse a policy of nonalignment with any world power.

Nehru was harshly criticized for his leniency in dealing with Red China. It was the only major country with which he could not reach his goal of peaceful co-existence. Even after signing the Sino-Indian Treaty on Tibet, China entered the northern border of India, a fact that Nehru kept hidden from parliament until five years later.

It is perhaps ironic that such a powerful head of state had been only mildly interested in government affairs at the onset of his career. As a young lawyer Nehru had joined the moderate party, representing it at the Bankepore Congress as a delegate. He then saw the congress as "a theatre where well-to-do English-educated Indians were playing the role of gentlemen politicians in their 'morning coats and 'wellpressed trousers,'" wrote Pandy.

Then in 1919, Gandhi organized the Satyagraha Sabha ("truthful effort") in reaction to the Rowlatt Bill just passed by the ruling British. The bill enabled the English to "short-circuit the processes of law in dealing with terrorists," Pandy explained, a bill that seemed to leave much room for interpretation. It was this movement of peaceful noncooperation with the British raj that spurred Nehru's interest in politics. In his autobiography *Toward Freedom,* Nehru stated: "I was afire with enthusiasm and wanted to join the Satyagraha Sabha immediately. I hardly thought of the consequences—law breaking, jail going, etc."

In 1920, Nehru visited the inhabitants of the Jumna River in Allahabad, an experience that furthered his commitment to politics. A Brahman, or member of the wealthy class, himself, Nehru had been unaware of just how wretched the conditions under which many of his countrymen survived. "That visit was a revelation to me," he wrote. "A new picture of India seemed to rise before me, naked, starving, crushed and utterly miserable. And their faith in us, casual visitors from the distant city, embarrassed me and filled me with a new responsibility that frightened me."

Nehru's sense of responsibility and firm commitment to Gandhi's philosophy of civil disobedience resulted in jail sentences many times throughout his life. In all, Nehru was imprisoned nine times for a total confinement of nine years. While in jail he became immersed in study, especially of writings on Marxism and Taoism. A prolific author, he also accomplished most of his writing while behind bars. In the preface to *Toward Freedom,* he wrote: "The primary object in writing these pages was to occupy myself with a definite task, so necessary in the long solitudes of jail life, as well as to review past events in India, with which I had been connected, to enable myself to think clearly about them. I began the task in a mood of self-questioning . . . [and] if I thought of an audience, it was one of my own countrymen and countrywomen."

Reviewing *Toward Freedom,* Margaret Marshall observed in *Nation:* "It is the impact of this double play of forces upon an intelligent, sensitive, and genuinely noble being which makes his remarkable autobiography one of the most absorbing personal histories of modern times." Concerning the writing itself, Charles Fleischer commented in the *New York Times:* "Since the style is the man, let it be promptly recorded that Nehru's autobiography is written in lucid, purest English, his deepest thoughts expressed in simplest speech. In a word, his style is so obviously sincere that the man's integrity is absolutely unquestionable." Clifton Fadiman noted in *New Republic* that while "his is not an autobiography of universal appeal . . . Nehru's book is one of the few available to English readers that really make clear history and meaning of the Indian Nationalist movement during the last thirty years."

The Discovery of India is Nehru's second autobiography. Isaac Rosenfelt commented, "There is a turgid feeling to *The Discovery of India* which must be attributed to the great gloom and greater injustice of Nehru's wartime imprisonment." John Bicknell described it as a "profound and illuminating document, not only in its exploration of the Indian heritage but especially for the light it throws on the character of a remarkably brilliant and complex personality."

Nehru was the father of the late Indira Gandhi, who served as the Prime Minister of India from 1966-77 and again from 1980 until her assassination in 1984.

AVOCATIONAL INTERESTS: Yoga, horseback riding, swimming, spinning yarn, reading, "mountains, running water, children, glaciers, good conversation, all animals except bats and centipedes."

BIOGRAPHICAL/CRITICAL SOURCES:

BOOKS

Chakrabarti, Atulananda, *Lonesome Pilgrim,* foreword by Hugh Tinker, Allied Publications, 1969.
Edwardes, Michael, *Nehru: A Pictorial Biography,* Viking, 1962.
Gopal, Sarvepalli, *Jawaharlal Nehru: A Biography,* Volume 1: *1889-1947,* J. Cape, 1975, Harvard University Press, 1976, Volume 2: *1947-1956,* J. Cape, 1980.
Hutheesing, Krishna Nehru, *We Nehrus,* Holt, 1967.
Karanjia, R. K., *The Mind of Mr. Nehru: An Interview,* Allen & Unwin, 1960.
Karkala, John B. Alphonso, *Jawaharlal Nehru,* Twayne, 1975.
Moraes, Frank, *Jawaharlal Nehru: A Biography,* Macmillan, 1956.

Nanda, B. R., editor, *Indian Foreign Policy: The Nehru Years*, University of Hawaii, 1976.

Nehru, Jawaharlal, *Toward Freedom*, John Day, 1941.

Nehru, Jawaharlal, *The Quintessence of Nehru*, introduction by K. T. Narasimha Char, Allen & Unwin, 1941.

Nehru, Jawaharlal, *Glimpses of World History*, John Day, 1942.

Nehru, Jawaharlal, *The Discovery of India*, John Day, 1946.

Nehru, Jawaharlal, *Nehru, the First Sixty Years*, edited with commentary by Dorothy Norman, John Day, 1965.

Pandey, Bishwa Nath, *Nehru*, Stein & Day, 1976.

Rao, *Nehru Legacy*, Popular Prakashan, 1971.

Roberts, Elizabeth Manchline, *Gandhi, Nehru and Modern India*, Methuen, 1974.

Sheean, Vincent, *Nehru: The Years of Power*, Random House, 1959.

PERIODICALS

American Historical Review, April, 1976.

Encyclopedia Americana, Americana, 1977.

English Historical Review, April, 1974.

Foreign Affairs, April, 1974.

Nation, March 1, 1941.

New Republic, September 23, 1946, January 28, 1967, June 19, 1971.

New Yorker, February 22, 1941, August 17, 1946, November 11, 1967.

New York Times, February 23, 1941, July 28, 1946, May 28, 1964.

Times Literary Supplement, September 21, 1973, January 10, 1986.

Washington Post, December 19, 1962.

*   *   *

NELSON, Alice Ruth Moore Dunbar   1875-1935
(Alice Dunbar, Alice Moore Dunbar, Alice Dunbar-Nelson, Alice Moore Dunbar-Nelson, Alice Ruth Moore)

PERSONAL: Born July 19, 1875, in New Orleans, La.; died September 18, 1935, in Philadelphia, Pa.; daughter of Joseph (a seaman) and Patricia (a seamstress; maiden name, Wright) Moore; married Paul Laurence Dunbar (a writer), March 8, 1898 (separated, 1902; died, 1906); married Henry Arthur Callis (a teacher), January, 1910 (divorced, 1911); married Robert J. Nelson (a journalist), April, 1916. *Education:* Attended Straight University, c. 1890; Cornell University, M.A.; postgraduate study at Pennsylvania School of Industrial Art and University of Pennsylvania.

CAREER: Writer. Worked as a teacher at schools in New Orleans, La., 1892-96, New York City, 1897, and Wilmington, Del., 1902-20, and at various black colleges. Co-founder of White Rose Mission (became White Rose House for Girls), in New York City, and of Industrial School for Colored Girls in Delaware; volunteer worker for Circle for Negro War Relief, 1918; member of field staff of Women's Committee on the Council of Defense; also member of Delaware's State Republican Committee, 1920; executive secretary for American Friends Interracial Peace Committee, 1928-31.

WRITINGS:

(Under name Alice Ruth Moore) *Violets, and Other Tales*, Monthly Review Press, 1895.

(Under name Alice Dunbar) *The Goodness of St. Rocque, and Other Stories*, Dodd, 1899.

(Editor, under name Alice Moore Dunbar) *Masterpieces of Negro Eloquence: The Best Speeches Delivered by the Negro From the Days of Slavery to the Present Time*, Douglass, 1914.

(Editor and contributor, under name Alice Moore Dunbar-Nelson) *The Dunbar Speaker and Entertainer*, J. L. Nichols, 1920.

(Under name Alice Dunbar-Nelson) *Give Us Each Day: The Diary of Alice Dunbar-Nelson*, edited and with introduction by Gloria T. Hull, Norton, 1984.

Work represented in anthologies, including *Negro Poets and Their Poems*, edited by Robert T. Kerlin, Associated Publishers, 1923, and *Caroling Dusk*, edited by Countee Cullen, Harper, 1927.

Author of unpublished novels "This Lofty Oak" and "Confessions of a Lazy Woman."

Author—probably under name Alice Moore Dunbar-Nelson—of column "Une Femme dit" in *Pittsburgh Courier*, 1926 and 1930, and of column "As in a Looking Glass" in *Washington Eagle*, 1926-30.

Contributor, often under name variations, to periodicals, including *A M.E. Church Review, Crisis, Daily Crusader, Education, Wilmington Journal Every Evening, Journal of Negro History, Leslie's Weekly, Messenger, Saturday Evening Mail, Smart Set, Southern Workman*, and *Opportunity*. Founder and co-editor of *Wilmington Weekly*, 1920.

SIDELIGHTS: Alice Ruth Moore Dunbar Nelson was probably the first black woman to distinguish herself in American literature. She was a versatile writer who produced short stories, poems, and a wide range of criticism, and she was also a staunch supporter of black rights, devoting herself—both in public and private—to furthering the causes of racial equality and world peace. Nelson is thus considered an important figure not only for her literary achievements but for her work in sociopolitical forums. It is her impressive array of accomplishments and efforts that has prompted writers such as *Ms.* reviewer Carolyn Heilbrun to hail her as "gifted and ambitious."

Nelson was born Alice Ruth Moore in 1875. In New Orleans she readily distinguished herself scholastically, and by age fifteen she had enrolled at the city's Straight University. There she trained for a teaching career but also studied nursing and stenography. In addition she played in local music groups—classical and popular—and edited the women's page of a black fraternity publication. Many of her experiences and observations inspired her first work, *Violets, and Other Tales*, which she published in 1895 after commencing her teaching career in New Orleans.

Violets, and Other Tales, which contains poems and essays in addition to short stories, at times focuses on the melancholic aspects of life and love. In the title story, a young woman gives her beloved a bouquet of violets and dies soon afterward. Later her married sweetheart happens upon the flowers but is unable to recall how he obtained them, whereupon his unsympathetic wife pitches the withered flowers into the fireplace flames. Also notable, though less characteristic of the collection, is "The Woman," an engaging essay supporting female independence and women's careers.

Soon after the publication of *Violets, and Other Tales* Nelson moved to Massachusetts with her family. She then began corresponding with Paul Laurence Dunbar, an increasingly famous writer who had reportedly become infatuated with Nelson upon spotting her photograph in a Boston periodical. Nelson and

Dunbar corresponded for two years before actually meeting in early 1897 as he prepared to undertake a reading tour of England. They became formally engaged during their brief encounter and secretly wed the next spring. In the interim Nelson taught in New York City and helped establish its White Rose Mission in Harlem.

While married to Dunbar, Nelson completed *The Goodness of St. Rocque, and Other Stories,* fourteen tales of Creole life in New Orleans. The collection is remembered for its vivid portraits of admirable individuals overcoming unfavorable circumstances. Among the noteworthy tales in the volume is the title work, in which a Creole woman resorts to both voodoo and Catholic ritual in an ultimately successful attempt to regain the love of a dashing fellow.

In 1902 Nelson and Dunbar separated. Nelson then traveled to Delaware and began teaching at both high school and college levels. For the next eighteen years Nelson lived and taught in Delaware. Dunbar died in 1906, and four years later Nelson married a fellow teacher. That marriage ended in 1911, however, and five years later she married again, this time to journalist Robert J. Nelson, with whom she remained for the rest of her life.

During this often turbulent period Nelson continued her literary career. She contributed short stories and poems to various periodicals and edited the volumes *Masterpieces of Negro Eloquence* and *The Dunbar Speaker and Entertainer,* which were principally intended for students. Included in the latter are some of her own writings, notably "I Sit and Sew," a poem in which she expressed her irritation at the general denigration of women's potential for contribution during the years of World War I. Dissatisfied with merely complaining, Nelson demonstrated her own usefulness by serving with the Circle of Negro War Relief in 1918 and then joining the Women's Commission on the Council of Defense, through which she organized relief efforts by black women in Southern states.

In the 1920s Nelson increased her involvement in social causes and politics. She supervised the activities of black women in Delaware's State Republican Committee in 1920 and executed similar responsibilities for the Democratic Party in New York City four years later. Toward the close of the decade she also served as executive secretary for the American Friends Interracial Peace Committee. But even during this period of political involvement she continued her writing career by appearing as a columnist in the *Pittsburgh Courier* and the *Washington Eagle* and by publishing poems and stories in periodicals such as the *Messenger* and *Crisis.* Her productivity remained steady until the end of the 1920s, when she published only one article in 1928 and another one in 1929. A 1932 article for *Wilmington's Journal Every Evening* became her only piece from that decade. She died three years later.

Although Nelson is sometimes considered merely a peripheral figure in the Harlem Renaissance of black literature, she is nonetheless esteemed for her daring advocacy of equal rights for women and blacks and for the consistently high quality of her poetry and prose. The distinguishing aspects—simplicity, precision, incisiveness—of her fiction and essays were also evident in her posthumously published *Give Us Each Day: The Diary of Alice Dunbar-Nelson.* Brent Staples, writing in the *New York Times Book Review,* recommended the diary for its insights into both the suffrage and black rights movements, observing that the work "lets us inside what was then a thriving national network of black women's social groups." Staples also contended that throughout the diary Nelson maintains "an entertaining haugh-

tiness" that seemed essential to her self-esteem. He called the posthumous work "a valuable contribution to women's letters."

BIOGRAPHICAL/CRITICAL SOURCES:

BOOKS

Bone, Robert, *Down Home: A History of Afro-American Short Fiction From Its Beginnings to the End of the Harlem Renaissance,* Putnam, 1975.
Brawley, Benjamin, *Paul Laurence Dunbar: Poet of His People,* University of North Carolina Press, 1936.
Dictionary of Literary Biography, Volume 50: *Afro-American Writers From the Harlem Renaissance to 1940,* Gale, 1987.
Dunbar-Nelson, Alice, *Give Us Each Day: The Diary of Alice Dunbar-Nelson,* edited and with introduction by Gloria T. Hull, Norton, 1985.

PERIODICALS

CLA Journal, March, 1976.
Ms., June, 1985.
New York Times Book Review, April 14, 1985.

*   *   *

NEMEROV, Howard (Stanley) 1920-

PERSONAL: Born March 1, 1920, in New York, N.Y.; son of David and Gertrude (Russek) Nemerov; married Margaret Russell, January 26, 1944; children: David, Alexander Michael, Jeremy Seth. *Education:* Harvard University, A.B., 1941.

ADDRESSES: Home—6970 Cornell Ave., St. Louis, Mo. 63130.

CAREER: Hamilton College, Clinton, N.Y., instructor, 1946-48; Bennington College, Bennington, Vt., member of faculty in literature, 1948-66; Brandeis University, Waltham, Mass., professor of English, 1966-68; Washington University, St. Louis, Mo., visiting Hurst Professor of English, 1969-70, professor of English, 1970-76, Edward Mallinckrodt Distinguished University Professor of English, 1976—. Visiting lecturer in English University of Minnesota, 1958-59; writer-in-residence, Hollins College, 1962-63. Consultant in poetry, Library of Congress, 1963-64; chancellor, American Academy of Poets, beginning 1976. *Military service:* Royal Canadian Air Force, 1942-44; became flying officer; U.S. Army Air Forces, 1944-45; became first lieutenant.

MEMBER: National Institute of Arts and Letters, American Academy of Arts and Letters, American Academy of Arts and Sciences (fellow), Phi Beta Kappa (honorary member), Alpha of Massachusetts.

AWARDS, HONORS: Bowdoin Prize, Harvard University, 1940; *Kenyon Review* fellowship in fiction, 1955; Oscar Blumenthal Prize, 1958, Harriet Monroe Memorial Prize, 1959, Frank O'Hara Memorial Prize, 1971, Levinson Prize, 1975, all from *Poetry* magazine; second prize, *Virginia Quarterly Review* short story competition, 1958; National Institute of Arts and Letters Grant, 1961; Golden Rose Trophy, New England Poetry Club, 1962; Brandeis Creative Arts Award, 1963; D.L., Lawrence University, 1964, and Tufts University, 1969; National Endowment for the Arts Grant, 1966-67; First Theodore Roethke Memorial Award, 1968, for *The Blue Swallows;* St. Botolph's Club (Boston) Prize for Poetry, 1968; Guggenheim fellow, 1968-69; Academy of American Poets fellowship, 1970; Pulitzer Prize and National Book Award, 1978, and Bollingen Prize, 1981, Yale University, all for *The Collected Poems of Howard Nemerov;* the first Aiken Taylor Award for Modern Poetry, 1987, from *Sewanee*

Review and University of the South; National Medal of Art, 1987, for promoting "excellence, growth, support and availability of the arts in the United States"; honorary degree from Washington and Lee University; named Poet Laureate of the United States.

WRITINGS:

POETRY

The Image and the Law, Holt, 1947.
Guide to the Ruins, Random House, 1950.
The Salt Garden, Little, Brown, 1955.
Small Moment, Ward Ritchie Press, 1957.
Mirrors and Windows, University of Chicago Press, 1958.
New and Selected Poems, University of Chicago Press, 1960.
Endor: Drama in One Act (verse play; also see below), Abingdon, 1961.
The Next Room of the Dream: Poems and Two Plays (includes the verse plays "Endor" and "Cain"), University of Chicago Press, 1962.
(Contributor) Ted Hughes and Thom Gunn, editors, *Five American Poets,* Faber, 1963.
The Blue Swallows, University of Chicago Press, 1967.
A Sequence of Seven with a Drawing by Ron Slaughter, Tinker Press, 1967.
The Winter Lightning: Selected Poems, Rapp & Whiting, 1968.
The Painter Dreaming in the Scholar's House (limited edition), Phoenix Book Shop, 1968.
Gnomes and Occasions, University of Chicago Press, 1973.
The Western Approaches: Poems, 1973-1975, University of Chicago Press, 1975.
The Collected Poems of Howard Nemerov, University of Chicago Press, 1977.
Sentences, University of Chicago Press, 1980.
Inside the Onion, University of Chicago Press, 1984.
War Stories: Poems about Long Ago and Low, University of Chicago Press, 1987.

Contributor of poems to numerous periodicals, including *Harvard Advocate, Kenyon Review, Poetry, New Yorker, Nation,* and *Polemic.*

OTHER

The Melodramatists (novel), Random House, 1949.
Federigo: Or the Power of Love (novel), Little, Brown, 1954.
The Homecoming Game (novel), Simon & Schuster, 1957.
A Commodity of Dreams and Other Stories, Simon & Schuster, 1959.
(Editor and author of introduction) Henry Wadsworth Longfellow, *Longfellow: Selected Poetry,* Dell, 1959.
"The Poetry of Howard Nemerov" (two audio cassettes), Jeffrey Norton, 1962.
Poetry and Fiction: Essays, Rutgers University Press, 1963.
(Author of foreword) Miller Williams, *A Circle of Stones,* Louisiana State University, 1964.
(Author of introduction) Owen Barfield, *Poetic Diction: A Study in Meaning,* McGraw-Hill, 1964.
(Author of commentary) William Shakespeare, *Two Gentlemen of Verona,* Dell, 1964.
Journal of the Fictive Life (autobiography), Rutgers University Press, 1965, reprinted with a new preface, University of Chicago Press, 1981.
(Editor and contributor) *Poets on Poetry,* Basic Books, 1965.
(Editor) Marianne Moore, *Poetry and Criticism,* Adams House & Lowell House Printers, 1965.

(Contributor) Sheldon Norman Grebstein, editor, *Perspectives in Contemporary Criticism,* Harper, 1968.
(Contributor) A. Cheuse and R. Koffler, editors, *The Rarer Action: Essays in Honor of Francis Fergusson,* Rutgers University Press, 1971.
Stories, Fables and Other Diversions, David R. Godine, 1971.
Reflexions on Poetry and Poetics, Rutgers University Press, 1972.
(Contributor) Robert Boyers, editor, *Contemporary Poetry in America: Essays and Interviews,* Schocken, 1975.
(Contributor) Shirley Sugarman, editor, *Evolution of Consciousness: Studies in Polarity,* Wesleyan University Press, 1976.
Figures of Thought: Speculations on the Meaning of Poetry and Other Essays, David R. Godine, 1978.
"Howard Nemerov" (sound recording), Tapes for Readers, 1978.
"Howard Nemerov" (sound recording), Tapes for Readers, 1979.
(Contributor) Arthur Edelstein, editor, *Images and Ideas in American Culture: The Functions of Criticism, Essays in Memory of Philip Rahv,* Brandeis University Press, 1979.
New and Selected Essays, with foreword by Kenneth Burke, Southern Illinois University Press, 1985.
The Oak in the Acorn: On Remembrance of Things Past and on Teaching Proust, Who Will Never Learn, Louisiana State University Press, 1987.

Contributor of essays, articles and reviews to literary journals, including *Hudson Review, Poetry, Atlantic, Partisan Review* and *Virginia Quarterly Review.* Contributor of short fiction to *Harvard Advocate, Story, Esquire, Carleton Miscellany, Reporter,* and *Virginia Quarterly Review.*

SIDELIGHTS: Howard Nemerov is a highly acclaimed poet appreciated for the range of his capabilities and subject matter, "from the profound to the poignant to the comic," James Billington remarked in his frequently quoted announcement of Nemerov's appointment to the post of United States poet laureate. A distinguished professor at Washington University in St. Louis since 1968, Nemerov writes poetry and fiction that engage the reader's mind without becoming academic, many reviewers report. Though his works show a consistent emphasis on thought—the process of thinking and ideas themselves—his poems relate a broad spectrum of emotion and a variety of concerns. As Joyce Carol Oates remarks in the *New Republic,* "Romantic, realist, comedian, satirist, relentless and indefatigable brooder upon the most ancient mysteries—Nemerov is not to be classified." Writing in the study *Howard Nemerov,* Peter Meinke states that these contrasting qualities are due to Nemerov's "deeply divided personality." Meinke points out that Nemerov himself has spoken of a duality in his nature in *Journal of the Fictive Life* in which he says that "it has seemed to me that I must attempt to bring together the opposed elements of my character represented by poetry and fiction." Comments Meinke, "These 'opposed elements' in Howard Nemerov's character are reflected in his life and work: in the tensions between his romantic and realistic visions, his belief and unbelief, his heart and mind."

If Nemerov harbors impulses toward both poetry and fiction, he expresses them as opposites suspended in balanced co-existence rather than dissonance. A direct expression of this equilibrium is his poem "Because You Asked about the Line between Prose and Poetry." Writes *Poetry* contributor Mary Kinzie, "It is about rain gradually turning into snow, but still acting like rain (only somehow lighter and thicker), until—there is suddenly snow flying instead of rain falling." As the poem states, "There came a moment that you couldn't tell. / And then they clearly flew instead of fell." Kinzie continues, "What clearly flew?

Clearly, the pieces of snow, now soft and crowded flakes," but these words also leave room to suggest the sudden upward flight of some dark swallows Nemerov had mentioned earlier in the poem. These birds, Kinzie says, are "the suggestive warrant for any kind of flight. . . . So is the poem launched. Not going straight to its goal—not falling like rain—a poem imperceptibly thickens itself out of the visible stream of prose." The choice—the crossing of the line that separates opposing impulses—is not consciously traceable, Nemerov told Melinda Miller of the *Washington Post:* "It's like a fairy tale. You're allowed to do it as long as you don't know too much about it."

The Harvard graduate's first book of poems, *The Image and the Law,* characteristically is based on opposed elements, on a duality of vision. As F. C. Golffing explains in *Poetry,* "Mr. Nemerov tells us that he dichotomizes the 'poetry of the eye' and the 'poetry of the mind,' and that he attempts to exhibit in his verse the 'ever-present dispute between two ways of looking at the world.'" Some reviewers find that this dichotomy leads to a lack of coherence in the verse. *New York Times* writer Milton Crane, for example, feels that the poems "unfortunately show no unity of conception such as their author attributes to them." The book was also criticized for being derivative of earlier modern poets such as T. S. Eliot, W. H. Auden, W. B. Yeats, and Wallace Stevens.

After reading *Guide to the Ruins,* Nemerov's second book of verse, *Saturday Review* contributor I. L. Salomon asserts that Nemerov "suffers from a dichotomy of personality." Within Nemerov, Salomon claims, an "instinct for perfection" and unity contends with a modern "carelessness in expression." Yet Crane notices not so much modern "carelessness" as praiseworthy modern sensibility; he believes that *Ruins* is "the work of an original and sensitive mind, alive to the thousand anxieties and agonies of our age." And Meinke contends that it is Nemerov's "modern awareness of contemporary man's alienation and fragmentation" combined with "a breadth of wit in the eighteenth century sense of the word" which "sets Nemerov's writing apart from other modern writers."

Like *Image and the Law* and *Guide to the Ruins, The Salt Garden,* when it first came out, drew criticism for being derivative. "The accents of Auden and [John Crowe] Ransom," observed Louis Untermeyer, "occasionally twist his utterance into a curious poetic patois." Similarly, Randall Jarrell found that "you can see where he found out how to do some of the things he does—he isn't, as yet, a very individual poet." Years later, when asked if his work had changed in character or style, he replied in *Poets on Poetry,* "I began and for a long time remained imitative, and poems in my first books . . . show more than traces of admired modern masters—Eliot, Auden, Stevens, [E. E.] Cummings, Yeats." Meinke, too, maintains that Nemerov in his early work was "writing Eliot, Yeats, and Stevens out of his system." Yet at the same time that Untermeyer and Jarrell faulted Nemerov for his imitation, like other readers, they were impressed by his growth as a poet. Jarrell commented that "as you read *The Salt Garden* you are impressed with how much the poet has learned, how well he has developed," while Hayden Carruth remarked, "Nemerov's new book is his third . . . and his best; steady improvement, I take it, is one sign of formidable ability."

The Salt Garden, many critics feel, marks the beginning of other changes in Nemerov's work as well. Meinke observes that in this volume "Nemerov has found his most characteristic voice: a quiet intelligent voice brooding lyrically on the strange beauty and tragic loneliness of life." In a review of *The Collected Poems of Howard Nemerov,* Willard Spiegelman, like Meinke, discovers in the poems from *The Salt Garden* "Nemerov's characteristic manner and tone." Spiegelman still finds opposed elements, but in balance; Nemerov's manner is "genuinely Horatian according to Auden's marvelous definition of looking at 'this world with a happy eye / but from a sober perspective.' Nemerov's *aurea mediocritas* [golden mean] sails between philosophical skepticism . . . and social satire on one side, and, on the other, an open-eyed, child-like appreciation of the world's miracles."

Another change which began with *Salt Garden* and continues in *Mirrors and Windows, The Next Room of the Dream,* and *The Blue Swallows* is Nemerov's growing concern with nature. In 1966, Nemerov wrote in *Poets on Poetry* of the impact of the natural world on his work: "During the war and since, I have lived in the country, chiefly in Vermont, and while my relation to the landscape has been contemplative rather than practical, the landscape nevertheless has in large part taken over my poetry." This interest in the landscape has led Chad Walsh to say of *Swallows* that "in its quiet lyricism and sensitivity to nature it suggests Robert Frost." The comparison to Frost, suggested by many other critics, is also made on the grounds that Nemerov, like Frost, brings philosophical issues into his poetry. As he says in *Poets on Poetry,* he is not so much an observer of nature as its medium, bringing into speech "an unknowably large part of a material world whose independent existence might be likened to that of the human unconscious, a sleep of causes, a chaos of the possible-impossible." Phrasing it differently in the poem "A Spell before Winter," Nemerov writes, "And I speak to you now with the land's voice, / It is the cold, wild land that says to you / A knowledge glimmers in the sleep of things: / The old hills hunch before the north wind blows."

A feature of the poems more frequently pointed out by critics is a witty, ironic manner and a serious, perhaps pessimistic, philosophy. James Dickey observes the seriousness that underlies Nemerov's wit. Nemerov, Dickey maintains, "is one of the wittiest and funniest poets we have. . . . But the enveloping emotion that arises from his writing is helplessness: the helplessness we all feel in the face of the events of our time, and of life itself. . . . And beneath even this feeling is a sort of hopelessly involved acceptance and resignation which has in it more of the truly tragic than most poetry which deliberately sets out in quest of tragedy." At the same time, Julia A. Bartholomay detects a somewhat different dichotomy. She contends that in Nemerov's poetry there is a basic dualism that "underlies the two different . . . attitudes which appear consistently in the poet's work. On the one hand, he is very much the witty, sophisticated man of his time. . . . Nemerov often views life with a humorous but bitter irony. . . . On the other hand, the poet perceives the world ontologically. His experience may be philosophical, subjective, lyrical, or even mystical." Bartholomay argues that Nemerov's double view is expressed in his poetry through the use of paradox. The paradoxes reflect the "divisiveness, fragmentation, complexity, and absurdity of modern existence."

Not all critics applaud the tragic irony which Dickey and many others find in Nemerov's poetry. Carruth, for example, comments: "No one would deny that famous and marvelous poems have been written in the manner of poetic irony. . . . But today this manner is an exceedingly tired poetic attitude. . . . And Nemerov's tired attitude is revealed in tired poetry: spent meters, predictable rhymes, and metaphors haggard with use." *New York Times* critic Thomas Lask also objects to Nemerov's irony, but for different reasons. He believes that in *Blue Swallows* it has turned bitter, expressing "loathing and contempt for man and his work." In contrast to both these views, Laurence Lieberman, writing in the *Yale Review,* feels that "Howard Nemerov has perfected the poem as an instrument for exercising brilliance of wit. Searching, discursive, clear-sighted, he has learned to make the poem serve his relaxed manner and humane insights so expertly, I can only admire the clean purposefulness of his statements, his thoughtful care, the measure and grace of his lines."

However strong his ironic voice, Nemerov has mellowed with age, according to many reviewers. Meinke claims that "Nemerov has progressed steadily in his poetry to a broader, more tolerant view, less bitter and more sad." Likewise, Harvey Gilman finds in a review of *Gnomes and Occasions* that "Nemerov's tone modulates as saving wit gives way to wistful contemplation, reminiscence, and prayer. The mask of irony is lowered and Nemerov writes a more sustained elegiac verse. . . . True, the epigrammatic manner remains in evidence . . . but the wit is here tinged with whimsy and warmth." Similarly, Spiegelman observes: "Nemerov, growing old, becomes younger as he adopts the manner of an ancient sage. Cynicism barely touches his voice; the occasional sardonic moments are offset by feeling and sympathy. . . . In the 40's and 50's Nemerov was rabbinically fixated on sin and redemption. What was, early on, a source of prophetic despair . . . becomes in the poems of his middle age the cause of poetic variety and energy, metaphysical delight, and emotional equilibrium." And Helen Vendler discerns in a critique of *Collected Poems* that as "the echoes of the *grand maitres* fade, the poems get steadily better. The severity of attitude is itself chastened by a growing humanity, and the forms of the earth grow ever more distinct."

Gnomes and Occasions indulges Nemerov's penchant for short, aphoristic verses in which the images carry the burden of persuasion. In these "gnomes," Nemerov achieves a "Biblical resonance," says Kenneth Burke in his introduction to Nemerov's early poems, which are still ranked with the best postwar American poetry. More than one critic has referred to Nemerov's writings as wisdom literature. For example, Helen Vendler reports in *Part of Nature, Part of Us* that Nemerov's "mind plays with epigram, gnome, riddle, rune, advice, meditation, notes, dialectic, prophecy, reflection, views, knowledge, questions, speculation—all the forms of thought. His wishes go homing to origins and ends." Scholars link this stylistic tendency to the poet's Jewish heritage. Meinke describes the early Nemerov as a "nonpracticing Jew engaged in a continual dialogue with Christianity . . . testing its relevance in the modern world." In addition to the influence of Dante and St. Augustine, that of W. B. Yeats leaves its mark on the poems, says *Dictionary of Literary Biography* contributor Robert W. Hill, "not so much in form or style as in subject matter and in a decidedly religious quality of the language." For instance, one of Nemerov's definitions of poetry given in "Thirteen Ways of Looking at a Skylark" states: "In the highest range the theory of poetry would be the theory of the Incarnation, which seeks to explain how the Word became Flesh."

Nemerov, however, does not reconstruct the world with imagination as other poets have done. Explains Hill, "While Yeats went about his way inventing new religion and culling the cabala for hints and signs, Nemerov's poems show him to be a critic of the secularizers: coming from the Jewish tradition, his sense of the decline of religion is not so easily pacified by new contrivances as Yeats's was. But the connections Nemerov feels with the seers of the past are clearly modern, clearly attached with the threads of the naturalistic modes, the beliefs in touchable things rather than in the untouchable." Thus Nemerov uses acts of the imagination not to alter the world but to make it known. To the extent that this process is magical, "Our proper magic is the magic of language," claims the poet, according to *Contemporary Authors Bibliography Series* contributor Gloria Young.

Poetry as a link between the material and spiritual worlds emerges as the theme of *Sentences*. In this volume, Nemerov achieves thematic coherence by organizing the poems into three sections, "Beneath," "Above," and "Beyond." Bonnie Costello, writing in *Parnassus: Poetry in Review,* relates that the sections "mark off, respectively, poems of low diction and subject (our social sphere of sex and power), poems of higher diction and subject (metaphysics and poetry), and those of middle diction and subject (our origin and fate)." Critics approve the last two sections more than the first, which they claim is beneath the level of quality they have come to expect from Nemerov. The section castigates the purveyors of low artistic, social and political values, relates Ronald Baughman in the *Dictionary of Literary Biography Yearbook: 1983.* "The reviewers damn the writer for accomplishing the goal which he has set for himself—the portrayal of man acting beneath dignity." Looking over the entire book, Baughman offers, "*Sentences* contains a wide range of poems, extending from the mocking, bitter verse of section one to the interesting but restrained appraisals of section two to the deeply moving contemplations of section three. The volume's theme—the order art gives to the randomness of life—develops with this movement from beginning to end. Nemerov's title is reminiscent of Stephen Spender's poem 'Subject: Object: Sentence,' in which Spender states, 'A sentence is condemned to stay as stated—/ As in *life-sentence, death-sentence,* for example.' As Howard Nemerov dramatizes his life and death sentences, he reveals his attempts to connect, through the power of his art, with the world below, nature above, and the spirit beyond."

The Collected Poems presents verse from all of the earlier volumes. Its publication in 1977 spurred a re-evaluation of Nemerov's works as a whole. Phoebe Pettingell notes in the *New Leader* that the book shows "a gradual intensifying of a unified perspective," the poet's obsession with the theme of "man's sometimes tragic, sometimes ludicrous relation to history, death and the universe." Robert B. Shaw, writing in the *Nation,* relates, "To what extent, he repeatedly wonders, is the world we see our own creation? . . . Is the poem a mirror reflecting the appearances of the world in responsible detail, or is it a window, a transparent medium through which we may see . . .? Or might it begin in one and with care and luck become the other? Nemerov never fully unravels these aesthetic and metaphysical knots. They provide him the material for endless reflection." Tom Johnson offers this assessment in the *Sewanee Review:* "Nemerov has written more incisively of science and its place in our imaginations than anyone else has yet managed to do in good (or even readable) poems. . . . The breadth of accomplishment and depth of insight are one's most striking impressions from first readings of the *Collected Poems,* enriched later by the humor, in intricacy, the grace." Shaw recommends *Collected Poems* to readers whose interest in poetry stems more from curiosity than from experience with the genre. "Such readers," Shaw says, "can expect to be charmed by the easy flow of Nemerov's reasoned discourse, and moved by those fine moments in his poems in which reason is overcome by awe."

Nemerov's prose has also been commended, especially for displaying an irony and wit similar to that of his poems. His novels, as Meinke remarks, "like his poems, . . . are basically pessimistic. The condition of man is not an enviable one: we act foolishly and understand imperfectly. Nemerov's dark viewpoint, which in his poetry is redeemed by beauty . . ., in his fiction is redeemed by humor." Meinke terms *The Melodramatists* "a highly successful first novel," and in the *Nation* Diana Trilling comments that after a slow start, it is "a considerable first novel—literate and entertaining, with a nice satiric barb." *Federigo: Or* the Power of Love and The Homecoming Game were also well received. For example, Richard Sullivan calls the latter book a "beautifully controlled satire" with characters "rendered with authentic irony," and Atlantic reviewer C. J. Rolo finds it has "wit, dash, and point."

Through the characters in these novels, Nemerov explores "the consequences of the overactive imagination," writes Carl Rapp in the Dictionary of Literary Biography: Novelists since World War II. Characters with romantic expectations of finding meaningful action and self-realization amid the social pressures of their times instead realize that they are the victims of their own fantasies. Thus, the novels, like the poetry, comment on the relationship between imagination and reality. Nemerov published his last novel The Homecoming Game (about a professor who discovers his limits when faced with opposing groups on campus) in 1957. Rapp suggests, "Nemerov has perhaps come to feel that the novelist himself, with his own incorrigible tendency to fantasize melodramatic scenes and situations, presents a spectacle as ridiculous as that of his own characters. In recent poems such as 'Novelists' and 'Reflexions of a Novelist,' he observes that it is, of course, the novelist who is preeminently the man with the overactive imagination, the egomaniac, the voyeur." Nemerov told Robert Boyers in a Salmagundi interview that he left off being a novelist when Bennington College chose to retain him as its poet and hired Bernard Malamud to be its novelist.

Though through with the novel form, Nemerov continues to work with prose in short stories and literary criticism. Like his poetry and fiction, Nemerov's essays have won for him the respect of many well-known writers and critics. To Figures of Thought: Speculations on the Meaning of Poetry and Other Essays, Benjamin DeMott responds: "Taken as a whole . . . these 'speculations' are uncommonly stimulating and persuasive. . . . [This book] communicates throughout a vivid sense of the possibility of a richer kind of knowing in all areas than we're in the process of settling for. . . . Like the high art it salutes, it hums with the life of things." Moreover, Joyce Carol Oates adds: "The book is a marvelous one, rewarding not only for what it tells us about poetry in general . . ., but for what it tells us about the processes of the imagination. Nemerov is, quite simply, a brilliant mind."

New and Selected Essays, a more recent collection of essays spanning thirty years of Nemerov's criticism, is also considered valuable. "It is the texture of [Nemerov's] thinking that is exhilarating, and not the Grand Propositions—though one of the latter (his favorite) is sturdy indeed: 'Poetry is getting something right in language.'. . . The theoretical essays and the studies of particular writers are the ones most wealthy in serviceable lore," offers Richard Wertime in the Yale Review. Deborah S. Murphy and Young state in the Contemporary Authors Bibliography Series that since "Nemerov is a poet who is continually changing and growing, becoming more complex in subject matter and apparently simpler in style," the body of his work has only begun to receive the serious critical attention it merits.

Nemerov's books have brought him every major award for poetry, including the National Book Award, the Pulitzer Prize, the Bollingen Prize, and the National Medal of Art. Regarding his fame, he told Jake Thompson of the Chicago Tribune, "You do the best you can and really don't worry about immortality all that much, especially as you have to be dead to achieve it. . . . Oh, you want praise and recognition and above all money. But if that was your true motive, you would have done something else. All this fame and honor is a very nice thing, as long as you don't believe it."

MEDIA ADAPTATIONS: The Homecoming Game was adapted as a play entitled "Tall Story" and filmed by Warner Bros. in 1959.

BIOGRAPHICAL/CRITICAL SOURCES:

BOOKS

Bartholomay, Julia A., The Shield of Perseus: The Vision and Imagination of Howard Nemerov, University of Florida Press, 1972.

Boyers, Robert, editor, Contemporary Poetry in America: Essays and Interviews, Schocken, 1974.

Boyers, Robert, editor, Excursions: Selected Literary Essays, Kennikat Press, 1975.

Contemporary Authors Bibliography Series, Volume 2, Gale, 1986.

Contemporary Literary Criticism, Gale, Volume 2, 1974, Volume 6, 1976, Volume 9, 1978, Volume 36, 1986.

DeMott, Robert J., and Sanford E. Marovits, editors, Artful Thunder: Versions of the Romantic Tradition in American Literature in Honor of Howard P. Vincent, Kent State University Press, 1975.

Dickey, James, Babel to Byzantium, Farrar, Straus, 1968.

Dictionary of Literary Biography, Gale, Volume 5: American Poets since World War II, 1980, Volume 6: American Novelists since World War II, Second Series, 1980.

Dictionary of Literary Biography Yearbook: 1983, Gale, 1984.

Donoghue, Denis, editor, Seven American Poets from MacLeish to Nemerov, University of Minnesota Press, 1975.

Duncan, Bowie, editor, The Critical Reception of Howard Nemerov: A Selection of Essays and a Bibliography, Scarecrow Press, 1971.

Howard, Richard, editor, Preferences, Viking, 1974.

Hungerford, Edward, editor, Poets in Progress: Critical Prefaces to Ten Contemporary Americans, Northwestern University Press, 1962.

Hutton, Charles, editor, Imagination and the Spirit: Essays in Literature and the Christian Faith Presented to Clyde S. Kilby, Eerdmans, 1971.

Kumin, Maxine, To Make a Prairie: Essays on Poets, Poetry and Country Living, University of Michigan Press, 1979.

Labrie, Ross, Howard Nemerov, Twayne, 1980.

Lieberman, Laurence, editor, Unassigned Frequencies: American Poetry in Review, 1964-1977, University of Illinois Press, 1977.

Maxfield, Melinda R., editor, Images and Innovations: Update 1970's, Center for the Humanities, Converse College, 1979.

Meinke, Peter, Howard Nemerov, University of Minnesota Press, 1968.

Mills, William, The Stillness in Moving Things: The World of Howard Nemerov, Memphis State University Press, 1975.

Nemerov, Howard, The Next Room of the Dream, University of Chicago Press, 1962.

Nemerov, Howard, Journal of the Fictive Life (autobiographical), Rutgers University Press, 1965, reprinted with a new preface, University of Chicago Press, 1981.

Nemerov, Howard, Poets on Poetry, Basic Books, 1966.

Nemerov, Howard, New and Selected Essays, Southern Illinois University Press, 1985.

Rosenthal, M. L., The Modern Poets: A Critical Introduction, Oxford University Press, 1961.

Vendler, Helen, Part of Nature, Part of Us: Modern American Poets, Harvard University Press, 1980.

Waggoner, Hyatt, American Poets from the Puritans to the Present, Houghton, 1968.

Wyllie, Diana E., *Elizabeth Bishop and Howard Nemerov: A Reference Guide,* Hall, 1983.

PERIODICALS

America, October 5, 1974, April 8, 1978, February 1, 1986, May 7, 1988.

American Book Review, March, 1979.

American Poetry Review, May/June, 1975, January, 1976.

American Scholar, summer, 1959, summer, 1968.

Antioch Review, spring, 1963, summer, 1987.

Atlantic, November, 1954, May, 1957, November, 1961, February, 1968.

Chicago Review, Volume 25, number 1, 1973.

Chicago Tribune, July 4, 1988.

Chicago Tribune Book World, March 29, 1981.

Christian Science Monitor, January 29, 1964.

Commonweal, February 13, 1959.

Encounter, February, 1969.

Georgia Review, winter, 1976, fall, 1985.

Harper's, September, 1963.

Hudson Review, summer, 1963, spring, 1964, spring, 1976, autumn, 1984.

Island, fall, 1966.

Journal of Aesthetics and Art Criticism, spring, 1979.

Kenyon Review, winter, 1952.

London Review of Books, February 21, 1985.

Los Angeles Times, June 19, 1987.

Massachusetts Review, spring, 1981.

Modern Language Notes, December, 1978.

Nation, July 13, 1963, November 8, 1975, February 25, 1978, November 11, 1978.

New Leader, December 5, 1977, April 30, 1984.

New Republic, June 23, 1958, April 28, 1973, April 8, 1978.

New Yorker, March 14, 1959, April 1, 1961.

New York Herald Tribune Book Review, March 1, 1959, July 30, 1961.

New York Times, August 1, 1947, May 21, 1950, March 3, 1957, March 30, 1968, April 28, 1968, December 26, 1978, June 5, 1987, June 11, 1987, May 18, 1988.

New York Times Book Review, April 3, 1949, May 21, 1950, July 17, 1955, February 8, 1959, March 1, 1959, January 8, 1961, July 21, 1963, November 8, 1975, December 18, 1977, April 16, 1978.

Parnassus: Poetry in Review, fall/winter, 1973, spring/summer, 1975, spring/summer, 1976, fall/winter, 1977, fall/winter, 1981.

Partisan Review, winter, 1961, winter, 1965.

Poet and Critic, Number 11, 1979.

Poetry, November, 1947, June, 1955, December, 1958, September, 1963, March, 1965, February, 1967, December, 1976, September, 1978, September, 1981, February, 1988.

Poets and Writers, May/June, 1987.

Prairie Schooner, spring, 1965.

Reporter, September 12, 1963.

Salmagundi, fall/winter, 1975, fall, 1978.

San Francisco Review of Books, July, 1984.

Saturday Review, July 1, 1950, May 21, 1955, September 27, 1958, February 21, 1959, February 11, 1961, July 6, 1963.

Sewanee Review, winter, 1952, spring, 1961, fall, 1968, summer, 1978, October, 1985, January, 1988.

Southern Review, winter, 1974, summer, 1975, fall, 1976, summer, 1979, winter, 1979.

Thought, summer, 1979.

Times Literary Supplement, February 19, 1960, June 11, 1976, October 6, 1978.

University of Windsor Review, spring, 1969.

Virginia Quarterly Review, spring, 1978, autumn, 1984, spring, 1988.

Washington Post, January 15, 1981, March 31, 1987, June 11, 1987.

Washington Post Book World, December 24, 1967, December 25, 1977, June 11, 1987, May 18, 1988.

Webster Review, spring, 1974, fall, 1980.

World Literature Today, summer, 1981, autumn, 1984, winter, 1986.

Yale Review, autumn, 1954, autumn, 1955, summer, 1961, summer, 1964, autumn, 1968, spring, 1976, summer, 1985.

OTHER

"One on One" (filmed interview), Kent State University Television Center, October 5, 1979.

* * *

NERUDA, Pablo 1904-1973

PERSONAL: Given name, Ricardo Eliezer Neftali Reyes y Basoalto; adopted the pseudonym Pablo Neruda at the age of 14, name legally changed, 1946; born July 12, 1904, in Parral, Chile; died September 23, 1973, of heart failure following an operation for cancer of the prostate, in Santiago, Chile; son of Jose del Carmen Reyes Morales (a railroad worker) and Rosa de Basoalto (a schoolteacher); married Maruca Hagenaar Vogelzang, 1930 (marriage ended); married Matilde Urrutia, 1951; children (first marriage): Malva Marina, a daughter (died, 1942). *Education:* Attended local schools at Temuco, Chile; attended Instituto Pedagogico (Santiago, Chile) in the early 1920s, and University of Chile, 1926. *Politics:* Communist (member of central committee of Chilean party).

ADDRESSES: Home—Marquez de la Plata 0192, Santiago, Chile; and Isle Negra, near Valparaiso, Chile.

CAREER: Went to Rangoon, Burma, as Chilean consul, 1927; consul in Colombo, Ceylon, 1929, Batavia, Java, 1930 (visiting China, Japan, and Indo-China); during the early 1930s he was consul in Buenos Aires, Siam, Cambodia, Anam, and Madrid; helped Spanish refugees in Paris, 1939; sent to Chilean Embassy, Mexico City, Mexico, 1939-41, consul, 1941-44; when he returned to Chile in 1945, he was elected to the Senate as a Communist; he wrote letters from 1947-49, charging President Gonzalez Videla with selling out to foreign investors and monopolists; threatened with arrest by the Chilean Supreme Court in 1948, he escaped to Mexico; also traveled in Italy, France, U.S.S.R., Red China; returned to Chile in 1953, after the victory of the anti-Videla forces; nominated for president on Chilean Communist Party ticket, 1970; Chilean ambassador to France, 1971-72. Came to New York for the PEN Congress, 1966. Member of World Peace Council, 1950-73.

MEMBER: Union de Escritores Chilenos (president, 1959-73), Modern Language Association of America (honorary fellow), International PEN.

AWARDS, HONORS: Third prize, provincial Juegos Florales competition, 1919, for "Communion ideal"; first prize for poetry in the Students' Federation spring festival, Instituto Pedagogico, 1921, for *La cancion de la fiesta;* honorary doctorate, University of Michoacan (Mexico), 1941; Premio Municipal de Literatura (Chile), 1944; Premio Nacional de Literatura (Chile), 1945; International Peace Prize, 1950; Lenin and Stalin Peace Prize, 1953; Litt.D., Oxford University, 1965; awarded Czechoslovakia's highest decoration, 1966; Nobel Prize in literature, 1971.

WRITINGS:

La cancion de la fiesta (poetry), Federacion de Estudiantes de Chile (Santiago), 1921.

Crepusculario (poetry), Nascimento (Santiago), 1923, 4th edition, Losada (Buenos Aires), 1971.

Viente poemas de amor y una cancion desesperada, Nascimento, 1924, definitive edition, 1932, 16th edition, Losada, 1972, translation by W. S. Merwin published as *Twenty Love Poems and a Song of Despair,* J. Cape, 1969.

El habitante y su esperanza (prose; also see below), Nascimento, 1925, 2nd edition, Ediciones Ercilla (Santiago), 1939.

(With Tomas Lago) *Anillos* (prose poems; also see below), Nascimento, 1926.

Tentativa del hombre infinito (poem; also see below), Nascimento, 1926, new edition, Editorial Orbe (Santiago), 1964.

Prosas de Pablo Neruda (prose), Nascimento, 1926.

El hondero entusiasta, 1923-1924 (poetry; also see below), Ediciones Ercilla, 1933, 3rd edition, 1938.

Residencia en la tierra (poetry and prose), Ediciones del Arbol (Madrid), Volume I (1925-31), 1933, Volume II (1931-35), 1935, published in one volume, Losada, 1944, 3rd edition, 1969.

Poesias de Yillamediana presentadas por Pablo Neruda, Cruz y Raya (Madrid), 1935.

Homenaje a Pablo Neruda de los poetas espanoles: Tres cantos materiales (poetry), Plutarco (Madrid), 1935, translation by Angel Flores published as *Tres cantos materiales: Three Material Songs,* East River Editions, 1948.

Sonetos de la muerte de Quevedo, presentados por Pablo Neruda, Cruz y Raya, 1935.

Espana en el corazon: Himno a las glorias del pueblo en la guerra (poetry; first printed by Spanish Republican soldiers on the battlefront; also see below), Ediciones Ercilla, 1937, 2nd edition, 1938.

Las furias y las penas (poetry), Nascimento, 1939.

(With Emilio Oribe and Juan Marinello) *Neruda entre nosotros* (prose), A.I.A.P.E. (Montevideo), 1939.

Homenaje a Garcia Lorca (prose), A.I.A.P.E., 1939.

Chile os acoge (prose), [Paris], 1939.

Un canto para Bolivar (poetry), Universidad Nacional Autonoma de Mexico, 1941.

(Contributor of poetry) *Presencia de Garcia Lorca,* Darro (Mexico), 1943.

Nuevo canto de amor a Stalingrado (poem), Comite de ayuda a Rusia en guerra (Mexico), 1943.

Canto general de Chile (poem), privately printed, 1943.

Cantos de Pablo Neruda (poetry), Hora del Hombre (Lima), 1943.

Cantico, La Gran Colombia (Bogota), 1943.

Pablo Neruda: Sus mejores versos, La Grand Colombia, 1943.

Saludo al norte y Stalingrado, privately printed, 1945.

Carta a Mexico, Fondo de Cultura Popular (Mexico), 1947.

Tercera residencia, 1935-1945 (poetry; includes *Espana en el corazon*), Losada, 1947, 5th edition, 1971.

Viajes al corazon de Quevedo y por las costas del mundo (prose), Sociedad de Escritores de Chile (Santiago), 1947.

28 de Enero, Partido Comunista de Chile, 1947.

Los heroes de carcon encarnan los ideales de democracia e independencia nacional, El Tranviario (Santiago), 1947.

La verdad sobre las ruputuras (prose), Principios (Santiago), 1947.

La crisis democratica de Chile, Hora del Hombre, 1947, translation published as *The Democratic Crisis of Chile,* Committee for Friendship in the Americas (New York), 1948.

Dura elegia, Cruz del Sur (Santiago), 1948.

Himno y regreso, Cruz del Sur, 1948.

¡Que despierte el lenador! (poetry), Coleccion Yagruma (Havana), 1948, translation published as *Peace for Twilights to Come!,* Jayant Bhatt for People's Publishing House (Bombay, India), 1950.

Alturas de Macchu-Picchu (poetry), Libreria Neira (Santiago), 1948, definitive edition, Nascimento, 1954, translation by Nathaniel Tarn published as *The Heights of Macchu Picchu,* J. Cape, 1966, Farrar, Straus, 1967.

Coral de ano nuevo para mi patria en tinieblas, privately printed, 1948.

Pablo Neruda acusa, Ediciones Pueblos Unidos (Montevideo), 1948.

Y ha llegado el monento en que debemos elegir, privately printed, 1949.

Gonzalez Videla, el Laval de America Latina: Breve biografia de un traidor, Fondo de Cultura Popular, 1949.

Dulce patria, Editorial del Pacifico (Santiago), 1949.

Neruda en Guatemala (prose), Saker-Ti (Guatemala), 1950.

Patria prisionera, Hora del Hombre, 1951.

A la memoria de Ricardo Fonseca, Amistad (Santiago), 1951.

Cuando de Chile, Austral (Santiago), 1952.

Poemas, Fundamentos (Buenos Aires), 1952.

Los versos del capitan: Poemas de amor (anonymously published until 3rd edition, 1963), privately printed in Naples, 1952, 7th edition, Losada, 1972, translation by Donald D. Walsh published as *The Captain's Verses,* New Directions, 1972.

Todo el amor (poetry), Nascimento, 1953.

En su muerte, Partido Comunista Argentino (Buenos Aires), 1953.

Poesia politica: Discursos politicos, two volumes, Austral, 1953.

Las uvas y el viento (poetry), Nascimento, 1954.

Odas elementales (first volume of "Elementary Odes"; also see below), Losada, 1954, 3rd edition, 1970.

Discurso inauguracion fundacion Pablo Neruda, Universidad de Chile (Santiago), 1954.

Alli murio la muerte, Ediciones del Centro de Amigos de Polonia (Santiago), 1954.

Regreso la sirena (poetry), Ediciones del Centro de Amigos de Polonia, 1954.

Viajes (prose), Nascimento, 1955.

Nuevas odas elementales (second volume of "Elementary Odes"; also see below), Losada, 1956, 3rd edition, 1971.

Oda a la tipografia (poetry), Nascimento, 1956.

Dos odas elementales, Losada, 1957.

Estravagario (poetry), Losada, 1958, 3rd edition, 1971, translation by Alastair Reid published as *Extravagaria,* J. Cape, 1972, Farrar, Straus, 1974.

Tercer libro de las odas (third volume of "Elementary Odes"), Losada, 1959.

Algunas odas (poetry), Edicion del 55 (Santiago), 1959.

Cien sonetos de amor (poetry), Losada, 1959, 6th edition, 1971, translation by Stephen J. Tapscott published as *100 Love Sonnets,* University of Texas Press, 1986.

Odas: Al libro, a las Americas, a la luz (poetry), Homenaje de la Asociacion de Escritores Venezolanos (Caracas, Venezuela), 1959.

Todo lleva tu nombre (poetry), Ministerio de Educacion (Caracas), 1959.

Navegaciones y regresos (poetry), Losada, 1959.

(With Federico Garcia Lorca) *Discurso al Alimon sobre Ruben Dario,* Semana Dariana (Nicaragua), 1959.

(With Pablo Picasso) *Toros: 15 lavis inedits,* Au Vent d'Arles (Paris), 1960.

Cancion de gesta (poetry), Imprenta Nacional de Cuba (Havana), 1960, 3rd edition, Siglo (Montevideo), 1968.

Oceana (poem), La Tertulia (Havana), 1960, 2nd edition, 1962.

Los primeros versos de amor (poetry), Austral, 1961.

Las piedras de Chile (poetry), Losada, 1961, translation by Dennis Maloney published as *The Stones of Chile,* White Pine, 1987.

Primer dia de La Sebastiana, privately printed, 1961.

Cantos ceremoniales (poetry), Losada, 1961, 2nd edition 1972.

Plenos poderes (poetry), Losada, 1962, 2nd edition, 1971, translation by Reid published as *Fully Empowered: Plenos poderes,* Farrar, Straus, 1975.

(With Mario Toral) *Poema con grabado* (poetry), Ediciones Isla Negra (Santiago), 1962.

La insepulta de Paita (poetry), Losada, 1962.

Con los catolicos hacia la paz, [Santiago], 1962, published as *Cuba: Los obispos,* Paz y Soberania (Lima), 1962.

(With Nicanor Parra) *Discursos: Pablo Neruda y Nicanor Parra* (prose), Nascimento, 1962.

Mensaje de paz y unidad, Internacionalismo proletario, [and] *El poeta de la revolucion* (addresses), Esclarecimiento (Lima), 1963.

(With Gustavo Hernan and Guillermo Atias) *Presencia de Ramon Lopez Velarde en Chile,* Universitaria (Santiago), 1963.

Memorial de Isla Negra (poetry), Volume 1: *Donde nace la lluvia,* Volume 2: *La luna en el laberinto,* Volume 3: *El fuego cruel,* Volume 4: *El cazador de raices,* Volume 5: *Sonata critica,* Losada, 1964, translation by Reid published as *Isla Negra: A Notebook,* bilingual edition, Farrar, Straus, 1980.

Arte de pajaros, Sociedad de Amigos del Arte Contemporaneo (Santiago), 1966, translation by Jack Schmitt published as *The Art of Birds,* University of Texas Press, 1985.

Una casa en la arena (poetry and prose), Lumen (Barcelona), 1966, 2nd edition, 1969.

La barcarola (poem), Losada, 1967.

Fulgor y muerte de Joaquin Murieta: Bandido chileno injusticiado en California el 23 de julio de 1853 (play), Zig-Zag (Santiago), 1967, translation by Ben Belitt published as *Splendor and Death of Joaquin Murieta,* Farrar, Straus, 1972.

(With Miguel Angel Asturias) *Comiendo en Hungria* (poetry and prose), 1968.

Las manos del dia (poetry), Losada, 1968, 2nd edition, 1970.

Aun: Poema, Nascimento, 1969.

Fin de mundo (poem), Losada, 1969.

La copa de sangre (poetry and prose), privately printed, 1969.

La espada encendida, Losada, 1970, 2nd edition, 1972.

Las piedras del cielo, Losada, 1970, translation by James Nolan published as *Stones of the Sky,* Copper Canyon, 1987.

Discurso pronunciado con ocasion de la entrega del premio Nobel de literatura, 1971, Centre de Recherches Hispaniques (Paris), 1972, translation published as *Toward the Splendid City: Nobel Lecture,* Farrar, Straus, 1974.

Cantos de amor y de combate (poetry), Austral, 1971.

Geografia infructuosa (poetry), Losada, 1972.

Cuatros poemas escritos en Francia, Nascimento, 1972.

Libro de las odas, Losada, 1972.

El mar y las campanas: Poemas, Losada, 1973, translation by William O'Daly published as *The Sea and the Bells,* Copper Canyon, 1988.

La rosa separada (poetry), Losada, 1973.

El corazon amarillo (poetry), Losada, 1974.

Elegia (poetry), Losada, 1974, published as *Elegia: Obra postuma,* Seix Barral, 1976.

Incitacion al Nixonicidio y alabanza de la revolucion chilena (poetry), Grijalbo (Barcelona), 1974, translation by Steve Kowit published as *Incitement to Nixonicide and Praise for the Chilean Revolution,* Quixote, 1974, 2nd edition, 1980.

Defectos escogidos (poetry), Losada, 1974.

Oda a la lagartija (poem), P. R. Martorell (Camp Rico de Canovanas), 1974.

El mal y el malo (twenty fragments from *Canto general*), P. Alcantara y V. Amaya, 1974.

Jardin de invierno, Losada, 1974, published as *Jardin de invierno: Obras postuma,* Seix Barral, 1977, translation by O'Daly published as *Winter Garden,* Copper Canyon, 1986.

Libro de las preguntas, Losada, 1974, published as *Libro de las preguntas,* Seix Barral, 1977.

Cartas de amor de Pablo Neruda (love correspondence), compiled by Sergio Lorrain, Ediciones Rodas (Madrid), 1974.

Confieso que he vivido: Memorias, Seix Barral (Barcelona), 1974, translation by Hardie St. Martin published as *Memoirs,* Farrar, Straus, 1977.

OMNIBUS VOLUMES

Seleccion (poetry), compiled by Arturo Aldunate, Nascimento, 1943.

Coleccion residencia en la tierra: Obra poetica, ten volumes, Cruz del Sur, 1947-48.

Canto general (poetry), Comite Auspiciador (Mexico), 1950, 5th edition in two volumes, Losada, 1971.

Poesias completas, Losada, 1951.

Los versos mas populares (poetry), Austral, 1954.

Los mejores versos de Pablo Neruda (poetry), [Buenos Aires], 1956.

Obras completas (complete works), Losada, 1957, 3rd updated edition in two volumes, 1968.

El habitante y su esperanza, El hondero entusiasta, Tentativa del hombre infinito, [and] *Anillos,* Losada, 1957, 4th edition, 1971.

Antologia, Nascimento, 1957, 4th enlarged edition, 1970.

The Selected Poems of Pablo Neruda, edited and translated by Belitt, Grove, 1961.

Antologia poetica, selected by Pablo Luis Avila, Gheroni (Torino, Italy), 1962.

Poesias, selected by Roberto Retamar, Casa de las Americas (Havana), 1965.

Antologia esencial, selected by Hernan Loyola, Losada, 1971.

Poemas immortales, selected by Jaime Concha, Quimantu (Santiago), 1971.

Obras escogidas (poetry), selected by Francisco Coloane, A. Bello (Santiago), 1972.

Antologia popular 1972, [Santiago], 1972.

Pablo Neruda (includes poems, Nobel prize acceptance speech, interview, and chronologies), Noroeste (Buenos Aires), 1973.

Poesia, two volumes, Noguer (Barcelona), 1974.

OTHER ENGLISH TRANSLATIONS

Selected Poems (from *Residencia en la tierra*), translated by Flores, privately printed, 1944.

Residence on Earth and Other Poems (includes "Residence on Earth I and II," "Spain in the Heart," "General Song of Chile," and "Recent Poems"), translated by Flores, New Directions, 1946.

Let the Splitter Awake and Other Poems (selected from *¡Que despierte el lenador!,* and *Canto general;* also see below), Masses & Mainstream, 1950.

Let the Rail-Splitter Awake (also see below), World Student News, 1951.

Twenty Love Poems; A Distaining Song, translated by W. S. Merwin, Grossman, 1961.

Elementary Odes (selections), translated by Carlos Lozano, G. Massa, 1961.

Residence on Earth (selections), translated by Clayton Eshleman, Amber House Press, 1962.

Bestiary/Bestiario: A Poem, translated by Elsa Neuberger, Harcourt, 1965.

Nocturnal Collection: A Poem, translated by Flores, [Madison, Wis.], 1966.

We Are Many (poem), translated by Reid, Cape Goliard Press, 1967, Grossman, 1968.

Twenty Poems (selected from *Residencia en la tierra, Canto general,* and *Odas elementales*) translated by James Wright and Robert Bly, Sixties Press, 1967.

A New Decade: Poems, 1958-1967, edited by Belitt, translated by Belitt and Reid, Grove, 1969.

Pablo Neruda: The Early Poems, translated by David Ossman and Carlos B. Hagen, New Rivers Press, 1969.

Selected Poems, edited by Nathaniel Tarn, translated by Anthony Kerrigan and others, J. Cape, 1970, Delacorte Press, 1972.

New Poems, 1968-1970, edited and translated by Belitt, Grove, 1972.

Residence on Earth (includes *Residencia en la tierra,* Volumes I and II, and *Tercera residencia*), translated by Donald D. Walsh, New Directions, 1973.

Five Decades: A Selection (Poems 1925-1970), edited and translated by Belitt, Grove, 1974.

Passions and Impressions, translated by Margaret S. Peden, Farrar, Straus, 1982.

Windows That Open Inward: Images of Chile, translated by Reid and others, White Pine, 1984.

Still Another Day, translated by O'Daly, Copper Canyon, 1984.

The House at Isla Negra, translated by Maloney and Clark Zlotchew, White Pine, 1988.

Let the Railsplitter Awake and Other Poems, translated by Waldeen, International Publishing, 1989.

Late and Posthumous Poems, 1968-1974, edited and translated by Belitt, Grove Press, 1989.

OTHER

(Translator into Spanish) William Blake, *Visiones de las hijas de Albion y el viajero mental,* Cruz y Raya, 1935.

(Translator into Spanish) William Shakespeare, *Romeo y Julieta,* Losada, 1964.

(Translator into Spanish) *Cuarenta y cuatro* (Rumanian poetry), Losada, 1967.

(Contributor) Robert Bly, compiler, *Neruda and Vallejo: Selected Poems,* translated by Bly and others, Beacon Press, 1971.

(Contributor) Walter Lowenfels, editor, *For Neruda, for Chile: An International Anthology,* Beacon Press, 1975.

(Contributor) Lloyd Mallan, editor, *Three Spanish American Poets: Pellicer, Neruda, Andrade,* translated by Mary Wicker, Gordon Press, 1977.

Also author of *Cartas de amor,* edited by Sergio Larrain, 1974, of *Cartas a Laura,* edited by Hugo Montes, 1978, of *Para nacer he nacido,* 1980, and, with Hector Eandi, of *Correspondencia,* edited by Margarita Aguirre, 1980; also author of *Poemas,* for Horizonte. Also editor and translator of *Paginas escogidas de Anatole France,* 1924. Contributor of poems and articles to numerous periodicals worldwide, including *Selva austral, Poetry,*

Nation, Commonweal, Canadian Forum, and *California Quarterly.* Work represented in many anthologies, including *Anthology of Contemporary Latin American Poetry,* edited by Dudley Fitts, New Directions, 1942; *Three Spanish American Poets: Pellicer, Neruda, and Andrade,* Sage Books, 1942; *Modern European Po-etry,* edited by Willis Barnstone, Bantam, 1966. Founder and editor with Manuel Altolaguirre of *El caballo verde para la poesia* (poetry periodical), six issues, 1935-36, and *Aurora de Chile,* 1938.

SIDELIGHTS: "No writer of world renown is perhaps so little known to North Americans as the Chilean poet Pablo Neruda," observed *New York Times Book Review* critic Selden Rodman in 1966. "Yet on a recent visit to New York he held a capacity audience enthralled at the Y.M.H.A.'s Poetry Center as he read—in Spanish—from his works. Only Dylan Thomas and Robert Frost (reading in English, of course) had evoked a similar state of euphoria or aroused the standing ovation that was accorded Neruda on that memorable night." Numerous critics consider Neruda the greatest poet writing in the Spanish language during his lifetime, although many readers in the United States find it difficult to disassociate his poetry from his fervent commitment to Communism. An added difficulty lies in the fact that Neruda's poetry is very hard to translate; the volume of his work available in English is small compared to his total output. Nonetheless, declared John Leonard in the *New York Times,* Neruda "was, I think, one of the great ones, a Whitman of the South."

Born Ricardo Eliezer Neftali Reyes y Basoalto, Neruda adopted the pseudonym under which he would become famous in his early teens. He grew up in the backwoods of southern Chile, in a frontier settlement called Temuco. The territory was harsh, a region where "vegetation covered a good part of the surroundings with thick foliage, and storms came from the sea," declared Salvadore Bizzarro in *Pablo Neruda: All Poets the Poet.* "Distant erupting volcanoes were a threat to the inhabitants. Outside of heavy rainfalls and frequent inundations, fires and earthquakes were the most feared calamities." Although his family, conditioned by the rugged atmosphere, did not themselves encourage Neruda's literary development, the budding writer received assistance from unexpected sources. Among his teachers "was the poet Gabriela Mistral, who would be a Nobel laureate years before Neruda," report Manuel Duran and Margery Safir in *Earth Tones: The Poetry of Pablo Neruda.* "It is almost inconceivable that two such gifted poets should find each other in such an unlikely spot. Mistral recognized the young Neftali's talent and encouraged it by giving the boy books and the support he lacked at home."

It was in this atmosphere and under this encouragement that Neruda composed his first poetry. By the time he finished high school, he had published in local papers and Santiago magazines, and had won several literary competitions. In 1921, he left southern Chile for Santiago to attend school, with the intention of becoming a French teacher. He was a rather indifferent student, however, and, as Duran and Safir explained, "love affairs, books, classes at the Instituto Pedagogico, daydreams, long hours spent looking at the sunset from his window on Maruri Street occupied most of his time. And writing." While in Santiago, Neruda completed one of his most critically acclaimed and original works, the cycle of love poems called *Viente poemas de amor y una cancion desesperada,* later published in English translation under the title *Twenty Love Poems and a Song of Despair*—a work that marked him as an important Chilean poet.

Viente poemas brought the author notoriety with its explicit celebration of sexuality, and, as Robert Clemens remarked in *Satur-*

day Review, "established him at the outset as a frank, sensuous spokesman for love." While other Latin American poets of the time used sexually explicit imagery, Neruda was the first to win popular acceptance for his presentation. Mixing memories of his love affairs with memories of the wilderness of southern Chile, he created a poetic sequence that not only describes a physical liaison, but also evokes the sense of displacement that Neruda felt in leaving the wilderness for the city. "Traditionally," stated Rene de Costa in *The Poetry of Pablo Neruda,* "love poetry has equated woman with nature. Neruda took this established mode of comparison and raised it to a cosmic level, making woman into a veritable force of the universe."

"In *20 poemas,*" reported David P. Gallagher in *Modern Latin American Literature,* "Neruda journeys across the sea symbolically in search of an ideal port. In 1927, he embarked on a real journey, when he sailed from Buenos Aires for Lisbon, ultimately bound for Rangoon where he had been appointed honorary Chilean consul." Duran and Safir explained that "Chile had a long tradition, like most Latin American countries, of sending her poets abroad as consuls or even, when they became famous, as ambassadors." Neruda was not really qualified for such a post, Duran and Safir assert; his spoken English (Rangoon was the capital of the British colony of Burma) was sparse and he had no real knowledge of a consul's business. Above all, he was unprepared for the squalor, poverty, and loneliness to which the position would expose him. "Neruda travelled extensively in the Far East over the next few years," Gallagher continued, "and it was during this period that he wrote his first really splendid book of poems, *Residencia en la tierra,* a book ultimately published in two parts, in 1933 and 1935." Neruda added a third part, *Tercera residencia,* in 1947.

Residencia en la tierra, published in English as *Residence on Earth,* is widely celebrated as containing "some of Neruda's most extraordinary and powerful poetry," according to de Costa. Born of the poet's feelings of alienation, the work reflects a world which is largely chaotic and senseless, and which—in the first two volumes—offers no hope of understanding. De Costa quoted the Spanish poet Garcia Lorca as calling Neruda "a poet closer to death than to philosophy, closer to pain than to insight, closer to blood than to ink. A poet filled with mysterious voices that fortunately he himself does not know how to decipher." With its emphasis on despair and the lack of adequate answers to mankind's problems, *Residencia en la tierra* in some ways foreshadowed the post-World War II philosophy of existentialism. "Neruda himself came to regard it very harshly," wrote Michael Wood in the *New York Review of Books.* "It helped people to die rather than to live, he said, and if he had the proper authority to do so he would ban it, and make sure it was never reprinted."

Residencia en la tierra also marked Neruda's emergence as an important international poet. By the time the second volume of the collection was published in 1935 the poet was serving as consul in Spain, where "for the first time," reported Duran and Safir, "he tasted international recognition, at the heart of the Spanish language and tradition. At the same time . . . poets like Rafael Alberti and Miguel Hernandez, who had become closely involved in radical politics and the Communist movement, helped politicize Neruda." When the Spanish Civil War broke out in 1936, Neruda was among the first to espouse the Republican cause with the poem *Espana en el corazon*—a gesture that cost him his consular post. He later served in France and Mexico, where his politics caused less anxiety.

Communism rescued Neruda from the despair he expressed in the first parts of *Residencia en la tierra,* and led to a change in his approach to poetry. He came to believe "that the work of art and the statement of thought—when these are responsible human actions, rooted in human need—are inseparable from historical and political context," reported Bizzarro. "He argued that there are books which are important at a certain moment in history, but once these books have resolved the problems they deal with they carry in them their own oblivion. Neruda felt that the belief that one could write solely for eternity was romantic posturing." This new attitude led the poet in new directions; for many years his work, both poetry and prose, advocated an active role in social change rather than simply describing his feelings, as his earlier oeuvre had done.

While some critics have felt that Neruda's devotion to Communist dogma was at times extreme—Leonard reported that "he drank Marxist slogans neat"—other have recognized the important impact his politics had on his poetry. Clayton Eshleman wrote in the introduction to Cesar Vallejo's *Poemas humanos/ Human Poems,* "Neruda found in the third book of *Residencia* the key to becoming *the* twentieth-century South American poet: the revolutionary stance which always changes with the tides of time." Gordon Brotherton, in *Latin American Poetry: Origins and Presence,* expanded on this idea, saying, "Neruda, so prolific, can be lax, a 'great bad poet' (to use the phrase Juan Ramon Jimenez used to revenge himself on Neruda). And his change of stance 'with the tides of time' may not always be be perfectly effected. But . . . his dramatic and rhetorical skills, better his ability to speak out of his circumstances, . . . was consummate. In his best poetry (of which there is much) he speaks on a scale and with an agility unrivalled in Latin America."

Neruda expanded on his political views in the poem *Canto general,* which, according to de Costa, is a "lengthy epic on man's struggle for justice in the New World." Although Neruda had begun the poem as early as 1935—when he had intended it to be limited in scope only to Chile—he completed some of the work while serving in the Chilean senate as a representative of the Communist Party. However, party leaders recognized that the poet needed time to work on his opus, and granted him a leave of absence in 1947. Later that year, however, Neruda returned to political activism, writing letters in support of striking workers and criticizing Chilean President Videla. Early in 1948 the Chilean Supreme Court issued an order for his arrest, and Neruda finished the *Canto General* while hiding from Videla's forces.

Although, as Bizzarro noted, "In [the *Canto General*], Neruda was to reflect some of the [Communist] party's basic ideological tenets," the work itself transcends propaganda. Looking back into American prehistory, the poet examined the land's rich natural heritage and described the long defeat of the native Americans by the Europeans. Instead of rehashing Marxist dogma, however, he concentrated on elements of people's lives common to all people at all times. Nancy Willard writes in *Testimony of the Invisible Man,* "Neruda makes it clear that our most intense experience of impermanence is not death but our own isolation among the living. . . . If Neruda is intolerant of despair, it is because he wants nothing to sully man's residence on earth." "In the *Canto,*" explained Duran and Safir, "Neruda reached his peak as a public poet. He produced an ideological work that largely transcended contemporary events and became an epic of an entire continent and its people."

In *Poetry,* James Wright summed up the *Canto*'s argument: "Appalled by loneliness I sought my human brothers among the living; I do not really object to their death, as long as I can share with them the human death; but everywhere I go among the living I find them dying each by each a small petty death in the midst of their precious brief lives. So I ascended to the ancient ruins of the city of Macchu Picchu in the Andes; and there I found that, however the lives of my human brothers may have suffered, at least they are all now dead together. . . . I love the poor broken dead. They belong to me. I will not celebrate the past for its perfect power over the imperfect living. 'I come to speak for your dead mouths.' The silent and nameless persons who built Macchu Picchu are alive in Santiago de Chile. The living are the living, and the dead the dead must stay."

Neruda returned to Chile from exile in 1953, and, said Duran and Safir, spent the last twenty years of his life producing "some of the finest love poetry in *One Hundred Love Sonnets* and parts of *Extravagaria* and *Barcarole;* he produced Nature poetry that continued the movement toward close examination, almost still shots of every aspect of the external world, in the odes of *Voyages and Homecomings,* in *The Stones of Chile,* in *The Art of Birds,* in *A House by the Shore,* and in *Sky Stones.* He continued as well his role as public poet in *Chanson de Geste,* in parts of *Ceremonial Songs,* in the mythical *The Flaming Sword,* and the angry *A Call for Nixonicide and Glory to the Chilean Revolution."*

However, at this time, Neruda's work began to move away from the highly political stance it had taken during the 1930s and toward a new type of poetry. Instead of concentrating on politicizing the common folk, Neruda began to try to speak to them simply and clearly, on a level that each could understand. He wrote poems on subjects ranging from rain to feet. By examining common, ordinary, everyday things very closely, according to Duran and Safir, Neruda gives us "time to examine a particular plant, a stone, a flower, a bird, an aspect of modern life, at leisure. We look at the object, handle it, turn it aroung, all the sides are examined with love, care, attention. This is, in many ways, Neruda . . . at his best."

In 1971, Neruda reached the peak of his political career when the Chilean Communist party nominated him for president. He withdrew his nomination, however, when he reached an accord with Socialist nominee Salvadore Allende. After Allende won the election he reactivated Neruda's diplomatic credentials, making him ambassador to France. It was while Neruda was serving in Paris that he was awarded the Nobel Prize for literature, in recognition of his oeuvre. Poor health soon forced the poet to resign his post, however, and he returned to Chile, where he died in 1973—only days after a right-wing military coup had killed Allende and seized power. Many of his last poems—some of them published posthumously—indicate his awareness of his death's approach. Fernando Alegria wrote in *Modern Poetry Studies,* "I think Neruda confronted the final enigma with total consciousness and solved it in terms of love and surrender to the materialistic dynamic of the world as he conceived it. What I want to emphasize is something very simple: Neruda was, above all, a love poet and, more than anyone, an unwavering, powerful, joyous, conqueror of death."

MEDIA ADAPTATIONS: Some of Neruda's work has been recorded, including "Pablo Neruda Reads His Poems in Spanish," Spoken Arts, 1972, Rafael de Penagos reading "Poesias escogidas," Discos Aguilar, 1972, and "Loretta Pauker Reads Extended Excerpts of 'Let the Rail Splitter Awake' [and] 'The Dead in the Square,' " Khalan Records, 1973. Neruda has also been recorded by the Library of Congress. Christopher Logue's twenty poems *The Man Who Told His Love* [Middle Scorpion Press, 1958] are based on some of Neruda's poetry and Rudolph

Holzmann's *Tres madrigales para canto y piano* [Editorial Argentina de Musica, 1946] sets Neruda's *Residencia en la tierra* to music.

AVOCATIONAL INTERESTS: Sailing.

BIOGRAPHICAL/CRITICAL SOURCES:

BOOKS

Benson, Rachel, translator, *Nine Latin American Poets,* Las Americas, 1968.

Bizzarro, Salvatore, *Pablo Neruda: All Poets the Poet,* Scarecrow Press, 1979.

Brotherton, Gordon, *Latin American Poetry: Origins and Presence,* Cambridge University Press, 1975.

Burnshaw, Stanley, editor, *The Poem Itself,* Holt, 1960.

Contemporary Literary Criticism, Gale, Volume 1, 1973, Volume 2, 1974, Volume 5, 1976, Volume 7, 1977, Volume 9, 1978, Volume 28, 1984.

de Costa, Rene, *The Poetry of Pablo Neruda,* Harvard University Press, 1979.

Duran, Manuel, and Margery Safir, *Earth Tones: The Poetry of Pablo Neruda,* Indiana University Press, 1981.

Eshleman, Clayton, translator and author of introduction, *Poemas humanos/Human Poems,* Grove Press, 1969.

Gallagher, David P., *Modern Latin American Literature,* Oxford University Press, 1973.

Garcia Lorca, Federico, *Obras completas,* Aguilar, 1964.

Neruda, Pablo, *Confieso que he vivido: memorias,* Seix Barral (Barcelona), 1974, translation by Hardie St. Martin published as *Memoirs,* Farrar, Straus, 1977.

Reiss, Frank, *The Word and the Stone: Language and Imagery in Neruda's "Canto General,"* Oxford University Press, 1972.

Willard, Nancy, *Testimony of the Invisible Man: William Carlos Williams, Francis Ponge, Rainer Maria Rilke, Pablo Neruda,* University of Missouri Press, 1970.

Woodbridge, Hensley C., and David S. Zubatsky, compilers, *Pablo Neruda: An Annotated Bibliography of Biographical and Critical Studies,* Garland, 1988.

PERIODICALS

Book Week, May 28, 1967.
Books, June, 1966.
Encounter, September, 1965.
Evergreen Review, December, 1966.
Modern Poetry Studies, spring, 1974.
Nation, July 1, 1966.
New Leader, July 3, 1967.
New Statesman, June 4, 1965.
New York Review of Books, October 3, 1974.
New York Times, June 18, 1966, August 1, 1966, March 4, 1977.
New York Times Book Review, July 10, 1966, May 21, 1967.
Poetry, June, 1947, February, 1963, October, 1967, June, 1968.
Ramparts, September, 1974.
Saturday Review, July 9, 1966, November 13, 1971.

—*Sketch by Kenneth R. Shepherd*

*   *   *

NEWBY, P(ercy) H(oward) 1918-

PERSONAL: Born June 25, 1918, in Crowborough, Sussex, England; son of Percy and Isabel Clutson (Bryant) Newby; married Joan Thompson, 1945; children: Sarah Jane, Katharine Charlotte. *Education:* Attended St. Paul's College, Cheltenham, England, 1936-38.

ADDRESSES: Home—Garsington House, Garsington, Oxford OX9 9AB, England. *Agent*—David Higham Associates, 5-8 Lower John St., London W1R 4HA, England.

CAREER: Fouad I University, Cairo, Egypt, lecturer in English literature, 1942-46; free-lance novelist, 1946-49; British Broadcasting Corp., London, England, producer in Talks Department, 1949-58, chief of Third Programme (now Radio Three), 1958-71, director of programs, 1971-75, managing director of radio, 1975-78. Chairman, English Stage Company, 1978-85. *Military service:* British Army, Royal Army Medical Corps, 1939-42; served in France and Egypt.

MEMBER: Society of Authors, Royal Society of Literature (fellow).

AWARDS, HONORS: Atlantic Award, Rockefeller Foundation, 1946; Somerset Maugham Prize, 1948, for *A Journey to the Interior;* Smith-Mundt fellowship, 1952; Yorkshire Post Fiction Award, 1968; Booker Prize, 1969, for *Something to Answer For;* Commander of the Order of the British Empire, 1972.

WRITINGS:

NOVELS

A Journey to the Interior, J. Cape, 1945, Doubleday, 1946.
Spirit of Jem (juvenile), illustrated by Keith Vaughan, foreword by Maia Wojciechowska, Lehmann, 1947, Delacorte, 1967.
Agents and Witnesses, Doubleday, 1947.
Mariner Dances, J. Cape, 1948.
Snow Pasture, J. Cape, 1949.
The Loot Runners (juvenile), Lehman, 1949, Macdonald, 1951.
The Young May Moon, J. Cape, 1950, Knopf, 1951.
A Season in England, J. Cape, 1951, Knopf, 1952.
A Step to Silence, J. Cape, 1952.
The Retreat, Knopf, 1953.
The Picnic at Sakkara, Knopf, 1955.
Revolution and Roses, Knopf, 1957.
A Guest and His Going, J. Cape, 1959.
The Barbary Light, Faber, 1962, Lippincott, 1964.
One of the Founders, Lippincott, 1965, new edition, Chivers, 1987.
Something to Answer For, Faber, 1968, Lippincott, 1969.
A Lot to Ask, Faber, 1973.
Kith, Little, Brown, 1977.
Feelings Have Changed, Faber, 1981.
Leaning in the Wind, Faber, 1986, Beaufort Books, 1987.

OTHER

(Author of introduction) A. W. Kinglake, *Eothen,* Lehmann, 1948.
Maria Edgeworth (criticism), A. Swallow, 1950, reprinted, Norwood, 1975.
The Novel, 1945-50, Longmans, Green, for British Council, 1951, reprinted, Richard West, 1978.
(Editor) *A Plain and Literal Translation of the Arabian Knight's Entertainments, Now Entitled "The Book of the Thousand and One Knights,"* translated by Richard Francis Burton, illustrated by W. M. Cuthill, Arthur Barker, 1950, published as *Tales from the Arabian Knights,* Pocket Books, c. 1951, reprinted, Washington Square, 1967.
Ten Miles from Anywhere, and Other Stories, J. Cape, 1958.
The Egypt Story: Its Art, Its Monuments, Its People, Its History, photographs by Fred Maroon, Abbeville Press, 1979.

The Warrior Pharaohs: The Rise and Fall of the Egyptian Empire, Faber, 1980.
Saladin in His Times (biography), Faber, 1983.

Former book reviewer for *Listener* and *New Statesman and Nation.*

SIDELIGHTS: When P. H. Newby first won the Booker Prize in 1969 for *Something to Answer For,* it was somewhat of a surprise to the critical community, which expected either Muriel Spark or Iris Murdoch to be awarded Britain's most remunerative literary prize. Newby had already written over a dozen novels at that time, and had been awarded the Atlantic Award in 1946 and the Somerset Maugham Prize in 1948 for his first novel, *A Journey to the Interior;* yet he was then, as he is now, a relatively unknown author. As Stanley Poss explains in *Critique: Studies in Modern Fiction,* "Newby has had neither a popular nor a critical success . . . because he puzzles the expectations of both camps. Enigmatic to the layman, 'traditional' (in his reliance on tangled plots) to the expert, he is truly, as a 1962 [*Times Literary Supplement*] article has it, a 'Novelist On His Own.' " Nevertheless, the author has become one of the most respected writers of his generation. In a *Dictionary of Literary Biography* article, E. C. Bufkin calls Newby "one of the most distinguished of the English novelists who began their careers immediately following World War II. . . . His sizeable body of work is notable for seriousness of themes, mastery of fictional techniques, and a style which—at once precise and suggestive, graceful and powerful—is capable of the subtlest as well as the broadest effects."

A thirty-year veteran producer and director for the British Broadcasting Corp., Newby calls himself a "weekend novelist," according to one *New York Times Book Review* writer; yet he has still managed to produce a steady stream of publications, most of which were written during the 1950s and 1960s. "[But] there is no link between the BBC and my writing really," the novelist tells Bolivar Le Franc in a *Books and Bookmen* interview. What did have a profound influence on Newby's writing was his four-year stay at Fouad I University in Cairo, Egypt, as a lecturer in English literature during World War II. "The central experience in my life was living in Egypt," Newby told *CA,* "where looking at the world through non-European and non-Christian eyes, my imagination was stimulated in a way it would not have been if I had remained in England." Although he has composed several novels that involve only English subjects, Newby reveals to Le Franc: "It's only when I detach myself from the British scene and in some way bring my Middle East experience into the novel I really think the thing comes alive."

From his first novel, *A Journey to the Interior,* to his more recent *Leaning in the Wind,* Newby has repeatedly returned to the subject of the Third World, its people, and its customs. In addition to his novels, he has written three nonfiction works about Egypt and the Middle East: *The Egypt Story: Its Art, Its Monuments, Its People, Its History, The Warrior Pharaohs: The Rise and Fall of the Egyptian Empire,* and *Saladin in His Time,* a biography about the Crusades-period Moslem leader. Newby's novels deal with the themes of appearance versus reality, misunderstanding and reconciliation, and the relationship between knowledge and innocence. Within these themes is the central idea in the author's work that "we never fully understand either our own behavior or that of other people," says G. S. Fraser in his *P. H. Newby.* Fraser concludes that the novelist's portrayal of this idea "is one of Newby's greatest gifts."

Several critics have divided Newby's fiction into different categories. Fraser classifies them as "early romanticism, comedy, and compassionate realism," while Poss distinguishes only two groups: "political comedies" and "romances." Both Fraser and Poss, however, consider the novelist's earlier works to be romances. The first of these books, *A Journey to the Interior,* is set in a fictional Middle East sultanate. Roger Winter, the recently widowed protagonist, travels to an Arabian country ostensibly to recover from typhoid. Actually, he is going on "a quest for health and life on both the physical and spiritual planes," writes Bufkin. While there, Winter falls in love with a woman named Nellie, who reminds him of his wife. The other half of the novel involves Winter's quest to find two men who have disappeared in the desert. Although the fate of these men remains a mystery by the end of the book, Winter's experiences while searching for them help him to understand himself and accept Nellie for who she is, rather than as a mere reflection of his dead wife.

"The qualities that P. H. Newby demonstrates in his first novel . . . ," asserts Frederick R. Karl in his 1962 book, *A Reader's Guide to the Contemporary English Novel,* "are characteristic of all his serious fiction: the discovery of a man's self through a journey or quest." Earlier novels by Newby also demonstrate what Fraser calls a "hallucinatory vividness," and, according to Poss, reveal the author's interest in the "myth-making part of writing." The central theme of several of these books, *Mariner Dances, The Snow Pasture,* and *The Young May Moon,* is concerned with the alienation and reconciliation between people. In Fraser's view, these works have several redeeming features, such as the "delicacy of natural description" in *The Snow Pasture,* and Newby's "surer hand . . . [in] getting inside a boy's mind" in *The Young May Moon;* but some reviewers like Karl believe they "lack vitality and intensity."

With *A Season in England,* Newby once again explores the theme of self-knowledge, and several reviewers have compared it to *A Journey to the Interior* because of this similarity. One difference, however, is that the protagonist, Tom Passmore, journeys from Egypt to England, rather than the other way around. Poss also notes that the tone of *A Season in England* "suggests that Newby's earlier beliefs in the possibilities of renewal of the psyche have diminished somewhat, or at least . . . he has come to believe that these possibilities do not always assert themselves in so splendid, perhaps even theatrical, a manner as in *A Journey to the Interior.*" *A Season in England* and the two novels that followed, *A Step to Silence* and *The Retreat,* "mark, though not dramatically, a steady progress in Newby's art," Fraser avers. "They handle tense and unpredictable situations with a new assurance."

Actually two parts of the same work, *A Step to Silence* and *The Retreat* contain a "darkness and exhaustion, madness and humorlessness not found elsewhere in the Newby canon," according to Bufkin. They also "display a firmer sense of moral pattern than Newby had so far achieved" at that time, says Fraser. Using the backdrop of the chaotic years before and during World War II, Newby presents a story of an equally chaotic relationship between an Englishman named Oliver Knight, his irrational Egyptian friend, Hesketh, and the two women they love. *The Retreat* ends tragically with the death of Hesketh's wife. Because Knight was alone with her when she died, Hesketh decides to write a letter confessing to the "murder" so that his friend would not be blamed; and he then commits suicide. Although the death of Hesketh's wife was due to natural causes, Knight decides to let himself be arrested for her murder. Together, writes Fraser, these two books present a recurring riddle in Newby's books in which "the madman protect[s] the almost excessively sane man and . . . the sane man . . . insist[s] on taking his own punishment."

After *The Retreat,* Newby's novels return to a lighter vein, though their subjects are still serious in nature. As Poss explains, the political comedies that followed *The Retreat* "turn on the 'Forsterian' question of how far can you go in getting to know a people whose class, race, religion, or whatever differ radically from your own." Other critics have noticed this influence as well, and Newby acknowledges this in his *Books and Bookmen* interview. "[The Picnic at Sakkara] owed a great deal to [E. M.] Forster's *A Passage to India,*" the novelist tells Le Franc. "Indeed," Newby continues, "Forster's attitude to the East is something I suppose has made a deep impression on me." However, one trait of Newby's work that distinguishes him from Forster is his use of humor when describing the clashes between cultures. It is a "sympathetic" type of comedy, though, says Fraser, who notes that Newby "is temperamentally incapable of writing corrective comedy, or satire."

The Picnic at Sakkara, Revolution and Roses, and *A Guest and His Going* comprise a trilogy that critics like Bufkin consider to demonstrate some of "Newby's best work, and most endearing." Setting these books during the last years of Farouk I's reign in Egypt, the Nasser revolution, and the Suez Canal crisis, the author brings together English and Egyptian characters to illuminate the differences in cultures. The two most prominent people in this trilogy, English professor Edgar Perry and his student, Muawiya Khaslat, are central to the first and third books, while *Revolution and Roses* focuses on the relationship between an English journalist and the Egyptian nationalist who courts her. Several critics feel, as Fraser does, that this second volume "is a much slighter work" than the other books in the trilogy. *The Picnic at Sakkara,* however, "is a masterly mixture generously flavored with irony," according to Bufkin, while V. S. Naipaul remarks in a *New Statesman* review that Newby "is wonderfully and intelligently inventive" in *A Guest and His Going.*

Contrasting the comical character of Muawiya, who is reminiscent of Hesketh in *A Step to Silence* and *The Retreat,* with the naive and high-principled Perry, Newby illustrates a fundamental difference in philosophy between East and West. Westerners tend to believe that the universe is unknowable, asserts the novelist, and, therefore, in an attempt to make sense of the world, they invent "little illusions of order," as *Twentieth Century Literature* contributor Francis X. Mathews phrases it. Mathews continues: "The Oriental, on the other hand, thinks he knows [about the world]. . . . His fantasy, which Newby terms 'the supreme Oriental luxury,' is founded on an instinctive acceptance of the improbable and the contradictory." With these contradictory views embodied in his characters, Newby adds a background set in a politically turbulent time to produce a "comic conflict between a fantastic society and fantastic individuals," says Mathews. "But beneath the laughter," the reviewer later adds, "is the same serious theme of the failure to connect," both on the personal and international level. *A Guest and His Going* ends with Perry's ultimate failure to communicate with Muawiya. But despite this defeat, Mathews concludes that "he has at least come to recognize his illusions for what they are."

Something to Answer For, also a political novel that deals with the theme of illusions, has "something of the vivid colour, violence, and mysteriousness of Newby's first two novels," reflects Fraser. A number of critics consider *Something to Answer For* to be the novelist's finest work to date. *New Yorker* contributor Wilfred Sheed calls the book "a first-rate novel about a major political subject." And a *Time* reviewer asserts: "*Something to Answer For* finds Newby at his often brilliant but racking best. If the reader does not mind getting his lumps, he will also come in for a fair share of illumination."

Something to Answer For is set in Egypt during the 1956 Suez Canal crisis. Jack Townrow is a small-time crook who has come to Port Said from Britain in order to take advantage of a widow who has recently received an inheritance. Being English, Townrow is a character who assumes, "as many English people do," according to Newby in a quote from Bufkin's essay, "that by and large the society he lives in is governed by good forces—forces that are operating wisely and well." But the struggle for control of the Suez Canal between the Egyptians, British, and French forces Townrow to realize that he is no more corrupt than his government. This, in turn, convinces him to reconsider his own conduct, and as a result he redefines his sense of morals.

Some critics, like *London Magazine* writer Michael Wilding, find this change of heart "a little unconvincing." Wilding believes that "a certain schematization of the moral positions ultimately limits *Something to Answer For.*" But Sheed feels that the juxtaposition between Townrow's conscience and the political issues at hand is well conceived. "This marshalling of all the resources of the human psyche to produce a universal historical consciousness is an enterprise worthy of Joyce," the reviewer observes. the skill with which the novelist combines issues in the political world with the problems of private morality prompts Bufkin to declare that *Something to Answer For* is "Newby's masterpiece: the richest in conception, the widest in scope, the most technically innovative, and the most assured of his novels."

With the exception of *Something to Answer For* and *A Lot to Ask,* a novel which, according to D. J. Enright in *Listener* "reads like a relatively austere replay" of its predecessor, most of Newby's more recent novels have a more comical tone reminiscent of *The Picnic at Sakkara.* Indeed, *One of the Founders* is "pure farce," attests Fraser. But Newby's other novels written after the 1960s are familiar combinations of serious themes with humorous overtones. For example, *Kith,* the story of a young man who falls in love with his uncle's beautiful Egyptian wife, is a "wise, sad, and very funny novel," according to *New York Times Book Review* contributor Sheldon Frank, who also calls the book "hilariously bleak."

Similarly, *Feelings Have Changed* is described in a *Times Literary Supplement* article by Alan Brownjohn as "a novel which is as carefully woven as it is mordantly witty." In this book, Newby ambitiously addresses the question of the meaning of life in, as *Spectator* contributor James Lasdun phrases it, "an elaborate pattern of coincidences involving [a] radio play, a priest, the two central couples, and the temples at Abu Sinbel in Egypt, with the purpose of showing that there is a rightness in the disposition in life, despite all its hardships." Although this blend of elements makes for an "absorbing book," as London *Times* critic Andrew Sinclair labels it, some critics feel that *Feelings Have Changed* is somewhat flawed. Lasdun, for example, asserts that there "is a certain lack of continuity between the very ordinary characters and the very extraordinary moral vision they are made to illuminate."

Leaning in the Wind has also received mixed reviews from critics. Some reviewers have complained that this novel, involving forgery, adultery, and 1970s African politics, has an unfocused plot. "It meanders without apparent purpose through a series of coincidences," claims *Times* contributor Isabel Raphael. In a completely contradictory *Library Journal* review, however, Bryan Aubrey holds that *Leaning in the Wind* has a "skillfully handled, highly ingenious plot." Furthermore, a *Publishers Weekly* writer concludes that the novel is "a story of fundamental human relationships, rendered with humor, sympathy, and feeling."

In taking all of the novelist's fictional works into consideration, Fraser concludes: "The final picture of life that emerges . . . from Newby's novels is that of life as rich, funny, but terrifyingly uncertain." It is this view of life which takes precedence over any other message, political or otherwise, in the author's writing. As Newby explains to Le Franc, "We're terribly vulnerable, weak animals in a cold and hostile universe. I mean, this is my view of life. Life is precarious. Life is hell and this is much more fundamental about a man than any thought about the particular social status he might happen to occupy." But despite life's seriousness, there is still room for levity. "Ever since *Picnic at Sakkara,*" Newby told *CA,* "I have tried to handle potentially tragic material in a light, even comic way. I have been called bleak by some who think they are paying me a compliment. I do not feel all that bleak; I am just trying to be realistic about the sometimes comfortless world we live in, and doing so, I hope, with charity."

BIOGRAPHICAL/CRITICAL SOURCES:

BOOKS

Bufkin, E. C., *P. H. Newby,* Twayne, 1975.
Contemporary Literary Criticism, Gale, Volume 2, 1974, Volume 13, 1980.
Dictionary of Literary Biography, Volume 15: *British Novelists, 1930-1959,* Gale, 1983.
Fraser, G. S., *P. H. Newby,* Longman, 1974.
Karl, Frederick R., *A Reader's Guide to the Contemporary English Novel,* Farrar, Straus, 1962.
T.L.S. 1962: Essays and Reviews from The Times Literary Supplement, Oxford University Press, 1963.

PERIODICALS

Best Sellers, April 15, 1969.
Books and Bookmen, January, 1969, June, 1969, July, 1969.
Book Week, July 2, 1967.
Book World, June 29, 1969.
British Book News, January, 1987.
Christian Science Monitor, August 3, 1967, June 5, 1969.
Critique: Studies in Modern Fiction, Volume 8, number 1, 1965, Volume 12, number 1, 1970.
Globe and Mail (Toronto), April 18, 1987.
Kirkus Reviews, February 1, 1988.
Library Journal, March 15, 1988.
Listener, November 14, 1968, May 3, 1973, September 25, 1980.
London Magazine, December, 1965, February, 1969.
London Review of Books, April 18, 1985.
Nation, April 28, 1969.
New Statesman, June 20, 1959, April 25, 1969.
Newsweek, August 15, 1977.
New Yorker, September 6, 1969.
New York Review of Books, June 5, 1969.
New York Times, April 19, 1953, August 10, 1977.
New York Times Book Review, April 19, 1953, May 11, 1969, August 7, 1977, August 26, 1984.
Observer, November 2, 1986.
Publishers Weekly, January 22, 1988.
Spectator, November 15, 1968, November 7, 1981, January 7, 1984.
Texas Studies in Literature and Language, spring, 1970.
Time, April 18, 1969.
Times (London), October 8, 1981, November 6, 1986.
Times Literary Supplement, April 6, 1962, December 4, 1969, May 11, 1973, April 8, 1977, October 9, 1981, March 9, 1984, December 12, 1986.
Twentieth Century Literature, April, 1968.

Wilson Library Bulletin, March, 1953.

—*Sketch by Kevin S. Hile*

*   *   *

NGUGI, James T(hiong'o)
See NGUGI wa Thiong'o

*   *   *

NGUGI wa Thiong'o   1938-
(James T[hiong'o] Ngugi)

PERSONAL: Original name, James Thiong'o Ngugi; born January 5, 1938, in Limuru, Kenya; married; children: five. *Education:* Makerere University, B.A., 1963; University of Leeds, B.A., 1964.

ADDRESSES: c/o William Heinemann Ltd., 15 Queen St., London W1X 8BE, England.

CAREER: Teacher in East African schools, 1964-70; University of Nairobi, Kenya, lecturer in English literature, 1967-69, later became senior lecturer and chairman of literature department. Creative writing fellow, Makerere University, 1969-70. Visiting lecturer, Northwestern University, 1970-71.

AWARDS, HONORS: Recipient of awards from the 1965 Dakar Festival of Negro Arts and the East African Literature Bureau, both for *Weep Not, Child.*

WRITINGS:

Homecoming: Essays on African and Caribbean Literature, Culture, and Politics, Heinemann, 1972, Lawrence Hill 1973.
Secret Lives, and Other Stories, Heinemann Educational, 1974, Lawrence Hill, 1975.
Petals of Blood (novel), Heinemann Educational, 1977.
(With Micere Githae Mugo) *The Trial of Dedan Kimathi,* Heinemann Educational, 1977, Swahili translation by the authors published as *Mzalendo kimathi,* c. 1978.
Mtawa Mweusi, Heinemann, 1978.
Caitaani mutharaba-ini, Heinemann Educational, 1980, translation by the author published as *Devil on the Cross,* Zimbabwe Publishing, 1983.
Writers in Politics: Essays, Heinemann, 1981.
Detained: A Writer's Prison Diary, Heinemann, 1981.
Njamba Nene na mbaathi i mathagu (juvenile) Heinemann Educational, 1982.
(Co-author and translator with Ngugi wa Mirii) *I Will Marry When I Want* (play), Heinemann, 1982.
Barrel of a Pen: Resistance to Repression in Neo-Colonial Kenya, New Beacon, 1983.
Decolonising the Mind: The Politics of Language in African Literature, Heinemann, 1986.
Njamba Nene and the Flying Bus (juvenile), translation by Waugui wa Goro, Africa World, 1989.
Njamba Nene's Pistol (juvenile), translation by Waugui, Africa World, 1989.
Matigari, translation by Waugui, Heinemann, 1989.

UNDER NAME JAMES T. NGUGI

The Black Hermit (play; first produced in Nairobi in 1962), Mekerere University Press, 1963, Humanities, 1968.
Weep Not, Child (novel), introduction and notes by Ime Ikeddeh, Heinemann, 1964, P. Collier, 1969.
The River Between (novel), Humanities, 1965.
A Grain of Wheat (novel), Heinemann, 1967, 2nd edition, Humanities, 1968.

This Time Tomorrow (play; includes "The Reels" and "The Wound in the Heart"; produced and broadcast in 1966), East African Literature Bureau, 1970.

CONTRIBUTOR TO ANTHOLOGIES

E. A. Komey and Ezekiel Mphahlele, editors, *Modern African Short Stories,* Faber, 1964.
W. H. Whiteley, editor, *A Selection of African Prose,* Oxford University Press, 1964.
Neville Denny, editor, *Pan African Short Stories,* Nelson, 1965.
Oscar Ronald Dathorne and Willfried Feuser, editors, *Africa in Prose,* Penguin, 1969.

OTHER

Contributor of stories to *Transition* and *Kenya Weekly News.* Editor of *Zuka* and *Sunday Nation* (Nairobi).

SIDELIGHTS: Novelist, dramatist, essayist, and literary critic Ngugi wa Thiong'o is East Africa's most prominent writer. Known to many simply as Ngugi, he has been described by Shatto Arthur Gakwandi in *The Novel and Contemporary Experience in Africa* as a "novelist of the people," for his works show his concern for the inhabitants of his native country, Kenya, who have been oppressed and exploited by colonialism, Christianity, and in recent years, by black politicians and businessmen. As *Africa Today* contributor D. Salituma Wamalwa observes: "Ngugi's approach to literature is one firmly rooted in the historical experience of the writer and his or her people, in an understanding of society as it is and a vision of society as it might be."

Throughout his career as a writer and professor, Ngugi has worked to free himself and his compatriots from the effects of colonialism, Christianity, and other non-African influences. In the late 1960s, for example, Ngugi and several colleagues at the University of Nairobi successfully convinced school officials to transform the English Department into the Department of African Languages and Literature. Shortly thereafter Ngugi renounced his Christian name, James, citing Christianity's ties to colonialism. He took in its place his name in Gikuyu (or Kikuyu), the dominant language of Kenya. Ngugi strengthened his commitment to the Kenyan culture in 1977, when he declared his intention to write only in Gikuyu or Swahili, not English. In response to a query posed in an interview for *Journal of Commonwealth Literature* concerning this decision, Ngugi stated: "Language is a carrier of a people's culture, culture is a carrier of a people's values; values are the basis of a people's self-definition—the basis of their consciousness. And when you destroy a people's language, you are destroying that very important aspect of their heritage . . . you are in fact destroying that which helps them to define themselves . . . that which embodies their collective memory as a people."

Ngugi's determination to write in Gikuyu, combined with his outspoken criticisms of both British and Kenyan rule, have posed threats to his security. In 1977 Ngugi's home was searched by Kenyan police, who confiscated nearly one hundred books then arrested and imprisoned Ngugi without a trial. At the time of his arrest, Ngugi's play Ngaahika Ndena ("I Will Marry When I Want"), co-authored with Ngugi wa Mirii, had recently been banned on the grounds of being "too provocative," according to *American Book Review* contributor Henry Indangasi; in addition, his novel *Petals of Blood,* a searing indictment of the Kenyan government, had just been published in England. Although Ngugi was released from prison a year later, his imprisonment cost him his professorship at the University of Nairobi. When his theatre group was banned by Kenyan officials in 1982,

Ngugi, fearing further reprisals, left his country for a self-imposed exile in London.

Ngugi chronicles his prison experience in *Detained: A Writer's Prison Diary,* and expresses his political views in other nonfiction works such as *Barrel of a Pen: Resistance to Repression in Neo-Colonial Kenya.* He has received the most critical attention, however, for his fiction, particularly his novels. Ngugi's first novel *Weep Not, Child* deals with the Mau Mau rebellion against the British administration in the 1950s, and his third novel *A Grain of Wheat* concerns the aftermath of the war and its effects on Kenya's people. Although critics describe the first novel as somewhat stylistically immature, many comment favorably on the universality of its theme of the reactions of people to the stresses and horrors of war and to the inevitable changes brought to bear on their lives.

In contrast, several reviewers believe that *A Grain of Wheat* fulfills the promise of Ngugi's first novel. *A Grain of Wheat* portrays four characters who reflect upon the events of the Mau Mau rebellion and its consequences as they await the day of Kenyan independence, December 12, 1963. G. D. Killam explains in his book *An Introduction to the Writings of Ngugi:* "Uhuru Day, the day when independence from the colonial power is achieved, has been the dream of each of these figures from their schooldays. But there is little joyousness in their lives as they recall over the four days their experiences of the war and its aftermath."

In their book *Ngugi wa Thiong'o: An Exploration of His Writings,* David Cook and Michael Okenimkpe praise the "almost perfectly controlled form and texture" of *A Grain of Wheat.* Killam comments: "A Grain of Wheat is the work of a writer more mature than when he wrote his first two books. . . . In *A Grain of Wheat* [Ngugi] takes us into the minds of his characters, sensibilities resonant with ambiguities and contradictions, and causes us to feel what they feel, to share in significant measure their hopes and fears and pain." Shatto Arthur Gakwandi similarly observes in *The Novel and Contemporary Experience in Africa:* "The general tone of *A Grain of Wheat* is one of bitterness and anger. The painful memories of Mau Mau violence still overhang the Kikuyu villages as the attainment of independence fails to bring the cherished social dreams." Gakwandi adds: "While the novel speaks against the harshness of colonial oppression, it is equally bitter against the new leaders of Kenya who are neglecting the interests of the peasant masses who were the people who made the greatest sacrifices during the war of liberation. Ngugi speaks on behalf of those who, in his view, have been neglected by the new government."

Petals of Blood, Ngugi's fourth novel, is considered his most ambitious and representative work. Like *A Grain of Wheat, Petals of Blood* describes the disillusionment of the common people in post-independence Kenya. Killam notes, however, that in *Petals of Blood* Ngugi "widens and deepens his treatment of themes which he has narrated and dramatized before—themes related to education, both formal and informal; religion, both Christian and customary; the alienation of the land viewed from the historical point of view and as a process which continues in the present; the struggle for independence and the price paid to achieve it." *Petals of Blood* is also described as Ngugi's most overtly political novel. A *West Africa* contributor notes an ideological shift in the novel "from the earlier emphasis on nationalism and race questions to a class analysis of society." Critics cite in particular the influence of both Karl Marx and Frantz Fanon, the latter of whom, according to Killam, "places the thinking of Marx in the African context." In *World Literature Written in English*

Govind Narian Sharma comments: "Whereas traditional religious and moral thought has attributed exploitation and injustice in the world to human wickedness and folly, Ngugi, analyzing the situation in Marxist terms, explains these as 'the effect of laws of social development which make it inevitable that at a certain stage of history one class, pursuing its interests with varying degrees of rationality, should dispossess and exploit another.' "

Petals of Blood concerns four principle characters, all being held on suspicion of murder: Karega, a teacher and labor organizer; Munira, headmaster of a public school in the town of Ilmorog; Abdulla, a half-Indian shopkeeper who was once a guerrilla fighter during the war for independence; and Wanja, a barmaid and former prostitute. "Through these four [characters]," writes Civia Tamarkin in the *Chicago Tribune Book World,* "Ngugi tells a haunting tale of lost hopes and soured dreams, raising the simple voice of humanity against the perversity of its condition." *American Book Review* contributor Henry Indangasi describes *Petals of Blood* this way: "Through numerous flashbacks, and flashbacks within flashbacks, and lengthy confessions, a psychologically credible picture of the characters, and a vast canvas of Kenya's history is unfolded."

Several reviewers note that Ngugi's emphasis on the economic and political conditions in Kenya at times overshadows his narrative. The *West Africa* contributor explains: "*Petals of Blood* is not so much a novel as an attempt to think aloud about the problems of modern Kenya: the sharp contrast between the city and the countryside, between the 'ill-gotten' wealth of the new African middle-class and the worsening plight of the unemployed workers and peasants." Charles R. Larson expresses a like opinion in *World Literature Today:* "*Petals of Blood* is not so much about these four characters (as fascinating and as skillfully drawn as they are) as it is about political unrest in post-independence Kenya, and what Ngugi considers the failures of the new black elite (politicians and businessmen) to live up to the pre-independence expectations." Foreshadowing Ngugi's 1977 arrest, Larson concludes, "In this sense *Petals of Blood* is a bold venture—perhaps a risky one—since it is obvious that the author's criticisms of his country's new ruling class will not go unnoticed."

Critics also maintain that this emphasis lends a didactic tone to the novel. Larson, for instance, comments in the *New York Times Book Review:* "The weakness of Ngugi's novel as a work of the creative imagination ultimately lies in the author's somewhat dated Marxism: revolt of the masses, elimination of the black bourgeois; capitalism to be replaced with African socialism. The author's didacticism weakens what would otherwise have been his finest work." *New Yorker* contributor John Updike similarly observes that "the characters . . . stagger and sink under the politico-symbolical message they are made to carry." *World Literature Today* contributor Andrew Salkey, on the other hand, offers this view: "It's a willfully diagrammatic and didactic novel which also succeeds artistically because of its resonant characterization and deadly irony. It satisfies both the novelist's political intent and the obligation I know he feels toward his art."

Despite these reservations, the majority of critics concur that *Petals of Blood* is an important literary contribution. Sharma, for example, writes that "Ngugi's *Petals of Blood* is a complex and powerful work. It is a statement of his social and political philosophy and an embodiment of his prophetic vision. Ngugi provides a masterly analysis of the social and economic situation in modern Kenya, a scene of unprincipled and ruthless exploitation of man by man, and gives us a picture of the social and moral consequences of this exploitation." Cook and Ikenimkpe state that *Petals of Blood* "stands as a rare literary achievement: with all its faults upon it, [it is still] a skillfully articulated work which in no degree compromises the author's fully fledged radical political viewpoint." Indangasis concludes: "In many senses, literary and nonliterary, *Petals of Blood* will remain a major but controversial contribution to African literature, and the literature of colonised peoples."

BIOGRAPHICAL/CRITICAL SOURCES:

BOOKS

Bailey, Diana, *Ngugi wo Thiong'o: The River Between, a Critical View,* edited by Yolande Cantu, Collins, 1986.
Contemporary Literary Criticism, Gale, Volume 3, 1975, Volume 7, 1977, Volume 13, 1980, Volume 36, 1986.
Cook, David and Michael Okenimkpe, *Ngugi wa Thiong'o: An Exploration of His Writings,* Heinemann, 1983.
Gakwandi, Shatto Arthur, *The Novel and Contemporary Experience in Africa,* Africana Publishing, 1977.
Killam, G. D., *An Introduction to the Writings of Ngugi,* Heinemann, 1980.
Ngugi wa Thiong'o, *Detained: A Writer's Prison Diary,* Heinemann, 1981.
Larson, Charles R., *The Emergence of African Fiction,* Indiana University Press, 1972.
Palmer, Eustace, *An Introduction to the African Novel,* Africana Publishing, 1972.
Palmer, Eustace, *The Growth of the African Novel,* Heinemann, 1979.
Robson, Clifford B., *Ngugi wa Thiong'o,* Macmillan (London), 1979.
Roscoe, Adrian, *Uhuru's Fire: African Literature East to South,* Cambridge University Press, 1977.
Tibble, Ann, *African/English Literature,* Peter Owen (London), 1965.
Tucker, Martin, *Africa in Modern Literature: A Survey of Contemporary Writing in English,* Ungar, 1967.

PERIODICALS

African Literature Today, Number 5, 1971, Number 10, 1979.
Africa Today, Volume 33, number 1, 1986.
American Book Review, summer, 1979.
Books Abroad, autumn, 1967, spring, 1968.
Books in Canada, October, 1982.
Chicago Tribune Book World, October 22, 1978.
Christian Science Monitor, October 11, 1978, September 5, 1986.
Iowa Review, spring/summer, 1976.
Journal of Commonwealth Literature, September, 1965, Number 1, 1986.
Listener, August 26, 1982.
Michigan Quarterly Review, fall, 1970.
New Republic, January 20, 1979.
New Statesman, October 20, 1972, July 24, 1981, June 18, 1982, August 8, 1986.
New Yorker, July 2, 1979.
New York Times, May 10, 1978, November 9, 1986.
New York Times Book Review, February 19, 1978.
Observer, June 20, 1982.
Times Literary Supplement, January 28, 1965, November 3, 1972, August 12, 1977, October 16, 1981, June 18, 1982, May 8, 1987.
Washington Post, October 9, 1978.
West Africa, February 20, 1978.
World Literature Today, spring, 1978, fall, 1978, spring, 1981, autumn, 1982, summer, 1983, winter, 1984, fall, 1987.
World Literature Written in English, November, 1979, autumn, 1982.

*   *   *

NICHOLS, Leigh
See KOONTZ, Dean R(ay)

*   *   *

NICHOLS, Peter (Richard) 1927-

PERSONAL: Born July 31, 1927, in Bristol, England; son of Richard George and Violet Annie (Poole) Nichols; married Thelma Reed (a painter), December 26, 1959; children: Abigail (deceased), Louise, Daniel, Catherine. *Education:* Attended Bristol Old Vic Theatre School, 1951-53, and Trent Park Teachers College, 1958-60. *Politics:* "Utopian socialist." *Religion:* None.

ADDRESSES: Agent—Margaret Ramsay Ltd., 14a Goodwin's Court, St. Martin's Lane, London WC2N 4LL, England.

CAREER: Professional actor, 1950-55; teacher, 1956-59; playwright, 1959—. Member of board of governors of Greenwich Theatre, 1971-75; member of Arts Council drama panel, 1973-76; visiting playwright at Guthrie Theatre, Minneapolis, MN, 1976.

MEMBER: Royal Society of Literature (fellow).

AWARDS, HONORS: Evening Standard, best play awards for *A Day in the Death of Joe Egg* in 1967, *The National Health* in 1969, and *Passion Play,* in 1981, best comedy award for *Privates on Parade* in 1978; John Whiting Award, 1969; Ivor Novello Award for best British musical, c. 1977, for *Privates on Parade;* Society of West End Theatres, best comedy award, 1978, for *Privates on Parade,* best musical award, 1983, for *Poppy;* Antoinette Perry Award ("Tony") for best revival, 1985, for *Joe Egg.*

WRITINGS:

PUBLISHED PLAYS

Promenade (produced on television, 1959), in *Six Granada Plays,* Faber, 1960.
Ben Spray (produced on television, 1961), in *New Granada Plays,* Faber, 1961.
The Hooded Terror (two-act; produced on television, 1963; produced on stage, 1964), [England], 1965.
The Gorge (produced on television, 1965), in *The Television Dramatist,* Elek, 1973.
A Day in the Death of Joe Egg (two-act; first produced in Glasgow, Scotland, at Citizens Theatre, 1967; also see below), Samuel French, 1967.
The National Health (two-act; first produced in London, England, at Old Vic National Theatre, 1969; also see below), Samuel French, 1970.
Forget-Me-Not Lane (two-act; first produced in London at Greenwich Theatre, 1973), Samuel French, 1971.
Chez Nous (two-act; first produced in London at Globe Theatre, 1974), Faber, 1974.
The Freeway (two-act; first produced in London at Old Vic National Theatre, 1974), Faber, 1975.
Privates on Parade (two-act; first produced in London at Aldwych Theatre, 1977), Faber, 1977.
(And director) *Born in the Gardens* (two-act; first produced in Bristol, England, at Bristol Old Vic Theatre Royal, 1979; produced in London at Globe Theatre, 1980), Faber, 1979.

Passion Play (two-act; first produced in London at Aldwych Theatre, 1981; produced as *Passion* on Broadway, 1983), Methuen, 1981.

Poppy (with music by Monty Norman; produced in London at Barbican Theatre, 1983), Heinemann Educational, 1982.

A Piece of My Mind (produced in Southampton at Nuffield Theatre, 1987), Heinemann Educational, 1988.

UNPUBLISHED PLAYS

Daddy Kiss It Better, produced in Yorkshire, 1968.

Neither Up nor Down, produced in London, 1972.

Beasts of England (based on works by George Orwell), produced in London, 1973.

Hardin's Luck (two-act; adapted from a work by E. Nesbit), first produced in London at Greenwich Theatre, 1977.

SCREENPLAYS

Catch Us if You Can/Having a Wild Weekend, Anglo Amalgamated, 1965.

Georgy Girl (adapted from the novel by Margaret Forster), Columbia, 1966.

Joe Egg (adapted from his play *A Day in the Death of Joe Egg*), Columbia, 1971.

National Health (adapted from his play *The National Health*), Columbia, 1973.

Privates on Parade (adapted from his play of the same title), Handmade Films, 1983.

Also author of *Changing Places,* 1984.

OTHER

Feeling You're Behind (autobiography), Weidenfeld & Nicolson, 1984.

Author of fifteen television plays and two adaptations of short stories for television.

WORK IN PROGRESS: A musical; a television series.

SIDELIGHTS: A Day in the Death of Joe Egg, Peter Nichols's first stage success, concerns two young parents coping with their mute, mongoloid child. It is also a comedy, noted *Time*'s T. E. Kalem, which places Nichols in the circle of contemporary British playwrights who treat serious subjects with a caustic, mordant sense of humor. In Kalem's view, "No one in contemporary theater orchestrates mordant laughter with a surer hand than . . . Nichols." Many reviewers focused on the comic strengths of the play; *Encounter* critic John Spurling praised the seriousness of its subject: "*Joe Egg* [gave] a hearty music-hall humour to a gloomy subject, but the basis of its considerable appeal for audiences was that it dealt in straightforward naturalistic terms with a topical problem—what is it like to have a spastic child?"

In his next play, *The National Health,* Nichols sets the action in a London hospital ward for the dying. Brendan Gill wrote in the *New Yorker:* " 'The National Health' . . . is a play about the physical and spiritual indignities of sickness, old age, and approaching death. . . . The dreadfulness of suffering and the still greater dreadfulness of the certain end to suffering hang in the antiseptic air. . . . Hard as it may be to believe, Mr. Nichols' play is an unbroken series of successful jokes: gallows humor of a kind that makes us simultaneously gasp and laugh. . . . Nichols' close, compassionate scrutiny of life and death heightened my sense of well-being instead of diminishing it."

The black comedy of *Joe Egg* and *The National Health* exemplified British theatre in the late 1960s, according to Kalem, and reflected a national mood about conditions of life in England.

For nearly two decades the London stage had been dominated by the angry, antiestablishment plays of writers like John Osborne (*Look Back in Anger*), but the change in dramatic tone, from hostility to a grim, mocking humor, corresponded to the decline of the welfare state. "Underlying that mockery is a sour nagging resentment of the present sorry state of England," Kalem contended. "Thus it is no unintended irony that *The National Health* is set in a hospital ward," where terminally ill patients meet their suffering without a loss of humor, however grisly. "Laughter," Kalem explained, "is a wonder drug by which man anesthetizes his consciousness" of dismal circumstances.

One criticism made against Nichols, that he does not fully exploit the dramatic potential of his plays, came from Stanley Kauffmann, whose review of *The National Health* appeared in the *New Republic:* "In all his work so far Nichols has shown irreverence for sentimentality and theatrical taboos but, fundamentally, not much more. He seems to bite bullets—in *Joe Egg* the anguish of having a brain-damaged child, in this play the implacability of the hospital beds waiting for every one of us—but he just mouths them for a while before he spits them out, he never really crunches. We keep waiting for the author's gravity as distinct from the subject's."

Ronald Bryden raised similar concerns in his review of *Chez Nous,* arguing that the conflict between gravity and farce, reality and fantasy, is central to the kind of plays Nichols writes. "Unfortunately," he remarked, "it becomes clear in *Chez Nous* that this recurring opposition expresses an equivalent tug-of-war within Nichols' talent." This time Nichols constructs a domestic comedy around two English couples, Liz and Dick, Diana and Phil, one visiting the other. In the middle of the quartet, though never seen onstage, is Liz and Dick's thirteen-year-old daughter, Jane, who turns out to be the mother of Phil's baby. This revelation comes early in the play and serves as the departure point for an examination of marriage, sexual relationships, and such contemporary subjects as pubescent liberation.

Bryden began his discussion of *Chez Nous* by observing that Nichols partly uses "plays as play: as fantasies exploring the alternatives to real life. The other half is . . . the realist who [reminds us] that you can have real emotions only about reality." In his estimation the central incident, Jane and Phil's parenthood, "is an improbability, a deliberate alternative to real life, engineered as a play-experiment to see what emotions one should have about it. Because it's unreal . . . most of the emotions it generates are unreal too. . . . I haven't said anything, I hope, which suggests that he's capable of writing a really bad play. But he spends far too much of his evening exploring all the unreal emotions. . . . His indulgence of fantasy has made things too artificial for . . . much conviction."

Some of the particular strengths of the play and Nichols's talent were described by Benedict Nightingale in his review for the *New Statesman:* "This is a very intelligent, careful play, which regards its protagonists with humour, horror, exasperation and compassion, though not always in equal proportion. . . . Diana and Phil prove rather more sympathetic—she for all her fastidiousness and melodramatics, he, with his ostentatious crudity, his pathetic yen for youth and craving for paternity. Their reconciliation, in which she unfurls the hysterectomy-scarred body she's always kept hidden, is unexpectedly moving, a declaration that affection can survive a mangling. As Nichols sees it, men are in thrall to their sexual drives, women doomed to humour them, but both sexes more tenaciously committed to marriage than they sometimes realise."

In *The Freeway* Nichols again joins fantasy and reality to launch an attack against rampant capitalism and acquisitiveness. Here he projects an England of the future in which all but the poorest own an automobile. Further, he envisions an eighty-mile-long traffic jam that lasts for three days on Britain's Fl, a colossal freeway running the length of the nation. Members of the aristocracy and working class are forced to contend with each other as well as with the lack of food, water, and sanitation. Kenneth Hurren of the *Spectator* stated, "Fl and the trouble that develops on it are a tortured metaphor for British democracy, class-ridden and acquisitive, careering along a freeway to disaster."

The Freeway fared less well with critics than Nichols's previous works. Hurren commented: "[Nichols] is a dramatist who has hitherto seemed possessed of as vivaciously original a comic talent as anyone presently operating in the theatre, and it is as surprising as it is dismaying to find that talent . . . foundering bleakly in contemplation of the menace of the motor car. . . . It would plainly be possible to develop the situation pretty humorously, but Nichols on this occasion seems to be altogether too embittered (he must have had some really terrible times in the Peugeot), and it is a measure, I suppose, of his desperation— and of the extraordinary fall in his standards of comedy—that he is reduced to the desolate business of trying to get a laugh or two out of people going to the lavatory in rather primitive circumstances."

In his review of the play Nightingale talked about some of the ideas Nichols raises: "We learn that individual self-indulgence can produce social misery; that labour tends to equate happiness with possessions, and that capital is only too glad to keep its power with the odd handout; that freedom, in short, may be slavery. But anyone who has read a little 19th-century history . . . will want to see more slippery questions tackled. . . . I found *The Freeway* not unenjoyable, a deliberately negative recommendation. As a play of ideas, it could be more provocative; as a comedy about people in a jam, more trenchant and amusing."

Passion Play, produced in New York as *Passion,* ranked among the best plays of the 1982-83 Broadway season, according to *New York Times* critic Frank Rich: "Nichols takes one of the oldest tales in the book—a middle-aged husband has an affair with a younger woman—and, with virtuoso writing and unsparing honesty, rocks the foundations of an audience's complacency." Nichols's innovation is to bring onstage, as separate entities, the private selves of his two protagonists, allowing the audience a rare glimpse behind the careful facades of the couple as their marriage dissolves. When, for instance, the husband first lies to his wife to cover up his affair, he remains placid on the outside while his private self capers around the stage in celebration. Observed Rich, "Nichols's plays demand dazzling direction and polished acting, in part because they almost always involve tricky theatrical devices" such as the dual personas in *Passion.* Although inspiring laughter at first, "the divided nature of the characters—and the juxtapositions of longing and heartbreak— become rending," Rich concluded. Similarly, a London *Times* reviewer, commenting on a London revival of the work, wrote that the "marvellous" play will "hit you dead between the eyes."

BIOGRAPHICAL/CRITICAL SOURCES:

BOOKS

Contemporary Literary Criticism, Gale, Volume 5, 1976, Volume 36, 1986.
Dictionary of Literary Biography, Volume 13: *British Dramatists since World War II,* Gale, 1982.

Kerensky, Oleg, *The New British Drama,* Hamish Hamilton. 1977.
Taylor, J. R., *The Second Wave,* Methuen, 1971.

PERIODICALS

Commonweal, March 15, 1968.
Encounter, January, 1975.
Hudson Review, summer, 1968.
Los Angeles Times, June 20, 1984, November 11, 1984, December 16, 1984.
Nation, February 19, 1968.
National Observer, February 12, 1968.
New Leader, February 26, 1968.
New Republic, November 2, 1974.
New Statesman, February 15, 1974, October 11, 1974.
Newsweek, February 12, 1968.
New Yorker, February 10, 1968, October 21, 1974.
New York Times, November 7, 1977, June 7, 1979, October 24, 1982, May 16, 1983, April 13, 1984, January 7, 1985, January 20, 1985, April 2, 1985, April 7, 1985, August 23, 1989.
Plays and Players, March, 1974.
Spectator, October 25, 1969, October 12, 1974.
Stage, June 8, 1972.
Time, October 21, 1974.
Times (London), April 23, 1984, May 10, 1984, March 11, 1987.
Times Literary Supplement, July 13, 1984.
Washington Post, July 17, 1969, July 27, 1969.

*   *   *

NIN, Anais 1903-1977

PERSONAL: First name is pronounced anna-*ees;* surname is pronounced *neen;* born February 21, 1903, in Paris, France; brought to the United States in 1914, became an American citizen; died January 14, 1977, of cancer, in Los Angeles, Calif.; daughter of Joaquin (a pianist and composer) and Rosa (a singer; maiden name Culmell) Nin; married Hugh Guiler (a banker; later, under the name Ian Hugo, a filmmaker and illustrator of Nin's books), 1920. *Education:* Attended public schools in New York; self-educated after grammar school.

CAREER: Writer. After leaving school at sixteen, worked as a fashion and artist's model; studied Spanish dance, giving one recital in Paris during the 1930s; studied psychoanalysis, then practiced under Otto Rank in Europe, and briefly in New York, during the mid-1930s, returning to France in 1935; established Siana Editions with Villa Seurat group (Henry Miller, Alfred Perles, Michael Fraenkel), about 1935; returned to United States in 1939; published her own books for four years under various imprints, principally Gemor Press. Frequent lecturer at colleges and universities, including Harvard University, University of Chicago, Dartmouth College, University of Michigan, University of California, Berkeley, and Duke University. Also taught creative writing and acted in films. Member of advisory board, Feminist Book Club, Los Angeles, and Women's History Library, Berkeley, Calif.

MEMBER: National Institute of Arts and Letters.

AWARDS, HONORS: Prix Sevigne, 1971.

WRITINGS:

NONFICTION

D. H. Lawrence: An Unprofessional Study, E. W. Titus (Paris), 1932, Spearman (London), 1961, A. Swallow, 1964.
Realism and Reality, Alicat, 1946.
On Writing, O. Baradinsky, 1947.

The Novel of the Future (also see below), Macmillan, 1968, reprinted, Ohio University Press, 1986.

Nuances, Sans Souci Press, 1970.

Philip K. Jason, editor, *Anais Nin Reader,* Swallow Press, 1973.

(With Duane Schneider) *An Interview with Anais Nin,* Village Press, 1973.

Evelyn Hinz, editor, *A Woman Speaks: The Lectures, Seminars, and Interviews of Anais Nin,* Swallow Press, 1975.

In Favor of the Sensitive Man and Other Essays, Harcourt, 1976.

NOVELS

Winter of Artifice, Obelisk Press (Paris), 1939, published as *Winter of Artifice: Three Novelettes,* A. Swallow, 1961, revised edition published as *Winter of Artifice* [and] *House of Incest* (also see below), P. Owen, 1974.

This Hunger, Gemor Press, 1945.

Ladders to Fire (also see below), Dutton, 1946, reprinted, Ohio University Press, 1959.

Children of the Albatross (also see below), Dutton, 1947.

The Four-Chambered Heart (also see below), Duell, 1950.

A Spy in the House of Love (also see below), British Book Centre (New York), 1954.

Solar Barque (also see below), A. Swallow, 1958, enlarged edition published as *Seduction of the Minotaur* (also see below), A. Swallow, 1961, reprinted, Ohio University Press, 1959.

Cities of the Interior (contains *Ladders to Fire, Children of the Albatross, The Four-Chambered Heart, A Spy in the House of Love,* and *Solar Barque*), A Swallow, 1959, reprinted, with *Seduction of the Minotaur* replacing *Solar Barque,* A. Swallow, 1961, published with an introduction by Sharon Spencer, Swallow Press, 1974.

JOURNALS

Gunther Stuhlmann, editor, *The Diary of Anais Nin* (also see below), Harcourt (first two volumes published in conjunction with Swallow Press), Volume 1: *1931-1934* (also see below), 1966, Volume 2: *1934-1939,* 1967, Volume 3: *1939-1944,* 1969, Volume 4: *1944-1947,* 1971, Volume 5: *1947-1955* (also see below), 1974, Volume 6: *1955-1966,* 1977, Volume 7: *1966-1974,* 1981 (published in England as *The Journals of Anais Nin,* P. Owen, Volume 1, 1966, Volume 2, 1967, Volume 3, 1970, Volume 4, 1972, Volume 5, 1974, Volume 6, 1977, Volume 7, 1980).

Duane Schneider, editor, *Unpublished Selections from the Diary* (contains excerpts from Volume 1 of *The Diary of Anais Nin*), D. Schneider Press, 1968.

Paris Revisited (contains excerpts from Volume 5 of *The Diary of Anais Nin*), Capra Press, 1972.

Rochelle Holt, editor, *Eidolons* (contains diary excerpts written in 1971), Ragnarok Press, 1973.

A Photographic Supplement to the Diary of Anais Nin, Harbrace, 1974.

The Early Diary of Anais Nin, Harcourt, Volume 1: *Linotte: The Early, Diary of Anais Nin, 1914-1920* (translated from the French by Jean L. Sherman), 1980, Volume 2: *1920-1923,* 1983, Volume 3: *1923-1927,* 1983, Volume 4: *1927-1931,* 1985.

Henry and June: From the Unexpurgated Diary of Anais Nin, Harcourt, 1986.

SHORT STORIES

Under a Glass Bell, Gemor Press, 1944, published as *Under a Glass Bell and Other Stories,* Dutton, 1948.

Collages (also see below), A. Swallow, 1964.

Waste of Timelessness, and Other Early Stories, Magic Circle Press, 1977.

Delta of Venus (erotica), Harcourt, 1977, published with photographs by Bob Carlos Clarke as *The Illustrated Delta of Venus,* W. H. Allen, 1980.

Little Birds (erotica), Harcourt, 1979.

AUTHOR OF INTRODUCTION

Henry Miller, *Tropic of Cancer,* Obelisk Press, 1934.

Bettina L. Knapp, *Antonin Artaud: A Man of Vision,* David Lewis, 1969.

John Pearson, *The Sun's Birthday,* Doubleday, 1973.

SOUND RECORDINGS

"An Evening with Anais Nin," Big Sur Recordings, 1972.

"Anais Nin Discusses The Diary of Anais Nin, 1944-1947, Volume IV, 'A Journal of Self-Discovery,' " Center for Cassette Studies, 1972.

"Craft of Writing," Big Sur Recordings, 1973.

"Anais Nin: The Author Explains the Purpose behind Her Writing," Center for Cassette Studies, 1975.

"Anais Nin in Recital: Diary Excerpts and Comments," Caedmon, 1979.

OTHER

House of Incest (prose poem), Siana Editions (Paris), 1936, Gemor Press (New York), 1947, A. Swallow, 1961.

(With John Boyce) *Aphrodisiac* (erotic drawings), Quartet Books, 1976.

Portrait in Three Dimensions (contains excerpts from *The Diary of Anais Nin, The Novel of the Future,* and *Collages*), Concentric Circle Press, 1979.

The White Blackbird, Capra Press, 1985.

Work is included in numerous anthologies. Contributor to periodicals, including *Massachusetts Review, New York Times, Village Voice, Saturday Review, Ms.,* and the *New York Times Book Review. Booster* and *Delta* (both Paris), society editor, 1937, associate editor, 1937-38, member of editorial board, 1939; *Two Cities,* general editor, 1959, honorary editor, 1960; member of advisory board, *Voyages.*

SIDELIGHTS: On a ship bound for New York from Barcelona in 1914, an eleven-year-old girl named Anais Nin began writing the journal that would gradually evolve into the most acclaimed work of her literary career, a journal that Henry Miller, writing in the *Criterion,* predicted would someday "take its place beside the revelations of St. Augustine, Petronius, Abelard, Rousseau, Proust, and others." Aboard the ship with young Anais were her two brothers, Thorvald and Joaquin, and her mother, Rosa Culmell Nin, a classical singer of Danish and French descent. Absent was Anais's father, Joaquin Nin. A respected Spanish composer and pianist, he was, Rosa told her children, on an extended concert tour; he would join them in New York City later. In fact, Joaquin had deserted his wife and three children forever. Suspecting the truth, Anais began her diary as an extended letter to her father, one intended to coax him back to his family.

For the first ten years of her life Anais had moved in some of Europe's most glittering circles. Her parents were both from aristocratic families, and their musical careers enabled them to associate with the finest artists of their day. While Anais enjoyed this cosmopolitan life, she was also shaken by her parents' private battles at home—violent arguments that stemmed from Joaquin's endless infidelities. When he finally deserted Rosa, she decided it would be best to take their children as far away from him as she possibly could. Although Anais had feared her harsh, critical father, she also idealized him and suffered keenly from his absence.

Trained only as a musician, Rosa Nin managed to support her children by taking in boarders and giving singing lessons in New York. The family led a life that was poor and drab compared to the one they had left behind them in Europe. Anais was isolated by her limited knowledge of English as well as by her deep sadness over the changes in her life. She turned to her journal for companionship and escape. "I hate New York," she confided in its pages at the age of eleven. "I find it too big, too superficial, everything goes too fast. It is just hell." Although filled with a strong desire for learning, Anais did poorly in school, preferring to educate herself by reading alphabetically through the books in the public library. When a teacher criticized her writing style as stilted, the sixteen-year-old dropped out of public school permanently. She remarked to her diary, "I leave . . . with the greatest pleasure in the world, the pleasure that a prisoner feels on leaving his prison after a sentence of a thousand years." When not studying in the library, Anais helped to support her family by working as a model for artists, illustrators and fashion designers.

Nin married Hugh Guiler, a banker, when she was twenty. Not long after their marriage, Guiler was transferred to a bank in Paris. Nin had been writing regularly in her journal since beginning it in 1914, but it wasn't until her return to Paris as an adult that she began to work seriously at writing for publication. As she struggled with her early fiction, she began to feel a powerful inner conflict between "her desire to be a woman—as she saw it, one who gives, is involved in relationships—and an artist—one who takes, is unfaithful and abandons loved ones (like her concert pianist father)," noted *New York Times Book Review* contributor Sharon Spencer. Nin felt unable to follow her artistic inclinations while also carrying out her duties as a banker's wife. Guiler's work kept the couple in conservative circles, and Nin, who craved the company of artists, found herself stifled by long hours spent in social intercourse with bank employees. But although she was beginning to "acknowledge disappointment with her marriage to the banker . . . Hugh Guiler," explained Spencer, Nin maintained a "madly romantic ideal of married love with remarkable tenacity."

In spite of her personal difficulties, Nin managed at this time to publish her first book, a commentary on D. H. Lawrence. Nin had been strongly influenced by Lawrence's style and "shared with him belief in the value of the subconscious, myth, progression, and the recognition of the physical," stated Benjamin Franklin V in the *Dictionary of Literary Biography*. While Nin's book *D. H. Lawrence: An Unprofessional Study* is still recognized as a sensitive and original discussion of the English novelist's work, its greatest importance was probably the change it helped bring about in Nin's private life. The lawyer she engaged to negotiate the contract for her book introduced her to a poor, unpublished American writer living in Paris, a man named Henry Miller, whose works *Tropic of Cancer* and *Tropic of Capricorn* would later be widely banned as obscene.

Miller lived in an underground world different from any Nin had ever known. His companions were the gangsters, prostitutes and drug addicts of Paris. He and his wife, June, lived a life of extremes, and it seemed to Nin that they were fully alive in a way that she was not. Franklin pointed out their differences in his essay: "Nin was personally elegant, Miller was not; she was selective, Miller voracious; in their writings Nin was implicit, Miller explicit; she was sensual, he sexual. But despite these and other differences Nin and Miller inspired each other, and each

performed as a sounding board for the other's ideas." As Nin became increasingly involved with Henry and June Miller, the tension she felt between her life as Hugh Guiler's wife and her life as Anais Nin the artist became intolerable. In 1932 she sought to resolve her conflicts through therapy with the prominent Parisian psychoanalyst, Rene Allendy, and later with Otto Rank, a brilliant though unorthodox student of Sigmund Freud.

Sharon Spencer believed that the insights Nin gained through "therapy with Otto Rank and a love affair with Henry Miller freed her to live a greatly expanded life—without sacrificing the marriage that had such great psychological and spiritual value for her." How she accomplished this is not known, for Nin heavily edited her published journals from those years and omitted all references to Hugh Guiler (at his request). It is known that he later established a secondary career as an artist and filmmaker under the pseudonym Ian Hugo. Nin appeared in some of his films, and his engravings illustrated some of her books. They remained legally married until her death, but they may have established an open relationship. During her lifetime, "Nin refused to discuss her marriage or even name her husband in interviews," revealed Rose Marie Cutting in *Anais Nin: A Reference Guide*. Psychoanalysis became a lifelong fascination for Nin. She studied it under Rank and eventually practiced with him in New York City. Its influence on her fiction was profound, for in all her novels she attempted to illustrate her characters' inner landscapes rather than to describe their external lives.

The first work to show evidence of Nin's liberation was a long prose poem entitled *House of Incest*. In a surrealistic style, the narrator recounts her nightmare of wounded souls, trapped by their unresolved inner conflicts in the dark, airless "house of incest." Only one inhabitant can find an exit from this sealed environment—a dancer who has lost her arms as punishment for clinging to all she loved in life. When she learns to accept her flaws, she is able to dance her way to the daylight outside the house. Incorporating Nin's own recurring dreams, *House of Incest* was symbolic of her feelings of suffocation from childhood traumas and her rebirth through psychoanalysis. "Nin's message is clear," explained Franklin in one of his *Dictionary of Literary Biography* essays. "The nature of man's existence is multiple and imperfect. Every individual has many parts, the sum of which is something less than one's ideal self. But if one ignores that multiplicity or demands perfection, that person will not be able to function in life. . . . Nin never expressed these basic concerns as eloquently or convincingly as she did in this first volume of her fiction, even though almost all the rest of her fiction is similar to it thematically." Franklin adds, "Such an esoteric book doubtless could not have been written or published in the United States at that time."

Indeed, Nin had trouble finding a publisher for *House of Incest* even in France. Eventually Nin, Miller and the other writers with whom they associated (a group sometimes called the Villa Seurat circle) established Siana Editions to publish their own works and those of other avant-garde writers. With the encouragement of the Villa Seurat writers, Nin's style continued to develop, and by the time she published *Winter of Artifice* in 1939, her prose showed much less of an obvious debt to surrealism. While *House of Incest* cautions against the danger of becoming trapped in one's dreams, *Winter of Artifice* stresses that "dreams have to be probed, not to the exclusion of conscious reality, but rather to nourish it," writes Franklin. The story centers on Djuna and her reunion with the father she has not seen for twenty years. Nin's narrative recreates Djuna's yearning to penetrate the many illusions with which both father and daughter have surrounded themselves. Little by little, she succeeds in exposing the true nature of their relationship.

Besides illuminating the psychological drama played out between Djuna and her father, Nin's intent in *Winter of Artifice* was to create prose that would provoke the immediate emotional response usually associated with music. Her success is unquestioned by Sharon Spencer, who wrote in *Collage of Dreams: The Writings of Anais Nin* that "*Winter of Artifice* is a mature work, very sophisticated technically, in which Anais Nin first fully displays her talent for adapting the structure of the non-verbal arts to fiction. It is a ballet of words in which music and movement are . . . skillfully balanced and . . . subtly interwoven." Bettina L. Knapp, in her critical volume entitled *Anais Nin,* praises the author's skillful use of "the literary devices of repetitions, omissions, ellipses, dream sequences, and stream-of-consciousness" that have the cumulative effect of "jarring the reader into a new state of awareness."

Both *House of Incest* and *Winter of Artifice* were well-received in Europe's avant-garde literary circles. But the rich cultural atmosphere that helped Nin to create those first books disintegrated as World War II drew closer. In 1939, Hugh Guiler was called back to the United States and Nin chose to accompany him. Just as she had in childhood, Nin found New York City cold and sterile in comparison to Europe. She also discovered that American publishers were unreceptive to her work, which they considered unhealthy, decadent surrealism. After a few years of consistent rejections by American publishers, Nin bought a secondhand, foot-operated printing press and began to set the type for her own books. In this way she produced limited editions of *House of Incest* and *Winter of Artifice,* as well as a volume of short stories, *Under a Glass Bell,* and another novel, *This Hunger.* In time she attracted the attention of Edmund Wilson, a highly-respected reviewer. He praised *Under a Glass Bell* in the *New Yorker:* "The pieces in this collection belong to a peculiar genre sometimes cultivated by the late Virginia Woolf. They are half short stories, half dreams, and they mix a sometimes exquisite poetry with a homely realistic observation. They take place in a special world, a world of feminine perception and fancy. . . . The main thing to say is that Miss Nin is a very good artist." It was through Wilson's influence that Nin was finally able to place her work with a commercial publisher in the United States.

In novels such as *Ladders to Fire, The Four-Chambered Heart* and *A Spy in the House of Love* Nin continued the exploration of the feminine psyche she had begun in *House of Incest* and *Winter of Artifice.* Her novels have a fluid quality, found *Spectator* contributor Emma Fisher, "because her female characters are all faces of Woman. . . . The characters melt and dissolve into each other," even exchanging names as they reappear from one novel to the next. William Goyen, who rated Nin "one of the most fiercely passionate practitioners of the experimental novel in America," stated in the *New York Times Book Review* that as Nin "follows the inner flow of her characters' drives and motivations . . . she occasionally directs the flow to the surface where she freezes it into something as plain and dazzling as ice." Reviews such as these helped to bring Nin greater acceptance in the United States.

But her fiction was still misunderstood and attacked by some critics, who objected to her experimental style as "murky and precious," to quote Audrey C. Foote in *Washington Post Book World.* "She covers her canvas too thickly," declared Herbert Lyons in the *New York Times Book Review.* "It tends to look like a used palette: the resulting abstraction is murky, meaningless

and too often in bad taste." Some reviewers felt that the absence of conventional plot and characters rendered Nin's books inaccessible. Others found her recurrent themes and characters tedious. For example, Blake Morrison wrote in his *New Statesman* review of the five-volume "continuous novel," *Cities of the Interior,* "Nin herself described *Cities of the Interior* as 'an endless novel,' and for anyone wading faithfully through 589 pages of such sub-Lawrentian wisdom as 'A breast touched for the first time is a breast never touched before' the description is going to sound all too appropriate."

In his *Dictionary of Literary Biography* essays, Franklin suggested that while Nin's fiction was very accomplished, it "was never popular, but understandably so: she wrote about psychological reality, not the surface reality that she called realism and that most readers desire." Franklin believed that "while her fiction may at first seem impenetrable because of its lack of surface reality, an attentive reading reveals a powerful psychological reality that is the hallmark of her writing." He concluded: "She was a great writer of psychological fiction. . . . Her work challenges the reader and involves him in the creative act."

When Nin finally did achieve widespread acceptance it was with the work she had never intended to publish—the diary she began on the ship to New York as an eleven-year-old girl. Writing in the journal had developed into an obsessive activity which Nin sometimes compared to a drug addiction. She eventually filled more than two hundred manuscript volumes with the record of her transatlantic crossings, relationships with artists both famous and unknown, struggles with publishers, and efforts toward artistic success and self-fulfillment. Many of those closest to her had at one time urged her to abandon her journal, including Allendy, Rank, and Miller. They felt that it was a hindrance to her career as a fiction writer, but the journal continued to grow. Eventually, Nin's supporters began to urge her to publish portions of it, believing that her finest writing was contained therein.

After long deliberation, Nin decided to go ahead with the project. Her aim in editing her personal journal was similar to her objective in fiction: to illuminate the drama of individual growth. Volume One of *The Diary of Anais Nin* appeared in 1966 and was received far more enthusiastically than any of the author's novels had been. Readers, particularly women and young people, identified strongly with Nin's quest for self-knowledge and personal freedom. Many critics called the *Diary* a far stronger literary work than anything Nin had published previously. For example, Jean Garrigue noted in the *New York Times Book Review:* "The best parts of this diary are written with a daylight energy and sharpness that are in marked contrast to the tangibilties and antennaed delicacy of Miss Nin's stories and novels. . . . This diary has the elusive fluidity of life. Its author-subject is neither moralizer nor judge but a witness, vulnerable, susceptible, subtle, critical. . . . It is a rich, various, and fascinating work."

Eventually seven volumes of *The Diary of Anais Nin* were published. Its success was summarized by Duane Schneider in the *Southern Review:* "*The Diary* stands as Miss Nin's most remarkable artistic achievement because its literary form provides the author with a more effective means to reveal her characters than her novels do. *The Diary* symbolizes a quest for complete self-introspection and understanding; the result of the quest is a coherent, organic, revelatory work of art." *Shenandoah* contributor Lynn Sukenick called Nin's diaries "books of wisdom which have elevated their author to the status of a sage and have had a healing effect on many of her readers."

The Diary of Anais Nin did receive some negative attention. Susan Manso remarked in the *New Boston Review* that the journal's size was "matched only by its vacuity," and Susan Heath wrote in *Saturday Review:* "Only the self-absorbed will be fascinated by this solipsistic quest for healing and wholeness, for they will see themselves in the mirror Miss Nin has held to her soul. And the disenchanted will recognize it as the tiresome work of a querulous bore who cultivates neurosis in hopes of achieving self-realization." But for the most part, *The Diary of Anais Nin* was accepted as an important document, both for Nin's insight into the development of individual personality and for her sketches of the many artists she associated with in her lifetime of world traveling.

After the publication of the *Diary*, Nin found herself in great demand as a lecturer. She became a controversial figure in the woman's movement, alternately praised for writing from a uniquely feminine perspective and denounced as a supporter of archaic feminine values. Asked by an interviewer for *East/West Journal* to explain why so many readers responded so strongly to her diary, Nin replied: "I believe that what unites us universally is our emotions, our feelings in the face of experience and not necessarily the actual experiences themselves. The facts were different, but readers felt the same way toward a father even if the father was different. So I think unwittingly I must have gone so deep inside what Ira Pogroff calls the personal well that I touched the water at a level where it connected all the wells together."

Anais Nin died of cancer in 1977 and, in accordance with her wishes, her ashes were scattered over the Pacific. After her death, the publication of two volumes of erotica she had written for a dollar a page while raising money to buy her printing press put her name on the *New York Times* bestseller list for the first time. *Delta of Venus* and *Little Birds* were praised by Alice Walker in *Ms.* as "so distinct an advance in the depiction of female sensuality that I felt, on reading it, enormous gratitude." Four volumes of journals predating those personally edited by Nin were also published after her death, completing what *Prairie Schooner* contributor Robert A. Zaller called "the odyssey of a great woman's life, a life which presents itself to us now as one of the most serious and important of our time."

The University of California has a large collection of Nin's papers and literary manuscripts, including her diaries. Much of Nin's published and unpublished work has also been collected at Northwestern University Library. *Under the Sign of Pisces,* a literary journal devoted to Anais Nin and her circle, is produced at Ohio State University. Nin's work is studied in Paris by the group Les Amis de Anais Nin.

MEDIA ADAPTATIONS: Walter Carrol adapted the short story "Under a Glass Bell" for a film of the same title in 1967. John McLean and Sharon Bunn adapted Volume 1 of *The Diary of Anais Nin* for a play entitled "The Voice of a Woman," first produced in Dallas, Texas at Poverty Playhouse, 1970. Danielle Suissa acquired film rights to *A Spy in the House of Love* in 1970.

BIOGRAPHICAL/CRITICAL SOURCES:

BOOKS

Anais Nin Observed: From a Film Portrait of a Woman as Artist, Swallow Press, 1976.
Authors in the News, Gale, Volume 2, 1976.
Contemporary Literary Criticism, Gale, Volume 1, 1973, Volume 4, 1975, Volume 8, 1978, Volume 11, 1979, Volume 14, 1980.
Cutting, Rose Marie, *Anais Nin: A Reference Guide,* G. K. Hall, 1978.
Dictionary of Literary Biography, Gale, Volume 2: *American Novelists since World War II,* 1978, Volume 4: *American Writers in Paris,* 1980.
Evans, Oliver, *Anais Nin,* Southern Illinois University Press, 1968.
Franklin V, Benjamin, *Anais Nin: A Bibliography,* Kent State University Press, 1973.
Franklin and Duane Schneider, *Anais Nin: An Introduction,* Ohio University Press, 1979.
Harms, Valerie, editor, *Celebration with Anais Nin,* Magic Circle Press, 1973.
Hinz, Evelyn J., *The Mirror and the Garden: Realism and Reality in the Writings of Anais Nin,* Harcourt, 1973.
Knapp, Bettina L., *Anais Nin,* Ungar, 1978.
Nin, Anais, *The Diary of Anais Nin,* Harcourt (first two volumes published in conjunction with Swallow Press), Volume 1: *1931-34,* 1966, Volume 2: *1934-1939,* 1967, Volume 3: *1939-1944,* 1969, Volume 4: *1944-1947,* 1971, Volume 5: *1947-1955,* 1974, Volume 6: *1955-1966,* 1977, Volume 7: *1966-1974,* 1981 (published in England as *The Journals of Anais Nin,* P. Owen, Volume 1, 1966, Volume 2, 1967, Volume 3, 1970, Volume 4, 1972, Volume 5, 1974, Volume 6, 1977, Volume 7, 1980).
Nin, *Paris Revisited,* Capra Press, 1972.
Nin, *The Early Diary of Anais Nin,* Harcourt, Volume 1: *Linotte: The Early Diary of Anais Nin, 1914-1920,* 1980, Volume 2: *1920-1923,* 1983, Volume 3: *1923-1927,* 1983, Volume 4: *1927-1931,* 1985.
A Photographic Supplement to the Diary of Anais Nin, Harcourt, 1974.
Realism, Reality and the Fictional Theory of Alain Robbe-Grillet and Anais Nin, University Presses of America, 1983.
Schneider, *Unpublished Selections from the Diary,* D. Schneider Press, 1968.
Schneider and Nin, *An Interview with Anais Nin,* D. Schneider Press, 1970.
Spencer, Sharon, *Collage of Dreams: The Writings of Anais Nin,* Swallow Press, 1977.
Spencer, Space, *Time and Structure in the Modern Novel,* New York University Press, 1971.
Stuhlmann, Gunther, editor, *Henry Miller: Letters to Anais Nin,* Putnam, 1965.
Zaller, Robert, editor, *A Casebook on Anais Nin,* World, 1974.

PERIODICALS

American Poetry Review, January-February, 1973.
Books Abroad, summer, 1963.
Books and Bookman, April, 1975.
Carleton Miscellany, fall/winter, 1973-74.
Chicago Review, Volume 24, number 2, 1972.
Chicago Tribune, April 8, 1979.
Chicago Tribune Book World, October 24, 1982.
Christian Science Monitor, November 1, 1978.
Contemporary Literature, spring, 1972.
Criterion, October, 1937.
L'Express, February 28, 1963.
Los Angeles Free Press, November 26, 1964.
Los Angeles Times Book Review, September 26, 1971, September 5, 1982, January 8, 1984.
Mademoiselle, March, 1965.
Mosaic, winter, 1978.
Ms., April, 1977, October, 1980.
Nation, July 24, 1954, November 30, 1974.

New Boston Republic, fall, 1976.
New Republic, June 15, 1974.
New Statesman, October 4, 1974, November 10, 1978.
New York Herald Tribune, May 1, 1966.
New York Times Book Review, November 29, 1964, April 24, 1966, July 17, 1966, November 23, 1969, January 16, 1972, September 9, 1973, April 14, 1974, June 27, 1976, July 10, 1977, August 13, 1978, April 8, 1979, June 16, 1985.
Outcast Chapbooks, number 11.
Oz, July, 1970.
Prairie Schooner, fall, 1962, summer, 1971, summer, 1972.
Saturday Review, November 30, 1946, May 7, 1966, July 22, 1967, May 4, 1974, May 29, 1976.
Second Wave, summer, 1971.
Shenandoah, spring, 1967, spring, 1976.
Southern Review, spring, 1970.
Spectator, January 20, 1979.
Times (London), August 12, 1985.
Times Literary Supplement, April 30, 1964, June 11, 1970, January 29, 1971, May 12, 1972.
Village Voice, January 6, 1975, July 26, 1976.
Vogue, October 15, 1971.
Washington Post Book World, October 29, 1978, August 29, 1985.
West Coast Review of Books, July, 1979.

OTHER

"Anais Observed" (film), Robert Snyder, 1973.

OBITUARIES:

PERIODICALS

Newsweek, January 24, 1977.
New York Times, January 16, 1977.
Time, January 24, 1977.
Washington Post, January 16, 1977.

*   *   *

NIVEN, Larry
    See NIVEN, Laurence Van Cott

*   *   *

NIVEN, Laurence Van Cott   1938-
    (Larry Niven)

PERSONAL: Born April 30, 1938, in Los Angeles, CA; son of Waldemar Van Cott (a lawyer) and Lucy (Doheny) Niven; married Marilyn Joyce Wisowaty, September 6, 1969. *Education:* Attended California Institute of Technology, 1956-58; Washburn University of Topeka, A.B., 1962; attended University of California, Los Angeles, 1962-63.

ADDRESSES: Home and office—3961 Vanalden, Tarzana, CA 91356.

CAREER: Writer, 1964—.

MEMBER: Science Fiction Writers of America.

AWARDS, HONORS: Hugo Awards, World Science Fiction Convention, for story "Neutron Star" in 1967, for novel *Ringworld* in 1971, for story "Inconstant Moon" in 1972, for story "The Hole Man" in 1975, and for novelette "The Borderland of Sol" in 1976; Nebula Award, Science Fiction Writers of America, 1970, and Ditmar Award, 1972, both for *Ringworld;* E. E. Smith Memorial Award, 1978; LL.D., Washburn University of Topeka, 1984.

WRITINGS:

UNDER NAME LARRY NIVEN; NOVELS

World of Ptavvs, Ballantine, 1966.
A Gift from Earth, Ballantine, 1968.
Ringworld, Ballantine, 1970.
(With David Gerrold) *The Flying Sorcerers,* Ballantine, 1971.
Protector, Ballantine, 1973.
(With Jerry Pournelle) *The Mote in God's Eye,* Simon & Schuster, 1974.
(With Pournelle) *Inferno,* Pocket Books, 1976.
A World Out of Time, Holt, 1976.
(With Pournelle) *Lucifer's Hammer,* Playboy Press, 1977.
The Magic Goes Away, Ace Books, 1978.
The Ringworld Engineers, Holt, 1980.
The Patchwork Girl, Ace Books, 1980.
(With Pournelle) *Oath of Fealty,* Simon & Schuster, 1981.
(With Steven Barnes) *Dream Park,* Ace Books, 1981.
(With Barnes) *The Descent of Anansi,* Pinnacle Books, 1982.
The Integral Trees, Ballantine, 1984.
(With Pournelle) *Footfall,* Ballantine, 1985.
The Smoke Ring, Ballantine, 1987.
(With Barnes and Pournelle) *The Legacy of Heorot,* Simon & Schuster, 1987.
(With Poul Anderson and Dean Ing) *The Man-Kzin Wars,* Baen Books, 1988.
(With Barnes) *Dream Park II: The Barsoom Project,* Ace Books, 1989.
(With Ing and S. M. Stirling) *Man-Kzin Wars II,* Baen Books, 1989.

STORY COLLECTIONS; PUBLISHED BY BALLANTINE, EXCEPT AS NOTED

Neutron Star, 1968.
The Shape of Space, 1969.
All the Myriad Ways, 1971.
The Flight of the Horse, 1973.
Inconstant Moon, Gollancz, 1973.
A Hole in Space, 1974.
Tales of Known Space, 1975.
The Long ARM of Gil Hamilton, 1976.
Convergent Series, 1979.
Niven's Laws, Owlswick Press, 1984.
The Time of the Warlock, SteelDragon, 1984.
Limits, 1985.

OTHER

(Contributor) Harlan Ellison, editor, *Dangerous Visions: 33 Original Stories,* Doubleday, 1967.
(Contributor) Reginald Bretnor, editor, *The Craft of Science Fiction,* Harper, 1976.
(Editor) *The Magic May Return,* Ace Books, 1981.
(Editor) *More Magic,* Berkley Publishing, 1984.

Work appears in anthologies. Contributor of short stories to *Magazine of Fantasy and Science Fiction, Galaxy, Playboy,* and other magazines.

SIDELIGHTS: Larry Niven's science fiction novels are speculations about the technologies of the future. Niven's speculations closely follow current trends in scientific research to their logical conclusions, while his visions of the future are usually optimistic. According to Raymond J. Wilson writing in the *Dictionary of Literary Biography,* "much of Larry Niven's fiction reveals a love affair with technology. Niven's protechnology heroes take the positive position that the problems raised by technology can be solved and are, in any case, a small price to pay for the benefits of technological advance." Niven's heavy emphasis on science is acknowledged by the author himself. Speaking to Jeffrey Elliot in *Science Fiction Review,* Niven explains: "I wait for the scientists' [research] results and then write stories about them. . . . I try to make my stories as technically accurate as possible." This devotion has paid off. Gerald Jonas states in the *New York Times Book Review* that "there is a certain type of science fiction story that is completely incomprehensible to the non-SF reader. Devotees know it as the 'hard science' story. . . . Devotees recognize Larry Niven as one of the masters of this rather specialized subgenre."

In *Ringworld* and *The Ringworld Engineers,* Niven extrapolates from current scientific speculation about creating artificial planets to imagine Ringworld, an artificial planet shaped like a giant hoop. It is a million miles wide, has a diameter of 190 million miles, and is built in orbit around a sun. Along its outer edge is a range of thousand-mile-high mountains to keep the atmosphere from spinning off as the planet rotates. The top surface of Ringworld—an area three million times larger than the surface of the Earth—has been terraformed to sustain life, while the underside is made of an incredibly strong material. Between Ringworld and the sun are a series of orbiting screens which serve to block sunlight at regular intervals to simulate night and day. The planet is, Bud Foote writes in the *Detroit News,* the "greatest of fictional artifacts."

Ringworld is based on speculations first made by prominent physicist Freeman Dyson. Dyson foresees a time when humanity will acquire the necessary technology to convert the gaseous planets of our solar system into heavier elements and use this material to construct a string of artificial planets in Earth's orbit. This project would provide mankind with more room for its expanding population. While strictly adhering to scientific possibility, Niven's *Ringworld* takes Dyson's idea a step further, envisioning a single huge planet rather than many smaller ones. As Niven states in *The Ringworld Engineers,* Dyson "has no trouble believing in Ringworld."

By the time the stories of *Ringworld* and *The Ringworld Engineers* take place, the builders of the planet are long dead, and Ringworld is populated by the barbarian descendants of the builders, who no longer understand the advanced technology which created their world. Because of the immense space available on the planet, an area impossible for any human to explore in a lifetime, a wide variety of races and cultures have evolved on Ringworld. In both books, this immense diversity is lavishly presented. In *Ringworld,* a human expedition crash-lands on the planet and is forced to journey across its width to safety, encountering many different peoples along the way. In *The Ringworld Engineers,* some stabilizer rockets which keep Ringworld in proper orbit have been removed by a culture using them to power their spaceships. An Earthling and an alien set out to find the repair center of Ringworld so they can make the repairs needed to get the planet back in orbit again. Their search takes them through a host of cultures. Speaking of *The Ringworld Engineers,* Galen Strawson of the *Times Literary Supplement* states that "the book is alive with detail. There is *rishathra,* sex between species; there are silver-haired vampires with supercharged pheromones; there are shadow farms and flying cities, quantities of different social forms and incompatible social *mores.* Faults of construction cease to matter in the steady stream of invention. This is in part a guidebook to (a minute fragment of) the Ringworld."

Niven had not originally intended to write a sequel to *Ringworld,* but the amount of interest science fiction readers showed in the award-winning novel, and certain technical questions they raised, eventually convinced him to write *The Ringworld Engineers.* Besides explaining a few engineering details about the planet's construction, *The Ringworld Engineers* also includes new ideas suggested by Niven's readers. As Strawson explains, Niven wrote the book "partly to answer questions and partly to incorporate details not of his own imagining." Because of this, Strawson sees a problem in the novel's structure. "The incidents [in *The Ringworld Engineers*] often seem set up to provide frames for the imparting of information about Ringworld's construction; so that although they are individually well conceived and executed, and jointly testify to Niven's remarkable powers of imagination, they fail to develop smoothly into one another." James Blish, writing in the *Magazine of Fantasy and Science Fiction,* finds fault with *Ringworld.* "The backdrop is a staggering invention," Blish believes, "but what is happening in the foreground is mostly conventional to the point of pettiness." Despite some criticism, the Ringworld books have proven enormously popular. Foote expresses the hope of many readers that "Niven does still more Ringworld books; it's a big world, and there is a lot of material there."

BIOGRAPHICAL/CRITICAL SOURCES:

BOOKS

Contemporary Literary Criticism, Volume 8, Gale, 1978.
Dictionary of Literary Biography, Volume 8: *Twentieth-Century American Science Fiction Writers,* Gale, 1981.
Niven, Larry, *The Ringworld Engineers,* Holt, 1980.
Platt, Charles, *Dream Makers, Volume II: The Uncommon Men and Women Who Write Science Fiction,* Berkley Publishing, 1983.

PERIODICALS

Analog, March, 1978, February, 1979.
Detroit News, April 20, 1980.
Future, Number 3, 1978.
Los Angeles Times Book Review, April 19, 1981, November 8, 1981, November 21, 1982.
Magazine of Fantasy and Science Fiction, September, 1971.
New Republic, October 30, 1976.
New York Times Book Review, January 12, 1975, October 26, 1975, October 17, 1976, November 13, 1977.
Science Fiction Review, July, 1978.
Times Literary Supplement, November 7, 1980.
Washington Post Book World, December 27, 1981, February 26, 1984.

*   *   *

NIXON, Richard M(ilhous) 1913-

PERSONAL: Born January 9, 1913, in Yorba Linda, Calif.; son of Francis Anthony (a store owner) and Hannah (Milhous) Nixon; married Patricia Ryan, June 21, 1940; children: Patricia (Mrs. Edward Finch Cox), Julie (Mrs. Dwight David Eisenhower II). *Education:* Whittier College, A.B. (with honors), 1934; Duke University, LL.B. (with honors), 1937. *Religion:* Society of Friends (Quaker).

ADDRESSES: Home—Saddle River, N.J. *Office*—26 Federal Plaza, New York, N.Y. 10278.

CAREER: Thirty-seventh president of the United States. Bewley, Knoop & Nixon, Whittier, Calif., general practice of law,

1937-42; Office of Emergency Management, Washington, D.C., attorney in tire rationing division, 1942; U.S. Representative from 12th District of California, serving on Education and Labor Committee, Select Committee on Foreign Aid, and Committee on Un-American Activities, 1947-50; appointed to vacant seat in U.S. Senate, 1950; U.S. Senator from California, serving on Labor and Public Welfare Committee and Expenditures in Executive Departments Committee, 1951-53; Vice-President of the United States, serving as chairman of President Eisenhower's Committee on Government Contracts, chairman of the Cabinet Committee on Price Stability for Economic Growth, and as the personal representative of the president on goodwill trips to fifty-four countries, 1953-61; Republican candidate for the presidency, with Henry Cabot Lodge as running mate, 1960; Adams, Duque & Hazeltine, Los Angeles, Calif., counsel, 1961-62; Republican candidate for governor of California, 1962; Mudge, Stern, Baldwin & Todd, New York City, member of firm, 1962-63; Nixon, Mudge, Rose, Guthrie & Alexander (later Nixon, Mudge, Rose, Guthrie, Alexander & Mitchell), New York City, partner, 1964-68; elected president of United States, with Spiro T. Agnew as vice-president, 1968, reelected to office with landslide majority vote of electoral college, 1972, resigned, 1974. Trustee, Whittier College, 1939-68; honorary chairman of Boys' Clubs of America. *Military service:* U.S. Naval Reserve, 1942-46; served in Pacific theatre of operations; became lieutenant commander.

MEMBER: French Fine Arts Academy (foreign associate member), Order of Coif.

WRITINGS:

The Challenges We Face (excerpts compiled from speeches and papers), McGraw, 1960.

Six Crises (autobiographical), Doubleday, 1962.

The Inaugural Address of Richard Milhous Nixon, Achille J. St. Onge, 1969.

Setting the Course, The First Year (policy statements), Funk, 1970.

U.S. Foreign Policy for the 1970's: Report to Congress, Harper, 1971.

A New Road for America (policy statements), Doubleday, 1972.

Four Great Americans (tributes to Dwight Eisenhower, Everett Dirksen, Whitney M. Young, and J. Edgar Hoover), Doubleday, 1973.

The Nixon Presidential Press Conferences, Earl M. Coleman, 1978.

RN: The Memoirs of Richard Nixon, Grosset, 1978.

The Real War, Warner Books, 1980.

Leaders, Warner Books, 1982.

Real Peace: A Strategy for the West, Little, Brown, 1983.

No More Vietnams, Arbor House, 1985.

1999: The Global Challenges We Face in the Next Decade, Simon & Schuster, 1988, published as *1999: Victory without War,* 1988.

In the Arena: A Memoir of Victory, Defeat and Renewal, Simon & Schuster, 1990.

Also author of yearly collections of State of the Union messages, news conference texts, messages to Congress, and major statements, published by Congressional Quarterly, 5 volumes, 1970-74; author of reports, speeches, addresses, official papers, and transcript collections published by U.S. Government Printing Office and other publishers.

SIDELIGHTS: When Richard M. Nixon first ran for public office over forty years ago, it was the start of a distinguished and highly visible political career that included terms as congress-

man, senator, vice-president, and eventually President of the United States. Nixon was frequently embroiled in controversy throughout his career, whether as a congressman investigating communism for the House Un-American Activities Committee in the late 1940s, or as a president criticized by liberals for U.S. involvement in Vietnam and by conservatives for establishing ties with Communist China. Nixon will most likely be known, however, for the scandal which drove him out of office in 1974; the Watergate break-in and cover up was tied to several members of his administration, and under threat of Congressional action, Nixon resigned the office. "Clare Boothe Luce once said that each person in history can be summed up in one sentence," Nixon related in a *Time* interview. "This was after I had gone to China. She said, 'You will be summed up, "He went to China." ' Historians are more likely to lead with 'He resigned the office.' "

Although Watergate ended his political career, Nixon has remained in the public eye with the publication of several books which focus on political issues and his own experiences. After recovering from a near-fatal bout of phlebitis in late 1974, as part of his "spiritual recovery" Nixon decided to write a personal account of his political career. *RN: The Memoirs of Richard Nixon* was published in 1978 to reviews that, while they differ in their assessment of the president himself, find the book interesting as a revelation of Nixon's character. *New York Times* critic Christopher Lehmann-Haupt, for example, observes that despite biases and flaws *RN* "remains a fascinating performance. Whether one dislikes it or admires it, the voice of the prose reflects its author more distinctly than does that of any other American political memoir I can think of offhand, and, for reasons both negative and positive, that voice continues to hypnotize throughout the book's 1,100 pages." "This is a tremendous book, rich in concrete detail, a major political event, and as close as we are ever likely to get to that *sui generis* political creature, Richard Nixon," Jeffrey Hart of the *National Review* similarly claims.

Many critics have noted, in the words of *New York Times Book Review* contributor James MacGregor Burns, that "most of this huge volume [Nixon] devotes to a long statement for the defense." As a result, the critic continues, "the fact that [Nixon's] accounts are highly selective, that he seeks to score points in a continuing debate with the news media and his other adversaries, that his judgments range from the contentious to the tendentious, should not surprise us." "But even [these] flaws of the book help to tell the story," Elizabeth Drew suggests in the *Washington Post Book World,* "the story of an individual whose mind worked in a certain way." Clive James likewise comments that *RN,* despite its subjective slant, "is not a mean book. Nixon's faults are all on view, but so is the fact that they are faults in something substantial," James writes in the *New Statesman.* "His claims to a place in history are shown to be not all that absurd," and his memoirs "constitute a readable book of no small literary merit and considerable human dignity." "For all of this book's predictable flaws," Drew concludes, "it is an interesting, sometimes even absorbing account that cannot be dismissed. Nixon is a major figure in our history, and here he gives us his own version of the years in which he dominated our national life."

Although his resignation removed Nixon from directly participating in political life, he considers that "for whatever time I have left, . . . what is most important is to be able to affect the course of events," as he remarked in *Time.* To that end, he has written several books on foreign policy; his first, 1980's *The Real War,* outlines the history and possible future of the Cold War, and "is a straightforward call for the United States to mobilize *all* its power—military, economic, political, Presidential, clandestine, intellectual, informational and especially will power—to combat the Soviet Union on a global scale," Flora Lewis summarizes in the *New York Times Book Review.*

Critics have faulted the book, however, both for what Lewis terms "a highly selective approach" to historical examples and for Nixon's combative tone. As *New York Review of Books* critic Ronald Steel states: "In this book instead of addressing himself seriously to the issues, [Nixon] panders to the public's anxieties. Instead of being constructive, he is once again being demolishing." And Philip Geyelin declares in the *Washington Post Book World* that *The Real War* overlooks Third World nationalism in order to emphasize fighting the communist threat; in addition, "what's missing here is any sense of how, as a practical matter, you do most of these things—where you get the money, for one thing, not to mention public or Congressional support." But, says David E. Kaiser in a *New Republic* article, "one need not share Nixon's assumptions or value his role in American history in order to find this book provocative. Much of its argument draws effectively on history, it says publicly what many foreign policy specialists probably believe but dare not reveal, and its world view has an inner consistency that forces every reader to examine his own basic assumptions."

Real Peace addresses some of the same issues as Nixon's previous work, but with a view towards detente rather than confrontation. "On balance," maintains Alvin Shuster in the *Los Angeles Times Book Review,* "[Nixon] has done well in taking critic issues before the country, in condensing and discussing them with a fair amount of clarity and force. There is no great writing here but he does manage to describe complex problems in understandable terms." Robert W. Tucker, however, feels that while Nixon's political assessments of the chances for "real peace" are interesting, he omits a concrete plan for attaining this peace. As the critic writes in the *New York Times Book Review:* "The need for Mr. Nixon's real peace can scarcely be denied. How to move toward it remains the great question." But critics such as Joseph Sobran find *Real Peace* more specific in its approach than *The Real War,* especially in the realm of Third World relations. As Sobran comments in the *National Review,* Nixon's new book "is an incisive, often profound manifesto for 'hard-headed detente,' written with aphoristic punch. . . . *Real Peace* contains the antidote to its own single mistake, and much wisdom and practical shrewdness besides. It is a book we need."

In *No More Vietnams* Nixon traces the history of foreign involvement in Vietnam and proposes policies that would prevent another setback against communism. "Besides aggressive self-justification," Toronto *Globe and Mail* writer William Thorsell notes, "this book aims to inspire renewed U.S. commitment to military intervention around the world to stop a voracious communism." " 'No More Vietnams' is two books," historian James Chace suggests in the *New York Times Book Review.* "The first is a highly selective history of the Vietnam War—a war, as he tells it, that we won. We then, however, 'lost the peace.' The second and more interesting book," the critic continues, is the chapter which outlines Nixon's program "to win the hearts and minds—and stomachs—of the third world." Echoing previous criticisms of Nixon's work, some reviewers have faulted the former president's interpretation of past events, citing a lack of specific attributions. As *Chicago Tribune* writer Raymond Coffey observes, despite some strong arguments, "the big problem with the book is that its version of Vietnam history . . . is so blatantly, so outrageously, self-serving that much of the weight and force of the Nixon prescription for the future . . . tend to be diminished."

Nevertheless, Steel admits, "Nixon is an intelligent man and many things in his book are thoughtful and challenging. He is always interesting to listen to, particularly on foreign policy, a field in which he has concentrated so much of his energies." Hart goes further in his praise, writing that *No More Vietnams* "is extraordinarily concise, providing, along with its strongly argued thesis . . . a history and an assessment of our Vietnam policy beginning with the Truman Administration in the immediate post-World War II period. Mr. Nixon's perspective here is presidential, his grasp of the history firm, and his judgments persuasive." "*No More Vietnams* is a very good book, in my opinion Richard Nixon's best, saving only the remarkable *Memoirs,*" Chilton Williamson, Jr., likewise states in the *National Review.* "Though frankly intended as a brief in defense of . . . American presence in Southeast Asia, as a history of a quarter-century of bitter warfare it develops and sustains sufficient consistency to extend its reach far beyond the bounds of mere apologia." "There is considerable intelligence in this polemic," concludes Thorsell, "enormous partisanship, useful insights, breathtaking self-delusion . . . , a feisty challenge to the media, and the crafty use of language."

1999: Victory without War is "important because it is a serious, cogently argued attempt to get American politicians . . . to look forward and to evolve a set of policies that will bring the United States, and the rest of the world, safely into the 21st century," as Paul Kennedy describes it in the *Washington Post Book World.* "Although written by a politician whose right-wing and anti-communist convictions are frequently in evidence, it nonetheless offers perspectives that ought to interest Democrats as much as Republicans." *1999,* according to Thorsell, "restates Nixon's fundamental thesis—that the Soviet drive for world domination remains the central fact of global politics, and that the United States is the Soviet Union's only real opponent." To that end, Nixon outlines potential U.S. strategies for dealing with not only the Soviet Union, but Europe, Asia, and third world nations. "He argues that one of the significant trends in the 21st century will be the rise of Western Europe, Japan and China to increasing importance in world politics, and he has a splendid chapter, both sympathetic and instructive, on the problems of the third world," *New York Times Book Review* contributor Marshall D. Shulman summarizes. This "effort to mark out a centrist position," the critic adds, "may contribute to the emergence of a more coherent consensus for American foreign policy."

Some reviewers, however, criticize the author for overlooking the effects of Soviet president Mikhail Gorbachev's reforms as well as the economic costs of pursuing a "victory without war" against the Soviets. The book, writes Stanley Hoffman in the *New Republic,* contains "an almost indiscriminate paranoia about the Soviet Union—and the absence of a political and financial price tag." "Nixon should stop trying so hard to sound like a statesman," James Fallows avers in the *New York Review of Books,* in favor of what the critic calls the former president's "canny, lawyerlike, poker-playing instinct for sizing up a situation and understanding the possibilities it allows." In contrast, Lehmann-Haupt, who finds Nixon's work full of "clarity, simplicity, and anecdotal appeal," believes that "what needs to be stressed is that in the main '1999' reflects what [Nixon's] admirers have always insisted is the better side of him. In short, if there is a residue of the political opportunist in these pages, it is by and large overwhelmed by the student of statecraft that he has aspired with such doggedness and energy to become." "If he is a prideful prisoner of traumatic experience, and moved too much by the desire for vindication, Nixon is also the most rigorous thinker who has inhabited the White House since John F. Kennedy," Thorsell similarly concludes. "His categorical view of the world need not be shared, but his voice should be heard. Again."

National Review contributor Herbert S. Parmet likewise praises the former president as "the most prominent, gifted, and contentious leader of post-World War II America," and terms 1990's *In the Arena: A Memoir of Victory, Defeat, and Renewal* "a useful introduction to [Nixon's] mind and personality." Consisting of a series of short chapters on various political and personal subjects, the critic continues, *In the Arena* "reveals Nixon the Elder, a long way from the Whittier lawyer, with a voice more mature but strikingly recognizable." This more personal tone, comments Lehmann-Haupt, is most likely due to Nixon's use of dictation in writing the book; "it is a more relaxed book," Lehmann-Haupt observes, and the chapters "read as if the author had unbuttoned his mind and set it free to gather wool." While this method allows the reader to glimpse and empathize with "a figure in many emotional guises," the critic adds, it also "prompts [Nixon] to refer to episodes in his career that have not only been dealt with at length in his previous books, but that are also covered repeatedly in the present volume." As a result, Roger Morris suggests in the *New York Times Book Review*, "what may distinguish the book most . . . are the aphorisms that flow from the resonant and authentic Nixon voice."

Nevertheless, some critics think that *In the Arena* devotes too much space to defending the author's political record and ideas. *Los Angeles Times Book Review* contributor John B. Judis, for instance, while noting that "there are sensible and interesting sections in this book," asserts that the book's "attempts at self-justification and its neo-Cold War policy prescriptions reflect a man who is still bedeviled by his past." *Washington Post Book World* writer Bob Woodward, however, believes that despite "the limitations of this book, and there are many, Nixon once again provides convincing evidence that he is a masterful student of world politics. He repeatedly digs for and finds examples of successful leadership, deftly isolating the powerful personality traits of Eisenhower, De Gaulle, Chou En-Lai and other giants. . . . Nixon is best writing about his intensely personal struggles (few better understand the importance of raw emotion in political life) and about the larger international scene he continues to study avidly." "This is, in most ways, a wistful book, suggesting what has been lost all around rather than beating to death the what-could-have-beens," concludes Parmet. "The spirit may be forced, but the closing tone is nevertheless upbeat and reflective. Nixon lives on; some will say he has returned, as if he ever disappeared."

"Despite one of the worst scandals in the history of the Presidency," Richard Bernstein states in the *New York Times*, Richard Nixon "has carved out a sizable niche for himself in the public arena with his reputation for realism and sagacity in public affairs." "There are few retired Washington giants," Paul Johnson similarly remarks in *Commentary*, that "keep themselves so well briefed on the state of the world, or who have more worthwhile observations to make about it." The critic adds that "there can be few men whose judgment of the American political scene is so shrewd and penetrating, as well as surprisingly objective. . . . He probably exercises more political influence than any other Western statesman not actually in office. Considering the depths of degradation from which he has climbed, this is a remarkable achievement." Returning from adversity is not an unusual achievement for Nixon, however, as he acknowledges in his latest memoir: "As I look back on the dark days after my resignation, my most vivid memory is of a conversation I had with Ambassador Walter Annenberg shortly after I returned to San

Clemente in 1974. He said, 'Whether you have been knocked down or are on the ropes, always remember that life is ninety-nine rounds.' Today, the battle I started to wage forty-three years ago when I first ran for Congress is not over. I still have a few rounds to go."

BIOGRAPHICAL/CRITICAL SOURCES:

BOOKS

Ambrose, Stephen E., *Nixon*, Simon & Schuster, Volume 1: *The Education of a Politician 1913-1962*, 1987, Volume 2: *The Triumph of a Politician 1962-72*, 1989.

Bernstein, Carl, and Bob Woodward, *All the President's Men*, Simon & Schuster, 1974.

Bernstein, Carl, and Bod Woodward, *The Final Days*, Simon & Schuster, 1976.

Brodie, Fawn M., *Richard Nixon: The Shaping of His Character*, Harvard University Press, 1983.

Casper, D. E., *Richard M. Nixon*, Garland Publishing, 1988.

Ehrlichman, John, *Witness to Power: The Nixon Years*, Simon & Schuster, 1982.

Frost, David, *"I Gave Them a Sword": Behind the Scenes of the Nixon Interviews*, Morrow, 1978.

Lukas, James Anthony, *Nightmare: The Underside of the Nixon Years*, Bantam, 1977.

Morris, Roger, *Richard Milhous Nixon: The Rise of an American Politician*, Henry Holt, 1989.

Nixon, Richard M., *Six Crises*, Doubleday, 1962.

Nixon, Richard M., *RN: The Memoirs of Richard Nixon*, Grosset, 1978.

Nixon, Richard M., *In the Arena: A Memoir of Victory, Defeat and Renewal*, Simon & Schuster, 1990.

Safire, William, *Before the Fall*, Doubleday, 1975.

Sulzberger, C. L., *The World and Richard Nixon*, Prentice Hall Press, 1987.

White, Theodore, *Making of the President 1972*, Atheneum, 1973.

White, Theodore, *Breach of Faith*, Atheneum, 1975.

Wills, Gary, *Nixon Agonistes*, Houghton, 1970, revised and enlarged edition, New American Library, 1979.

The Young Nixon, California State University Fullerton, Oral History Program, 1978.

PERIODICALS

Chicago Tribune, March 31, 1985.

Commentary, August, 1979, August, 1980, October, 1988.

Globe and Mail (Toronto), May 4, 1985, June 11, 1988.

Los Angeles Times Book Review, October 31, 1982, January 15, 1984, April 28, 1985, May 8, 1988, April 29, 1990.

Nation, July 8, 1978.

National Review, August 18, 1978, July 25, 1980, February 24, 1984, May 3, 1985, May 28, 1990.

New Republic, June 14, 1980, June 10, 1985, May 23, 1988.

New Statesman, June 8, 1978.

Newsweek, May 8, 1978, May 19, 1986.

New York Review of Books, June 29, 1978, June 26, 1980, May 30, 1985, July 21, 1988.

New York Times, June 8, 1978, March 15, 1985, March 28, 1985, April 11, 1988, April 9, 1990.

New York Times Book Review, June 11, 1978, May 25, 1980, October 31, 1982, January 29, 1984, April 7, 1985, April 17, 1988, April 29, 1990.

Saturday Review, June, 1980.

Spectator, July 15, 1978.

Time, June 9, 1980, April 2, 1990.

Times (London), April 17, 1986.

Times Literary Supplement, July 7, 1978, September 19, 1986, January 27, 1989.
Tribune Books (Chicago), April 15, 1990.
Washington Post, March 21, 1988.
Washington Post Book World, May 28, 1978, June 1, 1980, November 21, 1982, March 31, 1985, April 17, 1988.

*   *   *

NORDEN, Charles
 See DURRELL, Lawrence (George)

*   *   *

NORTH, Andrew
 See NORTON, Andre

*   *   *

NORTH, Anthony
 See KOONTZ, Dean R(ay)

*   *   *

NORTH, Milou
 See ERDRICH, Louise

*   *   *

NORTON, Andre   1912-
 (Andrew North; Allen Weston, a joint pseudonym)

PERSONAL: Given name Alice Mary Norton; name legally changed, 1934; born February 17, 1912, in Cleveland, Ohio; daughter of Adalbert Freely and Bertha (Stemm) Norton. *Education:* Attended Western Reserve University (now Case Western Reserve University), 1930-32. *Politics:* Republican. *Religion:* Presbyterian.

ADDRESSES: Home and office—1600 Spruce Ave., Winter Park, Fla. 32789. *Agent*—Russell Galen, Scott Meredith Literary Agency, 845 Third Ave., New York, N.Y. 10022.

CAREER: Cleveland Public Library, Cleveland, Ohio, children's librarian, 1930-41, 1942-51; Mystery House (book store and lending library), Mount Ranier, Md., owner and manager, 1941; free-lance writer, 1950—. Worked as a special librarian for a citizenship project in Washington, D.C., and at the Library of Congress, 1941. Editor, Gnome Press, 1950-58.

MEMBER: American Penwomen, Science Fiction Writers of America, American League of Writers, Swordsmen and Sorcerers Association.

AWARDS, HONORS: Award from Dutch government, 1946, for *The Sword Is Drawn;* Ohioana Juvenile Award honor book, 1950, for *Sword in Sheath;* Boys' Clubs of America Medal, 1951, for *Bullard of the Space Patrol;* Hugo Award nominations, World Science Fiction Convention, 1962, for *Star Hunter,* 1964, for *Witch World,* and 1968, for "Wizard's World"; Headliner Award, Theta Sigma Phi, 1963; Invisible Little Man Award, Westercon XVI, 1963, for sustained excellence in science fiction; Boys' Clubs of America Certificate of Merit, 1965, for *Night of Masks;* Phoenix Award, 1976, for overall achievement in science fiction; Gandalf Master of Fantasy Award, World Science Fiction Convention, 1977, for lifetime achievement; Andre Norton Award, Women Writers of Science Fiction, 1978; Balrog Fan-

tasy Award, 1979; Ohioana Award, 1980, for body of work; named to Ohio Women's Hall of Fame, 1981; Fritz Leiber Award, 1983, for work in the field of fantasy; E. E. Smith Award, 1983; Nebula Grand Master Award, Science Fiction Writers of America, 1984, for lifetime achievement; Jules Verne Award, 1984, for work in the field of science fiction; Second Stage Lensman Award, 1987, for lifetime achievement.

WRITINGS:

SCIENCE FICTION

(Editor) Malcolm Jameson, *Bullard of the Space Patrol,* World Publishing, 1951.
Star Man's Son, 2250 A.D., Harcourt, 1952, reprinted, Del Rey, 1985, published as *Daybreak, 2250 A.D.* (bound with *Beyond Earth's Gates,* by C. M. Kuttner), Ace Books, 1954.
Star Rangers ("Central Control" series), Harcourt, 1953, reprinted, Del Rey, 1985, published as *The Last Planet,* Ace Books, 1955.
(Editor) *Space Service,* World Publishing, 1953.
(Editor) *Space Pioneers,* World Publishing, 1954.
The Stars Are Ours! ("Astra" series), World Publishing, 1954, reprinted, Ace Books, 1983.
(Under pseudonym Andrew North) *Sargasso of Space* ("Solar Queen" series), Gnome Press, 1955, published under name Andre Norton, Gollancz, 1970.
Star Guard ("Central Control" series), Harcourt, 1955, reprinted, 1984.
(Under pseudonym Andrew North) *Plague Ship* ("Solar Queen" series), Gnome Press, 1956, published under name Andre Norton, Gollancz, 1971.
The Crossroads of Time ("Time Travel" series), Ace Books, 1956, reprint edited by Jim Baen, 1985.
(Editor) *Space Police,* World Publishing, 1956.
Sea Siege, Harcourt, 1957, reprinted, Del Rey, 1987.
Star Born ("Astra" series), World Publishing, 1957.
Star Gate, Harcourt, 1958.
The Time Traders ("Time War" series), World Publishing, 1958, reprinted, Ace Books, 1987.
Galactic Derelict ("Time War" series), World Publishing, 1959, reprinted, Ace Books, 1987.
(Under pseudonym Andrew North) *Voodoo Planet* ("Solar Queen" series; also see below), Ace Books, 1959.
Secret of the Lost Race, Ace Books, 1959, (published in England as *Wolfshead,* Hale, 1977).
The Beast Master ("Beast Master" series), Harcourt, 1959.
Storm over Warlock ("Planet Warlock" series), World Publishing, 1960, reprinted, Gregg Press, 1980.
The Sioux Spaceman, Ace Books, 1960, reprinted, 1987.
Star Hunter (also see below), Ace Books, 1961.
Catseye, Harcourt, 1961, reprinted, Del Rey, 1984.
Eye of the Monster, Ace Books, 1962, reprinted, 1987.
Lord of Thunder ("Beast Master" series), Harcourt, 1962.
The Defiant Agents ("Time War" series), World Publishing, 1962, reprinted, Ace Books, 1987.
Key out of Time ("Time War" series), World Publishing, 1963, reprinted, Ace Books, 1987.
Judgment on Janus, ("Janus" series), Harcourt, 1963, reprinted, Del Rey, 1987.
Ordeal in Otherwhere ("Planet Warlock" series), Harcourt, 1964, reprinted, Gregg Press, 1980.
Night of Masks, Harcourt, 1964, reprinted, Del Rey, 1985.
The X Factor, Harcourt, 1965, reprinted, Del Rey, 1984.
Quest Crosstime ("Time Travel" series), Viking, 1965, reprinted, Ace Books, 1981 (published in England as *Crosstime Agent,* Gollancz, 1975).

Moon of Three Rings ("Moon Magic" series; Junior Literary Guild selection), Viking, 1966, reprinted, Ace Books, 1987.

Victory on Janus ("Janus" series), Harcourt, 1966, reprinted, Del Rey, 1984.

Operation Time Search, Harcourt, 1967, reprinted, Del Rey, 1985.

Dark Piper, Harcourt, 1968.

The Zero Stone ("Zero Stone" series), Viking, 1968, reprinted, Ace Books, 1985.

Uncharted Stars ("Zero Stone" series), Viking, 1969.

Postmarked the Stars ("Solar Queen" series), Harcourt, 1969, reprinted, Fawcett, 1985.

Ice Crown, Viking, 1970.

Android at Arms, Harcourt, 1971, reprinted, Del Rey, 1987.

Exiles of the Stars ("Moon Magic" series), Viking, 1971.

Breed to Come, Viking, 1972.

Here Abide Monsters, Atheneum, 1973.

Forerunner Foray (Science Fiction Book Club selection), Viking, 1973.

(Editor with Ernestine Donaldy) *Gates to Tomorrow: An Introduction to Science Fiction,* Atheneum, 1973.

Iron Cage, Viking, 1974.

The Many Worlds of Andre Norton (short stories), edited by Roger Elwood, Chilton, 1974, published as *The Book of Andre Norton,* DAW Books, 1975.

Outside, Walker & Co., 1975.

(With Michael Gilbert) *The Day of the Ness,* Walker & Co., 1975.

Knave of Dreams, Viking, 1975.

No Night without Stars, Atheneum, 1975.

Perilous Dreams (short stories), DAW Books, 1976.

Voor Loper, Ace Books, 1980.

Forerunner ("Forerunner" series), Tor Books, 1981.

Voodoo Planet [and] *Star Hunter,* Ace Books, 1983.

Forerunner: The Second Venture ("Forerunner" series), Tor Books, 1985.

Flight in Yiktor ("Moon Magic" series), Tor Books, 1986.

"STAR KA'AT" SCIENCE FICTION SERIES; WITH DOROTHY MADLEE

Star Ka'at, Walker & Co., 1976.

Star Ka'at World, Walker & Co., 1978.

Star Ka'ats and the Plant People, Walker & Co., 1979.

Star Ka'ats and the Winged Warriors, Walker & Co., 1981.

FANTASY

Rogue Reynard (juvenile), Houghton, 1947.

Huon of the Horn (juvenile), Harcourt, 1951, reprinted, Del Rey, 1987.

Steel Magic, World Publishing, 1965, published as *Gray Magic,* Scholastic Book Service, 1967.

Octagon Magic, World Publishing, 1967.

Fur Magic, World Publishing, 1968.

Dread Companion, Harcourt, 1970.

High Sorcery (short stories), Ace Books, 1970.

Dragon Magic, Crowell, 1972.

Garan the Eternal (short stories), Fantasy Publishing, 1973.

Lavender-Green Magic, Crowell, 1974.

Merlin's Mirror, DAW Books, 1975.

Wraiths of Time, Atheneum, 1976.

Red Hart Magic, Crowell, 1976.

Yurth Burden, DAW Books, 1978.

Quag Keep, Atheneum, 1978.

Zarthor's Bane, Ace Books, 1978.

(With Phyllis Miller) *Seven Spells to Sunday,* McElderry, 1979.

Iron Butterflies, Fawcett, 1980.

Moon Called, Simon & Schuster, 1982.

Wheel of Stars, Simon & Schuster, 1983.

Were-Wrath, Cheap Street, 1984.

(Editor with Robert Adams) *Magic in Ithkar,* Tor Books, 1985.

(Editor with Adams) *Magic in Ithkar, Number 2,* Tor Books, 1985.

(Editor with Adams) *Magic in Ithkar, Number 3,* Tor Books, 1986.

(Editor with Adams) *Magic in Ithkar, Number 4,* Tor Books, 1987.

The Magic Books, Signet, 1988.

Moon Mirror, Tor Books, 1989.

(Editor with Martin H. Greenberg) *Catfantastic,* DAW Books, 1989.

"WITCH WORLD" FANTASY SERIES

Witch World, Ace Books, 1963, reprinted, 1978.

Web of the Witch World, Ace Books, 1964, reprinted, 1983.

Three against the Witch World, Ace Books, 1965.

Year of the Unicorn, Ace Books, 1965, reprinted, 1989.

Warlock of the Witch World, Ace Books, 1967.

Sorceress of the Witch World, Ace Books, 1968, reprinted, 1986.

Spell of the Witch World (short stories), DAW Books, 1972, reprinted, 1987.

The Crystal Gryphon (first volume in "Gryphon" trilogy), Atheneum, 1972.

The Jargoon Pard, Atheneum, 1974.

Trey of Swords (short stories), Ace Books, 1977.

Lore of the Witch World (short stories), DAW Books, 1980.

Gryphon in Glory (second volume in "Gryphon" trilogy), Atheneum, 1981.

Horn Crown, DAW Books, 1981.

'Ware Hawk, Atheneum, 1983.

(With A. C. Crispin) *Gryphon's Eyrie* (third volume in "Gryphon" trilogy), Tor Books, 1984.

The Gate of the Cat, Ace Books, 1987.

(Editor) *Tales of the Witch World,* Tor Books, 1987.

Four from the Witch World, Tor Books, 1989.

HISTORICAL NOVELS

The Prince Commands, Appleton, 1934.

Ralestone Luck, Appleton, 1938, reprinted, Tor Books, 1988.

Follow the Drum, Penn, 1942, reprinted, Fawcett, 1981.

The Sword Is Drawn (first volume of "Swords" trilogy; Junior Literary Guild selection), Houghton, 1944, reprinted, Unicorn-Star Press, 1985.

Scarface, Harcourt, 1948.

Sword in Sheath (second volume of "Swords" trilogy), Harcourt, 1949, reprinted, Unicorn-Star Press, 1985 (published in England as *Island of the Lost,* Staples Press, 1954).

At Sword's Points (third volume of "Swords" trilogy), Harcourt, 1954, reprinted, Unicorn-Star Press, 1985.

Yankee Privateer, World Publishing, 1955.

Stand to Horse, Harcourt, 1956.

Shadow Hawk, Harcourt, 1960, reprinted, Del Rey, 1987.

Ride Proud, Rebel!, World Publishing, 1961, reprinted, Juniper, 1981.

Rebel Spurs, World Publishing, 1962.

OTHER

(With Grace Hogarth, under joint pseudonym Allen Weston) *Murder for Sale* (mystery), Hammond, 1954.

(With mother, Bertha Stemm Norton) *Bertie and May* (biography), World Publishing, 1969.

(Editor) *Small Shadows Creep: Ghost Children,* Dutton, 1974.
The White Jade Fox (gothic), Dutton, 1975.
(Editor) *Baleful Beasts and Eerie Creatures,* Rand McNally, 1976.
Velvet Shadows (gothic), Fawcett, 1977.
The Opal-Eyed Fan (gothic), Dutton, 1977.
Snow Shadow (mystery), Fawcett, 1979.
Ten Mile Treasure (juvenile mystery), Pocket Books, 1981.
(With Enid Cushing) *Caroline,* Pinnacle, 1982.
(With Miller) *House of Shadows* (mystery), Atheneum, 1984.
Stand and Deliver, Tor Books, 1984.
(With Miller) *Ride the Green Dragon* (mystery), Atheneum, 1985.

Contributor to numerous periodicals and anthologies.

WORK IN PROGRESS: The Black Trillium, a novel, with fellow fantasists Marion Zimmer Bradley and Julian May.

SIDELIGHTS: Although she has penned numerous books of historical fiction and mystery, among other kinds, Andre Norton is best known and admired for her science fiction and fantasy. Although women writers were rare in the genre when she published *Star Man's Son, 2250 A.D.* in 1952, Norton quickly became a popular favorite, with some of her books selling over a million copies each. Despite frequent critical dismissal of her work as lacking complexity, both Norton's fans and peers have recognized her contributions to science fiction: she is one of the few writers to be awarded both the Science Fiction Writers of America's Grand Master Award and science fiction fandom's equivalent, the Gandalf Award.

"Those who know Miss Norton's work well appreciate her highly," notes a *Times Literary Supplement* writer. "She belongs to the group of writers whose books appear on the list for the young as a result of shrinkage in the adult novel, although her readers might be of any age over twelve." The critic adds that "the background of her stories is a literary one and includes myth and legend and the high tone and seriousness of epic, the dark and brooding matters of tragedy." Indeed, many critics have observed that solid research is the foundation of a Norton novel, a product of her early career as a librarian. As Francis J. Molson remarks in a *Dictionary of Literary Biography* essay: "The excitement and zest of great deeds or intrepid voyaging across galactic distances readers sense in Norton's science fiction and fantasy originate within her creative and prolific imagination, especially as it draws inspiration from and refashions material she has discovered in her extensive reading and research in history and related fields."

While critics may debate Norton's literary significance, many agree that her work has been overlooked for a variety of reasons. For instance, her first books were marketed toward juvenile readers, much as the early work of Robert Heinlein had been; thus, although they were read by all ages, Norton's novels were dismissed as relatively unimportant. Charlotte Spivack, however, proposes another explanation for Norton's lack of critical attention: "Her wide reading public has simply taken Andre Norton for granted, not as the author of a single masterpiece but rather as a steadily dependent writer who is always there with a couple of entertaining new paperbacks every year," as she writes in *Merlin's Daughters: Contemporary Women Writers of Fantasy.* "The would-be critic, on the other hand, is likely to be intimidated by the vast output and remarkable variety of this prolific writer."

Donald Wollheim similarly remarks in his introduction to *The Many Worlds of Andre Norton* that while science fiction and fantasy readers "may spend a lot of time discussing the sociology and speculations of the other writers, Andre Norton they read for pleasure. This is not to say that her works lack the depth of the others, because they do not," explains the critic. "But it is that these depths form part of the natural unobtrusive background of her novels." "It is possible that the pace and suspense of Norton's storytelling may so ensnare readers that they may overlook the themes or concerns her narratives embody," states Molson. But, the critic claims, "Norton's science fiction is actually serious on the whole—sometimes even explicitly earnest and didactic—as it dramatizes several themes and concerns. In fact, one theme, above all others, is pervasive in Norton's [work]: the centrality of passage or initiation in the lives of many of her protagonists."

Elisa Kay Sparks believes this theme figures prominently in Norton's work; in a *Dictionary of Literary Biography* essay, Sparks characterizes Norton's writings as "almost always . . . center[ing] on the process by which a somehow displaced, exiled, or alienated hero or heroine finds a new home or sense of community. From the first to the last her books insist on the necessity of cooperation between equals." "Frequently," relates Roger Schlobin in the introduction to his *Andre Norton: A Primary and Secondary Bibliography,* "the protagonists must undergo a rite of passage to find self-realization." The story of *Star Man's Son, 2250 A.D.* exemplifies this theme: a young mutant, scorned by a post-war society because of his differences, quests on his own to fulfill his father's legacy; in doing so, he discovers his own self-worth. As Molson describes it, the book "speaks directly and forcefully . . . through its convincing story of a boy's passage from a questioning, unsure adolescence to confident, assured young manhood."

It is this focus on the internal struggles of her characters that makes Norton's work interesting, suggests Schlobin in *The Feminine Eye: Science Fiction and the Women Who Write It.* "Norton's reverence for the self, especially as it seeks to realize its potentials . . . is one of the major reasons why her plots are always so exciting. Her protagonists have to deal not only with dangerous external forces but also with their own maturation and personal challenges," states the critic. One such protagonist appears in *Forerunner: The Second Venture,* a 1985 work. While *Fantasy Review* contributor Carl B. Yoke finds other aspects of the story disappointing, the main character Simsa "is one of those stubbornly-independent, highly resourceful, intuitive, and intelligent characters that many of us fans have come to expect and admire in Norton's work."

In resolving this theme of self-fulfillment, Norton's work frequently expresses another idea of importance to her work: that to understand oneself, a person must come to understand and accept others. "In Norton's novels the heroic quest for self-realization ends typically in union with another," maintains Spivack. "The resolution of inner conflict is androgynous. For Norton the integration of Self and Other is of supreme importance, whether the Other is gender or species." The critic elaborates, observing that in the "Magic" series of books for younger readers, "in each case the self-knowledge of the protagonist results not only from the admission of one's own weaknesses but also from the discovery of the Other as worthy of respect." Schlobin similarly comments in his bibliography that Norton's "resolutions are androgynous: within themselves or in union with another, [Norton's characters] find the ideal combination of male and female characteristics. Most of all," continues the critic, "they discover a sanctity of ideas and ethics, and they recognize their own places within the patterns and rhythms of elemental law and carry that recognition forward into a hopeful future."

For instance, in what is her most popular series, the novels of the "Witch World," the resolution of many of the books lies in the cooperation of male and female aspects. The Witch World includes a society of female witches who remain virginal as a means of sustaining their power; this dictate is later shown to be unnecessary and even detrimental to the witches. As Spivack interprets this, "in Norton's view neither sex is complete without the other; self-fulfillment involves union with the opposite sex. Furthermore," she adds, "the relationship between the sexes should be based on equality, not domination. . . . Wholeness through balanced union of male and female, especially on the plane of values, tends to eliminate the need for aggression. Norton is thus the first of the women fantasists to combine the themes of the renunciation of power, the depolarization of values, and the vindication of mortality." Characters who reject such compromises make up a great number of Norton's antagonists, states Sparks: "Norton consistently associates evil with the denial of such bonds, or with a lack of appreciation for individuality and liberty; opportunism, willful destructiveness, and the urge to dominate through the imposition of mechanized forms of control are characteristic attributes of her villains."

Indeed, it is the mechanical, non-individualistic aspects of science that frequently provide the conflict in Norton's work; "though many of her novels are set in the future," remarks Schlobin, "she has no special affection for the technological and, in fact, science is most often the antagonist in her fiction." Rick Brooks similarly notes in *The Many Worlds of Andre Norton* that "in the battle between technology and nature, Miss Norton took a stand long before the great majority of us had any doubts. . . . Technology is a necessary evil [in her work] to get there for the adventure and to get some of the story to work. And the adventure is as much to mold her universe to her views as to entertain," adds the critic. Norton revealed the reasons behind her distrust of technology to Charles Platt in *Dream Makers Volume II: The Uncommon Men and Women Who Write Science Fiction:* "I think the human race made a bad mistake at the beginning of the Industrial Revolution. We leaped for the mechanics, and threw aside things that were just as important. We made the transition too fast. I do not like mechanical things very much," the author explained. "And I don't like a lot of the modern ways of living. I prefer to do things with my hands; and I think everybody misses that. People need the use of their hands to feel creative." Brooks further notes: "Norton consistently views the future as one where the complexity of science and technology have reduced the value of the individual. . . . So Miss Norton is actually wrestling with the prime problem, that of human worth and purpose."

While some critics, such as Brooks, observe a higher purpose in Norton's writing, they consistently remark upon the author's ability to craft an entertaining tale. "Norton is above all committed to telling a story, and she tells it in clear, effective prose," asserts Spivack. "Not given to metaphors or lyricism, her style is focused on narrative movement, dialogue, and descriptive foreground. . . . Her scenes are moving and vivid, and both the outward action and inward growth are drawn convincingly and absorbingly." Molson concurs, calling Norton "a skilled teller of stories. . . . Characteristically, her stories, either science fiction or fantasy, are replete with incident; take place in the near or far future; feature alien or bizarre life forms, futuristic technology or exotic settings." In addition, the author not only provides her readers with new and exciting concepts but also with an opportunity to visualize these notions for themselves. As *Riverside Quar-*

terly contributor Barry McGhan summarizes, "[one critic] claims that a prime attraction of this author's writing is that she introduces many intriguing ideas that are never completely wrapped up at the end of the book, thus leaving something to be filled in by the reader's own imagination."

Yet for all Norton's skill in creating and presenting universes to her readers, she always includes ideas of substance in her fiction. "The sheer size of [Norton's] world, which is infinitely extended in time and space, and in which nothing is outside the bounds of possibility, is matched by the size of the themes she tackles," claims John Rowe Townsend in *A Sense of Story: Essays on Contemporary Writers for Children.* In a Norton novel, he adds, "there is always something beyond the immediate action to be reached for and thought about." Because of the breadth and scope of her work, maintains Brooks, "the chief value of Andre Norton's writing may not lie in entertainment or social commentary, but in her 're-enchanting' us with her creations that renew our linkages to all life." "Not only does she succeed in holding her reader," observes Spivack, "but her cosmos lingers in the mind, with its unforgettable images of alien species, jewels and talismans resonant with psychic powers, and magical transcendence of time and space. At the center of this original universe, with its startling variety of life forms, is the individual, alone, heroic, supremely important."

Another quality that makes Norton's science fiction memorable, as Wollheim states, is her ability to evoke the "sense of wonder" that characterizes much of the genre. "Andre Norton is at home telling us wonder stories. She is telling us that people are marvelously complex and marvelously fascinating. She is telling us that all life is good and that the universe is vast and meant to enhance our life to infinity. She is weaving an endless tapestry of a cosmos no man will ever fully understand, but among whose threads we are meant to wander forever to our personal fulfillment." The critic continues: "Basically this is what science fiction has always been about. And because she has always understood this, her audience will continue to be as ever-renewing and as nearly infinite as her subjects." Schlobin similarly concludes in *The Feminine Eye:* "Andre Norton, then, like all special writers, is more than just an author. She is a guide who leads us, the real human beings, to worlds and situations that we might very well expect to live in were we given extraordinary longevity. . . . The Norton future is an exciting realm alive with personal quests to be fulfilled and vital challenges to be overcome," Schlobin continues. "Is it any wonder that millions upon millions of readers, spanning three generations, have chosen to go with her in her travels?"

AVOCATIONAL INTERESTS: Collecting fantasy and cat figurines and paper dolls, needlework.

BIOGRAPHICAL/CRITICAL SOURCES:

BOOKS

Contemporary Literary Criticism, Volume 12, Gale, 1980.
Crouch, Marcus, *The Nesbit Tradition: The Children's Novel in England, 1945-70,* Benn, 1972.
Dictionary of Literary Biography, Gale, Volume 8: *Twentieth-Century American Science Fiction Writers,* 1981, Volume 52: *American Writers for Children since 1960: Fiction,* 1986.
Elwood, Roger, editor, *The Many Worlds of Andre Norton,* introduction by Donald Wollheim, Chilton, 1974, published as *The Book of Andre Norton,* DAW Books, 1975.
Magill, Frank N., editor, *Survey of Science Fiction Literature,* Volumes 1-5, Salem Press, 1979.

Platt, Charles, *Dream Makers Volume II: The Uncommon Men and Women Who Write Science Fiction,* Berkley Publishing, 1983.

Schlobin, Roger C., *Andre Norton,* Gregg, 1979.

Schlobin, Roger C., *Andre Norton: A Primary and Secondary Bibliography,* G. K. Hall, 1980.

Shwartz, Susan, editor, *Moonsinger's Friends: An Anthology in Honor of Andre Norton,* Bluejay Books, 1985.

Spivack, Charlotte, *Merlin's Daughters: Contemporary Women Writers of Fantasy,* Greenwood Press, 1987.

Staicar, Tom, editor, *The Feminine Eye: Science Fiction and the Women Who Write It,* Ungar, 1982.

Townsend, John Rowe, *A Sense of Story: Essays on Contemporary Writers for Children,* Lippincott, 1971.

PERIODICALS

Extrapolation, fall, 1985.

Fantasy Review, September, 1985.

Los Angeles Times, December 27, 1984.

New York Times Book Review, September 20, 1970, February 24, 1974, January 25, 1976.

Riverside Quarterly, January, 1970.

School Librarian, July, 1967.

Times Literary Supplement, June 6, 1968, June 26, 1969, October 16, 1969, July 2, 1971, April 18, 1972, April 6, 1973, September 28, 1973, July 16, 1976.

—*Sketch by Diane Telgen*

*   *   *

NOSILLE, Nabrah
See ELLISON, Harlan

*   *   *

NOVAK, Joseph
See KOSINSKI, Jerzy (Nikodem)

*   *   *

NYE, Robert 1939-

PERSONAL: Born March 15, 1939, in London, England; son of Oswald William and Frances Dorothy (Weller) Nye; married first wife Judith Preyed, 1959 (divorced, 1967); married second wife, Aileen Campbell (an artist, poet, and psychologist), 1968; children: (first marriage) Jack, Taliesin, Malory; (second marriage) Owen, Sharon, Rebecca. *Education:* Attended schools in England.

ADDRESSES: Home—Cork, Ireland. *Agent*—Anthony Sheil Associates, Ltd., 2/3 Morwell St., London WC1B 3AR, England; and Wallace, Aitken & Sheil, Inc., 118 East 61st St., New York, N.Y. 10021.

CAREER: Writer. Worked as a newspaper reporter, milkman, market garden laborer, and sanatorium orderly; *Times,* London, England, poetry critic, 1971—. Poetry editor, *Scotsman,* 1967—; fiction reviewer, *Guardian,* London. Writer in residence, University of Edinburgh, 1976-77.

MEMBER: Royal Society of Literature (fellow).

AWARDS, HONORS: Eric Gregory Award, 1963, for *Juvenilia 2;* Scottish Arts Council bursary, 1970, 1973, and publication award, 1970, 1976; James Kennaway Memorial Award, 1970, for *Tales I Told My Mother; Guardian* fiction prize, 1976, and Hawthornden Prize, 1977, both for *Falstaff.*

WRITINGS:

FOR CHILDREN

Taliesin (novel; also see below), Faber, 1966, Hill & Wang, 1967.

March Has Horse's Ears (short stories), Faber, 1966, Hill & Wang, 1967.

Beowulf: A New Telling (novel; also see below), illustrated by wife Aileen Campbell Nye, Hill & Wang, 1968 (published in England as *Bee Hunter: Adventures of Beowulf,* Faber, 1968, reprinted as *Beowulf, the Bee Hunter,* Faber, 1972).

Wishing Gold (novel; also see below), illustrated by Helen Craig, Macmillan (London), 1970, Hill & Wang, 1971.

Poor Pumpkin (short stories), Macmillan (London), 1971, published as *The Mathematical Princess and Other Stories,* Hill & Wang, 1972.

Cricket: Three Stories, pictures by Shelly Freshman, Bobbs-Merrill, 1975 (published in England as *Once upon Three Times,* Benn, 1978).

Out of the World and Back Again, illustrated by Joanna Troughton, Collins, 1977, published as *Out of This World and Back Again,* Bobbs-Merrill, 1978.

The Bird of the Golden Land, illustrated by Krystyna Turska, Hamish Hamilton, 1980.

Harry Pay the Pirate (novel), Hamish Hamilton, 1981.

Three Tales: Beowulf, Taliesin, Wishing Gold, Hamish Hamilton, 1983.

FOR ADULTS

Doubtfire (novel), Calder & Boyars, 1967, Hill & Wang, 1968.

Tales I Told My Mother (short stories), Hill & Wang, 1969.

(Contributor) *Penguin Modern Stories 6,* Penguin, 1970.

Lines Review 38 (includes four stories, poems, and a filmscript), [Edinburgh], 1971.

Falstaff: Being the "Acta Domini Johannis Fastolfe"; or, "Life and Valiant Deeds of Sir John Faustoff"; or, "The Hundred Days War," as told by Sir John Fastolf, K. G., to His Secretaries William Worcester, Stephen Scrope, Fr. Brackley, Christopher Hanson, Luke Nanton, John Bussard, and Peter Bassett—Now First Transcribed, Arranged, and Edited in Modern Spelling by Robert Nye (novel), Little, Brown, 1976.

Merlin (novel), Hamish Hamilton, 1978, Putnam, 1979.

Faust: Being the Historia von D. Johann Fausten dem Wietbeschreyten Zauberer und Schwartzkuenstler; or, History of Dr. John Faust the Notorious Magician and Necromancer, as Written by His Familiar Servant and Disciple Christopher Wagner, Now for the First Time Englished from the Low German (novel), Putnam, 1980.

The Voyage of the Destiny (novel), Putnam, 1982.

The Facts of Life and Other Fictions (short stories), Hamish Hamilton, 1983.

The Memoirs of Lord Byron (novel), Hamish Hamilton, 1989.

POEMS

Juvenilia 1, Scorpion Press, 1961.

Juvenilia 2, Scorpion Press, 1963.

Darker Ends, Hill & Wang, 1969.

Divisions on a Ground, Carcanet Press, 1976.

A Collection of Poems, 1955-1988, Hamish Hamilton, 1989.

PLAYS

(With William Watson) *Sawney Bean* (also see below; first produced in Edinburgh, Scotland, 1969, produced in New York, 1982), Calder & Boyars, 1970.

"Sisters" (also see below), first produced as a radio play by British Broadcasting Corp. (BBC Radio), 1969, first stage production in Edinburgh, Scotland, 1973.

"A Bloody Stupit Hole," BBC Radio, 1970.

"Reynolds, Reynolds," BBC Radio, 1971.

"Penthesilea" (adaptation of a play by Heinrich von Kleist; also see below), BBC Radio, 1971, first stage production in London, 1983.

The Seven Deadly Sins: A Mask (first produced in Stirling, Scotland, at the Stirling Festival, 1973), Omphalos Press, 1974.

"Mr. Poe: A Public Lecture with Private Illustrations," first produced in Edinburgh, Scotland, and London, 1974.

Three Plays: Penthesilia, Fugue, and Sisters, Marion Boyars, 1975.

(With Humphrey Searle) "The Devil's Jig" (play adaptation of a work by Thomas Mann), BBC Radio, 1980.

EDITOR

(And author of introduction) *A Choice of Sir Walter Raleigh's Verse,* Faber, 1972.

William Barnes of Dorset: A Selection of His Poems, Carcanet Press, 1973.

(And author of introduction) *A Choice of Swinburne's Verse,* Faber, 1973.

The Book of Sonnets, Oxford University Press (New York), 1976 (published in England as *The Faber Book of Sonnets,* Faber, 1976).

The English Sermon 1750-1850: An Anthology, Carcanet Press, 1976.

P.E.N. New Poetry I, Quartet Books, 1986.

WORK IN PROGRESS: A volume of collected poems.

SIDELIGHTS: Robert Nye is a writer of poetry, short stories, and novels for children and adults. He has also tried his hand at plays and scriptwriting, and has become a noted critic and editor, contributing reviews to the London *Times* and *Guardian.* Although his poetry and short stories have won the Eric Gregory Award and the James Kennaway Award respectively, Nye is best known for his novels *Merlin, Faust,* and *Falstaff;* the lattermost won the Hawthornden Prize in 1977 and was adapted for the stage. These books are examples of the author's tendency to borrow old story lines from myths and legends (usually of English, Welsh, and Celtic origin) and use literary and historical figures, reworking these two elements into tales with frequently humorous and ribald plots. Michael Wood in the *New York Review of Books,* along with other critics, compares Nye's style to that of French satirist Francois Rabelais, and London *Times* reviewer David Williams detects an influence of James Joyce in the author's work. Despite an early dissatisfaction with poetry, in 1988 the author told *CA:* "I . . . regard myself primarily as a poet." He further added that he writes prose "as a relief from the truth-telling which poetry requires of his adherents."

In a *Dictionary of Literary Biography* entry written by Elizabeth Allen, the author says his penchant for writing was first inspired by his mother, who, he relates, "was possessed of an innate peasant storytelling ability." By his early teens, Nye knew that he wanted to pursue a writing career. He decided against any further formal education after high school, concentrating instead on his poetry while working odd jobs to support himself and, later, his family. Though *Juvenilia 2* and *Darker Ends* were both well received by critics, these early poetry collections did not draw much income. His first collection of poetry, *Juvenilia 1,* was dismissed by critics, as one *Times Literary Supplement* article notes, for its "immaturity of attitude and elusiveness of meaning." This is not surprising, however, since Nye wrote many of the poems in *Juvenilia 1* while still a teenager.

According to the same article, by the time *Juvenilia 2* was written Nye's style had matured to the point where he could be called a "true poet." But after he published *Darker Ends* in 1969, the poet abandoned the genre for several years. In a 1967 *Books and Bookmen* interview, Nye explains his disenchantment with poetry: "Poetry on every side is announcing to all who still have an ear for its voice that it is a factitious and unsatisfactory means of expression." Instead, he says that he has turned to the novel because it "has in the last 50 years been surreptitiously taking over from poetry the field it once claimed as its own exclusive right." The field to which he refers is "the true history of the race: a permanent record of man's deepest moments of feeling, seeing, being."

Doubtfire, Nye's first novel, is faithful to his idea that novels should depict life poetically. It is "an exercise in word-imagery with allegorical overtones," describes Anthony Horner in *Books and Bookmen.* New Statesman contributor Gillian Freeman summarizes the book as being "a ranging exploration of the mind of an adolescent boy who, developing towards sexual maturity, is unable to sort out reality from fantasy." By telling the story from within the mind of a confused adolescent, Nye explores the nature of reality. "The Reality of Nye's intricately clever 'nowhere somewhere else' is not real because he teaches us that no reality is real," writes *Northwest Review* critic P. H. Porosky. "Madness, grotesque bizarreness replace so-called lucidity because, as Nye's characters learn, lucidity is really a fiction, a process of imagination, the minor image, or finally, . . . the poem." Porosky expresses frustration with Nye's obtuse, poetic approach in *Doubtfire,* remarking that "at times one wonders if there is any coherence at all." But in a London *Times* article Michael Wood brings to the reader's attention that not storyline, but "language is the hero" in *Doubtfire.* It is, says Wood, a "brilliantly sustained [book], . . . a poem-novel with careful syntax, proliferating pictures and a strong sense of the concrete."

Similarly, Nye's short stories are a departure from the norm, due to the author's unique use of language, characters, and plot. David Williams remarks that, as with *Doubtfire,* it is difficult to say what the stories in Nye's *Tales I Told My Mother* are about. He suggests that one will "probably get farther if he proceeds by way of similes rather than epitomes." To compose his stories, the writer uses a liberal mixture of characters and objects without much regard to the limitations of time, place, or reality. "Among other people and things," writes David Montrose in the *Times Literary Supplement,* Nye incorporates into his stories "various members of the Pre-Raphaelite Brotherhood, a Chinese giant, a reinterpretation of Chatterton's suicide, the Wandering Jew, and a lost novel by Emily Bronte." The reviewer concludes that *Tales I Told My Mother* displays "plenty of ingenuity." One original aspect of the book involves the way the author intertwines these elements to form an interconnected whole. In the *British Book News,* Neil Philip calls this approach to the short story "an immature 'experimental' attempt which nevertheless repays attention. Nye's prose is dazzling even at its most opaque, and his sheer delight in language is a delight for the reader, too."

His more recent collection of short stories, *The Facts of Life and Other Fictions,* also "confirms Nye's wonderful gift for language," asserts Montrose; but, the reviewer adds, the inventiveness of the author's earlier collection is lacking. Again, the author mixes various famous characters such as James Joyce and Anne Hathaway into the same storyline, but the plots in this case are unconnected and do not include "the dark imaginings" of

Tales I Told My Mother, says Montrose. However, he claims the story "Adam Kadmon" in *The Facts of Life* contains a previously undisclosed key to Nye's writing which "could almost be applied to the entire collection. The story, we learn, is 'a pack of lies'. . . . It has no other function or meaning."

This insight, when applied to Nye's *Falstaff,* explains this novel's content. With much extrapolation by the author, Shakespeare's comical character from *Henry IV* and *The Merry Wives of Windsor* dictates his own version of his life to several secretaries. Nye asks the reader to accept that, although Shakespeare tells us that Falstaff dies in *Henry IV: Part II,* his "death" was actually a ruse to avoid his creditors. Falstaff can then go on to describe what really happened at the Battle of Shrewsbury, the robbery at Gadshill, and other events from Shakespeare's plays, while adding many ribald adventures and explicit monologues about human bodily functions and parts of the corpulent storyteller's anatomy. In these memoirs Falstaff's character becomes heroic, logical, and noble. For example, he explains that he actually allowed Prince Hal to steal the booty from him at Gadshill because, as *Time* reviewer John Sklow puts it, any other course of action "would have destroyed the confidence of the next King of England." At the conclusion of the book, however, Falstaff confesses to a priest that his memoirs are really "lies about my whole life." The riddle comes when he adds: "But try & explain: some *true* lies?" Peter Conrad comments on this in the *Spectator:* "Falstaff's dying admission that his memoirs are a tissue of prurient lies only confirms his creative genius: he turns life into art, whereas Shakespeare can only make feeble art from the transcription of that life."

To *Village Voice* contributor Katherine Bouton, though, Falstaff's tales are "sometimes apt, but more often it is simply Shakespeare paraphrased." Bouton also finds the details of Falstaff's sexual exploits, which contain many suggestive puns, "tiresomely repetitive." She complains that there is "no plot or character development." West similarly believes that the rotund prevaricator "wears his welcome out." To a certain extent, Michael Wood supports this viewpoint; but he adds that the bawdiness in the novel "generally . . . takes on a rather attractive pathos, for we are rarely allowed to forget that Falstaff is not bragging, but *lying,* and that his 'cunterbury tales,' as he calls them, are a requiem for a life he never lived."

The two books which follow *Falstaff, Merlin* and *Faust,* are also largely based upon ribald adventures and incredible tales. Again, these novels borrow old, familiar stories and tell them from new perspectives. *Merlin* relates the events of the Arthurian legend from the viewpoint of the wizard, whom Nye describes as the offspring of a virgin and Satan. He is a kind of "failed Antichrist," who, when imprisoned in the crystal cave, "becomes the ultimate voyeur and cosmospectator," says *Times Literary Supplement Review* contributor T. A. Shippey. Mary Hope describes the book in the *Spectator* as "a gallimaufrey and hotch potch, linked by one splendid shaggy dog story." Like *Falstaff, Merlin* does not fall easily into the category of the novel because of its deemphasis of character and plot development. It is more of an exercise with "language, images, and psychological implications," asserts *Atlantic* contributor Phoebe-Lou Adams. As in the author's other books, *New Statesman* reviewer Helen McNeil says that the "giggling, scratching, farting, cursing, pissing, birching (lots of that), frigging, . . . only lead one away from any suspicion that these [characters] have ever lived or that they resemble us."

But even though "the novel fizzes along on a charge of multilevelled, inconsequential anecdote," comments Shippey, *Merlin* is "not as inconsequential as it looks." Through Merlin's eyes, the reader gains certain "sensational" insights which lead Shippey to believe that the moral of the story "is that the world is a book and the devil writes it . . . —an idea which all great Arthurians of the past would, I'm sure, find repugnant." Nevertheless, Nye does succeed in presenting this familiar story in a new way. Unhindered by any need to honor the Arthurian myth, the author is free to present a new perspective of the legend.

The author also brings originality to the legend of Faust through his customary shift in viewpoint, which in this case comes from Faust's protege Christopher (Kit) Wagner. Kit relates the last days of Faust before his contract with Satan expires and he is condemned to damnation in Hell. Contrary to Goethe's and Marlowe's versions, Nye's Faust is portrayed by Kit as a "chronic old lecher and drunken fool," according to *British Book News* reviewer Christopher Norris. The story relates the events of Faust's and Kit's travels as they journey to Rome "in a final bid to secure reprieve" from the Pope, writes *Spectator* critic Paul Ableman, but the trip deteriorates into a spree of debauchery which *Times Literary Supplement* reviewer J. B. Steane finds "tiresome, [especially] when 'come' cannot pass without a pun."

"The whole book," summarizes Norris, "is really a compendium of jokes, some of them told straight off on the flimsiest of narrative pretexts, others having a more subtle relation to the legend and tradition of Faust." He concludes that *Faust* is not a book "for the squeamish or custodians of moral sweetness and light." In Nye's version, however, the plot has "an original twist which gives the whole tale something of the nature of a metaphysical thriller with a surprise ending," says Ableman. It is, Norris adds, "a spirited piece of novelistic daring. A thoroughly enjoyable book."

In a combined review of *Falstaff* and *Faust,* Alan Franks concludes in the London *Times:* "These most ambitious novels could so easily have become inchoate . . ., but it is always the sheer vigour of Nye's language which pulls them back from the brink." Franks continues, "His is a highly individual diction, forever lancing its own pretensions with the use of tough, strangely timeless vernacular. The mixture of erudition and sheer belly mirth is potent indeed." Because his primary interest is poetry, Nye's continuing experimentations with language have tended to place plot and characterization in subordinate positions within his novels. This has sometimes made his work difficult for critics to interpret. In the *Dictionary of Literary Biography,* Allen summarizes Nye's writing as being "both traditional and highly individual: traditional in that he works with archetypal themes and myths available to all writers of story and legend both oral and literary, and individual in the forms in which he recreates them." It is this originality of form in perspective and language which has made Nye a noted contributor to English literature.

MEDIA ADAPTATIONS: Falstaff was produced as a radio play in 1981.

BIOGRAPHICAL/CRITICAL SOURCES:

BOOKS

Contemporary Literary Criticism, Gale, Volume 13, 1980, Volume 42, 1987.
The Dictionary of Literary Biography, Volume 14: *British Novelists since 1960,* Gale, 1983.

PERIODICALS

Atlantic, June, 1979.
Books and Bookmen, May, 1967, March, 1968.

British Book News, December, 1980, June, 1982.

Listener, February 29, 1968.

New Statesman, February 9, 1968, September 15, 1978.

New York Review of Books, January 20, 1977.

New York Times Book Review, November 7, 1976.

Northwest Review, summer, 1968.

Spectator, September 4, 1976, October 18, 1980, September 23, 1987.

Time, November 8, 1976.

Times (London), January 27, 1968, December 20, 1969, June 30, 1983, January 4, 1986.

Times Literary Supplement, July 26, 1963, September 15, 1978, October 17, 1980, June 17, 1983.

Village Voice, December 27, 1976.

O

OATES, Joyce Carol 1938-
(Rosamond Smith)

PERSONAL: Born June 16, 1938, in Lockport, N.Y.; daughter of Frederic J. (a tool and die designer) and Caroline (Bush) Oates; married Raymond Joseph Smith (an editor and former professor of English), January 23, 1961. *Education:* Syracuse University, B.A., 1960; University of Wisconsin, M.A., 1961.

ADDRESSES: Office—Ontario Review Press, 9 Honey Brook Dr., Princeton, N.J. 08540. *Agent*—Blanche C. Gregory, 2 Tudor City Place, New York, N.Y. 10017.

CAREER: Writer. University of Detroit, Detroit, Mich., instructor in English, 1961-65, assistant professor, 1965-67; University of Windsor, Windsor, Ontario, member of English department faculty, 1967-78; Princeton University, Princeton, N.J., writer in residence, beginning 1978, currently Roger S. Berlind Distinguished Professor.

MEMBER: American Academy and Institute of Arts and Letters, Modern Language Association, Phi Beta Kappa.

AWARDS, HONORS: National Endowment for the Arts grants, 1966, 1968; Guggenheim fellowship, 1967; O. Henry Award, Doubleday, 1967, for "In the Region of Ice," and 1973, for "The Dead"; Rosenthal Award, National Institute of Arts and Letters, 1968; National Book Award nomination, 1968, for *A Garden of Earthly Delights,* and 1969, for *Expensive People;* National Book Award for fiction, 1970, for *them;* O. Henry Special Award for Continuing Achievement, 1970 and 1986; Lotos Club Award of Merit, 1975; *Unholy Loves* was selected by the American Library Association as a notable book of 1979; *Bellefleur* was nominated for a *Los Angeles Times* Book Prize in fiction, 1980; St. Louis Literary Award, 1988; Rhea Award for the Short Story, Dungannon Foundation, 1990.

WRITINGS:

NOVELS

With Shuddering Fall, Vanguard Press, 1964.
A Garden of Earthly Delights, Vanguard Press, 1967.
Expensive People, Vanguard Press, 1967.
them, Vanguard Press, 1969, reprinted, Fawcett, 1986.
Wonderland, Vanguard Press, 1971.
Do with Me What You Will, Vanguard Press, 1973.
The Assassins: A Book of Hours, Vanguard Press, 1975.

Triumph of the Spider Monkey: The First Person Confession of the Maniac Bobby Gotteson as Told to Joyce Carol Oates (novella; also see below), Black Sparrow Press, 1976.
Childwold, Vanguard Press, 1976.
Son of the Morning, Vanguard Press, 1978.
Unholy Loves, Vanguard Press, 1979.
Cybele, Black Sparrow Press, 1979.
Bellefleur, Dutton, 1980.
Angel of Light, Dutton, 1981.
A Bloodsmoor Romance, edited by Karen Braziller, Dutton, 1982.
Mysteries of Winterthurn, Dutton, 1984.
Solstice, Dutton, 1985.
Marya: A Life, Dutton, 1986.
You Must Remember This, Dutton, 1987.
(Under pseudonym Rosamond Smith) *Lives of the Twins,* Simon & Schuster, 1988.
American Appetites, Dutton, 1989.
Because It Is Bitter, and Because It Is My Heart, Dutton, 1990.

STORIES

By the North Gate, Vanguard Press, 1963, reprinted, Fawcett, 1978.
Upon the Sweeping Flood and Other Stories, Vanguard Press, 1966.
The Wheel of Love and Other Stories, Vanguard Press, 1970.
Marriages and Infidelities, Vanguard Press, 1972.
The Goddess and Other Women, Vanguard Press, 1974.
Where Are You Going, Where Have You Been?: Stories of Young America, Fawcett, 1974.
The Hungry Ghosts: Seven Allusive Comedies, Black Sparrow Press, 1974.
(Fernandes/Oates) *The Poisoned Kiss and Other Stories from the Portuguese,* Vanguard Press, 1975.
The Seduction and Other Stories, Black Sparrow Press, 1975.
Crossing the Border: Fifteen Tales, Vanguard Press, 1976.
Night Side: Eighteen Tales, Vanguard Press, 1977.
All the Good People I've Left Behind, Black Sparrow Press, 1978.
The Lamb of Ahyssalia, Pomegranate, 1980.
A Sentimental Education: Stories, Dutton, 1981.
Last Days: Stories, Dutton, 1984.
Raven's Wing: Stories, Dutton, 1986.
The Assignation: Stories, Ecco Press, 1988.

Also author of a long short story, *Wild Nights,* published in limited edition by Croissant & Co., 1985. Contributor of short stories to anthologies, including O. Henry Awards Anthology, 1963, 1964, 1965, and 1987, *Best American Short Stories,* 1963, 1964, 1965, and *Fifty Best American Short Stories, 1915-1965.*

POEMS

Women in Love and Other Poems, Albondacani Press (New York), 1968.
Anonymous Sins and Other Poems (also see below), Louisiana State University Press, 1969.
Love and Its Derangements: Poems (also see below), Louisiana State University Press, 1970.
Angel Fire (also see below), Louisiana State University Press, 1973.
Love and Its Derangements and Other Poems (includes *Anonymous Sins and Other Poems, Love and Its Derangements,* and *Angel Fire*), Fawcett, 1974.
The Fabulous Beasts, Louisiana State University Press, 1975.
Season of Peril, Black Sparrow Press, 1977.
Women Whose Lives Are Food, Men Whose Lives Are Money: Poems, Louisiana State University Press, 1978.
Invisible Woman: New and Selected Poems, 1970-1972, Ontario Review Press, 1982.

Also author of limited editions, including *Dreaming America and Other Poems,* Aloe Editions, 1973, *The Stepfather,* Lord John Press, 1978, *Celestial Timepiece,* Pressworks, 1981, *Luxury of Sin,* Lord John Press, 1983, and *The Time Traveler,* Lord John Press, 1987.

NONFICTION

The Edge of Impossibility: Tragic Forms in Literature, Vanguard Press, 1972.
The Hostile Sun: The Poetry of D. H. Lawrence, Black Sparrow Press, 1973.
New Heaven, New Earth: The Visionary Experience in Literature, Vanguard Press, 1974.
Contraries: Essays, Oxford University Press, 1981.
The Profane Art: Essays and Reviews, Dutton, 1983.
On Boxing, Doubleday, 1987.
(With Eileen T. Bender) *Artist in Residence,* Indiana University Press, 1987.
(Woman) Writer: Occasions and Opportunities, Dutton, 1988.

PLAYS

"The Sweet Enemy," first produced Off-Broadway at Actors Playhouse, February 15, 1965.
"Sunday Dinner," first produced Off-Broadway at American Place Theater, October 16, 1970.
"Ontological Proof of My Existence," produced Off-Off-Broadway at Cubiculo Theater, February, 1972, published in *Partisan Review,* Volume 37, 1970.
Miracle Play, Black Sparrow Press, 1974.
Three Plays, Ontario Review Press, 1980.
"Presque Isle," first produced in New York at Theater of the Open Eye, April, 1984.
"Triumph of the Spider Monkey" (based on Oates's novella of the same title), first produced at the Los Angeles Theatre Center, October 31, 1985.

Also author of *In Darkest America; The Eclipse,* 1990.

EDITOR OR COMPILER

Scenes from American Life: Contemporary Short Fiction, Random House, 1973.

(With Shannon Ravenel) *Best American Short Stories of 1979,* Houghton, 1979.
Night Walks, Ontario Review Press, 1982.
First Person Singular: Writers on Their Craft, Ontario Review Press, 1983.
(With Boyd Litzinger) *Story: Fictions Past and Present* (textbook with instructor's guide), Heath, 1985.
(With Daniel Halpern) *Reading the Fights,* Holt, 1988.

OTHER

Contributor of fiction, poetry, and nonfiction to periodicals, including *New York Times Book Review, Michigan Quarterly Review, Mademoiselle, Vogue, North American Review, Hudson Review, Paris Review, Grand Street, Atlantic, Poetry,* and *Esquire.* Editor with husband, Raymond Smith, of *Ontario Review.*

WORK IN PROGRESS: Revising *The Crosswicks Horror,* a novel set in Princeton in 1906.

SIDELIGHTS: After two previous nominations, Joyce Carol Oates won the National Book Award for fiction in 1970. At 31, she was one of the youngest writers ever to receive that honor. Her winning novel, *them,* a fictional rendering of a poor Detroit family trapped in a cycle of violence and poverty, secured her reputation as one of the most talented young writers in America. But her storytelling gifts had been apparent from her very first book, *By the North Gate,* a short story collection published when she was only 25 years old. Since that collection appeared in 1963, Oates has published almost two books a year, dazzling readers with her versatility and sheer production. Her work includes more than twenty novels, sixteen short story collections, nine volumes of poetry, four books of literary criticism, three essay collections, several plays, and countless book reviews and articles. Oates has not limited herself to any particular genre or even to one literary style. She is equally at ease creating realistic short stories—for which she won an O. Henry Special Award for Continuing Achievement—or parodistic epics, of which the popular Gothics *Bellefleur, A Bloodsmoor Romance,* and *Mysteries of Winterthurn* are examples. She attracts readers because of her ability to spin suspenseful tales and to infuse the ordinary with terror; she attracts critics because she approaches her craft seriously and demonstrates a willingness to tackle subjects of social consequence. As Oates herself has stated, as quoted in a *Chicago Tribune Book World* discussion of her themes, "I am concerned with only one thing: the moral and social conditions of my generation."

Oates's fascination with society and man's role in it is more typical of nineteenth- than of twentieth-century novelists. "She recalls an old-fashioned idea of the novelist as one who does not occasionally unveil a carefully chiseled 'work of art' but who conducts a continuous and risky exercise of the imagination through the act of writing," notes *New York Times Book Review* contributor Thomas R. Edwards. In the tradition of nineteenth-century masters like Charles Dickens, Joseph Conrad, and Anthony Trollope, Oates is both prolific and serious. But while the Victorians were applauded for their productivity, modern novelists like Oates, whose production is high, are less likely to arouse praise than suspicion. The reason, Susan Wood explains in the *Washington Post Book World,* is that Oates "goes against the prevailing impulse in contemporary fiction toward the private and personal, a smallscale vision illuminated in the work of such a much-admired writer as Ann Beattie. . . . [Oates] is what I would call a 'social' novelist, interested in creating microcosms of the world that reflect the moral and philosophical questions encountered by man as he is in conflict with society, nature, God, history. What she admires in . . . novelists is passion, energy, the courage to take artistic and emotional risks; writing of Conrad's *Nostromo,* she is also speaking of herself: 'The creation of small, tidy, "perfect" works of art is by no means as tempting to the serious novelist as critics might like to think.' "

Oates's impatience with the less-is-more school of literary criticism stems in part from personal experience. She has sometimes been challenged by reviewers who think she writes too much. This small, but highly vocal, contingent questions her productivity and hints that "for a woman writer . . . such fecundity is positively indecent," to use Elaine Showalter's words from *Ms.* magazine. One objector is *Washington Post Book World* contributor Jonathan Yardley, who observed that if authors were "to be recognized solely for their productivity, then certainly Oates would get all the prizes; they'd have to invent new ones just for her. Every other week, it seems, the door to her aerie opens and a new book gusts forth." In a similar vein, *Time* contributor John Skow assaults Oates's "appalling prolificacy" and suggests "there has always been something off-putting about the fiction of Joyce Carol Oates." The implication seems to be that writers who wish to be taken seriously must limit themselves to a small number of publications, painfully eked out over a number of years. According to Showalter, "Some criticism is plainly envious; Oates herself has noted that 'perhaps critics (mainly male) who charged me with writing too much are secretly afraid that someone will accuse them of having done too little with their lives.' " Whatever its motive, this reaction may well represent a temporary backlash of no serious consequence to Oates's literary stature. Edwards dismisses the reaction as "unfair" and suggests, "With occasional exceptions (Joyce, Flaubert), we finally care most about novelists like Dickens, George Eliot, Balzac, Tolstoy, Hardy, James, Conrad, Lawrence or Faulkner whose work is copious enough to constitute a 'world,' and though no guarantees can be offered, energy like Joyce Carol Oates's may find an eventual reward."

If her tireless output sometimes attracts comment, so does the violence that seems to dominate her books. Over the years, however, Oates has become convinced that the real issue is probably her gender: she is a woman competing in a profession dominated by males. After participating in a writer's tour of Eastern Europe, during which she was regularly interrogated about her "distorted" vision of life, Oates addressed the question openly in a *New York Times Book Review* essay titled "Why Is Your Writing So Violent?": "It was once put to me directly, and no doubt has often been suggested by indirection, that I should focus my writing on 'domestic' and 'subjective' material, in the manner (for instance) of Jane Austen or Virginia Woolf, that I should leave large social-philosophical issues to men. The implication is that if Jane Austen and Virginia Woolf had lived in Detroit, they might have been successful in 'transcending' their environment and writing novels in which not a hint of 'violence' could be detected. . . . If they successfully resisted writing about large 'social issues' in their own times, it is implied, surely they would not have failed in this new and challenging context, and 'femininity' would not have to be despoiled. The question is always insulting. The question is always ignorant. . . . Since it is commonly understood that serious writers, as distinct from entertainers or propagandists, take for their natural subjects the complexity of the world, its evils as well as its goods, it is always an insulting question; and it is always sexist. The serious writer, after all, bears witness."

The world to which Oates bears witness has been described by Greg Johnson in *Understanding Joyce Carol Oates* as "a seething, vibrant 'wonderland' in which individual lives are frequently subject to disorder, dislocation and extreme psychological tur-

moil." Her protagonists range from indigent migrant workers to affluent suburbanites, from urban slum dwellers to distinguished visiting poets, and from religious zealots to feminist scholars, but they all share a common frame of mind. "All her characters," says Johnson, "regardless of background, suffer intensely the conflicts and contradictions at the heart of our culture." Because their afflictions are psychological, most of the actual violence occurs off-stage. "Oates is not concerned with the gory details," notes Michele Souda in the *Chicago Tribune Book World.* "That explicit sort of violence is kept at an amazing minimum, given her novels' various dark subjects. The violence of 'Angel of Light,' of 'them,' and of much of her work, is the violence *within*—the violence of that particularly furious, competitive tennis match, of superficial parties, of sex without love. Oates is not so much concerned with the violent *act* as with the violence that informs and distorts less apparently threatening acts, the ones that look clean, easy, legitimate."

A common misconception is that Oates's creative obsession with violence must stem from some unspeakable personal trauma. She is frequently questioned about her childhood: Was it tragic? Did she feel frightened all the time? Oates holds the modern obsession with psychoanalysis at least partly responsible for the confusion. "We seem to have inherited . . . the assumption that the grounds of discontent, anger, rage, despair—unhappiness in general—reside within the sufferer rather than outside of him," she says in her essay. In truth, Oates finds the day-to-day conditions of the real world more terrifying than any imagined nightmare. She believes man's inhumanity to man demands an extreme reaction. "A melancholy vision, a 'tragic' vision, [is] inevitable," Oates asserts in another *New York Times Book Review* article. "Uplifting endings and resolutely cheery world views are appropriate to television commercials but insulting elsewhere. It is not only wicked to pretend otherwise, it is futile."

Recognizing the malaise of the modern world, Oates transforms it into fiction. But the tenor of her private life is calm. She lives quietly with her husband of over 25 years, Raymond J. Smith, in a contemporary home several miles outside Princeton, New Jersey. (Formerly a professor of English, Smith runs the Ontario Review Press, a small publishing house that grew out of the *Ontario Review* journal he and Oates founded in 1974.) In addition to writing, editing, assisting her husband with the journal, and lecturing in creative writing at Princeton, Oates runs the household and maintains an active social life. She is enormously disciplined, devoting several hours each day to writing, and not too long ago began composing on a word processor. While the particulars of Oates's life make her "sound like any successful woman executive of the 1980s . . . she is most decidedly not like other people," says Showalter. "In the midst of a quite ordinary conversation about the news or television or the family, Oates often inserts remarks whose philosophical penetration makes the rest of us feel like amoebas in the company of a more highly evolved life form. She seems to be someone who is never blocked, whose unconscious is always available, who is most alive when she is writing and working. She has the uncanny personal power of genius."

Oates's special genius is the "ability to convey psychological states with unerring fidelity, and to relate the intense private experiences of her characters to the larger realities of American life," Johnson says. Her stories possess the authenticity of personal experience. "My writing is full of lives I might have led," Oates explained to *Boston Globe Magazine* contributor Jay Parini. "A writer imagines what could have happened, not what really happened." Oates ventures into explicit reminiscence in later novels such as *You Must Remember This,* while in her early work she sketches an emotional landscape that evokes her empathy with the poor. Many of her novels are set in the industrial midwest and Oates acknowledges her creative debt to her childhood.

A child of the Depression, Oates was born in Lockport, N.Y., on June l6, 1938, and raised on her grandparents' farm in nearby Erie County. Her father was a tool-and-die designer by trade, her mother, a housewife. Joyce was a bookish, serious child—radically different from her rowdy classmates at the one-room schoolhouse she attended—but she was always nurtured by her family. Early on, they recognized their daughter's extraordinary gifts. "She was always so hard-working, a perfectionist at everything," Carolina Oates, Joyce's mother, recalled to Parini. Even before she could write, Oates was a prolific storyteller. As a preschooler, she drew pictures to convey her narratives. She submitted her first novel to a publisher at the age of 15, but her manuscript about an addict who is rehabilitated by caring for a black stallion was rejected as "too depressing for the market of young readers," according to *Dictionary of Literary Biography* contributor Michael Joslin. After high school Oates won a scholarship to Syracuse University, graduating Phi Beta Kappa in 1960. She enrolled in graduate school at the University of Wisconsin the following term. There she met a young scholar named Ray Smith and within a year they married and moved to Texas. Smith pursued a Ph.D. and Oates, abandoning graduate studies, completed her first book of stories.

In the summer of 1962, the couple relocated to Detroit. That move lasted six years and, as Oates acknowledges in the *Michigan Quarterly Review*, made a tremendous creative impact: "If we had never come to the city of Detroit I would have been a writer (indeed, I had already written my first two books before coming here, aged twenty-three) but Detroit, my 'great' subject, made me the person I am, consequently the writer I am—for better or worse." So much of the fiction Oates wrote between 1963 and 1976 was inspired by the city and its suburbs that the author has acknowledged she can no longer "extract the historical from the fictional." But of all the novels and stories that center on Detroit, none has made a greater impact than her recollection of the 1967 race riots, Oates's National Book Award winner, *them.*

them is a social history that chronicles three decades in the life of the Wendall family, beginning in 1937 and culminating in the Detroit riots. The novel "is partly made up of 'composite' characters and events, clearly influenced by the disturbances of the long hot summer of 1967," Oates acknowledges, though she no longer suggests, as she did in an author's note that opens the book, that her protagonist Maureen Wendall was actually her former student and not a fictional character. That author's note, only later repudiated by Oates as a fiction in itself, describes the book as "a work of history in fictional form," and asserts that Maureen's remembrances shaped the story: "And so the novel *them,* which is truly about a specific 'them' and not just a literary technique of pointing to us all, is based mainly upon Maureen's numerous recollections. . . . It is to her terrible obsession with her personal history that I owe the voluminous details of this novel." Generally regarded as a self-contained work, *them* is also the concluding volume in a trilogy that explores different levels of American society: the migrant poor in *A Garden of Earthly Delights,* the suburban rich in *Expensive People,* and the urban working class in *them.* The focus of all three novels, as Oates explains in the *Saturday Review,* is a cross-section of "unusually sensitive—but hopefully representative—young men and women, who confront the puzzle of American life in different ways and come to different ends."

A story of inescapable life cyles, *them* begins with 16-year-old Loretta Botsford Wendall primping in front of her mirror on a Saturday night. "Anything might happen," she muses, innocently, never suspecting that the night will culminate in tragedy. After inviting her date to bed with her, Loretta is awakened by the sound of an explosion. Still half asleep, she realizes that her boyfriend has been shot in the head by Brock, her murderous brother. Screaming, she flees the house and runs into the street where she encounters an old acquaintance who is a policeman. Forced to become his wife in return for his help, Loretta embarks on a future of degradation and poverty. The early chapters trace Loretta's flight from her past, her move to Detroit, and her erratic relationships with her husband and other men. The rest of the book focuses on three of Loretta's children, especially Jules and Maureen, the two oldest, and their struggle to escape a second generation of violence and poverty.

" 'Them,' as literature, is a reimagining, a reinventing of the urban American experience of the last 30 years, a complex and powerful novel that begins with James T. Farrell and ends in a gothic dream; of the 'fire that burns and does its duty . . . ,' " says John Leonard in the *New York Times.* " 'Them' is really about all the private selves, accidents and casualties that add up to a public violence." *Christian Science Monitor* contributor Joanne Leedom also notes the symbolic importance that violence assumes and links it to the characters' search for freedom: "The characters live, love, and almost die in an effort to find freedom and to break out of their patterns. They balance on a precipice and peer over its edge. Though they fear they may fall, they either cannot or will not back away, for it is in the imminence of danger that they find life force. The quest in 'Them' is for rebirth; the means is violence; the end is merely a realignment of patterns."

Nowhere is the repetition of futile life cycles more clearly delineated than in the relationship between Loretta and her children. "The sixteen-year-old Loretta combing her hair before the mirror becomes the twenty-six-year-old Maureen; the mother's attempt at prostitution becomes the daughter's success. The Loretta-Brock relationship becomes the Jules-Maureen relationship, and Brock the murderer becomes Jules. The characters, so very unalike, beneath their surfaces are the same. The mother *is* the daughter, and all their lives are only random segments of a blind social continuum. They are them—those nameless others. And, by implication, so are we," writes a reviewer for the *Atlantic.*

Critics generally applaud the style in which *them* is written, noting that it starts off realistically, then veers into a naturalistic, at times almost gothic, tone. *New York Times Book Review* contributor Robert M. Adams compares its fluid prose to a nightmare that "admits few effects of distancing irony, no comforting perspectives" and commends the passages that describe Maureen's mental degeneration for their "hallucinating particularity." But *Saturday Review* contributor Benjamin DeMott criticizes this approach, arguing that it fails to provide the needed authorial distance. "The crudities and flatnesses of its characters' responses never are set in any perspective broader than their own," he maintains. Such minor objections have not diminished the novel's impact: it is widely accepted as one of Oates's best novels and a brilliant rendition of modern urban life.

Throughout the 1970s Oates continued her exploration of representative American people and institutions, artfully combining social analysis with vivid psychological portrayals. *Wonderland* probes the pitfalls of the modern medical community; *Do with Me What You Will* focuses upon the legal profession; *The Assassins: A Book of Hours* attacks the political corruption of Washington, D.C.; *Son of the Morning* traces the rise and fall of a religious zealot who thinks he's Christ; and *Unholy Loves* examines the shallowness and hypocricy of the academic community. In these and all her fictions, the frustrations and imbalance of individuals become emblematic of American society as a whole.

Oates's short stories of this period demonstrate similar concerns. Many critics judge her stories to be her finest work. "Her style, technique, and subject matter achieve their strongest effects in this concentrated form, for the extended dialogue, minute detail, and violent action which irritate the reader after hundreds of pages are wonderfully appropriate in short fiction . . . ," Michael Joslin observes in the *Dictionary of Literary Biography.* "Her short stories present the same violence, perversion, and mental derangement as her novels, and are set in similar locations: the rural community of Eden County, the chaotic city of Detroit, and the sprawling malls and developments of modern suburbia."

No single example can demonstrate Oates's mastery of the short story, but "Where Are You Going, Where Have You Been?" possesses characteristic strengths. One of the most frequently anthologized of all her stories, "Where Are You Going, Where Have You Been?" first appeared in 1966 and is generally considered a masterpiece of the short form. It is an allegorical tale of sexual initiation that depicts the seduction of an innocent young girl by an older man at the same time it demonstrates how familiar settings can assume strange and menacing proportions, how ordinary routines can shift into nightmares, and how peril lurks beneath the surface of the everyday.

The protagonist, 15-year-old Connie, is a typical teenager: she argues with her mother over curfews and hair spray, dreams about romantic love with handsome boys, and regards her older, unmarried sister as a casualty. One Sunday afternoon when her family is away, Connie is left home alone. The afternoon begins ordinarily enough, with Connie lazing about and drying her hair in the sun. "At this point," notes Johnson, "the story moves from realism into an allegorical dream-vision. Recalling a recent sexual experience as 'sweet, gentle, the way it was in movies and promised in songs,' Connie opens her eyes and 'hardly knew where she was.' Shaking her head 'as if to get awake,' she feels troubled by the sudden unreality of her surroundings, unaware—though the reader is aware—that she has entered a new and fearsome world." Shortly after this, a strange older man about 30 years old appears in a battered gold convertible. His name is Arnold Friend. Playful at first, Connie dawdles about accepting his invitation to take a ride. Friend becomes more insistent until, suddenly, it becomes very clear that what Friend has in mind is no ordinary ride. "It's real nice and you couldn't ask for nobody better than me, or more polite," Friend says. "I always keep my word. I'll tell you how it is, I'm always nice at first, the first time." He makes no attempt to follow Connie as she flees into the house, but he also makes it clear that the flimsy screen door between them is no real barrier. As Mary Allen explains in *The Necessary Blankness,* "his promise not to come in the house after her is more disturbing than a blunt demand might be, for we know he will enter when he is ready."

Writing in the *Hollins Critic,* Walter Sullivan describes the story as "an interlude of terror" that "builds fearfully toward a violence so unspeakable that it must happen offstage." Sullivan believes that the discrepancy between Connie's age and the stranger's "increases the tension and deepens the meaning of the story. . . . He is not what he seems, which is a familiar theme in modern fiction, and the car, the blaring radio, the clothes he has on, innocent symbols of a subculture under ordinary condi-

tions, are made evil by Friend's illegitimate intention. This is the true terror as all good writers understand: we may be frightened by the distortions of a dream landscape; but horror resides in the transformation of what we know best, the intimate and comfortable details of our lives made suddenly threatening." In a similar vein, Allen observes, "The story exhibits no violence. But it is more terrifying than those that do, with a fear that transforms familiar objects and the landscape in a way that suggests that they will never be quite normal again. A short passage of time is immense. Such treatment of the anticipation of violence is Oates's great strength."

Oates has always been sensitive to women's issues in her work, but this tale particularly lends itself to a feminist reading. "The story describes the beginning of a young and sexually attractive girl's enslavement within a conventional, male-dominated sexual relationship . . . ," explains Johnson. "As a feminist allegory, then, 'Where are You Going, Where Have You Been?' is a cautionary tale, suggesting that young women are 'going' exactly where their mothers and grandmothers have already 'been': into sexual bondage at the hands of a male 'Friend.' "

During the 1980s, Oates has continued her prolific odyssey, successfully exploring new avenues of storytelling and simultaneously experimenting with modern retellings of classical tales. In her 1981 novel, *Angel of Light,* for instance, Oates reshapes the classical Greek tragedy of the fall of the House of Atreus, transforming it into a contemporary study of public politics and personal betrayal. The novel met with positive reviews and widespread attention, but has been somewhat eclipsed by the books that came before and after it—*Bellefleur, A Bloodsmoor Romance,* and *Mysteries of Winterthurn*—commonly known as her Gothic series. These novels—among the most popular that Oates has written—parody the old-fashioned Gothics with "great intelligence and wit," according to Parini. "I like to call the novels parodistic,' " Oates told Parini. "They're not exactly parodies, because they take the forms they imitate quite seriously." Elaborate family sagas that span generations, the novels feature many of the stock elements of conventional Gothics, including ghosts, haunted mansions, and mysterious deaths. But the books are also tied to actual events. "I set out originally to create an elaborate, baroque, barbarous metaphor for the unfathomable mysteries of the human imagination, but soon became involved in very literal events," Oates explained in the *New York Times Book Review.* Her incorporation of real history into imaginary lives lends these tales a depth that is absent from many Gothic novels. Fanciful in form, they are serious in purpose, examining such sensitive social issues as crimes against women, children, and the poor as well as the role of family history in shaping destiny. For these reasons, Johnson believes that "the gothic elements throughout her fiction, like her use of mystical frameworks, serve the larger function of expanding the thematic scope and suggestiveness of her narratives."

Bellefleur, the first installment of the series, is a massive five-part novel that hopscotches back and forth through thousands of years of time and addresses the question of what it means to be an American. This theme is approached through the saga of the Bellefleurs, a rich and rapacious family with a "curse," who settle in the Adirondack Mountains. Interwoven with the exploits of this imaginary family are real people and events from nineteenth-century history, with appearances by abolitionist John Brown and president Abe Lincoln, who in this fiction fakes his own assassination in order to escape the pressures of public life.

In his front-page *New York Times Book Review* assessment of *Bellefleur,* the late John Gardner suggests that its plot defies easy summarization ("it's too complex—an awesome construction, in itself a work of genius"), but he does allow that "it's a story of the world's changeableness, of time and eternity, space and soul, pride and physicality versus love." *Los Angeles Times Book Review* contributor Stuart Schoffman calls the Bellefleurs' story "an allegory for America's: America the vain, the venal, the violent." Says *New York Times* critic John Leonard: "On one level, 'Bellefleur' is Gothic pulp fiction, cleverly consuming itself. . . . On another level, 'Bellefleur' is fairy tale and myth, distraught literature. . . . America is serious enough for pulp and myth, Miss Oates seems to be saying, because in our greed we never understood that the Civil War really was a struggle for the possession of our soul." Oates herself has acknowledged that the book was partially conceived as a critique of "the American dream," and critics generally agree that this dimension enhances the story, transforming the Gothic parody into serious art. Among the most generous assessments is Gardner's; he calls Bellefleur "a symbolic summation of all this novelist has been doing for 20-some years, a magnificent piece of daring, a tour de force of imagination and intellect."

Oates's second title in this series can best be labeled a Gothic romance. "This is Joyce Carol Oates at play, and at work, too, in 'A Bloodsmoor Romance,' a satirical comedy that accurately reproduces and parodies the 19th-century romance," notes Anatole Broyard in the *New York Times.* Over 600 pages in length, the novel is regarded by several critics as an elaborate joke, partially because of its highly self-conscious and pronouncedly ornate style. Authorial asides and breathless revelations limn the narrative—the story of "five sisters in search of love," according to the publisher's blurb. This tale of the four natural daughters of John Quincy Zinn and their adopted sister, Deirdre, is narrated by a local spinster, whose proper upbringing does not prohibit her from portraying a vivid picture of private Victorian sins.

Since its 1982 publication, *A Bloodsmoor Romance* has run the critical gauntlet, being alternately praised and denounced by reviewers. Alice Adams, one of its most enthusiastic supporters, proclaims *A Bloodsmoor Romance* "the finest novel yet by Joyce Carol Oates," in the *Los Angeles Times Book Review;* Denis Donoghue, on the other hand, declares the work "almost unreadable" in an extended essay in the *New York Review of Books.* Many who endorse the book interpret the black comedy as a tongue-in-cheek indictment of a cloying society dominated by hypocritical males. *A Bloodsmoor Romance*'s "real subject is the lot of women, especially the customs and attitudes that confined and oppressed them in the 19th century," writes *New York Times Book Review* contributor Diane Johnson. "Thus the book is a feminist romance with a lot of axes to grind." But, in direct response to Johnson's assessment, Donoghue writes: "If *A Bloodsmoor Romance* were offered as a serious account of the lot of women, then or now, it would be ludicrously inadequate to its theme. I think it wholly removed from such a concern. I see no merit in forcing upon the book the social density and public ramification which Joyce Carol Oates has taken care to exclude from it."

In Donoghue's eyes, the intellectual design of the novel interferes with its success in depicting characters. Oates, in parodying stock Victorian characters, has isolated her protagonists from the objective world and deprived them of genuine feelings. Instead, they relate only to other characters in other fictions. Thus, he concludes, Oates has written a book that requires "nothing but the rough-and-ready allusion to other books, books that have as their chief attribute the fact, thanks be to God, that nobody is required to care about them." In a somewhat softened version

of that sentiment, *Newsweek*'s Peter Prescott observes: "Of course in a spoof of romantic fiction the reader can't care for the characters; he waits for something bizarre to happen to them. The lack of caring, in so long a novel, becomes a burden, but as for the bizarre events Oates never fails us there."

For her third Gothic installment, Oates chose to write a thriller. *Mysteries of Winterthurn* is comprised of three different stories—the only three mysteries in the career of world-famous detective Xavier Kilgarvan that he has been unable to solve. Thus, what begins as a pastiche of nineteenth-century thrillers develops into a philosophical investigation of the larger, unsolvable mysteries of life. "What Oates is doing . . . is concocting radically ambiguous, undecidable stories, in which empirical hopes and metaphysical fears encounter each other head on, inscribed in one and the same set of signs," writes a *Times Literary Supplement* contributor. On the whole, reviewers appreciated the difficulty of the task Oates had set for herself in this novel, but expressed impatience with her continued use of archaic Gothic models and a desire for her return to more realistic forms.

Oates embarks on that return in *Solstice,* a psychological novel with a contemporary setting and modern-day concerns. "Solstice is a challenging book, rich, complex and dangerous," according to *Detroit News* contributor Peter Ross. "Like the best of Oates, it probes the deeper recesses of personality, illuminating the way with flashes of eroticism and psychological mystery." The story of how a friendship between two women develops into an obsession, *Solstice* dispells the naive feminist illusion that women are kinder to each other than men. Admired for its honest portrayal of female relationships, the book was generally well-received; all the same, it struck some reviewers as reading too much like a clinical case study to be fully satisfying as literature.

Virtually all of Oates's novels provoke conflicting responses that vary from reviewer to reviewer and book to book. Some critics extol her realistic works; others find her Gothic experiments most admirable. For almost any title one selects there are reviews that praise the work as representative of Oates's finest, while others lament its shortcomings. This pattern holds true as well for two related fictions of the 1980s—*Marya: A Life* and *You Must Remember This.* But there is also a consensus among some critics that these novels mark the achievement of a mature stage at which Oates successfully combines the best characteristics of her early and later work.

For instance, *New York Times* critic Christopher Lehmann-Haupt deems Marya "a fresh departure for Miss Oates—quieter, more controlled and realistic, and personal to the point of suggesting autobiography. It is as if she had consolidated whatever she learned from her rather recent experiments—the gothic excesses of 'Bellefleur,' 'A Bloodsmoor Romance,' and 'Mysteries of Winterthurn,' the nearly clinical psychological realism of 'Solstice'—and started over again on a smaller scale." Reviewing *You Must Remember This* for the *New York Times,* Michiko Kakutani similarly observes: "Miss Oates seems to have returned to the storytelling impulses that animated her first books; and in the wake of her uneven experiments with genre fiction . . . the result is a most felicitous one. Whereas such earlier novels as 'With Shuddering Fall,' 'Them' and 'Wonderland' held the author's penchants for the naturalistic and the Gothic in an uneasy balance, 'Remember' welds them together to create a portrait of family life in the 50s that is both recognizable and horrifying, mundane and disturbing."

Both books are coming-of-age novels set in upstate New York and both are more openly autobiographical than most of Oates's fiction. In her *CA* interview, Oates discusses how, in her own mind at least, the novels are paired, with Marya representing Oates's country experience and *You Must Remember This* reflecting her experience in the city. *New York Times Book Review* contributor Sven Birkerts believes the books are also linked in their representation of violence and that both represent a step forward in Oates's treatment of that theme: "The violence is now carried inward, where it has a chance of being countered by other psychic forces. The resulting prose is more complex and more tolerant of ambiguities, though the contest between tragic and redemptive forces has not yet been fought with the decisiveness that the highest art demands."

Throughout her writing career, Oates has distributed her energies among several projects, simultaneously producing novels and other types of books. Her recent foray into the arena of sports philosophy with the book-length essay *On Boxing* has been extremely well received and led to at least one television appearance as a commentator on the sport. Around this same time, Oates submitted a realistic mystery novel to a publisher under a pseudonym and had the thrill of having it accepted before word leaked out that it was Oates's creation. The stir that this revelation caused among her professional associates and the publicity it engendered in the press have made Oates wary. Though she plans to retain the pseudonym, she told *CA,* "I don't think I'll ever publish secretly again." Whatever path she chooses, Oates seems likely to continue her exploration of sociological themes. "Her achievement is all the more extraordinary when one considers that she is still in her forties and may now be viewed as entering the middle stage of her illustrious career," concludes Greg Johnson.

MEDIA ADAPTATIONS: Oates's short story "In the Region of Ice" was made into an Academy Award-winning short feature in the 1970s; "Daisy" was adapted for the stage by Victoria Rue and produced Off-Off-Broadway at the Cubiculo, February, 1980; "Where Are You Going, Where Have You Been?" was adapted for the screen as "SmoothTalk," a Spectrafilm release, directed by Joyce Chopra and produced by Martin Rosen, 1981; "Norman and the Killer" was also made into a short feature.

BIOGRAPHICAL/CRITICAL SOURCES:

BOOKS

Allen, Mary, *The Necessary Blankness: Women in Major American Fiction of the Sixties,* University of Illinois Press, 1974.
Authors in the News, Volume 1, Gale, 1976.
Bellamy, Joe David, editor, *The New Fiction: Interviews with Innovative American Writers,* University of Illinois Press, 1974.
Bender, Eileen, *Joyce Carol Oates,* Indiana University Press, 1987.
Bloom, Harold, editor, *Modern Critical Views: Joyce Carol Oates,* Chelsea House, 1987.
Contemporary Literary Criticism, Gale, Volume 1, 1973, Volume 2, 1974, Volume 3, 1975, Volume 6, 1976, Volume 9, 1978, Volume 11, 1979, Volume 15, 1980, Volume 19, 1981, Volume 33, 1985.
Creighton, Joanne V., *Joyce Carol Oates,* G. K. Hall, 1979.
Dictionary of Literary Biography, Gale, Volume 2: *American Novelists since World War II,* 1978, Volume 5: *American Poets since World War II,* 1980.
Dictionary of Literary Biography Yearbook: 1981, Gale, 1982.
Friedman, Ellen G., *Joyce Carol Oates,* Ungar, 1980.
Grant, Mary Kathryn, *The Tragic Vision of Joyce Carol Oates,* Duke University Press, 1978.
Johnson, Greg, *Understanding Joyce Carol Oates,* University of South Carolina Press, 1987.

Kazin, Alfred, *Bright Book of Life: American Novelists and Storytellers from Hemingway to Mailer,* Little, Brown, 1974.
Oates, Joyce Carol, *them,* Vanguard Press, 1969, reprinted, Fawcett, 1968.
Oates, *Where Are You Going, Where Have You Been?: Stories of Young America,* Fawcett, 1974.
Wagner, Linda W., editor, *Joyce Carol Oates: The Critical Reception,* G. K. Hall, 1979.
Waller, G. F., *Dreaming America: Obsession and Transcendence in the Fiction of Joyce Carol Oates,* Louisiana State University Press, 1979.

PERIODICALS

Atlantic, October, 1969, December, 1973.
Books and Bookmen, June, 1971.
Boston Globe Magazine, August 2, 1987.
Chicago Tribune Book World, September 30, 1979, July 27, 1980, January 11, 1981, August 16, 1981, February 26, 1984, August 12, 1984, January 13, 1985, February 23, 1986.
Christian Science Monitor, October 30, 1969.
Detroit News, January 15, 1964, May 21, 1972, November 13, 1977, July 27, 1980, October 11, 1981, October 17, 1982, March 11, 1984, February 3, 1985.
Globe and Mail (Toronto), February 11, 1984, April 25, 1987.
Hollin's Critic, December, 1972.
Los Angeles Times, April 2, 1981, February 18, 1986, October 13, 1986, November 7, 1986, August 7, 1987, January 31, 1988, July 21, 1988, December 9, 1988, April 16, 1990.
Los Angeles Times Book Review, August 12, 1980, September 19, 1982, January 8, 1984, September 30, 1984, January 6, 1985, March 1, 1987, August 16, 1987, January 15, 1989.
Michigan Quarterly Review, spring, 1986.
Ms., March, 1986.
Newsweek, September 29, 1969, March 23, 1970, August 17, 1981, September 20, 1982, February 6, 1984, January 21, 1985, March 24, 1986, March 9, 1987, August 17, 1987.
New Yorker, December 6, 1969, October 15, 1973, October 5, 1981, September 27, 1982, February 27, 1984.
New York Review of Books, December 17, 1964, January 2, 1969, October 21, 1971, January 24, 1974, October 21, 1982.
New York Times, September 5, 1967, December 7, 1968, October 1, 1969, October 16, 1971, June 12, 1972, October 15, 1973, July 20, 1980, August 6, 1981, September 18, 1982, February 10, 1984, January 10, 1985, February 20, 1986, February 10, 1987, March 2, 1987, March 4, 1987, August 10, 1987, April 23, 1988, December 21, 1988, March 30, 1990.
New York Times Book Review, November 10, 1963, October 25, 1964, September 10, 1967, November 3, 1968, September 28, 1969, October 25, 1970, October 24, 1971, July 9, 1972, April 1, 1973, October 14, 1973, August 31, 1975, November 26, 1978, April 29, 1979, July 15, 1979, October 7, 1979, July 20, 1980, January 4, 1981, March 29, 1981, August 16, 1981, July 11, 1982, September 5, 1982, February 12, 1984, August 5, 1984, January 20, 1985, August 11, 1985, March 2, 1986, October 5, 1986, March 15, 1987, August 16, 1987, January 3, 1988, October 2, 1988, January 1, 1989, January 15, 1989.
New York Times Magazine, July 27, 1980, January 3, 1988.
Saturday Review, October 26, 1963, November 28, 1964, August 5, 1967, October 26, 1968, November 22, 1969, October 24, 1970, June 10, 1972, November 4, 1972, August, 1981, March/April, 1985.
Time, January 3, 1964, November 1, 1968, October 26, 1970, August 25, 1980, August 17, 1981, October 4, 1982, February 23, 1987, August 31, 1987, January 9, 1989.

Times (London), February 11, 1982, April 4, 1985, January 8, 1987, June 10, 1987, June 11, 1987, August 30, 1989, April 11, 1990.

Times Literary Supplement, June 4, 1970, January 11, 1974, September 12, 1980, March 20, 1981, January 29, 1982, January 28, 1983, July 20, 1984, March 22, 1985, October 18, 1985, January 16, 1987, December 18, 1987, February 14, 1988, September 15, 1989.

Tribune Books (Chicago), March 1, 1987, July 19, 1987, April 18, 1988, December 18, 1988.

Village Voice, August 4, 1975, October 1, 1979, July 30, 1980, May 20, 1986.

Washington Post, October 15, 1971, September 18, 1978, August 18, 1986, December 16, 1987.

Washington Post Book World, February 22, 1981, August 16, 1981, September 30, 1984, January 6, 1985, February 23, 1986, November 30, 1986, March 8, 1987, January 8, 1989, April 8, 1990.

* * *

O'BRIEN, E. G.
See CLARKE, Arthur C(harles)

* * *

O'BRIEN, Edna 1936-

PERSONAL: Born December 15, 1936, in Tuamgraney, Ireland; daughter of Michael and Lena (Cleary) O'Brien; married Ernest Gebler (an author), 1952 (divorced, 1967); children: Sasha, Carlos (sons). *Education:* Attended Pharmaceutical College of Ireland.

ADDRESSES: Home—England. *Office*—c/o Duncan Heath Associates, 162-170 Wardour St., W1V 3AT. *Agent*—Robert Lescher, 155 East 71st St., New York, NY 10021.

CAREER: Novelist, playwright, and screenwriter.

AWARDS, HONORS: Kingsley Amis Award, 1962; *Yorkshire Post* novel award, 1971.

WRITINGS:

The Country Girls (novel; also see below), Knopf, 1960.
The Lonely Girl (novel), Random House, 1962, published as *The Girl with Green Eyes,* Penguin, 1970.
Girls in Their Married Bliss (novel), J. Cape, 1964, Houghton, 1968.
August Is a Wicked Month (novel), Simon & Schuster, 1965.
Casualties of Peace (novel), J. Cape, 1966, Simon & Schuster, 1967.
Zee and Company (novel), Weidenfeld, 1970.
Night (novel), Knopf, 1972.
Mother Ireland (nonfiction), photographs by Fergus Bourke, Harcourt, 1976.
Arabian Days (nonfiction), Quartet Books, 1977.
Johnny I Hardly Knew You (novel), Weidenfeld, 1977, published as *I Hardly Knew You,* Doubleday, 1978.
Seven Novels and Other Stories, Collins, 1978.
(Editor) *Some Irish Loving* (anthology), Harper, 1979.
James and Nora: A Portrait of Joyce's Marriage (nonfiction), Lord John Publishers, 1981.
The Country Girls Trilogy and Epilogue, Farrar, Straus, 1986.
Vanishing Ireland (nonfiction; photographs by Richard Fitzgerald), C. N. Potter, 1987.
The High Road (novel), Farrar, Straus, 1988.

SHORT STORIES

The Love Object, J. Cape, 1968, Knopf, 1969.
A Scandalous Woman and Other Stories, Harcourt, 1974.
Mrs. Rinehart and Other Stories, Weidenfeld & Nicolson, 1978.
A Rose in the Heart, Doubleday, 1979.
Returning: Tales, Weidenfeld & Nicolson, 1982.
The Dazzle (for children), illustrated by Peter Stevenson, Hodder & Stoughton, 1981.
A Christmas Treat (for children), illustrated by Stevenson, Hodder & Stoughton, 1982.
The Expedition (for children), Hodder & Stoughton, 1982.
The Rescue (for children), illustrated by Stevenson, Hodder & Stoughton, 1983.
A Fanatic Heart: Selected Stories of Edna O'Brien, foreword by Philip Roth, Farrar, Straus, 1984.
Tales for the Telling: Irish Folk and Fairy Stories (for children), illustrated by Michael Foreman, Atheneum, 1986.

PLAYS

A Cheap Bunch of Nice Flowers (produced in London, England, 1962), Elek, 1963.
A Pagan Place (produced on the West End at Royal Court Theatre, October, 1972), Knopf, 1970.
"The Gathering," first produced in Dublin, Ireland, 1974, produced in New York, NY, at Manhattan Theatre Club, 1977.
Virginia (first produced at Stratford, Ontario; produced in New York, NY at the Public Theater, 1985), Harcourt, 1981.
(Adaptor) "Madame Bovary" (based on the novel by Gustav Flaubert), produced at the Palace, Watford, England, 1987.

Also author of play, "The Keys of the Cafe."

SCREENPLAYS

"The Girl with Green Eyes" (based on O'Brien's novel *The Lonely Girl;* also see above), Lopert, 1964.
"Three into Two Won't Go," Universal, 1969.
"X Y and Zee" (based on O'Brien's novel *Zee and Company;* also see above), Columbia, 1972.

Also author of screenplays "A Woman at the Seaside" and "I Was Happy Here."

OTHER

Also author of "Flesh and Blood," 1987. Author of television plays "The Wedding Dress," 1963, "The Keys of the Cafe," 1965, "Give My Love to the Pilchards," 1965, "Which of These Two Ladies Is He Married To?," 1967, and "Nothing's Ever Over," 1968.

Contributor to *Oh! Calcutta!,* compiled by Kenneth Tynan, Grove, 1969. Also contributor to *New Yorker* and various English journals.

SIDELIGHTS: Edna O'Brien has been hailed by many critics as a champion of "the condition of women, especially their sexual repression." As James R. Frakes writes: "O'Brien thoroughly convinces me that she knows the mazed caverns of the mind and emotions of women driven by desperate love—the blind alleys, the slimy stalagmites and phallic formations, the harmless bats and deadly butterflies, the noxious wisps of nonsense songs, the smells of smoke."

One reason for this insightful portrayal of her characters is that O'Brien patterns the characters after herself. Vivien Raynor points out: "The women Edna O'Brien writes about have led lives similar to her own. They were born in Ireland around 1930 and left early to live among the foe. The Brits, the painted people.

A land where the king has piles. Usually they have married disastrously and have only a son or two to show for it." Agreeing with this assessment, Julia O'Faolian comments, in her review for the *New York Times Book Review:* "Miss O'Brien's range is narrow and obsessional. The larger world does not interest her. Her social settings are perfunctory. . . . Her sex and self-absorbed women are undisturbed by the day-to-day. Nothing intervenes to prevent their passion reaching boiling point. However, theirs never boils over. There is no explosion. No climax. This slice of life is chopped off more or less neatly and a few sentences of melancholy Stoicism tie it up."

But some people take offense at this typical character that O'Brien uses in her novels. They see the heroines as failures, chained to an inadequate man, "once fallen unable to rise, if they do totter to their feet, it is only to fall again." A reviewer for *Book World* described the usual O'Brien heroines as "women getting a kind of higher education at the hands of men. Jobs and professions notwithstanding, they are descendants of Byron's ladies, for whom love was their whole existence. . . . Her protagonists move gamely from one unsatisfactory man to the next, taking notes as they go. They have divested themselves of illusions and have assumed a bachelor bravado, letting the sexual chips fall where they may." Bernard Bergonzi agrees with these descriptions and feels: "If I were a woman I would be pretty disturbed by the way in which Miss O'Brien implicitly accepts and even reinforces traditional male prejudicies about women, of the kind advanced by the ideologues of European reaction and most available in English in the writings of Wyndham Lewis. This view of woman sees her as certainly biologically different from man and, in most respects, inferior; a creature rooted in matter, whose main function is reproductive and who is correspondingly mindless; quite incapable of rationality, judgment, or any form of intellectual activity."

However, Julia O'Faolian sees more to O'Brien's writings: "Although a feminist republic of free, responsible women might be tempted to ban Miss O'Brien's defeatist writings, they should rather, I think, be grateful to her. Her stories are bulletins from a front on which they will not care to engage, field reports on the feminine condition at its most acute. Only a woman fiction writer can safely and authentically explore feminine passivity to the full. She can experience it totally in her characters while protected from its virus by the fact that she is, qua writer, simultaneously active. Miss O'Brien explores with persuasive thoroughness."

"That O'Brien has been called a feminist develops not so much from an ideal or from a philosophical cause but from a realistic appraisal of the female condition and of the male-female relationship," Grace Eckley explains. "In the final analysis, loneliness and independence must be acknowledged as dominant themes in Edna O'Brien's fiction. Stresses, especially those of loneliness, most dramatically take the form of a quest for someone to love, and that person not only has a body but also reflects the protagonist's state of mind. . . . Still a second factor exposed by Miss O'Brien's literary stethoscope should cause more discomfort than this exclusive submergence in the love theme, and that is the thoroughness with which one's choice of someone to love defines the entire range of one's personality; it exposes a streak of masochism, describes one's pathetic ideals, or reflects conditions of loneliness."

BIOGRAPHICAL/CRITICAL SOURCES:

BOOKS

Contemporary Literary Criticism, Gale, Volume III, 1975, Volume V, 1976, Volume VIII, 1978, Volume XIII, 1980, Volume XXXVI.
Dictionary of Literary Biography, Volume XIV: *British Novelists since 1960,* Gale, 1983.
Eckley, Grace, *Edna O'Brien,* Bucknell University Press, 1974.

PERIODICALS

Atlantic Monthly, July, 1965.
Books, June, 1965.
Books and Bookmen, December, 1964.
Chicago Tribune Book World, December 9, 1984.
Globe and Mail (Toronto), December 17, 1988.
Los Angeles Times, April 3, 1979, December 16, 1988.
National Observer, June 21, 1965.
New York Review of Books, June 3, 1965, August 24, 1967.
New York Times, November 12, 1984.
New York Times Book Review, March 26, 1967, February 9, 1969, September 22, 1974, June 27, 1978, February 11, 1979, November 18, 1984, March 1, 1987, November 20, 1988.
New York Times Magazine, March 12, 1989.
People, April 17, 1978.
Publishers Weekly, December 26, 1986.
Saturday Review, June 5, 1965, March 25, 1967.
Times (London), October 14, 1988.
Times Literary Supplement, January 9, 1987, October 28, 1988.
Tribune Books, November 20, 1988.
Vogue, September 1, 1971.
Washington Post Book World, January 7, 1973, April 8, 1987, November 2, 1988.

*   *   *

O'CASEY, Sean 1880-1964
(Sean O'Cathasaigh)

PERSONAL: Birth-given name, John Casey; name Gaelicized to Sean O'Cathasaigh, c. 1909; surname Anglicized to O'Casey, 1923; born March 30, 1880, in Dublin, Ireland; self-exiled to England, 1926; died September 18, 1964, in Torquay, Devon, England; son of Michael (a clerk) and Susan (Archer) Casey; married Eileen Reynolds (an actress; stage name, Eileen Carey), 1928; children: two sons, Breon, Niall Ayamonn; one daughter, Shivaun. *Education:* Self-educated. *Religion:* Church of Ireland.

ADDRESSES: Home—Torquay, Devon, England.

CAREER: Playwright. Worked in ironmongery and hardware store, c. 1895-98; road worker, 1898-1910; laborer, 1910-23; secretary of Irish Citizen Army, 1913-14; full-time writer, 1924-64.

MEMBER: Gaelic League, St. Laurence O'Toole Pipers' Band (founding member).

AWARDS, HONORS: Hawthornden Prize, 1926.

WRITINGS:

PLAYS

"Cathleen Listens In" (one-act), first produced in Dublin, Ireland, at the Abbey Theatre, October 1, 1923.
"Nannie's Night Out" (one-act), first produced in Dublin at the Abbey Theatre, September 29, 1924.
The Plough and the Stars (four-act; first produced in Dublin at the Abbey Theatre, February 8, 1926), Macmillan, 1926.

The Silver Tassie (four-act; first produced on the West End at Apollo Theatre, October 11, 1929), Macmillan (London), 1928.

The Shadow of a Gunman (two-act; first produced in Dublin at the Abbey Theatre, April 9, 1923), Samuel French, 1932.

Juno and the Paycock (three-act; first produced in Dublin at the Abbey Theatre, March 3, 1924), Samuel French, 1932.

Within the Gates (four-scene; first produced on the West End at Royalty Theatre, February 7, 1934), Macmillan (London), 1933.

"A Pound on Demand" (one-act; first produced in New York City at American Repertory Theatre, January, 1947), published in *Five Irish Plays* (also see below), 1935.

"The End of the Beginning" (one-act; first produced in Dublin at the Abbey Theatre, February 8, 1937), published in *Five Irish Plays* (also see below), 1935.

Purple Dust (three-act; first produced in Boston, Mass., at Boston Tributary Theatre, December 6, 1944), Macmillan, (London), 1940, Dramatists Play Service, 1957.

The Star Turns Red (one-act; first produced in London, England, at Unity Theatre, March 20, 1940), Macmillan, (London), 1940.

Red Roses for Me (four-act; first produced in Dublin at Olympia Theatre, April, 1943), Macmillan (London), 1942, Macmillan (New York), 1943.

Oak Leaves and Lavender; or, A World on Wallpaper (first produced on the West End at Lyric Theatre, May 13, 1947), Macmillan (London), 1946, Macmillan (New York), 1947.

Cock-a-Doodle Dandy (three-scene; first produced in Newcastle upon Tyne, England, at People's Theatre, December 11, 1949), Macmillan (London), 1949.

"Hall of Healing," "Bedtime Story," and "Time to Go" (one-act plays; all first produced in New York City at Yugoslav-American Hall, May 7, 1952), all published in *Collected Plays* (also see below), 1949-52.

The Bishop's Bonfire: A Sad Play Within the Tune of a Polka (first produced in Dublin at Gaeity Theatre, February 28, 1955), Macmillan, 1955.

The Drums of Father Ned (first produced in Lafayette, Ind., 1959), St. Martin's, 1960.

Behind the Green Curtains [and] *Figuro in the Night* [and] *The Moon Shines on Kylenamoe* (three plays; all first produced Off-Broadway at Theatre de Lys, 1962), St. Martin's, 1961.

AUTOBIOGRAPHIES

I Knock at the Door: Swift Glances Back at Things That Made Me, Macmillan, 1939, adaptation by Paul Shyre as two-act play published as *I Knock at the Door,* Dramatists Play Service, 1958, original edition reprinted, Pan Books, 1971.

Pictures in the Hallway, Macmillan, 1942, adaptation by Shyre as two-act play published under same title, Samuel French, 1956 (first produced on Broadway at Playhouse Theatre, September 16, 1956), original edition reprinted, Pan Books, 1971.

Drums Under the Windows, Macmillan (London), 1945, Macmillan (New York), 1946, adaptation by Shyre published under same title, A. Meyerson, 1960.

Inishfallen, Fare Thee Well, Macmillan, 1949.

Rose and Crown, Macmillan, 1952.

Sunset and Evening Star, Macmillan, 1954.

Mirror in My House: The Autobiographies of Sean O'Casey, two volumes, (Volume 1 contains *I Knock at the Door, Pictures in the Hallway,* and *Drums Under the Windows;* Volume 2 contains *Inishfallen, Fare Thee Well, Rose and Crown,* and *Sunset and Evening Star*), Macmillan, 1956, published as

Autobiographies, two volumes, Macmillan (London), 1963, Carroll & Graf, 1984.

OTHER

(Under name Sean O'Cathasaigh) *Songs of the Wren,* [Dublin], 1918.

(Under name Sean O'Cathasaigh) *More Songs of the Wren,* [Dublin], 1918.

(Under name Sean O'Cathasaigh) *The Story of Thomas Ashe,* Fergus O'Connor, 1918.

(Under name Sean O'Cathasaigh) *The Story of the Irish Citizen Army,* Maunsel, 1919, reprinted, Talbot, 1971.

Windfalls: Stories, Poems, and Plays, Macmillan, 1934.

The Flying Wasp, Macmillan (London), 1937, reprinted, B. Blom, 1971.

The Green Crow, Braziller, 1956.

Feathers From the Green Crow, edited by Robert Hogan, University of Missouri Press, 1962.

Under a Colored Cap: Articles Merry and Mournful With Comments and a Song, St. Martin's, 1963.

Blasts and Benedictions (articles and stories), introduction by Ronald Ayling, St. Martin's, 1967.

The Sean O'Casey Reader: Plays, Autobiographies, Opinions, edited with an introduction by Brooks Atkinson, St. Martin's, 1968.

The Sting and the Twinkle: Conversations With Sean O'Casey, compiled by H. H. Mikhail, Barnes & Noble, 1974.

The Letters of Sean O'Casey, edited by David Krause, Macmillan, 1975.

OMNIBUS VOLUMES

Two Plays: Juno and the Paycock [and] *The Shadow of a Gunman,* Macmillan, 1925.

Five Irish Plays (contains "Juno and the Paycock," "The Shadow of a Gunman," "The Plough and the Stars," "The End of the Beginning," and "A Pound on Demand"), Macmillan, 1935.

Collected Plays (contains "Juno and the Paycock," "The Shadow of a Gunman," "The Plough and the Stars," "The End of the Beginning," "A Pound on Demand," "The Silver Tassie," "Within the Gates," "The Star Turns Red," "Purple Dust," "Red Roses for Me," "Halls of Healing," "Oak Leaves and Lavender," "Cock-a-Doodle Dandy," "Bedtime Story," and "Time to Go"), four volumes, Macmillan (London), 1949-52, St. Martin's, 1958.

Selected Plays (contains "The Shadow of a Gunman," "Juno and the Paycock," "The Plough and the Stars," "The Silver Tassie," "Within the Gates," "Purple Dust," "Red Roses for Me," "Bedtime Story," and "Time to Go"), introduction by John Gassner, Braziller, 1954.

Juno and the Paycock [and] *The Plough and the Stars,* Macmillan, 1957.

Three Plays: Juno and the Paycock, The Shadow of a Gunman, The Plough and the Stars, Macmillan (London), 1957, St. Martin's, 1960.

Five One-Act Plays (contains "The End of the Beginning," "A Pound on Demand," "Hall of Healing," "Bedtime Story," and "Time to Go"), St. Martin's, 1958.

Three More Plays (contains "The Silver Tassie," "Purple Dust," and "Red Roses for Me"), introduction by J. C. Trewin, St. Martin's, 1965.

The Complete Plays of Sean O'Casey, Macmillan, 1984.

Work represented in numerous anthologies.

SIDELIGHTS: Sean O'Casey rose from the Dublin slums to become one of the most esteemed dramatists of the twentieth century. When he was six years old his father died, leaving a family of thirteen to fend for themselves in Dublin. Sean, the youngest child in the family, suffered from a chronic eye disease that threatened him with blindness throughout his life. Because of this he was seldom able to attend school, but taught himself to read and write by the time he was thirteen. He became a drama enthusiast, Shakespeare and Dion Boucicault being his favorite authors, and performed in local theatre groups.

During his early years O'Casey supported himself by working as a common laborer. He soon became involved with the Irish struggle for freedom. He joined the Gaelic league, learned to speak, read, and write fluent Gaelic, and Gaelicized his name from John Casey to Sean O'Cathasaigh, under which his writings of that time were published. He also learned to play bagpipes and helped found the St. Laurence O'Toole Pipers Band.

When he was thirty O'Casey began to devote his energies to the Irish labor movement headed by Jim Larkin, helping to fight the appalling living and working conditions of his fellow workers. He served under Larkin as the first secretary of the Irish Citizen Army, wrote articles for the labor union's newspaper, and helped organize a transport strike in 1913. He resigned his post, however, in 1914 when he was unable to prevent a rival group, the Irish Volunteers, from weakening the labor union.

In his mid-thirties O'Casey returned to his previous interest in drama and began to write plays. He used this medium to express his concern for the effects of the Irish rebellion on average Dubliners like himself. His first play to be produced was "The Shadow of a Gunman," followed by "Juno and the Paycock" and "The Plough and the Stars." Kevin Sullivan remarked that O'Casey's "reputation for genius begins, and I think ends," with these three plays. "That in any event is the commonly accepted critical judgment on O'Casey which only his most fervent admirers . . . would care to dispute." In Robert Hogan's view, the negative reception of O'Casey's later plays may be attributed to most critics' aversion to original thought and their unquestioning acceptance of the cliche that "when O'Casey left for England, he left his talent behind him on the North Circular Road." Hogan himself believes "you can only prove the worth of a play by playing it," and having staged or performed in five of O'Casey's later plays he asserted that "most of O'Casey's late work is eminently, dazzlingly good."

O'Casey submitted several of his first playwriting attempts to the Abbey Theatre, which was run by William Butler Yeats and Lady Gregory. The Abbey finally accepted "The Shadow of a Gunman" for production in 1923. It was a tragedy of a poet and a peddler who become inadvertently involved in the guerrilla warfare of the Irish Republican Army (IRA) and the British soldiers in Dublin during 1920. A peddler, Seumas Shields, allows Donal Davoren, a struggling poet, to stay in his tenement room. Donal is mistaken by the neighbors for a brave IRA fighter. One of them, Minnie Powell, falls in love with the image of Donal as a romantic poet-gunman. A real patriot hides explosives in Seumas's room, and when guards raid the tenement Minnie moves the bombs to her room in order to save Seumas and Donal. As a result Minnie is arrested and then accidentally killed in a crossfire between Irish patriots and British guards.

Seumas's room is the setting for both acts of "The Shadow of a Gunman." It is cluttered with religious icons, pots and pans, a typewriter, flowers, and books. Bernice Schrank noted that "the setting creates an atmosphere of chaos congenial to the theme of breakdown which runs throughout the play." O'Casey's ex-plicit stage directions call for a messy room to imply the confused psychological states of Donal and Seumas, as well as the confusion of the country.

O'Casey's second play, "Juno and the Paycock," was considered by T. E. Kalem to be "one of the granitic masterworks of modern dramatic art." This tragicomedy studies the effects of Dublin' post-war disturbances on a tenement family in 1922. The head of the family is "Captain" Jack Boyle, who struts about from pub to pub like a peacock (paycock) while his wife Juno struggles to make ends meet at home. The family has no income because the Captain is unemployed, his son Johnny has been injured in the fight for independence, and his daughter Mary has joined the workers strike.

The family rejoices when Mary's suitor, lawyer Charlie Bentham, informs the Boyles that they are to inherit half the property of a rich relative. They begin to buy lavishly on credit. The Captain even promises to give up drinking and get a job. When the interpretation of the will turns out to be erroneous, Bentham skips town, creditors repossess the new merchandise, and Mary discovers she is pregnant.

The family's reaction to these events provides "a continuous contrast between the masculine and the feminine personages, from which the women emerge as far superior to the men because of their capacity for love, altruism, and wisdom," noted William A. Armstrong. "The men in the play are all deluded, self-centered, and hypocritical." The Captain and Johnny turn viciously against Mary when they learn of her pregnancy, and Bentham and another boyfriend desert her as well. Juno, on the other hand, is supportive and gives Mary sensible advice in her time of need.

Among the play's most noteworthy aspects, according to Armstrong, are its "modulated movement from the apparently comic to the grievously catastrophic," and the paralleling of domestic and national themes as represented by the treachery, desertion, and dissolution occurring both among the Boyles and among the Irish people. Bernard Benstock also praised the characterization of the Captain as "probably O'Casey's finest achievement," and the first presentation of a character type that he used in many of his later plays: "the indolent, self-indulgent braggart whom he saw at the crux of the paralytic condition in Irish life, but whose boisterous wit and elan always brought him at least halfway back to redemption."

The final drama of O'Casey tragicomic trilogy was "The Plough and the Stars," whose title was taken from the symbols on the Irish Citizen Army flag. This play occurs in 1915 and 1916, before and during the Easter Rebellion. The plot revolves around Nora Clitheroe, a young bride who is expecting a baby. She unsuccessfully tries to prevent her husband, Jack, from leaving to become a troop commander in the IRA. In his absence chaos ensues. The tenement neighbors join in the looting of Dublin. Nora loses her baby and goes mad, so when word comes that Jack has died in the fighting she cannot even be told. The play closes as a neighbor is fatally shot trying to protect Nora from stray bullets, and Nora cries for Jack's help, still unaware of his heroic death.

During the fourth Abbey performance of this play a riot broke out in the audience. Benstock observed that "the same Dubliners who were being dissected and lampooned in . . . [O'Casey's first two] comic tragedies sat in the theatre and roared at themselves, until the full brunt of O'Casey's satire struck home in *The Plough and the Stars.*" The blunt realism of O'Casey's depiction of sex and religion even offended some of the actors, and several refused to speak their lines.

Another reason for the uproar was that the people were accustomed to viewing Ireland as a fair land with the national fighters as hero-figures. But in "The Plough and the Stars" and his other plays the heroes are noncombatants, usually women who manage to survive the tragedies of war. "For O'Casey the essential reality of war, revolutionary or otherwise, no matter how splendid the principle for which it is fought, is pain, and pain dominates the last half of *The Plough and the Stars:* fear, madness, miscarriage, and death," noted Julius Novick. "No wonder the Nationalists rioted when the play was new; they did not want to see the seamy side of their glorious struggle."

Unhappy with the rioting, O'Casey moved to London in 1926. He continued to write, but his next play, "The Silver Tassie," was rejected by Yeats for production at the Abbey Theatre. Although most of the play was written in a naturalist style, in the second act O'Casey had used an expressionistic dream structure, a distorted setting, and stylized action. "Yeats told O'Casey that the play suffered from both inadequate technical prowess and imaginative unconvincingness," Richard Gilman related. O'Casey was bitter about the rejection and kept up a feud with Yeats for years because of it. He even published the correspondence concerning the rejection, claiming that Yeats had decided not to accept the play before he ever saw it. Denis Donoghue asserted: "Yeats made a critical error in rejecting the play, but the published correspondence shows that he was scrupulously honorable in reaching his decision. . . . The strongest argument against Yeats . . . is that *The Silver Tassie,* whatever its faults, was demonstrably superior to many of the plays that the Abbey had already accepted. But Yeats' critique of the play is formidable, and not all foolish or shallow."

After the rioting over "The Plough and the Stars" and Yeats's rejection of "The Silver Tassie," O'Casey was convinced that he could never achieve artistic freedom in Ireland. He remained in London, living "in stubborn exile a far remove from the people and places that fed his imagination and stirred his deepest feelings," reflected Kevin Sullivan. Although O'Casey never returned to Ireland, he and Yeats reconciled after several years, and his plays were once again produced at the Abbey Theatre.

When O'Casey began to write for the theatre he was a dedicated socialist, but Benstock said that despite this, "the early tenement plays are devoid of propagandistic evidence. He concentrated on real events, their complexities and their multiple acts on the people he knew, rarely showing his hand to his audience." William A. Armstrong noted that "the topical and the local elements in O'Casey's early plays are so strong that some critics belittled him as nothing more than a photographic realist who merely shuffled together for the stage familiar details of life in the Dublin slums during the time of the Troubles. This criticism is invalid, for O'Casey . . . has the myth-maker's great gift of discerning archetypal characters and situations, of distilling from everyday elements a quintessence of life far superior to the products of any documentary form of realism."

Even after his exile to England, O'Casey's "subject matter remained almost exclusively Irish, with only one or two exceptions, and for over thirty years he kept in touch with political and social changes in Ireland, mirroring them in his new plays and remaining a persistent critic of essential elements of Irish life under the Republic," Benstock noted. He continued to experiment with Expressionism in various themes from morality plays to comic fantasies. Although his use of stylization did not succeed in "The Silver Tassie," Joan Templeton declared that "the

techniques of Expressionism figure significantly in the success of the late comedies."

Among his more successful later plays were "Purple Dust" and "Cock-a-Doodle-Dandy." Most of these plays were comic pastorals containing the message that "merriment and joy are the primary virtues in a world that has denounced them too long," stated Joan Templeton. O'Casey often attempted to present a serious message through the comic mode, but this method did not always fare well. The "technique in these late comedies parallels that of the Dublin plays in their blend of the tragic and the pathetic with the wildly comic, but with strong elements of fantasy for leavening," Benstock noted. "Supernatural birds, superhuman heroes, mysterious priests who stir the youth to rebellion—all embodiments of the Life Force—take command in the more optimistic of the plays. . . . But in the more somber dramas, despite the many flashes of hilarity and song, the mood of bitterness predominates." Hogan said of the late plays that "by their verve, vitality, and brilliance, they and not the early masterpieces may ultimately prove to be O'Casey's great contribution to the theatre."

In 1939 O'Casey published the first book of his six-volume part-fictional autobiography. The autobiographies have many literary faults and have often been brushed aside as the work of an established writer's old age. But Gilman claimed that they were "perhaps the most durable of his contributions." In addition to providing valuable insight into O'Casey's personality and writing methods, these volumes contain many fascinating passages about important figures such as Yeats, Lady Gregory, T. P. O'Connor, and Bernard Shaw, and serve as important social documents of the period.

The Letters of Sean O'Casey supplements the autobiographies with numerous letters to, from, and about Sean O'Casey. Sullivan noted that the letters emphasize O'Casey's "generosity, his incredible energy and resilience," as well as his "perverse affection" for poverty "because it was *his* way of life," and his impatience "with any opinion that is not his own and, we suspect, precisely *because* it is not his own." Donoghue thought the letters presented O'Casey as "the most quarrelsome writer in Ireland, a notoriously quarrelsome country. . . . O'Casey brought his Ireland with him, and held on to its rancor wherever he happened to be; London, Devon, New York. He was always the man who was sacked from his first job." Nevertheless, a *New Yorker* critic concluded that "his grievances were, for the most part, real, and they are, even now, heartbreaking to read about."

Some critics have recently questioned O'Casey's place in literary history as one of the great modern playwrights. Richard Gilman contended that "O'Casey can't bear the weight of such an apotheosis. . . . There are too many bad and even deeply embarrassing plays in his oeuvre ('Within the Gates,' 'The Star Turns Red,' 'The Bishop's Bonfire,' et al.) and too many esthetic sins of naivete, rhetorical excess, sentimentality and tendentiousness in all but his very best work." Gilman suggested that O'Casey's reputation has less to do with his art than with other circumstances: "the sterility of the English-speaking theater in the twenties when he came to prominence with his 'Dublin' plays at the Abbey Theater; his ferocious battle with censorship; his own 'dramatic' story—slum childhood, self-education, lifelong near-blindness, self-exile."

Denis Donoghue declared that O'Casey's "career as an important dramatist came and went within five years. A man who writes *The Shadow of a Gunman* in 1923, *Juno and the Paycock* in 1924, *The Plough and the Stars* in 1926 and *The Silver Tassie* in 1928 should have the luck to continue writing good plays or the prudence to withdraw into dignity and silence. . . . But O'Casey lapsed into bad plays, hysterical essays, hectic reminiscences, blasts against the world, benedictions lavished upon communism, atheism, Welsh nationalism." Kevin Sullivan agreed, claiming that "the experimental plays . . . are interesting as experiments but hardly memorable as works of art. Sean O'Casey was above all a passionate man and his genius, if granted, is concentrated in this quality of his life which only occasionally carried over into the work."

Despite this criticism, Irma S. Lustig reminds us that "it is unjust to obscure O'Casey's farsightedness . . . by recalling only the strident means by which he was driven to express his views." "Politically a realist as well as a humanitarian, he predicted the global successes of socialism, especially if there were repeated wars. He foresaw the consequences of dividing Ireland, and the impossibility of 'classless' nationalist struggle. He challenged the exaltation of reckless violence." In striving to express his views, O'Casey developed "a voice of his own, a style of his own, and a body of artistic work that reflected his personality and thinking with flair and color," Benstock declared. "Sean O'Casey stands as Irish drama almost by himself—and one of the best dramatists writing in the English language in his time in any country."

BIOGRAPHICAL/CRITICAL SOURCES:

BOOKS

Armstrong, William A., *Sean O'Casey,* Longman, 1967.
Benstock, Bernard, *Sean O'Casey,* Bucknell University Press, 1970.
Contemporary Literary Criticism, Gale, Volume 1, 1973, Volume 5, 1976, Volume 9, 1979, Volume 11, 1979, Volume 15, 1980.
Dictionary of Literary Biography, Volume 10: *Modern British Dramatists, 1900-1945,* Gale, 1982.
Kilroy, Thomas, editor, *Sean O'Casey: A Collection of Critical Essays,* Prentice-Hall, 1975.
O'Casey, Eileen, *Cheerio, Titan: The Friendship Between George Bernard Shaw and Sean O'Casey,* Scribner, 1989.

PERIODICALS

Modern Drama, May, 1971, March, 1974.
MOSAIC, fall, 1977.
Nation, March 20, 1972, July 19, 1975.
New Republic, April 26, 1975.
Newsweek, January 15, 1973, March 31, 1975.
New Yorker, March 11, 1972, January 13, 1973, May 5, 1975.
New York Times Book Review, March 16, 1975.
South Atlantic Quarterly, summer, 1976.
Time, March 27, 1972, November 18, 1974.
Times Literary Supplement, January 2, 1976, August 14, 1981, April 19, 1985.
Village Voice, November 29, 1976.
Virginia Quarterly Review, summer, 1975.

*   *   *

O'CATHASAIGH, Sean
    See O'CASEY, Sean

*   *   *

O'CONNOR, (Mary) Flannery   1925-1964

PERSONAL: Born March 25, 1925, in Savannah, Ga.; died August 3, 1964, in Milledgeville, Ga., of lupus; daughter of Edward

Francis and Regina (Cline) O'Connor. *Education:* Women's College of Georgia (now Georgia College), A.B., 1945; State University of Iowa, M.F.A., 1947. *Religion:* Roman Catholic.

ADDRESSES: Home—Milledgeville, Ga. *Agent*— McIntosh, McKee & Dodds, 22 East 40th St., New York, N.Y. 10016.

CAREER: Author.

AWARDS, HONORS: Kenyon Review fellowship in fiction, 1953; National Institute of Arts and Letters grant in literature, 1957; first prize, O. Henry Memorial Awards, 1957, for "Greenleaf," 1963, for "Everything That Rises Must Converge," and 1965, for "Revelation"; Ford Foundation grant, 1959; Litt.D. from St. Mary's College, 1962, and Smith College, 1963; Henry H. Bellaman Foundation special award, 1964; National Book Award, 1972, for *The Complete Short Stories;* Board Award, National Book Critics Circle, 1980, for *The Habit of Being;* "Notable Book" citation, *Library Journal,* 1980, for *The Habit of Being.*

WRITINGS:

Wise Blood (also see below; novel), Harcourt, 1952.
A Good Man Is Hard to Find (stories; contains "A Good Man Is Hard to Find" [also see below], "The River," "The Life You Save May Be Your Own," "A Stroke of Good Fortune," "A Temple of the Holy Ghost," "The Artificial Nigger," "A Circle in the Fire," "A Late Encounter with the Enemy," "Good Country People," and "The Displaced Person"), Harcourt, 1955 (published in England as *The Artificial Nigger,* Neville Spearman, 1957).
(Contributor) Granville Hicks, editor, *The Living Novel,* Macmillan, 1957.
The Violent Bear It Away (also see below; novel), Farrar, Straus, 1960.
(Editor and author of introduction) *A Memoir of Mary Ann,* Farrar, Straus, 1961, reprinted, Beil, 1989 (published in England as *Death of a Child,* Burns & Oates, 1961).
Three by Flannery O'Connor (contains *Wise Blood,* "A Good Man Is Hard to Find," and *The Violent Bear It Away*), Signet, 1964, reprinted, New American Library, 1986.
Everything That Rises Must Converge (stories; contains "Everything That Rises Must Converge," "Greenleaf," "A View of the Woods," "The Enduring Chill," "The Comforts of Home," "The Lame Shall Enter First," "Revelation," "Parker's Back," and "Judgment Day"), Farrar, Straus, 1965.
Mystery and Manners: Occasional Prose, edited by Sally Fitzgerald and Robert Fitzgerald, Farrar, Straus, 1969.
The Complete Short Stories, Farrar, Straus, 1971.
The Habit of Being (letters), edited by S. Fitzgerald, Farrar, Straus, 1979.
Collected Works, Library of America, 1988.

O'Connor's writings have been translated into French, Italian, Portuguese, Spanish, Greek, Danish, and Japanese. Her work is represented in many anthologies and appears in periodicals, including *Accent, Mademoiselle, Critic,* and *Esquire.* An annual, *The Flannery O'Connor Bulletin,* was established in 1972.

O'Connor's papers are part of the permanent collection of the Georgia College Library.

SIDELIGHTS: A. L. Rowse called Flannery O'Connor "probably the greatest short-story writer of our time," and this opinion is not unique among critics. Though O'Connor's work has been compared frequently with that of Nathaniel Hawthorne, Nathanael West, and Fyodor Dostoevsky, among others, "as a person and a writer she was a complete original," wrote Josephine

Hendin. A religious writer who defined her "subject in fiction" as "the action of grace in territory held largely by the devil," O'Connor nevertheless believed good writing begins in a concrete "experience, not an abstraction." Her writing reflects this by being firmly rooted in her native South. Her Catholic family lived in Milledgeville, Georgia, since before the Civil War. "Ours is a real Bible Belt," she once said. "We have a sense of the absolute, . . . a sense of Moses' face as he pulverized the idols, . . . a sense of time, place and eternity joined." In his book *The Christian Humanism of Flannery O'Connor,* David Eggenschwiler said that "she insisted that the ultimate concerns of her art transcended the natural but that her art was primarily of the concrete world in which the transcendent was manifested. . . . She sought a more than worldly knowledge, not by knowing the world badly but by knowing it well."

Considering her limited output as a writer, the critical response to her canon has been extraordinary. More than a dozen books, chapters in many more, and hundreds of articles have been devoted to O'Connor's work. As Hendin noted in *The World of Flannery O'Connor,* the author produced "a body of work of remarkable uniformity and persistent design." Her themes have been identified by Stanley Edgar Hyman as the "profound equation of the mysteries of sex and religion, . . . change of identity, transformation, death-and-rebirth, . . . the perverse mother, . . . what Walter Allen . . . calls a 'world of the God-intoxicated,' [and] the transvaluation of values in which progress in the world is retrogression in the spirit."

O'Connor wrote: "I see from the standpoint of Christian orthodoxy. This means that for me the meaning of life is centered in our Redemption by Christ and that what I see in the world I see in relation to that." Andre Bleikasten, however, wrote of the "heresy" of Flannery O'Connor and warned that "O'Connor's public pronouncements on her art—on which most of her commentators have pounced so eagerly—are by no means the best guide to her fiction. As an interpreter, she was just as fallible as anybody else, and in point of fact there is much of what she has said or written about her work that is highly questionable. . . . The truth of O'Connor's work is the truth of her art, not that of her church. Her fiction does refer to an implicit theology, but if we rely, as we should, on its testimony rather than on the author's comments, we shall have to admit that the Catholic orthodoxy of her work is at least debatable. . . . Gnawed by old Calvinistic ferments and at the same time corroded by a very modern sense of the absurd, O'Connor's version of Christianity is emphatically and exclusively her own. . . . Flannery O'Connor was a Catholic. She was not a Catholic writer. She was a writer, and as a writer she belongs to no other parish than literature."

She was, however, a theological writer. As such, Ted R. Spivey explained, O'Connor dealt with violent and grotesque people because "man has in his soul a powerful destructive element, which often makes him behave in a violent and grotesque manner. . . . [Her writing is about] the existential struggle with the principle of destruction traditionally called the Devil." Numerous critics see this preoccupation with the demonic as a central characteristic of O'Connor's work. In opposition to this evil force O'Connor places a God whose "grace hits the characters in [her] stories with the force of a mugging," Hendin wrote. The climactic moments of grace in her stories and in her characters' lives have been described by Preston M. Browning, Jr., as "those moments when her characters undergo a traumatic collapse of their illusions of righteousness and self-sufficiency." As *Washington Post* critic William McPherson put it, "the question behind Miss O'Connor's stories is not whether God exists—he's there, all right—but whether men can bear it." Claire Katz summarized,

"it is the impulse toward secular autonomy, the smug confidence that human nature is perfectible by its own efforts, that she sets out to destroy, through an act of violence so intense that the character is rendered helpless, . . . [thus establishing] the need for absolute submission to the power of Christ." Hermione Lee of *New Statesman* echoed this view when she wrote, "Essentially, O'Connor's subject is acceptance: the point at which her sinners become aware of the awful unavoidability of Grace. All the stories drive towards an appointed end, often of horrifying violence. . . . The power of the work lies in its suppression of this severely orthodox subject beneath a brilliantly commonplace surface. . . . Its masterly realism springs from the life in Georgia, but its intellectual energy, and its penetration of grotesque extremes, derives from the faith."

Richard Poirier felt that this outlook contributed to O'Connor's major limitation, namely, "that the direction of her stories tends to be nearly always the same." *Hollins Critic* reviewer Walter Sullivan agreed but added, "what she did well, she did with exquisite competence: her ear for dialogue, her eye for human gestures were as good as anybody's ever were; and her vision was as clear and direct and as annoyingly precious as that of an Old Testament prophet or one of the more irascible Christian saints."

Her stories are not all terror and violence, however. There is also humor here, what Brainerd Cheney called "a brand of humor based on the religious point of view." James Degnan believed that O'Connor's was "a vision that clearly sees the tragedy of a world in which people are hopelessly alienated from each other, but a vision which stresses the comedy of such a world." In the introduction to *Everything That Rises Must Converge,* Robert Fitzgerald wrote, "There is quite a gamut of [comedy,] running from something very like cartooning to an irony dry and refined, especially in the treatment of the most serious matters." Kenneth L. Woodward likened O'Connor's "grimly Gothic humor" to that of William Blake.

In execution O'Connor's work "bears no relation whatever to the so-called 'art novel,' " noted Melvin Friedman. He explained, "Her novels and stories are in every sense traditionally constructed and make no use of the experimental suggestions of a Joyce, a Proust, a Faulkner, or even a Styron." He called her characters "almost all fanatics." Another critic, Louise Gossett, observed that "the bold lines of their portraiture . . . converge directly on the spiritual errors of the present. . . . When these lines are too direct, the fiction lapses into preaching." (O'Connor's letters reveal that she was aware of this problem. She wrote, "The novel is an art form and when you use it for anything other than art, you pervert. . . . If you do manage to use it successfully for social, religious, or other purposes, it is because you made it art first.")

It is the author's characters that rivet the attention of readers to her stories; Alice Walker noted that it was for O'Connor's characterizations "that I appreciated her work at first . . . these white folks without the magnolia . . . and these black folks without melons and superior racial patience, these are like the Southerners that I know." John Idol summed up Flannery O'Connor's fiction as follows: "In the twelve or fifteen of her best stories Miss O'Connor aptly blended satire and reverence, the concrete and the abstract, the comic and the cosmic, earning for herself a secure place among the writers of the Southern Renascence."

O'Connor's posthumously collected nonfiction has also earned praise. Granville Hicks wrote of *Mystery and Manners: Occasional Prose,* "I had read some of these lectures in one form or another, but until they were brought together I had not realized what an impressive body of literary criticism they constituted."

John Leonard wrote that *Mystery and Manners* "should be read by every writer and would-be writer and lover of writing. . . . [O'Connor] ranks with Mark Twain and Scott Fitzgerald among our finest prose-stylists." In 1972, O'Connor's *Complete Short Stories* won the National Book Award for fiction.

MEDIA ADAPTATIONS: A two-act play, "The Displaced Person," by Cecil Dawkins (first produced in New York at American Place Theatre, 1966) was based on five stories by Flannery O'Connor. A movie version of *Wise Blood* was directed by John Huston and released in 1980.

BIOGRAPHICAL/CRITICAL SOURCES:

BOOKS

Allen, Walter, *The Modern Novel,* Dutton, 1964.
Browning, Preston M., Jr., *Flannery O'Connor,* Southern Illinois University Press, 1974.
Contemporary Literary Criticism, Gale, Volume 1, 1973, Volume 2, 1974, Volume 3, 1975, Volume 6, 1976, Volume 10, 1979, Volume 13, 1980, Volume 15, 1980, Volume 21, 1982.
Dictionary of Literary Biography, Volume 2: *American Novelists since World War II,* Gale, 1978.
Dictionary of Literary Biography Yearbook: 1980, Gale, 1981.
Drake, Robert, *Flannery O'Connor,* Eerdmans, 1966.
Driskell, Leon V., and Joan T. Brittain, *The Eternal Crossroads: The Art of Flannery O'Connor,* University Press of Kentucky, 1971.
Eggenschwiler, David, *The Christian Humanism of Flannery O'Connor,* Wayne State University Press, 1972.
Feeley, K., *Flannery O'Connor: Voice of the Peacock,* Rutgers University Press, 1972.
Friedman, Melvin J., and Lewis A. Lawson, *The Added Dimension: The Art Mind of Flannery O'Connor,* Fordham University Press, 1966.
Gossett, Louise Y., *Violence in Recent Southern Fiction,* Duke University Press, 1965.
Hendin, Josephine, *The World of Flannery O'Connor,* Indiana University Press, 1970.
Hyman, Stanley Edgar, *Flannery O'Connor,* University of Minnesota Press, 1966.
Kazin, Alfred, *Bright Book of Life: American Novelists and Storytellers from Hemingway to Mailer,* Atlantic-Little, Brown, 1973.
Martin, C. W., *The True Country: Themes in the Fiction of Flannery O'Connor,* Vanderbilt University Press, 1969.
May, John R., *The Pruning Word: The Parables of Flannery O'Connor,* University of Notre Dame Press, 1976.
McFarland, Dorothy Tuck, *Flannery O'Connor,* Ungar, 1976.
Muller, Gilbert H., *Nightmares and Visions: Flannery O'Connor and the Catholic Grotesque,* University of Georgia Press, 1972.
O'Connor, Flannery, *Everything That Rise Must Converge,* introduction by Robert Fitzgerald, Farrar, Straus, 1965.
Orvell, Miles, *Invisible Parade: The Fiction of Flannery O'Connor,* Temple University Press, 1972.
Reiter, Robert E., editor, *Flannery O'Connor,* Herder, 1968.
Short Story Criticism, Volume 1, Gale, 1988.
Waldmier, Joseph J., editor, *Recent American Fiction: Some Critical Views,* Houghton, 1963.
Walters, Dorothy, *Flannery O'Connor,* Twayne, 1973.

PERIODICALS

America, March 30, 1957, October 17, 1964.
American Literature, March, 1974, May, 1974.
Arizona Quarterly, autumn, 1976.

Books and Bookmen, May, 1972.
Book World, February 11, 1979.
Catholic Library World, November, 1967.
Censer, fall, 1960.
Chicago Tribune, April 15, 1979.
Christian Century, September 30, 1964, May 19, 1965, July 9, 1969.
Commonweal, July 9, 1965, December 3, 1965, August 8, 1969.
Contemporary Literature, winter, 1968.
Critic, October-November, 1965.
Detroit News, March 25, 1979.
English Journal, April, 1962.
Esprit, winter, 1964 (entire issue).
Esquire, May, 1965.
Georgia Review, summer, 1958.
Hollins Critic, September, 1965.
Modern Age, fall, 1960.
Modern Fiction Studies, spring, 1973.
Ms., December, 1975.
New Republic, July 5, 1975, March 10, 1979.
New Statesman, December 7, 1979.
New York Herald Tribune Book Week, May 30, 1965.
New York Times, May 13, 1969, March 9, 1979.
New York Times Book Review, June 12, 1955, February 24, 1960, May 30, 1965, November 28, 1971, March 18, 1979, August 21, 1988.
Renascence, spring, 1965.
Saturday Review, May 12, 1962, December 16, 1962, May 29, 1965, May 10, 1969, November 13, 1971.
Sewanee Review, summer, 1962, autumn, 1963, spring, 1968 (entire issue).
Southwest Review, summer, 1965.
Spectator, August 30, 1968.
Studies in Short Fiction, spring, 1964, winter, 1964, winter, 1973, spring, 1975, winter, 1976.
Time, May 30, 1969, February 14, 1972, March 5, 1979.
Times Literary Supplement, September 12, 1968, November 21, 1980.
Washington Post, December 1, 1971.

*   *   *

ODETS, Clifford   1906-1963

PERSONAL: Born July 18, 1906, in Philadelphia, Pa.; died August 14, 1963, in Los Angeles, Calif.; son of Louis J. (a printer and company vice-president) and Pearl (Geisinger) Odets; married Luise Rainer (an actress), January 8, 1937 (divorced, May, 1940); married Bette Grayson (an actress), May 14, 1943 (died, 1954); children: (second marriage) Nora, Walt. *Education:* Attended secondary school in New York, N.Y. *Religion:* Jewish.

CAREER: Playwright. Left school at age fourteen; worked as actor in local New York City theatre groups, vaudeville performer, radio play and gag writer, and as radio broadcaster; acted character parts in traveling stock theatre productions and small parts in Broadway plays, 1923-28; played juvenile roles in New York Theatre Guild productions, 1928-30; founding member and actor with Group Theatre, New York City, 1930-35; screenwriter in Hollywood, Calif., 1935-37; returned to New York City and remained associated with Group Theatre, 1937-41; screenwriter and producer in Hollywood, 1941-61; worked in television, beginning 1961. Theatre director.

MEMBER: League of American Writers, Actors Equity Association, Dramatists Guild, Screen Writers Guild.

AWARDS, HONORS: New Theatre League award and Yale Drama Prize, both 1935, both for "Waiting for Lefty"; Award of Merit Medal from National Institute and American Academy of Arts and Letters, 1961.

WRITINGS:

PLAYS

Awake and Sing (three-act; first produced on Broadway at Belasco Theatre, February 19, 1935; copyrighted in 1933 under title "I Got the Blues"), Covici-Friede, 1935 (also see below).

Waiting for Lefty [and] *Till the Day I Die: Two Plays* (the former, one-act; the latter, seven-scene; both first produced on Broadway at Longacre Theatre, March 26, 1935), Covici-Friede, 1935 (also see below).

Paradise Lost (three-act; first produced on Broadway at Longacre Theatre, December 9, 1935), Random House, 1936 (also see below).

Golden Boy (three-act; first produced on Broadway at Belasco Theatre, November 4, 1937), Random House, 1937 (also see below).

Rocket to the Moon (three-act; first produced on Broadway at Belasco Theatre, November 24, 1938), Random House, 1939 (also see below).

Night Music: A Comedy in Twelve Scenes (three-act; first produced on Broadway at Broadhurst Theatre, February 24, 1940), Random House, 1940.

Clash by Night (two-act; first produced on Broadway at Belasco Theatre, December 27, 1941), Random House, 1942.

"The Russian People" (three-act; adapted from the play by Konstantin Simonov), first produced in New York, N.Y., at Guild Theatre, December 29, 1942.

The Big Knife (three-act; first produced on Broadway at American National Theatre and Academy, February 24, 1949), Random House, 1949 (also see below).

The Country Girl (three-act; first produced on Broadway at Lyceum Theatre, November 10, 1950), Viking, 1951, published as *Winter Journey*, Samuel French, 1955.

"The Flowering Peach" (three-act), first produced on Broadway at Belasco Theatre, December 28, 1954.

Also author of the unproduced plays "9-10 Eden Street," "The Silent Partner," "The Law of Flight," "By the Sea," "The Seasons," and "The Tides of Fundy."

OMNIBUS VOLUMES

Three Plays (contains "Awake and Sing," "Waiting for Lefty," and "Till the Day I Die"), Covici-Friede, 1935.

Six Plays of Clifford Odets (contains "Awake and Sing," "Waiting for Lefty," "Till the Day I Die," "Paradise Lost," "Golden Boy," and "Rocket to the Moon"), Modern Library, 1939, Grove Press, 1988.

Golden Boy, Awake and Sing [and] *The Big Knife*, Penguin, 1963.

SCREENPLAYS

"The General Died at Dawn" (adapted from the novel by Charles G. Booth), Paramount, 1936.

(And director) "None but the Lonely Heart" (adapted from the novel by Richard Llewellyn), RKO, 1944.

"Deadline at Dawn" (adapted from the novel by William Irish), RKO, 1946.

(With Zachary Gold) "Humoresque" (adapted from the short story by Fannie Hurst), Warner Brothers, 1946.

(With Ernest Lehman) "Sweet Smell of Success" (adapted from the novella "Tell Me About It Tomorrow" by Lehman), United Artists, 1957.

(And director) "The Story on Page One," Twentieth Century-Fox, 1960.

"Wild in the Country" (adapted from the novel *The Lost Country* by I. R. Salamanca), Twentieth Century-Fox, 1961.

Also author of the unproduced screenplays "Gettysburg" and "The River is Blue."

OTHER

The Time Is Ripe: The 1940 Journal of Clifford Odets, Grove Press, 1988.

SIDELIGHTS: A writer of the depression, Clifford Odets became an idol of the proletariat in the mid-1930s. Yet his own roots in the working class he treated so sympathetically in his works were not very deep: "I was a worker's son until the age of twelve," Odets once recalled. His father originally worked as a printer, but eventually came to own his own printing plant. When he moved his family to Philadelphia, the senior Odets continued to prosper in business. In contrast, young Clifford remained intent on pursuing a less conventional life by writing, giving poetry recitals, and acting in various companies. His refusal to pursue the family business combined with his devotion to writing at times provoked conflict in his family. Once Odets's obviously irate father smashed Clifford's typewriter. (Later, he replaced it.)

By 1930, Odets lived alone in New York City. There he grew increasingly aware of the destructive impact of the Great Depression as he observed the city's suffering masses. R. Baird Shuman reported that "as the depression continued, Odets grew more and more concerned about the plight of the working and middle classes. He looked about him for ways of ameliorating the widespread suffering and privation of the masses." Drawing on this sympathy, a sympathy he claimed first developed after reading Victor Hugo's novel *Les Miserables* in 1918, Odets wrote his first play, "9-10 Eden Street." Upon reading the play, Group Theatre associate Harold Clurman noticed most of the pain emitted from the work came from Odets himself. "Something in his past life had hurt him," Clurman speculated. "He was doubled up in pain, now, and in his pain he appeared to be shutting out the world." Whatever the source of his pain, Odets could not have been too encouraged about succeeding in acting or in writing—he "was not generally considered a gifted actor"; "9-10 Eden Street" was never produced.

Even Odets's association with the Group Theatre did not provide him enough influence to get his next play, "Awake and Sing," staged. Despite its interest in the work, the financially weak organization could not risk the chance of introducing an unproven playwright. Undaunted by this rejection, Odets wrote his next play, "Waiting for Lefty," for a New Theatre League play contest. It won, and was soon being played by the awarding organization on Sunday nights. This brief exposure precipitated a glorious introduction into the New York theatre world: within a year the most talked-about playwright since Eugene O'Neill had three plays running on Broadway.

"Waiting for Lefty" is "undoubtedly the most angry play which Clifford Odets had ever produced," claimed Shuman. Based on the incidents of the 1934 New York City cab strike, it is set on a practically bare stage, a meeting hall where the taxi drivers' union is gathered to take a strike vote. As the strike talks progress the union members, who have been seated among the audience, come forth to defend their position. In the process, flashback reveals the hardship in each of their financially desperate lives. With word that the absent Lefty, their militant representative, has been killed by an assailant, the workers fervently join together in chanting "Strike! Strike! Strike!" The play's impact is made even more shattering by Odets's skillful manipulation of events as they lead to a climax. As Joseph Wood Krutch pointed out, "The pace is swift, the characterization is for the most part crisp, and the points are made, one after another, with bold simplicity."

In judging "Waiting for Lefty," Krutch felt "there is no denying its effectiveness in achieving all it sets out to achieve." He conceded, however, that the play's "simplicity must be paid for at a certain price. The villains are mere caricatures and even the very human heroes occasionally freeze into stained glass attitudes. . . . No one, however, expects subtleties from a soap-box, and the interesting fact is that Mr. Odets invented a form which turns out to be a very effective dramatic equivalent of soapbox oratory."

Encouraged by the success of "Waiting for Lefty," the Group Theatre finally decided to run "Awake and Sing." Their decision was hardly a mistake: many critics include it among Odets's finest plays. "Awake and Sing" presented, with an "extraordinary freshness," the story of Ralph Berger as he frees "himself from his obsession with a purely personal rebellion against poverty which separates him from his girl and determines to throw himself with enthusiasm into the class struggle." Odets's ability in bringing life into his play fascinated Alfred Kazin: "In Odets's play there was a lyric uplifting of blunt Jewish speech, boiling over and explosive, that did more to arouse the audience than the political catch words that brought the curtain down. Everybody on that stage was furious, kicking, alive—the words, always real but never flat, brilliantly authentic like no other theater speech on Broadway, aroused the audience to such delight that one could feel it bounding back and uniting itself with the mind of the writer."

The Broadway success of Odets's proletariat themes brought him sudden critical attention. One critic called him "one of the few American playwrights who is worth thinking about at all." Many did think about him, but not so receptively; "Waiting for Lefty" was banned in seven cities. His suspected affiliations with the Communist party only increased the controversy surrounding him. Although Odets had belonged to the party for an eight-month span in 1934, he later quit, claiming it interfered with his freedom to write. He also joined in a delegation traveling to Cuba in 1935 to investigate conditions there. The group was deported by the Cuban government after the first day. Such activities helped create a "Communist" stigma around Odets which continued for many years: in the 1950s he testified at the Senate McCarthy hearings.

The much-anticipated fourth Odets play, "Paradise Lost," marked an unexpected turning point in his career. It failed miserably, but not before the success of his earlier works had made him an attractive candidate for a Hollywood screenwriting job. The decision racked Odets: he saw the lure of Hollywood and its promise of financial success shadowed by his devotion to the Group Theatre and its atmosphere of artistic freedom. Moved by the reasoning that he could help finance the Theatre with his Hollywood earnings, Odets decided to leave. In doing so, he incurred the scorn of many who accused him of abandoning his proletarian ideals for Hollywood's big money. Response to his first screenplay, "The General Died at Dawn," was made in the light of his plays. One critic asked, "Odets, where is thy sting?"

While the impact of the Hollywood move on Odets's career has been debated, at least one change is certain: his next plays gained a much broader audience. In "Golden Boy," Odets continued to probe the themes of his previous plays but kept his political and economic theories in the background. The story of a young Italian boy who abandons the fiddle for a fighting career, "Golden Boy" re-established Odets's reputation as a leading dramatist. Stark Young felt "his theatrical gift most appears . . . in the dialogue's avoidance of the explicit. The explicit, always to be found in poor writers trying for the serious, is the surest sign of a lack of talent. . . . Mr. Odets is the most promising writer our theatre can show." Viewing his career in retrospect, Walter Kerr affirmed that Hollywood had at least not stolen Odets's playwrighting sting: "Odets wrote *Golden Boy* at the height of his powers as an angry, moralizing neo-realist, and it remains his most successful play."

Drawing on his belief that "the more talented the Marxian dramatist the less sharply his plays are set from the best work of writers holding different political opinions," Krutch felt that in many respects Odets's next play, "Rocket to the Moon," was his finest. It was the last play to evoke major comparisons with his earlier Marxist works and their view of American life. Barry Hyams felt it similar to "Waiting for Lefty" and "Golden Boy," for these plays "did not attempt to speak *for* America. They spoke of America, of its indestructible good nature. . . . The shipping clerk could feel like Paul Bunyan. His nature was wedded to Walt Whitman. . . . His testament was that the human being not be nullified."

Odets's later plays were marked by moments of genuine praise but failed to capture the critical acclaim of the earlier works. "Night Music" was a "lyric improvisation . . . on the basic homelessness of the little man in the big city," wrote Harold Clurman. "It is charmingly sentimental, comically poetic, airy and wholly unpretentious." But, Clurman continued, "in *Night Music* Odets is far more wistful than angry." In "The Big Knife," a portrait of life in Hollywood, John Gassner thought Odets proved he "had lost none of his theatrical vigor and that no one writing realistic drama . . . can surpass his power to write with an explosive force and with a wild and swirling poetry of torment and bedevilment. . . . If *The Big Knife* is not a successfully realized play, . . . it is because Odets, a product of the agitated left-wing theatre of the 1930s, is heir to its major faults—to the tendency to put too much of the blame on society and too little on the individual." Another play, "The Country Girl," enjoyed tremendous success on Broadway and had "a certain honesty and considerable power." But still, said Clive Barnes, it was "by no means, a great play."

"The Flowering Peach," Odets's last play, marked a significant conclusion to his playwriting career as it confronted the author's declining political commitment. Shuman found in the play, a retelling of the Noah's ark story, evidence that "Odets seemed to find again the proper vehicle for what he wanted to say: . . . beyond hope and despair lies the desperate idea of *hope*." Gassner, on the other hand, expressed disappointment in these "doubts and vacillations. . . . It seemed as if Odets, with the example of generations of men before him, had given up hopes for a better world and is ready to accept humanity on its own second-best terms." Gerald Rabkin demonstrated, however, that the tone of acceptance inherent in "The Flowering Peach" can be interpreted differently. He believed "the significance of the play lies in the fact that Odets finally attempted to come to terms with the esthetic consequences of the loss of his political commitment. . . . The essence of *The Flowering Peach* is the acceptance of the loss of political faith. . . . Odets is basically concerned with man's reaction to cosmic injustice, his attempt to construct a means whereby he can *accept* this injustice. It is this concept of acceptance which dominates *The Flowering Peach.*"

In general, whatever faults there have been in Odets's plays have been transcended by his writing skill, especially in character presentation and language. "What has been impressive in Mr. Odets's plays," declared *Commonweal* reviewer Grenville Vernon, "has not been their ideas, which are pretty confused, or their structure, which has been pretty melodramatic, but the fact that the characterizations and the dialogue have a bite and an originality of turn which set them apart from the somewhat pallid characters and dialogues of most modern plays." Edith Isaacs, too, noticed "each of Odets's faults has almost its counterpart in creative quality. Against his extreme subjectiveness can be placed his wise desire to express the nature and the problems of the people that he knows. . . . Against the fact that he himself does most of the talking in his plays, there is the fact that the talk is exceptionally alive and theatrical, speech for an actor's tongue. Against the fact that the majority of his characters are cliches, the recognition that in almost every play there is at least one that is a real creation . . . one that has three dimensions and a soul."

While most critics at least respect Odets's contribution to the American theatre, there are some who feel he barely deserves that. John Simon called Odets "a well-meaning, mildly skillful hack, like the rest of our thirties dramatists. A hack who had lost his nerve." In a similar opinion, Brendan Gill declared: "The fact is that Odets has always been an absurdly overpraised playwright, and it is odd, looking back over his career, to recall the wringing of hands that took place when he seemed to abandon a lofty purpose on Broadway for the fleshpots of Hollywood; the dream factory was his proper milieu, and if he did not prosper there as an artist it is because there was little of the artist in him capable of prospering anywhere."

Undoubtedly, the events of the 1930s spurred Odets to write his plays of social impact. In a time when America thirsted for some sort of hope, his romanticism in plays offering hope for the individual mattered more than the inconsistencies inherent in them. As Allan Lewis noted, "These final exhilarating but inconsistent affirmations were requirements of the play of the depression, for actuality was full of heartbreak and terror." Inevitably, then, as the despair of the depressed thirties faded, a force that had provided the impact for Odets's plays was lost. "It is true that Odets took up other issues in certain works," admitted Malcom Goldstein, "particularly in his late plays; but whether subsidiary or paramount, class-consciousness is never absent, regardless of the year and the remoteness of his characters' concerns from money worries. Having taken a stand with the destitute proletariat, he could not recognize the fact of a rising employment index. After the first six plays . . . Odets's work dwindled in relevance to the age, until finally, after 1954, he could give the stage nothing at all."

BIOGRAPHICAL/CRITICAL SOURCES:

BOOKS

Brenman-Gibson, Margaret, *Clifford Odets: American Playwright,* Atheneum, 1982.
Clurman, Harold, *The Fervent Years,* Knopf, 1945, Harcourt, 1975.
Contemporary Literary Criticism, Gale, Volume 2, 1974, Volume 28, 1984.
Dictionary of Literary Biography, Gale, Volume 7: *Twentieth-Century American Dramatists,* 1981, Volume 26: *American Screenwriters,* 1984.
Downer, Alan S., editor, *American Drama and Its Critics,* Chicago University Press, 1965.
Dusenbury, Winifred Loesch, *The Theme of Loneliness in American Drama,* University of Florida Press, 1960.
Gassner, John, *Theatre at the Crossroads,* Holt, 1960.
Gould, Jean, *Modern American Playwrights,* Dodd, 1966.
Kazin, Alfred, *Starting Out in the Thirties,* Little, Brown, 1965.
Krutch, Joseph Wood, *The American Drama Since 1918: An Informal History,* Braziller, 1957.
Lewis, Allan, *American Plays and Playwrights of the Contemporary Theatre,* Crown, 1965.
Rabkin, Gerald, *Drama and Commitment,* Indiana University Press, 1964.
Shuman, R. Baird, *Clifford Odets,* Twayne, 1962.
Simon, John, *Singularities: Essays on the Theatre, 1964-73,* Random House, 1975.

PERIODICALS

American Quarterly, winter, 1963.
Commentary, May, 1946.
Commonweal, December 16, 1938, March 28, 1952, December 3, 1971.
Detroit News, February 28, 1982.
Drama Survey, fall, 1963.
Forum, May, 1949.
Los Angeles Times, February 24, 1983, September 1, 1988.
Nation, March 13, 1935, April 3, 1972.
New Republic, November 17, 1937, September 27, 1939, April 30, 1951.
New Yorker, January 22, 1938, March 25, 1972.
New York Times, December 24, 1971, March 16, 1972, May 31, 1978, January 8, 1984, March 9, 1984, March 18, 1984.
Saturday Review of Literature, December 9, 1950.
South Atlantic Quarterly, winter, 1970, spring, 1972.
Theatre Arts, April, 1939, October, 1954, September, 1955.
Time, June 8, 1970, March 26, 1984.
Times (London), September 10, 1984, April 6, 1989.
Tribune Books, August 21, 1988.

* * *

OE, Kenzaburo 1935-

PERSONAL: Surname is pronounced "*Oh*-way"; born January 31, 1935, in Ehime, Shikoku, Japan; married; children: two, eldest named Pooh. *Education:* Tokyo University, degree in French literature, 1959.

ADDRESSES: Home—585 Seijo-machi, Setagaya-Ku, Tokyo, Japan.

CAREER: Writer, 1957—.

AWARDS, HONORS: Akutagawa Prize from Japanese Society for the Promotion of Literature, 1958, for novella *Shiiku* ("The Catch"); Shinchosha literary prize from Shinchosha Publishing Co., 1964; Tanizaki prize, 1967.

WRITINGS:

IN ENGLISH

Shiiku (novella; title means "The Catch"), [Japan], 1958, translation by John Bester published in *The Shadow of Sunrise,* edited by Saeki Shoichi, Palo Alto, 1966.
Kojinteki na taiken (fiction), [Japan], 1964, translation by John Nathan published as *A Personal Matter,* Grove, 1968.

Man'en gannen no futtoboru (fiction; title means "Football in the First Year of Mannen), [Japan], 1967, translation by Bester published as *The Silent Cry,* Kodansha, 1974, reprinted, 1989.

Teach Us to Outgrow Our Madness (contains "The Day He Himself Shall Wipe My Tears Away," "Prize Stock," "Teach Us to Outgrow Our Madness," and "Aghwee the Sky Monster"), translation and introduction by Nathan, Grove, 1977.

The Crazy Iris and Other Stories of the Atomic Aftermath, translation by Ivan Morris and others, Grove, 1984.

FICTION; IN JAPANESE

Memushiri kouchi (title means "Pluck the Flowers, Gun the Kids"), [Japan], 1958.

Warera no jidai (title means "Our Age"), [Japan], 1959.

Okurete kita seinen (title means "Born Too Late"), [Japan], 1961.

Sakebigoe (title means "Screams"), [Japan], 1962.

Nichijo seikatsu no boken, [Japan], 1971.

Kozui wa waga tamashii ni oyobi, [Japan], 1973.

Seinen no omei, [Japan], 1974.

Pinchi ranna chosho, [Japan], 1976.

SHORT STORIES; IN JAPANESE

Oe Kenzaburo shu, [Japan], 1960.

Kodoku na seinen no kyuka, [Japan], 1960.

Seiteki ningen, [Japan], 1968.

Warera no hyoki o ikinobiru michi o oshieyo, [Japan], 1969, enlarged edition, 1975.

Oe Kenzaburo (volume from "Gendai no bungaku" series), [Japan], 1971.

Mizukara waga namida o nugui-tamau hi, [Japan], 1972.

Sora no kaibutsu Agui, [Japan], 1972.

ESSAYS; IN JAPANESE

Jizokusuru kokorozashi, [Japan], 1968.

Kakujidai no sozoryoku, [Japan], 1970.

Kowaremono to shite no ningen, [Japan], 1970.

Okinawa noto, [Japan], 1970.

Kujira no shimetsusuru hi, [Japan], 1972.

Dojidai to shite no sengo, [Japan], 1973.

Jokyo e, [Japan], 1974.

Bungaku noto, [Japan], 1974.

Genshuku na tsunawatari, [Japan], 1974.

Kotoba no yotte, [Japan], 1976.

OTHER

Sekai no wakamonotachi, [Japan], 1962.

Oe Kenzaburo zensakuhin, [Japan], 1966-67.

Oe Kenzaburo shu (volume from "Shincho Nihon bungaku" series), [Japan], 1969.

(Editor) Mansaku Itami, *Itami Mansaku essei shu,* [Japan], 1971.

Also author of *Hiroshima Notes* (essays), 1963, *The Perverts* (fiction), 1963, and *Adventures in Daily Life* (fiction), 1964.

SIDELIGHTS: Kenzaburo Oe became one of Japan's first authors ever to receive national recognition for his writing while still a university student. When he was awarded the prestigious Akutagawa Prize in 1958 for his novella *Shiiku* ("The Catch"), the twenty-three year old "automatically became Japan's *number one* young writer," stated Josh Greenfeld. "And with each succeeding work, both fictional and journalistic, his reputation as *number one* has grown to the point where . . . he is touted by the Japanese as their answer to Mailer, their send-up on Sartre, their oriental version of Henry Miller."

Despite his popularity, Oe has offended some Japanese critics with his controversial writing style, which, according to translator John Nathan, "treads a thin line between artful rebellion and mere unruliness." Rejecting the delicacy and elegant simplicity of traditional Japanese writers, Oe incorporated elements of Western style into his work. His long sentences, "crammed with adjectives and similes, . . . prod the reader along, constantly forcing him to make unexpected associations, or emphasizing the author's analytical self-awareness," said John Bester. In the preface to *A Personal Matter,* Nathan pointed out: "Oe consciously interferes with the tendency to vagueness which is considered inherent in the Japanese language. He violates its natural rhythms; he pushes the meaning of words to their furthest acceptable limits. . . . But that is to be expected: his entire stance is an assault on traditional values. The protagonist of his fiction is seeking his identity in a perilous wilderness, and it is fitting that his language should be just what it is—wild, unresolved, but never less than vital."

The most significant event of Oe's life occurred on August 15, 1945, when Emperor Hirohito announced over the radio that Japan had surrendered to the Allies. Young Oe and all Japanese children had been taught that the emperor was a living god and that it was their highest moral duty to die for him if so commanded. Upon hearing Hirohito on the radio, wrote Oe in "A Portrait of the Postwar Generation," "we were most surprised and disappointed by the fact that the Emperor had spoken in a *human* vŏice. . . . How could we believe that an august presence of such awful power had become an ordinary human being on a designated summer day?" This event became a frequent subject of his writing in later years, and by successfully capturing the confusion and quest for self-identity of post-war youth, Oe soon established himself as "the spokesman for an entire generation of young Japanese."

Western literature greatly influenced Oe's writings. At Tokyo University he studied the existentialist philosophies of Jean-Paul Sartre as well as the works of Blaise Pascal and Albert Camus. His favorite American authors were those whose heroes are searching for "personal freedom beyond the borders of safety and acceptance," authors such as Herman Melville, William Faulkner, and Norman Mailer. Oe was most inspired by Mark Twain's *Huckleberry Finn,* noted Nathan. "For Oe the single most important moment in the book was always Huck's agonized decision not to send Miss Watson a note informing her of Jim's whereabouts and to go instead to Hell. With that fearsome resolution to turn his back on his times, his society, and even his god, Huckleberry Finn became the model for Oe's existential hero."

The heroes of Oe's novels changed somewhat after 1964, when his first son, Pooh, was born with brain damage. "Until the advent of his first-born child, the quest for self-discovery took Oe's heroes beyond the boundaries of society into a lawless wilderness," observed Nathan. After Pooh's birth Oe began to write of heroes who "turn away from the lure of peril and adventure and seek instead, with the same urgency," a life of "certainty and consonance."

As a strong bond developed between Oe and his son, he wrote several partially autobiographical novels with the father of a brain-damaged child as protagonist. The first of these was *A Personal Matter,* the story of a twenty-seven-year-old man nicknamed Bird, whose wife gives birth to a deformed baby. The boy, looking like a two-headed monster, appears to have a brain hernia, and the doctors tell Bird that the baby will probably die or be a vegetable for life. Bird is so horrified that he chooses to let the baby die rather than face life tied to a retarded son. While his wife and child are in the hospital, Bird runs off to the apartment of a young widow friend, where he escapes into a world of fantasy, sex, and alcohol. He loses his teaching job after being so hung over that he vomits during a lecture. Meanwhile, the baby, being fed only on sugar water, refuses to die, so Bird takes him to an abortionist to have him killed. Suddenly, however, he changes his mind and returns the baby to the hospital. Doctors discover that the hernia is only a benign tumor and after successfully operating, they announce that the baby will be normal, though with a low IQ. Bird finds a new job and is reunited once more with his wife and child.

But the story is not as pretty as its ending might suggest. For example, D. J. Enright complained, "a fantastic amount of vomiting goes on, . . . and when Bird isn't actually vomiting, his stomach is generally heaving or churning." *Washington Post* reviewer Geoffrey Wolff declared that *A Personal Matter* "reeks of vomit and spilled whisky. Its surreal characters are all vegetables, cut off from history and hope. They define themselves by their despair. They use sex to wound and humiliate one another. They trick themselves with hopeless dreams of a new life, far away." Alan Levensohn surmised that this representation of mankind is Oe's way of suggesting that "the stunted existence Bird's baby will probably have, if Bird allows him to live, comes to seem terribly close to the existence which Bird and the others are making for themselves."

Several critics have noted that Oe compares Bird's personal disaster to the World War II nuclear holocaust. Wolff reflected: "Like the survivors of Hiroshima whose children were crippled in their mothers' wombs, Bird asks: Why? Who is to blame? Am I polluted? What grotesque signal has been delivered to me from Heaven?" Webster Schott noted that "Oe makes certain we understand that he is addressing the larger world beyond Bird's 'personal matter' by projecting his plot against nuclear tests, the defection of a Balkan diplomat and suicides galore." Oe also uses many symbols in the novel, added Schott, including Bird's baby, whose ruptured brain represents "a Japan that Burst its intellectual shell with a trauma."

Many reviewers were disappointed with the book's "cop-out fade-out" ending. "It is simply inconceivable that Bird could turn over so many new leaves in the space of the book's last few pages," Enright pointed out. "Even the most avid admirers of the happy ending in fiction . . . will find this one a miserable fraud." James A. Phillips commented that the epilogue completely undermines Oe's frank descriptions of sex and emotional turmoil. "To negate all this candor with a story-book ending leaves the reader with the feeling that being honest and baring your psyche is meaningless because ultimately you return to wishy-washy conventionality."

Wayne Falke theorized that the negative reactions of Western critics to Bird's final decision are due to cultural disparities. "Japan has a long tradition of accepting the inevitable which, in the West, is called resignation. . . . For the Japanese, to assume the responsibilities imposed upon one by one's superiors, by filial piety and the like, is an act of virtue. To maintain existent orders is preferable to change." Thus, when Bird chooses to remain with his wife and child, he is making the proper decision according to his own social structure. His actions are seen by Westerners, however, as taking the easy way out, because, according to Falke, "a more or less cheerful acceptance of circumstances is beyond our comprehension."

Despite their criticism of the book's ending, reviewers were receptive to the book as a whole. Several praised Oe's "crisp, pungent narrative" and "unaccommodating, sinewy, elliptical" style. John Hearsum remarked: "The prose is hard and brittle, the images like tiny nightmares. . . . The taut explosive style, and the images, make the book at some points as harrowing to read as some Japanese films are to watch. . . . It communicates the full terror of such a predicament, and confronts the arbitrary horror of the universe without any recourse to fancy techniques."

Another of Oe's translated books is *Teach Us to Outgrow Our Madness*. Two of its four short stories deal with brain-damaged children. In "Aghwee the Sky Monster," the father of a defective child helps arrange the child's death, then discovers that surgery would probably have saved its life. In the title story, a father becomes so close to his mentally retarded son that he is convinced he directly experiences any physical pain his son feels. Ivan Gold remarked that "no mere summary of the events of this brilliant story can convey the resonance and depth with which Oe is able to imbue the relationship."

Oe's focus on the "fierce, exclusive, isolating bond" with his son would "in a lesser writer be a fatal limitation," Nathan observed. But Oe has maintained his popularity. Some critics have even praised his concentration on the topic because his insight is so valuable to parents of retarded or autistic children. On the other hand, "obsession in and of itself is hardly a guarantee of literary quality," noted Gold. "But Oe is a supremely gifted writer . . . and able to 'fictionalize' the most significant elements of his life as can few others, and his work has enormous impact."

BIOGRAPHICAL/CRITICAL SOURCES:

BOOKS

Contemporary Literary Criticism, Gale, Volume 10, 1979, Volume 36, 1986.
Oe, Kenzaburo, *A Personal Matter,* translation by John Nathan, Grove, 1968.
Oe, Kenzaburo, *Teach Us to Outgrow Our Madness,* translation by Nathan, Grove, 1977.

PERIODICALS

Best Sellers, July 1, 1968, October, 1977.
Books Abroad, winter, 1969.
Christian Science Monitor, August 8, 1968.
Critique: Studies in Modern Fiction, Volume 15, number 3, 1974.
Hudson Review, autumn, 1968.
Japan Quarterly, October-December, 1973.
Life, August 16, 1968.
London Magazine, June, 1969.
Nation, August 5, 1968.
New Republic, August 17, 1968.
New Yorker, June 8, 1968.
New York Review of Books, October 10, 1968.
New York Times Book Review, July 7, 1968, September 8, 1985.
Studies in Short Fiction, fall, 1974.
Times Literary Supplement, October 26, 1984, April 28, 1989.
Voice Literary Supplement, October, 1982.
Washington Post, June 11, 1968.
Washington Post Book World, August 25, 1968, September 11, 1977.
World Literature Today, spring, 1978.

O'FAOLAIN, Julia 1932-
(Julia Martines)

PERSONAL: Surname is pronounced O'Fay-lawn; born June 6, 1932, in London, England; daughter of Sean (a writer) and Eileen (Gould) O'Faolain; married Lauro Martines (a professor and historian); children: Lucien Christopher. *Education:* University College, Dublin, received B.A. and M.A.; graduate study at Universita di Roma and Sorbonne, University of Paris.

ADDRESSES: Agent—Rogers, Coleridge & White, 20 Powis Mews, London W11 1JN, England; and International Creative Management, 40 West 52nd St., New York, N.Y. 10019.

CAREER: Writer, translator, and language teacher.

AWARDS, HONORS: Arts Council of Great Britain grant, 1981; *No Country for Young Men* was named to the Booker Prize short list.

WRITINGS:

(Translator, under name Julia Martines) Gene Brucker, editor, *Two Memoirs of Renaissance Florence: The Diaries of Buonaccorso Pitti and Gregorio Dati,* Harper, 1967.
(Translator, under name Julia Martines) Piero Chiara, *A Man of Parts,* Little, Brown, 1968.
We Might See Sights! and Other Stories, Faber, 1968.
Godded and Codded, Faber, 1970, published as *Three Lovers,* Coward, 1971.
(Editor with husband, Lauro Martines) *Not in God's Image: Women in History from the Greeks to the Victorians* (nonfiction), Harper, 1973.
Man in the Cellar (short stories), Faber, 1974.
Women in the Wall (novel), Viking, 1975.
Melancholy Baby, and Other Stories, Poolbeg Press, 1978.
No Country for Young Men (novel), Allen Lane, 1980, Carroll & Graf, 1986.
Daughters of Passion (short stories), Allen Lane, 1982.
The Obedient Wife (novel), Allen Lane, 1982, Carroll & Graf, 1985.
The Irish Signorina (novel), Allen Lane, 1984.

Contributor to anthologies, including *The Bodley Head Book of Irish Short Stories,* edited by David Marcus, Bodley Head, 1980, *The Penguin Book of Irish Short Stories,* edited by Benedict Kiely, Penguin, 1981, and *Fathers: Reflections by Daughters,* edited by Ursula Owen, Virago, 1983. Contributor of short stories and reviews to the London *Times, New Yorker, Kenyon Review, Saturday Evening Post, Vogue, Critic, Cosmopolitan, Irish Press, New York Times, Washington Post, Observer,* and other periodicals. Also contributor to "Kaleidoscope," a British Broadcasting Corporation radio program.

WORK IN PROGRESS: A novel set in the last years of papal Rome, before the city was annexed by Italy.

SIDELIGHTS: When Julia O'Faolain's book *Three Lovers* appeared, it was inevitable that comparisons between her novel and the work of her father, novelist and short-story writer Sean O'Faolain, would be made. But *Book World* critic J. R. Franks dismisses the issue by saying: "Yes, Julia O'Faolain is Sean's daughter. No, she does not write like her father. And maybe, if [*Three Lovers*] is a fair harbinger, she'll become the family-member whose name is used for identification." Franks's opinion is echoed by Sally Beauman, who notes in the *New York Times Book Review* that the author "writes firmly, with a voice all her own." Praising O'Faolain's "well planned, intelligent, concise" style, Beauman finds the author's writing "more

pointed than that of [her father] with a cold female eye for the egocentricities of masculine behavior."

Two of O'Faolain's notable works focus on women in history. *Not in God's Image: Women in History from the Greeks to the Victorians,* edited by O'Faolain and her husband, Lauro Martines, is described by a *Christian Century* writer as a collection of readings from primary sources that "documents the subjection of women in Western civilization." An *Economist* critic states that "as a source-book on the history of women, [*Not in God's Image*] stands in a class quite of its own. . . . The authors deal skillfully with the constant larding of hypocrisy, ranging from recipes for damaged maidenhoods to advice on concealing intellect." Mary Ellmann also admires the work, writing in the *New York Review of Books* that O'Faolain's effort is "distinguished by genuine scholarship. Its feminist sympathy is apparent . . . but it pursues the point by hard work, not by swishy emotion. And what a picture unfolds!"

Women in the Wall, a novel based on the life of Queen Radegund, who in the sixth century founded the monastery of the Holy Cross, is another example of O'Faolain's interest in women's place in history. But according to *Times Literary Supplement* critic Lalage Pulvertaft, by adapting such characters as Queen Radegund and St. Agnes, the author tampered with history to "try and answer fundamental questions about women's role in society." Pulvertaft faults O'Faolain's motives in writing *Women in the Wall:* "In her fashionable wish to explain visions as sexuality, vocations as perverted power mania, [the author] misses the nub of the matter; that God, through Christ, had challenged women as well as men to be individuals, even if this meant attacking the institutions of society."

Doris Grumbach, on the other hand, reviewing the book for *New Republic,* calls O'Faolain "a novelist of great talent whose interest has . . . come close to a Poe-ian obsession with immurement. . . . The force of language, the subtle and entirely successful recreation by means of it of the spirit as well as the events of Gallic life 13 centuries ago, at the end of the Roman era and the beginning of the Christian, make *Women in the Wall* a remarkably modern historical novel, poignant and powerful. It absorbs the reader into a time when women were chattels, when 'inherited land followed the spear not the spindle,'—into a time when the greatest conquerer was not of the flesh but of the spirit, when the full force of early Christianity made fanatics and saints of its believers."

With *No Country for Young Men,* O'Faolain "tackles the legacy of Republicanism in Southern Ireland through the story of one family," according to Hermoine Lee in the *Observer.* This story follows the efforts of an American sympathizer in Ireland who, while conducting research for a pro-Republican film, is drawn into the lives of a family whose members have involved themselves in the Irish cause for years. Writing a novel that spans three generations is "an ambitious undertaking," says Patricia Craig in the *Times Literary Supplement;* however, the critic finds the book somewhat "unsure of its own purpose. *No Country for Young Men* is not a political thriller, not a stark tragedy, not a documentary of social behaviour, not a story of personal relations, not a family saga, not a piece of historical fiction; but it contains . . . elements of all these."

Other critics, though, found more to praise in the novel. Lee, while acknowledging that "at times the novel edges toward lecture-topics," concludes nonetheless that the book's "strong grasp of the relation between a family and a national history transcends its occasional imaginative sagginess." The work "reflects a concern for the nation that emerged from the Troubles, and a worry about the new Troubles," states William Trevor in *Hibernea.* Trevor continues: "As a novel, it is old-fashioned in the very best sense, tidily knitting together its disparate strands, athletically leaping about in time and place, telling several stories at once." And *Guardian* reviewer Robert Nye, while noting that there "have been many novels about twentieth century Ireland and its problems," says that *No Country for Young Men* is "one of the very best books of its kind that it has ever been my pain and my pleasure to read."

Irish issues also surface in *The Obedient Wife,* but in a different setting. The tale of a Catholic housewife's infatuation with an Irish Catholic priest in Los Angeles, *The Obedient Wife* is "a novel about failures of instinct, as well as . . . social and conjugal failures," according to Patricia Craig in another *Times Literary Supplement* review. Craig adds: "There is plenty of scope for comedy in Julia O'Faolain's novel, but she has chosen not to present her material in a comic mode. . . . Instead she coolly assesses the circumstances and traits that have got her characters into their present predicament, and still more coolly allows their defects and misapprehensions to become apparent in the course of the narrative." *The Obedient Wife,* comments Craig, "is an exceptionally polished work; if its ending disappoints feminists, who require gestures of social rebelliousness from their fiction, just as Catholic readers used to require wholesomeness in theirs, it is none the less appropriate, in that it represents an assertion of the values its heroine has lived by."

O'Faolain is one of "the very few Irish writers who [is] truly international in range," declares Roger Garfitt in his contribution to the book *Two Decades of Irish Writing: A Critical Survey.* "Where she differs most sharply . . . from other Irish writers is in choosing to work from within the contemporary flux of modes and passions. Her characters generally have comparative economic freedom. . . . They do not escape, though, essentially the same challenges: only in their case the pressure comes from within, generally as a conflict between the direction of their own vitality and the assumptions of the way they have been brought up." Concludes Garfitt: "There is a power of mind behind her work, as well as an irreverently perceptive eye, that catches the intensity of human drives, the essential seriousness of the effort to live, without swallowing any of the trends in self-deception. She is an acute observer, who is involved at a level of concern deeper than the substance of her observations."

BIOGRAPHICAL/CRITICAL SOURCES:

BOOKS

Contemporary Authors Autobiography Series, Volume 2, Gale, 1985.
Contemporary Literary Criticism, Gale, Volume 6, 1976, Volume 19, 1981, Volume 47, 1988.
Dictionary of Literary Biography, Volume 14: *British Novelists since 1960,* Gale, 1983.
Dunn, Douglas, editor, *Two Decades of Irish Writing: A Critical Survey,* Dufor, 1975.
O'Faolain, Julia, *Women in the Wall,* Viking, 1975.
Rafroidi, Patrick, and Maurice Harmon, editors, *The Irish Novel in Our Times,* Volume 3, Publications de l'Universite de Lille, 1975-1976.

PERIODICALS

Best Sellers, May 1, 1971.
Book World, June 13, 1971.
Choice, December, 1973, October, 1975.
Economist, February 17, 1973.
Guardian, June 5, 1980.

Hibernea, June 5, 1980.
Listener, June 20, 1968, September 26, 1974, June 3, 1982.
London Magazine, September, 1968, November, 1970, October/November, 1974.
New Republic, May 10, 1975.
New Statesman, June 6, 1980, November 12, 1982.
New York Review of Books, November 1, 1973.
New York Times Book Review, May 9, 1971, December 1, 1985, July 20, 1986, February 1, 1987.
Observer, June 1, 1980.
Saturday Review, July 3, 1971.
Times Literary Supplement, April 4, 1975, June 13, 1980, July 23, 1982, October 26, 1984.

* * *

O'FAOLAIN, Sean   1900-

PERSONAL: Name originally John Francis Whelan, changed to Gaelic variant, 1918; born February 22, 1900, in Cork, Ireland; son of Denis and Bridget (Murphy) Whelan; married Eileen Gould, June, 1928; children: Julia, Stephen. *Education:* University College at Cork of National University of Ireland, B.A., 1921, M.A., 1925; Harvard University, M.A., 1929.

ADDRESSES: Home—17 Rosmeen Park, Dunlaoire, County Dublin, Ireland. *Agent*—A. P. Watt, 26/28 Bedford Row, London W.C.1, England.

CAREER: Fought in Irish Revolution, 1918-21; Irish Republican Army, director of publicity, 1923; Christian Brothers School, Ennis, Ireland, teacher, 1924; Princeton University, Princeton, N.J., and Boston College, Boston, Mass., lecturer in English, both 1929; St. Mary's College, Strawberry Hill, England, lecturer in English, 1929-33; full-time author, 1932—.

MEMBER: Arts Council of Ireland (director, 1957-59), Irish Academy of Letters.

AWARDS, HONORS: Commonwealth fellowship, 1926-28; John Harvard fellowship, 1928-29; Femina Prize nomination, 1932, for *Midsummer Night Madness and Other Stories;* D.Litt., Trinity College, Dublin, 1957.

WRITINGS:

SHORT STORIES

Midsummer Night Madness and Other Stories, Viking, 1932.
There's a Birdie in the Cage, Grayson, 1935.
The Born Genius: A Short Story, Schuman's, 1936.
A Purse of Coppers: Short Stories, J. Cape, 1937, Viking, 1938.
Teresa and Other Stories, J. Cape, 1947, published as *The Man Who Invented Sin and Other Stories,* Devin-Adair, 1948.
The Finest Stories of Sean O'Faolain, Little, Brown, 1957 (published in England as *The Stories of Sean O'Faolain,* Hart-Davis, 1958).
I Remember! I Remember! Stories, Little, Brown, 1962.
The Heat of the Sun: Stories and Tales, Little, Brown, 1966.
The Talking Trees and Other Stories, Little, Brown, 1970.
Foreign Affairs and Other Stories, Little Brown, 1976.
(With others) *One True Friend and Other Irish Stories,* Structural Readers, 1977.
Selected Stories of Sean O'Faolain, Little, Brown, 1978.
Collected Stories, three volumes, Constable, 1980-82, one volume, Little, Brown, 1983.

NOVELS

A Nest of Simple Folk, J. Cape, 1933, Viking, 1934.
Bird Alone, Viking, 1936.

Come Back to Erin, Viking, 1940, reprinted, Greenwood Press, 1972.

And Again?, Constable, 1979, Birch Lane Press, 1989.

BIOGRAPHIES

The Life Story of Eamon De Valera, Penguin, 1934.

Constance Markievicz; or, The Average Revolutionary, J. Cape, 1934, revised edition published as *Constance Markievicz,* Sphere Books, 1968.

King of the Beggars: A Life of Daniel O'Connell, the Irish Liberator, in a Study of the Rise of the Modern Irish Democracy, 1775-1847, Viking, 1938, abridged edition, Parkside Press (Dublin), 1945, reprinted, Greenwood Press, 1975.

De Valera, Penguin, 1939.

The Great O'Neill: A Biography of Hugh O'Neill, Earl of Tyrone, 1550-1616, Duell, Sloan & Pearce, 1942, reprinted, Mercier Press, 1970.

Newman's Way: The Odyssey of John Henry Newman, Devin-Adair, 1952 (published in England as *Newman's Way,* Longmans, Green, 1952).

Vive Moi! (autobiography), Little, Brown, 1964 (published in England as *Vive Moi! An Autobiography,* Hart-Davis, 1965).

TRAVEL

An Irish Journey, Longmans, Green, 1940.

A Summer in Italy, Eyre & Spottiswoode, 1949, Devin-Adair, 1950.

An Autumn in Italy, Devin-Adair, 1953 (published in England as *South to Sicily,* Collins, 1953).

OTHER

(Editor) *Lyrics and Satires from Tom Moore,* Cuala Press (Dublin), 1929, reprinted, Biblio Distribution Centre, 1971.

(Editor) *The Autobiography of Theobald Wolfe Tone,* Thomas Nelson, 1937.

She Had to Do Something: A Comedy in Three Acts (first produced in Dublin, 1937), J. Cape, 1938.

(Compiler) *The Silver Branch: A Collection of the Best Old Irish Lyrics, Variously Translated,* Viking, 1938, reprinted, Books for Libraries, 1968.

The Story of Ireland (history), Collins, 1943.

(Editor and author of foreword) Samuel Lover, *Adventures of Handy Andy,* Parkside Press, 1945.

(Author of preface) *D 83222, I Did Penal Servitude,* Metropolitan Publishing (Dublin), 1945.

The Train to Branbury (radio play; first broadcast in 1947), published in *Imaginary Conversations,* edited by Rayner Heppenstall, Secker and Warburg, 1948.

The Irish, Penguin, 1947, published as *The Irish: A Character Study,* Devin-Adair, 1949, revised and updated edition, Penguin, 1969, published as *The Story of the Irish People,* Avenel, 1982.

The Short Story (criticism and stories), Collins, 1948, Devin-Adair, 1951.

The Vanishing Hero: Studies in Novelists of the Twenties, Eyre & Spottiswoode, 1956, Little, Brown, 1957, published as *The Vanishing Hero: Studies of the Hero in the Modern Novel,* Grosset, 1957.

(Editor) *Short Stories: A Study in Pleasure,* Little, Brown, 1961.

Contributor of short stories and articles to numerous magazines, journals, and other periodicals. Editor, *Bell* (Irish periodical), 1940-45.

SIDELIGHTS: "Of all the significant O's in twentieth century Irish literature," notes Paul A. Doyle in *Best Sellers,* "Sean O'Casey is the most humorous and flamboyant, Liam O'Flaherty the most emotional and unpolished, Frank O'Connor the most satiric and whimsical, and Sean O'Faolain the most versatile and profound." One of modern Ireland's greatest chroniclers, O'Faolain has produced many memorable novels, short stories, and nonfiction works during his career, which spans more than fifty years.

Born John Francis Whelan in County Cork, Ireland, O'Faolain from an early age was inhibited, according to Gordon Henderson's *Dictionary of Literary Biography* article about the author, by "his father's unquestioning respect for authority, his mother's excessive piety, and the preoccupation both had with rising above their peasant-farmer origins." He was also influenced by the plays at the nearby Cork Opera House, and spent much of his time during his youth watching the dramatic presentations of such classics as *The Scarlet Pimpernel* and *The Prisoner of Zenda.* One play in particular had a dramatic effect on O'Faolain. Lennox Robinson's "The Patriot," a story set in an Irish shopkeeper's parlor, elicited a strong reaction from the boy. As O'Faolain relates in Henderson's article: "For years I had seen only plays straight from the West End of London. . . . Here was a most moving play about Irish peasants, shop-keeping and farming folk, men and women who could have been any one of my uncles and aunts down the country. It brought me strange and wonderful news—that writers could also write books and plays about the common everyday reality of Irish life."

Perhaps the most important event of O'Faolain's early years, however, was the Easter Rebellion of 1916. Although at first he opposed the uprising, motivated by his father's unwavering loyalty to the crown, O'Faolain soon became outraged at the brutal way the British forces "crushed the rebellion and then systematically executed its leaders," as Henderson puts it. "Fired with a new sense of nationalism," he continues, "[O'Faolain] was soon taking lessons in the Irish language and, at eighteen, joined other young men and women at a summer school for Gaelic speakers in the mountains of West Cork." At the same age, the young man unofficially changed his name from the anglicized John Whelan to the Gaelic Sean O'Faolain. He then joined the Irish Volunteers, an organization that later produced some members of the militant Irish Republican Army (IRA). And while O'Faolain eventually became involved with IRA activities—he was the group's publicity director at age twenty-three—the writer avoided the extreme, often violent tactics for which that organization would become infamous. "To have cast me for the role of a gunman would have been like casting me as a bull-fighter," explains O'Faolain in Henderson's piece. It was during this tumultuous period in Irish history that O'Faolain began his writing career.

The author's early works, including the novels *A Nest of Simple Folk* and *Bird Alone,* explore the lives of people caught up in various stages of "The Troubles." Leo O'Donnell, the lead character of *A Nest of Simple Folk,* for example, is seen over a period of sixty-two years, starting in 1854 and ending with the Easter Rebellion. O'Donnell, imprisoned for several years because of his Fenian involvement (the Fenians, an Irish nationalistic group, were established in the nineteenth century), "grows old futilely pursuing patriotic dreams," as Henderson writes, and passes his strong sense of Gaelic pride on to his nephew, Denis Hussey, a character modeled after O'Faolain himself. As both a political story and a poignant character study, *A Nest of Simple Folk* is "a memorable work, memorable as an instance of the power and passion of memory," according to Donat O'Donnell, reviewing the novel in *Renascence.*

Bird Alone, banned as obscene by Ireland's Censorship Board, opens with the elderly Corney Crone looking back over his life as a builder in Cork. The book focuses on his relationship with his grandfather, a staunch Fenian who helps shape young Crone's political viewpoint. Later, ostracized because of both his Irish activism and a scandal involving a woman who dies while giving birth to his child, Crone becomes a recluse, a "bird alone," living in an attic room.

"This is one of the very few modern novels . . . in which the treatment of character bears the stamp of a complete and subtle mastery," comments V. S. Pritchett about *Bird Alone.* In his *Christian Science Monitor* article, Pritchett continues: "The sympathy is profound to the point of tears—and they are often tears of that convinced laughter which comes when one says, These people are round, whole, real and lovable and yet have that quality of mysteriousness which leaves us . . . in questioning wonder before even those whom we know very well." The reviewer deems *Bird Alone* "the genre piece of a master." William Troy, on the other hand, has praise not for the characters in the novel, but for its setting. County Cork is presented, Troy declares in *Nation,* as "more real and interesting than any of its inhabitants. This is managed partly through the fluid poetic style and partly through a formal framework which makes possible the rapid transitions and vivid condensations of the memory." Troy does have criticism for *Bird Alone*—he says he received an impression "of conflicts unresolved, of ambiguities remaining suspended"—but he ultimately cites the book's "flowing current of exquisitely modulated language." This view is shared by *Boston Transcript* critic A. B. Tourtellot, who finds that the novel's "major flaw . . . is the inadequate treatment of the story as a story." However, Tourtellot concludes, *Bird Alone* is "a fine and rich book, but fine and rich chiefly because of the craftsmanship of its author and not because of the strength of the story."

Although his novels and books of criticism have been well received, O'Faolain is also generally regarded as an accomplished short-story writer. In his collections the author examines the many aspects of modern Irish life. "His stories are typically dense, lush, complex, and rich—his is not an art of understatement," finds Gary Davenport in a *Hudson Review* article. "[O'Faolain] has two major themes: what it means to be Irish, and what it means to be an Irish Catholic. [The author] is a loyal but critical Irishman; he is capable of denouncing Irish provincialism of both the nationalist and religious genres, but unlike [George Bernard] Shaw he denounces it from within: he lives in Ireland and he remains a Catholic. . . . And these stories are full to bursting of life. Landscape provides much of this richness—especially the fecund landscape of his native Cork: low thick clouds, endless rain, sodden earth. And the characters who live in this environment partake of its sense of being outside time."

"In regard to style," says Paul A. Doyle in his book *Sean O'Faolain,* "[the author] favors the technique of uniting suggestion and compression. He uses the words 'engrossed' and 'active' in reference to good style. The beginning of the narrative must at once establish the mood of the story and then the writer works carefully word by word, sentence by sentence, toward the total effect—the innermost illumination which is really the story . . . behind the story." Doyle notes: "The superior stories in [O'Faolain's collections] are characterized by subtlety, compassion, understanding, irony, and a perceptive awareness of the complexity of human nature. Themes and insights are suggested and implied rather than flatly stated, and the themes are significant. In these superior stories O'Faolain demonstrates authorial objectivity and detachment; he avoids description for its own

sake; and he successfully infuses a poetic mood—subdued and delicate—over the narratives. Overall, then, it may be affirmed that stories such as 'A Broken World,' 'The Man Who Invented Sin,' 'The Silence of the Valley,' 'Up the Bare Stairs'—to mention a few—exemplify considerable artistry and expert control of modern short story techniques."

"Although the tone in his stories is sometimes satiric," offers Henderson, "[the author] more often withholds judgement of his characters' actions or adopts the stance of an understanding observer. In this respect O'Faolain says he took [Anton] Chekhov as his model and acknowledges that he also learned from Chekhov to de-emphasize plot, advance the action indirectly by implication, strive for compression, and suffuse his stories with a poetic mood." O'Faolain's reputation as an important modern author, Henderson concludes, "rests most firmly on his short stories. . . . His later stories have won a wide popular audience in such mass-market circulation magazines as *Colliers, McCall's, . . .* and *Playboy.* Their popular appeal, however, does not reduce his stature as a writer of serious fiction. Like [James] Joyce and [Frank] O'Connor, he took the short story as he received it from [Guy de] Maupassant and Chekhov and transformed it into something uniquely his own and uniquely Irish."

O'Faolain's letters and manuscripts are collected at the Bancroft Library, University of California, Berkeley.

MEDIA ADAPTATIONS: Two of O'Faolain's short stories, "Mother Matilda's Book" and "The Man Who Invented Sin," were adapted into plays and broadcast by Granada Television Ltd. in England, August 19, 1970.

AVOCATIONAL INTERESTS: Travel and gardening.

BIOGRAPHICAL/CRITICAL SOURCES:

BOOKS

Contemporary Literary Criticism, Gale, Volume 1, 1973, Volume 7, 1977, Volume 14, 1980, Volume 32, 1985.
Dictionary of Literary Biography, Volume 15: *British Novelists, 1930-1959,* Gale, 1983.
Doyle, Paul A., *Sean O'Faolain,* Twayne, 1969.
Harmon, Maurice, *Sean O'Faolain: A Critical Introduction,* University of Notre Dame Press, 1966.
Keily, Benedict, *Modern Irish Fiction: A Critique,* Golden Eagle Books (Dublin), 1950.
O'Donnell, Donat, *Maria Cross: Imaginative Patterns in a Group of Modern Irish Writers,* Oxford University Press, 1952.
O'Faolain, Sean, *Vive Moi!,* Little, Brown, 1964.
Rippier, Joseph Storey, *The Short Stories of Sean O'Faolain: A Study in Descriptive Techniques,* Barnes & Noble, 1976.

PERIODICALS

Boston Transcript, October 10, 1936.
Chicago Tribune Book World, February 12, 1984.
Christian Science Monitor, August 12, 1936.
Dublin Magazine, April-June, 1955.
Hudson Review, spring, 1979.
Irish University Review, spring, 1976.
London Magazine, June, 1980.
Los Angeles Times, December 28, 1983.
Los Angeles Times Book Review, December 3, 1989.
Nation, January 24, 1934.
New Republic, February 15, 1939.
New Statesman, April 23, 1976, September 28, 1979.
Newsweek, January 8, 1962.
New York Times Book Review, May 12, 1957, January 25, 1976, November 26, 1978, October 30, 1983, September 17, 1989.

Renascence, autumn, 1950.
South Atlantic Quarterly, summer, 1976.
Time, June 26, 1976.
Times Literary Supplement, November 7, 1980, November 20, 1981, December 3, 1982.

* * *

O'FLAHERTY, Liam   1896-1984

PERSONAL: Born August 28, 1896, on Inishmore in the Aran Islands, Ireland; died September 7, 1984, in Dublin, Ireland; son of Michael and Margaret (Ganly) O'Flaherty; married Margaret Barrington (a writer), February, 1926 (marriage ended, 1932); children: Pegeen O'Flaherty O'Sullivan, Joyce O'Flaherty Rathbone. _Education:_ Attended Rockwell College, 1908-12, Blackrock College, 1912-13, and University College, 1913-14.

ADDRESSES: Agent—A. D. Peters Ltd., 10 Buckingham St., London WC2 N6BU, England.

CAREER: Writer. Founded the Irish Communist Party, 1922. Worked as a miner, lumberjack, hotel porter, and bank clerk in the United States and Canada. _Military service:_ Served in Irish Guards during World War I.

AWARDS, HONORS: James Tait Black Memorial Prize, 1926, for _The Informer;_ doctorate in literature from National University of Ireland, 1974; Allied Irish Bank—Irish Academy of Letters Award for literature, 1979.

WRITINGS:

NOVELS

Thy Neighbor's Wife, J. Cape, 1923, Boni & Liveright, 1924, Lythway Press, 1972.
The Black Soul, J. Cape, 1924, Boni & Liveright, 1925.
The Informer, Knopf, 1925, Harcourt, 1980.
Mr. Gilhooley, J. Cape, 1926, Harcourt, 1927.
The Assassin, Harcourt, 1928, Dufour, 1983.
The House of Gold, Harcourt, 1929.
The Return of the Brute, Mandrake Press, 1929, Harcourt, 1930.
The Puritan, J. Cape, 1931, Harcourt, 1932.
Skerrett, Long & Smith, 1932, Dufour, 1988.
The Martyr, Harcourt, 1933.
Hollywood Cemetery, Gollancz, 1935.
Famine, Random House, 1937, Godine, 1982.
Land, Random House, 1946.
Insurrection, Gollancz, 1950, Dufour, 1988.

SHORT STORIES

Spring Sowing, J. Cape, 1924, Knopf, 1926, Books for Libraries Press, 1973.
Civil War, Archer, 1925.
The Child of God, Archer, 1926.
The Terrorist, Archer, 1926.
The Tent and Other Stories, J. Cape, 1926.
The Fairy Goose and Other Stories, Faber & Gwyer, 1927, Gaige, 1928.
Red Barbara and Other Stories, Faber & Gwyer, 1928, Gaige, 1928.
The Mountain Tavern and Other Stories, Harcourt, 1929, Books for Libraries Press, 1971.
The Ecstasy of Angus, Joiner & Steele, 1931, Wolfhound, 1978.
The Wild Swan and Other Stories, Joiner & Steele, 1932.
The Short Stories of Liam O'Flaherty, J. Cape, 1937, abridged edition, New American Library, 1970.
Two Lovely Beasts and Other Stories, Gollancz, 1948, Devin-Adair, 1950.

Duil, Sairseal Agus Dill, 1953.
The Stories of Liam O'Flaherty, Devin-Adair, 1956.
Selected Stories, New American Library, 1958.
Short Stories, Brown, Watson, 1961.
Irish Portraits: Fourteen Short Stories, Sphere, 1970.
More Short Stories of Liam O'Flaherty, New English Library, 1971.
The Wounded Cormorant and Other Stories, Norton, 1973.
The Pedlar's Revenge and Other Stories, Wolfhound, 1976.
All Things Come of Age: A Rabbit Story, Wolfhound, 1977.
The Wave and Other Stories, Longman, 1980.

OTHER

Darkness (short story; limited edition), Archer, 1926.
The Life of Tim Healy, Harcourt, 1927.
A Tourist's Guide to Ireland, Mandrake Press, 1929.
Joseph Conrad: An Appreciation, E. Lahr, 1930, Haskell House, 1973.
Two Years (autobiography), Harcourt, 1930.
I Went to Russia (autobiography), Harcourt, 1931.
A Cure for Unemployment, E. Lahr, 1931.
Shame the Devil (autobiography), Grayson, 1934.
"Devil's Playground" (screenplay), Columbia, 1937.
"Last Desire" (screenplay), Lumen Films, 1939.
The Test of Courage, Wolfhound, 1977.
The Wilderness, Wolfhound, 1978, Dodd, 1987.

Also co-author of screenplay "The Informer," based on O'Flaherty's novel of the same title, 1935.

SIDELIGHTS: Criticism of Liam O'Flaherty's fiction is marked by a number of paradoxes. He has been both praised and condemned for his "Irishness" and his "anti-Irishness," his naturalism and his expressionism, and his existential awareness and his romantic idealism. While the sheer quantity of his writing could account for such differences in interpretation, the fact that they occur in discussions of the same works implies, rather, that O'Flaherty is a writer of greater complexity than is often acknowledged. William C. Frierson suggests that "the author's writings reflect the chaos of his life." And for a writer who has lived as everything from a hotel porter to a revolutionary fighter, wandering to places as far from Ireland as Canada and Rio de Janeiro, the life and the subsequent fiction could be chaotic indeed.

The setting for most of O'Flaherty's novels and short stories is Ireland, and his central characters are often Irish peasants deeply rooted in the land. James H. O'Brien points out that "collectively O'Flaherty's short stories describe two or three generations of life in the Aran Islands and the west of Ireland; perhaps they reach back even further, so little did life change in those areas until the end of the nineteenth century." Moreover, on the basis of a few of his novels (especially _The Informer_), he is thought of as a novelist of the Irish revolution.

On the other hand, as an early reviewer of _The Informer_ noted, O'Flaherty "never makes the common error . . . of falling into sentiment about Ireland or slipping out of the world of reality into that non-existent world of petulant, half-godlike and utterly fictitious Irishmen that other writers have created out of their false vision and saccharine fancy." Rather, he was part of a second wave of modern Irish writers, along with James Joyce and Sean O'Casey, who rebelled against the Celtic-revivalist ideals of Yeats and Synge. The fact that O'Flaherty was ultimately forced to leave Ireland and take up residence in England further separates him from the Irish literary tradition.

Nevertheless, one aspect of O'Flaherty's fiction grounds him solidly in an Irish tradition, specifically an oral tradition, and this is his ability as a storyteller. O'Brien explains, "In both novels and short stories, a Gaelic influence is manifest in the directness of narrative, the simplicity of language, and an elemental concern with primary emotions." In a review of *The Tent and Other Stories,* Edward Shanks saw this influence at work and remarked that O'Flaherty "sees directly and puts down directly what he sees. His best pieces, such as 'The Conger Eel,' have the character of pictures, simple and moving because they mean no more than they say."

A number of critics take exception to O'Flaherty's classification as a naturalist. O'Brien believes that "his purpose is not to present a realistic or naturalistic view of the Irish peasant. . . . Instead, O'Flaherty generally uses the simplicity of peasant life to depict elemental reactions and instincts." Frierson similarly writes: "Although naturalistic in his view of human depravity, in his brutality, and in his insistence upon physical reactions, Mr. O'Flaherty is too forceful to be pessimistic, too violent and too melodramatic to present us with a study of humanity. His distortions are those of the expressionist."

The expressionistic representation of violence and emotion is a characteristic other critics note. Frierson explains it further: "Everywhere there is primitive physical violence, reckless impulse, greed, and cruelty; and the full force of the author's dramatic fervor is exerted by riveting our attention upon physical manifestation of the strongest emotions." Sean O'Faolain also recognized the vital effect of "O'Flaherty's usual formula of a single character about whom the story swirls with such centrifugal force that one is swept out of incredulity by the excitement of feeling at the centre of a vortex." H. E. Bates maintains that "O'Flaherty, like Maupassant, saw life in a strong light, dramatically, powerfully. Energy alone is not enough, but the sensuous poetic energy of O'Flaherty was like a flood; the reader was carried away by it and with it, slightly stunned and exalted by the experience."

These different aspects of O'Flaherty's fiction—the Irishman turning away from yet remaining tied to Ireland, the realistic storyteller imbuing his tales with an intense expression of human emotion—are brought together by John Zneimer's interpretation. Comparing O'Flaherty to Dostoevski, Sartre, and Camus, Zneimer places him in an existentialist, as well as Irish, tradition. Because the Ireland in which O'Flaherty lived was an Ireland in which the old values and dreams were being destroyed by twentieth-century reality, O'Flaherty's Irishness and his existential awareness are inextricably tied. Zneimer writes, "He speaks in his novels about traditions that have failed in a world that is falling apart, about desperate men seeking meaning through violent acts." Thus Zneimer sees O'Flaherty's concern both with naturalistic details and the turbulence of human emotions as products of "his increasing awareness of man's mortality and ultimate annihilation in a universe that has no meaning and offers no consolation."

O'Flaherty turned his art, Zneimer concludes, into a religious quest, making his novels "spiritual battlegrounds whereon his characters . . . struggle to find meaning" in a meaningless world. O'Brien perceives this struggle, too, though he expresses it differently: "Beneath O'Flaherty's absorption in the physical, external world lies a belief in the evolutionary process, of men, especially artists, finding fulfillment in the struggle for perfection."

MEDIA ADAPTATIONS: Three of O'Flaherty's novels were filmed, including *The Informer,* directed by John Ford and starring Victor McLaglen, in 1935.

BIOGRAPHICAL/CRITICAL SOURCES:

BOOKS

Bates, H. E., *The Modern Short Story,* T. Nelson, 1945.
Contemporary Literary Criticism, Gale, Volume 5, 1976, Volume 34, 1985.
Dictionary of Literary Biography, Volume 36: *British Novelists, 1890-1929: Modernists,* Gale, 1985.
Dictionary of Literary Biography Yearbook: 1984, Gale, 1985.
Frierson, William C., *The English Novel in Transition, 1885-1940,* Cooper Square, 1965.
O'Brien, James H., *Liam O'Flaherty,* Bucknell University Press, 1970.
Zneimer, John, *The Literary Vision of Liam O'Flaherty,* Syracuse University Press, 1971.

PERIODICALS

London Mercury, August, 1926.
New Statesman and Nation, January 21, 1933.
New York Times Book Review, August 30, 1987.
Spectator, October 3, 1925.
Times Literary Supplement, January 1, 1982.

OBITUARIES:

PERIODICALS

Chicago Tribune, September 10, 1984.
Los Angeles Times, September 9, 1984.
New York Times, September 9, 1984.
Time, September 17, 1984.
Times (London), September 10, 1984.
Washington Post, September 9, 1984.

*   *   *

O'HARA, Frank   1926-1966

PERSONAL: Full name originally Francis Russell O'Hara; born June 27, 1926, in Baltimore, Md.; died July 25, 1966, in Mastic Beach, Long Island, N.Y., after being struck by a dune-buggy taxicab on Fire Island; buried in Green River Cemetery in Springs, Long Island, N.Y.; son of Russell J. and Katherine (Broderick) O'Hara. *Education:* Harvard University, A.B., 1950; University of Michigan, M.A., 1951. *Politics:* "Depends, independent I guess." *Religion:* None.

ADDRESSES: Home—790 Broadway, New York, N.Y. *Office*—Museum of Modern Art, 11 West 53rd St., New York, N.Y.

CAREER: Poet, playwright, and art critic. Museum of Modern Art, New York City, staff member, 1952-53; *Art News,* New York City, editorial associate, 1953-55; Museum of Modern Art, organizer of circulating exhibitions, 1955-60, assistant curator in department of painting and sculpture exhibitions, 1960-66. Poet and playwright in residence at Poet's Theatre, Cambridge, Mass., 1956; apprentice in stagecraft, Brattle Theatre, Cambridge. *Military service:* U.S. Navy, 1944-46.

AWARDS, HONORS: Hopwood Award, University of Michigan, 1951, for poetry; Ford Foundation fellowship, 1956; National Book Award, 1972, for *The Collected Poems of Frank O'Hara.*

WRITINGS:

POEMS

A City Winter, and Other Poems, Tibor de Nagy Gallery Editions, 1952.
Meditations in an Emergency, M. Alcover (Spain), 1956, Grove, 1957, 2nd edition, 1967.
Jackson Pollock, Braziller, 1959.
Second Avenue, Totem Press, 1960.
Odes, serigraphs by Michael Goldberg, Tiber Press, 1960, 2nd edition, Poets Press, 1969.
Lunch Poems, City Lights, 1964.
Featuring Frank O'Hara, [Buffalo, N.Y.], 1964.
Love Poems (Tentative Title), Tibor de Nagy Gallery Editions, 1965.
In Memory of My Feelings: A Selection of Poems, edited by Bill Berkson, Museum of Modern Art, New York, 1967.
Two Pieces, Long Hair Books (London), 1969.
Oranges, Angel Hair Books (New York), 1970.
The Collected Poems of Frank O'Hara, edited by Donald M. Allen, Knopf, 1971.
The Selected Poems of Frank O'Hara, edited by Allen, Knopf, 1974.
(With Bill Berkson) *Hymns of St. Bridget,* Adventures in Poetry, 1974.
Early Writing: 1946-1950, edited by Allen, Grey Fox Press, 1977.
Poems Retrieved: 1950-1966, edited by Allen, Grey Fox Press, 1977.

Also author of *The End of the Far West: 11 Poems,* 1974.

PLAYS

Try! Try!, first produced in Cambridge, Mass., at Poets Theatre, 1951.
Change Your Bedding, first produced at Poets Theatre, 1952.
The Houses at Fallen Hanging, produced at Living Theatre, 1956.
Awake in Spain (produced at Living Theatre, 1960), American Theatre for Poets, 1960.
The General's Return from One Place to Another (produced in New York City at Present Stages, 1964), [New York City], 1962.
Love's Labor (produced at Living Theatre, 1960), American Theatre for Poets, 1964.
Selected Plays, Full Court Press, 1978.

EXHIBITION CATALOGS

New Spanish Painting and Sculpture: Rafael Canogar and Others, Doubleday, for Museum of Modern Art, New York, 1960.
An Exhibition of Oil Paintings by Frankenthaler, Jewish Museum of the Jewish Theological Seminary of America, 1960.
Franz Kline, [Turin, Italy], 1963.
Arshile Gorky, Hermes (Bonn), 1964.
Robert Motherwell: With Selections from the Artist's Writings, Doubleday, for Museum of Modern Art, New York, 1965.
David Smith, 1907-1965, at the Tate Gallery, [London], 1966.
Nakian, Doubleday, for Museum of Modern Art, New York, 1966.
(With V. R. Lang) *A Day in the Life of the Czar, or I Too Have Lived in Arcadia,* produced in New York City at La Mama Etc., October, 1980.

OTHER

Hartigan and Rivers with O'Hara (an exhibition of pictures, with poems by O'Hara), Tibor de Nagy Gallery Editions, 1959.
Belgrade, November 19, 1963 (letter), Adventures in Poetry, c. 1972.
Art Chronicles 1954-66, Braziller, 1975.
Standing Still and Walking in New York (includes essays, criticism, and an interview with O'Hara), edited by Allen, Grey Fox Press, 1975.
Homage to Frank O'Hara, edited by Berkson and Joe LeSueur, Creative Arts Book (Berkeley, Calif.), 1980.

Also author of *Nature and New Painting,* Tiber Press; also author of dialogue for films; also author of unpublished short stories and of unfinished novel, *The 4th of July.* Contributor to books, including *New American Poetry,* edited by Allen, Grove, 1960. Contributor of poems to periodicals, including *Accent, Partisan Review,* and *New World Writing;* contributor of criticism to *Folder, Evergreen Review,* and *Kulchur.*

SIDELIGHTS: Frank O'Hara was described by Paul Carroll as "the first and . . . the best of the poets of the impure." Bill Berkson wrote of his work: "O'Hara has the ability, and the power, to use in a poem whatever occurred to him at the moment, without reflection. It is not that he lacked selectivity or discrimination, but rather that his poems grew out of a process of natural selection—discrimination conjoining civility of attention—so that any particle of experience quick enough to get fixed in his busy consciousness earned its point of relevance." O'Hara himself once said: "I don't think of fame or posterity (as Keats so grandly and genuinely did), nor do I care about clarifying experiences for anyone or bettering (other than accidentally) anyone's state or social relation, nor am I for any particular technical development in the American language simply because I find it necessary. What is happening to me, allowing for lies and exaggerations which I try to avoid, goes into my poems. I don't think my experiences are clarified or made beautiful for myself or anyone else, they are just there in whatever form I can find them. What is clear to me in my work is probably obscure to others, and vice versa. . . . It may be that poetry makes life's nebulous events tangible to me and restores their detail; or conversely, that poetry brings forth the intangible quality of incidents which are all too concrete and circumstantial. Or each on specific occasions, or both all the time."

O'Hara was one of the members of "The New York School" of poets, and collaborated in creative relationships with the "New York School Second Generation" painters in what were known as "poem paintings." After his death, his family and friends established the Frank O'Hara Foundation for Poetry and Art to recognize and assist poets, with eventual corresponding support for artists. The proceeds of *In Memory of My Feelings,* a limited edition volume, went to the Foundation for grants-in-aid to young writers.

BIOGRAPHICAL/CRITICAL SOURCES:

BOOKS

Allen, Donald M., *New American Poetry,* Grove, 1960.
Carroll, Paul, *The Poem in Its Skin,* Follett, 1968.
Contemporary Literary Criticism, Gale, Volume 2, 1974, Volume 5, 1976, Volume 13, 1980.
Dictionary of Literary Biography, Gale, Volume 5: *American Poets since World War II,* 2 parts, 1980, Volume 16: *The Beats: Literary Bohemians in Postwar America,* 2 parts, 1983.
Feldman, Alan, *Frank O'Hara,* Twayne, 1979.

Perloff, Marjorie, *Frank O'Hara: Poet among Painters,* Braziller, 1977.

Smith, Alexander, Jr., compiler, *Frank O'Hara: A Comprehensive Bibliography,* Garland, 1979.

Vendler, Helen, *Part of Nature, Part of Us: Modern American Poets,* Harvard University Press, 1980.

PERIODICALS

Art and Literature, spring, 1967.
Art in America, March, 1972, March, 1975.
Art News, September, 1966, January, 1968, May, 1974.
Audit/Poetry (special O'Hara issue), spring, 1964.
Christian Science Monitor, November 9, 1967, February 17, 1972.
Contemporary Literature, spring, 1976.
Iowa Review, winter, 1973, winter, 1974.
National Observer, July 10, 1967.
New Republic, January 1-8, 1972.
New Statesman, April 30, 1965.
Newsweek, January 22, 1968, December 20, 1971.
New York Review of Books, March 31, 1966.
New York Times, January 19, 1968, August 11, 1968.
New York Times Book Review, October 6, 1957, February 11, 1968, November 28, 1971.
Poetry, June, 1958, February, 1966, April, 1973.
Times Literary Supplement, January 27, 1978.
Village Voice, April 20, 1967, January 20, 1975, December 16, 1981.

OBITUARIES:

PERIODICALS

Antiquarian Bookman, September 5-12, 1966.
Newsweek, August 8, 1966.
New York Times, July 27, 1966, July 28, 1966.
Time, August 5, 1966.
Village Voice, July 28, 1966.

*   *   *

O'HARA, John (Henry) 1905-1970
(Franey Delaney)

PERSONAL: Born January 31, 1905, in Pottsville, Pa.; died of a heart attack April 11, 1970, in Princeton, N.J.; son of Patrick Henry (a physician) and Katherine Elizabeth (Delaney) O'Hara; married Helen Pettit, 1931 (divorced, 1933); married Belle Mulford Wylie, December 3, 1937 (died January, 1954); married Katherine Barnes Bryan, January 31, 1955; children: (second marriage) Wylie Delaney (Mrs. Dennis J. D. Holahan). *Education:* Attended Niagara Preparatory School, Niagara Falls, N.Y. *Religion:* None; raised as a Roman Catholic.

ADDRESSES: Home—Linebrook, R.D. 2, Princeton, N.J.

CAREER: Novelist and short story writer. *Pottsville Journal,* Pottsville, Pa., reporter, 1924-26; worked in Chicago, Ill., as an evaluating engineer, a boat steward, a steel mill worker, a soda jerk, an amusement park guard, a call boy and freight clerk for the Pennsylvania Railroad, and as a gas meter reader; worked in New York, N.Y., for various periodicals, including jobs as a rewrite man for the *Daily Mirror,* radio columnist (under pseudonym Franey Delaney) and movie critic for *Morning Telegraph,* staff member of *Time* magazine, reporter for *Herald Tribune,* and secretary to Heywood Broun; managing editor of *Pittsburgh Bulletin-Index;* became a press agent for Warner Bros., Hollywood, Calif.; film-writer, 1934 until mid-1940s. Appeared briefly as a reporter in the film "The General Died at Dawn," Paramount, 1936.

MEMBER: National Institute of Arts and Letters, Authors Guild, Dramatists Guild, Authors League of America, Screen Writers Guild, National Press Club, Silurians, Nassau Club (Princeton, N.J.), Field Club (Quogue, Long Island), Century Association, The Leash (New York), Raquet Club (Philadelphia), Beach Club (Santa Barbara), Loyal Legion (Pennsylvania commandery), National Golf Links of America (Southhampton, N.Y.), Kew-Teddington Observatory Society (Princeton), Hessian Relief Society (Princeton), Sigma Delta Chi.

AWARDS, HONORS: New York Critics Circle and Donaldson awards, 1952, both for musical "Pal Joey"; National Book Award, 1956, for *Ten North Frederick;* named honorary citizen of City of Philadelphia, 1961; Gold Medal Award of Merit for the Novel, 1964, American Academy of Arts and Letters.

WRITINGS:

NOVELS

Appointment in Samarra (also see below), Harcourt, 1934, reprinted with a new foreword by the author, Modern Library, 1953, Random House, 1982.
Butterfield 8 (also see below), Harcourt, 1935, Random House, 1982.
Hope of Heaven (also see below), Harcourt, 1938, Popular Library, 1973.
Pal Joey (also see below), Duell, 1940, Popular Library, 1976.
A Rage to Live, Random House, 1949, Popular Library, 1974.
The Farmers Hotel (novella; also see below), Random House, 1951, Popular Library, 1973.
Ten North Frederick, Random House, 1955, Popular Library, 1975.
A Family Party (novella), Random House, 1956.
From the Terrace, Random House, 1958, Popular Library, 1974.
Ourselves to Know, Random House, 1960.
The Big Laugh, Random House, 1962, Popular Library, 1977.
Elizabeth Appleton, Random House, 1963.
The Lockwood Concern, Random House, 1966.
The Instrument, Random House, 1967.
Lovey Childs: A Philadelphian's Story, Random House, 1969.
The Ewings, Random House, 1972.
The Second Ewings (fragment), Bruccoli Clark, 1977.

SHORT STORY COLLECTIONS

The Doctor's Son, and Other Stories (also see below), Harcourt, 1935, Hearst Books, c. 1962.
Files on Parade (also see below), Harcourt, 1939.
Pipe Night (also see below), preface by Wolcott Gibbs, Duell, 1945, Popular Library, 1974.
Hellbox, Random House, 1947, Popular Library, 1975.
Stories of Venial Sin, from Pipe Night, Avon, 1947.
The Great Short Stories of John O'Hara: Stories from The Doctor's Son, and Other Stories and Files on Parade, Bantam, 1956, Popular Library, 1973.
Selected Short Stories, Modern Library, 1956.
Assembly, Random House, 1961.
The Cape Cod Lighter: 23 New Short Stories, Random House, 1962.
49 Stories, Modern Library, 1962.
The Hat on the Bed, Random House, 1963.
The Horse Knows the Way, Random House, 1964.
Waiting for Winter, Random House, 1967.
And Other Stories, Random House, 1968.
The O'Hara Generation, Random House, 1969.

The Time Element, and Other Stories, Random House, 1972.
The Good Samaritan, and Other Stories, Random House, 1974.

OTHER

(Author of libretto) "Pal Joey" (two-act musical; based on O'Hara's novel of the same title; also see below), lyrics by Lorenz Hart, music by Richard Rogers, first produced on Broadway at Ethel Barrymore Theatre, December 25, 1940.

"Moontide" (screenplay), Twentieth Century-Fox, 1942.

Here's O'Hara (contains novels *Butterfield 8, Hope of Heaven,* and *Pal Joey;* and twenty short stories), Duell, 1946.

"On Our Merry Way" (screenplay; based on a story by Arch Oboler), Miracle Productions, 1948.

(With Hart) *Pal Joey: The Libretto and Lyrics,* Random House, 1952.

Sweet and Sour (essays), Random House, 1954, Popular Library, 1974.

Three Views of the Novel (lectures), [Washington], 1957.

Sermons and Soda-Water (three novellas), Volume 1: *The Girl on the Baggage Truck,* Volume 2: *Imagine Kissing Pete,* Volume 3: *We're Friends Again,* Random House, 1960.

Five Plays (also see below; contains "The Farmers Hotel," based on O'Hara's novel of the same title, "The Searching Sun," "The Champagne Pool," "Veronique," and "The Way It Was"), Random House, 1961.

Appointment in Samarra, Butterfield 8, [and] *Hope of Heaven,* Random House, 1963 (published in England as *Hope of Heaven, and Other Stories,* Hamish Hamilton, 1963).

My Turn (newspaper columns), Random House, 1967.

A Cub Tells His Story, Windhover/Bruccoli Clark, 1974.

"An Artist Is His Own Fault": John O'Hara on Writers and Writing, edited and with an introduction by Matthew J. Bruccoli, Southern Illinois University Press, 1977.

Remarks on the Novel (cassette recording), Bruccoli Clark, 1977.

The Selected Letters of John O'Hara, edited by Bruccoli, Random House, 1978.

Two by O'Hara (contains the unproduced play "Far from Heaven," and the unproduced screenplay "The Man Who Could Not Lose"), edited by Bruccoli and Carol Meyer, Harcourt/Bruccoli Clark, 1979.

Also author of play, "The Searching Sun," first produced in 1952. Author of columns "Entertainment Week," for *Newsweek,* 1940-42, "Appointment with O'Hara," for *Collier's,* 1954-56, and a column for *Holiday,* 1966. Contributor of over three hundred short stories to *New Yorker;* contributor to other periodicals.

SIDELIGHTS: The name of novelist and short story writer John O'Hara is not widely recognized today, but in the 1950s and 1960s he was one of the most popular, prolific, and financially successful authors in the United States. In the opinion of the majority of his critics, however, O'Hara's stories about upper-middle-class American social life in the first half of the twentieth century lacked the thematic depth and characterization of other authors whom he emulated: Ernest Hemingway, Sinclair Lewis, John Steinbeck, and F. Scott Fitzgerald. "Despite the great merit of his first novel [*Appointment in Samarra*] and his admirable accomplishments in the short-story form, including the *Pal Joey* sequence, O'Hara's reputation has been firmly nailed in place among the lower rungs on the ladder of literary prestige," remarked *Profiles of Modern American Authors* writer Bernard Dekle. A realist-naturalist writer, O'Hara emphasized complete objectivity in his books, writing frankly about the materialistic aspirations and sexual exploits of his characters. In order to simulate reality as much as possible, he also filled his novels with superfluous details, action, and characters. Critics often complemented the novelist on his "remarkable ear for language," as *John O'Hara* author Charles Child Walcutt called it, but felt his attention to details unimportant to plotting caused his books to lose focus. O'Hara biographer, Matthew J. Bruccoli, criticized this viewpoint of the author in his *The O'Hara Concern: A Biography of John O'Hara:* "The more-or-less grudging acknowledgement of O'Hara's 'surface reality,'" Bruccoli stated, "is intended to signal the absence of more profound qualities in his work. Fashionable critics look in vain for evidence of his commitment to relevant issues. O'Hara knew that such things have nothing to do with literature. His concern was to write truthfully and exactly about life and people." But "if it is impossible to say he was profound," as critics like *New York Times* contributor Robert F. Moss maintained, "[O'Hara] was something that, for a writer, is almost as important: irresistibly readable."

O'Hara was born to Irish Catholic parents in Pottsville, Pennsylvania, "a town dominated by a Protestant elite," according to *Dictionary of Literary Biography* contributor Charles W. Bassett. Patrick Henry O'Hara was a successful surgeon and prominent citizen in his community; his son John soon noticed, however, that there existed in Pottsville certain places where Irishmen, no matter how successful, were unwelcome. "O'Hara's Catholic faith declined in the face of Pottsville's elaborate demarcation according to wealth, class, and religion," Bassett related. Envious of the wealthy Protestants who were educated at Ivy League schools, O'Hara wanted to attend Yale himself, but was denied the opportunity when his father died unexpectedly and left the family with no money for such expenses. Instead, the future author spent a number of years working odd jobs, drinking heavily, and suffering through a brief, turbulent marriage with Helen R. Petit. His first break came when the *New Yorker* accepted some of his story submissions, which eventually encouraged O'Hara to begin his first novel. Although *Appointment in Samarra* was a great success and led to a lucrative career as a writer, O'Hara would never forget the social prejudices of Pottsville, and so this theme became dominant in his novels and short stories. "In one sense," commented James W. Tuttleton in his *The Novel of Manners in America,* "O'Hara's novels may thus be seen as the means by which he worked out his own ethnic resentment against the high and mighty in southeastern Pennsylvania."

Appointment in Samarra illustrates the tensions between the Irish Catholics and elite Protestants of the fictional town of Gibbsville, Pennsylvania, a city modeled after the author's own hometown, and in which many of his later stories would come to be set. The novel, which takes place in the 1920s, is about a Protestant Cadillac dealer, Julian English, who breaks the established social code of manners by throwing a drink in the face of an Irish bartender. This key turning point in the story marks the beginning of the end for English. He loses his other Irish customers, who regard English's behavior as an insult to their people, as well as his status as a true gentleman. The resulting loss of financial and social prestige eventually lead English to commit suicide. *Appointment in Samarra* was an instant popular success for the author, and went into five printings in its first year.

Reviewers in the 1930s, however, were shocked by the author's frank treatment of sex and social snobbery. In a 1934 *Saturday Review of Literature* article by Henry Seidel Canby, for example, the reviewer complained of a "thoroughgoing vulgarity in this book." Even one of O'Hara's literary idols, Sinclair Lewis, wrote in a following *Saturday Review of Literature* issue that "this book, for all the cleverness of is observation, the deftness of its tempo, the courage of its vocabulary, was inherently nothing but infantilism." Today, however, critics consider *Appointment in*

Samarra one of O'Hara's best works, often praising the concise plotting that the author would later sacrifice in his longer, more ambitious books. As a character study, *Appointment in Samarra* is also a stronger work than later O'Hara efforts. As Edmund Wilson, author of *Classics and Commercials: A Literary Chronicle of the Forties,* remarked: "*Appointment in Samarra* is a memorable picture both of a provincial snob, a disorganized drinking-man of the twenties, and of the complexities of the social organism in which he flourished and perished."

O'Hara's success with *Appointment in Samarra* opened a door for him as a writer for Paramount Studios in Hollywood, where his ability to write smooth dialogue was put to good use. Reviewers often praised O'Hara's talent in writing dialogue. Dekle, for instance, once noted that O'Hara "hears American speech with such unparalled accuracy and authenticity that his dialogue seems to have been recorded from life rather than written." According to Bassett, however, when it came to applying this skill to the screen "O'Hara was never . . . outstanding." Nevertheless, the experiences he had while in Hollywood proved to provide valuable material for his best-selling novels *Butterfield 8* and *Hope of Heaven.* Again, these works were unfavorably reviewed by critics. *Butterfield 8,* a book about a promiscuous woman whose desire to become respectable is thwarted by her bad reputation, was called "either pointless or puerile" by *Nation* reviewer Lionel Trilling. Interestingly, Trilling later changed his mind in a *New York Times Book Review* article. As other critics had noted, he complimented O'Hara this time on his understanding of "the complex, contradictory, asymmetrical society in which we live."

O'Hara's first attempt to write for the Broadway stage received more attention than his work for the film studios. "Pal Joey," an adaptation of the author's book of the same title, featured music by Richard Rodgers and Lorenz Hart, and was an immediate hit. Its 1952 revival, which won the New York Critics Circle and Donaldson awards, was an even bigger smash and has had more performances than any other Broadway revival. "Pal Joey"'s popularity was shared among critics and audiences alike this time, and O'Hara began to believe that he had "the right stuff for the stage, particularly the musical drama," related Bassett. "Potential directors and collaborators disagreed. . . . [His following plays] turn out to be alternately talky and dull, or melodramatic and incredible."

Between the publication of *Hope of Heaven* and *A Rage to Live,* O'Hara concentrated on his short story writing for the *New Yorker,* where his abilities were more appreciated. But the author, whose life had stabilized somewhat with his marriage to Belle Mulford Wylie and the birth of his daughter, became "restive under the widely held critical estimate that he was the master only of the stereotypically oblique *New Yorker* short story," reported Bassett. Therefore, he composed what became one of his most ambitious books, *A Rage to Live.* A lengthy novel about a marriage that is destroyed after the wife commits adultery, this novel addresses almost all of the author's concerns about social stratification, materialism, and the dangers of sexual passion. In a *New York Times Book Review* interview with Harvey Breit, the novelist asserted that *A Rage to Live* was a departure from all his previous work in that the "earlier books were special books about specialized people; but this is the big one, the overall one."

But many critics felt that the novel was poorly plotted and contained too many unnecessary details. One reviewer, Brendan Gill, called the book "discursive and prolix" and that it resembled "one of those 'panoramic,' three-or-four generation novels that writers of the third and fourth magnitude turn out in such disheartening abundance." The article, which appeared in the *New Yorker,* enraged O'Hara and caused him to break relations with the magazine for eleven years. *A Rage to Live* marked the beginning of a new phase in O'Hara's career in which his novels grew increasingly in length in his effort to, as he put it in his introduction to *Imagine Kissing Pete* in *Sermons and Soda-Water,* "devote my energy and time to the last, simple, but big task of putting it [the early twentieth-century American experience] all down as well as I knew how." Many reviewers, such as *Contemporaries* author Alfred Kazin, felt that the result of this objective was a book filled with irrelevant details and characters and demonstrated that O'Hara could no longer "keep a book under control." O'Hara considered himself a realist and repeatedly defended his approach by arguing that "actuality itself, the object of his mimetic art, lacked symmetry and 'discipline,' " reported Bassett. "Because O'Hara correlated his characters so closely with their milieu and its values," Bassett later added, "he expected his readers to *want* to understand that milieu as thoroughly as possible—hence, the 'irrelevancies.' "

Of the many lengthy novels that O'Hara wrote in the 1950s and 1960s, Bassett and other critics believed *Ten North Frederick* to be his "most successful 'big' novel"; and *New York Herald Tribune Book Review* contributor Milton Rugoff was impressed by "the evident maturity of the artist who composed it." The novel "is in a way a summation of O'Hara's concern with social status," related Rugoff. *Ten North Frederick* concerns the life of Joseph Chapin, a successful lawyer whose career, marriage, and political aspirations to become Governor of Pennsylvania have all been predetermined by his family's prominent social status. When Chapin overreaches the status that has been determined for him by aspiring to the presidency and having an affair with a woman half his age, he is destroyed. By the end of the novel, social pressures have forced him to break off his extramarital relationship, he has been cheated out of a one hundred thousand dollar campaign contribution, and he spends the rest of his life drinking himself to death. As Deborah A. Forczek observed in the *John O'Hara Journal, Ten North Frederick* clearly illustrates the novelist's belief that "social class distinctions were critical in determining an individual's fate."

Despite the fact that *Ten North Frederick* won a National Book Award, the sexual content of the novel caused it to be banned as obscene in Detroit and Albany. Sexuality had always been an important thematic part of O'Hara's works. Norman Podhoretz pointed out in his *Doings and Undoings* that the author believed "that a man is exhaustively defined by his observable behavior—by what is usually called his manner—and beyond that, by his sexual habits." But according to Bassett, the author's "vision of the mantislike female, ever ready to pounce on her sex-bewitched mate, waxes in the later fiction," as does "the sterile exploitiveness of lesbianism." The main female characters in such books as *From the Terrace, Ourselves to Know, Elizabeth Appleton,* and *Lovey Childs: A Philadelphian's Story* are drawn as conniving, snobbish, lubricious, and deadly in their ability to lure men toward self-destruction. In a 1975 *New Yorker* issue, however, a much more sympathetic Brendan Gill attributed O'Hara's treatment of his female characters to the novelist's Catholic upbringing. "Few of O'Hara's female characters are able to remain chaste for long," Gill observed; "he wrote about women and their sexual failings so often and with such relish that many reviewers accused him of seeing all women as nymphomaniacs. The truth is that his gloomy view of their weakness was but a manifestation of a profound and typically Irish Catholic disappointment" that women were not all virgins.

As O'Hara's emphasis on the sexual relationships of his characters increased, so did his concern for providing all the details he could about life in the first half of the twentieth century. This is especially evident in such works as *The Lockwood Concern* and *The Ewings,* both of which were critical failures. In a *Life* review of *The Lockwood Concern,* a book about the vision of a family's patriarchs to establish an enduring family dynasty, Conrad Knickerbocker averred that O'Hara's attention to "detail has become merely catalogue, and when the ephemera are stripped away his tales are lifeless." Characterization also became flatter in these books, according to a number of critics like Granville Hicks. "Except possibly in their sex lives," declared Hicks in a *Saturday Review* article, O'Hara's later characters "are dull people."

In his effort to write down everything he knew about twentieth century America, O'Hara's "output of words outran his considerable powers of invention," remarked *New York Times Book Review* critic Malcolm Cowley. A number of O'Hara's evaluators believed, therefore, that his shorter fiction was superior to his later novels. Short story collections like the author's *The Doctor's Son, and Other Stories* were highly acclaimed over the years. John Chamberlain, for example, glowingly reviewed *The Doctor's Son* in the *New York Times,* where he stated that in "any number of these stories, the transition from mimetic reporting to a turn of events that sharply illuminates basic character is very unobtrusively and skillfully made." Most of the stories in O'Hara's collections had been previously published in the *New Yorker,* and so when he broke relations with the magazine his short story output also diminished considerably. It was not until the publication of the three novellas comprising *Sermons and Soda-Water, The Girl on the Baggage Truck, Imagine Kissing Pete,* and *We're Friends Again,* that the writer returned to the *New Yorker* and the short story form.

Reviewers viewed these novellas to be some of the author's finest efforts. In the *Village Voice,* for instance, Sally O'Driscoll remarked that *Imagine Kissing Pete* "is probably his best work. . . . [It] has all O'Hara's important themes, distilled and condensed, without a wrong note anywhere." Douglas Robillard similarly asserted in an *Essays in Arts and Sciences* article that the last two novellas "should stand with the best fiction that O'Hara has written." *Sermons and Soda-Water* marked a new and superior phase in O'Hara's short story writing, according to critics like Robillard, who noted that the "stories he now wrote were exciting, moving, full of a great storyteller's most polished artistry." Books like *The Cape Cod Lighter, The Hat on the Bed,* and *The Horse Knows the Way* show the author's "practiced ease with the [short story] form," said Bassett, "and . . . the quality of all three of these collections is high, higher indeed than the achievement of his novels of the same era."

Many O'Hara critics now believe that it will be for his shorter works of fiction that the author will be remembered. Robert F. Moss, for one, concluded in the *New York Times Book Review* that the author's "lean, compact short stories have generally been more admired than his poorly focused novels"; and Robillard wrote that O'Hara's short fiction "will establish O'Hara in that great storytelling tradition that is very nearly the best thing in American literature." But in the opinion of other critics, one aspect of the writer's work that exists in both his short stories and his novels makes him a significant American author: his documentation of American social history. "Even those who disliked O'Hara's work," noted *New Republic* contributor Stanley Kauffman, "conceded that he was a sharp social historian, a ruthless investigator of sexual mores and a connoisseur of cultural data." "No one," declared George Steiner in the *Yale Review,* "has captured the relevant tones and shapes of American life with greater fidelity." O'Hara, however, disliked the label of social historian, and once said in a speech he gave in London in 1967, quoted in the *Dictionary of Literary Biography Documentary Series,* that being called a social historian was dangerous "because an author so described may begin to think of himself as a social historian and fall into the habit of writing like one."

O'Hara never got over the fact that he won few awards for his work, but he was proud that his books were frequently on the best seller lists. He told his audience in 1967 that "you must not expect modesty from me. I am just as aware as anyone else that my books have sold something like 15 million copies, and I could not have attained that circulation if I had not been readable." "O'Hara was given to immodest appraisals of his talent," reported *New York Times Book Review* critic James Atlas, "but his convictions about the scope and value of his work were by no means unjustified." John O'Hara, summed up a *Time* obituary, "was indisputably one of the major figures of 20th century American literature, but as indisputably, he was an author who never quite fulfilled the promise of his talent." But even though O'Hara was not a revolutionary writer, Christopher Lehmann-Haupt argued that it is not necessarily the "path-finders" and "experimenters" who will be remembered as it is "those who stake out their own territories and draw them so accurately as to give them lives of their own. If [this] is so, then John O'Hara's huge body of work may be around much longer than we had predicted."

The largest collection of John O'Hara's manuscripts and letters is kept at the John O'Hara study of Pattee Library at Pennsylvania State University.

MEDIA ADAPTATIONS: Three of O'Hara's novels have been adapted as films: "Ten North Frederick," starring Gary Cooper, 20th Century-Fox, 1958, "Butterfield 8," starring Elizabeth Taylor, Metro-Goldwyn-Mayer, 1960, and "From the Terrace," starring Paul Newman, 20th Century-Fox, 1960.

AVOCATIONAL INTERESTS: Golf, music.

BIOGRAPHICAL/CRITICAL SOURCES:

BOOKS

Aldridge, John W., *Time to Murder and Create: The Contemporary Novel in Crisis,* McKay, 1966.

Allen, Walter, *The Modern Novel,* Dutton, 1964.

Auchincloss, Louis, *Reflections of a Jacobite,* Houghton, 1961.

Breit, Harvey, *The Writer Observed,* World Publishing, 1956.

Bruccoli, Matthew J., *The O'Hara Concern: A Biography of John O'Hara,* Random House, 1975.

Carson, E. Russell, *The Fiction of John O'Hara,* University of Pittsburgh Press, 1961.

Concise Dictionary of American Literary Biography: The Age of Maturity, 1929-1941, Gale, 1989.

Contemporary Literary Criticism, Gale, Volume 1, 1973, Volume 2, 1974, Volume 3, 1975, Volume 6, 1976, Volume 11, 1979, Volume 42, 1987.

Dekle, Bernard, *Profiles of Modern American Authors,* Tuttle, 1969.

Dictionary of Literary Biography, Volume 9: *American Novelists, 1910-1945,* Gale, 1982.

Dictionary of Literary Biography Documentary Series, Volume 2, Gale, 1982.

Grebstein, Sheldon Norman, *John O'Hara,* Twayne, 1966.

Kazin, Alfred, *Contemporaries,* Atlantic/Little, Brown, 1962.

Kazin, Alfred, *Bright Book of Life: American Novelists and Storytellers from Hemingway to Mailer,* Atlantic/Little, Brown, 1973.

Long, Robert Emmet, *John O'Hara,* Ungar, 1983.

Madden, David, editor, *Tough Guy Writers of the Thirties,* Southern Illinois University Press, 1968.

O'Hara, John, *Sermons and Soda-Water,* Random House, 1960.

O'Hara, John, *Collected Stories of John O'Hara,* Random House, 1984.

Podhoretz, Norman, *Doings and Undoings,* Farrar, Strauss, 1964.

Tuttleton, James, *The Novel of Manners in America,* Norton, 1972.

Vidal, Gore, *Reflections Upon a Sinking Ship,* Little, Brown, 1969.

Voss, Arthur, *The American Short Story: A Critical Survey,* University of Oklahoma Press, 1973.

Walcutt, Charles Child, *John O'Hara,* University of Minnesota Press, 1969.

Wilson, Edmund, *Classics and Commercials: A Literary Chronicle of the Forties,* Farrar, Strauss, 1950.

PERIODICALS

America, October 12, 1985.
Books and Bookmen, April, 1968, August, 1970, May, 1974.
Chicago Tribune Book World, February 3, 1985.
Christian Science Monitor, November 30, 1967, December 19, 1968.
Detroit News, January 5, 1972.
Esquire, August, 1969, May, 1972.
Essays in Arts and Sciences, May, 1979.
John O'Hara Journal, winter, 1979-80.
Life, November 26, 1965.
Los Angeles Times, September 10, 1985.
Los Angeles Times Book Review, February 3, 1985.
Nation, November 6, 1935, January 20, 1969, October 6, 1969.
National Observer, January 1, 1967, December 23, 1968.
New Republic, April 13, 1938, November 11, 1940, February 26, 1972, October 5, 1974.
Newsweek, April 20, 1970.
New Yorker, August 20, 1949, September 15, 1975.
New Yorker Magazine, November 6, 1978.
New York Herald Tribune, November 25, 1958, November 24, 1961.
New York Herald Tribune Book Review, November 27, 1955, April 8, 1962.
New York Times, February 21, 1935, January 4, 1952, February 27, 1960, November 13, 1967, November 27, 1968, July 8, 1970, February 29, 1972, August 9, 1978, May 14, 1984, February 18, 1985.
New York Times Book Review, March 18, 1945, September 4, 1949 (interview), November 27, 1966, November 13, 1967 (interview), November 26, 1967, November 24, 1968, November 30, 1969, February 27, 1972, March 18, 1973, August 18, 1974, October 26, 1975.
Partisan Review, March, 1950.
Publishers Weekly, November 3, 1958 (interview).
Saturday Review, November 27, 1965, November 25, 1967, November 30, 1968, August 9, 1969, March 4, 1972.
Saturday Review of Literature, August 18, 1934, October 6, 1934.
Sewanee Review, summer, 1975.
Spectator, April 27, 1974.
Times Literary Supplement, August 24, 1967, May 28, 1976.
Village Voice, December 16, 1981, February 19, 1985.

Washington Post, July 16, 1969, February 25, 1972.
Washington Post Book World, November 19, 1967, November 24, 1968, February 20, 1972, February 10, 1985.
Yale Review, spring, 1961.

OBITUARIES:

PERIODICALS

Christian Science Monitor, April 23, 1970.
New York Times, April 12, 1970, April 13, 1970.
Publishers Weekly, April 20, 1970.
San Francisco Examiner, May 25, 1970.
Time, April 20, 1970.
Variety, April 15, 1970.
Washington Post, April 12, 1970, April 29, 1970.

—*Sketch by Kevin S. Hile*

*   *   *

OKIGBO, Christopher (Ifenayichukwu) 1932-1967

PERSONAL: Born in 1932, in Ojoto, Nigeria; killed August, 1967, in military action near Nsukka, Biafra (now in Nigeria); son of James (a school teacher) Okigbo; married wife, Sefi, in 1963; children: Ibrahimat (daughter). *Education:* University of Ibadan, B.A., 1956.

CAREER: Nigerian Department of Research and Information, Lagos, Nigeria, private secretary to the Minister, 1955-56; affiliated with Nigerian Tobacco Company and United Africa Company; Fiditi Grammar School, Fiditi, Nigeria, Latin teacher, 1959-60; University of Nigeria, Nsukka, assistant librarian, 1960-62; Cambridge University Press, Ibadan, Nigeria, West African representative, 1962-66; founder of small publishing company with Chinua Achebe in Enugu, Nigeria, 1967. Member of editorial staff of Mbari Press. *Military service:* Biafran Defense Forces, 1967; became major; killed in action.

AWARDS, HONORS: Dakar Festival of Arts first prize, 1966 (refused); posthumously awarded Biafran National Order of Merit.

WRITINGS:

POEMS

Heavensgate, Mbari Press (Ibadan, Nigeria), 1962.
Limits, Mbari Press, 1964.
Labyrinths, with Path of Thunder, Africana, 1971.
Collected Poems, with a preface by Paul Theroux and introduction by Adewale Maja-Pearce, Heinemann, 1986.

Also author of *Silences* and *Distances.* Contributor of poetry to periodicals, including *Transition* and *Black Orpheus.* Co-editor of *Transition.*

SIDELIGHTS: "There wasn't a stage when I decided that I definitely wished to be a poet," Christopher Okigbo once commented, "there was a stage when I found that I couldn't be anything else."

According to Paul Theroux in *Introduction to Nigerian Literature,* Okigbo was "an obscure poet, possibly the most difficult poet in Africa." Theroux suggests two approaches to Okigbo's work. One is to examine the words he used, many springing from his wide knowledge of other writers, and all having a special meaning in the context of his own work. The other is to "listen to his music." According to Theroux, one can hear three separate melodies in it: "the music of youth, the clamour of passage (that is, growing up) and lastly, the sounds of thunder."

Part of the complexity of Okigbo's poetry, according to Sunday O. Anozie in *Christopher Okigbo: Creative Rhetoric,* lies in the fact that "he is constantly exploring two irregular dimensions of myth . . . myth as a privileged religious mode of cognition" and myth, with totem, as "affective and even evaluative in a given cultural context." Anozie also cites the derivative nature of the poet's work, the "wide range of references to and echoes of other poets."

In Theroux's opinion, *Heavensgate* and *Limits* express the "music of growth," a music which also suggests the danger inherent in growing up. The bird imagery running through both poems is related to the speaker, the poet who appears in all of Okigbo's work and would seem to represent Okigbo himself. *Silences* and *Distances* speak of the disillusionments which can follow maturation and the loss of innocence. "It is safe to say that very few poems achieve the music and harmony that *Silences* does," Theroux commented. *Distances,* however, is characterized by pain, shocking images such as that of the "horizontal stone" which represents a morgue slab holding a corpse, and the repetition of the line, "I was the sole witness to my homecoming," indicating solitude at the attainment of maturity.

Okigbo felt none of the conflict between old and new that often seems to pose a problem for educated Africans. He often went back to his village for festivals and major religious ceremonies, and his own religion combined Christian and pagan elements. Interviewed by Marjory Whitelaw in *Journal of Commonwealth Literature,* he described the family shrine which housed their ancestral gods, the male Ikenga and the female Udo, whom he considered different aspects of the same force represented by the Christian god. Unlike others in his family, he never made sacrifices to these deities, but he declared: "My creative activity is in fact one way of performing these functions in a different manner. Every time write a poem, I am in fact offering a sacrifice." Okigbo's maternal grandfather, of whom he was believed to be a reincarnation, was the priest of a shrine to Idoto, the river goddess, and the poet's idea of his own priesthood is apparent in much of his writing.

In spite of this oneness with his background and the local themes and images which abound in his work, Okigbo did not adhere to the literary concept of negritude, which he felt, emphasized racial differences. He told Whitelaw: "I think I am just a poet. A poet writes poetry and once a work is published it becomes public property. It's left to whoever reads it to decide whether it's African poetry or English. There isn't any such thing as a poet trying to express African-ness. Such a thing doesn't exist. A poet expresses himself."

His interest in social and political change in his own country, however, formed an inseparable part of his work. Okigbo told Whitelaw of his conviction that the poet in any society could not examine his own identity in isolation, but that "any writer who attempts a type of inward exploration will in fact be exploring his own society indirectly." Okigbo's concern for humanity was perhaps best expressed in his commitment to the Biafran secession. He lost his life in August, 1967, fighting as a volunteer for the Biafran forces.

Anozie wrote: "Nothing can be more tragic to the world of African poetry in English than the death of Christopher Okigbo, especially at a time when he was beginning to show maturity and coherence in his vision of art, life and society, and greater sophistication in poetic form and phraseology. Nevertheless his output, so rich and severe within so short a life, is sure to place him among the best and the greatest of our time."

BIOGRAPHICAL/CRITICAL SOURCES:

BOOKS

Anozie, Sunday O., *Christopher Okigbo: Creative Rhetoric,* Evans Brothers, 1972.
Bing, Bruce, editor, *Introduction to Nigerian Literature,* Evans Brothers, 1972.
Contemporary Literary Criticism, Volume 25, Gale, 1983.
Egudu, Romanus N., *Four Modern West African Poets,* NOK Publishers International, 1977.

PERIODICALS

Books Abroad, spring, 1971.
Comparative Literature Studies, June, 1971.
Journal of Commonwealth Literature, July, 1968, July, 1970, June, 1972.

*   *   *

OLSEN, Tillie   1913-

PERSONAL: Born January 14, 1913, in Omaha, Neb.; maiden name, Lerner; daughter of Russian immigrants; father was Nebraska state secretary of Socialist Party; married Jack Olsen (a printer), 1936; children: Karla Olsen Lutz, Julie Olsen Edwards, Katherine Jo, Laurie. *Education:* High school graduate.

ADDRESSES: Home—1435 Laguna #6, San Francisco, Calif. 94115. *Agent*—Elaine Markson Literary Agency, 44 Greenwich Ave., New York, N.Y. 10011.

CAREER: Worked in industry and as typist-transcriber. Visiting professor, Amherst College, 1969-70, and University of Massachusetts, 1974; visiting instructor, Stanford University, 1971; writer in residence, Massachusetts Institute of Technology, 1973; International Visiting Scholar, Norway, 1980. Regents Lecturer, University of California, 1978.

AWARDS, HONORS: Stanford University creative writing fellowship, 1956-57; Ford grant in literature, 1959; O. Henry Award for best American short story, 1961, for "Tell Me a Riddle"; fellowship, Radcliffe Institute for Independent Study, 1962-64; National Endowment for the Arts grant, 1968; Guggenheim fellowship, 1975-76; award in literature, American Academy and National Institute of Arts and Letters, 1975; University of Nebraska, Doctor of Arts and Letters, 1979; Ministry to Women Award, Unitarian Women's Federation, 1980; Litt.D., Knox College, 1982.

WRITINGS:

Tell Me a Riddle: A Collection (stories), Lippincott, 1961, reprinted, Dell, 1989.
(Author of biographical interpretation) Rebecca Harding Davis, *Life in the Iron Mills* (nonfiction), Feminist Press, 1972.
Yonnondio: From the Thirties (novel), Delacorte, 1974, reprinted, Dell, 1989.
Silences (essays), Delacorte, 1978.
(Editor) *Mother to Daughter, Daughter to Mother: A Daybook and Reader,* Feminist Press, 1984.
(Editor with others) *Mothers and Daughters, That Special Quality: An Exploration in Photographs,* Aperture, 1989.

Short stories appear in more than seventy anthologies, including *Best American Short Stories,* 1957, 1961, and 1971, *Fifty Best American Stories, 1915-1965, Prize Stories: The O. Henry Awards, 1961, Norton Introduction to Literature,* 1977, *Elements of Literature,* 1978, and *The Modern Tradition,* 1979. Contributor to *Ms., Harper's, College English,* and *Trellis.*

A collection of Olsen's manuscripts is housed in the Berg Collection at the New York Public Library.

SIDELIGHTS: Tillie Olsen writes about those people who, because of their class, sex, or race, have been denied the opportunity to express and develop themselves. In a strongly emotional style, she tells of their dreams and failures, of what she calls "the unnatural thwarting of what struggles to come into being but cannot."

Olsen has published relatively little, citing her own life circumstances as the cause. She was forced to delay her writing for some twenty years while working at a number of jobs and raising four children. Her novel *Yonnondio* was begun during the depression but not finished until the early seventies. As Margaret Atwood writes in the *New York Times Book Review*, "few writers have gained such wide respect on such a small body of published work. . . . Among women writers in the United States, 'respect' is too pale a word: 'reverence' is more like it. This is presumably because women writers, even more than their male counterparts, recognize what a heroic feat it is to have held down a job, raised four children, and still somehow managed to become and to remain a writer."

Olsen's prose has been praised by a number of critics. A reviewer for the *New Yorker* writes that "the strength of Mrs. Olsen's writing is remarkable." Speaking of *Tell Me a Riddle,* R. M. Elman of *Commonweal* states that "there are stories in this collection which are perfectly realized works of art." Jack Salzman of *Book World* believes that "Tillie Olsen is one of the greatest prose stylists now writing" and calls her *Yonnondio* "a magnificent novel" and "the best novel to come out of the so-called proletarian movement of the '30s."

MEDIA ADAPTATIONS: Olsen's stories have been recorded by WBAI radio in New York City and by the Lamont Poetry Room at Harvard University. Some stories have been adapted for theatrical presentation.

BIOGRAPHICAL/CRITICAL SOURCES:

BOOKS

Contemporary Literary Criticism, Gale, Volume 4, 1975, Volume 8, 1980.
Contemporary Novelists, St. James Press/St. Martin's, 1986.
Dictionary of Literary Biography, Volume 28: *Twentieth-Century American-Jewish Fiction Writers,* Gale, 1984.
Dictionary of Literary Biography Yearbook: 1980, Gale, 1981.
Olsen, Tillie, *Silences,* Delacorte, 1978.
Ruddick, Sara, and Pamela Daniels, editors, *Working It Out,* Pantheon, 1977.

PERIODICALS

American Poetry Review, May/June, 1979.
Antioch Review, fall, 1978.
Atlantic, September, 1978.
Book World, April 7, 1974.
Chicago Tribune, October 29, 1961.
Christian Science Monitor, November 9, 1961, September 18, 1978.
Commonweal, December 8, 1961.
Los Angeles Times, May 15, 1980.
Ms., September, 1974.
Nation, April 10, 1972.
New Leader, May 22, 1978.
New Republic, November 13, 1961, March 30, 1974, December 6, 1975, July 29, 1978.
New Yorker, March 25, 1974.
New York Herald Tribune Books, December 17, 1961.
New York Times, July 31, 1978.
New York Times Book Review, November 12, 1961, March 31, 1974, July 30, 1978, June 19, 1983.
Publishers Weekly, November 23, 1984.
Story, Volume 1, number 1, 1964.
Studies in Short Fiction, fall, 1963.
Time, October 27, 1961.
Times (London), October 26, 1985.
Times Literary Supplement, November 14, 1980.
Village Voice, May 23, 1974, August 7, 1978.
Virginia Quarterly Review, fall, 1974.
Washington Post, September 11, 1978, March 30, 1980.
Yale Review, winter, 1979.

*   *   *

OLSON, Charles (John) 1910-1970

PERSONAL: Born December 27, 1910, in Worcester, Mass.; died after a short illness, January 10, 1979, in New York, N.Y.; son of Karl Joseph and Mary (Hines) Olson. *Education:* Wesleyan University, B.A., 1932, M.A., 1933; also studied at Yale University and Harvard University.

CAREER: Taught at Clark University, Worcester, Mass., at Harvard University, Cambridge, Mass., 1936-39, and at Black Mountain College, Black Mountain, N.C., serving as rector at Black Mountain, 1951-56; taught at State University of New York, Buffalo, 1963-65, and University of Connecticut, 1969.

AWARDS, HONORS: Received two Guggenheim fellowships; grant from Wenner-Gren Foundation, 1952, to study Mayan hieroglyphic writing in Yucatan; Oscar Blumenthal-Charles Leviton Prize, 1965; *Los Angeles Times* Book Award, 1984, for *The Maximus Poems;* American Book Award, Before Columbus Foundation, 1988, for *The Collected Poems of Charles Olson.*

WRITINGS:

Call Me Ishmael, Reynal & Hitchcock, 1947, Grove, 1958.
To Corrado Cagli (poetry), Knoedler Gallery (New York), 1947.
Y & X (poetry), Black Sun Press, 1948.
Letter for Melville (poetry), Melville Society, Williams College, 1951.
This (poem; design by Nicola Cernovich), Black Mountain College, 1952.
The Maximus Poems 1-10, Jargon, 1953, *11-22,* Jargon, 1956, Jargon/Corinth, 1960.
Mayan Letters, edited by Robert Creeley, Divers Press, 1953.
In Cold Hell, In Thicket, [Dorchester, Mass.], 1953, Four Seasons Foundation, 1967.
Anecdotes of the Late War (antiwar document), Jargon, c. 1957.
O'Ryan 2.4.6.8.10., White Rabbit Press, 1958.
Projective Verse (essay), Totem Press, 1959.
The Distances (poems), Grove, 1961.
Maximus, From Dogtown I, foreword by Michael McClure, Auerhahn, 1961.
A Bibliography on America for Ed Dorn, Four Seasons Foundation, 1964.
Human Universe, and Other Essays, edited by Donald Allen, Auerhahn, 1965.
Proprioception, Four Seasons Foundation, 1965.
O'Ryan 1, 2, 3, 4, 5, 6, 7, 8, 9, 10, White Rabbit Press, 1965.
Selected Writings, edited by Robert Creeley, New Directions, 1966.
Stocking Cap (story), Four Seasons Foundation, 1966.
Charles Olson Reading at Berkeley, Coyote, 1966.

West, Goliard Press, 1966.

The Maximus Poems IV, V, VI, Cape Goliard, in association with Grossman, 1968.

Pleistocene Man, Institute of Further Studies (Buffalo, N.Y.), 1968.

Causal Mythology, Four Seasons Foundation, 1969.

Letters for Origin, 1950-1956, edited by Albert Glover, Cape Goliard, 1969, Grossman, 1970.

Archaeologist of Morning (collected poems), Cape Goliard, 1970, Grossman, 1971, new edition, Grossman, 1973.

The Special View of History, edited by Ann Charters, Oyez, 1970.

Poetry and Truth: Beloit Letters and Poems, edited by George F. Butterick, Four Seasons Foundation, 1971.

Additional Prose, edited by Butterick, Four Seasons Foundation, 1974.

The Maximus Poems, Volume III, Grossman, 1974.

In Adullam's Lair, To the Lighthouse Press, 1975.

The Post Office, Grey Fox, 1975.

The Fiery Hunt and Other Plays, edited by Butterick, Four Seasons Foundation, 1977.

(With James Den Boer) *Olson-Den Boer: A Letter,* Christophers Books, 1977.

Muthologos: The Collected Lectures and Interviews, edited by Butterick, Four Seasons Foundation, 1978.

(With Robert Creeley) *Charles Olson and Robert Creeley: The Complete Correspondence,* eight volumes, edited by Butterick, Black Sparrow, 1980-87.

The Maximus Poems, edited by Butterick, University of California Press, 1983.

The Collected Poems of Charles Olson, edited by Butterick, University of California Press, 1987.

A Nation of Nothing but Poetry: Supplementary Poems, with an introduction by Butterick, Black Sparrow, 1989.

Author of dance-play "Apollonius of Tyana," 1951. Work is represented in anthologies, including *The New American Poetry: 1945-1969,* edited by Donald M. Allen, Grove, 1960, and *The Norton Anthology of Modern Poetry,* edited by Richard Ellmann and Robert O'Clair, Norton, 1973. Contributor to *Twice-A-Year, Black Mountain Review, Big Table, Yugen, Evergreen Review, Origin, Poetry New York,* and other periodicals.

SIDELIGHTS: In his influential essay on projective (or open) verse, Charles Olson asserts that "a poem is energy transferred from where the poet got it (he will have some several causations), by way of the poem itself to, all the way over to, the reader. Okay. Then the poem itself must, at all points, be a high energy-construct and, at all points, an energy-discharge." Form is only an extension of content and "right form, in any given poem, is the only and exclusively possible extension of content under hand. . . . I take it that PROJECTIVE VERSE teaches, is, this lesson, that that verse will only do in which a poet manages to register both the acquisitions of his ear *and* the pressures of his breath." Olson goes by ear, and his lines are breath-conditioned. The two halves, he says, are: "the HEAD, by way of the EAR, to the SYLLABLE/the HEART, by way of the BREATH, to the LINE." He believes "it is from the union of the mind and the ear that the syllable is born. But the syllable is only the first child of the incest of verse. . . . The other child is the LINE. . . . And the line comes (I swear it) from the breath. . . ." Robert Creeley explains thus: "What he is trying to say is that the heart is a basic instance not only of rhythm, but it is the base of the measure of rhythms for all men in the way heartbeat is like the metronome in their whole system. So that when he says the heart by way of the breath to the line, he is trying to say that it is in the line that the basic rhythmic scoring

takes place. . . . Now, the head, the intelligence by way of the ear to the syllable—which he calls also 'the king and pin'—is the unit upon which all builds. The heart, then, stands, as the primary feeling term. The head, in contrast, is discriminating. It is discriminating by way of what it hears." Olson believes that "in any given poem always, always one perception must must must MOVE, INSTANTER, ON ANOTHER!" So, all the conventions that "logic has forced on syntax must be broken open as quietly as must the too set feet of the old line."

Olson has thus rejected "academic" verse, with its closed forms and alleged artifice. Back to primal things, he says. The *Times Literary Supplement* notes that "culture, civilization, history (except history as personal exploration as in Herodotus) and, above all, sociology, are dirty words for him." Olson says: "It comes to this: the use of a man, by himself and thus by others, lies in how he conceives his relation to nature. . . . If he is contained within his nature as he is participant in the larger force, he will be able to listen, and his hearing through himself will give him secrets objects share. And by an inverse law his shapes will make their own way. . . . This is not easy. Nature works from reverence, even in her destructions (species go down with a crash). But breath is man's special qualification as animal. Sound is a dimension he has extended. Language is one of his proudest acts. . . . I keep thinking, it comes to this: culture displacing the state." M. L. Rosenthal comments: "The problem is to get back to sources of meaning anterior to those of our own state-ridden civilization and so to recover the sense of personality and of place that has been all but throttled."

Robert Duncan, in his essay "Regarding Olson's 'Maximus,' " writes: "Olson insists upon the active. Homo maximus wrests his life from the underworld as the Gloucester fisherman wrests his from the sea." Olson's striding poetic syllables, says Duncan, are "no more difficult than walking." Duncan traces Olson's aesthetics to nineteenth-century American sources: "I point to Emerson or to Dewey," writes Duncan, "to show that in American philosophy there are foreshadowings or forelightings of 'Maximus.' In this aesthetic, conception cannot be abstracted from doing; beauty is related to the beauty of a archer hitting the mark." A *Times Literary Supplement* reviewer observes that Olson's style is at times a "bouncy, get-in-with-it manner," often involving the "juxtaposition of a very abstract statement with a practical, jocular illustration of what the statement might imply." Writes Olson: "It's as though you were hearing for the first time—who knows what a poem ought to sound like? until it's thar? And how do you get it thar ezcept as you do—*you,* and nobody else (who's a poet? . . .)"

Anyone familiar with contemporary poetry would agree with Robert Creeley when he calls Olson "central to any description of literary 'climate' dated 1958." Olson's influence extends directly to Creeley, Duncan, Denise Levertov, and Paul Blackburn, and, as Stephen Stepanchev notes, Olson's projective verse "has either influenced or coincided with other stirrings toward newness in American poetry." He himself owes a great deal to Ezra Pound, William Carlos Williams, and Edward Dahlberg. The scope of Olson's work is "as broad as Pound's," writes Kenneth Rexroth. It is not simple poetry, much of it being fragmentary and experimental. But it has, says Rosenthal, "the power of hammering conviction—something like Lawrence's but with more brutal insistence behind it. It is a dogmatic, irritable, passionate voice, of the sort that the modern world, to its sorrow very often, is forever seeking out; it is not a clear voice, but one troubled by its own confusions which it carries into the attack."

Olson did not consider himself "a poet" or "a writer" by profession, but rather that nebulous and rare "archeologist of morning," reminiscent of Thoreau. He wrote on a typewriter. "It is the advantage of the typewriter that, due to its rigidity and its space precisions, it can, for a poet, indicate exactly the breath, the pause, the suspensions even of syllables, the juxtapositions even of parts of phrases, which he intends. For the first time the poet has the stave and the bar a musician has had. For the first time he can, without the convention of rime and meter, record the listening he has done to his own speech and by that one act indicate how he would want any reader, silently or otherwise, to voice his work."

BIOGRAPHICAL/CRITICAL SOURCES:

BOOKS

Allen, Donald M., editor, *The New American Poetry: 1945-1960,* Grove, 1960.
Contemporary Literary Criticism, Gale, Volume 1, 1973, Volume 2, 1974, Volume 5, 1976, Volume 6, 1976, Volume 9, 1978, Volume 11, 1979, Volume 29, 1984.
Dictionary of Literary Biography, Gale, Volume 5: *American Poets Since World War II,* 1980, Volume 16: *The Beats: Literary Bohemians in Postwar America,* 1983.
Olson: The Journal of the Charles Olson Archives, University of Connecticut Library, 1974—.
Rexroth, Kenneth, *Assays,* New Directions, 1961.
Rosenthal, M. L., *The Modern Poets,* Oxford University Press, 1965.
Stepanchev, Stephen, *American Poetry Since 1945,* Harper, 1965.

PERIODICALS

Black Mountain Review, Number 6, 1956.
Evergreen Review, summer, 1958.
Los Angeles Times Book Review, September 4, 1983.
Times Literary Supplement, November 25, 1965, September 30, 1988.
The Review, January, 1964.
Washington Post Book World, November 13, 1983, October 6, 1985.
West Coast Review, spring, 1967.

OBITUARIES:

PERIODICALS

Antiquarian Bookman, March 2-9, 1970.
New York Times, January 11, 1970.
Publishers Weekly, January 26, 1970.

*   *   *

O'NEILL, Eugene (Gladstone) 1888-1953

PERSONAL: Born October 16, 1888, in New York, N.Y.; died of pneumonia, November 27, 1953, in Boston, Mass.; buried December 2, 1953, in Forest Hills Cemetery, Boston, Mass.; son of James (an actor) and Mary Ellen (Quinlan) O'Neill; married Kathleen Jenkins, October 2, 1909 (divorced, 1912); married Agnes Boulton (a writer), April 12, 1918 (divorced, 1929); married Carlotta Monterey (an actress), July 22, 1929; children: (first marriage) Eugene Gladstone Jr.; (second marriage) Shane Rudraighe, Oona. *Education:* Attended Princeton University, 1906-07, and Harvard University, 1914-15. *Avocational interests:* Swimming, fishing, boating.

CAREER: Playwright. New York-Chicago Supply Co. (mail order firm), New York, N.Y., secretary, 1907-08; prospector in

Honduras, 1909-10; worked in father's theater company as assistant stage manager, 1910, and actor, 1912; sailor, and manual laborer in Buenos Aires, Argentina, 1910-11; *New London Telegraph,* New London, Conn., reporter, 1912. Co-manager of Provincetown Players, beginning in 1923.

MEMBER: Authors' League of America, American Academy of Arts and Letters, American Philosophical Society, National Institute of Arts and Letters, Dramatists' Guild, Irish Academy of Letters.

AWARDS, HONORS: Pulitzer Prize, 1920, for *Beyond the Horizon,* 1922, for *Anna Christie,* 1928, for *Strange Interlude,* and 1957, for *Long Day's Journey Into Night;* Gold Medal from National Institute of Arts and Letters, 1923; Litt.D. from Yale University, 1923; Nobel Prize in literature, 1936; New York Drama Critics Circle Award, 1957, for *Long Day's Journey Into Night.*

WRITINGS:

PLAYS

Thirst and Other One-Act Plays (contains *Fog, Recklessness, Thirst, Warnings,* and *The Web*), Gorham Press, 1914.
Thirst (first produced by Provincetown Players in Provincetown, Mass., at Wharf Theatre, August, 1916), published in *Thirst and Other One-Act Plays,* 1914 (also see above).
Fog (first produced by Provincetown Players in New York City at Playwrights' Theatre, January 5, 1917), published in *Thirst and Other One-Act Plays,* 1914 (also see above).
Bound East for Cardiff (one-act; first produced by Provincetown Players in Provincetown at Wharf Theatre, July 28, 1916, and in New York City at Playwrights' Theatre, November 3, 1916), published in *The Provincetown Plays, First Series,* F. Shay (New York), 1916, revised version published in *The Moon of the Caribbees and Six Other Plays of the Sea* (also see below).
Before Breakfast (one-act; first produced in New York City by Provincetown Players at Playwrights' Theatre, December 1, 1916), published in *The Provincetown Plays, Third Series,* F. Shay, 1916, published in *The Complete Works of Eugene O'Neill,* 1924 (also see below).
The Sniper (one-act; first produced by Provincetown Players in New York City at Playwrights' Theatre, February 16, 1917), published in *Lost Plays of Eugene O'Neill,* 1950 (also see below).
In the Zone (one-act; first produced in New York City by Washington Square Players at Comedy Theatre, October 31, 1917), published in *The Moon of the Caribbees and Six Other Plays of the Sea,* 1919 (also see below).
The Long Voyage Home (one-act; first produced in New York City by Provincetown Players at Playwrights' Theatre, November 2, 1917), published in *Smart Set,* October, 1917, published in *The Moon of the Caribbees and Six Other Plays of the Sea,* 1919 (also see below).
Ile (one-act; first produced in New York City by Provincetown Players at Playwrights' Theatre, November 30, 1917), published in *Smart Set,* May, 1918, published in *The Moon of the Caribbees and Six Other Plays of the Sea,* 1919 (also see below).
The Rope (one-act; first produced in New York City by Provincetown Players at Playwrights' Theatre, April 26, 1918), published in *The Moon of the Caribbees and Six Other Plays of the Sea,* 1919 (also see below).
The Moon of the Caribbees (one-act; first produced in New York City by Provincetown Players at Provincetown Playhouse, December 20, 1918), published in *Smart Set,* August, 1918,

published in *The Moon of the Caribbees and Six Other Plays of the Sea,* 1919 (also see below).

Gold (four-act; preliminary version of Act Four first produced as *Where the Cross Is Made* in New York City by Provincetown Players at Provincetown Playhouse, November 22, 1918, and published in *The Moon of the Caribbees and Six Other Plays of the Sea,* 1919 [also see below]; complete work first produced in New York City at Frazee Theatre, June 21, 1921), Boni & Liveright, 1921, extensively revised version published in *The Complete Works of Eugene O'Neill,* 1924 (also see below).

The Dreamy Kid (one-act; first produced in New York City by Provincetown Players at Provincetown Playhouse, October 31, 1919), published in *Theatre Arts,* January, 1920, published in *Contemporary One-Act Plays of 1921 (American),* Stewart Kidd, 1922, published in *The Complete Works of Eugene O'Neill,* 1924 (also see below).

The Moon of the Caribbees and Six Other Plays of the Sea (contains *Bound East for Cardiff, Ile, In the Zone, The Long Voyage Home, The Moon of the Caribbees, The Rope, Where the Cross Is Made*), Boni & Liveright, 1919.

Beyond the Horizon (three-act; first produced on Broadway at Morosco Theatre, February 3, 1920), Boni & Liveright, 1920.

Anna Christie (four-act; preliminary version produced as *Chris* in Atlantic City, N.J., March 8, 1920, and published as *Chris Christophersen,* Random House, 1982; final version first produced in New York City at Vanderbilt Theatre, November 2, 1921), published in *The Hairy Ape* [and] *Anna Christie* [and] *The First Man,* 1922 (also see below).

Exorcism (one-act; later destroyed by the author), first produced in New York City by Provincetown Players at Provincetown Playhouse, March 26, 1920.

The Emperor Jones (eight scenes; first produced in New York City by Provincetown Players at Provincetown Playhouse, November 1, 1920), published in *Theatre Arts,* January, 1921, revised version published in *The Emperor Jones* [and] *Diff'rent* [and] *The Straw,* 1921 (also see below).

Diff'rent (two-act; first produced in New York City by Provincetown Players at Provincetown Playhouse, December 27, 1920), published in *The Emperor Jones* [and] *Diff'rent* [and] *The Straw,* 1921 (also see below).

The Straw (three-act; first produced in New London, Conn., on November 4, 1921; produced in New York City at Greenwich Village Theatre, November 10, 1921), published in *The Emperor Jones* [and] *Diff'rent* [and] *The Straw,* 1921 (also see below).

The Emperor Jones [and] *Diff'rent* [and] *The Straw,* Boni & Liveright, 1921.

The First Man (four-act; first produced in New York City at Neighborhood Playhouse, March 4, 1922), published in *The Hairy Ape* [and] *Anna Christie* [and] *The First Man,* 1922 (also see below).

The Hairy Ape (eight scenes; first produced in New York City by Provincetown Players at Provincetown Playhouse, March 9, 1922), published in *The Hairy Ape* [and] *Anna Christie* [and] *The First Man,* 1922 (also see below).

The Hairy Ape [and] *Anna Christie* [and] *The First Man,* Boni & Liveright, 1922.

Welded (three-act; first produced in Baltimore on March 3, 1924; produced in New York City at Thirty-Ninth Street Theatre, March 17, 1924), published in *All God's Chillun Got Wings* [and] *Welded,* 1924 (also see below), extensively revised version published in *The Complete Works of Eugene O'Neill,* 1924 (also see below).

The Ancient Mariner (adapted from the poem "Rime of the Ancient Mariner" by Samuel Taylor Coleridge; first produced in New York City by Provincetown Players at Provincetown Playhouse, April 6, 1924), published in *The Unknown O'Neill,* 1988 (also see below).

All God's Chillun Got Wings (two-act; first produced in New York City at Provincetown Playhouse, May 15, 1924), first published in *American Mercury,* February, 1924, published in *All God's Chillun Got Wings* [and] *Welded,* 1924 (also see below).

All God's Chillun Got Wings [and] *Welded,* Boni & Liveright, 1924.

Desire Under the Elms (three-act; first produced in New York City at Greenwich Village Theatre, November 11, 1924), published in *The Complete Works of Eugene O'Neill,* 1924 (also see below), revised version published separately, Boni & Liveright, 1925.

The Complete Works of Eugene O'Neill (selection by the author, excluding several early plays; contains revised versions of many previously published plays), Boni & Liveright, 1924.

The Fountain (eleven scenes; first produced in New York City at Greenwich Village Theatre, December 10, 1925), published in *The Great God Brown, The Fountain, The Moon of the Caribbees, and Other Plays,* Boni & Liveright, 1926.

The Great God Brown (four-act; first produced in New York City at Greenwich Village Theatre, January 23, 1926), published in *The Great God Brown, The Moon of the Caribbees, and Other Plays,* Boni & Liveright, 1926.

Marco Millions (three-act; preliminary two-part, eight-act version published as *Marco's Millions* in *The Unknown O'Neill,* 1988 [also see below]; final version first produced on Broadway by Theatre Guild at Guild Theatre, January 9, 1928), Boni & Liveright, 1927.

Lazarus Laughed (four-act; preliminary version of Act I published in *The American Caravan: A Yearbook of American Literature,* Macaulay, 1927; final version first produced in Pasadena, California, at Pasadena Community Playhouse, April 9, 1928), Boni & Liveright, 1927.

Strange Interlude (nine-act; first produced on Broadway by Theatre Guild at John Golden Theatre, January 30, 1928), Boni & Liveright, 1928.

Dynamo (three-act; preliminary version first produced on Broadway by Theatre Guild at Martin Beck Theatre, February 11, 1929), final version, extensively revised, Liveright, 1929.

Mourning Becomes Electra (trilogy consisting of *Homecoming, The Hunted,* and *The Haunted;* first produced on Broadway by Theatre Guild at Guild Theatre, October 26, 1931), Liveright, 1931.

Ah, Wilderness! (four-act; three-act stage version first produced by Theatre Guild in Pittsburgh, Pa., at Nixon Theatre, September 25, 1933, and on Broadway at Guild Theatre, October 2, 1933, published by Samuel French, 1933), Random House, 1933.

Days Without End (four-act; first produced by Theatre Guild in Boston, Mass., December 27, 1933, and in New York City at Henry Miller Theatre, January 8, 1934), Random House, 1934.

The Iceman Cometh (four-act; first produced on Broadway by Theatre Guild at Martin Beck Theatre, October 9, 1946), Random House, 1946.

A Moon for the Misbegotten (four-act; first produced in Columbus, Ohio, by Theatre Guild at Hartman Theater, produced in New York City at Bijou Theatre, May 2, 1957), Random House, 1952.

Lost Plays of Eugene O'Neill (previously unpublished plays written before 1920; contains the one-acts *Abortion, The Movie Man, The Sniper,* and *A Wife for a Life,* and the three-act *Servitude*), introduction by Lawrence Gellert, New Fathoms Press, 1950.

Long Day's Journey Into Night (four-act; first produced in Stockholm, Sweden, at Kungliga Dramatiska Teatern, February 10, 1956, produced on Broadway at Helen Hayes Theatre, November 7, 1956), Yale University Press, 1956.

A Touch of the Poet (four-act; first produced in Stockholm at Kungliga Dramatiska Teatern, March 29, 1957, produced on Broadway at Helen Hayes Theatre, October 2, 1958), Yale University Press, 1957.

Hughie (one-act; first produced in Stockholm at Kungliga Dramatiska Teatern, September 18, 1958, produced on Broadway at Royale Theatre, December 22, 1964), Yale University Press, 1959.

More Stately Mansions (unfinished; edited versions first produced in Stockholm at Kungliga Dramatiska Teatern, September 11, 1962, produced in Los Angeles, Calif., at Ahmanson Theatre, September 12, 1967, published by Yale University Press, 1964), complete transcript, subtitled *The Unexpurgated Edition,* Oxford University Press, 1988.

The Calms of Capricorn (unfinished), transcription by Donald Gallup, Yale University Library, 1981, edited with additions by Gallup, Ticknor & Fields, 1982.

Eugene O'Neill: The Unfinished Plays (previously unpublished, incomplete works from 1940s; contains *The Visit of Malatesta, The Last Conquest,* and *Blind Alley Guy*), edited and annotated by Virginia Floyd, Ungar, 1988.

The Unknown O'Neill (includes the previously unpublished plays *The Personal Equation, Marco's Millions* [eight-act version], and *The Ancient Mariner,* with prose and poetry), edited by Travis Bogard, Yale University Press, 1988.

Eugene O'Neill: Complete Plays (includes the previously unpublished plays *Bread and Butter, Now I Ask You,* and *Shell Shock*), Library of America, 1988.

OTHER

(Author of introduction) Benjamine DeCasseres, *Anathema!,* Gotham, 1928.

(With Ralph Sanborn and Barrett H. Clark) *A Bibliography of the Works of Eugene O'Neill, Together With the Collected Poems of Eugene O'Neill,* Random House, 1931.

Inscriptions: Eugene O'Neill to Carlotta Monterey O'Neill, privately printed, 1960.

Poems, 1912-1944, edited by Donald Gallup, Yale University Library, 1979, revised, Ticknor & Fields, 1980.

Work Diary, 1924-1943, edited by Donald Gallup, Yale University Library, 1981.

Eugene O'Neill at Work: Newly Released Ideas for Plays (notebooks), edited and annotated by Virginia Floyd, Ungar, 1981.

"The Theatre We Worked For": The Letters of Eugene O'Neill to Kenneth Macgowan, edited by Jackson R. Bryer, Yale University Press, 1982.

"Love, Admiration, and Respect": The O'Neill-Commins Correspondence, edited by Dorothy Commins, Duke University Press, 1986.

"As Ever, Gene": The Letters of Eugene O'Neill to George Jean Nathan, Farleigh Dickinson University Press, 1987.

Selected Letters of Eugene O'Neill, edited by Travis Bogard and Jackson R. Bryer, Yale University Press, 1988.

Contributor to periodicals, including *Seven Arts* and *New York Times.* Associate editor and contributor to *American Spectator,* beginning in 1932.

MEDIA ADAPTATIONS: Anna Christie was adapted for a film of the same title, 1923, and for a film of the same title, starring Greta Garbo, 1930; *Strange Interlude* was adapted for a film of the same title, starring Clark Gable, MGM, 1932; *The Emperor Jones* was adapted for a film of the same title, starring Paul Robeson, United Artists, 1933; *Ah, Wilderness!* was adapted for a film of the same title, starring Lionel Barrymore, MGM, 1935, and for the film *Summer Holiday,* starring Mickey Rooney, MGM, 1948; *Bound East for Cardiff, The Moon of the Caribbees, In the Zone,* and *The Long Voyage Home* were adapted for the film *The Long Voyage Home,* directed by John Ford and starring John Wayne, United Artists, 1940; *The Hairy Ape* was adapted for a film of the same title, starring William Bendix and Susan Heyward, 1944; *Mourning Becomes Electra* was adapted for a film of the same title, starring Raymond Massey, Rosalind Russell, and Michael Redgrave, RKO, 1947; *Desire Under the Elms* was adapted for a film of the same title, starring Sophia Loren, Tony Perkins, and Burl Ives, Paramount, 1958; *Long Day's Journey Into Night* was adapted for a film of the same title, directed by Sidney Lumet and starring Ralph Richardson, Jason Robards, Katharine Hepburn, and Dean Stockwell, Embassy, 1962; *The Iceman Cometh* was adapted for a film of the same title, directed by John Frankenheimer and starring Lee Marvin and Fredric March, 1973.

WORK IN PROGRESS: An multi-play cycle spanning American history, tentatively titled "A Tale of Possessors Self-Dispossessed," was to include *A Touch of the Poet, More Stately Mansions, The Calms of Capricorn,* and perhaps as many as eight additional plays. A cycle of one-acts, "By Way of Obit," was to include *Hughie* and further works.

SIDELIGHTS: "I want to be an artist or nothing," wrote aspiring playwright Eugene O'Neill at the age of twenty-five. He pursued his goal relentlessly, and when he died forty years later he had written more than fifty plays, won the Nobel and several Pulitzer prizes, and earned his place as the first American dramatist of lasting, international stature. His work culminated with *The Iceman Cometh* and *Long Day's Journey Into Night,* two of the most powerful portraits of despair ever created for the stage. Despite such accomplishments O'Neill's reputation has always been mixed. The playwright, wrote Mary McCarthy in *Partisan Review,* has not "the slightest ear for the word, the sentence, the speech." "[He] is no thinker," wrote director Eric Bentley in *Kenyon Review.* "Look at the fruits of his thinking; his comparatively thoughtless plays are better." As biographer Frederic Carpenter observed, however, O'Neill's primary goal was not to be an intellectual playwright but an emotional one. "Our emotions are a better guide than our thoughts," Carpenter quoted him. "They are the deep undercurrent whereas our thoughts are often only the . . . surface reactions." Rarely successful as a poet or philosopher, he still excelled at conveying the anguish of being alive. O'Neill, wrote a *Time* reviewer, "[could] seize a blase Broadway crowd and wring it dry, half from fatigue, half from an emotional buffeting that no other American playwright ever inflicted on an audience. [He] could do what only a major artist can do: make his public share in the life of his private demons."

Until his mid-twenties O'Neill wrote little, but he encountered a great deal of pain that informed his later work. His torments began with his family, displayed as the Tyrone clan in *Long Day's Journey Into Night.* So painful and personal was this work that O'Neill would not allow it to be made public until after he was dead—preferably, not for decades after. O'Neill's father, James, rose from poverty to become one of nineteenth-century America's most popular actors. Obsessed with financial security, he toured the country for years performing *The Count of Monte Cristo,* a crowd-pleasing melodrama of betrayal, suffering, revenge, and triumph. Critics bemoaned the waste of his artistic talent, and, too late, he came to agree. As a young man James wed Mary Ellen Quinlan, known as Mary Tyrone in *Long Day's Journey* and as Ella during her lifetime. Born to wealth and educated in Catholic convent schools, Ella was ill prepared to marry an itinerant actor and became terribly isolated, shunned by women in conventional society and uneasy with free-wheeling show people. While recovering from Eugene's birth she became addicted to morphine and withdrew yet further. O'Neill's older brother Jamie was named for their father. Pampered as a child, Jamie became utterly irresponsible, fixated on his mother, and unable to accept any other women but prostitutes. With his father's influence he gained minor acting roles, but heavy drinking often ruined his performances. Surrounded by disappointment, O'Neill acquired what might be termed a "tragic sense of life": that people are doomed to suffer intensely, mocked by dreams they cannot attain. "None of us can help the things life has done to us," says Mary Tyrone. "They're done before you realize it, and . . . they make you do other things until at last everything comes between you and what you'd like to be, and you've lost your true self forever."

The young O'Neill shared his parents' transient way of life as he shuttled between hotels, looked to a maid as his second mother, and attended boarding schools. He noticed Ella's distractedness and feared she was going insane, but he did not learn of her addiction until he was fourteen. That year when the family gathered at their only real "home," a summer house in New London, Connecticut, Ella ran out of morphine and tried to drown herself. O'Neill promptly renounced his Catholic faith, since his mother's devotions had failed her. From then on, observers suggest, he considered himself an emotional outcast, seeking replacements for the mother and the God who had disappointed him. In *Long Day's Journey* O'Neill appears as "Edmund," actually the name of his brother who died in infancy. "It was a great mistake my being born a man, I would have been much more successful as a sea gull or a fish," Edmund says. "As it is, I will always be a stranger who never feels at home, . . . who must always be a little in love with death." O'Neill began to flout his parents' proprieties, as Jamie taught him about drinking, prostitutes, and iconoclastic writers. He soon discovered Friedrich Nietzsche, a German philosopher who said Christianity was in decline and offered a new faith based on confidence in one's inner resources. The West, Nietzsche suggested, believed too one-sidedly in rational thought, and he praised Dionysus, ancient Greek god of wine, as the patron of emotional release and spiritual awareness. O'Neill also valued the pessimism of Sweden's August Strindberg, whose plays mix love and hate as couples are joined in sexual desire and then battle each other for domination. For O'Neill, wrote biographer Louis Sheaffer, such plays were "pages from his own family history."

Meanwhile O'Neill's personal life brought him a full measure of unhappiness. After flunking out of Princeton University he eloped with Kathleen Jenkins, one of the few "respectable" young women he knew. Overwhelmed by marriage, he refused to live with his wife and their infant son, Eugene Jr. O'Neill's father found him work in an office, in the theater, and in a Central American gold-mining expedition, but O'Neill proved unenthusiastic until his father agreed to pay his passage on a tramp freighter. Enlisted to help the sailors, O'Neill found he enjoyed

the work and the companionship; moreover, observers suggest, the sea became like a new god to him, its vastness offering the promise that he could transcend his own existence. Ashore O'Neill continued to disintegrate. He identified morbidly with poor and rootless men, and after living in poverty in Buenos Aires he shipped back to New York City and moved into a wretched boardinghouse and barroom named "Jimmy-the-Priest's" for its poker-faced owner. "At Jimmy-the-Priest's," he later recalled, "I learned . . . not to sit in judgment on people." To receive a divorce under New York law, he arranged with his wife that he should be caught with a prostitute by her attorney. He then attempted suicide, surviving to find that he had tuberculosis.

Sent to a sanitarium to recover from his illness, O'Neill reassessed his life and decided to become a playwright. In 1914 he published his first one-act plays—once again using money from his father. O'Neill's apprentice works are generally mediocre and melodramatic, but as Travis Bogard observed in *Contour in Time,* they display basic themes that would dominate his later writings. Characters are manipulated by forces beyond their control; families are racked by conflict; those who betray their true nature are destroyed. Of particular note is *Bound East for Cardiff,* a play whose plausibility, focus, philosophical undercurrents, and careful use of emotion give it genuine power. The play unfolds aboard the S.S. *Glencairn,* where sailors watch over a dying shipmate. As the men converse they realize how the sea has bound them together and influenced their lives. The play succeeds despite its minimal plot, underscoring that O'Neill could build effective works entirely around the psychological interactions of his characters. The philosophical issues arise naturally from the setting. *Bound East for Cardiff* is not only the first proof of O'Neill's skill as a dramatist: it is also one of the first successes in realistic American drama.

But O'Neill often refused to work from his strengths—his ambitions outstripped his talent. He developed an experimenter's fascination with theatrical techniques and a wide-ranging imagination that often seemed unable to develop an idea slowly, plausibly, and completely. O'Neill's earliest mistake, Bogard contended, was to study play writing at Harvard University, where professor George Baker taught students how to craft saleable work for the commercial theater. O'Neill accepted Baker's opinion that *Bound East for Cardiff* was "not a play at all," apparently because it lacked the familiar plot devices of a conventional drama. Ignoring his natural flair for heartfelt emotion, O'Neill tried a new series of plays that would be more "impersonal," as Baker wished. The results, according to Bogard, are abhorrently shallow and mechanical: the worst is probably *Now I Ask You,* a drawing-room comedy that mocked the author's interest in Nietzsche. O'Neill's talent revived when he returned to the bars of New York, where he now often drank with the young intellectuals of Greenwich Village. His friends included Marxist writer John Reed and Reed's wife Louise Bryant, an advocate of free love with whom he had an affair. As with the sailors and drifters he knew, O'Neill seemed less interested in the Villagers' politics than in their quests for personal fulfillment. He particularly liked Terry Carlin, an old anarchist whose search for personal freedom had ended in quiet resignation. In the summer of 1916 the two men visited Provincetown, Massachusetts, where Carlin introduced O'Neill to the Provincetown Players, a group of theater enthusiasts from the Village who hoped to create an audience for innovative American drama. They were anxious for produceable scripts, and soon their summer theater—a shack on a Provincetown wharf—premiered *Bound East for Cardiff.* O'Neill had found his first appreciative audience, and when the

Players returned to New York for the winter they awaited more of his work.

With greater self-assurance O'Neill returned to themes he had explored before he met Baker. Seemingly driven by his own pain, he continued to fill his plays with unhappy marriages, madness, and death; but, surprisingly, his most effective early works were "Dionysian" evocations of the mysterious power of the sea and of human dreams. Three such plays—*In the Zone, The Long Voyage Home,* and *The Moon of the Caribbees*—once more involve sailors of the *Glencairn.* In *Caribbees,* the author's long-time favorite, the ship anchors off a Caribbean port while music wafts from shore. The sailors smuggle women and liquor aboard and engage in an orgy of mindless pleasure and brawling. The only unhappy man is pining for a lost girlfriend and refuses to participate. Like most of O'Neill's early works, the *Glencairn* plays were simple one-acts, ideally suited to a small company like the Provincetown Players. His success brought larger ambitions, and in 1918 he completed *Beyond the Horizon,* a full-length tragedy in which two brothers destroy themselves by ignoring their dreams. Robert Mayo, a young poet with wanderlust, decides to marry and tend the family farm; as a result his brother Andrew, who hoped to be a farmer, must work at sea. In the end Andrew is embittered and Robert welcomes his own untimely death, hoping to find poetry and transcendence beyond the grave. O'Neill waited two years to open the work on Broadway, achieving national fame and his first Pulitzer when it appeared in 1920. James O'Neill saw the work shortly before he died, and his approval helped to reconcile father and son.

O'Neill's lyrical realism peaked with *Anna Christie,* a 1921 romance that was one of his most popular plays. The title character, who falls into a life of prostitution on land, is redeemed by becoming a sailor's wife. Her fate confounds her immigrant father, a sailor who sent her inland to protect her from "dat old davil sea." O'Neill, Sheaffer observed, was disturbed to see his play become "a happy-ever-after which I did not intend." "Anna forced herself on me," the author wrote. "As she is the only one who knows exactly what she wants, she would get it." Thereafter O'Neill ceased to celebrate the dreamers of everyday life. Instead, observed Bogard, he embraced the new American doctrine of "Art Theatre," which questioned not only the light entertainment of James O'Neill's day but also a half-century of realism as perfected by dramatists in Europe. Seeking truths that lay beneath everyday reality, Art Theatre encouraged playwrights to compose philosophical works and to explore unusual techniques of presenting plays. Thus preoccupied, writers sometimes failed to communicate effectively with their audience. O'Neill's new obsessiveness even seemed to affect his marriage to writer Agnes Boulton. Agnes, who met O'Neill in a Village bar, was surprised to see him withdraw from the world in favor of his work. He looked to her for an all-encompassing love that she could not give—particularly after the births of their children, Shane and Oona.

Two of O'Neill's early "Art Theatre" plays were highly successful—a mixed blessing, Bogard notes, that encouraged his later excess. *The Emperor Jones* (1920) is a nightmarish monologue loosely inspired by the author's experience in the Central American jungle. Brutus Jones, a strong-willed black American laborer, takes control of a Caribbean island by exploiting the inhabitants' fear of magic and spirits. When his subjects revolt he escapes to the jungle, but he is overcome with terror and has a series of hallucinations—culminating in the appearance of a crocodile god—that make him easy prey for the rebels. The play was a huge success for the Provincetown troupe and offered the first major dramatic role for black actors on the white-dominated stage. In a similar vein, *The Hairy Ape* (1922) shows the emotional collapse of a workingman who is fiercely proud of his ability to shovel coal for a steamship's engines. Derided by a prim woman passenger, he rages at society for making him feel freakish. He tries to express his despair to both rich churchgoers and poor revolutionaries, then becomes wholly irrational and is crushed to death when he seeks the friendship of a gorilla at the zoo. Both plays convey emotional chaos through an atmosphere of unreality—the churchgoers, for instance, behave like automatons—but both are also based on real people whom O'Neill met during his wayfaring days. Even when O'Neill made broad statements about the human condition, he needed a realistic context to be most effective: "paradoxically," wrote Sheaffer, "he could soar only if he kept his feet on the ground."

Soon O'Neill's experiments were defeated by the scope of his own ambition: like Nietzsche, he wanted to resolve the world's religious unrest by finding a new faith. "The playwright today must dig at the roots of the sickness of today . . . the death of the Old God and the failure of science and materialism to give any satisfying new One," he wrote to drama critic George Nathan. "Anyone trying to do big work nowadays must have this big subject behind all the little subjects of his plays." In a series of grandiose, almost unproduceable works—including *Welded* (1924), *The Fountain* (1925), *The Great God Brown* (1926), *Lazarus Laughed* (1927), *Dynamo* (1929), and *Days Without End* (1934)—O'Neill portrayed various spiritual quests. In *Dynamo,* the alienated son of a minister embraces the false god of modern science, symbolized by an electrical power plant; in *Lazarus Laughed,* the biblical Lazarus arises from the dead to proclaim his freedom from the fear of mortality. Inspired by Art Theatre, O'Neill slighted realistic characterization in favor of his ideas. For dramatic power he used theatrical devices: a power-plant set for *Dynamo,* a booming laugh and crowds of followers for Lazarus, and an elevated poetic diction that he was ill-equipped to sustain. Repeatedly the plays failed even when the ideas were interesting. In *Welded,* for instance, playwright Michael Cape enacts the dilemma of O'Neill's second marriage—Cape wants a total spiritual union with his wife, while she fears for her individuality. "*Welded* is a finely conceived but over-intellectualized study, not a well-rounded three-dimensional drama about human beings," said biographer Barrett Clark. "It is the skeleton of a possibly fine play." Eventually O'Neill saw that Art Theatre had not served him well. "No more sets or theatrical devices as anything but unimportant background," he told Kenneth Macgowan. "Hereafter I will write plays primarily as literature to be read—and the more simply they read, the better they will act."

O'Neill's most successful work had continued to come from his forays into realism. *Strange Interlude* (1928), like *The Emperor Jones* and *The Hairy Ape,* combines artistic experiment with social reality. The play's dialogue is punctuated with "interludisms"—asides during which the characters describe their thoughts. This technique, O'Neill realized, was ideal for portraying the self-conscious intellectuals he had known in Greenwich Village. The play centers on Nina Leeds, modeled on the free-loving Louise Bryant. Nina searches narcissistically for the perfect man, and since he does not exist, she surrounds herself with men—a rich husband, an ambitious lover, a fatherly confidant, a son—each of whom gives her partial fulfillment. Eventually most of her men forsake her, and she realizes that life consists of quiet disappointment. As Carpenter observed, O'Neill's artistic vision had grown more pessimistic since the days of *Anna Christie,* and he now wrote of dreams gone wrong. *Strange Interlude* was an astonishing nine acts long, designed to rival the intricacy of a novel. When the play debuted on Broadway—complete with a dinner break—it was a massive success, partly because of the sheer novelty of its psychological revelations.

"Interludisms," O'Neill decided, were not a likely basis for more plays; historical drama, by contrast, became a lasting source of inspiration. As Bogard suggested, a period setting gave some much-needed structure to O'Neill's imaginings. *Desire Under the Elms* (1924) reveals the passions beneath the calm surface of a nineteenth-century New England farm family. "God's hard, not easy!" cries old patriarch Ephraim Cabot, toughened by years of labor. Meanwhile his passionate new wife has an affair with her adult stepson; in the shocking finale, she kills the illicit offspring of the affair, then goes hand-in-hand with her lover to prison. *Desire Under the Elms* was decried on moral grounds, but scandal only increased its popularity. Joseph Wood Krutch praised the play without trying to discover a redeeming social message. "The meaning and unity of [O'Neill's] work," he wrote in *Nation,* "lies not in any controlling intellectual idea and certainly not in a 'message,' but merely in the fact that each play is an experience of extraordinary intensity." In his next historical drama, *Mourning Becomes Electra* (1931), O'Neill consciously sought the intensity of ancient Greek tragedy. He adapted the "Oresteia" trilogy of Aeschylus—a tale of passion, murder, and divine retribution which, he observed, suggests "all the deep hidden relationships in the family." For O'Neill, the psychology of family life, not the ancient gods, determines each character's fate. When General Ezra Mannon returns to his New England home after the Civil War, he is killed by his adulterous wife Christine. Their daughter Lavinia ("Electra" in the old Greek version) thirsts for revenge and, with reluctant help from her brother Orin, she drives Christine to suicide. Brother and sister then make a futile effort to find peace in the dream-world of the South Seas. Soon they return to New England, where Orin kills himself and Lavinia confronts the ugly Mannon heritage by shutting herself inside the family homestead. When *Mourning Becomes Electra* debuted on Broadway in 1931, noted Carpenter, it garnered better reviews than any previous O'Neill work; nevertheless, the play closed fairly quickly and was seldom revived. "The very logical perfection of its artistic design," he explained, "may constitute its greatest fault": the characters are so relentlessly grim that they may lose the sympathy of the audience.

By the early 1930s O'Neill had written many plays about troubled families and spiritual quests. Biographers generally agree that his inspiration was autobiographical: he wished to deal with his "private demons" by using his life experience to make broad statements about human nature. Often his efforts proved lacking because he was unable to find a proper way to express his concerns. If O'Neill wrote too coldly in such plays as *Welded* and *Mourning Becomes Electra,* in other works he was probably too close to his subject. In 1920 he released *Exorcism,* a thinly veiled account of his suicide attempt, then withdrew the play and destroyed the scripts. He followed with *All God's Chillun Got Wings* (1924), a symbolic account of his parents' marriage that shows a black man ("Jim") and a white woman ("Ella") who struggle to love each other despite their differences. Unfortunately O'Neill could not dramatize the pain of the relationship without resorting to melodrama and reduced both characters to unconvincing madness. Finally, from 1932 to 1943, he wrote several openly autobiographical plays that are considered his finest work. As director Robert Brustein observed in *The Theatre of Revolt,* the author "had to write badly in order to write well."

Success gave O'Neill the leisure to write as he wished. *Strange Interlude* made him wealthy, and he used his money to leave Agnes and marry Carlotta Monterey, an actress well suited to the role of "great man's wife." As strong-willed as her husband, she both manipulated him and tended to his emotional needs; she also helped to fence off the outside world and allow O'Neill to withdraw deeply into himself. One morning in 1932, as he was mired in writing the philosophical drama *Days Without End,* he awoke with the idea for a nostalgic comedy loosely based on his youth in New London. Within a month he completed *Ah, Wilderness!,* a play which, he said, shows "the way I would have *liked* my boyhood to have been." The main character is Richard Miller, a good-natured seventeen-year-old who prompts a minor scandal by quoting "decadent" poetry to his girlfriend. Chastised by adults, he "rebels" by visiting a bar and a prostitute with a heart of gold. When he comes home drunk, his alcoholic Uncle Sid (Jamie) gently sees him to bed. Here images of O'Neill's tormented early years are transformed into figures of benevolence. Richard's father, for instance, is not based on the unhappy James O'Neill but on Fred Latimer, a hearty New London newspaper editor who shepherded the young O'Neill through a brief stint as a reporter. "It is as if," Carpenter observed, "the man who wrote the play were also watching over his characters to see that they did not follow his own dangerous path." *Ah, Wilderness!,* wrote Brustein, "prefigures [O'Neill's] transformation into an objective dramatic artist": only a mature writer, in full control of his material, could turn painful memories into a comedy with a life of its own.

Though O'Neill lived for twenty years after *Ah, Wilderness!* debuted in 1933, it was the last successful premiere he would see. Both his pessimism and his philosophizing were unsuited to the America of the Great Depression and World War II, when audiences craved dramas of social activism or positive statements about the national character. After *Days Without End* failed in 1934 he withdrew from the theater, more concerned with writing plays than seeing them produced. When he received the Nobel Prize in 1936, some found him unworthy, including *Saturday Review* critic Bernard De Voto. "What does he tell us, what does he show us, that we did not know before?" De Voto wrote. "Nowhere do we encounter the finality or the reconciliation of great art, nowhere is any fragment of human life remade for us in understanding." O'Neill's first new effort was "The Cycle," a projected cycle of eleven historical dramas called "A Tale of Possessors Self-Dispossessed." The saga would span American history, showing the gradual corruption of the country's idealism by greed. By 1939, after years of preparation, O'Neill was close to completing only one play, *A Touch of the Poet.* Frustrated and bored, he largely abandoned the Cycle in favor of his autobiographical dramas, beginning with *The Iceman Cometh.*

Set in a dingy New York barroom, *Iceman* centers on a group of steady drinkers like those O'Neill knew in his youth. Barman Harry Hope is based on a Villager who spent much of his life secluded in lodgings upstairs from his saloon. The patrons include Larry Slade, whose eloquent pessimism recalls that of failed anarchist Terry Carlin. Each of the regulars comforts himself with a hopeless "pipe dream": a politician awaits his public, a black man awaits interracial brotherhood, and so on. Into their world comes traveling salesman Theodore Hickman ("Hickey"), a besotted old friend who has suddenly become bright-eyed and energetic. With a salesman's skill and a preacher's zeal, Hickey convinces his friends to abandon their delusions in the name of truth. Having thus made them miserable, he proves himself to be the most deluded of all. In one of the most famous monologues in American drama, Hickey explains that he has shed his own delusion—guilt—by killing his wife, whose patient suffering made him feel guilty. He is immediately arrested, after which the patrons resume their drinking and dreaming, having decided that Hickey is insane. "All the old truisms of morality and philosophy seem suddenly to crumble," as Carpenter observed: if even the bringer of "truth" is a madman, what is left to believe in? "To hell with the truth!" says Larry Slade. "The lie of a pipe dream is what gives life to the whole misbegotten mad lot of us, drunk or sober." *The Iceman Cometh* has attracted more interest among literary critics than any other of O'Neill's works. Completed in 1940, it anticipated by a decade the flowering of existentialism, a philosophy holding that humanity must create its own sense of purpose in a godless and chaotic universe. By abjuring philosophy in favor of his own concrete experience, O'Neill had at last created an intellectual masterpiece. The seeming nihilism of *Iceman*, Bogard speculated, may have inspired O'Neill to write *Hughie*, a more hopeful one-act on a similar theme. In the lobby of a cheap New York hotel, Erie Smith tells the new night clerk about his predecessor—Hughie—who enjoyed Erie's posturing tales about the world of high-stakes gambling. The clerk tries to ignore Erie but finally relents. A sympathetic ear on a lonely night, O'Neill seems to suggest, is the only hope one person can offer another.

Next O'Neill turned to *Long Day's Journey Into Night*, the play he seems to have spent his life preparing to write. Night after night, according to Carlotta, he would leave his work tearful and exhausted. Abandoning his old experiments, O'Neill in *Long Day's Journey* observes the classic unities of time, place, and action, evoking years of misery in the events of a single day. The play is set in his family's New London summer house in 1912, just before he went to the sanitarium and became a playwright. As day begins the Tyrones try to be kind to each other, but ugly memories repeatedly emerge and inspire intensifying rounds of soul-searching, recrimination, and apology. The audience can hope that young Edmund may escape the family's despair, but the others are clearly trapped: James Tyrone Sr. by fear of poverty and regret for his wasted talent; Jamie by decadence and self-hatred; Mary by morphine and memories of her innocent girlhood. Finally that night the men watch helplessly as Mary appears in a drug-induced stupor, dragging her old wedding gown and recalling her lost youth. The Tyrones "become larger than their own small lives," wrote John Chapman in the *New York Daily News*. "They become humanity, looking for something but not knowing exactly what it is looking for." He declared: "This is O'Neill's most beautiful play. . . . And it is one of the great dramas of any time."

In contrast with Edmund's youthfulness, Jamie is the jaded villain of *Long Day's Journey Into Night*. "Kid. . . . Be on your guard," Jamie says, confessing that he introduced Edmund to alcohol and prostitutes out of a resentful urge to destroy him. Perhaps wishing to show more compassion for Jamie, who drank himself to death when their mother died, O'Neill wrote an epilogue to *Long Day's Journey* titled *A Moon for the Misbegotten*. The play is set in 1923, as an exhausted, middle-aged Jamie meets a hulking Irish-American farm girl named Josie Hogan. To compensate for her ugliness Josie claims vast sexual experience, but as an old fraud Jamie understands her lies at once. The two spend a chaste night discussing their sorrows and regrets. After Jamie leaves, Josie pronounces a sad blessing: "May you have your wish and die in your sleep soon, Jim, darling. May you rest forever in forgiveness and peace." Though criticized for an excess of sentiment, *A Moon for the Misbegotten* moved even the skeptical Mary McCarthy, who wrote in the *New York Times Book Review* that "this play exacts homage for its mythic powers, for the element of transcendence jutting up in it like a great wooden Trojan horse." As O'Neill composed *Misbegotten* he struggled against an increasing tremor in his hands. By the time he completed the play in 1943, his hands were virtually useless,

and he refused to dictate any new work to others. Having come to terms with his family, he wrote no more.

O'Neill's last years were as painful as anything he had known in his youth or created for the stage. Writing, biographers speculate, was a crucial emotional outlet for him, and once deprived of it he lost the will to live. He disowned two children: Oona had married Charlie Chaplin, an actor as old as her father, and Shane had become an aimless heroin addict. Meanwhile Eugene Jr. was unable to fulfill his early intellectual promise and committed suicide. Ill health compelled the O'Neills to sell their isolated California home in 1944; thereafter, to stay close to hospitals, they often lived in the sort of urban apartments O'Neill had hated ever since his father's days as a traveling actor. While living in New York in the mid-1940s O'Neill helped with rehearsals for *The Iceman Cometh* and *A Moon for the Misbegotten*, but both plays, in keeping with his fears, met with indifference from the general public. When *Misbegotten* failed during out-of-town tryouts he withdrew all his new work from further consideration, publishing *Misbegotten* only because he needed money. Carlotta, possibly concerned that O'Neill was losing interest in her, further isolated him from social contact, but he made few protests. The couple moved briefly to a home on the Massachusetts shore where they quarreled frequently. One winter night an ambulance was summoned to remove O'Neill, who had been found in the snow without a coat on, his leg broken. Some contend that he went to drown himself and fell on a rock. Temporarily estranged, the pair began legal proceedings against each other, but they soon reconciled and moved to O'Neill's last home, a Boston apartment where he stayed in seclusion. When he died in 1953, he seemed a figure from the distant theatrical past.

But O'Neill's reputation rapidly revived, virtually giving him a new career, as John Gassner observed. In 1956 director Jose Quintero, actor Jason Robards, and other newcomers staged an acclaimed Off-Broadway revival of *The Iceman Cometh*. To a new audience familiar with existentialism, the play seemed contemporary and important. Carlotta was so impressed that she had young Quintero direct the American premiere of *Long Day's Journey Into Night* the same year. The play garnered O'Neill's fourth Pulitzer and confirmed his status as America's greatest playwright. In his last plays, admirers declared, O'Neill had transcended stylistic weakness through the strength of his battered humanism. "He had the writer's one indispensable gift," wrote Joseph Wood Krutch in the *New York Times Book Review*. "He 'communicated'—the situation, the characters, and above all the depth of his concern with them." Krutch concluded: "An O'Neill who wrote better would have been a better O'Neill. But he will last longer and mean more than many who can, in the ordinary sense, write rings around him."

BIOGRAPHICAL/CRITICAL SOURCES:

BOOKS

Alexander, Doris, *The Tempering of Eugene O'Neill*, Harcourt, 1962.

Atkinson, Jennifer McCabe, *Eugene O'Neill: A Descriptive Bibliography*, University of Pittsburgh Press, 1974.

Authors in the News, Volume 1, Gale, 1976.

Berlin, Normand, *Eugene O'Neill*, Grove Press, 1982.

Bloom, Harold, editor, *Eugene O'Neill: Modern Critical Views*, Chelsea House, 1987.

Bogard, Travis, *Contour in Time: The Plays of Eugene O'Neill*, revised edition, Oxford University Press, 1987.

Bowen, Crosswell, *The Curse of the Misbegotten: A Tale of the House of O'Neill*, McGraw Hill, 1959.

Brustein, Robert, *The Theatre of Revolt: An Approach to the Modern Drama,* Little, Brown, 1964.

Cargill, Oscar, N. B. Fagin, and W. J. Fisher, editors, *O'Neill and His Plays: Four Decades of Criticism,* New York University Press, 1961.

Carpenter, Frederic I., *Eugene O'Neill,* revised edition, Twayne, 1979.

Clark, Barrett H., *Eugene O'Neill: The Man and His Plays,* Dover, 1947.

Dictionary of Literary Biography, Volume 7: *Twentieth-Century American Dramatists,* Gale, 1981.

Engel, Edwin A., *The Haunted Heroes of Eugene O'Neill,* Harvard University Press, 1953.

Falk, Doris V., *Eugene O'Neill and the Tragic Tension: An Interpretive Study of the Plays,* Rutgers University Press, 1958.

Floyd, Virginia, *The Plays of Eugene O'Neill: A New Assessment,* Ungar, 1984.

Frenz, Horst, *Eugene O'Neill,* Ungar, 1971.

Gassner, John, editor, *O'Neill: A Collection of Critical Essays,* Prentice Hall, 1964.

Gelb, Arthur and Barbara Gelb, *O'Neill,* Harper, 1962.

Griffin, Ernest G., *Eugene O'Neill: A Collection of Criticism,* McGraw Hill, 1976.

Miller, Jordan Y., editor, *Playwright's Progress: O'Neill and the Critics,* Scott Foresman, 1965.

Miller, Jordan Y., *Eugene O'Neill and the American Critic: A Summary and Bibliographical Checklist,* Archon Books, 1973.

O'Neill, Eugene, *Long Day's Journey Into Night,* Yale University Press, 1956.

Raleigh, John Henry, *The Plays of Eugene O'Neill,* Southern Illinois University Press, 1965.

Raleigh, John Henry, editor, *The Iceman Cometh: A Collection of Critical Essays,* Prentice Hall, 1968.

Ranald, Margaret Loftus, *The Eugene O'Neill Companion,* Greenwood Press, 1984.

Reaver, J. Russell, editor, *An O'Neill Concordance,* Gale, 1969.

Sheaffer, Louis, *O'Neill: Son and Playwright,* Little, Brown, 1968.

Sheaffer, Louis, *O'Neill: Son and Artist,* Little, Brown, 1973.

Tiusanen, Timo, *O'Neill's Scenic Images,* Princeton University Press, 1968.

Tornqvist, Egil, *A Drama of Souls: Studies in O'Neill's Supernaturalistic Technique,* Yale University Press, 1969.

Twentieth-Century Literary Criticism, Gale, Volume 1, 1978, Volume 6, 1982, Volume 27, 1988.

PERIODICALS

Kenyon Review, July, 1952.
Nation, November 26, 1924.
New York Daily News, November 8, 1956.
New York Times Book Review, August 31, 1952, September 22, 1957.
Partisan Review, November, 1946.
Saturday Review, November 21, 1936.
Time, November 15, 1968.

OBITUARIES:

PERIODICALS

Newsweek, December 7, 1953.
New York Times, November 28, 1953.
Time, December 7, 1953.

—*Sketch by Thomas Kozikowski*

ONETTI, Juan Carlos 1909-

PERSONAL: Born July 1, 1909, in Montevideo, Uruguay; son of Carlos and Honoria (Borges) Onetti; married Dolly Muhr, November, 1955; children: Jorge, Isabel.

ADDRESSES: Home—Gonzalo Ramfrez 1497, Montevideo, Uruguay.

CAREER: Writer of novels and short stories. Worked as editor for Reuter Agency in Montevideo, Uruguay, 1942-43, and in Buenos Aires, Argentina, 1943-46; manager of advertising firm in Montevideo, 1955-57; director of municipal libraries in Montevideo, beginning 1957.

AWARDS, HONORS: National Literature Prize of Uruguay, 1963; Ibera-American Award from William Faulkner Foundation, 1963; Casa de las Americas Prize, 1965; Italian-Latin American Institute Prize, 1972.

WRITINGS:

El pozo (also see below), Signo, 1939, enlarged and revised edition bound with *Seguido de origen de un novelista y de una generacion literaria* by Angel Rama, Editorial Alfa, 1965, 2nd revised edition, Arca, 1973.

Tierra de nadie (novel), Editorial Losada, 1941, reprinted, Editorial Seix Barral, 1979.

Para esta noche, Editorial Poseidon, 1943.

La vida breve (novel), Editorial Sudamericana, 1950, reprinted, Edhasa, 1980, translation by Hortense Carpentier published as *A Brief Life,* Grossman, 1976.

Un sueno realizado y otros cuentos (also see below), Numero, 1951.

Los adioses (novel; also see below), Sur, 1954, reprinted, Bruguera, 1981.

Una tumba sin nombre, Marcha, 1959, published as *Para una tumba sin nombre* (also see below), Arca, 1959, reprinted, Editorial Seix Barral, 1982.

La cara de la desgracia (novella; also see below), Editorial Alfa, 1960.

El astillero (novel), Compania General Fabirl Editora, 1961, reprinted, Catedra, 1983, translation by Rachel Caffyn published as *The Shipyard,* Scribner, 1968.

El infierno tan temido, Editorial Asir, 1962.

Tan triste como ella (also see below), Editorial Alfa, 1963, reprinted, Lumen, 1982.

Juntacadaveres (novel), Editorial Alfa, 1964, revised edition, Arca, 1973.

Jacob y el otro (also see below) [and] *Un sueno realizado y otros cuentos,* Ediciones de la Banda Oriental, 1965.

Cuentos completos, Centro Editor de America Latina, 1967, revised edition, Corregido, 1974.

Tres novelas (contains *La cara de la desgracia, Tan triste como ella,* and *Jacob y el otro*), Editorial Alfa, 1967.

Novelas cortas completas (contains *El pozo, Los adioses, La cara de la desgracia, Tan triste como ella,* and *Para una tumba sin nombre*), Monte Avila Editores, 1968.

La novia robada y otros cuentos (short stories including "La novia robada"; also see below), Centro Editor de America Latina, 1968, reprinted, Siglo Veintiuno Editores, 1983.

Los rostros del amor, Centro Editor de America Latina, 1968.

Obras completas, Aguilar, 1970.

La muerte y la nina (also see below), Corregidor, 1973.

Onetti (collection of articles and interviews), Troisi y Vaccaro, 1974.

Tiempo de abrazar y los cuentos de 1933 a 1950 (short stories), Arca, 1974.

(With Joaquin Torres-Garcia and others) *Testamento artistico,* Biblioteca de Marcha, 1974.
Requiem por Faulkner, Arca, 1975.
Tan triste como ella y otros cuentos (short stories), Lumen, 1976.
El pozo [and] *Para una tumba sin nombre,* Editorial Calicanto/ Arca, 1977, 2nd edition, Seix Barral, 1980.
Dejemos hablar al viento, Bruguera Alfaguara, 1979.
La muerte y la nina [and] *La novia robada,* Bruguera, 1980.
Cuentos secretos, Biblioteca de Marcha, 1986.
Presencia y otros cuentos, Almarabu, 1986.
Cuando entonces, Editorial Sudamericana, 1988.

Editor of *Marcha,* 1939-42, and *Vea y Lea,* 1946-55.

SIDELIGHTS: Although considered by a number of critics to be among the finest and most innovative novelists in South America, Juan Carlos Onetti is generally not well known outside of his homeland of Latin America. While praised and admired for their richness in imagination, creativity, and unique vision, Onetti's writings have also been described as fundamentally ambiguous, quite fragmentated, and often complex. As M. Ian Adams confirms in his book, *Three Authors of Alienation: Bombal, Onetti, Carpentier,* "Complexity and ambiguity are the major characteristics of Onetti's novels."

"Onetti's art is a strange aggregate of cultural characteristics and personal circumstances (some elusive, many contradictory and a few truly illuminating) none of which would really endear his writings to us were it not for the extraordinary nature of his style," states Luys A. Diez in *Nation.* Diez continues, "His prose has a genuinely hypnotic force, digressive and meandering, but quite without apparent *longueurs,* studded with linguistic quirks and poetic flights, economically terse and playfully serious; he teases the reader with alternate scenarios for a given situation to concentrate afterwards on a passing thought or a seemingly unimportant gesture."

Only two of Onetti's books have been translated into English. *The Shipyard,* though written after *A Brief Life,* was published first. It tells the story of Larsen, a shipyard worker who seeks to improve his social status by attaching himself to the shipyard owner's daughter. But he is unable to see that the society he aspires to has disintegrated, and the novel ends with his death. "Larsen moves through Onetti's pages as a figure virtually doomed to disaster," declares James Nelson Goodsell in the *Christian Science Monitor.* "Onetti is trying to evoke a picture of futility and hopelessness—a task which he performs very ably. . . . Onetti's purpose is to keep the reader absorbed, but to remain enigmatic. He succeeds admirably. [He] is a skillful writer whose prose is absorbing and demanding." And David Gallagher endorses *The Shipyard* in the *New York Times Book Review* as "a book which, for all its portentousness, few Latin American novelists have equaled."

The plot of *A Brief Life* is much more fantastical than that of *The Shipyard.* It concerns Juan Carlos Brausen, referred to as a "sort of Argentine Walter Mitty" by Emir Rodriguez Monegal in the *New York Times Book Review.* Brausen escapes from his many burdens by retreating from reality into a series of complex and often bizarre fantasy adventures. In *Review 75,* Hugo J. Verani calls *A Brief Life* "one of the richest and most complex novelistic expressions in Spanish-American fiction."

In a *Newsweek* review, Margo Jefferson writes that *A Brief Life* "is a virtuosic blend and balance of opposites: melodrama and meditation, eroticism and austerity, naturalism and artifice. . . . In Onetti's hands, the novel becomes an excursion into a labyrinth where the real and the imagined are mirror im-

ages. . . . Behind his sleight of hand is a melancholy irony—for all our efforts to escape a single life, we remain prisoners of a pattern, 'condemned to a soul, to a manner of being.' "

Because of its unique unfolding of plot, *A Brief Life* has received inevitable comparisons with the work of William Faulkner. Luys A. Diez notes in the *Nation* that "much of Faulkner's rich, dark sap flows through the meandering narrative." Diez also contends that "Onetti's novelistic magic, like Faulkner's, requires a certain amount of perseverance on the reader's part." And Monegal remarks that "in *A Brief Life,* Onetti's love for Faulknerian narrative is already evident."

Several critics have expressed their high regard for Onetti's skillful use of experimental narration. Zunilda Gertel writes in *Review 75* that "Onetti's narrative does not postulate an ideology or an intellectual analysis of the ontological. Instead, the existential projection of the 'I' is shown as a revelation within the signs imposed on him by literary tradition considered as ritual, not as reconciliation." Also writing in *Review 75,* John Deredita claims that *A Brief Life* "exhaustively tests the power of fantasy and fictional imagination as a counter to the flow of time. . . ." And Verani concludes that "Onetti does not emphasis the mimetic quality of narrative. The aim of his fiction is not to reflect an existent reality, a factual order, but . . . to create an essentially fabulated reality invested with mythic significance."

BIOGRAPHICAL/CRITICAL SOURCES:

BOOKS

Adams, M. Ian, *Three Authors of Alienation: Bombal, Onetti, Carpentier,* University of Texas Press, 1975.
Contemporary Literary Criticism, Gale, Volume 7, 1977, Volume 10, 1979.
Harss, Luis and Barbara Dohmann, *Into the Mainstream: Conversations with Latin-American Writers,* Harper, 1967.
Kadir, Djelal, *Juan Carlos Onetti,* Twayne, 1977.
Milian-Silveira, Maria C., *El primer Onetti y sus contextos,* Editorial Pliegos, 1986.

PERIODICALS

Christian Science Monitor, October 8, 1968.
Hispania 71, May, 1988.
Library Journal, March 1, 1976.
Nation, April 3, 1976.
Newsweek, February 16, 1976.
New Yorker, February 9, 1976.
New York Times Book Review, June 16, 1968, January 11, 1976.
Review 75, winter, 1975.
Saturday Review, January 24, 1976.

*　　*　　*

OPPENHEIMER, J(ulius) Robert   1904-1967

PERSONAL: Born April 22, 1904, in New York, N.Y.; died of throat cancer, February 18, 1967, in Princeton, N.J.; son of Julius (a textile importer) and Ella (an artist; maiden name, Friedman) Oppenheimer; married Katherine Puening Harrison, November 1, 1940; children: Peter, Katherine (Toni). *Education:* Harvard University, B.A. (summa cum laude), 1925; attended Cambridge University, 1925-26; University of Goettingen, Ph.D., 1927; postdoctoral study at Harvard University and California Institute of Technology, 1927-28, and University of Leiden and Polytechnic Academy, Zurich, 1928-29.

CAREER: University of California, Berkeley, and California Institute of Technology, Pasadena, 1929-47, began as associate professor, became professor of physics; director of U.S. atomic energy laboratory, Los Alamos, N.M., 1942-45; chairman of general advisory committee of United Nations Atomic Energy Commission, 1946-52; Princeton University, Princeton, N.J., director of Institute for Advanced Study, 1947-66.

MEMBER: American Physical Society (president, 1948), National Academy of Arts and Sciences, American Philosophical Society, American Academy of Arts and Sciences (fellow), Royal Society (fellow), Royal Danish Academy, Brazilian Academy, Japanese Academy (honorary member), Phi Beta Kappa.

AWARDS, HONORS: U.S. Medal for Merit, 1946; French Legion of Honor, 1958; Enrico Fermi Award from Atomic Energy Commission, 1963.

WRITINGS:

Science and the Common Understanding, Simon & Schuster, 1954.
The Open Mind, Simon & Schuster, 1955.
The Flying Trapeze: Three Crises for Physicists, Harper, 1969.
Lectures on Electrodynamics, Gordon & Breach, 1970.
Robert Oppenheimer: Letters and Recollections, edited by Alice Kimball Smith and Charles Weiner, Harvard University Press, 1980.
Uncommon Sense, edited by N. Metropolis and others, Birkhauser, 1984.
Atom and Void: Essays on Science and Community, Princeton University Press, 1989.

SIDELIGHTS: Often referred to as the "father of the atomic bomb," J. Robert Oppenheimer was instrumental in changing the nature of international defense and warfare. Though praised by the U.S. Government for his pioneering work in atomic research and honored for creating the weapon that helped hasten the end of World War II, Oppenheimer was later accused of disloyalty and declared a security risk by the country.

Oppenheimer first demonstrated his intellectual prowess as a student at New York's Ethical Culture School. Although adept in all his studies, he had a particular interest in science. At age eleven he was the only non-adult member of the New York Mineralogical Club, and at twelve he wrote and presented his first professional paper to his fellow mineralogists. Continuing his education, Oppenheimer studied physics at Harvard, where he completed his undergraduate courses in three years, graduating summa cum laude.

From Harvard he ventured to Cambridge University in England to study atomic theory with leading physicists of the day such as Joseph Thomson and Ernest Rutherford. His year at Cambridge, however, was a restless one. Assigned by Thomson to make metallic films used in testing the penetrating power of electrons, Oppenheimer found he was unskilled at the task. He became discouraged with his dream of being one of the first Americans to make a mark in the field of atomic research, a field dominated by the Germans, French, Danish, and English. He regained his self-confidence later when he transferred to Germany to begin his doctoral work at Goettingen, the world's principal center for atomic research. He received his doctorate in 1927 after submitting a thesis on quantum theory.

Returning to the United States, Oppenheimer took concurrent teaching positions at the California Institute of Technology (Caltech) and the University of California, Berkeley, where he developed the first school of theoretical physics in the United States. As a teacher, Oppenheimer was both feared and revered by his students. Though they recognized his genius, many of his students could not keep up with Oppenheimer's rapid pace in the classroom. Some students took their complaints to Berkeley's physics department chief, Raymond Birge, who also heard a complaint from Oppenheimer. Oppenheimer lamented that the class was not progressing because he had been moving *too slowly.* In Peter Michelmore's *The Swift Years: The Robert Oppenheimer Story,* Birge is quoted as saying, "It was my first intimation not only of the speed with which Oppenheimer's mind worked, but also of his complete failure at the time to realize how slowly, comparatively speaking, the minds of most other people worked."

Facing similar conflicts at Caltech, Oppenheimer once discovered that among the twenty-six students in his classroom, only one had registered for the class; the others were onlookers. After the first lecture, the sole registered student approached Oppenheimer and told him he could not survive Oppenheimer's pace. Oppenheimer replied: "Nonsense. You'll get good grades whatever happens. You have to; you're my only student." Three years later the student, Carl Anderson, won the Nobel Prize for discovering the positron, a positively charged particle that constitutes the antiparticle of the electron.

Though physics preoccupied him, Oppenheimer had a keen interest in languages, literature, and art. He cared little for world affairs, however, until the mid-1930s, when he heard of the Fascist movement in Italy and the abuse of Jews in Nazi Germany. Oppenheimer became interested in Communism, reading leftist newspapers, attending Communist rallies, and becoming friends with several party members. He later dismissed the party as ineffective, though he maintained the friendships he had formed for the rest of his life.

In 1943 Oppenheimer became part of a secret team of scientists and engineers who met in Los Alamos, New Mexico, to build the first atomic bomb. As the bomb neared completion, several of the men involved, especially Oppenheimer and Niels Bohr, began to contemplate the moral and political implications of creating a weapon powerful enough to level cities and kill tens of thousands of people. Hoping that the development and fear of such a destructive force would inspire world peace, Oppenheimer went to Washington and suggested that Russia, France, and China be informed of the bomb and help govern the weapon's use. He also expressed the concerted opinion of those at Los Alamos and elsewhere that the bomb should be detonated in order for its power and danger to be fully realized; they felt that only atrocities, not words, could demonstrate the bomb's potential.

On July 16, 1945, "Fat Man," one of two types of fission bombs manufactured at Los Alamos, was tested in the New Mexico desert. Oppenheimer said that as he watched the explosion, two lines from the Hindu *Bhagavad Gita* came to his mind. The first: "The radiance of a thousand suns." The second: "I am become death, The Shatterer of Worlds." The bomb, indeed, proved immensely destructive in actual use, destroying the Japanese cities of Hiroshima and Nagasaki in August, 1945. The world had never seen such a cataclysm, but those responsible for building the bomb were already planning a weapon of far greater power—the hydrogen bomb.

Oppenheimer and many of his colleagues were hesitant about making an H-bomb, arguing that further creation of nuclear weaponry would deter world peace. Their feelings were expressed by Oppenheimer, who upon accepting a presidential scroll for their work at Los Alamos predicted: "If atomic bombs are to be added as new weapons to the arsenals of a warring world, or to the arsenals of nations preparing for war, then the time will come when mankind will curse the name of Los Alamos and of Hiroshima." He later warned: "When we are blind to the evil in ourselves, we dehumanize ourselves, and we deprive ourselves not only of our destiny, but of any possibility of dealing with the evil in others."

In 1946 Oppenheimer wrote the Acheson-Lilienthal Report, calling for worldwide control of nuclear energy, and the Baruch Plan, which sought to control atomic power with supervision from the United Nations. The Soviet Union rejected both proposals. Oppenheimer continued his fight for atomic regulation, however, as chairman of the General Advisory Committee of the United Nation's Atomic Energy Commission (AEC) while concurrently serving as director of Princeton's Institute for Advanced Study.

When the Soviet Union tested its first atomic bomb in 1949, Oppenheimer and the AEC proposed development of smaller nuclear weapons rather than massive air-delivered nuclear bombs. Because of his hesitancy to recommend U.S. participation in a full-scale arms race, some began to question his loyalty to the United States. William Liscum Borden, an Air Force security officer, accused Oppenheimer of having been a Soviet espionage agent for the previous fourteen years, basing his accusation on Oppenheimer's doubts about the H-bomb and his relationships with Communists at Berkeley. Despite the fact that Oppenheimer's friendships with leftists were known of even before he was approved for the Los Alamos team, President Eisenhower, who had promised in his campaign to rid the government of subversives, revoked Oppenheimer's security clearance. Lewis Strauss of the AEC gave Oppenheimer the option of either resigning from the commission or requesting a hearing. Oppenheimer did the latter. The three-member hearing board decided that Oppenheimer's opposition to the building of the hydrogen bomb was not grounds for dismissal from the AEC, but ruled that he was a security risk. His continuous associations with people of questionable political affiliation, contended the board, demonstrated a "serious disregard for the requirement of the security system."

Some observers have felt that Oppenheimer was a victim of McCarthyism and the Cold War. "What the accusations that Oppenheimer was a Communist agent, a subversive opponent of the H-bomb, and a security risk really meant," proposed Christopher Lehmann-Haupt of the *New York Times*, "was that history had caught up with him. Conduct that was acceptable in the urgency of the hot war was not longer permissible in the stringency of the cold war. So in 1954 he was found 'guilty' of what he had been judged innocent when the A.E.C. gave him clearance in 1947." Geoffrey Woolf of *Newsweek* also noted the wave of McCarthyism that swept the United States at the time of Oppenheimer's hearing. Woolf then declared, "The security hearing was an act of consummate ingratitude toward a dedicated national servant, and it deprived the United States of a supremely valuable national resource."

Although his case was never reopened, Oppenheimer was somewhat vindicated in 1963 when he received the Enrico Fermi Award, the highest honor given by the AEC, to recognize scientific achievement and engineering in the development of atomic energy. Despite this acknowledgement, he was never again privy to secret, government information, and he returned to Princeton to resume his work.

Many of Oppenheimer' personal notes, letters, and thoughts are documented in *Robert Oppenheimer: Letters and Recollections.* One of his speeches in the book, "Secrecy and Science," explains his steadfast opinion that scientific achievements should be shared worldwide. It reads in part: "Secrecy strikes at the very root of what science is, and what it is for. It is not possible to be a scientist unless you believe that it is good to learn. It is not good to be a scientist, and it is not possible, unless you think that it is of the highest value to share your knowledge, to share it with anyone who is interested. It is not possible to be a scientist unless you believe that the knowledge of the world, and the power which this gives, is a thing of intrinsic value to humanity, and that you are using it to help in the spread of knowledge, and are willing to take the consequences."

In a *New York Times Book Review* critique of the collection of Oppenheimer's writings, Ronald Clark commented that "not even the Atomic Energy Commission doubted Oppenheimer's loyalty. Its members seem, rather, to have asked themselves whether he was the sort of man to wield the influence he did wield; or, perhaps more accurately, they asked whether he was, to use an English phrase, the sort of man to go tiger-shooting with. They decided 'no,' being helped in their decision by the weapons Oppenheimer too frequently left around for his enemies to pick up. These letters suggest that the answer should have been 'yes.' "

BIOGRAPHICAL/CRITICAL SOURCES:

BOOKS

Michelmore, Peter, *The Swift Years: The Robert Oppenheimer Story,* Dodd, 1969.
Rabi, I. I., Robert Serber, Victor F. Weisskopf, Abraham Pais, and Glenn T. Seaborg, *Oppenheimer,* Scribner, 1969.
Stern, Philip M., *The Oppenheimer Case: Security on Trial,* Harper, 1969.
Wilson, Thomas W., Jr., *The Great Weapons Heresy,* Houghton, 1970.

PERIODICALS

Nation, April 27, 1970.
New Republic, November 22, 1969.
Newsweek, November 10, 1969.
New York Review of Books, July 2, 1970.
New York Times, November 3, 1969.
New York Times Book Review, January 4, 1970.
Observer, June 13, 1971.
Washington Post, April 17, 1970.

OBITUARIES:

PERIODICALS

New York Times, February 19, 1967.
Time, February 24, 1967.
Times (London), February 20, 1967.

*   *   *

ORTEGA y GASSET, Jose   1883-1955

PERSONAL: Born May 9, 1883, in Madrid, Spain; died October 18, 1955, in Madrid; son of Jose Ortega y Munilla (a journalist and novelist) and Maria Dolores Gasset Chinchilla; married Rosa Spottorno y Topete, April 7, 1910; children: Miguel German, Jose, Soledad. *Education:* University of Madrid, licenciatura en filosofia y letras (M.A.), 1902, Ph.D., 1904; postgraduate study at universities of Leipzig, 1905, Berlin, 1906, and Marburg, 1906-07, 1911.

ADDRESSES: Home—Monte Esguinza 28, Madrid, Spain.

CAREER: Escuela Superior del Magisterio (normal school), Madrid, Spain, professor of psychology, logic, and ethics, 1908-10; University of Madrid, Madrid, professor of metaphysics, 1910-29 (resigned in protest against Spanish government), and 1930-36; representative of Province of Leon to Constitutional Parliament of Second Spanish Republic, 1931. Writer in exile in France, Netherlands, Argentina, and Portugal, beginning in 1936; University of San Marcos, Lima, Peru, professor of philosophy, beginning in 1941. Founder of Instituto de Humanidades (Madrid), 1948. Founder or co-founder of several publications, including *Faro* (title means "Beacon"); *Europa,* 1911; monthly journal *Espana* (organ of League for Political Education), c. 1914; newspaper *El sol,* 1917; founder and co-editor of literary monthly *La Revista de Occidente,* 1923-35.

MEMBER: League for Political Education (founder, c. 1914), Group at the Service of the Republic (co-founder, 1931), Pen Club (president).

AWARDS, HONORS: Scholarship from Spanish government for postgraduate study in Germany, 1906; elected to Royal Academy of Moral and Political Sciences, 1914; Gold Medal of City of Madrid, 1936; named to Bavarian Academy of Fine Arts, 1949; honorary doctorates from universities of Marburg and Glasgow, 1951.

WRITINGS:

Meditaciones del Quijote, Residencia de Estudiantes (Madrid), 1914, reprinted, Revista de Occidente en Alianza (Madrid), 1981, translation by Evelyn Rugg and Diego Marin published as *Meditations on Quixote,* Norton, 1961.

El espectador (title means "The Spectator"), Volumes 1 and 2, Renacimiento (Madrid), 1916, 1917, Volume 3, Calpe (Madrid), 1921, Volumes 4-8, Revista de Occidente, 1925-34, reprinted as one volume, Biblioteca Nueva (Madrid), 1950.

Personas, obras, cosas (title means "Persons, Works, Things"), Renacimiento, 1916, published as *Mocedades* (title means "Juvenilia"), Revista de Occidente, 1973.

Espana invertebrada (title means "Invertebrate Spain"), Calpe, c. 1921, reprinted, Revista de Occidente en Alianza, 1981, translation of selections by Mildred Adams published by Norton, 1937.

El tema de nuestro tiempo, Calpe, 1923, reprinted, Revista de Occidente en Alianza, 1981, translation by James Cleugh published as *The Modern Theme,* Harper, 1931.

La deshumanizacion del arte e ideas de la novela, Revista de Occidente, 1925, reprinted, Revista de Occidente en Alianza, 1984, translation by Helene Weyl published as *The Dehumanization of Art: Ideas on the Novel,* Princeton University Press, 1948.

La rebelion de las masas, Revista de Occidente, 1930, reprinted, Revista de Occidente en Alianza, 1981, translation by J. R. Carey published as *The Revolt of the Masses,* 1932, translation by Anthony Kerrigan published under the same title, with foreword by Saul Bellow, University of Notre Dame Press, 1986.

La mision de la universidad, Revista de Occidente, 1930, reprinted, Revista de Occidente en Alianza, 1982, translation by Howard Lee Nostrand published as *Mission of the University,* Norton, 1946.

La redencion de las provincias y de la decencia nacional (title means "The Redemption of the Provinces and National Decency"), Revista de Occidente, 1931, reprinted, Revista de Occidente Alianza, 1966.

Rectificacion de la Republica (title means "Rectification of the Republic"), Revista de Occidente, 1931.

Obras (title means "Works"), Espasa-Calpe (Madrid), 1932, reprinted with additions, 1943.

Pidiendo un Goethe desde dentro, Revista de Occidente, 1932, title essay translated by Willard R. Trask as "In Search of Goethe from Within" and included in *The Dehumanization of Art and Other Essays on Art, Culture, and Literature,* Princeton University Press, 1968.

Notas (title means "Notes"), Espasa-Calpe, 1938, reprinted with introduction by Julian Marias, Anaya (Salamanca), 1967.

Ensimismamiento y alteracion [and] *Meditacion de la tecnica* (title means "Self Contemplation and Alteration" [and] "Meditation on the Technical"), Espasa-Calpe Argentina, 1939, translation of *Ensimismamiento y alteracion* by Willard R. Trask published as "The Self and the Other" in *Partisan Review,* July, 1952, translation of *Meditacion de la tecnica* by W. Atkinson published as "Man the Technician" in *History as a System and Other Essays toward a Philosophy of History,* Greenwood Press, 1961 (also see below).

Ideas y creencias (title means "Ideas and Beliefs"), Espasa-Calpe Argentina, 1940, reprinted, Revista de Occidente, 1942.

El libro de las misiones (title means "The Book of Missions"), Espasa-Calpe Argentina, 1940, reprinted, Espasa-Calpe (Madrid), 1959.

Historia como sistema [and] *Concordia y libertad,* Revista de Occidente, 1941; *Historia como sistema* reprinted in *Historia como sistema y otros ensayos de filosofia,* Revista de Occidente en Aliaza, 1981; translation of *Historia como sistema* by W. Atkinson published in *History as a System and Other Essays toward a Philosophy of History,* Greenwood Press, 1961; translation of *Concordia y libertad* by Helene Wehl published as *Concord and Liberty,* Norton, 1946.

Castilla y sus castillos (title means "Castile and Her Castles"), Afrodisio Aguado (Madrid), 1942, reprinted, 1952.

Teoria de Andalucia (title means "Theory of Andalucia"), Revista de Occidente, 1942.

Man and Crisis, Revista de Occidente, 1942, translation by Mildred Adams published as *Man and Crisis,* Norton, 1958, published as *Entorno a Galileo* (title means "Concerning Galileo"), Revista de Occidente en Alianza, 1982.

Two Prologues, Revista de Occidente, 1944, first prologue reprinted in *Veinte anos de caza mayor* (title means "Twenty Years of Big-Game Hunting") by Eduardo Figueroa, Plus Altra (Madrid), 1948, translation of *Veinte anos* by Howard B. Wescott published as *Meditations on Hunting,* Scribner, 1986.

Obras completas, Revista de Occidente, volumes 1 and 2, 1946, volumes 3-6, 1947, Volume 7, 1961, volumes 8 and 9, 1962, volumes 10 and 11, 1969; volumes 1-11 reprinted, and Volume 12 published, by Alianza Editorial, Revista de Occidente, 1983.

Sobre la aventura y la caza (title means "On Adventure and the Hunt"), Afrodisio Aguado, 1949.

Papeles sobre Velazquez y Goya, Revista de Occidente, 1950, translation by Alexis Brown published in *Velazquez, Goya, and the Dehumanization of Art,* Studio Vista (London), 1972.

Estudios sobre el amor (title means "Studies on Love"), Aguilar (Madrid), 1950, reprinted, Revista de Occidente en Alianza, 1981, translation by Toby Talbot published in *On Love: Aspects of a Single Theme,* Meridian Books, 1960.

El hombre y la gente, Revista de Occidente, 1957, reprinted, Revista de Occidente an Alianza, 1981, translation by Willard R. Trask published as *Man and People,* Norton, 1963.

Meditacion de un pueblo joven (title means "Meditation on a Young Nation"), Revista de Occidente, 1958.

La idea de principio en Leibniz y la evolucion de la teoria deductiva, Revista de Occidente, 1958, reprinted by Revista de

Occidente en Alianza, 1981, translation by Mildred Adams published as *The Idea of Principle in Leibniz and the Evolution of Deductive Theory,* Norton, 1971.

Prologo para alemanes (title means "Prologue for Germans"), Taurus (Madrid), 1958, reprinted, 1974, translation by Philip W. Silver published in *Phenomenology and Art,* Norton, 1975.

Idea del teatro (title means "Idea of Theatre"), Revista de Occidente, 1958, reprinted in *Ideas del teatro y de la novela,* Alianza, 1982, translation of *Idea del teatro* by Philip W. Silver published in *Phenomenology and Art* (see above).

Kant, Hegel, Dilthey, Revista de Occidente, 1958, reprinted, 1973.

¿Que es filosofia?, Revista de Occidente, 1958, reprinted, Revista de Occidente en Alianza, 1982, translation by Mildred Adams published as *What Is Philosophy?,* Norton, 1960.

Apuntes sobre el pensamiento: su teurgia y su demiurgia (title means "Notes on Thinking: Its Creation of the World and Its Creation of God"), Revista de Occidente, 1959, reprinted, Revista de Occidente en Alianza, 1980, translation by Helene Weyl published in *Concord and Liberty* (see above).

Una interpretacion de la historia universal, Revista de Occidente, 1960, reprinted, Revista de Occidente en Alianza, 1980, translation by Mildred Adams published as *An Interpretation of Universal History,* Norton, 1973.

Meditacion de Europa (reprinted from *Obras completas,* Volume 9), Revista de Occidente, 1960.

Vives-Goethe, Revista de Occidente, 1961, reprinted, 1973.

Pasado y Porvenir para el hombre actual (title means "Past and Future for Man Today"; reprinted from *Obras completas,* Volume 9), Revista de Occidente, 1962, portions translated and published as "The Past and Future of Western Thought" in *Modern Age,* summer, 1958.

Mision del bibliotecario (y otros escritos afines) (title means "Mission of the Librarian [and Other Related Writings]"; reprinted from *Obras completas,* Volume 5), Revista de Occidente, 1962, portions translated by H. Muller and published as "Man Must Tame the Book" in *Wilson Library Bulletin,* 1936.

Unas lecciones de metafisica, Alianza, 1966, reprinted, Revista de Occidente en Alianza, translation by Mildred Adams published as *Some Lessons in Metaphysics,* Norton, 1969.

Origen de la filosofia, Revista de Occidente, 1967, reprinted, Revista de Occidente en Alianza, 1981, translation by Toby Talbot published as *Some Lessons in Metaphysics,* Norton, 1967.

La razon historia, Revista de Occidente, 1979, reprinted, Revista de Occidente en Alianza, 1983, translation by Philip W. Silver published as *Historical Reason,* Norton, 1984.

Investigaciones psicologicas, Revista de Occidente Alianza, 1982, translation by Jorge Garcia-Gomez published as *Psychological Investigations,* Norton, 1987.

¿Que es conocimiento? (title means "What Is Knowledge?"), Revista de Occidente en Alianza, 1984.

Contributor to numerous periodicals.

SIDELIGHTS: The significance of Jose Ortega y Gasset, whose world fame mainly stems from his controversial book *La rebelion de las masas* (*The Revolt of the Masses;* 1930) has always sparked debate. His most enthusiastic students believe that his philosophy is on a level "beyond which nothing has yet been achieved," as Julian Marias declares in *Ortega y Gasset,* while his critics see him as imprecise, inconsistent, literary rather than philosophical, and overly metaphorical in handling serious intellectual problems. Despite this critical split, Ortega y Gasset merits a place in history as both a major transitional figure between phenomenology and existentialism and as a key figure in Spanish culture. He aspired to elevate Spanish culture to match that of the rest of Western Europe, and in the first three decades of the twentieth century he indeed accomplished much toward achieving that goal.

During Ortega y Gasset's adolescence, Spain still reeled from losing its brief 1898 war with the United States. A group of writers, today known as the Generation of 1898, found that Spain's humiliation could be viewed as the symptom of a deeper national disease—demoralization—and that this sense of defeatism had actually preceded colonial defeat. As a young man Ortega y Gasset considered himself a member of the Generation of 1898, and he joined forces with such leading lights as Miguel de Unamuno and Antonio Machado in promoting the Europeanization of Spanish culture.

The Generation of 1898 was fortunate to have found a sympathizer in Ortega y Gasset. Breaking into print at an early age, he gave the group's writings ample publicity in his own articles, and he encouraged members to publish in the many magazines he founded to promote the moral and mental reform of Spanish society. Ortega y Gasset's writing style was so effective, his mode of presenting his ideas so attractive and persuasive, that, had he desired, he could have developed like his father into a brilliant journalist. Instead, in 1905 he decided to pursue postgraduate philosophy studies in Germany.

In his adolescence Ortega y Gasset had developed a passion for the works of German philosopher Friedrich Wilhelm Nietzsche, and he carried this enthusiasm with him to Germany when he went there at age twenty-two. At the University of Leipzig, where he was unable to secure admittance into classes of philology, he spent his days reading in the university library. He then went to Berlin, where he attended the public lectures of philosopher Georg Simmel. As a neo-Kantian, Simmel applied Immanuel Kant's philosophy—that knowledge is limited by perception—to an understanding of man and his relation to culture. Influenced by Nietzsche, Simmel enthralled Ortega y Gasset with his subtle ideas on life as a conflict between man—the creator of culture—and his own cultural products.

Late in 1906, Ortega y Gasset began studying at the University of Marburg under such Neo-Kantians as Hermann Cohen and Paul Natorp. From Cohen, Ortega y Gasset learned a sense of the drama associated with problems in philosophy along with the will to solve them with a system of disciplined ideas. Cohen based his own system on the discipline of modern physics, and he applied the logic of mathematics in solving philosophical problems. He believed that the mind could establish laws of conduct that would prove as valid for sciences of the spirit as Newton's laws are for the sciences of nature. Moreover, Cohen contended that the laws of nature and the laws of the spirit, when expressed in art, aroused a feeling for beauty, a sentiment valid as a law for all mankind. Cohen regarded individual life as an awareness and pursuit of the personal ideal, and he saw culture (logic, ethics, aesthetics) as the solution to the problem. But Ortega y Gasset, in considering culture, always returned to the problem of life, a self-conscious search for identity.

Through Natorp, a psychologist, Ortega y Gasset discovered the means of extending philosophy beyond neo-Kantian thought. Following the blueprint of Cohen, who intended to crown his own structure of ideas with psychology, Natorp built a two-part psychological system, one both descriptive and genetic. The first part described psychic experience; the second traced its causes.

After studying Natorp's ideas in 1912, Ortega y Gasset turned to the writings of one of Natorp's inspirations, Edmund Husserl, whose concept of psychic experience, particularly as explicated in *Logische Untersuchungen* (*Logical Investigations*), differed somewhat from Natorp's, and—as Julian Marias noted—provided the cornerstone for Ortega y Gasset's own philosophy. To the question, Who is the thinker of mathematical logic, the willer of logical ethics, the feeler of logical aesthetics?, Natorp responded, Spirit (or mind-in-general), thinking, willing, and feeling throughout history; and he added that psychology has the task of studying the mind-in-general. But Husserl held that the mind could be studied not only externally by psychology, but internally by phenomenology. Ortega y Gasset argued that what was real was the mind conceived as a natural object situated among other natural objects; toward these objects the mind constantly focused its attention, and from them it received endless stimuli. Thus Husserl's notion of the life-world was reflected in Ortega y Gasset's "I am myself and my circumstance," a statement that comprised both the first principle and summary of Ortega y Gasset's entire philosophy.

Ortega y Gasset reached this conclusion in 1914, the same year that he reconciled his enthusiasm for Germanic culture with his loyalty to native Spain. Inspired by the writings of Generation of 1898 leader Unamuno, Ortega y Gasset published *Meditaciones del Quijote* (*Meditations on Quixote*, 1914), which he intended as the first in a series of works noting universal values to be found in specific aspects of Spanish culture—Cervantes's view of life, the writings of Baroja and Azorin, and bullfighting, as examples. The book contained many philosophical insights, including the notion of human life as the frame of reference for all other realities; the idea of life as having nothing given to it except the problem of clarifying its own destiny; and the imperative to address this problem in view of concrete possibilities or circumstances.

Both Ortega y Gasset's conciliatory mood and the incomplete state of *Meditations* derived from his increased involvement in politics. In the fall of 1913 he founded a new political party, the League for Political Education, which he launched in a public lecture, "Vieja y nueva politica" ("Old and New Politics"). In his speech he claimed to live in a country of two Spains: Official Spain which was comprised of outworn institutions, the corrupt Parliament, the established political parties, the conservative press, and the ministries, and Vital Spain, which included the creative forces in the country, especially select minorities of intellectuals and the Spanish people. Old Spain, he declared, had crippled the country. New Spain, he added, might restore it. He attributed much of Spain's cultural deficiency to its lack of outstanding individuals and inspiring projects, and he defined a healthy society as one in which select minorities encourage the masses to willingly ignore their own private interests and enthusiastically collaborate. As the League's first priority Ortega y Gasset set the formation of an elite to educate the people in creative politics. But because he offered no concrete platform or program for the League, it dissolved in less than two years.

During the 1923 to 1930 military dictatorship of Miguel Primo de Rivera, Ortega y Gasset's intellectual creativity reached its peak. Unable to partake in politics, he wrote his most famous works. In 1925 he published a five-part series of articles titled "Hacia una antropologia filosofica" ("Toward a Philosophical Anthropology") in which he applied phenomenologist Max Scheler's idea of a basic science centered on man and his relationship to all other beings, and completed *Les deshumanizaci n del arte e ideas de la novela* (*The Dehumanization of Art*) which is respected by critics for its insights into the experimental—what

Ortega y Gasset called "dehumanizing"—art of the early twentieth century. During that same period of inspiration, he also borrowed from such thinkers as Martin Heidegger and Wilhelm Dilthey to further develop his own philosophy. The result was the explication of four basic principles, repeated in nearly every major work written by Ortega y Gasset after 1929: First, individual human life is the "root reality" to which all other realities must be referred and in which all others appear as in a framework; second, life is given to each human being as a problem to solve, as a "task" not finished beforehand, but needing to be done; third, life is a "decision" about what to do to be oneself; and fourth, life is a series of concrete possibilities from which to decide, and the possibilities, plural but not infinite in number, make up each individual's "circumstances."

The circumstances in which Ortega y Gasset unveiled his mature principles to the public represented a crowning moment of his life. This moment occurred in 1929, the year before the fall of the dictator Rivera, whose power diminished as a result of economic depression. When Rivera closed the University of Madrid, Ortega y Gasset protested by resigning as professor of metaphysics there, then rented a theater and sold tickets of admission to "What Is Philosophy?," the very course interrupted by the closure. In these lectures Ortega y Gasset expressed his four mature principles of human life and defined philosophy as universal knowledge, free of forejudgments. Because this knowledge relied on concepts, he saw philosophy as more akin to theology than to mysticism, which was unable to conceptualize union with God. He likened philosophy to sports—disciplined in accordance with internal rules requiring direct proof of every philosophical statement—and declared that life, with its four principles, is self-evident.

While teaching "What Is Philosophy?" Ortega y Gasset published parts of *The Revolt of the Masses* as separate articles. Like *¿Que es filosofia?* (*What Is Philosophy?*), a collection of the course lectures published in 1958, *The Revolt of the Masses* is a transitional work between anthropology and existentialism. Here Ortega y Gasset studied the character-type of the average European of his day. With every trait described, he passed judgment from the standpoint of his metaphysical principles of human life. Life was a task, a decision, and a repertory of possibilities, he declared, but the mass man was any person, whatever his social class, who performed no task and never innovated. His counter-type was the select individual, ever pioneering and perfectionistic.

The Revolt of the Masses is significant for its dire prophecies, made in the late 1920s, of what actually took place in the 1930s and 1940s. In retrospect, writes Jose Gaos in *Sobre Ortega y Gasset y otros trabajos de historia de las ideas en Espana y la America espanola,* "the prediction seems to have come true of the seriousness of the crisis, socialization, the reign of the masses—although in the face of facts like those represented by the *Duce* and the *Fuhrer,* there may be room for discussion about their susceptibility to direction from without, denied by Ortega y Gasset."

As if unmindful of his pessimism about the masses, Ortega y Gasset plunged back into politics after the fall of Primo de Rivera in January 1930. In February of 1931, Ortega y Gasset and writers Gregorio Maranon and Ramon Perez de Ayala founded the Group at the Service of the Republic, which resembled the earlier League for Political Education. The Group wanted Spain divided into ten large regions, each with its own local government, but all recognizing the sovereignty of the nation as a whole; it desired a strong central Parliament with as much authority as the executive to provide a system of checks and balances; it advocated a planned economy, designed to bring about agrarian reform; it supported a gradual but complete separation of Church and State; and it argued for a balanced budget as a first step to energetic public and private investment. On April 14, 1931, municipal elections in Madrid brought in the Second Spanish Republic, while voting out the monarchy. Surprised by the speed and peacefulness of the transition, Ortega y Gasset privately expressed uneasiness, though in his articles he hailed the simplicity with which the Republic had come into being.

Less than a year later, Ortega y Gasset's political aspirations ended as the result of an escalating disagreement. Minister of Labor Gabriel Maura questioned Ortega y Gasset's elitism, which was seen as incompatible with concern for the interests of workers. As recorded in his 1931 essay "Siguer los 'problemas concretas' " ("More on 'Concrete Problems' ") Ortega y Gasset merely responded with a sportive metaphor, suggesting that his service to the Republic was a form of aristocracy, which meant "fair play." In parliamentary debate over the emerging Constitution of the Republic, when his metaphorical style of speaking was attacked as false and affected, he defended its authenticity and claimed an unalienable right to practice, as he declared in *Rectificacion de la Republica* ("Rectification of the Republic"), "a poetic, philosophical, heart-felt, and merry politics." But Parliament was unresponsive to his wit and keen thought. As partisanship and extremism divided the Republic, Ortega y Gasset left politics in August 1932, and he dissolved the Group at the Service of the Republic the following October.

After leaving politics, Ortega y Gasset resumed his studies of Heidegger and Dilthey. History, Dilthey's favorite area of interest, dominated the last twenty years of Ortega y Gasset's thought. He attempted to make history a scientific discipline. Ortega y Gasset's justification for treating history as a science appeared in *Historia como sistema* (*History as a System;* 1941). Here Ortega y Gasset posed a historical problem, as always: humanity by the early twentieth century had lost confidence in natural science, once a replacement for religious faith. Now he wondered what life meant. Physics could not provide an answer; neither could any sciences that used its methods. Ortega y Gasset, following Dilthey, believed that the science of history could cure this crisis of faith, for history discovered the system of beliefs that guided man in deciding among possibilities for being himself—a process that was, after all, the task of life. For Ortega y Gasset, beliefs differed from mere ideas, or views of the world that man himself manipulated with full awareness. To understand the impact of subconscious beliefs on men's lives, it was only necessary to tell the story of their lives. Thus, Ortega y Gasset maintained, the science of history was the new science on which man must pin his faith. History told man what he was and clarified the meaning of his life. History could also guide his future: Once he learned the mistakes of the past, he would avoid them afterwards in the trial-and-error process that is living.

The year after publishing *History as a System,* Ortega y Gasset made an unpopular decision, one that prompted criticism from many Spaniards, for he fled Spain shortly after the outset of civil war there. Some critics, such as Pedro Cerezo Galan, feel that when Ortega y Gasset went into exile, he lost the power to speak as he had before. The books he wrote afterwards, declared Cerezo Galan in *La voluntad de aventura,* "lacked . . . the feel and breath of that circumstantial reality which blew like a clean wind throughout his best works."

From 1936 to 1945 Ortega y Gasset remained outside Spain. In France, the Netherlands, Argentina, and Portugal, he endured great hardships while desiring to write two long books, *Aurora de la razon historia* ("Dawn of Historical Reason") and *El hombre y la gente* (*Man and People,* 1957). In a prologue to *Ideas y creencias* ("Ideas and Beliefs"; 1940), he declared, "I have suffered misery, I have suffered long sicknesses of the kind in which death is breathing down your neck, and I should say that if I have not succumbed among so much commotion, it has been because the hope of finishing those two books has sustained me when nothing else would." Ortega y Gasset wrote merely a few pages of *The Dawn of Historical Reason,* mostly repeating ideas from *History as a System.* As for *Man and People,* in its final form was a lengthy course in sociology given in 1949 and 1950.

Far more revealing about Ortega y Gasset's life and times is *La idea de principio en Leibniz y la evolucion de la teoria deductiva* (*The Idea of Principle in Leibniz and the Evolution of Deductive Theory;* 1958), the book praised by Marias in *Ortega y Gasset* as the writer's best. The longest work he ever wrote, *The Idea of Principle in Leibniz* was left incomplete among his papers to be published after his death. Compared with its German sources—chiefly Husserl, Dilthey, and Heidegger—it is stimulating, often entertaining reading, filled with wordplay and jokes, and it shows Ortega y Gasset at his sharpest as an intellectual sportsman. Its theme is the history of the idea of principle. Ortega y Gasset began the work by translating into Spanish many notions from Heidegger's 1929 essay "Vom Weser des Grundes" ("On the Essence of Ground"), which explained how the philosophers Gottfried Wilhelm Leibniz, Kant, and Aristotle dealt with the idea of principle. Next Ortega y Gasset used his science of history to show that Aristotle, in handling principles, was inexact and "unprincipled," and he implied that Heidegger was similarly imprecise.

In *The Idea of Principle in Leibniz* Ortega y Gasset also objected to Heidegger's general tone, which he found too somber and anguished for philosophy. Among the Greeks, noted Ortega y Gasset, philosophy was a game of riddle-solving. Plato, for instance, often compared philosophy to sports and games. But Heidegger, when philosophizing about anguish and nothingness, seemed to make a sport of wallowing in despair, and his gloomy view of the world struck Ortega y Gasset as too narrow. "For that reason," wrote Ortega y Gasset in *The Idea of Principle in Leibniz,* "since my first writings, against the narrowness of a 'tragic sense of life' . . . I have counterposed a 'sportive and festive sense of existence,' which my readers—naturally!—read as a mere literary phrase."

Ortega y Gasset wanted to spend his final years in Madrid, the city of his birth and of his greatest triumphs, but on his return in 1945, according to Victor Ouimette in *Jose Ortega y Gasset,* he had to face "the hostility of the Church and the mistrust felt by the government of General Franco." He did extensive lecturing abroad in Germany and made appearances in Britain and Italy, with one visit, in addition, to the United States. Operated on for cancer on October 12, 1955, he died six days later. Controversy surrounded his death as it had so many aspects of his life. The Spanish press reported the visit to his home of the Jesuit Father Felix Garcia and the Archbishop of Saragossa. Had he converted to Catholicism at the last moment? Conservative factions contended that he had. But intimates of the philosopher, according to Guillermo Moron in *Historia politica de Jose Ortega y Gasset,* reported that he said, when the priests wanted to be admitted to confess him, "Let them allow me to die in peace."

BIOGRAPHICAL/CRITICAL SOURCES:

BOOKS

Abellan, Jose Luis, *Ortega y Gasset en la filosofia espanola: Ensayos de apreciacion,* Tecnos (Madrid), 1966.

Bayon, J., *Razon vital y dialectica en Ortega y Gasset,* Revista de Occidente, 1972.

Benitez, Jaime, *Political and Philosophical Theories of Jose Ortega y Gasset,* University of Chicago Press, 1939.

Brenan, Gerald, *The Spanish Labyrinth,* Cambridge University Press, 1960.

Cepeda Calzada, Pablo, *Las ideas politicas de Ortega y Gasset,* Alcala (Madrid), 1968.

Cerezo Galan, Pedro, *La voluntad de aventura: Aproximamiento critico al pensamiento de Ortega y Gasset,* Ariel (Barcelona), 1984.

Chamizo Dominguez, Pedro J., *Ortega y Gasset y la cultura espanola,* Cincel (Madrid), 1985.

Dilthey, Wilhelm, *Introduccion a las ciencias del espiritu,* translated by Julian Marias, 2nd edition, Revista de Occidente, 1966.

Duran, Manuel, editor and author of prologue, *Ortega y Gasset hoy,* Biblioteca Universitaria Veracruzana (Mexico), 1985.

Fernandez, Pelayo H., *La paradoja en Ortega y Gasset,* Jose Porrua Turanzas (Madrid), 1985.

Ferrater Mora, Jose, *Ortega y Gasset: An Outline of His Philosophy,* Yale University Press, 1963.

Gaete, Arturo, *El sistema maduro de Ortega y Gasset,* Compania General Fabril Editora (Buenos Aires), 1962.

Gaos, Jose, *Sobre Ortega y Gasset y otros trabajos de historia de las ideas en Espana y la America espanola,* Imprenta Universitaria (Mexico), 1957.

Garagorri, Paulino, *Introduccion a Ortega y Gasset,* Alianza (Madrid), 1970.

Garcia Astrada, Arturo, *El pensamiento de Ortega y Gasset,* Torquel (Buenos Aires), 1961.

Hanneman, Bruno, contributor, *Ortega y Gasset Centennial/Centenario Ortega y Gasset,* Jose Porrua Turanzas (Madrid), 1985.

Holmes, Oliver W., *Human Reality and the Social World: Ortega y Gasset's Philosophy of History,* University of Massachusetts Press, 1975.

Kern, Iso, *Husserl und Kant,* Nijhoff (The Hague), 1964.

L. Aranguren, Jose Luis, *La etica de Ortega y Gasset,* 2nd edition, Taurus (Madrid), 1959.

Lalcona, Javier F., *El idealismo politico de Ortega y Gasset,* Cuadernos para el Dialogo (Madrid), 1974.

Larrain Acuna, Hernan, *La genesis del pensamiento de Ortega y Gasset,* Compania General Fabril Editora (Buenos Aires), 1962.

Lopez Campillo, Evelyn, *La Revista de Occidente y la formacion de minorias, 1923-1936,* Taurus (Madrid), 1972.

Lopez-Morillas, Juan, contributor, *Intelectuales y espirituales,* Revista de Occidente (Madrid), 1961.

Marias, Julian, *El lugar del peligro; Una cuestion disputada en torno a Ortega y Gasset,* Taurus (Madrid), 1958.

Marias, Julian, *Ortega y Gasset,* 2 volumes, Alianza (Madrid), 1983.

Marrero, Domingo, *El centauro: Persona y pensamiento de Ortega y Gasset,* Imprenta Soltero (Puerto Rico), 1961.

Marrero, Vicente, *Ortega y Gasset, filosofo "mondain,"* Rialp (Madrid), 1961.

McClintock, Robert, *Man and His Circumstances: Ortega y Gasset as Educator,* Teachers College Press, 1971.

Menendez Pidal, Ramon, *La Espana del Cid,* Espasa-Calpe, 1967.

Molinuevo, Jose Luis, *El idealismo de Ortega y Gasset,* Narcea (Madrid), 1984.

Moron, Guillermo, *Historia politica de Jose Ortega y Gasset,* Ediciones Oasis (Mexico), 1960.

Moron Arroyo, Ciriaco, *El sistema de Ortega y Gasset,* Alcala (Madrid), 1968.

Niedermayer, Franz, *Jose Ortega y Gasset,* Colloquium Verlag (Berlin), 1959.

Orringer, Nelson R., *Ortega y Gasset y sus fuentes germanicas,* Gredos (Madrid), 1979.

Orringer, Nelson R., *Nuevas fuentes germanicas de ¿Que es filosofia? de Ortega y Gasset,* Consejo Superior de Investigaciones Cientificas (Madrid), 1984.

Ortega y Gasset, Jose, *Ideas y creencias,* Espasa-Calpe Argentina, 1940.

Ortega y Gasset, Jose, *The Idea of Principle in Leibniz and the Evolution of Deductive Theory,* Norton, 1971.

Ortega y Gasset, Jose, *The Modern Theme,* introduction by Jose Ferrater Mora, translated by James Cleugh, Harper, 1961.

Ortega y Gasset, Manuel, *Ninez y mocedad de Ortega y Gasset,* C.L.A.V.E. (Madrid), 1964.

Ouimette, Victor, *Jose Ortega y Gasset,* Twayne, 1982.

Paine, Stanley G., *The Spanish Revolution,* Norton, 1970.

Raley, Harold C., *Jose Ortega y Gasset: Philosopher of European Unity,* University of Alabama Press, 1971.

Rama, Carlos, *La crisis de la Espana del siglo XX,* Fondo de Cultura Economica (Mexico), 1960.

Rodriguez Huescar, Antonio, *Con Ortega y Gasset y otros escritos,* Taurus (Madrid), 1964.

Romero, Francisco, *Ortega y Gasset y el problema de la jefetura espiritual,* Losada (Buenos Aires), 1960.

Rukser, Udo, *Bibliographia de Ortega y Gasset,* Revista de Occidente (Madrid), 1971.

Salmeron, Fernando, *Las mocedades de Ortega y Gasset,* Colegio de Mexico, 1959.

Sanchez Villasenor, Jose, *Ortega y Gasset, Existentialist: A Critical Study of His Thought and His Sources,* translated by Joseph Small, Regnery, 1949.

Silver, Philip W., *Ortega y Gasset as Phenomenologist: The Genesis of "Meditations on Quixote,"* Columbia University Press, 1978.

Spiegelberg, Herbert, *The Phenomenological Movement: A Historical Introduction,* 2nd edition, 2 volumes, Nijhoff (The Hague), 1971.

Thomas, Hugh, *The Spanish Civil War,* Harper, 1961.

Twentieth-Century Literary Criticism, Volume 9, Gale, 1983.

Unamuno, Miguel de, *Obras completas,* 9 volumes, Escelicer (Madrid), 1966-71.

PERIODICALS

Aporia, number 3, 1981.

Azafea, number 1, 1985.

Comparative Criticism, number 6, 1984.

Cuadernos Salmantinos de Filosofia, number 8, 1981.

Cuenta y Razon, number 3, 1981.

Estudios, number 29, 2973.

Hispanic Review, number 47, 1979.

Journal of Aesthetics and Art Criticism, number 23, 1964.

Modern Language Notes, number 85, 1970, number 88, 1973, number 92, 1977.

Razon y Fe, June, 1941.

Revista de Occidente, number 140, 1974.

Romance Notes, number 17, 1976.

*   *   *

ORTON, Joe
See ORTON, John Kingsley

*   *   *

ORTON, John Kingsley   1933-1967
(Joe Orton)

PERSONAL: Born in 1933 in Leicester, England; murdered August 9, 1967. *Education:* Attended Royal Academy of Dramatic Art.

ADDRESSES: Home—London, England.

CAREER: Actor and playwright.

AWARDS, HONORS: London Critics Variety Award, 1964, for *Entertaining Mr. Sloane;* "Loot" was named best play of 1966 by *Evening Standard.*

WRITINGS:

PLAYS, UNDER NAME JOE ORTON

Entertaining Mr. Sloane (first produced in London at New Arts Theatre, May 6, 1964; produced on Broadway at Lyceum Theatre, October 12, 1965), Hamilton, 1964, Grove, 1965.
Crimes of Passion: The Ruffian on the Stair [and] *The Erpingham Camp* (both one-act plays; "The Ruffian on the Stair," first broadcast in London on BBC Radio, August 31, 1964; "The Erpingham Camp," first broadcast in London on Rediffusion Television, June 27, 1966; both produced in London at Royal Court Theatre, June 6, 1967; both produced in New York City at Astor Place Theatre, October 26, 1969), Methuen, 1967.
Loot (first produced in Cambridge, England, at Arts Theatre, February 1, 1965; produced on the West End at Jeannette Cochrane Theatre, September 27, 1966; produced on Broadway at Biltmore Theatre, March 18, 1968), Grove, 1967.
Funeral Games [and] *The Good and Faithful Servant* ("The Good and Faithful Servant," first produced in London at King's Head Theatre, March 17, 1967; "Funeral Games," produced with "The Ruffian on the Stair" in New York City at South Street Theatre, March 9, 1979), Methuen, 1970.
What the Butler Saw (first produced on the West End at Queen's Theatre, March 5, 1969; produced in New York City at McAlpin Rooftop Theatre, May 4, 1970), Samuel French, 1969.
The Complete Plays, Methuen, 1976, Grove, 1977.
Up Against It (unproduced screenplay; produced as a musical in New York City at Public Theatre, October, 1989), Methuen, 1979.

Also author of "Until She Screams," 1970, a sketch for Kenneth Tynan's *Oh! Calcutta!*

OTHER, UNDER NAME JOE ORTON

Head to Toe (novel), Blond, 1971.
The Orton Diaries, edited by John Lahr, Methuen, 1986.

SIDELIGHTS: While Joe Orton was being hailed by critics as the best modern writer of farce in English, audiences were walking out on performances of his plays. Orton was an iconoclast who dramatized the hypocrisy and perverseness of contemporary morality. As John Lahr wrote, "Orton's plays offend in order to instruct and heal. . . . [His] farces make an audience confront the schizophrenic patterns of their lives, rather than evade them." In this respect, he has been compared to Oscar Wilde, George Bernard Shaw, and Noel Coward.

The subject matter of Orton's plays is what viewers found offensive. For example, *Entertaining Mr. Sloane* is about a middle-aged brother and sister who protect their father's murderer because he is attractive and young and they want to sleep with him. In *Loot,* a mother's corpse is carefully guarded because also in the coffin is the plunder from a robbery. However, John Russell Taylor pointed out that "the key to Orton's dramatic world is to be found in the strange relationship between the happenings of his plays and the manner in which the characters speak of them." That is, while the occurrences on stage may be morally or conventionally outrageous, "the primness and propriety of what is said hardly ever breaks down."

Other critics have observed the same phenomenon. Keath Fraser noted Orton's knack for parodying "the manners which spring from an abyss between the characters' decorous language and their indecorous actions." Katharine J. Worth called this "the cool convention": the ability of style to keep feeling, or more particularly, violence and brutality, in its place. Harold Pinter described Orton's work as "brilliant and truly original. He has an instinctive grasp of construction."

That language is central to Orton's world view is confirmed by his imprisonment at one time for defacing library books. But language is central to his talent, too. Harold Clurman observed his ability to create dialogue "at once traditionally elegant and nasally obscene," and went on to say, "If you open your mouth in laughter at an Orton play, a spoonful of acid is dashed into it. His jokes are a preamble to murder."

Ironically, Orton himself was brutally murdered at the pinnacle of his career: he was thirty-four. As a result of his newly acquired success, Orton had been growing apart from Kenneth Halliwell, also a writer, with whom he had lived for fifteen years. Desperate, Halliwell killed Orton with a hammer, just as the character Pringle had put an end to his wife in Orton's own *Funeral Games,* noted Lahr. Then Halliwell took his own life with an overdose of nembutals. Lahr wrote: "Their deaths confirmed the vision of Orton's comedy, that reality is the ultimate outrage. Their epitaph was Orton's plays: a heritage of laughter created out of a lifetime's hunger for revenge."

BIOGRAPHICAL/CRITICAL SOURCES:

BOOKS

Contemporary Literary Criticism, Volume 4, Gale, 1975, Volume 13, 1980, Volume 43, 1987.
Dictionary of Literary Biography, Volume 13: *British Dramatists Since World War II,* Gale, 1982.
Joseph, F., editor, *Behind the Scenes,* Holt, 1971.
Lahr, John, *Astonish Me,* Viking, 1973.
Lahr, John, *Prick Up Your Ears: The Biography of Joe Orton,* Knopf, 1978 (also see below).
Taylor, John Russell, *The Second Wave,* Hill & Wang, 1971.
Worth, Katherine J., *Revolutions in Modern English Drama,* Bell, 1972.

PERIODICALS

Chicago Tribune, October 20, 1979, May 25, 1984, December 8, 1986.

Commonweal, October 23, 1970.
Los Angeles Times, February 4, 1983, May 13, 1987.
Modern Drama, February, 1972.
Nation, November 17, 1969, August 6, 1977.
New Boston Review, April/May, 1979.
Newsweek, April 20, 1987.
New York Times, March 9, 1979, March 10, 1985, February 19, 1986, February 23, 1986, April 7, 1986, April 14, 1986, April 12, 1987, April 17, 1987, March 9, 1989, October 15, 1989, December 5, 1989.
Sunday Times (London), November 22, 1970.
Time, September 15, 1967.
Times (London), November 6, 1986.
Times Literary Supplement, November 14, 1986.
Tribune Books (Chicago), July 26, 1987.
Washington Post, March 12, 1986, February 13, 1987, May 15, 1987.

OTHER

"Prick Up Your Ears" (film based on John Lahr's biography of Orton of the same title), Samuel Goldwyn Co., 1987.

*   *   *

ORWELL, George
    See BLAIR, Eric (Arthur)

*   *   *

OSBORNE, David
    See SILVERBERG, Robert

*   *   *

OSBORNE, George
    See SILVERBERG, Robert

*   *   *

OSBORNE, John (James) 1929-

PERSONAL: Born December 12, 1929, in London, England; son of Thomas Godfrey (a commercial artist) and Nellie Beatrice (a barmaid; maiden name, Grove) Osborne; married Pamela Elizabeth Lane (an actress), 1951 (divorced, 1957); married Mary Ure (an actress), November 8, 1957 (divorced, 1963); married Penelope Gilliatt (a drama critic and novelist), May 24, 1963 (divorced, 1967); married Jill Bennett (an actress), April, 1968 (divorced, 1977); married Helen Dawson, 1978; children: (third marriage) Nolan Kate. *Education:* "Worth no mention," writes Osborne, who left school at sixteen.

ADDRESSES: Home—The Water Mill, Hellingly, Sussex, England. *Agent*—Margery Vosper Ltd., 53A Shaftesbury Ave., London W. 1, England. *Office*—Woodfall Films, 27 Curzon St., London W. 1, England.

CAREER: Worked on trade journals *Gas World* and *Miller* for six months; was a tutor to juvenile actors in a touring group, later the group's assistant stage manager, and finally an actor specializing in characterizations of old men; made first stage appearance at Lyceum, Sheffield, England, in "No Room at the Inn," 1948; has appeared in "Don Juan," "Death of Satan," "Cards of Identity," "Good Woman of Setzuan," "The Apollo de Bellac," "The Making of Moo," and "A Cuckoo in the Nest." Playwright and producer; produced his first play at Theatre Royal,

Huddersfield, England, 1949; for two seasons co-managed a small theatrical company at seaside resorts; founder-director of Woodfall Films, 1958—; Oscar Lewenstein Plays Ltd., London, England, director, 1960—. Has appeared in films and television productions. Member of council, English Stage Co., 1968—.

MEMBER: Writers' Guild of Great Britain, Savile Club, Garrick Club.

AWARDS, HONORS: Evening Standard Drama Award, 1956 and 1965, for "A Patriot for Me," and 1968, for "The Hotel in Amsterdam"; New York Drama Critics Circle Award, 1958, for "Look Back in Anger," and 1965, for "Luther"; Tony Award, 1963, for "Luther"; Academy Award, 1963, for script for "Tom Jones"; *Plays and Players* best new play award, 1964, for "Inadmissable Evidence," and 1968, for "The Hotel in Amsterdam"; honorary doctorate, Royal College of Art, 1970.

WRITINGS:

A Better Class of Person: An Autobiography 1929-1956 (also see below), Dutton, 1981.
Too Young to Fight, Too Old to Forget, Faber, 1985.
The Meiningen Court Theatre, 1866-1890, Cambridge University Press, 1988.

A portion of the author's autobiography has also been adapted for television and published along with some of his other work as *A Better Class of Person* [and] *God Rot Tunbridge Wells,* Faber, 1985.

PLAYS

(With Stella Linden) "The Devil Inside Him," produced in Huddersfield, England, at Theatre Royal, May 29, 1950.
(With Anthony Creighton) "Personal Enemy," produced in Harrogate, England, at Grand Opera House, March 1, 1955.
Look Back in Anger (first produced in London, England, at Royal Court Theatre, May 8, 1956; produced on Broadway at Lyceum Theatre, October 1, 1957), S. G. Phillips, 1957, reprinted, Penguin, 1982.
(With Creighton) *Epitaph for George Dillon* (first produced in Oxford, England, at Oxford Experimental Club, February 26, 1957; produced in London at Royal Court Theatre, February 1, 1958; produced on the West End as "George Dillon," at Comedy Theatre, May 29, 1958; produced in New York at John Golden Theatre, November 4, 1958), Criterion, 1958.
The Entertainer (first produced in London at Royal Court Theatre, April 10, 1957; produced on the West End at Palace Theatre, September 10, 1957; produced on Broadway at Royale Theatre, February 12, 1958), Faber, 1957, Criterion, 1958, reprinted, Penguin, 1983.
The World of Paul Slickey (produced in London at Palace Theatre, May 5, 1959), Faber, 1959, Criterion, 1961.
Luther (first produced in London at Royal Court Theatre, July 27, 1961; produced on the West End at Phoenix Theatre, September 5, 1961; produced on Broadway at St. James Theatre, September 25, 1963), Faber, 1961, Criterion, 1962.
Plays for England: The Blood of the Bambergs [and] *Under Plain Cover* (both produced in London, 1963, and New York, 1965), Faber, 1963, Criterion, 1964.
Inadmissable Evidence (first produced in London at Royal Court Theatre, September 9, 1964; produced on the West End at Wyndham's Theatre, March 17, 1965; produced on Broadway at Belasco Theatre, November 30, 1965), Grove, 1965.

A Patriot for Me (produced in London at Royal Court Theatre, June 30, 1965; produced on Broadway at Imperial Theatre, October 5, 1969), Faber, 1966, Random House, 1970.

A Bond Honoured (adapted from Lope de Vega's *La Fianza Satisfecha;* produced in London at Old Vic, June 6, 1966), Faber, 1966.

Time Present [and] *The Hotel in Amsterdam* (both first produced separately in London at Royal Court Theatre, 1968; *Time Present* also produced on the West End at Duke of York's Theatre, July 1, 1968; *The Hotel in Amsterdam* also produced on the West End at New Theatre, September 5, 1968), Faber, 1968.

West of Suez (produced in London at Royal Court Theatre, August 17, 1971), Faber, 1971.

Hedda Gabler (adapted from Henrik Ibsen's play; produced in London at Royal Court Theatre, June 28, 1972), Faber, 1972, Dramatic Publishing Co. (Chicago), 1974.

A Sense of Detachment (produced in London at Royal Court Theatre, December 4, 1972), Faber, 1973.

The Picture of Dorian Gray: A Moral Entertainment (adapted from Oscar Wilde's novel; produced in London at Greenwich Theatre, February 13, 1975), Faber, 1973.

Watch It Come Down (produced in London at Old Vic, February 24, 1976), Faber, 1975.

The End of Me Old Cigar [and] *Jill and Jack: A Play for Television* (*The End of Me Old Cigar* produced in London at Greenwich Theatre, January 16, 1975), Faber, 1976.

Also editor of *Hedda Gabler and Other Plays,* by Henrik Ibsen.

TELEVISION PLAYS

"A Matter of Scandal and Concern," BBC Television, November 6, 1960, produced for stage in New York at New Theatre Workshop, March 7, 1966, published as *A Subject of Scandal and Concern: A Play for Television,* Faber, 1961.

The Right Prospectus: A Play for Television (broadcast in 1970), Faber, 1970.

Very Like a Whale (broadcast in 1970), Faber, 1971.

The Girls of Friendship (broadcast in 1972), Faber, 1972.

You're Not Watching Me, Mummy [and] *Try a Little Tenderness: Two Plays for Television,* Faber, 1978.

Also author of television plays "Billy Bunter," 1952, and "Robin Hood," 1953.

SCREENPLAYS

"Tom Jones" (produced by Woodfall Films, 1964), published as *Tom Jones: A Screenplay,* Grove, 1964, revised edition, 1965.

Also author of screenplays based on plays, including "Look Back in Anger," 1959, "The Entertainer," 1960, and "Inadmissable Evidence," 1968.

OTHER

(Contributor) Tom Maschler, editor, *Declaration,* Dutton, 1958.

(Translator) Walter Benjamin, *Origins of German Tragic Drama,* Verso, 1977.

Contributor to anthologies, including *Modern English Plays,* 1966, and *The Best Short Plays of the World Theatre, 1958-1967,* edited by Stanley Richards, 1968. Contributor to periodicals, including *Encounter, Observer,* and Times (London).

SIDELIGHTS: Prior to John Osborne's arrival on the scene, the British theatre consisted mainly of classics, melodramas, and drawing-room comedies. But in 1956, Osborne's third play and first London-produced drama, *Look Back in Anger,* shocked au-

diences and "wiped the smugness off the frivolous face of English theatre," as John Lahr puts it in a *New York Times Book Review* article. Set in a postwar Britain of uncertain prospects and a rising underclass, the play introduced a new phrase into the lexicon, "angry young man," personified by the story's antihero, Jimmy Porter.

As *Look Back in Anger* begins, Jimmy is a twenty-five-year-old working-class youth with a provincial university education and bleak hopes for the future. He frequently clashes with his wife, Alison, who comes from a more privileged background; the couple share their tiny flat with Cliff, Jimmy's partner in the sweet-shop business. A triangle forms among Jimmy, Alison, and Alison's friend Helena, who alerts Alison's parents to the squalor their now-pregnant daughter is living in and helps convince Alison to leave Jimmy. Helena, however, stays on and becomes Jimmy's mistress. As time goes on, Alison miscarries and, realizing her love for Jimmy, returns to the flat. Helena decides that she cannot come between Jimmy and his wife any longer and withdraws. Meanwhile, Cliff also leaves the flat in an attempt to better his lot. "And Alison's baby which could have taken Cliff's place in their triangular relationship will never be," Arthur Nicholas Athanason explains in a *Dictionary of Literary Biography* article. "Jimmy and Alison must depend more than ever now on fantasy games to fill this void and to achieve what moments of intimacy and peaceful coexistence they can in their precarious marriage."

With the immediate and controversial success of *Look Back in Anger,* continues Athanason, the author "found himself, overnight, regarded as a critic of society or, more precisely, a reflector of his generation's attitudes toward society. Needless to say, the concern and feeling for intimate personal relationships that are displayed in *Look Back in Anger* may indeed have social and moral implications. But what really moves Osborne in this play seems to be the inability of people to understand and express care for each other better—particularly in their language and their emotional responsiveness. What is new and experimental in British drama about [the play] is the explosive character of Jimmy Porter and his brilliant and dazzling vituperative tirades, in which a renewed delight in a Shavian vigor and vitality of language and ideas is displayed with virtuoso command." Noting a resemblance to Tennessee Williams' play *A Streetcar Named Desire,* Athanason labels *Look Back in Anger* "an intimate portrait of an extremely troubled working-class marriage (riddled with psychological problems and sexual frustrations), which was, in its way, a theatrical first for British drama."

The play received mixed reviews when it opened in London, apparently since some critics could not see beyond Jimmy's explosive character to examine the themes underlying the fury he directed against the social mores of the day. One critic who overwhelmingly approved of *Look Back in Anger* was Kenneth Tynan. It was his support that helped the play gain success. So impressed was Laurence Olivier with *Look Back in Anger* that the actor commissioned Osborne to write a play for him. The result was a drama—*The Entertainer*—which featured a leading role that is considered one of the greatest and most challenging parts in late twentieth-century drama.

In chronicling the life of wilting, third-rate music-hall comedian Archie Rice, Osborne was acknowledged to be reflecting in *The Entertainer* the fate of postwar Britain, an island suffering recession and unemployment, losing its status as an empire. "Archie is of a piece with the angry Osborne antiheroes of 'Look Back in Anger' and [the author's later play] 'Inadmissible Evidence,'" notes Frank Rich in a *New York Times* review of a revival of *The*

Entertainer. "He's a repulsive, unscrupulous skunk, baiting everyone around him (the audience included); he's also a somewhat tragic victim of both his own self-contempt and of a declining England. If it's impossible to love Archie, we should be electrified or at least antagonized by his pure hostility and his raw instinct for survival. Mr. Osborne has a way of making us give his devils their pitiful due."

The drama's allegory of fading Britain and Olivier's compelling portrayal of Archie made *The Entertainer* a remarkable success in its first production. However, when it was revived on Broadway in 1983 with Nicol Williamson as Archie, *New York Times* reviewer Walter Kerr observed that in the play Osborne "has first shown us, at tedious, now cliche-ridden lengths how dreary the real world has become—what with blacks moving in upstairs, sons being sent off to Suez, and everyone else sitting limply about complaining of it all. He has then had the drummer hit the rim of the snare as a signal that we're leaping over into music-hall make-believe—only to show us that it is exactly as dreary, exactly as deflated, exactly as dead as the onetime promise in the parlor. There is limpness in the living room and there is limpness before the footlights. . . . There is no transfusion of 'vitality,' no theatrical contrasts."

As Athanason explains, the author "owes a particular indebtedness to the turns and stock-character types of the English music-hall tradition, and, in *The Entertainer* particularly, he set out to capitalize on the dramatic as well as the comic potential of these values. For example, by conceiving each scene of this play as a music-hall turn, Osborne enables the audience to see both the 'public' Archie performing his trite patter before his 'dead behind the eyes' audience and the 'private' Archie performing a different comic role of seeming nonchalance before his own family."

Inadmissible Evidence presents another Osborne type in Bill Maitland, a contemporary London attorney who finds that his lusts for power, money, and women do little to fill the emotional voids in his life. Athanason describes the play as opening in a "Kafkaesque dream sequence set in a courtroom that foreshadows the fate of [Maitland,] on trial before his own conscience for 'having unlawfully and wickedly published and made known a wicked, bawdy and scandalous object'—himself. Although he pleads not guilty to the court's indictment of himself, his life is presumably the inadmissible evidence that he dares not produce in mitigation.

"Essentially a journey through the static spiritual hell of Maitland's mind, *Inadmissible Evidence* dramatizes a living, mental nightmare that culminates, as Maitland's alienation is pushed to its inevitable end, in a complete nervous breakdown," continues Athanason. "The play is principally a tour de force monologue for one actor, for its secondary characters are mere dream figures and metaphors that externalize the intense conflict going on within Maitland's disintegrating mind." The critic also feels that in this drama Osborne demonstrated his finest writing to date.

Osborne has written other notable plays, including *A Patriot for Me,* a fictional telling of the trial and last days of Hungary's infamous Captain Redl, who was framed for his homosexuality and pronounced an enemy of the state; and *Luther,* a biography of religious reformist Martin Luther, an antihero of his time. But the work that garnered perhaps the widest notice since the mid-1960s is not a play but a book: *A Better Class of Person,* the first volume of Osborne's autobiography.

In relating his life story through the age of twenty-six, Osborne caught the attention of critics for his caustic, even bitter, descrip-

tions of his home life, especially his relationship with his parents. Osborne's father, who worked intermittently in advertising, was a sickly figure who spent his last years in a sanitarium. His mother, a bartender, seems to be the focal point of the author's harshest remarks. Osborne "looks back, of course, in anger," remarks John Leonard in a *New York Times* article. "In general, he is angry at England's lower middle class, of which he is the vengeful child. In particular, he reviles his mother, who is still alive. Class and mother, in this fascinating yet unpleasant book, sometimes seem to be the same mean thing, a blacking factory."

If Osborne's memories are more bitter than sweet, a number of critics found that the author's hard-bitten style makes for an interesting set of memoirs. *Washington Post Book World* reviewer David Richards did not, indicating that "like the male characters in his plays, who fulminate against the sordidness of life, Osborne is probably a romantic *manque.* But it is often difficult to feel the real anguish under the relentless invective of his writing. *A Better Class of Person* is the least likeable of autobiographies, although it should, no doubt, be pointed out that affability has never been one of Osborne's goals."

More often, critics had praise for the book, as in *Newsweek* writer Ray Sawhill's view that the author "has an explosive gift for denunciation and invective, and what he's written is—deliberately, nakedly—a tantrum. . . . He can blow meanness and pettiness up so large that they acquire a looming sensuality, like a slow-motion movie scene. His savage relish can be so palpable that you share his enjoyment of the dynamics of rage. Osborne's memoirs constitute "the best piece of writing [the author] has done since 'Inadmissible Evidence,'" according to Lahr in his *New York Times Book Review* piece. "After [that play,] his verbal barrages became grapeshot instead of sharpshooting. He neither revised his scripts nor moderated his cranky outbursts. His plays, like his pronouncements about an England he could no longer fathom, became second-rate and self-indulgent. But 'A Better Class of Person' takes its energy from looking backward to the source of his pain before fame softened him. [The work proves that] John Osborne once again is making a gorgeous fuss."

As *Los Angeles Times* critic Charles Champlin points out, "There is nothing about stagecraft in 'A Better Class of Person,' but everything about the making of the playwright. The [author's *Look Back in Anger*] was abrasive and so is the autobiography. It is also, like the play, savagely well-written, vividly detailed, and corrosively honest, unique as autobiography in its refusal to touch up the author's image. He encourages us to find him impossible and absolutely authentic."

Commenting on the reaction to his life story, Osborne expresses surprise that people should find the book so extreme in its emotions. "Actually I consider myself rather reticent," the author told Roderick Mann in a *Los Angeles Times* interview. "I don't set out to say outrageous things, though that's the way they sometimes turn out. And people do get upset so easily."

BIOGRAPHICAL/CRITICAL SOURCES:

BOOKS

Banham, Martin, *Osborne,* Oliver & Boyd, 1969.
Brown, John Russell, editor, *Modern British Dramatists: A Collection of Critical Essays,* Prentice-Hall, 1968.
Brown, John Russell, *Theatre Language: A Study of Arden, Osborne, Pinter, Wesker,* Taplinger, 1972.
Carter, Alan, *John Osborne,* Oliver & Boyd, 1969.
Contemporary Literary Criticism, Gale, Volume 1, 1973, Volume 2, 1974, Volume 5, 1976, Volume 11, 1979.

Dictionary of Literary Biography, Volume 13: *British Dramatists Since World War II,* Gale, 1982.

Farrar, Harold, *John Osborne,* Columbia University Press, 1973.

Hayman, Ronald, *John Osborne,* Ungar, 1972.

John Osborne: A Symposium, Royal Court Theatre, 1966.

Osborne, John, *A Better Class of Person: An Autobiography 1929-1956,* Dutton, 1981.

Taylor, John Russell and others, *John Osborne: Look Back in Anger, a Casebook,* Macmillan, 1968.

Trussler, Simon, *John Osborne,* Longman, 1969.

Tynan, Kenneth, *Tynan on Theatre,* Penguin, 1964.

PERIODICALS

Drama: The Quarterly Theatre Review, winter, 1975, autumn, 1978.

Los Angeles Times, November 13, 1981, October 18, 1984, February 18, 1985.

New Republic, November 1, 1969.

Newsweek, December 14, 1981.

New Yorker, March 15, 1982.

New York Review of Books, January 6, 1966.

New York Times, November 5, 1981, January 21, 1983, January 30, 1983.

New York Times Book Review, November 8, 1981.

Times (London), October 15, 1981, May 1, 1983, May 13, 1983, August 10, 1983.

Times Literary Supplement, January 4, 1974, October 16, 1981, August 31, 1984.

Washington Post Book World, December 27, 1981.

*   *   *

OSCEOLA
See BLIXEN, Karen (Christentze Dinesen)

*   *   *

OUSMANE, Sembene   1923-

PERSONAL: Name cited in some sources as Ousmane Sembene; born January 8, 1923, in Ziguinchor, Casamance, Senegal. *Education:* Attended technical school; studied at Gorki Film Studios in early 1960s.

ADDRESSES: Home—c/o P.O. Box 8087, Yoff, Dakar, Senegal.

CAREER: Worked as fisherman in Casamance, Senegal, and as plumber, mechanic's aid, and bricklayer in Dakar, Senegal, before World War II; worked as docker and stevedore in Marseilles, France, in late 1940s; became union leader. Writer and filmmaker. *Military service:* Served in French Army during World War II.

AWARDS, HONORS: Literature prize from Dakar Festival of Negro Arts, 1966, for *Vehi-Ciosane ou Blanche-genese, suivi du Mandat;* prize from Cannes Film Festival, 1967, for "Le Noire de . . . "; special prize from Venice Film Festival, 1968, and award for best foreign film from Atlanta Film Festival, 1970, both for "Mandabi."

WRITINGS:

Le Docker noir (novel; title means "The Black Docker"), Nouvelles Editions Debresse, 1956.

Oh Pays, mon beau peuple! (novel; title means "Oh My Country, My Beautiful People"), Le Livre Contemporain, 1957.

Les Bouts de bois de Dieu (novel), Amiot-Dumont, 1960, translation by Francis Price published as *God's Bits of Wood,* Doubleday, 1962.

Voltaieque (short stories), Presence Africaine, 1962, translation by Len Ortzen published as *Tribal Scars, and Other Stories,* INSCAPE, 1974.

Vehi-Ciosane; ou, Blanche-genese, suivi du Mandat (two novellas), Presence Africaine, 1965, translation by Clive Wake published as *The Money Order, With White Genesis,* Heinemann, 1971.

Xala (novel; title means "Impotence"), Presence Africaine, 1973, translation by Clive Wake published as *Xala,* Lawrence Hill, 1976.

Dernier de l'empire (novel), Harmattan, 1981, translation by Adrian Adams published as *The Last of the Empire,* Heinemann, 1983.

Also author of the novel *Fat Ndiay Diop,* 1976.

OTHER PUBLISHED FICTION

"Le Noire de . . ." (short story), published in *Presence africaine* in 1961, translation by Ellen Conroy Kennedy published as "Black Girl" in *African Short Stories,* edited by Charles R. Larson, Macmillan, 1970.

Referendum (novel; first novel in *L'Harmattan* trilogy), published in *Presence africaine* in 1964.

SCREENPLAYS; AND DIRECTOR

"Le Noire de . . ." (adapted from Ousmane's story; also see above), Actualities Francais/Films Domirev of Dakar, 1966 (released in the United States as "Black Girl," New Yorker Films, 1969).

"Mandabi" (adapted from Ousmane's novella *The Money Order;* also see above), Jean Maumy, 1968 (released in the United States by Grove Press, 1969). "Emitai," Paulin Soumanou Vieya, 1971 (released in the United States by New Yorker Films, 1973).

"Xala" (title means "Impotence"), Societe Nationale Cinematographique/Films Domirev, 1974 (released in the United States by New Yorker Films, 1975). "Ceddo," released in the United States by New Yorker Films, 1978 (first released in 1977).

Also screenwriter and director of "Borom Sarret," 1964; "Niaye," 1964; "Tauw," 1970; and the unreleased film "Songhays," 1963.

OTHER

Contributor to periodicals, including *Presence africaine.* Founding editor of periodical *Kaddu.*

SIDELIGHTS: Sembene Ousmane is a respected Senegalese artist who has distinguished himself in both literature and film. He was born in 1923 in the Casamance region and attended school only briefly before working as a fisherman. After moving to Senegal's capital, Dakar, Ousmane found various jobs in manual labor. He worked in Dakar during the late 1930s, but when World War II began he was drafted by the colonial French into their armed forces, and he eventually participated in the Allied invasion of Italy. When the war ended Ousmane returned home to the Casamance area and resumed his early life as a fisherman. After a short period, however, he traveled back to France, where he found work as a stevedore on the Marseilles docks.

Ousmane's experiences as a dockworker provided background for his first novel, *Le Docker noir* ("The Black Docker"). In this work Ousmane wrote of a black stevedore who writes a novel but is robbed of the manuscript by a white woman. Much of the novel delineates the ensuing consequences of that incident. Although *Le Docker noir* proved somewhat flawed, it nonetheless represented an alternative career for Ousmane after a back injury rendered him unfit for dock work.

With *Le Docker noir* Ousmane sought to express the plight of many minorities including Spaniards and Arabs as well as blacks exploited and abused at the French dockyards. But while he specified afterwards that his perspective was that of the minority, and thus contrary to that of whites, Ousmane was quick to add that he was not advocating negritude, a black-pride movement that he dismissed as sentimental and narrow-minded in its emphasis. He remained, however, a champion of black rights in Africa.

Ousmane's concern over conflicting philosophies within Africa's black community is evident in his second novel, *Oh Pays, mon beau peuple!* ("Oh My Country, My Beautiful People"), which concerns the failings of an ambitious Senegalese farmer returning home after a long absence. Accompanied by his white wife, the farmer alienates himself from both whites and blacks, for both groups resent his interracial marriage and his efforts to modernize the community's farming system. Eventually the farmer's behavior becomes intolerable to the villagers, and he is killed.

Like *Le Docker noir, Oh Pays, mon beau peuple!* was written in French, but unlike the earlier novel, Ousmane's second work fared well throughout much of Europe and was even published in Japan. After completing *Oh Pays, mon beau peuple!* Ousmane spent a few years traveling in many of the countries where the novel was earning acclaim. He eventually left Europe, however, and visited Cuba, China, and even the Soviet Union, where he studied filmmaking at a leading studio.

In 1960 Ousmane published his third novel, *Les Bouts de bois de Dieu* (*God's Bits of Wood*), which became his first work to gain significant attention from English readers. *God's Bits of Wood* is a fictionalized account of a railroad workers' strike that stalled transportation from Dakar to Niger in late 1947 and early 1948. Much more ambitious than Ousmane's previous works, the third novel is a sweeping, epic-style account featuring several characters and spanning Senegal's political and social extremes. In 1970, when the novel appeared in English translation, *Times Literary Supplement*'s reviewer T. M. Aluko wrote that Ousmane's work "was a vivid rendering of the strike and the strikers." Aluko also cited Ousmane's particular skills as a novelist, declaring that he possessed "the ability to control a wide social panorama, without once losing sight of, or compassion for, the complexity and suffering of individuals."

Ousmane followed *God's Bits of Wood* with a short story collection, *Voltaieque* (*Tribal Scars*), and *Referendum,* the first part of a trilogy entitled *L'Harmattan* ("The Storm"). He then completed *Vehi-Ciosane; ou, Blanche-genese, suivi du Mandat* (*The Money Order, With White Genesis*), a volume comprised of two novellas. The book was an immense critical success, earning Ousmane the literature prize from the 1966 Dakar Festival of Negro Arts.

By the mid-1960s Ousmane was also working in film. In 1964 he completed his first notable work in that medium, the sociological study "Borom Sarret," and three years later he wrote and directed "Le Noire de . . ." ("Black Girl"), which detailed the degrading circumstances endured by an African servant in a French household. These films were shown together in New York City in 1969, and A. H. Weiler writing in the *New York Times* called both works insightful and provocative. Weiler also wrote that Ousmane's films derived from "the quiet distinctions of simplicity, sincerity and subdued anger toward the freed black

man's new burdens." In addition, Weiler contended that the works "put a sharp, bright focus on an emerging, once dark African area."

Ousmane enjoyed even greater acclaim as a filmmaker with "Mandabi," his adaptation of his own novella *The Money Order.* "Mandabi" is a comedy about a middle-aged fool, Dieng, who receives a considerable financial sum from a nephew in Paris. Much of the humor in "Mandabi" derives from Dieng's vain, foolhardy efforts to secure identification papers necessary for cashing the money order. In the course of his efforts Dieng is swindled, robbed, thrashed, and publicly humiliated by his greedy family and fellow citizens. Adding further to the humor is the actual behavior of Dieng, an arrogant dimwit who smugly parades about his village oblivious of the animosity he provokes. In the *New York Times,* Roger Greenspun noted as much when he wrote that because Dieng "is such a pompous fool, so blithely superior to his two wives, so gluttonous with his food and confident in his walk, his troubles seem deserved and funny." Greenspun described Ousmane's directorial style as "spare, laconic, slightly ironic" and added that he "displays a reticence towards his characters that grants him freedom from explicit moral judgment."

Humor did not figure in Ousmane's next film, "Emitai," which he completed in 1971. In this work he chronicles a conflict between Senegalese natives and French colonialists at the beginning of World War II. The conflict centers on the natives' opposition to French troops sent into the Senegalese village to commandeer several tons of rice. Neither faction particularly cherishes the rice: For the villagers it is intended for use in religious ceremonies; for the French, it is rendered unnecessary by a change in military tactics. Nonetheless, neither side concedes to the other, and the conflict is resolved with futile violence. In his *New York Times* review, Roger Greenspun found "Emitai" a refreshing, if sobering, counterpoint to the Hollywood adventure films of the 1930s and 1940s, observing that "the absolute ineffectiveness of massed spears against a few well-placed rifles should lay to rest the memories of a good many delicious terrors during Saturday afternoons at the movies." Greenspun also commended Ousmane's directorial reserve and subtlety and declared that the filmmaker's relatively detached style resulted in a film "that keeps surprising you with its ironic sophistication."

Ousmane's next filmmaking venture, "Xala," marked his return to comedy. In "Xala" he lampoons the increasing Westernization of African politics and business. The protagonist of "Xala" is El Hadji, a corrupt bureaucrat who also serves his community as an importer of fairly exotic goods, including whiskey, yogurt, and perfume. Like his Western counterparts, El Hadji wears costly European business suits, totes a briefcase, and continually confers with advisers and fellow bureaucrats. His corrupt ways, while causing no good to his community, have contributed greatly to his considerable prosperity. That prosperity, however, is undermined when El Hadji takes a third wife and discovers that he is suddenly impotent. Apparently the victim of a curse, El Hadji consults witch doctors, including one fellow who sports an expensive business suit while squatting in his hut. That witch doctor fails to cure El Hadji, but for a substantial sum another doctor is able to restore the bureaucrat's sexuality. Unfortunately, troubles continue to plague El Hadji when he is implicated in a corrupt business action and is dismissed, by equally corrupt fellow bureaucrats, from the community's chamber of commerce. More marital problems then ensue, for El Hadji fails to pay his witch doctor and is thus once again impotent. Another cure is then attempted, one in which El Hadji must remove his clothing and allow several cripples to spit on him. He complies, but a much greater catastrophe awaits him.

"Xala" was released in 1974, only months after Ousmane had published his novel of the same title. When the film was shown in the United States in 1975, it was commended in the New York Times as "an instructive delight" and as "cutting, radiant and hilarious." *Time*'s reviewer, Richard Eder, added that Ousmane's film was George Orwell's novel *Animal Farm* "applied to African independence." Similarly, Ousmane's novel *Xala* was cited by *Nation* reviewer Eve Ottenberg as a witty portrait of "the destruction of tribal values." She wrote that the themes of *Xala* allowed Ousmane "to show people at their most flawed, eccentric, energetic and comic."

Ousmane continued to probe cultural discontinuity in "Ceddo," his 1977 film about religious conflict in an unspecified African kingdom. This conflict is triggered when a Catholic king converts to Islam and brings a Moslem teacher into his band of advisers. The king's associates then convert to Islam, too, leaving only the common villagers outside the Islamic faith. Resentful of the king's changing policies, the villagers kidnap the king's daughter and thus force him to negotiate. During meetings between factions, the opportunistic Islamic teacher intercedes and precipitates the slaughter of all the non-Moslems. Vincent Canby, in his review for the *New York Times,* noted that the manner of "Ceddo" was "reserved, cool, almost stately." He confirmed that the obviously anti-Moslem film had been banned in Senegal, but Canby observed that the banning was prompted by a seemingly trivial aspect: Ousmane refused to render the spelling of the film's title to be consistent with his government's own spelling.

Ousmane's stature as an African artist has risen steadily since he published his first work in 1956. In the ensuing years he has used his art to protest injustice against blacks and to decry the increasing disintegration of black Africa's heritages. He has also established himself as a formidable filmmaker in a medium where commercial considerations are usually dominant over the artistic, and the critical acclaim accorded his films in the United States testifies to his wide appeal and considerable achievements. Ousmane's works thus transcend cultural specifics and assure him recognition as a leading artist of his time.

BIOGRAPHICAL/CRITICAL SOURCES:

BOOKS

Brench, A. C., *The Novelists' Inheritance in French Africa: Writing From Senegal to Cameroon,* Oxford University Press, 1967.
Dathorne, O. R., *African Literature in the Twentieth Century,* Heinemann Educational, 1976.
Silver, Helene and Hans M. Zell, editors, *A Reader's Guide to African Literature,* Africana Publishing, 1971.

PERIODICALS

Africa Report, February, 1963.
American Cinematographer, November, 1972.
Black Orpheus, November, 1959.
Cineaste, Volume 6, number 1, 1973.
Cinema Quebec, March/April, 1973.
Film Quarterly, spring, 1973.
Nation, April 9, 1977.
New Yorker, May 16, 1977.
New York Times, January 13, 1969, September 30, 1969, November 9, 1969, February 10, 1973, October 1, 1975, January 27, 1978.

New York Times Book Review, November 28, 1976.
Quarterly Review of Film Studies, spring, 1979.
Times Literary Supplement, October 16, 1970.
World Literature Today, winter, 1978.

*   *   *

OZ, Amos 1939-

PERSONAL: Given name Amos Klausner; born May 4, 1939, in Jerusalem, Israel; son of Yehuda Arieh (a writer) and Fania (Mussman) Klausner; married Nily Zuckerman, April 5, 1960; children: Fania, Gallia, Daniel. *Education:* Hebrew University of Jerusalem, B.A., 1963; St. Cross College, Oxford, M.A., 1970.

ADDRESSES: Home—Israel. *Agent*—Mrs. D. Owen, 28 Narrow St., London E. 14, England.

CAREER: Writer, 1962—. Has worked as tractor driver, youth instructor, school teacher, and agricultural worker at Kibbutz Hulda, Israel. Visiting fellow, St. Cross College, Oxford University, 1969-70. Writer in residence, Hebrew University of Jerusalem, 1975, and Colorado College, 1985. *Military service:* Israeli Army, 1957-60; also fought as reserve soldier in the tank corps in Sinai, 1967, and in the Golan Heights, 1973.

MEMBER: P.E.N. International, Hebrew Writers Association.

AWARDS, HONORS: Holon Prize for Literature, 1965; Israel-American Cultural Foundation award, 1968; B'nai B'rith annual literary award, 1973; Brehner Prize, 1978.

WRITINGS:

Artzot ha' tan (short stories), Massada (Tel Aviv), 1965, translation by Nicholas de Lange and Philip Simpson published as *Where the Jackals Howl, and Other Stories,* Harcourt, 1981.
Makom acher (novel), Sifriat Po'alim (Tel Aviv), 1966, translation by de Lange published as *Elsewhere, Perhaps,* Harcourt, 1973.
Michael sheli (novel), Am Oved (Tel Aviv), 1968, translation by de Lange in collaboration with Oz published as *My Michael,* Knopf, 1972.
Ad mavet (two novellas), Sifriat Po'alim, 1971, translation by de Lange in collaboration with Oz published as *Unto Death,* Harcourt, 1975.
Laga'at ba'mayim, laga'at ba'ruach (novel), Am Oved, 1973, translation by de Lange in collaboration with Oz published as *Touch the Water, Touch the Wind,* Harcourt, 1974.
Anashim acherim (anthology; title means "Different People"), Ha'Kibbutz Ha'Meuchad (Tel Aviv), 1974.
Har he'etza ha'raah (three novellas), Am Oved, 1976, translation by de Lange in collaboration with Oz published as *The Hill of Evil Counsel,* Harcourt, 1978.
Soumchi (juvenile), Am Oved, 1978, translation by Oz and Penelope Farmer published as *Soumchi,* Harper, 1980.
Be' or ha'tchelet he'azah (essays; title means "Under This Blazing Light"), Sifriat Po'alim, 1979.
Menucha nechonah (novel), Am Oved, 1982, translation by Hillel Halkin published as *A Perfect Peace,* Harcourt, 1985.
Po ve'sham b'eretz Yisra'el bistav 1982 (nonfiction), Am Oved, 1983, translation by Maurie Goldberg-Bartura published as *In the Land of Israel,* Harcourt, 1983.
(Editor with Richard Flantz and author of introduction) *Until Daybreak: Stories from the Kibbutz,* Institute for the Translation of Hebrew Literature, 1984.
Black Box (novel), translation by de Lange, Harcourt, 1988.
The Slopes of Lebanon (essays), translation by Maurie Goldberg-Bartura, Harcourt, 1989.

Also editor of *Siach lochamium* (title means "The Seventh Day"). Contributor of essays and fiction to periodicals in Israel, including *Davar.*

SIDELIGHTS: Author Amos Oz has spent his career examining the experience of the Jewish people in Israel. Through fiction and nonfiction alike, he describes a populace under emotional and physical siege and a society threatened by internal contradictions and contention. Himself a native-born Israeli (a *sabra*), Oz writes books that are "indispensable reading for anyone who wishes to understand . . . life in Israel, the ideology that sustains it, and the passions that drive its people," according to Judith Chernaik in the *Times Literary Supplement.* Immensely popular in his own country, Oz has also established an international reputation; translations of his books have appeared in more than fifteen languages, including Japanese, Dutch, Norwegian, and Rumanian. In a *New Republic* assessment of the author's talents, Ian Sanders notes: "Amos Oz is an extraordinarily gifted Israeli novelist who delights his readers with both verbal brilliance and the depiction of eternal struggles—between flesh and spirit, fantasy and reality, Jew and Gentile. . . . His carefully reconstructed worlds are invariably transformed into symbolic landscapes, vast arenas where primeval forces clash." *Times Literary Supplement* contributor A. S. Byatt observes that in his works on Israel, Oz "can write with delicate realism about small lives, or tell fables about large issues, but his writing, even in translation, gains vitality simply from his subject matter." *New York Review of Books* correspondent D. J. Enright calls Oz "his country's most persuasive spokesman to the outside world, the literary part of it at least."

"In a sense Amos Oz has no alternative in his novels but to tell us what it means to be an Israeli," writes John Bayley in the *New York Review of Books.* A *sabra* who grew up along with the young nation, Oz has seen military service in two armed conflicts—the Six Day War and the Yom Kippur War—and he has lived most of his adult life as a member of Kibbutz Hulda, one of Israel's collective communities. His fictional themes arise from these experiences and are considered controversial for their presentations of individuals who rebel against the society's ideals. *New York Times Book Review* contributor Robert Alter contends that Oz's work is "symptomatic of the troubled connection Israeli writers increasingly feel with the realities of the Jewish state." Chernaik elaborates on this submerged "interior wilderness" that Oz seems compelled to explore: "He hears and sees more acutely than most, and has an uncanny gift for recording the distinctive features of his world, juxtaposing the socialist dreams and apocalyptic visions of the early Zionists, the naive arrogance of the young, and the nightmares of the mad and embittered. The overwhelming impression left by his fiction is of the precariousness of individual and collective human effort, a common truth made especially poignant by a physical landscape thoroughly inhospitable to human settlement, and given tragic dimensions by the modern history of the Jews and its analogues in Biblical history." Oz himself told the *New Republic* that he tries to tap his own turmoil in order to write. His characters, he said, "actually want two different things: peace and excitement, excitement and peace. These two things don't get along very easily, so when people have peace, they hate it and long for excitement, and when they have excitement, they want peace."

A central concern of Oz's fiction is the conflict between idealistic Zionism and the realities of life in a pluralistic society. As a corollary to this, many of his *sabra* characters have decidedly ambivalent feelings towards the Arab population, especially Palestinians. *Commentary* essayist Ruth R. Wisse writes that in book after book, "Oz has taken the great myths with which modern Israel is associated—the noble experiment of the kibbutz, the reclamation of the soil, the wars against the British and the Arabs, the phoenix-like rise of the Jewish spirit out of the ashes of the Holocaust—and shown us their underside: bruised, dazed, and straying characters who move in an atmosphere of almost unalleviated depression. . . . Oz in his fiction specializes in exposing the darker motives and disturbed dreams of those who must sustain these structures on which the country stands." Nehama Aschkenasy offers a similar assessment in *Midstream:* "The collective voice is suspiciously optimistic, over-anxious to ascertain the normalcy and sanity of the community and the therapeutic effect of the collective body on its tormented member. But the voice of the individual is imbued with a bitter sense of entrapment, of existential boredom and nausea, coupled with a destructive surrender to the irrational and the antinomian." Needless to say, this theme is one of Oz's most controversial. *New York Times Book Review* correspondent Morris Dickstein notes that the author often "takes the viewpoint of the detached participant, the good citizen who does his duty, shares his family's ideals but remains a little apart, wryly skeptical, unable to lose himself in the communal spirit. . . . Oz is intrigued by the tension between community and offbeat individuality."

The kibbutz provides Oz with a common background and inspiration. Its lifestyle serves as a powerful symbol of the nation's aspirations, as well as a microcosm of the larger Jewish family in Israel, suffocatingly intimate and inescapable, yet united in defense against the hostile forces besieging its borders. Alter declares that nearly all of Oz's fiction "is informed by the same symbolic world picture: a hemmed-in cluster of fragile human habitations (the kibbutz, the state of Israel itself) surrounded by dark, menacing mountains where jackals howl and hostile aliens lurk. . . . This symbolic opposition is the vehicle for a series of troubled narrative meditations on the rationalist-idealist enterprise of socialist Zionism and, beyond that, on civilization and its discontents, for the jackals out there often find an answering voice in the jackal beneath the skin of those who dwell within the perimeter of civilization." According to *Jewish Quarterly* contributor Jacob Sonntag, the people of Oz's fiction "are part of the landscape, and the landscape is part of the reality from which there is no escape." If the landscape is inescapable, the bonds of family also offer little relief. Dickstein writes: "The core of feeling in Oz's work is always some sort of family, often a family being torn apart." *Los Angeles Times* correspondent Elaine Kendall similarly observes that Oz's fiction "confronts the generational conflicts troubling Israel today; emotional rifts intensified by pressure and privation. In that anguished country, the usual forms of family tension seem reversed; the young coldly realistic; the elders desperately struggling to maintain their belief in a receding ideal."

"Daytime Israel makes a tremendous effort to create the impression of the determined, tough, simple, uncomplicated society ready to fight back, ready to hit back twice as hard, courageous and so on," Oz told *Partisan Review.* "Nocturnal Israel is a refugee camp with more nightmares per square mile I guess than any other place in the world. Almost everyone has seen the devil." The obsessions of "nocturnal Israel" fuel Oz's work, as Mark Shechner notes in *Nation.* "In [Oz's] fiction," Shechner writes, "the great storms that periodically descend on the Jews stir up strange and possessed characters who ride the gusts as if in a dream: raging Zionists, religious fanatics poised to take the future by force, theoreticians of the millennium, strategists of the end game, connoisseurs of bitterness and curators of injustice, artists of prophecy and poets of doctrine." This is not to suggest, however, that Oz's work is unrelentingly somber or polemical.

According to Dickstein, the "glow of Oz's writing comes from the spare and unsentimental warmth of his own voice, his feeling for atmosphere and his gallery of colorful misfits and individualists caught in communal enterprises." Bayley likewise concludes: "One of the admirable things about Oz's novels is the humor in them, a humor which formulates itself in having taken, and accepted, the narrow measure of the Israeli scene. Unlike much ethnic writing his does not seek to masquerade as *Weltliteratur.* It is Jewish literature acquiescing amusedly in its new militantly provincial status."

Oz's accounts of his own childhood illustrate the stresses placed upon the young in modern Israel. He was born Amos Klausner in Jerusalem in 1939 and grew up "in a right-wing Zionist family, in a house filled with books," to quote the author from a *New Republic* interview. Oz's father was a librarian and expert on comparative literature, well versed in a dozen languages, but Oz grew up speaking only Hebrew. In *Partisan Review* he described his early years. "My father wanted me to become the archetype of the new Israeli: simple, blond, cleansed of Jewish neurosis, tough, gentile-looking," he said. "I was meant to be a new leaf altogether: a sabra, tough, simple, unambivalent." And yet, he told *New Republic,* he was also expected to "carry the Jewish genius, and bring honor to the family." At fifteen he rebelled against the scholarly atmosphere and his parents' bourgeois values. He joined Kibbutz Hulda, changed his name to Amos Oz, and undertook menial labor in the fields. A childhood yearning to be a writer could not be so easily expelled, however. Eventually Oz returned to Jerusalem to study at the Hebrew University; on holidays he returned to the kibbutz, where he was allowed to schedule time for writing among his other community duties. As his stories and novels began to sell, he was granted more and more days away from the fields in order to pursue his craft. He told *New Republic:* "In the end, when I look at myself, I am doing exactly what my father wanted me to do. In the kibbutz I look like one of the members, and yet I follow my forefathers. I deal with words. My escape was a full circle."

Oz is an unusual Israeli writer in that he has chosen to stay at the kibbutz throughout his career, even though the income from his royalties is substantial. As a member of the collective, he signs his paychecks over to the kibbutz treasurer, not keeping any fraction of them himself. Far from complaining, however, Oz feels that the system works to his benefit. "I don't have to live on advances," he told the *New York Times Book Review,* "I don't fill out income tax forms, I have no mortgage, I don't have to write book reviews or lecture, and the only essays I do are for rage. . . . It means a very modest standard of living, but I much prefer this life to existence in a literary aquarium." Nor does Oz overlook the opportunity the kibbutz offers him to study many personalities at close range. "I know a hell of a lot about the people in Hulda—their family history, secret pains, loves and ambitions," he told *Publishers Weekly.* "In this respect I am living in the middle of a rushing stream." Even when he was younger, he said in *Partisan Review,* the kibbutz "evoked and fed my curiosity about the strange phenomenon of flawed, tormented human beings dreaming about perfection, aching for the Messiah, aspiring to change human nature. This perpetual paradox of magnanimous dream and unhappy reality is indeed one of the main threads in my writing." Furthermore, he told the *Washington Post,* his fellow kibbutzniks react to his works in fascinating ways: "It's a great advantage, you know, to have a passionate, immediate milieu and not a literary milieu—a milieu of real people who tell me straight in my face what they think of my writing."

My Michael, a novel about the psychological disintegration of a young Israeli housewife, was Oz's first work translated and published in English. *New Republic* contributor Lesley Hazleton calls the book "a brilliant and evocative portrait of a woman slowly giving way to schizoid withdrawal" and "a superb achievement, . . . the best novel to come out of Israel to date." In *Modern Fiction Studies,* Hana Wirth-Nesher expresses the view that Oz uses his alienated protagonist "to depict the isolation and fear that many Israelis feel partially as a country in a state of siege and partially as a small enclave of Western culture in a vast area of cultures and landscapes unlike what they have known. . . . Both the social and spatial aspects of Jerusalem in this novel express symbolically the awe and insecurity of its inhabitants." Alter praises *My Michael* for managing "to remain so private, so fundamentally apolitical in its concerns, even as it puts to use the most portentous political materials." Indeed, *Washington Post Book World* reviewer Audrey C. Foote finds the work's message to be "a caustic repudiation of the cherished conception of the young *sabra* as invariably vigorous, dedicated, and brave." Paul Zweig claims in the *New York Times Book Review* that when *My Michael* was published in Israel shortly after the Six Day War, it proved "extremely disturbing to Israelis. At a time when their country had asserted control over its destiny as never before, Oz spoke of an interior life which Israel had not had time for, which it had paid no heed to, an interior life that contained a secret bond to the Asiatic world beyond its border." Controversial though it was, *My Michael* was a best-seller in Israel; it established Oz's reputation among his countrymen and gave him entree into the international world of letters.

Oz's first novel, *Elsewhere, Perhaps,* was his second work to be translated and published abroad. Most critics feel that the book is the best fictional representation of kibbutz life to emerge from Israel; for instance, *Jewish Quarterly* reviewer Jacob Sonntag writes: "I know of no other book that depicts life in the Kibbutz more vividly, more realistically or with greater insight." In the *Nation,* William Novak notes that the story of sudden violent events in the lives of three kibbutz families engages our sympathies because of the compelling sincerity and moral concerns of the characters, and because of the extent to which this is really the story of an entire society." *New York Times Book Review* correspondent A. G. Mojtabai stresses the realistic sense of conflict between military and civilian values portrayed in *Elsewhere, Perhaps.* According to Mojtabai, two perceptions of "elsewhere" are active in the story: "elsewhere, perhaps, the laws of gravity obtain—not here; elsewhere, perhaps in some kingdom by the sea exists the model which our kibbutz imperfectly reflects, a society harmonious, healthful, joyful, loving—not here, not yet." Novak concludes that the novel's publication in the United States "should help to stimulate American appreciation of contemporary Israeli literature and society."

"As a seamstress who takes different pieces of cloth and sews them into a quilt, Amos Oz writes short pieces of fiction which together form a quilt in the reader's consciousness," notes J. Justin Gustainis in *Best Sellers.* "Just as the quilt may be of many colors but still one garment, Oz's stories speak of many things but still pay homage to one central idea: universal redemption through suffering." Oz began his literary career as an author of short fiction; he has since published several volumes of stories and novellas, including *Where the Jackals Howl, Unto Death,* and *The Hill of Evil Counsel.* Aschkenasy suggests that the stories in *Where the Jackals Howl* "are unified by an overall pattern that juxtaposes an individual permeated by a sense of existential estrangement and subterranean chaos with a self-deceiving community collectively intent upon putting up a facade of sanity and buoyancy in order to deny—or perhaps to exorcise—the demons from without and within." Chernaik notes of the same book that the reader coming to Oz for the first time "is likely to find his perception of Israel permanently altered and shaped by these tales." The novellas in *Unto Death* "take as their theme the hatred that surrounds Jews and that destroys the hated and the haters alike," to quote Joseph McElroy in the *New York Times Book Review.* *Midstream* contributor Warren Bargad finds this theme one manner of expressing "the breakdown of the myth of normalcy which has been at the center of Zionist longing for decades: the envisioned State of Israel, with its promise of autoemancipation, which would make of the Jewish people a nation among nations. For Oz it is still an impossible dream."

In an assessment of Oz's nonfiction, Shechner describes what he calls the "two Amos Ozes." One, Shechner writes, is "a fiction writer with an international audience, the other an Israeli journalist of more or less hometown credentials. . . . Oz's journalism would seem to have little in common with the crepuscular world of his fiction. A blend of portraits and polemics, it is straightforward advocacy journalism, bristling with editorials and belonging to the world of opinions, ideologies and campaigns." Despite his sometimes bleak portrayal of his homeland in his fiction, Oz believes in Israel and expresses strong opinions on how it should be run. Alter notes: "In contrast to the inclination some writers may feel to withdraw into the fastness of language, the Oz articles reflect a strenuous effort to go out into Israeli society and sound its depth." Furthermore, according to Roger Rosenblatt in the *New York Times Book Review,* as a journalist, Oz establishes "that he is no ordinary self-effacing reporter on a quest, but a public figure who for years has participated in major national controversies and who regularly gives his views of things to the international press, 'ratting' on his homeland." *Washington Post Book World* contributor Grace Schulman suggests that Oz's journalism "may be the way to an esthetic stance in which he can reconcile the conflicting demands of artistic concern and political turbulence."

In the Land of Israel, a series of interviews Oz conducted with a wide variety of Israelis, is his best known work of nonfiction. Shechner claims that the book "provoked an outcry in Israel, where many saw the portraits of Jews as exaggerated and tailored to suit Oz's politics." The study does indeed present a vision of a pluralistic, creatively contentious society, "threatened as much by the xenophobia and self-righteous tribalism within as by enemies without," according to Gene Lyons in *Newsweek.* Christopher Lehmann-Haupt offers a similar opinion in the *New York Times.* "All together," he writes, "the voices of 'In the Land of Israel' serve to elucidate the country's complex ideological cross-currents. And conducted as they are by Mr. Oz, they sing an eloquent defense of what he considers a centrist position, though some of his critics might call it somewhat left-of-center. Mr. Oz has distilled his country's dilemma to the tragic realization that every human being faces, which is, as one old pioneer put it: 'To be without power is both a sin and a catastrophe. On the other hand, to live by force is no less a catastrophe, and maybe a sin, too.' " The book has disturbed American critics as much as their Israeli counterparts. Schulman notes: "Amos Oz writes of a country in turmoil. . . . Like a journey through the circles of Dante's Inferno, Oz's travels take him from despair to agony." *Atlantic* reviewer Irving Howe likewise contends that *In the Land of Israel* "sets one's mind reeling with speculations and anxieties." Lyons feels that the work is most valuable for what it shows the reader about Oz and his positions *vis a vis* his country's future. Lyons concludes: "Eloquent, humane, even religious in the deepest sense, [Oz] emerges here—and I can think

of no higher praise—as a kind of Zionist Orwell: a complex man obsessed with simple decency and determined above all to tell the truth, regardless of whom it offends."

Oz's novel *A Perfect Peace,* published in Israel in 1982 and the United States in 1985, returns to the modern kibbutz for its setting. The story revolves around two young kibbutzniks—one rebellious after a lifetime in the environment, the other an enthusiastic newcomer—and an aging politician, founder of the collective. According to Alter, the novel is "a hybrid of social realism and metaphysical brooding, and it gains its peculiar power of assertion by setting social institutions and political issues in a larger metaphysical context. There is a vivid, persuasive sense of place here . . . but local place is quietly evoked against a cosmic backdrop." *Times Literary Supplement* reviewer S. S. Prawer observes that the work holds the reader's attention by providing a "variety of boldly drawn characters who reveal themselves to us in and through their speech. . . . Oz's storytelling, with its reliance on journals and inner monologues, is pleasantly old-fashioned; he conscientiously underpins his construction with recurrent motifs and personal tics in the approved manner; and he conjures up the kibbutz environment in the sober prose that makes much of typical smells, sounds and sights." In a *New York Times Book Review* piece, Schulman contends that it is "on a level other than the documentary that this novel succeeds so well. It is concerned with inner wholeness, and with a more profound peace than respect between generations and among countries. . . . The impact of this novel lies in the writer's creation of characters who are outwardly ordinary but inwardly bizarre, and at times fantastic." "This is Oz's strangest, riskiest and richest novel to date," Rita Kashner notes in the *Washington Post Book World.* "He writes in his usual clean, blunt prose, his characters' voices ring true, and he creates a world which makes perfect sense, except that at its core is a series of impenetrable mysteries. . . . Oz has spent craftsman's years developing a tender, ironic humor and an accuracy of voice that serve him brilliantly here."

Critics find much to praise in Oz's portraits of the struggling nation of Israel. "Mr. Oz's words, his sensuous prose and indelible imagery, the people he flings living onto his pages, evoke a cauldron of sentiments at the boil; yet his human vision is capacious enough to contain the destruction and hope for peace," writes Richard R. Lingeman in the *New York Times.* "He has caught a welter of fears, curses and dreams at a watershed moment in history, when an uneasy, restless waiting gave way to an upsurge of violence, of fearsome consequences. The power of his art fuses historical fact and symbol; he makes the ancient stones of Jerusalem speak, and the desert beyond a place of jackals and miracles." Kendall concludes: "This land of Oz is harsh and unfamiliar, resisting interpretation, defying easy solutions. His Israel is a place few tourists ever see and visiting dignitaries rarely describe. There, tension is the only constant and the howling of the jackals ceases only to begin again each night. Oz writes about that tension and that sound: how it feels, what it does." In the *Saturday Review,* Alfred Kazin states that Oz's effect on him is always to make him realize "how little we know about what goes on inside the Israeli head. . . . To the unusually sensitive and humorous mind of Amos Oz, the real theme of Jewish history—especially in Israel—is unreality. When, and how can a Jew attain reality in the Promised Land, actually touch the water, touch the wind?" Chernaik feels that Oz is "without doubt a voice for sanity, for the powers of imagination and love, and for understanding. He is also a writer of marvellous comic and lyric gifts, which somehow communicate themselves as naturally in English as in Hebrew."

Hebrew is the language in which Oz chooses to write; he calls it a "volcano in action," still evolving rapidly into new forms. Oz likes to call himself the "tribal storyteller," as he explained in the *New York Times:* "I bring up the evil spirits and record the traumas, fantasies, the lunacies of Israeli Jews, natives and those from Central Europe. I deal with their ambitions and the powderbox of self-denial and self-hatred." In a *Washington Post* interview, he maintained that Israel would always be the source from which his inspiration would spring. "I'm fascinated," he said of his homeland. "Yes, indeed, I'm disgusted, appalled, sick and tired sometimes. Even when I'm sick and tired, I'm there. . . . It's my thing, if you will, in the same sense that William Faulkner belonged in the Deep South. It's my thing and my place and my addiction." Married and the father of three children, Oz continues to live and work at Kibbutz Hulda. He also speaks and travels frequently, bringing his personal thoughts to television and lecture audiences in Israel and abroad. Describing his creative impulses, Oz told the *New York Times:* "Whenever I find myself in total agreement with myself, then I write an article—usually in rage—telling the government what to do. But when I detect hesitation, more than one inner voice, I discover in me the embryo of characters, the seeds of a novel."

MEDIA ADAPTATIONS: My Michael was adapted as a film under the same title in Israel.

BIOGRAPHICAL/CRITICAL SOURCES:

BOOKS

Contemporary Literary Criticism, Gale, Volume 5, 1976, Volume 8, 1978, Volume 11, 1979, Volume 27, 1981, Volume 33, 1985, Volume 54, 1989.

PERIODICALS

Atlantic, December, 1983.
Best Sellers, October, 1978.
Chicago Tribune, December 7, 1989.
Commentary, July, 1974, April, 1984.
Jewish Quarterly, spring-summer, 1974.
Los Angeles Times, May 21, 1981, June 24, 1985, December 25, 1989.
Los Angeles Times Book Review, December 11, 1983.
Midstream, November, 1976, January, 1985.
Modern Fiction Studies, spring, 1978.
Nation, September 7, 1974, June 8, 1985.
National Review, April 20, 1984.
New Leader, January 6, 1975.
New Republic, November 29, 1975, October 14, 1978, June 27, 1981, July 29, 1985.
Newsweek, November 21, 1983, July 29. 1985.
New Yorker, November 18, 1974, August 7, 1978, August 19, 1985.
New York Review of Books, February 7, 1974, January 23, 1975, July 20, 1978, September 26, 1985.
New York Times, May 19, 1978, July 18, 1978, May 22, 1981, October 31, 1983, November 11, 1989.
New York Times Book Review, May 21, 1972, November 18, 1973, November 24, 1974, October 26. 1975, May 28, 1978, April 26, 1981, March 27, 1983, November 6, 1983, June 2, 1985, February 4, 1990.
Partisan Review, Number 3, 1982, Number 3, 1986.
Publishers Weekly, May 21, 1973.
Saturday Review, June 24, 1972, November 2, 1974, May 13, 1978.
Spectator, January 9, 1982, December 17, 1983, August 10, 1985.
Studies in Short Fiction, winter, 1982.

Time, January 27, 1986.
Times (London), August 1, 1985.
Times Literary Supplement, July 21, 1972, February 22, 1974, March 21, 1975, October 6, 1978, September 25, 1981, July 27, 1984, August 9, 1985, March 2, 1990.
Village Voice, February 14, 1984.
Washington Post, December 1, 1983.
Washington Post Book World, May 28, 1972, May 31, 1981, June 14, 1981, November 13, 1983, July 14, 1985.
World Literature Today, spring, 1982, spring, 1983, summer, 1984, autumn, 1986.

*   *   *

OZICK, Cynthia 1928-
(Trudie Vocse)

PERSONAL: Born April 17, 1928, in New York, N.Y.; daughter of William (a pharmacist) and Celia (Regelson) Ozick; married Bernard Hallote (a lawyer), September 7, 1952; children: Rachel Sarah. *Education:* New York University, B.A. (cum laude), 1949; Ohio State University, M.A., 1950.

ADDRESSES: Home—34 Soundview St., New Rochelle, N.Y. 10805.

CAREER: Novelist, essayist, critic, translator, and author of short fiction. Filene's Department Store, Boston, Mass., advertising copywriter, 1952-53; New York University, New York City, instructor in English, 1964-65; City College of the City University of New York, New York City, distinguished artist-in-residence, 1981-82. Taught fiction workshop at Chautauqua Writers' Conference, July, 1966.

MEMBER: PEN, Authors League of America, American Academy of Arts and Sciences, Phi Beta Kappa.

AWARDS, HONORS: National Endowment for the Arts fellow, 1968; B'nai B'rith Jewish Heritage Award, Edward Lewis Wallant Memorial Award, and National Book Award nomination, all 1972, all for *The Pagan Rabbi, and Other Stories;* Jewish Book Council Award, 1972, for *The Pagan Rabbi, and Other Stories,* and 1976, for *Bloodshed and Three Novellas;* American Academy of Arts Award for Literature, 1973; O. Henry First Prize Award in fiction, 1975, 1981, 1984, and 1989; Pushcart Press Lamport Prize, 1980; Guggenheim fellow, 1982; National Book Critics Circle Award nomination, 1982 and 1983; Mildred and Harold Strauss Livings grant, American Academy and Institute of Arts and Letters, 1983; honorary degrees from Yeshiva University, 1984, Hebrew Union College, 1984, Williams College, 1986, and Hunter College of the City University of New York, 1987; Distinguished Service in Jewish Letters Award, Jewish Theological Seminary, 1984; Distinguished Alumnus Award, New York University, 1984; PEN/Faulkner Award nomination, 1984; Phi Beta Kappa oration, Harvard University, 1985; Rea Award for the Short Story, Dungannon Foundation, 1986; National Book Critics Circle Award nomination, 1989, for *Metaphor and Memory.*

WRITINGS:

FICTION

Trust (novel), New American Library, 1966, reprinted, Dutton, 1983.
The Pagan Rabbi, and Other Stories, Knopf, 1971.
Bloodshed and Three Novellas, Knopf, 1976.
Levitation: Five Fictions, Knopf, 1982.
The Cannibal Galaxy (novel), Knopf, 1983.
The Messiah of Stockholm (novel), Knopf, 1987.

The Shawl (short story and novella), Knopf, 1989.

NONFICTION

Art and Ardor: Essays, Knopf, 1983.
Metaphor and Memory: Essays, Knopf, 1989.

CONTRIBUTOR

Erwin Glikes and Paul Schwaber, editors, *Of Poetry and Power: Poems Occasioned by the Presidency and by the Death of John F. Kennedy,* Basic Books, 1964.

Murray Mindlin and Chaim Bermont, editors, *Explorations: An Annual on Jewish Themes,* Quadrangle, 1968.

Harold U. Ribalow, editor, *My Name Aloud: Jewish Stories by Jewish Writers,* Yoseloff, 1969.

W. Moynihan, D. Lee, and H. Weil, editors, *Reading, Writing, and Rewriting,* revised and condensed edition, Lippincott, 1969.

Martha Foley and David Burnett, editors, *The Best American Short Stories, 1970,* Houghton, 1970.

Women in a Sexist Society, Basic Books, 1971.

Foley, editor, *The Best American Short Stories, 1972,* Houghton, 1972.

Harry Harrison and Brian W. Aldiss, editors, *Best SF: 1971,* Putnam, 1972.

The First Ms. Reader, Warner Books, 1973.

C. Shrodes, H. Finestone, and M. Shugrue, editors, *The Conscious Reader: Readings Past and Present,* Macmillan, 1974.

Pat Rotter, editor, *Bitches and Sad Ladies: An Anthology of Fiction by and about Women,* Harper's Magazine Press, 1975.

Prize Stories 1975: The O. Henry Awards, Doubleday, 1975.

Joyce Field and Leslie Field, editors, *Bernard Malamud: A Collection of Critical Essays,* Prentice-Hall, 1975.

Foley, editor, *The Best American Short Stories, 1976,* Houghton, 1976.

Simon Wiesenthal, *The Sunflower: With a Symposium,* Schocken, 1976.

All Our Secrets Are the Same: New Fiction from Esquire Magazine, Norton, 1976.

Irving Howe, editor, *Jewish-American Stories,* Mentor, 1977.

Jeannette Webber and Joan Grumman, editors, *Woman as Writer,* Houghton, 1979.

The Penguin Book of Jewish Short Stories, Penguin, 1979.

Familiar Faces: Best Contemporary American Short Stories, Fawcett-Crest, 1979.

Robert Detweiler and Glenn Meeter, editors, *Faith and Fiction: The Modern Short Story,* Books on Demand, 1979.

Pushcart Prize V: Best of the Small Presses, 1980-1981 Edition, Pushcart Press, 1980.

Howard Schwartz and Anthony Rudolf, editors, *Voices within the Ark: The Modern Jewish Poets,* Avon, 1980.

Hortense Calisher and Shannon Ravenel, editors, *The Best American Short Stories, 1981,* Houghton, 1981.

William Abrahams, editor, *Prize Stories, 1981: The O. Henry Awards,* Prentice-Hall, 1981.

Abrahams, editor, *Prize Stories of the Seventies: From the O. Henry Awards,* Doubleday, 1981.

Jack Dunn, editor, *More Wandering Stars: An Anthology of Jewish Fantasy and Science Fiction,* Doubleday, 1981.

Susan Cahill, editor, *Motherhood: A Reader for Men and Women,* Avon, 1982.

Pushcart Prize VII: Best of the Small Presses, 1982-1983 Edition, Pushcart Press, 1982.

John Updike and Ravenel, editors, *The Best American Short Stories, 1984,* Houghton, 1984.

Abrahams, editor, *Prize Stories 1984: The O. Henry Awards,* Doubleday, 1984.

The Jewish Bible: Thirty-seven American Authors, Harcourt, 1987.

Also contributor to *Gates of the New City,* Avon.

CONTRIBUTOR OF TRANSLATIONS

Irving Howe and Eliezer Greenberg, editors, *A Treasury of Yiddish Poetry,* Holt, 1969.

Howe and Greenberg, editors, *Voices from the Yiddish: Essays, Memoirs, Diaries,* University of Michigan Press, 1972.

Howe and Ruth Wisse, *The Penguin Book of Yiddish Verse,* Viking, 1987.

OTHER

(Author of foreword) Gertrud Kolmar, *Dark Soliloquy: The Selected Poems of Gertrud Kolmar,* Seabury, 1975.

(Author of foreword) Milton Hindus, editor, *The Worlds of Maurice Samuel: Selected Writings,* Jewish Publication Society of America, 1977.

(Author of introduction) Bill Henderson, editor, *Pushcart Prize XI: Best of the Small Presses, 1986-1987 Edition,* Pushcart Press, 1986.

Contributor to "About Books" column in *New York Times Book Review,* 1987. Contributor, under pseudonym Trudie Vocse, of article "Twenty-four Years in the Life of Lyuba Bershadskaya" to *New York Times Magazine.* Contributor of other articles, reviews, stories, poems, and translations to periodicals, including *Commentary, New Republic, Partisan Review, New Leader, New York Times Book Review, Ms., Esquire, New Yorker, American Poetry Review, Harper's,* and *New York Times Magazine.*

SIDELIGHTS: Cynthia Ozick is "an important voice in American fiction, a woman whose intellect . . . is so impressive that it pervades the words she chooses, the stories she elects to tell, and every careful phrase and clause in which they are conveyed," writes Doris Grumbach in the *Washington Post Book World.* An acclaimed novelist, short story writer, essayist, and critic, Ozick is best known for her fiction, and in this regard "few contemporary authors have demonstrated her range, knowledge, or passion," says Diane Cole in the *Dictionary of Literary Biography.* Described by Elaine M. Kauvar in *Contemporary Literature* as a "master of the meticulous sentence and champion of the moral sense of art," Ozick writes on a variety of subjects, often mixing such elements as fantasy, mysticism, comedy, satire, and Judaic law and history in a style that suggests a poet's perfectionism and a philosopher's dialectic. Although many of her works are steeped in Judaic culture and explore the conflict between the sacred and the profane, the epithet "Jewish writer"—as she has been called—is a misnomer according to many critics, including Ozick herself, who claims in *Art and Ardor* that the term is an oxymoron. Rather, to use the words of Robert R. Harris in *Saturday Review,* she is fundamentally a writer "obsessed with the words she puts on paper, with what it means to imagine a story and to tell it, with what fiction is. The result is a body of work at once as rich as Grace Paley's stories, as deeply rooted in Jewish folklore as Isaac Bashevis Singer's tales, [and] as comically ironic as Franz Kafka's nightmares."

While she has yet to attain the wide popularity of many bestselling authors, Ozick has attracted the attention of readers and reviewers of serious fiction ever since her first book, *Trust,* was published in 1966. Narrated by an anonymous young woman searching for real and psychological identity, *Trust* is a long, intricately plotted, literary novel about personal and political betrayal that, according to *New York Times Book Review* contributor David L. Stevenson and others, hearkens back to the tradition of Henry James, Joseph Conrad, and D. H. Lawrence. Martin Tucker points out in the *New Republic* that Ozick's "style, though shaped by the ancient moderns . . . is not self-consciously imitative. The outstanding achievement of her first novel is its play with words, its love of paradox." Other critics also praise Ozick's linguistic virtuosity in *Trust,* although several share Tucker's opinion that "sometimes the cleverness of her style is obtrusive." R. Z. Sheppard, for instance, writes in *Book Week* that *Trust* "introduces a novelist of remarkable intelligence, learning, and inventiveness—qualities that make the book an uncommonly rich reading experience, yet qualities so lavishly displayed they frequently hobble . . . Ozick's muse." Nevertheless, Sheppard believes Ozick "still manages a considerable achievement of passion and skill," and Tucker calls the novel "brilliant." Stevenson, moreover, hails the book as "that extraordinary literary entity, a first novel that is a genuine novel, wholly self-contained and produced by a rich, creative imagination."

Following *Trust,* Ozick published three award-winning collections of shorter fiction, *The Pagan Rabbi, and Other Stories, Bloodshed and Three Novellas,* and *Levitation: Five Fictions,* that firmly established her reputation as a writer of exceptional talent. In a *New York Times Book Review* article on the first of these collections, Johanna Kaplan says Ozick proves herself to be "a kind of narrative hypnotist. Her range is extraordinary; there is seemingly nothing she cannot do. Her stories contain passages of intense lyricism and brilliant, hilarious, uncontainable inventiveness—jokes, lists, letters, poems, parodies, satires." Reflecting on *Levitation* and the other two collections in the *New York Review of Books,* A. Alvarez concludes that Ozick is "a stylist in the best and most complete sense: in language, in wit, in her apprehension of reality and her curious, crooked flights of imagination. . . . Although there is nothing stiff or overcompacted about her writing . . . she . . . has the poet's perfectionist habit of mind and obsession with language, as though one word out of place would undo the whole fabric." Such quality of invention prompts John Leonard to call the title story of *Levitation* "a masterpiece" in the *New York Times,* and leads *New York Times Book Review* contributor Leslie Epstein to regard *The Pagan Rabbi, and Other Stories* and *Bloodshed and Three Novellas* as "perhaps the finest work in short fiction by a contemporary writer." Ozick's talent furthermore encourages *Newsweek*'s Peter S. Prescott to "fearlessly predict that when the chroniclers of our literary age catch up to what has been going on (may Ozick live to see it!), some of her stories will be reckoned among the best written in our time."

Because, as Kaplan notes, Ozick's range in these stories is so extraordinary, a brief summary cannot do them justice. Cole provides an indication of Ozick's stylistic virtuosity: "From page to page, Ozick will shift from an elevated Biblical inflection to the stilted Yiddish of the Russian immigrant to a slangy American vernacular; from sharply focused realism to fantastical flights into the supernatural. Magical transformations abound—of women into sea nymphs, trees into dryads, virile young poets into elderly androgynes." Similarly, Ozick's tales defy easy explication, in part because of their "thought-provoking dialectical quality," according to Harris and others. Carole Horn says in the *Washington Post Book World:* "You could think about the themes that run through 'Bloodshed,' 'Usurpation' and 'The Mercenary' at great length. . . . The more of the Jewish Idea, as Ozick calls it, you have at your command, the broader the levels of meaning you could explore. But you don't need that to find them interesting reading." Harris points out that because

Ozick "deals with ideas—many of them steeped in Jewish Law and history—her stories are 'difficult.' But by difficult I mean only that they are not in the least bit fluffy. No word, emotion, or idea is wasted. They are weighty, consequential tales, lightened and at the same time heightened by their visionary aspects. . . . Her stories are elusive, mysterious, and disturbing. They shimmer with intelligence, they glory in language, and they puzzle."

The most frequently discussed theme in these stories is that of idol worship. "Again and again," writes Cole, ". . . characters are torn between the opposing claims of two religions. One is always pagan, whether it be the worship of nature or the idolatrous pursuit of art, whereas the other—Judaism—is sacred." Kaplan, among others, sees this theme in its broadest theological sense, as a "variant of the question: what is holy? Is it the extraordinary, that which is beyond possible human experience—dryads ('The Pagan Rabbi') or sea-nymphs ('The Dock-Witch')? Or is the holiness in life to be discovered, to be seen in what is ordinarily, blindly, unthinkingly discounted?" But Eve Ottenberg, author of a *New York Times Magazine* profile of Ozick, maintains that this theme has its greatest impact in a specifically Jewish context. "Over and over again," states Ottenberg, "[Ozick's] characters struggle, suffer, perform bizarre feats, even go mad as a result of remaining or finding out what it means to remain—culturally, and above all, religiously—Jewish in a world that for the most part is hostile. Her characters are often tempted into worshiping something other than God—namely, idols. And this struggle marks her characters with a singular aloneness—the aloneness of people who are thinking a great deal about who they are, and for whom thinking, not doing, is the most emotional and engaging aspect of their lives."

Idol worship is also the principal theme of Ozick's two subsequent novels, *The Cannibal Galaxy* and *The Messiah of Stockholm.* In fact, "idolatry is Cynthia Ozick's great theme," announces Edmund White in a *New York Times Book Review* appraisal of *The Cannibal Galaxy.* "In stories, essays and . . . in her second novel she meditates on this deep concern—the hubris of anyone who dares to rival the Creator by fashioning an idol." Harold Bloom declares in the *New York Times Book Review* that the central point of Ozick's work culminating in *The Messiah of Stockholm* has been to somehow reconcile her need to create fiction with her desire to remain a follower of the Jewish tradition. "Ozick's vision of literature," writes Bloom, "is conditioned by her anxiety about idolatry, her fear of making stories into so many idols. And her most profound insight concerns her ambivalence about the act of writing and the condemnation of the religion of art, or the worship of Moloch. This insight comes to the fore when she asks herself the combative question that governs every strong writer: 'Why do we become what we most desire to contend with?' "

As Bloom reports, Ozick's reply to this question in her early essays "was immensely bitter," and the same could be said for her early stories. The novella "Usurpation," collected in *Bloodshed and Three Novellas,* is ostensibly "a tale against tale telling," according to *Time*'s Paul Gray and others. "The thoroughly Jewish concern in this work," states Ruth R. Wisse in *Commentary,* "is the writing of fiction itself, in . . . Ozick's view an inheritance from the Gentiles and by nature an idolatrous activity. Art—in the Western tradition of truth to fiction as its own end—is against the Second Commandment, she says, and anti-Jewish in its very impulse. As a Jewish artist . . . Ozick undertakes to subvert the aesthetic ideal by demonstrating its corrupting and arrogant presumption to truth."

Ozick has modified her position over time, though. "I've revised my thinking," she told Mervyn Rothstein of the *New York Times.* "The earlier way was an error. Now I have a better idea, I think, a larger, more penetrating thought—which I didn't come to myself. . . . Though the imagination does lead to the making of images, twist it up higher, require more of the imagination, put more pressure on it—and then and only then can you have monotheism. Because monotheism requires the highest possible imagination—in order to imagine that which no image can be made of, that which you cannot see, smell, touch. To imagine the unimaginable requires the hugest possible imagination."

Bloom considers Ozick's "triumph" in *The Messiah of Stockholm* to be "a developed awareness that her earlier view of art as idolatry was too severe. . . . The novel is a complex and fascinating meditation on the nature of writing and the responsibilities of those who choose to create—or judge—tales. Yet on a purely realistic level, it manages to capture the atmosphere of Stockholm and to be, at times, very funny indeed about the daily operations of one of the city's newspapers and Lar's [the protagonist's] peculiar detachment from everyday work and life."

In addition to these concerns, *The Messiah of Stockholm* has garnered praise for its stylistic vitality, a common characteristic of Ozick's work. Calling the book "a poetic yet often raucously comic epic" in Chicago *Tribune Books,* Mona Simpson maintains that "of course, no work of Ozick's can be talked about without first acknowledging the simple brilliance of her prose." John Calvin Batchelor insists in the *Washington Post Book World* that *The Messiah of Stockholm* "is a superb read, with prose so deft that were it fisticuffs the author would be forbidden by law to combat mortals." But perhaps the finest compliment comes from Michiko Kakutani in the *New York Times:* "What distinguishes 'The Messiah of Stockholm' and lofts it above your run-of-the-mill philosophical novel is the author's distinctive and utterly original voice. . . . Ozick possesses an ability to mix up the surreal and the realistic, juxtapose Kafkaesque abstractions with Waughlike comedy. Bizarre images . . . float, like figures in a Chagall painting, above precisely observed, naturalistic tableaux; and seemingly ordinary people suddenly become visionaries capable of madness or magic. The result is fiction that has the power to delight us and to make us think."

BIOGRAPHICAL/CRITICAL SOURCES:

BOOKS

Alexander, Edward, *The Resonance of Dust: Essays on Holocaust Literature and Jewish Fate,* Ohio State University Press, 1979.

Berger, Alan L., *Crisis and Covenant: The Holocaust in American Jewish Fiction,* New York State University Press, 1985.

Bestsellers 90, Issue 1, Gale, 1990.

Bloom, Harold, editor, *Cynthia Ozick,* Chelsea House, 1986.

Cohen, Sarah Blacher, *Comic Relief: Humor in Contemporary American Literature,* University of Illinois Press, 1978.

Contemporary Literary Criticism, Gale, Volume 3, 1975, Volume 7, 1977, Volume 28, 1984.

Dictionary of Literary Biography, Volume 28: *Twentieth-Century American-Jewish Fiction Writers,* Gale, 1984.

Dictionary of Literary Biography Yearbook, Gale, *1982,* 1983, *1983,* 1984.

Ozick, Cynthia, *Art and Ardor,* Knopf, 1983.

Pinksker, Sanford, *The Uncompromising Fictions of Cynthia Ozick,* University of Missouri Press, 1987.

Rainwater, Catherine and William J. Scheick, editors, *Three Contemporary Women Novelists: Hazzard, Ozick, and Redmon,* University of Texas Press, 1983.

Rainwater, Catherine and William J. Scheick, editors, *Contemporary Women Writers,* University of Kentucky, 1985.

PERIODICALS

Book World, June 19, 1966.

Chicago Tribune, September 17, 1989.

Chicago Tribune Book World, February 14, 1982, October 30, 1983.

Commentary, June, 1976, March, 1984, May, 1984.

Commonweal, December 2, 1966, September 3, 1971.

Contemporary Literature, spring, 1985, winter, 1985.

Critique, Volume 9, number 2, 1967.

Globe and Mail (Toronto), October 7, 1989.

Hudson Review, spring, 1984.

Los Angeles Times, March 11, 1987.

Los Angeles Times Book Review, May 29, 1983, September 18, 1983, October 8, 1989.

Nation, February 20, 1982, July 23-30, 1983.

New Republic, August 13, 1966, June 5, 1976.

Newsweek, May 10, 1971, April 12, 1976, February 15, 1982, May 30, 1983, September 12, 1983.

New York Review of Books, April 1, 1976, May 13, 1982, November 30, 1983, May 28, 1987.

New York Times, July 9, 1966, July 5, 1971, January 28, 1982, April 10, 1983, April 27, 1983, August 29, 1983, March 25, 1987, March 28, 1987, September 5, 1989, October 3, 1989.

New York Times Book Review, July 17, 1966, June 13, 1971, April 11, 1976, January 31, 1982, February 14, 1982, May 22, 1983, September 11, 1983, March 22, 1987, September 10, 1989.

New York Times Magazine, April 10, 1983.

Publishers Weekly, March 27, 1987.

Saturday Review, July 9, 1966, February, 1982.

Time, August 12, 1966, April 12, 1976, February 15, 1982, September 5, 1983.

Times (London), April 8, 1982.

Times Literary Supplement, January 26, 1967, April 23, 1982, January 20, 1984.

Tribune Books (Chicago), March 1, 1987.

Village Voice, February 10, 1982.

Washington Post Book World, June 6, 1971, March 13, 1977, February 28, 1982, July 3, 1983, September 25, 1983, March 8, 1987.

P

PACKER, Vin
See MEAKER, Marijane (Agnes)

*   *   *

PAGE, P(atricia) K(athleen) 1916-
(Judith Cape, P. K. Irwin)

PERSONAL: Born November 23, 1916, in Swanage, Dorset, England; immigrated to Canada, 1919; daughter of Lionel Frank (a Major General) and Rose Laura (Whitehouse) Page; married William Arthur Irwin, December, 1950; stepchildren: Neal A., Patricia J. Irwin Morley, Shelia A. Irwin Irving. *Education:* Attended Art Students' League, New York, N.Y., and Pratt Institute; studied art privately in Brazil and New York.

ADDRESSES: Home—3260 Exeter Rd., Victoria, British Columbia, Canada V8R 6H6.

CAREER: Poet and artist. Has held jobs as sales clerk and radio actress in Saint John, New Brunswick, filing clerk and historical researcher in Montreal, Quebec; script writer for National Film Board, Ottawa, 1946-50. Conductor of workshops at the Writers' Workshop, Toronto, Ontario, 1974-77, and University of Victoria, 1977-78. Member of the Advisory Arts Panel to the Canadian Council, 1976-79. Has had solo exhibitions of paintings (under name P. K. Irwin) at Picture Loan Society, Toronto, 1960, Galeria de Arte Moderna, Mexico City, 1962, and Art Gallery of Greater Victoria, 1965; participant in group exhibitions in Canada and Mexico; work is represented in collections, including National Gallery of Canada, Art Gallery of Ontario, Vancouver Art Gallery, Art Gallery of Greater Victoria, University of Victoria, and private collections in Canada and abroad.

AWARDS, HONORS: Received by Academia Brazileira de Letras (Rio de Janeiro); Life Member, League of Canadian Poets; Bertram Warr Award from *Contemporary Verse* (Vancouver), 1940; Oscar Blumenthal Award from *Poetry* (Chicago), 1944; Canadian Governor-General's Award in Poetry, 1954, for *The Metal and the Flower;* Officer of the Order of Canada, 1977; National Magazines Award (gold), 1985; D.Litt., University of Victoria, 1985; Canadian Authors' Association Prize for Poetry, 1987.

WRITINGS:

(Under pseudonym Judith Cape) *The Sun and the Moon* (novel), Macmillan, 1944.

As Ten as Twenty (poems), Ryerson, 1946.
The Metal and the Flower (poems), McClelland & Stewart, 1954.
Cry Ararat! Poems New and Selected, McClelland & Stewart, 1967.
(Contributor) John R. Colombo, editor, *How Do I Love Thee: Sixty Poets of Canada (and Quebec) Select and Introduce Their Favourite Poems from Their Own Work,* Hurtig, 1970.
The Sun and the Moon and Other Fictions, Anansi, 1973.
Poems (1942-1973): Selected and New, Anansi, 1974.
(Editor) *To Say the Least: Canadian Poets A-Z,* Press Porcepic, 1979.
Evening Dance of the Grey Flies (poetry and prose), Oxford University Press, 1981.
The Glass Air (poetry, drawings, and essays), Oxford University Press, 1985.
A Brazilian Journal (prose and sketches), Lester & Orpen Dennys, 1987.
A Flask of Sea Water (juvenile), Oxford University Press, 1988.

CONTRIBUTOR TO ANTHOLOGIES

R. Hambleton, editor, *Unit of 5,* Ryerson, 1944.
John Sutherland, editor, *Other Canadians,* First Statement Press, 1947.
A. J. M. Smith, editor, *Book of Canadian Poetry,* University of Chicago Press, 1948.
Desmond Pacey, editor, *A Book of Canadian Stories,* Ryerson, 1950.
Louis Dudek and Irving Layton, editors, *Canadian Poems, 1850-1952,* Contact, 1952.
Earle Birney, editor, *Twentieth Century Canadian Poetry,* Ryerson, 1954.
Smith and F. R. Scott, editors, *The Blasted Pine,* Macmillan, 1957.
Ralph Gustafson, editor, *The Penguin Book of Canadian Verse,* Penguin, 1958.
Robert Weaver, editor, *Canadian Short Stories,* Oxford University Press, 1960.
Layton, editor, *Love Where the Nights Are Long,* McClelland & Stewart, 1962.
Milton Wilson, editor, *Poetry Mid-Century,* McClelland & Stewart, 1964.
Smith, editor, *The Oxford Book of Canadian Verse,* Oxford University Press, 1965.
Dudek, editor, *Poetry of Our Time,* Macmillan, 1965.

Smith, editor, *Modern Canadian Verse,* Oxford University Press, 1967.

R. Beny, editor, *To Everything There Is a Season,* Longmans, Green, 1967.

Mary Alice Downie and Barbara Robertson, editors, *The Wind Has Wings,* Oxford University Press, 1968.

Douglas Lockhead and Raymond Souster, editors, *Made in Canada,* Oberon, 1970.

A. O. Hughes, editor, *Tribal Drums,* McGraw, 1970.

J. Michael Yates, editor, *Contemporary Poetry of British Columbia,* Sono Nis Press, 1970.

Oscar Williams, editor, *A Little Treasury of Modern Poetry,* 3rd edition, Scribner, 1970.

Ondaatje and Urquhart, editors, *The Broken Ark,* Oberon, 1971.

Goldberg and Wright, editors, *I Am a Sensation,* McClelland & Stewart, 1971.

D. Livesay, editor, *40 Women Poets of Canada,* Ingluvin Press, 1972.

Weaver and William Toye, editors, *The Oxford Anthology of Canadian Literature,* Oxford University Press, 1973.

Pacey, editor, *Selections from Major Canadian Writers,* McGraw, 1974.

Gary Geddes, editor, *Sookum Wawa,* Oxford University Press, 1975.

John Newlove, editor, *Canadian Poetry: The Modern Era,* McClelland & Stewart, 1977.

Geddes and Phyllis Bruce, editors, *15 Canadian Poets Plus 5,* Oxford University Press, 1978.

Douglas Daymond and Leslie Monkman, editors, *Literature in Canada,* Gage Educational Publishing, 1978.

Columbo, editor, *The Poets of Canada,* Hurtig, 1978.

Daryl Hine and Joseph Parisi, editors, *The Poetry Anthology, 1912-1977,* Houghton, 1978.

Joseph Perrine, editor, *Sound and Sense,* Harcourt, 1982.

Margaret Atwood, editor, *The Oxford Book of Canadian Verse,* Oxford University Press, 1982.

Jack David and Robert Lecker, editors, *Canadian Poetry,* New Press, 1982.

The World of the Stone Angel, Prentice-Hall, 1983.

Geoff Hancock, editor, *Illusion,* Aya Press, 1983.

Rosemary Sullivan, editor, *Stories by Canadian Women,* Oxford University Press, 1984.

The Norton Anthology of Literature by Women, Norton, 1985.

Leon Rooke and John Metcalfe, editors, *The New Press Anthology #2, Best Stories,* General Publishing, 1985.

Contributor to *Western Windows,* 1977, *The Norton Anthology of Poetry,* 3rd edition, and *An Anthology of Poetry in English,* edited by M. L. Rosenthal.

OTHER

Also author of script and commentary for "Teeth Are To Keep," an animated film. Author of a dramatized version of *The Sun and the Moon* for Canadian Broadcasting Corporation (CBC) radio. Author of *Personal Landscape, A Song Cycle,* with music by Bernard Naylor, for Arts National, CBC, and author of the libretto for *The Travelling Musicians,* with music by Murray Adaskin. Contributor to periodicals and little magazines, including *Alphabet, Artscanada, Canadian Forum, Canadian Literature, Canadian Poetry, Saturday Night, Contemporary Verse, The White Pelican, Ellipse, Queen's Quarterly, Blackfish, Northern Review, Ontario Review, Poetry, Reading, Tamarack Review, Voices, Ariel, Tuatara, West Coast Review, Poetry Australia,* and *Encounter* and *Observer* (both England). Editorial board, *Malahat Review,* formerly, co-editor of *Preview,* and regional editor for *Northern Review.*

SIDELIGHTS: Canadian poet P. K. Page is an artist in many senses of the word. She is also known as P. K. Irwin, the acclaimed painter, and as Judith Cape, the fiction writer. She was given the Governor General's award for her second book of poems, *The Metal and the Flower* (1953), and was made an Officer of the Order of Canada in 1977. In a *Canadian Literature* review, A. J. M. Smith places Page "among the fine poets of this century" and deems her poem "Arras" "the high point of a school of Canadian symbolist poets." Critics find a unity of vision in all her works. "Page is an almost entirely visual poet," writes *Canadian Literature* essayist Rosemary Sullivan, who believes that Page's line "I suffer shame in all these images" conveys "one of the deepest impulses of her work." Page also reaches out for a reality larger than and beyond the visible world. "Landscapes behind the eyes have appeared in Page's poems since her first collection in 1946. [In *Evening Dance of the Grey Flies*] they shine in the jewelled colouring of her intricately-wrought technique, a technique which has always been dazzling," Ann Mandel notes in a *Canadian Forum* review. Sullivan observes, "The discrepancy between the ideal world of the imagination, the potent world of dream, and the real world of the senses becomes one of her most obsessive subjects."

Sullivan reports that Page "began her poetic career with a reputation as a poet of social commitment and is probably still best known for the poems of the 1940s written while she was a member of the Montreal *Preview* group of poets." During that time, Montreal was the center of Canadian literary activity. The group, which included Page, Patrick Anderson, F. R. Scott, and many other poets, produced *Preview,* the literary magazine in which Page's earliest poems first appeared. According to *Canadian Literature* contributor S. Namjoshi, this group "had leftist leanings, and several of [Page's] poems reveal what may be termed a 'pro-proletarian' consciousness." However, Sullivan maintains that Page's "poetry has more to do with folklore, myth and archetype than with objective time, history and social fact." While the critic finds a "genuine compassion" for society's victims in Page's early poetry, Sullivan notes that "the poet's verbal facility betrays her. The attention she gives to metaphor distracts from the human dilemma that is her theme."

Poet and critic A. J. M. Smith reports in *Canadian Literature* that Page's experiences during the 1950s and early sixties stimulated her attention to detail. During those years, she accompanied her husband, a Canadian editor and diplomat, to Australia, Brazil, and Mexico. Though Page painted more than she published during this time, Smith believes "her painting and her poetry complemented one another: each . . . made the other better, or made it more deeply what it was. . . . And then the immersion in the language, landscape, and the mythology of the strange, intense, and perhaps intensely un-Canadian places had a stimulating and enriching influence on all her latest poems." Negative criticism of Page's poetry centers on the abundance of vivid images. "Each of Miss Page's stanzas is so crowded with new and exciting pictures, that . . . [each] seems . . . to require the attention of a whole poem," John Sutherland comments in the *Northern Review.* As Sullivan explains, Page "has such a remarkable verbal gift that the image-making process can become almost too seductive. . . . The poet is trapped by her remarkable responsiveness to nature." Page is so receptive to "sensual detail, to each 'bright glimpse of beauty,' that even the sense of self, of separateness from the world, seems threatened."

This threat is a major element in her novel and first book. The heroine in *The Sun and the Moon* empathizes so thoroughly with inanimate objects that she "becomes a rock, a chair, a tree, experiencing these forms of existence in moments of identity," Sullivan relates. "But there is an alternative rhythm where the self is invaded. . . . Not only her identity, but also the identity of the other is destroyed by her chameleon presence. . . . To control this invasion an extraordinary exertion of will is necessary. For the poet, this means a control through technique, verbal dexterity. But P. K. Page's greatest dilemma is to ensure that this control is not sterile, that language is explored as experience, not evasion."

Page's writings also discuss the danger of becoming trapped in the private world of the imagination. Namjoshi defines the "central persona" of Page's poetry as "the woman caught within the confines of her inner reality, her personal Noah's Ark, seeking some way to reconcile the internal and the external, to make a harmony out of the double landscapes." "That the artist must make the effort to mediate between the internal and the external is central to her poetry," the reviewer states. Namjoshi names the poem "Cry Ararat" Page's "most successful effort at bringing the private world and the external world into alignment. 'Ararat!' is the cry of the isolated individual trapped within the confines of his private ark." Mount Ararat symbolizes a resting place between the "flood" of detail in the physical world, and "the stifling closeness of his own four walls. He need not withdraw into his private world, nor is his individuality submerged in the flood." This poem lends its title to Page's third book of poems, *Cry Ararat!: Poems New and Selected*—a loan that Namjoshi deems "fitting," since the poem "is a definitive and serious investigation of [Page's] theme, and brings the dilemma postulated by her to a final resolution."

In *Evening Dance of the Grey Flies,* the poet's seventh book, *Times Literary Supplement* contributor Fleur Adcock recognizes the characteristic "spiritual quest which expresses itself in highly colorful visionary language." Kevin Lewis, writing in *Quill and Quire,* says of Page, "It is no small feat to write convincing poetry in such a thick, imagistic style. . . . She must stand as one of the premier poets in Canada simply because she has such a beautiful way with words." *Canadian Literature* contributor Tom Marshall concludes, "As poet and calligrapher, [Page] delights in details and images, but has learned . . . to subordinate whimsy to the . . . design or large metaphor that captures a sense of the macrocosm. . . . She is one of our best poets."

BIOGRAPHICAL/CRITICAL SOURCES:

BOOKS

Contemporary Literary Criticism, Gale, Volume 7, 1977, Volume 18, 1981.
Dictionary of Literary Biography, Volume 68: *Canadian Writers, 1920-1959,* Gale, 1988.
Frye, Northrup, *The Bush Garden,* Anansi, 1971.
Page, P. K., *Poems Selected and New,* Anansi, 1974.
Waddington, Miriam, editor, *Essays, Controversies and Poems,* McClelland & Stewart, 1972.
Woodcock, George, editor, *Poets and Critics: Essays from Canadian Literature, 1966-74,* Oxford University Press, 1974.

PERIODICALS

Canadian Forum, May, 1974, May, 1982, March, 1985, March, 1986.
Canadian Literature, autumn, 1970, autumn, 1971, spring, 1975, winter, 1976, winter, 1978.
Canadian Poetry: Studies, Documents, Reviews, spring/summer, 1979.
Globe and Mail (Toronto), June 27, 1987.
Malahat Review, January, 1978.
Northern Review, December/January, 1947.

Poetry, October, 1968.
Quill and Quire, January, 1982.
Times Literary Supplement, October 26, 1973, March 18, 1983.

*   *   *

PAGET-LOWE, Henry
See LOVECRAFT, H(oward) P(hillips)

*   *   *

PAGNOL, Marcel (Paul) 1895-1974

PERSONAL: Born February 25 (some sources say February 28), 1895, in Aubagne, France; died April 18, 1974; son of Joseph (a teacher) and Augustine (a seamstress; maiden name, Lansot) Pagnol; married Simone Collin, 1916; married second wife, Jacqueline Bouvier (an actress), October 6, 1945; children: (first marriage) two sons, one daughter; (second marriage) two sons. *Education:* Attended lycee Thiers, Marseilles, France; received degree in letters and teaching diploma from University of Montpellier.

CAREER: Teacher of English at school in Tarascon, France, 1912, and Pamiers sur Ariege and lycee Saint-Charles, Marseilles, France, 1914-17; professor at lycee Condorcet, Paris, France, 1922-29; playwright; novelist; screenwriter, director, and producer of motion pictures. Director of films, including "Angele," 1934, "Cesar," 1936, "Harvest," 1937, "The Baker's Wife," 1939, "The Well-Digger's Daughter," 1940, "Ways of Love," 1950, "Manon des sources," 1952, and "Letters From My Windmill," 1954. Producer of films, including "Marius," 1931, "Fanny," 1932, "Angele," 1934, "Cesar," 1936, "Harvest," 1937, "The Well-Digger's Daughter," 1940, "The Prize," 1950, "Manon des sources," 1952, "Carnival," 1953, and "Letters From My Windmill," 1954. Co-founder of *Fortunio* (literary magazine, later published as *Les Cahiers du sud*), 1911; founder of *Les Cahiers du film* (literary magazine), 1931; founder and head of Les Films Marcel Pagnol (motion picture company and film studio), 1934. French consul for Portugal in Monaco. *Military service:* French infantry, 1914-17; French army, 1940.

MEMBER: L'Academie Francaise, Societe des Auteurs et Compositeurs Dramatiques (president, 1944-46), Syndicat Autonome du Cinema Francais (honorary president).

AWARDS, HONORS: New York Film Critics awards for best foreign film, 1939, for "Harvest," and 1950, for "Ways of Love"; Grand Officier de la Legion d'Honneur.

WRITINGS:

PLAYS

(With Paul Nivoix) *Les Marchands de gloire* (four-act; first produced in Paris at the Theatre de la Madeleine, April 15, 1925), [Paris], 1926, reprinted with illustrations by Andre Bertran, Editions Pastorelly, 1976.
Jazz (four-act; first produced in Paris at the Theatre des Arts, December 26, 1926), [Paris], 1927, reprinted, Livre de Poche, 1975.
Topaze (four-act; first produced in Paris at the Theatre de Varietes, October 9, 1928), Fasquelle, 1930, reprinted, Presses Pocket, 1976, translation by Renee Waldinger published as *Topaze,* Barron's, 1958.
Marius (four-act; first produced in Paris at the Theatre de Paris, March 9, 1929), Fasquelle, 1931, definitive edition illustrated by Suzanne Ballivet, Editions Pastorelly, 1969.

Fanny (three-act; first produced in Paris at the Theatre de Paris, December 5, 1931), Fasquelle, 1932, definitive edition illustrated by Ballivet, Editions Pastorelly, 1970.

Cesar (adapted from Pagnol's screenplay of the same title; first produced in Paris at the Theatre de Varietes, December 18, 1946), Fasquelle, 1937, definitive edition illustrated by Ballivet, Editions Pastorelly, 1970.

Angele (adapted from Pagnol's screen adaptation of Jean Giono's novel of the same title), Fasquelle, 1953.

Judas (five-act; first produced in Paris at the Theatre de Paris, October 7, 1955), Grasset, 1956.

Also author or co-author of other stage plays, including "Catulle," 1913, "Ulysse chez les Pheniciens," 1918, "Un Direct au coeur," 1924, and "Fabian," 1956.

SCREENPLAYS

"Marius" (adapted from Pagnol's play of the same title), released in France, 1931, released in the United States as "Marius," Joinville/Paramount, 1933 (also see above).

"Fanny" (adapted from Pagnol's play of the same title), released in France, 1932, released in the United States as "Fanny," Les Films Marcel Pagnol/Siritzky International, 1948 (also see above).

(And director) "Angele" (adapted from Jean Giono's novel of the same title), Les Films Marcel Pagnol, 1934 (also see above).

Merlusse (released in France, 1935), [Paris], 1935, reprinted, edited with introduction and notes by Lucius Gaston Moffatt, Holt, 1937.

(And director) "Cesar," Les Films Marcel Pagnol, 1936, released in the United States as "Cesar," 1937 (also see above).

(And director) *Regain* (adapted from Giono's novel of the same title; released in France, 1937, released in the United States as "Harvest," French Cinema, 1939), [Paris], 1937, reprinted, illustrations by Suzanne Ballivet, Editions Pastorelly, 1973.

Le Schpountz (released in France, 1938), [Paris], 1938, reprinted, Livre de Poche, 1975.

(And director) *La Femme du boulanger* (adapted from Giono's novel *Jean le bleu;* released in France, 1939, released in the United States as "The Baker's Wife," La Societe des Films Marcel Pagnol, 1940), [Paris], 1938.

(And director) *La Fille du puisatier* (released in France, 1940, released in the United States as "The Well-Digger's Daughter," Les Films Marcel Pagnol/Siritzky International, 1946), [Paris], 1941, reprinted, 1973.

La Belle Meuniere (released in France, 1948), Editions Self, 1948, reprinted, Presses Pocket, 1978.

Cigalon (released in France, 1936), edited by John Braddock Sturges, Heath, 1948, reprinted, Presses Pocket, 1978.

(And director) "Jofroi" (one of three short films released under the title "Ways of Love"; adapted from Giono's story "Jofroi de la Maussan"), Joseph Burstyn, 1950.

"Le Rosier de Madame Husson" (adapted from Guy de Maupassant's story of the same title), released in France, 1950, released in the United States as "The Prize," Les Films Marcel Pagnol/Classic Pictures, 1952.

(And director) "Manon des sources," released in France, 1952.

"Carnival" (adapted from a play by Emile Mazaud), Gaumont, 1953.

(And director) *Trois Lettres de mon moulin* (adapted from stories by Alphonse Daudet; released in France, 1954, released in the United States as "Letters From My Windmill," Mediterranean/Tohan Pictures, 1955), Flammarion, 1954, re-

vised edition published as *Quatre Lettres de mon moulin,* Editions Pastorelly, 1979.

La Prere aux etoiles (released in France, 1942), Editions de Provence, 1974.

Nais (based on a work by Emil Zola; released in France, 1945), Presses Pocket, 1977.

Also author or co-author of other screenplays, including "Un Direct au coeur," 1933 (also see above), "L'Agonie des aigles," 1933, "Le Gendre de Monsieur Poirier," 1934, "L'Article 330," 1934, "Tartarin de Tarascon," 1934, "Monsieur Brotonneau," 1939, "La Dame aux camelias," 1962, and "Le Cure de Cucugnan" (for television), 1967.

COLLECTIONS

Oeuvres dramatiques: Theatre et cinema, Gallimard, 1954.

Marius [and] *Fanny* [and] *Cesar,* Le Club de Meilleur Livre, 1956.

Souvenirs d'enfance (contains *La Gloire de mon pere, Le Chateau de ma mere, Le Temps des secrets,* and *Le Temps des amours*), Editions Pastorelly, 1957-1977.

Oeuvres completes, Editions de Provence, 1964.

Oeuvres completes, Club de l'Honnete Homme, 1970.

La Belle Meuniere [and] *Le Rosier de Madame Husson,* Editions Pastorelly, 1978.

OTHER

La Petite Fille aux yeux sombres (novel), [France], 1919, reprinted, Julliard, 1984.

Pirouettes (novel), 1922, reprinted, Fasquelle, 1932, reprinted, Presses Pocket, 1979.

Notes sur le rire, 1927, reprinted, Nagel, 1947.

Le Premier Amour, 1946, reprinted, Editions de Provence, 1974.

Cinematurgie de Paris (addresses, essays, and lectures), [France], 1948, reprinted, Editions Pastorelly, 1980.

Critique des critiques, Nagel, 1949.

La Gloire de mon pere (title means "My Father's Glory"), Editions Pastorelly, 1957, definitive edition illustrated by A. Dubout, 1958, translation by Rita Barisse published with *My Mother's Castle* as *The Days Were Too Short,* Doubleday, 1960, reprinted as *My Father's Glory* [and] *Mother's Castle,* North Point Press, 1986.

Le Chateau de ma mere (title means "My Mother's Castle"), Editions Pastorelly, 1958, definitive edition illustrated by Dubout, 1960, translation by Barisse published with *My Father's Glory* (also see above) as *The Days Were Too Short,* Doubleday, 1960, reprinted as *My Father's Glory* [and] *My Mother's Castle,* North Point Press, 1986.

Le Temps des secrets (memoirs), Editions Pastorelly, 1960, translation by Barisse published as *The Time of Secrets,* Doubleday, 1962.

L'Eau des collines (two-volume novel adapted from Pagnol's screenplay "Manon des sources"), Editions de Provence, Volume 1: *Jean de Florette,* 1962, Volume 2: *Manon des sources,* 1963, translation of both volumes by W. E. van Heyningen published as *The Water of the Hills,* North Point Press, 1988 (both novels also published separately in French under titles *Jean de Florette* and *Manon des sources,* Editions de Provence, 1963; also see above).

Les Sermons de Pagnol, compiled by C. Norbert Calmels, Morel, 1967.

(Contributor) *Contes de Provence* (short stories), Dupuis, 1968.

Le Temps des amours (memoirs), postscript by Bernard de Fallois, Julliard, 1977, translation by Eileen Ellenbogen published as *The Time of Love,* H. Hamilton, 1979.

Confidences (vignettes), Julliard, 1981.

Inedits, edited by Jacqueline and Frederic Pagnol, Vertiges du Nord/Carrere, 1988.

Translator of various works into French, including several of William Shakespeare's plays and Virgil's *Eclogues.* Contributor to periodicals, including *Cahiers du cinema, Les Cahiers du film, Cinemonde,* and *New York Times Magazine.*

SIDELIGHTS: Marcel Pagnol's prosaic and cinematic renderings of life in southern France have secured his place in French culture and history. A respected playwright, screenwriter, filmmaker, and novelist, he is probably best remembered for his pioneering role in the development of French cinema. Pagnol earned acclaim as a playwright in the late 1920s and, with the advent of sound film, saw the motion picture as a medium that could redefine the art of theatre. With the profits from his early writings, Pagnol established the motion picture company Les Films Marcel Pagnol in 1934. Throughout the 1930s, some critics dismissed his cinematic efforts as "canned theatre"—merely filmed versions of stage productions. But Pagnol has since been credited with prefiguring the trend toward greater realism in film. His 1934 film "Angele," about a peasant girl who bears a child out of wedlock, is generally considered a forerunner of neorealism, the cinematic movement that flourished in Europe immediately after World War II.

Following his father's example, Pagnol began his career as an educator, teaching English in schools in his native Marseilles and writing original plays in his spare time. He achieved mild success with several stage productions in the early 1920s, but in 1928 he gained recognition as a distinguished playwright with "Topaze," his satire about an eccentric schoolteacher's transformation into a corrupt but contented tycoon. "Topaze" enjoyed a legendary two-year run in Paris and was followed by the even more successful "Marius," the first play in Pagnol's highly acclaimed "Marseilles Trilogy."

Consisting of "Marius," "Fanny," and "Cesar," the "Marseilles Trilogy" revolves around the three title characters: young Marius, who longs for a life on the sea; his father, Cesar, who owns a waterfront bar in Marseilles; and Fanny, a shellfish vendor in love with Marius. "Marius," first staged in 1929 and later adapted by Pagnol for the screen, traces the tumultuous love affair between Marius and Fanny. Overwhelmed by his passion for the sea, Marius cannot make a commitment to Fanny. Consequently, Fanny accepts a marriage proposal from Honore Panisse, a wealthy sailmaker thirty years her senior, and Marius goes off to sea. In the 1931 play "Fanny," released the next year as a film, Fanny learns that she is pregnant with Marius's child. The kindly Panisse is still intent upon marrying Fanny, provided they raise her child as their own. Marius returns from sea after the baby's birth and, learning that he is the boy's father, declares his love for Fanny. Fanny admits that she still loves Marius but refuses to leave her faithful husband, Panisse. Marius reluctantly heads back to sea. "Cesar," which Pagnol first wrote for the screen and directed in 1937 and later adapted for the stage, focuses on Cesariot, Fanny and Marius's now-adult son. Following the death of Panisse, Cesariot learns of his true parentage. His grandfather, Cesar, tells him of Marius's whereabouts, and Cesariot engineers a reunion between Marius and the widowed Fanny.

Pagnol's "Marseilles Trilogy" was a critical and popular success in France. While several British film critics objected to Pagnol's allegedly nonchalant treatment of premarital sex, all three films received international praise for their multifaceted characterizations and realistic evocations of Marseilles and its culture. Commenting on the enduring appeal of the films, Edward Baron

Turk asserted in *American Film:* "Escape, transgression, and promiscuity are not—in Pagnol's soothing scheme of things—challenges to prevailing order. They are instead the expression of eternal human drives that fit, approvingly, into a continuing age-old pattern of growing up." In addition, the critic deemed the trilogy "one of the most cherished love stories of our century" and "a monument of early sound filmmaking."

Many of the stylistic and thematic trends Pagnol established in his "Marseilles Trilogy" appear in his subsequent films. The 1937 award-winner "Harvest" concerns a good-hearted farmer who lives alone in a deserted village and falls in love with the victim of a gang rape. "The Baker's Wife," released in 1939, tells of a village baker's refusal to resume work until his wife—who ran away with a Marquis's shepherd—returns home. The 1940 film "The Well-Digger's Daughter" deals with a young girl who becomes impregnated by her aviator lover and is consequently disowned by her strict father. These and other films written and directed by Pagnol, including the 1954 adaptation "Letters From My Windmill," share a setting in the southern French countryside and feature simple characters, usually farmers or laborers, and happy endings. Pagnol received some criticism for his use of stock filming techniques and his seeming misogyny—New York state censors tried unsuccessfully to ban "Harvest" for its demeaning depiction of women. But the irony, dry humor, and earthy charm of his scripts won over many critics and reinforced Pagnol's reputation as both a pioneering filmmaker and a humanitarian capable of great sympathy and insight into life's joys and perils.

In 1952, Pagnol wrote and directed "Manon des sources," a four-hour film that is now generally considered his masterwork, and ten years later he adapted the film for the two-volume novel known in English as *The Water of the Hills* (also published in separate volumes as *Jean de Florette* and *Manon of the Springs). The Water of the Hills* tells of the innocent hunchback Jean's ill-fated struggle to create a simple and happy life for himself, his wife, and his small daughter, Manon, on a small patch of land in a Provencal village. A city denizen, Jean inherits the fertile strip of land from his mother, Florette, and, believing they will thrive on a rich and natural country lifestyle, moves his family there. Selfish and avaricious neighbors—wanting the land for themselves—block the spring on Jean's land, cutting off his water source. Jean dies trying to save his land. His daughter Manon, having remained in the country after Jean's death, grows up possessing what *Chicago Tribune* reviewer Constance Markey called a "oneness with nature." As a young woman, Manon avenges her father's death and finds peace among the villagers.

While several critics considered the plot contrived and predictable, most lauded the story for its raw appeal and fundamental nature. Deirdre Bair, writing in the *New York Times Book Review,* noted that *The Water of the Hills* "convey[s] all the color and texture of Provencal village life, custom, and landscape" and "flow[s] with brisk precision from initial tragedy to final ironic triumph." *Times Literary Supplement* contributor David Coward agreed, adding, "The novels are more sombre, more thoughtful than his original film, but Pagnol the mellow moralist is as ever the genial host and comic raconteur. He is a keen-eyed, sharp-eared observer, and lovers of eccentricity, the ridiculous, and human weakness are bidden to a feast."

As his filmmaking career slowed in the late 1950s, Pagnol began writing his autobiography. The project resulted in four volumes—*My Father's Glory, My Mother's Castle, The Time of Secrets,* and *The Time of Love*—collectively titled *Souvenirs d'enfance.* Each of the works was widely praised for its charm.

In the first two volumes, which were jointly published in 1960 as *The Days Were Too Short,* Pagnol recalls the summers he spent as a young boy with his family in a country farmhouse near Marseilles. A dissenting reviewer complained that the volumes were overly sentimental, but *New York Times Book Review* contributor S. N. Behrman captured the consensus of the critics, suggesting that *The Days Were Too Short* reflects Pagnol's "enormous gusto for life, his humor, sympathy and wit, his keen satiric sense and his inexorable eye for reality."

The Time of Secrets, Pagnol's third autobiographical volume, traces the author's growth into manhood, describing the heartbreak of adolescent love and his decision to forgo a life as a country farmer for study at the lycee. Deeming the work "an intermingling of the child's world and the benevolent satirist's judgment of it," Anna Balakian, writing in *Saturday Review,* proclaimed: "With Pagnol's faculty for glowing detail and subtle innuendo, autobiography becomes indeed creative writing." Pagnol's *The Time of Love,* written between 1959 and 1962 and posthumously published as the fourth of the *Souvenirs* volumes, details the author's school years at the lycee in Marseilles. Several critics again hinted that Pagnol may have infused his recollections with too much sentiment, thereby inflating the truth, but in an article for *World Literature Today,* Madeleine Rumeau-Smith judged the memoir a fitting testament to "the tender, naive and indulgent humor of Pagnol."

MEDIA ADAPTATIONS: Pagnol's novels *Jean de Florette* and *Manon des sources* were both adapted for films of the same titles by Claude Berri and Gerard Brach, directed by Berri, and produced by Pierre Grunstein, Renn-Films, 1986, released in the United States as "Jean de Florette" and "Manon of the Springs," Orion, 1987; several other works by Pagnol, including the play "Topaze," have been adapted for film.

BIOGRAPHICAL/CRITICAL SOURCES:

BOOKS

Castans, Raymond, *Il etait une fois,* Julliard, 1980.
The Motion Picture Guide, ten volumes, Cinebooks, 1986.

PERIODICALS

American Film, October, 1980.
Chicago Tribune, July 22, 1962, May 20, 1988.
New York Times, October 28, 1952, December 19, 1955.
New York Times Book Review, October 23, 1960, April 17, 1988.
Saturday Review, July 28, 1962.
Spectator, August 25, 1979.
Times Literary Supplement, December 23, 1960, March 23, 1962, February 26, 1988, June 10, 1988.
Washington Post Book World, November 30, 1986.
World Literature Today, spring, 1978, autumn, 1983.

*   *   *

PAIGE, Richard
See KOONTZ, Dean R(ay)

*   *   *

PAKENHAM, Antonia
See FRASER, Antonia (Pakenham)

*   *   *

PALEY, Grace 1922-

PERSONAL: Born December 11, 1922, in New York, N.Y.; daughter of Isaac (a doctor) and Mary (Ridnyik) Goodside; married Jess Paley (a motion picture cameraman), June 20, 1942 (divorced); second husband Robert Nichols (an architect and writer); children: (first marriage) Nora, Dan. *Education:* Attended Hunter College (now Hunter College of the City University of New York), 1938-39, and New York University. *Politics:* "Anarchist, if that's politics." *Religion:* Jewish.

ADDRESSES: Home—126 West 11th St., New York, N.Y. 10011; and Thetford Hill, Vt. 05074. *Office*—Department of Literature and Writing, Sarah Lawrence College, Bronxville, N.Y. 10708.

CAREER: Writer. Teacher at Columbia University and Syracuse University during the early 1960s; member of literature faculty at Sarah Lawrence College, Bronxville, N.Y., since 1966, and at City College of New York since 1983. Secretary, Greenwich Village Peace Center.

MEMBER: National Institute of Arts and Letters.

AWARDS, HONORS: Guggenheim fellowship in fiction, 1961; National Council on the Arts grant; National Institute of Arts and Letters Award for short story writing, 1970; nomination for PEN Faulkner Award for Fiction, 1986, for *Later the Same Day;* Edith Wharton Citation of Merit, New York State Writers Institute, 1986, naming Paley "first state author" of New York; National Endowment for the Arts senior fellowship, 1987.

WRITINGS:

The Little Disturbances of Man: Stories of Women and Men at Love, Doubleday, 1959, published with new introduction by A. S. Byatt as *The Little Disturbances of Man,* Virago, 1980.
Enormous Changes at the Last Minute (short stories), Farrar, Straus, 1974.
Leaning Forward, Granite Press, 1985.
Later the Same Day (short stories), Farrar, Straus, 1985.
(With Vera B. Williams) *Three Hundred Sixty-Five Reasons Not to Have Another War: 1989 Peace Calendar,* New Society, 1988.
(Author of preface) *A Dream Compels Us: Voices of Salvadoran Women,* South End Press, 1989.

Stories have been published in *Atlantic, Esquire, New Yorker, Ikon, Genesis West, Accent,* and other periodicals.

WORK IN PROGRESS: Short stories.

SIDELIGHTS: With just three books of short stories, Grace Paley has established her niche in the world of letters. Her distinctive voice and verbal gifts have captured the hearts of critics who praise her vision as well as her style. In short and sometimes plotless tales, she plumbs the lives of working class New Yorkers, mapping out what *New York Review of Books* contributing critic Michael Wood calls "a whole small country of damaged, fragile, haunted citizens." Rather than action, Paley relies on conversation to establish character, reproducing Jewish, Black, Irish, and other dialects with startling accuracy. *America* reviewer William Novak deems her "a writer's writer" who "focuses her talent and energy on the craft itself" and "observes the classic rules: she writes what she knows, she does not attempt too much, she shies away from any hint of cliche and tells a simple and honest story." Walter Clemons's assessment is even more generous; in a *Newsweek* review he proclaims her "one of the best writers alive."

The daughter of Russian immigrants who arrived in New York around the turn of the century, Paley was raised in the Bronx. At home, her parents spoke Russian and Yiddish, and Paley grew up under two cultures, influenced by the old world as well as the new. From her surroundings, she gleaned the raw material for her short stories, and both her Russian/Jewish heritage and her perceptions of New York street life pervade her work.

Though she enrolled for a time at Hunter College, Paley never completed her studies; she was, as her London publisher Virago reports, "too busy writing poetry and reading voraciously to finish school." She married young and during the 1950s began to write short stories. Her first collection, *The Little Disturbances of Man: Stories of Women and Men at Love,* was published when she was thirty-seven. An ardent feminist and active pacifist, Paley admits she is often distracted from writing by political causes. She has never finished a novel. "Art is too long and life is too short. There is a lot more to do in life than just writing," she explains.

With the publication of *The Little Disturbances of Man,* Paley began to attract critical attention. Initial sales were modest, but the collection drew a loyal following and good reviews. The *New Yorker* assessed Paley's writing as "fresh and vigorous," noting that "her view of life is her own." To *Kirkus Reviews* the collection seemed "alternately humorous and touching, simple and unaffected . . . a demonstration of a considerable talent."

The ten stories that comprise the volume focus on the inhabitants of a boisterous city neighborhood where, to use Paley's words, "dumbwaiters boom, doors slam, dishes crash; every window is a mother's mouth bidding the street shut up, go skate somewhere else, come home." Ordinary people in unexceptional circumstances, these characters demonstrate the way man deals with the "little disturbances" of life. In her introduction to the Virago edition of this volume, A. S. Byatt points out that "we have had a great many artists, more of them women than not, recording the tragedies of repetition, frequency, weariness and little disturbances. What distinguishes Grace Paley from the mass of these is the interest, and even more, the inventiveness which she brings to her small world."

The serio-comic tone of Paley's voice is unmistakable and, to some critics, the distinguishing characteristic of her art. "To venture a few pages into a Paley story is to be trapped by her unique idiom, dragged forward by her poetic logic, and whipped helplessly to the end on rollerskates of pain and laughter," notes Christopher Lehmann-Haupt in the *New York Times.* Writing in *Commonweal,* Ivan Gold says that her stories "give quirky, anguished, funny, loving, deep and antic glimpses into the hearts and lives of children, mothers, lovers, spouses divorced and abandoned, the ageing and the old, in a prose as resilient and unpredictable as one imagines the fate of her characters to be."

In "An Interest in Life," the set piece of the collection and the story from which the book's title is drawn, Paley's mode becomes clear. Initially the story of a husband's desertion of his wife and four children, it begins: "My husband gave me a broom one Christmas. This wasn't right. No one can tell me it was meant kindly." In a *Partisan Review* article, Jonathan Baumbach explains how "the matter-of-fact, ironic voice of the protagonist, Ginny, distances the reader from the conventions of her pathos, makes light of easy sentiment, only to bring us, unburdened by melodrama, to an awareness of the character as if someone known to us intimately for a long time. Ginny, in a desperate moment, writes out a list of her troubles to get on the radio show, 'Strike It Rich.' When she shows the list to John Raftery, a returned former suitor unhappily married to someone else, he points out to her that her troubles are insufficient, merely 'the little disturbances of man.' Paley's comic stories deal in exaggerated understatement, disguise their considerable ambition in the modesty of wit."

Unlike her later fiction, Paley's first book features several conventionally crafted stories that are narrated by a speaker who is not the author and built around a series of incidents that comprise the plot. "The Contest," "Goodbye and Good Luck," "An Irrevocable Diameter," and "A Woman Young and Old" belong to this category. Paley's other approach is more open and fragmentary and can be seen in "An Interest in Life" and "The Used-Boy Raisers," stories narrated respectively by Virginia and Faith, two women not unlike the author. Explains Byatt: "Faith and Virginia both appear elsewhere in Grace Paley's work, with their dependent children, their circumscribed lives, their poverty and resourcefulness, their sexual greed and their consequent continuing openness to exploitation by, and readiness to exploit, men. Their tales have no beginnings and ends, in the sense in which *An Irrevocable Diameter* has, or, best of the 'well-made tales,' *In Time Which Made a Monkey of Us All.* But they have beginnings and ends verbally, and they are brilliant, as the choice of the parts that make them is brilliant."

With the passage of time, Paley's reputation as a master storyteller spread, and continued reader interest led to an event that Walter Clemons characterizes as "almost without parallel in the forlorn history of short-story collections." In 1968, nine years after its hard cover publication by Doubleday, *The Little Disturbances of Man* was formally reissued by Viking, a *different* publisher.

Another six years would pass before the appearance of *Enormous Changes at the Last Minute,* Paley's second collection of short stories. But, as Ivan Gold reports, "during her literary lean years, Grace Paley's life was fat. She gave to the roles of wife and mother the profound, existential attention her readers would have been able to predict." In addition to her homemaking duties, Paley submerged herself in political activities—distributing anti-war pamphlets, marching on the Capitol, and traveling overseas to protest American involvement in Vietnam. "I think I could have done more for peace," she told *People,* "if I'd written about the war, but I happen to love being in the streets." Paley has also been involved in the women's movement and antimilitarist groups.

While the seventeen tales that make up Paley's second collection are not "war stories," they do reflect the moral imperative that informs her politics. "As a woman I'm trying to restore something to the scales, so that the woman can be seen—not as she has been," Paley explained to *Ms.* interviewer Harriet Shapiro. "It may come from my political feelings, but I think art, literature, fiction, poetry, whatever it is, makes justice in the world. That's why it almost always has to be on the side of the underdog."

Enormous Changes at the Last Minute not only plays off the title of Paley's first book, but also features the same setting and several of the same characters. Faith reappears with her boys Richard and Tonto and so does Johnny Raftery—his love affair with Ginny recounted this time from his mother's point of view. While William Novak finds the second collection "somewhat broader in range . . . more American and less parochial," he attributes the change to "subjects and themes rather than . . . the basic techniques of writing." For Novak, the crucial quality is still *how* Paley writes rather than what she is saying: "We are so accustomed to responding to fiction in terms of its themes and characters that we must reawaken our linguistic sensitivities when reading Grace Paley. The qualities and substances that give strength to most of our good writers are quite alien from her work."

Plot, for instance, figures in these stories almost as an afterthought. The tales are open-ended, fragmentary, and sometimes actionless. In a story called "A Conversation with My Father," Paley explains why. The piece begins with an ailing father's request to his daughter: "I would like you to write a simple story just once more . . . the kind deMaupassant wrote, or Chekhov, the kind you used to write." Though she would like to please him, the daughter reveals that she has always avoided plot "not for literary reasons, but because it takes all hope away. Everyone real or invented deserves the open destiny of life."

In the eyes of Michele Murray, however, Paley disregards her own requirement. "Even with the glitter of its style, over which Paley skates like some Olympic champion of language, *Enormous Changes* is a book of losses and failures," she writes in the *New Republic.* "It's not tragedy that weighs down these stories, it's no more than despair and repetition. Tragedy suggests depths and alternatives and is built into a world of choices. Paley's world . . . is severely limited, the world as given, without any imagined alternatives, only endless vistas of crumbling buildings, bedrooms opening onto air shafts, and a phalanx of old people's homes."

But Burton Bendow argues that Paley "is right to avoid looking tragedy in the face; she knows where her talent lies. It is, if not for comedy exactly, for virtuoso mimicry. I would guess," he continues in the *Nation,* "that the first thing she has in mind when starting work on one of her better stories is a voice. Definitely not a plot which would keep her to the straight and narrow and cramp her digressions, or a situation or a point of view or even a character, but a voice with a particular ring and particular turns of phrase." Paley herself told Shapiro that she "used to start simply from language. . . . I would write a couple of sentences and let them lay there. Not on purpose, but just because I couldn't figure out what was going to come next. I've always worked very blind."

Paley's technique may explain what academics sometimes call the "unevenness" of her writing. As Vivian Gomick writes in the *Village Voice:* "Her successes are intermittent, unpredictable, often unshapely and without wholeness; there is no progression of revelation, the stories do not build one upon another, they do not—as is abundantly clear in this new collection—create an emotional unity. On the other hand: Paley when she is good is so good that she is worth 99 'even' writers, and when one hears that unmistakable Paley voice one feels what can be felt only in the presence of a true writer: safe."

Paley's third collection of short stories, *Later the Same Day,* reintroduces characters present in earlier stories, including Faith. Michiko Kakutani notes in the *New York Times,* however, that "the people in this collection are older than before, more given to remembering love and ambition than experiencing it anew. Most of them, as the narrator of 'Love' observes, have settled into a 'homey life in middle age with two sets of bedroom slippers' and are trying to cope with the fact that their families and their sense of attachment have slowly dwindled." Kakutani also notes that "responsibility—to one's family, one's friends and to social ideals—remains the dominant concern of Mrs. Paley's characters." Paley's latest collection of stories confirms her reputation as one of the most respected storytellers in America. As William Logan comments in the *Chicago Tribune:* "I do not know if she is one of the masters of the short story—large claims have been advanced for writers whose talent is far inferior to hers. I know only that I return to her stories with more pleasure, and await them with more anticipation, than those of any of her contemporaries."

MEDIA ADAPTATIONS: A film written by John Sayles and based on three stories from *Enormous Changes at the Last Minute,* opened at the Film Forum in New York City, April, 1985.

BIOGRAPHICAL/CRITICAL SOURCES:

BOOKS

Authors in the News, Volume 1, Gale, 1976.
Contemporary Literary Criticism, Gale, Volume 4, 1975, Volume 6, 1976, Volume 37, 1986.
Dictionary of Literary Biography, Volume 28: *Twentieth Century American-Jewish Fiction Writers,* Gale, 1984.
Paley, Grace, *Enormous Changes at the Last Minute,* Farrar, Straus, 1974.
Paley, Grace, *The Little Disturbances of Man,* introduction by A. S. Byatt, Virago, 1980.
Paley, Grace, *Later the Same Day,* Farrar, Straus, 1985.

PERIODICALS

America, June 8, 1974.
Chicago Tribune, April 21, 1985.
Commonweal, October 25, 1968.
Harper's, June, 1974.
Kirkus Reviews, February 15, 1959.
Los Angeles Times, May 22, 1985.
Los Angeles Times Book Review, May 19, 1985.
Milwaukee Journal, May 5, 1974.
Ms., May, 1974.
Nation, September 10, 1973, May 11, 1974.
New Republic, March 16, 1974.
New Statesman, March 14, 1980.
Newsweek, March 11, 1974, April 15, 1985.
New Yorker, June 27, 1959.
New York Review of Books, March 21, 1974.
New York Times, February 28, 1974, April 10, 1985.
New York Times Book Review, April 19, 1959, March 17, 1974, April 14, 1985.
Partisan Review, spring, 1975.
People, February 26, 1979.
Publishers Weekly, April 5, 1985.
Saturday Review/World, March 23, 1974.
Skylines, April, 1986.
Time, April 29, 1974, April 15, 1985.
Times (London), November 7, 1985, September 26, 1987.
Times Literary Supplement, November 22, 1985.
Village Voice, March 14, 1974.
Washington Post, April 14, 1985.
Washington Post Book World, April 28, 1985.

*   *   *

PALINURUS
See CONNOLLY, Cyril (Vernon)

*   *   *

PANOVA, Vera (Fedorovna) 1905-1973
(Vera Veltman)

PERSONAL: Born March 20, 1905, in Rostov-on-Don, Russia (now U.S.S.R.); died March 4, 1973. *Education:* Attended schools in Russia.

CAREER: Novelist, short story writer, and playwright. Worked as journalist, 1922-46.

MEMBER: Soviet Writers Union, Congress of Soviet Writers.

AWARDS, HONORS: Stalin Prize, 1947, for *Sputniki,* 1948, for *Kruzhilikha,* and 1950, for *Yasni bereg.*

WRITINGS:

IN ENGLISH TRANSLATION

Sputniki (novel), [Moscow, U.S.S.R.], 1946, translation by Marie Budberg published as *The Train,* Knopf, 1949 (also see below).

Kruzhilikha (novel), [Moscow], 1948, translation by Moura Budberg published as *The Factory,* Putnam, 1949, reprinted, Hyperion Press, 1977.

Vremena goda (novel), [U.S.S.R.], 1954, translation by Vera Traill published as *Span of the Year,* Harvill, 1957.

Serezha (novel), [Leningrad, U.S.S.R.], 1956, translation published as *Time Walked,* Harvill, 1957, Arlington Books, 1959, published as *A Summer to Remember,* T. Yoseloff, 1962, translation of original Russian by Rya Gabel published as *On Faraway Street,* Braziller, 1968 (also see below).

Selected Works (contains "The Train," "Valia," "Volodia," and "Serezha"), translated by Olga Shartse and Eve Manning, Progress, 1976.

Seroyzha: Several Stories From the Life of a Very Small Boy, translated by Nicholas Bierkoff and Ann Krooth, Harvest, 1988.

OTHER

Yasni bereg (novel), [U.S.S.R.], 1949.

Izbrannye sochineniya (two-volume collection; contains "Sputniki," "Yasni bereg," "Serezha," "Kruzhilikha," and "Vremena goda"), [U.S.S.R.], 1956.

Metelitsa (play; first produced in 1942), [U.S.S.R.], 1957.

Sentimental'nyi roman (novel; title means "Sentimental Story"), [U.S.S.R.], 1958.

V staroi Moskve (play; first produced in 1940), Iskusstvo, 1958.

Ilia Kosogor (collection of plays; contains "Ilia Kosogor" [first produced in 1939], "V staroi Moskve," "Metelitsa," and "Devochki" [first produced in 1945]), [U.S.S.R.], 1958.

Valia [and] *Volodia* (two short stories), Pravda, 1960.

Evdokiia (fiction), [U.S.S.R.], 1960.

Rabochii poselok (collection; contains "Rabochii poselok," "Sasha," and "Rano utrom"), [U.S.S.R.], 1966.

Liki na zare, [U.S.S.R.], 1966.

Povesti, Lenizdat, 1966.

Pogovorim o strannostiakh liubvi (collection of plays), [U.S.S.R.], 1968.

Skazanie ob Ol'ge (juvenile), [U.S.S.R.], 1968.

Izbrannoe, [U.S.S.R.], 1972.

Zametki literatora (addresses, essays, and lectures), [U.S.S.R.], 1972.

Nashi deti, [U.S.S.R.], 1973.

O moei zhizni, knigakh i chitateliakh (biography), [U.S.S.R.], 1975.

Also author of "Provody belykh nochei" (play), first produced in 1961, and "Skolko let, skolko zim!" (play; title means "It's Been Ages!"), first produced in 1966.

Author of humorous sketches under pseudonym Vera Veltman. Work represented in anthologies, including *Contemporary Russian Drama,* edited by Franklin O. Reeve, Pegasus, 1968.

SIDELIGHTS: Vera Panova, a noted Russian novelist, received little formal education. Her father was killed in a boating accident when she was only five, leaving the family in financial difficulties. Panova worked in a laundry as a child and was an avid

reader. At age seventeen Panova began her writing career working for a Soviet newspaper. In the early 1930s she published several plays. She found drama too confining, however, and soon turned to writing fiction.

During World War II Panova was a correspondent on a hospital train, writing dispatches from interviews with wounded Soviet soldiers. She later drew from these experiences for her first novel, *The Train.* It was published in the Soviet Union in 1946 and became one of the most popular and successful novels about World War II.

The Train is a character study of a number of people who lived on a hospital train for several years during the war. The story explores how the war affected their lives and relates the adjustments to peacetime conditions. With a new national unity born out of the war, the Soviet people on Panova's train were forced to reassess their personal values and ethics.

The transition period from war to peace is the setting of Panova's second novel, *The Factory.* As in *The Train,* Panova again focuses on a group of people and how they are affected by external conditions, although this novel is set in a factory.

Panova received a public reprimand in 1954 following the publication of her next novel, *Span of the Year.* This novel concerns a corrupt Soviet official and a young criminal. Critics argued that such a thing would not exist or at least not escape punishment under their party system.

In these and later novels, Panova's style was decidedly feminine. She limited her themes to the human elements of a given situation and was commended for her characterizations of ordinary people and their lives. The major forces in her works are such things as love, compassion, child raising, and family relationships.

BIOGRAPHICAL/CRITICAL SOURCES:

PERIODICALS

New Statesman and Nation, January 22, 1949.
New Yorker, April 16, 1949.
New York Herald Tribune Book Review, June 28, 1959.
New York Herald Tribune Weekly Book Review, April 10, 1949.
New York Times, April 10, 1949.
Time, April 18, 1949.
San Francisco Chronicle, May 15, 1949.
Saturday Review of Literature, April 30, 1949.
Time, May 11, 1959.

OBITUARIES:

PERIODICALS

New York Times, March 6, 1973.

* * *

PARASOL, Peter
See STEVENS, Wallace

* * *

PARGETER, Edith Mary 1913-
(Ellis Peters)

PERSONAL: Born September 28, 1913, in Horsehay, Shropshire, England; daughter of Edmund Valentine and Edith (Hordley) Pargeter. *Education:* Attended schools in England.

ADDRESSES: Home—Parkville, 14 Park Lane, Madeley, Telford, Shropshire TF7 5HF, England. *Agent*—Deborah Owen Ltd., 78 Narrow St., Limehouse, London E 14 8BP, England.

CAREER: Pharmacist's assistant and dispenser in Dawley, Shropshire, England, 1933-40; full-time novelist and translator of prose and poetry from the Czech and Slovak. *Military service:* Women's Royal Naval Service, 1940-45; became petty officer; received British Empire Medal.

MEMBER: International Institute of Arts and Letters, Society of Authors, Authors League of America, Authors Guild, Crime Writers Association.

AWARDS, HONORS: Edgar Allan Poe Award for best mystery novel, Mystery Writers of America, 1961, for *Death and the Joyful Woman;* Gold medal, Czechoslovak Society for International Relations, 1968; Silver Dagger, Crime Writers Association, 1981, for *Monk's-Hood.*

WRITINGS:

Hortensius, Friend of Nero, Dickson, 1936.
Iron-Bound, Dickson, 1936.
The City Lies Foursquare, Reynal & Hitchcock, 1939.
Ordinary People, Heinemann, 1941, published as *People of My Own,* Reynal, 1942.
She Goes to War (novel), Heinemann, 1942.
The Eighth Champion of Christendom, Heinemann, 1945.
Reluctant Odyssey (sequel to *The Eighth Champion of Christendom*), Heinemann, 1946.
Warfare Accomplished, Heinemann, 1947.
The Fair Young Phoenix, Heinemann, 1948.
By Firelight, Heinemann, 1948, published as *By This Strange Fire,* Reynal & Hitchcock, 1948.
The Coast of Bohemia (travel), Heinemann, 1950.
Lost Children (novel), Heinemann, 1950.
Holiday with Violence, Heinemann, 1952.
This Rough Magic (novel), Heinemann, 1953.
Most Loving Mere Folly (novel), Heinemann, 1953.
The Soldier at the Door (novel), Heinemann, 1954.
A Means of Grace (novel), Heinemann, 1956.
The Assize of the Dying: 2 Novelletes (contains "The Assize of the Dying" and "Aunt Helen"), Doubleday, 1958 (published in England with an additional story, "The Seven Days of Monte Cervio," as *The Assize of the Dying: 3 Stories,* Heinemann, 1958).
The Heaven Tree, Doubleday, 1960.
The Green Branch, Heinemann, 1962.
The Scarlet Seed, Heinemann, 1963.
The Lily Hand and Other Stories, Heinemann, 1965.
A Bloody Field by Shrewsbury, Macmillan (London), 1972, published as *The Bloody Field,* Viking, 1973.
Sunrise in the West (first volume in "The Brothers of Gwynedd" sequence), Macmillan (London), 1974.
The Dragon at Noonday (second volume in "The Brothers of Gwynedd" sequence), Macmillan (London), 1975.
The Hounds of Sunset (third volume in "The Brothers of Gwynedd" sequence), Macmillan (London), 1976.
Afterglow and Nightfall (fourth volume in "The Brothers of Gwynedd" sequence), Macmillan (London), 1977.
The Marriage of Megotta, Viking, 1979.

UNDER PSEUDONYM ELLIS PETERS

Death Mask, Collins, 1959, Doubleday, 1960.
Where There's a Will, Doubleday, 1960 (published in England as *The Will and the Deed,* Collins, 1960), published as *The Will and the Deed,* Avon, 1966.

Funeral of Figaro, Collins, 1962, Morrow, 1964.
The Horn of Roland, Morrow, 1974.
Never Pick up Hitch-Hikers!, Morrow, 1976, bound with *Catch a Falling Spy* by Len Deighton and *More Tales of the Black Widowers* by Isaac Asimov, W. J. Black, 1978.

"FELSE FAMILY" DETECTIVE NOVELS SERIES; UNDER PSEUDONYM ELLIS PETERS EXCEPT AS INDICATED

(Under own name) *Fallen into the Pit,* Heinemann, 1951.
Death and the Joyful Woman, Collins, 1961, Doubleday, 1962.
Flight of a Witch, Collins, 1964.
Who Lies Here?, Morrow, 1965 (published in England as *A Nice Derangement of Epitaphs,* Collins, 1965).
The Piper on the Mountain, Morrow, 1966.
Black Is the Colour of My True-Love's Heart, Morrow, 1967.
The Grass Widow's Tale, Morrow, 1968.
The House of Green Turf, Morrow, 1969.
Mourning Raga, Macmillan (London), 1969, Morrow, 1970.
The Knocker on Death's Door, Macmillan (London), 1970, Morrow, 1971.
Death to the Landlords!, Morrow, 1972.
City of Gold and Shadows, Macmillan (London), 1973, Morrow, 1974.
Rainbow's End, Macmillan (London), 1978, Morrow, 1979.

"CHRONICLES OF BROTHER CADFAEL" MYSTERY SERIES; UNDER PSEUDONYM ELLIS PETERS

A Morbid Taste for Bones, Macmillan (London), 1977, Morrow, 1978.
One Corpse Too Many, Macmillan (London), 1979, Morrow, 1980.
Monk's-Hood, Macmillan (London), 1980, Morrow, 1981.
Saint Peter's Fair, Morrow, 1981.
The Leper of St. Giles, Macmillan (London), 1981, Morrow, 1982.
The Virgin in the Ice, Macmillan (London), 1982, Morrow, 1983.
The Sanctuary Sparrow, Morrow, 1983.
The Devil's Novice, Macmillan (London), 1983, Morrow, 1984.
Dead Man's Ransom, Morrow, 1984.
The Pilgrim of Hate, Macmillan (London), 1984, Morrow, 1985.
An Excellent Mystery, Morrow, 1985.
The Raven in the Foregate, Morrow, 1986.
The Rose Rent, Morrow, 1987.
The Hermit of Eyton Forest, Headline, 1987, Mysterious Press, 1988.
The Confession of Brother Haluin, Headline, 1988, Mysterious Press, 1989.
A Rare Benedictine (short stories), Headline, 1988, Mysterious Press, 1989.
The Heretic's Apprentice, Headline, 1989, Mysterious Press, 1990.
The Potter's Field, Headline, 1990.

CONTRIBUTOR

Alfred Hitchcock Presents: Stories Not for the Nervous, Random House, 1965.
Alfred Hitchcock Presents: Stories That Scared Even Me, Random House, 1967.
George Hardinge, editor, *Winter's Crimes 1,* St. Martin's, 1969.
A. S. Burack, editor, *Techniques of Novel Writing,* The Writer, 1973.
Hilary Watson, editor, *Winter's Crimes 8,* St. Martin's, 1976.
Hardinge, editor, *Winter's Crimes 11,* St. Martin's, 1979.
Hardinge, editor, *Winter's Crimes 13,* St. Martin's, 1981.

TRANSLATIONS FROM THE CZECH

Jan Neruda, *Tales of the Little Quarter* (short stories), Heinemann, 1957, reprinted, Greenwood, 1977.

Frantisek Kosik, *The Sorrowful and Heroic Life of John Amos Comenius,* State Educational Publishing House (Prague), 1958.

A Handful of Linden Leaves: An Anthology of Czech Poetry, Artia (Prague), 1958.

Joseph Toman, *Don Juan,* Knopf, 1958.

Valja Styblova, *The Abortionists,* Secker & Warburg, 1961.

(With others) Mojmir Otruba and Zdenek Pesat, editors, *The Linden Tree: An Anthology of Czech and Slovak Literature, 1890-1960,* Artia (Prague), 1962.

Bozena Nemcova, *Granny: Scenes from Country Life,* Artia (Prague), 1962, reprinted, Greenwood, 1977.

Joseph Bor, *The Terezin Requiem,* Knopf, 1963.

Alois Jirasek, *Legends of Old Bohemia,* Hamlyn, 1963.

Karel Hynek Macha, *May,* Artia (Prague), 1965.

Vladislav Vancura, *The End of the Old Times,* Artia (Prague), 1965.

Bohumil Hrabel, *A Close Watch on the Trains,* J. Cape, 1968.

Josefa Slanska, *Report on My Husband,* Macmillan (London), 1969.

Ivan Klima, *A Ship Named Hope: Two Novels,* Gollancz, 1970.

Jaroslav Seifert, *Mozart in Prague,* Artia (Prague), 1970.

OTHER

Also author of *The Horn of Roland,* bound with *Danger Money* by Mignon G. Eberhart and *The Romanov Succession* by Brian Garfield for the Detective Book Club by W. J. Black. Contributor of short stories to magazines, including *The Saint* and *This Week.*

SIDELIGHTS: Edith Pargeter, writing as Ellis Peters, has "recreated the world of England in the first years of the High Middle Ages" in her chronicles of Brother Cadfael, according to Andrew M. Greeley in the *Armchair Detective.* A twelfth-century crusader turned monk and herbalist, Brother Cadfael is the protagonist of a series of novels which mix historical background, romance, and detection, and which Greeley describes as "a fascinating reconstruction of the religion, the history, the social structure, the culture, the politics, and the lifestyle of England in the twelfth century." Set on the Welsh border near Shrewsbury, where Peters lives today, the books take place during the tumultuous reign of Stephen of England, when fighting between the king and his cousin the Empress Matilda (or Maud) racked the realm.

Peters's Cadfael novels have been compared with Umberto Eco's best-seller *The Name of the Rose,* which tells the story of another crime-solving monk in fourteenth-century Italy. The resemblence, however, is only superficial; seven Cadfael chronicles preceeded Eco's book, and Peters does not expound a theory of semiotics as Eco does. Her books are, in fact, "closer in spirit to the heroics of *The Black Arrow* or *Men of Iron,*" according to Geoffrey O'Brien in the *Village Voice,* and she lists Rudyard Kipling, Thomas Mallory and Helen Waddell among her literary influences. As Greeley points out, "Eco undoubtedly describes truth in his book. Ellis Peters, for her part, has only verisimilitude; and, as any storyteller knows, verisimilitude makes for a better story than truth and may, finally, at the level of myth and symbol, be even more true." Peters described herself to *CA* as "essentially a storyteller, and in my view no one who can't make that statement can possibly be a novelist, the novel being by definition an extended narrative reflecting the human condition, with the accent on the word 'narrative.' "

Many of the books in this series have classic boy-meets-loses-gets-girl subplots which, in some reviewers' opinions, overwhelm the elements of detective fiction. For example, T. J. Binyon comments in the *Times Literary Supplement* that "to include not one, not two, but three separate romances in *The Sanctuary Sparrow* seems excessive," and remarks that in *The Pilgrim of Hate,* "romance is gradually crowding out detection." Marcel Berlins states in the London *Times* that *An Excellent Mystery* has in fact "little mystery, though much chivalrous romance." Other commentators are not so troubled; the "twee little romances," as Margaret Cannon in the Toronto *Globe and Mail* calls them, are in her opinion used for effect, and do not interfere with the main story.

The "charmingly exotic (but not too exotic) background," as *Washington Post Book World* reviewer Joseph McLellan calls it, combined with Peters's grasp of characterization, forms a large part of the attraction these novels have for readers. Derrick Murdoch in the Toronto *Globe and Mail* defines their charm as "the manner in which the speech and usages of those ancient times are made to seem alive without unnecessary explanation." "Having read all the chronicles," Greeley states, "one feels that one has become part of a little section of England around Shrewsbury between 1137 and 1140, and that one knows the monks and the townsfolk and the squires and the nobility almost as though they were friends and neighbors." He continues, "Perhaps the greatest achievement of the Cadfael chronicles is Peters's ability to help us feel and accept the common humanity which links us to these inhabitants' world, so very different from our own."

Pargeter told *CA:* "Streams of consciousness and probings of the solitary, and usually uninteresting, human-soul-at-the-end-of-its-tether are not for me. Nor do I find vice and evil more interesting than virtue, and I hope my books go some way to defy and disprove that too-easily accepted judgement. It gives me great satisfaction that many times people have written to me to tell me, in varying terms, that I have made them feel better, not worse, about being human. That's all the acknowledgment I need."

MEDIA ADAPTATIONS: The Assize of the Dying was filmed under the title "The Spaniard's Curse"; *Death and the Joyful Woman* was presented on "The Alfred Hitchcock Hour"; *Mourning Raga* and *The Heaven Tree* were adapted for radio in 1971 and 1975, respectively; Pargeter's short story "The Purple Children" was produced on television in Canada and Australia.

AVOCATIONAL INTERESTS: Music (especially opera and folk), reading, theatre, art.

BIOGRAPHICAL/CRITICAL SOURCES:

PERIODICALS

Armchair Detective, summer, 1985.

Best Sellers, October 1, 1966, August 1, 1967, June 1, 1968, April 15, 1969, March 15, 1970, February, 1984, July, 1984, March, 1986, August, 1986, February, 1987.

Books and Bookmen, April, 1965, December, 1967, June, 1968, June, 1969, August, 1970.

Globe and Mail (Toronto), May 5, 1984, July 5, 1986, December 13, 1986.

Listener, May 19, 1983.

Los Angeles Times Book Review, January 31, 1982, February 26, 1984, October 27, 1985.

National Review, December 5, 1986.

New Yorker, November 5, 1984.

New York Times Book Review, May 9, 1965, November 6, 1966, August 13, 1967, May 26, 1968, September 26, 1982.

Observer, February 14, 1965, May 15, 1966, September 17, 1967, April 21, 1968, January 23, 1983, August 4, 1985.

Publishers Weekly, February 8, 1985.

Punch, May 29, 1968.

Spectator, March 5, 1965, June 3, 1966.

Time, August 17, 1987.

Times (London), January 21, 1983, July 11, 1985.

Times Literary Supplement, February 25, 1965, June 2, 1966, September 21, 1967, July 18, 1968, October 3, 1980, February 18, 1983, July 13, 1984, January 11, 1985, October 3, 1986, January 30, 1987.

Village Voice, July 16, 1985.

Washington Post Book World, January 31, 1981, June 21, 1981, May 16, 1982.

Wilson Library Bulletin, October, 1983.

* * *

PARK, Jordan
See POHL, Frederik

* * *

PARKER, Bert
See ELLISON, Harlan

* * *

PARKER, Dorothy (Rothschild) 1893-1967

PERSONAL: Born August 22, 1893, in West End, N.J.; died June 7, 1967; daughter of J. Henry and Eliza A. (Marston) Rothschild; married Edwin Pond Parker II, 1917 (divorced, 1928); married Alan Campbell (a motion picture actor and scenarist), October, 1933 (divorced, 1947); remarried Campbell, August, 1950 (died, 1963). *Education:* Attended Ms. Dana's School, Morristown, N.J., and Blessed Sacrament Convent, New York, N.Y. *Politics:* Generally far left.

ADDRESSES: Home—Volney Hotel, 23 East 74th St., New York, N.Y.

CAREER: Vogue, New York, N.Y., member of editorial staff, 1916-17; *Vanity Fair,* New York, N.Y., member of editorial staff and drama critic, 1917-20 (she was fired for writing unfavorable reviews of three important plays); *New Yorker,* New York, N.Y., book reviewer, writing "Constant Reader" column, about 1925-27; free-lance writer, 1927-67. Lived in Hollywood, Calif., for many years, beginning in the early 1930's, while writing for motion pictures and magazines; taught English at Los Angeles State College (now California State University, Los Angeles), about 1960. (She said that she didn't lecture; instead, "the students read things and then they fight. It's called discussion.") Founder, with Robert Benchley and Robert E. Sherwood, of the Algonquin Round Table in the Algonquin Hotel, New York, N.Y. (resigned during the 1930's).

AWARDS, HONORS: O. Henry Memorial Award, 1929, for short story "Big Blond."

WRITINGS:

(With George Chappell and Frank Crowninshield) *High Society,* illustrations by Anne Harriet Fish, Putnam, 1920.

Men I'm Not Married To; Women I'm Not Married To, Doubleday, Page, 1922.

Enough Rope (poems), Boni & Liveright, 1926, new edition, 1934.

Sunset Gun (poems), Boni & Liveright, 1928, new edition, 1934.

(With Elmer Rice) *Close Harmony, or The Lady Next Door* (play; originally copyrighted as "Soft Music," 1924, but never published or produced with that title; first produced as "Close Harmony" in New York at Gaiety Theater, December 1, 1924), Samuel French, 1929.

Laments for the Living (stories), Viking, 1930.

Death and Taxes (poems), Viking, 1931.

After Such Pleasures (stories), Viking, 1932.

Collected Poems: Not So Deep as a Well, Viking, 1936.

Here Lies (stories), Viking, 1939.

(With Arnaud d'Usseau) *Ladies of the Corridor* (play; first produced in New York at Longacre Theater, October 21, 1953), Viking, 1944.

OMNIBUS VOLUMES

Collected Stories, Modern Library, 1942.

Collected Poetry, Random House, 1944.

Dorothy Parker (selected poetry and prose), introduction by W. Somerset Maugham, Viking, 1944, revised and enlarged edition published as *The Portable Dorothy Parker,* 1973.

The Best of Dorothy Parker, Methuen, 1952.

Constant Reader (selected stories from the *New Yorker*), Viking, 1970.

A Month of Saturdays, Macmillan (London), 1971.

EDITOR

The Portable F. Scott Fitzgerald, Viking, 1945.

Cazenove Gardner Lee, *Lee Chronicle: Studies of the Early Generations of the Lees of Virginia,* New York University Press, 1957.

(With F. B. Shroyer) *Short Story: A Thematic Anthology,* Scribner, 1965.

UNPUBLISHED PLAYS

(Lyricist) "Round the Town" (revue), first produced in New York at Century Roof Theater, May 21, 1924.

(Contributor of sketches) "Shoot the Works" (revue), first produced in New York at George M. Cohan Theater, July 21, 1931.

(Contributor of sketches) "After Such Pleasures" (revue based on Parker's short stories; adaptation by Edward F. Gardner), first produced in New York at Bijou Theater, February 7, 1934.

(With Ross Evans) "The Coast of Illyria" (play based on the life of Charles Lamb), first produced in Dallas, 1949.

(Lyricist with John La Touche and Richard Wilbur) "Candide," first produced in New York at Martin Beck Theater, December 1, 1956.

SCREENPLAYS; ALL WITH HUSBAND, ALAN CAMPBELL

"Here is My Heart," Paramount, 1934.

"One Hour Late," Paramount, 1935.

"Big Broadcast of 1936," Paramount, 1935.

"Mary Burns, Fugitive," Paramount, 1935.

"Hands Across the Table," Paramount, 1935.

"Paris in Spring," Paramount, 1935.

"Three Married Men," Paramount, 1936.

"Lady Be Careful," Paramount, 1936.

"The Moon's Our Home," Paramount, 1936.

"Suzy," Metro-Goldwyn-Mayer, 1936.

"A Star is Born," United Artists, 1937.

"Sweethearts," Metro-Goldwyn-Mayer, 1938.

"Crime Takes a Holiday," Columbia, 1938.

"Trade Winds," United Artists, 1938.

"Flight into Nowhere," Columbia, 1938.

"Five Little Peppers and How They Grew," Columbia, 1939.

"Weekend for Three," RKO, 1941.

"Saboteur," Universal, 1942.

"A Gentle Gangster," Republic, 1943.

"Mr. Skeffington," Warner Bros., 1944.

"Smash-Up: The Story of a Woman," Universal, 1947.

"The Fan," Twentieth Century-Fox, 1949.

Parker also adapted for television her stories "The Lonely Leave," "A Telephone Call," and "Dusk Before Fireworks" for the Festival of Performing Arts, WNEW-TV, May 8, 1962.

Parker was a regular contributor to the *New Yorker* from its second issue, February 28, 1925, until December 14, 1957. She regularly contributed book reviews to *Esquire* for several years, beginning in 1958.

SIDELIGHTS: "Dorothy Parker was small, dark, and fragile, with a sharp, pretty face and an air of being almost too sensitive to what went on about her," wrote Anita Loos. It was this sensitivity that produced one of the sharpest, most biting wits in modern letters. Loos concluded that "Dorothy's presence anywhere tended to produce an atmosphere of tension." The *Time* reporter noted that "hers was the tongue heard round the world. . . . During the long Victorian era, wit had hardly been considered a feminine attribute. Dorothy Parker proved again that bitchiness could be the soul of wit."

Parker came to deplore the reputation accorded her wit. She once said that "it got so bad that they began to laugh before I opened my mouth." She held in similar contempt her reputation as a serious writer. She told her *Paris Review* interviewer that her play, *Ladies of the Corridor,* was "the only thing I have ever done in which I had great pride." (The play's Broadway run was only modestly successful.) She added that she "fell into writing, . . . being one of those awful children who wrote verses." She always referred to her rhyming as "verse"; "I cannot say poems," she told the *Paris Review.* "Like everybody was then, I was following in the exquisite footsteps of Miss Millay, unhappily in my own horrible sneakers. My verses are no damn good. Let's face it, honey, my verse is terribly dated—as anything once fashionable is dreadful now. I gave it up [her last published poem was written in 1944], knowing it wasn't getting any better, but nobody seemed to notice my magnificent gesture."

But her harsh self-derogation was enthusiastically contradicted by critics and acquaintances. ("Acquaintances," because Loos doubts that she had any real *friends;* "she had no belief at all in friendship and knew herself to be a lone wolverine.") Ogden Nash once wrote: "To say that Mrs. Parker writes well is as fatuous, I'm afraid, as proclaiming that Cellini was clever with his hands. . . . The trick about her writing is the trick about Ring Lardner's writing or Ernest Hemingway's writing. It isn't a trick." And Edmund Wilson found beauty in her work: "She is not Emily Bronte or Jane Austen, but she had been at some pains to write well, and she has put into what she has written a voice, a state of mind, an era, a few moments of human experience that nobody else has conveyed." Somerset Maugham wrote: "Perhaps what gives her writing its peculiar tang is her gift for seeing something to laugh at in the bitterest tragedies of the human animal." If Parker's laughter seemed merciless, it was because she truly believed that humor and compassion are inharmonious sentiments. Alden Whitman recalled Parker's own definition of her particular talent: "Humor to me, Heaven help me, takes in many things. There must be courage, there must be no awe. There must be criticism, for humor, to my mind, is encapsulated in criticism. There must be a disciplined eye and a wild mind. There must be a magnificent disregard of your reader, for if he

cannot follow you, there is nothing you can do about it." Whitman summarized: "Her lifelong reputation as a glittering, annihilating humorist in poetry, essays, short stories and in conversation was compiled and sustained brickbat by brickbat." (Although, Whitman added, she was not altogether without sentimentality; "she truly loved flowers, dogs and a good cry.")

Although many have called Parker's wit ageless, some critics attribute her immense success to the peculiarities of the 1930's and 1940's, her most expressive and influential years. The *Time* writer noted: "If one wonders what so captivated her contemporaries, the answer is probably that she viewed the period as it liked to picture itself: a time of grace and intelligence, when irony could conquer sentimentality and laughter would always overwhelm tears." Wilson, analyzing Parker's work in retrospect, concluded that her writing "has a value derived from rarity—a rarity like that of steel penknives, good erasers and real canned sardines, articles of which the supply has almost given out and of which one is only now beginning to be aware of how excellent the quality was." But Parker could never complain of a dearth of admirers (if she entered any complaint, it was that she was overrated). In 1931 Henry Seidel Canby wrote: "In verse of a Horatian lightness, with an exquisite certainty of technique, which, like the lustre on a Persian bowl, is proof that civilization is itself a philosophy, Dorothy Parker is writing poetry deserving high praise. . . . I suspect that one should quote Latin rather than English to parallel the edged fineness of Dorothy Parker's verse. This belle dame sans merci has the ruthlessness of the great tragic lyricist whose work was allegorized in the fable of the nightingale singing with her breast against a thorn. It is a disillusion recollected in tranquility where the imagination has at last controlled the emotions. It comes out clear, and with the authentic sparkle of a great vintage." Louis Kronenberger expressed similar admiration for her work in 1936, concluding that "there is no one else in Mrs. Parker's special field who can do half as much." And Alexander Woollcott, a fellow Algonquin Round Table luminary, wrote in the early 1940's: "Mrs. Parker's published work does not bulk large. But most of it has been pure gold and the five winnowed volumes of her shelf . . . are so potent a distillation of nectar and wormwood, of ambrosia and deadly nightshade, as might suggest to the rest of us that we all write far too much. Even though I am one who does not profess to be privy to the intentions of posterity, I do suspect that another generation will not share the confusion into which Mrs. Parker's poetry throws so many of her contemporaries, who, seeing that much of it is witty, dismiss it patronizingly as 'light' verse, and do not see that some of it is thrilling poetry of a piercing and rueful beauty."

Although Parker's formidable wit had found a large audience as early as 1927, her enthusiasm for politically liberal causes did not amuse certain United States authorities. Whitman reported that "from the late nineteen-twenties, when Mrs. Parker was fined $5 for 'sauntering' in a Boston demonstration against the execution of Nicola Sacco and Bartolomea Vanzetti, she was active in liberal causes. In the Spanish Civil War and afterward, she was national chairman of the Joint Anti-Fascist Refugee Committee and active in its behalf. This had repercussions in 1951 when she was cited, by the House Un-American Activities Committee, with 300 other writers, professors, actors and artists, for affiliation with what the committee designated as 'Communist front' organizations." In 1944 Edmund Wilson offered an explanation, if not an apology, for her activities: "A decade or more ago she went out to Hollywood and more or less steadily stayed there, and, once away from her natural habitat, New York, she succumbed to the expiatory mania that has become epidemic with film-writers and was presently making earnest appeals on behalf of those organizations which talked about being 'progressive' and succeeded in convincing their followers that they were working for the social revolution, though they had really no other purpose than to promote the foreign policy of the Soviet Union." Much later Parker spoke bitterly of her years in California: "I can't talk about Hollywood," she told the *Paris Review.* "It was a horror to me when I was there and it's a horror to look back on. I can't imagine how I did it. When I got away from it I couldn't even refer to the place by name. 'Out there,' I called it."

Parker frequently expressed a desire to be rich. When asked to name "the source of most of [her] work," she replied: "Need of money, dear." She explained: "I'd like to have money. And I'd like to be a good writer. These two can come together, and I hope they will, but if that's too adorable, I'd rather have money. I hate almost all rich people, but I think I'd be darling at it."

For the most part, Parker had as little respect for contemporary writers as for any other group. She admitted that she usually turned to older writers "for comfort" and cited *Vanity Fair* as her favorite novel. She added: "I was a woman of eleven when I first read it," and speculated that she has since read Thackeray's book "about a dozen times a year." But she would not discount younger writers without qualification. She told the *Paris Review* interviewer: "I will say of the writers of today that some of them, thank God, have the sense to adapt to their times. Mailer's *The Naked and the Dead* is a great book. And I thought William Styron's *Lie Down in Darkness* an extraordinary thing. The start of it took your heart and flung it over there. He writes like a god . . . I love Sherlock Holmes. My life is so untidy and he's so neat. But as for the living novelists, suppose E. M. Forster is the best, not knowing what that is, but at least he's a semifinalist, wouldn't you think?"

Edmund Wilson once noticed that all of Parker's books had "funereal titles," but that "the eye was always wide open and the tongue always quick to retort. Even those titles were sardonic exclamations on the part of an individual at the idea of her own demise." Indeed, Parker's suggestions for her own epitaph have become famous; perhaps "Excuse my dust" and "If you can read this, you've come too close" are most often quoted. When she died, more that fifty literary and theatrical acquaintances attended the brief funeral; it was Zero Mostel who remarked: "If she had had her way, I suspect she would not be here at all." In 1987, twenty years after her death, controversy arose over where Parker's ashes should be housed. Parker's lawyer, who had kept the ashes in his office, decided that her remains should have a permanent resting place. A possibility was the Algonquin Hotel in New York—where she had founded the literary Round Table—but the hotel rejected the idea as inappropriate.

Parker left the bulk of her estate to Martin Luther King, Jr.; upon his death, whatever remained went to the National Association for the Advancement of Colored People.

MEDIA ADAPTATIONS: "As Dorothy Parker Said," a musical revue based on her works, was first produced in London at Fortune Theatre, July 21, 1969, and "Speakeasy, An Evening Out With Dorothy Parker," a presentation of five of Parker's stories, was produced in New York at the American Place Theater, January 16, 1983. A one-woman show, "The Singular Dorothy Parker," was staged in New York at the Actors' Playhouse in April, 1985, with actress Jane Connell portraying Parker.

BIOGRAPHICAL/CRITICAL SOURCES:

BOOKS

Contemporary Literary Criticism, Volume 15, Gale, 1980.
Cowley, Malcolm, editor, *Writers at Work: The "Paris Review" Interviews,* Viking, 1957.
Dictionary of Literary Biography, Gale, Volume 11: *American Humorists, 1880-1950,* 1982, Volume 45: *American Poets, 1880-1945,* First Series, 1986, Volume 86: *American Short-Story Writers, 1910-1945,* First Series, 1989.
Keats, John, *You Might as Well Live,* Simon & Schuster, 1970.
Loos, Anita, *A Girl Like I,* Viking, 1966.
Meade, Marion, *Dorothy Parker: What Fresh Hell is This?,* Villard Books, 1988.
Short Story Criticism, Volume 2, Gale, 1989.

PERIODICALS

Books and Bookmen, April, 1971.
Chicago Tribune, July 23, 1987.
Christian Science Monitor, May 7, 1970.
Esquire, July, 1968.
McCall's, October, 1970.
Newsweek, October 12, 1970.
New York Times, December 13, 1936, June 8, 1967, June 10, 1967, June 27, 1967.
Saturday Review, June 13, 1931, November 4, 1933.
Time, June 16, 1967.
Washington Post, August 14, 1987.

*   *   *

PARKER, Robert B(rown) 1932-

PERSONAL: Born September 17, 1932, in Springfield, Mass.; son of Carroll Snow (a telephone company executive) and Mary Pauline (Murphy) Parker; married Joan Hall (an education specialist), August 26, 1956; children: David F., Daniel T. *Education:* Colby College, B.A., 1954; Boston University, M.A., 1957, Ph.D., 1970.

ADDRESSES: Home—Cambridge, Mass. *Agent*—The Helen Brann Agency, Inc., 157 West 57th St., New York, N.Y. 10019.

CAREER: Curtiss-Wright Co., Woodridge, N.J., management trainee, 1957; Raytheon, Co., Andover, Mass., technical writer, 1957-59; Prudential Insurance Co., Boston, Mass, advertising writer, 1959-62; Boston University, Boston, lecturer in English, 1962-64; Massachusetts State College at Lowell (now University of Lowell), instructor in English, 1964-66; Massachusetts State College at Bridgewater, instructor in English, 1966-68; Northeastern University, Boston, assistant professor, 1968-74, associate professor, 1974-76, professor of English, 1976-79; novelist, 1979—. Lecturer, Suffolk University, 1965-66. Co-chairman, Parker-Farman Co. (advertising agency), 1960-62. Film consultant to Arthur D. Little, 1962-64; consultant for television series based on his "Spenser" series, "Spenser: For Hire," 1985-88. *Military service:* U.S. Army, 1954-56.

MEMBER: Writers Guild of America.

AWARDS, HONORS: Edgar Allan Poe Award, Mystery Writers of America, 1976, for *Promised Land;* Litt.D., Northeastern University, 1987.

WRITINGS:

(With others) *The Personal Response to Literature,* Houghton, 1970.
(With Peter L. Sandberg) *Order and Diversity: The Craft of Prose,* Wiley, 1973.

(With John R. Marsh) *Sports Illustrated Weight Training,* Lippincott, 1974.

(With wife, Joan Parker) *Three Weeks in Spring* (nonfiction), Houghton, 1978.

Wilderness (novel), Delacorte, 1979.

Love and Glory (novel), Delacorte, 1983.

The Private Eye in Hammett and Chandler, Lord John, 1984.

Parker on Writing, Lord John, 1985.

(With Raymond Chandler) *The Poodle Springs Story,* Putnam, 1989.

Perchance to Dream, Putnam, 1991.

"SPENSER" DETECTIVE SERIES

The Godwulf Manuscript (also see below), Houghton, 1974.

God Save the Child (also see below), Houghton, 1974.

Mortal Stakes (also see below), Houghton, 1975.

Promised Land, Houghton, 1976.

The Judas Goat, Houghton, 1978.

Looking for Rachel Wallace, Delacorte, 1980.

Early Autumn, Delacorte, 1981.

A Savage Place, Delacorte, 1981.

Surrogate: A Spenser Short Story, Lord John, 1982.

Ceremony, Delacorte, 1982.

The Widening Gyre, Delacorte, 1983.

Valediction, Delacorte, 1984.

A Catskill Eagle, Delacorte, 1985.

Taming a Sea-Horse, Delacorte, 1986.

Pale Kings and Princes, Delacorte, 1987.

Crimson Joy, Delacorte, 1988.

Playmates, Putnam, 1989.

The Early Spenser: Three Complete Novels: The Godwulf Manuscript, God Save the Child, Mortal Stakes, Delacorte, 1989.

OTHER

Also author with wife, Joan H. Parker, of several television scripts for series "Spenser: For Hire." Contributor to *Lock Haven Review* and *Revue des langues vivantes.* Contributor of restaurant reviews to *Boston Magazine,* 1976.

MEDIA ADAPTATIONS: Film rights have been sold to many of the Spenser novels.

SIDELIGHTS: Robert B. Parker's "Spenser" series represents "the best American hardboiled detective fiction since Ross Macdonald and Raymond Chandler," according to *Armchair Detective* writer Anne Ponder. Parker's career as a novelist began only after he spent years producing ad copy and technical writing for various companies. At his wife's urging, he completed his Ph.D. and entered the teaching profession to gain more time for his own writing projects. "Being a professor and working are not the same thing," Parker explained to Wayne Warga in the *Los Angeles Times.* In a Toronto *Globe and Mail* interview with Ian Brown, Parker expressed his feelings about the university environment even more frankly: "The academic community is composed largely of nitwits. If I may generalize. People who don't know very much about what matters very much, who view life through literature rather than the other way around. . . . In my 14 or 16 years in the profession, I've met more people that I did not admire than at any other point in my life. Including two years in the infantry, where I was the only guy who could read."

It took two and a half years of writing in his spare time for Parker to complete his first fiction manuscript, but only three weeks for it to be accepted for publication. Parker's doctoral thesis had treated the classic detective fiction of Raymond Chandler and Dashiell Hammett, and his first novel, *The Godwulf Manuscript,* presented a detective in the tradition of Philip Marlowe and Sam Spade. A Boston policeman turned private eye after being fired for insubordination, Spenser is "a man's man, all six feet plus of him, a former professional fighter, a man who can take on any opposition," relates Newgate Callendar in the *New York Times Book Review.* The character's traditional toughness is balanced by his "honesty and his sensitivity," continues Callendar. "Spenser may be something of a smart aleck but only when he is faced with pomposity and pretension. Then he reacts, sometimes violently. He is educated and well read, though he never parades his knowledge. His girlfriend is the perfect woman, as smart as he is, and so he never has to chase around. Pushed as he is by his social conscience, he is sometimes dogged enough to seem quixotic."

Parker followed *The Godwulf Manuscript* with *God Save the Child, Mortal Stakes, Promised Land* and other Spenser novels. Their growing success soon enabled him to quit his teaching post and devote himself to writing full time. The author now estimates that it takes him three to five months to write a Spenser adventure. Many critics point to Parker's plotting as his weakness, but he is widely praised for his evocative descriptions, for his sharp, witty dialogue, and for introducing a more human, emotional tone to the hard-boiled detective genre. H. R. F. Keating comments in the London *Times* that in the Spenser books "there is a concern with human beings that rises at times to compassion and perhaps falls at other times to that commonish complaint among American novelists 'psychology showing through.' But the seriousness that this indicates is always well-compensated for by Parker's dialogue. Spenser is a wisecracking guy in the firm tradition of the Chandler shamus, and above and beyond this all the conversations in the books are splendidly swift and sharp." In her review of *Pale Kings and Princes, Washington Post Book World* writer Jean M. White concurs that "Parker . . . writes some of the snappiest and sauciest dialogue in the business," and she calls the book "lean and taut and crisply told with moments of genuine humor and genuine poignancy."

One of Parker's most notable departures from the detective novelists before him is Spenser's monogamous commitment to his psychologist lover, Susan Silverman. "By all the unwritten rules of private-eye fiction, that [relationship] should have handicapped Spenser's future literary prospects disastrously," declares Derrick Murdoch in the Toronto *Globe and Mail.* "Instead it has allowed him to develop into the most fully rounded characterization of an intelligent human being in the literature—a mixture of idealism, passion, strength, frailty and unselfish tenacity." In his book *Sons of Sam Spade, The Private-Eye Novel in the 70s: Robert B. Parker, Roger L. Simon, Andrew Bergman,* David Geherin also states his belief that the Spenser character has "grown significantly, especially in the area of self-knowledge, thanks in part to the frequent confrontations between his ever-deepening relationship with Susan. Even when she is absent . . . her presence is felt. . . . Parker's handling of Spenser's relationship with Susan effectively disproves Chandler's assertion that the love story and the detective story cannot exist in the same book. Not only do they coexist in Parker's novels, the love story adds an element of tension by serving as a poignant reminder of the vast distance that separates the mean streets from the quiet ones." A *Time* reviewer emphasizes, however, that for all the intellectual and romantic dialogue, Parker's novels never lack "slambang action."

"Robert B. Parker's influence on the [detective] genre is unquestioned," summarizes Margaret Cannon in the Toronto *Globe and Mail.* "Spenser liberated the PI from California, gave him a whole new line of inquiry, and taught him to love." Furthermore, "With each novel Parker has exhibited growing independence from his predecessors, confidently developing his own themes, characters, and stylistic idiom," concludes Geherin. "However, despite his innovative efforts, he has remained faithful to the conventions of the genre, so effectively laid down by his predecessors. He has thus earned for himself the right to be designated *the* legitimate heir to the Hammett-Chandler-Macdonald tradition, which, thanks to the efforts of writers like Parker, shows no signs of diminishing."

BIOGRAPHICAL/CRITICAL SOURCES:

BOOKS

Carr, John C., *Craft of Crime,* Houghton, 1983.
Contemporary Literary Criticism, Volume 27, Gale, 1984.
Geherin, David, *Sons of Sam Spade, The Private-Eye Novel in the 70s: Robert B. Parker, Roger L. Simon, Andrew Bergman,* Ungar, 1980.
Parker, Robert B., *Three Weeks in Spring,* Houghton, 1978.

PERIODICALS

Armchair Detective, fall, 1984.
Chicago Tribune, September 20, 1985, October 12, 1989.
Chicago Tribune Book World, June 28, 1987.
Clues: A Journal of Detection, fall/winter, 1980, spring/summer, 1984.
Critique, fall, 1984.
Globe and Mail (Toronto), May 12, 1984, June 6, 1984, June 15, 1985, June 21, 1986, May 13, 1989.
Los Angeles Times, January 26, 1981, March 20, 1981, June 21, 1982, January 17, 1984, February 16, 1986.
Los Angeles Times Book Review, July 6, 1986, May 10, 1987, May 14, 1989, October 19, 1989.
New Republic, March 19, 1977, November 4, 1978.
Newsweek, June 7, 1982, June 17, 1985, July 7, 1986.
New Yorker, July 13, 1987.
New York Times, January 21, 1981, September 20, 1985, July 2, 1987.
New York Times Book Review, January 13, 1974, December 15, 1974, November 11, 1979, August 2, 1981, May 1, 1983, May 20, 1984, June 30, 1985, June 22, 1986, May 31, 1987, April 23, 1989, October 15, 1989.
People, May 7, 1984.
Southwest Review, autumn, 1974.
Time, July 1, 1985, July 7, 1986, July 27, 1987.
Times (London), November 4, 1978, May 4, 1987.
USA Today, March 20, 1987.
Washington Post, May 17, 1983, March 7, 1984.
Washington Post Book World, April 15, 1984, June 15, 1986, June 21, 1987, May 21, 1989, October 8, 1989.

*   *   *

PARRA, Nicanor 1914-

PERSONAL: Born September 5, 1914, in Chillan, Chile; son of Nicanor P. (a teacher) and Clara S. (Navarette) Parra; married Ana Troncoso, 1948 (marriage ended); married Inga Palmen; children: seven. *Education:* University of Chile, degree in mathematics and physics, 1938; attended Brown University, 1943-45; studied cosmology at Oxford University, 1949-51.

ADDRESSES: Home—c/o Julia Bernstein, Parcela 272, Lareina, Santiago, Chile. *Office*—Instituto Pedagogico, Avenida Macul 774, Santiago, Chile.

CAREER: Poet and scientist. Secondary school teacher, 1938-43; University of Chile, Santiago, professor, 1947-52, direc-

tor of school of engineering, 1948—, professor of theoretical physics, 1952—. Visiting professor at Louisiana State University, 1966-67, and New York University, Columbia University, and Yale University, 1971; has given poetry readings in many countries, including the United States, Russia, Venezuela, Cuba, Peru, and Argentina.

AWARDS, HONORS: Premio municipal de poesia, Santiago, Chile, 1937, for *Cancionero sin nombre,* and 1954, for *Poemas y antipoemas;* Writers Union Prize, 1954; Premio Nacional de Literatura (national prize for literature), Chile, 1969, for *Obra gruesa;* Guggenheim fellowship, 1972; first Richard Wilbur prize for poetry, American Literary Translators Association and University of Missouri Press, 1984, for *Sermons and Homilies of the Christ of Elqui.*

WRITINGS:

IN ENGLISH TRANSLATION

Poemas y antipoemas, Nascimento, 1954, Catedra (Madrid), 1988, translation of selected poems by Jorge Elliot published as *Anti-poems,* City Lights, 1960.
Poems and Antipoems (bilingual selection of poems from other works), edited by Miller Williams, New Directions, 1967.
Obra gruesa, Editorial Universitaria, 1969, Editorial Andres Bello, 1983, translation by Williams of selected poems published as *Emergency Poems,* New Directions, 1972.
Sermones y predicas del Cristo de Elqui, Universidad de Chile Estudios Humanisticos, 1977, translation by Sandra Reyes published as *Sermons and Homilies of the Christ of Elqui* (bilingual edition; also see below), University of Missouri Press, 1984.
Nuevos sermones y predicas del Cristo de Elqui, Ganymedes, 1979, translation by Reyes published in *Sermons and Homilies of the Christ of Elqui,* University of Missouri Press, 1984.
Antipoems: New and Selected, edited by David Unger, translation by Lawrence Ferlinghetti and others, New Directions, 1985.

OTHER

Cancionero sin nombre (title means "Untitled Book of Ballads"), Nascimento, 1937.
La cueca larga (also see below), Editorial Universitaria, 1958, 2nd edition, 1966.
Versos de salon, Nascimento, 1962.
(With Pablo Neruda) *Discursos,* Nascimento, 1962.
La cueca larga y otros poemas, edited by Margarita Aguirre, Editorial Universitaria de Buenos Aires, 1964.
(Editor) *Poesia sovietica rusa,* Editorial Progreso, 1965.
Canciones rusa, Editorial Universitaria, 1967.
Poemas, Casa de las Americas, 1969.
Poesia rusa contemporanea, Ediciones Nueva Universidad, Universidad Catolica de Chile, 1971.
Los profesores, Antiediciones Villa Miseria (New York), 1971.
Antipoemas: Antologia (1944-1969), Seix Barral, 1972.
Artefactos/Nicanor Parra, Ediciones Nueva Universidad, Universidad Catolica de Chile, 1972, enlarged edition, 1972.
Poema y antipoema a Eduardo Frei, Editorial America del Sur, 1982.
Coplas de Navidad, Ediciones del Camaleon, 1983.
Poesia politica, Bruguera, 1983.
Nicanor Parra: Biografia emotiva (selected poems), compiled by Efrain Szmulewicz, Ediciones Rumbos, 1988.

Also author of *La evolucion del concepto de masa,* 1958; *Deux poemas,* 1964; *Tres poemas,* 1965; *Defensa de Violeta Parra,*

1967; (translator from the English) R. D. Lindsay and Henry Margenau, *Fundamentos de la fisica* (title means "Foundations of Physics"), 1967; *Muyeres,* 1969; and *Ejercicios respiratorios.*

SIDELIGHTS: Chilean poet Nicanor Parra, a contemporary of Pablo Neruda, inherited a poetic tradition that ensconced lofty themes in grandiose language. "Parra," declared *New York Times Book Review* contributor Alexander Coleman, "is an antipoet. Antipoets . . . dread the very idea of Poetry and its attendant metaphors, inflated diction, romantic yearning, obscurity and empty nobility." Poetry is not an elite pastime, but belongs to the less-privileged majority, he believes. Its proper subject matter is not truth and beauty, but the vulgar surprises of life that more often than not amount to a bad joke. His antipoems relate the ironies of life in ordinary speech made colorful by witty insights into the unpretentious characters he presents. Coleman describes Parra's tools as "irony, burlesque, an astringent barrage of cliches and found phrases, all juxtaposed in a welter of dictions that come out in a wholly original way, laying open everybody's despair." With these methods, says a *Publishers Weekly* reviewer, "Parra bids to break the barrier between the poem and the public." As a champion of accessible poetry, Parra has exerted a major influence on Hispanic literature.

Parra was born in southern Chile near the small town of Chillan in 1914. Having an interest in science and an aptitude for mathematics, he studied mathematics and physics at the University of Chile, advanced mechanics at Brown University in Rhode Island, and, with the aid of a British Council grant, cosmology at Oxford. Since 1948, he has been a professor of theoretical physics at the University of Chile. In addition to his professional activities, he has maintained an interest in American and British poetry, both of which have influenced his work. The factor which perhaps shaped his personal aesthetic the most, however, was having to write in the shadow of the Nobel Prize winner Neruda. Parra became an antipoet, says Emir Rodriguez Monegal in *The Borzoi Anthology of Latin American Literature,* "in order to negate the exalted conception of the poet that Neruda represented so grandly. The fact that he finally succeeded in creating a viable alternative confirms his unique gifts." Parra's antipoetry "is a prime example of a generational reaction to the styles and concerns of earlier poets: it negates the highly metaphorical, surrealistic style of the 1930s," Edith Grossman suggests in *Contemporary Foreign Language Writers.*

Though Parra's early books contain some surreal imagery, later books rely on manipulation of narrative structure to achieve their effects. "Using narrative devices but deflecting the normal expectations of the reader by interrupting and even cutting short the anecdotal flow, Parra 'deconstructs' the poem and finally achieves an almost epigrammatic structure that moves from one intense fragment of verbal reality to the next," Rodriguez Monegal suggests. In addition, the antipoet feels that poetry need not be musical to be good. He maintains that since man talks more than he sings, man should leave the singing to the birds. Another feature the antipoems borrow from prose is the presence of characters found in contemporary urban settings. Mobsters and nymphomaniacs, ragged and rough-talking bag ladies, pugilistic youth and frustrated office workers alike have their say in Parra's antipoems.

Another character that caught Parra's sustained attention was Domingo Zarate Vega, a construction worker who became a self-styled prophet in the 1920s. Parra borrows the folk legend's voice for all the poems in *Sermons and Homilies of the Christ of Elqui.* The result, says a *Georgia Review* contributor, "makes for a powerful, entertaining, and often quirky reading experience."

Doing for the figure of Christ what he has always done for Hispanic poetry, Parra demythologizes the Chilean prophet (and, by implication, other religious figures) by describing the profane conditions of their lives. Parra's Christ matter-of-factly jokes about his sackcloth robe and his breakfast of hot water. Later, he chides followers for giving the pages of the Bible and the Chilean flag a reverence that is inappropriate and impractical. Here, as in his other books, Parra shows the humor (and fury) to be gained from recognizing that people or objects traditionally considered sacred are not.

Parra's iconoclasm is so thoroughgoing that after poetry readings, he says "Me retracto de todo lo dicho" ("I take back everything I told you"). He also refuses to formulate a firm definition of antipoetry. He turns interviews into anti-interviews, frustrating most inquiries into his personal life and writing process, which he calls "a professional secret," Grossman reports. He has written that the thanks he gets for his freedom from tradition is to be declared *persona non grata* in literary circles. Yet many critics offer generally favorable impressions of Parra's work. In his *New York Times Book Review* piece about *Poems and Antipoems,* Mark Strand comments: "Parra's poems are hallucinatory and violent, and at the same time factual. The well-timed disclosure of events—personal or political—gives his poems a cumulative, mounting energy and power that we have come to expect from only the best fiction." In a *Poetry* review, Hayden Carruth adds: "Free, witty, satirical, intelligent, often unexpected (without quite being surrealistic), mordant and comic by turns, always rebellious, always irreverent—it is all these and an ingratiating poetry too."

Partisan Review contributor G. S. Fraser observes that among Hispanic writers, Parra possesses the liveliest wit. "I think that being a professor of mathematics may have given him the logical quickness which lies at the essence of wit," Fraser suggests. Grossman concurs that Parra "has brought to Hispanic literature a new vision of the expressive possibilities of colloquial Spanish." Strand points out, "It is the difference between Parra's antipoems and anybody else's that is significant. . . . To many readers Parra will be a new poet, but a poet with all the authority of a master."

BIOGRAPHICAL/CRITICAL SOURCES:

BOOKS

Contemporary Foreign Language Writers, St. Martin's, 1984.
Contemporary Literary Criticism, Volume 2, Gale, 1974.
Gottlieb, Marlene, *No se termina nunca de nacer: La poesia de Parra,* Playor, 1977.
Grossman, Edith, *The Antipoetry of Parra,* New York University Press, 1975.
Montes, Hugo, *Parra y la poesia de lo cotidiano,* Pacifico, 2nd edition, 1974.
Rodriguez Monegal, Emir, editor, *The Borzoi Anthology of Latin American Literature,* Volume 2: *The Twentieth Century—From Borges and Paz to Guimaraes Rosa and Donoso,* Knopf, 1986.

PERIODICALS

Arizona Quarterly, summer, 1967.
Books Abroad, summer, 1968.
Carleton Miscellany, spring, 1968.
Hudson Review, autumn, 1968, winter, 1972-73.
Nation, August 7, 1972.
National Observer, March 24, 1973.
New Statesman, November 8, 1968.
New York Times Book Review, December 10, 1967, May 7, 1972.

Partisan Review, summer, 1974.
Poetry, September, 1968.
Review, winter, 1971, spring, 1972.

—*Sketch by Marilyn K. Basel*

*   *   *

PARSONS, Talcott   1902-1979

PERSONAL: Born December 13, 1902, in Colorado Springs, Colo.; died May 8, 1979, in Munich, West Germany; son of Edward Smith (a Congregational minister, English professor, and president of Marietta College) and Mary Augusta (Ingersoll) Parsons; married Helen Bancroft Walker (an administrative assistant), April 30, 1927; children: Anne (deceased), Charles Dacre, Susan Pendrell Parsons Cramer. *Education:* Amherst College, A.B., 1924; London School of Economics and Political Science, graduate study, 1924-25; University of Heidelberg, Dr. of Phil., 1927. *Politics:* Independent.

ADDRESSES: Home—62 Fairmont St., Belmont, Mass. *Office*—330 William James Hall, Harvard University, Cambridge, Mass. 02138.

CAREER: Amherst College, Amherst, Mass., instructor in economics, 1926-27; Harvard University, Cambridge, Mass., instructor, 1927-36, assistant professor, 1936-39, associate professor, 1939-44, professor of sociology, 1944-73, professor emeritus, 1973-79, chairman of department, 1944-46, first chairman of department of social relations, 1946-56, member of staff of School for Overseas Administration, 1943-46. Visiting summer professor of sociology at Columbia University, 1933 and 1935, and University of Chicago, 1937; visiting professor of social theory, Cambridge University, 1953-54. Fellow, Center for Advanced Study in the Behavioral Sciences, 1957-58.

MEMBER: American Academy of Arts and Sciences (fellow), American Philosophical Society, American Sociological Association (president, 1949; secretary, 1960-65), Eastern Sociological Society (president, 1941-42), Chi Psi, Phi Beta Kappa.

AWARDS, HONORS: L.H.D., Amherst College, 1949; Dr. rer. pol., University of Cologne, 1963.

WRITINGS:

(Translator) Max Weber, *Protestant Ethic and the Spirit of Capitalism,* Scribner, 1930.
The Structure of Social Action, two volumes, McGraw, 1937, 2nd edition, Free Press, 1966.
(Editor and translator) Weber, *The Theory of Social and Economic Organization,* Oxford University Press, 1947.
Essays in Sociological Theory, Free Press, 1949, revised edition, 1973.
The Social System, Free Press, 1951.
(Editor with E. A. Shils, and contributor) *Toward A General Theory of Action,* Harvard University Press, 1951.
(With Robert F. Bales and Shils) *Working Papers in the Theory of Action,* Free Press, 1953.
(Co-author) *Family Socialization and Interaction Process,* Free Press, 1955.
(With Neil J. Smelser) *Economy and Society,* Free Press, 1956.
Structure and Process in Modern Societies, Free Press, 1960.
(Editor with others) *Theories of Society: Foundations of Modern Sociological Theory,* Free Press, 1961.
Social Structure and Personality, Free Press, 1964.
Societies: Evolutionary and Comparative Perspectives, Prentice-Hall, 1966.

(Editor with Kenneth B. Clark) *The Negro American,* foreword by President Lyndon B. Johnson, Houghton, 1966.
Sociological Theory and Modern Society, Free Press, 1967.
(Editor) *American Sociology: Perspectives, Problems, Methods,* Basic Books, 1968.
Politics and Social Structure, Free Press, 1969.
(Contributor) Philip Rieff, *On Intellectuals,* Doubleday, 1969.
(With others) *Socialization and Schools,* Harvard Educational Review, 1968.
The System of Modern Societies, Prentice-Hall, 1971.
(Compiler with Victor Lidz) *Readings on Premodern Societies,* Prentice-Hall, 1972.
(With Gerald Platt) *The American University,* Harvard University Press, 1973.
The Evolution of Societies, edited by Jackson Toby, Prentice-Hall, 1977.
Social Systems and the Evolution of Action Theory, Free Press, 1977.
Action Theory and the Human Condition, Free Press, 1978.
Talcott Parsons on Institutions and Social Evolution: Selected Writings, edited with an introduction by Leon H. Mayhew, University of Chicago Press, 1985.
Readings from Talcott Parsons, edited by Peter Hamilton, Tavistock, 1985.

SIDELIGHTS: Talcott Parsons was, according to the *New York Times,* "a towering figure in the social sciences" who was "responsible for the education of three generations of sociologists." Although Parsons "propounded abstract theories about human social systems that were highly controversial," the *Times* continues, "he achieved something like immortal status as a man of thought."

BIOGRAPHICAL/CRITICAL SOURCES:

BOOKS

Black, M., editor, *The Social Theories of Talcott Parsons,* Prentice-Hall, 1961.
Mitchell, William C., *Sociological Analysis and Politics: The Theories of Talcott Parsons,* Prentice-Hall, 1967.

OBITUARIES:

PERIODICALS

Newsweek, May 21, 1979.
New York Times, May 9, 1979.
Washington Post, May 12, 1979.*

*   *   *

PASOLINI, Pier Paolo   1922-1975

PERSONAL: Born March 5, 1922, in Bologna, Italy; found bludgeoned to death, November 2, 1975, in Ostia, Italy; son of Carlalberto (an officer) and Susanna (Colussi) Pasolini. *Education:* Earned Ph.D. from University of Bologna.

CAREER: Director of motion pictures; writer. Founder of Academiuta di lenga Furlana (Academy of Friulan Language); actor in "Il gobbo" and "Requiescant," in addition to many of his own screenplays. *Military service:* Served with Italian Army, 1943.

AWARDS, HONORS: Silver Bear Award, 1971, for "Il Decamerone"; Golden Bear Award, 1972; special jury prize from Cannes Film Festival, 1974; Karlovy Vary Festival award for "Accatone"; Viareggio Prize for *Le ceneri de Gramsci;* director award for "Edipo re."

WRITINGS:

NOVELS

Ragazzi di vita, Garzanti, 1955, 12th edition, 1963, translation by Emile Capouya published as *The Ragazzi,* Grove Press, 1968.

Una vita violenta (also see below), Garzanti, 1959, translation by William Weaver published as *A Violent Life,* J. Cape, 1968, reprinted edition by Bruce S. Kupelnick, Garland Publishing, 1978.

Il sogno di una cosa, Garzanti, 1962.

Teorema, Garzanti, 1968.

POETRY

Le ceneri di Gramsci, Garzanti, 1957, 5th edition, 1965.

L'usignolo della Chiesa Cattolica, Loganesi, 1958.

Passione e ideologia, 1948-1958, Garzanti, 1960.

La religione del mio tempo, Garzanti, 1961, 4th edition, 1963.

Poesia in forma di rosa, Garzanti, 1964, 2nd edition, 1964.

Poesie dimenticate, Societa Filologica Friulana, 1965.

(With Laura Betti) *Potentissima signora,* Loganesi, 1965.

Poesie, Garzanti, 1970.

Trasumanar e organizzar, Garzanti, 1971.

Tal cour di un frut: Nel cuore di un fanciullo, 2nd edition, Doretti, 1974.

La Nuova gioventu: Poesie friulane, 1941-1974, Einaudi, c. 1975.

Le poesie, Garzanti, 1975.

SCREENPLAYS

Accattone (released by Cino del Duca/Arco, 1961; adapted from own novel, *Una vita violenta*), Edizioni FM, 1961.

La commare secca, Zibetti, c. 1962.

Mama Roma (released by Arco/Cineriz, 1962), Rizzoli, 1962.

"La ricotta," Arco/Cineriz/Lyre, 1962.

"La rabbia," Opus, 1963.

Il vangelo secondo Matteo (released by Arco/Lux, 1964; released in the U.S. as "The Gospel According to St. Matthew"), Garzanti, 1964.

"Comizi d'amore," Arco, 1964.

"Sopraluoghi in Palestina," 1964.

"La terra vista della luna," Dino de Laurentis/United Artists, 1965.

Uccellacci e accellini (released by Arco, 1966), Garzanti, 1966.

Edipo re (released by Arco, 1967; released in the U.S. as "Oedipus Rex"; adapted from the tragedy by Sophocles), Garzanti, 1967.

"Che cosa sono le nuvole?," Dino de Laurentis, 1967.

"Le sequenza del fiore de corta," 1967.

"Teorema" (adapted from own novel), Aetus, 1968.

Medea (released by San Marco/Rosima Anstaldt/New Line Cinema, 1970; released in the U.S. as "Medea"; adapted from the tragedy by Euripides), Garzanti, 1970.

Ostia, Garzanti, 1970.

Il Decamerone (film in trilogy; also see below; released by Produzione Europee Associate/United Artists, 1971; released in the U.S. as "The Decameron"; adapted from the work by Giovanni Boccaccio), Cappelli, 1975.

I racconti di Canterbury (film in trilogy; also see below; released by United Artists; released in the U.S. as "The Canterbury Tales"; adapted from the work by Geoffrey Chaucer), Cappelli, 1975.

Il fiore delle Mille e una notte (film in trilogy; also see below), Cappelli, 1975.

Trilogia della vita (includes *Il Decamerone, I racconti di Canterbury,* and *Il fiore della Mille e una notte*), Cappelli, 1975.

Also author of screenplays "Porcile," 1969, "Appunti per un' Orestiade africana," 1970, "Salo, or 120 Days of Sodom," "On Any Street," "From a Roman Balcony," "Bell' Amore," "Woman of the River," "La donna del fume" (with Mario Soldati), "Il prigioniero della montagna" (with Luis Trenker), "Le notti de Cabiria" (with Federico Fellini), "La notte brava" and "Il bell'Antonio" (with Mauro Bolognini), "Il carro armato dell' settembre" (with Gianni Puccini), and "La ragazza in vetrina" (with Luciano Emmer).

OTHER

(Translator) Aeschylus, *Orestiade,* Einaudi, 1960.

(Contributor) Sam Waagenaar, *Donne di Roma,* Saggiatore, 1960.

(Contributor) Enzo Siciliano, editor, *Scrittori della realta dell'VIII al XIX secolo,* Garzanti, 1961.

L'odore dell'India, Loganesi, 1962.

(Translator) Titus Maccius Plautus, *Il vantone [di] Plauto,* Garzanti, 1963.

Ali dagli occhi azzurri, Garzanti, 1965, 2nd edition, 1976.

(Contributor) Gioacchino Colizzi, *Attalo,* Lara, 1968.

Affabulazione: Pilade (play; first produced in Taormina, Italy, at Greek Theatre, August 30, 1969), Garzanti, 1977.

(Compiler) *Canzoniere italiano* (anthology), two volumes, Garzanti, 1972.

Empirismo eretico, 2nd edition, Garzanti, 1972, translation by Ben Lawton and Louise K. Barnett published as *Heretical Empiricism,* edited by Barnett, Indiana University, 1988.

Calderon (play), Garzanti, 1973.

Il padre selvaggio, Einaudi, 1975.

La divina mimesis, Einaudi, c. 1975.

Scritti corsari, Garzanti, 1975.

Lettere agli amici, edited by Luciano Serra, Guanda, 1976.

Lettere luteranc, Einaudi, 1976.

Pasolini in Friuli, 1943-1949, Arti grafiche friulane, 1976.

Con Pier Paolo Pasolini (interview), edited by Enrico Magretti, Bulzoni, 1977.

Le belle bandiere: Dialoghi 1960-1965, edited by Gian Carlo Ferretti, Editori riuniti, 1977.

Mario Kicci, editor, *Pier Paolo Pasolini e Il Setaccio 1942-1943,* Cappelli, 1977.

I disegni 1941-1975, edited by Giuseppe Zigaina, Edizioni di Vanni Scheiwiller, 1978.

Lettere 1955-1975, Einaudi, 1988.

Also author of play "Orgia," 1969.

SIDELIGHTS: Pier Paolo Pasolini bore a great affinity with the poor. Upon being conscripted into the Italian Army only a week before its surrender to the German forces, Pasolini fled the ominous prison camps to Casarsa, a small impoverished town in the Friulan section of northern Italy. It was here that Pasolini wrote his early poetry, in the language of the district. He was sympathetic to the plight of the peasants, and joined them in their revolts against the notorious war lords. Pasolini learned a lesson in Casarsa that was to remain with him always: the frightening reality of class struggle.

Pasolini's first novel, *The Ragazzi,* gives evidence of this concern. Though drawing no conclusions, it is an almost clinical study of "the street urchins of Rome, specifically the ones who came of age in the disjointed and disillusioning years after the war, the way they were. Pasolini's ragazzi lie and steal. They are cruel and cynical; they despise authority, mock the church, experience sexual intercourse while still in short pants," reported Robert Crichton. The novel unleashed a fury of rage against the author. His readers were appalled at the audacity of Pasolini to imply that all the young people of Italy behaved in such a manner, for the Italian word *ragazzi* literally means youth in general.

In this novel, which was later produced as a film, Pasolini acted as a nonjudgmental, detached observer, unfeeling and unemotional, duly recording what he saw. In addition to this, the work has no discernible form, no unifying motif linking it all together. "This is not a novel," asserted Crichton, "but a loosely connected series of sketches, verbal pictures, unresolved short stories and fragments of life. . . . The result is an imbalanced mass of behavioristic description, whose intent is not to re-create a life, but to expose a condition of life." This, it seems, was Pasolini's crime. He broke Italian film tradition by revealing "a condition of life" long ignored, the wretched poor.

His next novel, *A Violent Life,* also involves the peasant class. The main character, the young Tomasso, lives a life of petty thievery. He is eventually caught by the police and imprisoned. When released, he decides to try an honest living only to be fired by his first employer when found to be tubercular. Still determined to make good, he joins the rescue operations of the slum in which he was raised that had recently been ravaged by flood. He dies in the attempt. "Fatalistic yet exuberant," remarked one reviewer, "the youngsters at the centre of his books are social outcasts for any number of reasons—through ignorance, through lack of the means or the will to change, through lack of sympathy, on anyone else's part, for their plight; above all though a social system that has totally excluded them, failed to harness their exuberance, failed to make anything of their possibilities."

Pasolini assumes the same stance in his films as in his novels: sober objectivity. He is the instrument through which we see that the reality of life is not always pleasant. A particularly sordid slice of life is chronicled in "Salo, or 120 Days of Sodom," one of his later films. Based on the Marquis de Sade's work of the same name, Pasolini's version takes place in fascist Italy rather than the original seventeenth century Swiss villa. The four "gentlemen" are presented by Pasolini as well-read and cultured intellectuals, a judge, a banker, a duke, and a bishop, who "exercise every conceivable form of torture and excess on innumerable victims," asserted Gideon Bachmann. "I have in no way tried to arouse sympathy, and in fact the film would lose its sting if I had," Pasolini disclosed to Bachmann. "In this I am also very true to de Sade: I have not shown victims whose side the viewer could be on. Pity would have been horrible as an element in this film, nobody would have stood for it. People who cry and tear their hair out would have made everybody leave the cinema after five minutes. In any case, I don't believe in pity." Above all, Pasolini strives for the stark and unidealized truth. "My ambition in making films," he has said, "is to make them political in the sense of being profoundly 'real' in intent: in choosing the characters, in that which they say and in that which they do . . . I do nothing to console, nothing to embellish reality, nothing to sell the goods."

"The Decameron" has become one of Italy's biggest money-making motion pictures of all time, and although enjoying somewhat less success in its U.S. release, it did meet with high critical acclaim. Based on ten stories from Boccaccio's fourteenth century work, the film "lyrically" interweaves the tales by means of a giant fresco. Characters slip in and out of the design almost at will, appearing in several tales. Due to its explicit sexuality, however, dissension arose among some reviewers. "Pier Paolo Pasolini's *The Decameron* strikes the senses like an early spirit of spring, and it's one of the most innocent dirty movies ever made," expressed Tom Shales. Kathleen Carroll disagreed, de-

scribing it as a "strangely lifeless film," and summarized: "In the end Pasolini proves only that he is a dull pornographer."

Pasolini's version of Euripides' *Medea* saw the film debut of operatic superstar Maria Callas, and while most reviewers agreed that she gave a surprisingly effective and artistic performance as the tragic heroine, they rendered decidedly opposing estimations on the screenplay itself. Paul Zimmerman, for example, announced "Medea" to be "educational, respectable, boring," but Vincent Canby protested, claiming the film "superb" and "full of eccentric imagination and real passion." Much of the controversy stemmed from Pasolini's rather loose adaptation of the original, but, as Canby noted, "Euripedes was not, after all, a movie maker."

BIOGRAPHICAL/CRITICAL SOURCES:

PERIODICALS

Best Sellers, December 1, 1968.
Film Quarterly, winter, 1973-74, winter, 1975-76.
Los Angeles Times, January 7, 1972.
Nation, December 6, 1975.
New Statesman, November 19, 1971.
New York Daily News, December 13, 1971.
New York Times, October 5, 1971, October 29, 1971.
New York Times Book Review, November 10, 1968.
Newsweek, September 13, 1971.
Observer Review, January 28, 1968.
Saturday Review, May 3, 1969.
Times Literary Supplement, February 8, 1968, September 12, 1968, October 12, 1973, October 31, 1975, February 13, 1976.
Variety, December 11, 1968, March 19, 1969.
Washington Post, February 11, 1972.

OBITUARIES:

PERIODICALS

New York Times, November 3, 1975.
Time, November 17, 1975.

　　　　　*　　*　　*

PASQUINI
　　See SILONE, Ignazio

　　　　　*　　*　　*

PASTERNAK, Boris (Leonidovich) 1890-1960

PERSONAL: Born February 10, 1890, in Moscow, Russia (now U.S.S.R.); died May 30, 1960, of cancer, in Peredelkino, U.S.S.R.; buried in Peredelkino, U.S.S.R.; son of Leonid Osipovich (a painter) and Rosa Isidorovna (a pianist; maiden name, Kaufman) Pasternak; married Yevgenia Vladimirovna Lurye Muratova (a painter), 1922 (divorced, 1931); married Zinaida Nikolayevna Neyhaus, 1934; children: (first marriage) Yevgeny; (second marriage) Leonid. *Education:* Attended Marburg University, 1912; received degree from Moscow University, 1913. *Religion:* Russian Orthodox.

CAREER: Writer, translator, and poet. Private tutor in Moscow, Russia, 1908 and 1913-15; clerk in chemical factory in the Urals, 1915-1916; librarian in the Library of the Commissariat for Enlightenment and Education.

MEMBER: Writers' Union (U.S.S.R), American Academy of Arts and Letters (honorary member).

AWARDS, HONORS: Nobel Prize for literature, 1958; Bancarella Prize, 1958, for *Doctor Zhivago;* Writers' Union turned the author's country home in Peredelkino into a museum and site for annual readings of poetry, 1988.

WRITINGS:

POETRY, EXCEPT AS NOTED

Blitzhetz tuchakh (title means "Twin in the Clouds"), [Russia], 1914.

Poverkh barerov (title means "Above the Barriers"), [Moscow], 1917.

Detstvo Luvers (title means "The Childhood of Luvers"), [Russia], 1919, translation by Robert Payne published as *Childhood,* Straits Times Press, 1941, translation by I. Langnas published as *The Adolescence of Zhenya Luvers,* Philosophical Library, 1961.

Sestra moia zhizn, [Moscow], 1923, translation by Philip C. Flayderman published as *Sister My Life: Summer, 1917,* Washington Square Press, 1967 (also published as *My Sister, Life;* see *OMNIBUS VOLUMES*).

Temy i variatsi (title means "Themes and Variations"), [Moscow], 1923, reprinted, Ardis, 1972.

Vysockaya bolezn (title means "The Lofty Malady"), [U.S.S.R], 1924.

Vozdushnye puti (short stories; title means "Aerial Ways"), [U.S.S.R.], 1925, reprinted, Ardis, 1976.

The Year 1905, [U.S.S.R.], 1926.

Leitenant Shmidt (title means "Lieutenant Schmidt"), [U.S.S.R.], 1927.

Spektorsky (autobiographical), [U.S.S.R.], 1931.

Okhrannaya gramota (autobiographical prose), [U.S.S.R.], 1931 (translation published as *Safe Conduct: An Autobiography;* see *OMNIBUS VOLUMES*).

Vtoroye rozhdenie (title means "Second Birth"), [U.S.S.R.], 1932.

Stikhotvoreniia v odnom tome (title means "Poetry in One Volume"), Association of Leningrad Writers, 1933.

Poemy (title means "Poems"), [Moscow], 1933.

Povest (autobiographical prose), [Leningrad], 1934, translation by George Reavey published as *The Last Summer,* illustrations by V. Konashevich, Avon, 1959, revised edition, introduction by Lydia Pasternak Slater, Penguin, 1976.

Stikhotvoreniia, [Moscow], 1936.

Na rannikh poezdakh (title means "On Early Trains"), [Moscow], 1943.

Zemnoy proster (title means "Terrestrial Expanse"), [Moscow], 1945.

Il Dottor Zivago (novel), translation by Pietro Zveteremich, Feltrinelli, 1957, translation by Max Hayward and Manya Harari published as *Doctor Zhivago* (also contains *The Poems of Yurii Zhivago,* translation by Bernard Guilbert Guerney), Pantheon, 1958, reprinted, Collins, 1982, published in U.S.S.R. in periodical *Novy Mir* (title means "New World"), January, 1988.

I Remember: Sketch for an Autobiography (autobiographical prose; translation by David Magarshack from the Russian manuscript "Autobiogratichesey ocherk,") Pantheon, 1959 (published in England as *An Essay in Autobiography,* translation by Manya Harari, Collins, 1959).

Kogda razgulyayetsya (title means "When the Skies Clear"), Collins, 1959, translation by Michael Harari published as *Poems, 1955-1959,* 1960.

Lettere agli amici georgiani (letters; translation by Clara Coisson from the Russian manuscript "Pis'ma k gursinskim druz'iam,") Einaudi, 1967, translation with notes and introduction by Magarshack published as *Letters to Georgian Friends,* Harcourt, 1968.

Slepaia krasavitsa (play), Collins, 1969, reprinted, Izd-vo Alagata, 1981, translation by Hayward and Manya Harari published as *The Blind Beauty,* Harcourt, 1969.

Boris Pasternak: Perepiska s Ol'goi Freidenberg (letters), edited with introduction and notes by Elliott Mossman, Harcourt, 1981, translation by Mossman and Margaret Wettlin published as *The Correspondence of Boris Pasternak and Olga Freidenberg, 1910-1954,* Harcourt, 1982.

Letters, Summer 1926 (correspondence of Rainer Maria Rilke, Marina Tsvetayeva, and Boris Pasternak), edited by Yevgeny Pasternak, Yelena Pasternak, and Konstantin M. Azadovsky, translated by Wettlin and Walter Arndt, Harcourt, 1985.

TRANSLATOR; FROM ENGLISH, EXCEPT AS NOTED

(From the Georgian) *Gruzinskie liriki,* [Moscow], 1935.

William Shakespeare, *Gamlet,* Molodaya Gvardia, 1940.

Shakespeare, *Antonii i Kleopatra,* [Moscow], 1944.

Shakespeare, *Romeo i Dzhul'etta,* Gos. izd-vo detskoi lit-ry, 1944.

Shakespeare, *Otello,* [U.S.S.R.], 1945.

(From the Georgian) *Gruzinski Poety,* [Moscow], 1946.

Shakespeare, *Genrikh IV,* [Moscow], 1948.

Vil'iam Shekspir (collection), Iskusstvo, 1949.

Shakespeare, *Korol' Lir,* [U.S.S.R.], 1949, published as *Korol' Lir: Tragediia piati aktakh,* Iskusstvo, 1965.

(With Samuil Marshak) Shakespeare, *Tragedii* (collection), [Moscow], 1951.

(From the German) Johann Wolfgang von Goethe, *Faust,* [Leningrad], 1953.

(From the Georgian) *Stikhi o Gruzii,* Izd-vo Soiuza pisateli Gruzii, Zaria vostoki, 1958.

(From the German) Johann Christoph Friedrich von Schiller, *Mariia Stiuart,* Goslitizdat, 1958.

Also translator of German works by Heinrich von Kleist and Rainer Maria Rilke; English works by Ben Jonson, Lord Byron, Percy Bysshe Shelley, and John Keats; Polish works by Juliusz Slowacki; Ukrainian works by Taras Grigorievich Shevchenko; and Hungarian works by Sandor Petofi.

OMNIBUS VOLUMES IN ENGLISH TRANSLATION

Boris Pasternak: The Collected Prose Works (contains *Safe Conduct, Il tratto di Apelle, Aerial Ways, Letters From Tula,* and *The Childhood of Luvers*), edited by Stefan Schimanski, translation by Beatrice Scott and Robert Payne, Lindsay Drummond, 1945.

Selected Poems, translation by J. M. Cohen, Lindsay Drummond, 1946.

Selected Writings (contains *Safe Conduct, Aerial Ways, Letters From Tula, The Childhood of Luvers, The Stranger,* and selected poems), New Directions, 1949, published as *Safe Conduct: An Autobiography and Other Writings,* 1958.

Poems, translation by Lydia Pasternak Slater, foreword by Hugh MacDiarmid, P. Russell, 1958, revised and enlarged edition, 1958.

Prose and Poems, edited by Schimanski, introduction by Cohen, revised edition, Benn, 1959.

Poems, translation by Eugene M. Kayden, University of Michigan Press, 1959, 2nd edition, revised and enlarged, Antioch Press, 1964.

In the Interlude: 1945-1960 (includes the poems from *Doctor Zhivago* and *When the Skies Clear*), edited and translated by Henry Kamen, foreword by Maurice Bowra, notes by George Katkov, Oxford University Press, 1962.

Fifty Poems, edited and translated by Slater, Barnes & Noble, 1963, published as *Poems of Boris Pasternak,* Unwin, 1984.

The Poems of Doctor Zhivago (contains the poems from *Doctor Zhivago*), translation and commentary by Donald Davie, Barnes & Noble, 1965.

Seven Poems, translation by George L. Kline, Unicorn Press, 1969, 2nd edition, 1972.

My Sister, Life; and Other Poems, edited and texts by Olga Andreyev Carlisle, photographs by Inge Morath, Harcourt, 1976.

Collected Short Prose (contains *Safe Conduct: An Autobiography, The Mark of Apelles, Letters From Tula, Without Love, The Childhood of Zhenya Luvers, Aerial Ways,* essays, and articles), edited with introduction by Christopher Barnes, Praeger, 1977.

Selected Poems, translated by Jon Stallworthy and Peter France, Allen Lane, 1982.

My Sister, Life [and] *A Sublime Malady,* Ardis, 1983.

The Voice of Prose (contains early prose and autobiography), edited by Barnes, Grove, 1986.

Works also represented in *The Poetry of Boris Pasternak, 1917-1959,* edited and translated by George Reavey, 1959, revised edition published as *The Poetry of Boris Pasternak, 1914-1960,* 1960.

OMNIBUS VOLUMES IN RUSSIAN

Izbrannye perevody, Sovietskii pisatel, 1940.

Sochineniya, four volumes, edited by G. P. Struve and B. A. Filippov, introduction by Vladimir Veidle, University of Michigan Press, 1961, Volume 1: *Stikhi i poemy, 1912-1932,* Volume 2: *Proza, 1915-1958: Povest, rasskazy, avtobiograficheski proizvedeniia,* Volume 3: *Stikhi 1936-1959; Stikhi dlia detei; Stikhi 1912-1957, ne sobrannye v knigi avtora; Atat'i i vystupeniia,* Volume 4: *Doktor Zivago.*

Stikhotvoreniia i poemy, Gos. izd-vo Khudozhestvennoi lit-ry, 1961.

Stikhotvoreniia i poemy, edited by L. A. Ozerov, introduction by A. D. Sinyavsky, Sovietski pisatel, 1965.

Stikhi, edited by Z. Pasternak and E. Pasternak, introduction by Korney Chukovsky, Khudozhestvennaya Literatura, 1966.

Stikhi, Khudozhestvennaya Literatura, 1967.

Izbrannoe v dvukh tomakh, two volumes, Khudozhestvennaya Literatura, 1985, Volume 1: *Stikhotvoreniia i poemy,* Volume 2: *Stikhotvoreniia.*

OTHER

La Reazione di Wassermann: Saggi e materiali sull'arte (addresses, essays, and lectures; includes translation of "Vassermanova reakciia" [title means "Wasserman Test"] originally published in periodicals in 1914), introduction by Cesare G. De Michelis, Marsilio [Padova, Italy], 1970.

Roger Martin du Gard, Gabriela Mistral, Boris Pasternak (selections from the works of these three Nobel laureates; also contains Nobel Prize announcements, presentation addresses, and acceptance speeches), A. Gregory, 1971.

Pasternak on Art and Creativity (addresses, essays, and lectures), edited by Angela Livingstone, Cambridge University Press, 1985.

Composer of "Sonata in B minor for Piano," 1905, and "Prelude in G-sharp minor," 1906; three musical compositions publicly performed in Moscow in 1976.

SIDELIGHTS: Nobel laureate Boris Pasternak was highly regarded in his native Russia as one of the country's greatest postrevolutionary poets. He did not gain worldwide acclaim, however, until his only novel, *Doctor Zhivago,* was first published in Europe in 1958, just two years before the author's death. Banned in Russia as anti-Soviet, Pasternak's controversial prose work was hailed as a literary masterpiece by both American and European critics, but its publication was suppressed in Russia until 1988. The attention focused on Pasternak and his work as a result of the *Zhivago* affair brought with it a renewed public interest in the author's earlier writings. Consequently, numerous English translations of Pasternak's entire canon, including his poetry, autobiographical prose, and *Doctor Zhivago,* became readily available in the Western world.

Born in 1890 to a cultivated, cosmopolitan Moscow family, Pasternak grew up in an atmosphere that fostered an appreciation of the arts and the pursuit of artistic endeavors. His father, Leonid, was a prominent Russian portrait painter and art teacher, and his mother, Rosa, was a former concert pianist who forfeited a promising musical career in the interest of her husband and children. The Pasternaks were part of an exclusive social circle that consisted of Russia's finest musicians, writers, and painters, including premier novelist Leo Tolstoy and composers Alexander Scriabin, Sergei Rachmaninov, and Anton Rubinstein. In the rich cultural surroundings of Pasternak's home, observed Gerd Ruge in *Pasternak: A Pictorial Biography,* "art was a normal activity which needed neither explanation nor apology and which could fill out and take possession of a man's whole life."

Pasternak was only four years old when he first met Tolstoy, who attended a concert at the Pasternaks' given by Boris's mother and two professors—a violinist and a cellist—from the Moscow Conservatory. In his 1959 memoir *I Remember: Sketch for an Autobiography,* Pasternak reflected on the impact of the music, especially that of the stringed instruments, played in Tolstoy's honor: "I was awakened . . . by a sweetly poignant pain, more violent than any I had experienced before. I cried out and burst into tears from fear and anguish. . . . My memory became active and my consciousness was set in motion. [From that time I] believed in the existence of a higher heroic world, which must be served rapturously, though it might bring suffering." The family's ongoing contact with Tolstoy—Leonid illustrated the author's novella *Resurrection* in 1898—culminated in "the forlorn station where Tolstoy lay dead in a narrow humble room," related Marc Slonim in the *New York Times Book Review.* According to Slonim, the author's moving recollections, brought to life at Tolstoy's wake and documented in *I Remember,* demonstrate how great a part "the creator of *War and Peace* [played] in the ethical formation of Pasternak, particularly in his developing attitude toward history and nature."

An encounter in 1903 with the celebrated composer Scriabin prompted the fourteen-year-old Pasternak to devote himself entirely to the composition of music. He eagerly embraced the study of music at the Moscow Conservatory and under composer Reinhold Glier but completely renounced his chosen vocation six years later. He attributed the need for this difficult and radical decision to his lack of both technical skill and pitch recognition, explaining in *I Remember,* "I could scarcely play the piano and could not even read music with any fluency. . . . This discrepancy between the . . . musical idea and its lagging technical support transformed nature's gift, which could have served as a source of joy, into an object of constant torment which in the end I could no longer endure." Pasternak not only resented his musical inadequacy but, despising any lack of creativity, perceived it as an omen, "as proof," he wrote in *I Remember,* that his devotion to "music was against the will of fate and heaven."

The author completely disassociated himself from music, cutting all ties to composers and musicians and even vowing to avoid concerts. Still, Pasternak would allow his love of music to color his writings, steeping both the poetry and prose he would later compose in a melodic air of rhythm and harmony. In *Boris Pasternak: His Life and Art,* Guy de Mallac cited Christopher Barnes's assessment of the writer's style: "It is no doubt to Scriabin that Pasternak, and we, are indebted for the poet's initial captivation by music, and for the development of his fine 'composer's ear' which is traceable throughout the strongly 'musical' poetry and prose."

De Mallac suggested that prevailing literary trends in early twentieth-century Russia also exerted a great influence on the impressionable adolescent. The beginnings of the Russian symbolist movement—a romantic reaction to realism that was advocated most notably by writer Alexander Blok—in the 1890s led to a reexamination of accepted artistic concepts. And as World War I approached, Pasternak would, for several years, associate himself with the futurists, a group of writers whose works were marked by a rejection of the past and a search for new forms. De Mallac pointed out that Pasternak was born into a world "of recurrent economic crises and political repression, dissent, and assassination. . . . [Russian czar Nicholas II's] reactionary stance . . . only fed the flames of political and social revolt and exacerbated the critical and hostile attitudes of the intelligentsia. . . . Pasternak . . . soon realized that the society he lived in was doomed to undergo radical upheavals."

Pasternak's early experiences—his development as a youth within a highly cultural milieu, the early associations with Tolstoy and Scriabin, his innate sensitivity and strongly superstitious nature, and the implications of the dawn of the Russian Revolution—combined to profoundly affect his development as a man and as a writer. After studying philosophy at Marburg University in 1912 under neo-Kantian scholar Hermann Cohen, who purported a philosophy of coherence and world order and abjured human intuition or irrationality, Pasternak again made an abrupt and radical change in his life, leaving Marburg that same summer. De Mallac noted that while Pasternak "did not absorb all of Cohen's theories, [the author] was influenced by the philosopher's monotheism and highly ethical standards." In her prologue to the 1976 edition of Pasternak's *My Sister, Life; and Other Poems,* Olga Andrevey Carlisle reaffirmed that although "philosophy was to remain an important element in his life, [after the summer of 1912] it was no longer [his] central concern." The experience of being rejected by a lover was the catalyst that turned Pasternak into a poet.

In 1912 Ida Davidovna, a young woman whom Pasternak had known since childhood, refused the author's proposal of marriage. De Mallac noted that for Pasternak, "creative self-renewal [was] directly induced by a stormy passion." The intensity of the experience with Davidovna, theorized de Mallac, affected Pasternak "so strongly that he soon made another decision: he would not marry a woman; he would divorce a profession. . . . Impelled by [a] new, poetic perception of the world, he began writing poetry." After traveling to Italy, Pasternak returned to Moscow to write.

Through his highly original poetry, Pasternak explores the many moods and faces of nature as well as man's place in the natural world. In his first collection of poems, the 1923 volume *My Sister, Life: Summer 1917,* the author asserts his oneness with nature, a credo which would guide all of his subsequent writings:

"It seemed the alpha and omega— / Life and I are of the same stuff; / And all year round, with snow or snowless, / She was like my alter ego / And 'sister' was the name I called her."

My Sister, Life is marked by the spirit of the revolution. De Mallac suggested that it was Pasternak's "sincere endeavor to apprehend the era's political turmoil, albeit in a peculiar mode of cosmic awareness." The poet evokes the ambience of prerevolutionary Russia in "Summer 1917," a poem which reduces the last weeks of peace before the war to days "Bright with wood sorrel . . . / When the air smelled of wine corks." Another poem from *My Sister, Life,* frequently but loosely translated as "The Racing Stars," captures with startling and unconventional imagery the moment in time when nineteenth-century Russian poet Aleksander Pushkin wrote his passionate poem "The Prophet": "Stars swarmed. Headlands washed in the sea. / Salt sprays blinding. Tears have grown dry. / Darkness brooded in bedrooms. Thoughts swarming, / While the Sphinx listens patiently to the Sahara." Robert Payne commented in *The Three Worlds of Boris Pasternak* that the author's "major achievement in poetry lay . . . in his power to sustain rich and varied moods which had never been explored before."

The 1920s and 1930s were years of transformation for Pasternak. By the end of 1923, he had married painter Yevgenia Vladimirovna and, upon the publication of a second outstanding collection of lyric poetry titled *Themes and Variations,* had established himself as one of Russia's most innovative and significant twentieth-century poets. The author had enjoyed a successful and prolific period through the early 1920s and supported the Russian Revolution at its inception, feeling the movement would be justified if it did not demand the sacrifice of citizens' individuality. But shortly after Joseph Stalin had seized power in the country in 1928, Pasternak wrote only sporadically, feeling stifled by pressure from the Communist government to adhere to the party's ideals in his writings. He chose instead to lose himself in the act of translating the works of foreign writers, including William Shakespeare.

Almost simultaneously, the author ended his association with the futurists, considering their concept of new poetry too narrow to accommodate his unique impressions and interpretations. As a conseqence of the break, Pasternak lost longtime friend Vladimir Mayakovski, the Russian futurist poet who glorified the Revolution and identified with the Bolshevik party, an extremist wing of the Russian Socialist Democratic party that seized supreme power in Russia through the revolt. Pasternak did not align himself with any other literary movement during his lifetime. Instead, wrote de Mallac, he worked "as an independent, if often isolated, artist, in pursuit of aims he would define for himself."

Several translations of Pasternak's early poetry and prose, including the 1931 autobiographical prose work *Safe Conduct,* began to appear in the United States in the late 1940s. Slonim echoed the majority of the critics when he commented on the inevitable futility of trying to capture the impact of the author's words, especially his poetry, in English translation: "In the case of Pasternak, whose poetry is complex and highly diversified, the perfect marriage of image, music and meaning can be rendered in English only with a certain degree of approximation." Andrey Sinyavsky pointed out in his piece for *Major Soviet Writers: Essays in Criticism* that "authenticity—the truth of image—is for Pasternak the highest criterion of art. In his views on literature and his practice as a poet he is filled with the concern 'not to distort the voice of life that speaks in us.' " Sinyavsky further asserted that the "fullness" of Pasternak's words—at times "light" and "winged," at times "awkward . . . choked and almost sobbing"—is achieved through the freedom with which he wrote in his native language: "In [his] naive, unaffected outpouring of words, which seems at first not to be directed by the poet but to carry him along after it, Pasternak attained the desired naturalness of the living Russian language."

Pasternak's highly metaphorical writing style made his early works somewhat difficult to understand. In *I Remember* the author looks with disapproval at what he termed the "mannerisms" of his youth. In an effort to make his thoughts and images clearer and more accessible to a larger audience, Pasternak worked after 1930 to develop a more direct and classical writing style. Many critics have cited his masterpiece *Doctor Zhivago* and its accompanying poetry as the culmination of these efforts.

De Mallac theorized that *Doctor Zhivago,* the work for which Pasternak is most famous, "was forty years in the making." According to the critic, "Pasternak called 1945 and 1946 his 'years of deep spiritual crisis and change.' " It was during this time that the author called began to weave the first draft of his impressions of the war and its effect on his generation with a highly personal love story—in the form of *Doctor Zhivago.*

In the fall of 1946, while married to his second wife, Zinaida Nikolayevna (his marriage to Yevgenia Vladimirovna had ended in divorce in 1931), Pasternak met and fell in love with Olga Ivinskaya, an editorial assistant for the monthly Soviet periodical *Novy Mir.* In her 1978 memoir *A Captive of Time,* Ivinskaya recalled that upon her arrival home from a lecture in which Pasternak read from his translations, she told her mother, "I've just been talking to God." Ivinskaya's admiration for the author was in sharp contrast to Zinaida's coolness, for as de Mallac documented, Pasternak's wife was "little attuned to [her husband's] spiritual and aesthetic pursuits. . . . Her rather brusque and authoritarian manner . . . was ill-oriented to his sensibilities. . . . Pasternak would seek from Ivinskaya the spiritual and emotional solace that his wife had not given him." Many critics have contended that the poems written during Pasternak's affiliation with Ivinskaya are among his best. One such poem was excerpted by Irving Howe in the *New York Times Book Review:* "I have let my family scatter / All my dear ones are dispersed, / And the loneliness always with me / Fills nature and my heart. . . . / You are the good gift of destruction's path, / When life sickens more than disease / And boldness is the root of beauty— / Which draws us together so close."

The author's affair with Ivinskaya coincided with the Russian Communist party's renewed attack on deviationist writers. Numerous sources suggested that Stalin showed an unusual tolerance for Pasternak—such special treatment may have stemmed from the author's work as a translator and promoter of Georgian literature, as Stalin was a native of Georgia. Howe reported that "there were rumors in Moscow that the dictator, glancing over a dossier prepared for Pasternak's arrest, had scribbled, 'Do not touch this cloud-dweller.' "

Pasternak's lover, however, was not afforded such consideration. Arrested in 1949 for having engaged in alleged anti-Soviet discourse with the author, Ivinskaya was convicted and sentenced to four years in a labor camp after refusing to denounce her lover as a British spy. As documented in *A Captive of Time,* she suffered systematic psychological torture at the hands of her captors. Pregnant with Pasternak's baby at the time of her imprisonment, Ivinskaya, promised a visit from the author, was instead led through prison corridors to a morgue. Fearing that Pasternak's body lay among the cadavers, she suffered a miscarriage.

Although Pasternak remained free, Howe reported that the author "all the while seems to have been haunted by guilt: toward his betrayed wife, toward his lover far off in a camp, toward his colleagues in Russian literature who had been cut down by the regime." Of Ivinskaya, as cited in *A Captive of Time,* Pasternak wrote: "She is all life, all freedom, / A pounding of the heart in the breast, / And the prison dungeons / Have not broken her will." Upon her release, Ivinskaya proclaimed her undying love to Pasternak, and, although he thought it best that they no longer see each other, she eventually won the author back.

Ivinskaya is generally regarded as the model for Lara, the heroine in *Doctor Zhivago.* De Mallac noted that when speaking with certain visitors, Pasternak often "equated" Lara with Ivinskaya. But the critic contended that "Lara is in fact a composite portrait, combining elements of both Zinaida Nikolayevna and Olga Ivinskaya." The novel itself was, as de Mallac indicated, "a 'settlement' of sorts" for Pasternak, an attempt to relate in a comprehensive volume of fictional prose the suffering and injustice he had witnessed during the years of the war.

Doctor Zhivago begins with the suicide of young Yuri Zhivago's father. The boy—whose name means "alive"—grows up in Czarist Russia, becomes a doctor, and writes poetry in his spare time. Zhivago marries the daughter of a chemistry professor and is soon drafted as a medical officer in the Revolution. Witnessing the frightening social chaos in Moscow, he leaves with his family upon the completion of his service for refuge in a hamlet beyond the Urals. Zhivago's life soon becomes complicated by the reappearance of Lara, a girl he had known years earlier. Lara has married Strelnikov, a nonpartisan revolutionary who is captured by the Germans and presumed dead. Zhivago is kidnapped by the Red partisans and forced into duty as a frontline physician in Siberia. Returning to the Urals following his release from servitude, he finds that his family has been exiled from Russia. He encounters Lara, whom he has loved since their first meeting, and they have a brief affair. Learning that she is endangered through her union with Strelnikov, who still lives, Zhivago convinces her to seek safety in the Far East with Komarovsky, the wretched lover of Lara's mother; Komarovsky had raped Lara when she was a teenager and then forced her to be his mistress.

Without his one true love, Zhivago goes back to Moscow a broken man. The willing submission of his former intellectual friends to Soviet policies sparks in him a growing contempt for the intelligentsia as a whole. "Men who are not free," he muses, "always idealize their bondage." Zhivago later dies on a street in Moscow. Lara, who, unbeknownst to Zhivago, had given birth to his child, "vanished without a trace and probably died somewhere, forgotten as a nameless number on a list that afterward got mislaid, in one of the innumerable mixed or women's concentration camps in the north."

Despite the implications of its plot, *Doctor Zhivago* is not ordinarily viewed as a political novel or an attack on the Soviet regime. (Pasternak proclaimed in *My Sister, Life* that he greatly "disliked" writers who "commit themselves to political causes," especially those "who make a career out of being Communists.") Rather, the book is judged by most critics as an affirmation of the virtues of individuality and the human spirit. In a review for *Atlantic Monthly,* Ernest J. Simmons contended that "it is the story of Russians from all walks of life who lived, loved, fought, and died during the momentous events from 1903 to 1929. . . . And the beloved, ineradicable symbol of their existence is Russia."

In an essay for *Major Soviet Writers,* Herbert E. Bowman quoted Pasternak as calling *Doctor Zhivago* "my chief and most important work." Critics have generally considered Zhivago to be an autobiographical character, Pasternak's second self. Slonim commented, "There is no doubt that the basic attitudes of [the] hero do reflect the poet's intimate convictions. [Zhivago] believes that 'every man is born a Faust, with a longing to grasp and experience and express everything in the world.' And he sees history as only part of a larger order."

Like Pasternak, Yuri Zhivago welcomes the Revolution in its infancy as a revitalizing agent with the potential to cleanse his native country of its ills. The character rejects the Soviet philosophy, though, when it becomes incompatible with "the ideal of free personality." Communists always talk of "remaking life," but "people who can talk in this way," claims Zhivago, "have never known life at all, have never felt its spirit, its soul. For them, human existence is a lump of raw material which has not been ennobled by their touch." To Yuri, life "is away out of reach of our stupid theories." Of the higher echelons within the Marxist regime Zhivago declares, "They are so anxious to establish the myth of their infallibility, that they do their utmost to ignore the truth." The truth for Zhivago is that all aspects of the human personality must be acknowledged and expressed, not denied or unduly restrained. In spite of the horrors and trials it depicts, the novel leaves what Slonim referred to as "the impression of strength and faith" existing "underneath the Communist mechanism."

Judged as a work of fiction, *Doctor Zhivago* is, according to many critics, technically flawed. Some reviewers maintained that while Pasternak was a master poet, his inexperience as a novelist is evident in both his flat expository style and his frequent use of coincidence to manipulate the plot of the book. Most reviewers, however, conceded that the book's honest tone supersedes any signs of structural awkwardness. David Magarshack commented in *Nation*, "If Pasternak's novel cannot compare as a work of art with the greatest Russian novels of the nineteenth century, it certainly excels them as a social document, as a work of observation of the highest order." Calling *Doctor Zhivago* "one of the great events in man's literary and moral history," Edmund Wilson concluded in the *New Yorker*, "Nobody could have written it in a totalitarian state and turned it loose on the world who did not have the courage of genius. . . . [Pasternak's] book is a great act of faith in art and in the human spirit."

In the summer of 1956 Pasternak submitted his manuscript of *Doctor Zhivago* to *Novy Mir*. The editorial board returned the manuscript to the author with a ten-thousand-word letter of rejection. Excerpted in the *New York Times Book Review*, the letter held that "the spirit of [the] novel [was] that of non-acceptance of the socialist revolution." The board further accused Pasternak of having "written a political novel-sermon par excellence" which was "conceived . . . as a work to be placed unreservedly and sincerely at the service of certain political aims." Although publication of *Doctor Zhivago* was suppressed in Russia, the manuscript was smuggled to the West where it was published, first in Italy by Feltrinelli, in 1957.

Despite the harassment he suffered in his own country, Pasternak enjoyed high acclaim in the West for his novel. In announcing the author's selection as the winner of the Nobel Prize for literature on October 23, 1958, the secretary of the Swedish Academy indirectly focused attention on *Doctor Zhivago* by citing Pasternak's achievements in both poetry and Russia's grand epic tradition. The resulting speculation that the award had, in fact, been given solely for *Doctor Zhivago*, and that the poetry had been mentioned only as a courtesy, immersed the author in a politically charged international controversy that continued

even after his death in 1960. While Pasternak initially accepted the award, cabling the message, as quoted in *Time*, that he was "infinitely grateful, touched, proud, surprised, [and] overwhelmed," he officially declined the prize six days later. In *A Captive of Time*, Ivinskaya admitted that she persuaded Pasternak to sign a repudiation "in view of the meaning given the award by the society in which [he] live[d]."

Nevertheless, Pasternak was expelled from the Soviet Writers' Union and deemed a traitor. Dusko Doder, writing in the *Los Angeles Times*, related some of the bitter attacks launched against Pasternak after he was named Nobel laureate. A union representative called the writer "a literary whore, hired and kept in America's anti-Soviet brothel." A government official referred to him as "a pig who has fouled the spot where he eats and cast filth on those by whose labor he lives and breathes." Communist propagandists urged that the novelist be banished from Russia. But following Pasternak's refusal of the award and his entreaty to Premier Nikita Khrushchev—in a letter, excerpted in the *New York Times*, he told the Soviet leader, "Leaving the motherland will equal death for me. I am tied to Russia by birth, by life and work"—the author was permitted to remain in his native country.

Pasternak died a disillusioned and disgraced man on May 30, 1960. As cited in his obituary in the *New York Times*, one of the poems from *Doctor Zhivago* provides for the author an appropriate epitaph: "The stir is over. . . . / I strain to make the far-off echo yield / A cue to the events that may come in my day. / The order of the acts has been schemed and plotted, / And nothing can avert the final curtain's fall. / I stand alone. . . . / To live life to the end is not a childish task."

In what Philip Taubman, writing in the *New York Times*, termed a "rehabilitation" that "has become perhaps the most visible symbol of the changing cultural climate [in the U.S.S.R.] under [Soviet Communist leader Mikhail] Gorbachev," Pasternak finally earned in death the recognition from his country that was denied him during his lifetime. The author was posthumously reinstated to his place in the Writers' Union on February 19, 1987. And, three decades after its original release, *Doctor Zhivago* was finally published in Russia in 1988, to be freely read and enjoyed as Pasternak had intended.

MEDIA ADAPTATIONS: Doctor Zhivago was adapted by Robert Bolt for a film of the same title, directed by David Lean, produced by Carlo Ponti, released by Metro-Goldwyn-Mayer, 1965; the novella *The Last Summer* and the poem *Spektorsky* were adapted by Craig Raine for the libretto to the opera *The Electrification of the Soviet Union*, music by Nigel Osborne, 1986.

BIOGRAPHICAL/CRITICAL SOURCES:

BOOKS

Brown, Edward J., editor, *Major Soviet Writers: Essays in Criticism*, Oxford University Press, 1973.

Conquest, Robert, *The Pasternak Affair: Courage of Genius*, Lippincott, 1969.

Contemporary Literary Criticism, Gale, Volume 7, 1977, Volume 10, 1979, Volume 18, 1981.

de Mallac, Guy, *Boris Pasternak: His Life and Art*, University of Oklahoma Press, 1981.

Dyck, J. W., *Boris Pasternak*, Twayne, 1972.

Erlich, Victor, editor, *Pasternak: A Collection of Critical Essays*, Prentice-Hall, 1978.

Gifford, Henry, *Pasternak: A Critical Study*, Cambridge University Press, 1977.

Gladkov, Alexander, *Meetings With Pasternak: A Memoir,* translated and edited with notes and introduction by Max Hayward, Harcourt, 1977.

Hughes, Olga Raevsky, *The Poetic World of Boris Pasternak,* Princeton University Press, 1974.

Ivinskaya, Olga, *A Captive of Time,* translation by Hayward, Doubleday, 1978.

Pasternak, Boris, *Doctor Zhivago,* translation by Hayward and Manya Harari, Pantheon, 1958.

Pasternak, *Safe Conduct: An Autobiography and Other Writings,* New Directions, 1958.

Pasternak, *I Remember: Sketch for an Autobiography,* translation by David Magarshack, Pantheon, 1959.

Pasternak, *My Sister, Life; and Other Poems,* edited by Olga Andreyev Carlisle, Harcourt, 1976.

Pasternak, *Collected Short Prose,* edited with introduction by Christopher Barnes, Praeger, 1977.

Pasternak, and Olga Freidenberg, *The Correspondence of Boris Pasternak and Olga Freidenberg, 1910-1954,* edited by Elliott Mossman, translation by Mossman and Margaret Wettlin, Harcourt, 1982.

Payne, Robert, *The Three Worlds of Boris Pasternak,* Coward, 1961.

Ruge, Gerd, *Pasternak: A Pictorial Biography,* McGraw, 1959.

PERIODICALS

Atlantic Monthly, September, 1958.
Canadian Forum, December, 1958.
Chicago Tribune, January 25, 1988.
Commonweal, November 14, 1958.
Los Angeles Times, January 4, 1983.
Nation, September 13, 1958.
New Republic, September 8, 1958.
New Yorker, November 15, 1958.
New York Times, June 23, 1982, February 24, 1987.
New York Times Book Review, September 7, 1958, December 7, 1958, April 5, 1959, November 1, 1959, November 12, 1967, February 5, 1978, June 27, 1982.
Saturday Review, September 6, 1958.
Spectator, September 5, 1958.
Time, September 15, 1958, October 19, 1959, March 6, 1979, August 18, 1980, August 9, 1982.
Times (London), December 12, 1983.
Times Literary Supplement, January 23, 1964.
Washington Post, May 17, 1988.
World Literature Today, autumn, 1977.

OBITUARIES:

PERIODICALS

Harper's, May, 1961.
Nation, June 11, 1960.
Newsweek, June 6, 1960.
New York Times, May 31, 1960, June 1, 1960, June 3, 1960.
Time, June 13, 1960.

*   *   *

PATCHEN, Kenneth   1911-1972

PERSONAL: Born December 13, 1911, in Niles, Ohio; died January 8, 1972; son of Wayne (a steel mill worker) and Eva Patchen; married Miriam Oikemus, June 28, 1934. *Education:* Attended University of Wisconsin, 1928-29.

ADDRESSES: Home—2340 Sierra Ct., Palo Alto, Calif.

CAREER: Writer of prose and of poetry. Made poetry-jazz appearances across the United States and in Canada, and poetry recordings for Cadence and Folkways albums. Artist, worked in the graphic arts, and originator of own limited editions books, more than eight hundred issued with individual painted covers. Exhibited paintings in various cities and at universities. Held many jobs in his youth, including working in a steel mill and migratory work in the United States and Canada.

AWARDS, HONORS: Guggenheim fellowship, 1936; Ohioana Book Award in poetry, 1944, for *Cloth of the Tempest;* Shelley Memorial Award, 1954; National Foundation on Arts and Humanities award, 1967, for lifelong contribution to American letters.

WRITINGS:

POETRY

Before the Brave, Random House, 1936, reprinted, Haskell House, 1974.
First Will and Testament, New Directions, 1939.
Teeth of the Lion, New Directions, 1942.
The Dark Kingdom, Harriss & Givens, 1942.
Cloth of the Tempest, Harper, 1943.
An Astonished Eye Looks Out of the Air, Untide Press, 1945.
Outlaw of the Lowest Planet, Grey Walls Press, 1946.
Selected Poems, New Directions, 1946, revised edition, 1964.
Pictures of Life and Death, Max Padell, 1947.
They Keep Riding Down All the Time, Max Padell, 1947.
Panels for the Walls of Heaven, Bern Porter, 1947.
CCCLXXIV Poems, Max Padell, 1948.
Red Wine and Yellow Hair, New Directions, 1949.
Orchards, Thrones and Caravans, Print Workshop, 1952.
Fables and Other Little Tales, Jonathan Williams, 1953.
The Famous Boating Party and Other Poems in Prose, New Directions, 1954.
Glory Never Guesses, privately printed, 1955.
Surprise for the Bagpipe Player, privately printed, 1956.
When We Were Here Together, New Directions, 1957.
Hurrah for Anything: Poems and Drawings, Jonathan Williams, 1957 (also see below).
Poemscapes, Jonathan Williams, 1958 (also see below).
To Say If You Love Someone, Decker Press, 1959.
Because It Is, New Directions, 1960 (also see below).
Love Poems, City Lights, 1960, published as *The Love Poems of Kenneth Patchen,* Kraus Reprint, 1973.
Poems of Humor and Protest, City Lights, 1960.
Selected Love Poems, Jargon, 1965.
Like Fun I'll Tell You, Jonathan Williams, 1966.
Hallelujah Anyway, New Directions, 1966 (also see below).
But Even So, New Directions, 1968 (also see below).
Love and War Poems, Whisper & Shout, 1968.
The Collected Poems of Kenneth Patchen, New Directions, 1969.
Aflame and Afun of Walking Faces, New Directions, 1970.
Wonderings, New Directions, 1971.
In Quest of Candlelighters, New Directions, 1972.
A Poem for Christmas, Artichoke, 1976.
The Argument of Innocence, Scrimshaw Press, 1977.
Still Another Pelican in the Breadbox, edited by Richard Morgan, Pig Iron Press, 1980.
What Shall We Do Without Us? The Voice and Vision of Kenneth Patchen, Sierra Book Club, 1984.

NOVELS

The Journal of Albion Moonlight, Max Padell, 1941, reprinted, New Directions, 1961.

The Memoirs of a Shy Pornographer: An Amusement, New Directions, 1945, reprinted, 1965.
Sleepers Awake, Max Padell, 1946, reprinted, 1969.
See You in the Morning, Max Padell, 1948.

PLAYS

"Now You See It (Don't Look Now)," produced Off-Off Broadway at Thresholds Theatre, December, 1966.
Patchen's Lost Plays, edited by Richard Morgan, Capra, 1977, reprinted, Borgo Press, 1988.

OMNIBUS VOLUMES

Doubleheader (contains *Poemscapes, Hurrah for Anything,* and *A Letter to God*), New Directions, 1966.
Out of the World of Patchen, New Directions, 1970, Volume I: *Because It Is,* Volume II: *But Even So,* Volume III: *Doubleheader,* Volume IV: *Hallelujah Anyway.*

SIDELIGHTS: Largely a self-taught writer, Kenneth Patchen never appeared to win widespread recognition from the professors at universities or many literary critics. As the *New York Times Book Review* noted: "While some critics tended to dismiss his work as naive, romantic, capricious and concerned often with the social problems of the 1930's, others found him a major voice in American poetry. . . . Even the most generous praise was usually grudging, as if Patchen had somehow won his place through sheer wrongheaded persistence."

The bulk of Patchen's followers were and still are young people. Kenneth Rexroth once pointed out that "during the Second World War and the dark days of reaction afterwards [Patchen] was the most popular poet on college campuses." One reason for the attraction of generations of college-age readers to Patchen may be the quality of timelessness of his beliefs and ideas. An article in the *New York Times* explained that Patchen's antiwar poetry—written in response to atrocities of World War II—was embraced by students protesting the Vietnam War in the late 1960s.

A writer for the *New York Times Book Review* once wrote that "there is the voice of anger—outspoken rage against the forces of hypocrisy and injustice in our world. Patchen sees man as a creature of crime and violence, a fallen angel who is haunted by all the horrors of the natural world, and who still continues to kill his own kind: 'Humanity is a good thing. Perhaps we can arrange the murder of a sizable number of people to save it.' "

In the 1950's Patchen become famous in poetry circles for reading his poetry to the accompaniment of jazz music.

BIOGRAPHICAL/CRITICAL SOURCES:

BOOKS

Contemporary Literary Criticism, Gale, Volume 1, 1973, Volume 2, 1974, Volume 18, 1981.
Dictionary of Literary Biography, Gale, Volume 16: *The Beats: Literary Bohemians in Postwar America,* 1983, Volume 48: *American Poets, 1880-1945, First Series,* 1986.
Rexroth, Kenneth, *Assays,* New Directions, 1961.
Rexroth, *American Poetry in the Twentieth Century,* Herder, 1971.
Walsh, Chad, *Today's Poets,* Scribner, 1964.
Wilder, Amos N., *Spiritual Aspects of the New Poetry,* Harper, 1940.

PERIODICALS

New York Times Book Review, February 2, 1958, June 22, 1958, October 20, 1968.

Poetry, September, 1958, February, 1965.
Saturday Review, July 12, 1958.
Yale Review, June, 1958.

OBITUARIES:

PERIODICALS

Newsweek, January 24, 1972.
New York Times, January 9, 1972, January 10, 1972.
Publishers Weekly, January 24, 1972.
Time, January 24, 1972.
Washington Post, January 10, 1972.

*   *   *

PATERSON, Katherine (Womeldorf) 1932-

PERSONAL: Born October 31, 1932, in Qing Jiang, China; daughter of George Raymond (a clergyman) and Mary (Goetchius) Womeldorf; married John Barstow Paterson (a clergyman), July 14, 1962; children: Elizabeth Polin (adopted), John Barstow, Jr., David Lord, Mary Katherine (adopted). *Education:* King College, A.B., 1954; Presbyterian School of Christian Education, M.A., 1957; postgraduate study at Kobe School of Japanese Language, 1957-60; Union Theological Seminary, New York, N.Y., M.R.E., 1962. *Politics:* Democrat. *Religion:* Presbyterian Church in the United States.

ADDRESSES: Home—Norfolk, Va.

CAREER: Public school teacher in Lovettsville, Va., 1954-55; Presbyterian Church in the United States, Board of World Missions, Nashville, Tenn., missionary in Japan, 1957-62; Pennington School for Boys, Pennington, N.J., teacher of sacred studies and English, 1963-65; writer.

MEMBER: Authors Guild, PEN, Children's Book Guild of Washington.

AWARDS, HONORS: American Library Association (ALA) Notable Children's Book award, 1974, for *Of Nightingales That Weep;* ALA Notable Children's Book award, 1976, National Book Award for Children's Literature, 1977, runner-up for Edgar Allan Poe Award (juvenile division), Mystery Writers of America, 1977, and American Book Award nomination, children's fiction paperback, 1982, all for *The Master Puppeteer;* ALA Notable Children's Book award, 1977, John Newbery Medal, 1978, Lewis Carroll Shelf Award, 1978, and Division II runner-up, Michigan Young Reader's Award, 1980, all for *Bridge to Terabithia;* Lit.D., King College, 1978; ALA Notable Children's Book award, 1978, National Book Award for Children's Literature, 1979, Christopher Award (ages 9-12), 1979, Newbery Honor Book, 1979, CRABbery (Children Raving About Books) Honor Book, 1979, American Book Award nominee, children's paperback, 1980, William Allen White Children's Book Award, 1981, Garden State Children's Book Award, younger division, New Jersey Library Association, 1981, Georgia Children's Book Award, 1981, Iowa Children's Choice Award, 1981, Massachusetts Children's Book Award (elementary), 1981, all for *The Great Gilly Hopkins;* U.S. nominee, Hans Christian Andersen Award, 1980; *New York Times* Outstanding Book List, 1980, Newbery Medal, 1981, CRABbery Honor Book, 1981, American Book Award nominee, children's hardcover, 1981, and children's paperback, 1982, all for *Jacob Have I Loved;* *The Crane Wife* was named to the *New York Times* Outstanding Books and Best Illustrated Books lists, both 1981; Parent's Choice Award, Parent's Choice Foundation, 1983, for *Rebels of the Heavenly Kingdom;* Irvin Kerlan Award, 1983, "in recognition of singular attainments in the creation of children's literature"; University of Southern Mississippi School of Library Service Silver Medallion, 1983, for outstanding contributions to the field of children's literature; nominee, Laura Ingalls Wilder Award, 1986; Regina Medal Award, Catholic Library Association, 1988, for demonstrating "the timeless standards and ideals for the writing of good literature for children."

WRITINGS:

JUVENILES

The Sign of the Chrysanthemum, Crowell Junior Books, 1973, reprinted, Trophy, 1988.
Of Nightingales That Weep, Crowell Junior Books, 1974.
The Master Puppeteer, Crowell Junior Books, 1976.
Bridge to Terabithia, Crowell Junior Books, 1977.
The Great Gilly Hopkins, Crowell Junior Books, 1978.
Angels and Other Strangers: Family Christmas Stories, Crowell Junior Books, 1979 (published in England as *Star of Night: Stories for Christmas,* Gollancz, 1980).
Jacob Have I Loved, Crowell Junior Books, 1980.
Rebels of the Heavenly Kingdom, Lodestar, 1983.
Come Sing, Jimmy Jo, Lodestar, 1985.
(With husband, John Paterson) *Consider the Lilies: Flowers of the Bible* (nonfiction), Crowell Junior Books, 1986.
Park's Quest, Lodestar, 1988.

TRANSLATOR

Sumiko Yagawa, *The Crane Wife,* Morrow, 1981.
Momoko Ishii, *Tongue-Cut Sparrow,* Lodestar, 1987.

Also translator of Hans Christian Andersen's *The Tongue Cut Sparrow,* for Lodestar.

OTHER

Who Am I? (curriculum unit), CLC Press, 1966.
To Make Men Free (curriculum unit; includes books, records, pamphlets, and filmstrip), John Knox, 1973.
Justice for All People, Friendship, 1973.
Gates of Excellence: On Reading and Writing Books for Children, Lodestar, 1981.
The Spying Heart: More Thoughts on Reading and Writing Books for Children, Lodestar, 1989.

Contributor of articles and reviews to periodicals.

SIDELIGHTS: In much of her fiction for young adults, Katherine Paterson focuses on "the difficult but enlightening processes through which young people who are prematurely left to their own resources become acquainted with the compromises and obligations that are necessary to survival in the adult world," characterizes Jonathan Yardley in the *Washington Post Book World.* Critics remark on Paterson's honesty in presenting these kind of situations to a young audience, finding that her characters confront their problems without ever giving up hope. But what reviewers think is even more remarkable is Paterson's ability to create realistic characters, believable settings, and thoroughly convincing dialogue. Although she develops a moral to some degree in her works, she does so without preaching. In a *Dictionary of Literary Biography* essay, M. Sarah Smedman comments on the author's skill: "The distinctive quality of Paterson's art is her colorful concision. Whether she is narrating or describing, her mode is understatement, her style pithy. She dramatizes, never exhorts, creating powerful scenes in which action subtly elicits and restrains emotional response. Gestures and dialogue are natural and real. Metaphors derive from the novel's setting and come alive through strong verbs and the often unnoticed but per-

fectly apt detail." Continues Smedman: "Paterson weaves plot strands and symbols seamlessly into tightly meshed stories in which each character, each episode, each image, each bit of dialogue helps to incarnate what the author is imagining." It is this ability to create an entire story that has endeared Paterson's writing to numerous readers and earned her two National Book Awards and Newbery Medals.

Paterson's background as a child in China and as a student in Japan has helped her create some of her memorable stories. Born in Qing Jiang, China, to missionary parents, Paterson often found herself an outsider in a foreign culture. When her family returned to the United States because of World War II, the author again felt a stranger because of her foreign experiences. As Smedman describes, "moving about between China and various locations in Virginia, North Carolina, and West Virginia, the young Paterson experienced a variety of cultures and almost continual change. Before she graduated . . . [from college] in 1954, she had attended thirteen schools." It was her sense of being an outsider, or a "weird little kid," as she has described herself, that led Paterson to writing. As she relates in her book *Gates of Excellence: On Reading and Writing Books for Children,* "The reader I want to change is that burdened child within myself. As I begin a book, I am in a way inviting her along to see if there might be some path through this wilderness that we might hack out together, some oasis in this desert where we might find refreshment, some sheltered spot where we might lay our burden down. This is done by means of a story—a story peopled by characters who are me but not simply me." This strong sense of being alien appears in Paterson's characters, making them people with whom her readers strongly identify.

Paterson's first three novels draw specifically on her knowledge of Japanese history and custom; *The Sign of the Chrysanthemum,* her first, takes place during the twelfth-century civil wars of Japan. In the midst of this chaos is Muna ("No Name"), a young orphan who embarks on a search for his samurai father and thus his identity and a place in society. Many critics comment on the aptness of setting that Paterson creates for this story: a *Kirkus Reviews* writer believes the story to be "suspended in delicate imagery" and "sustained by the carefully evoked setting." Even though one critic thinks some of the plot elements are melodramatic, most reviewers find them involving: "The story is exciting, moving, and unpredictable, and is presented with precision and economy of language," writes *Times Literary Supplement* contributor Graham Hammond. Similarly, Virginia Haviland notes in *Horn Book* that "the storytelling holds the reader by the quick pace of the lively episodes, the colorful details, and the superb development of three important characters." During the course of the novel, Muna comes to terms with his "namelessness" and forges an identity for himself, an ending many find honest. As the *Kirkus Reviews* writer remarks, the story will please readers with "a realistic, stoical resolution which leaves some questions . . . open-ended."

Paterson returns to twelfth-century Japan for *Of Nightingales That Weep,* her second novel. The story follows a female character this time: Takiko is the young daughter of a samurai whose life is disrupted by her mother's remarriage. Displeased with her mother's new husband, Takiko decides to fend for herself among the royal court. Paterson makes optimum use of her setting; "again the exquisitely reconstructed backgrounds and episodes and the gradual character development will induce admirers of historical fiction to share Takiko's experience," remarks a *Kirkus Reviews* contributor. Marcus Crouch was originally daunted by this setting, finding it alien; however, he writes in the *Junior Bookshelf* that "once started, *Of Nightingales That Weep* turns out to be a hypnotically dominating book." Reflecting this opinion, Jennifer Farley Smith observes that the author's "feeling for the rawness and vitality of history makes the events of eight centuries ago seem hauntingly relevant, humanly near," she says in the *Christian Science Monitor.* Patricia Craig, however, writing in *Books and Bookmen,* does not think *Nightingales* is as effective as Paterson's earlier novel, for "it has something of the formality and simplicity of a retold folk tale. Its moral message is clear." But Smedman believes the story is subtle: "Takiko's gradual recognition and appreciation of Goro's veiled, steadfast love and her wholehearted response are rendered strong and unsentimental through the Japanese setting with its indigenous religious and social rituals, folklore and superstitions; through energizing contextual imagery; and through gentle irony—all integrally fused in the structure of the novel."

Paterson's setting jumps to the famine of late eighteenth-century Japan for her National Book Award-winning novel *The Master Puppeteer.* The Hanaza, a Japanese puppet theater, is the backdrop for a mystery involving a Robin Hood type bandit and Jiro, who becomes a puppeteer's apprentice in hopes of both feeding himself and winning honor. In creating the mystery, Paterson "has blended a literate mix of adventure and Japanese history with a subtle knowledge of young people," remarks Diana L. Spirt in *Introducing More Books: A Guide for the Middle Grades.* In following Jiro's development with his masters in the theater and his parents in the streets, the author demonstrates her ability to "exploit the tension between violence in the street and dreamlike confrontations of masked puppet operators," comments a *Kirkus Reviews* writer, thus making the book more "lively and immediate" than its predecessors.

In addition to her praise for the book's method, Spirt states that the work, although set in a distant time and place, presents the idea that "young people living in historical times and belonging to other cultures often faced problems and had feelings similar to those of today's youth." Smedman echoes this assessment, noting that "many of the social and political issues of eighteenth-century Japan are contemporary, world-wide problems as well: the conflict between the upper and lower classes, the rights of the poor, and the degree to which the young are bound to conform to the values of their parents." But instead of creating a dull fable, Paterson places these issues within a mystery involving enough to be nominated for a Mystery Writers of America Edgar Award. As Smedman asserts, "the tension between suspense and horror, attraction and revulsion, life inside the theater and out, stage plays and human history propels the narrative action and equilibrates the reader's response."

In her first Newbery Award-winner, *Bridge to Terabithia,* Paterson uses a more familiar, contemporary setting to tell the story of two "weird little kids" who become fast friends. The focus of the book is on the developing friendship between Jesse and Leslie, two outsiders from widely different backgrounds. The two children spend much of their time creating a fantasy world, Terabithia, where they can share their imaginings and ideas. Many critics praise Paterson for creating a realistic boy-girl friendship, something "so curiously unsung in literature," remarks Jill Paton Walsh in the *Christian Science Monitor.* According to Walsh, *Bridge to Terabithia* contains "a real marriage of minds between children whose imaginative gifts cut off from others and bind them together." Similarly, Mrs. Hildagarde Gray observes in *Best Sellers* that the book is "not a love story of physical encounter but a fusion of souls and minds," something she finds "rare" in current works.

The portrayal of this relationship works well because of the sharply drawn protagonists; "Jess is trapped in the middle without advantages, just the character young readers will most readily identify with," comments Richard Peck in the *Washington Post Book World.* His friend Leslie is the daughter of liberal middle-class parents who choose to live in a poor neighborhood; because of their lifestyle, Leslie has "committed the crime of being different, a point the young reader will grasp well before the adult reviewer," adds Peck. Jack Forman concurs, writing in *School Library Journal* that "Jess and Leslie are so effectively developed as characters that young readers might well feel that they were their classmates." In addition, the book contains strong background detail that reinforces the believability of the story; "We are shown those unspoken yet accurately observed customs that govern school conduct," says *Times Literary Supplement* contributor Julia Briggs. "Accurate and convincing in its details of everyday life, school playground tussles, poverty and work," observes Walsh, the novel "is never banal."

The novel develops into a more complex story when Leslie is killed while attempting to enter Terabithia during a storm and Jesse is left to reconcile himself to her death. Jesse's struggle to accept death reflects the author's own experiences; just as Paterson was recuperating from cancer, her son's best friend was killed by lightning. As one way to deal with her son's grief, Paterson began writing the story; however, as she relates in *Gates of Excellence,* when the story arrived at that point "I found I couldn't let my fictional child die. I wrote around the death. I even cleaned the kitchen—anything to prevent this death from taking place." Spurred by the remarks of a friend, Paterson realized that it was her own death she was afraid to face, and after coming to grips with that idea, she was able to continue with the novel.

Similarly, rather than focusing on the lost friendship, *Bridge to Terabithia* "centers on the importance of life continuing after tragedy," remarks Bernice E. Cullinan in *Literature and the Child.* "Rather than being destroyed by his friend's death, Jesse builds on the legacy Leslie leaves him and continues Terabithia, passing it on to his younger sister, May Belle." Jesse lets go of his grief for Leslie, yet holds on to the strength and imagination she taught him. The result, writes Cullinan, is a "well-crafted novel [that] is both gripping and memorable, its images evocative. . . . It celebrates the vision of imagination and touches children's hearts." "Typical of a Paterson novel," notes Smedman, "*Bridge to Terabithia* insightfully penetrates the thought and feelings of children and adults." Concludes the critic: "The novel is wrought with the artistry characteristic of its author: the right word in the right place; the restraint of sentiment with wit; light ironic foreshadowing; the creation of a world through antithetical balance . . . ; imagery engendered by the setting and woven seamlessly into the fabric of the novel."

Paterson sets a more comedic tone with her next novel, *The Great Gilly Hopkins,* even though the subject is a foster child abandoned by her mother. The novel was inspired by the author's own stint as a foster mother; as she relates in *Gates of Excellence,* Paterson realized that she had been "regarding two human beings as Kleenex, disposable," because of their temporary situation. This led her to imagine the character of Gilly Hopkins, a girl who fights against any sign of care or affection from her temporary family by lying, swearing, and making herself disagreeable to all who come too close. While one reviewer finds this makes the character unpleasant for too long, Natalie Babbitt remarks in the *Washington Post Book World* that even though "Gilly is a liar, a bully, a thief, . . . because Paterson is interested in motivations rather than moralizing, the reader is free to grow very fond of her heroine—to sympathize, to understand, to identify with Gilly, and to laugh with her."

Babbitt also extends words of praise to the novel's other characters, commenting that "what Paterson has done is to combine a beautiful fairness with her affection for her creations, which makes them solidly three-dimensional." *New York Times Book Review* contributor Byrna J. Fireside also notes that the author "has a rare gift for creating unusual characters who are remarkably believable." Nevertheless, the critic feels that Paterson has overextended herself, "because too much is attempted in one book." Smedman differs, writing that the large cast of characters works to the book's advantage: "Gently, kindly, Paterson exposes stereotypical thinking and behavior of righteous but ineffectual social workers, school principals, teachers, and preachers, usually through estimable characters . . . who, transcending the type, frustrate Gilly's prejudices." Like the author's previous works, *The Great Gilly Hopkins* avoids the predictable ending; while Gilly meets her mother and is taken home by her grandmother, she belatedly realizes that she does care about her foster family. "Without a hint of the prevailing maudlin realism," summarizes a *Kirkus Review* writer, "Paterson takes up a common 'problem' situation and makes it genuinely moving, frequently funny, and sparkling with memorable encounters." This effective treatment of her subject earned Paterson a second National Book Award.

Paterson's second Newbery Award-winner, *Jacob Have I Loved,* "is a provocative and powerful story of an adolescent's submergence by and victory over her bitter jealousy of her twin sister," describes Smedman. Gail Godwin asserts that "the attractiveness of this novel lies in its author's choice of setting [and] how she uses that setting to intensify the theme of sibling rivalry." Set on the Chesapeake island of Rass, the story is told through the eyes of Sara Louise "Wheeze" Bradshaw, "an ugly duckling of such endurance and rough charm that readers should take to her immediately," observes *Washington Post Book World* contributor Anne Tyler. Sure that she is unloved because her talented, fragile twin gets all the attention, Wheeze must struggle to overcome her low self-esteem. Although the novel is written in the first person, "this is not a stereotypical good sister/bad sister story," notes Tyler. "It's convincingly complex, ambiguous." Paul Heins also finds the characterization to be effective; as he writes in *Horn Book,* "The author has developed a story of great dramatic power, for Wheeze is always candid in recounting her emotional experiences and reactions. At the same time, the island characters come to life in skillful, terse dialogue."

It takes several years for Wheeze to discover her own self-worth and her value to others; consequently, the last sections of the novel are related from Wheeze's adult perspective. Some critics feel these sections detract from the novel's impact; Tyler finds that "there's a change of pace that's difficult to adjust to" while a *Kirkus Reviews* writer thinks the swift resolution "tends to flatten the tone and blur the shape of the novel." But Smedman, writing in *Children's Literature in Education,* believes that this brief recounting is entirely appropriate: "The subsequent and final two chapters do compress many events and much time in a very little space. However, they are essential to complete the webbing of the stories; and their swiftness and brevity are entirely in keeping with the nature of the events they record." The critic adds: "Louise realizes the nature and power of love, which comes to her . . . instantaneously, with the concentrated force of a revelation."

Many reviewers observe an allusive element in *Jacob Have I Loved;* the title refers to the biblical story of the twins Jacob and

Esau. Heins feels that "the Biblical allusions add immeasurably to the meaning of the story and illuminate the prolonged—often overwhelming—crisis in the protagonist's life." Smedman also remarks upon this level of the story, finding it adds deeper meaning even if the reader does not accept the Christian idea behind it: "Paterson's subtle art incorporates the third dimension inobtrusively, to be discovered and to enrich the story. For those who do not discover it, the story still works. Without violating the norms of realism, though perhaps stretching them to include a coincidence more possible than probable, it incorporates the wisdom of myth and fairy tales."

With *Rebels of the Heavenly Kingdom,* Paterson "has written a more accomplished work of fiction, and certainly a deeper and more resonant one, than most of the novels written these days for an adult readership," states Jonathan Yardley in the *Washington Post Book World.* Paterson returns to the historical novel form, setting the story in mid-nineteenth-century China. "Magnificent and momentous," notes Smedman in the *Dictionary of Literary Biography,* "this starkly realisitic adventure-romance rewards discriminating readers with the poignant stories of Wang Lee and Mei Lin, two young people caught in the devastation wrought by fanatic warlords whose religious ideals are shot through with political ambitions." More directly involved with historical events, the story follows the two characters' participation in the "Heavenly Kingdom," a religious, patriotic movement rebelling against the country's overlords.

Because the plot is closely tied to actual events, some reviewers think that the quality of the novel is compromised. Ruth M. McConnell, writing in the *School Library Journal,* comments that Paterson "does not adequately integrate the historical facts into the story," and adds that "often the characters are vehicles for the theme rather than individuals in their own right." *New York Times Book Review* contributor Hazel Rochman concurs, observing that "at times the plot . . . seems manipulated to bring about Wang Lee's moral development; and too many characters are one-dimensional." In contrast to the criticisms that the characters appear distant, Walsh writes in the *Times Educational Supplement* that this separation is appropriate to the subjects of the novel: "If a certain strangeness in their manner of thinking distances us from [Paterson's] characters, . . . it is doubtless because she has accurately portrayed people who are indeed strange to us."

As with her other novels, *Rebels of the Heavenly Kingdom* is also praised for its honesty in addition to its ability to entertain. "It is one of the many strengths of Paterson's fiction that . . . she always has her gaze set firmly on the realities of life," remarks Yardley. He adds that in her novel "she gives us a wholly believable 19th-century China, and she gives us an experience that is entirely true to the way life works." Walsh echoes this opinion, noting that although it relates a tale of adventure and romance, "the book has not lost the profound moral seriousness that distinguishes Katherine Paterson's contemporary writing, for all its rapid pace and plot."

In *Come Sing, Jimmy Jo,* Paterson "provides an engaging fantasy about what it might be like to become famous," describes Campbell Geeslin in the *New York Times Book Review.* Nevertheless, the novel "provides something more than entertainment," says Geeslin, for it follows the problems of young James as he becomes involved in his family's country music act. From a poor Appalachian family, James is thrust into a world where he becomes "Jimmy Jo," a world that further confuses his school and family life. Paterson again brings her flair for recreating language to this story; as Stephen Fraser remarks in the *Christian*

Science Monitor, "what Katherine Paterson does so well is catch the cadence of the locale without sounding fake. There isn't a false note in her diction." Similarly, *Washington Post Book World* contributor Elizabeth Ward finds that "the remarkable thing about *Come Sing, Jimmy Jo* is the way Katherine Paterson is able to bring music to life through her prose, always a difficult thing for a writer to do convincingly." Adds Ward: "This is not just a story about country music. The whole book sings."

Even though they praise Paterson's recreation of the West Virginian atmosphere, some critics believe that the novel is not as realistic as her previous works. In the *Times Literary Supplement,* Neil Philip complains that "the story is in some ways rather trite, and not altogether convincing in its depiction of the working of the music business." Kristiana Gregory similarly remarks on the inconsistency of the book's conclusion: "The uplifting ending wraps everything into happily-ever-after, pleasant for sure, but not nearly as realistic as the rest of the book," the critic writes in the *Los Angeles Times Book Review.* In contrast, Fraser observes that "Paterson knows children, their fears and their joys. . . . This book is James's personal, inward journey, and it is deeply felt." And Ward thinks that *Come Sing, Jimmy Jo* reflects the quality of Paterson's other novels, for it "is full of what [Paterson] has called 'stronger themes,' the harsher aspects of human life which she feels children, too, need to read about." Concludes the critic: "At the same time it is as alive and hilarious as any book children are likely to read this year and in that, perhaps lies the 'stubborn seed of hope' she has promised always to plant for them."

"*Park's Quest,* her latest work, shows us Paterson at her best," comments Michele Landsberg in the *Washington Post Book World.* Park is the son of a pilot killed during the Vietnam War, and his "quest" to learn about his father is one he sees "as noble, and as important, as was the [Arthurian] knights' quest for the Holy Grail," describes *New York Times Book Review* contributor Alice McDermott. Park's mother, who refuses to discuss the child's father, agrees to send Park to visit his father's family in rural Virginia. In relating Park's unfamiliarity with his relatives, "Paterson is sharply observant and funny about the sheer awkwardness of daily life for the self-conscious prepubescent," notes Landsberg. Nevertheless, adds the critic, "she never makes the mistake of letting Park become narcissistically obsessed over trivia. Those small social agonies pale beside his wrenching curiosity about his father, his boyish triumphs, [and] his fear of [his] paralyzed grandfather." Similar to Paterson's other stories of personal searching, Park's "quest for knowledge about his father changes," relates McDermott, to something more realistic, a quest "for forgiveness."

Park's Quest also carries the mark of the author's other work in its believable portrayal of Park and his family. Observes Landsberg: "Character, in fact, is Paterson's great glory. Every word of dialogue falls as naturally as water, yet every word speaks volumes, revealing both adults and children as complex, interesting, ultimately lovable characters." And true to the Paterson tradition, *Park's Quest* deals with its protagonist's problems in a straightforward and honest manner. "No story of the Vietnam War, even one meant for children, can be made as simple and as noble as the war stories of old, or as the story of the quest for the Holy Grail," states McDermott. "Katherine Paterson clearly acknowledges this and in 'Park's Quest' she confronts the complexity, the ambiguity of the war and the emotions of those it involved with an honesty that young readers are sure to recognize and appreciate." Concludes the critic: "What is even more remarkable is that she has fashioned from this complexity a story

for young adults that does not offer an antidote, or even a resolution . . . but that speaks instead of the opportunity for healing."

In writing about complex issues in her fiction, Paterson often concludes her stories in what seems to be an unsatisfactory, or "unhappy," manner. When *Language Arts* interviewer Linda T. Jones asked her the reason for her unconventional endings, Paterson responded: "The books ended the way I thought the books had to end. That's not satisfying to anybody, but it seems to me that if you're really 'in' a story then the story seems to have a life of its own. The story seems to have necessities and its own ending. When children ask me, as they often do, why Leslie Burke had to die [in *Bridge to Terabithia*], I honestly feel that I had no choice in the matter." The author continued: "If you try to change what is the inevitable ending of that story, you violate the story and the reader will recognize that."

Remaining true to a story is important for Paterson, especially because of the important role she thinks fiction can play in a reader's life. As she writes in *Gates of Excellence,* "fiction allows us to do something that nothing else quite does. It allows us to enter fully into the lives of other human beings. But, you may argue, these are not real people, they are fictitious—merely the figments of one writer's imaginations." However, Paterson notes, a character can be "more real to us than the people we live with every day, because we have been allowed to eavesdrop on her soul." Because readers can involve themselves in different experiences through books, Paterson thinks that "books, fiction, give us practice in life that we've never had to live through before, so when the time comes, we have in a sense been through that experience before," she remarked to Jones. "The book is there in the background to comfort us and assure us that we can go through with this. Books are great vehicles of hope for us and help and instruct us in all the good ways."

BIOGRAPHICAL/CRITICAL SOURCES:

BOOKS

Children's Literature Review, Volume 7, Gale, 1984.
Contemporary Literary Criticism, Gale, Volume 12, 1980, Volume 30, 1984.
Cullinan, Mary, with Mary K. Karrer and Arlene M. Pillar, *Literature and the Child,* Harcourt, 1981.
Dictionary of Literary Biography, Volume 52: *American Writers for Children since 1960: Fiction,* Gale, 1986.
Paterson, Katherine, *Gates of Excellence: On the Reading and Writing of Books for Children,* Lodestar, 1981.
Peterson, Linda and Marilyn Solt, *Newbery and Caldecott Medal and Honor Books: An Annotated Bibliography,* Twayne, 1982.
Spirt, Diana, *Introducing More Books: A Guide for the Middle Grades,* Bowker, 1978.

PERIODICALS

Best Sellers, February, 1978, January, 1981, August, 1985.
Books & Bookmen, December, 1975, March, 1977.
Children's Literature in Education, autumn, 1983.
Christian Science Monitor, November 6, 1974, May 3, 1978, January 21, 1981, October 7, 1983, September 6, 1985.
Horn Book, October, 1973, December, 1980.
Junior Bookshelf, August, 1977, August, 1981.
Kirkus Reviews, November 15, 1973, October 1, 1974, January 15, 1976, September 1, 1977, February 15, 1978, November 1, 1980, November 15, 1981, June 15, 1983, May 15, 1985, September 1, 1986.
Language Arts, February, 1981.
Los Angeles Times Book Review, November 23, 1986.

New York Times Book Review, November 13, 1977, April 30, 1978, December 2, 1979, December 21, 1980, July 17, 1983, May 16, 1985.

School Library Journal, November, 1977.

Signal, May, 1982.

Theory into Practice, autumn, 1982.

Times Educational Supplement, September 30, 1983.

Times Literary Supplement, September 19, 1975, December 10, 1976, September 29, 1978, December 14, 1979, November 20, 1981, August 16, 1985, May 9, 1986.

Washington Post Book World, November 13, 1977, May 14, 1978, November 9, 1980, November 8, 1981, June 12, 1983, May 12, 1985.

* * *

PATON, Alan (Stewart) 1903-1988

PERSONAL: Surname rhymes with "Dayton"; born January 11, 1903, in Pietermaritzburg, South Africa; died of throat cancer, April 12, 1988, in Botha's Hill (near Durban), Natal, South Africa; son of James (a civil servant) and Eunice (James) Paton; married Doris Olive Francis, July 2, 1928 (died October 23, 1967); married Anne Hopkins, 1969; children: (first marriage) David Francis, Jonathan Stewart. *Education:* University of Natal, B.Sc., 1923. *Religion:* Anglican.

ADDRESSES: Home—Botha's Hill, Natal, South Africa.

CAREER: Writer. Ixopo High School, Ixopo, Natal, South Africa, teacher of mathematics and physics, 1925-28; Maritzburg College, Pietermaritzburg, Natal, teacher of mathematics, physics, and English, 1928-35; Diepkloof Reformatory, near Johannesburg, South Africa, principal, 1935-48; Toc H Southern Africa, Botha's Hill, Natal, honorary commissioner, 1949-58; University of Natal, Durban and Pietermaritzburg, Natal, president of the Convocation, 1951-55 and 1957-59; founder and president, Liberal Party of South Africa (originally the Liberal Association of South Africa before emergence as a political party; declared an illegal organization, 1968), 1958-68. Non-European Boys' Clubs, president of Transvaal association, 1935-48.

MEMBER: Royal Society of Literature (fellow), Free Academy of Arts (Hamburg; honorary member).

AWARDS, HONORS: Anisfield-Wolf *Saturday Review* Award, 1948, Newspaper Guild of New York Page One Award, 1949, and London *Sunday Times* Special Award for Literature, 1949, all for *Cry, the Beloved Country;* Benjamin Franklin Award, 1955; Freedom House Award (U.S.), 1960; Medal for Literature, Free Academy of Arts, 1961; National Conference of Christians and Jews Brotherhood Award, 1962, for *Tales from a Troubled Land;* C.N.A. Literary Award for the year's best book in English in South Africa, 1965, for *Hofmeyr,* and 1973, for *Apartheid and the Archbishop: The Life and Times of Geoffrey Clayton, Archbishop of Cape Town.* L.H.D., Yale University, 1954, Kenyon College, 1962, La Salle University, Philadelphia, 1986; D.Litt., University of Natal, 1968, Trent University, 1971, Harvard University, 1971, Rhodes University, 1972, Williamette University, 1974, University of Michigan—Flint, 1977, University of Durban/Westville, 1986; D.D., University of Edinburgh, 1971; LL.D., Witwatersrand University, 1975.

WRITINGS:

Meditation for a Young Boy Confirmed (poem), S.P.C.K., 1944, Forward Movement, 1954.

Cry, the Beloved Country (also see below), Scribner, 1948, recent edition, Macmillan, 1987.

"Cry, the Beloved Country" (screenplay; based on his novel of the same title), United Artists, 1951.

Too Late the Phalarope (Book-of-the-Month Club selection), Scribner, 1953, reprinted, Penguin, 1971.

The Land and the People of South Africa, Lippincott, 1955 (published in England as *South Africa and Her People,* Lutterworth, 1957), revised edition published under original title, Lippincott, 1972.

South Africa in Transition, Scribner, 1956.

Hope for South Africa, Praeger, 1959.

Tales from a Troubled Land (stories; also see below), Scribner, 1961 (published in England as *Debbie Go Home,* J. Cape, 1961, new edition, Penguin, 1965).

Hofmeyr (biography), Oxford University Press, 1964, abridged edition published as *South African Tragedy: The Life and Times of Jan Hofmeyr,* Scribner, 1965, new edition, Oxford University Press, 1971.

(With Krishna Shah) *Sponono* (play; based on three stories from *Tales from a Troubled Land;* first produced on Broadway at the Cort Theatre, April 2, 1964), Scribner, 1965.

Instrument of Thy Peace: The Prayer of St. Francis, Seabury, 1968, revised edition, 1982.

The Long View, edited by Edward Callan, Praeger, 1968.

For You Departed, Scribner, 1969 (published in England as *Kontakion for You Departed,* J. Cape, 1969).

(With others) *Creative Suffering: The Ripple of Hope,* Pilgrim, 1970.

Apartheid and the Archbishop: The Life and Times of Geoffrey Clayton, Archbishop of Cape Town, David Philip (Cape Town, South Africa), 1973, Scribner, 1974.

Knocking on the Door: Alan Paton/Shorter Writings, edited by Colin Gardner, Scribner, 1975.

Towards the Mountain: An Autobiography, Scribner, 1980.

Ah, But Your Land Is Beautiful (novel), Scribner, 1981.

(Author of foreword) Elsa Joubert, *Poppie Nongena,* Norton, 1985.

Journey Continued: An Autobiography, Scribner, 1988.

SIDELIGHTS: One of the earliest proponents of racial equality in his native South Africa, Alan Paton first came into the public eye in 1948 with his novel *Cry, the Beloved Country.* A landmark publication for its time, the novel follows the fate of a young black African, Absalom Kumalo, who, having murdered a white citizen, "cannot be judged justly without taking into account the environment that has partly shaped him," as Edmund Fuller writes in his book *Man in Modern Fiction: Some Minority Opinions on Contemporary American Writing.* The environment in question is typified by the hostility and squalid living conditions facing most of South Africa's nonwhites, victims of South Africa's system of apartheid.

"Three artistic qualities of *Cry, the Beloved Country* combine to make it an original and unique work of art," Edward Callan notes in his study *Alan Paton.* "First, the poetic elements in the language of some of the characters; second, the lyric passages spoken from outside the action, like the well-known opening chapter; and third, the dramatic choral chapters that seem to break the sequence of the story for social commentary, but which in fact widen the horizon of the particular segments of action to embrace the whole land, as well as such universal concerns as fear, hate, and justice."

In assessing Paton's work, Callan compares the author to American poet Robert Frost. Paton's art, says Callan, "is related to South Africa as Robert Frost's is to New England. Both of these writers work within the framework of an external landscape where they know all the flowers and shrubs, birds and animals, by their familiar names. As observers of the human inhabitants of these landscapes, both writers recognize the profound aspirations of human personality; and both communicate their insights in language that is fresh and simple, yet vibrant with meaning."

Paton followed *Cry, the Beloved Country* with another socially conscious novel, *Too Late the Phalarope.* This volume centers on a white Afrikaner, Pieter, whose youthful idealism has tragic consequences. The story hinges on Pieter's love affair with a black girl; according to Alfred Kazin in the *New York Times Book Review,* "Under the 'Immorality Act' of the country, sexual relations between whites and blacks are a legal offense." As Kazin goes on to explain, "Pieter is sent to prison, his father strikes [the youth's] name from the great family Bible and dies of shame, and the whole family withdraws from the community in horror at Pieter's crime 'against the race.' "

"Invariably, comparisons [of *Too Late the Phalarope*] with *The Scarlet Letter* and *Crime and Punishment* arise," as Fuller points out in another work, *Books with Men behind Them.* "Once Pieter has committed his act, there is no possible release for him but total exposure—a dilemma he shares in part with [*The Scarlet Letter*'s] Arthur Dimmesdale and [*Crime and Punishment*'s] Raskolnikov. Paton gives us a long sequence of superb suspense, arising out of guilty misunderstandings of innocent natural coincidences. But just as the death wish is commonly unconscious, so Pieter suffers an agonized dread of discovery, unconscious of the fact that it is that exposure and its consequences that have motivated him from the start."

A handful of nonfiction works and biographies followed Paton's second novel, but the author received more critical attention for his 1981 book, *Ah, But Your Land Is Beautiful,* which was his first novel in 28 years. The story opens with an act of quiet rebellion. An Indian teenager named Prem enters the Durban Library in Natal, South Africa, and sits down to read. Since she is not white, she is barred from using the facility. However, Prem defies the authorities, and her struggle ignites the embryonic anti-apartheid campaigns of the 1950s. The story goes on to trace the history of such organizations as the Liberal Party (of which Paton was president from 1958 to 1968).

As *Chicago Tribune Book World* reviewer Charles R. Larson sees it, the novel "fairly groans under the weight of human misery and havoc." He also states that "readers unfamiliar with the horrors of South African politics may be shocked to learn of apartheid legislation against racial mixing at every level of human contact—including funerals and religious services." "Paton's determination to expose injustice is so overwhelming that too often his characters have little life beyond their roles in his morality drama," John Rechy writes in a *Los Angeles Times Book Review* article. "Emphasizing their admirable hope and courage, he at times denies them the full, defining power of their rage. The unfortunate result is that the evil, too, becomes faceless; a disembodied voice of inquisition barking out injustice." But whatever artistic criticism he has for *Ah, But Your Land Is Beautiful,* Rechy concludes that he "respectfully [envies] Paton's courageous hopefulness, which has allowed him, at age 78 [at the time of publication] to continue to believe that justice may prevail in his beautiful land of entrenched evil."

Newsweek critic Peter S. Prescott sees in Paton's dispassionate style an advantage to the novel's message: the author "offers no diversions, no digressions, no scenes designed to build character, to set a time or place, except as they are shaped by his obsession with this appalling injustice. That in itself would make [*Ah, But Your Land Is Beautiful*] extraordinary; what makes it more so is his ability to keep such a story light and dramatic." In a similar vein, John Romano points out in a *New York Times Book Review* piece that in Paton's novel "individual human dilemmas are never swallowed up or diminished by the overarching political context of the story he is telling. Paton is relentless in his faith in the moral meaning of individual human experience." The author's faith, Romano adds, "is not a religious one, but a faith in the function, the usefulness of personal sympathy. . . . [Paton's] considerable practical contributions to political life in South Africa aside, his place in the literature of social protest has been secured by his steady devotion to the ideal of the empathetic imagination in fiction."

Originally Paton had hoped to make *Ah, But Your Land Is Beautiful* the first part of a trilogy of novels about South African race relations. Weakened by a heart condition, however, he concentrated on his autobiography. He finished the first volume, *Towards the Mountain,* in 1980, and the second, *Journey Continued,* just before his death in 1988. The books describe Paton's early years as an educator, when he observed the social inequities that prompted *Cry, The Beloved Country,* and his later involvement with the Liberal party, which dissolved in 1968 rather than purge its nonwhite members as the government demanded. In his last years Paton was criticized by many anti-apartheid activists because he opposed their efforts to pressure the government by discouraging foreign investment in South Africa. Such sanctions, Paton argued, would unduly punish South Africa's poorest blacks, and he decried even Nobel Prize-winning clergyman Desmond Tutu for supporting such a strategy. Though controversial, Paton saw his actions as consistent with a lifelong belief in progress through moderation and mutual understanding. As he wrote in *Journey Continued:* "By liberalism I don't mean the creed of any party or any century. I mean a generosity of spirit, a tolerance of others, an attempt to comprehend otherness, a commitment to the rule of law, a high ideal of the worth and dignity of man, a repugnance for authoritarianism and a love of freedom."

MEDIA ADAPTATIONS: "Lost in the Stars," a musical tragedy adapted for the stage by Maxwell Anderson from *Cry, the Beloved Country,* with music by Kurt Weill, was first produced on Broadway at the Music Box, October 30, 1949; a motion picture, "Lost in the Stars," based on the musical, was produced by American Film Theatre in 1974; the play, "Too Late the Phalarope," adapted by Robert Yale Libott from Paton's novel of the same title, was first produced on Broadway at the Belasco Theatre, October 11, 1956; the stage and screen rights to *For You Departed* have been sold.

BIOGRAPHICAL/CRITICAL SOURCES:

BOOKS

Callan, Edward, *Alan Paton,* Twayne, 1968, revised edition, 1982.
Contemporary Literary Criticism, Gale, Volume 4, 1975, Volume 10, 1979, Volume 25, 1983, Volume 55, 1989.
Fuller, Edmund, *Books with Men behind Them,* Random House, 1962.
Fuller, Edmund, *Man in Modern Fiction: Some Minority Opinions on Contemporary American Writing,* Random House, 1958.
Paton, Alan, *Towards the Mountain: An Autobiography,* Scribner, 1980.
Paton, Alan, *Journey Continued: An Autobiography,* Scribner, 1988.

PERIODICALS

Chicago Tribune Book World, February 28, 1982, May 9, 1985.

Detroit News, March 28, 1982.
Globe and Mail (Toronto), May 5, 1984.
London Review of Books, December 3, 1981.
Los Angeles Times, May 22, 1988.
Los Angeles Times Book Review, April 25, 1982, October 30, 1988.
New Republic, March 24, 1982.
Newsweek, March 15, 1982.
New York Times, July 13, 1981, April 2, 1988.
New York Times Book Review, August 23, 1953, April 16, 1961, April 4, 1982, November 20, 1988.
Times (London), November 12, 1981, August 26, 1989.
Times Literary Supplement, August 11, 1961, September 23, 1988.
Tribune Books, November 27, 1988.
Washington Post Book World, December 11, 1988.

OBITUARIES:

PERIODICALS

Chicago Tribune, April 13, 1988.
Los Angeles Times, April 12, 1988.
New York Times, April 13, 1988.
Times (London), April 13, 1988.
Washington Post, April 13, 1988.

*   *   *

PATTERSON, Harry   1929-
(Martin Fallon, James Graham, Jack Higgins, Hugh Marlowe)

PERSONAL: Some sources list given name as Henry; born July 27, 1929, in Newcastle-on-Tyne, England; holds dual English and Irish citizenship; son of Henry (a shipwright) and Henrietta Higgins (Bell) Patterson; married Amy Margaret Hewitt, December 27, 1958 (marriage ended, 1984); married Denise Lesley Anne Palmer, 1985; children: (first marriage) three daughters, one son. *Education:* Carnegie College, certificate in education, 1958; London School of Economics and Political Science, London, B.Sc., 1962. *Politics:* "Slightly right of center." *Religion:* Presbyterian.

ADDRESSES: Agent—David Higham Associates Ltd., 5/8 Lower John St., Golden Square, London W1R 4HA, England.

CAREER: Worked at a variety of commercial and civil service posts before resuming his education in 1956; Allerton Grance Comprehensive School, Leeds, England, history teacher, 1959-64; Leeds Polytechnic, Leeds, lecturer in liberal studies, 1964-68; James Graham College, New Farnley, Yorkshire, England, senior lecturer in education, 1968-69; Leeds University, Leeds, tutor, 1970-72; currently a full-time writer. Former member of Leeds Art Theatre. *Military service:* British Army, Royal Horse Guards, 1947-49.

MEMBER: Royal Economic Society (fellow), Royal Society of Arts (fellow), Crime Writers' Association.

WRITINGS:

Sad Wind from the Sea, Long, 1959.
Cry of the Hunter, Long, 1960.
The Thousand Faces of Night, Long, 1961.
Comes the Dark Stranger, Long, 1962.
Hell Is Too Crowded, Long, 1962, reprinted in paperback under pseudonym Jack Higgins, Fawcett, 1977.
Pay the Devil, Barrie & Rockliff, 1963.

The Dark Side of the Island, Long, 1963, reprinted in paperback under pseudonym Jack Higgins, Fawcett, 1977.
A Phoenix in the Blood, Barrie & Rockliff, 1964.
Thunder at Noon, Long, 1964.
Wrath of the Lion, Long, 1964, reprinted in paperback under pseudonym Jack Higgins, Fawcett, 1977.
The Graveyard Shift, Long, 1965.
The Iron Tiger, Long, 1966, reprinted in paperback under pseudonym Jack Higgins, Fawcett, 1979.
Brought in Dead, Long, 1967.
Hell Is Always Today, Long, 1968, reprinted in paperback under pseudonym Jack Higgins, Fawcett, 1979.
Toll for the Brave, Long, 1971, reprinted in paperback under pseudonym Jack Higgins, Fawcett, 1976.
The Valhalla Exchange, Stein & Day, 1976.
To Catch a King, Stein & Day, 1979.

Also author of stage play titled "Walking Wounded," 1987.

UNDER PSEUDONYM MARTIN FALLON

The Testament of Caspar Shultz, Abelard, 1962, reprinted in paperback under pseudonym Jack Higgins, Fawcett, 1978.
Year of the Tiger, Abelard, 1964.
Keys of Hell, Abelard, 1965, reprinted in paperback under pseudonym Jack Higgins, Fawcett, 1976.
Midnight Never Comes, Long, 1966, reprinted in paperback under pseudonym Jack Higgins, Fawcett, 1975.
Dark Side of the Street, Long, 1967, reprinted in paperback under pseudonym Jack Higgins, Fawcett, 1974.
A Fine Night for Dying, Long, 1969 reprinted in paperback under pseudonym Jack Higgins, Arrow, 1977.

UNDER PSEUDONYM JAMES GRAHAM

A Game for Heroes, Doubleday, 1970.
The Wrath of God, Doubleday, 1971.
The Khufra Run, Macmillan, 1972, Doubleday, 1973.
The Run to Morning, Stein & Day, 1974, published in England as *Bloody Passage,* Macmillan, 1974.

UNDER PSEUDONYM JACK HIGGINS

East of Desolation, Hodder & Stoughton, 1968, Doubleday, 1969.
In the Hour Before Midnight, Doubleday, 1969.
Night Judgment at Sinos, Hodder & Stoughton, 1970, Doubleday, 1971.
The Last Place God Made, Collins, 1971, Holt, 1972.
The Savage Day, Holt, 1972.
A Prayer for the Dying, Collins, 1973, Holt, 1974.
The Eagle Has Landed, Holt, 1975.
Storm Warning, Holt, 1976.
Day of Judgement, Collins, 1978, Holt, 1979.
The Cretan Lover, Holt, 1980.
Solo, Stein & Day, 1980.
Luciano's Luck, Stein & Day, 1981.
Touch the Devil, Stein & Day, 1982.
Exocet, Stein & Day, 1983.
Dillinger, Stein & Day 1983.
Confessional, Stein & Day, 1985.
A Jack Higgins Trilogy, Scarborough House, 1986.
Night of the Fox, Simon & Schuster, 1987.
A Season in Hell, Simon & Schuster, 1989.
Cold Harbour, Simon & Schuster, 1990.

UNDER PSEUDONYM HUGH MARLOWE

Seven Pillars to Hell, Abelard, 1963.

Passage by Night, Abelard, 1964, reprinted in paperback under pseudonym Jack Higgins, Fawcett, 1978.

A Candle for the Dead, Abelard, 1966, published in England under pseudonym Jack Higgins as *The Violent Enemy,* Hodder & Stoughton, 1969.

SIDELIGHTS: Harry Patterson told *CA:* "I look upon myself primarily as an entertainer. Even in my novel, *A Phoenix in the Blood,* which deals with the colour-bar problem in England, I still have tried to entertain, to make the events interesting as a story—not just the ideas [and] ethics of the situation. I believe that at any level a writer's only success is to be measured by his ability to communicate."

All of Patterson's books have been translated into Swedish, some into German, Italian, Norwegian, Dutch, and French. He spends his holidays on the continent "whenever possible," and is interested in the theater.

MEDIA ADAPTATIONS: Films have been made of several of Patterson's novels, including, *The Violent Enemy,* 1969, *The Wrath of God,* 1972, *The Eagle Has Landed,* Columbia, 1977, *To Catch a King,* Home Box Office, 1984, *Confessional,* 1985, and *A Prayer for the Dying,* Samuel Goldwyn Co., 1987.

BIOGRAPHICAL/CRITICAL SOURCES:

BOOKS

Bestsellers 89, Issue 3, Gale, 1989.

PERIODICALS

Chicago Tribune, August 4, 1982.
Los Angeles Times, August 29, 1980, September 5, 1985, January 29, 1990.
Los Angeles Times Book Review, July 6, 1980, September 25, 1983.
New York Times, July 28, 1982.
New York Times Book Review, September 5, 1982, January 18, 1987.
Publishers Weekly, August 27, 1979.
Times (London), October 20, 1986, December 4, 1986.
Washington Post, March 31, 1979, September 29, 1981, February 7, 1987.

* * *

PATTERSON, Henry
See PATTERSON, Harry

* * *

PAULING, Linus (Carl) 1901-

PERSONAL: Born February 28, 1901, in Portland, Ore.; son of Herman William (a pharmacist) and Lucy Isablle (Darling) Pauling; married Ava Helen Miller, June 17, 1923 (died December 7, 1981); children: Linus Carl, Jr., Peter Jeffress, Linda Helen, Edward Crellin. *Education:* Oregon State Agricultural College (now Oregon State University), B.S., 1922; California Institute of Technology, Ph.D., 1925; postdoctoral study at the universities of Munich, Copenhagen, and Zurich, 1926-27.

ADDRESSES: Home—Deer Flat Ranch, Salmon Creek, Big Sur, Calif. 93920. *Office*—Linus Pauling Institute of Science and Medicine, 440 Page Mill Rd., Palo Alto, Calif. 94306.

CAREER: Oregon State Agricultural College (now Oregon State University), Corvallis, assistant in quantitative analysis,

1919-20, assistant in chemistry and in mechanics and materials, 1920-22; California Institute of Technology, Pasadena, research associate, 1925-26, research fellow, 1926-27, assistant professor, 1927-29, associate professor, 1929-31, professor of chemistry, 1931-64, chairman of the division of chemistry and chemical engineering, 1936-58, director of Gates and Crellin Laboratories of Chemistry, 1936-58, member of board of trustees executive committee, 1945-48; Center for the Study of Democratic Institutions, Santa Barbara, Calif., research professor of the physical and biological sciences, 1963-67; University of California, San Diego, professor of chemistry, 1967-69; Stanford University, Stanford, Calif., professor of chemistry, 1969-74, professor emeritus, 1974—; Linus Pauling Institute of Science and Medicine, Palo Alto, Calif., president, 1973-75, fellow, 1973—.

Visiting lecturer in chemistry and physics, University of California, 1929-33, Massachusetts Institute of Technology, 1932; Foster Lecturer, University of Buffalo, 1936, 1953; George Fisher Baker Lecturer in Chemistry, Cornell University, 1937-38; Silliman Lecturer, Yale University, 1947; George Eastman Professor at Balliol College, Oxford, and Charles Lyall Lecturer at Exeter College, Oxford, 1948; Treat B. Johnson Lecturer, Yale University, 1953; Prather Lecturer, Harvard University, 1955; George A. Miller Lecturer, University of Illinois, 1956; Meade-Swing Lecturer, Oberlin College, 1956; Avogadro Commemoration Lecturer, Accademie dei Quaranta, Rome, 1956; National Institutes of Health lecturer, 1957; Beth Walton Moor Lecturer, Florida State University, 1958; Vanuxem Lecturer, Princeton University, 1959; Messenger Lecturer, Cornell University, 1959. Consultant to government agencies and research groups. *Wartime service:* Member of explosives division of U.S. National Defense Research Commission and official investigator for medical research committee of U.S. Office of Scientific Research and Development, 1942-45, member of U.S. Research Board for National Security, 1945-46; received U.S. Presidential Medal for Merit, 1948, "for exceptionally meritorious conduct in the performance of outstanding services to the United States from October, 1940, to June, 1946."

MEMBER: International Society of Hematology, International Society for Research on Nutrition and Vital Substances (honorary), International Society for the Study and Development of Human Relations (honorary), World Association of Parliamentarians for World Government, European Society of Haematology (honorary), American Chemical Society (president, 1949), American Philosophical Society (vice-president, 1951-54), American Association for the Advancement of Science (president, Pacific division, 1941-46), American Physical Society (fellow), American Association of Clinical Chemists (honorary), American Academy of Arts and Sciences, American Academy of Political Science, American Society of Naturalists, American Academy of Neurology, American Crystallographic Association, Mineralogical Society of America (fellow), National Academy of Sciences (chairman, chemistry section, 1940-45), Royal Institution of Great Britain (honorary), Chemical Society of London (honorary fellow), The Royal Society of London (foreign member), Oxford Natural Science Club (honorary), Royal Society of Arts (Benjamin Franklin Fellow), Society for Social Responsibility in Science, Weizmann Institute of Science (honorary fellow), The Harvey Society (honorary), Longshoremen, Shipsclerks, and Walking Bosses Division of the International Longshoremen's and Warehousemen's Union (honorary), Alpha Omega Alpha Honor Medical Society (honorary).

Institute of France, Academy of Sciences (correspondent, section of geology), Academie Nationale de Medecine de France (correspondent), Societe de Chimie Physique (France; honorary), Academie des Sciences, Inscriptions, et Belles Lettres de Toulouse (France; foreign member), Royal Society of Liege (Belgium; honorary fellow), Italian Chemical Society (honorary fellow), Academy of Sciences of Bologna (Italy; corresponding foreign member), Accademia Gioenia di Scienze Naturali di Catania, Sicily (Italy; honorary), The Academy of the Lynxes, Rome (Italy; foreign member), Bavarian Academy of Sciences, Mathematics-Natural Science Class (Germany; corresponding member), Deutsche Akademie der Naturforscher Leopoldina (Germany), Austrian Academy of Sciences (corresponding member), Swiss Chemical Society (honorary), Norwegian Academy of Science, Royal Norwegian Academy of Science, Royal Norwegian Scientific Society, Lisbon Academy of Science (Portugal; corresponding member), Soviet Academy of Sciences (U.S.S.R.; foreign member), Indian Academy of Sciences (honorary), National Institute of Sciences of India (honorary), Chemical Society of Japan (honorary), Chemical Society of Chile (honorary).

AWARDS, HONORS: National Research Fellow in chemistry, 1925-26; John S. Guggenheim Foundation fellow, 1926-27; Irving Langmuir Prize in pure chemistry from American Chemical Society (ACS), 1931; elected to National Academy of Sciences, 1933; William H. Nichols Medal from New York section of ACS, 1941; Willard Gibbs Medal from Chicago section of ACS, 1946; Theodore William Richards Medal from Northeast section of ACS, 1947; Davy Medal from The Royal Society of London, 1947; Louis Pasteur Medal from Biochemical Society of France, 1952; Page One Award for work on proteins from Newspaper Guild of New York, 1953; Nobel Prize for Chemistry from Nobel Foundation for "research into the nature of the chemical bond and its application to the elucidation of the structure of complex substances," 1954; Thomas Addis Medal from National Nephrosis Foundation, 1955; Amedeo Avogadro Medal from Italian Academy of Sciences, 1956; John Phillips Memorial Medal for contributions to internal medicine from American College of Physicians, 1956; Pierre Fermat Medal, 1957; Paul Sabatier Medal, 1957; gold medal from French Academy of Medicine, 1957; medal with laurel wreath for contributions to international law from International Grotius Foundation, 1957.

Named Rationalist of the Year by American Rationalist Federation, 1960; Cheers of the Year award from The Minority of One, 1960; grande medaille de vermeil from the City of Paris, 1961; Humanist of the Year award from American Humanist Association, 1961; Nobel Peace Prize, 1962; (with wife, Ava Helen Pauling) Janice Holland Peace Prize, 1962; Roebling Medal of the Mineralogical Society of America, 1967; Phi Beta Kappa Award in Science, 1971, for *Vitamin C and the Common Cold;* International Lenin Peace Prize from the Presidium of the Supreme Soviet of the U.S.S.R., 1972; U.S. National Medal of Science, 1974; 1977 Lomonosov Gold Medal from the Presidium of the Academy of the U.S.S.R. for work in chemistry and biochemistry, 1978; Award of Merit from the Decalogue Society of Lawyers, 1978; Chemical Sciences Award from the U.S. National Academy of Sciences, 1979; gold medal from the National Institute of Social Sciences, 1979; Annual Award from Women Strike for Peace, 1982; award for chemistry from Arthur M. Sackler Foundation, 1984; Priestley Medal for contributions to chemistry from ACS, 1984.

Rachel Carson Memorial Award from Lake Michigan Federation; gold medal from Rudolph Virshow Medical Society of New York; Modern Medicine Award for Distinguished Achievement from Modern Medicine Publications; Linus Pauling Medal from Puget Sound and Oregon sections of ACS; Gandhi Peace Prize; Eliasberg and Goedel Medallions in Anesthesiology; Vollum

Award; Dr. Martin Luther King, Jr., Medical Achievement Award for pioneering work in determining the cause of sickle-cell anemia; Grand Officer of the Order of Merit of the Italian Republic; Ordre du Merite Social de Belgique; Medal of the Senate of the Republic of Chile.

Numerous honorary degrees, including: Sc.D. from Oregon State College, 1933, University of Chicago, 1941, Princeton University, 1946, Cambridge University, 1947, University of London, 1947, Yale University, 1947, Oxford University, 1948, Brooklyn Polytechnic Institute, 1955, Humboldt University, 1959, University of Melbourne, 1964, University of Delhi, 1967, Adelphi University, 1967, Marquette University School of Medicine, 1969; Dr.h.c. from University of Paris, Sorbonne, 1948, University of Toulouse, 1949, University of Liege, 1955, University of Montpellier, 1958, Jagiellonian University, 1964, University of Warsaw, 1969, University of Lyon, 1970; M.A. from Oxford University, 1948; L.H.D. from University of Tampa, 1950; U.J.D. from University of New Brunswick, 1950; D.F.A. from Chouinard Art Institute, 1958; LL.D. from Reed College, 1959.

WRITINGS:

(With Samuel Goudsmit) *The Structure of Line Spectra,* McGraw, 1930, reprinted, 1963.

(With E. Bright Wilson, Jr.) *Introduction to Quantum Mechanics, With Applications to Chemistry,* McGraw, 1935, Dover, 1985.

The Nature of the Chemical Bond and the Structure of Molecules and Crystals: An Introduction to Modern Structural Chemistry, Cornell University Press, 1939, 3rd edition, 1960, shortened 3rd edition published as *The Chemical Bond: A Brief Introduction to Modern Structural Chemistry,* 1967.

General Chemistry, W. H. Freeman, 1947, 2nd edition, 1953, 3rd edition, 1970, recent edition, Dover, 1988.

College Chemistry: An Introductory Textbook of General Chemistry, illustrations by Roger Hayward, W. H. Freeman, 1950, 3rd edition, 1964.

Molecular Structure and Biological Specificity, American Institute of Biological Sciences, 1957.

No More War!, illustrations by Hayward, Dodd, 1958, enlarged edition, 1962, reprinted, 1983.

(With Hayward) *The Architecture of Molecules,* W. H. Freeman, 1964.

Science and World Peace, Indian Council for Cultural Relations (New Delhi), 1967.

Structural Chemistry and Molecular Biology, edited by Alexander Rich and Norman Davidson, W. H. Freeman, 1968.

(Editor) *Centennial Lectures: 1968 to 1969,* Oregon State University Press, 1969.

Vitamin C and the Common Cold, W. H. Freeman, 1970.

(Editor with David Hawkins) *Orthomolecular Psychiatry: Treatment of Schizophrenia,* W. H. Freeman, 1973.

(With son, Peter Pauling) *Chemistry,* W. H. Freeman, 1975.

Vitamin C, the Common Cold, and the Flu, W. H. Freeman, 1976, Berkley, 1981.

(With Ewan Cameron) *Cancer and Vitamin C: A Discussion of the Nature, Causes, Prevention, and Treatment of Cancer With Special Reference to the Value of Vitamin C,* Linus Pauling Institute of Science and Medicine, 1979.

(Author of introduction) Roger Walsh, *Staying Alive: The Psychology of Human Survival,* Shambhala, 1984.

How to Live Longer and Feel Better, Freeman, 1986.

Featured on sound recordings, including: *The Committed Scientist,* American Chemical Society, 1968; *Society and the Future,*

Science and the Future, American Chemical Society, 1976; and *Vitamin C and Cancer,* Big Sur Recordings, 1976.

Contributor of more than four hundred scientific papers and of more than one hundred articles on social and political issues, especially peace, to periodicals.

Associate editor of *Journal of the American Chemical Society,* 1930-40, of *Journal of Chemical Physics,* 1932-37, and of *Chemical Reviews.*

Member of editorial board, American Chemical Society "Monograph Series."

SIDELIGHTS: "Linus Pauling is one of that select group of individuals whose lives have made a discernible impact on the contemporary world," proclaimed the *Antioch Review* in 1980. Two years later, writing of Pauling in *Discover,* John Langone deemed Pauling "one of the world's most distinguished scientists, the only American chemist whose name is a household word." Pauling "calls himself a physical chemist," explained Horace Freeland Judson in an extensive 1978 *New Yorker* essay. "In over half a century in science," Judson continued, "in over five hundred scientific publications, Pauling has stretched that designation to cover everything from crystal structure and quantum mechanics, where he began, to molecular biology, molecular medicine, molecular psychiatry, and the structure of atomic nuclei." "The two-time Nobel laureate with the pioneering spirit has made headlines with countless achievements and an array of controversial causes," asserted Lidia Wasowicz in a 1985 *Chicago Tribune* report. "Pauling's contributions in such diverse fields as chemistry, molecular biology, immunology, genetic diseases, metallurgy and peace," Wasowicz assessed, "are part of textbook history."

A native of Portland, Oregon, Pauling was born in the first year of the twentieth century. He was, according to Ted G. Goertzel, Mildred George Goertzel, and Victor Goertzel, in their *Antioch Review* article, "very much a product of American culture and society," what Wasowicz termed "one of the last of a breed the American maverick." Pauling left Portland High School without a diploma following a dispute with the school's principal over American history course requirements; at age sixteen he enrolled at Oregon State Agricultural College and began to study what was already his abiding interest: chemistry. "I was simply entranced by chemical phenomena, by the reactions in which substances disappear and other substances, often with strikingly different properties, appear," Pauling wrote in *Daedalus.* He informed Judson: "I developed a strong desire to understand the physical and chemical properties of substances in relation to the atoms and molecules of which they are made up. This interest has largely determined the course of my research for fifty years."

After receiving his doctorate from the California Institute of Technology in 1925, Pauling traveled to Europe as a Guggenheim fellow to study with physicists pioneering quantum mechanics, a new concept in the investigation of the nature of matter. Working with Arnold Summerfield in Munich, Germany, Erwin Schroedinger in Zurich, Switzerland, and Niels Bohr in Copenhagen, Denmark, Pauling began to use the principles of quantum mechanics to solve the problem of how atoms and molecules chemically combine. He returned to the United States in 1927 and accepted a position as assistant professor at California Institute of Technology. A productive period in Pauling's life followed, for in the decade from 1926 to 1936, as Judson related, "Pauling and others working in the domain where physics shades into chemistry . . . were learning just how atoms are allowed in nature to behave in one another's intimate company."

"More than anyone else, Pauling has made the structure of molecules the central and most productive question of modern chemistry," Judson declared. In the 1920s and 1930s Pauling and his colleagues worked to understand the properties of chemical substances in relation to their structure. Applying the physics of quantum mechanics to the structure of molecules, Pauling arrived at his breakthrough theory of resonance in chemical bonding. "The principle of resonance states, for example," Judson explained, "that if a molecule can be described as having the bonds among its atoms arranged in either of two ways, then the molecule is to be considered as existing in both arrangements simultaneously." The theory of resonance, and other theories of chemical bonding, were described by Pauling in seven landmark articles published from 1931 to 1933. "By 1935," Pauling told Judson, "I felt that I had an essentially complete understanding of the nature of the chemical bond." Pauling's "investigation of the powers that bind substances," Wasowicz reported, constituted what Pauling considers "his greatest scientific contribution [and] revolutionized modern chemistry." In fact, Judson related, in the years following the publication of Pauling's ideas, "structures of the molecules of two hundred and twenty-five substances were determined in Pauling's laboratory . . . and a great many others in other laboratories." The basis for modern theories of chemical bonding, Pauling's ideas explained the properties of many complicated substances and led to the development of drugs, plastics, and synthetics. His concepts were brought together and published in the 1939 book *The Nature of the Chemical Bond,* deemed one of the most influential chemical texts of the twentieth century. "His definitive book," Langone asserted, "ensured the dominance of his theories for years to come."

Molecular biology and biochemistry began to interest Pauling in the mid-1930s, when he investigated the molecular structure of hemoglobin, a component of blood responsible for oxygen transfer. Pauling told Judson that in 1935 he "asked what the structure of the hemoglobin molecule should be in order to account for the way it takes up oxygen." Then, Pauling continued, he "began to speculate more generally about the properties of the large molecules found in living organisms and about the problem of the structure of proteins," the essential constituents of all living cells. By 1937 Pauling was determined to arrive at a detailed structural understanding of proteins, which are composed of amino acids—molecules that combine to form larger molecules called peptides, which, in turn, combine to form chains of polypeptides, the complex components of proteins.

Pauling's subsequent work in this area was redirected by the onset of World War II, when the chemist became a member of the consultative committee of medical research for the U.S. Office of Scientific Research and Development. In this wartime capacity Pauling, using his protein research findings, helped to produce, in 1942, the first synthetic antibodies from blood globulins. In synthesizing these antibodies, and in uncovering the molecular structure of antitoxins, he helped to advance the frontier of immunology. While working for government agencies Pauling also supervised a project that in 1945 developed a gelatin-derived substitute for plasma, an essential blood component. Similar lines of inquiry attracted the chemist at the close of World War II. In April, 1947, he received a grant to study organic proteins and the debilitating polio virus. By 1949 Pauling had discovered a structural fault in blood hemoglobin responsible for the blood disease known as sickle-cell anemia. This discovery, which, according to Langone, represented "the first direct linking of a disease to a molecular defect," established a chemical basis for genetic diseases and carried wide-ranging impact in the fields of medicine, biochemistry, genetics, and anthropology.

Pauling's research activities in the early 1950s revolved chiefly around the problem he had first identified in 1937, namely, trying to determine the structure of protein molecules. By 1948, Judson recounted, "Pauling had come to realize that there was a general argument . . . for supposing that the structure he wanted would be a helix," or spiral staircase form. In 1951 Pauling, in a culmination of fourteen years of work with amino acids and peptides, presented a model for protein molecules called the "alpha helix." Together with his colleague, Robert B. Corey, Pauling accurately delineated the atomic structure of several types of protein molecules, outlining the first configurations to show protein's correct three-dimensional atomic arrangement. Termed by Judson "a rare triumph," the discovery of the alpha helix protein structure led to important developments in disease control, plastics, and synthetic fibers.

To his life of research and academic pursuits Pauling added a new set of concerns when World War II's conclusion was precipitated by American use of newly developed atomic bombs. In 1946 Pauling became a member of the board of trustees of the Emergency Committee of Atomic Scientists, which favored international controls on the use and development of atomic energy. Fulfilling a pledge he wrote in 1947, Pauling included in every lecture a comment about the importance of world peace. The chemist publicly declared that radioactive fallout produced in nuclear weapons testing threatens humanity. He explained that the radiation from nuclear fallout elements like strontium 90 and carbon 14 enters the food chain and leads to adverse biological effects, both direct and hereditary, such as leukemia, cancer, physical defects, and mental retardation.

Because of his advocacy of world peace and his outspoken opposition to atmospheric testing of nuclear weapons, Pauling was denounced in the early 1950s as a Communist subversive by U.S. Senator Joseph McCarthy and was twice, in 1952 and 1954, refused a passport. "Even when accused of being un-American or a 'Communist sympathizer,' " the Goertzels wrote, "[Pauling] responded with an ironic smile and clever wit that consistently 'one-upped' his opponents." Pauling answered McCarthy's charges by denying that he was Communist and adding, "I am not even a theoretical Marxist." In an interview with Barbara Reynolds published in *USA Today* Pauling added a further twist, noting that he was also discredited in Communist-ruled Soviet Union: "Soviet chemists were forbidden to use my ideas in science, . . . which they said were incompatible with dialectical materialism." Pauling's wife played a major role in his crusade for world peace and nuclear disarmament, and when asked why he didn't abandon his efforts in the face of powerful attacks, the chemist told Wasowicz, "I continued because . . . I had to keep the respect of my wife." As Judson commented: "Pauling's political stand in the last years of the Truman Presidency seems mild now—a rather flamboyantly idealistic campaign against the Cold War, atomic weapons, and the development of the hydrogen bomb. In those days . . . Pauling's course required courage and principle."

"His politics had unpleasant consequences at the time," Judson continued. "At the end of April, 1952, Pauling was supposed to go to London to attend a meeting of the Royal Society [of London] on the structures of proteins, but at the last minute was refused a passport." By this time, Pauling had come to suspect that the helical form might also be the key to the structures of biochemical molecules other than proteins, especially nucleic acids, substances found in cell nuclei responsible for replicating and interpreting genetic messages. Scientists worldwide worked in the 1950s to determine the structure of one nucleic acid in particular, deoxyribonucleic acid (DNA), and new, clearer X-ray photographs of the molecule were available in the spring of 1952 to those who were able to attend the Royal Society meeting. Pauling's absence, termed a "scandal" by fellow scientists, deprived him of the opportunity to see the new DNA photographs. "Whether Pauling . . . could have learned enough [in London] to be the first to solve the structure of DNA is a question that must hang forever in the balance," Judson commented, for in 1953 James D. Watson and Francis Crick, scientists working in England with access to accurate photographs of DNA, solved the double-helix structure of the molecule, confirming Pauling's hunch. "There is no doubt whatever," Judson proclaimed, "that Pauling's lifetime of work on the structures of molecules provided information, insights, rules, techniques, and intellectual approaches that Watson and . . . Crick required" to formulate their history-making model of DNA. "The discovery of the structure of DNA by Watson and Crick," Judson continued, "was itself a tribute . . . to Pauling." When Pauling was asked why he didn't devote more of his research time to solving DNA's structure, Langone reported, the chemist replied, "Well, the fact is I didn't work harder at it partially because I had to put in so much time combating McCarthyism."

But Pauling's political views eventually gained acceptability, and Pauling himself gained widespread fame, in 1954, when he was awarded the Nobel Prize in Chemistry for "research into the nature of the chemical bond and its application to the elucidation of the structure of complex substances." By 1955 other scientists were joining Pauling in uncovering and warning of the dangerous genetic and pathological effects of radioactive fallout from atomic explosions. That year Pauling participated in the first international Pugwash Conference, a gathering composed of scientists supporting nuclear disarmament. When internationally respected theologian and physician Albert Schweitzer, himself a Nobel laureate, broadcast a mandate for a ban on nuclear weapons testing, the appeal lent support to a petition Pauling circulated in 1957 urging international cessation of nuclear testing. Ultimately signed by more than eleven thousand scientists, the petition was presented to the United Nations in 1958; two years later Pauling successfully defied a U.S. Senate internal security subcommittee demanding the names of those who had aided the chemist in circulating the petition.

No More War!, Pauling's popular book on disarmament, was first published in 1958. That year Pauling engaged in a televised debate with hydrogen-bomb architect Edward Teller and brought an unsuccessful suit against the U.S. Defense Department and the U.S. Atomic Energy Commission in an effort to halt atomic weapons tests. In the early 1960s Pauling continued his campaign, cabling his concerns to Soviet Premier Nikita Khrushchev in September, 1961, and joining an April, 1962, protest in Washington, D.C., to decry atomic weapons testing. An enlarged edition of *No More War!* was published in 1962, and in November of that year the book's author received nearly twenty-five hundred write-in votes in California's gubernatorial election. On October 10, 1963, the effective date for the provisions of a U.S.-Soviet nuclear weapons test ban treaty, Pauling was awarded the 1962 Nobel Peace Prize for his efforts on behalf of halting the testing of nuclear weapons, thus becoming the first recipient of two unshared Nobel prizes. Accepting the Peace Prize in December, 1963, Pauling called for an end to the research, development, and use of biological and chemical weapons. Explaining why, of his two Nobel prizes, he valued his Peace Prize more highly, Pauling told Wasowicz: "The Peace Prize came for work I was doing as a sacrifice—lecturing and writing, hundreds and hundreds of lectures about radioactive fallout and about nuclear weapons and the need to world peace. I was taking time away from things I really liked to do because of a sense of duty."

In 1963 Pauling left the California Institute of Technology, with which he had been affiliated for four decades, to work as a research professor at the Center for the Study of Democratic Institutions, where he pursued peace and disarmament causes. In 1965 the scientist circulated a letter signed by eight Nobel laureates urging American withdrawal from the escalating Vietnam conflict. Two years later Pauling joined political philosopher Herbert Marcuse, educator and linguist Noam Chomsky, pediatrician Benjamin Spock, and others, in a "call to resist illegitimate authority" that branded as unconstitutional U.S. involvement in Vietnam and urged resistance to the conscriptive military draft. Pauling encountered opposition to his scientific endeavors because of these political positions. According to Langone, "he was barred from receiving federal research grants for many years, and President [Richard] Nixon, counseled by the White House scientific advisers, twice denied him the National Medal of Science (it was finally awarded to him by President [Gerald] Ford in 1975)." Commenting on his political and social involvement, Pauling told Langone, "I believe in democracy, the people making decisions as a whole. I don't say, for instance, that the *scientist* should refuse to work on nuclear weapons. The *people* should refuse to allow these weapons of mass destruction to be developed—and because the scientist has a better understanding of such matters, he has the obligation to help, to the best of his ability, his fellow citizens to understand what the problems are."

Scientific research pursued by Pauling beginning in the 1960s included an investigation of the molecular mechanism of general anesthesia that led to a new theory of the way in which anesthetics interfere with consciousness. In linking the abnormal molecular structure of genes to hereditary diseases and mental retardation, Pauling helped to create the field of molecular biology, proposing the concept of "molecular disease." Pauling's inquiry into what he terms "orthomolecular" medicine—therapeutic alteration of body chemistry—coincided with his establishment, in the mid-1970s, of the Linus Pauling Institute of Science and Medicine, a nonprofit research institute at which Pauling oversees empirical confirmation of his orthomolecular theories. According to *Newsweek*, neither of Pauling's Nobel prizes "has brought him the celebrity his 'orthomolecular medicine' has." Pauling's claim for his theories, as articulated by the Goertzels, states that "perhaps all of modern, drug-oriented medicine could be replaced by 'orthomolecular' medicine, which treats the body entirely with natural substances."

As put forth in his popular books *Vitamin C and the Common Cold, Orthomolecular Psychiatry: Treatment of Schizophrenia, Cancer and Vitamin C,* and *Vitamin C, the Common Cold, and the Flu,* Pauling's proposals for mental and physical health describe a program of chemical balance within the body that includes the introduction into body chemistry of large amounts of various vitamins, including vitamin C, or ascorbic acid. Identified by the Goertzels as "part of a broad countercultural movement against established medicine and in favor of natural foods and remedies," Pauling's position on vitamin C maintains that, in the words of *Listener* critic Henry Miller, "while minute doses of ascorbic acid may prevent scurvy, enormously larger doses are required to sustain good health." Pauling also proposes vitamin therapy to prevent or cure the common cold, cancers, influenza, and certain mental diseases. In his *Saturday Review* discussion of Pauling's books on orthomolecular medicine, author and editor Norman Cousins explained that Pauling's theory "is built on the well-known fact that the human body neither manufactures

nor stores Vitamin C, yet cannot live without it. Therefore, he says, large amounts ought to be made available in case of need." Cousins noted Pauling's further claim that "massive doses of vitamins, with the emphasis on the Vitamin B family, plus ascorbic acid, enhance the body's ability to repair its 'orthomolecular' deficiencies and to provide for restored chemical balance in the brain." Cousins went on to characterize the reaction of the mental health establishment to Pauling's theories as "rigid to the point of being absurdly illogical in their opposition to megavitamin treatment."

Assessing *Vitamin C and the Common Cold,* Miller remarked that "the most disturbing thing about this highly unscientific book is the tenacious and emotive enthusiasm that Dr. Pauling brings to his profession of faith in ascorbic acid." Similarly, a critic quoted by Langone commented: "Twenty, thirty years ago, he was unerringly rational. Now his feelings about vitamin C are naive. He insists on taking a position that no self-respecting scientist would. There is absolutely no evidence, and Pauling's conclusions have not stood up." *Newsweek,* however, noted that while "the scientific establishment sees [Pauling] as something of a crank . . . he continues to push his unorthodox views, and no one has absolutely refuted them. Concluding his review, Cousins advocated serious consideration of Pauling's theories, arguing, "Whether the issue concerns the common cold or mental disease or any of the areas that have claimed Dr. Pauling's interest, he should be confronted only on the highest ground. Professional prerogatives or even tradition should not be allowed to outweigh the possibility that his work could lead to a genuine improvement in the human condition." Reviewing *Vitamin C, the Common Cold, and the Flu* in the *West Coat Review of Books,* critic Henry Zorich acknowledged, "When Pauling speaks, you've got to listen." And Pauling mentioned to Wasowicz the attitude of some colleagues, noting, "They have said that I've been right so often in the past that I'm probably right this time, too."

Whether proposing new avenues of scientific inquiry or espousing social and political causes, Pauling commands respect in his dual roles as scientist and humanitarian. "There is little danger when he is wrong and sometimes a great deal to be gained when he is right," the Goertzels wrote. "His unrelenting refusal to admit defeat," Wasowicz noted, "and his persistent crusades have, over the years, stirred up lingering hostilities of passionate proportions in some scientific and political circles—and a kind of folk-hero reverence elsewhere." Summarizing Pauling's career for Wasowicz, Stanford University chemist Haden McConnell averted: "His contributions are hard to total up because they are so many, so diverse and so profound. Time has passed, and nobody remembers how it all got started. But so many things a modern chemist uses in his day-to-day work can be traced back to Linus Pauling." Still active into his eighties as a lecturer, humanitarian crusader, researcher, and author of scientific papers, Pauling informed Wasowicz: "I'm always being asked if I won't write my autobiography. But I have so many other things to do. Hashing over old stuff doesn't interest me as much as making discoveries."

BIOGRAPHICAL/CRITICAL SOURCES:

BOOKS

Farber, Eduard, *Nobel Prize Winners in Chemistry, 1901-1961,* Abelard-Schuman, 1963.

Gray, Tony, *Champions of Peace,* Paddington Press, 1976.

Lipsky, Mortimer, *Quest for Peace: The Story of the Nobel Award,* A. S. Barnes, 1966.

Watson, James Dewey, *The Double Helix: A Personal Account of the Discovery of the Structure of DNA,* Atheneum, 1968.
Wintterle, John and R. S. Cramer, *Portraits of Nobel Laureates in Peace,* Abelard-Schuman, 1971.

PERIODICALS

Antioch Review, summer, 1980.
Chicago Tribune, April 18, 1985.
Daedalus, fall, 1970.
Discover, November, 1982.
Globe & Mail (Toronto), May 16, 1987.
Harper's Bazaar, May, 1983.
Listener, April 22, 1971.
Los Angeles Times Magazine, October 13, 1985.
New Republic, June 5, 1961.
Newsweek, November 15, 1954, July 4, 1960, October 21, 1963, September 29, 1975, October 27, 1980.
New Yorker, December 4, 1978.
Saturday Review, May 15, 1971.
USA Today, September 14, 1983.
Washington Post Book World, January 30, 1972.
West Coast Review of Books, March, 1977.

*   *   *

PAYNE, Alan
See JAKES, John (William)

*   *   *

PAZ, Octavio 1914-

PERSONAL: Born March 31, 1914, in Mexico City, Mexico; son of Octavio Paz (a lawyer) and Josephina Lozano; married Marie Jose Tramini, 1964; children: one daughter. *Education:* Attended National Autonomous University of Mexico, 1932-37. *Politics:* "Disillusioned leftist." *Religion:* Atheist.

ADDRESSES: Home—Lerma 143-601, Mexico 5, D.F., Mexico. *Office*—c/o *Vuelta,* Avenida Contreras 516, Tercer Piso, San Jeronimo 10200 DF, Mexico City, Mexico.

CAREER: Writer. Government of Mexico, Mexican Foreign Service, posted to San Francisco, Calif., and New York, N.Y., secretary at Mexican Embassy in Paris, beginning 1945, charge d'affaires at Mexican Embassy in Japan, beginning 1951, posted to Mexican Secretariat for External Affairs, 1953-58, Extraordinary and Plenipotentiary Minister to Mexican embassy, 1959-62, ambassador to India, 1962-68. Visiting professor of Spanish American literature, University of Texas at Austin and Pittsburgh University, 1968-70; Simon Bolivar Professor of Latin American Studies, 1970, and fellow of Churchill College, Cambridge University, 1970-71; Charles Eliot Norton Professor of Poetry, Harvard University, 1971-72. Regent's fellow at University of California, San Diego.

MEMBER: American Academy and Institute of Arts and Letters (honorary).

AWARDS,HONORS: Guggenheim fellowship, 1944; Grand Prix International de Poesie (Belgium), 1963; Jerusalem Prize, Critics Prize (Spain), and National Prize for Letters (Mexico), all 1977; Grand Aigle d'Or (Nice), 1979; Premio Ollin Yoliztli (Mexico), 1980; Miguel de Cervantes Prize (Spain), 1982; Neustadt International Prize for Literature, 1982; Wilhelm Heinse Medal (West Germany), 1984; T. S. Eliot Award for Creative Writing, Ingersoll Foundation, 1987; Tocqueville Prize, 1989.

WRITINGS:

POETRY

Luna silvestre (title means "Sylvan Moon"), Fabula (Mexico City), 1933.
¡No pasaran!, Simbad (Mexico City), 1936.
Raiz del hombre (title means "Root of Man"; also see below), Simbad, 1937.
Bajo tu clara sombra y otros poemas sobre Espana (title means "Under Your Clear Shadow and Other Poems about Spain"; also see below), Espanolas (Valencia), 1937, revised edition, Tierra Nueva (Valencia), 1941.
Entre la piedra y la flor (title means "Between the Stone and the Flower"; Nueva Voz (Mexico City), 1938, 2nd edition, Asociacion Civica Yucatan (Mexico City), 1956.
A la orilla del mundo y Primer dia; Bajo tu clara sombra; Raiz del hombre; Noche de resurrecciones, Ars (Mexico City), 1942.
Libertad bajo palabra (title means "Freedom on Parole"), Tezontle (Mexico City), 1949.
¿Aguila o sol? (prose poems), Tezontle, 1951, 2nd edition, 1973, translation by Eliot Weinberger published as *¿Aguila o sol?/ Eagle or Sun?* (bilingual edition), October House, 1970, revised translation by Weinberger published under same title, New Directions, 1976.
Semillas para un himno, Tezontle, 1954.
Piedra de sol, Tezontle, 1957, translation by Muriel Rukeyser published as *Sun Stone/Piedra de sol* (bilingual edition; also see below), New Directions, 1963, translation by Peter Miller published as *Sun-Stone,* Contact (Toronto), 1963, translation by Donald Gardner published as *Sun Stone,* Cosmos (New York), 1969.
La estacion violenta, Fondo de Cultura Economica (Mexico City), 1958, reprinted, 1978.
Agua y viento, Ediciones Mito (Bogota), 1959.
Libertad bajo palabra: Obra poetica, 1935-1958, Fondo de Cultura Economica, 1960, revised edition, 1968.
Salamandra (1958-1961) (also see below), J. Mortiz (Mexico City), 1962, 3rd edition, 1975.
Selected Poems of Octavio Paz (bilingual edition), translation by Rukeyser, Indiana University Press, 1963.
Viento entero, Caxton (Delhi), 1965.
Blanco (also see below) J. Mortiz, 1967, 2nd edition, 1972, translation by Weinberger published under same title, The Press (New York), 1974.
Disco visuales (four spatial poems), Era (Mexico City), 1968.
Ladera este (1962-1968) (title means "Eastern Slope (1962-1968)"; also see below) J. Mortiz, 1969, 3rd edition, 1975.
La centena (Poemas: 1935-1968), Seix Barral (Barcelona), 1969, 2nd edition, 1972.
Topoemas (six spatial poems), Era, 1971.
Vuelta (long poem), El Mendrugo (Mexico City), 1971.
Configurations (contains *Piedra de sol/Sun Stone, Blanco,* and selections from *Salamandra* and *Ladera este*), translations by G. Aroul and others, New Directions, 1971.
(With Jacques Roubaud, Edoardo Sanguinetti, and Charles Tomlinson; also author of prologue) *Renga* (collective poem written in French, Italian, English, and Spanish), J. Mortiz, 1972, translation by Tomlinson published as *Renga: A Chain of Poems,* Braziller, 1972.
Early Poems: 1935-1955, translations by Rukeyser and others, New Directions, 1973.
3 Notations/3 Rotations (contains fragments of poems by Paz), Carpenter Center for the Visual Arts, Harvard University, 1974.

Pasado en claro (long poem), Fondo de Cultura Economica, 1975, revised edition, 1978, tranlation included as title poem in *A Draft of Shadows and Other Poems* (also see below), New Directions, 1979.

Vuelta, Seix Barral, 1976.

(With Tomlinson; sonnets written by Paz and Tomlinson in Spanish and English) *Air Born/Hijos del aire,* Pescador (Mexico City), 1979.

Poemas (1935-1975), Seix Barral, 1979.

A Draft of Shadows and Other Poems, edited and translated by Weinberger, with additional translations by Elizabeth Bishop and Mark Strand, New Directions, 1979.

Selected Poems (biligual edition), translations by Tomlinson and others, Penguin, 1979.

Octavio Paz: Poemas recientes, Institucion Cultural de Cantabria de la Diputacion Provincial de Santander, 1981.

Selected Poems, edited by Weinberger, translations by G. Aroul and others, New Directions, 1984.

Cuatro chopos/The Four Poplars (bilingual edition), translation by Weinberger, Center for Edition Works (New York), 1985.

The Collected Poems, 1957-1987: Bilingual Edition, New Editions, 1987.

PROSE

El laberinto de la soledad (also see below), Cuadernos Americanos, 1950, revised edition, Fondo de Cultura Economica, 1959, reprinted, 1980, translation by Lysander Kemp published as *The Labyrinth of Solitude: Life and Thought in Mexico,* Grove, 1961.

El arco y la lira: El poema; La revelacion poetica; Poesia e historia, Fondo de Cultura Economica, 1956, 2nd edition includes text of *Los signos en rotacion* (also see below), 1967, 3rd edition, 1972, translation by Ruth L. C. Simms published as *The Bow and the Lyre: The Poem, the Poetic Revelation, Poetry and History,* University of Texas Press, 1973, reprinted, 1977, 2nd edition, McGraw-Hill, 1975.

Las peras del olmo, Universidad Nacional Autonoma de Mexico, 1957, revised edition, Seix Barral, 1971, 3rd edition, 1978.

Tamayo en la pintura mexicana, Universidad Nacional Autonoma de Mexico, 1959.

Cuadrivio: Dario, Lopez Velarde, Pessoa, Cernuda, J. Mortiz, 1965.

Los signos en rotacion, Sur (Buenos Aires), 1965.

Puertas al campo (also see below), Universidad Nacional Autonoma de Mexico, 1966.

Claude Levi-Strauss; o, El nuevo festin de Esopo, J. Mortiz, 1967, translation by J. S. Bernstein and Maxine Bernstein published as *Claude Levi-Strauss: An Introduction,* Cornell University Press, 1970 (published in England as *On Levi-Strauss,* Cape, 1970).

Corriente alterna, Siglo Veintiuno Editores (Mexico City), 1967, reprinted, 1980, translation by Helen R. Lane published as *Alternating Current,* Viking, 1973.

Marcel Duchamp; o, El castillo de la pureza, Era, 1968, translation by Gardner published as *Marcel Duchamp; or, The Castle of Purity,* Grossman, 1970.

Conjunciones y disyunciones, J. Mortiz, 1969, 2nd edition, 1978, translation by Lane published as *Conjunctions and Disjunctions,* Viking, 1974.

Mexico: La ultima decada, Institute of Latin American Studies, University of Texas, 1969.

Posdata (also see below) Siglo Veintiuno, 1970, translation by Kemp published as *The Other Mexico: Critique of the Pyramid,* Grove, 1972.

(With Juan Marichal) *Las cosas en su sitio: Sobre la literatura espanola del siglo XX,* Finisterre (Mexico City), 1971.

Los signos en rotacion y otros ensayos, edited and with a prologue by Carlos Fuentes, Alianza (Madrid), 1971.

Traduccion: Literatura y literalidad, Tusquets (Barcelona), 1971.

Aparencia desnuda: La obra de Marcel Duchamp, Era, 1973, new enlarged edition, 1979, translation by Rachel Phillips and Gardner published as *Marcel Duchamp: Appearance Stripped Bare,* Viking, 1978.

El signo y el garabato (contains *Puertas al campo*), J. Mortiz, 1973.

(With Julian Rios) *Solo a dos voces,* Lumen (Barcelona), 1973.

Teatro de signos/Transparencias, selection and montage by Rios, Fundamentos (Madrid), 1974.

La busqueda del comienzo: Escritos sobre el surrealismo, Fundamentos, 1974, 2nd edition, 1980.

El mono gramatico, Seix Barral, 1974, translation from the original Spanish manuscript published as *Le singe grammarien,* Skira (Geneva), 1972, translation by Lane of Spanish original published as *The Monkey Grammarian,* Seaver, 1981.

Los hijos del limo: Del romanticismo a la vanguardia, Seix Barral, 1974, translation by Phillips published as *Children of the Mire: Modern Poetry from Romanticism to the Avant-Garde,* Harvard University Press, 1974.

The Siren and the Seashell, and Other Essays on Poets and Poetry, translations by Kemp and Margaret Sayers Peden, University of Texas Press, 1976.

Xavier Villaurrutia en persona y en obra, Fondo de Cultura Economica, 1978.

El ogro filantropico: Historia y politica, 1971-1978 (also see below), J. Mortiz, 1979.

In/mediaciones, Seix Barral, 1979.

Mexico en la obra de Octavio Paz, edited by Luis Mario Schneider, Promexa (Mexico City), 1979.

El laberinto de la soledad; Posdata; Vuelta a El laberinto de la soledad, Fondo de Cultura Economica, 1981.

Sor Juana Ines de la Cruz; o, Las trampas de la fe, Seix Barral, 1982, translation by Peden published as *Sor Juana; or, The Traps of Faith,* Harvard University Press, 1988.

(With Jacques Lassaigne) *Rufino Tamayo,* Ediciones Poligrafia (Barcelona), 1982, translation by Kenneth Lyons published under same title, Rizzoli, 1982.

(With John Golding) *Guenther Gerzo* (Spanish, English and French texts), Editions du Griffon (Switzerland), 1983.

Sombras de obras: Arte y literatura, Seix Barral, 1983.

Hombres en su siglo y otros ensayos, Seix Barral, 1984, translation by Michael Schmidt published as *On Poets and Others,* Seaver Books, 1987.

Tiempo nublado, Seix Barral, 1984, translation by Lane with three additional essays published as *On Earth, Four or Five Worlds: Reflections on Contemporary History,* Harcourt, 1985.

The Labyrinth of Solitude, The Other Mexico, Return to the Labyrinth of Solitude, Mexico and the United States, The Philanthropic Ogre, translated by Kemp, Yara Milos, and Rachel Phillips Belash, Grove, 1985.

Arbol adentro, Seix Barral, 1987, translation published as *A Tree Within,* New Directions, 1988.

Convergences: Essays on Art and Literature, translation by Lane, Harcourt, 1987.

EDITOR

Voces de Espana, Letras de Mexico (Mexico City), 1938.

(With others) *Laurel: Antologia de la poesia moderna en lengua espanola,* Seneca, 1941.

Antologie de la poesie mexicaine, Nagel, 1952.

Antologia poetica, Revista Panoramas (Mexico City), 1956.

(And translator with Eikichi Hayashiya) Matsuo Basho, *Sendas de Oku,* Universidad Nacional Autonoma de Mexico, 1957, 2nd edition, Seix Barral, 1970.

Anthology of Mexican Poetry, translation of Spanish manuscript by Samuel Beckett, Indiana University Press, 1958, reprinted as *Mexican Poetry: An Anthology,* Grove, 1985.

Tamayo en la pintura mexicana, Imprenta Universitaria (Mexico City), 1958.

Magia de la risa, Universidad Veracruzana, 1962.

Fernando Pessoa, *Antologia,* Universidad Nacional Autonoma de Mexico, 1962.

(With Pedro Zekeli) *Cuatro poetas contemporaneos de Suecia: Martinson, Lundkvist, Ekeloef, y Lindegren,* Universidad Nacional Autonoma de Mexico, 1963.

(With others and author of prologue) *Poesia en movimiento: Mexico, 1915-1966,* Siglo Veintiuno, 1966, translation edited by Mark Strand and published as *New Poetry of Mexico,* Dutton, 1970.

(With Roger Caillois) *Remedios Varo,* Era, 1966.

(And author of prologue) Xavier Villaurrutia, *Antologia,* Fondo de Cultura Economica, 1980.

CONTRIBUTOR

In Praise of Hands: Contemporary Crafts of the World, New York Graphic Society, 1974.

Avances, Fundamentos, 1978.

Democracy and Dictatorship in Latin America: A Special Publication Devoted Entirely to the Voices and Opinions of Writers from Latin America, Foundation for the Independent Study of Social Ideas (New York), 1982.

Instante y revelacion, Fondo Nacional para Actividades Sociales, 1982.

Frustraciones de un destino: La democracia en America Latina, Libro Libre, 1985.

Weinberger, editor, *Nineteen Ways of Looking at Wang Wei: How a Chinese Poem Is Translated,* Moyer Bell, 1987.

TRANSLATOR

(And author of introduction) William Carlos Williams, *Veinte Poemas,* Era, 1973.

Versiones y diversiones (translations of poems from English, French, Portuguese, Swedish, Chinese, and Japanese), J. Mortiz, 1974.

Apollinaire, *15 Poemas,* Latitudes (Mexico City), 1979.

OTHER

"La hija de Rappaccini" (one-act play; based on a short story by Nathaniel Hawthorne; first produced in Mexico, 1956), translation by Harry Haskell published as "Rappaccini's Daughter" in *Octavio Paz: Homage to the Poet,* Kosmos (San Francisco), 1980.

(Author of introduction) Carlos Fuentes, *Cuerpos y ofrendas,* Alianza, 1972.

(Author of introduction) *Antonio Palaez: Pintor,* Secretaria de Educacion Publica (Mexico), 1975.

(Author of foreword) *A Sor Juana Anthology,* translation by Alan S. Trueblood, Harvard University Press, 1988.

One Word to the Other, Latitudes, 1989.

Contributor to numerous anthologies. Founder of literary review, *Barandal,* 1931; member of editorial board and columnist, *El Popular,* late 1930s; co-founder of *Taller,* 1938; co-founder and editor, *El Hijo Prodigo,* 1943-46; editor of *Plural,* 1971-75; founder and editor, *Vuelta,* 1976—.

SIDELIGHTS: Often nominated for the Nobel Prize, Mexican author Octavio Paz has a world-wide reputation as a master poet and essayist. Although Mexico figures prominently in Paz's work—one of his best-known books, *The Labyrinth of Solitude,* for example, is an comprehensive portrait of Mexican society— *Los Angeles Times* contributor Jascha Kessler calls Paz "truly international." *World Literature Today*'s Manuel Duran feels that Paz's "exploration of Mexican existential values permits him to open a door to an understanding of other countries and other cultures" and thus appeal to readers of diverse backgrounds. "What began as a slow, almost microscopic examination of self and of a single cultural tradition widens unexpectedly," Duran continues, "becoming universal without sacrificing its unique characteristic."

One aspect of Paz's work often mentioned by critics is his tendency to maintain elements of prose—most commonly philosophical thought—in his poetry and poetic elements in his prose. Perhaps the best example to support this claim can be found in Paz's exploration of India entitled *The Monkey Grammarian,* a work which *New York Times Book Review* contributor Keith Botsford calls "exceedingly curious" and describes as "an extended meditation on the nature of language." In separate *World Literature Today* essays critics Jaime Alazraki and Jose Miguel Oviedo discuss the difficulty they would have assigning the book to a literary genre. "It is apparent," Alazraki notes, "that *The Monkey Grammarian* is not an essay. It is also apparent that it is not a poem, at least not in the conventional sense. It is both an essay and a poem, or perhaps neither." Oviedo similarly states that the book "does not belong to any specific genre—although it has a bit of all of them—because it is deliberately written at the edge of genres."

According to Oviedo, *The Monkey Grammarian* is the product of Paz's long-stated quest "to produce a text which would be an intersection of poetry, narrative and essay." The fusion of opposites found in this work is an important element in nearly all Paz's literary production. In many instances both the work's structure and its content represent a blending of contradictory forces: *Renga,* for example, is written in four languages, while *Air Born/Hijos del Aire,* is written in two. According to *World Literature Today* contributor Frances Chiles, Paz strives to create in his writing "a sense of community or communion" which he finds lacking in contemporary society. In his Neustadt Prize acceptance speech reprinted in *World Literature Today,* Paz attempts to explain his emphasis on contrasting thoughts: "Plurality is Universality, and Universality is the acknowledging of the admirable diversity of man and his works. . . . To acknowledge the variety of visions and sensibilities is to preserve the richness of life and thus to ensure its continuity."

Through juxtapostion of contrasting thoughts or objects Paz creates a more harmonious world, one based on complementary association of opposites found in the Eastern concept of yin and yang. This aspect of Paz's thinking reveals the influence of his six-year stay in India as Mexican ambassador to that country. Grace Schulman explains Paz's proclivity for Eastern philosophy in her *Hudson Review* essay: "Although he had embraced contraries from the beginning of his writing career, [as] Mexican ambassador to India [he] found in Tantric thought and in Hindu religious life dualities that enforced his conviction that history turns on reciprocal rhythms. In *Alternating Current,* he writes that the Hindu gods, creators or destroyers according to their names and region, manifest contradiction. 'Duality,' he says, 'a basic feature of Tantrism, permeates all Hindu religious life: male and female, pure and impure, left and right. . . . In Eastern thought, these opposites can co-exist; in Western philosophy, they disappear for the worst reasons: far from being resolved into a higher synthesis, they cancel each other out.' "

Critics point to several repeated contrasting images that dramatically capture the essence of Paz's work. Ronald Christ, for example, comments in his *Nation* review of *¿Aguila o sol?/Eagle or Sun?* (the Spanish portion of which is the equivalent of the English expression "heads or tails?"): "The dual image of the Mexican coin which gives *Eagle or Sun?* its title epitomizes Paz's technique and credo, for we see that there is no question of eagle *or* sun rather of eagle *and* sun which together in their oppositeness are the same coin." Another of the poet's images which reviewers frequently mention is "burnt water," an ancient Mexican concept which appears in Paz's work in both Spanish and in the Aztec original, "atl tlachinolli." Schulman maintains that "burnt water" is "the dominant image of [Paz's] poetry" and finds that the image fulfills a role similar to that of the two sides of the coin in *Eagle and Sun?* She notes: "Paz sees the world burning, and knows with visionary clarity that opposites are resolved in a place beyond contraries, in a moment of pure vision: in that place, there are no frontiers between men and women, life and death." Chiles calls the Aztec combination of fire and water "particularly apt in its multiple connotations as a symbol of the union of all warring contraries."

Critics agree that Paz's great theme of a blended reality situates his work in the forefront of modern literature. As Christ notes: "By contraries then, by polarities and divergences converging in a rhetoric of opposites, Paz [has] established himself as a brilliant stylist balancing the tension of East and West, art and criticism, the many and the one in the figures of his writing. Paz is thus not only a great writer: he is also an indispensable corrective to our cultural tradition and a critic in the highest sense in which he himself uses the word." Enrique Fernandez similarly sees Octavio Paz as a writer of enormous influence. "Not only has he left his mark on world poetry, with a multilingual cortege of acolytes," Fernandez writes in a *Village Voice* essay, "he is a force to be reckoned with by anyone who chooses that modernist *imitaio Christi,* the Life of the Mind."

BIOGRAPHICAL/CRITICAL SOURCES:

BOOKS

Contemporary Literary Criticism, Gale, Volume 3, 1975, Volume 4, 1975, Volume 6, 1976, Volume 10, 1979, Volume 19, 1981, Volume 51, 1989.
Wilson, Jason, *Octavio Paz,* Twayne, 1986.

PERIODICALS

Hudson Review, autumn, 1974.
Interview, October, 1989.
Los Angeles Times, November 28, 1971.
Nation, August 2, 1975.
New York Times Book Review, December 27, 1981, December 25, 1988.
Times (London), June 8, 1989.
Village Voice, March 19, 1985.
World Literature Today, autumn, 1982.

—*Sketch by Marian Gonsior*

p'BITEK, Okot   1931-1982

PERSONAL: Born in 1931 in Gulu, Uganda; died July 19, 1982; son of a schoolteacher; married twice. *Education:* Attended King's College, Budo; Government Training College, Mbarara, teaching certificate; Bristol University, certificate of education; University College of Wales, LL.B.; Institute of Social Anthropology, Oxford, B.Litt., 1963.

CAREER: Taught school in the area of Gulu, Uganda, and played on the Ugandan national soccer team in the mid-1950s; Makerere University, Kampala, Uganda, lecturer in sociology, 1964; Uganda National Theater and Uganda National Cultural Center, Kampala, director, 1966-68; University of Iowa, Iowa City, fellow of international writing program, 1969-70, writer in residence, 1971; University of Nairobi, Nairobi, Kenya, senior research fellow at Institute of African Studies and lecturer in sociology and literature, 1971-78; University of Ife, Ife, Nigeria, professor, 1978-82; Makerere University, professor of creative writing, 1982; writer. Visiting lecturer at University of Texas, 1969. Founder of the Gulu Arts Festival, 1966, and the Kisumu Arts Festival, 1968.

AWARDS, HONORS: Jomo Kenyatta Prize for Literature, Kenya Publishers Association, for *Two Songs,* 1972.

WRITINGS:

POETIC NOVELS

Song of Lawino: A Lament, East African Publishing, 1966, Meridian Books, 1969.
Song of Ocol, East African Publishing, 1970.
Song of a Prisoner, Third Press, 1971.
Two Songs: Song of Prisoner [and] *Song of Malaya,* East African Publishing, 1971.
Song of Lawino and Song of Ocol, introduction by G. A. Heron, East African Publishing, 1972.

OTHER

Lak tar miyo kinyero wi lobo? (novel; title means "Are Your Teeth White? Then Laugh!"), Eagle Press, 1953.
African Religions in Western Scholarship, East African Literature Bureau, 1970.
Religion of the Central Luo, East African Literature, 1971.
Africa's Cultural Revolution (essays), introduction by Ngugi wa Thiong'o, Macmillan Books for Africa, 1973.
(Compiler and translator) *The Horn of My Love* (folk songs), Heinemann Educational Books, 1974.
(Compiler and translator) *Hare and Hornbill* (folktales), Heinemann Educational Books, 1978.

Contributor to periodicals, including *Transition.*

SIDELIGHTS: Eulogized as "Uganda's best known poet" in his London *Times* obituary, Okot p'Bitek had a distinguished career in the fields of sport, education, and the arts. While serving as a teacher in his native Uganda during the 1950s, he played on the country's national soccer team, going to the 1956 Summer Olympic Games in London, England. P'Bitek stayed in Great Britain to obtain degrees from several universities before returning to Uganda to teach at the college level. He published his first book, *Lak tar miyo kinyero wi lobo?* ("Are Your Teeth White? Then Laugh!"), in 1953, but it was the 1966 publication of his *Song of Lawino* that brought p'Bitek his first real acclaim. In the same year, p'Bitek was named director of the Uganda National Theater and Cultural Center. In this post he founded the successful Gulu Arts Festival, a celebration of the traditional oral history, dance, and other arts of his ancestral Acholi people. Due to political pressures, however, p'Bitek was forced from his directorship after two years. He moved to Kenya, where, with the exception of visits to universities in the United States, he remained throughout the reign of Ugandan dictator Idi Amin. After founding the Kisumu Arts Festival in Kenya and later serving as a professor in Nigeria, p'Bitek eventually returned to Makerere University in Kampala, Uganda. He was a professor of creative writing there when he died in 1982.

P'Bitek sought, in his role as cultural director and author, to prevent native African culture from being swallowed up by the influences of Western ideas and arts. He was particularly interested in preserving the customs of his native Acholi. While serving as director for the Uganda National Theater and Cultural Center, p'Bitek proclaimed in an interview with Robert Serumaga which appeared in *African Writers Talking:* "The major challenge I think is to find what might be Uganda's contribution to world culture. . . . [W]e should, I think, look into the village and see what the Ugandans—the proper Ugandans—not the people who have been to school, have read—and see what they do in the village, and see if we cannot find some root there, and build on this." He further explained to Serumaga his feelings about the influence of Western culture on his own: "I am not against having plays from England, from other parts of the world, we should have this, but I'm very concerned that whatever we do should have a basic starting point, and this should be Uganda, and then, of course, Africa, and then we can expand afterwards."

Song of Lawino, p'Bitek's most famous work, takes as its central issue the defense of Acholi tradition against the encroachment of Western cultural influences. Originally composed by p'Bitek in the Acholi (sometimes known as Lwo or Luo) language, he translated *Song of Lawino* into English before its publication. He put the English words to traditional Acholi verse patterns, however, and the result was pleasing to many critics. A reviewer in the *Times Literary Supplement* lauded p'Bitek's creation thus: "In rewriting his poem in English he has chosen a strong, simple idiom which preserves the sharpness and frankness of [its] imagery, a structure of short, free verses which flow swiftly and easily, and an uncondescending offer of all that is local and specific in the original."

Categorized as a poetic novel, *Song of Lawino* is narrated by an Acholi woman named Lawino who tells an audience her life story in the form of an Acholi song. Her main complaint is against her husband Ocol, who neglects her because of her adherence to Acholi ways. Ocol, in contrast, tries to become as westernized as possible, rejecting his culture as backward and crude. His negative feelings toward his background are further symbolized by his preference of his mistress, Clementina, over Lawino. Clementina is thoroughly westernized, from her name to her high-heeled shoes. Lawino tells us that her rival straightens her hair, uses lipstick, and "dusts powder on her face / And it looks so pale; / She resembles the wizard / Getting ready for the midnight dance." Lawino speaks disdainfully of what she perceives as unnatural behavior on the part of her husband and his mistress; in favorable opposition to this she praises the life of her village. Most critics agree that Lawino's loving descriptions of the simple Acholi rural activities and rituals leave the reader with no doubt as to whose side the author takes. As reported in the *Times Literary Supplement,* "It is Lawino's voice that we need to hear, reminding us of the human reality behind glib rejections of the backward, the primitive, the 'bush people.' " P'Bitek later wrote *Song of Ocol,* which purports to offer Lawino's husband's defense, but most reviewers concurred in believing that Ocol's words merely confirm Lawino's condemna-

tion of him. Another *Times Literary Supplement* critic judged that *Song of Ocol* "savo[rs] too much of a conscientious attempt to give a voice to an essentially dull, pompous, and vindictive husband."

P'Bitek's next poetic novels, published as *Two Songs: Song of Prisoner* [and] *Song of Malaya,* together won him the Kenya Publishers Association's Jomo Kenyatta Prize in 1972. *Song of Prisoner* relates the thoughts, both hopeful and despairing, of a political prisoner, and, according to the *Times Literary Supplement,* "its imagery has much of the freshness and inventive energy of Okot's best work." The narrator describes his cell as a cold, imprisoning woman and relates his feelings of betrayal, his fears of his lover's unfaithfulness, and his daydreams of merry-making. *Song of Malaya* is written in the persona of a prostitute and tells of the abuses she suffers. Judged slightly sentimental by some critics, the prose poem discusses, among other things, the irony in the fact that prostitutes are often rounded up and jailed by men who were their patrons the previous evening.

In his later years, p'Bitek's literary efforts turned primarily to translation. He published *The Horn of My Love,* a collection of Acholi folk songs in both Acholi and English translation, in 1974, and *Hare and Hornbill,* a collection of African folktales, in 1978. In *The Horn of My Love,* declared reviewer Gerald Moore in the *Times Literary Supplement,* "p'Bitek argues the case for African poetry as poetry, as an art to be enjoyed, rather than as ethnographic material to be eviscerated." The book contains ceremonial songs about death, ancient Acholi chiefs, and love and courtship. *Hare and Hornbill,* according to Robert L. Berner critiquing in *World Literature Today,* is divided roughly in half between tales of humans and tales of animals, including one about a hare seducing his mother-in-law. "P'Bitek is particularly qualified to deal with these tales," Berner proclaimed, and "reveals a thorough understanding of African folk materials."

BIOGRAPHICAL/CRITICAL SOURCES:

BOOKS

p'Bitek, Okot, *Song of Lawino: A Lament,* East African Publishing, 1966.
Pieterse, Cosmo, and Dennis Duerden, editors, *African Writers Talking,* Africana Publishing, 1972.

PERIODICALS

Times Literary Supplement, February 16, 1967, November 5, 1971, February 21, 1975.
World Literature Today, summer, 1979.

OBITUARIES:

PERIODICALS

Times (London), July 23, 1982.

*   *   *

PEAKE, Mervyn 1911-1968

PERSONAL: Born July 9, 1911, in Kuling, Central China; moved to England in 1923; died of Parkinson's Disease, November 18, 1968, in Burcot, Oxfordshire, England; son of Ernest Cromwell (a doctor and missionary) and Elizabeth (Powell) Peake; married Maeve Gilmore (a painter), 1937; children: Sebastian, Fabian, Clare. *Education:* Attended Eltham College and Royal Academy Schools.

ADDRESSES: Home—1 Drayton Gardens, London S.W. 10, England. *Agent*—David Higham Associates, 76 Dean St., Soho, London W.1, England.

CAREER: Author, poet, painter. *Military service:* British Army; served as engineer and official military artist during World War II; official illustrator of German concentration camp at Belsen.

MEMBER: Royal Society of Literature (fellow).

AWARDS, HONORS: Heinemann Award for Literature, 1951, for *Gormenghast* and *The Glassblowers.*

WRITINGS:

(Self-illustrated) *Captain Slaughterboard Drops Anchor,* Eyre & Spottiswoode, 1942, Macmillan, 1967.
The Drawings of Mervyn Peake, Grey Walls Press, 1945.
Titus Groan (also see below), Eyre & Spottiswoode, 1946.
(Self-illustrated) *Craft of the Lead Pencil,* Wingate, 1946.
(Self-illustrated) *Letters from a Lost Uncle,* Eyre & Spottiswoode, 1948.
Gormenghast (also see below), Eyre & Spottiswoode, 1950.
Mr. Pye, Heinemann, 1953, Overlook Press, 1984.
"The Wit to Woo," first produced at Arts Theatre, London, 1958.
Titus Alone (also see below), Eyre & Spottiswoode, 1959, new edition, 1970.
The Gormenghast Trilogy (contains *Titus Groan, Gormenghast,* and *Titus Alone*), Weybright & Talley, 1967, Overlook Press, 1988.
(With Brian W. Aldiss and J. G. Ballard) *The Inner Landscape,* Allison & Busby, 1969.
Mervyn Peake: Writings and Drawings, edited by wife, Maeve Gilmore, and Shelagh Johnson, St. Martin's, 1974.
Boy in Darkness, Exeter, 1976.
Peake's Progress: Selected Writings and Drawings of Mervyn Peake, edited by M. Gilmore, Allen Lane, 1979, Overlook Press, 1981.

POETRY

Shapes and Sounds, Chatto & Windus, 1940, reprinted, Village Press, 1974.
The Glassblowers, Eyre & Spottiswoode, 1945.
(Self-illustrated) *Rhymes without Reason,* Eyre & Spottiswoode, 1948.
(Self-illustrated) *Rhyme of the Flying Bomb,* Dent, 1962, Dufour, 1973.
Poems and Drawings, Keepsake Press, 1965.
A Reverie of Bone, and Other Poems, Bertram Rota, 1967.
A Book of Nonsense, Owen, 1972.
Selected Poems of Mervyn Peake, Faber, 1972.
Twelve Poems: 1939-1960, Bran's Head Books, 1975.

Also illustrator of numerous books.

SIDELIGHTS: Mervyn Peake's most popular work is the *Gormenghast Trilogy,* a singular gothic fantasy of tremendous proportions that is made up of the books *Titus Groan, Gormenghast,* and *Titus Alone.* A writer for the London *Times* described the trilogy as "an immensely long and detailed description of a house and its inhabitants who never could have existed, but are presented with such art that the reader cannot doubt their reality." R. G. G. Price of *Punch* thought that the trilogy is "about a closed world set in a vast castle governed by ancient rituals and peopled by eccentrics." Writing in *Critical Quarterly,* Ronald Binns stated that *Titus Groan* is "concerned with [the] lavish description of the decaying world of the castle and its environs, together with the dramatisation of a range of weird and eccentric characters." Speaking of the trilogy as a whole, he wrote: "It belongs to no obvious tradition [and] lacks an ordered structure." In similar terms, Michael Wood wrote in the *Observer* that *Titus*

Groan "is impossible to describe and therefore hard to recommend coherently." Ducan Fallowell of *Books and Bookmen* marvelled that Peake "can describe a rafter in two thousand words without introducing anything extraneous such as a pillar or even a beam, or boring you. . . . Two thousand words on a rafter? Which is only part of a roof, you know. And Peake describes the whole roof and the castle of which it is a part, a castle five miles long, describes all of it, and what goes on in and around it. Strange."

The trilogy chronicles the life of Titus Groan from his birth to maturity, although, as Robert Ostermann wrote in the *National Observer,* "to speak of these novels as being 'about' anything is as inadequate as saying *The Odyssey* is about a man trying to get home to his wife. Such fiction as this is first and foremost about itself. These novels are not an echo or an imitation of life. Their life is their own—a bizarre, often awe-full life. And it imposes itself with obsessive force on the reader." Wood found that Peake "presents a world which, like Kafka's, demands to be discussed in its own terms—the reverse of an allegory. It is a world of fantasy, . . . a closed, self-sufficient creation." Price echoed this judgment: "The books must be appreciated on their own terms outside the normal categories of fiction as a gigantic feat of sustained invention, a vicarious dream of extraordinary vividness, [and] a triumph of visual writing."

Writing in a lively prose, Peake populated his trilogy with a host of unique and colorful characters. "The people in *Titus Groan,*" Lin Carter wrote in *Imaginary Worlds,* "are monstrous caricatures portrayed with the gusto and violent energy of a Dickens." Philip Guerrard of *City of San Francisco* agreed that Peake used "Dickensian caricature." Stephen J. Laut believed that "the characters are as wild a collection of grotesques as one could find." "Mr. Peake's style," Ruth Teiser of the *San Francisco Chronicle* commented, "is marvelous to a degree. . . . His inventiveness, his ingenuity, and his humor are astonishing." Carter praised "the florid richness of the prose," while Ostermann noted Peake's "language and scenes [that] combine the lyrical and the monstrous."

Overall, the *Gormenghast Trilogy* is highly considered by several critics. Price called it an "odd minor masterpiece," and Ostermann judged it "an eccentric, poetic masterpiece." R. G. Davis of the *New York Times* remarked that "Peake liberates and elevates as well as charms." Writing in the *Spectator,* J. W. M. Thompson stated that Peake has "a secure place among that precious line of originals . . . who resist classification and fashion, and go their own ways."

MEDIA ADAPTATIONS: Titus Groan, Mr. Pye, and *Rhyme of the Flying Bomb* were adapted as radio plays; Peake's poems were adapted by James Milton and Polly Pen for the musical "Songs on a Shipwrecked Sofa," c. 1987.

BIOGRAPHICAL/CRITICAL SOURCES:

BOOKS

Batchelor, John, *Mervyn Peake: A Biographical and Critical Exploration,* Gerald Duckworth, 1974.
Carter, Lin, *Imaginary Worlds,* Ballantine, 1973.
Contemporary Literary Criticism, Gale, Volume VII, 1977, Volume LIV, 1989.
Dictionary of Literary Biography, Volume XV: *British Novelists, 1930-1959,* Gale, 1983.
Gilmore, Maeve, *A World Away: A Memoir,* Gollancz, 1970.
Gilmore, M. and Shelagh Johnson, editors, *Mervyn Peake: Writings and Drawings,* St. Martin's, 1974.
Mervyn Peake, 1911-1968, National Book League, 1972.

Metzger, Arthur, *A Guide to the Gormenghast Trilogy,* T-K Graphics, 1976.
Watney, John Basil, *Mervyn Peake,* St. Martin's, 1976.

PERIODICALS

Best Sellers, November 1, 1967.
Books and Bookmen, February, 1969, March, 1972, April, 1976, April, 1979.
Book World, January 7, 1968.
Cambridge Review, November 23, 1973.
City of San Francisco, February 17, 1976.
Contemporary Review, April, 1968.
Critical Quarterly, spring, 1979.
Detroit News, September 13, 1981.
Listener, December 19, 1974.
National Observer, November 6, 1967, December 11, 1967.
New Statesman, January 26, 1968, November 8, 1974, December 20, 1974, February 16, 1979.
New York Times, November 19, 1968, June 4, 1987.
Observer, April 14, 1968, September 27, 1970, January 28, 1979.
Revue des Langues Vivantes, Number 40, 1974.
Saturday Review, December 16, 1967.
Spectator, December 29, 1967, January 26, 1968, November 11, 1972.
Studio, September, 1946.
Times (London), November 19, 1968, August 5, 1978.
Times Literary Supplement, June 25, 1970, April 21, 1972, January 26, 1973, April 4, 1975.
Unisa English Studies, Volume XII, Number 1, 1974.

*   *   *

PEALE, Norman Vincent 1898-

PERSONAL: Born May 31, 1898, in Bowersville, Ohio; son of Charles Clifford (a physician and minister) and Anna (DeLaney) Peale; married Loretta Ruth Stafford, June 20, 1930; children: Margaret Ann (Mrs. Paul F. Everett), John Stafford (an ordained minister and philosophy professor), Elizabeth Ruth (Mrs. John M. Allen). *Education:* Ohio Wesleyan University, B.A., 1920; Boston University, M.A., 1924, S.T.B., 1924. *Politics:* Republican.

ADDRESSES: Home—1030 Fifth Ave., New York, N.Y. 12564; and "Quaker Hill," Pawling, N.Y. 12564. *Office*—1025 Fifth Ave., New York, N.Y. 10028.

CAREER: Ordained into Methodist Episcopal Church, 1922; *Morning Republican,* Findlay, Ohio, 1920, reporter; *Detroit Journal,* Detroit, Mich., 1920, reporter; pastor in Berkeley, R.I., 1922-24, Brooklyn, N.Y., 1924-27, Syracuse, N.Y., 1927-32; Marble Collegiate Reform Church, New York, N.Y., pastor, 1932-84; writer, 1937—. Chaplain, American Legion, Kings County, N.Y., 1925-27. Co-founder and member, Institutes of Religion and Health; co-founder, Foundation for Christian Living, 1940. Host of a weekly radio program on NBC, "The Art of Living," 1935—, a program on station WOR, 1954-84, and "American Character," 1975—, "Positive Thinking Network, with Norman Vincent Peale," 1981—, "The Angelus Hour," and television programs, "What's Your Trouble," and "Guideposts Presents Norman Vincent Peale." Lecturer on public affairs and personal effectiveness. President of Protestant Council of New York, 1965-69, and the Reformed Church of America, 1969-70. Acting chairman, committee for Constitutional Government; member of executive committee of Presbyterian Ministers Fund for Life Insurance, and trustee, Ohio Wesleyan Uni-

versity and Central College. Technical advisor for film, "One Foot in Heaven," Warner Brothers, 1963.

MEMBER: National Temperance Society (president), American Authors Guild, Lotos Club, Episcopal Actors Guild, Sons of the American Revolution, Ohio Society of New York (president, 1952-55), Rotary Club, Masons, Metropolitan Club, Union League, Alpha Delta, Phi Gamma Delta.

AWARDS, HONORS: Honorary degrees from many institutions, including Duke University, 1938, and Brigham Young University, 1967; numerous awards, including Freedoms Foundation award, 1952, 1955, 1959, 1973, 1974; Horatio Alger award, 1952; American Education award, 1955; Government Service Award for Ohio, 1956; National Salvation Army Award, 1956, 1957; Distinguished Salesman's Award from New York Sales Executives, 1957; International Human Relations Award from the Dale Carnegie Club International, 1958; Clergyman of the Year Award, Religious Foundation of America, 1964; Paul Harris Fellow Award from Rotary International, 1972; Distinguished Patriot Award from Sons of the American Revolution, 1973; Order of Aaron and Hur, Chaplains Corps, U.S. Army, 1975; All-Time Great Ohioan Award, 1976; Family of Man award, 1981, Treasure Award, 1984; Medal of Freedom National Award, 1983; Religion in Media Gold Angel, 1984; Caleb B. Smith Medal of Honor, Grand Lodge of Indiana, 1984; Bowery Savings Bank 150th Anniversary Distinguished New Yorker Award, 1984; International Rotary Award, 1984.

WRITINGS:

SELF-HELP BOOKS

The Art of Living (essays), Abingdon, 1937, new edition published as *The New Art of Living,* Worlds Work, 1975.
You Can Win (essays), Abingdon, 1939.
(With Smiley Blanton) *Faith Is the Answer: A Psychiatrist and a Pastor Discuss Your Problems,* Abingdon-Cokesbury, 1940, enlarged and revised edition, Guideposts Associates, 1955.
A Guide to Confident Living, Prentice-Hall, 1948, reprinted, Fawcett, 1975.
(With Blanton) *The Art of Real Happiness,* Prentice-Hall, 1950, revised edition, Fawcett, 1976.
(Author of introduction) *Guideposts* editors, *What Prayer Can Do,* Doubleday, 1953.
The Power of Positive Thinking, Prentice-Hall, 1952, reprinted, Fawcett, 1976, abridged edition published as *The Power of Positive Thinking for Young People,* Prentice-Hall, 1954.
Inspiring Messages for Daily Living, Prentice-Hall, 1955.
Stay Alive All Your Life, Prentice-Hall, 1957.
The Amazing Results of Positive Thinking, Prentice-Hall, 1959.
(Author of foreword) Blanton, *The Healing Power of Poetry,* Crowell, 1960.
The Tough-Minded Optimist, Prentice-Hall, 1961, revised edition published as *Positive Thinking for a Time Like This,* 1975.
Sin, Sex and Self-Control, Doubleday, 1965.
The Healing of Sorrow, Doubleday, 1966.
Enthusiasm Makes the Difference, Prentice-Hall, 1967.
You Can if You Think You Can, Prentice-Hall, 1974.
The Positive Principle Today: How to Renew and Sustain the Power of Positive Thinking, Prentice-Hall, 1976.
Positive Imaging, Revell, 1981.
Have a Great Day, Revell, 1984.
The Power of Living, Doubleday, 1990.

BOOKS ON THE LIFE OF CHRIST

The Coming of the King (juvenile), Prentice-Hall, 1956.
He Was a Child (juvenile), Prentice-Hall, 1957.
Jesus of Nazareth: A Dramatic Interpretation of His Life from Bethlehem to Calvary, Prentice-Hall, 1966.
The Story of Jesus (juvenile), Gibson, 1976.
The Positive Power of Jesus Christ, Tyndale, 1980.

EDITOR

Guideposts: Personal Messages of Inspiration and Faith, Prentice-Hall, 1948.
The Guideposts Anthology, Guideposts Associates, 1953.
Faith Made Them Champions, Guideposts Associates, 1954.
Sermon on the Mount, engravings by John de Pol, World, 1955.
Unlock Your Faith-Power, Guideposts Associates, 1957.
Guideposts to a Stronger Faith, Guideposts Associates, 1959.

OTHER

Adventures in the Holy Land, Prentice-Hall, 1963.
Norman Vincent Peale's Treasury of Courage and Confidence (anthology), Doubleday, 1970.
Bible Stories (juvenile), F. Watts, 1973.
Norman Vincent Peale's Treasury of Joy and Enthusiasm, Revell, 1981.
The True Joy of Positive Living (autobiography), Morrow, 1984.
My Favorite Quotations, Harper, 1990.

Also editor of several volumes of testimonials from *Guideposts* magazine. Also author of newspaper columns, "Confident Living" and "Positive Thinking." Contributor to periodicals, including *Christian Herald, Reader's Digest, Look.* Publisher and editor-in-chief, *Guideposts* magazine, New York City, 1945—; publisher with wife, Ruth Stafford Peale, of *PLUS: The Magazine for Positive Thinking.*

SIDELIGHTS: Norman Vincent Peale is "one of the most noted preachers of the century . . . [and] one of the most influential Americans of our age," writes a *Parade* contributor. One of the first religious leaders to recognize the potential of mass media, Peale has used books, television, and radio, along with the pulpit, to communicate to Americans his message of self-help through positive thinking and prayer. Peale is a dynamic speaker, and his sermons have helped increase membership in every church in which he has served. As minister for three years in a struggling Brooklyn congregation, Peale collected enough funds to build a new church, while raising membership from forty to nearly nine hundred. In 1932, he became pastor of the historic but decaying New York City Marble Collegiate Church, where he initially preached to five hundred people. But by the end of his fifty year pastorate, closed circuit television had been installed to accommodate the more than four thousand people attending the church.

Peale's primary success came with *The Power of Positive Thinking,* the most famous of his many books stressing the cultivation of a positive attitude as the key to happiness. As have many self-help writers, Peale happened upon his principles through working on his own problems. "I was a very shy, self-doubting boy," he told Miriam Berkley for *Publishers Weekly,* "and I put myself down all the time. It's a miserable way to live. I went out and I prayed and I told the Lord if he could turn a drunk into a sober person and a thief into an honest man, he could certainly help me get over this terrible thing. I struggled with it a long time, then got the answer. So I wrote a book. Since the answer was faith, I wanted faith in the title and called it *The Power of Faith.*" Peale disliked the book after finishing it, however, and threw it

in the waste basket. But, as Peale told Berkley, his wife, Ruth, retrieved the manuscript and took it to Myron Boardman of Prentice-Hall, who "came to me and said, 'Who do you want this book to be read by, church people?' I said 'No, everybody.' 'Well,' he said, '*The Power of Faith* won't do it.' " Boardman decided that 'positive thinking' was a recurrent theme in the book, and chose it for the title.

The Power of Positive Thinking soared to the top of the *New York Times* best seller list, where it remained for three years, breaking the previous all-time record set by Lloyd Douglas' novel, *The Robe.* As Georgia Dullea puts it in the *New York Times, The Power of Positive Thinking* "became a model for self-help books." Although "over the years, the concept of positive thinking has been variously dismissed by religious and secular critics as simplistic and selfish, as using religion to gain fame or wealth," observes Dullea, sales of the book have now topped fifteen million copies worldwide. Douglas T. Miller in the *Journal of Popular Culture,* explains the minister's approach to problems: "The underlying assumption of Peale's teaching was that nearly all basic problems were personal, the result of inner conflicts and especially 'negative thinking.' We 'manufacture our own unhappiness,' he told readers. 'By our thoughts and attitudes we distill out of the ingredients of life either happiness or unhappiness for ourselves.' 'Unhappiness' could be avoided by following one of his simple formulas. As he wrote in the introduction to *The Power of Positive Thinking,* 'you do not need to be defeated by anything . . . you can have peace of mind, improved health, and a never-ceasing flow of energy. . . . By using the techniques outlined here you can modify or change the circumstances in which you now live, assuming control over them. . . . You will become more popular, esteemed, and well-liked individual." Peale, while not overstating his book's literary merit, believes strongly in its message. "I don't think this is the greatest work of art or literature that ever came down the road," he told the *Parade* interviewer. "But it has sensible principles. If a person were to live by it, he wouldn't be free of trouble, but he'd know how to handle trouble. He'd have a good life."

Peale also broke new ground, and irritated some religious leaders, by using psychology in counseling parishioners. In the 1930s, Peale began working with psychiatrist Dr. Smiley Blanton to initiate a religio-psychiatric outpatient clinic, which eventually became the nonprofit Institutes of Religion and Health. Staffed by clergymen of all denominations, psychiatrists and social workers, the organization treats approximately six hundred patients a week at its New York City headquarters, and has established branches in Harlem, Chicago, and Green Bay, Wisconsin.

In a *Los Angeles Times* interview with Beth Ann Krier, J. Harold Ellens, the founder and editor of the *Journal of Psychology and Christianity* observes, "It is a very significant fact that Dr. Peale was three-quarters of a century ahead of the times with his emphasis on the relationship between psychology and religious experience. He saw psychology and Christian experience as very compatible . . . he had the courage to stand pat on this position in spite of the opposition of the entire Christian church for nearly half a century. His genius was that he . . . translated psychotheology into the language of the people."

Peale's message also appears monthly in *Guideposts* magazine. According to a *New Yorker* contributor, "Each month, *Guideposts* features inspiring stories of people who have walked up to adversity and kicked it." Founded by the Peales in conjunction with Lowell Thomas, Thomas E. Dewey, Raymond Thornburg, and Captain Eddie Rickbacker in 1945, the magazine started as a four-page spiritual newsletter for businessmen. It now runs forty-eight pages, with a circulation of about four and a half million and an estimated readership of fourteen and a half million. In 1940, the Peales founded the Foundation for Christian Living, which distributes Peale's numerous books and those of other writers, as well as publishing an inspirational magazine, *PLUS: The Magazine of Positive Thinking.*

Peale's autobiography, *The True Joy of Positive Living* sums up a lifetime of work spent in attempting to improve people's lives. While it is filled with anecdotes about the minister's acquaintances, both famous and unknown, "one emerges from it with little private knowledge of the public man," writes Berkley. But John Fraunces in *Best Sellers* finds *The True Joy of Positive Living* "an unconscious telling of how [Peale's] personality developed, and how this very unusual man came to be an integral part of the American scene. . . . In this book he makes it sound as if Christ himself were speaking rather than a practiced, polished preacher."

Oddly enough, Peale does not see himself as the outgoing, constantly cheerful figure that he portrays. "Oh, I live in misery," he told Dullea. "But I overcome it by affirmations, by 'imaging,' by positive thinking. I suppose the day I'm lying in my casket the minister could say, 'Here's a shy boy.' "

MEDIA ADAPTATIONS: Excerpts of *The Power of Positive Thinking* were recorded for RCA Victor in 1953.

BIOGRAPHICAL/CRITICAL SOURCES:

BOOKS

Authors in the News, Volume 1, Gale, 1976.
Davis, Elisabeth L., *Fathers of America,* Revell, 1958.
Gordon, Arthur, *Norman Vincent Peale: Minister to Millions,* Prentice-Hall, 1958.
Peale, Norman Vincent, *The Power of Positive Thinking,* Prentice-Hall, 1952.
Westphal, Clarence, *Norman Vincent Peale: Christian Crusader,* Denison, 1964.

PERIODICALS

American, June, 1949.
Best Sellers, November, 1984, August, 1986.
Booklist, February 1, 1982, August, 1984.
Cleveland Press, March 9, 1974.
Good Housekeeping, January, 1956.
Journal of Popular Culture, summer, 1975.
Los Angeles Times, June 5, 1988.
Los Angeles Times Book Review, December 9, 1984.
Newsweek, December 28, 1953.
New Yorker, February 25, 1985.
New York Times, May 26, 1988.
Parade, May 17, 1987.
Publishers Weekly, January 14, 1974, July 12, 1976, September 28, 1984.
Quarterly Journal of Speech, December, 1954.
Reader's Digest, February, 1954.
Time, November 1, 1954.
Washington Post Book World, October 17, 1982.
West Coast Review of Books, February, 1982.

PEARSON, Andrew Russell 1897-1969
(Drew Pearson)

PERSONAL: Born December 13, 1897, in Evanston, Ill.; died September 1, 1969, in Washington, D.C.; buried in Potomac, Md.; son of Paul Martin and Edna (Wolfe) Pearson; married Countess Felicia Gizycka, March 12, 1925 (divorced); married Luvie Moore, November 12, 1936; children: (first marriage) Ellen Pearson Arnold. *Education:* Swarthmore College, A.B., 1919. *Religion:* Quaker.

CAREER: Director of American Friends Service Committee in Serbia, Montenegro, and Albania, 1919-21; University of Pennsylvania, Philadelphia, instructor in industrial geography, 1921-22; Columbia University, New York, N.Y., lecturer in commercial geography, 1924; staff member, *United States Daily,* 1926-33, and *Baltimore Sun,* Baltimore, Md., 1929-32; author with Robert S. Allen of syndicated newspaper column "Washington Merry-Go-Round," 1932-42, sole author of column, beginning 1942, author with Jack Anderson, 1965-69. Occasional correspondent in Far East and Europe, 1922-31 and 1942-59; interviewed "Europe's Twelve Greatest Men" for newspaper syndicate, 1923, and also Premier Khrushchev, 1961 and 1963, President Tito, 1962, the King and Queen of Greece, and Premier Fanfani of Italy; accompanied President Kennedy to Venezuela and Colombia, 1962. Weekly radio commentator, beginning 1935. Organized Friendship Train to Europe, 1947-48; president, Food for Peace Committee, beginning 1961; secretary, America's Conscience Fund, beginning 1963; president of Washington, D.C., chapter, Big Brothers. *Military service:* U.S. Army, 1918.

MEMBER: International Platform Association (president, 1950), Overseas Writers, National Press Club, Circus Fans of America, Phi Beta Kappa, Kappa Sigma, Delta Sigma Rho, Cosmos Club (Washington, D.C.).

AWARDS, HONORS: LL.D., Harding College, 1945, and William Jewell College, 1948; Sigma Delta Chi national award for best Washington journalism, 1942; Father of the Year, 1948; Knights of Columbus International Gold Medal, 1948; French Legion of Honor; First Order Star of Solidarity (Italian Republic); Variety Club Heart of Gold Award, 1963; Pulitzer Prize nomination (with Jack Anderson) for national reporting, 1967, for articles on U.S. Senator Thomas J. Dodd.

WRITINGS:

UNDER NAME DREW PEARSON

(With Robert S. Allen) *Washington Merry-Go-Round,* Liveright, 1931.
(With Allen) *More Merry-Go-Round,* Liveright, 1932.
(With Constantine Brown) *The American Diplomatic Game,* Doubleday, Doran, 1935.
(With Allen) *The Nine Old Men,* Doubleday, Doran, 1937, reprinted, Da Capo Press, 1974.
(With Allen) *Nine Old Men at the Crossroads,* Doubleday, Doran, 1937, reprinted, Da Capo Press, 1974.
(With Jack Anderson) *U.S.A.: Second-Class Power?,* Simon & Schuster, 1958.
(With Anderson) *The Case against Congress,* Simon & Schuster, 1968.
(With Gerald Green) *The Senator* (novel), Doubleday, 1968.
(With Green) *The President* (novel), Doubleday, 1970.
Diaries: 1949-1959, edited by Tyler Abell, Holt, 1974.

Also author with Robert S. Allen of comic strip "Hap Hazard," 1941, and of radio program "News for the Americas," National

Broadcasting Co., Inc., 1941; author of television films "Report on the Holy Land," "Report on Alaska," and "The Gentle Persuaders." Editor of weekly newsletter, *Personal from Pearson,* beginning 1953. Contributor to magazines.

SIDELIGHTS: The most widely read columnist of his day, Drew Pearson specialized in reporting what the *New Republic*'s C. W. Gilbert once called "the gossip which the Capital loves to whisper but hates to see in print." At its peak, his "Washington Merry-Go-Round" feature ran in six hundred papers seven days a week, reaching an audience of about forty million people. During the course of his long career, Pearson's "aggressive, raucous, and occasionally sensational" exposes (as another *New Republic* writer described them) led some 275 people to file more than $200 million worth of lawsuits against the columnist, only one of which he lost—for $50,000. Vilified by those he attacked (including J. Edgar Hoover, Robert Kennedy, and Joseph McCarthy) and praised by those who escaped his eye for scandal, Pearson regarded himself as a "voice for the voiceless," or, as *Time*'s Michael Demarest stated, "a kind of national ombudsman." But his greatest contribution was not the *amount* of wrongdoing he exposed; more important, noted Demarest, was the fact that Pearson's "impassioned" approach to weeding out corruption in government circles established "a pattern of investigative reporting [that] permanently emboldened American journalism."

Heir to a crusading tradition that made its first appearance in America around the turn of the century, Pearson launched his career in 1931 when he teamed up with fellow reporter Robert S. Allen to produce an anonymous, gossipy account of behind-the-scenes life in Washington, *The Washington Merry-Go-Round.* Pearson, then with the *Baltimore Sun,* and Allen, a *Christian Science Monitor* bureau chief, packed their controversial book with inside material on the Hoover administration that their own papers had refused to publish. After they were revealed as the authors of *The Washington Merry-Go-Round,* both men were fired from their respective newspapers. A short time later, however, Pearson and Allen signed up with United Features to write a syndicated column (also called "Washington Merry-Go-Round") modeled after their original collaboration. The two men worked together on the column for the next ten years; when Allen joined the Army in 1942, Pearson began writing alone and continued to do so until the late 1950s when one of his investigators, Jack Anderson, became his associate. Anderson then took over the column after Pearson's death in 1969.

Most observers, even those who felt, such as Demarest, that Pearson "was often unfair, egotistical and quixotic" in his relentless pursuit of government figures, agreed that "for all his vanities and vendettas, [he] was a valuable man." The *Washington Post,* for example, remarked that "he was a moralist who was proud to be a muckraker," a man who exhibited "the conscience of a Quaker and the touch of a stevedore" during "his extraordinary career as the most successful, in many ways the most effective, and certainly the most controversial journalist of his time. . . . Most of the time he had the right targets and the right causes, and he brought to his crusades a powerful, innovative and relentless force." As the *New York Times Book Review* C. V. Shannon declared: "[Pearson] had the curiosity, the physical energy, the quickness of mind and the gritty determination to be on top of every story and to elbow himself to the front of every crowd that mark the journalist in his purest form." To the *Chicago Tribune Book World*'s Robert Sherrill, Pearson was simply "the greatest muckraker of all time. Woodward and Bernstein may have toppled Richard Nixon, but as practitioners of muckraking they are drab apprentices compared to Pearson. . . .

[But he] was not merely a muckraker; he was the embodiment of everything in the unregenerate press that politicians and corporate malefactors hate and fear—and grudgingly respect. Reporting was just one gun in his arsenal. He was also [, according to his longtime colleague Jack Anderson,] the 'maximum politic—part intelligence sleuth, part commentator, part lobbyist, part conspirator, part caucus-master.' In his quiet, Quaker fashion he could play dirty as hell."

Not everyone, however, was willing to overlook Pearson's "dirty play" as he set out to demonstrate that the end justifies the means. The *Saturday Review*'s M. W. Childs, for example, once noted that the columnist habitually displayed "an unfortunate self-righteousness, which comes out in his telling of his own propaganda exploits." This self-righteousness often led him to attack someone *before* he had proof of any criminal wrongdoing. While this may, in retrospect, seem unimportant to many in the case of a Senator Joseph McCarthy, there were times, as the *New Republic*'s Joseph Nocera pointed out, when "the vendettas, the politicking, the steady stream of columns were used on dozens of politicians far less evil than McCarthy."

One of these targets was James Forrestal, Roosevelt's secretary of the Navy and Truman's secretary of defense. Explained Joe Klein of the *New York Times Book Review:* "It wasn't that Forrestal had done anything specific or illegal to offend Pearson; it was merely that Pearson disliked his Wall Street, rightwing style, and *sensed* there was corruption somewhere in Forrestal's past." Over a period of several years, Pearson pursued Forrestal in a manner even Jack Anderson characterized as full of "low blows" that occasionally descended to the level of "poison gas." In the end, Nocera recalled, "Forrestal cracked, committed suicide, and a large portion of the blame was placed squarely on Pearson."

Whether they admired or despised him, most observers agree that there will never be another journalist quite like Drew Pearson. To Arthur Cooper of *Newsweek,* he was "that rare combination of showman and newsman, and every day his pungent blend of punditry and titillating gossip would set off quaking shocks on the Washington seismograph. He had the power to enrage presidents and unmake senators. . . . But unlike I. F. Stone, Drew Pearson was not content merely to exorcise the corruptors, grafters and scoundrels from the corridors of power. He demanded entree to those corridors himself in order to effect changes in government policy. Which is why Pearson was something more than a journalist—and something less." Concluded Cooper: "It is unlikely—and this may not be a bad thing—that any newsman will ever again wield as much influence as Pearson."

BIOGRAPHICAL/CRITICAL SOURCES:

BOOKS

Anderson, Jack, and James Boyd, *Confessions of a Muckraker: The Inside Story of Life in Washington during the Truman, Eisenhower, Kennedy and Johnson Years,* Random House, 1979.

PERIODICALS

American Political Science Review, June, 1935.
Atlantic Bookshelf, April, 1935.
Best Sellers, August 15, 1968, October 1, 1968, September 15, 1970.
Bookman, September, 1931.
Books, January 20, 1935, November 8, 1936.
Boston Transcript, January 19, 1935.

Chicago Tribune Book World, May 6, 1979.
Current History, December, 1936.
Forum, September, 1931, March, 1935.
Life, August 9, 1968.
Listener, February 6, 1975.
Nation, August 26, 1931, February 13, 1935, September 23, 1968.
National Observer, October 28, 1968.
National Review, December 31, 1968.
New Republic, August 12, 1931, December 23, 1936, October 13, 1958, October 5, 1968, June 30, 1979.
Newsweek, October 21, 1968, February 25, 1974.
New Yorker, September 28, 1968, February 25, 1974.
New York Herald Tribune Book Review, December 7, 1958.
New York Review of Books, February 13, 1969.
New York Times, July 26, 1931, January 27, 1935, September 2, 1972.
New York Times Book Review, July 28, 1968, March 17, 1974, May 20, 1979.
Outlook, July 29, 1931.
Review, July 28, 1968, March 17, 1974, May 20, 1979.
San Francisco Chronicle, October 13, 1958.
Saturday Review, October 18, 1958, November 9, 1968.
Saturday Review of Literature, September 5, 1931, January 19, 1935.
Spectator, January 18, 1975.
Survey, December 1, 1931.
Time, December 13, 1948, August 23, 1968, March 4, 1974.
Times Literary Supplement, August 29, 1935.
Washington Post, August 8, 1968, October 10, 1968, September 11, 1970.
Washington Post Book World, August 11, 1968, June 17, 1979.
Yale Law Journal, January, 1937.

OBITUARIES:

PERIODICALS

New York Times, September 2, 1969.
London Times, September 2, 1969.
Variety, September 3, 1969.
Washington Post, September 3, 1969.

*   *   *

PEARSON, Drew
See PEARSON, Andrew Russell

*   *   *

PEDERSEN, Knut   1859-1952
(Knut Hamsun, Knut Pedersen Hamsund)

PERSONAL: Born August 4, 1859, in Lom, Norway; died February 19, 1952, in Grimstad, Norway; married Bergljot Bech, 1898 (marriage ended, 1906); married Marie Andersen (an actress), 1909; children: (first marriage) Victoria; (second marriage) Tore, Arild, two daughters.

ADDRESSES: Home—Grimstad, Norway.

CAREER: Writer. Worked as clerk, peddler, shoemaker's apprentice, sheriff's assistant, schoolteacher, and construction worker in Norway, 1874-82; coal trimmer, country schoolteacher, salesman, longshoreman, civil servant, and road and farm worker in midwest United States, 1882-86; lecturer in Norway, 1886; lecturer in Minneapolis, Minn., harvester in North Dakota, and horse car conductor in Chicago, Ill., 1886-88; farmer in Norway, 1918-52.

AWARDS, HONORS: Nobel Prize for literature, 1920.

WRITINGS:

COLLECTED WORKS; UNDER PSEUDONYM KNUT HAMSUN

Samlede verker (fifteen volumes), Gyldendal, 1954-56.

NOVELS; UNDER PSEUDONYM KNUT HAMSUN

Den Gaadefulde (title means "The Mysterious One"), M. Urdal, 1877.
Bjoerger, privately printed, 1878.
Sult, [first published in 1890], A. Cammermeyer, 1899, translation by George Egerton published as *Hunger,* Knopf, 1920, reprinted, Rupa, 1949, translation by Robert Bly, with introduction by Isaac Bashevis Singer, published by Farrar, Straus, 1967.
Mysterier, Gyldendal, 1892, translation by Arthur G. Chater published as *Mysteries,* Knopf, 1927, translation by Gerry Bothmer published by Farrar, Straus, 1971.
Redaktoer Lynge (title means "Editor Lynge"), [first published in 1893], A. Cammermeyer, 1901.
Ny jord, [first published in 1893], A. Cammermeyer, 1900, translation by Carl Christian Hyllested published as *Shallow Soil,* Scribner, 1914.
Pan, af Loeitnant Thomas Glahn's papirer, [first published in 1894], A. Cammermeyer, 1901, translation by W. W. Worster published as *Pan,* Gyldendal, 1920, Knopf, 1921, translation by James W. McFarlane published as *Pan, From Lieutenant Thomas Glahn's Papers,* Artemis Press, 1955, Farrar, Straus, 1956.
Victoria: En kaerligheds historie, [first published in 1898], A. Cammermeyer, 1902, translation by Chatel published as *Victoria,* Knopf, 1923, translation by Oliver Stallybrass published by Farrar, Straus, 1969.
I aeventyrland (title means "In Wonderland"), 1903.
Svaermere, Gyldendal, 1904, translation by Worster published as *Dreamers,* Knopf, 1921 (published in England as *Mothwise,* Gyldendal, 1921).
Under hoestsjernen, [first published in 1906], translation by Worster published as *Under the Autumn Sky in Wanderers* (includes *A Wanderer Plays on Muted Strings;* also see below), Knopf, 1922 (also see below).
Benoni, Gyldendal, 1908, translation by Chater published as *Benoni,* Knopf, 1925 (also see below).
Rosa, af student Parelius' papirer (title means "Rosa: From Student Parelius's Papers"), Gyldendal, 1908, translation by Chater published as *Rosa,* Knopf, 1925 (also see below).
En Vandrer spiller med sordin, Gyldendal, 1909, translation by Chater published as *A Wanderer Plays on Muted Strings* in *Wanderers* (includes *Under the Autumn Sky*), Knopf, 1922 (also see below).
Den siste glaede, Gyldendal, 1912, translation by Paula Wiking published as *Look Back on Happiness,* Coward-McCann, 1940.
Boern av tiden, Gyldendal, 1913, translation by J. S. Scott published as *Children of the Age,* Knopf, 1924.
Segelfoss by, Gyldendal, 1915, translation by Scott published as *Segelfoss Town,* Knopf, 1925.
Markens groede, Gyldendal, 1917, translation by Worster published as *Growth of the Soil,* Knopf, 1920, Souvenir Press, 1989.
Konerne ved vandposten, Gyldendal, 1920, translation by Chater published as *The Woman at the Pump,* Knopf, 1928, trans-

lation by Stallybrass and Stallybrass published by Farrar, Straus, 1978.

Siste kapitel, Gyldendal, 1923, translation by Chater published as *Chapter the Last,* Knopf, 1929.

Landstrykere, Gyldendal, 1927, translation by Eugene Gay-Tifft published as *Vagabonds,* Coward-McCann, 1930, translation by McFarlane published as *Wayfarers,* Farrar, Straus, 1980.

August, Gyldendal, 1930, translation by Gay-Tifft published as *August,* Coward-McCann, 1931.

Benoni [and] *Rosa,* Knopf, 1932.

Men livet lever, Gyldendal, 1933, translation by Gay-Tifft published as *The Road Leads On,* Coward-McCann, 1934.

Ringen sluttet, Gyldendal, 1936, translation by Gay-Tifft published as *The Ring Is Closed,* Coward-McCann, 1937.

The Wanderer (contains *Under the Autumn Sky* and *A Wanderer Plays on Muted Strings*), translated by Stallybrass and Gunnvor Stallybrass, Farrar, Straus, 1975.

PLAYS; IVAR KARENO TRILOGY; UNDER PSEUDONYM KNUT HAMSUN

Ved rigets port (title means "At the Gate of the Kingdom"; first published in 1895), A. Cammermeyer, 1902.

Livets spil (title means "Game of Life"; first published in 1896), A. Cammermeyer, 1902.

"Aftenroede" (title means "Red of Evening"), 1898.

OTHER PLAYS; UNDER PSEUDONYM KNUT HAMSUN

"Munken Vendt" (title means "Vendt the Monk"), 1902.

"Droning Tamara" (title means "Tamara the Queen"), 1903.

Livet i vold, Gyldendal, 1910, translation by Graham Rawson and Tristan Rawson published as *In the Grip of Life,* Knopf, 1924.

OTHER; UNDER PSEUDONYM KNUT HAMSUN, UNLESS OTHERWISE NOTED

Fra det moderne Amerikas aandslive (essays), P. G. Philipsens, 1889, translation by Barbara Gordon Morgridge published as *The Cultural Life of Modern America,* Harvard University Press, 1969.

Siesta (short stories), 1897.

Kratskog (short stories; title means "Brushwood"), 1903.

Det vilde Kor (poetry; title means "The Wild Chorus"), 1904.

Stridende Liv (short stories; title means "Struggling Life"), 1905.

Dikte (poetry), 1921.

Artikler (articles), Gyldendal, 1939, reprinted, 1966.

Paa gjengrodde stier (memoirs), Gyldendal, 1949, translation by Carl L. Anderson published as *On Overgrown Paths,* Paul Eriksson, 1967.

Brev til Marie (correspondence), Aschehoug, 1970.

Contributor to periodicals—once, inadvertently, under pseudonym Knut Pedersen Hamsund—including *Ny jord* and *Samtiden.*

SIDELIGHTS: Knut Hamsun is considered to be the greatest novelist Scandinavia has ever produced. Certainly he is one of the very few Scandinavian writers—along with his fellow Norwegians, the playwright Henrik Ibsen and the novelist Sigrid Undset, and the Swedish playwright August Strindberg—who have acquired a truly international reputation. Hamsun was one of the pioneers of psychological literature and employed techniques such as stream-of-consciousness and interior monologue that would be associated in the twentieth century with Virginia Woolf and James Joyce, who used them *after* Hamsun did. Adept at portraying the "isolated individual"—himself—in the

1890s, Hamsun in his mature years turned his attention to the environment, producing "social novels" that capture the flavor of northern Norway while exposing the ills of industrialized society. Although his sympathy for Nazi Germany cast a pall over his reputation, Hamsun's literary innovations, his versatility, and his mastery of style in his more than thirty-five volumes ensure his place at the top of the Scandinavian Olympus.

Knut Hamsun was born Knut Pedersen in Lom, Gudbrandsdal, on August 4, 1859. When he was four years old his family moved to Hamaroey in Nordland, above the Arctic circle. The family was impoverished and moved because Hamsun's relatively wealthy uncle, who lived in Hamaroey, invited the Pedersens to farm property he owned.

In 1868, at the age of nine, Hamsun was separated from his family and taken to live with this uncle, Hans Olsen, who needed the boy's help at a post office he also ran. Because Hamsun's parents were in debt to Olsen, they could not intervene. Hans Olsen starved and beat his nephew, however, and Hamsun later attributed his chronic nervous difficulties to childhood malnutrition suffered while living with his uncle. Even in his last work, *On Overgrown Paths,* written at the age of eighty-nine, Hamsun referred to the suffering he endured in his uncle's home.

Hamsun finally escaped to Lom in 1874 and thereafter followed five years of wandering and itinerant work: he was a clerk in stores, a peddler in northern Norway, a shoemaker's apprentice, an assistant to a sheriff, and an elementary school teacher. These experiences provided the background for his fine novels of life in northern Norway.

In 1877 Hamsun published his first book, *Den gaadefulde* ("The Mysterious One"). The following year a poem, "Et gjensyn" ("A Reunion"), and a second novel, *Bjoerger,* were published. These early novels were the thinly disguised daydreams of a lonely youth cut off from family and society. The autobiographical nature of the works has been emphasized by Rolf Nyboe Nettum in *Konflikt og visjon: Hovedtemaer i Knut Hamsuns foifatterskap, 1890-1912* ("Conflict and Vision: Main Themes in Knut Hamsun's Authorship 1890-1912"), and the links between these early "daydreams" and the great outsider-novels of the 1890s have been exposed by Jan Marstrander in a Norwegian doctoral dissertation, *Livskamp og virkelighetsoppfatning i Knut Hamsuns tidligste forfatterskap* ("Existential Struggle and the Perception of Reality in Knut Hamsun's Earliest Works").

These early works have little value other than to offer insight into the psychological makeup of the adolescent Hamsun. It is no wonder that a young man who had been cut off from family at an early age, had been deprived of the company of his peers, and had moved from one temporary job to another should come to see himself as an outsider and outcast. His feelings of inferiority resulted from his lack of formal education and his humble position in society. In 1879 he left Nordland for the south, where he worked building roads, nearly starving in Oslo during the winter of 1879 and later during the winter of 1886. These experiences would bear fruit in the autobiographical novel *Hunger,* Hamsun's first major work.

While a construction worker in the early 1880s, Hamsun read voraciously in local libraries and began to hold literary lectures for small audiences. In 1882 he immigrated to America with dreams of literary success—dreams that were shattered. In America he found hard physical labor and no literary recognition. When a doctor told him he was dying of consumption, he returned, in the fall of 1884, to Norway, where he recovered and published an article on Mark Twain under the name of Knut Pedersen Hamsund. The "d" on the end of his surname was omitted by the printer and thereafter the Norwegian author was known as Knut Hamsun. During the summer of 1886, Hamsun again traveled as a literary lecturer, and in August of that year he returned to America, where he worked as a farm laborer, as a streetcar conductor in Chicago, and as a journalist in Minneapolis. In the summer of 1888, Hamsun left America permanently and settled in Copenhagen, where the first chapters of *Hunger* were published anonymously in the journal *Ny jord.* In 1889 Hamsun delivered anti-American lectures before the Students' Association in Copenhagen, and that year his lectures were published as a book, *On the Cultural Life of Modern America.*

His bitter experiences in America (the spirit of which he later contrasted with the self-sufficient quietism of the Near East) contributed significantly to Hamsun's increasingly reactionary political views. The environmental pollution, noise, and apparent superficiality of industrialized America would become permanent targets of Hamsun's ire in works written after the turn of the century. The importance of Hamsun's years in America for his development as author and citizen has been stressed by Harald S. Naess in *Hamsun og Amerika* ("Hamsun and America") and in his introductory biography, *Knut Hamsun.* In the 1920s Hamsun rescinded some of his more virulent comments on America and admitted that he had, in fact, learned much in that country. Naess theorizes that the irony and humor of Hamsun's social novels was learned in America from Mark Twain.

The year 1890 was pivotal for Hamsun. The full novel *Hunger* was published and made him famous, and an article, "Fra det ubevisste Sjeleliv" ("From the Unconscious Life of the Mind"), in the journal *Samtiden* presented his literary views. This article foreshadowed literary lectures that Hamsun would hold throughout Norway in 1891, lectures in which he attacked the "four greats" (Henrik Ibsen, Bjoernstjerne Bjoernson, Alexander Kielland, and Jonas Lie) of Norwegian literature and the naturalist literature of the 1880s. Hamsun argued that externals of plot were not important; rather, importance lay in the portrayal of the mind (even the subconscious) of one individual.

In this article Hamsun called for the abandonment of "types" and for the description of the modern, complex individual: "Now what if literature on the whole began to deal a little more with mental states than with engagements and balls and hikes and accidents as such? Then one would, to be sure, have to relinquish creating types, as all have been created before, 'characters' whom one meets every day at the fishmarket. . . . But in return . . . we would experience a little more of the secret movements which are unnoticed in the remote places of the soul, the capricious disorder of perception, the delicate life of fantasy held under the magnifying glass, the wandering of these thoughts and feelings out of the blue; motionless, trackless journeys with the brain and the heart, strange activities of the nerves, the whispering of the blood, the pleading of the bones, the entire unconscious life." In the same article, Hamsun describes phenomena that can be experienced by sensitive, impressionable individuals—"a sudden, unnatural staring in to locked kingdoms which open up"—and he stresses the importance of ephemeral sensations: "They are often too fleeting to be seized and held fast, they last a second, a minute, they come and go like blinking lights; but they have made a mark, produced a sensation, before they disappeared." Hamsun refers to such phenomena as "these almost imperceptible Mimosa-like movements of the soul." Having rejected the literature of social criticism of the preceding generation, Hamsun called for a new psychological literature.

In accordance with his stated literary views he produced several great novels during the 1890s: *Hunger,* 1890; *Mysteries,* 1892; *Pan,* 1894; and *Victoria,* 1898. In these works he attempted to illustrate his literary program. These novels all depict gifted outsiders, most of whom are poets and all of whom bear a striking resemblance to Hamsun himself. These heroes are self-destructive in erotic relationships, unsuccessful at integrating themselves into the community, lacking in family roots, and without prestige or self-esteem. One of them (Tangen of *Hunger*) flees the site of his suffering, two of them (Nagel of *Mysteries* and Glahn of *Pan*) commit suicide, and another, Johannes of *Victoria,* succeeds as a poet by renouncing love and accepting his isolation.

Hamsun himself can easily be identified in the protagonists of his early works: *Hunger* is an autobiographical account of experiences suffered in Oslo and Copenhagen; many of Hamsun's short stories are first-person accounts of real-life experiences; letters written by Hamsun parallel Nagel's statements in *Mysteries.* In fact, Tore Hamsun wrote in his biography of his father that "Nagel . . . is Hamsun himself." The wanderer in the second work of the wanderer trilogy, *A Wanderer Plays on Muted Strings* (1909), is even identified as "Knut Pedersen from Nordland." A knowledge of Hamsun's unhappy childhood and years of frustration, struggle, and starvation in Norway, Denmark, and America renders the desperation of such heroes as Tangen, Nagel, and Glahn even more poignant. Nagel calls himself "a stranger to existence" and "a foreigner among my fellow men." Not only are the heroes of the 1890s and the wanderer of the trilogy written in the first decade of the twentieth century outsiders, they are also curiously passive and seem to accept their unhappiness and failure without protest. Nettum has pointed out this self-destructive passivity in *Konflikt og visjon,* and the theme of the outsider has been thoroughly treated by Jan Marstrander in *Det ensomme menneske i Knut Hamsuns diktning* ("The Isolated Individual in Knut Hamsun's Fiction").

To portray effectively an individual from the inside out, Hamsun not only employed the technique of interior monologue but also devoted much space in his works of the 1890s to dreams, hallucinations, and descriptions of his protagonists' poetic creations. The action sometimes takes place on various planes of time, as in *Pan,* which records events that took place years before the central action of the book and ends with an epilogue after the hero's death. Fragments of memory or fantasy interrupt the narrative in many works. The novels of the 1890s were practical applications of Hamsun's views on literature as outlined in the article on the subconscious from 1890 and in the lectures of 1891. His techniques foreshadowed so much that has become standard fare in the twentieth century that Isaac Bashevis Singer wrote in the introduction to Robert Bly's translation of *Sult* (*Hunger*): "He [Hamsun] is the father of the modern school of literature in every respect—his subjectiveness, his fragmentarism, his use of flashbacks, his lyricism. The whole modern school of fiction in the twentieth century stems from Hamsun."

Although the autobiographical wanderer books—*Under the Autumn Star,* 1907; *A Wanderer Plays on Muted Strings,* 1909; and *Look Back on Happiness,* 1912—retained the outsider protagonist of the 1890s, Hamsun's work changed after the turn of the century. Instead of endeavoring to penetrate the mind of one individual with whom he identified, Hamsun now began to turn his attention to the outside world. From defense of the outsider he moved to criticism of the environment.

In 1893 he had written two realistic novels, *Editor Lynge* and *Shallow Soil.* After the negative reception that *Mysteries* received in 1892, Hamsun was bitter enough to strike back. Olav Thommesen, the editor of *Verdens gang,* accused Hamsun of being a charlatan, and *Editor Lynge,* the story of an unscrupulous, sensation-mongering newspaper editor, is widely considered to be a roman a clef attacking Thommesen. *Shallow Soil* rails at artists as a whole, portraying them as unprincipled parasites living off the naive businessmen who actually are the creative people.

After the turn of the century, social novels with an omniscient narrator became the norm. Among Hamsun's most popular works in Norway are those set in the northern part of the country, the locale of Hamsun's childhood and adolescence. In these novels Hamsun employs local dialect, irony, and humor. *Dreamers* appeared in 1904, followed in four years by *Benoni* and *Rosa.* *Children of the Age* was published in 1913 and two years later its sequel, *Segelfoss Town,* appeared. In 1917 *Growth of the Soil* came out, followed in the early 1920s by *The Women at the Pump* and *Chapter the Last.* Perhaps the most famous of the novels set in northern Norway comprise the August trilogy, published between 1927 and 1933: *Vagabonds, August,* and *The Road Leads On.* After those successful, colorful works, there appeared in 1936 a depressing story of the corruption of modern life, *The Ring Is Closed,* which confirmed a decline in Hamsun's creative powers. His last work, *On Overgrown Paths,* which appeared in 1949, was provoked by political events and was, like his first important work, *Hunger,* a first-person autobiographical account of personal suffering.

The reasons for Hamsun's change in focus and style after the turn of the century are numerous, but aging was a prime factor. Throughout his life Hamsun abhorred the aging process; it is perhaps a cruel wrong that he lived to be ninety-two years old. He believed that after the age of fifty, one was no longer a participant in but only a spectator to life. The autobiographical wanderer books, the first of which was written when Hamsun was forty-eight years old, reflect this attitude.

Perhaps because of his own unhappy childhood, Hamsun was always extremely fond of children and a champion of youth. In some of his short stories and sketches depicting scenes from his own childhood, he maintained that no adult ever suffers as much as an impressionable child does. In 1907, Hamsun delivered a lecture entitled "Aerer de unge" ("Honor the Young") at the Norwegian Students' Union in Oslo, in which he argued that the old should voluntarily make way for the young. After all, had not the elder statesmen of the literary establishment (Ibsen, in particular) tried to block Hamsun's path to success? Hamsun himself, once established as a famous author and secure financially, was extremely generous to younger, unknown writers. When in 1920 he was awarded the Nobel Prize for literature, his acceptance speech in Stockholm was a paean to youth; Tore and Marie Hamsun record that the sixty-one-year old author was bitter at not having received such recognition earlier when he was still young.

Throughout his works Hamsun's obsession with age is apparent: repulsive descriptions of senile old men, Mons and Fredrik Mensa, appear in the novel *Rosa,* and an entire dramatic trilogy of the 1890s—"At the Gates of the Kingdom," 1895; "The Game of Life," 1896; and "Twilight," 1898—laments the loss of youthful idealism and courage. The vital young rebel Kareno of the first play has, by the third play (in which he has reached the dread age of fifty), betrayed his ideals and compromised with the establishment for material comfort. Even more revealing of Hamsun's fears was the play "In the Grip of Life," which appeared in 1910, one year after he had married an actress twenty-three years his junior. The play portrays the moral decline of a

fortyish former actress who is married to a senile old man whom she continually betrays. Age caused Hamsun to turn his gaze away from the isolated individual; it is one of the primary factors in the alterations of style which marked his works of the twentieth century.

Other contributing influences on Hamsun's stylistic evolution were the changes in his personal and professional life: he married and became a father, acquired property, established roots, and achieved literary and financial success. Hamsun had married for the first time in 1898, when he was nearly thirty-nine. Having grown up without family and wandered rootlessly over two continents, he was not yet ready for responsibility, and although his first marriage to Bergljot Bech produced a daughter, Victoria, in 1902, the marriage was dissolved in 1906.

In 1909 Hamsun married the young actress Marie Andersen, whom he had met when she was rehearsing the role of Elina in "The Gates to the Kingdom." This marriage lasted until Hamsun's death, although the twenty-three-year age difference and Hamsun's difficult temperament caused frustration and disappointment on both sides. Marie had to give up the theatre when they married, and Hamsun insisted that they move to his farm, Skogheim, in northern Norway. Hamsun, the masterful portrayer of the rootless wanderer and isolated individual, became a family man and gentleman farmer. Thus his focus shifted, and he idealized the farmer, as in *Growth of the Soil.* In his second marriage he fathered two sons and two daughters. When life in the North proved to be too harsh, Hamsun bought the large farm, Noerholm, in southern Norway in 1918, and this estate remained his home until he died (it is still owned by his son Arild).

In addition to these significant changes in his personal life, Hamsun had achieved prestige and financial security, a clear influence on the stylistic development of his later works. He was no longer the struggling rebel, the outsider attempting to gain entry to the community and trying to establish a relationship with a "proud princess" he could never have. Now he was respected and had the opportunity to voice his opinions with the expectation that they would be heeded. Thus in his social novels, he tends to sermonize.

Still another theory for the change in Hamsun's style focuses upon a possible decline in his creative powers. Anna Sofie Hansen in *Hamsun og publikum* ("Hamsun and the Public") maintains that the Norwegian author lost his creative surge and, therefore, wrote relatively conventional narrative novels of a panoramic nature; in other words, diligence took the place of inspiration. However, many critics (Marstrander, Naess, Nettum) do not dismiss the later work in this way. The emphasis has shifted, they agree: since Hamsun was no longer a totally isolated individual without family, his need to focus upon himself lessened considerably. But that inspiration abandoned him is debatable; after all, *Vagabonds* is one of his best novels and yet dates from 1927. Moreover, because his last work returns to the format and atmosphere of his first, that final effort contradicts any possible claim that Hamsun could no longer be inspired.

Hamsun involved himself in psychoanalysis in 1926 when he consulted a psychiatrist in Oslo precisely because he feared that his creative powers had dried up. In this context it is worth noting that Hamsun's early traumas had been exorcised in effective works of art. The short story "Et spoekelse" ("A Ghost") describes an apparition that plagued the young Hamsun. A German psychiatrist, Dr. Eduard Hitschmann, in an article in *Imago* (1924) interpreted the story as the expression of a castration complex. Furthermore, a Norwegian psychiatrist, Trygve

Braatoey in *Livets cirkel* (1929), discussed Hamsun's "mother fixation" and the difficulties of his heroes in relating to women.

It is clear that Hamsun the outsider feared insanity, and his early heroes of the 1890s suffer most when they are accused of being "crazy." The accusation is made of the hero of *Hunger* by Ylajali, of Nagel by Dagny Kielland and Kamma in *Mysteries,* of Glahn by the doctor in *Pan,* and of Abel by Olga in *The Ring Is Closed.* Hamsun himself felt most deeply humiliated after the war by his incarceration in the Psychiatric Clinic in Oslo. He wrote in *On Overgrown Paths,* "I wanted to be in an ordinary prison."

An image that crops up in that final book and that had occurred in the first major work, *Hunger,* is that of the caged animal. The hero of *Hunger* does not like to see "animals in cages"; he obviously thinks of himself as such a curiosity to the ordinary, healthy people around him. The world is a zoo and he, like Hamsun himself, is one of the main attractions. During his interment in the Psychiatric Clinic, Hamsun complained that foreigners visited the institution to see "the locked-up animal," as he referred to himself. Similar phrases turn up in Hamsun's letters. He resented the crowds of the curious who would converge on Noerholm to "stare at the animal." Acutely stung by the psychiatrists' verdict of "permanently impaired mental faculties," he wrote his final book to expose the treatment he had received and to refute the doctors' findings. Thorkild Hansen in *Prosessen mot Hamsun* ("The Trial Against Hamsun") stresses that Hamsun became truly inspired only in times of suffering and adversity as he had in *Hunger* and in *On Overgrown Paths,* even though he had written many "uninspired" novels in between.

Knut Hamsun is known not only for his psychological portrayals of outsiders but also for his poetic descriptions of nature. Certainly nature was Hamsun's great consolation as a lonely child, and his early outsider protagonists flee to nature to heal the wounds inflicted on them by others. The hero of *Hunger* escapes to the forest and the cemetery, as did the young Hamsun. Nagel likewise seeks refuge in the woods, where he fantasizes about being united with nature and the cosmos after his death. He feels "related to every tree in the forest," and Glahn, the hunter, describes himself as "the son of the forest." Johannes of *Victoria* and the wanderer also spend much time communing with nature, which they and their creator regard as a compassionate force. Yet Hamsun's concept of nature evolved as he acquired roots. Instead of the forest and the wilderness, the ideal becomes the cultivated field, as in *Growth of the Soil.* Instead of compensation for human companionship, nature becomes evidence of God's miracle—growth. Hamsun's reverence for the soil increased after he himself became a farmer.

Throughout his life, Knut Hamsun represented the dichotomy between the artist and the citizen. In his works he constantly disparaged artistic activity that inevitably alienates the artist from his fellow men, and he glorified the simple life of tilling the soil. Yet Hamsun, even after he achieved financial security and had the opportunity to live a life close to the soil, could not do so. Instead of remaining on his farm, he often abandoned his wife and children to travel to hated cities in order to write more books. A foreman took care of the farm while Hamsun wrote books criticizing the artificiality of city life.

It is obvious that in his most famous tribute to the agricultural life, *Growth of the Soil,* Hamsun's affinity is not with the idealized pioneer Isak, but with the vagabond Geissler. Geissler's birthplace of Lorn and childhood memories are those of Hamsun and, like Hamsun, Geissler preaches the "correct" way of life but is unable to live it himself. He says to Isak, "I know what's right, but don't do it." And yet, Isak and Aksel Stroem could not succeed in the wilderness without the help of Geissler, who provides them with sophisticated farm machinery, shows them how to irrigate their farms, and protects them against the envious city folk. Geissler is truly the flesh-and-blood character in the book, while Isak seems to be a symbol rather than a real person. Even in the later social novels, an occasional complex character will emerge, such as Edevart in *Vagabonds* and *August.* Both Geissler and Edevart may be identified with Hamsun.

The dual (and incompatible) occupations of artist and farmer plagued Hamsun. In letters to his wife he regretted not having been just the boy from the neighboring farm; he often protested to the Norwegian Authors' Organization against being addressed as "Author, Knut Hamsun." He claimed to be "a farmer in Aust Agder." The conflict is represented in symbols and characters from the early works—Nagel is a violinist who pretends to be an agronomist—and finds allegorical expression in the short story "Hemmelig ve" ("Secret Suffering"). Hamsun appears to have been one of those driven in spite of himself to create works of art instead of living in the practical world he extolled.

Knut Hamsun's running feud with industrialization and his advancing age locked him into political views that went from conservative to reactionary. He had always admired Germany and hated England. In 1943 he wrote in *Aftenposten,* "I am deeply and passionately anti-English, anti-British, and I can't remember that I have ever been different." Before World War II, Hamsun had turned down the Goethe Prize of ten thousand marks from the city of Frankfurt "because I didn't want to reap advantage from being Germany's humble friend in Norway." As a former Nobel Prize winner, he was invited to state his opinions on the worthiness of future candidates, and in 1935 made himself unpopular by lobbying against awarding the Nobel Peace Prize to Carl von Ossietzky, a German Jew confined to a concentration camp in Hitler's Germany.

In May, 1940, when German troops entered Norway, Hamsun alienated his countrymen by printing an appeal to his fellow Norwegians in the May 4, 1940, issue of the paper *Fritt folk,* the organ of the Norwegian Nazi Party: "Norwegians! Throw down your weapons and go back home. The Germans are fighting for all of us." Throughout the war Hamsun continued to write articles in support of the Germans; in 1943 he met Hitler at Berchtesgaden, Austria, and after Hitler's death, when Hamsun knew all was lost, he nevertheless published a paragraph in praise of the fallen German leader.

Despite his affection for Germany, Hamsun did not refuse the many Norwegians who appealed to him during the war to intervene on behalf of their countrymen sentenced to death by the German authorities. Trying to save condemned Norwegians, Hamsun sent countless telegrams to the Nazi government; he appealed personally to Joseph Terboven, the "Gauleiter" for Norway, and was successful in securing the release of prisoners from concentration camps, notably the publisher Harald Grieg and the author Ronald Fangen. Fortunately for Hamsun's reputation, the 1943 interview with Hitler was recorded secretly by the latter's press chief. The purpose of Hamsun's visit to Hitler had been to bring about the removal of the sadistic Terboven. The elderly author became enraged when he realized that the timid interpreter was not translating everything he said, and the interview ended with Hitler in a rage and Hamsun in tears.

Hamsun's attitude before and during World War II has perplexed many of his readers. At first senility and mental deterioration seemed to provide the explanation, but the publication of *On Overgrown Paths* in 1949 contradicted this theory. An examination of Hamsun's life and work shows that his pro-German, anti-English stance was sincere and constant. During his travels in the Near East and America, Hamsun had encountered arrogant Englishmen who insulted him or ignored him. On the other hand, he had received free passage to America from the German captain of an oceanliner in 1882. From the earliest years of his career the Germans had appreciated his works, and he, in turn, admired German culture.

But perhaps most important of all, England was the ancient power, Germany the new one, healthy and full of vigor. There is a definite link between Hamsun's revulsion for old age and his hatred of England. In Hamsun's mind, England was the oppressive uncle, Germany the struggling, able youth. Sten Sparre Nilson in *En oern i uvaer: Knut Hamsun og politikken* ("An Eagle in the Storm: Knut Hamsun and Politics") explained the Norwegian writer's Nazi sympathies in terms of his hatred for Uncle Hans, who had oppressed him as a child. This theory is valid but does not tell the entire story. Consider the disappointment Hamsun felt over the "modern Norway" of the twentieth century—the one that persisted in admiring the English, the one which refused to follow Hamsun's example to colonize the northern part of the country, the one that refused to return to the simple life and virtues of the past.

The new Germany, however, seemed to be practicing what Hamsun preached: the peasant was glorified; women were to be modest and to confine themselves to "Kinder, Kueche, Kirche"; physical vigor and manliness were rewarded; education became secondary to physical labor; national customs were religiously elevated; and a sense of national solidarity and superiority was sought. How much Knut Hamsun knew about Nazi ideology is unclear, but he certainly knew that the Germans were the opposite of the English with their democracy, a system which had treated him, a spiritual aristocrat, unkindly. He knew that the Germans admired him, and it appeared that they agreed with him that civilization was evil and that closeness to the soil was tantamount to virtue.

When the war was over, Hamsun, his wife, and his two sons were arrested; Hamsun was incarcerated first in a hospital, then in an old folks' home, and finally in the Oslo Psychiatric Clinic. The worst experience was the stay in the clinic, where Hamsun, already deaf and almost blind, was subjected to interrogation and forced to write innumerable answers in failing light. There is no doubt that this experience undermined his health. As he stated bitterly in *On Overgrown Paths,* "I was a healthy human being; I was turned into jelly."

When Hamsun's case was repeatedly postponed, he wrote the prosecutor general asking to be brought to trial. He felt that, given the chance to speak in public, he would be cleared. In fact, when Hamsun was finally tried, the judge did acquit him, but the two lay judges, who were farmers from Hamsun's district, found him guilty, and their majority opinion decided the case. *On Overgrown Paths,* written in 1948 and published the following year, makes clear that Hamsun was not begging for sympathy: "I'm not defending myself at all. I am presenting this as an explanation, as information." He said that although he respected the law, he esteemed his own conscience more.

After the Norwegian Supreme Court upheld the verdict in 1948, Hamsun put down his pen for good. The last few years of his life were spent in isolation once again (because of his deafness and increasing blindness) on his now crumbling estate of Noerholm, where he died on February 19, 1952. *On Overgrown Paths,* his last work, had been proof of Hamsun's stubbornness and ability to remain true to himself. In it he had declared, "I am who I

am." Once again, at the very end of his life, he found himself isolated from family and countrymen, penniless, and attempting to explain himself to a hostile world.

Knut Hamsun's early literary theories and method of writing can be seen as a type of self-justification. Since he was obsessed with self, he rejected the outward-directed naturalist literature of the preceding generation. He criticized the literary establishment for being concerned with social criticism; only the individual counted, he felt. Since he was an isolated, unrecognized person of considerable gifts, he was determined to create the in-depth portrayal of such a person. Perhaps he called for a "new" literature because he himself was not capable of producing the "old" literature at the time of his breakthrough in the 1890s. His attitude toward the actual production of literature was clearly the traditional romantic one: inspiration engulfs the poet from without and makes him simply a recording instrument. According to a letter Hamsun wrote in 1908 to his German translator, Heinrich Goebel, the Norwegian author experienced inspiration as did his fictional progeny (the writer in *Hunger,* the composer Holmsen in *Children of the Age,* the painter in the short story "Solens soenn" ["Son of the Sun"]): "Every poet knows that poems come into existence under the relative pressure of mood. A sound hums inside of you, you see colors before your eyes, you feel something flowing inside you."

Certainly the manner in which his ideas came to him influenced Hamsun's views on literature. At first he advocated what he could do, but after the turn of the century he learned to compose works in the old "realistic" style, because the frustration and intensity of his youth had in large part evaporated. Given his early experiences of inspiration and considering the beauty of his prose poetry in *Pan,* it is ironic that Hamsun's poems—collected in *Det vilde kor* ("The Wild Chorus"), 1904—were unsuccessful and notably uninspired. His verse play "Munken Vendt" ("Friar Vendt") of 1902 had fared no better.

The exaggerated sense of the individual, of the self, is a defiance against others who do not understand or accept. Hamsun's innovations in literature may have resulted from his need for self-assertion. The sense of not fitting in sometimes produces a destructive rage, a desire to punish or get even. Therefore Hamsun attacked Ibsen and the older "greats," he called for an end to literary conventions (this would make way for uneducated newcomers like himself), he wrote on America as he did, he—the failed playwright—rejected drama as a literary form, he—the autodidact—was anti-intellectual and an enemy of formal education, and he found himself even more isolated politically.

The intensity of his individualism was such that it dictated Hamsun's literary views, was repeatedly mirrored in his best works, and doomed him to isolation from family, society, and nation. The need to reaffirm one's individuality makes itself seen in Knut Hamsun's literary theories and production as well as in his own life.

MEDIA ADAPTATIONS: Hunger was adapted for Swedish film by writer/director Henning Carlsen in 1966.

BIOGRAPHICAL/CRITICAL SOURCES:

BOOKS

Berendsohn, Walter A., *Knut Hamsun: Das unbaendige Ich und die menschliche Gemeinschaft,* Albert Langen, 1929.
Braatoey, Trygve, *Livets cirkel,* Cappelen, 1954.
Brynildsen, Aasmund, *Svermeren og hans deinon,* Dreyer, 1973.

Giersing, Morton, John Thobo Carlson, and Michael Westerg-aard-Nielsen, *Det reaktionaere oproer: Om fascismen Knut Hamsuns forfatterskab,* GMT, 1975.

Gustafson, Alrik, *Six Scandinavian Novelists,* Princeton University Press, 1967.

Hamsun, Tore, *Knut Hamsun,* Gyldendal, 1959.

Hansen, Anna Sofie, *Hamsun og publikum,* Berlingske Forlag, 1980.

Hansen, Thorkild, *Prosessen mot Hamsun,* Gyldendal, 1978.

Kierkegaard, Peter, *Knut Hamsun som modernist,* Medusa, 1976.

Landquist, John, *Knut Hamsun: Sein Leben und sein Werk,* Fischer, 1927.

Larsen, Hanna Astrup, *Knut Hamsun,* Knopf, 1922.

Marstrander, Jan, *Det ensomme menneske i Knut Hamsuns diktning: Betraktninger omkring Mysterier og et motiv,* Det Norske Studentersamfunds kulturutvalg, 1959.

Marstrander, Jan, *Livskamp og virkelighetsoepfatning i Knut Hamsuns tidligste forfatterskap,* [University of Oslo], 1982.

Naess, Harald S., *Knut Hainsun og Amerika,* Gyldendal, 1969.

Naess, Harald S., *Knut Hamsun,* G. K. Hall, 1984.

Nettum, Rolf Nyboe, *Konflikt og visjon: Hovedtemaer i Knut Hamsuns forfatterskap, 1890-1912,* Gyldendal, 1970.

Nilson, Sten Sparre, *En oern i uvaer: Knut Hamsun og politikken,* Gyldendal, 1960.

Oeysleboe, Olaf, *Hainsun g jennom stilen,* Gyldendal, 1964.

Rottern, Oeystein, *Knut Hamsuns Landstrykere: En ideologikritisk analyse,* Gyldendal, 1978.

Simpson, Allen, *Knut Hamsuns Landstrykere,* Gyldendal, 1973.

Tiemroth, Joergen, *Illusionens vej: Om Knut Hamsuns forfatterskab,* Gyldendal, 1974.

Twentieth-Century Literary Criticism, Volume 14, Gale, 1984.

Vige, Rolf, *Knut Hamsun's "Pan,"* Universitetsforlaget, 1963.

PERIODICALS

American Scandinavian Review, September, 1939.

Freeman, August 8, 1923.

New Republic, February 1, 1969, August 2, 1980, August 9, 1980.

New Statesman, April 29, 1922.

New York Herald Tribune Books, May 22, 1927, April 7, 1940.

New York Times Book Review, August 22, 1971.

PMLA, September, 1956.

Scandinavian Studies, August, 1960, February, 1964, November, 1966, spring, 1976, spring, 1981.

Scandinavica, November, 1974, November, 1980.

Smith College Studies in Modern Languages, October, 1921, January, 1922.

Studies in Short Fiction, winter, 1982.

Symposium, summer, 1982.

Times (London), July 1, 1989.

*   *   *

PEESLAKE, Gaffer
See DURRELL, Lawrence (George)

*   *   *

PERCY, Walker 1916-1990

PERSONAL: Born May 28, 1916, in Birmingham, Ala.; died of cancer in May, 1990; son of Leroy Pratt and Martha (Phinizy) Percy; married Mary Bernice Townsend, November 7, 1946;

children: Ann Boyd, Mary Pratt. *Education:* University of North Carolina, B.A., 1937; Columbia University, M.D., 1941.

ADDRESSES: Home—Old Landing Rd., Covington, La. 70433. *Agent*—McIntosh & Otis, Inc., 475 Fifth Ave., New York, N.Y. 10017.

CAREER: Author.

MEMBER: American Academy and Institute of Arts and Letters (fellow).

AWARDS, HONORS: National Book Award for fiction, 1962, for *The Moviegoer;* National Book Award nomination, 1966, for *The Lost Gentleman;* National Institute of Arts and Letters grant, 1967; National Catholic Book Award, 1971, for *Love in the Ruins; Los Angeles Times* Book Prize, 1980, National Book Critics Circle citation, 1980, American Book Award nomination, 1981, Notable Book citation from American Library Association, 1981, and P.E.N./Faulkner Award nomination, 1981, all for *The Second Coming; Los Angeles Times* Book Prize for current interest, 1983, for *Lost in the Cosmos: The Last Self-Help Book;* St. Louis Literary Award, 1986; Ingersoll Prize from Ingersoll Foundation, 1988.

WRITINGS:

FICTION

The Moviegoer, Knopf, 1961, reprinted, Avon, 1980.

The Last Gentleman, Farrar, Straus, 1966, reprinted, Avon, 1978.

Love in the Ruins: The Adventures of a Bad Catholic at a Time near the End of the World, Farrar, Straus, 1971, reprinted, Avon, 1978.

Lancelot, Farrar, Straus, 1977.

The Second Coming, Farrar, Straus, 1980.

The Thanatos Syndrome (Book-of-the-Month Club selection), Farrar, Straus, 1987.

NONFICTION

The Message in the Bottle: How Queer Man Is, How Queer Language Is, and What One Has to Do with the Other, Farrar, Straus, 1975.

Lost in the Cosmos: The Last Self-Help Book, Farrar, Straus, 1983.

Novel-Writing in an Apocalyptic Time (limited edition), Faust Publishing Company, 1986.

State of the Novel: Dying Art or New Science, Faust Publishing Company, 1988.

OTHER

(Author of introduction) William Alexander Percy, *Lanterns on the Levee: Recollections of a Planter's Son,* Louisiana State University Press, 1974.

Contributor of essays to scholarly journals and popular periodicals, including *Esquire, Commonweal, America, Harper's, Georgia Review, Saturday Review, Michigan Quarterly Review,* and *Personalist.*

SIDELIGHTS: Walker Percy is a highly respected American author who, through more than thirty years of writing, has balanced interesting, accessible fiction with serious ideas. With an "intellectual range and vigor few American novelists can match," to quote *New York Times Book Review* contributor Thomas LeClair, Percy seeks to understand the peculiar *angst* of the modern individual, adrift in the twentieth century. He uses novels to unite empirical practice with existentialist perception in the manner of some modern European writers, but his fictional milieus are invariably American—the fairways, subdivisions, and country clubs of the homogenized "New South" in which he lives. *Atlantic* essayist Richard Todd describes the author's theme as "the search for whatever it is that can banish despair" in this era when science and technology alleviate physical suffering but offer no solutions to spiritual crises. "Percy has spent his entire career debriding the same wound," Todd notes. "His work is narrow but it cuts deep." Since the publication of his National Book Award-winning novel *The Moviegoer* in 1961, the Alabama native has "claimed a position, never relinquished, as not only a major Southern novelist, but as one of the unique voices in American fiction," according to Malcolm Jones in the *New York Times Magazine.* As Charles Poore notes in the *New York Times,* Percy "shows us the modern world through the distorting mirrors that the modern world foolishly calls reality." Gail Godwin offers a concurrent description in the *New York Times Book Review.* "Walker Percy," Godwin writes, "has the rare gift of being able to dramatize metaphysics."

Epithets abound in critiques of Percy's work. The writer has been called "the moralist of the deep South," "the doctor of the soul," and even "the Dixie Kierkegaard." Simplistic as such appellations might seem, they nevertheless indicate Percy's central preoccupations: the nature of the cosmos and man's place in it, morality as opposed to mere civility, and sensitivity to the afflictions occasioned by the incomprehensibility of the self by itself. Jones claims that Percy "is one of our severest moralists, and one of our most philosophical novelists. . . . His [fictional] lawyers and doctors are not deaf to the imperatives of the past, but they are very much citizens of modern . . . America, all searching for an answer to the question Percy himself once posed in an essay: 'Why does man feel so sad in the twentieth century?' " Lewis Jerome Taylor, Jr., elaborates in *Commonweal:* "Percy has keen and perceptive eyes for the despair underlying the increasing disarray of society, its root cause and its possible cure. It is not, however, knowledge about reality as such that primarily concerns him but the way by which a person can come to himself and begin to live his own life. Percy is an existentialist. A delightful thing about him, and one that continually carries over into his fictional characters, is that he is a man . . . who seems somehow to have moved into the realm of freedom."

The "realm of freedom" from which Percy works is that of the Christian—specifically Roman Catholic—faith. "Walker Percy is a Christian novelist," explains Peter Prescott in *Newsweek,* "which is not to say that he's a Christian who writes novels—there's no shortage of those—but that he's a novelist who writes about Christian concerns." Having immersed himself in the works of Christian philosophers such as Soeren Kierkegaard and Gabriel Marcel, Percy strives to convey "the Christian truth to an age for which the traditional words have worn so smooth that they no longer take effect," in Taylor's words. In a *Georgia Review* interview, Percy explains how his faith gives perspective to his writing: "To me, the Catholic view of man as pilgrim, in transit, in journey, is very compatible with the vocation of a novelist because a novelist is writing about man in transit, man as pilgrim." *New York Times Book Review* contributor John Romano takes the view that this particular perspective of Percy's "does not mean that plot and character are merely pretexts for philosophical investigations. Rather it refers to what is at stake in the outcomes of events that are tracked and lives that are examined. And although his best characters are fully realized and knowable persons, although he has brought great and careful energy to bear upon the study of a particular region of the country at a historically discreet moment, what is at stake in Percy's fiction is not finally personal or local. Instead he is testing certain con-

cepts, traditional ones, such as the concept that one person might come to know and love another, and that language might actually assist rather than deter that process; or a concept that a life might be lived in some authentic relation to its own chief events . . . without the need to distort or repress or deny; or the concept that there are impulses, casual and shaping, that lie outside whatever scientific account we can take of ourselves."

Critics stress that Percy's Catholicism does not lead him to pen mere sermons exhorting the reader to seek Christian salvation. Instead, as Alfred Kazin notes in *Harper's,* Percy is "atypical" both as a Southerner and a Roman Catholic. "There is a singularity to his life," Kazin observes, "to his manifest search for a new religious humanism, there is a closeness to pain and extreme situations, that makes him extraordinarily 'sensitive'—to the existential theme of life as shipwreck—without suggesting weakness." In his fiction and nonfiction alike, Percy primarily diagnoses the American anomie, aware, as Kierkegaard was, that recognition of the presence of psychic woe is the first step to its cure. Prescott contends that Percy "writes about neurosis and existential terror, about malaise and the general breakdown of function in machines, in institutions and in people." Percy "started out, like any American writer, trying to capture ways of feeling," Richard Eder declares in the *Los Angeles Times Book Review.* "But Percy's hunt for contemporary pain led him to the mind. Our dramas may play out in our affections, our sex lives, our politics and in the exercise and adornment of our egos, but their roots are in our metaphysics." Addressing himself to Percy's methods in *Walker Percy,* Jac Tharpe explains that whatever may be his character, the author "has a finely wrought ironic mind, a healthy approach to human antics through satire, and a good sense of humor" on which to build philosophical ideas central to human awareness.

Percy's youth in the deep South was far from ordinary; events from his formative years and young manhood often serve as the experiences upon which his fiction is based. He was born in 1916 in Birmingham, Alabama, and he spent his childhood there. When Percy was thirteen, his father committed suicide. His mother died two years later in an automobile accident. Percy and his two brothers were then adopted by their father's cousin, William Alexander Percy, a wealthy and learned gentleman who lived in Greenville, Mississippi. Uncle Will, as they called him, was himself a writer whose poetic memoir, *Lanterns on the Levee: Recollections of a Planter's Son* was a popular exploration of postwar gentility in the South. As a teenager, Percy encountered intellectuals of all sorts in his adoptive parent's home—historians, novelists, psychologists, and poets all enjoyed the elder Percy's hospitality. From such stimulating surroundings Percy left for college in 1934, planning to pursue a career in medicine. He studied chemistry at the University of North Carolina and in due course was admitted to medical school at the Columbia College of Physicians and Surgeons. He received his medical degree from that institution in 1941, and that same year he began his residency at Bellevue Hospital in New York City.

As a working pathologist in New York, Percy was called upon to perform autopsies on indigent alcoholics, many of whom had died of tuberculosis. Within a year Percy contracted the dreaded lung disease himself; he spent most of the following three years in a sanatorium. While convalescing he explored the humanistic interests that he had been unable to pursue during his medical training—French and Russian literature, philosophy and psychology. In 1944 Percy had recovered sufficiently to return to Columbia to teach pathology, but he suffered a relapse and decided to quit medicine. The illness was somewhat fortuitous, because Percy had become deeply interested in a whole new realm of intellectual endeavor. He told *Bookweek:* "If the first great intellectual discovery of my life was the beauty of the scientific method, surely the second was the discovery of the singular predicament of man in the very world which has been transformed by this science. An extraordinary paradox became clear: that the more science progressed and even as it benefited man, the less it said about what it is like to be a man living in the world." Percy searched for a solution to this paradox and began to consider a career, however humble, through which he could expose the unique modern conundrum. Writing provided him the means to that end. His first published works were philosophical essays that appeared in scholarly journals; these essays dealt with self-estrangement in the twentieth century, its causes and ramifications. Having married in 1946 and converted to Roman Catholicism in 1947, Percy and his wife moved to New Orleans, and then to Covington, Louisiana, living on an inheritance from a relative. When one of his children was born deaf, Percy became fascinated by a branch of philosophy that has consumed him ever since—semiotics, the study of symbols and how they are used in human communication.

Percy wrote two unpublished novels before beginning *The Moviegoer.* He finally found his fictive niche, however, when he decided to follow Albert Camus's example and write about a character who serves as "an embodiment of a certain pathology of the twentieth century," to use his own words from the *Southern Review.* He told the *New York Times* that in order to write meaningful fiction he had to overcome the American tendency "to distinguish between our reflections on our universal predicament and what can be told in fiction. . . . The French see nothing wrong with writing novels that address what they consider the deepest philosophical issues." *The Moviegoer* was published in 1961 when Percy was forty-five, and although the publisher, Alfred A. Knopf, did little to promote the book, it was discovered and accorded the National Book Award. Most critics feel that *The Moviegoer* presents most of the themes with which Percy has concerned himself in subsequent fiction and nonfiction. "What we don't see in Percy's novels is the changing vision of the world that we often get from a writer who publishes while he is young, and then continues to write," notes Andre Dubus in *Harper's.* "With *The Moviegoer* we were in the hands of a mature writer whose theme had already chosen him. He has been possessed by it ever since, and that is why he is not truly repetitious. . . . It's not repetition we're hearing, but the resonant sound of a writer grappling with his theme."

In *The Moviegoer* and subsequent novels, Percy introduces the concept of *Malaise,* a disease of "depression and despair, intensified by the awareness of a moral and metaphysical wasteland in which intellectuals claim to have outgrown the rituals and beliefs of organized religion," according to Tharpe. *Everydayness,* a term coined by Binx Bolling in *The Moviegoer,* serves as a precursor to—or substitute for—the malaise itself. Tharpe describes this condition as "the drag of uneventful, unchallenging life for those living in an environment so successful in satisfying physical needs that it encourages a man to be a content animal." Percy's protagonists move from the realm of everydayness into a search for self that brings them first to a recognition of the defects in the cult of technology, then to the awareness of shallowness in their own lives. His characters "are well-bred Southern gentlemen who, although endowed with all the trappings of contemporary comfort, are haunted by the fear that they lead meaningless and inauthentic lives," writes Francine du Plessix Gray in the *New York Times Book Review.* "They are all the more doomed because their gentility curbs them from that searing self-questioning which might jolt them into admitting their despair

and exploring its roots." *Southern Review* essayist Richard Lehan suggests that Percy's fiction "takes place in a prolapsed workaday world, often cut off from the ordinary workaday world, where characters are haunted by the past and bound by the absurdity of their situation. To this, Percy adds two states of narrative consciousness—one of perception and another of reflection—and also a sense of the grotesque. . . . Percy's alienated man is lonely and unloved, an isolated consciousness."

Coincident with their sense of alienation and inauthenticity, Percy's characters come to perceive a wider failure of human communication, the displacement of meaningful language by an array of cliches and elitist or technical jargon. In *Walker Percy: Art and Ethics,* Michael Pearson writes: "Percy's books are studies of man's inability to speak to his fellow-man, and affirmations of man's potential to communicate, to be fully human. . . . Percy asks the reader to view the mystery of language, to see that it can screen the world from sight or it can be a lens to clarify reality." Needless to say, Percy's wayfarers also neglect the divine, and consequently are apt to objectify other human beings, using or abusing them without full awareness of their humanity. At a crucial point in his search, Tharpe notes, the Percy protagonist finds that "the world itself, made for his pleasure, has lost its value, though he cannot really escape it; and when he tries to live in it, he no longer has any familiarity with it or its ways. He cannot really operate at the transcendental realm, and his achievements and aspirations mean he is homeless in the immanent realm. Thus, he is more homeless and alienated than he ever was." According to *Dictionary of Literary Biography Yearbook 1980* contributor Joan Bischoff, this "cerebral main character shares many of the author's insights and obsessions: he is keenly aware of the paradoxes of being alive, the critical significance of language, and the corruption of contemporary American life."

How the individual has come to such an impasse in the twentieth century can be inferred from Percy's novels. The author also explores this conundrum in his nonfiction. Basically, Pearson explains, for Percy, "a careful look at language will point toward a clearer image of the human condition. All of his theories—linguistic, philosophical, and aesthetic—hinge on the central concept of symbolization. The germ of Percy's aesthetic theory begins with his disagreement with the behavioristic thesis that language can be explained as a stimulus-response mechanism. The flaw in the behavioristic thesis is that it makes no distinction between a sign and a symbol. . . . Naming sets human language apart from other forms of animal communication." In Percy's view, an investigation of the nature of language may yield a more spiritually satisfying theory about humankind than that currently propounded by the natural sciences. Scientific humanism, in fact, cannot adequately explain the sovereignty and individuality of human life, but it can serve to alienate man from his metaphysical strivings. Charles P. Bigger claims in *Walker Percy: Art and Ethics* that the author has, "with truly remarkable success, set himself to the task of restoring strangeness to the name and to ourselves, the users of names. Just as in his novels he has celebrated, often with comic irony, the violence and strangeness of man, so too through the resonance of the name he sets himself to uncover from the banalities of the behavioral sciences the peculiar mystery of being human."

A fresh perception of the uniqueness of language—of naming is one method by which to overcome the malaise. Percy told the *Michigan Quarterly Review:* "It is the artist who at his best reverses the alienating process by the very act of seeing it clearly for what it is and naming it, and who in this act establishes a kind of community. It is a paradoxical community whose members are both alone yet not alone, who strive to become themselves and discover that there are others who, however tentatively, have undertaken the same quest." No technology, however advanced, can substitute for the quest, he told the *Washington Post,* for such searching is "integral to the human condition." Pearson writes: "It is Percy's hope that literature can be 'news,' the message that will deliver man from despair. For Percy, the 'news' is the Christian, specifically Catholic, message, but Percy is also attempting to renew faith in man as a sovereign knower in a universe of experience. . . . Percy does not view literature as a means to an end, but as an articulation of the previously unnamed."

The malaise and the alienation of self can also be overcome by love—the acceptance of another individual as a co-celebrant of being. According to Lehan, life thus becomes "a search for shared consciousness, for a communion of mind, for the affirmation of self which can only be found in the reflection of the other." Several of Percy's novels end with marriages; most end with intimations of epiphany, a divine love that will aid in the recovery of being. *New Republic* contributor Jonathan Yardley finds that as Percy's tales unwind, "there is an ultimate accommodation, an acceptance of pain in its various forms balanced, or made possible, by a discovery of love." In *Walker Percy: An American Search,* Robert Coles writes: "Every Percy novel ends on Marcel's theory of concreteness. . . . Grand designs, brilliant projects or propositions are put aside in favor of a step toward a person and a specific kind of life (a beginning of it) with that person." Without evangelizing, Percy stresses the positive ramifications of faith, good works, and family. "Tradition, accumulated wisdom," Yardley concludes, "is the bedrock. The 'deep abscesses in the soul of Western man' can be removed not by technology or theory but by the most fundamental respect for human dignity and diversity."

In the *New York Review of Books,* Thomas Nagel asserts that *The Moviegoer* "remains Percy's purest and most exact description of that malady of extreme detachment from perception and action which allows the victim to make contact with reality only when he is first dislodged, with greater or less violence, from his accustomed perch." The first-person narrative reveals the life of Binx Bolling, a Southerner of genteel background who becomes sensitive to the malaise as he goes through his middle-class routines in New Orleans. Kazin calls the work "a lean, tartly written, subtle, not very dramatic attack on the wholly bourgeois way of life and thinking in a 'gracious' and 'historic' part of the South. But instead of becoming another satire on the South's retreat from its traditions, it [is], for all the narrator's bantering light tone, an altogether tragic and curiously noble study in the loneliness of necessary human perceptions." Coles notes that at certain points in the novel, "Percy's didactic intentions appear, but never disruptively. The reader is free to glide through and beyond, simply enjoying a witty and charming Binx as he recalls his past or makes his clever appraisals." *New York Review of Books* contributor Robert Towers expresses the opinion that *The Moviegoer* is "Percy's best work, a perfect small novel whose themes, though important, are never allowed to overload the fictional craft. It is a book redolent of its time and place, a book with a thickly sensuous texture that can accommodate both the banalities of contemporary New Orleans and the glamorous aspects of Binx's now meaningless heritage. It is full of expertly realized characters." In the *Mississippi Quarterly Review,* John F. Zeugner concludes: "*The Moviegoer* seems to have been composed in joy—a muted celebration of Bolling's departure from despair. Written in the first person, shaped with a tranquil irony, *The Moviegoer* hums with the exhilaration of a man who has argued his way out of darkness."

Will Barrett, the protagonist of both *The Last Gentleman* and *The Second Coming,* must also argue his way out of darkness, but he is impeded in the first book by anmesia and in the second by attacks of heightened memory that return him to his traumatic past. Although both novels re-present Percy's philosophical and moral views, they also reveal "a man of fiction who clearly [enjoys] the old-fashioned virtues of the trade—storytelling, the amusement and edification of readers through the novelist's ability to use his imagination, conjure up all sorts of people, events, predicaments," to quote Coles. Tharpe feels that Percy uses Barrett's peculiar mental state and his social milieu as springboards from which to attack "christendom, with its two moral failures, sexual indulgence and enslavement of blacks." Those two issues are certainly explored, particularly in *The Last Gentleman,* but *New York Times Book Review* correspondent Peter Buitenhuis finds another level of meaning in the fiction. *The Last Gentleman,* Buitenhuis writes, "succeeds brilliantly in dramatizing the contradictory nature of reality through characters who are at once typical of our condition yet saltily individual. Walker Percy's perception luminously lights up obscure depths of experience without at the same time explaining that experience easily away." In *The Second Coming* Barrett finally finds answers to his metaphysical quandary through his relationship with a young woman whose innovative use of language strengthens their bond. *Commonweal* reviewer Gerard Reedy writes: "The major change *The Second Coming* rings on the previous novels lies in its greater exploration of the peaceful, romantic images that have always been present in Percy's work and are here amplified to challenge, if not drown out, the discord of twentieth-century America." *Time* correspondent Paul Gray concludes that in all of its many convolutions, "*The Second Coming* is a meticulously crafted narrative, unobtrusively folding the distant past into a busy present."

Love in the Ruins and *The Thanatos Syndrome* also share the same protagonist—Dr. Tom More, a fictional descendant of the famous Tudor-era martyr, Sir Thomas More. Both works are set in the very near future; they reveal a morally bankrupt and politically polarized America where scientists use mechanical and technical means to distort human souls. Yardley contends that Percy's purpose "is not gloomy prognostication, though there is plenty of that. He is concerned with fantasizing the world as it now exists, with placing today's complaints in tomorrow's setting." *Saturday Review* contributor Joseph Catinella finds *Love in the Ruins* "a stunning satire conceived with mock-heroic intensity, peopled by absurd but recognizable human beings, and written with a gusto that makes most doomsday books look like effete comic strips." *The Thanatos Syndrome* finds More battling a group of scientists and social planners who contaminate public water supplies with a chemical that alters human nature. Malcolm Jones feels that the novel "slices deep with its uncompromising critique of the ethical, even religious pitfalls inherent in social engineering generally and euthanasia in particular." In a *Washington Post Book World* review, Yardley concludes that *The Thanatos Syndrome* is "a novel about ideas and issues that matter, a novel that looks beyond its own confines to the larger world outside, a novel that challenges the reader to think and imagine. . . . Its expansiveness and humanity are welcome reminders of what fiction can accomplish when it is written for more than the celebration of self or the adulation of a coterie."

Percy has also written two nonfiction books that present his semiotic explanation of the singular predicament of the self—*The Message in the Bottle: How Queer Man Is, How Queer Language Is, and What One Has to Do with the Other,* and *Lost in the Cosmos: The Last Self-Help Book. The Message in the Bottle* is a series of essays, some highly technical, that Percy wrote for journals over a period of twenty years; in the *Southern Review* Bigger calls it "an important work by a major novelist who is also even more impressive as a philosopher, one who lovingly seeks and strives for wisdom in and out of the conditions here and now with us in America." *Lost in the Cosmos* is clearly intended for a general audience. In a question-and-answer format, it presents a darkly humorous appraisal of the deficiencies in the comprehension of the self in an era when the sciences can explain everything else. Percy quietly mocks sex therapy, the "Phil Donahue Show," and efforts to contact extraterrestrial beings; he also explains his views on semiotics, using terms and diagrams the general reader can understand. *New Republic* reviewer Jack Beatty summarizes the work: "Our alienation from each other, our estrangement from religious faith, and our semiological pathos as the creature that can name everything in the cosmos except itself, have us in a permanently awful fix. Despite its subtitle, this book won't help, though it does contain one form of comfort: intellectual delight. It crackles with thought, ideas, exotic information." In *Time,* R. Z. Sheppard compares *Lost in the Cosmos* to Carl Sagan's *Cosmos,* a book that expresses hopes for an encounter with intelligent beings from outer space. "Percy's specialty is the gentle chiding of a generation that came of age blowing its mind and ended up blow-drying its hair," Sheppard writes. ". . . Percy's *Cosmos* is more challenging than Sagan's because the remote possibility of contacting extraterrestrials palls before a mankind that is alien to itself. Running off to the stars may be far simpler than exploring the black holes of human nature." Bigger offers this assessment of Percy's nonfiction in *Walker Percy: Art and Ethics:* "Percy once said that he wrote novels when he got philosophical cramps. One can say that his philosophy cures many philosophical cramps. By centering on one point, the mystery of naming as disclosing world, Percy has performed a remarkable service towards our recovery of strangeness. . . . The possibility of language discloses us as beings within and without the world."

Percy is inevitably considered a "Southern novelist," laboring within the tradition of William Faulkner, Eudora Welty, and Flannery O'Connor. Percy maintains, however, that a distinctive literature of the American South is not tenable as a concept in these days when regional impulses no longer mold the national character. "Faulkner and all the rest of them were always going on about this tragic sense of history, and we're supposed to sit on our porches and talk about it all the time," Percy told the *New York Times Book Review.* "I never did that. My South was always the New South. My first memories are of the country club, of people playing golf." Elsewhere in the *New York Times Book Review* the author added: "I lived a hundred miles from William Faulkner but he meant less to me than Albert Camus." Indeed, as Yardley sees it, "one does not immediately sense the South in Percy's work . . . because he is telling us that the South is not the South any more, that it has been absorbed into the crassness and possibly the hopelessness of America. Percy's South has been violated not by Sherman's marauders but by . . . the masters of commerce and technology." *Saturday Review* contributor Bruce Cook likewise notes that Percy's fiction "lacks the local color—the magnolias and honeysuckle—and the Faulknerian, Old Testament sensibility for which [Southern] writers are noted. He is essentially a philosophical novelist; but a rare one, for there is such a crisp clarity to his writing, and such a lot of humor, that it is quite without pretension."

This is not to say that Percy's fiction lacks all sense of region. Godwin writes: "By choice as well as inclination, Mr. Percy is primarily a novelist of ideas, but he is a fine novelist of manners,

too. He is uncommonly good at evoking the atmosphere and language of his region; he is dead on target when depicting the subtle, often devious locutions of Southern American talk." Nor does the author ignore the pertinent issues of modern Southern history, especially race relations, in his novels. "It's the great strength of Percy's fiction that he looks about him and sees a landscape of moral and emotional confusion, and refuses to offer handy sociological or economic wisdom by way of comforting explanation for it," Todd claims. "He speaks directly and challengingly to the private heart." In a *New York Review of Books* essay, V. S. Pritchett praises Percy for "moving about, catching the smell of locality, and for a laughing enjoyment between his bouts with desperation and loss. . . . The sense of America as an effluence of bizarre locality is strong."

For all its serious portent, Percy's fiction is nevertheless imbued with comedy, satire, and intimations that humankind's case is not completely hopeless. He is also considered an engaging stylist whose accessible prose facilitates understanding of deep issues. As Joyce Carol Oates observes in the *New Republic,* Percy "has been wonderfully alive to the sounds and textures and odors of life, and his ability to render the baffling solidity of the world [makes] his prose sing with vitality. . . . It [is] hardly abstract notions of freedom, determinism, existential *angst,* alienation, etc. that [makes] these novels so irresistible. They [are] artistically and humanly rich, and beautifully crafted." In the *New Republic,* Yardley also describes what he views as the best aspect of Percy's work: "For all its seeming despair, for all its sad irony and wicked satire, it resolves into affirmation. In a cynical age it may seem sentimental. Human community, neighborliness, rootedness in the land, simple decency and honesty—those qualities are often acknowledged today, if at all, with embarrassed smirks. But the point of Percy's work, of the laughter he directs at our posturings, is that they are the best we have to fall back on. That he finds we have not yet lost them despite it all, that he is still not without hope, is a good word in a bad time."

Percy's works are popular among discerning readers both in America and abroad; he told the *Los Angeles Times* he thinks this is the case because "people realize that I'm just as screwed up as they are, and the only difference between us is that I have a way of writing about it." The author said in the *New York Times* that the rewards for a long writing career come when a novelist is "able to say something that everybody knows and yet doesn't know that he knows. The reader reads it and says, 'Why, that's me. I hadn't thought about it. I didn't know anybody else felt that way.'"

BIOGRAPHICAL/CRITICAL SOURCES:

BOOKS

Broughton, Panthea Reid, editor, *The Art of Walker Percy: Stratagems for Being,* Louisiana State University Press, 1979.

Bryant, Jerry H., *The Open Decision: The Contemporary American Novel and Its Intellectual Background,* Free Press, 1970.

Coles, Robert, *Walker Percy: An American Search,* Little, Brown, 1978.

Contemporary Literary Criticism, Gale, Volume 2, 1974, Volume 3, 1975, Volume 6, 1976, Volume 8, 1978, Volume 14, 1980, Volume 18, 1981, Volume 47, 1988.

Dabbs, James McBride, *Civil Rights in Recent Southern Fiction,* Southern Regional Council, 1969.

Dictionary of Literary Biography, Volume II: *American Novelists since World War II,* Gale, 1978.

Dictionary of Literary Biography Yearbook: 1980, Gale, 1981.

Douglas, Ellen, *Walker Percy's "The Last Gentleman": Introduction and Commentary*, Seabury, 1969.

Hoffman, Frederick J., *The Art of Southern Fiction: A Study of Some Modern Novelists*, Southern Illinois University Press, 1967.

Hyman, Stanley Edgar, *Standards: A Chronicle of Books for Our Time*, Horizon, 1966.

Lawson, Lewis A. and Victor A. Kramer, editors, *Conversations with Walker Percy*, University Press of Mississippi, 1985.

Lehan, Richard, *A Dangerous Crossing: French Literary Existentialism and the Modern American Novel*, Southern Illinois University Press, 1973.

Luschei, Martin, *The Sovereign Wayfarer: Walker Percy's Diagnosis of the Malaise*, Louisiana State University Press, 1972.

Murray, Albert, *South to a Very Old Place*, McGraw, 1971.

Poteat, Patricia Lewis, *Walker Percy and the Old Modern Age: Reflections on Language, Argument, and the Telling of Stories*, Louisiana State University Press, 1986.

Sheed, Wilfrid, *The Morning After*, Farrar, Straus, 1971.

Tanner, Tony, *The Reign of Wonder: Naivety and Reality in American Literature*, Cambridge University Press, 1965.

Tanner, Tony, *City of Words: American Fiction 1950-1970*, Harper, 1971.

Tharpe, Jac, editor, *Walker Percy: Art and Ethics*, University Press of Mississippi, 1980.

Tharpe, Jac, *Walker Percy*, Twayne, 1983.

PERIODICALS

America, January 5, 1957, January 12, 1957, July 20, 1957.
American Scholar, summer, 1968.
Atlantic, August, 1971, March, 1977, July, 1980, April, 1987.
Bookweek, December 25, 1966.
Book World, May 16, 1971.
Carleton Miscellany, Volume XVI, 1976-77.
Centennial Review, winter, 1968.
Chicago Tribune Book World, May 29, 1983, March 29, 1987.
Colorado Quarterly, spring, 1972.
Commonweal, July 6, 1956, December 13, 1957, June 5, 1959, December 22, 1961, October 29, 1971, May 10, 1974, October 25, 1974, August 29, 1980.
Detroit News, May 3, 1987.
Esquire, December, 1977, April, 1980.
Georgia Review, fall, 1971, winter, 1977, fall, 1978.
Globe & Mail (Toronto), May 9, 1987.
Harper's, April, 1965, June, 1971, April, 1977.
Hollins Critic, October, 1973.
Horizon, August, 1980.
Journal of Religion, July, 1974.
Los Angeles Times, August 10, 1983.
Los Angeles Times Book Review, June 5, 1983, April 12, 1987.
Michigan Quarterly Review, fall, 1977.
Mississippi Quarterly, winter, 1974-75.
Modern Age, fall, 1980.
Nation, August 8, 1966, April 30, 1977, August 16, 1980.
New Leader, October 13, 1975.
New Republic, April 13, 1987.
New Orleans Review, May, 1976.
New Republic, June 18, 1966, May 22, 1971, July 19, 1975, February 5, 1977, July 5-12, 1980, July 11, 1983.
Newsweek, May 17, 1971, February 28, 1977, July 7, 1980, June 13, 1983.
New York, July 28, 1980.
New Yorker, July 22, 1961, September 11, 1971, May 2, 1977, October 2, 1978, September 1, 1980, June 15, 1987.

New York Review of Books, July 28, 1966, July 1, 1971, September 18, 1975, March 31, 1977, August 14, 1980.
New York Times, June 16, 1966, May 15, 1971, February 17, 1977, July 3, 1980, June 11, 1983, April 1, 1987.
New York Times Book Review, May 28, 1961, June 26, 1966, May 23, 1971, July 4, 1971, June 8, 1975, February 20, 1977, June 29, 1980, June 5, 1983, August 4, 1985, April 5, 1987.
New York Times Magazine, March 22, 1987.
Notes on Mississippi Writers, fall, 1971, spring, 1978, summer, 1979.
Novel, fall, 1972.
Partisan Review, summer, 1966, spring, 1973.
Prairie Schooner, summer, 1968.
Publishers Weekly, March 21, 1977.
Saturday Review, June 18, 1966, May 15, 1971, November 6, 1973, June 28, 1975, March 19, 1977, April 1, 1978.
Sewanee Review, autumn, 1973.
Shenandoah, spring, 1967, winter, 1972, winter, 1976.
South Atlantic Bulletin, May, 1972.
South Atlantic Quarterly, summer, 1969.
Southern Literary Journal, fall, 1973, fall, 1977.
Southern Quarterly, January, 1978, Volume XVIII, number 3, 1980.
Southern Review, spring, 1968, October, 1970, spring, 1973, autumn, 1977, winter, 1977, spring, 1978, winter, 1978, winter, 1984.
Southern Studies, summer, 1979.
Southern Voices, May-June, 1974.
Southwest Review, spring, 1974.
Spectator, February 14, 1981.
Time, May 19, 1961, February 1, 1963, May 17, 1971, March 7, 1977, July 14, 1980, June 20, 1983, March 30, 1987.
Times Literary Supplement, December 21, 1967, October 1, 1971, January 23, 1981.
Village Voice, July 9-15, 1980, June 14, 1983.
Virginia Quarterly Review, summer, 1977.
Washington Post, May 14, 1987.
Washington Post Book World, February 27, 1977, July 20, 1980, June 19, 1983, March 22, 1987.
World Literature Today, spring, 1981, spring, 1984.
Yale Review, winter, 1976.

OBITUARIES:

PERIODICALS

Newsweek, May 21, 1990.
Time, May 21, 1990.

*   *   *

PEREGOY, George Weems
    See MENCKEN, H(enry) L(ouis)

*   *   *

PERELMAN, S(idney) J(oseph)   1904-1979

PERSONAL: Born February 1, 1904, in Brooklyn, N.Y.; died October 17, 1979, in New York, N.Y.; son of Joseph (a machinist and merchant) and Sophia (Charren) Perelman; married Laura West (a writer), July 4, 1929 (died April 11, 1970); children; Adam, Abby Laura. *Education:* Brown University, B.A., 1925.

CAREER: Judge magazine, New York City, cartoonist and writer, 1925-29; *College Humor* magazine, New York City, cartoonist and writer, 1929-30; full-time writer, 1929-79; writer of motion picture scripts, 1930-56. Manager of radio program, "Author, Author."

MEMBER: Screen Writers Guild, Dramatists Guild, National Institute of Arts and Letters, Century Association.

AWARDS, HONORS: New York Film Critics award and Academy of Motion Picture Arts and Sciences award (Oscar) for best screenplay, 1956, for "Around the World in Eighty Days"; special National Book Award for his contribution to American letters, 1978.

WRITINGS:

Dawn Ginsbergh's Revenge, Liveright, 1929.

(With Quentin Reynolds) *Parlor, Bedlam and Bath,* Liveright, 1930.

Strictly from Hunger, foreword by Robert Benchley, Random House, 1937.

Look Who's Talking, Random House, 1940.

The Dream Department, Random House, 1943.

The Best of S. J. Perelman, Random House, 1944, reprinted, 1962, published as *Crazy Like a Fox* (also see below), Modern Library, 1947, reprinted, Vintage Books, 1973.

Keep It Crisp (also see below), Random House, 1946.

Acres and Pains (also see below), Reynal & Hitchcock, 1947, reprinted, Simon & Schuster, 1972.

Westward Ha! or, Around the World in Eighty Cliches, Simon & Schuster, 1947, reprinted, Da Capo, 1984.

Listen to the Mocking Bird, Simon & Schuster, 1949, reprinted, 1970.

The Swiss Family Perelman, Simon & Schuster, 1950.

A Child's Garden of Curses (contains *Crazy Like a Fox, Keep It Crisp,* and *Acres and Pains*), Heinemann, 1951.

The Ill-Tempered Clavichord, Simon & Schuster, 1952.

Hold That Christmas Tiger!, Hart, 1954.

Perelman's Home Companion: A Collector's Item (the Collector Being S. J. Perelman) of 36 Otherwise Unavailable Pieces by Himself, Simon & Schuster, 1955.

The Road to Miltown; or, Under the Spreading Atrophy, Simon & Schuster, 1957 (published in England as *Bite on the Bullet; or, Under the Spreading Atrophy,* Heinemann, 1957).

The Most of S. J. Perelman, introduction by Dorothy Parker, Simon & Schuster, 1958, reprinted, 1980.

The Rising Gorge, Simon & Schuster, 1961.

Chicken Inspector No. 23, Simon & Schuster, 1966.

(Author of introduction and notes with Richard Rovere) Fred L. Israel, editor, *1897 Sears Roebuck Catalogue,* Chelsea House, 1968.

Baby, It's Cold Inside, Simon & Schuster, 1970.

Vinegar Puss, Simon & Schuster, 1975.

Eastward Ha!, Simon & Schuster, 1977.

The Last Laugh, introduction by Paul Theroux, Simon & Schuster, 1981.

That Old Gang o' Mine: The Early and Essential S. J. Perelman, edited by Richard Marschall, Morrow, 1984.

Don't Tread on Me: The Selected Letters of S. J. Perelman, edited by Prudence Crowther, Penguin, 1987.

PLAYS

(Contributor of sketches) "The Third Little Show" (revue), produced in New York, 1932.

(Contributor of sketches with Robert MacGunigle) "Walk a Little Faster" (revue), produced in New York, 1932.

(With wife, Laura Perelman) "All Good Americans" (comedy; also see below), produced in New York, 1933.

(Contributor of sketches) "Two Weeks with Pay" (revue), toured, 1940.

(With Laura Perelman) *The Night Before Christmas* (comedy; also see below; produced in New York, 1941), Samuel French, 1942.

(With Ogden Nash) *One Touch of Venus* (comedy; produced in New York, 1943), Little, Brown, 1944.

(With Al Hirschfeld) "Sweet Bye and Bye" (comedy), produced in New Haven, Conn., 1946.

(With Ogden Nash) *The Beauty Part* (two-act comedy; first produced in New Hope, Pa., 1961; produced in New York, 1962), Samuel French and Simon & Schuster, 1963.

Also author, with Nathanael West, of "Even Stephen," a three-act satire written in 1934 but never produced.

SCREENPLAYS

(With Will B. Johnstone and Arthur Sheekman) "Monkey Business," Paramount, 1931, published in *The Four Marx Brothers in Monkey Business and Duck Soup,* Lorrimer, 1972, Simon & Schuster, 1973.

(With Bert Kalmar and Harry Ruby) "Horse Feathers," Paramount, 1932.

(With Jack McGowan and Lou Breslow) "Sitting Pretty," Paramount, 1933.

(With Laura Perelman) "Paris Interlude," adapted from their play "All Good Americans," Metro-Goldwyn-Mayer, 1934.

(With Laura Perelman, David Boehm, and Marguerite Roberts) "Florida Special," Paramount, 1936.

(With Laura Perelman) "Ambush," Paramount, 1939.

(With Laura Perelman) "Boy Trouble," Paramount, 1939.

(With Laura Perelman and Marion Parsonnet) "The Golden Fleecing," Metro-Goldwyn-Mayer, 1940.

(With James Poe and John Farrow) "Around the World in Eighty Days," adapted from the novel by Jules Verne, United Artists, 1956.

Also worked on the screen story for "Larceny, Inc.," based on his play "The Night Before Christmas," co-authored by Laura Perelman, 1942.

TELEVISION SCRIPTS

"The Changing Ways of Love," Columbia Broadcasting System (CBS-TV), 1957.

"Elizabeth Taylor's London," Columbia Broadcasting System (CBS-TV), 1963.

Also author of television special script "Aladdin," and of "Omnibus" series, NBC-TV, 1957-59.

CONTRIBUTOR

Louis G. Locke, William M. Gibson, and George W. Arms, editors, *Readings for a Liberal Education,* Rinehart, 1948, revised edition, 1952.

John Lincoln Stewart, editor, *The Essay: A Critical Anthology,* Prentice-Hall, 1952.

P. G. Wodehouse and Scott Meredith, editors, *Best of Modern Humor,* Metcalf, 1952.

Wodehouse and Meredith, editors, *The Week-end Book of Humor,* Washburn, 1952.

George Oppenheimer, editor, *The Passionate Playgoer: A Personal Scrapbook,* Viking, 1958.

Leslie A. Fiedler, editor, *Art of the Essay,* Crowell, 1958.

Earle R. Davis and W. C. Hummel, editors, *Reading for Opinions,* Prentice-Hall, 1960.

Alfred Kazin, editor, *The Open Form: Essays for Our Time,* Harcourt, 1961.

Also contributor to *Jewish-American Stories,* edited by Irving Howe, 1977.

OTHER

Regular contributor of essays to the *New Yorker,* 1931-39; contributor of essays to periodicals, including *Holiday, Travel and Leisure, McCall's, Saturday Evening Post, Country Book, Contact,* and *Life.*

SIDELIGHTS: S. J. Perelman, whose works are principally collections of his contributions to the *New Yorker,* was once considered "the funniest man alive," according to William Zinsser in a *New York Times Magazine* article. Sometimes hailed as a great writer of satire and criticism, Perelman was usually characterized simply as a humorist. A few days after the author's death, *New Yorker* editor William Shawn indicated in a *New York Times* obituary that Perelman was "one of the few remaining writers in America who devoted themselves wholly to humor. Over the years," said Shawn, "people often put pressure on him to write something they considered serious—a novel, say—but he was never diverted from doing what he apparently was born to do, which was to write short humor pieces."

The sheer volume of his output was "astounding," reported *Dictionary of Literary Biography* contributor Steven H. Gale, who indicated that 441 of Perelman's essays were eventually collected. The author himself wrote in his introduction to *The Most of S. J. Perelman,* a collection of thirty years of his work, that "if I were to apply for a library card in Paris, I would subscribe myself as a *feuilletoniste,* that is to say a writer of little leaves."

Perelman's prose style is best characterized by the imaginative use to which he put the English language or what he himself once described as "my preoccupation with cliches, baroque language, and the elegant variation," according to *New Republic* writer R. D. Rosen. In the opinion of Christopher Adcock, writing in another volume of the *Dictionary of Literary Biography,* Perelman's "gift for wordplay, evident in his books, plays, and scripts, helped shape twentieth-century American humor."

According to Herbert Mitgang in the *New York Times Book Review,* *New Yorker* colleague E. B. White once said of Perelman's style: "Sid had the greatest and most formidable vocabulary I have ever encountered. It was like an elaborate erector set, one word leading to another, joined to still another, to produce a truly remarkable structure." Shawn related that "people were so enormously entertained by him that they sometimes overlooked his great originality and his literary brilliance. He was a master of the English language, and no one has put the language to more stunning comic use than he did."

His facility with the English language made him a master parodist. According to Tom Wolfe in the *New York Times Book Review,* Perelman's "peculiar tone was a parody of the grandiloquence of the late 19th century prose that high school and college students were steeped in during his youth." Cartoonist Al Hirschfeld, a close friend and sometimes collaborator, remarked in the *New York Times* obituary that Perelman "was at his best when he was parodying or just taking the essence out of a thing that had already been accepted, like a movie or a novel or an advertisement; he didn't copy nature, he copied art."

Perelman's approach was usually eclectic; he was often praised for "the wondrous mixture of references and allusions to all areas of life," Gale wrote, "some familiar and some esoteric, often juxtaposed with one another." Louis Hasley in the *South Atlantic*

Quarterly described the author as having a "kangaroo mind." As William Zinsser indicated in the *New York Times Magazine,* after having read Perelman's early work, he "saw that anything was possible if a writer threw off the chains of logic and let his mind work by free association, ricocheting from the normal to the absurd and usually destroying, by the very unexpectedness of its angle, whatever trite or pompous idea had been there before."

As a boy, Perelman wanted to he a cartoonist, not a writer, and practiced drawing cartoons on the cardboard strips containing bolts of material in his father's dry goods store. But, according to Gale, the young Perelman was also "a voracious reader . . . [of] the variety of books that captured the attention of the youngsters of that time: the Toby Tyler books, *Graustark, Girl of the Lumberlost, Trail of the Lonesome Pine, The Mystery of Fu Manchu, The Winning of Barbara Worth, Scaramouche, Pollyanna,* and the novels of Charles Dickens. In many ways the style and subject matter of these books supply the foundation for Perelman's humor."

While at Brown University as a premedical student, he became a cartoonist for the *Brown Jug,* the campus humor magazine, and, according to Gale, "even though Perelman later became the magazine's editor and thus began to write for publication, his humor always contained the deceptive simplicity and somewhat stylized feeling of a cartoon." His artistic bent may also have affected his work habits. After viewing a collection of some two hundred of the author's manuscripts that are kept at the New York Public Library, Mitgang reported that Perelman, who was fastidious in his personal manner and dress, was also a fastidious craftsman: "Where changes were made in the typescripts, they were not written in by hand; instead, he rolled the page back into the typewriter and typed in the interlineations. Where whole paragraphs were revised, he pasted in the new material." All of his rudimentary notes were also typed.

When Perelman left Brown University in 1925, he accepted a contract to provide two cartoons and one humor piece per issue to *Judge,* a popular weekly periodical that Perelman told Zinsser was "the most insolvent of magazines. Its treasurer, Joseph Cooney, had a gray suit, and they painted the office gray to make him invisible. Hirelings waiting to he paid would see a red spot moving along the walls, but by the time they realized it was Cooney's ruddy face he was out the door." In 1930, Perelman moved on to *College Humor.* He told Maralyn Lois Polak in the *Philadelphia Inquirer* that during those years, he'd "write jokes that had nothing to do with my pictures, an intricate system of verbiage, founded on puns like 'I have Bright's disease, and he has mine!' Soon the captions of my drawings got longer and longer. Finally they displaced the drawings entirely."

It was at *College Humor* that "a style of his own began to emerge," Gale related. "I was beginning to develop a sense of parody," Perelman told Zinsser, "and of lapidary prose." Perelman's early style "shows the influence of many writers," Gale maintained. Over the years, the author mentioned having been influenced by such authors as George Ade, Stephen Leacock, Max Beerbohm, Robert Benchley, Ring Lardner, James Joyce, Raymond Chandler, E. M. Forster, and Henry David Thoreau, said Gale. "But as most great artists, Perelman had the ability to make what he borrowed his own, and to go beyond his source, even though, as he admits in a 1963 *Paris Review* interview, he 'stole from the very best sources.' "

Several of the author's pieces and cartoons from the very early *Judge* years, as well as a few cartoons from the *Brown Jug* university era, have been posthumously compiled in *That Old Gang o' Mine.* "The cartoons," according to Sherwin D. Smith in the *New York Times Book Review,* "begin as shameless imitations of John Held Jr.'s fake woodcuts and move on to parody Art Deco. The prose is lunatic free association to the point of Dada." While Smith felt that "by now, the ethnic jokes have become offensive," and that the work is "juvenilia," Peter de Vries pointed out in a *New Yorker* review of the book that "even in the sketches spun out on the obvious college-humor level of the era we see the wild free association, anarchic wordplay, maniacal non sequiturs, preposterous names and surrealist juxtapositions prescient of the accomplished pyrotechnician to come." As Stefan Kanfer wrote in *Time,* "the great edifice of his satire rests on these early pieces. He was a source and a delight even before he had learned control and timing."

In 1929, Perelman published his first actual book, *Dawn Ginsbergh's Revenge.* His own name was inadvertently left off the title page, but Groucho Marx provided a dust jacket blurb for the book. (Two years later, Groucho would remember Perelman when the Marx Brothers were searching for script material.) Most of the essays in this work originally appeared in *Judge,* and according to Gale, "some of the characteristic elements of Perelman's comic style are already evident. These early pieces are short, and they are not the work of a mature writer, but there are moments of Perelman at his best in the collection." In particular, Gale pointed out, parts of *Dawn Ginsbergh's Revenge* show "Perelman's predilection for having fun with the names of his characters, for punning, for incongruity, and for reversal."

The year following publication of *Dawn Ginsbergh's Revenge, Parlor, Bedlam and Bath* was published, and then seven years later, Perelman's collection *Strictly from Hunger* appeared in print with a foreword by Robert Benchley. In those intervening seven years, Perelman had begun writing for the *New Yorker* and had also moved to Hollywood to work on the scripts for several films, beginning with the Marx Brothers' "Monkey Business" and "Horse Feathers." Adcock maintained that the Marxes would prove to he "ideal performers of Perelman's material. He could introduce characters and situations at will, with no regard for logic, and Groucho Marx in particular was well suited for Perelman's wordplay."

Perelman apparently detested much of the movie industry culture although it provided him with writing material. He readily admitted "that the sole motivation for his connection with Hollywood was money," according to Gale, and Wilfrid Sheed explained in the *New York Review of Books* that "Hollywood proceeded to rub his Ivy League nose in it, and give him his best subject." Gale reported that in a 1963 *Paris Review* interview, Perelman "expressed his impression of the city and the industry as 'a dreary industrial town controlled by hoodlums of enormous wealth, the ethical sense of a pack of jackals, and a taste so degraded that it befouled everything it touched. I don't mean to sound like a boy Savonarola, but there were times, when I drove along the Sunset Strip and looked at those buildings, or when watched the fashionable film colony arriving at some premiere at Grauman's Egyptian, that I fully expected God in his wrath to obliterate the whole shebang. It was—if you'll allow me to use a hopelessly inexpressive word—*degoutant.*' "

Sheed noted that "the Marxes, who should have been his natural allies, and who perfectly rendered one half of his personality, revolted him almost as much as the moguls. Although he would later search the world for other gorillas, and better incongruities, he never found anything to match Hollywood in the Thirties. It was like first love. Although he whored after bizarre settings for the rest of his life, he could never recapture the shock of that first

encounter with savagery. It is no accident that the part of his memoirs [*The Last Laugh*] that works is set in Hollywood. He felt like a kid again."

Perelman's posthumously published *The Last Laugh* includes four chapters from his unfinished autobiography, "The Hindsight Saga," a takeoff on John Galsworthy's *The Forsyte Saga.* This section deals with Perelman's career in Hollywood and New York and relates his experiences with the Marx Brothers and such literary figures as humorist Dorothy Parker and his close friend and brother-in-law Nathanael West. According to Wolfe, the theme of much of "The Hindsight Saga" "is a familiar one in Hollywood memoirs: the sophisticated but needy artist from the East at the mercy of golden boors of the West such as [Mike] Todd and Herman Mankiewicz." J. A. Ward in the *Southern Review* stated that Perelman and Nathanael West "found in the show business milieu both an ideal metaphor for American culture in general and a set of rhetorical techniques suitable to their own fictional interests." Perelman would produce "hundreds of short stories, nearly all variants on the same subject," Ward said, "the hyper-literary naive who becomes entrapped into actual or quasi-show business situations dominated by manic tyrants."

An inveterate traveler, Perelman also wrote numerous essays and published several collections based on his journeys. *Westward Ha! or Around the World in Eighty Cliches,* published in 1948, was the first of several works devoted entirely to his travel experiences. It contains twelve selections that were originally published in *Holiday* magazine and that are considerably longer than his standard essay. The book chronicles an around-the-world trip the author undertook with Al Hirschfeld, a caricaturist from the *New York Times.* Not only is *Westward Ha!* Perelman's first volume concerned entirely with travel, Gale wrote, "it is also his best. The content is well balanced between providing insights to the writer (and exploring the human condition through the metaphor of travel) and commenting on the locales he visits." In all of his travel pieces, according to Gale "Perelman's primary concern is Perelman. He is his own best subject and it is often difficult to distinguish between reporting and fiction. . . . Accidents, mishaps, scraps, emotional reactions, relationships with his fellow travelers, how he sees himself in relation to the world around him—these are Perelman's subjects."

After Perelman's wife died, the author sold their Bucks County farm so that he could travel more freely, once remarking that "happiness is a paper bag of possessions in a room at the Mills Hotel," related Mitgang. Dissatisfied, he moved to London but returned to the United States two years later after finding London too civilized. At age 74, he attempted to reverse the eight-thousand-mile route followed in his award-winning film, "Around the World in Eighty Days," as he drove his 1949 MG across Europe from Paris, through the Middle East and India. He spent a month in Hong Kong attempting to have the car sent by train so that he could complete the journey through China. He would have been the first person to bring a privately owned car into Communist China since the takeover in 1949 but had to abandon the project when he was hospitalized with pneumonia.

Perelman's style and tone tempered in his later years. In his book *Baby, It's Cold Inside,* for example, Perelman "becomes introspective in his tone," according to Gale. He "seems to look upon his material with a somewhat sadder and wiser detachment than had been apparent previously." Reviewing the posthumously published *The Last Laugh,* Terry Teachout commented in the *National Review:* "The reader begins to suspect that Perelman had simply ceased to find the world particularly amusing by the time he wrote these pieces. Such a development will come as no surprise, since Perelman was never a good-humor man at any point in his long career."

In Zinsser's opinion, the change in Perelman's tone was both a product of his advancing years and the turbulent decades of the 1960s and 1970s. "The biggest difference," Zinsser wrote, "is not that humor has gone out of the humorist, but that the world has taken over his work. Life today has become so outlandish that it outstrips the writer's comic imagination. It is its own comment." In a 1975 *Philadelphia Inquirer* interview with Maralyn Lois Polak, Perelman expressed a similar view: "I think humor in America has greatly declined and may disappear entirely. It is not easy to satirize the absurd when the absurd has become official."

In the *New York Times* obituary, Al Hirschfeld commented that he couldn't think of anyone working in comedy who hadn't been influenced by Perelman. Writers as diverse as Woody Allen and E. B. White have credited Perelman as an early influence. In a *Listener* article, Allen recalled that he discovered Perelman when he was still in high school: "I came across certain pieces that he had written and I immediately was stunned by them. I thought they were just the best and the funniest things I had ever read. . . . What happens to you when you read Perelman when you're a young writer is fatal because his style seeps into you. He's got such a pronounced, overwhelming comic style that it's very hard not to be influenced by him." As reported by Zinsser, White acknowledged Perelman's influence in their early days and commented that "his pieces usually had a lead sentence or lead paragraph that was as hair-raising as the first big dip on a roller coaster: it got you in the stomach, and when it was over you were relieved to feel deceleration setting in. In the realm of satire, parody, and burlesque, he has, from the beginning, bowed to none."

Other humorists have expressed their admiration—even their envy—of Perelman's abilities. Writing in *Saturday Review,* Steve Allen indicated that upon reading Perelman's *The Road to Miltown; or, Under the Spreading Atrophy,* "the professional humorist is apt to experience sensations similar to those known to pianists who listen to an Art Tatum recording. He feels, in other words, like giving up." According to Zinsser, Robert Benchley once said that "it was just a matter of time before Perelman took over the dementia praecox field and drove us all to writing articles on economics." And in her *New York Times* review of *The Road to Miltown,* Dorothy Parker judged that Perelman "stands alone in this day of humorists. Mr. Perelman—there he is. . . . Lonely he may be—but there he is."

Some two hundred of Perelman's manuscripts are on file in the Berg Collection at the New York Public Library.

MEDIA ADAPTATIONS: "One Touch of Venus" was adapted into a film in 1948.

BIOGRAPHICAL/CRITICAL SOURCES:

BOOKS

Atkinson, Brooks, editor, *Tuesdays and Fridays,* Random House, 1963.
Authors in the News, Gale, Volume 1, 1976, Volume 2, 1976.
Brustein, Robert S., editor, *Seasons of Discontent,* Simon & Schuster, 1965.
Contemporary Literary Criticism, Gale, Volume 3, 1975, Volume 5, 1976, Volume 9, 1978, Volume 15, 1980, Volume 23, 1983, Volume 44, 1987, Volume 49, 1988.

Dictionary of Literary Biography, Gale, Volume 11: *American Humorists, 1800-1950,* 1982, Volume 44: *American Screenwriters, Second Series,* 1986.
Fowler, D., *S. J. Perelman,* Twayne, 1983.
Gale, S. H., *S. J. Perelman,* Garland Publishing, 1985.
Gilman, Richard, editor, *Common and Uncommon Masks,* Random House, 1971.
Lister E., *Don't Mention the Marx Brothers,* Book Guild, 1985.
Newquist, Roy, editor, *Conversations,* Rand McNally, 1967.
Perelman, S. J., *The Most of S. J. Perelman,* Simon & Schuster, 1958, reprinted, 1980.
Perelman, S. J., *The Last Laugh,* Simon & Schuster, 1981.
Plimpton, George, editor, *Writers at Work,* Viking, 1963.
Sheed, Wilfred, editor, *The Morning After,* Farrar, Straus, 1971.
Wain, John, editor, *Essays on Literature and Ideas,* Macmillan, 1963.
Wilk, M., *And Did You Once See Sidney Plain?,* Coalition of Publications for Employment, 1985.
Yates, Norris W., editor, *The American Humorist,* Iowa University Press, 1964.

PERIODICALS

Atlantic, May, 1957, December, 1970, August, 1981.
Books, August 8, 1937, August 11, 1940, January 31, 1943.
Book Week, June 18, 1944, September 15, 1946, October 16, 1966.
Book World, September 6, 1970.
Boston Globe, February 3, 1943, June 7, 1944.
Boston Transcript, August 7, 1937, September 7, 1940.
Chicago Sun, September 2, 1948.
Chicago Sun Book Week, September 7, 1947.
Chicago Sunday Tribune, January 27, 1957, September 24, 1961.
Chicago Tribune Book World, July 5, 1981, November 20, 1983.
Christian Science Monitor, September 20, 1949, January 25, 1962, September 1, 1966.
Commonweal, July 9, 1948.
Detroit News, August 23, 1981.
Guardian, October 5, 1962.
Harpers Bazaar, May 2, 1972.
Life, February 9, 1962.
Listener, July 20, 1978, November 15, 1979.
Los Angeles Times Book Review, July 19, 1987.
Nation, October 15, 1949.
National Review, November 27, 1981.
New Republic, September 1, 1937, September 23, 1940, December 8, 1952, March 29, 1975, November 4, 1981.
New Statesman, November 24, 1967.
Newsweek, January 7, 1963, October 3, 1966, October 2, 1972.
New Yorker, August 10, 1940, December 23, 1950, October 29, 1979, August 13, 1984.
New York Herald Tribune Book Review, August 10, 1947, August 8, 1948, October 2, 1949, November 26, 1950, October 26, 1952, November 6, 1955, January 20, 1957, November 12, 1961.
New York Review of Books, April 6, 1978, November 5, 1981, November 8, 1984.
New York Times, November 30, 1930, April 8, 1937, January 31, 1943, July 2, 1944, August 25, 1946, August 24, 1947, August 8, 1948, September 25, 1949, November 26, 1950, November 9, 1952, October 30, 1955, January 20, 1957, November 20, 1957, September 30, 1970, January 7, 1971, June 13, 1971, March 21, 1975, June 10, 1981, June 25, 1981, February 2, 1987, February 8, 1987, May 14, 1987, July 2, 1987.

New York Times Book Review, July 2, 1944, January 20, 1957, December 10, 1961, September 18, 1966, August 30, 1970, March 23, 1975, October 2, 1977, March 15, 1981, July 19, 1981, July 8, 1984, July 5, 1987.
New York Times Magazine, January 26, 1969.
Paris Review, fall, 1963.
People, July 27, 1987.
Philadelphia Bulletin, October 27, 1974.
Philadelphia Inquirer, March 30, 1975.
Publishers Weekly, May 19, 1975.
San Francisco Chronicle, August 17, 1947, August 8, 1948, September 23, 1949, November 22, 1950, October 30, 1952, January 20, 1957, September 20, 1961.
Saturday Review, January 3, 1953, February 2, 1957, September 23, 1961, November 19, 1966, March 22, 1975, March 22, 1977, October 15, 1977, July, 1981.
Saturday Review of Literature, July 12, 1930, July 31, 1937, August 17, 1940, February 13, 1943, July 8, 1944, September 21, 1946, August 9, 1947, August 7, 1948, November 26, 1949, December 16, 1950.
South Atlantic Quarterly, winter, 1973.
Southern Review, summer, 1976.
Spectator, October 5, 1962, May 27, 1978.
Springfield Republican, November 23, 1952, October 29, 1961.
Theatre Arts, September, 1944, August, 1948.
Time, August 12, 1940, February 1, 1943, June 19, 1944, August 26, 1946, August 18, 1947, September 19, 1949, October 13, 1961, April 7, 1975, August 6, 1984, August 10, 1987.
Times (London), September 24, 1981.
Times Literary Supplement, November 30, 1962, April 16, 1970, August 27, 1971, November 16, 1973, July 7, 1978, December 25, 1981, September 24, 1982, February 5, 1988.
Vogue, February 1, 1963.
Voice, July 17, 1984.
Washington Post, November 30, 1978, July 8, 1987.
Washington Post Book World, October 30, 1977, August 2, 1981, June 21, 1987.
Weekly Book Review, July 9, 1944, September 8, 1946.

OBITUARIES:

PERIODICALS

Chicago Tribune, October 18, 1979.
New York Times, October 18, 1979.
Washington Post, October 18, 1979.

*   *   *

PERSE, Saint-John
    See LEGER, (Marie-Rene Auguste) Alexis Saint-Leger

*   *   *

PETERS, Ellis
    See PARGETER, Edith Mary

*   *   *

PETERS, S. H.
    See PORTER, William Sydney

*   *   *

PETRY, Ann (Lane)   1908-

PERSONAL: Born October 12, 1908, in Old Saybrook, Conn.; daughter of Peter Clarke (a druggist) and Bertha (James) Lane; married George D. Petry, February 22, 1938; children: Elisabeth Ann. *Education:* University of Connecticut, Ph.D., 1931; attended Columbia University, 1943-44.

ADDRESSES: Home—Old Saybrook, Conn. *Agent*—Russell & Volkening, Inc., 551 Fifth Ave., New York, N.Y. 10017.

CAREER: James' Pharmacy, Old Saybrook and Old Lyme, Conn., pharmacist, 1931-38; *Amsterdam News,* New York City, writer and advertising saleswoman, 1938-41; *People's Voice,* New York City, reporter and editor of woman's page, 1941-44; writer.

MEMBER: P.E.N., Authors Guild, Authors League of America (secretary, 1960).

AWARDS, HONORS: Houghton Mifflin literary fellowship, 1946; Litt.D. from Suffolk University, 1983.

WRITINGS:

ADULT FICTION; PUBLISHED BY HOUGHTON, EXCEPT AS INDICATED

The Street (novel), 1946, reprinted, Beacon Press, 1985.
Country Place (novel), 1947, reprinted, Chatham Bookseller, 1971.
The Narrows (novel), 1953, reprinted, Beacon Press, 1988.
Miss Muriel and Other Stories (short stories), 1971.

JUVENILE; PUBLISHED BY CROWELL, EXCEPT AS INDICATED

The Drugstore Cat, 1949.
Harriet Tubman: Conductor on the Underground Railroad, 1955, reprinted, Archway, 1971 (published in England as *A Girl Called Moses: The Story of Harriet Tubman,* Methuen, 1960).
Tituba of Salem Village, 1964.
Legends of the Saints, 1970.

OTHER

Work is represented in anthologies. Contributor to magazines.

SIDELIGHTS: With the publication of *The Street* in 1946, Ann Petry became the first black female author to address the problems black women face as they struggle to cope with life in the slums. Following in what Arthur P. Davis calls "the tradition of hard-hitting social commentary which characterized the Richard Wright school of naturalistic protest writing," *The Street* tells the story of Lutie Johnson's attempts to shield herself and her young son from the world outside their tiny Harlem apartment. Though several critics, including those commenting in the *New Yorker* and the *Saturday Review of Literature,* felt that the novel was somewhat "overwritten," they agreed with the majority of their colleagues that it was well worth reading.

For instance, despite what he termed "a bad sag in the last third of the book which is almost fatal," the *New Republic*'s Bucklin Moon was moved enough by Petry's unflinching portrayal of violence and degradation to remark: "Mrs. Petry knows what it is to live as a Negro in New York City and she also knows how to put it down on paper so that it is as scathing an indictment of our society as has ever appeared. . . . To this reviewer Mrs. Petry is the most exciting new Negro writer of the last decade."

In his *New York Times* review, Alfred Butterfield noted that "Ann Petry has chosen to tell a story about one aspect of Negro life in America, and she has created as vivid, as spiritually and emotionally effective a novel as that rich and important theme has yet produced. . . . It deals with its Negro characters without condescension, without special pleading, without distortion of any kind. . . . [It overflows] with the classic pity and terror of good imaginative writing."

After *The Street,* Petry wrote two more novels, *Country Place* in 1947 and *The Narrows* in 1953. Each one, though, takes place not in the slums of New York City, but in small, middle-class New England towns, a change in locale that critic Carl Milton Hughes describes as the author's "assertion of freedom as a creative artist with the whole of humanity in the American scene as her province." In short, declares Hughes in *The Negro Novelist: 1940-1950,* "Petry's departure from racial themes and the specialized Negro problem add[ed] to her maturity."

But the change in locale did not bring about a corresponding change in plot. As she did in *The Street,* Petry continued to build her stories around the same basic themes of adultery, cruelty, violence, and evil. *Country Place,* for example, examines the disillusionment of a returned soldier, Johnnie Roane, who discovers in the midst of a terrible storm that the town gossip about his wife's infidelity is true; though shattered by the realization, Roane resists the impulse to kill her and her lover and decides instead to make a new life for himself in New York. *The Narrows,* on the other hand, deals with the tragic affair between a young, well-educated black man and a rich white girl—an affair that is doomed as soon as the townspeople, both black and white, find out about it.

Some reviewers, such as the *New York Herald Tribune Weekly Book Review*'s Rose Feld and Richard Sullivan of the *New York Times,* criticize *Country Place*'s occasional plot improbabilities as well as Petry's technique of switching the identity of her narrator in mid-story, but most regard it as a worthy follow-up to *The Street.* Said J. C. Smith of the *Atlantic:* "Most of the characters are well done, but, curiously enough, Johnny Roane, the hero, is not. . . . Taken as a whole, though, *Country Place* is a good story. . . . It preaches no sermons, waves no flags. It tells a plausible narrative of . . . some very human people." Feld cited "the feel of a small town, the integrity of dialogue, [and] the portrayal of Johnnie, of Glory, [and] of Mrs. Gramby" as being among the "exceedingly good" parts of *Country Place,* while Sullivan noted that "despite the violence of its events, [it is] a rather quiet book, carefully and economically phrased" and "full of fresh, effective writing."

Bradford Smith of the *Saturday Review of Literature,* however, criticizes Petry for never really developing her basic premise. He writes: "The book seems to say (though not for the first time) that humanity is as degraded in [a small town] as in Studs Lonigan's Chicago. The trouble is that, while the reader is made to understand the social forces which produced Studs Lonigan, there is no comparable explanation for Mrs. Petry's characters. Her 'good' people . . . are shadowy, while her 'bad' people lack motivation or background."

Petry's third novel, *The Narrows,* prompts Arna Bontemps to comment in the *Saturday Review:* "A novel about Negroes by a Negro novelist and concerned, in the last analysis, with racial conflict, *The Narrows* somehow resists classification as a 'Negro novel,' as contradictory as that may sound. In this respect Ann Petry has achieved something as rare as it is commendable. Her book reads like a New England novel, and an unusually gripping one." Admitting that in less skilled hands the theme "might have been merely sensational," the *New York Herald Tribune Book Review*'s Mary Ross concludes that Petry "builds a novel that has depth and dignity. There is power and insight and reach of imagination in her writing."

On the other hand, a *New Yorker* critic characterizes *The Narrows* as "an anguished book, written with an enormous amount of emotion and some thought, that does not quite succeed because there is far too much of it." A *Nation* reviewer seemingly agrees, stating that "one gets the impression of a hodge-podge of styles, structures, ideas."

Wright Morris, discussing *The Narrows* in a *New York Times* article, is critical of another aspect of the book. "[Petry's] canvas has depth and complexity," he began, "but the surface drama central to the tragedy is like a tissue of tabloid daydreams, projected by the characters." In his book *Black on White: A Critical Survey of Writing by American Negroes,* David Littlejohn agrees that Petry has always had "an uncomfortable tendency to contrive sordid plots (as opposed to merely writing of sordid events). She seems to require a 'shocking' chain of scandalous doings . . . on which to cast her creative imagination." Nevertheless, he states, "so wise is her writing, . . . so real are her characters, so total is her sympathy, that one can often accept the faintly cheap horrors and contrivances. . . . And if one allows himself to be overexcited by these intrigues . . . he misses, I think, the real treasures of Ann Petry's fiction."

Among these treasures, Littlejohn says, can be found a "solid, earned, tested intelligence," "a prose that is rich and crisp," and "characters of shape and dimension, people made out of love, with whole histories evoked in a page. . . . This, to me, the intelligence, the style, and above all the creative sympathy, is what sets Ann Petry . . . into a place almost as prominent and promising as that of [Richard Wright, James Baldwin, and Ralph Ellison]. She is not, of course, writing 'about' the race war. . . . But if an American Negro can, despite all, develop such an understanding of other people as Ann Petry's—and more prodigious still, *convey* that understanding—then let her write what *Peyton Place*-plots she will, she is working toward a genuine truce in the war."

Critique: Studies in Modern Fiction reviewer Thelma J. Shinn also has words of praise for Petry's ability to understand and depict people—not just black people, but all people who are weakened and disillusioned by poverty and by racial and sexual stereotypes. Writes Shimm: "Petry has penetrated the bias of black and white, even of male and female, to reveal a world in which the individual with the most integrity is not only destroyed but is often forced to become an expression of the very society against which he is rebelling. . . . Ann Petry does not ignore the particular problems of blacks; her portrayals . . . display potentiality enough for admiration and oppression enough for anger to satisfy any black militant. Her novels protest against the entire society which would contrive to make any individual less than human, or even less than he can be."

AVOCATIONAL INTERESTS: Gardening, sewing, cooking, writing poetry.

BIOGRAPHICAL/CRITICAL SOURCES:

BOOKS

Bone, Robert A., *The Negro Novel in America,* revised edition, Yale University Press, 1965.
Children's Literature Review, Volume 12, Gale, 1987.
Contemporary Literary Criticism, Gale, Volume 1, 1973, Volume 7, 1977, Volume 18, 1981.
Davis, Arthur P., *From the Dark Tower: Afro-American Writers from 1900 to 1960,* Howard University Press, 1974.
Hughes, Carl Milton, *The Negro Novelist: 1940-1950,* Citadel Press, 1953, reprinted, 1970.

Littlejohn, David, *Black on White: A Critical Survey of Writing by American Negroes,* Viking, 1966.
O'Brien, John, editor, *Interviews with Black Writers,* Liveright, 1973.

PERIODICALS

Atlantic, November, 1947.
Christian Science Monitor, February 8, 1946, August 19, 1971.
Commonweal, February 22, 1946.
Critique: Studies in Modern Fiction, Volume 16, number 1, 1974.
Nation, August 29, 1953.
New Republic, February 11, 1946.
New Yorker, February 9, 1946, October 11, 1947, August 29, 1953.
New York Herald Tribune Book Review, August 16, 1953.
New York Herald Tribune Weekly Book Review, October 5, 1947.
New York Times, February 10, 1946, September 28, 1947, August 16, 1953.
Pharmacy in History, Volume 28, number 1, 1986.
San Francisco Chronicle, August 26, 1953.
Saturday Review, August 22, 1953, October 2, 1971.
Saturday Review of Literature, March 2, 1946, October 18, 1947.
Times Literary Supplement, May 2, 1986.

*　　*　　*

PEVSNER, Nikolaus (Bernhard Leon)   1902-1983

PERSONAL: Born January 30, 1902, in Leipzig, Germany (now East Germany); died after a long illness, August 18, 1983, in London, England; son of Hugo and Anna Pevsner; married Carola Kurlbaum, 1923 (died, 1963); children: Thomas, Dietrich, Uta Hodgson. *Education:* Attended Universities of Leipzig, Berlin, Frankfurt, and Munich; Ph.D., 1924.

ADDRESSES: Home—2 Wildwood Ter., North End, London N.W.3, England.

CAREER: Dresden Gallery, Dresden, Germany, assistant keeper, 1924-28; University of Goettingen, Goettingen, Germany, lecturer in history of art and architecture, 1929-33; University of London, Birkbeck College, London, England, professor of the history of art, 1945-68, professor emeritus, 1968—; Cambridge University, Cambridge, England, Slade Professor of Fine Art, 1949-55, fellow of St. John's College, 1950-55, honorary fellow, 1967. Reith Lecturer, British Broadcasting Corp., 1968-69; Slade Professor of Fine Art, Oxford University, 1968-69; lecturer on tours in Canada, South Africa, Australia, and New Zealand. Art Editor, Penguin Books. Member, Royal Fine Art Commission, Historical Building Council, National Advisory Council for Art Education, National Council for Diplomas in Art and Design, and Advisory Board for Redundant Churches. British commissioner, Council of Europe Exhibition, 1971.

MEMBER: Royal Institute of British Architects (honorary associate member), Society of Antiquaries (fellow), Royal College of Art (honorary associate member), Victorian Society (chairman), British Council (member of arts panel), William Morris Society, American Academy of Arts and Sciences (honorary member), Academia de Belle Art (Venice; honorary academician), Akademie der Wissenschaften Goettingen (honorary fellow).

AWARDS, HONORS: Commander, Order of the British Empire, 1953; Howland Prize, Yale University, 1963; Royal Gold Medal for architecture, 1967; knighted, 1969; recipient of doctorates from University of Leicester, University of York, University of Leeds, Oxford University, University of East Anglia, and University of Zagreb.

WRITINGS:

Italian Painting from the End of the Renaissance to the End of the Rococo, Atheneum, 1927-30.
The Baroque Architecture of Leipzig, W. Jess, 1928.
Pioneers of the Modern Movement from William Morris to Walter Gropius, Faber, 1936, 2nd edition published as *Pioneers of Modern Design from William Morris to Walter Gropius,* Museum of Modern Art, 1949, revised edition, Penguin, 1960.
An Inquiry into Industrial Art in England, Cambridge University Press, 1937.
(With S. Sitwell and A. Ayscough) *German Baroque Sculpture,* Duckworth, 1938.
Academies of Art, Past and Present, Macmillan, 1940, reprinted with new preface by the author, Da Capo Press, 1973.
An Outline of European Architecture, Penguin, 1942, Scribner, 1948, 8th edition, Penguin, 1973.
The Leaves of Southwell, Penguin, 1945.
Visual Pleasures from Everyday Things: An Attempt to Establish Criteria by Which the Aesthetic Qualities of Design Can Be Judged (booklet), Batsford, 1946.
Matthew Digby Wyatt, Cambridge University Press, 1950.
Charles R. Mackintosh, Il Balcone (Milan), 1950.
High Victorian Design, Architectural Press, 1951.
The Englishness of English Art, British Broadcasting Corp., 1955, expanded and annotated edition, Praeger, 1956, reprinted, Penguin, 1976.
(Author of foreword and postscript) Michael Farr, *Design in British Industry: A Mid-Century Survey,* Cambridge University Press, 1955.
(With Michael Meier) *Gruenewald,* Abrams, 1958.
Christopher Wren, 1632-1723, Universe Books, 1960.
The Planning of the Elizabethan Country House, Birkbeck College, University of London, 1961.
(With others) *The Sources of Modern Art,* Thames & Hudson, 1962, published as *The Sources of Modern Architecture and Design,* Praeger, 1968.
The Choir of Lincoln Cathedral: An Interpretation, Oxford University Press, 1963.
(Contributor) Peter Ferriday, editor, *Victorian Architecture,* J. Cape, 1963.
(Author of introduction) *Maxwell Fry,* Monks Hall Museum, 1964.
(Author of foreword) Nicholas Taylor, *Cambridge New Architecture: A Guide to the Post-War Buildings,* privately printed, 1964.
Art Nouveau in Britain (exhibition catalog), [London], 1965.
(Editor with John Fleming and Hugh Honour) *The Penguin Dictionary of Architecture,* Penguin, 1966, 3rd edition, 1980, revised and enlarged version of original edition published as *A Dictionary of Architecture,* Allen Lane, 1975, Overlook Press, 1976.
Studies in Art, Architecture, and Design, Walker & Co., 1968, Volume 1: *From Mannerism to Romanticism,* Volume 2: *Victorian and After.*
Ruskin and Viollet-le-Duc: Englishness and Frenchness in the Appreciation of Gothic Architecture, Thames & Hudson, 1969.
Robert Willis, Smith College, 1970.
Some Architectural Writers of the Nineteenth Century, Clarendon Press, 1972.
Architecture as a Humane Art, College of Architecture and Design, University of Michigan, 1973.

(Editor with James Maude Richards) *The Anti-Rationalists: Art Nouveau Architecture and Design,* Harper, 1973.

(Editor) *The Picturesque Garden and Its Influence outside the British Isles,* Dumbarton Oaks, 1974.

(Contributor) Jane Fawcett, editor, *The Future of the Past: Attitudes to Conservation, 1174-1974,* Whitney Library of Design, 1976.

A History of Building Types, Princeton University Press, 1976.

"THE BUILDINGS OF ENGLAND" SERIES; PUBLISHED BY PENGUIN

Cornwall, 1951, 2nd edition, revised by Enid Radcliffe, 1970.

Nottinghamshire, 1951, 2nd edition, revised by Elizabeth Williamson, 1979.

Middlesex, 1952.

North Devon, 1952.

South Devon, 1952.

London, Except the Cities of London and Westminster, 1952, reprinted, 1969.

Hertfordshire, 1953, 2nd edition, revised by Bridget Cherry, 1977.

Derbyshire, 1953, 2nd edition, revised by Williamson, 1978.

County Durham, 1954.

Cambridgeshire, 1954, 2nd edition, 1970.

Essex, 1954, 2nd edition, revised by Radcliffe, 1965.

London: The Cities of London and Westminster, 1957, 2nd edition, 1962, 3rd edition, revised by Cherry, 1973.

(With Ian A. Richmond) *Northumberland,* 1957, reprinted, 1974.

North Somerset and Bristol, 1958, reprinted, 1973.

South and West Somerset, 1958.

Shropshire, 1958.

Yorkshire: The West Riding, 1959, 2nd edition, revised by Radcliffe, 1968.

Leicestershire and Rutland, 1959.

Buckinghamshire, 1960.

Suffolk, 1961, 2nd edition, revised by Radcliffe, 1975.

Northamptonshire, 1961, 2nd edition, revised by Cherry, 1973.

(With Ian Nairn) *Surrey,* 1962.

North-east Norfolk and Norwich, 1962.

North-west and South Norfolk, 1962.

Herefordshire, 1963.

(With Derek Simpson) *Wiltshire,* 1963, 2nd edition, revised by Cherry and Desmond Bonney, 1976.

(With John Harris) *Lincolnshire,* 1964.

(With Nairn) *Sussex,* 1965.

Yorkshire: The North Riding, 1966.

Berkshire, 1966.

(With Alexandra Wedgwood) *Warwickshire,* 1966.

(With David Lloyd) *Hampshire and the Isle of Wight,* 1967.

Cumberland and Westmorland, 1967.

Bedfordshire and the County of Huntingdon and Peterborough, 1968.

Worcestershire, 1968.

Lancashire, two volumes, 1969.

(With John Newman) *West Kent and the Weald,* 1969.

(With Edward Hubbard) *Cheshire,* 1971.

(With John Hutchinson) *Yorkshire: York and the East Riding,* 1972.

(With Newman) *Dorset,* 1972.

Staffordshire, 1974.

(With Jennifer Sherwood) *Oxfordshire,* 1974.

OTHER

Editor, "Pelican History of Art" series, Penguin, 1953-66. Member of editorial board, *Architectural Review.*

BIOGRAPHICAL/CRITICAL SOURCES:

BOOKS

Summerson, John, editor, *Concerning Architecture: Essays on Architectural Writers and Writing Presented to Nikolaus Pevsner,* Penguin, 1968.

OBITUARIES:

PERIODICALS

Chicago Tribune, August 20, 1983.

Los Angeles Times, August 20, 1983.

New York Times, August 20, 1983.

Time, August 29, 1983.

Times (London), August 19, 1983, August 25, 1983.

* * *

PHILLIPS, Jack
See SANDBURG, Carl (August)

* * *

PHILLIPS, Jayne Anne 1952-

PERSONAL: Born July 19, 1952, in Buckhannon, W.Va.; daughter of Russell R. (a contractor) and Martha Jane (a teacher; maiden name, Thornhill) Phillips; married Mark Brian Stockman (a physician), May 26, 1985; children: one son, two stepsons. *Education:* West Virginia University, B.A. (magna cum laude), 1974; University of Iowa, M.F.A., 1978.

ADDRESSES: Home—Brookline, Mass. *Agent*—Lynn Nesbit, International Creative Management, 40 West 57th St., New York, N.Y. 10019.

CAREER: Writer. Adjunct associate professor of English, Boston University, Boston, Mass., 1982; Fanny Howe Chair of Letters, Brandeis University, Waltham, Mass., 1986-87.

MEMBER: Authors League of America, Authors Guild, P.E.N.

AWARDS, HONORS: Pushcart Prize, Pushcart Press, 1977, for *Sweethearts,* 1979, for short stories "Home" and "Lechery," and 1983, for short story "How Mickey Made It"; Fels Award in fiction, Coordinating Council of Literary Magazines, 1978, for *Sweethearts;* National Endowment for the Arts fellowship, 1978 and 1985; St. Lawrence Award for fiction, 1979, for *Counting;* Sue Kaufman Award for first fiction, American Academy and Institute of Arts and Letters, 1980, for *Black Tickets;* O. Henry Award, Doubleday & Co., 1980, for short story "Snow"; Bunting Institute fellowship, Radcliffe College, 1981, for body of work; National Book Critics Circle Award nomination, American Library Association Notable Book citation, and *New York Times* Best Books of 1984 citation, all 1984, all for *Machine Dreams.*

WRITINGS:

Sweethearts, Truck Press, 1976.

Counting, Vehicle Editions, 1978.

Black Tickets (short stories), Delacorte, 1979.

How Mickey Made It (short stories), Bookslinger, 1981.

Machine Dreams (novel), E. P. Dutton/Lawrence, 1984.

Fast Lanes (short stories), Vehicle Editions, 1984, reprinted, E. P. Dutton/Lawrence, 1987.

CONTRIBUTOR TO ANTHOLOGIES

Henderson, editor, *The Pushcart Prize II: Best of the Small Presses,* Pushcart Press, 1978.

Joyce Carol Oates and Shannon Ravenel, editors, *The Best American Short Stories 1979: Selected from U.S. and Canadian Magazines,* Houghton, 1979.

Abrams, editor, *The O. Henry Awards: Prize Stories 1980,* Doubleday, 1980.

Henderson, editor, *The Pushcart Prize IV: Best of the Small Presses,* Pushcart Press, 1980.

Cassill, editor, *The Norton Anthology of Short Fiction,* Norton, 1981.

Henderson, editor, *The Pushcart Prize VII: Best of the Small Presses,* Pushcart Press, 1983.

Wolff, editor, *Matters of Life and Death,* Wampeter Press, 1983.

Woodman, editor, *Stories about How Things Fall Apart and What Happens When They Do,* Word Beat Press, 1985.

Henry, editor, *Ploughshares Reader: Fiction for the Eighties,* Pushcart Press, 1985.

Hills and Jenks, editors, *Esquire Fiction Reader,* Wampeter Press, 1985.

Jenks, editor, *Soldiers and Civilians: Americans at War and at Home,* Bantam, 1986.

Solomon, editor, *American Wives,* Signet/New American Library, 1986.

Norris, editor, *New American Short Stories,* New American Library, 1986.

Forkner and Samway, editors, *Stories of the Modern South,* Penguin, 1986.

Chipps and Henderson, editors, *Love Stories for the Time Being,* Pushcart Press, 1987.

Carver and Jenks, editors, *American Short Story Masterpieces,* Delacorte, 1987.

OTHER

Contributor of short stories to magazines, including *Granta, Grand Street, Esquire,* and *Rolling Stone.*

SIDELIGHTS: Jayne Anne Phillips "stepped out of the ranks of her generation as one of its most gifted writers," writes Michiko Kakutani in the *New York Times.* "Her quick, piercing tales of love and loss [demonstrate] a keen love of language, and a rare talent of illuminating the secret core of ordinary lives with clearsighted unsentimentality," Kakutani continues. Phillips began as a poet, and that influence is apparent in her prose. Her "use of language is richly sensuous," says Carol Rumens in the *Times Literary Supplement.* "She takes street slang all the way to poetry and back. . . . Few enough writers at any time have the power to take language and polish it until it is sharp and gleaming again." David Wilk, Phillips's first publisher, is quoted by David Edelstein of *Esquire* as stating that her prose is enhanced by "the specificity of her language, the closely controlled writing on emotion."

The short stories in *Black Tickets,* Phillips's first effort for a commercial press, fall into three basic categories: short stylistic exercises, interior monologues by damaged misfits from the fringes of society, and longer stories about family life. In these stories, notes Michael Adams in the *Dictionary of Literary Biography Yearbook: 1980,* "Phillips explores the banality of horror and the horror of the banal through her examination of sex, violence, innocence, loneliness, illness, madness, various forms of love and lovelessness," and lack of communication. These stories were drawn, observes James N. Baker of *Newsweek,* "from observations she made in her rootless days on the road," in the mid-

1970s when she wandered from West Virginia to California and back again, "then developed in her imagination."

"Most of the stories in *Black Tickets,*" states Thomas R. Edwards in the *New York Review of Books,* "examine the lives of people who are desperately poor, morally deadened, in some way denied comfort, beauty, and love." While some of these stories deal with alienation within families, others are "edgy, almost hallucinatory portraits of disaffected, drugged out survivors of the 60s," according to Kakutani in the *New York Times.* Stories of this genre in the collection include "Gem-crack," the monologue of a murderer driven by a voice in his head that he calls "Uncle," and "Lechery," the story of a disturbed teenaged girl who propositions adolescents. These are "brittle episodes of despair, violence and sex," declares *Harper's* reviewer Jeffrey Burke, characterized by "economy and fierceness [and] startling sexuality," in the words of Walter Clemons of *Newsweek.*

Other stories—the strongest of the collection, in some reviewers' opinions—focus on less unique individuals. They are about more or less ordinary people, in families, who are trying to love each other across a gap," according to Edwards. Stories such as "Home," "The Heavenly Animal," and "Souvenir" all deal with the problems of grown-up children and their aging parents: a young woman's return home forces her divorced mother to come to terms with both her daughter's and her own sexuality; a father attempts to share his life—Catholic senior citizens meals, car repairs—with his daughter and fails; a mother slowly dying of cancer still has the courage to comfort her daughter. In them, Edwards states, "Phillips wonderfully captures the tones and gestures in which familial love unexpectedly persists even after altered circumstances have made [that love] impossible to express directly."

While some reviewers—like Rumens, who calls the dramatic monologues in *Black Tickets* "dazzling"—enjoy Phillips's richly sensuous language, others feel the author's best work is found in the more narrative stories concerning the sense of alienation felt by young people returning home. Stone calls them "the most direct and honest of the longer works in the collection" and states that "the language in these stories serves character and plot rather than the other way around." "The strength in these stories," says Mary Peterson in the *North American Review,* "is that even narrative gives way to necessity: honesty gets more time than forced technique; language is simple and essential, not flashy; and even the hard truth, the cruel one, gets telling."

In his review of *Black Tickets* which appeared in the *New York Times Book Review,* John Irving remarks, "I hope Miss Phillips is writing a novel because she seems at her deepest and broadest when she sustains a narrative, manipulates a plot, develops characters through more than one phase of their life or their behavior. I believe she would shine in a novel." *Machine Dreams,* the next book in Phillips's oeuvre, is indeed a novel. In it, the author uses the family in much the same way she had in some of the stories in *Black Tickets.* The novel tells the story of the Hampson family—Mitch, Jean, their daughter Danner and son Billy—focusing on the years between World War II and the Vietnam War, although it does show glimpses of an earlier, quieter time in Jean's and Mitch's reminiscences. Essentially, it is the story of the family's collapse, told from the point of view of each of the family members.

In a larger sense, however, *Machine Dreams* is about disorientation in modern life, tracing, in the words of Allen H. Peacock in the *Chicago Tribune Book World,* "not only [the Hampson's] uneasy truce with contemporary America but contemporary America's unending war with itself." Mitch and Jean were raised in the days of the Depression, hard times, "but characterized by community, stability and even optimism. You could tell the good guys from the bad ones in the war Mitch fought," says Jonathan Yardley in the *Washington Post Book World. Machine Dreams* is, he concludes, "a story of possibility gradually turning into disappointment and disillusionment," in which the Hampson family's dissolution mirrors "the simultaneous dissolution of the nation." Peacock echoes this analysis, declaring, "This is the stuff of tragedy: disintegration of a family, disintegration by association of a society." Toronto *Globe and Mail* contributor Catherine Bush points out that the machine dreams of the title, "the belief in technology as perpetual onward-and-upward progress; the car as quintessential symbol of prosperity: the glamor of flight . . . become nightmares. Literally, the dream comes crashing down when Billy leaps out of a flaming helicopter in Vietnam." Bush notes that Vietnam itself, however, is not the cause of the dissolution; appropriately, she observes, Phillips "embeds the war in a larger process of breakdown."

Part of this tragedy lies in the characters' inability to understand or control what is happening to them. Kakutani explains: "Everywhere in this book there are signs that the old certainties, which Miss Phillips's characters long for, have vanished or drifted out of reach. Looking for love, they end up in dissonant marriages and improvised relationships; wanting safety, they settle for the consolation of familiar habits." For them, there are no answers, there is no understanding. "This fundamental inexplicability to things," states Nicholas Spice in the *London Review of Books,* "is compounded for Phillips's characters by their uncertainty about what it is exactly that needs explaining. Emerson's dictum 'Dream delivers us to dream, and there is no end to illusion' might aptly stand as the motto of the book."

In *Machine Dreams,* many reviewers recognize the strength and power of Phillips's prose. " 'Black Tickets' posed a dilemma" for readers, states Anne Tyler in the *New York Times Book Review.* "Was it so striking because it was so horrifying, or because it was so brilliantly written? With 'Machine Dreams' we don't have to ask. Its shocks arise from small, ordinary moments, patiently developed, that suddenly burst out with far more meaning than we had expected. And each of these moments owes its impact to an assured and gifted writer." She also rises to the technical challenge of using more than one point of view. As John Skow of *Time* magazine declares, "Phillips . . . expresses herself in all four [character] voices with clarity and grace." Geoffrey Stokes writes in the *Voice Literary Supplement,* "That *Machine Dreams* would be among the year's best written novels was easy to predict," and Yardley calls the novel "an elegiac, wistful, rueful book."

A theme of discontinuity and isolation from the past, similar to that of *Machine Dreams,* is expressed in *Fast Lanes.* Like *Black Tickets,* it is a collection of short stories, whose "structural discontinuities," in the opinion of Paul Skenazy in the *San Francisco Chronicle,* "mirror the disassociated lives Phillips sets before us." The book begins with "stories of youthful drift and confusion and gradually moves, with increasing authority, into the past and what we might call home," comments Jay McInerney in the *New York Times Book Review.* Many of the characters "are joined more by circumstances than by relationships"; they "lack purpose and authority," says Pico Iyer of *Time* magazine. "Their world is fluid, but they do not quite go under. They simply float." These are people, adds Kakutani, for whom "rootlessness has become the price of freedom, alienation the cost of self-fulfillment."

In some reviewers' opinions, *Fast Lanes* suffers in comparison with *Machine Dreams.* For instance, Kakutani states that although "these [first] pieces remain shiny tributes to [the author's] skills—they rarely open out in ways that might move us or shed light on history the way that . . . *Machine Dreams* did." David Remnick, writing for the *Washington Post Book World,* does find that the last two stories in the book—the ones most reminiscent of the novel—are "such strong stories that they erase any disappointment one might have felt in the other five. They are among the best work of one of our most fascinating and gritty writers, and there can be little disappointment in that." Chicago *Tribune Books* contributor Alan Cheuse similarly says that in these stories "you can see [Phillips's] talent grow and flex its muscles and open its throat to reach notes in practice that few of us get to hit when trying our hardest at the height of our powers."

Some of Phillips's best writing, concludes Marianne Wiggins of the *Times Literary Supplement,* concerns "the near-distant fugitive past—life in the great USA fifteen years ago," reflecting the unsettledness of that period in American life. In some ways her writing returns to themes first expounded by the poets and novelists of the Beat generation; *Los Angeles Times Book Review* contributor Richard Eder calls *Fast Lanes* "the closing of a cycle that began over three decades ago with Kerouac's 'On the Road,' " the novel about the post-World War II generation's journey in search of the ultimate experience. "It is the return trip," Eder concludes, "and Phillips gives it a full measure of pain, laced with tenderness." McInerney echoes this assessment, calling Phillips "a feminized Kerouac."

In an interview with Phillips for *Publishers Weekly,* Celia Gilbert remarks, "Phillips has always been obsessed by the rootlessness of her generation and the accommodations families have to make to changing times." She adds, "Writing about . . . people on the road and at loose ends, she reflected part of her generation's experience, the generation that was of college age in the '70s." Phillips herself summarized her vision in that same interview: "Unlike the people of the '60s, we didn't have a strong sense of goals, nor the illusion we could make a difference. They were very organized and considered themselves a community. Their enemy was an obvious one. By the '70s, people began to experience a kind of massive ennui. Kids dropping acid did it to obliterate themselves, not to have a religious experience. Only people with a strong sense of self came through. . . . In the '70s there was still enough security so that people felt they could be floaters. Now things are too shaky for that."

MEDIA ADAPTATIONS: Machine Dreams has been optioned for film.

BIOGRAPHICAL/CRITICAL SOURCES:

BOOKS

Contemporary Literary Criticism, Gale, Volume 15, 1980, Volume 33, 1985.
Dictionary of Literary Biography Yearbook: 1980, Gale, 1981.

PERIODICALS

Books & Arts, November 23, 1979.
Books and Bookmen, December, 1984.
Books of the Times, January, 1980.
Boston Review, August, 1984.
Chicago Tribune, September 30, 1979.
Chicago Tribune Book World, June 24, 1984, July 22, 1984.
Commonweal, October 19, 1984.
Detroit News, January 27, 1980, December 13, 1984.

Elle, April, 1987.

Esquire, December, 1985.

Globe and Mail (Toronto), July 28, 1984.

Harper's, September, 1979.

Kirkus Reviews, February 15, 1987.

Listener, December 13, 1984.

London Review of Books, February 7, 1985.

Los Angeles Times Book Review, July 9, 1984, April 19, 1987.

Ms., June, 1984, June, 1987.

New Leader, December 3, 1979.

New Republic, December 24, 1984, September 2, 1985.

New Statesman, November 9, 1984.

Newsweek, October 22, 1979, July 16, 1984.

New York Review of Books, March 6, 1980.

New York Times, June 12, 1984, June 28, 1984, January 6, 1985, April 4, 1987, April 11, 1987.

New York Times Book Review, September 30, 1979, July 1, 1984, March 17, 1985, May 5, 1985, May 3, 1987.

North American Review, winter, 1979.

Observer, October 28, 1984.

Publishers Weekly, May 9, 1980, June 8, 1984, February 27, 1987.

Quill and Quire, September, 1984.

San Francisco Chronicle, July 22, 1984, April 5, 1987.

Spectator, November 3, 1984.

Threepenny Review, spring, 1981.

Time, July 16, 1984, June 1, 1987.

Times Literary Supplement, November 14, 1980, November 23, 1984, September 11, 1987.

Tribune Books (Chicago), April 19, 1987.

Village Voice, October 29, 1979.

Voice Literary Supplement, June, 1984, February, 1986.

Wall Street Journal, July 25, 1984.

Washington Post Book World, December 21, 1979, June 24, 1984, April 26, 1987.

West Coast Review of Books, November, 1984.

* * *

PHILLIPS, Richard
See DICK, Philip K(indred)

* * *

PHILLIPS, Ward
See LOVECRAFT, H(oward) P(hillips)

* * *

PIAGET, Jean 1896-1980

PERSONAL: Surname is pronounced pee-ah-jhay; born August 9, 1896, in Neuchatel, Switzerland; died September 16, 1980, in Geneva, Switzerland; son of Arthur (a professor) Piaget; married Valentine Chatenay (a psychologist), 1923; children: Jacqueline, Lucienne, Laurent. *Education:* Universite de Neuchatel, B.A., 1915, Ph.D., 1918; postgraduate study at Universitaet Zurich, Universite de Paris, and the Sorbonne.

ADDRESSES: Office—Faculty of Psychology and Educational Sciences, University of Geneva, 3 Place de l'Universite, 1211 Geneva 4, Switzerland.

CAREER: Institut Jean Jacques Rousseau, Geneva, Switzerland (now Institut des Sciences de l'Education, University of Geneva), research psychologist, 1921-33, co-director, 1933-71; Un-

iversite de Neuchatel, Neuchatel, Switzerland, professor of philosophy, 1925-29; Universite de Geneve, Geneva, associate professor of the history of scientific thought, 1929-39, professor of sociology, 1939-52, professor of experimental psychology, 1940-71, professor emeritus, 1971-80; International Center of Genetic Epistemology, Geneva, founder and director, 1955-80. Director of International Bureau of Education, Geneva, 1929-67; professor of psychology at Universite de Lausanne, Lausanne, Switzerland, 1937-51; professor of psychology at the Sorbonne, 1952-63. Visiting lecturer at numerous universities in Europe and the United States.

MEMBER: Academie Internationale de Philosophie des Sciences, Institut Internationale de Philosophie, Union Internationale de Psychologie Scientifique, New York Academy of Science, Boston Academy of Arts and Sciences, Academie dei Lincei, Academie des Sciences de Bucarest, Academie des Sciences et Lettres de Montpellier, Academie Royale de Belgique, Association de Psychologie Scientifique de Langue Francaise, Societe Suisse de Logique et de Philosophie des Sciences, Societe de Psychologie de Espagne, Societe Suisse de Psychologie, Societe Neuchateloise des Sciences Naturelles, Federacion Columbiana de Psicologia.

AWARDS, HONORS: Prix de la Ville de Geneve, 1963; American Research Association award, 1967; American Psychological Association award, 1969; Prix Foneme, 1970; Erasmus Prize, 1972; Prix de l'Institut de la Vie, 1973. Honorary degrees from numerous universities, including Harvard University, 1936, the Sorbonne, 1946, University of Brussels, 1949, University of Oslo, 1960, Cambridge University, 1960, University of Moscow, 1966, Yale University, 1970, Temple University, 1971, and Yeshiva University, 1973.

WRITINGS:

IN ENGLISH TRANSLATION

Le Langue et la pensee chez l'enfant, Delachaux & Niestle, 1923, 7th edition, 1968, translation by Marjorie Worden published as *The Language and Thought of the Child,* Harcourt, 1926, 3rd revised edition, Humanities, 1959, reprinted, 1971.

(With others) *Le Jugement et le raisonnement chez l'enfant,* Delachaux & Niestle, 1924, 5th edition, 1963, translation by Worden published as *The Judgment and Reasoning in the Child,* Harcourt, 1928, published as *The Judgment and Reason in the Child,* 1929, reprinted, Littlefield, 1976.

Le Representation du monde chez l'enfant, Delachaux & Niestle, 1926, translation by Jean Tomlinson and Andrew Tomlinson published as *The Child's Conception of the World,* Harcourt, 1929, reprinted, Littlefield, 1975.

La Causalite physique chez l'enfant, Delachaux & Niestle, 1927, translation by Marjorie Worden Gabain published as *The Child's Conception of Physical Causality,* Harcourt, 1930.

Le Jugement moral chez l'enfant, Presses universitaires de France, 1932, 4th edition, 1973, translation by Gabain published as *The Moral Judgment of the Child,* Harcourt, 1932, reprinted, Free Press of Glencoe, 1966.

La Naissance de l'intelligence chez l'enfant, Delachaux & Niestle, 1936, 5th edition, 1966, translation by Margaret Cook published as *The Origins of Intelligence in Children,* International Universities Press, 1952, published as *The Origin of Intelligence in the Child,* Routledge & Kegan Paul, 1953, Norton, 1963.

La Construction du reel chez l'enfant, Delachaux & Niestle, 1937, 3rd edition, 1963, translation by Cook published as *Child's Construction of Reality,* Routledge & Kegan Paul,

1953, published as *The Construction of Reality in the Child,* Basic Books, 1954, reprinted, Ballantine, 1986.

(With Barbel Inhelder) *Le Developpement des quantites chez l'enfant: Conservation et atomisme,* Delachaux & Niestle, 1940, 2nd augumented edition, 1962, translation by Arnold J. Pomerans published as *The Child's Construction of Quantities: Conservation and Atomism,* Routledge & Kegan Paul, 1974.

(With Alina Szeminska) *La Genese du nombre chez l'enfant,* Delachaux & Niestle, 1941, 3rd edition, 1964, translation by C. Gattegno and F. M. Hodgson published as *The Child's Conception of Number,* Routledge & Kegan Paul, 1952, Norton, 1965.

La Formation du symbole chez l'enfant: Imitation jeu et reve, image et representation, Delachaux & Niestle, 1945, 2nd edition, 1959, translation by Gattegno and Hodgson published as *Play, Dreams, and Imitation in Childhood,* Norton, 1951, reprinted, Peter Smith, 1988.

(With others) *Les Notions de mouvement et de vitesse chez l'enfant,* Presses universitaires de France, 1946, translation by G. E. T. Holloway and M. J. Mackenzie published as *The Child's Conception of Movement and Speed,* Basic Books, 1970, reprinted, Ballantine, 1986.

(With Esther Bussmann, Edith Meyer, Vroni Richi, and Myriam van Remoortel) *Le Developpement de la notion de temps chez l'enfant,* Presses universitaires de France, 1946, 2nd edition, 1973, translation by Pomerans published as *The Child's Conception of Time,* Routledge & Kegan Paul, 1969, Ballantine, 1985.

La Psychologie de l'intelligence, Colin, 1947, translation by M. Piercy and D. E. Berlyne published as *The Psychology of Intelligence,* Routledge & Kegan Paul, 1950, Littlefield, 1976.

(With Inhelder) *La Representation de l'espace chez l'enfant,* Presses universitaires de France, 1948, translation by F. J. Langdon and J. L. Lunzer published as *The Child's Conception of Space,* Humanities, 1956.

(With Inhelder and Szeminska) *La Geometrie spontanee de l'enfant,* Presses universitaires de France, 1948, 2nd edition, 1973, translation by E. A. Lunzer published as *The Child's Conception of Geometry,* Basic Books, 1960.

(With Inhelder) *La Genese de l'idee de hasard chez l'enfant,* Presses universitaires de France, 1951, translation by Lowell Leake, Paul Burrell, and Harold Fishbein published as *The Origin of the Idea of Chance in Children,* Norton, 1975.

Logic and Psychology, translation by Wolfe Mays and F. Whitehead, Manchester University Press, 1953, Basic Books, 1957.

(With Inhelder) *De la logique de l'enfant a logique de l'adolescent,* Presses universitaires de France, 1955, translation by Anne Parson and Stanley Milgrom published as *The Growth of Logical Thinking from Childhood to Adolescence: An Essay on the Construction of Formal Operational Structures,* Basic Books, 1958.

Le Genese des structures logique elementaire: Classifications et seriations, Delachaux & Niestle, 1959, translation by Lunzer and D. Papert published as *The Early Growth of Logic in the Child: Classification and Seriation,* Harper, 1964.

Les Mecanismes perceptifs, Presses universitaires de France, 1961, translation by G. N. Seagrim published as *The Mechanisms of Perception,* Basic Books, 1969.

Comments on Vygotsky's Critical Remarks Concerning "The Language and Thought of the Child," and "Judgment and Reasoning in the Child," translated by Parson, M.I.T. Press, 1961.

(With Evert W. Beth) *Epistemologie mathematique et psychologie: Essai sur les relations entre la logique formelle et la pensee reele,* Presses universitaires de France, 1961, translation published as *Mathematical Epistemology and Psychology,* Gordon & Beech, 1966.

(With Paul Fraisse and Maurice Reuchlin) *Histoire et methode,* Presses universitaires de France, 1963, 3rd edition, 1970, translation by Judith Chambers published as *History and Method,* Basic Books, 1968.

(Editor with Fraisse) *Traite de psychologie experimentale,* Presses universitaires de France, 1963, 3rd edition, 1970, translation published as *Experimental Psychology: Its Scope and Method,* Basic Books, 1968.

Six etudes de psychologie, Gonthier, 1964, translation by Anita Tenzer and David Elkind published as *Six Psychological Studies,* Random House, 1967.

Sagesse et illusions de la philosophie, Presses universitaires de France, 1965, 3rd edition, 1972, translation by Wolfe Mays published as *Insights and Illusions of Philosophy,* World Publishing, 1971.

(With Inhelder) *L'Image mentale chez l'enfant,* Presses universitaires de France, 1966, translation by P. A. Chilton published as *Mental Imagery in the Child: A Study of the Development of Imaginal Representation,* Basic Books, 1971.

(With Inhelder) *La Psychologie de l'enfant,* Presses universitaires de France, 1966, 6th edition, 1975, translation by Helen Weaver published as *The Psychology of the Child,* Basic Books, 1969.

Biologie et connaissance: Essai sur les relations entre les regulations organiques et les processus cognitifs, Gallimard, 1966, reprinted, 1973, translation by Beatrix Walsh published as *Biology and Knowledge: An Essay on the Relations between Organic Regulations and Cognitive Processes,* University of Chicago Press, 1971.

On the Development of Memory and Identity, translation by Eleanor Duckworth, Barre, 1968.

John Amos Comenius on Education, Teachers College, 1968.

Le Structuralisme, Presses universitaires de France, 1968, 6th edition, 1974, translation by Chaninah Maschler published as *Structuralism,* Basic Books, 1970.

(With Inhelder) *Memoire et intelligence,* Presses universitaires de France, 1968, translation by Arnold J. Pomerans published as *Memory and Intelligence,* Basic Books, 1973.

L'Epistemologie genetique, Presses universitaires de France, 1970, translation by Duckworth published as *Genetic Epistemology,* Basic Books, 1972.

(With R. Garcie) *Les Explications causales,* Presses universitaires de France, 1971, translation by Donald Miles and Marguerite Miles published as *Understanding Causality,* Norton, 1974.

Science of Education and the Psychology of the Child, translation by Derek Coltman, Viking, 1971, reprinted, Penguin, 1977.

Psychology and Epistemology: Towards a Theory of Knowledge, translation by P. A. Wells, Viking, 1972.

The Principles of Genetic Epistemology, translation by Mays, Basic Books, 1972.

Ou va education, Denoel/Gonthier, 1973, translation by George-Anne Roberts published as *To Understand Is To Invest: The Future of Education,* Grossman, 1973.

The Child and Reality: Problems of Genetic Psychology, translation by Arnold Rosin, Grossman, 1973.

Main Trends in Interdisciplinary Research, Harper, 1973.

Main Trends in Psychology, Harper, 1973.

The Place of the Sciences of Man in the System of Sciences, Harper, 1974.

(With others) *Recherches sur la contradiction,* two volumes, Presses universitaires de France, 1974, translation by Derek Coltman published as *Experiments in Contradiction,* University of Chicago Press, 1981.

Adaptation vitale et psychologie de l'intelligence: Selection organique et phenocopie, Hermann, 1974, translation by Stewart Eames published as *Adaptation and Intelligence: Organic Selection and Phenocopy,* University of Chicago Press, 1980.

L'Equilibration des structures cognitives: Probleme central du developpement, Presses universitaires de France, 1975, translation by Arnold Rosin published as *The Development of Thought: Equilibration of Cognitive Structures,* Viking, 1977.

(With M. Amann) *Reussir et comprendre,* Presses universitaires de France, 1978, translation by Pomerans published as *Success and Understanding,* Harvard University Press, 1978.

The Grasp of Consciousness: Action and Concept in the Young Child, translation by Susan Wedgwood, Harvard University Press, 1976.

Sarah F. Campbell, editor, *Piaget Sampler: An Introduction to Jean Piaget through His Own Words,* Wiley, 1976, J. Atonson, 1977.

Howard E. Gruber and J. Jacques Voneche, editors, *The Essential Piaget,* Basic Books, 1977.

Behavior and Evolution, translation by Donald Nicholson-Smith, Pantheon, 1978.

Howard E. Gruber and J. Jacques Voneche, editors, *The Essential Piaget: An Interpretive Reference and Guide,* Basic Books, 1978.

Jeanette McCarthy Gallagher and J. A. Easley, Jr., editors, *Piaget and Education,* Plenum, 1978.

Jean-Claude Bringuier, *Conversations with Jean Piaget,* University of Chicago Press, 1980.

Massimo Piattelli-Palmarini, editor, *Language and Learning: The Debate between Jean Piaget and Noam Chomsky,* Harvard University Press, 1980.

Intelligence and Affectivity: Their Relationship during Child Development, translation by T. A. Brown and C. E. Kaegi, Annual Reviews, 1981.

Possibility & Necessity, two volumes, translation by Helga Feider, University of Minnesota Press, 1987.

(With Rolando Garcia) *Psychogenesis & the History of Science,* translation by Feider, Columbia University Press, 1988.

IN FRENCH

Recherche (novel), Edition la Concorde, 1918.

Classes, relations et nombres: Essai sur les groupements de la logistique et sur la reversibilite de la pensee, Vrin, 1942.

(With Marc Lambercier, Ernest Boesch and Barbara von Albertini) *Introduction a l'etude des perceptions chez l'enfant et analyse d'une illusion relative a la perception visuelle de cercles concentriques,* Delachaux & Niestle, 1942.

(With Lambercier) *La Comparaison visuelle des hauteurs a distances variables dans la plan fronto-parallele,* Delachaux & Niestle, 1943.

(With others) *Essai d'interpretation probabliste de la loi de Weber et de celles des concentrations relatives,* Delachaux & Niestle, 1945.

(With Inhelder) *Experiences sur la construction projective de la ligne droite chez les enfants de 2 a 8 ans,* Delachaux & Niestle, 1946.

Etude sur la psychologie d'Edouard Claparede, Delachaux & Niestle, 1946.

Le Droit a l'education dans le monde actuel, UNESCO, 1949.

(With M. Boscher) *L'Initiation au calcul: Enfants de 4 a 7 ans,* Bourrelier, 1949.

Traite de logique: Essai de logistique operatoire, Colin, 1949, 2nd edition published as *Essai de logique operatoire,* Dunod, 1972.

Introduction a l'epistemologie genetique, three volumes, Presses universitaires de France, 1950, 2nd edition, 1973.

Essai sur les transformations des operations logiques: Les 256 operations ternaires de la logique bivalente des propositions, Presses universitaires de France, 1952.

Les Relations entre l'affectivite et l'intelligence dans le developpement mental de l'enfant, Centre de Documentation Universitaire, 1954.

(With others) *L'Enseignement des mathematiques,* Delachaux & Niestle, 1955.

(Editor) *Etudes d'epistemologie genetique,* Presses universitaires de France, 1957.

(With Inhelder) *Le Developpement des quantites physiques chez l'enfant,* Delachaux & Niestle, 1962.

(With Fraisse, Elaine Vurpillot, and Robert Frances) *La Perception,* Presses universitaires de France, 1963.

(Editor with Maurice Patronnier de Gandillac) *Entretiens sur les notions de genese et de structure,* Mouton, 1965.

Etudes sociologiques, Librarie Droz, 1965.

Logique et connaissance scientifique, Gallimard, 1967.

La Psychologie de l'intelligence, A. Colin, 1967, 2nd edition, 1973.

Epistemologie et psychologie de l'identite, Presses universitaires de France, 1968.

(With others) *Epistemologie et psychologie de la fonction,* Presses universitaires de France, 1968.

Epistemologie des sciences de l'homme, Gallimard, 1970.

(With others) *Les Theories de la causalite,* Presses universitaires de France, 1971.

(With J. Bliss) *Les Directions des mobiles lors de chocs et de poussees,* Presses universitaires de France, 1972.

(With Bliss) *La Transmission des mouvements,* Presses universitaires de France, 1972.

La Formation de la notion de force, Presses universitaires de France, 1973.

(With Bliss) *La composition des forces et le probleme des vecteurs,* Presses universitaires de France, 1973.

(With A. Blanchet) *La Prise de conscience,* Presses universitaires de France, 1974.

Les Mecanismes perceptifs: Modeles probabilistes, analyse genetique, relations avec l'intelligence, 2nd edition, Presses universitaires de France, 1975.

Le Comportement, moteur de l'evolution, Gallimard, 1976.

(With Gil Henriques and I. Berthoud-Papandropoulou) *Recherches sur la generalisation,* Presses universitaires de France, 1978.

Recherches sur les correspondances, Presses universitaires de France, 1980.

CONTRIBUTOR

Troisieme cours pour le personnel enseignant, Bureau International d'Education, 1930.

Quatrieme cours pour le personnel enseignant, Bureau International d'Education, 1931.

C. Murchison, editor, *Handbook of Child Psychology,* Clark University Press, 1931.

Le Self-Government a l'ecole, Bureau International d'Education, 1934.

Le Travail par equipes a l'ecole, Bureau International d'Education, 1935.

UNESCO, Freedom and Culture, Columbia University Press, 1951.

(And author of introduction) *Conference internationale de l'instruction publique,* [Geneva], 1951.

E. G. Boring and others, *History of Psychology in Autobiography,* Volume 4, Clark University Press, 1952.

Swanson, Newcomb, and Hartley, editors, *Readings in Social Psychology,* Holt, 1952.

(And author of introduction) R. Girod, *Attitudes collectives et relations humaines,* Presses universitaires de France, 1952.

H. E. Abramson, *Conference on Problems of Consciousness,* Josiah Macy Foundation, 1954.

P. Osterrieth and others, *Le Probleme des stades en psychologie de l'enfant,* Presses universitaires de France, 1955.

P. H. Hock and J. Zubin, editors, *Psychopathology of Childhood,* Grune & Stratton, 1955.

J. de Ajuriaguerra and others, *Aktuelle Problem der Gestalttheorie,* Hans Huber, 1955.

J. Tanner and Inhelder, editors, *Discussions on Child Development,* Volumes 1-4, Tavistock, 1956, International Universities Press, 1958.

(And author of introduction) Jan Comenius, *Pages Choisies,* UNESCO, 1957, also published as *Selections,* UNESCO [Paris], 1957.

D. Katz, *Handbuch der Psychologie,* 2nd edition, Benno Schwabe, 1959.

(Author of introduction) M. Margot, *L'Ecole operante,* Delachaux & Niestle, 1960.

(And author of introduction) M. Nassefat, *Etude quantitative sur l'evolution des operations intellectuals,* Delachaux & Niestle, 1963.

(And author of introduction) Elaine Vurpillot, *L'Organisation perceptive,* Vrin, 1963.

(And author of introduction) Inhelder, *Le Diagnostic du raisonnement chez les debiles mentaux,* 2nd edition, Delachaux & Niestle, 1963.

(And author of introduction) John H. Flavell, *The Developmental Psychology of Jean Piaget,* Van Nostrand, 1963.

Richard E. Ripple and Verne N. Rockcastle, editors, *Piaget Rediscovered,* Cornell University School of Education, 1964.

(And author of introduction) T. Gouin Decarie, *Intelligence and Affectivity in Early Childhood,* translation by Elisabeth Brandt and Lewis Brandt, International Universities Press, 1965.

(And author of introduction) Millie Almy and others, *Young Children's Thinking: Studies of Some Aspects of Piaget's Theory,* Teacher's College Press, 1966.

(And author of introduction) *Dictionnaire d'epistemologie genetique,* Presses universitaires de France, 1966.

Marcia W. Piers, editor, *Play and Development: A Symposium,* Norton, 1972.

Richard I. Evans, *Jean Piaget: The Man and His Ideas,* Dutton, 1973.

OTHER

Contributor to *Proceedings of the International Congresses of Psychology,* Harvard Tercentenary Conference. Co-editor of *Revue Suisse de Psychologie* and *Archives de Psychologie.* Contributor to numerous periodicals, including *Mind, British Journal of Psychology, Initiation au Calcul, Scientific American, Enfance, British Journal of Educational Psychology, Revue Suisse Psychologie, Synthese, Methados, Diogene Traite de Psychologie Experimentale, Etudes d'Epistemologie Genetique, Journal de Psychologie Normale et Pathologique, Archives de Psychologie* (Geneva), *American Journal of Mental Deficiency, Acta Psychologica,* and *Annee Psychologique.*

SIDELIGHTS: Psychologist Jean Piaget spent most of his long and productive career studying the development of intelligent thinking in children. *Times Literary Supplement* contributor Keith Lovell called Piaget "one of the giants in the history of psychology," a tireless worker who gave the world "a wealth of brilliant and penetrating insights into the intellectual growth of children." In an era when much attention focused on abnormal or pathological behavior, Piaget became known for his descriptions of the normal processes that transform infants into rational, creative adults. His work took into account biological functions, environmental stimuli, and even philosophical theory to create a detailed picture of the stage development of human intellectual life. According to Howard Gardner in the *New York Times Book Review,* Piaget "realized a scientific career of unsurpassed fecundity" that is still gaining approval among modern educators and social scientists. Margaret A. Boden expressed a similar opinion in her work *Jean Piaget.* The psychologist's influence, noted Boden, "has been enormous, especially in his later years, by which time American experimental psychology had moved toward a philosophical base more congruent with his approach." Jerome S. Bruner put it more simply in a *New York Times Book Review* essay. To quote Bruner, Piaget remains "one of the two towering figures of 20th-century psychology."

Ironically, Piaget did not consider himself a child psychologist. He preferred the title "genetic epistemologist"—one who studies the mechanisms by which an organism learns. Richard Evans explained the term in *Jean Piaget: The Man and His Ideas.* "Genetic epistemology deals with the formation and meaning of knowledge and with the means by which the human mind goes from a lower level of knowledge to one that is judged to be higher," Evans wrote. "It is not for psychologists to decide what knowledge is lower or higher but rather to explain how the transition is made from one to the other. The nature of these transitions is a factual matter. They are historical, or psychological, or sometimes even biological." *New York Review of Books* essayist Rosemary Dinnage claimed that Piaget's "mighty project," the one that consumed him for sixty years, was "to trace, right into adulthood, the growth of all the major concepts that structure our world: time, space, causality, substance, number." By this means Piaget discovered that learning is not something poured into a child, but rather something a child helps to create through his or her own activities. In the *New Republic,* Robert Coles concluded: "His studies are meant to give us clues about how we get to be the somewhat knowing, thoughtful people we are. . . . [Piaget was] ever anxious to learn how it is we obtain our knowledge of the world—an acquisition that begins during the first days of life."

Piaget was born and raised in Neuchatel, Switzerland, the son of a college professor who specialized in the history of the Middle Ages. In *Jean Piaget: The Man and His Ideas,* Piaget described his childhood as not particularly happy; his mother suffered from mental illness, and partly out of fear of her condition he threw himself into rigorous scientific study at an early age. He was only eleven when he published his first paper—a short account of a rare part-albino sparrow he observed in his garden. From there he undertook the biological study of mollusks, a genera of great variety in Switzerland. While still in his early teens he was invited to assist the curator of Neuchatel's museum, and he began writing a series of papers on the mollusks in the museum's collection. His reputation became such that at the tender age of sixteen he was offered the directorship of another of Switzerland's mollusk collections—the board of trustees were not aware that he had yet to finish high school. In *Jean Piaget: The Man and His Ideas,* Piaget reminisced about the lasting importance of his work on mollusks, which he continued in college: "These studies, premature as they were, were nevertheless of great value for my scientific development; moreover, they functioned, if I may say so, as instruments of protection against the demon of philosophy. Thanks to them, I had the rare privilege of getting a glimpse of science and what it stands for, before undergoing the philosophical crises of adolescence. To have had early experience with these two kinds of problematic approaches constituted, I am certain, the hidden strength of my later psychological activity."

Eventually Piaget became less interested in pure biology and more consumed by the philosophical/psychological dilemma of "how we know." He turned to psychological study as a means to the end of developing a biologically-oriented theory on the nature and origins of knowledge. As Howard E. Gruber noted in the *New York Times Book Review,* Piaget "took up the study of the child as an approach to fundamental epistemological questions. To his surprise, this became a never-ending enterprise." In the 1920s, many people held the view that children were merely "little adults," who reasoned like grownups. While administering intelligence tests on his young subjects, Piaget came to realize that the "wrong" answers children gave to some questions were quite revealing. Boden explained: "These errors were not merely insignificant mistakes due to childish ignorance and uninformed guessing; rather, they suggested to Piaget's amazement that the logical structures of the child's mind are importantly different from those of adult knowledge. . . . Piaget decided to explore children's thinking further for the light it might throw on the nature and development of human knowledge in general: psychology, he thought, was 'the embryology of intelligence.' " Evans described the aim of Piaget's early experiments: "By testing the child's understanding of the physical, biological, and social worlds at successive age levels, Piaget hoped to find an answer to the question of how we acquire knowledge. In effect Piaget had created an experimental philosophy that sought to answer philosophical questions by putting them to empirical test."

Piaget summarized his findings on juvenile cognition in a series of books, beginning in 1923 with *Le langue et la pensee chez l'enfant* (translated into English as *The Language and Thought of the Child*). Although he later wrote that his early publications were premature—merely the groundwork for future theories—they "made Piaget's name and have probably been more widely read than anything he subsequently wrote," to quote Dinnage. In 1925 Piaget and his wife began their own family, and with the birth of their daughter Jacqueline, they embarked on a program of detailed observation of infant behavior. Boden declared that the result of this observation "was the theory of sensorimotor intelligence, published through the 1930s, which described the spontaneous development (well before the appearance of language) of a practical intelligence based in action, an intelligence that forms and is formed by the infant's nascent concepts of permanent objects, space, time, number, and cause." Put more simply, Piaget suggested that such humble infant acts as sucking and looking constitute the earliest manifestations of intellect, and that babies are born possessing structures with which to organize experience. Dinnage concluded that the birth of his own children made Piaget aware "of how much happened in children's lives before they even started to talk, and one of the main themes in all his work since then has been that intelligence can only grow through actual physical as well as mental engagement with the environment." The critic added that Piaget's books on his chil-

dren's growth "make up the only coherent account we have of the human being's experience in the first year of life."

"Piaget set himself the task of explaining how the mental structures of the newborn baby become the structures of the adolescent intellect," wrote P. G. Richmond in *An Introduction to Piaget.* "He knew these extreme conditions were not the same and that there must be changes in between which would explain how the first condition became the last." Taking issue with conceptions of heredity and passive accumulation of knowledge as the formative processes in children's cognition, Piaget contended that youngsters of all ages were active agents in their personal intellectual development. According to Evans, Piaget "spoke of learning as, in part, 'the modification of experience as the result of behavior.' He argued that the child's actions upon the world changed the nature of his experience. This is another way of stating the relativity of nature and nurture. If experience is always a product (to some extent) of the child's behavior, any modification of behavior as a result of experience must be relative to the child's actions. Human experience, then, must be relative to human action. . . . Piaget [argued] that the mind never copies reality but instead organizes it and transforms it, reality, in and of itself being . . . unknowable." Bruner felt that Piaget "made a profound mark on modern psychology by refocusing attention on man's sources of rationality, on the processes by which he achieves that rationality, and by showing how human intelligence at all levels of development can be described precisely and rigorously in terms of the underlying logic of the action through which intelligence expresses itself."

As his experience with children of all ages accumulated, Piaget was able to formulate a series of four major stages of mental growth. In the first, the "sensory-motor period," the infant is chiefly concerned with the mastery of objects—toys, blocks, and household items. This phase lasts roughly from birth to two years. The second stage, the "preoperational period," concerns the mastery of symbols, including those occurring in language, fantasy, play, and dreams. This period generally lasts until age six. From six to twelve, the child undergoes the "concrete operational period," during which he or she learns to master the concepts of numbers, classes, and relations, and how to reason about them. Finally, the adolescent enters the "formal operational period," a stage dominated by logical thought and the understanding of others' thinking. "One of Dr. Piaget's major contributions was his development of a theory that children pass through distinct stages of mental and emotional development," wrote J. Y. Smith in the *Washington Post.* "This home truth has been observed by other psychologists—and by numerous parents—but Dr. Piaget gave it a coherence that has had enormous implications not only for the development of clinical child psychology, but also for education." Piaget was criticized for the formality of his stage development plan, but he himself was careful not to tie the stages too closely to chronological ages, recognizing that individual children develop at different rates. Coles summarized Piaget's formulation: "If Freud has taught us how hard and even fierce a struggle each child must wage for sanity, emotional stability, self-respect, Piaget has given us a glimpse of the work that goes into the gradually obtained victory we all too readily tend to think of as a flat given: intelligence—meaning competence, judgment and perceptiveness with respect to the things of this world."

Because he was trained first as a biologist, Piaget sought to explain the development of intelligence as a biological adaptation to the environment—the human organism's way of maximizing its genetic potential. Boden contended that the scholar's "genetic structuralism in biology attempted a synthesis of the Darwinian stress on the organism's autonomy and the Lamarckian emphasis on the organism's adaptive response to the environment." Piaget's guiding principle was the movement toward "equilibrium," achieved through the two components of adaptation he called "assimilation" and "accommodation." Henry W. Maier explained the concepts in *Thinkers of the Twentieth Century.* "In Piagetian formulation," Maier stated, "equilibration involves the adaptive processes of assimilation and accommodation. A process of feedback and forecasting leads to an advancement in thinking. To put it in another way, events are understood or adjusted at first within the context of ongoing comprehension in order to make sense out of one's experience. Assimilation occurs at the expense of the input. Accommodation, in contrast, changes a person's understanding (and eventually the structure of comprehending) in order to adapt more fully and potentially reorganize one's conception of the world." Evans put it thus: "Piaget's answer . . . was that the child's ideas about the world were 'constructions' that involved both mental structures and experience. . . . While the changes with age imply the role of experience, their orderliness reflects an interaction between nature and nurture." Dinnage, too, concluded that "the crown of the theory . . . is that precisely as the individual's thinking evolves from infancy, so do species themselves evolve—both are concerned in a process of constant re-equilibration, of balancing accommodation to the environment with assimilation of it."

To quote Whitman, "the unfolding of Dr. Piaget's explanations occurred over a lifetime, so there were refinements as new evidence was sifted; but these did not alter his basic theories." Piaget was a prolific writer who spent at least four hours every day composing new text; his lifetime output has been estimated at more than one hundred books, chapters of books, published papers, and edited volumes. As Piaget's explorations of juvenile cognition became more complicated over the years, however, so did his writings. In the *New York Times Book Review,* David Elkind declared that as he did less of the interviewing of children himself, and as his theory became more systematic, Piaget's style "became more abstract and difficult to read. Moreover, he [made] no concessions to readers and [assumed] that they [would] understand his integration of biological, logical, philosophical and psychological concepts." Gardner similarly observed that Piaget's publications "are workaday at best, and often pose difficulties for colleagues and translators." Elkind added, though, that despite their difficulty, "the books are rewarding because on almost every page there are fresh insights into the ways children think about and see the world. For those who have the time and are willing to put in the effort, reading Piaget himself more than repays the investment."

Piaget's work has had broad implications for the fields of psychology, education, and philosophy. "Many experienced or gifted teachers have long applied Piaget's concepts in the classroom without giving conscious consideration to the matter," wrote Richmond. "In such cases Piaget's work lends systematic support to what is intuitively understood. In another sense, however, Piaget's work has greater value. The generality of his concepts, and the panoramic view of intellectual development he offers, can comment upon a diversity of educational matters." Boden addressed a different dimension of Piaget's study. "Psychologists," she claimed, "have given much attention to his theory of intelligence as interiorized action, to his vision of the mind as a continuously developing system of self-regulating structures that actively mediate and are transformed by the subject's interaction with the environment." Dinnage looked at Piaget's work from its philosophical perspective in her essay. The critic observed that from Piaget's perspective, "childhood is a long process of 'decentering,' abandoning the egocentric position until gradually 'the self is freed from itself and assigns itself a place as a thing among things, an event among events.' For Piaget this is noble: the great act of intellect, as central for the individual as when 'Copernicus ceased to believe in geocentrism and Einstein in Newtonian absolutes.'" Here, concluded Dinnage, "we find the unacknowledged moral mainspring of all [Piaget's] work."

If the intellectual establishment was slow to accept Piaget's theories, subsequent decades have enhanced the scholar's reputation. According to Evans, Piaget retained "the ambiguous position of the intellectual innovator" throughout his life, and therefore "it will probably be decades before his ideas become firmly rooted within the canons of psychology." Evans explained, however, that Piaget will be remembered just as Sigmund Freud has been, and for many of the same reasons. "The findings he . . . gleaned, and the theory he . . . constructed after more than forty years of studying the development of intelligence, are effecting a veritable Copernican revolution in our understanding of the growth and functioning of the human mind," Evans wrote. Boden likewise stated that modern developmental psychology "would be very different without him and, surely, considerably poorer." She added: "For all the criticisms that can justly be made of him, there is no question that Piaget is a modern master. At both observational and theoretical levels, his work has provided a stimulus to (or more appropriately perhaps, a seed of) our understanding of the development of intelligence that is without equal." *New York Times* correspondent John Leonard concluded that Piaget "asked the right questions and . . . what he observed of children getting to know space, time, cause and objectivity is an indispensable starting point for thinking about how the mind constructs the world." To quote Leonard further, Piaget's "is at least a humane psychology, stressing curiosity and competence."

BIOGRAPHICAL/CRITICAL SOURCES:

BOOKS

Atkinson, Christine, *Making Sense of Piaget: The Philosophical Roots,* Routledge & Kegan Paul, 1983.

Boden, Margaret, *Jean Piaget,* Viking, 1979.

Brainerd, J., *Piaget's Theory of Intelligence,* Prentice-Hall, 1978.

Brearly, Molly and Elizabeth Hitchfield, *A Teacher's Guide to Reading Piaget,* Routledge & Kegan Paul, 1966.

Bruner, Jerome S., *The Process of Education,* Harvard University Press, 1960.

Bruner, Jerome S., *Towards a Theory of Instruction,* Harvard University Press, 1966.

Butterworth, George, editor, *Infancy and Epistemology: An Evaluation of Piaget's Theory,* St. Martin's, 1982.

Cohen, David, *Piaget: Critique and Reassessment,* Croom Helm, 1983.

Dasen, Pierre R., editor, *Piagetian Psychology: Cross Cultural Contributions,* Gardner Press, 1976.

Egan, Kieran, *Education and Psychology: Plato, Piaget, and Scientific Psychology,* Columbia Teachers College Press, 1983.

Elkind, David and John Flavell, editors, *Studies in Cognitive Development: Essays in Honor of Jean Piaget,* Oxford University Press, 1969.

Evans, Richard I., *Jean Piaget: The Man and His Ideas,* Dutton, 1973.

Evans, Richard I., *Dialogue with Jean Piaget,* Praeger, 1981.

Flavell, John H., *The Developmental Psychology of Jean Piaget,* Van Nostrand, 1963.

Furth, Han, *Piaget and Knowledge: Theoretical Foundations,* Prentice Hall, 1969.

Gallagher, J. M. and Reid, D. K., *The Learning Theory of Piaget and Inhelder,* Brooks/Cole, 1981.

Geber, Beryl A., *Piaget and Knowing: Studies in Genetic Epistemology,* Routledge & Kegan Paul, 1977.

Gruber, Howard E. and J. Jacques Voneche, *The Essential Piaget: An Interpretive Reference and Guide,* Basic Books, 1978.

Holloway, G. E. T., *An Introduction to "The Child's Conception of Geometry,"* Routledge & Kegan Paul, 1967.

Hunt, J. McVicker, *Intelligence and Experience,* Ronald, 1961.

Inhelder, Barbel and Harold H. Chipman, editors, *Piaget and His School: A Reader in Developmental Psychology,* Springer-Verlag, 1976.

Kessen, William and Clementina Kuhlman, *Thought in the Young Child: Report with Particular Attention to the Work of Piaget,* Child Development Publications, 1960.

Kitchener, Richard F., *Piaget's Theory of Knowledge: Genetic Epistemology and Scientific Reason,* Yale University Press, 1986.

Labinowicz, E., *The Piaget Primer,* Addison-Wesley, 1980.

Liben, Lynn S., editor, *Piaget and the Foundations of Knowledge,* Erlbaum, 1983.

Maier, Henry, *Three Theories of Child Development,* Harper, 1965.

Malerstein, A. J., *A Piagetian Model of Character Structure,* Human Sciences Press, 1982.

Modgil, Sohan and Celia Modgil, *Jean Piaget: Consensus and Controversy,* Praeger, 1982.

Modgil, Sohan, and others, editors, *Jean Piaget: An Interdisciplinary Critique,* Routledge & Kegan Paul, 1983.

New Directions in Piagetian Theory and Practice, Erlbaum, 1981.

Phillips, J. L., *Piaget's Theory: A Primer,* W. H. Freeman, 1980.

Piattelli-Palmarini, Massimo, *Language and Learning: The Debate between Jean Piaget and Noam Chomsky,* Harvard University Press, 1980.

Pulaski, M. A. S., *Understanding Piaget,* revised edition, Harper, 1980.

Richmond, P. G., *An Introduction to Piaget,* Basic Books, 1971.

Ripple, Richard E. and Verne N. Rockcastle, editors, *Piaget Rediscovered,* Cornell University School of Education, 1964.

Seltman, Muriel and Peter Seltman, *Piaget's Logic: A Critique of Genetic Epistemology,* Allen and Unwin, 1985.

Shulman, Valerie L., and others, editors, *The Future of Piagetian Theory: The Neo-Piagetians,* Plenum, 1985.

Silverman, Hugh J., editor, *Piaget, Philosophy, and the Human Sciences,* Humanities Press, 1980.

Thinkers of the Twentieth Century, Gale, 1983.

Varma, Ved P. and Phillip Williams, editors, *Piaget, Psychology and Education: Papers in Honor of Jean Piaget,* Hodder & Stoughton, 1976.

Wadsworth, B. J., *Piaget's Theory of Cognitive Development,* Longman, 1979.

Wolff, Peter H., *The Developmental Psychologies of Jean Piaget and Psychoanalysis,* International Universities Press, 1960.

PERIODICALS

American Sociological Review, February, 1966.
Commonweal, April 5, 1968.
Education Digest, March, 1968.
New Republic, March 18, 1978.
New York Review of Books, December 21, 1978, October 23, 1980.
New York Times, January 25, 1980.
New York Times Book Review, February 11, 1968, August 1, 1976, May 14, 1978, October 19, 1980.

New York Times Magazine, May 26, 1968.
Saturday Review, May 20, 1967, April 20, 1968.
Times Educational Supplement, December 6, 1957.
Times Literary Supplement, August 22, 1968, September 4, 1969, June 25, 1970, March 17, 1972, June 2, 1972, August 11, 1972, June 29, 1973, August 19, 1977.
Yale Review, winter, 1987.

OBITUARIES:

PERIODICALS

Newsweek, September 29, 1980.
New York Times, September 17, 1980.
Time, September 29, 1980.
Times (London), September 18, 1980.

—*Sketch by Anne Janette Johnson*

* * *

PIERCY, Marge 1936-

PERSONAL: Born March 31, 1936, in Detroit, Mich.; daughter of Robert and Bert (Bunnin) Piercy; married third husband, Ira Wood, June 2, 1982. *Education:* University of Michigan, A.B., 1957; Northwestern University, M.A., 1958.

ADDRESSES: Home—Box 943, Wellfleet, Mass. 02667. *Agent*—Lois Wallace, Wallace Literary Agency, Inc., 177 East 70th St., New York, N.Y.

CAREER: Writer. Gives readings of her own poetry. Board member, Massachusetts Foundation for Humanities and Public Policy, Massachusetts Council on the Arts and Humanities, 1986—, and Massachusetts Arts Lottery Council, 1988—.

AWARDS, HONORS: Avery and Jule Hopwood Award of University of Michigan for poetry and fiction (minor award), and for poetry (major award); literature award, Governor's Commission on the Status of Women (Massachusetts); Borestone Mountain Poetry Award (twice); Orion Scott Award in Humanities; National Endowment for the Arts award, 1978.

WRITINGS:

POETRY

Breaking Camp, Wesleyan University Press, 1968.
Hard Loving, Wesleyan University Press, 1969.
(With Bob Hershon, Emmet Jairett, and Dick Lourie) *4-Telling,* Crossing Press, 1971.
To Be of Use, Doubleday, 1973.
Living in the Open, Knopf, 1976.
The Twelve-Spoked Wheel Flashing, Knopf, 1978.
The Moon Is Always Female, Knopf, 1980.
Circles on the Water: Selected Poems of Marge Piercy, Knopf, 1982.
Stone, Paper, Knife, Knopf, 1983.
My Mother's Body, Knopf, 1985.
Available Light, Knopf, 1988.

FICTION

Going Down Fast, Trident, 1969.
Dance the Eagle to Sleep, Doubleday, 1971.
Small Changes, Doubleday, 1973.
Woman on the Edge of Time, Knopf, 1976.
The High Cost of Living, Harper, 1978.
Vida, Summit, 1980.
Braided Lives, Summit, 1982.
Fly Away Home, Summit, 1984.

Gone to Soldiers, Summit, 1987.
Summer People, Summit, 1989.

OTHER

The Grand Coolie Damn, New England Free Press, 1970.
(With Ira Wood) *The Last White Class: A Play about Neighborhood Terror,* Crossing Press, 1979.
Parti-Colored Blocks for a Quilt, University of Michigan Press, 1982.
(Editor) *Early Ripening: American Women Poets Now,* Unwin Hyman, 1988.

Work represented in over 100 anthologies, including *Best Poems of 1967, New Women, The Fact of Fiction,* and *Psyche: The Feminine Poetic Consciousness.* Contributor of poetry, fiction, essays and reviews to *Paris Review, Transatlantic Review, Mother Jones, New Republic, Village Voice,* and *Prairie Schooner.* Most of Piercy's books have been translated into foreign languages, including French, Dutch, Italian, Japanese, Hebrew, German, Norwegian, Swedish, and Danish.

SIDELIGHTS: "Almost alone among her American contemporaries, Marge Piercy is radical and writer simultaneously, her literary identity so indivisible that it is difficult to say where one leaves off and the other begins," writes Elinor Langer in the *New York Times Book Review.* A prominent and sometimes controversial poet/novelist, Piercy first became politically active in the 1960s, when she joined the civil rights movement and became an organizer for SDS (Students for a Democratic Society). After a few years, she realized that the male power structure associated with the mainstream capitalist society was also operating in the anti-war movement and that women were being relegated to subservient work. In 1969, she shifted her allegiance to the fledgling women's movement where her sympathies remain.

Now she openly acknowledges that she wants her writing—particularly some of her poems—to be "useful." "What I mean by being of use," Piercy explained in the introduction to *Circles on the Water,* "is not that the poems function as agitprop or are didactic, although some of them are. . . . What I mean by useful is simply that readers will find poems that speak to and for them, will take those poems into their lives and say them to each other and put them up on the bathroom wall and remember bits and pieces of them in stressful or quiet moments. That the poems may give voice to something in the experience of a life has been my intention. To find ourselves spoken for in art gives dignity to our pain, our anger, our lust, our losses. We can hear what we hope for and what we most fear in the small release of cadenced utterance. We have few rituals that function for us in the ordinary chaos of our lives."

Piercy's moralistic stance, more typical of nineteenth than twentieth century writers, has alienated some critics, producing charges that she is more committed to her politics than to her craft. The notion makes Piercy bristle: "As a known feminist I find critics often naively imagine I am putting my politics directly into the mouth of my protagonist," she told Michael Luzzi in an interview reprinted in *Parti-Colored Blocks for a Quilt.* "That I could not possibly be amused, ironic, interested in the consonances and dissonances. They notice what I have created and assume I have done so blindly, instead of artfully, and I ask again and again, why? I think reviewers and academics have the fond and foolish notion that they are smarter than writers. They also assume if you are political, you are simpler in your mental apparatus than they are; whereas you may well have the same background in English and American literature they have, but add to it a better grounding in other European and Asian and

South American literatures, and a reasonable degree of study of philosophy and political theory."

Fellow feminist and poet Erica Jong has sympathized with Piercy's dilemma, writing in the *New York Times Book Review* that she is "an immensely gifted poet and novelist whose range and versatility have made it hard for her talents to be adequately appreciated critically."

Rather than propaganda, Piercy creates what she calls "character-centered fiction." As she explained to *CA:* "I start with a theme and work very very hard to develop well-rounded characters. For me, plot issues from character." And while she has always desired that her poems work for others, she told Richard Jackson that "it is as absurd . . . to reduce poems to political statements as it is to deny they have a political dimension."

Piercy's sense of politics is deep-rooted. She grew up poor and white in a predominantly black section of Detroit. Her mother was a housewife with a tenth-grade education; her father a millwright who repaired and installed machinery. From her surroundings, Piercy learned about the inequities of the capitalist system: "You see class so clearly there," she told Celia Betsky in the *New York Times Book Review.* "The indifference of the rich, racism, the strength of different groups, the working-class pitted against itself."

Piercy escaped the destiny of many of her contemporaries (unhappy marriages filled with unwanted children) by winning a scholarship to the University of Michigan. The first person in her family to attend college, she was an enthusiastic student, encouraged in her writing by winning several Hopwood awards. Still, professional success did not come easily. Ten years elapsed before she was able to give up a series of odd jobs and support herself by writing. Her first six novels were rejected, and she suspects that *Going Down Fast* found a publisher largely because of its lack of women's consciousness and its male protagonist.

Despite such resistance, Piercy kept writing political novels featuring female characters, often with backgrounds similar to her own. In 1973, she published *Small Changes,* a novel that *New Republic* contributing critic Diane Schulder calls "one of the first to explore the variety of life-styles that women . . . are adopting in order to give meaning to their personal and political lives." Addressing women's issues head on, this book conveys what *New York Times Book Review* contributing critic Sara Blackburn calls "that particular quality of lost identity and desperation, which, once recognized as common experience, has sparked the rage and solidarity of the women's liberation movement." In an essay she wrote for *Women's Culture: The Women's Renaissance of the Seventies,* Piercy describes the book as "an attempt to produce in fiction the equivalent of a full experience in a consciousness-raising group for many women who would never go through that experience." To demonstrate the way that female subjugation cuts across social strata, she includes both a working class woman, Beth, and a middle class intellectual, Miriam, as main characters.

In her depiction of these women, Piercy concentrates on what Catharine R. Stimpson calls "the creation of a new sexuality and a new psychology, which will permeate and bind a broad genuine equality. So doing, she shifts the meaning of small change," Stimpson continues in the *Nation.* "The phrase no longer refers to something petty and cheap but to the way in which a New Woman, a New Man, will be generated: one halting step after another. The process of transformation will be as painstaking as the dismantling of electrified barbed wire."

Widely reviewed by established magazines and newspapers, *Small Changes* received qualified praise. No critics dismiss the novel as unimportant, and most commend Piercy's energy and intelligence, but many object to the rhetoric of the book. "There is not a good, even tolerable man in the whole lot of characters," observes Margaret Ferrari in her *America* review. "While the women in the novel are in search of themselves, the men are mostly out to destroy themselves and anyone who crosses their paths. The three main ones in the novel are, without exception, stereotyped monsters." For this reason, Ferrari describes her reaction to the novel as "ambivalent. The realistic Boston and New York locales are enjoyable. The poetry is alluring and the characters' lives are orchestrated so that shrillness is always relieved. . . . In short, the novel is absorbing despite its political rhetoric."

After praising Piercy's "acute" social reportage and her compelling story line, Richard Todd raises a similar objection. "What is absent in this novel is an adequate sense of the oppressor," he writes in the *Atlantic*. "And beyond that a recognition that there are limits to a world view that is organized around sexual warfare. It's hard not to think that Piercy feels this, knows that much of the multiplicity and mystery of life is getting squeezed out of her prose, but her polemical urge wins out."

Piercy challenges the validity of such criticisms. "People tend to define 'political' or 'polemical' in terms of what is not congruent with their ideas," she told Karla Hammond in an interview reprinted in *Parti-Colored Blocks for a Quilt*. "In other words, your typical white affluent male reviewer does not review a novel by Norman Mailer as if it were political the same way he would review a novel by Kate Millet. Yet both are equally political. The defense of the status quo is as political as an attack on it. A novel which makes assumptions about men and women is just as political if they're patriarchial assumptions as if they're feminist assumptions. Both have a political dimension."

And a few reviewers concede their biases. William Archer, for instance, speculates in his *Best Sellers* review that "the special dimension of this book becomes apparent only through a determined suspension of one's preconceptions and a reexamination of their validity."

If *Small Changes* delineates the oppression of women, *Woman on the Edge of Time* affords a glimpse of a better world. The story of a woman committed to a mental hospital and her periodic time travels into the future, the novel juxtaposes our flawed present against a utopian future. "My first intent was to create an image of a good society," writes Piercy in *Women's Culture: The Women's Renaissance of the Seventies,* "one that was not sexist, racist, or imperialist: one that was cooperative, respectful of all living beings, gentle, responsible, loving, and playful. The result of a full feminist revolution." Despite a cool reception by critics, *Woman on the Edge of Time* remains one of Percy's personal favorites. "It's the best I've done so far," she wrote in 1981.

With *Vida,* her sixth novel, Piercy returns to the real world of the sixties and seventies, cataloging the breakdown of the revolutionary anti-war movement and focusing on a political fugitive who will not give up the cause. Named for its main character, Davida Asch, the novel cuts back and forth from past to present, tracing Vida's evolution from liberal to activist to a member of a radical Weatherman-type group called the Network. Still on the run for her participation in a ten-year-old bombing, Vida must contend with a splintered group that has lost its popular appeal as well as the nagging temptation to slip back into society and resume normal life. "The main action is set in the autumn of 1979," explains Jennifer Uglow in the *Times Literary Supple-*

ment, "as Vida faces divorce from her husband (turned media liberal and family man), her mother's final illness, her sister's imprisonment and the capture of an old colleague and lover. The pain of these separations is balanced against the hope offered by a new lover, Joel." At the story's close, Joel (a draft dodger) is captured by the F.B.I. and Vida, for whom the loss is acute, is not certain she can continue. But she does. "What swept through us and cast us forward is a force that will gather and rise again," she reflects, hunching her shoulders and disappearing into the night.

A former political organizer, Piercy writes from an insider's point of view, and critics contend that this affects the novel. "There is no perspective, there are not even any explanations," notes Elinor Langer in the *New York Times Book Review*. "Why we are against the war, who the enemy is, what measures are justified against the state—all these are simply taken for granted." And while a state of "war" may well exist between American capitalists and American radicals, the 1960s revolutionaries are not of the same caliber as the French Resistance workers or the Yugoslav partisans, according to *Village Voice* contributing reviewer Vivian Gornick. "Vida Asch and her comrades are a parody of the Old Left when the Old Left was already a parody of itself," she maintains.

Politics aside, reviewers find much that is praiseworthy in the novel. "The real strength of the book lies not in its historical analysis but in the power with which the loneliness and desolation of the central characters are portrayed," notes Jennifer Uglow. Lore Dickstein calls it "an extraordinarily poignant statement on what has happened to some of the middle-class children of the Sixties," in the *Saturday Review*. And Elinor Langer commends Vida as "a fully controlled, tightly structured dramatic narrative of such artful intensity that it leads the reader on at almost every page."

A strong protagonist and an engaging plot are also the components of *Fly Away Home,* Piercy's eighth novel. Thanks to these strengths, this oft-told tale of a woman's coming to awareness because of divorce becomes "something new and appealing: a romance with a vision of domestic life that only a feminist could imagine," says *Ms.* reviewer Ellen Sweet.

Though Daria Walker, the main heroine, is a traditional wife in a conventional role, Alane Rollings deems her "a true heroine. Not a liberated woman in the current terms of career-aggressiveness," Rollins continues in the *Chicago Tribune Book World,* "she is a person of 'daily strengths' and big feelings. When we first meet her, she is a success almost in spite of herself, a Julia Child-type TV chef and food writer, but more important to her, a loving wife and mother in a lovely home." Sweet calls her a "Piercy masterpiece."

Not everyone agrees with this assessment. Because Daria's self-awakening is tied to her growing awareness of her husband's villainy, and because Ross, the husband, is a sexist profiteer who exemplifies the inequities of the capitalist system, some critics suggest that "politics sometimes takes precedence over characterization," as Jeanne McManus puts it in the *Washington Post Book World*. "Daria's not only got to get her own life together but also take on a city full of white-collar real estate criminals who are undermining Boston's ethnic minorities. And she's not just a full-figured woman in a society of lean wolfhounds, but also a bleeding heart liberal, a '60s softy, in an age of Reaganomics. It's a pleasure when Piercy lets Daria sit back and just be herself, frustrated, angry or confused."

In an interview with Michael Luzzi, however, Piercy asserts that her "characters do have their own momentum and I can't force them to do things they won't do. Sometimes in the first draft, they disturb the neat outlines of the previously arranged plot, but mostly I try to understand them well enough before I start to have the plot issue directly out of the characters." And in the eyes of some critics, Piercy succeeds. As Sweet observes in *Ms.:* "The real plot [in *Fly Away Home*] is in Daria's growing awareness of herself and her social context."

In addition to her novels, Piercy has published books of poetry, each of which reflects her political sympathies and feminist point of view. "I am not a poet who writes primarily for the approval or attention of other poets," she explains in her introduction to *Circles on the Water,* and, in a letter to *CA,* she provides further insight into her work: "Usually the voice of the poems is mine. Rarely do I speak through a mask or persona. The experiences, however, are not always mine, and although my major impulse to autobiography has played itself out in poems rather than novels, I have never made a distinction in working up my own experience and other people's. I imagine I speak for a constituency, living and dead, and that I give utterance to energy, experience, insight, words flowing from many lives. I have always desired that my poems work for others. 'To Be of Use' is the title of one of my favorite poems and one of my best-known books."

Accessible to ordinary readers, Piercy's poetry recounts not only the injustices of sexism, but also such pleasures of daily life as making love or gardening. "There is always a danger that poems about little occurrences will become poems of little consequence, that poems which deal with current issues and topics will become mere polemic and propaganda, that poems of the everyday will become pedestrian," observes Jean Rosenbaum in *Modern Poetry Studies.* "To a very large extent, however, Marge Piercy avoids these dangers because most of her poetry contributes to and extends a coherent vision of the world as it is now and as it should be."

Writing in the *New York Times Book Review,* Margaret Atwood refers to Piercy's perception as "the double vision of the utopian: a view of human possibility—harmony between the sexes, among races and between humankind and nature—that makes the present state of affairs clearly unacceptable by comparison." In her poems, Piercy's outrage often explodes. "You exiled the Female into blacks and women and colonies," she writes in *To Be of Use,* lashing out at the mechanistic men who rule society. "You became the armed brain and the barbed penis and the club. / You invented agribusiness, leaching the soil to dust, / and pissed mercury in the rivers and shat slag on the plains, / withered your emotions to ulcers."

Though some critics maintain that Piercy at her angriest is Piercy at her best, the poet does not limit herself to negativism. She also writes of the strength that lies buried in all women and the ways it can be tapped. "Stretch out your hand," Piercy writes in *Hard Loving,* "stretch out your hand and look: / each finger is a snake of energy, / a gaggle of cranking necks. / Each electric finger conducts the world."

While her poetry "focuses on the social problems of America, it focuses also on her own personal problems," Victor Contoski explains in *Modern Poetry Studies,* "so that tension exists not only between 'us' and 'them,' but between 'us' and 'me.'" The following lines from "Doing It Differently," published in *To Be of Use,* demonstrate the way in which even private relationships are tinged by social institutions: "We will be equal, we say, new man and new woman. / But what man am I equal to before the law of court or custom? / The state owns my womb and hangs a

man's name on me / like the tags hung on dogs, my name is, property of. . . ." This is poetry both personal—that is, addressed from a particular woman to a particular man—and public, meaning that it is concerned with issues that pertain to all of society.

Playfulness, sensuality, and humor also figure in Piercy's poems, and one of the verses from *The Moon Is Always Female* even contains advice about writing: "The real writer is one / who really writes. Talent / is an invention, like phlogiston / after the fact of fire." Here, as in all her work, Piercy's fierce commitment to work shines through. She is dedicated to her craft and to her vision of a better future. "She rams on," writes Margaret Atwood in the *Nation,* "and the reader can only applaud."

BIOGRAPHICAL/CRITICAL SOURCES:

BOOKS

Contemporary Authors Autobiography Series, Volume 1, Gale, 1984.

Contemporary Literary Criticism, Gale, Volume 3, 1975, Volume 6, 1976, Volume 14, 1980, Volume 18, 1981, Volume 27, 1984.

Kimball, Gayle, editor, *Women's Culture: The Women's Renaissance of the Seventies,* Scarecrow, 1981.

Piercy, Marge, *Hard Loving,* Wesleyan University Press, 1969.

Piercy, *To Be of Use,* Doubleday, 1973.

Piercy, *The Moon Is Always Female,* Knopf, 1980.

Piercy, *Vida,* Summit, 1980.

Piercy, *Parti-Colored Blocks for A Quilt: Poets on Poetry,* University of Michigan Press, 1982.

Walker, Sue and Eugenie Hamner, editors, *Ways of Knowing: Critical Essays on Marge Piercy,* Negative Capability Press, 1984.

PERIODICALS

America, December 29, 1973.

Atlantic, August, 1971, September, 1973.

Chicago Tribune, April 10, 1984.

Chicago Tribune Book World, January 13, 1980, June 8, 1980, February 14, 1982, April 24, 1983, February 26, 1984.

Detroit Free Press, February 28, 1982.

Detroit News, February 24, 1980, March 21, 1982, March 4, 1984.

Los Angeles Times, December 15, 1988.

Modern Poetry Studies, Volume VIII, number 3, 1977.

Ms., July, 1978, January, 1980, June, 1982, March, 1984.

Nation, December 7, 1970, November 30, 1974, December 4, 1976, March 6, 1982.

New Republic, December 12, 1970, October 27, 1973, February 9, 1980.

New Statesman, May 18, 1979.

New Yorker, April 10, 1971, February 13, 1978, February 22, 1982.

New York Times, October 21, 1969, October 23, 1970, January 19, 1978, January 15, 1980, February 6, 1982, February 2, 1984.

New York Times Book Review, November 9, 1969, August 12, 1973, January 22, 1978, November 26, 1978, February 24, 1980, February 7, 1982, August 8, 1982, February 5, 1984.

Poetry, March, 1971.

Prairie Schooner, fall, 1971.

Publishers Weekly, January 18, 1980.

Saturday Review, March 1, 1980, February, 1982.

Times Literary Supplement, March 7, 1980, January 23, 1981, July 23, 1982, June 15, 1984.

Village Voice, February 18, 1980, March 30, 1982.
Washington Post Book World, January 27, 1980, February 7,
   1982, May 30, 1982, February 19, 1984.

*   *   *

PIERS, Robert
See ANTHONY, Piers

*   *   *

PILCHER, Rosamunde   1924-
(Jane Fraser)

PERSONAL: Born September 22, 1924, in Lelant, Cornwall, England; daughter of Charles (a commander in the Royal Navy)
and Helen (Harvey) Scott; married Graham Hope Pilcher (a
company director), December 7, 1946; children: Fiona, Robin,
Philippa, Mark. *Education:* Educated at public schools in England and Wales. *Politics:* Conservative. *Religion:* Church of
Scotland.

ADDRESSES: Home—Over Pilmore, Invergowrie, by Dundee
DD2 5EL, Scotland. *Agent*—Curtis Brown, 62-68 Regent St.,
London W1, England.

CAREER: Writer. *Military service:* Women's Royal Naval Service, 1942-46.

WRITINGS:

The Blue Bedroom and Other Stories, St. Martin's, 1985.
The Shell Seekers (novel), St. Martin's, 1988.
September, Thomas Dunne Books, 1990.

Also author of *Legacies,* 1987.

ROMANCE NOVELS

A Secret to Tell, Collins, 1955.
April, Collins, 1957.
On My Own, Collins, 1965.
Sleeping Tiger, Collins, 1967, St. Martin's, 1974.
Another View, Collins, 1969, St. Martin's, 1974.
The End of the Summer, Collins, 1971, St. Martin's, 1975.
Snow in April, St. Martin's, 1972.
The Empty House, Collins, 1973, St. Martin's, 1975.
The Day of the Storm, Collins, 1975.
Under Gemini, Collins, 1976.
Wild Mountain Thyme, St. Martin's, 1979.
The Carousel, St. Martin's, 1982.
Voices in Summer, St. Martin's, 1982.

ROMANCE NOVELS; UNDER PSEUDONYM JANE FRASER

Halfway to the Moon, Mills & Boon, 1949.
The Brown Fields, Mills & Boon, 1951.
Dangerous Intruder, Mills & Boon, 1951.
Young Bar, Mills & Boon, 1952.
A Day Like Spring, Mills & Boon, 1953.
Dear Tom, Mills & Boon, 1954.
Bridge of Corvie, Mills & Boon, 1956.
A Family Affair, Mills & Boon, 1958.
A Long Way from Home, Mills & Boon, 1963.
The Keeper's House, Mills & Boon, 1963.

PLAYS

(With Charles C. Gairdner) *The Dashing White Sergeant* (three-
   act; first produced in London, 1955), Evans, 1955.
"The Tulip Major," first produced in Dundee, Scotland, 1957.

Also author of *The Piper of Ordre,* with Gairdner, published by
Evans.

OTHER

Also contributor of many short stories to magazines in the
United States and Great Britain, including *Good Housekeeping,
McCalls, Redbook, Woman and Home, Woman,* and *Woman's
Own.*

SIDELIGHTS: British author Rosamunde Pilcher specializes in
"light reading for intelligent ladies," as she states in a *Publishers
Weekly* interview with Amanda Smith. Pilcher has written over
twenty novels, primarily in the romance genre, and in the past
ten years has sold more short stories to *Good Housekeeping* magazine than any other writer. She began her career writing what
she describes in the *Publishers Weekly* interview as "sort of
mimsy little love stories for Mills and Boon" under the pseudonym Jane Fraser. In search of a new image, Pilcher moved from
Mills & Boon to Collins, and from there to the American publisher St. Martin's, who published her bestselling novel *The Shell
Seekers* in 1988.

The Shell Seekers, Pilcher's longest and most complex work, focuses on Penelope Keeling, an independent, offbeat British
woman. Through flashbacks to the World War II era and the recent past, the reader learns of Penelope's idyllic childhood in
Cornwall, England, her hasty wartime marriage, her troubled relationship with two of her three children, and the unexpected
deaths of her mother and her one true love. Now comfortably
settled in a country cottage filled with items from this rich but
tragic past, Penelope draws strength and comfort from these
cherished possessions—particularly The Shell Seekers, a masterpiece painted by her father, Lawrence Stern—and from the simple pleasures of gardening, letter writing, and sharing meals with
friends and family.

Although *The Shell Seekers* is not autobiographical, the novel
loosely parallels Pilcher's life in several ways. For instance, Pilcher grew up near the artistic community of Cornwall, and like
Penelope, served in the Women's Royal Naval Service during
World War II. She also is related by marriage to Victorian
painter Thomas Millie Dow, who, as Laurel Graeber observes
in the *New York Times Book Review,* "could have been a contemporary of the fictional Lawrence Stern." Pilcher comments to
Graeber, "I did feel that I had put a lot of myself down on
paper. . . . I feel that if I had died the next day after writing
[*The Shell Seekers*], everyone would know exactly what happened."

The Shell Seekers was warmly received by critics. *Washington
Post* contributor Susan Dooley writes: "Pilcher's book is a story
about all the steps of love, from the first flush of gratitude at finding a winter aconite specking the snow to the awe of discovering
another person whose life fits into your own. There are no complex ideas or complicated events. And there are no trapezes set
up in the bedroom so the characters can astound the reader with
high-flying feats. *The Shell Seekers* is about ordinary people
doing ordinary things, and Pilcher has made that seem every bit
as important as it really is." *The Shell Seekers,* remarks a *Publishers Weekly* contributor, "is a satisfying and savory family
novel, in which rich layers of description and engagingly flawed
characters more than make up for the occasional cliche." *New
York Times Book Review* contributor Maeve Binchy comments
that the flashbacks "are done with the ease and charm of a kindly
friend showing you a photograph album: not a mammoth session
to glaze the eyes, but a gentle journey telling you these longed-for
facts about people you already know." She concludes: "It is a

measure of this story's strength and success that a reader can be carried for more than 500 pages in total involvement with Penelope, her children, her past and the painting that hangs in her country cottage. *The Shell Seekers* is a deeply satisfying story, written with love and confidence."

As a romance writer, Pilcher hasn't always received the respect she feels she deserves, but she hopes that the warm critical response and wide readership that *The Shell Seekers* received will enhance her reputation. She explains in *Publishers Weekly:* "All my life I've had people coming up and saying, 'Sat under the hair dryer and read one of your little stories, dear. So clever of you. Wish I had the time to do it myself.' I just say, 'Yeah, fine, pity you don't.' I've been beavering away. And now I'm hoping that nobody will ever, ever say that again."

BIOGRAPHICAL/CRITICAL SOURCES:

PERIODICALS

Library Journal, January, 1988.
New York Times Book Review, February 7, 1988.
Publishers Weekly, March 30, 1984, June 14, 1985, November 23, 1987, January 29, 1988.
Washington Post, January 12, 1988.
Writer, May, 1988.

*   *   *

PINCHERLE, Alberto 1907-
(Alberto Moravia)

PERSONAL: Born November 28, 1907, in Rome, Italy; son of Carlo (an architect and a painter) and Teresa (de Marsanich) Pincherle; married Elsa Morante (a writer), 1941 (divorced); married Dacia Maraini (a novelist), 1963 (marriage ended); married Carmen Llera, 1985. *Education:* Awarded high school diploma after passing equivalency tests, 1967.

ADDRESSES: Home—Lungotevere della Vittoria 1, Rome, Italy.

CAREER: Writer. Part-time editor for a publishing house. State Department lecturer in tour of U.S., 1955; lecturer at Queens College of the City University of New York, and other schools, 1964 and 1968.

MEMBER: International PEN (president, 1959), American Academy of Arts and Letters (honorary member), National Institute of Arts and Letters (honorary member).

AWARDS, HONORS: Corriere Lombardo Prize, 1945, for *Agostino;* Strega Literary Prize and Chevalier de la Legion d'Honneur (France), both 1952; Marzotto Award for Fiction, 1954; Viarreggio Prize, 1961, for *La Noia;* Commander de la Legion d'Honneur (France), 1984.

WRITINGS:

NOVELS

Gli indifferenti (also see below), Alpes (Milan), 1929, reprinted, Bompiani, 1976, translation by Aida Mastrangelo of original edition published as *The Indifferent Ones,* Dutton, 1932, translation by Angus Davidson published as *The Time of Indifference,* Farrar, Straus, 1953, reprinted, Greenwood Press, 1975.
Le ambizioni sbagliate, Mondadori (Milan), 1935, translation by Arthur Livington published as *The Wheel of Fortune,* Viking, 1937, translation by Davidson published as *Mistaken Ambitions,* Farrar, Straus, 1955.

La mascherata (also see below), Bompiani, 1941, reprinted, 1981, translation by Davidson published as *The Fancy Dress Party,* Secker & Warburg, 1947, reprinted, 1974.
Agostino: Romanzo, Documento (Rome), 1944, translation by Beryle de Zoete published in *Two Adolescents: The Stories of Agostino and Luca* (also see below), Farrar, Straus, 1950 (published in England as *Two Adolescents: Agostino and Disobedience,* Secker & Warburg, 1952).
Due cortigiane [and] *Serata di Don Giovanni* (novellas), L'Acquario (Rome), 1945.
La romana, Bompiani, 18947, translation by Lydia Holland published as *The Woman of Rome,* Farrar, Straus, 1949, reprinted, Manor Books, 1973.
La disubbidienza, Bompiani, 1948, reprinted, 1981, translation by Davidson of original edition published as *Disobedience,* Secker & Warburg, 1950, translation also published in *Two Adolescents: The Stories of Agostino and Luca,* Farrar, Straus, 1950 (published in England as *Two Adolescents: Agostino and Disobedience,* Secker & Warburg, 1952).
Il conformista, Bompiani, 1951, translation by Davidson published as *The Conformist,* Farrar, Straus, 1951, reprinted, Greenwood Press, 1975.
Il disprezzo, Bompiani, 1954, translation by Davidson published as *A Ghost at Noon,* Farrar, Straus, 1955.
Five Novels by Alberto Moravia: Mistaken Ambitions, Agostino, Luca, Conjugal Love, [and] *A Ghost at Noon* (also see below), Farrar, Straus, 1955.
La ciociara, Bompiani, 1957, translation by Davidson published as *Two Women,* Farrar, Straus, 1958.
La noia, Bompiani, 1963, translation by Davidson published as *The Empty Canvas,* Farrar, Straus, 1965.
L'attenzione: Romanzo, Bompiani, 1965, translation by Davidson published as *The Lie,* Farrar, Straus, 1966.
Io et lui, Bompiani, 1971, translation by Davidson published as *Two: A Phallic Novel,* Farrar, Straus, 1972 (published in England as *The Two of Us,* Secker & Warburg, 1972).
La vita interiore, Bompiani, 1978, translation by Davidson published as *Time of Desecration,* Farrar, Straus, 1980.

1934, Bompiani, 1982, translation by William Weaver published under same title, Farrar, Straus, 1982.

La tempesta (novella), Pellicanolibri (Catania), 1984.
L'uomo che guarda, Bompiani, 1985, translation by Tim Parks published as *The Voyeur: A Novel,* Secker & Warburg, 1986.

SHORT STORIES

La bella vita, Carabba (Lanciano), 1935, published as *La bella vita: L'Italia del consenso in undici racconti,* Bompiani, 1976.
L'imbroglio, Bompiani, 1937.
I sogni del pigro, Bompiani, 1940.
L'amante infelice, Bompiani, 1943.
L'epidemia: Racconti surrealistici e satirici, Documento, 1944.
L'amore coniugale, e altri racconti, Bompiani, 1949, reprinted, 1981, translation by Davidson of long story entitled "L'Amore coniugale" published as *Conjugal Love,* Secker & Warburg, 1951.
I racconti, Bompiani, 1952, reprinted, 1983, translation by Bernard Wall, Baptista Gilliat Smith, and Frances Frenaye published as *Bitter Honeymoon, and Other Stories,* Secker & Warburg, 1960, translation by Davidson published as *The Wayward Wife, and Other Stories,* Secker & Warburg, 1960.
Racconti romani (originally published in the Milanese newspaper *Corriere dell Sera*), Bompiani, 1954, translation by Da-

vidson of selections published as *Roman Tales,* Secker & Warburg, 1956, Farrar, Straus, 1957.

Nuovi racconti romani (originally published in *Corriere dell Sera*), Bompiani, 1959, reprinted, 1978, translation by Davidson of selections from original edition published as *More Roman Tales,* Secker & Warburg, 1963.

L'automa, Bompiani, 1963, translation by Davidson published as *The Fetish,* Secker & Warburg, 1964, published as *The Fetish, and Other Stories,* Farrar, Straus, 1965.

Cortigiana stanca, Bompiani, 1965, published as *Cortigiana stanca: Racconti,* 1974.

Una cosa e una cosa, Bompiani, 1967, translation by Davidson of selections published as *Command and I Will Obey You,* Farrar, Straus, 1969.

Racconti, edited by Vincenzo Traverse, Appleton, 1968, published as *Racconti di Albert Moravia,* Irvington, 1979.

Il paradiso (also see below), Bompiani, 1970, translation by Davidson published as *Paradise and Other Stories,* Secker & Warburg, 1971, published as *Bought and Sold,* Farrar, Straus, 1973.

Un'altra vita (also see below), Bompiani, 1973, translation by Angus Davidson published as *Lady Godiva and Other Stories,* Secker & Warburg, 1975, translation published as *Mother Love,* Panther, 1976.

Boh (also see below), Bompiani, 1976, translation by Davidson published as *The Voice of the Sea and Other Stories,* Secker & Warburg, 1978.

La cosa e altri racconti, Bompiani, 1983, translation by Parks published as *Erotic Tales,* Secker & Warburg, 1985.

PLAYS

(With Luigi Squazini) "Gli indifferenti" (adapted from his novel; published in *Sipario* [Milan], 1948), produced in Rome, 1948.

"Il provino," produced in Milan, 1955.

"Non approfondire" (one-act), produced, 1957.

Teatro (contains "La Mascherata" and "Beatrice Cenci"; also see below), Bompiani, 1958.

Beatrice Cenci (also see below; published in Italian in *Botteghe Oscure,* 1955), translation by Davidson, Secker & Warburg, 1965, Farrar, Straus, 1966.

Il mondo e quello che e (produced in Venice, 1966; adaptation by Albert Husson produced as "The World as It Is" in Paris at Theatre de l'Oeuvre, October, 1969), Bompiani, 1966.

Il dio Kurt (two-act with prologue; produced in Rome at Municipal Theatre of Aquila, 1969), Bompiani, 1968.

La vita e gioco (produced in Rome, 1970), Bompiani, 1969.

Also author of "La Mascherata" (adapted from his novel), c. 1956.

OTHER

La speranza: Ossia cristianesimo e comunismo, Documento, 1944.

(Editor) Leopardi Monaldo, *Viaggio di Pulcinella,* Atlanta (Rome), 1945.

Opera completa, seventeen volumes, Bompiani, 1952-67.

Un mese in U.R.S.S., Bompiani, 1958.

(With Elemire Zolla) *I moralisti moderni,* Garzanti, 1960.

(Editor with Zolla) *Saggi italiani,* Bompiani, 1960.

Un'idea dell'India, Bompiani, 1962.

L'uomo come fine e altri saggi (essays), Bompiani, 1964, translation by Wall of a selection published as *Man as an End—A Defense of Humanism: Literary, Social, and Political Essays,* Farrar, Straus, 1965.

La rivoluzione culturale in Cina ovvero il convitato di ietra, Bompiani, 1967, translation published as *The Red Book and the Great Wall: An Impression of Mao's China,* Farrar, Straus, 1968.

A quale tribu appartieni?, Bompiani, 1972, translation by Davidson published as *Which Tribe do You Belong To?,* Farrar, Straus, 1974.

Al cinema: Centoquarantotto film d'autor (reviews), Bompiani, 1975.

Quando Ba Lena era tanto piccola, Lisciani e Zampetti (Teramo), 1978.

Impegno controvoglia—Saggi, articoli, interviste: Trenta-cinque anni di scritti politici, edited by Renzo Paris, Bompiani, 1980.

Cosma e i briganti, Sellerio (Palermo), 1980.

Lettere del Sahara, Bompiani, 1981.

Opera, 1927-1947, Bompiani, 1986.

Passeggiate africane, Bompiani, 1988.

Also author of numerous screenplays, including "Un colpo di pistola," 1941, "Ultimo incontro," 1951, "La provinciale," 1952, "La romana" (based on his novel), 1955, "Racconti romani" (based on his stories), 1956, "La giornata balorda," 1960, "Agostino" (based on his novel), 1962, "Le ore nude," 1964, and "L'occhio selvaggio," 1967. Foreign correspondent for *La Stampa* and *Gazzeta del Popolo* (Turin), 1930-39; film critic for *La Nuova Europa,* 1944-46, and for *L'Espresso,* 1955—; co-editor with Alberto Carocci of bi-monthly magazine, *Nuovi Argomenti,* 1953—.

SIDELIGHTS: As a child Alberto Moravia used to recount stories to himself, sometimes only interrupting them for sleep and meals. Lonely and isolated, deprived at the age of nine of a normal childhood because of tuberculosis of the bone, he took refuge in his own imagination and in books. Moravia describes this illness as one of the most important events of his life; because of it he had to submit to and do things that healthy children do not usually encounter. "Our character is formed by those things we are constrained to do," he wrote later, "not by those things we do of our own accord." This enforced captivity undoubtedly encouraged the youngster in his literary career.

Although he denies being the author of a book of poems published when he was only thirteen that some reference sources attribute to him, Moravia's first book did appear while he was still a teenager. While he had planned to write a play, what emerged was a novel, *Gli indifferenti.* The story of Carla and her brother Michele and their gradual decline through indifference into moral indolence, the book "had one of the greatest successes in modern Italian literature," according to Joan Ross and Donald Freed in their *The Existentialism of Albert Moravia.* While the volume's subject matter shocked the readers of the time, it gave Moravia the thematic basis for a life's work. "More than anything [this first novel] irritated its readers by its stark portrayal of the decadence and moral rot of the middle-class Italian society of its day," notes Jane E. Cottrell in *Alberto Moravia.* "However, the decay of the middle class was only a secondary theme; its principal subject was the despair and alienation of people entrapped in what would later come to be known in literature as 'the absurd.' For in retrospect, *Gli indifferenti* can be seen as the first European existentialist novel. . . . Since his first novel, Moravia has explored again and again in his fiction the same ideas and themes."

In a *Paris Review* interview Moravia spoke about the acclaim that greeted *Gli indifferenti*'s publication: "It was one of the greatest successes in all modern literature. The greatest actually;

and I can say this with all modesty. There has never been anything like it. Certainly no book in the last fifty years has been greeted with such unanimous enthusiasm and excitement." Unfortunately, the first English edition, which appeared with the title *The Indifferent Ones,* was allegedly so badly translated that the book made little impact on the English-speaking world. A second translation, *The Time of Indifference,* fared much better. *New York Times* contributor Frances Keene wrote that Moravia's "ear for dialogue, for the rhythm of seemingly pointless banter, gives us the very edge of each one's weaknesses. There are no false passages even in the monologue of this book, which tears open today, as it did more than twenty years ago, the fourth wall of many a sterile menage." This translation, however, did not appear until 1953 by which time Moravia had already become known to American readers through a later novel, *La romana,* published in English as *The Woman of Rome.*

R. W. B. Lewis calls *The Woman of Rome* "on balance, a distinguished piece of fiction," and finds that it has a "lyrical reflectiveness" and "muffled nostalgia" which sets it apart from other realistic novels. Narrated in the first person, it reveals Moravia's competence as a craftsman as well as his gift for psychological acumen. The narrator, Adriana, is a young girl of working class origins who turns to prostitution as a way of life. "The uniqueness of Adriana," comments Sergio Pacifici, "consists precisely in her being able to find in promiscuous love the very strength to accept with cheerfulness an otherwise sordid existence." Pacifici goes on to point out that Adriana's observation that "everything was love and everything depended on love, . . . and if you did not have it, you could not love anyone or anything" representative of Moravia's "only genuinely positive answer to the problem of the incoherence and senselessness of life."

Moravia was attacked for his frank treatment of sex in these early novels as well as in his later fiction. Critics have accused him of immorality, lewdness, and obsessiveness. In fact, all of his works were placed on the Index in 1952. Carlo Goldini writes that in Moravia's fiction "we find ourselves in a world peopled with abnormal and morbid individuals obsessed by sensual and erotic preoccupations varying from natural sexual urges to unrestrained lust." And, on the same topic, Lewis has said, "Everything other than sex is, in the stories of Moravia, an extension of sex; or perhaps better, everything other than sex is sooner or later converted into it." In a letter to Lewis, Moravia admitted that "sex has been for me the key to many doors," but added that, when he first started to write, "there were only a few things which seemed to me solid and true and these things were connected with nature and the less objectionable and analysable and ineffable sides of the human soul. Among these things no doubt was sex, which is something primordial and absolute."

Despite such explanations Moravia feels the wrath of censors into his sixth decade as a writer. "Moravia has been identified with sex ever since the runaway success of *Woman of Rome* in 1947 established him as Italy's best-known novelist," observes Miranda Seymour in her *Spectator* commentary on the literary figure. "The sex-scenes in his . . . novel, *Time of Desecration,* were of such a singular nature that the French translators complained, the Italian Mary Whitehouse rose in wrath, and the Germans, not usually known for their puritanism, flatly refused to publish the book." Commenting on the same novel, *New York* magazine contributor Joshua Gilder notes, "Moravia's earlier stories were often brilliant little studies of erotic compulsion. But the erotic component has steadily drained away, until all we are now left with is the compulsion. *Time of Desecration* reads less like a novel than a case study of sexual pathology."

Stylistically, Moravia is not an innovator nor even a particularly polished writer. Charges that he "writes badly" or even "ungrammatically" are not infrequently levelled at him. In his *New York Times* review of *1934* Anatole Broyard observes, "Moravia has never had what might be called a style, but now he seems to have developed what could be described as an aggressive absence of style. A sentence like 'He resumed eating with intent, choleric voracity' suggests no language at all, neither in the original Italian nor the translator's English version." Lewis finds that Moravia "is usually happier with the short novel (and the short story) than with the novel proper; his resources and his themes appear to lack the variety and the inward momentum that novels require." Elaborating on this idea, Pacifici comments, "It is the less sustained genres of the short story and the novella that he has found a felicitous vehicle to dramatize, effectively and succinctly, the few themes close to his sensibility." Maurice Valency concluded, "The short tale is his specialty. In this form, at his best, he is absolutely unsurpassed."

Offering a defense to some criticism leveled at his work, Moravia once said, "Good writers are monotonous, like good composers. Their truth is self-repeating. They keep rewriting the same book. That is to say, they keep trying to perfect their expression of the one problem they were born to understand." Nevertheless, some critics fault Moravia for his constant repetition of themes and subject matter and contend that his later works lack the tautness and vigor of his earlier fiction. "Alberto Moravia is a one-book man in the saddest sense of all, " John Simon observes. "His first novel, *The Time of Indifference,* written when he was still in his teens, said his entire say in optimum form. Later works, for all their occasional diversionary tactics, revealed an obsessively narrow scope and a severely limited technique." Ross and Freed, however, believe that Moravia has improved as a writer over the years. "Moravia has gone beyond the bleak, sordid vision of *Time of Indifference,*" they note. "In subsequent works his perception has deepened and matured. Out of this intense vision we sense a true empathy for the condition of modern man."

Apart from his novels, novellas, and short stories, Moravia has written several plays, hundreds of film reviews, and published several collections of essays. *Man as an End,* the first group of his essays to appear in English, was well-received by reviewers. A *Kirkus Service* reviewer describes the volume as "the work of a vital, exciting and brilliant mind . . . and without doubt one of the most significant European imports in a decade." And Eliot Fremont-Smith writes: "What is moving here is the depth of Moravia's commitment to the cause of man; beyond this, these essays offer rare insights into men and letters, and demonstrate an energetic mind in purposeful and inspiring action." Moravia is a trenchant polemicist; his essays, whether philosophical, political, or critical will always provoke and stimulate. The prevailing feeling is, however, that his position in literature will be determined by his shorter fiction among which there are, perhaps, one or two near masterpieces, such as *Agostino. Time* has called him "one of the best writers in the world today," and Pacifici suggest that, if Moravia does rank with the genuine artist of our century, it is because "after years of writing, and despite the fact that time itself has not changed in any substantial way the *manner* of his writing, he has come closer to saying something about the condition of modern man."

MEDIA ADAPTATIONS: "The Wayward Wife," was made into a film by Mario Soldati and released by Embassy, 1955; *La romana* was filmed as "The Woman of Rome," directed by Luigi Zampa, 1956; *La noia* was filmed as "The Empty Canvas," directed by Vittorio de Sica, 1965; *Gli indifferente* was filmed as "Time of Indifference," 1965; *Il disprezzo* was filmed as "Le Mepris," by Jean-Luc Godard, 1965; *Il conformista* was filmed as "The Conformist," by Bernardo Bertolucci, 1970; *Il dio Kurt* and *Racconti romani* were also filmed.

BIOGRAPHICAL/CRITICAL SOURCES:

BOOKS

Chiaromente, Nicola, *The Worm of Consciousness, and Other Essays,* Harcourt, 1976.
Contemporary Literary Criticism, Gale, Volume 2, 1974, Volume 7, 1977, Volume 11, 1979, Volume 27, 1984, Volume 46, 1988.
Cottrell, Jane E., *Alberto Moravia,* Unger, 1974.
Heiney, D. W., *Three Italian Novelists,* University of Michigan Press, 1968.
Lewis, R. W. B., *The Picaresque Saint,* Lippincott, 1959.
Pacifici, Sergio, *A Guide to Contemporary Italian Literature,* Meridian Books, 1962.
Ragusa, Olga, *Narrative and Drama: Essays in Modern Italian Literature from Verga to Pasolini,* Humanities, 1976.
Ross, Joan, and Donald Freed, *The Existentialism of Alberto Moravia,* Southern Illinois University Press, 1972.

PERIODICALS

Atlantic, February, 1955.
Best Sellers, July 15, 1969.
Books Abroad, autumn, 1950, summer, 1969, winter, 1971.
Books and Bookmen, July, 1969.
Book Week, April 17, 1966.
Book World, September 22, 1968.
Christian Science Monitor, July 17, 1969.
Commonweal, October 22, 1965.
Life, April 28, 1972.
Listener, November 21, 1968.
London Magazine, October, 1968.
Modern Fiction Studies, Number 3, 1958.
Modern Language Journal, Volume 26, 1952.
Nation, April 5, 1971.
New Leader, April 19, 1971.
New Republic, October 26, 1968.
New York, May 23, 1983.
New Yorker, May 7, 1955.
New York Herald Tribune Book Review, October 7, 1951.
New York Review of Books, January 16, 1969.
New York Times, May 24, 1953, January 19, 1966, May 9, 1968, September 19, 1970, March 21, 1971, May 8, 1972, May 11, 1983.
New York Times Book Review, August 3, 1950, April 17, 1953, May 23, 1965, February 9, 1969, May 17, 1970, March 29, 1987.
Observer, December 22, 1985, November 23, 1986.
Paris Review, summer, 1954.
Saturday Review, August 23, 1969, February 13, 1971.
Spectator, November 15, 1968, November 16, 1985.
Stage, July 5, 1973.
Time, June 11, 1965, October 18, 1968.
Times Literary Supplement, September 20, 1965, September 19, 1968, June 5, 1969, November 14, 1986.
Virginia Quarterly Review, spring, 1953.
Washington Press Book World, January 26, 1986.

*   *   *

PINTA, Harold
See PINTER, Harold

PINTER, Harold 1930-
(David Baron, Harold Pinta)

PERSONAL: Born October 10, 1930, in Hackney, London, England; son of Hyman (a tailor) and Frances (Mann) Pinter; married Vivien Merchant (an actress), September 14, 1956 (divorced, 1980); married Lady Antonia Fraser (a writer), November, 1980; children: (first marriage) Daniel. *Education:* Attended Hackney Downs Grammar School, London, 1941-47; attended a few drama schools, including the Royal Academy of Dramatic Art for three months in 1948.

ADDRESSES: Agent—Judy Daish Associates, 83 Eastbourne Mews, London W2 6LQ, England.

CAREER: Poet and playwright. Became interested in theater when he played Macbeth at the age of sixteen; once worked as a "chucker-out" in a dance hall and as a waiter at the National Liberal Club; also worked as a dishwasher and a salesman; actor, using stage name David Baron, 1948-58, performing with Shakespearean repertory company in Ireland, 1950-52, with Donald Wolfit's Shakespearean company, The Bournemouth Repertory Company, and other repertory companies, 1952-58; still acts occasionally, now using his own name; director of plays, including some of his own, 1970—. Associate director, National Theatre, London, 1973—. *Military service:* None; conscientious objector (fined thirty pounds).

MEMBER: League of Dramatists, Modern Language Association (honorary fellow).

AWARDS, HONORS: Evening Standard drama award, 1961, Newspaper Guild of New York award, 1962, both for "The Caretaker"; Italia Prize for television play, 1963, for "The Lover"; two Screenwriters Guild Awards, for television play and for screenplay, both 1963; New York Film Critics Award, 1964, for "The Servant"; British Film Academy Award, 1965 and 1971; Commander, Order of the British Empire, 1966; New York Drama Critics Circle Award, Whitbread Anglo-American Theater Award, and Antoinette Perry (Tony) Award, all 1967, all for "The Homecoming"; Shakespeare Prize, Hamburg, West Germany, 1970; Writers Guild Award, 1971; Best New Play award, *Plays & Players,* 1971, and Tony Award nomination, 1972, both for "Old Times"; Austrian State Prize in Literature, 1973; New York Drama Critics Circle Award, 1980; Pirandello Prize, 1980; Common Wealth Award, Bank of Delaware, 1981; Elmer Holmes Bobst Award for Arts and Letters, 1985, for drama; has received honorary degrees from many institutions in the United Kingdom and the United States.

WRITINGS:

PRODUCED PLAYS AND SCREENPLAYS

"The Room" (also see below), first produced in Bristol, England at Bristol University Memorial Building, May 15, 1957; produced with "The Dumb Waiter" in London at Hampstead Theatre Club, January 21, 1960; produced in San Francisco at Encore Theatre, July 15, 1960; produced with "A Slight Ache" in New York at Writers Stage Theatre, December 9, 1964; produced on Broadway at Booth Theatre, October 3, 1967.
The Birthday Party: A Play in Three Acts (first produced in Cambridge, England at Arts Theatre, April 28, 1958; produced in Hammersmith at Lyric Theatre, May 19, 1968; produced in New York at Booth Theatre, October 3, 1967; also see below), Encore, 1959, Samuel French, 1960, 2nd revised edition, Eyre Methuen, 1981.

"The Dumb Waiter" (also see below), first produced in German translation by Willy H. Thiem in West Germany at Frankfurt-am-Main, February 28, 1959; produced with "The Room" in London at Hampstead Theatre Club, January 21, 1960; produced Off-Broadway with "The Collection" at Cherry Lane Theatre, November 26, 1962.

"A Slight Ache" (also see below), first produced as radio drama, for BBC Radio Third Programme, July 2, 1959; produced on stage in London at Arts Theatre Club, January 18, 1961; produced with "The Room" in New York at Writers Stage Theatre, December 9, 1964.

"Trouble in the Works" [and] "The Black and White" (also see below), first produced together as part of "One to Another" (revue) in Hammersmith at Lyric Theatre, July 15, 1959; produced on the West End at Apollo Theatre, September 23, 1959.

"Request Stop," "Last to Go," "Special Offer," [and] "Getting Acquainted" (also see below), first produced together on the West End as part of "Pieces of Eight" (revue) at Apollo Theatre, September 23, 1959.

"A Night Out" (also see below), first produced as radio drama for BBC Third Programme, March 1, 1960 (Pinter played a small role); produced on stage on the West End at Comedy Theatre, October 2, 1961.

The Caretaker: A Play in Three Acts (first produced in London at Arts Theatre Club, April 27, 1960 [Pinter played the part of Mick for four weeks in 1961]; produced in New Haven, Conn., at Schubert Theatre, September, 1961; produced on Broadway at Lyceum Theatre, October 4, 1961; also see below), Methuen, 1960, 2nd edition, 1962, reprinted, 1982.

"The Dwarfs" (also see below), first produced as radio drama for BBC Third Programme, December 2, 1960; produced on stage with "The Lover" in London at Arts Theatre Club, September 18, 1963; produced Off-Broadway with "The Dumb Waiter" at Abbey Theatre, May 3, 1974.

"Night School" (television drama; also see below), first produced for Associated Rediffusion Television, 1960.

"The Collection" (also see below), first produced as television drama for Associated Rediffusion Television, May 11, 1961; produced on stage on the West End at Aldwich Theatre, June 18, 1962; produced Off-Broadway with "The Dumb Waiter" at Cherry Lane Theatre, November 26, 1962.

"The Lover" (also see below), first produced as television drama for Associated Rediffusion Television, March 28, 1963; produced on stage with "The Dwarfs" in London at Arts Theatre Club, September 18, 1963; produced Off-Broadway at Cherry Lane Theatre, January 4, 1964.

"The Servant" (screenplay), Springbok-Elstree, 1963.

"That's Your Trouble" (radio drama; also see below), first produced for BBC Third Programme, 1964.

"That's All" (radio drama; also see below), first produced for BBC Third Programme, 1964.

"Applicant" (radio drama; also see below), first produced for BBC Third Programme, 1964.

"Interview" (radio drama; also see below), first produced for BBC Third Programme, 1964.

Dialogue for Three (radio drama; first produced for BBC Third Programme, 1964), published in *Stand,* Volume 6, number 3, 1963.

"The Guest" (screenplay; adapted from "The Caretaker"), Janus, 1964.

"The Pumpkin Eater" (screenplay; also see below), Rank, 1964.

The Homecoming: A Play in Two Acts (first produced in Cardiff, Wales, at New Theatre, March 22, 1965; produced on the West End at Aldwych Theatre, June 3, 1965; produced in

New York at Music Box Theatre, January 5, 1967), Samuel French, 1965, new revised edition, Karnac, 1968.

Tea Party (first produced as television drama for BBC Television, March 25, 1965; produced Off-Broadway with "The Basement" at Eastside Playhouse, October 15, 1968; also see below), Methuen, 1965, Grove, 1966.

"The Basement" (also see below), first produced as television drama for BBC Television, February 20, 1967; produced on stage Off-Broadway with "Tea Party" at Eastside Playhouse, October 15, 1968.

"Pinter People" (television interview and sketches), first produced for NBC-TV, December 6, 1968.

"The Quiller Memorandum" (screenplay; also see below), Twentieth-Century Fox, 1967.

"Accident" (screenplay; also see below), Cinema V, 1967.

"The Birthday Party" (screenplay), Continental, 1968.

Landscape (radio drama; first produced for BBC Third Programme, 1968; also see below), Pendragon Press, 1968.

"Night" (also see below), produced as part of "We Who Are About To . . .," in London at Hampstead Theatre Club, February 6, 1969; produced on the West End as part of "Mixed Doubles: An Entertainment on Marriage" (revised version of "We Who Are About To . . .") at Comedy Theatre, April 9, 1969.

"Landscape" [and] "Silence" (also see below), first produced on the West End at Aldwych Theatre, July 2, 1969; produced Off-Broadway at Forum Theatre, April 2, 1970.

"Sketches," first produced in New York at Actors Playhouse, November 3, 1969.

Old Times (first produced on the West End at Aldwych Theatre, June 1, 1971; produced in New York at Billy Rose Theatre November 16, 1971), Grove, 1971.

"The Go-Between" (screenplay; also see below), World Film Services, 1971.

"The Homecoming" (screenplay), American Film Theatre, 1971.

Monologue (television drama; first produced for BBC Television, 1973; also produced on stage), Covent Garden Press, 1973.

No Man's Land (first produced on the West End at National Theatre at the Old Vic, April 23, 1975), Grove, 1975.

"The Last Tycoon" (screenplay; also see below), Paramount, 1975.

Betrayal (first produced on the West End at the National Theatre, November 15, 1978; produced in New York at Trafalgar Theater, January 6, 1980), Eyre Methuen, 1978, Grove, 1979, revised edition, Methuen, 1980.

"Other Pinter Pauses" (revue), first produced in New York at Victory Gardens Studio Theater, December 17, 1979.

The Hothouse (first produced in London at Hampstead Theatre Club, May 1, 1980; produced in New York at Playhouse Theatre, May 6, 1982), Grove, 1980, revised edition, Methuen, 1982.

Family Voices: A Play for Radio (first produced as radio drama for BBC Radio Third Programme, January 22, 1981; produced on the West End at National Theatre, February 13, 1981; also see below), Grove, 1981.

"The French Lieutenant's Woman" (screenplay; also see below), United Artists, 1981, published as *The French Lieutenant's Woman: A Screenplay,* Little, Brown, 1981.

A Kind of Alaska: A Play (first produced at National Theatre, 1982; also see below), Samuel French, 1981.

Victoria Station (also see below), Samuel French, 1982.

Other Places (triple bill; first produced in London, 1982; includes "Family Voices," "A Kind of Alaska," and "Victoria Station"; also see below), Methuen, 1982, Grove, 1983, (revised version omitting "Family Voices" and including "One for the Road" [also see below], first produced at Manhattan Theater Club, April 17, 1984; produced in London, 1985).

"Betrayal" (screenplay), Twentieth-Century Fox/International Classics, 1983.

"Precisely" (sketch), first produced as part of "The Big One" in London, 1983.

One for the Road: A Play (first produced in Hammersmith at Lyric Theatre, March 16, 1984), Samuel French, 1984, Grove, 1986, revised edition, Methuen, 1985.

"Turtle Diary" (screenplay), United British Artists/Britannic, 1986.

Mountain Language (first produced on the West End at National Theatre of Great Britain, November, 1988; produced in New York at CSC Theater with "The Birthday Party," November, 1989), published in *Times Literary Supplement,* October 7, 1988.

Also author of "Langrishe, Go Down" (also see below), 1977, and of a screenplay based on Ian McEuen's *The Comfort of Strangers.*

COLLECTIONS

The Birthday Party and Other Plays (includes "The Birthday Party," "The Room," and "The Dumb Waiter"), Methuen, 1960, published as *The Birthday Party and The Room,* Grove, 1961.

A Slight Ache and Other Plays (includes "A Slight Ache," "A Night Out," "The Dwarfs," "Trouble in the Works," "The Black and White," "Request Stop," "Last to Go," and "Applicant"), Methuen, 1961.

The Caretaker and The Dumb Waiter, Grove, 1961.

Three Plays: A Slight Ache, The Collection, The Dwarfs, Grove, 1962.

The Collection and The Lover (includes a prose piece, "The Examination"), Methuen, 1963.

The Dwarfs and Eight Review Sketches (includes "The Dwarfs," "Trouble in the Works," "The Black and White," "Request Stop," "Last to Go," "Applicant," "Interview," "That's All," and "That's Your Trouble"), Dramatists Play Service, 1965.

Tea Party and Other Plays (includes "Tea Party," "The Basement," and "Night School"), Methuen, 1967.

The Lover, Tea Party, The Basement: Two Plays and a Film Script, Grove, 1967.

A Night Out, Night School, Revue Sketches: Early Plays, Grove, 1968.

Landscape and Silence (includes "Landscape," "Silence," and "Night"), Methuen, 1969, Grove, 1970.

Five Screenplays (includes "Accident," "The Caretaker," "The Pumpkin Eater," "The Quiller Memorandum," and "The Servant"), Methuen, 1971, revised version, omitting "The Caretaker" and substituting " "The Go-Between," Karnac, 1971, Grove, 1973.

Plays, four volumes, Methuen, 1975-81, published as *Complete Works* (with an introduction, "Writing for the Theatre"), Grove, 1977-81.

The French Lieutenant's Woman and Other Screenplays (includes "The French Lieutenant's Woman," "Langrishe, Go Down," and "The Last Tycoon"), Methuen, 1982.

Other Places: Three Plays (includes "A Kind of Alaska," "Victoria Station," and "Family Voices"), Grove, 1983.

OTHER

(Contributor) Harold Clarman, editor, *Seven Plays of the Modern Theater* (includes "The Birthday Party"), Grove, 1962.

(With Samuel Beckett and Eugene Ionesco) "The Compartment" (unreleased screenplay), published in *Project 1,* Grove, 1963.

Mac (on Anew McMaster), Pendragon Press, 1968.

(Editor with John Fuller and Peter Redgrove) *New Poems 1967: A P.E.N. Anthology,* Hutchinson, 1968.

Poems, edited by Alan Clodd, Enitharmon, 1968, 2nd edition, 1971.

Poems and Prose 1949-1977, Grove, 1978, revised edition published as *Collected Poems and Prose,* Methuen, 1986.

(With Joseph Losey and Barbara Bray) *The Proust Screenplay: A la recherche du temps perdu,* Grove, 1978.

I Know the Place: Poems, Greville Press, 1979.

(Editor with Geoffrey Godbert and Anthony Astbury) *A Hundred Poems by a Hundred Poets: An Anthology,* Methuen, 1986.

Also contributor of poems, under pseudonym Harold Pinta, to *Poetry London.*

WORK IN PROGRESS: A screenplay based on Fred Uhlman's novel *Reunion,* with Jerry Schatzberg.

SIDELIGHTS: In a February 1967 interview with the *New Yorker,* Harold Pinter, one of the foremost British dramatists since World War II, cryptically explains the geneses of three of his early plays: "I went into a room and saw one peron standing up and one person sitting down, and a few weeks later I wrote *The Room.* I went into another room and saw two people sitting down, and a few years later I wrote *The Birthday Party.* I looked through a door into a third room, and saw two people standing up and I wrote *The Caretaker.*" Since *The Room* opened in 1957, Harold Pinter's work has excited, puzzled, and frustrated audiences and academicians alike. Some have praised his work for its originality, while others have dismissed it as willfully obscure—responses evoked by the plays' unconventional plots and character development, their inexplicable logic and inconclusive resolutions, and their distinctive dialogue, echoing the inanities of everyday speech as well as its silences. In spite of their disparagers, Pinter's plays are frequently produced—in English and in translation—and continue to attract popular and scholarly attention.

Born October 30, 1930, at Hackney, East London, Pinter grew up in a working-class neighborhood, which, despite some dilapidated housing, railway yards, and a dirty canal, he remembered fondly in the *New Yorker* interview: "I actually lived in a very pleasant environment and in a very comfortable terraced house." However, like other English children who grew up in London during the air raids of World War II, he learned first hand of imminent and omnipresent terror, a theme which appears in much of his work.

Pinter's theatrical career started early. While attending Hackney Downs Grammar School, he won title roles in *Macbeth* and *Romeo and Juliet.* The *Hackney Downs School Magazine* records his dramatic debuts. Of young Pinter's Macbeth, the magazine's critic wrote in the summer of 1947: "Word-perfect, full-voiced, Pinter took the tragic hero through all the stages of temptation, hesitation, concentration, damnation. He gave us both Macbeth's conflicts, inner and outer, mental and military, with vigour, insight, and remarkable acting resource." The summer 1948 review of Pinter's Romeo, if somewhat less laudatory, points nonetheless to the young actor's flair for the dramatic: "Pinter again bore the heat and burden of the evening with unfailing vitality. . . . Perhaps he excelled where strong action reinforces the words—as where he flung himself on the floor of the Friar's cell in passionate histrionic abandon."

Both these reviews are remarkably prescient: what the young actor apparently learned, in part at least from playing Macbeth and Romeo, Pinter the playwright uses. His characters are at their most compelling when their conflicts are "inner" and "mental," unseeable and therefore frequently unnameable; his plots, despite their surface calm and minimal physical action, nonetheless demonstrate "histrionic abandon," the result of verbal brilliance and stunning visual imagery.

Along with acting, young Pinter displayed a talent for athletics: in 1948 he broke the school's record for the 220 yards and equaled the record for the 100 yards. He also played cricket, a game he continues to follow. Not surprisingly, therefore, sports have a special significance in his work. The characters in *No Man's Land,* for example, are named after famous cricket players, and squash in *Betrayal* is symbolically important to the play's meaning. In Pinter's screenplays, sports and sports imagery are similarly illuminating.

Besides his successes at play—both on field and on stage—the *Hackney Downs School Magazine* also records those of a literary bent: an essay and two poems, which attest to the young artist's sensitivity to language. In his essay, "James Joyce," published in the winter 1946 issue, Pinter discusses the novelist's poetic use of language: "and slowly the words subside into softness, softly drifting." His juvenile poetry features the alliteration, repetition, and play with language that appears in his adult work, drama and poetry alike.

Pinter's verbal acumen was also rewarded outside the world of belles lettres: it helped the young man ward off East End thugs, as Pinter recalled in a 1966 *Paris Review* interview with Lawrence M. Bensky: "I did encounter [violence] in quite an extreme form. . . . If you looked remotely like a Jew you might be in trouble. Also, I went to a Jewish club, by an old railway arch, and there were quite a lot of people often waiting with broken milk bottles in a particular alley we used to walk through. There were one or two ways of getting out of it—one was purely physical, of course, but you couldn't do anything about the milk bottles—*we* didn't have any milk bottles. The best way was to talk to them, you know, sort of 'Are you all right?' 'Yes, I'm all right.' 'Well, that's all right then, isn't it?' and all the time keep walking toward the lights of the main road." Manipulating language in order to shield oneself from physical or emotional harm without conveying rational information is a skill possessed by many of Pinter's dramatic characters.

Pinter left grammar school in 1947 and the following year received a grant to study acting at the Royal Academy of Dramatic Art (RADA). In *Pinter the Playwright* Martin Esslin records Pinter's memory of this experience: "I went to RADA for about two terms, then I left of my own free will, I didn't care for it very much. I spent the next year roaming about a bit." In fact, according to the *New Yorker* interview, he spent the next ten years writing—"Not plays. Hundreds of poems . . . and short prose pieces"—and acting: ". . . my experience as an actor has influenced my plays—it must have—though it's impossible for me to put my finger on it exactly. I think I certainly developed some feeling for construction . . . and for speakable dialogue." As an actor Pinter grew intimately familiar with the dramatic properties of the stage and the spoken word, and as a poet with the emotive possibilities of language.

In 1950 *Poetry London* published several of his poems under the pseudonym "Harold Pinta" (the Spanish or Portuguese form of "Pinter"), and the poet began work as a professional radio and television actor. In *Prose and Poetry, 1949-1977* Pinter declares that in 1951 he began a two-year stint with Anew McMaster's

touring company in Ireland, his "first job proper on the stage"; after returning from Ireland, Pinter (who in 1954 assumed the stage name of "David Baron") acted "all over the place in reps." In 1957 Harold Pinta, the poet, and David Baron, the actor, collaborated on a one-act play, *The Room,* the writing of which took Harold Pinter, the playwright, "four days, working in the afternoons," he told the *New Yorker.*

After *The Room,* Pinter's plays came fast. During 1957 he wrote *The Dumb Waiter,* a one-act play, and *The Birthday Party,* his first full-length play, which ran for only one week and got terrible reviews, with one notable exception—Harold Hobson's appraisal in the *Sunday Times:* "Now I am well aware that Mr. Pinter's play received extremely bad notices last Thursday morning. At the moment I write these lines it is uncertain even whether the play will still be in the bill when they appear, though it is probable it will soon be seen elsewhere. Deliberately, I am willing to risk whatever reputation I have as a judge of plays by saying that *The Birthday Party* is . . . a First, and that Mr. Pinter, on the evidence of this work, possesses the most original, disturbing and arresting talent in theatrical London."

Despite *The Birthday Party*'s predominantly dismal critical and commercial reception, Pinter continued during 1958 and 1959 to write plays for radio and stage—*A Slight Ache; The Hothouse* (which was not produced until 1980); revue sketches; and *A Night Out.* With his second full-length play, *The Caretaker,* the playwright received critical accolades. One of the more influential notices was Kenneth Tynan's in the *Observer:* "With *The Caretaker* . . . Harold Pinter has begun to fulfill the promise that I signally failed to see in *The Birthday Party* two years ago. The latter play was a clever fragment grown dropsical with symbolic content. . . . In *The Caretaker* symptoms of paranoia are still detectable . . . but their intensity is considerably abated; and the symbols have mostly retired to the background. What remains is a play about people." *The Caretaker* ran for twelve months in the East End and in October 1961 opened on Broadway, again to critical, but not commercial, success. In the *New York Times,* Howard Taubman wrote: "*The Caretaker* . . . proclaims its young English author as one of the important playwrights of our day."

Important and prolific, Pinter continued to write plays, short ones including *Night School* and *The Dwarfs, The Collection* and *The Lover, Tea Party;* and full-length ones, *The Homecoming,* which established Pinter's reputation as a major dramatist, *Old Times, No Man's Land,* and *Betrayal.* More recently, he has concentrated on short but intriguing theatrical pieces: *Family Voices, Victoria Station, A Kind of Alaska,* and *One for the Road.*

Although they cannot be easily classified according to dramatic schools, Pinter's plays nonetheless reflect movements in the British theatre of the last three decades, including realism, epic theatre, and absurdism. Early critics perceived the author of *The Room* and *The Birthday Party* to be a member of the "kitchen sink" school of realism, along with John Osborne, Shelagh Delaney, and other British playwrights who drew their characters from the working class, their sets from the provinces, and their dialogue from the patterns and sounds of regional speech. Especially in his first few plays, Pinter's lower-class characters with their Cockney idiom and their bleak settings recall the social, psychological, and linguistic verisimilitude found in "kitchen sink" drama. However, his is a surface realism. He is not essentially, as Esslin points out in *Pinter the Playwright,* a realistic dramatist: "This is the paradox of his artistic personality. The dialogue and the characters are real, but the over-all effect is one of mystery, of uncertainty, of poetic ambiguity." Nor does Pinter regard himself as belonging to this dramatic school: "I'd say what goes on in my plays is realistic, but what I'm doing is not realism," he declared in the *Paris Review* interview.

Of the prevalent strains of twentieth-century British drama, epic theater has appeared to have the least influence on Pinter. Unlike his contemporaries John Arden, Arnold Wesher, and Edmund Bond, dramatists who are greatly influenced by German playwright Bertolt Brecht, Pinter has, for the most part, eschewed such Brechtian conventions as protagonists who represent the working class and themes that are socially and politically timely. However, in *The Hothouse,* a farcical play set in a mental institution, and in *One for the Road,* a disturbing one-act play that takes place in a government retaining home, Pinter touches on social commentary—the insidious inanity of bureaucracies and the mechanistic sadism of totalitarianism—and, epic-like, appeals primarily to his audience's intellect rather than to its emotions.

However, in its usual predilection for examining the private rather than the social sphere, Pinter's work is perhaps most clearly influenced by the absurdists, particularly by Irish playwright and novelist Samuel Beckett, for whom Pinter expressed admiration in the *Paris Review* interview: "I think Beckett is the best prose writer living." Admittedly, the world of Pinter's *Betrayal* is not that of Beckett's *Endgame;* the disjunction within the former results from marital discord, within the latter from existential fragmentation. Nevertheless, as Esslin writes in *Pinter the Playwright:* "Existential adjustment, coming to terms with one's own being, precedes, and necessarily predetermines, one's attitude to society, politics, and general ideas. Like Beckett and [Franz] Kafka Pinter's attitude . . . is that of an existentialist: the mode of a man's *being* determines his *thinking.* Hence, to come to grips with the true sources of their attitudes, the playwright must catch his characters at the decisive points in their lives, when they are confronted with the crisis of adjustment to themselves." As in much of absurdist drama, the names and behaviors of Pinter's characters, the plays' props and sets, resonate symbolically—"Riley" in *The Room* and *Family Voices,* the matchseller in *A Slight Ache,* the statue of Buddha in *The Caretaker,* vases and olives in *The Collection,* for example. And although Stanley in *The Birthday Party* is not *Endgame*'s Hamm or Clov, he contains elements of both—blindness and entrapment—and his fate is similarly and existentially capricious.

Belonging to no single school, Pinter draws from each to create a body of work idiosyncratically and recognizably his own. Those dramatic elements that are identifiably "Pinteresque" include his characters' mysterious pasts, his theme of the intruder, and his use of language—textual and subtextual—and of silence. In *Pinter the Playwright* Esslin quotes a letter received by Pinter shortly after *The Birthday Party* opened: "Dear Sir, I would be obliged if you would kindly explain to me the meaning of your play *The Birthday Party.* These are the points I do not understand: 1. Who are the two men? 2. Where did Stanley come from? 3. Were they all supposed to be normal? You will appreciate that without the answers to my questions I cannot fully understand your play." Pinter is said to have replied: "Dear Madam, I would be obliged if you would kindly explain to me the meaning of your letter. These are the points which I do not understand: 1. Who are you? 2. Where do you come from? 3. Are you supposed to be normal? You will appreciate that without the answers to my questions I cannot fully understand your letter." Both query and response are telling. Traditional dramatic exposition and character development have accustomed theater audiences to expect playwrights to provide enough information about the past to make the characters' present situations and motivations explicable. Like the inquisitive letter writer, playgoers re-

quest of dramatic art the logic and order that like outside the theater denies. Pinter, along with many other twentieth-century dramatists, refuses his audience this luxury.

In *The Birthday Party,* for example, Stanley Webber lives as the only boarder in Meg and Petey Boles's boarding house. The play's central mystery, and therefore a large part of its dramatic tension, evolves from the relationship between Stanley and the two men, Goldberg and McCann, who arrive at the boarding house. From the start, questions about the past arise and remain unanswered. Who is Stanley Webber? Why is he vegetating at the Boles's? What is his relationship with Meg? With the promiscuous neighbor, Lulu? Is it, or is it not, his birthday? Is he, or is he not, a pianist? Why do Goldberg and McCann want to find him? Why do they take him, dressed "in a dark well cut suit and white collar," to Monty? Who is Monty? The more information the audience receives the more confused it becomes.

Because the past is unverifiable, all that viewers can know about a Pinter character is what they themselves discern. And this source or kind of information often does not satisfy audiences familiar primarily with conventional dramatic exposition, especially since Pinter's characters confuse their viewers with contradiction. Consequently, audiences remain uncertain of motivations and unable to verify what little they can surmise, a predicament that coincides with life outside the theater. How can we know, Esslin asks in *Pinter the Playwright,* with "any semblance of certainty, what motivates our own wives, parents, our own children?" We can't. And Pinter's drama impedes all our attempts to know, despite (or perhaps because of) the anxiety that this raising of unanswerable questions creates.

Equally unsettling both to audiences and the plays' central figures is the theme of the intruder who invariably enters the rooms, basements, flats, and houses of Pinter's characters and in some way disrupts the residents. At times the intruder is a stranger, such as Riley, who enters Rose's haven in *The Room;* the matchseller whom Flora and Edward invite into their home in *A Slight Ache;* Spooner, whom Hirst picks up at a pub in *No Man's Land.* At other times the intruder is a friend or family member; in *The Homecoming,* for example, Teddy returns with his wife to his father's home; in *The Basement,* Stott takes his lover to visit and old friend; and in *Old Times,* Anna visits her former roommate.

In an unsigned insert to the program brochure of a 1960 performance of *The Room* and *The Dumb Waiter,* Pinter addresses the theme of the inevitability of an intruder: "Given a man in a room and he will sooner or later receive a visitor. A visitor entering the room will enter with intent. If two people inhabit the room the visitor will not be the same man for both. A man in a room who receives a visit is likely to be illuminated or horrified by it. The visitor himself might as easily be horrified or illuminated. . . . A man in a room and no one entering lives in expectation of a visit." Physical, psychological, or emotional disruption caused by the intruder provides the dramatic tension of most of Pinter's plays. For example, in *Betrayal* Jerry intrudes into Robert and Emma's marriage by initiating an affair with his best friend's wife. In *Family Voices* Voice 1 intrudes as a roomer upon the Withers family, and he, in turn, is intruded upon—although he appears not to realize it—by Voice 2, his mother, who entreats him to return home, and by Voice 3, his dead father, who intrudes upon life. Deborah, the central character in *A Kind of Alaska,* also intrudes upon life by awakening after twenty-nine years: in a sense, she becomes an intrusion to herself—a middle-ages woman imposing herself upon the young girl who was afflicted with sleeping sickness those many years before. In a Pinter play, intrusion inevitably will occur.

The dramatist's uncannily realistic sounding dialogue, replete with the linguistic inanities (pauses, tautologies, nonverbal sounds, disjunctive responses) and the verbal acts (defense, acquiescence, coercion, aggression) of everyday conversation, is also typically "Pinteresque." Yet despite its surface realism, Pinter crafts his dialogue with a poet's tools, including the caesurae, or silences. Although it is often parodied by his detractors and imitated by his admirers, the explicitly assigned "Pinter-pause" is invariably meaningful, reflecting a number of responses including puzzlement (Gus's pondering over the mysterious menu in *The Dumb Waiter*), illumination (Aston's finally realizing that Davies will not allow him to remain as caretaker or boarder in *The Caretaker*), and retrenchment (Ruth and Lenny's engaging in a verbal duel for control in *The Homecoming*). Pinter's pauses comprise lines without words, lines that frequently speak as loudly as, or sometimes louder than, words.

Another silence—a noisy one—exists in Pinter's plays. In a speech delivered at the 1962 National Student Drama Festival in Bristol and published as the introduction to the first volume of the *Complete Works,* the playwright addresses this form of verbal hiatus: "There are two silences. One when no word is spoken. The other when perhaps a torrent of language is being employed. This speech is speaking of a language locked beneath it. That is its continual reference. The speech we hear is an indication of that which we don't hear. It is a necessary avoidance, a violent, sly, anguished or mocking smoke screen which keeps the other in its place. When true silence falls we are still left with echo but are nearer nakedness. One way of looking at speech is to say that it is a constant stratagem to cover nakedness." In order to cover their nakedness, Pinter's characters frequently discuss topics that have little to do with what is really on their minds: for instance, Rose in *The Room* chatters on about the weather and the apartment house in her attempt to reassure herself of the sanctuary of her room; Deeley, in *Old Times,* describes Kate's bathing habits to Anna in order to establish his intimacy with his wife and belittle the relationship between the two friends; and Robert, in *Betrayal,* discusses squash and lunch in a veiled assault on his wife. In instances such as these, language functions primarily on a subtextual level; it is not the meaning of the words that is essential, but how the characters use speech to bring about their different ends: to hide the pain of a relationship gone awry, the desperation of being lonely and homeless, the fear of relinquishing control. Unheard melodies in Pinter's language are often far less sweet than those heard.

Yet melodies heard can indeed be sweet. Lexical associations, *double entendre,* puns, exotic diction, onomatopoeia, and repetition—all poetic devices—call attention to the playwright's use of language. An early play written originally for radio and therefore dependent upon words alone to convey meaning, *A Slight Ache,* exemplifies Pinter's language at its most brilliant and meaningful. Language becomes this play's central theme: the character who possesses verbal acumen survives unscathed (as did young Pinter *en route* to his club in London's East End), while those who lose control over language are doomed.

Rich in sensory appeal and dense with imagery, this play has little action. A married couple, Edward and Flora, spend "the longest day of the year" at their country house. After breakfast, Edward notices a matchseller, who has apparently been there for "weeks," standing by the back gate. This day, however, Edward decides to invite the matchseller in to determine why he persists in remaining by the gate while making no attempt to sell his wares. The matchseller, who remains mute throughout the play, tacitly accepts the invitation, and Edward and Flora take turns playing host and hostess to their silent guest. During the course of the play, Edward grows increasingly weak and finally collapses on the floor; the matchseller, on the other hand, appears progressively rejuvenated. At play's end, Flora passes the tray of wet, useless matches to her prostrate husband and leaves with her new partner, the matchseller.

Of the names of Pinter's characters, Bernard Dukore writes in a 1981 *Theatre Journal* article: "Namesakes provide important clues that warrant attention, especially of a writer like Pinter, who carefully and precisely measures every aspect of his plays, including varying lengths and pauses. It is unlikely that he would be less sensitive to or painstaking with his character's name." Sometimes the names of Pinter's characters straightforwardly suggest personality traits (Bert Hudd, the monosyllabic, sadistic trucker of *The Room,* for example), but more often they signify allusively, often ironically (Dakore notes the "ruth-less" Ruth of *The Homecoming* returning to her husband's people as does the Old Testament Ruth before her). Flora's name suggests benevolent and fecund nature but her actions point to manipulative emasculation. She orchestrates her husband's demise.

Early in the play, Flora establishes her supremacy over Edward by acting the part of an indulgent parent, "calmly" correcting her husband while teaching him the plants' proper names: "Edward—you know that shrub outside the toolshed. . . . That's convolvulus." As though speaking to a small child, Flora also explains to her husband the need for the canopy, "To shade you from the sun." To label elements within one's environment is, in a sense, to control those elements and that environment. By naming the plants in her garden, Flora establishes dominance over her immediate environment. She also "names" Edward: she refers to him by his given name an inordinate number of times (considering they are the only two speakers in the play) and uses the faintly scatological sobriquet, "Weddie. Beddie Weddie." She also christens the matchseller: "I'm going to . . . call you Barnabas."

In contrast to his wife, Edward is unable to name the plants in his garden—a shortcoming Pinter points to in the play's opening dialogue: "You know perfectly well what grows in your garden," Flora states, and Edward replies, "Quite the contrary. It is clear that I don't." Nor can Edward recall the name of the squire's red-headed daughter, with whom he was enamored: "The youngest one was the best of the bunch. Sally. No, no, wait a minute, no, it wasn't Sally, it was . . . Fanny." Moreover, he calls lunch *petit dejeuner* (French for "breakfast") and rants at his guest for consuming "duck," although Flora has invited the matchseller to share a mid-day goose. Her husband's inability to label and thereby control his environment—garden or dining room—dooms him before his more able wife; he is fated to succumb to Flora and her new ally, the matchseller, who remains nameless to her husband.

As Edward grows weaker, he grows even less able to use language effectively. Early in the play he attempts fastidiousness in his choice of words: "It will not bite you! Wasps don't bite. . . . They sting. It's snakes . . . that bite. . . . Horseflies suck." Later he haltingly differentiates between a road and a lane: "It's not a road at all. What is it? It's a lane." Despite his efforts at linguistic precision, Edward loses control when confronted by the matchseller to whom he offers an inappropriately discriminating choice of drinks: "Now look, what will you have to drink? A glass of ale? Curacao Fockink Orange? Ginger beer? Tia Maria? A Wachenheimer Fuchsmantel Reisling Beeren Auslese?

Gin and it? Chateauneuf-du-Pape? A little Asti Spumanti? Or what do you say to a straightforward Piesporter Goldtropfschen Feine Auslese (Reichsgraf von Kesselstaff)?" Like the provocatively named plants—honeysuckle, convolvulus, clematis—in Edward and Flora's garden, these drinks amuse in the sexual suggestiveness and continental inclusiveness. Less comically, the list reflects Edward's growing anxiety. The language through which he earlier attempts denotative exactness in reference to wasps and lanes carries him away—from one exotic beverage to another. Toward the play's end, Edward is reduced to nonverbal communication: "Aaaaahhhh." Flora retains control over language. She endures.

Since *No Man's Land* in 1975, Pinter has relied less on verbal indulgence and more on elements of design to evoke meaning. The poet-playwright seems to be increasingly influenced by the scenarist-playwright, a change resulting perhaps from the requirements and possibilities of cinema. Over the years four of Pinter's plays have been filmed: *The Caretaker, The Birthday Party, The Homecoming,* and *Betrayal.* He has also written ten screenplays based on other writers' novels; all but one (*The Proust Screenplay*) have been filmed: *The Servant, The Pumpkin Eater, The Quiller Memorandum, Accident, The Go-Between, Langrishe, Go Down, The Last Tycoon, The French Lieutenant's Woman,* and *Turtle Diary.* Although this list appears disparate, it possesses internal logic. The playwright-scenarist adapts fiction whose themes and subjects are those of his own dramatic art: adultery; role reversal or role confusion; duplicity; physical, psychological and emotional cruelty; artistic stasis; homosexuality; and perverted birthday celebrations, to mention only a few of these motifs. Furthermore, like his plays, the novels he has adapted for the screen focus predominantly on character rather than on plot. Even in a spy thriller like *The Quiller Memorandum,* assassinations, attempted murders, and scenes of torture fade from memory more rapidly than do the characters. Another denominator common to the stage plays and screenplays is Pinter's exploration of time and memory, topics he has dealt with frequently since writing *Old Times* in 1970. Simple flashback accommodates the characters' memories in the screenplay versions of *The Pumpkin Eater* and *Accident;* but *The Go-Between, A la recherche du temps perdu,* and *The French Lieutenant's Woman* require more innovative techniques to deal with their sophisticated examinations of time. A technique Pinter uses in the screenplays—flashbacks interwoven with flashforwards—reappears in his play *Betrayal.* In short, Pinter's work in film expands upon the interests he explores on the stage.

Although Pinter is not essentially a comic writer, he does write very funny dialogue. When characters posture, as when Edward lists the contents of his liquor cabinet for the matchseller's benefit in *A Slight Ache,* Deeley flaunts his familiarity with the past to denigrate his houseguest in *Old Times,* or when Robert recounts his experience at the American Express office where he has just learned of his wife's affair with his best friend in *Betrayal,* their speeches are frequently comic, often extravagantly so. In *Pinter the Playwright,* Esslin reprints Pinter's 1960 response to an open letter "deploring the gales of laughter about the unhappy plight of the old tramp" in *The Caretaker:* "An element of the absurd is, I think, one of the features of the play, but at the same time I did not intend it to be merely a laughable farce. If there hadn't been other issues at stake the play would not have been written. . . . Where the comic and the tragic (for want of a better word) are closely interwoven, certain members of the audience will always give emphasis to the comic as opposed to the other, for by doing so they rationalize the other out of existence. . . . Where . . . indiscriminate mirth is found, I

feel it represents a cheerful patronage of the characters on the part of the merrymakers, and thus participation is avoided. This laughter is in fact a mode of precaution, a smoke-screen, a refusal to accept what is happening as recognizable. . . . From this kind of uneasy jollification I must, of course, disassociate myself. . . . As far as I'm concerned, *The Caretaker* is funny, up to a point. Beyond that point it ceases to be funny, and it was because of that point that I wrote it."

In *The Caretaker,* as in all of Pinter's plays, comic elements illuminate noncomic ones. On one hand, humor serves as a balm, easing audience discomfort at witnessing the characters' pain; on the other, it intensifies the discomfort by forcing pain into contiguity with laughter so that the distinctions between the two disappear, and the audience is left precariously straddling the fine line that separates the comic from the noncomic. In his best work, Pinter leaves his audiences at that moment when the plays cease altogether to be funny—when bright lights "photograph" the silent threesome in the final tableau of *Old Times* or fade as Hirst takes one last drink in *No Man's Land,* when the curtain falls on Max imploring Ruth to kiss him in *The Homecoming* or on Meg blissfully unaware that Stanley has been taken away in *The Birthday Party.* Ultimately, Pinter's plays emphasize that which is not comic, and despite their considerable humor, his vision is not a comic one.

Unquestionably, Harold Pinter is one of the major playwrights of his time. His work has greatly influenced a number of contemporary dramatists on both sides of the Atlantic; critics and scholars alike consider his six full-length works (*The Birthday Party, The Caretaker, The Homecoming, Old Times No Man's Land, Betrayal*) to be among the most important plays of the mid-twentieth century. In his more recent work, Pinter continues to experiment with possibilities of theater, to search for the exact verbal and visual image, and to strive for theatrical economy.

In a speech originally delivered in Hamburg, West Germany, in 1970 and published in the fourth volume of the *Complete Works,* the playwright declares: "The image must be pursued with the greatest vigilance, calmly, and once found, must be sharpened, graded, accurately focused and maintained, and the key word is economy, economy of movement and gesture, of emotion and its expression . . . so there is no wastage and no mess." Whether a woman clutches her eyes (*The Room*), a man drinks to stasis (*No Man's Land*) or a cabby sits silently in his taxi (*Victoria Station*), Pinter's dramatic images and the vision they embody remain in his audience's memories long after the stage lights have faded.

BIOGRAPHICAL/CRITICAL SOURCES:

BOOKS

Contemporary Literary Criticism, Gale, Volume 1, 1973, Volume 3, 1975, Volume 6, 1976, Volume 9, 1978, Volume 11, 1979, Volume 15, 1980, Volume 27, 1984.
Dictionary of Literary Biography, Volume 13: *British Dramatists since World War II,* Gale, 1982.
Esslin, Martin, *Pinter the Playwright,* Methuen, 1984.
Gale, Steven H. *Harold Pinter: An Annotated Bibliography,* G. K. Hall, 1978.
Kerr, Walter, *Harold Pinter,* Columbia University, 1967.
Pinter, Harold, *A Slight Ache and Other Plays,* Methuen, 1961.
Pinter, Harold, *Complete Works,* Volume 1, Grove, 1977.
Pinter, Harold, *Prose and Poetry, 1949-1977,* Grove, 1978.

PERIODICALS

Chicago Tribune, September 26, 1989.

Hackney Downs School Magazine, winter, 1946, summer, 1947.
Modern Drama, Volume 27, 1984.
New Yorker, February 25, 1967.
New York Times, October 5, 1961, October 15, 1961, October 6, 1989, November 9, 1989.
New York Times Magazine, December 5, 1971.
Observer, June 25, 1960.
Paris Review, fall, 1966.
Sunday Times (London), May 25, 1958.

*   *   *

PINTO, Peter
See BERNE, Eric (Lennard)

*   *   *

PIRSIG, Robert M(aynard) 1928-

PERSONAL: Born September 6, 1928, in Minneapolis, Minn.; son of Maynard E. (a professor) and Harriet (Sjobeck) Pirsig; married Nancy James (an administrator), May 10, 1954 (divorced August, 1978); married Wendy L. Kimball, December 28, 1978; children: (first marriage) Christopher (deceased November 17, 1979), Theodore; (second marriage) Nell. *Education:* University of Minnesota, B.A., 1950, M.A., 1958.

ADDRESSES: Office—c/o William Morrow and Co., Inc., 105 Madison Ave., New York, N.Y. 10016.

CAREER: Montana State College (now University), Bozeman, instructor in English composition, 1959-61; University of Illinois, Chicago, instructor in rhetoric, 1961-62; technical writer at several Minneapolis, Minn., electronic firms, 1963-67; Century Publications, Minneapolis, contract technical writer, 1967-73; writer. Minnesota Zen Meditation Center, member of board of directors, 1973—, vice-president, 1973-75. *Military service:* U.S. Army, 1946-48.

MEMBER: Society of Technical Communicators (past secretary and treasurer).

AWARDS, HONORS: Guggenheim fellowship, 1974; Friends of Literature Award, 1975; outstanding achievement award, University of Minnesota, 1975; American Academy and Institute of Arts and Letters Award, 1979.

WRITINGS:

Zen and the Art of Motorcycle Maintenance: An Inquiry into Values, Morrow, 1974.

Contributor to *New York Times Book Review.*

WORK IN PROGRESS: Anthropological research, intended to relate metaphysics of quality, as defined in first book, to cultural problems of today.

SIDELIGHTS: "*Zen and the Art of Motorcycle Maintenance* is an exciting autobiography that is at the same time a serious philosophical reflection on contemporary American culture," recounts Richard L. Rubenstein. "Pirsig tells of an extraordinary motorcycle journey he took during the summer of 1968 with his 11-year-old son Chris. . . . Pirsig takes a commonplace article of technological society and teaches us to see it as a simple yet profound image of ourselves and our world."

R. Z. Sheppard writes: "*Zen and the Art of Motorcycle Maintenance* is an unforgettable trip. It accelerates from the befuddle-

ments of transmission linkage through Pirsig's history of Western thought to the mysteries of divine madness with scarcely a wobble. The fact that much of Pirsig's torque-wrenched dissertation echoes the quandaries that some high-energy physicists have about the nature of matter is not of primary importance. What matters most is that he communicates how very much he cares about living as a whole man and how hard he has worked at it. Indeed, the special gift of the universal principle that Pirsig calls Quality is caring, even if one reaches for the heavens with grease on his hands."

George Steiner sums up his reaction to Pirsig's book in the *New Yorker:* "A detailed technical treatise on the tools, on the routines, on the metaphysics of a specialized skill; the legend of a great hunt after identity, after the salvation of mind and soul out of obsession, the hunter being hunted; a fiction repeatedly interrupted by, enmeshed with, a lengthy meditation on the ironic and tragic singularities of American man—the analogies with *Moby Dick* are patent. Robert Pirsig invites the prodigious comparison."

BIOGRAPHICAL/CRITICAL SOURCES:

BOOKS

Contemporary Literary Criticism, Gale, Volume 4, 1975, Volume 6, 1976.

PERIODICALS

Economist, November 30, 1974.
Harvard Economic Review, February, 1975.
New Statesman, November 15, 1974.
Newsweek, June 3, 1974.
New Yorker, April 15, 1974.
New York Times Book Review, March 30, 1975, March 4, 1984.
Science, January 24, 1975.
Time, April 15, 1974.

*   *   *

PLANTE, David (Robert) 1940-

PERSONAL: Born March 4, 1940, in Providence, R.I.; son of Anaclet Joseph Adolph and Albina (Bison) Plante. *Education:* Attended University of Louvain, Belgium, 1959-60; Boston College, B.A., 1961.

ADDRESSES: Home—38 Montagu Square, London W1, England. *Agent*—Deborah Rogers Ltd., 49 Blenheim Crescent, London W11, England; and Georges Borchardt, 136 East 57th St., New York, N.Y. 10022.

CAREER: Writer, living in England since 1966. English School, Rome, Italy, teacher, 1961-62; *Hart's Guide to New York,* New York, N.Y., researcher, 1962-64; Boston School of Modern Languages, Boston, Mass., teacher, 1964-65; teacher at St. John's Preparatory School, 1965-66; University of Tulsa, Tulsa, Okla., writer-in-residence, 1979-82; Cambridge University, Cambridge, England, visiting fellow, 1984-85.

AWARDS, HONORS: Henfield Fellow, University of East Anglia, 1975; British Arts Council grant, 1977; *The Family* was nominated for a National Book Award, 1979; Guggenheim grant, 1983; Prize for Artistic Merit, American Academy-Institute of Arts and Letters, 1983.

WRITINGS:

NOVELS, EXCEPT AS INDICATED

The Ghost of Henry James, Gambit, 1970.
Slides, Gambit, 1971.

Relatives, J. Cape, 1972, Avon, 1974.

The Darkness of the Body, J. Cape, 1974.

(Contributor) Giles Gordon, editor, *Beyond Words: Eleven Writers in Search of a New Fiction,* Hutchinson, 1975.

Figures in Bright Air, Gollancz, 1976.

The Family (first novel in trilogy), Farrar, Straus, 1978.

The Country (third novel in trilogy), Atheneum, 1981.

The Woods (second novel in trilogy), Atheneum, 1982.

Difficult Women: A Memoir of Three (nonfiction), Atheneum, 1983.

The Foreigner, Atheneum, 1984.

The Catholic, Atheneum, 1986.

The Native, Macmillan, 1988.

Works represented in anthologies, including *Penguin Modern Stories 1,* Penguin, 1969, and *Prize Stories 1983: The O. Henry Awards,* edited by William Abrahams, Doubleday, 1983. Contributor to periodicals, including *New Yorker, Paris Review, Modern Occasions, Transatlantic Review,* and *Tri-Quarterly.*

SIDELIGHTS: David Plante's writing has been abundant and variegated. *Publishers Weekly* critic John F. Baker indicates that Plante "began his writing life as a very deliberate experimentalist, has worked through in his most admired works to date, the trilogy *The Family, The Country,* and *The Woods,* to a form of intensely heightened naturalism, and has now branched out in *Difficult Women* into a kind of deadpan literary memoir." Plante's subsequent novels, *The Foreigner, The Catholic,* and *The Native,* continue the saga of the Francoeur family, the subject of his earlier trilogy, by focusing on the offspring as they attempt to come to terms with their heritage.

Although Plante is primarily a novelist, *Difficult Women: A Memoir of Three* is a nonfictional portrait of three literary figures, novelist Jean Rhys, feminist writer Germaine Greer, and literary hostess Sonia Orwell, George Orwell's widow. In the book, Plante examines his friendships with the three, friendships motivated in part by his interest in the women's "difficult" dispositions, but also by their standing in the literary world. Orwell was able to introduce Plante to many in her large circle of friends, including Rhys, and, in Plante's opinion, Rhys in particular represented the intellectual cafe society that flourished in Paris during the 1920s. Vivian Gornick writes in the *New York Times Book Review* that Plante describes "the spectacular exaggerations of will and character the three women embody." And according to *Saturday Review* critic Andrea Barnet, "Plante raises these psychological portraits to the narrative pitch of fiction. He brings each to life with a dramatic precision that is formidable." "It's as if Mr. Plante were staring out over a wild and rugged typography of femaleness and wondering how one lives in such a land," maintains Anatole Broyard in the *New York Times.*

Patricia Blake writes in *Time,* however, that "though he purports to have given them a sympathetic hearing, Plante seems curiously ambivalent, not only about this trio, but about the entire sex." *Harper's* critic James Wolcott also finds the book's tone offensive. Describing it as a "racy, chatty, celebrity-cruising memoir," he theorizes that Plante, "a writer's writer" held in high critical regard for his quiet literary accomplishments, "wanted to break out of his modest niche in the literary world and cut a larger swath." "The mistake," he writes, "was in taking such a tacky approach. In dishing Jean Rhys, Sonia Orwell, and Germaine Greer in *Difficult Women,* David Plante has not only nudged his lance into the sickly creature that was once chivalry, but he's done violence to his own respectable name."

Plante firmly established his literary reputation with his trilogy of novels that relates the story of the Francoeurs, a large, working-class, Roman Catholic family with a French-Canadian and partially American Indian heritage. Told from the viewpoint of the young writer son, Daniel, the novels describe his passage from adolescence to adulthood and his family's disintegration: his mother suffers a breakdown and becomes senile, while his father grows bitter and senile with old age and finally dies. The first novel of that trilogy, *The Family,* writes John Calvin Batchelor in the *Village Voice,* "represents a departure so radical and unprecedented from the experimental directions Plante has unsuccessfully worked" in his first five shorter novels "that one is obliged once again to assert that all things are possible for those who make-believe." With *The Family,* asserts Batchelor, Plante has returned to "a fictionist's primary responsibility—storytelling."

In such early experimental novels as *The Darkness of the Body,* Plante often left the details of character and setting deliberately vague, in order for the reader to focus upon the inner emotional life of the protagonists. And he frequently disregarded conventional narrative. His first novel, for instance, *The Ghost of Henry James,* is described by Baker as "a fragmented narrative that was a deliberate tribute to the master." "Plante has applied the Jamesian mood to a contemporary situation," writes Jonathan Yardley in the *New York Times Book Review,* and the result is something more or less than a novel, since, according to a *Times Literary Supplement* critic, it is also " 'a functional analysis' of the work of Henry James." The point of the exercise, writes Denis Donoghue in the *New York Review of Books,* "is to write the kind of story that James might write if he had the luck to live in 1970, free of social restraint."

Such experimentation can be found throughout Plante's earliest writing. *New York Times Book Review* critic Jonathan Strong indicates that the title of Plante's work *Slides* refers to "the 67 vignettes in which the story is told. They *are* slides (rather than home movies) because they each focus on one moment of tension that breaks off unresolved, leaving it for us to imagine what happens next." And in his fifth novel, *Figures in Bright Air,* Plante told Baker in an interview, "I'd got away from narrative altogether, trying to create something that reverberates, as music does."

However, not all reviewers agree with Batchelor that Plante's experimental efforts were completely "unsuccessful." A *Times Literary Supplement* reviewer comments in qualification that, in his earlier works, Plante "gives the impression of a talented writer somehow trapped by the elaborateness of his own ingenuities." Mary Sullivan in the *Listener* maintains that "*Slides* induces a series of satisfactions all the deeper for being not quite graspable." And although Richard Freedman in *Book World* describes *The Ghost of Henry James* as "overrich and too highly technicolored, festering in elegant decadence, and ideal for inhaling with a Campari-and-soda," *New York Times Book Review* critic Jonathan Yardley calls it "in many respects a remarkable piece of work." Plante's trilogy may represent a return to traditional narrative, but as Plante sees it, the books are not a repudiation of the experimental work, but instead, a logical progression from it. He indicated to Baker: "I always wanted to write [the trilogy], and in a way all my earlier work was an attempt to prepare myself for it, trying to learn a craft."

Batchelor believes *The Family* is a significant improvement over Plante's previous efforts. In *The Family,* he writes, Plante "has finally permitted his serious ideas to live in recognizable, admirable human beings who dream, build, brag, stumble, collapse and get up again." The book describes the emotional breakdown of Reena Francoeur, Daniel's mother, but in Batchelor's opinion, the story is about the father, Jim Francoeur, "a hard, taciturn, disciplined man who has worked unflinchingly for 40 years at the same tool shop. His temperament dominates the family; and it is his rise to near success as a foreman, a local Republican candidate, and a home-owner, and his fall to near hopelessness as an unemployed, heavily indebted, and cruelly, intractably frightened old man that defines the plot."

Plante uses "only the simple vocabulary of his working-class characters [to plunge] us into a hermetic, devout, French-Catholic world," writes Elizabeth Peer in *Newsweek.* This family situation is particularly "claustrophobic," maintains Anne Stevenson in the *Times Literary Supplement,* "contained as it is within a Catholic French-speaking parish in a Protestant New England city at a time (the late 1950s) when the old-fashioned life of the parish is under threat from the mass-making (or in this case, possibly, Mass-breaking) forces of American society."

"Plante is very good at creating this world," confirms Susan Wood in *Washington Post Book World,* "the weight of its oppression, as he describes the ugliness of the factories, the churches, the schools, the houses. One flinches at the conversations of Matante Oenone, Jim's sister, which tend toward lurid descriptions of poverty and death, or at the nuns' equally lurid descriptions of the sufferings of the saints and martyrs, and the passion of Christ. Also depressing are the long and detailed conversations within the family, those double binds in which conflicting messages of love and hate are so often sent." "Through the eyes of adolescent Daniel, the sixth son," states Peer, "we experience the unpredictable shifts of family chemistry."

Although the viewpoint in *The Family* is Daniel's, the story is told in the third person. In *The Country,* the Francoeur children are grown, and the events—the elderly Francoeurs' retreat into senility and the father's death—are related in the first person by Daniel who lives in London, returning only to visit. The book's subject, according to A. Alvarez in the *New York Review of Books,* "is the numbing grief grown children feel as they watch their parents descend into helplessness and death." *Washington Post Book World* critic Jonathan Yardley states that "the novel, like its subject, is neither glamorous nor sexy. Plante's prose is spare, measured, quietly insistent; though the novel is brief, it conveys the labored pace of a long dying. It also conveys both the ordinariness and the extraordinariness of dying, its universality and its uniqueness." The work is described in the *New York Times Book Review* by Mary Gordon "a haunting lament, a controlled cry of loss and knowledge won through language, sorrow, memory, impossible and comprehending love."

Despite its subject matter, "self-control dominates *The Country,*" writes *Time* reviewer Paul Gray. "Plante is a minimalist with language; his prose reduces events to small, discrete moments. He uses words less to evoke a scene than to catalogue it." "This flat style may look easy," the critic writes, "but what Plante accomplishes with it is not." *Nation* reviewer Brina Caplan points out that Plante's "narrator follows action and speech with the watchful precision of an Indian ancestor tracking game through the woods. No word is wasted, and every word reports something seen, heard or touched. As a result, *The Country* is written in spare prose that isolates the external facts of ordinary life, reminding us of their inherent order and gravity."

Calling Plante a "highly visual writer," *Newsweek* reviewer Jean Strouse indicates that he "gives the physical feeling of this world . . . along with the bleak, claustrophobic atmosphere of the senior Francoeurs' lives." *New Republic* critic Jack Beatty adds

that "it is Plante's grip on the objective method of narration, his commitment to what Henry James called scenic rendering, that allows him, in the long flashback at the country house, to turn from brother to brother and from mother to father in quick defining strokes of description and dialogue." "The novel," writes Strouse, "moves through small emblematic, almost ceremonial moments—as if you were watching a film in freeze frame with the sound off." Alvarez comments that "it is like watching a whole movie in slow motion: discreet movements, each frozen and complete in itself, and a slightly distorted soundtrack, full of Chekhovian gaps and silences, through which the characters mutely hint at feelings they do not otherwise care to articulate."

Yet Yardley maintains that "*The Country* has one unfortunate weakness. Its intensity occasionally lapses into humorlessness; when seriousness becomes solemnity, as Plante is inclined to let it do, what we get is huffing and puffing." And A. N. Wilson in the *Times Literary Supplement* prefers some of Plante's experimental fiction to *The Country,* which he finds overly realistic and subjective. He writes: "I do not know whether *The Country* is an insufficiently transformed piece of autobiography, or whether the failure is owing to the possibly delicate nature of his material." The novel, in his opinion, "lacks the crisp detachment and originality of mind displayed in David Plante's earlier novels *Relatives* and *The Ghost of Henry James.*"

Most reviewers, however, consider *The Country* a remarkable achievement. Beatty, for instance, concludes that "throughout the novel there are even hints that the world is lit by a mystery beyond death. This is suggested in an insistent imagery of light breaking into darkened rooms and illuminating the tops of trees at dusk; and it is made explicit early in the novel when Daniel sees his father standing alone in the woods [surrounded by his ancestors]. This preserving place seems to be a fusion of the Catholic notion of the communion of saints with Daniel's projection of his primordial Indian descent, and it surrounds the action of the novel like a ring of light from a far country to which all the characters are going. It adds a note of the numinous to this lovely painful book."

The completive novel of the trilogy, *The Woods,* was originally published last, but since it concerns Daniel's first two years of college and the intervening summers he spends at the lake where his family vacations, it should fall second chronologically, as it was written. A slim book, it is divided into three parts, "The Reflection," "The Woods," and "The War," which present three scenes from the young writer's life during a period when he fears being drafted into the army. In the novel, Daniel also comes to accept his homosexuality, but overall, according to Jack Beatty in *New Republic,* the work "is about the adolescent dread of selfhood and its loneliness." R. Z. Sheppard in *Time* writes that "few periods are as difficult to pin down as that brief limbo between the end of youth and the beginning of adulthood. The mysteries of the physical and the spiritual, the image and the imagination are fresh and beckoning."

Although *The Woods* is part of the trilogy, its concerns are dissimilar to those of *The Family* and *The Country.* Here, writes *New York Times Book Review* critic Edith Milton, "Mr. Plante is not interested in the sociology of Daniel's world or in the psychology of the people he shares it with; he explores instead the boundary between Daniel's ruthlessly insignificant everyday existence and the vast landscape of his inner apathy, examining through Daniel's eyes the proposition that matter and spirit are irreversibly divided from each other and that both are irrevocably alien to him."

Chicago Tribune Book World reviewer L. M. Rosenberg maintains that the book is built around "one peculiar but interesting question, namely: What does it mean to live inside a body?" "Central to the novel is the philosophical notion of body as idea," agrees Rosalind Belben in the *Times Literary Supplement,* "the body not confined to flesh and blood but a configuration projected by the mind into 'a space' outside." "The focus," writes Beatty, "is on Daniel's consciousness, specifically on his preoccupation with 'the space, large and empty' which he sees behind people as a kind of enveloping presence. (It is a version of the existentialist notion of 'the encompassing,' and while Daniel is drawn toward it as to a great mystery, readers who think existentialism vaporous will not pass page two.)"

"Young Daniel Francoeur, Plante's protagonist, feels what seems a uniquely Roman Catholic variety of metaphysical lust," maintains *Newsweek* critic Gene Lyons. "He craves not so much to make love as to uncover spiritual mysteries." *New York Review of Books* critic Robert Towers points out that "Plante manages to surround almost every object and every inconsequential event with a kind of luminescent space, like a halo. By following Daniel's attention as it moves very slowly from one thing to the next, he produces an effect of hallucinatory realism, in which each detail seems to exist in its own right, to have a quasimystical 'thingness' about it, quite apart from whatever significance it may or may not have in the larger picture."

The result is a paucity of active narrative. According to Milton, "leitmotifs create the real fictional texture of the novel, which has a surface almost without incident, indeed almost without narrative." And *Washington Post Book World* critic Jonathan Yardley considers that "texture" overly cerebral. In *The Woods,* he writes, "Plante has made the mistake of intellectualizing what is not, in point of fact, an intellectual or rational process: an adolescent's struggle to come to terms with a world considerably more ambiguous than he is capable, at this point, of understanding. Not merely does Daniel Francoeur spend too much time feeling sorry for himself, but he does so in thoughts and language that are quite implausible for one of his inexperience and immaturity."

Milton agrees that *The Woods* is not without fault, but argues that "it is also a brilliantly original work, intense, illuminating and compelling. Eccentric enough to be beyond the pale of most critical judgement, its virtues certainly are worth considerably more than its faults." As Le Anne Schreiber explains in the *New York Times,* Plante attempts to describe "states of mind so elusive that they can only be intimated; his is a world of vague apprehensions and diffuse longings, and to enter it is to feel perpetually suspended on the verge of something. Revelation seems imminent until one realizes that for David Plante the sense of imminent revelation is a permanent condition."

Plante continues the Francoeur saga with *The Foreigner, The Catholic,* and *The Native. The Foreigner* is narrated by a nameless nineteen-year-old critics suspect is Daniel, who sets off for a year of study in Paris determined to let go of his roots. He becomes involved with Angela, a black American woman, and her lover Vincent, and follows them to Spain, where they introduce him to the banality of the underworld. Harriett Gilbert in *New Statesman* called *The Foreigner* "a strange, uneven, unsettling book: initially, a superb account of late adolescent dislocation; progressively, something more disquieting and ruthless." In *The Catholic* Daniel tells of his homosexual relationships with his college roommate and a man he meets in a Boston bar who eventually rejects him.

The Native focuses on Philip, one of the seven Francoeur sons, who, in his attempt to free himself from his parents' religion and culture, marries a Protestant woman. He soon realizes that she is stupid and common and that their daughter yearns for the spurned spirituality of her father's youth. "By mapping out the ways in which beliefs, resentments and hopes are handed down, generation to generation, the ways in which love can mutate into hatred, neediness into rebellion, [Plante] creates a portrait of family that is as uncompromising as it is moving," Michiko Kakutani states in her *New York Times Book Review* critique of *The Native.* "Plante's understanding of the complicated, often perverse configurations that familial relationships can form remains unerring."

BIOGRAPHICAL/CRITICAL SOURCES:

BOOKS

Contemporary Literary Criticism, Gale, Volume 7, 1977, Volume 23, 1983, Volume 38, 1986.
Dictionary of Literary Biography Yearbook: 1983, Gale, 1984.

PERIODICALS

Books and Bookmen, May, 1971, July, 1972.
Bookseller, March, 1971.
Book World, November 1, 1970.
Chicago Tribune Book World, October 4, 1981, September 19, 1982, March 6, 1983.
Choice, March, 1971.
Contemporary Review, April, 1974.
Guardian Weekly, June 24, 1972, February 2, 1974.
Harper's, January, 1983.
Listener, March 19, 1970, March 18, 1971, June 15, 1972, February 7, 1974, April 1, 1976.
Los Angeles Times, October 2, 1984.
Nation, February 6, 1982.
New Republic, October 7, 1981, October 11, 1982.
New Statesman, March 13, 1970, March 12, 1971, June 16, 1972, February 1, 1974, April 2, 1976, March 13, 1981, February 4, 1983, November 9, 1984.
Newsweek, July 24, 1978, September 14, 1981, September 6, 1982.
New Yorker, September 20, 1982.
New York Review of Books, November 5, 1970, August 17, 1978, November 19, 1981, December 16, 1982.
New York Times, July 19, 1982, January 15, 1983, September 12, 1984, August 13, 1988.
New York Times Book Review, November 29, 1970, December 6, 1970, August 22, 1971, October 20, 1974, July 2, 1978, October 4, 1981, August 15, 1982, January 16, 1983, August 7, 1988.
Observer, March 15, 1970, March 14, 1971, June 18, 1972, January 27, 1974, April 4, 1976.
Publishers Weekly, June 29, 1970, June 7, 1971, August 26, 1974, December 24, 1982.
Saturday Review, September 2, 1978, March-April, 1983.
Spectator, March 14, 1970, March 27, 1971, February 2, 1974, April 10, 1976, February 6, 1982.
Time, October 12, 1981, August 2, 1982, February 7, 1983.
Times (London), January 27, 1983.
Times Literary Supplement, March 19, 1970, April 16, 1971, July 7, 1972, February 1, 1974, July 2, 1976, April 28, 1978, March 13, 1981, January 29, 1982, February 25, 1983.
Village Voice, April 23, 1979.
Voice Literary Supplement, February, 1983.
Washington Post Book World, August 27, 1978, September 27, 1981, August 8, 1982.

PLATH, Sylvia   1932-1963
(Victoria Lucas)

PERSONAL: Born October 27, 1932, in Boston, Mass.; committed suicide, February 11, 1963, in London, England; buried in Heptonstall, Yorkshire, England; daughter of Otto Emil (a professor) and Aurelia (a teacher; maiden name, Schober) Plath; married Ted Hughes (a poet), June 16, 1956 (separated, 1962); children: Frieda Rebecca, Nicholas Farrar. *Education:* Smith College, B.A. (summa cum laude), 1955; attended Harvard University, summer, 1954; Newnham College, Cambridge, Fulbright scholar, 1955-57, M.A., 1957. *Religion:* Unitarian Universalist.

ADDRESSES: Home—Court Green, North Tawton, Devonshire, England.

CAREER: Worked as a volunteer art teacher at the People's Institute, Northampton, Mass., while in college; served as guest editor with *Mademoiselle,* summer, 1953; taught English at Smith College, 1957-58; lived in Boston, 1958-59, and Yaddo, 1959; settled in London, England, 1959, then in Devon, England.

MEMBER: Phi Beta Kappa.

AWARDS, HONORS: Mademoiselle College Board contest winner in fiction, 1953; Irene Glascock Poetry Prize, Mount Holyoke College, 1955; Bess Hokin Award, *Poetry* magazine, 1957; first prize in Cheltenham Festival, 1961; Eugene F. Saxon fellowship, 1961; Pulitzer Prize in poetry, 1982, for *Collected Poems.*

WRITINGS:

POETRY

The Colossus, Heinemann, 1960, new version published as *The Colossus and Other Poems,* Knopf, 1962.
(Editor) *American Poetry Now* (supplement number 2 to *Critical Quarterly,*) Oxford University Press, 1961.
Uncollected Poems (booklet), Turret Books (London), 1965.
Ariel, Faber, 1965, Harper, 1966.
Wreath for a Bridal (limited edition), Sceptre Press, 1970.
Crossing the Water: Transitional Poems, Harper, 1971.
Crystal Gazer and Other Poems (limited edition), Rainbow Press (London), 1971.
Lyonnesse (limited edition), Rainbow Press, 1971.
Million Dollar Month (limited edition), Sceptre Press, 1971.
Winter Trees, Faber, 1971, Harper, 1972.
Collected Poems, edited by Ted Hughes, Harper, 1981.
Stings (drafts), Smith College, 1983.

Poetry included in anthologies, including *The New Yorker Book of Poems,* Viking, 1969. *Early Poems,* a collection of Plath's work, was published as the May, 1967, issue of *Harvard Advocate;* fifty of her early unpublished poems appeared in *Times Literary Supplement,* July 31, 1969.

OTHER

(Under pseudonym Victoria Lucas) *The Bell Jar* (novel), Heinemann, 1963, published under real name, Faber, 1965, Harper, 1971.
Three Women: A Monologue for Three Voices (radio play; broadcast on British Broadcasting Corporation in 1962; limited edition), Turret Books, 1968.
Letters Home: Correspondence, 1950-1963, selected and edited with a commentary by Aurelia Schober Plath, Harper, 1975.
The Bed Book (for children), Harper, 1976.

Johnny Panic and the Bible of Dreams: Short Stories, Prose, and Diary Excerpts, Harper, 1979.
The Journals of Sylvia Plath, edited by Hughes and Frances McCullough, Ballantine, 1983.

Contributor to *Seventeen, Christian Science Monitor, Mademoiselle, Harper's, Nation, Atlantic, Poetry, London Magazine,* and other publications.

SIDELIGHTS: When Sylvia Plath ended her life in 1963, she was already becoming a legend. Robert Lowell, who knew her when she audited a class he was teaching, recalls her as a "distinguished, delicate, complicated person" who gave no indication of what would come later. Her final achievement, he admits, startled him. Yet she was precocious as a child (her first published poem appeared in the *Boston Traveller* when she was eight-and-a-half), and A. Alvarez notes that while at college Plath "remorselessly" won all the prizes, and that beneath "a nervous social manner . . . she was ruthless about her perceptions, wary and very individual."

Alvarez believes that with the poems in *Ariel* Plath made "poetry and death inseparable. The one could not exist without the other. And this is right. In a curious way, the poems read as though they were written posthumously." Robert Penn Warren calls *Ariel* "a unique book, it scarcely seems a book at all, rather a keen, cold gust of reality as though somebody had knocked out a window pane on a brilliant night." George Steiner writes: "It is fair to say that no group of poems since Dylan Thomas's *Deaths and Entrances* has had as vivid and disturbing an impact on English critics and readers as has *Ariel.* . . . Reference to Sylvia Plath is constant where poetry and the conditions of its present existence are discussed." After her death, her reputation grew and she inspired younger poets to write as she did. But, as Steiner maintains, her "desperate integrity" cannot be imitated. "No artifice alone could have conjured up such effects," writes Peter Davison.

Like other major poets, Plath consistently courted death. She once said: "When I was learning to creep, my mother set me down on the beach to see what I thought of it. I crawled straight for the coming wave and was just through the wall of green when she caught my heels." At nineteen she first attempted suicide. In her final poems, writes Charles Newman, "death is preeminent but strangely unoppressive. Perhaps it is because there is no longer dialogue, no sense of 'Otherness'—she is speaking from a viewpoint which is total, complete. Love and Death, all rivals, are resolved as one within the irreversibility of experience. To reverse Blake, the Heart knows as much as the Eye sees." Alvarez believes that "the very source of [Plath's] creative energy was, it turned out, her self-destructiveness. But it was, precisely, a source of *living* energy, of her imaginative, creative power. So, though death itself may have been a side issue, it was also an unavoidable risk in writing her kind of poem. My own impression of the circumstances surrounding her eventual death is that she gambled, not much caring whether she won or lost; and she lost," he adds, only because the possibility of future poems has been lost. Steiner, however, believes that from these final poms she could never return.

As a very young poet Plath experimented with the villanelle and other forms. She had been "stimulated" by such writers as Lawrence, Joyce, Dostoevski, Virginia Woolf, Henry James, Theodore Roethke, Emily Dickinson, and later by Robert Lowell and Anne Sexton. She has been linked with Lowell and Sexton as a member of the so-called "confessional" school of poetry. Ted Hughes notes that she shared with them a similar geographical home land as well as "the central experience of a shattering of the self, and the labour of fitting it together again or finding a new one." And nothing more.

Although her first volume of poems is extremely accomplished, erudite, and imaginative, it was not yet entirely the product of an individual voice. Afterwards, Plath developed her technique until the tone of her poems was transformed. She later said: "I can't read any of the poems [in *The Colossus*] aloud now. I didn't write them to be read aloud. In fact, they quite privately bore me. Now these very recent ones—I've got to say them. . . . Whatever lucidity they may have comes from the fact that I say them aloud." Alvarez also notes that, in the poet's later works, the relevance of the experience recounted becomes terribly direct, and cites the poem "Ariel" as an example: "The rider is one with the horse, the horse is one with the furrowed earth, and the dew on the furrow is one with the rider. The movement of the imagery, like that of the perceptions, is circular. There is also another peculiarity: although the poem is nominally about riding a horse, it is curiously 'substanceless' to use her own word. You are made to feel the horse's physical presence, but not to see it. . . . It is as though the horse itself were an emotional state. So the poem is not about 'Ariel'; it is about what happens when the 'stasis in darkness' ceases to be static."

At such times, Plath was able to overcome the "tension between the perceiver and the thing-in-itself by literally becoming the thing-in-itself," writes Newman. "In many instances, it is nature who personifies her." Similarly, Plath uses history "to explain herself," writing about the Nazi concentration camps as though she had been imprisoned there. She said: "I think that personal experience shouldn't be a kind of shut box and mirror-looking narcissistic experience. I believe it should be generally relevant, to such things as Hiroshima and Dachau, and so on." Newman explains that "in absorbing, personalizing the socio-political catastrophes of the century, [the author] reminds us that they are ultimately metaphors of the terrifying human mind." Alvarez notes that the "anonymity of pain, which makes all dignity impossible, was Sylvia Plath's subject." Her reactions to the smallest desecrations, even in plants, were "extremely violent," writes Hughes. "Auschwitz and the rest were merely the open wounds." In sum, Newman believes, Plath "evolved in poetic voice from the precocious girl, to the disturbed modern woman, to the vengeful magician, to—*Ariel*—God's Lioness."

Plath's earlier poems, Ted Hughes reports, were written "very slowly, Thesaurus open on her knee, in her large, strange handwriting, like a mosaic, where every letter stands separate within the work, a hieroglyph to itself. If she didn't like a poem, she scrapped it entire. . . . Every poem grew complete from its own root, in that laborious inching way, as if she were working out a mathematical problem, chewing her lips, putting a thick dark ring of ink around each word that stirred for her on the page of the Thesaurus." After she had written "The Stones," the last poem she completed in America before becoming a complete exile, the poet repudiated everything prior to this work as juvenilia. With the birth of her first child in 1960, "she received herself," writes Hughes, "and was able to turn to her advantage all the forces of a highly-disciplined, highly intellectual style of education which had, up to this point, worked mainly against her. . . . The birth of her second child, in January of 1962, completed the preparation." In 1961 she wrote "Tulips" without consulting the thesaurus, "and at top speed, as one might write an urgent letter. From then on, all her poems were written in this way."

Newman considers Plath's only novel, *The Bell Jar,* a "testing ground" for her poems. It is, according to the critic, "one of the

few American novels to treat adolescence from a mature point of view. . . . It chronicles a nervous breakdown and consequent professional therapy in non-clinical language. And finally, it gives us one of the few sympathetic portraits of what happens to one who has genuinely feminist aspirations in our society, of a girl who refuses to be an *event* in anyone's life. . . . [Plath] remains among the few woman writers in recent memory to link the grand theme of womanhood with the destiny of modern civilization." She told Alvarez that she published the book under a pseudonym partly because "she didn't consider it a serious work . . . and partly because she thought too many people would be hurt by it."

The Bell Jar was published one month before Plath's death. After its publication she began to write poems with intense, almost demonic speed, as many as three per day. "One is reminded," Newman suggests, "of Beethoven's atonal explosions in the last quartets, of Turner's last seascapes as they became abstractionist holocausts. In the last poems, there is not the slightest gap between theory and realization, between myth and the concrete particular—they utterly escape the self-consciousness of craft." During the final week of her life Plath wrote five poems, all included in *Ariel.* Davison notes that these last poems are "a triumph for poetry . . . at the moment that they are a defeat for their author. . . . No matter to whom these may be addressed, they are written for nobody's ears except the writer's. They have a ritual ring, the inevitable preface to doom." Lowell calls the poet's final manner of feeling "controlled hallucination, the autobiography of a fever." "These last poems stun me," writes Anne Sexton. "They eat time."

Alvarez reports that Plath seemed convinced that the basis for her suffering was the death of her father when she was eight. The most powerful of her last poems, "Daddy," is explained by her as an "awful little allegory" that she had to act out before she was free of it. Steiner calls the poem an achievement in "the classic act of generalization, translating a private, obviously intolerable hurt into a code of plain statement, of instantaneously public images which concern us all. It is the 'Guernica' of modern poetry."

Hughes summarizes Plath's unique personality and talent: "Her poetry escapes ordinary analysis in the way clairvoyance and mediumship do: her psychic gifts, at almost any time, were strong enough to make her frequently wish to be rid of them. In her poetry, in other words, she had free and controlled access to depths formerly reserved to the primitive ecstatic priests, shamans and Holymen."

"Surveyed as a whole, . . . I think the unity of her opus is clear," the poet continued. "Once the unity shows itself, the logic and inevitability of the language, which controls and contains such conflagrations and collisions within itself, becomes more obviously what it is—direct, and even plain, speech. This language, this unique and radiant substance, is the product of an alchemy on the noblest scale. Her elements were extreme: a violent, almost demonic spirit in her, opposed a tenderness and capacity to suffer and love things infinitely, which was just as great and far more in evidence. Her stormy, luminous senses assaulted a downright, practical intelligence that could probably have dealt with anything. . . . She saw her world in the flame of the ultimate substance and the ultimate depth. And this is the distinction of her language, that every word is *Baraka:* the flame and the rose folded together. Poets have often spoken about this ideal possibility but where else, outside these poems, has it actually occurred? If we have the discrimination to answer this question, we can set her in her rightful company."

MEDIA ADAPTATIONS: A film version of *The Bell Jar* was produced by Avco-Embassy in 1978; *Letters Home* was adapted into a play by Rose Leiman Goldemberg and staged in 1979.

BIOGRAPHICAL/CRITICAL SOURCES:

BOOKS

Aird, E. M., *Sylvia Plath,* Harper, 1973.
Alvarez, A., *The Savage God: A Study of Suicide,* Weidenfeld & Nicolson, 1971, Random House, 1972.
Concise Dictionary of American Literary Biography: The New Consciousness, 1941-1968, Gale, 1987.
Contemporary Literary Criticism, Gale, Volume 1, 1973, Volume 2, 1974, Volume 3, 1975, Volume 5, 1976, Volume 9, 1978, Volume 11, 1979, Volume 14, 1980, Volume 17, 1981, Volume 50, 1988, Volume 51, 1989.
Dictionary of Literary Biography, Gale, Volume 5: *American Poets since World War II,* Volume 6, *American Novelists since World War II,* 1980.
Newman, Charles, editor, *The Art of Sylvia Plath: A Symposium,* Indiana University Press, 1970.
Steiner, N. H., *A Closer Look at Ariel: A Memory of Sylvia Plath,* Harper's Magazine Press, 1973.
Stevenson, Anne, *Bitter Fame: The Undiscovered Life of Sylvia Plath,* Houghton, 1989.
Wagner-Martin, Linda, *Sylvia Plath: A Biography,* Simon & Schuster, 1987.
Writers on Themselves, British Broadcasting Corporation, 1964.

PERIODICALS

Atlantic, August, 1966.
Critical Quarterly, Volume 7, number 1, 1965.
Ms., September, 1972.
New Republic, June 18, 1966.
Newsweek, June 20, 1966.
New York Times, October 9, 1979.
Partisan Review, winter, 1967.
Poetry, March, 1963, January, 1967.
Reporter, October 7, 1965.
Time, June 10, 1966.
Tri-Quarterly, fall, 1966.

*   *   *

PLICK et PLOCK
  See SIMENON, Georges (Jacques Christian)

*   *   *

PLIMPTON, George (Ames)   1927-

PERSONAL: Born March 18, 1927, in New York, N.Y.; son of Francis T. P. (a lawyer and former U.S. deputy representative to the United Nations) and Pauline (Ames) Plimpton; married Freddy Medora Espy (a photography studio assistant), March 28, 1968; children: Medora Ames, Taylor Ames. *Education:* Harvard University, A.B., 1950; King's College, Cambridge, B.A., 1952, M.A., 1954. *Politics:* Democrat. *Religion:* Unitarian Universalist.

ADDRESSES: Home—541 East 72nd St., New York, N.Y. 10021. *Office*—Paris Review, Inc., 45-39 171st Pl., Flushing, N.Y. 11358. *Agent*—Russell & Volkening, 50 West 29th St., New York, N.Y. 10001.

CAREER: Writer and editor. Editor of the *Lampoon* while at Harvard. Principal editor, *Paris Review,* 1953—, publisher, with

Doubleday & Co., of Paris Review Editions (books), 1965—. Associate editor, *Horizon,* 1959-61; contributing editor, *Sports Illustrated,* 1967—; associate editor, *Harper's,* 1972—; contributing editor, *Food and Wine,* 1978; member of editorial advisory board, *Realities,* 1978. Director, American Literature Anthology program, 1967—; chief editor of annual anthology of work from literary magazines for the National Foundation on the Arts and Humanities; adviser on John F. Kennedy Oral History Project. Instructor at Barnard College, 1956-58; associate fellow, Trumbull College, Yale, 1967. Occasional actor in films; journalistic participant in sporting and musical events. Honorary commissioner of fireworks, New York City, 1973—. Trustee, National Art Museum of Sport, 1967—, WNET-TV, 1973—, Police Athletic League, 1976—, African Wildlife Leadership Foundation, 1980—, Guild Hall, East Hampton, 1980—. *Military service:* U.S. Army, 1945-48; became second lieutenant.

MEMBER: Pyrotechnics Guild International, American Pyrotechniques Association, Explorers Club, NFL Alumni Association; clubs include Century Association, Racquet and Tennis, Brooks, Piping Rock, Dutch Treat, Coffee House, Devon Yacht, Travelers (Paris).

AWARDS, HONORS: Distinguished achievement award, University of Southern California, 1967; D.H.L., Franklin Pierce College, 1968.

WRITINGS:

The Rabbit's Umbrella (juvenile), Viking, 1955.
(Editor) *Writers at Work: The Paris Review Interviews,* Viking, Volume 1, 1957, Volume 2, 1963, Volume 3, 1967, Volume 4, 1976, Volume 5, 1981, Volume 6, 1984, Volume 7, 1986, Volume 8, 1988.
(Editor with Peter Ardery) *The American Literary Anthology,* Number 1, Farrar, Straus, 1968, Number 2, Random House, 1969, Number 3, Viking, 1970.
(Editor) Jean Stein, *American Journey: The Times of Robert Kennedy* (interviews), Harcourt, 1970.
(Editor) Stein, *Edie: An American Biography,* Knopf, 1982.
(Editor with Christopher Hemphill) Diana Vreeland, *D.V.,* Random House, 1984.
Fireworks: A History and Celebration, Doubleday, 1984.
(Editor) *Poets at Work,* Viking, 1989.
(Editor) *Women Writers at Work,* Viking, 1989.
The Best of Plimpton, Atlantic Monthly Press, 1990.

SPORTS WRITING

Out of My League (baseball anecdotes), Harper, 1961, reprinted, Penguin, 1983.
Paper Lion (football anecdotes), Harper, 1966.
The Bogey Man (golf anecdotes), Harper, 1968, reprinted, Penguin, 1983.
(Editor and author of introduction) Pierre Etchebaster, *Pierre's Book: The Game of Court Tennis,* Barre Publishers, 1971.
(With Alex Karras and John Gordy) *Mad Ducks and Bears: Football Revisited* (football anecdotes), Random House, 1973.
One for the Record: The Inside Story of Hank Aaron's Chase for the Home Run Record, Harper, 1974.
Shadow Box (boxing anecdotes), Putnam, 1977.
One More July: A Football Dialogue with Bill Curry, Harper, 1977.
(Author of text) *Sports!,* photographs by Neil Leifer, H. N. Abrams, 1978.
A Sports Bestiary (cartoons), illustrated by Arnold Roth, McGraw-Hill, 1982.

Open Net (hockey anecdotes), Norton, 1985.
The Curious Case of Sidd Finch (baseball novel), Macmillan, 1987.

OTHER

(With William Kronick) "Plimpton! Shoot-out at Rio Lobo" (script), American Broadcasting Companies, Inc. (ABC-TV), 1970.
"Plimpton! The Man on the Flying Trapeze" (script), ABC-TV, 1970.
(With Kronick) "Plimpton! Did You Hear the One About . . .?" (script), ABC-TV, 1971.
(With Kronick) "Plimpton! The Great Quarterback Sneak" (script), ABC-TV, 1971.
(With Kronick) "Plimpton! Adventure in Africa" (script), ABC-TV, 1972.
(Author of introduction) Bill Plympton, *Medium Rare: Cartoons,* Holt, 1978.
(Author of introduction) *Oakes Ames: Jottings of a Harvard Botanist, 1874-1950,* edited by Pauline Ames Plimpton, Harvard University Press, 1980.

SIDELIGHTS: The "career" section cited above does not do justice to George Plimpton's life. Authorities call Plimpton a "professional amateur," for, although writing is his primary occupation, he has also pitched in a post-season All-Star game in Yankee Stadium, held the position of third-string rookie quarterback for the Detroit Lions in 1963, taking the field in one exhibition game (and later playing with the Baltimore Colts against the Lions), golfed in several Pro-Am tournaments, briefly appeared in a basketball game for the Boston Celtics, boxed with former light heavyweight champion Archie Moore, and served as a goalie for the Boston Bruins hockey team in 1977 and the Edmonton Oilers in 1985. He also fought in a bullfight staged by Ernest Hemingway in 1954, and worked as a trapeze artist, lion-tamer, and clown for the Clyde Beatty-Cole Brothers Circus.

In less athletic activities, Plimpton developed a stand-up comedy routine and performed it in Las Vegas. He served as a percussionist with the New York Philharmonic and as a guest conductor of the Cincinnati Symphony. He has also been seen in films, including "Rio Lobo," where he played a bad guy shot by John Wayne, Norman Mailer's "Beyond the Law," and the film version of "Paper Lion." On television he has hosted specials and appeared in commercials, and since 1973 he has exercised his interest in pyrotechnics as honorary commissioner of fireworks for New York City.

Reviewers consider *Paper Lion,* Plimpton's book about his football adventures with the Detroit Lions, a classic of sports writing. It "is the best book written about pro football—maybe about any sport—because he captured with absolute fidelity how the average fan might feel given the opportunity to try out for a professional football team," explains Hal Higdon in the *Saturday Review.* The book attracted sports fans not only through its innovative concept—a writer actually taking the field with a professional team—but also through the author's command over language. "Practically everybody loves George's stuff because George writes with an affection for his fellow man, has a rare eye for the bizarre, and a nice sense of his own ineptitude," declares Trent Frayne in the Toronto *Globe and Mail.* "[Ernest] Hemingway . . . [once] said, 'Plimpton is the dark side of the moon of Walter Mitty.'"

Many writers echo Hemingway's statement. However, although Plimpton's adventures superficially resemble those of James Thurber's famous character, there are many differences between the two. "In his participatory journalism [Plimpton] has been described wrongly as a Walter Mitty, and he is nothing of the sort. This is no daydreaming nebbish," declares Joe Flaherty in the *New York Times Book Review.* Plimpton's adventures are tangible rather than imaginary. Yet, while Mitty in his dreams is a fantastic success at everything he undertakes, Plimpton's efforts almost invariably result in failure and humiliation. "Plimpton has stock in setting himself up as a naif . . . many of us are familiar with his gangling, tweedy demeanor and Oxford accent. He plays the 'fancy pants' to our outhouse Americana," Flaherty asserts. "George Plimpton doesn't want to be known as an athlete," explains Cal Reynard in the *Arizona Daily Star.* "He figures his role in sports is that of the spectator, but he wants to get closer to the game than the stands."

After more than twenty years of writing non fiction about sports, Plimpton published his first sports novel, *The Curious Case of Sidd Finch,* in 1987. Plimpton based the story on a *Sports Illustrated* article he had written for the 1985 April Fools Day issue about a former Harvard man-cum-Buddhist-monk, Siddhartha (Sidd) Finch, who can pitch a baseball half again as fast as any other pitcher in the history of the game—about 150 MPH. Plimpton's article claimed that Finch was about to sign with the New York Mets, and speculated about the impact an unhittable pitcher would have on the game of baseball. *The Curious Case of Sidd Finch* expands on the article, telling how Finch, after much self-doubt, is persuaded to play for the Mets and, on his return to Shea Stadium, pitches what former major league pitcher Jim Brosnan, writing in the *Washington Post Book World,* calls "THE perfect game"; he strikes out the entire batting lineup of the St. Louis Cardinals in perfect order.

Plimpton's reviewers have read *The Curious Case of Sidd Finch* with mixed feelings. Although Brosnan finds the novel "sort of like a shaggy-dog tale that once was a crisp one-liner," he continues, "*The Curious Case of Sidd Finch* is not the rollicking farce I'd hoped for, but it's worth a reading." Lee Green, writing in the *Los Angeles Times Book Review,* calls the book a "wonderfully wry and whimsical debut novel," while National League president and *New York Times Book Review* contributor A. Bartlett Giamatti states, "Mr. Plimpton's control is masterly," and adds, "[The baseball] culture is splendidly rendered with an experienced insider's knowledge, and the whole saga of Finch's brief, astonishing passage through big-league baseball is at once a parody of every player's as-told-to biography, a satire on professional sports, an extended (and intriguing) meditation on our national pastime and a touching variant on the novel of education as Sidd learns of the world."

Although his sports writing remains his best-known work, Plimpton's own interest centers on the small literary magazine he has edited since 1953. James Warren explains in the *Chicago Tribune,* "It's the Paris Review, not the chronicles of his own sporting foibles . . . that constitutes the soul—and takes up much of the time—of Plimpton's life." The *Paris Review,* unlike many other literary magazines, focuses on creative writing rather than criticism. Many famous American writers—including Jack Kerouac, Philip Roth, Henry Miller, and John Updike—have published first efforts or complete works in its pages.

Plimpton's interviews with writers about the craft of writing are a major attraction of the journal. It was the *Paris Review,* explains Nona Balakian in the *New York Times,* that first "developed a new kind of extended and articulate interview that combined the Boswellian aim with an exploration of the ideas of major contemporary writers on the art of fiction and poetry." "The thing that makes these interviews different from most interviews," writes Mark Harris in the *Chicago Tribune Book World*, "is that they go on long enough to get somewhere. If they do not arrive at the point I dreamily hoped for—creativity totally clarified with a supplementary manual on How To Write—they supply very good instruction nevertheless." The result, Balakian concludes, is "a heightened awareness of a writer's overall purpose and meaning."

MEDIA ADAPTATIONS: "Paper Lion," the story of Plimpton's experiences as a short-term member of the Detroit Lions football team, was filmed by United Artists in 1968. Alan Alda portrayed Plimpton, but the author himself also had a role—he played Bill Ford.

BIOGRAPHICAL/CRITICAL SOURCES:

BOOKS

Authors in the News, Volume 1, Gale, 1976.
Contemporary Literary Criticism, Volume 36, Gale, 1986.
Talese, Gay, *The Overreachers,* Harper, 1965.

PERIODICALS

Arizona Daily Star, March 24, 1974.
Book Week, October 23, 1966.
Chicago Tribune, December 22, 1986, June 15-June 16, 1987.
Chicago Tribune Book World, May 3, 1981, September 2, 1984, October 14, 1984, November 24, 1985.
Christian Science Monitor, December 5, 1968.
Commentary, October, 1967.
Detroit News, March 16, 1986.
Globe and Mail (Toronto), July 7, 1984, February 8, 1986, June 14, 1986.
Los Angeles Times, July 22, 1982, March 20, 1987.
Los Angeles Times Book Review, September 30, 1984, June 21, 1987.
Milwaukee Journal, November 12, 1974.
New Yorker, November 12, 1966.
New York Herald Tribune, April 23, 1961.
New York Review of Books, February 23, 1967, February 7, 1974.
New York Times, November 12, 1973, July 29, 1977, November 16, 1977, March 28, 1981, June 14, 1984, November 14, 1985, July 30, 1987.
New York Times Book Review, April 23, 1961, November 10, 1968, January 6, 1974, July 31, 1977, November 6, 1977, June 17, 1984, September 23, 1984, November 24, 1985, July 5, 1987.
Saturday Review, December 10, 1966, August 14, 1971.
Spectator, October 14, 1978.
Time, December 19, 1977, September 10, 1984, December 8, 1986, June 8, 1987.
Times Literary Supplement, December 1, 1978, January 21, 1983, December 21, 1984, August 2, 1985, September 5, 1986, March 20, 1987.
Tribune Books (Chicago), July 5, 1987.
Wall Street Journal, August 28, 1984.
Washington Post, January 7, 1986.
Washington Post Book World, May 27, 1984, September 2, 1984, June 21, 1987.

—*Sketch by Kenneth R. Shepherd*

*   *   *

PLOMER, William Charles Franklin   1903-1973

PERSONAL: Surname is pronounced to rhyme with rumour; born December 10, 1903, in Northern Transvaal, Africa; died September 21, 1973, in England; son of Charles (magistrate specializing in native affairs) and Edythe (Waite-Browne) Plomer. *Education:* Attended Rugby.

ADDRESSES: c/o Jonathan Cape, 30 Bedford Square, London W.C.1, England.

CAREER: Writer. After schooling returned to Africa, became farmer in Stormberg mountains, and joined a Settler's Association; lived in Johannesburg, and was a trader in Zululand; published the literary review *Voorslag* ("Whiplash") with Roy Campbell; spent two years traveling and teaching in Japan; returned to England through Manchuria, Siberia, Russia, and Poland; was offered Chair of English Literature at Imperial University, Tokyo (formerly held by Lafcadio Hearn), but refused it and, after visiting France, Germany, and Italy, went to live in Greece; later returned to England. *Military service:* Served with British Naval Intelligence, 1941-45.

MEMBER: International PEN, Royal Society of Literature (fellow), Kilvert Society (president), Byron Society (vice president), Society of Authors, Poetry Society (president, 1968-71).

AWARDS, HONORS: D.Litt., University of Durham; Queen's Gold Medal for Poetry, 1963; Commander of the Order of the British Empire, 1968; co-recipient with Alan Aldridge, Whitbread Literary Award for best children's book, 1973, for *The Butterfly Ball and the Grasshopper Feast.*

WRITINGS:

Turbott Wolfe, introduction by Laurens van der Post, Hogarth, 1925, Harcourt, 1926, reprinted, Oxford University Press, 1985.
I Speak of Africa, Hogarth, 1927.
Notes for Poems, Hogarth, 1927.
The Family Tree (poetry), Hogarth, 1929.
Sado, Leonard & Virginia Woolf (London), 1929, reprinted as *They Never Came Back,* Coward, 1932.
Paper Houses (stories), Coward, 1932.
The Case Is Altered, Farrar & Rinehart, 1932, revised edition, Chatto & Windus, 1970.
The Fivefold Screen (poetry), Hogarth, 1932.
The Child of Queen Victoria and Other Stories, J. Cape, 1933.
Cecil Rhodes, Appleton, 1933.
The Invaders, J. Cape, 1934.
Ali the Lion: Ali of Tebeleni, Pasha of Jannina, 1741-1822, J. Cape, 1936, published as *The Diamond of Jannina: Ali Pasha, 1741-1822,* Taplinger, 1970.
Visiting the Caves (poetry), J. Cape, 1936.
Selected Poems, Hogarth, 1940.
Double Lives: An Autobiography, J. Cape, 1943, Noonday Press, 1956, reprinted, Books for Libraries, 1971.
Dorking Thigh and Other Satires (poetry), J. Cape, 1945.
Four Countries, J. Cape, 1949.
Museum Pieces, J. Cape, 1952, Noonday Press, 1954.
Borderline Ballads (poetry), Noonday Press, 1955 (published in England as *A Shot in the Park,* J. Cape, 1955).
Coming to London (stories), edited by John Lehmann, Phoenix House, 1957.
At Home: Memoirs, Noonday Press, 1958, reprinted, Books for Libraries, 1971.
Collected Poems, J. Cape, 1960.
Taste and Remember (poetry), J. Cape, 1966.
(Translator) Ingrid Jonker, *Selected Poems,* J. Cape, 1968.
Celebrations, J. Cape, 1972.
(With Alan Aldridge) *The Butterfly Ball and the Grasshopper Feast,* J. Cape, 1973, Viking, 1975.

Collected Poems, J. Cape, 1973.
The Autobiography of William Plomer, Taplinger, 1975, new revised edition, 1976.
Electric Delights (collection of essays, poems, stories, and travel sketches), edited and introduced by Rupert Hart-Davis, David Godine, 1978.

EDITOR

(And author of introduction) H. Ichikawa, *Japanese Lady in Europe,* Dutton, 1937.
(And author of introduction) R. F. Kilvert, *Kilvert's Diary, 1870-1879,* three volumes, J. Cape, 1938-40, revised edition, 1961, reprinted, Penguin, 1984.
Herman Melville, *Selected Poems,* Hogarth, 1943.
W. D'Arfey, *Curious Relations,* J. Cape, 1945, Sloane, 1947, reprinted, Sphere Books, 1968.
New Poems, 1960-1961 (a PEN anthology), Transatlantic, 1961.
(And author of introduction) Richard Rumbold, *A Message in Code: The Diary of Richard Rumbold, 1932-1961,* Weidenfeld & Nicolson, 1964.

LIBRETTOS; ALL WITH BENJAMIN BRITTEN

Gloriana (opera in three acts), Boosey & Hawkes, 1953.
Curlew River: A Parable for Church Performance (based on *Sumidagawa* by Juro Motomasa), Faber Music, 1964.
The Burning Fiery Furnace: Second Parable for Church Performance, Faber Music, 1966.
The Prodigal Son: Third Parable for Church Performance, Faber Music, 1968.

SIDELIGHTS: Reviewing Plomer's first book, *Turbott Wolfe,* Walter Yust commented: "The 'story' is the least important portion of the book. The impressions of Turbott Wolfe, a good and thoughtful man torn by disillusion and with only a half faith in humankind, are rich and warm. Some are harsh but many are beautiful. His are the moods and honesty of a Dostoievsky and the delight in firm color of a Henri Rousseau." *Double Lives,* his autobiography, described an exciting epoch in South African history just before the turn of the century. "Here both his wit and his sympathy are fully engaged; his ability at characterization is in full play," wrote Elizabeth Barthelme. The *San Francisco Chronicle* reviewer pointed out that "the scenes shift from Victorian salons to the African bush. [The book] juxtaposes the amenities of a liberal England with the life on a frontier in which the racial conflicts present in Africa today were already foreshadowed." The *New York Times* commented on Paper Houses: "One cannot read very far in Mr. Plomer's book without observing that his stories are 'different,' that they attempt through the guise of fiction to adumbrate certain peculiar spiritual and mental attitudes of the Japanese, and that an unsensational honesty is behind every paragraph." Vincent Sheean stated that Plomer "writes whole pages of English prose, which for hard, solid beauty have not been surpassed since the early James Joyce."

Ernestine Evans wrote of *The Case is Altered:* "By the clear consciousness of its telling and the courage of its perceptions, no one can fail to be moved, in pain for the matter, and in pleasure for the manner, of its telling." According to H. C. Webster, *At Home: Memoirs,* a sequel to *Double Lives,* "deserves to rank with the best literary autobiographies that have come out of England."

MEDIA ADAPTATIONS: Gloriana was performed during the coronation celebration for Queen Elizabeth II in 1953. *Conversation with My Younger Self* was broadcast on the BBC Third Programme on December 12, 1962.

BIOGRAPHICAL/CRITICAL SOURCES:

BOOKS

Contemporary Literary Criticism, Gale, Volume 4, 1975, Volume 8, 1978.
Dictionary of Literary Biography, Volume 20: *British Poets, 1914-1945,* Gale, 1983.

PERIODICALS

Books, June 2, 1929, September 1, 1936.
Commonweal, December 28, 1956.
Literary Review, April 24, 1926.
New York Times, July 28, 1929, January 1, 1956, November 16, 1958.
New York Times Book Review, February 18, 1979.
San Francisco Chronicle, March 10, 1957.
Times Literary Supplement, March 21, 1929, December 28, 1984.
Washington Post Book World, January 14, 1979.

*   *   *

PLOWMAN, Piers
See KAVANAGH, Patrick (Joseph)

*   *   *

PLUM, J.
See WODEHOUSE, P(elham) G(renville)

*   *   *

POET OF TITCHFIELD STREET, The
See POUND, Ezra (Weston Loomis)

*   *   *

POHL, Frederik   1919-
(Elton V. Andrews, Paul Fleur, Warren F. Howard, Ernst Mason, James McCreigh, Donald Stacy; S. D. Gottesman, Lee Gregor, Cyril Judd, Paul Dennis Lavond, Scott Mariner, Edson McCann, Jordan Park, Charles Satterfield, Dirk Wilson, joint pseudonyms)

PERSONAL: Born November 26, 1919, in New York, N.Y.; son of Fred George (a salesman) and Anna Jane (Mason) Pohl; married Doris Baumgardt (divorced, 1944); married Dorothy Louise Lena (divorced, 1947); married Judith Merril (divorced, 1952); married Carol M. Ulf, September 15, 1952 (divorced, 1983); married Elizabeth Anne Hall (a professor of English), July, 1984; children: Ann (Mrs. Walter Weary), Karen (Mrs. Robert Dixon), Frederik III (deceased), Frederik IV, Kathy. *Education:* Attended public schools in Brooklyn, N.Y., "dropped out in senior year." *Politics:* Democrat. *Religion:* Unitarian.

ADDRESSES: Home and office—Palatine, Ill. *Agent*—Curtis Brown, Ltd., 575 Madison Ave., New York, N.Y. 10022.

CAREER: Writer. Popular Publications, New York City, editor, 1939-43; Popular Science Publishing Co., New York City, editor in book department and assistant circulation manager, 1946-49; literary agent, 1946-53; free-lance writer 1953-60; *Galaxy* Magazine, New York City, editor, 1961-69; Ace Books, New York City, executive editor, 1971-72; Bantam Books, New York City, science fiction editor, 1973-79. Staff lecturer, American Management Association, 1966-69; cultural exchange lecturer in science fiction for U.S. Department of State in Yugoslavia, Romania, and the Soviet Union, 1974; also lecturer at more than two hundred colleges in the United States, Canada, and abroad; represented United States at international literary conferences in England, Italy, Brazil, Canada, and Japan. Has appeared on more than four hundred radio and television programs in nine countries. County committeeman, Democratic Party, Monmouth City, N.J., 1956-69; trustee, The Harbour School, Red Bank, N.J., 1972-75, and First Unitarian Church of Monmouth City, 1973-75. *Military service:* U.S. Army Air Forces, 1943-45; received seven battle stars.

MEMBER: Science Fiction Writers of America (president, 1974-76), Authors Guild (Midwest area representative), British Interplanetary Society (fellow), American Astronautical Society, World SF (president, 1980-82), Authors Guild (member of council, 1975—), American Association for the Advancement of Science (fellow), World Future Society, American Civil Liberties Union (trustee, Monmouth County, N.J., 1968-71), New York Academy of Sciences.

AWARDS, HONORS: Edward E. Smith Award, 1966; Hugo Award, World Science Fiction Convention, 1966, 1967, and 1968, for best editor, 1974, for short story, "The Meeting," 1978, for best novel, *Gateway,* and 1986, for story "Fermi and Frost"; H. G. Wells Award, 1975; Nebula Award, Science Fiction Writers of America, 1977, for best novel, *Man Plus,* and 1978, for best novel, *Gateway;* John W. Campbell Award, Center for the Study of Science Fiction, 1978, for *Gateway,* and 1986, for *The Years of the City;* American Book Award, 1979, for *JEM;* Popular Culture Association annual award, 1982; guest of honor at science fiction convention in Katowice, Poland, 1987.

WRITINGS:

(Under pseudonym James McCreigh) *Danger Moon,* American Science Fiction (Sydney), 1953.
(With Lester del Rey under joint pseudonym Edson McCann) *Preferred Risk,* Simon & Schuster, 1955.
Alternating Currents (short stories), Ballantine, 1956.
(Under pseudonym Donald Stacy) *The God of Channel 1,* Ballantine, 1956.
(With Walter Lasly) *Turn the Tigers Loose,* Ballantine, 1956.
Edge of the City (novel based on screenplay by Robert Alan Aurthur), Ballantine, 1957.
Slave Ship, Ballantine, 1957.
Tomorrow Times Seven: Science Fiction Stories, Ballantine, 1959.
The Man Who Ate the World, Ballantine, 1960.
Drunkard's Walk, Ballantine, 1960.
(Under pseudonym Ernst Mason) *Tiberius,* Ballantine, 1960.
Turn Left at Thursday: Three Novelettes and Three Stories, Ballantine, 1961.
The Abominable Earthman, Ballantine, 1963.
The Case against Tomorrow: Science Fiction Short Stories, Ballantine, 1965.
A Plague of Pythons, Ballantine, 1965.
The Frederik Pohl Omnibus, Gollancz, 1966.
Digits and Dastards, Ballantine, 1966.
The Age of the Pussyfoot, Ballantine, 1969.
Day Million (short stories), Ballantine, 1970.
Practical Politics, 1972 (nonfiction), Ballantine, 1971.
The Gold at the Starbow's End, Ballantine, 1972.
(With Carol Pohl) *Jupiter,* Ballantine, 1973.
The Best of Frederik Pohl, introduction by Lester del Rey, Doubleday, 1975.
The Early Pohl, Doubleday, 1976.

Man Plus, Random House, 1976.
Gateway, St. Martin's, 1977.
The Way the Future Was: A Memoir, Ballantine, 1978.
JEM, St. Martin's, 1979.
Beyond the Blue Event Horizon, Ballantine, 1980.
Syzygy, Bantam, 1981.
The Cool War, Ballantine, 1981.
Planets Three, Berkley, 1982.
Bipohl, Two Novels: Drunkard's Walk and The Age of the Pussyfoot, Ballantine, 1982.
Starburst, Ballantine, 1982.
Starbow, Ballantine, 1982.
(Author of introduction) *New Visions: A Collection of Modern Science Fiction Art,* Doubleday, 1982.
Midas World, St. Martin's, 1983.
Heechee Rendezvous, Ballantine, 1984.
The Years of the City, Simon & Schuster, 1984.
The Merchant's War, St. Martin's, 1984.
Pohlstars, Ballantine, 1984.
Black Star Rising, Ballantine, 1985.
The Coming of the Quantum Cats, Bantam, 1986.
Chernobyl, Bantam, 1987.
The Annals of the Heechee, Ballantine, 1988.
Narabdela Ltd., Del Rey, 1988.
The Day the Martians Came, St. Martin's, 1988.
Homegoing, Del Rey, 1989.

Contributor, sometimes under pseudonyms, to *Galaxy, Worlds of Fantasy, Science Fiction Quarterly, Rogue, Impulse, Astonishing, Imagination, If, Beyond, Playboy, Infinity,* and other magazines.

WITH CYRIL M. KORNBLUTH

(Under joint pseudonym Cyril Judd) *Gunner Cade,* Simon & Schuster, 1952.
(Under joint pseudonym Cyril Judd) *Outpost Mars,* Abelard Press, 1952.
The Space Merchants, Ballantine, 1953, 2nd edition, 1981.
Search the Sky, Ballantine, 1954.
Gladiator-at-Law, Ballantine, 1955.
A Town Is Drowning, Ballantine, 1955.
Presidential Year, Ballantine, 1956.
(Under joint pseudonym Jordan Park) *Sorority House,* Lion Press, 1956.
(Under joint pseudonym Jordan Park) *The Man of Cold Rages,* Pyramid Publications, 1958.
Wolfbane, Ballantine, 1959, reprinted, Garland Publishing, 1975.
The Wonder Effect, Ballantine, 1962.
Our Best: The Best of Frederik Pohl and C. M. Kornbluth, Baen Books, 1987.

WITH JACK WILLIAMSON

Undersea Quest, Gnome Press, 1954.
Undersea Fleet, Gnome Press, 1956.
Undersea City, Gnome Press, 1958.
The Reefs of Space (also see below), Ballantine, 1964.
Starchild (also see below), Ballantine, 1965.
Rogue Star (also see below), Ballantine, 1969.
Farthest Star: The Saga of Cuckoo, Ballantine, 1975.
The Starchild Trilogy: The Reefs of Space, Starchild, and Rogue Star, Paperback Library, 1977.
Wall around a Star, Ballantine, 1983.
Land's End, St. Martin's, 1988.

EDITOR

Beyond the End of Time, Permabooks, 1952.

Star Science Fiction Stories, Ballantine, 1953.

Star Short Novels, Ballantine, 1954.

Assignment in Tomorrow: An Anthology, Hanover House, 1954.

Star of Stars, Doubleday, 1960.

The Expert Dreamer, Doubleday, 1962.

Time Waits for Winthrop, Doubleday, 1962.

The Best Science Fiction from "Worlds of If" Magazine, Galaxy Publishing Corp., 1964.

The Seventh Galaxy Reader, Doubleday, 1964.

Star Fourteen, Whiting & Wheaton, 1966.

The If Reader of Science Fiction, Doubleday, 1966.

The Tenth Galaxy Reader, Doubleday, 1967, published as *Door to Anywhere,* Modern Literary Editions, 1967.

The Eleventh Galaxy Reader, Doubleday, 1969.

Nightmare Age, Ballantine, 1970.

Best Science Fiction for 1972, Ace Books, 1973.

(With Carol Pohl) *Science Fiction: The Great Years,* Ace Books, 1973.

The Science Fiction Roll of Honor, Random House, 1975.

Science Fiction Discoveries, Bantam, 1976.

Science Fiction of the Forties, Avon, 1978.

Galaxy Magazine: Thirty Years of Innovative Science Fiction, Playboy Press, 1980.

Nebula Winners Fourteen, Harper, 1980.

(Co-editor) *The Great Science Fiction Series,* Harper, 1980.

(With son, Frederik Pohl IV) *Science Fiction: Studies in Film,* Ace Books, 1981.

Yesterday's Tomorrows: Favorite Stories from Forty Years as a Science Fiction Editor, Berkley, 1982.

(With wife, Elizabeth Anne Hill) *Tales from the Planet Earth,* St. Martin's, 1986.

(With others) *Worlds of If: A Retrospective Anthology,* Bluejay Books, 1986. SIDELIGHTS: "Like all the other great men in SF," writes Algis Budrys in the *Magazine of Fantasy and Science Fiction,* "Frederik Pohl is idiosyncratic, essentially self-made, and brilliant. Unlike many of the others, he has an extremely broad range of interests and education." As both an author and editor Pohl has been, Robert Scholes and Eric S. Rabkin assert in *Science Fiction: History, Science, Vision,* "One of few men to make a genuine impact on the science fiction field."

In the 1950s, Pohl wrote a number of influential books with the late C. M. Kornbluth in which they "pioneered and excelled in a completely new kind of science fiction," writes Charles Platt in *Dream Makers: The Uncommon People Who Write Science Fiction.* "They invented and played with 'Sociological SF'— alternate futures here on Earth, exaggerating and satirizing real-life social forces and trends." The best of these collaborations was *The Space Merchants,* a satirical look at a world ruled by advertising; the book was inspired by Pohl's own short stint in an advertising agency. In this world, "exploitation of resources, pollution of environment, and overpopulation are all rampant," Scholes and Rabkin point out, "while the advertisers use every device of behavior control including addictive substances in the products. The beauty of [the book] is that it manages to be absurd and at the same time frighteningly close to the way that many people actually think. The lightness of touch and consistency of imagination make it a true classic of science fiction." "This novel is the single work most mentioned when Pohl's fiction is discussed," Stephen H. Goldman of the *Dictionary of Literary Biography* explains. "It is on every critic's list of science fiction classics and has never been out of print since its first appear-

ance. While Pohl and Kornbluth produced other highly readable novels *The Space Merchants* remains their single greatest achievement."

As editor of *Galaxy* and later with Bantam Books, Pohl was a strong supporter of the 'new wave' writers in science fiction—writers who borrowed literary techniques from mainstream literature to use in their science fiction, while eliminating what they saw as the genre's cliches. Ironically, Pohl came under fire from some of these writers for being too conservative. "I published the majority of 'new-wave' writers," Pohl told Platt. "It wasn't the stories I objected to, it was the snottiness of the proponents. . . . The thing that the 'new wave' did that I treasure was to shake up old dinosaurs, like Isaac [Asimov], and for that matter me . . ., and show them that you do not really have to construct a story according to the 1930s pulp or Hollywood standards."

Some of the new wave's influence can be seen in Pohl's prize-winning novel *Gateway,* the story of the discovery of an ancient spaceport of the Heechee, a long-dead civilization. Each spaceship found at the port is operable, but so highly advanced that the propulsion system and the destination for which it is programmed are incomprehensible to humans. A few brave adventurers dare to travel in the ships in a kind of lottery system. "Occasionally," writes Goldman, "one of the Heechee ships lands at a site that is filled with undiscovered artifacts, and the human riders share in the financial rewards these discoveries can bring." At other times, the adventurers never return, or return dead. The story, Mark Rose of the *New Republic* finds, "conveys a vivid sense of the pathos and absurdity of human ignorance in attempting to exploit a barely understood universe." Patrick Parrinder of the *Times Literary Supplement* agrees: "The novel is remarkable for its portrayal of human explorers rushing into space in a mood of abject fear and greed, in machines they cannot understand or control."

The story of the spaceport and its hazardous explorations is interspersed with seriocomic scenes involving a guilt-ridden adventurer—an adventurer who made a fortune during a trip on which he was forced to abandon the woman he loves—and his computer psychoanalyst. "Pohl's touch is always light and sure," Rose comments, "and, indeed parts of the novel are extremely funny." Goldman notes that in *Gateway* "Pohl has finally balanced the demands of an imaginative world and the presentation of a highly complex character. . . . This balance has led to his most successful novel thus far." In *Gateway,* Roz Kaveney of *Books and Bookmen* believes, Pohl "successfully combined wit and humanity in a novel of character. [The result is] a highly competent, darkly witty entertainment." Other critics found the computer psychoanalyst a particularly believable character. "What makes this book so intriguing," Peter Ackroyd of *Spectator* writes, "is not its occasional satire and consistent good humor, but the fact that Pohl has managed to convey the insistent presence of the non-human, a presence which may indeed haunt our future."

Pohl's next novel, *JEM,* also won critical praise. Set in the near future when the Earth has been divided into three camps—People, Fuel, and Food—the novel tells the story of three bands of human colonists on another planet. When there is a war and a resulting social breakdown on Earth, the colony is suddenly independent and "must then find a way to reconcile its divisions, both among the colonists and between the colonists and the three excellently depicted native sapient species, if it is to survive," writes Tom Easton of the *Magazine of Fantasy and Science Fiction.* Gerald Jonas of the *New York Times Book Review* compares *JEM* to *The Space Merchants* because "*JEM* is also social satire—but without the humor." "It is essentially a political allegory," Alex de Jonge of *Spectator* observes, "describing the struggle between the world's three blocs . . . each attempting to colonize a planet."

The colonization of Jem repeats some mistakes made on Earth. "With systematic, undeviating logic," writes Budrys, "Pohl depicts the consequent rape of Jem. As each of the expeditions struggles to do its best, there are moments of hope, and moments of triumph. But they are all no more than peaks on a downhill slope. The ending of it all is so genuinely sad that one realizes abruptly how rarely SF evokes pure sorrow, and how profound Pohl's vision was in conceiving of this story." Russell Lord of the *Christian Science Monitor* found it is Pohl's "basically poetic imagination that elevates this novel to a high position among the author's works."

Joseph McClellan of the *Washington Post Book World* offers an insight into what has made Pohl's writing among the best in the science fiction field. "Pohl's work," McClellan writes, "offers science fiction at its best: basic human problems . . . woven deftly into an intricate plot; pure adventure happening to believable (if not deeply drawn) characters in surroundings almost beyond the borders of imagination; and at the end, when other questions have been laid to rest, the posing of a new question as unfathomable as time and space themselves."

BIOGRAPHICAL/CRITICAL SOURCES:

BOOKS

Aldiss, Brian, *Billion Year Spree: The History of Science Fiction,* Doubleday, 1973.
Amis, Kingsley, *New Maps of Hell: A Survey of Science Fiction,* Harcourt, 1960.
Carter, Paul A., *The Creation of Tomorrow: Fifty Years of Magazine Science Fiction,* Columbia University Press, 1977.
Contemporary Authors Autobiography Series, Volume 1, Gale, 1984.
Contemporary Literary Criticism, Volume 18, Gale, 1981.
Dictionary of Literary Biography, Volume 8: *Twentieth Century American Science Fiction Writers,* Gale, 1981.
Platt, Charles, *Dream Makers: The Uncommon People Who Write Science Fiction,* Berkley, 1980.
Pohl, Frederik, *The Way the Future Was: Memoir,* Ballantine, 1978.
Scholes, Robert and Eric S. Rabkin, *Science Fiction: History, Science, Vision,* Oxford University Press, 1977.
Walker, Paul, *Speaking of Science Fiction: The Paul Walker Interviews,* Luna Press, 1978.

PERIODICALS

Analog, February, 1977, January, 1979, December, 1979, May, 1980.
Books and Bookmen, November, 1979.
Christian Science Monitor, June 20, 1979.
Magazine of Fantasy and Science Fiction, March, 1978, September, 1979.
New Republic, November 26, 1977.
New Statesman, April 15, 1977.
New York Times, September 7, 1983.
New York Times Book Review, March 27, 1977, May 20, 1979.
Publishers Weekly, July 31, 1978.
Spectator, January 28, 1978.
Times Literary Supplement, January 14, 1977, January 27, 1978, May 14, 1983.
Tribune Books (Chicago), March 15, 1987.
Washington Post, October 4, 1987.

Washington Post Book World, March 14, 1980, November 23, 1980, July 25, 1982.

* * *

POLLITT, Katha 1949-

PERSONAL: Born October 14, 1949, in New York, N.Y.; daughter of Basil Riddiford and Leanora (Levine) Pollitt. *Education:* Radcliffe College, B.A., 1972.

ADDRESSES: Home—245 West 13th St., New York, N.Y. 10011.

CAREER: Writer.

AWARDS, HONORS: Award for best poetry from National Book Critics Circle, 1983, for *Antarctic Traveller;* grant from National Endowment for the Arts, 1984; Peter I. B. Lavan Younger Poets Award from Academy of American Poets, 1984; Arvon Foundation Prize from *Observer,* 1986; Guggenheim fellowship, 1987.

WRITINGS:

Antarctic Traveller (poetry), Knopf, 1982.

Contributor to periodicals, including *Atlantic Monthly, Mother Jones, Nation, New Republic, New Yorker, New York Times Book Review,* and *Yale Review.*

SIDELIGHTS: Katha Pollitt is considered among the most promising American poets of recent decades. She began publishing her verse extensively in the mid-1970s in prestigious magazines such as *Atlantic Monthly* and *New Yorker,* and when her poems were collected as the book *Antarctic Traveller,* she was quickly acclaimed as a refreshing voice in contemporary poetry. Dana Gioia, for instance, wrote in *Hudson Review* that Pollitt "has an extraordinarily good ear," while Richard Tillinghast noted in *Sewanee Review* that she "possesses a winning quality that Robert Fitzgerald has aptly characterized as 'serious charm.' "

Critics agree that one of Pollitt's most impressive skills is her ability to use visual imagery as a means of exploring human thought and emotion. Typically successful in this regard is "Five Poems From Japanese Paintings," in which largely descriptive verse conveys an appropriate sense of reflection or action. In the segment entitled "Moon and Flowering Plum," for example, Pollitt employs a brief description of nature as a means for subtly addressing the implications of indecisiveness and commitment. "What Pollitt wants, what she creates," declared Richard Howard in *Nation,* "is the alternative life, unconditioned, eagerly espousing all that is unknown." Howard added that in "Five Poems From Japanese Paintings," "the decorous is the decisive moment, indulged only to be twitched away from us with a teasing laugh."

But Pollitt's strengths are not exclusively visual. Her verse marks her as an insightful artist whose perspective encompasses both the personal and the universal. Her thematic interests are particularly evident in poems such as "Discussions of the Vicissitudes of History Under a Pine Tree," where the vividness of nature leads to a commentary on human change, and "Thinking of the World as Idea," in which an observation of early morning harbor activities prompts a brief reflection on dreams, poetry, and the world. Even more modest efforts such as "Intimation," in which an old song sparks a mysterious memory, and "Sonnet," where the poet delineates a lover's perceptions, expand beyond the poignancy of their strictly personal contexts and offer stirring insights into behavior, perception, and even memory.

For her evocative and all-encompassing poetry, Pollitt is often paired with Wallace Stevens. Bruce Bennett, writing about *Antarctic Traveller* for the *New York Times Book Review,* mentioned Stevens while noting that Pollitt seems preoccupied by the artistic process and the inevitabilities of existence. "Like Wallace Stevens," Bennett observed, "Pollitt contrasts life and art." Howard also noted similarities between Pollitt and Stevens, but added that Pollitt was unique in avoiding obfuscation in her depictions and interpretations of people and nature. "What gives the distinction, the special twist of idiom we call style," Howard declared, "is the perception of delight in the world entertained on its own terms."

Antarctic Traveller enjoyed immense critical success upon publication in 1982. Richard Tillinghast wrote in *Sewanee Review* that Pollitt had produced a "fine collection" and that her stance was "romantic, full of emotion and delicate sensibility, yet convincing." Similarly, Gioia wrote that Pollitt "is a poet to watch" and commented, "Her lines are almost always exactly right, and there is a sense of finish and finality to her work one rarely sees in poets young or old—the diction clean and precise, the rhythms clear and effective." But Pollitt had been getting positive reviews even before her book was published. In the 1981 volume *Bounds Out of Bounds,* author Roberta Berke hailed Pollitt as "a miniaturist who captures elusive subjects with great delicacy and concision." Berke added that Pollitt's poems "are unabashedly intelligent and often metaphysical" and that Pollitt "combines her awareness of contraries and her intelligence with a vivid imagination that impels her best work toward that 'Supreme Fiction' which was Wallace Stevens's goal."

Of course, not all critical comments were entirely free of objection. Both Tillinghast and *New Republic* reviewer Jay Parini complained about Pollitt's use of the second-person pronoun, a device that Parini called "an irritating mannerism passed around the various M.F.A. programs like the German measles." And both Gioia and *Georgia Review* critic Peter Stitt lamented Pollitt's occasional reluctance or inability to pursue the philosophical implications of some poems. But even Stitt, who was less enthusiastic than most reviewers, wrote that *Antarctic Traveller* signaled the continued existence of the "objective mode of lyric poetry." He added that Pollitt's "best poems have a spare delicacy reflective of a rigorous sense of decorum."

Aside from her poetry, Pollitt has written critical reviews for many publications, including *Nation, Mother Jones,* and the *New York Times Book Review,* and she has discussed writers ranging from playwright Christopher Durang to novelist Saul Bellow. In addition, she has produced essays, including a scathingly persuasive condemnation of surrogate mothering. This essay, published in *Nation* in 1987, refutes many of the assumptions regarding this controversial practice and explores its legal and moral ramifications in a manner that exposes inherent sexism and elitism. Pollitt has thus proven herself impressive in nonfiction as well as poetry.

BIOGRAPHICAL/CRITICAL SOURCES:

BOOKS

Berke, Roberta, *Bounds Out of Bounds: A Compass for Recent American and British Poetry,* Oxford University Press, 1981.
Contemporary Literary Criticism, Volume 28, Gale, 1984.

PERIODICALS

American Poetry Review, September, 1982.
Georgia Review, summer, 1982.

Hudson Review, winter, 1982-83.
Nation, March 20, 1982.
New Republic, April 14, 1982.
New York Times Book Review, March 14, 1982.
Poetry, December, 1982.
Washington Post Book World, February 21, 1982.

*   *   *

POPPER, Karl R(aimund) 1902-

PERSONAL: Born July 28, 1902, in Vienna, Austria; son of Simon Siegmund Carl (a barrister) and Jenny (Schiff) Popper; married Josefine Anna Henninger, April 11, 1930 (died November 17, 1985). *Education:* University of Vienna, Ph.D., 1928; University of New Zealand, M.A., 1938; University of London, D.Lit., 1948.

ADDRESSES: Office—London School of Economics and Political Science, University of London, London WC2, England.

CAREER: University of Canterbury, Christchurch, New Zealand, senior lecturer in philosophy, 1937-45; University of London, London School of Economics and Political Science, London, England, reader, 1945-49, professor of logic and scientific method, 1949-69, professor emeritus, 1969—. William James Lecturer in Philosophy, Harvard University, 1950; visiting professor, Institute for Advanced Studies, Vienna, 1956, University of California, Berkeley, 1962, University of Minnesota, 1962, Indiana University, 1963, New York University, 1963, Massachusetts Institute of Technology, 1963, and University of Denver, 1966; annual philosophical lecturer, British Academy, 1960; Herbert Spencer Lecturer, Oxford University, 1961 and 1973; Sherman Lecturer, University College, University of London, 1961; Farnum Lecturer, Princeton University, 1963; Arthur Holly Compton Memorial Lecturer, Washington University, St. Louis, 1965; Kenan University Professor, Emory University, 1969; Ziskind Professor, Brandeis University, 1969; Romanes Lecturer, Oxford University, 1972; Henry D. Broadhead Memorial Lecturer, University of Canterbury, 1973; Darwin Lecturer, Cambridge University, 1977; Tanner Lecturer, University of Michigan, 1978; Doubleday Lecturer, Smithsonian Institution, 1979; distinguished lecturer at other institutions in England, Australia, and New Zealand.

MEMBER: International Academy for Philosophy of Science (fellow), Academie Internationale d'Histoire des Sciences, Academie Europeenne des Sciences, des Arts, et des Lettres (member of British delegation), Institut de France, Academie Royale Belgique, American Academy of Arts and Sciences (honorary foreign member), British Academy (fellow), British Society for the History of Science (chairman of philosophy of science group, 1951-53), Aristotelian Society (president, 1958-59), British Society for the Philosophy of Science (president, 1959-61), Association for Symbolic Logic (member of council, 1951-54), Royal Institute of Philosophy (member of board, 1956—), Royal Society of New Zealand (honorary member), Royal Society of London (fellow), Phi Beta Kappa (Harvard chapter; honorary member).

AWARDS, HONORS: Center for Advanced Study in the Behavioral Sciences fellow, 1956-57; LL.D., University of Chicago, 1962, and University of Denver, 1966; knighted by Queen Elizabeth, 1965; Prize of the City of Vienna, 1965, for contributions to the moral and mental sciences; Salk Institute for Biological Studies visiting fellow, 1966-67; Lit.D., University of Warwick, 1971, University of Canterbury, 1973, and Cambridge University, 1980; University of Copenhagen Sonning Prize, 1973; Grand Decoration of Honour in Gold, Austria, 1976; American

Political Science Association Lippincott Award, 1976, for *The Open Society and its Enemies;* D.Litt., University of Salford, 1976, City University, London, 1976, and University of Guelph, 1978; Karl Renner Prize, 1978; Dr.rer.nat.h.c., University of Vienna, 1978; Dr.phil.h.c., University of Mannheim, 1978, and University of Salzburg, 1979; American Museum of Natural History Gold Medal, 1979, for distinguished service to science; Ehrenzeichen fuer Wissenschaft und Kunst, Austria, 1980; Dr.rer.pol.h.c., University of Frankfurt am Main; Order of Merit of the Federal Republic of Germany, member, 1980, Grand Cross second class, 1983; Prix Alexis de Tocqueville, 1984.

WRITINGS:

Logik der Forschung: Zur Erkenntnistheorie der modernen Naturwissenschaft, Springer Verlag, 1935, 8th revised and enlarged edition, J. C. B. Mohr, 1984, translation by author of original edition published as *The Logic of Scientific Discovery,* Basic Books, 1959, 11th revised edition, Hutchinson, 1983.

The Open Society and Its Enemies, Volume I: *The Spell of Plato,* Volume II: *The High Tide of Prophecy: Hegel, Marx, and the Aftermath,* Routledge & Sons, 1945, 14th revised edition, Princeton University Press, 1984.

The Poverty of Historicism, Beacon Press, 1957, 3rd edition, Routledge & Kegan Paul, 1961.

Conjectures and Refutations: The Growth of Scientific Knowledge, Basic Books, 1962, 5th edition, Routledge & Kegan Paul, 1974.

Objective Knowledge: An Evolutionary Approach, Clarendon Press, 1972, 7th revised edition, Oxford University Press (New York), 1983.

The Philosophy of Karl Popper, two volumes, edited by Paul A. Schilpp, Open Court, 1974, revised autobiographical section published separately as *Unended Quest: An Intellectual Autobiography,* Fontana, 1976.

(With John C. Eccles) *The Self and Its Brain,* Springer International, 1977, 4th edition, 1985.

Die beiden Grundprobleme der Erkenntnistheorie, Volume I, J. C. B. Mohr, 1980.

Postscript to the Logic of Scientific Discovery, Volume I: *Realism and the Aim of Science,* Volume II: *The Open Universe: An Argument for Indeterminism,* Volume III: *Quantum Theory and the Schism in Physics,* Hutchinson, 1982-83.

A Pocket Popper, Fontana, 1983.

Auf der Suche nach einer besseren Welt, R. Piper Verlag, 1984.

CONTRIBUTOR

Gesetz und Wirklichkeit, [Innsbruck], 1949.

Readings in Philosophy of Science, Scribner, 1953.

The State versus Socrates, Beacon Press, 1954.

Contemporary British Philosophy, Allen & Unwin, 1956.

British Philosophy in the Mid-Century, Allen & Unwin, 1957.

Observation and Interpretation, Butterworth & Co., 1957, Dover, 1962.

The Philosophy of History in Our Time, Anchor Books, 1959, revised edition, 1961.

Philosophy for a Time of Crisis: An Interpretation, with Key Writings by Fifteen Great Modern Thinkers, Dutton, 1959.

Theories of History, Free Press of Glencoe, 1959.

Society, Law, and Morality, Prentice-Hall, 1961.

Der Sinn der Geschichte, C. H. Beck, 1961.

Geist und Gesicht der Gegenwart, Europa Verlag, 1962.

Philosophy for a Time of Crisis, by Albert Einstein, E. M. Forster, Karl R. Popper, and Bertrand Russell, Kinseido, 1962.

Club Voltaire, Szczesny Verlag, 1963.

Plato: Totalitarian or Democrat?, Prentice-Hall, 1963.

The Philosophy of Rudolf Carnap, Open Court, 1964.

Theorie und Realitaet, J. C. B. Mohr, 1964.

Form and Strategy in Science, D. Reidel, 1964.

The Socratic Enigma, Bobbs-Merrill, 1964.

Human Understanding: Studies in the Philosophy of David Hume, Wadsworth, 1965.

Versaeumte Lektionen, Sigbert Mohn Verlag, 1965.

Philosophical Problems of the Social Sciences, Macmillan, 1965.

Mind, Matter, and Method: Essays in Honor of Herbert Feigl, University of Minnesota Press, 1966.

Quantum Theory and Reality, Springer Verlag, 1967.

Also contributor to *Logik der Sozialwissenschaften,* 1965.

OTHER

Contributor of more than 100 articles to philosophy and science journals. Member of editorial board, *British Journal for the Philosophy of Science, Ratio, Monist, Dialectica,* and *Erfahrung und Denken.*

WORK IN PROGRESS: Three additional volumes of *Die beiden Grundprobleme der Erkenntnistheorie.*

SIDELIGHTS: Regarded as a lucid, eloquent philosopher and one of the most distinguished of contemporary thinkers, Karl R. Popper is the author of "one of the most celebrated and controversial views of science to have been put forward in this century," writes Jonathan Lieberson in the *New York Review of Books.* Lieberson describes Popper as a logician of science who has denied that science employs induction, and who has claimed that what demarcates science from nonscience, in particular metaphysics, is that scientists seek the truth by vigorously trying to falsify their theories. "For Popper," explains Anthony Quinton in the *Times Literary Supplement,* "scientific rationality is not a routine of fact-collecting but an alternation of adventurous guessing followed by rigorous testing. Its capacity for being tested, being possibly shown to be false by experience, is what makes a theory scientific, rather than pseudoscientific like alchemy and psycho-analysis or protoscientific like the speculative atomism of the ancient Greeks."

Popper first articulated his view of "falsifiability" as the determining criterion of scientific knowledge in *Logik der Forschung,* his first book. Highly influential even in English-speaking countries, the 1935 work appeared in a series sponsored by the Vienna Circle of logical positivists, a group of philosophers at the University of Vienna who attempted to "purify" philosophy by discarding its metaphysical elements and making logic its organon. Though associated with the circle, Popper was not a member, as he disagreed with some of their principal doctrines. While Popper shared their belief that physical science is the most acceptable part of what is considered human knowledge, he rejected their traditional, Baconian view that scientific knowledge is acquired through induction. Popper maintained in *Logik der Forschung* that what makes a theory *scientific* is not its degree of probability based on the mechanical observation of numerous instances, but rather its ability to withstand determined efforts to refute, or falsify, it. He also believed the positivists were mistaken in dismissing metaphysics as nonsense, for although he too considered it nonscience, he claimed that metaphysics could anticipate science by suggesting falsifiable—hence, scientific—hypotheses.

Popper later translated *Logik der Forschung* as *The Logic of Scientific Discovery,* and the book has become a classic text on the scientific method. Discussing the English-language edition in the

Nation, N. R. Hanson proclaims that "without any doubt this is one of the most important books in philosophy of science ever written."

BIOGRAPHICAL/CRITICAL SOURCES:

BOOKS

Ackerman, Robert, *The Philosophy of Karl Popper,* University of Massachusetts Press, 1976.

Bunge, Mario, editor, *The Critical Approach to Science and Philosophy: Essays in Honor of Karl R. Popper,* Free Press of Glencoe, 1964.

Feyerabend, Paul K., *Against Method,* Schoken, 1978.

Lakatos, Imre and Alan Musgrave, editors, *Criticism and the Growth of Knowledge,* Cambridge University Press, 1970.

Levinson, Paul, editor, *In Pursuit of Truth: Essays on the Philosophy of Karl Popper on the Occasion of His Eightieth Birthday,* Humanities, 1982.

Magee, Bryan, *Karl Popper,* Viking, 1973 (published in England as *Popper,* Fontana, 1973).

O'Hear, Anthony, *Karl Popper,* Routledge & Kegan Paul, 1980.

Popper, Karl R., *Unended Quest: An Intellectual Autobiography,* Fontana, 1976.

Schilpp, Paul A., editor, *The Philosophy of Karl R. Popper,* two volumes, Open Court, 1974.

PERIODICALS

Archiv fuer Rechts und Sozialphilosophie, Volume XLVI number 3, 1960.

Manchester Guardian, January 16, 1959.

Nation, June 27, 1959.

New Scientist, Volume V, number 124, 1959.

New Society, September 12, 1963.

New York Review of Books, November 18, 1982, December 2, 1982.

Times (London), July 29, 1982.

Times Literary Supplement, December 3, 1982.

*   *   *

PORTER, Katherine Anne   1890-1980

PERSONAL: One source cites full name as Katherine Anne Maria Veronica Callista Russel Porter; born May 15, 1890, in Indian Creek, Tex.; died September 18, 1980, in Silver Spring, Md., of cancer; daughter of Harrison Boone and Mary Alice (Jones) Porter; first married at sixteen, divorced at nineteen; married second husband, Eugene Dove Pressly (employed with the American Consulate in Paris), 1933 (divorced April 19, 1938); married Albert Russel Erskine, Jr. (a professor of English), 1938 (divorced, 1942). *Education:* Educated in convent and private schools.

CAREER: Professional writer. Lecturer and teacher at writer conferences; speaker at more than 200 universities and colleges in the United States and Europe. Writer in residence, or member of the faculties of English, at Olivet College, 1940, Stanford University, 1948-49, University of Michigan, Ann Arbor, 1953-54, University of Virginia, 1958, and Washington and Lee University, where she was first woman faculty member in the school's history, 1959. Ewing Lecturer, University of California, Los Angeles, 1959; first Regents Lecturer, University of California, Riverside, 1961. Member, President Johnson's Committee on Presidential Scholars.

MEMBER: National Institute of Arts and Letters (vice-president, 1950-52), American Academy of Arts and Letters.

AWARDS, HONORS: Guggenheim fellowships, 1931 and 1938; first annual gold medal, Society of the Libraries of New York University, 1940, for *Pale Horse, Pale Rider;* Library of Congress fellow in regional American literature, 1944; chosen one of six representatives of American literature at International Expositions of the Arts in Paris, 1952; Ford Foundation grant, 1959-61; State Department grants for international exchange of persons to Mexico, 1960 and 1964; first prize, O. Henry Memorial Award, 1962, for "Holiday"; Emerson-Thoreau Bronze Medal for Literature, American Academy of Arts and Sciences, 1962; Pulitzer Prize, 1966, and National Book Award, 1966, both for *The Collected Stories of Katherine Anne Porter;* gold medal, National Institute of Arts and Letters, 1967; creative arts award, Brandeis University, 1971-72. Honorary degrees include D.Litt., University of North Carolina, 1949, Smith College, 1958, and Wheaton College; D.H.L., University of Michigan, 1954, and University of Maryland, 1966; D.F.A., LaSalle College.

WRITINGS:

My Chinese Marriage, Duffield, 1921.

Outline of Mexican Popular Arts and Crafts, Young & McCallister, 1922.

What Price Marriage, Sears, 1927.

Flowering Judas (story; Book-of-the-Month Club selection), Harcourt, 1930, 2nd edition with added stories published as *Flowering Judas, and Other Stories,* 1935.

(Translator and compiler) *Katherine Anne Porter's French Songbook,* Harrison Co., 1933.

Hacienda: A Story of Mexico, Harrison Co., 1934.

Noon Wine, Schuman's, 1937.

Pale Horse, Pale Rider (three novelettes), Harcourt, 1939.

(Translator) Fernandez de Lizardi, *The Itching Parrot,* Doubleday, 1942.

(Author of preface) Flores and Poore, *Fiesta in November,* Houghton, 1942.

The Leaning Tower, and Other Stories, Harcourt, 1944.

The Days Before: Collected Essays and Occasional Writings, Harcourt, 1952, revised and enlarged edition published as *The Collected Essays and Occasional Writings of Katherine Anne Porter,* Delacorte, 1970.

The Old Order: Stories of the South from Flowering Judas, Pale Horse, and the Leaning Tower, Harcourt, 1955.

Fiction and Criticism of Katherine Anne Porter, University of Pittsburgh Press, 1957, revised edition, 1962.

Ship of Fools (novel; Book-of-the-Month Club selection), Little, Brown, 1962, reprinted, 1984.

The Collected Stories of Katherine Anne Porter, Harcourt, 1965.

A Christmas Story, illustrations by Ben Shahn, Dial, 1967.

The Never Ending Wrong, Little, Brown, 1977.

Contributor to numerous magazines.

SIDELIGHTS: Although her output was relatively small, Katherine Anne Porter was one of the most recognized and acclaimed American writers of short fiction of the twentieth century. In 1966 she won both the Pulitzer Prize and National Book Award for *The Collected Stories of Katherine Anne Porter,* many of which were written between 1922 and 1940. Porter also authored one novel, *Ship of Fools,* which took over twenty years to write and was one of most awaited literary products of its day when published in 1962. Although the novel drew mixed reviews, Porter's reputation rests firmly on the strength of her short fiction, which is marked by an economy of style and a controlled portrayal of character and emotion. Laurie Johnston notes in the *New York Times* that Porter's "storytelling had a quality of translucence—a smoothly polished, surface objectivity that nevertheless moved the reader to share the underlying turmoil of her characters and their often frightening interrelationships." Robert Penn Warren went as far in the *Washington Post* to state that Porter "is certainly unsurpassed in our century or country—perhaps any time or country—as a writer [of] fiction in the short forms of story or novella. . . . Her work remains a monument to a tremendous talent—even genius. It is permanent."

"My whole attempt," Porter once wrote, "has been to discover and understand human motives, human feeling, to make a distillation of what human relations and experiences my mind has been able to absorb. I have never known an uninteresting human being, and I have never known two alike; there are broad classifications and deep similarities, but I am interested in the thumbprint. I am passionately involved with these individuals who populate all these enormous migrations, calamities; these beings without which, one by one, all the 'broad movements of history' could never take place. One by one-as they were born."

These feelings for humanity were reflected in Porter's writings, George Hendrick believes. He wrote in his 1965 book, *Katherine Anne Porter:* "Over the last four decades, Miss Porter's short stories have been marked by a mastery of technique, mind and society itself, without lapsing into popular cliches. No matter whether she has written about Mexicans, Texans, Irishmen, or Germans, one feels that she knows the people and their backgrounds perfectly; she has lived and relived the experiences and emotions so thoroughly that she has often written her stories and short novels in a matter of hours or days."

Although she considered herself primarily a writer, Porter had to adopt sidelines to make a living. At 21, she worked for a newspaper in Chicago and later played bit parts in movies. In 1921, she went to Mexico to study Aztec and Mayan art designs and became involved in the Obregon Revolution. All the while she continued to write, burning 'trunksful' of manuscripts. She once told a *Paris Review* interviewer: "I practiced writing in every possible way that I could. . . . This has been the intact line of my life which directs my actions, determines my point of view, profoundly affects my character and personality, my social beliefs and economic status and the kind of friendships I form. . . . I made no attempt to publish anything until I was thirty, but I have written and destroyed manuscripts quite literally by the trunkful. I spent fifteen years wandering about, weighted horribly with masses of paper and little else. Yet for this vocation I was and am willing to live and die, and I consider very few other things of the slightest importance."

James William Johnson feels that "had Miss Porter left those trunksful of manuscripts unburned, the objection [some critics have] based on volume could have been met. Yet this very act of selectivity is an indication of the guiding principle which has made her unique. Her critical judgment, as accurate and impartial as a carpenter's level, has limited her artistry in several ways. It has not permitted her to universalize but has confined her to being a 'witness to life.' Consequently her fiction has been closely tied to what she herself has experienced firsthand. The fact that Miss Porter's essays parallel her stories in theme—love, marriage, alien cultures—is significant in this light. Her artistic preoccupation with 'truth' has prevented the fictional generalizations often thought of as scope." Christopher Isherwood agrees and introduces this reservation: "She is grave, she is delicate, she is just—but she lacks altogether, for me personally, the vulgar appeal. I cannot imagine that she would ever make me cry, or laugh aloud."

But Porter had stern words for much of the "vulgar appeal" of some contemporary literature: "We are being sluiced at present with a plague of filth in words and in acts, almost unbelievable abominations, a love of foulness for its own sake, with not a trace of wit or low comedy to clear the fetid air. There is a stylish mob with headquarters in New York that is gulping down the wretched stuff spilled by William Burroughs and Norman Mailer and John Hawkes—the sort of revolting upchuck that makes the old or Paris-days Henry Miller's work look like plain, rather tepid, but clean and well-boiled tripe." As a retort to those who consider contemporary life to be alienated and meaningless, she said: "But I tell you, nothing is pointless, and nothing is meaningless if the artist will face it. And it's his business to face it. He hasn't got the right to sidestep it like that. Human life itself may be almost pure chaos, but the work of the artist—the only thing he's good for—is to take these handfuls of confusion and disparate things, things that seem to be irreconcilable, and put them together in a frame to give them some kind of shape and meaning."

MEDIA ADAPTATIONS: Ship of Fools was filmed by Columbia in 1965; *Noon Wine* was dramatized and filmed for television's "ABC Stage 67" in 1967; the movie rights to *Pale Horse, Pale Rider* were sold in 1970; Porter's short story "The Jilting of Granny Weatherall," was filmed for television and broadcast March 3, 1979, on Public Broadcasting Service's "American Short Story."

AVOCATIONAL INTERESTS: Outdoor life (Porter was the great-great-great granddaughter of Jonathan Boone, the younger brother of Daniel Boone), old music, medieval history, reading, cookery, gardening.

BIOGRAPHICAL/CRITICAL SOURCES:

BOOKS

Aldridge, John W., *Time to Murder and Create,* McKay, 1966.
Authors in the News, Volume 2, Gale, 1976.
Contemporary Literary Criticism, Gale, Volume 1, 1973, Volume 3, 1975, Volume 7, 1977, Volume 10, 1979, Volume 13, 1980, Volume 15, 1980, Volume 27, 1984.
Dictionary of Literary Biography, Gale, Volume 4: *American Writers in Paris, 1920-1939,* 1980, Volume 9: *American Novelists, 1910-1945,* 1981.
Dictionary of Literary Biography Yearbook: 1980, Gale, 1981.
Hardy, J. E., *Katherine Anne Porter,* Ungar, 1973.
Hartley, L. C., and G. Core, editors, *Katherine Anne Porter,* University of Georgia Press, 1969.
Hendrick, George, *Katherine Anne Porter,* Twayne, 1965.
Mooney, Harry John, editor, *The Fiction and Criticism of Katherine Anne Porter,* University of Pittsburgh Press, 1962.
Nance, William L., *Katherine Anne Porter and the Art of Rejection,* University of North Carolina Press, 1964.
West, Ray B., Jr., *Katherine Anne Porter* (pamphlet), University of Minnesota Press, 1963.
Wilson, Edmund, *Classics and Commercials,* Farrar, Straus, 1950.

PERIODICALS

Harper's, September, 1965.
New Republic, April 19, 1939, December 4, 1965.
New York Times, March 16, 1966.
New York Times Book Review, April 1, 1962.
Paris Review, Number 29, 1963-64.
Partisan Review, spring, 1966.
Sewanee Review, spring, 1974.
Twentieth Century Literature, April, 1967.
Virginia Quarterly Review, autumn, 1960.
Washington Post, May 15, 1970, May 18, 1981.

Washington Star, May 11, 1975.

OBITUARIES:

PERIODICALS

Chicago Tribune, September 20, 1980.
Newsweek, September 29, 1980.
New York Times, September 19, 1980.
Times (London), September 20, 1980.
Washington Post, September 19, 1980, September 20, 1980.

* * *

PORTER, William Sydney   1862-1910
(O. Henry, Oliver Henry, S. H. Peters)

PERSONAL: Middle name originally spelled "Sidney"; born September 11, 1862, in Greensboro, N.C.; died of cirrhosis of the liver, June 5, 1910, in New York, N.Y.; son of Algernon Sidney (a physician) and Mary Jane Virginia (Swaim) Porter; married Athol Estes, July 5, 1887 (died, July 25, 1897); married Sara Lindsay Coleman, November 27, 1907; children: (first marriage) Margaret. *Education:* Attended secondary school in Greensboro, N.C.

CAREER: Short story writer and poet. Worked in a drug store, Greensboro, N.C., c. 1877-82; worked on ranch, La Salle county, Tex., 1882-84; worked as a bookkeeper and draftsman, Austin, Tex., 1884-91; First National Bank, Austin, teller, 1891-94; owner of weekly newspaper *Rolling Stone,* Austin, 1894 (failed, 1895); *Daily Post,* Houston, Tex., columnist, 1895; fled to Honduras to escape indictment for embezzlement, 1896; returned to United States and convicted of embezzlement, 1897; inmate of Ohio State Penitentiary, 1898-1901; worked for *Pittsburgh Dispatch,* c. 1901-02.

WRITINGS:

SHORT STORY COLLECTIONS, EXCEPT WHERE NOTED;
UNDER PSEUDONYM O. HENRY

Cabbages and Kings (novel), McClure, 1904.
The Four Million (includes "The Gift of the Magi"), McClure, 1906.
The Trimmed Lamp, and Other Stories of the Four Million (includes "Brickdust Row," "The Guilty Party," "The Last Leaf," "The Lost Blend," "The Making of a New Yorker," and "The Trimmed Lamp"), McClure, 1907.
Heart of the West (includes "An Afternoon Miracle," "Hearts and Crosses," "Hygeia at Solito," and "The Princess and the Puma"), McClure, 1907.
The Voice of the City: Further Stories of the Four Million, McClure, 1908.
The Gentle Grafter, McClure, 1908.
Roads of Destiny (includes "Friends in San Rosario," "The Halberdier of Little Rheinschloss," "A Retrieved Reformation," and "Whistling Dick's Christmas Stocking"), Doubleday, 1909.
Options (includes "He Also Serves" and "Supply and Demand"), Harper, 1909.
Strictly Business: More Stories of the Four Million (includes "Past One at Rooney's"), Doubleday, 1910.
Whirligigs (includes "The Ransom of Red Chief "), Doubleday, 1910.
Let Me Feel Your Pulse, Doubleday, 1910.
Sixes and Sevens, Doubleday, 1911.
(And illustrator) *Rolling Stones* (includes "The Marquis and Miss Sally" and "An Unfinished Christmas Story"), Doubleday, 1912.

Waifs and Strays, Doubleday, 1917.
O. Henryana, Doubleday, 1920.
Postscripts (stories first published in Houston *Daily Post*), edited by Florence Stratton, Harper, 1923.
(And illustrator) *O. Henry Encore,* Upshaw, 1936.

Also author of *Seven Odds and Ends, Poetry and Short Stories,* 1920. Author of "Money Maze." Contributor to periodicals, including *McClure's* and New York *World.*

OMNIBUS VOLUMES

The Complete Writings of O. Henry, fourteen volumes, Doubleday, 1917.
The Ransom of Red Chief, and Other O. Henry Stories for Boys, edited by Franklin K. Mathiews, Doubleday, 1918.
The Biographical Edition, eighteen volumes, Doubleday, 1929.
The Best Short Stories of O. Henry, edited by Bennett A. Cerf and Van H. Cartmell, Modern Library, 1945.
O. Henry's Cops and Robbers: O. Henry's Best Detective and Crime Stories, edited by Ellery Queen, L. E. Spivak, 1948.
The Complete Works of O. Henry, two volumes, Doubleday, 1953.
The Stories of O. Henry, edited by Harry Hansen, Heritage Press, 1965.
Surprises: Twenty Stories by O. Henry, edited by Richard Corbin and Ned E. Hoopes, Dell, 1966.
O. Henry Stories: The American Scene as Depicted by the Master of Short Stories, Platt & Munk, 1969.
O. Henry Selected Stories, Franklin Library, 1978.
Collected Stories of O. Henry, edited by Paul J. Horowitz, Avenel Books, 1979.

OTHER

Letters to Lithopolis (letters written to Mabel Wagnalls), Doubleday, 1922.

Author of short story "The Miracle of Lava Canyon," 1897. Author with Franklin P. Adams of "Lo!," a play first produced in Illinois in 1909. Author of works under pseudonyms Oliver Henry and S. H. Peters.

SIDELIGHTS: William Sydney Porter, best known under the pseudonym O. Henry, created short, often humorous stories with ironic twists or surprise endings, a type still referred to as "the O. Henry style." Porter's critical reputation climbed to a dazzling high from approximately 1910 to 1930, when he became the most popular short story writer in American literature, considered the equal of Nathaniel Hawthorne, Edgar Allan Poe, and other great short-fiction writers. Yet his reputation plummeted during the 1940s and 1950s to an equally unrealistic low, when his technical virtuosity was dismissed as flashy trickery and his social consciousness as shallow sentimentality. Objective evaluations of Porter have been rare because of this extreme variance in his popular and critical reputations, a problem complicated by his controversial life. Indeed, as Arthur W. Page recalled in *The Country Life Press,* even Porter's fiction is "tame compared with the romance of his own life."

Porter's biography is unusually relevant not only as it affects his critical reputation but as it forms the basis for most of his stories. Born William Sidney Porter (he changed the spelling of his middle name to Sydney in 1898) on September 11, 1862, in Greensboro, North Carolina, Porter was raised by his grandmother and his aunt after his mother died and his father became absorbed in drinking and inventing a perpetual motion machine. Porter left school at age fifteen and worked as a pharmacist's assistant in Greensboro; both the town and the occupation would appear in fictional form in later stories. At age twenty he moved to Texas to escape symptoms of tuberculosis. Working on the La Salle County ranch and sleeping outdoors, he learned the Western dialect, customs, and mannerisms that would be reflected in almost one hundred Western stories. Five years later Porter eloped with Athol Estes, the model for the character of Della in his most famous story, "The Gift of the Magi." Athol gave birth to a son who died within hours and in 1889 to a daughter, Margaret. To support his wife and young child, Porter was forced to accept a position as teller at the First National Bank of Austin, which had extremely informal policies that led him either to fail to record or to steal a deposit. After three years, Porter resigned from the bank in 1894 to establish, write, and edit his own humor magazine, *The Rolling Stone.* This weekly periodical, which satirized local and national events, ceased publication after a little over one year, but Porter continued writing, working for the Houston *Daily Post* as a contributor of comic sketches and cartoons as well as serious critical pieces that reflected his growing mastery of word usage, mythological allusions, plot twists, and character types. However, the incident at the First National Bank of Austin haunted him. Although in 1895 a grand jury had failed to find sufficient evidence to indict him and the bank's owners had requested that charges be dropped, the bank examiner persevered, and Porter was arrested for embezzlement in 1896. While returning to Austin to stand trail, he fled to New Orleans, then to Honduras, but word that Athol's health was failing brought him back to Austin, where she died in July, 1897.

Porter was convicted of embezzlement on February 17, 1898, and sentenced to five years in the Ohio State Penitentiary, yet his guilt or innocence has never been firmly established. To his mother-in-law, as C. Alphonso Smith reported in *O. Henry Biography,* Porter insisted he was "absolutely innocent of wrong doing"—a scapegoat for lax banking practices. To friends such as Anne Partlan, according to Howard Sartin in *Southern Humanities Review,* he claimed to be shielding a bank official who had befriended him, as happens in his story "Friends in San Rosario." Some believed Porter used the money to finance *The Rolling Stone,* perhaps intending to repay it later. Porter himself refused to speak openly of the matter, and his few cryptic comments are intriguing but unenlightening. For example, as Smith noted, Porter once compared himself to the central character of British novelist Joseph Conrad's *Lord Jim:* "I am like Lord Jim, because we both made one fateful mistake at the supreme crisis of our lives, a mistake from which we could not recover"; but characteristically, Porter did not specify whether this mistake was taking the bank's money, covering up for a friend who had done so, or fleeing his trial, an action that many saw as a tacit admission of guilt.

Guilty or innocent, in the Ohio State Penitentiary Porter became familiar with many of the men whose stories he would later recreate in fiction, including Al Jennings, a bank and train robber Porter had met during his exile in Honduras, and the safecracker whose story he immortalized in "A Retrieved Reformation," which was adapted by Paul Armstrong into a hit play, "Alias Jimmy Valentine." The prison experience was deeply degrading for Porter, and he hid his time in the penitentiary from everyone, even his own daughter. Ironically, "Alias Jimmy Valentine" became so popular that it led to a vogue of "crook plays," then to the gangster films such as those of Edward G. Robinson and James Cagney. An additional irony was that the incarceration helped prepare Porter to become a professional writer, for his prison stay allowed him the time both to write and to pursue publication—his first story written in prison, "Whistling Dick's Christmas Stocking," appeared in *McClure's* in 1899. This was

also the first story he signed as "O. Henry," although he continued to use other pseudonyms such as Oliver Henry or S. H. Peters. The origin of the famous pen name is uncertain: various biographers have suggested that it was taken from the listing of French chemist Etienne-Ossian Henry in the *United States Dispensatory,* which Porter had used as a pharmacist; from the reply of a friend asked for a suitable first name—"Oh! I don't know"—or from the society column of a New Orleans newspaper. Whatever its derivation, Fred Abrams suggested in *Studies in Short Fiction,* "Porter's desire to adopt a pseudonym was undoubtably motivated by his desire to conceal the stigma of being a convict. His own vague explanations of the pseudonym in later years were a patent evasion of the truth." Making the most of his time in prison, Porter contributed to various magazines stories based on his experiences in the American South and West and in Central America, and he worked through a period of literary apprenticeship in which his style was transformed from journalism to genuine literature.

On July 24, 1901, Porter left prison, his sentence having been commuted to three years and three months for good behavior. After a brief period working for the *Pittsburgh Dispatch,* in April of 1902 he arrived in New York City, responding to the metropolis with love and awe, spending hours talking with characters of the city—gangsters, shopgirls, hobos, prostitutes, actors—and transmuting them into fiction that he sold at a rapid rate to magazines and newspapers. In December of 1903 Porter agreed to furnish one story each week to the New York *World,* an arrangement that continued until 1906. In 1904 alone he published seventy-five stories.

Despite this frenetic pace, in 1904 Porter also found time to publish his first book and only novel, *Cabbages and Kings.* Actually, the "novel" was composed of a previously published short story, "Money Maze," which comprised the plot and was broken into separate sections. To these sections Porter added other early stories (mostly set in Honduras, which he called "Anchuria"), simply changing the names of the characters. According to William Wash Williams in *The Quiet Lodger of Irving Place,* Porter fittingly described *Cabbages and Kings* as "a few of my South American stories strung on a thread." Although the novel was generally well received by critics and was praised as a realistic depiction of life in Honduras, it did not sell well, and a contemporary appraisal by Smith concluded that Porter's experimental novel was ultimately a failure: "It is not equal to the sum total of its seventeen constituent parts. It has unity, but it is the unity of a sustained cleverness carried to an extreme. Suspense is preserved but interest is sacrificed."

Porter followed *Cabbages and Kings* with a much more successful, straightforward collection of short stories set in New York City and entitled *The Four Million* (1906). The title was a satirical reference to the famous statement of New York society leader Ward McAllister that there were only four hundred people in New York City worth knowing—the wealthy elite who comprised the highest class of society. In titling his collection *The Four Million,* Porter implied that every individual among the four million who populated the city had a story worth telling, regardless of social position. In *Through the Shadows With O. Henry,* Al Jennings recalled Porter's philosophy: "The short story is a potent medium of education. It should combine humor and pathos. It should break prejudice with understanding. I propose to send the down-and-outers into the drawing-rooms of the 'get-it-alls,' and I intend to insure their welcome. All that the world needs is a little more sympathy. I'm going to make the American Four Hundred step into the shoes of the Four Million." This democratic approach caught the attention of the public, and critical acclaim followed as well. An unsigned review in the January, 1907, *Atlantic Monthly* encapsulated the fine points of *The Four Million:* "[Porter] knows his world well, but he sees it with eyes for its beauty as well as its absurdity. There is imagination as well as vision, and beyond his expert knowledge of our colloquial tongue he possesses in the background, to be used when needed, a real style."

In 1907, as well as marrying Sara Coleman, an old friend from Greensboro, Porter published one volume of New York stories, *The Trimmed Lamp,* and one of Western stories, *Heart of the West.* Other collections rapidly followed. In 1908, *The Voice of the City,* containing more tales of New York, and *The Gentle Grafter,* recounting stories he had heard in the penitentiary, were published. Continuing the hectic pace he had established, Porter produced two more volumes of stories in 1909, *Roads of Destiny* and *Options.* He also collaborated with Franklin P. Adams on a musical comedy, "Lo!," which closed after fourteen weeks. "Alias Jimmy Valentine," the play based on his story "A Retrieved Reformation," was a success in five countries and garnered high revenues for its dramatist, Paul Armstrong. The play, however, produced little for Porter, who had sold all dramatic rights for five hundred dollars.

By 1910 Porter was suffering from nervous exhaustion and ill health, as well as financial desperation caused by his own generosity and financial irresponsibility. He published one last collection, *Strictly Business,* and began planning an autobiographical novel. On June 5, Porter died of cirrhosis of the liver, a condition aggravated by his longtime drinking habit. At the time of his death he was the most popular short story writer in the world. As reported by Richard O'Connor in *O. Henry: The Legendary Life of William S. Porter,* he was eulogized by critics such as Hildegarde Hawthorne, who in the *New York Times* praised Porter's "humanism, the gallant humor, the technique of the surprise twists, the mechanism of his plotting." Several posthumous collections followed: *Whirligigs* (1910), *Sixes and Sevens* (1911), *Rolling Stones* (1912), and *Waifs and Strays* (1917).

Critical analysis of Porter's stories has often focused on his strong sense of place and the way in which he both portrays the realistic details and evokes the atmosphere of his chosen setting. His depiction of New York City appealed to critics such as Van Wyck Brooks, who in *The Confident Years: 1885-1915* observed, "New York was really O. Henry's own . . . because of his attitude towards it, the fresh curiosity with which he approached it, his feeling of wonder about it, on certain levels, all of which made for a literary virtue transcending his occasional cheapness and coarseness, his sometimes unbearable jocularity and meretricious effects." Many of the sights of New York City and the local hangouts that Porter frequented reappear in fictional guise in his stories, adding to their realism: Scheffel Hall at Seventeenth Street and Third Avenue was the beer hall in "The Halberdier of Little Rheinschloss"; Sherkey's saloon on Fourteenth Street was central to the action of "Past One at Rooney's" and "The Guilty Party"; Gramercy Park was the site of "The Trimmed Lamp"; and Healy's Cafe on Irving Place and Eighteenth Street became "Kenealy's Cafe" in "The Lost Blend." His scenes of Central America and of the American South and West were crafted with the same careful detail. E. Hudson Long in an essay collected in *A Good Tale and a Bonnie Tune* extolled the accuracy of Porter's western tales, claiming that his descriptions of the ranch houses and their furnishings were exact down to the water jars and that he captured and reproduced the customs relating to hospitality, smoking, holidays, entertainment, and law enforcement. In his detailed descriptions of the locales of his tales, Porter reflected the contemporary emphasis on realism.

Much as the settings of Porter's life were transformed in his fiction, so to were the people he had known recreated as his most famous characters. Even such an apparently unrealistic creation as the taxicab driver who used—and misused—multisyllabic words and the working-class Irish who read *The History of Greece* were based on actual individuals. In fact, the characters regarded by readers as most unlikely were often based on real people. The ex-cowboy bank examiner and his informal procedures in "Friends in San Rosario" had innumerable real-life counterparts, perhaps, of course, in Porter's own life; the charitable Curtis Raidler who adopts an ailing stranger in "Hygeia at Solito" was based on rancher Mont Woodward; the exaggerated pranks of the cowhands in "The Marquis and Miss Sally" rivaled the real tricks of cowmen like Gus Black; both the Cisco Kid, a Porter creation who became an American folk legend, and another character, King James, had their prototypes in such genuine desperadoes as John Wesley Hardin and King Fisher. One of Porter's characters that readers may find least believable is the chivalric outlaw Black Bill, who steals only from men, and only according to their ability to pay; yet this robber with a heart of gold faithfully echoed the actions of Texas outlaw Ham White.

Despite their realistic sources, Porter's characters are regarded by many critics as shallow and stereotypic. Eugene Current-Garcia proposed in *O. Henry (William Sydney Porter)* that most of Porter's principal characters are "pawns in human form, lacking the complexity of motives governing the lives of even simple human beings, lacking inner conflict and the power to act in ways consistent with their alleged make-up, lacking individuality. . . . There is little depth or complexity of meaning, as the actions and interactions of his characters remain largely on the surface of things. Usually a few basic passions are involved—love, hate, fear, greed—and the conflicts between them end in marriage or death, satisfaction or sorrow, which the reader must accept on faith, since little or no analysis of motives has been attempted. The characters, the great majority of whom are men, fall into a number of recognizable, conventionalized types—good guys and bad guys." While critics such as Archibald Henderson in *South Atlantic Quarterly* found characters like Jeff Peters, the gentle grafter, to be "truly American" figures, they must admit, as Henderson did, that "characterization very often passed into caricature." Yet Smith mentioned another possible reason for the scant attention given to character development in Porter's works, arguing that Porter concentrated instead on thematic content: "Character, plot, and setting were ancillary to the central conception—were but the concrete expressions of the changing ideas that he had in mind."

Criticism has also focused upon Porter's immense vocabulary and his acute sensitivity to word usage. Even such censorious critics as Fred Lewis Patee, who in *The Development of the American Short Story* condemned the "utter artificiality" of the speech of Porter's characters, had to admit Porter's "verbal precision and wide range of vocabulary," conceding that "not even [American realistic novelist] Henry James could choose words more fastidiously or use them more accurately." Porter's careful use of words was especially evident in his descriptive passages, which, as Current-Garcia noted, are "cunningly fitted into the structure of his narrative so that they are made to appear not simply gratuitous lingual ornaments but integral parts of the tale."

If Porter's word play revealed his joy in using language, his use of the surprise ending reflected his delight in the technique of storytelling. The surprise ending became the hallmark of the O. Henry style, and the question for the reader was not if there would be a surprise ending, but just what the surprise would be and how the author would contrive to bring it about. As Current-Garcia noted, Porter was skilled at using incongruity—"the juxtaposition of unexpected, inharmonious elements built into the structure of the story"—to create a conclusion that was the antithesis of the reader's expectation or of the conventional expectations of society. In stories like "The Gift of the Magi," the reader would believe that the expected reversal had already occurred and that the climax had been reached, only to be shocked by a double reversal. Porter's finest climaxes involved genuine paradoxes, and in capturing the paradoxical and irrational nature of life Porter was actually more realistic than many writers of his generation.

After the 1920s Porter's critical reputation experienced a precipitous decline. New short story techniques displayed by writers such as Sherwood Anderson and Ernest Hemingway, relying on simple declarative statements, caused Porter's more elegant style to appear outdated. In the 1940s and 1950s Porter's works were no longer considered worthy of consideration as serious literature. However, as Current-Garcia warned, "Just as the original adulation lavished upon O. Henry proved to be laughably excessive, so may the more recent deprecation of his work turn out to be both imperceptive and unjustified." In any event, Porter's popularity with the reading public has survived two decades of critical overestimation and more than five decades of scholarly neglect, and he retains a strong general readership. His works still appear in paperback editions and enjoy a prominent position on public library shelves; there have been at least forty radio and stage dramatizations, one hundred and thirty motion pictures, and forty television adaptations of Porter's work; and his stories have been translated into at least a dozen languages. Porter's enduring popularity may be another reason that objective critical estimates are so rare. As has happened with other fiction writers who won enormous popular acclaim in their own day—Rudyard Kipling and Arthur Conan Doyle, for example—the very intensity of the public adulation has turned away the critics, who tend to assume that popular literature is categorically worthless. Only in the case of British novelist Charles Dickens has this critical dictum been reversed, and then only within recent decades; perhaps Porter's readership can hope for a similar revival within the next hundred years.

Some critics have attempted to analyze Porter's phenomenal popular appeal. S. P. B. Mais, in *From Shakespeare to O. Henry: Studies in Literature,* summarized the positive estimates of Porter's work: "a range of fancy, an exuberance of humour, a sympathy, an understanding, a knowledge of the raw material of life, an ability to interpret the passing in terms of the permanent, an insight into individual and institutional character, a resolute and persuasive desire to help those in need of help—in a word, a constant and essential democracy." William Saroyan agreed in the *Kenyon Review* that the great appeal of Porter's stories lay in their democratic impulse, "concealing behind laughing language a profound love for the great masses of people who are frequently called the little people."

Yet many critics have steadfastly contended that Porter's approach is superficial, avoiding profound questions or glossing over the unpleasantness of life. N. Bryllion Fagan, in *Short Story Writing: An Art or a Trade?,* called Porter's stories "sketchy, reportorial, superficial, his gift of felicitous expression camouflaging the poverty of theme and character. The best of them lack depth and roundness, often disclosing a glint of a sharp idea unworked, untransmuted by thought and emotion." However, Current-Garcia replied, "One could hardly avoid seeing life's drabness: for O. Henry the point was to transcend it." H. J. Forman, in *North American Review,* also observed that one did not

come to Porter for philosophy, but that his "combination of technical excellence with whimsical, sparkling wit, abundant humor and a fertile invention is so rare that the reader is content." Other critics of Porter's own time, such as O. W. Firkins in *Modern Essays,* implied that Porter's understanding of human nature constituted a genuine contribution: "O. Henry had rare but precious insights into human destiny and human nature," although he "was apt to present his insight in a sort of parable or allegory, to upraise it before the eyes of mankind on the mast or flagpole of some vehement exaggeration." A more recent biographer, E. Hudson Long in *O. Henry: The Man and His Work,* affirmed that "O. Henry not only widened the experience of his readers, he restated the verities which exist wherever people continue to strive for truth and beauty in life. He was never unsympathetic, except with those who sought to deprive others of their rights as human beings, and his writings have in them feelings of compassion for the weakness of man, which, joined with his remarkable ability of expression, makes his stories at their best an influence for the furthering of these ideals."

Still, critical denigration of Porter has persisted. As O'Connor commented, "Both his strengths and weaknesses as a writer are held in contempt—his cleverness and his sentimentality, his mastery of technique, his facility at constructing plots, his trick endings, his hyperbolic humor." Even basically favorable critics such as Mais have admitted that Porter's best endings are scattered among "dull, pointless, or insipid" stories, the result of his constant attempt to produce fiction on demand for the ready cash their sales ensured. Summarizing critical objections, Mais cited Porter's "slap-dash style, his far-fetched metaphors and similes," his "impossible exaggerations" and his editorial intrusions, disagreeing with Forman over the delicacy of Porter's wit by arguing that it "degenerates only too often into buffoonery." Fagan wrote that "O. Henry's technique consisted mainly of a series of clever tricks," despite "his dexterity in performing them. . . . Admitting that through his superficial cleverness there occasionally glimmers an uncommon understanding of and a sympathy for the people whose destinies he juggles, the fact remains that his example is that of clever execution rather than artistic conception."

Such critics may have taken their cue from Porter himself. As reported by George MacAdam in *O. Henry Papers,* Porter observed to a friend, "I'm a failure. I always have the feeling that I want to get back somewhere, but I don't know just where it is. My stories . . . don't satisfy me. . . . It depresses me to have people point me out or introduce me as a 'celebrated author.' It seems such a big label for such picayune goods." While such statements may simply have reflected Porter's undeniable modesty and his self-effacing manner, they have encouraged critics such as Fagan to speculate, "That William Sidney Porter was himself greatly displeased with his accomplishment, that he even held it in contempt is attested by his prevailing cynical tone. He knew he was not creating art, that he was not giving the best there was in him. There was not time for that and editors did not want it, and with a bitterness that Mark Twain and Jack London shared to their dying day he continued to perform tricks." If it were truly the case that, as Porter himself seems to have felt, his work suffered from the pressures of creating for a livelihood, then, Fagan concluded, he "must be assigned his rightful position—among the tragic figures of America's potential artists whose genius was distorted and stifled by our prevailing commercial and infantile conception of literary values." It is also possible, though, that only the impetus of financial need drove the normally placid Porter to write, and without the pressure, he may not have created at all. Be that as it may, most critics agree with Current-Garcia that Porter was "more concerned with this problem of producing a weekly diet of light entertainment than with the more demanding problem of rendering artistically the manifold dramas inherent in Manhattan's domestic life."

Many critics have appreciated Porter's use of social themes. Some of these are rather sentimental, but, like Dickens, Porter was known for playing lightly but effectively on a sentimental theme. His representative motifs include reformation or rehabilitation, contrasting crime and authority; the disparity between wealth and poverty, often explored through the use of mistaken identity; and disguise and pretense. Some of his themes echo those of romantic writers such as Nathaniel Hawthorne: the miraculous influence of a little child, the contrast of appearance and reality, and the compensation for poverty and degradation by love and freedom. Indeed, Porter's poor and dispossessed are noble characters with an innate capacity for dignity and sacrifice. As Smith commented, two strata of society interested Porter most: "those who were under a strain of some sort, and those who were under a delusion. The first stirred his sympathy, the second furnished him with unending entertainment." In "The Making of a New Yorker," the character Raggles is a tramp, which Porter terms "only an elliptical way of saying he was a philosopher, an artist, a traveler, a naturalist, and a discoverer."

Just as he saw the integrity of the poor, Porter did not unquestioningly accept the worth of the wealthy but examined the ways in which they gained their riches. O'Connor cited Porter's theory that "the higher the level of society you explored the more deplorable was the state of morality. . . . His villains were more likely to be silk-hatted hypocrites who robbed banks from the inside, and let someone else suffer the consequences than honest working crooks." His humanitarianism was especially evident in his portrayal in tales like "An Unfinished Christmas Story" and "The Trimmed Lamp" of the single girls who worked in shops and factories, and he studied the details of their lives with sociological exactness. Stories such as "Brickdust Row" reflect the damaging effects of the slum environment while works like "The Guilty Party" focus on slum children, forced to play in the streets and defeated from the start. Porter even examined the exploitation of the American Indians in tales such as "Supply and Demand" and "He Also Serves." Smith summarized the unique contribution of Porter's sociological themes: "It is O. Henry's distinction that he has enlarged the area of the American short story by enriching and diversifying its social themes. In his hands the short story has become the organ of a social consciousness more varied and multiform than it had ever expressed before."

Current-Garcia defined four other premises, beyond the sociological ones, of the stories set in New York City: the reversal of fortune, discovery and initiation through adventure, the city as a spiritual plaything for the imagination, and the basic yearning of all human life. Firkins mentioned several types of plots: love stories in which divided hearts or simply divided persons are brought together by chance; hoax stories; prince and pauper stories, in which wealth and poverty meet; disguise stories; and complemental stories such as "The Gift of the Magi," in which the actions of two people complement each other with a perfect ironic balance. Significantly, Langford found a common theme in many of the stories Porter wrote while in prison: the vindication of a character who, like Porter at that time of his life, had lost his claim to respectability and even integrity. Ultimately, Smith suggested, all of Porter's stories "search for those common traits and common impulses which together form a sort of common denominator of our common humanity."

Unfortunately, few critics have considered the role of women in these love stories. Western tales such as "Hearts and Crosses," "The Marquise and Miss Sally," and "The Princess and the Puma" feature characters like Josefa, who can "put five out of six bullets through a tomato-can swinging at the end of the string," and Santa, who can rope one cow out of a mass of milling cattle. Such women are a refreshing contrast to the stereotypes prevalent in much of the popular literature at the turn of the century, but the contradictions in Porter's attitude towards women deserve further investigation. For example, in a story originally called "The Miracle of Lava Canyon" when it was written in 1897, a daring snake-charmer named Alvarita, as comfortable with gunplay as she is with serpents, meets a cowardly marshall while searching in the desert for her escaped giant python. When a desperado appears, the marshall is afraid until his eyes meet Alvarita's. From their glance the marshall gains the courage to dispatch the outlaw, only to have her fall into his arms, pretending to be frightened of a small garden snake. Yet in a revised version entitled "An Afternoon Miracle," Porter altered events so that Alvarita loses her bravery and becomes genuinely afraid of her former pets. Such a change may have many implications: that women lose their strength when they fall in love; that psychological attributes can be transferred completely from their possessor to another; and of course that women, to enter into relationship with men, must at least hide, if not utterly sacrifice, their self-reliance and individual strengths—in short, their identities. Perhaps Williams was correct in finding in Porter's works "a deep-seated distrust" for women; certainly such themes require critical attention.

The popularity of Porter's work has remained despite critical neglect. His democratic themes, his worthy poor, and his outlaws with hearts of gold have an appeal for the common reader that goes beyond social distinctions. As Current-Garcia observed, Porter's work contains a sense of the "oneness at the heart of things," the timeless appeal of which transcends his dated language. This essential faith in life's possibilities was reflected in Porter's remark when asked his opinion of the hereafter, as quoted by Smith: "For myself, I think we are like little chickens tapping on their shells." Through his consistent use of paradox and the reversal of the reader's expectations, Porter opened the minds of his readers to new possibilities. Despite his own and later critical estimates of his talent, Porter's work still fulfills this function, which he defined as the writer's central goal. Thus, both by his own standards and by those of sales figures and popular recognition, Porter's success as a literary artist remains undiminished.

Porter's work has been translated into at least twelve languages.

MEDIA ADAPTATIONS: Many of Porter's stories have been adapted into films and plays. Among the films are "The Texan," 1930, "The Return of the Cisco Kid," 1939, "The Gay Caballero," 1940, "The Girl From San Lorenzo," 1950, and "Hideout," 1949. "O. Henry's Full House," a collection of movies based on Porter's stories and released by Twentieth Century Fox in 1952, included "The Cop and the Anthem," "The Ransom of Red Chief," and "The Gift of the Magi." Among play adaptations are "Alias Jimmy Valentine," based on "A Retrieved Reformation," adapted by Paul Armstrong and produced in New York City in 1909, and "The Gift of the Magi" and "The Ransom of Red Chief," both adapted by Anne Coulter Martens. "Gifts of the Magi," a musical based on several Porter stories, was produced in New York City at the Lamb's Theater in 1985.

Many of Porter's stories have been adapted for television and for radio. In addition, several have been recorded on audio cassette and released by Miller-Brody Productions, including "The Gift of the Magi" and "The Last Leaf."

BIOGRAPHICAL/CRITICAL SOURCES:

BOOKS

Arnett, Ethel Stephens, *O. Henry From Polecat Creek,* Piedmont Press, 1962.

Boatright, Mody, and other editors, *A Good Tale and a Bonnie Tune,* Southern Methodist University Press, 1964.

Brooks, Van Wyck, *The Confident Years: 1885-1915,* Dutton, 1952.

Brown, Deming, *Soviet Attitudes Toward American Writing,* Princeton University Press, 1962.

The Country Life Press, Doubleday, 1919.

Current-Garcia, Eugene, *O. Henry (William Sydney Porter),* Twayne, 1965.

Davis, Robert H., and Arthur B. Maurice, *The Caliph of Bagdad,* D. Appleton, 1931.

Dictionary of Literary Biography, Gale, Volume 12: *American Realists and Naturalists,* 1982, Volume 78: *American Short Story Writers, 1880-1910,* 1989, Volume 79: *American Magazine Journalists, 1850-1900,* 1989.

Fagan, N. Bryllion, *Short Story Writing: An Art or a Trade?,* Thomas Seltzer, 1923.

Gallegly, Joseph, *From Alamo Plaza to Jack Harris's Saloon: O. Henry and the Southwest He Knew,* Mouton, 1970.

Jennings, Al, *Through the Shadows With O. Henry,* A. L. Bart, 1921.

Langford, Gerald, *Alias O. Henry: A Biography of William Sidney Porter,* Macmillan, 1957.

Long, E. Hudson, *O. Henry: The Man and His Work,* University of Pennsylvania Press, 1949.

Mais, S. P. B., *From Shakespeare to O. Henry: Studies in Literature,* Grant Richards, 1917.

Moose, Roy C., editor, *O. Henry in North Carolina,* University of North Carolina Library, 1957.

Morley, Christopher, editor, *Modern Essays,* Harcourt, 1921.

O'Connor, Richard, *O. Henry: The Legendary Life of William S. Porter,* Doubleday, 1970.

O. Henry Papers Containing Some Sketches of His Life Together With an Alphabetical Index to His Complete Works, Doubleday, 1924.

Patee, Fred Lewis, *The Development of the American Short Story,* Biblo & Tanner, 1975.

Sinclair, Upton, *Bill Porter: A Drama of O. Henry in Prison,* privately printed, 1925.

Smith, C. Alphonso, *O. Henry Biography,* Doubleday, 1921.

Stuart, David, *O. Henry: A Biography of William Sidney Porter,* Stein & Day, 1987.

Twentieth-Century Literature Criticism, Gale, Volume 1, 1978, Volume 19, 1986.

Williams, William Wash, *The Quiet Lodger of Irving Place,* Dutton, 1936.

PERIODICALS

American Literary Realism, 1870-1910, Number 1, 1967.
American Literature, Number 7, 1935, Number 44, 1973.
Atlantic Monthly, January, 1907.
Classical Journal, October, 1947-May, 1948, October, 1948-May, 1949.
Kenyon Review, Number 29, 1967.
Markham Review, Spring-Summer, 1984.
Mississippi Quarterly, Spring, 1981.
New Republic, December 2, 1916.
New York Times, June 5, 1985, December 18, 1985.

North American Review, May, 1908.
Prairie Schooner, Number 47, 1973.
Sewanee Review, April, 1914.
Shakespeare Association Bulletin, January, 1944.
South Atlantic Quarterly, July, 1923.
Southern Humanities Review, Number 10, 1976.
Studies in Short Fiction, Number 15, 1978.

*　　*　　*

POTOK, Chaim 1929-

PERSONAL: Born Herman Harold Potok, February 17, 1929, in New York, N.Y.; changed given name to Chaim, pronounced 'Hah-yim'; son of Benjamin Max (a businessman) and Mollie (Friedman) Potok; married Adena Sarah Mosevitzky, June 8, 1958; children: Rena, Naama, Akiva. *Education:* Yeshiva University, B.A. (summa cum laude), 1950; Jewish Theological Seminary, M.H.L., 1954; University of Pennsylvania, Ph.D., 1965.

ADDRESSES: Home—20 Berwick St., Merion, Pa. 19131.

CAREER: Writer. Ordained rabbi (Conservative), Jewish Theological Seminary, New York City, national director, Leaders Training Fellowship, 1954-55; Camp Ramah, Ojai, Calif., director, 1957-59; University of Judaism, Los Angeles, instructor, 1957-59; Har Zion Temple, Philadelphia, Pa., scholar in residence, 1959-63; Jewish Theological Seminary, member of faculty of Teachers' Institute, 1963-64; *Conservative Judaism,* New York City, managing editor, 1964-65; Jewish Publication Society, Philadelphia, editor-in-chief, 1965-74, special projects editor, 1974—. Visiting professor, University of Pennsylvania, 1983, Bryn Mawr College, 1985. *Military service:* U.S. chaplain in Korea, 1956-57; became first lieutenant.

MEMBER: Rabbinical Assembly, PEN, Authors Guild, Artists Equity.

AWARDS, HONORS: Edward Lewis Wallant Award and National Book Award nomination, both for *The Chosen;* Athenaem Award for *The Promise.*

WRITINGS:

NOVELS

The Chosen, Simon & Schuster, 1967.
The Promise (sequel to *The Chosen*), Knopf, 1969.
My Name Is Asher Lev, Knopf, 1972.
In the Beginning, Knopf, 1975.
The Book of Lights, Knopf, 1981.
Davita's Harp, Knopf, 1985.

OTHER

Jewish Ethics (pamphlet series), 14 volumes, Leaders Training Fellowship (New York), 1964-69.
The Jew Confronts Himself in American Literature, Sacred Heart School of Theology (Hales Corners, Wis.), 1975.
Wanderings: Chaim Potok's History of the Jews (nonfiction), Knopf, 1978.
Ethical Living for a Modern World, Jewish Theological Seminary of America (New York), 1985.

Contributor of short stories and articles to *Commentary, Reconstructionist, Moment, Esquire, American Judaism, Saturday Review, New York Times Book Review,* and other periodicals.

WORK IN PROGRESS: A novel.

SIDELIGHTS: Chaim Potok is familiar to many readers as the author of best-selling novels like *The Chosen* and *The Promise.* Less well known, though equally important to Potok, is his devotion to Judaism: he is an ordained rabbi and scholar of Judaic texts as well as a writer. Potok's attempts to reconcile these disparate commitments have resulted in frustration, yet he uses this to his advantage in his novels. As he comments to Elizabeth Duff in the *Philadelphia Inquirer,* "While this tension is exhausting, . . . it is fuel for me. Without it, I would have nothing to say."

Because of his Jewish heritage, Potok is frequently called an American Jewish writer. Although he understands the need for such labels, he prefers to be described as "an American writer writing about a small and particular American world," he writes in an essay in *Studies in American Jewish Literature.* His vision has enthralled readers of all kinds, due in part, according to *New York Times Book Review* contributor Hugh Nissenson, to Potok's "talent for evoking the physical details of this world: the tree-lined streets, the apartment filled with books, the cold radiators, the steaming glasses of coffee." Potok, however, attributes the success of his novels to the universality of his subject matter. "In the particular is contained the universal," he explains to Millie Ball in the *Times Picayune.* "When you write about one person or set of people, if you dig deeply enough, you will ultimately uncover basic humanity."

Raised in an Orthodox Jewish family, Potok was drawn to the less restrictive doctrine of Conservative Judaism as a young adult and was eventually ordained a Conservative rabbi. While his Judaic background has provided him with a wealth of material for his novels, it was and continues to be a source of conflict as well. Potok's interest in writing and literature, sparked by Evelyn Waugh's *Brideshead Revisited,* was opposed by both his family and teachers. His mother, for example, when told of his aspiration to write, remarked, " 'You want to be a writer? Fine. You be a brain surgeon on the side,' " Potok recalls to *Fort Lauderdale News* writer Linda Sherbert. The teachers at his Jewish parochial school responded similarly, disappointed that Potok would want to take time away from studying the Talmud to read and write fiction. Potok discusses these reactions in an interview with S. Lillian Kremer in *Studies in American Jewish Literature:* "There was anger. There was rage. I still experience it. There is something in the Jewish tradition which casts a very definite denigrating eye upon the whole enterprise of fiction. . . . Scholarship is what counts in the Jewish tradition, Talmudic scholarship, not the product of the imagination."

This conflict between religious and secular commitments is a recurring theme in Potok's novels. In his first book, *The Chosen,* Potok portrays Danny Saunders, a young man torn between fulfilling the expectations of his rabbi father and satisfying his own need for secular knowledge. The Saunders belong to the Jewish sect called Hasidism, whose members are "known for their mystical interpretation of Judaic sources and intense devotion to their spiritual leaders," according to S. Lillian Kremer in the *Dictionary of Literary Biography.* When Danny becomes an adult, he is expected to take on his father's role as *tzaddik,* which Nissenson describes as "a teacher, spiritual adviser, mediator between his community of followers and God, and living sacrifice who takes the suffering of his people—of all Israel—upon himself." To strengthen Danny's soul and thus prepare him "to assume the burdens of his followers," writes Kremer, Rabbi Saunders has raised Danny according to unusual Hasidic tradition which dictates that under certain circumstances, a father and son should speak only when discussing religious texts.

In direct contrast to the Saunders are the Malters: Reuven, who becomes Danny's close friend, and Reuven's father, who tutors Danny in secular subjects. As Orthodox Jews, the Malters "emphasize a rational, intellectual approach to Judaic law and theology," explains Kremer. Reuven's father recognizes the importance of Judaic scholarship, but he, unlike Rabbi Saunders, encourages his son to study secular subjects as well. Furthermore, Malter has built his relationship with Reuven on mutual love and respect, not suffering.

Though Danny's problems with his father are crucial to the narrative, *The Chosen* is more than a story of parental and religious conflict, according to Karl Shapiro, who writes in *Book Week—World Journal Tribune:* "The argument of the book concerns the level of survival of Judaism, whether it shall remain clothed in superstition and mysticism, or whether it shall convey the message of humanitarianism, with the secular Jew as the prophet of gentleness and understanding."

Like many first novels, *The Chosen* received mixed criticism from reviewers. *New York Times* contributing critic Eliot Fremont-Smith describes the book as "a long, earnest, somewhat affecting and sporadically fascinating tale of religious conflict and generational confrontation in which the characters never come fully alive because they are kept subservient to theme: They don't have ideas so much as they represent ideas." While *New Republic* contributor Philip Toynbee observes that Potok's prose has "too many exhausted phrases and dead words," he maintains that *The Chosen* "is a fascinating book in its own right. Few Jewish writers have emerged from so deep in the heart of orthodoxy: fewer still have been able to write about their emergence with such an unforced sympathy for both sides and every participant." Concludes Nissenson: "The structural pattern of the novel, the beautifully wrought contrapuntal relationship of the boys, and their fathers, is complete. We rejoice, and we weep a little, as at those haunting Hasidic melodies which transfigure their words."

Potok's third novel, *My Name Is Asher Lev,* is a variation "on an almost classic theme: the isolation of the artist from society," writes Thomas Lask in the *New York Times.* Despite its conventional theme, *My Name Is Asher Lev* has what Lask calls "a feeling of freshness, of something brand-new" which he attributes not to "the artist and his driving needs but [to] the society from which he is inexorably isolating himself: the intense, ingrown, passionate, mystical world of Hasidism."

The protagonist, Asher Lev, lives in a familial and spiritual environment similar to that of Danny Saunders. Asher's parents are devout Hasids, and his father is actively involved in rebuilding the Jewish community in Europe. Asher, however, is a gifted artist, and his father neither understands nor respects his artistry. While art is not expressly forbidden in the Hasidic tradition, it is considered "blasphemous at worst and mere indulgence of personal vanity at best," according to Kremer in the *Dictionary of Literary Biography.* The tenuous relationship between Asher and his father is strained further when Asher, as a part of his studies, learns to draw crucifixions and nudes.

Although Asher does not consciously reject his heritage, he finds it impossible to repress his artistic instinct. Lask observes that while both Asher and the Hasidic community do their "best to retain the old relationship, . . . there seems to be an artistic destiny greater than both of them." Asher's reluctance to abandon his religious tradition is a significant difference between Potok's characters and those of other American Jewish writers, according to Kremer. "They do not share the assimilationist goals of the Jews about whom Saul Bellow and Philip Roth write. . . . In the instances when Potok's characters enter the secular public world, they maintain orthodox private lives." Even after he has left his family and community, Asher identifies himself as an observant Jew. Thus, as John H. Timmerman observes in *Christian Century*, Asher "stands *not* in open rebellion against, but as a troubled seeker of, his place within a tradition."

Potok followed his fifth novel with his first nonfiction book, *Wanderings: Chaim Potok's Story of the Jews.* Although it is nonfiction, *Wanderings* is similar to Potok's novels, Jack Riemer suggests in *America.* "Just as there he really sought for his self in the guise of a story about a young man wrestling with modernity, so here he searches for his soul in the form of a confrontation with his roots and with his memories." Potok explains to Robert Dahlin in *Publishers Weekly:* "I went wandering inside my own tradition, its history. . . . And I didn't move on until I understood."

Wanderings, a lavishly illustrated book, is described by *Chicago Tribune Book World* contributor Dan Rottenberg as "a rare phenomenon: a coffee-table book with some real intellectual bite to it." Beginning with the family of Abraham, *Wanderings* traces 4,000 years of Jewish history. Potok portrays the Jews as a people who have cohabited with and been persecuted by many different civilizations throughout history, and who, despite their small population, have usually managed to survive their persecutors. According to Rottenberg, "what emerges from Potok's mixture of history, Scriptures, novelistic writing, and personal reminiscences is a portrait of Judaism as very much a living, breathing, kicking organism."

Several reviewers observe that Potok's training as a novelist serves him well in his first foray into nonfiction. Rottenberg, for example, writes: "The eye of the novelist can enhance our understanding of history, especially when the novelist is someone like Potok, whose fictitious work has always been firmly rooted in cultural and historical scholarship. . . . Potok is able to paint scenes for us, to put flesh on his characters, to speculate about their motives, without abandoning the detachment of the historian." *New York Times Book Review* contributor Alan Mintz describes *Wanderings* as "a mixed performance. Mr. Potok can produce a good, strong narrative that also maintains a sense of historical proportion; and his occasional evocations of settings and feelings do contribute to a fuller sense of the past. But often the pursuit of drama gets him into trouble and the writing becomes stylized." Michael J. Bandler, however, maintains in the *Christian Science Monitor* that "one cannot resist the temptation to observe without being facetious that as a historian, Potok solidifies his reputation as a fine novelist."

While Potok's sixth novel, *Davita's Harp,* is similar to his earlier works in setting and theme, it is his first story told from a female perspective. "That leap takes sensitivity and some daring, and Potok handles it well," writes *Detroit News* contributor Lisa Schwarzbaum. "*Davita's Harp* is a warm, decent, generous and patient exploration of important issues facing Jewish women today."

When the novel opens, Davita is eight years old. She is the daughter of a Jewish mother and a Christian father who have abandoned their respective religions and are now devoted Communists. Davita experiments with both faiths, but she is entranced by the Jewish rituals practiced by her neighbors and eventually embraces Orthodox Judaism. She soon realizes the limitations of her religion, however, when she is denied a prize as the best student in her parochial school graduating class solely because she is a girl.

A *Time* critic observes that "during the conflict between Davita's reverence for Hebraic tradition and her determination to make a place for herself, the narrative becomes far livelier and suggests possibilities for a worthier sequel." A similar opinion is expressed by Paul Cowan who comments in the *New York Times Book Review* that the first quarter of *Davita's Harp,* which concerns the political activities of Davita's parents, contains "some of Mr. Potok's most disappointing pages," but that "as Davita comes to life, so does the book." *Chicago Tribune Book World* contributor George Cohen, however, maintains that "it is an engrossing plot—Potok is a master storyteller—but much of the pleasure in reading 'Davita's Harp' is the beauty of the language."

Perhaps the harshest criticism of *Davita's Harp* is voiced by Andrew Weinberger, who comments in the *Los Angeles Times Book Review,* "The problem with this novel is that it is too predictable, too familiar. . . . Potok could do better, one feels, than to walk down this old road again." Nissenson, however, maintains: "It is not a paucity of imagination, but rather an obsession that brings Potok back, again and again, to these kinds of characters, this milieu. However, he chooses a different theme for every book. And in each one he probes a little deeper in an attempt to get at some essential truth about the human condition which is hidden among the Biblical scholars, the explications of Rashi, the yeshivas and the nearsighted kids that haunt him."

MEDIA ADAPTATIONS: "The Chosen," a Landau Productions movie based on Potok's novel of the same name, is distributed by Twentieth Century-Fox and stars Robbie Benson, Maximilian Schell, Rod Steiger, and Barry Miller; *The Chosen* was also adapted as a musical for the stage that first opened in New York City, December 17, 1987.

AVOCATIONAL INTERESTS: Oil painting, photography.

BIOGRAPHICAL/CRITICAL SOURCES:

BOOKS

Authors in the News, Gale, Volume 1, 1976, Volume 2, 1976.
Contemporary Literary Criticism, Gale, Volume 2, 1974, Volume 7, 1977, Volume 14, 1980, Volume 26, 1983.
Dictionary of Literary Biography, Volume 28: *Twentieth-Century American-Jewish Fiction Writers,* Gale, 1984.
Dictionary of Literary Biography Yearbook: 1984, Gale, 1985.

PERIODICALS

America, February 7, 1979.
Book Week—World Journal Tribune, April 23, 1967.
Chicago Tribune, December 1, 1987.
Chicago Tribune Book World, November 26, 1978, October 11, 1981, March 24, 1985.
Christian Century, February 17, 1982, May 16, 1984.
Christian Science Monitor, February 12, 1979.
CLA Journal, Volume 14, number 4, June, 1971.
Commentary, October, 1972, April, 1979, March, 1982.
Detroit News, March 17, 1985.
Fort Lauderdale News, March 22, 1976.
Los Angeles Times Book Review, November 8, 1981, May 26, 1985.
New Republic, June 7, 1967.
New Yorker, November 17, 1975, November 9, 1981.
New York Times, April 24, 1967, September 12, 1969, April 21, 1972, December 3, 1975, November 2, 1986, July 24, 1987, January 3, 1988, January 7, 1988.

New York Times Book Review, May 7, 1967, September 14, 1969, April 16, 1972, October 19, 1975, December 17, 1978, October 11, 1981, March 31, 1985.
Philadelphia Bulletin, May 16, 1974.
Philadelphia Inquirer, April 27, 1976.
Publishers Weekly, May 22, 1978.
Saturday Review, September 20, 1969, April 15, 1972.
Studies in American Jewish Literature, Number 4, 1985.
Time, October 19, 1981, March 25, 1985.
Times Literary Supplement, March 5, 1970, October 6, 1972, May 28, 1982.
Times-Picayune (New Orleans), February 25, 1973.
Washington Post, November 27, 1981.
Washington Post Book World, December 13, 1978.

*   *   *

POTTER, Dennis (Christopher George) 1935-

PERSONAL: Born May 17, 1935, in Joyford Hill, Gloucestershire, England; son of Walter and Margaret Constance (Wales) Potter; married Margaret Morgan (a journalist), 1959; children: one son, two daughters. *Education:* New College, Oxford, B.A. (with honors), 1959. *Politics:* Labour.

ADDRESSES: Home—Morecambe Lodge, Duxmere, Ross-on-Wye, Herefordshire 3199, England. *Agent*—Clive Goodwin, 79 Cromwell Rd., London S.W.7, England.

CAREER: British Broadcasting Corp. (BBC-TV), London, England, member of current affairs staff, 1959-61; London Daily Herald, London, 1961-64, began as feature writer, became television critic; London Sun, London, editorial writer, 1964; freelance playwright, author, and journalist, 1964. Labour candidate for Parliament from East Hertfordshire, 1964.

AWARDS, HONORS: Writer of the Year Awards from Writers Guild of Great Britain, 1966 and 1969; award from Society of Film and Television Arts, 1966; BAFTA Award, 1978, for "Pennies from Heaven," and 1980, for "Blue Remembered Hills"; Prix Italia, 1982, for "Blade on the Feather, Rain on the Roof, Cream in My Coffee"; honorary fellow, New College, Oxford, 1987.

WRITINGS:

PLAYS

"Vote Vote Vote for Nigel Barton," 1965, revised version incorporating "Vote Vote Vote for Nigel Barton" and "Stand Up, Nigel Barton" (also see below), produced in Bristol at Theatre Royal, November 27, 1968, published in *The Nigel Barton Plays: Two Television Plays,* Penguin, 1967.
"Stand Up, Nigel Barton," first televised, 1965, published in *The Nigel Barton Plays,* 1967.
Son of Man (first televised on British Broadcasting Corp. (BBC-TV), 1969, first produced in Leicester, 1969, produced in London at Round House Theatre, 1969), Deutsch, 1970.
"Lay Down Your Arms," first televised on Independent Television (ITV), May 23, 1970.
"Traitor," first televised on BBC-TV, October 14, 1971.
"Follow the Yellow Brick Road," 1972, published in *The Television Dramatist,* edited by Robert Muller, Elek, 1973.
"Only Make Believe," first televised, 1973, first produced in Harlow, 1974.
"Joe's Ark," 1974, published in *The Television Play,* edited by Robin Wade, BBC Publications, 1976.

Brimstone and Treacle (first produced in Sheffield at the Crucible Theatre, October, 1977; also see below), Eyre Methuen, 1978.
"Pennies From Heaven" (screenplay; adapted from the television series by Potter), Metro-Goldwyn-Mayer, 1981.
"Brimstone and Treacle" (screenplay; adaptation of Potter's stage play), 1982.
Sufficient Carbohydrate, Faber & Faber, 1983.
"Gorky Park" (screenplay adapted from the novel by Martin Cruz Smith), Orion, 1983.
Waiting for the Boat (three plays), Faber & Faber, 1984.
"Dreamchild" (screenplay), Curzon/Universal, 1985.
"Track 29" (screenplay based on Potter's television play "Schmoedipus"), Island Pictures, 1988.
The Singing Detective (sextet; produced on BBC-Television, November 9, 1986), Random House, 1988.

Also author of "The Confidence Course," 1965; "Alice," 1965; "Where the Buffalo Roam," 1966; "Emergency Ward Nine," 1966; "Message for Posterity," 1967; "A Beast With Two Backs," 1968; "The Bonegrinder," 1968; "Shaggy Dog," 1968; "Moonlight on the Highway," 1969; "Angels Are So Few," 1970; "Paper Roses," 1971; "Casanova" (six-play series), 1971; "A Tragedy of Two Ambitions" (adapted from story by Thomas Hardy), 1973; "Schmoedipus" (adapted from novel by Angus Wilson), 1974; "Late Call" (serial; adapted from novel by Wilson), 1975; "Double Dare," 1976; "Where Adam Stood" (adapted from *Father and Son* by Edmund Gosse), 1976; "Pennies From Heaven" (sextet), 1978; "The Mayor of Casterbridge" (adapted from novel by Hardy), 1978; "Blue Remembered Hills," 1979; "Blade on the Feather, Rain on the Roof, Cream in My Coffee," 1980; "Tender Is the Night" (sextet adapted from novel by F. Scott Fitzgerald), 1985; "Visitors," 1987; "Christabel" (quartet adapted from *The Past Is Myself* by Christabel Bielenberg), 1988; "Blackeyes," 1989.

OTHER

The Glittering Coffin (nonfiction), Gollancz, 1960.
The Changing Forest: Life in the Forest of Dean Today (nonfiction), Secker & Warburg, 1962.
Hide and Seek (novel), Deutsch, 1973.
Ticket to Ride (novel), Faber & Faber, 1986, Vintage Books, 1989.
Blackeyes (novel), Faber & Faber, 1987, Random House, 1988.

Also author of *Pennies from Heaven* (novel), 1982.

SIDELIGHTS: Dennis Potter's numerous television plays have earned him a reputation as "one of the major dramatists writing for the medium." His first effort, "Vote Vote Vote for Nigel Barton," is a tragicomedy about a young Labour candidate's campaign for public office. This work and its companion play, "Stand Up, Nigel Barton," were together adapted for the stage under the title "Vote Vote Vote for Nigel Barton." Jeremy Kingston praised Potter's skill in combining elements of the two plays, noting that "the mingling of Nigel's past with his present and the tension between public and private face work as strongly on the stage as I am told they did on [television]." *New Statesman* critic Benedict Nightingale disagreed, claiming that Potter "shuffled" the plays together "like two decks of cards." He commented further that the play's attack upon "stupid and irrelevant reactionaries" causes it to fail as a political commentary.

Many of Potter's works have generated controversy. His play "Son of Man" created a furor when it was first broadcast on BBC-TV and later when it was broadcast on KYW-TV in Philadelphia. Picketers protested that in the play Christ is portrayed as a "hippie." Potter's television play "Brimstone and Treacle" was also involved in conflict when BBC-TV decided against broadcasting it in response to protests by viewers of the BBC who considered the play too shocking for television. Those who feared censorship of the media, in turn, condemned the action of the BBC. The play was later produced for the stage and also published with a twenty-five-hundred-word introduction that presented the author's view of the quarrel. John Coleby, who reviewed the published version of the play, referred to it as "moving," "compelling," and "strong" but observed that "in the end the ingredients don't quite blend, the flavor is nondescript."

Potter also wrote the screenplay for "Pennies From Heaven," a film that impressed some critics and confused others with its combination of 1930's-musicals whimsy and Ingmar Bergman-like despair during the Depression. The *Chicago Tribune*'s Gene Siskel wrote, "One of the things we can make of [certain scenes] is that there was a huge gap between the grim realities of the Depression and the songs that were created in part to lift the nation's spirit." The *New York Times*'s Vincent Canby was less convinced of the film's merits. He conceded that some of the musical transitions—featuring actors lip-syncing songs by performers such as Bing Crosby—were "spectacularly effective," but added that Potter and director Herbert Ross have created a work that is "chilly without being provocative in any intellectual way." Canby cited one scene in which the male protagonist lip-syncs a woman's voice as "briefly funny," then added that "the merciless eye of the camera and the film's deliberate pacing drain all real wit and spontaneity from the sequence."

Another Potter screenplay, "Dreamchild," takes place in the 1930s, when an elderly Alice Liddell Hargreaves (the "Alice" of Lewis Carroll's *Alice in Wonderland* and *Alice through the Looking-Glass*) travelled to New York to receive an honorary degree. The unaccustomed pressures of American city life exhaust her and set her to dreaming about her childhood. Stephen Holden, writing in the *New York Times,* says that "Dreamchild" "paints the early 1930s in glowing storybook colors that complement the subtlety of the performances," and concludes that it is "a lovely, wistful little fairytale for adults." Gene Siskel, in the *Chicago Tribune,* states that the film "goes its own special with precision and consummate skill," and declares, "See this fascinating and troubling and beautifully acted movie and your reading of 'Alice' never will be the same."

BIOGRAPHICAL/CRITICAL SOURCES:

PERIODICALS

Chicago Tribune, December 22, 1981, January 10, 1986.
Christian Science Monitor, November 26, 1969.
Drama, autumn, 1978.
Encounter, February, 1974.
Listener, November 15, 1973.
Los Angeles Times, November 18, 1982, September 15, 1985, October 18, 1985.
New Statesman, December 6, 1968, November 2, 1973.
New York Times, December 11, 1981, October 4, 1985.
New York Times Book Review, October 15, 1989.
Punch, December 4, 1968, November 19, 1969.
Stage, October 21, 1971.
Times (London), December 9, 1983, February 14, 1984, September 9, 1986, October 1, 1987.
Variety, March 18, 1970.
Washington Post, January 17, 1986.

POTTER, Stephen   1900-1969

PERSONAL: Born February 1, 1900; died December 2, 1969, in London, England; son of Frank Collard and Elizabeth (Reynolds) Potter; married Mary Attenbourgh (a painter; divorced); married Heather Lyon, 1965; children: three sons. *Education:* Attended Merton College, Oxford.

CAREER: Secretary to playwright Henry Arthur Jones; lecturer in English literature at University of London, London, England, beginning in 1925; writer-producer for British Broadcasting Corp. (BBC), London, 1935-45. *Military service:* Coldstream Guards, special reserve, 1919.

WRITINGS:

The Young Man (novel), J. Cape, 1929.
D. H. Lawrence: A First Study, J. Cape, 1930.
Coleridge and S.T.C., J. Cape, 1935.
The Muse in Chains: A Study in Education, J. Cape, 1937, reprinted, Norwood Editions, 1978.
The Theory and Practice of Gamesmanship; or, The Art of Winning Games Without Actually Cheating, Hart-Davis, 1947, published as *Gamesmanship; or, The Art of Winning Games Without Actually Cheating,* Holt, 1948.
Some Notes on Lifemanship, With a Summary of Recent Research in Gamesmanship, Hart-Davis, 1950.
One-Upmanship: Being Some Account of the Activities and Teaching of the Lifemanship Correspondence College of One-Upness and Gameslifemastery, Holt, 1952.
Sense of Humour (anthology), Holt, 1954.
Christmas-ship; or, The Art of Giving and Receiving, Hart Press, 1956.
Potter on America, Hart-Davis, 1956, Random House, 1957.
Supermanship; or, How to Continue to Stay on Top Without Actually Falling Apart, Hart-Davis, 1958, Random House, 1959.
Steps to Immaturity (autobiography), Hart-Davis, 1959.
The Magic Number: The Story of "57," Max Reinhardt, 1959.
Three-Upmanship: The Theory and Practice of Gamesmanship; Some Notes on Lifemanship and One-Upmanship, Holt, 1962.
The Adventures of a Clasperchoice (juvenile), Lippincott, 1964.
Anti-Woo: The First Lifemanship Guide; The Lifeman's Improved Primer for Non-Lovers, With Special Chapters on Who Not to Love, Falling Out of Love, Avoidance Gambits, and Coad-Sanderson's Scale of Progressive Rifts, McGraw, 1965.
Golfmanship, McGraw, 1968 (published in England as *The Complete Golf Gamesmanship,* Heinemann, 1968).
The Complete Upmanship, Including Gamesmanship, Lifemanship, One-Upmanship, Supermanship, Hart-Davis, 1970.

Editor of *Selected Poetry and Prose,* by Samuel Taylor Coleridge, 1933, *Minnow Among Tritons: Mrs. S. T. Coleridge's Letters to Thomas Poole, 1799-1834,* 1934, and *Selected Poems of Coleridge,* 1935. Book and drama critic for various British magazines and newspapers, beginning in 1945; editor of *Leader* and *London Magazine,* 1949-51.

SIDELIGHTS: Stephen Potter was known for his development of and his books on the theory of gamesmanship. He believed that a "courteously clever" person could successfully defeat a talented opponent in any game. Potter was indirectly introduced to this technique by a colleague and tennis partner, Dr. Cyril Joad. During a game with two undergraduate students, Joad politely requested that they clearly state whether the ball landed in or out. This remark caught the students off guard and, as a result, they lost the game. Potter reasoned that their performance was hindered when their etiquette and sportsman-like conduct was questioned.

Potter's first books were scholarly: studies of D. H. Lawrence and Samuel Taylor Coleridge and a book on education. But when faced with unemployment during a fuel crisis in England in 1947, Potter turned to what he had always used successfully: gamesmanship. *The Theory and Practice of Gamesmanship* was published in 1947 and several other volumes followed during the next twenty years. B. V. Winebaum found *Some Notes on Lifemanship* to be "a mine of practical strategy, a highly mannered exercise in the study of manners." C. E. Vulliamy agreed and also commented, "The fun of Mr. Potter has the extraordinary merits of being subtle yet hilarious, concealed and open, allusive and self-evident; and how delightful it is to find a wit that is neither sick nor soured." In his review of *Golfmanship*, Rex Lardner noted: "[It is] fitting that Mr. Stephen Potter should produce a new text on modern gamesmanship—more subtle, sophisticated and precisely directed than the old. . . . Here are listed verbal ploys, sartorial ploys, fiduciary ploys. . . . Difficult situations are faced and questions answered. . . . This is a splendidly funny book."

Some critics, however, tired of the novelty of gamesmanship after the publication of several books on the subject. A *New Yorker* critic reported: "Admirers of Mr. Potter's [earlier books] may find that his methods and the point of view behind them don't seem as funny or as sharp as they once did, possibly because they are no longer surprising, or possibly because he is getting a little tired of his own joke." But Edmund Wilson defended Potter, noting that "what is so good in these books of Potter's is the brevity and compactness of the presentation. As in any practical manual, the principles are stated and concisely illustrated. Nothing goes on too long."

BIOGRAPHICAL/CRITICAL SOURCES:

PERIODICALS

Book World, January 5, 1969.
Christian Science Monitor, May 23, 1957, January 15, 1959.
Manchester Guardian, July 2, 1954.
Nation, September 26, 1959.
New Yorker, November 8, 1952.
Saturday Review of Literature, January 8, 1949.
Spectator, February 9, 1934.
Times Literary Supplement, November 17, 1950, October 10, 1952.

OBITUARIES:

PERIODICALS

Antiquarian Bookman, December 15, 1969.
Books Abroad, spring, 1970.
New York Times, December 3, 1969.
Publishers Weekly, December 15, 1969.
Time, December 12, 1969.

*   *   *

POUND, Ezra (Weston Loomis) 1885-1972
(William Atheling, The Poet of Titchfield Street, Alfred Venison)

PERSONAL: Born October 30, 1885, in Hailey, Idaho; died November 1, 1972, in Venice, Italy; buried in San Michele Cemetery on the island of San Giorgio Maggiore, Italy; son of Homer Loomis (a mine inspector in Idaho, later an assayer at the Phila-

delphia mint) and Isabel (Weston) Pound; married Dorothy Shakespear, 1914; lived with Olga Rudge for 12 years; children: Omar Shakespear, Mary Rachewilz. *Education:* Attended University of Pennsylvania, 1901-03; Hamilton College, Ph.B., 1905; University of Pennsylvania, fellow in Romantics, received M.A,, 1906.

CAREER: Writer, poet, critic. Wabash College, Crawfordsville, Ind., lecturer in French and Spanish, 1906; Regent Street Polytechnic Institute, London, England, teacher of literature; foreign correspondent in London for *Poetry* (Chicago), 1912-19; associated with H. L. Mencken's *Smart Set;* W. B. Yeats's unofficial secretary in Sussex, England, 1913-16; unofficial literary executor for Ernest Fenollosa, London, 1914; member of the editorial staff of *Mercure de France,* Paris, and of the British publications, *Egoist* and *Cerebralist;* founder, with Wyndham Lewis, of the Vorticist magazine, *BLAST!,* 1914; London editor of *The Little Review,* 1917-19; left London, 1921, and settled in Paris; Paris correspondent for *The Dial,* 1922; moved to Rapallo, Italy, 1925; founder and editor of *The Exile,* 1927-28; radio broadcaster in Rome until 1945; arrested by the U.S. Army in 1945 and charged with treason; after being declared insane and unfit to stand trial for his life, committed to St. Elizabeth's Hospital, Washington, D.C., until 1958; lived in Italy, 1958-72.

AWARDS, HONORS: Honorary degree from Hamilton College, 1939; *Dial* Award for distinguished service to American letters; Bollingen Library of Congress Award, 1949, for *The Pisan Cantos;* Academy of American Poets fellowship, 1963.

WRITINGS:

POETRY

A Lume Spento (also see below), privately printed in Venice by A. Antonini, 1908.
A Quinzaine for This Yule, Pollock (London), 1908.
Personae, Elkin Mathews (London), 1909.
Exultations, Elkin Mathews, 1909.
Provenca, Small, Maynard (Boston), 1910.
Canzoni, Elkin Mathews, 1911.
Ripostes of Ezra Pound, S. Swift (London), 1912, Small, Maynard, 1913.
Personae and Exultations of Ezra Pound, [London], 1913.
Canzoni and Ripostes of Ezra Pound, Elkin Mathews, 1913.
Lustra of Ezra Pound, Elkin Mathews, 1916, Knopf, 1917.
Quia Pauper Amavi, Egoist Press (London), 1918.
The Fourth Canto, Ovid Press (London), 1919.
(And translations) *Umbra,* Elkin Mathews, 1920.
Hugh Selwyn Mauberley, Ovid Press, 1920.
Poems, 1918-1921, Boni & Liveright, 1921.
A Draft of XVI Cantos, Three Mountains Press, 1925.
Personae: The Collected Poems of Ezra Pound, Boni & Liveright, 1926.
Selected Poems, edited and with an introduction by T. S. Eliot, Faber & Gwyer, 1928, Laughlin, 1957.
A Draft of the Cantos 17-27, John Rodker (London), 1928.
A Draft of XXX Cantos, Hours Press (Paris), 1930, Farrar & Rinehart, 1933.
Homage to Sextus Propertius, Faber, 1934.
Eleven New Cantos: XXXI-XLI, Farrar & Rinehart, 1934, published in England as *A Draft of Cantos XXXI-XLI,* Faber, 1935.
(Under pseudonym The Poet of Titchfield Street) *Alfred Venison's Poems: Social Credit Themes,* Nott (London), 1935.
The Fifth Decade of Cantos, Farrar & Rinehart, 1937.
Cantos LII-LXXI, New Directions, 1940.
A Selection of Poems, Faber, 1940.

The Pisan Cantos (also see below), New Directions, 1948.

The Cantos of Ezra Pound (includes *The Pisan Cantos*), New Directions, 1948, revised edition, Faber, 1954.

Selected Poems, New Directions, 1949.

Personnae: The Collected Poems of Ezra Pound, New Directions, 1950, published in England as *Personnae: Collected Shorter Poems,* Faber, 1952, new edition published as *Collected Shorter Poems,* Faber, 1968.

Seventy Cantos, Faber, 1950.

Section Rock-Drill, 85-95 de los Cantares, All'Insegna del Pesce d'Oro (Milan), 1955, New Directions, 1956.

Thrones: 96-109 de los Cantares, New Directions, 1959.

The Cantos (1-109), new edition, Faber, 1964.

The Cantos (1-95), New Directions, 1965.

A Lume Spento, and Other Early Poems, New Directions, 1965.

Selected Cantos, Faber, 1967.

Drafts and Fragments: Cantos CX-CXVII, New Directions, 1968.

From Syria: The Worksheets, Proofs, and Text, edited by Robin Skelton, Copper Canyon Press, 1981.

The Collected Early Poems of Ezra Pound, New Directions, 1982.

PROSE

The Spirit of Romance, Dent, 1910, New Directions, 1952, revised edition, P. Owen, 1953, reprinted, New Directions, 1968.

Gaudier-Brzeska: A Memoir Including the Published Writings of the Sculptor and a Selection from His Letters, John Lane, 1916, New Directions, 1961.

(With Ernest Fenollosa) *Noh; or, Accomplishment: A Study of the Classical Stage of Japan,* Macmillan (London), 1916, Knopf, 1917, published as *The Classic Noh Theatre of Japan,* New Directions, 1960.

Pavannes and Divisions, Knopf, 1918.

Instigations of Ezra Pound, Together with an Essay on the Chinese Written Character by Ernest Fenollosa, Boni & Liveright, 1920.

Indiscretions, Three Mountains Press (Paris), 1923.

(Under pseudonym William Atheling) *Antheil and the Treatise on Harmony,* Three Mountains Press, 1924, published under his own name, P. Covici, 1927, 2nd edition, Da Capo, 1968.

Imaginary Letters, Black Sun Press (Paris), 1930.

How to Read, Harmsworth, 1931.

ABC of Economics, Faber, 1933, New Directions, 1940, 2nd edition, Russell, 1953.

ABC of Reading, Yale University Press, 1934, New Directions, 1951, new edition, Faber, 1951.

Make It New, Faber, 1934, Yale University Press, 1935.

Social Credit: An Impact (pamphlet), Nott, 1935, reprinted, Revisionist Press, 1983.

Jefferson and/or Mussolini, Nott, 1935, Liveright, 1936.

Polite Essays, Faber, 1937, New Directions, 1940.

Culture, New Directions, 1938, new edition published as *Guide to Kulchur,* New Directions, 1952.

What is Money For?, Greater Britain Publications, 1939, published as *What Is Money For?: A Sane Man's Guide to Economics,* Revisionist Press, 1982.

Carla da Visita, Edizioni di Lettere d'Oggi (Rome), 1942, translation by John Drummond published as *A Visiting Card,* Russell, 1952, published as *A Visiting Card: Ancient and Modern History of Script and Money,* Revisionist Press, 1983.

L'America, Roosevelt e le Cause della Guerra Presente, Edizioni Popolari (Venice), 1944, translation by Drummond published as *America, Roosevelt and the Causes of the Present War,* Russell, 1951.

Introduzione alla Natura Economica degli S.U.A., Edizioni Popolari, 1944, English translation by Carmine Amore published as *An Introduction to the Economic Nature of the United States,* Russell, 1958.

Oro e Lavoro, Tip. Moderna (Rapallo, Italy), 1944, translation by Drummond published as *Gold and Work,* Russell, 1952, reprinted, Revisionist Press, 1983.

Orientamenti, Edizioni Popolari, 1944.

"If This Be Treason . . . " (four original drafts of Rome radio broadcasts), privately printed for Olga Rudge, 1948.

The Letters of Ezra Pound, 1907-1941, edited by D. D. Paige, Harcourt, 1950.

Patria Mia (written in 1913), R. F. Seymour (Chicago), 1950 (published in England as *Patria Mia and The Treatise on Harmony,* Owen, 1962).

Literary Essays of Ezra Pound, edited and with an introduction by T. S. Eliot, New Directions, 1954.

Lavoro ed Usura, All'Insegna del Pesce d'Oro, 1954.

Brancusi, [Milan], 1957.

Pavannes and Divagations, New Directions, 1958.

Impact: Essays on Ignorance and the Decline of American Civilization, edited and with an introduction by Noel Stock, Regnery, 1960.

EP to LU: Nine Letters Written to Louis Untermeyer, edited by J. A. Robbins, Indiana University Press, 1963.

Pound/Joyce: The Letters of Ezra Pound to James Joyce, edited by Forrest Read, New Directions, 1967.

Selected Prose, 1909-1965, edited by William Cookson, New Directions, 1973.

Ezra Pound and Music: The Complete Criticism, edited by R. Murray Schafer, New Directions, 1977.

"Ezra Pound Speaking": Radio Speeches of World War II, edited by Leonard W. Doob, Greenwood Press, 1978.

Letters to Ibbotsom, 1935-1952, National Poetry Foundation, 1979.

Ezra Pound and the Visual Arts, edited by Harriet Zinnes, New Directions, 1980.

Letters to John Theobald, Black Swan Books, 1981.

Pound-Ford, the Story of a Literary Friendship: The Correspondence between Ezra Pound and Ford Madox Ford and Their Writings about Each Other, New Directions, 1982.

Ezra Pound and Dorothy Shakespear: Their Letters, 1909-1914, New Directions, 1984.

Pound-Lewis: The Letters of Ezra Pound and Wyndham Lewis, New Directions, 1985.

Selected Letters of Ezra Pound and Louis Zukofsky, New Directions, 1987.

Pound the Little Review: The Letters of Ezra Pound to Margaret Anderson, New Directions, 1988.

TRANSLATOR

The Sonnets and Ballate of Guido Cavalcanti, Small, Maynard (Boston), 1912, published as *Ezra Pound's Cavalcanti Poems* (includes "Mediaevalism" and "The Other Dimension," by Pound), New Directions, 1966.

(Contributor of translations) *Selections from Collection Yvette Guilbert,* [London], 1912.

Cathay, Elkin Mathews, 1915.

Certain Noh Plays of Japan, Cuala Press (Churchtown), 1916.

Twelve Dialogues of Fontenelle, 1917.

(With Agnes Bedford) *The Troubadour Sings,* 1920.

Remy de Gourmount, *The Natural Philosophy of Love,* Boni & Liveright 1922.

Confucius, *To Hio: The Great Learning,* University of Washington Bookstore, 1928.

Confucius: Digest of the Analects, edited and published by Giovanni Scheiwiller, 1937.

Odon Por, *Italy's Policy of Social Economics, 1930-1940,* Istituto Italiano D'Arti Grafiche (Bergamo, Milan and Rome), 1941.

(Translator into Italian, with Alberto Luchini) *Ta S'eu Dai Gaku Studio Integrale,* [Rapallo], 1942.

Confucius, *The Great Digest [and] The Unwobbling Pivot,* New Directions, 1951.

Confucius, *Analects,* Kasper & Horton (New York), 1951, published as *The Confucian Analects,* P. Owen, 1956, Square $ Series, 1957.

The Translations of Ezra Pound, edited by Hugh Kenner, New Directions, 1953, enlarged edition published as *Translations,* New Directions, 1963.

The Classic Anthology, Defined by Confucius, Harvard University Press, 1954.

Richard of St. Victor, *Pensieri sull'amore,* [Milan], 1956.

Enrico Pea, *Moscardino,* All' lnsegna del Pesce d'Oro (Milan), 1956.

Sophocles, *Women of Tiachis* (play; produced in New York at Living Theatre, June 22, 1960), Spearman, 1956, New Directions, 1957.

Rimbaud, All' Insegna del Pesce d'Oro, 1957.

(With Noel Stock) *Love Poems of Ancient Egypt,* New Directions, 1962.

EDITOR

(And contributor) *Des Imagistes* (anthology; published anonymously), A. & C. Boni, 1914.

(And contributor) *Catholic Anthology, 1914-1915,* Elkin Mathews, 1915.

Passages from the Letters of John Butler Yeats, Cuala Press, 1917.

Ernest Hemingway, *In Our Time,* Three Mountains Press, 1924.

The Collected Poems of Harry Crosby, Volume Four, Torchbearer, [Paris], 1931.

Guido Cavalcanti, *Rime,* Marsano (Genoa), 1932.

Profiles (anthology), [Milan], 1932.

(And contributor) *Active Anthology,* Faber, 1933.

Ernest Fenollosa, *The Chinese Written Character as a Medium for Poetry,* Square $ Series, 1935.

(With Marcella Spann) *Confucius to Cummings: An Anthology of Poetry,* New Directions, 1964.

OTHER

Contributor to *British Union Quarterly, Townsman, Hudson Review, National Review, New Age* (under the pseudonym Alfred Venison), and other periodicals. Also wrote the score for "Le Testament," a ballet and song recital based on the poem by Francois Villon, 1919-21, first produced in its entirety at Gian Carlo Menotti's Festival of Two Worlds, Spoleto, July 14, 1965; wrote opera, "Villon," in the early 1920s, portions performed in Paris, 1924, and broadcast on the B.B.C., 1931 and 1962; wrote an unfinished opera, "Cavalcanti"; composer of several short pieces for the violin; transcribed medieval troubadour songs.

SIDELIGHTS: Of all the major literary figures in the twentieth century, Ezra Pound has been the most controversial; he has also been one of modern poetry's most important contributors. In an introduction to the *Literary Essays of Ezra Pound,* T. S. Eliot declared that Pound "is more responsible for the twentieth-century revolution in poetry than is any other individual." Four decades later, Donald Hall reaffirmed in remarks collected in *Remembering Poets* that "Ezra Pound is the poet who, a thousand times more than any other man, has made modern poetry possible in English." The importance of Pound's contributions to the arts and to the revitalization of poetry early in this century has been widely acknowledged; yet in 1950, Hugh Kenner could claim in his groundbreaking study *The Poetry of Ezra Pound,* "There is no great contemporary writer who is less read than Ezra Pound." Pound never sought, nor had, a wide reading audience; his technical innovations and use of unconventional poetic materials often baffled even sympathetic readers. Early in his career, Pound aroused controversy because of his aesthetic views; later, because of his political views. For the greater part of this century, however, Pound devoted his energies to advancing the art of poetry and maintaining his aesthetic standards in the midst of extreme adversity.

In his article "How I Began," collected in *Literary Essays,* Pound claimed that as a youth he had resolved to "know more about poetry than any man living." In pursuit of this goal, he settled in London from l908 to 1920, where he carved out a reputation for himself as a member of the literary avant-garde and a tenacious advocate of contemporary work in the arts. Through his criticism and translations, as well as in his own poetry, particularly in his *Cantos,* he explored poetic traditions from different cultures ranging from ancient Greece, China, and the continent, to current-day England and America. In *The Tale of the Tribe* Michael Bernstein observed that Pound "sought, long before the notion became fashionable, to break with the long tradition of Occidental ethnocentrism." In his efforts to develop new directions in the arts, he also promoted and supported such writers as James Joyce, T. S. Eliot and Robert Frost. The critic David Perkins, writing in *A History of Modern Poetry,* summarized Pound's enormous influence: "The least that can be claimed of his poetry is that for over fifty years he was one of the three or four best poets writing in English"; and, Perkins continues, his "achievement in and for poetry was threefold: as a poet, and as a critic, and as a befriender of genius through personal contact." In a 1915 letter to Harriet Monroe, Pound himself described his activities as an effort "to keep alive a certain group of advancing poets, to set the arts in their rightful place as the acknowledged guide and lamp of civilization."

Arriving in Italy in 1908 with only $80, Pound spent $8 to have his first book of poems, *A Lume Spento,* printed in June, 1908, in an edition of 100 copies. An unsigned review appearing in the May, 1909 *Book News Monthly* (collected in *Ezra Pound: The Critical Heritage*) noted, "French phrases and scraps of Latin and Greek punctuate his poetry. . . . He affects obscurity and loves the abstruse." William Carlos Williams, a college friend and himself a poet, wrote to Pound, criticizing the bitterness in the poems; Pound objected that the pieces were dramatic presentations, not personal expressions. On October 21, 1909, he responded to Williams, "It seems to me you might as well say that Shakespeare is dissolute in his plays because Falstaff is . . . or that the plays have a criminal tendency because there is murder done in them." He insisted on making a distinction between his own feelings and ideas and those presented in the poems: "I catch the character I happen to be interested in at the moment he interests me, usually a moment of song, self-analysis, or sudden understanding or revelation. I paint my man as I *conceive* him," explaining that "the sort of thing I do" is "the short so-called dramatic lyric." Pound continued to explore the possibilities of the dramatic lyric in his work, later expanding the technique into the character studies of *Homage to Sextus Propertius* and *Selwyn Mauberley* and of the countless figures who people the *Cantos.*

Pound carried copies of *A Lume Spento* to distribute when he moved to London later that year; the book convinced Elkin Mathews, a London bookseller and publisher, to bring out Pound's next works: *A Quinzaine for this Yule, Exultations* and *Personae.* Reviews of these books were generally favorable, as notices collected in *The Critical Heritage* reveal: Pound "is that rare thing among modern poets, a scholar," wrote one anonymous reviewer in the December, 1909 *Spectator,* adding that Pound has "the capacity for remarkable poetic achievement." British poet F. S. Flint wrote in a May, 1909 review in the *New Age,* "we can have no doubt as to his vitality and as to his determination to burst his way into Parnassus." Flint praised the "craft and artistry, originality and imagination" in *Personae,* although several other unsigned reviews pointed out difficulties with Pound's poems.

His first major critical work, *The Spirit of Romance,* was, Pound said, an attempt to examine "certain forces, elements or qualities which were potent in the mediaeval literature of the Latin tongues, and are, I believe, still potent in our own." The writers he discussed turn up again and again in his later writings: Dante, Cavalcanti, and Villon, for example. Pound contributed scores of reviews and critical articles to various periodicals such as the *New Age,* the *Egoist,* the *Little Review* and *Poetry,* where he articulated his aesthetic principles and indicated his literary, artistic, and musical preferences, thus offering information helpful for interpreting his poetry. In his introduction to the *Literary Essays of Ezra Pound,* T. S. Eliot noted, "It is necessary to read Pound's poetry to understand his criticism, and to read his criticism to understand his poetry." His criticism is important in its own right; as David Perkins pointed out in *A History of Modern Poetry,* "During a crucial decade in the history of modern literature, approximately 1912-1922, Pound was the most influential and in some ways the best critic of poetry in England or America." Eliot stated in his introduction to Pound's *Literary Essays* that Pound's literary criticism was "the most important contemporary criticism of its kind. He forced upon our attention not only individual authors, but whole areas of poetry, which no future criticism can afford to ignore."

Around 1912, Pound helped to create the movement he called "Imagisme," which marked the end of his early poetic style. In remarks first recorded in the March, 1913 *Poetry* and later collected in his *Literary Essays* as "A Retrospect," Pound explained his new literary direction. Imagism combined the creation of an "image"—what he defined as "an intellectual and emotional complex in an instant of time" or an "interpretative metaphor"—with rigorous requirements for writing. About these requirements, Pound was concise but insistent: "1) Direct treatment of the 'thing' whether subjective or objective 2) To use absolutely no word that did not contribute to the presentation 3) As regarding rhythm: to compose in sequence of the musical phrase, not in sequence of a metronome." These criteria meant 1) To carefully observe and describe phenomena, whether emotions, sensations, or concrete entities, and to avoid vague generalities or abstractions. Pound wanted "explicit rendering, be it of external nature or of emotion," and proclaimed "a strong disbelief in abstract and general statement as a means of conveying one's thought to others." 2) To avoid poetic diction in favor of the spoken language and to condense content, expressing it as concisely and precisely as possible. 3) To reject conventional metrical forms in favor of individualized cadence. Each poem, Pound declared, should have a rhythm "which corresponds exactly to the emotion or shade of emotion to be expressed."

The original Imagist group included just Pound, H. D. (Hilda Doolittle), Richard Aldington, F. S. Flint, and later William Carlos Williams. American poet Amy Lowell also adopted the term, contributing one poem to the 1914 anthology *Des Imagistes,* edited by Pound. In following years, Lowell sponsored her own anthologies that Pound thought did not meet his Imagist standards; and wishing to dissociate himself from what he derisively called "Amygism," he changed the term "Image" to "Vortex," and "Imagism" to "Vorticism." Writing in the *Fortnightly Review* of September 1, 1914, Pound expanded his definition of the image: "a radiant node or cluster, it is what I can, and must perforce call a VORTEX, from which, and through which, and into which ideas are constantly rushing." As a much more comprehensive aesthetic principle, Vorticism also extended into the visual arts and music, thus including such artists as the Englishman Wyndham Lewis and Henri Gaudier-Breska, a French sculptor.

Another important facet of Pound's literary activity was his tireless promotion of other writers and artists. He persuaded Harriet Monroe to publish T. S. Eliot's "The Love Song of J. Alfred Prufrock," calling it in a 1914 letter to Monroe "the best poem I have yet had or seen from an American." In 1921, he edited Eliot's *The Waste Land* (published 1922), possibly the most important poem of the modernist era. In a circular (reprinted in Pound's *Letters*) for Bel Esprit, the well-intentioned but ill-fated scheme to help support artists in need, Pound described the poetic sequence of Eliot's poem as "possibly the finest that the modern movement in English has produced." Eliot in turn dedicated the poem to "Ezra Pound, *il miglior fabbro*" (the better craftsman), and in his introduction to Pound's *Selected Poems* (1928) declared, "I sincerely consider Ezra Pound the most important living poet in the English language."

Pound was also an early supporter of the Irish novelist James Joyce, arranging for the publication of several of the stories in *Dubliners* (1914) and *A Portrait of the Artist as a Young Man* (1916) in literary magazines before they were published in book form. Forrest Read, in his introduction to *Pound/Joyce: The Letters of Ezra Pound to James Joyce,* reported that Pound described Joyce to the Royal Literary Fund as "*without exception* the best of the younger prose writers." Read declared that Pound "got Joyce printed" and "at critical moments Pound was able to drum up financial support from such varied sources as the Royal Literary Fund, the Society of Authors, the British Parliament, and the New York lawyer John Quinn in order to help Joyce keep writing." Richard Sieburth in *Istigatios: Ezra Pound and Remy de Gourment* noted, "Ever concerned about the state of Joyce's health, finances, and masterpiece-in-progress, Pound prevailed upon him to quit Trieste for Paris, thus setting in motion one of the major forces that would make Paris the magnet of modernism over the next decade. When Joyce and family arrived in Paris in July, Pound was there to help them settle: he arranged for lodgings, and loans . . . and introduced Joyce . . . to the future publisher of *Ulysses* (1922), Sylvia Beach."

Other writers Pound praised while they were still relatively unknown included D. H. Lawrence, Robert Frost, H. D., and Ernest Hemingway. In his *Life of Ezra Pound,* Noel Stock recalled that in 1925, the first issue of *This Quarter* was dedicated to "Ezra Pound who by his creative work, his editorship of several magazines, his helpful friendship for young and unknown . . . comes first to our mind as meriting the gratitude of this generation." Included among the tributes to Pound was a statement of appreciation from Ernest Hemingway: "We have Pound the major poet devoting, say, one-fifth of his time to poetry. With the rest of his time he tries to advance the fortunes, both material and artistic, of his friends. He defends them when they are attacked, he gets them into magazines and out of jail. He loans them money. He sells their pictures. . . . He advances them hospital expenses and dissuades them from suicide. And in the end a few of them refrain from knifing him at the first opportunity."

Pound's contributions to translation and his rapid critical and poetic development during the Vorticist years are reflected in *Cathay* (1915), translations from the Chinese. In a June, 1915 review in *Outlook,* reprinted in *The Critical Heritage,* Ford Madox Ford declared it "the best work he has yet done;" the poems, of "a supreme beauty," revealed Pound's "power to express emotion . . . intact and exactly." Sinologists criticized Pound for the inaccuracies of the translations; Wi-lim Yip, in his *Ezra Pound's Cathay,* admitted, "One can easily excommunicate Pound from the Forbidden City of Chinese studies"; yet he believed that Pound conveyed "the central concerns of the original author" and that no other translation "has assumed so interesting and unique a position as *Cathay* in the history of English translations of Chinese poetry." In *The Pound Era,* Kenner pointed out that *Cathay* was an interpretation as much as a translation; the "poems paraphrase an elegiac war poetry. . . . among the most durable of all poetic responses to World War I." Perhaps the clearest assessment of Pound's achievement was made at the time by T. S. Eliot in his introduction to Pound's *Selected Poems;* he called Pound "the inventor of Chinese poetry for our time" and predicted that *Cathay* would be called a "magnificent specimen of twentieth-century poetry" rather than a translation.

Hugh Selwyn Mauberley (1920) avoided the problems of being evaluated as a translation, since the title refers to a fictional rather than an historical poet. Yet this poem also suffered at the hands of readers who misunderstood the author's intent. In a July, 1922 letter to his former professor, Felix Schelling, Pound described *Propertius* and *Mauberley* as "portraits," his rendering of sensibilities. Propertius represents the character of a Roman writer responding to his age; Mauberley, the character of a contemporary British critic-poet. Both poems were, Pound told Schelling, his attempt "to condense a James novel" and both were extended dramatic lyrics. "Mauberley is a learned, allusive, and difficult poem, extra-ordinarily concentrated and complex," Michael Alexander observed in *The Poetic Achievement of Ezra Pound;* a central difficulty the poetic sequence presents is point of view. Most importantly, however, *Mauberley* served as Pound's "farewell to London" and showed, according to Alexander, "how profoundly Pound wished to reclaim for poetry areas which the lyric tradition lost to the novel in the nineteenth century—areas of social, public, and cultural life." The poem thus points toward the work that was to occupy Pound for the remainder of his life: the *Cantos.*

By the time Pound left London for Paris in December, 1920, he had already accomplished enough to assure himself a place of first importance in twentieth-century literature. Yet his most ambitious work, the *Cantos,* was scarcely begun. And for a time, it seemed that his long poem was stalled. He had written to Joyce in 1917, "I have begun an endless poem, of no known category . . . all about everything." His original first *Three Cantos* had been published in *Poetry* (1917) and his *Fourth Canto* in 1919. Cantos V, VI, and VII appeared in the *Dial* (1921) and "The Eighth Canto" appeared in 1922, but except for limited editions, no new poems appeared in book form for the next decade. *A Draft of XVI. Cantos* (1925) in an edition of only 90 copies came out in Paris, and *A Draft of XXX Cantos* in 1930; but commercial editions of the first thirty *Cantos* were not published in London and New York until 1933.

The significance of Pound's undertaking was recognized early. In a 1931 review for *Hound and Horn,* reprinted in *The Critical Heritage,* Dudley Fitts called the *Cantos* "without any doubt, the most ambitious poetic conception of our day." Three decades later, in "The Cantos in England," also reprinted in *The Critical Heritage,* Donald Hall concluded, "Pound is a great poet, and the *Cantos* are his masterwork." The long poem, however, presented innumerable difficulties to its readers. When *A Draft of XVI. Cantos* appeared, William Carlos Williams lamented in a 1927 issue of the *New York Evening Post Literary Review* (comments reprinted in *The Critical Heritage*), "Pound has sought to communicate his poetry to us and failed. It is a tragedy, since he is our best poet." Pound himself worried: "Afraid the whole damn poem is rather obscure, especially in fragments," he wrote his father in April, 1927. With fragmentary, telescoped units of information arranged in unfamiliar ways, the *Cantos* confounded critics. Fitts summarized two common complaints: "The first of these is that the poem is incomprehensible, a perverse mystification; the second that it is structurally and melodically amorphous, not a poem, but a macaronic chaos." And George Kearns in his *Guide to Ezra Pound's Selected Cantos* warned that "a basic understanding of the poem requires a major investment of time" since if "one wants to read even a single canto, one must assemble information from a great many sources." The first major critical treatment of Pound's work, Kenner's *The Poetry of Ezra Pound* (1951) paved the way for other serious scholarly attention, and intense critical activity in recent years has produced a host of explanatory texts designed to help readers understand and evaluate the *Cantos.*

Reestablishing a poetic tradition traced from Homer's *Odyssey* and Dante's *Divine Comedy,* the *Cantos* are a *modern* epic. In his 1934 essay "Date Line" (in *Literary Essays of Ezra Pound*), Pound defined an epic as "a poem containing history." He further declared, in *An Introduction to the Economic Nature of the United States* (1944; reprinted in *Selected Prose, 1909-1965*), "For forty years I have schooled myself, not to write an economic history of the U.S. or any other country, but to write an epic poem which begins 'In the Dark Forest,' crosses the Purgatory of human error, and ends in the light and 'fra i maestri di color che sanno' [among the masters of those who know]." Bernstein explained that Pound's concept of an epic determined many of the characteristics of the *Cantos:* "the principle emotion aroused by an epic should be admiration for some distinguished achievement," rather than "the pity and fear aroused by tragedy." Thus, the *Cantos* are peopled with figures Pound considers heroic. Historical characters such as the fifteenth century soldier and patron of the arts Sigismundo Malatesta, the Elizabethan jurist Edward Coke, Elizabeth I, John Adams, and Thomas Jefferson speak through fragments of their own writings. Embodying the ideals of personal freedom, courage, and independent thinking, they represented to Pound heroic figures whose public policies led to enlightened governing. Pound searched through the historical and mythical past as well as the modern world to find those who embodied the Confucian ideals of "sincerity" and "rectitude" in contrast to those who through greed, ignorance, and malevolence worked against the common good.

An epic also encompasses the entire known world and its learning; it is "the tale of the tribe." Thus, the *Cantos* were designed to dramatize the gradual acquisition of cultural knowledge. Pound's poem follows other epic conventions, such as beginning *in medias res* (in the middle) and including supernatural beings in the form of the classical goddesses. The structure is episodic and polyphonic, but the form is redefined to be appropriate for the modern world. Christine Froula in *A Guide to Ezra Pound's*

Selected Poems suggested that Pound's poem, "in its inclusion of fragments of many cultures and many languages, its multiple historical lines, its anthropological perspectives, remains a powerfully and often movingly expressive image of the modern world. It marks the end of the old idea of the tribe as a group who participate in and share a single, closed culture, and redefines it as the human community in all its complex diversity." The *Cantos* are, thus, "truly expressive of our perpetually unfolding perception and experience."

In an often quoted letter to his father in April, 1927, Pound explained that the "outline or main scheme" of the *Cantos* is "Rather like, or unlike, subject and response and counter subject in fugue: A.A. Live man goes down into world of Dead/C.B. The 'repeat in history'/B.C. The 'magic moment' or moment of metamorphosis, bust thru from quotidien into 'divine or permanent world.' Gods., etc." In the same letter, Pound also briefly outlined the themes—the visit to the world of the dead, the repetition in history, and the moment of metamorphosis—all of which have correspondences in three texts that served as his major inspiration: Dante's *Divine Comedy,* Homer's *Odyssey,* and Ovid's *Metamorphosis.* To these models, Pound added the teachings of Confucius, historical material, and information from his immediate experience. In *The Spirit of Romance* (1910), Pound had earlier interpreted the *Divine Comedy* both as a literal description of Dante's imagining a journey "through the realms inhabited by the spirits of the men after death" and as the journey of "Dante's intelligence through the states of mind wherein dwell all sorts and conditions of men before death." The *Cantos* also dramatize such a journey. "By no means an orderly Dantescan rising/but as the winds veer" (Canto LXXIV), the *Cantos* record a pilgrimage—an intellectual and spiritual voyage that parallels Dante's pursuit of enlightenment and Ulysses's search for his proper home. Alexander noted, "If the *Cantos* are not cast consistently in the form of a voyage of discovery, they are conducted in the spirit of such a venture, and continents or islands of knowledge, like Enlightenment America or Siena, or corners of Renaissance Italy, or China as seen via Confucianism, are explored and reported on." The journey in the *Cantos* occurs on two levels: one, a spiritual quest for transcendence, for the revelation of divine forces that lead to individual enlightenment; the other, an intellectual search for worldly wisdom, a vision of the Just City that leads to civic order and harmony. These goals, personal and public, are present throughout the poem; they also sustained the poet throughout his life.

Canto I introduces these controlling themes, presenting Odysseus's visit to the underworld, where he is to receive information from the spirits of the dead that will enable him to return home. The scene also serves as an analogy to the poet's exploration of the literature from the past in hopes of retrieving information that may be significant in his own time. Later Cantos present historical figures such as Sigismundo Malatesta and explore the relationship between creativity in the political and literary realms. By the 1930s, Pound was writing about banking and economic systems, and incorporating into the *Cantos* his own ideas about usury, which he identified as an exploitative economic system. Froula noted that the *Cantos* was "a verbal war against economic corruption, against literal wars, against materialism, against habits of mind that permit the perpetuation of political domination. It advocates economic reform as the basis of social and cultural reform, and it could not have held aloof from political reality."

Pound himself was also not aloof from political reality. An admirer of Mussolini, he lived in fascist Italy beginning in 1925. When the Second World War broke out, Pound stayed in Italy, retaining his American citizenship, and broadcasting a series of controversial radio commentaries. These commentaries often attacked Roosevelt and the Jewish bankers whom Pound held responsible for the war. By 1943, the United States government deemed the broadcasts to be treasonous. At war's end Pound was arrested by the United States Army and kept imprisoned in a small, outdoor wire cage at an Army compound near Pisa, Italy. For several weeks during that hot summer, Pound was confined to the cage. At night, floodlights lit his prison. Eventually judged to be mentally incompetent to stand trial, Pound was incarcerated in St. Elizabeth's Hospital in Washington, D.C. He was to stay in the hospital until 1958 when Robert Frost led a successful effort to free the poet. Ironically, while imprisoned by the Army in Italy, Pound completed the "Pisan Cantos," a group of poems that Paul L. Montgomery of the *New York Times* called "among the masterpieces of this century." The poems won him the Bollingen Prize in 1949.

Upon his release from St. Elizabeth's in 1958, Pound returned to Italy where he was to live quietly for the rest of his life. In 1969, *Drafts and Fragments of Cantos CX-CXVII* appeared, including the despairing lines: "My errors and wrecks lie about me/ . . .I cannot make it cohere." Speaking to Donald Hall, Pound described his *Cantos* as a "botch. . . . I picked out this and that thing that interested me, and then jumbled them into a bag. But that's not the way to make a *work of art.*" Poet Allen Ginsberg reported in *Allen Verbatim: Lectures on Poetry, Politics, Consciousness* that Pound had "felt that the Cantos were 'stupidity and ignorance all the way through,' and were a failure and a 'mess.' " Ginsberg responded that the *Cantos* "were an accurate representation of his mind and so couldn't be thought of in terms of success or failure, but only in terms of the actuality of their representation, and that since for the first time a human being had taken the whole spiritual world of thought through fifty years and followed the thoughts out to the end—so that he built a model of his consciousness over a fifty-year time span— that they were a great human achievement." In the end, Pound fulfilled his own requirement for a poet, as stated in his *Selected Prose, 1909-1965:* "The essential thing about a poet is that he build us his world."

BIOGRAPHICAL/CRITICAL SOURCES:

BOOKS

Alexander, Michael, *The Poetic Achievement of Ezra Pound,* University of California Press, 1979.

Bernstein, Michael, *The Tale of the Tribe: Ezra Pound and the Modern Verse Epic,* Princeton University Press, 1980.

Concise Dictionary of American Literary Biography: The Twenties, 1917-1929, Gale, 1989.

Contemporary Literary Criticism, Gale, Volume 1, 1973, Volume 2, 1974, Volume 3, 1975, Volume 4, 1976, Volume 5, 1976, Volume 7, 1977, Volume 10, 1979, Volume 13, 1980, Volume 18, 1981, Volume 34, 1985, Volume 48, 1988, Volume 50, 1988.

Dictionary of Literary Biography, Gale, Volume 4: *American Writers in Paris, 1920-1939,* 1980, Volume 45: *American Poets, 1880-1945, First Series,* 1986, Volume 63: *Modern American Critics, 1920-1955,* 1988.

Eliot, T. S., *Ezra Pound: His Metric and Poetry,* Knopf, 1917.

Froula, Christine, *A Guide to Ezra Pound's Selected Poems,* New Directions, 1982.

Ginsberg, Allen, *Allen Verbatim: Lectures on Poetry, Politics, Consciousness,* McGraw, 1975.

Hall, Donald, *Remembering Poets,* Harper, 1978.

Homberger, Eric, editor, *Ezra Pound: The Critical Heritage,* Routledge & Kegan Paul, 1972.

Kearns, George, *Guide to Ezra Pound's Selected Cantos,* Rutgers University Press, 1980.

Kenner, Hugh, *The Poetry of Ezra Pound,* New Directions, 1950.

Kenner, Hugh, *The Pound Era,* University of California Press, 1971.

Perkins, David, *A History of Modern Poetry: From the 1890's to the High Modernist Mode,* Harvard University Press, 1976.

Pound, Ezra, *The Spirit of Romance,* Dent, 1910, New Directions, 1952, revised edition, P. Owen, 1953.

Pound, Ezra, *Selected Poems,* edited and with an introduction by T. S. Eliot, Faber & Gwyer, 1928, Laughlin, 1957.

Pound, Ezra, *Literary Essays of Ezra Pound,* edited and with an introduction by T. S. Eliot, New Directions, 1954.

Pound, Ezra, *Pound/Joyce: The Letters of Ezra Pound to James Joyce,* edited by Forrest Read, New Directions, 1967.

Pound, Ezra, *Drafts and Fragments: Cantos CX-CXVII,* New Directions, 1968.

Pound, Ezra, *Selected Prose, 1909-1965,* edited by William Cookson, New Directions, 1973.

PERIODICALS

New York Times, July 9, 1972, November 4, 1972, November 5, 1972.

OBITUARIES:

PERIODICALS

Newsweek, November 13, 1972.
New York Times, November 2, 1972.
Publishers Weekly, November 13, 1972.
Time, November 13, 1972.

* * *

POWELL, Anthony (Dymoke) 1905-

PERSONAL: Surname rhymes with "Noel"; born December 21, 1905, in London, England; son of Philip Lionel William (an army officer) and Maude Mary (Wells-Dymoke) Powell; married Lady Violet Pakenham, daughter of fifth Earl of Longford, December 1, 1934; children: Tristram, John. *Education:* Balliol College, Oxford, B.A., 1926, M.A., 1944.

ADDRESSES: Home—The Chantry, near Frome, Somerset, England.

CAREER: Writer, 1930—. Affiliated with Duckworth & Co., Ltd. (publishing house), London, England, 1926-35; scriptwriter for Warner Brothers of Great Britain, 1936. Trustee of National Portrait Gallery, London, 1962-76. *Military service:* Welch Regiment, Infantry, 1939-41, Intelligence Corps, 1941-45; served as liaison officer at War Office; became major; received Order of the White Lion (Czechoslovakia), Order of Leopold II (Belgium), Oaken Crown and Croix de Guerre (both Luxembourg).

MEMBER: American Academy of Arts and Letters (honorary member), Travellers' Club (London), Modern Language Society (honorary member).

AWARDS, HONORS: Named Commander of Order of the British Empire, 1956, named Companion of Honor, 1988; James Tait Black Memorial Prize, 1958, for *At Lady Molly's;* W. H. Smith Fiction Award, 1974, for *Temporary Kings;* Bennett Award from *Hudson Review* and T. S. Eliot Award from Ingersoll Foundation, both 1984, both for body of work. D.Litt., University of Sussex, 1971, University of Leicester and University

of Kent, 1976, Oxford University, 1980, and Bristol University, 1982.

WRITINGS:

(Editor) *Barnard Letters, 1778-1884,* Duckworth, 1928.

Afternoon Men (novel), Duckworth, 1931, Holt, 1932, reprinted, Popular Library, 1978.

Venusberg (novel; also see below), Duckworth, 1932, Popular Library, 1978.

From a View to a Death (novel), Duckworth, 1933, reprinted, Popular Library, 1978, published as *Mr. Zouch, Superman: From a View to a Death,* Vanguard, 1934.

Agents and Patients (novel; also see below), Duckworth, 1936, Popular Library, 1978.

What's Become of Waring? (novel), Cassell, 1939, Little, Brown, 1963, reprinted, Popular Library, 1978.

(Editor and author of introduction) *Novels of High Society from the Victorian Age,* Pilot Press, 1947.

John Aubrey and His Friends, Scribner, 1948, revised edition, Barnes & Noble, 1963, reprinted, Chatto & Windus, 1988.

(Editor and author of introduction) John Aubrey, *Brief Lives and Other Selected Writings,* Scribner, 1949.

(Author of introduction) E. W. Hornung, *Raffles,* Eyre & Spottiswoode, 1950.

Two Novels: Venusberg [and] *Agents and Patients,* Periscope-Holliday, 1952.

(Author of preface) *The Complete Ronald Firbank,* Duckworth, 1961.

(Contributor) *Burke's Landed Gentry,* Burke's Peerage Publications, 1965.

Two Plays: The Garden God [and] *The Rest I'll Whistle,* Heinemann, 1971, Little, Brown, 1972.

(Contributor) Richard Shead, *Constant Lambert,* Simon Publications, 1973.

To Keep the Ball Rolling: The Memoirs of Anthony Powell, Volume 1: *Infants of the Spring,* Heinemann, 1976, published as *Infants of the Spring: The Memoirs of Anthony Powell,* Holt, 1977, reprinted, Penguin, 1984, Volume 2: *Messengers of Day,* Holt, 1978, Volume 3: *Faces in My Time,* Heinemann, 1980, Holt, 1981, Volume 4: *The Strangers Are All Gone,* Heinemann, 1982, Holt, 1983, abridged edition of all four volumes published as *To Keep the Ball Rolling,* Penguin, 1983.

(Author of introduction) Jocelyn Brooke, *The Orchid Trilogy,* Secker & Warburg, 1981.

O, How the Wheel Becomes It! (novella), New American Library, 1985.

The Fisher King (novel), Norton, 1986.

"A DANCE TO THE MUSIC OF TIME" SERIES; NOVELS; ALSO SEE BELOW

A Question of Upbringing, Scribner, 1951, reprinted, Warner Books, 1985.

A Buyer's Market, Heinemann, 1952, Scribner, 1953, reprinted, Warner Books, 1985.

The Acceptance World, Heinemann, 1955, Farrar, Straus, 1956, reprinted, Warner Books, 1985.

At Lady Molly's, Heinemann, 1957, Little, Brown, 1958, reprinted, Warner Books, 1985.

Casanova's Chinese Restaurant, Little, Brown, 1960, reprinted, Warner Books, 1985.

The Kindly Ones, Little, Brown, 1962, reprinted, Warner Books, 1985.

The Valley of Bones, Little, Brown, 1964, reprinted, Warner Books, 1985.

The Soldier's Art, Little, Brown, 1966, reprinted, Warner Books, 1985.

The Military Philosophers, Heinemann, 1968, Little, Brown, 1969, reprinted, Warner Books, 1985.

Books Do Furnish a Room, Little, Brown, 1971, reprinted, Warner Books, 1986.

Temporary Kings, Little, Brown, 1973, reprinted, Warner Books, 1986.

Hearing Secret Harmonies, Heinemann, 1975, Little, Brown, 1976, reprinted, Warner Books, 1986.

"A DANCE TO THE MUSIC OF TIME" OMNIBUS VOLUMES

A Dance to the Music of Time: First Movement (contains *A Question of Upbringing, A Buyer's Market,* and *The Acceptance World*), Little, Brown, 1963.

A Dance to the Music of Time: Second Movement (contains *At Lady Molly's, Casanova's Chinese Restaurant,* and *The Kindly Ones*), Little, Brown, 1964.

A Dance to the Music of Time: Third Movement (contains *The Valley of Bones, The Soldier's Art,* and *The Military Philosophers*), Little, Brown, 1971.

A Dance to the Music of Time: Fourth Movement (contains *Books Do Furnish a Room, Temporary Kings,* and *Hearing Secret Harmonies*), Little, Brown, 1976.

WORK IN PROGRESS: Miscellaneous Verdicts, a collection of criticism.

SIDELIGHTS: Novelist Anthony Powell has spent more than forty years chronicling the changing fortunes of Great Britain's upper class in the twentieth century. He is best known for his twelve-volume series "A Dance to the Music of Time," the longest fictional work in the English language. Published in installments over almost twenty-five years, "A Dance to the Music of Time" follows a number of characters from adolescence in 1914 to old age and death in the late 1960s. *New Yorker* contributor Naomi Bliven calls the series "one of the most important works of fiction since the Second World War," and *New Republic* reviewer C. David Benson describes the novels as "the most sophisticated chronicle of modern life we have." In the Toronto *Globe and Mail,* Douglas Hill observes that Powell "has had the good fortune to be in the right place at the right time and among the right people, and to be able to watch all this passing scene and transform the most apparently insignificant moments into the fabric of his fiction."

Newsweek correspondent Gene Lyons notes that Powell is "entirely provincial, yet not at all a snob, . . . an aristocratic man of letters in the best British tradition." Lyons continues: "He is a contemporary of that extraordinary group of English writers who were born during the first decade of this century." Indeed, Powell enjoyed close friendships with Evelyn Waugh, Cyril Connolly, and George Orwell, and he knew numerous other important writers, including Dylan Thomas and F. Scott Fitzgerald. Powell grew up in comfortable circumstances—he is a descendent of nobility—and was educated at Eton and Oxford. As Benson notes, however, the author's entire generation "was marked by having experienced the extinction of the privileged England of their childhoods which was replaced by a completely different post-war world." In his fiction Powell explores the extinction, or rather the metamorphosis, of the British upper class.

Powell graduated from Oxford in 1926 and took a job with Duckworth, a major publishing house in London. While he served as an editor at Duckworth, Powell began to write fiction of his own; eventually, Duckworth published four of his five early novels. *Dictionary of Literary Biography* contributor James

Tucker describes Powell's first few books as "entertaining, light, but not lightweight." Tucker also observes that in his early works Powell "appears to be interested in societies under threat, either from their own languor and foolishness or from huge political reverses or from calculated infiltration by arrivistes." Powell's first novel, *Afternoon Men,* has become his best known prewar work. A satire of the upper-middle-class penchant for aimlessness, *Afternoon Men* begins and ends with party invitations. Tucker contends that, in the novel, Powell "expertly depicts the banality of the lives under scrutiny by having characters talk with a remorseless, plodding simplicity, as if half-baked, half-drunk, or half-asleep after too many nights on the town."

Even though Powell's first five novels sold only several thousand copies apiece, by the 1930s the author "had come to be recognized as one of several significant novelists who had emerged in Britain since World War I," to quote Tucker. Like most Englishmen his age, however, Powell faced a cessation of his career when the Second World War began. He enlisted in the Welsh Regiment and then served four years with the Intelligence Corps as liaison to the War Office. When the war ended, Powell still did not return to fiction for some time. Instead, he wrote a comprehensive biography on John Aubrey, a seventeenth century writer and antiquary of Welsh descent. Only when *John Aubrey and His Friends* was completed did Powell return to fiction—but he did so in a grand way. Tucker writes: "Believing that many authors went on producing what were virtually the same characters in book after book, though with different names and in fresh circumstances, [Powell] wanted to break out from the confines of the 80,000 word novel. The *roman-fleuve* would allow him to recognize the problem openly and continue with established characters through successive volumes. During the late 1940s, while visiting the Wallace Collection in London, he saw Nicolas Poussin's painting *A Dance to the Music of Time* and felt he had at last found the theme and title of his work."

The Poussin painting depicts the four seasons as buxom young maidens, dancing under a threatening sky to music provided by a wizened, bearded man—Father Time. Powell's work, too, involves "dancers," a coterie of interrelated men and women living in modern Britain, whose lives intersect on the whims of fate. As Tucker notes, "scores of major characters dance their way in and out of one another's lives—and especially one another's beds—often in seemingly random style; yet when the whole sequence is seen together there is some sort of order. To put it more strongly than that would be wrong; but music and dance do imply a system, harmony, pattern."

Kerry McSweeney describes "A Dance to the Music of Time" in a *South Atlantic Quarterly* essay. According to McSweeney, the book's subject "is a densely populated swathe of upper-class, upper-middle-class, artistic, and Bohemian life in England from the twenties to the seventies. The vehicle of presentation is the comedy of manners. Attention is consistently focused on the nuances of social behavior, the idiosyncracies of personal style, and the intricacies of sexual preference. All of the characters in the series . . . are seen strictly from the outside—that is, in terms of how they choose to present themselves to the world." In the early volumes, the characters leave school to establish careers which are often less important than the whirl of social obligations. The middle volumes concern the years of the Second World War, and the later volumes send many of the characters to their deaths. In *The Situation of the Novel,* Bernard Bergonzi notes that "A Dance to the Music of Time" is "a great work of social comedy in a central English tradition" that "also conveys the cumulative sense of a shabby and dispirited society." A *Washington Post Book World* reviewer calls the series "an addictive social fantasy, strictly controlled by the author's sense of the ambiguity of human relationships and an indispensable literary style."

The action in "A Dance to the Music of Time" is revealed by Nicholas Jenkins, a non-participant observer who is happily married, urbane, and loyal to his values. From his vantage point in society, Jenkins describes the ascent of several power-hungry men—chief among them Kenneth Widmerpool—who become consumed by the perfection of their public images. Bliven contends that the series "subtly but ever more insistently contrasts the quest for power with the urge to create. The power seekers are killers and lovers of death, and the defenses against them are disinterestedness, playfulness, and, above all, artistic dedication." Tucker sees the tension between Jenkins and Widmerpool as "the difference between a man who is nothing but ambition, a sort of burlesque Faust, and another who represents enduring standards of humaneness, creativity, and artistic appreciation in a shoddy world."

"A Dance to the Music of Time" does not provide a continuous narrative; rather, it presents a series of minutely-observed vignettes, described with an understated prose. "What strikes one first about [the series]," Tucker writes in *The Novels of Anthony Powell,* "is its elaborate texture and seemingly cast-iron poise, qualities suiting the narrator's wisdom, favoured status, knowledge and assurance. . . . The prose is largely appositional: to borrow the mode, plain statement followed by commentary or modification or conjecture, so that the reader feels himself presented with a very wide choice of possible responses; the uncertainties of real life are caught. . . . This modulated dignity, mandarin with the skids under it, gives Powell's style its distinction." In the *New York Review of Books,* Michael Wood concludes that the most "persistent pleasure" to be gained from Powell's masterwork "is that of having your expectations skillfully and elegantly cheated: the musician plays a strange chord, or an old chord you haven't heard for a long time, even a wrong note now and then." Lyons makes the observation that "A Dance to the Music of Time" provides a remarkable steadfastness of vision—"the novel's closing pages, written 25 years after the opening, make so perfect a fit they might have been the product of a single morning's work."

Powell's series has found numerous champions in both Great Britain and the United States. *Chicago Tribune Books* reviewer Larry Kart, for one, calls "A Dance to the Music of Time" the "century's finest English-language work of fiction." In *The Sense of Life in the Modern Novel,* Arthur Mizener writes that the effect of the work "is a very remarkable one for the mid-twentieth century. It is as if we had come suddenly on an enormously intelligent but completely undogmatic mind with a vision of experience that is deeply penetrating and yet wholly recognizable, beautifully subtle in ordination and yet quite unostentatious in technique, and in every respect undistorted by doctrine." *Commonweal* contributor Arnold Beichman praises Powell's novels for their "great cosmic sadness about our lives," adding: "It is Powell's skill and power in depicting man's helplessness that makes [his] novels so unforgettable, so wonderfully sad." Speaking to the universality of "A Dance to the Music of Time," *National Review* correspondent Anthony Lejeune concludes that Powell "makes us see not only his world, but ours, through his eyes. Not only his characters, but our own lives and the lives which are constantly weaving and unweaving themselves around us, become part of the pattern, part of the inexplicable dance."

Powell has not been idle since the completion of "A Dance to the Music of Time." Since 1975 he has written a four-volume memoir, a novella entitled *O, How the Wheel Becomes It!,* and a novel, *The Fisher King.* In *The Novels of Anthony Powell,* Tucker suggests that one feels "a plea throughout Powell's books for the natural warmth and vitality of life to be allowed their expression. . . . The distinction of Powell's novels is that they engagingly look at surfaces and, at the same time, suggest that this is by no means enough. They will continually disturb the surface to show us much more. In their quiet way they direct us towards a good, practical, unextreme general philosophy of life." *Voice Literary Supplement* contributor Ann Snitow observes that Powell can be recommended "for his long, honorable battle with language, his unavoidable anxieties, his preference for kindness over gaudier virtues. If he's brittle, it's because he knows things break; he's never complacent in either his playfulness or his hauteur." Snitow concludes: "Powell's a writer who values humility—antique word—a virtue now so necessary, and even more rare and obscure, perhaps, than Powell himself."

BIOGRAPHICAL/CRITICAL SOURCES:

BOOKS

Allen, Walter, *The Modern Novel,* Dutton, 1965.
Bergonzi, Bernard, *The Situation of the Novel,* University of Pittsburgh Press, 1970.
Bergonzi, Bernard, *Anthony Powell,* Longman, 1971.
Contemporary Literary Criticism, Gale, Volume 1, 1973, Volume 3, 1975, Volume 7, 1977, Volume 9, 1978, Volume 10, 1979, Volume 31, 1985.
Dictionary of Literary Biography, Volume 15: *British Novelists, 1930-1959,* Gale, 1983.
Hall, James, *The Tragic Comedians,* Indiana University Press, 1963.
Karl, Frederick R., *A Reader's Guide to the Contemporary English Novel,* Farrar, Straus, 1962.
Mizener, Arthur, *The Sense of Life in the Modern Novel,* Houghton, 1964.
Morris, Robert K., *The Novels of Anthony Powell,* University of Pittsburgh Press, 1968.
Ries, Lawrence R., *Wolf Masks: Violence in Contemporary Poetry,* Kennikat, 1977.
Russell, John, *Anthony Powell, A Quintet, Sextet and War,* Indiana University Press, 1970.
Shapiro, Charles, *Contemporary British Novelists,* Southern Illinois University Press, 1965.
Spurling, Hilary, *Invitation to the Dance: A Guide to Anthony Powell's "Dance to the Music of Time,"* Little, Brown, 1978.
Symons, Julian, *Critical Occasions,* Hamish Hamilton, 1966.
Tucker, James, *The Novels of Anthony Powell,* Columbia University Press, 1976.

PERIODICALS

Atlantic, March, 1962.
Best Sellers, March 15, 1969.
Books and Bookmen, April, 1971, March, 1976, January, 1977.
Book Week, April 9, 1967.
Chicago Tribune Books, September 28, 1986.
Chicago Tribune Book World, July 19, 1981.
Christian Science Monitor, October 6, 1960, January 25, 1967, March 16, 1967, March 9, 1981.
Commonweal, July 31, 1959, May 12, 1967, May 30, 1969.
Contemporary Literature, spring, 1976.
Critique, spring, 1964.
Encounter, February, 1976.
Globe and Mail (Toronto), March 31, 1984.
Hudson Review, summer, 1967, spring, 1976, winter, 1981-82, autumn, 1984.

Kenyon Review, winter, 1960.
Listener, October 14, 1968, September 11, 1975, May 11, 1978.
London Magazine, January, 1969.
London Review of Books, May 18, 1983.
Los Angeles Times Book Review, May 22, 1983, November 6, 1983.
Nation, May 29, 1967, December 10, 1973, June 19, 1976.
National Review, December 7, 1973, June 11, 1976, January 11, 1985.
New Leader, November 26, 1973.
New Republic, September 24, 1962, April 22, 1967, October 27, 1973, June 11, 1977.
New Review, September, 1974.
New Statesman, June 25, 1960, July 6, 1962, May 19, 1980, May 21, 1982.
Newsweek, March 24, 1969, October 29, 1973, April 5, 1976, April 25, 1983, September 2, 1985.
New Yorker, July 3, 1965, June 3, 1967, May 10, 1976.
New York Herald Tribune Books, February 11, 1962.
New York Review of Books, May 18, 1967, November 1, 1973.
New York Times, March 14, 1968, March 13, 1969, September 8, 1971, February 17, 1972, February 4, 1981, November 16, 1984, September 23, 1986.
New York Times Book Review, January 21, 1962, September 30, 1962, March 19, 1967, March 9, 1969, October 14, 1973, November 1, 1973, April 11, 1976, February 8, 1981, June 26, 1983, January 22, 1984, October 19, 1986, February 21, 1988.
Observer Review, October 10, 1967, October 13, 1968, February 14, 1971.
Publishers Weekly, April 5, 1976.
Saturday Review, March 18, 1967, March 8, 1969, November 11, 1973, April 17, 1976.
Sewanee Review, spring, 1974.
South Atlantic Quarterly, winter, 1977.
Spectator, June 24, 1960, September 16, 1966, October 18, 1968, September 13, 1975, October 9, 1976, June 5, 1982.
Time, August 11, 1958, March 3, 1967, March 28, 1969, March 9, 1981.
Times (London), April 3, 1980, May 13, 1982, June 16, 1983, April 3, 1986.
Times Literary Supplement, October 17, 1968, March 28, 1980, June 24, 1983, September 21, 1984, April 4, 1986.
Twentieth Century, July, 1961.
Virginia Quarterly Review, summer, 1976, spring, 1978, autumn, 1985.
Voice Literary Supplement, February, 1984.
Washington Post Book World, April 4, 1976, May 30, 1976, October 9, 1977, September 17, 1978, January 18, 1981, October 12, 1986, December 13, 1987.
World Literature Today, summer, 1979.

—*Sketch by Anne Janette Johnson*

* * *

POWERS, J(ames) F(arl) 1917-

PERSONAL: Born July 8, 1917, in Jacksonville, Ill.; son of James Ansbury and Zella (Routzong) Powers; married Elizabeth Alice Wahl (a writer), April 22, 1946; children: Katherine, Mary, James, Hugh, Jane. *Education:* Attended Northwestern University, 1938-40. *Religion:* Roman Catholic.

CAREER: Worked as book store clerk, chauffeur, and insurance salesman. Editor, Illinois Historical Records Survey, 1938; creative writing teacher at St. John's University, Collegeville,

Minn., 1947, Marquette University, Milwaukee, Wis., 1949-50, University of Michigan, Ann Arbor, 1956-57, Smith College, Northhampton, Mass., 1965-66, and St. John's University, 1976—.

MEMBER: National Institute of Arts and Letters.

AWARDS, HONORS: National Institute of Arts and Letters grant, 1948; Guggenheim fellowship in creative writing, 1948; Rockefeller fellowship, 1954, 1957, 1967; National Book Award, 1963, for *Morte d'Urban;* nominated for National Book Award and National Book Critics Circle Award, both 1988, both for *Wheat That Springeth Green.*

WRITINGS:

Prince of Darkness and Other Stories (story collection), Doubleday, 1947, reprinted, Random House, 1979.
The Presence of Grace (story collection), Doubleday, 1956.
Morte d'Urban (novel), Doubleday, 1962, reprinted, Random House, 1979.
Look How the Fish Live (story collection), Knopf, 1975.
Wheat That Springeth Green, Knopf, 1988.

Work represented in anthologies. Contributor to *New Yorker, Nation, Partisan Review, Reporter, Collier's, Kenyon Review,* and other periodicals.

SIDELIGHTS: J. F. Powers's fiction examines the relationship between the religious and secular worlds. He is especially concerned, F. W. Dupee writes, with "the contradictions that beset Catholicism, in practice if not in theory, because of its claim to an earthly as well as a divine mission and authority." Leo J. Hertzel states Powers's primary theme as "the problem of how to put the Christian's traditional smiling contempt of the world into action in the grim, restricted society of organized modern America."

Powers often examines this problem within a clerical setting, where the differences between the religious and secular worlds are most pronounced. As Dupee states, Powers favors "the simple spectacle of priests going about the ordinary business of their professions." Powers's world, Stanley Poss writes, "is frequently clerical, in a very domestic way." This clerical setting is used, George Scouffas believes, because "the Church offers a ready-made, highly developed, . . . organized [and] historically weathered pattern of order. . . . Opposed to the Church is the 'world,' or disorder. . . . This setting-up of opposing forces represents a formalization of a basic paradox in reality and experience."

Powers employs a highly satiric style when depicting members of the clergy in their struggles with the secular world. "The priesthood," Naomi Lebowitz writes, "offers a particularly good stage for Powers's form of comedy, for it serves as a microcosm of sin and virtue magnified in conflict by conscience." Powers, as John V. Hagopian notes, is "known among his peers as a brilliant satirist." Hayden Carruth believes that Powers "has revived the satire of the Golden Age . . . within a modern context of style and attitude." Not all critics find Powers's satire admirable. Thomas Rowan, for example, calls it "mean-spirited" and suggests that Powers "has been peering too long at a few soiled pores on the face of the Catholic priesthood."

Although Powers's fiction is humorous, it also confronts and examines serious issues. A reviewer for *Time* comments that Powers is "the only man besides John Updike who can write about salvation and damnation in a world rapidly becoming trivialized by loneliness and loss of ardor." John P. Sisk admires Powers for his "ability to portray virtue in its complex relations with evil, an ability that includes, though it may go considerably beyond, the ability to confront ambivalence."

Summing up Powers's place in contemporary literature, Hagopian believes that Powers's "taut, understated ironies are out of step with current literary fashions, [and] as a consequence, Powers remains on the periphery of the literary stage, even though he is, as Frank O'Connor says, 'among the greatest of living story-tellers.' " Hagopian concludes that Powers works with "such immense skill and tough-minded compassion that his writing will surely endure."

BIOGRAPHICAL/CRITICAL SOURCES:

BOOKS

Contemporary Literary Criticism, Gale, Volume 1, 1973, Volume 4, 1975, Volume 8, 1978.
Evans, Fallon, editor, *J. F. Powers,* B. Herder, 1968.
Hagopian, John V., *J. F. Powers,* Twayne, 1968.
Hyman, Stanley Edgar, *Standards: A Chronicle of Books for Our Time,* Horizon Press, 1966.
Kazin, Alfred, *Contemporaries,* Atlantic, 1962.
Kellogg, Gene, *The Vital Tradition: The Catholic Novel in a Period of Convergence,* Loyola University Press, 1970.
The Picaresque Saint: Representative Figures in Contemporary Fiction, Lippincott, 1959.
The Short Story in America, 1900-1950, Regnery, 1952.
Whitbread, Thomas B., editor, *Seven Contemporary Authors,* University of Texas Press, 1966.

PERIODICALS

American Benedictine Review, March, 1964.
Atlantic, November, 1962, November, 1975.
Catholic World, September, 1952.
Commonweal, October 12, 1962.
Contemporary Literature, spring, 1968.
Critique, fall, 1958.
Encounter, November, 1963.
Esquire, December, 1975.
Homiletic and Pastoral Review, January, 1963.
Hudson Review, summer, 1976.
Kenyon Review, summer, 1958.
Los Angeles Times, September 15, 1988.
Minnesota Review, Volume 9, number 1, 1969.
Nation, September 29, 1962.
National Review, March 18, 1977.
New Leader, October 13, 1975.
New Republic, April, 1956, September 24, 1962, November 29, 1975.
Newsweek, October 13, 1975.
New York Review of Books, November 13, 1975.
New York Times, September 25, 1975.
New York Times Book Review, October 30, 1988.
Our Sunday Visitor, September 2, 1963.
Partisan Review, spring, 1963, spring, 1973.
Progressive, October, 1962, December, 1975.
Renascence, summer, 1965.
Sewanee Review, January, 1977.
Time, November 3, 1975.
Times Literary Supplement, October 28, 1988.
Tribune Books, August 14, 1988.
Twentieth Century Literature, July, 1968.
Virginia Quarterly Review, winter, 1976.
Washington Post Book World, August 14, 1988.
Worship, November, 1962.
Yale Review, December, 1962.

POWYS, John Cowper 1872-1963

PERSONAL: Surname is pronounced "*Po*-is"; born October 8, 1872, in Shirley, Derbyshire, England; came to United States, 1928; died June 17, 1963, in Merionethshire, Wales; son of Charles Francis (an Anglican clergyman) and Mary Cowper (Johnson) Powys; married Margaret Alice Lyon, 1896 (died, 1947); children: one son. *Education:* Corpus Christi College, M.A.

ADDRESSES: Home—Blaenau-Festiniog, Wales.

CAREER: Educator, critic, novelist, and poet. Lecturer in literature at universities in England, including Oxford and Cambridge; lecturer at universities in the United States, winters, c. 1904-34; lived in New York, 1928-34; returned to Wales, 1934; full-time writer, c. 1934-60.

AWARDS, HONORS: Honorary doctor of letters from University of Wales.

WRITINGS:

Odes and Other Poems, Rider & Co., 1896.
Poems, Rider & Co, 1899.
The War and Culture: A Reply to Professor Muensterberg, G. A. Shaw, 1914 (published in England as *The Menace of German Culture: A Reply to Professor Muensterberg,* Rider & Co., 1915).
Visions and Revisions: A Book of Literary Devotions, G. A. Shaw, 1915, reprinted, CORE Collection, 1978.
Wood and Stone: A Romance, G. A. Shaw, 1915.
Wolf's-Bane Rhymes (poems), G. A. Shaw, 1916.
Confessions of Two Brothers, Manas Press, 1916, reprinted, Scholarly Press, 1971.
One Hundred Best Books, G. A. Shaw, 1916.
Rodmoor: A Romance, G. A. Shaw, 1916, revised edition with preface by G. Wilson Knight, Colgate University Press, 1973.
Suspended Judgments: Essays on Books and Sensations, G. A. Shaw, 1916, reprinted, Norwood Editions, 1977.
Mandragora (poems), G. A. Shaw, 1917.
The Complex Vision, Dodd, 1920.
T. Seltzer, Samphire, 1922.
The Art of Happiness, Haldeman-Julius, 1923, reprinted, Village Press, 1974.
Psychoanalysis and Morality, J. Colbert, 1923, reprinted, Village Press, 1975.
Ducdame (novel), Doubleday, 1925.
The Religion of a Sceptic (essays), Dodd, 1925, reprinted, Village Press, 1975.
The Secret of Self Development, Haldeman-Julius, 1926, reprinted, Village Press, 1974.
The Art of Forgetting the Unpleasant, Haldeman-Julius, 1928, reprinted, Village Press, 1974.
The Meaning of Culture (essays), Norton, 1929, reprinted, Greenwood, 1979.
Wolf Solent (novel), Simon & Schuster, 1929, reprinted, Scholarly Press, 1971.
The Owl, the Duck, and—Miss Rowe! Miss Rowe! (short stories), Black Archer Press, 1930, reprinted, Village Press, 1975.
In Defence of Sensuality (essays), Simon & Schuster, 1930, reprinted, Village Press, 1974.
Dorothy M. Richardson, Joiner and Steele, 1931.
A Glastonbury Romance (novel), Simon & Schuster, 1932, reprinted, Overlook Press, 1987.
A Philosophy of Solitude (essays), Simon & Schuster, 1933, reprinted, Village Press, 1974.

Weymouth Sands (novel), Simon & Schuster, 1934, reprinted with an introduction by Angus Wilson, Rivers Press, 1973.

Autobiography, Simon & Schuster, 1934, reprinted, New Directions, 1960, revised edition with introduction by J. B. Priestley and notes by R. I. Blackmore, Colgate University Press, 1968.

Jobber Skald (novel), John Lane, 1935.

Maiden Castle (novel), Simon & Schuster, 1936, reprinted, Colgate University Press, 1966.

Morwyn; or, The Vengeance of God (novel), Cassell, 1937, reprinted, Sphere, 1977.

Enjoyment of Literature (essays), Simon & Schuster, 1938 (published in England as *The Pleasures of Literature,* Cassell, 1938).

Owen Glendower (novel), Simon & Schuster, 1940, reprinted, Chivers, 1974.

Mortal Strife, J. Cape, 1942, reprinted, Village Press, 1974.

The Art of Growing Old (essays), J. Cape, 1944.

Dostoievsky (essays), John Lane, 1946, reprinted, Haskell House, 1973.

Pair Dadeni; or, The Cauldron of Rebirth, Druid Press, 1946.

Obstinste Cymric: Essays 1935-1947, Druid Press, 1947, reprinted, Village Press, 1973.

Rabelais: His Life, the Story Told by Him, Selections Therefrom Here Newly Translated, and an Interpretation of His Genius and His Religion, Bodley Head, 1948, reprinted, Philosophical Library, 1951, reprinted, Village Press, 1974.

The Inmates (novel), Philosophical Library, 1952.

In Spite Of: A Philosophy for Everyman (essays), Philosophical Library, 1953.

Atlantis (essays), Macdonald, 1954, reprinted, Chivers, 1973.

The Brazen Head (novel), Colgate University Press, 1956.

Lucifer: A Poem, Macdonald, 1956.

Up and Out (contains "Up and Out" and "The Mountains of the Moon"), Macdonald, 1957, reprinted, Village Press, 1974.

Culture and Nature, edited by Ichiro Hara, Hokuseido Press, c. 1958.

Letters of John Cowper Powys to Louis Wilkinson, 1935-1956, Colgate University Press, 1958.

Culture and Life, edited by Hara, Hokuseido Press, c. 1958.

Homer and the Aether, Macdonald, 1959.

All or Nothing, Macdonald, 1960, reprinted, Village Press, 1974.

John Cowper Powys: A Selection From His Poems, edited with introduction by Kenneth Hopkins, Colgate University Press, 1964.

Letters From John Cowper Powys to Glyn Hughes, edited by Bernard Jones, Ore Publications, 1971.

Letters to Nicholas Ross, edited by Arthur Uphill, Bertram Rota, 1971.

William Blake, Village Press, 1974.

John Cowper Powys: Letters, 1937-1954, edited with introduction and notes by Iorwerth C. Peate, University of Wales Press, 1974.

Romer Mowl and Other Stories (contains "Romer Mowl," "The Spot on the Wall," and "The Harvest Thanksgiving"), edited by Bernard Jones, Toucan Press, 1974.

Two and Two, Village Press, 1974.

An Englishman Up-State, Village Press, 1974.

Real Wraiths, Village Press, 1974.

Letters of John Cowper Powys to His Brother Llewelyn, edited by Malcolm Elwin, two volumes, Volume 1: *1902-1925,* Volume 2: *1925-1939,* Village Press, 1975.

You and Me, Village Press, 1975.

Three Fantasies, Carcanet, 1986.

Also author of *Debate: Is Modern Marriage a Failure?,* with Bertrand Russell, 1930, and the novel *Porius: A Romance of the Dark Ages,* 1951. Contributor to periodicals, including *Dial, American Mercury,* and *Century.*

SIDELIGHTS: John Cowper Powys belonged to a very literary family. His mother was collaterally related to British poets William Cowper and John Donne. Of Powys's immediate family, six of his ten brothers and sisters also published books, although only two others, Llewelyn and Theodore Francis, achieved literary prominence.

It has been said of Powys's lectures and writings that they reveal more about him than about the intended subject. No matter how odd the characters, "nobody in a novel by Mr. Powys is ever as interesting as the author himself," observed Mark Van Doren. "His best book is still his 'Autobiography,' which is completely and frankly about himself, and where to be sure he confesses that he has made an art out of acting as if he were even more interesting than he is." But despite the autobiographical nature of all his work, Glen Cavaliero insisted that "far from being narrowly egoistic and inward-turning, [it] is a projection of the self into an autonomous world of the imagination which is accessible to everyone."

Powys published his first novel when he was forty-three years old, and continued a prolific writing career until his eighties. Many of his works deal with myths, cosmic fantasies, and the elemental forces of nature. *A Glastonbury Romance,* for example, is an adaptation of the myth that Joseph of Arimathea possessed the Holy Grail. In his writings Powys seeks to convey his personal philosophies and as a result the characters often seem to soliloquize instead of talk.

An important theme in Powys's writing is man's sexual nature. G. Wilson Knight assessed his treatment of the subject as "both unorthodox and traditional." Powys clearly presents man's obsession with the "bisexual . . . vision which, though transmitted through human figures, speaks from a dimension beyond the biological." His handling of human sexuality is strangely impersonal in that "there is a divergence from ordinary desire to a more refined but impersonal and cerebral fascination." In Knight's opinion, "probably [Powys's] most important contribution to our religious tradition is his insistence that 'no religion that doesn't deal with sex-longing in some kind of way is much use to us.'"

Powys tells us that he himself is half a woman and thus he can understand sexual matters from a woman's point of view. But as Knight pointed out, Powys's fictional women are generally presented as stereotypical "normal" girls and are less individualized than the male characters. The only in-depth female characters are "those who have, or touch, boylike attributes, such as Gladys in *Wood and Stone,* Philippa in *Rodmoor,* and Persephone Spear in *A Glastonbury Romance.*"

Most of Powys's novels are extremely long, and as Knight explained, "his mastery of the long sentence, like the wielding of a giant's club, tempts him, on occasion, too far." *Times Literary Supplement* called Powys a "self-indulgent writer . . . [who was] never fully master of the pace and cohesion of an entire novel," and complained about his "coyness or archness, his literary echoes, his use of capital letters, italics, hyphens, and exclamation marks to draw attention to what should be sufficiently challenging in itself."

On the other hand, many of the same critics who panned Powys also praised him as a genius for his eloquence, humor, and cunning irony. A *Times Literary Supplement* reviewer explained this paradox: "Powys is rather like life itself: you can object strongly to parts of it, and be often baffled for a meaning, but the sum total impresses."

BIOGRAPHICAL/CRITICAL SOURCES:

BOOKS

Breckon, Richard, *John Cowper Powys: The Solitary Giant,* K. A. Ward, 1969.

Cavaliero, Glen, *John Cowper Powys, Novelist,* Clarendon Press, 1973.

Collins, Harold P., *John Cowper Powys: Old Earthman,* Barrie & Rockliff, 1966.

Contemporary Literary Criticism, Gale, Volume 7, 1977, Volume 9, 1978, Volume 15, 1980, Volume 46, 1988.

De Wet, Oloff, *A Visit to John Cowper Powys,* Village Press, 1974.

Dictionary of Literary Biography, Volume 15: *British Novelists, 1930-1959,* Gale, 1983.

Hooker, Jeremy, *John Cowper Powys,* University of Wales Press, 1973.

Hopkins, Kenneth, *Powys Brothers: A Biographical Appreciation,* Fairleigh Dickinson University Press, 1967.

Humtrey, Belinda, *Essays on John Cowper Powys,* University of Wales Press, 1972.

Knight, George Wilson, *Saturnian Quest,* Harvester Press, 1978.

Miller, Henry, *Immortal Bard,* Village Press, 1973.

Powys, John Cowper, *Autobiography,* Simon & Schuster, 1934, reprinted, New Directions, 1960, revised edition, Colgate University Press, 1968.

Powys, *Confessions of Two Brothers,* Manas Press, 1916, reprinted, Scholarly Press, 1971.

Van Doren, Mark, *The Private Reader: Selected Articles and Reviews,* Holt, 1942.

PERIODICALS

Books and Bookmen, February, 1974, February, 1977, March, 1977.

Chicago Tribune, December 21, 1987.

Choice, June, 1975.

London Magazine, February/March, 1973.

Modern Fiction Studies, summer, 1976.

Times Literary Supplement, March 24, 1972, February 8, 1974, May 16, 1975.

*   *   *

PREVERT, Jacques (Henri Marie) 1900-1977

PERSONAL: Born February 4, 1900, in Neuilly-sur-Seine, France; died April 11, 1977, in Omonville-La-Petite, France; son of Andre (a clerk) and Suzanne (Catusse) Prevert; married Simone Dienne, April 30, 1925 (marriage ended); married Janine Tricotet, March 4, 1947. *Education:* Educated in Paris, France.

ADDRESSES: Home—Cite Veron, 82 Blvd. de Clichy, 75018 Paris, France.

CAREER: Poet, screenwriter, and dramatist. Exhibitions of his collages held in Paris, 1957 and 1982, and in Antibes, 1963. Appeared as an actor in several of his films.

AWARDS, HONORS: Grand Prix from Societe des Auteurs et Compositeurs Dramatiques, 1973; Grand Prix National from *Cinema,* 1975.

WRITINGS:

IN ENGLISH TRANSLATION

Paroles (poetry; title means "Words"), Editions du Point du Jour, 1945, revised and augmented edition, Gallimard, 1966, translation by Lawrence Ferlinghetti published as *Selections from 'Paroles,'* City Lights, 1958.

(With Albert Lamorisse) *Bim, le petit ane* (juvenile), Guilde du Livre, 1951, translation by Bette Swados and Harvey Swados published as *Bim, the Little Donkey,* Doubleday, 1973.

(Author of introduction) *Couleur de Paris,* illustrated with photographs by Peter Cornelius, La Bibliotheque des Arts, 1961, translation by Jonathan Griffin and Margaret Shenfield published as *Paris in Colour,* Thames & Hudson, 1962, Bramhall House, 1963.

(Author of preface) *Les Halles: L'Album du coeur de Paris,* illustrations by Romain Urhausen, Editions des Deux-Mondes, 1963, translation published as *Les Halles: The Stomach of Paris,* Atlantis Books, 1964, published as *Les Halles de Paris* (French, German, and English text), Moos, 1980.

Prevert II (anthology), translation by Teo Savory, Unicorn Press, 1967.

Les Enfants du paradis (screenplay), Lorrimer Publishing, 1968, translation by Dinah Brooke published as *Children of Paradise,* Simon & Schuster, 1968.

Le Jour se leve (screenplay), translation by Brooke and Nicola Hayden, Simon & Schuster, 1970.

To Paint the Portrait of a Bird—Pour faire le portrait d'un oiseau (juvenile; bilingual French/English text), translation by Ferlinghetti, Doubleday, 1971.

Words for All Seasons: Selected Poems, translation by Teo Savory, 1979.

Blood and Feathers: Selected Poems of Jacques Prevert, translation by Harriet Zinnes, Schoken, 1987.

POETRY

(With Andre Verdet) *Histoires* (title means "Stories"), Editions du Pre aux Clercs, 1946, reprinted, Gallimard, 1974.

Grand Bal du printemps (title means "Grand Ball of Spring"; also see below), illustrated with photographs by Izis Bidermanas, Guilde du Livre, 1951.

Charmes de Londres (title means "The Charms of London"; also see below), illustrated with photographs by Bidermanas, Guilde du Livre, 1952.

Lumieres d'homme (title means "Lights of Man"), Guy Levis Mano, 1955.

La Pluie et le beau temps (title means "Rain and Fine Weather"; also see below), Gallimard, 1955.

(With Joseph L. Artigas) *Miro,* Maeght, 1956.

(Contributor) Henry Decanaud, *La Pierre dans le souffle* (title means "The Stone in the Wind"), Seghers, 1959.

Poemes, edited by J. H. Douglas and D. J. Girard, Harrap, 1961.

Histoires et d'autres histoires (title means "Stories and Other Stories"), Gallimard, 1963.

Varengeville, illustrations by Georges Braque, Maeght, 1968.

Poesies (includes *Spectacle* [also see below] and *La Pluie et le beau temps*), Newton Compton, 1971.

Choses et autres (title means "Things and Others"), Gallimard, 1972.

Grand Bal du printemps [suivi de] *Charmes de Londres,* Gallimard, 1976.

Anthologie Prevert (anthology with French text), edited with English introduction and notes by Christiane Mortelier, Methuen Educational, 1981.

SCREENPLAYS

(With Paul Grimault) *La Bergere et le remoneur* (title means "The Shepherdess and the Chimneysweep"), Les Gemeaux, 1947.

Les Amants de Verone, Nouvelle Edition, 1949.

Guy Jacob, Andre Heinrich, and Bernard Chardere, editors, *Jacques Prevert* (anthology), Imprimerie du Bugey, 1960.

"Les Visiteurs du soir," published in *Deux Films francais: Les Visiteurs du soir* [and] *Le Feu follet,* edited by Robert M. Hammond and Marguerite Hammond, Harcourt, 1965.

Drole le drame (also see below), Balland, 1974.

Jenny; Le Quai des brumes: Scenarios, preface by Marcel Carne, Gallimard, 1988.

La Fleur de l'age; Drole de drame: Scenarios, Gallimard, 1988.

Also author of other screenplays, including "L'Affaire est dans le sac," 1932, "Ciboulette," 1933, "L'Hotel du Libre-Echange," 1934, "Un Oiseau rare," 1935, "Le Crime de Monsieur Lange," 1936, "Ernest le Revelle," 1938, "Le Soleil a toujours raison," 1941, "Les Visiteurs du soir," 1942, "Lumiere d'ete," 1943, "Sortileges," 1945, "Les Portes de la nuit," 1946, "Notre Dame de Paris," 1953, and "Les Amours celebres," 1961.

OTHER

Contes pour les enfants pas sages (juvenile; title means "Stories for Naughty Children"), Editions du Pre aux Clercs, 1947, reprinted, Gallimard, 1984.

(With Camilla Koffler) *Le Petit Lion* (title means "The Little Lion"), illustrated with photographs by Ylla, Arts et Metiers Graphiques, 1947.

(Contributor) Joseph Kosman, *Le Rendezvous: Ballet en trois tableaux* (piano scores), Enoch, 1948.

(With Verdet) *C'est a Saint Paul de Vence,* Nouvelle Edition, 1949.

Spectacle (poems, plays, and prose), Gallimard, 1949, reprinted, 1972.

Des betes (title means "Animals"), illustrated with photographs by Ylla, Gallimard, 1950.

Guignol (title means "Puppet Show"), illustrations by Elsa Henriquez, Guilde du Livre, 1952.

Lettres des Iles Baladar (title means "Letter from the Baladar Islands"), Gallimard, 1952.

L'Opera de la lune (title means "Moon Opera"), lyrics by Christiane Verger, Guilde du Livre, 1953, reprinted, Editions G. P., 1974.

(With Georges Ribemont-Dessaignes) *Joan Miro,* Maeght, 1956.

(With Ribemont-Dessaignes) *Arbres* (title means "Trees"), Gallimard, 1956, 2nd edition, 1976.

Images (title means "Pictures"), Maeght, 1957.

Dix-sept Chansons de Jacques Prevert (title means "Seventeen Songs by Jacques Prevert"), music by Joseph Kosma, Folkuniversitetets Foerlag, 1958.

Portraits de Picasso (title means "Portraits of Picasso"), illustrated with photography by Andre Villers, Muggiani, 1959, reprinted, Ramsay, 1981.

(Contributor) Ylipe, *Magloire de Paris,* Losfeld, 1961.

(With Max Ernst) *Les Chiens ont soif* (title means "The Dogs Are Thirsty"), Pont des Arts, 1964.

Jacques Prevert presente "Le Circle d'Izis" (title means "Jacques Prevert Presents 'The Circle of Izis' "), illustrated with photographs by Bidermanas, A. Sauret, 1965.

(With Helmut Grieshaber) *Carl Orff: Carmina burana,* Manus Presse, 1965.

Georges, illustrations by Ribemont-Dessaignes, Cagnes, 1965.

(Contributor) Alexander Calder, *Calder,* Maeght, 1966.

Fatras, illustrations by the author, Livre de Poche, 1966.

Prevert vous parle (title means "Prevert Speaks to You"), Prentice-Hall, 1968.

(Contributor) Cesare Vivaldi, *Mayo,* Instituto Editoriale Italiano, 1968.

Imaginaires (title means "Make-Believe"), A. Skira, 1970.

(With Andre Pozner) *Hebdomadaires* (interview; title means "Weeklies"), G. Authier, 1972.

(With Rene Bartele) *Images de Jacques Prevert* (title means "Pictures by Jacques Prevert"), Filipacchi, 1974.

Le Jour des temps, illustrations by Max Papart, Galerie Bosquet and Jacques Goutal Darly, 1975.

A travers Prevert (title means "Through Prevert"), Gallimard, 1975.

Soleil de nuit, Gallimard, 1980.

Pages d'ecriture (juvenile), Gallimard, 1980.

Couleurs de Braque, Calder, Miro, Maeght, 1981.

(Illustrator) Andre Pozner, *Jacques Prevert: Collages,* Gallimard, 1982.

La Cinquieme Saison, Gallimard, 1984.

Chanson des cireurs de souliers, illustrations by Marie Gard, Gallimard, 1985.

Chanson pour chanter a tue-tete et a cloche-pied, illustrations by Gard, Gallimard, 1985.

Also author of *Le Cheval de Troie,* 1946, *L'Ange garde-chiourme,* 1946, and *Vignette pour les vignerons,* 1951. Author of farces, pantomimes, ballets, and skits, including "Baptiste" (mime play) and "La Famille tuyau de poele" (title means "Top-hat Family"), 1935, and of lyrics for numerous popular songs, including "Les Feuilles mortes" (title means "Autumn Leaves"), set to music by Joseph Kosma. Work represented in numerous anthologies, including *Let's Get a Divorce,* edited by E. R. Bentley, Hill & Wang, 1958, and *Selections from French Poetry,* edited by K. F. Canfield, Harvey House, 1965. Contributor to *Coronet, Kenyon Review, Poetry,* and other periodicals.

SIDELIGHTS: On Jacques Prevert's death in 1977, Marcel Carne, the producer with whom Prevert collaborated on several major films, told the *New York Times* that Prevert was "the one and only poet of the French cinema. He created a style, original and personal, reflecting the soul of the people. His humor and poetry succeeded in raising the banal to the summit of art." Between 1937 and 1950 Prevert collaborated with Carne on eight major films and became one of France's most important screenwriters.

Prevert was a poet as well as a screenwriter, so the comparison Carne made between Prevert's cinematic work and poetry was not surprising. Prevert's general appeal as a poet was such that *New Republic* contributor Eve Merriman called the Frenchman "France's most popular poet of the 20th century." He began writing poetry in the early 1930s but did not see his first volume of poetry, *Paroles,* published until 1946. The book was a best-seller, selling hundreds of thousands of copies. In his biography *Jacques Prevert* William E. Baker noted that the titles of several of Prevert's early books of poetry—including *Paroles,* which means "Words"—"in a very general way" described the poet's stylistic tendencies: "*Paroles* because the poet has a genius for making all sorts of ordinary idiom highly expressive, *Spectacle* because his verbal tricks often correspond to the antics of a clown or a magician, and *La Pluie et le beau temps* [which means 'Rain and Fine Weather'] because the emotional tones of his symbols can have the classic simplicity of the summer-and-winter, sunshine-and-rain cycle of life and love."

BIOGRAPHICAL/CRITICAL SOURCES:

BOOKS

Baker, William E., *Jacques Prevert*, Twayne, 1967.
Contemporary Literary Criticism, Gale, Volume 15, 1980.

PERIODICALS

Modern Language Journal, October, 1949.
Times Literary Supplement, January 19, 1973.
Wisconsin Studies in Contemporary Literature, summer, 1966.

OBITUARIES:

PERIODICALS

AB Bookman's Weekly, June 20, 1977.
New Republic, July 9 & 16, 1977.
New York Times, April 12, 1977.

*   *   *

PRICHARD, Katharine Susannah 1883-1969

PERSONAL: Born 1883, in Levuka, Fiji; died October 2, 1969; daughter of Tom Henry (editor of *Fiji Times*) and Edith Isabel (Fraser) Prichard; married Hugo Throssell (an Army captain), 1919; children: Ric Prichard. *Education:* Educated in Australian schools.

ADDRESSES: Home—Greenmount, West Australia.

CAREER: Grew up in Australia, except for one period in Tasmania, and had first short stories published at eleven; later journalist for newspapers in Melbourne and Sydney and other Australian publications, and free-lance journalist in London, England, 1908 and 1912-16; fiction writer in Australia, 1916-1969.

AWARDS, HONORS: Hodder & Stoughton prize of one thousand pounds, 1924, for *The Pioneers; Art in Australia* prize, 1924, for short story, "The Grey Horse"; *Triad* award for a three-act Australian play, 1927, for *Brumby Innes; Bulletin* (Sydney) prize of five hundred pounds, 1928, for *Coonardoo.*

WRITINGS:

The Pioneers, Hodder & Stoughton, 1915, revised edition, Angus & Robertson, 1963.
Windlestraws, Holden & Hardingham, 1917.
The Black Opal, Heinemann, 1921.
Working Bullocks, Viking, 1927.
The Wild Oats of Han (juvenile), Angus & Robertson, 1928, revised edition, Lansdowne Press, 1968.
Coonardoo, the Well in the Shadow, J. Cape, 1929, Norton, 1930.
Haxby's Circus: The Lightest, Brightest Little Show on Earth, J. Cape, 1930, published as *Fay's Circus*, Norton, 1931.
Earth Lover (poems), Sunnybrook Press, 1930.
Kiss on the Lips, and Other Stories, J. Cape, 1932.
The Real Russia, Modern Publishers, 1934.
(With others) *Best Australian One-Act Plays*, edited by William Moore and T. I. Moore, Angus & Robertson, 1937.
Intimate Strangers, J. Cape, 1937.
Brumby Innes (three-act play), Paterson's Printing Press, 1940.
Moon of Desire, J. Cape, 1941.
(Editor with others) *Australian New Writing 1943-1945*, Current Books, 1943-1945.
Potch and Colour (short stories), Angus & Robertson, 1944.
The Roaring Nineties: A Story of the Goldfields of Western Australia, J. Cape, 1946.
Golden Miles, J. Cape, 1948.
Winged Seeds, J. Cape, 1950.
N'goola, and Other Stories, Australasian Book Society, 1959.

Child of the Hurricane (autobiography), Angus & Robertson, 1963.
On Strenuous Wings, edited by Joan Williams, Seven Seas Publishers, 1965.
Happiness: Selected Short Stories, Angus & Robertson, 1967.
Subtle Flame, Australasian Book Society, 1967.
Moggie and Her Circus Pony, F. W. Cheshire, 1967.

Also author of collection of short stories entitled *The Grey Horse*, 1924, and of play entitled "Bid Me To Love," 1974. Work anthologized in *The World's Greatest Short Stories*, Crown.

MEDIA ADAPTATIONS: The Pioneers was made into a motion picture in 1926.

SIDELIGHTS: Katharine Susannah Prichard's books have been translated into twelve languages, including Russian, Latvian, Hungarian, Slovak, Afrikaans, Armenian, and Chinese.

BIOGRAPHICAL/CRITICAL SOURCES:

BOOKS

Contemporary Literary Criticism, Volume 46, Gale, 1988.

*   *   *

PRIESTLEY, J(ohn) B(oynton) 1894-1984
(Peter Goldsmith)

PERSONAL: Born September 13, 1894, in Bradford, Yorkshire, England; died after a brief illness August 14, 1984, in Stratford-upon-Avon, England; son of Jonathan (a schoolmaster) Priestley; married Patricia Tempest (died, 1925); married Mary Holland Wyndham Lewis (marriage dissolved, 1952); married Jacquetta Hawkes (an archaeologist and writer); children: (first marriage) two daughters; (second marriage) two daughters, one son (Tom). *Education:* Trinity Hall, Cambridge, M.A. *Politics:* Leftist.

ADDRESSES: Home—Kissing Tree House, Alveston, Stratford-upon-Avon, England. *Agent*—A. D. Peters, 10 Buckingham St., Adelphi, London W.C.2, England.

CAREER: Novelist, playwright, essayist, and journalist. Began writing for newspapers in England at the age of sixteen; critic, reviewer, and essayist for various periodicals in London, beginning 1922; director of Mask Theatre, 1938-39. Lecturer on a U.S. tour in 1937; spent several winters in Arizona. Advisor on film scripts in Hollywood and England, and, during World War II, broadcast "Postscripts," a series of BBC radio talks. Appeared in semi-documentary "Battle for Music," a 1943 Strand/Anglo American film. United Kingdom delegate to two UNESCO conferences, 1946-47; one of originators of Campaign for Nuclear Disarmament (CND). Chairman of International Theatre Conferences at Paris, 1947, and Prague, 1948, British Theatre Conference, 1948, and International Theatre Institute, 1949. Member of National Theatre Board, 1966-67; former chairman of council on London Philharmonic Orchestra, and a director of *New Statesman* and *Nation. Military service:* British Army, Infantry, 1914-19; became commissioned officer; wounded three times.

MEMBER: Screenwriters' Association (London; president, 1944-45), Savile Club (London).

AWARDS, HONORS: James Tait Black prize for fiction, 1930, for *The Good Companions;* Ellen Terry Award for best play of 1947, for "The Linden Tree"; British Order of Merit, 1977; LL.D., St. Andrews University; D.Litt., Universities of Colorado, Birmingham, and Bradford.

WRITINGS:

FICTION

Adam in Moonshine, Harper, 1927.

Benighted, Heinemann, 1927, published as *The Old Dark House,* Harper, 1928.

The Good Companions (also see below), Harper, 1929.

(With Hugh Walpole) *Farthing Hall* (humorous romance), Macmillan, 1929.

Angel Pavement, Harper, 1930, reissued with foreword by Sinclair Lewis, Readers Club Press, 1942.

The Town Major of Miraucourt, Heinemann, 1930.

Faraway, Harper, 1932.

Albert Goes Through, Harper, 1933.

(With Gerald W. Bullett) *I'll Tell You Everything,* Macmillan, 1933.

Wonder Hero, Harper, 1933.

They Walk in the City [and] *The Lovers in the Stone Forest,* Harper, 1936.

The Doomsday Men: An Adventure, Harper, 1938.

Let the People Sing, Heinemann, 1939, Harper, 1940.

Black-Out in Gretley: A Story of and for Wartime, Harper, 1942.

Daylight on Saturday, Harper, 1943 (published in England as *Daylight on Saturday: A Novel About an Aircraft Factory,* Heinemann, 1943).

Three Men in New Suits, Harper, 1945.

Bright Day, Harper, 1946, reissued with new introduction by Priestley, Dutton, 1966.

Jenny Villiers: A Story of the Theatre, Harper, 1947.

Going Up; and Other Stories and Sketches, Pan Books, 1950.

Festival, Harper, 1951 (published in England as *Festival at Farbridge,* Heinemann, 1951).

The Other Place, and Other Stories of the Same Sort, Harper, 1953.

Low Notes on a High Level, Harper, 1954 (published in England as *Low Notes on a High Level: A Frolic,* Heinemann, 1954).

The Magicians, Harper, 1954.

Saturn over the Water: An Account of His Adventures in London, New York, South America, and Australia by Tim Bedford, Painter; Edited with Some Preliminary and Concluding Remarks by Henry Sulgrave; and Here Presented to the Reading Public, Doubleday, 1961.

The Thirty-First of June: A Tale of True Love, Enterprise, and Progress, in the Arthurian and Ad-Atomic Ages, Heinemann, 1961, Doubleday, 1962.

The Shapes of Sleep: A Topical Tale, Doubleday, 1962.

Sir Michael and Sir George: A Tale of COSMA and DISCUS and the New Elizabethans, Heinemann, 1964, published as *Sir Michael and Sir George: A Comedy of the New Elizabethans,* Little, Brown, 1966.

It's an Old Country, Little, Brown, 1967.

The Image Men, Volume 1: *Out of Town,* Volume 2: *London End,* Heinemann, 1968, published as single-volume edition, Little, Brown, 1969, volumes published separately, Penguin, 1969.

The Carfitt Crisis, and Two Other Stories, Heinemann, 1975.

PLAYS

Dangerous Corner (three-act; first produced on the West End, 1932; produced in New York, 1932), Heinemann, 1932, Samuel French, 1932.

The Roundabout (three-act comedy; first produced in 1933), Samuel French, 1933.

Eden End (three-act; first produced on the West End, 1934; produced Off-Broadway, 1935), Heinemann, 1934, Samuel French, 1935.

Laburnum Grove (three-act "immoral comedy"; first produced on the West End, 1933; produced on Broadway, 1935), Heinemann, 1934, Samuel French, 1935.

Cornelius ("a business affair in three transactions"; first produced on the West End, 1935), Heinemann, 1935, Samuel French, 1936.

Duet in Floodlight (comedy; first produced on the West End under Priestley's direction, 1935), Heinemann, 1935.

(With Edward Knoblock) *The Good Companions* (two-act; based on Priestley's novel of the same title; first produced on the West End, 1931; produced in New York, 1931), Samuel French, 1935.

Bees on the Boat Deck (two-act farcical tragedy; first produced on the West End, 1936), Heinemann, 1936.

(Under pseudonym Peter Goldsmith, with George Billam) *Spring Tide* (three-act; first produced on the West End, 1936), Heinemann, 1936.

I Have Been Here Before (three-act; first produced in London, 1937; produced in New York, 1938), Heinemann, 1937, Harper, 1938.

Mystery at Greenfingers ("comedy of detection"; first produced in 1938), Samuel French, 1937.

People at Sea (three-act; first produced on the West End, 1936), Heinemann, 1937, Samuel French, 1938.

Time and the Conways (three-act; first produced on the West End, 1937; produced in New York, 1938), Heinemann, 1937, Harper, 1938.

When We Are Married (three-act Yorkshire farcical comedy; first produced on the West End, 1938; produced on Broadway, 1939), Heinemann, 1938, Samuel French, 1940.

Johnson Over Jordan [and] *All About It* (the former a three-act morality play, first produced on the West End, 1939; the latter an essay), Harper, 1939, play published separately by Samuel French, 1941.

Desert Highway (two-act, with an interlude; first produced on Broadway, 1944), Samuel French, 1944.

They Came to a City (two-act; first produced on the West End, 1943), Samuel French, 1944.

How Are They at Home? (two-act topical comedy; first produced on the West End, 1944), Samuel French, 1945.

"Good-Night Children" (comedy; first produced on the West End, 1942), published in *Three Comedies,* Heinemann, 1945.

An Inspector Calls (three-act; first produced on the West End, 1946; produced on Broadway, 1947), Heinemann, 1947, Dramatists Play Service, 1948, abridged edition, Macmillan, 1966.

The Long Mirror (three-act; first produced in Edinburgh, 1945), Samuel French, 1947.

Music at Night (three-act; first produced on the West End, 1939), Samuel French, 1947.

The Rose and the Crown (one-act; first produced in 1947), Samuel French, 1947.

The Golden Fleece (three-act comedy; first produced in 1948), Samuel French, 1948.

(With Doris Zinkeisen) *The High Toby* (play for "toy theatre"; first produced in 1948), Penguin, 1948.

The Linden Tree (two-act; first produced on the West End, 1947; produced on Broadway, 1948), Samuel French, 1948.

Ever Since Paradise (three-act; first produced in London, 1947), Samuel French, 1949.

Home is Tomorrow (two-act; first produced on the West End, 1948), Heinemann, 1949, Samuel French, 1950.

(Author of libretto) *The Olympians* (three-act opera; score by Arthur Bliss; first produced in London at Covent Garden Theatre, 1949), Novello, 1949.

Bright Shadow (three-act "play of detection"; first produced in Palmer's Green, 1950), Samuel French, 1950.

Summer Day's Dream (two-act; first produced on the West End, 1949), Samuel French, 1950.

(With wife, Jacquetta Hawkes) *Dragon's Mouth* (dramatic quartet in two parts; first produced in London, 1952; produced Off-Broadway, 1955), Harper, 1952.

Mother's Day (one-act comedy; first produced in 1953), Samuel French, 1953.

Private Rooms (one-act comedy "in the Viennese style"; first produced in 1953), Samuel French, 1953.

Treasure on Pelican (three-act; first produced in London, 1952), Evans Brothers, 1953.

Try It Again (one-act), Samuel French, 1953.

A Glass of Bitter (one-act; first produced in 1954), Samuel French, 1954.

(With Hawkes) "The White Countess," first produced on the West End, 1954.

The Scandalous Affair of Mr. Kettle and Mrs. Moon (three-act comedy; first produced on the West End, 1955), Samuel French, 1956.

The Glass Cage (two-act; written for Crest Theatre, Toronto; first produced on the West End, 1957), Kingswood House (Toronto), 1957, Samuel French, 1958.

(With Iris Murdoch) *A Severed Head* (three-act; adapted from the novel by Murdoch; first produced on the West End, 1963), Samuel French, 1964.

Also author of "The Golden Entry," produced in 1955, "These Our Actors" and "Take the Fool Away," both produced in 1956, and "The Pavilion of Masks," first produced in 1963. Plays published in omnibus volumes and in anthologies.

ESSAYS

Papers from Lilliput, Bowes, 1922.

I for One, John Lane, 1923, Books for Libraries Press, 1967.

Talking, Harper, 1926.

J. B. Priestley (selected essays), Harrap, 1926.

Open House, Harper, 1927.

Apes and Angels, Methuen, 1928.

Selected Essays, edited by G. A. Sheldon, A. & C. Black, 1928.

The Balconinny, and Other Essays, Methuen, 1929, published as *The Balconinny,* Harper, 1930.

Self-Selected Essays, Harper, 1932.

The Secret Dream: An Essay on Britain, America and Russia (based on radio broadcasts, 1946), Turnstile Press, 1946.

Delight, Harper, 1949.

All About Ourselves, and Other Essays, selected and introduced by Eric Gillett, Heinemann, 1956.

Thoughts in the Wilderness, Harper, 1957.

Essays of Five Decades, selected, with a preface, by Susan Cooper, Little, Brown, 1968.

Outcries and Asides, Heinemann, 1974.

The Happy Dream, Whittington Press, 1976.

EDITOR

(And author of introduction) Thomas Moore, *Tom Moore's Diary* (selections), Cambridge University Press, 1925, Scholarly Press, 1971.

(And author of introduction and notes) *Essayists Past and Present: A Selection of English Essays,* Dial, 1925.

(And compiler) *The Book of Bodley Head Verse,* Dodd, 1926.

These Diversions (essay series), six volumes, Jarrolds, 1926-28.

Our Nation's Heritage (country anthology), Dent, 1939.

(And compiler and author of introduction) Charles Dickens, *Scenes of London Life from "Sketches by Boz"* (selections), Pan Books, 1947.

(And author of introduction) *Best of Leacock,* McClelland & Stewart, 1957 (published in England as *The Bodley Head Leacock,* Bodley Head, 1957).

(With O. B. Davis) *Four English Novels* (includes *Pride and Prejudice,* by Jane Austen, *The Pickwick Papers,* by Charles Dickens, *Return of the Native,* by Thomas Hardy, and *The Secret Sharer,* by Joseph Conrad), Harcourt, 1960.

(With Davis) *Four English Biographies* (includes *Shakespeare of London,* by Marchette Chute, *The Life of Samuel Johnson,* by James Boswell, *Queen Victoria,* by Lytton Strachey, and *The Edge of Day: Boyhood in the West of England,* by Laurie Lee), Harcourt, 1961.

(With Josephine Spear) *Adventures in English Literature,* Laureate edition, Harcourt, 1963.

OTHER

The Chapman of Rhymes (poems), Alexander Moring (London), 1918.

Brief Diversions (tales, travesties and epigrams), Bowes, 1922.

Figures in Modern Literature, Dodd, 1924.

The English Comic Characters, Dodd, 1925, new edition, Bodley Head, 1963, Dufour, 1964.

Fools and Philosophers: A Gallery of Comic Figures from English Literature, John Lane, 1925.

George Meredith, Macmillan, 1926.

Thomas Love Peacock, Macmillan, 1927, new edition, St. Martin's, 1966.

The English Novel, Benn, 1927, new revised and illustrated edition, Thomas Nelson, 1935.

Too Many People, and Other Reflections, Harper, 1928.

English Humour, Longmans, Green, 1929.

The Works of J. B. Priestley, Heinemann, 1931.

English Journey: Being a Rambling but Truthful Account of What One Man Saw and Heard and Felt and Thought During a Journey through England during the Autumn of the Year 1933, Harper, 1934.

Midnight on the Desert: Being an Excursion into Autobiography during a Winter in America, 1935-36, Harper, 1937 (published in England as *Midnight on the Desert: A Chapter of Autobiography,* Heinemann, 1937).

(With others) *First "Mercury" Story Book,* Longmans, Green, 1939.

Rain upon Godshill: A Further Chapter of Autobiography, Harper, 1939.

(Co-author) "Jamaica Inn" (screenplay; based on the novel by Daphne du Maurier), Mayflower/Paramount, 1939.

Britain Speaks (based on a series of radio talks to America, May 5 to September 24, 1940), Harper, 1940.

Postscripts (originally radio broadcasts), Heinemann, 1940, published as *All England Listened: The Wartime Broadcasts of J. B. Priestley,* introduction by Eric Sevareid, Chilmark, 1967.

Out of the People, Harper, 1941.

Britain at War, Harper, 1942.

(With Philip Gibbs and others) *The English Spirit,* edited and introduced by Anthony Weymouth, Allen & Unwin, 1942.

British Women Go to War, photographs by P. G. Hennell, Collins, 1943.

Russian Journey, Writers Group of the Society for Cultural Relations with the U.S.S.R., 1946.

Theatre Outlook, Nicholson & Watson, 1947.

(And co-producer) "Last Holiday" (screenplay), Associated British Picture Corp., 1950.

The Priestley Companion (selections), introduction by Ivor Brown, Penguin, 1951.

(With Hawkes) *Journey down a Rainbow* (travel sketches), Harper, 1955.

The Art of the Dramatist (lecture with appendices and discursive notes), Heinemann (Melbourne), 1957.

Topside; or, The Future of England (dialogue), Heinemann, 1958.

The Wonderful World of the Theatre, edited by David Lambert, designed by Germano Facetti, Garden City Books, 1959 (published in England as *The Story of the Theatre,* Rathbone, 1959), revised and enlarged edition, Doubleday, 1969.

Literature and Western Man: Criticism and Comment of Five Centuries of Western Literature, Harper, 1960.

William Hazlitt, Longmans, Green, for the British Book Council and the National Book League, 1960.

Charles Dickens: A Pictorial Biography, Thames & Hudson, 1961, Viking, 1962, published as *Charles Dickens and His World,* 1969.

Margin Released: A Writer's Reminiscences and Reflections, Harper, 1962.

Man and Time, Doubleday, 1964.

Lost Empires: Being Richard Herncastle's Account of His Life on the Variety Stage from November 1913 to August 1914, Together with a Prologue and Epilogue, Heinemann, 1965.

The Moments, and Other Pieces, Heinemann, 1966.

Salt is Leaving, Pan Books, 1966.

The World of J. B. Priestley, selected and introduced by Donald G. MacRae, Heinemann, 1967.

Trumpets Over the Sea: Being a Rambling and Egotistical Account of the London Symphony Orchestra's Engagement at Daytona Beach, Florida, in July-August, 1967, Heinemann, 1968.

The Prince of Pleasure and His Regency, 1811-20, Harper, 1969.

Anton Chekhov, A. S. Barnes, 1970.

The Edwardians, Harper, 1970.

Snoggle (juvenile fiction), Harcourt, 1972.

Victoria's Heyday, Harper, 1972.

Over the Long High Wall: Some Reflections and Speculations on Life, Death and Time, Heinemann, 1972.

The English, Heinemann, 1973.

A Visit to New Zealand, Heinemann, 1974.

Particular Pleasures: Being a Personal Record of Some Varied Arts and MAny Different Artists, Heinemann, 1975.

Found, Lost, Found, or, The English Way of Life, Heinemann, 1976.

Instead of the Trees (autobiography), Heinemann, 1977.

J. B. Priestley's Yorkshire, edited by William Reginald Mitchell, Dalesman, 1987.

Works also appear in omnibus volumes and collections. Also author of several screenplays, including "The Foreman Went to France," "Britain at Bay," and "Priestley's Postscripts." Author of television series, "You Know What People Are," of the program, "Lost City," in which he appeared, and of a television play "Anyone for Tennis?," produced by BBC-TV in 1968. Author of numerous booklets, and of introductory notes to numerous books. Contributor of essays, articles, sketches, reviews, and short stories to numerous periodicals and newspapers.

SIDELIGHTS: "At 72," a critic noted in a 1967 *Time* review of *It's an Old Country,* "J. B. Priestley is a British institution: a word-factory who has turned out 29 volumes of assorted nonfiction and 24 novels. Yet each successive effort manages to offer a number of odd little surprises. The first in this novel is that a man of Priestley's age should be at all interested in examining Swinging Britain; the second is that his study makes such jolly good entertainment." Entertainment and humor were Priestley's forte; called "Jolly Jack" by a number of British critics, he was frequently compared to Charles Dickens (although Priestley disliked the comparison) because of the "robust humour" of his style and the hosts of minor characters which crowded his novels. David Williams, John K. Hutchens, and Eric Rhode, among others, commented on Priestley's "Dickensian" streak. "In many respects," Frederick T. Wood asserted, "Mr. Priestley is the Dickens of the modern age. He epitomizes the spirit of the average Englishman of the twentieth century as Dickens did of the nineteenth; his stories, too, have the same air of free, hearty humour, the same spontaneity and inconsequentiality. . . . He writes with an understanding and a sympathy that speaks a depth of experience and a wide contact with humanity."

In spite of his prolific output, Priestley, according to John Gale, described himself as a lazy man. "I'm a professional writer, and I write," he told Gale. "I'm not a freak. Those who think writers shouldn't write are the freaks. One shouldn't start comparing oneself to better men, but think of the amount that Shakespeare wrote, or Dickens, or Tolstoy. Only in this age people don't write." Priestley lamented the lack of attention given fiction in general, and the novel in particular. In a 1967 *New Statesman* article he stated: "[The novel's] place has been taken in the literary pages (such as they are), in the bookshops, the library lists, the literate sector of the public mind, by ghost-written memoirs, biographies, tarted-up history and sodden slabs of sociology. . . . I have no dislike of facts. I rather enjoy them, and have spent many a cheerful hour just pottering about among statistics laid out like new towns. Every conscientious writer, I feel, should occasionally explore the figures and facts. But no genuine creative writer will ever imagine that here will be found the truth about people. . . . It is good fiction, so largely ignored now, that brings us so much closer to the real facts."

Although Priestley's work was immensely popular, he was not generally perceived as a literary giant, an impression some critics have challenged. As Colin Wilson remarked, "[after reading *The Edwardians,*] I found myself wondering again why it is that Priestley is so generally underrated. . . . Intelligence is not a word that critics associate with Priestley; they've got him typed as a pipe-smoking Yorkshireman with a slow, deliberate voice. In fact, the sheer range of his interests means that he can usually say something fresh and penetrating on almost any subject. If he was thirty years younger, he could do as Norman Mailer has done, and make a new reputation as a journalist social-commentator." Once labeled "an old-fashioned English radical" in a newspaper profile, Priestley was a master of the farce and of social satire. He poked fun at modern academia, communications, and what David Williams called "our sales-promotion world" in *The Image Men,* a later novel. Robert Cromie of *Book World* remarked that this volume was "a thing to read and enjoy, a volume to restore your slipping faith in the comic novel, a genre which I, at least, was beginning to fear was on the verge of becoming the literary equivalent of the passenger pigeon." John Braine similarly found the book "a romp, an excursion into jollity, an unashamed piece of escapism. It's the kind of entertainment which I for one relish more and more, and I hope that

Mr. Priestley wasn't serious when he said it would be his last novel."

But *The Image Men* was in fact the author's last novel, and its publication ended an era Priestley started in 1927 with *Adam in Moonshine.* "In 1929," he noted, "I helped to popularize the long novel by publishing *The Good Companions,* which had an enormous success both in England and America, and was followed by the almost equally successful *Angel Pavement.*" The latter, a best-seller when it appeared in the United States in 1930, has been reissued several times, a testimony to the durability and authenticity of Priestley's characterization of the common man. His "very sure skill in the portrayal of dramatic types," as Benjamin Ifor Evans observed, carried the author easily into drama, a career begun in 1932 with the West End production of his first play, *Dangerous Corner.* Since then Priestley has written over fifty plays (for various media), run his own producing company in London, and staged more than thirty plays, many of them his own. Evans wrote that "Priestley's range as a dramatist was unusual. . . . To all [his skills] was added in a number of the plays a rare, imaginative overtone. It was as if amid all the boldly drawn characters and the Yorkshire fun a sensitive and metaphysical mind was operating." The critic added that Priestley showed "a considerable command of the theatre as a technical instrument."

Priestley maintained that his dramatic works were strongly influenced by the time-theories of J. W. Dunne's *Experiment with Time* and *Serial Universe,* an interest evident in his earlier plays, especially *Time and the Conways* and *I Have Been Here Before.* Frederick Lumley, in his survey *New Trends in 20th Century Drama,* expressed the belief that Priestley's pre-war "time" plays were the product of the first of three distinct periods through which he moved as a playwright. The critic elaborated: "The second period belongs to his adherence to the Labour Party and the ardent faith he once had for Socialist utopias and ideals. Finally there is the 'in wilderness' period of disillusionment, when he realised that the City he wrote about was no longer to be reached through party politics, and, viewed from the wilderness, his common sense told him it was no longer practical. After being for so long a man who knew all the answers he has become a man of doubts; he still has his pipe in his mouth but it has gone out." Lumley concluded that "Priestley is a playwright who has attempted to break out of the conventions of the naturalistic drama, tending sometimes towards a modified form of expressionism, at other times breaking up the illusion of the box-realism deliberately, as in *Ever Since Paradise.* He would fly if he could, but he has not the power of poetry to sweep him over and beyond the immediate present. His blunt Yorkshire idiom and common-sense outlook make this alien to his character. Although an idealist, he is most successful when he realises his limitations; an intelligent thinker, he has not a serious mind. But he has a flare for the theatre, is masterly in his technique, generally topical, and a writer to whom good humour comes naturally."

Priestley himself attested to his moderate disposition, noting that "murderous thoughts don't visit me." He agreed with Lumley and Alan Trachtenberg that he "[couldn't] manage any real thinking. . . . If I have written more than most authors, this is not because I have been exceptionally industrious—I am in fact rather lazy—but because I can concentrate quickly on my work. On the other hand, I have never thought constructively. My mind moves in a series of intuitive flashes. Whenever I have sat down to work out a complicated plot, let us say, nothing has happened and I found myself wandering away from the notebook—I buy notebooks but never make proper use of them—to clean some pipes or search for a book. Then an idea jumps into my mind while I am shaving or in the bath."

In addition to the novelist and the dramatist in Priestley, "there is yet another side," as Richard Church said. "He is a master in the art of the essay . . . [and] a sound literary critic. He bases his judgment on his wide reading, as a conscious estimate, and on a native fairness and compassionate common-sense, as an unconscious estimate." "I think of myself as eighteenth century," Priestley explained to Harvey Breit in 1951. "Writers wrote everything then, essays, novels, plays, there was a variety, a professionalism." Dudley Carew of *Time and Tide* concurred with Church that Priestley "used the medium of the essay to write some of the best critical appreciations that have appeared in this century." To those who are familiar with Priestley the essayist, Carew maintained, "it is . . . his likeness, the impression that he himself, through his essays, has given us, which springs to the mind whenever his name or his work is mentioned. That is the broad figure with the pipe and the survival of the Bruddersford accent, inconspicuously dressed. . . . One who speaks his own mind and who, like the bluff, representative Englishman this all so misleadingly seems to add up to, enjoys a good grumble."

In a review of *Essays of Five Decades,* a selection covering the author's entire writing career, Trachtenberg likewise commented on the duality of Priestley's nature as expressed in his essays, in which "the inner life . . . [protests] against the drabness and conformity of increasingly organized modern life, including the beneficent bureaucracies of socialism. These simultaneous wishes, for social order and for personal anarchy, are the coordinates of Priestley's world, and their interplay might very well lay him down as a sentimentalist (a frequent accusation), or a bit of an old-fashioned grouch." As a result, David McCord found, the collection is "a comfortable book, a book to be at home in. There is a sense of Old Stability stalking through it." "It was an excellent notion to publish a selection of Mr. Priestley's essays covering the whole of his writing life," Malcolm Muggeridge concluded. "This is not just because he is a highly accomplished essayist—I should say about the most accomplished of our time—but also because the selection provides a sort of conspectus of him and his work."

MEDIA ADAPTATIONS: Several of Priestley's works have been made into motion pictures, including: *Benighted,* which was produced as "The Old Dark House" by Universal in 1932 and Columbia in 1963; *The Good Companions,* filmed as a musical in 1933 by Fox and in 1957 by Associated British-Pathe; "Sing As We Go," filmed by Associated Talking Pictures/Associated British Films in 1934; *Dangerous Corner,* a 1935 Radio Pictures film; "Look Up and Laugh," produced by Associated Talking Pictures/Associated British Films in 1935; "Laburnum Grove," filmed by Associated Talking Pictures/Associated British Films in 1936; *Let the People Sing,* produced by British National/Anglo American in 1942; "Somewhere in France," a 1943 United Artists production; "When We Are Married," produced by British National/Anglo American in 1943; "They Came to a City," filmed by Ealing in 1944; *An Inspector Calls,* a 1954 Associated Artists production; and *The Severed Head,* adapted by Iris Murdoch and filmed in 1970 by Winkast, and adapted by Frederic Raphael and produced for Columbia in 1971 by Alan Ladd, Jr.

A Theatre Guild radio production of *Laburnum Grove* was broadcast in 1948, and a television adaptation by Edward Mabley was produced on CBS in 1949; *Counterfeit,* adapted for television by Ellen Violett, was produced on CBS for U.S. Steel Hour on August 31, 1955. *The Good Companions* was also made into a stage musical with music by Andre Previn and lyrics by Johnny Mercer; in 1972 Leslie Sands produced and narrated an anthology of Priestley's dramatic works, entitled "J. B. Priestley's Open House," on the West End. Shortly after Priestley's death in 1984, his son Tom produced a Central-TV special, "Time and the Priestleys," incorporating interviews with and autobiographies of the author.

AVOCATIONAL INTERESTS: Painting, listening to music.

BIOGRAPHICAL/CRITICAL SOURCES:

BOOKS

Baker, Denys Val, editor, *Writers of Today,* Sidgwick & Jackson, 1946.
Breit, Harvey, *The Writer Observed,* World Publishing, 1956.
Contemporary Literary Criticism, Gale, Volume 2, 1974, Volume 5, 1976, Volume 9, 1978, Volume 34, 1985.
Cooper, Susan, *J. B. Priestley: Portrait of an Author,* Harper, 1971.
Dictionary of Literary Biography, Gale, Volume 10: *Modern British Dramatists, 1900-1945,* 1982, Volume 34: *British Novelists, 1890-1929: Traditionalists,* 1985, Volume 77: *British Mystery Writers, 1920-1939,* 1989.
Dictionary of Literary Biography Yearbook: 1984, Gale, 1985.
Evans, Benjamin Ifor, *English Literature between the Wars,* 2nd edition, Methuen, 1949.
Evans, Gareth Lloyd, *J. B. Priestley: The Dramatist,* Heinemann, 1964.
Hughes, David, *J. B. Priestley: An Informal Study of His Work,* Hart-Davis, 1958.
J. B. Priestley: An Exhibition of Manuscripts and Books, Humanities Research Center, University of Texas, 1962.
Lumley, Frederick, *New Trends in 20th Century Drama,* Oxford University Press, 1967.
Pogson, Rex, *J. B. Priestley and the Theatre,* Triangle Press, 1947.

PERIODICALS

Book World, October 6, 1968, May 11, 1969.
John O'London's Weekly (incorporated with *Time and Tide,* 1954), February 18, 1960.
Nation, November 18, 1968.
National Review, June 3, 1969.
New Statesman, January 6, 1967, February 24, 1967, May 5, 1967.
New York Times, January 2, 1978.
New York Times Book Review, April 22, 1951, May 30, 1954, October 27, 1968.
New York Times Magazine, January 4, 1948.
Observer Review, February 16, 1969, September 14, 1969.
Punch, November 20, 1968, October 20, 1970.
Stage, September 9, 1971, February 24, 1972.
Time, May 19, 1967.
Time and Tide, May 22, 1956.
Times Literary Supplement, February 22, 1968.

OBITUARIES:

PERIODICALS

Chicago Tribune, August 16, 1984.
Detroit Free Press, August 16, 1984.
Los Angeles Times, August 16, 1984.
Newsweek, August 27, 1984.
New York Times, August 16, 1984.
Time, August 27, 1984.
Times (London), August 16, 1984.

Washington Post, August 16, 1984.

*   *   *

PRITCHETT, V(ictor) S(awdon) 1900-

PERSONAL: Born December 16, 1900, in Ipswich, England; son of Sawdon (a businessman) and Beatrice (Martin) Pritchett; married second wife, Dorothy Roberts, October 2, 1936; children: (second marriage) Josephine (Mrs. Brian Murphy), Oliver. *Education:* Attended secondary school in Dulwich, England.

ADDRESSES: Home—12 Regents Park Terr., London N.W. 1, England. *Agent*—A. Peters, 10 Buckingham St., London WC2N 6BU, England.

CAREER: Writer, 1921—. Bookkeeper in the leather trade, London, England, 1916-20; freelance journalist for the *Christian Science Monitor* in France, Ireland, Spain, Morocco, and the United States, 1923-26; *New Statesman,* London, and *Nation,* New York, N.Y., literary critic, 1926-65, director, 1951-75. Christian Gauss Lecturer, Princeton University, 1953; Beckman Professor, University of California, Berkeley, 1960; writer in residence, Smith College, 1966; Zisskind Professor, Brandeis University, 1968; Clark Lecturer, Cambridge University, 1969; visiting professor, Columbia University, 1970.

MEMBER: PEN International (president, 1974-75), English PEN Club (president, 1970), Society of Authors (president), American Academy of Arts and Sciences (honorary foreign member), American Academy and Institute of Arts and Letters (honorary foreign member), Royal Society of Literature (fellow), Savile Club, Beefsteak Club.

AWARDS, HONORS: Royal Society of Literature Award, 1967, and Heinemann Award, 1969, both for *A Cab at the Door: A Memoir;* Commander of the British Empire, 1968, knighted, 1975; PEN Award for biography, 1974, for *Balzac;* "notable book of 1979" citation from *Library Journal,* 1980, for *The Myth Makers: Literary Essays.* Honorary degrees from Leeds University, 1971, Columbia University, Harvard University, and University of Sussex.

WRITINGS:

NONFICTION

Marching Spain, Benn, 1928.
In My Good Books, Chatto & Windus, 1942, reprinted, Kennikat, 1970.
The Living Novel, Chatto & Windus, 1946, Reynal, 1947, revised and expanded edition published as *The Living Novel, And Later Appreciations,* Random House, 1964.
(With Elizabeth Bowen and Graham Greene) *Why Do I Write?,* Percival Marshall, 1948.
Books in General, Harcourt, 1953, reprinted, Greenwood Press, 1981.
The Spanish Temper, Knopf, 1954, reprinted, Hogarth, 1984.
London Perceived, Harcourt, 1962, 2nd edition, 1963.
The Offensive Traveller, Knopf, 1964 (published in England as *Foreign Faces,* Chatto & Windus, 1964).
New York Proclaimed, Harcourt, 1965.
The Working Novelist, Chatto & Windus, 1965.
Shakespeare: The Comprehensive Soul, British Broadcasting Corporation (BBC), 1965.
Dublin: A Portrait, Harper, 1967.
A Cab at the Door: A Memoir (autobiography), Random House, 1968 (published in England as *A Cab at the Door: An Autobiography, Early Years,* Chatto & Windus, 1968).
George Meredith and English Comedy, Random House, 1970.

Midnight Oil (autobiography), Chatto & Windus, 1971, Random House, 1972.

Balzac (biography), Random House, 1974.

The Gentle Barbarian: The Life and Work of Turgenev (biography), Random House, 1977.

The Myth Makers: Literary Essays, Random House, 1979 (published in England as *The Myth Makers: Essays on European, Russian, and South American Novelists,* Chatto & Windus, 1979).

The Tale Bearers: Literary Essays, Random House, 1980 (published in England as *The Tale Bearers: Essays on English, American, and Other Writers,* Chatto & Windus, 1980).

(With Reynolds Stone) *The Turn of the Years,* Random House, 1982.

The Other Side of the Frontier: A V. S. Pritchett Reader, Robin Clark, 1984.

Man of Letters: Selected Essays, Chatto & Windus, 1985, Random House, 1986.

Chekhov: A Spirit Set Free (biography), Random House, 1988.

NOVELS

Clare Drummer, Benn, 1929.

Elopement into Exile, Little, Brown, 1932 (published in England as *Shirley Sanz,* Gollancz, 1932).

Nothing Like Leather, Macmillan, 1935.

Dead Man Leading, Macmillan, 1937, reprinted, Oxford University Press, 1985.

Mr. Beluncle, Harcourt, 1951, reprinted, Postway Press, 1972.

SHORT STORIES

The Spanish Virgin and Other Stories, Benn, 1930.

You Make Your Own Life, Chatto & Windus, 1938.

It May Never Happen and Other Stories, Chatto & Windus, 1945, Reynal, 1947.

The Sailor, Sense of Humor, and Other Stories, Knopf, 1956 (published in England as *Collected Stories,* Chatto & Windus, 1956), also published as *The Saint and Other Stories,* Penguin, 1966.

When My Girl Comes Home, Knopf, 1961.

The Key to My Heart: A Comedy in Three Parts (contains "The Key to My Heart," "Noisy Flushes the Birds," and "Noisy in the Doghouse"), Chatto & Windus, 1963, Random House, 1964.

Blind Love and Other Stories, Chatto & Windus, 1969, Random House, 1970.

(Contributor) *Penguin Modern Stories 9,* Penguin, 1971.

The Camberwell Beauty, Random House, 1975.

Selected Stories, Random House, 1978.

The Fly in the Ointment, Cambridge University Press, 1978.

On the Edge of the Cliff, Random House, 1979.

Collected Stories, Random House, 1982.

More Collected Stories, Random House, 1983.

EDITOR

Robert Louis Stevenson, *Novels and Stories: Selected,* Duell, Sloan & Pearce, 1946.

Turnstile One: A Literary Miscellany from the New Statesman and Nation, Turnstile, 1951.

Robert Southey, *The Chronicle of the Cid,* J. Enschede en Zonen for Limited Editions Club, 1958.

The Oxford Book of Short Stories, Oxford University Press, 1981.

Also editor of periodicals *This England, New Statesman,* and *Nation,* 1937.

OTHER

"Essential Jobs" (screenplay), 1942.

Author of weekly column, "Books in General," in the *New Statesman.* Contributor of essays to numerous periodicals, including *Nation, New York Times, New York Times Book Review, New York Review of Books, Holiday, English Review, New Yorker, Playboy,* and *Atlantic Monthly.*

SIDELIGHTS: Many observers consider V. S. Pritchett England's premier living man of letters. Pritchett's phenomenal career spans six decades and includes numerous volumes of literary criticism, fiction, biography, and nonfiction—all crafted for the discerning general reader. *New York Times Book Review* contributor Penelope Mortimer calls Pritchett "a veteran of the international literary establishment: a humanitarian and one of the greatest stylists in the English language." Mortimer adds that the author's "position in the world of letters is unassailable. . . . [His] reputation for excellence is unquestionable and secure." Knighted in 1975 for his service to British literature, Pritchett has spent a lifetime studying—and adding to—the Continental literary canon. According to Helen Muchnic in the *Saturday Review,* he is "the most cosmopolitan of literary critics. His range is broad, and he is always at home in the work he is writing about, whatever its place of origin, language, or century. . . . He likes to detect a writer's individuality in his work and to examine the special quality of his skill. His approach is essentially humanistic, and he writes with unassuming wisdom, perceptiveness, and charm." *Los Angeles Times Book Review* essayist Charles Champlin expresses a similar opinion: "V. S. Pritchett," writes Champlin, "Sir Victor since 1975, is the wise, foxy and kindly grandfather of present English letters: critic, biographer, essayist, novelist and, above all, one of the masters of the short story. . . . Pritchett is a matchless observer, but more: an appreciator of what he observes and, accordingly, a writer to be appreciated, profoundly."

Washington Post Book World correspondent Michael Dirda calls Pritchett's achievement "a triumph of the work ethic." Indeed, Pritchett has managed to write full-length books while maintaining a substantial schedule of monthly reviewing for a number of British and American periodicals. Such industry, writes Richard Locke in the *New York Times Book Review,* "suggests the preternatural energy of genius, and almost all this . . . work exhibits a fresh, compulsive curiosity and a vigorous prose style." Pritchett's career is characterized by its unusual length and also by the author's unconventional background. Largely self-educated, the son of working-class parents, Pritchett "rose by talent and force of will to gentility, a high personal civilization, and a distinguished literary career," to quote *Sewanee Review* contributor B. L. Reid. Walter Sullivan praises Pritchett in the *Sewanee Review* for his ability "to create a variety of backgrounds: he is not tied, as so many writers are, to a single and usually restricted world." Locke likewise contends that Pritchett "has the lower-middle-class Londoner's quick eye and sharp tongue and appetite for comedy. He's quick to spot pride, the cover-up, flummery, snobbery, cant. From his work he appears to be an emotional, intensely curious man—plucky, blunt, generous." Pritchett "seems to have been a virtuoso all his working life," writes Lynne Sharon Schwartz in the *Washington Post Book World.* "[He is] a luminous example of what it means to be timeless."

Pritchett himself has documented his unorthodox childhood in an award-winning narrative entitled *A Cab at the Door: A Memoir.* By his own account, his youth was not the sort which portended a career in letters. He was born in 1900 into genteel London poverty; his father, a constantly failing businessman, moved the family often in order to outrun debt collectors. Pritchett's schooling was consequently haphazard, although he did manage to learn French and German and cultivate a taste for literature. While still a young teen he came under the influence of a school teacher who encouraged him to write, and the youngster determined that he wanted to be a professional author. This career choice was unacceptable to his family—*New York Review of Books* essayist John Gross comments that Pritchett's father "jeered at his ambitions and grumbled about his ingratitude." At the age of fifteen Pritchett was forced to leave school for a position with a London leather wholesaler. The tedious office work was made bearable by the opportunity to observe the various colorful characters in the leather trade, and Pritchett spent most of his off-hours reading classical English and European literature. Finally, when he was twenty, Pritchett was granted a trip to Paris after a long illness that forced him out of work. He left for France secretly vowing never to return.

Reid writes: "All lives are hard but Pritchett's was harder than most. His family created him and by their lights nurtured him, but they very nearly killed him. . . . Writing . . . is something one must do for oneself, but few writers can have been so utterly self-made. Pritchett learned to write by reading and writing. No master, no old boys, pulled him along." Once out of sight of his family, Pritchett found life on his own in Paris an exhilarating experience. While working a number of odd jobs, he absorbed the culture and ambience of the city and continued his solitary regimen of reading. In 1921 his first three submitted pieces of writing were accepted by the *Christian Science Monitor.* Pritchett chose that particular periodical because his father was a Christian Scientist and because he himself had followed the faith—without much enthusiasm—for some years. With the promise of further work from the *Monitor,* he quit his regular jobs; however, assignments came slowly and paid low wages, so he eventually had to return to London, nearly penniless. *Dictionary of Literary Biography* contributor Harry S. Marks notes that Pritchett "left Paris after a two-year stay, having gained a large degree of freedom, self-confidence, and an expanded awareness of different cultures and national characteristics." He was to put this awareness to good use in the ensuing years, as the *Monitor* sent him to Ireland, Spain, and the Appalachian Mountain region of America as an investigative reporter.

Still in his mid-twenties, Pritchett began writing regular articles from the various countries to which he was assigned by the *Monitor.* He then began to use his impressions in books such as the nonfiction *Marching Spain* and the collection *The Spanish Virgin and Other Stories.* Meanwhile, he began to sell his travel essays and book reviews to the *Manchester Guardian* and the *New Statesman,* both prestigious forums for such a young writer. According to Champlin, Pritchett's "range of information and his perfect command of style stay constant, which is to say they were achieved early." Modest success also came early to Pritchett; both *Marching Spain* and *The Spanish Virgin* sold in excess of three thousand hardback copies, a much better showing than the publishers had anticipated. Marks observes, however, that the critics "were less than kind to Pritchett's early efforts at writing fiction." For several years Pritchett concentrated on writing novels rather than stories, and it is these works that received such cool reviews. Between 1929 and 1937 he published four novels, after which he opted almost exclusively for the short story format. As Valentine Cunningham notes in the *Times Literary Supplement,* by his own and his century's thirties, "Pritchett was well into his stride: a pace that, astonishingly, he's been able to maintain ever since. . . . From the start his trademark has been making human moments into epiphanies through mem-

orable phrases, vivid tags and scraps of ideolect captured by roaming and plundering the language registers of an extraordinary breadth of classes and sects, odd social crannies, dark and curious corners of behavior."

Pritchett's youth may not have prepared him for a conventional career in literary criticism, but it certainly gave him ample material from which to draw for fiction. To quote *Time* magazine correspondent Timothy Foote, the author's short stories "regularly throb with the same grotesque scenes and sensuous memories as his life, recollected with a comic clarity and shrewd indulgence." Many of Pritchett's stories chronicle the mundane lives of England's lower middle class, especially its older, more eccentric members. In *Books and Bookmen,* Jean Stubbs maintains that the writer "has a lively affection for the oddballs: seldom successful, physically and mentally scarred, stupid and shrewd, mean and kind and predatory, unconsciously ridiculous, tripped up by their virtues and hounded by their vices. But never once does he allow his compassion to slither into sentimentality, nor his listening eyes and seeing ears to persuade him into mere cleverness." Cunningham notes that what Pritchett celebrates "is the heroicism of banal life [as well as] ordinary people, made marginal and socially insignificant by provinciality or lack of intelligence, or by the chosen exiles of enthusiastic religiosity." Eudora Welty elaborates in the *New York Times Book Review:* "These are *social* stories," Welty writes. "Life goes on in them without flagging. The characters that fill them—erratic, unsure, unsafe, devious, stubborn, restless and desirous, absurd and passionate, all peculiar unto themselves—hold a claim on us that is not to be denied. They demand and get our rapt attention, for in their revelation of their lives, the secrets of our own lives come into view. How much the eccentric has to tell us of what is central!" Robert Kiely also observes in the *New York Times Book Review* that Pritchett's characters "are often middle-aged or old and living in moderate-to-desperate circumstances." The critic adds, however, that Pritchett "resists the temptation (possibly is not even tempted) to blast them off the face of the earth or transform them into heroes. But he shows us, and, furthermore, delights us, by making us believe in the human capacity to change and, particularly, to love." *New Republic* essayist William Trevor concludes that a foreign reader wishing to understand the English people "might profitably turn first to the stories of V. S. Pritchett. . . . He would meet the prejudices and pettinesses of that extraordinary island, the subtleties of its class system, the trailing mists of an empire that will not quite go away."

Some reviewers feel that Pritchett's stories offer scathing criticism of British middle-class mores. Others find the author preoccupied with individual lives, with the fantasies, illusions, and longings that transcend class or education. "Typically," declares Benjamin DeMott in the *New York Times Book Review,* "a Pritchett tale offers a minimum of two vividly defined, sprightly-tongued characters, much observable incident, and authoritative views of contemporary manners. . . . But Pritchett's creative energy usually spends itself not upon narrative ingenuities but upon climaxes in which surprising configurations of feelings stand revealed, born naturally from the movement of events, and unobtrusively correcting simplistic versions of our emotional insides. The effect is often that of ironic comedy, never harsh but never gullible." In the *New York Review of Books,* Denis Donoghue writes: "Mr. Pritchett's stories are invariably written in search of a character. They end when the character has been disclosed. Usually the story presents the character at one revealing moment, and it rarely concerns itself with other possibilities, later chapters, for instance, in a character's life. The short story is a happy form for Mr. Pritchett because he identifies character and nature; a man's character is his nature and it may be disclosed in a flash, the significant circumstances of a moment." *New York Times Book Review* correspondent Guy Davenport likewise observes that Pritchett's characters "are human wills desperately on their own; their dogged independence being the source of the comedy they generate. And it is the comedy of tolerant understanding, for Mr. Pritchett is a sane and immensely civilized writer. He is also a wonderfully invisible writer. Accomplished as he is with books and ideas . . . nothing resembling a thesis or political stance or philosophical notion appears in these stories. Mr. Pritchett is all eye, all ear. That an author so congenial and wise can tell such tales of human folly with never a blush nor a grumble is a triumph of good nature."

Stylistically, Pritchett's stories combine economical language and descriptive passages with a strong sense of the comic in human language and gesture. Pritchett "can peek and tell with the best of them," according to Carole Cook in the *Saturday Review.* "His hallmark is the airy gentleness of his touch as he lifts the veils." *New York Review of Books* essayist Jonathan Raban offers a more detailed appraisal. "The moral philosophy and the literary artifice by which [Pritchett's] characters are brought into being are cunningly hidden from the reader," Raban writes. "The seemingly inconsequential talkiness of tone, together with Pritchett's habitual air of just being a plain man with an anecdote to tell, are devices that conceal an art as rigorous and deeply thought out as that of Henry James. Beware of Pritchett's homespun manner: it is an elaborate camouflage." Similarly, *New Republic* contributor Edith Milton observes that underlying Pritchett's simple narratives and familiar settings "is the suggestion of wildly tangled contradiction. Pritchett's stories are full of mysteries and the unexplained fragments of relationships, which we are asked to intuit rather than understand. . . . These are stories which so delicately suggest the unseen, inner core by its shadow cast against the visible outside surface, that they succeed not only as works of fiction but as achievements of a profoundly poetic imagination." In the *New York Review of Books,* Frank Kermode calls Pritchett "in the best sense, very knowing. . . . He always knows how people speak, with their bodies as well as their tongues. Yet it seems wrong to say, as people do, that his primary concern is with the progressive unveiling of character. . . . [A] literal transfiguration of the commonplace seems to be Pritchett's central theme."

Recent compilations of Pritchett's fiction—including *Collected Stories, More Collected Stories,* and *On the Edge of the Cliff* have introduced the author to a new generation of readers and have enhanced his reputation amongst his peers. "Pritchett's literary achievement is enormous, but his short stories are his greatest triumph," claims Paul Theroux in the *Saturday Review.* "And one can say with perfect confidence that there is nothing like them in the language, because every short story writer of brilliance makes the form his own." Welty writes: "Any Pritchett story is all of it alight and busy at once, like a well-going fire. Wasteless and at the same time well fed, it shoots up in flame from its own spark like a poem or a magic trick, self-consuming, with nothing left over. He is one of the great pleasure-givers in our language." In the *Washington Post Book World,* Robertson Davies concludes that Pritchett's fictions "are all illuminated by understanding, and have the ring of truth. Every word and situation, every queer turn of events, carries conviction. This is literary achievement on a very high level, and what a relief it is from the tedious stream of stories about privileged people who have time and inclination for foolish mischief, usually of a sexual kind, and who are so frequently authors, or artists, or simply rich idlers, but who are invariably self-indulgent dullards." *New Re-*

public contributor William Trevor suggests that Pritchett "has probably done more for the English short story than anyone has ever done."

As a literary journalist, Pritchett strives to keep his essays free of academic cant and pedantic assertions—these, he feels, obscure literature and quell curiosity. His criticism, most of which has appeared initially in periodicals, has been collected in *The Myth Makers: Literary Essays, The Tale Bearers: Literary Essays,* and *Man of Letters: Selected Essays,* among others. Locke calls Pritchett the critic "a surviving link with the great tradition of English and European literature. Neither a scholar nor an intellectual in the New York or Continental sense, Pritchett is the supreme contemporary virtuoso of the short literary essay. . . . Pritchett is informal but never clubby, witty but never snide or snobbish, precise and always full of gusto—a true descendant of William Hazlitt." Reid likewise notes that no writer in years "has talked so clearly and wisely about the craft of writing and what might be called the moral psychology of the writer." *Times Literary Supplement* reviewer D. J. Enright sees Pritchett as the consummate teacher, offering his audience fresh insights. "In truth he does teach," Enright declares, "and by the direct method: journeying through literature, exploring, recording and sharing his findings in their immediate (though never naive) freshness and concreteness. He doesn't write down to the common reader; he writes at his own level, which *seems* to be that of the common reader, a figure whose actual existence in flesh and blood we may doubt but of whose nature and capacities we somehow have a pretty good idea." *Chicago Tribune* correspondent Stevenson Swanson concludes that Pritchett's "resourcefulness never flags in finding ways to communicate what it feels like to read a particular author, one of the most difficult tasks of a critic."

Pritchett enjoys probing the unity of a writer's life and art in his critical essays. He has also explored this theme in full-length biographies such as *Balzac, The Gentle Barbarian: The Life and Work of Turgenev,* and *Chekhov: A Spirit Set Free.* According to George Core in the *Sewanee Review,* to read Pritchett's criticism "is to understand the relation of the author's world to the life of his writing—or the writer's life to the world of his characters. Pritchett enters so thoroughly into the mind and work of the writer he criticizes that he all but vanishes." In Bayley's view, such perceptions "are fresh and invariably good-natured for it is by his kindliness and fellow-feeling that [Pritchett] goes on to reveal the real qualities of the writers under discussion. Of course he favors writers who take a real interest in human beings and the performances they create around themselves, because that is what, as a novelist and short-story writer, he does so well himself." *New Statesman* contributor A. S. Byatt states that the critic "likes to take the great, the outstanding, the enduring book and isolate the qualities that make it so. If biography helps, he tells us what we need to know; if political or cultural history is more useful, we have that; if perfectly chosen examples of style and pace are required, he provides them. He is supremely tactful, and never superfluous." A *Times Literary Supplement* reviewer similarly concludes that Pritchett's essay subjects "exist in their environments, writer and circumstance explaining each other, and these cross-explanations are surely what any reader wants to know about a writer. But there is also another and most compelling question that one practitioner inevitably puts to another: How did you do it? Mr. Pritchett has a keen professional eye for the technical tricks of his craft, the management and mismanagement of effects."

Pritchett's essays show the same straightforward prose and clarity of style that can be found in his fiction. To quote Core, the life of art "is conveyed by the vitality of V. S. Pritchett's prose and by his unflagging curiosity. The critical prose is less metaphorical, less involved with the idiom of the times and its walks. . . . In the criticism Pritchett speaks directly to the reader in a unique voice—quiet, measured, compelling." Dirda praises Pritchett for his qualities of "modesty, judiciousness, and good sense," adding: "The essays are clearly written and jargon-free; they emphasize the biographical and are sprinkled with apt quotations. . . . Throughout, one senses that Pritchett has done enormous homework, that he has read an author entire, and that he brings to bear, appropriately and illuminatingly, a lifetime of reading." John Gross in the *New York Times* notes a "prose at once ruminative and succinct, close-packed and compressed without being congested," and suggests that half of Pritchett's secret "lies in a style which does not only illumine or take on the color of its surroundings, but which provides its own satisfactions as well. It is as satisfying to come across the right words in the right order in a critical essay as it would be anywhere else." *London Magazine* correspondent John Mellors also cites Pritchett's essays for their careful use of the *mot juste*. "The best of Pritchett's reviews and criticisms are as enthralling as his short stories," Mellors writes. "Nothing is either a priori or ex cathedra. . . . He observes and describes, simplifies and sympathizes, and finally illuminates by a combination of common sense and brilliant insight. . . . Above all, he has the knack of helping the common reader . . . to clarify apparent obscurities and discrepancies in an author's work."

It can be argued that Pritchett is best known as a critic and that his essays are widely read and respected by others in his field. *Chicago Tribune Book World* contributor Robert W. Smith contends that Pritchett's criticism "still stands unsurpassed. It has sweep and cogency and charm. And always surprise." Davies feels that Pritchett's nonfiction work "is a fine balance in the hurly-burly of weekly publishing. Critics like Pritchett belong to the small body of serious lovers of literature who will not compromise with standards that reach beyond the enthusiasms of the immediate present." Cunningham writes: "Matured long ago past the stage of having to strain for a young reviewer's smartness, V. S. Pritchett's criticism practices wisdom. Wisdom comes so naturally to his reviewing pen, in fact, that we end up taking his crisply sage reflections, his most assentable asides, the continual evidencing of hard-schooled and well-tried gumption, almost for granted. Well-put insights pile up." R. W. B. Lewis offers perhaps the most cogent appreciation of Pritchett in a *New Republic* review. "Pritchett's well-modulated prose is a constant pleasure," Lewis declares; "it is never self-admiring and never out of keeping with its subject. . . . He occupies today a nearly solitary position as a literary critic in the great tradition—standing between literature and human society to greet the books as they come, passing the word back and forth."

Few workers in any line of business sustain careers into their seventies. Pritchett has labored well into his late eighties, publishing a biography of Chekhov and continuing his reviewing almost on a full-time basis. Theroux observes that the affable Pritchett "has a hiker's obvious health, a downright manner, an exuberant curiosity and the sort of twinkle that puts one in mind of a country doctor—that spirit-boosting responsiveness that works cures on malingerers." In the *Detroit News*, Sheldon Frank also notes that Pritchett is "a man invigorated by growing old, alive and open to the world in a way a child should envy." Pritchett lives in the Camden Town district of London, and although he sometimes complains about his work load, he is still able to communicate enthusiasm for his surroundings, his essay subjects, and the world of letters in general. According to William Abrahams in

the *New Republic*, the pleasure Pritchett takes in writing "translates itself into the pleasure one takes in reading him—the opportunity to acquaint oneself with a temperament that is humane, an intelligence that is acute and a technique that is masterly." Locke calls Pritchett "incontestably one of the happy few, a man seemingly blessed in life and work. He still regards literature as a personal communication, a social act, a performance and a mark of character. This is certainly not the only way to read and write, but it carries the cultural momentum and authority of a great tradition with it; and Pritchett deserves our warmest homage and thanks, particularly in an age of rising literary technocrats and declining literary culture and continuity."

BIOGRAPHICAL/CRITICAL SOURCES:

BOOKS

Contemporary Fiction in America and England, 1950-70, Gale, 1976.
Contemporary Literary Criticism, Gale, Volume 5, 1976, Volume 13, 1980, Volume 15, 1980, Volume 41, 1987.
Dictionary of Literary Biography, Volume 15: *British Novelists, 1930-1959,* Gale, 1983.
Pritchett, V. S., *A Cab at the Door: A Memoir,* Random House, 1968 (published in England as *A Cab at the Door: An Autobiography, Early Years,* Chatto & Windus, 1968).
Pritchett, V. S., *Midnight Oil,* Chatto & Windus, 1971, Random House, 1972.
Solotaroff, Theodore, *The Red Hot Vacuum and Other Pieces on Writing in the Sixties,* Atheneum, 1970.

PERIODICALS

Atlantic, August, 1971.
Books and Bookmen, December, 1969, November, 1985.
Chicago Tribune, July 9, 1986.
Chicago Tribune Book World, May 27, 1979, May 23, 1982.
Detroit News, May 30, 1982, October 30, 1983.
Listener, July 19, 1979, August 5, 1982.
London Magazine, April/May, 1975, July, 1980.
Los Angeles Times, March 16, 1983.
Los Angeles Times Book Review, May 23, 1982, September 11, 1983, June 29, 1986.
Modern Fiction Studies, summer, 1978.
Nation, October 2, 1967, May 8, 1972, December 31, 1973, May 10, 1975, August 16-23, 1986.
New Leader, December 31, 1979.
New Republic, May 11, 1968, May 6, 1972, October 19, 1974, April 23, 1977, July 8, 1978, July 19, 1980, August 2, 1982.
New Statesman, May 18, 1979.
Newsweek, April 22, 1968, May 16, 1977, May 29, 1978, May 10, 1982.
New Yorker, May 1, 1965, October 29, 1973, May 30, 1977, June 11, 1979, June 9, 1980, June 28, 1982, April 8, 1985, June 9, 1986.
New York Herald Tribune Book Review, April 25, 1954.
New York Review of Books, July 1, 1965, September 14, 1967, February 13, 1969, March 12, 1970, July 20, 1972, October 4, 1973, March 20, 1975, September 15, 1977, August 17, 1978, February 7, 1980, June 12, 1980, June 24, 1982, June 26, 1986.
New York Times, May 5, 1977, May 28, 1979, June 28, 1979, October 31, 1979, April 24, 1982, August 31, 1983, December 16, 1985.
New York Times Book Review, April 25, 1954, April 18, 1965, August 13, 1967, April 28, 1968, December 1, 1968, January 25, 1970, April 30, 1972, October 14, 1973, September 15, 1974, May 22, 1977, June 25, 1978, June 3, 1979, No-

vember 18, 1979, June 29, 1980, May 30, 1982, September 18, 1983, May 4, 1986.

New York Times Magazine, December 14, 1980, March 13, 1983.

Observer, June 21, 1970, December 15, 1985.

Publishers Weekly, April 10, 1972.

Saturday Review, June 26, 1965, April 6, 1968, May 4, 1968, March 14, 1970, May 6, 1972, October 19, 1974, May 14, 1977, July 8, 1978, December, 1979, May, 1982.

Sewanee Review, summer, 1975, spring, 1977, spring, 1981.

Spectator, October 12, 1974, June 25, 1977, January 7, 1984.

Time, May 17, 1968, August 3, 1970, September 16, 1974, May 23, 1977, November 12, 1979, May 5, 1980.

Times (London), June 25, 1981, February 11, 1984, June 4, 1988.

Times Literary Supplement, February 4, 1965, April 1, 1965, August 17, 1967, February 22, 1968, November 6, 1969, December 18, 1970, October 22, 1971, September 14, 1973, October 25, 1974, June 24, 1977, May 12, 1978, January 18, 1980, February 29, 1980, September 26, 1980, June 25, 1982, November 4, 1983, August 17, 1984, November 22, 1985.

Tribune Books (Chicago), October 16, 1988.

Washington Post Book World, April 30, 1972, June 12, 1977, May 27, 1979, November 18, 1979, December 9, 1979, May 25, 1980, April 25, 1982, October 9, 1983, June 22, 1986, October 23, 1988.

—*Sketch by Anne Janette Johnson*

*   *   *

PROPHET, The
See DREISER, Theodore (Herman Albert)

*   *   *

PROUST, (Valentin-Louis-George-Eugene-)Marcel 1871-1922
(Marc Antoine, Dominique, Echo, Horatio)

PERSONAL: Born July 10, 1871, in Auteuil, France; died of pulmonary infection (one source says pneumonia and bronchitis), November 18, 1922, in Paris, France; buried at Pere-Lachaise Cemetery (French national cemetery), Paris, France; son of Adrien (a medical doctor and professor) and Jeanne (Weil) Proust. *Education:* Attended Ecole Libre des Sciences Politiques, 1890; Sorbonne, University of Paris, licence es lettres, 1895.

ADDRESSES: Home—44 rue Hamelin, Paris, France.

CAREER: Writer. Mazarine Library of Institut of France, Paris, librarian, 1895-1900. Co-founder of *Le Banquet,* 1892. *Military service:* French Army, 1889-90; served in infantry.

AWARDS, HONORS: Goncourt Prize from Goncourt Academy, 1919, for *Within a Budding Grove;* named to French Legion of Honor, 1920.

WRITINGS:

Oeuvres completes de Marcel Proust (ten volumes; title means "Complete Works of Marcel Proust"), Nouvelle Revue Francais, 1929-36.

"A LA RECHERCHE DU TEMPS PERDU" (SEVEN-PART NOVEL: TITLE MEANS "IN SEARCH OF LOST TIME"), 1913-27, TRANSLATION PUBLISHED AS "REMEMBRANCE OF THINGS PAST," 1922-31

Part 1: *Du Cote de chez Swann* (two volumes), Grasset, 1913, translation by C. K. Scott-Moncrieff published as *Swann's Way,* Holt, 1922.

Part 2: *A l'ombre des jeunes filles en fleurs* (three volumes; title means "In the Shade of Young Girls in Bloom"), Nouvelle Revue Francais, 1919, translation by Scott-Moncrieff published as *Within a Budding Grove,* T. Seltzer, 1924.

Part 3: *Le Cote de Guermantes* (two volumes; second volume includes first portion of *Sodome et Gomorrhe;* also see below), Nouvelle Revue Francais, Volume 1, 1920, Volume 2, 1921, translation by Scott-Moncrieff published as *The Guermantes Way,* T. Seltzer, 1925.

Part 4: *Sodome et Gomorrhe* (four volumes; title means "Sodom and Gomorrah"; first volume contains second portion of *Le Cote de Guermantes;* also see above), Nouvelle Revue Francais, 1922, translation by Scott-Moncrieff published as *Cities of the Plain,* A. & C. Boni, 1927.

Part 5: *La Prisonniere* (two volumes), Nouvelle Revue Francais, 1923, translation by Scott-Moncrieff published as *The Captive,* A. & C. Boni, 1929.

Part 6: *Albertine disparue* (two volumes; title means "Albertine Missing"), Nouvelle Revue Francais, 1925, translation by Scott-Moncrieff published as *The Sweet Cheat Gone,* A. & C. Boni, 1930, revised translation by Terence Kilmartin published as *The Fugitive* (also see below).

Part 7: *Le Temps retrouve* (two volumes), Nouvelle Revue Francais, 1927, translation by Frederick A. Blossom published as *The Past Recaptured,* Random House, 1934, translation by Andreas Mayer published as *Time Regained,* Chatto & Windus, 1970.

All seven parts of *A la recherche du temps perdu* reprinted in three volumes by Gallimard, 1954, translation by Scott-Moncrieff and Blossom reprinted in two volumes by Random House, 1960, translation by Scott-Moncrieff and Mayer revised by Kilmartin and published in three volumes by Random House, 1981.

Un amour de Swann (chapter from *Du Cote de chez Swann*), published by Gallimard, 1919, translation by Scott-Moncrieff published as *Un amour de Swann,* Macmillan, 1965, revised translation by Kilmartin published as *Swann in Love,* Random House, 1984.

OTHER NOVELS

Jean Santeuil (three volumes), preface by Andre Maurois, Gallimard, 1952, translation by Gerard Hopkins published as *Jean Santeuil,* Simon & Schuster, 1956.

TRANSLATOR AND COMMENTATOR

John Ruskin, *La Bible d'Amiens* (translation of *The Bible of Amiens*), Mercure de France, 1904.

John Ruskin, *Sesame et les lys* (translation of *Sesame and Lilies*), Mercure de France, 1906, introduction translated by William Burford and published as *On Reading,* Macmillan, 1971.

On Reading Ruskin: Prefaces to "La Bible d'Amiens" and "Sesame et les Lys" With Selections from Notes to the Translated Texts, translated and edited by Jean Autret, William Burford, and Phillip J. Wolfe, Yale University Press, 1987.

LETTERS

Comment debut a Marcel Proust: Lettres inedites, Nouvelle Revue Francais, 1925.

Lettres inedites, Bagneres-de-Bigorre, 1926.

Caresse Crosby and Harry Crosby, editors and translators, *Forty-seven Unpublished Letters From Marcel Proust to Walter Berry,* Black Sun Press, 1930.

Correspondance generale de Marcel Proust, six volumes, Plon, 1930-36.

Lettres a la N.R.F., Gallimard, 1932.

Lettres a un ami, recueil de quarante-et-une lettres inedites addresses a Marie Nordlinger, 1889-1908, Editions du Calame, 1942.

Lettres a Madame C., J. B. Janin, 1946.

A un ami: Correspondance inedite, 1903-1922, Amiot-Dumont, 1948, translation by Alexander Henderson and Elizabeth Henderson published as *Letters to a Friend,* Falcon Press, 1949.

Mina Curiss, translator and editor, *Letters of Marcel Proust,* introduction by Harry Levin, Random House, 1948.

Lettres a Andre Gide, Neuchatel, 1949.

Lettres de Marcel Proust a Bibesco, Guilde du Livre, 1949.

Philip Kolb, editor, *Marcel Proust: Correspondance avec sa mere,* Plon, 1953, translation by George D. Painter published as *Marcel Proust: Letters to His Mother,* Rider, 1956, Citadel Press, 1958.

Kolb, editor, *Marcel Proust et Jacques Riviere: Correspondance, 1914-1922,* Plon, 1954.

Kolb, editor, *Lettres a Reynaldo Hahn,* Gallimard, 1956.

Kolb, editor, *Choix de lettres,* Plon, 1965.

Kolb, editor, *Lettres retrouvees,* Plon, 1966.

Comment debut a Marcel Proust, Gallimard, 1969.

Kolb, editor, *Correspondance de Marcel Proust,* numerous volumes, Plon, 1970—.

Michael Raimond, editor, *Correspondance Proust-Copeau,* University of Ottawa, 1976.

Kolb, editor, *Correspondance Marcel Proust-Jacques Riviere (1914-1922),* Gallimard, 1976.

Kolb, editor, *Selected Letters,* Volume 1: *1880-1903,* translation by Ralph Mannheim, Doubleday, 1983, Volume 2: *1904-1909,* translation by Terence Kilmartin, Oxford University Press, 1989.

OTHER

Les Plaisirs et les jours (prose and poetry), preface by Anatole France, Calmann Levy, 1896, translation of prose by Louise Varese published as *Pleasures and Regrets,* Crown, 1948, reprinted, Dufour, 1986 (also see below).

Pastiches et melanges (articles), Nouvelle Revue Francais, 1919 (also see below).

Chroniques (articles), Nouvelle Revue Francais, 1927 (also see below).

Gerard Hopkins, editor and translator, *Marcel Proust: A Selection From His Miscellaneous Writings* (contains material from *Pastiches et melanges* and *Chroniques;* also see above), A. Wingate, 1948.

Justin O'Brien, editor and translator, *The Maxims of Marcel Proust* (contains material from *A la recherche du temps perdu;* also see above), Columbia University Press, 1948, reprinted as *Aphorisms and Epigrams From "Remembrance of Things Past,"* McGraw, 1964.

Contre Sainte-Beuve (essays), Gallimard, 1954, translation by Sylvia Townsend Warner published as *On Art and Literature, 1896-1919,* Meridian Books, 1958 (published in England as *By Way of Sainte-Beuve,* Chatto & Windus, 1958).

Pleasures and Days (includes material from *Pleasures and Regrets;* also see above), translated by Varese, Hopkins, and Barbara Dupee, Doubleday, 1957, reprinted, Fertig, 1978.

Against Sainte-Beuve and Other Essays, translation by John Sturrock, Penguin, 1988.

Also author of *Portraits de peintre* (poetry), 1896, and of prefaces to other volumes.

Contributor, sometimes under pseudonyms Marc Antoine, Dominique, Echo, and Horatio, to periodicals including *Le Banquet* and *Figaro.*

SIDELIGHTS: Marcel Proust is generally considered the greatest French novelist of the twentieth century. His reputation, which derives exclusively from the importance of his multivolume novel *Remembrance of Things Past,* is that of a dazzling stylist, analytical thinker, and social observer. His novel is founded on his powers of meticulous recollection and his ability to shape those memories into a compelling—some might even say exhausting—account of one man's search for his past. This search leads the narrator, and reader, into a world of charm and deceit, virtue and perversion. E. M. Forster, in his *Abinger Harvest,* called Proust's novel "an epic of curiosity and despair," while Edmund Wilson wrote in *Axel's Castle* that *Remembrance of Things Past* was "one of the gloomiest books ever written." But Andre Maurois, in his biography *Proust: Portrait of a Genius,* reconciled Proust's seemingly unending inquisitiveness with his profound melancholy by noting that the former constitutes Proust's salvation from the latter. "Proust, like Shakespeare, had plumbed the extremes of human misery," wrote Maurois, "but, like Shakespeare, found . . . serenity in Time Regained."

Proust was born in 1871 of bourgeois parents. His father was a noted physician who had distinguished himself in his efforts to combat the spread of cholera from Persia, and Proust's mother was a highly educated Jewish woman known for her charm and humor. As a child Proust enjoyed significant attention and affection from his mother, and more than one biographer has remarked on their seeming inseparability. Aside from sharing similar interests—reading, taking walks—Proust and his mother were bound by considerations for his tenuous health. He continually suffered indigestion, and at age nine he experienced the first of innumerable asthma attacks. The sources of these attacks seemed countless: anxiety, exhaustion, and insomnia, as well as more familiar causes such as dust, dampness, and smoke, all seemed to prompt traumatic breathing. Young Proust, moody and obsessive, learned to manipulate his parents, particularly his mother, with his health problems, exploiting their reluctance to administer punishment for tantrums or defiant behavior.

Once in school Proust distinguished himself with honors despite his often poor health. In his early school years he was frequently mocked by classmates for his feminine features and delicacy, but he eventually won the admiration of some of these same students for his literary precocity. Among his closest friends at the Lycee Condorcet, from which he graduated in 1889 with distinctions in composition and classical languages, were Daniel Halevy and Jacques Bizet, son of the famed composer Georges Bizet. In 1888 Proust and his two friends collaborated on the journals *La Revue verte* and *La Revue lilas,* with Proust serving as both contributor and as scathing copyeditor for his less talented friends. His own writings, which include an autobiographical account of contemplation, reveal an early penchant for ornamentation and inquisitive thinking. His interest in the latter continued during his final school year when he studied idealists such as Immanuel Kant. For Proust, Kant proved inspirational, prompting speculations on metaphysics and human behavior. Biographer Richard Barker has even suggested in *Marcel Proust* that during this time the impressionable Proust "formed mental habits that were to remain with him for the rest of his life."

Upon graduating from the Lycee Condorcet Proust decided to pursue a career as a writer. But first he had to fulfill his military obligations. Laws at the time stipulated five years of service for eligible Frenchmen, but exceptions were made for educated citizens willing to purchase their own equipment. For citizens such as these, the required period was reduced to one year, and it was for such a term that Proust enlisted in 1889. In the French Army Proust's poor physical health proved only a slight liability, and he avoided certain rigors by ingratiating himself with his commanding officer. During his service, however, Proust did suffer bouts of depression, including a particularly traumatic period following the death of his grandmother. But his health was generally favorable. And although he was stationed in Orleans, Proust indulged his interest in high society by occasionally accompanying a new friend, Gaston de Caillavet, to receptions and parties in Paris.

Proust continued to patronize Parisian society after leaving the French Army in 1890. Through Gaston de Caillavet's mother, Madame Arman de Caillavet, Proust met author Anatole France, who was the principal guest in her salon. At this time Proust also infiltrated the circle gathered by Genevieve Straus, mother of his old schoolmate Jacques Bizet and thus widow of the composer Georges Bizet. Straus's next husband was a wealthy lawyer who installed her among antique furnishings in a vast apartment on Paris's Boulevard Haussmann. Proust greatly admired Madame Straus, who was known for her cutting wit, and biographers such as Barker and George D. Painter have speculated that young Proust even entertained notions of a sexual relationship with his acerbic hostess. Other prominent Parisians visited by Proust were Madame Aubemon de Nerville, whose own salon had earlier featured Anatole France, and Laure Hayman, formerly mistress to one of Proust's great-uncles. Despite a modest allowance, Proust lavished gifts on Hayman, and some biographers acknowledge that his interest in her was sexual as well as social. "It would not have been the first nor the last time that Proust's relations with women were physical," Painter noted in his biography *Marcel Proust.* Still another romantic interest of Proust's was Jeanne Pouquet, fiance of his friend Gaston de Caillavet. His flirtatious, excessively complimentary manner—defined as "Proustifying" by his friends—sometimes angered de Caillavet. But by 1893, when his two friends married, Proust had lost interest in other women and had shifted his romantic concerns, as Painter observed, to other men.

During this initial period of extensive socializing Proust published his first writings in a modest magazine, *Le Banquet,* which he founded with Jacques Bizet, Daniel Halevy, and a few other friends. Proust's early writings are mostly anecdotes or short reviews focusing on Paris society, and they often reveal his intentions as an effusive social climber. His collaborators at *Le Banquet* sometimes protested Proust's use of the publication for overt pandering to hostesses such as Countess Adheume de Chevigne, whom he flatteringly portrayed in hope of an introduction to the aristocracy. One such trite piece by Proust eventually prompted action from *Le Banquet*'s Femand Gregh, who published a brief notice disassociating the staff from Proust's comments.

While writing for *Le Banquet* Proust placated his concerned parents by studying law at the Sorbonne. After completing his studies, though, he avoided entering the field and began studying philosophy. At this time Proust also wrote several fictional pieces for *La Revue blanche,* which had acquired *Le Banquet*'s staff. Proust's new writings—sensitive character studies with vaguely erotic overtones—showed a marked improvement over his earlier society reports. But he followed these writings with an article on the flamboyant Count Robert de Montesquiou, whose mediocre poetry was apparently prized by Proust. The article on Montesquiou was intended as the first in a series, but various editors rejected Proust's excessively flattering portrait, and he consequently abandoned the series.

Proust began collecting his contributions to *Le Banquet* and *La Revue blanche,* and in 1896 he published these writings, along with additional stories, as *Les Plaisirs et les jours.* Despite a laudatory preface credited to Anatole France—it was actually written by Arman de Caillavet—the book's sales were minimal and even failed to return the cost of publication. And reviews were generally bland or negative, dismissing Proust's style as precious and his all-enveloping sentence structure as convoluted and confusing. But in retrospect *Les Plaisirs et les jours,* which was published in English as *Pleasures and Regrets,* is considered prophetic of Proust's later masterpiece, *Remembrance of Things Past.* In his biography Barker concedes that *Les Plaisirs* is "not entirely successful" but added that it contains "the raw material for a work of art," and Milton Hindus, in his *Reader's Guide to Marcel Proust,* is particularly attentive to themes of jealousy and sexual transgression in the stories of *Les Plaisirs.* These themes, dominant in *Remembrance,* were first explored by Proust in tales such as "A Young Girl's Confession," which concerns envy and sexual indiscretion, and "Violante," which details the foul repercussions of high-society life and sexual indulgence.

After publishing *Les Plaisirs* and an insignificant verse collection, Proust resumed work on a more ambitious literary project: a vast, autobiographical novel elaborating the themes of his earlier work. For the next few years Proust devoted himself to this work, ultimately writing more than one thousand pages. This novel, published only posthumously as *Jean Santeuil,* failed to cohere, but it provided a clear indication of the skill and talent that Proust would later use in producing his masterpiece. Themes such as obsessive jealousy and ostensibly perverse sexuality are readily evident in *Jean Santeuil,* and whole episodes of the later *Remembrance* are introduced in the earlier novel in a manner almost entirely duplicated in the later work. More importantly, as Barker indicated, *Jean Santeuil* served as Proust's forum for developing and refining a writing style "so completely transparent that it would reveal with absolute accuracy the most minute observations." This style, justifiably complex in its ornate detail, would become a hallmark of *Remembrance of Things Past.*

Proust socialized extensively in the late 1890s. An affair with Reynaldo Hahn, a musician, had ended tempestuously in 1897, but Proust apparently found other lovers, and he remained a frequent visitor to the salons of de Caillavet and newfound aristocratic acquaintances. But his activities were increasingly undermined by poor health and related problems. He suffered from asthma attacks, usually as he prepared for sleep. The ensuing insomnia prompted him to experiment with allegedly sleep-inducing drugs. But some of these drugs were addictive, and their frequent use led to prolonged melancholy. Proust's mother cautioned him against dependence on these drugs, and as an alterative she took him on seaside vacations. When circumstances dictated occasional separation, Proust and his mother corresponded daily. Her letters posed queries about his health, while his missives detailed his various ailments.

But these discomforts did not prevent Proust's involvement in the Dreyfus scandal that shook France at this time. Alfred Dreyfus was a Jewish captain in the French Army, and in 1895 he was imprisoned on Devil's Island after his conviction for attempting to deliver secret documents to Germany. Few French citizens objected to the original verdict, though Dreyfus's alleged treason caused some embarrassment in the Jewish community. In 1896 new evidence indicated that a Major Esterhazy, and not Dreyfus, was guilty of the treasonous act. Major Joseph Henry, whose charwoman had discovered the original evidence, began forging new evidence against Dreyfus, ostensibly to protect the army's already tainted reputation. But when Dreyfus's brother Mathieu published the evidence against Esterhazy, the army was compelled to try the new suspect. Esterhazy's surprising acquittal in 1898 resulted in public outcry from French intellectuals, who accused the French military of anti-Semitism in keeping Dreyfus on Devil's Island. Proust was among the first members of this protest group—known collectively as Dreyfusards or Revisionists—and he joined such prominent artists as Anatole France and Emile Zola in petitioning for Dreyfus's retrial. Major Georges Picquart, who had discovered the evidence against Esterhazy, was eventually tried for his own allegedly subversive behavior, but his eccentric manner while testifying only further obscured the facts, and he too was found guilty.

The Dreyfus scandal exerted a powerful effect on Parisian' society. Aristocratic circles, largely Christian and nationalist, remained supportive of French authority, while bourgeois groups often rallied behind the Dreyfusards. Proust, who frequented salons of both social strata, sought to alleviate tension by inviting supporters of both sides to a party that occurred remarkably free of hostility. He also continued as an active Dreyfusard despite conflicting social ties, and his interest intensified when Major Henry's forgeries were exposed. For Proust and other Dreyfusards, Henry's folly represented the turning point in the entire scandal. The French military, despite its own commitment to the original verdict against Dreyfus, was compelled to try Henry, who promptly killed himself. Proust, at this point, was lobbying for the release from prison of Major Picquart, who had been imprisoned for allegedly protecting Dreyfus. The Dreyfusards' efforts eventually proved successful, for by 1899 Picquart was free and the French Government decidedly pro-Dreyfus. The largely anti-Semitic Nationalists staged a final conflict when Jules Guerin, secretary-general of the Anti-Semitic League, secured himself with weapons and challenged the Dreyfusards to attack his headquarters. This action, however, resulted in only minimal violence, and Guerin finally surrendered to police and fire fighters.

Despite the French Government's newfound support for Dreyfus, he was once again found guilty when tried by the French Army. But Proust was now confident that the state would not condone such a verdict. He was correct, for the French president then pardoned Dreyfus, who returned to the French mainland a broken, tragic figure. Barker, in his biography, wrote that for Proust, who was half-Jewish, the Dreyfus scandal would remain a cherished memory "of a long and bitter struggle against the forces of anti-Semitism, carried to a successful conclusion."

In the early 1900s Proust's literary interest turned to English critic John Ruskin. Since late 1899 Proust had been reading Ruskin's works in French translation and contributing studies on Ruskin to periodicals such as *Le Figaro* and *Le Mercure de France.* Recognizing that Ruskin's intricate, detailed style resembled his own, Proust resolved to translate Ruskin's work into French. He began with Ruskin's *The Bible of Amiens,* a discussion of art and architecture in the Amiens region of France. Proust worked on the translation for more than three years, delving into Ruskin's canon and traveling to Amiens and even to Venice to see those artworks referred to by Ruskin in various volumes. But upon publication in 1904 Proust's translation met with little success and was accorded only minimal attention in the French publications. A subsequent translation of Ruskin's *Sesame and Lilies* fared similarly, aside from an unusually praiseworthy account in *Le Figaro,* which Proust was dismayed

to discover had gone unread by his friends. In a letter, he complained that most educated Parisians "are incapable of reading even so much as a newspaper." This comment, cited in Barker's biography, is indicative of Proust's disappointment at the reception given the product of his intense labor.

Proust's health during these years remained unstable, but problems such as asthma and depression were doubtless exacerbated by his increasingly eccentric behavior. In an attempt to ease the breathing difficulties resulting from asthma, he burned medicinal powders, and to stabilize the air in his bedroom he forbade servants from dusting there. Thus the room was often full of smoke and dust, two agents detrimental to asthmatics. For his insomnia Proust ingested trional, which he often misused by taking in the morning as his surroundings became increasingly lively. This rendered the trional ineffective and plunged Proust into further anxiety. His efforts to sleep in the morning seemed strange to his mother, who tried to conduct household matters as if her son kept usual hours. This allegedly unsympathetic behavior frustrated and angered Proust, who criticized her in letters delivered from his gloomy bedroom. In 1903 Proust was further shaken by the death of his father, who had been a respected physician and professor. For Proust, the death was particularly devastating since he felt guilty over his failure to realize his father's hopes and intentions. After the funeral Proust devoted a long bereavement to completing the first Ruskin translation, which he dedicated to his father.

Following the death of his father Proust adopted a more conciliatory tone in writing to his mother. He maintained his nocturnal lifestyle but vowed to work toward keeping normal hours. In 1904, continuing with his efforts to regulate his life, Proust sought medical assistance in combating asthma. His physician diagnosed Proust's affliction as anxiety-related and advised him to enter a German clinic, where he would undergo a treatment similar to that used with drug addicts. Proust demurred, then began considering a similar clinic in Switzerland. He decided to pursue treatment in Switzerland after finishing his translation of Ruskin's *Sesame and Lilies,* but in the fall of 1905 his plans were dashed when his mother fell ill with uremia. She died soon afterward, whereupon Proust entered another period of mourning. Toward the end of 1905, however, he decided to take a cure, but in Paris. His treatment consisted, at least in part, of staying in bed and eating as often and as much as possible. After several weeks, Proust abandoned the ludicrous process.

Without his parents to support him Proust was forced to seek cheaper living accommodations. But in 1906 he moved into a costly apartment on a busy, tree-lined boulevard that guaranteed noise, dust, and pollen. Despite its entirely unsuitable nature, the apartment appealed to Proust, for it had once been owned by a relative and was thus known by his late mother. The idea of living in an apartment familiar to his mother powerfully appealed to Proust, and so he moved despite the obvious liabilities. Eventually the apartment located on the Boulevard Haussmann became notorious for its disheveled, dark, dusty interior and its inconvenient air temperature. The place was disheveled because Proust refused to arrange to clean furniture for fear of stirring dust, and it was dark because he slept during the daytime and thus kept the curtains closed to sunlight. Finally, the air temperature was disturbing to visitors because of Proust's bizarre belief that it was healthier to remain cold in the winter and hot in the summer. Therefore he kept the windows open in the winter and slept under heavy blankets in the summer. For Proust this apartment, particularly its gloomy, filthy bedroom, which he lined with cork to muffle sound, constituted his chief environment for the next thirteen years.

In 1907 Proust began reworking the nearly eighty notebooks that composed *Jean Santeuil.* While organizing this material he also produced an autobiographical/critical volume, *Contre Sainte-Beuve,* which included long accounts derived from the *Jean Santeuil* notes. In *Contre Sainte-Beuve* Proust challenged the aesthetic principles of French critic Charles Augustin Sainte-Beuve, who believed that contemporary literature was best comprehended through an understanding of its writers. Proust argued that literature existed independently—inspired from unfathomable depths within the writer—and that Sainte-Beuve's method was superficial. Aside from its critical passages, though, *Contre Sainte-Beuve* contained lengthy digressions on memory and love, the two major themes of *Remembrance of Things Past,* and the earlier work, which was published only posthumously, is now read chiefly as a precursor to the later masterpiece.

While writing *Contre Sainte-Beuve* Proust was already shaping the *Jean Santeuil* material into *Remembrance.* Working constantly, he re-structured his narrative around the theme of memory and began writing anew from a first-person perspective. The result was *Swann's Way,* the first volume of *Remembrance. Swann's Way* begins with the narrator, Marcel, noting, "For a long time I used to go to bed early." He discusses the effects of dreams, then reveals his desire to retrieve his past. This revelation is followed by a childhood recollection in which Marcel and his parents are visited by a family friend, Charles Swann. Marcel recounts how, on this particular visit from Swann, he was forced by his father to withdraw without receiving a kiss from his mother. Marcel retires sorrowfully to his bedroom. But his father, realizing his son's distress, eventually sends Marcel's mother to his room and even allows her to sleep there. The opening segment, entitled "Overture" by translator C. K. Scott-Moncrieff but untitled by Proust, concludes with the famous tea-and-madeleine incident, in which the narrator tastes a pastry dipped in tea and is immediately overwhelmed by memories of his childhood. His subsequent recollections constitute, along with attendant analysis, the remainder of *Remembrance of Things Past.*

In "Overture" Proust introduces *Remembrance*'s principal themes: memory and possessive love. In *Swann's Way*'s longest single section, "Swann in Love," he depicts the destructive force of such love in recounting Swann's social decline. This decline is precipitated by his love for Odette, a manipulative courtesan who drives Swann to acts of obsessive jealousy, much to the amusement of bourgeois hostess Madame Verdurin. Swann realizes his folly only after dreaming of Odette and the Verdurins, whereupon he acknowledges having wasted his life and his love on a woman with whom he was incompatible. *Swann's Way* ends with a transitional section leading into *Within a Budding Grove,* the second volume of *Remembrance of Things Past.*

Upon completing *Swann's Way* Proust labored to secure a publisher, even venturing from his cork-lined room to press for the book's acceptance. But each publisher rejected the work: some were opposed to the book's length, especially since it was merely part of a larger work; others were nonplussed by Proust's intricate prose and his penchant for detail. One such editor even wrote to Proust's brother. "My dear friend," the editor conveyed, "perhaps I am dense but just don't understand why a man should take thirty pages to describe how he rolls about in bed before he goes to sleep." After multiple rejection Proust decided to publish *Swann's Way* at his own expense. This proved a costly gambit when, at the proofreading stage, Proust appended whole pages to the galleys and filled their margins, thus effectively re-writing the entire manuscript.

Proust's personal life at this time was hardly conducive to the demands of writing and revising. Suffering from insomnia, weight loss, and even dental pain, he hired his lover, Alfred Agostinelli, as his live-in secretary. But Agostinelli had a wife and her constant presence thwarted Proust's creativity and his romantic inclinations. As tensions at Proust's apartment peaked in 1913, he left for a brief vacation. His respite was hardly calming, however, for he traveled with the Agostinellis. Proust eventually convinced Agostinelli to return with him to Paris without Mrs. Agostinelli. But once home Proust again succumbed to his various ailments. Bedridden, he inexplicably contemplated another vacation.

Swann's Way received publication in late 1913 and brought more anguish to Proust. Critics generally agreed that he possessed sensitivity and a keen perception, but they also complained that he lacked artistic judgment—that the sentences rambled interminably, thoughts turned confusing, and the entire work required drastic reduction. For Proust, who had dreamed of winning a literary prize for his work, the reviews were devastating.

Proust suffered further hardship in 1914 when his lover, Agostinelli, fled the gloomy, prison-like confines of the Boulevard Haussmann apartment and began training as an airplane pilot. Proust was crushed by Agostinelli's desertion, and he begged him to return. But Agostinelli continued his training, and he died that spring when he lost control of his plane and crashed at sea. Before Proust could recover from his grief, he executed a series of stock maneuvers that ravaged his finances. Later that year the French economy collapsed, and World War I followed.

During the war Proust continued writing *Remembrance of Things Past.* The second volume, *Within a Budding Grove,* awaited publication by the *Nouvelle Revue Francais,* and the third volume, *The Guermantes Way,* approached completion. These two volumes, more chronological than *Swann's Way,* depict Marcel's early loves and chart his rise in society. In the final section of *Swann's Way,* Marcel befriends Charles Swann's daughter, Gilberte, while playing on the Champs-Elysees. *Within a Budding Grove* continues with this friendship, noting Marcel's attempts to manipulate her and perpetuate their relationship through lies and various contrivances. This segment of the novel features an obsessive analysis of dying love and is considered one of the finest episodes in all of *Remembrance.* Two other important characters are introduced in *Within a Budding Grove:* Robert de Saint-Loup, a military man who provides Marcel with an important introduction into high society, and Baron de Charlus, a flamboyant homosexual—based on Montesquiou—who presumes to serve as Marcel's mentor. The end of the second volume concerns Marcel's budding love for Albertine, one of several girls he meets while vacationing seaside.

In *The Guermantes Way,* emphasis shifts from romance to high society, and much of this volume consists of dinner parties. Here Marcel begins infiltrating Parisian society and meets acquaintances of the revered Guermantes clan. During a long sequence depicting one such party, the Dreyfus affair is discussed in detail, with Baron de Charlus offering a bizarre, somewhat anti-Semitic defense of the convicted Jewish officer, Dreyfus. Among other guests, banal activities are discussed in merciless detail. Allusions are also made to homosexuality, a dominant theme of subsequent volumes. *The Guermantes Way* ends with a pair of tragedies. Marcel's grandmother suffers a stroke and is subsequently plagued with temporary blindness and deafness. Her inept physician's cures, including leeches and morphine injections, drive her to suicide, at which she fails. And her eventual death, though expected, exerts a devastating effect on Marcel. The other tragedy involves Charles Swann, who reveals to the Duke and Duchess de Guermantes that he is dying of cancer. This is the famous "Red Shoes" episode, in which the Duke de Guermantes dismisses Swann's revelation and expresses greater concern for the shoes his wife is donning for a party.

Proust was surprisingly active during the war. While struggling with asthma, failing vision, and other ailments, he nonetheless managed to venture from seclusion to maintain social ties and visit more recent acquaintances. He also attended symphonic concerts and even frequented all-male brothels. But when the war ended he faced another trauma. His finances were dwindling, and his other resources were few. Then his apartment house was sold and he had to find another home. In 1919, suffering from asthma and distraught from upheaval, he moved into a furnished apartment on the Rue Laurent-Pichat. This place was so noisy that Proust resorted to drugs to temper his anxieties and sustain him as he worked. He lived here less than one year before moving again, this time to an extremely unsatisfactory apartment—too expensive, *too* dark, too small—where he continued writing and rewriting the final volumes of *Remembrance of Things Past.*

In the ensuing volumes of his masterpiece Proust continued charting the narrator's experiences in high society and portraying romantic love as futile and disappointing. *Remembrance*'s fourth volume, *Cities of the Plain,* begins with Marcel discovering Baron de Charlus in a homosexual act. The sequence develops into a long, historical/scientific analysis of homosexuality and its implications. The novel also includes episodes devoted to more social gatherings and portrays two loves: that of the baron for a callous violinist and that of Marcel for his childhood friend Albertine. Baron de Charlus's relationship develops into a pathetic farce; his callous lover manipulates and abuses him into humiliation. Marcel's love for Albertine, which provides the key drama in the next two volumes, is similarly hopeless, as Marcel grows increasingly suspicious of Albertine's previous relationships with other women.

Marcel's relentless desire to expose Albertine's lesbianism—behavior that echoes Charles Swann's earlier actions against Odette in *Swann's Way*—comes the focal point of *The Captive* and of the first half of *The Sweet Cheat Gone* (retitled *The Fugitive*). In these two volumes Proust exhaustively explores love's more insidious aspects: jealousy and infidelity, manipulation and exploitation. Social intrigue is also represented in the Verdurin's scheme to disrupt Baron de Charlus's relationship with violinist Charles Morel, a member of their circle, and in Marcel's efforts to ingratiate himself with the Duke and Duchess de Guermantes. In *The Sweet Cheat Gone* Marcel also learns of Albertine's accidental death, whereupon he becomes obsessed with establishing her lesbian past. Other important episodes in this volume include Marcel's visit to Venice, where he meets characters from his past, and his discovery that Robert Saint-Loup, his friend from years earlier, also engages in homosexual practices.

The Past Recaptured, the concluding work in *Remembrance of Things Past,* unites the characters and themes of preceding volumes. It begins with Marcel visiting his childhood friend Gilberte—daughter of Charles Swann and Odette—and her husband, Robert Saint-Loup. Marcel marvels at the couple's perverted behavior, notably the homosexual husband's flagrant womanizing, which is apparently designed to conceal further his actual preference for men. Marcel also discovers that the Verdurins, once considered vulgar, bourgeois pretenders to high society, are now key social figures. He then withdraws from society and enters a sanitorium to better contend with his tuberculo-

sis. The narrative subsequently turns to Parisian society during World War I and focuses particular attention on Baron de Charlus's experiences at all-male brothels. Following another withdrawal to a sanitorium, Marcel returns to Paris—the war has ended—and discovers that the aristocratic Guermantes and the coarse Verdurins have joined through marriage, thus forever compromising French high society. At a costume party, Marcel is stunned to realize the effects of age on the various celebrants, most of whom he can no longer recognize. It is at this party that Marcel's memories are triggered by seemingly insignificant details. Like the tea and madeleine of *Swann's Way,* these details prompt flooding memories that overwhelm and inspire Marcel. He then reveals his intentions to record his past experiences and sensations in the homage to time that will become, presumably, *Remembrance of Things Past.*

Summarizing *Remembrance of Things Past,* as more than one critic has conceded, is impossible. Its riches—vivid characters, astounding insights, elaborate descriptions—spread across such length, more than thirty-three hundred pages in a 1982 edition of the English translation, indicate that mere plot synopsis must necessarily prove superficial and inadequate to any true appreciation or understanding of the work. Some critics, including biographer George Painter, have even speculated that Proust's masterpiece transcends the novel genre and is more accurately an elaborate memoir. *Remembrance of Things Past,* according to Painter, was intended by Proust as "the symbolic story of his life" and thus "occupies a place unique among great novels in that it is not, properly speaking, a fiction, but a creative autobiography."

Proust did not live to see his entire work published. He did receive greater acclaim, however, winning the prestigious Goncourt Prize for *Within a Budding Grove* in 1919. But even this honor was not without its attendant controversy, as some critics suggested that Proust, at age forty-nine, was too old for an honor intended for young writers. Other critics rallied to Proust's defense, claiming that *Within a Budding Grove*—and *Swann's Way*—signified the presence of a great, innovative artist. Even critics objecting to *Swann's Way* conceded that they had been rash, and affirmed that *Within a Budding Grove* was indication of a major work. But by 1922, with the final three volumes still to be published, Proust was too weak to take an active interest in his newfound celebrity. Already wracked with numerous complaints, including dizziness, slurred speech, and impaired vision, Proust fell desperately ill after contracting a cold that autumn. A disastrous adrenalin injection only compounded his problems, and by November he was near death. On November 18, 1922, Proust, in delirium, declared that a large, black figure loomed near his bedroom door. A final injection by his brother, a doctor, proved futile, and that evening Proust died.

In the years since Proust's death *Remembrance of Things Past* has increased in stature, and it now ranks among the century's greatest works. The English translation, largely written by C. K. Scott-Moncrieff, is similarly praised as a masterpiece of its kind, and it has exerted considerable influence since its volumes began appearing in the early 1920s. Joseph Conrad, in a letter to Scott-Moncrieff in 1923, concluded that the appeal of Proust's work lies in its "inexplicable character." Conrad wrote: "It appeals to our sense of wonder and gains our homage by its veiled greatness. I don't think there ever has been in the whole of literature such an example of the power of analysis, and I feel pretty safe in saying that there will never be another."

MEDIA ADAPTATIONS: "Swann in Love," a chapter from Swann's Way, was adapted by Peter Brook, Jean-Claude Carriere, and Marie-Helene Estienne for the film "Swann in Love," directed by Volkor Schloendorff, 1984.

BIOGRAPHICAL/CRITICAL SOURCES:

BOOKS

Albaret, Celeste, *Monsieur Proust,* edited by Georges Belmont, translated by Barbara Bray, McGraw, 1976.

Alden, Douglas W., *Marcel Proust and His French Critics,* Russell, 1973.

Ames, Van Meter, *Proust and Santayana: The Aesthetic Way of Life,* Russell, 1964.

Barker, Richard H., *Marcel Proust,* Criterion Press, 1958.

Bell, Clive, *Proust,* Hogarth Press, 1928.

Bell, William Stewart, *Proust's Nocturnal Muse,* Columbia University Press, 1962.

Bersani, Leo, *Marcel Proust: The Fictions of Life and Art,* Oxford University Press, 1965.

Brady, Patrick, *Marcel Proust,* Twayne, 1977.

Cirard, Rene, editor, *Proust: A Collection of Critical Essays,* Prentice-Hall, 1962.

Cocking, J. M., *Proust,* Yale University Press, 1956.

Dictionary of Literary Biography, Volume 65: *French Novelists, 1900-1930,* Gale, 1988.

Forster, E. M., *Abinger Harvest,* Harcourt, 1936.

Fowlie, Wallace, *A Reading of Proust,* Anchor Books, 1964.

Graham, Victory, *The Imagery of Proust,* Blackwell, 1966.

Green, F. C., *The Mind of Proust: A Detailed Interpretation of "A la recherche du temps perdu,"* Cambridge University Press, 1949.

Haldane, Charlotte, *Marcel Proust,* Arthur Barker, 1951.

Hindus, Milton, *The Proustian Vision,* Columbia University Press, 1954.

Hindus, Milton, *A Reader's Guide to Marcel Proust,* Noonday Press, 1962.

Hughes, Edward J., *Marcel Proust: A Study in the Quality of Awareness,* Cambridge University Press, 1983.

Kazin, Alfred, *The Inmost Leaf: A Selection of Essays,* Harcourt, 1955.

Kilmartin, Terence, *A Reader's Guide to "Remembrance of Things Past,"* Random House, 1983.

Leon, Derrick, *Introduction to Proust: His Life, His Circle, His Work,* Kegan Paul, 1940.

Lesage, Laurent, *Marcel Proust and His Literary Friends,* University of Illinois Press, 1958.

March, Harold, *The Two Worlds of Marcel Proust,* University of Pennsylvania Press, 1948.

Maurois, Andre, *Proust: Portrait of a Genius,* translated by Gerard Hopkins, Harper, 1950.

Miller, Milton L., *Nostalgia: A Psychoanalytic Study of Marcel Proust,* Houghton, 1956.

Moss, Howard, *The Magic Lantern of Marcel Proust,* Macmillan, 1962.

Painter, George D., *Marcel Proust* (two volumes), Chatto Windus, 1959, Random House, 1978.

Price, Larkin B., editor, *Marcel Proust: A Critical Panorama,* University of Illinois Press, 1973.

Quennel, Peter, editor, *Marcel Proust, 1871-1922: A Centenary Volume,* Weidenfeld & Nicolson, 1971.

Rogers, B G., *Proust's Narrative Technique,* Librairie Droz, 1965.

Sansom, William, *Proust and His World,* Thames & Hudson, 1973.

Scott-Moncrieff, C. K., editor, *Marcel Proust: An English Tribute,* T. Seltzer, 1923.

Shattuck, Roger, *Proust's Binoculars: A Study of Memory, Time, and Recognition in "A la recherche du temps perdu,"* Random House, 1963.

Spagnoli, John, *The Social Attitude of Marcel Proust,* Publications of the Institute of French Studies, Columbia University, 1936.

Strauss, Walter A., *Proust and Literature: The Novelist as Critic,* Harvard University Press, 1957.

Twentieth-Century Literary Criticism, Gale, Volume 7, 1982, Volume 13, 1984, Volume 33, 1989.

Wilson, Edmund, *Axel's Castle: A Study in the Imaginative Literature of 1870-1930,* Scribner, 1931.

PERIODICALS

Harper's, September, 1981.
Hudson Review, winter, 1958-59.
Los Angeles Times, January 18, 1988.
Modern Language Review, January, 1962.
New Republic, September 21, 1932.
Newsweek, June 29, 1981, October 1, 1984.
New Yorker, October 12, 1981.
New York Times, December 28, 1947, June 5, 1987.
New York Times Book Review, July 11, 1971, May 3, 1981, May 29, 1983.
Sewanee Review, spring, 1932.
Time, October 15, 1984.
Times Literary Supplement, September 25, 1987, October 7, 1988, October 13, 1989, November 24, 1989.
Washington Post, October 8, 1987.

* * *

PROVIST, d'Alain
See DIOP, Birago (Ismael)

* * *

PROWLER, Harley
See MASTERS, Edgar Lee

* * *

PTELEON
See GRIEVE, C(hristopher) M(urray)

* * *

PUCKETT, Lute
See MASTERS, Edgar Lee

* * *

PUIG, Manuel 1932-1990

PERSONAL: Born December 28, 1932, in General Villegas, Argentina; died July 22, 1990, in Cuernavaca, Mexico; son of Baldomero (a businessman) and Maria Elena (a chemist; maiden name, Delledonne) Puig. *Education:* Attended University of Buenos Aires, beginning 1950, and Centro Sperimentale di Cinematografia, beginning 1955; studied languages and literature at private institutes. *Religion:* None.

ADDRESSES: Home—Rio de Janiero, Brazil. *Office*—c/o Erroll McDonald, Vintage Books, 201 East 50th St., New York, N.Y. 10022.

CAREER: Translator and Spanish and Italian teacher in London, England, and Rome, Italy, 1956-57; assistant film director in Rome and Paris, France, 1957-58; worked as a dishwasher in London and in Stockholm, Sweden, 1958-59; assistant film director in Buenos Aires, Argentina, 1960; translator of film subtitles in Rome, 1961-62; Air France, New York, N.Y., clerk, 1963-67; writer, 1967—. *Military service:* Argentina Air Force, 1953; served as translator.

AWARDS, HONORS: La traicion de Rita Hayworth was named one of the best foreign novels of 1968-69 by *Le Monde* (France); best script award, 1974, for "Boquitas pintadas," and jury prize, 1978, for "El lugar sin limites," both from San Sebastian Festival; American Library Association (ALA) Notable Book, 1979, for *The Kiss of the Spider Woman; Plays & Players* Award for most promising playwright, 1985, for "Kiss of the Spider Woman."

WRITINGS:

La traicion de Rita Hayworth, Sudamericana (Buenos Aires), 1968, reprinted, Casa de las Americas, 1983, translation by Suzanne Jill Levine published as *Betrayed by Rita Hayworth,* Dutton, 1971, reprinted, 1987.

Boquitas pintadas (also see below), Sudamericana, 1969, translation by Levine published as *Heartbreak Tango: A Serial,* Dutton, 1973.

The Buenos Aires Affair: Novela policial, Sudamericana, 1973, translation by Levine published as *The Buenos Aires Affair: A Detective Novel,* Dutton, 1976.

El beso de la mujer arana (also see below), Seix-Barral (Barcelona), 1976, translation by Thomas Colchie published as *The Kiss of the Spider Woman,* Knopf, 1979.

Pubis angelical (also see below), Seix-Barral, 1979, translation by Elena Brunet published under same title, Vintage, 1986.

"El beso de la mujer arana" (play; adapted from his novel; also see below), first produced in Spain, 1981, translation by Allan Baker titled "Kiss of the Spider Woman," first produced in London at the Bush Theatre, 1985, produced in Los Angeles at the Cast Theatre, 1987.

Eternal Curse upon the Reader of These Pages, Random House, 1982, Spanish translation by the author published as *Maldicion eterna a quien lea estas paginas,* Seix Barral, 1982.

Sangre de amor correspondido, Seix Barral, 1982, translation by Jan L. Grayson published as *Blood of Requited Love,* Vintage, 1984.

Bajo un manto de estrellas: Pieza en dos actos [and] *El beso de la mujer arana: Adaptacion escenica realizada por el autor* (plays; also see below), Seix Barral, 1983.

Under a Mantle of Stars: A Play in Two Acts, translation by Ronald Christ, Lumen Books, 1985 (produced in the original Spanish as "Bajo un manto de estrellas").

(Contributor) G. W. Woodyard and Marion P. Holt, editors, *Drama Contemporary: Latin America,* PAJ Publications, 1986.

Mystery of the Rose Bouquet (play; produced at the Bush Theatre, 1987, produced in Los Angeles, Calif., at Mark Taper Forum, November 16, 1989), translation by Baker, Faber, 1988 (produced in the original Spanish as "Misterio del ramo de rosas").

Also author of screenplays for "Boquitas Pintadas," adapted from his novel, 1974, "El lugar sin limites," adapted from Jose Donoso's novel, 1978, and "Pubis angelical." Contributor to various periodicals, including *Omni.*

WORK IN PROGRESS: Production of his screenplay "Seven Tropical Sins" by David Weisman's Sugarloaf Films company; developing a musical comedy with Weisman, "Chica Boom!"; the book for a musical version of *The Kiss of the Spider Woman.*

SIDELIGHTS: As a boy growing up in rural Argentina, novelist Manuel Puig spent countless hours in the local movie house viewing screen classics from the United States and Europe. His enchantment with films led him to spend several years pursuing a career as a director and screenwriter until he discovered that what he wanted to write was better suited to fiction; nevertheless, Puig's work is saturated with references to films and other popular phenomena. "[But] if Puig's novels are 'pop,' " observes Jonathan Tittler in his *Narrative Irony in the Contemporary Spanish-American Novel,* it is because "he incorporates into his fiction elements of mass culture—radionovelas, comic books, glamour magazines, and in *Betrayed by Rita Hayworth,* commercial movies—in order to unveil their delightfully insidious role in shaping contemporary life." Puig echoes the design of these media, "us[ing] those forms as molds to cast his corny, bathetic material in a form displaying a witty, ironic attitude toward that material," notes Ronald Christ in *Commonweal.* Ronald Schwartz concurs with this assessment; writing in his study *Nomads, Exiles, and Emigres: The Rebirth of the Latin American Narrative, 1960-80,* the critic contends that Puig employs "the techniques of pop art to communicate a complex vision of his own world. It is [the] cinematic influence that makes *Betrayed by Rita Hayworth* and Puig's subsequent novels some of the most original contemporary Latin American narratives."

In *Betrayed by Rita Hayworth,* "the idea of the novel is simple: the drama and pathos of moviegoing as a way of life in the provinces, where often people get to respond to life itself with gestures and mock programs taken over from film," describes *New York Times Book Review* contributor Alexander Coleman. The story is narrated primarily through the eyes of Toto, a young boy born in the Argentinian pampas, and recounts the everyday life of his family and friends. "The novel's charm," claims *Newsweek* writer Walter Clemons, "is in the tender gravity with which Puig records the chatter of Toto's family and neighbors. Kitchen conversations, awkwardly written letters and flowery schoolgirl diary entries . . . combine to evoke lives of humblest possibility and uncomplaining disappointment."

While this description may sound gloomy, states Coleman, nevertheless *Betrayed by Rita Hayworth* "is a screamingly funny book, with scenes of such utter bathos that only a student of final reels such as Puig could possibly have verbally re-created [it] for us." "Above all, Puig has captured the language of his characters," D. P. Gallagher reports in his *Modern Latin American Literature,* and explains: "There is no distance separating him from the voices he records, moreover, for they are the voices that he was brought up with himself, and he is able to reproduce them with perfect naturalness, and without distortion or parodic exaggeration. That is not to say that his novels are not very polished and very professional," the critic continues. "Like all the best Latin American novels . . . , they are structured deliberately as fictions. But the authenticity with which they reflect a very real environment cannot be questioned."

Puig's next novel, *Heartbreak Tango,* "in addition to doing everything that *Rita Hayworth* did (and doing it better, too) actually proclaims Puig not only a major writer but a major stylist whose medium brings you both the heartbreak *and* the tango," Christ declares in *Review 73.* Bringing together letters, diaries, newspapers, conversations, and other literary artifices, *Heartbreak Tango,* as *New York Times* reviewer Christopher Lehmann-Haupt relates, "reconstructs the lives of several Argentine women, most of whom have in common the experience of having once passionately loved a handsome, ne'er-do-well and doomed young man who died of tuberculosis." Mark Jay Mirsky comments in the *Washington Post Book World* that at first "I missed the bustle, noise and grotesque power of *Betrayed by Rita Hayworth.* The narrative of *Heartbreak Tango* seemed much thinner, picking out the objects and voices of its hero [and] heroines with too obvious a precision." Nevertheless, the critic admits, "as we are caught up in the story, this taut line begins to spin us around."

Michael Wood, however, believes that it is this "precision" which makes *Heartbreak Tango* the better novel, as he details in a *New York Review of Books* article: "*Heartbreak Tango* seems to me even better than Puig's earlier *Betrayed by Rita Hayworth* because its characters' moments are clearer, and because the general implication of the montage of cliche and cheap romance and gossip is firmer." The critic adds that "the balance of the new book," between irony and sentimentalism, "is virtually perfect." Gallagher presents a similar opinion in the *New York Times Book Review,* noting that "it has been said that [*Heartbreak Tango*] is a parody, but that underestimates the balance between distance and compassion that Puig achieves. His characters are camp, but they are not camped up, and their fundamental humanity cannot be denied." Despite this serious aspect, the critic remarks that *Heartbreak Tango* "is a more accessible book than its predecessor without being less significant. It is compelling, moving, instructive and very funny." "At the same time," concludes David William Foster in *Latin American Literary Review,* "no matter how 'popular' or 'proletarian' the novel may appear to be on the surface, the essential and significant inner complexity of [*Heartbreak Tango*], like that of *Betrayed by Rita Hayworth,* bespeaks the true artistic dimensions of Puig's novel."

"The appearance of Manuel Puig's new novel, *The Buenos Aires Affair,* is especial cause for celebration," Ronald De Feo asserts in the *National Review,* "not only because the book makes for fascinating reading, but also because it demonstrates that its already highly accomplished author continues to take chances and to grow as an artist." Subtitled *A Detective Novel,* the story takes place in the city and investigates a kidnapping involving two sexually deviant people. "It is not devoid of the lucid and witty observation of absurd behaviour that characterized" *Heartbreak Tango,* maintains a *Times Literary Supplement,* "but it is altogether more anguished." As Toby Moore elaborates in another *Times Literary Supplement* review, "Puig's subject is the tangle made up of love and sexual desire. . . . In *The Buenos Aires Affair* the anxieties and inhibitions of the two characters are so great that they never get to a point of love; all they have is the dream of sex which obsesses and torments them."

The author sets this psychological drama within the framework of a traditional thriller; "what makes Puig so fascinating," writes *New York Times Book Review* contributor Robert Alter, is "the extraordinary inventiveness he exhibits in devising new ways to render familiar material." De Feo, however, faults the author for being "a shade too inventive, [for] we are not always convinced that [these methods] are necessary. But," the critic adds, "the book is more intense, serious, and disturbing than the other novels, and it is a welcome departure for this searching, gifted writer." And the *Times Literary Supplement* writer claims that *The Buenos Aires Affair* "is technically even more accomplished than the previous novels, and Sr Puig is able to handle a wide variety of narrative devices in it without ever making them seem gratuitous."

Shortly after the publication of *The Buenos Aires Affair* in 1973, Puig found it more difficult to remain in Argentina; *Affair* had been banned (presumably because of its sexual content), and the political situation was becoming more restrictive. This increasingly antagonistic climate led Puig to a self-imposed exile, and

is reflected in what is probably his best-known work, *The Kiss of the Spider Woman.* Set almost entirely in an Argentinian jail cell, the novel focuses on Valentin, a radical student imprisoned for political reasons, and Molina, a gay window dresser in on a "morals" charge, who recounts his favorite 1930s and '40s movies as a means of passing time. "In telling the story of two cellmates, Puig strips down the narrative to a nearly filmic level—dialogue unbroken even to identify the speakers, assuming we can project them onto our own interior screens," relates Carol Anshaw in the *Voice Literary Supplement.* "If this insistent use of unedited dialogue tends to make the book read a bit like a radio script, however," observes *New York Times Book Review* contributor Robert Coover, "it is Mr. Puig's fascination with old movies that largely provides [the novel's] substance and ultimately defines its plot, its shape. What we hear," the critic continues, "are the voices of two suffering men, alone and often in the dark, but what we see . . . [is] all the iconographic imagery, magic and romance of the movies." The contrast between the two men, who gradually build a friendship "makes this Argentinian odd couple both funny and affecting," Larry Rohter states in the *Washington Post Book World.* But when Molina is released in hopes that he will lead officials to Valentin's confederates, "the plot turns from comedy to farce and Puig's wit turns mordant."

In addition to the continuous dialogue of the jail cell and surveillance report after Molina's release, *The Kiss of the Spider Woman* contains several footnotes on homosexuality whose "clumsy academic style serves to emphasize by contrast that the two prisoners' dialogue is a highly contrived storytelling device, and not the simulation of reality you may take it to be at first," comments Lehmann-Haupt. Because of this, the critic explains, the book becomes "a little too tricky, like a well-made, 19th-century play." Other reviewers, however, find *The Kiss of the Spider Woman* "far and away [Puig's] most impressive book," as Anshaw says. "It is not easy to write a book which says something hopeful about human nature and yet remains precise and unsentimental," Maggie Gee remarks in the *Times Literary Supplement.* "Puig succeeds, partly because his bleak vision of the outside world throws into relief the small private moments of hope and dignifies them, partly through his deft manipulation of form." Schwartz similarly concludes that *The Kiss of the Spider Woman* "is not the usual jumble of truncated structures from which a plot emerges but, rather, a beautifully controlled narrative that skillfully conveys basic human values, a vivid demonstration of the continuing of the genre itself."

Inspired by a stay in New York, *Eternal Curse on the Reader of These Pages* was written directly in English and, similar to *The Kiss of the Spider Woman,* is mainly comprised of an extended dialogue. Juan Jose Ramirez is an elderly Argentinian living in exile in New York and Lawrence John is the irritable, taciturn American who works part-time caring for him. But as their dialogues progress, Lehmann-Haupt notes, "it becomes increasingly difficult to tell how much is real and how much the two characters have become objects of each other's fantasy life." *Los Angeles Times Book Review* critic Charles Champlin, although he believes these dialogues constitute a technical "tour de force," questions "whether a technical exercise, however clever, [is] the best way to get at this study of conflicting cultures and the ambiguities in the relationship."

Gilbert Sorrentino similarly feels that *Eternal Curse* is "a structural failure, . . . for the conclusion, disastrously, comments on and 'explains' an otherwise richly ambivalent and mysterious text." The critic continues in the *Washington Post Book World:* "It's too bad, because Puig *has* something, most obviously a sense that the essential elements of life, life's serious 'things,' are precisely the elements of soap opera, sit-coms, and B-movies." But Lehmann-Haupt thinks *Eternal Curse* is "more austere and intellectually brittle than any of [Puig's] previous books, [and] less playful and dependent on the artifacts of American pop culture," and calls the novel a "fascinating tour de force." "Puig is an artist, . . . and his portrait of two men grappling with their suffering is exceedingly moving and brilliantly done," declares William Herrick in the *New Leader.* "Strangely, the more space I put between the book and myself, the more tragic I find it. It sticks to the mind. Like one cursed, I cannot find peace, cannot escape from its pain."

Echoing themes of Puig's previous work, maintains *Nation* contributor Jean Franco, "politics and sexuality are inseparable in *Pubis Angelical,*" the latest of Puig's novels to be published in the United States. Alternating the story of Ana, an Argentinian exile dying of cancer in Mexico, with her fantasies of a 1930s movie star and a futuristic "sexual soldier," *Pubis Angelical* speaks "of the political nightmares of exile, disappearance, torture and persecution," describes Franco, "though as always in Puig's novels, the horror is tempered by the humor of his crazy plots and kitsch stage props." "Puig is both ruthless and touching in his presentation of Ana's muddled but sincere life," states Jason Wilson in the *Times Literary Supplement;* "and if he is sometimes too camp, he can also be very funny." The critic elaborates: "His humour works because he refuses to settle for any single definition of woman; Ana is all feeling and intuition . . . although she is also calculating, and unfeeling about her daughter." But while Ana's advancing cancer and the problems of her dream counterparts are severe, "however seriously Puig is questioning gender assumptions and behavior his voice is never a solemn one," Nick Caistor claims in the *New Statesman.* "The work as a whole fairly bristles with ingenuity and energy," Robert Towers writes in the *New York Review of Books;* "the thematic parallels between the three texts seem almost inexhaustible, and one finishes the novel with a sense of having grasped only a portion of them." Nevertheless, the critic faults *Pubis Angelical* for being "an impressive artifact rather than a fully engrossing work of fictional art."

Steve Erickson likewise criticizes the novel, commenting in the *New York Times Book Review* that "what's amazing about 'Pubis Angelical' is how utterly in love it is with its own artificiality." The critic adds that "the novel fails most devastatingly" in the portrayals of Ana's fantasies: "There's nothing about their lives to suggest that . . . they have a reality for her." While Jay Cantor similarly believes that "it isn't till the last quarter of the book that the fantasies have sufficient, involving interest," he acknowledges in the *Los Angeles Times Book Review* that "there is an audacity to Puig's method, and an intellectual fire to Puig's marshaling of motifs that did then engage me." "In any case, whatever the whole [of the novel] amounts to, each individual part of 'Pubis Angelical' develops its own irresistible drama," counters Lehmann-Haupt. "Though it takes an exercise of the intellect to add them together, they finally contribute to what is the most richly textured and extravagant fiction [Puig] has produced so far."

"Less interested in depicting things as they might be, and concerned with things as they are, Puig does not resort to make-believe," Alfred J. MacAdam asserts in *Modern Latin American Narratives: The Dreams of Reason.* "His characters are all too plausible, . . . [and their lives] simply unfold over days and years until they run their meaningless course." It is this ordinary, commonplace quality of life, however, that the author prefers to investigate, as he told the *Washington Post*'s Desson

Howe: "I find literature the ideal medium to tell certain stories that are of special interest to me. Everyday stories with no heroics, the everyday life of the gray people." And films play such a large role in his work because of the contrast they provide to this mundane world: "I think I can understand the reality of the 1930s by means of the unreality of their films," Puig remarked in a *Los Angeles Times* interview with Ann Marie Cunningham. "The films reflect exactly what people dreamed life could be. The relationships between people in these films are like the negative of a photograph of real life." "I can only understand realism," the author further explained to *New York Times* writer Samuel G. Freedman. "I can only approach my writing with an analytical sense. . . . I can write dreams, but I use them as part of the accumulation of detail, as counterpoint." Because of his realistic yet inventive portrayals, contends Schwartz, "Manuel Puig is a novelist moving in the direction of political commitment in his depiction of the provincial and urban middle class of Argentina, something that has never before been attempted so successfully in Latin American letters." The critic concludes: "Clearly, Puig, thriving self-exiled from his native country, is an eclectic stylist, a consummate artist."

MEDIA ADAPTATIONS: The Kiss of the Spider Woman was made into a film by Brazilian director Hector Babenco in 1985 and starred Raul Julia, William Hurt (in an Oscar-winning performance), and Sonia Braga.

BIOGRAPHICAL/CRITICAL SOURCES:

BOOKS

Contemporary Literary Criticism, Gale, Volume 3, 1975, Volume 5, 1976, Volume 10, 1979, Volume 28, 1984.

Gallagher, D. P., *Modern Latin American Literature,* Oxford University Press, 1973.

MacAdam, Alfred J., *Modern Latin American Narratives: The Dreams of Reason,* University of Chicago Press, 1977.

Schwartz, Ronald, *Nomads, Exiles, and Emigres: The Rebirth of the Latin American Narrative, 1960-80,* Scarecrow, 1980.

Tittler, Jonathan, *Narrative Irony in the Contemporary Spanish-American Novel,* Cornell University Press, 1984.

PERIODICALS

Chicago Tribune Book World, April 15, 1979.

Commonweal, June 24, 1977.

Latin American Literary Review, fall, 1972.

Los Angeles Times, January 30, 1987, February 3, 1987, November 16, 1989, November 17, 1989.

Los Angeles Times Book Review, June 20, 1982, December 28, 1986.

Nation, April 18, 1987.

National Review, October 29, 1976.

New Leader, June 28, 1982.

New Statesman, October 2, 1987.

Newsweek, October 25, 1971, June 28, 1982.

New York Review of Books, December 13, 1973, January 24, 1980, December 18, 1986.

New York Times, November 28, 1973, April 23, 1979, June 4, 1982, September 25, 1984, August 5, 1985, December 22, 1986, October 25, 1988.

New York Times Book Review, September 26, 1971, December 16, 1973, September 5, 1976, April 22, 1979, July 4, 1982, September 23, 1984, December 28, 1986.

Review 73, fall, 1973.

Times (London), August 23, 1985.

Times Literary Supplement, November 6, 1970, August 31, 1973, September 21, 1984, October 16, 1987, August 11-17, 1989.

Voice Literary Supplement, April, 1989.
Washington Post, November 16, 1985.
Washington Post Book World, November 25, 1973, April 22, 1979, August 1, 1982.
World Literature Today, winter, 1981.

—*Sketch by Diane Telgen*

*   *   *

PURDY, James (Amos) 1923-

PERSONAL: Born July 17, 1923, in Ohio; son of William and Vera Purdy. *Education:* Attended University of Chicago and University of Puebla, Mexico.

ADDRESSES: Home—236 Henry St., Brooklyn, N.Y. 11201.

CAREER: Writer. Lawrence College (now University), Appleton, Wis., faculty member, 1949-53; worked as an interpreter in Latin America, France, and Spain; United States Information Agency lecturer in Europe, 1982.

AWARDS, HONORS: National Institute of Arts and Letters grant in literature, 1958; Guggenheim fellow, 1958, 1962; Ford Foundation grant, 1961; *On Glory's Course* nominated for PEN-Faulkner Award, 1985; received Rockefeller Foundation grant.

WRITINGS:

NOVELS

63: Dream Palace (also see below), William-Frederick, 1956.
Malcolm (also see below), Farrar, Straus, 1959.
The Nephew (also see below), Farrar, Straus, 1961.
Cabot Wright Begins, Farrar, Straus, 1964.
Eustace Chisholm and the Works, Farrar, Straus, 1967, reprinted, Carroll & Graf, 1986.
Jeremy's Version, Doubleday, 1970.
I Am Elijah Thrush, Doubleday, 1972.
The House of the Solitary Maggot, Doubleday, 1974.
Color of Darkness [and] *Malcolm* (also see below), Doubleday, 1974.
In a Shallow Grave, Arbor House, 1976.
Narrow Rooms, Arbor House, 1978.
Dream Palaces: Three Novels (contains *Malcolm, The Nephew,* and *63: Dream Palace*), Viking, 1980.
Mourners Below, Viking, 1981.
On Glory's Course, Viking, 1984.
In the Hollow of His Hand, Weidenfeld & Nicolson, 1986.
The Candles of Your Eyes, Viking, 1986.
Garments the Living Wear, City Lights Books, 1989.

STORY COLLECTIONS

Don't Call Me by My Right Name and Other Stories (also see below), William-Frederick, 1956.
63: Dream Palace: A Novella and Nine Stories (contains *63: Dream Palace,* and *Don't Call Me by My Right Name and Other Stories*), Gollancz, 1957.
Color of Darkness: Eleven Stories and a Novella (contains *63: Dream Palace, Don't Call Me by My Right Name Other Stories,* and two stories), New Directions, 1957.
Children Is All (stories and plays), New Directions, 1962.
An Oyster Is a Wealthy Beast (a story and poems), Black Sparrow Press, 1967.
Mr. Evening: A Story and Nine Poems, Black Sparrow Press, 1968.
On the Rebound: A Story and Nine Poems, Black Sparrow Press, 1970.

A Day after the Fair: A Collection of Plays and Stories, Note of Hand, 1977.
The Candles of Your Eyes and Thirteen Other Stories, Owens, 1988.

POEMS

The Running Sun, Paul Waner Press, 1971.
Sunshine Is an Only Child, Aloe Editions, 1973.
Lessons and Complaints, Nadja, 1978.
Sleep Tight, Nadja, 1979.
The Brooklyn Branding Parlors, Contact/II, 1985.

PLAYS

"Cracks," produced in New York City, 1963.
Wedding Finger, New Directions, 1974.
Two Plays (contains "A Day at the Fair" and "True"), New London Press, 1979.
Scrap of Paper [and] *The Berrypicker,* Sylvester & Orphanos, 1981.
Proud Flesh, Lord John Press, 1981.

Also author of play "Mr. Cough and the Phantom Sex," 1960.

RECORDINGS

"Eventide and Other Stories," Spoken Arts, 1968.
"63: Dream Palace," Spoken Arts, 1969.

OTHER

(Contributor) James Laughlin, editor, *New Directions in Prose and Poetry 21,* New Directions, 1969.

Contributor to over fifty books and to magazines, including *Mademoiselle, New Yorker,* and *Commentary.*

SIDELIGHTS: After his short stories were rejected by every magazine to which he submitted them, James Purdy published his first two books with a subsidy publisher in 1956. He sent copies of these subsidy books—the novel *63: Dream Palace* and the collection *Don't Call Me by My Right Name and Other Stories*—to a number of prominent literary figures, hoping to create some interest in his writing. The resulting interest was far more than he had expected. Dame Edith Sitwell, the English poet, wrote back to Purdy, calling several of his short stories "superb: nothing short of masterpieces" and his novel "a masterpiece from every point of view." Because of her admiration for Purdy's work, Sitwell spoke to the publishing firm of Gollancz and persuaded them to issue an English edition of Purdy's books. The Gollancz edition, combining both of his subsidy books into a single volume entitled *63: Dream Palace: A Novella and Nine Stories,* was well reviewed in England and launched Purdy's literary career. The same material, plus two additional stories, was published in America as *Color of Darkness: Eleven Stories and a Novella* in 1957.

Purdy first made his reputation, a *Times Literary Supplement* reviewer explains, because he wrote "in a style, a tone, that was as direct and natural as someone talking . . . and through eyes that belonged exclusively to him. You may dislike a writer's vision, but if he has one that is unique, you must admit his talent: it is the only sure sign of originality." Purdy's unique vision has been expressed in a variety of ways. As Henry Chupack emphasizes in his book *James Purdy,* he has "created many worlds; and each with its own discernible and distinct features." This variety makes Purdy a difficult writer to categorize. Stephen D. Adams writes in his book *James Purdy* that his "originality and extraordinary talents cannot be neatly inventoried. . . . To portray him as the author of an eccentric body of fiction, as a part of some movement or fashionable literary trend, or as a novelist who essentially mocks the capacities of art, is to deny the complexities of his individual voice."

A continuing concern with the crippling effects of the American family on its children marks all of Purdy's work. His early books portray orphans or runaways who are exploited or abused by older characters, while his more recent novels examine the destructive relationships between family members. The failure of love is behind the failure of the family in Purdy's work, Frank Baldanza writes in *Centennial Review,* resulting in children "who, as adults, pass on the anguished, lonely legacy to their own offspring. . . . Purdy's vision is somber and frightening." This vision is defined by Chupack as being the essence of postwar America. Chupack writes: "Behind [postwar America's] facade of great material wealth lay a vast spiritual wasteland of loveless lives and hellish marriages; from such barren marriages came children who, as a rule, were treated cruelly by their parents and by other adults; rape and homosexuality were engaged in by those who, denied love in their own lives, sought it in antisocial actions; and most ironic of all, the quest for wealth and the possession of it did not result in happiness."

Purdy distances himself from his fictional material while still involving his readers emotionally with his characters. He relates often violent or horrifying events in a flat, ironic prose to create a black comedy that transcends its melancholic subject matter. Writing in the *Village Voice,* Debra Rae Cohen explains that Purdy's narrative voice "cleaves to the rhythms proper to the world it creates, but keeps you aware, by its very pervasiveness, of the bemused, sardonic intelligence behind it all. . . . In the black humor of his artificial America, he seems sometimes as distanced as a puppeteer."

Critical reaction to Purdy's work ranges from high praise from such writers as Gore Vidal, Marianne Moore, Dorothy Parker, and John Cowper Powys to outright dismissal by other observers. A writer for the *Times Literary Supplement* admits that "there has always been a good deal of critical confusion about [Purdy]. As a writer, he has existed at extremes of praise and disparagement." Jerome Charyn also remarks on this critical polarity. Writing in the *New York Times Book Review,* Charyn explains that Purdy "exists in some strange limbo between adoration and neglect," although Charyn judges him to he "one of the very best writers we have." The English writer Francis King, in an article for the *Spectator,* notes the lack of critical acceptance Purdy has received. "Although," King writes, "he strikes me as a writer of far greater originality and power than [Saul] Bellow, [Philip] Roth, or [John] Updike, James Purdy has only rarely received his due in his native America." Critical reaction in Europe has generally been kinder to Purdy, particularly in France, England, and Italy.

In a letter to *CA,* Purdy states that his literary stature has been determined by the existing literary establishment, which is unsympathetic to his kind of writing. Purdy explains: "Reviewing in America is in a very bad state owing to the fact that there are no serious book reviews, and reputations are made in America by political groups backed by money and power brokers who care nothing for original and distinguished writing, but are bent on forwarding the names of writers who are politically respectable. There are also almost no magazines today which will print original and distinguished fiction unless the author is a member of the New York literary establishment. Reputations are made here, as in Russia, on political respectability, or by commercial acceptability. The worse the author, the more he is known."

Having what Warren French and Donald Pease in the *Dictionary of Literary Biography* call a "haunting, nightmarish quality," Purdy's first novel, *63: Dream Palace,* tells of two orphaned brothers who leave West Virginia to live in Chicago. Living in a big city for the first time, Fenton and Claire unknowingly associate with people who wish to exploit them. In his attempts to support the sickly Claire, Fenton moves from theft to prostitution to drugs, ultimately strangling Claire while under the influence of drugs.

The book was inspired by Purdy's own youth. "I left home at an early age and went to Chicago. It was the first big city I had ever known, and was unprepared for its overwhelming confusion," Purdy writes in the *Contemporary Authors Autobiography Series.* But *63: Dream Palace* is "biography . . . transformed into a supreme fiction that sails close-hauled in one direction to out-and-out naturalism, and in the other to surrealistic fable," as Robert K. Morris writes in the *Nation.* Morris concludes by describing the novel as "at once a marvelous and depressing tale, as lucid and total an allegory of despair as one could imagine."

The short stories of Purdy's other early book, *Don't Call Me by My Right Name,* are, Anthony Bailey of *Commonweal* believes, "a novel departure in the craft of the short story." Bailey finds that Purdy's achievement in these stories makes "the work of many highly skilled writers seem extremely dependent on literary convention and, in doing so, [Purdy] has made fresh contact with moral reality." Similarly, William Bittner of *Nation* thinks Purdy's work "seems to be more what the short story might have been had it developed continuously from [Edgar Allan] Poe, [Nathaniel] Hawthorne, and [Herman] Melville. Purdy, at any rate, is that rare bird in this age of reportorial fiction, a writer who creates."

The critical acclaim for Purdy's work continued with the release of the novel *Malcolm* in 1959. The book tells the story of a fifteen-year-old boy who is abandoned at a posh hotel by his father. Making the acquaintance of an astrologer, Mr. Cox, Malcolm is given a list of addresses of people he should visit and the advice, "Give yourself up to things." The people Malcolm visits, Donald Cook writes in the *New Republic,* try "to use him and to possess him." "The themes of '63: Dream Palace,' " Jean E. Kennard explains in *Number and Nightmare: Forms of Fantasy in Contemporary Fiction,* "are more fully developed in . . .Malcolm. Using the picaresque novel pattern of a young man setting out to learn about life through a series of adventures, Purdy ironically tells the story of a young man who is used by everyone he meets and learns nothing." Though Cook admits "there is a great deal of depravity and perversity" in the novel, he believes that Purdy has the "ability to touch upon these things with gentleness and wit, and thereby to provide new illuminations."

Malcolm is eventually pressured into marriage with a nymphomaniac nightclub singer and dies, as Purdy writes in the novel, of "acute alcoholism and sexual hyperaesthesia." Billed as a comic novel by its publisher, *Malcolm* evokes laughter that "sounds a little like the beginning of a death rattle," R. W. B. Lewis writes in the *New York Herald Tribune Book Review.* Lewis places *Malcolm* in the "fine old comic picaresque tradition" and calls Purdy "a writer of exceptional talent, who must be acknowledged in the company say, of Saul Bellow and Ralph Ellison." Paul Herr of the *Chicago Review* also praises the novel. "With the publication of *Malcolm,*" Herr states, "James Purdy has left no doubt that he is a writer of integrity with a voice of his own."

Kennard argues that *Malcolm* is primarily concerned with "the failure of communication." This failure is dramatized by the contradictory language of Purdy's characters and the self-negating scenes between them. "Characters reply to each other in a series of nonsequitors . . .," Kennard reports. "Just as individual sentences cancel each other out, so too the action of the novel progressively unmakes itself. All relationships disintegrate. . . . Malcolm is eventually found drifting aimlessly from one place to another." Tony Tanner, writing in *City of Words: American Fiction, 1950-1970,* also sees this process of dissolution in *Malcolm.* "In the world in which . . . Malcolm finds himself," Tanner writes, "sense is continually dissolving in contradictions. There is nothing stable enough or meaningful enough around him to enable him properly speaking to 'begin'. . . . He passes through changing scenes but, instead of thickening into identity and consolidating a real self, his life is really a long fading."

In an article for *Critique: Studies in Modern Fiction,* Charles Stetler finds this dissolution—"the disturbing themes of loneliness and lack of identity in the bizarre nightmare of modern existence," as he calls it—the subject matter of what is essentially a parody. "Without question," Stetler writes, "*Malcolm* is a story of a young man confronting adulthood, for initiation is its central theme. [But Purdy] has offered us a sport on that type, using the genre to satirize it, with a wry approach to form as well as content. Viewed this way, the satire of an already cheerless book is deepened, and the blackness of its humor becomes more pervasive, more complete, and more grim." This parody ultimately extends to the death of Malcolm at book's end. There is some doubt surrounding Malcolm's death, with the coroner and undertaker both claiming there was no body in Malcolm's coffin. "Thus," Stetler writes, "if nothing proves that Malcolm is dead, nothing, likewise, guarantees that Malcolm ever lived, in any sense of the word. Instead of the novel being an allegory of a young everyman, it is more an allegory of no man—the way Purdy sees modern man."

In *The Nephew,* Purdy continues to write of characters who have no fixed identity. This time, though, his primary character never appears in the novel. Cliff Mason, missing in action in the Korean War, becomes the subject of a memorial book being compiled by his Aunt Alma, who raised him after his parents died. Her research into Cliff's life ends inconclusively. As Martin Tucker writes in *Commonweal;* "she discovers she knows almost nothing about the only person she has loved." But her search for Cliff reveals much about the secret sorrows and fears of her neighbors and friends in the small town in which she lives, and what little new she does discover about Cliff strongly suggests that he was homosexual. Her search, French and Pease comment, "results not in recovering the boy, but in exposing the banal hidden secrets of her neighbors and leading them to a new apprehension of each other." As in *Malcolm,* where a dissolution takes place in the narrative, "the action of [*The Nephew*] is a movement towards the void. . . . The reader is taken towards nothing as each piece of information gleaned contradicts what has gone before," Kennard writes.

Several observers see *The Nephew* and its story of a search for a dead relative as merely a structure in which Purdy explores small town life, satirizing the conventions of contemporary America. Herbert Gold, writing in the *New Republic,* finds that "the plot is a mere excuse for a curious parody of a Norman Rockwell illustration or an Edgar Lee Masters poem," while French and Pease point out that the town of Rainbow Center in which Alma lives is "a half-American-gothic, half-Ozlike community." "Purdy's aim," Curtis Harnack explains in the *Chicago Sunday Tribune,* "is leveled at America's values and beliefs, at contemporary society itself."

This literary assault utilizes a variety of writing styles and genres, all of which Purdy employs with great skill. "From humor to pathos, from farce to caricature or to straight narrative," William Peden writes in the *Saturday Review,* "Mr. Purdy is in constant control of his material. . . . If any doubts exist concerning Mr. Purdy's unique abilities, this slender, unpretentious, thoroughly admirable novel should dispel them." Calling *The Nephew* "a small work of authentic fictional art," Lewis claims that Purdy "has demonstrated a range and variety in his steadily strengthening talent—one of the most decisive literary talents to have appeared since the last war—to which one happily sees no obvious bounds."

With his next two novels, *Cabot Wright Begins* and *Eustace Chisholm and the Works,* Purdy met with strong opposition from what he calls, in his *CA Autobiography Series* article, the "essentially stuffy New York establishment." *Cabot Wright Begins* concerns a Wall Street heir who becomes a rapist. After he is captured and imprisoned, Cabot Wright decides to compose his memoirs, hiring a woman writer to help him. But the woman's experiences with the publishing world, which is not interested in the truth of Wright's situation but with a commercial version of it, force her to abandon the project. A third of the novel's length deals with the problems involved in writing Cabot's biography and the reaction the manuscript receives. It is this satirical look at the publishing world, what French and Pease call "Purdy's frontal assault on what he regards as a decadent literary establishment and the vulgarities of a culture shaped by advertising," that inspired, some critics feel, the negative reaction to the novel. The reviewer for the *Times Literary Supplement* revealed, for example, that one of the novel's characters, a critic named Doyley Pepscout, was based on an actual New York critic. Or so the critic, who attacked the book, believed.

Other reviewers also criticized *Cabot Wright Begins.* Stanley Edgar Hyman writes in *Standards: A Chronicle of Books for Our Time* that "Purdy is a terrible writer, and worse than that, he is a boring writer." Theodore Solotaroff, in his *The Red Hot Vacuum and Other Pieces on the Writing of the Sixties,* finds that "the first two thirds or so of *Cabot Wright Begins* is a cool, mordant, and deadly accurate satire on American values, as good as anything we have had since the work of Nathanael West. . . . But having sprung his indignation, Purdy eventually allows it to get out of hand. Losing the objectivity of his art, he continues to pour it on and pour it on."

Despite such criticism, the book received positive comments from a number of observers. These include Tanner, who states that *Cabot Wright Begins* "gathers together all the themes opened up or touched on in Purdy's earlier work and explores them with a subtlety and humour and power which makes this, to my mind, not only Purdy's most profound novel but one of the most important American novels since the war." The *Times Literary Supplement* critic describes *Cabot Wright Begins* as "not only the most savage of satires on the American way of life . . .; it is also an extremely funny book."

Purdy's next novel, *Eustace Chisholm and the Works,* was again met with derision from "the anaesthetic, hypocritical preppy, and stagnant New York literary establishment," as Purdy writes in his *CA Autobiography Series* article. It was the book's sympathetic portrayal of homosexual love that Purdy believes caused the furor. "Such love," he writes in his *CA Autobiography Series* article, "unless treated clinically or as a documentary cannot be tolerated by the New York literary Powers-That-Be." One negative review was by Nelson Algren who, in *Critic,* finds little merit in *Eustace Chisholm and the Works.* He calls it a "fifth-rate *avant-garde* soap opera" and claims that "what makes the book such a deadly bore, what makes the reader's mind boggle, is that the author is unaware of anything preposterous about men who believe so firmly in both prayer and faggotty that they can go from sex to penitence without getting off their knees."

Revolving around Eustace Chisholm, a bisexual would-be poet, the novel tells of several love relationships, including that between Eustace and his wife, Carla, between Daniel Haws and Amos Ratcliffe, and between Maureen O'Dell and Daniel Haws. "Homosexuals comprise most of the characters in *Eustace Chisholm and the Works,*" Robert K. Morris writes in the *Nation,* "but homosexuality is not really the subject. The world of the pervert has been blown up to accommodate the larger themes of alienation, isolation and lovelessness." Similarly, Rachel Trickett of the *Yale Review* calls *Eustace Chisholm and the Works* an "appalling fable of the impossibility of love, with the violent depiction of the frustration and martyrdom of a romantic homosexual passion, and its brutally comic presentation of heterosexual promiscuity and abortion."

Several critics see the novel's early pages as weaker than its conclusion. Wilfred Sheed of the *New York Times Book Review,* for example, finds "the first part of this story [to be] told on a note of shrill facetiousness. . . . But slowly, and one might guess, diffidently, the book becomes a little more serious. . . . The whole last section is a purple feast of sadomasochism. It is also a risky and serious piece of writing, which waives the extenuations of humor, and is possibly the best writing Purdy has ever done." Morris, too, sees a change in the narrative during the course of the novel. "What begins as the whimpering and whining of unrequited lovers moves toward a crescendo of suffering," Morris writes, "and what starts as a vague, troubled dream becomes an excursion in nightmare."

But French, writing in his *Season of Promise,* praises *Eustace Chisholm and the Works* in its entirety. After reading Purdy's earlier fiction, he explains, "I was scarcely prepared for the violently compressed power, the exhausting vehemence, the almost superhuman exorcism of the wanton evil that destroys many innocents that set Purdy's new effort far apart from the whining and the cocktail chatter that often passes for serious fiction. I was staggered by Purdy's tale." Trickett concludes that the novel "is conceived and executed with the most elaborate artistry . . . The book has brilliance and originality."

Since writing *Eustace Chisholm and the Works,* Purdy has turned to stories inspired by the tales he heard as a child from his grandmother and great-grandmother. These stories are set in rural Ohio and concern the farmers and small-town inhabitants of the region. In *Jeremy's Version, The House of the Solitary Maggot, Mourners Below,* and *On Glory's Course,* Purdy transforms his ancestors' remembrances into fiction. This change in subject matter, French and Pease maintain, is characterized by "less spectacular yet even more frightening tales of the South and Midwest, employing regional vernaculars to present intensive, brooding, in-depth studies of small groups of pathetic figures spotlighted against uncluttered pastoral settings."

Jeremy's Version is set in the small Ohio town of Boutflour and examines the relationships that bind together the Fergus family. "The action is violent, gothic, but mostly kept in the family," the *Times Literary Supplement* reviewer comments. Wilfred Fergus is an irresponsible father; his wife, Elvira, raises their three sons on her own; and the sons are trying to work out their own lives in the stifling atmosphere of their rural community. Though Purdy's subject matter has changed, there is much similarity between this novel and previous ones. As in his previous novels,

Purdy remains concerned with the fate of young people abused and exploited by their elders. And as in *The Nephew* and earlier works, he uses a memoirist to relate his story. This time it is a 15-year-old boy who is writing a novel based on the remembrances of an older character and on a diary written by a third character.

Guy Davenport sees Purdy as working in a familiar genre, the American gothic, but using it to express his own vision. "It is a novel which, in a sense, has been written many times before; practically every scene is wonderfully nostalgic rather than new," he writes in the *New York Times Book Review.* "This effect is deliberate and masterfully exploited." The gothic elements in the novel include, the *Times Literary Supplement* reviewer states, "two possible rapes, lost fortunes, drink, fights, 'unspoken of' crimes, lurid revelations about small town sex, scandals, climactic effects, a son's attempt to shoot his mother and a canvas of characters drawn, mostly, in blood." Through these gothic elements, J. R. Lindroth writes in *America,* Purdy "succeeds in evoking the appalling difficulties involved in raising a family in a small town. Financial pressures, sibling rivalries, Oedipal conflicts, dissipate the illusion of a Utopian existence in rural America." Davenport believes Purdy explores the stifling effects of family life in *Jeremy's Version.* Purdy shows that "character is a role written for us by our families; only in loneliness and desperation do we dare leave the stage. . . ." Davenport writes. "All the characters . . . are trying to wake up and live . . .; their tragedy is that they do not know what this means, and remain as bewildered as children on a dull afternoon who want something, but do not know what they want."

The House of the Solitary Maggot is set in Prince's Crossing, not far from Boutflour, the setting of *Jeremy's Version.* Prince's Crossing is a place, Purdy explains in the novel, no longer on the maps because it is now too small to constitute a village. It is, writes Irving Malin of the *New Republic,* "a ghostland, . . . filled with people unable to accept the facts of daily life, obsessed by bright visions of glory, fame and love. They are sleepwalkers." The novel is narrated by Eneas Harmond, a hermit who listens to Lady Byethewaite speak into a tape recorder about the history of her family. The tape recording is meant for Lady Byethewaite's great-great-nephew. This narration combines Harmond's story with that of Lady Byethewaite and joins "the voices of past and present" as well, Malin states. The ruin eventually brought upon Byethewaite's three sons—fathered by a Mr. Skegg, a local magnate (pronounced "maggot" by the locals)—is caused by "the irresponsibility of the presumed parents and the inability of the sons to cope with their own emotions," French and Pease write.

Several reviewers find that Purdy's prose transcends the tragedy and squalor of his story. "It has a strange sense of poetry—the poetry of the seedy, the run-down, the decayed and corrupt," writes Douglas Dunn in the *Glasgow Herald.* "The achievement of the book—and I think it is very considerable—is that Purdy's prose and phrase-making elevate the emotional squalor of his story and its characters to a level of effect that is hauntingly beautiful and pure." Calling *The House of the Solitary Maggot* a "mythic and disturbing novel," Malin believes that Purdy transcends his material by using its familiar elements while simultaneously rejecting them. "Purdy," Malin states, "writes a conventional novel but, too shrewd to simply imitate past masters, gives us distinctive, nightmarish patterns, as if he accepts and rebels against 'traditional' images."

Mourners Below continues Purdy's interest in Midwestern settings, being set in a nameless location referred to only as "our town" by Purdy. The novel centers on the Bledsoe family: Eugene Bledsoe, his son Duane, and Duane's two half-brothers, Douglas and Justin, recently killed in an unspecified war. Duane is visited by the ghosts of his brothers and comes to feel that Justin, whom he closely resembles, is urging him to carry out his wishes. Before joining the army Justin had an affair with the wealthy Estelle Dumont, and now he wants Duane to rekindle this relationship for him. Duane is first pushed into attending a masquerade at Estelle's home and then, when the party is over, into seducing her. After leaving Estelle the next morning, Duane is set upon by two ruffians who, thinking they are attacking Justin, rape him. "The story that Mr. Purdy is telling," observes King, "is in the nature of a macabre fairy-tale or parable." Similarly, T. O. Treadwell of the *Times Literary Supplement* finds that "the meaning of *Mourners Below* lies on the symbolic, even allegorical level." Writing in the *Chicago Tribune Book World*, Lyle Rexer calls *Mourners Below* "a rural fairy tale, whose fantastic events conceal a psychomythic crisis, in this case the reconciliation of innocence and temporality."

Although there is a mythic level to the novel, King explains that it is "otherwise realistic in its depiction of the life of the small Mid-West town in which all these bizarre, supernatural happenings take place." Julia M. Klein of the *New Republic* believes that Purdy creates "a world where the supernatural merges with the real, [and he] illuminates a reality whose core, if not its contours, matches our own." Because the novel ends with Duane raising the child he has fathered with Estelle, Cohen sees a final twist in the story from the fantastic to the realistic. "Purdy winds up the novel," Cohen writes, "with a deft change of scale; turning, by implication, the small end of the telescope on his characters, he transforms the grotesque and outlandish back into the mundane."

This combination of the real and fantastic parallels Purdy's blending of the comic and bleak as well. "While the grief of *Mourners Below* is very real indeed," Gary Krist writes in the *American Book Review*, "it is touched by an inimitable quality of absurdity and deadpan excess. The morbid background of silence and death is only an instrument of Purdy's essentially comic vision." This view is shared by Klein, who defines the first third of the novel as "a skillful psychological portrait" of Duane's father and the rest of the book as "something wilder and more comic—and finally more terrible."

Krist concludes that *Mourners Below* is "one of [Purdy's] best novels." Klein believes that the novel "recapitulates many of Purdy's concerns—with small-town families in crisis, the explosiveness of contained emotion, the marriage between the dead and the living. Purdy sees to the heart of relations between the sexes. . . . He celebrates the bonds between brothers, between father and son, even as he underlines the near impossibility of intimacy."

On Glory's Course, nominated for the PEN-Faulkner Award in 1985, is set in the Midwestern town of Fonthill during the 1930s. It is a "sexually repressed town," as Michael Dirda describes it in the *Washington Post,* in which Adele Bevington is an elegant and wealthy woman with a "sinful" past. Some thirty years earlier, Adele was forced to give up for adoption her illegitimate son. She has been searching for him ever since, convinced that he is alive and well and still living somewhere in Fonthill.

Marked by a style that attempts to capture the speaking rhythms of the period, *On Glory's Course* has met with some criticism from several reviewers who feel the attempt fails. Robert J. Seidman of the *New York Times Book Review,* for example, thinks the "idiom so ponderous" that Purdy's characters "have trouble speaking their lines." Roz Kaveney of the *Times Literary Supplement* finds the dialogue "wearisomely convoluted and stilted." But Carolyn See of the *Los Angeles Times* argues that the sometimes portentous language is appropriate to the novel's time period. While she admits that at first a reader may believe he is "being made part of an experiment with words," See explains that a more flamboyant speech was common at the time: They "didn't just gossip about you, they resorted to calumny. And people didn't scold or even chide, they were apt to repeat an objuration."

Despite his objections to the novel, Seidman concedes that "Adele, the embattled town rebel, has courage and wit, even stature" and "Purdy does mount a few hilarious comic scenes." Kaveney, too, finds some merit in *On Glory's Course.* "The novel," he writes, "is partly redeemed by the way Purdy keeps the reader turning pages." See maintains that she "recognized a couple of those ironing-board tirades [found in the novel]; others who do may love this book."

Evaluations of Purdy's achievement often place him among the finest of American writers. The late Edith Sitwell wrote in the *New York Herald Tribune Book Review* that "James Purdy will come to be recognized as one of the greatest living writers of fiction in our language." Purdy, Chapuck believes, "is a writer of marvelous power, who has made us think deeply and seriously about the human condition." Similarly, Paul Bresnick finds in an article for the *New York Arts Journal,* "Purdy has the uncanny ability to compel us to experience emotional states we are thoroughly unfamiliar with. He alerts us to impulses we thought we had successfully murdered or buried. He sensitizes us to new (or rather, submerged) areas of our souls." Charyn calls Purdy "one of the most uncompromising of American novelists," while King feels "that a small, perpetually radioactive particle of genius irradiates the mass of the work he has produced over the years." Purdy is especially admired by other writers, including Marianne Moore, Paul Bowles, William Carlos Williams, Edward Albee, and Angus Wilson. His books have been translated into 22 languages, his poems have been set to music, and in 1975, the Modern Language Association of America devoted an entire seminar to Purdy's work.

Still, Purdy is little known by the American public. As he told *CA* in a letter: "This is an age of exhibitionists, not souls. The press and the public primarily recognize only writers who give them 'doctored' current events as truth. For me, the only 'engagement' or cause a 'called' writer can have (as opposed to a public writer) is his own vision and work. It is an irrevocable decision: he can march only in his own parade."

This approach has gained Purdy a wider readership abroad than in his native America. Speaking of a tour he made for the United States Information Agency in 1982 to Israel, Finland, and Germany, Purdy recalls in the *CA Autobiography Series* the welcome he received: "My reception in these countries was enthusiastic beyond my expectations, and it was brought home to me again that my stories reach some deep note in readers who are receptive and open."

MEDIA ADAPTATIONS: Malcolm was adapted as a play by Edward Albee and published by Dramatists Play Service in 1966; some of Purdy's poems have been set to music by Richard Hundley and Robert Helps; the story "Sleep Tight" was filmed by Inquiring Systems, Inc.; a film version of *In a Shallow Grave,* adapted by Kenneth Bowser, was released by Skouras Pictures in 1988.

BIOGRAPHICAL/CRITICAL SOURCES:

BOOKS

Adams, Stephen D., *James Purdy,* Barnes & Noble, 1976.
The American Novel: Two Studies, Kansas State Teachers College of Emporia, Graduate Division, 1965.
Chupack, Henry, *James Purdy,* Twayne, 1975.
Contemporary Authors Autobiography Series, Volume 1, Gale, 1984.
Contemporary Literary Criticism, Gale, Volume 2, 1974, Volume 4, 1975, Volume 10, 1979, Volume 28, 1984.
Dictionary of Literary Biography, Volume 2: *American Novelists since World War II,* Gale, 1978.
French, Warren, *Season of Promise,* University of Missouri Press, 1968.
French, Warren, editor, *The Fifties: Fiction, Poetry, Drama,* Everett/Edwards, 1971.
Hyman, Stanley Edgar, *Standards: A Chronicle of Books for Our Time,* Horizon Press, 1966.
Kennard, Jean E., *Number and Nightmare: Forms of Fantasy in Contemporary Fiction,* Archon Books, 1975.
Kostelanetz, Richard, editor, *On Contemporary Literature,* Avon, 1964.
Langford, Richard E., editor, *Essays in Modern American Literature,* Stetson University Press, 1963.
Laughlin, James, editor, *New Directions in Prose and Poetry 26,* New Directions, 1973.
Lehmann, John and Derek Parker, editors, *Edith Sitwell, Selected Letters,* Macmillan (London), 1970.
Malin, Irving, *New American Gothic,* Southern Illinois University Press, 1962.
Moore, Harry T., editor, *Contemporary American Novelists,* Southern Illinois University Press, 1964.
Purdy, James, *63: Dream Palace,* William-Frederick, 1956.
Purdy, James, *Malcolm,* Farrar, Straus, 1959.
Schwarzschild, Bettina, *The Not-Right House: Essays on James Purdy,* University of Missouri Press, 1969.
Solotaroff, Theodore, *The Red Hot Vacuum and Other Pieces on the Writing of the Sixties,* Atheneum, 1970.
Tanner, Tony, *City of Words: American Fiction, 1950-1970,* Harper, 1971.
Waldmeir, Joseph S., editor, *Recent American Fiction: Some Critical Views,* Michigan State University, 1963.
Weales, Gerald, *The Jumping-off Place: American Drama in the 1960's,* Macmillan, 1969.

PERIODICALS

America, February 27, 1971.
American Book Review, May-June, 1982.
American Literature, November, 1974.
Andy Warhol's Interview, December, 1972.
Antioch Review, spring, 1962, spring, 1971.
Best Sellers, June 15, 1967, June, 1978.
Book Week, October 18, 1964, May 9, 1965, May 28, 1967.
Bulletin of Bibliography, January-March, 1971.
Centennial Review, summer, 1974.
Chicago Review, autumn-winter, 1960.
Chicago Sunday Tribune, October 9, 1960.
Chicago Tribune Book World, August 23, 1981, January 5, 1986.
Commonweal, January 17, 1958, October 16, 1959, October 21, 1960, January 4, 1963.
Contemporary Literature, autumn, 1970, summer, 1974.
Critic, August-September, 1967.
Critique: Studies in Modern Fiction, Volume 14, number 3, 1973.
Glasgow Herald, January 8, 1986.

Life, June 2, 1967.
London Magazine, February-March, 1973.
Los Angeles Times, December 18, 1977, March 26, 1984.
Los Angeles Times Book Review, October 5, 1986.
Nation, January 1, 1958, November 19, 1960, March 23, 1964, October 9, 1967, June 9, 1969, May 15, 1972.
National Review, February 26, 1963, September 1, 1972.
New Republic, November 9, 1959, October 3, 1960, November 17, 1962, October 26, 1974, July 18, 1981.
New Statesman, May 7, 1960, January 17, 1986.
Newsweek, October 12, 1970.
New York Arts Journal, April-May, 1978.
New York Herald Tribune Book Review, December 29, 1957, October 1, 1959, November 6, 1960, November 18, 1962.
New York Review of Books, November 5, 1964.
New York Times, December 29, 1957, January 9, 1966, May 6, 1988.
New York Times Book Review, October 6, 1957, September 27, 1959, October 9, 1960, May 21, 1967, June 2, 1968, November 15, 1970, February 8, 1976, April 23, 1978, July 26, 1981, February 26, 1984, October 19, 1986, September 6, 1987, October 29, 1989.
Partisan Review, fall, 1972.
Penthouse, July, 1974.
Publishers Weekly, June 19, 1981.
Queen's Quarterly, summer, 1962.
Renascence, winter, 1963.
San Francisco Chronicle, October 18, 1959.
Saturday Review, January 25, 1958, September 26, 1959, November 26, 1960, November 17, 1962, August 5, 1967, June, 1981.
Southern Review, summer, 1974.
Spectator, April 29, 1960, May 19, 1984, March 1, 1986.
Time, December 9, 1957, October 17, 1960.
Times (London), May 10, 1984.
Times Literary Supplement, May 6, 1960, June 10, 1965, March 28, 1968, June 4, 1971, August 31, 1984, March 8, 1985, February 19-25, 1988.
Tribune Books (Chicago), July 5, 1987.
Tri-Quarterly, fall, 1967.
Twentieth Century Literature, April, 1969, fall, 1982.
University of Dayton Review, summer, 1974.
Village Voice, July 22, 1981.
Virginia Quarterly Review, spring, 1963, autumn, 1967, autumn, 1972.
Washington Post, August 1, 1981, March 2, 1985.
Wilson Library Bulletin, March, 1964.
Wisconsin Studies in Contemporary Literature, summer, 1965.
Yale Review, spring, 1968.

*   *   *

PUZO, Mario   1920-

PERSONAL: Born October 15, 1920, in New York, N.Y.; son of Antonio (a railroad trackman) and Maria (Le Conti) Puzo; married Erika Lina Broske, 1946; children: Anthony, Joey, Dorothy, Virginia, Eugene. *Education:* Attended New School for Social Research and Columbia University.

ADDRESSES: Home—Long Island, N.Y. *Agent*—Candida Donadio and Associates, Inc., 111 West 57th St., New York, N.Y. 10019.

CAREER: Variously employed as messenger with New York Central Railroad, New York City, public relations administrator with U.S. Air Force in Europe, administrative assistant with

U.S. Civil Service, New York City, and editor-writer with Magazine Management; author. *Military service:* U.S. Army Air Forces, during World War II; served in Germany.

AWARDS, HONORS: Academy Awards, American Academy of Motion Picture Arts and Sciences, and Screen Awards, Writers Guild of America, West, Inc., for best screenplays adapted from another medium, 1972, for "The Godfather," and 1974, for "The Godfather: Part II."

WRITINGS:

The Dark Arena (novel), Random House, 1955, revised, Bantam, 1985.
The Fortunate Pilgrim (novel), Atheneum, 1964.
The Runaway Summer of Davie Shaw (juvenile), illustrated by Stewart Sherwood, Platt & Munk, 1966.
The Godfather (novel; also see below; Literary Guild and Book-of-the-Month Club selections), Putnam, 1969.
(Contributor) Thomas C. Wheeler, editor, *The Immigrant Experience: The Anguish of Becoming an American,* Dial, 1971.
"The Godfather" Papers and Other Confessions, Putnam, 1972.
Inside Las Vegas (nonfiction), photographs by Michael Abramson, Susan Fowler-Gallagher, and John Launois, Grosset, 1977.
Fools Die (novel; Book-of-the-Month Club selection), Putnam, 1978.
The Sicilian (novel), Linden Press, 1984.

Contributor of articles, reviews, and stories to *American Vanguard, New York, Redbook, Holiday, New York Times Magazine,* and other publications.

SCREENPLAYS

(With Francis Ford Coppola) "The Godfather" (based on Puzo's novel of same title), Paramount, 1972.
(With Coppola) "The Godfather: Part II," Paramount, 1974.
(With George Fox) "Earthquake," Universal, 1974.
(With others) "Superman," Warner Bros., 1978.
(With David Newman and Leslie Newman) "Superman II," Warner Bros., 1981.

Also author of "The Cotton Club."

WORK IN PROGRESS: Screenplay for "The Godfather: Part III," for Paramount.

SIDELIGHTS: "Late in 1965 a Putnam editor stopped in at Magazine Management's offices, overheard [Mario] Puzo telling Mafia yarns and offered a $5,000 advance for a book about the Italian underworld," *Time* reports. The result is *The Godfather,* and "the rest," as *Time* notes, "is publishing history." *The Godfather* has been phenomenally successful; it has sold over thirteen million copies, spawned two Academy Award-winning movies, and made Puzo a wealthy, famous, and sought-after novelist and screenwriter.

The fame and the money are particularly important to Puzo. Prior to *The Godfather* he had written two critically well-received but commercially unsuccessful novels. In *Time,* Puzo relates an incident that occurred in 1955, shortly after the publication of his first novel, *The Dark Arena:* "It was Christmas Eve and I had a severe gall-bladder attack. I had to take a cab to the Veterans Administration Hospital on 23rd Street, got out and fell into the gutter. There I was lying there thinking, here I am, a published writer, and I am dying like a dog. That's when I decided I would be rich and famous." *The Godfather,* he states in *"The Godfather" Papers and Other Confessions,* was written "to make money. . . . I was 45 years old and tired of being an art-

ist." Nevertheless, as Robert Lasson of the *Washington Post Book World* contends, "Puzo sat down and produced . . . a novel which still had enormous force and kept you turning the pages." Others agree. *The Godfather* became the best-selling novel of the 1970s, outselling that decades' other blockbusters— *The Exorcist, Love Story,* and *Jaws*—by millions.

Puzo's story details the rise of Don Vito Corleone, the fall of his sons Sonny and, especially, Michael, the Mafia's peculiar behavior code and honor system, and the violent power struggle among rival "families." To some reviewers, Puzo's tale is a symbolic treatment of the corruption of the American dream. Although not all critics view the novel so seriously, most agree with Polly Anderson in the *Library Journal* that "the book is well written, suspenseful and explodes in a series of dramatic climaxes." *Newsweek*'s Pete Axthelm calls Puzo "an extremely talented storyteller" and states that *The Godfather* "moves at breakneck speed without ever losing its balance." And a critic for the *Saturday Review* contends that "Mario Puzo has achieved the definitive novel about a sinister fraternity of crime."

Several reviewers have noted the realism and believability of the book's settings and characters. "He makes his frightening cast of characters seem human and possible," according to the *Saturday Review* critic. And in another *Saturday Review* article, "A Mafioso Cases the Mafia Craze," Vincent Teresa, who apparently knows his subject, praises the author for portraying the Godfather as a fair and compassionate administrator of justice: "Puzo also showed the compassion of a don, the fair way Corleone ruled. That's the way most dons are. . . . If you go to a don . . . and you've got a legitimate beef . . . and it proves to be the truth, you'll get justice. That's what makes the dons so important in the mob. They rule fair and square."

Such remarks have given rise to the suspicion that Puzo's knowledge of the Mafia and its people is firsthand. The author disclaims this rumor in *"The Godfather" Papers and Other Confessions* by explaining that the book is based on research and anecdotes he had heard from his mother, an Italian immigrant, and on the streets. Still, the doubts persisted. Real-life underworld figures began approaching Puzo, convinced that he had some sort of link to organized crime. "After the book became famous, I was introduced to a few gentlemen related to the material," the author states in *Time.* "They were flattering. They refused to believe that I had never had the confidence of a don."

While most critics praise *The Godfather*'s realism, others have chastised Puzo for presenting his subjects in too favorable a light. These critics contend that because Puzo consistently justifies Don Vito's violent actions and solutions, certain readers have found the character and his family worthy of compassion and esteem. "The author has chosen to portray all Godfather's victims as vermin and his henchmen as fairly sympathetic," *Esquire*'s Barton Midwood asserts, "and in this way the book manages to glamorize both the murderer himself and the [imbalanced] economy in which he operates." In *Critical Inquiry,* John G. Cawelti voices a similar complaint. "Throughout the story," the reviewer writes, "the Corleone family is presented to us in a morally sympathetic light, as basically good and decent people who have had to turn to crime in order to survive and prosper in a corrupt and unjust society." Puzo addresses this issue in a *Publishers Weekly* interview with Thomas Weyr. He expresses surprise at the positive response accorded the Corleones, particularly Vito: "I was awfully surprised when people loved the Godfather so much. I thought I showed him as a murderer, a thief, a villain, a man who threw babies in the oven. . . . So I was astounded when I was attacked for glorifying the Mafia. It's a little tricky. I think it is a novelist's job not to be a moralist but to make you care about the people in the book."

After *The Godfather* and *"The Godfather" Papers and Other Confessions* Puzo focused his attention on screenwriting, first as co-author of "The Godfather" and "The Godfather: Part II," then as co-author of "Earthquake," "Superman," and "Superman II." Special effects, rather than story or plot, highlight the last three films. Pauline Kael of the *New Yorker* comments: "You go to 'Earthquake' to see [Los Angeles] get it, and it really does. . . . 'Earthquake' is a marathon of destruction effects, with stock characters spinning through it." A *Time* critic finds that "Superman," for which Puzo wrote the first draft, is "two hours and fifteen minutes of pure fun, fancy and adventure." Garnering far more serious attention are "The Godfather" and its sequel.

The first film covers the period from the mid-1940s to the mid-1950s, when Michael takes command of the "family"; the second film charts the youth and early manhood of the original Godfather, Vito, and contrasts his coming-of-age with Michael's. Vincent Canby of the *New York Times* remarks that "the novel is a kind of first draft—an outline of characters and an inventory of happenings—that has only now been finished as a film." In another *New Yorker* review, Kael deems "The Godfather" "the greatest gangster picture ever made" and praises the "metaphorical overtones that took it far beyond the gangster genre." Part II, according to Kael, is even more "daring" in "that it enlarges the scope and deepens the meaning of the fist film." The critic maintains that "the second film shows the consequences of the actions of the first; it's all one movie, in two great big pieces, and it comes together in your head while you watch."

Although Puzo is given co-author status for both screenplays, Francis Ford Coppola's direction and interpretation are credited with giving the films their "epic" quality. "[Coppola] turns 'The Godfather: Part II' into a statement, both highly personal and with an epic resonance, on the corruption of the American dream and on the private cost of power," Paul D. Zimmerman writes in *Newsweek*. Puzo is the first to agree. "Coppola fought the battle for the integrity of the movies; if it weren't for him, they would have been 30's gangster pictures," he tells Herbert Mitgang in a *New York Times Book Review* interview. " 'Godfather' is really his movie." Yet, Kael notes, "There was a Promethean spark" in Puzo's novel that afforded Coppola "an epic vision of the corruption of America." Kael adds, "Much of the material about Don Vito's early life which appears in Part II was in the Mario Puzo book and was left out in the first movie, but the real fecundity of Puzo's mind shows in the way this new film can take his characters further along and can expand . . . the implications of the book."

In October of 1978 Puzo's long-awaited fourth novel, *Fools Die,* was published. The headlines and cover stories surrounding its publication began in June—four months before the first hardcover edition went on sale—when New American Library paid an unprecedented $2.2 million for the paperback rights, plus $350,000 for the reprint rights to *The Godfather.* In spite of the hoopla concerning this record-setting price, or perhaps because of it, critical reaction to *Fools Die* has been mixed. "It seems a publishing event rather than a novel," Roger Sale opines in the *New York Review of Books.* In a *New Republic* review, Barbara Grizzuti Harrison offers a similar appraisal, claiming that "it is a publishing event (though hardly a literary one)." And the *Village Voice*'s James Wolcott asks: "In all this commotion, a fundamental question has gone unasked. . . . Has anyone at Putnam actually *read* this book?"

The action of *Fools Die* moves from Las Vegas to New York to Hollywood, purporting to "give us the inside skinny" on gambling, publishing, and movie-making, according to *Washington Post Book World*'s William McPherson. Harrison adds that "the events loosely strung together in this . . . book are meant to dramatize ambition, power, and corruption. I say *meant* to," she explains, "because Puzo, through the offices of his narrator John Merlyn, keeps reminding the reader that these are his themes, as if we might otherwise forget." Geoffrey Wolff of *New Times* airs a corresponding complaint: "Because he won't trust a reader to remember the climaxes of a few pages earlier, he recapitulates the plot, as though *Fools Die* were a serial, or a television series." Wolff suggests that "perhaps Puzo doesn't trust a reader to remember what he has just written because he himself has such trouble remembering what he has just written." The critic goes on to detail several contradictory descriptions given throughout the novel concerning characters' appearances, habits, and lifestyles. Wolcott also notes that "there are discrepancies in Puzo's *narrative* as gaping as crevasses."

Wolcott further criticizes the novel's structure and syntax: "The novel seems to have evolved from manuscript to book without anyone daring . . . to make sorely needed corrections. . . . Tenses are jumbled, punctuation is eccentric . . ., and the author never quite masters the use of the participle phrase." Wolff attacks the book's "slipshod craftsmanship," and *Newsweek*'s Peter S. Prescott states, "Structurally, *Fools Die* is a mess."

Despite such less-than-favorable reviews, the novel has been a popular success (it was the third highest selling hardcover novel of 1978), and Prescott and others admit that *Fools Die* can be entertaining, humorous, and, in some instances, inspired. "I had a fine time reading it," Prescott writes. "Its many stories, developed at varying lengths, are slickly entertaining." *Time* comments: "*Fools Die* contains the sort of mini-dramas and surprises that keep paperback readers flipping pages; a man wins a small fortune at baccarat and blows his brains out; a straightforward love affair turns baroque with kinky sex; an extremely cautious character makes a stupid and fatal error." Moreover, Prescott finds: "Puzo here reveals an unsuspected talent for gross comedy. . . . In [the character] Osano, the most famous living American novelist, he has written an inspired caricature of our own dear Norman Mailer."

"I wrote *Fools Die* for myself," the author tells Mitgang. "I wanted to say certain things about gambling, Las Vegas and the country." According to David Robinson of the *Times Literary Supplement,* Puzo is quite successful at capturing the flavor and feel of Las Vegas: "The first and best section of *Fools Die* is set in Las Vegas. Puzo's forte is the neo-documentary background; and . . . his portrayal of [that city] has the appearance of authenticity." *Time* agrees: "Puzo's description of Las Vegas, its Strip, showgirls, characters, and the variety of ways one can lose money swiftly and painlessly, are carried off with brio. The green baize world of casino management has never seemed more professional, entertaining and lethal."

In general, critics contend that the jury is still out regarding Puzo's status in American literature. They agree that his first two novels display great promise (Frederic Morton of the *New York Herald Tribune Book Review,* for example, finds that *The Dark Arena* "reveals Mr. Puzo to be a writer of power and precision," and the *New York Times Book Review*'s David Borloff judges *The Fortunate Pilgrim* "a small classic"), but suggest that *The Godfather* and *Fools Die* are too commercial. Nevertheless, *Times* concludes: "If Mario Puzo never writes another word he will already have earned the title of Godfather of the Paperbacks. . . . Puzo's *The Godfather* and 'an offer you can't refuse' have already become part of the language. This may find him a niche in American letters. He is already assured a place in American numbers."

AVOCATIONAL INTERESTS: Gambling, tennis, Italian cuisine, and dieting.

MEDIA ADAPTATIONS: The Sicilian was adapted for the screen by Steve Shagan and directed by Michael Cimino for Twentieth Century-Fox, 1989.

BIOGRAPHICAL/CRITICAL SOURCES:

BOOKS

Contemporary Literary Criticism, Gale, Volume 1, 1973, Volume 2, 1974, Volume 6, 1976, Volume 36, 1986.
Green, Rose B., *The Italian-American Novel,* Fairleigh Dickinson University Press, 1974.
Madden, David, editor, *Rediscoveries,* Crown, 1972.
Puzo, Mario, *"The Godfather Papers" and Other Confessions,* Putnam, 1972.
Wheeler, Thomas C., editor, *The Immigrant Experience: The Anguish of Becoming An American,* Dial, 1971.

PERIODICALS

Chicago Tribune, June 19, 1981.
Commonweal, May 6, 1955, June 4, 1965.
Critical Inquiry, March, 1975.
Esquire, February, 1971.
Library Journal, April 1, 1969.
Life, July 10, 1970.
Los Angeles Times, February 14, 1987, October 23, 1987.
McCall's, May, 1971.
Nation, June 16, 1969.
New Republic, November 18, 1978.
Newsweek, March 10, 1969, December 23, 1974, September 18, 1978, January 1, 1979.
New Times, October 2, 1978.
New York, March 31, 1969.
New Yorker, December 12, 1974, December 23, 1974.
New York Herald Tribune Book Review, March 6, 1955.
New York Review of Books, July 20, 1972, October 26, 1978.
New York Times, February 27, 1955, March 12, 1972, March 16, 1972, June 19, 1981, November 22, 1984, June 5, 1986, May 22, 1987.
New York Times Book Review, January 31, 1965, February 18, 1979.
People, July 3, 1978.
Publishers Weekly, May 12, 1978.
Saturday Review, February 26, 1955, January 23, 1965, March 15, 1969, January 20, 1973.
Time, March 13, 1971, December 16, 1974, August 28, 1978, November 27, 1978.
Times (London), May 3, 1985.
Times Literary Supplement, December 1, 1978.
Village Voice, September 4, 1978.
Washington Post, March 12, 1970, October 23, 1987, October 24, 1987.
Washington Post Book World, March 9, 1969, April 9, 1972, September 24, 1978.

*   *   *

PYM, Barbara (Mary Crampton)   1913-1980

PERSONAL: Born June 2, 1913, in Oswestry, Shropshire, England; died January 11, 1980, in England; daughter of Frederic Crampton (a solicitor) and Irena (Thomas) Pym. *Education:* St. Hilda's College, Oxford, B.A. (with honors), 1934. *Religion:* Church of England.

ADDRESSES: Home—Barn Cottage, Finstock, Oxford, England.

CAREER: Novelist. International African Institute, London, England, 1946-74, began as staff member, became assistant editor of *Africa* and of the "Ethnographic and Linguistic Surveys of Africa" series. *Military service:* Women's Royal Naval Service, serving in England and Italy, 1943-46.

MEMBER: Society of Authors, P.E.N.

AWARDS, HONORS: Quartet in Autumn was a finalist for the Booker McConnell Prize, 1977; *A Glass of Blessings* was cited as an American Library Association notable book, 1980.

WRITINGS:

NOVELS, EXCEPT AS INDICATED

Some Tame Gazelle, J. Cape, 1950, reprinted, 1978, Dutton, 1983.
Excellent Women, J. Cape, 1952, reprinted 1977, Dutton, 1978.
Jane and Prudence, J. Cape, 1953, reprinted, 1979, Dutton, 1981.
Less Than Angels, J. Cape, 1955, Vanguard, 1957, reprinted, J. Cape, 1978, Dutton, 1980.
A Glass of Blessings, J. Cape, 1958, reprinted, 1977, Dutton, 1980.
No Fond Return of Love, J. Cape, 1961, reprinted, 1979, Dutton, 1982.
Quartet in Autumn, Macmillan (London), 1977, Dutton, 1978.
The Sweet Dove Died, Macmillan (London), 1978, Dutton, 1979.
A Few Green Leaves, Dutton, 1980.
An Unsuitable Attachment, Dutton, 1982.
A Very Private Eye: An Autobiography in Diaries and Letters (autobiography), edited by sister, Hilary Pym, and Hazel Holt, Dutton, 1984.
Crampton Hodnet, Dutton, 1985.
An Academic Question, Dutton, 1986.
Civil to Strangers and Other Writings (collected fiction), edited by Hazel Holt, Dutton, 1988.

SIDELIGHTS: During the 1950s, England's Barbara Pym was a quietly successful novelist of manners. Her fictional domain was the British drawing room—a genteel world that she populated with solitary women, fickle clergymen, and bumbling anthropologists. Very little actually happened to these characters, but Pym evoked their miniature crises with a perception and wit that reminded reviewers of Jane Austen. When the 1960s arrived, so did a new literary trend toward more "contemporary" novels, and—as Francis King explains in *Books and Bookmen*—"her publishers underwent both a change of direction and a change of feeling about her work. They were not interested in the next of her novels, and, worse, no other publisher could be persuaded to be interested." Pym's literary career languished for sixteen years until, in 1977, her name appeared twice in a *Times Literary Supplement* poll of the most underrated writers of the century. Around the same time Pym submitted a new novel ("as churchy as I wished to make it") to a different publisher and, with the appearance of *Quartet in Autumn,* launched her comeback. She was able to complete several novels before her death from cancer at age sixty-six, and she lived to see much of her earlier work reprinted.

In addition to writing fiction, Pym did editorial work at the International African Institute, a non-profit organization for the study of African languages and culture. There she shared an office with Hazel Holt, a colleague who soon became a close friend and, after Pym's death, her literary executor. When demand arose for a volume about Pym's life, it was Holt who (with Hilary Pym's assistance) compiled and edited Barbara Pym's correspondence in *A Very Private Eye: An Autobiography in Diaries and Letters.* Writing in the preface, Holt explains how "in the endless afternoons of office life and in our free time, we talked about her books and the characters she had created . . . so that the world of the novels soon became as much a part of our lives as the real world." While Pym was a "capable and conscientious editor" for the African institute, Holt reports that she "had no real interest in Africa as such, being far more fascinated by the anthropologists and linguists than by the subjects they were studying. She created a comic world around them, embroidering the few facts she knew about the various authors and reviewers into a splendid fantasy so that it was often difficult to remember what was real and what was not. ('I couldn't ask W. if his Mother was better because I couldn't remember if we'd invented her.')" These inventions often found their way into Pym's books, which abound with the quirks and foibles of anthropologists.

In not just her characterizations but in all aspects of her books, Pym "was strictly true to what she knew. There are almost no children in her fiction, no politics or worldly intrigue, and very few excursions abroad," reports *Time*'s Martha Duffy. Herself a single woman, Pym wrote compassionately of women alone, "excellent women," as she called them in her critically acclaimed novel of that title, "who are not for marrying." Timid, self-conscious, church-attending spinsters, these women "wade at the edge of life while others swim into the current that leads to husbands or professional status," continues Duffy.

Because the lives of Pym's characters are unremittingly routine, the emphasis in her books is psychological. Events are less important than the way they are perceived, as A. N. Wilson explains in the *Times Literary Supplement:* "All the people in [Pym's novels] are completely realistic: the sort of people we meet every day of our lives and never particularly notice. . . . By *noticing* them in such detail, Miss Pym's art endows them with a significance which they could never possess in life, so that what sound—if they are described outside the context of the book—to be mild and uneventful moments really come over as quite strong."

Edith Milton believes that Pym "has a genius for slanting her view of the restricted lives of her characters so that they shine, still, with reflections of an ancient greatness that the world they live in no longer affords. The bygone mysteries of the Church of England and the lost snobberies of empire return as ghostly and gently comic echoes of themselves in the habits and pretensions of Barbara Pym's people, who," Milton continues in the *New York Times Book Review,* "are no longer quite appropriate to the present day."

Mildred Lathbury, heroine of *Excellent Women,* is a case in point. A clergyman's daughter whose idea of rebellion is to attend a "high" Anglican mass where incense is burned, Mildred divides her time between St. Mary's Church and a charitable organization for impoverished gentlewomen. Still in her early thirties, she already seems resigned to spinsterdom and willingly accepts her role as a supporting player in other people's crises. In times of trouble, Mildred is always ready to provide a cup of hot tea—a woman "capable of dealing with most of the stock situations or even the great moments of life—birth, marriage, death, the successful jumble sale, the garden fete spoiled by bad weather." The plot of the novel revolves around a shallow young

officer and his anthropologist wife who have taken up residence in the flat below Mildred's and whose crumbling marriage she is soon called upon to save. That burden, as well as her circumspect role as peacemaker in several other romantic conflicts, comprises the bulk of the story. Events move so slowly that, as John Updike notes in his *New Yorker* review, "it would be hard to imagine a more timid world than that of 'Excellent Women,' or a novel wherein closer to nothing happens."

Though uneventful, Barbara Pym's novels provide a milieu well suited to her style. "High comedy needs a settled world, ready to resent disturbance," writes Penelope Fitzgerald in the *London Review of Books,* "and in her nine novels Barbara Pym stuck serenely to the one she knew best. . . . This meant that the necessary confrontations must take place at cold Sunday suppers, little gatherings, visits, funerals, and so on, which Barbara Pym, supremely observant in her own territory, was able to convert into a battleground." Victoria Glendinning says that in *Excellent Women,* "Pym's technique for comic effect is to glide over the pain of big happenings and to make much of the disproportionate impact of tiny ones." Writing in the *New York Times Book Review,* Glendinning continues: "Thus, when the marriage of Mildred's friends, the Napiers, is breaking up and she is more involved than she finds comfortable, we are told that 'the effects of grief and shock are too well known to need description.' Yet at a parish meeting, when Mildred asks whether the statutory cup of tea is really necessary, the distress and dismay of the other ladies is fully acknowledged, for this matter of the tea was 'the sort of question that starts a landslide in the mind.' "

In *Excellent Women,* as in all of Pym's books, there is a serious message beneath the veneer of humor. "Mildred's narrative moves with such wit and verve that it takes a while to recognize how deeply unfunny the novel is at heart," writes Harriet Rosenstein in *Ms.* "She cannot stop uttering chipper little ironies at her own expense, cannot demand that somebody be genuinely concerned with her. Knowing soon enough that she is expendable— merely 'excellent,' that is—Mildred nonetheless assists in their foolish dramas because she wants to matter to the men she helps, all of them unworthy of her, and she finally knows that too. The book is really about what happens when a woman's defenses against both hope and hopelessness are blown away, about loneliness and making do."

Rosenstein's interpretation of *Excellent Women* evokes its darker side, but there is evidence in the novel that Mildred relishes her freedom. On one occasion she is invited to dine at home with an eminent—if humorless—anthropologist named Everard Bone, but she turns him down, seemingly blind to his romantic interest. We learn that they get married in a later book, but for now Mildred happily accepts her single condition: "As I moved about the kitchen getting out china and cutlery, I thought, not for the first time, how pleasant it was to be living alone," she admits at the novel's end. Responsive to this brighter note, John Updike concludes that the book "is a startling reminder that solitude may be chosen, and that a lively, full novel can be constructed entirely within the precincts of that regressive virtue, feminine patience."

Following the publication of *Excellent Women,* Pym produced four more books, each opening onto what Philip Larkin called "England in the 1950s, and the lives of youngish middle-class people, educated rather above the average and sometimes to a background of High Anglicanism, who find for the most part that the daily round, the common task, doesn't quite furnish all they at any rate do ask. . . . Throughout the novels runs the theme that if we are to live at all we must turn, however hesitatingly and with whatever qualifications, to someone else.'' Penelope Fitzgerald identifies three kinds of conflicts in Barbara Pym's novels: ''growing old . . .; hanging on to some kind of individuality, however crushed, however dim; and adjusting the vexatious distance between men and women.''

Pym's exploration of these themes was interrupted in 1963 when the manuscript for *An Unsuitable Attachment* came back from an editor at Jonathan Cape with a note that it would not be published. ''It may be,'' Pym wrote in a letter to Philip Larkin reprinted in *A Very Private Eye,* ''that this novel is much *worse* than my others, though they didn't say so, giving their reason for rejecting it as their fear that with the present cost of book production etc. etc. they doubted whether they could sell enough copies to make a profit.'' The literary climate of the ''Swinging Sixties'' was the root of the problem, but Pym ''felt that it was her failure as a writer that was the reason for her rejection, . . . and for a while she mistrusted her own talents as well as her critical judgement,'' Holt reports. ''She started several novels, one with an academic setting which she thought might be more 'publishable'— but she was never satisfied with them and they were never completed or revised. At no time, in spite of suggestions made to her by well-meaning friends, would she ever compromise and write in a style or form that was not her own.'' (The academic novel was published posthumously as *An Academic Question* and welcomed by Pym's admirers, including *Chicago Tribune*'s Ruth Lopez, who notes that the book's contemporary main character ''really is not very different from the 'excellent women' in [Pym's] other books.' '')

Five years later, in 1968, Pym completed *The Sweet Dove Died* but was unsuccessful at finding a publisher. ''Not the kind of novel to which people are turning,'' one house wrote. During this time, Pym continued her work as an assistant editor of *Africa.* She underwent a successful operation for breast cancer in 1971 and returned to her job until 1974, when failing health forced her to retire. It was then that she completed, ''for her own enjoyment and for that of her friends,'' as Holt reports, a novel that ''had been simmering in her mind for some time about four elderly people in an office and the effect of retirement upon two of them.'' With the memory of failure still strong in her mind, Pym had little real hope of publication, and the manuscript for *Quartet in Autumn* was initially rejected. But when both Philip Larkin and Lord David Cecil cited her in the *Times Literary Supplement* as one of the most underrated writers of the age, there was a renewed interest in her work and, in 1977, Macmillan published what many consider her finest novel.

A serious story with comic overtones, *Quartet in Autumn* traces ''a beautifully calm and rounded passage in and out of four isolated individuals as they feebly, fitfully grope toward an ideal solidarity,'' according to John Updike. The lives of the four are uniformly bleak. Letty and Marcia are spinsters without families, Norman is a small, spiteful bachelor who harbors deep resentments against blacks and automobiles, and Edwin is a widower who spends all his free time visiting Anglican churches. As the story opens they are working together at an unspecified office job, their tasks so insignificant that the department will be eliminated upon their retirement. In fact, at the luncheon given to honor Letty's and Marcia's years of service, it becomes ridiculously apparent that not even the company officials are sure of their function. The situation becomes poignant when the reader realizes that this inconsequential drudgery is the focal point of their lives.

After retiring, Letty—the only self-aware character in the novel and one who evokes comparisons to Mildred of *Excellent Women*—tries hard to keep up appearances, but Marcia, always eccentric, lapses into madness, hoarding milk bottles, dreaming of the surgeon who performed her mastectomy, and slowly starving herself to death. When Marcia dies, Norman, Edwin, and Letty find their tenuous relationship strengthened and, by the novel's close, Letty speculates that all that has happened ''at least . . . made one realize that life still held infinite possibilities for change.''

Despite the upbeat ending, Karl Miller finds the novel depressing. ''Marcia is precisely evoked, and so is Letty,'' he writes in the *New York Review of Books.* ''But, it looks as if the imagination of the victim, of the celibate, which has informed her fiction is less lively here, less hopeful, and the story of these poor things is not a rich one.'' John Updike, however, expresses a different view. ''Miss Pym's portrait, from within, of a 'shopping bag lady,' showing the exact, plausible thought processes behind such mad actions as leaving trash in libraries, and attempting to dig up a dead cat, is an achievement.'' Harriet Rosenstein agrees, noting that Pym ''has set down these tiny, terminal lives with such loving particularity that they count as much to us as to the people living them.'' And Richard Boeth maintains in *Newsweek* that ''precisely because of the unimaginative, churchy, circumscribed nature of their lives, they are ideally suited to the purpose—as Jane Austen's provincials were to her quite similar purpose.''

That purpose includes a keen awareness of the double standard for men and women—an awareness that manifests itself in irony and runs throughout Pym's books. Thus, when Letty loses her apartment, Edwin isn't worried: '' 'Oh, a woman can deal with these things easily enough,' he reminded Norman in a rather sharp tone. 'There's no need to make the kind of fuss you or I would make if we were faced with such a situation.' '' Recurring behavior of this sort may be what prompts Philip Larkin to suggest in a *Times Literary Supplement* article that in all Pym's novels, ''it is the men who come off worst: grotesquely insensitive . . .; automatically stingy . . .; or perhaps simply selfish.'' In his *Punch* review, A. L. Rowse is more specific: ''They don't notice much (Miss Pym notices *every*thing); they assume that the whole meal is for them; they will take the last chocolate biscuit on the plate; men are not nearly so good at secrets as women; husbands will assume that their wives vote the same way as they do.'' Because of the insights the novels provide into the inequities between the sexes, Larkin believes ''no man can read them and be quite the same again.''

The success of *Quartet in Autumn* guaranteed a market for *The Sweet Dove Died* and a subsequent novel entitled *A Few Green Leaves.* It was not until the author had died, however, that the ''lost'' manuscript of *An Unsuitable Attachment* was discovered among her papers and posthumously published in 1982. The book that had originally been rejected by Jonathan Cape now received many good reviews, including high praise from *New York Times Book Review* critic Edith Milton, who called it ''a paragon of a novel, certainly one of her best, witty, elegant, suggesting beyond its miniature exactness the vast panorama of a vanished civilization.'' What she is writing about, according to Mary Cantwell, is the same theme she has always explored, ''the human need to be linked—whether to another human being, a cat or . . . the stability promised by a house with 'nice things' in it. She does so,'' continues Cantwell in the *New York Times,* ''without ever raising her voice, pounding home a point or slumping into sogginess, and she is, as her fans have been saying, quite something.''

"I suspect," concludes Bruce Allen in the *Chicago Tribune Book World,* "that her books will continue to speak to us for a very long time."

MEDIA ADAPTATIONS: Excellent Women was serialized for the British Broadcasting Corporation's "Woman's Hour"; British television rights to *Quartet in Autumn* have been purchased by Ken Taylor; *A Very Private Eye* was adapted by Hazel Holt into a one-woman play.

AVOCATIONAL INTERESTS: Reading, domestic life, cats.

BIOGRAPHICAL/CRITICAL SOURCES:

BOOKS

Contemporary Literary Criticism, Gale, Volume 13, 1980, Volume 19, 1981, Volume 37, 1986.
Dictionary of Literary Biography, Volume 14: *British Novelists since 1960,* Gale, 1983.
Dictionary of Literary Biography Yearbook: 1987, Gale, 1988.
Pym, Barbara, *Excellent Women,* J. Cape, 1952.
Pym, Barbara, *Quartet in Autumn,* Macmillan (London), 1977.
Pym, Barbara, *A Very Private Eye: An Autobiography in Diaries and Letters,* edited by Hazel Holt and Hilary Pym, Dutton, 1984.

PERIODICALS

Books and Bookmen, July, 1978.
Chicago Tribune, August 26, 1986.
Chicago Tribune Book World, August 1, 1982.
Commonweal, May 8, 1981.
Detroit News, April 15, 1979.
Globe and Mail (Toronto), August 11, 1984.
Harper's, August, 1983.
Hudson Review, autumn, 1980, autumn, 1981.
London Review of Books, November 20-December 4, 1980.
Los Angeles Times, July 22, 1982, August 16, 1983, July 23, 1985.
Los Angeles Times Book Review, October 12, 1980, May 24, 1981, August 5, 1984, September 14, 1986, February 7, 1988.
Ms., May, 1979, June, 1982.
New Statesman, September 23, 1977, August 15, 1980, February 19, 1982.
Newsweek, October 23, 1978, April 16, 1979, April 14, 1980, January 19, 1981, January 24, 1983, July 23, 1984.
New Yorker, February 26, 1979, May 24, 1982, January 17, 1983, September 5, 1983.
New York Review of Books, November 9, 1978.
New York Times, May 10, 1982, January 1, 1983, August 5, 1983, June 14, 1984.
New York Times Book Review, December 24, 1978, February 1, 1981, June 20, 1982, February 13, 1983, July 31, 1983, July 8, 1984, January 17, 1988.
Publishers Weekly, October 12, 1984, October 4, 1985.
Punch, October 19, 1977.
Time, October 9, 1978, September 26, 1983, June 24, 1985.
Times (London), February 18, 1982, July 19, 1984, June 20, 1985.
Times Literary Supplement, March 11, 1977, July 7, 1978, July 18, 1980, February 26, 1982.
Tribune Books (Chicago), January 3, 1988.
Washington Post Book World, April 6, 1980, June 20, 1982, January 14, 1983, August 21, 1983, June 9, 1985, September 28, 1986, January 17, 1988.

OBITUARIES:

PERIODICALS

Publishers Weekly, March 14, 1980.

* * *

PYNCHON, Thomas (Ruggles, Jr.) 1937-

PERSONAL: Born May 8, 1937, in Glen Cove, Long Island, N.Y.; son of Thomas Ruggles (an industrial surveyor) and Katherine Frances Bennett Pynchon. *Education:* Cornell University, B.A., 1958.

CAREER: Writer. Lived in Greenwich Village for one year after graduating from college; worked for Boeing Aircraft, Seattle, Wash., on a house organ; went to Mexico to finish his first novel; later moved to California. *Military service:* U.S. Navy, two years (interrupted his college studies).

AWARDS, HONORS: William Faulkner novel award, 1963, for *V.;* Rosenthal Foundation Award from National Institute of Arts and Letters, 1967, for *The Crying of Lot 49;* National Book Award, 1974, for *Gravity's Rainbow* (refused); Howells Medal from National Institute and American Academy of Arts and Letters, 1975, for body of work.

WRITINGS:

V. (novel; portions of Chapter 3 first appeared in another form as a short story, "Under the Rose," in the *Noble Savage,* number 3; another part was first published in *New World Writing*), Lippincott, 1963.
The Crying of Lot 49 (novel; sections first published as "The World [This One], the Flesh [Mrs. Oedipa Maas], and the Testament of Pierce Inverarity," in *Esquire,* December, 1965; another section in *Cavalier*), Lippincott, 1966.
Gravity's Rainbow (novel), Viking, 1973.
(Author of introduction) Richard Farina, *Been Down So Long It Looks Like Up to Me,* Penguin Books, 1983.
Slow Learner (short story collection), Little, Brown, 1984.
Vineland (novel), Little, Brown, 1990.

Also author of several short stories published by Aloes Books, including *Mortality and Mercy in Vienna,* 1976, and *Low-Lands,* 1978. Contributor of short stories and essays to periodicals, including *New York Times Magazine, New York Times Book Review, Cornell Writer, Holiday, Cornell Alumni News, Saturday Evening Post,* and *Kenyon Review.*

SIDELIGHTS: Perhaps the most significant biographical fact about Thomas Pynchon is his anonymity. Pynchon is so reticent about himself and so wary of publicity that it is unclear even what he looks like: the most recent published photographs of him come from his high school annual. For a time it was commonplace to compare him with J. D. Salinger, another famous American novelist who evades public scrutiny, but the comparison proved inadequate: Salinger, at least, can be located, while Pynchon keeps even his whereabouts a secret from everyone but his closest and most loyal friends. A former Cornell classmate, Jules Siegel, hinted in a 1977 *Playboy* article that this reclusiveness stems from the kind of paranoia that characteristically informs Pynchon's fiction (and has been termed "Pynchonesque"), but other evidence suggests that in his personal life this daring and iconoclastic writer is merely intensely private and intensely shy.

Three short occasional pieces that Pynchon wrote in the 1980s provide some information about his development as a writer.

The first of these, an introduction to the 1983 reissue of Richard Farina's novel, *Been Down So Long It Looks Like Up to Me,* is largely made up of reminiscences about the days when Pynchon and Farina were undergraduates at Cornell University. Pynchon pictures himself as an admirer and to some extent a follower of the late poet, songwriter, folksinger, and fiction writer, who knew not only the best parties but also "coeds I had lusted after across deep lecture halls." Some of Pynchon's former professors construe the relationship rather differently, however. "Farina was the performer," Walter Slatoff, professor of English at Cornell, recalled in a recent conversation. "Pynchon watched. He was always on the sidelines, but that was because he was taking everything in." In a 1963 article, "The Monterey Fair," collected in *A Long Time Coming and a Long Time Gone,* Farina himself represented Pynchon as essentially an observer, who skulked on the periphery of the action in dark glasses while evading reporters from *Life* magazine who were already trying to get a story on the newly famous author of *V.*

If Pynchon spent a great deal of time watching during those years, he was also listening. In the 1984 introduction to a collection of early short stories, *Slow Learner,* he refers to his most serious youthful fault as "Bad Ear" and lists the writers Jack Kerouac and the Beats generally, Saul Bellow, Herb Gold, and Philip Roth, who helped him develop his perception of voices by showing him "how at least two very distinct kinds of English could be allowed in fiction to exist." He also confirms thematic influences that various critics have noted as consistently important in his work: Niccolo Machiavelli's *The Prince,* Norbert Wiener's expositions of information theory, *The Education of Henry Adams,* and Karl Baedeker's guides. And he asserts his preoccupation with mortality, perhaps the single most resonant theme in his fiction. "When we speak of 'seriousness' in fiction," he observes, "ultimately we are talking about an attitude toward death—how characters may act in its presence, for example, or how they handle it when it isn't so immediate." This concern with mortality underlies Pynchon's fascination with the apparently abstract notion of entropy: the tendency for any system to move from a state of order to one of disorder. "Certain processes, not only thermodynamic ones but also those of a medical nature, can often not be reversed," he notes dryly, and adds, "Sooner or later we all find this out, from the inside."

The insistence that real understanding comes "from the inside" informs the *Slow Learner* introduction, in which Pynchon derides his early tendency toward abstraction and "literariness." But the self-castigation seems unduly harsh, for erudition has always served passion and compassion in his writing. In a 1984 *New York Times Book Review* essay, "Is It O.K. to Be a Luddite?," Pynchon observes that reactions against technological developments tend to be motivated less by ignorance and superstition than by the awareness that technology tends to centralize means of control. *Gravity's Rainbow,* especially, is built around this recognition and around an attendant development that may promise a highly qualified basis for hope: "If our world survives, the next great challenge to watch out for will come . . . when the curves of research and development in artificial intelligence, molecular biology and robotics all converge. Oboy. It will be amazing and unpredictable, and even the biggest brass, let us devoutly hope, are going to be caught flat-footed." Such observations reinforce the implication that Pynchon's own investigations into "artificial intelligence, molecular biology and robotics" derive from an overriding concern with the unprecedented complexities and dangers of a contemporary world brought into being by a chain of social and scientific revolutions, and with the situation of human beings whose capacity for integrity and action is severely limited by the power structures that result.

It remains true, however, that Pynchon's work strikes many readers as intensely difficult. This difficulty needs emphasizing inasmuch as it is not an extrinsic characteristic—one that a more careful author could have avoided, or one that the reader can circumvent with a good plot summary. Indeed, much of the difficulty arises precisely because Pynchon's plots resist summarization, just as his narrators resist reduction to a single identifiable voice and his range of reference seems virtually endless. The radical disruptions sometimes amounting to outright denials of narrative sequence in *Gravity's Rainbow* led the Pulitzer Prize editorial board to refuse to grant the fiction award to Pynchon for that novel, although the nominating jurors—writers Elizabeth Hardwick, Benjamin De Mott, and Alfred Kazin—who recommended the award had been unanimous in their choice. While the controversy was raging, however, Edward Mendelson was writing in the *Yale Review,* "Pynchon is, quite simply, the best living novelist in English," and was ranking *Gravity's Rainbow* with James Joyce's *Ulysses* and Thomas Mann's *The Magic Mountain* as one of the greatest novels of the twentieth century. It is clear that difficulty may provoke reflection as well as reaction. Pynchon still has vocal detractors, but as Khachig Tololyan writes in the *New Orleans Review,* "It is no longer possible to be seriously interested in contemporary American literature and yet to claim jauntily that one 'just can't get through' Thomas Pynchon's books."

In fact, the structural difficulty central to these books early became a theme, so that to a degree all Pynchon's novels are about difficulties in reading—and about "reading" as a metaphor for all the ways in which people try to make sense of the world in which they find themselves. In Pynchon's work, the act of reading parallels the act of deciphering a world problematically constructed of codes. Treating *The Crying of Lot 49,* Frank Kermode observes in an essay collected in Seymour Chatman's *Approaches to Poetics,* "What Oedipa is doing is very like reading a book," and the statement applies as well to Herbert Stencil in *V.* and to any number of questing heroes in *Gravity's Rainbow.* The notion of "reading" experience as a way of discerning meanings occurs as early as the 1960 short story "Entropy," in which, as Joseph Tabbi observes in a *Pynchon Notes* article, the undergraduate Pynchon is already working to create an imaginative order in art that would engage randomness and indeterminacy in modern life and in the changing physical world." In *V.,* published in 1963, apparent randomness and indeterminacy are qualities of the fictional universe that confronts the reader as well as the characters, and the central action of the quest is disconcertingly similar to the reader's own act of interpretation.

In a wider sense, "reading" is the process by which people make a story out of experience and call it history. As Tony Tanner remarks in his article "V. and V-2," collected in Edward Mendelson's *Pynchon: A Collection of Critical Essays,* V. is very much aligned with the short story "Entropy" in its concern for the possible running-down of history, for a gradual decline, which the narrator terms decadence. But while Pynchon's work "is certainly about a world succumbing to entropy, it is also about the subtler human phenomena the need to see patterns which may easily turn into the tendency to suspect plots." Tanner's synopsis plays on a double meaning inherent in the word "plot." In one sense a plot is a story line, the bare outline of "what happens" in a work of fiction. In another sense, however, a plot is a conspiracy, an underlying story of secret manipulation that reveals "what really happened." Insofar as history is "plotted" it may entail both of these meanings: if it tells a story it may do so precisely because someone has created that story, arranged things to produce certain results. A conspirator and an author clearly have something in common if the pun is taken seriously. Perhaps history itself has authors. Perhaps crucial events take place because somebody planned things that way.

V. is "about" plotting in this disturbing sense inasmuch as it raises questions about history within its own structure. The chapters taking place in the narrative present, in the years 1956 and 1957, are punctuated by chapters set at various times in the previous three-quarters of a century. The jumps between "past" and "present" are violent and to some extent unexplained. In some cases the reader can be reasonably sure that one of the protagonists, Herbert Stencil, is narrating the "historical" story, but in other cases it is radically unclear where the story is coming from or why it occurs at this point in the "present" action. The problem of connections thus becomes a major concern of the reader, who in making sense of Pynchon's novel is suddenly immersed in the same enterprise as Stencil himself.

Stencil's activity, a form of quest, involves looking through segments of recent history for manifestations of a woman known to him only as *V.* In the process Stencil serves as a persona of the reader, for as Melvyn New notes in the *Georgia Review*, "While Herbert Stencil searches for clues to the meaning of the woman *V.*, accumulating his notecards, his sources, his linkages, we, as readers, parallel his activity, making our own accumulations, driven by the same urge to fit the pieces together, to arrive at the meaning of the novel *V.*" The central dilemma of this quest depends on the double meaning of "plot." If the connections that Stencil discerns between the events of history are real, they seem to be evidence of a conspiracy bringing the twentieth century to a state of apocalyptic decadence, a situation analogous to the entropic run-down posited by thermodynamic theory as the terminus of the physical universe. If these connections are not real, but only projected out of a need to find order in the events of history, historical events become meaningless: uncaused and unmotivated, and causing and motivating nothing in the present.

Several critics have argued that one or the other of these alternatives is sanctioned by the author. For instance, Richard Patteson writes in *Critique*, "A primary source of tension in *V.* lies in the conflict between the attempt to discover or create form and the overwhelming tendency toward formlessness in the universe." Despite his emphasis on the tension engendered by this conflict, Patteson seems to find in "formlessness" Pynchon's view of the true state of affairs, with the consequence that "If some of the pieces—the essential ones, the vital connections—are imagined by Stencil, then no plot really exists." On the other hand, David Richter in *Fable's End: Completeness and Closure in Rhetorical Fiction* believes that Pynchon intended the connections to be real ones, for "What Pynchon was attempting to do in *V.* is nothing less than an explanation of the course of Western civilization in the twentieth century and a philosophy of its fate." In these terms, Richter argues, the novel is a failure because it "fails to justify, much less make a virtue of, its paralyzing complexity." A third possibility, proposed by Molly Hite in *Ideas of Order in the Novels of Thomas Pynchon,* is that the search for sequential connections joining "past" chapters to each other and implying causal linkages culminating in the narrative "present" is a bogus quest that exposes the limited preconceptions behind judgments of historical causality. The important relations in the book and in the world of the book are relations of resemblance. Hite argues: "Historical episodes resemble each other, but this resemblance does not signal an underlying 'plot.'. . . The important thing about resemblances is that they can be recognized; it is al-

ways possible, if highly unlikely in Pynchon's view, that someone will learn."

The critical dispute over the significance of connections in *V.* is inevitably a self-conscious one, underscoring the awareness that *V.* is to at least an extent about the sort of thing that critics do. As Richard Poirier writes in his *Twentieth Century Literature* essay, "In Pynchon's novels the plots of wholly imagined fictions are inseparable from the plots of known history or science. More than that, he proposes that any effort to sort out these plots must itself depend on an analytical method which, both in its derivation and in its execution, is probably part of some systematic plot against free forms of life." Thus by the same token that *V.* is about itself it points outside itself. As Poirier observes, the world articulated by the writings of historians and scientists seems similarly "plotted" and requires us to "read" it in similar ways. Pynchon employs this paradigm of the world as a text again in his second novel, *The Crying of Lot 49,* a book in some respects simpler in structure, and therefore commensurately easier to read, than *V.* (Pynchon does not seem to prize the relative lucidity and economy of this work as much as many of his reviewers. In the introduction to *Slow Learner* he identifies *The Crying of Lot 49* as a story "which was marketed as a 'novel,' and in which I seem to have forgotten most of what I thought I'd learned up till then.")

The Crying of Lot 49 has only one protagonist, another quester with the quest-hero's resonant name of Oedipa, and only one line of action, which remains resolutely chronological. Readers are thus largely spared the task of making connections within the story and left to observe the spectacle of the hero making her own connections which is to say either discerning them in or projecting them onto a satirically envisioned landscape of Southern California at mid-century. The parodic quality of *V.* is if anything intensified in *The Crying of Lot 49,* where Oedipa Maas (the surname means "more" in Spanish and is close to "measure" in German) is joined by Manny DiPresso, Stanley Koteks, Genghis Cohen, and a rock group called the Paranoids. Manfred Puetz suggests in his study *The Story of Identity* that Pynchon's characters tend to be stereotypical and "curiously one-dimensional" precisely because of the interpretive dilemmas in which they find themselves: "they remain caught in their situations" and "act out the same obsessions in compulsive repetitiveness." Certainly the metaphors of entrapment that confine Oedipa also define her. She is most memorably a princess in a tower weaving a tapestry that comes to constitute the world.

Like *V., The Crying of Lot 49* is concerned with the "plot" of history, embodied in the force that might be behind a spectral underground association called the Tristero. The novel is also more explicit than *V.* in its assertion of decoding activities as characteristic of scientific thinking and to this end uses the concept of entropy as an aspect of both physics and information theory. As Ann Mangel notes in an essay appearing in *Mindful Pleasures: Essays on Thomas Pynchon,* "By building his fiction on the concept of entropy, or disorder, and by flaunting the irrelevance, redundancy, disorganization, and waste involved in language, Pynchon radically separates himself from earlier twentieth-century writers, like [William Butler] Yeats, [T. S.] Eliot, and Joyce." But this antimodernism becomes productive, a critique of the modernist rage for order and in the process an exemplary postmodernism, inasmuch as it sees in the order of closed artistic systems an analogue of the conditions for entropic rundown. Mangel continues, "the complex, symbolic structures [that the modernists] created to encircle chaotic experience often resulted in the kinds of static, closed systems Pynchon is so wary of."

The publication of *Gravity's Rainbow* in 1973 secured Pynchon's reputation. The controversy over the Pulitzer was widely publicized and criticized, with many readers regarding the editorial board's decision as comparable to acts of the repressive power structure that the novel painstakingly documents. In addition *Gravity's Rainbow* won the National Book Award (Pynchon refused it, sending "Professor" Irwin Corey, a self-proclaimed master of double-talk, to the awards ceremony as his surrogate) and the William Dean Howells Award of the American Academy of Arts and Letters for the best novel of the decade. Both the acclaim and the hostility that this book engendered testify to its innovations. As Tololyan observes in his *New Orleans Review* article, it surpasses many traditional definitions "of what can be considered literary," upsetting "narrow generic and modal categories" of criticism and refusing "to fulfill a set of expectations nurtured by reading the great novels of the nineteenth century, or the slighter fictions of our time."

One index of the scope of *Gravity's Rainbow* is certainly the fact that it has been reviewed in *Scientific American* and discussed at length in *Technology and Culture.* In the latter journal Joseph Slade hails Pynchon as "the first American novelist to accept the duty of which [Aldous] Huxley speaks," the duty "to seek powerful means of expressing the nature of technology and the crises it has generated." In a study entitled *Readings from the New Book of Nature: Physics and Metaphysics in the Modern Novel,* Robert Nadeau identifies these crises with the collapse of "the Newtonian world view, which features along with the Western mind itself either-or categorical thinking, simple causality, immutable law, determinism, and discrete immutable substances"; but Alan Friedman, writing in Charles Clerc's collection *Approaches to "Gravity's Rainbow,"* finds more recent scientific world views equally unsatisfactory: "Unfortunately, the visions from science do not provide more hopeful guides away from the horrors *Gravity's Rainbow* reveals in life and death. Doctrinaire acceptance of any of these visions proves as sterile as the nonscience-related images that obsess characters." Richard Poirier's review in *Saturday Review of the Arts* suggests that, on the contrary, scientific data permeate the book not to provide solutions to conceptual difficulties but to compound these difficulties by offering yet another tradition to which the language can allude. The central symbol of the novel, the V-2 rocket, is thus even more overdetermined than central symbols tend to be; it is "Moby Dick and the Pequod all in one, both the Virgin and the Dynamo of Pynchon's magnificent book."

Poirier goes on to comment, "More than any living writer, including Norman Mailer, [Pynchon] has caught the inward movements of our time in outward manifestations of art and technology so that in being historical he must also be marvelously exorbitant," and the "exorbitant" quality of *Gravity's Rainbow* may constitute its greatest threat to traditional ideas of the "literary." In the Charles Clerc anthology, Joseph Slade points to Pynchon's "faith in the unity of Creation"; but a number of other critics see in *Gravity's Rainbow* a work constituted in opposition to existing notions of unity, and especially in opposition to the unity of the artistic work celebrated by the earlier masters of literary modernism. For example, Brian McHale, writing in *Poetics Today,* calls *Gravity's Rainbow* a "postmodern text" that subverts the emphasis on coherence of the "modernist reading" it seems to elicit. Charles Russell concurs that the novel pushes at conventional boundaries and notes in his essay in the Clerc collection, "Indeed, Gravity's Rainbow is but one manifestation of a widespread literary fascination with the nature and limits of aesthetic and social language during the past two decades." And John Muste, writing in *Boundary 2,* finds in the circular image of the mandala (a preoccupation of the southwest African Herero characters prominent in the novel) an emblem of the reader's situation. "Confronted with a text which contains a veritable cornucopia of clues," he observes, "we search diligently and sometimes desperately for ways of arranging these clues in a meaningful pattern. *Gravity's Rainbow* invites, even demands, such efforts, and steadfastly rebuffs them. It gives nothing away. At the center of the mandala rests that infuriating empty circle, that refusal to impose meaning or to confirm either our fondest wishes or our direst fears."

Yet the "infuriating empty circle" that seems to repel the reader's attempts to arrive at a coherent interpretation of *Gravity's Rainbow* is not an ultimately negative cipher for any of these critics. The structure of this novel seems to enact its thematic concerns with a vengeance, so that characters, situations, and events proliferate beyond control or limit. Within the novel, however, controls and limits are rarely benign, and characters tend to be free to the extent that they evade other people's attempts to define them. Louis Mackey observes in his *Sub-Stance* essay that in the same way the tone of narration undermines "every ingredient of form—myth, symbol, archetype, history, allegory, romantic quest, even the ritual sanctities of science," and that consequently the refusal to be pinned down into wholly determinate meanings is part of the novel's achievement: "The language—this is the secret of its mastery—is not master of itself. It has renounced self-mastery, so that there is no 'authentic' text of *Gravity's Rainbow.* . . . Whatever it says garrulously and disconcertingly fails to make the point. And that of course is the point."

"The point" that Mackey reaches may well strike many readers as excessively intellectual, for the same reason that some reviewers found the book as a whole formidably erudite but unrewarding as an experience. "The literary reviewers have treated the novel as seriously as it deserves," writes Philip Morrison in a *Scientific American* article reprinted in Mendelson's *Pynchon: A Collection of Critical Essays;* "it is a brilliant book, but be warned, that glow is icy cold." Others clearly revel in the characterization (Scott Simmon notes in "A Character Index: Gravity's Rainbow," published in *Critique,* that there are over 300 characters who are developed in some detail), in the multiple voices of a narrative that shifts without warning from slangy Americanism to the high-minded musings of German idealism to oddly private reflections and reminiscences, and in the rich interplay of themes that are represented as constituting the entire legacy of Western culture. And some critics argue that *Gravity's Rainbow* is most exhilarating in its refusal to yield a single "authorized" reading. "And out of this dismantling a promise?" inquires Charles Russell, who goes on to propose a tentative answer: "The art of fragments—whether they portend death or revitalization—this is the final gift of Pynchon. It is an anarchic vision that promises either freedom or impotence, creation or mindless pleasures." "Mindless Pleasures" was Pynchon's original title for *Gravity's Rainbow;* this title suggests that for the author himself the book was something other than and something more than an intellectual tour de force.

The publication of *Gravity's Rainbow* marked the beginning of a seventeen-year silence interrupted only by the 1984 realease of *Slow Learner,* a collection of five previously-published short stories. In 1990, however, Pynchon reentered the literary mainstream with *Vineland,* a novel taking its title from the fictional northern California county in which it takes place. Focusing on a group of 1960s beatniks after they lived through the disillusionment of the following decade into the television-dominated culture of the 1980s, *Vineland* features a pot-growing handyman, landscaper, and former rock singer named Zoyd Wheeler, his teenaged daughter Prairie, and Frenesi Gates, his ex-wife. The book's complex plot begins with Zoyd's being forced into hiding when a prosecutor from Washington D.C. (and Frenesi's jealous former lover) tries to kidnap Prairie in an attempt to resume his relationship with Frenesi, who has disappeared. Unlike Pynchon's previous novels, *Vineland* contains numerous references to popular culture and alludes to many fewer scholarly, literary, or historical ideas. Critics trace, however, Pynchon's trademark themes of entropy and paranoia, and many comment on the wit, humor, and extraordinary facility with language that Pynchon demonstrates in the novel.

While finding much about *Vineland* to praise, reviewers generally agree that Pynchon's much-anticipated novel does not surpass either *Gravity's Rainbow* or *The Crying of Lot 49* as his best work. "*Vineland* won't inspire the same sort of fanatic loyalty and enthusiasm that *Gravity's Rainbow* did," asserts David Strietfeld in *Fame,* who quips, "The new novel has got a much more mainstream flavor. . . . Call it Pynchon Lite." Expressing severe criticism is *Listener's* John Dugdale, who feels that *Vineland's* grounding in contemporary American life detracts from the importance of Pynchon's themes: "[*Vineland*] is an unsatisfactory, stripped-down novel lacking the internal tension which sustained its predecessors: the interplay between abstract concepts and human stories, past art and modern lives, the scholarly and the streetwise. By misguidedly choosing to quit the literature of ideas, Pynchon robs his writing of both its vitality and its distinctiveness." But Paul Gray, writing in *Time,* is more appreciative of *Vineland* and its portrait of betrayal, conformity, materialism, and shallowness: "It is, admittedly, disquieting to find a major author drawing cultural sustenance from *The Brady Bunch* and *I Love Lucy* instead of *The Odyssey* and the Bible. But to condemn Pynchon for this strategy is to confuse the author with his characters. He is a gifted man with anti-elitist sympathies. Like some fairly big names in innovative fiction, including Flaubert, Joyce and Faulkner, Pynchon writes about people who would not be able to read the books in which they appear. As a contemporary bonus, Pynchon's folks would not even be interested in trying. That is part of the sadness and the hilarity of this exhilarating novel."

BIOGRAPHICAL/CRITICAL SOURCES:

BOOKS

Bestsellers 90, Issue 2, Gale, 1990.
Chatman, Seymour, editor, *Approaches to Poetics,* Columbia University Press, 1973.
Clerc, Charles, editor, *Approaches to "Gravity's Rainbow,"* Ohio State University Press, 1983.
Contemporary Fiction in America and England 1950-1970, Gale, 1976.
Contemporary Literary Criticism, Gale, Volume 2, 1974, Volume 3, 1975, Volume 6, 1976, Volume 9, 1978, Volume 11, 1979, Volume 18, 1981, Volume 33, 1985.
Cooper, Peter L., *Signs and Symptoms: Thomas Pynchon and the Contemporary World,* University of California Press, 1983.
Cowart, David, *Thomas Pynchon: The Art of Allusion,* Southern Illinois University Press, 1980.
Dictionary of Literary Biography, Volume 2: *American Novelists since World War II,* Gale, 1978.
Farina, Richard, *A Long Time Coming and a Long Time Gone,* Random House, 1965.
Farina, Richard, *Been Down So Long It Looks Like Up to Me,* introduction by Thomas Pynchon, Penguin Books, 1983.
Fowler, Douglas, *A Reader's Guide to "Gravity's Rainbow,"* Ardis, 1980.

Harris, Charles B., *Contemporary American Novelists of the Absurd,* College and University Press, 1972.
Hendin, Josephine, *Vulnerable People: A View of American Fiction since 1945,* Oxford University Press, 1978.
Hite, Molly, *Ideas of Order in the Novels of Thomas Pynchon,* Ohio State University Press, 1983.
Hyman, Stanley Edgar, *Standards: A Chronicle of Books for Our Time,* Horizon Press, 1966.
Kazin, Alfred, *Bright Book of Life: American Novelists and Storytellers from Hemingway to Mailer,* Little, Brown, 1973.
Kostelanetz, Richard, *On Contemporary Literature,* Avon, 1964.
Lehan, Richard, *A Dangerous Crossing: French Literary Existentialism and the Modern American Novel,* Southern Illinois University Press, 1973.
Levine, George and David Leverenz, editors, *Mindful Pleasures: Essays on Thomas Pynchon,* Little, Brown, 1976.
McConnell, Frank, *Four Postwar American Novelists: Bellow, Mailer, Barth, Pynchon,* University of Chicago Press, 1977.
Mendelson, Edward, editor, *Pynchon: A Collection of Critical Essays,* Prentice-Hall, 1978.
Nadeau, Robert, *Readings from the New Book on Nature: Physics and Metaphysics in the Modern Novel,* University of Massachusetts Press, 1981.
Newman, Robert D., *Understanding Thomas Pynchon,* University of South Carolina Press, 1986.
Olderman, Raymond M., *Beyond the Waste Land: A Study of the American Novel in the 1960s,* Yale University Press, 1972.
Pearce, Richard, editor, *Critical Essays on Thomas Pynchon,* G. K. Hall, 1981.
Plater, William M., *The Grim Phoenix: Reconstructing Thomas Pynchon,* University of Indiana Press, 1978.
Puetz, Manfred, *The Story of Identity: American Fiction of the Sixties,* Metzlersche Verlagsbuchhandlung, 1979.
Pynchon, Thomas, *Slow Learner,* Little, Brown, 1984.
Richter, David H., *Fable's End: Completeness and Closure in Rhetorical Fiction,* University of Chicago Press, 1974.
Schaub, Thomas H., *Pynchon: The Voice of Ambiguity,* University of Illinois Press, 1981.
Scholes, Robert, *The Sounder Few: Essays from the "Hollins Critic,"* University of Georgia Press, 1971.
Schultz, Max F., *Black Humor Fiction of the Sixties: A Pluralistic Definition of Man and His World,* Ohio University Press, 1973.
Scotto, Robert M., *Three Contemporary Novelists: An Annotated Bibliography of Works by and about John Hawkes, Joseph Heller, and Thomas Pynchon,* G. K. Hall, 1977.
Siegel, Mark R., *Pynchon: Creative Paranoia in "Gravity's Rainbow,"* Kennikat, 1978.
Slade, Joseph W., *Thomas Pynchon,* Warner Books, 1974.
Tanner, Tony, *City of Words: American Fiction 1950-1970,* J. Cape, 1971.

PERIODICALS

Boundary 2, Volume III, 1975, Volume V, number I, 1976, Volume VIII, 1980, Volume IX, number 2, 1981.
Chelsea Review, December, 1969.
Chicago Tribune Book World, April 8, 1984.
Commentary, September, 1963, September, 1973.
Commonweal, July 8, 1966.
Contemporary Literature, summer, 1974, autumn, 1977, autumn, 1979, spring, 1980.
Critical Quarterly, Volume LXIII, 1976.
Critique, Volume VI, 1963-64, Volume X, number 1, 1967, Volume XIV, number 2, 1972, Volume XVI, number 2, 1974, Volume XVIII, number 3, 1977.

Fame, winter, 1990.
Genre, Volume V, 1972.
Georgia Review, Volume XXXIII, number 1, 1979.
Globe and Mail (Toronto), June 30, 1984, January 20, 1990.
Harper's, March, 1975.
International Fiction Review, Volume IV, 1977.
Liberation, October 11, 1985.
Listener, February 1, 1990.
Literature/Film Quarterly, Volume VI, 1978.
London Magazine, Volume X, number 7, 1970.
Los Angeles Times, December 10, 1989.
Los Angeles Times Book Review, May 6, 1984, December 31, 1989.
Modern Fiction Studies, Volume XXIII, 1977.
Nation, September 25, 1967, July 16, 1973, February 26, 1990.
New Leader, May 23, 1966.
New Orleans Review, Volume V, 1977.
New Republic, Volume CLXVIII, 1973.
New Statesman, October 11, 1963, April 14, 1967.
Newsweek, April 1, 1963, May 2, 1966, May 20, 1974, April 9, 1984, January 8, 1990.
New York Herald Tribune Books, April 21, 1963.
New York Review of Books, June 23, 1966, March 22, 1973.
New York Times, March 29, 1984, December 26, 1989.
New York Times Book Review, April 21, 1963, April 28, 1963, May 1, 1966, July 17, 1966, March 11, 1973, April 15, 1984, October 28, 1984, January 14, 1990.
Notes on Modern American Literature, Volume IV, 1979.
Partisan Review, Volume XXX, 1963, Volume XXXIII, 1966, Volume XXXVI, 1969, Volume XL, 1973, Volume XLII, 1975.

Paunch, Volume XL-XLI, 1975.
Perspectives on Contemporary Literature, Volume II, 1976.
Playboy, March 7, 1977.
PMLA, Volume XCII, 1978.
Poetics Today, Volume I, numbers 1-2, 1979.
Punch, April 26, 1967.
Pynchon Notes, February, 1984, fall, 1984.
Renascence, Volume XXXII, number 2, 1980.
Saturday Night, August, 1966.
Saturday Review, April 30, 1966.
Saturday Review of the Arts, Volume I, number 3, 1973.
Southern Humanities Review, Volume XVIII, number 4, 1984.
Sub-Stance, Volume XXX, 1981.
Technology and Culture, Volume XXIII, 1982.
Time, April 23, 1984, January 15, 1990.
Times (London), January 10, 1985, February 3, 1990.
Times Literary Supplement, October 11, 1963, January 11, 1985, February 2, 1990.
Tribune Books, January 14, 1990.
Tri-Quarterly, winter, 1967.
Twentieth Century Literature, Volume XXI, number 2, 1975, Volume XXV, number 1, 1979.
Virginia Quarterly Review, summer, 1963, autumn, 1970.
Washington Post, December 6, 1989.
Washington Post Book World, April 22, 1984, January 7, 1990.
Yale Review, Volume LXII, 1973, Volume LXVII, 1975.

*   *   *

PYTHON, Monty
 See CLEESE, John (Marwood)

Q

QIAN Zhongshu
See CH'IEN Chung-shu

* * *

QUASIMODO, Salvatore 1901-1968

PERSONAL: Surname is accented on second syllable; born August 20, 1901, in Modica, Sicily, Italy; died of a brain hemorrhage, June 14, 1968, in Naples, Italy; buried in Famedio, Milan, Italy; son of Gaetano (a state inspector) and Clotilde (Ragusa) Quasimodo; married Maria Cumani (a dancer), 1948; children: Orietta, Alessandro. *Education:* Polytechnic study in Rome, Italy. *Religion:* Roman Catholic.

ADDRESSES: Home—Corso Garibaldi 16, Milan, Italy.

CAREER: Worked as a technical designer for a construction firm, 1920-24, and in hardware store, 1924-26; junior official in the State Civil Engineers Bureau, traveling in Calabria, Sardinia, and Lombardy, Italy, 1926-29; began writing seriously, and worked briefly as a secretary for the publishing house of Mondadori in Milan during 1929; *Il Tempo* (magazine), Milan, Italy, assistant editor and drama critic, 1938-40; Giuseppe Verdi Conservatory, Milan, Italy, professor of Italian literature, 1941-64.

MEMBER: Accademia Nazionale di Luigi Cherubini (Florence; corresponding member), Academy of American Arts and Sciences, Akademi der Kuenste zu Berlin, Academie Internationale des Sciences Politiques de Geneve, Accademia Italiana di Scienze Biologiche e Morali.

AWARDS, HONORS: Etna-Taormina International Poetry Prize (shared with Dylan Thomas), 1953; Tor Margana Prize; Viareggio Prize, 1958, for *La terra impareggiabile;* Nobel Prize for Literature, 1959; laureate honoris causa, Oxford University, 1967.

WRITINGS:

IN ENGLISH TRANSLATION

The Selected Writings of Salvatore Quasimodo, edited and translated by Allen Mandelbaum, Farrar, Straus, 1960.
Salvatore Quasimodo: Poems, Wesleyan University, 1960.
(Editor with Carlo Golino) *Contemporary Italian Poetry: An Anthology,* 1962, reprinted, Greenwood, c. 1981.

The Poet and the Politician, and Other Essays, translated by Thomas Bergin and Sergio Pacifici, Southern Illinois University Press, 1964.
Selected Poems, translated by Jack Bevan, Penguin, 1965.
To Give and to Have, and Other Poems, translated by Edith Farnsworth, H. Regnery, 1969.
Debit and Credit, translated by Jack Bevan, Anvil Press Poetry, 1972.

Works represented in anthologies, including *1001 Poems of Mankind,* compiled by Henry W. Wells, Tupper & Love, 1953; *The Promised Land and Other Poems,* edited by Sergio Pacifici, Vanni, 1957; *The Penguin Book of Italian Verse,* edited by George Kay, Penguin, 1958.

IN ITALIAN

Acque e terre (poems; title means "Water and Earth"), Edizioni di Solaria (Florence), 1930.
Oboe sommerso (title means "Sunken Oboe"), Circoli (Genoa), 1932.
Odore di eucalyptus e altri versi, Antico Fattore (Florence), 1933.
Erato e Apollion, Scheiwiller (Milan), 1936.
Poesie, Primi Piani (Milan), 1938.
Ed e subito sera (title means "And It's Suddenly Evening"), Mondadori, 1942, 5th edition, 1971.
Con il piede straniero sopra il cuore (title means "With the Alien Foot on Our Heart"), Costume (Milan), 1946.
Giorno dopo giorno, Mondadori, 1947, 7th edition, 1961.
La vita non e' un sogno (poems; title means "Life Is No Dream"), Mondadori, 1949, 7th edition, 1966.
Billy Budd (libretto), Suvini e Zerboni, 1949.
Il falso e vero verde: Con undiscorso sulla poesia (title means "The False and True Green"), Mondadori, 1956, 4th edition, 1961.
La terra impareggiabile (title means "The Matchless Earth"), Mondadori, 1958, 5th edition, 1962.
Poesie scelte, edited by Roberto Sanesi, Guanda (Parma), 1959.
Petrarca e il sentimento della solitudine, All'insegna del pesce d'oro (Milan), 1959.
Tutte le poesie, Mondadori, 1960, 8th edition, 1970.
L'amore di Galatea (libretto), Edizioni Teatro Massimo (Palermo), 1960.
Il poeta e il politico e altri saggi, Schwarz, 1960.
Scritti sul teatro, Mondadori, 1961.
Nove poesie (poems), Franco Riva (Verone), 1963.

Dare a avere: 1959-1965 (poems; title means "Giving and Having: 1959-1965"), Mondadori, 1966.
(Author of introduction) Domenico Cantatore, *Cantatore,* Maestre (Rome), 1968.
Un anno di Salvatore Quasimodo: Lettere aperte, Immordino, 1968.
Le opere: Poesia, prosa, traduzioni, edited by Guido di Pino, Unione Tipograficoeditrice Torinese, 1968.
Le lettere d'amore di Quasimodo, edited by Guido Le Noci, Appolinaire, 1969.
Poesie e discorsi sulla poesia, edited by Gilberto Finzi, Mondadori, 1971.

Also author of *Xavier Bueno,* Edizioni Galleria Santa Croce.

TRANSLATOR INTO ITALIAN

Lirici Greci, Edizioni di Corrente, 1940, 7th edition, Mondadori, 1963.
Virgil, *Il fiore delle Georgiche,* Gentile (Milan), 1942.
Catullus, *Carmina,* [Milan], 1945.
Homer, *Traduzioni dall' Odissea,* Rosa e Ballo, 1945.
John Ruskin, *La Bibbia di Amiens,* Mondadori, 1946.
Aeschylus, *Le coefore* (also see below), Bompiani, 1946.
Sophocles, *Edipo re* (also see below), [Florence], 1946.
William Shakespeare, *Romeo e Giulietta,* Mondadori, 1948.
William Shakespeare, *Macbeth,* Einaudi (Turin), 1952.
William Shakespeare, *Riccardo III,* Mondadori, 1952.
Pablo Neruda, *Poesie,* Einaudi, 1952, 3rd edition, 1967.
Sophocles, *Elettra* (also see below), Mondadori, 1954.
Catullus, *Canti,* Mondadori, 1955.
William Shakespeare, *La tempesta,* Einaudi, 1956.
Moliere, *Tartuffe,* [Milan], 1957.
e. e. cummings, *Poesie scelte* (also see below), All'insegna del Pesce d'oro, 1957.
William Shakespeare, *Otello,* Mondadori, 1958.
Ovid, *Dalle metamorfosi,* All'insegna del Pesce d'oro, 1959.
Euripides, *Ecuba,* Mondadori, 1963.
Conrad Aiken, *Mutevoli pensieri* (also see below), Scheiwiller (Milan), 1963.
Tragici greci (includes *Le coefore, Elettra,* and *Edipo re*), Mondadori, 1963.
William Shakespeare, *Drammi,* Mondadori, 1963.
Euripides, *Eracle,* Mondadori, 1966.
William Shakespeare, *Antonio e Cleopatra,* Mondadori, 1966.
Dall' Antologia Palatina, Mondadori, 1968.
Homer, *Iliade: Episodi scelti,* Mondadori, 1968.
Yves Lecomte, *Il gioco degli astragali,* Moneta (Milan), 1968.
(And compiler) *Da Aiken e Cummings* (includes *Mutevoli pensieri* and *Poesie scelte*), Mondadori, 1968.
Leonida di Taranto (with essay by Carlo Bo), Lacarta, 1969, limited edition (translations only, edited by Guido Noci), Apollinaire, 1970.
(And editor) Paul Eluard, *Donner a voir,* Mondadori, 1970.

Also translator of Biblical writings.

EDITOR

(With L. Anceschi) *Lirici minori del XIII e XIV secolo,* [Milan], 1941.
Lirica d'amore italiana, Schwarz, 1957.
Poesia italiana del dopoguerra, Schwarz, 1958.
Fiore dell'Antologia Palatina, Guanda (Bologna), 1958.
Tudor Arghezi, *Poesie,* Mondadori, 1966.
Michel Angelo Buonarroti, *L'opera completa de Michelangelo pittore,* Rizzoli, 1966, 5th edition, 1969.

SIDELIGHTS: "His voice is not only unique in contemporary European poetry," wrote Francis Golffing, "but it is a voice of rarest distinction: absolutely free of rhetorical inflation, at once generous and fastidious, *'unfashionable'* yet representative of an entire generation. . . . Quasimodo is the least vapid of poets, even as he is one of the purest by those exigent standards to which Mallarme, Rilke, and Valery have accustomed us." C. M. Bowra noted that Quasimodo "writes with an unusual sensibility about nature and with a keen understanding about the more elusive moods of the human spirit. He never says too much or tries to pass beyond the limits of his themes. He is intimate, discerning, sensitive, but he has not yet found the extraordinary power which is all the more impressive for being held in strict control and is now his most characteristic gift." The simplicity of his free verse was deceptive. A reviewer in the *Yale Review* wrote: "At first glance [his] poetry may seem somewhat minor and monotonous. However, some careful examination will reveal Quasimodo's rare gift for delicacy of phrasing and tightness of structure."

His early poems tended to be subjective and nearly experimental. Though his work showed great continuity through the years, after 1940 it became less personal, more aware of external events. Bowra wrote: "Quasimodo is a classical poet who has absorbed the best modern devices and combines order, economy and clarity with a full measure of inventive surprise. Though he eschews the more traditional forms of Italian verse and in his earlier work favored short lines, his work has now an impressive, majestic movement which owes not a little to the great masters of his language. . . . [He now stands] in his own strength as a poet who is both Italian and European, both contemporary and universal."

BIOGRAPHICAL/CRITICAL SOURCES:

BOOKS

Angioletti, Annamaria, *E fu subito sera,* Marotta (Naples), 1969.
Birolli, x. Beuno, Cantatore, De Chirico, Esa D'albisola, Fabbri, Manzu, Marino C., Mastroianni, Migneco, Rossello, Rossi, Sassu, Sotilis, Unsellini, Tamburi visti da Salvatore Quasimodo, Edizioni Trentadue (Milan), 1969.
Contemporary Literary Criticism, Volume 10, Gale, 1979.

PERIODICALS

Books Abroad, winter, 1960.
Christian Science Monitor, June 9, 1960.
London Magazine, December, 1960.
New York Herald Tribune Book Review, July 10, 1960.
New York Times Book Review, November 15, 1959, July 3, 1960.
Reporter, December 10, 1959.
Saturday Review, November 7, 1959, June 1, 1960.
Yale Review, September, 1960.

OBITUARIES:

PERIODICALS

New York Times, June 15, 1968.
Times (London), June 17, 1968.
Washington Post, June 15, 1968.

*   *   *

QUEEN, Ellery
   See DANNAY, Frederic and STURGEON, Theodore (Hamilton) and VANCE, John Holbrook

QUENEAU, Raymond 1903-1976
(Sally Mara)

PERSONAL: Born February 21, 1903, in Le Havre, France; died October 25, 1976, in Paris, France; son of Auguste (a businessman) and Josephine (Mignot) Queneau; married Janine Kahn, 1934; children: Jean-Marie. *Education:* University of Paris, licence es lettres, 1926.

ADDRESSES: Office—Gallimard, 5 rue Sebastien-Bottin, 75007 Paris, France.

CAREER: Comptoir national d'escompte (bank), Paris, France, employee, beginning 1927; Gallimard (publishing house), Paris, reader, 1938-39, secretary general, beginning 1941, director of *Encyclopedie de la Pleiade,* 1955-75. Member of l'Academie Goncourt (literary jury), 1951-76. Founder, with Francois Le Lionnais, of Ouvroir de litterature potentielle ("Oulipo"). *Military service:* Served in Algeria and Morocco as a Zouave, 1926-27, and in French army, 1939-40; became corporal.

MEMBER: Academie de l'humour, American Mathematical Society, College of 'pataphysique.

AWARDS, HONORS: Prix de l'Humour Noir for *Zazie dans le metro.*

WRITINGS:

IN ENGLISH TRANSLATION

Le Chiendent (novel), Gallimard, 1933, reprinted, 1974, enlarged edition with an article by Jean Queval and notes by Nicole Onfroy, Bordas, 1975, translation by Barbara Wright of first French edition published as *The Bark Tree,* Calder & Boyars, 1968, New Directions, 1971.

Un Rude hiver (novel), Gallimard, 1939, translation by Betty Askwith published as *A Hard Winter,* Lehmann, 1948.

Pierrot mon ami (novel), Gallimard, 1943, reprinted, 1965, translation by J. McLaren Ross published as *Pierrot,* Lehmann, 1950.

Loin de Rueil (novel), Gallimard, 1944, reprinted, 1967, translation by H. J. Kaplan published as *The Skin of Dreams,* New Directions, 1948, reprinted, H. Fertig, 1979.

Exercises de style, Gallimard, 1947, revised edition, 1973, translation by Wright published as *Exercises in Style,* Gabberbocchus, 1958, reprinted, New Directions, 1981.

(Compiler) Alexandre Kojeve, editor, *Introduction a la lecture de Hegel,* Gallimard, 1947, abridged translation by James H. Nichols, Jr. published as *Introduction to the Reading of Hegel,* Basic Books, 1969.

(Under pseudonym Sally Mara) *On est toujours trop bon avec les femmes* (also see below), Editions du Scorpion, 1947, translation by Wright published under author's real name as *We Always Treat Women Too Well: A Novel,* New Directions, 1981.

Le Dimanche de la vie (novel; also see below), Gallimard, 1951, reprinted, 1973, translation by Wright published as *The Sunday of Life,* Calder, 1976, New Directions, 1977.

Zazie dans le metro (novel), Gallimard, 1959, reprinted, 1977, translation by Wright published as *Zazie,* Harper, 1960.

Cent mille milliards de poemes (novel), Gallimard, 1961, reprinted, 1981, translation published as *One Hundred Million Million Poems* (bilingual edition), Kickshaws (Paris), 1983.

Les Fleurs bleues (novel), Gallimard, 1965, enlarged edition with introduction and notes in English edited by Wright, Methuen, 1971, translation by Wright published as *The Blue Flowers,* Atheneum, 1967 (published in England as *Between*

Blue and Blue, Bodley Head, 1967), reprinted, New Directions, 1985.

Le Vol d'Icare, Gallimard, 1968, translation by Wright published as *The Flight of Icarus,* New Directions, 1973.

Raymond Queneau: Poems, translated by Teo Savory, Unicorn Press, 1971.

Pounding the Pavement, Beating the Bushes, and Other Pataphysical Poems (bilingual edition), translation by Savory of poems from *Courir les rues, Battre le campagne,* and other volumes (also see below), Unicorn Press, 1986 (published in England as *Pataphysical Poems,* 1986).

NOVELS

Gueule de Pierre (also see below), Gallimard, 1934.

Chene et chien (title means "Oak and Dog"; novel in verse; also see below), Denoel, 1937.

Odile, Gallimard, 1937, reprinted, 1969.

Les Enfants du limon (title means "Children of the Earth"), Gallimard, 1938.

Les Temps meles (title means "Mixed-up Times"; also see below), Gallimard, 1941.

Saint Glinglin (revision of *Gueule de Pierre* and *Les Temps meles*), Gallimard, 1948.

(Under pseudonym Sally Mara) *Journal intime* (also see below), Editions du Scorpion, 1950.

Also author of *A la limite de la foret,* 1947, *Le Cheval troyen,* 1948, and *Un conte a votre facon,* 1968.

POETRY

Les Ziaux (also see below), Gallimard, 1943.

Une Trouille verte, Editions de Minuit, 1947.

L'Instant fatal (also see below), Gallimard, 1948.

Petite cosmogonie portative (title means "A Portable Little Cosmogony"; also see below), Gallimard, 1950.

Si tu t'imagines, 1920-1951 (title means "If You Imagine"), Gallimard, 1952, revised edition published as *Si tu t'imagines, 1920-1948,* 1968.

Le Chien a la mandoline (title means "The Dog on the Mandolin"), Verviers, 1958, enlarged edition, 1965.

Sonnets, Editions Hautefeuille, 1958.

Variations typographiques sur deux poemes de Raymond Queneau (title means "Typographic Variations of Two Poems by Raymond Queneau"), [Paris], 1964.

L'Instant fatal, precede de Les Ziaux, Gallimard, 1966.

Courir les rues, Gallimard, 1967.

Battre le campagne, Gallimard, 1968.

Chene et chien (includes *Chene et chien,* revised version of *Petite cosmogonie portative,* and *Le Chant de Styrene*), Gallimard, 1968.

Fendre les flots (title means "Parting the Waters"), Gallimard, 1969.

Bonjour Monsieur Prassionos, G. A. Parisod, 1972.

OTHER

Les derniers jours (title means "The Last Days"), Gallimard, 1936, reprinted with a preface by Olivier de Magny, Societe Cooperative (Lausanne), 1965.

Bucoliques, Gallimard, 1947.

Joan Miro; ou, Le poete prehistorique (title means "Joan Miro; or, The Prehistoric Poet"), A. Skira, 1949.

(With Queval) *Rendez-vouz de juillet* (title means "Rendezvous in July"), Chavane, 1949.

Batons, chiffres, et lettres (title means "Sticks, Figures, and Letters"), Gallimard, 1950, revised and enlarged edition, 1965.

(Editor with A. J. Arberry and others) *Les Ecrivains celebres* (title means "Famous Writers"), three volumes, L. Mazenod, 1951-53, 3rd edition, 1966.

(Editor) *Anthologie des jeunes auteurs* (title means "Anthology of Young Authors"), Editions J.A.R., 1955.

(Editor) *Histoire des litteratures* (title means "History of Literatures"), three volumes, Gallimard, 1955-58.

(Compiler) *Pour une bibliotheque ideale* (title means "For an Ideal Library"), Gallimard, 1956.

Lorsque l'espirit (title means "When the Spirit"), Collection Q., 1956.

(Contributor) *Le Declin du romantisme: Edgar Poe* (title means "The Decline of Romanticism: Edgar Poe"), L. Mazenod, 1957.

Les Oeuvres completes de Sally Mara (title means "The Complete Works of Sally Mara"; contains *On est toujours trop bon avec les femmes, Journal intime,* and "Sally plus intime" [title means "More Intimate Sally"]), Gallimard, 1962.

Entretiens avec Georges Charbonnier (title means "Interviews with Georges Charbonnier"), Gallimard, 1962.

Bords: Mathematiciens, precurseurs, encyclopedistes, Hermann, 1963.

Une Histoire modele (title means "A Model History"), Gallimard, 1966.

Texticules, Galerie Louise Leiris, 1968.

Raymond Queneau en verve (title means "Raymond Queneau at His Best"), P. Horay, 1970.

De quelques langages animaux imaginaires et notamment du langage chien dans "Sylvie et Bruno" (title means "Of Several Imaginary Animal Languages, Notably the Dog Language in 'Sylvie and Bruno' "), L'Herne, 1971.

Le Voyage en Grece (title means "Voyage to Greece"), Gallimard, 1973.

Morale elementaire (title means "Elementary Ethics"), Gallimard, 1975.

(With Elie Lascaux) *Correspondance Raymond Queneau-Elie Lascaux,* Gallimard, 1979.

Contes et propos (fiction), Gallimard, 1981.

Une Correspondance: Raymond Queneau-Boris Vian, Association des Amis de Valentin Bru, 1982.

Journal, 1939-1940, suivi de Philosophes et voyous, edited by A. I. Queneau and J.-J. Marchand, Gallimard, 1986.

Also author of "En passant" (play), 1944, and *La Litterature potentielle,* 1973; author of screenplays, including, "Monsieur Ripois," 1954, "La Mort en ce jardin," 1956, (with others) "Un Couple," 1960, and "La Dimanche de la vie" (adapted from his novel of the same title), 1967. Also translator of works by Maurice O'Sullivan, Sinclair Lewis, George du Maurier, and Amos Tutuola. Author of column, "Connaissez-vous Paris?," for *L'Intransigeant,* 1936-38, and of weekly column for *Front National,* 1940-45.

SIDELIGHTS: French novelist and poet Raymond Queneau blended the complex linguistic and narrative patterns of James Joyce, the use of colloquial language of Louis-Ferdinand Celine, and the inane humor of Alfred Jarry to produce an unique brand of writing. The roots of Queneau's style can be traced to the beginning of his career in the 1920s and his involvement with Andre Breton and the Surrealist movement which so influenced the Parisian literary milieu of the era. Queneau's work reflects the Surrealist rebellion against established societal values and emphasis on the irrational forces of the subconscious mind. His novels and poems reveal a deep preoccupation with the problem of language, a concern that often came to be the most important feature of his writing.

Queneau believed that written French had become completely disassociated from the spoken form of the language and, therefore, strove to reproduce spoken rather than written French in his work. He described this new form of language as "le neo francais." "In Queneau's hands," noted Tom Bishop in the *Saturday Review,* "language—vocabulary, spelling, syntax—is manipulated, squeezed, and pulled until it fairly explodes and becomes a 'neo-language' of slang and colloquialisms." Not only did Queneau use language usually heard in the streets of Paris in his books, but he also delighted in stretching language to its utmost limits. Germaine Bree and Margaret Otis Guiton concluded in their assessment of Queneau appearing in *An Age of Fiction: The French Novel from Gide to Camus* that the author wrote in "Queneau-ese" and noted that his readers would find his works so "full of puns, coined words, polysyllables, alliterations and phonetic ornaments" that saying that he wrote in French would be inaccurate. According to *French Studies* contributor Christopher Shorley, "Queneau's commitment to language in all its manifestations is perhaps the most consistent single element in his works."

Queneau also experimented with the printed word and the structure of the novel. Some examples of his innovations include changing typefaces throughout the course of a novel, illustrating a debate going on within a character's mind by dividing a page into two columns, using a short poetic line to represent the rhythm of dialogue, and employing made-up punctuation marks. In *Exercises de style* he recounts a brief anecdote about an ordinary encounter on a bus in ninety-nine different ways, changing styles as well as genres as he tells the incident in prose, in free verse, as a sonnet, and as a play. *The Flight of Icarus* is another example of his experimentation with the novel. The text includes a spoof of mystery stories and a play with seventy-four scenes. In *French Review,* Robert Henkels, Jr. called the work "neither fish nor fowl, . . . it explores several topics, and dabbles with several genres all at once." *Listener* contributor Ronald Bryden observed that it was "less novel than intellectual comic-strip: a daisy-chain of dialogue 'frames' ballooned with puns and in-jokes." Vivian Kogan observes in her *Dictionary of Literary Biography* essay that Queneau's probing of the novelistic form "invites the reader to view all of literature as a series of permutations that have no ultimate or 'authentic' text as their origin. . . . His intentions are therapeutic rather than destructive of literature; his purpose is to rid literature of its rusty, crusty conventions."

It was not until 1959 with publication in France of his *Zazie dans le metro* (published in English translation in 1960 as *Zazie*) that Queneau attained international fame as a novelist. This novel—the story of eleven-year-old Zazie who visits her uncle in Paris and surprises him with her use of foul language—included the experimentation in language and zany comedy that readers had come to expect from Queneau. Although *Zazie* was popularly acclaimed, it was unevenly reviewed by U.S. critics. In his *Critical Essays,* Roland Barthes discussed the confusion surrounding the book as well as his own admiration for it: "*Zazie dans le metro* is really an exemplary work: by vocation, it dismisses both . . . the serious and the comic," Barthes noted. "Which accounts for the confusion of our critics: some have taken it seriously as a serious work of art, suited to exegetical decipherment; others, judging the first group grotesque, have called the novel absolutely frivolous . . . ; still others, seeing neither comedy nor seriousness in the work, have declared they did not understand. But this was precisely the work's intention—to wreck any dialogue about it, representing by the absurd the elusive nature of language." In *Zazie,* Vernon Hall, Jr. observed in *Lively Arts and Book Review,*

Queneau appears "intoxicated with a vocabulary partially picked up from the streets, partially invented, [and] he passes on this intoxication to his . . . readers."

Queneau's inimitable use of language is also found in his poetry, most of which has been overlooked by the English-speaking world. In 1986 Teo Savory, one of Queneau's translators, brought out an English-language edition of a selection of his poems written from 1943 to 1969; *Pounding the Pavements, Beating the Bushes, and Other Pataphysical Poems* appeared with Savory's hopes of correcting this situation. These poems reveal the similarities between Queneau the novelist and Queneau the poet. As a poet he used features also found in his fiction: colloquial language, phonetic spelling, and invented words; but in his poetry he was able to add another comic dimension with his playful use of rhyme. *Times Literary Supplement* contributor Peter Reading quoted a portion of one of the translated poems: "Ah when I was young/ how happy I was! Like/ a lizard in the sun/ looking at my toenails." Reading pointed out another similarity between Queneau's poetry and the fiction in "the existence of a number of different possible readings" in many of the poems. This is reminiscent of Queneau's *Exercises in Style* with its multiple retellings of the same incident and also of the writer's *Morale elementaire* (title means "Elementary Ethics"), a collection containing both prose and verse poems set in columns across the page which can be read in several directions either individually within a column or across all the columns on the page. Reading pointed out that in Queneau's poetry "often the starting-point is purposely minimal and the real subject-matter becomes the language"—a statement which also could be made about Queneau's fiction, in which critics observed characters and content taking a subordinate position to linguistic experimentation.

Queneau's playful use of language has made translation of his work difficult. A *Times Literary Supplement* reviewer commented: "Translation is, in a sense, the whole of Raymond Queneau's art. The task of translating him in turn into an alien language and cultural context is virtually impossible." Reviewers, however, have generally praised Barbara Wright for her attempts to capture in English the spirit of the slang and puns which dominated his work. Those critics, such as Hall and Laurent LeSage, who found the translations lacking the same impact as the original works still seemed to agree that even in English translation Queneau was worth reading. LeSage, for example, noted in his *Saturday Review* essay on *Zazie* that "for French readers, recognition of the familiar under Queneau's distortions made the charm of the book. This, alas, is not for us. But the exotic can have its charm, too, and if Queneau's caricatures are for us bereft of living models, we may find them none the less fascinating for it. Freed of all contingencies, they become pure figures of fun and their story a fantasy taking place on the moon."

MEDIA ADAPTATIONS: Zazie was made into a film by Louis Malle in 1960.

BIOGRAPHICAL/CRITICAL SOURCES:

BOOKS

Barthes, Roland, *Critical Essays,* Northwestern University Press, 1972.
Bree, Germaine, and Margaret Otis Guiton, *An Age of Fiction: The French Novel from Gide to Camus,* Rutgers University Press, 1957.
Contemporary Literary Criticism, Gale, Volume 2, 1974, Volume 5, 1976, Volume 10, 1979, Volume 42, 1987.
Dictionary of Literary Biography, Volume 72: *French Novelists, 1930-1960,* Gale, 1988.

PERIODICALS

French Review, October, 1975.
French Studies, October, 1981.
Listener, July 5, 1973.
Lively Arts and Book Review, December 11, 1960.
Saturday Review, October 15, 1960.
Times Literary Supplement, May 25, 1967, September 19, 1968, March 7, 1986.

OBITUARIES:

PERIODICALS

AB Bookman's Weekly, January 3, 1977.
New York Times, October 26, 1976.

—*Sketch by Marian Gonsior*

*   *   *

QUIROGA, Horacio (Sylvestre)   1878-1937
(Guillermo Eynhardt)

PERSONAL: Born December 31, 1878, in Salto, Uruguay; committed suicide by taking poison while suffering from cancer, February 19, 1937, in Buenos Aires, Argentina; interred in Salto, Uruguay; son of an Argentine vice-consul; married Ana Maria Cires, December 30, 1909 (committed suicide, December, 1915); married second wife, Maria Elena, July, 1927 (separated); children: (first marriage) Egle (daughter), Dario; (second marriage) one child. *Education:* Attended University of Montevideo.

CAREER: Writer. Colegio Nacional, Buenos Aires, Argentina, Spanish teacher, 1903; member of Argentine Government commission studying Jesuit ruins in Misiones, Argentina, in early 1900s; cotton farmer in Chaco, Argentina; Escuela Normal, Buenos Aires, professor of Spanish language and literature, 1906-11; justice of the peace and official recorder, San Ignacio, Argentina; farmer, charcoal maker, and distiller in Misiones; employed at Uruguayan consulates in Buenos Aires, beginning c. 1917, and San Ignacio, 1932.

MEMBER: El Consistorio de Gay Saber.

WRITINGS:

Los arrecifes de coral (poems and stories; title means "Coral Reefs"), originally published in 1901, published with essays by Carlos A. Herrera MacLean and Antonio M. Grompone, C. Garcia & cia (Montevideo, Uruguay), 1943.
Las sacrificadas, cuento excenico en cuatro actos (four-act play; title means "The Sacrificed"), "Buenos Aires" Cooperativa Editorial Limitada, 1920.
Diario de viaje a Paris, introduction and notes by Emir Rodriguez Monegal, Numero (Montevideo), 1950.
La vida en Misiones, prologue and notes by Jorge Ruffinelli, Arca (Montevideo), 1969.
Sobre literatura, prologue by Roberto Ibanez, notes by Ruffinelli, Arca, 1970.
Epoca modernista, prologue by Arturo Sergio Visca, notes by Ruffinelli, Arca, 1973.

FICTION

Historia de un amor turbio (title means "The Story of a Troubled Courtship"), originally published in 1908, Babel (Buenos Aires, Argentina), 1923, reprinted, Barreiro y Ramos (Montevideo), 1968.
Cuentos de amor, de locura y de muerte (title means "Stories of Love, Madness, and Death"; includes "Nuestro primer ci-

garro," "El meningitis y su sombra," "Una estacion de amor," "La muerte de Isolda," "Buques suicidantes," "El almohadon de pluma," "El solitario," and "La gallina degollada"), originally published in 1917, Babel, 1925, reprinted, Bello (Santiago, Chile), 1984.

Cuentos de la selva, originally published in 1918, C. Garcia y cia, 1940, reprinted, Juventud (La Paz, Bolivia), 1982, translation by Arthur Livingston published as *South American Jungle Tales,* illustrations by A. L. Ripley, Duffield, 1922.

"El salvaje" y otros cuentos (title means "'The Savage' and Other Stories"; includes "El salvaje," "La realidad," "Reyes," "La navidad," "La pasion," "Corpus," "La reina italiana," "Los cementerios belgas," "Estefania," "La llama," "Fanny," "Lucila Strinberg," "Un idilio," "Tres cartas y un pie," and "Cuento para novios"), Biblioteca Argentina de Buenas Ediciones Literarias (Buenos Aires), 1920, reprinted, Alianza (Madrid, Spain), 1982.

Anaconda (contains "Anaconda," "El simun," "Gloria tropical," "El yaciyatere," "Los fabricantes de carbon," "El monte negro," "En la noche," "Polea loca," "Dieta de amor," and "Miss Dorothy Phillips, mi esposa"), originally published in 1921, reprinted, Biblioteca Argentina de Buenas Ediciones Literarias, 1930, reprinted, Alianza, 1981.

El desierto (title means "The Wilderness"; contains "El desierto," "Un peon," "Una conquista," "Silvina y Montt," "El espectro," "El sincope blanco," "Los tres besos," "El potro salvaje," "El leon," "La patria," and "Juan Darien"), Babel, 1924, reprinted, Losada (Buenos Aires), 1974.

"La gallina degollada," y otros cuentos, Calpe (Madrid), 1925, reprinted, Centro Editor de America Latina (Buenos Aires), 1967, translation by Margaret Sayers Peden published as *The Decapitated Chicken," and Other Stories,* introduction by George D. Schade, illustrations by Ed Lindlof, University of Texas Press, 1976.

Los desterrados: Tipos de ambiente (title means "The Exiled"; contains "El ambiente: El regreso de Anaconda," "Los tipos: Los desterrados," "Van-Houten," "Tacuaramansion," "El hombre muerto," "El techo de incienso," "La camara oscura," and "Los destiladores de naranja"), originally published in 1926, Biblioteca Argentina de Buenas Ediciones Literarias, 1927, reprinted, Losada, 1983, translation by J. David Danielson and Elsa K. Gambarini published as *"The Exiles" and Other Stories,* University of Texas Press, 1987.

Pasado amor (title means "Bygone Love"), Biblioteca Argentina de Buenas Ediciones Literarias, 1929, reprinted, Losada, 1981.

Mas alla (title means "The Great Beyond"; contains "Mas alla," "El vampiro," "Las moscas," "El conductor del rapido," "El llamado," "El hijo," "La senorita Leona," "El puritano," "Su ausencia," "La bella y la bestia," and "El ocaso"), originally published in 1934, [Buenos Aires], 1935, reprinted as *El mas alla,* Losada, 1964.

Our First Smoke, translated from the Spanish "Nuestra primer cigarro" by Annmarie Colbin, Vanishing Rotating Triangle, 1972.

"The Flies," in *Review 76,* 1976.

Also author of *El crimen del otro* (title means "Another's Crime"; includes "El crimen del otro," "La justa proporcion de las cosas," "La princesa bizantina," and "Hashish"), 1904, and *Los perseguidos* (title means "The Pursued"), 1905.

LETTERS

Cartas ineditas de Horacio Quiroga, [Montevideo], 1959.

Cartas ineditas, edited with notes by Arturo Sergio Visca, Biblioteca Nacional, Departamento de Investigaciones (Montevideo), 1970.

El mundo ideal de Horacio Quiroga [y cartas ineditas de Quiroga a Isidoro Escalera], edited by Antonio Hernan Rodriguez, Centro de Investigacion y Promocion Cientifico-Cultural, Instituto Superior del Profesorado Antonio Ruiz de Montoya (Posadas, Argentina), 1971.

Cartas desde la selva, Gente Nueva (Havana, Cuba), 1971.

Cartas de un cazador, Arca, 1986.

OMNIBUS VOLUMES

Cuentos (stories), C. Garcia y cia, 1937.

Horacio Quiroga: Sus mejores cuentos (stories), edited with introduction and notes by John A. Crow, Cultura (Mexico), 1943, reprinted with prologue by Mario Rodriguez Fernandez, Nascimento (Santiago), 1971.

Cuentos escogidos (stories; contains "Nuestro primer cigarro," "La insolacion," "El alambre de pua," "Yaguai," "Anaconda," "Los fabricantes de carbon," "En la noche," "Los pescadores de vigas," "La voluntad," "El simun," "A la deriva," "El hombre muerto," "El yaciyatere," and "Tacuara-Mansion"), prologue by Guillermo de Torre, [Madrid], 1950.

"El regreso de Anaconda," y otros cuentos (stories; title means "'The Return of Anaconda,' and Other Stories"), Universitaria de Buenos Aires, 1960.

Anaconda. El salvaje. Pasado amor, Sur (Buenos Aires), 1960.

Cuentos (stories; contains "El potro salvaje," "Juan Darien," "El regreso de Anaconda," "El desierto," "Los desterrados," "El hombre muerto," "Los destiladores de naranja," "Las moscas," "El hijo," "El conductor del rapido," "El almohadon de plumas," "Los inmigrantes," and "Una bofetada"), edited with introduction by Ezequiel Martinez Estrada, Casa de las Americas (Havana), 1964.

Seleccion de cuentos (stories), two volumes, edited by Emir Rodriguez Monegal, [Montevideo], 1966.

Obras ineditas y desconocidas, edited by Angel Rama, Arca, 1967—.

De la vida de nuestros animales (stories), prologue by Mercedes Ramirez de Rossiello, notes by Jorge Ruffinelli, Arca, 1967.

Novelas cortas, two volumes, Arca, 1967.

"A la deriva" y otros cuentos (stories; title means "'Drifting' and Other Stories"), Centro Editor de America Latina (Montevideo), 1968.

Cuentos, 1905-1935 (stories), prologue by Rama, notes by Ruffinelli, Arca, 1968.

Los cuentos de mis hijos (stories), Arca, 1970.

El desafio de las Misiones (stories; contains "A la deriva," "Anaconda," and "Los desterrados"), introduction by Angel L. Grenes, Casa del Estudiante (Montevideo), 1977.

Novelas completas (contains "Historia de un amor turbio," "Las fieras complices," "El mono que asesino," "El hombre artificial," "El devorador de hombres," "El remate del imperio romano," "Una caceria humana en Africa," and "Pasado amor"), Ediciones del Atlantico (Montevideo), 1979.

Cuentos completas (stories), two volumes, Ediciones la Plaza, 1979.

Mas cuentos (stories), introduction by Arturo Souto Alabarce, Porrua, 1980.

"El sincope blanco" y otros cuentos de horror (horror stories), Valdemar Ediciones (Madrid), 1987.

OTHER

Work represented in anthologies, including *A World of Great Stories,* edited by Hiram Haydn and John Cournos, Crown, 1947; *Classic Tales From Spanish America,* edited and translated by William E. Colford, Barron's, 1962; and *Spanish American Literature Since 1888 in Translation,* edited by Willis Knapp Jones, Ungar, 1963. Contributor to Salto periodicals under pseudonym Guillermo Eynhardt, 1897-98. Founder and editor of journal *Revista del Salto,* 1899.

SIDELIGHTS: Known for his preoccupation with the themes of madness and death and his vivid depictions of the jungle, Horacio Quiroga won acclaim as one of the greatest short story writers of Latin America. His fiction was considered closely linked to the violence and tragedy that punctuated his life. Several of his relatives and friends died in accidents—one at Quiroga's hands—or committed suicide; Quiroga himself experienced recurring bouts of illness, which led to his own suicide at the age of fifty-eight, and both his marriages failed. The personal element deemed strongest in his work, however, was his jungle experience. Born in Uruguay, Quiroga spent much of his life in Argentina's wild Misiones region, which became the foundation of some of his best-known writings. Observed Jefferson Rea Spell in *Contemporary Spanish-American Fiction,* "It is [Quiroga's] ability to transfer to his pages the atmosphere of Misiones, the scene of so many of his joys and sorrows, that catches the attention of his readers and gives him distinction as a writer." Critics such as Jean Franco, writing in *An Introduction to Spanish-American Literature,* recognized Quiroga's contribution to "the art of the short story" also. Assessed Franco, "He can certainly be counted one of the Latin-American masters of the genre."

Quiroga began his writing career as part of the *modernista* school of Spanish-American literature at the turn of the century. The movement was characterized by its rejection of naturalism in favor of innovative language, meter, and rhyme. Quiroga's involvement included founding a short-lived modernist journal, *Revista del Salto,* writing a volume of modernist stories and verse, *Los arrecifes de coral,* and founding the school's first Uruguayan group, El Consistorio de Gay Saber. He had become interested in modernism through acquaintance with Argentine poet Leopoldo Lugones, and it was through Lugones that Quiroga ultimately found his own literary niche—Lugones headed the historical commission with which Quiroga first visited Misiones to study Jesuit ruins in 1903.

With his second book, the 1904 collection *El crimen del otro,* Quiroga began to move away from modernism. He adopted a more realistic, detail-oriented prose and revealed his lifelong fascination with madness, horror, and death—macabre concerns that suggested a literary kinship with Gothic writer Edgar Allan Poe. In addition to modernistic tales such as "La princesa bizantina," the volume contains stories powerfully influenced by Poe. For instance, Poe's "Cask of Amontillado" provides the framework for the title story: Quiroga's mentally unbalanced characters discuss the classic tale and eventually enact its climactic scene, one character interring the other alive. Reflected Ernesto Montenegro in the *New York Times Book Review,* Quiroga "seems to hold a strong predilection for those states of mind not yet out of the twilight of reason or already drifting beyond the world of consciousness. . . . Still, his stories are seldom gruesome and never lugubrious. Almost always a sardonic humor plays a light accompaniment to his more fearsome imaginings." Like Poe, Quiroga earned a reputation as a craftsman of the short story, creating vivid images and skillfully evoking atmosphere with a few carefully chosen words. Remarked John Eu-

gene Englekirk in his book *Edgar Allan Poe in Hispanic Literature:* "No other Hispanic prose writer has so vividly expressed the spirit of Poe's tales as has Horacio Quiroga. . . . [He] has fortified himself with Poe's magic art of availing himself of every possible means for creating the effect desired. . . . That is why Quiroga, like Poe, can hold his reader's interest in tales that under another's pen would fail utterly."

Quiroga earned his first widespread popularity with *Cuentos de amor, de locura y de muerte,* published in 1917, which was also his first book to feature Misiones. Noted Spell, "The stories [Quiroga] wrote in Misiones . . . brought him a very enviable reputation as a *cuentista,*" or storyteller. *Cuentos de amor* contains "fifteen of the most representative," including stories closely identified with events from Quiroga's life, dark stories demonstrating the continued influence of Poe, and the first jungle stories, in which Quiroga's depiction of the conflict between man and nature is considered central. Poisonous and nonpoisonous snakes, rabid dogs, tropical rain and heat, and the Parana River are among the jungle elements on which the plots hinge. In the setting of Misiones, Franco suggested, "an accident or a moment of carelessness can change a normal working day into a fierce struggle for life. It was this that fascinated Quiroga." In the jungle, Englekirk asserted, Quiroga "uncovered untold treasures with which to bring into original and masterful display those characteristics that had, up to this time, been employed on imaginary themes of a decidedly Poesque trend."

Two of the stories without a specific Misiones slant also impressed critics: "El solitario" ("The Solitaire") and "La gallina degollada" ("The Decapitated Chicken"). According to Spell, they "come as near meeting the requirements of an artistic short story as anything that Quiroga wrote." The first describes a jeweler who suffers with a vain and unfaithful wife, until he kills her with a scarf pin she had coveted; the second, "the most tragic story that Quiroga wrote," relates how several mentally deficient children, after seeing a cook behead a chicken, kill their sister. Wrote Spell, "Both are told in a very direct and straightforward manner; each creates a very definite mood; the plots, though simple, are well constructed . . . and the characters . . . are well delineated." With such stories, judged Englekirk, Quiroga "emerged, at last, as a master of the short story and as a truly original writer."

Quiroga frequently featured animal protagonists in his fiction, notably in the jungle fables of *Cuentos de la selva* and *Anaconda,* which were aimed at children and adults, respectively. Stories such as "Anaconda," in which a group of snakes, disagreeing among themselves, try to prevent scientists from making an antivenin that will render their sole weapon useless, dramatize "the struggle . . . between the undisciplined, bold forces of savagery and the snares of civilization," assessed Montenegro. Spell deemed "Anaconda" Quiroga's masterpiece. "In nothing else that he has written can there be found such a large number of excellent qualities," the critic maintained, lauding the "intensely individual" setting, precise characterization, simple and effective style, and sympathy Quiroga evokes in the reader. Celebrated as among Quiroga's best writing, the collections prompted favorable comparisons to the works of British writer Rudyard Kipling. Montenegro, for example, likened Quiroga's social satire to Kipling's while commending Quiroga's "superior learning in natural history and more direct contact with his subject." *Cuentos de la selva* was Quiroga's first book to be translated into English, appearing as *South American Jungle Tales* in 1922.

In his 1926 collection, *Los desterrados: Tipos de ambiente,* Quiroga depicted the "exiles" of the jungle—frontiersmen, drunkards, laborers, and eccentrics who made the wilderness their home. Notable is "El hombre muerto" ("The Dead Man"), judged one of Quiroga's best stories and singled out by George D. Schade, in his introduction to *The Decapitated Chicken, and Other Stories,* for its tight structure, precise diction, and skillful use of "suggestion and implication, rather than outright telling." The story focuses on the thoughts of a farmer dying because he accidentally wounded himself with a machete; unable to accept his fate, he continues to make plans for his farm until, ultimately, his self-awareness is vanquished by death. According to Schade, "El hombre muerto" exemplifies Quiroga's "magnificent treatment of death"—it is told in a "natural and matter-of-fact" manner and achieves "a high degree of emotional intensity." Other stories in the collection feature the widow of a drunken judge who had a photograph made of her husband's corpse, the boa constrictor from the earlier "Anaconda," and a delirious, drunken father who mistakes his daughter for a rat and kills her.

Published in 1934, Quiroga's final story collection was the somber and, to some reviewers, even morbid *Mas alla.* One story, reminiscent of "El hombre muerte," describes a man who awaits death after falling and breaking his back; another shows a father who, though hallucinating, has an accurate precognition of his son's death. In the title story, two lovers commit suicide and are reunited after death, only to be separated without knowing what awaits them. Other tales describe a train engineer going insane; a man who, obsessed by a deceased actress, commits suicide to be with her; and a woman in an insane asylum. In Spell's opinion, the book was strongly shaped by "the troubles that marred the last years of [Quiroga's] life—domestic dissensions, financial difficulties, and ill health." The critic felt that Quiroga's preoccupation with death and suicide and his return to the theme of insanity seemed "not only to indicate an unhealthy state of mind but to presage his own tragic end."

Critics have expressed a range of opinions regarding Quiroga's literary talent. Although some criticized his work for being undisciplined and uneven in quality, many agreed with William Peden, who stated in *Review,* "At their best, Quiroga's stories succeed as entertainment, as art, as commentary on the human situation." Spell, who found the total impact of Quiroga's work "slight," nonetheless acknowledged that the handful of outstanding stories was "enough to entitle him to international fame." Praise for Quiroga's technical skills came from various sources, including Schade, who found Quiroga "a master craftsman," and Franco, who acknowledged him as a significant regional writer and short story master. And if Quiroga's writing seemed narrowly focused on the bizarre and macabre, it also proved memorable. Commented Peden: "Quiroga's stories pass what to me is perhaps the ultimate test of a work of fiction, that of memorableness. Quiroga is a master of the stunning effect, the vivid detail, the unforgettable scene that linger painfully in the reader's consciousness, as real as remembrances of past injustices or unhealed wounds."

BIOGRAPHICAL/CRITICAL SOURCES:

BOOKS

Englekirk, John Eugene, *Edgar Allan Poe in Hispanic Literature,* Instituto de las Espanas, 1934.
Franco, Jean, *An Introduction to Spanish-American Literature,* Cambridge University Press, 1969.
Peden, Margaret Sayers, editor, *The Latin American Short Story: A Critical History,* Twayne, 1983.
Quiroga, Horacio, *"The Decapitated Chicken," and Other Stories,* University of Texas Press, 1976.

Rodes de Clerico, Maria E. and Ramon Bordoli Dolci, *Horacio Quiroga: Antologia, estudio critico y notas,* Arca, 1977.
Spell, Jefferson Rea, *Contemporary Spanish-American Fiction,* University of North Carolina Press, 1944.
Twentieth-Century Literary Criticism, Volume 20, Gale, 1986.

PERIODICALS

Hispania, September, 1972.
New York Times Book Review, October 25, 1925.
Review, winter, 1976.

—*Sketch by Polly A. Vedder*

* * *

QUOIREZ, Francoise 1935-
(Francoise Sagan)

PERSONAL: Born June 21, 1935, in Cajarc, France; daughter of Pierre (an industrialist) and Marie (Laubard) Quoirez; married Guy Schoeller, March 13, 1958 (divorced, 1960); married Robert James Westhoff, January 10, 1962 (divorced, 1963); children: (second marriage) Denis. *Education:* Attended Sorbonne, University of Paris.

ADDRESSES: c/o Ramsay, 9 rue Racine, Cherche-Midi, 75006 Paris, France; and c/o Editions Flammarion, 26 rue Racine, 75006 Paris, France.

CAREER: Writer. Director of film "Les Fougeres bleues," 1976.

AWARDS, HONORS: Prix des Critiques, 1954, for *Bonjour tristesse.*

WRITINGS:

UNDER PSEUDONYM FRANCOISE SAGAN; NOVELS, EXCEPT AS INDICATED

Bonjour tristesse, Julliard, 1954, translation by Irene Ash published under same title, Dutton, 1955, reprinted, Popular Library, 1974.
Un Certain Sourire, Julliard, 1956, translation by Anne Green published as *A Certain Smile,* Dutton, 1956.
Dans un mois, dans un an, Julliard, 1957, translation by Frances Frenaye published as *Those without Shadows,* Dutton, 1957.
Aimez-vous Brahms?, Julliard, 1959, translation by Peter Wiles published under same title, Dutton, 1960.
Les Merveilleux Nuages, Julliard, 1961, translation by Green published as *The Wonderful Clouds,* Murray, 1961, Dutton, 1962.
La Chamade, Julliard, 1965, translation by Robert Westhoff published under same title, Dutton, 1966.
Le Garde du coeur, Julliard, 1968, translation by Westhoff published as *The Heart Keeper,* Dutton, 1968.
Un peu de soleil dans l'eau froide, Flammarion, 1969, translation by Terence Kilmartin published as *A Few Hours of Sunlight,* Harper, 1971 (translation by Joanna Kilmartin published in England as *Sunlight on Cold Water,* Weidenfeld & Nicolson, 1971).
Des bleus a l'ame, Flammarion, 1972, translation by J. Kilmartin published as *Scars on the Soul,* McGraw, 1974.
Un Profil perdu, Flammarion, 1974, translation by J. Kilmartin published as *Des yeux de soie: Nouvelles* (short stories), Flammarion, 1975, translation by J. Kilmartin published as *Silken Eyes,* Delacorte, 1977.
Lost Profile, Delacorte, 1976.
Le Lit defait, Flammarion, 1977, translation by Abigail Israel published as *The Unmade Bed,* Delacorte, 1978.

Le Chien couchant, Flammarion, 1980, translation by C. J. Richards published as *Salad Days,* Dutton, 1984.

Musique de scenes (short stories), Flammarion, 1981, translation by Richards published as *Incidental Music,* Dutton, 1985.

La Femme fardee, Jean-Jacques Pauvert aux Editions Ramsay, 1981, translation by Lee Fahnestock published as *The Painted Lady,* Dutton, 1983.

Un Orage immobile, Jean-Jacques Pauvert aux Editions Ramsay, 1983, translation by Christine Donougher published as *The Still Storm,* Allen (London), 1984, Dutton, 1985.

De Guerre lasse, Gallimard, 1985, translation by Donougher published as *A Reluctant Hero,* Dutton, 1987.

Un Sang d'aquarelle, Gallimard, 1987.

PLAYS

Chateau en Suede (comedy; title means "Castle in Sweden"; first produced in Paris at Theatre d'Atelier, March, 1960), Julliard, 1960.

Les Violons parfois (two-act; first produced in Paris at Theatre Gymnase, 1961), Julliard, 1962.

La Robe mauve de Valentine (first produced at Theatre des Ambassadeurs, 1963), Julliard, 1963.

Bonheur, impair, et passe, Julliard, 1964.

Le Cheval evanoui [and] *L'Echarde* (title means "The Fainted Horse" [and] "The Splinter"; first produced together in Paris at Theatre Gymnase, September, 1966), Julliard, 1966.

Un Piano dans l'herbe (two-act comedy; title means "A Piano in the Grass"; first produced in Paris at Theatre d'Atelier, October 15, 1970), Flammarion, 1970.

Il fait beau jour et nuit (title means "It's Nice Day and Night"), Flammarion, 1979.

"*L'Exces contraire,*" produced in Paris at Bouffes-Parisiens, 1987.

Also author of play "Zaphorie," 1973.

FILMSCRIPTS

(With Alain Cavalier) "La Chamade" (based on author's novel of same title), co-produced by Les Films Ariane, Les Productions and Artistes Associes, and P.E.A. (Rome), 1969.

(Author of dialogue with Philippe Grumbach) "Le Bal du Comte d'Orgel" (based on novel by Raymond Radiguet), produced by Les Films Marceau-Cocinor, 1970.

(With Jacques Quoirez and Etienne de Monpezat) *Le Sang dore des Borgia* (television film), Flammarion, 1977.

Also author of "Dans un mois, dans un an" (based on author's novel of same title) and, with Claude Chabrol, "Landru."

OTHER

Toxique (autobiographical fragments), illustrated by Bernard Buffet, Julliard, 1964, translation by Frenaye published under same title, Dutton, 1964.

(With Federico Fellini) *Mirror of Venus,* photographs by Wingate Paine, Random House, 1966.

(With Guillaume Hanoteau) *Il est des parfums* (nonfiction), J. Dullis, 1973.

Responses: 1954-1974 (interviews), J.-J. Pauvert, 1974, translation published as *Nightbird: Conversations with Francoise Sagan,* Crown, 1980.

(Author of introduction and commentary) *Brigitte Bardot,* Flammarion, 1975, translation by Judith Sachs published as *Brigitte Bardot: A Close-Up,* Delacorte, 1976.

Avec mon meilleur souvenir (memoir), Gallimard, 1984, translation by Donougher published as *With Fondest Regards,* Dutton, 1985.

La Maison de Raquel Vega: Fiction d'apres le tableau de Fernando Botero, Editions de la Difference, 1985.

(Author of preface) George Sand and Alfred de Musset, *Lettres d'amour,* Hermann, 1985.

Sarah Bernhardt: Le Rire incassable, Robert Lafont, 1987, translation by Sabine Destree published as *Dear Sarah Bernhardt,* Holt, 1988.

The Eiffel Tower: A Centenary Celebration, Vendome, 1989.

Also author, with Michael Magne, of scenario for ballet "Le Rendez-vous manque" (title means "The Broken Date"), first produced in Monte Carlo, January, 1958; author of commentary for a volume of photographs of New York City; writer of lyrics for singer Juliette Greco.

SIDELIGHTS: Described by critic Brigid Brophy as "the most under-estimated presence in postwar French writing," Francoise Sagan has tried for more than twenty years to live up to—or live down, depending on one's point of view—the reputation she established in the 1950s as the precocious author of *Bonjour tristesse.* Born into an upper-middle-class family and educated in private and convent schools in France and Switzerland, Sagan was a mere eighteen years old when, having failed the examinations that would have allowed her to continue her studies at the Sorbonne, she sat down one August day in 1953 and began working on a novel. Bored and eager to placate her parents, she completed a manuscript (parts of which she read to friends in order to gauge their reactions) in only three weeks; in it she told the bittersweet story of Cecile, a worldly seventeen-year-old girl who plots to break up her philandering father's sudden engagement to his former mistress by subtly pitting her against his current mistress.

Considered rather shocking in its time (more for its disturbing *amorality* than for its *immorality*), *Bonjour tristesse* ("Hello Sadness") met with immense commercial and critical success after its release in the spring of 1954. Its astonishing reception made Sagan a celebrity virtually overnight; people quickly came to regard her as a spokesperson for a whole generation of bored and blase young adults. This particular assumption, formulated so early in Sagan's career, combined with her well-known fondness for the "good life"—namely gambling, dancing, drinking, and driving fast, expensive sports cars (preferably in her bare feet)—convinced many readers and critics that she was living the aimless, cynical, and ultimately self-destructive type of life she described with such obvious insight and authority. It is a reputation that has plagued her throughout her career, making it impossible for some critics to take her work seriously while others, such as the *Washington Post Book World*'s L. J. Davis, admit to feeling "a persistent, uneasy, and half-baffled sense that she is really up to more than she seems to be, that behind the mask there lurks a shrewd seriousness of intent that defies and perhaps even deliberately mocks analysis."

For the most part, the plots and characters of a typical Sagan novel are interchangeable. Each story depicts a confrontation between young and old, either in the form of a middle-aged man and his much younger mistress or, less often, a middle-aged woman and her young lover. The scene of this confrontation is usually a place frequented by the idle rich, occasionally on the Riviera, even once in the Florida Keys and once in Southern California, but mostly in the nightclubs, salons, and theaters of Paris. Despite the glamorous locales, however, action and physical description are kept to a bare minimum; instead, Sagan focuses on the interrelationships between her characters as each one leads a life seemingly devoid of a past, a future, or a purpose. As the title of her first novel suggests, an atmosphere of sadness, disillusionment, resigned pessimism, loneliness, and cynicism permeates Sagan's stories. Though her characters are constantly in pursuit of pleasure, they are fully aware that true happiness, assuming they ever experience it, is a transitory state at best, liable to vanish at a moment's notice. Furthermore, as *Bonjour tristesse*'s Cecile concludes after her father Raymond's fiancee (Anne) commits suicide (Cecile had led her to believe that Raymond no longer loved her), what a person *thinks* will result in happiness or satisfaction often has precisely the opposite effect. All of these painful discoveries are related in a prose style that critics have compared to that of the great classical French writers: subdued, non-judgmental, precise, and deceptively simple and spare, almost to the point of austerity. Yet in mood, Sagan's stories reflect the feelings of malaise and doubt that were prevalent among educated, upper-class French youth in the 1950s and 1960s.

As it had the year before in Paris, *Bonjour tristesse* overwhelmed critics when it appeared in an English translation in 1955. A typical reaction was that of Rose Feld, who wrote in the *New York Herald Tribune Book Review* that "some may find it shocking and immoral, but none will gainsay that here is a talent extraordinary not only for its maturity of style but for its adult perceptiveness of human character." A *Saturday Review* critic, noting that the novel was "sensational yes; but skillfully and quietly done," had special praise for Sagan's accurate portrayal of the "confused feelings" of adolescence. The *Atlantic*'s Charles J. Rolo remarked that "the novel has about it such a solid air of reality that I originally suspected a sizable element might be autobiographical," but he was pleased to discover that "in fact, it is a genuine work of the imagination, which makes it all the more impressive." The *Nation*'s Haakon Chevalier felt that it was nothing short of a "miracle" for one so young to have written a novel that "transcends its subject matter, as in classic tragedy."

Even those who found the work flawed in several respects admitted that Sagan was definitely a talented writer. As John Raymond of the *New Statesman and Nation* observed: "It has been suggested that this novel is slick and meretricious. Personally I do not find it so. Setting aside Mlle. Sagan's extraordinary precocity, the book seems to me a considerable achievement, a work of art of much beauty and psychological perception. If the writer alters anywhere, it is, I think, in her melodramatic ending and, perhaps even more, in her portrait of Anne, who never quite comes alive except as a paragon and as a victim. But with the father and daughter Mlle. Sagan excels."

The *New York Times*'s Marcel Arland called *Bonjour tristesse* "a charming story," but declared that "the theme lacks probability. . . . The plot savors of the artificial, the characters are a little too conventional and slightly superficial. All the same, the fact remains that the writer disarms us and that her book is light and fragile and pleasant to read from beginning to end (or almost so)."

V. P. Hass of the *Chicago Sunday Tribune*, however, did not agree. Though he described it as "a brilliant, casually decadent little novel," he reported being "repelled" by the "glossy rottenness" and "carnality" of the story. *Commonweal*'s Nora L. Nagid declared that, in addition to being "as preposterous a book as one is likely to come across," it was "childish and tiresome in its singleminded dedication to decadence." Somewhat less offended, a *Times Literary Supplement* critic dismissed it as "only at one remove from the more banal form of romantic novelette."

Finally, John Metcalf of the *Spectator* commented: "[*Bonjour tristesse*] is a clever schoolgirl's version of Colette, pretentious, precocious and—for all its avowed lack of moral fibre—priggish. . . . Mlle. Sagan does not lack for effrontery. It will be interesting to see what comes next."

What came next was *A Certain Smile,* the story of a brief but passionate affair between a twenty-year-old Sorbonne student and a married man who is twice her age. For the most part, reviewers felt that it was a worthy successor to *Bonjour tristesse. Commonweal*'s Anne Fremantle, for example, found Sagan's second novel "as deceptively simple as her first, and written in that quiet, uncluttered prose that she has now perfected at the age of twenty, and with an economy and skill most writers wish they could achieve at three times her age." Peter Quennell of the *Spectator* concluded that the new novel was "decidedly better than the first; and, while [Sagan] has reaffirmed her existing qualities, many of the faults that marred *Bonjour tristesse* have been quietly dropped overboard."

Several critics, however, noted enough similarities between the two novels to suggest that perhaps Sagan was already displaying a tendency to limit herself thematically and stylistically. While granting that staging a "repeat performance" of a book like *Bonjour tristesse* "in itself is quite an achievement," a *Times Literary Supplement* reviewer declared that "one is still inclined to think she has been lucky in the extent of the interest and the excitement she has aroused." Hass, commenting once again in the *Chicago Sunday Tribune*, wrote that "it's all very Gallic, but I found [*A Certain Smile*] unwholesome and rather revolting. . . . One hopes that Miss Sagan, having worked this profitable lode twice, will turn her unquestioned talent to something of greater moment." After praising Sagan's writing for its "exceptional economy and elegance," the *Atlantic*'s Phoebe Adams also expressed a desire to see her branch out artistically, stating: "If there is any cause for concern in *A Certain Smile,* it is the lack of a sign that the author has tried to expand her view, vary her methods, or explore more deeply in the minds of her characters. *A Certain Smile* is a bull's-eye, true enough, but on the same range and the same target [as *Bonjour tristesse*]."

These last few comments more or less sum up the opinions critics have held on Sagan's work since 1956. Almost without exception, they have become progressively more bored and annoyed by her unwillingness or inability to depart from the rigid pattern established in *Bonjour tristesse* and *A Certain Smile.* Though Marjorie Perloff of the *Washington Post Book World* characterizes all of her subsequent work as little more than "pulp fiction," the reaction of the *Atlantic*'s Rolo to *Those without Shadows* is a somewhat more typical one: "After her remarkable first book, which had a core of genuine feeling, Mlle. Sagan has slid into progressive apathy. Her present novelette has nothing to say. . . . For all her literary skills and graces, which are considerable, her juvenile world-weariness has become tiresome."

Aimez-Vous Brahms?, for instance, though hailed by some as the work of a "mature artist," elicited its share of negative comments as well. "There are times when Mlle. Sagan writes so appallingly that one would like to shoot the pen out of her hand," declared Patrick Dennis in the *Saturday Review.* "At other times her perception, her economy, and her utter style leave one speechless with admiration. . . . [But] she is all style with absolutely nothing to say." Praising Sagan's skill at "exploring and defining the territory of sexual attraction and experience," the *New York Herald Tribune Book Review*'s Feld admitted that "this is no small gift but with repetition and without enrichment of other worlds . . . it grows thin with usage. The promise offered by

[Sagan's] first book seems to be bogging down in works that are contrived or designed for, popular erotic appeal. On that level, they're good but it's not good enough for her."

Some sixteen years later, in 1976, reviewers such as the *Times Literary Supplement*'s Victoria Glendinning were still writing: "Sagan has in her time said some wry things about love; in *Lost Profile,* the insights are thin on the ground. . . . To her contemporaries, her early work was indeed 'sophisticated and erotic.' But now she is still writing for adolescents of the 1950s, hung-up on father figures, mad about puppies." The *Spectator*'s Duncan Fallowell agreed with this assessment of *Lost Profile.* Describing Sagan's fictional world as "a narrow mix of sympathy and arrogance," he stated that "writing *Bonjour tristesse* Miss Sagan had an excuse for such a self-opinionated heart. To find that in her tenth novel . . . she has advanced her profundity not at all, is still playing the cramped teenager trying to escape Daddy, comes as something of a shock." Anatole Broyard of the *New York Times* merely noted: "The precocious adolescent who burst upon the world murmuring 'hello, sadness,' is now a writer of shamelessly happy love stories. Perhaps French sophistication has outlived its usefulness."

In 1974, the publication of *Scars on the Soul,* an intermingling of fiction, personal reflection, and autobiography, prompted some critics to conclude that Sagan had become nearly as dissatisfied with her own work as they had. While the book's novel portion, in which Sagan resurrects two characters from one of her plays and chronicles their romantic escapades, is judged to be only marginally interesting, its personal revelations surprised many readers, especially in light of Sagan's characteristic reluctance to discuss her private thoughts. In these nonfiction sections, the author self-mockingly describes "the revulsion, the boredom, the distaste I now feel for a way of life that until now, and for very good reasons, had always attracted me." Meditating on paper about her past and her work, she wonders how to write this particular novel, and even whether to write it at all.

Broyard, for one, seems to wish she hadn't. He writes: "Deft, spare, understated, subtle, disciplined, classic—these are the words critics have used to praise the novels of Francoise Sagan. She possessed to an uncommon degree, they said, the typically French flair for nuance. She could sketch in a character in a gesture, immortalize him or her in a line or two of dialogue. Her sentences were as well shaped as a Chanel suit. She dealt in essences, light and sensuous as a perfume. National pride preened itself on her. . . . Now, in *Scars on the Soul,* Miss Sagan has exposed the woman behind the novels and very nearly destroyed her own myth. The book is a very flimsy novella padded out by alternating chapters of 'self-portrait.' [This] nonfiction part of the book paradoxically discards all those qualities for which Miss Sagan was esteemed. . . . [They] are replaced by a coy pomposity and page after page of puerile philosophizing."

Commenting in the *New Yorker,* John Updike observes that the novel portion of *Scars on the Soul* displays "a dainty wit [and] a parody of decadence. . . . The book reads easily; it is company. The author's cry of personal crisis . . . feels sincere. . . . However, there is about *Scars on the Soul* an arrogant flimsiness that invites a quarrel. . . . Mlle. Sagan has for fabric only the shreds and scraps of a world she has come to despise." Noting that her defense of the bored and idle rich who people her stories "rings hollow," Updike concludes: "We have indeed come a long, heavy way from *Bonjour tristesse,* with its sparkling sea and secluding woods, its animal quickness, its academically efficient plot, its heroes and heroines given the perfection of Racine personae by the young author's innocent belief in glamor. Her present

characters seem—by this retrospect—degenerate forms of the incestuous affection between Cecile and her father in *Bonjour tristesse.* . . . Mlle. Sagan—at this juncture in her career, at least—has ceased to love herself, and has lost with love the impetus to create a fictional world."

In a final comment, a *New York Times Book Review* critic echoes Updike's remarks regarding Sagan's failure to charm and move readers as she once did. Calling attention to the reissue of *Bonjour tristesse* and *A Certain Smile* (timed to coincide with the publication of *Scars on the Soul*), he reports that the passage of time has not altered the fact that they are "effortlessly, economically, elegantly told tales." But time has made its mark in other ways, he concludes. "The existentialist overtones, the overlay of 'French decadence' seems *deja vu,*" the reviewer notes. "Since then, Anglo-Saxons, even Americans, have come a long way."

MEDIA ADAPTATIONS: In 1958, *Bonjour tristesse* was filmed by Columbia Pictures Industries, Inc., and *A Certain Smile* was filmed by Twentieth Century-Fox Film Corp. *Aimez-vous Brahms?* was filmed as "Goodbye Again" by United Artists Corp. in 1961.

BIOGRAPHICAL/CRITICAL SOURCES:

BOOKS

Brophy, Brigid, *Don't Never Forget: Collected Views and Reviews,* Holt, 1966.
Contemporary Literary Criticism, Gale, Volume 3, 1975, Volume 4, 1976, Volume 9, 1978, Volume 17, 1981, Volume 36, 1986.
Cowley, Malcolm, editor, *Writers at Work,* Viking, 1958.
Dictionary of Literary Biography, Volume 83: *French Novelists since 1960,* Gale, 1989.
Hourdin, Georges, *Le Cas Francoise Sagan,* Editions du Cerf, 1958.
Sagan, Francoise, *Toxique,* Julliard, 1964, translation by Frances Frenaye published under same title, Dutton, 1964.
Sagan, Francoise, *Des bleus a l'ame,* Flammarion, 1972, translation by Joanna Kilmartin published as Scars on the Soul, McGraw, 1974.
Sagan, Francoise, *Responses: 1954-1974,* J.-J. Pauvert, 1974, translation published as *Nightbird: Conversations with Francoise Sagan,* Crown, 1980.

PERIODICALS

Atlantic, April, 1955, September, 1956, November, 1957, August, 1962, May, 1974.
Best Sellers, November 15, 1968, May 1, 1971, February, 1978, April, 1979.
Books and Bookmen, January, 1975.
Catholic World, December, 1956.
Chicago Sunday Tribune, April 24, 1955, August 19, 1956, March 13, 1960.
Chicago Tribune, May 4, 1986.
Commonweal, May 13, 1955, September 14, 1956, November 29, 1957.
Detroit News, February 13, 1983.
Globe and Mail (Toronto), July 30, 1988.
Holiday, January, 1969.
Listener, March 25, 1976.
Los Angeles Times, November 7, 1980, August 24, 1984.
Los Angeles Times Book Review, February 6, 1983, September 1, 1985.
Manchester Guardian, August 14, 1956.
Nation, August 13, 1955.
New Republic, August 20, 1956.

New Statesman, October 26, 1957, February 27, 1960, March 19, 1976, October 14, 1977.

New Statesman and Nation, May 21, 1955.

New Yorker, March 5, 1955, November 2, 1968, August 12, 1974, May 10, 1976, November 21, 1977, December 25, 1978.

New York Herald Tribune Book Review, February 27, 1955, August 19, 1956, October 27, 1957, March 13, 1960.

New York Times, February 27, 1955, August 19, 1956, October 27, 1957, April 15, 1974, April 22, 1976, January 27, 1983.

New York Times Book Review, March 13, 1960, November 13, 1966, November 10, 1968, April 14, 1974, October 30, 1977, December 10, 1978, February 6, 1983, March 11, 1984, September 9, 1984.

San Francisco Chronicle, August 12, 1956, October 28, 1957, March 11, 1960, July 9, 1962.

Saturday Review, March 5, 1955, August 18, 1956, October 26, 1957, March 12, 1960, July 14, 1962.

Spectator, May 20, 1955, August 17, 1956, February 19, 1960, March 27, 1976.

Springfield Republican, March 13, 1955, April 10, 1960.

Time, October 28, 1957, March 14, 1960, May 20, 1974, April 27, 1981, January 31, 1983, September 3, 1984.

Times (London), May 26, 1983, May 17, 1984, September 9, 1987, February 13, 1989.

Times Literary Supplement, May 27, 1955, August 24, 1956, February 26, 1960, December 8, 1961, October 27, 1966, March 19, 1976, May 18, 1984, July 6, 1984, August 2, 1985.

Tribune Books (Chicago), July 31, 1988.

Washington Post, February 4, 1983.

Washington Post Book World, April 11, 1975, April 28, 1974, July 6, 1975.